# INVESTIGATING CRIMES

# INVESTIGATING CRIMES
## AN INTRODUCTION

**ALFRED R. STONE**
Texas Department of Public Safety

**STUART M. DeLUCA**

HOUGHTON MIFFLIN COMPANY    BOSTON
Dallas    Geneva, Illinois    Hopewell, New Jersey
Palo Alto    London

*Dedicated to Oleta and Joan,*
*whose tolerance and patience*
*appear boundless*

Drawings by Steve Horst

Printed in the U.S.A.

Library of Congress Catalog Card Number: 79-88446
ISBN: 0-395-28525-9

# CONTENTS

# Unit III
## DEALING WITH THE PEOPLE

*Investigating Crimes* is designed for use in criminal investigation courses offered at colleges, universities, and police academies.

In developing this text, we have tried above all to be realistic and practical, to include everything a police investigator must know while excluding anything that would have no utility in the real world of police operations. In doubtful cases, we have been especially generous with information that does not seem to be readily available in other police literature.

It is futile to teach people things they don't need to know. Police investigators rarely perform elaborate instrumented analyses of evidence; those procedures are performed by technicians (if they are available at all). Similarly, fingerprint classification and analysis is a rare and noble art with very limited utility in most investigations; when needed, it can and should be done by properly trained technicians.

By the same token, it is unfair to teach people only part of what they need to know, and it is unrealistic to expect people to transfer and adapt what they have learned in one context into an altogether different context. Police investigators do need to know something more about the effective use of communications, records, information sources, and other resources than has been offered in the standard textbooks of the past.

Our task has been complicated by the fact that police organizations in general, and their investigative components in particular, are presently undergoing a transitional period from the traditional, specialist-oriented structures that have been conventional in large police agencies for the past fifty years or so, to less rigid structures that rely more heavily on the use of patrol officers and other generalists to conduct nearly all investigations. We heartily agree with the current thinking that the new, less rigid structures will improve the efficiency and productivity of police investigations. Our problem is that we don't know what kind of working environment today's student will enter a year or two years or five years from now. Therefore, we have tried as much as possible to present the material in a way that will be equally valid and useful for the generalist investigator (such as a patrol officer who has investigative responsibility for all but the most serious crimes) and for the specialist detective. If we have leaned in one direction or the other, it would be toward the generalist; in the future, we anticipate that more and more police agencies will expect patrol officers to conduct all but the rarest and most complex investigations, often with the assistance of investigative generalists who are familiar with a wide range of scientific techniques.

The book is divided into five units. Before the first unit, we have included an introductory chapter which presents an overview of law enforcement as society's response to the problem of crime, and places criminal investigation in that context. There is nothing much in the introductory chapter that the pre-service student of law enforcement will find new or surprising, but it ought to serve as a useful refresher for the practicing police officer who is undertaking a course in investigation on an in-service basis. In either case, the chapter will orient (and perhaps caution) the student to the authors' assumptions and biases.

Unit I places criminal investigation in its context in terms of the national law enforcement system and in terms of the administrative and operational structures most often found in local police agencies.

Units II, III, IV, and V present the essential steps in the investigative process, more or less in chronological order. Unit II concerns the immediate tasks of the investigator at the scene of a reported crime, including the acquisition and preservation of physical evidence.

Unit III concerns the investigator's duties with respect to the people involved in a crime other than the perpetrator. While the importance of physical evidence cannot be denied, the fact is that the investigator gathers the most immediately useful information from *people,* not *things,* and that most of those people are to be found at or near the crime site: victims, witnesses, and bystanders. Chapter 7 deals specifically and rather extensively with the special problems of dealing with crimes of physical violence. Chapter 8 concerns a very different sort of problem, one that seems to plague and exasperate even the most experienced investigator: dealing with the news media at a crime scene.

Unit IV is predicated on the assumption that most investigations will not end at the crime scene and that the investigator must draw on a variety of resources to conclude the case successfully. Among those resources, described in separate chapters, are: police communications systems, the

criminalistics and pathology laboratories, records and information systems, and personal information sources (particularly informants).

Unit V is intended to guide the investigator in the concluding phases of an investigation, prior to the arrest of a suspect; indeed, in this unit we assume that the perpetrator has not yet been identified.

Unit VI brings the investigative process to its ultimate conclusion: the arrest, interrogation, and trial of the suspect. Since property searches away from the scene of the crime often occur at this stage of the investigation, a chapter on this subject is included. The four chapters in this unit have been prepared with great care to reflect the constitutional and legal principles of arrest, interrogation, search, and courtroom procedure as they are currently understood and practiced.

Throughout the book, we have tried to include several devices that will help both the student and the instructor.

Each chapter begins with a brief quiz, *Study Clues.* The quiz is intended as an informal pre-test of the student's existing knowledge of the subjects covered in the chapter; in addition, we hope the student's curiosity and interest in the material might be piqued by the questions (especially those he or she can't answer correctly). The answers are printed on the next left-hand page, so the students can test themselves independently. Thus, students who can answer all the questions correctly already know much of the essential information in the chapter and probably can assimilate the rest by simply skimming over the material.

Several chapters contain a section headed *Investigator's Notes.* In general, the material in these sections is supplemental to the main text and has been set apart because it may be useful to the student (or, for that matter, to the practicing investigator) on a reference basis.

A hypothetical investigation, *The Burglary at 1209 Main Street,* is described in four "acts" at different points in the book. The purpose in presenting this fictitious case is to illustrate the application of the theory we offer in the text.

Each chapter concludes with a set of objective questions, *Review of the Evidence* (mostly multiple-choice and true/false), covering the major points in the chapter and a set of discussion questions, *Topics for Investigation.* The objective questions are intended to be challenging but fair, and to reflect accurately whether the student has acquired the information presented in the chapter. The discussion questions, while they are related to the chapter's contents, are *not* intended as a test of knowledge. Rather, they are offered to encourage the students to apply the information in the chapter to the real world, to expand their imaginations and their perceptions of police science, and to consider the problems of criminal investigation in the broadest possible context. Some of the discussion questions could serve as the basis for independent or group projects; other questions may stimulate the students to reconsider some of their assumptions and presuppositions about criminal investigation in particular and law enforcement in general. Naturally, there are no "right answers" to any of the discussion questions.

There are four appendixes. The first one offers a summary of the metric system of measurement. We have included this information because it is our opinion that police officers—particularly investigators and criminalistics personnel—should adapt to the metric system as rapidly as possible. For the same reason, all measurements in the text are given first in metric units and then, parenthetically, in conventional units (approximated in many cases); measurements in the illustrations are given *only* in metric units. We have no doubt that the metric system ultimately will supplant the conventional system in the United States, and, since the metric system is infinitely more convenient, more conducive to accuracy, and more useful than the traditional system, we hope the change will come soon.

The second appendix is a glossary of law enforcement terms used in criminal investigations. Most of the definitions are given in the text in essentially the same form; we have merely gathered them all together in one place for convenient reference.

The third appendix is a bibliography. We make no claim that it is exhaustive or comprehensive, nor that every item in it will prove valuable to the reader. These are, however, the sources that have proven useful to us.

The fourth appendix is a reference chart of investigative techniques that are most likely to be useful for each of the types of crime listed in the FBI's Uniform Crime Reports index system.

Anyone who would even consider the creation of a new college textbook, whether in law enforcement or in some other field, first must enlist the help of as many friends, colleagues, and associates as possible. Without their assistance and support, the task is overwhelming and ultimately impossible. In our case, we have been blessed with an abundance of generous help and unsparing cooperation, for which we are profoundly grateful. We can only hope that the results, for which we assume all responsibility (or blame if need be), will justify the efforts devoted to assisting us by the individuals and agencies mentioned below.

Steve Horst's illustrations add a great deal to the appearance and clarity of the text; Harry Kieke, a darkroom magician, somehow made usable prints out of the most unpromising negatives; Ms. Jackie Foreman transformed mumbled dictation tapes into the first draft of the text; and Ms. Ethel Munson, librarian (now retired) for the Texas Department of Public Safety, was always willing to help track down one more reference or elusive fact.

Many of the photographs were taken by the authors, with the cooperation and assistance of the Austin, Texas, Police Department; the Texas Department of Public Safety; the University of Texas at Austin; Bill Alford, News Director, KTVV Television, Austin; Jeff Bruce, Managing Editor, *Austin American-Statesman;* Beverly Williams Daughtry, publisher, *Elgin* (Texas) *Courier;* Honorable Richard E. Scott, Justice of the Peace, and Donald R. Nesby, Constable, Travis County Precinct One.

Other photographs were provided for our use by the Texas Department of Public Safety, the Dallas Police Department, Southwestern Institute of Forensic Sciences, Eastman Kodak Company, Polaroid Corporation, and Dektor Counterintelligence and Security, Inc.

Special mention must be made, and our deep gratitude must be expressed for the assistance given freely by Leonard Hancock, Chief, Temple Police Department, and his staff, especially Major W. A. Lange and Captain J. David Wilde. They not only provided photographs and copies of forms from their files, they also provided nearly all the models in the posed photographs taken by the authors to illustrate various investigative procedures and techniques; those models were, in fact, Temple Police Department officers and the hospitable citizens of that city.

The following people reviewed our manuscript in its various stages of development, and we are grateful for the advice and criticism they offered: Warren W. Bundy, Schenectady County Community College; Ronald J. Waldron, Federal Bureau of Prisons; Fred E. Whitmore, Long Beach City College; John B. Wolf, Union College, Cranford, New Jersey; and Roy J. Wright, Illinois Central College.

LAW ENFORCEMENT OFFICERS in the United States are faced with a bewildering variety of problems:

- They are expected to stop the rising tide of crime, although no one pretends to understand why criminal behavior continues to flourish.
- They are expected to protect law-abiding citizens from threats to life and property. At the same time they must show great sensitivity to the constitutional rights and the human predicament of the supposed criminal.
- They are expected to be better educated and more professional than their predecessors, even though they must deal every day with the most unsavory elements of society.
- They are expected to display unwavering tact, unfailing courtesy, and unblemished integrity, in spite of the ever increasing dangers to their own lives and well-being.

It is almost a wonder that anyone wants to be a police officer. Yet, astoundingly, many police agencies find that they have more applicants than vacancies and that many of the prospective recruits are bright young people who see police work not as a menial task for social misfits but as a challenging opportunity to serve the community.

This text is intended as an introduction to one aspect of police work: the investigation of crime. But before we begin to examine the details of that all-important specialty, it may be helpful to outline the background for law enforcement in general.

## WHY DO CRIMES OCCUR?

The earliest known forms of social organization arose in part to solve the problem of protecting the individual member of a social group from both natural disasters and calamities caused by human beings. For example,

through cooperation with others, individuals could provide against starvation when weather or disease destroyed part of the crops. In the same way, by banding together for mutal protection, individuals could repel invaders from neighboring tribes or communities.

As social organizations evolved in the dim past, another function became important: establishing and enforcing codes of acceptable conduct. These codes were the forerunners of our modern concept of criminal law.[1]

Today's criminal law is infinitely more complex and more formally structured than those early codes. Nevertheless, the purpose is the same: to protect the members of the social unit from attacks on their persons, their property, and their essential liberty.[2] Those who fail to abide by the law are branded criminals and are subject to various kinds of *sanctions*, or penalties.

But if criminal laws are intended to protect everyone's most essential rights, why do some people become criminals? Why cannot everyone simply live in peace and harmony with one another?

## WHY PEOPLE COMMIT CRIMES

Unfortunately, there is no simple answer to this question. This does not mean that nobody has tried to determine the answer; philosophers, politicians, poets, and scientists all have attempted to produce sensible answers.[3] The trouble is that no single answer seems to be a valid explanation for all the different types of crime. Even for a particular criminal incident, it is nearly impossible to settle on a single explanation as the true cause. Some crimes are simply inexplicable, no matter what theory one uses.

Where does this leave the police officer? Some say that a police officer should not worry about why people commit crimes; the police officer's job is to arrest criminals, not to understand them. Unfortunately, that approach generally leads to ineffectual, slipshod police work and unhealthy police attitudes. A police officer must try to understand not only the criminal, but all of the people in the community with whom the officer interacts. Only through that understanding can the police officer live up to society's expectations of its law enforcement system.[4]

For example, the officer should recognize that many crimes are caused by the victims themselves. There are a number of ways in which this can occur:

- The victim may have instigated or provoked the crime. Quite often, the "victim" of an assault actually started the fight, or at least brought it on by taunts or verbal abuse.
- The victim may have invited the crime, perhaps inadvertently. Many people habitually leave their keys in their cars, but complain bitterly when the cars are stolen.
- The victim may have been a participant in the crime. This is especially common in cases involving prostitution, gambling, loan shark rackets, and similar criminal behavior.
- The victim may have been in collusion with the criminal. Most so-called confidence games are simply frauds that depend on the willing cooperation of the victim.
- The victim may be among the large segment of the population that tolerates criminal behavior as long as it does not happen to them. The failure of the public to report criminal activity is one of law enforcement's greatest problems.
- The victim may be so apathetic and helpless that he or she does nothing to prevent a crime. The majority of serious crimes against property occur in the nation's slums and ghettoes; the victims are people whose energies are entirely taken up by the struggle to survive, and they often have so little that they make almost no effort to protect themselves. Many slum residents feel that they live in territory that cannot be defended, so they do not even try.[5]

## PUBLIC ATTITUDES AND CRIME

One contributing factor in the failure or refusal of many people to report crime is the ineffectiveness of the police. Some people feel that they have been treated with indifference or outright hostility by the police. Many people fear reprisal if they report crimes, and some people even fear that the reprisal will come from the police themselves. Perhaps a majority of the population believes that the police are incompetent or ineffectual, especially when dealing with relatively minor crimes. In all such cases, of course, the problem is circular: the failure of citizens to cooperate with the police simply makes the police that much less effective.[6]

Many crimes, especially property crimes, occur at the interface between poverty and affluence. The crime rates among populations where virtually everyone is poor—for example, in many of the underdeveloped nations—remain relatively low; the people are too busy staying alive to prey on their equally poor neighbors. Similarly, property crime is fairly unusual among people who are equally affluent. But where the very poor and the comparatively rich exist side by side, both the temptation and the opportunity for illegal activity become overwhelming.[7]

Finally, crime is most common in unstable populations: where people move so often that they do not know their neighbors, where restless young people lack parental guidance and supervision, where social and moral values are changing rapidly, where ethnic

*An invitation to crime. Much publicity has been given to the probable consequences of leaving keys in the ignition, yet many people persist in this careless practice.*

groups with extremely different social habits come into conflict.

### CRIME'S EFFECT ON THE COMMUNITY

Crime is not only a problem for law enforcement agencies; it is a social calamity that affects the entire community. The rising incidence of crime reflects failures not only by the police, but also by the schools, churches, social service agencies, and other social institutions. Unfortunately, spreading the blame does not solve the problem. When more and more crimes occur, when the criminals are not caught—or, having been caught, are not kept from repeating their crimes—the public naturally looks to the criminal justice system and demands answers to hard questions.[8]

From beginning to end, the kind and quality of law enforcement and criminal justice that the system provides will determine the kind and quality of social life that the community enjoys. Thus, the demands that society places on police officers are not unreasonable; they are inescapable.

### WHAT IS CRIME?

In simplest terms, a *crime* is a violation of a law. Laws are made by the United States Congress, by state legislatures, by city governments (in the form of ordinances), and sometimes by county governments.

### KINDS OF LAWS

Fortunately, not all laws have to be enforced by the police. Lawmakers distinguish between *civil* laws, which concern relationships and transactions between individuals; *regulatory* or *administrative* laws, which concern governmental processes; and *criminal* laws, which generally concern individual behavior that affects the entire community.[9]

These distinctions are far from clear-cut, and there is a good deal of confusion about the kinds of actions that fall into one category or another. Some types of behavior may involve all three kinds of laws, and there are many instances in which the biggest problem faced by the police is determining whether a criminal law has been broken and, if so, which one.

A somewhat stricter definition can be applied to criminal laws: a violation of a law is a crime if—and only if—the lawmaking body has specified that the violator, once convicted, may be punished either by fine or by imprisonment. By this definition, for example, a law that provides only for the payment of damages to a victim would not involve a crime; it would be a civil matter. Similarly, a law that provides only for the loss or suspension of some privilege, such as a business license, would be considered a regulatory or administrative law. This kind of definition is helpful, but there are still plenty of "gray areas" and overlapping laws to produce confusion.

*A police officer may be responsible, at least in theory, for enforcing some fifteen thousand criminal laws.*

### KINDS OF CRIMES

There are more than three thousand federal laws that concern crimes, and the number of criminal laws at the state and local levels may be four or five times as great. In theory, every police officer should be aware of every criminal law, the precise definition of the criminal behavior, and the kinds of evidence necessary to identify and convict a violator. In reality, however, most police officers deal with no more than a few hundred specific crimes.

Criminal laws can be classified in all sorts of ways for different purposes. The most commonly used system is the one developed by the Federal Bureau of Investigation (FBI) with the assistance of several committees composed of police officials and law enforcement experts. This system is used to prepare the FBI's annual *Uniform Crime Reports* (UCRs), statistical summaries assembled from data reported by almost all police agencies in the country.

The UCR classification is divided into Part I crimes, often called "major crimes," and Part II crimes, which some people call "minor crimes," although several of the offenses in this category can involve serious loss or damage to the victim.

The Part I offenses are criminal homicide, forcible rape, robbery, aggravated assault, burglary, larceny or theft (excluding robbery and fraud), and motor vehicle theft.

The Part II offenses are simple assault, arson, forgery and counterfeiting, fraud, embezzlement, dealing in stolen property, vandalism, weapons offenses, prostitution, statutory rape and other sex offenses, narcotic drug offenses, gambling, offenses against the family or children, driving while under the influence of alcohol or narcotics, liquor law offenses (other than drunkenness), drunkenness, disorderly conduct, vagrancy, all other violations of state or local laws, and juvenile crimes. Arrests on general suspicion, when no particular crime is alleged, are also reported under Part II.

In looking over the list of Part I and Part II offenses, one might consider how many of these terms the average citizen would be able to define. Given a particular instance of criminal behavior, most people would have a good deal of trouble deciding which category of offense was involved. Indeed, many police officers—even experienced ones—share this problem. Yet making that decision is sometimes a crucial step in identifying and ultimately convicting the criminal.

## THE INCIDENCE OF CRIME

The crimes that concern Americans the most are those that affect their personal safety at home, at work, or on the street. In particular, people fear attack from strangers: mugging, assault, rape, and murder.[10]

In fact, some 70 percent of all willful murders, two-thirds of aggravated assaults, and the majority of rapes are committed by relatives, friends, or acquaintances of the victims—people that the victim knew and trusted.[11] According to some studies, the risk of serious attack from spouses, family members, and friends is almost twice as great as the chance of attack from strangers. Juvenile gangs—widely regarded as the terror of their communities—are involved in less than 4 percent of aggravated assaults.[12]

Nearly one-third of all criminal arrests in the United States are for drunkenness. Almost half of all arrests are for that one crime plus other crimes against public order: gambling, liquor law violations, prostitution, vagrancy, and the like. Of the serious crimes reported (including those for which no arrest is obtained), the great majority involve burglary, nonviolent theft, and theft of motor vehicles. In 1976, the FBI reported the following statistics for Part I crimes (based on both reported offenses and arrests):[13]

| OFFENSE | REPORTED INCIDENTS | OFFENSES PER 100,000 PERSONS |
|---|---|---|
| Murder | 20,600 | 9.7 |
| Forcible rape | 55,210 | 26.1 |
| Robbery | 441,290 | 208.8 |
| Aggravated assault | 452,720 | 214.2 |
| Burglary | 3,020,700 | 1,429.0 |
| Larceny (theft) | 5,227,700 | 2,473.0 |
| Motor vehicle theft | 973,800 | 460.6 |

These are the crimes that most concern the public, the ones that draw the most zealous response from the police and constitute the "crime waves" reported in newspaper headlines. And yet, statistically, they are by far the smaller part of the criminal problem in American society. The average police officer deals far more often with the supposedly minor crimes listed in Part II of the UCRs.[14]

Such statistics are small comfort to anyone who is a victim of *any* crime. To the victim, even a presumably minor violation may be a personal catastrophe. People who are afraid to walk the streets of their own neighborhoods do not care to be told that the statistics are on their side.

And yet the fact is that the average person has less than a 2.5 percent chance of being the victim of the most common serious crime—simple larceny—in any given year. It is essential that both law enforcement officials and patrol officers on the beat know and understand these facts.

Whatever the statistics may be for each category of crime in a given year, there is widespread agreement that both the number of criminal offenses and the *crime rate* (the number of offenses per 100,000 persons) are constantly increasing. Quite often it is the increase, not the raw number of offenses, that sends the editorial writers running to their typewriters. Furthermore, it is the increase that frustrates law enforcement agencies and endangers their credibility in the eyes of the public.[15]

Increasing crime rates should not be belittled, and there is nothing to be gained by trying to explain them away. However, it is important to keep them in perspective and try to understand them. For example, in a recent year, the burglary rate increased 17.6 percent over the previous year; the actual number of offenses reported increased 18.5 percent over the previous year. The average citizen's exposure to the risk of burglary had apparently increased by about one-sixth in one year.[16]

But look more closely at the reported rates. For every 100,000 people in the United States, there were 1,429 reported burglaries, or a total of 3,020,700 burglaries in the entire country. According to the FBI, about 62 percent (1,872,834) of the reported burglaries were of residences. If we assume that the FBI's term *residence* and the term *household,* as defined by the U.S. Census Bureau, are similar, then we can see how likely it would be for any given household to be burglarized in that particular year. According to the Census Bureau, there were in that year about 69,000,000 households in the country;[17] thus, the chance that any one of them would be burglarized was 1 in 37, or about 2.7 percent.

How much did the increased burglary rate affect the average citizen? The FBI says that burglaries had increased by 18.5 percent over the previous year, which means that the prior year's total must have been about 2,550,000. If the proportion of residential burglaries had not changed drastically, there must have been about 1,581,000 of them. The Census Bureau says that there were about 68,250,000 households in that previous year. Using these figures, the chance of a given household's being burglarized during that previous year was 1 in 43, or 2.3 percent. The 0.4 percent difference is too small to be significant and may be due to the imprecise figures we have been using.

Does this mean, then, that residential burglary was a trivial problem in those particular years? Of course not. What it does mean is that crime statistics must be placed in the proper perspective and not simply taken at face value. This is especially true when percentages are used and even more so when a percent of change is used. This is where editorial writers (and other people who get unduly excited) go wrong.

Suppose, for example, that two murders are reported in a particular year in a small town of ten thousand persons. During the next year, the town's population has increased by five hundred persons (5 percent) and three murders occur—an increase of 50 percent. Imagine the headlines: "Murder rate up ten times as much as population!"

Obviously, any change in a small number will result in a large percent of change; the reverse is true for a large number. This is one reason the FBI uses "crime rate" figures—the number of incidents for every 100,000 people. But this, too, is only a partial solution and can result in very misleading figures simply because the volume of serious crimes is so small in comparison to the size of the population.[18]

## BEING REALISTIC ABOUT CRIME

Having looked at crime statistics with a skeptical eye, we can see that it does not take very much to produce what appears to be a horrendous increase in the crime rate. Consider the list of factors that contribute to crime: overcrowded slums, economic deprivation, social disruption, racial and ethnic conflict, disparities between poverty and affluence in the same community, population mobility, family disintegration, changing social and moral values, and so on. Economists and sociologists tell us that every one of these factors has changed for the worse in recent years. It is hardly any wonder that the volume and rate of crime have increased; indeed, we might well wonder why the increase has not been much larger.

There has always been too much crime. There has never been a period in American history when crime was not a major social concern, although there have been brief periods when some communities were relatively free of crime. In fact, there are still communities today where serious crime is extremely rare. As might be expected, these are more or less isolated, very stable communities in which most of the people share common attitudes, accept the existing social and economic order, and realize that the chances of committing a serious crime and remaining undetected would be very small.

In most of the United States, the amount of crime changes constantly, day and night, month to month, and place to place. These changes are important to society because they determine what kinds of laws are needed and how much support should be given to law enforcement agencies. The changes are equally important to law enforcement officials because they determine the best ways to deploy personnel and other resources.

## WHAT SHOULD BE DONE ABOUT CRIME?

What America does about crime depends ultimately on how Americans see crime, for the government of a free society can act only in response to the desires of the governed. People have many different opinions and attitudes about crime. Most people worry about just the kind of crime they are least likely to experience: violent attack by a stranger. Shoplifting, which directly affects every consumer's pocketbook, does not seem to concern anyone very much—even the shopkeepers who are the immediate victims.

The lines along which the nation as a whole takes specific action against crime will be those that the public believes to be necessary. Unfortunately, proposed solutions to the crime problem, like other social ideas, tend to run in cycles and fads. At various times, it has been popularly believed that crime could not be solved by the criminal justice system at all, that only the elimination of causes, such as slum conditions and poverty, would reduce the crime rate. At other times it has been believed that the best cure for crime would be extremely severe punishment of offenders. More recently, it has been argued that the severity of punishment is relatively unimportant, but that swift and certain punishment has a strong deterrent effect.

The American public has been incredibly tolerant of its criminal justice system. The fact is that the system has not served the nation very well. The public expresses concern and sometimes voices insistent demands for improvement, but most people seem to expect their local police to be rather inefficient at best and slightly corrupt at worst. Most people assume that prisons do not work—at least, not in terms of rehabilitating offenders. Yet the public is willing to spend money to build new prisons, although it is unwilling to spend money to improve the existing ones.

In a recent study, hypothetical criminal cases were presented to 50 judges in three northeastern states. One judge "sentenced" a convicted felon to 3 years in prison. Given exactly the same information, another judge "sentenced" the same felon to 20 years in prison and a $65,000 fine. In other cases used in the study, prison sentences handed down to the same offender for the same offense varied so widely that some judges would have put an individual in prison for twice as long as another judge would. Not only did different judges vary in the severity of the sentences they gave, but each judge varied unpredictably from case to case, with no consistent pattern appearing, except that 2 of the 50 judges were "consistently severe."[19]

Apparently, even those at the top of the criminal justice system are very confused about what the system is supposed to do and what methods are most effective. It is no wonder that law enforcement personnel at the lower echelons and the general public are even more confused. And there are few signs that the confusion will be dispelled soon. Both the public and politicians seeking office agree that crime is one of the most serious domestic problems. Public concern about crime is mounting.

The public has every right to be concerned. Any level of crime is too much for the immediate victims. However, there is not much prospect of reducing crime drastically; in fact, some sociologists believe that a certain level of criminal activity is unavoidable, and perhaps even healthy, in any society.[20]

The worst mistake that the public makes is to blame the police for the high level of crime. Crimes are not caused by the inadequacies or the inefficiencies of the police. The notion that the police can somehow *prevent* crime has been badly overestimated (even by the police themselves).[21]

It is equally mistaken to blame lenient courts, indulgent prisons, or the levels of permissiveness and moral decadence in society. Some of the harshest, most totalitarian societies in the world are battered by crime that is far more pervasive and violent than anything we have experienced in the United States; there are also more tolerant and unrestrained societies than ours in which crime is relatively infrequent.

Reducing the level of criminality in society requires, first and foremost, a willingness by its citizens to abide by the existing laws. The laws, however, must be worthy of acceptance; unjust and unnecessary laws must be removed from the books. It is not possible for the public to respect and trust a legal system that too often seems arbitrary and irrational.[22]

The second requirement is that the laws must be applied and enforced consistently. The degree of severity or leniency in the criminal justice system probably is less important than the consistency of enforcement. People are more inclined to respect and observe laws if it is generally understood that everyone will be treated equally. Otherwise, the unequal application of the laws suggests favoritism, irrationality, and arbitrariness, all of which diminish the public's trust and confidence.

The average citizen encounters the law only in the person of the police officer. To most people, the police officer *is* the law made manifest. The officer's conduct, concern for the individual citizen, and basic decency are the primary factors by which most people measure the law's fairness and honesty. In a very real sense, the quality of our society depends on the success of individual police officers.

## WHAT IS THE ROLE OF THE CRIME INVESTIGATOR?

This book will serve as an introduction to one of the most highly respected and frequently misunderstood functions of law enforcement: the investigation of crimes. No matter what your present or future position in law enforcement may be, an understanding of the principles of criminal investigation will serve you well and, more important, will enable you to serve your community effectively.

In most police departments, criminal investigation is the specific responsibility of middle-level officers, those with the title of

*The responsibility for effective criminal investigation is shared by detectives and patrol officers. Frequent communication, both formal and informal, must take place between both sections of a police agency.*

detective or investigator and the rank of sergeant, lieutenant, or captain. According to conventional theory, patrol officers do not investigate crimes; they merely respond to a complaint, prepare a preliminary report, and provide the investigators with an initial body of information. In practice, however, patrol officers are a crucial part of the investigative team, and they should know at least enough about criminal investigation to keep from destroying or eliminating important evidence. Therefore, a good patrol officer should be as familiar as a homicide lieutenant with the principles outlined in this book.[23]

When a crime is reported or discovered and the police officer arrives on the scene, a number of important actions must be taken almost simultaneously. First, lives and property must be protected from any further loss or damage. Next, bystanders and curious on-lookers must be kept out of the immediate crime scene. Third, steps must be taken to ensure that no physical evidence at the crime scene is lost, destroyed, or tainted. It is at this point that too many investigations are thwarted before they even begin.

Police science today is highly advanced. Criminalists have at their command sophisticated equipment and techniques by which they can reconstruct a criminal event, identify a suspect, and in many cases tie the suspect to the event. However, none of this is possible if the physical evidence has been mutilated by a patrol officer tramping through the crime scene.

One of the tragedies of modern police work is that too little use is made of scientific investigation. Proper and thorough investigations are too often reserved only for the most spectacular crimes. Routine crimes such as residential burglaries, muggings, and the like are given only cursory attention. We hope that the study of this text will convince you that *every* crime deserves proper investigation. We believe that there might be many instances in which the proper investigation of a routine offense could be the essential element in preventing future, perhaps more serious, crimes.[24]

We also agree wholeheartedly with the noted criminalist Jay Cameron Hall, a veteran of more than forty years of police work, who says, "The chief goal of criminalistics is to pin the criminal to the scene of his crime—if guilty—or to exonerate him if innocent. Ideally, the forensic scientist [and, we would add, the police investigator], above all else, should seek truth."[25]

Seeking truth is no easy task, especially in a cluttered and confusing world awash with crime and tragedy. Police officers are under enormous pressure to solve every crime, arrest someone, and get the criminals off the streets and into the prisons where they belong. There are more cases than a detective could ever hope to solve, and there is never enough time to give each case the attention that it deserves. Under these conditions it is all too easy to forget about seeking truth and just to look for someone to toss in the bucket. According to a survey taken a few years ago, as many as 10 percent of felony convictions in this country are "questionable": the wrong persons may be in prison. One wonders how many of those erroneous convictions are the result of slipshod investigations.

In summary, then, this is a book about seeking truth, the first requisite for fairness and honesty in our criminal justice system. As you study the specific techniques and procedures we describe, bear in mind that it will be up to you to see that they are used properly

for one goal: to defend the innocent and to apprehend the guilty.

## REFERENCES

1. Edwin H. Sutherland and Donald R. Cressey, *Criminology*, 9th ed. (Philadelphia: J. B. Lippincott, 1974), p. 298.

2. Macklin Fleming, *Of Crime and Rights* (New York: W. W. Norton, 1978), pp. 42–45.

3. Norval Morris and Gordon Hawkins, *The Honest Politician's Guide to Crime Control* (Chicago: University of Chicago Press, 1970), p. 37. Richard D. Knudten, *Crime in a Complex Society* (Homewood, Ill.: Dorsey Press, 1970). See chaps 11, 12, and 13 for discussion of various theories to explain crime. Sutherland and Cressey, Fleming, and Morris and Hawkins also discuss this subject.

4. Samuel Walker, *A Critical History of Police Reform* (Lexington, Mass.: Lexington Books, D. C. Heath, 1977), p. 173.

5. President's Commission on Law Enforcement and the Administration of Justice, "The Challenge of Crime," in *Police Administration: Selected Readings*, ed. William J. Bopp (Boston: Holbrook Press, 1975), pp. 13–15.

6. Fleming, p. 19.

7. Morris and Hawkins, p. 36.

8. Knudten, p. 38.

9. Fleming, p. 26.

10. Fleming, p. 15.

11. U.S. Federal Bureau of Investigation [FBI], *Crime in the United States: Uniform Crime Reports*, annual (Washington, D.C.: U.S. Department of Justice, 1976), pp. 10–17.

12. Morris and Hawkins, p. 76.

13. FBI, 1977, p. 15.

14. Morris and Hawkins, pp. 3–6.

15. Knudten, pp. 12–13. Walker, p. 23, notes that the general level of crime actually has *decreased* during the past hundred years in the United States, contrary to popular opinion.

16. FBI, 1975, p. 29.

17. U.S. Bureau of the Census, *Statistical Abstracts of the United States*, annual (Washington, D.C.: U.S. Department of Commerce, 1975), table 50.

18. Morris and Hawkins, pp. 32–34.

19. "Tests Show Justice Uneven," Associated Press dispatch in the Austin *American-Statesman*, Austin, Tex., September 10, 1975.

20. Fleming, pp. 58–59.

21. Morris and Hawkins, p. 87.

22. Walker, p. 14.

23. Fleming, pp. 150–151.

24. Walker, p. 172.

25. Jay Cameron Hall, *Inside the Crime Lab* (Englewood Cliffs, N.J.: Prentice-Hall, 1974), p. 16.

# UNIT I

## CRIMINAL INVESTIGATION IN LAW ENFORCEMENT

STUDY CLUES

1. True or false: Investigating crimes is the central business of every law enforcement agency.

2. Approximately how many different law enforcement agencies would have jurisdiction in a typical medium-sized American city?
   a. one
   b. between two and five
   c. about ten
   d. more than one hundred
   e. more than five hundred

3. True or false: Even if several different agencies have jurisdiction in the same geographic area, each is responsible for specific types of offenses; there is no overlapping or duplication.

4. Which of the following is *not* generally considered a proper role or function for a police officer to undertake?
   a. keeping the peace and preserving public order
   b. intervening in social crises
   c. advising citizens of their legal rights and responsibilities in noncriminal situations
   d. assisting the public in nonemergency situations
   e. protecting lives and property against possible crimes

5. *Criminal investigation* generally means
   a. identifying the person responsible for an offense that has been reported to police.
   b. discovering criminal acts that have not already been reported.
   c. gathering information about persons who are suspected of involvement in crimes.
   d. evaluating information which seems to show that an arrested person is not guilty of a particular crime.
   e. all of the above.

FOR MANY PEOPLE, investigating crimes—"detective work"—is the most exciting, glamorous part of law enforcement. Mystery stories in which a clever, perceptive hero unravels a complex set of circumstances to identify a criminal have a long tradition in literature and to this day are a popular type of mass-culture novel. Newspapers, magazines, books, radio, television, and movies all glorify the detective who outwits and catches the cunning thief or brazen murderer. People enjoy the thrill of the hunt, the tracking down of an elusive quarry.

Unfortunately, Art is not always Truth. The reality of criminal investigation is that it is almost always a tedious, frustrating business that ends in failure far more often than in success. Furthermore, it is rarely carried out by the lone detective stalking the prey. Although crimes are sometimes solved by the detective's hunches or by a brilliant insight that turns a commonplace object into a crucial clue, typical detective work more often involves endlessly interviewing apathetic citizens, poring over musty files, and reading terse reports written in the dry, technical language of overworked laboratory personnel.

Criminal investigation is an important activity in most law enforcement agencies, but for many smaller agencies it is only one of the duties assigned to every officer. Some large agencies have dozens or even hundreds of highly trained and talented specialists for each type of criminal investigation; other agencies must fit their investigative work into the routines of patrolling, traffic control, and other general-purpose tasks; still other agencies do very little detective work at all.[1]

Crime investigators in law enforcement agencies rarely work alone. Modern investigative theory holds that it is usually preferable for a single individual to be responsible for the overall direction of a given investi-

*Crime fiction fascinates the public, but the image of the detective is often very unrealistic.*

gation. However, except for relatively minor cases or in very small agencies, the supervising investigator works closely with other detectives, patrol officers, criminalistics technicians, records and data specialists, and personnel in other agencies.[2]

## AGENCIES AT EVERY LEVEL

The number of different governmental agencies that have law enforcement powers and responsibilities continues to grow every year, as Congress, federal regulatory agencies, state legislatures, and local governments decide that new laws are needed and assign the job of enforcing the laws to different agencies.

The result is that in almost every community in the United States, dozens or even hundreds of different agencies have some kind of law enforcement responsibility, either as their primary purpose or as an adjunct to their main business.

A *police agency*, or primary law enforcement agency, is one whose principal duties are enforcement of criminal laws, investigation of crimes, and apprehension of criminals. Police agencies include the Federal Bureau of Investigation, the Secret Service, state police and highway patrols, county sheriffs, and municipal police departments.

A *regulatory agency* is one whose primary duty is to develop rules for some specific area of public activity, such as a type of business or profession. Most regulatory agencies have the power to enforce their own regulations by applying sanctions (such as fines or other penalties) against violators. Strictly speaking, a regulation is not a law; laws can be made only by legislators. But if a regulation is enforced as though it were a law, the distinction is not very important to most people. Also, some regulatory agencies are empowered to enforce specific laws, either civil or criminal, in addition to their own regulations.

A third kind of law enforcement agency is neither a police agency nor a regulatory agency; we will call it a *co-agency*. A co-agency is one whose primary purpose is to provide some kind of service to the public; but in order to provide that service, it has the power to make and enforce regulations or to enforce laws. Local and state public health agencies are examples of co-agencies.

An agency's *jurisdiction* means, first, the geographic area within which it has the right to function and, second, the kinds of laws or regulations that it has the power to enforce.

ANSWERS TO STUDY CLUES
1. False   2. d   3. False   4. c   5. e

Both meanings of the term are extremely important.

Police agencies generally have a well-defined geographic jurisdiction; outside of their own area, they have no police powers except in a few special circumstances. Within their geographic jurisdiction, however, most police agencies have very broad enforcement responsibilities. They enforce all of the criminal laws and, in most cases, a variety of noncriminal regulations.

Regulatory agencies and co-agencies, on the other hand, may or may not have limited geographic jurisdiction, but they are always limited to specific areas of the law or types of regulated activity. Some agencies of this sort are responsible for enforcing only one particular law.

The question of jurisdiction is important because when a criminal event is discovered or reported, it is necessary to determine not only who committed the crime, but also what crime was committed and which agency has jurisdiction. It is very common for a single criminal event to involve violations of several different criminal laws and noncriminal regulations; sometimes one person or group of persons commits a series of separate criminal offenses in a number of different locations. To make the matter even more complicated, different laws assign geographic jurisdiction differently among the various enforcement agencies—and some kinds of behavior might be criminal in one jurisdiction but not in another. Thus, it is not unusual for three or four agencies to be involved in basically the same criminal investigation and for each agency to claim the right to arrest the criminal.

Such duplication and overlapping of jurisdiction is a serious problem in law enforcement even under the best of circumstances. It is an intolerable situation if the agencies refuse or fail to cooperate with one another.

## A SELECTED LIST OF LAW ENFORCEMENT AGENCIES

The following list, although it is by no means exhaustive, includes most of the agencies or types of agencies that have law enforcement responsibilities at each level of government.

| NAME OF AGENCY | TYPE OF AGENCY | GEOGRAPHIC JURISDICTION | LAW ENFORCEMENT AND INVESTIGATIVE ROLE AND RESPONSIBILITIES |
|---|---|---|---|
| **FEDERAL AGENCIES** | | | |
| Federal Bureau of Investigation | Police | Entire U.S. | Primary federal police agency. Enforces some 200 laws assigned to it by Congress, including most federal criminal laws. |
| Organized Crime and Racketeering Unit | Police | Entire U.S. | Branch of Office of U.S. Attorney General. Assists federal, state, and local police by coordinating investigations of organized crime, vice activities. |
| Immigration and Naturalization Service | Regulatory | Entire U.S. | Enforces laws dealing with entry of foreign citizens into the U.S., process by which foreign citizens obtain U.S. citizenship. |
| Drug Enforcement Administration | Regulatory | Entire U.S. | Enforces laws concerning marijuana, narcotics, other dangerous or controlled drugs. Assists police agencies in drug investigations and arrests. |
| U.S. Marshals | Co-agency | Entire U.S. | Primary duty is to assist federal courts by serving legal papers, taking custody of federal prisoners, and so on. Marshals have some police powers but are rarely involved in investigations. |
| Secret Service | Police | Entire U.S. | Branch of Treasury Department. Originally established to combat counterfeiting and forgery of federal documents; now also responsible for protection of President and other high officials. |

| NAME OF AGENCY | TYPE OF AGENCY | GEOGRAPHIC JURISDICTION | LAW ENFORCEMENT AND INVESTIGATIVE ROLE AND RESPONSIBILITIES |
|---|---|---|---|
| Internal Revenue Service | Regulatory | Entire U.S. | Enforces all domestic tax laws, investigates possible violations. One of its divisions is the Bureau of Alcohol, Tobacco, and Firearms, which enforces tax laws pertaining to these items as well as all federal laws regulating their manufacture, sale, and use. |
| Bureau of Customs | Regulatory | Entire U.S., mainly at ports of entry, borders | Enforces laws requiring taxes ("duty") to be paid on merchandise brought into the U.S.; also enforces laws prohibiting entry of certain items ("contraband"). |
| Bureau of Chief Postal Inspector | Co-agency | Entire U.S. | Enforces laws concerning items that must not be mailed (such as explosive objects) and illegal use of mails (such as mail fraud). Postal Service is a semi-independent corporation, not a government agency, but postal inspectors still have some police investigative powers. |
| Coast Guard | Regulatory | All coastal and inland waters | Enforces laws against smuggling and other illegal activities on coastal borders; also regulates boating, maritime industry. |
| National Park Service; Fish and Wildlife Service | Regulatory | National parks, wildlife refuges, recreation areas | Enforce laws and regulations governing recreational use of parks, conservation of fish and wildlife. |
| Food and Drug Administration | Regulatory | Entire U.S. | Enforces laws concerning manufacture and sale of all foods for human consumption, prescription and nonprescription drugs, some cosmetics. |
| Public Health Service | Co-agency | Entire U.S. | Assists states in developing and enforcing sanitation laws; enforces public health laws (mostly for sanitation) on fed- |

| NAME OF AGENCY | TYPE OF AGENCY | GEOGRAPHIC JURISDICTION | LAW ENFORCEMENT AND INVESTIGATIVE ROLE AND RESPONSIBILITIES |
|---|---|---|---|
| Public Health Service | Co-agency | Entire U.S. (Cont'd.) | eral property, in interstate transportation, and in certain other special areas. |
| Social and Rehabilitation Service | Co-agency | Entire U.S. | Administers welfare programs (some of which are also administered by Social Security Administration); investigates fraud or abuse of welfare system. |
| Department of Transportation | Co-agency | Entire U.S. | Enforces laws dealing with transportation through Federal Aviation Administration, Federal Railroad Administration, National Highway Traffic Safety Administration. |
| Border Patrol | Police | Land borders | Enforces laws concerning passage between the U.S. and Mexico or Canada. |
| Nuclear Regulatory Commission | Regulatory | Entire U.S. | Enforces laws governing mining, processing, use, and disposal of radioactive materials. |
| Commission on Civil Rights | Regulatory | Entire U.S. | Enforces laws protecting civil rights of citizens, including laws against racial and sexual discrimination. |
| Environmental Protection Agency | Regulatory | Entire U.S. | Enforces laws against pollution or destruction of natural environment. |
| Federal Reserve System | Co-agency | Entire U.S. | In cooperation with three federally operated bank insurance corporations, Federal Reserve System enforces laws governing banking industry, combats fraud, embezzlement, and other banking crimes. |
| Federal Trade Commission | Regulatory | Entire U.S. | Enforces laws governing business activity, laws against consumer fraud, unfair competition, and improper business practices. |
| Securities and Exchange Commission | Regulatory | Entire U.S. | Regulates all aspects of securities industry (stock exchanges). |

| NAME OF AGENCY | TYPE OF AGENCY | GEOGRAPHIC JURISDICTION | LAW ENFORCEMENT AND INVESTIGATIVE ROLE AND RESPONSIBILITIES |
|---|---|---|---|
| Interstate Commerce Commission | Regulatory | Entire U.S. | Regulates all business activity that goes beyond borders of a single state. Duties partly overlap those of Federal Trade Commission. |
| Occupational Safety and Health Administration (OSHA) | Regulatory | Entire U.S. | Enforces extensive laws designed to protect health and safety of workers in all industries. |

## STATE AGENCIES

| | | | |
|---|---|---|---|
| State Police | Police | Within the state | Some states have no state-wide general police agency; criminal law enforcement is left to counties and cities. Most states have police, however, who are responsible for criminal investigation, highway traffic laws, and various related matters. |
| Office of the Attorney General | Police | State | Usually the highest state official with direct law enforcement responsibilities. Also acts as attorney for the state in noncriminal matters. Many have active, well-organized staffs for investigation of organized crime, consumer fraud, and so on. |
| State Militia (National Guard) | Co-agency | State (May be placed under federal control by order of the President) | Headed by the Adjutant General. Has no law enforcement duties, but assists local police in major emergencies. |
| Parks agencies | Co-agency | State | Usually employ rangers with specific, though limited, police powers. |
| Liquor Control agencies | Regulatory | State | Enforce state laws governing transportation, sale, and use of alcoholic beverages; sometimes involved in related law enforcement. |
| Organized Crime Commission | Varies | State | Some states have highly organized, full-time staffs who |

| NAME OF AGENCY | TYPE OF AGENCY | GEOGRAPHIC JURISDICTION | LAW ENFORCEMENT AND INVESTIGATIVE ROLE AND RESPONSIBILITIES |
|---|---|---|---|
| Organized Crime Commission (Cont'd.) | Varies | State | investigate organized crime. Other states have only a loosely structured citizens' advisory committee or none at all. |

Most state agencies are organized along lines that closely parallel the federal government's regulatory and service agencies, because many federal programs are administered through counterpart agencies at the state level. However, states also have their own unique governmental structures and agencies. Various regulatory and co-agencies may be concerned with gambling, sporting events, credit transactions, conservation of specific resources (water, petroleum, and so forth) at the state level.

## COUNTY AGENCIES

| Office of the Sheriff | Police | County | Every state provides for a sheriff as primary police agent outside of incorporated cities. Many sheriffs work alone, without a single deputy; others, in major metropolitan areas, have hundreds of deputies organized as a full-fledged police force. |
|---|---|---|---|
| Office of the Constable | Varies | County | In most states, comparable to federal marshals: assists courts, serves legal papers, and so forth. In some states, constables have broad law enforcement powers and duties. Most authorities consider the position obsolete and feel it should be either redefined or eliminated. |

Regulatory and co-agencies: In most states, county governments are not well organized or developed; regulatory and service functions are performed by state agencies. However, some large metropolitan counties offer the same array of services and carry out the same regulatory duties as the state-level agencies.

## LOCAL AGENCIES

| Police Department | Police | Within the city limits | General responsibility for enforcement of all criminal laws and local ordinances. |
|---|---|---|---|

| NAME OF AGENCY | TYPE OF AGENCY | GEOGRAPHIC JURISDICTION | LAW ENFORCEMENT AND INVESTIGATIVE ROLE AND RESPONSIBILITIES |
|---|---|---|---|
| Special police units | Police | Varies | Some large cities have independent police agencies to patrol and protect specific areas, such as parks, harbors, and subway systems. |

Regulatory and co-agencies: Most cities have counterparts of state agencies. In addition, some cities have a variety of other regulatory and service agencies, some of which have limited law enforcement or investigative responsibilities—for example, school systems, hospital and medical facilities, zoning and property development control agencies, building inspection agencies, utility agencies, animal control agencies, noise abatement agencies, public transportation, and services for the elderly.

The information in this table was compiled from several sources. The *Reader's Digest Almanac* (Pleasantville, N.Y.: Reader's Digest Association, annual) contains an excellent list of all federal agencies and their principal purposes. This information is subject to change due to the frequent efforts to reorganize the federal bureaucracy.

There may be well over a hundred government agencies—federal, state, county, and municipal—investigating crimes and enforcing laws in a single community. Such a situation can create chaos if the various investigators trip over one another, withhold information, and squabble over the right to charge an alleged violator.

On the positive side, however, the sheer number of investigative and enforcement agencies can provide the primary police agency with valuable assistance and support. No police officer ever has too much help; on the contrary, most police officers never have enough help. However, a police officer who knows which agency has expertise in what areas and which agency is willing to share information (with proper respect for the rights and privacy of citizens) will find potentially dozens of avenues for productive investigation.

Tracking down a suspected criminal by checking with the water department, the state unemployment agency (Did she file a change-of-address card to ensure that she would continue to receive her unemployment checks?), and the Veterans' Administration (Where is his home town? Could he be headed for it?) may seem a far cry from the lonely, dogged pursuit of the movie detective. However, that kind of interagency cooperation is the foundation on which many successful investigations are made.[3]

Cooperation of this sort does not always come automatically. Some agencies must abide by laws and regulations that limit the kinds of information they can divulge, even to the police. And some law enforcement agencies guard their independence with a tenacity that would do credit to a miser. If you wait until you must have a vital piece of information that can be obtained only from one

*Criminal Investigation in Law Enforcement*

source, you may find the door shut. If your own agency maintains a policy of keeping secrets from other agencies, you can hardly expect to be greeted with open arms. Inter-agency cooperation is a process that must be developed and maintained consistently on a day-to-day basis. To put it another way, it is up to you to be sure that your telephone works in both directions.

## INTRA-AGENCY COOPERATION

If cooperation between the various law enforcement agencies is sometimes a problem, surely there ought to be ample cooperation within a single agency. It is hard to imagine why personnel in one division of a police department would withhold information from their colleagues in another division.

And yet it happens. The fact that it happens is inexcusable, but the reasons are numerous: jealousy and rivalry among the various sections (an all-too-common symptom of misguided or incompetent leadership), lack of systematic procedures for sharing information, and, in too many cases, simple ignorance—especially ignorance of the proper roles and functions of the various personnel in different sections.

### MULTIPLE ROLES OF THE POLICE

Modern police officers and the agencies that employ them serve multiple roles. In small agencies, these roles are divided among a few individuals, each of whom must be responsible for many jobs. Even in very large metropolitan police departments, duties are usually divided between the *specialists*, who have one particular responsibility, and the *generalists*, particularly the patrol officers, who fulfill a number of different roles.[4]

• A police agency must keep the peace by controlling and suppressing disorderly conduct and disruptive behavior.

• A police agency must protect the lives and property of citizens by anticipating possible criminal acts and preventing them.

• A police agency must intervene in social crises, such as family disturbances, trade disputes, and public demonstrations, to see that they do not get out of hand and that the individuals are guided to appropriate sources of relief or assistance.

• A police agency must aid the public by providing directions, by guiding traffic, by directing individuals to other agencies that can assist them in specific ways, and by helping old people cross the street.

• A police agency must detect and investigate crimes, identify and apprehend the suspected perpetrator, and gather evidence that demonstrates the guilt of the accused.[5]

### THE PATROL FORCE AND INVESTIGATION

The heart of almost all police agencies is the patrol force: officers who circulate throughout the community, on foot or in vehicles, often for eight hours at a time. When a crime is reported, it is usually a patrol officer who is dispatched to make the initial investigation. The patrol officer must determine, tentatively, what sort of crime has been committed, how serious it is, what evidence is likely to be at the crime scene, and whether specialist investigators should be brought in at once, at some later time, or not at all. Some crimes are actually detected by the patrol officer, and occasionally a patrol officer interrupts a crime while it is still in progress.[6]

In every instance, the patrol officer needs to know what kinds of evidence to look for and how to gather it. At the very minimum, the patrol officer must know enough to avoid

*Patrol officers are almost always the first to arrive at the scene of a crime. The actions they take in the first few minutes after they arrive may determine whether the investigation will succeed or fail.*

disturbing, tainting, or obliterating evidence. The officer may have no further part in the investigative process; in a large agency he or she might never even find out the results of an investigation except by sheer chance. Nevertheless, the patrol officer must have a very clear, thorough understanding of what the specialist investigators do.

### THE INVESTIGATOR'S ROLE

The duties of the criminal investigator, whether a specialist or a generalist, are complex. In mystery novels, the nature of the crime and most of the major circumstances are usually set out in advance; all that the detective must do is put the clues together and identify the criminal. Once the criminal has been arrested, the detective's role is finished.

In real life, of course, it is not that simple. First, the investigator must determine whether a crime has occurred. That is not always as easy as it sounds. Sometimes the person who reports a crime exaggerates what has

happened or is confused and upset enough to overlook the true extent of the crime. In many cases, investigators themselves must detect crimes that otherwise would never be reported, perhaps because the victims are unaware of the crime, or because the victims prefer not to make the crime known (a common occurrence with business or "white-collar" crimes), or, especially in vice cases, because the "victim" is a willing participant.

Once the nature of the crime has been determined, the investigator must learn enough about the circumstances to be able to identify the person responsible. Gathering evidence always has this one goal: correctly identifying the person, or group of persons, who committed the crime.[7]

Along the way toward that goal, the investigator may spend a good deal of time investigating persons who are suspected of being involved in a crime or series of crimes, even if the crime itself has never been detected or reported, as, for example, in the case of many vice offenses.

*Criminal Investigation in Law Enforcement*

At the same time, the investigator is likely to obtain evidence that seems to show that a suspected criminal is *not* guilty of a particular crime. Such evidence can never be overlooked; it must be scrupulously checked, verified, and evaluated. A police investigator has a constitutional obligation to attempt to keep an innocent person from being brought into court and charged with a crime and to make sure that legitimate evidence in an accused person's favor (what we will call *contra-evidence* although the terms *negative evidence* and *defense evidence* are sometimes used) is made available to the defense and to the court for its consideration.

The detective stories are correct in one respect: the investigative role ordinarily ends when the accused has been arrested and all of the evidence has been turned over to the appropriate prosecuting official, unless additional evidence is needed or unexpectedly appears. Although the investigator will have to testify at the trial of the accused, he or she can get into trouble by becoming personally involved in seeing that the accused is convicted and punished.

These divisions of responsibility are based on centuries of human experience in guaranteeing the rights of free citizens, in developing efficient police operations, and in accommodating all the varieties of human social behavior. The major responsibility of a police agency is to enforce the law by apprehending suspected criminals and presenting them, along with supporting evidence, for trial. No police officer has a duty—or, for that matter, a right—to interpret what the law should be, to advise a citizen about the law (except in the limited sense of informing a suspect of constitutional rights and explaining the legal nature of the offense with which the person is charged), or to determine what punishment should be given to a guilty party.

REFERENCES

1. V. A. Leonard, *The Police Detective Function* (Springfield, Ill.: Charles C Thomas, 1970), pp. 3–4.

2. George D. Eastman, ed., *Municipal Police Administration* (Washington, D.C.: International City Management Association, 1969), p. 25.

3. Leonard, pp. 45–49.

4. Leonard, p. 5.

5. Eastman, pp. 3–4.

6. Gwynne Peirson, *Police Operations* (Chicago: Nelson-Hall, 1976), p. 5.

7. *Criminal Investigation* (Gaithersburg, Md.: International Association of Chiefs of Police, 1971), pp. 8–9.

## REVIEW OF THE EVIDENCE

1. True or false: The FBI is the federal government's only police agency.
2. An agency that has the power to enforce its own regulations by applying sanctions against violators is
   a. a police agency.
   b. a regulatory agency.
   c. a municipal agency.
   d. a co-agency.
   e. none of the above.
3. An agency's *jurisdiction* may refer to the geographic area in which it operates or to
   a. the court to which it is assigned.
   b. the size of its enforcement staff.
   c. the types of sanctions that it can apply.
   d. the kinds of laws or regulations that it can enforce.
   e. none of the above.
4. Indicate which of the following are police agencies (P), regulatory agencies (R), and co-agencies (C).
   a. Federal Bureau of Investigation
   b. Immigration and Naturalization Service
   c. Internal Revenue Service
   d. Organized Crime and Racketeering Unit
   e. Nuclear Regulatory Commission
   f. Occupational Safety and Health Administration
   g. Federal Trade Commission
5. Which of the following statements is *not* true with regard to state police agencies?
   a. In some states they have no criminal law enforcement responsibility.
   b. In some states the state police and the state highway law enforcement agencies are separate.
   c. In some states the state police are responsible for both criminal and traffic law enforcement.
   d. In some states the state police are the only criminal law enforcement agency.
   e. Usually they have jurisdiction anywhere within their state.
6. What state agency is often headed by an adjutant general?
   a. state police
   b. state treasury
   c. state militia
   d. prosecuting attorneys
   e. penal institutions
   f. none of the above
7. Which of the following kinds of law enforcement agents serves, in most states, a very limited law enforcement role and is regarded by many authorities as obsolete?
   a. sheriff
   b. constable
   c. magistrate

d. special police unit

e. district attorney

8. True or false: All government agencies are required by law to provide any information in their files to the police.

9. What is the first responsibility of the crime investigator?

    a. to put all the clues together and identify the criminal

    b. to detect unreported crimes

    c. to disprove the validity of contra-evidence

    d. to determine whether a crime has been committed

    e. none of the above

10. *Contra-evidence* is

    a. evidence in an accused person's favor.

    b. evidence that proves conclusively who committed a crime.

    c. worthless evidence that wastes an investigator's time.

    d. misleading claims made by the defense.

    e. none of the above.

## TOPICS FOR INVESTIGATION

1. As legislative bodies pass new laws and assign enforcement responsibilities to different agencies, the extent of overlapping and duplicated jurisdiction grows. Should all violations of the law be made crimes and all jurisdiction be given to police agencies? To what extent should overlapping and duplication be reduced, and how?

2. The text states: "The reality of criminal investigation is that it is almost always a tedious, frustrating business that ends in failure more often than in success." Study the FBI's Uniform Crime Reports for a recent year and compare the clearance records for the Part I violations. Why do some crimes have much higher clearance rates than others? What are some reasons for the dismal clearance record for property crimes?

3. When three or four different agencies are involved in essentially the same criminal investigation and each agency claims the right to arrest and bring the criminal to trial, on what basis should the dispute be resolved?

4. Many states have organized-crime commissions. These agencies range from loosely structured citizens' advisory committees to highly developed, independent investigative and enforcement agencies. What type of structure is most desirable and why?

5. List all the kinds of information usually available within a police agency. Which kinds of information should be made available routinely to other government agencies? Which information should be made available only under special restrictions? Which information should not be made available to anyone outside of the police department? In questionable cases, who should make the final decision? (Note: In actual practice, these matters are often subject to state or local laws.)

## CHAPTER 2

# ORGANIZATION OF CRIME INVESTIGATION AGENCIES

---

### STUDY CLUES

1. Which of these factors can influence the administrative organization of a law enforcement agency?
    a. the agency's jurisdiction
    b. the agency's size
    c. traditional organizational structure and arrangements
    d. the types of crimes investigated
    e. all of the above

2. True or false: The principal investigator personally undertakes all activities related to the investigation of a crime.

3. The decision about how much effort to expend in solving a particular crime may be based on
    a. public pressure to solve the crime.
    b. the amount of available personnel.
    c. the likelihood that the criminal will repeat the crime.
    d. the social status of the suspected criminal or of the victim.
    e. the value of the loss to the victim.
    f. all of the above.
    g. only b and c above.

4. True or false: The value of the loss to a victim from a crime can be determined by logical, objective methods.

5. One of the *disadvantages* of organizational structure that allows personnel to specialize in investigating a particular type of crime is
    a. increased expertise in a certain type of investigation.
    b. increased rivalry among investigative units.
    c. increased ease of communication among members of each investigative unit.
    d. improved allocation of personnel.
    e. none of the above.

6. True or false: All violations of the law must be reported to the police by the public before an investigation can begin.

7. True or false: After a patrol officer arrives at the scene of a reported crime, his or her role in the investigation may be very great or very small, depending on the policy of the officer's agency.

8. In which of the following ways do special investigative units (such as narcotics units, organized crime units, or juvenile units) differ from regular investigative sections of an agency?
   a. number of personnel assigned to the unit
   b. extensive use of undercover work
   c. responsibility to report directly to a high official rather than to middle-level supervisors
   d. need to keep all operations completely secret from other sections of the agency
   e. greater familiarity with technical methods of investigating crimes

THROUGHOUT THIS BOOK we will emphasize the theory that every police officer is an investigator. The principles and techniques of investigating crimes should be thoroughly understood and regularly practiced by every officer, whether he or she is assigned to the detective bureau, patrol, traffic, jail, or community relations.

## GENERAL PRINCIPLES OF ORGANIZATION

When a crime has been reported to or discovered by the police, someone must be responsible for conducting the investigation of that crime. Assigning this responsibility is essentially a matter of management. Usually the assignment is predetermined by the administrative arrangements that exist in the agency.[1]

The administrative organization of criminal investigation varies enormously from agency to agency. Several factors can influence the arrangement that an agency has and, thus, determine how investigative assignments are made.[2]

## FACTORS THAT INFLUENCE ORGANIZATIONAL STRUCTURE

The agency's jurisdiction has a lot to do with the way in which the agency is organized. In this context, geographic jurisdiction is not as important as the kinds of laws and regulations that the agency enforces. An agency of broad jurisdiction, such as a police agency, is organized very differently from an agency with limited jurisdiction, such as a liquor control agency.

The agency's size is a major factor. Small agencies have few options in their organization; large agencies have more opportunities and temptations to develop an elaborate hierarchy of specialists, supervisors, and ancillary functions.

Another factor is harder to define. It is the combination of management philosophies, theories of police science, and traditions which determine to some extent how police agencies are organized. Tradition is a dominant influence. Police science as a formal body of knowledge is a relatively new development. It has been only in recent years that much attention has been paid to the question of how a police agency should be organized and administered. The vast majority of senior police officials have come up through the ranks within the same agency. Although they may have attended seminars and workshops on police administration, they are most familiar and comfortable with the arrangements they have known throughout their careers; usually they are extremely reluctant to make drastic changes. Thus, there is a kind of built-in conservatism that discourages any major deviations from the "tried-and-true" methods, most of which were invented years ago in response to conditions that may not be relevant today.[3]

On the other hand, in agencies that experience substantial change in administrative organization, the motivating influence may be a current fad in management theory, political expediency, or something other than a clear and coherent philosophy of police science.[4]

### ASSIGNING INVESTIGATIVE RESPONSIBILITY

However an agency is organized, someone must investigate each crime that comes to the agency's attention. If the investigation is to succeed, the responsibility must be fixed on one particular person.

This does not mean that the person responsible for an investigation must do all of the work alone. A successful investigation may require many different talents and skills. However, it is important for one person to take charge and assume the direction of the team's effort. We will call this person the *principal investigator*, or supervising investigator, regardless of whether the person is a

ANSWERS TO STUDY CLUES
1. e   2. False   3. f   4. False
5. b   6. False   7. True   8. b and c

patrol officer, a higher-ranking detective, or someone assigned to the criminalistics lab or another support service.

The principal investigator decides, at least tentatively, what crime has been committed, what kinds of evidence should be sought, and what evidentiary leads should be pursued. This individual also assumes responsibility for coordinating all intra-agency or inter-agency efforts. It is the principal investigator's business to keep track of all of the evidence, to make all necessary reports or see that they are made, to receive information from other sections or other agencies, and to request assistance from others when it is needed.[5]

In any extensive investigation, many crucial decisions must be made: which leads to follow up, which suspects or witnesses to interview (and, sometimes, which ones to believe), when to present the case to the prosecutors, whether and when to ask for search or arrest warrants, and so on. All these decisions should be made by the principal investigator in consultation with other members of the investigative team and with the approval of superior officials. Finally, the principal investigator decides when a case can be closed, either because all relevant evidence has been found and the guilty person has been turned over to the prosecutors or because there is not enough evidence available to justify pursuing the case any further.

Often the principal investigator must decide how much effort should be expended on a given case. This may be the most difficult, and perhaps the most crucial, decision of all.

### ALLOCATING INVESTIGATIVE RESOURCES

The objective of any criminal investigation is to identify the perpetrator and to prove to the satisfaction of a judge or jury that the ac-

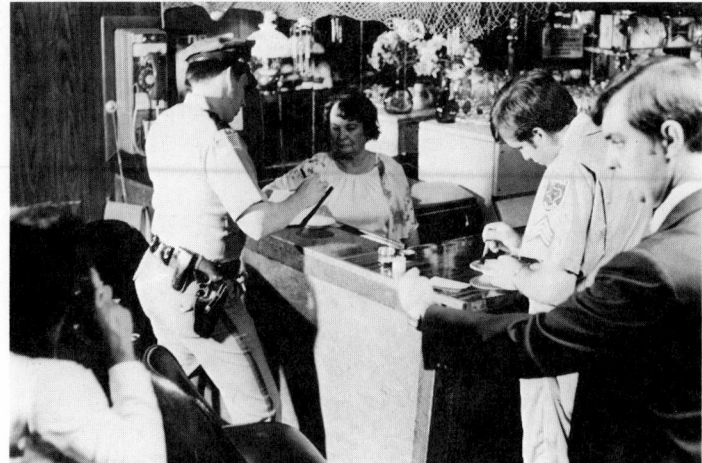

*In every case, one person must have the responsibility of acting as the principal investigator; this person should direct the other officers and technicians at the crime scene as they interview witnesses, take photographs, and gather evidence.*

cused person is the only one who could have committed the crime. Sometimes there is little doubt as to the perpetrator: the criminal is caught red-handed in the act of committing the crime, or a suspect admits to the crime, or the evidence is overwhelmingly conclusive. Unfortunately, it is much more common for the offender to be unknown and the evidence to be scant or inconclusive. Those are the cases that require hard decisions.

Ideally, every criminal case should be followed to its perfect conclusion, the conviction of the guilty party. But police agencies are notoriously understaffed and overworked. With rare exceptions, a police agency cannot afford to devote more than a small portion of its resources—its personnel, equipment, and funds—to any one case.

In theory, there are no "small" crimes. Every crime is a major calamity to its victim, whether the loss involves a stolen bicycle, a million dollars' worth of jewelry and securities, or a human life. The mere fact that a law exists should make clear the community's considered judgment that a certain kind of behavior is not to be tolerated. Any violation

of any law should be treated with seriousness and diligent effort by the police.

The everyday reality, however, is that the police make constant judgments about the seriousness of the crimes that come to their attention and, therefore, the degree of effort that will be expended in investigating each crime.[6] Some of the factors that influence these judgments are legitimate and necessary. Other factors are inappropriate and should be resisted by a conscientious investigator.

The legitimate factors center on two major questions:

• What impact does the crime have on the immediate victim and on the community as a whole, either because of the seriousness of the crime or because of the likelihood that it will be repeated?

• Is there a reasonable chance that the police will be able to identify, apprehend, and convict the perpetrator?

Hardly anyone would disagree that a crime involving the loss of the victim's life is more serious than, say, a crime that merely annoys or inconveniences the victim (for example, an

*Public pressure, often expressed and reflected in newspaper headlines, sometimes influences the effort police spend in solving particular kinds of crime.*

obscene telephone call). Most people would agree, too, that the embezzlement of a bank, resulting in the loss of thousands of dollars, is more serious than the shoplifting of a fifty-cent bag of candy. It is not very hard to decide the relative degree of effort that should be spent in investigating these extremely different cases.

The problem arises when the values involved either are very similar or are not so obvious. For example, should equal investigative effort be devoted to solving the stabbing death of a wino behind a bar and the murder in a hotel room of a prominent business executive who had registered under a fictitious name? Should equal effort be expended on two auto theft cases if one car was a twenty-year-old jalopy owned by an unemployed transient and the other car was a brand-new sedan owned by the mayor? Police investigators consider such questions every day.

Unfortunately, their decisions are not al-ways based on legitimate considerations. The most common illegitimate factor is public pressure—illegitimate because the public may have a faulty perception of the true seriousness of various crimes and may respond to purely emotional influences.[7]

Every law enforcement agency is utterly dependent on the public for support in thousands of ways, both tangible and intangible. It follows that the agency is vulnerable to the community's demands that a particular crime or type of crime be given more or less attention than the police feel is justified.[8]

The sources of public pressure are not hard to identify. They usually include politicians (the elected officials to whom the police agency must answer), the news media, and individual citizens. Citizens may apply pressure directly, by writing letters or making telephone calls to senior police officials, or indirectly, by contacting political leaders or by forming organizations and conducting public demonstrations.[9]

The reasons that public pressure is exerted in a particular case are not always so easy to determine. Some crimes receive disproportionate public attention because of the social status of the victim. Sometimes the spectacular nature of the crime itself arouses public revulsion and concern, especially if there is a strong sexual element to the crime or if the victim is exceptionally undeserving (as in the murder of a child). Sometimes the reason for the public's interest is quite obvious, for example, when a series of unsolved residential burglaries has occurred. In other cases the public's motives are less clear, especially when the pressure is for *less* enforcement instead of more, for example, when the community objects to vigorous enforcement of pornography or gambling laws.

It is important for the police to understand and, as much as possible, resist such illegitimate pressures. Unfortunately, such pressures often are irresistible. The police are forced to waste precious time and effort on certain investigations, while neglecting other similar and equally important cases.

## ADMINISTRATIVE ORGANIZATION

Although the administrative arrangements within police agencies vary considerably, certain patterns are common enough to be called typical. In this section, we shall describe some of these patterns which, with variations and adaptations to meet local needs, can be found in almost every police agency.

### LIMITED-JURISDICTION AGENCIES

As noted in Chapter 1, some law enforcement agencies are devoted entirely to a single law or type of law, although their geographic jurisdiction may include the whole country. The Secret Service is one example and there are many others at the federal and state levels, although they are less common at the local level.

The administrative structure of a limited-jurisdiction agency usually is very simple (Figure 2.1). An executive heads the agency, usually with some support staff; below that level, the personnel are divided into a number

FIGURE 2.1
A LIMITED-JURISDICTION AGENCY

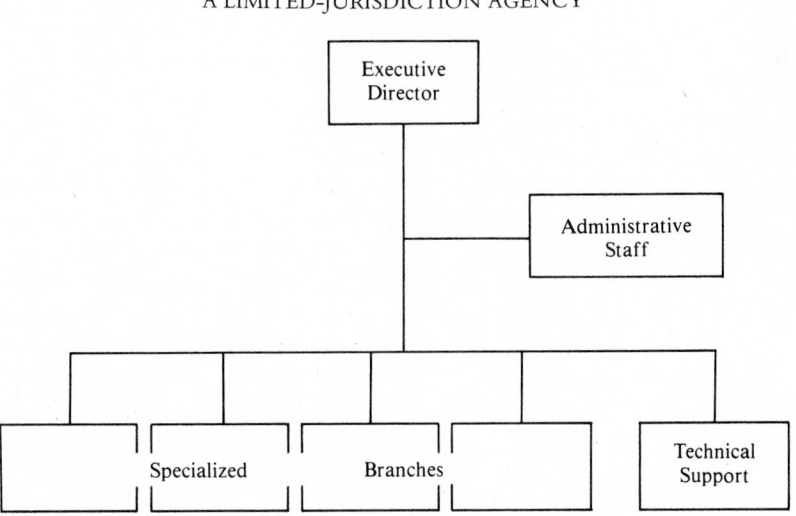

of specialized branches, each of which is responsible for all enforcement activities regarding a particular law or a particular type of crime. Usually there are also separate branches for the various technical and support services. It is rare for such an agency to have any generalist branches comparable to the patrol division of a local police department.

FIGURE 2.2
A SMALL GENERAL-JURISDICTION AGENCY

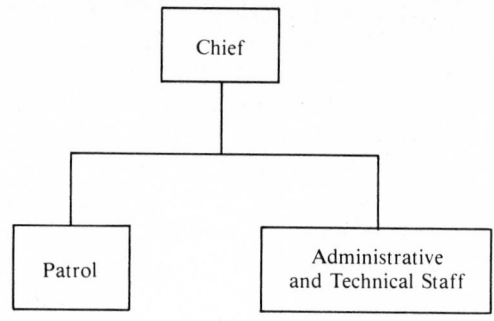

## SMALL GENERAL-JURISDICTION AGENCIES

A *general-jurisdiction agency* is one that, like most police departments, has broad responsibility for enforcement of all sorts of criminal laws as well as miscellaneous service functions. The great majority of police agencies in the United States are very small: a staff of fifty people or less and sometimes as few as one or two people. With so few personnel available, specialization simply is not practical (Figure 2.2). If there are enough people in the agency—at least twenty-five or so—one or two of them might be assigned exclusively to investigation, but those persons would be responsible for *all* investigations that are beyond the capabilities of the patrol officers. Even in a very small agency, some personnel are necessarily assigned to administrative and staff duties; the rest are assigned to patrol.[10]

## LARGE GENERAL-JURISDICTION AGENCIES

At the opposite extreme are the very large police agencies—those that have a thousand or more employees; an agency that has more than two hundred employees would be considered a large agency.

There are about 250 large agencies in the United States, and about 50 of those are very large. Altogether, there are more than 13,000 municipal and county police agencies in the country, so obviously the vast majority have fewer than 200 employees.

A large agency has both the opportunity and, presumably, the need to devote a portion of its resources to specialized criminal investigations. With more employees, a large agency also has a greater need to provide for lines of communicating and reporting and for the exercise of supervision. In short, the organization chart becomes considerably more complicated.

Typically, below the chief executive of the agency and the administrative staff is at least one level of senior supervisory officers. A common pattern is to divide the agency into three major sections: patrol, criminal investigations, and technical services (although the terminology may vary). The patrol section may be further subdivided, either in terms of geography—into different precincts—or in terms of duty shifts. Sometimes a separate branch of the patrol section is assigned exclusively to traffic law enforcement, and sometimes a fourth major section is devoted to traffic.

Some very large agencies duplicate this entire structure in each precinct, so that every precinct has its own patrol, investigation, traffic, and technical services units.

There are as many ways to divide the criminal investigations section (often called the detective bureau) as there are ways to classify crimes. Actually, most large agencies have evolved not according to carefully conceived plan, but rather as a long series of spur-of-the-moment decisions. The chart shown in Figure 2.3 is by no means intended as a model, but merely provides an example of what often exists.[11]

Some of the most interesting administrative patterns are those that have been developed by medium-sized police departments—those in the range of fifty to two hundred employees.

Many of these agencies, as might be expected, are merely scaled-down versions of the large agencies. As a small agency begins to grow and more elaborate administrative mechanisms are needed, it is only natural for

FIGURE 2.3
A LARGE GENERAL-JURISDICTION AGENCY

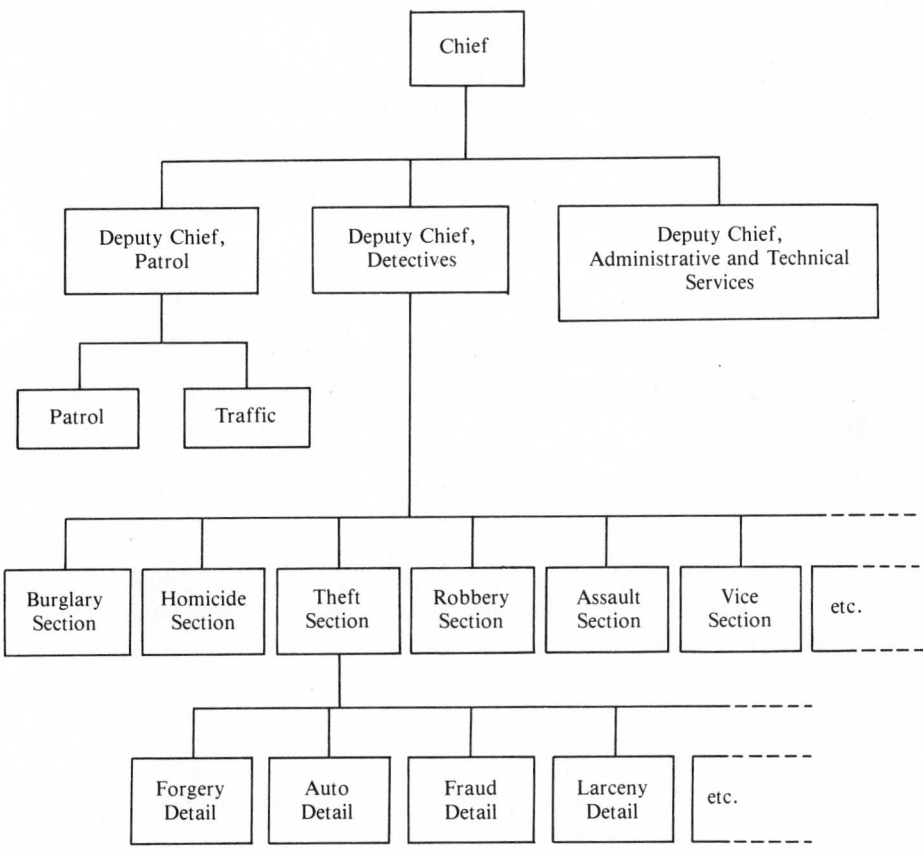

the administrators to follow the most familiar model. Not only is this the traditional way to proceed, but there is some ego satisfaction in seeing one's agency emulating the "big guys" in the nearest major city. Thus, the familiar pattern consists of three main sections, assigned to patrol, technical services, and investigation, the latter being further divided into a number of specialties. The number of subsections usually is limited only by the number of personnel who can be put into these categories. Some consideration also may be given to the specific needs of a community; the crimes that occur most often are most likely to have an entire section devoted to them, and comparatively rare crimes are combined in one way or another.

This traditional administrative pattern is not wholly unjustified. Assigning personnel according to categories of crime enables each investigator to become very experienced in the techniques and methods used to investigate the crimes for which he or she is responsible. There are, however, some serious disadvantages to this type of organization.

The major disadvantage is the obvious pitfall in any kind of specialization. A person may know a great deal about one specialty but not much about anyone else's work. The specialist may do a splendid job as long as the crime fits the investigator's conventional frame of reference, but may be completely lost if the problem involves two or more areas of specialization, for example, a homicide resulting from the armed robbery of a narcotics dealer.

Furthermore, the specialist has a natural tendency to become emotionally as well as intellectually attached to the area of expertise. The homicide detective may have no interest in the problems of the burglary detail. After a while, in fact, the homicide detective may come to think that burglary detectives really

are not very important. Soon such attitudes lead to strong intersectional jealousies and conflicts. If a case arises in which both the homicide and the burglary detectives ought to be involved, they may have a very hard time working together.

Another problem with excessive specialization is that it can lead to the misallocation of personnel. The smallest number of people that a section can contain is one. However, there are bound to be times when there are very few homicides to be investigated by the homicide detective but more armed robberies than the robbery detective can handle. Some of the overflow could be shifted onto the homicide detective's desk, but in practice that is not done very often.[12]

One way to deal with the pitfalls of specialization is to move people around from one section to another periodically. In theory, this at least prevents the personnel from becoming too fond of their work and too narrow in their attitude. However, this eliminates the one presumed benefit of specialization: allowing an individual to develop exceptional skill and experience in a particular kind of investigation. People-shuffling seems to avoid a direct answer to the real question: are the benefits of specialization greater than the costs in terms of narrowed attitudes and poor allocation of resources?[13]

Some medium-sized agencies have faced the question squarely, and their answer is no. Instead of the typical large-agency pattern of specialized sections, these medium-sized agencies have evolved new patterns to meet their special needs.

One simple solution is to follow the common practice of dividing the entire agency into the usual three main sections, but to keep all of the detectives together as "semigeneralists." New cases can be assigned to whomever is free or by some plan of rotation. A detective might work on a homicide on one day, a forgery on the next day, and residential burglaries during the rest of the week.[14]

A somewhat more elaborate system, based on a similar concept, breaks down the distinction between the patrol and the investigative functions. Under this plan, the investigative section is deliberately kept very small. The personnel in the patrol section are trained in investigative techniques and conduct the major part of all crime investigations. Detectives step in only when an investigation becomes unusually elaborate or time consuming; otherwise, the detectives serve as overall coordinators, assisting the patrol officers when necessary.

There are many possible variations to this plan. One of its advantages is that it can be adapted to meet local needs, personal preferences, and relative strengths and weaknesses of a particular agency's personnel.

One variation is shown in Figure 2.4. This is the organization chart, considerably condensed and simplified, for a city police department in a community of about fifty thousand people. The department has 110 employees, of whom 90 are commissioned police officers. Two-thirds, or 60, of the commissioned officers are assigned to the patrol section. However, of the 20 officers assigned to each patrol shift, 2 or 3 are "patrol officer–investigators." They have no specific beat, no district to patrol. They are key figures in the plan.

The criminal investigation section consists of nine officers: a captain, a lieutenant, four sergeants, and three more patrol officer–investigators. Three of the sergeants are "semi-specialized": one is particularly responsible for investigating crimes against persons (assaults, homicides, rapes); one works mostly on forgeries, bad checks, and credit card

FIGURE 2.4
A MEDIUM-SIZED GENERAL-JURISDICTION AGENCY

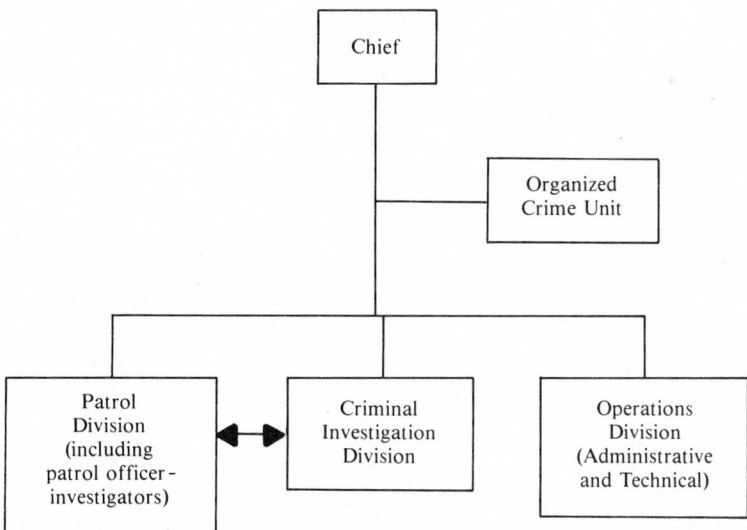

abuses; the third works mainly on other types of property crimes, such as residential burglaries. The fourth sergeant, a trained polygraph operator, assists any of the other three sergeants who needs help. For that matter, any of the four might assist another on a particular case or take over part of an excessive workload. The three patrol officer–investigators in the investigation section generally handle juvenile crimes and family problems but they, too, assist the sergeants when necessary.

One other special feature of this plan is the organized crime unit (OCU). This unit consists of a sergeant, three patrol officer–investigators, and an assistant district attorney. They are responsible for all organized crime investigations, including narcotics trafficking, prostitution, gambling, loan frauds, and so on. The OCU reports directly to the Chief of Police rather than to the investigation section. This is an unusual arrangement for a relatively small agency, but it meets the particular needs of the community.

The other 17 commissioned officers (those not in patrol, investigation, or OCU) are assigned to various technical support and administrative duties.

The system works in this way: When a crime is reported, the patrol officer who arrives first at the scene assumes immediate responsibility for any investigation. If it seems that the investigation can be completed quickly, that individual handles it alone. If necessary, one of the patrol officer–investigators will cover the first officer's district during that time.

If the investigation cannot be completed quickly—say, in an hour or two—the patrol officer may turn it over to one of the patrol officer–investigators for follow-up. If there is no urgency to the investigation, the patrol officer or the patrol officer–investiga-

tor may put off the follow-up until a later time when other duties are not so pressing. Almost all routine investigations and virtually all misdemeanor cases are handled from initial response to arrest by the personnel in the patrol section.

Only if the crime is a major one or if the investigation is likely to be extremely complex will it be turned over to the investigation section, where it will be assigned to one of the patrol officer–investigators or sergeants there. Of course, all investigations are reported to the investigation section as a matter of routine, and the detectives are always available to lend guidance or whatever assistance may be needed.

This plan might not work in every community. The system requires a high degree of flexibility and coordination, and it depends heavily on adequate training of all personnel. However, if such a plan can be made to work, it seems to offer a number of advantages over the traditional pattern.[15]

## OPERATIONAL ORGANIZATION

Regardless of the administrative pattern of organization within a police agency, certain functions still must be carried out. Whether the agency is small or large, limited or general in jurisdiction, these functions tend to be very similar and to be distributed in similar ways.

Violations of criminal laws must come to the attention of the agency. Either the violations must be reported by the public (most often by the victim or by someone acting in the victim's behalf) or the violations must be discovered by the law enforcement agents themselves.

As soon as a crime is reported or discovered, the police agency must respond as quickly as possible to prevent any further loss or damage to the victim. In fact, the possibility of danger to the victim should be the single most important factor in determining how quickly the police respond to a reported crime. For example, if two reports are received simultaneously, one concerning a burglary that occurred several hours earlier and the other concerning a traffic accident with injuries, the traffic accident should be handled first. The burglary will wait.

Once the scene of the crime and the victims are secured against further loss or damage, the business of investigation can begin: collecting evidence, interviewing the victims and witnesses, and so on.

Although we feel that the patrol-oriented type of organization described in the last section has considerable merit, the fact remains that most police agencies of whatever size are organized along traditional lines. Therefore, the operational procedures we will describe from now on apply to a traditional system and would have to be modified somewhat if patrol officers are to play the major role in most investigations.[16]

## RESPONSIBILITIES OF THE PATROL OFFICER

The first response to a reported crime is almost always made by a patrol officer. Most reports are received by the police over the telephone. The switchboard operator gives the information to a dispatcher who, by radio, assigns a patrol officer to handle the call. The patrol officer may have very little information about the nature of the reported crime.

When the officer arrives at the scene of a reported crime, the immediate task is to protect both the victims, if they are present, and the scene itself. Usually the criminal has left the scene before the police arrive, but the officer must never assume that this is the case; if the criminal is still at the scene, the officer's own life and the lives of the people present may be in jeopardy.

Next, the officer must make a quick assessment of the overall situation. The person who reported the crime (the *complainant*) may or may not be present. If the complainant, a victim, or witnesses are present, the officer should locate these persons, obtain identification, and ask what has happened. Based on the accounts of the complainant, the victim, and any immediate witnesses, as well as the officer's observation of the crime scene, the patrol officer makes a tentative assessment of what crime has occurred. Was it a burglary (forced entry into a building) or a robbery (unlawful taking of property from another

person), or did an estranged husband reclaim his clothes and personal belongings? This initial assessment will determine what kinds of evidence should be sought at the crime scene and may have considerable bearing on whether the patrol officer should call in an investigator immediately or merely report the incident later.

From the time the patrol officer first arrives at the crime scene, attention must be paid to protecting the scene against the loss or contamination of evidence. Naturally, if a victim is injured, emergency medical treatment of the victim is more important; otherwise, nothing at all should be disturbed.

How far the patrol officer goes in investigating the crime will depend entirely on the rules and policies of the police agency involved. Some agencies expect the officer to do nothing more than conduct initial interviews of the victim and immediate witnesses. The results of these interviews are then reported to the investigators, either immediately by telephone or police radio or later in written form. Other agencies expect the patrol officer to conduct at least a cursory preliminary investigation. This may involve locating and identifying physical evidence, such as tools, weapons, items of clothing, or other objects at the scene. The patrol officer may be expected to take photographs of the scene to record its initial appearance. Rarely would a patrol officer be expected to look for trace evidence such as fingerprints, physiological stains (blood, semen, and the like), soil, or threads, unless that officer will be responsible for the continuing investigation. However, if the officer observes any such traces in the course of the preliminary investigation, careful note should be made of their existence, location, and possible value as evidence.

Some agencies' rules are based on the theory that the first person to arrive at the scene has the best opportunity to uncover evidence and therefore should continue the investigation as long as it is productive. This might mean spending an hour or two at the crime scene. The opposite philosophy is that patrol officers have no business interfering with investigative work and that they are as likely to foul up the scene as they are to uncover usable evidence. Agencies that adopt this philosophy expect the patrol officer to devote attention to protecting the scene until competent investigators arrive. The patrol officer should touch nothing and should return to the regular beat as soon as the investigators get there, unless the officer's help is needed to control bystanders or automotive traffic.[17]

We tend to agree with the first opinion: the patrol officer should do just as much investigating as time and circumstances permit. Evidence at a crime scene has a bad habit of getting lost quickly; the sooner it is identified and recovered, the better. Assuming that the officer is competent and adequately trained, there is no reason for a patrol officer to turn into a piece of furniture on arriving at the scene of a crime. (However, regardless of what we think, each police officer must abide by the rules and procedures that have been established in his or her own agency.)

In any case, unless the perpetrator of the crime is already known and the facts of the criminal event are readily apparent, at some point the patrol officer must either call for the investigators or discontinue the investigation and file a written report. Either way, the crime now becomes a case for the investigators to solve.

RESPONSIBILITIES
OF THE INVESTIGATOR

Cases are assigned to police investigators by various means. Occasionally, a complainant may call a detective directly to report a crime. This sometimes happens when the crime occurred several hours earlier and has just been discovered. Otherwise, most cases come to the investigators' attention as a result of a telephone or radio call or a written report from the patrol officer who initially responded to the complaint.

The nature of the crime may determine which investigator handles a case, especially in smaller agencies where each detective specializes in certain kinds of cases. In larger agencies the nature of the crime simply determines which section of the detective bureau will receive the report. Within that section, cases are assigned by the senior officer on duty, either by rotation or by rather arbitrary decisions about which detective is most capable of handling each case.

Once a case has been assigned to the investigator (who then becomes the principal investigator), the first task is to evaluate the crime report as it was received. If the report has come from a patrol officer, either by telephone or radio or in written form, it probably will be reasonably complete and reliable. However, if the report has come directly from a complainant or victim, it must be regarded with some suspicion. Is the information accurate? Is there enough information so that the investigator has a fairly good understanding of how the crime occurred? Is the complainant's definition of the crime appropriate? Most people have only very fuzzy notions of the distinctions between, for example, a burglary, a robbery, and a theft. However, those distinctions may influence the way in which an investigation is pursued.

If it is a major crime, especially a crime of violence, the investigator should visit the scene as soon as possible. Victims and witnesses should be interviewed extensively. Any and all physical evidence, especially trace evidence, must be identified, collected, and removed from the scene for further examination. The scene must be photographed from every conceivable angle; measurements must be taken and sketches drawn. These procedures may take several hours, but no step should be overlooked or slighted.

The task of the investigator is to establish that one particular person or group of persons committed certain actions and, in doing so, violated certain laws. Three specific questions are relevant:

- *Who* committed the crime?
- *What actions* were committed in the course of the crime?
- *What law* was violated?

Every criminal law contains two main parts: a statement of what specific human actions are prohibited and a statement of what penalties may be imposed on anyone who commits those actions. The statement of prohibited behavior must be very clear so that any reasonably intelligent person will know what is prohibited. The actions that, taken together, constitute a crime are known as the *elements* of the crime.

In addition, in order to convict someone for a violation of the law, it is necessary to convince a judge or jury that the accused—and no one else—committed the prohibited actions voluntarily or, in some instances, acted with reckless disregard for the probable consequences of certain behavior. Thus, the voluntary or reckless nature of the criminal's behavior is an additional element of the crime.

In short, the investigator must "prove the elements" of the crime. Sufficient evidence must be obtained, and the investigator must have enough understanding of the evidence to prove that the elements of the crime actually existed and that the accused person was the perpetrator of the crime.[18] Fortunately, the investigator will rarely have to do all this alone. Except in the very smallest agencies in remote rural areas, the police investigator will be able to call on a number of other people for assistance.

## RESPONSIBILITIES OF THE TECHNICAL SPECIALISTS

Two main types of technical specialists are especially helpful to investigators: the technicians and scientists in the criminalistics laboratory and the personnel who maintain all kinds of criminal and identification records. There are others as well, whom we will encounter as we go along.

*Criminalistics,* a term that we have already used several times, is the science of discovering and evaluating evidence related to a crime (and a *criminalist* is a person who practices the science of criminalistics). The definition is unwieldy and rather vague, because there are no precise limits to this field of endeavor; on the contrary, the horizons of criminalistics are constantly expanding.

Another way of looking at criminalistics is to define it as the combination of many different scientific disciplines and techniques for the purpose of investigating crimes. Almost all of the techniques used in criminalistics have been borrowed or adapted from other branches of science. For example, chemical analysis and mass spectroscopy are techniques that are used not only in the crime lab, but also in the geology lab, the industrial chemical lab, and even the astronomical observatory. Fingerprint analysis and firearms examination both owe their existence to the development of microscopic study techniques used in the biological sciences and in structural physics.

The point is that all kinds of scientific techniques and processes can be applied to the specific purpose of identifying and evaluating evidence that might be connected to a crime. Chemical analysis, spectroscopy and spectrography, impression casting, fingerprint examination (or *dactyloscopy*), photography, comparative microscopy, and analysis of physiological fluids are some of the more common procedures used in the criminalistics laboratory. However, other techniques can also be used to solve a crime, and it is often up to the criminalist to invent or discover a technique suitable to the investigative problem.

As a general rule, the criminalist should be guided mainly by the needs of the principal investigator. The investigator, by the same token, must make those needs known to the criminalist. It is not enough for the investigator to send a pile of evidence bags and envelopes down to the lab with a note that says, "Found these at scene of murder—see what you can make of them." The investigator should tell the criminalist the circumstances of the crime and whatever else is known about the criminal event. Certainly the criminalist needs to know, as precisely as possible, where the evidence was found, and under what circumstances. Photographs showing the location of the evidence before its removal should be provided to the criminalist. Finally, the investigator should indicate what kind of information is needed from the criminalist. Unless the investigator asks the right questions, the criminalist may waste a great deal of time hunting for the wrong answers. Some kinds of evidence may be subjected to several different types of analysis depending on exactly what information is required, and sometimes performing one type of analysis can destroy the evidence so that another type of analysis cannot be performed.[19]

The criminalist, however, must be careful not to be trapped into accepting all of the investigator's assumptions and judgments too quickly. There is always the possibility that the evidence will tell a completely different story about what happened and who committed the crime. The criminalist's job is to learn as much as possible from the available evidence—not to prove the investigator's pet theory. The criminalist should be guided, not stampeded, by the investigator.

The role of the records and identification (R&I) personnel is different from that of the crime lab, but no less important. Most police agencies accumulate enormous stores of records. The productive use of these records has solved many crimes; in one case, for example, a parking ticket was used to track down the so-called Son of Sam murderer in New York City.

The sheer volume of police records, however, makes their use extremely difficult. In television dramas, if a detective finds a fingerprint at the scene of a crime, the case is solved; all that remains is to match the print to the right criminal in the department's files. In reality, that almost never happens. If you have in hand a fingerprint that you suspect came from the perpetrator of a crime but you have no idea who that person might be, you might have to compare it with many thousands of other prints before you could find a match. When you consider that every human being has ten distinctly different fingerprints, you can see that the task of matching an unknown print to a duplicate—which might or might not be somewhere in the files—is an overwhelming task.

Of course, if you have any idea of who the criminal might be, that simplifies the task considerably. This is where the R&I specialists come in. By knowing how their files are organized and how to find information in the files, they may save you endless hours of fruitless searching. This is true whether the subject is fingerprints, crime reports, mug shots, M.O. (modus operandi) files, or anything else.

Again, like the personnel in the criminalistics lab, the R&I staff must depend on the principal investigator for guidance. Only the investigator knows what to look for; the R&I personnel tell the investigator how to look, and sometimes they do the looking.

## SPECIAL INVESTIGATIVE UNITS

Many police departments, especially the larger ones, have investigative sections in addition to the main detective bureau. These special units usually are devoted to a particular type of crime problem that requires unusual expertise or that, by its nature, demands some kind of special handling. Typical special investigative units are organized crime units, narcotics units, juvenile crime units (which are sometimes combined with crime prevention units), and consumer protection and business crime units.

Since these special units are formed to meet unique local needs, no one pattern can be called typical for all of them. However, there are some common characteristics and some fairly representative examples that will provide an idea of what you might find in a given agency.

### ORGANIZED CRIME AND NARCOTICS UNITS

Organized crime units and narcotics units are often very similar; the major difference lies in the range of their interests. Both depend heavily on "deep undercover" work: police officers attempt to infiltrate the underworld circles in which crimes are planned and conducted, gather as much information as possible, and make possible the arrest of the key figures who are responsible for the most serious abuses. The arrests themselves are often made by regular detectives as a result of information passed along to them by the undercover officers.

In many departments, the OCU and the narcotics unit report directly to the Chief of Police or to another high-ranking official, rather than to the detective bureau. Indeed, in some large agencies, the personnel of these units are not well known even to their fellow police officers. Deep undercover agents work and sometimes live in a world that is far removed from ordinary reality, a world in which suspiciousness that borders on paranoia is a normal reaction. It can be a world of great danger.Unfortunately, the practice of extreme secrecy can itself be dangerous. There have been instances in which undercover agents and regular police officers have unwittingly engaged in gun battles with one another.

Even though the agents in these units typically have little direct contact with the regular investigators, the special agents must be able to pass information to the regular officers and vice versa. The communication system must be carefully worked out in advance to ensure that the information is properly handled.

### JUVENILE CRIME UNITS

Juvenile crime units work at nearly the opposite end of the crime spectrum: their concern is to identify potential criminals before their careers in crime are fully launched. Juvenile crime officers routinely handle such matters as truancy, vandalism, juvenile mischief, and misdemeanors involving juveniles. They are often involved in working with juvenile gangs, youth programs, schools, and social workers. Sometimes the officers find it necessary to intercede directly in family crises; in those cases, close cooperation between the officer, the social worker or other counselor, and the school may help to keep a young person from drifting away from the family and into a life of crime.

Sometimes juvenile crime officers receive information that has great value to the detective bureau. Even though a juvenile is not directly involved in a crime, he or she might know someone who is engaged in criminal activity and might pass that information along to the officer. Similarly, the detectives may learn of a young person who is involved in criminal activity of some sort; by giving that information to the officers, the detective may avoid having to deal with that youth later on.

### CONSUMER PROTECTION AND BUSINESS CRIME UNITS

Until very recently, police agencies avoided having anything to do with consumer protection or most business crimes; such matters were settled in the civil courts. However, new laws have been passed in many states and at the federal level; the laws have defined and redefined certain kinds of activity as crimes rather than as civil matters. The police have been forced to deal with these problems even though they can be extremely complicated and delicate.

Most consumer protection problems involve allegations of fraud: the consumer bought something that turned out to be unsatisfactory. It is not always easy to tell whether the merchant deliberately cheated the consumer or whether the consumer simply failed to make an intelligent purchase. Sometimes the answer is obvious, as when the goods are blatantly shoddy or the service is clearly dishonest. Unfortunately, that is not always the case. Consumer protection investigators may have to do a good deal of detective work just to find out whether a crime has been committed or whether it is all

*Sometimes an investigation is necessary in order to determine whether any crime has been committed, or whether it is just a misunderstanding between the merchant and the customer.*

a misunderstanding. Quite often, the best solution is to try to get the two parties to settle the matter between themselves.

Business crimes are another type of problem. Fraud is only one type of business crime; others include embezzlement, conversion (improperly using property that has been entrusted to one's care), violations of securities trading laws, espionage and sabotage, invasion and piracy, and computer crimes.

Obviously, such crimes are very different in nature from the usual burglary or street mugging. To make matters worse, business executives often prefer not to let the police know when they have been victimized, partly because of the damage to their egos and, perhaps, their business reputations, and partly out of fear that public disclosure will make them vulnerable to similar attacks in the future. When the police are called on to deal with a business crime, the investigator must display a level of skill and knowledge that is sometimes far greater than is necessary for ordinary police work.

These are not the only types of special investigative units that can be formed. When an unusual need exists in a community, or when an opportunity exists for the police to develop a unique service, the formation of a special unit may be justified. When that occurs, the most serious problem for the regular investigators, and for the agency as a whole, will be to ensure that there is adequate provision for communication and coordination between the special unit and the regular detectives.

## REFERENCES

1. George D. Eastman, ed., *Municipal Police Administration* (Washington, D.C.: International City Management Association, 1969), p. 25.

2. Eastman, pp. 18–19.

3. Samuel Walker, *A Critical History of Police Reform* (Lexington, Mass.: Lexington Books, D. C. Heath, 1977), p. 169.

4. Walker, p. ix.

5. *Criminal Investigation* (Gaithersburg, Md.: International Association of Chiefs of Police, 1971), p. 17.

6. Eastman, pp. 136–137.

7. David J. Bordua and Albert J. Reiss, Jr., "Environment and Organization: A Perspective on the Police," in *The Police: Six Sociological Essays*, ed. David J. Bordua (New York: John Wiley, 1967), p. 37.

8. Eastman, pp. 3–4.

9. V. A. Leonard, *The Police Enterprise* (Springfield, Ill.: Charles C Thomas, 1971), p. 16.

10. Eastman, p. 28.

11. Eastman, pp. 33–37.

12. V. A. Leonard, *The Police Detective Function* (Springfield, Ill.: Charles C Thomas, 1970), p. 5.

13. Eastman, pp. 19–22.

14. Eastman, p. 28.

15. This description and the information in the Investigator's Notes 2 were obtained in a personal interview with Chief Leonard Hancock, Temple, Texas, Police Department, October 10, 1977.

16. Leonard, *The Police Detective Function*, p. 8.

17. Richard H. Fox and Carl L. Cunningham, *Crime Scene Search and Physical Evidence Handbook* (Washington, D.C.: U.S. Department of Justice, National Institute of Law Enforcement and Criminal Justice, 1973), pp. 12–13.

18. Paul B. Weston and Kenneth M. Wells, *Criminal Evidence for Police* (Englewood Cliffs, N.J.: Prentice-Hall, 1971), p. 1.

19. *Criminal Investigation*, p. 9.

## REVIEW OF THE EVIDENCE

1. The person who is responsible for all aspects of a criminal investigation is
   a. the criminalist.
   b. the patrol officer.
   c. the complainant.
   d. the principal investigator.
   e. none of the above.
2. True or false: Only an officer of detective rank or higher can be considered a supervising investigator.
3. Which of the following factors should influence a decision about the allocation of resources to a particular investigation?
   a. the seriousness of the crime
   b. editorials criticizing the police agency
   c. the likelihood that the crime will be repeated
   d. the social status or prominence of the victim
   e. the likelihood that the case can be solved
   f. all of the above
   g. none of the above
4. True or false: Public pressure on a law enforcement agency always involves a demand for stricter enforcement and more efficient investigation of crimes.
5. Which kind of agency usually has no generalist branches in its administrative organization?
   a. small general-jurisdiction agencies
   b. limited-jurisdiction agencies
   c. large general-jurisdiction agencies
   d. co-agencies
   e. medium-sized general-jurisdiction agencies
6. Of the 13,000 police agencies in the United States, how many have fewer than 200 employees?
   a. 250
   b. all of them
   c. 10,000
   d. 6,500
   e. 12,750
7. The major advantage of the traditional pattern of administrative organization is that
   a. investigators can become very proficient within their area of specialization.
   b. it is more efficient than other systems.
   c. senior officers have more opportunities for advanced training and education.
   d. new officers do not require special education, since it is the most familiar system.
   e. it ensures an even distribution of the workload.
8. True or false: The police must respond to complaints and reports of crime in the order in which they are received so that there can be no accusation of favoritism.

9. The actions that, taken together, constitute a crime are known as
   a. the law.
   b. the elements of the crime.
   c. the perpetrator of the crime.
   d. the consequences of the crime.
   e. evidence.
10. Indicate which of the following tasks should be performed by the patrol officer (P) on arriving at the scene of a reported crime; by the principal investigator (I); by the criminalistics technician (C); by the records and identification technician (R); and by an officer in a special investigative unit (S).
   a. classify a fingerprint according to a standardized system based on common characteristics
   b. decide which of several techniques should be used to analyze or examine an item of evidence
   c. attempt to infiltrate groups that are suspected of criminal activities
   d. make a tentative assessment of the nature of a crime
   e. decide what kinds of evidence should be sought

## TOPICS FOR INVESTIGATION

1. Why is it so important for one individual to assume the responsibility of being the principal investigator? Could this responsibility be shared by two or more officers so that they could do twice as much work in a given period of time?
2. According to the text, there is a built-in conservatism in many police agencies that reinforces the traditional system of organization; on the other hand, agencies that try to follow a more innovative course may be subject to fads and fashions of management theory and police science. Which of these forces—traditionalism or faddishness—might be more destructive of a police agency in the long run?
3. Do you agree with our definitions of the "legitimate" and the "illegitimate" factors that can influence the allocation of resources for an investigation? Should the likelihood that an investigation will succeed determine the amount of effort that goes into the investigation? Should the police, as public servants paid by taxes, pay attention to the public's concern about crime? What other factors, legitimate or otherwise, should influence these decisions?
4. In what ways are law enforcement agencies dependent on public support? What can an agency do to reduce that dependency and, thus, protect itself from unreasonable public pressures?
5. Do you agree with Chief Hancock's statement, "Most departments should do away with detective divisions"?

# Unit II
## THE INITIAL
## INVESTIGATION

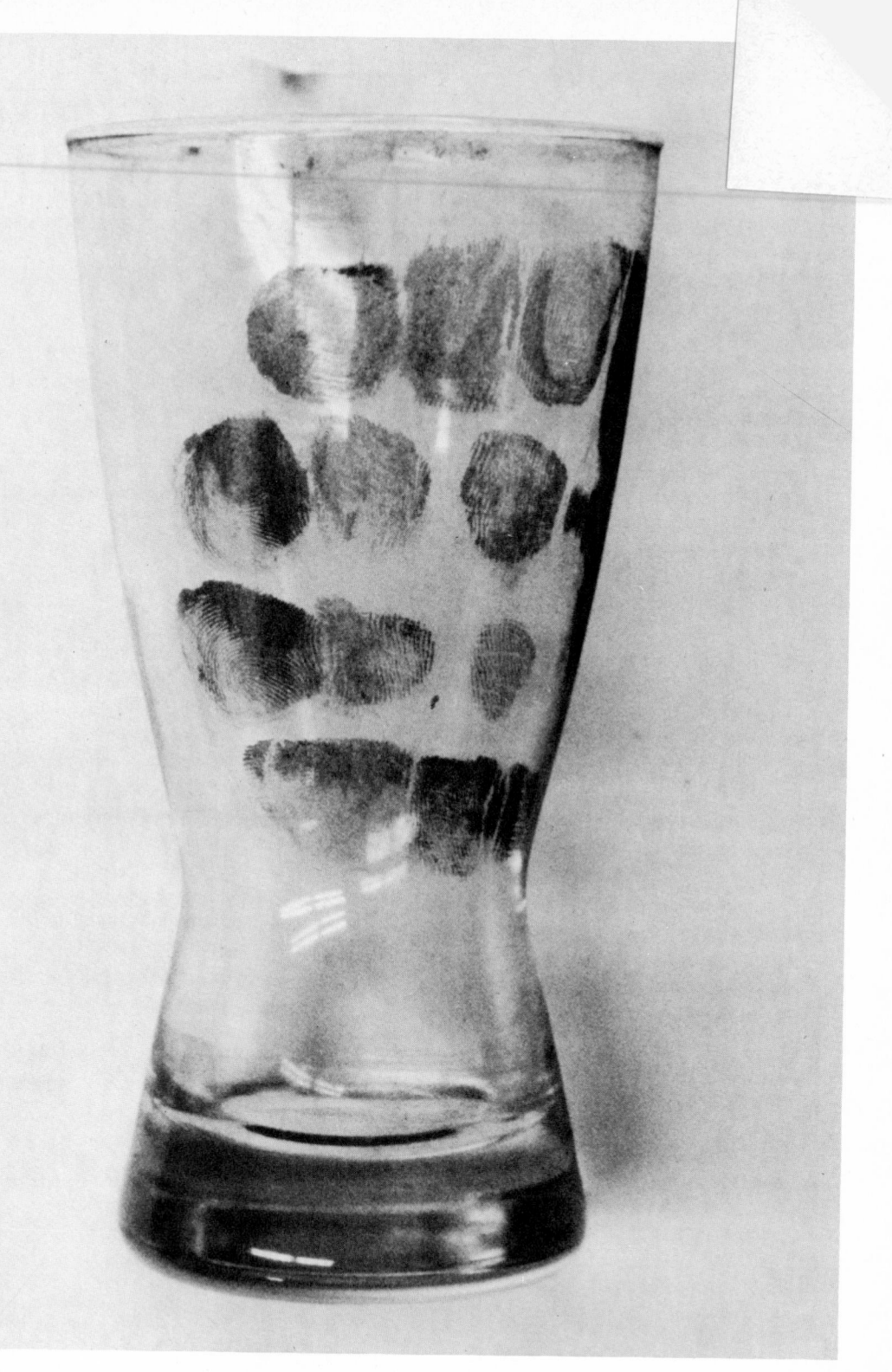

# CHAPTER 3

## WHEN A CRIME IS REPORTED

---

STUDY CLUES

1. The scene of a crime must be sealed in order to
    a. preserve the integrity of evidence.
    b. prevent witnesses and bystanders from leaving.
    c. protect the constitutional rights of suspects.
    d. trap the criminal at the scene.
    e. establish the nature of the crime.
2. True or false: No one has a right to keep a police officer from entering the scene of a reported crime.
3. When a crime is reported, the switchboard operator must obtain what essential information?
    a. the identity of the perpetrator
    b. the names of all known witnesses
    c. the location of the crime
    d. the general nature of the crime
    e. a description of any property that was stolen
4. True or false: An officer responding to a report of a crime should always use the siren and flashing lights on the patrol car to get there as quickly as possible.
5. A standard object is one that
    a. has been found at the scene of a crime.
    b. is identical in every way to an unknown object.
    c. is very common and unimportant.
    d. comes from a known source and, therefore, can be compared with an unknown object.
    e. has been supplied to the police by its manufacturer for purposes of comparison and identification.
6. True or false: A patrol officer should rely on other people to summon an ambulance or other assistance, rather than take the time from more important duties at a crime scene.

A CRIMINAL INVESTIGATION BEGINS when the crime is discovered by or reported to the police. In fact, most major crimes are not discovered by the police and never would be investigated if someone did not report them. Many authorities believe that only a small percentage of property crimes (burglaries and thefts) are ever reported.[1]

Very few serious crimes are reported while the event is occurring. The exceptions are assaults and armed robberies, which are sometimes reported by witnesses who happen to observe the crime in progress, and burglaries of buildings that are protected by alarm systems.

Typically, major crimes are reported by the victim after the criminal has left the scene—sometimes several hours or even several days after the event.

*Whoever takes the initial report of a crime must obtain as much information as possible*

## TAKING THE INITIAL REPORT

Whoever takes the initial report must try to get as much information as possible. Because most crimes are reported by telephone to the police department's emergency switchboard, the responsibility for obtaining the initial information usually rests on the switchboard operator or dispatcher.

The operator or dispatcher often cannot obtain as much information as the police would like to have. Sometimes the victim is too rattled to be coherent or does not yet know exactly what has happened. Sometimes the caller is not the victim, but is instead a witness or other concerned citizen who wants to make the crime known but does not want to be involved any further.

The essential information that the switchboard operator or dispatcher must obtain includes:

• the general nature of the crime: whether it is an assault, a burglary, a murder, or whatever;

• the location at which the crime occurred: a street address, if possible, or at least a location specific enough that an officer can go directly to the scene without wasting time in trying to find it.

In addition, the person who receives the initial report should try to obtain the following information:

• What is the identity of the caller? Is it the victim or a witness? What is the caller's name, telephone number, and relationship to the crime?

• What is the basis for the report? Did the caller witness the crime directly or discover it after the fact? If the caller is not the victim, where is the victim now?

• Was the perpetrator or a likely suspect observed at the scene? If so, does the caller know the identity of the perpetrator? Can the caller describe the suspect in detail? Where did the perpetrator go after the event? Can the caller describe the getaway car, if any?

All this information must then be relayed to a police officer, usually by police radio. Depending on the size of the agency and the operating procedures it has adopted, serious crimes may be brought to the attention of the detectives by the switchboard operator or dispatcher; sometimes other senior officers also must be notified. In most cases, the usual procedure is to send a patrol officer to investigate the reported crime.

Once in a while, someone will approach a police officer on the street and report a crime. The officer should obtain the same kind of information that the switchboard operator would try to get, even if the crime is reportedly still in progress. It is a serious and possibly fatal mistake for a police officer to rush off to the scene of a reported crime without having as much information as is available.

## ARRIVING AT THE SCENE

In spite of the emphasis we have put on getting plenty of information during the initial report, the patrol officer or detective who responds to it must guard against relying excessively on that information. The person who reported the crime might be mistaken or might be willfully lying.

ANSWERS TO STUDY CLUES
1. a    2. False    3. c and d    4. False
5. d    6. False

First of all, there is always a possibility that the crime is still in progress. The responding police officer must be prepared for this possibility and must be ready to defend against being attacked on arriving at the scene. No police officer should ever approach the scene of a reported serious crime without having backup assistance immediately available.

Even if the criminal event has ended, the perpetrator might still be at the scene. The criminal may not have had time to flee and may be trapped by the police officer. Sometimes the criminal will hide at the scene or nearby or will mingle with the witnesses and other bystanders. Once in a great while the criminal will report a crime as a means of averting suspicion. All these possibilities must be considered while approaching the scene of a crime.

Once the officer is satisfied that the criminal is not present and that there is no immediate danger, the investigation of the crime proceeds. Immediately on arriving at the scene, the officer should make a deliberate visual sweep of the entire area. This may take only a few seconds, but it should always be done. The officer should especially notice three things: the general arrangement of the scene, the people present, and the relative positions of all the objects at the scene.[3]

Because every crime scene is unique, it is hard to generalize about what to look for. In scanning the general arrangement of the scene, the officer should try to get an overall impression that will be helpful in understanding what took place. If the scene is outdoors, the officer should notice the entrances to and exits from the area: How does a person get here? Where does a person go when leaving here? The officer also should notice what buildings or other physical structures are nearby: could the criminal have come out of that doorway, or fled down those cellar steps?

*The Initial Investigation*

# HOW TO APPROACH
# A CRIME SCENE

## USING FLASHING LIGHTS
## AND SIREN

The flashing lights and siren on a police vehicle serve one purpose: to assist the officer in getting through traffic quickly and safely. These devices can be badly misused, so most agencies have specific policies about them. Generally those policies require the officer to limit their use as much as possible.[2]

A siren should be turned off as far as practical from the reported scene of a crime, never less than two or three blocks away, unless there continues to be heavy traffic close to the scene. It is better to be delayed a few seconds by traffic than to advertise one's arrival when there is a possibility that the criminal is still at or near the scene.

At night, the same advice applies to flashing lights. In the dark, flashing lights are noticeable from a much greater distance than during daylight hours.

## APPROACHING A DOORWAY

No officer should *ever* walk right up to the door at a reported crime scene. The criminal may be behind the door, waiting to attack the first person who arrives.

The wrong way to approach a door is shown in Figure 3.1. The officer walks up to the center of the door and knocks. If someone inside intends to attack the officer, usually the assailant will fire a weapon or hurl an object through the center of the door.

The right way is shown in Figure 3.2.

FIGURE 3.1
THE WRONG WAY TO
APPROACH A DOOR

FIGURE 3.2
THE RIGHT WAY TO
APPROACH A DOOR

The officer approaches at an angle, staying as far as possible from the center of the door, and stands to one side of the doorway itself. It helps to stand sideways to the door, too, because this somewhat reduces the target area of the body.

An officer approaching alone should stand on the lock side of the door, rather than the hinge side. As Figure 3.3 shows, by standing on the hinge side, the officer becomes visible to anyone inside as soon as the door is opened slightly. By standing on the lock side, the officer has a chance to evaluate the situation after the door has been opened; the person inside is forced to come out toward the officer.

When two officers approach a door together, one should stand on either side. If there is any available shelter, it is better for the officer on the hinge side to stand away from the building about 3 to 4 meters (10 to 12 feet); this gives the officer a better view into the room as the door is opened. However, if there is

FIGURE 3.3
STANDING ON THE PROPER SIDE OF A DOOR

**A. Standing on the Hinge Side**

**B. Standing on the Lock Side**

*The Initial Investigation*

no shelter, the officer on the hinge side should remain flattened against the building until the door begins to open. As the door opens and the officer is able to see into the room, it will be easier to deal with any weapon that is thrust out through the doorway. The partner, out of sight of the criminal, also should be prepared to help (Figure 3.4).

If the crime took place in a business establishment, what kind of business is it? Again, where are the entrances and exits, and where do they lead? What businesses are next door? Is the main area a large, open space, or is it cluttered and crowded with display counters and merchandise?

Similar questions must be asked in a residence: What rooms are immediately adjacent to the room in which the crime took place?

FIGURE 3.4
TWO OFFICERS APPROACHING A DOOR

Notice that the officer on the hinge side has taken advantage of the shelter provided by the hedge.

*When a Crime is Reported*

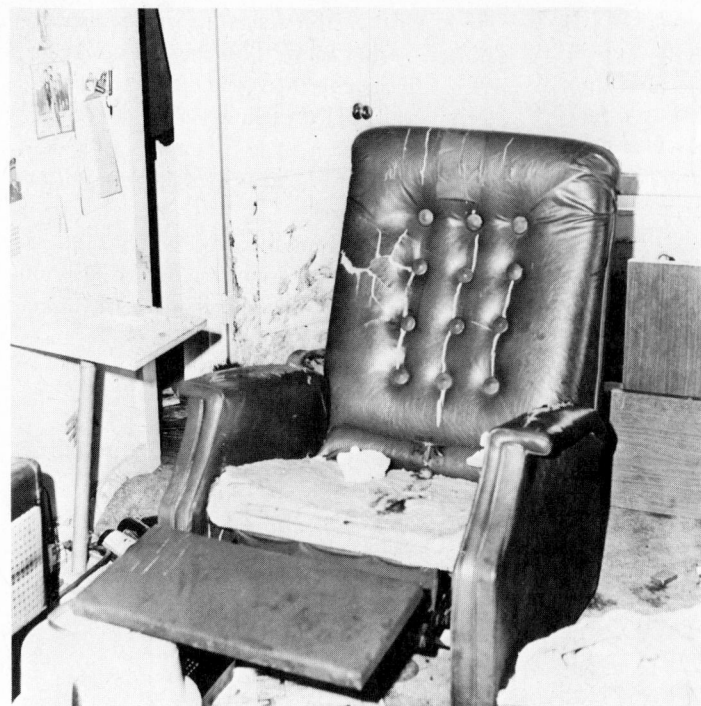

*Upon arriving at the crime scene, the officer first must make a "visual sweep" of the area. What information could be obtained from this scene, and what questions should be raised? (Photo courtesy of Temple, Texas, Police Department)*

Are windows and doors open or closed, locked or unlocked? Who lives next door? Is the scene of the crime a living room, a kitchen, a bedroom?

Not all of these questions can be answered in the few seconds that a visual sweep requires. In fact, one purpose of the sweep is to raise these questions, which the officer must answer later.

A second objective of the visual sweep is to notice all the persons present at the scene. Eventually the police officer must identify each person and determine what relationship, if any, the person had to the crime.

The third purpose of the visual sweep is to notice all the physical objects at the scene and their relative positions. In a crowded or cluttered scene, this may prove to be a difficult challenge. The officer should especially con- centrate on anything that seems to be out of place: a piece of furniture, or even a small object such as an ashtray or vase, that does not look as if belongs in its present location. Such objects may have been moved during the course of the crime and thus might have some value as evidence. Some other objects deserve special attention, too: Are lamps and light fixtures turned on or off? Is a radio, tele- vision, or phonograph turned on? Are win- dow shades or drapes open or closed? The answers to such questions may prove helpful in understanding how the crime occurred.

All this information should be accumulated during a very brief, but thorough and con- scientious, scan of the scene. No part of the scene should be overlooked even though the whole process may take no more than two or three seconds.

At this time it is extremely important that nothing be touched or moved unless it hinders the officer's access to the scene or poses some immediate danger to the officer, victim, or bystanders. The positions of things may be important clues in themselves and should not be altered. The officer may have to restrain the natural impulse to rearrange things and the well-meaning efforts of witnesses and bystanders to straighten up any mess or clutter.[4]

## PROTECTING PEOPLE AND PROPERTY

As soon as the police officer's initial assessment of the crime scene is completed, attention can be given to protecting the people at the scene while simultaneously protecting the scene itself from tampering or contamination.[5]

In any violent crime the first priority must be to ensure that the victim receives all necessary medical aid.[6] Sometimes this means that the police officer must render first aid, although this should be avoided, when possible, because the officer has other things to do. The officer should quickly examine the victim, determine the apparent extent and type of injuries, then summon an ambulance either by telephone or police radio. This should be done even if someone else has already called for an ambulance. The confirming call may avoid time-wasting confusion, and it creates an immediate record of the fact that, in the officer's judgment, medical help was required. If the victim's injuries are life threatening, it may not be possible to wait for an ambulance; the police officer must either begin first-aid procedures or find someone at the scene who is competent to do so.

If the victim, witnesses, or others are in jeopardy because of some condition of the crime scene—for example, a fire, a leaking gas line, a live electrical wire, or a bomb threat—either the dangerous condition or the people or both must be removed. Additional assistance may be needed; in this case the officer should use the telephone or radio to ask for help from the fire department, bomb squad, electrical company, or other appropriate agency. Even if such help has already been requested by someone else, it is a good idea to make a confirmation call, because this creates a record of the officer's assessment of the situation at the crime scene.

Everything that has been described so far can and must be done within the first two or three minutes after the officer's arrival on the scene. Once these duties have been taken care of, the officer is ready to proceed with the investigation. The next step is to protect the evidence.

## PROTECTING THE SCENE AND EVIDENCE

The scene of a crime, whether major or minor, seems to have an irresistible appeal. Everyone wants to know what happened, and sometimes it seems that everyone wants to be a detective. This applies not only to the victim and witnesses, who have a legitimate reason for being present, but equally to uninvolved bystanders and passers-by. A violent crime often attracts a crowd from blocks around. Even police officers and other officials, who ought to know better, sometimes invade, disrupt, and contaminate a crime scene without meaning to do so.

The only solution is to adopt an absolutely inflexible rule: get everyone out and keep them out. Victims, witnesses, and all others should be removed from the crime scene as quickly as possible. At an outdoor scene, move them away from the actual location of the crime's occurrence; at an indoor scene, take them outdoors or to an adjacent room, preferably one that was not used by the criminal for entry or exit.[7]

In the process of moving everyone away from the scene, the officer should obtain quick identifications; each person's name and the reason for being at the scene should be sufficient. Uninvolved bystanders should be screened and, if they have no legitimate business at the scene, they should be sent on their way.

Is there a danger of losing a valuable witness, or even the criminal or an accomplice, by sending people away too quickly? Yes, there is. However, there are a few ways that an officer can quickly size up the bystanders and decide which ones should be sent away. One method is to use reverse psychology. Those individuals who are most in the way, who seem most determined to tramp through the scene, are the *least* likely to have been involved in the crime. However, those who hang back and calmly watch the proceedings or who seem to be making an effort to be inconspicuous should be regarded with some suspicion. The officer should request identification and should make a note of the person's name, address, and telephone number before sending the person away. If there is any serious reason to think that the person might be involved in the crime or if the person continues to behave in a suspicious manner, he or she should be asked to remain at the scene.

As soon as everyone has been removed from the immediate scene of the crime, the scene should be sealed. At an outdoor scene, this may require setting up ropes or other barriers, or perhaps using cooperative bystanders to establish a barrier line. An indoor scene usually can be sealed off simply by closing a door or by stationing another police officer or cooperative bystander at the entrance. Regardless of the method used, the scene should remain sealed until the officer is ready to begin the search for evidence or until a detective arrives and relieves the patrol officer of responsibility.[8]

## A CONSTITUTIONAL PROBLEM

At this point we must back up a bit and discuss a rather rare, but potentially serious, problem.

When a police officer first arrives at the scene of a reported crime, there must be no question whatsoever of the officer's identity and purpose. Even though wearing a full uniform, police badge, and name tag, the officer must announce that he or she is a police officer before entering any residence or any nonpublic area of a place of business. This is doubly important for a plainclothes officer.

A law enforcement officer may not enter a home or the private sections of a business establishment without the express permission of the owner or the legal custodian of the property, unless the officer has a valid search warrant or has actually observed a crime in progress and has reason to believe that the perpetrator will flee or that someone's life or property may be in danger.[9]

We will discuss this matter in greater detail in Chapter 17. Our point here is that a police officer responding to a call may not barge into someone's home or place of business. Usually there is no problem; the victim or other persons present at the scene will gladly admit the officer. However, there may be a problem if the perpetrator of the crime or an accomplice is still at the scene or if the victim is engaged in some kind of criminal activity that the police might discover.

If one encounters such a situation, there is

nothing to be done except to post an officer near every entrance to the building to observe anyone who leaves or enters. Meanwhile, the officer in charge should call (by telephone or radio) and report the situation to a superior officer or detective, who may then take the necessary steps to obtain a search warrant.

Until a warrant is obtained, the police officers may not enter the premises unless they have some reason to believe that a crime is being committed. Reasons for such a belief might include the following: the officer sees an apparent armed robbery taking place inside a grocery store; the officer hears a person screaming for help; there is evidence of a fire or other physical danger; someone who appears to be responsible and reliable informs the officer that a crime is taking place. In any of these cases, forced entry might be justifiable; however, there is a chance that if the officer forces entry, any resulting arrest will be invalidated in court.

These restrictions do not apply in a public place. As a general rule, any place that is outdoors, that is open to public view, and to which the public ordinarily has access is defined as a *public place* even if the property is owned by some private individual. A vacant lot could be considered a public place in this sense. Any place that is owned by the public through some agency of the government is a public place, whether indoors or outdoors; however, employees of a public agency may have some individual rights of privacy within an area such as their own offices.[10] Whether some locations are considered public or private may be difficult to determine. A vacant lot surrounded by a high, locked fence probably would not be considered a public place. A farmer's field, separated from the highway by nothing more than a barbed wire fence and a row of trees, might or might not be considered public by a court.

Business establishments pose another problem. Usually, those areas within a commercial building where public business is transacted are considered public places; examples include the sales area of a store, the lobby of an office building, the dining room of a restaurant, and so on. However, a private office, a storeroom, the kitchen of a restaurant, and other parts of a business to which the public ordinarily does not have access probably would not be considered public places by a court. Furthermore, an area regarded as a public place during the day might be considered private property at night, when locked up.

We raise the issue at this point for a simple reason: any evidence that is improperly or illegally obtained will not be admissible in court. This rule can have far-reaching consequences.

For example, suppose the police receive a report that a man is beating his wife. A patrol officer is dispatched to the address; a man answers the door and refuses to admit the officer. Fearing that the woman might have been battered into unconsciousness or even beaten to death, the officer pushes into the house. Once inside, the officer does not find a woman who has been beaten, but on the coffee table in the living room there is a package of white powder which may be heroin. At this point the officer has no legal grounds to arrest the man. If an arrest is made, the case will be thrown out of court because the only evidence—the package of suspected heroin— was obtained illegally. The officer had no legal right to enter the house.

A police officer who arrives at the scene of a reported crime must always act in such a way that the constitutional rights of the victim, the witnesses, and the presumed criminal are protected. Otherwise, solving the crime will be merely an exercise in futility.

## THE INTEGRITY
## OF EVIDENCE

Once the police officer has entered the scene of a crime legally, every effort must be made to preserve the integrity of all possible evidence. That is one of the two main reasons for sealing the scene; the other is to prevent evidence from being removed or destroyed, either deliberately or accidentally.[11]

In order for physical evidence to be admitted in a trial, someone must be able to testify about where the evidence was found, in what condition it was, and what relationship it had to the criminal event. Furthermore, someone must be able to testify that there is no possibility that the evidence has been altered or tampered with in any way from the moment of its discovery until its presentation in court.[12] The rationale for this requirement is obvious. Evidence has no value in determining the guilt or innocence of the accused if there is any possibility, however remote, that someone has tampered with it.

A related problem, and another reason for sealing the crime scene as quickly as possible, is the contamination of the scene with *nonevidence*, or false evidence. Much of the valuable physical evidence at a crime scene is in the form of fingerprints, footprints, tool marks, clothing threads, and physiological fluids. A good deal of this trace evidence is microscopic, and therefore it is difficult to find and identify. If the scene of a crime is preserved intact from the time at which the crime was committed until the search for trace evidence begins, it is reasonable for the investigator to assume that all of the traces found at the scene are actually related to the crime in some way. However, if witnesses, bystanders, and others trample through the scene, they will leave behind their own traces. The task of the investigators and criminalists will be enormously compounded, because they will have to sort out all of that nonevidence to distinguish it from genuine evidence.

Imagine, for example, how frustrating it would be to spend several hours matching the only fingerprint found on a weapon just to discover that it belonged to a careless police officer.

## IDENTIFICATION
## OF EVIDENCE

Every single physical object in and around the scene of a crime represents potential evidence. The problem lies not in finding evidence, but in understanding and using it.[13]

People cannot walk through a room without leaving behind abundant proof of their presence. Soil, ashes, and sometimes liquid matter are transferred between their shoes and the floor or carpet. Threads, soil, hair, and debris of various kinds are transferred between their clothes and anything that people touch or brush against. Perspiration, saliva, and chemical traces from cosmetics such as perfume, aftershave lotion, or hair preparations may be left behind on upholstered furniture.[14]

Every action that a criminal commits leaves behind some evidence. If a tool is used to pry open a window or door, there are the marks made by the tool. If the victim is struck by any sort of weapon—a blunt instrument, a knife, a bullet, or even a fist—there will be characteristic marks that might be used to trace the weapon. Poisonous liquids, powders, and gases, as well as narcotic substances, leave behind telltale chemical residues.

Occasionally a criminal leaves behind personal possessions, such as clothing or other personal effects. Sometimes, if the crime was committed impulsively, the criminal leaves behind fingerprints. Even attempts to avoid leaving behind such obvious evidence fail:

gloves worn to avoid leaving fingerprints may instead leave threads or an impression of the thread pattern of the tips of the fingers.

The investigator's problem is twofold: First, it is necessary to determine the meaning of each item of evidence, including all of the minute, often microscopic traces that we have just mentioned. What does each bit of evidence have to do with the crime? Second, the investigator must identify the evidence, determining its relationship to the specific individual—criminal or victim or witness—who left it at the scene.[15]

The concept of *identity* is a subtle one (Figure 3.5); too often the word is used incorrectly or too loosely. Two objects can be said to be identical when they are alike in every characteristic. In the strictest sense, no two objects are ever identical; there are some characteristics, however minor, by which they could be distinguished. Fortunately, the police are not usually concerned with a strict definition of identity. The police want answers to questions like these: Did this chip of glass come from that broken window? Did this clump of soil come from that shoe? Did this thread come from that sweater? Whose fingerprint is this?[16]

For our purposes, then, we can say that an object has been *identified* when it can be shown that it has a sufficient number of characteristics that are like a known object, or *standard*. The key concept is that an unknown object is compared with a known object. The police find that the unknown object and the known object have a certain number of characteristics that are alike. Based on reason and experience, they are able to say that it would be extremely unlikely for the unknown object to be identified with any other object. Thus, they conclude that the unknown object is identified with the known object.

For example, a fingerprint (the unknown)

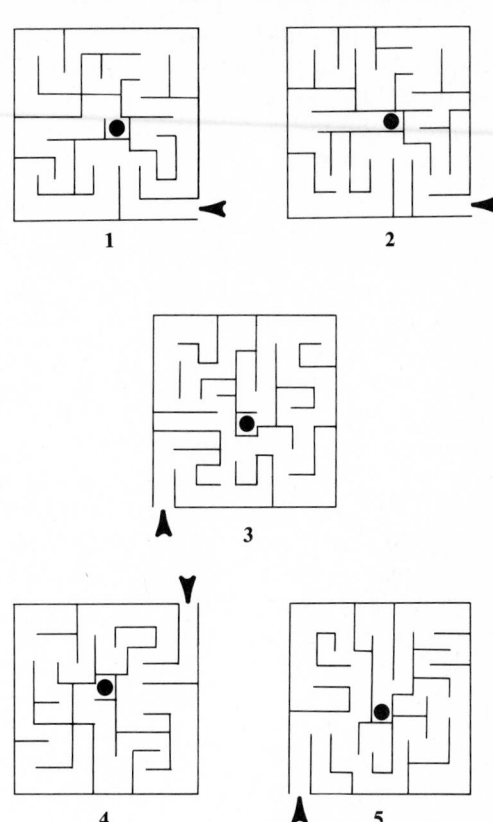

FIGURE 3.5
THE CONCEPT OF IDENTITY

Two of these five mazes are **identical**.
Which two?

found at the scene of a crime is compared with a printed record of many other fingerprints (the standards). The unknown fingerprint matches a number of characteristics of the recorded fingerprint that was taken several years ago from an accused burglar. The greater the number of characteristics that are found to be similar between the unknown print and the standard one, the more confident the police can be that the unknown fingerprint comes, in fact, from the previously accused burglar. The police know from reason and past experience that no two people ever have identical fingerprints; in fact, no two fingers on the same hand have identical pore and ridge patterns.

Notice, also, that in this example the absence of any contrary evidence is most important. If the unknown print contained characteristics that were substantially unlike the standard print, the police would be forced to conclude that the two could not have come from the same person—no matter how much they might be alike.

Here is another example: A chip of glass is found in the shoe of a suspected burglar. The police know that a window was broken by a burglar to gain entry into a store. When the unknown chip is compared with the known window, the chip exactly fits the jagged edge of the broken pane. This is known as a *jigsaw fit*, and it is considered one of the best kinds of physical evidence.[17] Furthermore, laboratory examination shows that the chip and the broken window are both the same color, refract (bend) light to the same angle, and contain the same mixture of silica and other materials. Actually, the jigsaw fit alone would be enough to lead the police to believe that the chip has been properly identified. The additional tests remove all reasonable doubt: the chip came from the window.

Of course, our examples have been easy ones. Good, usable fingerprints are not often found at the scene of a crime. Even if the criminal has been careless enough to leave fingerprints, they may be so fragmentary or smudged that there are too few clear characteristics for an identity to be established. At best, partial fingerprints might prove useful as contra-evidence.

A more common and more serious problem is the lack of a known, or standard, object with which an unknown object can be compared. Traces of soil from a criminal's shoes may be left behind, for example, but unless the investigator has some notion about where that bit of soil might have been picked up on a suspect's shoes, the sample may not be too useful. Sometimes that sort of evidence becomes valuable only after a suspect has been located. In this instance, the soil trace found at the crime scene might eventually be identified with soil that still clings to a suspect's shoes.[18]

The fact that some evidence becomes useful only during the later stages of an investigation reinforces the idea that all evidence must be protected from possible contamination. In the example just mentioned, suppose that the soil sample found at the crime scene is handled carelessly. Several days later, a suspect is located and a pair of shoes is recovered. It would be extremely helpful if the soil on the suspect's shoes could be compared with the soil sample from the crime scene but, unfortunately, the unknown sample has been misplaced. When it is found, there is no way to be certain that the sample has not been contaminated. Even if the sample from the crime scene and the sample from the suspect's shoes were found to be identical in every respect, the suspect's attorney could claim quite correctly that the unknown sample could have come from anywhere.

Having discussed the preliminary steps and the important precautions that a police officer must take on arriving at the scene of a crime, let us review these procedures. To do so, we shall describe a hypothetical case from the police officer's point of view. The officer's thoughts are in italics. Notice what the officer does, says, and observes.

# THE BURGLARY
## AT 1209 MAIN STREET

Patrol unit Baker-9 is on routine patrol when the following radio message is received: "Baker-9, see the manager at 1209 Main. Reported burglary. 1209 Main. Code 1."

Baker-9—Patrol Officer Dale Cole—drives at normal speed (code 1) to the address, pulling into a parking space across the street from the building. The building is a three-story brick apartment house with common walls between it and similar buildings on either side. There are two windows on each of the upper two floors; the ground floor has one window next to the entrance. There is no fire escape on the front of the building.

*No burglar could have used those windows for entry or exit. If there was a burglar, either he used an entry at the back of the building or he walked through the front door.*

Officer Cole walks up to the front entrance, double-checking to be sure it is the right address. The front door is locked; in order to get in, one must ring a buzzer and wait to be admitted by someone inside. *The mailboxes and the buzzer buttons look to be in fairly good shape, so they probably work. Some of the boxes have names on them and others don't, but the manager's box is clearly marked.* (Sometimes criminals gain entry to a building like this by pressing several buttons at random. When someone answers through the intercom system, the criminal just says, "Delivery boy!" There is a good chance that one of the residents will carelessly hit the switch that unlocks the front door, giving the criminal access to the whole building.)

The officer presses the button on the manager's mailbox. After a few moments, the manager answers through the intercom.

OFFICER: This is Officer Cole of the Police Department. I'm responding to a call about a burglary.

The manager pushes the button that unlocks the front door; Officer Cole enters the building. *If the burglar went in or out through this door, there won't be much chance of finding fingerprints or other traces; too many other people might have come through here since the burglary.*

The manager's apartment is on the first floor next to the foyer. A man is standing in the doorway.

OFFICER: Are you the manager of this building?

MANAGER: Yes, Officer, I'm Mr. Davis. I'm the one who called. Someone broke into apartment 3-C.

OFFICER: Okay, would you please show me where that is?

The manager leads Officer Cole up a narrow, dimly lit flight of stairs to the second floor, down a corridor, and up another flight to the third floor. At the second-floor landing, Officer Cole notices the arrangement of the apartments. *There appear to be four apartments on each floor: two at the front, one at the back, and one along the side. The side apartments must not have any windows at all. The open stairwell and the long corridor make our footsteps echo pretty loudly. If anyone came along here, unless he made an extreme effort to be quiet, there's a good chance that*

*someone in one of these apartments
would hear.*

OFFICER: Is there a fire escape on the back of the building?

MANAGER: No. The building itself is fireproofed, and it's small enough that we don't have to have a fire escape.

OFFICER: Is there a back door on the ground floor?

MANAGER: Yes, and there's also stairs down to the basement and an outside entrance through the laundry room.

OFFICER: Are those entrances kept locked?

MANAGER: The back door is locked to the outside, but it's got a panic bar on the inside. I try to keep the laundry room door locked, but the tenants leave it unlocked sometimes when they're going in and out. I'm always after them about it.

*As they reach the third-floor landing, Officer Cole looks around. There are four doors from the corridor, the same arrangement as on the second floor. Three of the doors are closed; the door to one of the front apartments is open. All of the doors appear to be in good condition—sturdy and tight fitting, with modern locks.*

OFFICER: Which apartment was broken into, Mr. Davis?

MANAGER: The front one, here—the one with the door open.

OFFICER: Are the tenants at home now?

MANAGER: No, I haven't seen them since yesterday.

OFFICER: Did you find the door open like that?

MANAGER: No, I opened it with my passkey. Mrs. Logan—the lady who lives here—she asked me to adjust her stove. When I saw what a mess the place

was, I went right back downstairs and called you.

*Inside the apartment are two women and a little boy, about four years old. They appear to be straightening the apartment.*

OFFICER: Ladies, would you come out of the apartment, please? Please leave everything just the way you found it.

MANAGER: Officer, this is my wife, Mrs. Davis, and this is Mrs. Torres and her little boy. They live next door.

OFFICER: Who are the tenants in this apartment?

MANAGER: Mr. and Mrs. Logan, a real nice young couple. They don't have any children.

OFFICER: All right, I'd like everyone to stay out of the apartment now. Mrs. Davis and Mrs. Torres, if you'd like to wait in Mrs. Torres's apartment, I'll want to talk to you in a few minutes. Mr. Davis, would you wait here, please.

While the manager waits in the hallway, Officer Cole makes an initial assessment of the suspected crime scene.

*The door from the corridor opens into a single, rather large room, about fifteen by twenty feet. There are two doors from this room in the wall at the left. At the far end of the room—the front of the building—there's an archway into what appears to be a breakfast nook; there must be a kitchen off to the left, too. The one window in the front wall is in the living room. The living room contains a sofa— possibly a sofa bed—two chairs, a coffee table, and bookshelves along the long wall. The room is bright, clean, and basically in good order. The sofa cushions are in place. Some newspapers, magazines, and articles of clothing are strewn around on the floor. A table lamp has been knocked askew. There's a tele-*

vision stand in the corner, but no TV on it. There's also a vacant space on the bookshelves, large enough to have held a stereo or a radio.

OFFICER: Mr. Davis, do you happen to know where Mr. Logan works?

MANAGER: I think he's some kind of mechanic. I guess it's on the lease papers he signed.

OFFICER: What about Mrs. Logan? Does she work?

MANAGER: I think so, but I don't know where. She's usually not here during the day.

OFFICER: Would you please look up those lease papers and see if you can find out where Mr. Logan works?

While Mr. Davis goes back downstairs, Officer Cole enters the apartment and walks directly across the main living area in order to see into the breakfast nook and kitchen.

*There are dishes in the sink, and the remains from breakfast are still on the table. On the kitchen counter are a toaster, a coffee pot, and a small electric broiler. The cupboard doors over the counter are standing open. It's strange that a burglar would go through the cupboards but would ignore these small appliances, any of which could be sold for five or ten bucks. There's a broken cup lying on the floor in front of the refrigerator, at the far end of the kitchen. A mark on the wall, directly above the broken cup, could have been made by the cup striking the wall.*

Officer Cole next returns to the main room to check the two doors that lead from it. One door is slightly ajar, so the officer uses a pencil to pry it open, rather than handle the doorknob. The door opens into a small bathroom. *The room is clean and well ordered, except that the sink is dirty. There are fresh stains of what appears to be oil or grease, along with smaller stains that look like blood. On the ledge at the back of the sink is an open box of adhesive bandages. A towel has been dropped on the floor between the sink and the toilet; it, too, appears to have grease and blood stains on it.*

Officer Cole next checks the other door, but it is closed tightly so there is no need to disturb it now. The officer looks around the room once more, then returns to the corridor outside the apartment. It is time to begin interviewing the manager and the two women. And Officer Cole has a lot of questions for Mr. and Mrs. Logan, the tenants.

We shall discontinue our narrative for now, but we shall come back to 1209 Main Street in later chapters.

As you should realize, this hypothetical crime scene presents a number of problems. Has Officer Cole been able to determine the nature of the crime, if any, yet? What investigative questions have been developed? Where should the officer begin to look for specific evidence? In your opinion, should Officer Cole continue the investigation or call for the detectives?

In the next two chapters, we shall discuss physical evidence: what it is, how to find it, and how to handle it. However, as you can see from the case we have been discussing, often the next step in an investigation is to interview the victim and any witnesses at the scene. The information obtained from the interviews may help to determine what evidence should be sought. Techniques of interviewing will be the subject of Chapter 6.

## REFERENCES

1. Ronald J. Waldron, et al., *The Criminal Justice System* (Boston: Houghton Mifflin, 1976), pp. 356–357.

2. Gwynne Peirson, *Police Operations* (Chicago: Nelson-Hall, 1976), pp. 100–101.

3. Richard H. Fox and Carl L. Cunningham, *Crime Scene Search and Physical Evidence Handbook* (Washington, D.C.: U.S. Department of Justice, National Institute of Law Enforcement and Criminal Justice, 1973), p. 15.

4. Fox and Cunningham, p. 12.

5. *Criminal Investigation* (Gaithersburg, Md.: International Association of Chiefs of Police, 1971), p. 15.

6. Fox and Cunningham, p. 12.

7. Peirson, p. 89.

8. Paul B. Weston and Kenneth M. Wells, *Elements of Criminal Investigation* (Englewood Cliffs, N.J.: Prentice-Hall, 1971), pp. 12–14.

9. *Criminal Investigation*, pp. 115–120.

10. Edward C. Fisher, *Search and Seizure* (Evanston, Ill.: Traffic Institute, Northwestern University, 1970), pp. 31–36.

11. Fox and Cunningham, pp. 12–13.

12. Weston and Wells, *Elements of Criminal Investigation*, p. 7.

13. Paul L. Kirk, *Crime Investigation*, 2d ed. (New York: John Wiley and Sons, 1974), p. 3.

14. Kirk, p. 2.

15. *Criminal Investigation*, p. 12.

16. Fox and Cunningham, p. 3.

17. Kirk, p. 263.

18. Peirson, p. 111.

# REVIEW OF THE EVIDENCE

1. Which of these types of crime is most likely to be reported to the police while the crime is still in progress?
    a. a forgery
    b. a daytime burglary of a residence
    c. an assault
    d. a homicide
    e. an embezzlement
2. True or false: When a citizen stops a police officer on the street to report a crime, the officer should go to the scene as quickly as possible in hopes of catching the criminal, rather than waste time by asking the citizen for detailed information.
3. On which side of a door should a police officer stand when he or she arrives at the scene of a reported crime?
    a. the lock side
    b. the hinge side
    c. neither; he or she should stand at the center of the door, facing it squarely
4. Which of the following is *not* one of the purposes of a visual sweep of the crime scene?
    a. to gain an overall impression of the scene
    b. to identify the perpetrator
    c. to raise questions that the investigator will attempt to answer later
    d. to notice all the persons present
    e. to notice all the physical objects at the scene and their relationships or relative positions
5. True or false: Whenever possible, a police officer should avoid giving first aid to the victim of a violent crime.
6. Who should be allowed to remain at a crime scene while evidence is being sought and collected?
    a. the victim, witnesses, and anyone else directly involved in the criminal event
    b. only police officers and other authorized officials
    c. suspicious bystanders
    d. only the investigating officer and technicians under the investigator's supervision
    e. no one at all
7. True or false: Anyone who hangs back at the fringes of a crowd of bystanders, trying to look inconspicuous or unconcerned, should be regarded with suspicion and asked for identification.

8. Police officers may enter a home or other private place without permission under which of the following conditions?
   a. if they have a search warrant
   b. if someone has reported a crime at the location
   c. if they actually observe a crime in progress
   d. if they observe something indicating that a person's life is in danger
   e. if they think that there might be some evidence of criminal activity at the location

9. An unknown object is said to be *identified* if
   a. the investigator knows what it is.
   b. it belonged to the perpetrator.
   c. it shares a sufficient number of common characteristics with a known, or standard, object.
   d. it is identical in every detectable way with another object.
   e. it is found at a crime scene or in a suspect's possession.

10. One of the best kinds of physical evidence is
   a. trace evidence.
   b. a partial fingerprint.
   c. broken glass.
   d. a jigsaw fit.
   e. a soil sample.
   f. a standard object.

## TOPICS FOR INVESTIGATION

1. Most authorities agree that only a small percentage of property crimes are ever reported to the police. Some authorities believe that even violent crimes are badly underreported. Why are serious crimes not reported? Should laws be passed that would require citizens to report any crime that they know about?

2. Approaching the scene of a reported crime is one of the most dangerous parts of a police officer's job. Some officers wear bulletproof vests and other garments or devices in an effort to reduce the danger. However, many police officials fear that such garments or devices make officers more complacent and careless. Do you think police officers should use such garments or devices?

3. A police officer may be able to send bystanders and other people away from the scene of a crime, but how should an officer deal with other officials or with a victim who wants to "play detective" and refuses to leave the scene?

4. Evidence that was obtained improperly cannot be introduced into a criminal trial, even if it means that the accused criminal must go free. This is known as the *exclusionary rule*. Why would this rule apply in the hypothetical case described in the text, in which heroin was discovered in a man's living room? What is the purpose of the exclusionary rule?

5. Did Officer Cole have proper permission or some other legal basis to enter the Logans' apartment? What if Mr. or Mrs. Logan should object to people having entered their apartment when they were not there?

## CHAPTER 4

# RECORDING
# AND REPORTING
# EVIDENCE

STUDY CLUES

1. True or false: Evidence is anything that tends to affirm or deny either the guilt or the innocence of the accused.
2. Indicate which of the following would be direct evidence (D) and which would be circumstantial evidence (C).
   a. a witness who saw the accused at the scene of a crime an hour before it occurred
   b. a television set, found in the suspect's possession, bearing the same serial number as one that was stolen in a burglary
   c. a witness who says that the suspect and the victim quarreled frequently
   d. a soil sample that was found on the suspect's shoes and is almost identical to soil taken from the scene of the crime
   e. testimony of a witness who saw the crime and identifies the suspect as the perpetrator
3. A threatening letter written by the accused to the victim would be
   a. direct evidence.
   b. impression evidence.
   c. trace evidence.
   d. documentary evidence.
   e. testimonial evidence.
4. True or false: It is often helpful to return to the scene of a crime several times during the course of an investigation to search for additional evidence.
5. An offense report is
   a. a printed form on which the official documentation of a case is recorded.
   b. the initial report to the police of a suspected crime.
   c. the investigator's field notes.
   d. a list of physical evidence found at a crime scene
   e. all of the above.
6. True or false: Photographs of a crime scene should be taken only by a qualified photographic specialist.
7. Photographs of a crime scene should show which of the following?
   a. the general locality, such as adjacent buildings
   b. the overall crime scene
   c. specific details or places within the crime scene that have evidential value
   d. all of the above
   e. none of the above

AFTER A POLICE OFFICER has arrived at the scene of a reported crime and has completed the preliminary steps described in Chapter 3, it is time to begin searching for the evidence that will lead to a complete understanding of the crime and, hopefully, to the apprehension and conviction of the criminal.

The search for evidence obviously is a crucial stage in a criminal investigation. Indeed, some people consider "investigating" and "searching for evidence" to be synonymous, as though the other steps of the investigation did not exist or matter. Although most people have a general understanding of the importance of evidence and what it is, a few technical points about the nature of evidence should be understood before we discuss the procedures for locating and recording it.

## WHAT IS EVIDENCE?

Our legal system is based largely on what is known as the *adversary system*. A criminal trial under this system is a highly specialized form of debate or argument. One side, representing the public, argues that the accused person has committed a crime and therefore should be punished. The other side, the defendant, denies the accusation.[1] Furthermore, the U.S. system specifies that the burden of proof rests on the prosecution. This means that the prosecution, representing the public, must persuade the judge or jury that the accused person is guilty beyond any reasonable doubt. The defendant does *not* have to prove innocence; it is necessary only to argue that there is some reason to doubt the prosecutor's argument. Strictly speaking, a defendant does not have to present witnesses or evidence, testify, or do anything at all. It is entirely up to the prosecutor to present sufficient evidence to persuade the jury (or, if there is no jury, the judge).[2]

There are many rules governing the way in which evidence must be presented in court. The prosecutor cannot simply say to the jury, "We believe that so-and-so is guilty for the following reasons . . ." The prosecutor must present evidence to demonstrate the reasons that the accused is believed to be guilty.

Physical evidence can be presented in a criminal trial only through the testimony of witnesses.[3] The prosecutor cannot hold up a gun and say, "This gun was found at the scene of the crime. We later learned that this gun was used to shoot the victim and that the gun was owned by the defendant." Instead, the prosecutor must introduce a witness who is prepared to say, "I found this gun at the scene of the crime, in such-and-such a place. I am quite certain that it is the gun I found." The same witness, or perhaps another one, must then say, "I tested this gun, using standard and reliable procedures that have been used many times before, and found that there was good reason to believe that the same gun fired a bullet into the victim." Finally, there must be a witness who can say, "I checked the serial number on the gun and found that it was registered to the defendant, according to the official records maintained for this purpose," or, perhaps, "I sold this gun to the defendant on the day before the crime was committed." As you can see, each small bit of evidence must be presented through the *testimony*, or statement, of a witness who has personal, immediate knowledge of the facts.[4]

In almost every criminal case that comes to trial, the police officers who investigated the crime are among the most important witnesses. The judge and jury expect a police officer to be thorough, objective, and reliable in presenting testimony: to say exactly what the officer knows about the crime, how that information was learned, and how reasonable conclusions were made. The officer must live up to those expectations by being prepared to explain, in great detail, the methods and procedures used to locate, examine, and preserve all the evidence that could be found in connection with the crime.

*Evidence,* then, is anything that tends to affirm or to deny either the argument that the accused is guilty or the argument that the accused is innocent.[5] The testimony of witnesses who personally observed the crime is evidence. So is the testimony of witnesses who were not present during the crime but have some other personal knowledge of the crime, the victim, or the accused. Police officers' testimony about the way in which they conducted their investigation is evidence.

Physical objects can be evidence. Weapons, tools, and other material things that were used to commit the crime; clothing, hair, fingerprints, footprints, and personal effects belonging to either the victim or the perpetrator and helping to demonstrate how the crime took place and who was present; photographs or drawings of the crime scene; castings or other kinds of reproductions of impressions found at the crime scene—all of these are different types of evidence.

Not all of the physical evidence that might be found at the crime scene is useful and usable in court. Sometimes objects or traces (such as fingerprints, bloodstains, and the like) turn out to have no real connection with the crime at all, or the connection simply cannot be proved. Some evidence may be very valuable in leading the investigator to the guilty party, but for one reason or another (possible contamination, for example) cannot be used in court. Sometimes evidence turns out to be worthless because its significance or connection with the crime cannot be understood—for example, a fragmentary fingerprint that does not match any known suspect.

## GLOSSARY OF TYPES OF EVIDENCE

There are many different ways to classify or describe the different types of evidence, depending on the purposes to be served. Rather than limiting our discussion to one particular system of categories, we shall use various terms. Here is a brief glossary of some of the terms that we may use:

*Circumstantial evidence.* Information or objects that concern facts about the crime, the suspect, or the victim and suggest a relationship among them, but that do not specifically demonstrate the events of the crime. This would include, for example, the testimony of a witness who saw the accused enter the scene of a crime, the testimony of a gun dealer who claims to have sold a gun to the accused, or testimony that the accused and the victim argued frequently and violently. Generally, circumstantial evidence suggests but does not prove conclusively that the accused could have committed the crime. (See also *indirect evidence.*)[6]

*Direct evidence.* Physical objects or the testimony of witnesses that bear directly on the criminal event. Examples are a gun that was found in the suspect's possession and that, according to appropriate tests, was used to shoot the victim; a television set bearing the same serial number as the set stolen in a burglary; or the testimony of a witness who was present at the crime, saw it occur, and is able to identify the perpetrator.[7]

*Documentary evidence.* Any sort of record, form, letter, note, or other document—any means of conveying recorded information—that has some demonstrable connection to the

ANSWERS TO STUDY CLUES
1. True   2a. C   2b. D   2c. C   2d. C
2e. D   3. d   4. False   5. a   6. False   7. d

*The Initial Investigation*

crime. For example, this could be a threatening letter written by the accused to the victim (or by the victim to the accused, for that matter); a pawnbroker's ledger showing the serial number of a gun sold to the accused and later found at the crime scene; a fraudulent check allegedly written by the accused; or the address of the crime scene, scribbled on a memo pad found in the defendant's motel room. Usually, a document is something written or printed on a piece of paper; strictly speaking, however, a photograph, motion picture film, video tape, audio tape recording, or even data stored electronically in a computer might constitute *documents* in the same sense.[8]

*Impression evidence.* A mark made in or on a solid surface. This would include scratches made in a metal window screen or a wood window sill by a burglar's tools; tire tracks left on the dirt driveway leading to the crime scene; or fingerprints, palm prints, bare footprints, or even lip prints left by the perpetrator of a crime.

*Indirect evidence.* Information concerning the victim, the suspect, or the general circumstances of the crime or the crime scene, but not having a direct connection to the crime itself. Examples are a list of the victim's friends and acquaintances; the fact that the crime scene is a house of prostitution; or the information that a known suspect, who has fled the scene, works for a taxicab company and has not yet received his weekly paycheck.

*Physical evidence.* Any material object, of any size or form, that can be shown to have some connection to a crime. Physical evidence may include the *instruments* of the crime (weapons, tools, or other devices used to commit the crime); the *fruits* of the crime (stolen goods, money, or anything else that comes into the possession of the criminal as a result of the crime); *contraband* (anything, such as drugs or gambling devices, that cannot be possessed legally); or circumstantial evidence.

*Trace evidence.* Physical evidence that is left at the scene of a crime by the perpetrator, usually unwittingly, or that can be used to identify the perpetrator. In this sense, if a burglar accidentally drops a wallet at the scene of a crime, the wallet would be considered trace evidence. Ordinarily, however, trace evidence is very small matter: fingerprints and other inadvertent impressions, hair, soil, physiological fluids (such as blood or semen), stains, broken glass, and so on. Most trace evidence must be examined under a microscope or by some kind of laboratory analysis for its value to be realized.

One other kind of evidence deserves special attention: what we have called contra-evidence. *Contra-evidence* is any evidence that appears to contradict the weight of all the other evidence accumulated and, thus, casts doubt on whether a suspect is truly guilty. Suppose there are two eyewitnesses who claim to have seen the suspect fire a pistol at the victim, as well as various other kinds of evidence to connect the suspect to the crime—but the only fingerprint found on the gun does not belong to the suspect. The fingerprint would be contra-evidence.

We will discuss in a later chapter how contra-evidence should be treated in preparing a case for trial. For now, let us simply repeat what we said in Chapter 1: contra-evidence must not be overlooked, ignored, or discarded; it must be scrupulously checked, verified, and evaluated until the contradiction is somehow resolved.

THE CHAIN OF CUSTODY

In Chapter 3, we briefly discussed the concept of the integrity of evidence. We pointed out that evidence is useless if there is any chance that it has been contaminated or if its original source is uncertain. One of the most important ways to ensure the integrity of evidence is to establish and maintain an unbroken chain of custody.[9]

The *chain of custody* is simply a clear record of where each item of evidence has been from the time it was discovered until it is presented in court (Figure 4.1). The chain is broken if there is any time when no one knows where the evidence was or what was being done to it.

The chain begins when an investigator decides that a certain object might have value as evidence. A record of the object, including its description and its location, must be made immediately, and the investigator must assume custody of the object by actually taking

FIGURE 4.1
THE CHAIN OF CUSTODY

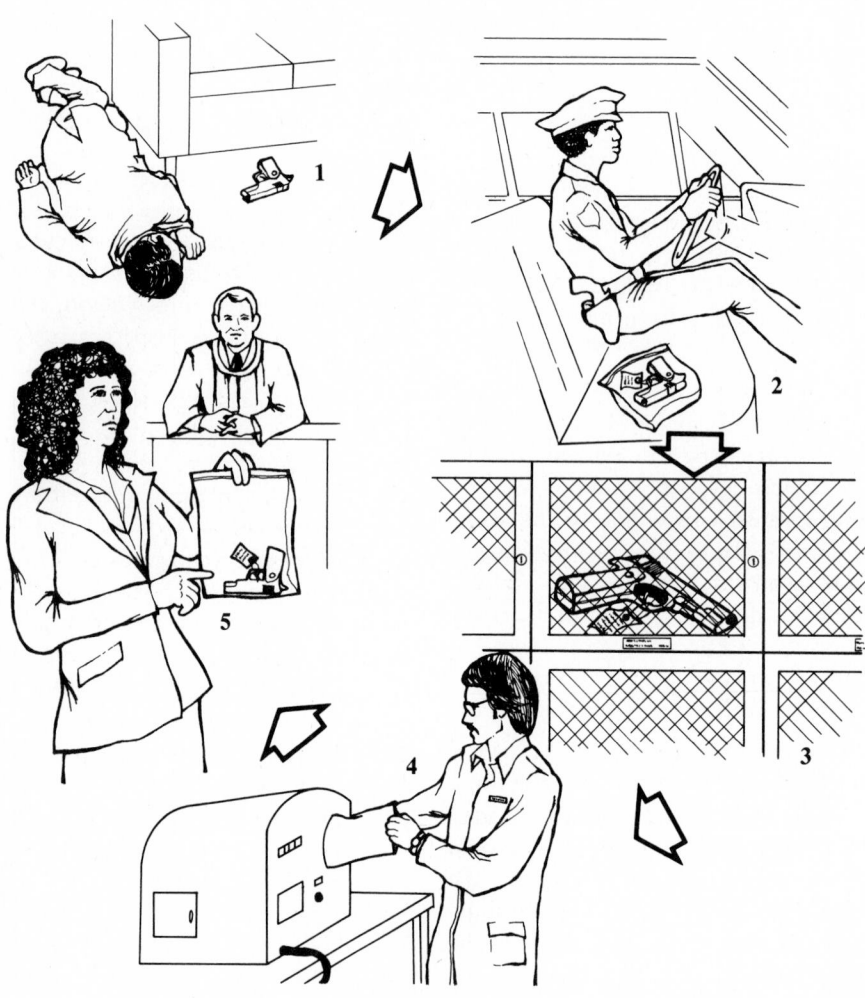

*The Initial Investigation*

it into possession. A record must be made of everything that is done with the object: where it is taken, where and how it is stored, to whom it is given and for what purposes. If it is delivered to a laboratory, for example, the transfer must be recorded, showing to whom the object has been entrusted. That person then takes custody and must keep equally clear, complete records of the object's location until it is returned to the investigator.

If an object is left unattended or unguarded for even a few seconds, a defendant could argue that it is not valid evidence: someone could have contaminated it with false or misleading traces or could have substituted one object for another.

Most police agencies provide evidence lockers in which physical evidence can be stored without breaking the chain of custody and without requiring each officer to carry around all the evidence from all the cases that might be in progress at any given time. Many agencies have a centralized evidence room with a police officer as an attendant; the attendant acts as the custodian for all the evidence placed in the room. A better, but somewhat more expensive, arrangement is for each police officer to have a separate locker in which evidence can be kept. The lockers might even have two keys, one of which would be kept by the individual officer and the other kept by the attendant, both keys being required to open the lock.

## EVALUATING EVIDENCE

Not all evidence is "good" evidence. The investigator's purpose in seeking and examining evidence is to arrive at a true and full understanding of the criminal event: who committed the crime, how, and perhaps why. The evidence that contributes to that understanding will be used in court to persuade the jury or judge that the accused is guilty, provided that the evidence has not been compromised or contaminated and provided that the officer is able to explain the source and meaning of the evidence.

Evidence serves the same functions for a police officer that symptoms do for a physician. Just as some physicians are better at recognizing symptoms and arriving at correct diagnoses, so some investigators seem to have the knack of finding and understanding the evidence that they need to reach a proper conclusion. Conversely, there are some physicians who "diagnose" an illness by trying different remedies until one of them works, assuming that the patient lives long enough. The equivalent in criminal investigation is the "investigator" who overlooks valuable evidence, collects evidence that is of little value, chases wild geese, and waits for the criminal to make a confession.

There is no simple, step-by-step method, no magic recipe or formula that we can give to help an investigator distinguish between genuine evidence and that which is worthless. That kind of discrimination comes from experience, and a little talent cannot hurt. We can suggest only that the investigator overlook nothing. At the scene of a crime, everything that might be useful evidence should be noticed, recorded, collected, and analyzed. Once the investigator has left the scene of the crime, one might as well assume that any evidence that was overlooked or neglected will no longer exist. Almost without exception, the investigator cannot go back later; it would be impossible to state with any certainty that the neglected evidence is uncompromised and uncontaminated, if it is still there at all.

The time to decide which evidence is useful and which is not comes after all the potential evidence has been collected and analyzed and after all the available witnesses have been questioned. Only then is the investigator likely to have a sufficient understanding of the crime to decide what evidence is needed and which items, originally thought to be evidential, have no bearing on the case.[10]

There is no such thing as too much evidence. Most investigations fail because too little evidence is considered, even when the evidence was readily available. It naturally follows that if the investigator is to collect everything that might be useful and then sort it out later, there must be a complete, detailed, and very accurate record of what items have been removed from the scene, where they were found, and what their connection to the crime might be. Without these records the investigator will not be able to make sense of the evidence later; furthermore, without such records the investigator is incapable of testifying adequately about the evidence in court.

Keeping good records is a fundamental part of the investigator's job. Just as a plumber requires the right wrenches, a crime investigator requires the right record-keeping equipment.

## THE NOTEBOOK

The documentation of every crime investigation begins with the investigator's *field notes*—the information that is recorded when an officer responds to the initial report of the crime. The field notes are the ultimate source of information about what the investigator saw, heard, did, and learned. They will guide the course of the investigation to its conclusion, and they will be used in court as the basis for the investigator's testimony.[11]

As a general rule, the notes themselves are not considered official documents; as such, they are not open to public view, they are not subject to *subpoena* (a court order that certain evidence be presented), and they are not introduced as evidence in a trial. Their purpose is mainly to refresh the investigator's memory as the investigation proceeds, especially when the officer testifies in court.[12]

Unfortunately, some police officers have excessive faith in the reliability of the unaided memory, and thus they fail to write down on paper the greater part of what they see, hear, do, and learn. Later—perhaps hours, days, weeks, months, even years later, when a case comes to trial—the information no longer exists and cannot be recaptured.

We offer, therefore, a simple standard for an officer to decide what should go into field notes: the notes should be so complete that if the investigator were hit by a truck tomorrow, another officer who had just moved from another state could pick up the investigation without faltering. This is, of course, a somewhat idealized standard and will not always be maintained. However, the closer you can come to it, the more proficient and reliable you will be as an investigator.

### SIZE OF THE NOTEBOOK

Field notes should be kept in a notebook so that they can be properly organized for immediate access and reference. A very few police agencies provide a standardized notebook and printed note forms; in most cases, the type of notebook and the method of recording information are left up to each officer.[13]

Unfortunately, police officers have long-standing prejudices about notebooks. One is that a notebook should be as small as possible—preferably small enough to fit into a buttoned shirt pocket. That size may be handy, but it is certainly much too small to record useful information in detail. This prejudice is so widespread that it deserves some comment. Part of the rationale behind it is

*The Initial Investigation*

*A tape recorder can be used as an "electronic notebook" to record the investigator's observations at the crime scene.*

later be played back or neatly transcribed and summarized as many times or in as many different ways as necessary.[14]

The sad fact is that feelings about tape recorders run so high that certain police agencies have been showered with abuse for merely requesting funds to buy tape recorders. Those rare agencies that have somehow managed to acquire the equipment usually are not able to use it with full effectiveness because of the public's suspicious attitude. Of course, hiding the recorder and using it surreptitiously to avoid a public fuss only reinforces the feeling on all sides that tape recorders are somehow inherently evil. We hope that this attitude will change. A tape recorder should be used openly whenever a victim, witness, or suspect is being interviewed or interrogated, and it can replace a notebook for recording the officer's observations and findings at the crime scene (though a notebook is still required for sketching). It is certainly no more "immoral" to record the voice of an interview subject than it is to write down what the person says—and the recording is invariably more complete and more accurate.

unfortunate because, used properly, a tape recorder can be an enormously valuable tool. The prejudice stems from the association of tape recorders with eavesdropping, spying, and invading others' privacy. There is also a deep-seated belief that any tape recording can be easily altered to distort the information it contains. That is not true: the alterations can almost always be detected. Besides, handwritten notes can be altered, too. Furthermore, handwritten notes are never as detailed or as accurate as a verbal account recorded on tape. In addition to its use in interviewing witnesses, a hand-held cassette tape recorder can keep a running narrative of everything that crime investigators observe and do at a crime scene. The recorded information could

## PHOTOGRAPHY

The effective use of photography in criminal investigation has not yet reached its potential, although photographs have been used extensively in investigation for several decades. Part of the problem is that too often photography is left to the specialists who are called in only for major crimes, and they are frequently called in too late.[15]

Crime scene photography should be the responsibility of every investigator, including the first officer to reach the scene. In order for this potential to be achieved, however, every police officer must acquire some basic

*Four types of cameras. Left: a 4-by-5-inch view camera; center rear: a 35 mm single-lens reflex (SLR) camera; right: a 2 ¼-by-2 ¼-inch view camera; center foreground: a 26 mm snapshot camera. (Photo courtesy of Harry E. Kieke)*

understanding of photography and the operation of cameras.

### TYPES OF CAMERAS

Photographic equipment can be classified in many different ways. For our purposes, we shall divide all types of cameras into three categories: large-format, 35mm, and snapshot.

Large-format cameras include the 4-by-5-inch view cameras, which were once standard equipment for newspaper and police photography and are still common. Other cameras that we consider large-format are 2¼-by-2¼-inch cameras and twin-lens reflex cameras, because the film used in all of them is relatively large in size. This means that a picture taken by one of these cameras can be enlarged several times with very little loss of detail and sharpness; occasionally this capability can play an important role in discovering or understanding evidence. However, technological advances in the manufacture of film and cameras have greatly reduced the differences between large-format cameras and smaller-format cameras, such as 35mm cameras, so

that the larger cameras are no longer clearly superior. The larger cameras are comparatively bulky, awkward to use, and expensive, so there is nothing much to recommend them for police work today.

The universal standard for almost all professional photography is the 35mm camera, especially those with single-lens reflex viewing (usually abbreviated to SLR). An enormous variety of kinds of film is available for these cameras. In addition, the cameras themselves are available in a vast array of styles, suiting almost any conceivable purpose or budget. Many 35mm SLR cameras are designed so that the lenses can be interchanged, permitting the same camera body (and the same roll of film) to shoot a series of pictures from several different perspectives. Most 35mm films are fine enough to be enlarged several times before noticeable loss of picture quality results; 35mm slides can be projected onto the largest screen. Finally, the cameras are small, compact (except when fitted with very long lenses), and easy to use; some of the more expensive models are nearly as automatic and foolproof as a cheap snapshot camera but produce far better results.

Snapshot cameras, such as the Instamatic type (which uses 26mm film) and the "pocket" type (which uses 10mm film), are often recommended for use by patrol officers because of their very low cost, convenient size, and easy operation. Unfortunately, these advantages are gained at the expense of photographic quality. Most snapshot cameras have plastic lenses, which provide a very inferior picture. The film size is so small that enlargements at high magnifications are rarely satisfactory (especially since the original negative is not very good). Because snapshot cameras are intended for amateur use, only a few films are available in the appropriate sizes and those films do not include the better-quality types that are widely available in the 35mm size. In general, we conclude that a snapshot camera is better than no camera at all, but just barely.[16]

### FILM TYPES

Photographic films can be divided neatly into three main categories: black-and-white print film, color print film, and color slide film. Other characteristics of a particular film— what size it is, whether it is paper-backed or acetate-backed, and whether it is sold as cut sheets or as rolls—depend mainly on the type of camera in which the film will be used.[17]

Should a crime investigator take black-and-white pictures, color prints, or color slides? The final decision depends mainly on the anticipated use of the photograph. This was not always true. Until fairly recently, only black-and-white films were readily available at reasonable cost and offered both the grain quality and the light responsiveness, or *speed,* that police photography requires. Today, however, excellent color-print and color-slide films are available for almost any purpose, particularly in the 35mm size.

For example, it is extremely important for investigative photographs to be taken under *available light*—whatever light is available at the crime scene. Because most crimes take place indoors and in other locations with relatively poor light, available-light photography requires a high film speed. Otherwise, the shutter must be kept open so long in order for the film to gather enough light that the picture cannot turn out as sharp as necessary. Older high-speed films were so grainy that the picture quality suffered tremendously, and under poor light only black-and-white film would be practical at all. Today, the choice should depend on how the pictures will be used, because there are high-speed color films that will produce pictures equal in quality to most black-and-white films.

Black-and-white prints are very inexpensive, are easy to process, and often show details that might be obscured by colorful patterns. On the other hand, color film is not terribly expensive and it sometimes shows details that black-and-white film would miss. Some types of color films can be processed locally, in a police agency's own lab or by any local photo studio. Other types of color films require more elaborate processing in a sophisticated laboratory, which introduces complications into the chain of custody that ought to be avoided.

There is one special circumstance that the investigator ought to be aware of: if the crime scene is especially gory or gruesome, color photographs may not be permitted in court because of the "inflammatory and prejudicial" effect that they might have on a jury.[18]

Of course, the best and simplest solution to the dilemma is to do both: photograph the scene extensively with both color and black-and-white film. If this is not practical, color slide film might be the best compromise; not only is the color slide useful in itself, but either black-and-white or color prints can be made from the slide with negligible losses in picture quality.[19]

### INSTANT PHOTOGRAPHY

Some police agencies like to use *instant* (or self-developing) photography because there is no concern about having the film lost or destroyed in processing and the results of each photograph can be seen immediately.

There are two manufacturers of instant photographic systems: Polaroid and Kodak. Polaroid has made instant cameras and films for many years and offers an extensive line of both cameras and films for many different purposes. Kodak began marketing its instant cameras a few years ago and makes essentially just one line and one type of film, aimed clearly at the amateur market.

The professional type of cameras and films made by Polaroid are as good in quality and as versatile as any other professional photographic equipment, so instant photography has much to recommend it for criminal investigation. The only real drawbacks are that the film is very expensive and the cameras, especially the professional models, tend to be rather bulky and awkward.[20]

### ARTIFICIAL LIGHTING

As we have already mentioned, investigative photographs ought to be taken under available light. At the very least, overall pictures of the entire crime scene must be taken with available light at whatever combination of shutter speed and aperture will give the best results.

However, sometimes the scene is so poorly lit that important details cannot be photographed with existing light. This is quite often true for such details as impression evidence or objects that happen to lie in shadows. Some sort of artificial light must be used to make these details visible.[21] The simplest solution is to move an ordinary lamp into the area to be photographed. This may raise the level of illumination enough to permit a good picture without seriously changing the natural appearance of things. If that still is not enough, a photographic light must be used. The general types of photographic lighting are photoflood lamps, flashbulbs, and electronic flash units.

Photoflood lamps are ordinary incandescent lamps made to use high wattages and produce a great deal of light. Typical photoflood lamps range from 200 watts to 1,000 watts or more. Usually the lamps are held in special reflectors that concentrate the light in the desired direction. One or two photoflood lamps of 200 watts will provide adequate light for color photography in a 3-meter-square room.

Flashbulbs are also incandescent lamps, but they are filled with highly combustible metallic filaments. When current is applied the lamp bursts into flame inside its glass envelope. The result is a short but very intense flash of light. Although flashbulbs are inexpensive and somewhat more convenient to use than photoflood lamps (which must be held in place by mounting them on a light tripod or clipping them to an object in the room), flashbulbs have two big drawbacks. First, they can be used only once. Second, the light they produce is very harsh and, because the flash unit is almost always mounted directly onto the camera, all the light comes from one direction. The result is often that surfaces facing the camera are overly illuminated, but the sides of objects are thrown into dark shadows.

Electronic flash units use a sort of fluorescent lamp that, like a flashbulb, provides a brief, intense burst of light. The main advantage of the electronic flash is that it can be used over and over again. Most electronic flash units are battery-powered, but some can be connected to an adapter or charger that operates off a standard electrical outlet.

Electronic flash units are often designed to be mounted on the camera. When this is done, the result is often the same as that produced by flashbulbs: the light all comes from one direction, so some surfaces are overilluminated and others are plunged into shadow. For investigative work the flash unit should be equipped with a long cord so that it can be held away from the camera. It is usually better to aim the flash at the ceiling, floor, or a wall, to "bounce" the light onto the object being photographed and thus produce a softer, more even illumination. When a single small object is to be photographed, the flash unit should be held at an angle, ordinarily about 45 degrees with respect to the camera and the object itself.

Some new, relatively expensive flash units are specifically designed either to vary the amount of light they produce, depending on the distance from the camera to the subject, or to bounce the light off nearby walls or the ceiling. Other electronic flash units are designed for automatic remote control. The "slave," or remote unit, has a light-sensitive cell that acts as a trigger. When the flash unit attached to the camera is fired, its light triggers the remote unit and causes it to fire as well. This all happens quickly enough that the effect is of a single burst of illumination from two sources. Three or even four flash units can be operated simultaneously in this way. Thus, electronic flash units can be used in the same manner as photofloods, if the photographer can get someone to hold the remote units at the proper locations or can mount them on tripods.

Figure 4.3 shows the proper placement of artificial lighting units, such as photofloods or remote-controlled electronic flash units, to illuminate an object or small area of a room.

## PHOTOGRAPHIC REFLECTORS

As our discussion of artificial lighting suggests, sometimes it is more important to achieve a proper distribution of light than just to add more light. One way to get a fairly even distribution of light is to "bounce" a flash off a wall or ceiling. However, this is not always practical, especially if the surface is too dark to reflect much light or if the nearest surface is too far away.

Photographers frequently use reflectors of various sorts to control the distribution of light. All kinds of photographic reflectors are available, including some elaborate ones made of aluminum and other metallic foils. But even a simple reflector can mean the difference between a good, clear photograph and a muddy mess. Anything that reflects light can be used as a photographic reflector. For example, a simple rectangle of glossy white cardboard or posterboard will serve the purpose very well.

The proper placement of a reflector depends on far too many factors to be discussed here. If a constant light source, such as a photoflood lamp, is used, a little experimentation will soon determine the proper placement. If an intermittent source, such as flashbulbs or an electronic flash unit, will be used, the photographer ought to imagine where the light from the flash will fall and how it can be redirected by a reflector to produce the desired effect. The effort will not always succeed but a little experience will produce more successes than failures, and sometimes there will be no other way to obtain a photograph of a vital clue.

## FIGURE 4.3
## PLACEMENT OF ARTIFICIAL LIGHTING

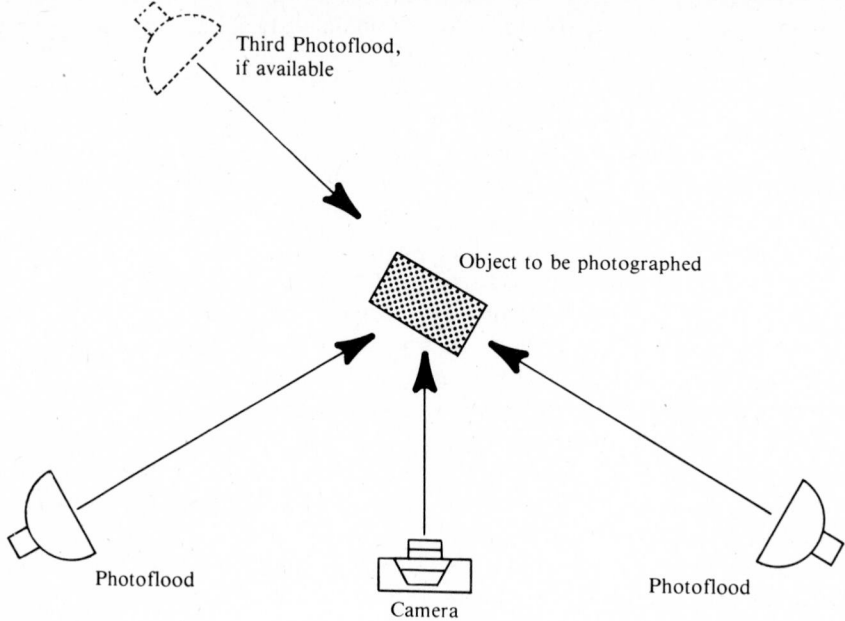

Third Photoflood,
if available

Object to be photographed

Photoflood

Camera

Photoflood

## PHOTOGRAPHING
THE CRIME SCENE

Over the years there has been a running debate over whether photography should precede or follow visual examination of the crime scene, taking of measurements, and sketching. The simple solution is that the two processes should take place more or less simultaneously.

If a single investigator is handling the whole investigation, he or she can enter the crime scene, make notes and sketches, then take up a camera and snap a few pictures before moving on, provided that the camera is small and compact enough. If this procedure seems to be unwieldy, an equally good alternative is the two-person procedure: two officers should work literally side by side, one

making notes and sketches while the other takes photographs.

Either way, the point is that the notes, sketches, and photographs should virtually duplicate one another. Each of the three methods of recording information should provide a complete portrayal of the crime scene and of each item of evidence.[22]

Some agencies continue to require that crime scene photography be done by a specialist. In that case, it may be necessary for the visual examination of the scene to proceed before the photographer arrives. Extra precautions must be taken to ensure that nothing is touched or moved out of place before the scene has been photographed; otherwise, not only will the evidence be contaminated, but there may be discrepancies between the in-

*The Initial Investigation*

vestigator's notes, the sketches, and the photographs. When pointed out by a defense attorney in court, such discrepancies can invalidate all the evidence that has been so painstakingly accumulated.[23]

The photographs of a crime scene should show three things; the general locality, the overall scene, and the specific objects or places within the scene that may have evidential value.[24]

The *general locality* means the area around the crime scene. That might include the exterior of the building, hallways and adjacent rooms that are not part of the crime scene itself, and so on. For an outdoor crime scene, the entire surrounding area should be photographed, including any nearby buildings or open fields.

Locality photographs are often overlooked but they can be crucial to a case. For example, a few years ago a young woman claimed that she had been raped in an open field. The case did not come to trial for many months, during which time the area where the alleged crime occurred was developed into a thriving residential community. The defense claimed that no rape had occurred, that the supposed victim was a willing participant. If she had resisted, the defense said, her screams would have been heard by someone in one of the nearby homes. However, when photographs of the locality were presented by the prosecution, the jury could easily see that at the time of the crime there were no buildings for more than a mile around. The rapist was convicted.

No crime scene is permanent. Often, by the time a case comes to trial, the scene has been so altered that a reconstruction would be impossible. Photographs (and, to a lesser extent, sketches) are the only evidence that can show the scene as it actually looked.

After the general locality has been photographed, pictures are taken of the *crime scene* itself: the room or rooms or the outdoor area where the crime took place. Pictures should be taken from a variety of angles and locations. In a room, for example, at least one picture should be taken from each corner and from each entrance. If the sequence of the criminal event is known, photographs should be taken of the point of entry, each place where a significant part of the event occurred, and the point of exit.

Finally, detailed photographs must be taken of every object or place in the crime scene that has any connection with the criminal event. All physical objects that have, or might have, some value as evidence must be photographed in the exact location and position where they are found. Stains, impressions, and other trace evidence also must be photographed before any effort is made to remove or reproduce them.

The photographer should make a note of each picture as it is taken. This record should include the following:

- the precise location from which the photograph was made
- the direction in which the camera was aimed
- the principal object that was photographed or the purpose of the picture
- the technical information about the picture: the shutter and aperture settings, lens focal length, and type of artificial lighting used, if any
- the type of camera and type of film
- the photographer's name and badge number

Each page of notes should be marked with a heading showing the case number (or any other unique identifying number), the type of crime being investigated and the address or other information about the location.[25]

## TWO SPECIAL-PURPOSE CAMERAS

### FINGERPRINT CAMERAS

It is extremely difficult to get a good photograph of a fingerprint or any other small impression or stain with an ordinary camera. A close-up lens attachment can be used on a 35mm camera, but then lighting remains a problem.

Fingerprint cameras, manufactured by several companies, are designed specifically to solve this problem. A fingerprint camera is simply an ordinary camera to which a special lens has been attached in a boxlike housing. The housing, which usually also contains a light unit, is exactly the right size; when the end of the housing is placed against the object to be photographed, a clear image will be formed on the film (Figure 4.4).[26]

The only special precaution to be taken with a fingerprint camera is that the end of the housing must be pressed flush against the object containing the impression and the camera must be held steady. Occasionally a fingerprint is found on an object of such complex shape or in such an awkward position that a fingerprint camera cannot be used conveniently.

Most fingerprint camera housings are large enough to permit placement of an identification card within the picture area without covering up any part of the fingerprint. The card should include the date, time, place, and investigator's name or initials. If there is enough room, the note should include the nature of the object on which the print was found.

Fingerprint cameras also can and should be used to record other types of impressions, stains, and other small evidence that would be hard to photograph with an ordinary camera.

### KODAK EKTAGRAPHIC VISUALMAKER

In the absence of a fingerprint camera, a Kodak Ektagraphic Visualmaker can serve the same purpose (Figure 4.5). The Visualmaker is a kit containing an Instamatic (26mm) camera and two framelike devices. Each frame has a clamp at one end, into which the camera is locked. When the camera is in place, a supplementary close-up lens fits over the camera's own lens. The rest of the frame serves to hold the camera at the correct distance from the object to be photographed, which is placed opposite the camera. There is even a built-in reflector that distributes light from a flashcube on the camera over the surface being photographed. The two frames in the kit are of different sizes so that different-sized objects can be photographed at appropriate distances. The smaller frame should produce acceptable images of fingerprints and other small impressions, and the larger frame can be used for almost any physical evidence that can be held in one's hand.

The Visualmaker kit is not extremely expensive, but it may be too expensive to provide one for every investigator. Many schools have the kit, as do advertising agencies and other places that produce slide programs frequently.

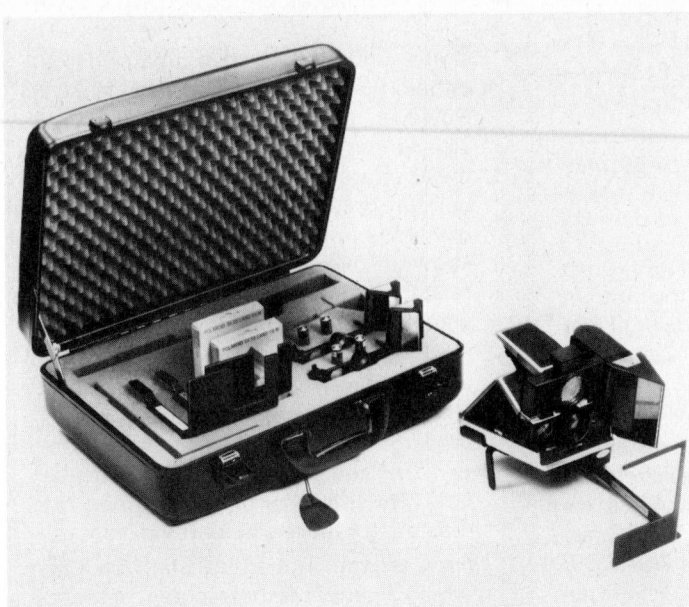

## FIGURE 4.4
## A POLAROID CV-70 KIT

*This portable system for precision close-up photography, using SX-70 Land cameras, is useful for photographing figerprints. The system uses three close-up lenses with matching color-coded focusing frames for life-size, 2X and 3X magnification. The Kit includes a Polatronic flash unit and is contained in a lightweight aluminum case with the capacity to hold camera and all accessories, as well as several SX-70 film packs. (Photo courtesy of Polaroid Corporation)*

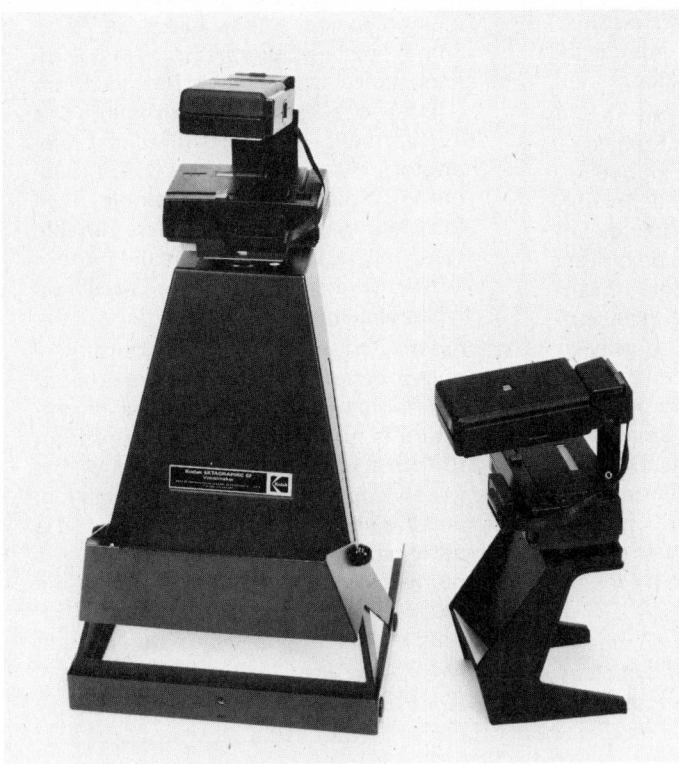

## FIGURE 4.5
## A KODAK EKTAGRAPHIC
## VISUALMAKER KIT

*This model comes complete with an electronic flash unit, and a pistol-type grip can be used to hold the small camera holder. (Photo courtesy of Eastman Kodak Co. Note: "Kodak," "Ektagraphic," and "Visualmaker" are all registered trademarks of the Eastman Kodak Co.)*

The following list of terminology may serve the uninitiated as a brief guide to photography.[27]

*Aperture.* The opening through which light passes in order to strike the film. On better cameras, the aperture is built into the lens and is adjustable. On simple snapshot cameras, the aperture may be merely a hole in the shutter blade.

*ASA number (film speed).* An index number that indicates the film's responsiveness to light. Low-speed films are rated below ASA 50; moderately fast films, between ASA 50 and ASA 200; fast films, above ASA 200. A fast film can produce usable pictures under poor lighting; a slow film, however, has finer grain and other qualities and thus can be enlarged to higher magnifications.

*Color balance.* The responsiveness of a film to the various portions of the color spectrum. Color films are designed for specific lighting conditions. If an outdoor (daylight) film is used under incandescent light, the picture will be orange tinted (too "warm"). If an indoor (incandescent or tungsten) film is used outdoors, the result will be bluish-gray or purplish (too "cold"). Filters can be used to compensate for the wrong film, but the filters cut down on the amount of light passing through the lens. Outdoor film should be used under fluorescent light or with electronic flash, while indoor film should be used with photofloods, flashbulbs, and ordinary incandescent lighting.

*Depth of field.* The range of distances, away from the camera, within which all objects remain in focus. As a rule, short (wide-angle) lenses have greater depth of field than do long (telephoto) lenses. However, the aperture setting (f-stop) also affects depth of field: the smaller the aperture (the *higher* the f-stop number), the greater the depth of field. Depth of field is important when you wish to show an overall scene or a number of related objects within a scene, and you want all of them to remain in focus.

*f number (lens speed).* An index of the lens's efficiency in transmitting light. Generally, the f number also represents the largest aperture (lowest f-stop number) that can be used on that particular lens. Thus, the *lower* the number, the "faster" (or more efficient) the lens.

*Focal length.* The optical size of a lens, which determines the apparent perspective of the pictures it produces. Usually marked inside a lens barrel as "F = 35mm" or "F = 50mm." For 35mm cameras, typical lenses would be 6 to 25mm ("fish-eye"); 25 to 40 (wide-angle); 45 to 65 (normal); 70 to 150 (medium telephoto); 150 to as much as 1,600 (telephoto). Most lenses have a single, fixed focal length; however, there are variable focal-length lenses, often called *zoom lenses,* available for some sizes and types of cameras.

*f-stop.* The size of the aperture (see above) is expressed as an *f-stop number* or *f number.* On better cameras, the aperture is adjustable over a range from f/1.0 to f/16 or f/32. The difference between one f-stop, or marked position, and the next is that half as much light is admitted at the higher number; the stop numbers represent ratios involving the diameter of the aperture. Thus, an aperture of f/4 admits twice as much light as f/5.6.

*Light meter.* A photoelectric device for

measuring the amount of light that is available in order to determine the proper aperture and shutter settings. Some of the more expensive cameras have built-in light meters. However, a built-in meter can read the light only as it reaches the camera from the entire scene in front of the lens; sometimes it is more valuable to know the amount of light being reflected from a single object in the scene, in which case a separate meter should be used.

*Range-finder viewing.* A viewing system, used to aim and focus a camera, in which images from two openings on the front of the camera are superimposed in a single view finder. Through the use of mirrors and prisms, the system is designed so the two images correspond exactly and look like a single image when the lens is properly focused.

*Shutter.* The part of a camera that opens to admit light at the proper moment—when a button is pressed, for example. On better cameras the length of time that the shutter remains open can be varied; this is known as *shutter speed.* A fast shutter speed tends to produce a sharp picture. However, for any given amount of light, as the shutter speed increases, the aperture also must be increased, which *reduces* the depth of field. Thus, to increase depth of field, shutter speed must be reduced.

*Single-lens reflex viewing (SLR).* A viewing system in which the photographer is able to see the subject through the camera's lens while aiming and focusing. Through-the-lens viewing is accomplished by an arrangement of mirrors and prisms that can be rather bulky. However, it is the only system that enables the photographer to see exactly what will be recorded on the film.

## THE PHOTOGRAPHER'S STANDARD

In photographing small objects of evidence or such things as tire tracks—when the dimensions are important, but would not be obvious from the picture alone—many photographers like to include a ruler or other measuring device in the picture. This is a helpful technique, as anyone who views the photograph can easily see the size of the object by comparing it to the ruler. Furthermore, enlargements can be made to the actual size of the object simply by enlarging the picture until the ruler is accurately reproduced.[28]

In the absence of a suitable ruler, especially for very small objects, any common item of known size (a coin, for example) can be placed in the picture area. Such items serve as a standard in roughly the same sense as the standard against which an unknown bit of evidence is compared. Some care must be exercised in the choice of photographic standards, however. Paper clips, for example, come in a great variety of sizes and thus would be worthless for this purpose.

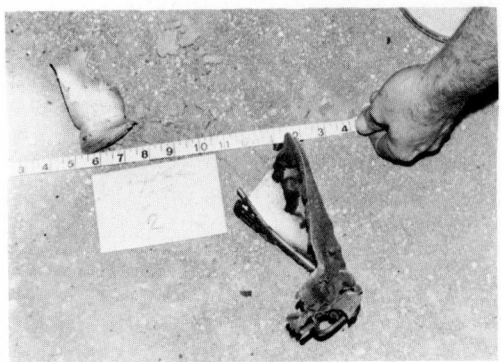

*The use of a photographic standard. Notice that an identification card also has been included in the scene. (Photo courtesy of Temple, Texas, Police Department)*

Some courts will not allow photographs to be introduced as evidence if they contain any "foreign object," anything other than the items actually found at the scene of a crime. The easiest way to solve this problem is to take two shots, one with the standard and one without.[29]

When including a standard object such as a ruler in the photograph, the photographer must be sure that it is exactly perpendicular to the camera's direction; otherwise, the standard will be distorted by perspective.

## MOTION PICTURES AND VIDEO TAPE

Sometimes it is helpful to photograph a crime scene in such a way that a sequence of events could be reproduced visually. This is often true in particularly complicated crimes, in which a series of separate incidents took place within an overall criminal event or in which the movements of the criminal and the victim must be understood. The circumstances obviously call for some sort of motion picture.

Motion pictures can be useful not only to show sequences and movements, but to show relationships between stationary objects as well. For example, suppose the crime scene is a very large room. The body is found at one end of the room near a doorway; the supposed murder weapon is a fireplace tool, taken from the fireplace at the opposite end of the room. No matter how many still pictures are taken, it will be difficult to simulate the relationship between the location of the body and the place from which the murder weapon was taken. However, this relationship could be shown very easily by placing a motion picture camera somewhere between the two locations, starting the camera at the fireplace, then turning the camera toward the location of the body (*panning* the room).

Motion pictures have provided good results in some investigations, and every once in a while they receive a lot of publicity. However, their use is still rare for several reasons. Motion picture cameras are not especially expensive, but the film is. Also, some special skill and experience are required of the person taking the pictures if the results are to be usable.

Perhaps the most serious problem is the processing of the film. Some kinds of motion picture film can be processed locally by the police agency or by a local commercial film processor. However, the processing requires expensive, bulky, and sophisticated equipment attended by well-trained technicians. Very few police agencies will find motion pictures valuable enough to justify that kind of expense. Sending the film away for processing is, of course, unacceptable because of the disruption of the chain of custody and because of the possibility of loss or damage to the film. [30]

There is one alternative that might be considered if a case virtually demands the use of motion pictures. Most television stations have appropriate cameras, used mostly for news gathering, which they might be willing to lend to the police. Indeed, they might be willing to have one of their photographers take the pictures, under immediate supervision of the investigator. Best of all, many television stations have their own film processing equipment on the premises, so the chain of custody can remain unbroken.

Another alternative is to use video tape instead of motion pictures. In fact, video tape has a few advantages over film. Some of the newer videotape cameras are capable of producing good pictures under very low light in black-and-white or in color, depending on the camera. The biggest advantage, of course, is that video tape does not require any processing. The pictures can be seen while they are being recorded and immediately afterward.

There are other advantages to video tape. The tape can be played back as often as desired, up to several hundred showings with most good-quality tape. However, once it is determined that a particular tape is no longer needed, it can be erased and reused. The video tape itself is not terribly expensive; compared to motion picture film, it is quite cheap.

The two major drawbacks to video tape are the equipment and the "magnetic tape prejudice." Videotape equipment is expensive, comparatively bulky, and fairly delicate. The minimum equipment required is a camera and a recorder; when the tape is played, a television set also is needed. Although the equipment is now much more compact and far lighter than it used to be, even the smallest recorder weighs around 12 kilograms (about 25 pounds). Although some recorders can be battery operated, the batteries do not last long, and household current should be used whenever possible. Thus videotape recording involves carrying the camera, the recorder, a cable connecting the two, and perhaps a separate electrical adapter and its cable. All of this can be a lot for one person to handle, especially in a crowded crime scene.

The magnetic tape prejudice that we discussed with regard to audio tape recording applies almost equally to video tape. Many people are suspicious of any kind of magnetic tape because of the presumption that it could be altered in some way. Actually, altering a video tape is not easy. It is not possible to edit a video tape by physically cutting the tape and splicing it back together, as can be done with audio tape and with motion picture film. If this is done with video tape, the result will be an obvious disruption of the picture and sound and possible damage to the delicate recording and playback mechanism. Video tape can be edited, of course, but only with expensive and sophisticated equipment, and even then a good deal of skill is required before an undetectable edit can be made.

If the integrity of a videotape recording is a serious problem, there are two simple solutions. One involves adding a device called a *date-time generator*. This device is connected to the recorder so that whenever a recording is made, the date and time are added to the picture from the camera. When the recording is played back, the date and time are seen superimposed over the picture, usually along the top or the bottom of the screen. Once the date and time have been recorded, it would be impossible to edit the picture information without disrupting the date-time sequence. A simpler antitampering technique is to include a clock in the scene. It would take consummate skill for anyone to edit a video tape so perfectly that the hands of a clock in the background remain unaffected.

More elaborate antitampering devices could be developed, but they hardly seem necessary, especially as the chain of custody can be maintained much more securely with a video tape than with a reel of motion picture film.

## MEASUREMENT AND NOTETAKING

We have already discussed the crucial importance of field notes and have suggested the hit-by-a-truck-tomorrow standard for completeness. Now let us consider what information the notes should contain.

Each time a new case is started, the principal investigator should prepare a set of notes, beginning with a summary of the information available at the outset. This would include the investigator's name and other identifying information (badge number, agency, division, or precinct, as appropriate); the nature of the alleged offense; the location of the alleged offense's occurrence; the name of the victim, if known; and the name of the complainant, if different from the victim. If a case number, offense number, or some other identifying number has already been assigned to the case, it should appear on this initial page of notes and should be repeated on each succeeding page.

After this summary page, there should be at least one page of notes recording the officer's initial impressions of the crime scene. The time of arrival at the scene should be recorded along with the names of every individual already present at the scene (with the address and telephone number of each potential witness). The description of the crime scene can be put in fairly general terms at this point, but should include precise information about the location and the general circumstances.[31]

Now the detailed measuring, notetaking, sketching, and photographing begin. Hereafter, the field notes can be divided into five main sections:

1. Descriptions accompanying sketches, including measurements

2. Descriptions accompanying photographs, including measurements, when appropriate

3. Descriptions of each item of physical evidence found at the scene or elsewhere

4. Summaries of interviews with the victim, witnesses, and suspects

5. Any other information obtained through direct observation, from other investigators, or from technical services such as criminalistics labs

## THE ROLE AND VALUE OF SKETCHES

If adequate photographs are made of a crime scene, it may seem redundant to make detailed sketches of the same things. However, the photographs and the sketches serve somewhat different purposes. They complement each other, and both are equally important.

A drawing or sketch is the simplest, most effective way to show distances and to identify items of evidence in their original locations at the scene. A sketch shows relationships, while a photograph shows details of appearance. One great advantage of a sketch is that the details that can distract from clarity are eliminated: only the most significant information is recorded in a visual form that permits easy, rapid comprehension. During the later stages of an investigation, and especially in court, the combination of accurate sketches and good photographs can help to reproduce the crime scene with great clarity and vividness.[32]

It is not necessary for the investigator to be an accomplished artist or draftsman. The investigator's sketches do not have to be in accurate scale; however, scale drawings are not difficult to make, especially if graph paper is used. Aesthetic excellence is far less important than simplicity and clarity. Occasionally it may be helpful to have a trained artist prepare finished drawings for presentation in the courtroom, but this is not often necessary. If they are accurate, the officer's original sketches may be sufficient, and their very simplicity gives them an air of authenticity that can be persuasive to a jury.

The measurements shown in the drawings and listed in the notes must be accurate. Proper measuring tools must be used and proper measuring techniques must be followed. Otherwise, the value of the evidence can be challenged in court, sometimes with devastating effects on the prosecution's case.

### TOOLS AND TECHNIQUES FOR MEASURING

The basic tool for measurement at the crime scene is the flexible steel ruler or tape measure. A steel measure is preferred because it will not stretch, as a fabric tape will.

Two or three steel tape measures of different sizes, such as 2.5, 10, and 25 meters (or 8, 25, and 50 feet) should cover almost every situation. Smaller steel rulers also should be available, although they are more useful as standard objects for photography than as devices for measuring evidence at the crime scene. Rulers of 15 centimeters, 50 centimeters, and 1 meter (or 6 inches, 1 foot, and 1 yard) are likely to be useful. Smaller measurements, which might require such devices as calipers, dividers, or micrometers, ought to be done in a laboratory rather than in the field.[33]

By the time an investigator is ready to take measurements of the crime scene, chances are that at least one other officer will have arrived to assist. However, if an officer is forced to do the measuring alone, either nylon-filament strapping tape or aluminized tape ("duct tape" or "gaffer's tape") can be used to hold one end of the measuring device securely in place. If this procedure is followed, the officer must check and recheck both ends of the tape to be sure that the anchored end has not come loose, throwing off the measurements. At an outdoor scene a small stake or nail can be used to anchor the free end of the tape in hard soil, or a heavy object (a brick or a rock, for example) can serve as an anchor.

Some police officers like to ask a bystander to assist in taking measurements. One reason for this is that the helpful bystander later can be called to testify about the procedures used in taking measurements, confirming the officer's testimony. However, other police authorities point out that having a bystander act as an assistant can backfire; you might not be able to locate the bystander later, or the person might turn out to be undependable as a witness.

Whatever method you use, it is important that the measurements be accurate. An error of ½ centimeter over a distance of ½ meter would be barely acceptable. Over a distance of 5 meters, the error should be no more than 1 centimeter; from 5 to 10 meters, no more than 2 centimeters. Beyond 10 meters the amount of error should be no more than one-half of 1 percent.

One way to ensure accurate measurements and to show the precise locations of objects in a sketch is to use the *triangulation system*. The first step is to determine reference points within the scene. These reference points should be obvious and more or less permanent features, such as the corners of a room or a large tree in a field. Since most rooms are approximately rectangular, only four reference points are usually needed. At an outdoor scene, or in a very irregularly shaped room, reference points should be chosen with care to include the whole area of the crime scene within a shape that is as close to rectangular as possible.

Once the reference points have been established (and marked on the sketch), it is a simple matter to measure the location of each item of evidence from two different reference points. The distances between the reference points themselves are also measured and shown on the sketches, so each item of evidence is located at one corner of a triangle (Figure 4.6); there can be little doubt about its exact place in the crime scene if these meas-

FIGURE 4.6
THE TRIANGULATION SYSTEM

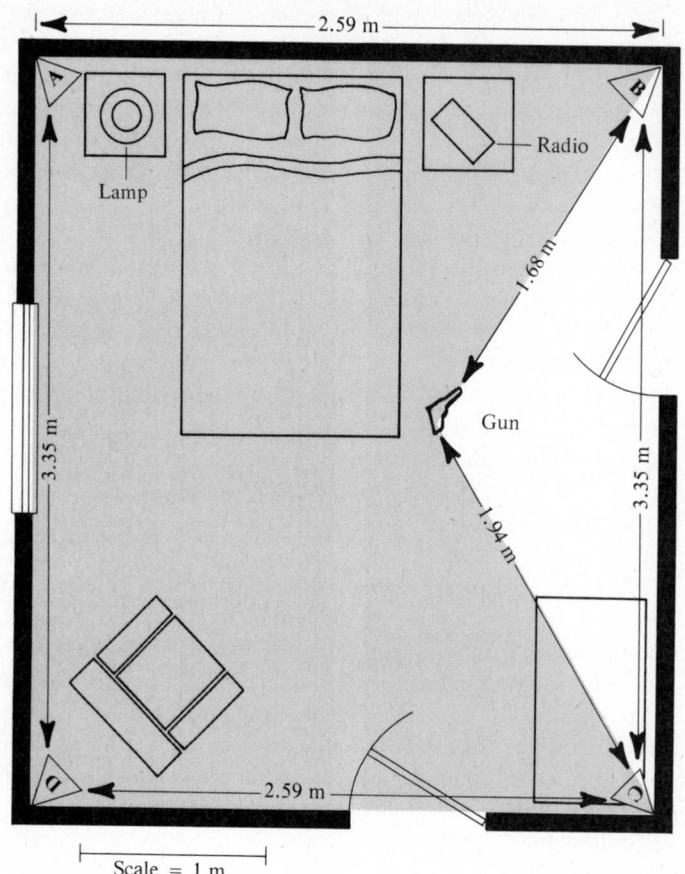

Lamp

Radio

Gun

Scale = 1 m

urements are accurately recorded in the investigator's sketches and notes.[34]

### SKETCHING PROCEDURES

Whether the sketches of the crime scene are made by the same person who does the photography or by a second person, they should be done at approximately the same time and, as much as possible, in the same order. If two people are involved, the principal investiga-tor should do the sketches and direct the photographer. The two forms of visual record should complement each other and should be made in the same sequence: first, the general locality; next, an overall view of the crime scene; finally, the specific details. If the scene is extremely complex—involving, say, several rooms in a home or office building—or if the criminal event took place at several different locations, each location or portion of the scene should be separately sketched and the relationships between them shown on a master sketch.[35]

The sketches can take different forms: the plan, the elevation drawing, the "all-walls view," the "exploded view," and the detail drawing. Each form serves somewhat different purposes.

**The plan.** Almost everyone is familiar with a floor plan, a drawing of a home or other building that shows the locations of the walls, doorways, windows, and furniture. A *plan* is simply a drawing that shows the locations and relationships of things as they are arranged on the ground or floor (Figure 4.7). It is a two-dimensional view, as if seen from a great height.

**The elevation drawing.** An *elevation drawing* is the vertical counterpart of a plan: it shows the locations and relationships between objects against a vertical surface such as a wall (Figure 4.8). In some elevation drawings, only the vertical surface itself (that is, the wall) is shown; in other elevations, the objects near a wall might be shown in relationship to the vertical surface.

**The all-walls view.** It is sometimes helpful to show the plan and several elevations of a single room all on one sketch. This can be done by laying the baseline of each elevation against the corresponding points on the plan. The result is a drawing that shows the room as if it were flattened out on the page.

This is easy enough to do if the room has

FIGURE 4.7
A PLAN

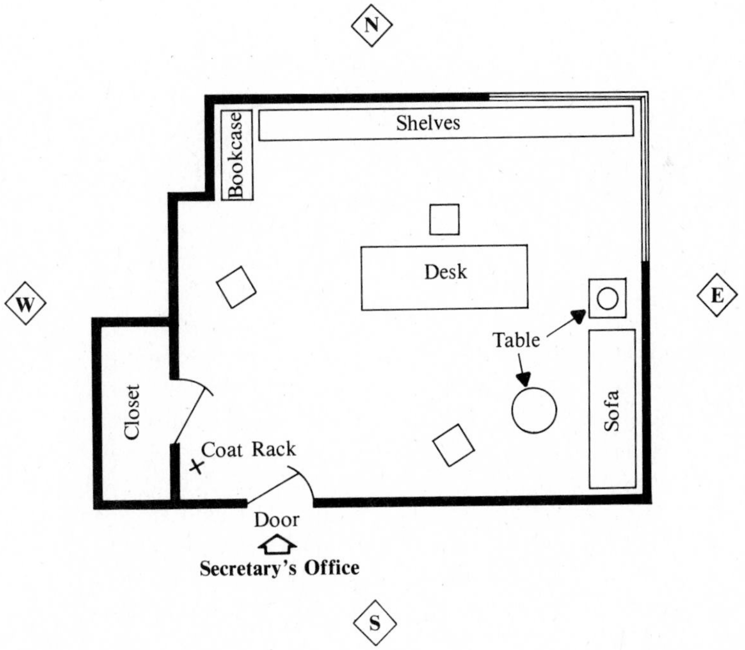

FIGURE 4.8
ELEVATIONS

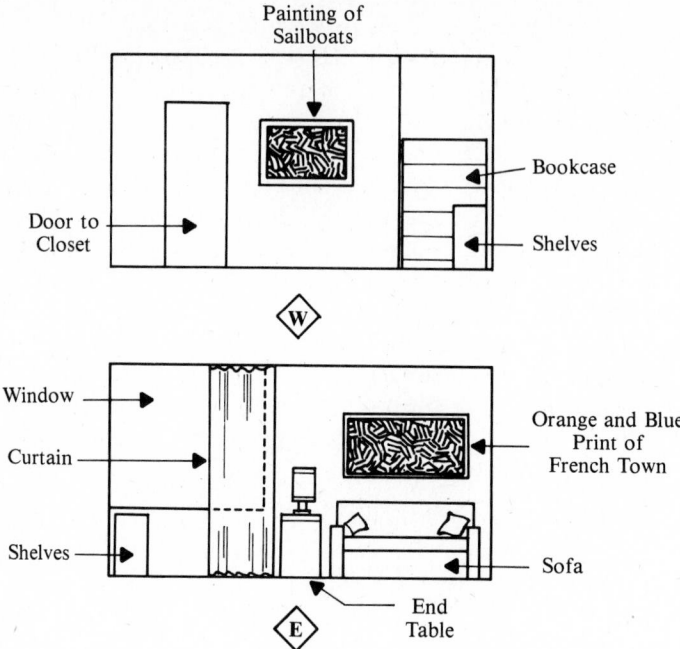

a fairly simple rectangular shape, but such is not always the case. Usually, unimportant surfaces can be omitted from the all-walls view; in Figure 4.9, a short jog in one wall has been left out without seriously affecting the value of the sketch.

**The exploded view.** An all-walls view is a two-dimensional sketch or, rather, a combination of several two-dimensional views. Sometimes, however, a scene is just too complicated for this form to be satisfactory. In that case, an exploded view might be used. The *exploded view* is three-dimensional, but it is made up of the same components that we have already described: the plan and the elevations. The difference is that they are shown at an angle, as if in perspective, with

arrows to connect the various pieces in their proper relationships (Figure 4.10). Developing a good exploded view is tricky and requires some practice; however, when no other form of drawing will show the relationships properly, even a poorly drawn exploded view might be better than none.

**The detail drawing.** There is normally no need for the investigator to make elaborate sketches of the individual items of evidence. If the evidence is small enough to be removed, it can be photographed and then taken to the laboratory for careful measurement and examination. If the evidence is too large or is fixed in place and cannot be removed, the photographs alone may be sufficient. Castings or other reproductions also can record large or immovable items of evidence.

Occasionally, however, an investigator may need to make a drawing of some detail of evidence that, for one reason or another, cannot be photographed, removed to the laboratory, or reproduced by casting.

A *detail drawing* should be a three-dimensional view of the object, isolated from its surroundings. Two or more separate drawings may be needed to show all sides or surfaces. For investigative purposes, a detail drawing should not be made in normal perspective. Instead, an *isometric* drawing should be made. This means that each line in the drawing is done to the same scale (Figure 4.11). The result will look very odd to the eye because we expect to see things in normal perspective; we assume, for instance, that the line across the back of a cube will appear shorter than the line across the front. However, for use in an investigation, it is more

FIGURE 4.9
"ALL-WALLS" VIEW

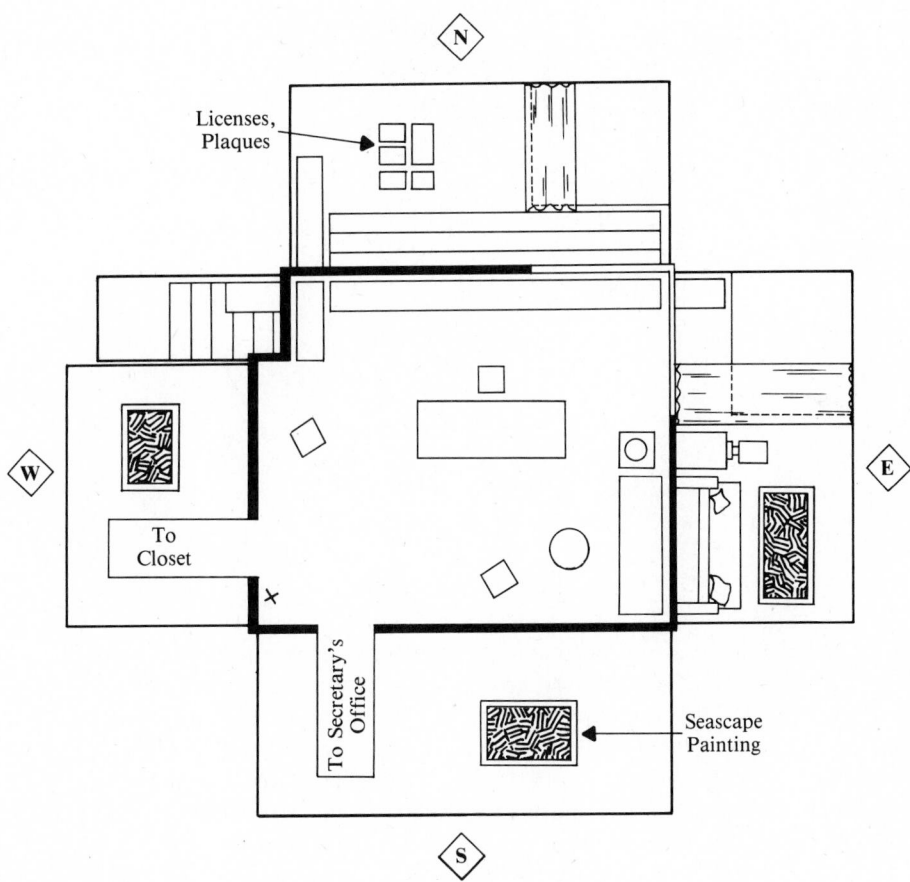

FIGURE 4.10
"EXPLODED" VIEW

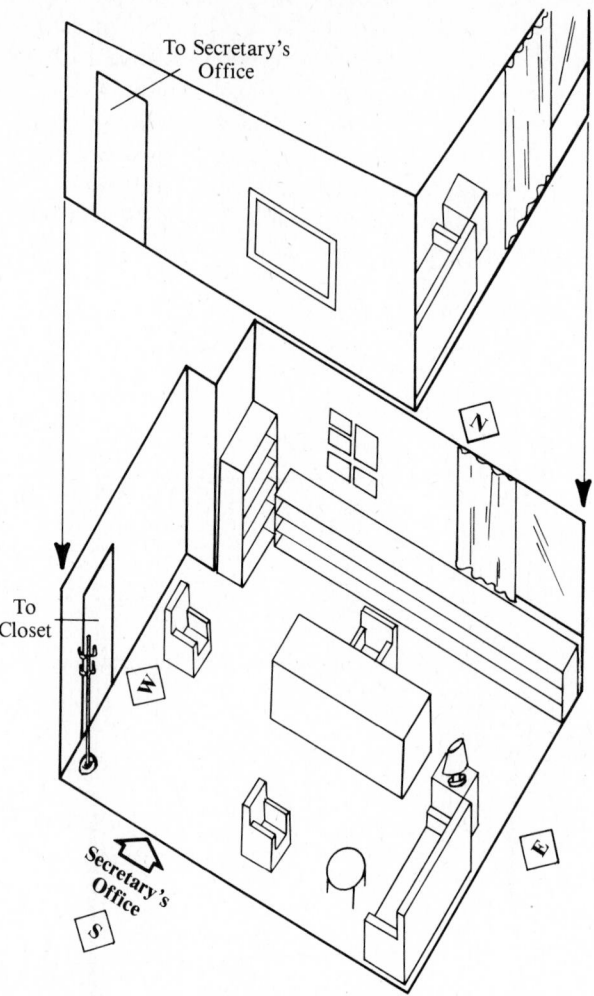

To Secretary's
Office

To
Closet

Secretary's
Office

important that the scale of the drawing be maintained consistently. If the isometric drawing is so distorted that the object seems almost unrecognizable, a separate sketch can be made in normal perspective.

**Importance of sketches.** Making all of these sketches and drawings can be a time-consuming task. Certainly, the time spent on them should be proportional to the importance of the case. However, the chore of sketching must not be slighted. Even with dozens of excellent photographs and ample physical evidence, complete and accurate sketches can provide the road map that guides the investigator to a true understanding of the crime.

FIGURE 4.11
ISOMETRIC DETAIL DRAWING

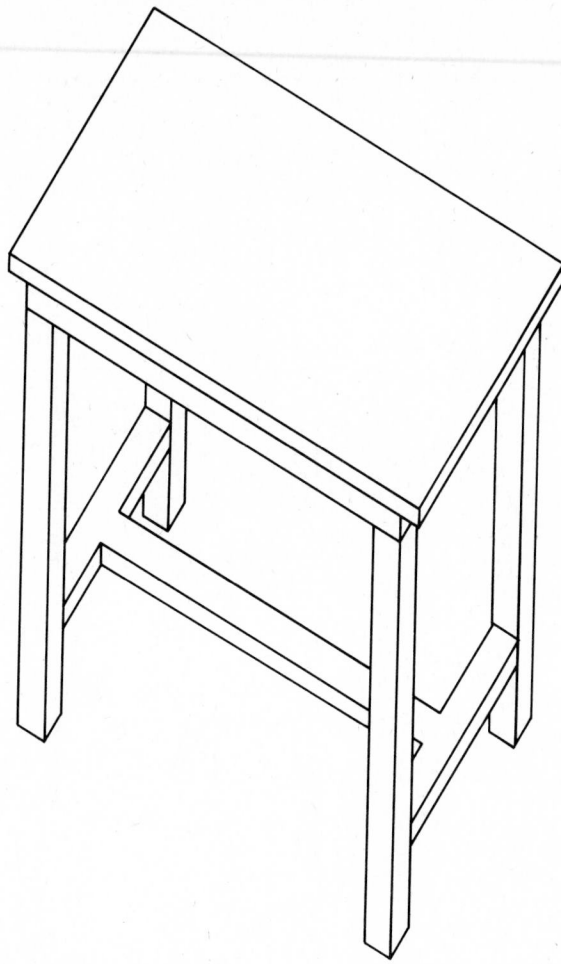

SKETCH NOTATIONS

Sketches are easier to draw and simpler to understand if a standardized set of symbols or a code is used for common elements. A key to the code or symbols should be kept permanently in the notebook; if necessary, a copy of the key might be included in the file for each case.

All measurements should be shown directly on the sketch, with arrows connecting the points from which the measurements were made (Figure 4.12). This must be done with some care to keep the sketch from becoming overcrowded and messy.

For each sketch, there should be a complete description of what the sketch is intended to

FIGURE 4.12
SKETCH WITH MEASUREMENTS

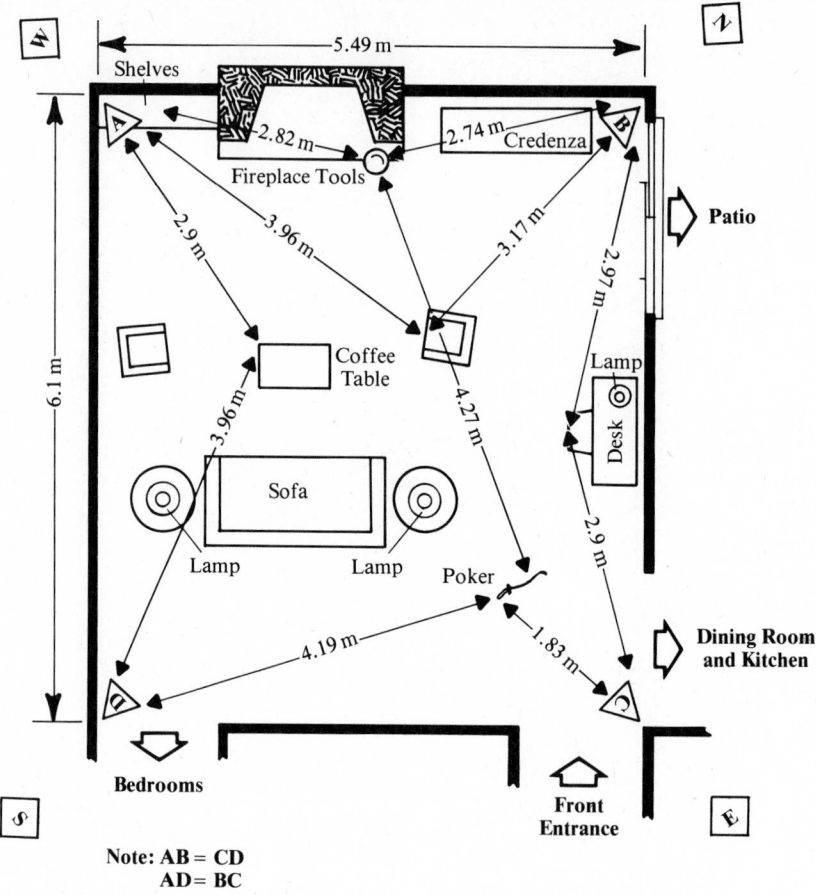

Note: AB = CD
AD = BC

represent and what it contains. There should be a heading that relates the sketch to the case, and the name of the person who made the sketch should be indicated. If a binder notebook is used, the notes for a sketch can be written either on the back of the sketch or on the facing page. If the latter procedure is used, it should be followed consistently, all pages should be numbered in sequence, and all of the pages for a single case should be stapled together so that nothing can be misplaced. Every measurement shown in the sketch should be listed in the notes, stating the object measured, the dimensions, and the points from which the measurements were taken. If the triangulation system is used, the reference points should be shown distinctively on the sketch (for example, capital letters inside a triangle); these symbols can then be used in the accompanying notes (Figure 4.13).

FIGURE 4.13
NOTES DESCRIBING A SKETCH

(p.8)  Homicide - 3/8/78   #62114
312 Woods Lane

Sketch: Living room
Major dimensions (A)(B) = 5.49m = (C)(D)
(A)(D) = 6.1m = (B)(C)

Locations of evidence:
broken corner of
coffee table — 2.9m from (A)
3.96m from (D)

blood on cushion of chair - 3.96m from (A)
3.17m from (B)

desk chair (see summary) - 2.97m from (B)
2.9m from (C)

fireplace poker - 1.83m from (C), 4.19m from (D)
4.27m from fireplace toolrack

fireplace tools - 2.82m from (A)
2.74m from (B)

ACT II
THE BURGLARY
AT 1209 MAIN STREET

Do you remember the case that Officer Cole was investigating back in Chapter 3? If you have forgotten some of the details, you may wish to refresh your memory by referring back to pages 67 through 69.

Here are the sketches that Officer Cole has made in the course of investigating the suspected burglary (Figure 4.14). As you might expect, Officer Cole uses our system of sketching and notetaking; drawings are at the right, and notes for each drawing are on the facing pages of the notebook.

*Recording and Reporting Evidence*

# FIGURE 4.14
## OFFICER COLE'S SKETCHES

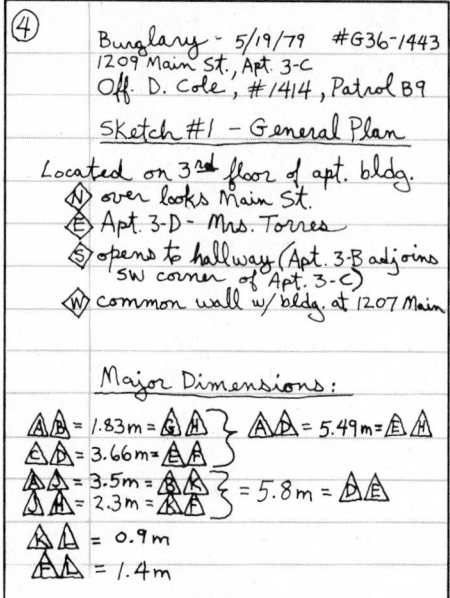

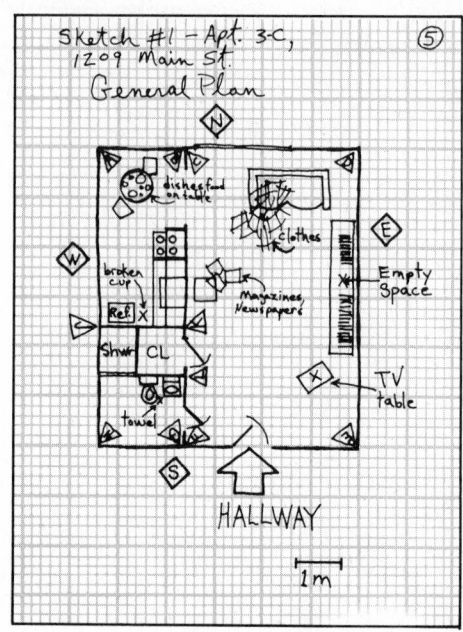

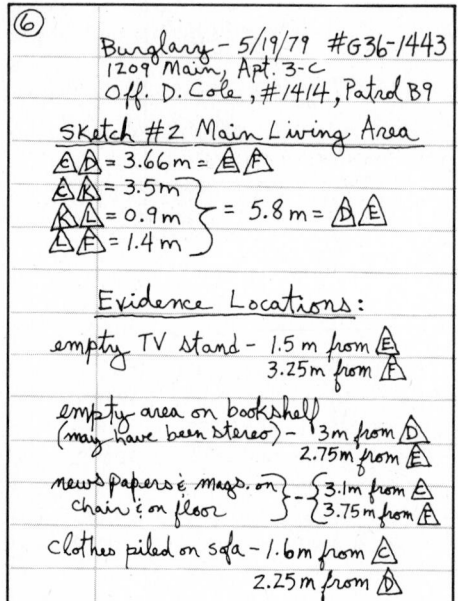

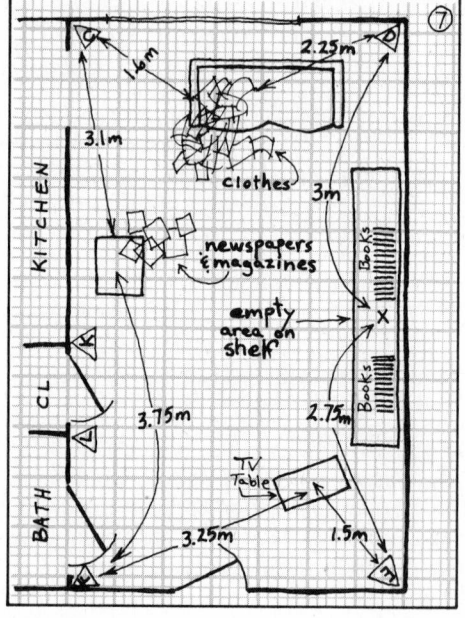

*The Initial Investigation*

**⑧**

Burglary - 5/19/79 #G36-1443
1209 Main, Apt. 3-C
Off. D. Cole, #1414, Patrol B9

Sketch #3 Kitchen

△A △B = 1.83 m = △A △A
△A △A = 3.5 m = △A △B

Evidence Locations

Breakfast food, dishes
on table — 0.75 m from △A
1.5 m from △A

Broken cup on floor — 1.12 m from △A
0.84 m from △A

Note: 1.62 m above broken cup,
scratch and chipped plaster
on wall.

Note: Some of cupboard doors
found open; could not determine
whether anything was missing.

---

**⑨**

Sketch #3 – Kitchen

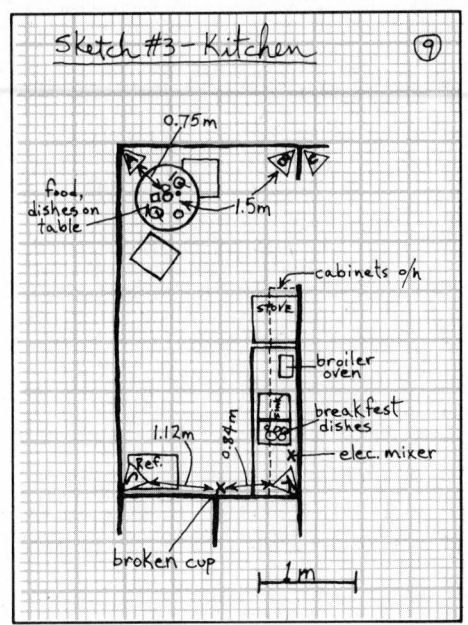

0.75m

food,
dishes on
table

1.5m

cabinets o/h

store

broiler
oven

breakfast
dishes

elec. mixer

1.12m  0.84m

Ref.

broken cup

|__1m__|

---

**⑩**

Burglary - 5/19/79 #G36-1443
1209 Main, Apt. 3-C
Off. D. Cole, #1414, Patrol B9

Sketch #4 – Bathroom

△G △H = 1.83 m   △A △M = 0.85 m
△G △L = 1.53 m

Evidence Locations

Dirty towel — possible
blood stains — 1.25 m from △G
0.65 m from △A

Not shown on this sketch:

Stains in sink — appear to be
grease and blood

Box of adhesive bandages on
back of sink — grease marks
on box

See sketch #5

---

**⑪**

Sketch #4 – Bathroom

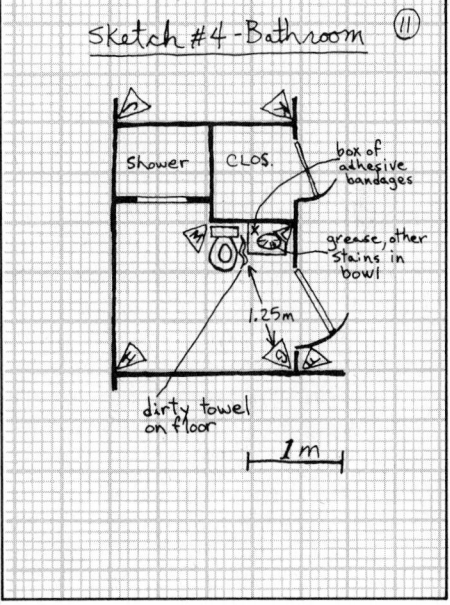

Shower   CLOS.

box of
adhesive
bandages

grease, other
stains in
bowl

1.25m

dirty towel
on floor

|__1m__|

FIGURE 4.14
OFFICER COLE'S SKETCHES (CONT'D)

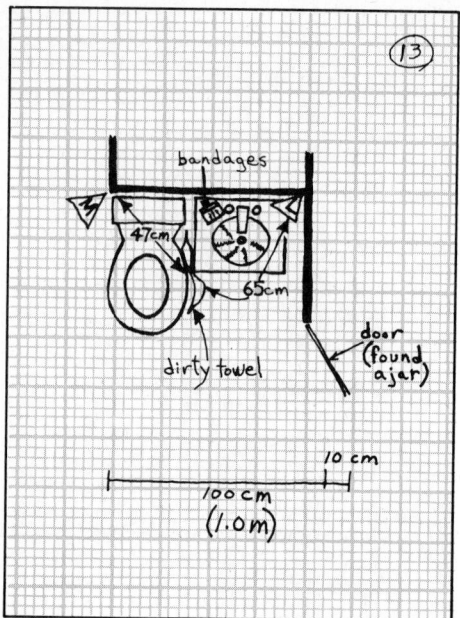

Burglary - 5/19/79 #G36-1443
1209 Main, Apt. C-3
Off. D. Cole, #1414, Patrol B9

Sketch #5 - Bathroom detail
△Ⓜ = 0.85m
Dirty towel (on floor) - 65 cm from △
47 cm from Ⓜ

Stains in sink - equally distributed
around bowl; center of bowl
31 cm from △, 63 cm from Ⓜ

Box of adhesive bandages on
back of sink, 41 cm from △
42 cm from Ⓜ

## EVIDENCE RECORDS

In addition to the notes for sketches and photographs, the field notes should contain a record of each item of physical evidence found at the scene or, later in the course of the investigation, anywhere else.[36]

Each item should be described as carefully and as thoroughly as possible. Material objects such as weapons, tools, or items of clothing should be described in terms of their nature, type, manufacturer and model, color, size, and anything else that individualizes the item. The location of the item when it was first discovered is of critical importance. Finally, the notes should describe each item's condition when it was found: broken, soiled, torn, stained, or whatever.

When the evidence list has been completed, it should be checked against the notes for the sketches. Each item ought to appear in both places. If it is not in both places, either it was omitted accidentally from one list or the other, or there is some reason that it is not shown on the sketch. An explanation for the discrepancy should be written into the notes.

Before leaving the crime scene, the investigator should take a few moments to review all of the notes carefully. Errors, discrepancies, or omissions should be corrected immediately; if the correction is obvious (such as a scratched out word or phrase), it should be initialed by the officer. Once the investigator has left the scene, the field notes must not be changed even if it is later discovered that some detail is wrong. The field notes themselves should be treated as if they were evidence and should be protected from any tampering or contamination.

## OFFENSE, EVIDENCE, AND SUMMARY REPORTS

The investigator's field notes and sketches form the basis not only for courtroom testimony, but also for the official documents by which a criminal investigation is recorded. These documents include the original offense report, an evidence list or report, and in many cases periodic summary reports of new information or evidence. Many agencies provide standardized printed forms for each purpose; if not, however, some systematic form should be followed.

The offense report may be as short as a single sheet or as long as necessary to include all essential information about a case. The report should include at least the following information:

1. The date and time of the original complaint or discovery of the suspected crime; the name of the complainant or the officer who discovered the crime and initiated the investigation

2. The names of the officers who initially responded to the complaint; their time of arrival at the scene

3. Address or other description of the location where the crime occurred or was discovered

4. Name, home address, and description of the victim (age, sex, ethnic group, occupation, and so on)

5. Apparent nature of the alleged or suspected crime

6. Name, badge number, and agency, precinct, or service division of the principal investigator

7. Same information for every other police officer who participates in the investigation

8. List of witnesses, including name, address, phone number, and other identifying information as needed; a brief indication of

what information each witness possesses (present at the scene, saw perpetrator fleeing, or whatever)

9. List of all physical evidence recovered at the scene; its apparent significance if known; notes on approximately where it was found, who found it, how it was marked, and what was done with it (in whose custody it was placed or to what laboratory or other location it was taken)

10. Narrative description of the investigation, including in summary form all that is known about the criminal event: who did what, how, to whom, and why[37]

One of the greatest misconceptions about these official forms is that they should be written in stilted, legalistic language. Some agencies insist that the writers use a third-person style, which presumably conveys an impression of detached objectivity. Unfortunately, that style also leads the writer into twisted and unnatural phrasing that can completely obscure meaning.

An offense report does not have to be a literary masterpiece, but it does have to be clear, concise, and accurate. Simple language works best. The investigator should write down what was seen, heard, done, and learned.[38]

Unless the agency's policy is absolutely inflexible on this point, it is far better for the report to be written in the first person: "I arrived at the scene with my partner, Officer Jones, and met the storekeeper at the front door. She introduced herself as Ms. A. Brown." This is infinitely more understandable than the following: "This officer arrived at the reported location in company with Officer Jones, whereupon this investigator and Officer Jones encountered Ms. A. Brown, who identified herself as being the proprietor of the business establishment at said location, and who was awaiting the arrival of said officers at the entrance thereto."

The offense report should not include the investigator's opinions or conclusions about the nature of the offense. It is not up to the investigator, generally, to make a final decision about whether the crime was a homicide, manslaughter, or self-defense, for example. All that the investigator has to do is write down what has been learned; the information will speak for itself, and the proper officials will be able to determine what crime has occurred. However, this does not mean that the investigator should not have an opinion; on the contrary, an understanding of the nature of the crime will play a major part in determining how the investigation should proceed. [39]

The evidence report should contain essentially all the information that was recorded in the field notes for each item of evidence. Again, there is usually a standardized form for this purpose. However, significant information about a piece of evidence should not be omitted just because the form does not ask for it; the people who make up forms cannot foresee every conceivable circumstance.

Offense and evidence reports ordinarily are prepared as soon as possible after the initial stage of the investigation has been completed. The officer who writes the reports should take plenty of time and ensure that the reports are thorough, clear, and accurate. The reports should be checked carefully against the field notes to be certain that there are no discrepancies or significant omissions. An incomplete, inaccurate, or incomprehensible report is worse than none at all. Or, to put it in more positive terms, a good report is the beginning of a good investigation. It is worth taking the time and effort to do it right.

## REFERENCES

1. Paul B. Weston and Kenneth M. Wells, *Criminal Evidence for Police* (Englewood Cliffs, N.J.: 1971), Prentice-Hall, pp. 2–5.

2. Weston and Wells, *Criminal Evidence,* p. 5.

3. Weston and Wells, *Criminal Evidence,* p. 6.

4. Weston and Wells, *Criminal Evidence,* p. 18.

5. V. A. Leonard, *The Police Detective Function* (Springfield, Ill.: Charles C Thomas, 1970), p. 50.

6. Weston and Wells, *Criminal Evidence,* pp. 107–115.

7. *Criminal Investigation* (Gaithersburg, Md.: International Association of Chiefs of Police, 1971), p. 79.

8. Weston and Wells, *Criminal Evidence,* p. 101.

9. *Criminal Investigation,* pp. 102–108.

10. Gwynne Peirson, *Police Operations* (Chicago: Nelson-Hall, 1976), pp. 110–111.

11. *Criminal Investigation,* pp. 15–16.

12. Richard H. Fox and Carl L. Cunningham, *Crime Scene Search and Physical Evidence Handbook* (Washington, D.C.: U.S. Department of Justice, National Institute of Law Enforcement and Criminal Justice, 1973), p. 34.

13. Fox and Cunningham, p. 34.

14. Fox and Cunningham, p. 34.

15. Paul L. Kirk, *Crime Investigation,* 2d ed. (New York: John Wiley and Sons, 1974), p. 85.

16. Kirk, pp. 19, 86; *Criminal Investigation,* p. 95.

17. Kirk, pp. 94–96.

18. Weston and Wells, *Criminal Evidence,* p. 104.

19. Kirk, p. 21.

20. Kirk, p. 87.

21. Kirk, pp. 96–100.

22. Paul B. Weston and Kenneth M. Wells, *Elements of Criminal Investigation* (Englewood Cliffs, N.J.: Prentice-Hall, 1971), pp. 15–16.

23. *Criminal Investigation,* p. 94.

24. Fox and Cunningham, p. 43.

25. Leonard, p. 51.

26. Kirk, p. 20.

27. Kirk, pp. 90–94; see also any of the numerous inexpensive guides and handbooks for amateur and professional photographers published by the Eastman Kodak Company, the Petersen Publishing Company, and others.

28. Weston and Wells, *Elements of Criminal Investigation,* p. 17.

29. *Criminal Investigation,* p. 96.

30. Kirk, p. 102.

31. Weston and Wells, *Elements of Criminal Investigation,* pp. 14–15.

32. Fox and Cunningham, p. 35.

33. Fox and Cunningham, p. 38.

34. *Criminal Investigation,* p. 92.

35. Weston and Wells, *Elements of Criminal Investigation,* pp. 18–21.

36. Fox and Cunningham, pp. 32–34.

37. Leonard, pp. 100–103.

38. *Criminal Investigation,* p. 23.

39. *Criminal Investigation,* p. 22.

## REVIEW OF THE EVIDENCE

1. True or false: Only the testimony of witnesses who personally observed a crime (including the victim) can be presented in a trial.

2. Contra-evidence is
   a. microscopic material.
   b. evidence that should be ignored.
   c. worthless or misleading evidence.
   d. evidence that seems to contradict the majority of the other available evidence.
   e. evidence that, when properly considered, leads to a correct understanding of the entire criminal event.
   f. none of the above.

3. True or false: An investigator's notebook must be small enough to fit into a buttoned pocket.

4. Which of the following could serve as a partial substitute for an investigator's notebook?
   a. photographs of the crime scene
   b. sketches of the crime scene
   c. magnetic tape recordings
   d. the offense report
   e. physical evidence

5. True or false: Handwritten field notes are usually more detailed and accurate than a verbal account recorded on tape.

6. A special camera with a housing over the lens, often with its own built-in light unit, is
   a. a single-lens reflex camera.
   b. a fingerprint camera.
   c. a range-finder camera.
   d. a large-format camera.
   e. none of the above.

7. Motion pictures or video tape should be used
   a. to maintain the chain of custody.
   b. to show relationships among various objects or places within the crime scene.
   c. to show a sequence of events.
   d. to prove that the evidence has not been contaminated.
   e. for all of the above reasons.
   f. for none of the above reasons.

8. Which of the following should *not* be considered as one of the main sections of an investigator's field notes?
   a. descriptions and measurements accompanying sketches
   b. descriptions and measurements accompanying photographs
   c. a description of each item of physical evidence
   d. a narrative summary of the investigation, phrased in the first person, unless agency rules require a third-person style

  e. summaries of interviews with witnesses

  f. any other information obtained by the investigator

9. The triangulation system is

  a. a method of drawing in which all lines are made the same length.

  b. a method of producing videotape pictures in three colors.

  c. a system of measuring distances from predetermined reference points.

  d. a system used to aim and focus a type of camera.

  e. none of the above.

10. Which of these should *not* be included in the offense report?

  a. a list of witnesses

  b. names and badge numbers of all police officers who have assisted in an investigation

  c. the date and time of the original complaint

  d. a list of physical evidence

  e. the investigator's assessment of the nature of the crime

### TOPICS FOR INVESTIGATION

1. The text suggests the hit-by-a-truck-tomorrow standard for an investigator's field notes. Is this standard realistic and practical? Is it necessary?

2. How can police officers and agencies overcome the so-called magnetic tape prejudice among themselves and the general public?

3. A complete investigative photography kit, costing anywhere from $500 to $2,000, would include a good 35mm camera, a couple of lenses, photographic lighting equipment, a fingerprint camera, and miscellaneous accessories. Bearing these costs in mind, should every patrol unit be equipped with such a kit? If not, which of the various alternatives (purchase of cheaper cameras, use of photographic specialists, and so on) would be most desirable?

4. Many agencies require all investigative photography to be done by specialists. Should they also have specialist artists to do all crime-scene sketches? How can specialists, both photographers and artists, be most effective as support for field investigations?

5. Police officers often grumble about the amount of paperwork they are expected to do. Are the requirements that we have discussed in this chapter—field notes, sketches, offense reports, evidence lists, summary reports, and so on—reasonable or excessive? What could be done to reduce the burden of paperwork without sacrificing investigative quality? Does paperwork detract from or interfere with a police officer's ability to conduct an investigation?

# CHAPTER 5
## ACQUIRING, COLLECTING, AND PRESERVING EVIDENCE

STUDY CLUES

1. Criminal instruments, fruits of a crime, and contraband are examples of
    a. circumstantial evidence.
    b. contra-evidence.
    c. direct evidence.
    d. trace evidence.
    e. testimonial evidence.
2. True or false: Friction-ridge impressions are formed whenever one of the contact surfaces of the body is pressed against another surface.
3. The five zones of a crime scene are the route of approach, point of entry, crime site, point of exit, and route of departure. A suspect's vehicle might include which of these zones?
    a. routes of approach and departure
    b. points of entry and exit
    c. the crime site
    d. all of the above
    e. none of the above
4. True or false: The only kind of casting material that is useful for investigation is plaster of paris.
5. Which of the following statements are true?
    a. All investigators should have the same standard kit of materials and tools for collecting, marking, and preserving evidence.
    b. All friction-ridge impressions can be classified as "latent prints."
    c. Sometimes fingerprints can be found on and "lifted" from human skin.
    d. The pattern of a stain and its location on a garment may be just as important as the nature of the stain.
    e. Impression evidence may be found on the nose of a spent bullet.

IN THE LAST TWO CHAPTERS we have discussed at some length the procedures for locating, identifying, and recording evidence and we have described the nature of evidence in general terms. In this chapter we will be much more specific about the kinds of evidence that should be sought at a crime scene and the ways in which it should be collected and preserved for an investigation. In other words, we will describe what to look for, where to look for it, and what to do with it when you have found it.

So far, everything we have said about the search for evidence has concerned the investigation at the scene of a crime. In many cases, perhaps the great majority, that is the only locale where evidence is sought. However, it is often necessary to seek evidence at other locations, especially places associated with the suspected perpetrator.[1] The principles that we have outlined apply equally to those instances. The only important difference is that the search for evidence away from the crime scene may take place under hostile circumstances; suspects, especially if they are guilty, almost certainly do not want any evidence to be found. Much more care must be taken to ensure that only appropriate evidence is collected and that the constitutional rights of suspects are scrupulously observed. These are matters that we shall cover later, primarily in Chapter 17.

For now, we shall concentrate on the search for evidence at the crime scene.

## WHAT TO LOOK FOR

Both direct and indirect evidence should be sought at the crime scene. Direct evidence relates specifically to the criminal event. Indirect evidence concerns the victim or the perpetrator but has no immediate connection to the criminal event. Circumstantial evidence is a form of indirect evidence that suggests a relationship between the perpetrator and the event, but does not necessarily prove that a particular individual committed the crime. All these types of evidence are likely to be found at the scene in the form of physical objects.

### DIRECT EVIDENCE

Three kinds of direct evidence may be found:

• Objects that by their nature, placement, or condition indicate that a crime has occurred. For example, a dead body by itself does not prove that a crime has occurred; however, the condition (or sometimes the placement) of the body and of other objects in the vicinity may show that the person was murdered. A safe whose door has been removed by explosives would almost always be evidence that a crime (safecracking or burglary of a safe) has been committed.

• Objects that indicate how the crime occurred. Most of the direct evidence at a crime scene usually falls into this category: weapons, tool marks, documents, ordinary objects (such as furniture) that are out of their usual place, and so on.

• Criminal instruments, fruits of a crime, and contraband that can be connected to an individual. There are many physical things whose mere possession is illegal; called *contraband,* these include certain drugs, tools made or modified specifically for use in burglary, gambling devices, and some kinds of weapons. Many other things are legal to own except when they are connected to a crime: firearms, for example, or personal property that has been stolen. If any of these objects are found at a crime scene or elsewhere, they are direct evidence. If the objects contain traces of an individual, such as fingerprints, then that individual ordinarily becomes a suspected criminal.

## INDIRECT EVIDENCE

Much of the evidence that can be found at a crime scene is indirect, especially circumstantial evidence. There are four major categories of such evidence:

• Traces of the criminal. These include anything that the perpetrator left behind which can be used to show that a certain person was at the scene and, sometimes, that certain actions, which may have been connected to the crime, were performed.

• Objects that might have been transferred from the scene or the victim to the perpetrator. For example, soil, paint, glass fragments, and other debris might be picked up by the criminal in the course of the crime. Hair, blood, skin particles, clothing fibers, and other material could be transferred from the victim to the perpetrator of an assault. If any such material is found later on the person or clothing of a suspect, there is good reason to believe that the suspect was at the scene. However, in order to establish that relationship, the necessary standards must be obtained at the crime scene. Otherwise, for example, soil found in the suspect's shoes would be meaningless as evidence.

• Objects that suggest the victim's activities prior to the crime or imply how the crime occurred. Sometimes there is so little direct evidence at the scene of a crime that the investigator must back up and begin to reconstruct the events that preceded the crime itself. Knowing the victim's activities prior to the crime may lead, indirectly, to the perpetrator or, at least, to a clearer understanding of how the crime took place.

• Objects that suggest ways to locate a suspect. Objects found at the scene may have no clear connection with the victim, the perpetrator, or the crime itself, but they may help to develop investigative avenues that might ultimately lead to the perpetrator. For example, suppose a book of matches found at the scene has no fingerprints, handwritten notes, or other markings that indicate conclusively a connection with either the victim or the suspect. However, if the matchbook contains advertising for a nightclub, it may be that either the victim or the perpetrator frequents that night club. In the absence of any better evidence, it could be worth checking to see whether any of the nightclub's employees knew the victim or had any other knowledge of the crime.

The foregoing list of types of evidence has been arranged more or less in priority order. In acquiring, collecting, and preserving evidence, especially at a crime scene, one should place the greatest emphasis on direct evidence. After that, the most useful indirect evidence would be traces of the perpetrator. Next in value would be debris that might have been transferred from the scene or victim to the perpetrator. The other two categories of indirect evidence deserve the least attention from the investigator, except when all other kinds of evidence are lacking or insufficient.

## THE FORMS OF PHYSICAL EVIDENCE

The various forms of physical evidence, discussed very briefly in Chapter 4, will now be examined in greater detail. These are the specific, material things that an investigator should look for at the scene of a crime. Nine forms of physical evidence are discussed in the following pages.

**Impressions: friction-ridge prints.**
Human skin is made up of several layers of living cells. The cells closest to the surface are called the *epidermis*. The epidermal cells directly on the surface usually are dead and fall off easily, while at a slightly lower level within the epidermis new cells are being formed constantly. The epidermis varies in thickness and in form. Over most of the body it is around 0.5 to 1.0 centimeters thick; it is

*The fingerprint files of the FBI in Washington, D.C. Each file console contains several thousand cards. Matching a single unknown print to one of these millions of cards could take years of effort. (Photo courtesy of FBI)*

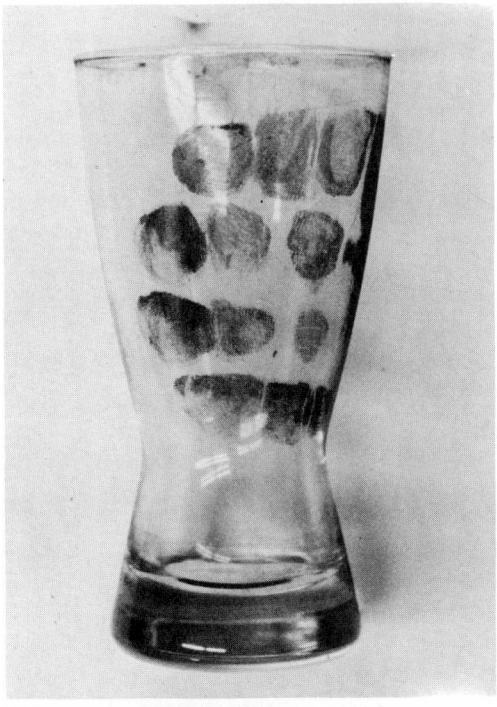

*Fingerprints found on a drinking glass. It is unusual to find a nearly complete set of prints in one place, but if the thumb print can be found on this glass, too, the set can be classified under the Henry system and possibly matched to a known print in the files. (Photo courtesy of Dallas, Texas, Police Department)*

relatively smooth and soft. However, the transparent covering over the cornea of the eye and the hard shell of the fingernails and toenails are also composed of epidermal cells.

To the crime investigator, the most interesting and significant areas of the body are those places where hair cells are absent: the palms of the hands, the inner surfaces of the fingers, the soles of the feet, and the lips. In those places, the epidermal cells grow in patterns composed of ridges and valleys. The ridges serve a useful purpose: they keep the skin from sliding when it is pressed against another surface, thus providing traction for the hands' grip, for example. Because these ridges are constantly rubbed against everything that is touched by the hands, feet, and lips, they are known as *friction ridges*.

Sweat and oil, produced in the subcutaneous layer below the epidermis, collect in the valleys between the ridges; dust, grease, and other debris also collect there. When the ridged skin is pressed against any surface, some of this viscous debris is transferred to the surface, and thus an impression of the ridge-and-valley pattern is left behind.[2]

Friction-ridge patterns are absolutely unique to each individual. Thus, an impression found on a given surface can be matched to the pattern found on the skin of a particular individual, and it can be said with near certainty that the individual at some time touched the surface where the impression was found. There are only two requirements for the friction-ridge pattern to be made useful as evidence: first, it must be found and recorded in visible form; second, it must be matched to the individual who left the impression. Both requirements pose certain difficulties.

**Impressions: tire and shoe prints.** Much of the value of friction-ridge impressions lies in the fact that the patterns are unique to particular individuals. Some manufactured objects also have patterns that may be unique, or nearly so, and that may be found in the form of impressions at a crime scene.

Tire and shoe prints are often valuable as evidence. Both tires and shoes are made in an enormous variety of shapes, sizes, and styles by different manufacturers. Both tire treads and the heels of shoes (and sometimes the soles as well) are formed by the manufacturer in ridged patterns for the same reason that such patterns appear on the contact surfaces of human skin: to improve traction.

Tire and shoe prints are most likely to be found in moderately soft soil or mud. Sometimes they can be found as a track through some fairly thick or viscous liquid such as oil, grease, or blood. Occasionally a tire or a shoe will collect debris in its pattern and will transfer the debris to a hard surface, such as a floor or driveway, leaving a reasonably clear

*Tire tracks in sand. These tracks are clear enough to permit matching with a suspect's vehicle. What other information might be obtained from this set of tracks? (Photo courtesy of Texas Department of Public Safety)*

impression of the pattern. In any of these cases, the tire or shoe print can be recorded or reproduced as evidence that might be matched to the original object that was the source of the impression.[3]

**Impressions: tool marks.** Whenever two objects are pressed with some force against each other, the harder object will leave an impression on the softer object. A careful examination of the impression may produce a pattern that can be matched to the object that caused the impression.[4]

For example, when a screwdriver or pry bar is used to force open a latch or a window,

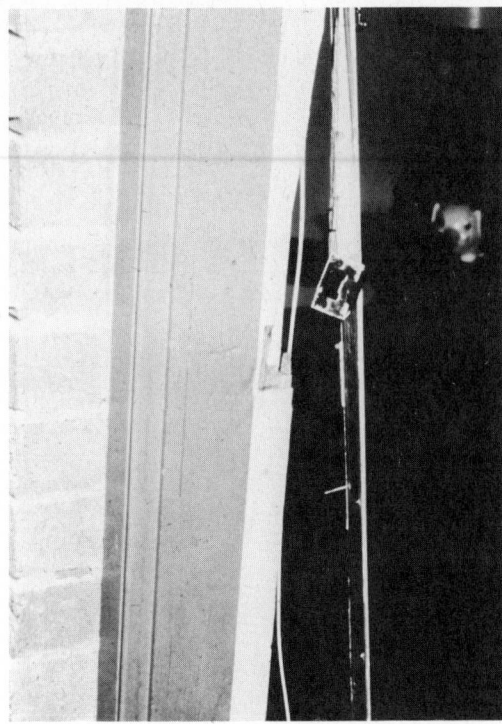

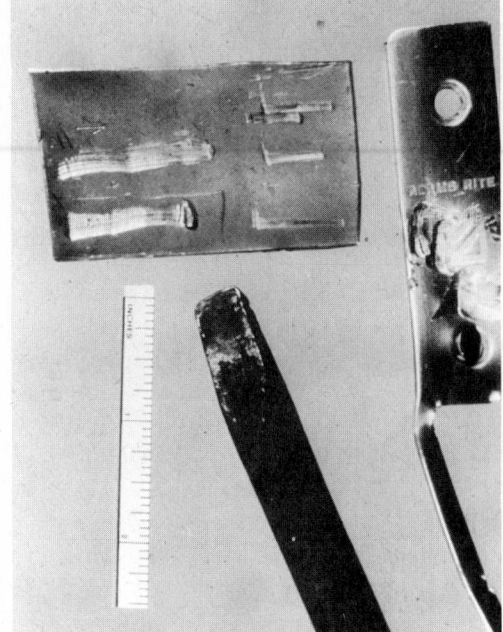

*After a prying tool was recovered from suspects, a comparison sample was made by pressing the tool against a plate of soft lead. The striker plate taken from the burglary scene is at right. Notice also that a photographer's standard has been included in this picture, alongside the tool, to indicate its size. (Photo courtesy Southwestern Institute of Forensic Sciences, Dallas, Texas)*

*Burglars entered this home by prying the door away from its frame, doing considerable damage to the frame. The striker plate, seen hanging by one screw to the splintered frame, bears a clear impression of the prying tool. (Photo courtesy of Southwestern Institute of Forensic Sciences, Dallas, Texas)*

the tool usually leaves scratches on the metal or wood surfaces. To the naked eye, the scratches may seem uniform and undistinguished. However, examining the scratches under a microscope may reveal minute characteristics that can be attributed to the peculiar, distinctive shape of the tool that made them. Even though a casual glance at two screwdrivers suggests that they are identical, a microscopic examination of the striking surfaces will show that there are small defects and markings caused either by the manufacturing process or by normal wear. These small defects and markings produce unique patterns.

The science of firearms examination (sometimes mistakenly called "ballistics") relies almost entirely on the fact that when a firearm is used, tool marks (in a broad sense) are left on the cartridge and the bullet.

**Impressions: fabric and other superficial marks.** The principle mentioned above—whenever two objects are pressed together, the harder one will leave an impression on the softer one—applies equally to objects that are not rigid. For example, if a piece of fabric is pressed against a surface containing a fairly soft coating, such as wax or paint, the pattern of the fabric will be left behind as an impression. This fact is quite often overlooked by criminals who, hoping to avoid leaving their fingerprints, inadvertently leave clear impressions of the gloves they wore.

Almost anything can leave superficial markings or impressions, but fabrics are of special interest because, as with fingerprints, tire prints, and tool marks, it is often possible to match the impression with the object that made it. Fabrics, like tires and shoes, are manufactured in a great variety of styles and patterns; two different areas of the same garment sometimes have different thread patterns. Many crimes have been solved by matching a fabric pattern found at the scene to a garment worn by the suspect.[5]

Jewelry, fragments of broken glass or metal, and writing instruments (pens, pencils, typewriters, and the like) are among the other kinds of objects that sometimes produce significant impression evidence.

*The scratch marks on the edge of the hood of this automobile were made by cloth, when the car struck a pedestrian. (Photo courtesy of Southwestern Institute of Forensic Sciences, Dallas, Texas)*

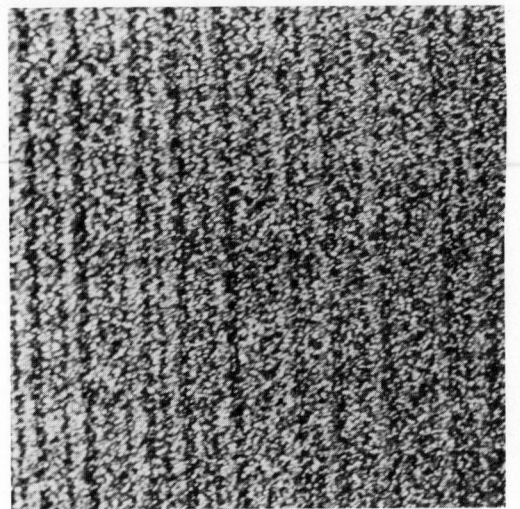

*Microscopic examination of this piece of cloth indicates that it made the impression on the auto hood shown at left, thereby demonstrating that the automobile struck the person who was wearing this garment. (Photo courtesy of Southwestern Institute of Forensic Sciences, Dallas, Texas)*

result in a good match with the garment from which the fiber came.

By the same token, whole garments, cloth fragments, and loose fibers are sometimes found on the suspect or nearby. If these cloth items can be matched to the victim or to the crime scene, they can serve as important evidence.[6]

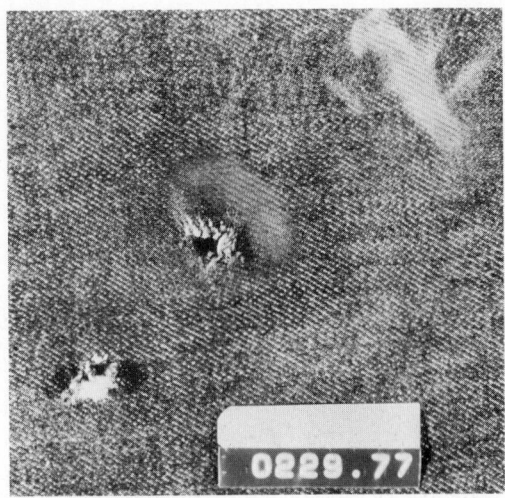

*Cloth evidence found at a crime scene. This one piece of evidence tells a great deal about the crime; the depression around the bullet hole at center contains powder residue from the barrel of the weapon, while the white smear at upper right is residue from the cylinder. The hole at lower left is an exit hole. The distance from the cylinder to the barrel end suggests not only the size of the weapon, but the manufacturer and model. (Photo courtesy of Southwestern Institute of Forensic Sciences, Dallas, Texas)*

**Clothing, cloth, and loose fibers.** Aside from the fabric impression that may be made by a piece of cloth, the cloth itself, found at the scene of a crime, might be significant as evidence. Criminals frequently tear their clothes in the course of their surreptitious or violent activity, leaving behind cloth fragments that might be matched later to the whole garment. Occasionally an entire garment or a cloth item such as a handkerchief might be accidentally left behind by a criminal. Even when such items are not found at the scene of a crime, there are almost always loose fibers that have fallen off the criminal's clothing. Under the right circumstances, careful examination of the fibers may

**Weapons, tools, and other gross objects.** Anything that the criminal carried to the crime scene and left behind, used in the course of the crime, or removed from the crime scene (even if the removal itself was not illegal) may be useful as evidence. The most obvious examples are the weapons used to commit a physical assault and the tools used to gain entry during the criminal event.

Any object at the scene of a crime that does not clearly belong there should be regarded as potentially valuable trace evidence. Besides clothing, criminals have been known to leave behind their wallets, jewelry, personalized checks, credit cards, flashlights, radios and other small appliances, cigarette lighters and matchbooks, cigarette or cigar butts, and all sorts of other items that can be traced to their owners.

A special subcategory is food left behind by the criminal. If the criminal remains at the scene for any length of time, he or she may eat or drink something and leave behind either the partially consumed food item or the wrapper. Aside from the obvious trace evidence that might be left on the wrapper (such as fingerprints), a partially consumed piece of food might retain an impression of the criminal's teeth. In this case the impression might be traced, quite literally, to the mouth of the source. If nothing else, food items may suggest something about the perpetrator's habits and tastes. There is also the possibility that saliva left on partially consumed food or on a beverage container could be analyzed to indicate the criminal's blood type, although this is not likely to be successful.

**Debris.** This category includes almost everything that can be accidentally transferred onto a person's body, clothing, or other objects and moved from one place to another. Debris usually is significant as in-

*Burglar tools left behind at the scene of an attempted safe-cracking. Burglars often leave their tools at the scene because getting caught with the tools in their possession would be incriminating. (Photo courtesy of Dallas, Texas, Police Department)*

direct or circumstantial evidence. It is either brought to the scene of the crime by the criminal or it is picked up at the scene and carried away by the criminal.

Incidentally, as you read other works on police science, you may find some confusion over the terms *trace* and *debris*. Some criminalists and writers use the word *trace* to mean any very small evidence, regardless of its source or meaning—which is approximately what we mean by *debris*. Other writers often include fingerprints, fluid stains, and tool marks as trace evidence. As we have defined the word, and as we shall try to use it consistently, *trace evidence* means specifically *traces of the criminal:* anything that the criminal leaves behind, regardless of its nature or its size, which could be used to identify a suspect. Thus, trace evidence is not necessarily debris, and debris is not necessarily trace evidence.

One common type of debris evidence is soil. Soil can be analyzed for the presence of distinctive mineral components and organic (vegetable) matter. Soils vary so much in their composition that they are highly useful for identification. Detectable variations occur from one place to another over distances of less than one meter and at different levels that are only a few centimeters apart. Thus, soil found on the suspect may be traced to a specific location with a high degree of precision. Similarly, soil found at the scene of a crime might indicate the usual whereabouts or the recent activities of the criminal.[7]

Vegetable matter other than soil also may be valuable if the material can be identified as something fairly rare or specific to a particular location. Such materials might include leaves, flowers, and other plant parts, pollen, seeds, spores, molds, decayed matter, and even traces of organic chemicals such as insecticides or herbicides.[8]

Glass and plastic fragments are frequently found at a crime scene, especially when entry has been forced by breaking a window or when violent activity has resulted in broken objects. Identifiable particles may be found in the suspect's cuffs or pockets or be embedded in clothing and objects carried by the criminal. Examination of glass and plastic fragments may even lead to a jigsaw fit, the most persuasive kind of evidence possible.[9] Paints, plaster, enameled metal, and other coatings often produce chips and other particulate debris that can be analyzed and matched.[10]

Humans and other animals continuously shed hairs and dead skin particles. These items, too, can be analyzed and matched to the individual (or animal) who left them behind.[11]

**Fluids and stains.** Many kinds of fluids and stains may be found at the scene of a crime and determined to have value as evidence. All fluids and stains can be divided into those of physiological origin and those of nonphysiological origin.

Physiological fluids include blood, semen, urine, saliva, perspiration, mucus, and other fluids, all of which are excreted or expelled from the body under various circumstances. With proper analysis, these fluids may be traced to their source. The most obvious example is blood typing: almost any sample of blood, no matter how small, can be analyzed to determine its type within the ABO classification system. Other classification systems also can be used sometimes, although they may require a larger sample.[12]

Semen, saliva, and other body fluids often contain blood components that can be typed in the same way as blood itself. If this is not possible (some people do not excrete blood components in these other fluids), the fluid still may be analyzed. For example, it is now possible to analyze semen for its genetic components, yielding an identification that can be vastly more helpful than an ordinary blood typing.[13]

Nonphysiological fluids and stains are harder to develop as evidence, especially if they are available only in small amounts. However, sometimes such materials as alcohol, oil, grease, medicines, and even water can yield evidential information. If nothing else, the mere presence of these materials may

*In this crime scene, the pattern of the blood stains is itself an important clue in understanding how the crime occurred. (Photo courtesy of Temple, Texas, Police Department)*

say something about the criminal's habits, activities, or usual occupation.[14]

**Documents.** As we mentioned earlier, anything used to convey information can be regarded as a document. Ordinarily this would include any handwritten, typewritten, or printed matter on paper. Under unusual circumstances, a photograph, tape recording, or even information in a computer memory could constitute a document.

Documents may have value as evidence either for the content itself (the information contained in the document) or for the medium by which the content is conveyed (the paper, ink, type impression, or whatever). Sometimes impressions such as fingerprints can be found on a document even though the impression is essentially irrelevant to the document's contents.

Documents often serve as direct evidence of such crimes as forgery, passing bad checks, counterfeiting, embezzlement, fraud, extortion, and so on. In other cases, the document provides indirect evidence of some kind.[15]

## WHERE TO LOOK

A crime scene includes the specific location at which a crime occurred and the immediately surrounding areas through which the perpetrator passed while approaching the scene and leaving it. In all, there are five *zones,* each of which is likely to contain certain kinds of evidence: the route of approach, the point of entry, the crime site, the point of exit, and the route of departure. In addition, the body of a victim of violent attack can be considered a part of the crime scene, and a vehicle associated with a crime is a specialized sort of scene.

### THE ROUTE OF APPROACH

In order for a criminal to commit a crime, first he or she must get to the place where the crime is to be committed. The course taken is the *route of approach.* This route has no specific beginning point. Generally, the farther one goes from the scene of the crime, the less probable it becomes that one will find evi-

*The Initial Investigation*

dence. There is, however, no fixed rule for determining how far to go.

Most routes of approach are public places (in a broad sense). That is, a criminal approaches a potential crime scene by way of public streets, sidewalks, driveways, building lobbies, and hallways that are ordinarily open to the public. Unfortunately, this means that it is almost impossible to discover and identify evidence, because it has been contaminated by the passage of the general public.

However, when the route of approach includes areas that are relatively isolated, whether they are public or private property, the chances of finding useful evidence increase. For example, if a burglar crosses the victim's backyard (especially if the yard is fenced), there is a good possibility of finding trace evidence, impressions, gross objects, and so on.

Therefore, if the route of approach is reasonably uncontaminated, look for such evidence as vehicle tracks, shoe prints, bare footprints, and objects that may have been left behind by the perpetrator. Notice places like gate latches or railings that might contain impression evidence; a criminal might not think to put on gloves until actually entering the crime scene. Bushes and other large plants, especially if they are thorny or rough-barked, might contain torn cloth or fibers from the criminal's clothing. If the route of approach includes a stretch of sandy, soft, or muddy soil, a number of samples ought to be taken for possible matching with debris on a future suspect's clothing or shoes. Any unusual vegetable matter also should be noticed and sampled.

Of the five zones of a crime scene, the route of approach is ordinarily the least likely to be productive of evidence. Nevertheless, evidence may be found in this area and a careful search is worthwhile, particularly if the evidence found in the other zones is scant or unreliable.

*Each of the items in this photograph is an example of a document that could be used as evidence.*

## THE POINT OF ENTRY

The second zone within a crime scene is the specific place at which the criminal entered the locale of the crime. The point of entry is easily defined for a building; but if the crime occurred outdoors, the point of entry may be rather vague or arbitrary. For an outdoor crime, the point of entry may be regarded simply as an extension of the route of approach, and the same kinds of evidence should be sought.

For an indoor crime, the point of entry assumes a good deal of importance. One must determine immediately whether entry was made with or without force. An unforced entry implies one of several things: perhaps the victim was careless about protecting the property, or the victim willingly admitted the criminal, or the criminal had some legitimate reason to have access to the building. An unforced entry usually provides little in the way of evidence unless the criminal has carelessly left behind fingerprints on a door, hardware, or supporting structure.

A forced entry is another matter entirely. If a door or window was pried open, there are tool marks that must be carefully photographed and, if possible, reproduced by casting. In some cases it may be possible to remove the whole surface on which the tool marks appear so that the marks themselves can be examined under a microscope. If there is any broken glass, all the broken pieces should be collected. If possible, the remainder of the broken pane should be removed from its frame and kept as evidence.

All surfaces should be checked for fingerprints and cloth impressions. If there is broken glass, it is very possible that the criminal was cut by it; a thorough check should be made for bloodstains on and around the point of entry. Torn cloth and cloth fibers also are likely to be found.

Although gross objects are not often found at the point of entry, occasionally a criminal will break a tool, such as a screwdriver or pry bar, and drop it at the scene. It also sometimes happens that a wallet or other object will fall from the criminal's pocket, unnoticed, while the criminal is engaged in forcing entry.

## THE CRIME SITE: INDOORS

The specific place where the criminal event occurred is the site of the crime, the third zone of the crime scene and, for obvious reasons, the most productive locale for evidence.

The site should be studied carefully to determine the sequence in which events took place. Depending on the nature of the crime, a criminal event may involve only one specific, limited action by the criminal, or it may involve a long series of separate actions that cover a relatively large physical space. In the absence of a witness or a coherent account from the victim, it may be extremely difficult to determine what actions were committed and in what order. However, this information is of great value, so the attempt must be made.

• What parts of the room or rooms did the criminal pass through? Debris evidence transferred from the criminal to the locale may be found there.

• What objects did the criminal touch or handle in the course of committing the crime? Those objects should be examined carefully for impression evidence, debris, and other traces.

• What objects might the criminal have touched or brushed against accidentally? Impressions and other traces are most likely to be found on such objects, rather than on things that were handled deliberately.

Any gross objects found at the site (personal effects, tools, weapons, and so on) should be regarded as evidence unless the investigator can establish that the object belongs in the scene. Fluids and stains are almost certain to be found if the crime involved a violent attack on a person. Garments, pieces of cloth, and cloth fibers may be present. Any broken object is certain to leave fragments that must be collected and examined.

If documentary evidence is to be found, it will almost certainly be found somewhere at the crime site (or later at the suspect's place of residence). Suicide notes, threatening letters, extortion notes, forged or fraudulent documents, notes or books containing names and addresses, letters indicating a relationship between the victim and the suspect, financial documents—all may be located at the crime site.

### THE CRIME SITE: OUTDOORS

An outdoor crime scene poses a great many problems for the investigator, primarily because much of the evidence will be lost in the natural environment. Impressions and debris are especially difficult to identify in an outdoor scene and may be inseparable from the soil, vegetable matter, and other normal surroundings. Nevertheless, the effort must be made to locate and identify any such evidence that exists and to separate it from the environmental background.

Garments, torn cloth, and cloth fibers assume special importance at an outdoor scene because they are comparatively easy to separate from the natural surroundings. Fluids and stains also should be sought and carefully collected. Blood and other physiological fluids can be analyzed even if they have seeped into the soil. Samples of the soil, vegetable matter (especially if it is unusual), and other environmental debris should be collected, as such materials are almost certain to have

transferred onto the clothing or person of the criminal.

Conducting a search of a large outdoor area can be a complicated, time-consuming procedure. Because communications play a major role in coordinating a large-scale search, we will put off a discussion of the subject until Chapter 9, which deals with communications.

### THE VICTIM OF ATTACK

In a sense, the body of a victim is also a part of the site of a crime and should be treated as such. Whether or not the attack is lethal, any person who is violently attacked invariably bears all kinds of evidence.[16]

The position of a corpse is potentially important as evidence in itself and should be carefully recorded in both photographs and sketches. An attempt should be made to determine whether the body's final location is actually the place where the person was attacked or whether the body was moved to that spot after death occurred.

The nature and location of all wounds and marks on the victim's body should be noted. Photographs of wounds and other marks are especially important if the victim is still alive, because the wounds will soon heal and no longer be available for examination. Fluids and stains are likely to be found on the body, on garments, and on surrounding surfaces. Both the location and the nature of the substances are important. Sometimes the pattern of a bloodstain, for example, can tell a great deal about how the crime occurred.

Debris should not be overlooked, especially on a corpse. Loose hairs, soil, glass or metal fragments, and cloth fibers all may prove valuable. Once the body has been moved, however, such evidence is likely to be lost.

## THE POINT OF EXIT

Just as criminals must enter a crime site, so must they leave it. The point of exit is not always the same as the point of entry, so it often requires separate study. The kinds of evidence likely to be found at the point of exit include mostly traces, impressions, and debris.

There are important differences between the point of entry and the point of exit that affect the kinds of evidence to be sought. Usually criminals leave the scene of a crime as quickly as possible. In this haste, they are likely to be much more careless than they were when entering the site. Torn clothing, cuts on the hands and elsewhere, and inadvertent impressions such as fingerprints may result. It is not unusual for a fleeing criminal to drop weapons, tools, and stolen merchandise at or near the point of exit, but it is unusual for the criminal to stop, go back, and pick up what has been dropped.

It is unlikely that a criminal will have to "break out" by forcing a door or window. If the preferred escape route is blocked for some reason, chances are that the criminal will use the route of entry instead. If there are indications of a forced exit, an effort should be made to explain why the criminal found it necessary to use force.

## ROUTE OF DEPARTURE

Continuing in flight from the crime site, the criminal passes through the fifth zone of the crime scene, the route of departure. Like the route of approach, this zone often involves public areas where any evidence is almost certain to be contaminated, if it can be discovered at all. However, a comparatively isolated route of departure may yield some evidence, especially in the form of tire or shoe prints and various kinds of debris. There is a fair chance that the criminal will leave behind weapons, tools, and other gross objects along the route of departure, either accidentally (dropping them in haste) or deliberately (throwing them away or hiding them to avoid discovery). The route of departure, therefore, may be a more fruitful area in which to seek evidence than the route of approach.

## VEHICLES

Automobiles, trucks, and other vehicles are quite often involved in crimes. The nature of the crime has a lot to do with the role that a vehicle may have played and the kinds of evidence that may be found in or on the vehicle.[17]

In some cases the vehicle may have been the site of the crime. This would be the case when a violent assault or rape took place inside an automobile. In such cases the interior of the vehicle should be examined for evidence in essentially the same manner as an indoor crime scene. Impressions (fingerprints and cloth impressions in particular) should be sought on all surfaces where they might be found. Fluids and stains are especially important in such cases and must be collected even if it is necessary to rip up the upholstery. Debris such as hair, cloth fibers, soil, and vegetable matter are certain to be found.

If a vehicle is the crime site, the point of entry (which usually is also the point of exit) deserves special attention. Some kind of impression evidence, either fingerprints or cloth impressions, will be found on the glass, on the metal surfaces of the door, and sometimes on the door handle. Torn cloth and cloth fibers are often found on the door latch and on sharp edges. It also may be helpful to collect a sample of the grease on the edge of the door; comparable grease may have transferred to the criminal's clothing.

In other cases, the vehicle is not so much

the site as the instrument of the crime: for example, a hit-and-run or an assault by motor vehicle. Most states' laws provide harsh penalties for leaving the scene of a traffic accident without identifying oneself and offering to render aid if it is needed; this is the crime of hit-and-run. Notice that the accident itself may be completely innocent: the crime occurs *after* the accident, when the criminal chooses to flee. In contrast, an assault with a motor vehicle consists of a deliberate effort by a driver to cause a collision with another vehicle or with a pedestrian, with the intention of causing damage to property or to person.

In either case, the fact of a collision must be established, and it must be shown that the suspected vehicle was involved in the collision. Possible evidence includes cloth impressions or fingerprints (from the victim if the vehicle struck a person), paint smears or chips transferred from one vehicle to another or from the vehicle to a person, impressions of the object struck, and debris of all sorts (especially glass and metal fragments).

However, merely establishing that a particular vehicle was involved in the collision is not enough. The investigator also must be able to demonstrate that the alleged criminal was driving the vehicle at the time of the collision. Thus, a careful examination of the interior, paying special attention to the driver's seat and the vehicle's controls (steering wheel, pedals, knobs, and so forth), is required. Again, impression evidence is likely to be found on the windows and on the metal surfaces of the driver's door.

Finally, a vehicle may have been used simply to transport the criminal to and from the scene of the crime. In this case, the vehicle could be regarded as part of the route of approach and route of departure. The main problem for the investigator is to prove that the vehicle had some connection with the crime. The connection can be established quite well if tools of the crime, weapons, or fruits of the crime (stolen goods, for example) are found in the vehicle. Otherwise, the connection might be established by finding debris that can be traced back to the crime site or to the victim. Soil, vegetable matter, hairs, and cloth fibers are the types of debris that may prove useful; if the crime involved a forced entry or any destruction of property, glass or metal fragments also may be found in the criminal's vehicle.

One caution must be given with regard to seeking evidence in a vehicle: overlook nothing. Criminals show considerable ingenuity in hiding contraband, the fruits of crime, and weapons or tools within their vehicles. An automobile is a complex and intricate machine that offers dozens of places for concealment. Evidence (especially contraband, such as narcotics) has been found taped to the underside of a fender, hidden inside a tubeless tire, suspended on a string in the fuel tank or radiator, stashed inside the empty cabinet of a radio or tape deck, and even taped to the inside of the air cleaner. Recently a young man found that the heater did not work very well in a car he had bought the previous summer. A mechanic soon discovered the cause of the problem: three bags of marijuana stashed inside the heater's fan. Luckily, the young man was able to persuade the authorities that the marijuana was not his.

## HANDLING, MARKING, AND PACKAGING EVIDENCE

So far, we have discussed the kinds of evidence that may be found at a crime scene and the places to look for it. In earlier chapters we explained the need to establish and maintain

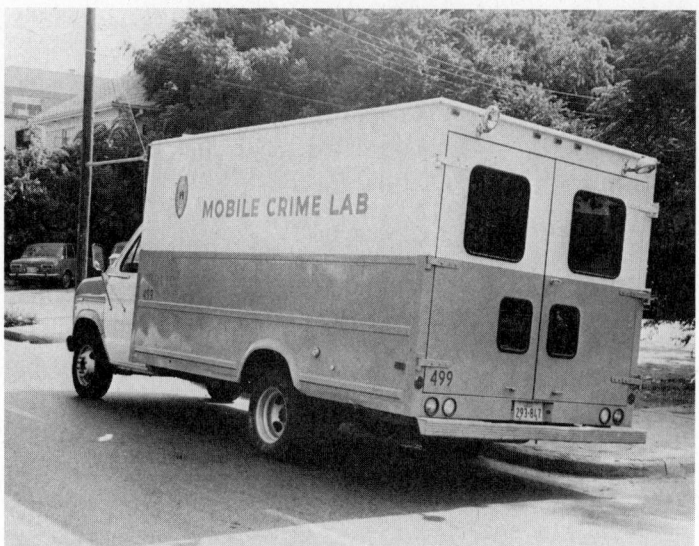

*This mobile crime lab enables technicians to bring sophisticated equipment directly to the crime scene.*

a chain of custody for all physical evidence in order to avoid any possibility of contamination that would render the evidence meaningless. You also should have a good understanding of the importance of recording every bit of evidence in photographs, sketches, and notes.

We have arrived, thus, at the crucial point at which the evidence must be physically removed from the scene of the crime and preserved for later examination, analysis, and possible presentation in court. What the investigator does at this point will determine whether the evidence that has been found is valuable in identifying and convicting the criminal—or becomes useless junk.

### BASIC EQUIPMENT

Each investigator develops a set of materials and tools for collecting, marking, and preserving evidence, based on personal experience and methods of operation. Some of the items in this list ought to be available to every law enforcement officer and should be con-

sidered standard equipment in every patrol vehicle, as basic as the radio and shotgun; other items are likely to be available only to investigative specialists. Many larger agencies now have mobile crime labs that are fully equipped to dismantle the entire crime scene, remove and analyze every conceivable form of evidence, and perform many kinds of technical examination on the spot. Although such facilities are very nice to have, they are ordinarily used only for the most spectacular or serious crimes; routine investigations still must be carried out by less sophisticated methods.[18]

**Manipulative instruments.** The investigator's kit should include several instruments for examining and handling small items. Tweezers, wooden tongs, a high-quality magnifying glass, and various kinds of scraping tools are basic. A small spatula, such as a putty knife, is handy. Hobbyists' knives (such as X-Acto knives, which offer a variety of interchangeable blades and handles) are especially useful, as are several small spoons.[19]

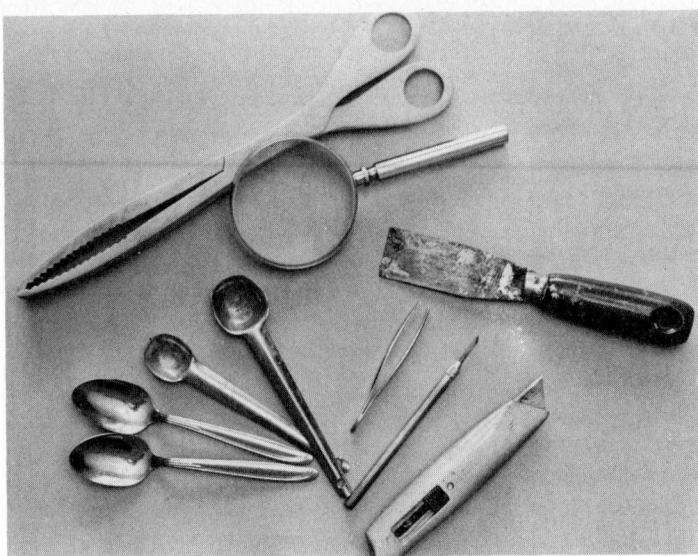

*Manipulative instruments: wooden tongs, a magnifying glass, a putty knife, several spoons, tweezers, a small X-Acto knife, and a mat knife. (Note: X-Acto is a registered trademark.)*

**Filtered vacuum cleaner.** A battery-powered, hand-held vacuum cleaner is particularly appropriate for picking up all sorts of debris. A full-sized vacuum, though more powerful and effective, may prove cumbersome in many situations. Regardless of the type of equipment chosen, it must be filtered. Several types of filtering devices are marketed specifically for investigative use. Typically, they consist of a filter holder that is placed somewhere between the nozzle at the end of the machine's wand and the opening to the dustbag. Disks of filter paper are placed in the holder. After an area has been swept for debris, the filter paper must be carefully removed from the holder. The debris is then dumped off the paper into an envelope or vial; usually the paper itself is placed in the container along with the debris. The filter paper should never be reused, and it must be changed for each area within the crime scene that is swept.[20]

**Brushes.** In addition to the vacuum cleaner and filter device, or sometimes in place of them, several small brushes should be available for sweeping up debris. Sometimes the debris is found in locations where a vacuum cannot reach. Two or three soft-bristle watercolor brushes, a toothbrush or typewriter cleaning brush, and a small whiskbroom make up a good assortment. Care must be exercised to ensure that all the debris is removed from the brush after each use; otherwise, the brush itself could contaminate the next area that is swept.

**Thread.** A spool of white (undyed) cotton thread should be kept in a clean, tightly sealed container. The thread can be used to collect blood and, sometimes, other fluids.

**Evidence containers.** Each item of evidence must be placed in its own separate container. Sometimes this means that a large number and variety of containers are needed. Several types of envelopes should be available, including manila (kraft paper) envelopes in two or three sizes, paper envelopes (letter size), and glassine envelopes (the small, cellophanelike envelopes that hold photo-

*Collecting instruments: a whisk broom, a typewriter brush, several watercolor (soft-bristle) brushes; white cotton thread (used to collect liquid blood).*

*Evidence containers. The evidence kit should include a variety of containers—envelopes, plastic wrapping materials, vials and bottles, and so forth—in several sizes. They should be kept in a clean, tightly sealed box or case, so that they will not become contaminated before they are needed.*

graphic negatives and postage stamps). Polyethylene bags, such as those sold as liners for trash cans, are very handy for all kinds of bulky evidence. A quantity of small vials or test tubes are needed for the storage of liquid materials and debris as well as a few larger bottles for bulkier materials; each vial, tube, or bottle must have a tight-fitting stopper or cap. Cardboard boxes are useful for larger objects; the boxes can be stored flat to take up as little room as possible. Last, but not least, a roll of brown (kraft) wrapping paper and a small roll of glazed white paper (butcher paper) should be included. This list certainly

*The Initial Investigation*

does not exhaust the possibilities; many investigators may wish to include other types of evidence containers.[21]

**Fingerprint kit.** One of the most indispensable tools is the fingerprint kit, used to develop and remove friction-ridge prints and, sometimes, other impressions. Many kinds of kits are available from commercial sources. Whether bought in that form or assembled by the investigator, the kit should contain two kinds of print powder (light-colored and dark-colored), very soft brushes for distributing the powder, one or two kinds of tape to remove the powdered print, and appropriate containers, cards, and labels. Some print kits also include small vials of the chemicals necessary to develop prints that have been absorbed into paper or fabrics.[22]

**Casting materials.** Plaster of paris has been used by law enforcement agents for many years to make castings of impressions such as tire tracks or shoe prints, and it remains the most useful all-around casting material. Therefore, the evidence kit should contain a box or plastic bag of dry plaster, a small mixing bowl, a wooden spatula for mixing and spreading the wet plaster, and several sheets of reinforcing material (wire screen is most often used). A small roll of piano wire or picture-hanging wire also may help, either to reinforce a large cast or to form handles for the convenient handling of the cast. A small container of dry tempera paint powder in a fairly dark color also may prove useful on occasion. In addition to these materials for plaster casting, other casting materials should be included, because plaster, though it has a wide range of uses, does not reproduce microscopic details well (such as those found in tool marks). All kinds of casting materials are offered commercially for law enforcement use and many investigators have discovered their own favorite casting materials. As there is not enough space in this text to cover the subject thoroughly (and new developments would probably make the discussion obsolete in a matter of months), you should consult the books, monographs, and journal articles devoted specifically to casting.[23]

**Labels.** Finally, the evidence kit should include several kinds of labeling materials, including adhesive-backed paper labels, a roll of white adhesive tape, index cards, a china marking pen, and some kind of engraving tool, such as a metal scribe.

## IMPRESSIONS: FRICTION-RIDGE PRINTS

Friction-ridge prints are often visible to the naked eye, especially those found on glass or metal surfaces or impressed into shallow pools of blood, grease, and other fluid or semifluid materials. In other instances, blood or some other highly visible material on the subject's hand is the medium by which the impression is made; this is often true when the criminal is cut while forcing entry to the crime scene.

Other prints, however, are not so readily visible. These are called *latent* prints because they can be made visible by certain techniques. Some people refer to all friction-ridge impressions as latent prints, but the term is inaccurate when used that broadly.

A latent print must be made visible and a visible print must be made transferable before either kind of print can be preserved as evidence. Fortunately, the same procedure can be used with either a latent or a visible print, as shown in Figure 5.1. The most common and reliable technique is to spread a thin layer of very fine powder over the print; the powder adheres to the greasy residue that forms the print. This technique works well for almost all kinds of impression prints except those that are formed in blood or other fluid

FIGURE 5.1
MAKING A LATENT PRINT VISIBLE

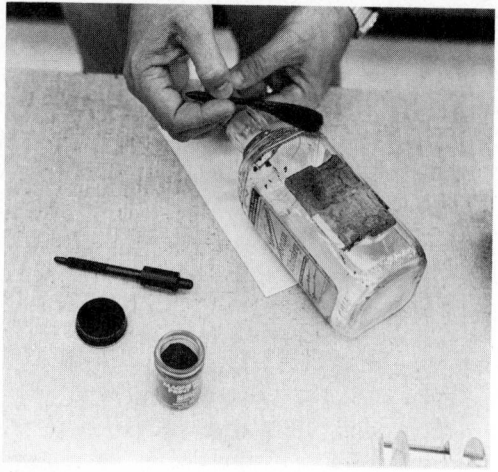

*This technique is simple in theory but requires some skill in practice. Print powder is gently spread over the surface where a latent print is likely to be found, then carefully brushed away to reveal the print.*

material that is still damp: first the liquid must be dried (after a sample has been removed for separate testing).[24]

There are several kinds of powders made commercially for crime investigators and sold as fingerprint powder. Generally the powders are sold in kits, containing a white or very light gray powder for use on dark surfaces and a black or dark gray powder for use on light surfaces. If commercial powders are not available and prints must be located quickly, other substances could be used, such as finely ground pencil lead (graphite), charcoal, or talcum powder.

Print powder is not difficult to use, but some care must be exercised to avoid obliterating the print. The usual technique is to sprinkle the powder onto a fine, soft brush. The brush is then dusted very lightly over the print or, if the print is not visible, over the area where prints are expected to be, trying to achieve thorough coverage of the area in a thin, even layer. Usually the print becomes partly visible at once, for the powder clings to the residue. Once the location and general shape of the print have been determined, the remaining superfluous powder can be gently whisked away. Sometimes a second light dusting with powder is necessary to make all the lines in the print clearly distinguishable.

Most investigators consider blowing the dust away to be a poor practice. Not only is it messy, but there is a chance that saliva and moisture from the mouth will settle on the print, possibly destroying it. However, some investigators like to use a small air bulb to blow the powder off the exposed print, rather than dusting it off with a brush. Such bulbs are sold by camera stores for cleaning the delicate interior parts of a camera.

Once a print has been rendered visible and stable, it should be photographed immediately. Depending on the type of camera used and the overall situation, it is a good idea to include in each photograph a note or label giving the identification of the crime being investigated, the object on which the print was found, its location within the crime scene, and the name or initials of the investigator. A standard object, such as a small coin or ruler, can be included in the photograph as well, if there is enough room. However, one photograph should be taken of the print without any notes, standard objects, or anything else.

If the object is small enough to be easily transported, it should be marked for future identification and packaged. It is always preferable to have fingerprints "lifted" in the laboratory, where the process can be done with great care, rather than in the field. The kind of marking chosen will depend mainly on the nature of the object. In general, it is best to attach a label on a piece of string if this can be done so that the label cannot come loose. The next best method is to scratch or inscribe the investigator's initials into the surface of the object in a location that will be easy to find but that will not interfere with any laboratory examination of the object. Note that initials should be used, not a meaningless symbol such as $X$.

In packaging the object for transportation, one must employ a method to ensure that the fingerprint is not wiped off. It may be possible to place the object in a cardboard box and surround it with packing material so that it cannot shift. Another technique would be to surround the print area with a "dam" of cardboard, modeling clay, or even a crumpled sheet of tissue paper held in place with tape. A sheet of wrapping paper can be stretched tightly over the dam and taped in place for further protection.

The print-bearing object should be taken to the lab and examined as quickly as possible. Friction-ridge prints are very perishable. Although it is theoretically possible to develop latent prints that are a week or more old, in practice the difficulties are very great and the results usually very poor.

Sometimes, however, it is not practical to transport the object to the lab for examination. This might be the case when there is no lab that exclusively serves the investigator's agency, when the lab is known to have an unmanageable backlog of work, or when the crime being investigated is relatively minor or routine and will not merit the services of the lab. In those cases, it is worthwhile for the investigator to lift the prints in the field, in the hope that the prints may prove valuable when a suspect is found.

The basic technique is to use a transparent adhesive-backed tape to remove the pattern of powder-laden grease from the surface and transfer it to a stiff card. Again, the technique is not very difficult, but it does require some care and skill. Many investigators use an ordinary cellophane tape or frosted tape (such as 3M Scotch Magic Tape) to lift prints. Such tapes work well enough, but have one serious drawback: the adhesive material interacts with the greasy residue of the print, and in a few days the print disappears. Commercial fingerprinting tapes are made with adhesives that dissolve the print much more slowly, but even the best of the commercial tapes will retain a usable print for no more than a few weeks. Once the print has dissolved, only the photographs remain as evidence.

To transfer, or lift, a print, a length of tape is stretched over the print area. One end of the tape should be anchored to the surface of the object outside of the print area. The tape then can be pulled taut, without pulling so hard as to stretch or tear the tape, and placed evenly over the print. *Once any part of the tape touches the print, the tape must not be smoothed out,* because this will destroy the print pattern. The tape should be lifted by peeling up one end and pulling it straight away from the object without letting the tape curl back. The tape containing the print is then moved immediately to a stiff card (white for a black-powder print, black or dark gray for a white-powder print) and laid onto the card in the same manner that the tape was placed over the print: anchor one end, then lay the tape down onto the card without stretching and without smoothing it (Figure 5.2).

Some commercially made fingerprinting tapes are designed differently. Instead of having the adhesive material on a clear tape, the adhesive is spread on the stiff card. The card is then laid over the print area and pressed down gently. Once the powder has been embedded into the adhesive on the card, a

FIGURE 5.2
LIFTING A FINGERPRINT

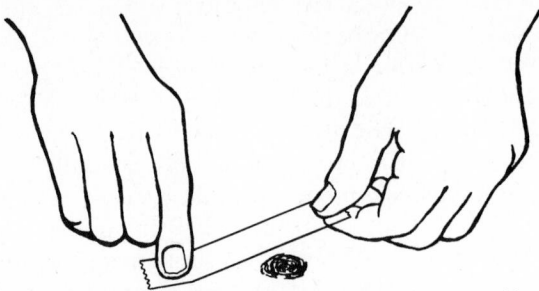

A. First, anchor one end of the tape, stretch the tape over the print area, and lay the tape down over the print. Do not smooth out the tape once contact is made.

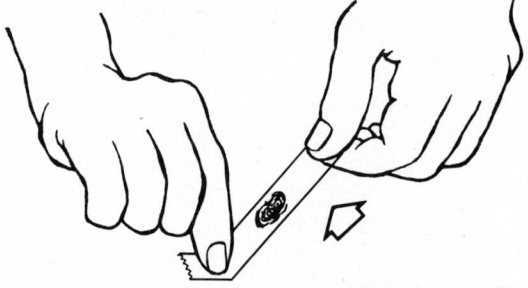

B. Lift the unanchored end of the tape, pulling it straight back from the print. Do not let the tape curl.

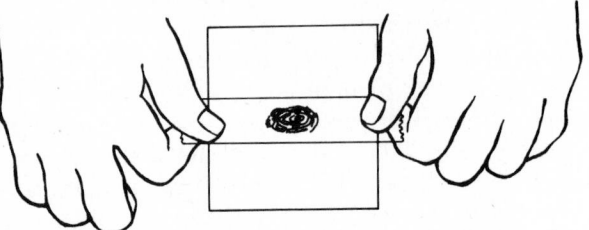

C. Place the tape containing the lifted print onto a stiff card of the appropriate color (white for a black-powder print, dark gray or black for a white-powder print).

clear film is placed over it as a protective cover. This system has the advantage of reducing the chances of distorting the print by mishandling the flexible tape; however, it can be more difficult to press the stiff, adhesive-covered card onto a print if the print-bearing surface is curved or irregular in shape.

Special care must be taken when a print or group of prints is too large to be transferred on a single tape. The two or three pieces of tape needed to lift the print should be laid onto the print area together, so that their edges precisely touch or very slightly overlap; gaps between the edges of the tape must

## FIGURE 5.3
## LIFTING A LARGE PRINT

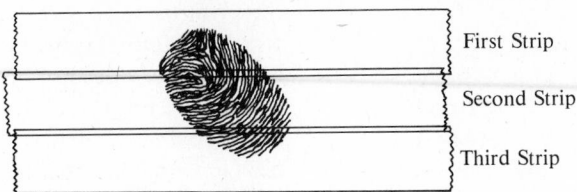

First Strip

Second Strip

Third Strip

A. Be certain that the edges of the strips of tape touch or slightly overlap. Do not leave gaps between them.

First Strip      Second Strip      Third Strip

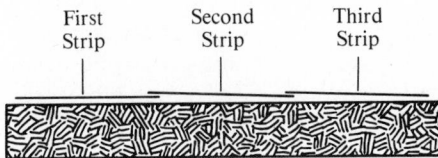

B. The **last** piece of tape laid over the print should be the **first** piece of tape removed.

be avoided. Once all the tape has been laid down and the entire print is covered, the last piece of tape should be removed first, to avoid disturbing the overlapping sections, as shown in Figure 5.3.

Another method can be used to lift fingerprints that are found on curved surfaces or in inaccessible locations. Instead of adhesive tape, a special nylon spray is used. First, the print area should be outlined with a thin material such as masking tape or two to three layers of cellophane tape. The aerosol material (sold commercially by several companies) is sprayed over the print area and allowed to dry. A fairly thick film will form over the print. Once the film dries, it is virtually transparent and can be carefully peeled off and transferred to a card or piece of glass.

A problem arises in attempting to identify and remove fingerprints from absorbent materials such as cloth, paper, and human skin. Since the print is composed of grease, perspiration, and similar oils or liquids, it is ab-

sorbed more or less rapidly into the surface of absorbent materials. Powders brushed onto the surface have nothing to cling to and, thus, are ineffective. Instead, it is necessary to use some chemical agent that will react to the organic matter that is always found in prints.

There are several kinds of chemicals used for this purpose and a variety of techniques for applying them. In general, these techniques are unlikely to be successful in the field; they should be employed in the laboratory by experienced technicians. If it is very probable that usable prints will be found on a piece of fabric, paper, or similar absorbent material, the object should be taken to the lab without delay. Similarly, if there is good reason to think that prints might be found on the skin of a victim, the effort to locate and develop those prints should be made in the hospital clinic or, for a corpse, in the morgue. Realistically, the chance for success in all such efforts is rather low, but under some circumstances, such as a very serious crime and a lack of other evidence, the effort may be worthwhile.[25]

## IMPRESSIONS: TIRE AND SHOE PRINTS

The second type of impression evidence, tire and shoe prints, can be extremely difficult to collect and preserve. Much depends on the location and the type of surface where they are found.[26]

Impressions in well-packed soil are certainly the easiest to remove, provided that the impression is deep enough. It is a very lucky investigator who finds prints that were made in shallow mud that has since dried to a sturdy consistency. Prints in very soft or sandy soil may absolutely defy the investigator's attempts to get a good casting. Prints found as a track through grease, liquids, or dust on a hard surface such as a driveway or floor are nearly impossible to preserve intact. Such prints should be carefully photographed from several angles, including directly overhead, and at least one set of photographs should contain a standard object, such as a meter stick or ruler. Even if it is possible to preserve prints by casting, the first step should be photography.

Sometimes it is hard to get a clear photograph of an impression in soil because there is not enough visual contrast between the high and low surfaces. If a light is set at an angle, better contrast can be achieved by creating sharp shadows. However, the resulting image is somewhat distorted and it may be difficult for anyone examining the photographs to tell exactly where the edges are. A better technique is to heighten the contrast by adding an appropriate material to the impression. This can be done simply by sprinkling dry, powdered plaster into the print area until the pattern becomes more readily visible. The powder should be spread into as thin a layer

as possible, covering only the lowest surfaces. Later, when wet plaster is poured into the print to make a casting, the dry powder will be absorbed into the cast. If a light-colored powder does not help—for example, if a shallow print is found in light-colored soil—powdered dry tempera paint can be used instead of dry plaster. The tempera, too, will be absorbed into the wet plaster casting; the result may be a funny-looking cast, but the print is not harmed.

Once photographs have been obtained, the casting can begin.[27] First, a border should be placed around the area of the print, using strips of wood, heavy cardboard, or some other appropriate material. The border should be close enough to the print area to avoid wasting plaster, but far enough from the edges of the impression that the pattern will not be distorted.

The plaster should be mixed according to the manufacturer's directions to make a thick, smooth paste, by adding small quantities of dry powder to water in a mixing bowl. A wooden spatula or spoon is used to stir the mixture until it has a thick, creamy consistency, similar to machine-made soft ice cream. The mixture is then carefully poured from the bowl into the print area and spread into an even layer. Smoothness is especially important, as any air bubbles or lumps trapped in the plaster will distort the pattern of the cast or cause the cast to break, either of which means a great waste of effort, a worthless cast, and probably the destruction of useful evidence. The casting process is shown in Figure 5.4.

If the print is very large, the plaster should be spread over the entire area in a thin layer, rather than being pushed into a thick layer in one area. Additional layers can be added without harm, but a usable cast cannot be made in patches. If the print is so large (for

## FIGURE 5.4
## MAKING A PLASTER CASTING

A. Mix an appropriate quantity of plaster in a small bowl by adding the dry plaster to water until the mixture is smooth, creamy in texture.

B. Pour or spoon the plaster mix into the impression. Use a spoon or spatula to spread the plaster evenly over the whole impression area. Add more plaster in layers as needed.

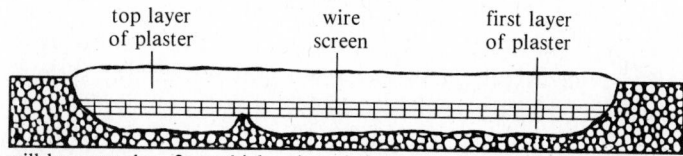

top layer          wire          first layer
of plaster         screen        of plaster

C. If the cast will be more than 2 cm thick, wire reinforcement is needed. Lay wire screen onto the plaster when it is about 1.5 cm thick, then add more plaster on top. Wire handles can be inserted into the cast in the same manner.

example, a very long tire track) that it cannot be covered with a single layer, no matter how thin, it would be better to cast the impression in several sections, each separate cast overlapping the next by a few centimeters.

Several layers of plaster can be poured on top of one another to form a finished cast about two centimeters or so in thickness. If the impression is so deep that a thicker cast is required, or if the surface area covered by the cast is more than about 100 square centimeters, the cast should be reinforced with wire screen. This is done very simply by placing the screen into the wet plaster when it is about 1½ centimeters thick, then adding another layer of plaster on top of the screen.

Once the desired thickness of the cast has been achieved, one may be tempted to press down on the plaster and be sure that the material has covered all of the desired detail. This is not a good idea; any pressure applied to the top of the cast may force the plaster at the bottom to ooze into the soil, spoiling the whole project. Wet plaster ordinarily is heavy enough to settle into all the grooves and crevices of a tire or shoe print without additional pressure.

Haste in removing the plaster casting also can lead to wasted effort. Ample time should be allowed for the plaster to dry: at least ten or fifteen minutes for a thin cast, as much as a half-hour to an hour for a thicker cast. Actually, the hardening of the plaster depends less on dryness than it does on a crystallization process. As the plaster crystallizes, the casting will feel warm; as soon as it is cool, it should be hard enough to be gently removed. While the plaster hardens, the investigator should initial the back of the cast and mark it with the identification of the case, the location, and the date.

Once the cast has hardened, it should be removed carefully, so that the original impression is disturbed as little as possible. The cast should be inspected at once to be sure that it is an accurate reproduction. Loose soil or debris should be gently brushed off. The casting process may distort the original impression to such a degree that a second attempt at reproduction cannot be made. However, until the investigator is satisfied that the cast is accurate or that the impression is ruined, the possibility of an additional casting should be maintained.

One caution regarding tire prints: The circumference of an ordinary automobile tire may be anywhere from 1½ to 2 meters, and truck tires may have a circumference of as much as 3 meters. A tire print that is only a few centimeters long represents just a small portion of the tire's surface. The investigator should be sure to cast as much of the tire's circumference as possible. It is especially helpful to get a casting long enough to show a recurring pattern or mark, such as a broken tread. This gives a clear indication of the tire's size, which may be helpful in determining the type of vehicle involved. A knowledge of the tire's circumference, its tread width, and its tread pattern should be sufficient to indicate a very narrow range of possible suspect vehicles.

Another point, often overlooked if an investigator is careless and hasty, is the fact that most vehicles (except for motorcycles and bicycles) have at least four different tires. A single tire print may be insufficient for the positive identification of a given vehicle, but castings from four prints that match all four tires on a suspect's vehicle would be difficult to refute.

Once a plaster cast has been made, it should be wrapped and placed in a protective box, suitably labeled. The impression surface of the cast should never be touched with a knife, screwdriver, or any other hard instrument; if dirt clings to the impression, it can be removed with a damp sponge.

## IMPRESSIONS: TOOL MARKS

The value of tool marks and other fine impressions as evidence rests largely on the possibility of matching microscopically small details in the impression with corresponding irregularities on the tool or device that caused the impression. Plaster of paris is not a suitable material for reproducing these marks because the relatively large crystalline structure of the plaster will not permit the very fine detail to be re-created. Of course, tool marks should be carefully photographed, even

*Microscopic comparison of tool marks. At left is the mark made on a door striker plate taken from the crime scene; at right, comparison marks from a suspected tool, made by pressing the tool against a soft lead plate. The pattern of striations (tiny grooves made in the tool by wear, etc.) strongly suggests that the suspected tool was, in fact, used in the burglary. (Photo courtesy of Southwestern Institute of Forensic Sciences, Dallas, Texas)*

though photographs are not likely to convey the details that are needed for microscopic examination.

The best procedure by far is to take the object bearing the impressions to the laboratory. There, the markings themselves can be examined under the microscope and recorded by microphotography. Sometimes it is even worth the effort to remove a portion of a door frame or window (with the owner's permis-sion, of course) to preserve tool marks for laboratory examination.

If the object simply cannot be transported to the laboratory, the only alternative is to make a casting. Any number of materials can be used for this purpose, including several that are produced commercially for law enforcement agents. Many investigators have developed a repertoire of casting materials and techniques for different purposes, using

*Acquiring, Collecting, and Preserving Evidence*

dental wax, silicone rubber, a plasticlike substance called *moulage,* other plastics, and soft or meltable metals (such as Wood's metal). All these casting materials have distinctive properties, various advantages and disadvantages, and specific methods of application. Because there are so many different techniques and because new casting materials are constantly being discovered or developed, we shall make no attempt to describe them here. We strongly urge every student of investigation to experiment with many different casting techniques.[28]

Whatever casting technique is used, the end product should be a clear, accurate and highly detailed reproduction of the mark or impression. Sometimes, when the impression is deep enough and undistorted, the casting is actually a duplicate of the object (such as the tip of a screwdriver) that made the mark. After a casting has been made, appropriate identifying marks should be inscribed directly into the cast. The casting should then be carefully packaged, the package should be clearly labeled, and the object should be transported to the laboratory.

### IMPRESSIONS: FABRIC AND OTHER SUPERFICIAL MARKS

Most fabric impressions and any other superficial marks caused by contact between two surfaces under pressure should be treated in the same way as tool marks. Photographs must be taken of the impression at the crime scene. If possible, the object itself should be transported to the laboratory for close examination. If that is not possible and if the impression is of sufficient evidential value, a casting should be made in the field, using a material that reproduces fine detail.

Sometimes a good deal of ingenuity must be shown by the investigator to obtain a reproduction of a superficial impression. For example, occasionally a mark is found in a relatively soft surface. Any attempt to apply the usual casting materials would almost certainly destroy the impression and perhaps even damage the underlying surface. Of course, the more casting methods an investigator knows, the better the chances of being able to choose a method that is suitable for almost any situation.

There are, however, a few tricks that can help. They all have the same objective: to stabilize the impression and the surface on which it is found so that a usable reproduction can be made.

One of the simplest ways to stabilize an impression is to spray it with a plastic aerosol material. Among the materials that can be used for this purpose are the DuPont Krylon acetate sprays, which are available in several forms. Clear lacquer also can be used for this purpose; the type sold as fingernail polish is especially suitable for small impressions. Another good lacquer type of product for extremely delicate impressions is artists' fixative, which is sold by art supply stores; usually it is applied with some kind of atomizer spray. Once an impression and its underlying surface have been stabilized, the normal casting methods can be applied.

### CLOTHING, CLOTH, AND FIBERS

Garments are often important as evidence or they are likely to bear evidence, especially in cases involving violent attack. As a general rule, in any investigation of an assault, rape, attempted homicide, or homicide, every effort should be made to obtain the clothing that was worn by the victim at the time of the criminal event. Garments usually are less important in other types of crime, although occasionally a burglar or thief will accidentally leave behind an article of clothing.

FIGURE 5.5
AIR DRYING WET GARMENTS

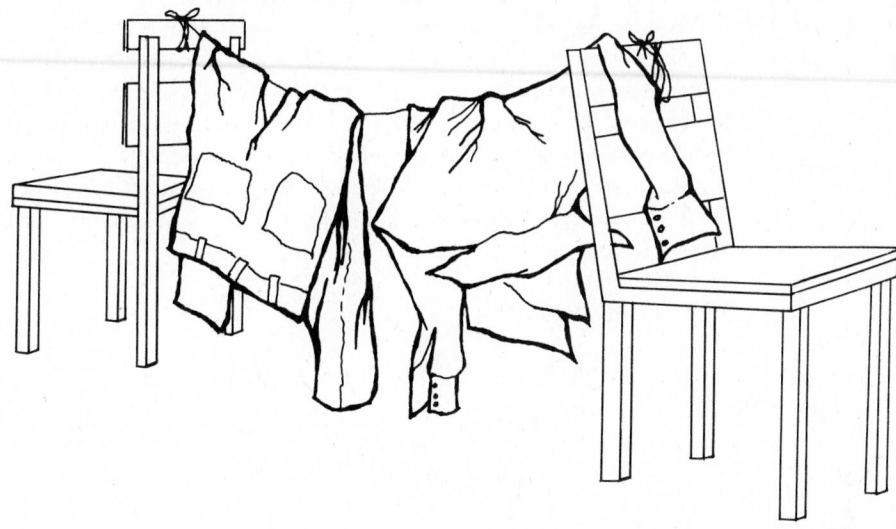

One of the most important kinds of evidence often found on garments is physiological fluids and stains. These materials almost always can be attributed to either the criminal or the victim. We will discuss later how such fluids and stains should be treated; for now, however, we will merely point out that any fluid or stain on a garment should be preserved with great care. The natural urge of the victim or the victim's friends and relatives to launder the soiled clothing must be restrained.

Wet clothing or a garment that has a wet stain on it must be handled with some care. The pattern of the stain and its location on the garment may be just as important as the nature of the stain. For that reason, the garment should not be folded and wrapped until the stain is completely dry. Instead, the garment should be hung across a line, if possible, or across the back of a wood or metal chair (not an upholstered chair, which might absorb the fluid), as shown in Figure 5.5. Air drying is the only acceptable method of stabilizing a stain. The stained area should not touch or rub against anything else until the stain is completely dried.

Once the garment has been dried, debris evidence can be removed from it. A simple way to do this is to hold the garment above a large sheet of clean wrapping paper and shake the garment vigorously. Most of the loose debris will fall onto the paper; whatever does not fall off probably will remain intact until the garment has been examined microscopically. The wrapping paper should either be carefully folded and sealed into a package, or the debris may be transferred into another container. Another approach to the removal of debris from a garment is to vacuum it with a vacuum cleaner equipped with a filter trap. This procedure will remove much more debris than mere shaking. Furthermore, vacuuming will make it possible to tell where on the garment most of the debris was found if each part of the garment is vacuumed separately.

After loose debris has been removed, the garment should be carefully folded. In folding, one should exercise care to avoid placing a crease through any stained area; the staining material may crack and flake off or may be transferred to another part of the garment. The folded garment can be packaged in wrapping paper, a clean kraft paper bag (such as a shopping bag), or a manila envelope. Both the garment and the package should be labeled.

Individual pieces of cloth, such as torn scraps that may have come from the criminal's clothing, usually require no special processing. However, they should not be handled by the investigator with bare hands since perspiration and other oils on the hands could destroy microscopic evidence. The easiest way to handle a small piece of cloth is with tweezers or wooden tongs. If these are not available, a clean piece of wrapping paper should be held between the investigator's fingers and the cloth evidence.

The cloth can be placed in an envelope, bottle, or vial, depending on its size, and the container properly labeled. Large pieces of cloth can be marked for identification by pinning or tying a label onto the material. Very small pieces of cloth should not be marked since the marking itself could damage latent evidence such as invisible laundry marks, chemical traces, or microscopic debris.

Individual cloth fibers are likely to be found mixed with other debris, such as loose soil, hair, and so on. When this is the case, the fibers can be treated in the same manner as the other debris (see below). Occasionally, however, a loose fiber is found by itself or comes to the investigator's attention apart from the surrounding debris. The loose thread might be found snagged on a windowsill where a burglar entered, or caught under the headlight rim of a suspected hit-and-run car, or clinging to the upholstered chair in which a murder victim was found. In any case, the fiber by itself may have substantial value as evidence. It should be removed with a pair of tweezers, taking care not to break the thread, and placed in a vial or small envelope. The container should be sealed and labeled as usual.

## WEAPONS, TOOLS, AND OTHER GROSS OBJECTS

Almost any kind of physical object might be associated with a crime. Typically, such objects include any sort of weapon, tools used to effect entry or to carry out some other phase of the crime, contraband, stolen goods, and the like. When such objects have been identified as prospective evidence, the first step should be to treat the object as a surface on which friction-ridge prints or other impressions may be found. Even if such impressions are not found, other trace evidence might be on the object (debris, fluids, or stains). Some portion of the object itself may have made an impression, such as a tool mark, elsewhere in the crime scene. All such possibilities should be considered thoroughly.

Any physical object that may have evidential value should be handled in a way that avoids unnecessary contact with its surface. Some portion of its surface will have to be touched in order to pick up and move the object. However, contact should be kept to an absolute minimum, and the handler should avoid any part of the surface likely to bear impressions or other trace evidence.

One special caution applies here: Contrary to some fictional detectives' practices, a pencil should *never* be placed in the barrel of a

FIGURE 5.6
LIFTING A HANDGUN

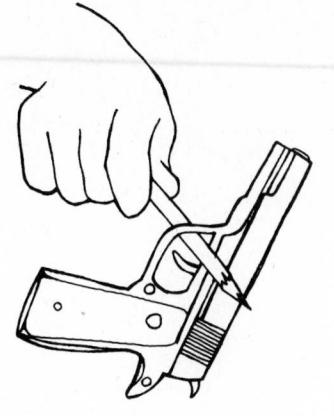

A. Place a pencil through trigger guard.

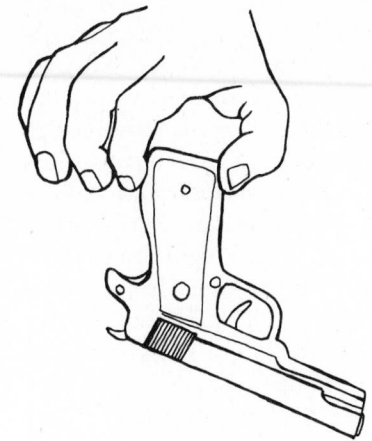

B. Grasp trigger guard or butt of gun.

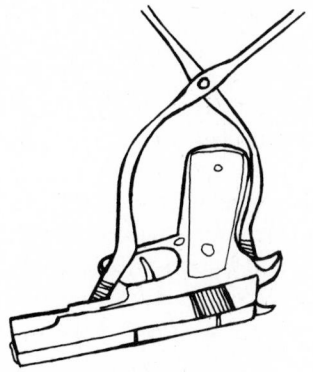

C. Lift with wooden or metal tongs.

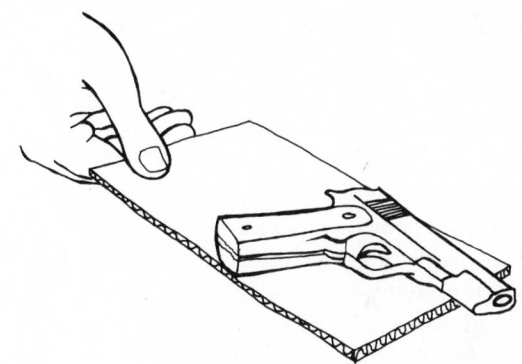

D. Slide stiff cardboard under gun.

handgun in order to lift it without touching the grip or trigger. The pencil not only would disturb the powders that are likely to be found in the muzzle of the gun, but certainly would distort the microscopically fine markings within the barrel, which are essential for firearms comparison. Most handguns can be picked up and moved by grasping them with the trigger guard between the thumb and forefinger. If the gun is too heavy for this, a pencil can be placed through the trigger guard and used to hoist the weapon. If there is no trigger guard, the gun can be lifted by grasping the butt of the grip between thumb and forefinger, as shown in Figure 5.6.[29]

Wrapping the weapon in a clean handkerchief, wrapping paper, or anything else is a poor idea, too, because of the likelihood that any fingerprints on the weapon will be rubbed off. If the weapon is too heavy or bulky for any of the methods suggested above, it would be better to slide a piece of stiff cardboard under the weapon and lift it.

Because weapons are almost always crucial evidence in a criminal case, they must be marked with special care. A label tied to the weapon is always a good idea. However, it is also wise to inscribe the investigator's initials somewhere on the weapon so that there will be no doubt about the weapon's identity. On a handgun, the initials might be inscribed on the heel of the butt or on the barrel just in front of the trigger. Both are locations where prints and other traces are unlikely to be found unless the weapon was used as a bludgeon; in that case the butt should not be used for marking. On a knife, a good place to inscribe is the blade just below the hilt; again, however, be sure that there are no particles of debris clinging to the hilt that might be disturbed by the marking process.[30]

Bullets and cartridge cases also must be treated with some special precautions. When the trigger is pulled on a firearm, the cartridge is struck by metal parts; an explosion occurs; the bullet is propelled out through the barrel, whose fine markings scratch the bullet as well as giving it a spiraling spin. All these events result in what amount to tool marks on the bullet and on the cartridge. These marks can be immensely valuable in demonstrating that a particular bullet was fired from a particular gun.

Before any cartridge is removed from the place where it is found, the location must be determined with absolute precision. Even the *orientation* of the cartridge (the direction in which the open end is lying) may be important. Often, the position of the cartridge can be a clue in determining the exact placement of the weapon when it was fired, or, at least, when the spent case was ejected.

A cartridge is likely to bear fingerprints as well as the impression of the firing pin and,

*A bullet recovered from a crime scene. Even though the bullet itself is severely deformed, the scratchlike markings—caused by the irregularities in the weapon's barrel—are clearly visible and might be used to identify the weapon used. (Photo courtesy of Temple, Texas, Police Department)*

often, chamber markings and scratches from the ejection mechanism. The best way to pick it up is to hold it loosely in a soft cloth such as a handkerchief. The investigator's initials (or, if the case is too small, some other unique symbol) should be inscribed inside the open end of the cartridge, if possible, or otherwise on the outside, as close to the open end as practical.

A bullet should never be pried out of any object in which it is lodged. If the bullet is located inside a plaster or wood surface, it can be removed by cutting out the area surrounding the bullet itself. If the object in which the bullet is lodged is small enough, the whole object should be taken to the laboratory. Once the bullet has been collected, it, too, should be handled carefully in a soft cloth— not held by tweezers or any other comparatively hard object. If the shape of the bullet has not been distorted, initials may be inscribed on the base; otherwise, it is better not to try to mark the bullet but simply to place it in a sealed, labeled container. Even a badly distorted bullet may still contain markings that can be matched to the *rifling* (the spiral pattern of grooves and ridges) within the weapon's barrel. Fabric and other impressions are often found on the nose of a bullet.

Shotgun pellets are more difficult to recover and a good deal less likely to be traceable to a particular weapon. However, the effort to recover them still should be made, especially if it seems to be possible to recover all or nearly all of the shot from a single shell. Less care needs to be exercised in recovering the pellets, because they almost certainly will not bear any rifling marks or other impressions. The shell, however, is another matter; it usually does contain valuable impressions and should be handled as carefully as a cartridge or bullet.[31]

### DEBRIS

Debris can be found throughout the crime scene, from the route of approach to the route of departure and everywhere in between. The problem in collecting debris is twofold: first, to be reasonably sure that the material collected has some value as evidence; second, to ensure that the location at which the material is collected has been fully identified so that one can establish the meaning of the debris as evidence. There would be no point in running a vacuum cleaner over the entire area of a crime scene and dumping all of the debris into a single container. Unless the investigator knows where the debris was found and what its possible source might be, it is utterly meaningless.

The first step in collecting valuable debris evidence, then, is to determine where to look and why. Are you looking for material that might have been left behind by the criminal? In that case, the area immediately surrounding the point of entry may be valuable, especially if entry was forced. The site of the

criminal event also should yield productive evidence. On the other hand, are you looking for standards against which to compare debris that you may find, later, on the suspect? If so, the place to look is wherever the criminal is most likely to have come into direct contact with an undisturbed environment. The route of approach and the peripheral areas of the crime site may be productive, but the point of entry and the crime site itself cannot be considered undisturbed locations.

Ultimately, the search for debris evidence amounts to a sampling procedure in which each appropriate area is swept separately. The extent of the search will depend on such factors as the seriousness of the crime, the degree to which a particular suspect is already known, and the nature of the crime. For a major crime for which other evidence is lacking, it may be profitable to sample each of the five zones of the scene as well as the body and clothing of the victim (if there was any violence) and the interior of any vehicle involved. Again, each specific location must be swept individually and the debris collected at each place must be put in a separate container, carefully marked to show where the material was found.

One category of debris evidence requires special comment. Soil samples are frequently taken along the routes of approach and departure, particularly when tire prints or shoe prints are found, and at almost every outdoor crime scene. A soil sample can be immensely valuable if it is properly collected; otherwise, it may have little or no value as evidence. The investigator should bear in mind that the value of a soil sample depends mostly on its individuality. Fortunately for crime investigators, soils vary from one place to another in ways that can be detected fairly readily. Samples taken only a meter apart may prove to be remarkably different in composition, and it is the difference that counts. Thus, a good deal of care must be exercised in selecting the place where the sample is to be collected.[32]

Some sampling sites are obvious: the bottom of a shoe print or tire print, for example, or the ground directly below a window that was forced open. In other cases, the investigator may be faced with a large area through which the criminal might have passed; choosing the right place to sample may require some imagination and ingenuity. No investigation can be successful on the basis of a single sample. On the contrary, samples should be taken at each place where the criminal might have come into contact with the environment, and a small number of additional samples should be taken at some distance from the immediate crime scene for use as comparison standards (for example, another part of the yard where, presumably, the criminal did not pass through).

In collecting a soil sample, one usually has no difficulty in obtaining a large enough volume of material. However, care must be exercised to avoid digging too deeply. Usually the criminal came into contact only with the surface. Soil only a few centimeters below the surface might have a very different composition, which could lead to substantial errors in trying to obtain a good match. Therefore, the material should be scraped up with a spoon, spatula, or similar tool, not dug out of the ground.

Gunpowder is another type of debris evidence that presents some problems. Many myths about gunpowder residues have been perpetuated in detective fiction. One myth is that an investigator can tell, merely by looking for powder burns on a suspect's hands, whether the person has fired a weapon within a given period of time and, if so, what type of weapon. Another myth is that the distance between a weapon and the victim can be read-ily determined by studying the pattern of powder traces on the victim. Fictional detectives perform these computations with the speed and confidence of fortunetellers. In truth, powder debris may be very valuable in some investigations and very misleading in others.

Not all firearms leave a powder residue on the hand that held the gun. Under some circumstances the powder might be sprayed onto the criminal's clothing, but not the hand. The criminal might wrap the weapon in a blanket, pillow, or other material to muffle the explosion, in which case the powder might never reach the hand at all. And firearms do not always spray powder onto the victim, even when the muzzle is very close to the victim's flesh. In many cases the markings on the victim's skin are not powder burns at all, but real burns caused by the gases created during combustion. In that case, a study of the burn may or may not indicate the distance of the weapon. The results might be very ambiguous.

Despite these reservations, it is nonetheless true that powder residues associated with a firearm can be valuable evidence. Quite often it is not the powder itself but the pattern of its distribution that will be meaningful. Any suspected powder residue or burn should be photographed extensively and carefully. After that, a sample of the powder should be collected, sealed in a suitable container, and appropriately labeled.[33]

## FLUIDS AND STAINS
Any liquid or semiliquid substance found at a crime scene is almost certain to be of some evidential value, even if it is nothing but plain water.

Material that is still in a liquid state is relatively easy to locate and collect. The simplest way is to scoop it up in an open vial, test tube, or bottle. If the liquid pool is not deep enough for this technique, one alternative is to collect the liquid on absorbent filter paper.

Blood can be collected on white cotton thread, a spool of which should be in the investigator's kit. A length of thread is unwound from the spool and dragged through the blood, several times if necessary, until it is fairly well saturated with the liquid. The thread can then be placed in a vial. If the unsaturated end of the thread, by which it was held, is left hanging out of the vial when the stopper is put in or the cap screwed on, the thread will hang relatively flat in the vial instead of bunching up at the bottom (Figure 5.7).

FIGURE 5.7
COLLECTING BLOOD ON COTTON THREAD

A. Unwind a length of thread (from 10 cm to 30 cm depending on the quantity of blood available). Drag the thread through the pool of blood until the thread is well saturated.

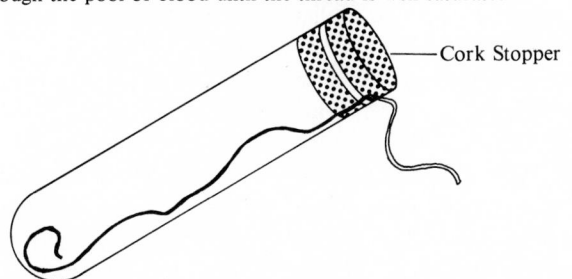

Cork Stopper

B. Place the thread in a vial, test tube, or bottle. Leave the unsaturated end hanging out of the vial.

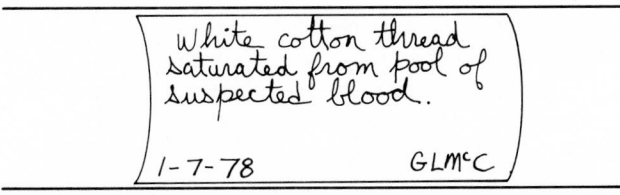

White cotton thread saturated from pool of suspected blood.

1-7-78          GLMᶜC

C. Label vial appropriately.

Dried pools of fluid and fluid stains that are only slightly damp are much more difficult to collect. Usually the only good way to collect them is to remove the whole object or cut away the appropriate portion and take it along to the laboratory. Unfortunately, this is not always practical or permitted by the owner of the object. The next-best method is to scrape as much of the stain as possible off the object onto a clean piece of paper (filter paper works nicely). If scraping is used, do not scrape too deeply, or a lot of irrelevant debris will be collected from the surface of the stained object. A comparatively blunt scraping device, such as the edge of a spoon or a metal spatula (such as a putty knife) is preferable to a knife blade.

A special problem is that sometimes stains are not readily observable. Blood may have been washed away either deliberately, to hide a crime, or accidentally when water or some other liquid has been spilled. Sometimes blood seeps into crevices where it cannot be seen. Other physiological fluids, especially semen, dry to a white or clear powder that may be hard to identify.

Any garment or object on which a stain is suspected because of the nature of the crime should be taken to the laboratory for examination. Chemical tests can determine the presence of blood, semen, and other physiological or nonphysiological fluids even after a garment has been washed thoroughly several times. If latent stains are suspected at the crime scene, similar chemical tests can be used to detect and identify the substance. These tests are either simple but not very reliable, or they are reliable but not very simple. Generally, it is best to obtain the help of a skilled laboratory technician, even if there will be some delay before the technician can arrive at the crime scene. Latent stains usually do not go away; unlike other kinds of evidence, they can be detected at the crime scene after a passage of several days or even weeks. Of course, any delay will require sealing the crime scene for a longer period of time to avoid contamination of the evidence.

## DOCUMENTS

The collecting and handling of documentary evidence in the field ought to pose no special problems. Whether a document is useful as evidence depends on its nature, content, the likelihood of its having been handled by the victim or criminal, and the location where it was found (which might indicate, for example, that it was left behind accidentally by the criminal). All these factors should be more or less obvious when the document is first found.

Documents, including paper ones, should be handled as little as possible, since latent prints may be discovered on them and developed in the laboratory. However, the contents of the document or the instruments used to create it (pen, ink, typewriter) are usually of most interest to the investigator.[34]

Naturally, every document should be marked for identification. Authorities differ over whether the investigator's mark should be placed on the face of the document, where it can be easily recognized, or in a location such as the back of the document, where it cannot interfere with the study of the document itself. In any case, the marking should be clear, readily recognized, and placed where it will not contaminate the evidence. Each item of documentary evidence should be separately packaged in an appropriate, properly labeled container. Paper documents should never be folded or rolled up; they should be packaged just the way they are found. If necessary, a piece of stiff cardboard should be included in the package to prevent any damage to the document.

Too often, valuable documents are not recognized as such by investigators. As we have mentioned before, anything that conveys information can be considered a document: not only printed or written information on paper, but also photographs, audio tapes, and so on.

Carbon paper and carbon typewriter ribbons (the kind that are used once and then discarded) are often overlooked, but they can yield all kinds of information about a suspect's or victim's activities. Even when a sheet of carbon paper has been used several times, some information can be gleaned as long as the individual letters can be made out.

Even burned paper documents should be carefully collected. Paper burns at a relatively high temperature, and thus even when a deliberate effort is made to destroy it, some portion of the paper may remain intact. If nothing else, the type of paper and perhaps the composition of the ink, pencil lead, or typewriting might be determined.

### WOUNDS AND MARKS ON THE VICTIM OF ATTACK

Every victim of any violent assault, whether living or dead, should be examined by a physician as soon as possible. Some states now require an autopsy in every case of death in which the circumstances are not known beyond all reasonable doubt—essentially, any death that occurs outside of a physician's immediate care. Even if there is a strong presumption of natural or accidental death, an autopsy ought to be performed, whether or not the law requires it. Too often the emotional response of the victim's friends or relatives is permitted to block a necessary autopsy, partly because so many people believe, erroneously, that an autopsy leaves the corpse grossly disfigured.[35]

A victim who survives an assault usually can describe the attack both thoroughly and accurately, but this is not always the case. Recently, for example, a series of women were attacked by a rapist who strangled his victims until they were unconscious, but still alive. Most of the victims were attacked while asleep, and although they knew that they had been assaulted, they could furnish almost no information about the attacker. Even when the victim seems to be able to provide a coherent account of the incident, an examination by a competent physician (preferably one with a good background in criminal investigation) may provide important details and corroboration.

Before the physician's examination or an autopsy, the investigator's study of the victim should be as thorough as circumstances permit. Each wound or mark of struggle should be identified, photographed, and described in the investigator's notes. The position of the wound or mark on the body should be particularly noted, along with the size and depth of the mark and its apparent cause.

When a corpse is discovered, the position of the body should receive the investigator's full attention because it may reveal a great deal about the sequence of events that led to the death. In general, wounds can be understood only when they are considered in relation to the final position of the body.

Scratch marks, particularly if they occur as parallel streaks, almost always indicate fingernail scratches. If a suspect can be identified and located quickly, there is a good chance that skin particles can be found under the criminal's fingernails; the skin particles may be identifiable as having come from the victim. Conversely, in any violent attack in which the attacker and the victim came into direct contact, the victim's fingernails should be scraped for skin particles and other debris. Often the victim will have scratched the attacker without even being aware of having done so.

Victims usually bear other kinds of debris and trace evidence. Obtaining this evidence is not always easy when the victim is still alive. Usually the victim is extremely upset and anxious to complete the investigative process as quickly as possible. However, if the investigator is sensitive to this desire and explains patiently the possible value of the evidence, chances are good that the victim will cooperate.[36]

The first step is for the victim to change clothes, and a private place should be available for this procedure. The victim should be instructed to remove each garment carefully. If possible, the victim should stand on a large sheet of clean wrapping paper while removing the garments. As the victim removes each garment, it should be either allowed to drop onto the wrapping paper or hung over the back of a chair. Any garment that has a wet stain should be hung on a line or on a metal or wood chair. After the victim has completely changed clothes, the garments should be left where they are; the victim should not pick up the garments and take them to the investigator. Instead, the investigator should retrieve the garments, handling and packaging them as we have discussed previously.

These procedures should be followed for any victim of a violent crime—except rape. A rape victim should be asked not to change clothes until she is examined by a physician. The likelihood is so great that important debris evidence will be found on the garments, especially on the underclothes, that they should be removed only by someone—such as a nurse or doctor—who can do it with proper care. For the same reasons, protection and preservation of debris evidence, the rape victim should be wrapped in a robe, long coat, or blanket while being transported to the hospital or clinic where the examination is to be performed.

Debris evidence may very well be found on the victim's body itself, especially in violent crimes involving close physical contact. With rare exceptions, the investigator will have no opportunity to collect such evidence. The physician who examines the victim should be instructed to look for such evidence, to collect it, and to preserve it in the proper manner.

If the victim refuses to be examined, which often is the case, the investigator might suggest ways that the victim can locate and collect debris evidence, but the chances of getting anything useful are very slim.

Later, especially in Chapter 10, we will discuss some of the laboratory procedures for developing and analyzing evidence. This information will suggest not only the kinds of evidence that can be valuable, but also some of the reasons for the elaborate collection and preservation procedures that we have described in this chapter.

We have now explored most of the procedures that must be used in seeking physical evidence, particularly at the scene of a crime. If you were Officer Cole, investigating the suspected burglary at 1209 Main Street (Chapter 3), by now you would have accumulated a fairly large pile of potential evidence. You would have your field notes, sketches of the crime scene (Chapter 4), and probably two or three rolls of film containing photographs of the scene. You would have pieces of the broken coffee cup from the kitchen, the greasy towel from the bathroom, and probably the box of adhesive bandages. You might have fingerprints from various locations including the door handles, the kitchen table, the cupboard doors, and the television table. You would have collected samples of the stains in the bathroom sink as well as debris from the kitchen and main living room. You would have at least a large box full of potential evidence.

Of course, you still would not know for sure whether a crime had actually been committed and, if so, what crime. If your investigation has followed the same sequence as these chapters, you have not yet collected one of the best kinds of evidence: the statements of witnesses.

Our next chapter deals with just that subject, interviewing witnesses, victims, and bystanders.

### REFERENCES

1. Paul L. Kirk, *Crime Investigation,* 2d ed. (New York: John Wiley and Sons, 1974), p. 35.
2. Kirk, pp. 60–61.
3. Paul B. Weston and Kenneth M. Wells, *Elements of Criminal Investigation* (Englewood Cliffs, N.J.: Prentice-Hall, 1971), p. 30.
4. Weston and Wells, *Elements of Criminal Investigation,* pp. 34–35.
5. Kirk, pp. 120–123.
6. Kirk, pp. 117–120.
7. Richard H. Fox and Carl L. Cunningham, *Crime Scene Search and Physical Evidence Handbook* (Washington, D.C.: U.S. Department of Justice, National Institute of Law Enforcement and Criminal Justice, 1973), p. 80.
8. Kirk, p. 310.
9. Kirk, chap. 22.
10. Kirk, p. 240.
11. Kirk, p. 143.
12. Fox and Cunningham, p. 60.
13. Kirk, p. 207.
14. Kirk, pp. 229–232.
15. Kirk, pp. 470–472.
16. Kirk, p. 43.
17. Fox and Cunningham, pp. 24–27.
18. Weston and Wells, *Elements of Criminal Investigation,* pp. 23–25.
19. Kirk, p. 26.
20. Kirk, pp. 23–25.
21. Kirk, p. 26.
22. Kirk, pp. 22–23.
23. Kirk, pp. 28–29.
24. Fox and Cunningham, pp. 51–57.
25. Fox and Cunningham, p. 57.
26. Kirk, pp. 74–84.
27. Fox and Cunningham, pp. 134–143.
28. Kirk, pp. 51–58.
29. Fox and Cunningham, pp. 84–85.
30. Fox and Cunningham, pp. 86–95.
31. Weston and Wells, *Elements of Criminal Investigation,* pp. 26–27.
32. Kirk, p. 277.
33. Kirk, pp. 405–409.
34. Fox and Cunningham, p. 155.
35. Weston and Wells, *Elements of Criminal Investigation,* pp. 38–39.
36. Fox and Cunningham, pp. 27–28.

## REVIEW OF THE EVIDENCE

1. Nine specific types of physical evidence are listed and discussed in this chapter. Which of these is *not* one of them?
   - a. tool marks
   - b. debris
   - c. friction-ridge prints
   - d. clothing, cloth, and loose fibers
   - e. the positions of objects and the relationships between them
   - f. weapons, tools, and other gross objects
   - g. tire and shoe prints
   - h. documents
   - i. fabric and other superficial impressions
   - j. fluids and stains

2. True or false: Whenever two objects are pressed together with sufficient force, the softer object will leave an impression on the harder one.

3. An *unforced* entry to a crime scene suggests which of the following?
   - a. The victim was careless about protecting the property.
   - b. No crime was committed.
   - c. The victim willingly admitted the criminal.
   - d. The criminal had some legitimate reason to have access to the building.
   - e. The victim probably was engaged in some kind of criminal activity.

4. As used in this text, the term *trace evidence* refers specifically to
   - a. anything that the criminal left behind at the scene of a crime.
   - b. any evidence that must be examined under a microscope.
   - c. tire or shoe prints.
   - d. debris evidence.
   - e. all of the above.

5. True or false: Friction-ridge impressions are left only on hard, smooth surfaces such as metal or glass.

6. True or false: Most people, but not all, excrete blood components into other physiological fluids such as semen, saliva, and perspiration.

7. Rate the five zones of a crime scene according to the likelihood that valuable evidence will be found in each zone. Use a scale from 1 to 5, with 1 representing the most productive zone.
   - a. route of approach
   - b. point of entry
   - c. crime site
   - d. point of exit
   - e. route of departure

8. True or false: The body of a victim of violent attack should be considered and treated as a part of the crime site.

9. Where should each of the following types of evidence be marked by the investigator for future identification?
   a. a garment
   b. a handgun
   c. a plaster cast of a shoe print
   d. a bullet
   e. a paper document

10. Fill in the blank: The value of a ——— depends mostly on its individuality. Samples taken only a meter apart may prove to be remarkably different in composition, and it is the difference that counts.
    a. physiological fluid stain
    b. friction-ridge impression
    c. thread pattern
    d. wound or mark on the victim's body
    e. soil sample

## TOPICS FOR INVESTIGATION

1. Study the sketch of a crime scene and accompanying notes shown below. Using only this information, list the five zones of the crime scene and the types of evidence that you would look for in each zone. Bear in mind that a crime scene could have more than one crime site.

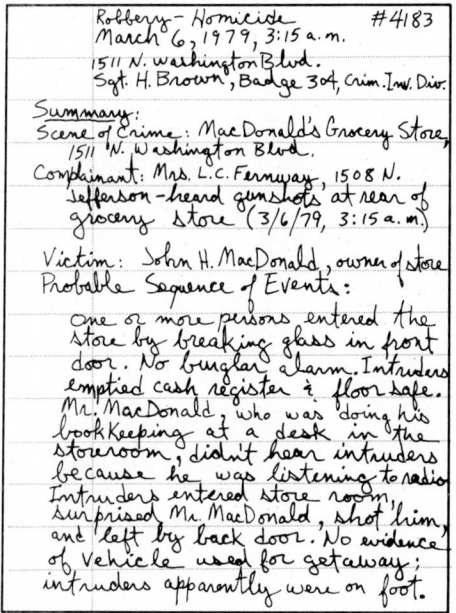

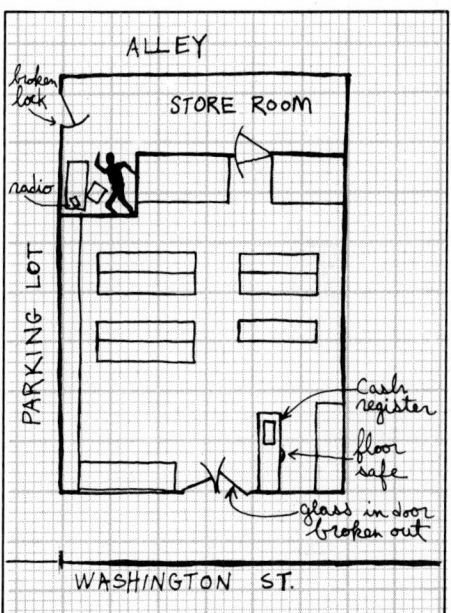

2. Why is a jigsaw fit considered the most persuasive kind of evidence possible? What sorts of evidence are likely to display a jigsaw fit or its equivalent?
3. Victims of crimes, even of violent crimes, are not always cooperative with the police. A victim may refuse to submit to a physical examination or to permit the investigator to remove items of evidence. What can be done to encourage a hostile victim to be more cooperative? Should the police have the authority to compel a victim to cooperate? If so, what kinds of cooperation should the police be able to require?
4. Only a few states require an autopsy in cases of a questionable death. Most states merely require an *inquest,* a legal hearing that is conducted by a magistrate or coroner and at which testimony of witnesses and other evidence may be produced. But the most obvious kind of evidence—an autopsy—is not mandatory. Should all states require an autopsy? If so, under what circumstances and with what limitations? To what extent should the wishes and sensitive feelings of the victim's family and close friends be respected?
5. Which of the procedures described in this chapter are intended primarily to maintain the chain of custody, and which are intended to protect evidence from contamination? Do these complicated and time-consuming procedures interfere with or detract from the more basic purposes of an investigation, locating and identifying the perpetrator?

# Unit III

## Dealing With
## The People

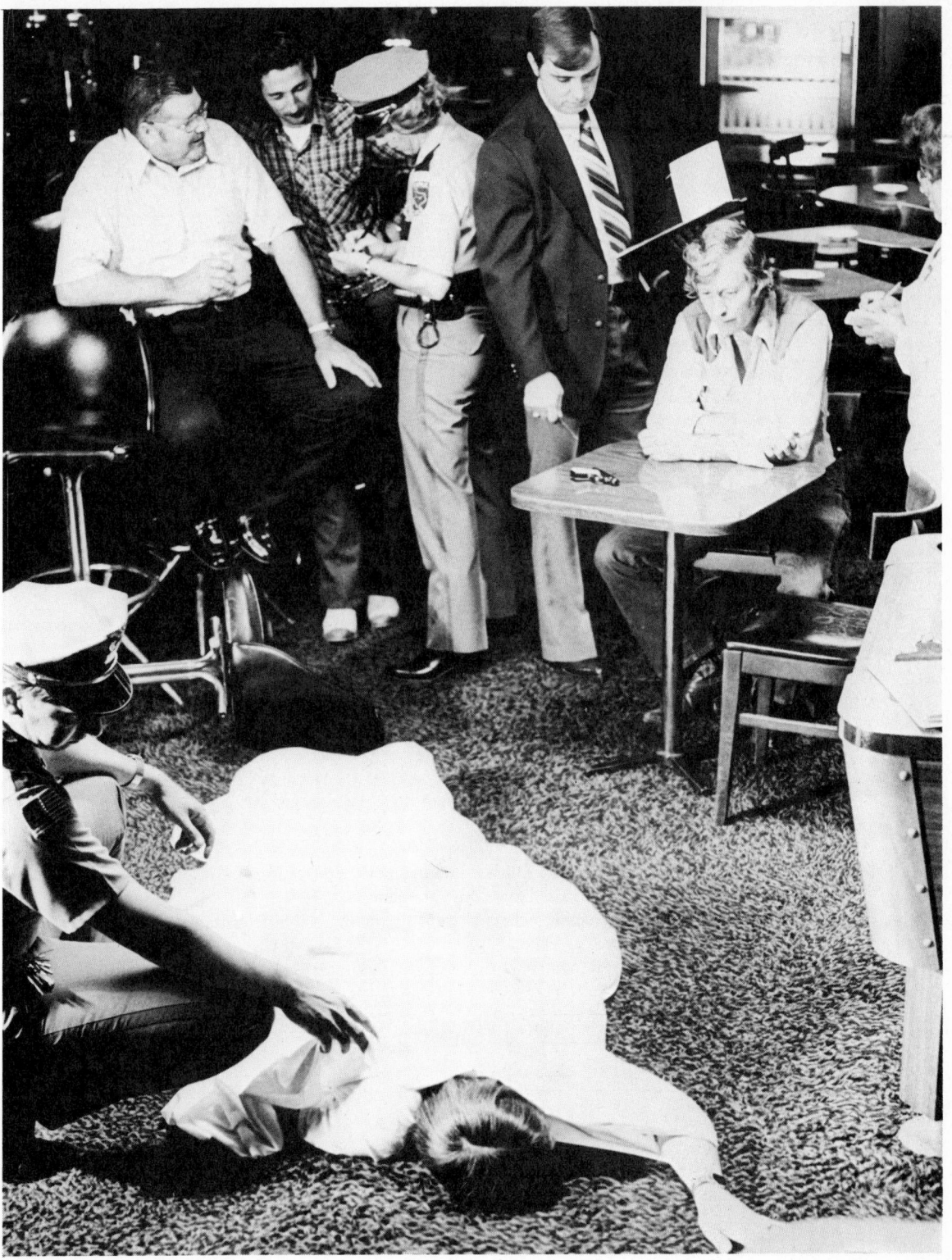

# CHAPTER 6

## VICTIMS, BYSTANDERS, AND WITNESSES

5. Which of the following techniques should *not* be used when interviewing witnesses?
   a. allowing the witness to talk at length, giving a complete account of the crime
   b. making deliberate misstatements while summarizing what a witness has said to you
   c. telling a witness that another witness's statement is contradictory and asking the witness to clarify the discrepancy
   d. interviewing all witnesses separately, in privacy
   e. telling a witness, "We already know what happened, but I'd like you to confirm some of the details for me"
6. True or false: Victims are sometimes hostile or reluctant because they feel guilty about having been attacked.

EVIDENCE IS NOT LIMITED to physical objects, debris, and so forth that can prove a certain person committed a certain crime. The testimony of witnesses, too, is valuable evidence. Except in the very simplest and most minor cases, both types of evidence are required in order for the perpetrator to be convicted. Physical evidence can be introduced only if there is a witness who can explain its origin and significance. The police officers and various technical experts provide much of this testimony, but juries (and judges, too) often feel more confident that a "nonexpert" witness's testimony is truthful and objective, since the police and their experts might be prejudiced against the defendant. Furthermore, physical evidence found at the scene of a crime may be impossible to interpret unless the investigator can compare the evidence with a witness's account of the crime.[1]

For both of these reasons, the testimony of witnesses, including the victim and any bystanders at the crime scene, is vital to the criminal investigation. The investigator must attempt to find out what these people know about the criminal event.

The testimony of witnesses cannot always be taken at face value. The victim of a crime could hardly be considered completely neutral and unbiased toward the criminal, and crime victims are often emotionally upset, confused, or mistaken about what has taken place. Bystanders who happened to be at the scene of the crime and other witnesses who presumably know something about the crime also may be biased either in favor of the suspect or otherwise, and they may be honestly mistaken about what they think they know. Gaining information from victims and witnesses is never easy. However, there are some techniques and procedures that can help to make the job a little simpler and much more productive.

Before discussing those techniques, we need to make a distinction between an interview and an interrogation. Both terms apply to a structured, controlled effort by an investigator to gain information from another person: a victim, bystander, witness, or suspect.

Generally speaking, only suspects are interrogated. Victims, witnesses, and others are interviewed. The difference between the two terms is that an *interview*, though it should follow some plan or outline, begins with no preconceived notions about the information to be learned. Thus, an interview tends to be somewhat less formal in structure and more casual in style. An *interrogation,* however, is an attempt to gain certain specific information; the questions usually follow a carefully planned and rather rigid structure. The kind of information sought might include corroboration of what the investigator already has learned or an admission or confession from a suspect. Logically, interviews are conducted early in an investigation, when little or nothing is known about the criminal event. During the later stages of the investigation, when a good deal of evidence has been accumulated and the investigator needs merely to confirm what has been discovered, the style of questioning will be more along the lines of an interrogation.

This chapter is concerned primarily with the techniques of the interview. Later, in Chapter 16, we will discuss the procedures for an interrogation.

## QUALITIES OF AN INTERVIEWER

Successful interviews are conducted by good interviewers. Careless or misguided interviewers rarely get the information that they need. Often, they leave the witnesses with such a poor impression of the police that other investigators, attempting to fill in the gaps, will be met with hostility or indifference. Thus, a bad interviewer not only fails to obtain essential information, but also "spoils" the witnesses so that no one else can get the information either.

The qualities of a good interviewer are numerous. No one has all of these qualities at the beginning of a law enforcement career,

ANSWERS TO STUDY CLUES
1. b    2. All of them    3. False    4. a
5. c    6. True

but everyone can develop them through experience, training, and effort. Some of these desirable qualities are sufficiently obvious that discussion is unnecessary. In order to be a good interviewer, the investigator must be knowledgeable, objective, self-confident, patient, persistent, tactful, adaptable, alert, and thorough. In addition, there are certain qualities of a good investigative interviewer that do require some explanation.

### COMPASSION

The interviewer must be compassionate. This does not mean simply that the investigator should sympathize with the victim (although certainly that should be true). We mean something deeper than that. Police officers deal every day with people surviving in the worst imaginable circumstances: people who teeter perpetually on the brink of extinction through grinding poverty and the degrading effects of alcoholism, drug addiction, emotional disturbance, mental as well as physical disability, and criminality. Often it is difficult to tell the victims from the criminals, the predators from their prey. It takes a strong, self-assured person to face such constant wretchedness without losing a sense of proportion and reality.

Sociologist William Ker Muir, Jr., describes a compassionate police officer as having "the tragic view." By this, Muir means that the police officer believes that all human beings are essentially alike, that human nature is a mixture of both good and bad elements in each of us, and that anyone might fall into circumstances that would produce an evil response. It is this attitude, Muir claims, that enables a police officer to deal with each person as an individual deserving sympathy and respect.[2] Muir says that police officers who lack the tragic view fall prey to "dualism," which he defines as the belief that the world

*Dealing with the People*

is made up of good people and bad people, the former requiring protection and the latter deserving neither pity nor concern. Police officers who have this attitude soon find that they are classifying more and more people as "bad" and fewer people as "good" until they no longer care for, or about, anyone.[3]

In dealing with the victims as well as the perpetrators of crime, Muir's tragic view is indispensable. Criminals and some victims, too, are often not very nice people. They can be cruel, mean-tempered, irresponsible, and erratic. One of the principal hallmarks of the true professional in law enforcement is the ability to deal with all people with genuine concern, respect, and dignity. Anyone who cannot meet that standard will be a poor interviewer and perhaps does not belong in law enforcement at all.

## ARTICULATENESS

Another essential quality of the investigative interviewer is articulateness. Police officers must deal not only with people in the lowest strata of society, but also with those in the highest echelons. Investigators must be able to converse comfortably and appropriately with all kinds of people. They must be able to use words, grammar, and ideas that are suitable to the other person's emotional and intellectual capacities. Police officers should enjoy talking about anything at any time, and they should be able to express their own feelings, ideas, and experiences without hesitation or awkwardness.[4] Many times, the key in getting another person to talk, especially about an unpleasant experience, is the ability to put the other person's feelings into words. Even a simple, trite phrase, such as "What a terrible thing to have happened to you!" lets the victim of a crime know that the investigator understands and cares about the victim's feelings. The victim knows that it is all

right to express his or her own feelings about what has happened; this is the first step in getting useful information.

## A SKEPTICAL ATTITUDE

A third basic quality of the successful interviewer is a skeptical attitude. Most people are not very observant or perceptive about the things that go on around them. Furthermore, human memory is not perfectly accurate under the best of circumstances. A police officer, even while being compassionate and sympathetic, must not forget that the information received from witnesses is never entirely, absolutely true. It is the investigator's job to discover the truth by comparing information from as many different sources as possible, discarding what is found to be inaccurate and reinforcing what is correct.

## OPEN-MINDEDNESS

Finally, a police officer must be open-minded throughout an investigation. If an investigator begins with a preconceived notion about how a crime has occurred or who committed the crime, there is a natural, subconscious tendency to prove oneself right. Too often, such preconceptions can lead to the total disregard for truth.

It is relatively easy to begin an investigation with an open-minded attitude, but maintaining that attitude becomes increasingly more difficult as the investigation proceeds. Once a suspect has been identified, there is an overwhelming temptation to ignore or overlook any evidence that suggests that the suspect is innocent. The only way for an investigator to avoid this tendency is to remember constantly that the evidence must be followed, wherever it leads.

The loss of open-mindedness is especially disastrous when an officer is interviewing witnesses. A witness will sense the fact that the officer has some preconceived idea about the crime; from that moment on, the witness will be completely unreliable. Some witnesses will try to say whatever the officer wants to hear, whether or not it is truthful. Other witnesses will have the opposite reaction: they will deliberately choose to withhold information. Much of the hostility that witnesses display toward the police is based on their belief that the police are prejudiced or dishonest. Anything an interviewer does to confirm that belief will destroy the witness's potential usefulness.

Again, we must point out that no one has all these qualities in perfect proportion. They must be developed, cultivated with the same deliberate care as skill in collecting evidence or technical mastery of firearms examination. Furthermore, these qualities must be sincere. An investigator cannot pretend to be open-minded, patient, or compassionate; the witness will sense the insincerity and will conclude that the officer is dishonest.

## CONSTITUTIONAL ASPECTS OF THE INTERVIEW

Under U.S. law, all citizens have a legal obligation to assist the police by providing any information that the police require to enforce the law. The only limitation is that citizens cannot be compelled to testify against themselves. This is known as the "right against self-incrimination."[5]

The basic principle is set out in the Fifth Amendment to the U.S. Constitution and is also defined in the constitutions of all but two of the states (Iowa and New Jersey). The specific application of the principle and its many implications have been further defined through court decisions and individual laws.

Ordinarily, witnesses (especially the victims of crime) cannot use the Fifth Amendment as a reason for refusing to provide information. The right against self-incrimination applies only to persons accused of crimes, and the circumstances under which this right can be invoked are narrowly limited. However, if victims or other witnesses refuse to provide information for fear that it could lead to criminal charges against them, there is very little that an investigator can do about it. Any effort to compel witnesses to give information is unlikely to be productive.

There is another principle that the investigator also must recognize: the right of privacy or, as the great Supreme Court Justice Louis Brandeis put it, "the right to be let alone."[6] Actually, there is nothing in the U.S. Constitution and very little in state constitutions or other laws about the right of privacy. However, the Supreme Court and lower courts have consistently held that such a right is implied in the Constitution and in the body of common law that forms the basis for the legal system. Therefore, a right of privacy is assumed to exist even though it is only vaguely defined and its exact limits are uncertain.

From a practical point of view, the right of privacy means that an investigator cannot compel a possible witness to give information unless the investigator has ample reason to believe that the witness has some direct connection to a crime. Even then, victims of crimes are presumed to have a right not to complain, even though this right has no real legal basis.

In brief, then, the constitutional right against self-incrimination and the presumed right of privacy severely limit the ability of an investigator to obtain information from an unwilling witness. Realistically, an investigator can obtain useful information only from willing, cooperative witnesses.

## WHO ARE THE WITNESSES?

We have used the terms *victims, bystanders,* and *witnesses* rather loosely; now it is time to define them.

A *witness* is anyone who has knowledge about a crime or about a suspect, any person who has information that may be useful to the police. A further distinction is made between *primary witnesses,* those who have personal knowledge of the criminal event, and *secondary witnesses,* those who know little or nothing about the crime itself but who have some information about the victim, the perpetrator, a potential suspect, or some circumstance relating to the crime.

A *victim* is a person who is directly affected by a criminal event. This may be the person or family whose property was stolen or destroyed through criminal action, or it may be the person who was criminally attacked. In the case of a homicide, the word *victim* usually is applied only to the dead person; however, we consider the immediate family and sometimes other close associates also to be victims.

A *bystander* is a person who is present at the scene of a crime but did not observe the criminal event itself or arrived after the crime was committed. In other words, a bystander has little direct, personal knowledge of the crime, but some bystanders may be good secondary witnesses.

## LOCATING WITNESSES

One of the first tasks of an investigator arriving at the scene of a reported crime is to locate as many potential witnesses as possible. We mentioned this important duty briefly in Chapter 3; now we shall look at it in more detail.

### WITNESSES AT THE CRIME SCENE

Anyone who is present at the scene must be regarded as a potential witness. Thus, the first step in locating witnesses is to screen those present, to separate the true witnesses from the mere bystanders.

At an indoor crime scene, usually few people are present when the police arrive. All people at the scene should be required to identify themselves; names and addresses should be recorded in case they must be contacted later. One or two simple questions may be enough to distinguish between the primary witnesses and the bystanders: "Were you here when the robbery occurred?" or "Did you see what happened here?" Those who give a positive answer should be asked to remain at the scene; those who give a negative answer may be permitted to leave but should be told that they might be contacted later by a detective.[7]

Sometimes, especially at an outdoor crime scene, a large crowd will have gathered by the time the police arrive. In that case, the task of sorting out witnesses from bystanders is somewhat more difficult. Time may not permit even a cursory check of every person present. As a general rule, people on the fringes of the crowd are least likely to be witnesses and therefore can be sent on their way without bothering to get an identification. Those closest to the crime site should be checked and briefly questioned. At the same time, the caution that we suggested in Chapter 3 should be remembered: anyone who seems to be anxious to leave the scene or who appears to be making a special effort to remain inconspicuous should be regarded with suspicion and should not be allowed to leave without having been fully identified.[8]

## LOCATING ADDITIONAL WITNESSES

Sometimes the problem is not too many potential witnesses but not enough. In such a case, two techniques may be helpful in locating additional witnesses.

The first is the physical search. Starting at the site of the crime, the investigator attempts to find anyone who was near the crime scene at the time of the criminal event. For example, if the crime took place in a single-family residence, the next-door neighbors would be interviewed, then the neighbors across the street and behind the house (on the next street) and finally, other neighbors on the same block. If the crime took place in an apartment building, first the investigator would interview everyone living on the same floor, then the people on the immediately adjacent floors, and then the people who live along the apparent routes of approach and departure.[9]

The second technique is to have each witness suggest additional witnesses. This technique is sometimes useful in cases involving a violent attack, although it is less valuable for common property crimes such as burglary. As a potential witness is interviewed, the investigator might ask such questions as "Do you know anyone who would have had some reason to commit this attack?" or "Who else, besides you, knew that the victim was going to be here at this time?" Similar questions can be formulated according to the particular circumstances of the crime.[10]

A third technique is used far less often than these, but once in a great while it can be productive. The technique is to find witnesses who are related to the crime scene by time rather than by physical proximity or by some association with the victim. However, locating these time-related witnesses is tedious.

For example, in almost every residential neighborhood there are people who pass through the area every day at just about the same time: delivery persons, postal carriers, people on their way to or from work, and so on. Other people also pass through the area regularly, but not every day: sanitation workers, meter readers, route salespeople. If the time that a crime occurred is known with some precision, it may be possible to locate secondary witnesses by waiting for them in the vicinity of the crime scene at the appropriate time of day. Usually this will require a surveillance of the area over a period of several days just to identify the people who pass through on a regular basis. Obviously, this is a time-consuming and tedious technique, which is why it is not used very often.[11]

## SEPARATING THE WITNESSES

Once the people at a crime scene have been identified, it is extremely important to separate them as much as possible. The purpose is to discourage them from discussing the crime among themselves. If the crime is *fresh*—that is, if it has just occurred—all available witnesses should be interviewed immediately, before the search for physical evidence is undertaken. However, if a fairly long period of time has elapsed, the opposite procedure may be used: the search for physical evidence first, followed by the questioning of witnesses.

The reason for these procedures is that witnesses have a tendency to "compare notes" about the experience they have shared. In doing so, usually without realizing it, they arrive at a mutual understanding about what has happened. They may decide to forget cer-

*Dealing with the People*

tain details from their own perceptions; if no one else saw it that way, they figure that it must not have happened that way. The story that they arrive at may be extremely consistent and coherent, but not entirely true.

If the investigator can keep the witnesses from comparing notes, there are likely to be several accounts of the crime, all of which vary somewhat. Often it is the discrepancies and contradictions that are most significant. The information obtained from witnesses then can be checked against the physical evidence. Although not all contradictions will be resolved, the interpretation of the evidence will be guided by the effort to explain the discrepancies between the witnesses' stories.[12]

On the other hand, if the witnesses already have had ample opportunities to compare notes and develop a common story, deliberately or otherwise, there is nothing to be gained by hurrying to interview them. Instead, the examination of the physical evidence provides the investigator with a basis for interview questions. After studying the physical evidence, the investigator may have a clear concept of how the crime occurred, but usually there will be many points of uncertainty. These uncertainties serve during the interviews both as reference points for the investigator's questions and as ways to discover inconsistencies in the witnesses' accounts.

For example, you may recall that in the hypothetical investigation in Chapter 3, the investigator discovered a broken cup on the kitchen floor. While interviewing the building manager, the manager's wife, and the next-door neighbor, Officer Cole might ask each of them, "Did you notice a broken cup on the kitchen floor? Do you happen to know how it might have gotten broken?" The officer could also ask the neighbor, "Do you recall hearing any sounds that might indicate an argument or fight? Do you remember hearing anything being thrown against the kitchen wall?"

## INTERVIEWING THE COOPERATIVE WITNESS

Before interviewing any witness, the investigator must make an assessment of the witness's willingness to be cooperative. In general, victims and witnesses who were present during the crime are likely to be cooperative, because they are anxious to have the criminal caught and punished.[13] Bystanders may be somewhat less cooperative, especially if they feel that they do not know anything important about the crime and would prefer not to be involved. However, these general observations certainly do not always apply: victims and witnesses may be extremely hostile or indifferent, and bystanders may be unusually cooperative.

Reluctant, hostile, or indifferent witnesses require special treatment, which we shall discuss shortly. For now, we shall concentrate on witnesses who are willing to cooperate with the investigator.

### QUESTIONING IN ISOLATION

Each witness must be interviewed in isolation, physically separated from other witnesses and police officers as much as possible. If the investigator can take the witness into a separate room, so much the better. Two or more investigators working together should interview the witnesses separately and simultaneously, then compare notes among themselves and, if necessary, reinterview the witnesses.

Separating witnesses from others during questioning is extremely important for several reasons. First, it ensures that the witness can give full, undivided attention to the investigator's questions without being distracted by hectic activity at the crime site. Second, if the witness is confused or emotionally upset, isolation may help to spare the witness from unnecessary embarrassment. Third, isolation means that the witness is not influenced by the presence of anyone else at the scene and may feel free to say things that could be embarrassing or even dangerous in front of someone else. Fourth, isolation ensures that each witness will have no way of knowing what other witnesses have said and thus will be unable to slant testimony in any particular direction.[14]

The importance of isolation in interviewing witnesses can be illustrated by a simple story, one that has been repeated many times over. The police received a call that there had been a shooting at a neighborhood tavern. When they arrived, they found a man lying on the floor, the victim of a gunshot wound. There were about two dozen people in the tavern, almost all of whom must have been present when the fatal shot was fired. However, as soon as the gunshot victim was discovered, one of the patrol officers looked around the room and demanded, "Who saw what happened? Who shot this man?" No one answered. The officer then confronted each individual in the tavern, in front of everyone else, and asked, "Did you see who shot this man?" Every single person denied having seen the attack. Some claimed to have had their backs turned; others claimed to have walked in after the shooting. Nearly half the people in the tavern claimed that they were in the restroom at the time of the shooting— in spite of the fact that the restroom could accommodate only two people. No one would even admit to having called the police.

It is impossible to say why this particular incident occurred. Certainly, distrust of the police is one explanation. Perhaps the people in the bar were afraid for their own lives, or perhaps they felt that the victim deserved his fate. Whatever the explanation, the problem might have been avoided if the police officers had questioned each person in privacy.

### THE QUESTION SEQUENCE

In each interview, questions should be asked in a definite, planned sequence. This not only helps the investigator to organize the information in the field notes, but it also helps the witness to remember details that otherwise might be overlooked.

The first group of questions should be designed primarily to obtain positive identification of the witness, including name, address, place of employment, telephone numbers at work and at home, and relationship (if any) to the victim. This group of questions also may clarify the witness's relationship to the crime, including why the witness was present at the crime scene, whether the witness is an acquaintance of the victim or the perpetrator, and so on. If the witness is nervous, upset, or uncertain, these initial questions can be combined with reassuring comments that have a calming effect.[15]

Next, the witness should be asked a very generalized question, such as "Can you tell me exactly what you saw take place here?" Usually the witness will give a complete, overall account of the event. The investigator must *not* interrupt to ask for clarification or explanation of details, but should let the witness talk as long as he or she wishes. If the witness runs out of words or seems to lose track of the subject or begins to ramble about irrelevant matters, the investigator may steer

*Dealing with the People*

the conversation back to the subject with a prompting question, such as "After that, what happened next?"

Usually the investigator should not take notes during this phase of the interview but instead should concentrate on getting an overall impression of the event from this witness's point of view. Notetaking at this point might distract the witness or contribute to uneasiness.[16]

Once the witness has completed the general account of the crime, the investigator should go back through the entire sequence of events, asking for additional information about particular details: "Where did you first see the attacker? Which door did he enter by? What was the color of his shirt and pants? Did he hold the gun in his right hand or his left hand?" During this second series of questions, extensive notes should be taken.

A third round of questioning often is needed to clarify any points of uncertainty or to correct any possible errors, contradictions, and inconsistencies. The investigator must be especially tactful during this round, even with a cooperative witness, to avoid giving the impression of not believing the witness or of arguing with the witness's account of the crime. Instead, the investigator must reassure the witness that the police are interested only in understanding everything correctly, just as the witness saw it.[17]

As a general rule, the investigator should never contradict or argue with a witness. The investigator may know that the victim was shot in the head, and a witness may claim to have seen the gun placed against the victim's stomach as the shot was fired, but there is no point in arguing. The witness either is honestly mistaken or has decided to try to confuse the investigator. Or, perhaps, the witness *did* see a shot fired into the victim's stomach, in

which case the corpse needs to be examined more closely.

The sequence of questioning outlined above serves several purposes. First, it helps both the investigator and the witness to organize the information mentally. Second, the sheer repetition often causes a witness to reveal inconsistencies or contradictions, caused either by a deliberate effort to distort the account or by honest mistakes.

At the end of each series of questions, the investigator should offer a summary of what the witness has said. With a genuinely cooperative witness, the summarizing helps to reassure the witness that the investigator understands the testimony. However, the summarizing also can be used as a device to detect a lying witness or one who is thoroughly confused. This is done by introducing into the summary one or two "mistakes" or "misunderstandings," that is, deliberate misstatements by the investigator. A truthful, alert witness will immediately correct these mistakes, while an untruthful witness might overlook them or even agree to them.

One final point should be made about interviewing a cooperative witness: as a rule, the investigator should never reveal information to a witness about the testimony of other witnesses or the physical evidence that has been discovered. On the other hand, witnesses (especially victims) have a legitimate interest in knowing how the investigation is proceeding. Therefore, the investigator must be tactful and skillful in evading the witness's questions, while recognizing the legitimate basis for the witness's curiosity. Any brusque or officious behavior on the part of the investigator—such as "I'm asking the questions here; you just give me the answers"— will very quickly turn a cooperative witness into a hostile one.

One of the kinds of information most often sought by the investigator is a description of the criminal. Unfortunately, most investigators ask for only the most rudimentary information: what was the criminal's height and weight, hair color, skin color, and color or style of clothing?

The common experience of all police officers indicates that such descriptions are notoriously inaccurate. Witnesses who were within a few feet of the perpetrator often disagree strongly about basic physical characteristics of the criminal, things that ought to be obvious to everyone. Such inaccuracy is usually attributed to the emotional instability, lack of perception, or stupidity of the witness. However, a contributing factor is the poor questioning technique of the investigator.

The most effective technique is to ask a general question followed by a series of specific questions, especially suggestive questions of the either-or type.

For example, the investigator might begin by asking, "Can you describe the person who committed the crime?" The answer that the witness gives is not important and should not be written down; the question merely serves to focus the witness's attention on the subject.

The next question might be, "Was he about as tall as I am, or shorter, or taller?" If the answer is ambiguous, the witness might be asked to compare the criminal to other people who are immediately present, such as another police officer, or to someone else who is well known to the witness, such as a relative or close friend. Similar questions will establish the criminal's approximate weight and build.

The questions then should be very detailed and should follow a logical pattern, such as starting at the head and working down to the feet. The exact wording of the questions is not as important as their form and their specific, highly detailed nature. The following list of questions may be taken as an example of the form that should be followed.

• Was his hair blond, brown, or black? Was it straight, wavy, curly, or kinky? Did he have a crew cut or other distinctive hair style? Did his hair extend beyond the tops of his ears, to his shirt collar, or to his shoulders?

• Was his skin light or dark? Was it yellowish, olive, chocolate brown, or bluish-black? Was his skin clear and smooth or rough? Did you notice any signs of acne, scars, tattoos, prominent moles or liver marks, warts, or any other disfiguring marks on his face?

• Was his forehead high, narrow, sloping, or unusually broad? Was the head itself round, flat-topped, egg-shaped, or bulging in either the front or back? Was there any baldness or a receding hairline? Did you notice any grayness at the temples? What kinds of wrinkles did you see on the face, especially around the eyes?

• Were the eyes prominent, sunken, widely or narrowly spaced? Were they round or almond-shaped? Was there anything unusual in the way the criminal looked at things: a vacant stare, a tendency for the eyes to wander, a glazed look, or anything like that?

• Was the nose long, pointed, flat, wide, or crooked? Did it look as though it might ever have been broken?

• Was the mouth small, average, or large? Were the lips full, thick, overhanging, protruding, or puffy? Were they pink, dark red, pale, or bluish? Were there any irregularities in the teeth: stained color, crookedness, overbite or underbite, missing teeth, braces, obvious dentures, or metal crowns? Were there any sores or blisters on the lips or around the mouth?

• Was the chin receding, jutting, or flat? Was it pointed, rounded, or square? Was it a double chin, dimpled, or cleft?

• Did the criminal have a moustache, beard, or other facial hair? (If possible, the witness should be shown pictures of various types of facial hair and asked to pick out the picture that most closely resembles the criminal's facial hair.)

• Was the neck long, slender, short, or thick? Was the Adam's apple prominent or depressed? Did the criminal stand so that his head was upright on his shoulders or did his head hang forward or cocked to one side?

• Were the shoulders small, narrow, heavy, round or stooped, sloping, or unequal? Were there any major irregularities: a humpback, dropped shoulder, or protruding shoulder blade? How would you describe the criminal's posture: upright, slouching, rigid, or staggering?

• Was the chest flat, narrow, pigeon-chested, or broad? Was the stomach flat, bulging, overhanging, or unusually thin? Were the hands long, narrow, flat, stubby, or meaty? Did you notice any irregularities: arthritic knuckles, twisted fingers, or missing fingertips? Were there any scars, tattoos, or other marks on the hands, wrists, or arms?

• What color shirt or jacket was worn? What was the style? Was it long- or short-sleeved? How was it fastened in front: buttons, snaps, zipper, ties? Or did it have a closed front, like a pullover? Was there any stitching or embroidery?

Were there any words, symbols, or pictures printed or stitched on the fabric? Where were the pockets located? Were they patch pockets, slanted, covered with a flap, or zippered?

• What color were the slacks and what was the general style? What kind of fabric were they made of? Was there a belt and, if so, what kind of buckle did it have? Where were the pockets and what was their shape? Did the pants have a zipper, buttons, or snaps?

• What color were the shoes: brown, black, white? Were they low shoes or boots? Were they a distinctive style, such as tennis or soccer shoes, wing tips, western boots, combat boots? Did they have regular soles or rubber soles? Were the heels normal in height or built-up? Was there anything distinctive about the stitching or decorations on the shoes or boots?

Similar questions can be asked, if appropriate, about the criminal's hat or headgear, gloves, outerwear, and anything the criminal carried or displayed.

The answers to these questions can often provide a detailed and accurate picture of the suspect. Sometimes a witness is surprised to realize that the detailed impression does not entirely agree with the superficial, generalized impression given earlier. The investigator should reassure the witness that this is often the case.

## INTERVIEWING THE RELUCTANT OR HOSTILE WITNESS

People can have many different reasons for not wishing to give information to the police. Faced with a reluctant or hostile witness, the investigator must attempt to discover which reasons might apply.

## WHY WITNESSES ARE UNCOOPERATIVE

Some people simply do not wish to be involved in a criminal investigation. They might feel that their involvement will be time-consuming; it could cost them money if they have to take time off from work, or it could merely be inconvenient. They may have so little confidence in the ability of the police that they prefer not to waste their time by helping.

Witnesses often fear retaliation from the criminal if they cooperate with the police. This is especially true when the crime is committed in a relatively close-knit community, such as a ghetto or an ethnic neighborhood, and even more so when the witness knows the criminal. Occasionally, witnesses might fear retaliation from other people in the community.

Victims of crime often have irrational responses that can include extensive bouts of paranoia. They may be extremely fearful that the criminal will attack again. Some victims are even afraid of reprisals from the police themselves. Victims of violent crimes sometimes respond, paradoxically, by feeling guilty: they blame themselves for having been attacked. All of these irrational fears can be aggravated if the investigator is judgmental in attitude or acts in an aggressive or overbearing manner.

Finally, it is not unusual for witnesses, including victims, to be reluctant or hostile because of their own guilt. They might have some complicity in the crime itself, in which case they have no wish to discuss it. More often, the witness or victim is involved in some other criminal activity and is fearful that the police will discover their other crimes while investigating the immediate crime.

It can be extremely difficult to dissipate these fears and it is not always possible to succeed. However, the effort must be made, because a reluctant or hostile witness may have information that is not available from any other source.[18]

## HOW TO ENCOURAGE COOPERATION

If a witness seems reluctant or mildly hostile, the investigator must take time during the initial stage of questioning to deal with the problem. The investigator should explain carefully the importance of the witness's testimony and the way in which that testimony will be used. The investigator should make clear that everything the witness says will be kept confidential until the suspect is caught and brought to trial. However, the investigator also should state that the witness might have to testify in court.

Appeals to a witness's sense of civic pride or responsibility are effective once in a while. Another approach is to point out that unless the criminal is caught, other people are likely to suffer from the same crime. Threats, even very mild or implied ones, are almost never effective.

One approach that is often very effective is to ask the witness merely to confirm what the police already know. The investigator should approach the witness with an elaborate show of self-confidence and decisiveness, treating the witness's testimony as not especially important or valuable. The investigator might say, "We've got a pretty good idea of what happened here, but I'd like you to check me on a couple of the details." This is followed by a very generalized summary of the information that has been obtained from the physical evidence and other interviews. Only details that would be obvious to a casual bystander should be included in the summary.

Again, as in summarizing for a cooperative witness, the investigator might include a few deliberate misstatements. Human nature is such that people feel an enormous compulsion to impress others with their personal knowledge and to ensure that their own perceptions are accepted by others. Thus, following a summary containing a few mistaken details, even the most reluctant or hostile witness is likely to blurt out, "No, that's not what happened at all!" After that, the witness may be eager to talk.

The summarizing device serves another purpose, too. A witness with a guilty conscience may be reluctant to speak up until it becomes apparent that the police already know most of the story. The witness may then decide that the testimony is not important enough to keep secret any longer and will give the police whatever additional details they want.[19]

If these devices fail and the witness is still reluctant or hostile, the interview should be discontinued. Sometimes a witness will decide to cooperate after having had a chance to think over the situation. Later, perhaps, the investigator will have gained enough information from other sources to use the summarizing technique more successfully. Sometimes it turns out that a hostile witness's testimony is not needed anyway. Or, if it is and if the investigator has a fairly clear idea of what the testimony would be, legal proceedings can be instituted by the prosecutor to compel the witness's testimony under oath.

WHEN A
WITNESS ASKS FOR
FAVORS OR PROTECTION

Never, under any circumstances, should an investigator bargain for information with a reluctant or hostile witness. Police officers have no legal right to offer leniency, immunity from criminal charges, or any other kind of favor in return for information. Furthermore, if they make such a promise, they must attempt to keep it—which usually cannot be done—or they will soon have a reputation in the community as liars. Either way, the officers have needlessly jeopardized their personal integrity and the credibility of their agencies.

If a witness asks for such a favor, the only proper response is to say, "Right now, we're only investigating this particular crime. If you know anything about it, we will be grateful for your help and I will see that your cooperation is made known to the proper authorities." A witness who insists on making a deal should be taken by the officer to the prosecutor's office. If any deal is to be made, it will have to be made by the district attorney or an equivalent official—not by a police officer.

Another sticky problem is the witness who asks for protection against possible reprisals. In this case, the investigator must make a number of difficult judgments: Is the witness's fear justified? Does the witness know enough about the crime to warrant special protective efforts? How much protection would be required and for how long?

If the investigator decides that the witness's fears are justified, the matter should be referred to higher authorities, including the district attorney or other prosecuting official. Decisions about whether to offer protection and what kind of protection should be offered cannot be made by the investigator without consulting higher officials. In these circumstances, the investigator must be fully honest with the witness about what can and cannot be done. The explanation, however, should include the fact that the criminal will have no way of knowing just how cooperative the witness was. In fact, the more cooperation the witness gives, the more probable it becomes that the criminal will be caught and thus will be unable to retaliate against the witness.

## INTERVIEWING SECONDARY WITNESSES

A secondary witness is someone who has little or no direct knowledge of the crime but does have some other knowledge that is needed by the police. A secondary witness may be someone who knows the victim or a suspected perpetrator or an individual who knows some circumstance surrounding the crime. Secondary witnesses are often found by one of the two methods that we have mentioned: a physical search in the vicinity of the crime or the questioning of primary witnesses. Less often, secondary witnesses are found through the time-related search already discussed. Another way of locating secondary witnesses is through public appeals, a method that we will describe in Chapter 8.

The questioning of a secondary witness usually is not as elaborate nor as formal as the questioning of a primary witness. In most cases, only a few specific questions are asked of a secondary witness. Secondary witnesses typically are not aware of the significance of the information that they have. A person might have heard a loud noise in the middle of the night and never realized that it was a gunshot or a burglar blowing a safe. Criminals often go about their ordinary, routine affairs without attracting any special notice from their neighbors. Thus, secondary witnesses rarely come forward to offer information to the police; unless the police locate them and ask the right questions, the information is never discovered.

The search for secondary witnesses usually is motivated by the fact that some key piece of information is missing. It may be some important detail about the crime itself or simply the whereabouts of the principal suspect. Only in a rare case for which little physical evidence and no primary witnesses are available would the police try to find a secondary witness who can provide a generalized account of the crime.

The nature of the information being sought determines the kinds of questions that should be asked. When a potential secondary witness has been located, the investigator first must ask the usual questions to establish the witness's identity, relationship to the victim or suspect, and so on. Then the investigator asks for the specific information needed. A simple, direct question is the best way to get a simple, direct answer. Usually there is nothing to be gained by asking misleading or vague questions or by trying to trick a secondary witness into giving useful information. On the contrary, such tactics may confuse the witness or arouse suspicion; in that case an otherwise cooperative witness may become reluctant or hostile.

Sometimes a secondary witness will ask for an explanation for the interview. This is especially common when the investigator asks questions about a witness's friends or relatives, who may be either the victims or the suspects in the crime. Again, neither brusqueness nor evasiveness will be productive. Unless the witness is given a satisfactory explanation, the likelihood of cooperation declines drastically.

Fictional detectives usually respond to such requests by saying, "It's just a routine investigation." Unfortunately, that phrase has appeared so often in fiction that it serves to reinforce, rather than to dispel, the witness's suspicions. Consequently, this phrase should *never* be used.

Honesty is the best policy. At the same time, the investigator should not give any specific, detailed information about the crime

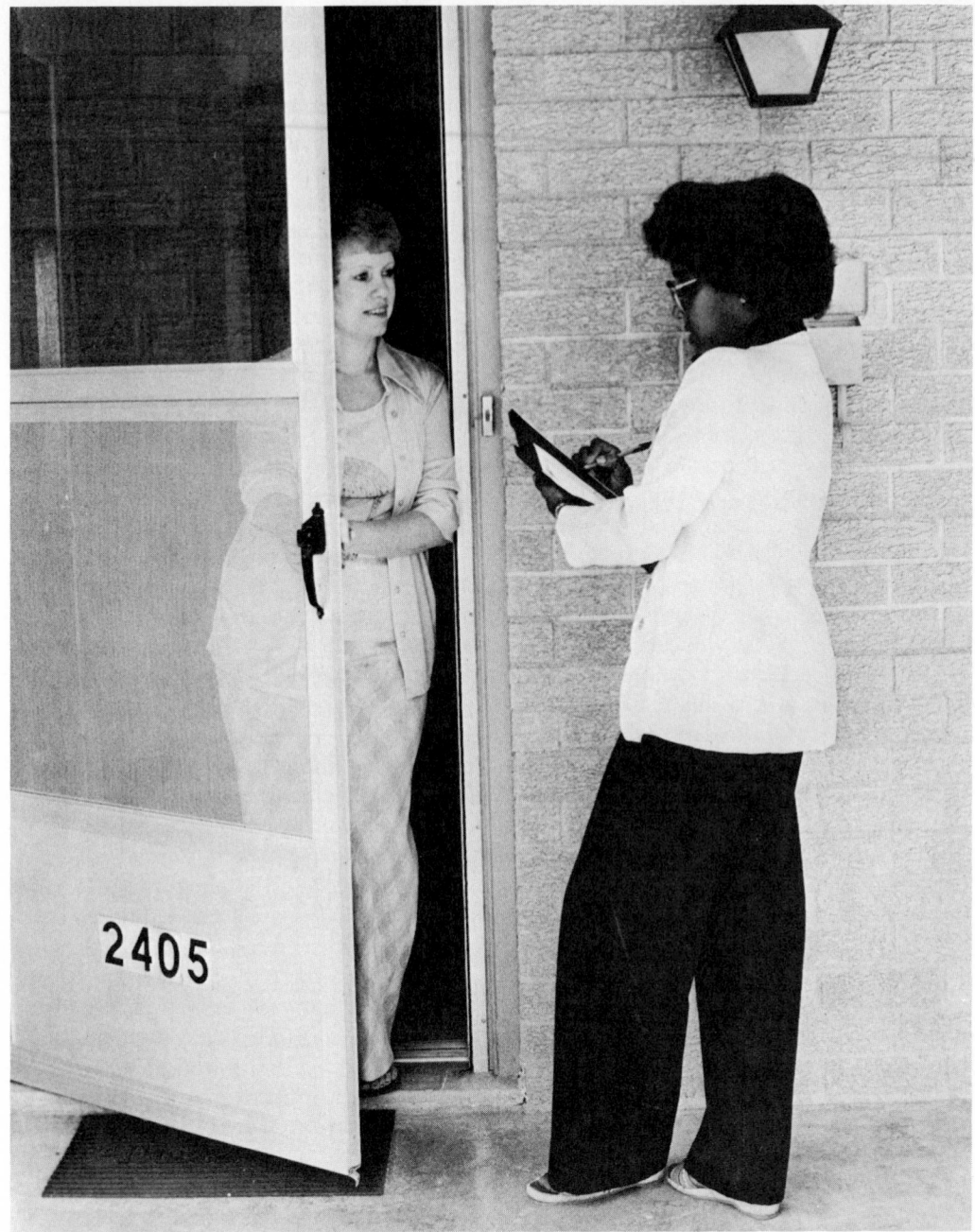

*Secondary witnesses often do not realize the significance of their information, which might include the one fact needed to solve a case. It is up to the investigator to locate every secondary witness and to ask the right questions to prompt the witness to give useful information.*

or the progress of the investigation. Instead, the investigator might say, "We're investigating a crime, and we think you might have seen the criminal leaving the scene." If information is sought about a suspect, the investigator could explain, "We're looking for ——— because we understand that she might be in some trouble and we need to find her before anything worse happens."

If the potential witness persists in asking for a detailed explanation, the investigator should treat the questions directly: "I can understand why you're interested in all of this, but I'm not permitted to tell you any more of the details." If the witness is not satisfied and continues to ask prying questions, another good technique is to confront the witness: "Why are you asking me about that?"

Such exchanges should not be allowed to go on for long. If the witness will not cooperate, break off the interview. However, if it seems probable that the witness has useful information, one effective technique is to send another investigator to conduct a second interview (after careful coaching by the principal investigator). If possible, the second interviewer should be a higher-ranking police officer or a member of the prosecutor's staff. Ultimately, legal proceedings could be used to compel testimony under oath, but that is rarely necessary.

## WRITTEN AND SIGNED STATEMENTS

So far, all the interviews that we have described involved oral questioning of the witnesses and notetaking by the investigator. An audio tape recorder in this stage of the investigation could be very helpful, but unfortunately such equipment is rarely used.

Most police agencies do not require that witnesses' statements be reduced to writing or that they be signed, though some agencies do have such regulations. As a general rule, we feel that written or signed statements are usually unnecessary and could be misinterpreted by witnesses. Once they have signed something, even something as informal as field notes, witnesses may feel legally bound to uphold the same story even if they later realize that a mistake was made about some crucial detail. Most people have very little knowledge of or understanding about police procedures. They may be badly intimidated by something so "official" as a signed statement.

On the other hand, a signed statement can be a very effective way to ensure that a reluctant or hostile witness will not back away from the testimony. Here again, a difficult judgment must be made by the investigator. Asking the witness to give a signed statement might frighten the person into refusing to help at all. On the other hand, it might impress the witness with the seriousness and importance of giving truthful testimony. Naturally, the investigator should not even mention a signed statement until the initial field interview has been completed and then only if a statement is really necessary.

If a signed statement is necessary and the witness agrees to give one, it should be taken at the police station. The procedure for a witness's signed statement is similar to, though simpler than, the procedure followed for a suspect. The witness and investigator should meet in a small, fully enclosed room, away from the distraction of other people and activities. If a stenographer must be present, he or she should be seated behind the witness and should be as unobtrusive as possible. A better practice is to have the stenographer in an adjacent room, listening to the interview by means of a microphone and speaker system. Another alternative is to tape-record the interview and have the stenographer transcribe the tape. Even better, the interview could be tape-recorded and also written down by a stenographer.

Whatever method is used, the result should be a neatly typed transcript of the entire interview. The investigator and the witness should read through the transcript together and mark any corrections on each copy; all corrections should be initialed by both the witness and the investigator. Finally, the witness should sign the statement, preferably in the presence of a notary public.[20]

Occasionally, a witness will ask to have a lawyer or some other person present during a formal interview. A witness has no legal grounds for making such a request, but usually there is no reason to deny it. If the investigator senses that the witness merely wants some kind of reassurance, probably no harm will be done in agreeing to the request.

## REFERENCES

1. Gwynne Peirson, *Police Operations* (Chicago: Nelson-Hall), 1976, p. 116.

2. William Ker Muir, Jr., *Police: Streetcorner Politicians* (Chicago: University of Chicago Press, 1977), p. 51.

3. Muir, pp. 178–181.

4. Muir, p. 227.

5. Fred E. Inbau and Marvin E. Aspen, *Criminal Law for the Police* (Philadelphia: Chilton, 1969), pp. 124–125.

6. *Olmstead v. U.S.,* 277 U.S. 438, 478 (1928).

7. Paul B. Weston and Kenneth M. Wells, *Elements of Criminal Investigation* (Englewood Cliffs, N.J.: Prentice-Hall, 1971), p. 45.

8. James R. Waters and Sheree A. McGrath, *Introduction to Law Enforcement* (Columbus, Ohio: Charles E. Merrill, 1974), p. 82.

9. Weston and Wells, *Elements of Criminal Investigation,* p. 46.

10. Weston and Wells, *Elements of Criminal Investigation,* p. 48.

11. Weston and Wells, *Elements of Criminal Investigation,* p. 47.

12. Peirson, p. 117.

13. Weston and Wells, *Elements of Criminal Investigation,* p. 51.

14. Peirson, p. 117.

15. Weston and Wells, *Elements of Criminal Investigation,* pp. 49–50.

16. Waters and McGrath, p. 83.

17. Weston and Wells, *Elements of Criminal Investigation,* pp. 53–56.

18. Weston and Wells, *Elements of Criminal Investigation,* p. 45.

19. Weston and Wells, *Elements of Criminal Investigation,* p. 52.

20. Weston and Wells, *Elements of Criminal Investigation,* pp. 56–57.

## REVIEW OF THE EVIDENCE

1. Indicate which of these descriptions apply to an interview of a witness (W), to an interrogation of a suspect (S), or to both (B).
   a. is a structured, controlled effort to gain information from another person
   b. begins with no preconceived notions about the information to be learned
   c. usually follows a carefully planned and rather rigid series of questions
   d. is less formal in structure and more casual in style
   e. is usually conducted during the later stages of an investigation to confirm information that has been discovered earlier

2. "The tragic view" that police officers should have, according to one sociologist, means
   a. a belief that some people are basically good and others are basically bad.
   b. a belief that most people's lives end in misfortune.
   c. a belief that all people are essentially a mixture of good and bad elements.
   d. a belief that all people are inherently evil.
   e. a belief that victims of crime deserve more sympathy and respect than criminals.

3. True or false: People who enjoy talking and who are able to express their own feelings and ideas often make good investigators.

4. Individuals cannot be compelled to testify against themselves. This principle, expressed in the U.S. Constitution, is known as
   a. the right against self-incrimination.
   b. the right not to complain.
   c. the right of privacy.
   d. freedom of expression.
   e. the right of habeas corpus.

5. As defined in the text, a victim would always be what kind of witness?
   a. cooperative
   b. primary
   c. productive
   d. articulate
   e. secondary

6. True or false: When several witnesses give an account of a crime that is completely consistent and coherent, the investigator can assume that the account is true in every respect.

7. Which of the following is *not* one of the reasons for interviewing witnesses in isolation?
   a. to ensure that the witness is not distracted by hectic activity at the crime site
   b. to spare the witness from embarrassment
   c. to intimidate the witness so that he or she will be less likely to lie
   d. to keep the witness from being influenced by what other witnesses say
   e. to give the witness an opportunity to say things that could be embarrassing or dangerous if other people heard them

8. True or false: It is essential for the investigator to force witnesses to clarify all contradictions or inconsistencies in their statements.

9. If a witness asks questions about the crime or the progress of the investigation, the interviewer's first response should be
    a. to say that it is none of the witness's business.
    b. to give a general or vague answer, recognizing the legitimate basis for the witness's curiosity.
    c. to tell the witness, "This is just a routine investigation."
    d. to ask why the witness wants to know about it.
    e. to tell the witness, "I'm not allowed to answer questions like that."
10. Which of the following statements is or are true?
    a. Some people do not want to be involved in a criminal investigation because they do not believe that the police will be able to solve the case.
    b. Some witnesses are afraid of retaliation from the police, from the criminal, or from other people in the community if they cooperate.
    c. Some witnesses are hostile because they are involved in some kind of criminal activity that they are afraid will be discovered.
    d. Victims often feel guilty about having been attacked.
    e. All of the above are true.
    f. None of the above is true.

## TOPICS FOR INVESTIGATION

1. Witnesses are sometimes hostile or reluctant because of their lack of confidence in the police. What can a law enforcement agency do to prevent this? Why would some people fear reprisals from the police for reporting a crime or giving truthful statements to an investigator? What would such attitudes—even if they are unfounded—say about a law enforcement agency?
2. Why should an investigator go to great lengths to avoid giving a witness any detailed information about a crime or the progress of an investigation, especially if the witness has a legitimate reason for wanting to know?
3. Which of the qualities of a good interviewer do you consider most important? Which of them should apply equally to all police officers? Are there other important qualities that should be added to the list?
4. Do you agree with the sociologist Muir's ideas about the tragic view? What are some implications of this idea for other areas of a police officer's job, such as crime prevention, treatment of suspects, or treatment of convicted offenders and ex-offenders?
5. Victims and witnesses have a legal obligation to provide information to the police. However, the presumed right of privacy and the right not to complain seriously undermine the effectiveness of that obligation. Why do these vague "rights" exist? Since these presumed rights have no constitutional basis, should they be eliminated by new laws reinforcing the legal duty to cooperate with the police?

# CHAPTER 7
## CRIMES OF VIOLENCE

STUDY CLUES

1. How is the crime of assault different from the crime of murder?
   a. A weapon is used to commit a murder; an assault does not require a weapon.
   b. Assault victims usually know their attackers; murder victims usually do not.
   c. An assault victim survives the attack; a murder victim does not.
   d. An assault is an attack that occurs during the commission of another crime; a murder does not have to involve another crime.
   e. All of the above are correct.
2. True or false: A crime investigator must devote full attention to the task of solving the crime without being distracted by a victim's irrational emotional responses.
3. Which of the following is *not* part of a victim's response to a violent assault?
   a. a tendency to blame others, including the police, for failing to prevent the attack
   b. feelings of vulnerability and helplessness
   c. feelings of guilt and self-blame
   d. denial that the incident occurred at all
   e. none of the above
4. True or false: In the most common type of murder, the victim and the murderer are complete strangers.
5. Rape differs from most other crimes in which of the following ways?
   a. It is usually provoked or initiated by the victim.
   b. The burden of proof rests mostly on the victim, who must prove that a crime occurred.
   c. The victim must be prepared to undergo a long series of attacks on her dignity, self-respect, and integrity.
   d. The investigator must be more skeptical and impersonal than usual.
   e. All aspects of the investigation can be conducted by the police without outside help.
6. Which of these statements are true?
   a. More than one-fourth of murder victims are close relatives of the murderer.
   b. Well-planned murders, which are solved only by the skill and ingenuity of the investigator, are the most common type of violent assault.
   c. Maniacal and sadistic murders often occur in series and receive prominent attention in the news media.
   d. The motive usually is the single most important clue in solving a murder case.
   e. Most victims and murderers share the same sociological background.

ANY INVOLVEMENT IN A CRIME is emotionally disturbing. This is true for everyone who has any connection at all with a criminal event: the victim and the perpetrator, immediate witnesses, family and friends of the victim, and even the police officers.

Consider, for example, your own emotional response to a very simple, minor, and routine law enforcement event: being given a traffic ticket. If you have ever been stopped for speeding or another relatively minor offense, you might recall your feelings at the time. Most people feel a mixture of guilt, embarrassment, and anger. They often consider themselves to be the victims of bad luck or of an arbitrary authority that has unfairly disrupted their lives.

The more serious the crime, the more powerful and devastating is the emotional response both of the victim and of the person who committed the crime. The feelings of these two parties may be more similar than you would expect. That does not mean that a criminal deserves the same sympathy that we normally give to a victim, but it suggests that a police officer must anticipate and allow for these reactions.

## THE PSYCHOLOGY OF THE VICTIM

In this chapter we shall deal specifically with the psychological and sociological aspects of the most serious kinds of crime: violent physical assault and sexual assault. Our purpose is to gain some insights into how the victims and the perpetrators come to be in those circumstances, how the victims respond emotionally to their misfortune, and how these psychological and sociological factors affect the way in which one must pursue the essential tasks of an investigation.

Ordinarily, people become victims because of some specific event in their lives, such as a crime that is committed against them, illness, or bodily injury. However, other individuals become "victims" by self-definition: they feel frightened, confused, and unable to cope with their own normal affairs. Both kinds of victims experience similar feelings.

Most people become victims of crime through circumstances over which they have no control. Others become victims through carelessness or by placing themselves in dangerous and crime-provoking situations.

Perhaps the most damaging part of being a victim is the sense of powerlessness and vulnerability. Many victims feel that they have no control over the forces that threaten them. Some respond to this feeling by abandoning any attempt to care for themselves, to plan and regulate their own daily lives. Others react in the opposite way, by trying to rebuild their defenses and make them impregnable; this can mean shutting out the rest of the world as much as possible and having no contact with other people.[1] An excessive belief in supernatural phenomena or luck, witchcraft, and other superstitions also can result from a victim's attempts to deal with the sense of powerlessness.

### THE INABILITY TO MAKE PLANS

Planning is a crucial type of human activity, even such simple planning as making up a shopping list or deciding to awaken at eight o'clock. Plans are intended to eliminate uncertainty and to ward off accidents or other disruptions. When such ordinary plans fail because a crisis, such as a crime, intervenes, then the feeling of helplessness is reinforced. People who feel that they are victims often

*When a crisis such as a crime disrupts people's plans, they may feel an overwhelming sense of futility and powerlessness. (Photo courtesy of Texas Department of Public Safety)*

refuse to make any kind of plans at all. They may appear to be vague, confused, and unable to commit themselves to any sort of agreement or appointment.

Such people are difficult to deal with because one cannot depend on them to do anything, even if they have promised to do it. They may become extremely withdrawn or erratic in their behavior, although they often seem calm or even unusually serene. Because they feel victimized, some people become locked into these behavioral patterns for long periods of time. In a way, they are refusing to accept responsibility for their own lives because they feel that life is too unpredictable for their efforts to have much effect.

Although this is a typical pattern for people who feel victimized, it is not the only pattern

ANSWERS TO STUDY CLUES
1. c    2. False    3. e    4. False
5. b and c    6. a, c, and e

of response. Furthermore, there can be very wide variations in the degree to which the victims of crime react.

### THE GUILT RESPONSE

Another factor that greatly complicates the police officer's job is the feelings of guilt that many victims have. This may seem surprising or even paradoxical at first, but an examination of how our culture handles mishaps reveals the origin of the victim's guilty feelings.

Children learn early in life that they must take precautions against all sorts of accidents, even those that could be regarded as unavoidable. If a child is hurt on the playground, knocks over a glass of milk at the dinner table, or suffers any of the countless routine misfortunes of childhood, the accident often results in some kind of punishment. The child may be scolded for carelessness or misbehavior, or other children may ridicule the child for clumsiness. In any case,

*Dealing with the People*

*People learn early in life that they are held responsible for mishaps. As adults, they often feel guilty when they are the victims of crime. (Photo by Julie O'Neil)*

children soon learn that they are at fault whenever they suffer any kind of mishap. These experiences are internalized at an early age and carried into adult life.

In many instances self-criticism is fully justified. Some people do provoke or invite misfortune, including criminal attack. Certainly, each person must assume some responsibility for self-protection. Sheer carelessness and negligence provide criminals with abundant opportunities. However, it is also true that no one deserves to be criminally assaulted, no matter how careless the person was or how provocative his or her behavior might have been. Furthermore, the victim's feelings of guilt can interfere seriously with the immediate need to assist the police in their investigation and can lead to other inappropriate emotional responses.[2]

One frequent result of excessive guilt on the part of the victim is a hostile reaction to the police. The victim may feel that the police are present in a punitive or blaming role—in essence, in place of the victim's parents. Anything that a police officer does in a suspicious or accusatory manner will be perceived as a threat to the victim. The investigator must learn how to defuse these feelings, while still maintaining objectivity and impartiality.[3]

A primary task of the investigator, often, is to provide psychological "first aid" to the victim and even to witnesses.

### FOUR STAGES OF EMOTIONAL RESPONSE

The feelings of vulnerability and helplessness, of the futility of planning, and of guilt are common to all victims throughout their emotional reaction to a crime. In addition, victims tend to go through four stages of overt emotional response. These stages may overlap to a considerable degree and there may be a stronger tendency toward one phase or another, but the investigator should learn to recognize each stage.

**Denial.** The first stage is *denial:* the victim refuses to admit that the crime has happened. Often this feeling is put into words very directly; the victim may say, "I can't believe this is real," or, "This can't be happening to me!" Sometimes the victim insists, "This is somebody's idea of a joke." The denial response is one way that the victim attempts to rationalize or to postpone feelings of guilt, inadequacy, and vulnerability. If the investigator reacts by insisting that the victim face the facts or by exhibiting anger, the victim may be propelled even deeper into the denial response. Instead, the investigator should express sympathy and concern, but gently direct the victim's attention to the details of the event.

An important variation of the denial response is exhibited by the victim who fails to display any emotions. The victim knows and admits that the crime has occurred, but refuses to accept the fact emotionally. The victim may seem extremely matter-of-fact and self-controlled in a recitation of the sequence of events, almost as if describing something that happened to another person. Often the description is flat, colorless, very well organized, but vague and lacking in detail.

Such an emotional denial cannot last indefinitely. At some point the victim must release the repressed emotions, and the sooner the better. Unfortunately, there is no way for the investigator to know when the release will occur or what might trigger it. Sometimes a few words of kindness or sympathy from the investigator will produce an emotional release. In other instances, an innocent question that the victim interprets as harsh or accusatory will produce an explosive reaction.

**Blaming.** Once the victim admits, both intellectually and emotionally, that the crime has occurred, the second stage of response, *blaming,* is entered.

Our system of criminal law is based on the assumption that each person is responsible for his or her own actions. When a crime occurs, the person responsible must be identified and held accountable. In this sense, the whole function of law enforcement is to blame the right person for each crime.

However, the emotional response of a victim may be indiscriminate. The victim may lash out in all directions, assigning blame to anyone: friends, neighbors, even casual acquaintances. The victim may make seemingly bizarre statements: "It's all my neighbors' fault! If they hadn't turned off their porch light, the criminal wouldn't have dared to sneak into my bedroom!" In part, this blaming response is an effort by the victim to reassign the guilt that he or she feels for failing to avoid being victimized.

The police themselves are often blamed for failing to prevent the crime. Sometimes the victim displays towering anger toward the police: "If you weren't so busy chasing speeders, you could patrol my neighborhood and stop these criminals!" There is no good way to answer such a complaint without further antagonizing the victim. Instead, an officer should understand the emotional basis for the remark and should respond in a sympathetic fashion, perhaps by saying, "Yes, I wish we could catch all of them before they do these things to people."

The best psychological first aid for the blaming response is to reassure the victim, quietly and confidently, that the criminal is the only person responsible for the crime, that the police will devote their best efforts to finding the criminal, and that, once caught, the criminal will be duly punished. Nothing should be said to encourage the victim to project blame inappropriately; such remarks as "All these hippies should be rounded up and shot!" deserve no answer.

It is important to recognize that the blaming response stems largely from the victim's self-blame or feelings of guilt. Therefore, no matter how irrational a victim may become in blaming other people for his or her misfortune, the police officer should not point out that the victim is partly at fault. Any such comment will merely inflame the situation even more. On the other hand, if the victim seems to be completely absorbed in self-recrimination, it may be effective to point out that it is the criminal, not the victim, who is responsible for the crime. The effect may be to provoke a siege of blaming responses, but at least the potentially destructive guilt cycle may be broken.

Ultimately, the investigator must attempt to redirect the victim's attention to the immediate problem: providing information that the police can use to apprehend the perpetrator of the crime.

**Anger.** At some point, the blaming response usually evolves into a generalized *anger* on the part of the victim; this is the third stage of emotional reaction. The degree and depth of anger vary considerably. Sometimes the victim is merely depressed and irritable; sometimes the victim becomes violently aggressive. The victim may become surly, unresponsive, and totally uncooperative. Drastic threats of vengeance may be expressed against the criminal, if the victim knows who it was, or against the world in general. The efforts of the police to apprehend the criminal may be ridiculed with biting sarcasm. Even mild-mannered, good-natured individuals may become hostile and belligerent.

This stage of the victim's response can only be weathered. There may be very little that

the police officer can do to redirect the victim's anger into productive channels. If the anger response is particularly acute, the investigator may have to suspend normal work for a time in order to restrain the victim, to keep him or her from acting out aggressive impulses. This is the only stage in the victim's response that may demand a strongly authoritarian response from the police. Sometimes, when there seems to be a danger that the victim's anger has gotten out of control, a few sharp words can be effective. Even mild threats may be necessary: "You are not going after your attacker at all, because if you do, we'll have to put you in jail! We will take care of her in the proper, legal way, but you've got to cooperate so we can do our job."

**Integration.** Finally, once the victim has worked through all of the foregoing stages, the last phase is *integration*. This means that the victim has come to terms with the criminal event as a disruption of his or her life. A healthy integration must include intellectual and emotional acceptance of the fact that the crime has occurred, but that it is only one event in a person's life. The victim has regained a feeling of control over his or her environment and personal behavior, and has regained self-respect.

**Variations in the victim's response.** No two people ever respond to an event in quite the same way. Some victims pass through all four stages of emotional reaction with surprising speed and relatively little damage. Others may take several days, weeks, or even months to work through their responses. A few victims, especially victims of sexual assault, never entirely recover.

Occasionally a victim will go through all four stages and then, for no apparent reason, go through them again. Thus, the police officer should not be overly surprised if a victim seems to bounce back and forth from one stage to another, or suddenly flares up into a blaming or anger response again.[4]

**Dealing with the victim's responses.** Police officers frequently express resentment over having to deal with victims' irrational responses, especially when anger or hostility is directed toward them. A police officer is not expected to be a psychoanalyst or therapist. Unfortunately, that kind of professional help usually is not available to the victim when it is needed most: immediately after the crime has occurred. Instead, it is the police officer, and especially the principal investigator, who is nearest at hand. The nature of the investigative task dictates that cooperation must be obtained from the victim. It just is not possible to ignore the victim until the person has calmed down. Like it or not, the burden falls on the police officer to provide the information, reassurance, and psychological support that the victim must have.

## RAPE OR SEXUAL ASSAULT

According to some psychologists, the human emotional structure is designed specifically to sustain and promote three basic *drives* or fundamental needs: self-preservation, preservation of the species through procreation, and self-expression. Almost every sort of human activity or behavior is connected directly to one or more of these three drives.

Our own culture is often criticized for being obsessed with sex. Whether or not that criticism is justified, it is certainly true that a very large part of our value system, our shared heritage of moral codes, and our legal system is devoted to the control of sexual activity. In opposition to these restraining factors, our society provides many influences that promote, enhance, and encourage sexual

behavior. Inevitably, people get caught in the crosscurrents between those factors which promote sexual activity and those which discourage or inhibit it. When people are unable to deal with these powerful forces, one result is sexual crime.

There has been a running debate in our country for at least the past hundred years over what kinds of sexual activity should be defined as criminal. The debate may continue for many years; however, one point is not seriously questioned: sexual acts committed by force will not be tolerated.

The strongest, most punitive laws in most states are reserved for murder, kidnapping, and rape. There is widespread agreement throughout our society that a man should not be permitted to force a woman to submit to sexual intercourse.[5] Other kinds of sexual attack are treated with similar seriousness, but there are many areas of uncertainty. For example, some states have rewritten their rape laws so that it is possible for a woman to be convicted for raping a man. Other states have changed the law so that a man can be convicted of raping his wife; generally, the rape laws do not apply in such a situation, for the laws make the assumption that a woman implicitly consents to sexual relations when she marries. Homosexual activity, prostitution, and sexual activity involving minors are other areas in which the law seems less certain today than it was only a few years ago.[6]

For our purposes, we shall confine our discussion to any case in which a person complains of a violent or forceful sexual attack, regardless of the gender of the parties involved or their other relationships. Most of what we have to say will be equally applicable whether or not a crime, technically defined, was committed. We shall be particularly concerned with the most common type of sexual crime that requires police investigation: rape.

## DEFINITIONS OF RAPE

*Rape* can be defined simply as the carnal knowledge of a female, forcibly and against her will. The strict legal definition varies from state to state and is subject to change, but the most common rape statutes provide for several specific elements:

1. There must have been sexual intercourse between the attacker and the victim. In some states, this is interpreted to mean that penetration of the vagina has occurred; in other states, actual penetration is not required; and in a few states, the mere disrobing of the victim may be sufficient.

2. The victim must be someone other than the attacker's wife. Again, this part of the law has been revised in some states to protect wives from being forced to submit to sexual relations. However, remember that some states do not require a formal wedding ceremony for a marriage to exist. It is possible for a woman to become legally a man's wife without intending or realizing it if she lives with him and regularly consents to a sexual relationship.

3. There must be evidence that the victim did not consent to any sexual activity and in fact resisted the attacker. Resistance does not have to be proved if it can be shown that the woman was incapable of resisting because she was drugged, asleep, unconscious, or otherwise incapacitated. Some women are assumed to be incapable of either giving or denying consent: women who are mentally defective, emotionally disturbed, or less than a certain age (which varies from state to state, as low as 12 or 14 years old and as high as 18 years old). This element also is satisfied if it is proved that the woman was tricked or coerced (by a threat of violence, for example).

Merely reviewing the definition of rape produces a strong feeling of revulsion in many people. It is not hard to understand the overwhelming nature of the victim's emotional response to such an attack. When one considers that a rape often is brutal and vicious and that the victim's life is in great danger, it becomes hard to imagine how a rape victim could avoid a profound reaction.

## DEALING WITH THE VICTIM'S EMOTIONAL RESPONSE

Unfortunately, for too many victims the crime itself is only the beginning of the ordeal. Unlike most of our laws concerning serious crimes, the rape law by its very nature involves only two individuals: the attacker and the victim. Except in the comparatively rare case of a gang rape, ordinarily there are no witnesses and relatively little in the way of physical evidence (although great strides have been made in recovering and using what little evidence is available). A charge of rape often becomes a matter of her word against his. The attacker may admit to having had sexual relations with the victim, but may claim that the woman consented or even initiated the activity.

The situation is different in several ways from most criminal cases. In spite of our tradition and our legal principle of innocence until guilt is proven, people have a strong tendency to assume that anyone accused of a crime is in fact guilty. In rape cases, however, this is not always true. On the contrary, many people tend to be extremely skeptical about a charge of rape, especially if the accused attacker does not have a criminal record. People are often suspicious that the woman has made the accusation out of spite or malice or has deliberately accused one man of rape in order to hide her sexual involvement with another man. Thus, the burden of proof lies not just on the prosecution—it rests specifically on the victim.[7]

Largely because of this tendency to blame the victim (or, at least, the victim's fear that this will happen), an estimated 50 to 90 percent of all rapes are never reported to the police. Even when rape is reported, the arrest and conviction rates are not very encouraging. In 1976, for example, only 52 percent of reported rapes were cleared by arrest, and only a third of those accused of rape were convicted of that crime.[8]

These factors must be kept in mind when dealing with the victim of a rape or any other serious sexual assault. Not only has the victim suffered a traumatic event, but now the victim must be prepared to undergo a long series of attacks on her (or his) dignity, self-respect, and integrity.

The police officer must make every effort to demonstrate compassion, understanding, and respect for the victim's feelings. The skepticism and objectivity essential to any investigation should not be thrown over, but the investigator must be extraordinarily careful not to display an attitude that the victim might perceive as threatening or hostile. A callous or impersonal attitude on the part of the investigator is not only unproductive, but actually cruel and unprofessional.

*A rape crisis center volunteer. In addition to providing assistance to victims of sexual attack, many rape crisis centers conduct public education campaigns to inform the public about sexual behavior and to help prevent sexual crimes. (Photo by Julie O'Neil)*

### THE RAPE CRISIS CENTER

Thousands of communities, large and small, now have rape crisis centers to help the police as well as the victims of sexual assaults. There are many variations in the organizational structure of rape crisis centers, but generally a center has a minimal paid staff and a large corps of volunteers. The volunteers are trained to help the victim overcome the emotional trauma of an attack. Concern for the victim is undeniably the center's first priority, but the volunteers are also trained to work with the police. Often the volunteers know more about the proper investigative procedures than the average patrol officer knows, and many volunteers are well versed in the legal ramifications of a rape case.

Most rape crisis centers advertise their services throughout the community, using mass media, posters, and similar means. As a result, rape victims often contact the rape crisis center before contacting the police or anyone else. The usual policy of a rape crisis center is to notify the police only if the victim permits it. Some police officials resent this policy and the "interference" of the nonprofessional volunteers, but in fact the policy is essential in order to gain the trust of the victim at a crucial time. Many rape cases would not be reported or discovered at all if it were not for the existence of the rape crisis center. Furthermore, if the victim initially refuses to go to the police, the volunteers usually continue their efforts to persuade the victim to change her mind.

Conversely, wherever an effective rape crisis center exists, it should be standard police policy that when a rape victim initially contacts the police department, the center is notified immediately. Some agencies go even further: when a rape is reported, a rape crisis center volunteer rides with the patrol officer who responds to the call.

Whichever agency is contacted first, it is vitally important for the victim to have a medical examination as soon as possible. We shall come back to this subject later; for now, the point is that either the police or the rape crisis center volunteer must make every effort to persuade the victim to consent to an examination.

Once in a while a rape victim goes on her own to a hospital emergency room before contacting the police or rape crisis center. Procedures and policies must be worked out in advance whereby the emergency room staff will notify the center or the police or both. Cooperation must be continuously maintained among all three entities.

Regardless of which agency is contacted first, it is usually best to let the rape crisis center volunteer take the lead in dealing with the victim. The investigator should stay out of the way until the victim has worked out her immediate emotional reactions. However, the investigator should remain on the scene to ensure that the investigation is not needlessly contaminated or complicated. For example, the victim should not be permitted to take any drugs or medication except by a doctor's instructions, and then preferably after the medical examination.

The victim should be persuaded *not* to change clothes before going to the hospital. A friend, relative, or the volunteer should bring a change of clothing to the hospital. The investigator must obtain the clothing that was worn at the time of the attack; it should be collected, prepared, and packaged for transfer to the laboratory as described in Chapter 5.

As a rule, it is desirable to have the examination take place in a public (city- or county-operated) hospital or clinic, rather than in a private physician's office or a privately owned hospital. The staff of a public hospital are usually better trained to deal with rape cases and probably will have accumulated some experience with them. A private physician, however, usually lacks experience in such matters and may be extremely reluctant to become involved in a criminal investigation or to testify in court about the results of the examination. If the victim insists on being examined by her own physician, those desires must be honored. However, the investigator should meet with the physician just prior to the examination and offer suggestions on the procedures that will be helpful to the investigation. The rape crisis center volunteer may be a strong ally either in persuading the victim to go to a public hospital or in persuading the physician to be cooperative.

If your community does not yet have a rape crisis center, no effort should be spared to get one started. The program does not have to be elaborate or expensive in a small community; a few trained volunteers can be kept on call for the occasional rape case. Existing social service agencies, either governmental or voluntary, may be able to provide the nucleus of the staff and assistance in organizing the program. If it just is not possible to organize a rape crisis center, perhaps because of opposition or apathy in the community, the next best alternative is to organize a special training and consultation program for all police personnel. Help for this purpose should be available from social service agencies, psychologists, psychological social workers, ministers, and other practitioners in the helping professions.

## THE RAPE INVESTIGATION

The investigative procedures for rape cases are essentially the same as those for any other crime and follow the outline given in Chapters 3, 4, and 5.

Quite often the victim knows the attacker; in this case, trace evidence is sought at the crime scene to confirm the identification. If the attacker is unknown, the search for trace evidence must be exhaustive and must cover all five zones of the crime scene. A special effort must be made to locate three particular types of trace evidence: blood, semen, and hair. The victim herself is likely to be a site for all three; it would be very hard to prove the elements of rape if none of these types of evidence could be found in the pubic area.

In addition, at the crime site the investigator should collect samples of any debris that might have been transferred to the attacker. If the assailant can be apprehended fairly soon, within a few hours of the attack, there is an excellent chance that the corresponding debris can be found on the suspect's clothing, body, vehicle, and personal effects.

The medical examination is absolutely indispensable to a rape investigation. If the victim refuses to submit to the examination, the investigation cannot proceed. In fact, any unnecessary delay in obtaining the examination will reduce the likelihood of finding conclusive evidence. It is particularly important not to let the victim bathe or otherwise clean up before the examination. She should be taken to the hospital exactly as the attacker left her, unless emergency medical care is needed for serious injuries.

We shall not describe in detail the medical procedures used in a rape examination. This information is readily available in medical textbooks and journals and in law enforcement materials, and it should be common knowledge to any emergency room staff.[9] In brief, the medical examination will begin with a taking of a *history*. Usually this does not mean a long account of the patient's past medical experience, but includes basic information about the patient, pre-existing medical conditions, and a summary of how the present medical problem—the rape—occurred.

The patient is then disrobed and examined by the physician in the presence of a nurse; at least one of the medical personnel should be female. Any injuries, such as cuts or bruises, are treated immediately. Someone on the medical staff or a police photographer should take photographs of all injuries, and they should be thoroughly described in the physician's notes. Soil, physiological fluids, hair, or other debris on the victim must be carefully collected by the medical staff and preserved for criminalistic study. Fingernail scrapings also should be collected since the victim may have scratched the attacker during the struggle.

The physician usually will be able to determine whether the victim has experienced sexual intercourse within recent hours, and any injuries to or near the vagina will be noted. In the past, it was important to determine whether the victim was virginal before the alleged rape (except in the case of a victim who was married or previously married). It was assumed that an unmarried woman who was not virginal might have an "unchaste character," which threw considerable doubt on the allegation of rape. Today, however, this assumption is not ordinarily made, and the question of virginity is irrelevant—except that if the woman is still virginal when examined, presumably there was no penetration and, under some state laws, there could not have been a rape.

An effort also will be made to collect any semen that might still be in the vagina or cervix. The presence of semen containing live (*motile,* or moving) sperm is considered positive proof of recent intercourse; but the absence of sperm, alive or otherwise, is not necessarily evidence that there was no intercourse. Analyses of any semen that is found may be useful in identifying the attacker.

Interviewing a rape victim poses many problems because of the victim's emotional condition. It is not always possible nor desirable to wait until the victim is completely calm and other phases of the investigation, such as the search for physical evidence and the medical examination, have been completed. On the other hand, these important steps must not be delayed. As a result, the interview is likely to be carried out on a catch-as-catch-can basis. This may mean a disjointed, poorly organized interview, but that cannot be helped. Again, the rape crisis center volunteer, if he or she has been properly trained, should provide much assistance in getting information from the victim.

## PHYSICAL ASSAULT AND MURDER

Fictional murderers are always very clever people who plan their crimes with a good deal of forethought and cunning. Only the superior intelligence and intuition of the detective prevent the crime from going unsolved. The key clue in solving a fictional murder is almost always the interpretation of the culprit's motive, which is never obvious but always highly significant. Greed, jealousy, and revenge are the common motives in fictional murders.

On the other hand, the murders that gain the most prominence in the news media are almost the exact opposite in character. Banner headlines and feverish editorials are reserved for murders that are random, bizarre, and essentially motiveless; usually the murderer turns out to be emotionally disturbed, if not legally insane. Often the murderer and the victim are complete strangers. Typical examples might be the "Son of Sam" murders in New York and the "Hillside Strangler" murders in Los Angeles.

The characteristics given to fictional murderers provide dramatic vividness and suspense to the story. The spectacular, inexplicable murders that dominate headlines for weeks at a time arouse a great deal of fear among the general population. But in real life, neither the cleverly premeditated murders nor the bizarre, irrational murders are the kind that the police encounter most often.[10]

### THE TYPICAL MURDER

Most murders are committed by people of average or somewhat below-average intelligence. Murderers often are emotionally disturbed to some degree, but the disturbance may not be obvious even to close friends and relatives. Usually murders are not planned in advance, and the criminals make no deliberate preparations to evade capture. The murderer and the victim almost always know each other to some degree. More than one-fourth of all murders are committed by close relatives of the victims. The criminal event usually occurs spontaneously as the result of a brief impulse for motives that seem trivial.

However, the conditions preceding the crime often include sporadic violence, erratic behavior, and emotional tensions that may have been mounting over a long period of time.[11]

We shall discuss the factors that impel a person to commit a murder in more detail shortly. At this point, we shall concentrate on the victims of murder. In general, the same considerations will apply to the victims of any serious physical assault, the only difference being that the victim of an assault survives the attack.[12]

The victim of murder often is the spouse, parent, child, or sibling of the attacker. In 1976, this was true in more than 27 percent of the reported cases. In another 54 percent of reported cases, the victim and the attacker were friends, neighbors, or acquaintances.[13] Both parties in these cases shared the same socioeconomic status and usually were alike in educational attainment, intellectual capacities, and emotional adjustment. Many studies have indicated that all four of these factors tend to be very deficient among both murderers and their victims.[14] The great majority of murders involve men as both perpetrator and victim, with women infrequently playing either role. Most victims of murder and murderers are between the ages of 18 and 30.[15]

The picture that arises from this jumble of statistics is that murder is the product of a relationship between two people, a relationship that has become mutually destructive. They probably live under circumstances that produce overwhelming psychological pressures: poverty, ignorance, shabby and overcrowded housing, and total or substantial unemployment. It is extremely difficult for people from healthy backgrounds to comprehend the effects of these factors on an individual's drive for self-preservation and self-expression.[16]

In combination with these sociological factors, some individual factors are also common among both victims and murderers: alcohol and drug abuse, emotional instability, a history of unsatisfactory interpersonal relationships, and physical or mental disease. Both parties may have had occasional involvements in relatively minor crime; however, only about one-fifth of all murders occur in the course of other crimes (most often robberies).[17]

The overwhelming majority of murders are committed with handguns. Other firearms (rifles and shotguns), knives, and personal weapons (hands, fists, feet) are also frequently used to commit murders; other weapons are rarely involved.

Taking all of these factors into account, we can construct a theoretical typical murder case. Two young men in a bar, usually in a ghetto neighborhood, fall into an argument. Almost certainly the young men know each other; they are likely to be close relatives. Chances are that they argue frequently about the same things. One or both of them may have a long history of minor scrapes with the police and a reputation for a violent, uncontrolled temper. This time, however, one of them has a gun or a knife, and suddenly, without warning, the weapon is displayed and used. Pure chance frequently dictates which of the pair becomes the victim and which the murderer.[18] The immediate motives for such murders are often astonishingly trivial. Murders have been committed over a parking place, a domino game that the murderer thought was too noisy, and a negligible amount of money. Jealousy and sexual entanglements figure in a high percentage of murders.[19]

The investigator of a murder must recognize the factors that we have described. The motive for the crime often is not important

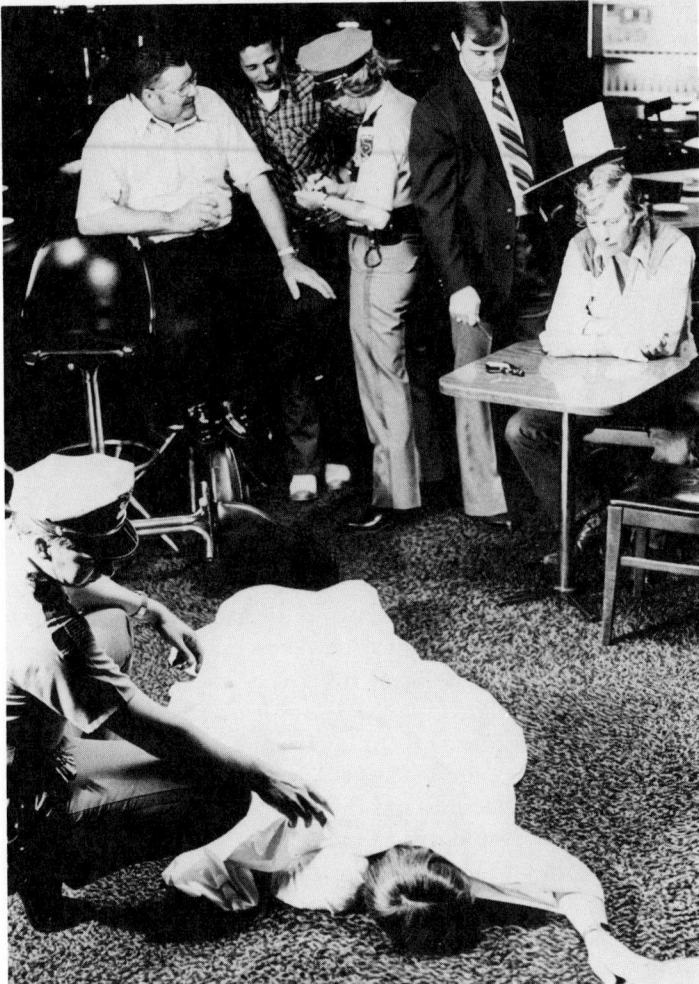

*The typical murder. Both the victim and the murderer are male, between 18 and 30 years old; they have known each other for a long time. Before the murder, they were drinking; an argument broke out between them; one of them produced a weapon—often a cheap handgun—and, in a moment, the other was killed.*

in identifying the perpetrator, although it may be important in securing a conviction because juries usually want some explanation for a violent act. Almost always, the attacker is someone the victim knew quite well, and the relationship between them is equally well known to many other people: their families, friends, neighbors, and casual acquaintances. Sometimes the secondary witnesses show surprise not that the murder has occurred but

that it was delayed for so long. Often they are surprised to learn which of the parties was the victim and which was the murderer.

In a sense, the person who is killed is not the sole victim of a murder but merely the primary victim. The real victims of a murder are the other people who are immediately affected by the death: the family and intimate friends. We might even call them *secondary victims.* Their psychological response to the crime is likely to be very similar, both in nature and in intensity, to the reactions of a direct or primary victim of other types of crime. The same sequence of denial, blaming, anger, and eventual integration can be expected, as well as the same underlying elements of fear, helplessness, guilt, loss of self-respect, and so on. The investigator, therefore, must approach secondary victims in the same way that primary victims would be treated.

## ATYPICAL MURDERS

Of course, not all murders follow the pattern we have described. Atypical murders can be classified into four main categories: planned murders, maniacal murders, sadistic murders, and terroristic murders. Each category has its own characteristic victims and perpetrators, and each requires a distinctive investigative approach.

**Planned murder.** What we call *planned murder* is most like the murders in popular fiction. Such murders are extremely rare but they do sometimes occur. The distinguishing feature of a planned murder is the unusual degree of care exercised by the murderer to escape detection. This exceptional forethought is shown by the absence of physical evidence at or near the crime site. Frequently, the crime takes place well out of public view so that there are no witnesses. Sometimes the circumstances of the crime are difficult to determine, and there may be a good deal of confusion about the exact manner of death.

As with a typical murder, the victim and the perpetrator of a planned murder usually have a well-established relationship prior to the crime; indeed, the motive for murder usually grows out of that relationship. As in fictional mysteries, discovering the motive may be the key to identifying the perpetrator. Much will depend on the interviews that the investigator conducts with the secondary victims and secondary witnesses, for it is only through these interviews that the motive is likely to be revealed.

Many carefully planned murders are the work of hired murderers; in this case the chances of identifying and convicting the perpetrator are depressingly small. Hired murderers are used by organized criminals to carry out their intergang warfare, to enforce their vicious authority, and occasionally to gain revenge against some "civilian" (a noncriminal) who has somehow aroused the wrath of the gangsters. Despite the low odds of success, all murders should be investigated with every intention of identifying the perpetrator and securing a conviction. The traditional attitude of some police agencies that gang murder is not a police problem as long as it is confined to gangsters does not reflect well on an agency's professionalism.

**Maniacal murder.** The essential characteristic of a *maniacal murder* is its repetition. Maniacal murders often occur in series, sometimes over a period of several years. The victims and the murderer may be complete strangers, although sometimes a maniacal murderer will establish some kind of relationship with the victims; a sexual relationship is not unusual. The murders frequently show a degree of premeditation, involving more or less elaborate attempts to disguise the fact of murder, eliminate physical evidence, and elude capture. Usually the victims of a maniacal murderer are very much alike; for example, they might all be middle-aged, blonde-haired, overweight women, or they might all be elderly men who live alone. In fact, the similarity of the victims may be the key element in capturing a maniacal murderer. The "Hillside Strangler" in the Los Angeles area is an example of a maniacal murderer.

**Sadistic murder.** *Sadistic murderers,* on the other hand, strike completely at random in an irrational and unpredictable manner. Although the victims might be similar in some respects, the real characteristic of a sadistic murderer is the similarity in the manner of committing the crime. Like maniacal murders, sadistic murders often take place in a series. The crime itself is frequently brutal and vicious, involving savage mutilation of the corpse. Sadistic murders occasionally are connected to other serious crimes, including armed robberies, burglaries, and rapes. Sometimes it is apparent that the associated crime is little more than a pretext for the murder itself.

Identifying a sadistic murderer is extremely difficult because of the sheer unpredictability of the murderer's behavior. Physical evidence may be relatively abundant, because the sadistic murderer may make little effort to conceal it. However, without a suspect with whom the evidence can be matched, identification is almost impossible. Secondary victims and secondary witnesses are not very helpful, since usually there was no prior relationship between the victim and the attacker.

Solving a sadistic murder case usually depends on luck more than anything else. Occasionally a victim survives the attack and can identify the attacker; sometimes a witness happens to observe the attack. More often, a sadistic murderer is captured in connection with other criminal activity or because a connection can be made to a previous conviction.

**Terroristic murder.** *Terroristic murders* are distinguished by their being the result of some sort of conspiracy or group activity. Political assassination and juvenile gang warfare are both examples of terroristic murder. Again, such cases are extremely difficult to solve. The difficulty is compounded by the fact that the whole group shields the perpetrator.

Often some kind of relationship exists between the victim and the terroristic attacker, but they might not know one another personally; their association arises out of their membership in their respective groups. Sometimes, however, terroristic murders are carried out at random with no particular intended victim. Juvenile gangs and extremist political factions are most often involved in such random killings.

Generally, terroristic murders can be solved only if a member of the group responsible for the murder can be persuaded to give the police incriminating evidence. Otherwise, the chances of using physical evidence or the testimony of other witnesses to identify and convict a terroristic murderer are very slim.

**Combined types of murder.** It should be understood that these four categories are not completely exclusive. A maniacal murderer may also be sadistic; terrorists, especially those who carry out politically motivated assassinations, usually plan their violent acts with compulsive precision. Our purpose in suggesting these four categories is to offer the investigator some guidance in choosing the techniques that are most likely to be productive.

## THE EVOLUTION OF VIOLENT OFFENDERS

So far, we have discussed some of the characteristics of both victims and perpetrators of violent crimes. It is equally important for the investigator to have a thorough understanding of how people become rapists or murderers. Our intent is not to generate sympathy for violent offenders, but rather to gain some insights that can be helpful in identifying and even predicting violent behavior.

## SOCIOLOGICAL AND ENVIRONMENTAL FACTORS

As we have already said, most violent offenders share with their victims an unhealthy sociological background: they are poor, poorly educated, unemployed or only sporadically employed at menial jobs, and often afflicted with a variety of illnesses. These factors are so widely understood and documented that they do not need repeating.[20]

What is not so widely understood by people who have never experienced such an environment is the sheer, overwhelming futility that dominates these individuals' lives. Living in filthy, overcrowded, and deteriorating buildings, the ghetto dweller's energies are concentrated on the urgent and constant struggle to survive. If a person has little education and an unimpressive work record, there is little chance for finding satisfying employment, and jobs are not readily available in the ghetto, anyway. Physical illness is a constant threat to the individual's well-being. Mental retardation and emotional illness are equally common.

Alcoholism, drug use, prostitution, gambling, petty thievery and burglary, and random violence make up a large part of everyday reality for the ghetto dweller. Although the vast majority of ghetto dwellers are or try to be law-abiding, they are motivated more by the will to retain their self-respect than they are by respect for the law.[21]

Under these conditions, many ghetto dwellers resemble the victims of crime, whom we discussed earlier. They share a generalized sense of helplessness and vulnerability, a feeling that they are incapable of controlling their own lives or the events around them. The difference is that the victims of crime usually recover; people in the ghetto have no chance to recover, because the conditions that produce their victimization never change.

These sociological and environmental conditions finally produce a deadening of moral values and sensibilities, a desperate urge to survive in the face of unremitting danger, and a sense of futility. In combination with alcohol or drug abuse, physical illness, or emotional illness, the product can be persons who feel very little responsibility for their behavior, have virtually no self-esteem or self-respect, and are intimately familiar with many forms of common crime.

It is the individual's specific response to this environment that determines whether the individual becomes an offender. After all, most people in even the worst imaginable circumstances do not become criminals, much less violent criminals.[22] Those who do become criminals rarely make a conscious, deliberate decision to adopt a life of crime. What happens is that a young person, surrounded by examples of rampant vice and petty crime and faced with the futility of trying to avoid an unpleasant future, concludes that the risks involved in drug trafficking, burglary, or purse-snatching are outweighed by the potential rewards. The first criminal episode may occur on an impulse or under the influence of like-minded peers or as a result of drinking or drug usage. Such initial crimes are almost always successful; the chance of being apprehended by the police is very small. Thus, the incipient criminal is encouraged to try again. Soon he or she finds that criminal behavior has become habitual, and that it is a very hard habit to break. Relationships with law-abiding friends and family are strained, if not fully ruptured; soon the young criminal associates with and is influenced by only others in the same straits.[23] It is a sad comment on the structure of our society that some ghetto youths discover their only real success in a life of crime.

Young people who drift into crime in the way we have just described often make a conscientious effort to avoid violence. However, their own desperation and fear lead them to commit their first act of violence in connection with their other crimes. Perhaps an intended robbery victim fights back or they are discovered in the course of a burglary; perhaps they encounter violence in the course of drug trafficking or prostitution. The young criminal's first episode of violence is likely to be rationalized as an unavoidable act committed in self-defense. Thereafter, violent attacks may occur more and more frequently as part of the criminal's pattern of behavior.

## COMPULSIVE SEXUAL OFFENDERS

Sex offenders are less likely to follow this sequence of slow evolution into a life of crime. People who commit sexual offenses, especially violent ones, are far more likely to be responding to psychological compulsions.

The psychology of sex is far too broad a subject to be treated here, although it certainly deserves study by every law enforcement agent. But there are a few points that we wish to touch upon.

**Violent sexual offenders.** *Compulsive behavior* is behavior that the individual is powerless to prevent. Rape, incest, child molestation, exhibitionism, and other criminal sexual activities are almost always the result of compulsions caused by emotional disturbances.

A compulsive sexual offender may seem completely normal in every respect. Often the offender is a productive, respectable member of the community. Friends and family members have no inkling of any criminal activity. Usually compulsive, violent sexual offenders are not involved in other kinds of criminal behavior, which increases the difficulty in identifying them. The exception is the individual whose life is so thoroughly degraded by alcoholism, drug abuse, or association with criminality (especially vice) that sexual crime develops as a small part of the overall pattern of criminal behavior.

One characteristic of the compulsive offender is the repetition of the offense. Acting under psychological compulsion, the offender repeats the attack again and again with little or no variation. In this respect, the compulsive sex offender closely resembles the maniacal murderer; indeed, maniacal murders often are a result of sex-related compulsions, and violent, compulsive sexual offenses often stop just short of murder.

**Nonviolent sexual offenders.** Most so-called nonviolent sexual crimes are not a product of compulsive behavior. The most important exceptions are *exhibitionism* (indecent exposure) and *voyeurism* (window-peeping and similar offenses), both of which indicate some sort of emotional disorder. However, these offenses are obviously far less dangerous than any kind of violent assault, and there is little evidence that exhibitionists or voyeurs also engage in violence.

Because our laws have not kept pace with changing moral values and concepts of normal or proper sexual behavior, many people engage in behavior that is classified in most states as criminal. These states retain laws that a large part of the population considers obsolete or inappropriate, yet the laws remain unchanged either because they are overlooked or because there is vehement opposition to change. Ordinarily these laws are ignored by the public and the police alike. However, under certain circumstances (for example, if the illegal behavior becomes a public scandal) the police are unable to ignore the law or overlook behavior that appears to be illegal.

Homosexuality, adultery, fornication (sexual relations between unmarried persons), and a great variety of sexual activities that are widely regarded as normal or harmless may be illegal. Unfortunately, this means that many people routinely engage in illegal activities that they consider normal and unobjectionable.

## SOCIOPATHOLOGICAL OFFENDERS

The term *sociopathology* means diseased or perverted relationships with other people. In brief, a sociopath is a person who is incapable of establishing or maintaining a healthy relationship with others. (Such people used to be called psychopaths but that terminology is no longer generally accepted.)[24]

There appears to be no single cause for sociopathology. The term suggests some kind of emotional illness, but currently there is no particular psychological or psychiatric explanation for the development of a sociopath. Some, but not all, sociopaths display the effects of mental defects, including retardation or organic brain damage. Other sociopaths are able to maintain the appearance of a normal, productive, respectable, and law-abiding life. Some display a great deal of ingenuity and shrewdness, although generally sociopaths are not well educated.

A few years ago, a genetic peculiarity was thought to be a possible explanation for sociopathology. Scientists discovered that some males have an atypical chromosome, one that contains the sex-determining genes. Instead of the usual arrangement of one female, or X, chromosome and one male, or Y, chromosome, these men had one X and two Y's. When it was discovered that this odd arrangement could be found in a significantly high percentage of criminals convicted of violent crimes, the conclusion was drawn that the extra Y chromosome caused or contributed to the sociopathological behavior.

Today, however, this theory is far less widely accepted. No one ever came up with a sensible explanation of how this small genetic peculiarity could influence overt behavior. Furthermore, the same peculiarity has been found in many men who are by no means sociopaths, and many convicted violent offenders have been found to be free of this particular genetic oddity. Perhaps some future research will show that there really is a connection between hereditary factors and criminal behavior, but for now the XYY theory is given little credit.

One reason that hereditary factors are suspected is that sociopathological behavior often is seen at an early age. Children as young as five or six years old sometimes display the wanton recklessness, aggressiveness, and disruptive impulsiveness considered typical of adult sociopaths. It is too much to say that this kind of behavior indicates the predestination of a child to criminality: some children grow out of it and become law-abiding citizens, while some adults identified as sociopaths have no known history of troublesome childhoods. However, the similarity in the behavior of disruptive children and of sociopathological adults is so marked that it can hardly be ignored.

Although sociopathology is a fairly broad term covering a range of behavior patterns, a general picture of the sociopath can be drawn. Sociopaths are characterized by impulsive, often extremely reckless activities. They disregard not only the lives and welfare of others, but also their own. They are fiercely aggressive with little or no clear provocation.

The sociopath is incapable of sustaining a normal, satisfying relationship with another person. Paradoxically, male sociopaths are sometimes extremely attractive to women, especially women who believe that they can reform them.[25] Long-lasting, volatile relationships often exist between sociopathological sadists (people who derive pleasure from hurting others) and masochists (people who derive pleasure from being hurt). Wife beating and child abuse are typical aspects of sociopathological behavior, although neither kind of violence is restricted to sociopaths.

Another important characteristic of the sociopath is the diversity of criminal behavior. As we have mentioned, young people sometimes progress through a sequence of increasingly more serious crimes. Most confirmed criminals tend to specialize in a particular type of crime. Sociopaths, in contrast, commit every sort of crime indiscriminately, from shoplifting to mayhem. An unrestrained sociopath can wreak havoc on an entire community. Sociopaths are sometimes responsible for maniacal, sadistic, and terroristic murder sprees.

In a sense, a sociopath is not really compulsive; there is no emotional pressure or tension compelling the individual to act in a vicious or criminal manner. On the contrary, unlike the compulsive sexual offender, the sociopath is defined as a person who lacks any compulsions, including the normal compulsions of conscience and self-respect. A sociopath is utterly incapable of giving or receiving love, sympathy, or respect. A sociopath acts purely on impulse and is therefore completely erratic and unpredictable. Finally, most sociopaths appear to be incapable of learning from their own experiences. Neither harsh punishment nor the more enlightened forms of rehabilitative therapy seem to be effective on the true sociopath. Such people typically

spend the greater part of their adult lives enmeshed in our criminal justice system.

INSANITY AND THE LAW

Neither the compulsive sexual offender nor the sociopath is likely to be regarded as "insane" under the U.S. system of law. Both kinds of offenders are usually considered responsible for their criminal acts, even though it is understood that they have little ability to modify their own behavior.

Nevertheless, "insanity" is a legitimate defense against any criminal charge. If a person can prove that he or she is "insane" or was "insane" at the time of the alleged crime, the laws in every state dictate that the person cannot be convicted. Some states require the "insane" person to be committed to a mental institution and treated for the "insanity," but other states have no such requirements: the "insane" offender is simply set free.

The significance of this discussion for the investigator is that the evidence gathered at the crime scene and thereafter may have considerable bearing on whether the plea of "insanity" is successful. The police have no interest in preventing a successful plea of "insanity" if it is truly justified. On the contrary, the whole community is better off if the person is treated, instead of being warehoused in a prison. But the plea of "insanity" can be abused. Often it is raised in very serious cases in which there is no other reasonable defense.

No one factor nor any one predetermined set of factors defines legal "insanity." The absence of erratic behavior does not in itself mean that the person is legally sane. On the other hand, the fact that a crime shows some degree of premeditation and cunning does not in itself eliminate the possibility of "insanity." All the circumstances of a crime, including the apparent motive or lack of one, must be considered in determining whether the accused was "insane."

There are three sources of evidence: the physical evidence, the testimony of witnesses, and the observations of the police officer. The first two have been described and discussed already; if the investigator has kept adequate records of all physical evidence and of all testimony, these records will include material that bears on the question of "insanity."

Unfortunately, investigators often forget or fail to record their own observations of the accused. It should be standard practice for the investigator to prepare a summary of observations of the suspect's behavior, actions, mannerisms, and other characteristics from the time at which the suspect is apprehended until the suspect is placed in custody to await trial. The summary should include specific examples of the suspect's behavior that illustrate unusual calmness, nervousness, excitability, erratic behavior, and so forth. Sometimes these records are every bit as important as the record of what the suspect said.

One caution must be mentioned, however: the investigator must avoid putting into these records any conclusions about the suspect's mental state. Medico-legal terms such as *sociopath, compulsive,* or *psychotic* may be extremely misleading when they are brought up during a trial. Concrete facts should be left to speak for themselves.

### DEVELOPMENT AND USE OF THE PSYCHOLOGICAL PROFILE

Anything that an investigator can learn about the perpetrator of a crime is likely to help in identifying and apprehending a suspect. The best evidence is that which points directly to a single individual: fingerprints, for example.

Eyewitness testimony, personal knowledge of the offender, and similar direct evidence is next best.

When these kinds of evidence are not available, apprehension of a suspect depends on the ingenuity and skill of the investigator. Physical evidence or the circumstances of the crime may suggest something about the habits, occupation, or other characteristics of the criminal; secondary witnesses also may contribute valuable information. Sometimes, however, all of the leads wind up in dead ends.

The psychological makeup of the offender should not be overlooked. Some crimes have been solved only because the investigator was able to understand the kind of person involved: the offender's environmental background, attitudes, values, motivations, and idiosyncrasies. Taken together, these factors constitute a person's *psychological profile.*

Few police officers have the extensive knowledge of psychology required to develop a psychological profile without outside help. Besides, the nature of the task suggests that the more people that participate, the better the results will be. Developing a psychological profile should be a group effort.

There is hardly a community in the United States that is completely lacking in resources for this task. Even in a small rural community the investigator should be able to find a local psychologist or psychiatrist, a psychological social worker, a physician with some background in psychiatry, or a member of the clergy who has taken advanced courses in psychology. It is enormously helpful if such individuals also have some past experience with criminal offenders. Former parole officers or retired parole board members might be added to the group.

A psychological profile can be developed in several ways. The most common proce-

*Developing a psychological profile is a group effort that can provide the investigator with valuable clues to an unknown suspect's identity.*

dure is to bring together all the resource people who are willing to help. The investigator should provide each resource person with a summary of the known facts about the crime; if possible, this should be done a few days in advance, so that they have time to acquaint themselves with the case. When the resource people are brought together, the investigator should present all of the evidence and information that is available. Sometimes apparently minor or trivial details can be significant to the resource advisers, so no detail should be overlooked. After the investigator's presentation, the advisers are free to ask questions, which the investigator answers as completely as possible. Ultimately, the advisers arrive at a consensus opinion about the psychological characteristics of the unknown perpetrator.

A different procedure must be used if it is impossible to bring all the advisers to a single meeting (for example, if consultants from a nearby city are to participate). In that case, the investigator should visit each adviser individually, present a written summary of the case,

and supply additional details orally. Each consultant then should prepare a written opinion of the offender's psychological profile. As soon as all of the written opinions are received, the investigator should make copies and circulate the copies to every adviser. This enables them to prepare a second opinion, responding to or incorporating the insights of the other consultants. If wide areas of disagreement remain, this step could be repeated a second or third time, until a consensus emerges.

A great deal of useful information can be obtained through a psychological profile, including information that does not have a direct bearing on the offender's mental or emotional condition. Although each profile will differ in its details and certain information may already have been obtained from direct evidence, here are some of the elements that might be included in the profile:

• A physical description of the offender. How old is the offender? How big? Is the offender of the same ethnic group as the victim or a different ethnic group? Is the offender unusually strong or weak? Does anything suggest physical deformity or handicap?

- The offender's background. What is the offender's most probable occupation? Does the offender live in the same community or neighborhood as the victim? What can be inferred about the offender's habits or lifestyle?
- The offender's mental capacities. Is the offender above or below average in intelligence? How well educated is the offender?
- The offender's emotional condition. Does the offender appear to suffer from specific symptoms of emotional disease, such as psychosis, or from neurotic compulsions? What can be inferred about the offender's family history, relationships with other people, general level of emotional adjustment or maturity, ability to deal with frustration, and so forth?

Sometimes the psychological advisers or consultants can provide an amazingly detailed description of the offender, so detailed that the investigator would almost recognize the offender on the street. Unfortunately, that is not always true; sometimes the effort to develop a psychological profile fails. Even worse, the profile may turn out to be inaccurate or misleading, and that can hinder the prosecution's efforts to convict the actual perpetrator. The investigator must remember that the profile represents only the opinions of the advisers, and opinions can be very wrong. Nonetheless, even taking into consideration these reservations and limitations, a psychological profile can be useful. In some cases, until a suspect is identified, the profile is the only really useful evidence of any kind.

## REFERENCES

1. William Ker Muir, Jr., *Police: Streetcorner Politicians,* (Chicago: University of Chicago Press, 1977), pp. 66–67.

2. John M. MacDonald, M.D., *Rape: Offenders and Their Victims* (Springfield, Ill.: Charles C Thomas, 1971), pp. 93–96.

3. MacDonald, pp. 96–98.

4. MacDonald, pp. 98–103.

5. Richard D. Knudten, *Crime in a Complex Society* (Homewood, Ill.: Dorsey Press, 1970), p. 55.

6. Knudten, p. 120.

7. U.S. Law Enforcement Assistance Administration [USLEAA], *Crimes and Victims* (Washington, D.C.: U.S. Department of Justice, 1974), p. 12.

8. U.S. Federal Bureau of Investigation [FBI], *Crime in the United States: Uniform Crime Reports,* annual (Washington, D.C.: U.S. Department of Justice, 1976), p. 161.

9. MacDonald, pp. 103–108.

10. USLEAA, p. 5.

11. Norval Morris and Gordon Hawkins, *The Honest Politician's Guide to Crime Control* (Chicago: University of Chicago Press, 1970), p. 40.

12. USLEAA, p. 5.

13. FBI, p. 10.

14. Edwin H. Sutherland and Donald R. Cressey, *Criminology,* 9th ed. (Philadelphia: J. B. Lippincott, 1974), p. 22.

15. FBI, pp. 10–11.

16. USLEAA, pp. 19–21.

17. FBI, p. 10.

18. Knudten, p. 147.

19. Knudten, p. 149.

20. M. Philip Feldman, *Criminal Behavior: A Psychological Analysis* (London and New York: John Wiley, 1977), p. 70.

21. Feldman, pp. 83–84.

22. Knudten, p. 17.

23. Knudten, p. 69.

24. Feldman, pp. 170–171, defines, and uses rather extensively, the term *psychopath,* contrary to the current practice in the United States.

25. MacDonald, p. 83.

## REVIEW OF THE EVIDENCE

1. Which of the following kinds of behavior might result from a victim's feelings of vulnerability or helplessness?
    a. blaming the police for failing to prevent the crime
    b. shutting out the rest of the world and avoiding any contact with other people
    c. vowing to take revenge against the criminal
    d. denying that the crime has occurred
    e. all of the above

2. True or false: The victims of crime often feel guilty and blame themselves because, as children, they were taught to do so.

3. An investigator says, "Look here, that kind of talk isn't going to do you any good. Why don't you just calm down and give me the information I need, so we can catch the person who did this to you?" This might be an appropriate response to which of the following statements by a victim?
    a. "This must be somebody's idea of a sick joke!"
    b. "It's all my own fault! If I had just gotten better locks put on all the doors, it never would have happened!"
    c. "I know where I can get a gun. I'll find the guy who did this, and I'll fix him so he'll never do it again!"
    d. "I pay good money for taxes to pay for the police department. If you people were doing your job, this wouldn't have happened to me!"
    e. None of these statements deserves that reply.

4. True or false: Helping the police to catch the rapist usually is the highest priority of a rape crisis center.

5. During a rape investigation, which of the following should *not* be done?
    a. The police should contact the rape crisis center and ask a volunteer to assist them.
    b. The victim should be given a chance to change clothes and clean up before being taken to the hospital for a medical examination.
    c. The medical examination should be conducted in the emergency room of a public hospital rather than in a private physician's office.
    d. Photographs should be taken of all wounds or injuries.
    e. The search for physical evidence should be as thorough as that made for any other crime.

6. Which of the following statements are true of the typical murder?
    a. The victim and the murderer are relatives, close friends, or acquaintances.
    b. The murder weapon is a handgun.
    c. The victim or murderer or both has a long history of minor scrapes with the police.
    d. The victim and the murderer have had a healthy, productive relationship until the time of the murder.
    e. The victim and the murderer come from very different socioeconomic backgrounds.

7. True or false: Secondary victims of a murder are likely to have emotional reactions that are completely different from the response of the primary victims of other crimes.

8. Which of the following statements would apply to a planned murder (P), a maniacal murder (M), a sadistic murder (S), or a terroristic murder (T)?
   a. The murderer strikes at random in an irrational and unpredictable manner.
   b. Hired murderers, working for organized crime, are sometimes responsible.
   c. Sometimes the circumstances of the crime and the manner of death are very difficult to determine.
   d. Such murders result from a conspiracy or a group activity.
   e. A sexual relationship between the murderer and the victims is not unusual.
   f. Some kind of relationship exists between the victim and the murderer, but often they do not know each other personally.
   g. Discovering the motive may be the key to the identification of the perpetrator.
   h. The murders occur in a series, and the victims are all very much alike.
   i. The crime associated with the murder often appears to be merely a pretext for the violent assault.

9. "They are incapable of sustaining a normal, satisfying relationship with other people. They are characterized by impulsive, often extremely reckless behavior. They may be fiercely aggressive with no clear provocation." These descriptions apply to
   a. compulsive sexual offenders.
   b. persons who are legally insane.
   c. sociopaths.
   d. typical murderers.
   e. all of the above.

10. A psychological profile is used
   a. to prove that the accused criminal is guilty.
   b. to learn something about an unknown suspect.
   c. to establish the sanity of a defendant.
   d. to discover the motive for a murder or assault.
   e. to treat the victim of violent crime.

### TOPICS FOR INVESTIGATION

1. The text describes the evolution of a criminal as a process by which young people, especially those who live in a ghetto or other circumstances of poverty and deprivation, gradually become involved in crime. What could be done by a law enforcement agency to prevent this evolutionary process? Is this the responsibility of the police or of some other agency of government?

2. Is it fair to expect a police officer to give psychological first aid to the victim of a crime? Should officers receive special training in psychology so that they will be better equipped for this role? How should a police officer deal with a victim who does not respond to such first aid and who does not seem to progress normally through the four stages of emotional response?

3. Suppose you were a member of the state legislature and you were assigned to a committee that is drafting a new rape statute. How should the crime of rape be defined? What penalties do you feel would be appropriate for rape? Should there be different

*Dealing with the People*

degrees of seriousness with different penalties? What could be done to protect the rights of both the victim and the accused offender, but at the same time to reduce the victim's ordeal?

4. Is it reasonable to say that such socioeconomic factors as poverty, poor housing, poor education, and so on *cause* violent crimes? Would the elimination of these factors result in the elimination of violent crime? What are some of the implications of the statement that "some ghetto youths discover their only real success in a life of crime." Is this true? If so, what could be done about it, and by whom?

5. How should society deal with compulsive offenders, sociopaths, and habitual criminals? Should the definition of insanity be broader or narrower than it is now? To what extent should our legal system make allowance for offenders whose intellectual, emotional, or moral capacities are diminished or impaired? What do you think of the requirement that criminals who are insane must be treated for their insanity?

## CHAPTER 8

# DEALING
# WITH THE
# NEWS MEDIA

STUDY CLUES

1. Deadlines are most important to which of the following journalists?
   a. television reporters
   b. radio reporters
   c. metropolitan daily newspaper reporters
   d. rural weekly newspaper reporters
   e. all of the above

2. At a large, metropolitan daily newspaper, which of the following personnel is most likely to decide how much coverage ought to be given to a particular story?
   a. the publisher
   b. the reporter
   c. the city editor
   d. the managing editor
   e. the editor in chief

3. What kind of news organization often sends two reporters to cover every story?
   a. large metropolitan newspapers
   b. smaller television stations
   c. larger television stations
   d. radio stations
   e. small-town newspapers

4. Which of the following is true about an *unattributed statement*?
   a. The reporter does not know who said it.
   b. The reporter does not know whether it is true.
   c. The information must not be published.
   d. The person who made the statement does not wish to be identified.
   e. The reporter refuses to disclose the source of the information.

5. True or false: Reporters, photographers, and camera operators should never be allowed to interview the victims and witnesses of a serious crime.

THE RELATIONSHIP BETWEEN law enforcement agencies and the news media has a long and sometimes disagreeable history. Ideally, police officers and local journalists ought to have a productive, cooperative relationship, for the fact is that they depend on each other. In practice, however, the relationship between the two groups is often marked by suspicion, deliberate mutual interference, and outright hostility.

Our interest in this chapter is not to promote better public relations between the police and the news media. That is the duty of a law enforcement agency's public information officer, community relations section, or top officials, but it is not a primary concern of the investigator. Rather, we are interested in exploring ways that the investigator can make good use of the news media not only to inform the community, but also to obtain information. Countless crimes have been solved and criminals apprehended only because a member of the public provided information to the police in response to a newspaper article or television news account.

Before we discuss the specific relationship that should exist between the police and the news media, some background information is needed. Police officers will be more successful in dealing with the news media if they have some understanding of how journalists operate.

## ORGANIZATION AND FUNCTIONS OF THE NEWS MEDIA

In the United States, news organizations are primarily local in their operation and orientation. This is not always true in other countries, many of which have a limited number of news media (primarily newspapers and television stations) that serve the whole country and that are sometimes controlled directly by the national government. Because the U.S. news media have a local orientation, and because the news media are vigorously competitive even in small communities, news about significant crime is given prominent attention.

There are many similarities between the organizational structures of broadcast news agencies (radio and television stations) and of newspapers. The reason for this is mostly historical: when broadcasting first developed, newspaper journalists were hired to staff the budding news departments, and they carried along their old habits and concepts. Only in recent years has broadcast journalism begun to develop along its own lines, but the similarities still outweigh the differences.

### NEWSPAPERS

All newspapers are organized along essentially the same lines, from the largest metropolitan dailies to the smallest country weeklies. The differences result from the smaller staffs of the smaller organizations: several functions must be combined and carried out by each person. In fact, many rural weekly newspapers are written, edited, and published by a staff of only two or three people.

A newspaper's organizational structure is divided into two major parts: the editorial department and the administration, which includes advertising, production (the printing of the paper), circulation, and all of the usual operations that any business requires: bookkeeping, promotion, purchasing, and so on. On any well-organized newspaper, the editorial department is completely independent of the other business functions.

The chief executive of a newspaper is the publisher. On many newspapers, this individual plays an important role in setting ed-

itorial policy, especially when the publisher owns the newspaper or a major share of it. However, when the newspaper is part of a chain owned by a distant corporation or when the newspaper's stock is owned by the general public, the publisher may be concerned solely with the business aspects of the paper and may have little or nothing to say about editorial matters.

The editorial department usually is headed by an editor in chief (sometimes simply called the editor). The functions of this person also vary somewhat. On some large newspapers, the editor in chief is basically a manager who sets general policies and exercises indirect control over the editorial operation. On other newspapers, especially smaller ones, the editor is deeply involved in day-to-day or even minute-to-minute decisions about which sto-

ries to cover and how much prominence to give each story.

On a large newspaper with a number of sections within the editorial department (national news, local news, sports, features, and so on), the managing editor coordinates the various departments and assigns each of them space within each edition.

The local news department, often called the metro or city department, is under the direction of the city editor. This person makes most of the initial decisions about which stories to cover and how much coverage to give them. The city editor gives reporters their assignments and guides them in the development of their stories.

Finally, at the bottom of the organization chart are the reporters themselves. A reporter's job is to gather information, organize it, and write a story that is comprehensible, thorough, accurate, and interesting. On some newspapers the reporters are also responsible for obtaining photographs, al-

ANSWERS TO STUDY CLUES
1. a and d   2. c   3. b   4. d   5. False

*The office of a small-town weekly newspaper. The editor-publisher (at left, with back to camera) helps paste up the page layouts while, in the background, one reporter retypes copy and the editor-publisher's daughter types up the advertisers' bills. (Photo courtesy the Elgin Courier, Elgin, Texas)*

though most major newspapers have a separate staff of photographers who work under the editors' and reporters' direction.

A newspaper story can originate from any of several sources. All newspapers receive a constant flow of *news releases*—stories and announcements written by official agencies, community organizations, and commercial enterprises about their activities and forthcoming events. Some newspapers publish news releases just as they are received if the release is deemed newsworthy and reasonably well written. More often a reporter is assigned to develop a story based on the information contained in the news release.

Other stories are generated by tips or suggestions from the general public, by regular sources of information or "informants" who have an established relationship with a reporter (not unlike police informants), or perhaps by people who feel that they have a particular grievance or problem. Some newspapers rely heavily on *stringers,* people who are paid a small fee to submit occasional reports or suggestions for stories.

Almost all newspapers provide extensive coverage of police activities and crime news. Most city editors or their subordinates have a radio receiver to monitor police, fire department, and ambulance service broadcasts. Thus, when a major event occurs, the editor hears about it at the same time that the patrol officer does. In some larger cities, the public safety agencies have set up a special radio service with transmitters in each agency's public information office and with receivers at each news organization, so that the news media can be alerted whenever there is a major event.

However a story originates, the person responsible for writing it in publishable form is the reporter. Some newspapers assign one or two reporters exclusively to the coverage of police news (the so-called police beat), although this is a less common practice today than it used to be.

Crime investigators and reporters are simultaneously natural allies and natural adversaries. For both of them, success in carrying out their duties depends on getting and using accurate information. Both operate under certain tensions and pressures, including the conflicting demands to work against time and yet to be thorough.

Actually, the pressure of time can be more severe for newspaper reporters than police investigators. The police ordinarily are not faced with inflexible deadlines. Although investigators want to apprehend a criminal as quickly as possible, it is far more important to gain the extra bit of information that will assure a conviction. For reporters, however, the deadline may be a constant problem. Axioms of journalism claim that the best story is worthless ten minutes after deadline and that there is nothing as stale as yesterday's news. Under these circumstances, reporters often have little choice but to get a story written before the deadline, even if they are not fully satisfied with the quantity or the accuracy of the information.

The story deadlines for each edition of a newspaper are set by the managing editor. Usually there are several deadlines for each edition, earlier times being set for feature materials and stories taken from the national or international wire services. The deadline for major local news usually represents the latest possible time that still allows for the story to be edited and prepared for publication.

The most inflexible deadlines are those maintained by newspapers that publish relatively few editions. For example, a weekly newspaper published every Friday morning may have its deadline on Tuesday afternoon. Anything that happens on Wednesday or Thursday is likely to be overlooked because it is too late for this week's paper and too early

for next week's. Similar problems are faced by reporters on daily newspapers that publish only one or two editions every day; missing a deadline may mean that a story will have gone stale by the time the next edition is published. However, in the larger cities a newspaper may publish as many as six or eight editions at various times throughout the day, and deadlines assume somewhat less importance.

Competition between the news media also contributes to the urgency of the reporter's work. The pressure to get a "scoop," to be the first news agency to cover a major story, is not as intense as it once was. Today few reputable, competent journalists will jeopardize accuracy in order to beat out their rivals. However, that element of competition does still exist and occasionally influences a reporter's behavior.

### THE BROADCAST MEDIA

Most of the same needs and conditions apply to broadcast journalists as to newspaper reporters. However, broadcast reporters have the additional burden of getting not only the facts of each story, but also the sounds and, for television broadcasting, the visual information.

Radio journalism is all but a dying craft in most communities. Even in the larger cities, many radio stations devote very little of their resources and efforts to local news coverage. They are content to spend three or four minutes of every hour reading brief news accounts taken directly from the wire services or from the news departments of affiliated television stations. However, some radio stations still maintain active news departments. Many larger cities have one or more radio stations that are devoted exclusively to news broadcasting and have large and well-organized news-gathering staffs.

A radio station's news operation usually is headed by a news director, who may have several other duties as well in a small station. Usually the reporters work directly under the news director's supervision. The news announcers, who actually read the news broadcasts, may or may not also serve as reporters.

The chief distinguishing feature of radio journalists is their tape recorders. Radio news personnel are under great pressure to get some kind of sound for every major story. Because reporters almost always arrive at the scene of a crime or any other story long after the event itself, they depend almost entirely on interviews with people involved in the event. This has a major influence on the way in which they operate and behave.

Most television stations devote a much larger portion of their resources and energies to news than do radio stations. Even comparatively small television stations almost always have a staff of reporters to cover local news events. A larger station may have as many people on its news staff as the local newspaper has in its editorial department.

The manager of a television news department may be called the news director or the news producer. In a very large department there may be an executive producer directing the whole operation and individual producers for each news program. Other managerial personnel may include one or more associate producers, assignment editors, and editors in charge of special areas, such as wire services, network features, and business news. Sports and weather coverage usually operate independently of the news staff.

Almost all television stations have a minimum of two half-hour news programs each day, usually between 5 and 7 P.M. and again at 10 or 11 P.M. (depending on which time zone the station is in). In addition, many stations have one or more 5- to 15-minute news

*A broadcast news car. The microwave antenna, when connected to a transmitter in the station wagon, can transmit "live" or videotape-recorded pictures and sound to the studio several miles away. (Photo courtesy KTVV Television, Austin, Texas)*

programs early in the morning and at noon. Each of these regular news programs usually includes a combination of local news, national and international news, feature stories, sports, and weather reports. Some stations also have special reports on business news or other areas of interest. Some stations have news-magazine or discussion programs that deal with specific topics in greater depth than is possible in regular news broadcasts.

Again, like newspapers, television and radio news organizations obtain stories and story ideas from many sources, not the least of which is a radio monitor for public safety broadcasts. In some communities, television reporters race to the scene of every major crime or traffic accident; occasionally they manage to reach the scene before the police do. This is an extremely dangerous practice, which the police must discourage strongly.

Newspaper and radio reporters are often resentful of television journalists, because the latter dominate the scene of a news event. Partly this is due to the highly competitive attitude of television news organizations, and partly it is an unavoidable effect of television news-gathering processes.

The main characteristic of television journalism is that it requires a reporter–camera operator team. At least two people are assigned to cover every story. At smaller stations each news team usually consists of two reporters; they exchange roles from one story to the next, acting alternately as the on-camera reporter and as the camera equipment operator. Larger stations usually have a camera crew, generally consisting of a camera operator and a sound equipment operator, accompanying each reporter. The largest stations and the major networks use a crew of four or five people under the direction of a producer who functions as the primary journalist; the reporter is merely an on-camera performer who relates the story that has been developed and organized by the producer.

Some television stations rely heavily on 16-millimeter motion picture cameras for news gathering. This camera is small, convenient to operate, and relatively inconspicuous, yet it produces excellent pictures when it is operated skillfully. Sound may be recorded on a separate machine synchronized to the camera, or it may be recorded magnetically inside the camera.

Most stations now have at least one video tape unit for news coverage. This is often called *electronic news gathering,* or ENG. The primary advantage of ENG is speed: because the video tape does not need to be processed and because editing can be accomplished quickly and easily by electronic means, a report can be put together in a matter of a few minutes. Video tape is also less expensive

At left, a television reporter with 16 mm film equipment; at right, a reporter with videotape equipment. Both types of equipment can record sound along with pictures. Film equipment has become less common because of the advantages of new, more compact videotape cameras and recorders.

than film. The major disadvantage of ENG is that the portable video tape equipment, though it is substantially more compact than earlier models, is still bulky and awkward to handle. A news team using ENG is more obtrusive than a film crew at a news event and may have a hard time working in confined quarters.

Television news reports have developed over the years into a very specific pattern that meets the particular needs of the standard television news program. Though it is flexi-

*Dealing with the People*

ble enough to vary in some important details, this pattern has an unvarying basic structure. Coverage of any news event almost always includes some silent film or video tape showing the general locale and, if the event is still going on when the news team arrives, the activities at the scene. The reporter's narration is recorded separately after the silent footage has been edited; this is called a *voice-over.* If there is dramatic activity at the news scene, such as a fire or a crime in progress, live sound may be recorded along with the silent footage.

The reporter also tries to obtain an interview with someone directly involved in the news event, such as the police investigator, a victim, or an eyewitness. If this is not possible, the reporter may interview a secondary witness, a police spokesperson, or anyone else who appears to have some information about the event. Usually the purpose of the interview is not to obtain information, but merely to put the information in someone else's mouth.

Finally, the reporter usually does a *stand-up*—a summary of the story or a comment on its significance, delivered directly to the camera. The stand-up may introduce the report or come at its conclusion, once all the film or video tape has been edited into final form. The reporter who covers a story also usually writes the *lead-in,* the brief introduction read by the news announcer in the studio during the news program.

The television reporter's job is much more complicated than that of the newspaper or radio reporter and is additionally burdened by the need to accommodate the film or video tape equipment. A newspaper reporter needs nothing more than a pad of paper and a pencil, and a radio reporter's tape recorder is relatively unobtrusive. It is no wonder that newspaper and radio journalists complain that they are elbowed out of the way by the pushy television people.

Television reporters are also much more deadline-conscious than most radio reporters or newspaper journalists. A television news story usually has only two chances to appear: on the dinner-hour news and on the late-evening news. Many smaller stations operate under a single deadline; if a story is not ready for the dinner-hour news, it will not be shown on a late-evening program, either. Before a story can be used, the film must be processed and edited or the video tape must be checked and then edited; the voice-over and lead-in must be written; the whole story must be timed to the very second; and whoever is in charge of the news program, either the news director or the producer, must schedule the story into the limited time that is available. It is a curious paradox that television gives the greatest sense of immediacy and timeliness to the news, yet in fact the deadlines for television news stories are sometimes an hour or two earlier than the deadlines for the equivalent edition of a newspaper.

## JOURNALISTS' ETHICS AND POLICE RESPONSIBILITIES

In recent years, many criticisms have been directed toward journalists. Reporters have been accused of being ideologically biased, unfair, inaccurate, incompetent, and generally irresponsible. Some criticism is justified and some may have been intended maliciously, but a large part of it stems from a lack of understanding of the nature and purposes of journalism in the United States.

The history of our free press goes back well before the American Revolution and today incorporates the nonprint, electronic media as well as newspapers and magazines. An elaborate body of ethical traditions, which have grown up during that long history, have great power over modern journalists. Journalists' ethics are self-imposed, and it would be pointless to deny that ethical restraints are sometimes overlooked by irresponsible or overzealous reporters, but by and large the principles are maintained by self-regulating mechanisms.

## THE ADVERSARY RELATIONSHIP

From the perspective of the crime investigator, the most important principle of journalists' ethics is the paramount status of the *adversary relationship.*

Journalism in the United States has its very roots in the need to rally public indignation against official corruption and injustice. Colonial newspapers played a vital role in support of the American Revolution by ensuring that the improprieties of the British government were vividly publicized. It is no accident that freedom of the press is one of the guarantees set out in the very first sentence of the Bill of Rights. Today, journalists interpret this special status to mean that they have a special mission to discover and expose any improper activities of the government. The adversary relationship applies equally to the local police department and to the national Congress or the President.

Critics of the news media, including police officials, often complain that reporters should support their government. Actually, reporters often go to great lengths to establish and maintain a friendly relationship with the police and other governmental agencies, since it is only through such relationships that the reporter can obtain needed information. Reporters can be placed in an extremely uncomfortable dilemma when friends in "high places" might be guilty of improprieties. Some reporters have no qualms about betraying such friendships, feeling that their ethical obligation to their readers or viewers—that is, to the general public—invariably transcends their responsibility to their friends. In fact, in such circumstances reporters may feel personally betrayed and unfairly manipulated by their former friends.

On balance, the interests of both the police and the community are best served if some distance is maintained between the law enforcement agency and the news media. The relationship should be cooperative, because cooperation works to everyone's advantage. However, the police are mistaken if they expect uncritical support or, even worse, favored treatment from reporters.

## THE RIGHT TO KNOW

A necessary consequence of the adversary relationship and of the freedom of the press guaranteed by the Constitution is the journalists' belief in the public's *right to know.*

Briefly stated, the *right to know* means the public's right to complete, prompt, and accurate information disclosing any and all activities, policies, or decisions of any public body. Journalists consider themselves to be the primary conduit through which the right to know is expressed. There is nothing in the Constitution that specifically addresses this issue, but the courts, legislatures, and executive branches of both national and state governments historically have upheld this principle. The federal government and many states now have "sunshine laws" or "freedom-of-information laws," which explicitly define the kinds of information to which journalists and the public must have unrestricted access.

There are some limits to the freedom-of-information laws. Generally, information that is potentially damaging to national security or to the maintenance of public order, information that is potentially embarrassing to an innocent private citizen, or information that has great economic significance to a private business does not have to be disclosed. Sometimes the right to know and the right of privacy conflict; the courts have vacillated in their decisions about which right is more important.

As a rule, law enforcement agencies are required to provide journalists with almost any information that a reporter requests except the identity of suspected offenders who are not actually in custody and the specific nature of the evidence against them. Police departments in most states also are not required to open their investigative files, their records of prior convictions and suspected criminal activity, or any other files that might contain misleading information that would embarrass innocent citizens or otherwise trample on the right of privacy. There are, however, circumstances under which reporters might obtain a court order giving them access to such sensitive information—for example, if a reporter suspected that damaging evidence of police abuses might be buried in the files. Although information about investigations that are currently in progress may be exempt from reporters' inquiries, almost all other information about police operations may be treated as public knowledge.

### PROTECTION OF SOURCES

Police officers can be frustrated to the point of agony when reporters, the champions of the public's right to know, turn around and refuse to give the police information that could help lead to the apprehension of a criminal. Yet protecting one's sources is another essential principle of journalistic ethics. A number of reporters have voluntarily served time in jail rather than reveal the sources of their information, even though they were ordered to do so by the courts.

Reporters reason that the right to know applies to public agencies such as the police, but not necessarily to private individuals and organizations, including themselves. Furthermore, they argue that the exposure of an informant might serve the short-term interests of justice, but in the long run would discourage other informants from giving information to journalists for fear of similar exposure. Therefore, they hold, the overriding interests of the public are best served if journalists are given the same privileges of confidentiality as members of the clergy or attorneys.

Some state legislatures have accepted this argument and have passed laws protecting the "privileged communications" of journalists. But other states have laws that expressly deny that such a privilege exists. There is no federal law on the subject at all, although several proposals have been introduced in Congress, and eventually such a law might exist. Court decisions at both state and federal levels have varied.

Until this principle is either ratified by a consistent body of law or discarded altogether, the police can expect to have little cooperation or success in gaining access to a reporter's sources of information. Reporters are not easy to intimidate, and many have shown themselves willing to suffer the indignities of jail rather than sacrifice their principles.

### UNATTRIBUTED AND BACKGROUND INFORMATION

Because of the principle of the public's right to know, a reporter feels justified in doing anything necessary in order to obtain information. In fact, the more effort that a public official or agency expends to keep information secret, the harder a reporter is likely to work to get the information and make it public. Nothing arouses a reporter's curiosity faster than the simple statement, "I'm not going to tell you."

Yet reporters feel an absolute moral obligation to respect the wishes of any source who says, "I'll tell you what you want to know, but you mustn't publish the fact that I told you," or "This information is for your use as background, but you mustn't publish any of it at this time."

There is a rational explanation for these strictures. A reporter maintains credibility by presenting not only the facts of a story, but some evidence indicating that the facts are accurately presented. The best way to do this is to attribute each major statement to a specific source. This is especially necessary when a statement represents opinion or conjecture rather than an observed fact.

For example, most editors would not allow a reporter to say, "Jones probably knew the assailant, who evidently murdered her in the course of robbing her wall safe." Instead, the reporter would say, "The police believe that Jones may have known the assailant. According to Lieutenant Smith of the Homicide Squad, Jones's wall safe was found empty, which suggests to the police that robbery was the motive for the slaying."

Suppose, however, that Lieutenant Smith does not wish to be quoted by name in the newspaper as the source for this information. If Smith tells the reporter, "Please don't attribute this to me," the reporter might say, "According to a spokesman for the Police Department, Jones's wall safe . . ." This is known, in the terminology of journalism, as an *unattributed statement*.

Going further, the police might prefer to say nothing in public about the possible motive for the slaying. In that case, Lieutenant Smith should not say, "We have no ideas about the motive," because eventually this will be shown up as a falsehood. Instead, Smith might say, "We don't want this to be published, because we may need this information to find the suspect. But we believe that the motive for the slaying was robbery." Now the reporters will feel a moral compulsion to refrain from publishing this *background information*.

There is one qualification to this principle: If the reporter feels that the information should be published in spite of the request to keep it secret, he or she may go to great lengths to find an independent source. For example, the reporter might ask the victim's family if they have any opinions about the motive. If someone else says, "Well, we all think the murderer robbed poor Jones's wall safe," the reporter may feel free to publish this statement and attribute it to the independent source.

QUESTIONS OF
TASTE, ACCURACY, AND
FAIRNESS

Aside from the general principles that we have outlined already, many other considerations influence how journalists work and what kinds of stories they publish or broadcast.

One must remember that journalism is an intensely competitive business in many communities. Not only do newspapers compete with other newspapers and television stations with other television stations, but the various media compete against each other as well. The ground rules for this competition are established by unspoken agreement among the different media in each community, and these

*Dealing with the People*

unwritten rules largely determine the quality of news coverage that a community receives.

In some communities the media compete for speed—to see who can get the stories first. In other communities the basis for competition may be accuracy and thoroughness, or "quality" journalism. Sensationalism is the basis for competition in a few communities: a constant diet of gory, spectacular, and scandalous stories. Some of the other bases for competition include a record of community service (which can lead to an uncritical attitude of constant praise for local government), imaginative investigation to discover hidden corruption, an emphasis on "good news" and positive stories, or a desire to make the news dramatic and entertaining (which can lead to the elimination of important but less exciting stories). There are also communities in which the news media compete along ideological lines, each one adopting a particular political philosophy or cause, or writing for one segment of the community.

All these forms of competition can lead to excess. When that happens, journalists lose their sense of perspective. Reasonable standards of taste, accuracy, and fairness are sacrificed in favor of scoring points against the competition. The police are very likely to get caught in the crossfire unless they recognize the problem and develop ways to protect themselves.

## THE RESPONSIBILITIES OF THE INVESTIGATOR

A crime investigator's first obligation is to solve the crime and apprehend the criminal. Beyond that, the investigator has an obligation to protect the victim from further harm and an obligation to assist the courts in the pursuit of justice.

The investigator's duty to cooperate with the news media obviously falls rather low on the list of priorities. However, cooperation can work two ways. By helping the journalists to get the information that they need, the investigator may encourage the journalists to share information that they have with the police. It is not unusual for reporters to have access to informants who would never willingly help the police. Sometimes frightened witnesses or an accomplice with a guilty conscience will give evidence to a reporter that otherwise would never come to light. Finally, it is sometimes true that a reporter, by virtue of superior ingenuity or simple luck, will discover information that has eluded the police investigator.

Ideally, a reporter should pass along all such information to the police before publishing it. The police might already have the information and also have a good reason for keeping it secret. Premature publicity has wrecked more than one criminal investigation.

The police cannot ignore the principle of the public's right to know. In practical terms, this means that the police should supply as much information as the journalists ask for. However, the investigator should assume responsibility for determining how much of this information is made public.

There is no perfect way to keep information secret from journalists. The use of unattributed statements may help, because journalists prefer not to rely on such statements if they can avoid it. Often the best way to keep information from being published is to give the information freely—but specify that it is meant for background only. If a reasonable explanation of the need for secrecy is given, the reporters are likely to feel obligated to maintain the confidence. Care must be exercised to ensure that reporters do not get confidential information from victims, witnesses, and other sources. This can be a difficult problem if a number of reporters have invaded the crime scene or if reporters show up at the crime scene after the police have left. Victims and witnesses should be cautioned not to discuss the details of a crime with anyone other than an attorney or police officer.

The investigator has an absolute responsibility to protect the scene of a crime from invasion by reporters or anyone else. No journalist or camera crew should be permitted to enter a crime scene until all physical evidence has been removed and all victims and witnesses have been interviewed by the investigator. After that, the reporters should be given free access to the scene, but only limited access, in the presence of the investigator, to the victims or witnesses. Sometimes these rules must be enforced vigorously to protect the scene from overzealous reporters.

Physical evidence should not be discussed with reporters, especially after it has been removed from the crime scene for examination. Details about a crime that remain hidden from public knowledge are often significant during the interrogation of potential suspects.

Victims and witnesses also must be protected. Reporters intent on getting a story are occasionally callous and exploitative in their treatment of victims. Both victims and witnesses may be emotionally overwrought and fearful of public notice, especially if they are going through the self-blaming stage of their emotional response to the crime. The investigator should be watchful for indications of insensitivity on the part of reporters and should step in if the victim or a witness is being abused.

Victims of violent crime should never be photographed or filmed for the benefit of reporters. This applies equally to murder victims and survivors of violent assault. The use of gory or sensationalistic photographs and film by the news media goes far beyond any right to know and constitutes an invasion of privacy.

Suspects, too, deserve some consideration when they are apprehended. A suspected or convicted criminal should not be completely stripped of human dignity and forced to parade like a zoo animal. Reporters should be given a reasonable opportunity to obtain a limited number of photographs and a few minutes of film or video tape footage. If the suspect is willing, a brief news conference might be arranged either on a preplanned basis or under more spontaneous circumstances. The news media must not be allowed to hound a suspect; harassment or embarrassing questions should be prohibited. Aside from simple human decency, the investigator also should consider that some criminal cases have been thrown out of court on the grounds that prejudicial publicity has precluded a fair trial.

Some of these problems may be avoided if the reporters feel that they have ample access to the investigator for whatever information they need. Much depends on the investigator's reputation for fairness, understanding of the journalists' needs, and willingness to be as cooperative as possible. An investigator who refuses to talk to reporters at all or who attempts to manipulate them by giving evasive, misleading, or unresponsive answers to their questions merely encourages the abuses that we have discussed.

## POSITIVE USES OF THE NEWS MEDIA

The basic mechanism for conveying information to the news media is the interview. Just as the investigator interviews witnesses to obtain information about a crime, reporters interview the investigator for the same

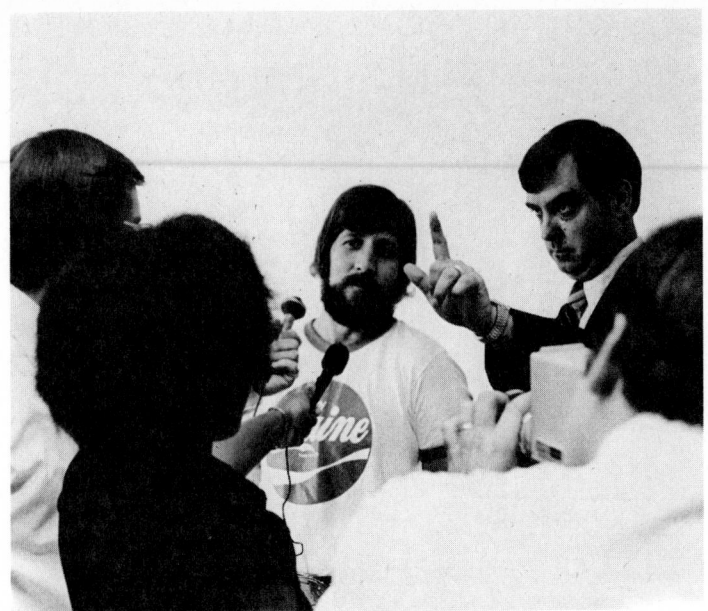

purpose. There are, however, some striking differences in technique and procedure.

Reporters covering an immediate news story ordinarily do not have the luxury of individual interviews with the principal witnesses. Instead, all the reporters attempt to interview the same person or small group of people simultaneously. For the person being interviewed, the result can be a bewildering flood of questions shouted from a dozen different sources at once. Camera lenses and microphones may be stuck into the interviewee's face by a jostling, shifting mob of reporters while flashguns pop and blinding lights flash on and off erratically.

The only way to reduce the chaos is to take charge of the interview. Sometimes, for unusually major crimes, it is a good idea to call for help: specifically, a public information officer or community relations specialist who can deal with the reporters until the investigator has time to give them proper attention.

Usually, however, the investigator must handle the situation alone.

We shall assume that the police have managed to keep all reporters out of the crime scene and away from the witnesses while the initial investigation is conducted. Physical evidence has been removed, witnesses have been interviewed, and nothing more remains to be done at the crime scene. Waiting outside, not at all patiently, are reporters from the local newspapers, television stations, and radio stations. When the investigator steps outside to meet with the reporters, several microphones will be thrust forward. The small black ones attached to tape recorders belong to the radio reporters; they have a natural need to get their microphones as close to the interviewee's lips as possible, because that helps to assure better sound quality and eliminate background noises. The bigger microphones attached to thicker cables belong to the television reporters; usually each micro-

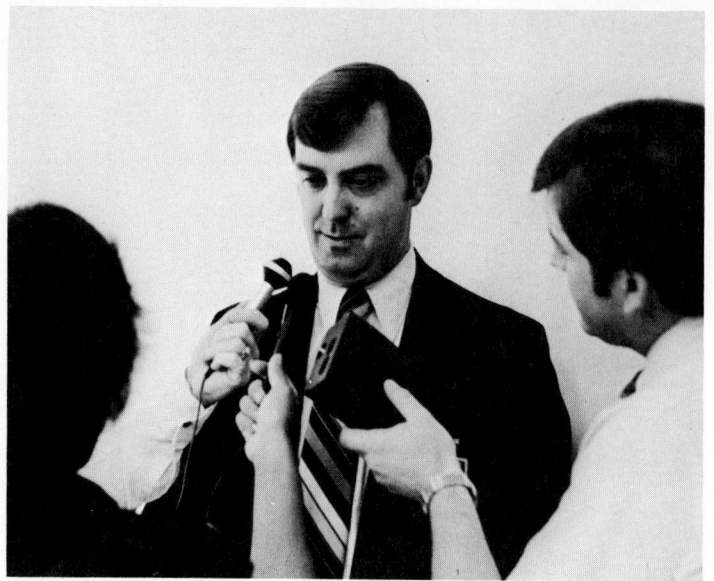

*Being interviewed by a group of reporters can be a bewildering, annoying experience. The investigator must take charge of the interview, accommodating the reporters by providing information they need, without compromising or interfering with the investigation.*

phone is labeled with the channel number of the station. The television people are not especially concerned about sound quality; they push their microphones forward to be sure that the channel number appears in the picture.

If you try to shrink back, away from the microphones, or push them away, you will find that they are shoved at you with renewed energy. The reporters are not trying to stick you in the eye or knock out your teeth; they are just doing their job. The best response is to stand still. This also helps the camera operators.

You may be bombarded with questions as soon as you step out in front of the reporters and they turn on their equipment. If you try to respond to all the questions, you will have lost control already. Instead, be quiet for a minute until the first wave of questions has passed. Then identify yourself, clearly and slowly: name, rank, and agency. Give a brief, coherent account of the crime, trying to keep

it to not more than three or four sentences. Then, without pausing, give a somewhat more detailed account, including any details that you are willing to have published or broadcast.

The first summary of the crime is mostly for the benefit of the radio reporters, who may use it in its entirety, and for the benefit of anyone who arrived late and does not yet know approximately what has happened. The second, more detailed account is for the newspapers and, mostly as confirmation, for the television people.

Once you stop, the questions will start again. If everyone is shouting at once, do not get rattled; listen patiently until you hear all of a question, then answer it. Try to pick out the person who asked the question and turn in that direction as you answer, especially if it is a television or radio reporter.

If you want your answer to be an unattributed statement or "background only," say so, clearly and unmistakably, *before* you

*Dealing with the People*

answer. Answer each question as directly and as succinctly as possible, and speak at a fairly rapid rate; slow, thoughtful speech sounds both boring and downright stupid on radio and television broadcasts.

Do not be surprised if you are asked the same questions over and over again with slight variations. This is because each television and radio reporter wants to record your answer to his or her question, not to some other reporter's question—but, of course, they all want the same information. Within reasonable limits, repeat your answers as often as the questions are repeated.

If the reporters wish to interview the victim or a witness and if you are willing to permit it, you should introduce the interviewee and try to control the questioning. This helps to reassure the witness and to prevent unnecessary exploitation. You may be able to get away with just a brief statement by the victim or witness recounting the crime from his or her point of view and perhaps one or two questions from the reporters.

After this, reporters may be admitted to the crime scene if it is a public place or if the owner of the property agrees. Radio reporters are not likely to be interested in anything more than a quick glance around the premises. Television crews may be a problem because of their bulky equipment and hot lights; however, they are very concerned about keeping out of one another's way because they do not want to show another station's reporters in their own film or tape. Newspaper photographers may be more of a nuisance, but if all evidence has been removed and if the journalists do not abuse other people's property, no special restrictions should be necessary.

You may be asked to do a separate interview with each television station's reporter within the crime scene. Usually this is a rea-sonable request and should be granted. The interview will rarely last more than about a minute, because that is as much time as is likely to be available in the news program.

After you are done with the radio and television people, you are likely to be approached by the newspaper reporters again, either as a group (rarely more than two or three reporters) or as individuals. Unless there is some pressing business elsewhere, the time should be given to answer all questions. You are likely to find that the newspaper reporters' questions are much more extensive than those of other reporters, because the newspaper can devote more space to the details of the story. Sometimes, however, the newspaper reporter merely wants to confirm such details as the spelling of names, the time of the criminal event, and so on.

## PREPLANNED NEWS CONFERENCES

Occasionally an investigator may desire to convey information to the news media about an ongoing investigation. One way to do this is to hold a news conference. A news conference also may be useful if the local news media indicate a continuing interest in the progress of an investigation. Rather than attempting to deal with each reporter who calls for information or requests an interview, the investigator can bring everyone up to date at one time at a news conference.

If the agency has a public information officer or a community relations section, their help should be solicited. The first step is to notify all the news media that the conference will be held at a predetermined time and place. The best time for a news conference is between 10 A.M. and noon or between 1 and 3 P.M.; reporters may not be available at other hours because of conflicts with their other work or with deadlines.

A written statement should be prepared before the news conference so that copies can be provided to everyone who attends. The statement should contain the essential information that is to be conveyed during the conference; it should be read aloud by the investigator or by an appropriate police official, depending on the agency's policy. Questions then should be handled—preferably by the investigator, who should know the answers—in essentially the same manner as in an interview.

A news conference should be called whenever there is a major development in a case of great public interest, such as the apprehension of a suspect or the discovery of important evidence. By calling a news conference, the investigator ensures that the public receives accurate information rather than rumors and speculation. The conference also ensures that the police will not be accused of giving the information selectively to favored reporters.

Sometimes a news conference can be useful when there is nothing to report. The investigator can make a direct appeal to the public, asking that any previously unknown witnesses come forward. If there is any sort of sketch or composite drawing of a suspect, it can be released to the news media in this manner. Many cases have been broken as a direct result of just such a news conference.

### THE SCHEDULED TELEVISION SERIES

Because news conferences have been so successful in bringing public attention to bear on unsolved crimes, a few agencies have experimented with regular, scheduled television programs devoted specifically to current criminal investigations. One such program has been carried on British television for several years and imitated in a number of other European countries. The idea has not caught on in the United States in spite of our presumed obsession with crime and violence. However, the Albuquerque, New Mexico, police department has conducted such a program during the past two years and has reported spectacular success with it.

The idea behind the program is simple enough: on a regular basis, perhaps once a month or once a week, a police representative discusses two or three unsolved crimes with a television journalist. Usually only cases that have reached an investigative dead end are used on such programs.

The program may be as elaborate in format as the participants wish. Some programs of this sort even include a dramatic re-enactment of the crime by actors. It might be appropriate and desirable to include interviews with the original victims or witnesses. Slides, photographs, and actual physical evidence might be shown.

Police agencies in the United States have had so little experience with regularly scheduled television programs that we cannot give an unqualified recommendation. However, we feel that the idea has some promise and, if carried out with taste and sensitivity, it could be extremely helpful.

### REFERENCES

The material in this chapter is based on the authors' personal experiences and observations. There are a number of good sources of information about public relations in police administration, but, surprisingly, there seems to be nothing at all on dealing with the news media in the course of an investigation.

## REVIEW OF THE EVIDENCE

1. News media in the United States give prominent attention to news about significant crimes partly because of
   a. their local orientation.
   b. their sensationalistic attitudes.
   c. their uncritical attitude toward the police.
   d. the traditional freedom of the press.
   e. none of the above.
2. Stories written by official agencies, community organizations, and commercial enterprises and sent to the news media are called
   a. stringers.
   b. public announcements.
   c. news conferences.
   d. news releases.
   e. informants.
3. The chief distinguishing feature of radio journalists is
   a. their urgent need to meet deadlines.
   b. their tape recorders.
   c. their lack of interest in interviews.
   d. their pushiness at a news scene.
   e. all of the above.
4. Why do television reporters almost always work in teams of two or more people?
   a. because their equipment is too bulky for one person to handle
   b. so that they are sure to get all the information
   c. so that one reporter can appear on camera while the other person operates the equipment
   d. so that they can alternate between operating the camera and reporting
   e. so that they can compete against the other news media by dominating the news scene
5. True or false: Reporters generally are idealogically biased, unfair, inaccurate, incompetent, and irresponsible because their historical traditions require them to be.
6. Journalists believe that they have a special mission to expose corruption and impropriety; this principle is called
   a. privileged communications.
   b. the adversary relationship.
   c. the public's right to know.
   d. freedom of the press.
   e. protection of their sources.

7. "Sunshine laws" in some states provide for
   a. unlimited access by reporters to any and all government records.
   b. the right of reporters to keep their sources of information confidential.
   c. access to most government records, although some restrictions exist to protect the right of privacy.
   d. jail sentences for any reporter who refuses to disclose sources of information.
   e. none of the above.
8. According to the text, a reporter might try to find an independent source for which of the following reasons?
   a. because the police refuse to give any information
   b. because the police have asked that certain information be treated as background only, but the reporter thinks that it should be published
   c. because he or she wishes to find someone who can contradict the information that the police have given
   d. because the police have asked that the information be published only on an unattributed basis
   e. because he or she wants to get information that the police do not have
9. True or false: A crime investigator's first obligation is to inform the public about significant crimes that occur.
10. If an investigator has reached a dead end and the crime is still unsolved, which of the following would be appropriate ways to generate new leads?
    a. hold a news conference
    b. issue a news release
    c. appear on a scheduled television series about crime
    d. all of the above
    e. none of the above

## TOPICS FOR INVESTIGATION

1. What should a police officer do if it seems that a particular reporter consistently disregards police requests that information be treated as background only or be published as unattributed statements?
2. According to the text, "on any well-organized newspaper, the editorial department is completely independent of the other business functions." Why would this be necessary for a well-organized newspaper? If the editorial and the other business departments of a newspaper are not kept separate, what would be some of the probable consequences in the way news is handled? Does the same principle apply to broadcast news organizations?
3. Both the adversary relationship and the concept of the public's right to know are derived from journalistic traditions that began during the Colonial era. How are these two traditions related to one another? Are these traditions still appropriate and necessary today?
4. A few states have enacted laws to define and uphold a reporter's right to protect sources; a few other states have enacted laws that specifically deny any such right. Most states,

however, have no laws on the subject at all. What is the law in your state? What do you think the law should be?

5. Under what specific circumstances should the police ask journalists to treat information on an unattributed or background-only basis? What would be the probable result if this kind of treatment is requested constantly? Should a police agency insist that all contacts between police officers and the news media be approved in advance by senior officials and that all interviews be given only by a designated public information officer or other spokesperson?

# UNIT IV
## THE INVESTIGATOR AND SUPPORT SERVICES

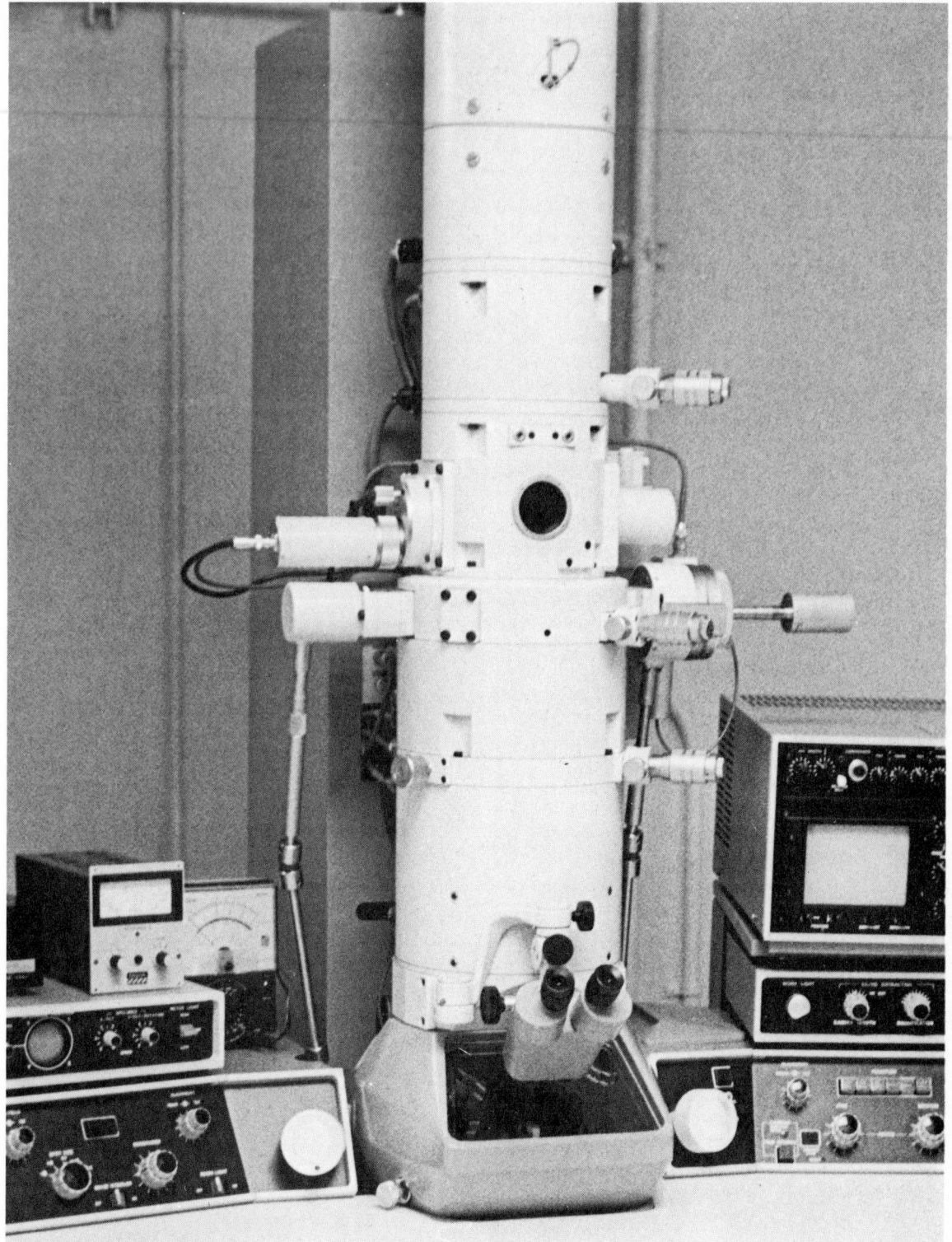

# CHAPTER 9
## COMMUNICATIONS IN INVESTIGATION

1. Most police communications systems have been developed primarily to serve
   a. investigators.
   b. the general public.
   c. administrators.
   d. patrol officers.
   e. none of the above.

2. The most common police radio systems have how many channels?
   a. one
   b. two
   c. three
   d. four
   e. five

3. The essential characteristic of a computer-aided police dispatching system is that
   a. all dispatching is done by the computer.
   b. there is a computer in every patrol vehicle.
   c. all communications must be in computer code.
   d. there is a computer terminal in every patrol vehicle.
   e. the dispatcher makes assignments by computer instead of by radio.

4. True or false: A teletype message can be sent only between two terminals that are permanently connected to each other.

5. A centralized, computer-based file of criminal records for use by a number of law enforcement agencies is known as
   a. CIC.
   b. CBCS.
   c. CADS.
   d. duplex system.
   e. none of the terms above.

6. In searching for physical evidence, which technique or techniques would be appropriate for a hilly, densely wooded area?
   a. spiral search
   b. strip or line search
   c. aerial search
   d. grid search
   e. surveillance

7. The major problem in the use of radio for a surveillance operation is
    a. the inability to keep unauthorized persons from overhearing radio communications.
    b. the lack of equipment designed for this special purpose.
    c. the excessive use of confusing codes.
    d. the fact that radio equipment is very conspicuous and therefore easily detected by the suspect.
    e. inadequate sharing of information between agencies.

THE ART AND SCIENCE of police communications have come a long way since the early days of this century, when young boys were hired as runners to carry messages from the precinct house to the foot patrolmen on their beats.[1] Yet, somehow the communications revolution has skipped over the detective bureau in most law enforcement agencies.

Typically, a crime investigator works in virtual isolation from the other elements of the department. Newly reported crimes are brought to the investigator's attention several hours or even a few days after the initial report and the patrol officer's preliminary investigation. Each case is assigned to one investigator (or, in some departments, a pair of investigators) who assumes sole responsibility for developing and following up leads, identifying and apprehending a suspect, and bringing the case to its legal conclusion.

Investigators rarely share information about the cases that they are working on; when they do, the information usually is idle gossip about some peculiar or spectacular aspect of a case.[2] An investigator may solicit information from other sections of the department, such as the records and identification bureau or the criminalistics lab, but even then the form and the substance of the communication are likely to be poorly organized and inefficient. Sometimes communicating is more trouble than it is worth.

These conditions are especially unfortunate because an effective, well-organized communications system can contribute substantially to the investigative operation. The problem is not a lack of technology, or "hardware," organized in a rational manner; rather, the problem too often is that the investigator fails to make use of the facilities and capabilities that are readily available.

Poor communication is most common in law enforcement agencies that are organized into separate patrol and investigative units, especially if the investigators are further divided into specialized categories. Agencies organized for patrol-oriented investigation tend to make better use of their communications capabilities, perhaps because teamwork and effective communication are recognized as indispensable to a patrol operation.[3]

In fact, most police communications systems have been developed primarily to serve the patrol function. Special efforts may be needed to adapt the communications system to the needs of the investigator, but they can pay large dividends in the long run.

## POLICE COMMUNICATIONS SYSTEMS

Before the widespread adoption of telegraphic and radio communications systems, police patrol officers were very much on their own. At the beginning of each shift, the foot patrolmen met at the station house for inspection and general instructions. Once they left the station to take up their walking beats, they were completely responsible for anything that occurred within their districts. They had no means to summon help from other officers, nor could the station notify the foot patrolmen of crime reports or complaints except by sending a messenger out to find them.[4]

The earliest form of police communications system was the telegraphic call box. Messages could be transmitted between the station house and the patrolman by means of Morse code—provided that the patrolman was at the call box to receive and transmit information. Later, telephone call boxes were introduced, greatly improving the efficiency of communications, but still requiring the presence of the patrol officer at a particular place. Elaborate signal systems, using flashing lights, loud gongs, and other devices, were installed to attract the patrol officer's attention when a message was waiting, but such systems worked only when the officer was within sight or hearing of the call box. Mostly, the signal systems served to draw crowds of curious citizens.[5]

Automotive police patrols were established in some cities before 1910, but police radio systems did not appear until after 1920. Even then, the first efforts were often very crude. For example, Detroit began to operate an experimental radio system in 1921. However, because there were no legal provisions for radio transmitters to be licensed to police agencies at that time, the Detroit system was licensed as a commercial broadcasting station. Between police calls, the station was required to broadcast "entertainment programs," which consisted mostly of the police department's band. The experiment did not last long.[6]

A more serious flaw in the early radio systems was their one-way operation. Messages could be broadcast from the central transmitter to the mobile receivers, but there was no provision for the patrol officer to request additional information or even to confirm that the message had been received. This defect was remedied in some departments by equipping patrol cars with both receivers and transmitters—two separate devices, both relatively expensive and extremely unreliable.

Eventually, dependable two-way radio equipment was developed. Today it is hard to imagine a police vehicle without its compact, trustworthy radio.

PATROL RADIO SYSTEMS

Even after mobile receivers and transmitters were combined into a single device, many police radio systems continued to use two separate frequencies for each communications channel. Such systems are called *duplex*. One frequency is used to transmit messages from a central dispatching point to the mobile units; the second frequency carries messages from the mobile units to the central station. The only real advantage of this system is that messages can flow in both directions simultaneously. Usually the dispatcher's receiver is separate from the transmitting circuits. Thus, for example, the dispatcher can receive an urgent message from a mobile unit in the midst of a long transmission. But the mobile units ordinarily are designed to operate only in one mode at a time, either receiving or transmitting, and most of the radio's circuitry serves both functions.

ANSWERS TO STUDY CLUES
1. d    2. a    3. d    4. False    5. a
6. b and d    7. a

The frequencies available for police radios are scarce and badly overcrowded, and the advantages of the duplex system are relatively minor. Most police radio systems today are *simplex* systems; that is, each unit is capable of both transmitting and receiving on the same frequency, though not at the same time. Simplex systems not only conserve scarce frequencies, but also permit each mobile unit to hear the transmissions of every other mobile unit within receiving range. Because of this mobile-to-mobile capability, in addition to base-to-mobile and mobile-to-base capabilities, simplex systems are often called *three-way* radios.[7]

The great majority of police radio systems use only one channel. For most small agencies, one channel is sufficient. In fact, in many parts of the country a half-dozen small agencies may operate on the same channel, sometimes using a single transmitter served by four or five separate dispatching centers. Though obviously economical, these arrangements depend on a high degree of intra- and interagency coordination to avoid chaos.

Most larger agencies have multichannel systems. Typically, a jurisdiction is divided into two or more geographic districts, and patrol units in each district are dispatched over a particular channel. A multichannel system greatly reduces the amount of radio traffic that each mobile unit must receive and thus reduces confusion. Of course, a multichannel system also means that patrol officers in one district may be unaware of events in an adjacent district, and this can lead to problems. Resolving these problems is the responsibility of the dispatchers.

Some agencies use all their channels for patrol dispatching. But often at least one channel is set aside as a command or tactical channel. This channel may be used for administrative communications between super-

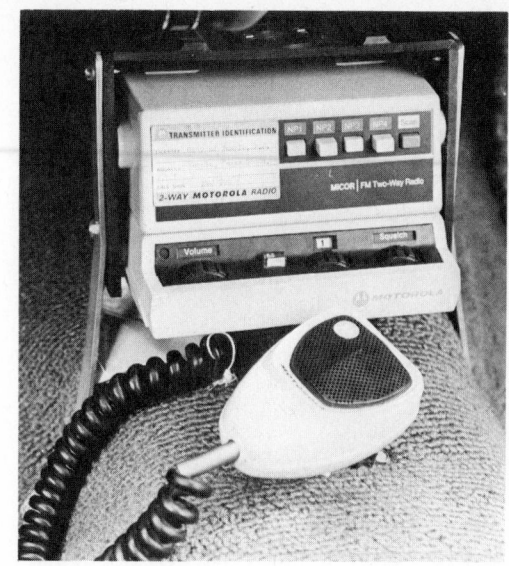

A modern, multichannel (simplex system) mobile radio in a patrol vehicle. (Photo courtesy of Temple, Texas, Police Department)

visory officers, for lengthy conversations between a single patrol unit and a supervisor or the central station, or for specialized purposes such as coordination between several units that are involved in surveillance, raids on crime sites, and so forth.

In many large urban areas, there is also an interagency or metro channel that is shared by all of the law enforcement agencies in the area. Sometimes nonpolice agencies (such as fire departments, ambulance services, and city or county officials) also have access to the metro channel. The metro channel is intended for coordination of activities that involve several different agencies: civil disasters, widespread forest or range fires, major traffic accidents, and the like. In some instances, the smaller agencies in an area may use the metro channel as their dispatching channel.

## COMPUTER-AIDED DISPATCHING

The most important and most basic change in police communications systems since the advent of mobile radio has been introduced in very recent years: it is called *computer-aided dispatching,* or CAD. Although the advantages of a CAD system are most impressive, the equipment is considerably more expensive than a conventional police radio system. Therefore, only a few departments have been able to install the computerized systems, usually with the help of federal grants or other special funding.

The essential characteristic of a CAD system is the use of a mobile computer terminal in each police vehicle, either in place of or in addition to the conventional radio. The mobile terminal consists of a keyboard and a display. The keyboard may be *alphanumeric* (similar to a typewriter keyboard, having separate keys for each letter and number), or it may be designed only for numerical data and a few codes (like a push-button telephone keyboard or an electronic calculator). The display unit in some CAD terminals consists of either a televisionlike screen or a printer similar to a teletype machine; some CAD terminals have both types of display. Voice radio circuits may be included in the CAD terminal; in this case a separate radio is unnecessary.

The police dispatcher operates a similar terminal in most CAD systems. The dispatcher types out messages on the keyboard; the message is transmitted by radio to the mobile units (or, in some systems, coded signals are used to transmit a message only to a specific mobile unit or a small group of units) and is reproduced on the mobile terminal's display. The mobile officer can acknowledge receipt of the message by pressing a code button or can use the keyboard to request additional in-

formation, report results of an investigation, and so on. If the officer happens to be away from the vehicle when the message is received, it will be waiting on the printer when the officer returns. Terminals with only a televisionlike display usually have some provision to store messages until the officer returns to the vehicle and asks for them.

Even if a CAD system does only what we have described, the advantages over voice communication are obvious. A great deal of information can be transmitted in written form, with more speed and far less chance of misunderstandings than in oral form. Furthermore, because the radio signals are in digital, electronic form, they are almost completely protected from interception by unauthorized persons. Someone who wants to listen in on the police communications would have to have an expensive CAD terminal to do so, and the terminal would have to accommodate the various types of coding signals that some CAD systems employ to limit a transmission to a particular mobile unit or group of units.

Some CAD systems do much more than we have just described. One sophisticated system operates as an automated dispatcher. When a complaint or crime report is received at the police station, the telephone operator enters the information into a computer console. Then, according to a predetermined program, the computer analyzes the complaint to assess its relative priority, the patrol district in which the complaint was reported, and the patrol unit that should be assigned to respond, plus any units needed for back-up. For some types of complaints, the computer can consult its memory bank (or even other computers) to determine what type of response may be required or even whether it is likely to be a false alarm. All of this is accomplished in fractions of a second.

The computer then displays on the dispatcher's terminal a proposed assignment of one or more patrol units to respond to the call. If the dispatcher agrees with the proposed assignment, merely pressing a button causes the message to be transmitted automatically to the mobile terminals. The dispatcher, however, can override the computer's proposed assignment and can transmit other messages to the mobile units at any time; in practice, this is rarely necessary.

CAD systems also can be connected into an interagency network for coordinated, multi-agency activities of nearly unlimited complexity. When everything is working properly and when the equipment has been properly programmed, the CAD computer never forgets, never gets too busy with other chores, and never gets rattled by excitement or tension.

Another important advantage of a CAD system, especially for investigative personnel, is that the mobile terminal can be given direct access to the agency's computerized crime and identification records as well as regional, statewide, and national Crime Information Centers (CICs). Using a conventional radio system, a patrol officer who has stopped a suspicious vehicle must verbally request "wants, warrants, and DMV" on the vehicle license plate and the occupants of the vehicle. The dispatcher then must enter the request into a computer or teletypewriter or, perhaps, must look the information up manually. The process can take several minutes, and important information can be overlooked. With a properly designed CAD system, the patrol officer can have immediate, direct access from the patrol vehicle to the agency's computer or to the distant CIC computers. Usually an answer comes back almost as fast as the officer can type in the request.

As experience is gained with CAD systems, and as more sophisticated versions are developed and put into service, there are likely to be many additional features and refinements. Some agencies already are installing automatic vehicle locators, which keep a central computer continuously informed of the location of every police unit. Automatic locators have been developed in the past for conventional radio systems, but they proved to be much more expensive than they were worth. However, when combined with automated dispatching, the locator system could make a great deal of sense.

Again, the greatest barrier to the widespread adoption of CAD systems is their initial cost, which can be enormous. However, since the turn of the century, the trend in electronic technology has been a steady flow of more sophisticated devices and a constant reduction in costs. It seems likely that CAD systems—perhaps devices more exotic than anything we can imagine today—will be as common in police communications thirty years from now as conventional two-way radio is today.[8]

### INTRA-AGENCY COMMUNICATIONS SYSTEMS

It is a curious paradox of police communications that a patrol officer in a vehicle halfway across town can be informed by radio of a crime, but a detective sitting in an office only a hundred feet from the radio room may not hear about the crime until two days later. Actually, a fellow detective sitting at an adjacent desk will probably *never* hear about the crime unless it is somehow outside of the ordinary.

In the vast majority of police agencies, intra-agency communication either is oral or depends on hand-delivered messages. If there is any systematic organization of intra-agency communications, the system is probably designed for administrative and supervisory purposes—to keep track of personnel assignments, workloads, and budgetary matters—rather than for investigative and enforcement purposes.[9]

Consider, for example, the handling of a routine crime report. The initial report comes in from the victim by telephone; the telephone operator fills out a complaint card and hands it or sends it by conveyor belt to the dispatcher. The dispatcher relays the information by radio to a patrol unit and then sets the card aside. The patrol officer responds to the call, conducts some sort of preliminary investigation, then reports back to the dispatcher. The dispatcher picks up the complaint card, indicates what action (if any) was taken by the patrol officer, and puts the card in a stack to be delivered later to a file clerk or sends the card by conveyor belt or pneumatic tube to the records and identification (R&I) bureau. Sometimes information from the complaint card is transferred to cross-reference cards, but usually the card is just filed away.

At the end of each shift or whenever it is convenient, the patrol officer turns in the preliminary investigation report. It may sit on someone's desk for several hours, but eventually it is hand-delivered to the detective bureau. Sometime later the case is assigned to a detective who then sees the report for the first time. In order to study the original complaint, the detective must either visit the R&I bureau in person or call a file clerk and ask that the card be delivered. In order to see whether similar crimes have been committed in the same neighborhood, whether the same victim has experienced similar crimes before, or whether a known suspect has a prior criminal record, the detective must visit the R&I

bureau in person or communicate by phone, describing the information needed and hoping that the clerk will be able to find it.

Admittedly, some agencies have made improvements in their internal communications systems. Even a manual file system, if it is well designed and organized, can improve the chances that needed information will be found, sooner or later. Nevertheless, the great majority of agencies continue to operate in the manner that we have just described. It is not surprising that, according to one study, more than 70 percent of all crime reports simply accumulate on the detectives' desks and receive no follow-up investigation at all.[10]

Improving intra-agency communications is a massive task. Few agencies have the resources or the inclination to undertake it. However, the general outline of an improved internal communications system should be fairly apparent.

Investigators should be made aware of every crime report as soon as it is received and should have access to the patrol officer's preliminary investigation report as soon as the investigation is completed. They should have direct, immediate access to summaries of recent crime activity and to all internal crime records. They should be familiar with the general level of criminal activity in the jurisdiction, including crimes for which they have no personal investigative responsibility. In brief, *criminal activity does not take place in a vacuum, and there is no reason that investigative activity should, either.*

It would be difficult, though possible, to develop this kind of internal communications system using only hand-written messages, hand delivery, and mechanical systems of conveyor belts and pneumatic tubes. A better solution is computerization, even though it is extremely expensive. Fortunately, the CAD systems that we have described for pa-

*Most police communications systems are designed to serve the needs of patrol and administration, not investigation. (Photo courtesy of Temple, Texas, Police Department)*

trol operations lend themselves readily to extension into the investigative offices. As CAD systems become more common, there is a good chance that computer terminals will sprout on detectives' desks.

### INTERAGENCY NETWORKS

Interagency communication has received a good deal of attention in recent years with rewarding results. Some fairly elaborate interagency communication networks have been established using telephone, teletype, and computer-based systems, not to mention the interagency radio systems already described. These interagency systems have proved to be immensely valuable to investigators.[11]

Most investigators maintain their own list of telephone numbers of helpful agencies, including law enforcement agencies with adjacent or overlapping jurisdictions and nonpolice agencies of various kinds: city and county welfare offices, bank clearing-houses, utility companies, and so on. Experienced investigators have found that an hour or so spent on the telephone can produce dozens of productive leads, especially when a suspect is known but his or her whereabouts are not.

Besides the public (or "common") telephone system, investigators sometimes have access to "dedicated" telephone lines connecting several different agencies. These "hot lines" are used primarily to summon emergency assistance, such as the fire department or ambulance service. However, sometimes dedicated lines maintain close communications between a local police department and the county sheriff, state police, and police departments in adjacent towns. Although the hot lines are used mostly to coordinate patrol activities, they also can serve the investigator who needs information from another agency or who needs to forward information to another agency. One advantage of a dedicated

*A police teletype terminal. Information is entered on the keyboard at right, checked on the video screen, then transmitted. Information is received on the printer at left. (Photo courtesy of Temple, Texas, Police Department)*

line is that usually there is no doubt about the identity and authority of the caller; if someone calls on a dedicated line that connects only to the sheriff's office, it is reasonable to assume that the caller really is a deputy sheriff and not an impostor.

Teletype networks have been used by police agencies since about 1915 and were preceded by telegraph systems using Morse or other codes. Originally, these systems were used for intra-agency communications between a headquarters station and the precinct offices or station houses located around a city or between the state police headquarters and the various district barracks. However, it was not long before interagency telegraph and teletype networks were established.

A teletype communications system, just like a telephone system, can use either common lines or dedicated lines. Systems using common lines are frequently called *Telex*, which is the trademark name of Western Union's common-carrier teletype network,

although similar services are offered by other companies. In a Telex system, the person who wishes to send a message first identifies the station being called, either by using a telephonelike dial or by typing the station's "address" on a keyboard. A connection is then made exclusively between the sending unit and the called unit.

Private-line teletype networks can employ a similar switching system so that a sending unit is connected to only one called unit (what is known as a switched, point-to-point system), or messages can be sent from any one unit to all the other units in the system (an unswitched, point-to-multipoint system). Some elaborate systems are designed so that a message can be sent from one point to a specific group of points, similar to a telephone conference call. Finally, teletype systems can be two-way or one-way in design, although one-way systems are not very common.

The most frequent use of a teletype system is to disseminate crime information to various districts within a single agency or to other agencies. For example, when a crime occurs in town A and the suspect is believed to have fled toward town B, a teletype message will be sent from A to B, requesting that the suspect be picked up. More generalized warnings about criminal activity also can be transmitted rapidly from place to place. The principal advantage over the use of a telephone for the same purpose is that the teletype message is in written form; a great deal of information can be conveyed with relatively small chance of misunderstanding, and the agency receiving the message has an accurate copy of the information for further dissemination or for record keeping.

During the early 1960s, the Federal Bureau of Investigation began to establish a National Crime Information Center, using computers to centralize the Bureau's enormous files of crime data. The FBI encouraged the states to establish their own CICs, and by the late 1960s most states had at least started to do so, partly because of the availability of federal funds for the purpose. Today there are not only the NCIC and state CICs in every state, but also some regional (less-than-statewide) CICs serving major metropolitan areas. We will describe these operations in more detail in Chapter 11; our point here is that these computerized centers are now fully operational, providing an enormous store of essential data that is available by telephone, teletype, or correspondence.

In fact, even these ordinary means of communication could be eliminated. A remote computer terminal can be connected directly to a distant computer by telephone line or by microwave radio. The computer terminal operator can converse with a computer in the next room, across town, or on a distant continent, all with equal ease and nearly equal speed. In fact, the computers themselves can be programmed to share information on their own initiative. You might ask your local agency's computer for information. It discovers that the information is not in its own memory banks, so it automatically transmits an inquiry to the state or national CIC, obtains an answer, and displays the answer on your terminal—and you would never know that the information came from hundreds or thousands of miles away.

There is virtually no limit to the potential capabilities of a computer-based communications system. When a system has been designed properly, personnel have been trained adequately, and appropriate information has been put into the computer's memory, the possibilities are enormous. For the present, these possibilities remain mostly unrealized. The CICs themselves are in operation, and they have already proved themselves to be of inestimable value. More elaborate and sophisticated systems will come in due time, despite the expense.

However, no matter how impressive the hardware may be, it is still nothing but a collection of blinking lights and pretty push buttons until someone—a crime investigator, for example—puts it all to good use.

## INVESTIGATIVE COMMUNICATIONS

The primary function of a crime investigator could be defined in terms of information. The investigator's task is to collect information from various sources, to process it in several ways, and ultimately to apply the information to answer certain questions: who committed a particular crime? how? and why? Anything that enables an investigator to collect more information, to collect it more rapidly, or to process it more effectively will enhance the investigator's ability to function.[12]

## NATIONAL LAW ENFORCEMENT TELECOMMUNICATIONS SYSTEM

Nearly instantaneous communication is possible between any two law enforcement agencies in the United States—including agencies at the local, state, and federal levels—thanks to the National Law Enforcement Telecommunications System (NLETS).

The NLETS network consists of a switched teletype line connecting all 50 states, the District of Columbia, and Puerto Rico, as shown in Figure 9.1. The switching center is located in Phoenix, Arizona; from that point, main trunk lines branch out to the state police headquarters in every state and to the federal agencies in Washington. Lines reach the local level through switching subcenters at each state's capital.

Because the system is based on conventional teletype equipment, it is completely compatible with existing teletype networks. Furthermore, in many cases it is possible to integrate the NLETS lines and an agency's computer so that direct access to criminal records can be provided. Through NLETS, any participating agency can obtain information directly from the National Crime Information Center (NCIC), operated by the FBI, and from most state CICs as well.

There are strict and fairly complicated rules governing the kinds and the format of messages that can be transmitted over the NLETS lines. For example, personnel vacancies cannot be advertised on NLETS. However, the system can be used for other kinds of administrative messages and almost any sort of crime information. The format rules and operating procedures can be learned by anyone who is reasonably familiar with a teletype machine. Although most departments employ trained operators to handle NLETS messages, there is no reason that an investigator could not acquire the basic skills to send and receive inquiries.

Ordinarily, NLETS is *not* used for routine inquiries about suspects' criminal records, identifications, and the like. These matters can be handled by correspondence with NCIC or the appropriate state CIC, rather than tying up valuable time on the teletype network. In general, NLETS is intended for occasions when an agency needs to disseminate crime information to a number of other agencies, to announce that a particular suspect is wanted or that a warrant has been issued for a certain person, to broadcast descriptions of stolen vehicles or stolen property (provided that a warrant exists to seize the property), and to convey important administrative information directly to another agency. Requests for vehicle license searches, for information about outstanding warrants on a particular person, and for help in locating an individual for some emergency reason (such as a death in the person's family) may be transmitted on the NLETS network, but only to the specific agencies that are likely to be concerned.

The investigator's greatest enemy is not the skill and cunning of criminals, but rather the passage of time. Research has shown that the great majority of crimes are solved in the preliminary investigation or not at all.[13] Once

FIGURE 9.1
NATIONAL LETS NETWORK (NLETS)

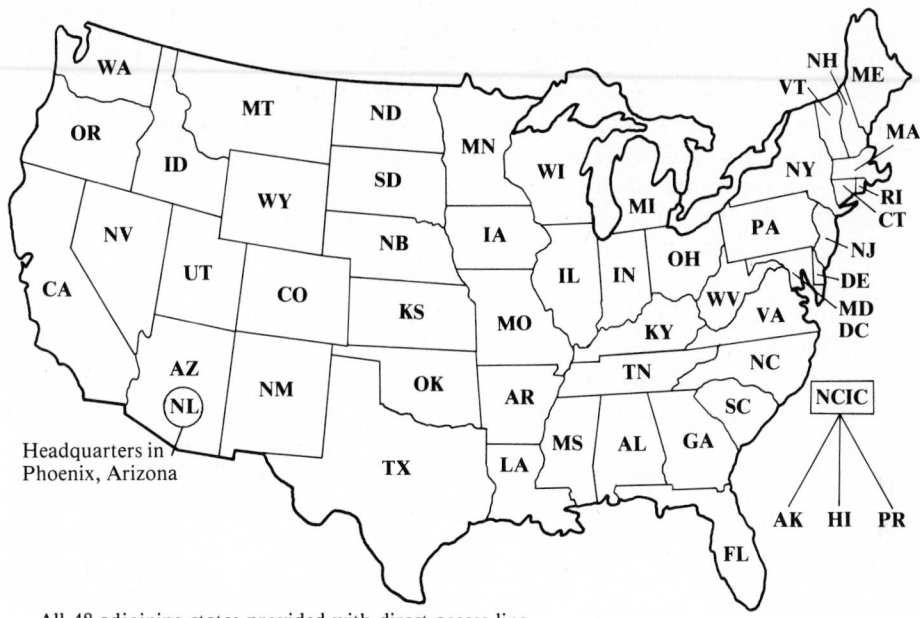

All 48 adjoining states provided with direct access line
to switcher in Phoenix, Ariz. **NCIC** provides
switching to and from Alaska, Hawaii and Puerto
Rico

a crime has been committed, the information about the crime (evidence) begins to disappear. The memories of victims and witnesses become steadily less reliable; physical evidence fades away or becomes hopelessly contaminated. Most minor crimes are never solved, because each investigator is responsible for too many investigations at once and thus cannot devote enough time to any one of them. Unless the victim or a witness can identify the perpetrator or the perpetrator's identity becomes known by sheer accident, the crime is never solved.

The solution to this dilemma is to do everything possible to provide the investigator with as much useful information as exists, as quickly as the information becomes known. Information is transferred from one person to another or from one place to another by means of various kinds of communications systems. The system might consist of an elaborate electronic network of computers or, on the other hand, it might merely consist of handwritten notes passed from the patrol officers to the detectives.

## THE INITIAL REPORT OF A CRIME

Regardless of the administrative and functional organization of a law enforcement agency, the personnel who are responsible for investigating crimes should be notified of every crime that occurs as soon as it has been reported. Very few agencies have arranged their communications systems to meet this objective. Even when sophisticated CAD systems are in operation, in most cases the investigators are not included in the system. Crime reports still reach their desks several hours or days after the fact.

It is not necessary for the detectives to respond immediately to every crime report, since that would merely duplicate the patrol officers' function and would interfere with the detectives' ability to pursue the time-consuming aspects of an investigation. However, if a detective is notified of every crime when it is reported, some characteristic may be recognized that would indicate the most appropriate response.

For example, an investigator might be working on a group of cases involving supermarket robberies. Suppose there have been several robberies with a common element: the robbers fled on foot in the direction of a nearby apartment building where, presumably, they had left their getaway car. If the investigator is notified immediately when another supermarket robbery is reported, he or she might advise the dispatcher to send one patrol unit to the supermarket and a back-up unit to the nearest apartment building. In this example, the information possessed by the investigator would be combined with the information possessed by the dispatcher, resulting in a response that neither party would have taken alone. It would not do much good if the investigator heard about the latest supermarket robbery several hours after the initial report.

According to existing theories of police procedure, the investigator should have sent a memo to all the dispatchers, advising them of the characteristic element that has been discovered in the series of supermarket robberies. Theoretically, then, whenever a dispatcher has a report of another such robbery, appropriate action could be taken. The problem is that investigators may find dozens of significant characteristics in the cases on which they are working. A truly perceptive and conscientious investigator could bury the dispatchers under a mound of memos, all of which would be forgotten immediately since the dispatchers already have plenty of other things to think about. Any such one-way information system is inevitably doomed to failure.

The communication must be two-way. Not only should the investigator be informed immediately when a crime is reported, but it is just as important for the investigator to be able to influence the response to that report. Sometimes the investigator may wish to give special instructions or suggestions to the dispatcher; sometimes the investigator may be able to provide the patrol officer with information that will influence the preliminary investigation. Once in a while the investigator may decide to intervene directly and conduct the preliminary investigation, especially in the most serious cases.

Many agencies, especially the smaller ones, already have an informal policy of notifying either detectives or supervisory officials when a serious crime, such as a murder, is reported. Our point is that the policy should be formalized, it should be made an integral part of the communications system, and it should apply to *every* crime, even the most insignificant ones. The battle against crime demands teamwork and coordination. It does not make sense to keep half of the team on the bench until the game is all but lost.

FIGURE 9.2
A STRIP OR LINE SEARCH PATTERN

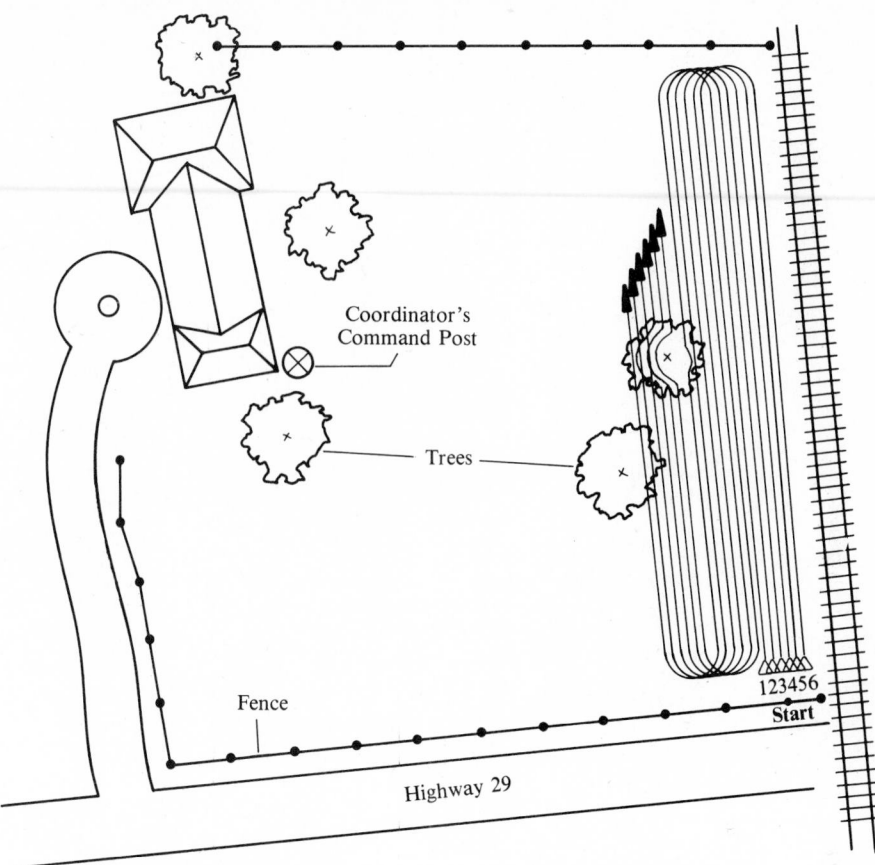

A variation of the strip or line search is the grid pattern (Figure 9.3). The only difference is that after the area has been completely searched in successive strips in one direction, the squad reassembles and conducts a second search at 90 degrees to the first search pattern.

If there are enough personnel available for two or more squads, they can be deployed in various ways. Two squads could be used to conduct a grid search simultaneously. This method can cause some confusion since the two squads will cross each other's paths constantly, but the confusion can be reduced by proper coordination between the squad leaders. An alternative is to have the two squads cover the same territory twice, sending the second squad into the search area over the same path that the first covered, but separating them by a two- or three-minute interval. This may be desirable when the search area is covered with dense underbrush or when there is concern over the possibility that one

FIGURE 9.3
A GRID SEARCH PATTERN

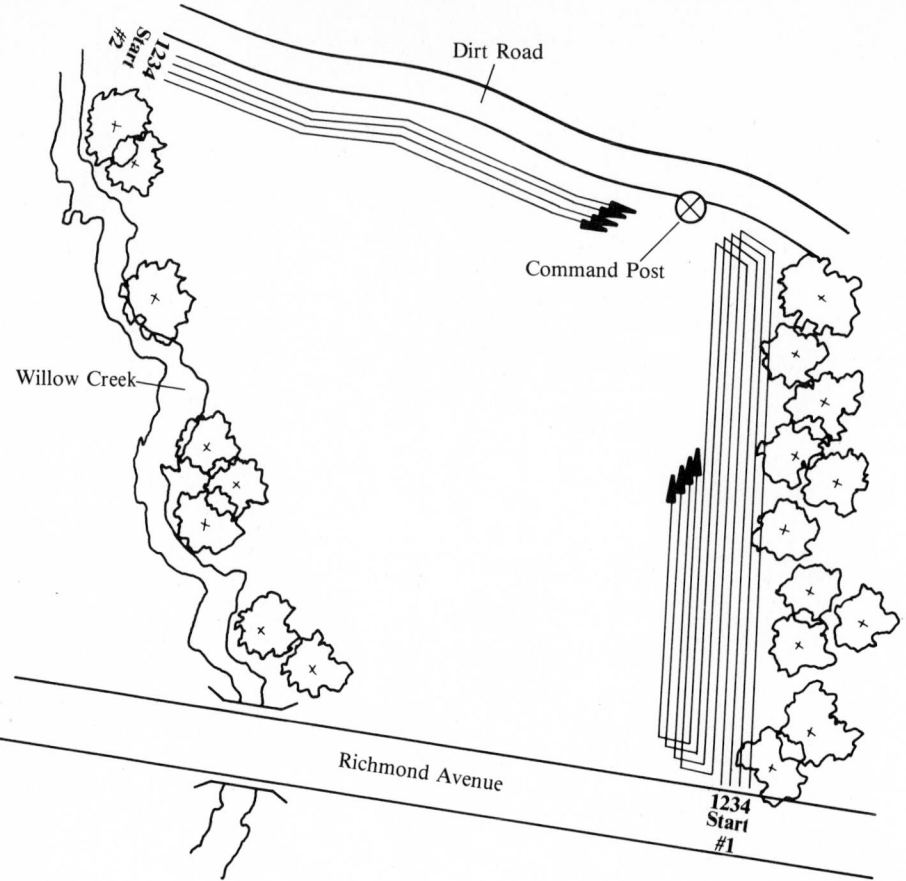

Dirt Road

Command Post

Willow Creek

Richmond Avenue

1234
Start
#2

1234
Start
#1

team will miss important evidence. Finally, the search area can be divided into two or more sections, each of which is examined by a separate squad. This greatly reduces the time required for the search, but care must be exercised to ensure that no part of the area is inadvertently missed because everyone thought that someone else would cover it.

The spiral search pattern is especially advantageous when the area to be searched is very irregular in shape, but the terrain is rea- sonably flat and uncluttered (Figure 9.4). It is a particularly good pattern when only one squad of searchers is available. The basic procedure is to line up the squad at one corner of the search area, just as for the strip or line pattern. However, instead of having the squad march back and forth across the area, the squad should proceed in a spiral pattern, following the contours of the area's boundaries, until they reach the center of the area. If the squad's path is carefully controlled by

*The Investigator and Support Services*

FIGURE 9.4
A SPIRAL SEARCH PATTERN

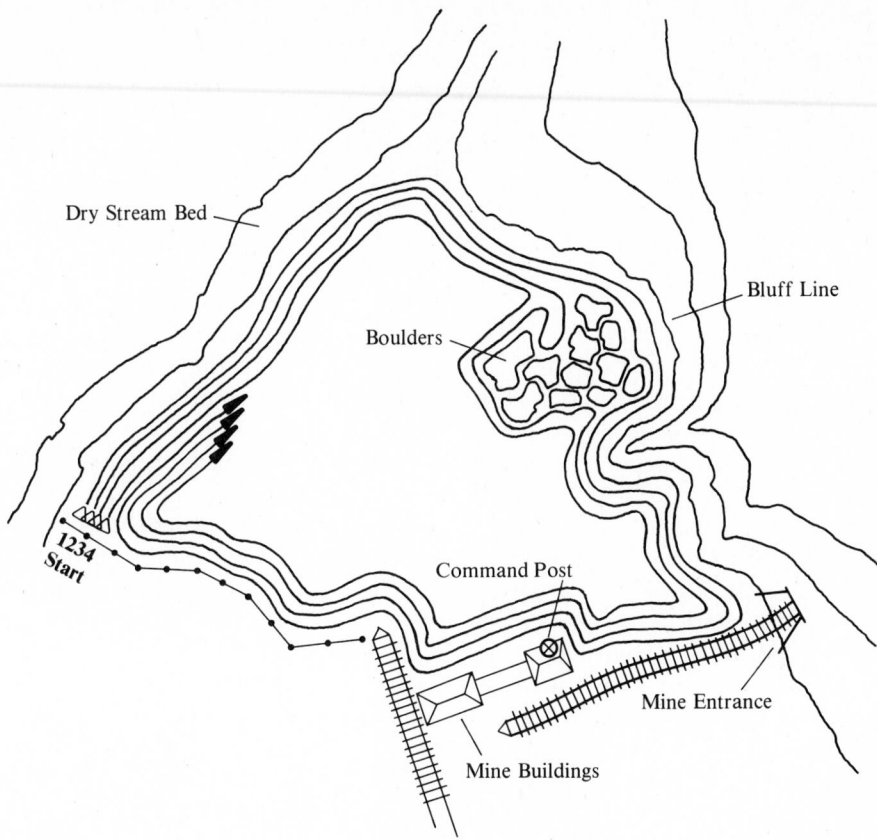

Dry Stream Bed

Bluff Line

Boulders

1234
Start

Command Post

Mine Entrance

Mine Buildings

the squad leader and the search coordinator, it will be almost impossible for any portion of the search area to be missed.

Unfortunately, the spiral pattern may not work as well where the terrain is very rough or hilly or where there are many obstructions and obstacles (buildings, trees, and the like) because of the difficulty in controlling the squad's path. In those cases, a strip or line pattern is probably preferable.

Regardless of the search pattern selected, good communications will contribute sub-

stantially to the ease and efficiency of the operation. The search coordinator should remain at a single location, preferably one from which it is possible to see the whole search area and follow the progress of the search teams. The squad leader is responsible for maintaining the discipline of the squad and for maintaining communication with the search coordinator.

Whenever any potential evidence is discovered by a squad member, the squad leader should relay this information to the search coordinator. Ordinarily, the evidence must not be removed from the place where it was found until it has been examined and photographed, and its location precisely measured, by the search coordinator or an assistant. Sometimes, especially if several pieces of evidence are being sought, it is desirable for the search squad merely to mark the evidence, then move on while the search coordinator or an assistant performs the other steps preparatory to the removal of the evidence.

## THE CONTINUING INVESTIGATION

As we have mentioned, almost all criminal investigations end right where they begin: the taking of the preliminary report. In an ideal world, this would not be true. Investigators would continue to investigate every reported crime until the perpetrator was identified, apprehended, and convicted. Unfortunately, in this less-than-ideal world, continuing investigations are conducted only when the crime is exceptionally serious or when nearly conclusive evidence has been discovered during the preliminary investigation. Even the existence of conclusive evidence is not enough to guarantee a follow-up investigation if the crime was relatively routine or petty.

Nevertheless, throughout this text we shall assume something closer to the ideal state: every crime is investigated until the case is solved or until every effort to solve it has been exhausted.

Again, we emphasize that the investigator's function is to collect, analyze, and act on information, which can be received only through direct observation or through some kind of communications system. Since every investigator's capacities for direct observation are limited by nature, communications systems must play a crucial role in the investigative process.

Perhaps the dominant communications system consists of written matter: reports, memoranda, and file cards. The investigator should have the preliminary investigative report, in written form, as a bare minimum. Sometimes it is helpful to compare the preliminary report with the original complaint. The principal investigator may add more information as a result of a follow-up examination of the crime scene, interviews with witnesses, or other observation. Information also might be obtained from other investigators who are working on similar cases, the crime analysis unit (if the agency has one), the criminalistics laboratory, and various other internal sources.

Another important communications system is the telephone. Investigators should keep in close touch with their counterparts in nearby agencies to compare and share information about similar crimes or patterns of criminal activity in their respective jurisdictions. Once a suspect has been identified, telephone calls to utility companies, employers, and other potential information sources can help the investigator to learn the suspect's whereabouts and habits.

The victims and witnesses of a crime should not be neglected as potential sources of information, even after they have been thoroughly interviewed. Sometimes a victim or witness will remember some minor detail that was overlooked at the time of the original interview. Ordinarily, a person will not bother to call the police just to add a seemingly trivial bit of information, although it could be the one fact that the investigator needs to identify or locate the perpetrator. It is up to the investigator to keep in touch with the victims and witnesses, and an occasional phone call serves the purpose well (besides reassuring the victims that the police are doing their best to solve the case).[15]

## SURVEILLANCE

Investigators sometimes require specialized communications systems for purposes outside of routine investigations, and surveillance is one such situation. Surveillance ordinarily is used in three general circumstances:

1. When a particular person is suspected of a certain crime or of unknown criminal behavior, surveillance is used to observe the person's activities for evidence of criminal actions.

2. When a particular person is suspected of a crime but the person's whereabouts are unknown, locations at which the person might appear (such as a residence) are observed or other individuals who have some relationship to the suspect (members of the suspect's family or suspected accomplices, for example) are observed in hopes of apprehending the suspect.

3. When it is believed that criminal activities are taking place or might take place at a given location, the location may be observed in order to learn the identities of the persons who frequent it or to detect any criminal activity that occurs.

All three forms of surveillance require specific, unique investigative techniques. For example, surveillance of an individual suspect might involve following the person on foot or by vehicle. Usually it is important for the suspect to be unaware of the surveillance, which might involve several different police personnel. The third type of surveillance, on the other hand, might require police personnel working undercover to infiltrate the criminal activity, while other agents remain outside the suspected criminal location.

In any case, the activities of all police personnel involved in a surveillance must be coordinated. This coordination usually is accomplished by radio. Since most police radio systems are not designed for this purpose—they are designed primarily for patrol dispatching—adaptations may be necessary.

The major problem in the use of radio for surveillance is the need to maintain security. Inexpensive radio receivers that monitor all standard police frequencies are readily available to the public. Many people listen to their police monitors for their personal entertainment; they enjoy the vicarious experience of police activity. Naturally, anyone who is involved in some sort of planned criminal activity will take the precaution of buying a police monitor in order to keep track of the locations of patrol units and, after the crime, the progress of investigative efforts. State laws and local ordinances have been passed to prohibit the use of police monitors, but federal courts generally have struck down such laws as improper because they conflict with federal law. Besides, such laws are virtually unenforceable and would be ignored by criminals anyway. The result is that every police officer should assume that whenever the police radio is used, the message will be overheard by all sorts of unauthorized listeners. Although this is mostly a nuisance in patrol work, it can be a very serious matter in investigative work and can be extremely dangerous to the unwary officer.[16]

There is no perfect solution to the problem of unauthorized listeners. If an agency has only one police frequency, investigative activities such as surveillance can be carried out on the same frequency as patrol dispatching. In fact, this can help to make the surveillance activity less obvious, if the coordinating messages are phrased and timed to resemble patrol dispatch and response messages.

If an agency has several frequencies, usually one of them will be reserved for administrative and investigative use. It is very helpful if this command or tactical channel is in an entirely different part of the radio frequency spectrum from the patrol channels. For example, if the agency uses VHF radio for its patrol channels (either "low band," around 37 mHz, or "high band," around 155 mHz), the command channel might be in the UHF band (around 450 mHz). Some of the cheaper police monitors are not equipped to receive UHF frequencies, but even when they are so equipped, criminals might be unaware that the agency uses those frequencies.

Whatever radio channel is chosen for investigative communications, all messages should be in some kind of code. The use of any code presupposes that all personnel involved in the activity are aware of the code. Standard codes, such as the APCO "10-Code," should not be used for investigative purposes, since the probability is too high that unauthorized listeners will be at least as familiar with them as the police personnel are. In fact, number-based codes are not very useful at all in investigative work because of the likelihood of misunderstandings.

The best codes use plain words with prearranged special meanings. A simple grammar can be established for most situations with only a dozen or so code words. Each word should represent one of the persons involved in the activity (the suspect, any other individuals with whom the suspect interacts, and each of the police personnel), one of the places where the activity will occur, and one of the various types of actions that are anticipated (arrival of the suspect, completion of a criminal transaction, departure of an undercover officer from the crime scene, the decision to move in and make an arrest, and so on). The list of code words should be kept to a minimum, not only to reduce the memorization task, but also to avoid confusion or misunderstandings. It does not matter at all whether the coded messages sound intelligible or sensible as long as the personnel involved in the operation understand them.

Oral codes should not be used for very long. It is best to make up an entirely new code for each new operation. If any operation lasts longer than two or three days, the code should be changed. Of course, it is essential for everyone involved in the operation to be alerted to the changes; every change increases the risk of misunderstandings or confusion.

Following is a simplified verbal code for an operation involving surveillance of a home where gambling activity is believed to be taking place:

## CODE GRAMMAR
## FOR A SURVEILLANCE OPERATION

### PERSONS

Primary suspect—Hot dog (Owner of residence)
Gambling equipment operators—Peanuts
Guards at front and rear doors—Hamburgers
Gambling customers—Popcorn
Lt. Adams—Eagle (Principal investigator and commander of surveillance operation)
Sgt. Baker—Hawk (Undercover investigator)
Patrol Unit C-10—Chicken
Patrol Unit D-11—Dove

### LOCATIONS

Front of residence—Parking lot
Front door—Ticket booth
Rear of residence—South side
Back door—Goal line
Main gambling room—End zone
Kitchen—Locker room
Bathroom—Press box

### ACTIONS

To be in place for observation—To sleep
To enter front door—To buy tickets
To enter back door—To score a touchdown
To gamble—To dance
To arrest, take into custody—To eat

EAGLE: "Is everyone sleeping?"

CHICKEN: "Chicken sleeping in the parking lot."

DOVE: "Dove sleeping on the south side."

EAGLE: "Roger. Hawk, buy your ticket."

HAWK: "Roger, Eagle." (Several minutes later) "Eagle, Hawk. I'm in the press box. There's a hot dog in the locker room, two hamburgers in the ticket booth, and one at the goal line. About ten popcorn dancing in the end zone. Only two peanuts tonight."

EAGLE: "Roger, Hawk. Chicken, buy your ticket and eat the hamburgers in the ticket booth. Dove, score your touchdown and eat the hamburger on the goal line. Hawk, can you eat the hot dog?"

HAWK: "Roger."

EAGLE: "Count five and go."

---

Mechanical and electronic devices can provide a measure of security on police radio frequencies. The most common such devices are called *scramblers*. Several different types are available commercially, each having somewhat different features and characteristics. Basically, all serve the same functions: the radio signal between the transmitter and the receiver is distorted so that it cannot be reproduced as intelligible speech by an unauthorized receiver.

Any scrambling system requires not only a scrambling device on the transmitter, but also an unscrambling device on each receiver. Usually these devices are fairly expensive, so most agencies are inclined to equip a relatively small number of vehicles with unscramblers. That is fine as long as only those vehicles are involved in an investigative operation. Unfortunately, if a unit without a scrambler is needed, the scrambling system is no longer usable. Generally speaking, effective scrambling systems are too cumbersome for use on walkie-talkies. In spite of these drawbacks, these systems can be useful in some investigative operations and should be considered as an alternative to awkward oral codes. Continued improvement in scrambling technology should lead to less cumbersome devices at lower costs, and perhaps someday they will be considered standard equipment for all police radio systems.

Computer-aided dispatching systems and, in general, any radio system that uses digital signals in place of voice-radio signals would not need scramblers to keep unauthorized listeners from overhearing conversations since the signals are scrambled, in effect, by the computer system. Even though the intention in converting the information to digital signals is not to keep the information secret, the result is to do just that. Anyone who wants to intercept and understand the signals would have to have a computer terminal of the same type as the police; and they are too expensive for most people to buy, as well as being available only from limited sources.

## GIGO AND NINO

Any communications system is only as good as the information that it contains and transfers from person to person or from place to place. If the information is wrong, incomplete, or irrelevant to the receiver's needs, useful communication cannot take place.

Computer scientists and communications engineers have a term that expresses this concept perfectly: *GIGO,* which means "garbage in, garbage out." In short, the quality of the information that a person extracts from a communications system cannot be any better than the quality of the information that someone else put into the system.

Actually, GIGO is not the only problem in police communications. An even bigger problem is the failure of crime investigators to take advantage of the communications facilities that are readily available to them. This failure is compounded by the fact that too many agencies ignore the communications needs of investigators. The most sophisticated facilities are reserved for patrol work, not for investigation. We certainly do not intend to slight the importance of patrol work, but we do believe that criminal investigation could be made more effective if investigators were included in the communications network from beginning to end.

Investigators cannot be expected to use information that they do not have. If no information is put into the system, none will come out—a condition we might call *NINO,* or "nothing in, nothing out."

## REFERENCES

1. Alan Burton, *Police Telecommunications* (Springfield, Ill.: Charles C Thomas, 1973), p. 4.

2. Peter W. Greenwood, Jan M. Chaiken, and Joan Petersilia, *The Criminal Investigation Process* (Lexington, Mass.: D.C. Heath, 1977), p. 15. This is a report of a comprehensive study by the Rand Corporation of criminal investigation practices of U.S. police agencies.

3. Paul M. Whisenand and Tug T. Tamaru, *Automated Police Information Systems* (New York: John Wiley, 1970), pp. 100–108.

4. Burton, p. 29.

5. Burton, pp. 30–32.

6. Burton, p. 38.

7. Burton, pp. 64–65.

8. George D. Eastman, ed., *Municipal Police Administration* (Washington, D.C.: International City Management Association, 1969), p. 274.

9. Eastman, pp. 56–57.

10. Eastman, p. 136.

11. Whisenand and Tamaru, p. 45.

12. Whisenand and Tamaru, p. 117.

13. Greenwood, Chaiken, and Petersilia, p. 118.

14. Paul B. Weston and Kenneth M. Wells, *Elements of Criminal Investigation* (Englewood Cliffs, N.J.: Prentice-Hall, 1971), pp. 10–12.

15. Greenwood, Chaiken, and Petersilia, chap. 12. This chapter describes in detail a survey of victims to determine whether they received adequate feedback from the police, and whether they would like to have received more information.

16. Eastman, pp. 250–251.

1. True or false: Law enforcement agencies that are organized for patrol-oriented investigation tend to make less effective use of their communications facilities than do agencies that have separate patrol and investigative functions.

2. A duplex radio system is one that
    a. enables personnel in vehicles to communicate directly with one another (sometimes called three-way radio).
    b. is used by many small agencies in the same area.
    c. requires separate receivers and transmitters in each vehicle.
    d. uses two different frequencies for each channel.
    e. allows two or more channels to operate on the same frequency.

3. A metro channel is used for
    a. administrative or supervisory communications within an agency that has several radio channels.
    b. coordination of activities that involve several different agencies.
    c. broadcasts to all patrol vehicles in all districts of a city.
    d. communications involving only nonpolice agencies, such as the fire department or ambulance service.
    e. computerized dispatching.

4. The most valuable characteristic of a computer-aided dispatching system is that
    a. all information is transmitted in "written" form.
    b. each vehicle is equipped with a computer whose memory contains all of the agency's crime records.
    c. dispatching assignments are made automatically by the computer, eliminating the expense of human dispatchers.
    d. detectives can be assigned to perform preliminary investigations of all reported crimes, instead of relying on patrol officers to do investigations.
    e. the computer can tell the exact location of every vehicle at all times.

5. The network of interagency teletype communications that connects police agencies and computerized crime data banks is called
    a. NCIC.
    b. CAD.
    c. NLETS.
    d. GIGO.
    e. Telex.

6. True or false: The investigator's greatest enemy is the passage of time.

7. Which of the following usually would *not* be required for a wide-area search for evidence?
    a. one or more squads of four to six officers
    b. multichannel, police-band portable radios
    c. a search coordinator (usually the principal investigator)
    d. a map or sketch of the search area
    e. evidence collection and photography equipment

8. The dominant type of communications system in police work usually is
    a. written.
    b. radio.
    c. telephone.
    d. oral.
    e. computerized.
9. True or false: Once the initial interview has been obtained, there is little need for the investigator to contact the victim or witnesses during the course of an investigation.
10. What is the most practical way to keep unauthorized listeners from overhearing police communications during a surveillance operation?
    a. rely on written communications instead of radio
    b. use only UHF frequencies that cannot be received by unauthorized persons
    c. use scramblers on all police radios
    d. use a standard, established numerical code, such as the APCO "10-Code"
    e. use a prearranged word code

### TOPICS FOR INVESTIGATION

1. How does a law enforcement agency's organizational structure affect the agency's use of communications? What changes in organizational structure would be likely to result in more effective communications? Is better communication a sufficient reason to adopt a particular organizational structure?
2. Why are most police communications systems designed primarily to serve the patrol function? How could a communications system be designed primarily for the investigative function, yet also be appropriate for patrol purposes and needs?
3. Suppose a police department decides to divide its jurisdiction into four patrol districts, but the agency can afford only three-channel radios. Should one channel be used as an administrative or tactical channel, or should all three channels be used for patrol in order to reduce the radio traffic on each channel?
4. A computer-assisted dispatching system is very expensive. Who benefits the most from a CAD system: patrol officers, investigators, or administrators? If you had to decide between installing a CAD system or spending the same amount of money to hire five more investigators in a medium-sized agency, which would you choose?
5. Why are law enforcement agencies so slow to develop efficient intra-agency communications systems, but so eager to install improved interagency systems?
6. Discuss this statement: "Criminal activity does not take place in a vacuum, and there is no reason that investigative activity should, either." Do you agree with the statement? What are the implications of this statement with regard to communications or to the investigator's role and functions?
7. Discuss the value of NLETS by itself, of CICs by themselves, and of both together. What can each system contribute to an investigation?
8. List every way an investigator can overcome the greatest enemy: time. Which of these ways can the investigator implement alone? Which require changes in organizational structure? Which require changes in communications systems?

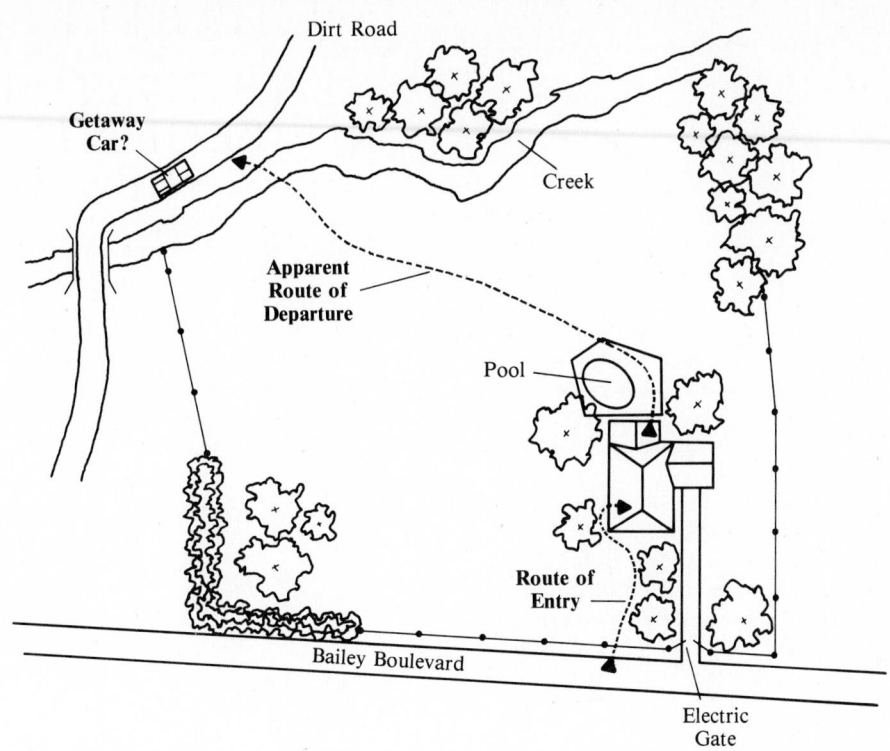

Dirt Road

Getaway Car?

Creek

**Apparent Route of Departure**

Pool

**Route of Entry**

Bailey Boulevard

Electric Gate

9. The above diagram is of an area to be searched for evidence in a burglary-homicide investigation. The perpetrator's route of approach and route of departure are shown on the sketch. The evidence being sought includes the murder weapon (a small-caliber handgun) and an unknown quantity of jewelry thought to have been stolen during the burglary, before the victim surprised the burglar and was shot. Other physical evidence also might be present. Design a search pattern for two four-person search squads.

10. You are in charge of a narcotics investigation. Three people (two men and a woman) are suspected drug dealers. The woman and one of the men live together; the other male suspect's residence is not known. An undercover agent, assisted by an informant, will enter the known residence, attempt to buy some narcotics, then leave. If the buy is successful, the surveillance team, which consists of six officers in three police vehicles, can move in and make an arrest. Design a verbal code grammar for this operation.

## CHAPTER 10

# LABORATORY
# AND TECHNICAL
# SERVICES

STUDY CLUES

1. True or false: It is the investigator's responsibility to tell the crime lab technicians what kind of information is needed before they examine the physical evidence from a crime.
2. For any particular bit of physical evidence, three basic questions must be answered. They are:
    a. What is its chemical composition?
    b. What is it?
    c. Where and by whom was it manufactured?
    d. Who is its rightful owner?
    e. Where did it come from?
    f. What is its relationship to the crime?
    g. In whose possession was it found?
    h. Does it contain traces of the perpetrator?
3. True or false: It is always essential to know the exact nature of any item of physical evidence.
4. A criminalist is
    a. any police officer assigned to investigate crimes.
    b. a student of criminology.
    c. any technical expert who assists investigators in developing evidence.
    d. an employee of the FBI.
    e. a technician who specializes in discovering evidence.
5. True or false: A coroner is always a physician.
6. The most versatile and most often used tool in the crime lab is
    a. the spectrophotometer.
    b. the gas chromatograph.
    c. the electron microscope.
    d. the chemical analysis machine.
    e. the medium-power microscope.
7. An inquest is held to determine
    a. what were the cause, manner, and time of death.
    b. whether there is sufficient evidence to issue a warrant for an arrest.
    c. who is a murder suspect.
    d. whether an autopsy is necessary.
    e. who has the legal right to sign a death certificate.
8. True or false: The investigation of arson is primarily the responsibility of the fire department, not the police.

AFTER THE PRELIMINARY INVESTIGATION at the scene of a crime has been completed, after all the reports have been written and filed, what happens next?

The fact that few cases are investigated to their conclusion does not mean that the effort to collect evidence and to prepare a thorough preliminary report is wasted. All physical evidence of every crime, however minor, should be kept intact until the case is closed or until a determination is made that the case is fundamentally unsolvable. Evidence from a minor crime might prove to be crucial in solving a more serious incident six months or a year later. Similarly, a suspect arrested for a serious crime might be linked to several previous, unsolved minor crimes.

If nothing else, evidence and information concerning minor crimes should be analyzed continually by individual investigators or by a separate crime analysis unit to determine whether a pattern of criminal behavior can be ascertained. Since the operation of the crime analysis unit generally involves various kinds of crime records, we shall discuss them more thoroughly in Chapter 11.

Plenty of cases do deserve and require follow-up investigation, either because they are highly solvable or because they involve a clear danger to the community. In general, every case that is solved—that is, a particular suspect is known, often on the basis of an identification made by a victim or witness at the scene of the crime—will require some kind of follow-up investigation before the suspect can be brought to trial. In this and the next several chapters, we shall be concerned mostly with these follow-up investigations.

physical evidence and testimonial evidence of victims and witnesses. At the conclusion of the preliminary phase, the investigator usually has a substantial quantity of this raw evidence. Some of it will form the foundation for legal charges against the suspect. Some, while useless in court, may be helpful to the investigator in identifying or locating a suspect; and some will prove to be totally useless. But the investigator has no way of knowing in advance which items are which.

The process of converting raw evidence into something more useful is called *developing* the evidence. The term refers to both physical and testimonial evidence, but it especially applies to the former. The responsibility for developing evidence rests entirely on the investigator. Fortunately, he or she has help in carrying out this task. Developing physical evidence depends largely on the services of several different kinds of technical specialists: criminalistics laboratory technicians, firearms examiners, medical examiners and pathologists, and records and identification technicians, to name a few.[1]

The investigator cannot simply bundle up a pile of evidence, ship it off to the lab, and expect the technicians to decide who committed the crime, how, and why. The technicians must know what kinds of information the investigator needs so that they can perform the appropriate tests or analytical procedures. Ordinarily, an investigator is not expected to be able to perform the analyses, but must know what kinds of tests are possible and appropriate so that the right questions can be asked. Asking the wrong questions usually results in getting the wrong answers or no answer at all.

## DEVELOPMENT OF EVIDENCE

The preliminary phase of an investigation is devoted largely to acquiring evidence, both

## THE THREE BASIC QUESTIONS

For any particular bit of physical evidence, whether it is a fingerprint, a burglar's tool, or a cloth fiber, the investigator usually wants to know three things: *what* is it, *where* did it come from, and *how* is it related to the crime?

To avoid confusion, we shall use three specific terms for the kinds of information that answer these three basic questions.

• A piece of evidence is *characterized* if we know what it is. A friction-ridge print is characterized if we know that it is a human fingerprint, probably from the person's left hand. A fragment of broken glass is characterized if we know that it is the sort of glass used in headlights, it is of a certain color and density, and it has a certain refractive index. A fiber is characterized if we know the kind of cloth it came from, its color, and the sort of garment that might be made of that kind of cloth. A fiber also could be characterized by the nature of the material: cotton, nylon, polyester, and so on.

• A piece of evidence is *identified* if we know where it came from.[2] As explained in Chapter 3, the identification of an unknown bit of evidence ordinarily depends on a comparison with a known, or standard, bit of similar material. Thus, a fingerprint is identified if we know that it came from the suspect because it matches (at several major, easily recognized points) a fingerprint taken directly from the suspect's hand. The fragment of broken glass is identified if we know that the broken headlight on the suspect's vehicle is made of glass that is essentially the same in color, density, and refractive index. A cloth fiber is identified when we know that it came from the victim's slacks.

• A piece of evidence is *rationalized* if we know how it is related to the crime. This is often the most difficult question to answer, because the range of answers is nearly infinite and there is no simple, logical way to arrive at an answer in every instance. The fingerprint might be rationalized most easily; it is related to the crime because the perpetrator presumably touched the object on which the fingerprint was found (for example, a cash register key) during the course of the criminal event. The fragment of broken glass might be rationalized if we know that the headlight was broken during a collision between the suspect's vehicle and the victim's body and if we found the glass fragment embedded in the victim's clothing. The cloth fiber might be rationalized if we understand that during the course of a rape the fiber was transferred from the victim's slacks to the suspect's clothing, where we later found it. These rationalizations, however, are relatively easy ones. Sometimes a piece of evidence, even when it has been both characterized and identified, utterly defies rational explanation. It is important to understand that rationalizing a piece of evidence does not mean making a wild guess or a flimsy, speculative explanation. It means reaching a rational conclusion, fully supported by other related evidence (including testimonial evidence), that can be successfully presented and defended in court.

It is not at all unusual for the answers to these three questions to produce contra-evidence or nonevidence, instead of the evidence that the investigator is seeking. For example, the fingerprint found on the cash register key might turn out to be identified as *not* belonging to the suspect if it does not match any of the suspect's known fingerprints. In that case, either the fingerprint has been improperly rationalized (perhaps it came not from the perpetrator of the crime, but from someone else who touched the key at another time) or the wrong person is suspected. In either case, it

ANSWERS TO STUDY CLUES
1. True    2. b, e, and f    3. False    4. c
5. False    6. e    7. a    8. False

is contra-evidence for demonstrating the guilt of the suspect. Similarly, the cloth fiber might prove to be characterized and identified as having come from the suspect's shirt. In this case, since it was found on the suspect's trousers, it is worthless as evidence: it demonstrates neither the guilt nor the innocence of the suspect.

For some kinds of evidence, a complete characterization is impossible or unnecessary, provided that the evidence can be successfully identified and rationalized. For example, soil debris might be found clinging to a suspect's shoes. It does not make the slightest difference whether the soil is chemically analyzed if it can be shown that the soil is identical to the soil in the garden below the window where the burglar entered the building. In fact, a chemical analysis might be relatively worthless, because many different soils are chemically similar but very different in their mechanical or physical structure. (Here you can see how asking the wrong question would produce the wrong answer. Suppose that the investigator asks the laboratory for a chemical analysis of the two samples of soil—one taken from the suspect's shoes and the other taken from the garden. In performing the analysis, just as the investigator requested, the laboratory might destroy the two samples. The investigator will receive a chemical analysis of the two samples, but there will be no way of knowing whether they both came from the same place!)[3]

### THE ROLE OF THE CRIMINALIST

Developing physical evidence requires the services of many different kinds of technical experts. The term *criminalist* applies generally to all of them, whether they perform their duties within a criminalistics laboratory or in some other setting.[4]

Like investigators, criminalists can be organized within a law enforcement agency in several different ways. The complexity and sophistication of the administrative arrangement often increase with the size of the agency. In smaller agencies, all the technical support personnel are likely to work in a single, centralized crime lab. Larger agencies are more likely to have a separate section or unit devoted specifically to fingerprint examination and identification, firearms examination, analysis of physical evidence, and so forth. One especially important group of criminalists usually is found outside of and completely separate from the law enforcement agency: the medical examiners.

### MEDICAL EXAMINERS, AND CORONERS

Most states require every county to have a designated official who serves as the coroner. The coroner's specific responsibility is to determine, for legal purposes, the time, manner, and cause of every death.

The great majority of deaths are either natural or accidental and occur to persons under the care of a physician. In those cases, the physician informs the coroner of the death and certifies that the death took place at a certain time, that the death was natural, and that the death was caused either by a naturally arising medical problem or by an accidental injury. Unless there is some good reason to question the physician's judgment, the coroner ordinarily accepts the physician's death certificate as valid.

However, if a person dies while not under the supervision of a physician or if there is any reason to suspect that the death resulted from a suicide or a homicide, the coroner is required to issue a legal ruling.

A coroner does not have to be a medical doctor. In fact, most coroners are not physicians, but are justices of the peace or magistrates. In a few states, a sheriff, police chief, or some other official may serve as a coroner. Obviously, these officials must rely on medical assistance to arrive at their legal judgments. In many counties, medical advice is provided by whichever local physician happens to be available. Some counties pay a local physician a modest fee to serve part-time as the official medical examiner or pathologist.

Many of the larger metropolitan areas have a full-time coroner–medical examiner who is most often a pathologist, that is, a physician who specializes in studying the nature of diseases and death. A few of these independent coroner's departments have fairly extensive staffs of medical examiners, laboratory technicians, and various specialists.

Whether there is a separate, full-time coroner's department or a county or city official who serves as coroner for specific cases, the coroner's function is not part of the police agency's responsibility. Nevertheless, the information resulting from a competent, thorough medical examination usually has an important bearing on the investigation of a suicide, murder, or other questionable death. We shall discuss some of the techniques and operations of the medical examiner later in this chapter.

### THE CRIMINALISTICS LABORATORY: OUTSIDE RESOURCES

Many small law enforcement agencies do not have the money and personnel to operate a full-time criminalistics laboratory and, in fact, do not need one because they experience few crimes that require a complete investigation. When such a crime does occur, the only alternative may be for the investigator to perform many of the technical procedures that ordinarily would be carried out by a highly trained, experienced specialist. When a major crime occurs, the investigator's ability to analyze and develop physical evidence may be inadequate.

For many years, the Federal Bureau of Investigation has provided criminalistics laboratory services for local police agencies. The FBI's criminalistics services have earned an exceptionally high reputation. Undeniably, the FBI has made many contributions to the advancement of criminalistics science. Furthermore, many skilled technicians from police departments across the nation owe their competence to the training that they have received at the FBI labs and schools. The only drawback to relying on the FBI's technical services is that evidence must be delivered to the labs for analysis. Usually this means that the evidence must be sent through the mails, causing a delay of at least several days. And the FBI's laboratories are sometimes swamped with work, which can mean even longer delays.

Many state police agencies also have established centralized criminalistics laboratories that provide services to local law enforcement agencies. The range of services offered and the quality of those services vary considerably. Again, there are delays in delivering evidence to a centralized laboratory and further delays if the laboratory is overburdened.

Some large metropolitan police departments are willing to provide technical services to other agencies in their area. In addition, regional crime labs have been established on a cooperative basis by groups of small departments that could not afford to maintain separate laboratories on their own. These regional labs, unfortunately, are still rare.[5]

Many investigators have discovered that there are resources within their own community, though outside the usual law enforcement circles, that can provide help with particular investigative problems. Teachers at nearby colleges or universities, local physicians, or private medical laboratories may be able to perform the kinds of analysis that the investigator needs. However, if these outside resources are used, the investigator must be extraordinarily careful to maintain the chain of custody, to prevent any conceivable contamination or loss of evidence, and to ensure that the analysis of evidence is undertaken from a criminalistic point of view. The investigator must bear in mind that the college professor, physician, or medical laboratory technician usually has very little understanding of the legal implications of physical evidence and may not realize the significance of the information needed.

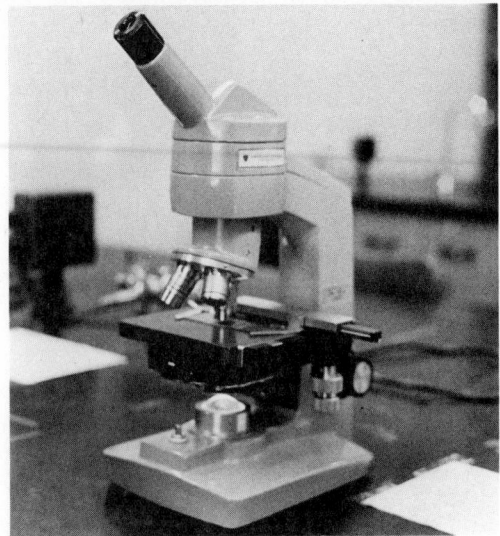

*A simple microscope. Used extensively in the crime lab to examine potential evidence.*

## LABORATORY INSTRUMENTS AND DEVICES

Modern criminalistics laboratories may contain a bewildering array of exotic equipment, much of it fabulously expensive,[6] that seems to provide detailed answers to impossible questions with miraculous speed and accuracy. Sometimes police officials (who are, after all, only human) can be overwhelmed with the glamor of the latest electronic wizardry. The truth is that much of the fancy equipment is very limited in its usefulness for criminalistics tasks. The great majority of crime lab procedures are carried out by routine, mundane, and decidedly unglamorous processes.

Some of the instruments and devices commonly used in criminalistics laboratories deserve description.

*Microscope.* The standard, medium-power microscope is by far the most versatile and most often used crime lab tool. In addition, various kinds of specialized microscopes serve particular purposes. A *comparison microscope* is designed to combine images from two separate slides into a single image; usually the two images are presented side by side, and in some comparison microscopes one image can be superimposed over the other. The device is used to compare many kinds of unknown evidence with known or standard samples. For example, a bullet recovered from a crime scene can be displayed immediately next to a bullet fired from a known weapon; the enlarged images of the two bullets can be placed side by side to compare the fine markings on one with the comparable markings on the other. A *polarizing microscope* is designed to study the way in which light passes through a thin layer of material. Sometimes the degree or direction of polarization reveals the internal structure of the material, which may tell a lot about the material's composition.[7] Usually a piece of evidence can be examined

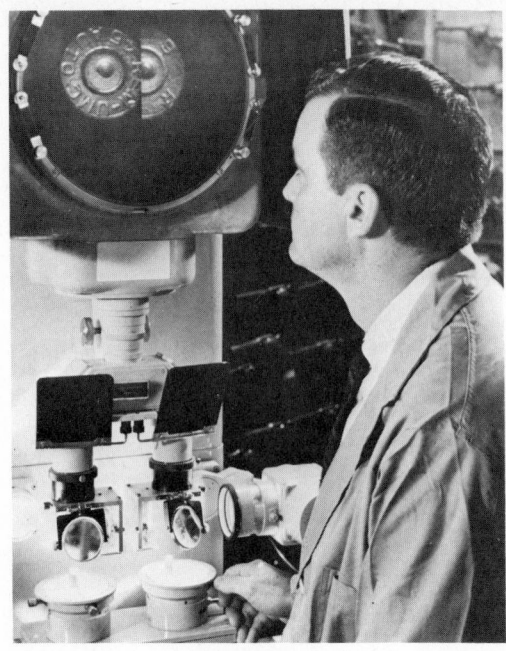

*A comparison microscope. Used to examine an unknown sample alongside a known, or standard, sample. (Photo courtesy the FBI)*

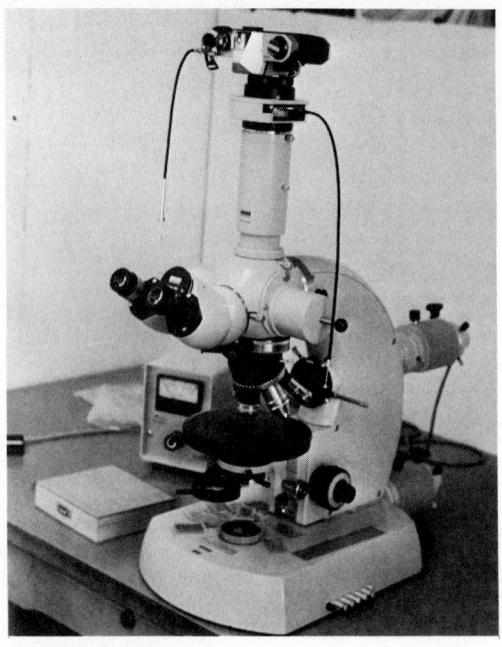

*A polarizing microscope (sometimes called a petrographic microscope). Used to study the crystalline structure of minerals and mineral-like materials.*

*A photograph taken through a comparison microscope. Two different cartridges are being compared; the markings indicate that both were fired from the same weapon. (Photo courtesy of Texas Department of Public Safety)*

*The Investigator and Support Services*

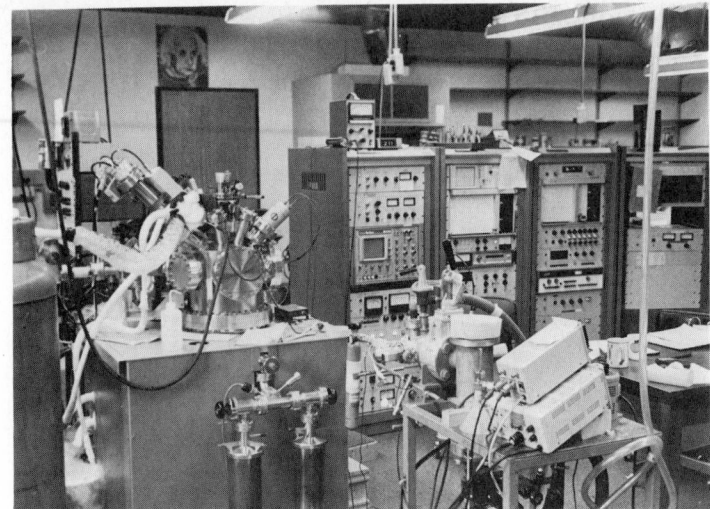

*One of the most elaborate and sophisticated spectrographs. The sample is placed in the chamber at left-center; the results are analyzed by the computers in the background and printed on the recording graphs (the white squares in the computer bank).*

under a microscope without damaging the evidence itself. But occasionally a thin layer or a small piece must be removed from a bulky item of evidence for microscopic examination.

*Spectroscope.* The basic principle of this device is rather simple. The sample material is slowly heated until combustion occurs. The light from the flame is then passed through a prism, which causes the light rays to be distributed along a spectrum. Since each chemical element produces a characteristic spectral pattern, the pattern can be used to detect the chemical components of the unknown material. However, there are three drawbacks. First, the spectral pattern shows that certain elements are present but it does not indicate their relative quantities. Second, the spectral patterns can be overwhelmingly complicated when complex chemical compounds are present, so this kind of analysis is helpful mostly for relatively simple minerals, metals, and inorganic materials. Third, since the sample must be burned, some material is unavoidably destroyed. The last problem is not

too serious, because only a small amount of material is required if the technician is skillful. A *spectrograph* is a related instrument, consisting of a spectroscope and a device to record the spectral pattern for later examination.

*Spectrophotometer.* This device does not require burning or any other destructive process, but it produces results similar to those of a spectroscope. In the spectrophotometer, light (from a lamp) passes through a prism so that only light rays of a single color are focused onto the material to be analyzed. Detectors measure the amount of this monochromatic (single-color) light that is reflected from the material. Each chemical element has a natural, characteristic pattern of light-absorbing and light-reflecting ability; these patterns are known from past experience. Thus, the amount of light of a given color that the material reflects indicates the presence of various elements. The spectrophotometer is sensitive and reliable enough to be used for very complex compounds, such as organic materials, and it is nondestructive. But it, too, in-

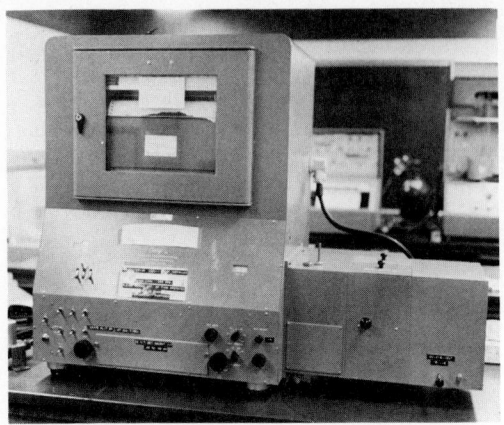

*A spectrophotometer. The sample is placed in the chamber at right; the results are printed on the recording graph at the top of the console.*

dicates only the presence of certain elements and not their relative quantities. The results can be difficult to interpret, so some errors are bound to occur.

*X-ray diffraction analysis (*also called *crystallography).* Quite often the chemical composition of a substance is not as important as its physical characteristics. This is often true for mineral and metallic compounds; several different compounds might have similar chemical compositions, but very different physical properties because of their internal crystalline structure. X-ray diffraction analysis determines the crystalline structure by focusing a stream of x rays into the substance and then photographing the pattern of the x rays that are deflected by the structure. X-ray diffraction analysis ordinarily is nondestructive.[8] This technique, incidentally, was used to discover the structure of DNA, the basic component of genes.

*Electron microscope (EM)* and *scanning electron microscope (SEM).* These devices are among the most exotic and expensive types of equip-ment found in criminalistics laboratories, and their presence is rare because of their cost. Both the EM and the SEM are designed to enlarge images far beyond the capabilities of any visible-light microscope. This is accomplished by aiming a stream of electrons at the sample and detecting the electrons that are reflected from the material. In a sense, the electron beam is used in place of a beam of light. The EM or SEM is intended for studying extremely minute bits of evidence, such as pollen spores or dust particles. It also can be used, under certain circumstances, to study the internal structure of transparent or translucent material, such as organic tissue. Usually, analysis by an electron microscope is nondestructive. However, it is sometimes necessary to cut or shave off a small bit of material from the main body of the evidence.[9]

*Neutron activation analysis.* When it is necessary to know not only the chemical compo-

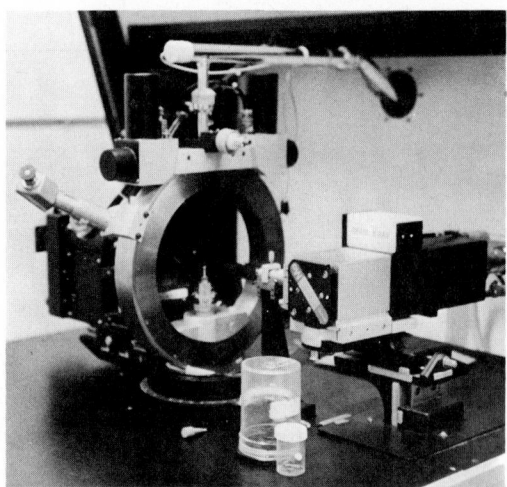

*An x-ray diffraction analyzer. The sample is placed on a holder at the center of the metal ring; x-rays from the device at right bombard the sample and are collected electromagnetically.*

An electron microscope. This very sophisticated model is capable of providing both transmission and scanning types of electron microscopy; the results appear on the small gray screen to the right of the vertical column, and can be recorded on photographic film.

nents of a substance, but also their relative quantities, neutron activation analysis can be used; however, this technique also requires extremely expensive equipment. A stream of neutrons is focused on the substance being studied. The substance absorbs some of the neutrons, changing the chemical elements into slightly radioactive forms. The radiation that emanates from the substance is then analyzed by sensitive detectors. The amounts and types of radiation induced by the neutron stream indicate both the presence and the relative amounts of the various chemical elements in the material. Neutron activation analysis is destructive of the evidence, it requires extremely expensive equipment, and the results, while sufficiently sensitive and accurate for the study of organic materials, are subject to a fairly wide margin of error.[10]

*Chromatography.* This is a general term that applies to several related techniques. The simplest form is *paper chromatography,* which is used only for analyzing liquid samples. A standard reacting agent is placed on a piece of absorbent filter paper and the unknown liquid sample is poured onto the paper. As the sample liquid is absorbed by the paper, it reacts with the standard agent. Different chemical substances within the sample will react at different rates and at varying distances from the point at which the sample was first placed on the paper. The result is a targetlike series of concentric rings, often in a variety of brilliant colors (thus the name *chromatography,* which means "color-writing"). The ring patterns are compared with known standard patterns to determine the chemical make-up of the sample.

Paper chromatography is a relatively simple technique that requires no special instruments or equipment. However, it works only if the investigator has some idea of the type of substance that the sample contains, so that the proper reacting agents can be used. Paper chromatography is sometimes used for quick field tests of suspected narcotics and poisons. Although the evidence is destroyed by the test procedure, only a minute sample is required.[11]

*Gas chromatography* is a much more sophisticated and complex procedure, requiring specialized equipment. In *gas-solid chromatography* (GSC), the sample material is placed in the instrument and heated to the point of combustion. The combustion gases are mixed with a neutral "carrier" gas and then carried into a column packed with a solid reacting agent. As in paper chromatography, the sample in the GSC reacts to the solid agent at different rates according to the chemical components of the sample. These reactions are identified by detectors and recorded on a graph. *Gas-liquid chromatography* (GLC) works the same way as GSC, the only difference being that the reaction column contains a liquid agent instead of a solid agent. Regardless of which type is used, the gas chro-

*A gas chromatograph. The sample is analyzed inside the console at left; the results are printed on the recording graph at right-center.*

matograph can provide not only an analysis of the chemical substances in the sample, but the relative quantities as well. The devices are commonly used to analyze organic materials, including physiological fluids. Although the sample material is destroyed in the testing, only a very small quantity is needed.[12]

*Chemical analysis.* Four of the instruments and techniques that we have just described can determine the chemical components of an unknown substance. Each of the four (spectroscope, spectrophotometer, neutron activation analysis, and chromatography) has certain limitations and certain applications for which it is especially well suited. In addition, the classical techniques of analytical chemistry can be used to determine the presence and relative quantities of chemical elements or compounds in an unknown sample.

Chemical analysis is not a single technique, but an entire body of techniques that have been developed over the past several centuries. In general, these techniques involve exposing the unknown substance to various known substances in an effort to induce a chemical reaction. The nature, rate, or results of that reaction indicate the nature of the unknown substance. When performed with some skill, these analytical techniques can be extremely specific and accurate. However, there are several limitations. First of all, the chemist must have some idea of the probable nature of the unknown substance; otherwise, there is no way to know where to start, and a good deal of time will be wasted on fruitless trial and error. Second, most chemical analysis techniques require a relatively large sample, many times larger than the samples needed for instrumented analysis such as that performed by a spectroscope or a GLC. Finally, almost all chemical analysis procedures are destructive in nature.

*Equipment for conventional chemical analysis. Such equipment is not as expensive as more exotic devices, but the classical techniques are time-consuming and almost always require destruction of the sample.*

Even with these limitations, classical chemical analysis is a standard part of a criminalistics laboratory's services. The fancy instruments are exciting to work with, but almost anything that they can do could be done by more traditional methods; the traditional methods simply take longer and require a larger sample.

## CAPABILITIES OF THE CRIME LAB

### IMPRESSIONS: FRICTION-RIDGE PRINTS

Fingerprints, palm prints, and footprints can be characterized by simple visual examination. Depending on the size of the print or the number of digits represented and the clarity of the print, it is usually possible to tell which hand (or which foot) made the impression. The existence of any deformities (for example, crooked or missing digits) usually can be determined by visual examination, and sometimes it is possible to determine that the person who left the print was wearing jewelry of a particular type or shape. Lip prints are somewhat harder to characterize; usually the characterization is based on the place at which the prints are found (such as the rim of a glass). Human friction-ridge prints are markedly different from those made by most other animals, the only important exceptions being the other primates (apes and chimpanzees); so unless there is some reason to believe otherwise, humanlike prints are assumed to have human origins.

Visual examination of footprints and hand prints may suggest the physiology of the person who left the impression. Although there are no direct correlations between hand or foot size and overall body structure, the range of variations is reasonably limited. Thus, for example, a small hand print would suggest a woman or child, whereas a large hand print would suggest a large man.

Identification of friction-ridge prints depends almost exclusively on microscopic examination, using either a medium-power standard microscope or a comparison microscope. Prints can be identified by direct comparison if a known standard is available. Otherwise, little can be done with footprints, lip prints, and palm prints. Fingerprints can be classified according to any of various schemes that depend on the presence and location of certain recognizable patterns of the ridges. The classification then can be compared with a large volume of other classified prints in either a manual or a computerized file. Fingerprint classification and file searches will be discussed in greater detail in Chapter 11.

Before friction-ridge prints can be examined, first they must be found. Sometimes this requires specialized laboratory procedures. Any object on which prints might be found should be delivered to the laboratory for examination. Most latent prints are developed and lifted by the methods described in Chapter 5. However, latent prints on absorbent surfaces, such as paper, cloth, or skin, require a different technique. The basic technique is to apply some chemical substance that will react with the organic chemicals in the oily secretions, perspiration, and other residues that form the impression. Several different chemicals can be used for this purpose, and they can be applied in various ways, depending mostly on the nature of the surface on which latent prints are suspected.[13]

## IMPRESSIONS: TIRE AND SHOE PRINTS

These large-scale impressions usually can be characterized and identified by simple visual examination and comparison with known standards. Visual examination usually is sufficient to detect irregularities, deformities, and other unusual characteristics in a tread pattern that will be helpful in making an identification based on comparison. Enlarged photographs are often useful in performing such examinations and comparisons.

One specialized laboratory test may be useful, but it requires examination of the impression at the crime scene by a competent technician. The test involves a device known as a *penetrometer,* which measures the degree to which the soil was compacted by the weight of the object or person that caused the impression. This information suggests the size of the person or vehicle involved. Penetrometer testing must be performed before any attempt is made to take a plaster cast of the impression. Unfortunately, the use of the penetrometer may disturb the impression, destroying the possibility of making a useful casting.

## IMPRESSIONS: TOOL MARKS

Impressions left by common tools (such as blunt instruments, knives, burglary tools, and so forth) usually are characterized and identified by examination under either a medium-power standard microscrope or a comparison microscope. Occasionally a high-power microscope may be used to detect minute irregularities in a tool impression. Many technicians like to use a microscope with an adjustable compound lens (often called a "zoom lens") that enables them to go from low to high power without moving the sample.

Markings on firearms bullets and cartridges or shells are also considered to be tool marks. Usually the type of weapon involved and its caliber can be determined by simple visual examination of the bullet or cartridge, since only certain kinds of ammunition fit certain kinds of firearms. Microscopic examination of the bullet or cartridge is necessary to reveal the fine markings that are produced in the firing chamber and in the rifle barrel when the weapon is fired. Microscopic examination also may reveal impressions on the nose of the bullet that can be compared with the surfaces through which the bullet passed; for example, it is often the case that a bullet will retain an impression of the thread pattern of the clothing worn by the person who was shot. This information might be useful if the bullet passed completely through the victim's body and lodged in a wall or fell to the floor or if it passed through more than one body.

The central question in any firearms examination is this: What weapon fired this bullet? Although visual and microscopic examination may be used to characterize the bullet or cartridge (that is, to determine the type of weapon involved), no identification is possible unless the weapon itself is recovered. The simplest way to identify a sample bullet with a known bullet is to test-fire the weapon, recover the test bullet intact, and compare it with the sample bullet. However, it must be realized that the tool marks left by a given weapon can change over a period of time. If the weapon is damaged (either accidentally or deliberately), repaired, exposed to severe weathering or rusting, or otherwise altered significantly, identification may be impossible. There are now many types of handguns that are designed with interchangeable barrels, further confusing the prospects of identifying a bullet with the weapon from which it was fired.[11]

One potential type of information should not be overlooked. Automatic weapons have some sort of ejection mechanism to remove a spent cartridge from the firing chamber before the next cartridge is moved into place.

*The availability of interchangeable barrels for some handguns reduces the possibility of determining that a particular weapon fired a bullet recovered from the crime scene.*

Each type of weapon has its own characteristic ejection mechanism. If spent cartridges are found at the crime scene, and if the locations at which they are found have been carefully recorded, it may be possible to reconstruct the circumstances of the crime by test-firing the recovered weapon and carefully studying the ejection pattern. Figure 10.1 shows how this can be done.

## IMPRESSIONS: FABRIC AND OTHER SUPERFICIAL MARKS

These miscellaneous impressions usually are characterized and identified by visual and/or microscopic examination and by comparison with a known standard. For example, a fabric impression can be studied to determine the type of fabric that caused the impression (size

FIGURE 10.1
RECONSTRUCTING A CRIME BY STUDYING
EJECTION PATTERN OF SUSPECT'S WEAPON

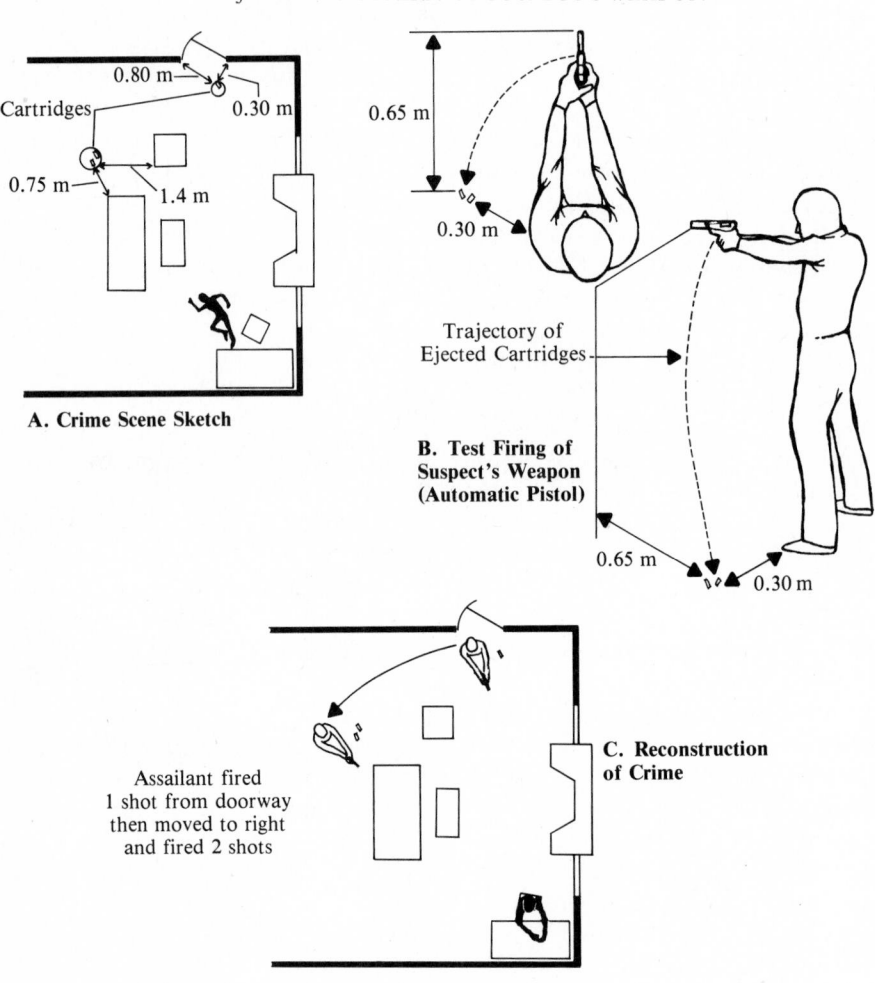

0.80 m
Cartridges
0.30 m
0.75 m
1.4 m

**A. Crime Scene Sketch**

0.65 m
0.30 m

Trajectory of
Ejected Cartridges

**B. Test Firing of
Suspect's Weapon
(Automatic Pistol)**

0.65 m
0.30 m

Assailant fired
1 shot from doorway
then moved to right
and fired 2 shots

**C. Reconstruction
of Crime**

of the individual threads; closeness and pattern of the weave), the presence of any unique decorative stitches or embroidery, and the type of garment that probably was involved. By far the most valuable result of any examination of miscellaneous impression evidence is comparison with a known standard; if there is no known standard, identification is very unlikely.

Teeth marks are exceptionally useful because of the uniqueness of each person's dentition. Much can be learned by a close examination of teeth marks: the person's jaw size, which suggests the person's overall physiology; the general state of health of the teeth, including the presence of dental fillings, bridgework, or other evidence of professional care; and, if the teeth marks are found on food items, something about the person's eating habits. It is possible to make an accurate identification of the person who left teeth marks at a crime scene by comparing the impressions with a dentist's records. Of course, this can be done only if the investigator has some idea of who the person might be; otherwise, it would be necessary to compare the impressions with every record in the files of every dentist within a given area. However, if the impression reveals extensive dental treatment—such as large partial dentures, orthodontic appliances, and so on—it might be helpful to have the impression studied by a group of dentists who are active in professional organizations or who teach in a local dental school. Since each dentist develops a personal style of work, it is sometimes possible for one dentist to recognize another's work.

## CLOTHING, CLOTH, AND LOOSE FIBERS

Recognizable garments can be characterized and sometimes identified by simple visual ex-

*Many commercial laundries use visible markings, such as the customer's name, instead of the invisible markings that can be seen only under ultraviolet light.*

amination. Identification is difficult because any given garment is unique; even though most garments are manufactured in very large quantities, there is not really such a thing as a standard sample. However, it is sometimes possible to identify a garment in other ways. For instance, a garment might be identified by comparing it with a photograph of the suspect in which the suspect is wearing the same garment. The garment might bear a label or some other visible, unique marking. Furthermore, a garment can be compared with a witness's description of it. Although this may not lead to a positive identification, it can lead to excluding an item as evidence; for example, if the witness said that the suspect wore a red shirt, a green shirt found in the suspect's closet obviously is not the one being sought.

Any garment that might have evidential value should be examined under a microscope to detect trace evidence such as debris or physiological stains. Garments also should be examined under an ultraviolet light, especially if the garment is of a type that normally must be dry-cleaned. Many laundry and dry cleaning establishments mark garments with invisible numbers or symbols that can be seen only under ultraviolet light. The purpose, of course, is to ensure that the garment is returned to its rightful owner. Each establishment has its own unique marking system, and many establishments keep a record of which markings correspond to what customer. Some communities have ordinances requiring laundries to use such marking systems and to provide the records to the police on request. However, this practice is not as common now as it once was, partly because the prevalence of synthetic fabrics (which are easily cleaned at home) has substantially reduced the public's dependence on commercial laundries.

The size and overall characteristics of a garment may suggest a great deal about a suspect. Even a relatively unimportant garment, such as a glove or sock, suggests the person's sex and physical size, although these inferences can be misleading and should not be considered anything more than speculation. A garment also might tell something about a person's lifestyle and personal habits.

A torn piece of cloth can be characterized by visual or microscopic examination to determine the thread pattern, type of fabric, and kind of garment or object from which the cloth most likely came. Torn cloth should be inspected under ultraviolet light in case a portion of a laundry mark is present, although that is rather unlikely. Identification of a torn piece of cloth usually is based on a comparison by visual or microscopic examination; sometimes a jigsaw fit can be found.

Loose fibers usually can be characterized by microscopic examination. Most fibers are readily distinguishable under a low- or medium-power microscope; an experienced examiner should have little trouble in recognizing fibers from different kinds of plants, synthetic fibers, or almost any sort of spun thread. Standard reference works are available to assist in the recognition of the fiber type. The color of the fiber also can be determined with little difficulty, sometimes by simple visual examination.

It may be possible to determine under microscopic examination whether a fiber was cut, torn, or pulled from a larger body of cloth. This information may help in rationalizing the fiber as evidence and even in understanding something about the criminal event. An indication of physical damage also may be useful in identifying the fiber if a known piece of cloth with corresponding damage is found.

Most of the fibers found at a crime scene are likely to be white cotton or a blend of cotton and a common synthetic fiber. These materials are so common that such fibers are usually useless as evidence.[15]

## WEAPONS, TOOLS, AND OTHER GROSS EVIDENCE

Most items of substantial size are readily characterized by visual examination and are just as readily identified by direct comparison with a known standard or with a witness's description. All items that might have value as evidence should be examined microscopically for the presence of debris, latent prints, or other useful traces. Otherwise, usually there is very little that needs to be done with such items in the laboratory. Firearms, of course, may be subject to examination in order to determine the identity of bullets or cartridges found at the crime scene; likewise, tools may be needed for comparison with tool mark impressions.

A criminalistics laboratory often proves its worth in the study of debris. No criminal can avoid leaving behind trace debris at the scene of a crime and taking along debris from the crime scene. In fact, criminals usually are unaware of the presence and significance of debris evidence. Unfortunately, too many crime investigators also seem to be unaware of the need to collect debris evidence and have it examined in the laboratory.

**Soil.** Visual examination of soil debris is sufficient to determine the sample's color, luster, and general type. Fairly large soil samples can be examined visually to determine the cleavage or fracture of solid particles (that is, the way the particles naturally divide when struck). Soil debris can be examined under a microscope to determine the crystal form, particle size, presence of fossil or vegetable matter, and presence of coal or other distinctive particles. All of these factors are useful

in characterizing the sample and identifying it on the basis of a known standard.

The simplest and, according to some authorities, the most useful type of instrumented examination is a density analysis.[16] The sample is carefully pulverized and then placed in a test tube or column containing a series of liquids of different densities. The particles of different densities will sort themselves out, floating on top of the various liquids, as illustrated in Figure 10.2. The relative quantity of particles at each level is likely to be characteristic of a particular soil. Experience with thousands of soil samples has shown that particle densities at a particular location are virtually unique; variations can be found only a few centimeters apart. Thus, if two soil samples are found to have nearly the same density distributions, it is likely that the samples are identical (came from the same place). If the samples do not have the same distributions, it is almost certain that they

FIGURE 10.2
SOIL DENSITY ANALYSIS

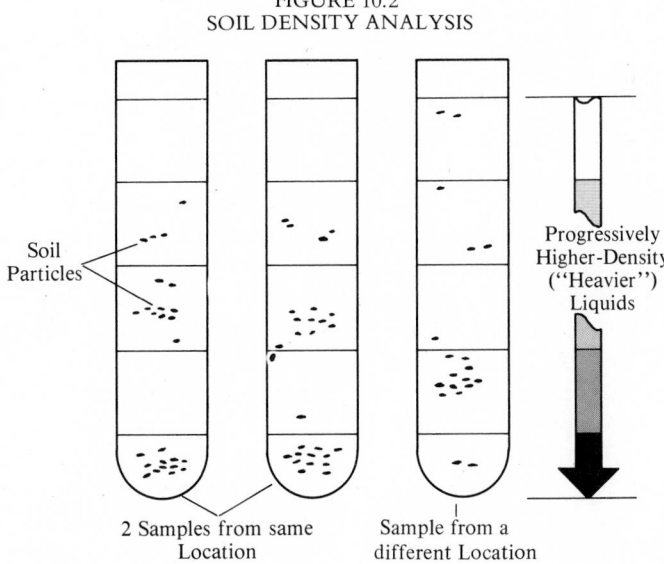

Soil Particles

Progressively Higher-Density ("Heavier") Liquids

2 Samples from same Location

Sample from a different Location

came from two different places. Although density analysis does not provide a complete characterization of a soil sample, sometimes it is enough to provide an identification.[17]

There are, of course, more elaborate ways to characterize and identify soils. Various instruments can be employed to analyze a soil's magnetic properties, hardness, solubility in water and various other liquids, fluorescence (either natural or induced by the introduction of chemical agents), crystal structure, and the presence of minute levels of radioactivity. X-ray diffraction analysis is often used to determine crystal structure, because that is more uniquely characteristic of different soils than is chemical composition. Yet another characterizing technique is *differential thermal analysis:* the sample is slowly heated and the resulting combustion reactions are studied. Of course, a sample can be chemically analyzed by either classical analytic techniques or one of the various analytical instruments, such as the gas chromatograph; however, chemical analysis is rarely necessary or helpful.[18]

**Vegetable (organic) matter.** Identification, and sometimes characterization, of vegetable matter such as seeds, leaves and pollen may be possible on the basis of visual or microscopic examination, especially if the sample is relatively whole and undamaged. Fragmentary or badly damaged vegetable matter is more difficult to characterize and identify, but good results may be obtained with a medium- or high-power microscope capable of revealing the internal structure of the material. Gas chromatography, neutron activation analysis, or spectrophotometric analysis can be used to characterize the sample by determining its component substances. The classical techniques of chemical analysis ordinarily would not help in studying organic materials except to detect minute amounts of anomalous substances, such as poisons.

**Chemical traces.** When very small quantities of unknown chemical substances such as liquids or stains are found, they should be examined first under a microscope for the presence of characteristic crystals or other physical structures. Paper tests, such as phenolphthalein tests to detect and differentiate between acids and bases, and paper chromatography may be used if the sample is large enough and if its general nature is known. Since these tests require the sample to be absorbed into the paper, there is the danger of losing the sample without gaining much information.

All sorts of instrumented tests can characterize and identify chemical traces. X-ray diffraction analysis, neutron activation analysis, spectroscopic and spectrophotometric examination, and gas chromatography all can be used. If all else fails or if none of these instruments are available, classical techniques can be attempted.

**Glass and plastic fragments.** Most of the same tests used for soil debris are applicable to glass and hard plastic fragments. In addition, this kind of debris can be examined visually or microscopically to determine the color, the presence of a pattern molded into the surface, and similar characteristics of the manufacturer's design.

Three particular characteristics deserve special study: the fracture pattern, stress pattern, and refractive index.[19] The fracture pattern for a fairly large pane or sheet of glass can be determined by visual examination. As shown in Figure 10.3, when a projectile strikes a sheet of glass, the impact fracture (or hole) produced is larger on the side *opposite* from the point of impact. The size and shape of a hole are determined by the nature of the projectile, the force of the impact, and the type of glass involved. If two of these three factors are known (for example, the na-

FIGURE 10.3
EXIT SIDE OF IMPACT HOLE IN GLASS
LARGER THAN ENTRANCE SIDE

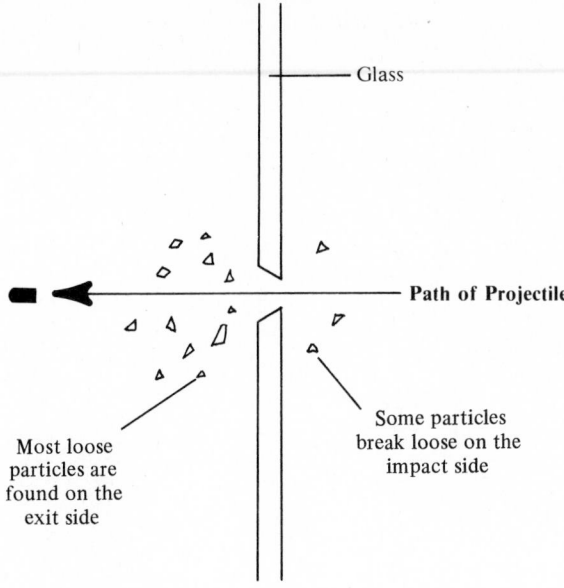

ture of the projectile and the impact force), it may be possible to calculate the third factor within a reasonable margin of error.

Usually when glass is struck with substantial force, the fracture extends from the point of impact in a radiating, weblike pattern. If a second impact occurs, the radiating lines from the second point of impact will extend only as far as the fracture lines from the first impact, as shown in Figure 10.4. Therefore, one can determine the sequence of several successive impacts by noticing which fracture lines are intercepted by previous lines.[20]

Most hard plastics behave in much the same way as glass, and, indeed, most varieties of glass contain plastic components or layers (such as the safety glass used in automobiles). However, some hard plastics will shatter or break along a straight line when struck with sufficient force, instead of fracturing in the way that glass does. These peculiarities can be used to characterize and identify the plastic material.

Stress patterns can be examined under a microscope, perhaps using a polarizing filter to make the lines clearer. As shown in Figure 10.5, around the point at which glass is struck there usually is a series of ringlike markings. These markings are caused by the tendency of the glass's crystal structure to bend, thus absorbing the force of the blow. Different varieties of glass and plastic exhibit different stress patterns. Also, if the characteristics of the glass are known or can be determined, sometimes it is possible to estimate the force of the impact that produced the stress pattern.

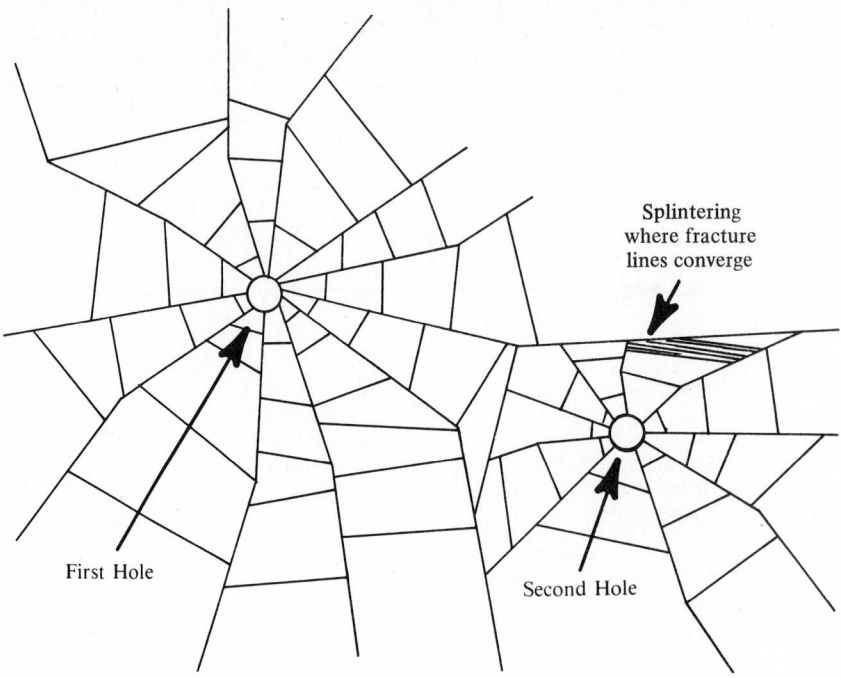

Splintering
where fracture
lines converge

First Hole

Second Hole

FIGURE 10.5
STRESS MARKS IN GLASS

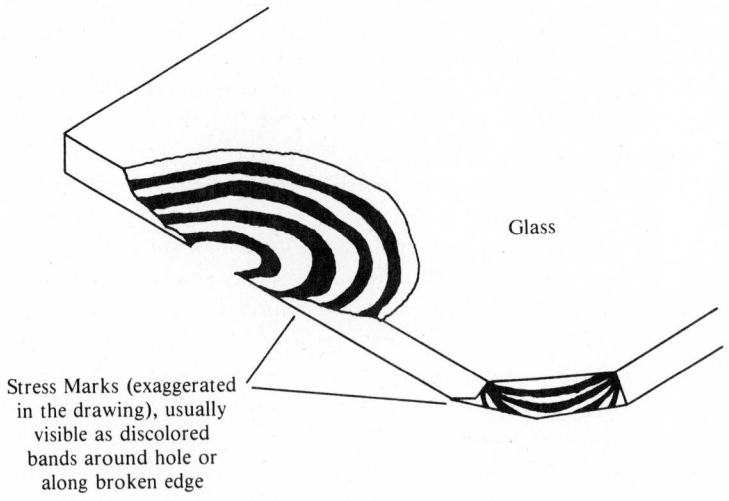

Glass

Stress Marks (exaggerated
in the drawing), usually
visible as discolored
bands around hole or
along broken edge

The refractive index is another important characteristic of glass and most hard plastics; it is a measurement of the material's tendency to cause light rays passing through the material to bend. Although there are special instruments to measure the refractive index in a standardized way, it is easy to see the approximate effect. Simply place a piece of glass a few centimeters in front of a sheet of graph paper, aim a strong flashlight through the glass at a 45-degree angle, and mark on the paper the approximate edges of the beam of light. Now do the same thing with a second sample of glass (preferably one from an entirely different source). You probably will find that the edges of the flashlight beam strike a different place on the graph paper because of the difference in the refractive abilities of the two types of glass. Naturally, the instruments used to measure refractive index are a great deal more precise and reliable than this simple demonstration.[21]

**Paint, plaster, enamel chips, and similar coatings.** The visible color of a paint or enamel chip is easily determined by comparing the sample with a standard color chart. A spectrophotometer can determine the composition of the pigment. The sample also may be analyzed in a gas chromatograph to ascertain its chemical composition. Since different manufacturers use particular formulas to make their paints and since many of these formulas are available in standard reference works, it may be possible to determine not only what type of paint it is, but also who made it, where it was sold, and how it is usually used.

Chips that contain several layers of paint or other material are especially useful. It is a simple matter to identify an unknown sample by comparing the colors and the sequence of layers with a known standard. The chances that samples from two different sources would have exactly the same colors in exactly the same sequence are very slight. However, care must be exercised when comparing chips of automobile enamel, since there may be several thousand vehicles with the same layers of metal sealant, rust inhibitor, undercoating, and final coating.

**Hair and skin particles.** Hair can be characterized as either human or animal. Sometimes it is possible to determine what kind of animal a hair came from, for different species of animals have fairly characteristic hair structures. If a hair is human, it is often possible to determine whether it came from a person's head or from another part of the body. The color of a hair can be compared with standard references or with a known sample; however, hairs from different parts of the same body vary quite a bit in color, so hair cannot be identified solely on the basis of color. Fortunately, it may be possible to identify an unknown hair sample by comparing its structure with a known sample. All this information can be obtained by examining the hair under a medium-power microscope. When the identification of a hair sample is of the utmost importance, a scanning electron microscope might be selected to study its internal structure and physical properties in great detail.

Hair often contains various sorts of debris, such as globules of grease, cosmetics, oily secretions from the body, and dust. This debris can be removed from the hair (often while the hair is being examined under a microscope) and studied separately. If there is a possibility that the hair came from a person who was poisoned, either accidentally or otherwise, the sample should be subjected to neutron activation analysis or gas chromatographic analysis, either of which will detect the presence of the metallic compounds that are present in almost all powerful poisons. Finally, hair often contains blood components. Thus the hair sample can be treated as if it were a blood sample, resulting in a typing according to the ABO or other classification system.[22]

**Physiological fluids.** There is some argument among criminalists over physiological fluids: should they be studied in the crime lab or should they be referred to a medical laboratory for analysis? The advantage to the latter procedure, of course, is that a medical laboratory is more accustomed, and should be better equipped, to deal with physiological materials. The main disadvantage is that the medical lab may be unaware of the legal implications of handling evidence—maintaining the chain of custody and so forth. While we shall not take sides in the argument, we would point out that it may be easier to coach medical technicians on the proper way to safeguard evidence than it would be to train crime lab technicians in the rather elaborate techniques of medical pathology. In any case, what really matters is the results, regardless of who produces them.

Blood is the most common and usually the most important kind of physiological fluid serving as evidence of a crime. At the crime scene a careful record should be made of the distribution of blood—drops, spatters, streaks, or pools—in relation to the site and the victim. Much is known about the physical behavior of blood, and a study of the distribution pattern can reveal important information about the circumstances of the crime.[23]

A blood sample can be tested by simple chemical means to determine whether the blood is human or animal. Microscopic examination of the sample may determine the presence of unusual cell structures, which may identify the source of the blood by comparison with a known sample.

Invariably, whenever blood is present as evidence, someone wants to know the blood type. This information may or may not prove useful, but it would be hard to imagine any laboratory routine that did not include blood typing at some point.[24] Blood typing, or classification, depends on the fact that every individual's blood contains various genetic components that help the body to recognize, and thus to attack or repel, foreign organisms. An Austrian physician working in the United States, Karl Landsteiner, discovered in about 1900 that blood from different people reacted in different ways to two particular types of foreign organisms. He deduced that human blood might contain either of two blood components, or *factors* (Type A and Type B), or both of them (Type AB), or neither of them (Type O). Thus, there were four basic types of blood. Landsteiner's discovery had great significance for the practice of medicine, since it explained why transfusions of blood were sometimes successful and sometimes disastrous. Blood could not be transfused from a donor whose blood type did not match the receiver's without great danger to the receiver *unless* the donor had type O blood, which would not cause the unwanted reaction.

Scientists soon learned that these blood types were transmitted genetically, from parents to offspring, according to the laws of inheritance worked out by Gregor Mendel in the late nineteenth century. In short, one's blood type depends, in a complex way, on the blood types of one's parents. This fact has helped to settle innumerable controversies and lawsuits concerning parentage.

From the crime investigator's point of view, the ABO blood classification system is sometimes, but not always, sufficient. For example, if blood is found at the crime scene and presumed to be from a cut on the suspect's hand, simple laboratory procedures may determine that it is Type A blood. If the suspect has Type B blood, it is very likely that the wrong person is suspected. On the other hand, if the suspect does have Type A blood, the identification is far from complete since millions of other human beings also have Type A blood. (In fact, Type O is the most common of the four blood types; Type A is relatively common, Type B fairly uncommon, and Type AB rather rare.)

The ABO system, however, is not the only means of typing blood. Landsteiner and a number of other researchers soon discovered other blood factors that could be used to classify human blood. The most important of these is the so-called Rh factor. This factor is either present or absent in any given individual, although it is present in the great majority of humans (and in Rhesus monkeys, in which it was first found). There are also M and N factors, at least one of which must be present, but either of which can be present in either of two forms. Thus, an individual might have Type M, Type n, Type MN, Type Mn, Type mN, and so on.

Blood typing is simple in theory but tedious in practice, because it involves placing a small amount of the unknown sample in solution with known standards and then waiting to see whether certain reactions take place. Classification by the ABO system is done routinely, and an Rh classification can be performed with relatively little fuss. However, a more extensive typing—for example, one using the MN system—would be justified only if the identification of the blood source is absolutely vital and if there is little or no other evidence on which an identification can be based.[25]

Besides typing and the sorts of analysis described above, the only other test that might be performed on a blood sample is a chemical analysis with, typically, a gas chromatograph. This might be done if there is reason to suspect the presence of anomalous substances, such as the metallic compounds characteristic of poisons.

Semen is the second most important type of physiological fluid that may have evidential value. Semen can be characterized by a simple chemical test involving the application of a small amount of acid phosphatase, which causes the semen to react in a particular, readily identifiable way. The semen sample also may be examined under a medium-power microscope to detect any sperm that are present. The proportion of live (still moving) sperm to dead sperm cells in a semen sample can be taken as a rough indication of the length of time since the semen was ejaculated, although the life span of the sperm can vary considerably according to environmental factors (the surrounding temperature in particular) and individual variations.

Semen and all other types of physiological fluids—in fact, any sort of physiological matter, such as skin cells, hair particles, and so on—can be treated as if they were blood to determine the individual's blood types. However, the absence of particular blood factors does not necessarily mean that these factors are absent in the person's blood. About 80 percent of the human population secrete blood components into all body cells, including body fluids, but the remaining 20 percent do not. Consequently, fluids or tissues from these "nonsecretors" will yield no information about the person's blood type.

Besides blood and semen, most other physiological fluids can be characterized with reasonable accuracy by a simple test: the fluid (sometimes mixed with a neutral carrier such as water) is sprayed into the flame of a gas burner. Each general type produces an identifiable color of flame and an odor. The test is not absolutely reliable, but when performed by a competent and experienced technician it should be adequate to distinguish between perspiration, urine, mucus, and saliva. If it is essential for an identification to be made on the basis of one of these fluids, the sample can be analyzed by gas chromatography (to detect inorganic chemicals) or by a process called *electrophoresis,* which detects protein components.

**Nonphysiological fluids.** Most nonphysiological fluids, such as oil, grease, and other organic or inorganic compounds, can be treated in the same manner as chemical traces (see above). Poisons or suspected poisons, medicines, and illegal drugs can be characterized and/or identified by paper chromatography, various chemical tests in which the unknown sample is mixed with known reactants, or instrumented analysis (gas chromatography or spectrophotometry).

**Miscellaneous stains.** Most stains are merely dried liquids and may be treated the same way that liquid samples are, except that the stain must be removed from the background surface first; this is commonly done by dissolving the stain in water or alcohol.

Cosmetic stains deserve special attention because of the enormous variety of cosmetics worn by both men and women. There is a good chance that a cosmetic stain can be identified on the basis of comparison with a known standard, such as a sample obtained from the suspect. Cosmetics come in liquid form (usually an aromatic agent combined with various activating ingredients, depending on its nature or purpose, and held together by water, alcohol, or other liquid binder) or powder form (the same aromatic and activating ingredients applied to finely ground minerals, usually magnesium silicate,

commonly known as talc). Sometimes complex organic compounds such as lanolin or chlorophyll are mixed into the cosmetic preparation; other cosmetics, such as deodorants, may contain a variety of metallic compounds such as aluminum chlorohydrate.

Cosmetic stains should first be examined visually. The color, texture, and liquid or powdery nature of the sample should be noted. Beyond that, probably the simplest procedure would be gas chromatography, which should give a detailed analysis of all its components. If a gas chromatograph is not available, the sample might be subjected to standard chemical tests, spectroscopic examination, or spectrophotometric analysis. Neutron activation analysis also can be used, but it is even less likely to be available than gas chromatography.[26]

## DOCUMENTS

Paper documents can be examined visually, with the naked eye or under a low-power microscope, to determine the color, texture, general type, and other characteristics of the paper and the presence of physical damage (cuts, tears, abrasion, burns or singe marks, signs of crumpling, folds, and the like). The sample can be compared with reference samples, which are easily obtained from companies that distribute printing papers and stationery. The better grades of stationery usually contain a watermark lightly embossed into the paper's surface during the manufacturing process; it ordinarily contains the name of the manufacturer and the brand name of the paper style, both of which may be clues to the source of the paper or may allow identification of the sample by comparison with a known standard.

Writing or other marks on a paper document should be examined visually. It is usually easy to determine the kind of writing instrument that made the impression. Pencil marks are recognizable by the color and texture of the markings and by the ease with which they can be removed by a soft eraser. Fountain pens use a liquid ink consisting of carbon or other coloring agents held in a water or oil base; the fluid is absorbed into the paper and resists all efforts at removal. Ballpoint inks, on the other hand, contain coloring agents held in a greasy binder and can be readily removed by scraping with a sharp knife. The inks used in nylon-tip and felt-tip pens usually are watery, like fountain-pen inks.

Typewritten and printed material is distinguished chiefly by the consistent quality of the letter shapes. Typewriters form impressions by impacting the letter shape through a ribbon. A nylon or cotton ribbon is impregnated with a fluid ink, which is absorbed into the paper's surface and cannot be removed easily. An acetate ribbon is backed with a carbon-based coating; this ink can be smeared or scraped off with a sharp knife.

The two most common types of printing are letterpress and offset lithography. Letterpress printing uses a relatively fluid ink that tends to be absorbed into the paper's surface. Offset lithography uses a thick, grease-based ink that sometimes can be scraped off the paper with a sharp knife.

Sometimes it is hard to distinguish a typewritten mark from a printed mark. The simplest method is to look for a badly formed letter, such as a letter that is partly broken or one that is not properly located on the line. If the misshapen or mislocated letter recurs consistently, the document was probably typewritten. However, if the same letter is misshapen or mislocated only once or twice, it is more likely that the document was printed. Unfortunately, this method is not foolproof, since the document could have been typewritten originally and then reproduced by offset lithography.

Besides letterpress and offset lithography, there are any number of other ways to print or reproduce written material: mimeograph, spirit duplicator (such as the popular Ditto machine), hectograph, and a profusion of copying processes. Space does not permit us to discuss each of these reproduction techniques; however, documents that have been produced by any of these techniques should be recognizable to an experienced technician.

Handwritten material often must be examined in an effort to identify the person who wrote the document. The technique is very simple: the questioned or unknown sample must be compared with a known sample, usually obtained from the suspect. However, this technique should not be attempted by amateurs or inexperienced investigators. Handwriting analysis, or graphoanalysis, is a highly refined art that demands talent, experience, and skill. (Graphoanalysis, by the way, should not be confused with "graphology," the pseudoscience that purports to study a person's character or personality by examining handwriting.)

Documents frequently must be examined to determine whether they have been altered or damaged in some way. Whenever any kind of impression is made on paper, the paper's fibers are permanently rearranged. Therefore, it is usually possible to detect the original impression even if the surface markings have been erased or covered over, provided that the paper itself has not been significantly damaged, for example, by dissolving the written image in a liquid. If the paper is held under an ultraviolet light, the erased impression may become visible. If the original markings have been covered over with a different type of ink, an infrared lamp may be used. Its light will be reflected to different degrees by the different kinds of ink. The evidence of the altered document may be recorded by photographing the document on special film that is sensitive either to ultraviolet or to infrared radiation.

## MEDICAL EXAMINATION OF VICTIMS OF VIOLENCE

As we said earlier, state laws provide for someone to serve as the coroner and to make legal judgments in all cases of questionable deaths. In many counties, the coroner is a magistrate or a law enforcment official who relies on whatever medical assistance is available in order to make these judgments; other counties have a part-time pathologist or medical examiner, usually a physician who has a private practice in the community. Most of the larger metropolitan areas have a full-time coroner who usually is a physician trained in pathology and who may be assisted by a staff of medical examiners (physicians) and laboratory personnel.

The coroner's department can be an immensely valuable resource to a law enforcement agency in the investigation of all crimes of violence, not just homicides. If there is no full-time medical examiner, the police should assume the responsibility for finding or developing a suitable alternative. A part-time county pathologist may be willing to serve on a voluntary or a token-fee basis; if not, another physician in the community may be capable of acting in this capacity. If the community has a public hospital, the physician in charge of the emergency room would be a good choice to assist the police with medical examinations. Most victims of violent crimes are likely to be treated in the emergency room, so it should be relatively easy to acquaint the emergency room staff with the procedures necessary to acquire and preserve evidence.

In Chapter 5 we described the basic procedures for treating the victim of a violent crime as a part of the crime scene, in terms of collecting evidence. In Chapter 7 we discussed in more detail the treatment of rape victims. You may wish to review those sections at this point. Briefly, the basic principle is that every effort should be made to recover evidence from the body of the victim. Usually there will be various kinds of debris evidence, some of which may prove to be traces of the perpetrator. In addition, a careful record must be made of all wounds or marks caused by the attack or by a struggle between the attacker and the victim. The physician who examines the victim should be able to determine what kind of weapon caused each wound. Of course, the victim's testimony is the most significant evidence about the criminal event.

Any violent or questionable death of a human being requires the most thorough and competent investigation that a law enforcement agency can provide. The medical examination is an indispensable part of such an investigation. The investigator should have a full understanding of what can be reasonably expected from a medical examination.

From a legal point of view, every human death is regarded as an event that must be satisfactorily explained by some competent authority. Physicians are entrusted with the responsibility of preparing and certifying an explanation of deaths that occur among patients under their immediate care and supervision. However, whenever a physician is unable to explain a person's death, either because the cause of the death is not known with certainty or because the person was not under a physician's care, the responsibility is assumed by the officially designated coroner.

This is true even when there is no direct evidence of violence or foul play.

There are four basic questions that must be answered whenever a person dies: the identity of the dead person, the time of death, the cause of the death, and the manner of the death.

Many people become confused about the latter two terms, but the distinction between them is absolutely vital. The *manner of death* is a specific legal characterization; in most states, there can be only four categories: natural death, accidental death, homicide, or suicide. The *cause of death* is a medical characterization; it is a description of the bodily processes that resulted in the termination of life and the events that precipitated or led to those bodily processes.

There usually is a clear relationship between the manner and the cause of death. If the cause of death is a disease or pathological condition of the body, such as arteriosclerosis leading to a heart attack, the manner of death presumably would be natural. If the cause of death is massive hemorrhaging as a result of injuries received in an automobile collision, ordinarily the manner of death would be accidental.

However, these relationships are not always so simple and clear-cut. For example, the automobile collision might have been caused by deliberate sabotage of one of the vehicles involved in the accident; in this case the manner of death would be homicide. Or if one of the drivers involved in the collision was intoxicated at the time, the laws of some states provide that the death would be considered a homicide.

The very word *homicide* is confusing to many people. The word has a very precise legal meaning: any death that is caused by a person other than the deceased. Not all homicides are unlawful; in most states, homicide is legally justified if it is necessary to defend one's own life or to protect another person from physical harm. Homicide also may be justifiable if it is committed by a law enforcement agent in the course of carrying out official responsibilities and duties.

A homicide is unlawful if it is the result of substantial negligence or reckless behavior (such as driving while intoxicated); such homicides generally are classified as *manslaughter*. Depending on the degree of negligence or recklessness involved, manslaughter may be treated as a serious misdemeanor or as a relatively minor felony.

A homicide committed with malice—with the specific intention of taking a person's life—and with some degree of premeditation or deliberate action or one that is the direct result of some other criminal activity is *murder*. Most states vary the penalty according to the degree of malice or deliberateness, but any form of murder is treated as a felony.

Some of the most perplexing and difficult death investigations are those involving suicide (the taking of one's own life). Many people feel an overwhelming moral repugnance toward the very idea of suicide. Consequently, they are extremely reluctant to accept the possibility that a friend or member of their family could have taken his or her own life. Physicians and others in the medical professions often have strong feelings about suicide. Legal authorities are convinced that a substantial percentage of suicides are improperly reported as either natural or accidental deaths, because physicians either refuse to accept deaths as suicidal or choose to hide the fact deliberately. On the other hand, accidental deaths can be inaccurately reported as suicides because of confusing circumstances surrounding the death. Sometimes an intentional murder is carefully planned to resemble a suicide.

It is virtually impossible for a medical examiner to make a competent judgment about the cause and manner of death without performing an autopsy. Consequently, most states require an autopsy to be performed in every case of violent or questionable death. A coroner may be reluctant to insist on an autopsy if the family of the deceased objects strenuously, especially if the coroner is not a physician. In such cases, the police should be prepared to demand that the legal requirements be satisfied; otherwise, they will be unable to pursue the criminal investigation for which they may be responsible. This kind of controversy is extremely unpleasant and could be politically expensive for a law enforcement agency, but the alternative is to neglect the agency's obligation to the whole community.

An autopsy must be conducted by a physician. It begins with a careful visual examination of the body. The physician notes all wounds, marks, deformities, and other unusual conditions and records their precise location on the body. Measurements are taken of the body's weight and height. The condition of the skin, general muscle tone, coloration, and so forth also are noted. The torso is then opened surgically and the condition of the vital organs is determined. Samples are taken of physiological fluids, tissues from various parts of the body, and contents of the stomach. If any of the vital organs is apparently involved in the cause of death (for example, a suspected heart attack), that organ may be removed for more thorough scrutiny. The cranial cavity also may be opened for examination if the brain or one of the other organs of the head may have been involved.

This exhaustive examination of the body is only the first step in the autopsy. The second step is the laboratory study of the physiological fluids and tissues. The procedures are essentially the same as those that we have already described.

An autopsy is not complete until the medical examiner is prepared to certify an explanation of the manner and cause of death. Occasionally this means that the medical examiner will withhold judgment until the police have reached at least tentative conclusions about the circumstances of the death. If the medical examiner remains unwilling or unable to certify the cause and manner of death, or if the examiner's judgment is questioned by someone who has a legitimate interest in the matter, an *inquest* may be held. The coroner presides over the inquest; there may or may not be a jury, depending on the state's laws and the coroner's preference. All parties who have some knowledge of the circumstances of the death are required to present their evidence or opinions. The coroner or the jury then arrives at a legal decision.

The time of death is often a crucial factor to the crime investigation, and it is one of the factors usually left to the judgment of the medical examiner or coroner. Unfortunately, determining the time of death is neither as easy nor as precise as it appears to be in fiction. Fictional coroners often determine the time of death by the degree of rigor mortis that the corpse displays. It is certainly true that every corpse becomes progressively rigid. However, there is an enormous range of individual variation in the process. It simply is not possible for a medical examiner to make an accurate, reliable determination of the time of death on the basis of rigor mortis. Instead, the time of death is determined by studying the overall circumstances of the death and the medical condition of the corpse.

For example, the contents of the corpse's stomach are often decisive in fixing the time of death. If the time of the person's last meal can be learned, the examiner may be able to judge (within a reasonable margin of error) the length of time between the last meal and the death from the degree to which the contents of the last meal have been digested.

Many other factors can be taken into account in establishing the time of death. Still, unless there is a dependable witness, this determination must be regarded as somewhat speculative and subject to error. The investigator will be lucky if the medial examiner is willing to specify a time within a range of four to eight hours or, if the corpse is discoverred after substantial decomposition has occurred, within a range of several days.[27]

The identification of a dead body is another matter. It is almost always possible to discover the identity of an unknown corpse even if the corpse has been extensively mutilated, dismembered, or decomposed, provided that sufficient investigative effort is expended.

The first step in identifying an unknown body usually is to obtain the corpse's fingerprints. Unless the hands are severely damaged or decomposed, this poses no real problem. The prints are then classified and compared with available known prints, concentrating particularly on the prints of missing persons and of anyone likely to be found in the circumstances or location where the corpse was discovered. Needless to say, the garments worn by the deceased and any jewelry or other personal effects found on or near the body provide important clues to identification.

The medical examiner or a mortician may be able to prepare the corpse for photographing so that the body (especially the face) has a natural appearance. This will make it easier to identify the corpse by comparing this photograph with others of the person.

If these steps fail, identification can be made on the basis of dental records (again, provided that there is some idea of the corpse's identity). In rare cases, it is possible to obtain an identification on the basis of physiological fluid or tissue samples by comparison with known standards. Another possibility, when the corpse is extensively decomposed, is artistic reconstruction of the facial features. In essence, this means making a plaster or papier-mâché model of the corpse's skeleton and then sculpting a presumed likeness over the model in clay, plaster of paris, or some other suitable material. Artistic reconstruction is not something that an amateur should attempt, because it requires the skills and talent of an artist and the scientific knowledge of an anatomist and an anthropologist. The results are unavoidably subject to a large margin of error. Nevertheless, in the absence of any other evidence, artistic reconstruction might provide the only lead toward an identification.

## OTHER LABORATORY SERVICES

The kinds of services that we have described for the criminalistics laboratory and for the medical examiner are adequate for nearly all crime investigations. However, once in a great while an investigation may require other types of highly specialized technical assistance. Few police agencies have the resources to maintain a staff and facilities for these rarely needed skills. However, sometimes a criminalistics technician will acquire expertise in these exotic areas out of personal interest and curiosity. Otherwise, the investigator will have to find someone in the community or in another agency who can provide the desired service.

## VOICE-PRINT ANALYSIS

During the late 1950s and early 1960s, scientists were attempting to discover a way that people could talk to computers. They realized that this involved two distinct processes: first, the computer must be able to recognize and react to the words spoken by different people; second, the computer must be able to convert electrical signals, representing information, into sounds that would be intelligible to people. So far, neither step has been accomplished with more than modest success, although scientists at dozens of research centers are still working on it. Nevertheless, the scientists made one important discovery of interest to crime investigators. They found that human voice patterns could be recorded as tracings on a graph. Furthermore, they found that these tracings were absolutely unique for each individual, regardless of the words that the person spoke. The graph tracing, in short, could serve as a "print" of the voice and, properly analyzed and interpreted, could provide an infallible means of determining whose voice was represented. Experiments further revealed that the voice print remained reliable even if the person attempted to disguise his or her voice or if the voice was altered by illness, stress, or other conditions.

Voice-print analysis, therefore, can be used to identify a person purely on the basis of the sound of the person's voice. The analysis is reliable even when the voice is heard over a telephone or on a tape recording. Evidence based on voice-print analysis has been accepted in court for both criminal and civil trials. The only special requirement (other than having the appropriate equipment and a skilled, experienced analyst) is that there must be a known sample of the person's voice with which to compare the unknown sample.[28]

## RE-CREATION OF LATENT ENGRAVINGS

Serial numbers and other identifying marks are often engraved into metal surfaces such as the engine block in a motor vehicle, a gun barrel, and the chassis of an electrical appliance. Thieves and other criminals remove the engraved markings to reduce the likelihood that the stolen goods can be identified. However, when identifying marks are stamped or engraved into metal, the surface's entire crystalline structure is affected. Usually the criminal succeeds in scratching away only the visible markings on the surface; the effects of the original stamping or engraving process remain as *latent engravings*.

The latent engravings can be reconstructed by various processes in the crime laboratory. The reconstruction process generally involves exposing the metal surface to a mild acid. The acid etches the surface more rapidly where the crystalline structure was disturbed by the original engraving process. Thus, in a matter of seconds, the original markings become visible again. Electrolytic etching works in essentially the same way and accomplishes the same purpose, but employs an electric current passing through the acid solution to speed up the etching.

## ARSON, INCENDIARY, AND EXPLOSIVES EXAMINATION

Many police departments are very reluctant to investigate arson or other crimes involving incendiary (fire-producing) or explosive devices. Even though the fire department naturally has a good deal of interest in these matters, they are crimes and thus are the responsibility of the police as well. Instead of being shunned by both the police and the fire department, the investigation of arson and incendiary or explosive crimes should be an area of mutual support and cooperation.

*Arson and incendiary crimes have become increasingly common in recent years. Police and fire investigators must work together to stop these devastating crimes.*

Arson and bomb experts should be able to determine the nature of the incendiary or explosive material and the method of ignition (the starting of the fire or the setting off of the bomb). The materials involved are highly volatile, which means that they are extremely unstable chemically. The examination of the crime scene and of any physical evidence found at the scene must carried out without delay; otherwise, the evidence may literally evaporate.

Incendiary and explosive devices may have fairly elaborate triggering mechanisms, often depending on timing devices or some sort of remote control. The criminals who specialize in arson and incendiary crimes tend to employ the same type of triggering device repeatedly. Thus, a careful study of the construction of the triggering device may be useful in identifying the perpetrator.[29]

# REFERENCES

1. Richard H. Fox and Carl L. Cunningham, *Crime Scene Search and Physical Evidence Handbook* (Washington, D.C.: U.S. Department of Justice, National Institute of Law Enforcement and Criminal Justice, 1973), p. 1.

2. Fox and Cunningham, pp. 6–8.

3. Paul B. Weston and Kenneth M. Wells, *Elements of Criminal Investigation* (Englewood Cliffs, N.J.: Prentice-Hall, 1971), pp. 73–74.

4. Jay Cameron Hall, *Inside the Crime Lab* (Englewood Cliffs, N.J.: Prentice-Hall, 1974), p. 16; Fox and Cunningham, p. 2.

5. Fox and Cunningham, pp. 174–185, provide a national directory of criminalistics laboratories, most of which are willing to provide services to agencies in nearby communities.

6. Hall, p. 50.

7. Raymond C. Murray and John C. F. Tedrow, *Forensic Geology* (New Brunswick, N.J.: Rutgers University Press, 1975), pp. 39–40.

8. Murray and Tedrow, pp. 140–145.

9. Hall, pp. 60–62; Murray and Tedrow, pp. 41–42, 137–139.

10. Hall, p. 94; Murray and Tedrow, pp. 155–156.

11. Hall, pp. 148–150.

12. Hall, p. 31.

13. Fox and Cunningham, p. 57.

14. Fox and Cunningham, p. 91.

15. Hall, p. 97.

16. Hall, p. 86.

17. Murray and Tedrow, pp. 112–117.

18. Murray and Tedrow, pp. 69–72, 133–136.

19. Hall, pp. 76–82.

20. Fox and Cunningham, p. 152.

21. Murray and Tedrow, p. 84.

22. Fox and Cunningham, p. 75.

23. Fox and Cunningham, p. 63.

24. Fox and Cunningham, pp. 4–5.

25. Fox and Cunningham, pp. 60–62; Hall, pp. 103–105.

26. Murray and Tedrow, p. 92.

27. John J. Horgan, *Criminal Investigation* (New York: McGraw-Hill, 1974), pp. 294–295.

28. Weston and Wells, pp. 77–79.

29. Fox and Cunningham, pp. 132–133.

## REVIEW OF THE EVIDENCE

1. Match each of the following terms with the definition given in this chapter.
   - i. Characterization
   - ii. Identification
   - iii. Rationalization
   - a. the origin of an item of evidence
   - b. the chemical analysis of an item of evidence
   - c. the physical description of the perpetrator
   - d. the nature of an item of evidence
   - e. the investigator's explanation of the suspect's motive for committing the crime
   - f. the legal responsibility for a homicide
   - g. the relationship between the item of evidence and the crime
   - h. whether a homicide is legal or illegal

2. True or false: Only a coroner has the legal authority to sign a death certificate.

3. Many small police agencies rely on the FBI's criminalistics service. The primary disadvantage to this practice is that
   - a. it takes too long.
   - b. the chain of custody is broken.
   - c. it is too expensive.
   - d. only a few standard services are available.
   - e. the evidence is often lost in the mail.

4. What kind of laboratory instrument is used to examine two items of evidence simultaneously?
   - a. electron microscope
   - b. binocular microscope
   - c. polarizing microscope
   - d. comparison microscope
   - e. low-power microscope

5. Which of the following instruments would be most useful in determining the chemical composition of a small amount of evidence that is thought to be organic in nature?
   - a. spectrograph
   - b. x-ray diffraction analyzer
   - c. electron microscope
   - d. neutron activation analyzer
   - e. gas-liquid chromatograph

6. A penetrometer might be used to study
   - a. tire or shoe prints.
   - b. fingerprints.
   - c. soil debris.
   - d. physiological fluids.
   - e. tool marks.

7. True or false: It is always possible to identify a bullet if the weapon is recovered.

8. The value of soil density analysis depends on the fact that
    a. different soils have different chemical compositions.
    b. soils are composed of varying proportions of particles that have different densities.
    c. the analysis can be performed rapidly in the field without special equipment.
    d. soil densities are approximately the same everywhere.
    e. the density of the soil indicates the weight of the object that made the impression.
9. True or false: Classical techniques of chemical analysis always should be used before more elaborate and expensive instrumented analysis is attempted.
10. True or false: When a projectile strikes a sheet of glass, the hole produced is larger on the side opposite from the point of impact.
11. Which of the following statements is true?
    a. Blood typing usually results in a positive identification.
    b. The ABO system is the only reliable means of classifying blood types.
    c. Blood typing is a complex procedure that requires sophisticated equipment because of the many different factors involved.
    d. Blood typing is the only way to distinguish between human and animal blood.
    e. All of the above are true.
    f. None of the above is true.
12. True or false: A coroner is responsible for certifying the cause and manner of death only when there is evidence of violence or foul play.
13. Which of the following statements is true?
    a. The *manner of death* is a legal characterization of a death according to one of four categories.
    b. The time of death often cannot be determined with a high degree of precision.
    c. The *cause of death* is a definition of the bodily processes that resulted in the termination of life.
    d. An autopsy may be conducted only by a physician.
    e. All of the above are true.
    f. None of the above is true.
14. True or false: Once serial numbers or other engraved markings have been removed from a metal surface, it usually is impossible to re-create them.

## TOPICS FOR INVESTIGATION

1. Since many small police agencies cannot afford to hire a staff of crime lab technicians, should investigators learn to perform the laboratory procedures themselves so that they will not have to depend on outside sources for help?
2. Laboratory analysis of evidence often produces contra-evidence or merely results in showing that the evidence is meaningless or useless. What should the investigator do to keep from wasting the laboratory's time and energy on such unproductive work?
3. Should state laws require every county to have a full-time, qualified medical examiner to serve as coroner?

4. If you were responsible for the budget of a police department with twenty-five officers and you had to choose between hiring one more investigator and contributing an equal amount of money to establish a regional crime lab, which would you choose?

5. Aside from the standard, medium-power microscope, which type of crime lab equipment seems to be most valuable?

6. On the chart below, indicate which types of laboratory examination would be appropriate for each type of evidence. Under Instrumented Analysis, indicate what type of instrument or technique should be used: spectroscope, spectrophotometer, x-ray diffraction analyzer, electron microscope, scanning electron microscope, neutron activation analyzer, paper chromatography, gas-solid chromatography, gas-liquid chromatography, chemical analysis techniques, penetrometer, density analysis, differential thermal analysis, or refractive index analysis. You may add other techniques, if necessary.

| TYPE OF EVIDENCE | VISUAL EXAMINATION | MICROSCOPE EXAMINATION | INSTRUMENTED ANALYSIS |
|---|---|---|---|
| Friction-ridge prints | | | |
| Tire and shoe prints | | | |
| Tool marks | | | |
| Fabric, other superficial marks | | | |
| Clothing, cloth, loose fibers | | | |
| Weapons, tools, gross objects | | | |
| Soil debris | | | |
| Vegetable (organic) matter | | | |
| Chemical traces | | | |
| Glass, plastic fragments | | | |
| Paint, plaster, enamel, coatings | | | |
| Hair and skin particles | | | |
| Physiological fluids | | | |
| Nonphysiological fluids | | | |
| Miscellaneous stains | | | |
| Documents | | | |

7. Why is every human death "regarded as an event that must be satisfactorily explained by some competent authority"? Because physicians sometimes make mistakes in certifying natural or accidental deaths and occasionally cover up suicides, should their authority to sign death certificates be transferred to the coroner for all deaths?

8. Since voice prints are as unique as fingerprints and therefore are valuable for purposes of identification, should law enforcement agencies establish voice-print files on a routine basis?

9. Why are many police departments reluctant to investigate arson? Should this responsibility be held primarily by the police or by the fire department?

10. In your opinion, what is the single most valuable contribution that science and technology could make to improve the capabilities of the criminalistics laboratory?

# CHAPTER 11

# RECORDS
# AND THEIR
# MANAGEMENT

IMAGINE, FOR A MOMENT, that a law enforcement agency is a sort of giant computer. The input-output devices are the patrol officers, undercover officers, telephone operators, and various other "peripheral" elements that receive and dispense information and carry out instructions. The detective is the central processing unit; following a predetermined program of rational procedures, the central processing unit (CPU) receives information, analyzes it, combines it with other information already in the system's memory, and either stores the results for future reference or initiates certain actions.

One of the most crucial elements in any computer system is its memory. The size and design of the memory determine the system's ability to absorb and use information. If the memory is too small for the system's needs, essential information will be lost because the CPU has no place to put it. If the memory is too large or too elaborate, vital decisions may be delayed because it takes the CPU too long to obtain information. Somehow, a computer's memory must be designed so skillfully that it is just the right size to contain all the information necessary and at the same time to deliver the information in an appropriate form without undue delay whenever it is requested.

But this book is not about computers; it is about criminal investigation. In a law enforcement agency, the memory is the records and identification section; and its function is as vital as that of a computer memory.

### ROLE OF THE RECORDS AND IDENTIFICATION SECTION

In most police agencies, the records and identification section must serve a variety of purposes, some of which may seem to be in conflict. One of the R&I section's roles is administrative. The records of complaints handled, offenses investigated, arrests made, and police services rendered to the community are important because they enable the department's administrators to make management decisions: where and how to deploy the personnel and other resources at their disposal. These records also permit administrators to supervise the activities of the agency's personnel. Since most police personnel work more or less on their own, without higher-ranking officials peering over their shoulders, the only tool of supervision available to the administrators is the review of formal reports and other records. Finally, many of the records that may be maintained by the R&I section are essentially administrative in nature: inventories of the department's equipment and property, vehicle maintenance logs, personnel assignments, and all sorts of other "housekeeping" matters.[1]

A second function of the R&I section is to maintain records that satisfy various legal requirements. For its own security and protection, a community gives the police the authority to deprive individual citizens of their liberty, to seize private property, and, when necessary, to use force—even deadly force—in order to obtain compliance with the law. When granting this authority, however, the community also imposes a number of restrictions on when and how that authority may be exercised. Only by producing accurate, complete records of their activities can the police demonstrate that they have used their authority properly and have scrupulously observed all the legal restrictions. The records kept by the R&I section are indispensable in meeting this need.

As important as these administrative and legal functions are, they should not overshadow the investigative role of the R&I section. Unfortunately, in too many police agencies, especially the smaller ones, that is exactly what happens: the R&I section becomes merely a passive repository of administrative and legal paperwork. Files are established and maintained to suit the convenience of administrators and to produce summaries of the agency's activities, but not to provide the vital details of specific incidents that an investigator needs to solve a crime.[2]

Arranging the department's memory to serve an active role in investigation is much more difficult. The heart of the difficulty is that no one can know in advance exactly what information might be needed in the future. The solution to a case might hinge on a small detail about the location at which a crime was committed, the people involved in the crime (both perpetrator and victim), or the methods by which the crime was carried out. The information may very well be buried somewhere in the files; but unless the investigator can find it when it is needed, it might as well not exist at all.

## THE WELL-ORGANIZED R&I SECTION

No model design for an R&I section would be equally suitable for every agency. The agency's size, its jurisdiction, and the kind of community that it serves all have a bearing on the kind of memory it needs. However, some common characteristics apply to nearly every police department, however large or small.

Experts on police administration are unanimous in their opinion that the R&I section and the communications section should be as closely related as possible. In small depart-

*No one knows exactly what information might be needed at some time in the future or for what purpose. If the information cannot be found when it is needed, it might as well not exist.*

ments, these two sections often can be combined into a single unit.[3] In very small agencies—those with fewer than 25 police officers—one person might serve as telephone operator, radio dispatcher, and records clerk. Larger agencies will require more people, but the same functions might be shared among them; there are many advantages for a fairly small agency in cross-training personnel to handle several different tasks so that the absence of a single individual does not cripple the agency. But eventually, as a department grows larger, more and more specialization becomes inevitable, and the communications

ANSWERS TO STUDY CLUES
1. False    2. b    3. g    4. c    5. c

and record-keeping functions are divided into two distinct units.

One of the most serious problems in establishing and maintaining an effective R&I section is the need to strike a balance between accessibility and security.[4] The information in the records system must be available to investigators, to administrators, and often to the general public. Citizens (or their lawyers) will need copies of accident reports, traffic citations, warrants, arrest records, and offense reports for their own use in courts or to satisfy the requirements of their insurance companies. In many departments, the R&I section also operates as the agency's public service desk—the main counter in the lobby of the police headquarters. However, the need for accessibility sometimes conflicts with the need for security. If all of an agency's vital records are kept in one place that is open to the public, they are an inviting target for anyone who wishes to disrupt police activities. The records must be protected from unauthorized tampering and from simple misplacement, whether deliberate or accidental.

Again, there is no perfect, universal solution. Each agency must find its own way to make the records accessible while simultaneously keeping them secure. We mention the problem here because the way in which this is done may affect the value of the records to the investigator. The investigator must be able to obtain information with as little delay as possible. Administrators and citizens usually can afford to wait a few minutes while someone finds a particular report, but an investigator—especially a patrol officer at the scene of a crime—needs information *immediately*, not half an hour from now. The investigator also must be confident that the information is complete and accurate, that no one has tampered with it or lost some part of it.[5]

All investigative records should be kept in one place or, at least, under the direct control of one management unit. The several sections of a law enforcement agency must not be permitted to establish their own separate files. If they do, inevitably there will be information in one section's files that could have solved a problem for another section if the latter had known that it existed.

## TYPES OF INVESTIGATIVE RECORDS

The exact contents of the R&I section's files will depend on the size, jurisdiction, and administrative philosophy and policies of the agency. However, law enforcement responsibilities and activities are similar enough that we can outline the most common kinds of records.

### CASE REPORTS

Every police case begins with a complaint from a victim or a notification from a citizen that a crime has occurred. Usually this notice comes by means of a telephone call. Whoever receives the telephone call should immediately record the information on a standard *complaint form,* which may be anything from a three-by-five-inch index card to a full-size sheet of paper. The form should include the essential details of the complaint or reported offense: where the apparent crime was committed, what happened, to whom, and who may have been the perpetrator. One important bit of information is the *case number,* which usually is stamped on the printed form. The case number will identify this particular case from then on; the number also will connect all of the other documents that might be generated during the course of an investigation, arrest of a suspect, and eventual prosecution.[6]

LOCATION OF INCIDENT

NATURE OF INCIDENT

COMPLAINANT – VICTIM

APD-CB

PHONE NO.

CLR.

ARR.

DISP.

ADDRESS

REC.

BACK-UP UNIT

DISP

ARR.

CLR.

BACK-UP OFFICER

O OLD     O 1. JUST OCCURED     O 2. IN PROGRESS     O

UNIT     OFFICER     EMP NO.

OFFENSE NO

SHIFT        DISTRICT
#1 O     #3 O
#2 O     OTHER O

REPORT AREA

SELF INITIATED O
ASSIGNMENT O

| ARREST | CLEARED BY |
|---|---|
| 1. ARREST CUSTODY O | 1. OFFENSE O |
| 2. ARREST RELEASE O | 2. SUPPL. OFF. O |
| 3. CITATION O | 3. MISC. INCIDENT O |
| 4. NO ARREST O | 4. RADIO CARD REPT. O |

| RECEIVED BY | DISPATCHED BY |
|---|---|

'n 0051   REV (1-78)     DD-H 18160

*A complaint form. This form is completed by the telephone operator, or whoever takes the original complaint. Later, it will be key-punched for use in a computer. (Courtesy Austin, Texas, Police Department)*

Usually the complaint form is held by the communications section while a patrol officer is dispatched to investigate the complaint. As soon as the initial investigation is completed, the complaint form is forwarded to the R&I section, where it is filed. The filing of the complaint form establishes the initial record of the case. If the complaint forms are generated in numerical order and filed in the same order, they also reflect the chronological sequence in which the complaints have been received.

Every complaint or reported offense should be recorded in exactly the same way. If an officer personally observes a crime in progress or if a crime is reported to an officer on the street, the offense should be reported to the communications section as soon as possible so that a complaint form can be recorded and a case number assigned. In a few large agencies, the R&I section, rather than the communications section, issues a case number under these circumstances.

Meanwhile, back at the scene of the crime, the patrol officer or detective who conducts the initial investigation must prepare an *investigative report*. This report, which we described in Chapter 4, amounts to a summary of the information in the investigator's own field notes. Most agencies use a printed form for the initial investigative report, which also may be known as an *offense report*. Some agencies have designed a variety of different forms for different kinds of offenses. The purpose is to ensure that vital information appropriate to the nature of the offense is recorded and that relatively unimportant details

*At right: An offense report form. This is the permanent record of a criminal offense and of the investigation. (Courtesy Austin, Texas, Police Department)*

## OFFENSE REPORT
**POLICE DEPARTMENT**
City of Austin  **CITY OF AUSTIN, TEXAS**

| 1. Offense No. | 2. Offense (Type) | 3. Classification After Investigation |
|---|---|---|

| 4. Victim's Name (Firm's Name If Business) | 5. Residence Address | Zip Code | 6. Res. Phone | 7. Bus. Phone |
|---|---|---|---|---|

| 8. Victim's Occupation | Race | Sex | Age | D.O.B. | 9. Date & Time Occurred |
|---|---|---|---|---|---|

| 10. Location:   Number   Street   Apt. # | 11. Date & Time Police Arrived | 12. Type of Premises Where Occurred |
|---|---|---|

| 13. Weapon, Instrument or Means of Attack | 14. How Means of Attack Used | 15. If Victim Hospitalized—Where |
|---|---|---|

| 16. Nature of Injuries and Where on Body | 17. Offender's Relationship to Victim |
|---|---|

| 18. Type Property Damaged or Taken | 19. Property / Evidence: Recovered ☐ Photographed ☐ Tagged ☐ | 20. Fingerprints Taken | 21. Operation I.D. # |
|---|---|---|---|

| 22. Victim's Vehicle   Yr-Make-Series-Body Style     Color | License-Yr-State | Vin |
|---|---|---|

Offense No.

### MOTOR VEHICLE THEFT

| 23. Other Identifying Marks-Damage-Decals-Etc. |
|---|

| 24. Name of Registered Owner | 25. Residence Address | 26. Res. Phone | 27. Bus. Phone |
|---|---|---|---|

| 28. Name of Last Driver | 29. Residence Address | 30. Res. Phone | 31. Bus. Phone |
|---|---|---|---|

| 32. Locked | 33. Ign. Locked | 34. Key In Car | 35. Owner Has Key | 36. Checked:   Leaving   Pound ☐  Repo ☐   Scene ☐ |
|---|---|---|---|---|

| 37. Lien Holder—Finance Co. | 38. Address | 39. Phone | 40. Payment Current  Yes ☐  No ☐ | 41. Date of Last Payment |
|---|---|---|---|---|

| 42. Insurance Co. or Agent | 43. Address | 44. Phone |
|---|---|---|

### BURGLARY

| 45. Exact Point of Entry Into Building | 46. Exact Point of Exit |
|---|---|

| 47. If Safe Burglary: Name of Safe, Serial Number and Size |
|---|

### FORGERY

| 48. Person Who Accepted Document | 49. Name of Bank | 50. Signature on Face |
|---|---|---|

| 51. Document Payable To | 52. Other Names (Company, Etc.) | 53. Names Endorsed on Back |
|---|---|---|

| 54. Offender Prepared Check in Victim's Presence: ☐ Yes. ☐ No. / Endorsed: ☐ Yes. ☐ No. | 55. Identification Used—Type & Number | 56. Type of Document |
|---|---|---|

| 57. Document I.D. No. | 58. Date on Document | 59. Amount of Check | 60. Receipt Given For Document  ☐ Yes.  ☐ No. |
|---|---|---|---|

**61. PROPERTY DESCRIPTION AND NARRATIVE:** Describe all property involved (lost, stolen, abandoned, found, etc.) first. Then begin a narrative description of the incident being reported. Detailed investigative information will be placed on supplementary pages.

Report Made by ............................................................................................... Coded ..........

   Name & Emp. No.        Typist's Emp. No.      Time & Date Rec'd      Time & Date Typed      Emp. No.

Approved by ................................................. Assigned to ............................ Indexed ..........

           Emp. No.                    Emp. No.        Emp. No.

PD-0001  (2-77)

(which might be crucial for another kind of offense) are left out. Typically, an agency might have different forms for crimes against persons, crimes against property, traffic accidents, crimes involving vehicles (auto theft, for example), miscellaneous crimes, and non-crime police services.

The investigative report or offense report should be submitted to the R&I section as soon as possible so that it can be filed with the original complaint form. If further investigation or other action, such as an arrest away from the scene of the crime, is required, a copy of the offense report may be placed in the appropriate departmental channels. It may be taken directly to a detective or it may first go through various administrators for assignment. Sometimes, especially in smaller departments and those that adhere to the patrol-investigator plan, the officer who conducted the initial investigation is responsible for follow-up work; in this case a copy of the offense report should remain in the officer's notebook.

As a case progresses, every step of the investigation and follow-up should be recorded on appropriate forms. It is the investigator's responsibility to see that the file is kept up to date, complete, and accurate. Again, printed forms may be available for *supplemental investigative reports,* or they may be prepared on plain paper. Some agencies require that a follow-up form be inserted in the file at regular intervals even if the form simply reads, "No progress." This is a way of checking to be sure that unsolved cases are not forgotten or ignored.

Every case file should be closed at some point by the decision of a responsible official of the department. The record of that decision should be the last item in each case file. The *closing report* may indicate that the case is "unsolved, no further information

available" or "closed by arrest." It is important to bear in mind, though, that a closed case can be reopened at any time if additional information is discovered or if the arrested person turns out not to have been the perpetrator.

The primary value of the case file is that it should contain all of the essential information about each incident. Whenever an investigator begins work on a new case, it is a good idea to check the files for similar cases. Sometimes information uncovered in one investigation, even if it failed to result in an arrest, will help to solve a later case.[7]

FIELD INTERVIEW
REPORTS

In the past, patrol officers were expected to spend a good deal of time conducting "field interviews" of "suspicious persons." The idea was that the patrol officer would stop anyone who seemed in any way suspicious or unusual. The citizen would be required to produce identification and an explanation for being present on the street. This information would be recorded by the police officer, including the person's name and address. Later, if a crime were reported in the same neighborhood, that individual might be rounded up and questioned as a possible suspect.

In recent years, the courts have taken a dim view of this kind of police activity. Citizens, unless their behavior clearly suggests that they have committed a crime or intend to do so, have every right to go about their business without police interference. The mere fact

At right: *A supplemental report form. This form is used to record additional information as the investigation continues. (Courtesy Austin, Texas, Police Department)*

| 1. OFFENSE NO. | SUPPLEMENTARY OFFENSE REPORT | | OFFENSE NO. |
|---|---|---|---|
| 2. OFFENSE REPORTED | | 3. CLASSIFICATION AFTER INVESTIGATION | |
| 4. ORIGINALLY CLASSIFIED AS | | 5. VICTIM'S NAME | |
| 6. VICTIM'S ADDRESS | | 7. DATE REPORTED | |

8. NARRATIVE:

Report
Made by ............................................................................................................ Coded ........................
       Name & Emp. No.        Typist's Emp. No.     Time & Date Rec'd.     Time & Date Typed     Emp. No.

Approved by ...................................................... Assigned to ........................................................ Indexed ....................
             Emp. No.                         Emp. No.     Emp. No.

| No. _____ | **POLICE DEPT. FIELD INTERROGATION REPORT** | | | | | | |
|---|---|---|---|---|---|---|---|

A field interview form. This card is filled out by any officer, following a field interview or interrogation. (Courtesy Temple, Texas, Police Department)

that persons seem unusual to a police officer does not mean that they ought to be suspected of being criminals. This kind of police practice can lead to all sorts of abuses. Furthermore, since few cities maintain foot patrols except in very limited areas, police officers generally are less familiar with the individuals who live in a given neighborhood or have legitimate business there.

Nevertheless, field interviews do still take place. For example, a patrol officer might observe someone forcing open a locked door at the back of a house. This certainly would be a suspicious circumstance that demands investigation. Suppose, however, that the individual claims to be the sister of the woman who lives there and gives a convincing explanation of her reason for breaking into the house. Under these circumstances—there being no evidence to indicate that a crime is being committed—the patrol officer would be justified in demanding that the person produce identification, but no other action would be taken. The incident should be recorded not as a complaint or offense, but as a field interview. The field interview report should be forwarded to the R&I section at the earliest opportunity. If the owners of the house later reported a burglary, the record of the field interview might lead directly to the perpetrator.

Of course, field interview reports are absolutely worthless unless investigators go to the trouble of checking through them. Conversely, it will not do investigators much good to check the field interview files unless the information is readily available. The key to availability, not only for field interview files but for *all* investigative records, is adequate cross-indexing.

## EVIDENCE AND PROPERTY INVENTORIES

Each item of physical evidence that is collected at the scene of a crime or anywhere else must be properly recorded. These records, too, should be maintained by the R&I section. The records are vital to the prosecution of the offender, since the chain of custody of the evidence must be established. Also, it is always possible that evidence found in connection with one case will prove to be valuable in the investigation of another crime, especially if the two cases happen to be similar.

Besides evidence, other kinds of property in the custody of the police also must be in-

| TEMPLE POLICE DEPARTMENT PROPERTY FORM | FILE NO. | | OFFENSE NO. | |
|---|---|---|---|---|
| Property Obtained From | | Address | | |
| Location of Property (Where Obtained) | | | Reason for Storage | |
| ITEM NO. | QUANTITY | Description of Property (Serial No., Marks, Condition, etc.) | | |

| Item No. | Date | Relinquished By | Received By | Reason |
|---|---|---|---|---|
| Item No. | Date | Relinquished By | Received By | Reason |
| Item No. | Date | Relinquished By | Received By | Reason |
| Item No. | Date | Relinquished By | Received By | Reason |

I CERTIFY THAT I AM LEGALLY ENTITLED TO THE ABOVE PROPERTY AND THAT I RECEIVE THE ABOVE PROPERTY AS IS.

NAME (TYPED) _____ SIGNED _____

RELEASING OFFICER _____

APC-1

*A property record form. This card is used to record any physical property, including evidence, being held by the police. (Courtesy Temple, Texas, Police Department)*

ventoried and properly recorded. This might include confiscated contraband or fruits of a crime (which are also evidence, of course); found property, whose rightful owner is unknown; personal property taken from arrested suspects and held until they are released; and any other property that belongs to some citizen but happens to be in the care of the police. Investigators who are working on property crime cases should get into the habit of checking through the property inventory files periodically just on the chance that items connected with a crime might turn up.[8]

### ARREST REPORTS

Whenever a suspect is arrested, either on a warrant obtained from a magistrate or otherwise, an *arrest report* must be completed by the officer who actually makes the arrest. The report includes a fairly complete physical description of the arrestee, the circumstances of the arrest, and the nature of the charges against the suspect. Other spaces on the arrest report (which is almost always a printed form) will be used to record court appearances, release on bail, and final disposition of

the case. Most R&I sections maintain a separate file for arrest reports.

Again, an investigator should check arrest reports to look for persons who have been accused in the past of crimes similar to the offense currently being investigated. Most criminals, especially those who commit property crimes and relatively minor crimes (such as vice offenses), specialize in a specific type of crime, which they commit in a habitual pattern. This information should be included on the arrest report, unless the agency maintains a separate modus operandi file.

### MODUS OPERANDI FILES

Criminologists have recognized for many years that criminal behavior tends to follow habitual patterns. Many criminals leave highly identifiable "trademarks" when they commit an offense. For example, a safecracker may have a particular method of removing or disabling the lock on a safe; a rapist may repeatedly employ the same approach or disguise to gain the confidence of victims. All of these characteristics are summarized by the term *modus operandi* or, more simply, *M.O.*, which means "method of operation."

# TEMPLE POLICE DEPARTMENT ARREST REPORT

| Last Name | First Name | Middle Name | Aliases | TPD No. |
|---|---|---|---|---|

| Address | City & State | Race | Sex | Hair | Eyes | Height | Weight |
|---|---|---|---|---|---|---|---|

| Age | D.O.B. | Place of Birth | Occupation | Place of Employment |
|---|---|---|---|---|

| Social Security No. | Drivers License No. | State | Type | Other ID Nos. |
|---|---|---|---|---|

Scars, Marks, Amputations and Tattoos

| Time and Date of Arrest | Searched By | Arresting Officer(s)-Badge No(s) | Booking Officer-Badge No. |
|---|---|---|---|

| Time and Date of Warning | Officer Giving Warning | Response to Warning (Exact Words) |
|---|---|---|

| Name of Complainant | Address of Complainant | Phone No. |
|---|---|---|

| Name (Next of Kin) | Relation | Address | Phone No. |
|---|---|---|---|

| Called Attorney: | Date | Time | Other Phone Calls |
|---|---|---|---|

| Place Arrested | Block Number of Street or Avenue | District & Grid No. |
|---|---|---|

| Vehicle | Year | Make | Model | License No. | Stored At |
|---|---|---|---|---|---|

| Currency $ | Change $ | Checks $ | Total $ | Belt | Medication, if any |
|---|---|---|---|---|---|

| Wallet | Watch | Rings | Keys | Knife | Lighter |
|---|---|---|---|---|---|

Other Items Not Classified

I certify that the above is a correct list of items removed from my possession at the time I was placed in jail.  **X**

I have received all of the above listed property this          day of                                                                              19

Signed **X**                                                              Time                              Date

How Released - Cash Bond - P.R. Bond - Include Bonding Agency          Releasing Officer

Final Disposition

| OFFENSE OR ARREST NUMBER | OFFENSE(S) CHARGED | BOND | COMPLAINT OR WARRANT NO. |
|---|---|---|---|
|  | 1. |  |  |
|  | 2. |  |  |
|  | 3. |  |  |
| FINGERPRINTED BY: | PHOTOGRAPHED BY: | ENTERED IN LEDGER BY: | |

**PARTICULARS OF ARREST**

Developing an effective M.O. file is not easy, because the information is difficult to classify beyond the obvious division into categories by offense. Nevertheless, a well-designed and constantly maintained M.O. file can be enormously valuable to the investigator, sometimes more valuable than any of the other files. By comparing the M.O. of a current case with the file, an investigator may be able to narrow the search for evidence, concentrating on a particular suspect.

There is a danger, however, that must be pointed out. The mere fact that two offenses present similar M.O.'s does not prove anything; the similarity might be merely coincidental. Professional criminals often teach their methods to novices who may imitate their masters with considerable success. Furthermore, whenever a crime is highly publicized, there is a strong possibility that the M.O. will be mimicked by other criminals. That is one reason the police must be extremely cautious about revealing too many details of a crime that is still under investigation. A similarity of M.O.'s might lead the investigator to believe that the same person committed both offenses or a series of offenses, but hard evidence still must be sought.[9]

CRIMINAL HISTORY FILES

A criminal history file is closely related to both the arrest report and the M.O. files, but all three serve slightly different purposes and ought to be maintained separately.

The criminal history file ordinarily is arranged alphabetically by the names of convicted criminals and sometimes subdivided

At left: *An arrest report form.*
*(Courtesy Temple, Texas, Police Department)*

by categories of offenses. Each file card or folder may contain copies of the arrest reports, warrants, court disposition records, and other information pertaining to the individual. Some agencies keep a much simpler criminal history file, containing only a list of the offenses for which the person has been convicted. The arrest reports and other records are kept completely separate. In either case, the criminal history file should include a complete physical description of the offender, a list of all known aliases, past addresses, names and addresses of family members and other known associates, and any other information that might help in locating the person.

Unless care is taken to keep the file up to date, the criminal history file can get completely out of hand. The file should be completely checked every year, or more often in a large agency, and purged of records of persons who are dead, imprisoned for life with little or no likelihood of parole, or unlikely to appear in the community again. Some agencies divide their criminal history files into active and inactive sections, the latter containing the records of individuals who are unlikely to run afoul of the law in the future.

VEHICLE FILE

Many agencies maintain a file record for every vehicle that is in any way involved in criminal activity. This might include vehicles used by criminals in the commission of crimes, stolen vehicles, vehicles involved in major traffic crimes (such as a hit-and-run accident or felony driving while intoxicated), and even vehicles that are merely owned by known or suspected criminals. Again, these files can grow to monstrous proportions unless they are regularly purged of obsolete and useless information.

TEMPLE POLICE DEPARTMENT
Temple, Texas

NAME _____     SEX _____

ADDRESS _____     RACE _____

_____       DOB _____

FBI _____      TPD _____

FPC _____      DPS _____

| DATE | NUMBER | CHARGE | DISPOSITION |
|------|--------|--------|-------------|
|      |        |        |             |
|      |        |        |             |
|      |        |        |             |
|      |        |        |             |
|      |        |        |             |
|      |        |        |             |
|      |        |        |             |
|      |        |        |             |
|      |        |        |             |
|      |        |        |             |
|      |        |        |             |
|      |        |        |             |
|      |        |        |             |
|      |        |        |             |
|      |        |        |             |
|      |        |        |             |
|      |        |        |             |
|      |        |        |             |

TPD #  O-12

LEAVE THIS SPACE BLANK

FPC

NAME _____ _____ _____
ALIAS _____

NO _____ RACE _____ SEX _____

**RIGHT HAND**

| 1. THUMB | 2. INDEX FINGER | 3. MIDDLE FINGER | 4. RING FINGER | 5. LITTLE FINGER |

**LEFT HAND**

| 6. THUMB | 7. INDEX FINGER | 8. MIDDLE FINGER | 9. RING FINGER | 10. LITTLE FINGER |

HAIR _____ EYES _____ HEIGHT _____ WEIGHT _____ AGE _____ DATE OF BIRTH _____
DPS·NO _____ FBI NO _____
PRISONER'S SIGNATURE
FINGERPRINTS TAKEN BY | DATE PRINTS TAKEN | NOTE AMPUTATIONS | X

**LEFT** FOUR FINGERS TAKEN SIMULTANEOUSLY | L. THUMB | R. THUMB | **RIGHT** FOUR FINGERS TAKEN SIMULTANEOUSLY

*A fingerprint card. (Courtesy Texas Department of Public Safety)*

## ACCIDENT REPORTS

State laws and local ordinances require most traffic accidents to be reported if there is substantial property damage or any personal injury. The accident may be reported by the individuals involved without police assistance; more often, the drivers will notify the police and ask for an investigation on the scene. Either way, a report should be filed.

Accident reports generally are of limited interest to investigators except when the accident involved a major traffic crime.

## PERSONAL IDENTIFICATION FILES

There is little doubt that personal identification files can be quite valuable to investigators. Unfortunately, that value is sometimes overstated in popular fiction and the news media. Very few crimes are solved by match-

*At left: A criminal history record form. (Courtesy Temple, Texas, Police Department)*

ing a single fingerprint found at the scene of a crime with a filed print or by showing mug shots of random criminals to eyewitnesses. Instead, personal identification files are consulted primarily to confirm the identity of a known suspect or to connect the suspect to several related crimes.

**Fingerprint files.** If you were to ask average citizens what would be found in a police R&I section's records, most likely they would answer immediately, "Fingerprints!" No other single aspect of police science has become so deeply embedded in the public's imagination.

Certainly, fingerprint files are valuable and almost every police agency maintains them. The value of fingerprints rests on the fact that every print is completely unique; this is true not only for fingerprints, but equally for palm prints, toe prints, sole prints, and even lip prints. The very uniqueness of fingerprints is directly due to the complexity of the friction-ridge patterns on the skin, which in turn makes it almost impossible to classify fingerprints in such a way that an unknown sample can be compared with a filed print.

This does not mean that the effort to classify fingerprints has not been made. The most widespread classification scheme is the Henry system, which was developed by Sir Edward Henry, a British criminologist.[10] Henry published his classification system in 1900; since then, it has been modified, adapted, extended, and elaborated any number of times, but the basic system is used by the Federal Bureau of Investigation and almost every state and local police agency in the United States and the rest of the English-speaking world.[11]

The Henry system depends on recognizing in a fingerprint one of three major patterns, each of which has two or three major subclassifications; beyond that, a fingerprint is classified according to such details as the number of ridges between two certain points, the presence or absence of certain details, or even the distance between two types of detail[12] (see Investigator's Notes 8). All of these factors are described according to a code formula that applies not to any one finger but to all ten fingers, including any missing digits. Once the fingerprints have been classified by the Henry formula, they may be filed in a coded sequence.[13]

Obviously, this system is extremely complicated. A good deal of skill and practice are required before a person can classify fingerprints by the Henry system with any confidence. Even then, the whole process is so complicated that small mistakes are inevitable, and two different experts are very likely to choose different classifications for the same set of fingerprints.

From an investigator's point of view, the Henry system is not very helpful except that once known suspects have been taken into custody, their fingerprints can be compared

---

### INVESTIGATOR'S NOTES 8
### FINGERPRINT CLASSIFICATIONS

There are three principal groups of ridge patterns used to describe, classify, and compare fingerprints (and, infrequently, toe prints as well). These primary categories are shown in Figures 11.1–11.3.

Within each of these major classifications, there are various subclassifications, depending on whose system one selects; for example, in the Henry system, there is only one type of loop, but there are at least two types of arches and five or six types of whorls.

More important than the subclassifications are the *Galton details,* named after Sir Francis Galton, who first developed a systematic way of describing fingerprint details and whose work formed the basis of the Henry system. The location, the number, and sometimes the relative positions of the Galton details distinguish one print from another—or show that two prints are identical. A few of the Galton details are illustrated in Figure 11.4.

---

with the filed prints to determine their true identity and to connect them to a criminal history, if they have one. The likelihood of finding a full set of ten fingerprints at a crime scene, all prints being clear enough to permit classification, is virtually nonexistent.

Efforts have been made to develop a system of classifying single prints, but again the complexity overwhelms the task. Part of the problem is that a fingerprint contains no inherent point of reference. Usually a fingerprint found at a crime scene, or anywhere else that it has been left accidentally, represents only part of the whole pattern. There is nothing in a partial print that clearly indicates the

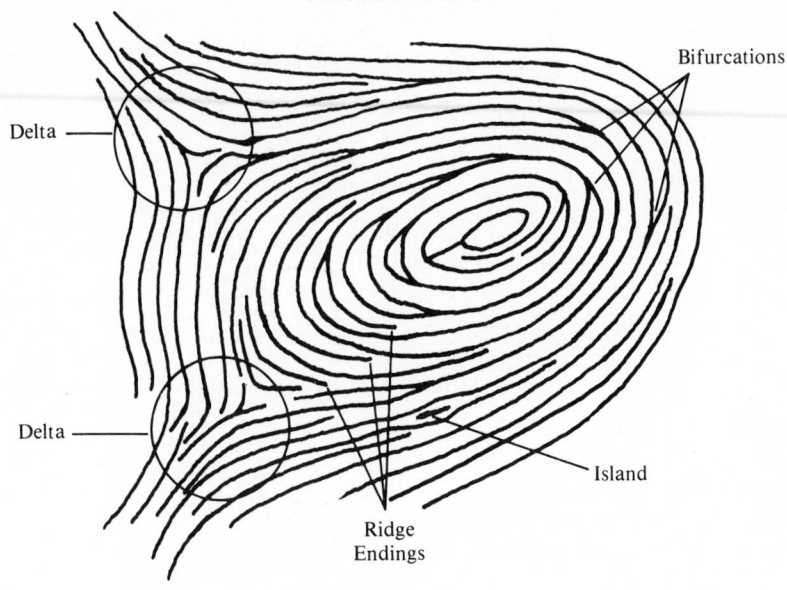

FIGURE 11.1
WHORL PATTERN

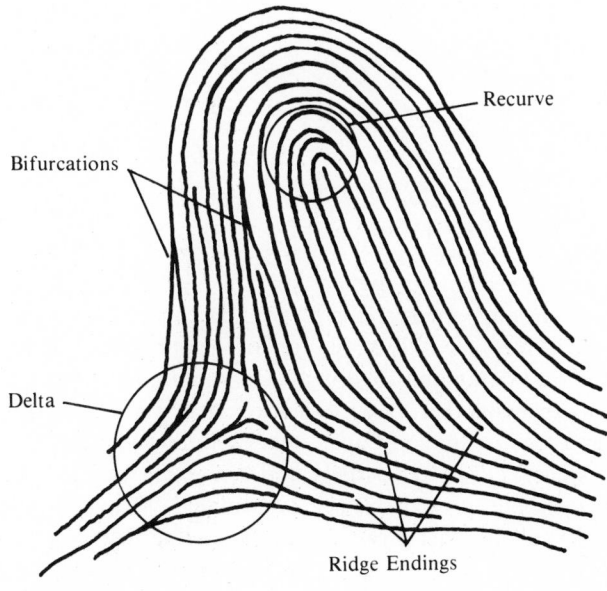

FIGURE 11.2
LOOP PATTERN

FIGURE 11.3
ARCH PATTERNS (TWO TYPES)

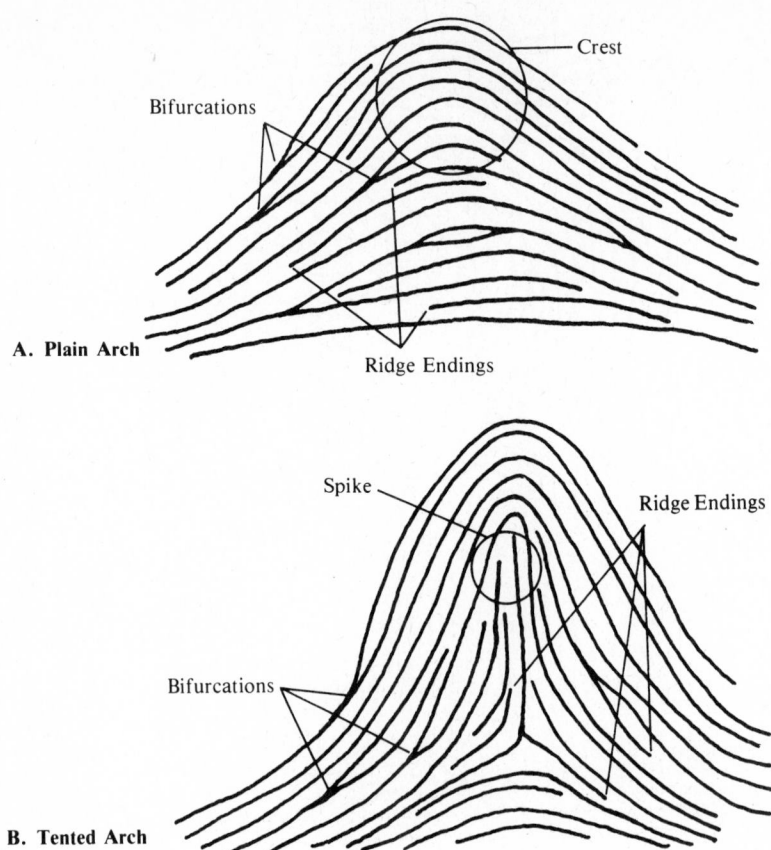

A. Plain Arch

B. Tented Arch

center of the pattern, or one edge, or even the direction of the pattern. Thus, the only way to compare two prints is to compare the relative positions of minute details that may or may not be present and may or may not appear in both impressions. Ultimately, the only good way to perform the comparison is to examine both prints side by side. Trying to locate a print in a file by describing a "found," unknown print is analogous to trying to find your pet fish in the ocean.[14]

Criminologists continue to search for a solution that would enable an investigator to take an unknown print found at a crime scene and locate its twin in a file of any given size. Automated techniques, employing computers and perhaps microfilm, may someday be the answer.[15]

FIGURE 11.4
GALTON DETAILS

**A. Overlapping Recurves or Staples**

**B. Bifurcation**

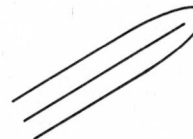

**C. Rod (End of ridge) Enclosed in Recurve or Staple**

**D. Enclosure**

**E. Island**

**Photograph files.** The limitations that apply to fingerprint files also apply to photo files. Most agencies maintain extensive files of the photographs of the faces of arrestees—so-called mug shots—supplemented by photos of known or suspected criminals from various external sources, such as the FBI. However, there is not any very good system of classification that would permit the photographs to be arranged logically. Usually the photos are filed by the subjects' names, perhaps subdivided by offense categories and perhaps further subdivided by some scheme of classifying M.O.'s. Photos are used most often to confirm a suspect's identity, to connect a suspect with a criminal history, or to link a suspect with related or similar cases. Once in a while, recent photos of a known suspect and others may be used for a "photo line-up" when a witness is unable or unwilling to attend a genuine line-up; however, this technique has limited value.

One obvious problem with photographs, aside from the impossibility of their classification, is that a person's appearance may change drastically from time to time or may seem to have changed when the person is seen under different circumstances. A change of hair style or color, changes in facial hair, or even such minor changes as the presence or absence of a suntan can destroy a witness's ability to recognize a suspect. Over any significant period of time, such as five or ten years, almost everyone's appearance changes enough that an old photograph has very little value for purposes of identification.

There is, however, one other possible purpose of a photo file. If a suspect has been identified on the basis of physical evidence or information from a witness, or if the suspect is known to the victim, but his or her whereabouts are unknown, a file photo might be circulated to patrol officers and other police units in the hope that someone will recognize the suspect on the street. The photo should never be more than five years old unless the suspect is between 25 and 40 years of age; during that period most people's appearance does not change too radically. Before the photo is circulated, witnesses should be asked to describe any major changes in the suspect's appearance: hair style, facial hair, new scars, and so on. If there have been major changes, it may be preferable to have an artist make a sketch of the suspect's current appearance instead of circulating a misleading photo.

NOTE: Do **NOT** Use Arrest
Sheet For Information
Below. Question Prisoner.
Use **NO** Other Source.

# PHYSICAL DESCRIPTION
## IDENTIFICATION SECTION
### AUSTIN, TEXAS POLICE DEPARTMENT

**APD NO.**_____

NAME _____ MAIDEN NAME _____

ALIASES _____ NICKNAME (S) _____

| SEX | RACE | HAIR | EYES | HT. | WT. | D.O.B. | AGE |
|-----|------|------|------|-----|-----|--------|-----|

OCCUPATION _____ EMPLOYER'S NAME & ADDRESS _____

BIRTH PLACE CITY & STATE _____ RESIDENCE STREET-CITY-STATE _____

WIFE'S FULL MAIDEN NAME & ADDRESS _____

ADDITIONAL NEXT OF KIN RELATION-NAME-ADDRESS _____

SCARS  {LEFT ARM & HAND}  I—_____

{RIGHT ARM & HAND}  II—_____

{FACE HEAD & NECK}  III—_____

{BODY AND DEFORMITIES}  IV—_____

## USE INK AND NEATLY CHECK ANY ITEM(S) THAT DESCRIBES THE PRISONER.

**BUILD (4)**
— 1 THIN
— 2 MEDIUM
— 3 HEAVY
— 4 OBESE (FAT)
— 5 MUSCULAR

**HAIR COLOR (5)**
— 1 LIGHT BROWN
— 2 DARK BROWN
— 3 BLACK
— 4 BLOND
— 5 PARTLY GREY-GREYING
— 6 GREY-WHITE-SILVER
— 7 RED
— 8 FROSTED

**HAIR TYPE (6)**
— 1 BALD OR SHAVED
— 2 THIN & RECEDING
— 3 WAVY, CURLY OR KINKY
— 4 BUSHY
— 5 CREW CUT
— 6 LONG
— 7 STRAIGHT
— 8 SIDEBURNS
— 9 WIG

**EYE COLOR (7)**
— 1 BROWN
— 2 BLUE
— 3 HAZEL OR GREEN
— 4 GREY
— 5 MAROON
— 6 MIXED

**EYE DEFECT (8)**
— 1 WEARS GLASSES
— 2 MISSING
— 3 CROSSED
— 4 BLIND LEFT
— 5 BLIND RIGHT
— 6 BULGING
— 7 SQUINTS OR BLINKS
— 8 GLASS EYE
— 0 NONE

**SPEECH (9)**
— 1 STUTTERS OR LISPS
— 2 FOREIGN
— 3 POOR GRAMMAR
— 4 SLOW
— 5 SOUTHERN DRAWL
— 6 TALKS FAST
— 7 NORTHERN
— 8 NATIVE OR NORMAL
— 9 MUTE

**DEFORM & AMPS (10)**
— 1 HUNCHBACK OR BOWLEGGED
— 2 LEFT ARM, HAND & FINGERS
— 3 RIGHT ARM, HAND & FINGERS
— 4 LEFT LEG & FOOT
— 5 RIGHT LEG & FOOT
— 6 EAR
— 7 FACE
— 8 LEFT HANDED
— 0 NONE

**TATOOS (11)**
— 1 LEFT ARM
— 2 RIGHT ARM
— 3 LEFT WRIST OR HAND
— 4 RIGHT WRIST OR HAND
— 5 FINGER
— 6 BIRTH MARK (NOT ON FACE)
— 7 BODY
— 8 NEEDLE MARKS
— 0 NONE

**SCARS (12)**
— 1 BURN
— 2 LEFT FACE
— 3 RIGHT FACE
— 4 NOSE
— 5 CHIN OR LIP
— 6 FOREHEAD OR EYEBROW
— 7 NECK
— 8 ARM
— 9 WRIST, HAND OR FINGERS
— 0 NONE

**TEETH (13)**
— 1 GOLD
— 2 MISSING
— 3 CHIPPED, BROKEN OR DECAYED
— 4 STAINED
— 5 PROTRUDING
— 6 PARTED OR SPREAD
— 7 CLEAN & WHITE
— 8 NO TEETH
— 9 FALSE

**EARS (14)**
— 1 PROTRUDING
— 2 CAULIFLOWER
— 3 HEARING AID
— 4 CLOSE TO HEAD
— 5 LARGE
— 6 SMALL
— 7 NORMAL; NOT OUTSTANDING
— 8 DEAF
— 9 PIERCED

**NOSE SHAPE (15)**
— 1 BROKEN OR CROOKED
— 2 FLAT
— 3 LONG
— 4 PUG (UP)
— 5 HOOKED (DOWN)
— 6 SMALL
— 7 NORMAL; NOT OUTSTANDING
— 8 LARGE

**FACIAL FEATURES (16)**
— 1 POCKMARKED OR ACNE
— 2 BIRTHMARK
— 3 FRECKLED
— 4 MOLE
— 5 THICK EYEBROWS
— 6 NOTICEABLE CHIN OR JAW
— 7 THICK LIPS
— 8 DIMPLES
— 9 BEARD, MUSTACHE OR GOATEE
— 0 NONE

DATE PRINTED _____

TIME PRINTED _____ : _____ AM-PM

PRINTED BY (SIGN) _____ # _____

## FOR IDENTIFICATION USE ONLY.

RIGHT INDEX

**BIRTH YEAR (1)**
— 1 0000-1915
— 2 1916-1925
— 3 1926-1935
— 4 1936-1940
— 5 1941-1945
— 6 1946-1950
— 7 1951-1955
— 8 1956-1960
— 9 1961-1965

**HEIGHT (2)**
— 1 TO 5-6
— 2 5-6 TO 5-11
— 3 OVER 5-11

**WEIGHT (3)**

MALE
— 1 TO 130 LBS
— 2 131 TO 160
— 3 161 TO 200
— 4 OVER 200

FEMALE
— 1 TO 100 LBS
— 2 101 TO 120
— 3 121 TO 140
— 4 141 TO 160
— 5 OVER 160

**CRIME (17)**
— 1 ROBBERY
— 2 SEX OFFENSE-ARSON
— 3 FORGERY-FRAUD
— 4 NARCOTICS
— 5 THEFT
— 6 AUTO THEFT
— 7 ASSAULT-MURDER
— 8 BURGLARY
— 9 MISCELLANEOUS

A mug shot card. (Courtesy Austin, Texas, Police Department)

MUG SHOT

APD # _____

NAME _____
ALIAS _____
ADDRESSES _____
_____
_____

DRIVERS LICENSE _____
_____ DOB _____
AUTOMOBILES _____
_____
_____
_____

OCCUPATIONS _____
_____

ASSOCIATES _____
_____

OTHER INFORMATION _____
_____

ORGANIZATIONS _____

PD 0027                SEE REVERSE SIDE

**Noncriminal identification files.** Usually the fingerprint files and photo files are made up mostly of records obtained when suspects are arrested. The records are retained on the theory that the same person may commit other crimes in the future. These records are often supplemented by additional prints and photos circulated by the FBI or other state and local police agencies. In addition, many agencies maintain extensive fingerprint and photo files of individuals who have no criminal record or known association with crime. These records should be kept completely separate from the criminal identification (ID) files.

Noncriminal ID records generally are created when the police agency is empowered by state law or local ordinance to issue licenses to taxicab drivers, liquor dealers, or people engaged in any number of other occupations. In addition, noncriminal ID records may be derived from applications for employment for the police department itself, the fire department, ambulance service, private secu-

At left: *A physical identification record form. (Courtesy Austin, Texas, Police Department)*

rity companies, or any other agency in which security is a major consideration.

It is very difficult to say whether the maintenance of all these noncriminal ID files is worth the effort. Many police officials believe that the files are indispensable, not so much for suggesting criminal suspects, but for identifying accident victims, unknown dead bodies, and the like. Many law enforcement authorities have urged that a national file of fingerprints of every adult citizen be established for just such purposes.[16]

On the other hand, perhaps one set of filed prints in ten thousand is ever needed for such purposes, and photo files are no more likely to be helpful. Some people are deeply suspicious of any effort by law enforcement agencies to maintain files on presumably innocent citizens, regardless of the intended purpose of the files. Insistence on any sort of universal fingerprinting would certainly evoke massive hostility and resentment.

All things considered, noncriminal ID files may be largely a waste of valuable time and resources. We think that in the future police officials may decide to put those resources to more productive uses.

## CROSS-INDEXES

Even a small police agency may develop a massive volume of information in its R&I files. Much of this information will never be used by anyone for anything, except perhaps in statistical summary form. However, somewhere in the files may be the one bit of information that an investigator needs to solve a criminal case.

Theoretically, it is possible for an investigator to look through all the files as part of each investigation. The impracticality of such a procedure is obvious; even in a small agency, each investigation would take weeks. And then the investigator would probably be so bored that the very item needed to crack the case would be overlooked.

The alternative is to provide the investigator with some kind of guidance that makes it possible to find just the information desired, no matter where it might be in the file. In a manual records system (one made up of paper documents stored in filing cabinets), guidance is provided by some sort of cross-indexing system. In an automated or computerized records system, the cross-indexing may be an inherent part of the system, which is one of the features that make such a system so valuable.[17]

A manual cross-indexing system usually relies on simple three-by-five-inch index cards. The cards are made up by the R&I personnel, not by the patrol officer or the investigator, when a complaint report, offense report, investigative report, arrest report, or any other record is filed. Creating and filing cross-index cards is a tedious, time-consuming task, but it can produce great dividends.

At least three major indexes should be prepared, but some agencies maintain four or more. One index is the name file. Each card contains the name of a person who in any way has come to the attention of the police: sus-pect, arrestee, victim, complainant, witness, or field interviewee. In addition to the person's name, the card should contain the person's address, telephone number, and occupation. Each incident that brought the person to the agency's attention and the date of each incident should be recorded. Some agencies add new information to existing name cards (for example, if a person is the victim of two different crimes on separate occasions), while others prefer to establish a new card for each incident, filing the new card directly behind the old one. Also, some agencies file together the names of individuals, businesses, aliases, and anything else that can be said to have a name (such as public events). Other agencies limit the name file to persons' names or maintain separate files for the various categories of names. This file can become fairly complex, for individual names might be cross-indexed within the index to the names of businesses, aliases, and so on.

A second type of cross-index is the location file. Here, each card contains an address, street intersection, or other distinctive place within the agency's jurisdiction where any incident involving police activity has occurred. The incident listed on a location card might be a crime, a traffic accident, or some sort of noncriminal police service. For example, some agencies might include fires and ambulance calls on their location cards. Again, successive incidents at one location might be recorded all on one card or on separate cards filed in chronological order.

Most agencies also cross-index their files by incident classifications. The incident classification cards are very brief summaries of the complaint reports or offense reports; each card gives the nature of the incident, the names of the people involved, the location, and the date. The cards are then filed in some orderly sequence according to the nature of the incident. The classification scheme found in the FBI's Uniform Crime Reports often is the basis for classifying the incident cards, although the UCR system may not provide as many classifications as an agency will need. Within each classification, cards are arranged chronologically.

Every index card should contain the case number for each incident that is recorded. This is how the numbering system proves its value, since it immediately connects the index card to the complaint form, the offense report, the supplementary reports, the arrest report, evidence forms, and every other record associated with a case.

Some agencies establish other index files as well. For example, incidents may be indexed by time of day and day of the week; a card would be made up for each reported incident and filed under, say, "Friday, 5:00 to 6:00 A.M." This file would serve two purposes: first, it would be helpful in determining whether there is a distinctive pattern of incidents at certain times of the day or on certain days of the week; second, it would allow the locating of other records if an investigator knew that a certain incident happened at a particular time, but did not know where the incident took place or who was involved. Of course, essentially the same information could be obtained from the agency's daily bulletins, but perhaps not so easily, especially in a very large agency.

## BULLETINS AND SUMMARIES

Almost every law enforcement agency prepares a daily bulletin (sometimes called a log or a police blotter) listing all of its activities in chronological sequence. Ideally, the bulletin should be prepared as early as possible each morning. It should include all of the previous day's activities; many agencies also use it as a sort of internal newsletter to advise personnel of significant events on that day's schedule. Copies should be circulated to every member of the agency, from the chief to the patrol officers.

In a large agency the daily bulletin can become overwhelming. Very few police officers are likely to take the time to read through a dozen or more pages of information at the beginning of each day's work. Instead, the information should be subdivided, perhaps by district or precinct.

The daily bulletins generally form the basis for weekly or monthly summaries of police activities. These summaries are intended primarily for administrative purposes and sometimes for public information; they are of interest to investigators only insofar as they reflect trends or patterns of criminal activity.[18]

## CURRENT WANTS AND WARRANTS

Every police officer in a law enforcement agency, especially the investigators, should be aware at all times of the contents of the *current wants and warrants file*. This file should contain three main types of records: the names and descriptions of all individuals wanted as suspects, witnesses, or even victims in connection with crimes currently being investigated; the names and descriptions of all persons for whom an arrest warrant has been issued; and the descriptions of all vehicles being sought by the police in connection with a crime (either because the vehicle itself is stolen or because the vehicle is thought to be driven or owned by a suspected criminal).

This information must be kept separate from all other files because the information must be immediately accessible. When a patrol officer observes someone who is behav-

```
WANTED                                        WANTED

LAST            FIRST           MIDDLE       APD No.

OFFENSE WANTED FOR                            OFFENSE NO

RACE    SEX   AGE    DOB     HEIGHT   WEIGHT   HAIR    EYES

OTHER DESCRIPTION OR I.D.
DRIVING:
          COLOR    YEAR   MAKE    LICENSE  YR.   STATE NO.

WARRANT NO.        COURT        JUDGE        TELETPYE NO.

VICTIM/COMPL.              ADDRESS          DATE REPORTED

PD 0093              CR SUPERVISOR                DATE
```

*A current wants and warrants card. (Courtesy Austin, Texas, Police Department)*

ing suspiciously, there is not time for a clerk to search through voluminous files; the patrol officer must be warned without delay if the suspicious person is a wanted criminal.

Current wants and warrants customarily are exchanged among law enforcement agencies in adjacent communities or jurisdictions. Unfortunately, some agencies—especially the very small ones and sometimes the very large ones—tend to become careless about distributing wants and warrants information to neighboring agencies. Investigators, above all other personnel, should assume the responsibility for seeing that wants and warrants are appropriately distributed and that their own agency's files are properly maintained.

It is just as important for the wants and warrants file to be kept up to date. When a suspect is arrested, a stolen vehicle is found, or a want or a warrant is no longer valid, all agencies that received the original notice should be informed. A wants and warrants file must contain only those records that are current and valid; otherwise, embarrassing and potentially dangerous mistakes can be made. Again, investigators should assume

much of the responsibility for canceling their own wants and warrants, even though the R&I section may be expected to carry out this routine task.[19]

## INFORMATION FROM OTHER SOURCES

Many criminal cases do not begin and end entirely within a single law enforcement agency. Most cases involve at least the law enforcement agency, the prosecutor's office, and the court system. Some cases also involve law enforcement agencies in adjacent communities or at the state or federal levels, other governmental agencies of various sorts, and, ultimately, a corrections agency. Since all these agencies must cooperate in order to bring a case to a successful conclusion, it is vital that information be shared freely among all of them.[20]

### NCIC AND NLETS

Information sharing among law enforcement agencies has been enormously enhanced by the establishment of the National Crime Information Center (NCIC), the National Law

Enforcement Telecommunications System (NLETS), and the state or regional counterparts of these entities.

The National Crime Information Center is essentially a nationwide, computerized R&I section operated by the Federal Bureau of Investigation. The NCIC computers contain the same kind of information that would be found in any well-organized local R&I section: criminal history files, personal identification files (mostly fingerprints, photographs, and M.O.'s), and current wants and warrants, both for persons and for vehicles. The information is gathered from the FBI itself, all other federal law enforcement or investigative agencies, and any state or local agency that wishes to participate. Similarly, the information is available from the computers to any legally authorized law enforcement agency that wants it. Requests for information from NCIC can be submitted by letter, telegram, telephone call, or even direct computer-to-computer connection.[21]

To ensure faster communication between NCIC and the thousands of local agencies, the federal government established NLETS, which we described in Chapter 9. One of the main advantages of NLETS is that a local police department can almost simultaneously inform adjacent agencies about a major criminal event, ask the state and national Crime Information Centers (CICs) for any information that they might have on the suspect, and pass the information along to neighboring departments. When used properly, the combination of NLETS, NCIC, and their state counterparts eliminates the advantage that a criminal has in being able to leave the scene of the crime quickly.

Several federal agencies besides the FBI are directly connected to the NLETS network. These agencies include the Treasury Department (Secret Service and the Bureau of Alcohol, Tobacco, and Firearms), the Department of the Army, the Department of the Navy, the Drug Enforcement Administration, and the Postal Inspection Service. Each of these agencies will respond to inquiries for the kind of information that they ordinarily possess.

## OTHER FEDERAL AGENCIES

Besides the agencies that can be contacted through NLETS, all the other federal agencies listed in Chapter 1 have information that might be of value to an investigator. Most of these agencies have regional offices and, sometimes, subregional offices in large cities around the country. Inquiries often can be routed through a regional or subregional office by the agency's own teletype or telephone network. This can save time and ensure that an inquiry is given prompt attention. Otherwise, the quickest way to obtain information is by direct telephone call.

## STATE AGENCIES

State law enforcement agencies are key elements in both NCIC and NLETS. All states have their own Crime Information Centers or operate one cooperatively with an adjacent state; they are all computerized and compatible with NCIC. In addition, the NLETS network has a "point of entry" in every state, almost invariably at the headquarters of the state police agency. From this point of entry, the statewide teletype networks branch out to reach local agencies. Similarly, any local police agency should be able to reach any other local agency in the same state by teletype, either by direct contact or through the state's NLETS control center.

In some states, a number of nonpolice, law-enforcement-related agencies are accessible through the state teletype network.

These agencies might include the Attorney General's Office, district or county attorneys (prosecutors), the state's corrections agency, the Adjutant General (state militia), and so forth. In other states, these agencies must be reached by more conventional methods, such as telephone, telegram, or mail. In addition, every state government has dozens of non-law-enforcement agencies that maintain various sorts of information that could be valuable to an investigator. Usually these agencies, too, must be reached by conventional means.

## THE COURTS

Investigators should be especially concerned with information about court proceedings. Unfortunately, this kind of information is rarely arranged for the convenience of police detectives, and sometimes it is almost impossible to obtain.

After an investigator has pursued a case to its solution, identified the person thought to be the perpetrator of a crime, arrested the suspect, and turned over the case to a prosecutor, naturally the final outcome is of professional interest. It is neither unusual nor inappropriate for an investigator to work closely with the prosecutors in order to be certain that the evidence is complete for a proper presentation of the case in court.

Furthermore, every investigator should maintain a general awareness of the present status of known or suspected criminals in the community. At any given moment, there may be a handful or several hundred offenders who are in jail or released on bond—being processed through the various hearings before trial, being tried, awaiting sentencing, and so on—and many convicted criminals may have been recently released either on parole or on completion of a prison sentence. It would be impossible for every investigator

to know the whereabouts of every criminal at all times. However, it should be possible for the police to keep track of criminals who are within the criminal justice process—between arrest and release. We shall discuss the various aspects of the court processes later, especially in Chapter 18. For now, we shall simply outline the means by which an investigator can keep track of an arrestee.

When a suspect is arrested, an arrest record is created. Usually the suspect is fingerprinted and photographed; these documents are checked against local, state, and national records to be certain that the suspect has been correctly identified and to learn whether there are any outstanding wants or warrants for the suspect. Meanwhile, the suspect is temporarily lodged in a police lock-up or local jail; a jail record is created.

Not long after arrest—almost always within a few hours—the suspect must be brought before a magistrate, advised of his or her constitutional rights, and formally charged with a crime. The arresting officer must satisfy the magistrate that there is enough evidence to justify holding the suspect in jail. In most states, the magistrate must decide at this point on the type or amount of bail. If the suspect is able to post the required bond, he or she may be released at once. Otherwise, the suspect returns to the lock-up to await trial. If it is expected that the trial will be delayed for a fairly long time or if the local lock-up is crowded, the suspect may be transferred to a county jail and placed in the custody of the sheriff. All these actions are reflected in the records of the magistrate's clerk. If the prisoner is transferred or released, that fact should be shown on the jail record card. The prosecutor's office also should have a complete record of these procedures. The investigator or arresting officer ordinarily is not notified of these events automatically.

Sometime after the initial appearance before a magistrate, the prisoner will be brought before whichever court will conduct the trial; this could be the municipal court, justice of the peace court, or county or district court. Often there are several such courts with overlapping or duplicate jurisdictions, and the assignment of a case to a particular court may be purely arbitrary. By this time the investigator should have turned the case over to a prosecutor. At the pretrial hearing, the prisoner will be given an opportunity to plead guilty or to demand a full trial. The prosecutor may be required to present at least the major elements of evidence against the defendant. If bail has not been set previously, it will be set at this point; in many relatively minor cases the defendant may be released without bail.

The investigator rarely will be informed of all these proceedings unless he or she goes to the trouble of tracking down the information. The prosecutor's office should be able to tell the investigator where the prisoner is and what will happen next. Otherwise, this information may be available from the clerk for the court with jurisdiction over the case or from the jail in which the prisoner is being held, unless the defendant is free on bail.

If the case goes to trial, the investigator will be informed by the prosecutor, because—except in rare cases—the investigator will be expected to testify. However, sometimes this information is transmitted in a rather casual form. In some communities the prosecutor merely sends to the police a copy of the weekly or monthly court docket, leaving it up to the police to determine which officers will be needed for which trials and on what days.

After trial, regardless of the outcome, the defendant usually disappears, as far as the police are concerned. If convicted, the criminal may be given a suspended sentence or probation, or may be sentenced to the amount of time already served (in essence, released without further punishment), or may be sent off to a state correctional institution. Eventually, the convicted criminal almost always returns to the community either on parole or on completion of the prison sentence. Again, investigators are almost never informed of these events. Information about sentencing may be available from the prosecutor's office or from the court clerk. Information about probationers and parolees should be available from the local probation office. Some state correctional institutions routinely inform local law enforcement agencies about the release of offenders who have completed their sentences or have been paroled; most institutions do not. More than one police officer has been astonished to discover that a fresh criminal case is the work of a convicted offender who was sent off to the state prison only a few months ago.

It is probably unfair to expect individual police investigators to keep track of every arrestee from the moment of arrest to the final release from prison. Most investigators are doing well if they keep up with their current cases. The responsibility for making this information available to local law enforcement agents, in timely and accessible form, should be assumed by the courts, the prosecutors, and the correctional officials. Unfortunately, no state has developed and implemented a system to do all that.[22]

## CRIME ANALYSIS UNITS

As we have mentioned several times, criminal activity often occurs in recognizable patterns. Not only do individual criminals repeat their offenses habitually, but there are also

*The primary role of the Crime Analysis Unit is to determine trends and patterns of criminal behavior; this information then must be given to both investigative and patrol personnel so that they can act on it. (Reproduced with permission of A.T. & T. Co.)*

should work very closely with investigators, and vice versa.

The CAU may function in a number of ways. For example, when there has been a series of crimes of a particular type—such as rapes, armed robberies, or residential burglaries—the CAU might study and compare the individual incidents to see whether there are common elements of the M.O. The common element could be a similarity among the different victims, or a trademark of the criminal, or merely the fact that all of the crimes have occurred within a restricted geographic area. Often this kind of crime analysis can indicate whether the series of crimes was committed by a single offender or by several different individuals.

Geographic patterns are often significant. Criminals frequently prey on people in their own neighborhoods. In other cases, criminals may take advantage of some unique situation that creates a special opportunity; for example, a criminal may use public transportation to reach an area in which there is a high concentration of liquor stores, massage parlors, or some other type of target.

Occasionally the CAU can actually predict where a criminal is most likely to strike next. Again, such predictions are based on the fact that criminals tend to follow habitual patterns. Some criminals establish certain criteria for their targets. For instance, a criminal might decide that drive-in grocery stores located in residential neighborhoods are especially vulnerable. Having set this conscious criterion, the criminal methodically robs one drive-in grocery after another—without realizing that a distinctive geographic sequence is being followed. The CAU, comparing the offense reports from a string of drive-in grocery robberies, might realize that only stores in residential neighborhoods are being robbed and that they are all within a few

general trends and even "fashions" in criminal behavior.

The people who occupy the fringes of society associate with one another and influence one another's behavior. When one criminal successfully holds up a liquor store, a growing epidemic of liquor-store holdups may follow. In much the same way, a particular type of crime can become "unfashionable" as soon as the police make a few significant arrests. The key to stopping a rash of crimes is to spot the pattern early and devote concerted efforts to making those significant arrests.

Most medium-sized or large police agencies have a special unit whose primary responsibility is to study crime reports in order to detect patterns and trends in criminal behavior. These *crime analysis units* (CAUs) blocks of a major expressway. The CAU might conclude that two or three particular stores are most likely to be the next targets. A close patrol of those potential targets might result in an on-the-spot arrest.

A crime analysis unit functions as a sort of superinvestigator, comparing information from a number of different cases rather than concentrating on solving a single case. To a large extent, every investigator should try to be an individual crime analysis unit, looking for indications of common elements among the various cases that are being investigated. Unfortunately, it is a human failing—not just of investigators but of most people—to be unable "to see the forest for the trees." The formally established CAU is designed specifically to look for "forests." If both the CAU and the individual investigator have ready access to accurate information and if they maintain good communication between themselves, the CAU can be helpful in letting the investigator know which "trees" to look out for.

## COMPUTERIZATION

So far in this chapter, the records systems that we have described have been based on manual records: individual sheets of paper, index cards, and printed forms stored in some kind of filing cabinet. More and more, these manual systems are being replaced with records systems that are automated or computerized.[23]

### ADVANTAGES AND DISADVANTAGES OF MANUAL SYSTEMS

The trend toward automation and computerization promises enormous dividends both in reducing the costs of police administration and in increasing the effectiveness of law enforcement. However, that promise is not al-ways fulfilled. Some agencies might be advised to stick with a manual system.

A manual system has two primary advantages. First, as long as the volume of records remains relatively small, a manual system is less expensive than even the simplest semi-automated system. All automated systems require some sort of special equipment and special procedures for filing and retrieving records. The equipment usually is costly to install, and the specialized procedures may impose continuing costs. Second, almost anyone of moderate intelligence and education can be trained to handle a manual records system. Automated systems may require more highly trained personnel. Not only does this mean higher costs, but the complexity of operating an automated system may mean that untrained individuals—patrol officers, investigators, and other police personnel—must depend on the trained staff to perform all of the filing and retrieval tasks.

The principal disadvantage of a manual system is that the retrieval of information becomes increasingly more difficult as the volume of records grows. The information takes longer to find and sometimes it cannot be found at all. Eventually the cost of time-consuming file searches and elaborate cross-indexing procedures may outweigh the economies of simple printed forms and filing cabinets. At that point, some kind of automation is necessary.

### SEMI-AUTOMATED RECORDS SYSTEMS

One of the simplest kinds of semi-automated systems employs edge-punched cards. Each record—complaint form, offense report, personal ID record, and so on—is prepared on a stiff card that has a row of small holes around all four edges. The holes themselves are coded to represent indexing categories, such as the type of incident or the location. After a card has been filled out, the appropriate holes are enlarged in order to extend to the edge of the card.

Sorting a stack of edge-punched cards is easy. A long rod is placed through the hole position for the desired index category and the stack of cards is lifted by the rod, as shown in Figure 11.5. The cards that have that particular hole punched out to the edge of the card will fall out of the stack. The cards that fall from the first sorting can be resorted in the same way again and again until, finally, the stack is reduced to the one card or small number of cards that fit all the criteria.

Of course, there is a limit to the number of index categories that can be accommodated; the limit is the number of holes present around the edge of the cards. Also, the sorting procedure can become tedious when three

FIGURE 11.5

EDGE-PUNCHED CARD SYSTEM

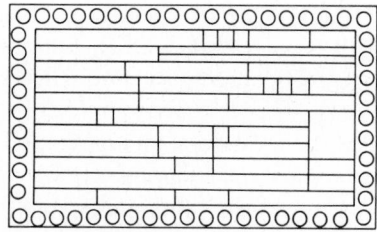

**A. An edge-punched card**

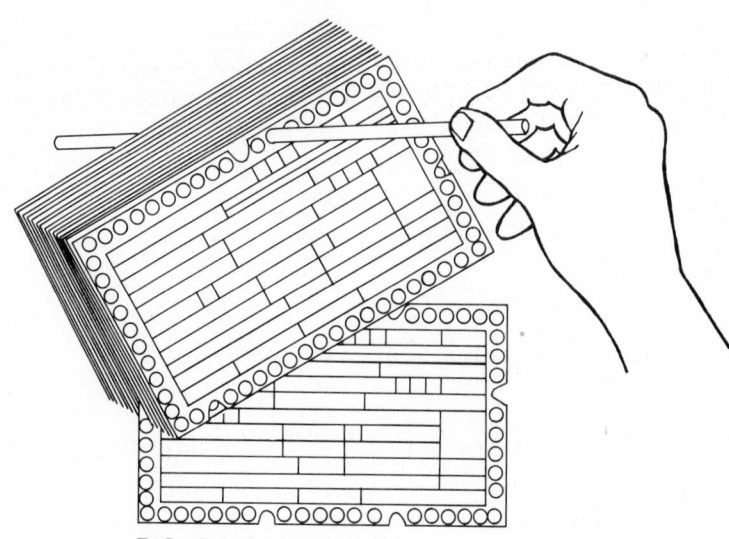

**B. Sorting edge-punched cards**

or four sortings are required to find the needed item of information. All the cards must be refiled manually, and there is always the danger that cards will be misfiled or lost.

Many law enforcement agencies have turned to microfilm as an alternative to manual records. Unfortunately, microfilm is a good solution to reducing the administrative costs of maintaining a large filing system, but it is often a poor solution to the problems of indexing and retrieving records.

The problem is that microfilmed records cannot be read without the help of a microfilm reader. This complicates the task of searching through the files to find a particular item of information. Some forms of microfilm, such as microfilm reels, are particularly troublesome, because the records are unavoidably filed in a rigid, unchangeable sequence. Microfiche (sheets of microfilm, usually four by six inches in size, that contain anywhere from 20 to 150 individual images) is much handier for records that are naturally grouped together, such as case files, since all documents associated with a single case can be placed on a single sheet.

There are computerized microfilm indexing systems that help to reduce the difficulties of retrieving information. These systems typically depend on coding the microfilmed records with some sort of index marks along the edges of the film. When a particular record must be found, the code numbers are entered at a simple keyboard. The microfilm reader then searches for the corresponding index marks on the reel of microfilm. These systems work reasonably well, but all the coding and indexing must be done, with perfect accuracy, when the record is filmed; the indexing cannot be changed later without a great deal of trouble. Furthermore, the index itself must be maintained (usually in manual form) separately from the microfilm files.

## FULLY AUTOMATED RECORDS SYSTEMS

Very few law enforcement agencies are able to afford complete computerization of their records. Even the largest agencies usually maintain most of their records in manual or semi-automated forms (especially microfilm).[24] Computerization means that information is stored in some sort of electronic memory. The information first must be translated from the original paper forms into an electronic code. The coded signal is transferred to the computer's memory. However, there are several different kinds of computer memory, and the kind determines the accessibility of the information in the system.

The most expensive type is an *on-line memory:* some kind of storage device that is permanently connected to the rest of the com-

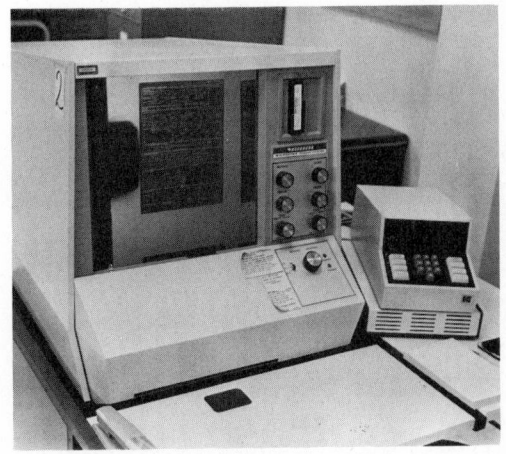

*An automated microfilm system. The control panel at right operates the computerized search system, which locates a particular record on a reel of film according to an index number. The index, of course, must be kept separately, either in manual form or in a separate computer memory.*

puter. Magnetic cores and magnetic disks are most often used for on-line memory. An on-line memory has one great advantage: all the information stored in it is available virtually on a moment's notice. The great disadvantage of on-line memory is that it is limited to the storage capacity of the particular device used. The only way to increase the storage capacity is to add more devices, and they are very expensive. For this reason, on-line memory is rarely chosen to store extensive files of information; more often, the on-line memory provides only temporary storage.

*Off-line memory* devices include punched cards, magnetic tape, some kinds of magnetic disks, and various other devices. Even small tape cassettes, like those that fit audio tape recorders, can provide off-line computer memory. In terms of the cost for each item of information stored, these types of memory are considerably less expensive than on-line devices. Furthermore, additional information can be stored by merely adding another stack of cards, or another tape, or another unit of the storage medium.

The problem, of course, is that information can be retrieved from any one of these devices only when it is connected to the rest of the computer. Since it is time-consuming and cumbersome to switch back and forth from, say, one tape to another, requests for information must be handled in batches: all requests for information from a particular tape are handled at one time. That is not much help when a patrol officer is standing in the street and checking to see whether a particular vehicle is wanted somewhere. Off-line memories are best suited to permanent storage of infrequently used records and to all sorts of administrative purposes for which speed of retrieval is not important.

Computerized police records systems have other disadvantages, too. Most law enforcement agencies that use computers must share them with other governmental agencies, such as the city's accounting office or personnel

*Computer memory devices. At left are several tape drives, any of which can be connected to the central processing unit (CPU) at any time, and the tapes can be removed and replaced. In the background are several rows of disk drives, all of which are connected to the CPU at all times, thus serving as on-line memory units.*

department. Often, the computer itself is located some distance from the police department. This can result in serious problems of both security and reliability.

In spite of all the problems and disadvantages, it seems evident that law enforcement agencies will rely more and more heavily on computers in the future. Unquestionably, computerization is the only way to handle the tremendous volume of information that modern police practice requires. A well-designed computer system can be an indispensable ally to the investigator, once the investigator learns how to use the system effectively.

## THE IDEAL SYSTEM

As far as we know, no police department in the country has a truly ideal computerized records system. However, just to demonstrate what such a system could do and what it might look like, we shall describe what we imagine to be a typical police case in a few years.

1:30 P.M.: The switchboard operator at police headquarters receives a complaint from the owner of Adams Liquors, 1569 North Street, that she has been robbed. The operator enters the complaint into the computer keyboard. The computer checks to see what patrol units are closest to the scene. Baker-6 is closest and is available, so the computer signals Baker-6 (through the unit's within-vehicle terminal) to respond to the call.

While Baker-6 is en route, the computer checks to see whether the Adams Liquor robbery is a significant crime. First, the computer searches its memory for any other crimes at the same location; finding none, it checks for other liquor store robberies in the same part of town. Four such robberies have occurred within the past two weeks. The computer immediately checks to see which detective is responsible for investigating the

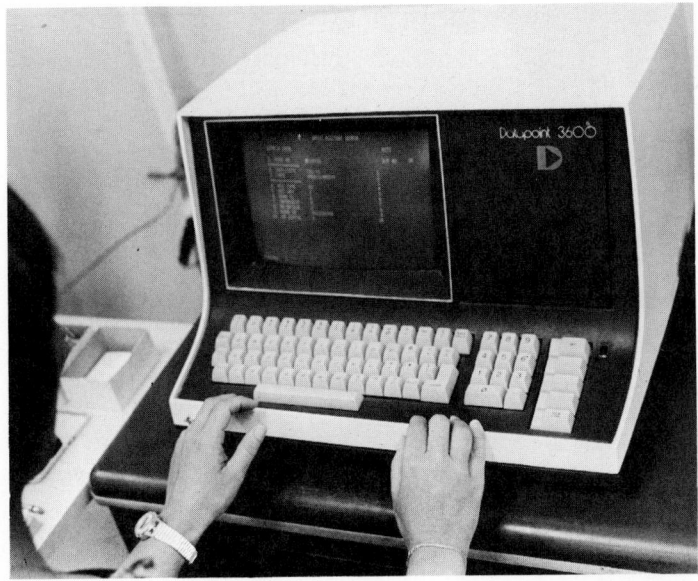

*Computerization offers the only solution to the information needs of the police. Someday, computer terminals like this one may be common on detectives' desks.*

previous four robberies; it is Sergeant Davis. The computer transmits a signal to Sergeant Davis's desk-top terminal, advising the detective of the robbery at Adams Liquors.

1:35 P.M.: Baker-6 arrives at the scene. Meanwhile, however, the computer has already provided Baker-6 with a summary of the information available about the other four robberies in the vicinity. Baker-6 uses this information to guide the interview with Ms. Adams and the other witnesses and to aid in the search for physical evidence. Fortunately, a customer who witnessed the crime is able to give Baker-6 a thorough description of the criminal. Baker-6 immediately transmits the description to the computer by the terminal within the patrol vehicle.

1:40 P.M.: The computer searches its memory for a potential suspect who matches the witness's description and who has a past record of similar robberies. One possible suspect comes up, but, on cross-checking this name, the computer discovers that he is already in jail on other charges. Nevertheless, the computer relays all this information to Sergeant Davis's terminal.

1:45 P.M.: Davis returns from doing field work on another case. The detective's desk-top terminal is displaying a signal light indicating that an important message is waiting in its local memory. Davis taps a couple of buttons, and the information about the Adams Liquors robbery and the similar cases appears on the display screen. Puzzled, Davis waits for more details from Baker-6.

2:00 P.M.: Baker-6, having completed the initial investigation, reports all available information through the in-vehicle terminal. The computer immediately begins analyzing the information and cross-checking it with its memory, while simultaneously relaying information to Davis. The Sergeant sees

something interesting in Baker-6's report: the victim and the witnesses all agree that the robber spoke with a pronounced Boston accent. Davis recalls that the nonsuspect, the one who is already in jail, also had a Boston accent. Using the desk-top terminal, Davis asks the computer whether the nonsuspect has any close relatives, such as a brother or son, or other close associates living in town. The computer quickly displays a list, drawn from the prisoner's criminal history file, of the nonsuspect's relatives and known associates. Yes, the prisoner has a brother who is only a year younger. The computer also gives Davis the brother's last known address.

There is not enough reason to consider the younger brother a definite suspect. If there were, Davis could use the computer to request an arrest warrant. Instead, Davis decides that some discreet questioning would be appropriate.

2:10 P.M.: Davis informs the computer that the younger brother, Edward Franklin, is to be regarded as a possible suspect in the Adams Liquors case and that Franklin should be observed, but not apprehended. The computer relays this information to all patrol units in the vicinity of Franklin's last known address. Meanwhile, the computer gives Davis the names and telephone numbers of Franklin's immediate neighbors. Davis calls each neighbor and asks a few questions about Franklin's whereabouts and activities. Most of the neighbors are not helpful, but one neighbor says that Franklin seems to have a lot of money to spend in local taverns and that he comes and goes at all hours of the day and night. In fact, the neighbor says, Franklin just drove up a few minutes ago in his big, flashy sedan. The neighbor gives Davis a description of the car.

Davis immediately runs the vehicle's description through the computer. It replies

322

that those license plates are supposed to be on a small foreign station wagon and that the description of Franklin's car matches either of two large sedans that were reported stolen about a month ago.

2:15 P.M.: Davis has everything necessary for a warrant now. The detective informs the computer that Edward Franklin is a suspect, wanted for armed robbery and auto theft. The computer prepares a warrant and relays it to the terminal in a magistrate's office, along with a summary of the information already known about Franklin. The magistrate's secretary prepares the actual warrant on paper; meanwhile, the magistrate signals the computer that the warrant is approved. The computer so informs Davis and immediately dispatches a patrol unit to pick up Franklin.

2:20 P.M.: Patrol unit Baker-9 arrives at Franklin's home. Franklin is apprehended while still counting the loot from the Adams Liquors robbery. Baker-9 also impounds Franklin's car; its engine number matches that of one of the stolen vehicles.

2:30 P.M.: Franklin is booked into the police jail, again with the computer's help. Meanwhile, Sergeant Davis is busy accumulating information from the computer about the other four liquor store robberies, the stolen car, and any other crimes that could be related. All this information will be handy when the detective interrogates the suspect in a few minutes. By that time, the computer will have checked Franklin's personal identification and will have looked for any other crimes that Franklin might have committed.

Someday, everything that we have just described may be considered ordinary and routine. There is nothing spectacular about this fictitious case, and such a computer is well within the range of current technology.

But consider what would be required for the same sequence of activities without the computer. First, Baker-6's investigative report probably would not have reached Sergeant Davis until the next day; it might even have gone to another detective who did not know about the other four armed robberies. Even if Davis had gotten the case and had made the connection to the other four robberies, it would have taken a good deal of searching through files to find Franklin's older brother as a possible suspect—and then more time to discover that the older brother was already in jail.

In fact, the only part of this whole story that reflects current police practice is the check on Franklin's car. Other than that, each step would take a minimum of several hours and very likely a day or two, following present law enforcement procedures. Instead, using our ideal system, Detective Davis acted as a central processing unit in partnership with a real computer and did the job in an hour.

## REFERENCES

1. George D. Eastman, ed., *Municipal Police Administration* (Washington, D.C.: International City Management Association, 1969), p. 146.

2. Peter W. Greenwood, Jan M. Chaiken, and Joan Petersilia, *The Criminal Investigation Process* (Lexington, Mass.: D. C. Heath, 1977), pp. 70–72.

3. Eastman, p. 247.

4. Eastman, p. 253.

5. Paul M. Whisenand and Tug T. Tamaru, *Automated Police Information Systems* (New York: John Wiley, 1970), p. 4.

6. Eastman, p. 254.

7. Greenwood, Chaiken, and Petersilia, pp. 12–14.

8. Eastman, pp. 270–274.

9. Maurice J. Fitzgerald, *Handbook of Criminal Investigation* (New York: Arco, 1969), pp. 119–125.

10. Harrison C. Allison, *Personal Identification* (Boston: Holbrook Press, 1973), p. 8.

11. Allison, chaps. 15, 16; Andre A. Moenssens, *Fingerprint Techniques* (Philadelphia: Chilton, 1971), chap. 6.

12. Allison, pp. 125–130.

13. Moenssens, pp. 160–164.

14. Moenssens, chap. 7.

15. Moenssens, pp. 243–251.

16. Allison, pp. 345–348.

17. Eastman, pp. 265–266.

18. Eastman, pp. 266–267.

19. Eastman, p. 263.

20. Whisenand and Tamaru, pp. 8–16.

21. Whisenand and Tamaru, pp. 37–40.

22. Eastman, pp. 268–270.

23. Whisenand and Tamaru, p. 5.

24. Whisenand and Tamaru, chap. 3.

## REVIEW OF THE EVIDENCE

1. One of the most serious problems in establishing and maintaining an effective R&I section is
    a. keeping administrative and legal records separate from investigative records.
    b. ensuring that the public has no access to confidential police records.
    c. keeping a balance between accessibility and security.
    d. covering the expense of both manual and automated record-keeping systems.
    e. avoiding the resentment that most people feel about the records kept by the police.

2. True or false: Supplemental investigative reports are prepared after the preliminary investigation only when a case has been solved.

3. Information about a suspect's habitual pattern of criminal behavior would most likely be found in
    a. the case file.
    b. the M.O. file.
    c. the personal identification file.
    d. the arrest reports file.
    e. the field interview file.
    f. all of the files mentioned above.
    g. none of the files mentioned above.

4. Which of the following files would be *least* helpful to the investigator if the identity of the perpetrator of a crime is not known?
    a. the M.O. file.
    b. the criminal history file.
    c. the incidents cross-index.
    d. the fingerprint file.
    e. the field interview file.

5. The most widely used system for classifying fingerprints is
    a. the Henry system.
    b. the edge-punched card system.
    c. the computer.
    d. the cross-index.
    e. the modus operandi system.

6. The primary purpose of a cross-indexing system is
    a. to reduce the volume of records that must be kept.
    b. to enable the investigator to identify suspects on the basis of their habitual patterns of criminal behavior.
    c. to aid the records clerks in summarizing information for administrative use.
    d. to inform patrol officers of any outstanding wants or warrants on a suspect.
    e. to guide the investigator in locating information in the main files.

7. Which of the following types of indexes should be included in any cross-indexing system?
   a. name index
   b. chronological index
   c. location index
   d. incident classification index
   e. numerical index
8. True or false: The responsibility for canceling a want or warrant notice rests with the investigator.
9. What would be the first place that an investigator should check to determine whether an arrested suspect has been released on bail?
   a. NCIC
   b. the jail record card
   c. the magistrate's clerk
   d. the prosecutor's office
   e. the R&I section
10. Edge-punched cards are one type of
   a. on-line memory.
   b. microfilm index.
   c. semi-automated records system.
   d. cross-indexing system.
   e. off-line memory.

TOPICS FOR INVESTIGATION

1. A police department's own records may be used by governmental officials or journalists to criticize the performance of police officers. Should efforts be made to ensure that only favorable information is found in records accessible to outsiders? What responsibility do individual officers have to prepare reports in a way that will reflect favorably on the department?
2. Under the laws of your state, which police records *must* be made available to any citizen on request? Which records *may* be made available under certain circumstances? And which records *may not* be made available except to other law enforcement personnel? How well are these laws implemented by local law enforcement agencies?
3. Discuss the use of field interview reports. Why have the courts "taken a dim view" of this police practice? Under what circumstances would a field interview be appropriate or inappropriate?
4. To what extent should police departments discontinue maintaining noncriminal ID files?
5. What should law enforcement agencies do to improve communications and record keeping in coordination with the courts and prosecutors' offices? What responsibility do individual police officers have in this regard? Although a computerized ideal system is probably unattainable, what could be done to improve the flow of information, and what would be the most important step?

# CHAPTER 12

## PERSONAL SOURCES OF INFORMATION

STUDY CLUES

1. True or false: The saying "Police officers are only as good as their sources" reflects an outmoded concept that has no validity in modern police work.
2. Which of the following steps should an investigator take to encourage patrol and public contact officers to pass along useful information?
   a. Make sure that individual officers, however helpful, are not singled out for rewards or attention just for doing their job.
   b. Insist that all patrol units use field interview report forms to report any suspicious circumstances or activities that they have observed.
   c. Circulate memos describing information needed to solve current cases.
   d. Recommend helpful officers for departmental commendations.
   e. Contact patrol units directly to discuss current investigations.
   f. Do all of the above.
   g. Do none of the above.
3. In some agencies, tactical units serve only in short-term crisis situations. In other agencies, tactical units are used primarily for
   a. routine investigations that do not require a detective's expertise.
   b. intensive patrol or surveillance of trouble areas.
   c. nonpolice services, such as VIP protection or funeral escorts.
   d. investigations of organized crime.
   e. the planning of departmental operations.
4. True or false: When dealing with tips, one ought to heed this rule: investigate the informant first; then investigate the information.
5. One of the most serious problems in dealing with paid informants is that
   a. police officers are not paid well enough to afford the use of informants.
   b. they are always unreliable because they are only interested in the money.
   c. it is illegal to pay an informant for information about criminal activity.
   d. the informant may be tempted to do something dangerous just to earn more money for information.
   e. there is no written record of payment and, therefore, no evidence of the source of information.

ONE OF THE OLDEST CLICHÉS in law enforcement is that "police officers are only as good as their sources." The cliché is still valid today, although it does not mean quite what it did in the past.

The bulk of all police work used to be performed by the beat patrolman. That individual was held personally accountable for everything that happened on his beat while he was on duty. A crime was considered a personal challenge to the patrolman's effectiveness and honor. One of the most crucial ways for a patrolman to maintain his effectiveness was to be thoroughly familiar with everyone and everything on the beat. The patrolman cultivated friendships among the shopkeepers, the tradespeople, the housewives, and even the children on his beat. In return for the security and protection offered by the patrolman, members of the community would pass along to him any information that they had gained about any sort of criminal activity.

Successful patrolmen became detectives when they were no longer young enough or strong enough to pound a beat every day. They brought with them their widespread networks of confidants and informants, the most vital asset that a detective could have. Investigating a crime generally meant finding someone who knew something about the crime and was willing to talk.

Many police officers try to function in the same way today. However, the nearly universal use of automotive patrols instead of foot patrols, the greatly increased mobility of the population in general and of the criminal element in particular, and the increasing development of scientific methods of crime investigation all have reduced the police officer's reliance on a network of informants as the basis for effective investigation.[1] On one hand, these traditional sources of information are far less available and valuable than they once were. On the other hand, law enforcement relies much more heavily on the sources of information that we have described: physical evidence, testimony of victims and witnesses, public contact through the news media, rapid intradepartmental and interdepartmental communications, scientific examination of evidence in the crime laboratory, and an elaborate system of record keeping, cross-indexing, and data retrieval.

This is not to say, however, that the more personal sources of information ought to be ignored. On the contrary, an investigator must not overlook *any* potential source of information. In this chapter, we shall look at some of the ways in which an investigator can develop and use informal networks of information sources both within and outside the law enforcement agency itself.

## SOURCES WITHIN THE DEPARTMENT

Every law enforcement agency is made up of a number of elements, as we saw in Chapter 2. We have tried to emphasize throughout this text the importance of establishing and maintaining a close working relationship among all these elements. To do so requires constant, consistent effort; the effort pays off when the steady flow of information among the various elements produces the one key fact, lead, or clue that results in the solution to a criminal case.

### PATROL, TRAFFIC, AND PUBLIC CONTACT UNITS

In almost all police agencies, well over half of the personnel are assigned to patrol work, either general patrol or traffic patrol. In medium-sized and large agencies some personnel usually are assigned to various public contact units: crime prevention, community relations, public information, and the like.

All of these units have in common the fact that their work involves constant contact with the public. General patrol and traffic patrol officers are on the street, in their vehicles or on foot, every day. A major part of their job is to learn to recognize suspicious circumstances and individuals. The other public contact units, although they are less often on the street, have many opportunities to receive information from the public about suspicious, possibly criminal activities.

Significant information is supposed to be recorded on field interview reports or other formal documents. However, in practice a great part of the information is never recorded, because the police officer either fails to realize its significance or feels that filling out the paperwork is too much bother.

There are three things that the investigator can do to take full advantage of the information resources of the department's public contact units.

• The investigator can make sure that the patrol and other units are aware of the information needed to solve current cases. This can be done through formal memoranda circulated to all units, informal notes or bulletins, or briefings at the roll call at the start of each shift.

• The investigator can take the initiative in soliciting information from all elements of the department. Field interview reports and other documents should be checked regularly, but that is only a beginning. Personal

communication should not be overlooked. For example, if the investigator is working on a group of residential burglaries in a particular neighborhood, the patrol units who work in that neighborhood should be asked about any suspicious individuals or activities that they might have observed but failed to report.

• The investigator can ensure that other units receive full credit and some gesture of appreciation when they provide useful information. Nothing is more effective in encouraging better communication than a simple word of thanks, especially if it is expressed in the form of an official commendation or other notice of a job well done.

## TACTICAL UNITS

Special tactical units serve a great range of purposes in different police agencies. Some departments have permanently established tactical patrol units whose function is to reinforce the regular patrol units in areas where there has been a recent upsurge of crime activity or to provide intensive surveillance of particular types of businesses that have recently been the target of an exceptional number of crimes: banks or jewelry stores, perhaps. This sort of tactical unit is sometimes called a *strike force.*

Other departments have no permanent tactical units, but provide special training to selected individuals, regardless of their ordinary assignment, who respond to short-term crises such as a sniper, a suspect who is holding hostages, or a bomb threat. An example of this second type of tactical unit is the well-known Special Weapons and Tactics (SWAT) Team of the Los Angeles Police Department. This kind of tactical unit rarely would have useful information for investigators because of the transitory, highly concentrated nature of the job.

ANSWERS TO STUDY CLUES
1. False    2. c, d, and e    3. b    4. False
5. d

*Roll-call briefings are one of the most effective ways for the investigator to share information with patrol officers.*

The first type of tactical unit, however, can provide invaluable assistance. The very nature of intensive patrol work, which is the major function of this kind of tactical unit, demands that the tactical officers know what they are looking for. Investigators ought to participate in making decisions about the deployment of tactical units from the very beginning: what kinds of cases the unit will be used for, where they will be used, what activities they will undertake on their own initiative, and so on. It is both foolish and potentially dangerous for investigators and tactical units to operate completely independently, as they do in some agencies; they are bound to get in each other's way.

In some departments the tactical unit's assignments are produced by the crime analysis unit, in consultation with undercover units working on vice, organized crime, or drug law enforcement. Other investigators may be left out of the decision-making process entirely. Such an arrangement ignores the interrelated quality of most criminal activity. Drug abusers commit robberies and burglaries; vice offenders associate with other petty criminals; organized criminals are deeply involved in all sorts of crime, particularly such businesslike activities as disposing of stolen property.

Thus, for example, a tactical unit might be called on to perform intensive surveillance of a residence where drug transactions take place, according to undercover agents. During the surveillance the tactical officers might observe expensive property, such as stereos and television sets, being taken into and out of the residence by suspected drug offenders. Such information could be immensely valuable to detectives working on burglaries. In this instance, the tactical officers would have an obligation to pass the information along to the detectives. However, it is equally important for the detectives to keep the lines of communication open so that this sort of information will be passed along.

## UNDERCOVER UNITS

One of the most fruitful sources of information may be a department's undercover units. Police undercover units most often are assigned to special crime control sections concerned with long-term investigations of vice, drug offenses, and organized crime. Occasionally they may conduct investigations of business crimes or some other problem. The essence of undercover work is that the agent infiltrates the criminal group itself, gathering information about the individuals involved until there is sufficient evidence to arrest key figures.

Obviously, an undercover agent's true identity must remain a secret. Some agents continue to work underground year after year, building one case after another against their criminal associates. Occasionally an agent even arranges to be "arrested" so that other criminals will not become unduly suspicious about the agent's apparent immunity from police attention. But ordinarily an undercover agent's identity is not widely known even among other police officers.

Maintaining communication between detectives and undercover agents is extraordinarily difficult but absolutely essential. Every undercover agent must have at least one route of contact with a supervisor or other police officer, partly so that information can be passed along as the agent discovers it and partly so that this individual can protect the agent if the latter's safety is endangered. The investigator must be satisfied to use whatever communication channel is available, even though it may be indirect and awkward. Direct contact with an undercover agent is utterly forbidden, except in the most urgent situations, because of the danger to the agent's life.

Similarly, an investigator must exercise discretion and common sense in asking an undercover agent to make inquiries about criminal activities. An undercover agent cannot ask too many questions without arousing suspicion, nor can the agent divert time and attention from one investigation, which may have taken several months to develop, in order to conduct another investigation on behalf of the detective.

Once in a while, it may be possible for undercover agents to initiate an investigation specifically for a detective. Usually this is possible only when an undercover agent has recently completed an assignment and is temporarily available for new work and when the case to be pursued fits into the agent's background of underground associations. For example, the investigators might be working on an unsolved murder that they believe to be connected with drug trafficking. If there is an undercover narcotics agent available, the agent might be asked to develop contacts with the murder victim's former associates. Here again, the detective must be realistic; too much should not be expected from the agent, who may not be able to gain the confidence of the intended targets of the investigation. Furthermore, undercover investigations are often very time-consuming. The detective must avoid putting undue pressure on the undercover agent to produce quick results, for patience and persistence are more likely to lead to success.

## EXTERNAL SOURCES OF INFORMATION

Despite all the scientific progress in discovering and developing physical evidence, the investigation of crime would be extraordinarily difficult if detectives never received information from tipsters, informants, and ordinary citizens. Fortunately, the flow of information is relentless, sometimes nearly reaching flood proportions. The investigator's problem is not only to encourage people to report information, but to make the best use of the information that is received.

## VOLUNTARY, NONCRIMINAL INFORMANTS

We mentioned in Chapter 6 the importance of secondary witnesses, people who happen to know something about a crime or about the participants in a criminal event even though they were not present when the crime was committed. In essence, all informants are secondary witnesses. However, there are important differences in the kinds of people who play this role in an investigation.

Investigators frequently receive information from individual citizens who were not present during a crime, do not personally know the victim or the perpetrator, and are not themselves involved in any sort of criminal activity, but who happen to know something about the criminal event. For example, the citizen may have observed a suspicious person or vehicle in the vicinity of the crime or may have seen the victim and a potential suspect arguing in some public place. Just as often, the secondary witness knows the victim or the offender personally, although the witness may be completely innocent of any criminal activity. After all, criminals must live someplace, buy groceries and other necessities, and generally come and go in their own neighborhoods. It is not unusual for other people to become suspicious of a neighbor who seems to have no visible means of support, but who always has plenty of money to spend, wears flashy clothes, and drives a strange variety of automobiles.[2]

Noncriminal volunteer informants often try to remain anonymous when they report their suspicions or observations to the police.

This desire for anonymity stems from a wish to avoid becoming involved in other people's problems, for fear of becoming the victim of retaliation or having to waste a good deal of time on matters that are of no personal concern. Unfortunately, the informant's desire for anonymity leaves the investigator in an awkward situation. It is nearly impossible to evaluate information without knowing who the source is and, in particular, whether the source is reliable. For this reason, the investigator must try to break down the barrier of anonymity without losing potentially valuable information.[3]

When someone calls with an anonymous tip, a detective should get the information first. Let the informant say everything he or she wants to say before asking any questions. Then, as in any other interview with a witness, summarize the information that has been given and try to elicit more details. Often the nature of the details will suggest the informant's identity.

Once all the information has been obtained, explain that every effort will be made to verify the information and thank the informant for having fulfilled an important duty of a citizen. However, you should explain, it may be very difficult to use the information without knowing the informant's identity. Point out that *only* you need to know who the informant is and that this information will not be revealed to anyone else. You might say casually, "I'll check this out right away, but I may need to get back with you on the details. Could I have a phone number where I can reach you during the day?" Once the informant gives a phone number, there should be no problem in getting a name to go with it.

Sometimes a secondary witness offers information that will be crucial to the prosecution of an offender. In this case, you must warn the informant that the information will have to be presented in court and that only the informant can present this testimony.[4] Otherwise, you might point out, it is likely that the offender will go free and will continue to prey on innocent citizens. Attempt to reassure the informant that every effort will be made to protect his or her identity and safety until the offender is behind bars. However, as we have said before, a police officer must be extremely careful not to make promises that cannot be kept. When a witness demands protection, the utmost caution and discretion must be exercised.

Not all noncriminal volunteer informants wish to remain anonymous. In fact, some informants are positively determined to attract attention to themselves. They might even go so far as to call newspaper reporters and brag about having given the police a tip that broke the case. Police officers also become familiar with well-meaning but eccentric citizens who see criminals hiding under every bush and lurking on every street corner. Such people pester detectives with all sorts of worthless "tips," especially during highly publicized investigations.

There are no easy guidelines or fixed rules to help the beleaguered detective sort out the productive leads from the unproductive. Unfortunately, every tip must be regarded as conceivably useful unless it is inherently contradictory or so trivial that it would contribute little or nothing to an investigation even if it were verified.

The detective must beware of ignoring tips from "unreliable" sources. After all, it is entirely possible that the most obnoxious crank might happen to stumble on the one fact that will solve a difficult case. Here, the rule reads: Investigate the information, not the informant. Tips from previously unreliable

sources might require more follow-up verification than a tip from a reliable source. Of course, if there is a great volume of information to be checked, common sense dictates that the tips from presumably reliable sources should be checked first, and those from unreliable sources should be left for last.

## HABITUAL INFORMANTS

So far, we have been talking about tips from individual citizens who are essentially secondary witnesses and who may never have volunteered information to the police before. There are also people who become regular or habitual informants, and some special procedures need to be established to cultivate these valuable contacts.

People volunteer information for a great variety of reasons, not all of which are obvious. Some people are motivated by a simple desire to see justice done, to assist the police, or to rid the community of criminals.[5] A few individuals develop a "detective complex." If they have provided useful, reliable information once or twice and have been rewarded with a gesture of appreciation, they come to see themselves as amateur detectives or volunteer police officers. Some departments encourage this attitude through formal programs of auxiliary police or police buddies, while many departments work just as hard to discourage amateur police buffs.[6]

The amateur detective can hardly be overlooked. Some of these individuals become so zealous that, unless restrained, they can interfere with legitimate police activities and seriously endanger themselves. On the other hand, these individuals may become valuable as extra eyes and ears for the police investigator if they are handled properly.

The rules for dealing with amateur detectives are simple:

*The investigator should agree to any reasonable precaution to protect an informant's identity, including meting the informant in out-of-the-way locations. (Photo by Julie O'Neil)*

1. Always express appreciation for information that a citizen provides and indicate that the tip will be followed up for verification. If an informant provides information that leads to the solution of a case, the investigator should take the time to let the informant know about it and to express thanks.

2. If an informant expresses concern about safety and security, the investigator should offer reassurance. The informant may feel more secure if a code name is used; the investigator should agree without hesitation and actually might suggest it. Other reasonable steps should be accepted to protect the informant's identity. However, excessively elaborate procedures for contacting an informant, passwords, secret codes, and so on should be avoided; they waste time, generate confusion and misunderstandings, and provide no real protection to anyone.

3. The informant must be made to understand that his or her only role is to provide information—*not* to participate in police activities such as surveillance, property searches, or arrests. Furthermore, the information belongs to the police department and not just to one investigator. The investigator must make it clear that the information will be reported in official documents and that other officers will be aware of it. Other officers might even have occasion to contact the informant directly at some time in the future. This procedure protects not only the detective but also the informant, in case the investigator should leave the police force or for some other reason become unavailable.

## PAID INFORMANTS

One of the most common sources of controversy and misunderstandings is the use of paid informants by the police. However, it seems to be a fact of life that some people are motivated only by greed; without the tangible reward of money they will not cooperate with the police or anyone else.

Some police agencies devote fairly large sums of money to networks of paid informants, and it appears that some informants actually earn a living, though meager, by supplying tips for cash. As long as the information is reliable and useful, many police authorities consider this practice justified.[7]

One danger is that when an informant depends on police money, there is inevitably a temptation to earn more and more money by supplying more and more information. This may lead the informant into extremely dangerous situations in the effort to produce information that would be valuable to the police. Less adventurous informants may solve the same problem by making up information or by creating situations that they can exploit, perhaps by entrapping their otherwise innocent associates.

From the investigator's point of view, the use of a paid informant creates a number of dilemmas. First, how much should an informant be paid? Some authorities say that the payment should be kept small so that the informant is not encouraged to rely on such payments as a major source of income. Other authorities fear that if payments are too small, the informant will feel little loyalty to the police or may be tempted to "raise the ante" by the improper methods that we just mentioned. Obviously, there is no easy answer and no generally accepted scale of payments.

Once an agency makes a policy decision to permit payments to informants, some safeguards must be established. The idea of cash payment should *never* be suggested by the investigator. When an informant suggests or demands payment for information, the investigator should respond by indicating that the matter must be approved by higher officials. A written record should be made of the nature of the information offered and of the amount of compensation requested by the informant. There should be a standard voucher form for this purpose. The voucher should be submitted to the investigator's superiors for approval. If payment is approved, the detective should obtain the required amount in cash from the department's business office. When payment is made, the informant should be required to provide a receipt, preferably by signing the voucher. A code name or alias may be used on the voucher, but in that case the informant should be told that his or her true identity is recorded elsewhere.

Some agencies will pay for information only after the information has been checked out and verified. This seems to be preferable to payment in advance, but it may not always be possible. Besides, the informant may not be at fault if the information turns out to be inaccurate.

Again, the informant must be made to understand that the information belongs to the police department as a whole, not just to one detective. When appropriate, the informant must be told that he or she might be called on to testify in court; ordinarily this is avoided, since it almost certainly compromises the informant's future usefulness.

One final caution is necessary: under no circumstances should a police officer ever pay for information out of his or her own pocket. To do so places the officer's personal integrity and reputation in serious jeopardy and may open a Pandora's box of legal and ethical problems. Besides, police officers are not paid that well.

**RECEIPT**

For and in consideration of the sale and delivery to the Temple Police Department Organized Crime Unit of information or evidence identified as follows:_____

_____

_____

I hereby acknowledge receipt of_____
dollars and_____ cents ($_____paid to
me by_____, agent
of the Temple Police Department Organized Crime Unit
Date:_____Signature:_____
Witness:_____
(If Any)

*A voucher form for payments to informants. (Courtesy Temple, Texas, Police Department)*

### CRIMINAL INFORMANTS

Criminals do not live in a vacuum. They have day-to-day lives apart from their criminal activity. Furthermore, most criminals associate with other individuals who are also involved in criminal activity. They share information about their past and future exploits; they often work together to carry out particular crimes; and some criminals operate illicit businesses such as fencing, dealing in weapons, and manufacturing burglary tools for purchase by other criminals.

It is not unusual for a petty criminal to decide to betray a criminal associate by giving information to the police. The informant may have any of several motives: fear of an associate whose violent behavior goes beyond the bounds of what is acceptable even among criminals, fear of being caught and punished for one's own misdeeds, or revenge for some real or imagined injury or insult. Discovering the motive is important to the investigator since it is a key factor in evaluating the informant's reliability; otherwise, there is a chance that the investigator will be deceived into serving as a tool of the informant.[8]

Criminal informants often try to hide their own involvement in crime. Usually the truth can be learned if the investigator simply remembers to ask the informant, "How do you happen to know what you've just told me?" If the informant refuses to answer or answers evasively, the investigator should be persistent without being unduly harsh. It may help to say something like this: "What you've just told me is important, and we will pursue it. We're very interested in getting a conviction in this case. However, if you are personally involved in any way, you'd better let me know about it now. If it comes out later, there won't be anything we can do to help you."

The investigator must be fully aware of the complex legal situation here. The police do not have the right or the authority to overlook or to forgive any crime that comes to their attention. It is absolutely improper and legally dangerous for a police officer to tell an informant, "If you'll give us information about so-and-so's crime, we'll forget about yours."

At the same time, however, the informant has the right to avoid self-incrimination. If the informant reveals some personal responsibility for criminal behavior, the police have no real choice but to arrest the informant and give the required constitutional warnings (the so-called Miranda warnings, which we will discuss in Chapter 15). Of course, unless this is done with great care and discretion, the informant may be frightened into silence. On the other hand, if the police fail to warn the informant properly, anything further that the informant says will be unusable as evidence, at least as far as making a case against the informant. A clever criminal might take advantage of this situation by revealing incriminating information about the activities of a *lesser* criminal, while simultaneously compromising the police investigation of more serious crimes.

Finally, the police have no authority to promise an informant freedom from prosecution, leniency, or anything else. Criminal informants often try to make a deal by offering information about other crimes in return for having their own offenses overlooked. The only deal that the police can offer is a promise to ensure that the informant's cooperative attitude is brought to the attention of the court. The police also may suggest to the prosecutor that charges against the informant be reduced or that leniency be recommended. However, it is up to the prosecutor to accept these suggestions, and ultimately it is up to the court to give or withhold leniency.[9]

There is one more step that can be taken by the court, but it should be reserved for unusual circumstances. If an individual has information about a serious crime but refuses to divulge the information because of his or her own minor involvement in the same crime, the court may grant *immunity from prosecution*. This means simply that the informant cannot be prosecuted on the basis of self-incriminating information. Immunity,

however, is a two-edged sword. Again, a clever criminal sometimes will arrange to be given immunity, supposedly to be able to reveal information freely about someone else's serious offenses, but really to avoid being prosecuted for his or her own crimes. Furthermore, juries sometimes consider testimony from immune witnesses to be suspect; so without solid evidence from other sources, there might not be a conviction anyway.

In summary, getting information from a criminal informant brings the investigator into a dense thicket of legal problems. Nevertheless, such information often is indispensable. As long as the investigator remains aware of the problems and proceeds with the full knowledge and guidance of higher authorities, the problems can be resolved.

Additional problems arise when an informant offers information about a crime that is being planned rather than a crime that has already taken place. Sometimes this happens when a petty criminal is being coerced into helping an associate commit a crime that the informant does not want to take part in or when the informant realizes that the planned crime is more dangerous or more serious than it first appeared. Generally, the police cannot act against someone who is merely planning a crime. It helps to know that a crime is being planned, but the police must wait until the offense is actually committed.

The dilemma is that the informant must be allowed—even encouraged—to carry out his or her part in the planned crime. Otherwise, it is highly likely that the plan will be dropped or substantially changed. But the police have no authority to condone any crime, however small. Further, the investigator must make certain that the informant's actions are not unreasonably dangerous, that the informant does not profit from the crime, and that the crime will not result in permanent harm to some innocent citizen. It is one thing to allow a planned burglary to proceed so that the burglars can be caught in the act, but the police certainly could not let a planned murder or arson be carried to the point of threatening someone's life or property.

Finally, the investigator must be certain that the informant did not initiate the planned crime and draw other people into the plan, for whatever purpose. In that case, the fact that the police were aware of the crime in advance but let it proceed so that arrests could be made would constitute *entrapment*.

If there is any doubt at all about a situation in which an informant tells an investigator about a planned crime, it may be better to disrupt the plan instead of allowing it to be executed with unforeseeable consequences. The simplest way to disrupt the planned crime is to arrest the informant or one of the other reported parties to the crime for an unrelated, minor offense. Another method is to give the target of the planned crime extraordinarily intensive protection. Most real-life criminals, unlike the criminal masterminds of popular fiction, can be frightened off rather easily if they see that carrying out their plans will be riskier than they had anticipated.

## THE INVESTIGATOR'S PERIPHERALS

At the beginning of Chapter 11, we described the police detective as the equivalent of a computer's central processing unit, or CPU, which receives information from a variety of remote devices, manipulates the information, stores it in memory, retrieves it again, and then uses the remote devices—known to computer operators as *peripherals*—to carry out certain actions. One important difference between a human detective and a computer is that the computer's central processing unit can accommodate only a certain number of peripherals, limited to the number of connections that the CPU is capable of making. A human detective, however, can have as many peripherals as there are people in the agency and in the community. All that the detective must do is to make the connections.

### REFERENCES

1. Peter W. Greenwood, Jan M. Chaiken, and Joan Petersilia, *The Criminal Investigation Process* (Lexington, Mass.: D. C. Heath, 1977), p. 23.

2. John J. Horgan, *Criminal Investigation* (New York: McGraw-Hill, 1974), p. 128.

3. Horgan, p. 127.

4. J. Shane Creamer, *The Law of Arrest, Search, and Seizure,* 2d ed. (Philadelphia: W. B. Saunders, 1975), p. 29.

5. Maurice J. Fitzgerald, *Handbook of Criminal Investigation* (New York: Arco, 1969), p. 47.

6. Paul B. Weston and Kenneth M. Wells, *Criminal Evidence for Police* (Englewood Cliffs, N.J.: Prentice-Hall, 1971), p. 206.

7. Greenwood, Chaiken, and Petersilia, p. 24.

8. Fitzgerald, p. 46.

9. Weston and Wells, p. 207.

# REVIEW OF THE EVIDENCE

1. True or false: The SWAT Team of the Los Angeles Police Department is an example of a tactical unit that would be unlikely to have information useful to investigators.

2. It is difficult for investigators to work with undercover agents because
   a. undercover investigations are often very time-consuming.
   b. undercover agents rarely come across information that would be valuable to investigators.
   c. undercover agents work in absolute secrecy and have no contact with other police officers.
   d. undercover agents are not trained in investigative techniques.
   e. giving information to investigators would reveal an undercover agent's identity.

3. How should an investigator deal with someone who offers information, but wishes to remain anonymous?
   a. Disregard the information because it is probably unreliable.
   b. Try to trick the informant into revealing his or her identity.
   c. Insist that the informant identify himself or herself before accepting any information.
   d. Accept the information without attempting to get the informant's identity.
   e. First get the information and then try to persuade the informant to reveal his or her identity.

4. True or false: A tip from a previously unreliable source should be ignored, because investigating it would be a waste of time.

5. If an informant expresses concern about personal safety, the investigator should
   a. arrange for whatever police protection is desired by the informant.
   b. explain to the informant that retaliation by criminals is rare and that police protection is too expensive to be supplied routinely.
   c. agree to use a code name, but not an elaborate set of codes or passwords.
   d. insist that the informant give all information immediately so that the criminal can be caught, thus eliminating any possible danger.
   e. disregard whatever the informant says, since it is obviously unreliable.

6. A paid informant should be required to
   a. reimburse the department if the information turns out to be false.
   b. sign a voucher or receipt when paid.
   c. testify in court in exchange for the payment offered by the police.
   d. encourage his or her associates to plan and carry out crimes and then inform the police so that the criminals can be caught in the act.
   e. do all of the above.
   f. do none of the above

7. True or false: An investigator generally can tell whether a criminal informant is trying to hide his or her own criminal activities.

8. Immunity from prosecution can be granted by
   a. the investigator.
   b. higher-ranking police officials.
   c. the prosecutor.
   d. a judge.
   e. a jury.
9. When a criminal informant tells the police about a crime that is being planned,
   a. the informant should be warned not to carry out his or her part in the planned crime.
   b. everyone involved in planning the crime should be arrested at once.
   c. the informant should be paid to encourage future tips.
   d. the investigator should explain that no one can be arrested until the crime has been committed, but that the information will be helpful if the crime takes place.
   e. the informant should be given immunity from prosecution.
10. True or false: The police should never attempt to disrupt a planned crime, because that will only endanger the informant and give the criminals a chance to refine their plans, reducing their risk and improving their likelihood of success.

## TOPICS FOR INVESTIGATION

1. List the ways by which an investigator could show appreciation to other police personnel who have provided useful information. Should a police agency establish a formal reward system for this purpose?
2. In some police departments, the tactical unit operates under the patrol division; in others, it is part of the crime analysis unit; in still others, it is a completely separate unit. Should a tactical unit be assigned to the criminal investigation section (detective bureau)?
3. What can investigators do to encourage citizens who have helpful information to come forward, without unduly encouraging cranks and eccentrics?
4. How should an investigator handle a police buff or amateur detective who has provided information that has helped to solve a difficult case, but who now seems to have become overzealous, endangering his or her own life?
5. How much should an informant be paid?

# Unit V

## THE CONTINUING INVESTIGATION

## CHAPTER 13

# PUTTING
# THE PIECES
# TOGETHER

STUDY CLUES

1. A crime is solved when
   a. the stolen property has been recovered.
   b. the perpetrator has been identified.
   c. all evidence has been collected, developed, and evaluated.
   d. the suspect has been convicted.
   e. all of the above have occurred.
   f. none of the above has occurred.
2. True or false: The perpetrator of a crime can be identified by any of six different methods.
3. After all the physical evidence has been analyzed, victims and witnesses have been interviewed, and all other sources of information have been checked, if a suspect still has not been identified, there is a good chance that
   a. the crime is not important enough to warrant further investigation.
   b. the crime never will be solved.
   c. the suspect will confess.
   d. the solution has been overlooked somewhere in the mass of evidence.
   e. there was no crime.
4. True or false: The reason that a crime was committed (the motive) might be an important clue in identifying the perpetrator.

ONE OF THE MOST REWARDING ASPECTS of criminal investigation is the intellectual challenge of tackling a difficult case that seems, at first glance, unsolvable. For many detectives, this is a distinctly personal challenge in which they pit their skill, training, knowledge, and resourcefulness against the criminals' cunning.

Many crimes are "no contest": the offender is easily identified in one way or another. Unfortunately, many other criminal cases are no contest for just the opposite reason: the detective does not have the slightest chance of success. Often there is not enough evidence for the detective to work with or the crime is too minor (compared with other crimes) to justify spending a good deal of time in order to develop meager evidence.[1]

This chapter deals specifically with those cases in which there is a genuine contest and the detective has enough evidence and enough time to pursue the case to its conclusion. Although such cases are relatively infrequent, the principles that underlie a thorough investigation should be applied to every case, however minor.

The essence of the detective's job is to obtain information from many different sources and to assemble that information into a logical, coherent account of how the crime was committed and by whom. The process is similar to putting together a jigsaw puzzle—except that the pieces may be scattered all over town.

## IDENTIFICATION OF THE PERPETRATOR

A crime is solved when the perpetrator has been identified. After that, the detective still may be responsible for apprehending the suspected perpetrator and for assisting in the prosecution of the offender, but normally the crime is considered solved even if the suspect is acquitted (unless some new evidence appears, demonstrating that the suspect is truly innocent).

There are only six ways by which a perpetrator can be identified.[2]

1. Someone who was present during the criminal event may identify the perpetrator. This may be the most common method by which crimes are solved, since the overwhelming majority of serious crimes are committed by individuals who were known to the victim before the criminal event. Even when the victim is unable to identify the perpetrator, quite often a primary witness can do so. Sometimes the victim or a witness can give the offender's name, address, and other detailed information.

Among the people who might be present at the criminal event and who almost certainly could identify the offender are the offender's accomplices and associates.[3] An *accomplice* (anyone who assists another person in committing a crime) may decide to betray the primary offender out of fear—either fear of the offender's turning against the accomplice or fear of having to bear the full responsibility for the crime while the principal offender goes free. Criminals often have a falling-out after a major crime or a series of crimes because of an argument over the division of the spoils or for similar reasons.

The offender's *associates* (friends or members of the criminal's family who are not participants in the crime) are less often present during the criminal event; however, if they happen to be there, they would be capable of identifying the perpetrator. Their willingness to do so might be based on fear again or perhaps on concern for the well-being of the offender and a desire to keep the offender from getting into more serious trouble.

2. A secondary witness may provide information that leads or points to the perpetrator. Secondary witnesses include informants, neighbors, and anyone else who was not actually present during the criminal event, but who has some information about the crime or the various participants. Often, the secondary witness does not realize the significance of the information. Sometimes the detective does not realize it, either, until a detail from one witness is put together with a bit of physical evidence, a vague description from a primary witness, and a few cautious inferences—all of which add up to the identification of the perpetrator.

3. Physical evidence may lead to the identification of a suspect. As we have said earlier, the usefulness of physical evidence in identifying the offender is somewhat overrated. Usually physical evidence is most important in developing an understanding of how a crime occurred and, once a suspect has been identified, tying the suspect to the scene of the crime. However, physical evidence does occasionally lead to an identification. Criminals have been known to leave behind such obvious clues as a wallet containing their name and address or a tool marked with their initials. Once in a great while, a single fingerprint is enough.

4. Circumstantial or other indirect evidence may lead to a particular suspect. The way in which the crime was committed may suggest a relationship between the criminal and the victim, for example, or it might lead to identification of the suspect on the basis of modus operandi (M.O.) records. Sometimes the detective is able to discern a clear, consistent pattern in a series of crimes, enabling the police to predict when and where the next crime in the series is most likely to occur. The offender might then be caught in the act. In a sense, the suspect has been "identified" even though no one knows who it is until the next crime in the series occurs.

5. A person who is not a suspect in the crime under investigation or is one of several possible suspects may admit a key fact that could be known only by the perpetrator. It is not unusual for criminals to give themselves away inadvertently while undergoing questioning about some other, unrelated crime or while being interviewed as a possible witness. Such an admission is *not* the same as a confession; by itself, an admission is not sufficient to convict the suspect. However, a crucial admission often is enough to identify a prime suspect.[4]

6. Finally, an individual may confess to a crime, whether or not the individual was a suspect at the time of the confession. Criminals who are being interrogated in connection with one crime often confess to a variety of other crimes. And it sometimes happens that the detective will begin an interview with someone who is thought to be a possible witness, only to have that individual confess to the crime.

Confessions play a relatively minor role in criminal investigation today. We shall explore the reasons that this is true and the role of the confession in modern police investigations in Chapter 16.

### SYSTEMATIC REVIEW OF THE EVIDENCE

A detective's job would be a lot easier if every crime solved itself, if the victim or another witness could identify the offender or if the offender walked into the police station and surrendered. However, real life is not like that.

ANSWERS TO STUDY CLUES
1. b    2. True    3. d    4. True

In the last ten chapters, we have described in detail the steps and procedures that an investigator should follow to recognize, obtain, preserve, and develop physical evidence, to locate and interview witnesses, to exchange information with other police officers and agencies, and to take advantage of the many other information resources that may be available. By this time, for any substantial investigation the detective should have amassed a great quantity of material. If the suspected perpetrator still has not been identified, there is a good chance that the solution is buried somewhere in the mass of evidence that has been accumulated. If not, at least reviewing the evidence will help the detective to determine what evidence is missing and what further investigative steps might be taken.[5]

One of the skills that an investigator must have is the ability to draw sound, logical *inferences* from the available evidence. An inference is not a guess, a hunch, a presumption, or an opinion. An inference is a conclusion based on rational thought, taking into consideration all the known facts and nothing else.[6]

For example, suppose you see a friend walking out of Grog's Department Store. The evidence indicates that she has been in the store, but you do not have enough information to say whether your friend has been shopping there or was in the store for some other reason. However, as you approach your friend, you notice that she is carrying a box reading "Grog's Dept. Store"; a sales slip is taped to the corner. Now it would be reasonable to infer that your friend bought something in the store: all the available evidence points to that conclusion.

Bear in mind, however, that not all inferences turn out to be true. For instance, your friend might have gone to Grog's to return a gift that was purchased for her by someone else. One of the most challenging aspects of criminal investigation is the fact that evidence often lends itself to two or more different interpretations, especially when only a few facts are available. The investigator must constantly guard against leaping to conclusions and overlooking evidence that happens not to fit a certain theory or interpretation of events.

## THE CASE REVIEW OUTLINE

A criminal investigation is an attempt to answer two simple questions: Who did it, and how? One way to answer those major questions is to ask a series of subsidiary questions, each of which should be answerable on the basis of the evidence that has already been acquired. The series of questions should represent a logical approach to the problem and, in particular, should force the investigator to consider as many interpretations of the known facts as can be imagined. The case review outline will serve as an example of the way in which a detective might systematically review the evidence in a case for which no suspect has been identified or there are several potential suspects.

1. Who was present at the criminal event?
   a. The perpetrator: one person or more than one?
   b. The victim: one person or more than one?
   c. The witnesses
      i. Have all the known witnesses been interviewed?
      ii. Could there be any unknown witnesses?
      iii. Could there be any persons who are not aware that they witnessed a crime (unwitting witnesses)?

    iv. Are there any witnesses who are unwilling to give information? Could any of them be accomplices or associates of the perpetrator?

2. What sequence of events occurred?
   a. Did the perpetrator enter the scene with the intent to commit a crime or did that intent arise after the perpetrator arrived there?
   b. Where, when and how did the perpetrator enter the scene?
   c. Did the perpetrator do anything at the scene before actually committing the crime?
   d. What crime was committed (in general or common terms—the legal definition can come later)?
   e. How was the crime committed? What actions did the perpetrator take? What, if anything, did the victim do to avoid, prevent, interrupt, or defend against the crime?
   f. What did the perpetrator do immediately after committing the crime, that is, before leaving the scene?
   g. How, where, and when did the perpetrator leave?
   h. Where did the perpetrator go after the crime?

3. What kind of person committed the crime?
   a. Physical description, if available
   b. Psychological profile, if one has been developed
   c. Peculiar habits or idiosyncrasies that can be identified from physical evidence, circumstances of the crime, or testimony
   d. Inferences that can be drawn about the perpetrator
      i. Does the perpetrator appear to be a professional or habitual criminal?
      ii. What unique characteristics are ev-

ident from the modus operandi? Is there a similar M.O. on file?
   e. Possible or known relationship of the perpetrator to the victim
      i. According to the victim's testimony
      ii. According to the witnesses' testimony
      iii. Inferred from circumstances of the crime

4. Why was this crime committed?
   a. Direct gain
      i. How much was gained? Was property of greater value overlooked? Were only certain kinds of property taken?
      ii. How will the gain be secured? Will the perpetrator have to dispose of the property, or will the perpetrator keep the property for personal use?
   b. Emotional satisfaction
      i. Revenge
      ii. Jealousy
      iii. Sexual passion
      iv. Brutal or sadistic impulse
      v. Fear: Of the victim? Of someone else?
   c. Relationship to other crimes
      i. Was this one of a series of similar crimes committed by the same person?
      ii. Could this crime have occurred as the consequence of some other (possibly undiscovered) crime committed either by the perpetrator or by the victim?
   d. Irrational or undiscoverable motives

5. Who had an opportunity to commit the crime?
   a. What physical capability (unusual strength or endurance, very large or very small physical stature) or other

physical characteristic (for example, the crime was committed by a left-handed person) is indicated?

b. Who normally would have access to the crime scene or to the victim for legitimate purposes?

c. Who would know the victim's routine activities or whereabouts? Would that knowledge create a special opportunity for someone to commit the crime?

6. What will the perpetrator do next (after the crime)?

a. Flee
   i. By what means? When? To where?
   ii. How might the perpetrator be recognized?

b. Dispose of stolen property or instruments of the crime
   i. Where and when could this be done?
   ii. How can the property or instruments be recognized and recovered?

c. Commit additional crimes
   i. Will the perpetrator commit the same crime or a similar crime?
   ii. Will this crime lead to other related crimes, either by the perpetrator or by someone else (for example, retaliation by the victim or the victim's friends)?

d. Attempts to conceal the crime and the perpetrator's identity
   i. What efforts to conceal have already been made?
   ii. What additional efforts could have been made at the time of the crime or shortly thereafter?
   iii. What renewed efforts at concealing identity could the perpetrator make now, knowing that the crime has been discovered?

7. What is the evidence for each answer given to the above questions?

a. Which answers are based on physical evidence?
   i. What is the evidence and how was it obtained or developed?
   ii. Could it be rationalized (interpreted) in any different way?

b. Which answers are based on the testimony of the victim, primary witnesses, or secondary witnesses?
   i. Is there reasonable certainty that the testimony is valid?
   ii. Could the testimony be interpreted or understood in any different way? Could any contradictions in testimony be resolved differently? If so, what would be the result?

c. Which answers are based on indirect or intangible evidence, such as circumstantial evidence?
   i. Have any of the circumstances of the crime been overlooked or given insufficient weight?
   ii. Is there any way in which the circumstances could be interpreted—no matter how implausible it seems—that would fit the known facts but give a different understanding of the crime?

8. What facts are missing?

a. Is it likely that physical evidence has not been discovered or has been overlooked?

b. Is it likely that the victim or a witness possesses additional information that has not yet been offered?

c. Does it appear that some of the testimony of the victim or a witness may be false or misleading?

d. What investigative steps can be taken to supply the missing evidence or account for its absence and to correct misleading testimony?

## ACT III
## THE BURGLARY
## AT 1209 MAIN STREET

We discussed this hypothetical burglary at 1209 Main Street in Chapters 3 and 4. Now let us bring the investigation up to date and apply the case review outline to the evidence that has been accumulated by Officer Cole.

First, reread the description of Officer Cole's initial assessment and observations of the scene (pages 67 to 69). Next, study the sketches of the scene made by Officer Cole (pages 105 to 108). Portions of the rest of the case file compiled by Officer Cole follow on the next several pages. Read this material with care; then see how many of the questions in the case review outline you can answer.

To conserve space and to keep from boring you unnecessarily, we have greatly condensed the material that would appear in the case file. Only the most significant information is presented. For example, since we already have provided an account of Officer Cole's initial assessment of the crime scene, that part of the preliminary investigative report has been omitted. In place of the full transcript of each interview with a witness, we will rely on Officer Cole's summaries. You may assume that we have not left out anything that would change the conclusions that might be drawn in this investigation.

### CITY POLICE DEPARTMENT PRELIMINARY REPORT OF INVESTIGATION

| | |
|---|---|
| CASE NO: | G36-1443 |
| INV: | D. Cole, #1414 |
| DATE: | 19 May 1979 |

On 19 May 1979, I was assigned to patrol district B-9. At 9:25 A.M., I was directed by radio to investigate a burglary complaint at 1209 Main Street. I arrived at that address at 9:32 A.M. 1209 Main Street is a three-story, brick apartment building.

[Officer Cole's initial assessment follows here.]

After completing this initial assessment, I interviewed Mrs. Eva Torres, Latin female, age 43, 5'10", 175 lbs., black hair with gray flecks, light brown skin. Mrs. Torres resides in Apt. 3-D, next to the Logan apartment. Mrs. Torres's son, Hector, age 5, was the only other person present in her apartment during the interview. (See Interview Transcript #1, attached.)

Mrs. Torres said that she knew nothing about a burglary of the Logan apartment until Mr. Davis, the manager, knocked on her door at about 9:15 this morning and asked if she knew where the Logans were. She didn't. At Mr. Davis's request, Mrs. Torres entered the Logan apartment. Mrs. Davis was in the apartment at that time, straightening up some clothes, newspapers, and other items that were scattered about the living room. Mrs. Torres helped Mrs. Davis by picking up some newspapers and magazines that were lying on the floor next to an armchair; she was doing this when I arrived.

Mrs. Torres said that she hadn't seen the Logans since the day before. She described the Logans as a "quiet, very nice black couple" who usually spent their evenings watching TV or listening to "rock" or "country" music on their stereo.

I asked Mrs. Torres whether she had heard any unusual sounds or disturbance yesterday in the Logan apartment. She answered reluctantly that she heard the sounds of an argument yesterday morning (18 May) at about 7:00 A.M. She said that she couldn't make out any words distinctly, but she heard the voices of both Mr. and Mrs. Logan, arguing. She heard no other voices. The argument seemed to last only a few minutes. At about 7:30 A.M., she heard the door of the Logans' apartment slam; that was about the time Mr. Logan usually went to work. About ten or fifteen minutes later, she heard the Logans' door open and close again, and she assumed that Mrs. Logan also had gone to work. Mrs. Torres said that she doesn't know where Mr. and Mrs. Logan are employed.

I asked Mrs. Torres whether she had heard any other sounds or unusual activity in or around the Logan apartment since yesterday. She said she had not heard anything until this morning. At about 8:30 A.M., she heard footsteps on the stairs and in the hall and then the door of the Logan apartment being opened and closed. At first she thought either Mr. or Mrs. Logan had returned, but after a few minutes the person apparently left the apartment. At about 8:45 A.M., she heard the footsteps of two people entering the apartment. A few minutes later, she heard one person leave the apartment and go down the stairs. She heard nothing more until 9:15 A.M., when Mr. Davis came to her door. She then realized that the people whom she had heard entering and leaving the Logan apartment earlier must have been Mr. and Mrs. Davis.

Mrs. Torres had nothing further to add.

I next interviewed Mrs. Karen Davis, white female, age 52, 5'6", 115 lbs., yellow blonde (apparently dyed), mottled light skin. This interview was conducted in Mrs. Torres's apartment; no one other than Mrs. Davis and myself was present. (See Interview Transcript #2, attached.)

Mrs. Davis said that she didn't know the Logans at all, that they were "just one of the tenants" to her, and that they paid their rent on time and never caused any trouble. Mrs. Davis said that she had not seen either of the Logans for "at least a week," but added that she didn't "keep track of all the tenants."

Mrs. Davis said that she was busy in her apartment (1-A) this morning a few minutes before 9:00 A.M. Her husband had gone upstairs sometime earlier, perhaps about 8:00 A.M., to perform various minor maintenance chores in the building. He came back downstairs shortly before 9:00 A.M. and told his wife that the Logan apartment was "all tore up, like somebody ransacked the place." Mrs. Davis said that she went upstairs to the Logan apartment with her husband just after 9:00 A.M. She said that the apartment was "a complete mess, with clothes and junk strewn all over it," dirty dishes on the table and in the sink, and so forth. She said that she told her husband to call the police because she thought there might have been a burglary; Mr. Davis then went back downstairs and called the police. However, Mrs. Davis said that she now believes there was no burglary; for all she knows, the Logans "live like this all the time." She said that she was sorry to cause so much trouble over "nothing."

I asked Mrs. Davis whether she had suggested that her husband solicit Mrs. Torres's help in straightening up the Logan apartment. Mrs. Davis said no; Mrs. Torres had just appeared at the door of the Logan apartment at about 9:15 A.M. and volunteered to straighten up. Mrs. Davis denied that she was straightening up the apartment; she said that that was Mrs. Torres's idea. Mrs. Davis had nothing more to add.

I then interviewed Mr. Winston Davis, the building manager. Mr. Davis is a white male, age 55, 5'8", 125 lbs., brown and gray hair, balding, sallow complexion. This interview was conducted in the hallway outside the Logan apartment; no other person was present. (See Interview Transcript #3, attached.)

Mr. Davis said that the Logans were a "pleasant young couple" who were always polite, always paid their rent on time, never caused trouble, and rarely made complaints or demands. He said that he had not seen Mr. or Mrs. Logan for the past day or two. He showed me a lease contract for Apt. 3-C, signed by Gary L. Logan, who gave his place of employment as Truck Works Garage, 216 E. First Ave.

Mr. Davis said that Mrs. Logan had left a note on his door two days ago, asking him to adjust the burners on the gas stove in Apt. 3-C. Mr. Davis said that he had intended to do that this morning as part of his usual round of minor "fixing chores" and had gone to the third floor after changing some light bulbs in the second floor hallway. He said it was about 8:45 A.M. when he entered the Logan apartment, using his master key. He said that the apartment was "pretty messy" when he entered it, but that he "didn't think much about it" until he entered the kitchen and found dirty dishes on the table and in the sink. This struck him as peculiar, he said, because "the Logans always seemed so neat; I couldn't figure them to be so messy." He said that he then went back downstairs and told his wife about what he had found. She accompanied him back upstairs and went into the Logan apart-

ment with him. However, it was her opinion, according to Mr. Davis, that the Logans were simply "that kind of people." Mr. Davis insisted that there might have been either a burglary or some kind of violent fight, and he decided to call the police. However, before doing so, he decided to ask Mrs. Torres whether she knew anything about the condition of the Logans' apartment. He said that she "claimed" not to know anything, but she followed him back into the Logan apartment and began "picking things up off the floor." Mr. Davis said that he then went downstairs to his own apartment and called the police at about 9:15 A.M. He had nothing further to add.

I returned to the Logan apartment and took 20 photographs (see Investigative Photography Record, attached). I also made measured sketches of each room; these sketches are now in my notebook. I labeled and collected three items of evidence:

#C-1: Broken coffee cup
#C-2: Box of adhesive bandages
#C-3: Cloth towel (found on bathroom floor)

I used a cotton swab to collect some of the grease and blood material found in the bathroom sink. The swab was placed in a vial and marked #C-4. No other physical evidence was removed from the apartment.

I dusted several areas for fingerprints, including the section of the bookcase where there appeared to be something missing (scratch marks on the shelf and an outline in the fine layer of household dust suggest that there had been an object of about 20 cm by 40 cm on the shelf), the TV stand, the doorknobs of the bathroom and closet doors, and the entire upper surface of the bathroom sink. Two reasonably clear fingerprints were found on the rim of the sink. No other usable prints were obtained from any location. No other trace evidence was sought or obtained.

In the course of this examination of the apartment, I opened the door next to the bathroom door; it led to a fairly large closet. In the closet were various items of both men's and women's clothing, as well as an ironing board, broom, miscellaneous household implements, and other personal property.

I did not disturb the two piles of clothing in the living room (one by the sofa; the other by the armchair). They seemed to consist of both men's and women's clothing of various sorts.

I left the Logan apartment at 10:52 A.M. I reported by radio an unknown crime, possible burglary or theft, with unknown suspects. I requested 10-6 [investigation of a complaint] out of district so that I could interview Mr. Logan; permission was granted. I drove to Truckworks, a garage that specializes in servicing large trucks, at 216 E. First Avenue. I found that Mr. Logan was in fact employed there and was at work at the time. The owner of the garage, Mr. Carey, gave me permission to interrupt Mr. Logan's work and allowed us to meet in his (Mr. Carey's) office.

I interviewed Gary Lawrence Logan, black male, age 28, 5'10", 155 lbs., black hair, brown eyes, medium brown skin, driver's license #9988776. The interview was conducted in Mr. Carey's office with no other person present. (See Interview Transcript #4, attached.)

I told Mr. Logan that I was investigating the possibility of "a problem," because Mr. Davis had expressed concern over the Logans' unexplained absence. Mr. Logan became very agitated and said that Mrs. Davis was a "snoopy, spying old biddy who has nothing better to do than butt into other people's lives." I told Mr. Logan that I had just come from his apartment and that it seemed "not to be in good order." I said that someone might have broken into the apartment and asked him whether he knew any other reason for it to be "messed up."

Mr. Logan seemed very concerned at this report. He then told me that he and his wife, Helen K. Logan, had had an argument the day before, at breakfast. He said that his wife had criticized him for leaving grease marks on the sink and a towel when he had washed his hands after coming home from work late on the previous night (17 May). This criticism led to an exchange of angry words, which culminated in his wife's throwing a coffee cup at him. The cup missed him, but struck the kitchen wall; a broken piece of the china had hit Mr. Logan on the cheek, causing a small cut. He said that he then went to the bathroom, washed and bandaged the cut, and left the apartment. He said that he hadn't gone back since then, but "probably would" in a few days, either to reconcile with his wife or to remove his clothes and other belongings. I asked him whether he had taken anything with him when he left the previous morning. He said that he had taken only his jacket and the "clothes on [his] back."

I asked Mr. Logan if he knew the present whereabouts of his wife. He said that she probably had gone home to her mother, Mrs. Opal Peterson, 9224 W. Douglas Ave.

I asked Mr. Logan if he would meet me at his apartment during his lunch hour, a few minutes after noon, so that we could determine whether anything was missing. He agreed to do so.

I went to a pay telephone and called Mrs. Peterson's home. I spoke to Mrs. Peterson, Mrs. Logan's mother. She confirmed that Mrs. Logan had "come back home" the previous day, but at the present time Mrs. Logan was at work. She is a waitress at the Quickstop Café, 7604 N. Raleigh Blvd., according to Mrs. Peterson. (There is no transcript of this telephone conversation.)

At 11:24 A.M., I requested and was given permission for 10-7 [out-of-service]. After eating lunch, I called 10-8 [in-service] and requested continuance of 10-6, returning to district; this was approved. I drove back to 1209 Main Street and met Mr. Logan at that address at 12:10 P.M.

Mr. Logan and I went directly to his apartment. He used his key to open the door, which I had left locked. On entering the apartment, Mr. Logan expressed surprise at its condition. At first he thought that his wife must have "thrown things around" in anger or perhaps she wanted to spite him. Then he said that the TV set and a stereo receiver-phonograph were missing. He described the TV as a 15-inch color set, manufacturer Trueview, model and serial numbers unknown. He said that it had a walnut-grain plastic case and a chip broken out of the corner just below the tuning knob. He described the stereo as a combination radio receiver and phonograph, manufacturer Soundgood, model and serial numbers unknown. He said that it had two small speakers attached by six-foot wires and a transparent plastic dust cover.

I asked Mr. Logan to look through the rest of the apartment; he did so and reported that nothing else seemed to be missing. He suggested that his wife might have taken the stereo and the TV, which were the only two items of any value that they owned. He expressed surprise when he discovered that she hadn't taken her clothes from the closet.

With Mr. Logan's permission, I used the telephone in the apartment to call Mrs. Logan at the Quickstop Café. The manager was at first reluctant to let me speak to her, since it was the café's rush hour; but when I explained the nature of the call, he agreed.

I told Mrs. Logan that I was calling from her apartment, that Mr. Logan was present, and that we were concerned because of the condition of the apartment. She expressed surprise and said that it was "not that bad" when she had left the previous morning. She admitted that she and her husband had had a fight and that she had left hastily, not bothering to clear the breakfast dishes from the table. But otherwise, she said, the apartment had been in good order. I asked her what items she had taken from the apartment with her. She said that she had taken only the clothes she was wearing and a jacket. She had intended to return after work that evening, to pick up her other things, but had gotten into a long conversation with her mother and was too tired to bother. She had nothing further to add. (There is no transcript of this telephone conversation.)

Before we ended our conversation, Mrs. Logan asked to speak to her husband. Mr. Logan came to the telephone and appeared to be engaged in an intimate conversation with his wife. I got the impression that she apologized to him and that he accepted the apology. He told her that the TV and stereo had been stolen from the apartment. Before ending the conversation, he said that he would see her later.

I asked Mr. Logan if he could explain

the disorderly condition of the apartment and the missing appliances, but he had nothing further to add. He and I left the apartment together at 12:41 P.M., and I called 10-8 at 12:42 P.M.

*P.O. Dale Cole #1414*

## CITY POLICE DEPARTMENT
### REPORT OF LABORATORY EXAMINATION

| | |
|---|---|
| CASE NO.: | G36-1443 |
| DATE: | 24 May 1979 |
| REPORT BY: | O. Ross, Lab. Tech. |
| REQUESTED BY: | Cole, #1414 |

| Item Examined | Findings |
|---|---|
| 1. Item #C-1, Coffee cup, marked "Kitchen, Apt 3C, 1209 Main, 19 May 79, D Cole" | Common-grade china coffee cup, silica glaze (beige), mfr. unknown. Side of cup opposite handle shows breakage, 11 cm along rim, 3 cm vertically; cracking consistent with cup having been dropped from a considerable height onto a hard surface or with a blow of substantial force (more than 2 kg/cm²). Residue in cup: coffee, sugar; no foreign substances. |
| 2. Item #C-2, Metal box, marked "Bathrm, Apt 3C, 1209 Main, 19 May 79, D Cole" | Small box of adhesive bandages of common commercial quality; hinged metal lid. Box contained assortment of wrapped bandages, various sizes. 3 clear fingerprints found on back of box. No other significant marks or substances. |
| 3. Item #C-3, Cloth towel, marked, "Bathrm, Apt 3C, 1209 Main, 19 May 79, D Cole" | Cloth towel, 80% cotton, 20% polyester fiber, common variety, white in color. Residues on towel consist of petroleum-based grease and oil with carbon black inclusions, various minor components, typical of greases and oils used in automotive lubricants; small quantity of blood, human, type A, Rh+, no other typing attempted; small quantities detergent, perfuming agents, etc., typical of household soaps, shampoos, cosmetics. |

*Putting The Pieces Together*

4. Item #C-4, Cotton swab, marked "Residue from bathrm sink, Apt 3C, 1209 Main, 19 May 79, D Cole"

(Cotton swab used only to carry residue evidence) Residue consists of petroleum-based greases and oils, essentially the same as those found on towel (Item #C-3); also, small quantity of blood, human, type A, Rh+, no other typing attempted.

Present Location of Evidence:

Items C-I, C-2, and C-3 returned to Off. Cole at officer's request. Item C-4 destroyed in testing. END OF REPORT.

*O. Ross, Lab Technician*

CITY POLICE DEPARTMENT
INTEROFFICE MEMORANDUM

DATE:     21 May 79
FROM:     Central Records, S. Walker, Sgt.
TO:       PO Dale Cole, B District
SUBJECT:  Identifications, re Case No. G36-1443

At your request, we have completed records checks on the individuals listed with the following results:

Logan, Gary Lawrence, B/M, 28, 5-10/155, Blk/Brn, Med Brn. DL 9988776. No wants/warrants. Traffic record only.

Logan, Helen Katherine (Peterson), B/F, 27, 5-7/110, Blk/Gry, Med Brn. DL 9412303. No wants/warrants. No record.

Davis, Winston Francis, W/M, 55, 5-8/125, Brn/Grn, Light. DL 8877665. No wants/warrants. Complainant, 9 Sep 78, tenant disturbing peace. Complainant, 3 Apr 78, tenant resisting eviction. Complainant, 15 Mar 78, prowler in alley. Apprehended in gambling raid, 21 Jun 76, no charges filed. Arrested, 11 May 74, misdemeanor theft, acquitted.

Davis, Karen Elizabeth, W/F, 56, 5-6/115, Wht/Brn, Med. No DL. No wants/warrants. Complainant, 29 Jun 78, tenant disturbing peace (Invg. Off. reported family disturbance; no action taken). Arrested, 4 Jul 72, public intoxication and disturbing peace, convicted and fined.

Torres, Eva Juanita Portales, W/F, 43, 5-10/175, Blk/Brn, Lt. Brn. No DL. No wants/warrants. No record.

END OF REPORT

*S. Walker, Sgt., C.R.B.*

*The Continuing Investigation*

Of course, not every crime is as complicated as the burglary (if that is in fact what it was) at 1209 Main Street. And some crimes are much more complicated. It would be rare for a relatively minor crime like this one to be so thoroughly investigated. However, if you examine all of the evidence carefully, you should be able to develop a reasonable, logical theory of the case that points to one or more potential suspects. In fact, you might be able to develop two or three equally reasonable theories.

## REFERENCES

1. Peter W. Greenwood, Jan M. Chaiken, and Joan Petersilia, *The Criminal Investigation Process* (Lexington, Mass.: D. C. Heath, 1977), p. 121.

2. John J. Horgan, *Criminal Investigation* (New York: McGraw-Hill, 1974), p. 6.

3. Edwin H. Sutherland and Donald R. Cressey, *Criminology*, 9th ed. (Philadelphia: J. B. Lippincott, 1974), pp. 261–264.

4. Paul B. Weston and Kenneth M. Wells, *Criminal Evidence for Police* (Englewood Cliffs, N.J.: Prentice-Hall, 1971), p. 194.

5. George D. Eastman, ed., *Municipal Police Administration* (Washington, D.C.: International City Management Association, 1969), pp. 136–137.

6. Weston and Wells, p. 108.

## REVIEW OF THE EVIDENCE

1. The most common method by which crimes are solved is
    a. physical evidence that leads to the identification of a suspect.
    b. circumstantial or indirect evidence that leads to a suspect.
    c. a confession by the perpetrator.
    d. an identification of the perpetrator by someone present during the criminal event.
    e. information offered by a secondary witness, which leads to the perpetrator.
2. Which of the six ways of identifying a perpetrator was *not* listed in Question 1?
3. Physical evidence is most important for what purpose(s)?
    a. understanding how the crime occurred
    b. identifying the perpetrator
    c. recovering stolen property
    d. tying a suspect to the scene of the crime
    e. identifying potential witnesses
4. True or false: A crucial admission usually is sufficient to convict the suspect.
5. The case review outline is
    a. a systematic, logical series of questions.
    b. one of the ways to identify the perpetrator.
    c. a report that should be prepared by the investigator.
    d. a type of indirect evidence.
    e. a summary of witnesses' testimony.
6. Which of the following questions should *not* be considered by the investigator during a case review, using the outline presented in this chapter?
    a. whether there was more than one perpetrator
    b. whether there might be unwitting witnesses
    c. whether one of the "witnesses" is actually an accomplice or associate of the perpetrator
    d. whether one of the witnesses has deliberately withheld information
    e. whether all the legal elements are present for the apparent crime
7. True or false: The perpetrator's activities after the crime occurred generally are of no great interest to the investigator.
8. True or false: The identification of a suspect must be based on solid physical evidence, not the investigator's inferences or interpretation of the crime.
9. One of the major values of the case review outline is that
    a. it invariably points to the guilty suspect.
    b. it reveals whether the witnesses have told the truth.
    c. it helps the investigator to organize the preliminary investigative report.
    d. it helps the investigator to determine what additional facts or evidence might be needed.
    e. it ensures that the investigator has not overlooked any physical evidence at the crime scene.

10. An admission is
    a. the same thing as a confession.
    b. a statement by a suspect of a fact that could be known only by the perpetrator.
    c. a statement by a witness that points to the guilty suspect.
    d. a statement by the victim that no crime has occurred.
    e. a report prepared by the investigator.

### TOPICS FOR INVESTIGATION

1. Consider the Burglary at 1209 Main Street by means of the outline below, indicate which facts are based on which kind(s) of evidence, and answer each question.

| | Physical Evidence | Testimony | Inference |
|---|---|---|---|
| a. Who was present at the criminal event? | | | |
| b. What sequence of events occurred? | | | |
| c. What kind of person committed the crime? | | | |
| d. Why was the crime committed? | | | |
| e. Who had an opportunity to commit the crime? | | | |
| f. What will the perpetrator do next? | | | |
| g. What is the evidence? | | | |
| h. What facts are missing? | | | |

2. If you were Officer Cole, whom would you consider as a potential suspect? What would be the next step in your investigation? What additional physical evidence would you like to have, if it exists?

3. The case review outline is intended for one's own use, to help organize one's thinking. Would it be a good idea to require an investigator to complete a report, following this outline, before authorizing a case to be declared "closed, unsolved"?

# CHAPTER 14
## WHEN A SUSPECT
## HAS BEEN IDENTIFIED

---

STUDY CLUES

1. True or false: Once a suspect has been identified by one of the six methods listed in Chapter 13, it is unnecessary to obtain identifications by any other methods.
2. Testimony from a witness might not be usable if the witness is incompetent. In the legal sense, incompetence would result from
   a. the witness's being less than 18 years old.
   b. the witness's being mentally defective.
   c. the witness's having a reputation for dishonesty.
   d. the witness's not being an expert on the subject to be presented in court.
   e. all of the above.
   f. none of the above.
3. True or false: The spouse of a defendant cannot be forced to testify unless he or she wishes to do so.
4. True or false: If a witness is legally competent, the jury is required to believe the witness's testimony.
5. Evidence that is unimportant or contributes very little to an understanding of a case, even though it is true, would be inadmissible because it is
   a. incompetent.
   b. irrelevant.
   c. prejudicial.
   d. immaterial.
   e. inflammatory.
6. True or false: Evidence should be presented to show the extent of the victim's suffering or other consequences of the crime, in order to arouse the jury's hostility toward the defendant.
7. Behavior can be criminal—even though it was not completely intentional—if it was criminally
   a. negligent.
   b. justifiable.
   c. reckless.
   d. mistaken.
   e. ignorant.
8. A lesser included offense is an offense that
   a. the defendant did not mean to commit.
   b. is not illegal.
   c. is more serious than the crime for which adequate evidence is available.
   d. is not specifically defined by law.
   e. contains some but not all of the elements of the most serious offense that could be charged.

AFTER A SUSPECT HAS BEEN IDENTIFIED, one might think that the investigative phase of the criminal justice process has come to an end. But, on the contrary, that is when the investigation shifts into high gear. Criminal cases are won or lost after the investigation has focused on one particular individual, and the most important evidence often is not discovered until then.[1] There is always the possibility that the wrong person has been identified, or even that the right person has been identified but for the wrong reasons. It is the investigator's responsibility to see that all of the available evidence clearly indicates the guilt of the accused to the exclusion of all other possible suspects.

The investigation continues not only after a suspect has been identified, but even after a suspect has been arrested. A thorough investigation should continue right up to the time of the trial if there is any reason at all to doubt the guilt of the accused. In exceptional cases, an investigation might be continued even after the accused has been convicted and sentenced.[2]

As we said in Chapter 13, there are only six ways that a suspect can be identified. They are

• identification by a person who was present at the criminal event (victim, witness, or associate of the perpetrator)
• identification by a secondary witness
• identification through physical evidence
• identification through circumstantial or other indirect evidence
• admission of guilty knowledge by an individual
• confession.

It is entirely possible to obtain a conviction on the basis of identification by only one of these six methods. However, the use of two or more methods increases the likelihood that the suspect is truly the perpetrator. There-

fore, once a suspect has been identified by one method, the investigator should attempt to obtain identification by as many additional methods as possible. Physical evidence and circumstantial evidence usually provide opportunities to do this. Sometimes reinterviewing the primary witnesses or finding additional secondary witnesses also will lead to *corroborating* evidence, or evidence that tends to confirm the validity of the original identification.

The investigator may very well have to seek additional evidence even though a large quantity has been developed already. More often, the necessary information is present in the available evidence. The investigator's task is to evaluate and arrange the evidence so that the essential information is presented in a logical, comprehensible manner.

## RE-EVALUATING THE EVIDENCE

### PHYSICAL EVIDENCE

The list of physical evidence should be reviewed and compared with the investigator's initial report of the crime. Laboratory reports concerning each item of physical evidence also should be studied. Briefly, the investigator should ask three questions about each item:

• What does the item show?
• What is its logical connection to the crime?
• What is its connection to the suspect?

### WITNESSES' TESTIMONY

The testimony of witnesses also must be reevaluated in the same manner. Until now, we have been concerned mostly with the content of witnesses' testimony; at this point, the investigator also must consider the competency and the reliability of the testimony.

The system of criminal justice in the

United States is based on the assumption that the truth about any event can be learned only by weighing the testimony of various people who claim to have knowledge about it.[3] There are legal penalties that can be imposed on people who deliberately offer false testimony, but the system also recognizes that people often are mistaken in their perceptions and in their memories of an event. Many safeguards have been built into the system to eliminate testimony that is likely to be false or mistaken. Although these safeguards will apply ultimately to the trial of the accused suspect, it is the investigator's responsibility to screen out testimony that is legally unacceptable.

For example, there are various laws that prohibit testimony from witnesses who are *incompetent*, that is, people who are incapable, unqualified, or unfit to offer truthful evidence.[4] A person who suffers a permanent mental defect such as emotional instability, mental retardation, or brain damage usually would not be allowed to testify. A person can be declared incompetent because of some temporary incapacity, too, such as intoxication by alcohol or drugs or a physical illness or injury that made the person at the time of the crime *or* will make the person at the time of the trial unable to give a true account of the criminal event.

Children pose a special problem with regard to competency. In most states a child can testify as a witness in a criminal case, but the child's competency can be questioned by either the prosecution or the defense. The judge presiding over the trial must be satisfied that the child is competent as a witness before the child's testimony can be introduced.

ANSWERS TO STUDY CLUES
1. False    2. b.    3. True    4. False
5. d.    6. False    7. a and c    8. e

Even though a person is inherently competent, he or she might be legally incompetent as a witness because of laws that give certain individuals *immunity* or *privilege*.[5]

This kind of immunity is not the same as, but is certainly related to, the immunity from prosecution discussed briefly in Chapter 12. Here the term *immune* means that the witness cannot be compelled to testify at all unless he or she wishes to do so. A spouse of the accused is immune to the legal power of both the prosecution and the defense to compel testimony. Even though there might be good reason to believe that the husband or wife of the accused knows something about the crime, neither the prosecution nor the defense can force the spouse to testify in court. On the other hand, the spouse may testify if he or she wishes to do so and can present testimony that is damaging to the defendant.

The word *privilege* generally refers to communications that pass between two people who have a special relationship to each other and that society, as a whole, does not wish to disrupt. Thus, a witness cannot testify about privileged communications even if he or she wishes to do so, unless the defendant specifically waives the privilege.

Confidential conversations between the defendant and a spouse are privileged. So are conversations between a member of the clergy and a member of the same church, between a doctor (including a psychiatrist, dentist, or chiropractor) and a patient, or between a lawyer and a client; the member of the clergy, doctor, or lawyer may not testify about such a conversation. The privilege, however, extends only to conversations that are within the scope of the individual's professional responsibilities. Ministers, doctors, or lawyers can testify about conversations with persons who had no professional relationship with them, and under certain circumstances they can testify about conversations that were not related to the professional services that they customarily render. Furthermore, ministers, doctors, and lawyers have the same obligation as any other citizen to report incidents of crime that come to their attention, to prevent crimes that are being planned or that are likely to occur, and to deliver to the police any physical evidence of a crime that comes into their possession. In short, the privilege of confidentiality is not completely limitless; a criminal cannot say just anything to a minister, doctor, or lawyer and expect it to be kept confidential.

Aside from the matter of competency and the related questions of legal immunity and privilege, there is still a need to determine whether a witness is *reliable*. The investigator should learn something about the reputation of anyone who may be called as a witness against the suspect. In general, citizens are assumed to be reliable unless there is some reason to believe otherwise. Among those reasons might be past criminal behavior by the witness, emotional instability or other mental defect, or merely a reputation in the community for dishonesty or lack of integrity.

When evidence is presented in a trial, the jury is expected to decide whether to believe it at all and, if so, to what extent. Therefore, the defendant's attorney will attack the credibility, or believability, of each of the prosecution's witnesses. Long before the trial, the investigator should determine whether each witness is believable.

• Is the testimony reasonably logical and coherent? Is it internally consistent and is it consistent with the other evidence in the case (both physical evidence and testimony of other witnesses)? Does the testimony make sense?

*The courtroom. Every aspect of the investigator's work will face its ultimate test in this arena.*

• How did the witness come to know the information presented in the testimony? If the witness claims to have observed certain events, is there any reason to doubt that he or she was capable of making that observation?[6]

• What expertise does a witness have? As a general rule, a witness may not present testimony containing an opinion about anything or representing a conclusion or inference. A witness can testify only about facts, such as events, which were observed personally or about which he or she has some direct knowledge.

An expert witness is not limited by the above rule.[7] An expert witness can present conclusions, opinions, or observations about anything within the range of the witness's qualifications as an expert. For example, a witness could testify that he saw the defendant run from a store, jump into a waiting car, and drive off at high speed. The witness could not testify that "the defendant drove the car with unusual skill, as if he were a racing car driver," unless he were qualified to make such a judgment because of special expertise in evaluating drivers or in automobile racing.

Since all physical evidence must be introduced by a witness who can testify about its origin, nature, and significance, the use of expert witnesses is extremely important. Almost all of the prosecution's expert witnesses are police personnel, technicians, and professional people who are employed by the police to carry out specific parts of an investigation, such as the laboratory examination of evidence. However, once in a while a primary witness to a crime or some secondary witness who is not employed by the police might be qualified as an expert witness. Expert witnesses often make a strong impression on the jury; consequently, the defense will try especially hard to discredit or disqualify the expert. Before any expert witness is called on, the investigator must be certain that the witness's qualifications are more than sufficient for the testimony that the witness will offer.[8]

## ADMISSIBILITY OF EVIDENCE

Just as there are safeguards to keep incompetent witnesses from testifying, there are other safeguards to prevent improper or misleading testimony or physical evidence from being introduced during a trial. Most of these latter safeguards are in the form of *rules of evidence*. Although some rules are embodied in laws passed by state or federal legislatures, most of them have been established by the courts themselves.[9]

Evidence cannot be admitted in a criminal trial if it has been illegally obtained. It is up to the investigator, in assembling the evidence against an accused suspect, to see that all the evidence has been acquired legally and properly. Evidence, whether physical objects or witnesses' testimony, also cannot be admitted if it is irrelevant, immaterial, or incompetent. These rules are a good deal more ambiguous and therefore harder to apply than the rule that excludes illegally obtained evidence.

The question of *relevance* concerns the basic purpose of any criminal trial.[10] The trial is held to determine whether one person, the accused, committed a certain crime at a certain time and place. Only evidence that tends to prove or disprove those specific facts may be introduced. As a general rule, evidence about the defendant's personal integrity, reputation, peculiar behavior or appearance, or other criminal activities in the past cannot be introduced. Similar kinds of evidence about the victim or about the place where the alleged crime was committed could not be introduced; for example, in a burglary trial the fact that the "residence" at which the alleged burglary took place was a house of prostitution could not be introduced unless that fact had some direct bearing on the nature of the crime.

There is an important exception to this general rule. Evidence about a person's reputation, including criminal involvements other than the immediate case, can be introduced to discredit the testimony of any witness. Thus, if the accused defendant chooses to testify in an effort to convince the jury that he or she is innocent, the prosecutor can present evidence that the defendant has been convicted of the same crime in the past, has a reputation for a violent temper, and so on. However, if the defendant does not testify, such evidence is considered irrelevant.

Evidence is *immaterial* if it is simply unimportant in considering the true facts of the case or if it is so vague or ambiguous that it contributes nothing to the jury's understanding of the facts. In the example in which a witness offers an opinion about the suspect's exceptional driving skill, that evidence might be admissible on the grounds of the witness's qualifications as an expert. But the evidence still might be inadmissible if the suspect's driving skill has no particular bearing on the crime that was allegedly committed—unless the fact that the defendant is a former racing driver is one of the factors used to identify him.[11]

Finally, evidence is *incompetent* if it is inherently misleading, untrue, or invalid or if the witness is not competent to present it (usually because the witness lacks the qualifications as an expert to testify about the nature or significance of the evidence). For example, suppose that the defendant is accused of committing a robbery. The victim has testified that the robber appeared to have a pistol tucked under his shirt, but that he never actually displayed the weapon. The prosecutor could not ask the witness to identify a pistol taken from the suspect's home, because there is no competent testimony that the same pistol, or any other pistol, was in the robber's possession at the time of the crime.[12]

Another set of rules of evidence deals with the problems of *prejudicial and inflammatory* evidence. Evidence may be introduced only if it tends to prove or disprove the facts concerning the alleged crime. Evidence cannot be introduced simply to show the extent of the victim's suffering or the other consequences of the crime or to describe any other circumstances that would merely arouse the jury's hostility toward the defendant.

For example, photographs of the victim of a beating might be admissible, since they tend to prove that the crime was committed and they may contain important information about the manner of the crime, the weapon, and so on. However, the same kind of photographs might be considered inadmissible if they showed the victim several weeks after the crime and were introduced merely to indicate that the victim continued to suffer. Photographs taken at the crime scene might be inadmissible if they display a great deal of blood or anything else that would be unduly disgusting to ordinary citizens, because such photographs would arouse prejudicial feelings in the jury. Color photographs of victims of violent crimes are often excluded for this very reason; and this is why black-and-white photographs should be available. On the other hand, the color photographs might be admitted if the prosecutor can convince the judge that the photographs contain important evidence that cannot be produced in any other way.

Obviously, the question of prejudicial and

inflammatory evidence involves subjective judgments and, to a degree, matters of individual taste and tolerance. An investigator must rely on the judgment of the prosecutor and other officials, since the investigator's own personal standards may be very different from the standards applied in court.

One other set of rules of evidence often plays a part in criminal trials: the hearsay and best evidence rules. The *hearsay rule* concerns testimony about information that the witness claims to have obtained from another person.[13] In general, hearsay evidence is not admissible for the simple reason that the source of the information cannot be cross-examined by the defendant's attorney. Therefore, a witness can testify only about his or her personal knowledge of an event. For example, a witness would not be allowed to say, "The defendant's wife told me that her husband had plenty of money because he had just robbed a liquor store." The hearsay rule applies to testimony about written matter, too. A witness could not say, "I found a note from the defendant in which she said she would be leaving town for a while because she had just killed her boyfriend."

There are exceptions to the basic hearsay rule that permit hearsay evidence to be introduced under certain circumstances. One important exception is the *dying declaration rule.* If a person believes that he or she is about to die, anything that the person says can be related by a witness later in court. The reason for this exception is that people who believe they are close to death have little motivation for lying and, in fact, may feel a strong compulsion to tell the truth. Of course, the credibility of the witness who relates the dying declaration still could be challenged and the validity of the statement itself might be questioned, but usually the statement would be admissible.[14]

The mere fact that a person is dead would not justify allowing a witness to relate anything that the person said. In order for the statement to be admissible, it must have been made at a time when the person had reason to believe that death was imminent. In fact, the person who made a dying declaration might still be alive, and yet the statement, related by a witness, would be admissible. What matters is that the person who originally made the statement thought that he or she was about to die at the time.

Another exception to the hearsay rule is that a witness who was an accomplice of the defendant (in legal terms, a *co-conspirator* in the crime) can testify about statements allegedly made by the defendant. This exception may apply even if the co-conspirator did not actually participate in the crime, but merely helped to plan it.[15]

There are several other exceptions to the hearsay rule, but they are highly technical in nature and therefore of more interest to lawyers than to investigators. In practical terms, an investigator simply needs to be aware of the hearsay rule. As long as witnesses are able to testify about events on the basis of their personal knowledge and observation, the hearsay rule is not a major problem.

The *best evidence rule* is closely related to the hearsay rule; it specifically concerns written documents and records. Put very simply, the best evidence for the content and meaning of a written document is the document itself, not a witness's description or explanation of it. A document is presumed to mean exactly what it says, neither more nor less. Ordinarily this rule is important only in civil cases involving contracts, real estate deeds, and so forth. However, occasionally a criminal case—for example, one involving fraud or conspiracy—might be based on various types of documents.[16]

In almost any extensive criminal investigation, there is a good chance that some evidence will be inadmissible because it was improperly obtained (or, more likely, because there is no way to prove that it was properly obtained); because it is irrelevant, immaterial, or incompetent; because it is prejudicial and inflammatory; or because it is based on hearsay. Each item of evidence that is to be introduced during the trial must pass all of these tests.

Inadmissible evidence is not entirely worthless, of course. Sometimes it is the inadmissible evidence that leads to the identification of a suspect. Unfortunately, merely knowing that someone committed a crime is not the same thing as proving it in court. Often an investigator must work diligently to make certain that crucial evidence is admissible and, conversely, that all the evidence needed to prove the guilt of the accused is available for trial.

## CONTRA-EVIDENCE

Ever since we introduced the term in Chapter 1, we have warned against disregarding or ignoring contra-evidence: any evidence that tends to disprove the guilt of the accused.

Contra-evidence can take many forms. It can be physical evidence, testimony, or circumstantial evidence. For example, if the only fingerprints found on a murder weapon are not those of the suspect, that is contra-evidence. If the victim says that the attacker was dark-haired, but the suspect is blond, that is contra-evidence. If the suspect claims to have been at a movie with two friends at the time of the crime, that is a common type of contra-evidence known as an *alibi*.[17]

Contra-evidence may be found at the crime scene, or it may appear in the testimony of witnesses. Suspects themselves usually offer all sorts of contra-evidence in the effort to show their innocence. Regardless of the source, all contra-evidence must be treated as if it might be valid. The investigator must be prepared to demonstrate that each item of contra-evidence has been carefully considered and has been found to be invalid for some good reason.

## DETERMINING THE OFFENSE

### DEFINITION OF THE CRIME

During the early stages of an investigation the investigator need not be overly concerned with defining the exact nature of the crime. It is sufficient to know the general type of crime that has been committed. However, once the suspect has been identified, the exact nature of the crime becomes important.

Human behavior is criminal if, and only if, it is clearly prohibited by a specific law. Furthermore, not all prohibited behavior is criminal. Behavior is criminal only if the law stipulates that a person convicted of such behavior will be punished by a fine, or by imprisonment in a jail or penitentiary, or by both a fine and imprisonment. Before a person can be convicted of violating a criminal law, a judge or a jury must be persuaded that the person committed the prohibited act as specified by the law.

As we have already seen in the process of investigating crimes, criminal behavior is complex. A single crime involves a series of steps: approaching the scene, entering the scene, interacting with the victim, committing the crime itself, and leaving the scene. We have tried to isolate each step so that it can be examined carefully by the investigator. In the same way, criminal laws define crimes in terms of a number of specific *elements* of behavior. In order for a person to be convicted of a crime, the prosecutor must prove to the satisfaction of the judge or jury that all of these elements were present in the criminal episode.

## GENERAL ELEMENTS

There are certain general elements that must be present for a crime to have been committed. First, the perpetrator of the crime must be mentally and physically capable of committing the crime; a person who is mentally incompetent or unable to control his or her behavior cannot be guilty of a crime.[18]

A person can be found guilty of a crime only if he or she acted voluntarily. Usually this means that the person must have intended to commit the act, must have known that he or she was committing the act, and must have known that the act was wrong. Behavior may be criminal even if it is not completely intended: for example, if a person is *reckless* (acts in a manner likely to cause harm, but disregards the consequences) or *criminally negligent* (acts in a manner that a person should know will be harmful, but ignores the risk).[19]

There must be a direct relationship between the action of the accused and the resulting crime. As the Texas criminal code puts it, "A person is criminally responsible if the result would not have occurred but for his conduct . . . unless [some other] cause was clearly sufficient to produce the result and the conduct of the actor was clearly insufficient" (*Texas Penal Code*, Title 2, Chapter 6, Section 6.04).

There are circumstances under which a person might have committed a crime unwittingly or unintentionally; in such a case the person probably would not be found guilty. If the perpetrator acted on the basis of some reasonable belief that turns out to have been mistaken, and if it was the mistake that resulted in a crime, the person is not guilty.

For example, suppose a person buys a used car at a price that is low, but not suspiciously low. The seller gives the buyer a bill of sale and a certificate of title. Later, the police arrest the buyer for receiving stolen property; the car was stolen, the certificate of title was fraudulent, and the bill of sale was forged. Under the circumstances, unless there is some evidence to show that the buyer knew that the car was stolen, the buyer would not be convicted of any crime. Indeed, the buyer is as much a victim as the rightful owner of the car.[20]

If a person acts under *duress* (threat of force or injury or any other sort of compulsion) or is deluded into believing that the action is not criminal, there is no crime. And, generally, a person cannot be held guilty of a crime if the action taken was intended to defend someone's life, safety, or property or to prevent a greater crime from being committed, provided that the action was reasonable under the circumstances and that excessive force (especially deadly force) was not used wantonly or merely to protect property.

All these general elements address the question of the criminal's state of mind at the time of the alleged offense. In summary, a person commits a criminal act only if the specified criminal behavior is carried out "with a guilty mind," either intentionally and knowingly or recklessly or negligently, and only if the person is mentally and physically capable of controlling his or her behavior.

Behavior that otherwise would be criminal may be legally innocent if the perpetrator meets certain requirements. For example, the use of force is permitted to protect a person's life, to protect property, or to carry out the duties of a law enforcement agent. The laws in each state define the specific circumstances under which force can be used. Many states also define the extent to which physical force may be used by a parent, teacher, guardian, or any other person to discipline a child. Certain individuals might have a privilege or even a definite obligation to act in certain ways that ordinarily would be criminal, depending on the state's law.

Again, the investigator must determine whether there is any evidence to suggest that the suspected criminal acted under some kind of privilege or legal justification. The absence of such a factor is one of the general elements of the crime.

### SPECIFIC ELEMENTS

Beyond the general elements described above, each criminal statute defines the specific elements that must exist in order for a crime to have been committed. There certainly is not enough space in this book to list all of the elements for all of the various kinds of behavior that might be prohibited by the states' criminal codes. Instead, we shall examine one criminal statute from one state: the Texas law defining the crimes of kidnapping and false imprisonment.

*Sec. 20.01. Definitions. In this chapter:*
*(1) "Restrain" means to restrict a person's movements without consent, so as to interfere substantially with his liberty, by moving him from one place to another or by confining him. Restraint is "without consent" if it is accomplished by:*
  *(A) force, intimidation, or deception; or*
  *(B) any means, including acquiescence of the victim, if he is a child less than 14 years of age or an incompetent person and the parent, guardian, or person or institution acting in loco parentis [in a parent's place] has not acquiesced in the movement or confinement.*
*(2) "Abduct" means to restrain a person with intent to prevent his liberation by:*
  *(A) secreting or holding him in a place where he is not likely to be found; or*
  *(B) using or threatening to use deadly force.*

*(3) "Relative" means a parent or stepparent, ancestor, sibling. or uncle or aunt, including an adoptive relative of the same degree through marriage or adoption.*

*Sec. 20.02. False Imprisonment. (a) A person commits an offense if he intentionally or knowingly restrains another person.*
*(b) It is an affirmative defense to prosecution under this section that:*
  *(1) the person restrained was a child less than 14 years of age;*
  *(2) the actor was a relative of the child; and*
  *(3) the actor's sole intent was to assume lawful control of the child.*
*(c) An offense under this section is a Class B misdemeanor unless the actor recklessly exposes the victim to a substantial risk of serious bodily injury, in which case it is a felony of the third degree.*
*(d) It is no offense to detain or move another under this section when it is for the purpose of effecting a lawful arrest or detaining an individual lawfully arrested.*

*Sec. 20.03. Kidnapping. (a) A person commits an offense if he intentionally or knowingly abducts another person.*
*(b) It is an affirmative defense to prosecution under this section that:*
  *(1) the abduction was not coupled with intent to use or to threaten to use deadly force;*
  *(2) the actor was a relative of the person abducted; and*
  *(3) the actor's sole intent was to assume lawful control of the victim.*
*(c) An offense under this section is a felony of the third degree.*

*Sec. 20.04. Aggravated Kidnapping. (a) A person commits an offense if he intentionally or knowingly abducts another person with the intent to:*
  *(1) hold him for ransom or reward;*
  *(2) use him as a shield or hostage;*
  *(3) facilitate the commission of a felony or the flight after the attempt or commission of a felony;*

*(4) inflict bodily injury on him or violate or abuse him sexually;*

*(5) terrorize him or a third person; or*

*(6) interfere with the performance of any governmental or political function.*

*(b) An offense under this section is a felony of the first degree unless the actor voluntarily releases the victim alive and in a safe place, in which event it is a felony of the second degree.*

Notice several important facts about this criminal statute and its logical structure. First of all, the statute begins with carefully worded definitions of the key terms used in the law itself. These definitions contain elements of the crime, just as the rest of the statute does.

For example, in accusing a suspect of false imprisonment, it would be necessary to show that the suspect restricted the victim's movements without consent. Since the lack of consent is specified as an element of the definition, it would be necessary to show that the perpetrator used force, intimidation, or deception to restrain the victim. As stated in this law, the key element in the crime of false imprisonment is that the victim has been restrained without consent. The law also lists certain circumstances in which it is permissible to restrain someone: specifically, one may restrain a child under 14 years of age if the actor (perpetrator) is a relative (as defined in the statute) whose intentions are legal. Similarly, the key element in the crime of kidnapping is that the victim has been abducted. The difference between abduction and restraint is found in the definitions; thus, in order to gain a conviction for kidnapping rather than for false imprisonment, it would be necessary to prove that the perpetrator held the victim in a secret place or used (or threatened to use) deadly force.

The law goes one step further and defines the crime of aggravated kidnapping. The key elements of this more serious crime are spelled out in a brief list, any one of which is sufficient to increase substantially the seriousness of the crime. Interestingly, the law closes by reducing the penalty if the kidnapper releases the victim unharmed, but only if the kidnapper does so voluntarily. Elsewhere in the Texas criminal code, the word *voluntary* is defined in such a way that action taken in the face of imminent capture by the police or in an attempt to avoid capture or punishment is not considered voluntary at all.

A detective investigating a case that generally would be considered a kidnapping must decide exactly what elements of the crime existed and, just as important, which of the elements can be proved in court by the available evidence. Ultimately, the final decision will be made by higher officials, probably the prosecutor. However, the investigator must make at least a tentative determination of the offense so that the proper evidence can be prepared.

## LESSER INCLUDED OFFENSES

The logical structure of the law is especially important at this point because quite often it is not possible to present adequate evidence for the most serious crime that the suspect has committed.

Suppose, for example, that you are investigating a case in which a man has abducted another man and demanded ransom. Under the Texas law this would constitute aggravated kidnapping. However, suppose that you have no evidence (physical or otherwise) that the ransom demand actually was made, and the suspect claims that the abduction was just a practical joke that backfired. Since you cannot prove all the elements of aggravated kidnapping, do you merely turn the suspect loose? Of course not; you charge him with a *lesser included offense*—simple kidnapping, in this case.

The concept behind the lesser included offense is that every criminal action contains a number of elements. If all of the elements are present in a particular event, the most serious crime has been committed; if some but not all of the elements are present, a less serious crime has been committed. In other words, the less serious offense is included in the more serious crime. Most criminal laws are very clear about how these lesser offenses are pyramided within the larger offense.

For example, a suspect might be charged with burglary in the first degree, burglary in the second degree, theft, or merely criminal trespassing, depending on what evidence is available. Similarly, a case of assault could range from a Class C misdemeanor (the least serious category of crimes) to a third-degree felony, depending on exactly what elements are present in the crime and which of them can be proved in court.

### MULTIPLE OFFENSES

For cases in which a single criminal event took place, the decision about what crime should be charged ordinarily is based on the availability of evidence. In general, the prosecutor will file the most serious charge for which there is adequate evidence.

However, some criminal events involve multiple offenses. For instance, the criminal illegally entered a home at night, vandalized part of the home, and removed some valuable property; while leaving the residence, the burglar was surprised by the owners, who were returning home; at this point the burglar shot and killed them. There might be ample evidence to charge the perpetrator with burglary, criminal mischief (or vandalism in some states), theft, and murder.

Some states have laws that determine what offenses can be charged in such a case. In many states the fact that the murder was committed during the course of another crime would automatically mean that the burglar would be charged with first-degree murder. However, usually it is the prosecutor who decides what charges to file.

In the past, prosecutors often would accuse a defendant of as many crimes as possible in a single charge, hoping to overwhelm the jury with a catalogue of sins. But today the tendency is to be more selective. For one thing, the prosecutor must prove the elements of every crime charged; if the charge is overburdened with a variety of offenses, this task may be all but impossible. There is some danger of confusing the jury by offering too much evidence on too many different points; one possible result is the jury's becoming sympathetic toward the poor, beleaguered defendant. If some of the charges are not adequately proved, the judge might intervene and dismiss those charges for insufficient evidence; this, too, makes a poor impression on the jury. Finally, there is the possibility that, regardless of the weight of the evidence, the jury will acquit the defendant altogether; in this case the defendant can never again be accused of any of the crimes charged.

For all these reasons, most prosecutors prefer to charge a suspect only with the one particular crime for which the evidence is most persuasive. This may not be the most serious crime that was committed. The theory is that any conviction is better than none at all; and once the accused has been convicted on one charge, it may be possible to bring the other charges in a separate trial.

However, there is one drawback to the principle of charging only the offense for which the evidence is most persuasive and holding additional charges for future use. Some recent court decisions have held that the constitutional protection against double jeopardy (being tried more than once for the same offense) applies to the criminal *event,* not to the specific criminal charge. At this time, such rulings have been obtained mostly in state courts; federal courts have not been clear on the matter. Thus, in some states the prosecutor must try the accused for all offenses connected to a single event, because there will not be an opportunity to bring additional charges at a later time. Here again, the nature and validity of the evidence will determine which charges can be brought and which must be disregarded.

The prosecutor's strategy may be somewhat different when the suspect is accused of a series of offenses at different times and places. The protection against double jeopardy would not apply to such a case. For example, if the suspect is accused of having committed ten different burglaries, one could hold ten separate trials (one for each offense) or combine all the offenses into one trial. Some states, however, do not permit charges to be combined in this fashion.

The prosecutor may decide to charge the suspect with one of the offenses for which there is good evidence, although it is not necessarily the best evidence or even the most serious offense. The theory behind this strategy is that if a conviction is obtained on a relatively weak case, the probability is increased of winning convictions on all the other cases. This likelihood might induce the defendant to plead guilty to some or all of them. Even if a conviction is not obtained on the relatively weak case, the defendant knows that stronger cases are being held in abeyance, and, therefore, the defendant may be eager to bargain for reduced charges in return for a plea of guilty.

Again, all these considerations of strategy must be decided by the prosecutor, but the prosecutor must rely on the recommendations of the investigator and on the investigator's presentation of the evidence. It is not enough for the investigator to deliver a file full of notes and documents and expect the prosecutor to sort it all out.

## COORDINATING WITH THE PROSECUTOR

Most larger police agencies have well-defined procedures for preparing criminal cases and delivering them to the prosecutor. But if there are no established policies, at least certain minimal steps should be taken by the investigator.

After the investigator has completely evaluated all the available evidence, filled in any missing points, checked out all the contra-evidence, and determined which elements of a specific criminal offense can be proved, a summary of the case should be prepared.[21] The summary should contain the investigator's statement of how the crime occurred: what specific actions were taken by the perpetrator, the victim, and any other participants. Attached to the summary should be a list of the physical evidence pertaining to the crime and a list of the testimony obtained from all pertinent witnesses. Even evidence that in the investigator's judgment is irrelevant or misleading should be included in the list, and special attention should be given to any contra-evidence; if necessary, explanatory notes may be added for irrelevant or misleading evidence or for contra-evidence.

The investigator's case summary should be reviewed by at least one higher official of the police department. The supervisor may be able to point out weaknesses, inconsistencies,

*During the conference with the prosecutor's staff, the investigator should present a summary of the case, describing all the evidence available to prove that the accused suspect committed the crime.*

or accidental omissions that the investigator has overlooked. These problems should be corrected before the case summary is delivered to the prosecutor.

After the summary has been approved by the supervisor, the investigator should arrange for a conference with an appropriate member of the prosecutor's staff (usually an assistant district attorney who handles criminal cases). During this conference, which might involve not only the investigator and the prosecutor but the supervising police official and other officials as well, the investigating officer should present the case summary and explain it in detail, describing the evidence that is available, any and all contra-evidence, and any evidence that has been set aside as irrelevant or misleading. At all times, the police must be completely candid with the prosecutor about any weaknesses in the case.

Following this conference, the prosecutor decides what charges will be brought against the suspect and arranges for a trial. The prosecutor also may decide that additional evidence is needed. Usually the investigator is notified of this requirement, though some prosecutors have their own investigative staffs to take over the case at this point.[22]

One very important decision should be made jointly by the prosecutor's staff and the police officers: the timing of an arrest.[23] Many times, the investigator-prosecutor conference will be held before an arrest has been made. As we shall see in the next chapter, it is often desirable to wait until the last possible moment before making an arrest.

Once the arrest has been made, there may be very little chance of obtaining additional evidence, because the suspect and his or her associates will do everything possible to destroy evidence or keep it from being found. Witnesses who were previously cooperative may be reluctant to say anything more for fear of retaliation from the defendant; witnesses who were hostile before the arrest are likely to be even more hostile if they feel sympathy for the accused. Because the timing of an arrest is so crucial to the success of a case and, in fact, because the entire arrest procedure is of the utmost importance, we shall discuss it in detail in the following chapter.

## REFERENCES

1. Peter W. Greenwood, Jan M. Chaiken, and Joan Petersilia, *The Criminal Investigation Process* (Lexington, Mass.: D. C. Heath, 1977), p. 167.

2. Greenwood, Chaiken, and Petersilia, pp. 237–238.

3. Ronald J. Waldron, et al., *The Criminal Justice System* (Boston: Houghton Mifflin, 1976), pp. 26–27.

4. Paul B. Weston and Kenneth M. Wells, *Criminal Evidence for Police* (Englewood Cliffs, N.J.: Prentice-Hall, 1971), pp. 15–16.

5. Weston and Wells, *Criminal Evidence,* pp. 16–17.

6. Weston and Wells, *Criminal Evidence,* p. 20.

7. Weston and Wells, *Criminal Evidence,* pp. 39–41.

8. Waldron, et al., p. 210.

9. Paul B. Weston and Kenneth M. Wells, *Elements of Criminal Investigation* (Englewood Cliffs, N.J.: Prentice-Hall, 1971), p. 7.

10. Weston and Wells, *Criminal Evidence,* p. 9.

11. Weston and Wells, *Criminal Evidence,* p. 10.

12. Weston and Wells, *Criminal Evidence,* p. 10.

13. Weston and Wells, *Criminal Evidence,* chap. 3.

14. Weston and Wells, *Criminal Evidence,* p. 27.

15. Weston and Wells, *Criminal Evidence,* p. 35.

16. Weston and Wells, *Criminal Evidence,* p. 102.

17. Weston and Wells, *Criminal Evidence,* p. 225.

18. A. C. Germann, Frank D. Day, and Robert J. Gallati, *Introduction to Law Enforcement and Criminal Justice,* rev. ed. (Springfield, Ill.: Charles C Thomas, 1973), p. 227.

19. Weston and Wells, *Criminal Evidence,* p. 226.

20. Weston and Wells, *Criminal Evidence,* p. 227.

21. Greenwood, Chaiken, and Petersilia, pp. 171–175.

22. Greenwood, Chaiken, and Petersilia, p. 67.

23. Waldron, et al., p. 32.

# REVIEW OF THE EVIDENCE

1. Many safeguards have been built into our legal system to eliminate witnesses' testimony that is likely to be
   a. damaging to the defendant.
   b. incredible.
   c. false or mistaken.
   d. unimportant.
   e. privileged.
2. The competence of a child to testify as a witness must be decided by the
   a. jury.
   b. prosecutor.
   c. defendant's attorney.
   d. investigator.
   e. judge.
3. Immunity means that
   a. the witness is temporarily or permanently incapable of testifying truthfully.
   b. the witness cannot be forced to testify unless he or she wishes to do so.
   c. the evidence cannot be introduced even if the witness is willing to testify.
   d. the defendant cannot be found guilty of the offense charged.
   e. the witness is an expert and, therefore, is permitted to express opinions.
4. True or false: When evidence is presented in a trial, the jury must decide whether to believe it at all and, if so, to what extent.
5. Evidence cannot be admitted in a criminal trial if
   a. the witness is not an expert.
   b. it is irrelevant, incompetent, or immaterial.
   c. it is prejudicial or inflammatory.
   d. it has been illegally obtained.
   e. all of the above are true.
   f. none of the above is true.
6. Evidence that ordinarily would be considered irrelevant may be introduced
   a. if it will discredit the testimony of a witness.
   b. if it is immune or privileged.
   c. if it tends to prove or disprove the guilt of the accused.
   d. if it is a dying declaration.
   e. if no other evidence is available.
7. In cases involving violent crimes, black-and-white photographs should be available as evidence because
   a. they show details more clearly than color photos.
   b. color photos might be considered inflammatory.
   c. they are more likely to arouse the jury's sympathy for the victim.
   d. they contain important evidence that cannot be produced in any other way.
   e. several copies can be made inexpensively for the jury to examine.

8. The hearsay rule concerns
   a. testimony from a witness who was not present during the crime.
   b. testimony about documents.
   c. testimony about information that a witness claims to have obtained from someone else.
   d. testimony about the witness's personal knowledge of the crime.
   e. testimony about the witness's opinion as an expert.
9. True or false: A defendant's alibi is an example of contra-evidence.
10. A person can be found guilty of a crime only if
    a. the person was mentally and physically capable of committing the crime.
    b. the person acted voluntarily.
    c. there is a direct relationship between the action of the accused and the resulting crime.
    d. the person knew that the action was a crime.
    e. the person was not acting under duress or compulsion.
    f. the person had no legal privilege or justification for committing the action.
    g. all of the above are true.
    h. none of the above is true.

### TOPICS FOR INVESTIGATION

1. Most of the matters discussed in this chapter are the proper concern of the prosecutor. Why should a police officer do the prosecutor's job? Is it a waste of time to consider these issues, because the prosecutor makes the final decisions?
2. Suppose that your only primary witness to a serious crime was drunk at the time. What could you do to ensure that the witness's testimony would be both admissible and believable?
3. Suppose that you have investigated a particularly gruesome violent crime. There are a number of witnesses who can identify the suspect, and one of them is the victim's six-year-old child. Should the child testify in court?
4. Why are certain conversations legally privileged? Should they be? Should privilege be extended to include conversations between a news reporter and a criminal or between an employer and an employee? Are there any circumstances under which the privilege should be suspended?
5. Why is evidence about the defendant's personal reputation or past criminal behavior considered irrelevant and therefore inadmissible? Should the jury not be allowed to know what kind of person the defendant is?
6. Suppose that you have investigated a serious crime and are certain that you have the guilty party. The trial starts tomorrow. While reviewing your notes one last time, you discover an important piece of contra-evidence that has been overlooked. As far as you know, neither the prosecutor nor the defendant is aware that this evidence exists. What would you do?
7. Under our legal system, the prosecution must prove all of the elements of a crime in order to obtain a conviction. Which element is most difficult to prove?

8. Citizens and police officers often are incensed when a criminal is allowed to plead guilty to a lesser included offense rather than standing trial for a more serious offense. Should prosecutors be required by law to bring a defendant to trial for the most serious offense for which there is ample evidence?

9. Some courts have held that the constitutional protection against double jeopardy applies to the criminal event, not to the specific offense charged. Do you agree with this judicial theory? How would it affect the investigator's responsibility?

10. Is it a good idea for prosecutors to have their own investigative staffs, separate from the police department? Why or why not?

# UNIT VI
## CONCLUDING
## THE INVESTIGATION

# CHAPTER 15
# THE ARREST

STUDY CLUES

1. True or false: In most states a law enforcement officer has the legal power to arrest someone on "suspicion" without specifying a particular crime.
2. The main purpose of prearrest surveillance is
    a. to identify the suspect.
    b. to arrest the suspect on sight.
    c. to identify the suspect's accomplices.
    d. to observe the suspect's normal pattern of habitual activities.
    e. to obtain evidence about the suspect's criminal activities.
3. True or false: Once a suspect becomes convinced that the police are no longer investigating a particular crime, locating that person will be nearly impossible.
4. True or false: An unplanned arrest usually occurs when a police officer is suddenly confronted with a wanted suspect in a situation that demands action.
5. The legal process that permits a wanted suspect to be returned from the jurisdiction where an arrest took place to the jurisdiction where the crime was committed is called
    a. extradition.
    b. direct pursuit.
    c. extraterritoriality.
    d. interagency cooperation.
    e. double jeopardy.

THE ARREST OF A SUSPECT is, in most police officers' minds, the culmination of the criminal investigation and the goal toward which they work. Being able to make an arrest, they feel, is the ultimate test of success. In the entire process, from the detection of a crime until the final verdict, there is no more critical and delicate step than the arrest. Before an arrest can be made, hundreds of hours may have been spent in investigating a crime. After the arrest, hundreds or even thousands of additional hours of police work—not including the time spent by prosecutors, jury members, witnesses, and officials of the court—will be invested in the investigative and judicial processes to obtain a conviction.

Why, then, should an arrest be treated with so much urgency that it is often mishandled? Surely the arrest deserves just as much forethought and planning as any other phase of the criminal investigation. Yet, far too often, a poorly executed arrest results in the dismissal or reduction of charges against a guilty suspect.[1] Furthermore, the arrest is by far the most dangerous action taken by a police officer. Guilty or innocent, the suspect feels an overwhelming compulsion to avoid being taken into custody. Even criminals who are otherwise nonviolent may be lured into violence by an improperly executed, poorly planned arrest.[2]

The alternative is a *planned arrest:* an arrest that is carefully designed to bring a suspect into custody with minimal danger to the police officer, to the suspect, and to innocent bystanders.

## DEFINITION OF AN ARREST

Although the definition varies somewhat from state to state, in general an arrest is a detention of a citizen in which the person is taken into custody, accused of a crime, and presented to an appropriate court.[3] Legally, an arrest has only one justification: to ensure that the accused will be present when the question of guilt is tried in court.[4] An arrest may have a secondary function was well: it prevents the criminal from continuing to violate the law, at least for whatever time the arrestee remains in custody. Some people believe that the power of arrest should be used specifically for this purpose whenever the police suspect that a citizen is engaged in criminal conduct. However, this concept of *preventive detention* is inescapably opposed to the principle of presumed innocence.

One function of the arrest should never be tolerated: the use of arresting authority to punish or harass suspected criminals or simply unpleasant and undesirable persons, when there is no evidence that they are guilty of a particular crime. Undeniably, police authorities have abused the power of arrest in this way, and some continue to do so. In many other countries, where the presumption of innocence is not a basic part of the legal system, this is normal police practice. Under our Constitution and the concepts of individual liberty that we profess to believe in, the exercise of arresting authority in the absence of clear and convincing evidence of guilt is completely unacceptable. That is why a citizen who is arrested illegally has every right to sue the offending police officer and, under certain circumstances, the government agency involved for false arrest. Any police officer who misuses the power of arrest is likely to face stern disciplinary action within the agency.

Some legal authorities believe that an arrest occurs any time a police officer exercises the authority to stop a citizen from doing whatever that individual wishes to do, including walking away from the police officer.[5] Even if the police officer says and does nothing that involves coercion or force, the mere fact that the officer could use coercion means that the citizen has no choice and, thus, the detention is not "voluntary."[6] In contrast, most police officers, with the full support of their agencies' regulations, make a clear distinction between an arrest and a field interrogation or field interview. To most officers, an arrest is a definite situation: it occurs when an officer says to a suspect, "You are under arrest for the crime of such-and-such."

This question—when does an arrest actually occur?—is crucial because if an arrest is made improperly, the accused almost certainly will go free, no matter how much evidence of guilt might exist. The arrest cannot be made until there is enough evidence to justify it. On the other hand, an arrest cannot be delayed by a police officer in order to continue questioning the suspect without giving the so-called *Miranda warning* (which usually results in the loss of all cooperation by the suspect).

The timing of the arrest is not the only critical issue. Indeed, each step in the arrest process must be carried out properly; otherwise the arrest will be invalid, the suspect will be free, and it will not be possible to bring a guilty criminal to justice.

Briefly, the laws of arrest, as defined by the Constitution, federal and state statutes, and court decisions, mean that:

1. The right of a police officer to stop a citizen on the street, to ask questions, and to search the person or property is severely limited. There must be either a warrant for the person's arrest or some probable cause to believe that the person either has committed a crime or is about to do so.

2. The right against self-incrimination (Fifth Amendment) and the right to legal counsel (Fourteenth Amendment provision of due process) are fundamental and apply throughout the criminal process. Thus, as soon as the police believe that a certain person is guilty of a crime, they are obligated to protect that person's constitutional rights.[7] The police must take special steps to ensure that any citizen accused of a crime is aware of those rights and is able to invoke them; thus, the *Miranda* warning is required.

3. Any failure to protect the accused's constitutional rights, either through an improper search or an improper arrest, is almost certain to doom any effort to prosecute. Improperly obtained evidence, no matter how damaging, is useless. The most sordid criminal, if improperly arrested, will be set free.

## THE ARREST WARRANT

There is one simple way for the police officer on the street to avoid many problems with both searches and arrests: get a warrant first. A warrant is an official order issued by a magistrate that instructs the police officer to conduct a search, seize certain property, or arrest a particular person.

The Fourth Amendment states the minimum requirements for a valid warrant: "no warrants shall issue, but upon probable cause, supported by oath or affirmation, and particularly describing the place to be searched, and the persons or things to be seized." The two essential elements here are the requirement of of "probable cause, supported by oath or affirmation," and the requirement of a precise, or particular, description.

There is no simple definition of *probable*

ANSWERS TO STUDY CLUES
1. True    2. d    3. False    4. True    5. a

## LANDMARK DECISIONS: ARRESTS

The Fourth and Fifth Amendments to the Constitution define the fundamental laws of arrest in the United States. These laws, however, are subject to interpretation by the Supreme Court. Here are some of the most significant cases decided by the Supreme Court concerning police arrests:

*Brown v. Mississippi* (1936). The Fifth Amendment applies to state cases as well as federal cases and prohibits the use of a confession that was obtained by coercion.

*Ashcraft v. Tennessee* (1944). The mere fact that a person is detained can have the same effect as coercion and can, therefore, invalidate a confession.

*Mallory v. United States* (1957); *Haynes v. Washington* (1963). The accused may not be interrogated at length before being presented to a magistrate for arraignment or being allowed to contact family or counsel. The fruits of such improper interrogations are not admissible during the trial.

*Massiah v. United States* (1964). An accused person must have the benefit of legal counsel before being interrogated. Furthermore, a confession is inadmissible on the basis of a single "technical" violation, not the totality of circumstances.

*Escobedo v. Illinois* (1964). An accused person in state as well as federal cases is entitled to counsel "as soon as the process shifts from investigatory to accusatory"—that is, as soon as there is probable cause to accuse the citizen of a crime. (In *Gideon v. Wainwright* [1963] the Court had ruled that states must provide counsel to indigent defendants in all criminal cases, not just capital cases.) These decisions mean that a crucial factor is the moment when an arrest is *possible,* because there is sufficient evidence to accuse the suspect of a crime.

*Miranda v. Arizona* (1964). The constitutional guarantees must be explained to an accused person as soon as the suspect is taken into custody, not at some later time when the accused is presented to a magistrate. Furthermore, those guarantees must contain specific elements: the right to remain silent; the right to be advised by legal counsel; the right to have legal counsel even if the accused cannot afford to hire a lawyer; and the right to cooperate in one part of an investigation or interrogation without waiving the right to remain silent at some later time (in short, the right to change one's mind about cooperating).

*Whiteley v. Warden* (1971, reaffirming earlier decisions). In general, a police radio broadcast of a description of a wanted fugitive is sufficient probable cause for an officer to arrest the person on sight. However, if the broadcast itself is not based on sufficient evidence to justify an arrest, the arrest is not valid.

*cause.* Generally, the term means "a reasonable ground of suspicion supported by circumstances sufficiently strong in themselves to warrant a cautious man in the belief that the accused person is guilty of a particular offense."[8] In other words, there must be some circumstance that would cause an objective person to agree that the suspect probably is guilty of a certain crime. If a person is observed by a police officer in the act of committing a crime, the requirement of

Came to hand the_____day of_____, 19_____, at_____o'clock_____M.,

and executed on the_____day of_____, 19_____, at_____o'clock_____M.,

by_____

I actually and necessarily traveled_____ miles in the service of this warrant, in addition to any other process in this cause during the same trip.

Fees:

Serving Warrants . . . . $_____

$_____ Chief of Police, Peace Officer's
Sheriff's, or other Peace Officer's Signature

$_____ City of_____, County

of_____, Texas

---

No._____

### IN MUNICIPAL COURT
Temple, Texas

## THE STATE OF TEXAS
VS.

_____

_____

# Warrant of Arrest

Issued _____ day

of _____ 197_____

Judge of the Municipal Court
City of Temple, Texas

THE STATE OF TEXAS )
COUNTY OF BELL )

IN MUNICIPAL COURT
**CITY OF TEMPLE**

# THE STATE OF TEXAS

TO THE CHIEF OF POLICE OR ANY PEACE OFFICER OF THE CITY OF TEMPLE, TEXAS OR ANY SHERIFF OR CONSTABLE OR OTHER PEACE OFFICER OF THE STATE OF TEXAS, GREETINGS:

YOU ARE HEREBY COMMANDED to arrest................................................................................if to be found

in your city or county and bring............................before me,.................................................................
Judge of the Municipal Court of the **City of Temple**, at my office in Temple, Texas, in said Bell County, instanter, then and there to answer THE STATE OF TEXAS and the CITY OF TEMPLE, for an offense

against the laws of said State and City, to-wit:......................................................................................

........................................................................................................................................................

........................................................................................................................................................

........................................................................................................................................................

.................................................................................................of which offense..........he..........

accused by the written complaint under oath of.....................................................................................
filed before me.

HEREIN FAIL NOT, but of this Writ make due return, showing how you have executed the same.

Witness my official signature, this............day of.................................................................. 197......

—————————————————————
Judge of the Municipal Court
City of Temple, Texas

---

probable cause is amply satisfied.[9] In fact, anything that occurs within a police officer's presence can provide probable cause for an arrest. *Presence* means not only within sight, but also within the range of the senses, including the senses of hearing, touch, smell, or even taste.

Any reasonably persuasive evidence about crimes that occurred outside of the officer's

presence may be sufficient to establish probable cause. Usually this means that a victim, witness, or informant tells the police officer about a crime and either identifies the perpetrator or describes him or her well enough to enable the officer to identify the suspect at a later time.[10] Physical evidence or even circumstantial evidence can supply probable cause if it points unmistakably to a certain suspect.

The other requirement for a warrant is *particularity*. The person to be arrested must be described as thoroughly as possible: for example, name, age, and home address. If this much information is not available, a warrant

*An arrest warrant. (left: front and back of warrant; above: inside) (Courtesy Temple, Texas, Police Department)*

can be issued on the basis of a physical description that is precise enough that the average, neutral observer would be able to distinguish the suspect from the general population of those with similar height, weight, and complexion.

Obtaining an arrest warrant is not very complicated. The police officer simply writes out the warrant and presents it to any magistrate. Standard printed forms usually are available, although a warrant can be written or typed on plain paper. The magistrate may question certain elements of the warrant, especially the probable cause and particularity.[11] The magistrate then either denies the warrant or signs it.

The person subject to arrest has the right to see and examine the warrant. The police officer ought to have the warrant in possession when the arrest is made. However, if the subject does not press this right and consents to the arrest, the mere fact that a warrant exists is sufficient. Also, if the subject of an arrest warrant might flee (as is often the case), any police officer who knows of an existing warrant may perform the arrest without having the warrant itself; it can be shown to the arrestee later.

When an arrest warrant is executed, the accused person must be informed of the nature of the criminal charge and the *Miranda* warning must be given. Most police agencies provide every officer with a "*Miranda* card" containing the precise wording that the agency prefers, although minor variations in wording do not invalidate the warning. The following is a typical *Miranda* warning.

*You are under arrest. Before you answer any questions or make any statements, it is my duty to advise you of your rights and to warn you of the consequences of waiving those rights. One: You have the right to remain silent and not say anything. Two: Any oral or written statement that you make can and will be used against you in court. Three: You have the right to have a lawyer present to advise you before and during any questioning by police officers or attorneys representing the state. Four: If you are too poor to hire a lawyer, the court will appoint one for you, free of charge, and your lawyer can advise you before or during any questioning. Five: You can decide to talk to anyone and you can stop talking to them at any time you want. Six: The above rights are continuing rights that can be urged by you at any stage of the proceedings.*

Some agencies require the arresting officer to ask the suspect to sign a copy of the *Miranda* warning. However, the arrestee cannot be forced to sign anything and usually will refuse to do so.

## ARRESTS WITHOUT A WARRANT

The procedures described so far represent the ideal, proper arrest of an accused citizen. Four basic steps have occurred:

- Probable cause was established.
- The person accused of the crime was properly identified, reducing the chance that the wrong person would be arrested.
- A warrant was obtained from a magistrate to authorize the arrest.
- At the time of the arrest, the arrestee's fundamental constitutional rights were protected by the *Miranda* warning.

Under certain circumstances one, but only one, of those four steps may be omitted: obtaining a warrant. Depending on the laws of a given state, police officers may carry out certain arrests without a warrant, provided that the other three steps are performed exactly as if a warrant were issued.

In some states an arrest without a warrant

*A Miranda warning card. (Courtesy Temple, Texas, Police Department)*

may be made only for a felony or for a breach of the peace.[12] A breach of the peace usually is defined as a misdemeanor, but it differs from other misdemeanors in an important way: it disturbs public order or decorum. Generally, an arrest cannot be made without a warrant for other misdemeanor offenses. There are other restrictions, too. The offense must be committed in the officer's presence, or it must be reported to the officer by a credible person *and* there must be reason to believe that the offender is about to escape or that the offense will continue. Otherwise, there is no reason for the officer not to go before a magistrate and obtain a warrant.

## ARRESTS ON SUSPICION

In the past, most states permitted an arrest on suspicion with very few restrictions or qualifications about what constituted suspicion. Many states still have broadly worded laws, such as the following:

*Any peace officer may arrest, without a warrant, persons found in suspicious places and under circumstances which reasonably show that such persons have been guilty of some felony or breach of the peace, or threaten or are about to commit some offense against the law.*

Used wisely, this broad power enables police officers to prevent crimes before they occur and, sometimes, to capture offenders before the crime has been discovered. Used unwisely, the power to arrest on suspicion permits police officers to harass innocent citizens, inevitably leading to diminished public respect for the law and for the police agency.

## THE PLANNED ARREST

### THREE CRITERIA

Not every arrest can be fully planned (later in this chapter, we shall deal with unplanned arrests). However, the arrest should be planned in nearly every case for which three basic criteria are met:

- The crime took place at some time in the past; since then, it has been thoroughly investigated.
- The investigation has resulted in the identification of a particular suspect with enough evidence of the suspect's guilt that an arrest warrant has been obtained.
- The suspect's whereabouts are known.

If the first two criteria have not been satisfied, the investigation should continue until there is enough evidence for an arrest warrant. If the third criterion is unmet, the investigator's efforts obviously must be devoted to locating the suspect.

Remember, every criminal lives somewhere. Every criminal must eat, sleep, and pass the time doing something. Every criminal associates with other people: family, friends, or accomplices. Almost without exception, people eventually return to familiar places and familiar patterns of living. Once a criminal becomes convinced that the police are no longer actively investigating a particular crime, usually that individual shows up at his or her known place of residence and favorite bars, clubs, or other places of amusement. A criminal flees or hides only in the belief that someone is in pursuit.

Once the whereabouts of the suspect are known, the arrest can be planned. Notice that we do not recommend that the suspect be arrested on sight. An arrest warrant can be executed at any time. So as long as the suspect's whereabouts are known, there is no reason to rush.

A planned arrest contains two major stages: the surveillance of the suspect and the execution of the arrest.

### PREARREST SURVEILLANCE

Surveillance ordinarily is regarded as part of the investigation prior to identification of a suspect. However, careful surveillance should be part of the arrest process as well. The purpose of prearrest surveillance is to observe the suspect's normal pattern of habitual, noncriminal activities so that the execution of the arrest can be planned. How does the suspect spend the day? Where does the suspect go to buy food or to find amusement and entertainment? Who usually accompanies the suspect away from his or her home?

All this information can be gathered in a day or two, at most, by merely observing the suspect. The surveillance must be surreptitious, of course; usually it is carried out by plainclothes officers in unmarked vehicles. At least two or three officers in different vehicles should work together in order to reduce the likelihood that the suspect will notice someone is watching.[13]

Elaborate disguises, such as utility trucks or delivery vans, are more appropriate for TV shows than for actual police work, although once in a while a disguise might be justified. The danger is that the disguise may call attention to itself. For example, a television repair truck parked for several hours in a low-income neighborhood might arouse suspicion, because very few people in such a neighborhood could afford to have a TV repairman come to their homes.[14]

If there is any indication that the suspect has become aware of the surveillance, it should be discontinued at once. After a few minutes, another officer in a different vehicle should take it up again.

The prearrest surveillance does not have to take very long; a few hours may be sufficient. The purpose is to gather just enough information to determine the best time and place to execute the arrest safely and effectively. Once that information has been obtained, the investigator is ready to advance to the next stage.

### EXECUTION OF THE ARREST

The safest place to execute an arrest is out in the open, away from the suspect's residence. Ideally, the suspect should be alone, far away from any vehicle or other place where weapons could be hidden, and far away from other people. The place of arrest should be chosen

### SURVEILLANCE TECHNIQUES

The term *surveillance* covers a number of related techniques that are sometimes used by investigators. Briefly, any surveillance consists of observing a person or place in a covert manner—that is, without letting the subject know that the surveillance is taking place. There are three basic types of surveillance: visual observation, undercover infiltration, and electronic surveillance.

### OBSERVATION

Visual observation can be either fixed or moving. Fixed observation ordinarily is used to keep watch over a particular place, such as a suspect's residence or a location where criminal activities may be ongoing. For fixed observation, usually the surveillance must be performed from outside the building. A short-term surveillance lasting only a few hours can be conducted by placing officers in parked cars or on foot in the area.[15] If the surveillance will last more than a day or

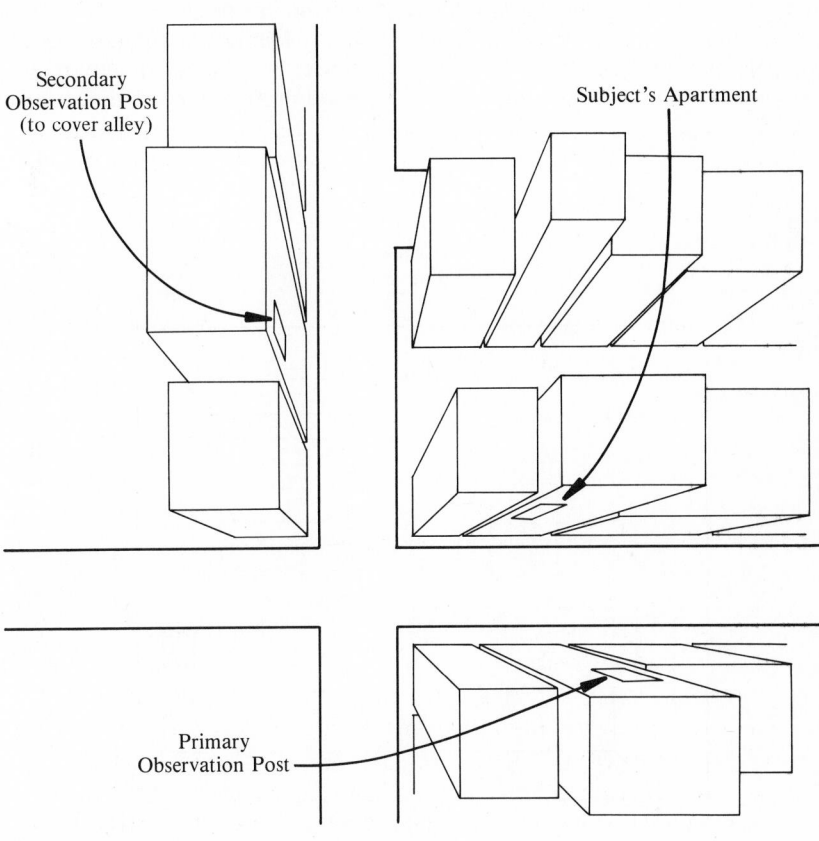

FIGURE 15.1
FIXED OBSERVATION POST, EXTERNAL

Secondary Observation Post (to cover alley)

Subject's Apartment

Primary Observation Post

two, it is better to rent a room, apartment, or office space in a nearby building. The observation post must have a clear view of the subject building. If there is more than one entrance, two or more observation posts might be required, as shown in Figure 15.1.

Fixed observation of a prospective crime site, such as a liquor store or a drive-in grocery in an area where there has been a spate of armed robberies, may require an observation post inside the building.[16] The observation post must be selected to give a clear, unobstructed view of the entrances and the point at which the crime is likely to occur. Officers must have rapid, easy access to and from the observation post, preferably by at least two different routes so they cannot be pinned down or trapped (Figure 15.2). If there is no suitable observation area, it may be possible to put up temporary partitions in an appropriate location. The partitions can be fitted with one-way glass windows and with signs indicating that the store is being remodeled.

Moving observation is almost always used for surveillance of a suspect or of the suspect's associates. The subject may be followed on foot, by vehicle, or in both ways. In any case, a successful moving surveillance requires a minimum of two officers and preferably three or four.

A moving perimeter plan (described on pages 396–398) may be attempted in surveillance operations, although it is primarily used in pursuit situations. The *leapfrog* technique is more often employed in surveillance. Two or more officers follow the subject, but only one officer is in close contact (that is, close enough to observe the subject con-

FIGURE 15.2
FIXED OBSERVATION POST, INTERNAL

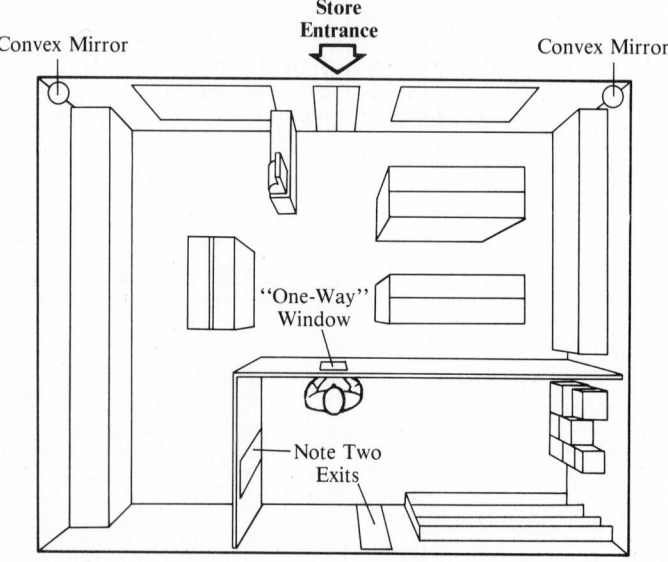

FIGURE 15.3
MOVING SURVEILLANCE

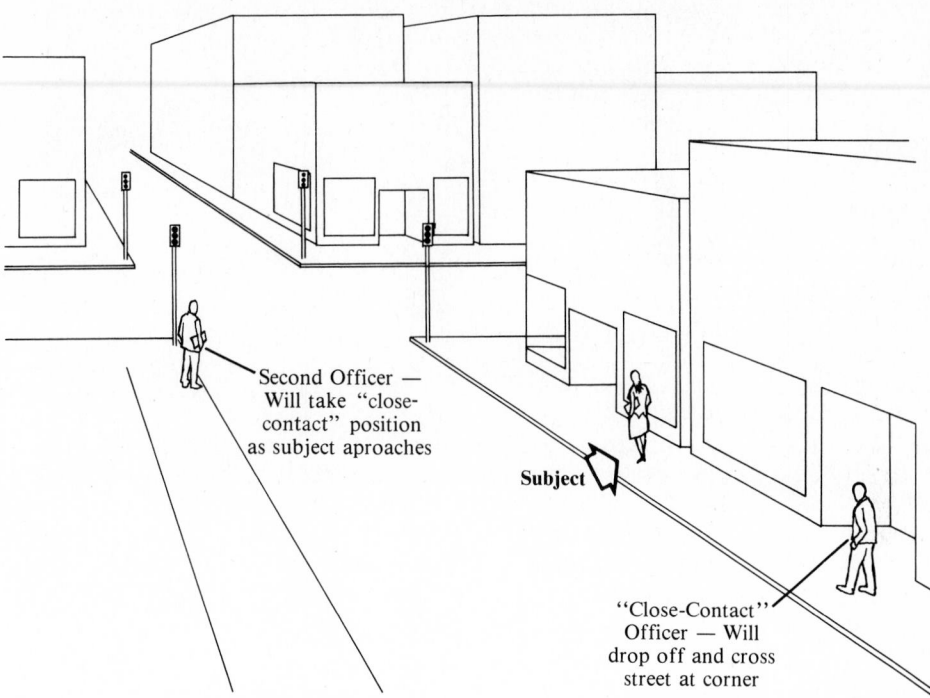

Second Officer —
Will take "close-
contact" position
as subject aproaches

**Subject**

"Close-Contact"
Officer — Will
drop off and cross
street at corner

stantly) at any time. After staying close to the subject for a block or so, that officer drops off and a second officer takes the close position. The first officer either follows at a distance, out of the subject's sight, or moves ahead of the subject by vehicle or by an alternative route, as shown in Figure 15.3. By frequently changing the officer in the close position, the surveillance team can follow for a considerable distance with little likelihood that the subject will be aware of being followed.[17]

### UNDERCOVER INFILTRATION

Undercover surveillance is almost never used in ordinary criminal investigations. When it is attempted, specially trained undercover agents, rather than the regular investigator, usually conduct the surveillance. For additional discussion of undercover surveillance, see page 332.

### ELECTRONIC SURVEILLANCE

The simplest form of electronic or automatic surveillance is the use of photographic devices to observe an area in which criminal activity is anticipated.[18] The automatic cameras seen in bank lobbies are an obvious example. Still, motion picture, or television cameras are alternatives; each has its advantages and disadvantages. One advantage of

*Video surveillance equipment can be used in any public place and has been used successfully in some investigations. It is most often valuable in long term, undercover operations.*

television is that the pictures can be viewed while they are being taken, using remote monitors. The images also can be recorded on video tape simultaneously. Since the tapes can be erased and reused if they are not needed, there is no waste in continuous recording, which would be impractically expensive with motion pictures.

Photographic surveillance can be maintained in any public area without intruding on anyone's privacy rights. However, any other form of electronic surveillance raises serious questions of constitutionality and propriety. As a general rule, no electronic surveillance should be used outside of a public place except under court order. Even then, the surveillance should be kept to the ab-

solute minimum required in order to obtain the specific evidence needed. The use of electronic surveillance for a "fishing expedition" in the hope of turning up some sort of evidence is not only improper, but almost always unproductive and unreasonably expensive.[19]

A wiretap is any sort of device that intercepts telephone calls to a given line. A wiretap can be used with the consent of the person who rents the line or under a court order. Some wiretap devices are completely undetectable by the telephone user. Automatic tape recorders, which begin recording whenever there is activity on the line, can provide an unattended wiretap.

There are all sorts of audio devices suitable for surveillance, including extraordinarily sensitive microphones, miniaturized radio transmitters, and so forth. Court orders for the use of such devices are hard to get and the results (if any) usually are not admissible in court. However, any conversation can be recorded with the consent of any one party to the conversation, and the recordings usually would be admissible as evidence against other parties to the conversation.

A complete record or log should be kept for every surveillance operation, indicating who or what was observed, what period of time it covered, and what the results were.[20]

to give the suspect little or no opportunity to escape by ducking into a building or by running. Once the place of arrest has been selected, the time of arrest is dictated by the suspect's normal habits. If the suspect's habits are irregular or are not thoroughly known, it may be necessary to keep the suspect under surveillance until he or she approaches a preselected location; then the investigator must move swiftly to execute the arrest.

Every arrest should be made by at least two officers. If there is any reason to think that the suspect might flee or offer resistance, the arrest team should include at least three and preferably four officers. However, it is not ordinarily desirable to bring in too many "troops"; the sudden presence of an unusual number of police vehicles will alert the suspect before all personnel can be brought into position, and it is too difficult to coordinate a large number of personnel. If the suspect is unusually dangerous and almost certain to resist, it is better for a small number of officers to make the initial approach. Additional personnel can be kept in reserve, out of sight

but within easy reach if they are needed. One officer, usually the principal investigator who is responsible for the entire case, must be in command of the arrest. Radio contact must be maintained continuously among all the personnel involved.

As the suspect approaches the selected place of arrest, one or two officers should move into position ahead of the suspect. Depending on the nature of the location, these officers might be 50 to 100 feet or as much as half of a city block from the arrest site. Another officer should move in behind the suspect and should immediately approach from the rear. The command officer then approaches the suspect directly, usually by driving up alongside the suspect, parking, and walking up to that individual. (Figure 15.4.) Naturally, this simplified procedure must be adapted to the particular circumstances. One or two additional officers might have to be placed along possible routes of escape, such as the entrances to stores or buildings.

As each officer approaches the suspect, the officer must be prepared to take shelter if the suspect suddenly becomes frightened and displays a weapon. However, if the arrest is executed properly, the suspect will not be aware of what is happening until it is all over. This element of surprise is by far the greatest protection that the police officers can have.

If the suspect is in a vehicle, it is unwise to attempt an arrest until the suspect has reached a destination and parked the vehicle. There is a good chance that some sort of weapon is hidden in the vehicle and can be reached quickly. Once the suspect leaves the vehicle, he or she is limited to the few weapons that can be hidden on the body. In brief, the police officer is far less vulnerable to attack and the suspect has fewer opportunities to escape when the arrest is made while the suspect is on foot.

FIGURE 15.4
A PLANNED ARREST

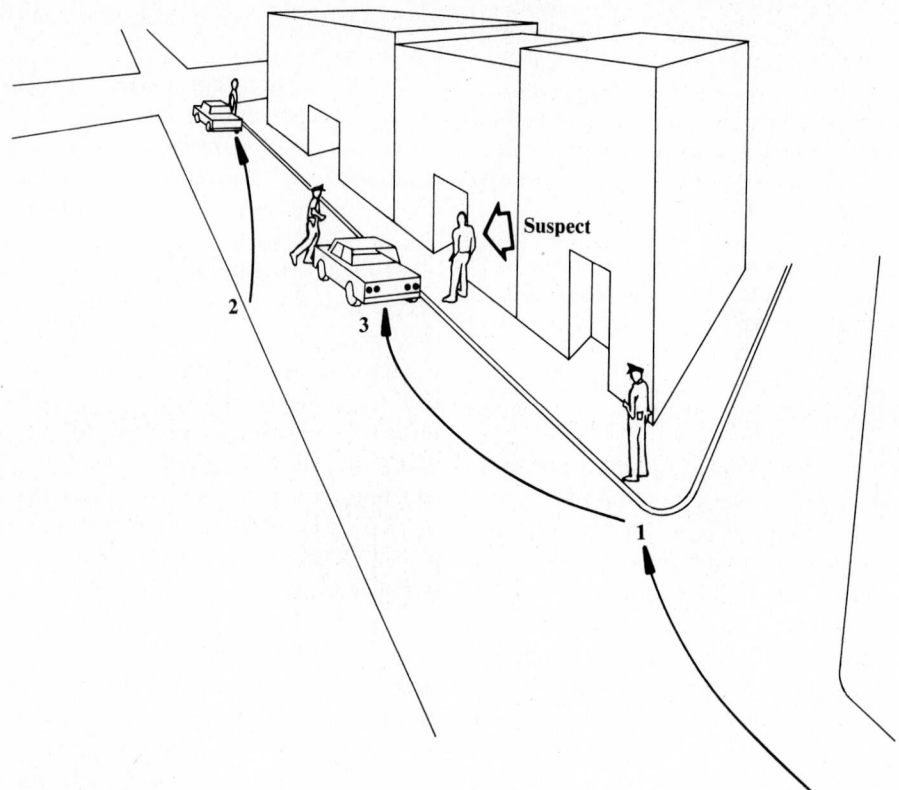

1. Command officer
   drops off trailing officer
   while . . .

2. Covering officers move into
   position ahead of suspect;
   then . . .

3. Command officer approaches
   suspect and makes arrest.


(NOTE: In the situation shown here, the command
officer should determine ahead of time that the
entrance doors to the three apartment buildings are
ordinarily locked, so the suspect cannot escape by
running into one of those buildings.)

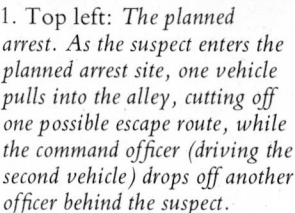

1. Top left: *The planned arrest. As the suspect enters the planned arrest site, one vehicle pulls into the alley, cutting off one possible escape route, while the command officer (driving the second vehicle) drops off another officer behind the suspect.*

3. Bottom left: *The command officer announces that the suspect is under arrest and recites the Miranda warning.*

2. Top right: *The suspect now has no route of escape; the command officer pulls up to the curb and approaches the suspect while the trailing officer approaches from behind.*

4. Bottom right: *The suspect is briefly but thoroughly searched, handcuffed, and removed from the scene. The entire arrest can be accomplished in less than two minutes.*

## THE FLEEING SUSPECT

Occasionally it is necessary to pursue a suspect who is fleeing in a vehicle. As dangerous as this procedure is, the danger can be reduced considerably if the police refuse to be drawn into a high-speed chase. The key to avoiding a high-speed chase—which endangers the police officers, the suspect, and anyone who may happen into the path of the chase—is to keep track of the suspect from a distance. The easiest way to do this is from the air: a helicopter or small aircraft can observe the suspect's vehicle and keep officers on the ground continuously informed of the suspect's location. Unfortunately, aircraft are not available to most small and medium-sized departments; and even when they are available, the cost of airborne surveillance may be regarded as excessive for relatively routine arrests.

An alternative method of pursuing a fleeing suspect without a high-speed chase is the *moving perimeter plan.*[21] The objective of this technique is not to keep the suspect's vehicle continuously in sight, but instead to establish moving observation points along the various routes that the suspect might take. Several police vehicles will have to be involved, and they must all be under the command of an officer who has a thorough knowledge of the community's streets.

From any given location, a suspect must follow one of a limited number of alternative routes. A police vehicle must be placed along each of these alternative routes to observe whether the suspect vehicle passes by. The command vehicle should follow the suspect vehicle at a considerable distance, so there is little likelihood that the suspect will be aware of being followed. As the suspect passes one of the perimeter vehicles, the command officer must be notified. The perimeter then must be rearranged, as quickly as possible, along the suspect's new route.

This can be accomplished most easily in a city that has a regular grid pattern of streets. As shown in Figure 15.5, as few as four police vehicles may be required to operate a moving perimeter: the command vehicle following the suspect, a lead vehicle waiting for the suspect to pass by, and two vehicles traveling along the parallel streets. If the suspect turns down a side street, the perimeter vehicle should be able to observe and report the change of direction.

The moving perimeter plan is more difficult to operate in a city whose streets are laid out irregularly. There may be a number of alternative routes that the suspect might take,

*The best way to avoid a high-speed chase is to keep the suspect in view from a helicopter or small airplane. Units on the ground can be directed to close off escape routes or to follow the suspect unobtrusively. (Photo courtesy Texas Department of Public Safety)*

396

FIGURE 15.5
THE MOVING PERIMETER PLAN

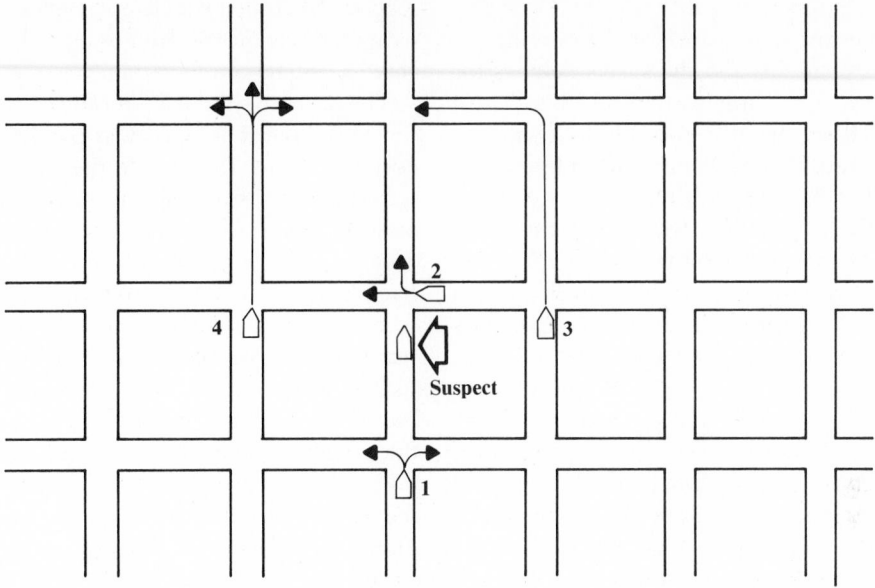

1. As soon as Suspect's direction of travel is determined, this vehicle will move to one of the side streets, while . . .

2. This vehicle moves into the "close-contact" position following the suspect and informing others of the Suspect's position and direction of travel; meanwhile, . . .

3. This vehicle moves ahead (assuming Suspect continues straight) and will take the "close-contact" position at the next intersection; or, if Suspect turns left, will continue along the parallel street, while . . .

4. This vehicle will either continue along the parallel street, or take up the trailing or "close-contact" position if the Suspect turns.

and each route must be covered by one or more perimeter vehicles. The number of officers involved in the operation can be reduced if it is possible to guess the suspect's most likely destination, but this increases the risk that the suspect will take an unexpected turn and elude the pursuers altogether.

It is essential to the success of the moving perimeter plan that the suspect remain unaware of the pursuit. The perimeter vehicles should make no effort to interfere with the suspect's movement; the object is to observe, not intercept. In fact, marked patrol cars can be used. When the suspect sees a patrol car that does not give chase, the suspect may conclude that no one is in pursuit. This is almost certain to induce the suspect to slow down and drive in a normal manner in order to avoid drawing attention. (Of course, this is not an appropriate procedure for pursuing reckless or intoxicated drivers for traffic violations; in such cases, the highest priority is given to stopping the driver.)

If airborne surveillance or the moving perimeter plan fails and the suspect eludes the pursuers, all is not lost. The investigator should have a pretty good idea of the suspect's probable destination. Most likely, the suspect will either return home or will go to a favorite place where friends and associates can be found. The temptation to brag about having evaded capture is very strong. What a pleasant surprise if the investigator is there, waiting for the suspect's arrival!

### CONCLUDING THE ARREST

Regardless of the method used, the objective is the same: execute the arrest out in the open, when the suspect least expects it and has the least opportunity to escape, to obtain a weapon, or to enlist the aid of friends in resisting the arrest.

When the suspect is approached, every effort must be made to remain calm and nonthreatening. Weapons should not be displayed unless there is some good reason to expect violent resistance. If the arrest has been properly planned, it will take several seconds for the suspect to understand what is happening, long enough for the command officer and the back-up officer to take complete charge of the situation. As long as they remain calm, the suspect probably will remain calm, too.

On approaching the suspect, the command officer first must offer identification. The suspect is then informed of the existence of an arrest warrant, or the other basis for the arrest, and the *Miranda* warning is given.[22] Standard police practice dictates that the suspect be searched and handcuffed at this point. However, if the suspect is properly hand-

cuffed (with the hands behind the back, palms outward), a search is not necessary, since the suspect will not be able to reach a hidden weapon. If handcuffs are not used, a reasonably thorough search certainly is required.[23]

The suspect should be removed from the site of the arrest as rapidly as possible to reduce the chance that one of the suspect's associates will observe the arrest and interfere or warn other associates. The entire procedure—approaching the suspect, identifying oneself as police, announcing the arrest, searching and/or handcuffing the prisoner, reading the Miranda warning, and placing the suspect in a police vehicle—should take barely more than a minute. The attitude of the officers should be one of calm, self-confident determination. Ideally, passers-by on the street should be unaware that anything out of the ordinary is taking place.

Not every planned arrest will proceed smoothly. The suspect may turn out to be more desperate and more willing to resist violently than was anticipated, or the suspect may choose to flee. Either response is likely to occur exactly when the command officer approaches the suspect and is most vulnerable. The back-up officers are responsible for protecting the command officer. They must be prepared to assist at the first indication of trouble. At the same time, the back-up officers must do what they can to keep innocent passers-by from interfering or from getting caught in any possible danger. The officers also must be careful not to place themselves in each other's area of responsibility. If the suspect flees, the back-up officers must be ready to cut off the route of escape. However, if pursuing the suspect might expose the officers themselves or innocent civilians to danger, it is better to let the suspect go and to begin more careful plans for another arrest at a later time.

There is no procedure that can completely eliminate the danger inherent in making an arrest. The procedure that we have outlined will not work perfectly every time. However, it is intended to reduce the danger by reducing the likelihood that the suspect will be tempted to resist or flee from the arrest. Much depends on the psychological element of surprise and thus on the skillful and well-timed actions of the officers involved.

## THE UNPLANNED ARREST

There are occasions when a planned arrest simply is not possible. In general, an unplanned arrest occurs when something unexpected happens: the police officer is suddenly confronted with a wanted suspect in a situation that demands immediate attention.

No police officer should initiate an arrest for a serious crime without at least one back-up officer immediately present. The only exception to this rule would be a situation in which the lives of innocent citizens are endangered and the officer is able to complete the arrest without increasing the danger or exposing himself or herself to even greater risk. Certainly there are people who are sociopathic or emotionally overwrought and who will inflict mayhem on anyone within their reach until they are stopped. In that case, a police officer is obliged to use whatever tactic is necessary to protect the lives of others, even at the cost of the officer's own life.

However, the average criminal suspect is unlikely to resort to violence unless frightened or provoked into it. If the suspect has not actually harmed anyone, no matter how threatening his or her behavior may be, there is a good chance of reducing the danger by reducing the tensions that otherwise might trigger violence.

It is rare for a police officer to interrupt a serious crime while it is in progress, but this does happen occasionally. Often the officer is as surprised as the criminal. Under these circumstances, the officer must do everything possible either to take control of the situation immediately or, if that is not feasible, to "retreat and regroup." Physical retreat from the scene may or may not be necessary. The officer may be able to stall long enough to regain control, perhaps by talking to the criminal.

During this initial period of confused confrontation, the officer must give the criminal an *apparent* route of escape. A criminal who feels cornered and trapped is most likely to commit random acts of violence. However, most criminals who are given a chance to flee the scene will do so. If the apparent escape route leads the criminal directly into the hands of back-up officers, so much the better. If not, at least the officer is still able to pursue the suspect. An officer lying wounded on the floor, or worse, is of little use to anyone.

If the officer is able to take charge of the situation, a call for back-up assistance must be made at the very first opportunity. While waiting for the back-up to arrive, the officer should be wary about proceeding with the arrest single-handedly; it may be better just to keep the situation stable without taking the chance of provoking or frightening the criminal into dangerous actions. With modern communications, it should never take more than two or three minutes for back-up personnel to respond.

These generalized guidelines will not apply to every situation. Even if we had twice as much space in this book, it would be impossible to discuss all the circumstances in which an officer might have to take direct, effective action, because every situation is unique. Ultimately, everything depends on the officer's alertness, experience, training, and ability to make nearly instantaneous decisions.

## THE FUGITIVE SUSPECT

### MOBILITY AND THE CRIMINAL

One of the great boons of our modern technological society is the unrivaled system of rapid, economical transportation available to everyone. In the United States the public enjoys a freedom of mobility that is unimaginable in many parts of the world.

Of course, the criminal enjoys the same benefits. It is entirely possible for a criminal to commit a crime, leave the scene by automobile, board a commercial jet plane, and arrive in another city halfway around the world before the crime is even discovered. More modestly, a criminal can commit a crime in a neighborhood far from his or her own residence and, in a few minutes, travel by boulevard and expressway to the other side of town.

It is the criminal's mobility—the ability to commit crimes outside of one's own neighborhood and to remove oneself quickly from the immediate vicinity of the crime—that places such a heavy burden on the investigative function of the police. If criminals were confined to their own immediate neighborhoods, it would be much harder for them get away without being seen by someone who knew them.

The fact is that despite the mobility that criminals enjoy, most of them do not stray very far from home. Crime rates are higher in some neighborhoods than in others for the simple reason that most criminals prey on their own neighbors. Unfortunately, the criminals who range most widely are the very ones who are hardest to catch, because they

*Criminals enjoy the same mobility as everyone else. Sometimes they are able to travel halfway across the country before their crimes are discovered.*

6. Creamer, p. 50.

7. Creamer, p. 34.

8. Ronald J. Waldron, et al., *The Criminal Justice System* (Boston: Houghton Mifflin, 1976), p. 41.

9. Creamer, p. 7.

10. Sidney H. Asch, *Civil Rights and Responsibilities under the Constitution* (New York: Arco, 1970), pp. 93–94.

11. Paul B. Weston and Kenneth M. Wells, *Criminal Evidence for Police* (Englewood Cliffs, N.J.: Prentice-Hall, 1971), p. 183.

12. A. C. Germann, Frank D. Day, and Robert R. J. Gallati, *Introduction to Law Enforcement and Criminal Justice,* rev. ed. (Springfield, Ill.: Charles C Thomas, 1973), pp. 101–102.

13. Paul B. Weston and Kenneth M. Wells, *Elements of Criminal Investigation* (Englewood Cliffs, N.J.: Prentice-Hall, 1971), p. 69.

14. John J. Horgan, *Criminal Investigation* (New York: McGraw-Hill, 1974), pp. 117–118.

15. Horgan, pp. 113–114.

16. Horgan, pp. 119–122.

17. Weston and Wells, *Elements of Criminal Investigation*, p. 69.

18. Horgan, pp. 122–124.

19. Weston and Wells, *Elements of Criminal Investigation*, p. 70.

20. Horgan, p. 112.

21. Horgan, p. 116.

22. Waters and McGrath, pp. 102–105.

23. Waters and McGrath, p. 112.

24. Waters and McGrath, p. 109.

25. Germann, Day, and Gallati, p. 231.

26. Germann, Day, and Gallati, p. 229.

27. Waters and McGrath, p. 110.

## REVIEW OF THE EVIDENCE

1. If charges against an arrested person are dismissed during the trial because there was no probable cause before an arrest, can the person be charged again for the same crime on the basis of evidence found after the first arrest?

2. Legally, an arrest has only one reasonable purpose. What is it?
   a. to keep the accused from committing further crimes
   b. to punish the criminal
   c. to ensure that the accused will be present when the trial is held
   d. to enable the police to gather evidence
   e. to permit accurate identification of the accused

3. Which of the following are *not* necessary for a planned arrest to be conducted?
   a. The crime has been thoroughly investigated.
   b. The suspect's whereabouts are known.
   c. The suspect is known to be violent and dangerous.
   d. A warrant for the arrest has been issued.
   e. The suspect's normal, noncriminal habits are known in complete detail.

4. The police officer is least vulnerable to attack and the suspect has the least chance to escape when
   a. back-up officers execute the arrest.
   b. the arrest is made while the suspect is on foot.
   c. the suspect is at home.
   d. the suspect is in a vehicle.
   e. the suspect has an apparent route of escape.

5. True or false: The key to avoiding a high-speed chase is to keep track of the suspect from a distance.

6. Which of the following elements must be included in the *Miranda* warning?
   a. the right to remain silent
   b. the right to counsel before and during questioning
   c. the right to compulsory process to obtain favorable witnesses
   d. the right to free counsel if the defendant is poor
   e. the right to change one's mind about cooperating

7. True or false: During a moving perimeter pursuit, the suspect must be aware at all times that the police have cut off all possible routes of escape.

8. When a police officer unexpectedly confronts a criminal, the officer must either take control of the situation *or*
   a. back down, retreat, and "regroup."
   b. call for back-up assistance.
   c. draw and use a weapon.
   d. arrest the criminal at once.
   e. try to keep the criminal from escaping.

9. The phrase "reasonable ground of suspicion supported by circumstances sufficiently strong in themselves to warrant a cautious man in the belief that the accused person is guilty of a particular offense" refers to
   a. probable cause.
   b. arrest on suspicion.
   c. particularity.
   d. ex post facto laws.
   e. none of the above.
10. Under certain circumstances, a private citizen can perform a legal arrest. Under which of the following circumstances is this true?
   a. when a misdemeanor warrant has been issued
   b. when a felony is committed in the citizen's presence
   c. when there is probable cause
   d. when a person who has committed a breach of the peace might escape
   e. none of the above

### TOPICS FOR INVESTIGATION

1. Although the Supreme Court has decided that preventive detention laws are unconstitutional, in some cases it is possible for the same results to be obtained by setting bail so high that the arrestee cannot obtain a bond. Thus, a potentially dangerous criminal can be kept off the streets while awaiting trial. Discuss the appropriateness of this procedure in a society that claims to believe that every citizen is innocent until proved guilty in a court of law.
2. Most police departments consider a case closed once an arrest has been made and someone has been accused of the crime. Even if the person is later released because of some technical flaw in the arrest, or if the accused is acquitted, usually the case is not reopened. Should it be? Bear in mind that the same person cannot be charged again for the same crime.
3. Under what circumstances would a planned arrest, as described in this chapter, be impractical or dangerous? What alternative procedures would be more practical or less dangerous, and why?
4. In most states, a citizen has a right to resist an illegal arrest. The police, on the other hand, have the authority to use force to execute an arrest. Discuss the implications and potential consequences of these conflicting laws, and suggest what the police officer can do to reduce the problem.
5. Describe three situations in which an unplanned arrest might occur, including (a) a situation in which the officer completes the arrest without assistance; (b) a situation in which the officer takes control and waits for back-up assistance; and (c) a situation in which the officer allows the suspect to escape.
6. The concepts of direct pursuit and extradition are necessary only because police officers' authority is restricted to their own geographical jurisdiction. Would it be better to give all law enforcement officers unrestricted jurisdiction so that these cumbersome laws and procedures would not be needed?

# CHAPTER 16
## INTERROGATING THE SUSPECT

1. What is generally the *least* important goal of an interrogation?
   a. obtaining admissions
   b. obtaining a confession
   c. filling in gaps in the evidence
   d. obtaining corroboration of evidence and testimony
   e. obtaining information about possible related crimes

2. Evidence that tends to confirm the truth or validity of other evidence is
   a. corroboration.
   b. an admission.
   c. a confession.
   d. interrogation.
   e. contra-evidence.

3. True or false: A suspect who appears eager to talk is more likely to be innocent than a suspect who is hostile and uncooperative.

4. At what point is the investigator entitled to insist on a formal interrogation?
   a. before the arrest
   b. immediately after the arrest
   c. during presentation of the case before a magistrate
   d. after the suspect's release on bail
   e. after denial of bail for the suspect
   f. all of the above
   g. none of the above

5. Which of the following statements is true?
   a. A polygraph machine distinguishes between true and untrue statements made by the suspect.
   b. A voice stress analyzer always should be used without the subject's knowledge.
   c. Results of a polygraph examination usually are not admissible in court.
   d. It is impossible to "fool" a polygraph machine.
   e. All of the above are correct.
   f. None of the above is correct.

CENTURIES AGO, when the concept of criminal law first began to develop, the confession of a suspected criminal played a crucial role in the trial. In some countries suspects could not be convicted unless they confessed to the crime. They could, however, be convicted *solely* on the basis of their confessions. The testimony of witnesses was considered relatively unimportant, and physical evidence was virtually unheard of. Naturally, under these circumstances criminals were very reluctant to confess. Methods of encouraging confessions thus became increasingly vigorous, finally resulting in the brutal forms of torture that we now regard with horror: the rack, the "iron maiden," immersion in water, and so forth.

By the eighteenth century, most of these grotesque forms of torture had fallen into disuse, but physical methods of coercion, such as beating or whipping, were not uncommon. Subtler techniques of psychological intimidation were also highly favored, especially the practice of holding a prisoner in complete isolation for weeks, months, or even years.

The Fifth Amendment to the Constitution of the United States was intended specifically to discourage such practices by eliminating the confession as a primary goal of criminal law enforcement. The amendment secures the right of the accused not to be "compelled to be a witness against himself." This right is known as the freedom from self-incrimination.[1]

Unfortunately, the fact that the Fifth Amendment is part of the basic law of the United States has not succeeded in stopping the practice of seeking involuntary confessions from suspects. So-called third-degree tactics of physical and psychological coercion or intimidation have been used throughout the nation's history.[2]

The courts have held repeatedly and consistently that a confession is worthless unless the accused has given it voluntarily. Nevertheless, even today there are occasional complaints of "police brutality" in response to aggressive and sometimes coercive interrogators who are seeking a confession.

In modern criminal justice processes, a confession simply is not that important. It is a rare case that can be solved only by a confession and an even rarer case that can result in a conviction based solely on a confession. A conviction is obtained by producing evidence, both direct and circumstantial, backed up by competent testimony. If there is sufficient evidence, a confession is not necessary. Conversely, a confession without sufficient evidence is almost worthless.

Certainly, a confession has some value and should not be ignored. However, an investigator should aim for other, more important goals that may be attained by interrogating a suspect. If investigators direct their efforts only at gaining a confession, those goals are unlikely to be achieved.

## THE ROLES OF INTERROGATION

To put the subject of confessions into proper perspective, note that it is only one of the five goals of every interrogation. These goals are

- obtaining a confession
- obtaining admissions
- obtaining corroboration
- filling in gaps in the evidence
- obtaining information about related crimes.

A *confession* is a statement by the accused that he or she committed a certain crime. By itself, the statement is meaningless because it might not be true, even if the suspect believes it is true. The confession must include a sufficient number of details that can be checked against known evidence to persuade a jury that the confession is valid.

The great problem with confessions is that they are so often false yet they can be very persuasive to a jury. Jurors who have little personal experience with crime or criminal psychology will find it difficult to understand that people do, indeed, confess to crimes they did not commit. Sometimes a false confession is the result of police intimidation.[3] Perhaps even more often, however, a false confession is the product of a confused or distorted mind. To make sure that a confession is valid, the investigator should attempt to get a number of details from the suspect; the details can then be checked for accuracy against known evidence.

Despite its drawbacks, a valid confession obviously can be a considerable help to the prosecution—*if* the confession was obtained in strict accordance with the law, *if* the confession was given freely without any hint of coercion or intimidation, *if* the criminal does not at some later time decide to recant or deny the confession, and *if* most of the details in the confession are in agreement with the available evidence. A confession that fails any one of these tests should not be relied on and probably should not be introduced during the trial at all.

A confession is not the only information that can be obtained through interrogation of a suspect.[4] One of the most important things that can be obtained is an *admission*, a statement by the accused admitting the truth of some fact or circumstance that connects the accused to the crime.

ANSWERS TO STUDY CLUES
1. b   2. a   3. False   4. g   5. c

An admission is not a confession, although, strictly speaking, a confession is an admission.[5] The accused does not admit to having committed the crime but does admit something that is known from the available evidence about the crime. For example, the accused might admit to having been at the scene of the crime or to having known the victim; the accused might admit ownership of the murder weapon or burglary tool. Any such admission suggests that the suspect may be guilty, but proves nothing.

An admission may be deliberate or *inadvertent* (accidental or unknowing). If the investigator asks, "Do you know Blank, the victim?" the suspect's admission, "Yes, I know Blank," would be a deliberate admission: the suspect knows that Blank was the victim because the investigator said so. On the other hand, the investigator might ask, "Do you know Blank?" The suspect might or might not know that Blank is the victim. If the suspect admits to knowing Blank, that would be an inadvertent admission. Of course, the mere fact of knowing the victim is not very strong evidence of guilt, but it could be one element in a conclusive chain of evidence. The investigator must verify each admission, like each confession, by checking it against known evidence and the testimony of witnesses.

Often the most important value of an admission is that it provides *corroboration*, that is, confirmation of the truth of some other piece of evidence. For example, if the suspect admits to having been at the scene of a crime, the admission would corroborate the fact that fingerprints found at the scene were those of the suspect. Notice that corroboration usually works both ways: the presence of the fingerprints also corroborates the suspect's admission.[6]

*Concluding the Investigation*

Physical evidence often must be corroborated by someone's testimony before its relevance to the crime can be completely understood. The testimony of witnesses *always* must be corroborated either by physical evidence or by the testimony of other witnesses; one witness's statement, by itself, usually is not sufficient to persuade a jury. Therefore, one of the principal purposes of the interrogation of a suspect is to corroborate as much of the evidence as possible, both physical evidence and the testimony of witnesses.

A suspect also may help the investigator to fill in gaps in the chain of evidence or may help to explain the significance of evidence that otherwise was not properly understood. Even though the suspect may neither confess nor make any admissions that are especially damaging, the information provided by the suspect, often inadvertently, may strengthen the prosecutor's case considerably.

Last, but far from least, an interrogation may be used to establish a suspect's involvement in crimes other than the one for which charges have been filed. As we have pointed out in earlier chapters, criminals often commit a series of similar crimes over a period of time. This is especially common for property crimes. Once the investigator is satisfied that a strong case has been built against a suspect in one case, it is always a good idea to try to find out whether the same person has committed any of several similar crimes.

These five goals—obtaining a confession, obtaining admissions, obtaining corroboration, filling in gaps in the evidence, and obtaining information about related crimes—apply to every interrogation of a prisoner. The importance of each goal varies from case to case and, thus, so should the proportion of effort devoted to each purpose. However, some effort should be devoted to each one.[7]

An investigator once spent several hours interrogating a hostile, belligerent suspect. The suspect refused to confess to or admit anything even though physical and testimonial evidence was overwhelming. The suspect revealed little that would corroborate the existing evidence, but luckily there were no major gaps in the chain of evidence that needed to be filled. Finally, the investigator decided that further questioning would be pointless. Just before sending the suspect back to a jail cell, the investigator blurted out, "Haven't you ever done anything like this before?" The suspect, overwhelmed by guilt, broke down and poured out a long and harrowing tale of burglaries, robberies, rapes, assaults, and other crimes.

## LEGAL RIGHTS OF PRISONERS

One of the most difficult aspects of a police officer's professional development is learning to regard criminals as ordinary human beings. Some police officers never do learn, and because of their failure, they damage the reputation of their agency and of the police profession in general.

The source of the problem is that criminals frequently are not very pleasant people. They often have committed acts that are extremely repugnant to most people. A natural tendency for the police officer, dedicated to upholding the law, is to sympathize with the innocent victim and to feel hostility toward the criminal. Certainly the criminal makes little effort to hide any feelings of hostility toward the police, and thus the officer may feel no inclination to suppress similar feelings toward the criminal.

Most police officers know better than to behave in an unprofessional manner in public, where someone might observe them. However, once the suspect has been taken into custody and is no longer in public view, it is extremely difficult for some officers to resist the temptation to express their hostilities. Such officers attempt to excuse their behavior by assuming that criminals deserve to be treated brutally—a belief that is shared, unfortunately, by large segments of the community.

There are, however, a number of very good reasons not to adopt such an attitude.

• Once professional discipline has broken down, the situation can get completely out of control. If an officer is not prevented from treating a prisoner roughly, the next prisoner may be treated even more savagely. In flagrant cases of police brutality, especially if a prisoner has died under mysterious circumstances while in custody, it is very likely that numerous instances of less extreme abuse have gone unpunished in the past.

• An unprofessional attitude contributes to the dangerous "us-against-them" perspective that police officers sometimes fall into. Remember that *criminals are not "the enemy."* Criminals are often as pitiable as their victims. The police officer's duty is to identify the criminal so that society can protect itself through the processes of criminal justice. It is not the police officer's duty to take revenge on the criminal on society's behalf.

• Inhumane treatment by the police ultimately becomes public knowledge. Many people feel that if the police fail to abide by the law, they are no better than the criminals on the other side of the bars. If there is a widespread belief that the police themselves are brutal and unprofessional, respect for the law is greatly diminished.

• Inhumane treatment of prisoners is counterproductive. A guilty suspect may have all charges dismissed if there is evidence

of improper arrest or custody. Furthermore, if criminals expect brutal treatment while in custody, they will resist being arrested that much more desperately and violently.

• Inhumane treatment of any sort and to any degree is illegal. In most cases, the purpose of pretrial detention in police custody is merely to ensure that the accused will appear for trial; it is *never* intended as a form of punishment for the alleged crime. Therefore, a suspect in custody is legally entitled to be treated with the same courtesy and dignity that would be given to any other presumably law-abiding citizen. Furthermore, a prisoner in police custody has a number of specific constitutional and legal rights designed to ensure that improper treatment does not occur.

## PRESENTATION BEFORE A MAGISTRATE

The suspect must be taken before a magistrate at the earliest possible time after the arrest, which usually means immediately after the suspect has been booked. If the arrest occurs at night or during a weekend, when a magistrate is not available, the appearance may be delayed no longer than until the next time the magistrate's court is open for business. Any unnecessary delay will invalidate the arrest: the suspect will go free.

If the suspect has not had an opportunity to confer with an attorney prior to the initial appearance before a magistrate, the latter must see that time is given for this purpose before proceeding any further. Then three tasks must be accomplished. First, the magistrate must make sure that the suspect has been given the *Miranda* warning; usually the magistrate accomplishes this by repeating the warning in its entirety. Second, the suspect must be informed of the nature of the accusation. Third, bail must be set.

Once the bail is set, the defendant may post a bond and be released immediately. De-

*A suspect must be brought before a magistrate as soon as possible after the arrest. The suspect is entitled to have a defense attorney present during this appearance; if the suspect does not already have an attorney, one will be appointed by the court at this time.*

pending on state law and the particular case, the bond may be in the form of cash deposited with the court, or it may be merely a written promise by the defendant to appear for trial. Most states permit professional bail bondsmen to guarantee a bond in return for a fee paid by the defendant, a practice that has been eliminated in some states because it can lead to abuses.

If not released on bail at the time of the presentation before a magistrate, the suspect usually is returned to the jail.

### OTHER RIGHTS OF PRISONERS

Prisoners cannot be held *incommunicado* (prevented from communicating with others).[8] They must be given a reasonable opportunity to contact friends or family, to inform them of their whereabouts and to arrange for legal assistance or bail. Although some police de-

partments still maintain the traditional "one phone call" rule, many departments no longer rigidly interpret this rule.

A prisoner is entitled to consult with an attorney at any time. The police must not do anything to interfere with the prisoner's access to an attorney or the attorney's access to the prisoner, and they must make some provision for the accused and the attorney to confer in private.

Freedom from self-incrimination is by far the most important of the suspect's rights. As expressed in the *Miranda* warning, this includes the right to remain silent, the right to have counsel during questioning, the right to cooperate at one time and to discontinue cooperation or to refuse to cooperate at another time, and the right to know that any statement is likely to be used against the accused in court.[9] The suspect may *waive* (give up or relinquish) any of these rights voluntarily, but may then invoke them again at any time.[10]

WAIVER OF
THE DEFENDANT'S
RIGHTS

If a suspect chooses to waive any of these rights, especially the right to remain silent, the investigator must be prepared to demonstrate in court that the waiver was made voluntarily. Otherwise the suspect might claim later that the police used coercion or deception to obtain information against the prisoner's will.

One way to document a waiver is to have witnesses present when the suspect volunteers to answer questions. There are, however, two problems with this method: first, the witnesses, usually other police officers, might not be believed by a jury; second, an interrogation is conducted most effectively if only the interrogator and the suspect are present.

Another solution is to ask the prisoner to sign a document stating that the right to remain silent is waived. Unfortunately, very few prisoners are willing to sign anything. Besides, once again, the prisoner can always choose to cease cooperating, regardless of what has been signed.

A third solution is to have the prisoner's attorney present during questioning. The attorney is then a witness to the voluntary cooperation of the suspect and, if it occurs, to the suspect's decision to stop cooperating. The drawback is that the attorney usually will advise the prisoner to say nothing. Even if the prisoner agrees to answer some questions, the attorney will interrupt the interrogation whenever a sensitive or potentially damaging question is asked.

Given all these considerations and reservations, one may wonder whether interrogation of a prisoner is possible at all. That is exactly our point: in modern police practice, under the legal restrictions that exist today, interrogation of a suspect is extremely difficult and usually not very productive. Thus, it is a great mistake for the investigator to rely on getting the truth from a suspect to solve the case.

## PSYCHOLOGY OF PRISONERS

Surprisingly, some prisoners are not only willing but actually eager to talk. Others will say nothing at all, even when it might be in their best interests to cooperate. The investigator must guard against forming any conclusions about a suspect's guilt or innocence purely on the basis of the prisoner's cooperation.

The most obvious reason to remain silent is that the suspects are guilty and do not want to provide the police with any information that might later prove to be damaging. However, sometimes suspects who are truly innocent also remain silent. They may feel intimidated and uncertain about how to prove their innocence. Some individuals feel a general hostility toward the police, which causes them to be uncooperative, perhaps even belligerent or aggressive, although they could demonstrate their innocence rather easily. Another possibility is that the suspects, though innocent of the particular crime being investigated, are guilty of some other crime and are afraid to say anything for fear of inadvertently exposing this fact.

An innocent suspect, of course, is likely to be anything but silent. Most people who have been arrested for a crime that they did not commit feel compelled to protest their innocence vigorously. It is extremely important for the police officer to acknowledge the

*Concluding the Investigation*

suspect's protestations and to offer reassurance that, if the suspect is truly innocent, the best course to follow is to cooperate and have trust in the criminal justice process. If the officer responds to the protestations with scorn or contempt, the innocent suspect is likely to become vehemently indignant and may decide to take extremely rash and sometimes disastrous action to obtain freedom from custody.

The guilty suspect, too, is likely to claim innocence. Some suspects are incredibly ingenious at developing one or more alibis in the attempt to "prove" their innocence. Unfortunately, the investigator has little choice but to attempt to verify every alibi that a suspect offers, no matter how improbable it may seem. As frustrating, aggravating, and time-consuming as this process may be to the investigator, checking out the suspect's alibis may eventually be productive. Once the investigator has disposed of all the alibis, the suspect may decide to tell the truth, if only out of sheer exhaustion. Even if this does not happen, sometimes a false alibi can reveal useful information, such as an inadvertent admission concerning the suspect's whereabouts or activities.

Some guilty suspects will talk with apparent candor and at great length. They may begin by attempting to act innocent and cooperative, especially if they have concocted some elaborate alibi that they believe is foolproof. Sooner or later, however, as long as the suspect continues to talk and the investigator continues to ask patient, thoughtful questions, the suspect is almost certain to begin making damaging admissions.

Sometimes a suspect does not even try to make up an alibi, but immediately confesses to the crime. In fact, suspects have been known to confess readily to crimes that had not previously been discovered, especially when the individual has been involved in a series of crimes.

Bear in mind, however, what we said earlier about false confessions. Not only do innocent people sometimes confess to crimes that they have not committed, because of some mental confusion or a desperate desire for attention, but occasionally guilty suspects will make *false confessions*, that is, confessions to crimes that they did not commit. They may do this in the hope of thoroughly confusing the police, thereby possibly destroying the prosecution's efforts to gain a conviction. They may also do so out of confusion or in an attempt to protect their criminal associates. Investigators must be careful not to be fooled by false confessions.

## INTERROGATION TECHNIQUES

Whether or not a prisoner intends to be cooperative, every interrogation amounts to a psychological battle between the interrogator and the suspect. There is no way to avoid this fact: it is inherent in the situation. However, there are ways to reduce the level of "warfare" and even to take advantage of it by creating and maintaining the proper psychological setting for the interrogation.

### WHEN TO INTERROGATE

The worst possible time to interrogate a suspect is at the time of arrest, especially if the arrest takes place at the scene of the crime. Both the suspect and the arresting officer are naturally tense and excited.

If there is a definite, known suspect, but insufficient evidence to justify an arrest, the investigator might try to interrogate to establish probable cause—usually with little chance of success. Whether or not the suspect has been interrogated to establish probable cause, once the decision has been made to arrest a suspect, the officer should complete the arrest as quickly as possible.

As soon as probable cause has been established, the arresting officer is legally required to give the *Miranda* warnings to the suspect before continuing (or beginning) the interrogation. Failure to do so almost certainly will invalidate the arrest. The *Miranda* decision also protects the suspect's right to confer with an attorney and to be brought before a magistrate without unnecessary delay; again, continued questioning could invalidate the arrest.

Informal questioning may be possible while transporting the prisoner to the police station or jail before booking.[11] Usually this possibility depends on whether the prisoner voluntarily talks with the arresting officer. If the prisoner does initiate a conversation, the questioning should be low-key, unaggressive, and as informal as possible. At this time a suspect is probably too concerned about his or her immediate fate to be capable of answering any but the most routine questions.

Once the prisoner arrives at the police station or jail, the process of booking and presenting the suspect to a magistrate will absorb all the avilable time; ordinarily there will be few opportunities for interrogation. After the appearance before the magistrate, in most cases the suspect will post a bond and will be released from custody. Most suspects will be only too eager to leave the police station as quickly as possible. The investigator might ask the suspect to answer a few questions, but the suspect cannot be compelled to do so.

There are two ways that opportunities for interrogation are created, but only one of these ways can be controlled by the investigator. If the investigator feels that interrogation is essential, the arrest can be planned for a time when it will not be possible to present the suspect before a magistrate for several hours. In most small towns and medium-sized cities, magistrates hold court only during normal business hours. If the suspect is arrested during the evening or on the weekend, a magistrate will not be available for at least several hours. The investigator may take advantage of this fact by planning the arrest appropriately. Of course, there is no guarantee that the suspect will agree to an interrogation. In larger cities, magistrates generally are available 24 hours a day, so there is no advantage to be gained by scheduling the arrest for the weekend or evening.

The other opportunity for interrogation arises only if the magistrate can be persuaded (usually by the assistant district attorney or other prosecutor who presents the case) that bond should be set fairly high or should be denied. In most states, bail can be denied only for defendants in cases of *capital crimes*, that is, offenses for which one possible punishment is death; and in some states, bail can be denied if the defendant has been convicted of a felony previously or is already out on bail, awaiting trial on another charge.[12] However, even if bail cannot be denied outright, magistrates often can be persuaded to set the amount of bail higher than the defendant will be able to pay. If the defendant is unable to post bond and thus is returned to jail, the investigator may ask the suspect to submit to questioning. The suspect has every right to refuse, of course, but often a suspect will feel that it is better to spend a few hours in an interrogation room rather than in a jail cell.

Even when a prisoner has been released on bond, the possibility of interrogation is not entirely lost. The investigator may find that the suspect's attorney is willing to permit an interrogation (with the attorney present) and will encourage the suspect to agree to it. The attorney may feel that being cooperative will

414

work to the suspect's benefit in the long run. Besides, by having the suspect interrogated, the attorney may find out something about the prosecution's evidence.

It is unwise for the investigator to be too eager to interrogate a prisoner. An interrogation that is held when the suspect is frightened, tense, emotionally upset, tired, or for any reason uncomfortable is unlikely to be very productive. Besides, any of those conditions could increase the odds that the suspect will claim coercion or mistreatment—not only invalidating the interrogation itself but possibly causing the whole case to be dismissed.

The best procedure is to wait until the prisoner has had a reasonable chance to calm down, to adjust to the sudden and often frightening loss of freedom, and to recover physically as well as emotionally from the ordeal of arrest and booking. The prisoner should be well rested and as comfortable as circumstances permit; injuries or medical problems of any sort should be attended to before any questioning is considered.[13]

Most of all, the suspect should be given plenty of time to think about his or her fate. In the past, many police officers thought it better to catch the suspect off guard and not to allow the suspect a chance to think up a good defense against the charges. Actually, just the opposite is true. Very few suspects are able to conceive of an elaborate, coherent defense. More often, a suspect will consider all sorts of possibilities, ranging from total refusal to cooperate (perhaps even fantasizing an attempt to escape from jail) to the opposite extreme, a full confession in the hope of winning sympathy and mercy. The more time that a suspect has to consider all these possibilities, the more uncertain he or she will become about which is the best strategy. It is this very uncertainty that the investigator can exploit during interrogation to reach the truth.

## WHERE TO INTERROGATE

We have already mentioned the possibility of questioning the prisoner informally, en route from the scene of arrest to the police station or jail. Actually, that sort of informal questioning can be conducted during the entire time that the suspect is in the investigator's immediate custody: in the investigator's office, the booking room, and even in the corridors while moving from one place to another. However, a thorough, formal interrogation requires a more appropriate setting. Most police stations have some sort of interrogation room. If there is no such designated facility, the investigator will have to use an office, conference room, or whatever else is available.

The ideal interrogation room should resemble the one shown in Figure 16.1. The room should be fairly small, not more than about three meters (roughly ten feet) square. Within reason, the smaller the room, the better: a room one-fourth of that size would be adequate. The lighting should be even, free from glare and fairly bright. The only furniture in the room should be two reasonably comfortable chairs and perhaps a small table or stand. Good ventilation is important, especially if the suspect is permitted to smoke.

The suspect should be seated facing away from the door. A window with one-way glass should be set fairly high in one wall so that other officers can observe the interrogation without distracting the suspect. A microphone connected to a tape recorder and, perhaps, a small speaker for the benefit of observers should be concealed behind a grille. The purpose of concealing the microphone is not to deceive the suspect, but merely to avoid distractions.

FIGURE 16.1
AN INTERROGATION ROOM

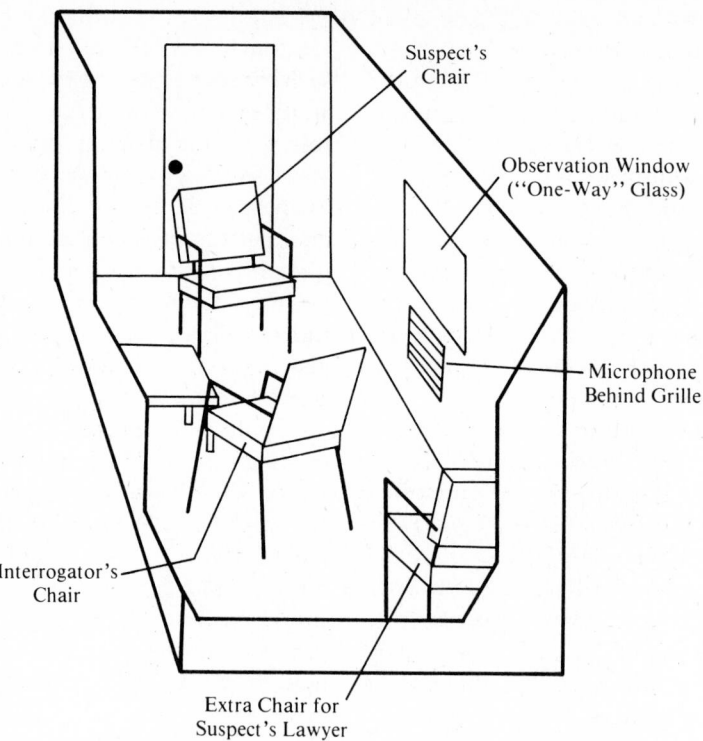

Suspect's Chair

Observation Window ("One-Way" Glass)

Microphone Behind Grille

Interrogator's Chair

Extra Chair for Suspect's Lawyer

Of course, a third chair must be provided if the suspect's attorney is present. However, no one else should be in the room during the interrogation. If the agency's policy requires all interrogations to be recorded in shorthand, the stenographer should listen by means of the microphone and a small speaker or earphone. Usually it is more practical to tape-record the interrogation and then to have the tape transcribed.

## WHO SHOULD INTERROGATE

Interrogating a suspect is a delicate psychological task that should be performed by someone who is well qualified. There are many different opinions about the best person to conduct an interrogation. The principal investigator might be the best choice. This individual certainly would know more about the case than anyone else and, presumably, would be able to ask the most pertinent questions. However, not all investigators are equally skilled at conducting an interrogation, especially a difficult one involving a hostile or recalcitrant suspect. Furthermore, the suspect may feel especially resentful toward the officer who is directly responsible for solving the case and making the arrest. Consequently, some police authorities believe that sensitive interrogations should be conducted by a highly trained specialist who has the temperament for this difficult task.[14]

If a specialist is used, the investigator should provide the interrogator with a carefully planned set of questions and a thorough summary of the facts of the case. The investigator should observe the interrogation from outside the room. Periodically the interrogator should find some pretext for leaving the room (perhaps to get the suspect a cup of coffee or a soft drink or to take a phone call); during these brief breaks the investigator and the interrogator may confer on the progress of the interrogation and on additional questions that might be asked.

Once in a while, in especially difficult cases, it may be desirable for two interrogators to work more or less in relay fashion: one interrogator conducts a portion of the questioning, then leaves the room and is replaced by the second interrogator. This method is successful sometimes because the two interrogators can use different styles of questioning; perhaps one can be friendly, while the other is more aggressive. However, it is tempting and easy to overdo this technique to the point of badgering the suspect and thus completely losing the suspect's cooperation.

## HOW TO CONDUCT THE INTERROGATION

There are no magic formulas or rules for interrogating a suspect. Much depends on the suspect's attitudes and emotional condition. Whoever conducts the interrogation must be adept at picking up hints about the subjects that the suspect wants to talk about or, at least, is willing to discuss. Skill in interrogation, like so many other facets of police work, must be developed through practice, experience, and sensitivity to human feelings and behavior. But there are some general guidelines and a few specific suggestions that we can offer.[15]

First, begin each interrogation session by repeating the *Miranda* warning. This may seem completely unnecessary, since the warning already has been given when the arrest was made and again when the suspect was presented before the magistrate. However, this step must not be omitted. By including the *Miranda* warning in the interrogation process itself, you are establishing your concern for the suspect's constitutional rights and you are removing any reasonable justification for the suspect to claim that coercion or deception was used.[16]

The next step in any interrogation is to get the suspect to talk. At this point, it does not matter what the suspect talks about. One way to start is to ask, "Is there anything you would like to ask me?" It is likely that innumerable questions are whirling around the suspect's mind. This surprising beginning, probably the opposite of the suspect's expectations, may be enough to trigger a torrent of questions: What's going to happen to me? How soon is there going to be a trial? What makes you think I did it? These questions should be answered candidly and as fully as possible, without revealing the nature or extent of the evidence in the case.

Another approach is to discuss general topics that are likely to be of interest or concern to the suspect. One such topic would be the suspect's background, family, and friends. Typical questions would include these: Where do you originally come from? How long have you lived here? What do you do for a living? Such questions are intended primarily to allow the suspect to relax and to begin talking without fear of giving away information concerning the alleged crime. The answers to the questions also may provide a skilled interrogator with important clues about the suspect's intellectual capacity, lifestyle, emotional make-up, and personal history, especially the people or things that are important to the suspect.[17]

Once the suspect begins to relax, the interrogator can focus attention directly on the criminal event. One way to do this is to say, "Look, we already know what happened. Now I'd like you to tell me your side of the story."

After such a question, the interrogator should simply sit back and wait. The suspect may take a very long time to answer or may respond by saying, "I don't know what you're talking about," or offering an equivalent denial. By remaining silent, the interrogator places a psychological burden on the suspect to say *something*. The result may be further denial or perhaps a long, concocted alibi. But once in a while, just to end the silence, the suspect will give in and either confess or begin making admissions that may lead to a confession. If the silence lasts longer than a minute or so (which can seem interminable under the circumstances), the interrogator might repeat the question or rephrase it in a somewhat more specific manner: "We know you were at the scene of the crime. Why don't you tell me what you were doing there?"

Eventually, this kind of questioning should lead to the suspect's story—a version of the event that places the suspect in the most favorable light. The suspect may claim to have been an innocent bystander or merely a minor accomplice. Again, the suspect may offer a purely fictitious alibi. Sometimes the suspect will give an account of the crime that is essentially correct, but includes some justification or rationalization for the criminal behavior.

This story should be accepted by the interrogator as if it were unquestionably true. The interrogator might even thank the suspect for being so cooperative and express sympathy or concern for the suspect or an understanding of the suspect's plight. If the story is clearly an alibi, the interrogator should promise to check it out immediately. It may even be desirable to go to the door of the interrogation room, to ask another officer, "check this is out right away," and to outline the suspect's alibi. Actually, the other officer should do no such thing; verification of the alibi is the responsibility of the principal investigator and can wait until the interrogation has been concluded. The purpose of this ploy is to establish in the suspect's mind that the alibi is being checked. If it is false, the suspect will suppose that the falsehood may be revealed at any moment.

The next stage of the interrogation is detailed questioning. Depending on what kind of alibi the suspect has offered and how closely the alibi matches the known facts about the crime, the interrogator may begin by attempting to reconcile the discrepancies. If the alibi is completely far-fetched, the interrogator should concentrate on any aspects of the crime that should be known to the suspect even if the alibi were true. For example, the suspect might claim to have been at a movie while the murder was committed. The interrogator still could ask whether the suspect knew the victim, had ever been at the scene of the crime, owned a weapon similar to the murder weapon, and so on.

After some time has passed, the interrogator should go back over the suspect's alibi: "I want to get it straight in my own mind." In the example cited above, the interrogator could ask, "What movie did you say you went to? Did you go by yourself or with someone else? Were there a lot of people in the theater that night? Had you ever seen that movie before? Do you go to a lot of movies

*Concluding the Investigation*

like that? How did you get to the theater—by car, on foot, or how? Where did you go after the movie? How late was that?"

This sort of detailed questioning can continue indefinitely. For the most part, the questions should be indirect and nonthreatening. The attitude of the interrogator should be the same as that suggested by the introductory question: "We already know what happened; we just want to hear your side of the story."

The interrogator must be especially alert to any discrepancies or inconsistencies in the suspect's answers. Some mistakes of fact or inconsistencies are perfectly natural; even an innocent person is likely to be rattled and to have lapses of memory. When the suspect becomes aware of such a mistake, the interrogator should be sympathetic and reassuring. There is no point in pouncing on the suspect and saying, "Ah-ha! First you said you ate a hot dog at the movie and now you claim it was popcorn! You're obviously lying through your teeth!" However, the interrogator should keep coming back to the areas of inconsistency: "Let's be sure we have all of this right."

The general sequence of questions should be very much like the sequence that we suggested in Chapter 6 for interviewing witnesses. You may wish to review that section.

IF THE SUSPECT
CONFESSES

When a suspect confesses to the crime being investigated, great care must be taken to ensure that the entire confession is documented for presentation in court. There are several ways to do this.

Some investigators are fond of handwritten confessions. Their theory is that a confession in the suspect's own handwriting is more persuasive to a jury than a document that obviously was typed by a stenographer. Unfortunately, there have been instances when a suspect has repudiated a handwritten confession, claiming that the interrogator dictated what was to be written. Furthermore, many suspects are barely literate; they would have a hard time writing a detailed account of a complex series of emotion-charged events. The confession is likely to be so incoherent and so filled with errors in grammar, spelling, and syntax that the jury will find it incomprehensible.

An alternative procedure is to discontinue normal questioning and ask the suspect to dictate a straightforward statement. This statement may be taken down in shorthand by a stenographer or tape-recorded; in either case, it is transcribed separately from the rest of the interrogation. The typed transcript is then read by the suspect, necessary corrections are made, and the statement is signed by both the suspect and the interrogator.[18] The stenographer's original shorthand notes or the tape recording should be preserved as supporting evidence.

The neatly typed, signed statement is very appealing to prosecutors and usually very persuasive to a jury. However, it is not immune to attack by the defendant's attorney, who may claim that the interrogator unduly influenced the suspect in the wording of the statement. A detailed narrative is an inherently artificial device, since people normally do not talk about their actions and behavior in a straightforward, coherent manner. If any part of the statement turns out to be false, misleading, inconsistent with other evidence, or inadmissible for some technical reason, the whole document might be thrown out.

For these reasons, perhaps the best approach is to keep the confession within the context of the entire interrogation. All of the interrogation should be recorded, either by shorthand or on tape, and transcribed from beginning to end. Again, the stenographer's original notes or the tape should be preserved as evidence; under certain circumstances, the tape itself might be presented in court. This procedure enables the prosecution to demonstrate that the whole interrogation process was conducted fairly and properly. Even if some portions of the transcript are ruled inadmissible for some technical reason, it is unlikely that the entire interrogation would be kept out; in fact, portions that otherwise might be inadmissible may be allowed on the grounds that they are necessary to show the context in which the confession was obtained.

If the full-transcript method of documenting the confession is selected, care must be exercised by the interrogator. Once the suspect has made a clear statement confessing the crime, the interrogator should inform the suspect once again that such a statement is a confession, that it has been recorded, and that it will be used in court. The suspect then can be asked to repeat the confession in detail. The interrogator should guide the suspect's statement by asking appropriate questions, but must be careful not to lead the suspect unnecessarily. For example, a question such as "What did you do last Friday evening, the twelfth, between seven and nine o'clock?" is preferable to "Did you go to Blank's Liquor Store last Friday evening between seven and nine o'clock?" However, the first question might be too vague and might cause the suspect to ramble about all sorts of irrelevant subjects; in this case the second question could be offered to focus the suspect's attention. The interrogator should not put words in the suspect's mouth; it is much better to let the suspect tell the story, rather than asking a question like "Did you go to Blank's Liquor

Store last Friday at 7:45 P.M. for the purpose of committing an armed robbery?"

There is no need to have the suspect sign the transcript of the interrogation. If the suspect later recants or denies that the interrogation took place, the stenographer's original shorthand notes (and the stenographer's testimony) or the tape recordings should be ample evidence to corroborate the transcript. Nor should minor errors of fact in the transcript be corrected. Again, it is perfectly natural for people to make mistakes or to suffer lapses of memory; the presence of small errors of detail are likely to increase, rather than decrease, the credibility of the suspect's statement. In fact, correcting minor errors will be more trouble than it is worth and may introduce questions about whether the police improperly manipulated the questioning of the suspect. Of course, major errors or inconsistencies must be corrected, or some reasonable explanation must be made when the evidence is presented. The transcript should be completely free of typographical errors and free of errors in grammar, punctuation, and so on, insofar as possible without distorting the actual words of the suspect.[19]

### WHAT TO ASK ABOUT RELATED CRIMES

Whether or not the suspect confesses to the crime that is immediately under investigation, it is always a good idea to ask questions about related crimes. However, the interrogator should deal with one crime at a time. Otherwise, the suspect (and the interrogator) might become confused about which crime is being discussed.

Opening up the conversation to include other crimes can be tricky. If the suspect has been involved in other crimes, he or she has probably considered the possibility that this additional guilt will be discovered. But if the suspect has not been involved in any other crimes, the reaction might be, "Now they're trying to pin every unsolved crime in the book on me." In either case, the suspect might be frightened into complete silence.

An indirect approach might be effective. Instead of asking, "By the way, did you also commit the armed robbery of Blank's Liquor on last Friday night?" the interrogator might ask, "Are you familiar with Blank's Liquor Store at Fifty-first and Main Street?" The one question that should not be asked in this context is "Where were you last Friday night between seven and nine o'clock?" The reason for this warning is that this question has become a cliché in movies and mystery fiction and is commonly understood to be an accusation. An alternative approach would be to ask the question directly, "Who robbed Blank's Liquor Store last Friday?" The interrogator might even add, "The robbery of Blank's was done in very much the same way as the one you committed last night, and the description of the robber fits you pretty well."

This process can continue indefinitely until every potentially related case has been discussed, one by one. General questions can be asked, too: "Have you committed any other crimes that we might not know about?" or "Is this the first time you've been involved in a crime?" Every interrogation should end with the open question "Is there anything else you'd like to tell me about?"

Under no circumstances should an interrogation last so long that the suspect becomes exhausted or shows signs of discomfort because of hunger or thirst. If at any time the suspect asks to take a rest or asks that the interrogation stop, those requests must be honored immediately.

## THE USE OF "LIE DETECTORS"

There are many myths and misunderstandings about so-called lie detecting equipment, especially the most common type, which is known as the polygraph.

The word *polygraph* simply means "multiple writer," referring to the fact that the machine is designed to record several types of information simultaneously. Specifically, the device records information about the physiological state of the person being interviewed: blood pressure, respiration, the electrical conductivity of the skin (an indirect way of measuring perspiration), and so on.[20] In principle, a polygraph is not much different from comparable devices used for medical purposes or for the remote telemetry of the physical condition of astronauts and test pilots.

The use of a polygraph to "detect lies" stems from the fact that when people tell lies, they ordinarily feel some kind of emotional response that is unavoidably expressed through changes in their physiological state. Thus, a polygraph cannot distinguish between a lie and a truthful statement; it merely records the fact that a person's physiological condition indicates that an emotional response occurred at a given time.[21]

Another kind of device has been developed recently for the same purpose. This device is called a *voice stress analyzer*. Its inventors claim that it, too, detects lies (or, more accurately, emotional reactions) by detecting variations in a person's voice that are caused by stress. The voice stress analyzer offers several advantages over the polygraph; it is a much more compact device, and it does not have to be connected directly to the subject. In fact, the manufacturers claim that the voice stress analyzer is equally effective when used in the presence of the subject or when used on the tape-recorded voice of the subject. If these claims can be verified and demonstrated under appropriate conditions, the device may become common very rapidly.

In either case, more depends on the skill of the person who operates the device than on the machine itself.[22] No machine known to science can read a person's mind. Neither the polygraph nor the voice stress analyzer can detect a false answer unless the right question is asked.

Furthermore, the polygraph records *all* emotional reactions. People who are being interviewed in connection with a crime naturally are emotionally upset. A skillful polygraph operator can distinguish between normal or innocent emotional responses and those that indicate lying. This is done through the examiner's choice of questions, the order in which questions are asked, and various other controlled factors designed to produce characteristic response patterns. Finally, it is the examiner's interpretation of the polygraph tracings (or the voice stress analyzer's indications) that matters. The machine does not indicate that a person has lied; it merely shows a variation in blood pressure or breathing rate or a change in voice tension.

The use of a lie detector is subject to the suspect's consent, as is the interrogation. No suspect can be compelled to submit to a polygraph test. A voice stress analyzer presumably could be used without the suspect's knowledge, but that would be very likely to lead to a complaint that the suspect's rights were violated and thus would jeopardize the whole case.

If a suspect agrees to undergo a polygraph examination, a trained, highly qualified polygraph operator must be used. The investigator and the examiner should work out together the questions to be presented by the

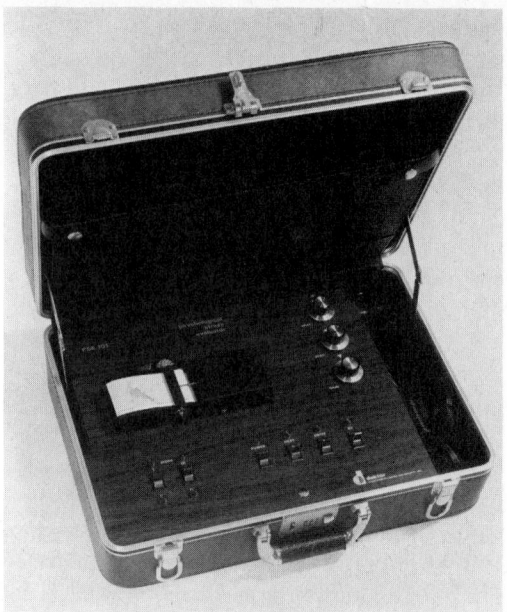

A voice stress analyzer. This device, called Psychological Stress Evaluator, Model PSE-101, has been used with success by some police agencies. (Photo courtesy of Dektor Counterintelligence and Security, Inc.)

examiner; of course, the examiner should have a thorough summary of the known facts in the case. Usually a polygraph examination should be conducted after an ordinary interrogation.[23]

It should be emphasized that the use of lie detecting devices can be risky, especially if the operator of the equipment is poorly trained or incompetent. In essence, lie detection is a process that attempts to use one's emotional reactions against oneself. The more deeply involved a suspect is in a crime, the greater the degree of emotional stress that he or she is likely to feel. The misapplication of lie detecting can lead to false or misleading results and can have devastating psychological effects on the suspect.

Any use of a lie detector comes perilously close to violating the suspect's freedom from self-incrimination, which is one reason that the results of a polygraph examination are not admissible in court even if the suspect submitted to the examination voluntarily.[24] An examination conducted at the suspect's request by an examiner retained by the suspect's attorney is another matter; the results of such an examination might be presented in court, although this happens rarely.

Interrogation does not make the case for an investigator. When conducted skillfully, interrogation can clarify the issues and it can open up new avenues of investigation about the crime under investigation and, perhaps, other related crimes that might have been committed by the same person. However, nothing that is said or done during an interrogation can change the inescapable fact that convictions are won on the basis of evidence, physical evidence and the testimony of qualified witnesses.

## REFERENCES

1. Sidney H. Asch, *Civil Rights and Responsibilities under the Constitution* (New York: Arco, 1970), p.115.

2. A. C. Germann, Frank D. Day, and Robert R. J. Gallati, *Introduction to Law Enforcement and Criminal Justice,* rev. ed. (Springfield, Ill.: Charles C Thomas, 1973), p. 115.

3. Paul B. Weston and Kenneth M. Wells, *Criminal Evidence for Police* (Englewood Cliffs, N.J.: Prentice-Hall, 1971), p. 195.

4. John J. Horgan, *Criminal Investigation* (New York: McGraw-Hill, 1974), p. 58.

5. Weston and Wells, *Criminal Evidence for Police*, p. 194.

6. Horgan, p. 72.

7. Horgan, p. 59.

8. Asch, pp. 116–117.

9. Horgan, p. 60.

10. Weston and Wells, *Criminal Evidence for Police*, p. 200.

11. Horgan, pp. 66–67.

12. Asch, p. 143.

13. Paul B. Weston and Kenneth M. Wells, *Elements of Criminal Investigation* (Englewood Cliffs, N.J.: Prentice-Hall, 1971), p. 64.

14. Horgan, pp. 61–62.

15. Horgan, pp. 64–65. The author compares two very different interrogating styles, "the logical approach" and "the emotional approach."

16. J. Shane Creamer, *The Law of Arrest, Search, and Seizure,* 2d ed. (Philadelphia: W.B. Saunders, 1975), p. 31.

17. Horgan, p. 59.

18. Horgan, p. 73.

19. Weston and Wells, *Elements of Criminal Investigation*, p. 67.

20. Horgan, p. 78.

21. Weston and Wells, *Elements of Criminal Investigation*, p. 75.

22. Horgan, p. 79.

23 Weston and Wells, *Elements of Criminal Investigation*, pp. 76–77.

24. Horgan, p. 80.

1. True or false: The Fifth Amendment prevents the use of a confession as evidence in a criminal trial.
2. The best way to determine the validity of a confession is to
    a. place the suspect under oath.
    b. ask the suspect to sign a waiver.
    c. have one or more witnesses present.
    d. corroborate it on the basis of physical evidence and other testimony.
    e. present it to a magistrate.
3. Mistreatment of a prisoner usually occurs because
    a. criminals are unpleasant people.
    b. criminals are protected by a number of laws and constitutional provisions.
    c. they are considered innocent until they are proven guilty.
    d. some police officers consider them to be "the enemy."
    e. most people naturally sympathize with the innocent victim.
4. Which of the following is *not* one of the purposes for bringing a prisoner before a magistrate?
    a. to set bond
    b. to ensure that the prisoner has been given the *Miranda* warning
    c. to inform the suspect about the nature of the evidence accumulated by the police
    d. to ensure that the prisoner has an opportunity to hire an attorney or to have one appointed by the court
    e. to inform the suspect of the charges
5. True or false: A suspect may decide to stop cooperating during an interrogation even after signing a waiver of the right to remain silent.
6. When a suspect offers an obviously fictitious alibi, the interrogator should
    a. accuse the suspect of lying.
    b. pretend to believe it, but investigate it later (after completing the interrogation) to be sure that it is false.
    c. suspend the interrogation immediately, until the alibi can be investigated.
    d. ignore it.
    e. question the suspect closely about every detail of the alibi until the suspect admits that it is a lie.
7. True or false: A skillful interrogator should never reveal any information to a suspect, but should direct all questions to the immediate topic of the crime being investigated.
8. The use of a polygraph to "detect lies" is based on
    a. the fact that when people tell a lie, they ordinarily feel some kind of emotional response.
    b. the fact that when a person lies, usually there is some change in physiological condition.
    c. the device's ability to record changes in the subject's physiological state.
    d. the polygraph operator's or examiner's skill in distinguishing between normal emotional reactions and those that indicate a lie.
    e. all of the statements above.
    f. none of the statements above.

9. What part should the principal investigator play in the polygraph examination?
    a. The investigator should assist the examiner in formulating questions.
    b. The investigator should conduct the examination.
    c. The investigator should be present, but should not participate in any way.
    d. The investigator should interpret the results.
    e. The investigator should not be present and has no significant role in the procedure.
10. True or false: The results of a polygraph examination are never admissible in court.

### TOPICS FOR INVESTIGATION

1. In the past, a confession usually was admitted as evidence in a criminal trial, but the jury was instructed to decide whether the confession was voluntary and to what extent it was credible. Under current rules of evidence, the judge must decide in advance whether a confession was voluntary and, therefore, admissible before it is introduced as evidence. Why has this change of procedure been made? Is the current procedure necessary to protect the defendant's rights, or is it an unnecessary restriction on police investigative practices?
2. Should the interrogation of a suspect be videotaped?
3. Discuss this statement: "criminals are not 'the enemy.'" Why is the "us-against-them" attitude described in the text as "dangerous"? Why should police officers be expected to remain calm, polite, and objective when they are faced with arrogant, belligerent, or hostile conduct on the part of criminals? Are these expectations reasonable or unreasonable, considering the fact that police officers are only human and have the same emotional responses that anyone else would have under similar circumstances?
4. One technique sometimes used by interrogators is to tell the suspect, in detail, all of the evidence that has been accumulated, in the hope of persuading the suspect that a conviction is inevitable and that there is no point in lying or refusing to confess. Is this a good technique or not?
5. When should a suspect be asked to submit to a polygraph examination and for what purposes?

# CHAPTER 17
## PROPERTY SEARCHES

1. True or false: The most important test of the constitutionality or legality of a search is whether it produces incriminating evidence.
2. Usually a search warrant may be used
   a. within five days after it is issued.
   b. at any time by any police officer.
   c. at the place to be searched only when the suspect is present.
   d. only by the officers who are specifically listed in the warrant.
   e. by any magistrate.
3. In a "stop-and-frisk" search, the officer:
   a. must have personal knowledge that the suspect has committed a particular crime.
   b. may not reach into or under the suspect's outer clothing unless a weapon appears to be hidden in or under the clothing.
   c. must give the *Miranda* warning before beginning the search.
   d. should ask the suspect to sign a waiver giving consent to the search.
   e. should remember to ask the suspect to empty his or her pockets, purse, briefcase, and the like.
4. True or false: The primary purpose of a search incidental to an arrest is to make sure that the arrestee does not have a weapon hidden within reach.
5. Which of the following persons could *not* give valid consent for a voluntary search?
   a. the suspect's spouse, if he or she lives with the suspect
   b. the suspect's mother or father, if the suspect is less than 18 years old
   c. the suspect's employer, if the place to be searched is the suspect's work area
   d. the landlord of the apartment building where the suspect rents an apartment
   e. the suspect's roommate in an apartment
6. If evidence of a crime is found in a public place, in circumstances that indicate that it has been abandoned, an officer is legally entitled to
   a. seize the evidence and remove it.
   b. arrest the suspect for abandoning evidence.
   c. obtain a search warrant for the place in which the evidence was observed.
   d. return the evidence to its rightful owner.
   e. search the suspect for additional evidence.

THE EVIDENCE FOUND at the scene of a crime often is all that is needed to identify, charge, and convict the suspect. But when the perpetrator of a crime takes the evidence away from the scene, yet another task is set for the investigator. The evidence must be found, wherever it is, and brought before the court. Otherwise the likelihood of convicting the perpetrator is greatly reduced.

Performed correctly, a property search and seizure is an indispensable part of a successful investigation. Nothing is quite as persuasive to a jury as the information that incriminating evidence—the murder weapon or the stolen property—was found hidden in the suspect's closet. However, if a property search is performed improperly or carelessly, it is almost equally certain that the guilty person will go free and that the innocent will continue to suffer. We saw in Chapter 15 that an arrest is worthless unless it is made in strict compliance with a complex set of legal rules and procedures. The same is true for property searches and seizures, for the same reason: the Bill of Rights was intended specifically to limit police powers, to prevent the abuse of those powers, and to guarantee to everyone the maximum degree of personal liberty.[1]

## CONSTITUTIONAL LIMITATIONS ON SEARCHES

The Fourth Amendment has the most direct bearing on property searches and seizures; it reads as follows:

*The right of the people to be secure in their persons, houses, papers, and effects, against unreasonable searches and seizures, shall not be violated, and no warrants shall issue, but upon probable cause, supported by oath or affirmation, and particularly describing the place to be searched, and the persons or things to be seized.*

The wording of this amendment is so clear and definite that there seems to be little room for misunderstanding or interpretation. Yet, the amendment has been treated like every other part of the Constitution: its exact meaning in specific cases has been and continues to be subject to change from time to time because of the decisions of the Supreme Court and the lesser branches of the judicial system.

In brief, the courts have held that the privacy and liberty of the citizen are paramount and, therefore, that *no* search is "reasonable" under the Fourth Amendment unless it is carried out under a valid search warrant issued by a magistrate who has objectively decided that the police officer knows exactly what evidence is being sought and has good reason to believe that it will be found in a particular place. There are only three exceptional situations in which a warrant is not needed for a search and one additional situation in which a warrant is not needed for property (such as evidence) to be seized. We shall deal with these limited exceptions later; for now, we want to stress that a search for evidence almost always requires a warrant.

The rule for searches is very different from the rules of arrest. An arrest can be made with or without a warrant, depending on many circumstances; in general, the factors that would enable an officer to obtain an arrest warrant are also sufficient to permit a warrantless arrest. However, that is not true for searches and property seizures. The fact that a warrant could have been obtained, but was not, does not justify a warrantless search; on the contrary, it supplies a good reason to throw out any evidence that was produced.[8]

### PROPER EVIDENCE AND MERE EVIDENCE

At one time, the Supreme Court ruled that there was a difference between "proper evi-

Nearly all major property search cases are based on interpretation of the Fourth Amendment. These are some of the landmark decisions of the Supreme Court on this subject:

*Weeks v. United States* (1914). Property seized in violation of the Fourth Amendment cannot be presented as evidence in a federal criminal case no matter how incriminating it might be.[3] This is known as the *exclusionary rule;* under the *Weeks* decision, it did not necessarily apply to state cases.

*Carroll v. United States* (1925). The police might be justified in searching an automobile without a warrant since the vehicle could be moved out of their reach before a warrant could be obtained. Nevertheless, there must be probable cause to believe the vehicle contains contraband (or other evidence) *before* the search takes place. This decision has been extended to include other circumstances in which quick action must be taken to prevent the removal or destruction of evidence.

*Wolf v. Colorado* (1949). The basic principles of the Fourth Amendment must apply in state cases as well as federal cases, but the exclusionary rule was not considered an "integral part" of Fourth Amendment protection and therefore did not necessarily apply at the state level.

*Mapp v. Ohio* (1961). The exclusionary rule applies to all criminal cases at every level.[4]

*Frazier v. Cupp* (1969). If two or more persons jointly own certain property, it is necessary to obtain the permission of only one owner before conducting a search without a warrant (a voluntary search). Any evidence found can be used to prosecute any of the owners, including those who did not agree to the search.[5]

*Davis v. Mississippi* (1969). Fingerprints are evidence and thus are subject to the same rules as any other evidence.

*Chimel v. California* (1969). When an arrest is made, the police officer has a right to search the area immediately surrounding the arrestee—more specifically, "the area into which the arrestee can reach"—but only for the limited purpose of detecting weapons that the arrestee could use to injure the police officer, to commit suicide, or to make an escape or for the purpose of finding evidence that otherwise would be destroyed or lost.[6]

Between 1964 and 1972, the Court issued a series of rulings that give the police even narrower powers to search a person before an arrest. These are known as stop-and-frisk rules. In essence, the rule is that a police officer can "frisk" a person for the sole purpose of determining whether the person has a weapon that could be used against the officer or someone else, even though the person is not under arrest.[7]

dence," evidence that had a clear and unmistakable connection to a crime, and "mere evidence," items that might have some connection to a crime but whose connection was not obvious at first glance (*Gouled v. United States*) [1921]. The Court decided that a warrant could be issued for proper evidence, and such items could be seized when found. But a warrant could not be issued for mere evidence, and, with some exceptions, mere evidence could not be seized.

This ruling produced endless confusion and controversy. The definition of proper evidence included such items as contraband, fruits of a crime, and instruments of a crime; everything else was to be regarded as mere evidence unless there were clear and compelling circumstantial reasons to believe that the item had a clear connection to a crime.

These very ambiguous rules remained in effect until 1967, when the Court reversed itself and abandoned the mere evidence concept *(Warden of Maryland Penitentiary v. Hayden)*. The court said that the mere evidence concept had arisen out of a misunderstanding; the Court in *Gouled* had intended to prevent "general search warrants," in which the police seek permission to conduct an exploratory search for whatever evidence might be found. Such searches are clearly prohibited by the Fourth Amendment. However, there was no reason to believe that certain kinds of property should be exempt from seizure as mere evidence if in fact they demonstrated some part of the guilt of the accused.[9]

Unfortunately, the proper evidence–mere evidence distinction had already become law in many states, and some of those laws still exist. Consequently, in those states a search warrant can be issued only for the instruments of a crime, fruits of a crime, or contraband. Whether mere evidence can be seized in the course of an otherwise valid search depends on the exact wording of the state law.

## THE RULE OF PARTICULARITY

Another important rule in searches and seizures is drawn straight from the Fourth Amendment, which says that a warrant must "particularly" describe the place to be searched and the persons and things to be seized.

There are really two requirements here. First, the investigator must know exactly what evidence is being sought; second, the investigator must know where the evidence is likely to be found. You cannot search a suspect's home just to see what might be found there. Nor can you search an entire neighborhood of homes in hope of turning up a murder weapon or some other item of evidence.[10] Usually the address of the house to be searched is sufficient, but if the location is an apartment or office, the apartment or room number must also be stated.

Similarly, the nature of the evidence being sought determines the degree of particularity that is necessary. For example, it would be hard to justify a warrant request for "an unknown quantity of cash stolen from Blank's Liquor Store." How could the investigator possibly know whether money found in the suspect's home had come from the liquor store or from some other source? On the other hand, a warrant probably would be issued for "an unknown quantity of narcotics," since any quantity of any sort of narcotic drug would be contraband.[11]

## PROBABLE CAUSE

In Chapter 15 we discussed the concept of probable cause for an arrest and how it is established. By and large, the same principles apply to searches and seizures.[12] There must be some reasonable grounds for believing that a particular type of evidence will be found in a particular place before the search is begun. The probable cause must exist first. The fact that evidence is found during a search does *not* establish probable cause.

Probable cause may be based on a tip from

an informant, the officer's own direct observation of illegal or suspicious activity, or a logical inference drawn from known facts and other evidence already obtained.[13]

## THE SEARCH WARRANT

A search warrant is an order from a judge or magistrate directing a police officer to search for a particular object or type of object in a particular place and, if the object is found, to seize it and bring it back to the court. Any magistrate can issue a search warrant. Ordinarily a search warrant is issued only at the request of a police officer; however, there is no legal requirement for the request, and a magistrate can issue a warrant on his or her own initiative.

Obtaining a search warrant in advance is not an absolute guarantee that evidence will be admissible. As a practical matter, the courts realize that not all magistrates are equally strict in considering probable cause, particularity, and other requirements of a valid warrant. Even after a warrant has been issued, the officer must be able to demonstrate that the search was conducted in compliance with the warrant and with other complicated rules. However, if the officer has acted in good faith in requesting a warrant, if there are no gross irregularities in the warrant itself, and if the conduct of the search was reasonable, the evidence is likely to be admitted.[14]

### WHEN TO OBTAIN A WARRANT

A search for evidence away from the scene of a crime must be planned and carried out just as carefully as an arrest. Physical evidence is critically important in convicting a criminal.

File No._____

IN MUNICIPAL COURT IN
AUSTIN TRAVIS COUNTY
TEXAS

THE STATE OF TEXAS

vs.

_____

_____

SEARCH WARRANT

Issued the_____ day of_____,
A.D. 19____.

_____
Judge of the Municipal Court in
Austin, Travis County, Texas

*A search warrant (above: front of warrant; right: back; p.432: inside) (Courtesy Temple, Texas Police Department.)*

Every effort must be made to ensure that the necessary evidence will be found in a manner that is consistent with the legal principles that we have been discussing.

Like the arrest of a suspect, an evidence search must not be initiated too hastily. However, evidence is far more likely to disappear forever than is a suspect. Most criminals are very much aware of the danger to their freedom if they are caught with incriminating evidence in their possession. There are, however, some types of crimes in which evidence is available more or less continually. This is true of most types of organized crimes: narcotics distribution, gambling, prostitution, and so on. There often is a degree of organization in property crimes as well, since most stolen goods ultimately are sold to "fences" who ship the merchandise to a distant city or to another part of the same city and resell the goods to presumably innocent citizens.

When the investigator is dealing with a crime that probably was committed by someone who is not involved in organized criminal activity (this usually is true for violent crimes), the timing of a search becomes more

AFFIDAVIT FOR SEARCH WARRANT (FOR CONTROLLED SUBSTANCE) FOR PRIVATE RESIDENCE

THE STATE OF TEXAS
COUNTY OF _____

Before me, the undersigned authority, on this day personally appeared the undersigned affiants, who being by me severally sworn, upon their oaths state, that: A certain building, house and place, occupied and used as a private residence, located in _____ County, Texas, described as _____

_____

(Give street name and number, and name of city or town, or accurate description and location of place)

and being the building, house or place of _____

_____

(Give full name or describe person accurately or state if unknown)

is a place where we each have reason to believe and do believe that said party so occupying and using, as a private residence, the said building, house and place has in _____ possession therein controlled substance, as that term is defined by law, and contrary to the provisions of law, and for the purpose of the unlawful sale thereof, and where such controlled substance are unlawfully sold; that on or about the _____ day of _____, A.D., 19_____,

_____

(Here state facts and information showing probable cause)

_____, Affiant

_____, Affiant

Subscribed and sworn to before me, by the within named affiants, on this the _____ day of _____,
A.D. 19_____.

_____
Judge of the Municipal Court in Austin,
Travis County, Texas

THE STATE OF TEXAS                    IN THE NAME AND BY THE AUTHORITY OF THE
COUNTY OF _____                        STATE OF TEXAS

To the Sheriff or any Peace Officer of _____ County, GREETING:

Whereas, the above complaint on oath and in writing, in accordance with law, has this day been made before me, alleging that the premises described as in the foregoing affidavit situated in said _____ County, Texas, and being the premises of _____

_____

is a place where controlled substance, described in the foregoing affidavit, are unlawfully sold, and possessed for the purpose of sale, and whereas, the particular grounds and probable cause for this warrant to issue are set forth in the said affidavit, which is made a part hereof, upon examination of the same by me, I am satisfied that the grounds exist and that probable cause is shown, and I believe in its existence and do so hereby find.

You are therefore hereby commanded to search forthwith the above described premises and persons found thereon for any said controlled substance, as that term is defined by law, unlawfully possessed, and possessed for the purpose of the unlawful sale thereof, and if any such controlled substance be found at any time within three days of the issuance hereof, upon or in said building, house or place so used as a private residence, you are hereby further commanded to seize all such controlled substance, and containers thereof; And you are hereby further commanded to arrest the said _____, the person accused of the unlawful possession, sale and equipment.

Herein fail not, but have you then and there this warrant within three days from its issuance with your return thereon showing how you have executed the same.

WITNESS my hand, this _____ day of _____, A.D. 19_____.

_____
Judge of the Municipal Court in Austin,
Travis County, Texas

Form 174
Rev 9-17-73

If a search must be conducted with the suspect present, there should be no one else present, neither criminal associates of the suspect nor innocent bystanders. The police officers must remember that they are invading the suspect's territory. If the suspect is surrounded by friends and associates, that puts the suspect at a considerable psychological advantage. Innocent bystanders might be used as hostages or shields if violence erupts. Only careful planning by the search team can reduce the psychological disadvantages under which they must function.

### APPROACHING AND ENTERING THE SEARCH SCENE

Members of the search team should be deployed around the building, as unobtrusively as possible, so that they can observe anyone leaving in a hurry. Unless there is a likely prospect of violence, one officer should approach the main entrance alone while at least one other officer provides cover. If the likelihood of violence is greater than usual, the approach should be make by two officers in the manner outlined in Investigator's Notes 3 (Chapter 3).

The officer should obtain the identity of the person who answers the door. If the person is not the suspect in the case, the officer should ask for the suspect. If the suspect is not present, the officer next should ask the person to state his or her relationship to the suspect (spouse, member of the family, landlord, friend, or whatever).

Some attempt should be made to gain entrance without using the warrant, provided that the person who answers the door has the necessary authority. If this attempt fails, the officer should present the warrant, explain its significance, and express the intention to enter and search the premises. Usually there will be no further resistance and the officer will be admitted.[18]

As soon as the door is open, the officer should signal to the other members of the search team by hand signal or walkie-talkie.

Those members of the team who are deployed at the front of the building should enter at once. Those at the rear or sides should wait until they are admitted through the other entrances to the building.

Once inside, the search team first must locate and identify every person in the building. This must be done with care because someone with violent intentions could be waiting behind every closed door. One officer should remain near the front entrance while the second walks through the entire building, checking each room, and admits any other members of the team through the side or rear entrances.

As soon as the premises have been secured and all occupants are identified, the search itself can begin. If possible, one member of the team should remain at the front entrance, perhaps questioning the person who answered the door. The other members of the team should proceed through the building according to their prearranged plan.

METHODS OF SEARCH

A good deal of thought must go into the search procedure because it must be limited to the specific evidence stated in the warrant. For example, if the warrant specifies that the object being sought is a television set, the officers must look only where a television set might be hidden: in closets, but not in kitchen cabinets or in dresser drawers. Some kinds of evidence, such as narcotics or a handgun, could be hidden almost anywhere; thus the officers would be entitled to remove the covers from appliances, dismantle exposed plumbing or air conditioning ducts, or even pry up loose floorboards.[19]

The search must be completed in a reasonable length of time, but *reasonable* is a relative term. It would take only a few seconds to search for a stolen automobile in the suspect's garage, but it might take two days to search through a large house for a suspected murder weapon.[20]

Once the evidence specified in the warrant has been found, the search must stop. There is no legal reason to continue the search. However, until that time, any evidence found during the course of a search may be seized even if it was not specified in the warrant (depending on the state's mere evidence laws). The search should be planned so that all the places searched are appropriate to the evidence stated in the warrant, but the most likely place is searched last. Otherwise, the opportunity to find unexpected evidence may be lost.

When any item of evidence is found, it must be treated in the way that we described in Chapters 4 and 5. The evidence must be photographed in place; measurements and sketches should be recorded; the evidence itself must be labeled, handled carefully, and packaged for delivery to the laboratory. A list of the items removed from the premises should be signed by the investigator and by the suspect or other person present. One copy should be retained by the investigator and the other copy left with the suspect or other person. If the search is conducted while no one other than the police is present, a copy of the evidence list should be left in a conspicuous place on the premises and another copy should be mailed or delivered to the suspect or the owner of the property.

CAREFUL
TREATMENT OF
PROPERTY

Care must be given to other people's property. During the search the property should be disturbed as little as possible. Pieces of furniture or other personal effects that are moved during the search should be returned to their original position; anything that is dismantled, opened, or otherwise disturbed should be restored to its previous condition.[21]

The way in which a search is conducted reflects the professionalism of the police officers involved. Sloppiness or carelessness with other people's property indicates poor discipline and an unprofessional attitude. Furthermore, every citizen, even the vilest criminal, is entitled to have his or her personal property treated with care and respect. The fact that a person might have committed a crime does not give the police any privilege to mistreat that individual's property.

Finally, the police officer must bear in mind that the suspect may have family or friends who also live on the premises being searched, and there would be no justification for destroying their property. To do so would merely breed resentment and hostility toward all law enforcement, attitudes that would spread through the suspect's circle of family and acquaintances and into the community. When police officers behave in a lawless and irresponsible manner, no matter what justification they think they have, the end result is merely more crime and violence in the community.

## STOP-AND-FRISK SEARCHES

A stop-and-frisk search involves a police officer who encounters a citizen in a public place and decides, on some reasonable basis, that the citizen might be engaged in or planning to commit a crime. The officer has the legal authority to stop the citizen, request identification, and inquire about the person's business.

The level of probable cause required to justify a stop-and-frisk search is very low. Nevertheless, there must be some reasonable basis for the officer to decide to stop a particular person. Although a tip from an informant could provide the probable cause, more often it is based on the officer's own observation of the citizen's behavior, which, in the officer's opinion, evokes suspicion.[22]

The mere fact that an officer feels justified in stopping a person and demanding identification, however, does not necessarily justify a frisking. There must be something about the citizen's appearance or behavior suggesting that the person might be armed. Only in that case is the officer entitled to conduct a brief search of the person to look for weapons that might be used against the officer or someone else.[23]

The frisking must be limited to external clothing. Only if something that might be a weapon is felt through the clothing can the officer reach into or under the clothing and withdraw the object. The shapes of most weapons are readily recognized through a layer or two of clothing, although bulky overcoats or sweaters may pose a problem.

It is not sufficient to pat down the clothing. Instead, the officer should press one hand tightly against the person's body and run the hand up and down along the arms, ribs, chest, back, and each side of the legs. Next, the officer should grasp a fold of cloth between the thumb and fingers and squeeze it tightly; this should be done at each location where weapons are likely to be hidden: at the wrists, the armpits, the waistline just above the front of the hips, the small of the back, the inner thighs, and around the ankles.

If the person being frisked has long or bushy hair, attention should be paid to the hair itself and to the collar. Knives, long steel pins, and other stabbing weapons are sometimes hidden in the hair or under the collar. There even have been instances in which small handguns were concealed in thick,

bushy hair. These areas should not be searched by hand, for a nasty puncture wound could result. Instead, the officer should probe the suspect's hair and the collar under the hair with a pencil or similar object.

If there is adequate reason to frisk a person who is not otherwise a criminal suspect, there is adequate reason to do it carefully and thoroughly. An incomplete, perfunctory frisking is insufficient to protect the officer and serves only to irritate the citizen, possibly provoking the violence that it is meant to avoid.

At the same time, the officer must not be excessively rough or abusive. Every effort must be made to keep from embarrassing the citizen unnecessarily. If possible, the person should be taken away from curious bystanders, both to avoid humiliating the person who is to be frisked and to avoid the possibility that bystanders might decide to interfere and rescue a friend.

As a matter of simple courtesy and respect for the citizen's dignity, it is desirable that male officers search only males and female officers search only females. However, if an occasion arises when a back-up officer of the appropriate gender is not available and if there is good reason to believe that an officer might be endangered if the person is not frisked, the search should be carried out in the same professional, thorough, and dignified manner that is always used.

Any evidence found during a stop-and-frisk search can be seized and might serve as probable cause for an arrest and a more thorough search.

A person being frisked cannot be made to empty pockets, open a purse or briefcase, or otherwise submit to a complete personal search: the stop-and-frisk search must be limited to the external clothing unless a weapon is distinctly felt under the clothes.

## SEARCH INCIDENTAL TO ARREST

The rules permit somewhat more latitude when a suspect is arrested. Regardless of whether the arrest itself is performed with a warrant, an officer is entitled to conduct a very thorough search of the arrestee's person and, according to the *Chimel* decision, the area within the arrestee's reach.[24] Any evidence found during the search may be seized, although the primary purpose of the search is to discover any weapons hidden on the arrestee's person or within reach.

The personal search at the time of arrest should be similar in technique to a frisking, but more thorough. The officer is entitled to reach into or under external clothing as reasonably necessary. The arrestee should be required to empty pockets, purse, briefcase, or other hand-held belongings so that the contents can be inspected.[25] It is better to have the suspect empty a purse, camera case, or other container, removing the items one by one and placing them where they can be inspected by the officer; there is always the chance that the container itself is booby-trapped, endangering any unwary person who tries to search it.

The search incidental to an arrest must be contemporaneous with the arrest itself; that is, the two events must be closely connected in time. Ordinarily, the arrest would come first, although the arrest and search can be carried out simultaneously or the search could begin before the arrest. However, it is *not* permissible for the arrest to take place as a result of the search, nor can an arrest be made for the sole purpose of justifying the search. There must be probable cause for the arrest, and preferably an arrest warrant, before the search begins.[26]

It is a cardinal rule of police practice that an armed suspect should never be placed in a police vehicle. The importance of this rule is obvious, and so is the danger of ignoring the rule carelessly. However, an arrested suspect usually should be handcuffed before being placed in the vehicle, and a properly handcuffed prisoner is incapable of reaching or using any weapon hidden on the body.

Aside from the search of the suspect's body and personal belongings, the *Chimel* decision allows the officer to search the vehicle or premises immediately surrounding the prisoner.[27] Ordinarily, the search must not exceed the area into which the prisoner could reach. This might include the room in which the person is taken into custody; outdoors, a radius of three meters or so (eight to ten feet) probably would be considered reasonable.[28] If the person is arrested while seated in a vehicle, the whole of the passenger compartment could be searched, including the spaces under the seats if they could be reached without removing the seats themselves. The trunk and other parts of the vehicle could not be searched at this time, although a warrant for such a search probably could be obtained later. Passengers in the vehicle could not be searched unless they, too, are under arrest; however, they could be frisked.[29]

It is standard police practice for all prisoners to be searched thoroughly when they are brought to the jail or station lock-up; this search, too, is considered reasonable under the *Chimel* decision. Once in a while, such a search will produce evidence such as narcotics that may be of interest to the investigator, but normally the booking search is more a concern of the jail custodian.

## VOLUNTARY SEARCHES

There is no need for the police officer to have a warrant, probable cause, or any other jus-

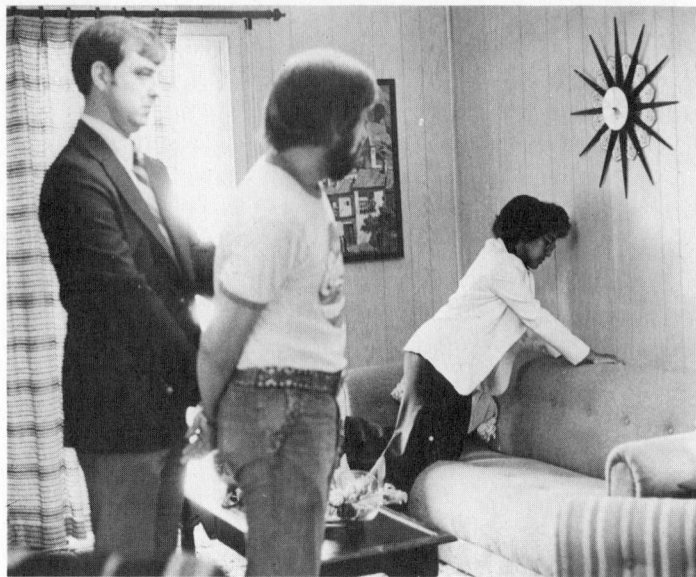

tification if the owner of the property consents to a search. Any police officer may search any property in any manner for any length of time if the owner permits it. Any item of evidence may be seized and removed if the owner permits it.[30] Obviously, a voluntary search is extremely desirable to the investigator because of this tremendous latitude. Unfortunately, carrying out a legally valid voluntary search is even harder than you might suppose.

First, there is the problem of determining who has the legal right or authority to permit the search. The owner of the place to be searched always has this authority.[31] If there are two or more people who jointly own the same property, any one of them can allow the police to search it, even if another owner disagrees or is unaware of the search.[32] If the place to be searched is an apartment, hotel room, business office, or other rented quarters that are actually occupied by a tenant, the legal owner of the building does *not* have the

authority to permit a search; instead, the tenant is considered the owner for this purpose.[33]

An employee or agent of the owner may act in the owner's place to give permission for a search if the employee or agent ordinarily would have the right to enter the place to be searched in the absence of the owner.[34] However, this kind of situation can become extremely complicated.

A parent always has the right to act for a dependent child; in most states, a child is considered a dependent until age 18. However, if the child does not live at home, the dependency might not exist. Anyone who is legally authorized to act as the custodian or guardian for a person who is physically or mentally incapacitated could permit a search of the dependent's premises.[35] In certain cases, a person is legally empowered to act *in loco parentis* (in the parents' place) with respect to a child or to a person who is physically or mentally incapacitated. For example, the chief administrator of a boarding school could authorize the search of a child's room without the child's consent or knowledge.[36]

In any of the situations that we have described, it may prove impossible to determine whether a particular person has the necessary authority to permit a legal search. When in doubt, get a warrant; no other rule is easier to remember and more likely to avoid trouble.

Once the legal authority to permit a search has been established, the officer's next task is to obtain the consent. The key word in a voluntary search is *voluntary*. The courts have maintained that a person's actions are voluntary only if the person is aware of the probable consequences of those actions and is equally capable of preventing them. In other words, a voluntary search is not voluntary if the person is unaware of the likely results or is under any sort of compulsion.[37]

In practical terms, this means that the investigator must explain three things to the owner:

• Why the search is to be conducted and what kind of evidence is being sought

• What will be done with any evidence that is found (specifically, that it will be used in court to demonstrate the guilt of the accused, who may or may not be the owner)

• That the owner has a legal right to deny permission for the search, to limit the search to certain places, or to discontinue the search at any time.[38]

The officer must not do anything that suggests coercion in any form. The time-honored cliché of detective fiction, "Why don't you just let me look around a little? If you haven't done anything wrong, you don't have anything to hide, right?" would completely invalidate a voluntary search because it amounts to psychological coercion and deception.

Many police agencies require their officers to obtain a signed waiver from anyone who permits a voluntary search. The waiver includes a statement that the person signing it has the legal authority to permit the search, understands the nature and purpose of the search, and chooses to waive the right to withhold permission. If a waiver is not used, questions about whether the search was truly voluntary will be raised in court, and the issue could come down to whether the judge believes the police officer or the owner. In such a situation, the court is obligated to assume that the search was not voluntary unless the police can prove otherwise.[39]

## SPECIAL CIRCUMSTANCES

There are a few circumstances in which the constitutional rights of citizens are not a factor, do not apply, or must be set aside.

### EXTREME AND IMMINENT DANGER

If lives or property are in extreme or imminent danger, it is not necessary to obtain a search warrant or anyone's permission nor is it necessary for an officer to give notice of the intention to enter before breaking into a place, searching for the source of potential danger, and seizing any evidence that might be found in the course of the search.[40] For example, if the police receive a tip from a reliable informant that a bomb has been set in a private building, the urgent need to find and remove the bomb is clearly superior to the legal niceties. Similarly, if an armed suspect is holding hostages or is firing a weapon from a building, the police do not need a warrant or anyone's permission to enter the building by force and to search for and seize the suspect and any evidence that might be discovered.[41]

## SEIZURE OF EVIDENCE
## IN A PUBLIC PLACE

A search warrant is unnecessary when evidence is found in a public place because, in a legal sense, there is no search.[42] The evidence may be seized and removed even if the owner objects.

However, property that is not evidence in itself (such as a suitcase) may be searched only if it has been abandoned or the owner consents. The *abandoned property* rule can apply to various situations. For example, if an apartment, hotel room, or rented office appears to be unoccupied, the landlord or building manager may give permission to search it on the assumption that the previous tenant has abandoned the property. The same rule could apply to a suspect's own home if there is reason to believe that the suspect has fled and does not plan to return. If the home is vacant for several days, utilities have been turned off, and some personal property has been removed, it might be reasonable to assume that the home has been abandoned.

Any property that is left unattended in a public place is assumed to be abandoned, whether or not it is in plain view. For example, if a weapon is thrown into a stream or hidden under some bushes in a park, it is considered to be abandoned and may be seized. However, if an item is left in a public place under circumstances which indicate that the owner intends to reclaim it, and if there is nothing about the item itself that is obviously illegal or connected with a crime, the abandoned property rule would not apply. For example, if a suspect asks another citizen, "Watch my suitcase for a minute while I go into the restroom," the suitcase is not abandoned and could not be searched or seized even if the police believe that it might contain contraband or other evidence.[43]

Evidence of a clearly illegal nature or with an obvious connection to a crime may be seized at any time if it is observed in plain view by a police officer. If a police officer walking down the street glances into a house and sees what appears to be a quantity of narcotics and drug paraphernalia sitting on the living room floor, the officer does not need to get a search warrant before entering the house and seizing the contraband. The same principle applies if evidence is left in plain sight inside an automobile or other vehicle, in the yard around the home, or in any place where it can be seen by anyone who passes by.

An important element in determining whether evidence is in plain view is whether the police officer has made any special effort to look for it. In the case of the narcotics seen through a front window, the plain view rule would not apply if the officer had climbed a ladder and peered in through a second-story window. Furthermore, the rule applies only when an officer has the legal right (either as a police officer or merely as a citizen) to be in the place from which the evidence is observed. For example, everyone has a right to walk by a house on a public sidewalk. However, if the house is set back on the lot away from the sidewalk and is surrounded by a fence, the officer could not climb over the fence, cross the yard, peer in through the window, and then claim that the evidence was in plain view. Despite these restrictions, the courts have been generous in allowing the police to use cameras, binoculars, flashlights, searchlights, and other devices to aid them in seeing things that are presumed to be in plain view.[44]

Plain view does not necessarily mean the officer's visual sense; any of the officer's senses might detect evidence that could be regarded as being in plain view. Ordinarily this would include hearing or smelling something; it is hard to imagine a situation in which an officer tasted or felt something that unexpectedly turned out to be evidence.

## DISPOSITION
## OF SEIZED EVIDENCE

After any seizure of evidence, whether the result of a search or the discovery of evidence in the special circumstances that we have just discussed, it is of paramount importance that the evidence be preserved for use in court. All evidence must be recorded and handled properly so that the chain of custody remains unbroken and there is no chance of contamination.

Problems arise when stolen property is recovered from a suspected thief. Naturally, the rightful owners want their property back, especially if the owners have not yet gone to the trouble and expense of replacing the stolen item. Unfortunately, convicting the thief will be all but impossible unless the stolen item is presented in court as evidence. If the property is returned to its rightful owner, it might not be available weeks or months later when the trial is finally held, and there certainly would be doubts about contamination or even about the identity of the property. Furthermore, people who have recovered their stolen property sometimes lose all interest in helping the police and may balk at being asked to testify in court.

As a rule, therefore, no property should be returned to its rightful owner until it is certain that the item will not be needed as evidence in court.[45] Large items such as a refrigerator or an automobile usually would not be brought into the courtroom anyway, but would be represented by photographs. If a number of separate items are involved, such as a quantity of stolen clothing or jewelry, it may be possible to return all but one or two

*A warrant is not needed if evidence is in plain sight.*

of the items to the owner, retaining only a sample for use as evidence.

The problem is more complicated when a quantity of merchandise is discovered in the possession of a suspect who may have committed several separate crimes, such as a string of burglaries. Usually it will be possible to convict the suspect for only one or two of the crimes. The property involved in those particular crimes certainly can be returned to the rightful owners after the trial. However, the police have no legal basis for returning property to rightful owners if no crime has been proved in court. Fortunately, the laws of most states provide for the settlement of "disputed possession" or "disputed ownership" cases through a relatively simple hearing process before a judge. The police are not directly involved in this process, but may be asked to provide information about the person claiming rightful ownership of the disputed property.[46]

Contraband does not have to be returned to anyone since, by definition, it is something that no one may possess legally.[47]

Items seized as instruments of a crime usually belong to the suspect. After trial, if the accused is convicted, most states demand that the instruments of a crime be forfeited. The law providing for the forfeiture usually indicates what is to be done with the forfeited property; typically, the police are given authority to sell the item at auction and turn the proceeds over to the city or county treasury. In some cases, the forfeiture of an automobile or other vehicle that was used in carrying out a crime is a more severe penalty than the prison sentence imposed on the convicted criminal.

---

ACT IV

## THE BURGLARY AT 1209 MAIN STREET

CITY POLICE DEPARTMENT
SUPPLEMENTAL REPORT OF
INVESTIGATION

CASE NO: G36-1443
INV: D. Cole, #1414
DATE: 20 May 1979

On May 20, 1979, I was assigned to patrol unit B-9. At approximately 10:05 A.M., I was directed to call Gary L. Logan, by telephone, at his place of employment. I did so at approximately 10:15 A.M. Mr. Logan, who was the victim of an apparent burglary that I investigated yesterday, told me that he and his wife returned to their apartment last night (19 May) and were surprised to

---

find clothes and other personal belongings "thrown around the living room." Mr. Logan sounded angry. He asked me to meet him at the apartment during the noon hour, and I agreed.

I arrived at the apartment building at 1209 Main Street at 12:15 P.M. I noticed Mr. Logan's auto parked in front of the building. At the front door, I pressed the intercom button for the Logan apartment; Mr. Logan answered, I identified myself, and Mr. Logan admitted me to the building by electric remote-controlled lock.

When I entered the lobby of the apartment building, I saw Winston Davis, who was known to me as the manager of the building. Mr. Davis had his back turned to me; he was walking down the corridor toward a door that I believe leads to the basement of the building. Mr. Davis was bent over as if he were carrying a heavy object. I said, "Hello," and he turned toward me. When he saw me, he gave no greeting, but hurried toward the door at the end of the corridor and fumbled with the doorknob. I said, "Here, Mr. Davis, let me give you a hand," and I approached him to assist with the door.

Mr. Davis said over his shoulder, "Thanks anyway, but I've got it." As he turned slightly, I saw that he was carrying what appeared to be a television set. I said, "Is that a television set, Mr. Davis?" He stopped and seemed to be uncertain about whether to continue. He turned toward me a little more and I could see that the television set was a portable model, that the nameplate below the controls on the front of the set read "Trueview," and that the lower right-hand corner of the cabinet was chipped.

I said, "Just a minute, Mr. Davis. May I see what you're carrying, please?" Mr.

---

Davis turned to face me. I said, "That looks a lot like the television Mr. Logan described. Is this the Logans' TV?"

Mr. Davis answered, "I don't know. I just found it down in the basement, and I brought it upstairs to find out who it belongs to. It was under a pile of paint rags."

I suggested that we go into the Davises' apartment, call Mr. Logan by telephone, and ask him to come down to identify the television set. Mr. Davis agreed to do this. Because he seemed to be having trouble carrying the heavy TV, I offered to take it from him and he allowed me to do so. I followed Mr. Davis into his apartment and placed the TV set on a coffee table at his suggestion.

At this point, Karen Davis—the wife of Mr. Davis—entered the room from another part of the apartment. On seeing me, Mrs. Davis said very loudly, "What is he doing here? Get him out of here. What's the matter with you?" Mr. Davis said, "Shut up, Karen. It's too late. He already saw the TV set."

I then asked Mr. Davis if he would like to call Mr. Logan. He declined, but suggested that I could do so. I obtained the telephone number from Mr. Davis's tenant list, which is posted on the telephone stand near the entrance to the kitchen. I called Mr. Logan, who was waiting for me in his apartment on the third floor, and asked him to come down to the Davises' apartment. As soon as the telephone call was completed, Mrs. Davis came out of the kitchen and said to me, "Officer, I sure do hope that is the Logans' television. Isn't it lucky that we found it so soon?" I agreed with this statement and then asked, "Who found the set?" Both Mr. and Mrs. Davis answered at the same time, "I did," and then Mr. Davis added, "Well, I guess she

saw it first, but I'm the one who went and got it."

Mrs. Davis said, "I was down in the laundry room and I saw it hidden behind one of the washing machines. I think it was that Mrs. Torres's washing machine, but I'm not sure."

Mr. Logan then arrived at the front door to the Davis apartment and was admitted by Mr. Davis. Mr. Logan examined the television set and said, "That's my TV, all right. That crack on the front is from when I dropped it when we were moving in. Also, the antenna terminal on the back is broken. That's from when my wife's little brother tripped over the antenna wire and pulled it loose."

I thanked Mr. Logan and asked him to go back upstairs and wait for me for a few minutes. He agreed to do so and asked if we had found his stereo yet. The Davises said nothing, so I said that it had not yet been found.

After Mr. Logan had left, I informed Mr. and Mrs. Davis that they were under arrest for the theft of the television set. I read them the *Miranda* warning. Neither volunteered to waive their right to remain silent. I asked them to be seated on the sofa in their living room while I made another phone call; I called Burglary Division and informed Sgt. Edwards of the arrest. At my request, Sgt. Edwards agreed to send a back-up unit and transportation for the prisoners.

After completing this phone call, I asked the Davises for permission to search their apartment, explaining that I wanted to look for the stereo. This request was refused by Mrs. Davis; Mr. Davis said nothing.

Patrol units B-7 and S-23 arrived at approximately 12:45 P.M. Sgt. Henry (S-23) gave the Davises the *Miranda* warnings again and turned them over to Off. King (B-7) for transportation to the station. I asked Sgt. Henry whether it would be all right to search the Davis apartment as a search incidental to the arrest. Sgt. Henry said that this would be improper, but Sgt. Edwards, in Burglary, would be able to obtain a warrant to search the apartment and other areas in the building. I then tagged the television set as evidence; Sgt. Henry and I proceeded to leave. We were met in the lobby by Mr. Logan. I explained to him what had happened and told him that we would have to keep the TV set temporarily as evidence and that Sgt. Edwards or another officer would be in touch with him soon regarding the stereo. This was agreeable to Mr. Logan, who said he needed to get back to work.

I left the apartment building at 12:52 P.M. and returned to the station to file this and related reports.

END OF SUPPLEMENTAL REPORT

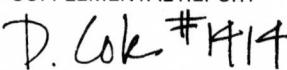

## REFERENCES

1. Edward C. Fisher, *Search and Seizure* (Evanston, Ill.: The Traffic Institute, Northwestern University, 1970), p. 11.

2. J. Shane Creamer, *The Law of Arrest, Search, and Seizure,* 2d ed. (Philadelphia: W. B. Saunders, 1975), pp. 4–5.

3. Fisher, pp. 245–247.

4. Fisher, p. 9.

5. Fisher, p. 120.

6. Creamer, p. 50.

7. Creamer, p. 40.

8. Creamer, p. 59.

9. Fisher, pp. 92–93.

10. Creamer, p. 7.

11. Fisher, pp. 152–154.

12. Fisher, p. 63.

13. Creamer, p. 13.

14. Creamer, p. 14.

15. Creamer, p. 66.

16. Fisher, p. 158.

17. Fisher, pp. 160–161.

18. Creamer, pp. 66–67.

19. Creamer, p. 62.

20. Creamer, p. 68.

21. Fisher, pp. 166–167.

22. Creamer, p. 40.

23. Creamer, p. 40.

24. Fisher, p. 204.

25. Fisher, pp. 190–192.

26. Fisher, p. 182.

27. Creamer, pp. 70–73.

28. Fisher, p. 199.

29. Fisher, pp. 207–211.

30. Creamer, p. 84.

31. Creamer, p. 86.

32. Fisher, pp. 120–121.

33. Fisher, p. 121.

34. Fisher, p. 125.

35. Fisher, pp. 122–123.

36. Fisher, pp. 124–125.

37. Fisher, pp. 111–113.

38. Creamer, p. 85.

39. Fisher, pp. 104–111.

40. Creamer, pp. 76–77.

41. Fisher, pp. 233–239.

42. Fisher, p. 51.

43. Fisher, p. 54.

44. Fisher, pp. 56–57.

45. Fisher, p. 283.

46. Fisher, p. 284.

47. Fisher, pp. 284–286.

1. True or false: The fact that a search warrant could have been obtained, but was not, may be sufficient reason to exclude from trial any evidence that the search produced.

2. Even when the police have a search warrant, they should try to obtain the permission of the property owner before conducting a search because
   a. a warrant is legal only when the owner agrees to it.
   b. they are less likely to be sued for abusing their police powers.
   c. evidence is worthless unless ownership of the incriminating item can be established.
   d. a voluntary search is not subject to as many restrictions as a search under a warrant.
   e. a search without the owner's permission might be considered unreasonable by a jury.

3. Generally, probable cause for a search may be established by
   a. a tip from an informant.
   b. an officer's observation of suspicious behavior.
   c. logical deductions based on existing evidence and known facts.
   d. the officer's observation of a suspect's illegal actions.
   e. all of the above.
   f. none of the above.

4. True or false: Once a search warrant is served, the search should continue until all possible evidence has been located and seized, whether or not the items were mentioned in the warrant, since it is impossible to get a second warrant to search the same place again.

5. A search incidental to an arrest may be made:
   a. immediately after the arrest.
   b. at any time after the arrest.
   c. only by the arresting officer.
   d. after the arrestee's booking into the jail or station lock-up.
   e. only under a valid warrant or owner's consent.

6. Which of the following places or areas can be searched under the rules for a search incidental to an arrest?
   a. the passenger compartment of the suspect's vehicle, if the suspect was in the vehicle at the time of the arrest
   b. the room in which the suspect is arrested
   c. the suspect's clothing and person
   d. any purse, briefcase, suitcase, box, or other container carried by the suspect
   e. the suspect's desk drawers, if the suspect is arrested in his or her office
   f. all of the above
   g. none of the above

7. Before valid consent for a voluntary search can be obtained, the owner of the property must be told
   a. the nature and purpose of the search and of the evidence being sought.
   b. that the owner has the right to refuse or to limit permission.
   c. that the evidence will be used in court to demonstrate the suspect's guilt.

  d. that if the suspect is innocent, giving consent will help to show a cooperative attitude.

  e. all of the above.

  f. none of the above.

8. True or false: Extreme and imminent danger to lives or property is the only legal justification for entering without notice and searching for evidence without a warrant or the owner's permission.

9. Which of the following would not be an example of abandoned property that could be searched and/or seized without a warrant?

  a. an apartment that has been vacated by the tenant, but still contains some of the tenant's belongings

  b. a suitcase left in a locker in a bus station

  c. a shoebox containing stolen money buried in the back yard of the suspect's home

  d. a gun thrown out the window of a moving car

  e. blood-stained clothing found in a garbage can in the alley behind the suspect's home.

10. The first thing that should be done with evidence seized under a search warrant is to

  a. deliver it to the magistrate who issued the warrant.

  b. return it to its rightful owner.

  c. place it in storage.

  d. deliver it to the criminalistics lab for study.

  e. introduce it in the trial of the suspect.

## TOPICS FOR INVESTIGATION

1. If the exclusionary rule were abolished, what other method could be used to enforce the Fourth Amendment guarantees?

2. Do you agree that searching for and seizing evidence when neither the suspect nor the owner of the property is present should be considered reasonable or should a rule be adopted that would require the police to conduct a search only in the presence of the owner of the property?

3. If a search is conducted under a search warrant issued by a magistrate, but the trial judge decides that the warrant was not valid, should the exclusionary rule be used to keep the evidence from being admitted?

4. Should a citizen have the right to refuse to submit to a stop-and-frisk search? If a citizen does refuse or resists being searched, is that resistance in itself probable cause for a more thorough search? What if the citizen tries to flee? How much force should an officer be permitted in conducting a stop-and-frisk search?

5. According to the *Chimel* decision, the primary reason to allow the police to search a suspect and nearby areas at the time of arrest is to protect the officers from a possible hidden weapon. Is this the only justification for such a search that, in your opinion, meets the Fourth Amendment standard of reasonableness?

6. How much good does it do to get a signed waiver before beginning a voluntary search, since the person who signed the waiver can change his or her mind at any time?

7. Suppose a college student, over 18 years old, lives at home. Could the police search the student's bedroom with only the consent of the student's parents?

8. Review Officer Cole's supplemental report in "The Burglary at 1209 Main Street—Act IV." Did Officer Cole act in accordance with the rules and laws that we discussed in this chapter? How did Officer Cole establish probable cause for the arrest of the Davises? Did Officer Cole violate the rules for a voluntary search by entering the Davis apartment? What if the missing stereo had been lying in plain sight on the dining room table of the apartment? Could Officer Cole have searched the Davis apartment under the search incidental to arrest rules or any other search and seizure rules? Or was Sergeant Henry correct in believing that a warrant was needed? Why did Officer Cole not even frisk the Davises prior to or at the time of the arrest? By the way, do you think the Davises are guilty of a crime? Why or why not?

# CHAPTER 18

## THE INVESTIGATOR IN CRIMINAL COURT

AFTER A SUSPECT has been arrested and charged with a crime, the investigator's role changes significantly. No longer is the principal investigator completely responsible for the case. Instead, the investigator is at most an aide to the prosecutor. Now the prosecutor is in charge, making all the important decisions. Sometimes the police investigator is ignored altogether.

However, during the period between the arrest and the trial and during the trial itself, there is much that the investigator can do to help the prosecutor. By working together, they are both more likely to achieve their common goal of convicting the guilty criminal.

## BASIC STEPS IN THE TRIAL PROCESS

Bringing a criminal to justice is a complex, often time-consuming affair. The path from suspicion to accusation to conviction is filled with obstacles and checkpoints designed to ensure that anyone wrongfully accused of a crime is set free at the earliest possible moment. It is not inappropriate to regard each major step as a hurdle that must be crossed.

### INDICTMENT OR INFORMATION

The formal accusation of the suspect is contained in the *indictment* (or presentment), if it is reviewed and approved by a grand jury, or in an *information,* if it is submitted by the prosecutor directly to a judge.

Reviewing proposed indictments is one of the major functions of a grand jury. Ordinarily an indictment is prepared in advance by the prosecutor and offered to the grand jury, which may refuse to issue it (a "no-bill") or may approve it (a "true bill").

An indictment can be presented and issued either before or after a suspect has been ar-

rested. If the indictment is issued before an arrest, usually the indictment is sealed when it is delivered to the court. This means that the name of the accused is not made public until an arrest has been made. In rare instances, a sealed indictment can be issued even though the name of the accused is not yet known. This procedure is employed occasionally in cases involving continuing crimes, such as vice or narcotics trafficking, when the police have accumulated evidence against several conspirators, but do not yet know the names of all of them.

Ordinarily an indictment is sought only after the suspect has been arrested. If the suspect was arrested at the scene of the crime or as a result of direct pursuit, there would have been no opportunity to obtain an indictment ahead of time. Even when the suspect is identified after a prolonged investigation, usually it is quicker and easier to obtain an arrest warrant from a magistrate, make an arrest, and then present the case to a grand jury, rather than seeking an indictment before the arrest.[1]

Some states have abolished the grand jury altogether and use only the process of information. Other states allow an accusation to be filed either by indictment or information, depending on the seriousness of the crime or some other factor. A few states still require an indictment for all felonies and most serious misdemeanors. Where an information is used, it is simply a matter of preparing the formal accusation and presenting it to the appropriate court. The judge reviews the information and, if it is in order, accepts it.[2]

### ESTABLISHMENT OF VENUE

One of the most important steps in the pre-trial process is setting *venue.* Venue simply means "the place where the crime was committed." According to the Constitution, a criminal is entitled to be tried in the judicial district where the alleged crime occurred. The purpose of this provision is to prevent the government from hauling the defendant into a courtroom hundreds of miles away, which would make it very difficult to present witnesses on the defendant's behalf.

In the great majority of cases, venue is easily established. Usually there is no question about where the crime was committed and, therefore, which court has jurisdiction. Sometimes, however, establishing venue can be a problem. For example, a person might be accused of committing a series of crimes over a relatively large geographic area. In which court should the trial be held? Or the criminal might have abducted a victim from one county, shot the victim in another county, and dumped the dead body out of the car in a third county. In which court should this criminal be tried?

Most states have complicated rules for deciding such questions. In general, a case should be tried where the best evidence against the defendant has been found and where the appropriate witnesses are available, all else being equal. If a series of crimes took place, the prosecutor with the strongest evidence usually will take the offender to trial first. If the accused is acquitted, the prosecutors in other jurisdictions may then file charges for the offenses committed in their areas.

The investigator often plays an important role in determining which court has venue, since the evidence must show where the crime took place. Any mistake in establishing venue could result in a mistrial. If the mistake is not discovered until late in the trial process, a retrial in the proper court may be impossible.

Sometimes a defendant will ask for a change of venue. This simply means that the defendant prefers to be tried in a court outside of the jurisdiction in which the alleged crime took place. The only reason for such a request to be granted is the possibility that there is so much prejudice against the defendant within the true venue that a fair trial would be impossible. Defendants who are seeking a change of venue often will introduce evidence that the news media have publicized the alleged crime so extensively that the people in the community are already convinced of the defendant's guilt. Judges are extremely reluctant to grant a change of venue, because moving a trial to a distant court is expensive, is inconvenient, and places a severe burden on the prosecution. However, if there is ample reason to believe that there is widespread prejudice against the defendant, a change of venue will be approved. Again, the police investigator's actions may have an important bearing on this decision. If the investigator is careless or irresponsible in providing information to the news media, excessive prejudicial publicity about the crime and the defendant may make a change of venue unavoidable.[3]

PRETRIAL HEARING

After the accused has been arrested and presented to a magistrate, the case is assigned to a particular court for trial. Within a few days, the judge assigned to the case holds a *pretrial hearing* (also called a preliminary hearing). This is an important step in which the evidence against the accused will be reviewed.

The judge considers the evidence, assuming it to be true. If it is deemed insufficient for the charges, either the charges must be

ANSWERS TO STUDY CLUES
1. False   2. b   3. False   4. b   5. f

*Concluding the Investigation*

reduced to some lesser included offense or the accused may be set free. If the judge considers the evidence to be sufficient, the case may proceed.[4]

During the pretrial hearing, the defendant is given the first opportunity to enter a *plea,* or a formal answer to the charges. There are four possible pleas: not guilty, guilty, nolo contendere, or no plea at all.[5]

A plea of *not guilty* means that the defendant denies the charge and wishes to have the case tried. A plea of *guilty* means that the defendant admits the charge, waives the right of trial, and is ready to be sentenced; however, it is not unusual for the judge to disregard a guilty plea and insist on a trial if, in the judge's opinion, there is any possibility that the defendant is not guilty or has been coerced or deceived into pleading guilty.

The plea of *nolo contendere* (a Latin phrase that means "I do not contest it") means that the defendant, though not admitting guilt, does not wish to be tried and is willing to accept whatever punishment the court imposes. This plea is not often entered in ordinary criminal cases, so it does not normally concern the investigator. If the defendant enters *no plea* at all ("standing mute"), the judge is required by law to enter a plea of not guilty.

Another part of the pretrial hearing reinforces the defendant's rights. The judge usually recites the *Miranda* warnings once again and ensures that the defendant has satisfactory counsel. If the defendant has not had an opportunity to confer with an attorney, the hearing will be postponed or suspended until this has been done.

The most important part of the pretrial hearing, from the point of view of both the prosecutor and the investigator, is the presentation of the prosecutor's evidence. The prosecutor must inform the court of the na-

ture of the case against the defendant and of the primary points of evidence. Usually it is not necessary to present witnesses; the prosecutor merely tells the court what the witnesses have said. However, the defense may challenge the prosecution and insist that witnesses be produced; in this case there is no alternative to the presentation of witnesses in order to give testimony and to be cross-examined by the defense.[6]

It is not legally necessary for the prosecutor to offer every bit of evidence during the pretrial hearing, only enough is required to show the reason for believing the defendant to be guilty. The defense usually presents no evidence during the hearing, but may challenge the prosecution's evidence; if the defense has an especially significant witness, such as someone who can establish a strong alibi, the witness may be called to testify. More important, the defense learns the main elements of the prosecutor's evidence and therefore gains an opportunity to prepare rebuttal evidence for the trial.

Finally, the pretrial hearing is an opportunity for both sides to introduce various legal *motions:* requests that the judge decide specific matters of law or of trial procedure. The number and variety of pretrial motions has grown enormously in recent years, partly as a result of heightened concern for the constitutional rights of criminal defendants and partly in an effort to settle as many issues as possible before the trial itself begins.[7]

The defendant may waive the pretrial hearing in order to get the trial underway as quickly as possible. Usually this is done only if the defense believes that the prosecution's case is weak; the defense does not want to give the prosecutor more time to discover new evidence or additional witnesses, thereby strengthening the case.

## PLEA BARGAINING

At any stage of the pretrial procedure, the prosecutor and the defense may engage in *plea bargaining*. In essence, a plea bargain is an agreement between the two sides that the prosecutor will ask for a certain kind of punishment if the defendant will plead guilty, thereby avoiding the necessity of a trial.

Plea bargaining is a topic of great controversy in criminal justice circles, controversy that we have no intention of settling or even of furthering in this text. However, this is one step in the trial process that, in our opinion, the investigator should ignore altogether. It is up to the prosecutor, not the investigator, to decide whether a reduced charge and a comparatively light sentence serve the ends of justice.

We might add, however, that some extremely interesting statistics were developed in a study of the investigative process by the Rand Corporation. Two different law enforcement agencies were studied; in department A, most criminal investigations were unusually thorough and well documented, while in department B most cases were handled in a routine, slipshod manner. Of the cases studied, almost 89 percent of the defendants charged by department A were convicted of the original charges; only about 11 percent pleaded guilty to lesser charges (which suggests plea bargaining), and none had the charges dismissed. However, in department B only about 44 percent of the defendants were convicted of the original charges, 23 percent pleaded guilty to lesser charges, and another 23 percent had the charges dismissed. It seems fair to conclude, then, that the answer to the problem of plea bargaining for light sentences is to conduct an investigation so thoroughly that conviction on the original charge is virtually inescapable.[8]

## ARRAIGNMENT AND PLEA

The last step in the pretrial process is the *arraignment*. The defendant is brought into the court once again to be formally charged and to enter a formal plea. If there are any pretrial issues that were not settled at the earlier hearing, they must be settled now.[9]

The significance of the arraignment has been greatly reduced since the increased use of an early pretrial hearing and the invention of the other steps in the pretrial process. In the past, the arraignment might have been the first time that the defendant heard the accusation. Now, however, the arraignment is largely a formality, the outcome of which has been settled in advance. If a plea bargain has been agreed on by both sides, it is presented at the arraignment. The judge has the option to accept the agreed-on plea or to reject it and is not necessarily bound to impose the sentence that was agreed on.[10]

In states where arraignment has become virtually an empty ceremony, the trial begins immediately after the defendant enters a not guilty plea. In most states, there may be an interval of a week or so between arraignment and trial.

## THE INVESTIGATOR AND THE PROSECUTION

### ASSEMBLY AND DELIVERY OF EVIDENCE

The first step in preparing a case for prosecution is the preparation of the case report that we described in Chapter 14. At that time, we were concerned with assembling the evidence prior to filing charges and making an arrest. However, the case report also will be the basis for the final report delivered to the prosecutor prior to the trial. The only difference is that the final report should contain any new evidence or information, and any errors in the previous report should be corrected. In particular, the final case report should contain the results of any additional investigations requested by the prosecutor or, if necessary, an explanation if a requested investigation was not conducted or produced no useful results.[11]

All physical evidence in the case should be removed from storage, carefully checked to be sure that it is properly marked for identification, packaged to ensure that it will not be damaged, and delivered to the prosecutor. Naturally, a receipt must be obtained to maintain the chain of custody. If the prosecutor has no facilities for storing evidence, it should be kept in police custody until the day that it is actually to be introduced in the trial, but the investigator still must check well in advance to be sure that it is ready. More than once, police officers have had to admit, to their enormous embarrassment, that crucial evidence could not be found at the last minute.

## WITNESSES

Some prosecutors prefer to have their own staffs locate and interview witnesses one last time before a trial. However, if the prosecutor does not take the initiative, the principal investigator should.

First and foremost, every witness must be found. It is not unusual for witnesses to "get lost" between the time of the crime and the time of the trial, perhaps months later. Rarely will a witness think to notify the police of a change of address, even when the police have asked the witness to do so. Sometimes a trial must be postponed until a crucial witness can be found, although judges are extremely reluctant to do this.

Once the witness is found, the investigator should inform the witness of the date, time, and place for the trial. It is well worth the effort to reinterview the witness at this point. Many witnesses need to have their memories refreshed by discussing the events of the crime, which may have taken place several months ago. The mere act of talking about the incident will generally serve this purpose. However, if a witness seems to have a serious problem in remembering some parts of the event or says things that clearly contradict the known facts and the witness's former testimony, it is not improper for the investigator to remind the witness of the previous statements. It may even be helpful to read to the witness a transcript of the original interview.

However, the investigator must not put words into a witness's mouth. A witness may have a legitimate reason for changing a story or may have decided not to cooperate any further. Any attempt by the investigator to intimidate or coerce the witness will backfire, certainly producing a hostile witness and possibly ruining the whole case if the witness complains to the judge.

Both sides have the power to subpoena a reluctant witness, but this power is used only if the witness's testimony is absolutely vital. However, it is not unusual for a witness to ask for a subpoena, since some employers will not permit the witness to take time off from work otherwise. The investigator should make sure that any such request is honored by the prosecutor. Some prosecutors and defense attorneys routinely subpoena all witnesses, even though it is not necessary for those who willingly testify.

Again, some prosecutors prefer to take all these steps on their own. They may feel that witnesses will be more comfortable talking to lawyers rather than to police officers, or that staff members trained in the law will be better able to evaluate the witness's ability to present testimony. If so, the investigator should stay out of the prosecutor's way but offer to provide any assistance needed.

## SURPRISE CONTRA-EVIDENCE

Once the trial is underway, the investigator often serves only to deliver evidence, to provide transportation for witnesses, and to testify at the appropriate time.

However, there is always the possibility that the defense will introduce new contra-evidence during the trial. We do not wish to overstate the likelihood that this will happen; very few criminal trials resemble the high drama of legal epics on television. Furthermore, it is not considered proper legal procedure for either side to introduce new, unexpected evidence in the middle of a trial, unless the evidence has just been discovered. If the defense discovers contra-evidence that provides a genuine alibi for the defendant, the prosecutor should be informed of it outside of the courtroom so that a new plea bargain can be struck or, if the evidence clearly shows the defendant's innocence, the charges may be dropped.

Nevertheless, it does sometimes happen that the defense will uncover new evidence that casts substantial doubt on the defendant's guilt. Occasionally a witness will blurt out something that contradicts the known facts or that puts the case in a different light. Usually these sudden revelations turn out to be red herrings, but there is always the possibility that newly discovered contra-evidence will demonstrate the defendant's innocence.

Any unanticipated contra-evidence introduced during a trial must be investigated immediately by the principal investigator. If the surprise evidence is very significant, it may even be necessary to ask for a recess in the trial until a proper investigation can be completed;

of course, this decision must be left up to the prosecutor.

Because there is the possibility of surprise evidence in any criminal trial, it is an excellent idea for the principal investigator to be in the courtroom throughout the entire trial. Most investigators are sufficiently conscientious to do this, but some consider a routine trial to be a boring waste of time. Boring it may be, but time is never wasted by an investigator who does the whole job.

## GIVING TESTIMONY

Testifying in court is just as much a part of a police officer's job as gathering evidence, interviewing witnesses, making arrests, or practicing on the firing range. It is hard to imagine any criminal trial in which the principal investigator or the arresting officer would not be an essential witness for the prosecution.

Nevertheless, many police officers resent and dislike the obligation to appear in court. Testifying always involves the risk that the officer's competence, integrity, and professionalism will be attacked by the defense. It is only natural to avoid such challenges to one's ego.

There are two things that the officer can do to reduce the likelihood of being personally humiliated in court (and of losing the case against the defendant). First, the officer can learn as much as possible about the trial procedure, in order to understand what is going to happen and why. Second, the officer can be prepared to make the best possible presentation of evidence.

## PREPARATION

Unless the prosecutor specifically asks the investigator to appear in uniform, civilian clothes should be worn. Clothing should be conservative and comfortable, and one's overall appearance should be neat and clean. Jewelry should be kept to an absolute minimum. In particular, the officer should not wear any pins, rings, or other insignia associated with political, religious, or fraternal organizations.

Before testifying, the investigator should meet one last time with the prosecutor (in a place removed from the courtroom). The prosecutor should be able to specify exactly what information and evidence the officer will be expected to present. If there are any areas of uncertainty, they should be discussed until both the officer and the prosecutor have a clear understanding of what the officer is able to say truthfully. It is just as important for the officer to know what points the prosecutor does not want to bring up, perhaps because another witness will be able to testify on those points more effectively. The prosecutor also may be able to advise the officer about probable defense tactics and the way in which they should be handled.

The final step in preparation should be an exhaustive review of the officer's personal field notes. The notes are the basis and original source for the entire case. Every point of the officer's testimony must be consistent with the notes made at the time that the information was first discovered. There are both advantages and disadvantages in taking one's notes to the witness stand, but in either case the officer must be completely familiar with every fact, measurement, and detail recorded in the notes as well as the information in all the reports, summaries, and records of the case.

## PRESENTATION BEFORE A GRAND JURY

For most police officers, testifying before a grand jury is a far less anxiety-producing experience than testifying in a trial. Indeed, many officers regard the grand jury as merely an extension of the prosecutor's office and, therefore, as being "on our side." Although this is not an accurate perception, neither is it particularly harmful.

A police officer testifying before a grand jury should confine the testimony to personal knowledge based on direct observation and physical evidence. Reasonable conclusions may be drawn but they must be firmly rooted in the evidence. Speculation and unsubstantiated theories or hunches are likely to have serious repercussions.

When testifying before the grand jury, the officer should have personal field notes and other documents in hand. Not only will this help to avoid lapses of memory or unintentional misstatements, but it also will create in the jurors' minds an impression of professionalism and thoroughness. There is no danger of giving the defense access to the notes, since the defense ordinarily does not participate in the grand jury proceeding.

## PRESENTATION DURING THE TRIAL

While testifying, the officer should avoid distracting mannerisms or gestures that might indicate nervousness, evasiveness, or indifference to the proceedings. All answers should be directed to the jury in a firm, clear voice. The only other person who should be addressed by the officer is the judge, if a problem arises or if there is a question about the proper procedure.

Every question must be answered unless one of the attorneys objects; in this case the witness should remain silent until the judge rules on the objection and, if the objection is overruled, instructs the witness to answer. Sarcasm, scornful comments, or other words or expressions that display any attitude or

*It is important for a police officer to present a good appearance while testifying. Neat, conservative attire, with no distracting jewelry, helps to make the right impression. Even more important is the officer's thorough preparation and professional attitude.*

duty as a witness is to present evidence, not to comment on it or to express feelings about it.

A witness is entitled to have aids to the memory such as notes or documents, and these would include the investigator's field notes and other records. Such materials are not subject to the usual rules of evidence, but they are subject to examination by both attorneys. In other words, if you use your field notes while testifying, the defense counsel has the right to examine them.

Strictly speaking, the right of examination applies only to those notes actually consulted by a witness. However, it is not always possible to put a precise limitation on what the defense counsel can look at, since the officer might refer to any of the notes that are actually present. Therefore, if you decide to bring your notes to the witness stand, bring only those that apply to the case being tried and only those that will be necessary to refresh your memory on the points about which you will testify. For example, there is

no requirement that you bring all your notes from the case just because you need your field sketches and measurements.

When notes are used, be sure that everything in them is consistent with your testimony and with the other evidence in the case or, if there are any inconsistencies, that you can explain them in a logical, reasonable manner.

## DIRECT EXAMINATION

When each witness takes the stand for the first time, the opposing side has the right to challenge the witness's qualifications to testify. Ordinarily this right is not used when the witness will testify only about personal knowledge and observation. But a challenge can be expected when a witness is presented as an expert who is competent to offer opinions, to draw conclusions, and generally to evaluate and interpret the evidence. The investigator and other police personnel often are presented as expert witnesses, and thus their qualifications must be established.

The prosecutor will ask the officer to state his or her name, rank, and assignment within the police agency. Several questions will be asked about the officer's experience and training and about any awards or commendations that the officer has received.

The defense counsel then may challenge the officer's expertise, usually by concentrating on the number of cases that the officer has investigated in the past or the number of arrests that the officer has made for the same type of crime. There is no magic number of past experiences that qualifies a person as an expert. The prosecutor should point out that the officer has been tested and evaluated by senior officials of the agency and has been found to be competent; otherwise, the officer never would have been assigned to perform the investigation.

Once the witness's qualifications have been established, the prosecutor begins direct examination. The goal is to present the officer's evidence as clearly and completely as possible. The relevance, materiality, and competence of the evidence must be shown before each new item of evidence is offered; the process by which this is done is called "building a foundation for the evidence."

For example, suppose that you are going to testify that you arrested the defendant on the charge of armed robbery based on a radio broadcast in which you were given a description of the suspect's vehicle. Before the prosecutor asks you about the arrest itself, you will be asked a long series of questions about the radio broadcast, your location when you first saw the suspect vehicle, your ability to see the vehicle clearly, your ability to distinguish a particular vehicle from others of similar style and color, and so on. You will be asked to describe, step by step, how you stopped the suspect vehicle, how you approached the suspect, how you verified the

suspect's identity, and what you did to determine that the defendant was in fact the person who had been described in the radio broadcast as an armed robber. Often the questions will seem tedious. However, if the prosecutor is successful in building a strong foundation for your evidence, you will be that much better prepared to withstand the defense counsel's attacks later.

Ordinarily, leading questions cannot be asked on direct examination. A leading question is one that suggests a particular answer, such as "When you saw the suspect's vehicle approaching you, did you recognize it as the car described in the radio broadcast? Was it a blue 1975 Ford sedan with Illinois license plates?" Instead, the witness must be asked questions that are relatively open-ended; "Why did you decide to stop this particular car when you saw it approaching you? What kind of car was it?"

This rule is not as rigidly enforced when an expert witness is testifying. The reason is that the expert's opinions and the reasons for those opinions are more important than the expert's observations of ordinary facts. Thus, the prosecutor (or the defense counsel) is allowed to lead the expert witness more rapidly through the presentation of simple facts. The rules against leading questions may be invoked, however, when an expert is asked to state an opinion or conclusion.

A leading question is not the same as a loaded question. A loaded question is one that cannot be answered without saying something that is either misleading or embarrassing; the classic example is "Have you stopped beating your children yet?" A loaded question is always improper and generally will not be permitted; a leading question is improper most of the time, but not always.

Any witness's testimony is likely to be interrupted from time to time by the opposing counsel's objections. This is often very irritating to the witness, especially when the objections come in the midst of a long, complicated series of questions. However, the defense counsel has not only a right to object to improper questions, but a legal and ethical obligation to do so (the prosecutor, of course, has the same right and obligation during the cross-examination of the witness). If the counsel fails to object to an improper question when it is asked, nothing can be done to correct the error afterward.

Objections can be raised for a number of reasons. The objection might be to a question that is misleading, irrelevant, immaterial, or leading. Many objections are intended to challenge the witness's competence to state a fact based on personal knowledge or to state an opinion as a qualified expert. Objections also are raised about points of legal procedure and rules of evidence.

These interruptions and disruptions are extremely aggravating, but they cannot be helped. The police officer on the witness stand must remain calm and unperturbed while the judge and the lawyers do their job. It will not help for the officer to display annoyance or impatience. If an objection is overruled, the judge will instruct the witness to answer the question. If there has been a lengthy argument over the objection, the attorney will repeat the question first. However, if the objection is sustained, the attorney must ask a different question. In either case, the officer should answer the question just as if there had been no interruption. Under no circumstances should an officer attempt to sneak in testimony that the judge has ruled to be improper.

### CROSS-EXAMINATION

After the prosecutor has completed the direct examination of the witness, the defense coun-

sel begins cross-examination. The cross-examination must be restricted to the issues that have been raised during the direct examination. Questions can be asked about the facts themselves (as related by the witness), about the witness's competence to observe the facts or to hold the opinions that the witness has expressed, and about the witness's general competence.

Leading questions can be used more freely in this process than during direct examination. This can lead an unwary officer into a common trap. For example, the officer may have testified that the suspect's vehicle was a blue 1975 Ford sedan. Later, the defense counsel may ask, "Now, Officer Adams, when you saw this car approaching you in a driving rainstorm, with a heavy stream of traffic passing you in both directions, did you realize at once that this light bluish-gray car was the vehicle that had been described in a radio broadcast sometime earlier?" A simple affirmative answer to such a question would not be very convincing. Fortunately, a witness always has the right to give a full answer in his or her own words, even if the attorney demands a yes-or-no answer. The way to deal with such a question is to say, "Yes. However, at that time it was no longer a driving rainstorm; the rain had let up. Also, the car was definitely blue in color, not gray, and it was a 1975 Ford sedan with Illinois license plates. As I said earlier, I had written down this description when it was given over the radio about five minutes earlier."

Occasionally an attorney may act impatient and interrupt the witness, insisting, "Just answer the question with yes or no!" If the defense counsel does this to an officer, usually the prosecutor will object. If the prosecutor fails to object, the witness should answer the question first, then complain to the judge in a respectful manner, "Your Honor,

*Cross-examination by the defense attorney can be a traumatic experience. The only remedy is to remain calm and take ample time before answering each question.*

I'm afraid my answer to that question may have been misleading. I would like to give a more complete answer."

On the other hand, a witness under cross-examination may not go beyond the question that has been asked. For example, if the defense counsel asks, "Was it raining at that time?" the witness would not be allowed to reply, "Yes, but the sun was shining through a break in the clouds and the street lights were on, so I could see everything clearly." Such an answer would produce an objection from the defense counsel that the witness was "unresponsive" and a rebuke from the judge.

### INTRODUCTION OF EXHIBITS AND PHYSICAL EVIDENCE

Either the prosecutor or the defense counsel will present exhibits to assist a witness in testifying and will offer physical evidence that is relevant to the issues in the trial. Physical evidence is often presented first as an exhibit.

The procedure is very simple. At an ap-propriate point the attorney will present an object and ask the witness, "Do you recognize this object? Will you please explain what it is?" If it is an exhibit designed to assist in presenting testimony, the witness might say, "This is a drawing that was made by a police artist, based on my sketches of the crime scene, showing the locations of the major items of evidence." In the same way, if it is an item of physical evidence, the witness might say, "This is a pistol that I found under the driver's seat in the defendant's automobile."

An object presented as an exhibit to assist a witness in testifying does not have to be introduced as evidence. Once an item is introduced into evidence, it becomes a permanent part of the trial record and must be available for the jury to examine later. If an exhibit is challenged on the grounds of relevance, materiality, or competence, or if the attorney who offers the item decides that it has not made a very good impression on the jury, it may be withdrawn.

# DEFENSE TACTICS

## GOALS OF THE DEFENSE COUNSEL

It is important to remember that the defendant does not have to prove his or her innocence. In theory, the defense does not have to prove anything; the prosecution must prove the defendant's guilt beyond all reasonable doubt. Thus, the principal goal of the defense is to raise doubts in the jurors' minds.

However, defense lawyers know that the presumption of innocence is only a legal theory, and, in fact, most people are inclined to think that anyone who is charged with a crime is likely to be guilty. Therefore, the defense must overcome this attitude by persuading the jury of two things: first, that the defendant might not have committed the crime, and second, that the police are mistaken for a particular reason. The second point is often easier to establish than the first, provided the defense can persuade the jury that the police are incompetent or malicious or both. Once a jury is convinced that that is the case, it is much easier to convince them that the defendant is innocent.

## PURPOSES OF THE DEFENSE'S ATTACK

Every question asked by the defense counsel has a definite purpose; a competent attorney will not waste time with random questions, hoping to turn up some unexpected weakness in the prosecution's case.

It is not a good idea for the police officer who is testifying to try to figure out the motive behind each question; the officer is likely to guess wrong, and the question still must be answered truthfully. However, many questions can be answered in more than one way, especially when an expert witness is offering opinions and conclusions. An awareness of the defense's purpose may help the witness to avoid giving answers that are ultimately misleading and that contribute to the defense's goals.

**The witness's competence.** Many of the questions posed by the defense will be intended to reveal the officer's lack of competence. Bear in mind that a witness can be incompetent in more than one sense. Usually the defense will try to show not that the officer is mentally deficient, but that the officer has had insufficient training, little experience in investigating complex cases, and so on.

The defense also may argue that while the officer is generally competent, for some reason he or she is not competent to offer the facts or opinions presented in direct testimony. For example, the defense could ask questions to show that the officer could not have seen the suspect's vehicle clearly or that a pistol owned by the defendant could not have been the murder weapon despite the firearms examiner's opinion.

**The methods used in the investigation.** Many of the defense counsel's questions will attack the methods used by the police to investigate the crime, identify the suspect, and effect the arrest. The defense will suggest that the methods were inappropriate, that the results of laboratory examinations are not conclusive (perhaps they could be interpreted differently by equally experienced investigators), or that the methods were incomplete. The defense may be fairly knowledgeable about standard investigative procedures and may ask such questions as "Did you conduct a paraffin test on the defendant's hands, face, and clothing at the time of arrest? Why not? If you had conducted such a test, wouldn't the results have shown that the defendant probably had not fired a gun?" Unless the officer has good, reasonable answers, not only will these questions suggest that the police are incompetent, but they may suggest that the police rushed to conclusions in their eagerness to arrest someone.

**Lack of probable cause.** Since the Supreme Court and the lower courts have placed increasing emphasis in recent years on the necessity of having probable cause prior to an arrest or search, this is a favorite point of attack for defense attorneys. The officer should expect to face such questions as these: "Why did you decide to stop this particular car and not any of the other cars that were going by at the time? Was this the only blue Ford sedan you saw that day? Did you stop all the others? At what point, and for what reason, did you decide to search the suspect? Did you decide to arrest the defendant before or after the search? Had you already read the *Miranda* warnings before the search?"

These can be troublesome questions; if not answered carefully, the whole case can be lost in a moment. Remember, there must have been probable cause *before* a search or an arrest. If a warrant was the basis for either the search or the arrest, the defense naturally has to attack the warrant rather than the officer's judgment; this is the best reason for obtaining a warrant whenever possible.

The officer also must be careful not to overstate the probable cause. Remember that, legally, the *Miranda* warnings must be given as soon as there is sufficient reason to arrest the suspect. If the officer testifies during the trial that there was probable cause for an arrest, but that the arrest was delayed while the suspect was questioned and searched, this would be even worse than having had too little probable cause. Probable cause does not mean certain proof; it merely means that the officer had some good reason to be suspicious and, therefore, performed the reasonable steps necessary to either confirm or allay that suspicion.

**Mistaken identity and contradictory evidence.** Whenever possible, the defense will try to show that the officer might be mistaken about the identity of the suspect or of some crucial item of evidence. It is a rare case that does not have some contradictory evidence or testimony for the defense to exploit; in the real world, events do not resolve themselves into nice, neat patterns. There is no point in trying to avoid or cover up contradictions, since the defense will seize on them as proof that the police are prejudiced against the poor, hapless defendant. Instead, the officer should answer a question about contradictions honestly: "I don't know why the other witness said that the assailant was blond, when everyone can see that the defendant has dark hair." Ultimately, it is the prosecutor's responsibility, not the officer's, to resolve contradictions to the jury's satisfaction.

**Prejudice and hasty conclusions.** If the defense can persuade the jury that the police in general or the individual officer had some prejudice against the defendant, this alone may be enough to raise reasonable doubt in the jurors' minds. One way to accomplish this purpose is to show that there was, or might have been, evidence of the defendant's innocence but that the police failed to investigate it. Another way to suggest prejudice is to ask questions about the officer's personal feelings and attitudes toward people of the defendant's ethnic group, age, and so on: "Tell me, Officer Adams, do you feel uneasy about patrolling the slum area where the defendant lives? In your opinion, are most young people like the defendant more or less likely to be involved in drug abuse than, say, a middle-aged, middle-class citizen like yourself?"

The only way to deal with this sort of question is to be able to answer truthfully that just as much effort was spent trying to demonstrate the defendant's innocence as was spent on proving guilt. That is why we have insisted throughout this book that all contra-evidence must be investigated thoroughly and every alibi must be checked out, no matter how ridiculous or unlikely it seems.

## AGGRESSIVE VERSUS FRIENDLY QUESTIONING

The attitude of the defense counsel is as much a part of the attorney's technique as the questions that are asked. Many attorneys see a trial not so much as a rational debate, but more as a dramatic contest in which they must act out a role for the benefit of the jury.

One role the defense attorney can play is that of the stalwart defender of the oppressed. The attorney hopes to convince the jury that the defendant is really the victim of the police, who in their excessive zeal and disregard for truth and justice have trampled on the poor defendant's rights. The attorney's questions are aggressive almost to the point of open hostility; with every question the attorney is suggesting to the jury, "You see? The cop is obviously lying!"

Aggressive questioning can take several different forms, depending partly on what the judge will let the attorney get away with. One technique is to throw a series of questions at the witness as rapidly as possible; as soon as the witness starts to answer a question, the attorney interrupts with the next question. Another technique is to ask a long, complicated question, often containing several misleading statements, and then to demand a yes-or-no answer. A third technique is to keep going over the same point, again and again, with slightly rephrased questions, in hope of forcing the witness to contradict earlier testimony. Yet another technique is "sudden silence": the attorney asks a question as if it were extremely significant, although in fact it may relate to a fairly minor point; after the witness answers, the attorney will glare at the witness with an expression that

suggests utter disbelief, but will say nothing, as if expecting the witness to offer some further explanation.

The best way to counter all these aggressive techniques is the same: to remain calm, answer each question as clearly and thoroughly as possible, and then say no more. A witness is entitled to a few moments to consider an answer before stating it. When questions are being fired in rapid succession, stop answering. Wait a full three seconds (count silently to six) after each question. If the defense counsel objects to the slow answers, so much the better; there is no rule that sets a time limit on a witness's answers.

As we said earlier, a witness always has the right to explain an answer if a simple yes-or-no answer would be incomplete or misleading. If a question is unusually complicated, be sure that you understand it before you try to answer. If parts of the question seem inherently contradictory or misleading, ask the attorney to repeat the question. If the question actually contains two or more questions, answer each of them in order; do not answer only the last one. If questions are repeated over and over, answer them patiently over and over again, being especially careful not to add anything that you have not said before nor to leave out anything significant. Sooner or later, the defense counsel will give up and will move on to another point, or the prosecutor will object to the badgering.

The best response to the sudden silence technique is to remain equally silent. Answer each question as it is asked, and then say nothing more; just sit patiently until the next question is asked. Above all, never respond to the defense counsel's aggressiveness with anger or annoyance.

Not all defense attorneys adopt the aggressive attitude. Some choose the opposite extreme of undue friendliness. In effect, they are suggesting to the jury, "Obviously there's been some unfortunate misunderstanding here, but we good-hearted folks will get it all straightened out eventually." Meanwhile, the "friendly" attorney hopes to lull the witness into a false sense of confidence, catch the witness in some minor misstatement or contradiction, and then pounce on it as proof of the misunderstanding. The friendly attorney often uses the repetitive question technique. Some attorneys deliberately appear to be bumbling and uncertain, not only to mislead the witness, but also to arouse the jury's sympathy in the hope that that sympathy will be transferred to the defendant.

Regardless of the defense attorney's antics (prosecuting attorneys sometimes use very similar tactics for essentially the same reasons), the police officer must not rise to the bait. A courteous and respectful attitude, regardless of provocation, is much more likely to gain the respect and confidence of the jury. There is no reason for the police officer to feel hostility toward the defense attorney, who has a job to do and does it as well as he or she can. In our system of justice the defense attorney is indispensable. It is the function of the attorney not to attack you but to challenge you, to force you to do your job to the best of your ability, and in so doing to protect the rights and the freedom of both the victim and the accused.

## OBJECTIVITY

In the introductory chapter of this book, we pointed out that the crime problem is very real and serious in the United States today, but it is not always the problem that people think it is. The great majority of reported crimes are relatively minor; serious crimes are actually infrequent, considering the size and diversity of our population. Furthermore, the most serious crimes, such as murder and rape, are most often committed by friends, acquaintances, and even relatives of the victims. In short, crime is not what it seems to be. Much of what appears to be logical and commonsensical turns out to be wrong.

Law enforcement is a profession that tries to establish orderly routines for the discovery of surprises. The practitioners of this profession are, for the most part, men and women who take their responsibility seriously. The essence of the investigator's job is to discover who perpetrated a given crime and to gather sufficient evidence to prove it in court. It is a job that demands a certain level of intellectual effort and imagination along with a great deal of persistence and a whole host of technical skills. More than anything else, however, the job of criminal investigator requires a certain attitude.

Some would call this attitude *skepticism:* a tendency to disbelieve whatever appears to be true until there is overwhelming, tangible proof. While skepticism certainly is part of the investigator's intellectual armor, we believe that the ideal investigator must go beyond skepticism to objectivity. By this, we mean that the investigator must avoid making judgments, taking sides, or favoring one person over another. It is hard not to be sympathetic toward the victim of a crime, and that sympathy naturally produces the opposite feelings toward the perpetrator. This natural antagonism toward the offender may be reinforced if the criminal turns out to be a generally unpleasant person, as many of them are.

The danger is that the investigator will respond to these normal emotional reactions rather than to the evidence itself. Consequently, mistakes are made. Charges are brought against the wrong person, or, worse yet, the investigation is mishandled out of haste and overzealousness so that the guilty offender must be set free.

You cannot and should not avoid feeling sympathy for the victims of crime. However, you must not let that sympathy override the professional discipline and sound judgment by which successful investigations are made. The key word, again, is objectivity. To discover the truth, you must be prepared for surprises, because the truth often is not what you thought it would be. The person who reported a crime may be the perpetrator. The victim may be more guilty than the offender. The suspect may be innocent. The most ridiculous alibi may be true.

It is relatively easy to be open-minded when you begin an investigation. However, as evidence is discovered, as the victim's suffering becomes apparent, as the offender's sordid and despicable behavior becomes known, you will find it harder to keep that objectivity. The ultimate test comes in the courtroom. If you see a trial as some kind of contest that you will win or lose, depending on the jury's verdict, then you have already lost.

Guilty criminals do go free, not because of unfair court decisions or misguided juries but because of inadequate police investigations. We would like to think that the skills, techniques, and procedures described in this text will enable you to conduct a successful investigation every time. However, all the skills, techniques, and procedures in the world will do you no good if you lose your objectivity.

The converse is also true: if you keep your objectivity and a healthy dose of skepticism, and if you are given the time to do your work properly, there is no crime that will remain unsolved forever and no criminal who will avoid just punishment.

## REFERENCES

Most of the contents of this chapter, concerning the officer in the courtroom, is based on unpublished training materials developed by the Texas Department of Public Safety, Austin, Texas. Another excellent reference is C. A. Pantaleoni, *Handbook of Courtroom Demeanor and Testimony* (Englewood Cliffs, N.J.: Prentice-Hall, 1971).

1. Ronald J. Waldron, et al., *The Criminal Justice System* (Boston: Houghton Mifflin, 1976), p. 208.

2. A. C. Germann, Frank D. Day, and Robert R. J. Gallati, *Introduction to Law Enforcement and Criminal Justice,* rev. ed. (Springfield, Ill: Charles C Thomas, 1973), pp. 239–240.

3. Germann, Day, and Gallati, p. 240.

4. Waldron et al., pp. 45–46.

5. Germann, Day, and Gallati, pp. 243–244.

6. Germann, Day, and Gallati, pp. 240–241.

7. Waldron et al., p. 47.

8. Peter W. Greenwood, Jan M. Chaiken, and Joan Petersilia, *The Criminal Investigation Process* (Lexington, Mass.: D. C. Heath, 1977), pp. 182–190.

9. Germann, Day, and Gallati, p. 243.

10. Waldron et al., p. 147.

11. Paul B. Weston and Kenneth M. Wells, *Elements of Criminal Investigation* (Englewood Cliffs, N.J.: Prentice-Hall, 1971), pp. 110–111.

## REVIEW OF THE EVIDENCE

1. The police investigator's principal function during a trial is
    a. to present the evidence against the accused.
    b. to make certain that the defendant is present.
    c. to perform any investigations requested by the judge or jury.
    d. to assist the prosecutor.
    e. to ensure that the spectators remain orderly.
2. A sealed indictment may be issued by a grand jury when
    a. there is not enough evidence for a regular indictment.
    b. the accused is not guilty.
    c. the prosecutor wishes to keep the evidence secret.
    d. the accused is well known and would be embarrassed by a public indictment.
    e. the accused has not yet been arrested.
3. True or false: If the defendant pleads guilty, the judge is required by law to accept the plea.
4. The phrase "building a foundation for the evidence" refers to
    a. admission of physical evidence during the trial.
    b. objection to the testimony of a witness.
    c. all the questions asked during direct examination.
    d. questions designed to establish the relevance, materiality, and competence of evidence.
    e. protection of the evidence from accidental loss.
5. True or false: While testifying, a witness should speak directly to the members of the jury.
6. If an attorney objects to a question and the judge sustains the objection, the witness should
    a. answer the question immediately.
    b. wait for the judge to instruct the witness to answer the question.
    c. wait three seconds and then answer the question as if there had been no interruption.
    d. attempt to sneak in the evidence at the next opportunity.
    e. wait for another question to be asked.
7. The primary goal of the defense is
    a. to persuade the jury that the police are mistaken, incompetent, or prejudiced against the defendant.
    b. to prove that the defendant could not have committed the crime.
    c. to convict the defendant.
    d. to fool the jury into believing that the defendant is innocent.
    e. to use legal tricks and loopholes to keep the prosecution from succeeding.
8. True or false: It is the responsibility of the prosecutor, not of the police officer, to resolve any contradictions in the evidence to the jury's satisfaction.

9. The best way for a witness to respond to repetitive questioning is
   a. to ignore the questions until the attorney goes on to another subject.
   b. to answer in the same way each time, giving exactly the same information, no matter how many times the question is asked.
   c. to answer the question more fully each successive time that it is asked, adding more details until the attorney is satisfied.
   d. to complain to the judge.
   e. to ask the prosecutor to object.
10. True or false: As an investigation progresses and more evidence accumulates, it becomes easier to be objective about the case.

## TOPICS FOR INVESTIGATION

1. Since a defendant is not required to take an active part in a trial, why is it necessary for every criminal defendant to have an attorney, often at public expense?
2. Several states have abolished the grand jury as a mechanism for reviewing accusations in criminal cases. Do you agree that the grand jury system is obsolete and unnecessary?
3. Before a trial begins, the defense has the right to examine the prosecution's evidence. Does this "right of discovery" unfairly hamper the prosecution? Should the prosecutor have the same right to "discover" the defense's evidence?
4. In what way does the presence of the public in the courtroom serve to protect the defendant's rights? Are there circumstances in which the public's presence might have the opposite effect? Should the public and news media be excluded from spectacular trials in order to prevent disruption of the proceedings or distraction of the jury? Should television cameras be allowed to film or to videotape criminal trials?
5. Why would it matter whether a police officer wears civilian clothes or a uniform while testifying in a trial? Should not a police officer be proud of the uniform and eager to wear it in public?
6. Suppose that you are reviewing your field notes in preparing to testify. In your notes of the preliminary investigation you discover a bit of evidence, overlooked until now, that might indicate that the defendant is innocent. The trial is already underway. Should you take your notes with you when you testify?
7. You are the principal investigator in a murder case that has attracted a tremendous public furor. The district attorney, who is struggling to be re-elected, has decided to go for the death sentence. In your investigation you have found clear evidence of extenuating circumstances; at most, the defendant might be guilty of negligent manslaughter. The court-appointed defense attorney has made no effort to investigate and therefore is not aware of your evidence. The prosecutor has instructed you to forget it. What should you do?
8. If police officers are expected to remain objective and uninvolved during the course of their work, how and when are they permitted to express their natural emotions about their work? How can an officer know when he or she is losing objectivity or is merely reacting in a normal way to extremely emotion-laden situations?

# The Metric System

FOR MORE THAN TWO CENTURIES the United States has used a hodgepodge of various systems of measurement, inherited mostly from medieval England, while the rest of the world gradually adopted the metric system. Within another generation, it is likely that the traditional system will no longer be considered acceptable for precise measurement. Law enforcement personnel will also have to adopt the metric system if they want their measurements to have any credibility.

Throughout this text, we have given measurements in metric units, parenthetically including rough approximations in conventional units. In sketches, illustrations, and supplementary material, measurements have been given only in metric units.

You will learn the metric system more rapidly if you use it independently, rather than trying to convert or "translate" metric units into conventional units and vice versa. However, for those who have not yet learned the metric system and who still need to translate, here is a table for converting the measurements most often used in police work.

## LENGTH

| | | |
|---|---|---|
| 1 inch (in.) | = | 2.54 centimeters (cm) |
| 1 foot (ft) | = | 30.48 centimeters |
| | = | 0.305 meters (m) |
| 1 yard (yd) | = | 0.914 meters |
| 1 mile (mi) | = | 1,609 meters |
| | = | 1.609 kilometers (km) |
| 1 centimeter | = | 0.394 inches |
| 1 meter | = | 39.37 inches |
| | = | 3.281 feet |
| | = | 1.094 yards |
| 1 kilometer | = | 0.621 miles |

## AREA

| | | |
|---|---|---|
| 1 square inch (sq in.) | = | 6.45 square centimeters (cm²) |
| 1 square foot (sq ft) | = | 929.03 square centimeters |
| 1 square yard (sq yd) | = | 0.836 square meters (m²) |
| 1 acre (A.) | = | 4,046.4 square meters |
| | = | 0.4046 hectares (ha) |
| 1 square mile (sq mi) | = | 1,581 hectares |
| | = | 2.59 square kilometers (km²) |
| 1 square centimeter | = | 0.155 square inches |
| 1 square meter | = | 10.76 square feet |
| | = | 1.196 square yards |
| 1 hectare | = | 1,196,000 square yards |
| | = | 2.471 acres |
| 1 square kilometer | = | 247.11 acres |
| | = | 0.386 square miles |

## WEIGHT

| | | |
|---|---|---|
| 1 ounce (oz) | = | 28.35 grams (g) |
| 1 pound (lb) | = | 453.6 grams |
| | = | 0.4536 kilograms (kg) |
| 1 ton (t) | = | 907.2 kilograms |
| | = | 0.9072 metric tons, or tonnes (t) |
| 1 gram | = | 0.035 ounces |
| 1 hectogram (hg) | = | 3.53 ounces |
| 1 kilogram | = | 35.27 ounces |
| | = | 2.204 pounds |
| 1 metric ton | = | 2,205 pounds |
| | = | 1.102 tons |

## METRIC PREFIXES

One advantage of the metric system is that conversion from one quantity to another within each system of units can be made by merely changing the prefix to the basic unit. The prefixes are based on Greek and Latin mathematical words. Here are the most commonly used prefixes.

| | |
|---|---|
| milli- | 1/1,000 |
| centi- | 1/100 |
| deci- | 1/10 |
| deca- | × 10 |
| hecto- | × 100 |
| kilo- | × 1,000 |

# GLOSSARY OF INVESTIGATIVE TERMS

**Accomplice.** Any person who knowingly and willingly assists a criminal in planning or carrying out a crime.

**Admission.** A statement by a suspect or defendant, admitting the truth of some fact or circumstance that connects the person to a crime, but does not by itself indicate that the person committed the crime. See *confession*.

**Alibi.** A statement by a suspect or defendant that, if true, indicates that the person could not have committed an alleged crime.

**Arraignment.** The formal presentation of an accusation to the arrested person and the individual's response to the charge, prior to a trial.

**Arrest.** The detaining and taking of a person into custody to be accused of a crime and presented to the appropriate court.

**Associate.** Any friend, relative, or acquaintance who maintains a relationship with a criminal; an associate may or may not be involved in criminal activities. See *accomplice*.

**Autopsy.** The medical examination of a deceased person to learn the time, cause, and manner of death and, sometimes, the identity of the deceased.

**Bail.** Surety posted by a prisoner in the form of a cash bond or personal pledge to guarantee that the prisoner will return to court at the appointed time for trial.

**Blood typing.** A method of classifying blood samples according to the presence of various genetic components, such as the A, B, or Rh factors.

**Breach of the peace.** A misdemeanor offense that disturbs public order or decorum or that tends to produce or incite violence.

**Bystander.** A person who is present at the scene of a crime, but who has no personal knowledge of the criminal event.

**Case report.** The complete, official record of a criminal case.

**Chain of custody.** A record of the whereabouts of an item of evidence from the time that it was discovered until it is presented in court.

**Characterize evidence.** To determine the nature or character of unknown evidence: what it is.

**Chemical analysis.** Any method used to determine the chemical composition of unknown material; especially, methods that rely on studying the reactions of the unknown material to known, standard chemical agents.

**Chromatography.** Any of several methods used to determine the chemical composition of unknown material by causing it to react with known substances and studying the colors of the reactions produced thereby; the simplest form is *paper chromatography*. See *gas chromatography*.

**Closing report.** The official document in which the reasons are given for closing a criminal case report, e.g., "closed by arrest" or "unsolved, no further information available."

**Co-agency.** An agency of government whose primary purpose is to perform some public service, but which also has the power to make and enforce regulations or to enforce laws.

**Comparison microscope.** A microscope

designed to permit the viewing of two items at once; for example, it is employed to compare unknown evidence with a known standard.

**Competence of evidence.** The inherent validity of the evidence or testimony. Evidence that is not competent may be inadmissible.

**Competence of a witness.** (1) The legally defined capacity of a person to present testimony; usually, a person is assumed to be competent unless incompetence is shown. (2) The ability of a witness to testify on the basis of personal knowledge and observation or, for opinion testimony, on the basis of expertise. See *incompetence*.

**Complainant.** The person who reports a crime to the police.

**Computer-aided dispatching (CAD).** A radio communications system in which a mobile computer terminal in each patrol vehicle receives, stores, and transmits messages in digital code from and to a computer-based, automated dispatching center.

**Confession.** A statement in which a person admits having some direct involvement in a crime. See *admission*.

**Continuing investigation.** That portion of a criminal investigation after the preliminary investigation has ended, but before the suspect has been identified.

**Contraband.** Any physical matter whose mere possession is prohibited by law.

**Contra-evidence.** Evidence indicating that a suspect might not be guilty.

**Coroner.** A public official, who may or may not be a physician, responsible for determining the time, cause, and manner of death and the identity of the deceased in all cases of violent or questionable death.

**Corroboration.** Information or evidence that confirms the validity of other known evidence.

**Crime.** A violation of a law for which the legal penalty includes a fine or imprisonment or both; more generally, antisocial behavior that affects the interests of the whole community.

**Elements of a crime.** The actions that, taken together, constitute a crime according to the law.

**Part I crime.** In the Uniform Crime Reports, a classification of crimes that includes the most serious offenses, such as homicide, rape, armed robbery, and burglary.

**Part II crime.** In the Uniform Crime Reports, the less serious crimes for which less complete data are recorded.

**Crime analysis unit (CAU).** A unit of a police agency responsible for studying patterns of criminal activity in order to recommend the allocation of personnel and other resources to disrupt or prevent the activities of criminals.

**Crime Information Center (CIC).** Any of the facilities maintained by state police agencies, or the National Crime Information Center (NCIC) maintained by the Federal Bureau of Investigation, in which records of criminals, criminal activities, and related matters are stored in computers for rapid access and dissemination to authorized law enforcement agencies on request.

**Crime rate.** A measure of criminal activity; the number of incidents of a certain type of crime in a given community over a given period of time, divided by the population of the community at that time; usually the number of incidents per 100,000 people.

**Crime scene.** The general area or location in which a crime has occurred.

**Crime site.** The exact place at which a criminal act was committed within a crime scene.

**Criminal history.** A record of the past activities, known associates, and identifying characteristics of a known or suspected criminal.

**Criminalistics.** The science of discovering and evaluating evidence related to a crime.

> **Criminalistics laboratory.** A scientific laboratory, usually operated by a police agency, for the study, discovery, development, and evaluation of evidence.

**Criminal negligence.** Action that a person should have known would cause harm to others, but that the person performed without attempting to avoid or reduce the risk to others.

**Crystallography.** See *x-ray diffraction analysis*.

**Differential thermal analysis.** A method of identifying evidence (especially soils) by comparing the reactions produced by slowly burning the unknown sample and a known sample.

**Direct evidence.** See *evidence*.

**Direct pursuit.** The legal doctrine under which police officers are permitted to continue pursuing a fleeing suspect even when the suspect travels beyond the officers' proper jurisdiction.

**Double jeopardy.** Prosecuting the same person twice for the same crime. This is forbidden by the United States Constitution.

**Duplex radio system.** A radio communication system using one frequency for base-to-mobile transmissions and another frequency for mobile-to-base transmissions. See *simplex radio system*.

**Electron microscope.** A device used to study the internal structure of material or the nature of very small material by the use of beams of electrons instead of beams of light. A *scanning electron microscope* (SEM) is a variation of this device.

**Entrapment.** Police behavior that induces a citizen into committing a criminal act in order that the police may arrest the citizen. This is forbidden by the United States Constitution.

**Evidence.** Anything that tends either to affirm or to deny a certain belief or argument, such as the belief that the accused is guilty of a crime.

> **Circumstantial evidence.** Information or objects that concern facts about a crime, the suspect, or the victim and that suggest a relationship among them, but do not specifically demonstrate the events of the crime.

> **Debris evidence.** Physical evidence of various sorts, including microscopic matter, that might be transferred between the victim and the perpetrator or between the perpetrator and the crime scene.

> **Direct evidence.** Physical objects or the testimony of witnesses that bear directly on the criminal event.

> **Documentary evidence.** Any sort of record or means of conveying recorded information that has some connection with a crime.

> **Gross evidence.** Any relatively large physical object, as distinguished from traces, impressions, debris, and other small matter.

> **Impression evidence.** Any mark made on a solid surface that indicates or demonstrates some fact of a criminal event.

> **Indirect evidence.** Information concerning the victim, a suspect, or the general circumstances of a crime or crime scene, but not having a direct connection to the crime itself. See *evidence: circumstantial evidence*.

> **Physical evidence.** Any object or matter that has a relationship to a criminal event.

> **Trace evidence.** Physical evidence that is left at the scene of a crime by the perpetrator, usually inadvertently.

**Exclusionary rule.** The legal principle that evidence obtained illegally or improperly is not admissible during a trial.

**Extradition.** The legal procedure by which a criminal suspect who has fled from the jurisdiction in which the alleged crime took place can be arrested in another jurisdiction (such as another state) and returned to face the criminal charge.

**Federal Bureau of Investigation (FBI).** The primary federal police agency; a division of the United States Department of Justice.

**Felony.** A crime for which the penalty imposed on offenders may include a sentence in prison or capital punishment.

**Field interview.** An interview conducted by a patrol officer or an investigator with a citizen whose behavior appears suspicious, but who is not a suspect in any particular crime; also called a *field interrogation*.

**Field notes.** Information recorded by an investigator during the course of an investigation, as a basis for official reports and, eventually, for the officer's testimony in court. These are usually kept in handwritten form in a notebook.

**Fingerprint analysis.** The study of fingerprints and other friction-ridge prints as evidence related to a crime; the classification of fingerprints for the purpose of identifying individuals.

**Firearms examination.** The study of firearms (including their bullets, cartridges, shells, and other related matter) as evidence related to a crime; often mistakenly called *ballistics*, which is merely the study of the trajectories of missiles.

**Fracture pattern.** The manner in which glass or any brittle material breaks when struck or penetrated by a projectile. This may be studied to characterize or identify the material or to rationalize the event that produced the fracture.

**Friction-ridge prints.** Impressions made by contact between the ridged surfaces of skin and any surface; they include fingerprints, palm prints, footprints, toe prints, and lip prints.

**Fruits of a crime.** Anything that comes into a criminal's possession as a result or benefit of a crime.

**Galton detail.** Any of several types of patterns, or elements of those patterns, that may be recognized in fingerprints and may be used for purposes of analysis, classification, comparison, or identification. These were first established by Sir Francis Galton (1822–1911).

**Gas chromatography.** Any of several methods used to determine the nature and quantities of the chemical components of unknown material by exposing the material to standard substances during combustion of the sample and studying the reactions produced thereby; often, *gas-liquid chromatography* (GLC) or *gas-solid chromatography* (GSC). See also *chromatography*.

**Hearsay evidence.** Testimony by a witness concerning information that the witness claims to have learned from another person. With some exceptions, it is usually inadmissible in a trial.

**Henry system.** A systematic procedure for analyzing and classifying fingerprints, used by the FBI and most American police agencies and developed by Sir Edward Richard Henry.

**Identification of evidence.** (1) Comparison of an unknown object or sample of matter with a known or standard object or sample, to determine whether they have a number of characteristics in common; knowledge of the source of unknown evidence: where it came from. (2) Information concerning the name, origin, and true description of a person, such as a suspect.

**Immunity of a witness.** A legally defined condition under which a witness may not be compelled to testify in a criminal court, or may be exempted from testifying about certain matters, or may be exempted from prosecution for offenses in which the witness may have been directly involved.

**Incommunicado.** Prevented from communicating with other persons.

**Incompetence (of a witness).** The inability of a person to offer legally acceptable or truthful testimony, either because of some incapacity of the individual or because the person could not know the desired information.

**Indictment.** The legal presentation of an accusation that a person has committed a crime, reviewed and either approved *(true bill)* or disapproved *(no bill)* by a grand jury. See also *information.*

**Inference.** A conclusion based on rational consideration of the known facts and available evidence. See *evidence: circumstantial evidence.*

**Informant.** Any person who provides information to a police officer concerning a particular crime or criminal activity in general. Individual may be paid or unpaid.

**Information.** The legal presentation of an accusation that a person has committed a crime, delivered to a magistrate by the prosecutor. See *indictment.*

**In loco parentis.** With regard to a child or a mentally or physically incompetent person, this means "having the place of a parent," including the rights and duties of parents.

**Inquest.** A legal proceeding, conducted by a coroner or a magistrate, to determine the time, cause, and manner of death and, sometimes, the identity of the deceased in cases of questionable deaths.

**Instrument of a crime.** Any object, such as a tool or other device, used by the perpetrator in the course of a crime.

**Interrogation.** A highly structured effort to obtain specific information from the suspected perpetrator of a crime. See *interview.*

**Interview.** A structured and controlled but relatively informal effort to elicit information from the victim of or a witness to a crime. See *interrogation.*

**Investigator.** A person who investigates crimes; usually a police officer, although some prosecutors also have investigators on their staffs.

> **Generalist investigator.** A police officer who investigates many different types of crimes and who may have other duties as well; for example, a patrol officer.
>
> **Principal investigator.** The individual who is assigned the responsibility for conducting or coordinating all aspects of the investigation of a particular crime.
>
> **Specialist investigator.** An investigator who is responsible only for certain types of criminal investigations.

**Jigsaw fit.** Comparison of an unknown piece of evidence with a known piece of evidence, in which the unknown piece precisely fits into a broken section of the known piece.

**Jurisdiction.** (1) The geographic area within which a government agency (such as a police department) has authority to function. (2) The kinds of laws or regulations that an agency has the authority to enforce.

**Latent engraving.** Patterns in the crystalline structure of metal objects, created when the object's surface was engraved. The patterns may be re-created even if the original engraving has been obliterated to prevent identification of the object.

**Latent print.** Any friction-ridge impression that is not readily visible, but can be rendered visible by proper methods of examination. Sometimes the term is mistakenly applied to all friction-ridge impressions, visible or otherwise.

**Laundry mark.** An indelible mark applied by commercial laundries to their customers' garments. The mark may be visible only under ultraviolet light and is used to identify the customer who owns the garment.

**Lesser included offense.** A criminal offense that, as defined by law, has some but not all of the elements of a more serious offense.

**Magistrate.** A public official, usually a judge or justice of the peace, who has any of various judicial and quasi-judicial functions under state or federal law, such as issuing warrants, arraigning and examining prisoners, conducting hearings, etc.

**Materiality of evidence.** The degree of importance or value of evidence or testimony in determining the facts and issues being debated in a trial. Evidence that is not sufficiently material may be inadmissible.

**Medical examiner.** A physician who acts as coroner or who assists a coroner in determining the time, cause, and manner of death and the identity of the deceased in cases of violent or questionable death; also called a *pathologist* (a physician who studies the nature of diseases and death).

***Miranda* warning.** A statement of an accused person's essential constitutional rights, which police officers are required to recite at the time a person is arrested or whenever there is probable cause to arrest the person; named for *Miranda v. Arizona,* a Supreme Court decision that established this rule.

**Misdemeanor.** A criminal offense for which the maximum penalty imposed on offenders may include a fine, a sentence in jail, or both.

**Modus operandi (M.O.).** The distinctive methods or patterns of behavior of a criminal who commits a series of similar crimes.

**Moving perimeter plan.** A procedure used to maintain surveillance of a suspect or other person without interfering with the person's movement, usually when the subject is in a vehicle.

**Murder.** The deliberate or unlawful taking of human life.

**Maniacal murder.** A series of murders committed in a repetitive pattern, often with some degree of premeditation and care to avoid detection.

**Planned murder.** A criminal homicide that the perpetrator has carefully planned in advance and with particular care to avoid being detected.

**Sadistic murder.** One or more murders carried out in a brutal, savage manner, often with few precautions to avoid detection. Sometimes it is committed in connection with another crime, such as armed robbery, which may serve merely as a pretext for the murder.

**Terroristic murder.** Murder carried out as a conspiracy or group activity and often directed at a specific victim or group of victims. Sometimes it is motivated by political or religious ideology.

**National Law Enforcement Telecommunications System (NLETS).** A private, switched teletype network connecting virtually all federal, state, and local police agencies for the rapid dissemination of information, notices, and requests for information concerning criminal activity and related law enforcement matters.

**Neutron activation analysis.** A method used to determine the nature and quantity of the chemical components of unknown material by bombarding the material with neutrons, thus causing the material to be somewhat radioactive, and by studying the pattern of radioactivity.

**No bill.** See *indictment.*

**Nolo contendere.** A Latin phrase that means "I do not contest"; used by the defendant in a plea to an accusation, it has the same effect as a plea of guilty but does not concede guilt.

**Offense report.** The official report of a crime investigation; usually the report includes the initial complaint and a summary of the preliminary investigation. See *case report*.

**Organized crime unit (OCU).** A division of a police agency whose primary responsibility is to investigate organized criminal activity, such as gambling, narcotics trafficking, prostitution, loan frauds, and the like. Often the OCU is administratively separate from the criminal investigation unit and reports directly to a high-level official of the agency.

**Particularity.** The constitutional requirement that property to be searched or seized or a suspect to be arrested must be described with sufficient clarity and specificity that the property or person can be readily distinguished from other similar property or persons.

**Patrol-oriented investigation.** An administrative organizational plan in which nearly all crimes are investigated by patrol officers, and only the most serious or complex cases are referred to specialists.

**Penetrometer.** A device used to determine the weight of an object that produced an impression in soil or another relatively soft surface.

**Period for service.** The period of time, usually five days, during which a warrant must be served. This generally applies to search warrants, not to arrest warrants.

**Perpetrator.** The person who has committed a criminal act.

**Physiological fluid.** Any fluid substance derived from a person's body, such as blood, semen, or perspiration.

**Point of entry.** The place at which a criminal actually enters a crime scene.

**Point of exit.** The place at which a criminal leaves the crime scene.

**Polarizing microscope.** A microscope designed to study the internal structure of materials by transmitting polarized light through the object.

**Police agency.** A primary law enforcement agency; an agency of government whose main responsibility is to enforce criminal laws, investigate crimes, and apprehend criminals.

**Polygraph.** A device used to record changes in a person's physiological state (blood pressure, respiration, etc.) during interrogation or interview to indicate when the subject is lying; often called a *lie detector*.

**Prejudicial evidence.** Evidence or testimony that, although true, has the effect of unfairly or excessively influencing the emotions of the jury, usually against the defendant. Such evidence also may be called *inflammatory,* and it may be inadmissible.

**Preliminary investigation.** The initial investigation of a crime, usually at the crime scene, involving collection of evidence and interviewing of the victim and/or witnesses.

**Presumption of innocence.** The legal principle that a person who has been accused of a crime must not be considered or treated as if the person were guilty until guilt has been determined in a proper trial. See also *preventive detention*.

**Preventive detention.** The use of the power of arrest to hold a suspected criminal in jail in order to prevent the person from committing additional crimes. This practice has been held to conflict with the constitutional doctrine of the *presumption of innocence* (see this term also).

**Privileged communications.** A legally defined condition that forbids certain communications between a witness and another person to be divulged in court; for example, conversations between a doctor and a patient are privileged and cannot be revealed by the doctor.

**Probable cause.** A condition in which there is reason to suspect that a person is guilty of a particular crime or that particular evidence will be found at a certain place.

**Proof beyond a reasonable doubt.** The legal requirement for a conviction of an accused criminal; the amount of evidence necessary to obtain a conviction.

**Property search.** An effort by a police officer to locate evidence in a place that is ordinarily private, in accordance with a search warrant, except under certain limited circumstances.

**Prosecutor.** A public official, usually bearing the title of district attorney, county attorney, or state's attorney, or an assistant to that official who represents the state in criminal trials and presents the case against the defendant.

**Psychological profile.** A description of a person, often an unknown suspect, indicating the person's character, personality, and other characteristics and based on inferences drawn from direct evidence by a panel of experts in psychology and related sciences.

**Rape crisis center.** A community service agency, often staffed largely by volunteers, that counsels and otherwise assists victims of sexual attacks. Most rape crisis centers work in close cooperation with the police.

**Rationalize evidence.** To understand the relationship between an item of evidence and the criminal event.

**Recklessness.** Action taken by a person without regard for the probable risk or injury to others. See *criminal negligence*.

**Refractive index.** The degree to which a light beam bends as it passes through glass or any other transparent material. This may be used to characterize or identify the material.

**Regulatory agency.** An agency of government whose primary duty is to develop and enforce rules for some specific area of public activity. Often regulatory agencies have the power to impose sanctions, such as fines, on violators of the agency's rules.

**Relevance of evidence.** The relationship between evidence or testimony and the issues being debated in a trial. Evidence that is not relevant may be inadmissible.

**Route of approach.** The route taken by a criminal before entering the crime scene. See *point of entry*.

**Route of departure.** The route taken by a criminal after leaving the crime scene. See *point of exit*.

**Scrambler.** An electronic device that renders a radio signal unintelligible to unauthorized listeners, thus protecting the security of communications.

**Search.** Any effort by a law enforcement agent to find a person or property that is not in plain sight or in a public place.

**Search warrant.** See *warrant*.

**Simplex radio system.** A radio communications system using the same frequency for base-to-mobile, mobile-to-base, and mobile-to-mobile transmissions; sometimes called a *three-way radio* system. See *duplex radio system*.

**Sociopathology.** Diseased or perverted relationships with other people, such that the sociopath is incapable of establishing or maintaining a healthy relationship with others.

**Soil density analysis.** A method of identifying soil samples by comparing the distribution of particles from unknown and known samples when the particles are placed in liquids of varying densities.

**Spectrophotometer.** A device used to create and study the reflection of light beams of different frequencies from unknown materials to determine the material's chemical composition. See *spectroscope*.

**Spectroscope.** A device used to create and

study the spectral pattern of light produced by combustion of material, thereby revealing the chemical composition of the material. See *spectrophotometer*.

**Spectrograph.** A device that both produces and records the spectral pattern of light created by the combustion of material.

**Spiral search.** A searching pattern used to locate evidence over a large area, usually outdoors, in which the search team follows a spiral path from the perimeter to the center of the area. See *strip search*.

**Standard.** An object or matter whose identity is known and which can be used for comparison with and identification of unknown evidence.

**Photographer's standard.** An object of known size that is placed in a photograph alongside the evidence to indicate its true size.

**Statement.** A written record of a witness's or suspect's testimony. It may be either handwritten by the witness or suspect or prepared by a stenographer, and it may be signed by the witness or suspect.

**Stop–and–frisk rule.** The legal rule that permits a police officer to perform an extremely limited search of a person who is not a suspect in any particular crime, but whose behavior seems to be suspicious.

**Stress pattern.** The manner in which materials react to unusual stress, such as being struck or penetrated by a projectile. Stress patterns may be studied to characterize or identify the material or to rationalize the event that produced the stress.

**Strip search.** (1) A pattern for searching a large area, usually outdoors, in which the search team follows a straight path from one side of the area to the other, then turns around and searches a second strip, etc.; also called a *line search*. (See *spiral search*.) (2) A thorough search of a prisoner, usually during the booking process, in which the prisoner is required to remove all clothing.

**Surveillance.** Any of several techniques or procedures used by police officers to observe a person or place, usually covertly, in order to gather information or evidence about criminal activity.

**Suspect.** A person who is believed to be the perpetrator of a crime.

**Tactical unit.** A unit of a police agency with specific, limited anticrime responsibilities.

**Testify.** To present information in court as a witness.

**Testimony.** Evidence presented orally by witnesses during a trial or other legal proceeding; more generally, the information given orally by a witness, victim, suspect, or any other person.

**Tool mark.** An impression left by a hard object on a softer surface, usually because the harder object was used as a tool to carry out a crime. In a sense, the rifling marks left on a bullet also can be regarded as tool marks.

**Triangulation system.** A system for measuring the locations of objects at a scene by establishing several reference points around the perimeter of the scene, then giving the distance from each object to at least two reference points.

**True bill.** See *indictment*.

**Undercover investigation.** The use of police agents to infiltrate a criminal organization in order to gather evidence of continuing crimes. Usually the agent adopts a fictitious identity.

**Uniform Crime Reports (UCR).** Statistical summaries of reported crimes and law enforcement activity, compiled from data reported by almost all police agencies in the country and published annually by the FBI under the title *Crime in the United States*.

**Vacuum filter trap.** A screen or filter

placed in the nozzle or suction hose of a vacuum cleaner to trap debris evidence for recovery from the crime scene, victim's clothing, etc.

**Venue.** The legal jurisdiction in which an alleged crime was committed.

**Victim.** A person who is directly affected by a crime.

> **Secondary victim.** A person who is affected by a crime indirectly, such as the family or friends of a murder victim.

**Visual sweep.** An overall visual assessment of a crime scene, made by the investigator immediately on arrival at the scene.

**Voice-print analysis.** A method used to identify a speaker when only the person's voice is available (e.g., a recorded voice of unknown or uncertain origin) by comparing the frequency pattern and other characteristics of the unknown voice with a known sample.

**Voice stress analyzer.** A device that purportedly detects and indicates changes in a person's emotional state due to such factors as lying, as reflected by changes in a person's vocal pattern. See also *polygraph*.

**Voluntary.** Of one's own free will and choice; not as a result of coercion, deception, or intimidation.

**Want.** A notice that a police agency "wants" a particular person or is searching for a particular vehicle in connection with a criminal investigation. See *warrant*.

**Warrant.** A legal order, issued by a magistrate, instructing a police officer to search and/or seize certain property or to arrest a certain person. See *want*.

**Witness.** Any person who has knowledge about a crime or suspect.

> **Primary witness.** A person who has direct, personal knowledge about a criminal event.

**Secondary witness.** A person who has some information concerning the victim, perpetrator, or circumstances of a crime, but no direct knowledge of the criminal event itself.

**X-ray diffraction analysis.** A method used to study the internal structure of material by bombarding the material with x rays and recording their pattern of transmission through the material. Also called *crystallography*.

# BIBLIOGRAPHY

Alex, Nicholas. *New York Cops Talk Back.* New York: John Wiley, 1976. An extensive survey of the attitudes of New York City police officers, written by an investigative journalist, concentrating on patrol officers' dissatisfactions and grievances.

Allison, Harrison C. *Personal Identification.* Boston: Holbrook Press, 1973. Comprehensive discussion of fingerprint examination and classification systems, physical description of suspects, and other aspects of identification.

Asch, Sidney H. *Civil Rights and Responsibilities under the Constitution.* New York: Arco, 1970. Good review of the Bill of Rights and other constitutional provisions, and how they have been interpreted by the courts and applied to both civil and criminal matters.

Bopp, William J., ed. *Police Administration.* Boston: Holbrook Press, 1975. The report of the President's Commission on Law Enforcement and the Administration of Justice, and other brief essays on administration.

Bordua, David J., ed. *The Police: Six Sociological Essays.* New York: John Wiley, 1967. The essay by Albert J. Reiss, Jr., and David J. Bordua, "Environment and Organization: A Perspective on the Police," is especially interesting.

Burton, Alan. *Police Telecommunications.* Springfield, Ill.: Charles C Thomas, 1973. A thorough review of the history of police use of telegraph and radio systems, but this book does not include in much detail some of the most recent advances.

Clark, Ramsey. *Crime in America.* New York: Simon and Schuster, 1970. This essay by the former Attorney General of the United States criticizes the present criminal justice system and offers some very general suggestions for reform.

Creamer, J. Shane. *The Law of Arrest, Search, and Seizure,* 2d. ed. Philadelphia: W. B. Saunders, 1975. An extremely convenient and comprehensive handbook, describing the basic constitutional principles, important court decisions, and their implications for police activities.

Cressey, Donald R. *Theft of the Nation.* New York: Harper and Row, 1969. An authoritative discussion of organized crime, emphasizing the history and organization of the Mafia.

*Criminal Investigation.* Gaithersburg, Md.: International Association of Chiefs of Police, 1971. A comprehensive handbook on investigative techniques, but very dated in approach and procedures.

Eastman, George D., ed. *Municipal Police Administration.* Washington, D.C.: International City Management Association, 1969. Although intended primarily for administrative and managerial officials, this volume of essays contains several sections on the organization and management of police investigative functions.

Feldman, M. Philip. *Criminal Behaviour: A Psychological Analysis.* London and New York: John Wiley, 1977. This British psychologist attempts to identify and describe each of the various kinds of criminals on the basis of their personal psychology and the

ton, D.C.: U.S. Department of Commerce, 1975.

U.S. Federal Bureau of Investigation. *Crime in the United States*. Annual. Washington, D.C.: U.S. Department of Justice, 1976.

U.S. Law Enforcement Assistance Administration. *Crimes and Victims*. Washington, D.C.: U.S. Department of Justice, 1974. An attempt to define methods of studying the victims of crime: how victims respond, the effects of crime on victims, and so forth.

von Hirsch, Andrew. *Doing Justice*. New York: Hill and Wang, 1976. A report of a blue-ribbon panel, The Committee for the Study of Incarceration, self-appointed to examine the failings of the correctional system. The Committee concluded that the correctional system is all right, but the criminal justice system is at fault.

Waldron, Ronald J., et al. *The Criminal Justice System*. Boston: Houghton Mifflin, 1976. An introductory textbook, thorough and well organized.

Walker, Samuel. *A Critical History of Police Reform*. Lexington, Mass.: Lexington Books, D. C. Heath, 1977. The author believes that police reforms have failed in the past because of political interference, public apathy, and a tendency toward faddishness among police administrators.

Waters, James R., and Sheree A. McGrath. *Introduction to Law Enforcement*. Columbus, Ohio: Charles E. Merrill, 1974. A very elementary but comprehensive overview of law enforcement practices.

Weinreb, Lloyd L. *Denial of Justice*. New York: Free Press, 1977. A critical review of police practices and court decisions in relation to constitutional guarantees.

Weston, Paul B., and Kenneth M. Wells. *Criminal Evidence for Police*. Englewood Cliffs, N.J.: Prentice-Hall, 1971. A comprehensive study, from a legal viewpoint, of criminalistics and investigative procedures.

Weston, Paul B., and Kenneth M. Wells. *Elements of Criminal Investigation*. Englewood Cliffs, N.J.: Prentice-Hall, 1971. A brief handbook on basic investigative techniques.

Whisenand, Paul M., and Tug T. Tamaru. *Automated Police Information Systems*. New York: John Wiley, 1970. Much of the book is extremely technical in approach, emphasizing information theory and analysis of records systems. However, there are chapters on the practical use of modern communications and recordkeeping equipment that would be of more general interest.

# REFERENCE CHART OF
# INVESTIGATIVE TECHNIQUES

The investigative procedures described in this text apply to virtually all criminal investigations, regardless of the type of crime. However, there are variations in the way these procedures are applied, in the sequence of investigative steps that are to be taken, and in the relative importance of the various kinds of evidence that may be acquired, depending on the type of crime being investigated. Furthermore, some types of crime require specialized investigative techniques, or the use of special resources, that would not be needed for most crime types.

In this reference chart, we have listed the techniques that are most likely to be useful for each of the types of crime in the FBI's Uniform Crime Reports index system. Under the heading, *Interview,* we list the persons who should be interviewed in the approximate order that the interviews should be held, and we list the kinds of information that the investigator should attempt to obtain from each interview. For more information on interviewing techniques, see pages 165–177. We have used the following abbreviations for the different classes of potential interviewees:

**VI**   Victim; the person immediately and directly affected by the criminal act

**SV**   Secondary victim; usually the family of the victim, or other person(s) indirectly affected by the criminal act; applies particularly to murder, kidnapping, and arson

**PW**   Primary witness; a person who was present during the criminal event or who has other direct, personal knowledge of the crime

**SW**   Secondary witness; a person who was not present during the crime but who has some knowledge of the suspect, victim, or circumstances of the crime; may include an informant

Under the heading, *Evidence Search,* we list the places where physical evidence is most likely to be found, in the approximate order in which the search should be conducted, and the types of evidence that the investigator should seek. For more information on searching for evidence, see pages 115–129. We have used the following abbreviations for the different places where physical evidence may be found:

**CRS**   The crime site; the place where the crime was committed

**RAP**   The route of approach used by the perpetrator to arrive at the crime scene

**PEN**   The point of entry used by the perpetrator to enter the crime scene

**PEX**   The point of exit at which the perpetrator left the crime scene

**RDE**   The route of departure used by the perpetrator in fleeing from the crime scene

**VIC**   The body of the victim

**VEH**   Any vehicle involved in the crime, such as the perpetrator's vehicle

Under the heading, *Special Techniques,* we list additional investigative procedures that are likely to be useful or, in some cases, necessary for particular types of crime. Where appropriate, we have included page references to the portion of the text where we have discussed these techniques in more detail.

The boldface numbers indicate the approximate value that the different types of evidence are likely to have in the investigation of each type of crime. (Where two items are given the same value, in most cases they are related; for example, for the crime of homicide, the discovery of the instrument of the crime is given a value of **3.** If the weapon involved in the crime is a firearm, and if it is recovered, it is subject to firearms examination, which is also given a value of **3.** These values are entirely relative, and the actual value of a particular item of evidence will depend on the particular crime being investigated; however, the values we have assigned may be helpful in determining the priorities given to the effort to obtain the various types of evidence. (**1** represents the highest probable value.)

The types of crime listed in this chart, and the definitions of each type of crime, have been adapted from the FBI Crime Index. All seven Part I crimes are listed, plus thirteen of the twenty-one Part II offenses. We have excluded those offenses that are not ordinarily subject to investigation: weapons violations, liquor law violations, common drunkenness, vagrancy, and so forth. We have also added two types of crime that are not included in the Crime Index: kidnapping and extortion. Both are relatively rare offenses, but they do require intensive investigation.

| CRIME TYPE | INTERVIEW | | EVIDENCE SEARCH | | SPECIAL TECHNIQUES |
|---|---|---|---|---|---|
| | WHO | WHAT TO ASK | WHERE | WHAT TO LOOK FOR | |
| **HOMICIDE** (Unlawful taking of human life) [pp. 191–195] [*Note:* The first object of investigation is to determine whether death was due to unlawful act.] | SV | 5 Identity of any person who might have reason to kill victim | **CRS PEX PEN RDE RAP** | 2 Traces of perpetrator<br>3 Instruments of the crime | 1 Medical examination of victim [pp. 280–283]<br>3 Firearms examination, if firearms used and weapon is recovered [pp. 267–268] |
| | PW | 4 Description of assailant<br>6 Sequence of events of the crime | **VIC** | 1 Traces of perpetrator | |
| **RAPE** (Sexual intercourse by force or deception) [pp. 186–191, 197] | VI | 2 Description of assailant<br>5 Sequence of events of the crime | **VIC** | 1 Traces of perpetrator<br>3 Evidence that a crime was committed | 1 Medical examination of victim [pp. 190–191] |
| | | | **CRS PEN VEH** | 4 Traces of perpetrator | |
| **ROBBERY** (Taking of money or property by force or threat of force) | VI | 1 Description of assailant<br>6 Sequence of events of the crime; M.O. | **CRS** | 3 Traces of perpetrator | 5 Identifiable goods may be located through pawn shops or through known dealers in stolen goods. [See *stolen property*, below.] |
| | PW | 2 Description of assailant | **RDE** | 4 Traces of perpetrator<br>5 Instrument or fruits of crime (sometimes lost or abandoned by fleeing offender) | |

| | | | | | |
|---|---|---|---|---|---|
| **AGGRAVATED ASSAULT** (Assault with intent to kill or to commit serious bodily injury) | **VI** | **1** Description or, if known, identity of perpetrator<br>**6** Sequence of events of the crime | **CRS** | **2** Traces of perpetrator<br>**4** Instrument of the crime | **3** Medical examination of victim [pp. 280–283] |
| | **PW** | **7** Description of assailant | **PEN** **PEX** **RDE** **RAP** | **5** Traces of perpetrator<br>**5** Instrument of the crime | |
| | | | **VIC** | **3** Traces of perpetrator | |
| **BURGLARY** (Unlawful entry into home or business to commit theft or another felony) | **VI** | **2** Identities of possible suspects (disgruntled employees, etc.)<br>**3** List of stolen objects | **CRS** **PEN** **PEX** **RDE** | **1** Traces of perpetrator<br>**4** Instruments of crime<br>**6** Fruits of crime (sometimes lost or abandoned) | [*Note:* In some states, it is important to establish the time of the offense, since penalties are higher for nighttime burglary than for daytime burglary.] |
| | **SW** | **5** Suspicious persons in area | | | |
| **LARCENY, THEFT** (Taking of property by stealth; includes purse-snatching, pocket picking, shoplifting, etc.) | **VI** | **3** Description of stolen property<br>**5** Description of persons observed near property prior to its disappearance | **CRS** | **1** Traces of perpetrator | **3** Identifiable goods may be located through pawn shops or through known dealers in stolen goods. [See *stolen property,* below.] |
| | | | **PEX** **RDE** | **2** Traces of perpetrator<br>**6** Fruits of crime | |
| | **PW** | **4** Description of suspect | | | |
| **MOTOR VEHICLE THEFT** (Taking of a motor vehicle without owner's consent) | **VI** | **1** Description of vehicle<br>**5** Identities of possible suspects | **VEH** | **2** Traces of perpetrator, if vehicle recovered | **3** Circumstances of the crime may help to establish M.O.: Was vehicle locked? What type of vehicle was stolen?<br>**6** Check known dealers in stolen vehicles and parts. [See *stolen property,* below.] |
| | **PW** **SW** | **4** Description of suspicious persons | | | |

| CRIME TYPE | INTERVIEW | | EVIDENCE SEARCH | | SPECIAL TECHNIQUES |
|---|---|---|---|---|---|
| | WHO | WHAT TO ASK | WHERE | WHAT TO LOOK FOR | |
| **SIMPLE ASSAULT** (Assault in which no deadly weapon was used) | VI ⎫ PW ⎭ | 1 Identity or description of assailant 3 Sequence of events of the crime | VIC ⎫ CRS ⎭ | 2 Traces of perpetrator | 4 Medical examination if victim seriously injured; otherwise, photographs of wounds |
| **ARSON** (Willful or malicious burning of property, with or without intent to defraud) [pp. 284–285] | VI | 3 Identities of possible suspects (disgruntled employees, etc.) 6 Victim's possible motive for arson (financial problems, etc.) | CRS | 2 Traces of perpetrator 1 Instruments of the crime | 1 Fire inspector should be able to determine where and how fire started; may recover part of incendiary device. M.O. is often helpful in identifying likely suspects. |
| | PW | 5 Suspicious persons in area | PEN ⎫ PEX ⎬ RDE ⎭ | 2 Traces of perpetrator | |
| | SW | 4 Identities of possible suspects 4 Victim's possible motive | | | |
| **FORGERY, COUNTERFEITING** (Presentation of false document to defraud) | VI | 1 Description of perpetrator 2 Sequence of events of the crime; M.O. | CRS | 4 Traces of perpetrator | 3 Examination and laboratory analysis of false document may reveal traces of perpetrator, other evidence. |
| | | | Document | 3 Traces of perpetrator | |

| Crime | | | | | Notes |
|---|---|---|---|---|---|
| **FRAUD** (Obtaining money or property by false pretenses) | VI | 1 Description of perpetrator<br>3 Sequence of events of the crime; M.O. | CRS | 2 Instruments of the crime (may include documents) | 2 Examination and laboratory analysis of fraudulent document may reveal traces of perpetrator, other evidence.<br>3 M.O. is often helpful in identifying possible suspects. |
| | PW<br>SW | 4 Description of perpetrator | | | |
| **EMBEZZLEMENT** (Misuse or taking of money, property entrusted to one's care) | VI | 1 Identity of suspect<br>3 Sequence of events, circumstances of the crime | CRS | 2 Instruments of the crime (may include documents) | 2 Audit of victim's records may reveal methods of perpetrator, other evidence. |
| **STOLEN PROPERTY OFFENSES** (Buying, possession, and selling of stolen property) | PW<br>SW | 2 Identity of suspect<br>3 Suspect's activities | CRS | 4 Instruments of the crime<br>1 Stolen property<br>4 Fruits of the crime (money, etc., received from sale of stolen goods) | 1 Undercover investigation is often successful in discovering routes of transmission of stolen goods. |
| **VANDALISM** (Willful or malicious destruction of property) | VI | 4 Identities of possible suspects<br>5 Time and circumstances of the crime | CRS | 1 Traces of perpetrator<br>3 Instruments of the crime | 2 In random vandalism, such as tire-slashing, M.O. and geographic pattern of repeated offenses may lead to suspects. |
| | PW | 2 Description of suspects | PEN<br>PEX<br>RDE | 6 Traces of perpetrator<br>7 Instruments of the crime | |
| **PROSTITUTION** (including related offenses, such as procuring, solicitation, etc.) | PW<br>SW | 4 Identities of suspects<br>4 Suspects' activities | CRS | 2 Instruments of the crime (such as documents showing lists of clients, records of receipts, etc.) | 1 Investigation usually requires undercover agent to pose as customer.<br>3 Accused prostitute may identify procurer, other accomplices. |

| CRIME TYPE | INTERVIEW | | EVIDENCE SEARCH | | SPECIAL TECHNIQUES |
|---|---|---|---|---|---|
| | WHO | WHAT TO ASK | WHERE | WHAT TO LOOK FOR | |
| **DRUG OFFENSES** (Possession, use, and sale of illegal drugs or other substances) | PW SW | 1 Identities of suspects 2 Suspects' activities | CRS | 3 Instruments of the crime (drugs, drug paraphernalia) | 3 Laboratory analysis of suspected drug is essential. 4 Investigation often requires undercover agent to pose as customer. 4 Accused drug user may identify dealer. |
| **GAMBLING** (Illegal operation of or participation in games of chance for money or other tangible goods) | PW SW | 2 Identities of suspects 3 Suspects' activities | CRS | 4 Instruments of the crime 5 Fruits of the crime (including documents showing receipts, gambling debts, etc.) | 1 Investigation often requires undercover agent to pose as customer. |
| **OFFENSES AGAINST THE FAMILY** (Spouse or child abuse or neglect; other offenses against the family usually are not subject to criminal investigation) | VI | 2 Circumstances of the crime | VIC | 1 Nature and extent of injuries | 1 Medical examination of victim is essential. [*Note*: Criminal investigation should be coordinated with public welfare agency, juvenile court.] |
| | SW | 3 Previous injuries to victim 4 Suspect's usual behavior | CRS | 5 Instruments of the crime (if any weapons were used) | |

| Offense | | | | |
|---|---|---|---|---|
| **NONVIOLENT SEX OFFENSES** (Homosexual offenses, statutory rape, other sex offenses) | PW<br>SW | 1 Identities of suspects<br>2 Suspects' activities | | 1 Investigation usually depends entirely on complaint of a primary witness; for statutory rape, treat as if it were forcible rape. [See *rape*, above.] |
| **DRIVING WHILE INTOXICATED** (Operation of motor vehicle while under influence of drugs or alcohol) | PW | 3 Identification of suspect<br>5 Suspect's activities | VEH — 4 Instruments of the crime (intoxicating substances or empty container) | 1 Medical examination of suspect or breathalyzer test to establish presence of intoxicant in bloodstream<br>2 Standard agility and sobriety tests |
| **KIDNAPPING** (Abduction, false imprisonment, holding for ransom, etc.) [pp. 269–270] | VI | 2 Identity or description of suspect(s)<br>3 Sequence of events of the crime | CRS * — 4 Traces of perpetrator; 5 Instruments of the crime (such as ransom note) | 1 Request immediate assistance of FBI; comply with all demands of kidnappers; do not attempt to rescue hostage or arrest kidnapper until hostage is free *or* there is evidence of extreme imminent danger to hostage. |
| | SV<br>PW | 6 Circumstances of the crime<br>7 Identities of possible suspects | CRS** VEH — 4 Traces of perpetrator; *Place from which victim was taken; **Place where victim was held | |
| **EXTORTION** (Blackmail; demand for money, goods, or services under duress or threat of violence) | VI | 1 Description of suspect(s)<br>2 Circumstances of the crime | Documents — 4 Traces of perpetrator; 5 Instruments of the crime | 3 If extortion is continuing, victim may assist police in "setting up" suspect.<br>4 Voice-print analysis of telephone call from extortionist may be valuable. |

role of flashing lights and siren in, 57

and the visual sweep, 56–60

Arson, 284–285

Artificial lighting and police photography, 86–88

*Ashcroft v. Tennessee,* 382

Associates (of a criminal), 345

Autopsy

procedures for, 282

and wounds, 151

Available light in police photography, 85

Bail

and suspect interrogation, 414

and suspect's legal rights, 410–411

Ballistics, 119

Bargaining with witnesses, 173

Best evidence rule, 366

Blood

collection of, 148–150

as fluid evidence, 123

lab analysis of, 276–277

typing of, 276–277

Brandeis, Louis, 164

Broadcast news media and the investigator, 210–213, 218–222

*Brown v. Mississippi,* 382

Brushes, 131–132

Bulletins, 311

Bullets

microscopic identification of, 267

recovery of, 146–147

as weapons evidence, 146–147

Business crime, 48

Bystanders

defined, 165

removal from the crime scene, 61–62

as source of evidence, 161

Cameras

fingerprint cameras, 90–91

Kodak Ektagraphic Visualmaker, 90–91

large-format cameras, 84

and police photography, 90–93

snapshot cameras, 85–86

in television journalism, 212

terms for, 92–93

35mm cameras, 84–85

*see also* Photography

Carbon paper, 151

*Carroll v. United States,* 428

Cartridges

and friction-ridge prints, 146

location of, 146

microscopic analysis of, 267–268

as weapons evidence, 146

Case assignment, 43

Case number

and case report, 293

in cross index, 311

Case reports

and case number, 293

and closing report, 296

and complaint form, 293–294

and investigative report, 294, 296

and offense report, 294–296

in prosecution, 454–455

as records, 293–296

Case review outline

and case study, 347–357

example of, 350–356

questions in, 347–349

Case solving, 344–359

and case review outline, 347–357

inferences in, 347

and suspect identification, 345–346

Case summary, 372–373

Casting materials

cautions about, 140

as equipment, 133

and fabric marks, 142

methods for use of, 138–140

and tire and shoe impressions, 138–140

and tool marks, 141–142

types of, 141–142

Chain of custody, 77–79

Characterization, of evidence, 256–257

Chemical analysis

of friction-ridge prints, 266

and lab instruments, 265

Chemical traces, 272

Chemicals

and invisible fluids, 150

and lifting prints, 137–138

# MOSBY'S
# Pharmacology in Nursing

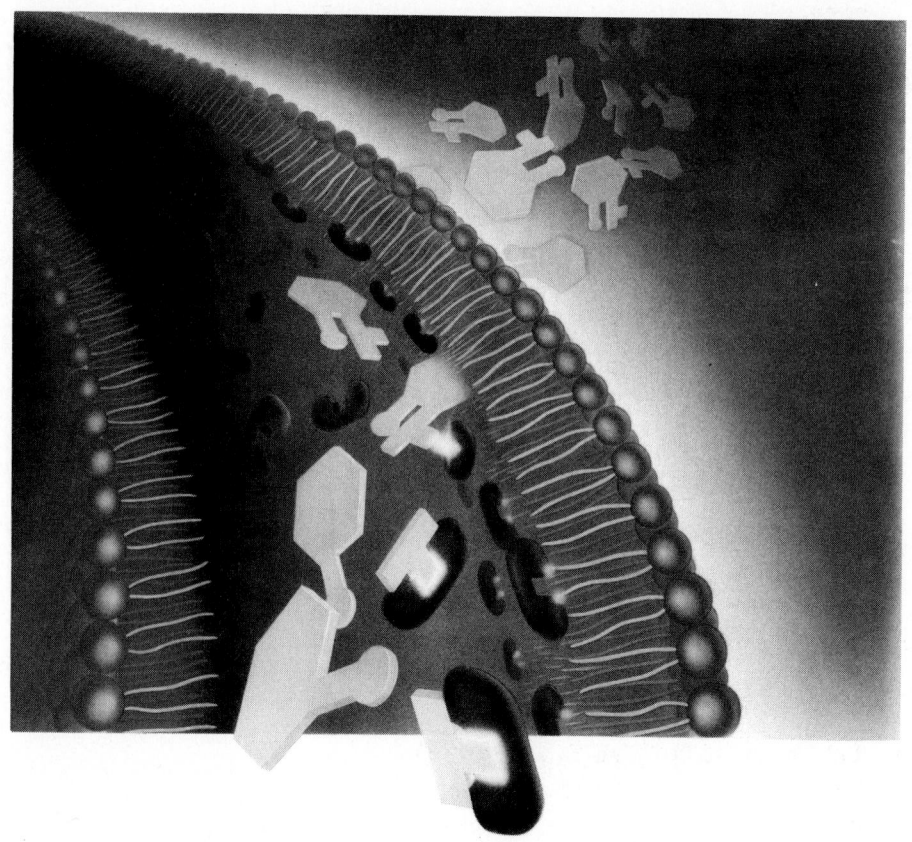

**COVER ILLUSTRATION:** ASPIRIN AND PAIN RELIEF

The color illustration on the cover, which is reproduced in black and white here, shows the process of pain relief with use of aspirin and other nonsteroidal antiinflammatory drugs (NSAIDs). The salicylate molecule of aspirin (shown in blue) provides pain relief by inhibiting the synthesis of prostaglandin, an agent that sends pain messages to the central nervous system.

Prostaglandin is created when the enzyme cyclo-oxygenase (shown in red) attaches itself to fatty acids (shown in yellow), which line the outer surface of the cell membrane. The active portion of the salicylate molecule attaches itself to the enzyme, thus preventing an enzyme–fatty acid bond and resulting in pain relief or analgesia.

# MOSBY'S
## Pharmacology
## in Nursing

**Leda M. McKenry,** **Ph.D., R.N.**
Faculty, University of Massachusetts, Amherst, Massachusetts;
Principal, Center for Advanced Nursing Studies, Kent, England

**Evelyn Salerno,** **Pharm.D., R.Ph.**
Adjunct Professor, University of Miami School of Nursing, Miami, Florida;
Director of Pharmacy Services, Hospice, Inc., Miami, Florida

*with 150 two-color illustrations*

**Mosby**
**Year Book**

St. Louis  Baltimore  Boston  Chicago  London  Philadelphia  Sydney  Toronto

**Mosby**
**Year Book**
Dedicated to Publishing Excellence

Executive editor: Don Ladig
Managing editor: Robin Carter
Developmental editor: Linda Wendling
Project manager: Mark Spann
Production editors: Stephen C. Hetager, Maureen Kenison,
　Barbara Terrell, Kathy Wiegand
Designer: Julie Taugner
Original illustrations by: Mark Swindle
Cover illustrator: © Ron Boisvert


EIGHTEENTH EDITION

Previous editions copyrighted 1936, 1940, 1942, 1945, 1948, 1951, 1955, 1960, 1963, 1966, 1969, 1973, 1976, 1979, 1982, 1986, 1989

Printed in the United States of America

Mosby–Year Book, Inc.
11830 Westline Industrial Drive
St. Louis, Missouri 63146


**Library of Congress Cataloging-in-Publication Data**

Mckenry, Leda M.
　　Mosby's pharmacology in nursing. — 18th ed. / Leda M. Mckenry,
　Evelyn Salerno.
　　　p.　　cm.
　　Includes bibliographical references and index.
　　ISBN 0-8016-3199-8
　　1. Pharmacology. 2. Nursing. I. Salerno,
Evelyn. II. Title.
　III. Title: Pharmacology in nursing.
　　[DNLM: 1. Pharmacology—nurses's instruction.　QV 4 M47m]
　RM301.M39　1991
　615'.1—dc20
　DNLM/DLC
　for Library of Congress
　　　　　　　　　　　　　　　　　　　　　91-33721
　　　　　　　　　　　　　　　　　　　　　CIP


GW/VH　9　8　7　6　5　4　3　2　1

# Consultants

**Jean Krajicek Bartek,** Ph.D., R.N., C.A.R.N
Assistant Professor,
University of Nebraska Medical Center,
Omaha, Nebraska

**Leah Cleveland,** Ed.D., R.N.
Professor,
Saddleback College,
Mission Viejo, California

**Marilyn Newcomer Culp,** M.N., R.N.
Assistant Professor,
Southern Oregon State College,
Ashland, Oregon

**Susan Waldrop Donckers,** Ed.D., R.N.
Associate Professor,
Radford Veterans Administration Hospital,
Radford, Virginia

**Patti Eisenberg,** M.S.N., R.N., C.S.
Clinical Specialist, Nutritional Support,
Jewish Hospital of St. Louis,
St. Louis, Missouri

**Kay Gaehle,** M.S.N.(R.), R.N.
Nursing Faculty,
Barnes College,
St. Louis, Missouri

**Mary B. Gardner,** M.S., R.N.
Lecturer,
Assumption College,
Worcester, Massachusetts

**Sondra Giordano,** M.S., R.N.
Assistant Professor,
Dutchess Community College,
Poughkeepsie, New York

**Karolyn W. Givens,** Ed.D., R.N.
Assistant Professor,
Radford University,
Radford, Virginia

**Margaret A. Gray,** M.N., O.C.N., R.N.
Clinical Nurse Specialist, Associate Professor,
Northeast Louisiana University,
Monroe, Louisiana

**Marcia Hill,** M.S.N., R.N.
Manager,
Dermatologic Therapeutics,
Methodist Hospital,
Houston, Texas

**Regina Jennette,** M.A., M.S.N., R.N.
Professor,
Coordinator of Nursing,
West Virginia Northern Community College,
Wheeling, West Virginia

**Barbara Johnston,** M.S., R.N.
Assistant Professor,
Molloy College,
Rockville Centre, New York

**Marilee Kuhrik,** M.S.N., R.N.
Faculty,
Barnes College,
St. Louis, Missouri

**Linda Lane Lilley,** M.S.N., R.N., O.C.N.
Assistant Professor,
Old Dominion University,
Norfolk, Virginia

**Sharon Liversidge,** B.S.N., R.N.
Nursing Instructor,
Vancouver Community College,
Vancouver, British Columbia

**Suzanne E. Malloy,** M.S.N., B.S.N., R.N.
Assistant Professor,
San Jose State University,
San Jose, California

**Lori Mangels,** Ph.D.
Research Associate,
University of Michigan,
Department of Pharmacology,
Ann Arbor, Michigan

**Jacqueline Maxwell,** M.S., R.N.
Instructor,
Foothills Hospital School of Nursing,
Calgary, Alberta

**Shirley Moore,** M.S., M.S.N., R.N.
Faculty,
Barnes College,
St. Louis, Missouri

**Judith L. Myers,** M.S.N., R.N.
Assistant Professor,
St. Louis University,
St. Louis, Missouri

**Barbara Ogden,** M.S.N., R.N.
Assistant Professor,
Faculty Liaison,
University of Florida,
Gainesville, Florida

**Michele Poradzisz,** M.S., R.N.
Instructor,
De Paul University,
Chicago, Illinois

**Gregory A. Reed,** Ph.D.
Assistant Professor,
University of Kansas Medical Center,
Kansas City, Kansas

**Susan A. Reed,** M.S.N., R.N., R.N.C.S.
Clinical Nurse Specialist,
Fort Howard Veterans Administration Medical Center,
Baltimore, Maryland

**Margaret Anne Reilly,** M.S., Ph.D.
Associate Professor,
College of New Rochelle School of Nursing,
New Rochelle, New York

**Carol M. Riscin,** B.S., R.N.
Level I Faculty,
Baptist Medical System School of Nursing,
Little Rock, Arkansas

**Barbara Scheiper,** M.S.N., R.N., C.S.
Executive Director,
Managed PsychCare Provident Counseling,
St. Louis, Missouri

**Frank J. Traeger,** Ph.D., M.A.
Assistant Professor,
Orange County Community College,
State University of New York,
Middletown, New York

**Richard E. Watters,** R.N., M.Ed.
External Studies Coordinator,
Edith Cowan University,
Perth, Australia

**Rita Yaeger,** M.A., M.S.N., R.N.
Professor,
West Virginia Northern Community College,
Wheeling, West Virginia

**Bonnie Young,** B.S.N., R.N.
Instructor,
Sharon Regional Health System School of Nursing,
Sharon, Pennsylvania

**Sheila J. Rankin Zerr,** R.N., M.Ed.
Visiting Assistant Professor,
University of Victoria,
Victoria, British Columbia

# Preface

*Mosby's Pharmacology in Nursing* is unique in several ways. First is its long history of providing nurses with a sound basis for the clinical application of pharmacology (see Publisher's Historical Perspective). Second is the book's usefulness as both a text and a reference. Because of its strong pedagogical features and clear, accessible approach, the book has enjoyed tremendous success as a textbook for students who, when confronted with some of the more rigorous content of their pharmacology course work, find our organization and presentation helpful. *Mosby's Pharmacology in Nursing* has additional appeal as a pharmacology reference because of its thorough coverage of pharmacologic principles and its emphasis on clinical nursing management. This makes the book useful both as a primary textbook and as a clinical reference for later use. Also unique is our comprehensive Instructor's Resource Manual, which, at over 400 pages, contains an unusual selection of teaching resources and strategies designed specifically to encourage students' engagement in the content and their active participation in the teaching/learning process.

## THE REVISION IS ESPECIALLY THOROUGH

This edition has been thoroughly revised and updated to include more than **50 new drugs** recently approved by the FDA—including many 1991 approvals and several investigational drugs. Despite the many pharmacologic advances and the large number of new drugs, an effort has been made to keep the book a manageable size. This was accomplished by condensing some material, deleting outdated information, and tailoring content to the knowledge base required of the nurse.

---

### PUBLISHER'S HISTORICAL PERSPECTIVE

*Mosby's Pharmacology in Nursing* has a tradition of providing the nursing student, educator, and practicing nurse with thorough and up-to-date pharmacology and nursing management.

In all of its previous editions, the book has sold nearly 2,000,000 copies, making it the most widely used and successful nursing pharmacology textbook ever published.

Currently in its eighteenth edition, *Pharmacology in Nursing* has its roots in *A Textbook of Materia Medica for Nurses* by A.L. Muirhead, published in 1919. In 1936 Hugh Alister McGuigan became the primary author, at which time the book was renamed *Materia Medica and Pharmacology*. In 1940 Elsie E. Krug joined McGuigan as coauthor, a role she was to hold until 1948 when she became the primary author. The book was renamed *Pharmacology in Nursing* in 1955, after ten successful editions.

---

The **drug monograph format** of the previous edition has been extensively reorganized. The text within monographs is in narrative form, with fewer headings and a more user-friendly flow. This was done to encourage students to actually read the material rather than scan a column of numerous headings, as is typically done with reference books. To promote ease of use, some discussions have been subdivided, as appropriate, into logical headings for each individual drug or drug group as follows: mechanism of action, indications, pharmacokinetics, side effects/adverse reactions, significant drug interactions, dosage and administration, and pregnancy safety category. These headings are used only within the lengthier or more complex discussions, to help organize the information.

Another major modification of the previous edition of *Mosby's Pharmacology in Nursing* is the expansion of nursing content. Nursing has been strengthened throughout to give the reader a stronger clinical focus. Each drug group or individual drug discussion ends with a **Nursing Management** section, which is subdivided, as appropriate, into nursing process headings: assessment (including nursing diagnoses); intervention; education; and evaluation. The planning step of the nursing process is not included; the implementation step is subdivided into intervention and education for emphasis. This format has been used because the text deals with the generalities of various clients receiving specific agents, rather than with unique individual clients for whom specific goals could be established. For example, the assessment of any client receiving a particular drug should be much the same with respect to the agent that client is receiving. Planning and client outcomes, however, are quite specific for each individual client.

The nursing management sections also address drug therapy specific to geriatric, pediatric, and other special client populations. Also included are explicit instructions to clients concerning self-medication. This approach adds to the nurse's expanding role in client education as an integral part of the administration of drugs.

Also new to this edition is the incorporation of **case studies** for all major drug groups at the ends of selected chapters. The case studies present commonly encountered clinical scenarios and a series of interactive questions to encourage application of key clinical content. Cases are included on topics such as polypharmacy in the elderly, pain management, hypertension, and Parkinson's disease—there are 14 cases in all.

**Geriatric implications** of drug therapy have been expanded and highlighted in boxes to reflect the special needs of this growing population group. Likewise, **pediatric implications** are boxed for emphasis within selected chapters. This new edition also features an up-to-date **new chapter** on immunosuppressants and immunomodulators that addresses medications and disorders affecting the immune system, including specific management of the AIDS client.

More than **150 two-color illustrations** are included, many of which are original and have been created for this edition. Like the cover illustration, many of these new illustrations depict the process of how drugs work in the body, to help students visualize the mechanism of drug action and apply this understanding to the administration of medications.

In response to feedback from pharmacology instructors, we have moved the **key terms lists** to the beginning of each chapter. Placing these terms at the beginning of a chapter allows a quick review of essential terminology and makes the student aware of what to look for or expect in that chapter.

## MANY SUCCESSFUL FEATURES HAVE BEEN RETAINED FROM THE PREVIOUS EDITION

The book is divided into **two major parts.** Part One, "Basic Concepts of Pharmacology," consists of three units. The first unit deals with the principles of pharmacology, and the second with the relationship of these principles to the nursing process. The third unit focuses on the biopsychosocial aspects of pharmacology, including psychologic and cultural aspects of drug therapy, drug therapy across the life span, and substance misuse and abuse. Part Two, "Clinical Aspects," is composed of the broad pharmacologic units that have been retained and modified from the preceding edition. This section, which makes up the largest portion of the book, consists of sixteen units, almost all of which focus on major drug categories.

Our **focus** is on basic concepts of pharmacology, with special emphasis on the role of the nurse in developing a comprehensive approach to the clinical application of drug therapy through use of the **nursing process.** With the increasing importance of pharmacology for the professional nurse, many nursing programs now offer specialized course work as a separate part of the curriculum. In this context, our goal remains to update and expand the scientific foundation that will provide the learner with rationales for clinical practice. Examples of sample **care plans,** including **nursing diagnoses,** are given for major drug classifications to provide guidance for the reader.

**Chapter objectives** are included at the beginning of each chapter to help students get an overview of material presented and to help them focus on important material. For easy identification or review, key terms are set in boldface type where defined in the text. **Summary tables** and **boxes** providing material of further interest are included throughout the book to supplement, reinforce, or help the student make comparisons among similar drugs.

## THE ANCILLARY PACKAGE IS DESIGNED TO FACILITATE LEARNING

An extensive ancillary package has been developed to provide a complete teaching resource for faculty in either integrated or separate pharmacology courses. This ancillary package includes an **Instructor's Resource Manual** that has been expanded and enhanced with a variety of new features. This manual includes: learning objectives; key terms; chapter outlines in a unique three-column format with teaching strategies and collaborative learning activities; an index to disorders discussed in the text; 24 case studies with interactive questions in a worksheet format for student use; 75 additional worksheets reproducible for classroom use; a 400-question testbank in NCLEX case-study format; 50

transparency masters taken from illustrations in the text-book; and an answer key. *A Quick Medication Administration Reference,* packaged with each copy of *Mosby's Pharmacology in Nursing,* includes 64 pages of useful reference data, such as adminstration techniques, drug compatibilities, abbreviations, conversions, weights, measures, client teaching information, and life span considerations. Also available is a **lecture video** that demonstrates the "Five Rights of Medication Administration." For instructors who would prefer not to use photocopies or would like their students to have a separate study guide, we have prepared a **Student Learning Guide** that includes the 75 student worksheets and 24 case studies found in the Instructor's Resource Manual. This learning guide is available only as a special package with the text, at an additional nominal cost. All of these ancillaries have been planned specifically to enable instructors of either integrated or separate pharmacology courses to make the most effective use of time both inside and outside the classroom. The ancillary package is also geared to encourage student involvement and to facilitate comprehension of key content related to pharmacology for nurses.

## ACKNOWLEDGMENTS

Many people have been involved throughout the revision process. We wish to thank the many editors and associates at Mosby–Year Book, especially Don Ladig, our editor and guide. With much gratitude we also thank Robin Carter, who worked so diligently alongside us on an almost daily basis. Her efforts, organizing talents, and support were invaluable during the revision process. During production Steve Hetager did an outstanding job supervising the details necessary to produce our book. Julie Taugner has our special gratitude for her meticulous attention to the design of the book and its package.

We also appreciate the efforts of Judy Myers, who generously shared her professional expertise and developed the case studies in the text. We sincerely thank Linda Wendling for her developmental work and her adept managing of the Instructor's Resource Manual. Likewise, we thank Sheila Rankin Zerr of the University of Victoria for updating the discussions of Canadian legislation. We are sincerely grateful to the instructors who made contributions to the Instructor's Resource Manual: Margaret Burns of Loma Linda University, Loma Linda, California, who contributed 10 case studies; Jane Hartsock of Minneapolis Community College in Minneapolis, Minnesota, who wrote the student worksheets; and Linda Lane Lilley of Old Dominion University in Norfolk, Virginia, who prepared the testbank. And last but by no means least, we are grateful to our families, friends, and colleagues for their patience, support, and encouragement.

We continue to welcome your suggestions and constructive criticisms in regard to *Mosby's Pharmacology in Nursing.* In the past, your comments have been most useful in the development of an improved, relevant pharmacology textbook, and we hope this open dialogue will continue with this and future editions.

*Leda M. McKenry*

*Evelyn Salerno*

# Brief Contents

# Detailed Contents

# Part One

# BASIC CONCEPTS

# Principles of Pharmacology

# Chapter

## ⟫1 Orientation to Pharmacology

### INTRODUCTION

Pharmacology is a living science; that is, it is the study of drug effects within a living system. It deals with all drugs in society today—legal or illegal, prescription or nonprescription (over-the-counter), to prevent disease or to cure or treat illness—drugs in any context. The pharmacologic agents available today have controlled and, in some instances, cured cardiac disease, hypertension, cancer, psychiatric illness, polio, and hundreds of other illnesses. The result has been improved quality of life and, perhaps, extension of the life span. Medications also can potentially

**FIGURE 1-1**   Bas-relief shows temple scene in which physician-god, daughter Hygeia, and symbolic snake cure patients in their sleep. *(From The National Archeological Museum, Athens, Greece. Used with permission.)*

harm the client, which is reflected by the fact that the term "pharmaceutical" is actually derived from the Greek word for poison (Siler et al, 1982). Therefore, the nurse should understand thoroughly any medication before giving it to a client. The nurse must know the usual dose, route of administration, indication(s), significant side effects and adverse reactions, major drug interactions, and appropriate nursing assessment, planning, implementation, and evaluation techniques necessary to safely administer the drug.

A number of terms are fundamental to the knowledge base of nurses. The box on p. 6 lists some basic terms; more are added when appropriate throughout the book.

## HISTORICAL TRENDS

Primitive peoples believed that disease was caused by evil spirits inhabiting the body. This thought persisted throughout the Egyptian period of medicine. Asclepios, who lived between 600 and 700 BC, was considered to be the principal Greek God of healing. He combined religion and healing in a temple setting and his large family represented health or medical idealogy. For example, his wife Epione soothed pain. His daughter Hygeia, the goddess of health, represented the prevention of disease; and Panacea, another daughter, represented treatment. His large temple settings were used to treat both the rich and poor to cure their illnesses (see Figure 1-1).

In the mid fifth century BC, Hippocrates advanced the idea that disease resulted from natural causes and could only be understood through study of natural laws. He believed the body had recuperative powers and saw the health care provider's role as assisting the recuperative process. Called the Father of Medicine, Hippocrates influenced the principles that control the practice of medicine today. Building on the teachings and practices of Hippocrates, Galen (131 to 201 AD) established a system of medicine and pharmacy that was recognized as the supreme authority for several hundred years.

The decline and fall of the Roman Empire marked the beginning of the medieval period (400 to 1580 AD). Germanic barbarians overran Western Europe and reverted to a medicine of folklore and tradition, similar to that of the Greeks before Hippocrates.

At the same time Christian religious orders built monasteries that became repositories for all learning, including pharmacy and medicine. They aided the sick and needy with

## PHARMACOLOGY TERMS

**drug** any substance used in the diagnosis, cure, treatment, or prevention of a disease or condition. The United States Food and Drug Administration (FDA) definition of *drug* also includes any substance listed in *The United States Pharmacopeia* (or *The British Pharmacopoeia*) and all substances, other than foods or devices, capable of altering body structure or function. The terms *medication, medicine, medicinal,* and *medicament* are also used.

**action of a drug** chemical changes or effects that a drug has on body cells and tissues.

**adverse reaction** an unintended and undesirable response to a drug.

**indication** an illness or disorder for the treatment of which a specific drug has a documented usefulness.

**nonprescription or over-the-counter (OTC) drugs** drugs that may be purchased without a prescription.

**pharmacodynamics** what drugs do to the body and how drugs interact with body tissue.

**pharmacogenetics** hereditary influences on an individual's response to a drug or drug category; possible basis for idiosyncratic (unexplainable) drug responses.

**pharmacokinetics** what the body does to a drug, that is, how a drug is altered as it travels through the body; its absorption, distribution, special tissue binding or affinity, metabolism, and excretion.

**prescription drugs** drugs requiring a prescription to be dispensed.

**side effect** an additional effect of a drug that is not necessarily the primary purpose of giving the drug. Side effects may be desirable or undesirable.

---

good food, rest, and medicinals from their monastery gardens.

The Arabs' interest in medicine, pharmacy, and chemistry was reflected in the hospitals and schools they built, the many new drugs they contributed, and their formulation of the first set of drug standards.

In 1240 AD Emperor Frederick II declared pharmacy to be separated from medicine. However, pharmacy was not truly established separately until the sixteenth century, when Valerius Cordus wrote the first pharmacopeia to be printed as an authoritative standard. Paracelsus, professor of physics and surgery at Basel, denounced "humoral pathology" and substituted the idea that diseases were actual entities to be combated with specific remedies. He improved pharmacy and therapeutics for succeeding centuries, introducing new remedies and reducing the overdosing so prevalent in that period.

In the seventeenth and eighteenth centuries great progress was made in pharmacy and chemistry. The first London pharmacopeia appeared in 1618. Many preparations that were introduced are still in use today, including tincture of opium, coca, and ipecac. In 1785 Englishman William Withering introduced infusion of digitalis for heart disease. Edward Jenner made his first public inoculation with smallpox vaccine in 1796.

During the nineteenth century, pharmaceutical chemistry emerged. Serturner's discovery of the alkaloid morphine in 1815 led to research on many vegetable drugs; quinine, strychnine, atropine, codeine, and others were found as a result. Ether and chloroform were first used as general anesthetics in the 1840s. The French *Codex* was issued in 1818 and was the first of the important national pharmacopeias. It was followed by the United States' *Pharmacopeia* in 1820, that of Great Britain in 1864, and Germany's in 1872.

Accurate study of dosage in the nineteenth century led to the establishment of large-scale manufacturing plants to produce drugs. Fewer drugs were prescribed, and knowledge of their expected action became more precise. Rational medicine had begun to replace empiricism.

In 1907 Ehrlich introduced salvarsan for syphilis; Banting followed in 1922 with the discovery of insulin for diabetes mellitus. The sulfonamides, penicillin, and other antibiotics revolutionized the treatment of infectious diseases. Cortisone was first used in 1949 and opened a new era in medical science. In 1955 and 1961 new poliomyelitis vaccines showed similar success.

In the late 1950s oral contraceptives were introduced and had widespread effects on the per capita birth rate and sexual mores. More recently, research has discovered new classes of drugs that the body itself produces, for example, interferon, enkephalins, and endorphins.

Between now and the year 2000, the trends in health care and pharmaceutics will focus on the following:

1. Consumer health education expansion—consumers will continue to seek information on preventive health care matters through computer software programs and other educational resources. People are motivated to take responsibility for health, disease prevention, and lowered costs for medical care.

2. Research—the thrust of research will be directed to finding new treatments, cures, or methods to prevent disease processes that limit the growth, everyday living, or average life span of the individual. Specific areas addressed will be preventing and treating heart attacks, stroke, and other devastating diseases of the cardiovascular system; reversing or curing viral diseases, with a primary focus on acquired immune deficiency syndrome (AIDS); dealing successfully with the muscular atrophic disease states; treating psychiatric illnesses; eliminating infectious disease; and, hopefully, making major in-roads to combat the 100 or more diseases known as cancer.

3. Orphan drugs—research will be expanded to provide new incentives to develop drugs for the individuals suffering from rare, chronic diseases, research that is

usually unprofitable. In 1983 the FDA established an Orphan Drug Act that provides grants to encourage this research. Among the disorders benefiting from this research are hepatic porphyria, hemophilia, leprosy (Hansen's disease), Cushing's syndrome, and Tourette's disorder. Over 20 new drugs have already been approved to treat some of these disease states, while more than 140 drugs are still under study (Tatro, 1988).

As a result of the current and projected trends, the health care consumer will be asking for more information; one of the persons most often questioned is the nurse. The nurse will take on greater responsibility for professional judgment in the administration and supervision of drug therapy as new products—usually more potent, more complex, and, therefore, with greater potential for toxicity—appear on the market. Therefore, nurses must know about and use drug information resources to better care for their clients.

## THE SCOPE OF NURSING MANAGEMENT

Drugs can help or harm. Nurses, physicians, and clinical pharmacists are held legally responsible for safe and therapeutically effective drug administration. Specifically, nurses are liable for their actions and omissions and for those duties they delegate to others, who may include medication technicians, pharmacy technicians, practical nurses, or even physicians. They are personally responsible—legally, morally, and ethically—for every drug they administer or have administered, no matter who actually prescribed it. Indeed, all members of a health team may be held liable for a single injury to a client. The increase in litigation against nurses and physicians indicates that society tolerates only a minimal margin of error in relation to human life. Claims have been brought against health professionals for drug errors that caused loss of life and permanent injury. When claims against health professionals are supported with evidence that the conduct of one or more health professionals helped to bring about the loss or injury, those parties may be held liable. The law, a legal and social norm, requires health professionals to be safe and competent practitioners and permits compensation to those harmed or injured.

However, the law is a protective force for the knowledgeable, competent, and responsible nurse. Nurses who are determined to safeguard patients from drug-induced harm will, for example:

- Use correct techniques and precautions
- Observe and chart drug effects explicitly
- Keep their knowledge base current
- Refer to authoritative sources in professional literature and to pharmacologists, pharmacists, and other respected colleagues
- Question a drug order that is unclear or that appears to contain an error
- Refuse to administer or refuse to allow others to order or administer a drug if there is reason to believe it will be harmful

The law, in turn, protects such nurses from unfair litigation.

Much remains to be learned about the actual mode of action as well as effects from prolonged use of many commonly prescribed drugs. Furthermore, there is increasing concern about drug-induced disease. Fortunately, drug therapy for most conditions or for illness prevention is temporary. However, some diseases require lifelong use of drugs to sustain life (such as insulin for diabetes mellitus) or prolonged use to maintain relatively normal physiologic or psychologic functioning (such as phenobarbital for seizure disorders).

Nurses are entrusted with potent and habit-forming drugs, and they must not abuse or misuse this trust. Used respectfully and intelligently, drugs are comforting and lifesaving. Used unwisely or with undue dependence, they can lead to tragedy. The nurse who combines diligent and intelligent observation with moral integrity and factual knowledge is a safe and competent practitioner and a credit to the nursing profession.

In addition, the nurse must establish with the client a "therapeutic alliance," a respectful and trusting relationship to facilitate the highest level of self-care attainable. The client is the most important participant in the team effort for safe and effective drug administration. Clients are not expected to be submissive, acquiescent, and nonquestioning followers of the health team's instructions, but must be motivated to assume responsibility for their own care; nurses must recognize that the power to comply is ultimately the client's. All the nurse's knowledge, skill, and ability are brought to bear on the establishment of a therapeutic alliance to facilitate the most appropriate level of self-care related to medications.

Pharmacology applies knowledge from many different disciplines, including anatomy and physiology, pathology, microbiology, organic chemistry and biochemistry, mathematics, psychology, and sociology. Thus, clinical drug therapy can be considered an applied science. The thousands of drugs available present a formidable study if they had to be approached as individual agents. Fortunately drugs can be systematically classified into a reasonable number of drug groups based on chemical, pharmacologic, or therapeutic relatedness. Understanding the characteristic effects of a particular class of drugs at the subcellular, tissue, organ, or functional system level permits a student or practitioner to extrapolate information to a wide variety of drugs. A typical representative drug can be selected and studied and its specific characteristics compared to others in the same class. Gradually, the individual builds a knowledge base.

Lists of drugs, dosages, and their indications should not be regarded as dogma. Laboratory research and new scientific methods of evaluation are constantly generating new information. Occasionally there are reports that a drug, even an old and trusted one, is suspected of causing mutations, birth defects, cancer, or less serious secondary effects. Not only nursing students but also practicing nurses are challenged by the proliferation of drugs; most of the drugs on the market today were developed recently. Change is the only constant in pharmacology.

Pharmacology books must be kept up-to-date in the nurse's library. In addition, official current literature on drugs must be followed carefully, since new drugs only slowly make their way into more permanent literature. For the nurse working in a hospital or health service, physicians, instructors, in-service educators, and pharmacists will be on hand to help. In a more isolated practice, greater personal effort will be required to maintain currency. In any case, nurses must pay close attention to the drug therapy of their clients.

Learning is an active process. Therefore clinical experience with drugs is invaluable, for it enables the student to:

1. Note which drugs are most commonly used to treat certain diseases or specific signs and symptoms
2. Note the frequency with which certain drugs are administered
3. Observe which drugs are most effective in relieving particular signs and symptoms
4. Witness individual differences in clients' reactions to a specific drug
5. Relate knowledge obtained from authoritative sources to real-life situations

Regardless of what is to be learned, reasoning and the ability to analyze and synthesize information are prerequisites to understanding. These cognitive skills, along with perceptual skills, permit a student to see meaningful relationships, make comparisons, and determine significance, all of which are essential for sound decision making in nursing.

## THE NURSING PROCESS AND DRUG ADMINISTRATION

The *nursing process* is a systematic method for identifying actual or potential health care problems or impediments to the activities of daily living. It points the way to rational nursing actions and objective evaluation of care.

The direction of the nursing process is fairly universal in the field, although its structure may vary from the widely used pattern of four phases or steps: (1) assessment of data (which may culminate in a nursing diagnosis), (2) planning, (3) implementation, and (4) evaluation.

To apply the nursing process to drug therapy, nurses *assess* the medication needs of their patients partly in terms of how these needs are matched by the prescriber's orders. The result of this assessment by the nurse is the nursing diagnosis. Nurses make *plans,* which include goals that directly relate to their *nursing diagnoses.* The stage is then set for *implementing* the goals, using specific, rationale-

based nursing actions. Such actions might simply be the preparation and administration of a medication as ordered or they might include steps to withhold a dose and obtain a changed order. The final step is the *evaluation* of the outcome in terms of the original goals. Each time a nursing process is evaluated, nurses' knowledge bases increase and become more valuable.

The nursing process is discussed in more detail in Unit Two: The Nursing Process and Pharmacology.

## GOALS OF THIS TEXT

This text orients the reader to nursing pharmacology and therapeutics by presenting a firm theoretic foundation and a practical approach to drug therapy applicable in many settings—the home, the clinic, the extended care facility, the office, the classroom, and the hospital.

Part One provides general principles, theories, and facts about all drugs and their administration. Practical information is presented on how the nursing process is integrated with pharmacology, and general principles of action are given to facilitate a student nurse's learning in both academic and clinical environments. The rest of the book presents specific drug information about clinical applications and nursing management. Thus this book can be used both as a text and as a reference.

To find information about a particular drug in this book:

1. Look it up in the index
2. When you find the information about the drug, refer back to the beginning of the chapter or unit and read the material that precedes the specific discussion

Reading only the pages listed in the Index for the drug will illuminate only the drug's specifics, out of context and without necessary fundamental information about that class of drugs. Reading the background information offers an overall view and places the drug information into an understandable framework.

The specific drug information summarizes what is needed to administer drugs safely and competently. Each discussion is titled with some of the common names by which the particular drug is known. (Chapter 3 explains the various types of names and forms of drugs.) The names of drugs that are available in Canada but not in the United States are followed by a maple leaf symbol (✹).

The **mechanism of action** explains how the drug acts at the biochemical or cellular level to produce its therapeutic effects. The officially approved therapeutic purpose of the drug or the conditions for which it is used are detailed under **indications.** The **pharmacokinetics** section specifies how the drug is absorbed, distributed, associated with tissue, biotransformed or metabolized, and excreted. The section entitled **side effects / adverse reactions** details most of the common secondary effects that may be experienced when the drug is administered. The **significant drug interactions** section names drugs whose concurrent administration requires caution because the concomitant use may lead to an effect different from that of either drug when used alone. The **dosage and administration** section presents currently approved dosages as well as dosing intervals and frequency. It must be noted that not all drugs have been tested for safety and efficacy in administration to the elderly, pregnant women and those who are breastfeeding, or children; the **pregnancy safety** section in each monograph lists the FDA pregnancy safety category. Routes and special techniques for drug preparation are also listed here in each monograph.

## Nursing Management Sections

The nursing management sections describe distinctive nursing measures:

Assessment: data gathering about an individual's experience with medications and/or identifying preexisting medical conditions that might influence the choice of dosage of drug

Intervention: special handling, timing of doses, and other significant aspects of the actual administration of a drug

Education: client teaching for the highest level of self-care related to medication administration

Evaluation: the ongoing monitoring of the client for safe and effective drug therapy

Safe, therapeutically effective drug administration is a major responsibility of nurses. It depends on sound, current knowledge of medications and careful monitoring of their effects on clients. Ongoing laboratory and clinical research modifies and enlarges available drug information, necessitating continual effort to keep one's knowledge up-to-date. The mode of action of many commonly prescribed drugs, effects of their prolonged use, and the possibility of drug-induced disease are yet to be completely understood. There are many sources of current drug information, but even the most diligent student of these sources requires clinical experience to develop competence in drug administration. Few areas of nursing demand more intellectual curiosity, integrity, factual knowledge, and motivation to use reference sources.

## SUMMARY

Pharmacology, the study of drug effects within a living system, has held importance for humanity through the ages, since it has always been linked to our concept of health and illness. It is a field of ever-increasing importance for nursing.

Because nurses are held by law to be responsible for the drugs which they administer, they should maintain a current knowledge base and be competent in the assessment, planning, implementation, and evaluation of the client's nursing care. The goal of this text is to assist the learner to achieve that knowledge and competency within pharmacology.

## BIBLIOGRAPHY

Atkinson LD and Murray ME. (1983). Understanding the nursing process, ed 2. New York: Macmillan Publishing Co.

Carlson JH et al. (1982). Nursing diagnosis. Philadelphia: WB Saunders Co.

Carpenito LJ. (1989/90). Nursing diagnosis: application to clinical practice, ed 3. Philadelphia: JB Lippincott Co.

Cox MB. (1987). Medication errors: what level of risk is acceptable? Nurse Patient Law, June, p. 1.

Cox HC et al. (1989). Clinical applications of nursing diagnoses. Baltimore: Williams & Wilkins.

Doenges ME et al. (1989). Nursing care plans: nursing diagnoses in planning patient care. Philadelphia: FA Davis Co.

Griffith-Kenny JW and Christenson PJ. (1986). Nursing process: application of theories, frameworks, and models, ed 2. St Louis: The CV Mosby Co.

Ivey M et al. (1984). Pharmacotherapeutics in primary care. New York: Elsevier North Holland, Inc.

La Monica EL. (1985). The nursing process: a humanistic approach, Menlo Park, CA: Addison-Wesley Publishing Co, Inc.

Leake CD. (1975). An historical account of pharmacology to the twentieth century. Springfield, Ill: Charles C Thomas, Publisher.

Lyons AS and Petrucelli II RJ. (1978). Medicine: an illustrated history. New York: Harry N Abrams, Inc.

Marriner A. (1982). The nursing process: a scientific approach to nursing care, ed 3. St Louis: The CV Mosby Co.

Murchison IA and Nichols TS. (1970). The legal foundations of nursing practice. New York: Macmillan Publishing Co.

Parks BR Jr. (1988). Orphan drugs . . . pharmaceutical products that may be commercially available in other countries but not in the United States, Pediatr Nurs 14(2):152.

Roger FB. (1972). A syllabus of medical history. Boston: Little, Brown & Co, Inc.

Siler WA et al. (1982). Death by prescription. Tallahassee, Fla: Rose Publishing Co, Inc.

Tatro DS. (1988). Orphan drugs, Facts & Comparisons Drug Newsletter 7(4):25

Trombitas ID et al. (1986). Monitoring the world's published literature for adverse drug experiences, Drug Inf J 20(1):57.

Yura H and Walsh MB. (1987). The nursing process: assessing, planning, implementing, evaluating, ed 5. East Norwalk, Conn: Appleton-Century-Crofts.

*Chapter*

# 2 Legal Foundations

## INTRODUCTION

Since the beginning of time, people have searched for substances to treat illness and cure disease. The oldest prescriptions known were found on a clay tablet, written by a Sumerian physician about 3000 BC, or nearly 5000 years ago.

Many remedies of past civilizations lacked the information we take for granted today, such as the strength of the substances in a preparation or even the ingredients themselves. For example, an Egyptian doctor's cure for night blindness was the "liver of ox, roasted and crushed;" or to cure blindness itself, one was instructed to mix a pig's eye with antimony, red ocher, and honey and pour the mixture into the blind person's ear (Modell and Lansing, 1967). These prescriptions were written about 1500 BC and clearly illustrate the knowledge gap that existed within even the basic sciences of anatomy and physiology. This type of medical practice, although perhaps not always as inappropriate, extended well into the nineteenth century. Standards for preparation, identification of ingredients, proof of effectiveness and safety, and government interventions are largely developments of the twentieth century.

## UNITED STATES DRUG LEGISLATION

Before 1906 patent medicines and remedies were sold by medicine men in traveling wagon shows, drugstores, and mail order and by doctors, real or self-titled. Such products were not required to list ingredients on the label, so many contained drugs such as opium, morphine, heroin, chloral hydrate, and alcohol. Many persons (especially infants) were reportedly injured, became addicted, or died as a result of the dangerous ingredients or their quantities in these preparations.

In 1906 the first federal **Pure Food and Drug Act** was passed to protect the public from adulterated or mislabeled drugs. The law required the drug company to declare on the package label the presence of 11 identified (some of which were in the list just mentioned) dangerous and perhaps addicting drugs. This first law had limitations that were used by the patent medicine dealers for their own gain. For example:

1. False and misleading claims about the curative value of the product were not allowed *on the package,* which was described as a bottle, label, or wrapper that encircled the bottle. Claims made in advertisements, newspapers, or drug almanacs, by word of mouth, or on signs in store windows were not covered. Unscrupulous nostrum dealers took full advantage of this oversight.
2. Serial numbers were required for products containing any of the 11 dangerous drugs, and each label was to bear the words "Guaranteed Under the Food and Drugs Act." This meant that the dealer had registered his product and was legally responsible for it if it was improperly sold under this act. However, many patent medicine dealers implied that this was the government seal of approval. In response to this abuse, this clause was abolished in 1919.
3. Only drugs sold in interstate commerce (made in one state and sold to persons living in other states) were covered. Drugs made and sold within one state did not fall under the jurisdiction of this law.

The Food and Drug Act of 1906 designated *The United States Pharmacopeia* and *The National Formulary* as official standards and empowered the federal government to enforce

**FIGURE 2-1**  Patent medicines and remedies from the turn of the century.

them. Drugs were required to comply with the standards of strength and purity professed for them, and labels had to indicate the kind and amount of morphine or other narcotic ingredients present.

In 1912 Congress passed the Sherley Amendment, prohibiting use of fraudulent therapeutic claims.

A further update of the drug legislation occurred in 1938 with the passage of the federal Food, Drug, and Cosmetic Act. More than 100 deaths had occurred in 1937 as a result of ingestion of a diethylene glycol solution of sulfanilamide. This preparation had been marketed as an "elixir of sulfanilamide" without investigation of its toxicity. Under the 1906 law the only charge that could be made against the drug was that it was mislabeled, since it was labeled an "elixir" and the drug failed to meet the definition of an elixir as an alcoholic solution. The 1938 act prevented the marketing of new drugs before they had been properly tested for safety by requiring the manufacturer to submit an investigational new drug exemption to the government for review of safety studies before a product could be sold.

The Durham-Humphrey Amendment of 1952 further changed the 1938 drug act as it related to legend (prescription) drugs and refills, as follows:

1. Legend drugs could be dispensed by prescription only (see box on p. 12).
2. Legend drug prescriptions could not be refilled without physician authorization.
3. Some legend drugs could be prescribed by oral or telephone instructions.
4. With certain limitations, refills could also be authorized by oral or telephone means.

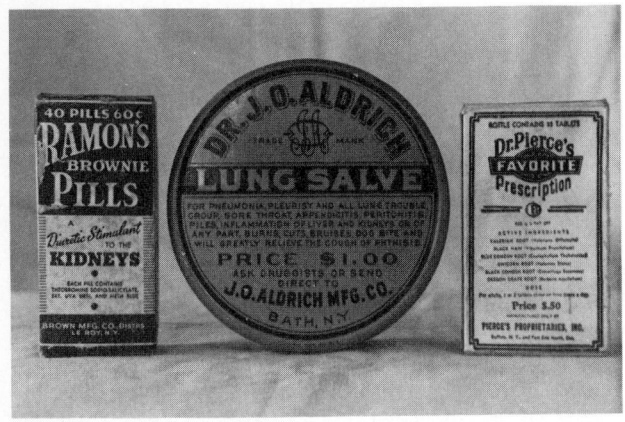

**FIGURE 2-2**    Patent medicines and remedies from the turn of the century.

---

## LEGEND DRUGS

**Legend drugs** must bear the legend "Caution: Federal law prohibits dispensing without prescription." These include all drugs given by injection as well as the following:

1. Hypnotic, narcotic, or habit-forming drugs or derivatives thereof as specified in the law
2. Drugs that, because of their toxicity or method of use, are not safe unless they are administered under the supervision of a licensed practitioner (physician or dentist)
3. New drugs that are limited to investigational use or new drugs that are not considered safe for indiscriminate use by the public

---

This amendment also recognized a second class of drugs, over-the-counter drugs (OTCs), for which prescriptions are not required.

In 1958 Senator Estes Kefauver of Tennessee began a senate investigation into the drug industry when it became known that the drug companies were making huge profits and that some drug promotion was false or misleading. This investigation received little support until given impetus by the thalidomide tragedy, although for the United States it was more a might-have-been catastrophe than a real one. Thalidomide, a hypnotic marketed in Europe, was found to be responsible for severe deformities in babies whose mothers had taken the drug during the early stages of pregnancy. These events led to passage of the Kefauver-Harris Amendment in 1962.

The Kefauver-Harris Amendment required proof of both safety and efficacy before a new drug could be approved for use. This meant that all drugs introduced under the safety-only criterion in effect from 1938 to 1962 had to be evaluated. To do this the FDA signed a contract with the National Academy of Sciences and its research arm, the

National Research Council (NAS/NRC), in 1966 to study all supporting data for all therapeutic claims. This program of study was called the Drug Efficacy Study Implementation (DESI). Early in the study it was agreed that each drug would be rated for effectiveness in each of its stated indications according to the following categories:

*Effective:* substantial evidence of effectiveness.
*Probably effective:* additional evidence required to rate the drug effective.
*Possibly effective:* eventual effectiveness possible, but little evidence of efficacy at the present time.
*Ineffective:* no substantial evidence of effectiveness.

Other rating categories have been formulated since that time:

*Ineffective as a fixed combination:* even though one or more components might be effective if used alone, the product is not acceptable in fixed dosage combination for reasons of safety or because there is no evidence of contribution of each component to claimed effect.
*Effective but:* although effective there is an appropriate qualification or restriction imposed on the drug, which is still under consideration by the NAS/NRC and the FDA; the drug is effective for some recommended uses but not for all, requiring labeling changes.
*Exempt:* less than effective, but a decision on whether to remove drug from the market is deferred pending completion of additional clinical studies.
*Effectiveness to be determined:* products not evaluated by NAS/NRC, which are undergoing FDA evaluation for effectiveness.
*Effective/new safety issue:* products never reviewed by the DESI process, which have now been discovered to have some harmful potential.

Thousands of drugs and therapeutic claims have been evaluated and "ineffective" drugs have been withdrawn from the market. Those rated as "possibly effective" or "probably effective" are being withdrawn or reformulated; however, a drug may remain on the market while claims are being modified and scientific data collected to substantiate the claims. Drugs in the "probably effective" and "possibly effective" categories must be upgraded to the "effective" category within time limits set by the FDA or the claims and drug withdrawn. On the other hand, the system allows the prescribing of an approved drug as therapy for a disorder for which the drug has not been FDA approved. The drug may be a fairly common one, and informed consent for this nonresearch application of the drug need not be obtained. (See the box on p. 13 for a summary of important legislation.)

### Over-the-Counter Drug Review

The over 300,000 OTC drug products currently available contain approximately 700 active ingredients. In 1972 the FDA assembled an advisory review panel to perform an ingredient review, asking primarily the following:

1. Are the stated ingredients recognized as safe and effective for consumers to self-medicate?

## IMPORTANT DRUG LEGISLATION (U.S.)

| | |
|---|---|
| Food, Drug and Cosmetic Act of 1938 | Mandated that drug manufacturers must test all drugs for harmful effects and that drug labels must be accurate and complete |
| Wheeler-Lea Act of 1938 | Defined criteria for nonfraudulent advertising |
| Durkham-Humphrey Amendment of 1952 | Distinguished more clearly between drugs that can be sold with or without a prescription and those that cannot be refilled |
| Drug Amendment of 1962 (Kefauver-Harris Act) | Tightened controls over drug safety and statements about adverse reactions and contraindications; drug testing methods; and drug effectiveness criteria |
| Controlled Substances Act of 1970 (Comprehensive Drug Abuse Prevention Act of 1970) | Categorized controlled substances based on their relative potential for abuse |
| Drug Regulation Reform Act of 1978 | Shortened the drug investigation process to release drugs sooner to the public |

2. Are the labeling, indications, dosage instructions and warnings sufficient? If they were found lacking, appropriate recommendations were to be developed.

This study, completed in 1983, found that approximately one third of the ingredients reviewed were safe and effective for labeled indications. Ingredients found particularly or potentially dangerous were either transferred to prescription status only (such as hexachlorophene, an antibacterial topical product with a potential for inducing neurologic toxicities) or removed entirely from the market. An example of the latter was camphorated oil or camphor liniment, which may be mistakenly taken orally for cod liver oil or castor oil, resulting in serious toxicity and even death. The benefits of this product did not outweigh the serious risks associated with its availability, so it was removed from the market.

## Prescription Drugs Switched to OTC Drug Status

The review panels and other interested parties suggested switching a number of prescription drugs to nonprescription drug categories, since such products were deemed to be safe for self-treatment by consumers without professional guidance. Examples of drugs that were changed from prescription to OTC status include diphenhydramine (Benadryl), which is now an active ingredient in OTC antihistamines and antitussive and hypnotic medications, and chlorpheniramine maleate (Chlor-Trimeton), which is now an OTC

antihistamine. Topical hydrocortisone is now available as an antipruritic and sodium fluoride rinse as an anticaries agent. A number of other products have been tentatively approved for OTC marketing in the future.

## Control of Opioids (Narcotics) and Other Dangerous Drugs

*Narcotic and drug abuse laws.* The Harrison Narcotic Act, passed in 1914, was the first federal law aimed at curbing drug addiction or dependence. This was the first narcotic act passed by any nation. It established the word "narcotic" as a legal term. This act regulated the importation, manufacture, sale, and use of opium and cocaine and all their compounds and derivatives. Marijuana and its derivatives were also subject to this act, as were many synthetic analgesic drugs that proved to produce or sustain either physical or psychologic dependence.

This act and other drug abuse amendments now have only historical import, since they have been superseded by the Comprehensive Drug Abuse Prevention and Control Act of 1970,* also called the **Controlled Substances Act** (CSA), which became effective May 1, 1971. This law was designed to provide "increased research into, and prevention of, drug abuse and drug dependence; to provide for treatment and rehabilitation of drug abusers and drug dependent persons; and to strengthen existing law enforcement authority in the field of drug abuse." This law is also designed to improve the administration and regulation of the manufacturing, distributing, and dispensing of **controlled substances** by legitimate handlers of these drugs to help reduce their widespread dispersion into illicit markets.

The CSA classifies controlled substances solely according to their compared use and abuse potentials. Drugs are classified into numbered levels or schedules from Schedule I to Schedule V (Table 2-1). Drugs with the highest abuse potential are placed in Schedule I; those with the lowest potential for abuse are in Schedule V. These classifications are flexible. Drugs may occasionally be added or be changed from one schedule to another without new legislation. It might be anticipated, for example, that marijuana might be changed to another schedule if and when it is accepted for use in treating the nausea that may occur with cancer chemotherapy or for treatment of glaucoma. Some drugs with potential for dependence, such as ethanol and certain analgesics, are not listed as controlled substances. In practice, states may differ in their implementation of the Controlled Substances Act. Anyone handling controlled substances should follow the more inclusive or stringent requirements of the laws, federal or state.

In July 1973, the Drug Enforcement Administration

---

*Current regulations can be obtained from the nearest Regional Director, Drug Enforcement Administration, or from the Drug Enforcement Administration, Department of Justice, Post Office Box 28083, Central Station, Washington, DC 20005.

**TABLE 2-1** Schedule of controlled substances

| Schedule | Characteristics | Dispensing restrictions | Examples (partial list) |
|---|---|---|---|
| I | High abuse potential<br>No accepted medical use—for research, analysis, or instruction only<br>May lead to severe dependence | Approved protocol necessary | Heroin, marijuana (cannabis), tetrahydrocannabinols, LSD, mescaline, peyote, psilocybin, methaqualone |
| II | High abuse potential<br>Accepted medical uses<br>May lead to severe physical and/or psychologic dependence | Written Rx necessary (signed by the practitioner)—only emergency dispensing permitted without written Rx (only required amount may be prescribed for emergency period)<br>No Rx refills allowed<br>Container must have warning label* | Opium, morphine, hydromorphone, meperidine, codeine, oxycodone, methadone, secobarbital, pentobarbital, amphetamine, methylphenidate, cocaine, and others |
| III | Less abuse potential than drugs in Schedules I and II<br>Accepted medical uses<br>May lead to moderate/low physical dependence or high psychologic dependence | Written or oral Rx required<br>Rx expires in 6 months<br>No more than 5 Rx refills allowed within a 6-month period<br>Container must have warning label* | Preparations containing limited quantities of, or combined with, one or more active ingredients that are noncontrolled substances: codeine, hydrocodone, morphine, dihydrocodeine or ethylmorphine, and nonnarcotic drugs such as derivatives of barbituric acid except those that are listed in another schedule, glutethimide, methyprylon, chlorphentermine, paregoric, and others |
| IV | Lower abuse potential compared to Schedule III<br>Accepted medical uses<br>May lead to limited physical or psychologic dependence | Written or oral Rx required<br>Rx expires in 6 months with no more than 5 Rx refills allowed<br>Container must have warning label* | Barbital, phenobarbital, chloral hydrate, meprobamate, fenfluramine, chlordiazepoxide, diazepam, oxazepam, clorazepate, flurazepam, lorazepam, dextropropoxyphene, pentazocine, mazindol, alprazolam, and others |
| V | Low abuse potential compared to Schedule IV<br>Accepted medical uses<br>May lead to limited physical or psychologic dependence | May require written Rx or be sold without Rx (check state law) | Medications, generally for relief of coughs or diarrhea, containing limited quantities of certain opioid controlled substances |

Courtesy Winthrop Laboratories, New York, N.Y. Modified from Ruggieri N.L.: Drug Therapy 10(12):58-64, 1980, and the DEA pharmacist's manual—an informational outline of the Controlled Substances Act of 1970, U.S. Dept. of Justice, Washington, DC, June 1980. (Data apply to federal CSA and Uniform Controlled Substances Act; state laws may differ.)
*Caution: Federal law prohibits the transfer of this drug to any person other than the patient for whom it was prescribed.

(DEA) in the Department of Justice became the nation's sole legal drug enforcement agency; it replaced the Bureau of Narcotics and Dangerous Drugs.

***Possession of controlled substances.*** It is unlawful for any person to possess a controlled substance unless it has been obtained by a valid prescription or order or unless its possession is pursuant to actions in the course of professional practice. It is a federal offense to transfer a drug listed in Schedule II, III, or IV to any person other than the patient for whom the drug was ordered.

Drug suppliers and hospitals—as well as physicians, pharmacists, and nurses—are individually and collectively responsible for accounting for inventory and management of the flow and distribution of controlled substances. Institutional control of the flow of controlled substances is maintained by carefully recorded checks of the balance on hand, supplies added, and doses administered. The nurse who is responsible for stock supplies of all drugs in each area of an agency usually orders the anticipated prescriptions each morning from the pharmacy. Control is maintained by actual counts of doses of each controlled substance by designated nurses at the beginning and end of each shift or workday. High accountability is demanded of the nurses who do this counting as well as all who handle controlled substances during the work period. Doses are recorded and tallied on a special form supplied by the pharmacy department (and also on a client medication recording form). Thus, each dose is accounted for as it is administered, discarded, wasted, or withheld. All doses of controlled substances should be kept in double-locked cabinets or other secured areas, with the keys in the custody of a designated nurse.

Although these protocols may seem to entail a needless waste of time, they are necessary to safeguard the control of drug flow. Routine delays caused by searching for the narcotics keys or by balky locks, key fumbling, and special recording forms should be counter-balanced by the efficient use of nursing time in client assessments and skilled administration techniques. Evaluation of the delays in the process and mechanisms to rectify them should be performed by nurses as part of their problem-identification and problem-management roles.

## Additional Regulatory Bodies or Services

***Food and Drug Administration.*** The Food and Drug Administration is charged with the enforcement of the federal Food, Drug, and Cosmetic Act. Seizure of offending goods and criminal prosecution of responsible persons or firms in federal courts are among the methods used to enforce the Act.

In addition, pharmaceutical firms must report at regular intervals to the FDA all adverse effects associated with their new drugs. The FDA also has an adverse-reaction reporting program with approximately 450 cooperating reporting sources. All health professionals are encouraged to relate an unusual occurrence or unusually high number of occurrences associated with a drug, its formulation, or packaging, and so forth. Communication may be made directly to the FDA by telephone and by completing a Drug Experience Report form. A response from the FDA will follow. The purpose of this program is to detect reactions that have not been revealed by previous clinical or pharmaceutical studies. Changes in the drug may be required, or it may be withdrawn from the market as was the drug benoxaprofen in 1982.

***Public Health Service.*** The Public Health Service is an agency that is part of the U.S. Department of Health and Human Services. One of its many functions is the regulation of biologic products. This refers to "any virus, therapeutic serum, antitoxin, or analogous product applicable to the prevention, treatment, or cure of diseases or injuries of man." The Public Health Service exercises control over these products by inspecting and licensing the establishments that manufacture them and by examining and licensing the products as well.

***Product liability.*** In a majority of the states the rule of strict manufacturer's liability has been adopted. This doc-

trine holds manufacturers liable for injuries caused by defects in their products, drugs, or devices. **Product liability** exists (1) if a product is defective or not fit for its reasonably foreseeable uses, (2) if the defect arose before the product left the control of the manufacturer, and (3) if the defect caused some person harm. If these three criteria are met, the manufacturer must pay money damages for the harm unless the liability can be shifted to some other party. Anyone harmed by a defective product has the right to sue the manufacturer for compensation.

Harm may be caused if the drug contains an ingredient whose danger is not commonly known or if it contains an ingredient known to be harmful that one would not reasonably expect to find in such a product. Drugs containing potentially harmful ingredients must provide on the label warnings concerning its use; otherwise, the product will be considered defective and the manufacturer liable for resulting harm to unusually susceptible persons who unknowingly use it. Whether or not a product is defective depends on its compliance with current reasonable standards of safety. Manufacturers are legally responsible for knowing the effects of their products. If an unknown risk could have been discovered through a reasonable amount of research, the manufacturer will be held liable for any resulting harm.

Since nurses are accountable, they will want to stay alert to defects in the drugs they administer. Despite manufacturers' quality assurance programs, drug products are susceptible to errors in the manufacturing, packaging, and delivery processes. Although detection of chemical defects is usually outside the nurse's province, detection of observable physical defects is not. Nurses should learn to be keenly aware of physical characteristics of the drugs they administer and make comparisons before administering them. For example, unusual discoloration, other inconsistencies, precipitates, or foreign bodies in parenteral fluids should be considered suspect. Such observations warrant withholding the drug and contacting the pharmacy department or other authoritative source. It might mean that an entire stock supply or batch is defective. Recall of defective drugs is necessary to prevent patient harm.

Occasionally, human error can be expected to cause the wrong medication to be dispensed from the pharmacy. Again, the nurse is responsible for every medication administered. In this case the nurse who administers the wrong drug and the pharmacist who labeled it may both be held liable for any resulting patient harm. This liability has been sustained in the courts on several occasions. Helpful color photographs of many drug formulations can be found in a section of the *Physicians' Desk Reference* when such a question arises. Pharmacists may also provide verification.

## CANADIAN DRUG LEGISLATION

In Canada, the Health Protection Branch (HPB) of the Department of National Health and Welfare is responsible for administration and enforcement of the Food and Drugs Act, as well as the Proprietary or Patent Medicine Act and the Narcotics Control Act. These acts are designed to protect the consumer from health hazards and fraud or deception in the sale and use of foods, drugs, cosmetics, and medical devices. Canadian drug legislation began in 1875 when the Parliament of Canada passed an act to prevent the sale of adulterated food, drink, and drugs. Since that time foods and drugs have been controlled on a national basis.

***Canadian Food and Drugs Act.*** In 1953 the present Canadian Food and Drugs Act was passed by the Senate and House of Commons of Canada. Since that time the law has been amended often. The Act stipulates that no food, drug, cosmetic, or device is to be advertised or sold to the general public as a treatment, preventive, or cure for certain diseases listed in Schedule A of the Act. Among the diseases included in the list are alcoholism, arteriosclerosis, and cancer. When it is necessary to provide adequate directions for the safe use of a drug used to treat or prevent diseases mentioned in Schedule A, that disease or disorder may be mentioned on the labels and inserts accompanying the drug. In addition, the Act prohibits the sale of drugs that are contaminated, adulterated, or unsafe for use and those whose labels are false, misleading, or deceptive. According to the Act, drugs must comply with prescribed standards as stated in recognized pharmacopeias and formularies listed in Schedule B of the Act, or according to the professed standards under which the drug is sold. Recognized pharmacopeias and formularies include the following:

*Pharmacopoea Internationalis*
*British Pharmacopoeia*
*The United States Pharmacopeia/The National Formulary*
*Pharmacopée Française*
*The Canadian Formulary*
*British Pharmaceutical Codex*

The legend Canadian Standard Drug or the abbreviation CSD must appear on the inner and outer labels of a drug to signify that it meets the standards prescribed for it.

Sale of certain drugs is prohibited unless the premises where the drug was manufactured and the process and conditions of manufacture have been approved by the Minister of National Health and Welfare. These drugs are listed in Schedules C and D and include injectable liver extracts, all insulin preparations, anterior pituitary extracts, radioactive isotopes, antibiotics for parenteral use, serums and drugs other than antibiotics prepared from microorganisms or viruses, and live vaccines. Distribution of samples of drugs is also prohibited, with the exception of distribution to duly licensed individuals such as physicians, dentists, or pharmacists. Schedule F of the Act contains a list of drugs that can be sold and refilled only on prescription. Refills may be permitted at specified intervals but cannot exceed 6 months. Drugs listed in Schedule F include the antibiotics, hormones, and tranquilizers. They must always be properly and clearly labeled and include directions for use. Labels on containers of Schedule F drugs must be marked with the

---

### CANADIAN PRESCRIPTION AND RESTRICTED DRUGS

| Category | Description |
|---|---|
| **Prescription Drugs** | |
| Schedule F | May be used only after professional consultation; includes over 200 drugs, identified by Pr on the label |
| Schedule G (also called "controlled drugs") | Affect the central nervous system (stimulants, sedatives); identified by C on the label |
| **Restricted Drugs** | |
| Schedule H | Available only to institutions for research; they present dangerous physiologic and psychologic side effects and have no recognized medical use |

---

symbol Pr (prescription required). These drugs cannot be advertised to the general public other than giving the name, price, and quantity of the drug. (See the box above for a summary of Canadian prescription [Schedule F and G] and restricted [Schedule H] drugs.)

*Controlled drugs* are those listed in Schedule G of the Act and include amphetamines, barbituric acid and its derivatives (barbiturates), and phenmetrazine. Controlled drugs must be marked with the symbol ⟨C⟩ in a clear and conspicuous color and size on the upper left quarter of the label. The proper name of the drug must appear on the labels either immediately preceding or following the proprietary or trade name. Controlled drugs can be dispensed only on prescription.

When a controlled drug is dispensed by prescription, the labels must carry the following:

1. Name and address of the pharmacy or pharmacist
2. Date and number of the prescription
3. Name of the person for whom the controlled drug is dispensed
4. Name of the practitioner
5. Directions for use
6. Any other information that the prescription requires be shown on the label

Prescriptions for controlled drugs cannot be refilled unless at the time the prescription was issued, the practitioner so directed in writing and specified the number of times it could be refilled and the dates for, or intervals between, refilling. All information on the labels must be clearly and prominently displayed and readily discernible. Controlled drugs cannot be advertised to the general public.

*Designated drugs* are the following controlled drugs: (1)

amphetamines, (2) methamphetamines, (3) phenmetrazine, and (4) phendimetrazine. Physicians may prescribe a designated drug for the following conditions: (1) narcolepsy, (2) hyperkinetic disorders in children, (3) mental retardation (minimal brain dysfunction), (4) epilepsy, (5) parkinsonism, and (6) hypotensive states associated with anesthesia. Permission can be obtained to prescribe amphetamines for clients with diagnoses other than those listed.

*Restricted drugs* are those listed in Schedule H of the Act and include the hallucinogenic drugs lysergic acid diethylamide (LSD), diethyltryptamine (DET), dimethyltryptamine (DMT), and dimethoxyamphetamine (STP; DOM). Sale of these drugs is prohibited. These drugs may be obtained for research by a qualified investigator if authorized by the Minister of National Health and Welfare. Precautions must be taken to ensure against loss or theft of a restricted drug.

The following are some of the additional requirements to be found in the Canadian Food and Drugs Act.

1. Labels of drugs must show:
   a. Proper name of the drug immediately preceding or following the proprietary or brand name
   b. Name and address of the manufacturer or distributor
   c. Lot number of the drug
   d. Adequate directions for use
   e. Quantitative list of medicinal ingredients and their proper or common names
   f. Net amount of drug
   g. Common or proper name and proportion of any preservatives used in parenteral drugs
   h. Expiration date if the drug does not maintain its potency, purity, and physical characteristics for at least 3 years from the date of manufacture
   i. Recommended single and daily adult dose; if the drug is for children the label must state: "Children: As directed by physician" or:

   | Age in Years | Proportion of Adult Dose |
   | --- | --- |
   | 10-14 | One-half |
   | 5-9 | One-fourth |
   | 2-4 | One-sixth |
   | Under 2 | As directed by physician |

   j. A warning that the drug be kept out of the reach of children and any precautions to be taken (e.g., *"Caution:* May be injurious if taken in large doses for a long time. Do not exceed the recommended dose without consulting a physician." Warning is to be preceded by a symbol—octagonal in shape, red in color, and on a white background)
   k. Contraindications and side effects of nonprescription drugs
   l. On and after July 1, 1974, the drug identification number assigned to the drug, preceded by the words "Drug Identification Number" or the abbreviation "D.I.N."; to be shown on the main labels of a drug sold in dosage form (i.e., one ready for use by the consumer)
2. Other specific regulations, such as:
   a. Manufacturers must be able to demonstrate that a drug in oral dosage form represented as releasing the drug at time intervals actually is released and available as represented

   b. Oral tablets must disintegrate within 45 minutes. Enteric-coated tablets must not disintegrate for 60 minutes when exposed to gastric juice but must disintegrate within an additional 60 minutes when exposed to intestinal juices
   c. Drugs containing boric acid or sodium borate as a medicinal ingredient must carry a statement that the drug should not be administered to infants or children under 3 years of age
   d. Safety factors such as sterility and absence of pyrogens must be assured in parenteral drugs

The regulations allow the government to withdraw from the market drugs found to be unduly toxic. New drugs introduced to the market must have shown effectiveness and safety in human clinical studies to the satisfaction of the manufacturer and the government.*

**Canadian Narcotic Control Act.**   The regulations of the Canadian Narcotic Control Act govern the possession, sale, manufacture, production, and distribution of narcotics. The Canadian Narcotic Control Act was passed in 1961 and revoked the Canadian Opium and Narcotic Act of 1952. The 1961 Act has been amended a number of times.

Only authorized persons can be in possession of a narcotic. Authorized persons include a licensed dealer, pharmacist, practitioner, person in charge of a hospital, or a person acting as an agent for a practitioner. A licensed dealer is one who has been given permission to manufacture, produce, import, export, or distribute a narcotic. Practitioners include persons registered under the laws of a province to practice the profession of medicine, dentistry, or veterinary medicine. However, persons other than these may be licensed by the Minister of National Health and Welfare to cultivate and produce opium poppy or marijuana or to purchase and possess a narcotic for scientific purposes. Members of the Royal Canadian Mounted Police and members of technical or scientific departments of the government of Canada or of a province or university may possess narcotics in connection with their employment. A person who is undergoing treatment by a medical practitioner and who requires a narcotic may possess a narcotic obtained on prescription. This person may not knowingly obtain a narcotic from any other medical practitioner without notifying that practitioner that he or she is already undergoing treatment and obtaining a narcotic on prescription.

All persons authorized to be in possession of narcotics must keep a record of the name and quantity of all narcotics received, from whom narcotics were obtained, and to whom narcotics were supplied (including quantity, form, and dates of all transactions). In addition, they must ensure the safekeeping of all narcotics, keep full and complete records on all narcotics for at least 2 years, and report any loss or theft within 10 days of discovery.

---

*For more specific information, see *Health Protection and Drug Laws* from Supply and Services Canada, Canadian Government Publishing Centre, Ottawa, Canada KIA 059.

The schedule of the Act lists those drugs, their preparations, derivatives, alkaloids, and salts that are subject to the Canadian Narcotic Control Act. Included in the schedule are opium, coca, and marijuana. Before a pharmacist legally may dispense a drug included in the schedule or medication containing such a drug, he or she must receive a prescription from a physician. A signed and dated prescription issued by a duly authorized physician is essential in the case of all narcotic medication prescribed as such or any preparation containing a narcotic in a form intended for parenteral administration. Medications containing a narcotic and two or more nonnarcotic ingredients may be dispensed by a pharmacist on the strength of a verbal prescription received from a physician who is known to the pharmacist or whose identity is established. Prescriptions of any narcotic drug may not be refilled.

There is one exception to the prescription requirement. Certain codeine compounds with a small codeine content may be sold to the public by a pharmacist without a prescription. In such instances the narcotic content cannot exceed 8 mg per tablet or 20 mg/28 ml. In products of this kind, codeine must be in combination with two or more nonnarcotic substances and in recognized therapeutic doses.

Additionally, items of this nature are required to be labeled in such a fashion as to show the true formula of the medicinal ingredients and a caution to the following effect: "This preparation contains codeine and should not be administered to children except on the advice of a physician." These preparations cannot be advertised or displayed in a pharmacy. It is also unlawful to publish any narcotic advertisement for the general public.

Labels of containers of narcotics must legibly and conspicuously bear the proprietary and proper or common name of the narcotic, name of the manufacturer and distributor, the symbol *"N"* in the upper lefthand quarter, and net contents of the container and of each tablet, capsule, or ampule.

Although the administration of the Canadian Narcotic Control Act is legally the responsibility of the Department of National Health and Welfare, the enforcement of the law has been made largely the responsibility of the Royal Canadian Mounted Police. Prosecution of offenses under the Act is handled through the Department of National Health and Welfare by legal agents specially appointed by the Department of Justice.

The Narcotic Control Act defines a narcotic addict as "a person who through the use of narcotics has developed a desire or need to continue to take a narcotic, or has developed a psychological or physical dependence upon the effect of a narcotic." A person brought into court for a narcotic offense may be placed in custody by the court for observation and examination. If the person is convicted of the offense and found to be a narcotic addict, the court can sentence him or her to custody for treatment for an indefinite period.

Amendments to this Act place special restrictions on methadone. No practitioner can administer, prescribe, give, sell, or furnish methadone to any person unless the practitioner has been issued an authorization by the Minister of National Health and Welfare.

***Application to nursing.*** A nurse may be in violation of the Canadian Narcotic Control Act if he or she is guilty of illegal possession of narcotics. Ignorance of the content of a drug in the nurse's possession is not considered a justifiable excuse. Proof of possession is sufficient to constitute an offense. Legal possession of narcotics by a nurse is limited to times when a drug is administered to a client on the order of a physician, when the nurse is acting as the official custodian of narcotics in a department of the hospital or clinic, or when the nurse is a client for whom a physician has prescribed narcotics. A nurse engaged in illegal distribution or transportation of narcotic drugs may be held liable, and heavy penalties are imposed for violation of the Canadian Narcotic Control Act.

Certain rules for controlled drugs, apart from general rules for prescription drugs, apply in most health agencies:

1. A PRN (an as-required-for-pain order for narcotics) must be rewritten every 72 hours.
2. A standing order (i.e., drug dose administered by the nurse for the physician without obtaining a signed order) is not permitted for narcotic drugs.
3. In an emergency situation a verbal order is permitted if the nurse documents the nature of the emergency in the chart and the nurse validates the order within 24 hours.
4. When a narcotic drug is administered to a client, the nurse must record the date, time of administration, client's name, physician's name, and signature of the nurse.
5. When a client refuses a dose of narcotic, it should be placed in the sewage system in the presence of a witness. If a dose of the drug is contaminated or wasted, the nurse should make an entry in the records book explaining how the dose was disposed of; a witness should then sign the entry.
6. All controlled substances stored on nursing units must be kept in locked cabinets so that only authorized personnel have access to them.

## STANDARDIZATION OF DRUGS

Drugs may vary considerably in strength and activity. Drugs obtained from plants, such as opium and digitalis, may fluctuate in strength from plant to plant and from year to year, depending on where the plants are grown, the age at which they are harvested, and how they are preserved. Since accurate dosage and reliability of a drug's effect depend on uniformity of strength and purity, standardization is necessary. The technique by which the strength and purity of a drug are measured is known as **assay.** The two general types of assay method used are chemical and biologic.

Chemical assay is a chemical analysis to determine the ingredients present and their amounts. A simple example would be the determination of the concentration of hydrochloric acid in a solution to be used medically.

Opium is known to contain certain alkaloids (*active principles* was the older term), and these may vary greatly in different preparations. The United States official standard demands that opium must contain not less than 9.5% and not more than 10.5% of anhydrous morphine. Opium of a higher morphine content may be reduced to the official standard by admixture with opium of a lower percentage or with certain other pharmacologically inactive diluents such as sucrose, lactose, glycyrrhiza, or magnesium carbonate.

In the case of some drugs, either the active ingredients are not known or there are no available methods of analyzing and standardizing them. These drugs may be standardized by biologic methods—**bioassay.** Bioassay is performed by determining the amount of a preparation required to produce a defined effect on a suitable laboratory animal under certain standard conditions. For example, the potency of a certain sample of insulin is measured by its ability to lower the blood sugar of rabbits. The strength of a drug that is assayed biologically is usually expressed in units. For example, insulin injection possesses a potency of not less than 95% and not more than 105% of the potency stated on the label, expressed in U.S.P. insulin units. Both the unit and the method of assay are defined, so that national and sometimes international standards exist.

**Drug standards in the United States.** Since 1980, the only official book of drug standards in the United States is *The United States Pharmacopeia* (USP). Any drug included in this book has met high standards of quality, purity, and strength. Drugs meeting these criteria can be identified by the letters U.S.P. following the official name. The U.S.P. is revised every 5 years by a group of elected scientific experts from a variety of fields, including nursing, pharmacy, pharmacology, and chemistry, to name a few, and by consumers.

The history of the standard reference books in the United States is interesting. The U.S.P., first published in 1820, has over the years been revised and published mainly by physicians. *The National Formulary* (N.F.) was established in 1888 by the American Pharmaceutical Association, and through the years it has been the project of pharmacists. In 1906 when the first Food and Drug Act was enacted, both of these privately issued compendia, the U.S.P. and the N.F., were established as the official standards by the United States government. In 1974 the United States Pharmacopeial Convention purchased *The National Formulary* from the American Pharmaceutical Association; beginning in 1980 the only official book of drug standards in the United States was *The United States Pharmacopeia.*

Although numerous additional reference books and guides are available on the market, two very valuable resources for drug information in a clinical setting are *U.S.P. Dis-*

*pensing Information* and the *American Hospital Formulary Service* (AHFS) *Drug Information* book. The U.S.P.-DI contains information for both the health care provider and the client. The professional volumes provide important information about a drug's indications, pharmacokinetics, precautions, dosing, warnings, and side effects. The volume containing client information on drugs is used to teach patients about their medications. (The advantage of using this volume is that photocopies used in a health care setting do not require any prior permission to distribute. Automatic permission is granted to professionals who copy a limited quantity of monographs from this volume to distribute directly to their patients, free of charge.) The U.S.P-DI is issued annually, with regular supplement updates during the year. AHFS *Drug Information* is issued by the American Society of Hospital Pharmacists. It contains a comprehensive, evaluative approach to individual drugs. Not infrequently, it reviews some of the newer or investigational uses of medications. Both references are highly recommended as resources to the nurse, pharmacist, or physician.

***Drug standards in Great Britain and Canada.*** The *British Pharmacopoeia* (B.P.) is similar to the U.S.P. in its scope and purpose. Drugs listed in the B.P. are considered official and subject to legal control in the United Kingdom and those parts of the British Commonwealth in which the *British Pharmacopoeia* has statutory force. It is published by the British Pharmacopoeia Commission under the direction of the General Medical Council. Dosage is expressed in metric system, although in some cases dosage is indicated in both metric and imperial systems.

*The United States Pharmacopeia* is used a great deal in Canada, and some preparations used in Canada conform to the U.S.P. instead of the B.P. because many of the drugs used in Canada are manufactured in the United States.

The *British Pharmaceutical Codex* (B.P.C.) is published by the Pharmaceutical Society of Great Britain. In general, it resembles *The National Formulary.*

*The Canadian Formulary* contains formulas for preparations used extensively in Canada. It also contains standards for new drugs prescribed in Canada but not included in the *British Pharmacopoeia.* The publication has been given official status by the Canadian Food and Drug Act.

*The Physician's Formulary* contains formulas for preparations that are representative of the needs of medical practice in Canada. It is published by the Canadian Medical Association.

## INTERNATIONAL DRUG CONTROL

International control of drugs legally began in 1912 when the first "Opium Conference" was held at The Hague. International treaties were drawn up legally obligating governments to (1) limit to medical and scientific needs the manufacturing of and trade in medicinal opium, (2) control the production and distribution of raw opium, and (3) establish a system of governmental licensing to control the manufacture of and trade in drugs covered by the convention.

In 1961 government representatives formulated the "Single Convention on Narcotic Drugs," which became effective in 1964. This Act consolidated all existing treaties into one document for the control of all narcotic substances by:

1. Outlawing their production, manufacture, trade, and use for nonmedicinal purposes
2. Limiting possession of all narcotic substances to authorized persons for medical and scientific purposes
3. Providing for international control of all opium transactions by the national monopolies (countries designated to produce opium, such as Turkey) and authorizing production only by licensed farmers in areas and on plots designated by these monopolies
4. Requiring import certificates and export authorizations

An **International Narcotics Control Board** was established to enforce this law. Since enforcement is an immense task, it is impossible to prevent illicit trafficking in drugs. For example, during a 1-year period it was estimated that 1200 tons of opium were circulated in the illicit market when 800 tons were considered sufficient for world medical needs. Laws need to be frequently updated and strictly enforced, but the unfortunate fact is that financial support for regulation and enforcement is sometimes not equal to the task.

## INVESTIGATIONAL DRUGS

The multibillion dollar pharmaceutical industry is constantly screening substances with potential for marketability as new drugs. Prospective drugs may take years and huge amounts of capital to progress through the following FDA-required testing sequence:

A. Animal studies, to ascertain
   1. Toxicity
     a. Acute toxicity—as determined by the **LD 50** (the dose that is lethal to 50% of the animals). This is known as the median lethal dose
     b. Subacute toxicity
     c. Chronic toxicity
   2. **Therapeutic index**—the ratio of the median lethal dose to the median effective dose
   3. Modes of absorption, distribution, metabolism (biotransformation), and excretion of the substance
B. Human studies
   1. Phase I—initial pharmacologic evaluation
   2. Phase II—limited controlled evaluation
   3. Phase III—extended clinical evaluation

A noteworthy lack of correlation exists between levels of toxicity in animals and adverse effects in humans. In addition, many symptoms of adverse effects in animals simply cannot be determined in animals. A partial list of common human symptoms that are not measurably distinguishable in animals includes such effects as dizziness, nausea, drowsiness, nervousness, indigestion, headache, and weakness.

*FDA approval process.* The FDA approval process and specifications are as follows:

1. IND **(Investigational New Drug)**—if a pharmaceutical company or individual desires to investigate a new drug substance or an old drug for a new indication or at a different, unapproved dosage in humans, an IND application must be completed and submitted to the FDA. The IND will include evidence of drug safety by providing animal or clinical information, proof of the investigator's qualifications to perform this research, and evidence of the drug product's proven quality and strength. The investigation covered under the IND is divided into three phases:

  Phase I—initial pharmacologic evaluation. A small number of normal individuals (usually volunteers) will take the drug so that the investigators can determine the pharmacokinetics of the agent (absorption, distribution, metabolism, routes of elimination or excretion). Blood tests, urine analysis, vital signs, and specific monitoring tests are performed during this phase.

  Phase II—limited controlled evaluation. Now the drug will be administered at gradually increasing dosages to selected individuals with the targeted disease. For example, if the product is believed to have antihypertensive properties, individuals with documented hypertension would be chosen for this phase. During this phase, the individual will be closely monitored for drug effectiveness and for side effects. If no serious side or adverse effects occur, the study will progress to phase III.

  Phase III—extended clinical evaluation. The drug is now ready for testing in various centers in the United States in larger numbers of individuals. Standards (protocols) have been developed and are to be followed at all investigative sites. The three objectives for this phase are: (1) clinical effectiveness, (2) drug safety determination, and (3) establishment of tolerated dosage or dosage range.

Several other factors are involved with this program. First, the investigator reports to the FDA after completion of each phase and needs its approval before progressing to the following phases. Second, a double-blind study may be instituted, usually in phase II or phase III. A double-blind study involves the administration of the research drug or a placebo (such as milk sugar) and/or a marketed drug with the same pharmacologic effects as the drug being studied. All of the products are formulated to look the same and then packaged, usually by code numbers. Generally no one involved with the study knows which bottle of medicine the client is taking: the study drug (the active drug) or the placebo. Therefore bias will be eliminated and the evaluation will be done accurately, on the basis of therapeutic response. (The codes and content identification sheets are usually sealed and locked up by the chief investigator or pharmacist, with instructions to break the code only in an emergency.)

2. NDA **(New Drug Application)**—following the completion of phase III of the IND and assuming the data collected indicate that the new drug is very promising, investigators will submit all the collected data to the FDA. After careful review of the

information, the FDA may approve or reject the NDA. If the NDA is approved, the drug product can be marketed for the selected indication in the dosing schedules, as studied. If the NDA is rejected, the FDA may require additional studies or information before reconsideration.

3. ANDA (**Abbreviated New Drug Application**) (for generic drug approval)—generic formulations of currently marketed medications are not usually required to repeat all the previous steps before marketing. A company is required to prove that its product can produce the same therapeutic effects as the already marketed drug. Although nearly all generic drugs require the ANDA, the FDA may require different methods to prove generic equivalency, depending on the drug. For example, chlordiazepoxide (Librium) and amitriptyline (Elavil) require in vivo studies—that is, the generic drug must be given to humans and blood and urine studies data should be equivalent to data obtained when the name brand product is given, according to statistical analysis. Other drug products, such as chlorpheniramine (Chlor-Trimeton) and dexamethasone (Decadron) only need to prove that the manufacturing process is in compliance with Good Manufacturing Practice guidelines and that their quality control standards are equivalent. In other words, testing in humans is not required for the latter drugs. Thus the FDA establishes the criteria according to the drug product, the possibility of bioequivalency problems, or the lack of such problems. Drugs marketed before 1938, such as chloral hydrate and phenobarbital, do not require an approved ANDA before marketing.

The nurse should be aware of several of the limitations of the testing and marketing process. First, the number of persons studied is often limited; it usually averages between 500 and 3000. The studies are conducted for a limited time, and often certain types of individuals are excluded, including infants, children, pregnant women, persons with multiple disease states, and, frequently, geriatric individuals. If a drug is considered safe and effective during the time of study, with the previously mentioned limitations, it is marketed. Once marketed, the drug will be used in much greater numbers of clients, probably for longer periods, and it is inevitable that the drug will be reported to produce additional effects (possibly therapeutic but often adverse) that were not noted during the trial studies.

Therefore, a phase IV, or postmarketing surveillance period, has been advocated to monitor and tabulate information about new drugs in order to disseminate it to health care professionals and consumers. This is a more difficult phase to supervise, since it depends on the voluntary reports of persons in the medical field. The importance of this phase should not be underestimated, since it will affect many more people than the previous three phases combined. (See the box on classifications for newly approved drugs.)

***Informed consent.*** All participants in experimental drug studies should be true volunteers and not subjected to any coercion. **Informed consent** should be obtained from them only after they have been given careful explanation of the purpose of the study, procedures to be used, and risks involved. New drug studies in children and psychiatric pa-

## FDA CLASSIFICATIONS FOR NEWLY APPROVED DRUGS

To assist the professional in immediately classifying new drug entities, the FDA has developed the following method of drug classification. A number and a letter are assigned to each new drug at the IND phase or at the NDA review by the FDA. The manufacturer has a right to contest this classification and have it changed before the final classification is established.

**Numerical Classification:**

1. A new molecular drug
2. A new salt of a marketed drug
3. A new formulation or dosage form not previously marketed
4. A new combination not previously marketed
5. A drug that is already on the market, a generic duplication
6. Product already marketed by the same company (This designation is used for new indications for a marketed drug.)

**Letter Classification:**

A— Drug offers an important therapeutic gain.
B— Medication offers a modest therapeutic gain over drugs already on the market.
C— Drug offers little or no therapeutic gain over other marketed drugs.
M— Drug marketed in a foreign country.
R— Drug has individual unique conditions for approval that are outlined in NDA approval letter.
T— Drug has toxicity problem (such as carcinogenicity in animals).
U— Drug is apt to be used for treatment of children.
D— Drug has less safety or is less effective as compared with marketed drugs but has a compensating virtue (such as being available for persons who have not responded to or are unable to tolerate the alternative available drugs on the market).
P— The important feature of the product is the container or package, not the drug.

The above classification is available by request from the Freedom of Information Staff at the Bureau of Drugs (Food and Drug Administration, 5600 Fishers Lane, Rockville, MD 20857).

tients require special consideration. Beginning in 1983, new rules stipulated that both children's and parents' consent are required for research involving children if it is funded by the Department of Health and Human Services. In addition, these researchers must follow more rigorous guidelines to protect a child's rights. The rights of human participants in medical research have come to be protected under the umbrella of the **Nuremberg Code.** This code was developed under the aegis of American physicians as a result of the post–World War II trials at Nuremberg of Nazi physicians who had conducted experiments on political prisoners without their consent. The Code states essentially that:

1. Truly voluntary consent of the human subject is critical
2. The experiment must be proved to be valid or made possible only through the use of human subjects
3. The results and risks are justified by the study
4. Unnecessary suffering, death, or disability will be avoided
5. The experiment will be conducted in a careful and professional manner by scientifically qualified persons
6. The subject or investigator may terminate the experiment at any point that it is felt unendurable or impossible

Additionally, any experimental drug trials using humans, which are supported by the U.S. Department of Health and Human Services, must also meet federal guidelines for the protection of participants. Institutions supporting such investigational research have review boards that evaluate aspects of the research as it affects human subjects and that formally approve or disapprove research proposals accordingly.

***Pregnancy safety categories.*** Before using any drug during pregnancy, the expected drug benefits should be considered against the possible risks to the fetus. While the FDA has established the following scale to indicate drugs that may have documented problems in animals and/or humans during pregnancy, for many drugs this information is unknown. For drugs with published classifications, though, the physician and/or health care provider should carefully review any precautionary information before using the drug product.

Category A—Studies indicate no risk to the fetus.

Category B—Studies indicate no risk in animal fetus; information in pregnant women is not available.

Category C—Adverse effects reported in animal fetus; information in pregnant women is not available.

Category D—Possible fetal risk in humans reported. But considering potential benefit versus risk may, in selected cases, warrant the use of these drugs in pregnant women.

Category X—Fetal abnormalities and positive evidence of fetal risk in humans is available from animal and/or human studies. These drugs should not be used in pregnant women.

## NURSES AND DRUG RESEARCH

Nurses involved in research projects concerning human subjects, whether tangentially or directly, must be knowledgeable about the precepts of the Nuremberg Code and must protect clients by being ever alert to the possibility of subtle slip-ups in protocol or oversights in adherence to the tenets of the Code. The most important elements of the Code relate to subjects' rights to informed consent and to participation

that is without coercion and fully voluntary. Although these rights would seem to be naturally assumed, they have occasionally been abrogated in the past (for example, instances of forced sterilization of retarded persons and of uninformed inoculations of military personnel with experimental drugs).

Informed consent refers to the written consent to an experimental procedure by individuals after they have received full and adequate explanation of the procedure itself, their full role in it, the expected effects, and the risks. This particular consent is heir to the flaws of other client consents: the information conveyed may be incomplete or not delivered in nonmedical language or perhaps presented at a time when the individual is sleepy or sedated and not fully cognizant of the ramifications of what is being signed. It is the nurse's obligation to ensure that this does not happen and that it is the researcher or the physician, not the nurse, who gives full explanation and answers pertinent questions.

Expanding roles in nursing often include nurses on the team researching experimental drug development. Indeed, more nurses than ever before are conducting research of their own, much of it clinical even if not directly related to investigational drugs, using human subjects. Because of a healthy professional commitment to client well-being, nurses may find themselves caught in an ethical conflict. They likely may feel ambivalent about clients' right to know (vis-a-vis the Patients' Bill of Rights) and yet be uncomfortably aware that too much information may unduly influence a person's behavior or condition in some way and thereby adversely influence the variable under study. This area of ethics awaits further study.

Nurses involved in clinical drug studies should be fully informed about the study and the drug under investigation. All information available to the physician, researcher, or pharmacist should also be available to the nurse. Ethical and legal responsibilities mandate that a nurse's actions be based on adequate knowledge and skill and that clients be protected from foreseeable harm. This necessitates that the nurse know the recommended dosage range and route of administration, the desired therapeutic effect, and the undesired and toxic effects. Throughout the entire investigation the nurse must strictly adhere to the protocols of the study. Recordings of all observations should be as precise as possible, for they will have a direct influence on the study outcome.

## NURSING LEGISLATION

Nursing practice is regulated not only by the previous drug standards and legislation but also by individual state nurse practice acts; joint policy statements among the state nursing associations, medical associations, and hospital associations; and institutional and agency policies. Institutions and agencies may set policies that interpret more specifically those actions allowable under state nursing practice acts, but they may not modify, expand, or restrict the intent of such acts. Personal and professional ethical standards further govern actual nursing decisions and judgments in practice.

The nurse practice acts of individual states define conditions under which nurses may be licensed to practice professionally. One of their functions is to protect the public from unskilled, undereducated, and unlicensed nurses and to delineate clearly the scope of nursing as a health care profession. Another function is to protect nurses by defining clearly their responsibilities and freedoms. Every state nurse practice act includes laws and regulations on reciprocity and suspension or revocation of nurse licenses.

***Changing nursing roles.*** Clearly the traditional roles of the nurse are changing and expanding along with newer techniques and approaches to drug therapy. These expanding roles often find the nurse in activities beyond traditionally accepted nursing practices, which challenge the judgment and accountability of the nurse legally. Two such areas are prescription writing and certain modes of drug administration.

Prescribing medications has been, in the past, a purely medical function as determined by state law, while medication administration has usually been delegated to nurses and occasionally to licensed pharmacists and other trained personnel. In reality, astute nurses have been indirectly prescribing for many years, using diplomatic ploys with physicians to attend to changing patient needs: "Will you write an order for Dulcolax for Mrs. Rommel? She hasn't had a bowel movement for 3 days." Now, certain expanding roles in nursing, along with increased education and expertise (e.g., certification as nurse practitioner by the American Nurses' Association), raise the issue of legalizing the prescribing function of nurse practitioners.

Two reports acknowledged this need, one from the American Medical Association in 1970 and the other from the Department of Health, Education and Welfare in 1971. Both clearly state that the prescribing of medications "may be the practice of medicine when carried out by a physician and the practice of nursing when carried out by the nurse." Several states as a result of this change have amended their nurse practice acts. These amendments have predominantly given authorization to the nurse practitioner to write prescriptions according to established protocols or under physician supervision or collaboration. In 28 states, nurse practitioners have legislative authority to prescribe as of January, 1989.

Other states have nurse-prescribing bills pending. Many states and institutions therein have developed protocols for designating the types of clients to be treated by nurse practitioners. They have also developed formularies to aid in their selection of prescribed drugs and to provide reviews of their prescribing activities, usually by periodic chart audits. One evaluative study of 1000 nurse practitioner-generated prescriptions demonstrated high levels of accuracy, accountability, and legibility. Of these prescriptions 25% were for relief of discomfort, 25% were for contraceptive purposes (one fourth of these were for diaphragms), 40% were for antibiotics, 6% were written to treat chronic stabilized disorders, and a small number were prescribed by the physician consultant for controlled substances. Non-prescription preparations such as Pepto-Bismol, aspirin, and vitamin supplements were also recommended by nurse practitioners. Of the drugs ordered 99% were consistent with the related protocol. There was no evidence of any complications arising from the medication prescribed, and all were deemed appropriate in terms of safety and therapeutic usefulness. It is of interest to note that the ratio of drug prescriptions to clients was lower among the nurse practitioners than among the physicians.

The AMA Socioeconomic Monitoring System has ascertained that physicians who employ nurse practitioners or physicians' assistants are able to charge less for visits and to manage about 20% more client visits per week than those who do not. Physicians who employ nurse practitioners report that they are generally pleased. Those physicians who were polled stated that they fully expected that more nurse practitioners would be part of the health care delivery system in the future and that this would be for the better. The plethora of studies attesting to the nurse practitioner's functional effectiveness, safety, and acceptance by the client may offer one solution to the high costs, long waits, and depersonalization in health care today.

Drug administration was, for a very long period in health care history, a function of physicians only. In fact, nurses were kept ignorant of the medications the client might be receiving. Gradually, medication administration became an interdependent function. Now, nurses find that they are increasingly taking responsibility for suggesting and selecting drugs, their dosages, and regulation. For example, in specialty units of some acute care hospitals, nurses assume responsibility for titrating the infusion rate and the dosage of potent antihypertensive medications against blood pressure parameters. They frequently are responsible for titrating intravenous (IV) fluids to replace gastrointestinal drainage milliliter for milliliter. In the past, nurses were authorized to administer large-volume continuous IV infusions. Nurses now also administer medications by small-volume intermittent IV infusion (by "piggyback" or "rider"). Furthermore, although the procedure is not generally legitimized as a nursing function, some hospitals, particularly in their specialized care units, authorize nurses to give very small-volume, undiluted medications either directly into a vein by IV "push" or into IV tubing.

Generally, changing roles and functions and the laws that govern them are not enacted simultaneously. Usually a time lag exists between the adoption of a new function and official approval. Thus nurses who prepare and inject admixtures intravenously, whatever the delivery system, are breaking new legal ground. Such procedures are potentially more risky than other medication procedures, and nurses who perform them are probably placing themselves in a tenuous legal position unless (1) they are qualified by virtue of adequate training, education, and experience and (2) there exists written sanction. Policies should be drawn up jointly by the administration of the hospital or agency and nursing representatives. These policy statements should carefully delineate the roles of nurses and physicians and present guidelines for these procedures. They should include a list of drugs and routes to be used only by physicians and a list of criteria for permitting nurses to give medications by an IV route or other system. Currently, a trend exists for pharmacy department personnel to draw up and mix admixtures in large-volume IV solutions before delivering the medication to the nursing area. This procedure is done under controlled conditions in agency pharmacies, with the goal of reducing IV solution contamination.

Basically, at the implementation stage, three conditions should be met before a nurse may legally begin to administer a medication by any mode:

1. The medication order must be valid
2. The physician and nurse must be licensed
3. The nurse must know the purpose, actions, effects, and major side and toxic effects of the drug

A valid order is one that leaves no room for doubt as to the medication prescribed, its dose and route, dosing interval, and the prescriber's name/signature. Moreover, the drug must also be deemed appropriate for that specific client. Since nurses are legally, morally, and ethically responsible for their actions, they must assess the medication order for its preciseness, accuracy, and appropriateness.

The medication order must be written and worded in such a way that it is correct, complete, legible, and clearly understandable. If it is not, clarification must be sought from the prescriber. Creating a healthy, open, questioning atmosphere in the prescriber-nurse relationship avoids the very real hazard lurking behind "guessing," "assuming," and "not wanting to bother the doctor."

Although not every medication given in error results in actual client harm, the potential always exists. It is wise to avert such incidents by clarifying the prescribing situation in the following ways.

*Verbal order.* A physician's order is given verbally (often at a client's bedside), such as "Just give her a little Mylanta." It is then appropriate to remind the prescriber that nurses cannot give medication unless the order is in writing. If the order is not written at that time, it is often forgotten. If the medication has already been given and it has not been "signed for" by the prescriber, it is illegal until the order is written and signed. Managing this before the prescriber leaves the area is often not possible.

*Telephone order.* An order given over the telephone can easily be miscommunicated, misinterpreted, or not clearly

heard, and such an order often remains too long unsigned by the prescriber. Many institutions have a specific policy that limits acceptance of verbal or telephone orders to emergency situations only. In any event, the prescriber should sign all orders as soon as possible. Nursing students should not be held responsible for following or transcribing *any* unsigned telephone or verbal orders.

*Incomplete order.* Orders that are not complete in medication name, dose, route, time, or signature must be clarified and completed before administration. Orders for medications to be given by the IV route are the ones most often found incomplete; frequently the rate of infusion is the part missing from the order.

*Incorrect or inappropriate order.* The order may be judged by the nurse to be incorrect or inappropriate for the client (for example, a dose too high for the client of low body weight or impaired renal function as evidenced by low creatinine clearance, or a medication ordered for a client with a recent myocardial infarction that is noted to have secondary effects of tachycardia or dysrhythmias). Here, the situation may be quite intimidating to the nurse, who is now in the position of challenging the judgment of the physician at the risk of incurring embarrassment, job threat, or both. Of course, such intimidation is not justifiable. It is the nurse's or nursing student's absolute right and responsibility to question *any* proposed action that is potentially harmful to a client. Often physicians and some nurses (and many consumers) are under the mistaken impression that nurses who merely act by following a physician's order are absolved from any untoward results of that act. Actually, *no one can relieve a nurse of responsibility for actions;* to carry out an order that the nurse knows to be incorrect constitutes negligence. To change an order by modifying any part of it, if done without consultation with the prescriber, is similarly illegal.

If an order is believed to be in error, some suggested actions are as follows:

1. Validate the order by consulting an authoritative reference source (see Chapter 5 for suggested drug data references).
2. If the order is apparently incorrect, objectively report the conflicting facts and discuss it with the prescriber in a factual, nonblaming manner.
3. If the prescriber still wants the medication given as ordered after the nurse's objections have been raised, can the nurse give the medication if the prescriber takes full responsibility? Again, *no one* can release nurses from full responsibility for every medication they give just because they are acting under a physician's order. To do so is to court a suit for negligence. This fact must be made clear to the prescriber as the rationale for the nurse's refusal to medicate.

If the prescriber chooses to administer the medication personally after the nurse refuses to do so in the belief that it could be potentially harmful to the client, the nurse should see that the facts of the situation are made known to the immediate supervisors, and consultation should be sought if necessary. If the drug is given, the medication record should reflect that it was the prescriber who gave it.

*Invalid order.* Orders signed by medical students, physicians' assistants, or nurse practitioners are not legally accepted as having been signed by a duly licensed physician (this is the wording of most nursing practice acts) and should not be implemented until a physician actually signs it (or the law is changed). Validity of orders written and signed by a nonlicensed intern or resident may be equivocal, depending on local law or policy.

*Order for unfamiliar drug.* Orders for a medication that is unfamiliar to the administering nurse must stimulate a nearly reflex reaction to "look it up" or to "ask the pharmacist." Administration of an unfamiliar drug while remaining in ignorance of its actions, its intended and side effects, and its adverse reactions (at the very minimum) is considered nursing negligence if it results in harm to the client. For instance, a nurse was found liable when a 3-month-old infant died after being given an injectable form of digoxin instead of the pediatric elixir. In another instance, a nurse was found negligent when prolonged infiltration of a levarterenol (Levophed) infusion went unobserved, causing permanent injury.

## Safeguards

Astute nurses are not only alert to the set limits of functioning but also to the quality of functioning within those limits. Although legal suits can be initiated when a nurse exceeds the limits of accepted practice, few have actually been instituted. However, more can be anticipated in the near future as the public becomes more aware of nurses' liability. Most suits, however, are brought by clients or their families who feel they have been subjected to behavior or to a procedure that was not of the quality of practice reasonably expected of someone with a nurse's professional education and experience and under the particular circumstances. This is identified legally as malpractice. The nurse can take safeguards against malpractice resulting from errors of medication administration by observing the **Five Patient Rights:**

1. The *right medication* (the one that was prescribed and one that is not contraindicated)
2. The *right patient* (not someone else's medication by mistake, or one that is similar in appearance)
3. The *right dosage* as prescribed and appropriate (it may involve simple mathematical computations)
4. The *right form, route, and technique* as prescribed
5. The drug at the *right time* (usually within half an hour of the time indicated and at beneficial intervals as ordered)

The following are examples of nursing actions that support and facilitate the meeting of these expectations:

1. Refusing to allow administration of a drug against good nursing judgment
2. Preparing medications in a quiet, undisturbed environment conducive to thoughtfulness and accuracy
3. Comparing the information on the medication ticket or Kardex with the prescriber's order and medication chart to prevent wrong dosage, double-dosing, or the like
4. Looking up information about all new or unfamiliar drugs before administering them
5. Reading medication labels three times—when taking drug container from its storage place, when preparing the dose, and when returning the drug container to its storage place
6. Carefully calculating dosage as necessary, especially when working with decimals
7. Administering only drug doses that were self-prepared
8. Positively identifying the client by comparing the arm band and the name on the medication ticket or medication administration record
9. Listening intently to clients when they question the administration of a particular drug, its color, size, dosage, or a possible allergy; clients frequently give nurses crucial data in this manner
10. Recording the administration of each dose as soon as possible
11. Observing carefully for side and toxic effects, reporting them, and documenting actions taken

Probably the most powerful fundamental force at work in the actual implementation of right and proper nursing practice is the nurse's own concept of ethical and moral correctness and responsibility. The American Nurses' Association (1985), the Canadian Nurses' Association (1980), and the International Council of Nurses (1973) have adopted similar codes of ethics for nurses, which can serve as a guide to standards of conduct, relationships, and practice. At the core of any such professional code is that its precepts spring from the reality that the client is a person with rights and dignity not to be subsumed under the needs or rights of any other person or the machinations of the institution or society at large. For example, clients have every right to know necessary information about a drug they are receiving and to refuse to take it after having been given the courtesy of an explanation, no matter what the consequences.

For the nurse's part, accountability is a term that has gained increasing import, particularly as related to pharmacotherapeutics. Nurses are no longer considered to be merely "physicians' handmaidens" or to be accorded "umbrella protection from litigation" by the physician and the institution. Nurses are increasingly expected to take the responsibility for and be answerable for the service they provide or make available.

In summary, basic guidelines to litigation-free, professional nursing practice and to medication administration in particular include:

1. Knowing the limitations of nursing practice in the community through awareness of the agency policies,

joint medical and nursing practice statements, nursing practice acts, and state and federal laws; then abiding by them

2. Knowing the limitations of one's own skills, expertise, knowledge, and experience and never exceeding them
3. Informing involved personnel of and documenting thoroughly and carefully all happenings related to client care, especially those with potential legal implications
4. Maintaining a professional, caring, and collaborative relationship with clients and their families. Aside from this approach being proper, it can act to dissolve potential dissatisfaction of clients with health care, with the institution, or with its policies.

## NURSING MANAGEMENT

Early in a nursing career, the study of legal issues related to the administration of medications can seem a somewhat less than fascinating exercise. However, as the nurse builds practical experience, this study will prove its worth time and time again. Laws, acts, codes, and regulations shaping pharmacologic practice provide the boundaries for safe practice. Experience proves that knowing the accepted scope of nursing practice of one's nation, state, locale, and institutional community provides security and support for the nurse who aspires to provide harm-free care. Legal statutes only guide; nurses have to translate these guides into action. Often what guides best within legal constraints is the individual nurse's judgment based on his or her own code of ethics, professionalism, and sense of accountability. A fundamental precept is that what is best for the client usually turns out to be best for the nurse.

There are few hard and fast rules in nursing practice. Many specific questions about legalities in drug administration must be answered, and the answer is often, "It depends . . . ." This should not act to immobilize nurses and prevent them from acting in healthy, assertive ways. If they function within the accepted boundaries of practice, continue to stretch for new knowledge, and act accountably for the benefit of their clients, little exists that can harm their clients, themselves, their professional reputations, or their jobs. The sureness that comes with experience flourishes as they exercise these skills. And exercising these skills often demands that they stand up for what is right in client care despite pressures in the situation generated by time constraints or by others who want them to "just get on with it." Being human, nurses will occasionally fail to use the best judgment or to be perfect. This is reasonable, but it is also reasonable for nurses to aspire to structure their practice in ways that make it difficult to fail.

The neophyte nurse may be somewhat shaken by the wealth of background information necessary to safe practice. The more experienced nurse will probably grapple with the temptation to become complacent and to make dangerous

assumptions about the limits of his or her practice. Both need equally to continue to read and question to improve the quality of their decisions, whether the issues stem from legal, ethical, or moral considerations.

The state of the art of drug development, evaluation, and prescribing, although sophisticated and well regulated in theory, may in practice be sometimes inadequate. Moreover, since all chemical substances such as drugs create side effects, adverse reactions, and interactions and many have been identified as having questionable efficacy, it becomes increasingly compelling to avoid medicating, when feasible, and to substitute rational nursing measures. For example, nursing interventions to promote comfort, if instituted effectively and early in the pain cycle, can often substantially reduce pain so that "as necessary" medications become less necessary.

## SUMMARY

Although substances to treat illness and cure disease have always existed, it wasn't until the twentieth century that the need to standardize and regulate such substances became apparent. In the United States the Pure Food and Drug Act of 1906 was the first to limit false and misleading claims for drugs, but only those for interstate commerce. It also established *The United States Pharmacopeia* and *The National Formulary* as official standards for drugs. Further legislation in 1938 required the testing of drugs for safety, and in 1952 the requirements for distinction between legend drugs and OTCs were established. Since that time, both types of preparations have proliferated and there is constant review to ensure their safety and efficacy.

The Harrison Narcotic Act of 1914 was the first law passed by any nation to regulate opium and other substances producing drug dependence. Currently such drugs are governed by the Controlled Substances Act, which in addition to other regulation, classifies controlled substances into their compared use and abuse potentials. This law influences the daily routine of many nurses, since the controlled substances count is performed at the beginning and end of every shift in settings where supplies of these drugs are maintained. Other protections in effect for consumers are the reporting of drug reactions by clinicians to the FDA, the regulation of biologic products by the Public Health Service, and the legislation of product liability by many states.

In Canada similar legislation exists for the protection of its citizens. Although often amended, the Canadian Food and Drugs Act of 1953 stipulates the standards for drugs through a variety of pharmacopeias and formularies; prohibits the sale of unsafe drugs and those with misleading labels; and, in general, regulates biologicals, legend, controlled, and designated drugs. The Canadian Narcotic Control Act of 1961 governs the possession, sale, manufacture, production and distribution of narcotics. By this Act a nurse can only be in legal possession of a narcotic when administering a drug on the order of a physician, acting as the official custodian of narcotics in a hospital/clinic, or being a client for whom a physician has prescribed a drug.

Because drugs vary in strength and activity, standardization is necessary to ensure uniformity of strength and purity by either chemical or biologic assay. The only official book of drug standards in the U.S. is *The United States Pharmacopeia,* whereas Canada uses the U.S.P., *The Canadian Formulary,* and the *British Pharmacopeia.*

The progress of any drug from concept to acceptance in general practice is a lengthy and costly one. The FDA approval process ensures that each drug progresses sequentially from being classified as an Investigational New Drug with an initial pharmacologic evaluation, a limited controlled evaluation, and an extended clinical evaluation. If promising, a New Drug Application is submitted to the FDA for approval. If approved, then a postmarketing surveillance period follows. All participants in the experimental studies of this process should have given informed consent. Because nurses have increasing contact with clinical drug studies, they need to understand the precepts of the Nuremberg Code and be alert to the protection of patients' rights.

Nurses in their practice are not only regulated by the legislation previously discussed, but also by the nurse practice acts of the individual state in which they practice. These statutes define the scope of nursing practice as a health care profession within that state. As the roles of nurses are changing and expanding in drug therapy, many states are allowing nurse practitioners to prescribe within limitations. But even for nurses without a practitioner qualification, medication administration has become more of an interdependent function. Three conditions are essential for the administration of any drug by a nurse: (1) the physician and the nurse must be licensed; (2) the medication order must be valid; and (3) the nurse must be knowledgeable about the drug. In addition, nurses can safeguard themselves from errors of medication administration by observing the Five Patient Rights. With increasing accountability for their role in pharmacotherapeutics, nurses should be aware of guides to litigation-free, professional nursing practice.

## BIBLIOGRAPHY

American Nurses' Association. (1985). Code for nurses with interpretive statements. Kansas City, Mo: The Association.

Bailey-Allen AM. (1987). The legal aspects of medications, Orthop Nurs 6(1):65.

Berlin CM Jr. (1987). The use of drugs during pregnancy and lactation, Public Health Rep (suppl), July-Aug p. 53.

Bigbee JL et al. (1984). Prescriptive authority for nurse practitioners: a comparative study of professional attitudes, Am J Public Health 74(2):162.

Blake JB, editor. (1968). Safeguarding the public: historical aspects of medicinal drug control. Baltimore: The Johns Hopkins University Press.

Canadian Nurses' Association. (1980). CNA code of ethics: an ethical basis for nursing in Canada. Ottawa: The Association.

Colen BD. (1988). Killing with kindness: should the terminally ill become guinea pigs for a storm of untested drugs? Health 20(1):6.

Corbett KM and Lynch LC. (1984). Professional nursing issues in the administration of investigational antiarrhythmic medications, Heart Lung 13(4):395.

Creighton H. (1986). Law every nurse should know, ed 5. Philadelphia: WB Saunders Co.

Feldman EG, editor. (1986). Handbook of nonprescription drugs, Washington DC: American Pharmaceutical Association.

Farley D. (1987/1988). Getting outside advice for the "close calls" . . . advise FDA about the safety and effectiveness of drugs and biological products, FDA Consum 21(10):14.

Farley D. (1987/1988). How FDA approves new drugs, FDA Consum 21(10):6.

Fischer RG. (1987). The meaning of FDA approval. Pediatr Nurs 13(5):360.

How each state stands on legislative issues affecting advanced nursing practice (1989). Nurse Pract 14(1):27.

Johnson JM. (1986). Clinical trials: new responsibilities and roles for nurses, Nurs Outlook 34(3):149.

Kallet A and Schlink FJ. (1933). 100,000,000 guinea pigs: dangers in everyday foods, drugs, and cosmetics. New York: The Vanguard Press, Inc.

Marchette L. (1984). Experimental drugs: where do you stand legally? RN 47(3):23.

Miwa LJ et al. (1986). Adverse drug reaction program using pharmacist and nurse monitors, Hosp Formul 21(11):1140.

Modell W and Lansing A. 1967. Drugs. New York: Life Science Library, Time Inc.

Rosenaur J et al. (1984). Prescribing behaviors of primary care nurse practitioners, Am J Public Health 74(1):10.

Schulmeister L. (1987). Litigation involving oncology nurses, Oncol Nurs Forum 14(2):25.

Snow B. (1988). Diogenes sheds new light on FDA regulatory action, Database 11(2):72.

Stillwell S. (1986). Ensuring safe, effective drug therapy, Nursinglife 6(6):30.

Todd B. (1986). Is tampering detectable? Geriatr Nurs 7(6):333.

United States Pharmacopeial Convention. (1991). USPDI: United States pharmacopeia drug index: drug information for the health care provider, vol 1, ed 11. Rockville, Md: United States Pharmacopeial Convention, Inc.

Young JH. (1961). The toadstool millionaires: a social history of patent medicines in America before federal regulation, Princeton, NJ: Princeton University Press.

# Chapter

# 3 Drug Preparations and Formulations

## CHAPTER OBJECTIVES

*After studying this chapter, you should be able to meet the following objectives and define the terms below.*

1. Describe the difference between chemical, generic, and trade names of drug products.

2. Differentiate between alkaloid, glycoside, gum, resin, and oil.

3. Describe the difference between permissive and mandatory drug substitution in the United States.

4. Name the four main sources of drug and biologic products.

5. Explain the importance of properly storing medication according to the manufacturer's specifications.

6. Identify nursing measures for proper drug storage and distribution.

7. Identify common pharmaceutical preparations and dosage forms.

8. Discuss delivery systems available for the administration of medications.

## KEY TERMS

**alkaloid,** page 30

**brand name,** page 29

**chemical name,** page 28

**efficacy,** page 36

**generic name,** page 29

**glycoside,** page 30

**gum,** page 30

**negative drug formulary,** page 29

**nonproprietary name,** page 29

**oil,** page 30

**potency,** page 36

**proprietary name,** page 29

**resin,** page 30

**trade name,** page 29

## NAMES OF DRUGS

As a drug passes through the investigational stage and the stages when it becomes accepted and marketed, it collects and keeps as many as three different types of names. The first is the chemical name, the second is the generic or nonproprietary name, and the third is the trade name.

The **chemical name** is a precise description of the drug's chemical composition and molecular structure. It is particularly meaningful to the chemist. For example, the chemical name of one of the commonly prescribed antibiotics is 4-dimethylamino-1,4,4a,5,5a,6,11,12a-octahydro-3,6,10,12,

12a-pentahydroxy-6-methyl-1, 11-dioxo-2-napthacenecarboxamide. Its generic name is tetracycline and it is also sold under a number of trade names—Achromycin, Mysteclin, and Panmycin, among others.

The **generic** or **nonproprietary name** is often assigned by the manufacturer with USAN (the United States Adopted Name Council of the U.S.P.) approval to denote a general class of pharmacologically similar drugs as designated by the U.S.P. The generic name is often derived from the chemical name and a simpler form. The generic name is not as easily remembered as the trade name, and thus is not as frequently selected by prescribers. However, the use of generic names is widely advocated to avoid confusion between trade names that are similar. The drug that is packaged under the generic name usually has the same therapeutic efficacy. In addition, it is much less expensive than the trade name drug, often costing only one-third to one-half as much. The **trade name, brand name,** or **proprietary name** is designated by the drug company selling it and is copyrighted; it is a proper noun and the first letter is capitalized. Trade names of drugs discussed in this book will be found enclosed in parentheses following the generic name.

Skilled marketing specialists work to give each of their company's drugs an easily spelled, short trade name that in some way communicates its major action or ingredient. To promote sales of the trade name drug, extensive advertising is usually necessary, involving considerable expense borne mainly by the consumer. However, much of the research in new drugs is done in laboratories of reputable drug firms; and, to realize a legitimate return for the cost of research, drug companies need to patent their products and have exclusive rights to their manufacture and sale.

Health care–related organizations have recognized the growing confusion among the public, health care providers, and prescribers resulting from the proliferation of "new" drugs and multiple names for each. Many of these "new" drugs are reformulations of established drugs (some whose patents may have expired after 17 years) designed to capitalize on an existing market. The United States Adopted Name Council of the U.S. Pharmacopeia Committee and the World Health Organization are working to facilitate world-wide standardization of drug names, and the AMA-USP Nomenclature Committee and the American Pharmaceutical Association are working to create simpler, more useful generic names through the use of more logical syllables. It is anticipated that these approved names will eventually be adopted as the official drug nomenclature.

## DRUG SUBSTITUTION

Nearly every state has a drug substitution law that either permits or mandates substitution on the part of the pharmacist, although the physician retains the prerogative to require the dispensing of a particular brand drug. In permissive states the physician must give express permission

---

> **FLORIDA NEGATIVE DRUG FORMULARY LIST**
> **(as of January, 1990)***
>
> 1. digoxin
> 2. digitoxin
> 3. quinidine gluconate
> 4. theophylline (controlled release)
> 5. warfarin (coumadin)
> 6. conjugated estrogens
> 7. erythromycin base
> 8. chlorpromazine (oral dosage forms)
> 9. dicumarol
> 10. phenytoin
> 11. nitrofurantoin
> 12. levothyroxine sodium

*This list may change in response to the publication of new information or evidence that can alter previous reviewed data.

for substitution by either signing a special section on the prescription form or by checking the correct phrase on the prescription. If substitution is not wanted, the physician may note this by writing "Dispense as written," "Brand necessary," or "Medically necessary."

In states with a mandatory law, the pharmacist is required to dispense approved, less expensive, generic drugs to the patient. Several exceptions apply in such situations; for example, the consent of the client may be required before substitution, or the physician may mark the individual prescription with a term that prohibits substitution, such as "Medically necessary." Some states, such as Florida, have enacted a **negative drug formulary,** a list of drugs that have a proven potential for different bioavailabilities or therapeutic problems and that may not be substituted for trade name drugs. If the physician orders a brand name for these products (see box above for Florida listing), then only that specific brand may be dispensed. If the physician orders any of these products by a generic name, which incidentally, is not recommended, then the pharmacist must select a product that is FDA approved and that has an NDA or an abbreviated new drug application number.

## SOURCES OF DRUGS

Drugs and biologic products have been identified or derived from four main sources: (1) plants, examples of which are digitalis, vincristine, and colchicine; (2) animals and humans, from which drugs such as epinephrine, insulin, and ACTH are obtained; (3) minerals or mineral products, such as iron, iodine, and Epsom salts; and (4) chemical substances made in the laboratory. The drugs made of chemical substances are pure drugs, and some of them are simple substances, such as sodium bicarbonate and magnesium hydroxide. Others are products of complex synthesis, such as the sulfonamides and the adrenocorticosteroids.

*Active constituents of plant drugs.* The leaves, roots, seeds, and other parts of plants may be dried or otherwise processed for use as medicine and, as such, are known as crude drugs. Their therapeutic effect is caused by the chemical substances they contain. When the pharmacologically active constituents are separated from the crude preparation, the resulting substances are more potent and usually produce effects more reliably than does the crude drug. Some of the types of pharmacologically active compounds found in plants, grouped according to their physical and chemical properties, are alkaloids, glycosides, gums, resins (balsams), and oils.

1. **Alkaloids** are organic compounds composed of carbon, hydrogen, nitrogen, and oxygen. They are alkaline in nature and are chemically combined with acids in the laboratory to form water-soluble salts, such as morphine sulfate and atropine sulfate. Synthetic alkaloids formulated in the laboratory have activity similar to plant alkaloids.

2. **Glycosides** are active plant substances that, on hydrolysis, yield a sugar plus one or more additional active substances. The presence of the sugar is not necessary for the action of the glycosides, but it is believed to increase the solubility, absorption, permeability, and cellular distribution. An important cardiac glycoside used in medicine is digoxin.

3. **Gums** are plant exudates. When water is added, some of them will swell and form gelatinous masses. Others remain unchanged in the gastrointestinal tract, where they act as hydrophilic (water-attracting) colloids; that is, they absorb water, form watery bulk, and exert a laxative effect. Agar and psyllium seeds are examples of natural laxative gums, while methycellulose and sodium carboxymethylcellulose are synthetic colloids. Gums are also used to soothe irritated skin and mucous membranes.

4. **Resins** are semisolid or solid plant exudates. The sap of certain trees also contains resin. Resins are not used as commonly today in medicine as they were in the past.

5. **Oils** are highly viscous liquids and are generally of two kinds, volatile or fixed. A volatile oil imparts an aroma to a plant; because of their pleasant odor and taste, these oils were frequently used as flavoring agents. Peppermint oil and clove oil are examples of volatile oils occasionally used in medicine. Fixed oils are generally greasy and do not evaporate easily, unlike volatile oils. Olive oil is a fixed oil used in cooking, while castor oil is an example of a fixed oil used in medicine.

## DRUG CLASSIFICATION

Drug classification can be approached from two perspectives, by clinical indication or by body system. This book uses both approaches where appropriate. Examples of drugs classified by clinical indication include:

Chapter 16—Central nervous system stimulants
Chapter 22—Skeletal muscle relaxants
Chapter 61—Other antimicrobial drugs and antiparasitic drugs

An example of drugs classified by body system is:

Unit Four—Drugs affecting the central nervous system

These drug groupings can assist the nurse to understand and memorize many of the individual agents available for drug therapy. Learning pharmacology becomes easier when one understands the common characteristics of each drug classification and when a prototype drug within each group is studied thoroughly. When a new drug becomes available, the nurse will then be able to associate it with its drug classification and make inferences about many of its basic qualities before reading about its specific properties. Learning which of its qualities are different from the prototype drug and its dosage is extremely helpful.

Nurses need not be overwhelmed by long, involved drug names. Certain syllables can suggest information, such as the suffix "-caine" and its association with anesthetics; the syllable in cortisone derivatives "-cort-"; "ceph-," relating to cephalosporin-type antibiotics; and so on. The basic information to be learned about each major drug includes its generic name and one trade name, the category to which it belongs, its clinical uses, its mechanism of action, side effects and toxic effects, and other specifics associated with the nurse's role in administration of, evaluation of, and client teaching about that drug. "Looking it up" should become second nature to the nursing student as well as the practicing nurse, who should also encourage or initiate the development of a nurses' library shelf and a file of informative inserts about drugs frequently used in the clinical area. *Nurses are professionally, morally, legally, and personally responsible for every dose of medication they administer.*

## PHARMACEUTICAL PREPARATIONS

Pharmaceutical preparations are the formulations that make a drug suited to various methods of administration. They may be made up by the pharmacist but more often are prepared by the pharmaceutical company from which they are purchased. The nurse who is informed about various preparations can make more astute judgments about their individual applications and appropriate recommendations to the prescriber when necessary.

The box on p. 31 details common preparations and their various applications.

## ALTERNATE DRUG DELIVERY SYSTEMS

Innovative advances in scientific technology and computerization provide impetus for the development of increasingly sophisticated drug delivery systems, particularly in the treatment of diabetes mellitus and cancer. However,

---

### Various Forms of Drug Preparations*

**Preparations for Oral Use**

*Liquids*

Aqueous solutions (substances dissolved in water and syrups)

Aqueous suspensions (solid particles suspended in liquid)

Emulsions (fats or oils suspended in liquid with an emulsifier)

Spirits (alcohol solution)

Elixirs (aromatic, sweetened alcohol and water solution)

Tinctures (alcohol extract of plant or vegetable substance)

Fluidextracts (concentrated alcoholic liquid extract of plant or vegetables)

Extracts (syrup or dried form of pharmacologically active drug, usually prepared by evaporating solution)

*Solid*

Capsules (soluble case [usually gelatin] that contains liquid, dry, or beaded drug particles)

Tablets (compressed, powdered drug(s) in small disk)

Troches/lozenges (medicated tablets that dissolve solwly in mouth)

Powders/granules (loose or molded drug substance for drug administration, with or without liquids)

**Preparations for Parenteral Use**

Ampules (sealed glass container for liquid injectable medication)

Vials (glass container with rubber stopper for liquid or powdered medication)

Cartridge/Tubex (single-dose unit of parenteral medication to be used with a specific injecting device)

*Intravenous infusions (suspended on hanger at bedside)*

Glass bottles, flexible collapsible plastic bags, and semirigid plastic containers in sizes from 150 to 1000 ml used for continuous infusion of fluid replacement with or without medications

Intermittent intravenous infusions—usually a secondary IV setup of a small plastic or glass bottle (volume between 50 to 250 ml) to which medication is added. It runs as a "piggyback," hung separately from the primary IV infusion via a secondary administration tubing set usually for a period of 20 to 120 minutes. The primary IV solution is run during the time between medication doses.

Heparin lock—a port site for direct administration of intermittent IV medications without the need for a primary IV solution

**Preparations for Topical Use**

Liniments (liquid suspensions for lubrication that are applied by rubbing)

Lotions (liquid suspensions that can be protective, emollient, cooling, astringent, antipruritic, cleansing, etc.)

Ointment (semisolid medicine in a base for local protective, soothing, astringent, or transdermal application for systemic effects [such as nitroglycerin, scopolamine, estrogen])

Paste (thick ointment primarily used for skin protection)

Plasters (solid preparations that are adhesive, protective, or soothing)

Creams (emulsions that contain an aqueous and an oily base)

Aerosols (fine powders or solutions in volatile liquids that contain a propellant)

**Preparations for Use on Mucous Membranes**

Drops are aqueous solutions with or without gelling agent to increase retention time in the eye. Drops used for eyes, ears or nose

Topical instillation of an aqueous solution of medications usually for topical action but occasionally used for systemic effects, including enemas, douches, mouthwashes, throat sprays, and gargles

Aerosol sprays, nebulizers, and inhalers deliver aqueous solutions of medication in droplet form to the target membrane, such as bronchial tree (e.g., bronchodilators)

Foams are powders or solutions of medication in volatile liquids with a propellant, such as vaginal foams for contraception

Suppositories usually contain medicinal substances mixed in a firm but malleable base (cocoa butter) to facilitate insertion into a body cavity (e.g., rectal or vaginal)

**Miscellaneous Drug Delivery Systems**

Intradermal implants are pellets containing a small deposit of medication that are inserted in a dermal pocket. Designed to allow medication to leach slowly into tissue. Usually used to administer hormones such as testosterone or estradiol

Micropump system is a small, external pump attached by belt or implanted that delivers medication via a needle into a continuous steady dose. Insulin, anticancer chemotherapy, and opioids are examples

Membrane delivery systems are drug-laden membranes that are instilled in the eye to deliver a steady flow of medications, such as pilocarpine or corticosteroids

*Also see text.

# Directions for use of
# *Carpuject*®
### Sterile Cartridge-Needle Units

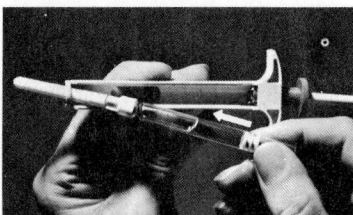

**1** Insert CARPUJECT Sterile Cartridge-Needle Unit, needle end first, into open side of holder.

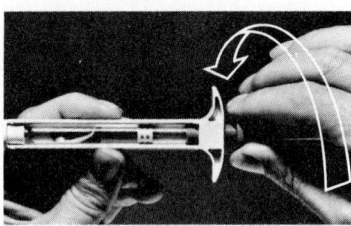

**2** Advance and engage blue locking screw and turn *clockwise* beyond initial resistance until it will no longer rotate.

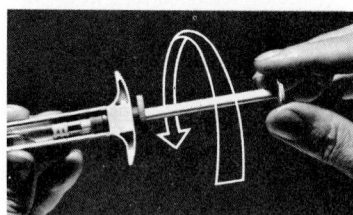

**3** Advance plunger rod and screw *clockwise* onto threaded insert in rubber plunger.
*To maintain sterility, leave needle guard in place until just before use.*

Prepare CARPUJECT unit for administration in a normal manner, ie, remove needle guard, dispel air from cartridge, and proceed with injection.

**FIGURE 3-1** Directions for use of Carpuject sterile cartridge-needle units with self-contained medication. *(Courtesy Winthrop-Breon Laboratories, New York, NY.)*

medical devices are not subject to the same rigorous evaluation or regulation as are drugs. Some examples of these technologies include implanted drug deposits, membrane drug delivery systems, and needle-syringe pump assemblies.

Implanted capsules of a progestin hormone, called the norplant method, are being tested for contraceptive efficacy. Implantation takes 15 minutes and is immediately effective. Contraceptive effects are said to last 5 to 7 years.

Prefilled medication cartridges with special administration injector units (plastic or metal syringes) are marketed under at least two trade names, Carpuject and Tubex. While both systems were primarily developed to help the nurse control and administer special medications, such as nar-

cotics (opioids), the Tubex closed injection system was recently developed to reduce the risk of an accidental self-injection by health care professionals (especially after administering an injection to a person that may be infected with the human immunodeficiency virus [HIV] or other blood-born microorganisms/pathogens). The Centers for Disease Control (CDC) has recommended that health care workers should not recap used needles and that disposable syringes, needles, and other sharp items should be placed in puncture resistant containers after client use, for both safety and proper collection for disposal. Figures 3-1 and 3-2 illustrate the directions for use of a Carpuject and the closed Tubex system.

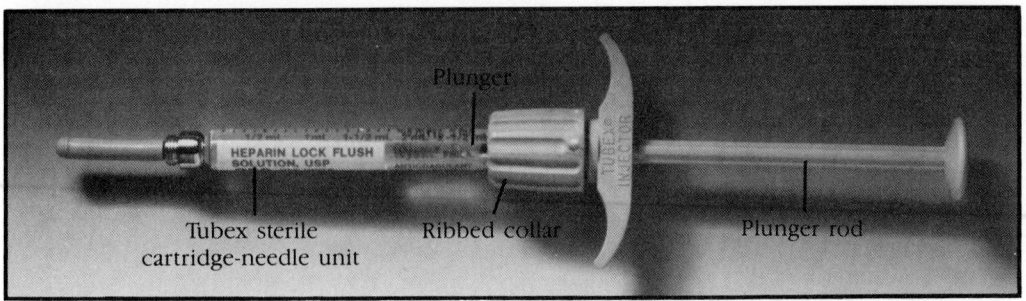

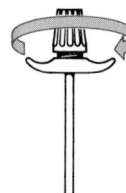

### How to load

1. Turn the ribbed collar to the "open" position until it stops.

### How to administer

Method of administration is the same as with conventional syringe. Remove needle cover by grasping it securely; twist and pull. Introduce needle into patient, aspirate by pulling back slightly on the plunger, and inject.

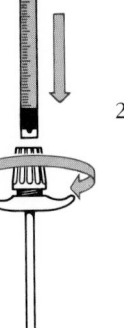

2. Hold injector with the open end up and fully insert the Tubex sterile cartridge-needle unit.

Firmly tighten the ribbed collar in the direction of the "close" arrow.

### How to unload and discard used unit

1. Do not recap the needle. Disengage the plunger rod.

2. Hold the injector, needle down, over a needle disposal container and loosen the ribbed collar. Tubex cartridge-needle unit will drop into the container.

Discard the needle cover.

The Tubex injector is reusable; do not discard.

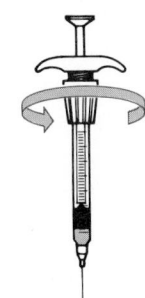

Thread the plunger rod into the plunger of the Tubex sterile cartridge-needle unit until slight resistance is felt.

The injector is now ready for use in the usual manner.

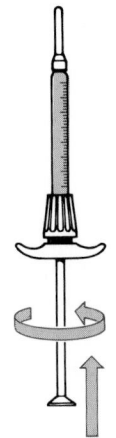

**FIGURE 3-2**  Directions for use of Tubex closed-injection system. *(Courtesy Wyeth-Ayerst Laboratories, Philadelphia, Pennsylvania.)*

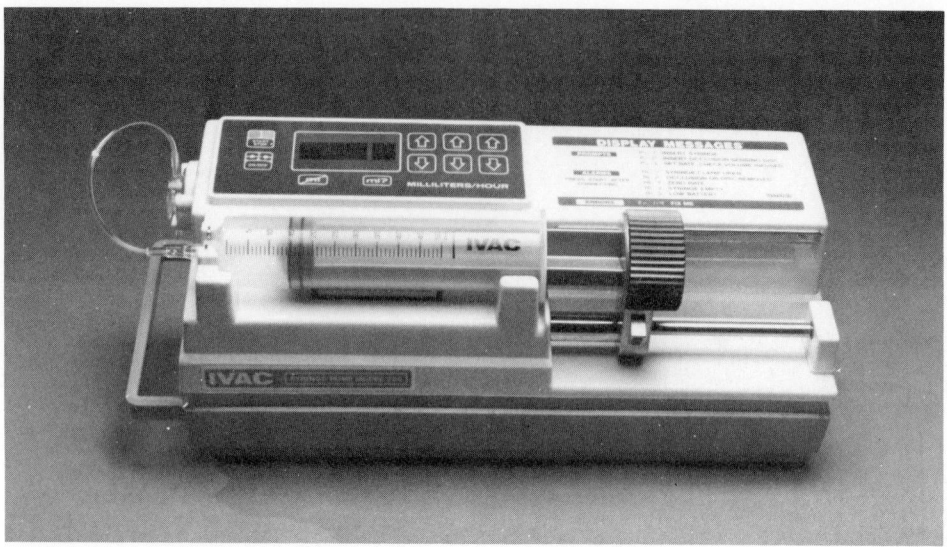

**FIGURE 3-3**   Microcomputer-controlled larger-volume syringe pump for use when medication or fluids of up to 50 ml need to be administered with accuracy and at a constant rate. *(Courtesy IVAC Corp., San Diego, Calif.)*

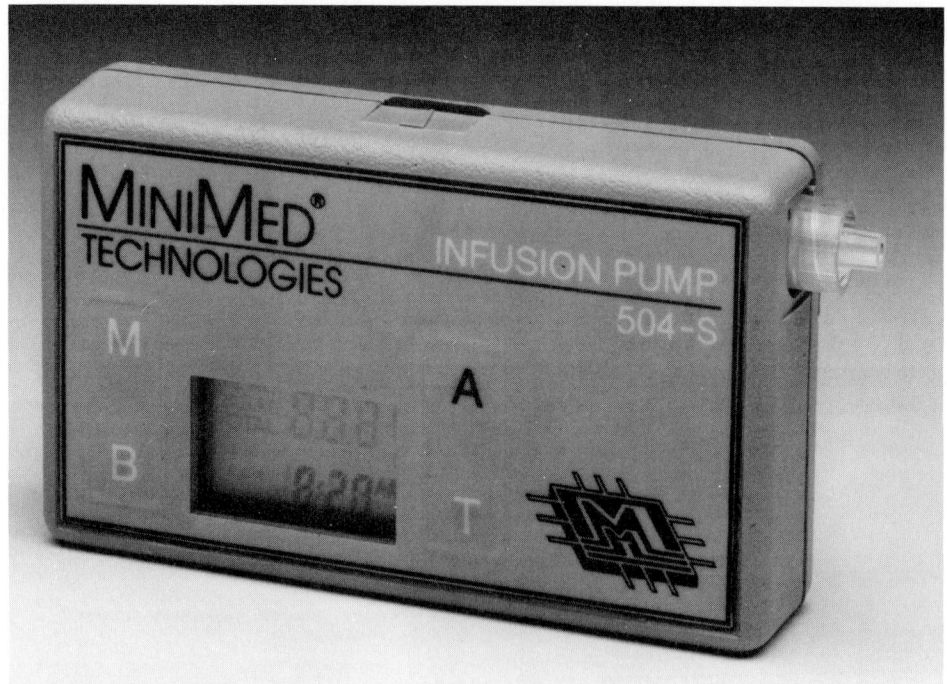

**FIGURE 3-4**   MiniMed Insulin Syringe. This pump (Infusion Pump 504-S) is one of the smallest and lightest available—it weighs only 3.1 ounces. The pump is easy to wear under clothing, carry in pockets, or attach to belts. Its features include a water-resistant package, long battery life (monthly change of batteries), and an alarm system to warn the user of an occlusion, an empty syringe, a runaway infusion, or a low or depleted battery. The unit can be preprogrammed for four basal variation rates in 24 hours, thus providing flexibility for the user. A 24-hour hotline is available to answer any questions on diabetes and the pump therapy. *(Courtesy MiniMed Technologies, Sylmar, Calif.)*

Small pumps weighing about half a pound are now available as portable infusion systems for continuous drug treatment of certain type I diabetic or cancer clients. The systems currently approved and in use generally consist of a battery, a programmable electronic "brain," an electric motor and pump, and a syringe, all of which are detachable as a unit from the small needle kept in place either in subcutaneous abdominal or thigh tissue (for diabetes) or by Silastic catheter inserted into an artery supplying the malignant tumor. These programmable pumps allow for various flow rates and an on-off feature. For clients with varying clinical needs, such a device appears to be quite efficient (Paice, 1987). Some systems are designed to be worn externally over clothing, stored in a pocket, or suspended from a belt or a neck chain (Figures 3-3 and 3-4). See also Figure 3-5 for Sof-set, cannula procedure.

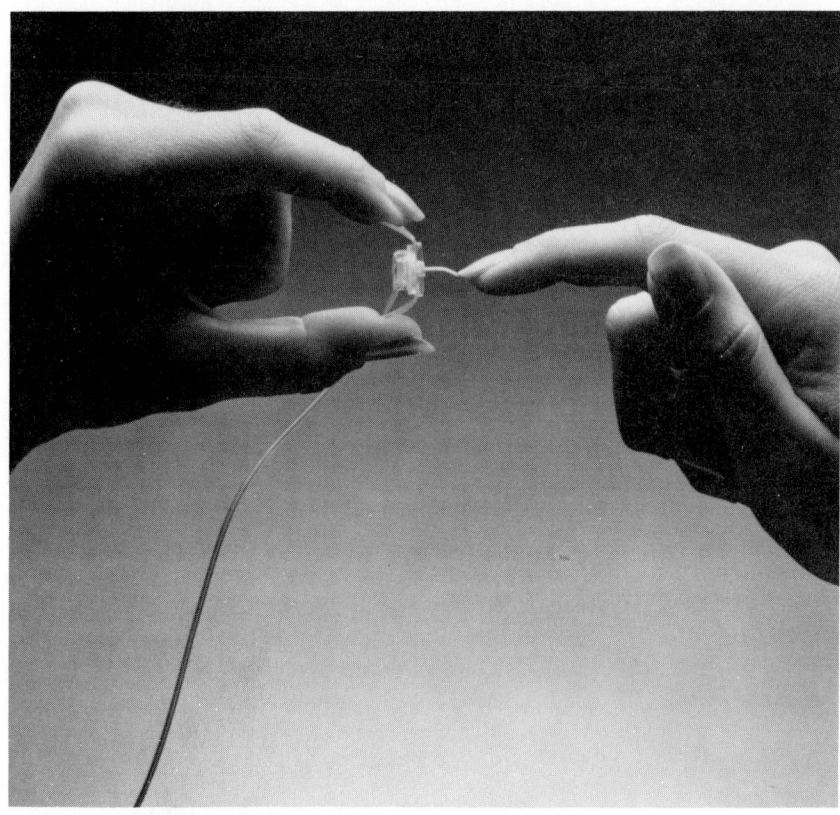

**FIGURE 3-5**  Sof-set, a soft teflon cannula and tubing that is inserted by needle, which is then withdrawn so the pump can operate without one. This product has a special adhesive dressing that inhibits bacterial growth. *(Courtesy MiniMed Technologies, Sylmar, Calif.)*

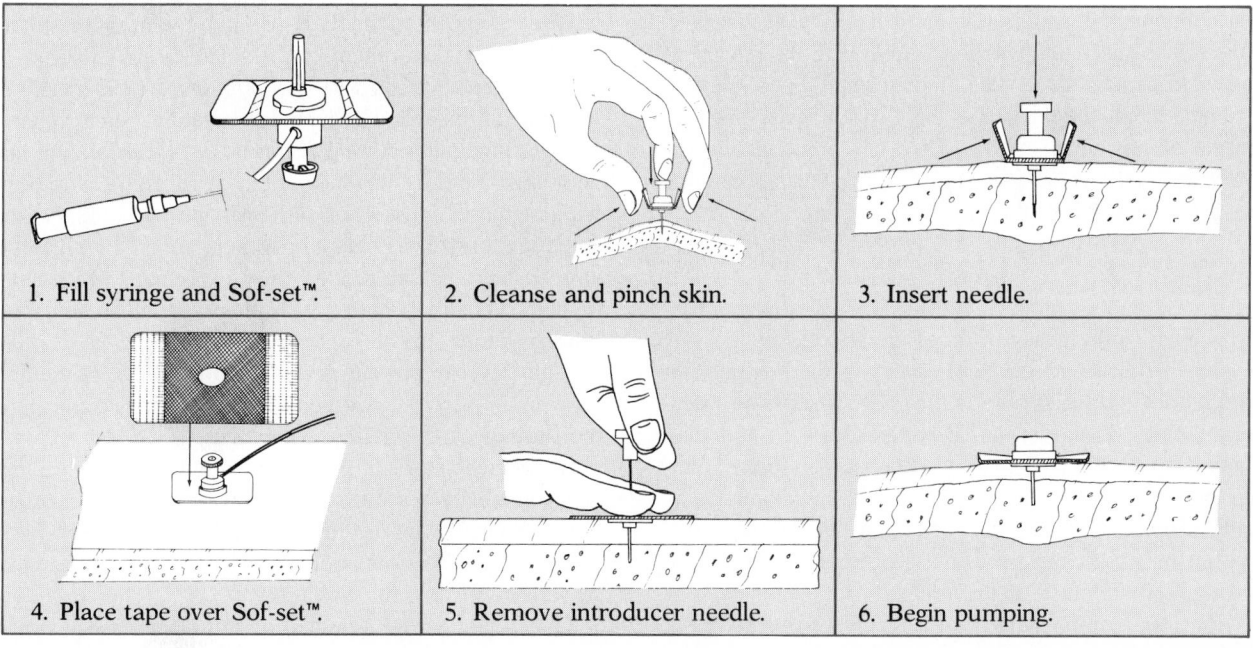

1. Fill syringe and Sof-set™.

2. Cleanse and pinch skin.

3. Insert needle.

4. Place tape over Sof-set™.

5. Remove introducer needle.

6. Begin pumping.

A patient-controlled analgesia (PCA) pump is used to control chronic and acute pain in home or hospital settings. It not only may be programmed for continuous administration, client activated, and clinician activated delivery, but it also records all bolus attempts (successful and unsuccessful) made by the client. Thus the nurse and physician are able to evaluate the appropriateness of the medication therapy and determine when the client is not receiving adequate medication. The pump is light-weight (about 15 ounces) and is worn by the client; thus it will not impair ambulation by mobile clients. For an illustration of a PCA pump, see Figure 12-3 (p. 218).

Topical ointment applications of nitroglycerin have been used to treat anginal pain for some time, and now microquantitative assay capabilities make possible precise unit dosages using transdermal modes. These products contain topical nitroglycerin in small unit-dose adhesive bandages that slowly release the medication over a 24-hour period. Some of them employ a semipermeable, rate-controlling membrane placed next to the skin (on the upper body, usually a hair-free area of the chest); others disperse the nitroglycerin evenly throughout a gel matrix. Nitrodisc, Nitro-Dur, and Transderm-Nitro are some trade name products. Similarly, motion sickness is treated with scopolamine (Transerm-V); duration of effects of one application behind the ear is about 3 days.

The student should be aware that new systems are similar to new drugs on the market—that is, widespread use often uncovers information or problems that were not previously documented. For example, reports have indicated that tolerance develops rapidly to the nitroglycerin patches, which can result in decreased effectiveness in as little as a 2-week time period (Abramowicz, 1984; Parker, 1985).

Investigational studies indicate nitroglycerin patches are more effective if dosed intermittently, that is 12 hours on and 12 hours off the medication. The tolerance that occurs with continuous dosing is less apt to occur with the intermittent dose schedule. Therefore, following the release of a new drug delivery system, monitoring is necessary to document therapeutic response and also the development of adverse or unwanted effects. Then new methods can be researched to offset or reduce any clinical setbacks with the delivery system (Gibaldi, 1988).

## DRUG STABILITY AND STORAGE

The potency and efficacy of drugs are affected by the way they are handled and stored. **Potency** is the strength per milligram of drug. **Efficacy** is the drug's maximum therapeutic ability. Deterioration, decomposition, or alteration of any drug or chemical compound begins as soon as it has been produced and proceeds gradually. Eventually this may result in altered effectiveness or toxicity of the drug, and this fact must be considered in the ordering, storing, dispensing, and administering of drugs.

Most drugs can be stored on the stock supply shelves or in the medication cart, but some must be stored according to specific manufacturer's directions (on the label or package insert) to retard deterioration (e.g., live vaccines, most reconstituted drugs, and most suppositories). Many drugs change composition or potency when exposed to light, heat, moisture, or gases in the environment. The U.S.P. has defined the nomenclature used in instructions for prevention of changes from heat:

Freeze: store below 0° C (32° F)

Store in a cold place: temperature no higher than 15° C (59° F)

Refrigerate: 2° to 15° C (36° to 59° F)

Avoid excessive heat: temperature no higher than 40° C (104° F)

Medication refrigerators should be used soley for the storage of drugs and related necessities and should be cleaned out regularly, with expired drugs being returned to the pharmacy. At least one thermometer should be inside to monitor temperature maintenance.

The appropriate storage of drugs on the nursing unit is a nursing responsibility, usually with the guidance and supervision of pharmacy staff.

Amber-colored containers protect some medications (such as furosemide and nitroglycerin) against deterioration by light. This fact and its significance should be pointed out to clients who are self-medicating and who might otherwise transfer medications to a different container (to take to work, on vacation, and the like). Storage in a closed cabinet or other dark place should also be advised. If it is feasible, clients should be given information about how to tell if their medication has deteriorated (nitroglycerin no longer tingles under the tongue), and they should be told that the medication may need replacement if storage requirements have been abridged or if the medication's appearance or effects have changed.

Certain drugs given intravenously are significantly light-sensitive: amphotericin B; B complex vitamins; cisplatin; daunorubicin; doxorubicin; the essential amino acid for injection, NephrAmine; and nitroprusside. These should be checked for visible signs of deterioration, such as color change, precipitation, or gas formation. Deterioration may neutralize the drugs or make them toxic, and it may occur without these signs. Thus nitroprusside and amphotericin solutions for infusions should be kept covered with foil or an amber plastic bag (not a brown paper bag, which is not light-protective). Unless freshly prepared, all the other solutions should also be kept covered.

Tight lids can prevent degradation or change of the drug form or its active constituents by preventing exchange of moisture or gases within the container.

Clients who store drugs at home should be reminded that they *must* be stored out of reach of children—particularly those under 5, who are insatiably curious and may mimic adults' drug-taking behavior. The drug's childproof cap may serve only to slow the child down.

The expiration dates printed on drug labels mean simply

**TABLE 3-1**   Storage requirements of selected intravenous drugs

| Drug | Stability after reconstitution at | | |
|------|--------------------|-------------|-----------|
| | Room temperature* | Refrigeration | If frozen |
| cefamandole (Mandol) | 24 hr | 96 hr | 6 mo |
| cefazolin sodium (Ancef, Kefzol) | 24 hr | 96 hr | 3 mo |
| cefoperazone sodium (Cefobid, Cefobine) | 24 hr | 120 hr | 3 to 5 wk, depending on concentration and parenteral solution used |
| sterile cefoxitin sodium (Mefoxin) | 24 hr | 48-168 hr | Up to 30 wk, depending on method of preparation |
| cephalothin sodium (Keflin, Ceporacin) | 12 hr (IM use) | 96 hr | 3 mo |
| moxalactam (Moxam) | 24 hr | 96 hr | 3 mo |

Data from U.S.P.-DI, volume I, 1991.

Recommended temperatures: room temperature: 25° C (77° F); refrigeration temperature: 5° C (41° F); frozen: −20° C (−4° F).

that the drug contained is probably at its peak effectiveness until some point in time around that date. Since quality controls in drug production are subject to error rates similar to all other control programs, pharmaceutical companies tend to estimate these expiration dates somewhat conservatively. Thus, the drug is not instantly rendered useless or harmful by that date, but the effectiveness of the therapy may be gradually diminished and the drug may produce inadequate or occasionally toxic results some time after the printed date. The nurse should not administer doses from an outdated lot of drug or container; a fresh supply must be obtained.

Certain precepts should guide the way clients' drugs are stored, distributed, and accounted for. Health care agencies have developed policies that, with variation, support these precepts as rules for client protection and prevent nurses from making errors. In addition, rational nursing judgments must enter into decision making, allowing departure from these rules as a wise and necessary choice, but this should never be undertaken lightly. It should also be a practice to consult other expert personnel or authorities.

The following guidelines are not necessarily listed in order of importance.

1. All medicines should be kept in a special place, which may be a cupboard, closet, or room. The area should not be freely accessible to the public.
2. Narcotic drugs and those dispensed under special legal regulations must be kept in a locked box or compartment (many states require double locks) and accounted for at the end of each shift. Any dose that is wasted or discarded must be attested to by another nurse by initialing of such a notation.
3. In some hospitals each client's medicines are kept in a designated place on a shelf or compartment of the medicine cupboard or room or in a drawer of the medication cart. Such an arrangement means that the nurse must be careful to keep the client's medicines in the right area and to make certain that,

when the client leaves the hospital, the medicines are returned to the pharmacy.
4. If stock supplies are maintained, they should be arranged in an orderly manner. Preparations for internal use should be kept separate from those used externally.
5. Some preparations, such as serums, vaccines, certain suppositories, certain antibiotics, and insulin, need to be kept on a refrigerator shelf, not on the door nor in or near the freezer compartment, to maintain a more constant cool temperature.
6. Labels of all medicines should be clean and legible. If they are not, they should be sent to the pharmacist for relabeling. *Nurses should not label or relabel medicines.*
7. Bottles of medicines should always be stoppered and protected from light, heat, and high humidity as necessary.

Many intravenous drugs require a diluent to dissolve the medication, which then can be added to a larger-volume solution for administration. The storage times for such medications can vary, depending on the following:

1. The expiration date on the package for the fresh package of medication stored under the specific instructions of the manufacturer
2. The expiration time period allotted for the dissolved medication
3. The expiration time period allotted for the dissolved medication added to a larger volume of solution

To obtain accurate information for an individual drug, the reader is referred to the drug's package insert or the U.S.P.-DI. Table 3-1 illustrates storage requirements and expiration times, even within the same drug classification (cephalosporin antibiotics).

## NURSING MANAGEMENT

Close attention to all drugs the nurse administers helps the nurse learn to identify them, tailor their application, and spot errors before they occur. Expertise is built in just this fashion. Learning names of drugs, their formulations, and

## MEDICATIONS THAT SHOULD NOT BE CRUSHED

The following is a partial listing of drugs that should not be crushed.* Whenever possible, it is suggested that if a liquid dosage form of the medication is available, it should be used instead of a crushed tablet. Coated tablets generally should not be crushed because the coating was applied for a specific reason, such as (1) to prevent stomach irritation (e.g., Dulcolax Tablet); (2) to prevent destruction by stomach acids (e.g., Ananase) (3) to produce a prolonged or extended effect (e.g., Dimetapp) or (4) to avoid an unwanted reaction (e.g., chloral hydrate in capsule has a very bitter taste and Povan tablet will stain the mouth red; Kaon tablets may produce a burning effect on sensitive mucosa).

| | | |
|---|---|---|
| Afrinol Repetabs | Donnatol Extentab | Nitroglycerin tab |
| Allerest Capsule | Drixoral tablet | Nitrospan capsule |
| Aminodur Duratab | Ecotrin tablet | Ornade Spansule |
| Artane Sequel | E-Mycin tablet | Quinaglute Duratab |
| ASA Enseals | Entozyme tablet | Quinidex Extentab |
| Azulfadine Entab | Feosol tablet | Slow K tablet |
| Bellergal-S Tablet | Feosol Spansule | Sudafed SA Capsule |
| Compazine Spansule | Ferro Grad-500 Tab | Theo-Dur tablet |
| Diamox Sequel | Isordil Sublingual | Ten-K |
| | Kaon tablet | Trental |

*From Mitchell, 1987; Segal, 1986; Mitchell and Pawlicki, 1989.

their pharmacologic actions is best done in small increments and in a systematic way by making associations between information about a known drug in a classification, its close analogues, and clients cared for. The learning value of analysis and synthesis of these data in actual practice far outweighs that of memorizing long lists of unrelated drugs and their properties. Nurses in emergency departments and in community health are frequently challenged to identify medications from clients' personal unlabeled pill boxes or containers. Often many varieties of drugs and pieces of tablets are mixed together. Clients are often unable to assist in indentification of their drugs, having never been properly educated by the health care system. The *Physicians' Desk Reference* for prescribed drugs, the *Physicians' Desk Reference for Nonprescription Drugs* and the U.S.P.-DI Patient Advice volume provide actual photographs of drugs, which will assist the nurse in making visual identification. In addition, manufacturers often place letters and/or numbers designating an identification code on their solid oral dosage forms. Although these markings may not be meaningful to the practicing nurse, pharmacists and local drug information centers can provide assistance in the identification of generic and trade products from them. Difficult identification problems may be referred to the FDA Drug Listing Branch or the FDA Division of Poison Control, both in Rockville, Maryland. Refer to Table 3-1 for descriptions and examples of some various drug forms now on the market. Various common routes of drug administration are discussed in Chapter 6.

In relation to drug preparation and formulation, the nurse can tailor the nursing intervention to individual client needs. For example, if a topical foam application is seen to be ineffective when it "runs" off the site, an available ointment, cream, or film form may be recommended as more adherent.

If a small child or an elderly client has difficulty swallowing pills, the drug form can be changed in collaboration with the prescriber to an equivalent dosage in liquid form. Such suggestions fall well within the province of nursing care.

If there is no liquid form of a drug available and another route is not feasible, some capsules or tablets may be physically altered to facilitate swallowing. Some capsules may be opened and some tablets crushed to a fine powder and mixed with a small amount of food, such as applesauce, pudding, or custard. Crushing can be done in several ways (it is not necessarily a sterile procedure): by placing the tablet in the bowl of one spoon and crushing with another spoon or by using a paper-lined mortar and a pestle or a special crushing device. A cold food such as ice cream or applesauce will tend to subdue a medication's bitter or oily taste. If the medication is added to a small amount of food, the client should be informed so that it may be entirely consumed on the first mouthful and none of the medication wasted or left unconsumed should the client refuse the rest. Medications should not be added to essential foods for children. Liquid or powdered medication in water may be instilled into a client's nasogastric tube after flushing the tube with a small amount of water, followed by additional water (total: approximately 60 ml). It is wise to medicate via nasogastric tube between tube feedings, if possible, so that drug-food interactions may be avoided and absorption improved. Sustained-release tablets often have layered coatings to delay dissolution and absorption of the drug over time (e.g., Theo-Dur); sustained-release capsules often contain similarly coated beads of the drug (Ornade Spansules). No sustained-release drug form should be crushed, chewed, or vigorously mixed with food for administration, because of the risk of overdosage when all of the drug is released for absorption at one time. Enteric-coated tablets (such as

Dulcolax) contain drugs that could be neutralized or irritating if dissolved in stomach acids; they are intended to dissolve in the small intestine. Enteric-coated medication should be taken whole, on an empty stomach, with a full glass of water to ensure rapid passage to the small intestine. These, as well as certain other drug forms, because of their special construction, should not be crushed for administration. See the box on p. 38 for selected medications that should not be crushed.

Therapeutic effects of drugs also depend on their potency. Thus their freshness at the time of administration may depend on awareness of the expiration dates and the ways the drugs are stored, capped, and used. Gross deterioration and manufacturing defects may manifest themselves in unusual consistency (such as viscosity of liquids and crumbling of tablets) and in changes in color, odor, or sediment. Any deviation from the expected appearance of a drug should be discussed with the pharmacy department and possibly reported to the manufacturer and the FDA. In any event the suspected drug should not be administered or ignored. Childproof caps, although they deter curious investigation and accidental poisonings, do prevent easy opening, especially by arthritic hands and individuals with impaired vision. Clients can request regular caps from the pharmacist.

The growing wealth of drugs from which to prescribe challenges physicians in the field as much as it does nurses and nurse practitioners. Nurses find themselves increasingly in the position of making suggestions and, in some instances, actually prescribing. Recommendations may relate to the medication itself, the dose, the route, or the scheduled timing of doses. This is a highly professional interdisciplinary obligation with which the practicing nurse and the physician should become comfortable.

## SUMMARY

Each drug is identified by three names: chemical; generic (nonproprietary), generally a simplification of the chemical name; and trade or brand name (proprietary), under which the pharmaceutical company markets the drug. Because generic drugs are less expensive than trade name drugs, most states allow pharmacists to substitute them for trade name drugs within limitations.

Plants, animals and humans, minerals, and chemical substances are the four sources of drugs. Pharmacologically active compounds derived from plants are alkaloids, glycosides, gums, resins, and oils.

Drugs are classified either by clinical indication or by body system. Drug classifications facilitate the nurse's understanding of pharmacology by allowing the conceptualization of the common characteristics of each grouping and prototype drug and the association of new drugs with a classification as these drugs become available.

As well as being familiar with various forms of drug preparations, the nurse should be knowledgeable about alternate delivery systems for drugs. Implantable capsules, portable pumps, and dermal patches are just some of the systems that make the administration of medications safer and more convenient.

The maintenance of potency and efficacy of drugs through proper storage and handling is a nursing responsibility. The nurse should follow the guidance of the health care agency's policies for the storage, distribution, and accounting for of drugs. Close attention to the medications the nurse administers assists the nurse in learning to identify them, individualize their application, and detect errors before they occur.

## BIBLIOGRAPHY

Abramowicz M. (1984). Nitroglycerin patches, Med Letter 26(664):59.

Birdsall C et al. (1987). How safe are generic drugs? Am J Nurse 87(4):431.

Florida Board of Pharmacy. (1990). Negative drug formulary, Chapter 21S-5. Tallahassee, Fla.

Fredholm N et al. (1984). Insulin pumps: the patient's verdict, Am J Nurs 84(1):36.

Gibaldi M (1988). Drug administration: tolerance, perspectives, Clin Pharm 6(8):57.

Goodman L et al, editors. (1990). Goodman and Gilman's The pharmacological basis of therapeutics, ed 8. New York: Macmillan Publishing Co.

Hagle ME. (1987). Implantable devices for chemotherapy: access and delivery, Semin Oncol Nurs 3(2):96.

Harris LC et al. (1987). Implantable infusion devices in the pediatric patient: a viable alternative, J Pediatr Nurs 2(3):174.

Knox LS. (1987). Implantable venous access devices, Crit Care Nurse 7(1):70.

McLaughlin-Hagan M. (1987). Devices for administering cancer drugs, AAOHN J 35(4):172.

Mitchell JF. (1987). Oral dosage forms that should not be crushed, Hosp Pharm 24(1):91.

Mitchell JF and Pawlicki KS. (1989). Update to the 1987 revision of "Oral dosage forms that should not be crushed," Hosp Pharm 24(1):91.

Nitroglycerin patch long-term use should include treatment-free interval. (1985). The Pink Sheet, FDC Rep 47(46):3.

Pageau MG et al. (1985). New analgesic therapy, Nursing '85 15(4):47.

Paice JA. (1987). New delivery systems in pain management, Nurs Clin North Am 22(3):715.

Parker J. (1985). Cited in Nitroglycerin patches don't prevent nitrate tolerance in angina patients, Am Pharm NS25(7):20.

Pepper GA. (1986). Revolution in dosage forms, Nurse Pract 11(5):76.

Perrault RM et al. (1987). Intraperitoneal chemotherapy, Nursing 17(9):112.

Powers J. (1989). Stat news, Sept, Florida Pharmacy Association.

Segal C. (1986). To crush or not to crush, Hosp Formul 21(8):882.

Speciale JL and Kaalaas J. (1985). Infuse-a-port: new path for IV chemotherapy, Nursing '85 15(10):40.

Strauss S and Sherman M. (1985). Regulations pertaining to expiration dating of drug products, US Pharmacist 10(4):40.

Turco SJ. (1986). Trends and new developments in recent IV delivery systems, CINA J 2(1):4.

United States Pharmacopeial Convention. (1991). USPDI: United States pharmacopeia drug index: drug information for the health care provider, vol, 1 ed 11. Rockville, Md: United States Pharmacopeia Convention, Inc.

Waldman SD et al. (1987). Troubleshooting intraspinal narcotic delivery systems, Am J Nurs 87(1):63.

Williams PJ. (1989). How do you keep medicines from clogging feeding tubes? Am J Nurs 89(2):181.

*Chapter*

 *4* # Principles of Drug Action

## CHAPTER OBJECTIVES

*After studying this chapter, you should be able to meet the following objectives and define the key terms.*

1. Discuss the three general properties of drugs.

2. Explain current theories of drug action: drug-receptor interaction, drug-enzyme interaction, and nonspecific drug interaction.

3. Describe the physiologic processes mediating drug action.

4. Cite examples of drug properties that influence pharmacokinetics.

5. Describe the three phases of drug activity: pharmaceutical, pharmacokinetic, and pharmacodynamic.

6. Describe nursing management related to client variables altering drug responses.

7. List unusual and adverse responses to drug therapy.

8. Identify nursing assessments that can be used to detect actual or potential adverse drug reactions.

## KEY TERMS

**absorption,** page 45

**bioavailability,** page 48

**biotransformation,** page 50

**buccal,** page 47

**dissolution,** page 43

**distribution,** page 48

**enteral,** page 46

**excretion,** page 51

**half-life,** page 55

**iatrogenic,** page 57

**intramuscular,** page 47

**intrathecal,** page 47

**intravenous,** page 47

**loading dose,** page 45

**maintenance dose,** page 45

**parenteral,** page 47

**receptor,** page 53

**subcutaneous,** page 47

**sublingual,** page 47

## INTRODUCTION

Since the number of drugs used in medical therapy is increasing tremendously, the nurse's responsibilities concerning these agents have also expanded. To approach the level of knowledge needed to meet these increased responsibilities, all health professionals must develop a fundamental theoretical framework within which to study and apply an understanding of drug therapy.

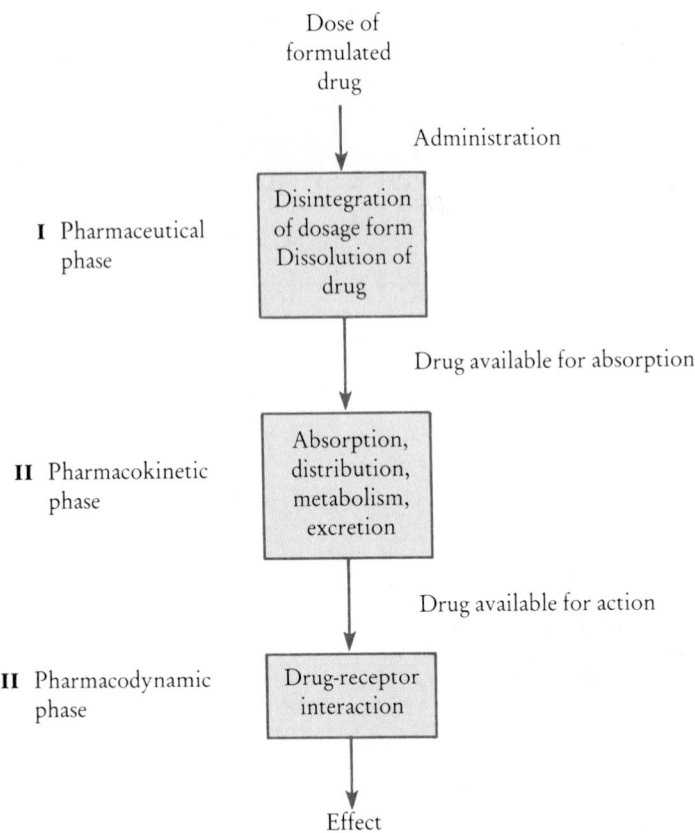

Dose of
formulated
drug

Administration

**I** Pharmaceutical
phase

Disintegration
of dosage form
Dissolution of
drug

Drug available for absorption

**II** Pharmacokinetic
phase

Absorption,
distribution,
metabolism,
excretion

Drug available for action

**III** Pharmacodynamic
phase

Drug-receptor
interaction

Effect

**FIGURE 4-1** Phases affecting drug activity.

Nurses have traditionally administered drugs to clients. Today, in many health care delivery settings, the nurse's responsibility has shifted to ensuring safe administration of drugs by a variety of specially educated health workers and to observing and interpreting the client's response to drug therapy. However, the moral, ethical, and legal responsibility for drug administration remains the nurse's.

This chapter presents theories of drug action, physiologic processes mediating drug action, variables affecting drug action, and unusual and adverse responses to drug therapy. The nurse can transfer this knowledge to care of the unique problems of individual clients.

## GENERAL PROPERTIES OF DRUGS

As stated earlier, a drug is a chemical that interacts with a living organism to produce a biologic response. This text deals with drugs administered in doses that obtain therapeutic, prophylactic, or diagnostic effects. These effects are achieved by some underlying biochemical and/or physiologic interaction between the drug and a functionally important tissue component (usually a receptor) in the body. Thus it is important to recognize the following general properties of drugs.

1. *Drugs do not confer any new functions on a tissue or organ in the body; they only modify existing functions.*

Therefore the effects of drugs can be recognized only by alterations of a known physiologic function or process. Alteration in function is achieved by drugs that can replace, interrupt, or potentiate a physiologic process in specialized tissues. The following are examples: drugs used to treat anemia can replace iron to restore the adequate production of red blood cells. Atropine, on the other hand, can interrupt the rate of salivation in preoperative patients, which is an essentially abnormal state but a necessary one to decrease the surgical risk of aspiration. Finally, the administration of a cathartic can potentiate the rate of evacuation of the large intestine.

2. *Drugs in general exert multiple actions rather than a single effect.* Consequently, drugs may, in varying degrees, produce undesirable responses because of their potential to modify more than one function of the body. These unwanted effects may be avoided somewhat by administering more specific or more selective drugs. For example, metaproterenol is a selective beta$_2$ adrenergic agent used to produce bronchodilation. Yet a common side effect is beta$_2$ mediated muscle tremors.

3. *Drug action results from a physicochemical interaction between the drug and a functionally important molecule in the body.* Some drugs act by combining with a small molecule (e.g., antacids neutralize gastric acid) or producing alteration of cell membrane activity (e.g., local anes-

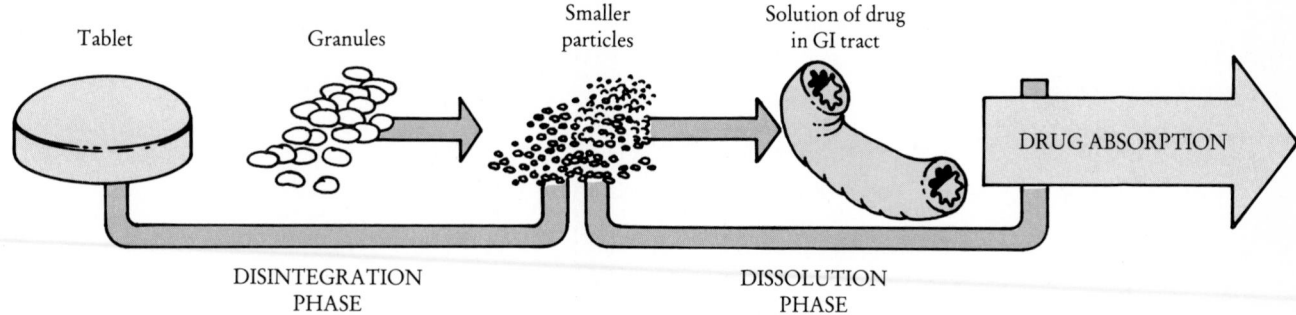

**FIGURE 4-2**  Phases of solid drug absorption.

thetics). However, the major mechanism by which drugs interact is by combining with macromolecular components of tissues, such as receptors.

## MECHANISMS OF DRUG ACTION

To produce its optimal desired or therapeutic effects, a drug must reach appropriate concentrations at its site of action. This means that the molecules of the chemical compound must proceed from their point of entry into the body to the tissues with which they react. In addition, the magnitude of the response depends on the dosage and the time course of the drug in the body. Therefore the concentration of the drug at its site of action is influenced by various processes, which may be divided into three phases of drug activity: pharmaceutical, pharmacokinetic, and pharmacodynamic. The sequential order of these phases is depicted in Figure 4-1.

### Pharmaceutical Phase

Pharmaceutics is the study of the ways in which various drug forms influence pharmacokinetic and pharmacodynamic activities. The drug may appear in solid form (tablet, capsule, or powder) or in liquid form (solution or suspension).

**Dissolution** refers to the rate at which a drug goes into solution. After ingestion, a solid drug (tablet or capsule) must first disintegrate before it becomes readily soluble in the body fluids. Following this process, the active drug ingredient is then free to enter solution. Thus the drug form is important, for the more rapid the rate of dissolution, the more readily the compound crosses the biologic membrane to achieve absorption. Obviously, oral drugs in liquid form are more rapidly available for gastrointestinal absorption than those in solid form (see Figure 4-2 and the box below it).

### Pharmacokinetic Phase

Pharmacokinetics is the study of the concentration of a drug during the processes of absorption, distribution, biotrans-

---

**ABSORPTION OF PREPARATIONS**

| | |
|---|---|
| Liquids, elixirs, syrups | Fastest |
| Suspension solutions | |
| Powders | |
| Capsules | |
| Tablets | |
| Coated tablets | |
| Enteric-coated tablets | Slowest |

---

formation, and excretion. The concentration that a drug attains at its site of action is influenced by four primary factors: the rate and extent to which a drug is (1) absorbed into body fluids, (2) distributed to sites of action or storage areas, (3) biotransformed or metabolized to breakdown products (metabolites), and (4) excreted from the body by various routes (see Figures 4-1 and 4-3).

### *Properties That Influence Pharmacokinetic Activity*
#### Physiochemical Properties of Drugs

In general, drugs exist as weak acids or weak bases. Moreover, in body fluids they appear in either ionized or nonionized forms. The ionized (polar) form is usually water soluble (lipid insoluble) and does not diffuse readily through the cell membranes of the body. By contrast, the nonionized (nonpolar) form is more lipid soluble (less water soluble) and is more apt to cross the cell membranes. The influence of pH on these compounds is discussed under Absorption in this chapter.

#### Physiochemical Properties of Cell Membranes

The extent to which a drug attains pharmacokinetic activity (absorption, distribution, biotransformation, and excretion) depends on the rate at which drugs cross the cell membrane. The membrane consists of a bimolecular layer of lipids that contain protein molecules, which are irregularly dispersed throughout the lipid bilayer. The protein molecule itself may act as a carrier, an enzyme, a receptor,

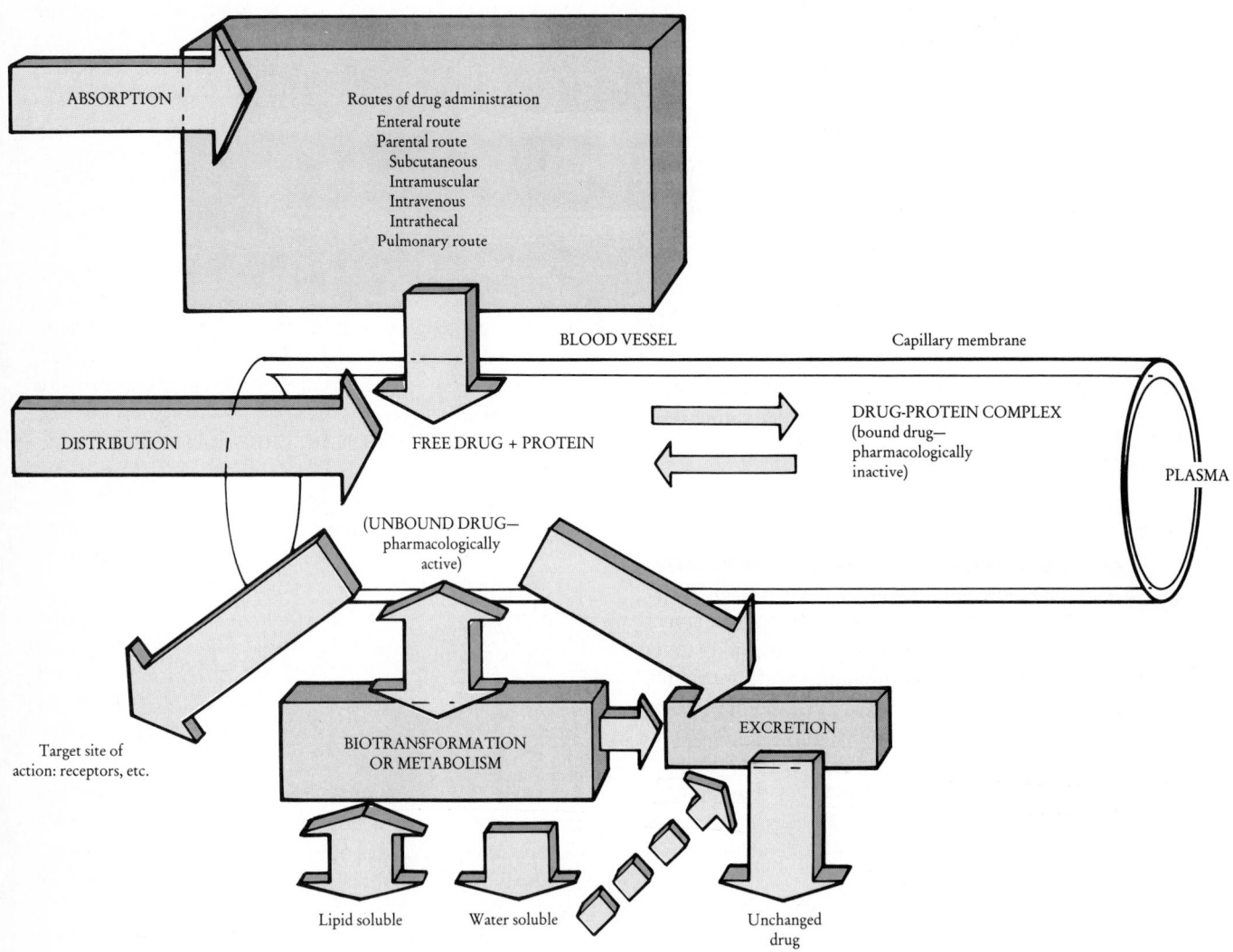

**FIGURE 4-3**  Schema of pharmacokinetic phase of drug action, showing absorption, distribution, biotransformation, and excretion of drugs. Note that only free drug is capable of movement for absorption, distribution to the target site of action, biotransformation, and excretion; the drug-protein complex represents bound drugs; and because the molecule is large, it is trapped in the blood vessel and serves as a storage site for the drug.

or an antigenic site. The drugs that are lipid (fat) soluble can pass through the lipid membrane, but those that are water soluble cannot. In this instance, the membrane, which appears to contain pores, permits the passage of small water-soluble substances such as urea, alcohol, electrolytes, and water itself.

Drug molecules, when free to move to sites of action, are transported from one body compartment to another by way of the plasma. However, free movement can be somewhat limited because these various sites are enclosed by membranes. Barriers to drug transport may consist of a single layer of cells, such as the villus in intestinal epithelium, or several layers of cells, such as skin. Nevertheless, in order for the drug to gain access to the interior of a cell or a body compartment, it has to penetrate cell membranes.

All the physiologic processes mediating drug action—absorption, distribution, metabolism, and excretion—are predicated on two physiochemical properties: passive transport and active transport.

*Passive transport.* Passive transport of drugs occurs when the membrane is not required to generate energy to carry out the process.

Passive transport, or passive diffusion, is the random movement of a substance from a region of higher concentration to a region of lower concentration until equilibrium is established at the membrane. With this method of transport, the membrane does not actively take part in the transport. The vast majority of drugs are transported via this mechanism.

*Carrier or active transport.* Moderate-sized water-soluble molecules as well as moderate-sized ions, including the ionic form of most drugs, do not readily enter cells but require some means of transport. Carrier transport, or active transport, is believed to be conducted by "carriers" that form complexes with drug molecules on one surface of the membrane, carry them through the membrane, and then dissociate from them. The dynamics of active transport are similar to that of facilitated diffusion except that in this type of transfer an energy source is required. It involves the movement of drug molecules against the concentration gradient (from areas of low concentration to areas of high concentration) or, in the case of ions, against the electrochemical potential gradient such as occurs with the "sodium pump." Active transport is usually more rapid than passive diffusion.

## Pharmacokinetic Activities
### Absorption

**Absorption** is a process that involves the movement of drug molecules from the site of entry into the body to the circulating fluids. Absorption begins at the site of administration and is essential to the three subsequent processes—distribution, metabolism, and excretion. The rate of drug absorption is significant because it determines when a drug becomes pharmacologically available in exerting its action. Of importance is that both the duration and the intensity of drug action are greatly influenced by the rate of this process. Accordingly, this type of response depends on the selection of the *route* of administration, the *dose* of the drug, and the *dosage form* (tablet, capsule, or liquid) of the agent administered.

***Variables that affect drug absorption.*** The rate and extent to which a drug is absorbed are influenced by the following:

1. Nature of the absorbing surface (cell membrane) through which the drug must traverse. The drug molecule may pass through a single layer of cells (intestinal epithelium), in which case transport is faster than when it traverses several layers of cells (skin). In addition, the size of the surface area of the absorbing site is another important determinant of drug absorption. Generally, the more extensive the absorbing surface, the greater the absorption of the drug and the more rapid its effects. Anesthetics are absorbed immediately from the pulmonary epithelium because of the vast surface area. Absorption from the small intestine, which offers a massive absorbing area, is more rapid than from a smaller absorbing surface, such as the stomach.

2. Blood flow to the site of administration. Circulation to the site of administration is a significant factor in the absorption of drugs. A rich blood supply (sublingual route) enhances absorption, whereas a poorly vascular site (subcutaneous route) delays it. A patient in shock, for example, may not respond to intramuscularly administered drugs because of poor peripheral circulation. Drugs injected intravenously, on the other hand, are placed directly into the circulatory system and are totally available. This route of administration is desirable when speedy drug effects are necessary, but it carries the potential danger of achieving temporarily toxic responses in vital organs such as the heart or the brain. Therefore, to prevent deleterious effects, some drugs must be injected slowly. In addition, the decreased peripheral blood flow in patients with congestive heart failure or circulatory shock may cause a significant reduction in the rate of transport of injected drugs to the target tissues, thereby considerably altering their efficacy.

3. Solubility of the drug. Again, to be absorbed, a drug must be in solution. The more soluble the drug, the more rapidly it will be absorbed. Moreover, because cell membranes contain a fatty acid layer, lipid solubility is a valuable attribute of drugs to be absorbed from certain areas—for example, the alimentary tract and the placental barrier. Chemicals and minerals that form insoluble precipitates in the gastrointestinal tract, such as barium salts, or drugs that are not soluble in water or lipids cannot be absorbed. Parenterally administered drugs prepared in oily vehicles, such as streptomycin, will be absorbed more slowly than drugs dissolved in water or isotonic sodium chloride.

4. pH. When in solution, drugs are a mixture of ionized and nonionized forms. The nonionized drug is lipid soluble and readily diffuses across the cell membrane: the ionized drug is lipid insoluble and nondiffusible. A drug that is acidic (e.g., aspirin) becomes relatively undissociated in an acid environment such as the stomach and therefore can readily diffuse across the membranes into the circulation. In contrast, a basic drug tends to ionize in the same acid environment and is not absorbed through the gastric membrane. The reverse occurs when a drug is in an alkaline medium. (See Figure 4-4.)

5. Drug concentration. Drugs administered in high concentrations tend to be more rapidly absorbed than drugs administered in low concentrations. In certain situations, a drug may be initially administered in large doses that temporarily exceed the body's capacity for excretion of the drug. In this way, active drug levels are rapidly reached at the receptor site. Once an active drug level is established, smaller daily doses of the drug can be administered to replace only the amount of the drug excreted since the previous dose. The initial and temporary overloading doses of the drug are priming, or **loading, doses,** while the smaller daily doses are **maintenance doses.** Such manipulation of drug dosage is frequently used, for example, with digitalis and steroid preparations in acute situations.

6. Dosage form. Drug concentration can be manipulated by pharmaceutical processing. It is possible to combine an active drug with a resin or another substance from which it is only slowly released or to prepare a drug in a vehicle that offers relative resistance to the digestive action of stomach contents (enteric coating). Enteric coatings on drugs are used for the following reasons: (1) to prevent decomposition of chemically sensitive drugs by gastric secretions (penicillin G and erythromycin are unstable in an acid pH), (2) to

pH effects on drug molecules:

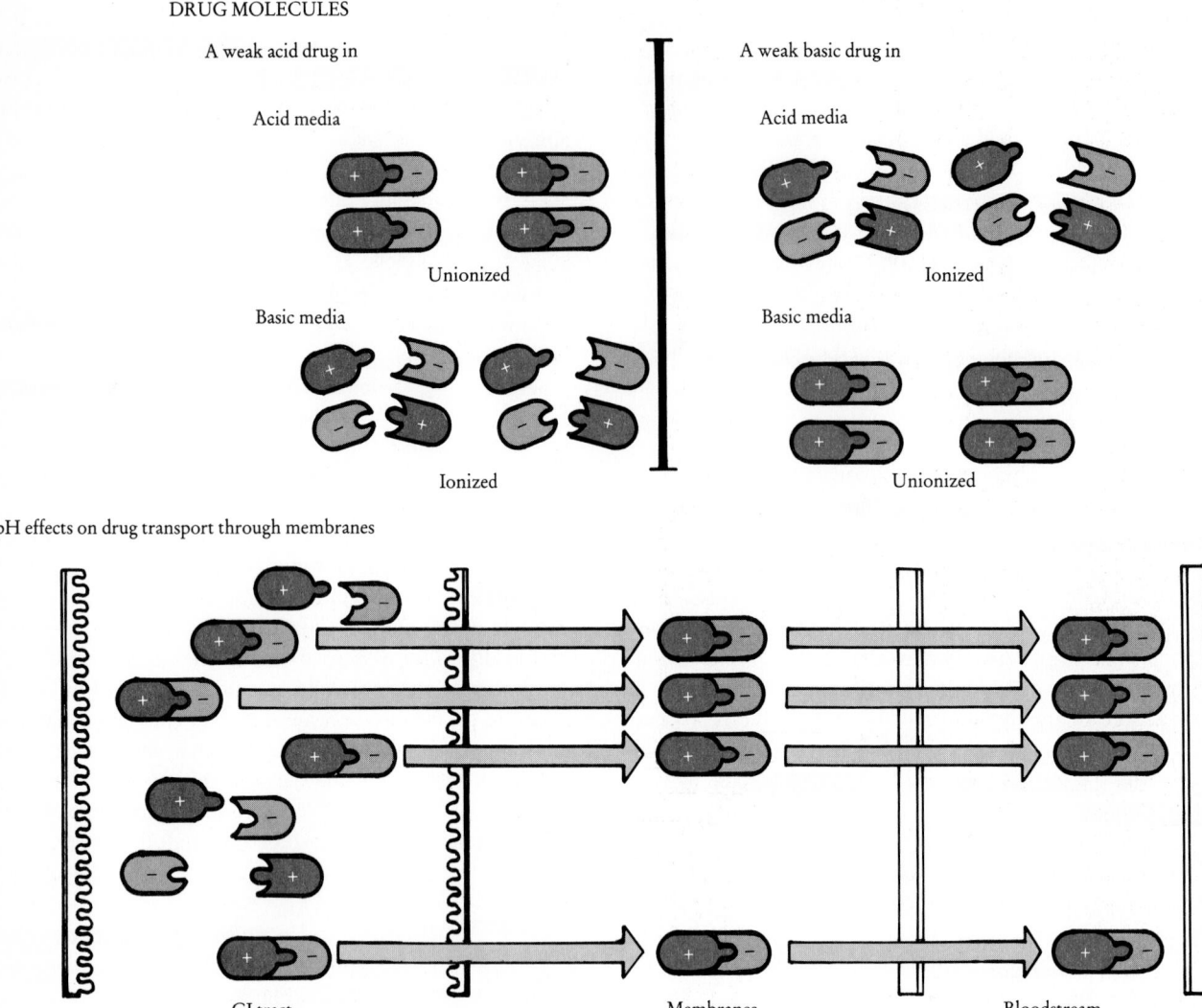

**FIGURE 4-4**  Effect of pH on drug ionization and transport.

prevent dilution of the drug before it reaches the intestine, (3) to prevent nausea and vomiting, and (4) to provide delayed action of the drug.

***Routes of drug administration.*** The mode of drug administration affects both the rate at which onset of action occurs and the magnitude of the therapeutic response that results. Therefore the choice of the route of administration is crucial in determining the suitability of a drug for an individual client. For example, a client who is vomiting will have little or no appreciable gastrointestinal absorption of a drug when it is administered orally. Obviously, parenteral administration would be more beneficial in obtaining a therapeutic drug response.

Drugs are given for either their local or systemic effects. The local effect of a drug usually occurs at the immediate site of application, in which case absorption is a disadvan-

tage. By contrast, when a drug is given for a systemic effect, absorption is an essential first step before the agent appears in the circulation and is distributed to a location distant from the site of administration.

A drug may enter the circulation either by being injected there directly—intravenously—or by absorption from depots in which it has been placed. The routes of drug administration can be classified into the following categories: (1) enteral (drugs administered along any portion of the gastrointestinal tract), (2) parenteral—subcutaneous, intramuscular, intravenous, intrathecal, (3) pulmonary, and (4) topical (see Figure 4-3.)

***Enteral route.*** Generally, oral ingestion, or the **enteral** route, is the most commonly used method of giving drugs. It is also the safest (because the drug may be retrieved), most convenient, and most economical route of administration. However, the frequent changes of the gastrointestinal environment produced by food, emotion, and physical activity make it the most unreliable and slowest of the commonly used routes. Drugs are absorbed from several sites along the gastrointestinal tract.

*Oral absorption.* The oral cavity is lined with mucous membranes that consist of epithelial cells. These cells secrete saliva to begin digestion of food. Although the oral cavity possesses a thin lining, a rich blood supply, and a slightly acidic pH, little absorption occurs in the mouth. On the other hand, despite its small surface area, the oral mucosa is capable of absorbing certain drugs as long as they dissolve rapidly in the salivary secretions. The oral mucosa absorbs drugs by the **sublingual** and **buccal** routes. In sublingual administration the drug is placed under the tongue to permit tablet dissolution in salivary secretions. Nitroglycerin is administered in this manner, and the patient is advised to refrain as long as possible from swallowing the saliva containing the tablet form of the drug. Because nitroglycerin is nonionic with a high lipid solubility, the drug readily diffuses through the lipid mucosal membranes. Following absorption, it enters the systemic circulation without preliminary passage through the liver. Accordingly, absorption is rapid, and the effects of the drug may become apparent within 2 minutes. In buccal administration the drug (tablet) is placed between the teeth and the mucous membrane of the cheek. Some hormones and enzyme preparations are administered by this route. The drug is absorbed rapidly and enters the general circulation directly without passing through the portal circulation. Both sublingual and buccal routes avert drug destruction by gastrointestinal fluids and the liver.

*Gastric absorption.* Although the stomach has a rich blood supply and large surface area, which provide excellent potential for drug absorption, it is not an important site for this process. The length of time a substance remains in the stomach is a significant variable in determining the extent of gastric absorption. This is governed by the pH of the drug and gastric motility.

In the stomach the pH is low (about 1.4); and drugs such as the barbiturates, which are slightly acidic, tend to remain nonionized and thus are readily absorbed into the circulation. Morphine and quinine are slightly basic; they ionize in the stomach and thus are poorly absorbed. A large majority of drugs are weak bases and on entry into the small intestine are absorbed because of the alkaline pH of the environment.

Generally, slowing the gastric emptying rate decreases drug absorption and vice versa. This is the reason so many drugs are administered on an empty stomach with sufficient water (8 ounces) to ensure their rapid passage into the small intestine, where drug absorption is increased because of the larger surface area available to the dissolving drug. Since some drugs cause gastric irritation, they are usually given with food. In addition, after drug administration, the client should be encouraged to lie on the right side to hasten gastric emptying time (time required for the drug to reach the small intestine). Prolongation of emptying time increases the risk of destruction of unstable drugs (acetaminophen [Tylenol]) by gastric juices.

*Small intestinal absorption.* The small intestine with its many villi has a larger absorption area than the stomach. Also, it is highly vascularized. Drugs that are poorly soluble in the stomach pass into this region. Drug absorption occurs mostly in the upper part of the small intestine. The pH of the intestinal fluid is alkaline (7 to 8) and strongly influences the rate of absorption of the nonionized basic drugs. Increased intestinal motility caused, for example, by diarrhea or cathartics may decrease exposure to the intestinal membrane and thereby diminish absorption. Prolonged exposure, on the other hand, allows more time for absorption.

*Rectal absorption.* The surface area of the rectum is not very large, but drug absorption does occur because of extensive vascularity. In addition, drugs administered rectally are not subjected to hepatic alteration, since the blood that perfuses this region bypasses the liver. Some disadvantages to rectal administration of drugs include erratic absorption because of rectal contents, local drug irritation, and uncertainty of drug retention.

*Parenteral route.* The **parenteral** route refers to the administration of drugs by injection. It is the most rapid form of systemic therapy.

*Subcutaneous.* A **subcutaneous** injection means that a drug is given beneath the skin into the connective tissue or fat immediately underlying the dermis. This site can be used only for drugs that are not irritating to the tissue; otherwise severe pain, necrosis, and sloughing may occur. The rate of absorption is slow and can provide a sustained effect.

*Intramuscular.* **Intramuscular** administration means that a drug is injected into the skeletal muscle. Absorption occurs more rapidly than with subcutaneous injection because of greater tissue blood flow.

*Intravenous.* The **intravenous** route produces an immediate pharmacologic response because the desired concentration of drug is injected directly into the bloodstream, thereby circumventing the absorption process. Drugs should be administered slowly to prevent adverse effects.

*Intrathecal.* **Intrathecal** administration means that a drug is injected directly into the spinal subarachnoid space, bypassing the blood-brain barrier. Many compounds cannot enter the cerebrospinal fluid or are absorbed in this region very slowly. When rapid effects of drugs are desired, as in spinal anesthesia or in treatment of acute infection of the central nervous system, this route may be used.

*Pulmonary route.* To ensure that normal gas exchange of oxygen and carbon dioxide is continuous in the lungs, drugs must be in the form of gases or fine mists (aerosols) when they are administered by inhalation. The lungs provide a large surface area for absorption, and the rich capillary network adjacent to the alveolar membrane may tend to promote ready entry of medication into the bloodstream. Drugs such as bronchodilators, mucolytics, and antibiotics are administered by various inhalation devices (nebulizers, pressure tanks) that propel the agents into the alveolar sacs and produce primarily local effects and at times unwanted systemic effects.

*Topical route.* Absorption of drugs applied topically to the skin and mucous membranes of various structures in the body is generally rapid.

*Skin.* Usually drugs applied to the skin are employed as topical remedies to produce a local effect. Only lipid-soluble compounds are absorbed through the skin, which acts as a lipid barrier. To prevent adverse effects from systemic absorption of toxic chemicals, only an intact skin surface should be used. Massaging the skin enhances absorption of the drug because capillaries become dilated and local blood flow is increased as a result of the warmth created by the friction of rubbing.

*Eyes.* Administration of drugs in the eye produces a local effect on the conjunctiva or anterior chamber. Eyeball movements promote the distribution of drug over the surface of the eye.

*Ears.* Administration of drops into the auditory canal may be chosen to treat local infection or inflammatory conditions of the external ear.

***Bioavailability.*** **Bioavailability** refers to the percentage of active substances in a drug that is absorbed and becomes available to the target tissue following administration. Thus drugs are biologically equivalent if they attain similar concentrations in blood and tissues at similar times; they are therapeutically equivalent if they provide equal therapeutic effectiveness in clinical trials. Of importance is the similarity of the absorption and therapeutic performances of drugs, which can be altered markedly by the ingredients and method of manufacture of an agent. Furthermore, different brands of the same drug can vary, and even different lots from a single manufacturer may show different levels of effectiveness. Thus the FDA is paying more attention to drug preparation and trying to ensure that the bioavailability of a drug conforms to uniform standards. Both the proportion of active drug and the percentage of its absorption are essential to attain therapeutic equivalence among all chemically similar drugs.

## Distribution

Once a drug is absorbed into the bloodstream, it is immediately distributed throughout the body by the circulation of the blood. **Distribution** is defined as the transport of a drug in body fluids from the bloodstream to various tissues of the body and ultimately to its site of action (see Figure 4-5). The rate at which a drug enters the different areas of the body depends on the permeability of capillaries for the drug's molecules. As already discussed, lipid-soluble drugs can readily cross capillary membranes to enter most tissues and fluid compartments, whereas lipid-insoluble drugs re-

quire more time to arrive at their point of action. However, cardiac functions also affect the rate and extent of distribution of a drug; specifically, cardiac output (amount of blood pumped by the heart each minute) and regional blood flow (amount of blood supplied to a specific organ or tissue) determine how much time is required. Most of the drug is first distributed to organs that have a rich blood supply: heart, liver, kidney, and brain. Afterward, the drug enters organs with a poor blood supply, which include muscles and fat.

***Drug reservoirs.*** Storage reservoirs allow a drug to accumulate by binding to specific tissues in the body. This sustains the pharmacologic effect of a drug at its point of action. The body's storage reservoirs involve two general types of drug pooling: plasma protein binding and tissue binding.

*Plasma protein binding.* On entry into the circulatory system, drugs may become attached to proteins, mainly albumin contained in the blood. Thus, as free drug enters the plasma, it binds to the protein to form a drug-protein complex. This combination can also be reversed:

$$\text{Free drug} + \text{Protein} \rightleftarrows \text{Drug-protein complex}$$

The formula indicates that equilibrium is established between the amount of free drug and the amount of drug that is bound to protein (drug-protein complex). Protein binding decreases the concentration of free drug in the circulation, thereby limiting the amount that travels to the site of action. The protein albumin molecule is too large to diffuse through the membrane of the blood vessel, so the bound molecule is trapped in the bloodstream and pharmacologically inactive. It becomes a circulating drug reservoir or storage depot (see Figure 4-5).

The equilibrium process is dynamic. As free drug is eliminated from the body, the drug-protein complex begins to dissociate so that more free drug is released to replace what is lost. As a result, the fact that the body temporarily stores the drug molecules in the drug-protein complex allows the drug to be available for a longer period of time. For example, a sulfonamide is highly bound to protein; and because free drug molecules are released slowly from the bound form, the antiinfective action of the antibiotic is long-lasting.

*Degree of drug binding.* Plasma protein binding is expressed as a percentage, which refers to the percent of total drug that is bound. Among the *highly protein-bound* drugs are bishydroxycoumarin (Dicumarol), which is 98% bound, and propranolol, which is 90% bound. Accordingly, a ratio exists between free and bound drug. In the case of propranolol this means that in a given period of time, 90% is bound to plasma proteins and only 10% of free drug is available for therapeutic use, eventual biotransformation, and excretion. Therefore if more than 10% of the drug is free to act within this same period of time, toxicity is likely to occur. Pentobarbital is 40% protein bound and represents a *moderately bound* drug, whereas guanethidine is only 1%

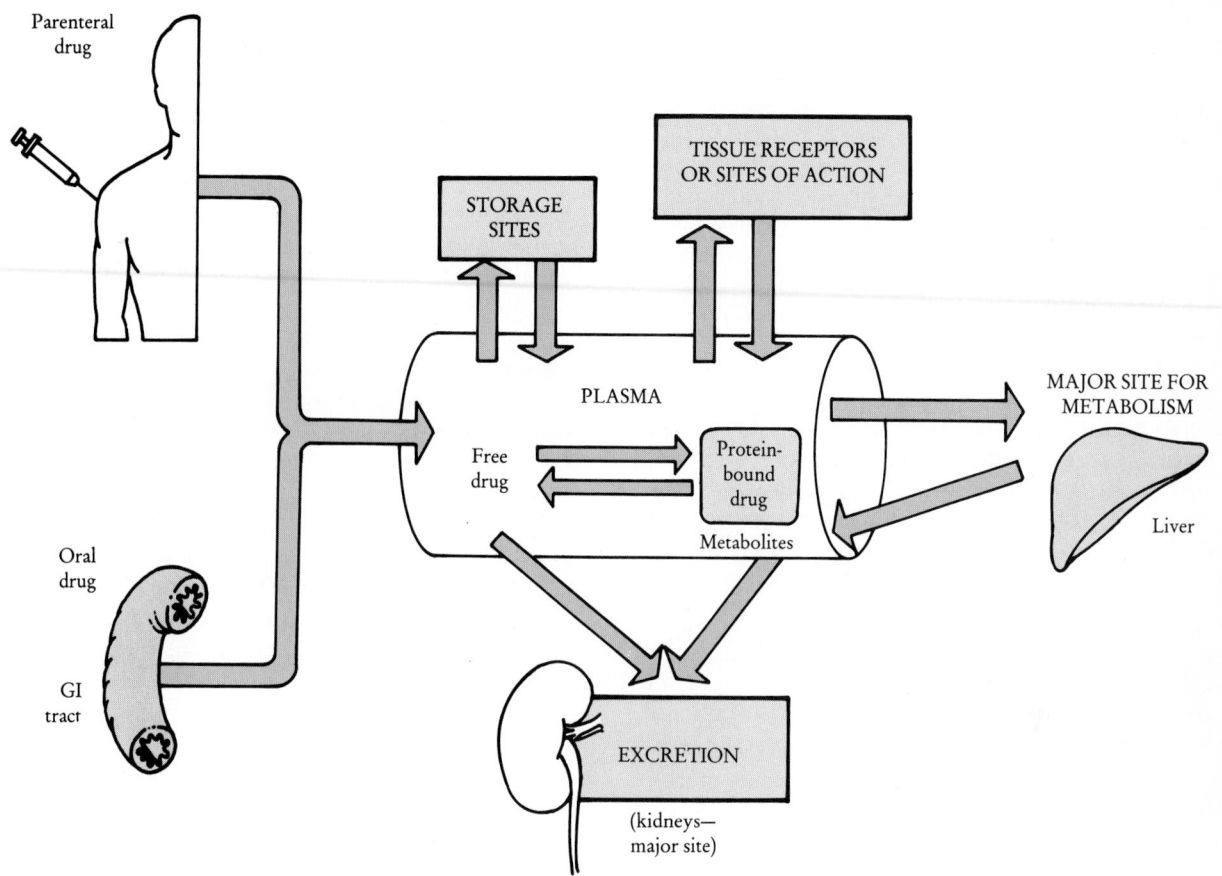

**FIGURE 4-5**   Drug transport in the body.

to 8% protein bound and is a *low-bound* drug.

*Competition for binding sites.* Since albumin and other plasma proteins provide a number of binding sites, two drugs can compete with one another for the same site and displace each other. This competition may have dangerous consequences if particular combinations of drugs are administered. For example, serious problems can arise when a client who is satisfactorily stabilized on maintenance doses of warfarin, an anticoagulant, is simultaneously given aspirin, an analgesic. The aspirin may displace some of the protein-bound warfarin, thereby increasing the free drug level and causing severe hemorrhage. Because warfarin is normally highly protein bound, its continued administration may raise the concentration of free drug, causing further severe adverse reactions. Therefore the nurse must be alert to the potential dangers of drug interactions occurring when multiple agents are prescribed concurrently.

*Hypoalbuminemia.* Hypoalbuminemia is characterized by low levels of albumin in the blood. Either hepatic damage, such as cirrhosis of the liver, or some type of body cavity drainage may cause hypoalbuminemia. Furthermore, failure of the liver to synthesize enough of the plasma proteins needed to bind drugs means that more free drug is available for distribution to tissue sites. Therefore when a client is given the normal dosage of a drug that depends on plasma binding, more of the free form of drug is allowed into the circulation, resulting in possible overdosage and toxicity. Clients who require drugs that depend on protein binding for distribution generally receive albumin replacement. Meanwhile, the drug dosage is adjusted until the normal level of the plasma protein is reported.

*Tissue binding*

*Fat tissue.* Lipid-soluble drugs have a high affinity for adipose tissue, which is where these drugs are stored. Moreover, the relatively low blood flow in fat tissue makes it a stable reservoir for drugs. As an example, a lipid-soluble drug such as thiopental may stay in low concentrations in body fat for as long as 3 hours following administration. If this drug is given again before it is all excreted, it can produce a cumulative effect, since an additional amount of the agent will be stored in the fat tissue.

*Bone.* Some drugs have an unusual affinity for bone. For example, the antibiotic tetracycline accumulates in bone after being absorbed onto the bone-crystal surface. The drug is stored in the crystal lattice of bone. Tetracycline can interfere with the growth of bones when it accumulates in skeletal tissues of the fetus (by crossing the placenta from the mother) or young children. When the drug is distributed

---

## FETAL DRUG EFFECTS

Two major types of drug effects occur in the fetus. When given during the first trimester of pregnancy, some drugs induce aberrant development of organs and systems during the formation of these structures. This type is known as a teratogenic drug, which is defined as an agent that causes physical defects in a developing embryo. Many drugs that cause anomalies are known to cross the placenta and exhibit teratogenicity.

The second type of drug affects the second half of pregnancy as well as delivery, causing respiratory depression in the newborn because of the underdeveloped capacity of the infant to biotransform the drug and excrete it.

The rate of maternal blood flow to the placenta limits the availability of the drug to the fetus. Because passage of drugs is delayed, drugs take action in the mother more rapidly than in the fetus. This fact explains why an alert infant can be delivered to an anesthetized mother, provided that delivery occurs within 10 to 15 minutes of the time the drug is administered to the mother. Long-term administration of drugs to the mother, however, may produce adverse effects on the fetus. For example, infants born to mothers dependent on narcotics or cocaine manifest withdrawal symptoms after delivery and removal from the flow of the products through the mother.

Unfortunately the teratogenic effects of many drugs have not been adequately studied. Also, a potentially dangerous drug may be administered to a woman who is not aware of her pregnancy. It should be assumed that any drug will be able to pass the placental barrier, and the nurse must advise pregnant women not to take any drug without consulting the physician. Drugs should be administered during pregnancy only when the advantages greatly outweigh the potential risks to the fetus.

---

to unerupted teeth in a fetus or young child, discoloration of teeth results. Brownish pigmentation of permanent teeth also may result if this drug is given during the prenatal period or early childhood. See the box above for specific actions of drugs in fetal tissues.

***Barriers to drug distribution.*** Specialized structures, which are made up of biologic membranes, can serve as barriers to the passage of drugs at certain sites in the body. These include the blood-brain barrier and the placental barrier.

***Blood-brain barrier.*** The blood-brain barrier is a special anatomic arrangement that allows distribution of only lipid-soluble drugs (e.g., general anesthetics, barbiturates) into the brain and cerebrospinal fluid. Actually, the barrier is made up of a row of capillary endothelial cells joined by continuous tight intercellular junctions. The capillaries are covered by a fatty sheath of glial cells. Consequently, compounds that are strongly ionized and poorly soluble in fat

cannot enter the brain. Thus antibiotics that cross the blood-brain barrier with difficulty cannot be used to treat infections of the central nervous system. However, if a drug is instilled intrathecally, it bypasses the blood-brain barrier and directly treats the bacterial infection.

***Placental barrier.*** The membrane layers that separate the blood vessels of the mother and fetus constitute the placental barrier. In addition, tissue enzymes in the placenta can metabolize some agents (e.g., catecholamines) by inactivating them as they travel from the maternal circulation to the embryo. Despite the thickness of the structure, it does not afford complete protection to the fetus. Unlike the blood-brain barrier, the nonselective passage of drugs across the placenta to the fetus is a well-established fact. Although lipid-soluble substances preferentially diffuse across the placenta, the barrier is also permeable to a great number of lipid-insoluble drugs. Consequently, many agents intended to produce a therapeutic response in the mother also may cross the placental barrier and exert harmful effects on the developing embryo. Among the drugs easily transported across the placenta are steroids, narcotics, anesthetics, and some antibiotics.

### Biotransformation or Metabolism

Following absorption and distribution of a drug, the body eliminates the drug, first by biotransformation and then by excretion. **Biotransformation** (metabolism) chemically inactivates a drug by converting (transforming) it into a more water-soluble compound, or metabolite, that can be excreted from the body (see Figure 4-3). The liver is the primary site of metabolism of drugs, but other tissues also may be involved in this process, namely the plasma, kidneys, lungs, and intestinal mucosa.

***Hepatic biotransformation.*** After distribution to their sites of action, most drugs undergo metabolic changes or biotransformation. The chemical alterations are produced by microsomal enzyme systems, located largely in the liver, which consist of endoplasmic reticula, a series of membranes that appear as a network of canals within the cells. The microsomal enzymes usually affect biotransformation of lipid-soluble, nonpolar drugs. To increase polarity, they undergo one or both of two general types of chemical reactions. One type of transformation consists of oxidation, hydrolysis, or reduction. These chemical reactions result in increased polarity and water solubility of drug molecules. The second type, called *conjugation,* involves the union of the polar group of a drug with another substance in the body—glucuronide, glycine, methyl, or other alkyl groups. The conjugated molecule also becomes more polar, more water soluble, and therefore more excretable. These responses generally produce a loss in pharmacologic activity and occasionally are referred to as *detoxication reactions.*

Individuals vary considerably in the rates at which they metabolize drugs. The microsomal enzyme system can be depressed by conditions that affect hepatic function, such as starvation and obstructive jaundice. Individuals with liver disease, severe cardiovascular dysfunction, or renal problems may be expected to suffer from prolonged drug metabolism. Infants with immature metabolizing enzyme systems and the aged with degenerative enzyme function are major groups that experience depressed biotransformation. Genetically determined differences also affect metabolism. Some drugs (e.g., procainamide, hydralazine, and isoniazid) are metabolized by the acetyltransferase system. This system divides the population into "rapid acetylators" and "slow acetylators." The rapid acetylators metabolize a greater proportion of a drug dose than do the slow acetylators. The rapid acetylators may develop reactions caused by the metabolic products of a drug, whereas the slow acetylators may appear more sensitive to a drug by experiencing severe toxic effects. For example, an individual who is a slow acetylator and who is receiving procainamide is apt to develop a lupus-like syndrome, which is a serious adverse response.

If drug metabolism is delayed, cumulative drug effects may be expected and may be manifested as excessive or prolonged responses to ordinary doses of drugs. If drug metabolism is stimulated, a state of apparent drug tolerance is produced. A number of substances cause increased activity by hepatic microsomal enzymes, including CNS depressants, xanthines, pesticides, food preservatives, and dyes. Repeated administration of some drugs may stimulate the formation of new microsomal enzymes. This is thought to be the case with some hypnotic drugs, whose effect diminishes with prolonged administration.

*Hepatic first-pass effect.* Orally administered drugs absorbed from the gastrointestinal tract normally travel first to the portal system and then to the liver before entering the general circulation. However, some drugs may first be taken up by the hepatic microsomal enzyme system, so that a significant amount is metabolized before the drug ever reaches the systemic circulation. Consequently, only a small fraction of the dose is available for distribution to produce a pharmacologic effect. Thus the hepatic first-pass effect is defined as an initial biotransformation of drug (on passage through the liver from the portal vein) that produces a loss of pharmacologically active molecules. In some cases, the hepatic first-pass effect may result in complete elimination of the drug without the production of any pharmacologic activity. Hence a drug with an extensive hepatic first-pass effect is administered parenterally to bypass the liver, thereby preventing initial biotransformation.

## Excretion

A drug continues to act in the body until it is biotransformed or excreted. Drug molecules—intact, changed, or inactivated—ultimately must be removed from their sites of action by physiologic channels involving mechanisms of excretion. **Excretion** is a process whereby drugs and pharmacologically active or inactive metabolites are eliminated from the body, primarily through the kidneys.

### Organs of excretion

*Kidneys.* Excretion via the kidneys remains by far the most important route of drug elimination. Some drugs are expected almost unchanged in the urine, while other drugs are so extensively metabolized that only a small fraction of the original chemical substance is excreted intact.

Excretion is accomplished through passive glomerular filtration, active tubular secretion, and partial reabsorption (see Figure 4-6). The availability of a drug for glomerular filtration depends on its concentration in unbound form in plasma. Free, unbound drugs and water-soluble metabolites are filtered by the glomeruli, whereas protein-bound substances do not pass through this structure. After filtration, lipid-soluble compounds are not excreted; instead, they are reabsorbed by the tubular nephron and reenter the systemic circulation. The water-soluble compounds, on the other hand, fail to be reabsorbed and therefore are eliminated from the body.

Urinary pH varies between 4.6 and 8.2 and affects the amount of drug reabsorbed in the renal tubule by passive diffusion. Weak acids are excreted more readily in alkaline urine and more slowly in acidic urine; the reverse is true for weak bases. In cases of poisoning by weak organic acids such as aspirin or phenobarbital, alkalinizing the urine can result in increased urinary drug excretion. Raising the pH of the urine causes weak acids to become ionized, and subsequently these agents are excreted.

Urine may be alkalinized by administering sodium bicarbonate or tromethamine (Tham-E). By contrast, high doses of vitamin C or ammonium chloride acidify the urine and promote the excretion of basic drugs. By altering the pH of urine, increased elimination of certain drugs can be facilitated, thus preventing prolonged action or overdosage of a toxic compound (see Table 4-1).

Another technique to alter the rate of excretion of a drug is to produce a competitively blocking effect. As an example, probenecid may be used to block the renal excretion of penicillin; this prolongs the effect of the antibiotic by maintaining a higher therapeutic plasma level.

Drugs may also be eliminated through the use of extracorporeal dialysis, which was originally designed to substitute for renal function in cases of severe but temporary

**TABLE 4-1**   Effect of urinary pH on drug excretion

| Weak acids | Weak bases |
|---|---|
| Phenobarbital | Amphetamines |
| Salicylates | Meperidine |
| Streptomycin | Quinidine |
| RATE OF EXCRETION IS: | RATE OF EXCRETION IS: |
| Increased in alkaline urine | Increased in acid urine |
| Decreased in acid urine | Decreased in alkaline urine |

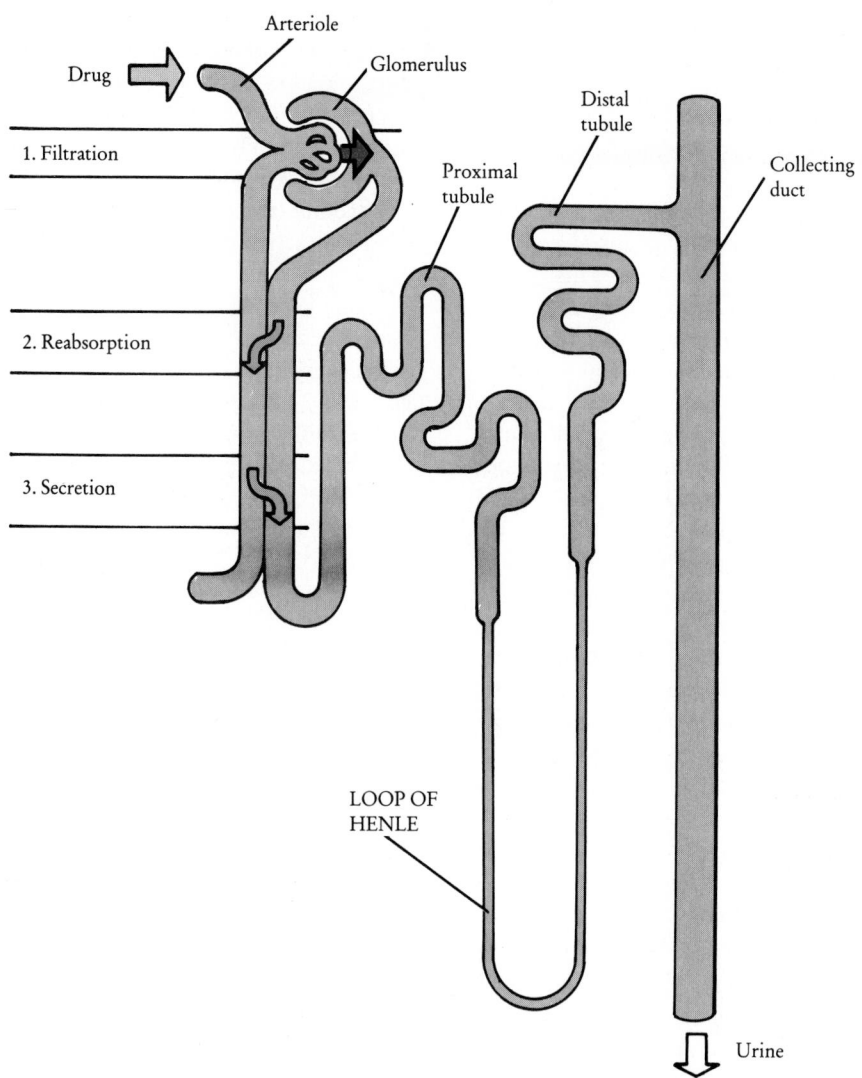

**FIGURE 4-6**  The drug excretion process.

renal shutdown. Overdosage of drugs may lead to just such a situation. By an artificial process resembling glomerular filtration, dialysis can achieve rapid reduction of high plasma levels of a drug. As a general rule, substances that are completely or almost completely excreted by the normal kidney can be removed by hemodialysis. Such substances include some CNS stimulants and depressants, some non-narcotic analgesics, and metals.

*Intestine.* Although the major route of excretion of drugs is the kidney, many agents are eliminated through the intestine by biliary excretion. After metabolism by the liver, the metabolite is secreted into the bile and passed into the duodenum. It is then eliminated with the feces. Certain drugs such as fat-soluble agents may be reabsorbed by the bloodstream and returned to the liver. This is the enterohepatic cycle. These compounds are later excreted by the kidney.

*Lungs.* Most of the drugs removed by the pulmonary route generally are intact and not metabolites. Agents such as gases and volatile liquids (general anesthetics) that are administered through the respiratory system usually are eliminated by the same route. On inspiration, these agents enter the bloodstream and, after crossing the alveolar membrane, are distributed by the general circulation. The rate of gas loss depends on the rate of respiration. Therefore exercise or deep breathing, which causes a rise in cardiac output and a subsequent increase in pulmonary blood flow, promotes excretion. By contrast, decreased cardiac output, such as that occurring in shock, prolongs the period of time for drug elimination. Other volatile substances such as ethyl alcohol and paraldehyde, which are highly soluble in blood, are excreted in limited amounts by the lungs. The remaining amounts are largely metabolized in the liver and excreted in urine. However, these compounds can be easily detected because the individual expires the gases into the atmosphere.

*Sweat and salivary glands.* The excretion of drugs through sweat and saliva is relatively unimportant. This process depends on diffusion of lipid-soluble drugs through the epithelial cells of the glands. The elimination of drugs and their metabolites into sweat may be responsible for causing side effects such as dermatitis and several other skin reactions. Drugs excreted in the saliva are usually swallowed and undergo the same fate as other orally administered agents. Furthermore, certain compounds that are given intravenously also may be excreted into saliva and cause the individual to complain of the "taste of drug."

*Mammary glands.*  Many drugs or their metabolites cross the epithelium of the mammary glands and are excreted in breast milk. Breast milk is acidic (pH 6.5), and therefore basic compounds such as narcotics (e.g., morphine and codeine) achieve high concentrations in this fluid. On the other hand, diuretics, barbiturates, sulfonamides, and other weak acids will be less concentrated in breast milk. A major concern arises over the transfer of drugs from mother to their breastfed babies. Although small quantities of any drug may be obtained in this manner, a cumulative effect can occur because of the undeveloped metabolizing system of the infant. Thus the nursing mother should be warned against taking any drug, because of its potential for reaching her infant. If medication is essential for the mother's health, the risk to the neonate can be diminished if the drug is given immediately after breastfeeding.

## Pharmacodynamic Phase

Pharmacodynamics is the study of the mechanism of drug action on living tissue. It is concerned with the response of tissues to specific chemical agents at various sites in the body. The effects of drugs can be recognized only by alterations of a known physiologic function. That is, drugs modify physiologic activity but do not confer any new function on a tissue or organ in the body. The goal of drug therapy is to attain a therapeutic effect in an individual. Therefore, in this context, drugs are used for cure of disease, symptomatic relief of symptoms, diagnosis, and also prevention of disease or undesirable conditions.

### Theories of Drug Action

The means by which drugs produce an alteration in function at their action is known as the mechanism of action. The mechanism of action of most compounds is believed to involve a chemical interaction between the drug and a functionally important component of the living system. Most drugs produce their effects by one of the following ways:
1. Drug-receptor interaction
2. Drug-enzyme interaction
3. Nonspecific drug interaction

**Drug-receptor interaction.**  Structural specificity is an essential postulate of the receptor theory of drug action. This theory hypothesizes that drugs are selectively active substances that have a high affinity for a specific chemical group or a particular constituent of a cell. In essence the

---

### DRUG-RECEPTOR INTERACTION TERMS

**affinity**  the propensity of a drug to bind or attach itself to a given receptor site.

**efficacy**  (intrinsic activity) the drug's ability to initiate biologic activity as a result of such binding.

**agonist**  a drug that combines with receptors and initiates a sequence of biochemical and physiologic changes; possesses both affinity and efficacy.

**antagonist**  an agent designed to inhibit or counteract effects produced by other drugs or undesired effects caused by cellular components during illness.

**competitive antagonist**  an agent with an affinity for the same receptor site as an agonist; the competition with the agonist for the site inhibits the action of the agonist; increasing the concentration of the agonist tends to overcome the inhibition. Competitive inhibition responses are usually reversible.

**noncompetitive antagonist**  an agent that combines with different parts of the receptor mechanism and inactivates the receptor so that the agonist cannot be effective regardless of its concentration. Noncompetitive antagonist effects are considered to be irreversible or nearly so.

**partial agonist**  an agent that has affinity and some efficacy but that may antagonize the action of other drugs that have greater efficacy. Not infrequently, antagonists share some structural similarities with their agonists.

---

drug-receptor interaction theory states that a certain portion (active site) of the drug molecule selectively combines or interacts with some molecular structure (reactive site on the cell surface or within the cell) to produce a biologic effect. Thus a **receptor** is a reactive cellular site with which a drug can interact to produce a pharmacologic response. The relationship of a drug to its receptor has often been likened to that of the fit of a key into its lock. The drug represents the key that fits into the lock or receptor. Thus some sort of reciprocal or complementary relationship exists between a certain portion of the drug molecule and the receptor site of the cell.

It has been postulated that the drug molecule with the best fit to the receptor will produce the greatest response from the cell. It has been suggested that there must be some force that attracts a receptor and holds it in combination with a specific drug long enough to produce a pharmacologic response. It is believed that drug receptor binding may result from the formation of chemical bonds—hydrogen, covalent, ionic, or van der Waals forces—between the receptors on the cell and the active site of the drug. Following absorption, a drug gains access to the receptor after it leaves the bloodstream and is distributed to tissues that contain receptor sites. (See the box above for terms used in this theory of drug action.)

The rate theory of drug action assumes that the most

important factor determining drug activity is the rate at which drug-receptor combinations take place. It is concerned with an intensity of effect. It postulates that if a drug-receptor complex dissociates rapidly, it has high efficacy. Conversely, if there is slow dissociation, there is firm binding, prolonged occupancy, and low efficacy. Thus, drug antagonism is associated with slow kinetics and drug agonism with fast kinetics.

**Drug-enzyme interaction.**  An interaction between drug and cellular enzyme is the second way by which drugs produce their effects. Enzymes are indispensable biologic catalysts that control all biochemical reactions of the cell. Drugs can inhibit the action of a specific enzyme and alter a physiologic response. For example, neostigmine, an agent used to manage the muscle weakness in myasthenia gravis, acts chemically by combining with acetyl cholinesterase to prevent this enzyme from inactivating acetylcholine at the neuromuscular junction.

Drugs that combine with enzymes are thought to do so by virtue of their structural resemblance to an enzyme's substrate molecule (the substance acted on by an enzyme). A drug may resemble an enzyme's substrate so closely that it can combine with the enzyme instead of with the normal substrate. Drugs resembling enzyme substrates are termed "antimetabolites" and can either block normal enzymatic action or result in the production of other substances with unique biochemical properties. The antimetabolites, then, become the receptor for the drug. However, although enzymes may be receptors, not all receptors are enzymes. An example of an antimetabolite is the anticancer drug methotrexate.

**Nonspecific drug interaction.**  Some drugs demonstrate no structural specificity and presumably act by more general effects on cell membranes and cellular processes. These drugs may penetrate into cells or accumulate in cellular membranes, where they interfere, by physical or chemical means, with some cell function or some fundamental metabolic processes.

Cell membranes are complex lipoprotein structures that regulate the flow of ions and metabolites in a highly selective manner, thereby maintaining an electrochemical gradient between the interior and exterior surfaces of the cell. Structurally nonspecific drugs are exemplified by the general anesthetics, which are lipid-soluble compounds of unrelated chemical structure but with similar properties. It is believed that general anesthetics alter the properties of lipids in cell membranes of nerves rather than act on specific receptors.

Other structurally nonspecific drugs may act by biophysical means that do not affect cellular or enzymatic functions. Drugs acting as a result of their obvious physical properties include the ointments and emollients. Hydrophilic indigestible substances exert a cathartic effect because of their physical action on the bowel. Examples of true chemical reactions that produce biologic effects are the interaction of

---

### PLASMA LEVEL PROFILE TERMS

**onset of action or latent period** interval between the time a drug is administered and the first sign of its effect

**termination of action** point at which a drug effect is no longer seen

**duration of action** period from onset of drug action to the time when response is no longer perceptible

**minimal effective concentration** lowest plasma concentration that produces the desired drug effect

**peak plasma level** highest plasma concentration attained from a dose

**toxic level** plasma concentration at which a drug produces serious adverse effects

**therapeutic range** range of plasma concentrations that produce the desired drug effect without toxicity (the range between minimal effective concentration and toxic level)

**loading dose** bolus of drug given initially to attain rapidly a therapeutic plasma concentration

**maintenance dose** the amount of drug necessary to maintain a steady therapeutic plasma concentration

---

a molecule such as lead with an antidotal drug and the neutralization by antacid drugs of hydrochloric acid present in gastric juice. Neither is considered a receptor interaction because no macromolecular tissue elements are involved. Detergents, alcohol, oxidizing agents such as hydrogen peroxide, and phenol derivatives such as Lysol are also structurally non-specific and act by irreversibly destroying the functional integrity of the living cell.

## Drug-Response Relationship

After it is administered, each drug has its own characteristic rate of absorption, distribution, biotransformation, and excretion. These can be analyzed by performing a plasma level profile. In many instances nurses are required to monitor serum drug levels to help the physician determine the dosage, scheduling, and route of administration for an individual patient. These data also provide information concerning the degree of therapeutic effectiveness so that potential adverse reactions can be predicted, thereby preventing serious clinical problems.

**Plasma level profile of a drug.**  The plasma or serum level profile graphically demonstrates the relationship between the plasma concentration of a drug and the level of the therapeutic effectiveness over a course of time. After one dose is administered, the time course of the amount of drug in the body depends on the rates of absorption, distribution, metabolism, and elimination. For example, the drug in Figure 4-7 has an onset of action of approximately 2 hours, peak level at 5 hours, and a 6 hours duration of

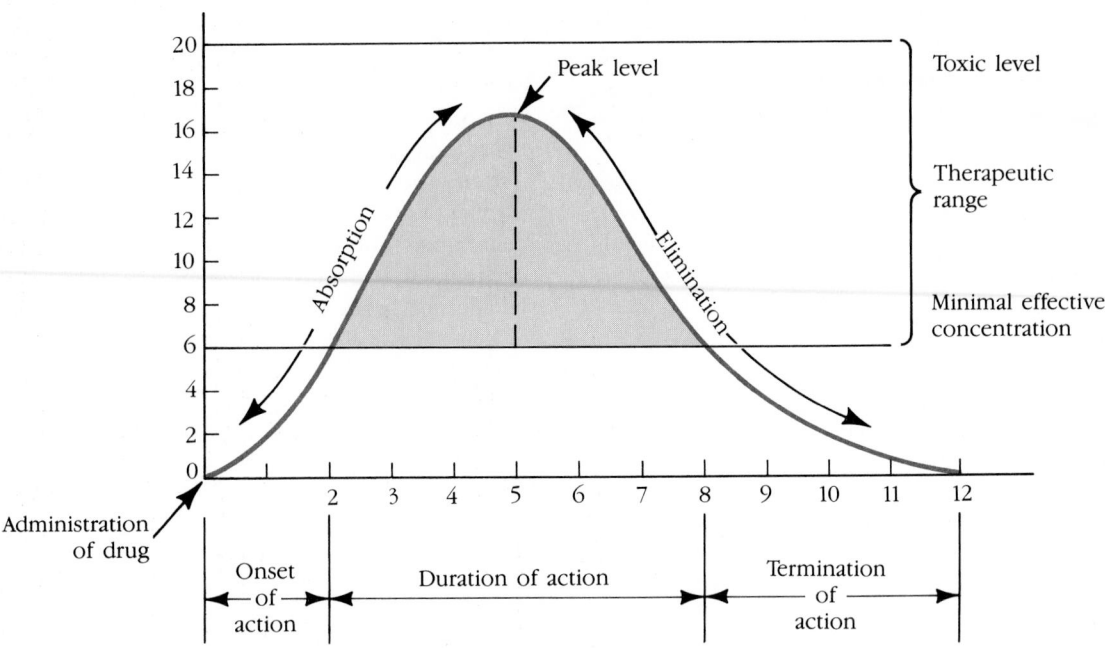

**FIGURE 4-7** Plasma level profile of a drug.

action or effect. By monitoring the plasma level of a compound, the efficacy and safety of drug therapy can be more closely controlled. The box on p. 54 lists important terms used in plasma level profiles and explains their interrelationships.

***Biologic half-life.*** The rate of biotransformation and excretion of a drug determines its biologic **half-life** (t½). Moreover, the duration of a dosage can be demonstrated by the biologic half-life, which is defined as the time required to reduce to one half that amount of unchanged drug that is in the body at the time equilibrium is established. The half-life of each drug is different. One with a short t½, such as 2 or 3 hours, will need to be administered more often than one with a long t½, such as 12 hours.

The half-life does not change with the drug dose; it always takes the same amount of time to eliminate one half of the drug present in the body. If, for example, 10,000 units of a drug are administered and that drug has a half-life of 4 hours, then 5000 units of the drug will be excreted in 4 hours. In the next 4 hours, 2500 units will be excreted, with 1250 units more being excreted in the third 4-hour period. In hepatic dysfunction, in which drug metabolism is impaired, or in renal disorders, in which elimination may be prolonged, the half-life of a drug is lengthened. This usually necessitates reduction of drug dosage.

***Therapeutic index.*** The therapeutic index (TI) provides a quantitative measure of the relative safety of a drug. It represents a ratio between two factors: (1) lethal dose (LD 50), which is the dose of a drug that is lethal in 50% of laboratory animals tested, and (2) effective dose (ED 50), which is the dose required to produce a therapeutic effect

in 50% of a similar population. The therapeutic index is calculated as follows:

$$TI = \frac{LD\ 50}{ED\ 50}$$

The closer the ratio is to 1, the greater the danger involved in administration of that drug to human beings. Obviously, in the human the dose that promotes a side effect or the first sign of a toxic response is of greater importance than the therapeutic index of the drug, since the physician's major concern is avoiding even an isolated fatality caused by drug toxicity.

## ADVERSE RESPONSES TO DRUGS

Drugs can react in the body to produce unpredictable, harmful, and sometimes unexplainable responses. No drug is totally safe and absolutely free of toxic effects. Sometimes these effects are immediately apparent. At other times they may take weeks or months to develop. Some adverse reactions are relatively mild; others can be fatal. With the increasing numbers of drugs being used, the incidence of adverse reactions has increased and is presently a significant problem in medical therapeutics.

### Predictable Adverse Responses

Some factors alter the response to drug therapy. Deviant drug reactions can frequently be traced to the predictable influence of such variables. The nurse must be cognizant of characteristics that modify cell conditions and, therefore, the activity of a drug. These characteristics include age, body mass, sex, environmental milieu, time of administration, pathologic state, genetic factors, and psychologic factors (see Table 4-2).

*Age.* It is generally recognized that children and elderly persons are highly responsive to drugs. Infants often have immature hepatic and renal systems and, therefore, incomplete excretory and metabolic mechanisms. Aged individuals may demonstrate different responses to drug therapy

because of deterioration of hepatic and renal function, which is often accompanied by concurrent disease processes, such as cardiovascular disease. Modification of dosage for children may be calculated on the basis of body weight or surface area.

*Body mass.* The relationship between body mass and amount of drug administered influences the distribution and concentration of a drug. To maintain a desired drug concentration in individuals of various sizes, drug dosage must be adjusted in proportion to body mass. For a given dose

**TABLE 4-2**   Factors altering drug responses

| Factor and pertinent description | Nursing considerations |
| --- | --- |
| Age<br>    Infants—immature body systems<br>    Children—dosage adjustment usually necessary<br>    Elderly—depressed hepatic and renal systems | Modify dosages. Children have a different physiologic profile and body mass distribution. Thus, dose per kilogram is individualized. It could be more or less than in an adult. Elderly clients may also have concomitant physical conditions that alter drug effects; altered excretion mechanism may also require less drug or different scheduling of medication. |
| Body mass<br>    The greater the volume of distribution, the lower the concentration of drug in the body compartments<br>    Calculation: average adult dose based on drug quantity that will produce a particular effect in 50% of population between the ages of 18 and 65 and weighing about 150 pounds (70 kg) | Adjust dosage in proportion to body mass. For children, dosage frequently is determined on the basis of amount of drug per kilogram of body weight or body surface area. |
| Sex<br>    Women—smaller than men; definite differences during pregnancy and in relative proportions of fat and water; drugs vary by water or fat solubility | Allow for size differential and whether a drug is water or lipid soluble. Avoid drugs during pregnancy unless an absolute necessity exists. |
| Environmental milieu<br>    Mood and behavior modified by (1) drug itself, (2) personality of the user, (3) environment of the user, and (4) interaction of these three factors; other factors: sensory—deprivation or overload; physical environment—cold vs heat, oxygen deprivation (altitude) | Be aware of the physical situation of the client with regard to heat and cold, interactions with other individuals, drug effects, and the way the client generally reacts to situations. |
| Time of administration<br>    Food—presence or absence<br>    Biologic rhythms—sleep-wake cycle, drug-metabolizing enzyme rhythms, corticosteroid secretion rhythm, blood pressure rhythms, circadian (24-hour) cycle in absorption and urinary excretion; also rhythm of drug receptor susceptibility | Give irritating drugs when food is in the client's stomach. Follow manufacturer's recommendations.<br>Make every effort to understand the client's normal and abnormal rhythms and seek possible relationships between the client's biologic rhythms and reactions to drug therapy.<br>Administer drugs at same time of day.<br>Altered body cycles (shift workers) may result in altered response to a drug. |
| Pathologic state<br>    Presence and severity of pathologic state—pain intensifies need for opioids; anxiety may produce resistance to large doses of tranquilizing drugs; presence of circulatory, hepatic, and/or renal dysfunctions interferes with physiologic processes of drug action | Take into account any pain, disease, or altered metabolic state of the client and adjust dosage accordingly. |
| Genetic factors<br>    Genetically determined abnormal susceptability to a chemical, or "idiosyncratic" response | Be aware that any client may show an idiosyncratic response. Always monitor closely, especially when beginning therapy, for abnormal susceptibility. Be aware of common drug idiosyncrasies. |
| Psychologic factors<br>    Symbolic investment in drugs and faith in their efficacy<br>    Placebo effect<br>    Hostility toward or mistrust of medicine or health personnel | Be aware of the attitude and the impression the nurse creates at the time of drug administration, and use them to enhance the drug's effects. |

of drug, the greater the volume of distribution, the lower the concentration of drug reached in various body compartments. Since the volume of interstitial and intracellular water is related to body mass, weight has a marked influence on the quantitative effects produced by drugs. The average adult drug dose is calculated on the basis of the drug quantity that will produce a particular effect in 50% of persons who are between the ages of 18 and 65 and weigh about 150 pounds (70 kg). Therefore, particularly for children and for very lean and for very obese individuals, drug dosage is frequently determined on the basis of amount of drug per kilogram of body weight or body surface area.

***Sex.*** Differences in drug effects related to the variable of sex result, in part, from size differences between men and women. Women are usually smaller than men, which will lead to high drug concentrations if dosage is prescribed indifferently. Demonstrable differences also exist in relative proportions of fat and water in the bodies of men and women, and some drugs may be more soluble in one or the other. Some authorities also indicate that subjective factors regarding drug effects may vary with sexual differences, stating that women are more suggestible to drug effects than men. This, however, is a controversial hypothesis.

Since drugs taken by a pregnant woman might affect the uterus and/or the fetus as a result of placental transfer, the use of drugs is best avoided during pregnancy unless an absolute necessity exists.

***Environmental milieu.*** Drugs affecting mood and behavior are particularly susceptible to the influence of the individuals environment. With such drugs one has to consider effects in light of four factors: (1) the drug itself, (2) the personality of the user, (3) the environment of the user, and (4) the interaction of these three components. Sensory deprivation and sensory overload may also affect responses to drugs. Physical environment can modify drug effects. For example, temperature affects drug activity: heat relaxes peripheral vessels and thus intensifies the actions of vasodilators, while cold has the opposite effect. The relative oxygen deprivation at high altitudes may increase sensitivity to some drugs.

***Time of administration.*** It is well known that drugs are absorbed more rapidly if the gastrointestinal tract is free of food and that irritating drugs are more readily tolerated if there is food in the stomach.

Although the theory is highly speculative, if findings from drug research on animals are applicable to humans, the time of drug administration in relation to human biologic rhythms can significantly affect the response to various drugs. It seems quite plausible that in humans the sleep-wake rhythm, deep sleep and dreaming sleep cycle, drug-metabolizing enzyme rhythms, corticosteroid secretion rhythm, blood pressure rhythms, and circadian (24-hour) variation in absorption and urinary excretion contribute to the effective, ineffective, adverse, or toxic response to particular drugs. There may also be a circadian rhythm in drug receptor susceptibility. Chronopharmacology and chronotoxicology are new areas of interest, and the frequency with which drug rhythm reports are appearing in the literature is increasing. The nurse should make every effort to understand the client's normal and abnormal rhythms and seek to determine possible relationships between the client's biologic rhythms and reactions to drug therapy.

***Pathologic state.*** The presence of a pathologic condition and the severity of symptoms may call for careful consideration of the type of drug administered and for adjustment in dosage. For example, the presence of severe pain tends to increase a client's requirement for opiates, and an extremely anxious individual can prove resistant to very large doses of tranquilizing and sedating drugs. Aspirin administered to a client with a fever will produce a decrease in temperature, whereas a client taking the drug for its analgesic effects will show no temperature change at all. Larger doses of insulin may be required for the client with diabetes whose condition is complicated by fever or infection. In addition, it bears repeating that the presence of circulatory, hepatic, and/or renal dysfunctions will interfere with the physiologic processes of drug action.

***Genetic factors.*** Genetic differences may alter greatly the response of individuals to a number of drugs. Such differences may arise from genetically conditioned deficiencies in drug metabolism or in receptor sensitivity. These pharmacogenetic abnormalities often manifest themselves as "idiosyncrasies" and may be mistakenly diagnosed as drug allergies. For example, some individuals may lack pseudocholinesterase activity in their plasma. If they receive an injection of succinylcholine, which is normally hydrolyzed by plasma cholinesterase, they may become paralyzed and remain that way for a long time. The field of pharmacogenetics is of great interest, since it may provide a rational explanation for many so-called drug idiosyncrasies.

***Psychologic factors.*** The client's symbolic investment in drugs and faith in their effects strongly influence and usually potentiate drug effects. The placebo effect is an outstanding example of how strong motivation can influence the emergence of desired drug effects. Conversely, hostility and mistrust of medicine and health personnel can diminish drug effects. It is important for nurses to realize that their attitudes and the impressions created at the time of drug administration may influence the therapeutic result.

## Iatrogenic Responses

Generally, the term **iatrogenic** diseases refers to adverse effects produced unintentionally in the treatment of a client. Iatrogenic diseases induced by drugs manifest themselves in five major groups: (1) blood dyscrasias, such as agranulocytosis, thrombocytopenia, aplastic anemia, and bone marrow depression; (2) hepatic toxicity, which is common and may take the form of biliary obstruction, hepatitis-like syndromes, and hepatic necrosis; (3) renal damage, particularly glomerular damage, which is a significant toxic effect of a number of drugs, including some antibiotics; (4) teratogenic effects, or drug effects causing malformations in the fetus as a result of placental transfer or drugs taken by a pregnant woman; and (5) dermatologic effects, such as acne, psoriasis, eczema, maculopapular rashes, and, rarely, erythema multiforme. By carefully monitoring a client's response to a drug, the nurse in some instances may be able to avert an iatrogenic disease.

In addition to these common and well-known drug-induced diseases, numerous other iatrogenic syndromes are specific to certain drugs. Ulceration of the gastrointestinal tract, for example, is a common result of long-term therapy with drugs such as aspirin, steroids, and potassium chloride. The relationship between oral contraceptive agents and thromboembolic phenomena is another untoward effect that may eventually be defined as an iatrogenic disease.

## Unpredictable Adverse Responses

Adverse drug reactions are one way of characterizing unpredictable and sometimes unexplainable drug responses that have not been optimally, clearly, and distinctly defined. The most common and best defined adverse drug reactions are the following. (See also the accompanying box.)

Drug allergy is an altered state of reaction to a drug, resulting from previous sensitizing exposure and the development of an immunologic mechanism. Substances foreign to the body act as antigens to stimulate the production of antibodies or immunoglobulins. Later, when a previously sensitized individual is again exposed to the foreign substance, the antigen reacts with the antibodies in ways that are damaging to body tissues. The antigen-antibody complex is not directly responsible for the manifestations of allergy. Rather, the complex reacts with various tissues and cells of the body by processes not clearly understood and causes them to release certain substances (for example, histamine), which then provoke the symptoms of allergy.

Allergic reactions may manifest themselves as a variety of symptoms, ranging from minor skin rashes to fatal hypotension. Reactions may be localized or widespread, and the symptoms can appear immediately or within hours to day after drug administration.

Immediate reactions occur within minutes of exposure to the chemical to which the person has been previously sensitized. Immediate and severe reactions are called anaphylactic reactions and are frequently fatal if not recognized and treated quickly. Signs and symptoms are severe, occur suddenly, and produce shock. The most dramatic form of anaphylaxis is sudden, severe bronchospasm, vasospasm, severe hypotension, and rapid death. Signs are largely caused by contraction of smooth muscles and may begin with irritability, extreme weakness, nausea, and vomiting and may proceed to dyspnea, cyanosis, convulsions, and cardiac arrest. Antihistamine drugs, epinephrine, and bronchodilators are indispensable in the treatment of anaphylactic shock.

Mild allergic reactions may be characterized by the development of a rash, angioedema, rhinitis, fever, asthma, and pruritus. Some allergic reactions are delayed and may appear anywhere from 7 to 14 days after initial administration of the drug. *Delayed reactions* are frequently analogous to *"serum sickness"* and are characterized by angioedema, arthralgia, fever, lymphadenopathy, and splenomegaly. Contact dermatitis, which results from direct skin contact with the eliciting drug, is also a delayed allergic response.

An individual who has had a mild allergic response to a particular drug should avoid reexposure to that drug and, optimally, should have skin tests performed in order to more definitely diagnose the response. Reinstitution of therapy with the same drug in a client who manifests allergic reactions is always dangerous, since an anaphylactic reaction may occur.

The term *hypersensitivity* is frequently used synonymously with allergy, but it is inappropriate because it is frequently confused with other kinds of adverse drug reactions. Since there is a lack of precision to defining hypersensitivity, avoiding use of the term may be wise.

*Idiosyncrasy* is any abnormal or peculiar response to a drug that may manifest itself by (1) overresponse or abnormal susceptibility to a drug; (2) underresponse, demonstrating abnormal tolerance; (3) a qualitatively different effect from the one expected, such as excitation after the administration of a sedative; or (4) unpredictable and unexplainable symptoms. Idiosyncratic reactions are generally thought to result from genetic enzymatic deficiencies that lead to an abnormal mechanism of metabolizing drugs. This term has been used rather vaguely to describe drug reactions that are qualitatively different from the usual effects obtained in the majority of patients and that cannot be attributed to drug allergy.

*Tolerance* is said to exist when there is a decreased physiologic response to the repeated administration of a drug or a chemically related substance. It is a reaction that necessitates an excessive increase in dosage to maintain a given therapeutic effect. Drugs well known for their propensity to produce tolerance are tobacco, opium alkaloids, nitrites, barbiturates, and ethyl alcohol. The actual mechanism of tolerance is unknown. In some instances, prolonged administration of some drugs somehow induces the synthesis of extra drug-metabolizing enzymes in the liver, which may account for the client's increased ability to tolerate larger drug doses than previously. *Cross tolerance* between related chemicals (such as between alcohol and some anesthetics) is a well-documented phenomenon. It is quite clear, however, that not all cases of tolerance are attributable to a drug's increased rate of metabolism. For example, the remarkable tolerance to morphine cannot be caused by its more rapid metabolic degradation.

*Tachyphylaxis* refers to a quickly developing tolerance to

---

## DRUG RESPONSES

---

| | |
|---|---|
| Drug allergy | Altered state of reaction resulting from previous sensitization and development of immunologic mechanism; body treats drug as an antigen and produces antibodies that react in ways harmful to body tissues |
| | Manifestations range from minor skin rashes to fatal anaphylaxis, are local or widespread, occur immediately or within hours to days following administration |
| | Life-threatening reactions: called anaphylactic reactions and are frequently fatal; signs and symptoms severe, occur suddenly, and produce shock; symptoms include sudden severe bronchospasm, vasospasm, severe hypotension, and death in the most severe form of anaphylaxis; signs are caused by contraction of smooth muscle and may begin with irritability, extreme weakness, nausea, and vomiting; may proceed to dyspnea, cyanosis, convulsions, and cardiac arrest; *Treatment:* antihistamine drugs, epinephrine, bronchodilators |
| | Mild reactions: rash, angioedema, rhinitis, fever, asthma, pruritus; may be immediate or appear 7 to 14 days after first administration of drug; delay reminiscent of "serum sickness" and characterized by angioedema, arthralgia, fever, lymphadenopathy, splenomegaly; also includes contact dermatitis; *Treatment:* avoid reexposure to that drug; skin tests may be performed to definitely diagnose response; do not reinstitute the therapy, since an anaphylactic response may then occur |
| Idiosyncrasy | Abnormal or peculiar response to drug; may be (1) overresponse or abnormal susceptibility, (2) underresponse that shows abnormal tolerance, (3) qualitatively different response than that expected, or (4) unpredictable or unexplainable response |
| Hypersensitivity | An exaggerated response to a drug; often incorrectly used as synonymous with allergy; usually idiosyncratic, not a true antigen-antibody reaction as seen with allergies |
| Tolerance | Decreased physiologic response to the repeated administration of a drug or chemically related substance |
| | Excessive increase in dosage required to maintain the required therapeutic effect |
| | Tolerance mechanism unknown; sometimes an effect resulting when prolonged administration of some drugs induces the synthesis of extra drug-metabolizing enzymes in the liver |
| Tachyphylaxis | Quickly developing tolerance to the rapid, repeated administration of drug |
| Cumulation | Results when the body cannot metabolize one dose of drug before another dose is administered; that is, drug is excreted more slowly than it is absorbed and the concentration of drug within the body rises; requires adjustment of the dosage to avoid toxic effects brought on by the accumulation of drug in the body |
| | Reaction can occur rapidly or insidiously |
| Drug dependence | A state in which intense physical or emotional disturbance is produced if a drug is withdrawn; previously termed *habituation* or *addiction;* can be physical or psychic (See Chapter 9) |
| Drug interaction | Effects of one drug are modified by the prior or concurrent administration of another drug, thereby increasing or decreasing the pharmacologic action of one or both drugs; may be beneficial or detrimental |
| Drug antagonism | Conjoint effect of two drugs is less than the sum of the drugs acting separately |
| Summation (addition) | Combined effect of two drugs produces a result that equals the sum of the individual effects of each agent, $1 + 1 = 2$; combination allows the administration of a lower dose of each drug, with a resultant decrease in adverse reactions |
| Synergism | Combined effect of drugs is greater than the sum of each individual agent acting independently; $1 + 1 = 3$ or more |
| Potentiation | Concurrent administration of two drugs in which one drug increases the effect of the other drug |

the rapid, repeated administration of a drug. It is quick in onset, and the client's initial response to the drug cannot be reproduced, even with larger doses of the drug.

*Cumulation* occurs when the body cannot metabolize one dose of a drug before another dose is administered. In other words, when drugs are excreted more slowly than they are absorbed, each new dose adds more to the total quantity in the blood and organs than is lost in the same amount of time by excretion. Unless drug administration is adjusted, sufficiently high concentrations can be reached to produce

toxic effects. Cumulative toxicity can occur rapidly, as dramatically illustrated in ethyl alcohol intoxication, or it can occur insidiously, as is the case in poisoning with heavy metals, such as lead. The latter is stored in many body tissues and deposited in bones, therefore having prolonged effects on the body while accumulation continues.

*Drug dependence* is the term preferred over the previous terminology of "habituation" and "addiction." The World Health Organization has suggested the use of the term *dependence* in conjunction with the drug being described (e.g., barbiturate dependence or opiate dependence). Dependence can be physical or psychic. Physical dependence refers to a state of physiologic adaptation to a drug that manifests itself by intense physical disturbance when the drug is withdrawn. Psychic dependence is a state of emotional reliance on a drug to maintain a sense of well-being. Its manifestations may range from a mild desire for a drug, to craving, to compulsive use of the drug. Drug dependence is explored in greater breadth and depth in Chapter 9.

*Drug interaction* occurs when the effects of one drug are modified by the prior or concurrent administration of another drug, thereby increasing or decreasing the pharmacologic action of each. Drug interactions may be either beneficial (e.g., probenecid prolongs the action of penicillins) or detrimental (e.g., aspirin increases the action of anticoagulants, causing hemorrhage).

*Drug antagonism* occurs when the conjoint effect of two drugs is less than the sum of the drugs acting separately.

*Summation (addition)* occurs when the combined effect of two drugs produces a result that equals the sum of the individual effects of each agent. The mathematical response is $1 + 1 = 2$. For example, codeine and aspirin both act as analgesics and when given together provide greater relief of pain than when either one is used alone. This combination allows the administration of a lower dosage of each drug, with a resultant decrease in adverse reactions.

*Synergism* describes a drug interaction in which the combined effect of drugs is greater than the sum of each individual agent acting independently. Mathematically the response is $1 + 1 = 3$. This can be exemplified by the use of a combination of drugs in treating hypertension. Each of the drugs lowers blood pressure, but in different ways; however, the combined effect produces a greater decrease in hypertension than if either drug were given alone.

*Potentiation* refers to the concurrent administration of two drugs in which one drug increases the effect of the other drug.

## NURSING MANAGEMENT

The nurse's responsibilities in the administration of drugs require more than memorization of specific drugs, their actions, and their dosages. Rather, effective implementation depends on a sound comprehension of the theories of drug action, constituting knowledge that the nurse can transfer to the individual client, each with a specific diagnosis and definable individual needs. Such a background necessitates the understanding of theories of drug action, physiologic processes mediating drug action, variables affecting drug action, and unusual and adverse responses to drug therapy.

On entry into the body, a drug initiates a series of physiologic events before it reaches its site of action. The extent of drug absorption depends on the form in which the drug appears. Tablets or capsules must first disintegrate and then be dissolved in solution before absorption through the intestinal membrane can occur. However, the nurse should never crush an enteric-coated tablet, because the coating protects it from destruction by the acid pH of the stomach. To maintain its effectiveness, the drug appears in this form so it can disintegrate and dissolve in the alkaline pH of the intestine. Drugs that irritate the gastric mucosa must also be coated.

To obtain the maximal pharmacokinetic benefit of a drug, the time of administration is another important concern of the nurse. Oral drugs should be given ½ hour before meals with a glass of water (8 ounces). It is important to remember that the presence of food, which delays stomach emptying, tends to diminish the therapeutic effect of the drug. Occasionally, an agent must be administered with meals to prevent gastrointestinal irritation. The nurse should anticipate a rapid response when a drug is given intravenously, because the full dosage is placed directly into the bloodstream, thus bypassing the need for absorption.

Individuals with hepatic dysfunction are susceptible to drug overdosage, especially if the drug is highly bound to plasma proteins. Adverse responses can be prevented by the administration of albumin. In addition, the nurse should be alert to the client's response to a drug if there is a renal disorder. Since most agents are excreted by the kidneys, the client should be observed for a cumulative effect that may result from the continued administration of the drug. Usually drug dosage is adjusted in individuals with hepatic or renal disorders so that adverse effects will be prevented.

In instances when the nurse is required to monitor serum drug levels, careful observations of the client's response to the drug provide information that aids the physician in determining the dosage of a drug, the frequency of administration, and the route of administration. The data are essential for promoting the optimal therapeutic benefit to the client and at the same time preventing potential adverse reactions.

Finally, the nurse should alert a pregnant woman about the danger of taking medications and, to prevent teratogenic effects, advise her to check with a physician before taking any drug. In addition, if a medication is required, the lowest possible dose of the prescribed drug should be administered.

## SUMMARY

Drugs, as chemicals that interact with a living organism to produce biologic responses, do so according to certain theories of drug action, physiologic processes mediating drug action, variables affecting drug action, and unusual and adverse responses to drug therapy. For general properties, drugs modify only existing functions and exert multiple actions rather than a single effect. These actions result from a physicochemical interaction between the drug and a functionally important molecule in the body.

To produce the desired effect, a drug must have an appropriate concentration at its site of action. This concentration is influenced by a number of processes, which can be divided into three phases: pharmaceutical, pharmacokinetic, and pharmacodynamic. The pharmaceutical phase focuses on the form of the drug, solid or liquid, and its dissolution to achieve absorption. The pharmacokinetic phase is concerned with the concentration of the drug influenced by the processes of absorption, distribution, biotransformation, and excretion. Absorption involves the movement of drug molecules from the site of entry into the body to the circulating fluids. The following factors influence absorption: the nature of the absorbing surface through which the drug must pass, blood flow to the site of administration, solubility of the drug, pH, drug concentration, and dosage form. Drugs may be given for their local or systemic effect. The routes of drug administration may be classified as enteral; parenteral-subcutaneous, intramuscular, intravenous, intrathecal; pulmonary; and topical. Distribution is the transport of a drug in body fluids to various tissues of the body and ultimately to the site of action. It is influenced by the body's storage reservoirs for drugs, plasma protein binding and tissue binding, as well as barriers to drug distribution, such as the blood-brain barrier and the placental barrier. In biotransformation the liver, as primary site for drug metabolism, inactivates the drug by converting it to a metabolite which can be excreted from the body. Excretion, elimination of the pharmacologically active or inactive metabolites from the body, is primarily through the kidneys with some elimination through the intestine, lungs, mammary glands, and sweat and salivary glands.

The pharmacodynamic phase is concerned with the response of tissues to specific chemical agents at various sites in the body. The mechanism for action between the drug and a functionally important component of the living system may be a drug-receptor interaction, drug-enzyme interaction, or a nonspecific drug interaction. Because each drug has its own characteristic pharmacokinetic activity, it may be necessary to monitor clients by obtaining a plasma level profile of the drug. The biologic half-life and therapeutic index of a drug also provide information to help the physician determine the dosage, scheduling, and route of administration for an individual client.

No drug is totally safe; it can sometimes react in the body to produce unpredictable and harmful effects. However, some identifiable factors do alter the response to drug therapy: age, body mass, sex, environmental milieu, time of administration, pathologic state, genetic factors, and psychologic factors. The adverse effects caused unintentionally by treatment are known as iatrogenic disease. With drug therapy, iatrogenic disease is manifested in five major effects: blood dyscrasias, hepatic toxicity, renal damage, teratogenic effects, and dermatologic effects. Other, and somewhat unpredictable, adverse effects may be evidenced as drug allergy, idiosyncrasy, tolerance, tachyphylaxis, cumulation, drug dependence, drug interaction, drug antagonism, summation, synergism, potentiation, and immediate reactions, such as anaphylaxis.

It is important that the nurse understand the principles involved in drug action and their influence on nursing practice to enable the administration of medication with the greatest safety and efficacy.

## BIBLIOGRAPHY

Clark JB et al. (1990). Pharmacological basis of nursing practice, ed 3. St Louis: Mosby–Year Book, Inc.

D'Arcy PF et al. (1987). Drug-antacid interactions: assessment of clinical importance, Drug Intell Clin Pharm 21(7/8):607.

DiPiro JT et al. (1989). Pharmacotherapy: a pathophysiologic approach. New York: Elsevier Science Publishing Co., Inc.

Franse VL et al. (1988). Drug-nutrient interactions in a Veteran's Administration Medical Center teaching hospital, Nutr Clin Pract 3(4):145.

Gilman AG et al, editors. (1990). Goodman and Gilman's The pharmacological basis of therapeutics, ed 8. New York: Macmillan Publishing Co.

Goth A and Vessell ES. (1984). Medical pharmacology: principles and concepts, ed 11. St Louis: The CV Mosby Co.

Green GR et al. (1988). Circumventing penicillin allergy, Patient Care 22(8):43.

Hansten PD and Horn JR. (1989). Drug interactions: clinical significance of drug-drug interactions. Philadelphia: Lea & Febiger.

Josephs C. (1987). The side-effects and interactions of drugs in elderly patients, Geriatr Nurs Home Care 7(3):17.

Kirk E et al. (1987). Effects of alcohol on the central nervous system: implications for the neuroscience nurse, J Neurosci Nurs 19(6):32.

Koch-Weser J. (1983). Drug administration in hepatic disease, N Engl J Med 309:1616.

Kolcaba K et al. (1989). Geropharmacology treatment, J Gerontol Nurs 15(5):29.

Lamy PP. (1980). Prescribing for the elderly. Littleton, Mass: PSG Publishing Co., Inc.

Levinson RS and Allen LV. (1976). Physiological and pharmaceutical factors that affect the bioavailability of drugs, Cont Educ Guide Pharm 1(3):1.

Martin RB. (1976). Drug interactions, Cont Educ Guide Pharm 1(1):1.

Porterfield L. (1988). Principles of drug action, AD Nurse 3(3):11.

Ramsey R. (1988). Adjusting drug dosages for critically ill elderly patients, Nursing 18(7):47.

Rousseau P. (1987). Pharmacologic alterations in the elderly, Hosp Formul 22(6):543.

Santo-Novac D et al. (1989). Rx: take caution with drugs for elders, Geriatr Nurs 10(2):72.

Schultz NJ. (1987). Principles of drug therapy, J Enterostom Ther 14(5): 212.

Schwartz RH and Yaffe SL, editors. (1980). Drug and chemical risks to the fetus and newborn. New York: Alan R Liss, Inc.

Skelly AH et al. (1987). Insulin allergy in clinical practice, Nurse Pract 82(39):44.

Stockley L. (1981). Drug interactions. London: Blackwell Scientific Publications, Inc.

Vore M et al. (1986). Common adverse drug interactions, Hosp Med 22(10):94.

Willis J. (1987). "The pill" may not mix well with other drugs, FDA Consum 21(2):26.

Winter ME at al. (1987). Essentials of therapeutic drugs monitoring, Physician Asst 11(7):79.

*Unit 2*

# The Nursing Process and Pharmacology

*Chapter*

# 5  Assessment, Nursing Diagnosis, and Planning

## INTRODUCTION

The **nursing process** is applied to drug therapy to develop a systematic, organized approach to handling the wealth of data about clients and their drugs. It provides direction for rational nursing actions to manage problems related to drug therapies. Conceptually, the nursing process itself continues to be in a healthy state of evolution as nurse researchers and practitioners develop and test nomenclature and theories.

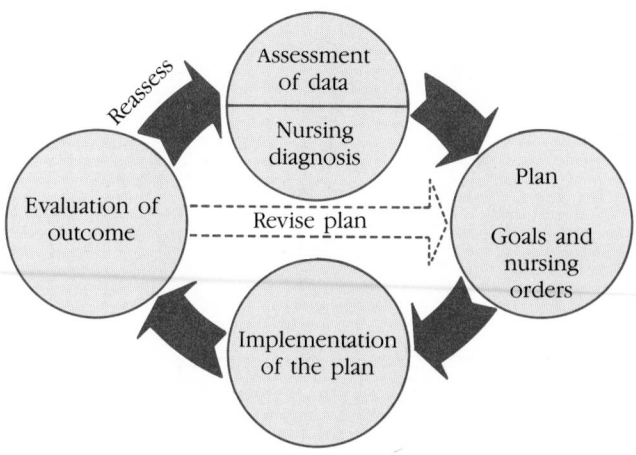

**FIGURE 5-1**   The nursing process.

Although current literature may not be in absolute agreement about all of the terminology or the distinctive phases in the nursing process, its concepts become more completely defined and more widely accepted with each passing year. The nursing process, however, is certainly a viable and practical organizing tool to apply to client care.

The nursing process was the foundation of high-quality clinical practice long before it had been conceptualized and given a name. Its process and phases are analogous to scientific and problem-solving methods. Although other variations exist, in this book it is described here in four phases: (1) assessment, culminating in nursing diagnoses, (2) planning, (3) implementation, and (4) evaluation. Figure 5-1 diagrams these phases or steps, which are discussed in this chapter and in Chapter 6. It should be kept in mind that the steps of the nursing process have an ongoing, cyclic nature—no step should be considered completed or static.

## ASSESSMENT

The assessment phase of the nursing process is both the first phase and a continuous phase that ends only on discharge of the client. During assessment of data, all the facts relating to clients and their drug therapy, relationships with others, the health history, and the environment are collected and organized so that the nurse can begin to make inferences about any problem in drug therapy. The data that are collected and analyzed form the basis for development of a nursing diagnosis.

The client's status and the assessment data derived from these indicated sources are constantly changing. Nursing diagnostic statements will change as well. In collaboration with the physician, these changes may result in revision of the medical plan, such as drug deletions, additions, or dosage changes.

Nurses must have a sound base of knowledge about a client's disorder and drugs being administered, as well as the skill to use references to answer questions that arise.

The ability to ask questions and seek answers about the data collected will form a solid foundation for the planning, implementation, and evaluation phases of the nursing process.

## Drug History Guidelines

Taking a **drug history** can be extremely useful for gathering data about an individual's experience with medications. Obtaining a comprehensive drug history requires a combination of nursing knowledge, interviewing skills, and a review of specific drug reference resources, whenever necessary. A drug history should explore the client's usage of prescription medications, usage of over-the-counter (OTC) drugs, self-treatment with herbal or home remedies, general and specific health history, and when possible, specific cultural factors that influence individual drug therapies. Figure 5-2 shows a sample drug history form.

A thorough drug history can provide extremely useful information for the entire health care team. For example, it can:

1. Explain a mysterious new symptom reported in the client.
2. Provide clues about unreported chronic disorders.
3. Reveal learning needs or concerns regarding client compliance with therapy.
4. Provide information crucial to prevent drug interactions, allergies, or side or toxic effects.
5. Help interpret laboratory tests reliably.
6. Identify the potential for drug-drug and drug-food interactions.

When a nurse is taking a drug history, it is important to communicate at the level of understanding appropriate for the client. Medical terminology may be confusing to the non-medically trained person; therefore the nurse should be familiar with local observances and, when applicable, ethnic or cultural expressions for specific diseases, illnesses, symptoms, and/or other information.

Open-ended questioning is preferred to direct "yes" or "no" questions during an interview. For example, to obtain information about a client's use of analgesics, a "yes" or "no" question would be: "Do you take analgesics? If 'yes,' name them." If the person is unsure of the meaning of the term *analgesia,* a "no" answer might be the natural response. The question can be reworded to ask, "What do you take when you have pain, such as a headache, backache, muscle sprain, or other type of ache or pain?" and the more descriptive information the nurse is seeking may then be forthcoming. Questions concerning over-the-counter drugs must often be accompanied by reminders from the interviewer. Commonly used product names or currently advertised brands may be suggested to jog the memory of the client. For example, aspirin is an ingredient in hundreds of OTC preparations; therefore simply asking the client if he or she consumes aspirin may limit the answer to only products

DRUG HISTORY

Patient's name _____ Sex _____ Age _____ Date of interview _____
Occupation                                                                Physician

Diagnosis and past history (if relevant)
    Frequency of meals?                                      Special diet, prescribed
                                                                 or self-imposed:
Allergies/drug reactions (food and/or drugs; describe reaction, approximate date, and action taken or outcome):


Close family members with drug allergies (relationship, drug, and reaction):

Type/daily consumption                                     Smoking (type and amount):
    of alcohol:


*Over-the-counter medications:*
(List medications, dose, frequency, and when last dose was taken for following:)
Constipation (laxatives):
Diarrhea (antidiarrheal):
Gastric upset (antacids):
Pain, headache (analgesics):
Cold medication (antihistamine, decongestants):
Cough medicine (syrups/other forms):
Drugs for sleep:
Drugs to stay awake:
Drugs for menstrual conditions in premenopausal women:
Drugs for nerves:
Drugs for fluid retention:
Do you use any salt substitutes (obtain brand name; Morton Lite Salt, CoSalt, etc.)
Do you use any food supplements? Name and quantity per day:
Do you buy health food store products? Obtain complete listing and daily consumption.

Do you take vitamins? Note type, strength, and amount per day:

Current prescribed medications; include name, strength, and daily dosage:

Prescription medications taken during the previous three months:


Nurse _____

**FIGURE 5-2**  Sample drug history.

labeled as aspirin. Suggesting trade name products, such as Anacin, Bufferin, or Alka Seltzer, would expand the possibility of obtaining a more thorough drug history.

If the interview is performed in the client's living quarters, the nurse should ask to see medications. Many individuals, especially the elderly, forget to report all the medications they have on hand for self-medicating purposes. Also the storage place for medications should be noted, since this may be important information if a potentially hazardous site is used. Storage in a bathroom cabinet or over a kitchen sink or stove may adversely affect many medications. Areas of heat and moisture are not recommended as proper storage areas for most drugs.

Evaluating the client's knowledge about proper disposal of drugs (via the sink or toilet), ability to read and understand the labels on medication, and ability to locate expiration dates is part of assessing the individual's ability to safely store and consume medications. Studies have indicated that many persons (from one third to one half of various elderly populations) cannot read or do not understand drug package labels. This high incidence clearly indicates an area of concern that requires nursing assessment.

Information should also be obtained on the individual's general life-style, consumption of alcohol, use of caffeine-containing products, and smoking habits. All these factors may affect or modify a typical drug response. (See the section on drug interactions in this chapter for further information.)

## Client and Environmental Data

Client and environmental data are collected from clients, their friends, or their relatives by subjective and objective observations. In addition to observation of clients and their environment, interactions of clients with others and notes from the history and physical examination sections of the chart are used as sources. At the initial interview the practitioner notes a client's past health history and does a physical examination to assess the client's current status. The resulting prioritized problem list directs the therapeutic approach.

Before compiling the nursing data base, rapport must be established if transfer of relevant information is to be made freely. Information obtained in the client's history and physical examination should be reviewed to select pertinent data. The nurse needs to gather data in certain areas to assess appropriateness of the planned drug therapy. If drug dosage and route of administration are not carefully selected, alterations in the various systems may result in either an increased or exaggerated drug effect or a decrease in drug response. Table 5-1 lists the major factors to be evaluated and pertinent data to be obtained.

## Current Client Drug Data

Drug data include information derived from the prescriber's orders or prescription and that gained from assessment of the drugs' effects on the patient, based on observation, vital signs, and laboratory reports. The characteristics of the drugs administered and the way the prescriber orders them have an impact on the client's nursing care.

### Drug Orders and Prescriptions

"Medicating" a client begins when the medication is suggested and authorized by a legally sanctioned prescriber, usually a licensed physician or dentist. These two professionals are currently the only ones legally allowed to initiate medication plans in all states. In several states, nurse practitioners or physicians' assistants have also been given that function legally; in other states this is under consideration. The practicing nurse should be aware of and follow the limitations outlined in the state nurse practice act.

The prescriber's orders are meant for the one who dispenses the medication. There are two different formats, the prescription blank and the order sheet. The prescription blank is given to the outpatient and is to be filled by a community pharmacist; it may look similar to Figure 5-3.

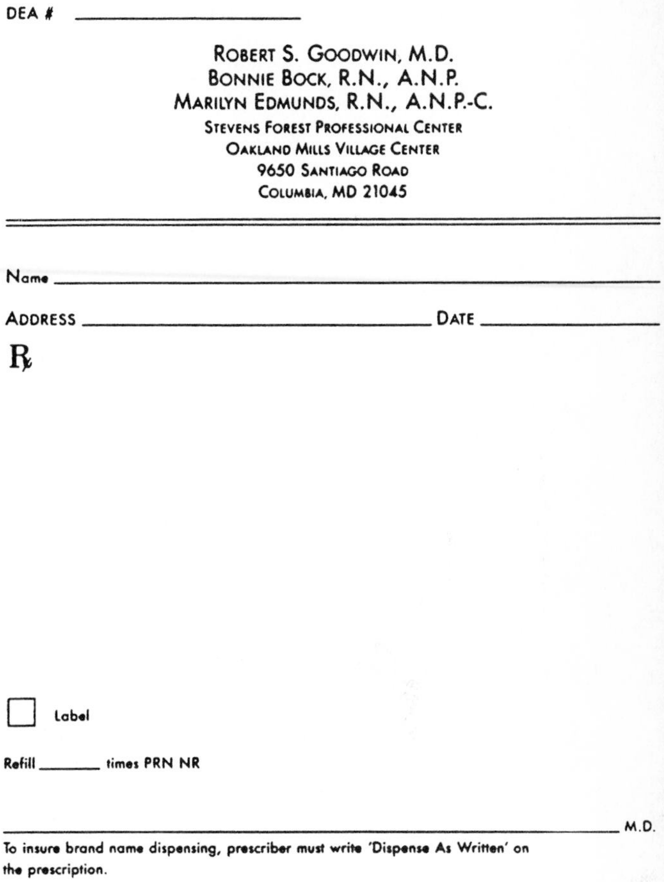

DEA # _____

ROBERT S. GOODWIN, M.D.
BONNIE BOCK, R.N., A.N.P.
MARILYN EDMUNDS, R.N., A.N.P.-C.
STEVENS FOREST PROFESSIONAL CENTER
OAKLAND MILLS VILLAGE CENTER
9650 SANTIAGO ROAD
COLUMBIA, MD 21045

Name _____

ADDRESS _____ DATE _____

℞

☐  Label

Refill _____ times PRN NR

_____ M.D.

To insure brand name dispensing, prescriber must write 'Dispense As Written' on the prescription.

**FIGURE 5-3** Example of a prescription blank. *(From Edmunds MW [1990]. Introduction to clinical pharmacology, St Louis: Mosby–Year Book, Inc.)*

For clients in an institutional setting, the order is written on an order sheet found in the client's chart (Figure 5-4). It is filled by the pharmacy within the institution or contracted for by the institution and sent to the medication area on the client's floor for access by the client's medication nurse.

The prescriber's order has seven elements that should be present and identifiable. These elements are included in the box below on the "Five Rights" of medication administration. All parts of the order should be legible and clearly

| **FIVE RIGHTS OF MEDICATION ADMINISTRATION** | |
|---|---|
| **Rights** | **Elements of Medication Order** |
| Right patient | 1. Client's name |
| | 2. Date order written |
| Right drug | 3. Medication name |
| Right dose | 4. Dosage |
| Right route | 5. Route |
| Right time | 6. Frequency |
| | 7. Prescriber signature |

**TABLE 5-1**   Client and environmental data

| Factor | Questions for evaluation | Rationale |
|---|---|---|
| Medical diagnosis | Are the drugs ordered clinically indicated and corroborated by the best judgments according to authoritative literature? | The client must be protected from wrongful harm; the administering nurse may be held legally accountable. |
| Age | Has the client's age been considered? Have drug reactions occurred in the past? | The very young and the elderly are subject to a wide range and great intensity of side and adverse effects because of reduced functioning of body systems that absorb, transport, affect the metabolism of, and excrete drugs (see also Chapter 8). |
| Body mass | Was the dosage assessed in relation to total body weight, body surface area (weight-to-height ratio), and lean body mass? | For prescribing purposes, the person up to 12 years old is usually considered a child and given a pediatric dosage. The dose is based on the different physiologic and pharmacokinetic factors in the neonate, infant, or older child. The average weight of a 12-year-old child is about 90 pounds; an "average" adult weighs 150 pounds. An adult at or near the weight of 90 pounds who receives the "average adult dose" may exhibit signs of overdosage. |
| Inherited factors | Have genetic differences (pharmacogenetic variations) in enzyme production or destruction, which may cause apparent therapeutic failure or secondary effects when a drug is metabolized too rapidly, too slowly, or incompletely, been considered? | Many aberrant reactions (termed *idiosyncrasy*) are often acutely caused by genetic abnormalities. An example is the lack of the enzyme glucose-6-phosphate dehydrogenase, found in a small percentage of people of Mediterranean descent (Italians, Greeks, Arabs, and Sephardic Jews) and in about 10% of American black males, less often in black females. Fava beans and medications such as aspirin, antimalarials, and sulfonamides, if taken by these susceptible people, may cause hemolytic anemia. Also, hypersensitivity (allergy) to specific medications often correlates with a tendency to other common allergies to certain foods, grasses, trees, molds, or animal dander. |
| Coexisting conditions | Are there disorders that affect any of the major body systems, especially those of the gastrointestinal tract or the circulatory, hepatic, or renal system, that will interfere with normal digestion, absorption, transport, metabolism, degradation, and detoxification or excretion of the drugs prescribed? | Impaired capacity for biotransformation may alter drug action and increase the possibility of toxic effects or therapeutic failure. Pregnancy or breastfeeding precludes administration of all but essential medications (see Chapter 8). |
| Compliance | Is there a past history or other factors indicating that the client, if self-medicating, will not follow medication instructions? (See Chapter 7 for full discussion of client compliance.) | Attitudes and behavior conducive to positive health behavior depend on psychosocial, cultural, economic, cognitive, and physical factors—how the client views and values health and illness; how the client understands or accepts illness; what he or she knows about the drug in question; how he or she relates to the health care surroundings, system, and practitioners; how the client assigns control and decision making; whether the client communicates and thinks logically; how he or she has been educated; and whether he or she has manipulative skills, among others. Studies show that having faith in a therapy has a decidedly favorable effect on its outcome. A subtle approach is needed to evaluate these parameters. |

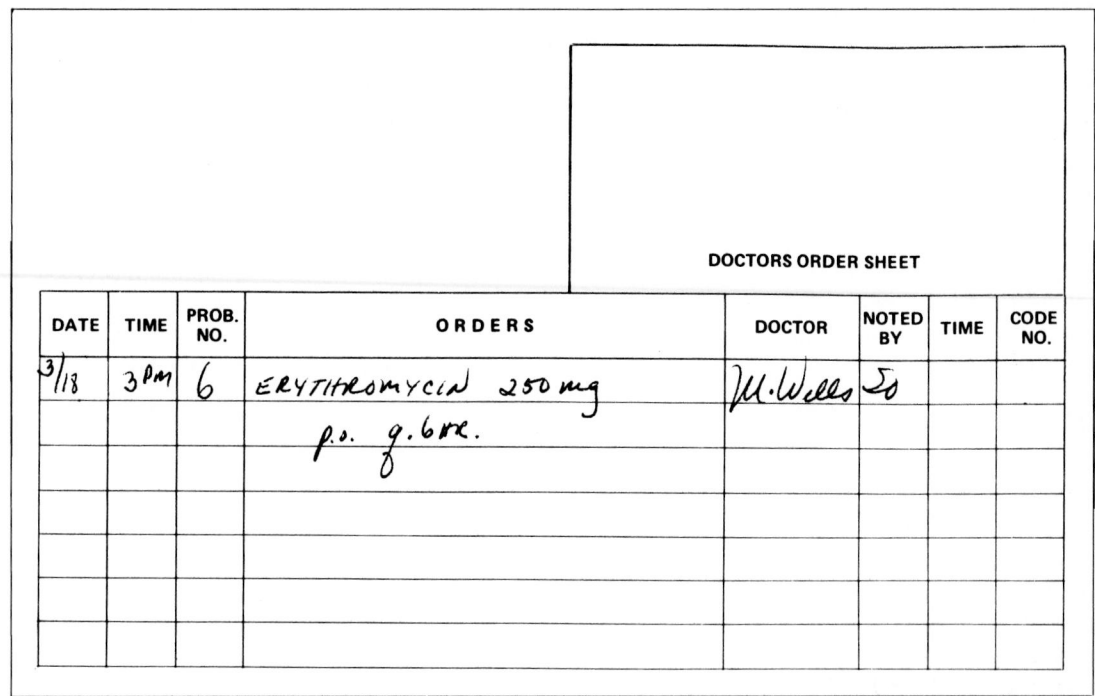

| DATE | TIME | PROB. NO. | O R D E R S | DOCTOR | NOTED BY | TIME | CODE NO. |
|------|------|-----------|-------------|--------|----------|------|----------|
| ³/18 | 3 PM | 6 | ERYTHROMYCIN 250 mg p.o. q.6hr. | M. Wells | So | | |
| | | | | | | | |
| | | | | | | | |
| | | | | | | | |
| | | | | | | | |
| | | | | | | | |

**FIGURE 5-4** Example of an order sheet.

expressed. If there is any doubt, the prescriber must be contacted to validate or clarify. Obviously, to administer a drug under questionable instructions is to risk harm to the client in an area with a high potential for error (see Chapter 6).

Safe nursing practice is to follow approved procedures in the particular work environment and to administer only drugs that are ordered in writing. Nursing students should be aware of special limitations imposed on their actions by the educational and/or clinical institution. In particular, they should be advised to follow only written orders. However, sometimes a verbal or telephoned order from a physician, often in response to the nurse's telephoned request, is unavoidable. When this occurs, it is best to copy the order as it is being given, then verify it by repeating it back to the sender. Verbal or telephoned orders should be rare, involving circumstances of some urgency rather than convenience. Such an order must be clearly communicated and noted on the client's chart by the nurse. The physician must countersign it, usually within 24 hours in most institutions, *to be legal*. Allowing the order to remain unsigned is careless and negligent because it violates both the law and institutional policy. This allows a precarious period of nursing vulnerability to malpractice charges (See Chapter 2.)

### Types of Drug Orders

It is probably obvious by now that, although outpatients are free to medicate themselves with any medication accessible, once an individual is admitted to a clinical institution, usually neither the client nor the nurse may legally administer any medication without a written order.

Contents of the prescriber's orders dictate the conditions under which the ordered drug may be administered. Several types of orders follow.

***Routine order.*** The most common type is the **routine order,** which means that the drug as ordered is to be regularly administered until a formal discontinuation order is written or until a specified termination date is reached. Automatic termination or "automatic stops" may be explicit in agency policy. Automatic stop policies may be mandated for institutional accreditation or licensure requirements, or they may be applied variously by institutions. Such policies act as a stimulus to the prescriber to evaluate continued need for those drugs that require especially close attention.

***Prn order.*** Prn drugs are to be administered by the nurse only "as necessary." Within the other criteria specified by the order, the decision of when to medicate is left to the nurse's judgment. This type has implications for nursing autonomy similar to protocol orders.

Medications to reduce the perception of pain make up the bulk of **prn orders.** Keen nursing assessments of pain are required to carry out these prn orders appropriately. (See Chapter 11 for specifics for the evaluation of pain.) It is sufficient to note that pain is a very complex phenomenon, influenced by factors of subjectivity, emotions, and age, among others. The most dependable guide is that the pain is what and when the client says it is; assumptions by the nurse are not as reliable. Research has demonstrated that patients are frequently undermedicated for pain. Children especially are frequently left to suffer, undermedicated for pain, under the assumption that their pain is less severe than it seems.

***Single order.*** A **single order** is to be administered only once, at the time indicated. An example is a preoperative medication.

***Stat order.*** A **stat order** is a single order that is to be administered immediately.

***Protocol.*** A **protocol** is a set of criteria that serves as a directive under which medication may be given. Protocols may typically be one of two types: standing orders or flow diagram protocols. Standing orders are officially accepted sets of orders (not only for medications) to be applied routinely by nurses to the care of clients with certain conditions or under certain circumstances (e.g., as part of admission orders in some critical care units). Flow diagram protocols are criteria that give nurse practitioners guidelines for administration of certain treatments and medications on the basis of patient variables. These protocols provide the widest scope for application of nursing judgment and decision making of all the types of orders. Criteria and direction may be either very specific, for those with limited expertise or responsibility, or less specific and allow for greater latitude, self-reliance, and sophistication in decision making.

### Assessment of Medication Orders

***Client.*** Every possible effort should be made to ensure that the client receives the intended medication in the manner planned by the prescriber. Toward this end, clients with similar names should be widely separated in the health care setting, and all their paperwork must be clearly distinguishable. An identifying arm band must be kept on every client and compared to identifying information that accompanies each dose of medication.

***Date.*** The date that a medication order was written must be checked against other information for accuracy or for confirmation of when the last dose is to be given.

***Medication.*** The medication's name may be written either in generic or trade name form. The client should know the name of the medication if it is agency policy. If it is not, then nurses in the agency should be actively working with administrative leaders to reverse the policy. Clients should be told the names of their drugs while hospitalized so they can reasonably be expected to follow self-administration orders successfully at home! It is dangerous to keep clients ignorant of their medications. Exact names and dosages are crucial information for attending physicians to know if, for example, emergency treatment is needed.

***Dosage and frequency.*** Drug dosages should be given as prescribed in the medication order unless nursing judgment detects, for example, that the size of the dose ordered falls outside the range of usual limits or that there are intervening factors in the patient-dosage, its frequency, or the route of administration. The drug would then not be administered and would be held until the nurse consults the prescriber on the question.

During the development of a drug the manufacturer makes determinations in regard to optimal range of dosage, frequency, and effective route for administration for most people. These are based on the known pharmacokinetics of the drug. For example, a drug that routinely undergoes biotransformation slowly may remain in the body system longer and produce more prolonged effects than another drug. Therefore it may effectively be given on a once-a-day basis, but a drug that is excreted rapidly may need to be given every 4 hours around the clock if effective tissue levels of the drug are to be maintained. Nursing judgments must be made in order to align an individual client's medication schedule with agency policy at appropriate intervals or to keep to a single schedule to meet a specific drug requirement (before or after meals) or a special need of the client. Some reasons to individualize administration time include client convenience and avoiding disturbing the client's rest, sleep, meals, visiting hours, other activities, or treatments. Rationales for other modifications in the medical plan should be discussed with the prescriber.

***Route.*** Every medication order should include a specified route for administration. Making assumptions in this area is negligent. However, choice of the actual *site* of administration of injectables is a nursing or nurse-patient decision. For example, subcutaneous, intramuscular, and intravenous sites to avoid include any areas of obvious injury, disease, or lesions, even if minor; any that are noticeably erythematous (reddened), vesicular (blistered), open and weeping or pustular, ecchymotic (bruised), or scarred; and those previously overused for injection. Such areas may have impaired circulation or may be adversely affected by the injection itself or by the material injected. Injection sites are rotated to avoid tissue damage from injections. (Details may be found in Chapter 6.)

The ordered route of administration should routinely be assessed as to its efficacy, feasibility, or practicality. The oral route would naturally be precluded for the client who is nauseated or vomiting, for example. Prior consultation with the prescriber must be made before administering a drug by a different route, because dosage or other factors may have to be readjusted if bioavailability is affected by such changes.

### *Evaluation of Primary and Secondary Effects*

The ultimate effects of drugs on the body can be divided into two types. The main purpose of administering a medication is to use its primary, or therapeutic effect. All other consequences can be considered secondary effects, largely unintended and often nontherapeutic. Figure 5-5 illustrates the association between common terms that are used to describe the relative severity of secondary effects.

Drugs are developed and formulated to promote special effects; therefore the appearance of secondary effects demonstrates a continuing challenge to drug manufacturers. The crux of this problem is that most drugs cannot be made

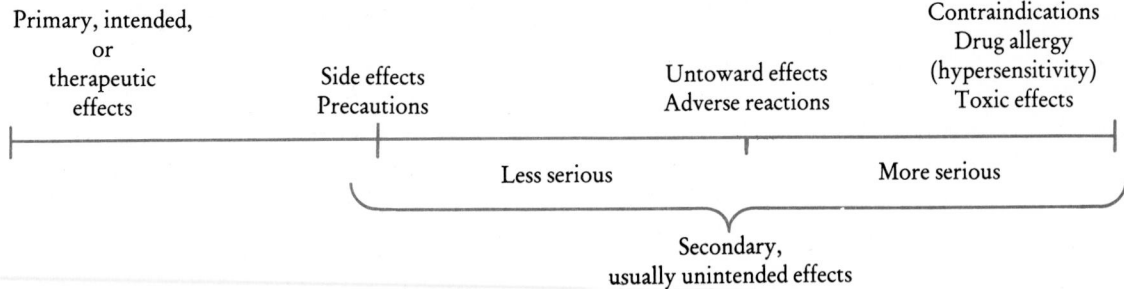

**FIGURE 5-5** Terms indicating relative severity of medication effects—a continuum.

selective enough to be targeted at only one body system, organ, tissue, or cell. When the drug is circulated or distributed to other areas, reactions may range in severity from merely inconvenient or annoying side effects to very serious adverse effects. On the other hand, a side effect may actually be the sought-after primary effect under certain circumstances or may be exploited by the prescriber as a therapeutic effect along with the primary effects. For example, diphenhydramine (Benadryl) is an antihistamine that produces a high incidence of drowsiness or sedation-type side effects. If this antihistamine is prescribed for an irritable child afflicted with an itching, poison ivy rash, the effect of sedation becomes a desired secondary effect. But if diphenhydramine is prescribed for an allergic reaction in a person who handles dangerous machinery or drives a commercial vehicle for a living, this side effect is undesired. In such instances, the physician should probably select an antihistamine with a sedative side effect that is considerably reduced.

Primary and secondary effects are often dose related— that is, directly related to increases in dosage—or they may be related to the duration of that specific therapy.

In the assessment phase of the nursing process, it is essential to discover any **contraindications** to a drug's administration. A contraindication to administration of a drug has potential to be more harmful than do side effects and adverse reactions, which may be discerned only in the evaluation phase (see Chapter 6), after the administration of the drug. It is essential that the medicating process be assessed with regard to each medication's clinical indications and potential efficacy and any contraindications, especially any allergy to the drug or any pathologic condition, etc., that would preclude its administration (see boxed material).

An allergic history of any sort, even if unrelated to the medication, must be explored to rule out and prevent any possible allergic reaction. The occurrence of drug allergy reactions is extremely individualized, unpredictable except for history, and not usually closely dose related. The reaction may result in a very serious and life-threatening situation. Consequently the drug must not be given. Reactions may vary from mild rash to severe exfoliative dermatitis and from asthma to anaphylactic shock. They may include urticaria, angioneurotic edema, and drug fever.

---

### MEDICATIONS FREQUENTLY IMPLICATED IN ALLERGIC REACTIONS

**Antibiotics:** penicillin (the most common cause of drug-induced anaphylaxis), cephalosporins, tetracyclines, streptomycin, erythromycin, neomycin, nitrofurantoin, and sulfa drugs (very frequently)

**Other drugs:** aspirin, hydantoins, acetaminophen, tolbutamide, gold salts, phenylbutazone, phenothiazines, histamines, aminopyrine, iodides, iron dextran, methylergonovine, quinidine, dipyrone, aminosalicylic acid, thiouracil, tranquilizers, anesthetics such as benzocaine (particularly troublesome because they are frequently used for application topically to irritated or delicate mucous membranes), tetracaine, procaine, lidocaine, and cocaine

**Diagnostic agents** such as iodinated contrast media (e.g., dye for IVP), iopanoic acid (Telepaque), sulfobromophthalein (BSP), dehydrocholic acid (Decholin), Congo red dye

**Biologicals** such as antitoxins, vaccines, gamma globulin, insulin, ACTH, enzymes, and their preservatives such as thimerosal, parabens, and antibiotics

---

An allergic drug response is caused by a specific reaction between a drug and the immune system. Most drugs are organic molecules with molecular weights of less than 1000 daltons, a dalton being an arbitrary unit of mass, equivalent to $1.657 \times 10^{-24}$ g. Such small molecules act as haptens; that is, they take on the ability to act as an allergen (to cause hypersensitivity or allergic reactions) only if they become bound to a carrier protein. This happens when the drug or its metabolite combines with tissue or plasma proteins to form the drug-protein complex, the complete allergen, necessary to stimulate the immune response and provoke an allergic response. At initial exposure to the drug, allergic persons may exhibit a latent period of 10 to 20 days before the hypersensitivity reaction occurs. Reactions to reexposure to the drug may occur sooner, even immediately.

It is essential to place alerting stickers or notations regarding the client's allergic history in the chart, Kardex, or other places according to agency policy. These locations need to be checked before any medications are given. Records may denote "no known allergy" (NKA), but usually this refers to drugs. Since a correlation often exists between one allergic response and the development of another, the client's description of *any* past allergic manifestations—to drugs, inhalants, contactants, foods (typically: eggs, orange juice, chocolate, shellfish, strawberries), or whatever—must be clarified and evaluated. Often the client erroneously defines an unexpected response as an allergic one. For example, the nausea following a meperidine (Demerol) injection may be labeled an allergic reaction by the patient, when in actuality it is likely to be only a normal, if exaggerated, side effect. Correcting such misinformation with the client and in the records may become important because it makes that drug available for therapy when necessary. Before any questionable medications are administered, nurses should specifically inquire about previous experiences with these agents and, if necessary for a client who has many allergies, discuss with the prescriber the need for a test dose. Special methods for those who must take medication to which they are allergic (e.g., aspirin, local anesthetics, or contrast media in diagnostic agents) include pretreatment medication in the form of antihistamines, prednisone, and ephedrine or cautiously increasing dosages of the allergy-provoking drug under supervision.

Other contraindications to drug therapy must be assessed before administration; evidence of other secondary effects usually appears only after the fact.

## Drug Interactions

The complexity of modern pharmacotherapy is nowhere more obvious than in the ever-growing list of drugs that interact nontherapeutically with one another, with foods, and with fluids and that distort laboratory test results. That these chemical substances will interact with or potentiate one another is not surprising; this fact should always be kept in mind when medications appear either ineffective or harmful or when the accuracy of laboratory tests is crucial.

Variables influencing drug interaction include (1) intestinal absorption, (2) competition for plasma binding, (3) drug metabolism or biotransformation, (4) action at the receptor site, (5) renal excretion, and (6) alteration of electrolyte balance. The following are examples of these variables' effects that interact nontherapeutically with other drugs, food, juices, and other liquids and distort many laboratory test results:

1. Intestinal absorption: foods or antacids that contain calcium, magnesium, or aluminum may complex or bind tetracycline, resulting in reduced absorption of the antibiotic.
2. Competition for plasma protein binding: tolbutamide

can be displaced from its binding on plasma proteins by bishydroxycoumarin, resulting in severe hypoglycemia. Many drugs are weak acids that are bound largely to plasma proteins. These weak acids may compete for binding sites on plasma proteins, thus increasing the free, active drug, which may have potent effects.

3. Drug metabolism or biotransformation: the monoamine oxidase inhibitors prevent the biotransformation of tyramine, which is present in aged cheese, liver, overripe fruit, and fermented meat (sausage, bologna, pepperoni, salami).
4. Action at the receptor site: numerous examples exist of one drug intensifying or antagonizing the action of another drug at the receptor site. For example, the antihistaminics decrease many effects of histamine, while cocaine increases the actions of epinephrine.
5. Renal excretion: probenecid inhibits the renal clearance of penicillin.
6. Alteration of electrolyte balance: the thiazide diuretics may cause hypokalemia, which predisposes to digitalis toxicity.

Not all drug interactions are dangerous; some are relatively insignificant or even beneficial. Tables listing known drug interactions should be posted in the medication area as references for nurses.

### Drug-Drug Interactions

Some drugs commonly involved in clinically significant drug-drug interactions include coumadin, tricyclic antidepressants (MAO inhibitors), aminoglycosides, amphetamines, corticosteroids, digitalis glycosides, diuretics, sulfonamides, alcohol, antihypertensives, beta blockers, and theophylline. Before any such medication is given, an appropriate source should be consulted to assess the drug, its mechanism, and any other medications given concurrently to determine the probability of interactions developing. This text gives this information in the context of specific drug monographs.

### Other Drug Interactions

***Drug-induced malabsorption of foods and nutrients.*** Drugs that change gastric or intestinal motility can alter the digestion or absorption of certain nutrients. Important drugs that affect these changes are stimulant cathartics and mineral oil and, at the other extreme, anticholinergics and narcotics. Long-term use of diuretics to treat such conditions as congestive heart failure can lead to serious potassium depletion. If the potassium loss is not corrected in clients taking digitalis, the heart may overrespond to the usual dose of digitalis. Some oral contraceptives impair folic acid absorption in undernourished clients.

***Food-induced malabsorption of drugs.*** Fatty foods or foods low in fiber will delay stomach emptying by up to 2 hours, which may result in delayed and/or reduced drug absorption. Several medications, though, such as griseofulvin and possibly spironolactone, exhibit enhanced bioavailability (absorption) following a high-fat meal. Many tetracyclines can form insoluble complexes in the gastrointestinal tract if given at the same time as foods or drugs containing ions of calcium, aluminum, magnesium, or iron. Thus, administering tetracycline medication along with milk-based tube feedings or common antacids should be avoided. Ascorbic acid from citrus fruits or juices enhances absorption of iron, but carbonated soft drinks or acid juices (fruit or vegetable) can cause drugs to dissolve more quickly in the stomach than in the intestine or can neutralize them, thereby changing the intended rate or completeness of absorption.

Milk, coffee, eggs, tea, whole-grain breads and cereals, dietary fiber, and foods containing bicarbonates, carbonates, phosphates, or oxalates may all reduce iron absorption if given concurrently. Iron products should be spaced at least 1 hour before or 2 hours after the mentioned food substances are given.

*Alteration of enzymes.* Enzyme alterations, either induction or inhibition, may affect the metabolism of a food or drug. The natural extract of licorice is chemically similar to that of steroids; and therefore if taken in excess, licorice can cause hypokalemia, retention of sodium and water with resultant hypertension, and alkalosis. Ingestion of large amounts would be contraindicated for clients who are concurrently taking potassium-losing diuretics or who have cardiovascular disease.

Likewise, consumption of large amounts of foods high in vitamin K (such as liver and green leafy vegetables) may reduce or antagonize the effectiveness of oral anticoagulants. Difficulty in maintaining the desired anticoagulant response with appropriately prescribed dosages indicates the need for an assessment of food and drug consumption.

Monoamine oxidase inhibitors (tricyclic antidepressants) act by inhibiting the breakdown of norepinephrine, a vasopressor substance. This excess norepinephrine is then stored in the neurons. The ingestion of certain tyramine-containing foods (aged cheeses, beef and chicken liver, pickled herring, broad beans, canned figs, bananas, avocados, soy sauce, active yeast preparations, beer, sherry in large quantities, Chianti wine, chocolate, anchovies, caffeine, mushrooms, raisins, sausages, dried fish, tuna fish, cola drinks, and many fermented foods) may elevate the quantity of norepinephrine to toxic levels, thereby precipitating hypertensive crises. OTC cold remedies containing ephedrine, phenylephrine, and phenylpropanolamine and amphetamines in general can act similarly, releasing stored quantities of norepinephrine. The net effect can be a headache, sudden climb in blood pressure to dangerous levels, cardiac arrhythmias, or intracranial bleeding.

*Alcohol consumption.* Of the more than 100 most frequently prescribed drugs, more than half contain at least one ingredient known to interact adversely with imbibed alcohol. An interaction is probable if the drug is known to affect the central nervous system or is metabolized by the liver. The effects are dose-related, and whether quantities of alcohol are used habitually, chronically, or only occasionally often makes a distinct difference in the direction of interactive effects. Patterns of alcohol consumption will likely have a bearing on the client's concurrence with drug treatment and follow-through as well. Alcohol consumption should be limited or totally avoided if a client is taking narcotics, tranquilizers, sedatives, and other CNS depressant—type drugs, which may cause additive or synergistic respiratory and CNS depression. Thus it is obvious that patterns of alcohol consumption are important when a history is being taken.

The fact that many elixirs and tinctures are liquid formulations of drugs dissolved in alcohol is significant, especially in the assessment of pharmacotherapy for children. These preparations must be reassessed and cannot be assumed to have the same rates and degrees of absorption as the same drugs in aqueous solution, since bioavailability may be altered.

*Cigarette smoking.* The main pharmacokinetic effect of heavy cigarette smoking is the lowering of drug plasma levels by induction of microsomal enzyme systems responsible for increased drug metabolism or excretion. The rate of theophylline breakdown is increased, necessitating an increase in dosage of from 1½ to 2 times the average dose. The usual doses of other drugs have diminished effectiveness in the heavy cigarette smoker—for example, the antidepressant imipramine; analgesics such as pentazocine, antipyyrene, phenacetin, and proproxyphene; vitamins C, $B_{12}$, and $B_6$; and the influenza vaccine. The absorption rate of insulin by the subcutaneous route is twice as slow as usual. Smoking also interacts with glutethimide, furosemide and propranolol. CNS depression and drowsiness are less frequent with diazepam (Valium), and drowsiness is reduced with chlorpromazine (Thorazine). When smoking is combined with use of estrogens, the risk of heart attack, stroke, and other circulatory disorders increases. Laboratory test results may also be somewhat outside the range of normal, depending on the duration of smoking history and inhalation practices. The white cell count is increased (in the absence of clinical infection); hemoglobin concentration, hematocrit, and red blood cell size are increased; and clotting time is reduced. Some investigators of cigarette smoking have found an abnormal increase in cholesterol, and others have found carcinoembryonic antigen levels as high as for persons with colon cancer, yet without other evidence of it. Therefore smokers can be expected sometimes to exhibit more numerous drug therapy "failures" or adverse effects, or they may even have fewer or different reactions to drugs than do nonsmoking patients. Certain laboratory test results must be interpreted in light of cigarette smoking history.

*Food-initiated alteration of drug excretion.* Changes in the pH of urine caused by food (making the urine overly

## ALLERGIC REACTIONS TO FOOD ADDITIVES

Allergic reactions have been reported following ingestion of food additives, such as monosodium glutamate (MSG), tartrazine, and sulfites. Tartrazine and sulfites are also used as additives, preservatives, and/or antioxidants in various medications. The most serious adverse reaction, resulting in some reported deaths, occurred most often in asthmatic patients. Current lists of foods and drug products containing tartrazine and sulfites should be reviewed in assessing reported allergic reactions. (See Appendix C.)

acidic or alkaline) can have a significant effect on the excretion rates of some drugs, since pH influences the ionization of weak acids and bases. A drug will diffuse more easily from the urine back into the blood in its nondissociated state, thereby prolonging drug action. Thus action of acidic drugs is prolonged when urine is acidic. Although it is quite difficult to override the kidneys' ability to regulate urine pH, an alkaline ash or acid ash diet, whether by purpose or not, can drive urinary pH above 8 or below 5, creating a medium for potential drug reactions. Continued taking of many antacid tablets each day in concert with quinidine administration was seen in one instance to create quinidine intoxication by shifting urinary pH toward the base and causing a serious arrhythmia necessitating hospitalization.

### Drug Incompatibilities

Interactions occurring when drugs are mixed before administration, as in a single syringe or in intravenous fluids, are termed drug **incompatibilities.** Drugs that are physically incompatible may produce unwanted changes through processes such as liquefaction, deliquescence, or precipitation. Chemical incompatibilities may result when ingredients interact to form new compounds or are neutralized. If drug incompatibilities are anticipated, separate administration routes should be sought. Some drugs are highly incompatible in solution with many other drugs. Since solution incompatibilities are frequently time dependent, fewer difficulties may be associated with mixing drugs in one syringe than in IV solutions; both drugs should be administered as soon after mixing as possible. Examples of drugs that are noted for interacting incompatibly with many other drugs in a syringe and that therefore should be administered alone include chloridiazepoxide, diazepam, pentobarbital, phenobarbital, phenytoin, secobarbital, and sodium bicarbonate.

Many drugs have explicit manufacturer's instructions for preparation (dilution and method of adding to selected IV parenteral solutions), which should be closely followed. A check for drug compatibility is indicated before two or more drugs are added to the same IV solution. Standard IV parenteral drug charts and guides are available for reference use. Many hospital pharmacies are providing an IV preparation service that screens for incompatibilities before preparation and delivery to the nursing area.

With the increase in the number of potent drugs and the variety of combinations, use of the pharmacist's expertise in a controlled environment is probably a wise policy. If the nurse is required to prepare IV solutions on the nursing unit, then adequate references, including a list of incompatibilities, should be posted in the area where the nurses perform this duty. Open communication on a regular basis with the pharmacy department is necessary in order to obtain new or additional information and/or assistance, whenever necessary.

## Sources of Drug Data

Any nursing process will be only as effective as the knowledge base and the analytic thought that go into it. Logic and judgment improve as the nurse's information base is perfected, partly as experience is tested against knowledge. Nowhere is ongoing self-learning more essential than in nursing pharmacotherapeutics. The "need to know" escalates, for example, when a nurse who is responsible for administering medications is confronted with an order for an unfamiliar drug or by an unexpected client symptom not usually associated with the diagnosis.

Realistically, it is not possible to know everything about all medications on the market, even those that nurses use frequently. Therefore, knowing where to get essential information as it becomes required is important. Various reference sources exist, each with its own emphasis, yet most are not completely adequate to meet the specialized needs of nursing pharmacotherapeutics.

### *Drug Information References*

The following are references frequently used as drug information sources by nurses.

*Physicians' Desk Reference* (P.D.R.) (Oradell, N.J.: Medical Economics Co., Inc.) is the most commonly consulted reference in clinical settings. It is a concise compilation of specific information similar to that found enclosed with medication as it comes from the pharmaceutical distributor (package inserts). As such, it is of limited value for the nursing process, since it is written in "medicalese," lacks any nursing methodology, and lists long strings of secondary effects without regard to relative frequency or severity. It is probably best used as a quick reference with another source handy to fill in information gaps. However, both the P.D.R. and package inserts can be considered to give an

FDA-approved and reliable discourse on drugs' clinical indications and safe ranges of dosages. The P.D.R. also lists the telephone numbers of pharmaceutical manufacturers to consult for specific questions or emergencies and to report adverse reactions.

Users of this information for the purpose of prescribing should be aware that individual cases may allow for variation in use and dosage of a drug, even to exceed suggested dosage range, but that such individual variation should have a valid rationale. When this source is being used, it should be borne in mind that the material it contains is submitted by the pharmaceutical company producing the drug. Other references provide unbiased drug information, including expanded areas of clinical drug use and application, which is preferable to the utilization of a pharmaceutical industry–supported reference.

*American Hospital Formulary Service* (Bethesda, Md., American Society of Hospital Pharmacists) is an objective overview in monograph form of nearly every available drug in the United States. It is kept current by periodically released supplements, and it includes extensive drug information. It is highly recommended as a source of drug information.

*A.M.A. Drug Evaluations* (Chicago, American Medical Association) is a source of information about specific drugs, even those that are being used for valid clinical applications different from those that have been approved thus far.

Nursing journals such as *American Journal of Nursing, Nursing92* (etc.), and *R.N.* offer both general and specific drug information in nursing terms and with a nursing perspective.

Many *nursing pharmacology texts* such as this one follow the same approach as the nursing journals but also include a greater depth of information about physiology and pathology of specific medication uses. Some offer only drug highlights for quick reference use.

*FDA Drug Bulletin* (Rockville, Md., Department of Health and Human Services, Public Health Service) is a free six-page newsletter published several times a year to inform health professionals about the results of recent FDA reviews of various drugs (usually common ones) and their new clinical findings. Each issue also includes a form for reporting unusual clinical experiences with drugs.

*Physicians' Desk Reference for Nonprescription Drugs* (Oradell, N.J., Medical Economics Co., Inc.) was first published in 1980 in recognition of the proliferation of over-the-counter drugs and the public's growing health awareness and interest in participating in self-care management. The format is similar to that of the P.D.R., with identifying photographs of the drugs, pharmaceutical company addresses, and descriptions of individual drugs and compounds. It also includes a section on the self-care of minor health problems.

*Handbook of Nonprescription Drugs* (Washington, D.C.,

American Pharmaceutical Association) deals with OTC drug information in general categories. Each chapter presents the relevant physiologic background first and concludes with a table comparing specific drugs.

The *National Formulary* (N.F.) (Rockville, Md.) is now combined with the *United States Pharmacopeia* (U.S.P.). The U.S.P. was the official reference recognized by the Federal Pure Food and Drug Act of 1906 and is still a required reference book for pharmacies in the United States. Its primary focus is drug sources, chemistry, physical properties, tests for identity, purity, assay, and official storage requirements. Hence its usefulness is directed more toward the pharmaceutical industry and pharmacists than toward the nursing profession.

*United States Pharmacopeia Dispensing Information* (Easton, Pa., U.S. Pharmacopeial Convention, Inc.) is a reference first published in 1980 to meet the needs of those involved in dispensing and administration, to themselves or others, *after* the prescription has been written and filled. The information on each drug includes its category, precautions to consider, side effects, information to tell the client, dosage forms, and labeling. A volume entitled "Advice for the Patient" is written in nontechnical language and provides pertinent essentials about the drug, a description of its ramifications, and methods of tailoring its administration to life-style. A major advantage of this reference is the manner in which it presents side effects—that is, the incidence potential (rare to common)—and it clearly states which ones should be reported to the physician. It is a highly valuable source for nurses.

*The Pharmacological Basis of Therapeutics* (AG Gilman, LS Goodman, and A Gillman, editors; New York: MacMillan, Inc.) is a thorough and respected reference text that is considered an authoritative source for those learning or working with pharmacology. It is not geared especially for nurses, nor does it contain specifics related to nursing pharmacotherapeutics, but it is an excellent reference work.

## Other Drug Information Sources

Drug information centers are located throughout the United States to disseminate information about the clinical uses of drugs and related equipment. Both general and specific information can be obtained, with advice based on scientific literature. A team of specially trained pharmacists is available, and these centers are often located within a large medical center setting. Many difficult pharmacologic questions related to client care can be dealt with quickly by contacting the nearest Drug Information Center.

Drug manufacturers, package inserts, and pharmacists located in hospitals, skilled care facilities, and other agencies also provide similar information.

Agencies frequently furnish similar sources of information. The area or floor where a nurse works often has a card file of package inserts; ideally, a nursing library shelf on

**TABLE 5-2** Nursing diagnoses and related interventions

| Type | Definition | Focus of nursing interventions |
|---|---|---|
| Actual (is present) | Validated major s/s* | To reduce or eliminate or promote positive diagnoses |
| High risk (may happen) | Presence of high-risk factors | To prevent onset |
| Possible (may be present) | Suspected to be present | To obtain additional data to rule out or confirm |

From North American Nursing Diagnosis Association (NANDA) taxonomy, 1990.
*s/s, Signs and symptoms.

each floor contains pharmacology information and other material of interest. Any nurse can initiate the development of such material and request funds or supplies. The agency nursing inservice or education department is responsible for promoting ongoing and updated learning and can facilitate audiovisual aids, references, or a seminar program. Building a personal library and maintaining its currency are also important professional activities.

No text is a complete source of all the pharmacology information necessary for nursing practice. The nurse must gather reliable information from various sources to meet clinical needs.

## ANALYSIS OF DATA

When data from the nursing assessment have been collected, the next phase is **analysis**—the critical evaluation of information to determine its meaning and importance. As with all phases of the nursing process, analysis is continuous. It is the process of interpreting data based on sound pharmacologic and nursing principles.

To facilitate analysis, the nurse may follow several steps. Initially, data are organized into categories. Categorization is accomplished by use of a planned systematic assessment, and gaps in data are noted. Once identified, missing information can then be obtained to complete the assessment. Accepted standards and norms are then applied to determine discrepancies between what is and what should be or could be, and conclusions are drawn regarding what actual, possible, or potential problems may be present. The culmination of analysis is the identification of specific areas toward which nursing care may be directed and may include a nursing diagnosis.

## NURSING DIAGNOSIS

The American Nurses' Association has defined a **nursing diagnosis** as a description of an actual or potential health problem that nurses are capable of treating and licensed to treat. One criterion is that it features a problem for which nursing care provides the most appropriate treatment. Basically, a nursing diagnosis should be a summary statement

to "engineer the uncertainty out of a patient care situation and thus minimize the number of incorrect inferences."*

The nursing profession is actively working toward standardization of nursing process terminology to facilitate communication among practitioners. A current aim is to classify groups of nursing diagnoses so that patterns will emerge, leading to categories of diagnoses. The North American Nursing Diagnosis Association (NANDA) has endorsed a classification of nursing diagnoses by human response patterns with approved terminology (Kim and others, 1990). Whenever possible, diagnostic statements used in this book are drawn from the list of NANDA-approved nursing diagnoses. The NANDA list and other widely circulated lists are not considered complete, but rather, nurses are encouraged to test them and develop new ones. See box for current list of NANDA-approved nursing diagnoses.

Several examples of nursing diagnoses follow. Note that there could be countless ways to convey the same thoughts, all equally correct; variations can arise from differences among individuals constructing the diagnoses and from the wording chosen. A nursing diagnosis includes two main components: a description of altered health status and an inferred reason for it. The main presenting symptom may also be included in the statement. The following list presents some sample nursing diagnoses:

Possible alteration in urinary elimination: urinary retention related to antihistamine therapy

Altered comfort: nausea/vomiting related to chemotherapy

High risk for alteration in bowel elimination: diarrhea related to antibiotic administration

Fluid volume excess: edema related to steroid therapy

Noncompliance: failure to refill prescriptions related to inadequate financial resources to buy drugs

See the box for those NANDA-approved nursing diagnoses more commonly seen as a result of drug therapy, noted by the asterisks.

A nursing diagnosis forms the basis for the design of the subsequent phases of the nursing process: planning, implementation, and evaluation. The diagnosis differentiates between actual, potential, and possible problems. Table 5-2

---

*Shamsky, S.L., and Yanni, C.: In opposition to nursing diagnosis: a minority opinion, Image: J. Nurs. Scholarship. 15(2):47, 1983.

## NINTH NORTH AMERICAN NURSING DIAGNOSIS ASSOCIATION (NANDA) APPROVED NURSING DIAGNOSES

*Activity intolerance
*Activity intolerance, high risk for
 Adjustment, impaired
 Airway clearance, ineffective
*Anxiety
*Aspiration, high risk for
 Body image disturbance
 Body temperature, altered, high risk for
*Breastfeeding, effective
 Breastfeeding, ineffective
*Breathing pattern, ineffective
 Cardiac output, decreased
 Communication, impaired verbal
*Constipation
 Constipation, colonic
 Constipation, perceived
 Coping, defensive
 Coping, family: potential for growth
 Coping, ineffective family: compromised
 Coping, ineffective family: disabling
*Coping, ineffective individual
 Decisional conflict (specify)
 Denial, ineffective
*Diarrhea
 Disuse syndrome, high risk for
 Diversional activity
 Dysreflexia
 Family processes, altered
*Fatigue
 Fear
 Fluid volume deficit (1)
 Fluid volume deficit (2)
*Fluid volume deficit, high risk for
*Fluid volume excess
*Gas exchange, impaired
 Grieving, anticipatory
 Grieving, dysfunctional
 Growth and development, altered
*Health maintenance, altered
*Health seeking behaviors (specify)
*Home health management, impaired
 Hopelessness
 Hyperthermia
 Hypothermia
 Incontinence, bowel
 Incontinence, functional
 Incontinence, reflex
 Incontinence, stress
 Incontinence, total
 Incontinence, urge
*Infection, high risk for

 Injury, high risk for
*Knowledge deficit (specify)
*Mobility, impaired physical
*Noncompliance (specify)
*Nutrition, altered: less than body requirements
 Nutrition, altered: more than body requirements
 Nutrition, altered: high risk for more than body requirements
*Oral mucous membranes, altered
 Pain
 Pain, chronic
 Parental role conflict
 Parenting, altered
 Parenting, altered, high risk for
 Personal identity disturbance
*Poisoning, high risk for
 Post-trauma syndrome
 Powerlessness
*Protection, altered
 Rape-trauma syndrome
 Rape-trauma syndrome: compound reaction
 Rape-trauma syndrome: silent reaction
 Role performance, altered
 Self-care deficit, bathing/hygiene
 Self-care deficit, dressing/grooming
 Self-care deficit, feeding
 Self-care deficit, toileting
 Self-esteem disturbance
 Self-esteem, chronic low
 Self-esteem, situational low
*Sensory/perceptual alterations (specify visual, auditory, kinesthetic, gustatory, tactile, olfactory)
*Sexual dysfunction
*Sexuality patterns, altered
*Skin integrity, impaired
*Skin integrity, impaired, high risk for
*Sleep pattern disturbance
 Social interaction, impaired
 Social isolation
 Spiritual distress (distress of the human spirit)
 Suffocation, high risk for
*Swallowing, impaired
 Thermoregulation, ineffective
*Thought processes, altered
 Tissue integrity, impaired
*Tissue perfusion, altered (specify renal, cerebral, cardiopulmonary, gastrointestinal, peripheral)
 Trauma, high risk for
 Unilateral neglect
 Urinary elimination, altered patterns
*Urinary retention
 Violence, high risk for: self-directed or directed at others

*Nursing diagnoses more commonly seen with drug therapy. Nursing diagnoses approved in 1990.

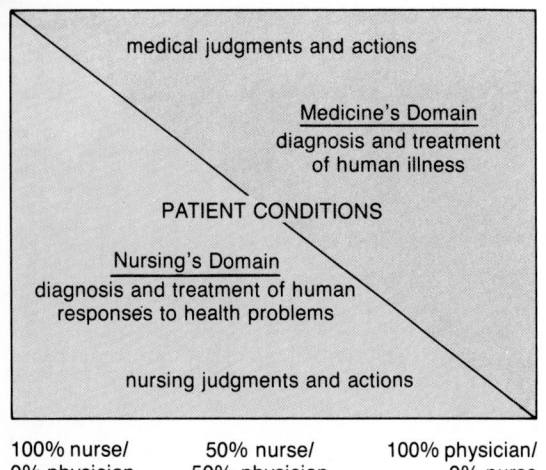

| 100% nurse/ | 50% nurse/ | 100% physician/ |
| 0% physician | 50% physician | 0% nurse |
| responsibility | responsibility | responsibility |

**FIGURE 5-6**   Nursing and medical responsibilities. *(From McLane AM, editor. [1987]. Classification of nursing diagnoses: proceedings of the Seventh Conference, St Louis: The CV Mosby Co.)*

defines each type and the corresponding focus of interventions.

## Nature of Nursing Actions

Nursing interventions may be categorized into three domains: **dependent** (or delegated), **collaborative,** and **independent.** Medicine diagnoses and treats pathologic or cellular responses, while nursing diagnoses and treats the human response (Sanford, 1987). Those activities legally requiring a physician directive, or dependent interventions, may constitute a significant portion of nursing practice related to pharmacology. A significant number of interventions require collaboration between nurses and other health care providers. Client conditions require differing ratios of medical (or other health care provider) and nursing input (Figure 5-6). Neither nurses nor other health-care providers possess exclusive responsibility for diagnosis and treatment of collaborative problems. Each group maintains its own responsibility throughout its involvement with the client. The independent domain involves the diagnosis and treatment of problems that are primarily nursing in nature. The nurse identifies these problems and assumes primary responsibility for ordering needed interventions.

## Utility of Nursing Diagnosis

By describing human responses, nursing diagnosis distinguishes nursing from other health care disciplines. Nursing diagnoses are most useful in the independent domain. Their use provides a focus for goals and interventions: a nursing diagnosis is a clear, concise description of a problem that is uniquely addressed by nurses. The development of nursing

diagnoses has added much to the refinement and description of nursing care by providing structure, focus, and language for clear communication.

Because of the early stage of development of nursing diagnosis, implementation of nursing diagnoses is hampered by divergent views, conceptual controversies, and confusing terminology. The nursing profession's health-related, strength-oriented emphases are not easily addressed by currently accepted nursing diagnoses, and it may be unrealistic to expect nursing diagnoses to describe all of nursing practice. Much of the nurse's role in pharmacotherapeutics encompasses the dependent and collaborative domains, areas not thoroughly addressed by nursing diagnoses. Throughout this textbook, the use of nursing diagnosis is encouraged but not forced upon situations in which it is inappropriate. As the evolution of nursing diagnosis continues, application to pharmacotherapeutics will become increasingly appropriate and useful.

## PLANNING FOR DRUG THERAPY

The planning phase of the nursing process has two parts, setting goals (or **outcome criteria**) and specific plans for interventions that will implement the goals. The planning to meet the pharmacotherapeutic nursing needs of clients should be characterized by an orientation to (1) the client, (2) resources in the environment, and (3) the future. These in turn should be characterized by a balance between the real and the ideal.

Goals associated with medication needs of patients may be stated in many ways to encompass these three orientations. They must actually be stated (e.g., in the nursing care plan) to provide communication with the rest of the staff and to give clear direction for the subsequent implementation and evaluation phases. Otherwise, implementation and evaluation of the nursing care will be based on vague events and partially remembered and incomplete actions.

Goals are objectives to be met sometime in the future. Therefore the use of the words "will be" in the goal statement is appropriate. An approximation of time limits for the goal to be accomplished should be included in the statement to provide a way of measuring progress toward the goal, whether short term, intermediate, or long term: "by date of discharge," "in 3 days," "by 2 PM today," and so forth. The time limit should be the best estimate, not an edict carved in stone. The goal should be client oriented in that it *should describe what the client's condition or behavior will be at the outcome of nursing care,* not what the nurse intends to *do* for the client. For example, a goal is best stated as "Client will demonstrate understanding of drug regimen before discharge from the hospital," rather than "To promote understanding of the drug regimen by the time of discharge from the hospital." See the sample nursing care plan illustrating client-oriented outcome criteria on page 79. If the goal de-

Selected nursing diagnoses related to client-oriented outcome criteria

| Nursing diagnosis | Goals/expected outcomes | Nursing interventions |
|---|---|---|
| Knowledge deficit related to her new drug regimen of digoxin, furosemide, and potassium chloride | Before discharge Ms. Strauss will: State the action of each drug and how it relates to her cardiac status. Identify at least three untoward reactions that should be reported to her health care provider. Weigh herself accurately and report results to nurse. Demonstrate the ability to take her own pulse accurately. | 1. Discuss with Ms. Strauss the action of each drug and how it relates to her cardiac status. 2. Instruct her about possible side/adverse effects of each drug. 3. Instruct her to report to her health care provider symptoms such as palpitations, resting pulse rate of <60 or >100, sudden change in weight, anorexia, nausea, or lethargy. 4. Discuss the importance of weighing daily and reporting a weight gain of 2 pounds or more. 5. Instruct in pulse-taking, using daily practice. 6. Include her significant other/care taker in the teaching, if possible. 7. Provide her with written instructions concerning all of her care as a guide for her use at home. |

scribes only what nurses do, they could work diligently to promote a client's understanding of a drug regimen, and success would merely be measured in the evaluation of what procedures were performed; yet the client may never have actually learned, which is the intent of the goal.

The nurse can prevent the blurring of the distinction between goals and interventions—two entirely different phases of the nursing process—by stating outcome criteria in terms of behavioral objectives for the client. If criteria are stated in words that depict nursing interventions or actions, such as "prevent," "provide," "promote," or "maintain," then evaluation of care becomes more an appraisal of what the nurse did by intervening than of the client's condition.

Finally, outcome criteria related to each nursing problem or diagnosis identified earlier may be ranked in priority to meet the client's needs.

The rest of the planning phase lays the ground work for carrying out specific actions in the implementation phase. Such plans for nursing actions should be supportable by applicable principles from the arts, sciences, and humanities, which are the foundations of nursing.

Development of a positive, accountable attitude through goal setting and planning for each nursing action strengthens what nurses do for clients and why. Outcome criteria and specific planning provide documentation for peers and preclude legal challenge, while first and foremost guiding the selection of appropriate caring actions. The completed abbreviated nursing care plan, as a blueprint for action, can be entered in writing in the Kardex or on the client's chart and makes up the plan for nursing management.

## SUMMARY

Although its structure and terminology may change, the nursing process remains an extremely useful clinical tool.

It should be approached as a framework for organizing client care in creative and satisfying ways.

Professional nurses enhance their decision-making skills by carefully critiquing their clients' medication plans and maintaining a strong knowledge base about medications, including their indications, mechanisms, pharmacokinetics, and dosages.

The quality of nursing assessment relies on the nurse's ability to observe significant cues, to make sound inferences, and to recognize the client's individuality and establish rapport. Thus a nurse can develop a valid diagnosis, establish realistic goals with the client, and shape an effective nursing plan.

Medication administration is a highly visible, legal function of nurses. Since it depends heavily on the structure and content of prescriber's orders, conscientious assessment of the drug order becomes a very healthy habit. Professional accountability for all disciplines demands open collaboration on questions about clients' medication orders and plans.

Underlying the routine of assessing medication therapy is the major goal of preventing harm. Assessment should emphasize preventing the client from receiving drugs that will interact, be incompatible, or evoke an allergic response; drugs that will not be degraded or excreted adequately; or drugs that will be transferred to a nursing infant or fetus. Creative nursing consists of finding ways to reschedule or space intervals between dosages of interactive drugs. If there is any question about pregnancy or breastfeeding, administration of a drug should be suspended and the prescriber contacted for consultation. Unfortunately, the early part of pregnancy, when it may still be unsuspected, is one of the most potentially dangerous periods for teratogenesis (birth defects, miscarriage). If the mother's disorder is serious enough, drug therapy may have to be maintained nonetheless. This may occasionally also be true for a client with a contraindicating concomitant disorder or organ system impairment. Reactions caused by incompatibilities in solution may be avoided or minimized if drugs are administered as soon as possible after mixing. Allergic reactions, if anticipated, are usually grounds for a prescriber's decision to change drugs. However, a nurse is often the one who notes the offending allergenic substance via a client's history and other data. Again, effective nursing assessment can improve compliance, enhance therapeutic outcomes, and avoid negative secondary effects.

The nursing assessment culminates in the identification of specific problems (actual, possible, or potential). Interventions by the nurse to address identified problems may involve physician-directed (or dependent) interventions, collaborative interventions with other health care providers, or interventions that are solely the domain of nurses. Those problems falling within the independent nursing domain are best described by the nursing diagnosis, a concise statement of a problem that is uniquely addressed by nurses.

After the identification of problems and the formulation of a nursing diagnosis, goals in the form of outcome criteria are established. A specific plan is developed to direct nursing care toward meeting the goals. The development of goals and clear planning form the basis for implementing and evaluating nursing care.

## BIBLIOGRAPHY

American Hospital Formulary Service. (1989). AHFS drug information '89. Bethesda, Md: American Society of Hospital Pharmacists, Inc.

Anthony ML et al. (1988). Nursing intervention: independent or not? Nurs Manage 19(12):14.

Atkinson LD and Murray ME. (1986). Understanding the nursing process, ed 3. New York: Macmillan Publishing Co.

Barash DA. (1987). For this nurse, action was the answer . . . prepared a medication handbook for her unit, Nursinglife 7(2):43.

Bell SK. (1980). Guidelines for taking a complete drug history, Nursing '80 10(3):10.

Bressler R. (1987). Multiple drug use in an elderly man, Hosp Formul 22(7):111.

Brunckhost L et al. (1989). Who's using nursing diagnoses? Am J Nurs 89(2):267.

Carey KW, editor. (1984). Nursing now: drug interactions. Springhouse, Pa: Springhouse Corp.

Carnevali DL. (1983). Nursing care planning: diagnosis and management. Philadelphia: JB Lippincott Co.

Carpenito LJ. (1989/90). Nursing diagnosis: application to clinical practice. ed 3. Philadelphia: JB Lippincott Co.

Cohen MR. (1987). Improperly mixed IV additives, Nursing 17(5):16.

Cooper JW. (1987). Drug related problems in nursing home patients: contraindications to drug usage, Nurs Homes 36(3)5.

Cooper JW. (1987). Adverse drug reactions and interactions in a nursing home, Nurs Home 36(4):7.

Foote AW et al. (1989). Nursing diagnosis: a strategy for teaching etiologies, J Neurosci Nurs 21(5):305.

Fagerman KE et al. (1988). Drug compatibilities with enteral feeding solutions administered by tube, Nutr Clin Pract 8(5):31.

Franse VL et al. (1988). Drug-nutrient interactions in a VAMC teaching hospital, Nutr Clin Pract 3(4):145.

Gordan M. (1987). Nursing diagnosis: process and application, ed 2. New York: McGraw-Hill Book Co.

Gilman AG et al, editors. (1990). Goodman and Gilman's The pharmacological basis of therapeutics. ed 8. New York: Macmillan Publishing Co.

Glange WD, Anderson KN, and Anderson LE, editors (1990). Mosby's medical, nursing, and allied health dictionary, ed 3. St Louis: The CV Mosby Co.

Green GR et al. (1988). Circumventing penicillin allergy, Patient Care 22(8):43.

Griffith JW and Christensen PJ. (1986). Nursing process: application of theories, frameworks, and models, ed 2. St Louis: The CV Mosby Co.

Hadaway L. (1988). Nursing diagnosis applied to IV nursing practice, J Intravenous Nurs 11(2):109.

Hansted PD. (1989). Drug interactions, ed 6. Philadelphia: Lea & Febiger.

Hussar DA. (1986). Geriatric drug interactions. East Hanover, NJ: American Society of Consultant Pharmacists and Sandoz Pharmaceuticals.

Hylnka J. (1987). More and more, nurses are learning about BC's drug and poison information centre, RNABC News 19(2):10.

Inquiry services—USA. (1988). Nursing 18(4):149.

Intravenous drug hazards: interactions, absorption, and inadequate mixing. (1988). Geriatr Nurs 9(1):20.

Kolcaba K et al. (1989). Geropharmacology treatment, J Gerontol Nurs 15(5):29.

Lee M et al. (1981). Tartrazine-containing drugs, Drug Intell Clin Pharm 15(10):782.

Loebl S & Spratto G. (1989). The nurse's drug handbook, ed 5. New York: John Wiley & Sons, Inc.

Major drug-information centres across Canada. (1988). Nursing 18(4):152.

Martin ME. (1989). Oral antibiotics for treatment of patients with chronic osteomyelitis, Orthop Nurs 8(3):35.

McCord MA. (1988). Relating nursing diagnosis to drug therapy, Nursing 18(10):80.

North American Nursing Diagnosis Association. (1989). Classification of nursing diagnosis: proceedings of the eighth conference. St Louis: The CV Mosby Co.

Osis M. (1986). Scheduling drug administration: drug and food interactions, Gerontion 1(5):8.

Otto SE et al. (1988). Nursing diagnosis: challenge for intravenous nursing practice, J Intravenous Nurs 11(4):245.

Rosenberg JM et al. (1986). Pharmacist-operated drug information centers in the US, Am J Hosp Pharm 44(3):337.

Ryan KA. (1989). Standardized care plans for IV therapy, J Intravenous Nurs 12(2):94.

Sanford S. (1987). Administrative applications of nursing diagnosis, Heart Lung 16(6):600.

Tatro DS. (1987). Searching at patient care locations: the Drug Information Center at Stanford University Hospital extends its services to computer searches in satellite pharmacies, Health On Line 2(10):1.

Ted Tse CS and Bernstein IL. (1982). Adverse reactions to tartrazine, Hosp Formul 17(12):1625.

Todd B. (1987). Cigarettes and caffeine in drug interactions, Geriatr Nurs 8(2):97.

Truiitt CA et al. (1982). An evaluation of a medication history method, Drug Intell Clin Pharm 16:592.

United States Pharmacopeial Convention. (1990). Drug information for the health care provider, ed 10. Rockville, Md: United States Pharmacopeial Convention.

Vanderbosch TM et al. (1986). Tailoring care plans to nursing diagnoses, Am J Nurs 86(3):313.

Vore M et al. (1986). Common adverse drug interactions, Hosp Med 22(10):94.

*Chapter*

# 6 Implementation and Evaluation

## CHAPTER OBJECTIVES

*After studying this chapter, you should be able to meet the following objectives and define the key terms.*

1. Identify the essential components of a written medication order.

2. Describe the factors considered in establishing the dosage, dosing intervals, and scheduling of medication.

3. Cite methods used to measure the correct dosage or rate of administration.

4. Identify specific procedures used to maintain client safety during the preparation and administration of medications.

5. Differentiate between systemic effects and local effects of medications.

6. Cite the advantages and disadvantages of the various routes of medication administration.

7. Identify the landmarks for the administration of medications via the intramuscular route.

8. Cite the reasons for modifying administration methods for psychiatric clients and other clients with special needs.

9. Discuss the rationale for teaching clients about their prescribed medication regimens.

10. Discuss the importance of evaluation in the nursing process.

## KEY TERMS

**apothecary system,** page 91

**compliance,** page 112

**drug potency,** page 87

**duration of action,** page 87

**household system,** page 92

**hypodermoclysis,** page 102

**infiltration,** page 105

**infusion controllers,** page 88

**infusion pumps,** page 88

**inhalation,** page 97

**insufflation,** page 97

**intermittent infusion,** page 107

**IV infusion,** page 106

**IV injection,** page 105

**latency,** page 87

**maximum effect,** page 87

**metric system,** page 90

**quality assurance,** page 112

**therapeutic index,** page 87

**time for maximum effects,** page 87

**Z-track method,** page 104

# IMPLEMENTATION

The implementation phase of the nursing process consists of putting goals into action. It is the actual giving of care as prescribed by the nursing care plan or nursing orders. The nurse, guided by the nursing care plan (formal or informal), with goals clearly in focus, can initiate proposed actions in an orderly way. The best chance for success lies in clear, frequent communication and collaboration with the client since any goal or action not viewed by clients as congruent with their own goals will decrease participation.

The implementation phase in drug therapy comprises all the steps of the administration of medications. It includes collaborating with the prescriber and medicating clients according to prescribers' orders, preparing drugs (including any necessary arithmetic calculations), techniques and procedures (with modifications for individual client situations), alertness to errors, recording medications given, and teaching clients about their drugs. Evaluation of goals follows and, depending on the specific goal, most often relates to some aspect of drug effects. Outcomes are measured and compared with the criteria established in the goals during the planning phase. Broader evaluation is done by nursing audit committees that critique the quality of nursing care administered to groups of clients, as well as individuals.

To perform all the functions of the nursing process, nurses must have strong interpersonal, cognitive, and psychomotor skills. Nursing actions are the product of foundational work in the psychosocial as well as the biologic and physical sciences.

## Drug Administration

The nursing function that is most closely identified with nursing by the public, and the one carrying the most legal vulnerability, is that of administering medications. It requires much preparation, a solid knowledge base, skilled decision-making abilities, and close attention to the "Five Rights" (see Chapter 5).

Technically, written medical orders are the only legal means for the administration of medications by nurses. Written orders constitute permanent legal records of the prescriber's plans and can be submitted as evidence in case of litigation. Thus, nurses must routinely ensure that (1) each order is appropriate, accurate, and complete and (2) the order is followed unerringly to completion, for nurses are held legally accountable for every dose of medication they administer. Free flow of communication between prescriber and nurse is crucial to fulfillment of this responsibility. Nurses must be ready to consult with the prescriber as necessary to clarify, understand, or suggest medication therapy as needed. Assertiveness is a quality that must be developed by professional nurses if they are to deal from an appropriate position of strength within the health care system to promote their clients' best interests while achieving equity for their own contributions.

---

## CHECKING TRANSCRIPTION

**Which Medication?**

Is it quinine sulfate (a medication for leg cramps) or quinidine sulfate (a cardiac depressant)? Pentobarbital or phenobarbital? Digoxin or digitoxin? Ornade or Ornase?

**Which Dose?**

Is it a loop of an *f, g,* or *q,* or another zero?

*Vital signs q 4 h*
*Gentamycin 60 mg IV 6 h*

**Anything Missing?**

Does Halcion i HS mean 0.125 mg or 0.25 mg?

---

What is the process by which a prescriber's order is translated into the administration of a medication? It is first transcribed by a ward clerk, nurse manager (or nursing care coordinator), or primary nurse from an order sheet onto the Kardex, medication administration record (MAR) (Figure 6-1), or medication ticket or card (Figure 6-2). Accuracy in transcription of the medication order to the medication administration record is essential. If the order has been transcribed by a ward secretary, it should be verified by a nurse, who can then better relate the medication to the client and the diagnosis. The nurse must check the dosage of the medication and the age of the client, check for drug interaction possibilities and for allergies, and ensure the completeness and clarity of the order to prevent error (see box). Whatever the question concerning the physician's order, legally it can only be clarified with the physician who has written the order. Verifying an order with another physician who happens to be present or with a nursing colleague does not suffice.

The drug is requested in a daily supply from the institution's pharmacy department. When the supply arrives, it is stored in the medication room either as stock supply to meet general needs of clients on the floor or in an individual client's own medication box or drawer of a medication cart.

The nurse administers a drug by following the order as written on the medication cart, ticket, or MAR. Because of space limitation, physicians, pharmacists, and nurses rely on pharmacologic abbreviations or symbols for communication. These are often from the Latin and are universally used. Table 6-1 includes the most commonly used abbreviations, along with some symbols common to clinical practice. Although apothecary symbols are sometimes used, they

Lorenzo, Joseph
M144444 8/15/55
Dr. Powell

MEDICATION RECORD

| INIT | DO / SD | RD / NSD | MEDICATION DOSE, ROUTE, FREQUENCY | TOUR | TIME INTERVAL | DATE 3/10 | DATE 3/11 | DATE 3/12 | DATE 3/13 | DATE 3/14 | DATE 3/15 | DATE 3/16 |
|---|---|---|---|---|---|---|---|---|---|---|---|---|
| L | 3/2 | | Erythomycin | N | 12-6 | 12 6 | 12 6 | | D/C | X | X | X |
| M | | | enteric coated | D | 12 | 12 | 12 | | | | | |
| M | 3/12 | | 250 mg q6hr. p.o. | E | 6 | 6 | | | | | | |
| | | | | N | | | | | | | | |
| | | | | D | | | | | | | | |
| | | | | E | | | | | | | | |
| | | | | N | | | | | | | | |
| | | | | D | | | | | | | | |
| | | | | E | | | | | | | | |
| | | | | N | | | | | | | | |
| | | | | D | | | | | | | | |
| | | | | E | | | | | | | | |
| | | | | N | | | | | | | | |
| | | | | D | | | | | | | | |
| | | | | E | | | | | | | | |
| | | | | N | | | | | | | | |
| | | | | D | | | | | | | | |
| | | | | E | | | | | | | | |
| | | | | N | | | | | | | | |
| | | | | D | | | | | | | | |
| | | | | E | | | | | | | | |
| | | | | N | | | | | | | | |
| | | | | D | | | | | | | | |
| | | | | E | | | | | | | | |
| | | | | N | | | | | | | | |
| | | | | D | | | | | | | | |
| | | | | E | | | | | | | | |
| | | | | N | | | | | | | | |
| | | | | D | | | | | | | | |
| | | | | E | | | | | | | | |

RECOPIED BY: DATE:

—Medication given
O—Medication Omitted—Explanation on Nurses' Notes.
D/C—Medication Discontinued. In addition to this record, anticoagulant and Diabetic records are also maintained
D.O.—Date ordered
S.D.—Stop date
N.S.D.—New stop date

ALLERGIES:

Penicillin

SIGNATURES

| | N | D | E | N | D | E | N | D | E | N | D | E | N | D | E | N | D | E | N | D | E |
|---|---|---|---|---|---|---|---|---|---|---|---|---|---|---|---|---|---|---|---|---|---|
| SIGNATURES | J. Jones R.N. | M. Whitehead RN | T. Grey R.N | J. Jones RN | M. Whitehead RN | | | | | | | | | | | | | | | | |

**FIGURE 6-1** Sample medication administration record (MAR).

| | |
|---|---|
| **Name:** | *Lorenzo, Joseph* |
| **Room & bed:** *212²* | **Date started:** *3/18* |
| **Dr.:** *Wells* | |
| **Noted by:** *J. Over Rn* | |
| **Medication & route:** *Erythromycin enteric coated 250mg* | |
| *p.o. q.6hr* | |
| | |
| **Time:** *12-6-12-6* | |

**FIGURE 6-2** Transcription of a medication order onto the Kardex or a medication card or ticket.

**TABLE 6-1**  Common abbreviations and symbols related to medication administration*

| Abbreviation | Unabbreviated form | Meaning | Abbreviation | Unabbreviated form | Meaning |
|---|---|---|---|---|---|
| a | ante | before | OU | oculus uterque | each eye |
| ac | ante cibum | before meals | pc | post cibum | after meals |
| ad lib | ad libitum | freely | PM | post meridiem | after noon |
| AM | ante meridiem | morning | PO | per os | by mouth, orally |
| bid | bis in die | twice each day | prn | pro re nata | according to necessity |
| c̄ | cum | with | pt | patient | patient |
| cap | capsule | capsule | q | quaque | every |
| cc, cm³ | cubic centimeter | cubic centimeter (ml) | qd | quaque die | every day |
| clt | client | client | qh | quaque hora | every hour |
| D/C or DC | discontinue | terminate | q4h, q4° | every 4 hours | every 4 hours around the clock |
| elix | elixir | elixir | | | |
| g, gm | gram | 1000 milligrams | qid | quater in die | four times each day |
| gr | grain | 60 milligrams | qod | quaque aliem die | every other day |
| gtt | gutta | drop | qs | quantum satis | sufficient quantity |
| h, hr | hora | hour | ® | right | right |
| hs | hora somni | at bedtime | ℞ | receipt | take |
| IM | intramuscular | into a muscle | s̄ | sine | without |
| IV | intravenous | into a vein | SL | sub linguam | under the tongue |
| IVPB | IV piggyback | secondary IV line | SOS | si opus sit | if necessary |
| kg | kilogram | 2.2 lb | ss | semis | a half |
| KVO | keep vein open | very slow infusion rate | stat | statim | at once |
| Ⓛ | left | left | SC, SQ | subcutaneous | into subcutaneous tissue |
| L | liter | liter | tbsp | tablespoon | tablespoon (15 ml) |
| μg, mcg | microgram | one millionth of a gram | tid | ter in die | three times a day |
| mg | milligram | one thousandth of a gram | TO | telephone order | order received over the telephone |
| mEq | milliequivalent | the number of grams of solute dissolved in one milliliter of a *normal* solution | tsp | teaspoon | teaspoon (4 or 5 ml) |
| | | | U | unit | a dosage measure for insulin, penicillin, heparin |
| min or m | minim | minim (1/15 or 1/16 ml) | VO | verbal order | order received verbally |
| ml, mL | milliliter | one thousandth of a liter | ĭ, ĭĭ | one, two | one, two (as in "gr ĭ," "gr ĭĭ") |
| ng | nanogram | one billionth of a gram | ℨ | dram | 4 or 5 ml |
| | | | ℥ | ounce or fluid-ounce | ounce (30 milliliters) |
| ō | no or none | no or none | × | times | as in two times a week |
| OD | oculus dexter | right eye | > | greater than | greater than |
| OS | oculus sinister | left eye | < | less than | less than |
| os | os | mouth | = | equal to | equal to |
| OTC | over-the-counter | nonprescription drug | ↑, ↗ | increase or increasing | increase or increasing |
| | | | ↓, ↙ | decrease or decreasing | decrease or decreasing |

*It is recommended that certain abbreviations be abandoned if they are found to be confusing.

**TABLE 6-2**   Drug abbreviations

| | |
|---|---|
| ACTH | adrenocorticotropic hormone |
| ASA | acetylsalicylic acid (aspirin) |
| CPZ | chlorpromazine |
| DES | diethylstilbestrol |
| DM | dextromethorphan |
| $D_5W$ | 5% dextrose in water |
| $D_5S$ | 5% dextrose in normal saline |
| DSS or DOSS | dioctyl sodium sulfosuccinate |
| DW | distilled water |
| EC | enteric coated |
| ETH & C | elixir terpin hydrate with codeine |
| Fe | iron |
| 5-FU | 5-fluorouracil |
| FUD | floxuridine |
| HC | hydrocortisone |
| K | potassium |
| KCl | potassium chloride |
| LOC | laxative of choice |
| MOM | milk of magnesia |
| 6-MP | 6-mercaptopurine |
| MS | morphine sulfate |
| MTX | methotrexate |
| Na | sodium |
| NS | normal saline |
| NTG | nitroglycerin |
| PAS | para-aminosalicyclic acid |
| PB | phenobarbital |
| PCN | penicillin |

are frequently misinterpreted and may be used incorrectly. The nurse should convert the apothecary measure to a metric measure when transcribing the medication order. In addition, prescribers should be encouraged to use the metric system to avoid errors. Abbreviations are a key to communication in the busy health field and should be learned. In addition, a number of physicians also use abbreviations for ordering specific medications. (See Table 6-2.) Because of the danger of misinterpretation, the use of variant or nonstandard abbreviations should be avoided. The nurse should review the approved abbreviation listing for the specific health agency.

When transcribed, the physician's order must contain all the elements described in Chapter 5. It must contain the *full name* of the patient (and bed location—for example, room 212, bed 2); the *date* the order was written; the *medication name, dosage, route,* and *frequency;* and, according to agency policy, the *name* or *initial* of the nurse responsible for the transcription. (See Figure 6-2).

## Types of Drug Delivery Systems

There are several approaches to distributing and dispensing drugs to clients in an institutional setting: the floor stock system, individual client prescription orders, unit dose drug distribution, and a combination of these. In the floor stock system, all medications except those infrequently used are stored in bulk on the nursing unit in the medication room. The disadvantages of this system are the increased potential for medication errors because of the large array of stock medications to choose from, the economic loss caused by misplaced or forgotten charges and expired drugs to be returned, the need for frequent total drug inventorying, and the storage problems inherent in crowded medication rooms. In addition, because of fear of contamination, the bottles of unused drugs must often be discarded, not allowing the client for whom the drug was originally ordered to receive financial credit for drugs not administered. The individual order method of dispensing each type of medication daily to individual clients is an improvement, but it is rather unwieldy and time consuming. A combination of floor stock and individual orders is generally superior but has the disadvantages of both systems.

Single-dose packages of drugs are dispensed in the unit dose drug distribution method. Each oral dose, for example, may be a tablet encased in a blister pack or a paper tear-off strip of tablets. This packaging is said to be the safest and most economical method of drug distribution.

The advantages of using the unit dose system far outweigh the disadvantages. The most important advantages are increased medication safety and decreased errors, since drug computations are largely eliminated. The drug is already properly labeled and does not have to be prepared. All the nurse needs to do is deliver the package to the client, where it is opened at the bedside and administered. This may permit clients to check on their own drugs and be assured of proper medication and dosage. Unit dose packaging also decreases chances of deterioration and permits giving financial credit to the client for drugs not used. Disadvantages include increased cost to set up the system and the need for additional pharmacy personnel to fill new orders and resupply the client's units each 24 hours. The administration of new and stat medication orders may be delayed while the medication order is sent to the pharmacy, filled, and then delivered back to the nurse rather than being immediately available on the unit. To avoid delays, emergency medications are often kept on each client unit for immediate access.

Strip packages make narcotic counting easier for nurses, since all packages in the strip are numbered. This also prevents contamination caused by pouring narcotic tablets into the hands for counting, which is a grossly improper technique. Prefilled unit dose disposable syringes are also available. Their advantages are:

1. Accuracy of dosage
2. Sterile product
3. Sharp needle
4. Elimination of suspected source of serum hepatitis (needle)
5. Less danger of drug absorption by personnel handling the drugs

6. Immediate availability of drug for use
7. Only medicine used is charged to client
8. Reduced likelihood of pilferage of narcotics
9. Less waste by breakage or incomplete use

Unit dose dispensing systems in hospitals may be centralized, decentralized, or a combination of both. In the centralized system the pharmacist and the pharmacy are located in a central area from which drugs are distributed to client care areas. In the decentralized system, clinical pharmacists and satellite pharmacies are located in client care areas and drugs are prepared and distributed to clients from those particular areas. In the combined system, medications are prepared in a central area, with clinical pharmacists assigned to various client care areas to oversee drug therapy, thus providing safer and more controlled drug ordering and drug distribution.

Medication carts are used in some hospitals for distributing unit doses to the nursing unit and to the client's bedside. Each client has a drawer or tray for medications, which is restocked by the pharmacy staff.

## Role of the Clinical Pharmacist

A present trend of drug delivery is toward more extensive use of clinical pharmacists stationed in nursing areas to work closely with physicians, nurses, and dietitians. Since pharmacists are educated in the compounding, dispensing, and control of drugs, they can be an invaluable resource for assistance in solving pharmacologic problems. Nurses frequently consult them about medication administration methods, dosages, drug identification, and secondary effects. Statistically, they are consulted by all health care disciplines, most often about antiinfectives, analgesics, and cardiovascular drugs. The health care system today demands more of this kind of interdisciplinary collaboration and shared expertise for the benefit of all, especially the client.

Hospital pharmacies can have special "clean rooms" and specially filtered air for compounding various parenteral solutions. A pharmacist or supervised designee may be responsible for putting all additives into intravenous solutions and checking all such solutions for compatibility reactions.

## Role of the Nurse

Regardless of changes in ordering, distributing, or administering drugs, nurses are still responsible for their clients' care 24 hours a day. Advanced technology and the release of more potent drugs on the market make it crucial for the nurse to be better informed on drugs and their actions. Nurses must make observations of clients and their response to drug therapy, determine whether prn orders are to be given, and consult with prescribers about withholding, discontinuing, or changing drugs. They continue to take histories, to teach clients about drugs and their effects, to work collaboratively with pharmacists, and to help clients plan drug therapy after returning home.

## Preparing to Administer Drugs

### Dosages, Dosing Intervals, and Scheduling

Understanding the medical rationale for selection of a particular dosage and frequency of administration requires a basic understanding of the drug in question. Within limits, increasing a drug's dose or frequency of administration increases pharmacologic effect but can also increase the risk of side and adverse effects. The various relationships involved can be represented as follows:

Optimal dosages → dose-response relationship
Optimal frequencies → time-response relationship

The variables to deal with in dose-response relationships are defined as follows:

**Drug potency:** absolute amount of drug required to produce a desired effect

**Therapeutic index:** relative margin of safety; the ratio of lethal dose to effective dose

**Maximum effect:** greatest response possible regardless of dose given

Time-response relationships deal with these variables:

**Latency:** time necessary for peak effect

**Time for maximum effect:** time after administration for the drug's effect to peak

**Duration of action:** length of drug effect

These last variables are affected by route used, pharmacokinetics involved, and individual client biorhythms.

To avoid wide fluctuations in the serum concentration of a drug, doses are given at appropriate intervals to avoid drug accumulation and toxicity. If the dosage interval is too short, drug accumulation with potential for toxicity will occur. If it is too long, serum concentration will drop because the drug will continue to be excreted and not replaced. Drugs with very short half-lives (see Chapter 4 for a discussion of drug half-life) will not accumulate if they are given orally and frequently, since very frequent doses are needed to achieve a steady state. Drugs with very long half-lives are often given once a day.

In drug studies, dosing relationships are interpreted on the basis of a normal curve, and dosages and dosing intervals are derived for treating the ideal "average" person in a population. This explains why certain medications with relatively long half-lives can usually be given once a day. Likewise, it explains why a drug scheduled to be given every 6 hours should not be expected to be as effective for most people if it is given arbitrarily four times a day during daylight hours. It is less likely that optimal serum levels or tissue levels will be maintained by the latter schedule. It also explains why, although dosage and dosing intervals have been studied statistically, drug therapy regimens must continually be reassessed for individual needs. Some people will always fall outside the "average" range in responding to a drug. In addition, dosing intervals may be modified in consideration of client convenience and the effect on compliance.

Times to administer routine medications may be determined by agency policy. For example, qid drugs may be routinely given at 10 AM, 2 PM, 6 PM, and 10 PM, or at 9 AM, 1 PM, 5 PM, and 9 PM, and so forth. Special units, such as pediatrics, have other medication hours to coincide with the special needs of their clients. Based on client convenience and the need to avoid mealtimes or other activities that might interfere with either drug administration or its pharmacokinetics, nurses may choose autonomously to vary the times (but not the intervals) if the decision is based on solid rationale. For example, calcium supplements might be given at bedtime rather than 9 AM on a daily schedule because calcium is better absorbed at night. Drugs administered once daily can usually be given according to a flexible schedule, perhaps just before or after a treatment that would interfere with a dosing time, such as a client's trip off the nursing unit to the physical therapy department or x-ray department. Drugs should be administered to clients as close to the time indicated as possible, but obviously a nurse cannot medicate each of a group of assigned clients at exactly the same time. Agency policies may vary, but usually they stipulate administration within ½ hour before or after the indicated time. Exempt from this flexibility are stat or one-time-only drug orders, such as those given before diagnostic procedures or surgery, and those medications administered at the most frequent intervals, such as q2h or q4h.

Drug effects are monitored by the prescriber and the nurse according to either *direct assessment* (by observation for clinical responses) or *indirect assessment* (by laboratory values or serum concentrations of the drug). Nurses, because of their unique presence and expertise, are most capable in assisting the prescriber to make keen assessments of clients' responses.

## Dosage Measurement

When the specified amount of a drug is not prepackaged in single unit doses, the nurse must be able to choose from among the sometimes numerous drugs for the client the right drug and the right dose. If the drug is formulated in units that are multiples of the dosage ordered, whether tablet or liquid, the computation to determine the correct dose is simple. If, however, the drug does not come in units that are multiples of the dose prescribed, if the drug must be dissolved in water, or if the order is written in the apothecary system and the drug is available only in metric units, dosage calculations will be necessary.

Flow rate calculations are necessary for certain therapies in order to set the proper amount for the desired dose effect. Intravenous infusions necessitate careful flow rate calculation. These therapies should be ordered by the prescriber in definitive amounts and rates. (See Chapter 71.)

The rate of replacement fluids with or without other additives by IV infusion may be regulated in one of two basic

---

### EXAMPLES OF CLINICAL IMPLICATIONS OF DRUG DOSING

Blood levels of steroids administered between 7:30 AM and 8:30 AM may most closely match levels as they would occur normally.

Most antibiotics and antihypertensives should be administered around the clock to achieve a steady state in the bloodstream.

Anticoagulant dosages should be titrated with tests of the client's own partial thromboplastin time or a similar determination.

Diuretics should not be administered late in the day or before appointments, when urinary urgency would be inconvenient for the client.

---

ways. One is by a simple *roller clamp* on the tubing, which can be manually adjusted to deliver the number of drops per minute that will provide the prescribed total amount over the prescribed time. Given the total volume of solution to be infused, the total number of minutes the solution is to be infused, and the drop factor (number of drops per milliliter that the tubing delivers—a small number that varies among tubing manufacturers and is found on the back of the tubing box), the prescribed drops per minute can be calculated and the set regulated by counting drops in the drip chamber of the tubing. A simple formula for IV flow rate calculation can be found in Exercise 11 later in this chapter. Details of regulating by manual clamps, the most common mode, may be found in a basic nursing text such as Potter and Perry (1989). (See Bibliography.)

Another way that infusions can be made to run more precisely is by the use of instrumentation such as IV controllers and pumps. These can be used in situations that require more accurate titration of infusion fluids or nutrients than is provided by hand-adjusted roller clamps, which can allow up to a 5% error in flow rate within the first 15 minutes of flow and other variations thereafter. One study in a Boston hospital revealed that 37% of the hospitalized clients who died from drug-related causes did so from fluid overload or potassium excess (potassium is a frequent additive to intravenous infusions). Increased use of instrumentation for regulating IV flow rates can be predicted in the future.

Most of the instrumentation to regulate infusions consists of various applications of either **infusion controllers** or **infusion pumps.** These small, boxlike devices are attached to IV poles. The infusion tubing is strung for regulation of rate to ensure automatic delivery of solutions at preselected rates or volumes. CAUTION: For instruments that can accommodate either macrodrip or microdrip tubing, the tubing must be appropriate for the drop factor used to calculate drop rate. A rate calculated on the basis of microdrip tubing but accidentally administered by macrodrip could seriously overdose or overhydrate a client.

Infusion controllers (Figure 6-3) work simply by utilizing the force of gravity. Controllers are not capable of delivering rates with the accuracy of infusion pumps (which may be more useful in special situations in which rises in back pressure are transmitted to the fluid in the tubing; such is the situation in arterial infusions or when the client is a restless child or a woman in labor). However, unlike infusion pumps, IV controllers will not pump fluid into interstitial tissue if the infusion needle infiltrates. Controllers are useful in 80% to 85% of cases calling for intravenous therapy.

Infusion pumps are of at least two kinds, both delivering infusion fluids under positive pressure: (1) nonvolumetric ("infusion pumps"; Figure 6-4), which measure fluid volume delivery by drop rate (not as accurate since drop volume may vary), and (2) volumetric ("volume pumps," which can measure very precisely even smaller volumes of infusion solution by milliliter per hour. This latter pump is especially useful for small children, total parenteral nutrition, and the administration of potent drugs by continous IV infusion (such as streptokinase, dopamine, or nitroglycerin). Alarm readout messages (e.g., "Fix Me") may be displayed on the front panel of the instrument.

Similar instrumentation is made by several different manufacturers, which use various physical principles to sense pressures and amount of pump fluid and read out the flow-rate settings and the like. Their capabilities include greater

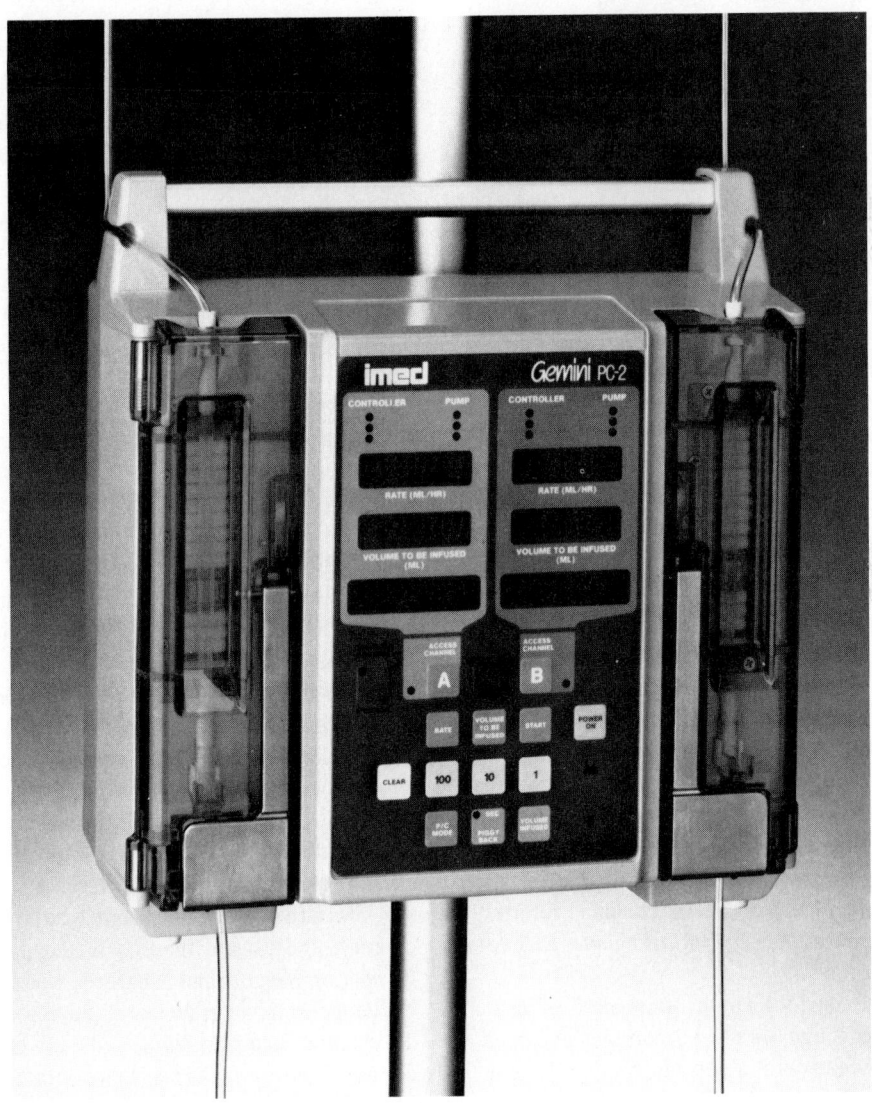

**FIGURE 6-3**  Intravenous controller for the simultaneous regulation of a primary or main intravenous infusion and a secondary, intermittent medication infusion. *(Courtesy IMED Corp., Warner-Lambert Co., Morris Plains, N.J.)*

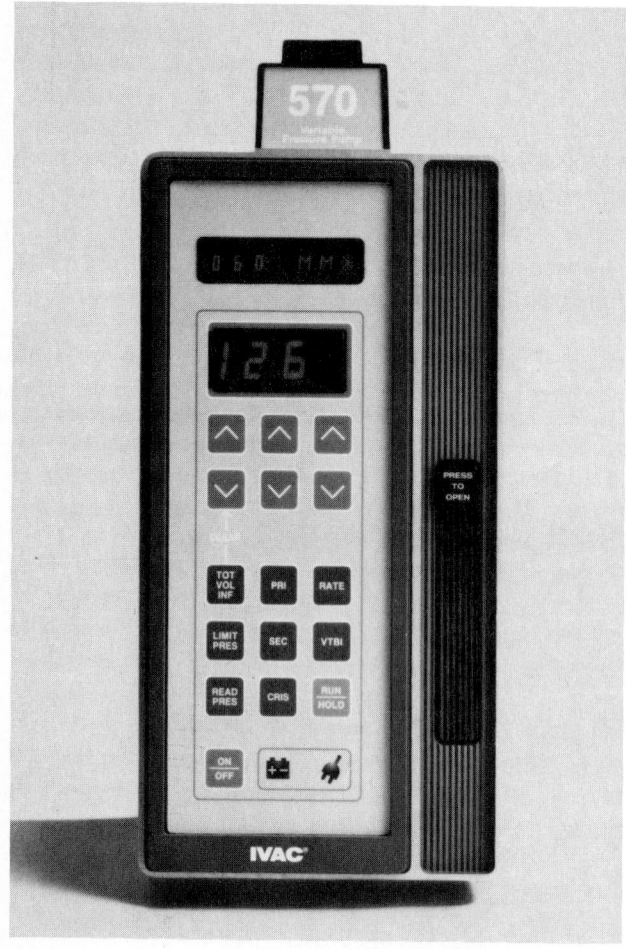

**FIGURE 6-4** Infusion pump used when positive pressure provided by peristaltic action on the tubing produces the preset drop rate. *(IVAC 570 type; courtesy IVAC Corp., San Diego, Calif.)*

accuracy than other modes of infusion delivery systems and alarms to warn of blocked tubing, air in the tubing, or empty solution containers. All this capability sounds ideal, but like all mechanical devices, infusion pumps are subject to malfunction and therefore require continued watchfulness by nurses to ensure reliability and to maintain personal contact with the purpose of it all—the client. There is currently a growing body of literature on this type of equipment. Its intricacy presents nurses with still another challenge, although not an insurmountable one. The reader is referred to the excellent references at the end of this chapter to learn more.

Oxygen therapy is also ordered in units of flow rate. Oxygen is a medication that should be administered with care, especially to a client with a chronic obstructive pulmonary disorder or one who requires longer-than-usual continuous oxygen supportive therapy. Regardless of the delivery equipment (nasal cannula or "prongs," nasal catheter, mask, or tent), the oxygen order should specifically state the desired flow, usually in liters per minute (e.g., 2 to 4 L/min) and, if necessary, by concentration desired. Regulation is usually by a flow meter calibrated in liters per minute, which is attached to a jar of oxygen-humidifying sterile distilled water to alleviate the drying effect of oxygen on respiratory mucosa.

Frequently, oxygen is ordered to be given "prn" or "on standby" for the client who can be anticipated to have occasional bouts of dyspnea or chest pain caused by coronary insufficiency. Full, continuous oxygen therapy for more than 24 hours can have serious consequences, since oxygen works to fuel oxidative body processes; certain tissues (especially lung and retinal tissues in the newborn) may literally burn themselves out. Clients with a history of chronic obstructive pulmonary disorders may also be at risk if the rate of flow routinely exceeds about 2 L/min. The bodily oxygen sensors in these clients have become accustomed to lower-than-normal blood oxygen levels accompanied by higher carbon dioxide levels. Their sensors have adapted to regulating respiratory excursions via higher-than-normal carbon dioxide levels. If these sensors are suddenly flooded with normal or high oxygen levels and correspondingly reduced carbon dioxide levels, the drive to initiate respiration is reduced or eliminated. Thus clients with chronic obstructive pulmonary disease may stop breathing if oxygen is delivered at or above the usual flow rates.

Most dosage calculations, however, deal with computing numbers of tablets to give or with changing from one unit of measurement to another. A dosage problem may be as simple as giving 10 grains of acetylsalicylic acid from a container of 5-grain tablets. It is almost as easy to figure out how many milliliters of morphine sulfate one must give if the container is labeled "15 mg = 1 ml" and the order reads "10 mg morphine sulfate SC." Complexity builds when the units of measurement in the medication order must be converted to a different type of unit in which the drug is available.

Currently three systems of measurement are in use for administering medications: the metric system (the most widely adopted and the most convenient), the apothecary system (which is being phased out), and the household system (the least accurate and not widely used except in home settings).

***Metric system.*** The **metric system** of weights and measures was invented by the French at the end of the eighteenth century, and toward the end of the nineteenth century the Bureau of Weights and Measures was formed and given the challenge to develop metric standards for international use. The United States finally joined the worldwide trend toward adoption of the metric system with the enactment of the Metric Conversion Act of 1975.

The basic metric units of measurement are the meter, the liter, and the gram. The *meter* is the unit for linear measurement, the *liter* for capacity or volume, and the *gram* for weight. A meter is a little longer than a yard; a liter is a little more than a quart; and a gram is a little more than the weight of a steel paper clip.

The metric system is a decimal system; the basic units can be divided into 10, 100, or 1000 parts; or the basic units can be multiplied by 10, 100, or 1000 to form secondary units that differ from each other by 10 or some multiple of 10. The names of the secondary units are formed by joining Greek or Latin prefixes to the names of the primary units (Table 6-3). Subdivisions of the basic units are made by moving the decimal point to the left, and multiples of the basic units are indicated by moving the decimal point to the right.

The meter is the unit from which the other metric units are dervied. Centimeters and millimeters are the chief linear measures used in hospital work. Measurement of the size of body organs is made in centimeters and millimeters, and the sphygmomanometer used to measure blood pressure is calibrated in millimeters of mercury. There are approximately 2.5 cm (25 mm) in 1 inch.

The liter is the unit of capacity or volume and is equal to approximately 1000 cc or 1000 ml. The weight of a liter of water at 4° C is 1 kg. Because of the way it was originally defined, a liter is actually 1000.028 cc. However, *in practice the cubic centimeter and the milliliter are considered equal.* The difference is so small that it is of no importance except in determinations of extreme precision.

Fractional parts of a liter are usually expressed in milliliters or cubic centimeters. For example, 0.6 liter would be expressed as 600 ml or 600 cc. Multiples of a liter are similarly expressed; 2.4 liters would be 2400 ml or cc. The abbreviation cc is in the process of being dropped and is considered obsolete; either ml or mL may be used, according to the National Bureau of Standards.

The gram is the metric unit of weight that is used in weighing drugs and various pharmaceutical preparations. Originally the unit of measurement for weight was the kilogram, but this proved too large to meet the practical needs of the pharmacist. The gram equals the weight of 1 ml of distilled water at 4° C.

The approved abbreviation for gram is g; G as the abbreviation for gram is no longer approved, since it conflicts with the abbreviation for the prefix *giga*. Gm is also not approved by the National Bureau of Standards.

As a review of Table 6-3 indicates, a decigram is 10 times greater than a centigram and 100 times greater than a milligram. To change decigrams to centigrams, one multiplies by 10; to change decigrams to milligrams, one multiplies by 100. To change milligrams to centigrams, one divides by 10; to change milligrams to decigrams, one divides by 100; to change milligrams to grams, one divides by 1000; and so forth. To figure out how many micrograms (μg) of medication there are in 1 milliliter, one determines how many milligrams are in a liter (or 1000 ml). The resulting

**TABLE 6-3**  Metric prefixes, meanings, and relationships

| Prefix | Meaning |
| --- | --- |
| Giga | Billions |
| Kilo* | Thousands |
| Hecto | Hundreds |
| Deka | Tens |
| Base units of meter, liter, gram | One unit |
| Deci | Tenths |
| Centi* | Hundredths |
| Milli* | Thousandths |
| Micro* | Millionths |
| Nano | Billionths |

*Prefixes most commonly encountered in nursing.

number is the same as the number of micrograms in 1 milliliter.

The style of notation proposed by the International System of Units (referred to as SI) from the National Bureau of Standards is recommended except when it conflicts with proper English language norms:

Units are not capitalized (gram, not Gram).

No period should be used with abbreviations of units (ml, not m.l. or ml.).

A single space should be left between the quantity and the symbol (24 kg, not 25kg).

Large numbers may be separated into groups of three numbers, without comma (25 000, not 25,000).

Except in the apothecary system, only decimal notation should be used, not fractions (0.25 kg, not ¼ kg).

Numerical quantities less than 1 should have a zero placed to the left of the decimal point (0.75 mg, not .75 mg).

Abbreviations should not be pluralized (kg, not kgs).

Nurses need the foregoing as part of their knowledge base not only to use in preparing medications but also to interpret laboratory data (some are reported in milliliters, others in deciliters or nanograms, and so forth), to weigh clients (kilograms instead of pounds), and to figure flow rates of IV infusions. (Refer to the table of abbreviations and symbols, Table 6-1, as necessary.)

Until the metric system is fully accepted in clinical practice, nurses will deal with all three systems of measurement: metric, apothecary, and household (Table 6-4). The nurse can extract a few crucial relationships to memorize. These data can then be readily inserted where applicable as part of a formula or as half of a ratio-and-proportion equation often used for dosage calculation. A suggested practical list of equivalents that nurses should know is presented in Table 6-4.

***Apothecary system.*** Only a few medications are now available in units of the **apothecary system.** It is less convenient and less precise than the metric system. The basic unit of weight is the *grain,* which is derived from the age-old standard of weight of a single grain of

**TABLE 6-4** Common approximate equivalents of weights and measures

| Metric | Apothecary | Household |
|---|---|---|
| WEIGHT | | |
| 1 kg* | 2.2 pounds | |
| 1000 mg = 1 gram* | gr xv | |
| 60 mg* (occasionally seen as 65 mg) | gr î | |
| 30 mg | gr ss (one half) | |
| 1 μg (mcg) = 0.001 mg | | |
| VOLUME | | |
| | 4 quarts | 1 gallon |
| 1000 ml* = approx 1 liter = 1000 cc | Approx 1 qt | 1 quart |
| 500 ml | Approx 1 pint (½ qt) | 16 ounces |
| 240 or 250 ml | ℥ viii (8 fluidounces)† = approx ½ pint | 1 cup or 1 glass |
| 30 ml* = approx 30 cc | ℥ î (1 fluidounce) | 2 tbsp |
| Approx 16 ml = approx 16 cc | ʒ iv (4 fluidrams) | 1 tbsp |
| Approx 8 ml | ʒ ii (2 fluidrams) | 2 tsp |
| 4 to 5 ml | ʒ î (1 fluidram) | 1 tsp |
| 1 ml* = approx 1 cc | Minims xv or xvi | Minims cannot be compared with drops |

*These equivalents may be committed to memory for ready application to dosage problems.
†Note the small difference in the symbols for fluidounce and fluidram.

wheat, a weight now variously accepted as approximately equivalent to 60 or 65 mg (60 mg is the more widely accepted of the two). Other units of weight commonly used in the apothecary system are the dram, the ounce, and the pound.

The basic unit of fluid volume is the *minim,* approximately equal to the volume of water that would weigh a grain, a very small amount, about 0.005 or 0.006 ml. Other volume measures, which may also be considered household measures, are the pint and the quart.

In written prescriptions, the placement of abbreviations and the type of numerals used in the apothecary system follow a more complex arrangement than in the metric system. In the apothecary system, the abbreviation is placed before the numeral. Whole numerical quantities usually are expressed in roman numerals (e.g., gr x for 10 grains). Fractional quantities are usually expressed by arabic numerals rather than by decimals (e.g., gr x ¼, not gr 0.25, for one-quarter grain). When comparing fractional amounts, remember that the larger the bottom number (the denominator), the smaller the quantity involved, given the same numerator. In other words, gr ½₀₀ is a smaller quantity than gr ½₅₀.

**Household systems.** Household measures include the glass, cup, tablespoon, teaspoon, and drops; pints and quarts are often included in this system as well as in the apothecary system. Recent changes in hospital reimbursement policies (e.g., DRGs [Diagnosis-Related Groups]), which have shortened hospital stays and correspondingly lengthened convalescence at home, and the increasing geriatric population have expanded the numbers of people under care at home. Because standardized measurements of household equipment usually do not exist in the home, the community health nurse may not have access to accurately calibrated

measuring devices in the home. For example, the average teacup or coffee cup can hold from 5 to 9 ounces or more, not the accepted 8 ounces or half pint. The average household teaspoon can hold 4 to 5 ml or more of liquid medication rather than the standard 5 ml. A drop and a minim *cannot* be considered equivalents, since drop size will vary with the viscosity of the medication even when measured by an approved dropper. Therefore any listing of houshold measurements on a table of equivalent measures must be considered only approximations. Depending on the situation (e.g., medicating infants) and the need for precise dosage, such measures may or may not be adequate. Clients may need to obtain precise measuring instruments from the local pharmacy or the visiting nurse for medication administration at home.

### Dosage Calculation

Challenges to the mathematical skills of nurses occur infrequently in the administration of medications. An equation can be set up to apply what the nurse has learned about a few crucial equivalents and how that relates to what needs to be solved—all in a logical sequence or relationship. Calculators may not be appropriate in the nursing unit, for they tend to have exasperating battery failures or to "disappear" from busy hospital units and nursing homes. It is more reliable to develop and maintain a basic competence in mathematical calculations.

Following are some typical exercises to do, accompanied by explanations and answers. These exercises assume a working knowledge of decimals, fractions, and a ratio-and-proportion approach to problem solving. Again, if you are used to working with another method that works as well, use it instead—just check your answers and rationale with the following.

## Exercises

1. If a drug is ordered in units different from the units on hand, the order must be mathematically translated into the units available. Thus if the medication order is written in terms of milligrams, yet the client's drug is supplied in grams, you must translate the needed dose into grams.

*Question:* A drug is ordered to be given in the amount of 1500 mg. how many grams would you give?

*Answer:* Knowing that there are 1000 mg in a gram, set up the ratio in logical sequence. The logic of the relationships ("this is to this as that is to that") remains constant in a ratio-and-proportion approach, but which of the relationships is set down first in the equation does not matter. Some people set down first, on the left side of the equation, the relationship between what has been ordered or what information is wanted in the problem and the unknown quantity, or $x$. Then on the right side of the equation they set down the known equivalents, the conversion factors, or the "givens." Once set up, the equation is solved by multiplying the means (middle adjacent numbers) by the extremes (numbers on each end):

$$1500 \text{ mg}:x = 1000 \text{ mg}:1 \text{ g}$$
$$1000x = 1500$$
$$x = 1.5 \text{ g}$$

*Question:* A dosage of 30 ml of cough syrup is ordered to be given qid. The label on the bottle of medication states that it contains a total of 240 cc. How many cubic centimeters would you give?

*Answer:* You need to know that 30 ml is roughly equivalent to 30 cc.

*Question:* 10 mEq of potassium chloride (KCl) is to be added to an IV infusion solution. KCl is available for this application in vials of 40 mEq/20 ml. How many milliliters would you give?

*Answer:* Again set up the equation in logical sequence, possibly starting with the desired ingredient and the unknown quantity.

$$10 \text{ mEq}:x = 40 \text{ mEq}:20 \text{ ml}$$
$$40x = 200$$
$$x = \frac{200}{40} = 5 \text{ ml}$$

2. Sometimes medication for injection comes in powdered or concentrated liquid form and must be dissolved (reconstituted) or diluted before it can be injected. Most often directions as to how much diluent (dissolving or diluting solution) and what kind should be added by needle and syringe are on the label of the container of the drug. All that the nurse needs to know to determine the amount to give is on the label.

*Question:* A certain antibiotic has been ordered "750 mg IV." The drug comes in a 10-g multiple-dose vial (there is more than enough of the drug in the vial for one dose) in powdered form. The label reads, "Add 7.2 ml sterile water or sodium chloride solution for injection to yield 10 ml of reconstituted drug." After the diluent has been added, how many milliliters would you give?

*Answer:* 10 ml now contains 10 g; thus 1 ml equals 1 g. You should already know or be able to refer to a listing of standard equivalents to find out that 1 g equals 1000 mg. You may

then start the equation by setting down the relationship between what you want to give and the volume that contains it. Then follow the same sequence of relationship on the other side of the equation which denotes what is available in which volume.

$$750 \text{ mg}:x = 1000 \text{ mg}:1 \text{ ml}$$
$$1000x = 750$$
$$x = \frac{750}{1000} = 0.75 \text{ ml}$$

Whenever a drug appears in concentrated form (powder or liquid), after the appropriate diluent has been added and well dispersed or dissolved, the same mathematical approach can be used, no matter what the size of the finished solution. NB: Do not fall into the trap of including the amount of *diluent* anywhere in your equation.

3. *Question:* The quantity of a certain medication is ordered as "gr xv," and the tablets on hand are in gr v dosage. How many tablets should be given?

*Answer:*

$$\text{gr } 15:x = \text{gr } 5:1 \text{ tablet}$$
$$5x = 15$$
$$x = \frac{15}{5} = 3 \text{ tablets}$$

4. *Question:* One quart bottle of potassium permanganate has been sent up from the pharmacy. The treatment order reads that a pint of potassium permanganate is used in each treatment of the client's skin condition. How much solution will be left after the first treatment?

*Answer:* One pint. You should know that 2 pints make 1 quart.

5. *Question:* How many pints should be requested from the pharmacy if a medication is to be given in 4-ounce doses three times a day for 2 days?

*Answer:* You need to know that 16 ounces are in 1 pint. Total number of ounces for the course of therapy = $4 \times 3 \times 2$ = 24 oz, or 1½ pints.

6. *Question:* A client's medication has been ordered based on body weight. If the client weighs 150 pounds, how many kilograms is that?

*Answer:* You need to know that 1 kg is equal to 2.2 pounds.

$$150 \text{ lb}:x = 2.2 \text{ lb}:1 \text{ kg}$$
$$2.2x = 150$$
$$x = \frac{150}{2.2} = 68.2 \text{ kg}$$

7. *Question:* Atropine sulfate gr $\frac{1}{150}$ is ordered. How many tablets would you give if the available supply is in tablets of 0.2 mg?

*Answer:* First you need to know that 1 grain is equivalent to 60 mg; then you can find how many milligrams are equivalent to gr $\frac{1}{150}$. Second, you need to find out how many tablets will provide the milligram equivalent of gr $\frac{1}{150}$.

$$\text{gr } \tfrac{1}{150}:x \text{ (mg)} = \text{gr } 1:60 \text{ mg}$$
$$x = 60\left(\frac{1}{150}\right)$$
$$x = \frac{60}{150} = 0.4 \text{ mg}$$

The second step may certainly be done without pencil and paper, but it is more likely to be accurate if not calculated in the head.

$$0.4 \text{ mg}:x = 0.2 \text{ mg}:1$$
$$0.2x = 0.4$$
$$x = \frac{0.4}{0.2} = 2 \text{ tablets}$$

8. *Question:* You may also be confronted with the reverse of the preceding question. How many grains would you give if 0.6 mg scopolamine has been ordered?
   *Answer:*

$$0.6 \text{ mg}:x \text{ (gr)} = 60 \text{ mg}:\text{gr } 1$$
$$60x = \frac{0.6}{60}$$
$$x = \text{gr } 0.01 = \text{gr } \frac{1}{100}$$

9. *Question:* Codeine gr ss is ordered; how many milligrams would you give?
   *Answer:* You need to know that the symbol "ss" indicates the quantity one half.

$$\text{gr } \frac{1}{2}:x \text{ (mg)} = \text{gr } 1:60 \text{ mg}$$
$$x = 60 \left(\frac{1}{2}\right)$$
$$x = \frac{60}{2} = 30 \text{ mg}$$

10. *Question:* The client is to take 6 ounces of magnesium sulfate solution, and the calibrations on the available measuring device are in milliliters. How many milliliters would you give?
    *Answer:* You need to know that 1 ounce is equivalent to 30 ml.

$$6 \text{ oz}:x \text{ (ml)} = 1 \text{ oz}:30 \text{ ml}$$
$$x = 6 \times 30$$
$$x = 180 \text{ ml}$$

11. Although some practitioners may not technically consider IV infusions to be medications, we will practice figuring IV infusion rates here.

    The amount of IV solution to be infused during a given length of time is the IV flow rate. It is dictated by the prescriber's order, which should give the total amount of fluid and the number of milliliters that should be infused over each 1-hour period or less *or* the number of drops per minute that should be infused. Some prescribers are still writing IV orders that give only the total volume of solution to be infused (e.g., 1000 ml) over a longer period (e.g., 8 hours). Technically, such information is inadequate and the order should be clarified.

    If the order does not spell out the rate of flow in drops per minute, the following formula may be used to figure this out:

$$\frac{\text{Total number of milliliters to be infused}}{\text{Total number of minutes infusion is to run}} \times \text{Drop factor}$$
$$= \text{Rate in drops per minute}$$

*Question:* If an order is given for 1000 ml D₅W to run for 8 hours and the drop factor is 10 drops per milliliter for the particular tubing used (other types deliver 15 drops or 60 drops—often used to infuse children), how fast should the IV infusion be set to run?
*Answer:*

$$\frac{1000 \text{ ml}}{480 \text{ min}} \times 10 = x$$
$$\frac{100}{48} \times 10 = 20.8 \text{ drops (gtt)/min} = 21 \text{ gtt/min}$$

A bit more challenging are some of the mathematics involved with IV rates for infusion pumps. These pumps are often used for giving drugs whose dosages must be calculated more closely.
*Question:* Dopamine 400 mg is ordered to be added to 250 cc D₅W to be infused at a rate of 350 μg/min. It is to be regulated by a volumetric infusion pump that is calibrated to deliver the fluid in units of cubic centimeters per hour. At how many cubic centimeters per hour should the pump be set?
*Answer:* Here you are asked to convert the "language" of one flow rate to the language of another. First you need to know that 1 μg is equal to 0.001 mg, so:

$$350 \text{ μg}:x = 1 \text{ μg}:0.001 \text{ mg}$$
$$x = 0.350 \text{ mg or } 0.35 \text{ mg}$$

Thus 0.350 mg is being infused every minute. Now you need to calculate the rate per hour. That is, if 0.35 mg is infused every minute, how many milligrams will be infused per hour?

$$x:60 \text{ min} = 0.35 \text{ mg}:1 \text{ min}$$
$$x = 60 \times 0.35$$
$$x = (350)0.01$$
$$x = 21 \text{ mg}$$

Now convert to cubic centimeters per hour:

$$21 \text{ mg}:x\text{(cc)} = 400 \text{ mg}:250 \text{ cc}$$
$$400x = 21 \times 250 = 5250$$
$$x = 13.125 \text{ or } 13 \text{ cc/hr}$$

12. *Question:* 30 mg of a drug for three times a day dosing has been ordered for a child who weighs 15 kg and is 90 cm tall. The recommended 24-hour total pediatric dosage is 90 to 150 mg/m². Is the ordered dose safe or unsafe for this child? Refer to the West nomogram (see Figure 9-2).
    *Answer:* According to the nomogram, a line drawn from points indicating 90 cm and 15 kg crosses the body surface area (BSA) column at the 0.62 point. This means that the child's body surface area is about 0.62 m². Multiply 0.62 by each of the numbers indicating the drug's range of safety to see if the ordered 24-hour dosage is within that range.

Some rules of thumb will become more important as the metric system predominates.

Place a zero to the left of the decimal point when there is no integer in the decimal.

Carry out problems to the hundredths place, and then round off only in the final answer.

Use judgement in rounding off numbers. The smaller the answer (the lower the number), the more significant the relative change in the answer made by rounding off.

Many excellent nursing texts are available that one can use to develop and practice arithmetic skills necessary in the administration of medications. (See the references at the end of this chapter.) Much more practice is necessary than is presented here for introductory purposes.

## Procedures and Techniques of Administration

Accurate and full identification of the client before each dose of medication is given ensures that the right person gets the right medication. Using the client's full name on all paperwork and in all references helps prevent mixups, as does being alert to similarities in names and geographically separating people with similar names. Nurses should not rely on memory to identify clients. *Checking the client's name on the arm band or name tag* against the name on the accompanying medication ticket is the *most reliable* mode of identification. Asking the client his or her name and comparing it with the name on the medication ticket, Kardex, or MAR is not foolproof. For example, a client may give his name as "William" (first name), and then be given medication intended for "Mr. Williams" (last name). Checking the client's name by calling it out and waiting for a corroborating answer is particularly risky; in a sleepy state, clients have been known to answer to almost any name. Reliance on names on bed tags or labels is dangerous because clients are often away from their beds; a bed can be inadvertently occupied by another client who is in a groggy state after returning, for example, from a laboratory test. Asking a family member is not foolproof either; a distraught family member may respond inappropriately. Again, the *surest* way to identify a client before giving medication is to *check the arm band* or *identifying tag*. In an institutional setting, medications should not be administered to any client not wearing an identification band or tag. Each institution has a policy for the replacement of identification bands or tags inadvertently removed or lost, and this policy should be complied with and the band or tag restored before any medications are administered. One exception might be in the case of an emergency, in which a delay might be detrimental. Even in an emergency the client's identity should be verified by some method before drug administration.

Before administering medications, the nurse must also make sure that the drug order has not been changed in any way (e.g., discontinued or dosage changed) from what appears on the medications ticket or MAR. It is also wise to check the medication administration record to see that the dose about to be given has not already been given by someone else caring for the client (such as the private duty nurse or nursing student). Individual agency policies spell out the checking procedure to be used; these policies should be followed routinely to avoid error.

The following are recommended guidelines for distributing or administering drugs to clients.

1. When preparing or giving medicines, concentrate your whole attention on what you are doing. Do not permit yourself to be distracted while working with medicines.
2. Make certain that you have a written order for every medication for which you assume the responsibility of administration. (Verbal and telephone orders should be written out and signed by the prescriber as soon as possible. These orders should be used only in limited circumstances and not for the convenience of the prescriber.)
3. Make a habit of reading the label of the medicine and comparing it to the MAR carefully at least three times: first, when removing the drug from the supply drawer or medication cart; second, when placing the medication in a souffle cup, ounce cup, or syringe; and third, just before administering it to the client, before the container is discarded.
4. Make certain that the data on the medicine card or MAR corresponds exactly with the prescriber's written order and with the label on the client's medicine. If the card system is used, a card should accompany each dose. Sometimes skipping a dose of medicine may be as dangerous as an overdose.
5. Never give a medicine from an unlabeled container or from one on which the label is not legible.
6. If you must in some way calculate the dosage for a client from the preparation on hand and you are uncertain of your calculation, verify your work on paper by having some other responsible person—an instructor, nurse in charge, or pharmacist—check it. In some hospitals certain drug dosages (e.g., insulin) are routinely verified by another nurse. Whenever the result of a calculation calls for more than two units of a drug to make a dose, double check the calculation. It is highly unusual for more than two units of a single drug to be administered in a single dose.
7. Measure quantities as ordered, using the proper equipment: graduated containers for milliliters, fluidounces, or fluidrams, minim glasses or calibrated syringes for minims, and droppers for drops. When measuring liquids, hold the container so that the line indicating the desired quantity is on a level with the eye. The quantity is read when the lowest part of the concave surface of the fluid (meniscus) is on this line.
8. Dosage forms such as tablets, capsules, and pills should be handled so that the fingers do not come into contact with the medicine. Use the cap of the container to guide or lift the medicine into the medicine glass or container you will be taking to the bedside of the client.
9. Avoid waste of medicines. Medicines tend to be expensive; in some instances a single capsule may cost the client several dollars. Dropping medicine on the floor is one way of being wasteful.
10. When pouring liquid medicines, hold the bottle so that the liquid does not run over the side and obscure the label. This is known as "palming the label." Wipe the rim of the bottle with a clean piece of paper tissue before replacing the stopper or cover.
11. Always prepare an IV admixture before you label the container, and verify the dosage on the emptied additive container when labeling the IV container.

12. When preparing an injection, always label the syringe immediately. Keep the vial with the syringe, and do not rely on memory to determine what solution is in which syringe.

13. Never administer medication prepared by another person. In doing so, you accept the responsibility for accuracy, dose, correct medication, and so forth. If the person who prepared the medication has made an error, you are accountable for any harm done to the client.

14. If a client expresses doubt or concern about a medication or the dosage of a medication, reassure the client as well as yourself by rechecking to make certain that there is no error, before the medication is administered. You may need to recheck the order, the label on the medicine container, or the client's chart. The astute and caring nurse also recognizes that a client who refuses medication has the right to do so and that this behavior is giving a message about expressed or unexpressed feelings. The understanding nurse is not content to simply chart that the client refused 10:00 AM medication. The client should be able to talk about whatever feelings caused the behavior; this will help the client feel that his or her reaction, whatever it may be, is accepted. You thus provide the client opportunities to exercise some control over the environment.

15. Assist weak or helpless clients to take their medications. Do so as patiently and unhurriedly as possible.

16. Many liquid medicines should be diluted with water or other liquid. This is especially desirable when medicines have a bad taste. Exceptions to this rule include cough medicines that are given for a local effect in the throat. The client (in the sitting position) should be supplied with *at least 100 ml of water* for swallowing solid forms such as tablets or capsules, unless the individual is allowed only limited amounts of fluid. This will facilitate dissolution and reduce gastric irritation, if any. Esophageal erosion caused by an adherent tablet or pill has been reported when inadequate amounts of water were given.

17. *Remain with the client until the medicine has been taken.* Most clients are very cooperative about taking medicines when the nurse brings them. However, sometimes clients are more ill than they appear and have been known to hoard medicines until they have accumulated a lethal amount and then take the entire amount, with fatal results. In some instances, however, clients may be permitted to keep medicines at their bedsides and take them as necessary, such as nitroglycerin and antacids. In fact, in some controlled situations in which clients self-administered medications, client satisfaction improved and nursing staff members felt that they had more time to instruct clients about their medications and not just distribute them (Anderson and Poole, 1983).

18. Stay, for at least 5 minutes, with the client receiving the first dose of an IV medication, especially antibiotics, and monitor closely for adverse effects.

19. Do not leave a tray or cart of medicines unattended. If you are in a client's room and must leave, take the tray of medicines with you. Similarly, do not leave the medication cart unattended in the hall; take it into the client's room with you.

20. Never chart a medicine as having been given until it has been administered. Nursing students should check the chart before giving a medication. MARs should document all medications, including prn's, one-time-only medications, and special drugs (e.g., heparin), in one place to allow the nurse to consider incompatibilities and/or duplications of similar drugs. The name of the drug, the dosage, the time of administration, and the route of administration should be noted on the medication record in the chart. In the recording of parenteral medications, the site of injection is always included. The patient's response, adverse as well as intended, to the medication should be recorded in the progress notes or nursing notes.

21. Always verify a drug's route of administration. Sometimes preparations for a specific route of administration may be used for another route. For example, Mycostatin suppositories developed for vaginal use may be used as an oral troche for an oral yeast infection, or some parenteral preparations may be diluted for oral use, such as vancomycin when indicated for pseudomembranous colitis. In this latter example and with other drugs, do not put oral drugs in syringes used for injection. Oral syringes that cannot accommodate a needle should be used to prevent accidental parenteral injection of an oral preparation.

22. Within an institutional setting, any unused medication should be returned to the pharmacy. According to institutional policy and in some states, the law requires the unused portion to be credited to the client's account. If it can be used for another client, the pharmacy will verify that it has been stored correctly and relabel it.

23. Borrowing medications from one client's supply for another client is not appropriate and leads to dosing errors. Only medications issued by the pharmacy and labeled for a specific client should be used for that client, except in the case of a stock medication kept on the nursing unit. Medications brought into the hospital by a client should be returned home with a family member or, if they are to be utilized in the institutional setting, sent to the hospital pharmacy to be verified and relabeled.

All medicine containers and trays should be scrupulously clean, and water supplied immediately after the medicine should be fresh. Carelessly prepared medicines and lack of consideration in the way a medicine is handed to a client can convey a demeaning or insulting message, whether intended or not.

When a medicine with an unpleasant taste is given, it is better to admit that it may be unpleasant than to make a client feel that his or her reaction is grossly exaggerated or silly. The nurse can attempt to improve the taste by diluting the medicine (if possible) or by offering chewing gum or hard candy immediately after the medicine.

If an injection is likely to sting or hurt, it is honest to tell the client beforehand. The client who is told is also more likely to deal with the pain more effectively than one who is not told. It is better to tell a child just before the injection rather than much beforehand, so that there is little time for the child to anticipate and grow anxious, thereby actually increasing the pain.

The route of administration of a drug is determined by its physical and chemical properties, the condition or status of the client, the desired action of the drug, its speed of absorption, and the rapidity of response desired. As a rule, drugs are administered for either local or systemic effects (see Chapter 5). Some drugs given locally may produce both local and systemic effects if they are partly or entirely absorbed; some drugs are applied for local absorption yet are targeted solely for systemic effect, such as nitroglycerin, ointment hormones, and scopolamine. There has been an increasing awareness that many more substances are absorbed through the skin than was previously believed. Toxic incidents in infants exposed to topically applied dermal medication are increasing. Some of these drugs are boric acid, iodides, hexachlorophene, corticosteroids, and rubbing alcohol. Care is advised in use of any topically applied drug on infants' skin. Yet a drug may be injected into a joint cavity and have little or no effect beyond the tissues of that structure.

### Administration for Local Effects

**Application to skin.** Medications are applied to the skin primarily for the following effects:

1. *Astringent:* resulting in vasoconstriction, tissue contraction, and decreased secretions and sensitivity, thereby counteracting inflammatory effects
2. *Antiseptic* or *bacteriostatic:* to inhibit growth and development of microorganisms
3. *Emollient:* for a soothing and softening effect to overcome dryness and hardness
4. *Cleansing:* for the removal of dirt, debris, secretions, or crusts

These medications may be applied in the form of a lotion, tincture, ointment or cream, foam, wet dressing, tampon, bath, or soak. The effectiveness of medicinals applied to the skin for local effect is limited by the fact that highly specialized layers of skin resist penetration of many (but not all) foreign substances to protect the internal body environment. Topical absorption is increased when the skin is thin or macerated, when there is increased drug concentration, when there is prolonged contact of the drug with the skin, or when the drug is combined with a solvent-penetrant (e.g., dimethyl sulfoxide [DMSO] and acyclovir are under study for topical use in this way). See information, presented in Chapter 68, on topical drugs and the instillation of eyedrops and eardrops.

**Application to mucous membranes.** Drugs are well absorbed across mucosal surfaces, and therapeutic effects are easily obtained. However, mucous membranes are highly selective in their absorptive capacity and vary in sensitivity. To produce the same effects, a drug applied to oral (buccal or sublingual) mucosa may be twice as concentrated as that applied to nasal mucosa, while its concentration may be reduced one fourth to one half for application to delicate membranes of the eye or urethra. Aqueous solutions are quickly absorbed from mucous membranes, whereas oily liquids are not. Oily preparations should not be applied to nasal or respiratory mucosa by sprays or nebulae, since the droplets of oil may be carried to terminal portions of the respiratory tract and retained there, causing lipoid pneumonia.

Respiratory mucosa may be medicated by means of inhalation or insufflation. The **inhalation** method utilizes sprays or nebulae, whereby the drug is sprayed into the throat by a nebulizer; aerosols are delivered by a flow of air or oxygen under pressure to disperse the drug throughout the lower respiratory tract. In the **insufflation** method a fine powder is blown or sprayed onto nasal mucosa. Drugs so administered tend to have both a local respiratory and a systemic effect. The respiratory mucosa offers an enormous surface of absorbing epithelium. If the drug is volatile and chemically absorbable and if there is more in the inspired air than in the blood, the drug is instantaneously absorbed. This fact is of significance in emergencies. Amyl nitrite, oxygen, and carbon dioxide are examples of volatile and gaseous agents that are given by inhalation.

Drugs in suppository form can be used for their local effects on the mucous membranes of the vagina, urethra, or rectum. Packs and tampons may be impregnated with a drug and placed in a body cavity; these are used particularly in the nose, ears, and vagina. Drugs may also be painted or swabbed on a mucosal surface, instilled (e.g., a vaginal douche), or administered via irrigation or injection (such as intralesional injection for psoriasis or local intraarterial injection for cancer).

### Administration for Systemic Effects

Drugs that produce a systemic effect must be absorbed into the bloodstream and carried to the cells or tissues capable of responding to them. The route of administration used depends on the nature and amount of drug to be given, the desired rapidity of effect, and the general condition of the client. Routes selected for systemic effect include the following: skin, oral, sublingual, rectal, and parenteral (injection). Routes of parenteral administration include the intradermal (or intracutaneous), subcutaneous, intramuscular, intravenous, intraspinal (or intrathecal), and sometimes intraarticular, intracardiac, intrapericardial, intraosseous, and intraperitoneal.

**Oral administration.** Oral administration is the safest, most economical, and most convenient way of giving medicines. Therefore it is the preferred route unless some distinct advantage is to be gained by using another way. Most drugs are absorbed from the small intestine; only a few are absorbed from the stomach and colon. This explains the ineffectiveness of cathartics and enemas in the attempt to remove most toxins and overdoses in cases of poisoning.

Following oral administration, drug effects are *slower* in onset and *more prolonged* but *less potent* than when drugs are given parenterally. Thus when a steady-state in pharmacokinetics is desired, it is often more closely approached with oral than with parenteral administration. When rapid, high dosages are needed as loading doses or in emergencies, the parenteral route may be used. Strategies for wise pain care, if carefully tailored to individual needs, can exploit these characteristics of oral and parenteral routes for analgesics. For the client in low-level or chronic pain, the oral route for analgesics can be more successful than other routes in promoting a steady state (fewer oscillations) in pain relief. Acute pain may submit to an initial dose of analgesic by the parenteral route, followed by oral doses. Altered effects from oral administration may result from (1) variation in absorption as a result of drug composition, gastric or intestinal pH and motility, food content, or a pathologic condition within the gastrointestinal tract or (2) alteration of the drug resulting from its retention, inactivation, or partial destruction by the liver if the drug traverses the hepatic circulation before entering the general circulation.

Disadvantages of oral administration of certain drugs are that (1) they may have an objectionable odor or taste or be bulky to swallow, (2) they may harm or discolor the teeth, (3) they may irritate the gastric mucosa, causing nausea and vomiting, (4) they may be aspirated by a seriously ill or uncooperative individual, (5) they may be destroyed by digestive enzymes, and (6) they may be inappropriate for some clients, such as those who must be given nothing by mouth.

***Sublingual administration.*** Drugs given sublingually are placed under the tongue, where they should be retained until dissolved and absorbed. The thin epithelium and rich network of capillaries on the underside of the tongue permit both rapid absorption and rapid drug action. In addition, there is greater potency than with oral administration, since the drug gains access to the general circulation without traversing the liver or being affected by gastric and intestinal enzymes. Many of the same effects apply also to *buccal* administration, whereby a tablet is held in the mouth in the pocket between gums and cheek for local dissolution and absorption.

The number of drugs that can be given sublingually is limited (e.g., nitroglycerin tablets). The drug must dissolve readily, and the client must be able to cooperate; the client must understand that the drug is not to be swallowed and that taking a drink must be avoided until the drug has been absorbed. However, usually little harm is done if a sublingual drug is inadvertently swallowed; effects may be neutralized or delayed slightly.

***Rectal administration.*** Rectal administration of certain preparations can be used advantageously when the stomach is nonretentive or traumatized, when the medicine has an objectionable taste or odor, or when it can be changed by digestive enzymes. It is also a reasonably convenient and safe method of giving drugs when the oral method is unsuitable, as when the individual is either a small child (or infant) or is unconscious. Rectal administration is contraindicated, however, if the anal area is irritated, or if diarrhea, rectal bleeding, or hemorrhoids are present.

Use of the rectal route avoids irritation of the upper gastrointestinal tract (however, aminophylline suppositories often irritate the rectal mucosa) and may promote higher bloodstream drug titers because venous blood from the lower

part of the rectum does not traverse the liver. The suppository as a drug vehicle is often superior to the retention enema because the drug is released at a slow but steady rate to ensure a protracted effect. One disadvantage of the retention enema is unpredictable retention of the drug; another is that some of the fluid may pass above the lower rectum and be absorbed into the portal circulation. An evacuant enema before administration of rectal medication is usually advisable to ensure that there is no fecal bulk in the rectum to obstruct free flow of the medicated enema or the action of a suppository. The amount of solution that can be given rectally is usually small.

Refrigerated suppositories will soften and cannot be inserted if they are handled or carried in the pocket for even a brief period. Cold running water will restore rigidity to suppositories. To be retained for effective therapy, suppositories and enema tubing must be inserted beyond the internal anal sphincter (2 to 3 inches). The dose of a suppository drug form cannot be divided by cutting the suppository in sections because the active drug constituent may not be evenly distributed.

***Parenteral administration.*** Strictly speaking, parenteral administration means administration by any route other than oral; thus technically it could be defined to include topical or inhalation administration. In practical usage, however, parenteral usually means administration by the use of a needle (see Table 6-5).

Parenteral administration of drugs includes all forms of drug injection into body tissues or fluids using a syringe and needle or catheter and container (Figures 6-5 and 6-6). Drugs given parenterally must be sterile, readily soluble and absorbable, and relatively nonirritating. Since parenteral administration of drugs can be hazardous, precautions are required: (1) aseptic technique must be used to avoid infection and (2) accurate drug dosage, proper rate of injection and proper site of injection are essential to avoid harm such as lipodystrophy (atrophy or hypertrophy of subcutaneous fat tissue), abscesses, necrosis, skin slough, nerve injuries, prolonged pain, or periostitis. *An injected drug is irretrievable,* and an error in dosage or method or site of injection is not easily corrected.

With drugs given parenterally (as compared with orally), (1) the onset of drug action is more rapid (except as noted previously), (2) the dosage is often similar, since drug potency remains unaltered, and (3) the cost of drug therapy may be greater. Parenteral administration of drugs requires specialized knowledge, aseptic technique, and manual skill to ensure safety and therapeutic effectiveness. Most methods of parenteral administration may be performed by the nurse, but some are usually done only by a physician. The nurse should know and adhere to agency policy. Clients and family members may also learn to administer injections.

***Intradermal.*** Intradermal or intracutaneous injection means that the injection is made into the upper layers of the skin almost parallel to the skin surface (Figure 6-7). The

**TABLE 6-5**  Suggested injection guides

| Route | Common areas | Region | Needle sizes* | Volume injected (ml) | | Examples of medications by this route |
|---|---|---|---|---|---|---|
| | | | | Average | Range† | |
| Intradermal (intracutaneous) | Skin (corium) | Inner aspect of mid forearm or scapula | 26 or 27 gauge × ⅜ in | 0.1 | 0.001 to 1.0 | Tuberculin, allergens, local anesthetics |
| Subcutaneous | Beneath the skin | Lateral upper arms; thighs; abdominal fat pads except the 1-in area around umbilicus and tissue over bone; upper back; upper hips | 25 to 27 gauge × ½ to ⅝ in‡ | 0.5 | 0.5 to 1.5 | Epinephrine (non-oily), insulin, some narcotics, tetanus toxoid, vaccines, vitamin $B_{12}$, heparin |
| Intramuscular | Gluteus medius | Dorsogluteal | 20 to 23 gauge × 1½ to 3 in‡ | 2 to 4 | 1 to 5 | Most intramuscular and Z-track injections |
| | Gluteus minimus | Ventrogluteal | 20 to 23 gauge × 1½ to 3 in‡ | 1 to 4 | 1 to 5 | All intramuscular medications |
| | Vastus lateralis | Anterolateral midthigh | 22 to 25 gauge × ⅝ to 1 in‡ | 1 to 4 | 1 to 5 | Almost all intramuscular medications |
| | Deltoid | Upper arm below shoulder | 23 to 25 gauge × ⅝ to 1 in‡ | 0.5 | 0.5 to 2 | Vaccines, absorbed tetanus toxoid, most narcotics, epinephrine, sedatives, vitamin $B_{12}$, lidocaine |
| Intravenous bolus | Cephalic and basilic veins | Dorsum of hand and forearm; antecubital fossa | 18 to 23 gauge × 1 to 1½ in | 1 to 10 | 0.5 to 50 (or more by continuous infusion) | Antibiotics, vitamins, fluids and electrolytes, antineoplastics, vasopressors, corticosteroids, aminophylline, blood products |

Modified from Newton M and DW, (1979). Guidelines for handling drug errors, Nursing '79 9(7):18.

*Needles used for withdrawing medication from a container should be changed before injecting medication drawn (1) from ampules, because irritating medication may cling to needle (filter-needles should be used to withdraw medication from ampules) and (2) from vials, because needles are dulled after insertion through rubber tops; disposable needles are thus labeled "for one-time use only."

†Administration of the largest volumes listed here should be avoided if possible by dividing the dose and using different sites or by using another route in consultation with prescriber.

‡See text for discussion of factors influencing choice of needle length.

amount of drug given is small, and absorption is slow. This method is used to advantage in testing for allergic reactions and for giving small amounts of a local anesthetic. In a test for allergic reactions, minute amounts of the solution to be tested are injected just under the outer layers of the skin. The medial surface of the forearm and the skin of the back are the sites frequently used. These injections are best made with a fine, short needle (26 or 27 gauge) and a small-barrel syringe (such as a tuberculin syringe) (Figure 6-8).

*Subcutaneous (SC).*  Small amounts of drug in solution are given subcutaneously usually by means of a 25-gauge (or thinner) needle and syringe. The needle is inserted

through the skin with a quick movement, but the injection is made slowly and steadily (Figure 6-9). The nurse should slightly withdraw the plunger of the syringe before injecting the drug, to make sure that a blood vessel has not been entered. The angle of insertion should usually be 45 to 60 degrees (but can be any angle from 30 to 90 degrees, depending on needle length and depth of fat pads), and insertion should be made on the fat pads of the abdomen, the outer surface of the upper arm, the anterior surface of the thigh, or occasionally the lower abdominal surface (heparin). In these locations there are fewer large blood vessels, and sensation is less keen than on the medial surfaces of

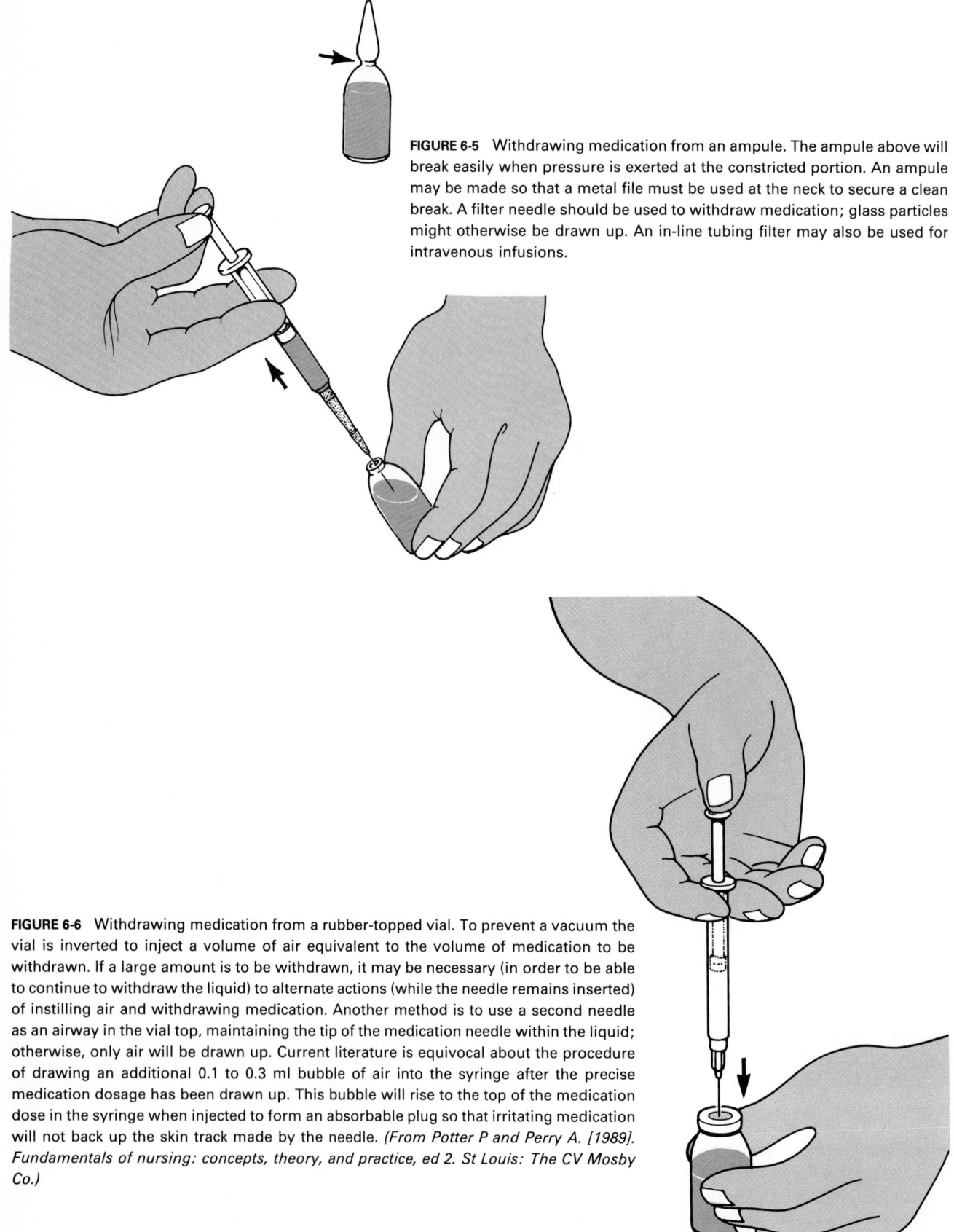

**FIGURE 6-5** Withdrawing medication from an ampule. The ampule above will break easily when pressure is exerted at the constricted portion. An ampule may be made so that a metal file must be used at the neck to secure a clean break. A filter needle should be used to withdraw medication; glass particles might otherwise be drawn up. An in-line tubing filter may also be used for intravenous infusions.

**FIGURE 6-6** Withdrawing medication from a rubber-topped vial. To prevent a vacuum the vial is inverted to inject a volume of air equivalent to the volume of medication to be withdrawn. If a large amount is to be withdrawn, it may be necessary (in order to be able to continue to withdraw the liquid) to alternate actions (while the needle remains inserted) of instilling air and withdrawing medication. Another method is to use a second needle as an airway in the vial top, maintaining the tip of the medication needle within the liquid; otherwise, only air will be drawn up. Current literature is equivocal about the procedure of drawing an additional 0.1 to 0.3 ml bubble of air into the syringe after the precise medication dosage has been drawn up. This bubble will rise to the top of the medication dose in the syringe when injected to form an absorbable plug so that irritating medication will not back up the skin track made by the needle. *(From Potter P and Perry A. [1989]. Fundamentals of nursing: concepts, theory, and practice, ed 2. St Louis: The CV Mosby Co.)*

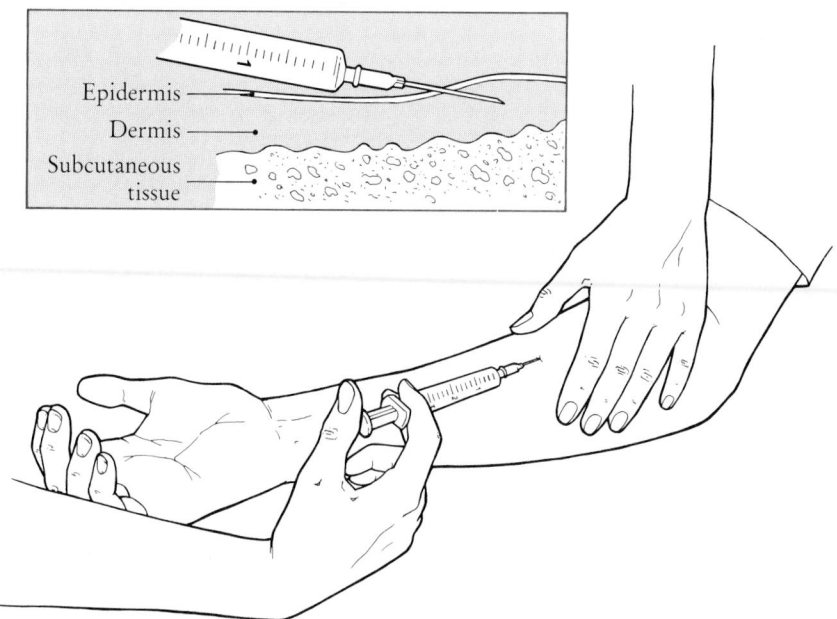

**FIGURE 6-7**   Intradermal injection. The needle penetrates epidermis and goes into dermis but not subcutaneous tissue. (Note that the skin is not pinched up.)

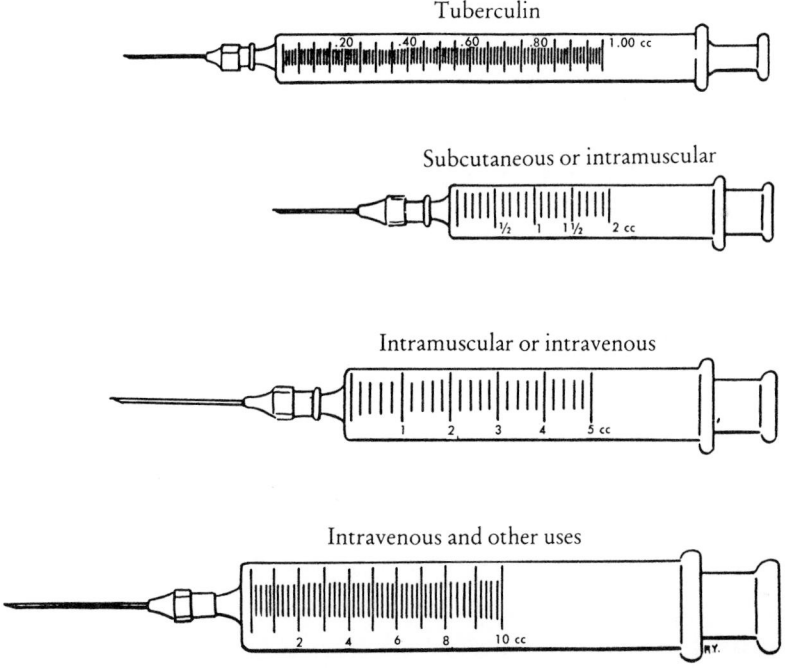

**FIGURE 6-8**   These syringes are used to accurately measure varying amounts of liquids and liquid medications. The uppermost syringe is known as a tuberculin syringe and is graduated in 0.01 cc (ml). It is a syringe of choice for administration of very small amounts. The 2 cc syringe is the one commonly used to give a drug subcutaneously or intramuscularly. It is graduated in 0.1 cc. The larger syringes are used when a larger volume of drug is to be administered intramuscularly or intravenously; for withdrawing blood for laboratory testing; or for obtaining urine specimens from urinary catheters (20 cc syringes may be preferred for the last two uses). These syringes and needles are not drawn to scale (e.g., the tuberculin syringe is much thinner and shorter than the others).

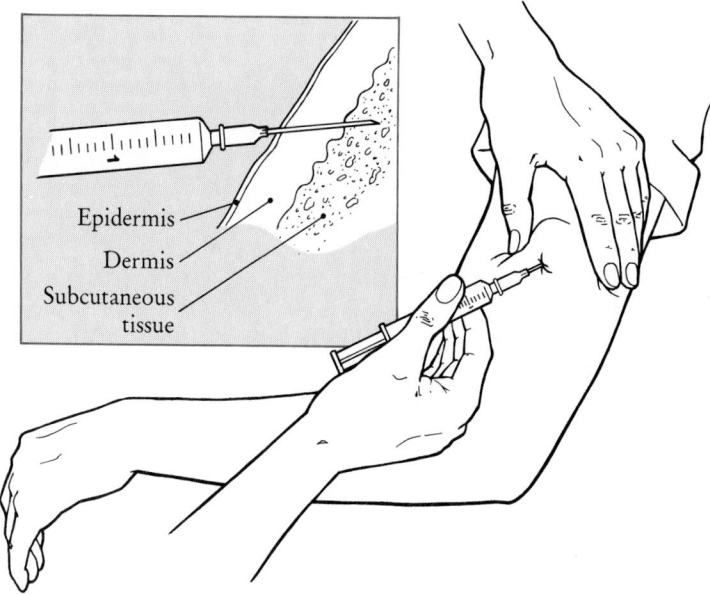

**FIGURE 6-9** Subcutaneous injection. The skin surface has been cleansed, and the syringe is held at the angle at which the needle will penetrate subcutaneous tissue. The left hand is used to pinch the arm gently but firmly. When the needle has been inserted into the subcutaneous tissue, the tissue of the arm is released and the solution is steadily injected. Based on the client's condition or the medication to be injected, nursing judgment may dictate a different angle or an approach different from pinching up the skin.

the extremities. Massage of the part after injection tends to increase the rate of absorption but should be avoided after injection of some drugs, such as heparin, to minimize bruising as the drug spreads through the tissues. Disposable syringes and needles contribute to aseptic safety of the procedure but also to cost and problems of storage and disposal. Subcutaneously injected medicines are limited to drugs that are highly soluble and nonirritating and to solutions of limited volume (ideally no more than 1 ml).

Irritating drugs given subcutaneously can result in the formation of sterile abscesses and necrotic tissue, especially if injections are made repeatedly in the same site. Care should be exercised to avoid contamination and to rotate sites. Subcutaneous injections are not effective in individuals with sluggish peripheral circulation (i.e., the client in shock).

The introduction of large amounts of solution (500 to 1000 ml in adults) into subcutaneous tissues is known as **hypodermoclysis.** Isotonic solutions of sodium chloride or glucose are administered this way. The needle is longer than that used for a regular subcutaneous injection, and it is inserted into areas of loose connective tissue such as that under the breasts, in the upper surfaces of the thighs, and in the subscapular region of the back. Fluids must be given slowly to avoid overdistention of the tissues. Hyaluronidase is sometimes added to the solution to facilitate the spread and absorption of fluid by decreasing the viscosity of the ground substance in connective tissues.

Most prescribers prefer IV infusion of fluids to hypodermoclysis because the amount of absorption is more readily determined.

*Intramuscular (IM).* Deeper injections are made into muscular tissue, through the skin and subcutaneous tissue, when a drug is too irritating to be given subcutaneously. Irritation may also occur with some drugs given intramuscularly. Larger doses can be given by intramuscular injection—up to 5 ml—than by subcutaneous injection. SC or IM absorption is delayed in circulatory collapse (i.e., shock states); the IV route is then chosen.

A drug may be given intramuscularly in an aqueous solution, an aqueous suspension, or a solution or suspension of oil. Suspensions form a depot of drug in the tissue, and slow, gradual absorption usually results. Two disadvantages are sometimes encountered when preparations in oil are used: the client may be sensitive to the oil, or the oil may not be absorbed. In the latter case, incision and drainage of the oil may be necessary. Few drugs are formulated in oil.

Criteria for selection of a safe intramuscular injection site include distance from large, vulnerable nerves, bones, and blood vessels and from bruised, scarred, or swollen previous injection or infusion sites. The type of needle used for IM injection depends on the site of the injection, the condition of the tissues, the size of the client, and the nature of the drug to be injected. Needles from 1 to 1½ inches in length are common. The usual gauge is 21 to 23 (*the larger the number, the finer the needle*). Fine needles can be used for

A

B

C

D

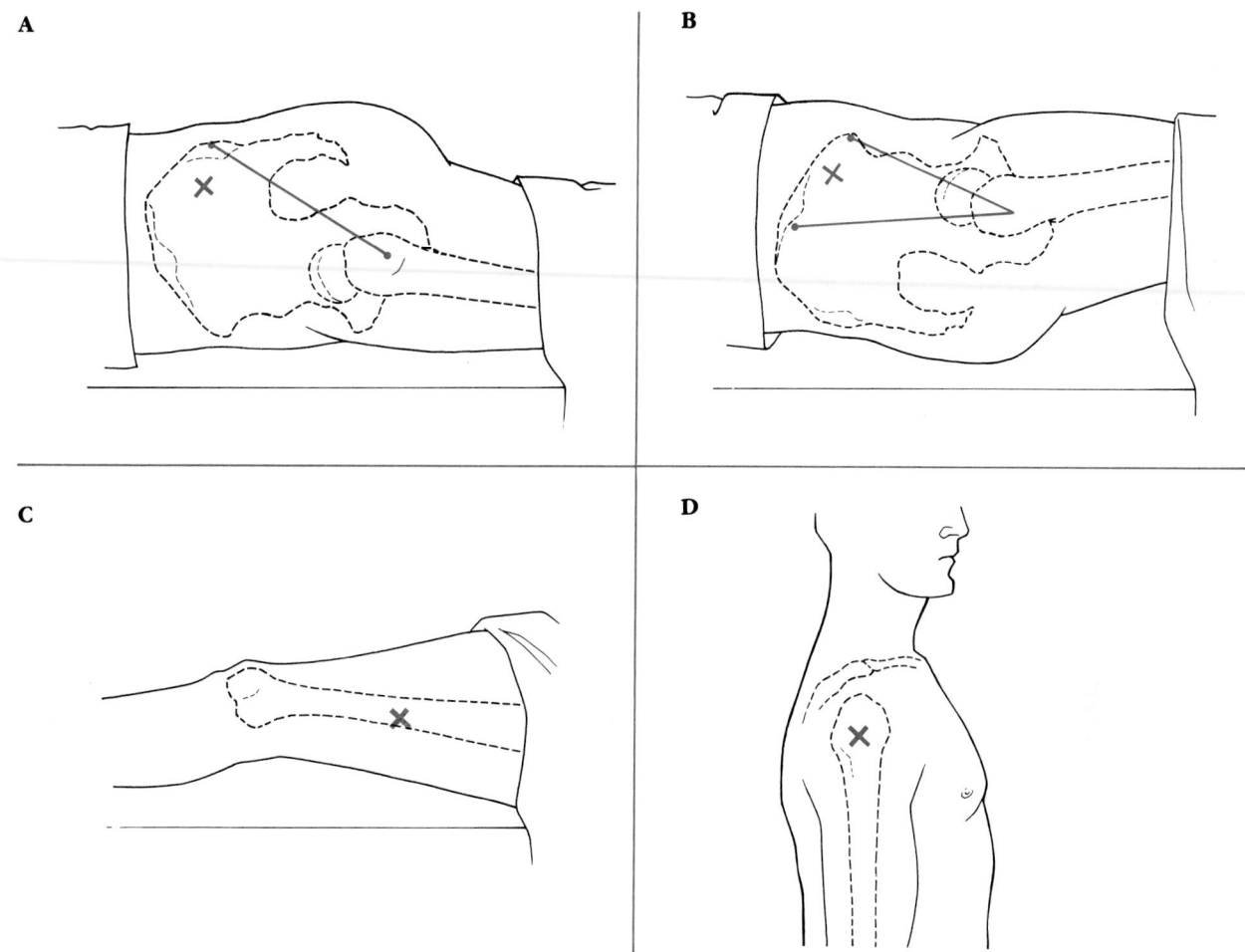

**FIGURE 6-10** Intramuscular injection. **A,** Dorsogluteal site, located anterior to the diagonal line from the trochanter to the posterior iliac spine. An injection near the middle of the buttocks may result in an injury to the sciatic nerve. The needle is inserted with a quick firm movement, entering perpendicular to the skin. After aspiration to make certain the needle is not in a blood vessel, the solution is injected slowly and steadily. **B,** Ventrogluteal intramuscular injection site. The V fans out from the greater trochanter between the anterior iliac spine and iliac crest. The injection site (X) is centered at the base of the triangle. **C,** Vastus lateralis (midlateral thigh) intramuscular injection site—a handsbreadth below the greater trochanter and a handsbreadth above the knee and halfway between the front and side of the thigh. **D,** Mid-deltoid intramuscular injection site—below the acromion and lateral to the axilla.

thin solutions and heavier needles for suspensions and oils. Needles for injection into the deltoid area should be ⅝ to 1 inch in length, the gauge again depending on the material to be injected. The deltoid can readily absorb up to 2 ml of drug. For many IM injections the gluteals are preferred because of fewer nerve endings and less discomfort at this site. The needle must be long enough to avoid depositing the solution of drug into the subcutaneous or fatty tissue. The depth of insertion depends on the amount of subcutaneous tissue and will vary with the weight of the client.

It is essential to locate the appropriate landmarks to delimit the areas safe for injections (Table 6-4 and Figure 6-10). IM injections may be given into such clearly defined areas of musculature as the gluteal region of the lower back (provides slowest absorption), the deltoid area, and the anterolateral thigh. At first it seems to most nursing students that the fleshy part of the buttock is a logical intramuscular site. It is not, since underneath, centrally, and running diagonally is the sciatic nerve, which if damaged can result in permanent leg paralysis. Every attempt must be made to avoid this area.

There are now two acceptable ways to map appropriate IM sites in the gluteal region. The formerly used method of dividing the gluteus medius into imaginary quadrants and injecting into the upper outer quadrant is out of favor be-

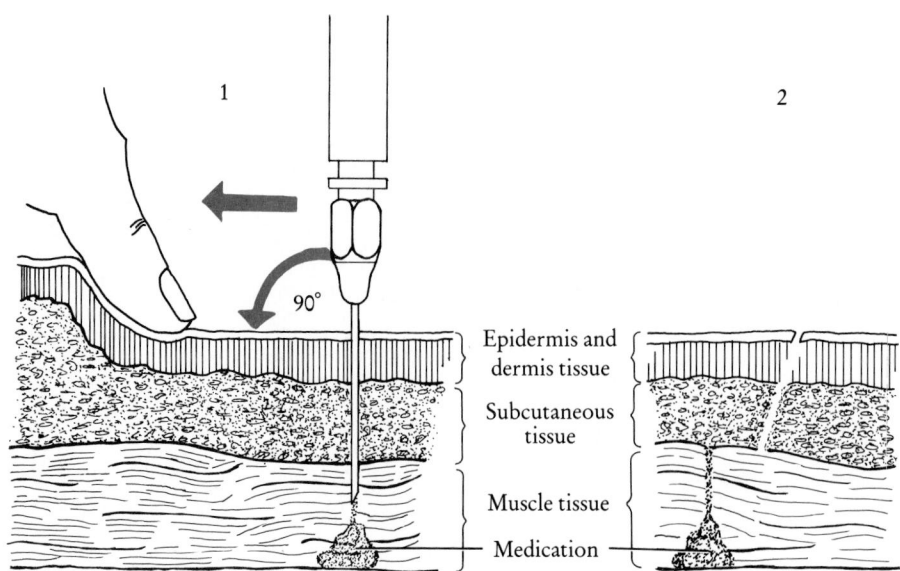

**FIGURE 6-11**  Z-track intramuscular injection method, which is useful for administration of medication known to cause pain or permanent staining of superficial tissues. *1,* The skin is stretched to one side and medication injected as usual, perpendicular to the skin surface, *2,* Needle is then removed and the skin allowed to return to resting position, sealing off the deposited medication from the track made by the needle. The site is not massaged in this method.

cause it does not necessarily prevent an injection into the sciatic nerve, especially if its course runs abnormally in an individual.

The nurse can best locate the *dorsogluteal site* (the muscle underneath is the gluetus medius) by asking the client to lie face down and exposing the entire area so that the landmarks and injection site can be clearly located. The proper site for this injection is outlined by an imaginary diagonal line drawn from the area of the greater trochanter of the femur to the posterior iliac spine. The injection should be given at any point between that imaginary straight line and below the curve of the iliac crest (hipbone) (see Figure 6-10, *A*).

The *ventrogluteal site* can be made accessible with the client in a supine, prone (which is awkward), or sidelying position. This site is used for IM injections in either children or adults and could be used more often than it is. To locate it on the left side, the nurse should palpate for the left greater trochanter with the right palm, point the right index finger to the anterior superior iliac spine, and extend the middle finger toward the iliac crest. The injection should be made into the center of the V formed between the index and middle fingers (see Figure 6-10, *B*). The left hand is likewise used to detect landmarks in the right hip.

Either of the two gluteal sites is preferred for the **Z-track method,** an injection method useful for administration of medication known to cause pain or permanent staining of superficial tissues (see Figure 6-11).

The *mid-deltoid area* is the muscular area in the arm formed by the rectangle bounded on the top by the edge of the shoulder and on the bottom by the beginning of the

axilla (see Figure 6-10, *D*). The deltoid muscle has a considerably higher blood flow than the other IM injection sites and, for rapid onset, is the area of choice for many small-volume (2 ml or less) medications.

The *vastus lateralis* is a muscular area in the upper outer leg. The potential area for injection is a long rectangular area just lateral to the frontal plane of the thigh. Its top boundary is found about one handsbreadth below the greater trochanter, and the bottom boundary is about one handsbreadth above the knee (see Figure 6-10, *C*). This area can accommodate volumes of medication the same size as the gluteus medius and is distant from any major blood vessels or nerves, but injection here may be more painful than in the buttocks.

Relaxation and comfort may be enhanced during an IM injection into the gluteal muscles if the client lies in a prone position with a pillow under the legs just below the knees, and in a toes-in position (to relax the buttocks). The side-lying position is an alternative. To prevent local postinjection complications (such as discomfort, scars, abscesses), no two injections should be made in the same spot during a course of treatment. Injection sites should be rotated and the site for each intramuscular injection should be recorded on the clinical record. (See Figure 6-12).

For the IM injection, the needle and syringe assembly is held as if it were a dart while the other hand stretches taut the skin of the injection site. The nurse can test sensitivity of the area by tapping it with the fingers. If the muscle mass underlying the injection site is inadequate to accommodate the length of the needle, the flesh may instead be pinched

| INTRAMUSCULAR INJECTION RECORD | | 1 | 2 | 3 | 4 | 5 | 6 | 7 |
|---|---|---|---|---|---|---|---|---|
| Site | | 1 | 2 | 3 | 4 | 5 | 6 | 7 |
| Right arm | A | | | | | | | |
| Left arm | B | | | | | | | |
| Right thigh | C | | | | | | | |
| Left thigh | D | | | | | | | |
| Right buttock | E | | | | | | | |
| Left buttock | F | | | | | | | |

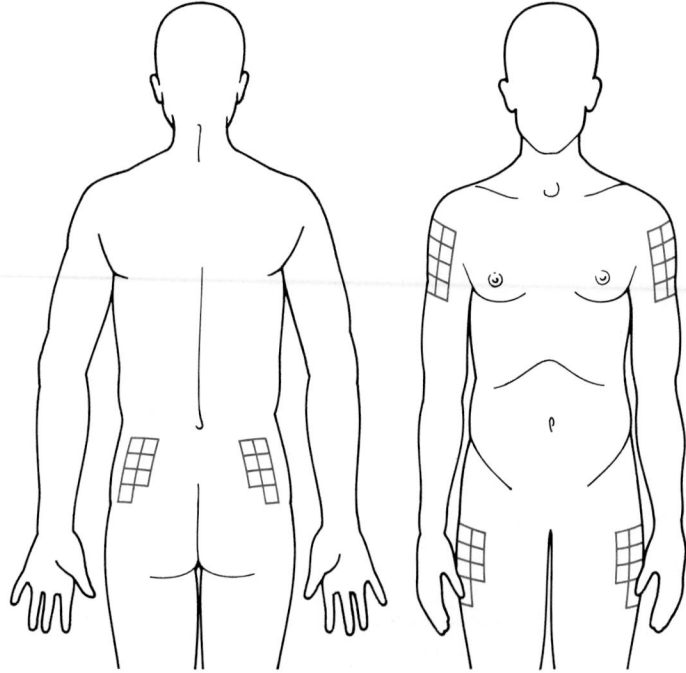

**FIGURE 6-12** Anatomic chart for the rotation of intramuscular injections. The chart may be kept with the MAR, nursing Kardex, or care plan to provide a reference for the nurse administering medications.

up before needle insertion. The injection should be made *perpendicular to the skin surface,* from a distance of about 2 inches, in one quick motion. If possible, the needle should not be inserted to its full depth and a small portion of needle should be left accessible above the skin so that the needle might be retrieved should it break, a very rare event. It is necessary to make certain that the needle is not in a blood vessel, thus causing the unintended deposit of medication into the bloodstream instead of muscle tissue (also very unusual). This is ascertained by pulling out the plunger *slightly* after the needle is in place in tissue (termed "aspiration"). A slight pinkish tinge to the medication may be seen close to the needle hub or a small amount of blood may enter the barrel of the syringe, if the needle is in a blood vessel rather than in tissue. If this is the case, needle and medication-filled syringe should be withdrawn and discarded before continuing. In certain instances injection of oily or particulate medicines or killed bacteria by such an inadvertent IV administration could result in a serious emergency.

Contrary to popular belief, needle puncture of the skin is not always the prime source of discomfort associated with injections, although a dull needle such as one inserted through a vial's rubber stopper will certainly contribute to pain. Also, it is not the length of the needle that causes pain, but the diameter; a 3-inch needle will hurt no more than a ⅝-inch one if the diameter is similar. Except for the psychologic aspect of anxiety about needles, most injection pain is thought to occur from stretching of tissue (pain

receptors in the skin) as it accommodates the volume of the drug; from irritation from the drug itself; from unsteadiness in the injector's technique, which results in jiggling of the needle during overly slow insertions; during aspiration; while the injector is reaching for the antiseptic swab at completion; or from wet antiseptic on the skin during insertion. Firm pressure applied to the needle-tissue juncture with an antiseptic swab will prevent discomfort as the needle is withdrawn. Massaging the site (except after heparin, iron dextran products, and others) acts to disperse the medication and may also reduce any discomfort.

*Intravenous (IV).* When an immediate effect is desired, when for any reason a drug cannot be injected into other tissues, or when absorption may be inhibited by poor circulation, the drug may be given directly into a vein as an *injection* or as an *infusion.* The technique of this method requires skill and asepsis, and the drug must be highly soluble and capable of withstanding sterilization. This method is of great value in emergencies. The dose and amount of absorption can be determined with accuracy. However, the rapidity of absorption and the fact that there is no recall once the drug has been given constitute dangers worthy of consideration. From this standpoint it is one of the least safe methods of administration. Precautions must be taken to prevent extravasation of drug or fluids into surrounding tissue (**infiltration**).

In **IV injection** ("IV push") a comparatively small amount of solution (also referred to as a bolus) is given by means of a syringe into IV tubing, into a heparin lock, or directly

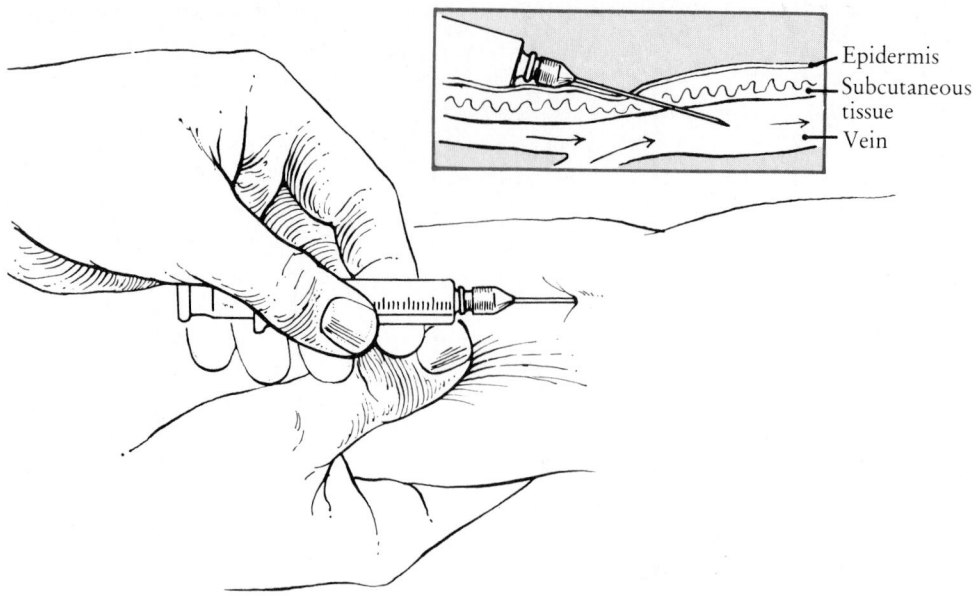

Epidermis
Subcutaneous tissue
Vein

**FIGURE 6-13**   Intravenous injection. The skin has been cleansed with a solution of alcohol. Thumb of right hand holds the skin taut. Withdrawal of blood indicates needle is in the vein. Solution is injected slowly and steadily.

into a vein over a 1- to 7-minute period. The drug is dissolved in a suitable amount of normal (physiologic) saline solution or some other isotonic solution. The injection is usually made into the median basilic or median cephalic vein at the bend of the elbow (Figure 6-13). However, another large accessible vein may be used. Factors that determine the choice of vein for IV therapy are related to the thickness of the skin over the vein, the closeness of the vein to the surface, the presence of a firm support (bone) under the vein, and the need to use a larger vein for concentrated or irritating substances. The veins in the antecubital fossa are readily accessible, although the veins of the back of the hand are also sometimes used for infusions. Leg veins are avoided because of their potential for phlebitis.

A vein that is normally distended with blood is much easier to enter than a partially collapsed one. A tourniquet is drawn tightly around the extremity proximal to the IV site to distend the vein, the air is expelled from the syringe, and the needle is introduced pointing proximally, bevel up. A few drops of blood aspirated into the syringe indicate that the needle is in the vein; the tourniquet is then removed and the solution injected slowly. As in all types of injections, the needle, syringe, and solution must be sterile; hands must be scrupulously washed, and antiseptic must be applied to the insertion site and allowed to dry. An IV bolus dose is the method of choice for rapidly administering drugs in an emergency because it is a reliable way to achieve optimal drug blood levels rapidly. It is also the way to administer certain IV medications that may be incompatible in solution: digoxin, diazepam, furosemide, diazoxide, certain anticancer drugs, and diagnostic agents in dye form. A 20-gauge

needle is commonly used for IV push or bolus doses.

Many drugs given intravenously must be given slowly to avoid cardiac, neurologic, or respiratory changes. Only drugs for which the nurse knows the dosage rate should be given IV, to avoid a potentially fatal problem.

In **IV infusion,** a larger amount of fluid is given, usually starting with 1 L. The solution flows by gravity from a graduated glass bottle or plastic bag through tubing, connecting tip, and needle or catheter into a vein. Or it may be infused with an IV controller or pump.

Infusions are most commonly given to relieve tissue dehydration, to restore depleted blood volume, to dilute toxic substances in the blood and tissue fluids, to supply electrolytes or drugs, to provide an IV line if an emergency is anticipated, or to provide a fluid challenge to evaluate kidney function.

The fluid is usually given slowly to prevent reaction or fluid overload, which may impair cardiac or pulmonary function, especially in elderly clients or those with cardiac disease. Ordinarily 8 hours are required for every 1000 ml of fluid, depending on the condition of the client and the nature of and reason for the solution. For children the rate will be slower and is determined by age, weight, and urinary output.

See Unit 18 for discussion of various IV infusion solutions and parenteral nutrition, and Chapter 30 for discussion of blood products.

A number of commercial solutions are used in IV replacement therapy. Some solutions contain not only salts of sodium and potassium but also salts of calcium and magnesium. Vitamins are also added to IV fluids when necessary.

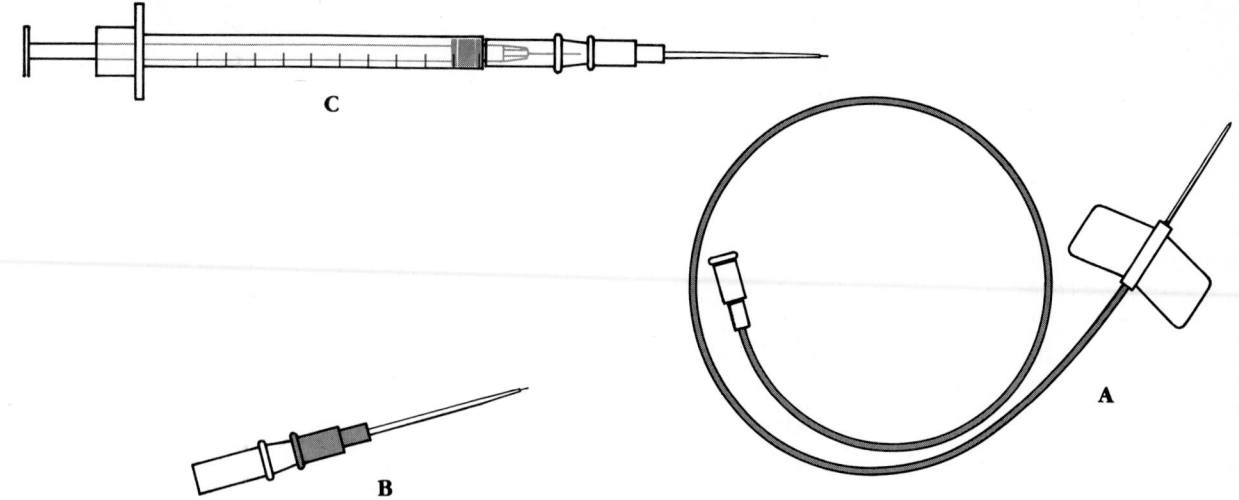

**FIGURE 6-14** IV needles. **A,** Butterfly needle. **B,** Over-needle catheter. **C,** Cannula (through-the-needle catheter).

Total parenteral nutrition (TPN) or hyperalimentation is the infusion of an individual's total basic nutritional needs via an infusion catheter into a large central vein and/or into a peripheral one. The choice of site depends partly on the phlebitis-causing potential of the medium. Fat emulsions have a much lower potential for causing phlebitis than hypertonic dextrose solutions used for TPN.

Whole blood and blood products are likewise given intravenously to restore depleted blood volume as well as constituents of the blood. Blood products should be introduced through IV tubing that has been primed with a normal saline infusion solution rather than dextrose solution, which would cause "stickiness" of red blood cells, causing them to clump artificially, possibly clogging the needle or causing hemolysis. Insertion of an 18-gauge or larger needle when blood products are expected to be infused will help minimize trauma to cells. Tubing should also be of the sort that incorporates a filter to trap cell particles and clumped cells to prevent them from circulating or clogging the needle.

Some drugs, such as antibiotics, are administered by **intermittent infusion** (known as "IV piggyback" [IVPB] or "IV rider" in some parts of the United States). They are given via a setup that is secondary to the primary IV infusion and that is hung in tandem and connected to the primary setup.

Most intermittent diluted drug infusions are meant to have a total infusion time of 20 or 30 minutes to 1 hour, depending on factors such as package insert instructions related to the amount of diluent required and the potential for vein wall irritation by the drug. Again, references for more detailed information can be found at the end of this chapter.

Particulate matter (which can consist of tiny chunks of rubber stoppers or glass slivers from ampules) in IV infusion solutions is disturbingly common. It can be introduced during manufacture, during changing of the solution bottle, or

during administration of a medication. One study showed that all twelve antibiotic injectables tested contained extraneous particles. The resulting potential for phlebitis is high. It is recommended that in-line filtering devices be used for all IV therapy. Optimal filtration is provided by 0.22-μm filters; most organisms, except certain strains of *Pseudomonas* and the viruses, are filtered out by 0.45-μm in-line filters. To prevent injection of larger particles, disposable needles with 5-μm filters can be used to draw medication up.

Stainless steel scalp-vein needles ("butterfly needles") produce lower rates of infection and phlebitis, but plastic catheters (over-needle catheters) or cannulaes (through-the-needle catheters) tend to decrease the incidence of infiltration and work best when an infusion needle will be in place for a long period (see Figure 6-14). Advantages and disadvantages must be weighed at the time of insertion. (See Table 6-6.)

IV devices that are inserted only by a physician are the subclavian through-the-needle catheter and the Hickman catheter. The subclavian through-the-needle catheter (12 inches or 30 cm) is used when poor venous access prohibits the use of peripheral veins or when irritating solutions must be infused directly into a large central vein to avoid phlebitis. The Hickman catheter is implanted surgically and is utilized for long-term IV therapy.

Although starting infusions and drawing blood were traditionally the duty of physicians, many nurses today perform these functions, especially in critical care areas. Probably one of the most effective approaches is the preparation of IV teams whose sole job is to maintain, remove, and replace IV needles, catheters, and so forth. However, such teams may prove to be a mixed blessing; even though they become very proficient at their job, they also may serve to further fragment a client's care.

**TABLE 6-6**   Intravenous needles in common use by nurses

| IV needle | Length of needle | Length of tubing | Indication |
|---|---|---|---|
| Wing-tip or scalp-vein needle (E-Z Set or Butterfly) | ½ to 1¼ in (1.3 to 3.1 cm) | 3 to 12 in (7.5 to 30 cm) | Client in stable condition; IV fluids or medications of short duration; intermittent IV push injections, indefinite period of time |
| Over-the-needle catheter (Abbocath, Jelco, or Angiocath) | Varies | 1¼ to 5½ in (3.1 to 13.8 cm); 1¼ to 2 in (3.1 to 5 cm) most commonly used | Client in unstable condition (needs large volume replacement); only available veins are poor; caustic medications to be administered |
| Through-the-needle catheter (Intracath) | 1½ to 2 in (3.8 to 5 cm) | 8 to 36 in (20 to 90 cm) | Client has poor venous access; long-term IV therapy; extremely caustic medications (continuous chemotherapy, total parenteral nutrition) |

Table 6-7 lists data to assess for IV needle site complications and suggests concomitant nursing interventions.

*Intrathecal.* Intrathecal (into a sheath) injection is also known as intraspinal, subdural, subarachnoid, or lumbar injection. The technique is the same as that required for a lumbar puncture. Nurses do not usually directly administer drugs intraspinally. However, the filling of a drug reservoir of an implanted intraspinal delivery system may be required. Special training of the nurse is needed, and the manufacturer's instructions should be followed closely.

•  •  •

In addition, drugs are occasionally administered by intracardiac, intrapericardial, intraperitoneal, intraarticular and intraosseous injections; however, institutional policy may not allow nurses to administer drugs by these routes.

### Psychiatric Clients and Special Situations

**Psychiatric clients.** Giving medicines to a psychiatric client may assume pronounced symbolic meanings. Meaningful interpersonal relationships are generally found outside medical situations. Psychiatric clients, however, frequently are unable to develop such relationships and look to health care providers for security and affection. Even then, their emotional deprivation may be concealed by an appearance of hostility or disdain.

In addition, immediate personal needs of the client and their current symptoms will influence the situation. Overwhelming anxiety, depression to the point of suicide, pain of an uncanny nature, or distortions of thought that constantly separate the client from others demand of the nurse much care in any contact. To the individual in a state of psychologic disequilibrium, that which is taken by mouth

or given by injection may hold threats and symbolic meanings rarely noted by other clients. The fear of poisons or supernatural effects of capsules or the suggestions of witchcraft ascribed to a needle often reach a high degree unless the nurse is able to understand the client's concerns and respond appropriately. The psychiatric clients' tendency toward impulsiveness and increased emotional sensitivity must constantly be kept in mind. The complexity and subtle implications inherent in administering medications to psychiatric clients make strong and persistent demands on professional nursing awareness, wisdom, and judgment. Although very successfully employed otherwise, nursing aides or mental health aides unlicensed as registered nurses are in a perilously unsafe position if they administer medications to psychiatric clients.

No practical suggestions can take the place of the techniques practiced by the psychiatric nurse, but the following factors should be considered in the general handling of medications for the psychiatric client:

1. Drugs for use in emergencies must be anticipated and readily available.
2. Medicines should be given in paper, not glass, containers. The psychiatric client is often so impulsive that all possible precautions must be taken to avoid accidents, and glass is always a potential suicide weapon.
3. Precautions should be used whenever drugs are administered or stored.
4. *The nurse must remain with the client until oral medications have been swallowed.* This principle is basic in the giving of all medications but of particular importance to the depressed and suicidal client; such individuals may conceal capsules in the mouth for long periods, only to hoard them until a lethal

**TABLE 6-7**   Common intravenous needle site complications

| Needle site data | Infiltration | Clot over needle opening or obstruction | Phlebitis | Infection at site of needle insertion |
|---|---|---|---|---|
| Color | Pale | No change | Red | Red over site |
| Temperature | Cool to cold | No change | Warm to hot | Warm at site |
| Swelling | Rounded | None | Cordlike vein path | Small amount at site |
| Pain | Yes, usually | None | Yes | None usually |
| Flow | Slowed or stopped | Slowed or stopped | No change or may be slowed | No change |
| Nursing actions | Tourniquet proximally (flow continues—infiltration)<br><br>Lower bottle (blood in tubing—no infiltration)<br><br>Discontinue IV<br><br>Call IV team<br><br>Get order for warm compresses and elevate part | Check for infiltration<br><br>Reposition arm<br><br>Raise IV container, close clamp, coil tubing, release quickly<br><br>Call IV team | Discontinue IV *usually* Call IV team<br><br>Note irritating solution (Valium, Keflin, KCl running too fast)<br><br>Warm compresses; elevate and immobilize part | Do not discontinue IV until IV team advice has been sought or physician has been notified (it may be the only vein available for essential infusion) |

supply has been accumulated. Frequently, measures such as piercing the capsule case and staying with the client until the drug is dissolved or using liquid preparations will ensure the actual ingestion of the drug.

5. It is often necessary not only to urge psychiatric clients to take medication but also to insist on its acceptance. The psychiatric client is frequently an indecisive, emotionally confused individual who tends to doubt everything. These clients often press the nurse for detailed information about a drug prescribed and frequently rebel because of minor discrepancies in information. Paradoxically, however, they comply quickly if a positive yet interested attitude is demonstrated without undue explanation.

6. It is of utmost importance to report all drug refusals to the prescriber in charge. In the meantime it is frequently also important to persuade the client to take the medicine. Omission of doses may cause the blood level of psychotropic drugs to be lowered so that larger doses than usual may eventually be needed. IM administration of psychotropic drugs assists in calming the client within a relatively short period of time, so that oral preparations may then be given. The oral route of administration is preferred and should be reinstituted as soon as possible.

### Special situations

*Swallowing difficulty.*   The following suggestions are for clients who have difficulty swallowing oral medications. If the cause is a diminished swallow reflex, however, the drug should be given by another route after consultation with the prescriber.

1. Have the client drink some water *just before* taking the medication and drink only a small amount *with* the medication. *Following* the drug, at least 100 ml of liquid should be taken.

Clients are capable of taking fluids more easily if they are in Fowler's position (upright sitting position).

2. Instruct the client to place the tablet at the midpoint of the tongue and toss it back to the throat with the water. For the hemiplegic client, place the tablet on the unaffected side of the tongue for swallowing.

If the head is tipped slightly forward, the act of swallowing follows more naturally; choking is more likely when the head is tilted back. Initiation of the mechanical act of swallowing may be facilitated by massaging the laryngeal prominence (Adam's apple) or the area just under the chin.

Medications may be crushed (except enteric-coated or sustained-action forms), or capsules may be opened and contents sprinkled on a small portion of easy-to-swallow food such as applesauce or gelatin desserts. The client should be told about this procedure and instructed to eat the medicated contents first so that very little remains unadministered if the rest is refused. This approach for children should be used cautiously, since the particular food may be rendered distasteful and be rejected by the child in the future.

Medications may be liquefied for drinking by the addition of water, or they may be administered by instillation into the mouth next to the cheek by a large syringe with or without a short tubing attached.

*Suggestions for clients with a tracheostomy tube in place.*   The tube should have a cuff, and it should be inflated whenever any substance is taken by mouth, in order to prevent it from accidentally entering the lungs. If there is an external attachment in place to allow the patient to talk, a T-piece should be substituted. After the medication has been swallowed, the cuff is deflated after suctioning is performed.

*Suggestions for administering medications to clients with a nasogastric (NG) or gastrostomy tube.* Follow the procedure for administering tube feedings, with these additional precautions.

1. Check placement of the tube before giving medications or tube feedings.
2. Give medications and tube feedings at separate intervals in case the stomach contents must be aspirated or the tube irrigated later.
3. Assess for potential drug-food interactions (penicillin G and most tetracyclines) if you must administer drugs with a feeding, just as you would with any oral drugs. See Chapter 3 for cautions about tablet crushing. If appropriate, a paste made with a few drops of mineral oil added to the crushed tablets, then mixed with water and instilled down the tube, is thought to keep the drug from sticking to the tube.
4. Crush and administer the medication first, before the feeding; flush the tubing before and after the medication to prevent the drug from sticking to the inside of the tube.
5. Afterward, position the client upright and turned slightly to the left side if the medication is for local effect in the stomach (e.g., antacids) and should remain there for a time.

## Preventing and Reporting Errors

It may help to be aware of some of the pitfalls with regard to medication administration. The accompanying box recounts actual errors related to medication administration to call attention to some common but careless nursing acts.

To prevent medication administration errors, the following guidelines should be observed:

1. Question the calculations or order if it appears that multiple tablets or several vials are necessary to prepare a single dose.
2. Carefully read all labels for *all* the "Five Rights," including the drug's name—the pharmacist can make a mistake, too, by sending the wrong medication.
3. Be wary about ambiguous orders or drug names, or drug names that include numerals. Consult with the prescriber if in doubt.
4. Be alert to unusually large dosages or excessive increases in dosages ordered.
5. When in doubt, check the order with the prescriber, a pharmacist, and the literature. Check even simple calculations with a peer.
6. Double-check with an allergic client about all new drugs as they are added to the treatment plan.
7. Routinely refer to drug interaction charts. Commit common interactive drugs to memory.
8. Question the use of nonstandard abbreviations and symbols; do not use them yourself.
9. Read the package insert carefully for specific instructions when giving a drug for the first time.
10. Do not use slang names or colloquialisms that may be unfamiliar to others.
11. Do not decipher illegible orders or make assumptions. Do not accept incomplete orders. Obtain a clear copy from the prescriber.

---

### ERRORS IN MEDICATION ADMINISTRATION

1. Not knowing why a medication was to be administered caused one nurse to irrigate a client's bladder with a topical astringent-antiinflammatory agent, Burow's solution, instead of the genitourinary antibiotic irrigant distributed by a manufacturer of a similar name. In another instant this caused another nurse to delay giving a dose of medication essential to recuperation after cancer chemotherapy because she believed it to be "just a vitamin" instead of folinic acid.
2. Not identifying clients by their arm bands caused several nurses to give medication to the wrong individuals in the right beds. One of the nurses even asked a client his name, which turned out to be similar to another client's. One nurse called out her client's name, and the wrong person responded. The result was the same—they all got the wrong medication.
3. Not checking with the prescribing physician caused one nurse to give her patient 30 ml of milk of magnesia every hour rather than every night because she misinterpreted the "qn" (an unacceptable abbreviation) order for "qh". Another nurse gave 2.5 mg of digoxin instead of 0.25 mg; although the order was wrong, the nurse did not recognize that it was excessive. The result was that the client received a toxic dose of medication.

---

12. Do not accept verbal or telephone orders except in an emergency. Nursing students should refer such requests to other practicing staff nurses.
13. Question a drug form used in an unfamiliar way (e.g., suspensions are usually given orally; an IV drug form ordered to be administered by feeding tube).
14. Question an unusual single order containing more than one drug.
15. Mistakes seem to breed other errors. It is axiomatic that when one thing goes wrong in a client's care, other mishaps follow inexorably. No one knows why.
16. Stay alert! Question! Learn!

In a large Michigan hospital, medication errors accounted for almost 41% of the incidents with potential for a lawsuit. Nursing errors accounted for 65% of these medication errors. Wrong dosage headed the list. Many computer programs for updating dosage calculation skills now exist, and more are on the way. Innumerable helpful instructional materials, including programmed learning texts, are available; some are listed at the end of the chapter. All personnel who, as part of their jobs, must calculate dosages should be alert for gaps in their mathematical competence. To double-check calculations with others when uncertain and to maintain proficiency by practice are practical, professionally necessary actions. This assumes another essential step: that all calculations are *written down* on paper to be checked.

To err is human. However, to admit its possibility and one's susceptibility is essential. To safeguard one's client as well as one's reputation and psyche, the first step in a suspected medication error is to backtrack to double-check one's actions or computations to see if an error occurred. Next is the step requiring the most accountability: to consult one's instructor or superior to inform him or her and to gain perspective and objective support. The client's prescriber should also be informed. Actions to correct drug effects and to normalize the client's condition follow. Precise, objective documentation of the event and the circumstances is made both on the chart and on a special form, the incident report. This report is an intraagency communication that is analyzed by the agency's risk management personnel to develop procedures for preventing the same or similar incidents.

## Client Teaching

Updating clients and keeping them informed about their treatment and other necessary information should be an ongoing activity that occurs naturally during any interaction with clients. Teaching should be a part of the plan in any nursing process. It may be a formal plan (e.g., a diabetic teaching program), or it may be a simple impromptu discussion based on a question the client raises.

Although teaching-learning interactions between client and nurse are among the most necessary and professionally demanding, teaching clients is not as visible as bathing them, taking their vital signs, or giving them injections. When it is done, it may not be seen as important enough to be noted in nursing progress notes. However, success in client learning has a direct bearing on success in convalescence at home. Strong rationales for teaching clients come from the many state nurse practice acts that define teaching as a necessary part of nursing, thereby giving it the power of a state mandate: one could be sued for not teaching clients. Accreditation committees recognize the importance of client teaching and look for documentation when they visit. Thus the resistance of other disciplines to client teaching by nurses is becoming less of an issue than it was in the past. Studies show that nurses actively engage in discussions about medications: 66% discuss them with physicians at least once a week, and 85% discuss them with clients monthly; 95% of the clients followed nurses' recommendations and passed them along to others.*

Basic to any learning are the following tenets:

1. Clients must be ready to learn. If they are in pain, about to be discharged, or emotionally upset, they will be too distracted to assimilate information.
2. The atmosphere must be conducive to learning. Privacy, some quiet, and a rapport between the nurse and the client that is facilitated by understanding of cultural or personal differences all aid the dynamics of learning.
3. Information must be presented at the level of clients' under-

standing. The nurse should find out what they already know and start from there.
4. Information should be presented beginning with the simple and building to the complex. Too much too fast will overwhelm clients. A good starting place is responding to a client's questions. The goal is to meet the client's learning needs, *not* the nurse's need to teach.
5. Learning and motivation will be enhanced by rewarding positive behavior. For example, relief of pain after clients put into use new learning will be its own reward; sometimes verbal rewards, such as a compliment on performing a procedure well, can be effective motivation.
6. Active participation should be encouraged at each step.
7. Specific feedback from clients is necessary to evaluate if learning has taken place. It is not enough just to "tell" clients over and over again. Return demonstration is perhaps the best way to evaluate the degree of success achieved in teaching.

Clients need to learn the following about their medications: the names of the medications (write them down), what they are for and how to recognize the proper effects (in very specific ways), some of the major secondary effects (expected and tolerable, and those representing toxicity), what to do if they miss a dose, how to store the medication, how to take it (e.g., with meals), and whom to call if there is a problem. It can be expected that clients will forget many of the instructions; a printed fact sheet or checklist to take home will be helpful to many clients and should augment the verbal explanation. Chapter 10, "Client Teaching for Self-medication of Medications" discusses this essential role of nursing in greater detail.

## Recording Drug Administration

Recording the administration of each dose of medication as soon as possible after it is given leaves a documented record if there is any question as to whether the client received the dose. Otherwise, the client may inadvertently receive a second dose from another nurse or nursing student. The busy nurse who "double-pours" (prepares two doses at one time—an illegal practice) may also be tempted to record the second dose at the same time the first dose is recorded. Medications should not be recorded (charted) before they are actually given, because something may come up to prevent that dose from being administered. Then the medication record, which is a legal document, will have to be corrected carefully and perhaps an incident report filed.

Several different forms are used to record medications for each client. These forms usually include areas to note each medication name, date, dose, route, and time, and the administering nurse's initials (see Figure 6-1). Extra notations may be added in certain instances. For example, when digitalis is given, the apical and radial pulses taken just before administration may be noted ("AP, 78; RP, 76"). If the pulses are found to be outside the normal limits established by that agency, the medication should not be given, the record should be marked "held" and initialed, and the prescriber should be consulted. Clients also have the right to refuse treatment, including medications, and sometimes do, despite explanations. "Refused" is then noted in the appropriate spot on the medication record, with the reason for the client's refusal. Medication may also be recorded as "discarded" or "wasted" if only part of it was administered and the rest had to be discarded (as in a prefilled syringe), or if the medication was dropped or contaminated. If the medication is a controlled substance, its disposal must be witnessed and initialed in the special record for this drug.

Routine (or continuous) daily medications usually are recorded on one type of form. Once-only, loading dosages, prn medications, and stat medications should be recorded on the same MAR. Administration of a controlled substance is recorded both on the prn medication sheet and on that particular drug's sheet (which includes a running tally of the balance of the controlled substance). A notation should usually be made in the progress notes on the client's chart relating to the assessment of the need for the administration of any prn medication and the client's response to its effects.

Potential for error in drug administration is almost limitless. Some mistakes of significance can be rectified if discovered and acted on quickly. Also, if an error was properly reported and appropriate actions were taken, courts tend to look more kindly on the nurse than if these were not done. Courts generally recognize the humanness of people, including nurses, and recognize the potential for error in clinical practice.

## EVALUATION

Evaluation is the completing step in the nursing process, which facilitates the delivery of high-quality nursing care in regard to pharmacotherapeutics. While planning nursing care and establishing goals, the nurse determines what kind of evaluation will take place and when and how it will be done. Clear and specifically stated goals make it easy to determine whether the intended outcomes have been achieved, or the degree of achievement. Evaluation includes both subjective and objective data. When evaluating the nursing care for a client undergoing drug therapy, the nurse looks at several areas:

1. Therapeutic response to the drug
2. Secondary or unwanted effects
3. Compliance/self-medication with accuracy
4. Learning

In evaluating therapeutic response, the nurse must have a clear understanding of the therapeutic goals. Evaluation may center on a reduction of symptoms, decreased frequency of attacks, enhanced organ function, elimination of infection, or a multitude of other goals. Evaluation looks for a drug's therapeutic response, but it is also directed toward detection of *any* response that may be attributed to the drug. An awareness of the pharmacology of the drug used and potential effects guides this evaluation. **Compli-**

ance refers to following the prescribed regimen correctly. In the hospital setting, evaluation may look at nursing care (was the drug administered in the correct dose and at the right time, with appropriate precautions?), while evaluation of outpatients is directed toward the client. Research indicates that at least one fourth of all outpatients fail to follow prescribed drug therapy correctly. Finally, the nurse will have to determine if educational goals are being met. Often, clients can report back what they have been told, yet be unable to apply this knowledge. Asking hypothetical questions and observing return demonstrations are helpful techniques for evaluation of learning.

In addition to the evaluation by the individual nurse or nursing team of the client's progress toward the goals and expected outcomes of nursing care, health care agencies also evaluate the process of medication administration, in general, as an important aspect of nursing care provided by that agency. Standards by which to evaluate care are developed from within the health care organization and may also be suggested by external organizations. The Joint Commission on Accreditation of Healthcare Organizations (JCAHO) is an organization that offers voluntary accreditation to health care agencies throughout the United States based on standards that are "recognized as representing a contemporary national consensus on quality patient care that reflects changing health care practices and current health care delivery trends" (JCAHO, 1990). Within the JCAHO standards for nursing services regarding policies and procedures, guidelines are set forth concerning medication administration in an effort to ensure safe nursing practice. They stipulate that the nursing department or service of a health care organization have policies and procedures to govern medication administration and that these "should specify, in accordance with applicable law and regulation and pertinent medical staff rules and regulations, who may give orders for drugs; who may accept verbal orders for drugs and when the orders must be authenticated by the prescribing practitioner; who may verify orders for drugs and how this must occur; who may supervise the administration of medications; and who may administer these medications, which medications they may administer, and how these individuals are to be supervised, if necessary (JCAHO, 1986). These policies and procedures serve to protect both client and nurse by setting forward the roles and responsibilities of all the members of the health team for the administration of medications. Nursing practice can then be evaluated to determine whether the care provided to clients was in keeping with the agency's policies and procedures.

The American Society for Hospital Pharmacists (1982) has also suggested indicators for evaluating the administration of medications as part of the nursing **quality assurance** process.

1. The drug is administered in the ordered dose.
2. The drug is administered by the ordered route.

3. The drug is administered by the ordered site.
4. The drug is administered at the ordered rate.
5. The drug is administered in the ordered drug form.
6. The drug is administered by the ordered schedule.
7. The drug is administered using the correct technique.

These indicators may be incorporated into a process of monitoring and evaluation by which nursing professionals examine the care they provide, determine possibilities for improvement of their practice, and take necessary action.

## SUMMARY

The implementation phase of the nursing process with regard to drug therapy begins when the nurse takes action to attain the goals established as described in Chapter 5. Nursing interventions are directed at the actual administration of drugs, which includes the preparatory steps as well as the subsequent recording of drug administration.

The traditional Five Rights—to ensure the right client, the right medication, the right route, the right dose, and the right time—are still reliable criteria for competent, safe, and individualized medication administration. So that nurses who are eager to provide high-quality care might have some of their penetrating questions answered, some of the theoretical bases for selection of drug dosages and dosing intervals have been included in this chapter. Examples have been presented of typical kinds of dosage calculations that sometimes challenge nurses, even those who have been practicing for a long time. Answers and explanations have also been included. Common drug routes and sites have been detailed and illustrated. Specialized and personalized nursing care of the psychiatric client, incorporating basic tenets of comfort, dignity, honesty, and patience when medications are given, has been discussed. Special helps have been presented for medication administration to those with a tracheostomy or nasogastric tube.

Evaluation of nursing functions in medication administration includes a critique of one's own techniques, but it is not limited to that. The environment should be made conducive to high-quality care by the nurse's efforts toward thoughtful and safe medication administration. Enough time must be set aside, and double-checking of calculations should be routine. Careful identification of clients is essential to ensure that the right person receives the medication as intended. Since nurses are in the position of being on the client care scene and taking care of clients as no one else does, they are uniquely placed to detect even subtle secondary drug effects, interactions, or incompatibilities.

Prevention of errors in medication administration is crucially important to nurses, since it is an area fraught with much potential for irreversible harm to clients. Alert attention to all of the details of medication administration, including client comments, must be maintained so that safety is not abridged and clients obtain the most beneficial effects of the drugs they take. Recording a drug dose is the final act of communication; it signifies that the drug was given and assures accountability by the nurse who "signs for it."

In short, the actual act of administering medications—the implementation or intervention phase of the nursing process—demands a solid knowledge base, well-practiced skills, commitment to continuous learning, and intense, unremitting concentration to sustain the best interests of the client. Potential for error is rife; medication administration cannot be a casual act or the risk will escalate.

Evaluation of therapeutic effects, secondary effects, compliance with the prescribed regimen, and client learning follows the implementation phase of the nursing process. It allows the nurse to determine if goals were met and measures the effectiveness of nursing care.

## BIBLIOGRAPHY

American Society for Hospital Pharmacists (ASHP). (1982). ASHP standard definition of a medication error, Am J Hosp Pharm 39:321.

Anderson K and Poole C. (1983). Self-administered medication on a postpartum unit, Am J Nurs 83(8):1178.

Bailey-Allen AM. (1987). The legal aspects of medications, Orthop Nurs 6(1):65.

Bickal T. (1987). A protocol for the diagnosis and treatment of extrapyramidal symptoms of neuroleptic drugs, Nurs Pract 12(1):25.

Brandt M et al. (1988). A severity index for medication errors, Nurs Manage 19(8):80 I.

Brim S. (1989). A quick guide for home use of inhalant medications, Pediatr Nurs 15(1):87.

Brown CS et al. (1987). Association between type of medication instruction and patients' knowledge, side effects, and compliance, H & CP 38(1):55.

Brubakken KM. (1989). Preoperative antibiotic administration: a case for interdisciplinary monitoring, J Nurs Qual Assur 3(2):69.

Carr DS. (1989). New strategies for avoiding medication errors, Nursing 19(8):38.

Caserta JE. (1987). It's a jumble—no; it's a maze—no; it's your client's medication shelf . . . medication management in the home, Home Health Nurse 5(1):1.

Chaplin G et al. (1985). How safe is the air bubble technique for IM injections?, Nursing '85 15(9):59.

Clayton M. (1987). The right way to prevent medication errors, RN 50(6):30.

Conti A et al. (1988). Performance on a mathematics/drug calculation test: relationship to subsequent reported medication errors, J Nurs Staff Dev 4(2):54.

Cooper JW. (1987). Drug-related problems in nursing homes: medication errors, Nurs Homes 36(2):13.

Cox MB. (1987). Medication errors: what level of risk is acceptable? Nurse Patient Law, June, p 1.

Davidhizar RE. (1987). Beliefs, feelings and insight of patients with schizophrenia about taking medication, J Adv Nurs 12(2):177.

Davis NM et al. (1987). Learning from mistakes: medication errors to avoid, Nursing 17(5):84.

DeMonaco HJ. (1988). IV drug delivery: new technologies for consideration, J Intravenous Nurs 11(5):316.

Fuqua RA et al. (1988). What we know about medication errors: a literature review, J Nurs Qual Assur 3(1):1.

Gardner C. (1987). Risk management of medication errors. I. NITA 10(3):187.

Gardner C. (1987). Risk management of medication errors. II. NITA 10(4):266.

Gilman A et al. (1990). Goodman & Gilman's The pharmacological basis of therapeutics, ed 8. New York: Macmillan Publishing Co.

Girotti MJ et al. (1987). Medication administration errors in an adult intensive care unit, Heart Lung 16(4):449.

Green LM. (1987). Calculation of dosage and infusion rate in continuous intravenous medication, J Post Anesth Nurs 2(3):210.

Harnden L. (1988). Disciplinary responses to nurses' medication errors, Dimen Health Serv 65(4):26.

Henrietta G. (1987). Lab tests you can't overlook, Nursing 17(3):48.

Henrietta G. (1987). Lab tests you can't overlook . . . certain drugs can cause physiologic problems. I. Nursing 17(2):56.

Hull RL. (1987). Prospective changes in drug administration, Nursing 17(1):54.

Implement program to control medication errors. (1988). Hosp Risk Manage 10(7):92.

Joint Commission on Accreditation of Healthcare Organizations. (1990). Committed to quality: an introduction to the joint commission on accreditation of healthcare organizations, Oakbrook Terrace, Ill: The Commission.

Joint Commission on Accreditation of Hospitals. (1986). A guide to JCAH nursing services standards. Chicago: The Commission.

Koska MT. (1989). Quality watch. Drug errors: dangerous, costly and avoidable, Hospitals 63(11):24.

Manthey M. (1989). Just what are doctors' orders anyway?, Nurs Manage 20(1):26.

McCort BA. (1987). Nursing math—no problem!, AD Nurse 2(5):14.

McGovern K. (1988). 10 golden rules for administering drugs safely, Nursing 18(8):34.

McNeilly JL. (1987). Medication errors: a quality assurance tool, Nurs Manage 18(12):53.

Mooney MA. (1987). Use of adult education principles in medication instruction . . . what do registered nurses know, J Contin Educ Nurs 18(3):89.

National Bureau of Standards, US Department of Commerce. (1977). The international system of units (SI), Special Pub No 330.

Nortridge JA. Calculating IV medications with confidence, Nursing 17(9):55.

Oriol MD et al. (1986). Involuntary commitment and the right to refuse medication, J Pyschosoc Nurs Ment Health Serv 24(11):15.

Pauca AL. (1988). Constant-rate drug infusions: two methods of preparation, AANA J 56(6):537.

Peck KR et al. (1988). Intraosseous infusions: an old technique with modern applications, Pediatr Nurs 14(4):296.

Pelletier LR et al. (1988). Method of medication administration: effect on error rates, J Nurs Adm 18(4):29.

Perry AG and Potter PA. (1990). Clinical nursing skills and techniques: basic, intermediate and advanced, ed 2. St Louis: Mosby–Year Book, Inc.

Pill-swallowing maneuver. (1987). Consultant 27(10):55.

Poster EC et al. (1988). Primary versus functional medication administration: monitoring and evaluating medication error rates, J Nurs Qual Assur 2(2):68.

Potter PA and Perry AG. (1989). Fundamentals of nursing, ed 2. St Louis: The CV Mosby Co.

Pullar T et al. (1989). Patients' knowledge concerning their medications on discharge from hospital, J Clin Pharm Ther 14(1):57.

Rasic E et al. (1989). A new system for managing medication errors, Nurs Manage 20(5):102.

Saunders A et al. (1988). Mixing premedication drugs in the syringe, Aust Nurses J 17(9):38.

Sesin P et al. (1987). New England Deaconesss guidelines for the administration of IV drugs. III. NITA 10(3):224.

Sesin P et al. (1987). New England Deaconess guidelines for the administration of IV drugs. I. NITA 10(1):17.

Sheridan M. (1988). Developing a tool for appraisal of nurse's knowledge regarding medications, J Contin Educ Nurs 19(2):84.

Stefos K. (1989). Administering drugs safely. I. Nursing 19(5):126.

Stull JC et al. (1988). Flow rate variability from electronic infusion devices, Crit Care Med 16(9):888.

Tesfa A. (1989). Drug therapy in elderly patients: diagnosis of drug-related problems, Recent Adv Nurs, no 23, p 45.

Testerman EJ. (1988). IV drug administration guidelines: a simplified format, J Intravenous Nurs 11(3):188.

Weintraub M. (1987). P & T policy issues: patients who refuse significant drugs, Hosp Formul 22(9):757.

Whittaker N. (1987). Finding the right answer . . . drug calculation, Senior Nurse 6(6):33.

Wieland D et al. (1987). Medication errors: what happens afterward?, Nursinglife 7(2):41.

Winter ME et al. (1987). Essentials of therapeutic drug monitoring, Physician Assist 11(7):79.

Worrell PJ et al. (1989). Posology: the battle against dosage calculation errors, Nurse Educ 14(2):27.

Zuckerman IH et al. (1988). Drug monitoring: an essential component of home care quality, Caring 7(1)10:54.

# Unit 3

## Biopsychosocial Aspects of
## Pharmacology

*Chapter*

# 7 Psychologic and Cultural Aspects of Drug Therapy and Self-Treatment

---

## CHAPTER OBJECTIVES

*After studying this chapter, you should be able to meet the following objectives and define the key terms.*

1. Discuss the influence of culture and psychological beliefs on drug therapy.

2. Discuss on a symbolic level what drugs mean to clients.

3. Identify factors that affect client compliance.

4. Differentiate between the advantages and disadvantages of self-treatment using nonprescription medication.

## KEY TERMS

**cultural background,** page 116
**health beliefs,** page 116
**placebo,** page 118

**Cultural background,** ethnic practices, psychological beliefs, and tradition influence both health beliefs and treatment results. Effectively caring for clients from different cultural groups requires an understanding of the predominant ethnic-specific influences and an assessment of the individual client to determine how those cultural influences affect health needs. Since nearly 2000 cultures and subcultures exist, it is impossible for the nurse to have a working knowledge of all of them. Instead, nurses and other health care professionals should study the predominant cultural groups in their communities. The literature from transcultural nursing and anthropology (see bibliography listing) provides valuable insights into various health care beliefs and practices.

**Health beliefs** and practices related to pharmacology are evident in all cultures. Some similarities exist in the way the use of drugs is perceived, most often regarding the value that the appropriate use of medications is to reach optimal health. Although most individuals share common views regarding life patterns, significant differences occur in values, beliefs, and attitudes. Clients bring to health settings psychological and cultural differences in perceptions of masculine and feminine roles, in rural and urban backgrounds, in ethnic groups, and in social classes that influence drug usage. To administer medications effectively and to teach clients self-administration require an understanding of the predominant cultural influences within the community, a knowledge base of the psychologic aspects, and an assessment of the individual client to determine how these influence health needs.

# PSYCHOLOGIC ASPECTS

Every drug administered to a client has a symbolic meaning and a potential psychologic effect in addition to its pharmacodynamic action. A drug not only alters the function or structure of some part of the body, but it may also influence the behavior, sense of well-being, and mental state of the client. Psychologic responses of clients to symbolism may mimic pharmacologic reactions, adverse effects, or even allergic reactions to drugs. A profound reaction may be observed in clients receiving placebos.

Medications tend to be more effective when individuals believe in their capacity to get well, when they have a strong desire to get well, and when they believe that the health personnel expect the medication to be effective and say so. Clients' past and present conditioning to drugs, illness, hospitals, nurses, and other health personnel as well as their health goals are determinant factors in the response to drugs. Nurses must remember that among the major deterrents to successful drug therapy are divergent goals of the client and the health personnel. An accurate appraisal of the client's goal in seeking health advice and therapy is important to planning and implementing an effective plan of care.

## Symbolic Meaning of Drugs to Clients

Medications may be a symbol of help to the client. This meaning is strengthened and drug effectiveness enhanced when physicians or nurses suggest to a client that a particular drug will be of benefit or help. Repeated suggestions to the client that the drug is beneficial further reinforce its therapeutic value. This is similar to the relief a mother's kiss gives to her child's pain; the assurance it gives makes the child feel better. Investigation of the effects of drugs on the mind has resulted in the conclusion that some drugs are effective only in the presence of an appropriate mental state.

Drugs may also be viewed as symbols of danger. Clients may interpret cure as a serious threat to their emotional security if illness is being used to meet a need for dependence. Taking medication may also be objectionable if there is a strong need to exhibit an image of independence; adverse reactions may even result. The client may complain of dry mouth, nausea, vomiting, palpitation, fatigue, and other vague feelings of discomfort. The individual may resist taking the medication, refuse to have the prescription refilled, or even throw the drug away.

Many people have ambivalent feelings about taking medications. An expressed desire to regain health may coexist with an unconscious reluctance to give up the secondary gains of the sick role. These gains can include freedom from responsibilities and extra attention. Individuals may report secondary drug effects or find reasons why they cannot take the medication to retain these benefits.

Clients may harbor unsubstantiated notions about medications. Some believe a medication is too strong or not needed any longer, and therefore may refuse to take the drug, decrease its amount at any one time, or decrease the number of times it is taken. This behavior may be suspected when a drug known to be effective for a specific condition is ineffective in a particular client with that condition.

A client who believes the drug is too weak may take the drug too often, request the drug more often than prescribed, or continue drug therapy for longer than prescribed. Some clients will increase the amount of drug taken, believing "if one dose is good, two will be better." Symptoms of overdosage may then develop.

Some fantasies concerning resistance evolve from fears. Individuals tend to fear radioactive drugs such as $^{32}P$ or $^{131}I$ and to fear dependence on drugs that have antidepressant, analgesic, or sedative effects. Although few people today believe in cure-all remedies, some have blind faith in a certain medication and prefer taking that drug rather than make an alteration in their life-style.

Clients who believe they are allergic to a certain drug, for real or imagined reasons, are likely to react with fear or panic when administration of that drug is contemplated. A detailed personal history and (if possible) tests for drug allergy should be used to corroborate or refute the client's belief. Rejection of a client's claim of allergic response without evidence is an unwise assessment of data and negligent, to say the least.

The route of administration of a drug and the financial cost of treatment as well as a client's conscious and unconscious attitudes toward drugs, physicians, nurses, illness, and so on influence the extent, duration, and intensity of the client's response to medication. Studies indicate that when a client is angry, resentful, or hostile, certain medications used in usual doses may not be effective.

A client's illness may affect the emotional response to a drug. When the illness is short, recovery complete, and medical and drug expense not too great, the client tends to have a positive reaction to drugs, hospitals, and health and nursing personnel. Strong negative reactions toward drugs or health personnel result when clients are falsely reassured that they will make a quick and complete recovery, when drugs are both ineffective and expensive, or when symptoms of allergy, side or toxic effects, or overdosage occur. Preparing clients for the realistic limitations of drugs, for side and adverse effects, and for drug expense tends to create reasonable expectations.

In any chronic illness a client may suddenly rebel against ill health and resist therapy with life-sustaining medications. When this occurs, clients may be testing to see if they are really dependent on the drugs, or they may be attempting a real or symbolic act of self-destruction. A stressful event or decision may be the root cause. Exploring the client's underlying fears and concerns is essential. Support, caring, or objective assistance in coping will be necessary.

To avoid causing the client unnecessary concern or to deflect time-consuming questions, many health care providers are reluctant to present any negative aspects when teaching client's about drugs. A clear, nonthreatening explanation about the purpose of the medication and how it may affect them is the least clients deserve. On the whole, most clients prefer knowing the potential risks of drug therapy; this knowledge also tends to increase their participation and to engender trust. Litigation could also ensue if clients suffer harm from unrecognized secondary effects of a drug because they were not informed. The nurse should be aware that some people do not want to know details of their treatment, and some are very suggestible.

It is just as important to *listen intently to what the client says* about the medication, the feelings associated with it, and the condition for which it has been prescribed. Then the health care provider can begin to see the situation from the client's point of view and develop an understanding of the client's motivation to seek health care. Does the individual see the treated condition as a physical threat? How much of a threat? How susceptible? How much control does the client want to exert over the condition? How probable is it that such control will reduce the threat adequately? Until these concerns and other personal factors are at least briefly explored, the success of treatment is uncertain.

## Effects of Drugs on the Mind

Many common drugs have a secondary effect on the client's mind. Drugs may interfere with judgment, mood, sense of values, motor ability, and coordination. Certain antihistaminics used to treat allergies may decrease alertness and cause drowsiness, depression, and predisposition to accidents. Antihypertensive agents may cause depression. Barbiturates and tranquilizers may induce inattentiveness and confusion and reduce initiative. Drug-induced depression calls for discontinuance or a decreasing dosage of the offending drug. Clients should be watched for self-destructive tendencies, since pharmacologic literature has abundant examples of those with drug-induced depressions who have attempted suicide.

## Placebo Therapy

In the past when a physician had no medicine to offer a client who expected treatment, a "sugar pill," or **placebo,** was given to placate the sick individual. A placebo is any treatment—medication, surgical or diagnostic procedure, or nursing action—that elicits a client's response simply because of its intent rather than its known active properties. A placebo is most often a formulation of a pharmacodynamically inert substance such as lactose or sugar, distilled water, normal saline, or a small dose of an innocuous substance such as a vitamin. In medicine, placebos are employed in one of two ways: in experimental drug studies (e.g., before the drug's approval by the FDA) or, much more rarely, to satisfy a client's unwarranted demand for a particular medication when in the considered judgment of the prescriber withholding a dose will impede psychologic or physical health.

Some documented facts about placebos follow.

- In one large study of placebo effects, 36% of the individuals with 1-day postoperative pain reported satisfactory relief. In another study, half the clients who had had wisdom teeth extracted were given morphine, the other half a saline injection. One third of this placebo group also reported significant pain relief. Thus placebos can work against severe pain in some instances. Furthermore, pain relief with administration of a placebo does not mean the client did not have real pain.

- The placebo response may result from objective physiologic and biochemical changes in the body as well as a change in the client's subjective complaints. This response can vary considerably from one client to another, but in published studies it is reported to be fairly consistent, about 20 to 40% of clients have a placebo response (Katzung, 1987).

- People who have positive responses to placebos are not especially anxious, gullible, or neurotic. They are people who are able to use their mental and physiologic capacity to obtain pain relief from a placebo. Statistically, they are likely to be college graduates with independent, responsible life-styles.

- Of 15 individuals 13 obtained pain relief despite being told outright that they were getting a placebo that had helped other clients. Given the right supportive environment, honesty may still be the best policy.

- A nurse cannot legally administer any drug, even a placebo, without a prescriber's order.

Although giving a placebo can, on occasion, be amazingly effective, it should never be administered lightly. Placebos are usually prescribed for extremely unusual situations where no other course of action seems viable. Because most people respond to honest, straightforward rationales, prescribers who value an open relationship with their clients will not write an order or prescription when it is not warranted, and they will explain the rationale behind their decision. Philosophically, most nurses seem to agree and, if given a choice, choose to administer the ordered placebo only after all other alternatives have been thoroughly explored.

## CULTURAL INFLUENCES ON HEALTH CARE

Published anthropologic and transcultural studies have offered nurses extensive information on how to assess cultural factors in their clients. Creative cultural measures for improved therapeutics and comfort are available in numerous books and research articles (Henderson, 1981; Bullough, 1982; Shubin, 1980).

Dr. M.L. Leininger (1978), a nurse-educator credited as

the major voice of the transcultural strand in nursing, has suggested asking questions such as the following to assess a client's cultural influences: "Could you tell me about yourself and your family?" "How do you keep well?" "What made you become ill?" If the nurse has gained the confidence of the client and family, feelings and beliefs will be more openly discussed. If the nurse treats this information with respect and incorporates some of the important aspects in the nursing care plan, then the client is apt to respond more readily to therapy.

Many cultural groups avoid standard American medicine until either their herbal or home remedies are totally ineffective or they have become acutely ill. Haitian, Hispanic, Cuban, Vietnamese, Samoan, Jamaican, Chinese, American Indian, and other clients generally follow this practice. Nurses should be aware of this reluctance to seek standard medical care. When the need arises, such individuals should be counseled on appropriate methods to use in seeking health care.

In an institutionalized setting, diets palatable and/or acceptable to the individual can be problematic. Many private and some public hospitals have recognized this problem and offer ethnic meals as alternatives to the standard fare. Dietary concerns are also intertwined with cultural beliefs. For example, many ethinic groups (Italian, Mexican, Cuban, and others) believe they need their own cultural foods to help hasten the recovery process. Discussing food preferences and preferred methods of preparation with clients is often very important for the well-being of the client.

The common process of leaving ice water at bedside for the administration of medications is a procedure we take for granted today. Some cultures though, such as the Chinese, Chinese-Americans, and Israelis, believe cold drinks are unhealthy for the sick person and may therefore avoid this fluid intake. This preference should be discussed with the individual and, if medically acceptable, hot tea or an alternate substitute should be provided.

## SELF-TREATMENT

Public interest in self-care management is at an all-time high, as exemplified by the numerous self-care books and clinics that now abound. One of the most effective and inexpensive ways to counteract rising health care costs may be through expanded, educated self-care management. Studies show that half the people visiting a general practitioner have already started a self-treatment plan that helps more than 60% of the time. If these people were also helped to learn when to seek medical supervision and how to follow treatment advice wisely, they would have a still greater potential for health.

Nurses, with their commitment to collaboration with the client to further health, can educate clients, as can pharmacists, physicians, and many other health care professionals. Consumer information pamphlets abound, even printed by the FDA in large type for the visually impaired, offer valuable advice about drug interactions, health foods, and nonprescription pain relievers.

Development of the science of public health has led to the realization that the state of a nation's health does not depend exclusively on the interplay between professional medical practice on the one hand and bacteria, malignancy, and other causes of disease on the other. The influence on community health of the individual's personal attempts at self-treatment or at life-style alterations has frequently been ignored or underestimated.

Drugs sold without prescription can induce sleep or wakefulness, relieve pain or tension, or supply the body with vitamins and minerals. Remedies can be purchased for any part of the body. Sales of prescription and nonprescription (or OTC) drugs have established the pharmaceutical industry as a continually growing multi-billion dollar industry. Concern over the use of home remedies and self-medication is not new, but rather continues to be a controversial subject.

## Self-Treatment Using Herbal Remedies

Treating illness with a natural remedy, such as herbal products, dates back to the earliest records of mankind. The belief that a simple herbal or folk medicine can cure or prevent many health problems is believed and practiced in many of our societies today. While some of the prominent medications used today originated from plant sources, such as digitalis from foxglove and vincristine or vinblastine from periwinkle, home brewing of such plants can be extremely dangerous.

Use of herbals, or the back-to-nature movement, has largely evolved from the frequent warnings issued on food additives, preservatives, or products that are said to have cancer-causing substances in them. This movement has spawned into a multi-million dollar enterprise that no longer only appeals to specific cultural or ethnic groups but is widespread in our population. The proliferation of health food stores, natural organic vegetables, and pharmacies and other outlets selling organic vitamins, cosmetics, etc., are indicative of this attraction.

Since a number of these herbal remedies can be harmful and because their use may lead to hospitalization, the nurse should be familiar with some of the more toxic agents. Table 7-1 contains lists of selected, unsafe herbs, herbals that should not be formulated and used as a food, beverage, or drug (Larkin, 1983). Table 7-2 is a list of herbal teas with the potential effects and/or dangers associated with their usage (Herbert, 1982).

The reader should be aware that safety does not imply effectiveness. Efficacy depends on the ailment and the quality and dose of the herbal used. Efficacy cannot be determined with home preparation of herbs. Because many herbals are sold as food products, they are rarely evaluated for any therapeutic value (or claim) or harmlessness.

**TABLE 7-1**   Selected unsafe herbals

| Botanical name | Common names | Comments |
|---|---|---|
| *Arnica montana* | arnica flowers, Wolf's-bane, mountain tobacco, Flores Arnicae | Substances extracted affect the heart and vascular systems. Arnica is extremely irritating and can induce a toxic gastroenteritis, nervous system disturbances, extreme muscle weakness, collapse, and perhaps, death |
| *Artemisia absinthium* | wormwood, absinthe, madderwort, absinthium, Mugwort | Contains a narcotic poison (oil of wormwood); can cause nervous system damage and mental impairment |
| *Atropa belladonna* | belladonna, deadly night-shade | Considered a poisonous plant that contains the toxic alkaloids of atropine, hyoscyamine, and hyoscine. Anticholinergic symptoms range from blurred vision, dry mouth, and inability to urinate to unusual behaviors and hallucinations |
| *Aesculus hippocasteranum* | buckeyes, horse chestnut, aesculus | Contains coumarin glycoside, aesculin; may interfere with normal blood clotting; a toxic plant |
| *Conium maculatum* | hemlock, conium, spotted hemlock, spotted parsley, St. Bennet's herb, spotted cowbane, fool's parsley | Contains toxic alkaloid coniine and perhaps, four other related alkaloids |
| *Lobelia inflata* | lobelia, Indian tobacco, wild tobacco, asthma weed, emetic weed | Toxic plant that contains lobeline plus other alkaloids; excessive use of plant or its leaves or fruit extracts can result in severe vomiting, pain, sweating, paralysis, decreased temperature, collapse, coma, and death |
| *Vinca major* *Vinca minor* | periwinkle, vinca, greater or lesser periwinkle | Contain toxic alkaloids (vinblastine, vincristine) that are cytotoxic and may cause liver, kidney, and neurologic damage |

**TABLE 7-2**   Toxic reactions reported with herbal teas

| Proposed usage | Herbal tea | Potential toxic effect |
|---|---|---|
| Appetite stimulant, anodyne, carminative, antispasmodic | chamomile | In persons allergic to ragweed, chrysanthemums, etc., it can cause skin rash and severe hypersensitivity reactions including anaphylaxis |
| Cathartic or laxative | buckthorn bark, senna leaves, dock roots, aloe leaves | Severe diarrhea may occur (aloe is a strong irritant commonly used to treat constipation in large animals) |
| | Burdock root | May cause anticholinergic symptoms of toxicity |
| Diuretic | juniper berries | Gastrointestinal tract irritant |
| | shave grass or horsetail plants | Contain nicotine and thiaminase (When consumed by horses and other grazing animals, they produce anorexia, loss of muscle control, excitability, diarrhea, seizures, coma and death. Beri-beri type symptoms resulting from a thiamine deficiency have been reported in sheep given shave grass) |

## Self-Treatment Using Nonprescription Drugs

***Advantages.*** The individual has a right to practice self-medication. Throughout history the public has searched for medicines to relieve ailments and has tried almost every natural material known in the battle against pain, discomfort, and disease.

That the public is health conscious is evident by the number of OTC and nonprescription drugs available. Many ailments are minor and temporary, and the client wants to eliminate discomfort as quickly as possible. Minor ailments do not always require the expertise of a physician; but be-

cause many nonprescription drugs can interact with prescription drugs, it is best to check with a doctor or pharmacist. Minor complaints can be successfully treated by nonphysicians. Indeed, if individuals sought medical advice for every minor ailment (colds, headaches, minor wounds, temporary gastrointestinal upsets, or minor burns), health care providers would be unable to attend to individuals who need professional medical care. However, self-medication, if misused or abused, can be harmful. See the box above on the general benefits and risks of OTC medications. Risks can be reduced by professionally implemented client teach-

## GENERAL BENEFITS AND RISKS OF OVER-THE-COUNTER MEDICATIONS

### Benefits

Occasional use of certain simple preparations can be highly effective for specified minor, usually self-limiting conditions.

Cost is low in relation to prescription drugs, and the cost of a physician's visit is eliminated.

The client regains some control over personal health care.

Directions and some possible secondary effects are listed on the label.

Condition is immediately treatable. OTC medications are as accessible as the nearest store supply, and a wait for a physician's appointment is eliminated.

### Risks

Treatment depends on client judgment in differentiating a minor condition from a major, more complex one and in selecting appropriate medication.

Signs and symptoms of a serious condition may be masked by the medication.

Costs in the long run may be higher if a serious condition progresses while improperly treated.

Substances taken as OTC drugs are not always viewed as "drugs" with potential for harm, and dosing may be exceedingly casual.

Available combination preparations very often contain useless or harmful stimulants or depressants (caffeine or alcohol) and allergy-producing preservatives in addition to the active ingredient.

Professional advice to integrate the drug into an overall plan (e.g., to prevent interactions) is absent unless all drugs are obtained from one source that keeps a drug profile on clients.

Dosage may be too low to be effective, risking decisions by the client to overdose or delay needed professional treatment.

Many do not read labels, and most label print is too small for easy reading, even with glasses, by those with failing eyesight.

Professional follow-up for other conditions may be avoided unknowingly.

OTC drug self-treatment promotes the idea that there is a "magic bullet" for every ailment, major or minor, and that no discomfort should be tolerated.

OTC drug containers are especially vulnerable to criminal package tampering if they are kept accessible on shelves or are not in tamper-proof containers.

**TABLE 7-3** Common useful over-the-counter preparations*

| Medication (examples) | Use |
|---|---|
| Analgesic balm or ointment (Banalg, Ben-Gay) | Minor muscle aches and pain |
| Analgesic tablets (aspirin, acetaminophen) | Headaches, minor aches, pain, and fever |
| Antacids (Mylanta, Maalox) | Indigestion, upset stomach |
| Antidiarrheal (Kaopectate, Pepto Bismol) | Mild, uncomplicated diarrhea |
| Antihistamines (Benadryl, Chlortrimeton) | Allergies, allergic rhinitis |
| Antiseptics, liquid (hydrogen peroxide, isopropyl alcohol) | Hydrogen peroxide—minor cuts, scrapes and wounds; alcohol—sprains or muscle strain |
| Mouthwash (Gly-Oxide) | Oral wound cleansing product for minor dental inflammation or irritations |
| Throat lozenges (Cepacol) | Minor sore throat |
| Skin lotion (calamine lotion) | Insect bites, minor itching, poison ivy |
| Contraceptives (spermicides, condoms) | Prevention of unwanted pregnancy or sexually transmitted diseases |
| Ipecac syrup | Accidental poison treatment |
| Laxatives, mild (Milk of Magnesia) | Constipation |
| Motion or travel sickness preparations (Bonine, transdermal scopolamine) | Prevention of dizziness, nausea, vomiting |
| Nasal decongestants (Sudafed) | To reduce nasal stuffiness resulting from colds or allergies |
| Sunburn and other burn treatments (A&D ointment, Nupercainal cream or ointment) | To treat minor burns or prevent sunburn |

*The client should read the container label carefully; and if there are any questions, the advice of the pharmacist or health care provider should be sought.

ing. See Table 7-3 for a recommended basic inventory for a home medicine cabinet.

***Disadvantages.*** Most preparations available before the twentieth century were either harmless vegetable concoctions or narcotic-laced nostrums. Modern chemistry and pharmacology produced literally thousands of preparations for self-medication. Some are quite effective for certain minor ailments, some are potentially dangerous, and some are worthless. Americans are generally overmedicated. They have developed a casual attitude toward drug use and believe every discomfort or disorder requires chemical treatment.

Today, OTC drugs can be bought in drugstores, supermarkets, restaurants, and vending machines. Annually, this is a $5 to $6 billion industry. Widespread sales promotion via the media encourages self-medication. Since the hazards are generally insufficiently detailed in advertisements and commercials, persistent abuse of medications and resultant toxic effects are fairly common. Many drugs tested as being harmless can actually cause serious secondary effects. Aspirin may upset the gastrointestinal tract or cause bleeding; one 5-grain aspirin impairs platelet aggregation to some extent for up to 1 week. Serious, complex problems can develop from vitamin and mineral overuse (with vitamin A or D overdosage, for example). Habitual use of certain laxatives may prevent absorption of fat-soluble vitamins or cause colon atony so that the treatment perpetuates constipation. Few established dosage limits exist for the use of OTCs by the pregnant or breast-feeding woman, and effects on the fetus and neonate may be extremely harmful. Therefore *no drug of any sort should be taken by a pregnant or breast-feeding woman until a health care provider is consulted*. Many OTC drugs are intended only for adults, not for children; the dosage should not simply be altered for administration to children. Additionally, *the prescriber should be consulted before the client takes any drug that may have caused a previous allergic reaction*.

Often, a surprising lack of critical judgment is employed when evaluating a newly marketed drug. Typically there is an initial overreaction, especially to new OTC or well-marketed prescription drug: a "honeymoon phase" occurs when the agent is introduced with fanfare and used and prescribed somewhat casually for a time. Then when longer-term results are apparent and new secondary reactions are discovered, its reputation suffers for a while, and its use may be overcautiously controlled. After another time period, use again builds to a more moderate level as the prescribers and the public recognize that judicious use under specified circumstances is the rational approach.

Habitual self-medication with nonprescription drugs may mask a serious condition, prevent diagnosis, endanger the individual's life, or create long-term, expensive medical problems. Health care providers have an obligation to understand how taking medication "fits" with clients' understandings, attitude, and life-styles. The accompanying box outlines how to understand and explore the risk-benefit ratio when consumers are contemplating the use of nonprescription drugs. An additional factor for consideration is cultural influences on self-treatment behaviors.

## Cultural Influences on Self-Treatment Behaviors

While research on the elderly and on their consumption of nonprescribed medications is limited and in some instances conflicting, a study conducted on the four predominant cultural groups in Miami reported important implications for the nurse and other members of the health care team (Salerno, 1985). The cultural groups studied via a descriptive survey design were Hispanics, Haitians, American blacks, and Caucasian Americans.

This study reviewed the factors influencing the elderly of these groups to choose and use OTC substances. An added feature was the development of a Self-Medicating Behavior Safety Scale (SMBS). This scale was applied to all persons interviewed (110 subjects), and a numerical value for safety was calculated for each client. The pharmacist-investigator reviewed all questionnaires and extracted data to answer the question: "Was there any difference between the cultures for potential for misuse or abuse of OTC medications?"

The following data were extracted from this study:

1. The Haitian elderly reported the highest number of health problems, but the greatest usage of OTC products was reported by the Caucasian subjects. The mean usage per group was Caucasian, 7.4; Black American, 4.4; Haitian, 5.8; and Hispanic, 2.4.

    One should be cautious in applying self-reported health information, however. The nurse should be aware of the "yea-saying" tendencies of minority groups when they are asked about their health or health care attitudes, meaning the answer is often an effort to please a member of the dominant group and/or health care provider. This behavior is much greater for minorities of Spanish heritage than for others. Scott (1978) reported that the Cuban population seems to be more highly motivated toward preventive medicine and tends to report fewer illnesses than do other minority groups. Lopez-Aquires (1984) advises caution with the use of the traditional measure of self-reported health perception among Hispanics, since their findings indicate that Hispanics significantly underestimate their objective health problems and conditions.

2. The ability to read and understand the label of a typical OTC (generic) cold medicine was tested on all individuals. The findings here were particularly alarming. Over 50% of the subjects could not read or comprehend the package label. Other studies (Knapp and Knapp, 1980; Robinson and Stewart, 1981) reported 33% of their subjects also had this problem. This high incidence has explicit implications for all health care personnel working with the elderly. Many geriatric clients may need help in choosing an appropriate OTC medication and with specific instructions concerning the proper way to take the medication.

3. The influencing factors reported to affect their choice of OTC products were significantly different with the four groups. While all relied highly on the suggestions of others, professionals included, the Caucasians reported a high reliance on reading materials, television, radio, and self-knowledge influencing their choice of OTC products. This has been supported by other researchers (Knapp, 1980). American blacks indicated that availability of OTC medications was very important, while the Haitians reported self-knowledge as the most important factor. Nearly all cultural groups utilized drugstores or pharmacies as their primary site to purchase OTC preparations.

4. The most common types of OTC products used by all groups were gastrointestinal (antacids, antidiarrheals and laxatives) and analgesics (aspirin and acetamin-

ophen products). Interestingly, the Caucasian subjects reported a high usage of vitamins while the Haitians reported a high usage of herbals and teas. The latter was not a major report of the other groups. But this finding is not surprising, as Scott (1978) reported that many Haitians self-treat with herbs and home remedies before orthodox health care is sought.

5. Statistics concerning forgetfulness in taking medications was also significant between all four groups. Each group used memory as the most common system used to remember to take medication. The Caucasian group reported they tended to use memory less and relied on special devices or systems to help them remember, yet they had the greatest incidence of forgetting to take their medications.

6. The evaluation of abuse and misuse of nonprescribed medications was largely dependent on the items listed in the Self-Medicating Behavior Safety Scale. While the researchers reported no differences between the four groups studied, the group mean was only 8.4 (The scale ranged from 1 to 15 with 15 [100%] being the highest and safest score possible.) The lowest score for safety, 7.6 (51%), was recorded by the Haitian group, 8.03 by Caucasians, 8.63 by Hispanics, and 10.9 (73%) by black Americans. The overall findings were in the low to low-average range for safety for all four groups.

A review of items #4 and #5 of the SMBS indicated that 56% of all subjects in the study used OTC medications inappropriately. The Caucasian group, at 81% inappropriate usage, was the highest. The latter was mainly demonstrated in inappropriate use of vitamins and health food products, with dosages in excess of U.S. RDAs,* and in some instances, approaching megadosages. Examples quoted from the article (Salerno, 1985) include:

One individual believed all OTC substances were "foods"; and she not only consumed large amounts of such products, but also advised all her friends to do the same. Another interviewee reported taking vitamin K tablets to treat "blood spots" or "skin bruises." Many unapproved indications were offered as reasons for consuming nonprescribed substances by all four groups interviewed. Examples included taking vitamin C "to help the eyes" or "whenever it rains"; Milk of Magnesia tablets "whenever dizzy"; Pepto Bismol for "hard stools"; Alka-Seltzer for "throat allergies"; Bufferin for "indigestion or greasy food"; and aspirin "to clean out the stomach" or "for heat in the stomach." While some expressions were endemic to a specific culture, the basic need for guidance and valid professional advice was evident.

7. Other potentially dangerous situations noted included a number of drug-drug interactions, such as the frequent use of antacids by clients taking digoxin, cimetidine, tetracycline, or others; the use of OTC sympathomimetics in hypertensive patients; and the use of alcohol by clients taking aspirin, nitrates, antihypertensives, and CNS depressants. Many clients were not aware of the possible interactions or the alternate methods (spacing drugs apart with antacids) employed when using such medications. Foreign drugs were being taken along with American medications, and in several instances, duplicate consumption of the same medications under different names was identified.

Another study performed in California concerned Chinese and Hispanic elders and OTC drug usage. Race was determined to be the important variable in the use of OTC preparations in this project. The Chinese elderly who were interviewed preferred topical preparations to treat pain, while the Hispanic group used mostly internal analgesics. Hispanics used more OTC products than the Chinese, an average of 3.8 to 2, respectively. One reason cited was, perhaps, their broad definition of the term "nerves." Hispanics tend to define nerves as nervousness, anxiety, restlessness, palpitations, high blood pressure and insomnia (Hess, 1986). With such a wide variety of illnesses defined as "nerves," the preparations used may also be varied, depending on the person's symptoms and his or her perception of etiology.

Because in China many folk remedies usually consist of a single dose of a liquid preparation, taking tablets or capsules on a regular schedule would perhaps be confusing to the older Chinese client. This may be the reason this group prefers teas and topical remedies.

The nurse should be aware of possible cultural influences on medicating behaviors of their clients. Such information may be used to guide the nurse to ask the right questions during the initial history, to be aware of possible reasons for noncompliance or lack of adherence to a therapeutic drug regimen, and to help identify specific areas needing additional client teaching.

## Legal Controls Over Nonprescription Drugs

Self-treatment with drugs and home remedies has always existed, but legislative controls are relatively recent. Control over nonprescription drugs has steadily increased in Canada, most European countries, and the United States. Drug laws are not intended to restrict arbitrarily the availability of drugs for self-medication but to make drug consumption safer and more effective, reserving legend drugs (those for prescription) for the more sophisticated and more potent formulations or for those with complex instructions. During very recent years there has been a change. The U.S. FDA has approved the change of several prescription drugs (e.g., some low-dose, tablet bronchodilators and certain topical cortisone preparations) to nonprescription status (Table 7-4).

Many nonprescription drugs have limited potency,

---

*U.S. Recommended Daily Allowances published by FDA (Davidson, 1990).

**TABLE 7-4**   Prescription drugs now marketable as over-the-counter drugs

| Generic/trade name | Indication(s) |
| --- | --- |
| brompheniramine (Dimetane) | Antihistamine |
| chlorpheniramine (Chlortrimeton) | Antihistamine |
| dexbrompheniramine (Disophrol, Drixoral SA) | Antihistamine |
| diphenhydramine (Benadryl, Nytol, Benylin, Vicks Formula 44) | Antihistamine, sleep aid, cough medicine |
| doxylamine succinate (Unisom) | Sleep aid |
| dyclonine (Sucrets) | Anesthetic lozenge |
| hydrocortisone (Cortaid, Wellcortin) | Topical antipruritic |
| ibuprofen (Advil, Nuprin) | Oral analgesic, antiinflammatory agent; also used for menstrual cramps |
| miconazole (Micatin) | Antifungal agent |
| oxymetazoline (Afrin, NTZ) | Nasal decongestant |
| oxymetazoline (OcuClear) | Eye-vasoconstrictor agent |
| povidone-iodine sponge (E-Z 241 Scrub) | Antimicrobial agent |
| sodium fluoride rinse (Fluorigard, ACT) | Anticaries dental rinse |
| triprolidine (Actidil, Actifed) | Antihistamine |
| xylometazoline (Otrivin) | Nasal decongestant |

whereas prescription agents are considerably stronger. Thus analgesics such as aspirin are available for the relief of minor aches and pains, but agents such as morphine that relieve visceral pain are not available without a prescription. A nonprescription drug, like a prescription drug, must be proved safe and effective in the conditions for which it is recommended. This rule has resulted in the withdrawal of many harmful and ineffective agents from the market. Nonprescription medicines must be safe and effective within a wide range of dosage. This provides wide protection against misuse. Most drugs capable of causing dependence, addiction, or abuse are no longer available across the counter. Many nonprescription drugs are of low toxicity and pose little threat to the average consumer when directions are followed, but many others do, especially if the consumer is allergic, pregnant, or breastfeeding or has disorders other than the one being treated.

According to law, all nonprescription drugs must show this information on their labels:

1. Name of the product
2. Name and address of the manufacturer, packer, or distributor
3. Net contents of the package
4. Active ingredients and the quantity of certain ingredients
5. Name of any habit-forming drug contained in the prescription
6. Cautions and warnings needed for the protection of the user
7. Adequate directions for safe and effective use

Drugs purchased in a grocery store or supermarket or from mail-order houses or vending machines do not always allow access to professional advice as needed from a pharmacist, who is usually on the premises when purchases are made from drug stores or pharmacies. Pharmacists are able to observe the drug-buying habits of their customers, keep a drug profile or drug history on each customer, and explain and advise consumers when a visit to the physician or prescriber is necessary. A well-run pharmacy can make a valuable contribution to the health of a community.

## SUMMARY

Medications tend to be more effective when clients believe in their own capacity to get well and in the drug itself. An accurate assessment of clients' past and present conditions to drugs, illness, hospitals, nurses, and other health care personnel, as well as their own health beliefs and practices, all influence their response to drug therapy. This assessment is most important in planning and implementing an effective care plan.

Since many clients avoid standard American medicine until either their home remedies or over-the-counter self-treatments are totally ineffective or they become acutely ill, it is essential that the nurse be aware of these practices and be prepared to counsel and support clients on appropriate methods to use in seeking health care. Although self-treatment using nonprescription drugs has its advantages for the treatment of minor complaints, consumers need a greater awareness of the risks of such medications.

With the proliferation of OTC products, legislative controls are increasing to make nonprescription drug consumption safer and more effective.

Clients should be reminded that nonprescription drugs are not curative but offer only symptomatic relief and that a health care provider should be seen when treated conditions are persistent or recurrent or when unusual reactions occur.

## BIBLIOGRAPHY

Abramowicz M. (1979). Toxic reactions to plant products sold in health food stores, Med Lett Drugs Ther 21(528):29.

Bernal H. (1988). In home medication checks with diabetics, Home Health Care 6(5):14.

Brown CS et al. (1987). Association between type of medication instruction and patient's knowledge, side effects, and compliance, Hosp & Comm Psychiatry 38(1):55.

Bullough VL and Bullough B. (1982). Health care for the other Americans. New York: Appleton-Century-Crofts, Inc.

Cluff LE. (1985). Patient compliance: changing patterns of disease and health care costs, Hosp Formul 20:503.

Cooper CR. (1982). Herbal remedies, Hosp Formul 17(10):1387, 91.

Davidson DE, editor. (1990). Handbook of nonprescription drugs, ed 9. Washington, DC: American Pharmaceutical Association.

DeSantis L. (1988). Cultural factors affecting newborn and infant diarrhea, J Pediatr Nurs 3(6):391.

Gilman A et al, editors. (1990). Goodman & Gilman's The pharmacological basis of therapeutics, ed 8. New York: MacMillan Publishing Co.

Henderson G and Primeaux M. (1981). Transcultural health care. Menlo Park, Calif: Addison-Wesley Publishing Co, Inc.

Henry ML et al. (1989). Herbal overdose in a renal transplant recipient, Resident & Staff Physician 35(1):88.

Herbert V and Barrett S. (1982). Vitamins & "health foods": the great American hustle. Philadelphia: George F Stickley Co.

Hess P. (1986). Chinese and Hispanic elderly and OTC drugs, Geriatr Nurs 7(6):314.

Hill MN. (1986). Drug compliance, Nursing '86 16(10):50.

Hogan III RP. (1983). Hemorrhagic diathesis caused by drinking an herbal tea. JAMA 249(19):2679.

How the Rx-to-OTC trend has expanded the US OTC market. (1988). Pharmacy Times 54(6):130.

Katzung BG. (1987). Basic and clinical pharmacology, ed 3. Norwalk, Conn: Appleton & Lange.

Knapp D and Knapp D. (1980). The elderly and nonprescribed medication, Contemp Pharm Practice 3(2):85.

Larkin T. (1983). Herbs are often more toxic than magical, FDA Consumer, HHS Pub No (FDA) 86-1112.

Leininger M. (1979). Transcultural nursing '79. New York: Masson Publishing USA, Inc.

Leininger M. (1978). Transcultural nursing: concepts, theories, and practices, New York: John Wiley & Sons.

Lopez-Aquires W et al (1984). Health needs of the Hispanic elderly, J Am Geriatr Soc, p 191.

Martinez RA. (1978). Hispanic culture and health care: fact, fiction, folklore. St Louis: The CV Mosby Co.

Orque MS et al. (1983). Ethnic nursing care, a multicultural approach, St Louis: The CV Mosby Co.

Robertson MHB. (1987). Folk health beliefs of health professionals, West J Nurs Res 9(2):257.

Robinson JD and Stewart RB. (1981). Elderly, understanding their nonprescription needs, Amer Pharm ns21(11):48.

Salerno E, Ries D, et al. (1985). Self-medicating behaviors, Fla J Hosp Pharm 5(3):13.

Scott CS. (1978). Health and healing practices among five ethnic groups in Miami, Florida. In Bauwens E, The anthropology of health, St Louis: The CV Mosby Co.

Shubin S. (1980). Nursing patients from different cultures, Nursing '80 10(6):78.

US Pharmacopeial Convention. (1991). Advice for the patient, ed 11. Rockville, Md: Mack Printing Co.

Wood CS. (1979). Human sickness and health: a biocultural view, Palo Alto, Calif: Mayfield Publishing Co.

# 8 Drug Therapy Across the Life Span

## KEY TERMS

**carcinogenic,** page 127

**fetal alcohol syndrome,** page 128

**infant,** page 126

**mutagenic,** page 127

**neonate,** page 126

**teratogenic,** page 127

## INTRODUCTION

The effects of pharmaceutical agents vary in clients of different ages. The reasons for these differences are complex. Understanding the rationale behind these effects will assist the nurse to administer medications safely and evaluate their responses appropriately, regardless of the client's age. In addition, the client's age might also determine special techniques of administering medication to provide greater safety for the client. In this chapter special factors related to child-bearing clients, neonates, infants and children, and the elderly are discussed. These are, of course, artificial categories because life is a continuum in which development, maturity, and then degeneration occur without any distinct demarcation. Individuals mature and decline and/or have special needs at different ages, at different rates, and under different circumstances, which affect drug response in characteristic ways. The child-bearing client, the **neonate** (birth to about 1 month of age), the **infant** (1 month to 2 years), the older child, and the geriatric client all have unique needs and nursing considerations based on both physiologic and psychosocial developmental levels.

## CHILD-BEARING CLIENTS

Any substance ingested or absorbed by a woman is likely to reach the fetus by way of maternal circulation or to be transferred to the breast-fed neonate by way of breast milk if the substance is in sufficient concentration and is well distributed. Thus drugs taken by the mother potentially can cause serious harm to the fetus or neonate. No drug is known to be *absolutely* safe for the developing embryo, but some oral medications that are inactivated in the mother's stomach or not absorbed by the maternal gastrointestinal tract are assumed to be relatively safe. However, many drugs and other substances have yet to be identified as harmful to the fetus.

Considerations for drug therapy in the child-bearing client center on the effects of drugs administered to the mother on the developing fetus or nursing infant. The child-bearing client takes, on average, four or more drugs (other than vitamins) during pregnancy, and the fetal effects of these drugs are unknown. Shepard (1982) has indicated that there are more than 600 substances with some degree of "teratogenicity," or ability to cause developmental abnormalities of offspring when taken by a parent, based on experiments in animals. Only about 25 are known to cause human malformations.

Parents now ask health professionals more questions than in the past. Nurses are called on to supply accurate information, provide rationales, discuss the options available, and support parents' decisions. Prescribers and parents may have to make difficult choices between the benefits to the mother and the risks to the fetus or neonate. A judgment may need to be made between the risks to both if the mother's illness is not treated by a certain drug and the risks to the fetus if the drug is administered. This dilemma illustrates the absolute necessity for nurses to keep up to date in their drug knowledge and highly skilled at information retrieval from reliable sources. Parents should make the ultimate decision, with informed, sensitive input from all appropriate health professionals.

## Drug Transfer to the Fetus

Pregnancy does not seem to have much effect on drug absorption from the gastrointestinal tract, but protein binding is decreased, freeing more drug for placental transfer. Biotransformation of drugs in the liver is probably delayed in pregnancy, but renal excretion may be more rapid because renal blood flow increases dramatically as a result of increased cardiac output and glomerular filtration rate. (See Chapter 4.)

At the placental interface, transfer of drugs and other substances is affected primarily by simple diffusion and partly by active transport. Transfer across the placenta depends on the chemical properties of the drug: its molecular weight, spatial configuration, protein-binding capabilities, $pK_a$ (the point when half the amount of drug in the body is ionized and half is nonionized; see Chapter 4, Figure 4-4) and lipid solubility, as well as its distribution and concentration gradient. The potential for transfer is proportional to the period of time the drug remains in the maternal bloodstream. Transfer is greater during late gestation because of enhanced uteroplacental blood flow, increased placental surface at the interface, thinner membranes separating maternal blood flow and placental capillaries, and an increased proportion of free drug available to the circulation. Pathologic processes in the placenta, such as inflammation, degener-

---

### DRUGS THAT CROSS THE PLACENTA RAPIDLY*

| | |
|---|---|
| ampicillin | meperidine |
| barbiturates | penicillin G |
| cephalothin | phenytoin |
| diazepam | propranolol |
| ethanol | salicylates |
| kanamycin | streptomycin |
| lidocaine and other local anesthetics | sulfonamides |
| | tetracycline |

*Especially if administered intravenously.

---

ation, or partial separation, can increase blood flow and thus drug transfer. Not much is known about drug metabolism in the placenta itself, but it is thought to be a less active process. Certain drugs can alter placental enzyme activity necessary for degradation of substances and for energy-dependent transport mechanisms.

Many drugs are carried across the placenta within minutes, especially if administered intravenously (see box above). Thus the historical concept of the placenta as a completely protective barrier to circulating substances must be discarded. Most drugs that cross the placenta stabilize in the fetus at a level between 50% and 100% of the maternal level. Some (such as diazepam and local anesthetics) stabilize at levels even higher than the mother's blood levels. However, continued exposure of the fetus to a drug is more important than the rate of placental transport.

Within the fetus, drug effects may be more significant and prolonged than in the mother because of (1) probable lower enzyme concentrations and enzymatic reaction rates of drug metabolism and (2) slower excretion rates. Fetal excretion of drugs takes place via maternal resorption and by excretion by the fetal kidneys into amniotic fluid, which, under ordinary circumstances, the fetus often swallows.

On occasion, various fetal complications such as anemia and syphilis exposure have been actively treated by drugs in utero. The drug delivery routes chosen have been either the passive, transplacental approach or direct instillations into the amniotic fluid. These modes are still controversial.

It is, however, well documented that many unintended fetal drug doses via maternal circulation produce harmful fetal effects. The embryo or fetus runs the risk of developing the usual side or toxic effects, just as the mother does. Also, doses can be lethal or **teratogenic** (causing fetal organ defects), **mutagenic** (causing genetic mutation), or **carcinogenic** (causing or accelerating the development of cancer, sometimes much later). An example of the last is the precancerous or cancerous cell changes discovered in youths whose mothers took the hormone diethylstilbestrol (DES) during pregnancy.

---

### DRUGS THAT ARE CONTRAINDICATED IN PREGNANT WOMEN*

| | |
|---|---|
| aminopterin | oral contraceptives |
| sodium iodide (I 125, I 131) | clomiphene |
| | measles vaccine |
| iodinated glycerol | mumps vaccine |
| diethylstilbestrol (DES) | rubella vaccine |
| | smallpox vaccine |
| chlorotrianisene | vitamin A, high doses (25,000 |
| dienestrol | units or more daily) |
| estradiol | isotretinoin |
| estrogens, conjugated | menadione |
| estrone | menadiol |
| ethinyl-estradiol | phencyclidine |
| mestranol | |

*These are listed in category X on the FDA pregnancy scale.

---

### ALCOHOL AND THE CHILD-BEARING CLIENT: FETAL ALCOHOL SYNDROME

Although the public is becoming aware of the hazards of using drugs during pregnancy, many people do not include alcohol in the category of drugs. The teratogenic effects of intrauterine alcohol exposure on the fetus are well documented. Heavy use of alcohol by the child-bearing client has been associated with retarded growth, a pattern of congenital anomalies, and neurologic dysfunction of the infant. These effects seem to be dose related, so that the greater the maternal alcohol consumption during pregnancy, the more severe the infant's symptoms. Although the exact mechanism of fetal alcohol syndrome (FAS) has not yet been specified, studies have demonstrated that counseling to decrease maternal alcohol intake has a beneficial effect on the health of both mother and infant. The nurse must be aware of clients who are at risk of FAS and be prepared to provide client education, counseling, and referral.

---

Every embryo undergoes a series of precisely programmed steps from cell proliferation, differentiation, and migration to organogenesis. The critical periods for drug effects on the fetus are the first 2 weeks of rapid cell proliferation, when drug exposures can be lethal to the embryo, and the third through the tenth weeks of pregnancy, when the axial skeleton, muscles, limbs, and organs are developing most rapidly.

An unfortunate example is the hypnotic drug thalidomide, which caused abnormal limb development (phocomelia) in many children whose mothers were administered the drug during pregnancy. Beyond the tenth week of pregnancy, the results are more likely to be physiologic or behavioral alterations and delays in growth.

Abuse of cocaine by pregnant women has resulted in reports of frequent miscarriages, fetal hypoxia, and low-birth-weight infants in the United States. In utero, cocaine exposure has induced fetal tremors, strokes, and an increase in stillbirth rates. Exposed infants are also at high risk for developing congenital heart disease, skull defects, and other congenital malformations. The newborn often has symptoms of increased irritability, increased respiratory and heart rates, diarrhea, irregular sleeping patterns, and poor appetite. It has been reported that behavioral patterns of infants born from cocaine-abusing mothers may also be affected— that is, they may have poor attention spans and a decrease in organizational skills (Hall et al, 1990). In an attempt to protect the unborn fetus, or to punish the mother of a child born with the medical complications resulting from cocaine abuse, the courts, or the legal system, has in many cases intervened.

Advice that all drugs be avoided during pregnancy and breast-feeding cannot always be followed. Some maternal conditions (e.g., hypertension, epilepsy, diabetes, and infection) place both mother and fetus in serious jeopardy if left untreated. Although authoritative literature and drug package inserts routinely warn that drugs have not been tested for use in pregnancy, during breast-feeding, or for infants, much empiric data and some research data are accumulating. The FDA now rates drugs as to their safety for use during pregnancy. This rating is discussed in Chapter 2. (See the box above for drugs that are contraindicated in pregnant women.)

Obvious legal and ethical problems associated with research experiments on such vulnerable subjects and with obtaining consent have delayed the generation of necessary data. Well-controlled research, although fraught with ethical dilemmas in research design, is undeniably needed. Nurses are well positioned to participate in this important research, and they should do so.

Certain categories of drugs are expressly contraindicated during pregnancy or are used only when the risk-benefit situation has been carefully considered and thoroughly discussed with the client. These are listed in the box. Some drugs considered relatively safe during pregnancy, depending on the situation, are listed in Table 8-1. However, their use should be severely curtailed, being limited to only those pregnant women whose life or that of the fetus would be in jeopardy without drug treatment. One variable to be considered is the dose that reaches the embryo or fetus. This depends on the maternal dosage, the maternal volume of distribution, and the metabolic clearance rate of the mother. The fetal gestational age at time of exposure, duration of therapy planned, fetal and maternal genotypes, and any other drugs administered concurrently are also factors in prescribing decisions. Dosages, dosing intervals, and duration of treatment may be manipulated carefully to avoid harmful effects. Ethyl alcohol, especially at or near time of conception, is associated with the **fetal alcohol syndrome,**

**TABLE 8-1**   Some drugs considered relatively safe for use in pregnancy

| Agent | Recommendations and cautions* | Agent | Recommendations and cautions* |
|---|---|---|---|
| ANALGESICS | | ANTIHYPERTENSIVES | |
| acetaminophen | Considered safest analgesic during pregnancy | methyldopa | Safest of antihypertensives during pregnancy (especially as substitute for diuretics in pregnancy for diastolic blood pressure >110 mm Hg in the third trimester) |
| ANTIASTHMATICS | | hydralazine | Safest for hypertensive crises in pregnancy |
| cromolyn sodium | Relatively safe | | |
| metaproterenol (aerosol) | Relatively safe for mild, intermittent episodes: avoid oral form | ANTIINFECTIVES | |
| theophylline | Relatively safe if blood levels are closely monitored | cephalosporins | Safe during pregnancy |
| | | erythromycin | For use as substitute for penicillin hypersensitivity |
| ANTICOAGULANTS | | metronidazole | Not to be used during the first trimester |
| heparin | For use during first trimester; use caution if given during last trimester | miconazole | Relatively safe |
| | | penicillin and derivatives | Relatively safe |
| ANTICONVULSANTS | | ANTITHYROID DRUGS | |
| phenobarbital | Can cause malformations: for use only if necessary to maintain seizure control; if given during pregnancy, monitor neonate during first 24 hours for neonatal coagulation defect (bleeding) | propylthiouracil | For use only if absolutely necessary (e.g., for hyperthyroidism); use lowest dose possible |
| | | ANTITUBERCULOSIS DRUGS | |
| ANTIDIABETICS | | rifampin | Relatively safe |
| insulin | Relatively safe; drug of choice | ethambutol | |
| ANTIEMETICS | | CARDIAC GLYCOSIDES | |
| pyridoxine | Relatively safe for morning sickness | digoxin | Relatively safe; maternal plasma levels should be closely monitored. Dosages may be increased toward the end of gestation and decreased for 6 weeks after delivery |
| doxylamine | For use as necessary for severe nausea or vomiting | | |
| prochlorperazine | | | |
| trimethobenzamide | | | |
| cyclizine | | | |
| meclizine | | | |

*Recommendations are likely to change; therefore, manufacturers' package inserts should always be consulted. No drugs are known to be *absolutely* safe during pregnancy. The use of many substances, including most drugs not on this list, should be carefully considered by the obstetrician as to risks and benefits. See drug monographs for specific drug information; see also bibliography. Consult references for sources of information about drugs in this table.

which produces both growth and mental retardation (see box on p. 128). Other very common substances such as aspirin, vitamin supplements, caffeine, and nicotine are suspected to cause adverse reactions in the fetus.

One difficulty with these and other substances is that effects on the embryo may occur before the woman is aware that she is pregnant. Women of child-bearing age who are not using contraceptives and who are sexually active should be prescribed for carefully and should be instructed to use over-the-counter medications cautiously. Education and prevention are considered the best therapy.

▷**Nursing Management:**
**Medication Administration in Childbearing Clients**

Most nursing goals related to these topics should be aimed at ensuring that parents know that any foreign substance absorbed by the mother may have lifelong effects on the child. A balance must be maintained between protecting the

child and dealing constructively with the family; creating unnecessary family concern is not appropriate. Essential to these aims is cooperating with the prescribing clinician, providing an environment for free exchange of information, and, if possible, forestalling parental feelings of guilt or fear associated with drug administration, whether planned or inadvertent. The following information should be conveyed.

1. Potential harm to the child resulting directly from substances the mother is exposed to and potential danger to both mother and child if treatment is not begun must both be weighed. These decisions must be made with the prescriber whenever exposure to an unfamiliar substance or drug is contemplated. Not everything is known at this time about effects on the child; and as more information becomes available, accepted guidelines may change.

2. Over-the-counter medications and other common substances such as aspirin, high-dose or multiple vitamin supplements, alcohol, caffeine, and nicotine may also have detrimental effects on the fetus.

**TABLE 8-2**   Pharmacokinetics that influence drug dosing

| Physiologic process | Neonate | Type of drugs affected |
|---|---|---|
| **ABSORPTION** | | |
| Gastric pH | Increased to 6 to 8 for first 24 hours; then usually a 10- to 15-day achlorhydria | Acid-labile drugs, such as oral penicillin better absorbed <br> Oral forms of phenobarbital or phenytoin: reduced bioavailability |
| Gastric emptying time | Prolonged, usually 6 to 8 hours | Oral absorption of penicillin increased; phenytoin, phenobarbital decreased |
| **DISTRIBUTION** | | |
| Total body water (TBW) content | 75% to 79% | Average adults have about 60% TBW and 25% to 45% fat |
| Adipose (fat) content | 5% to 12% | Vast differences in drug distribution across the age span <br> Water-soluble drugs have a larger volume of distribution in newborns, while fat-soluble drugs have considerably less <br> Drug dosage adjustments largely based on this factor |
| Protein binding | Decreased | Highly protein-bound drugs require dose adjustment to avoid toxicity |
| **METABOLISM** | | |
| Liver metabolism | Decreased | Potent or potentially toxic drugs requiring liver metabolism are slowly metabolized; lower doses are necessary for such drugs (especially chloramphenicol and theophylline, among others) |
| Microsomal enzymes | Low | |
| **EXCRETION** | | |
| Glomerular filtration | Decreased | Drugs excreted by filtration or secretion will accumulate in the neonate; dose adjustments necessary (especially aminoglycosides and digoxin) |
| Tubular secretion | Decreased | |

3. Any presciption written by a professional who is not a specialist in the care of pregnancies or nursing mothers should be evaluated by an obstetrician or pediatrician. The prescription may need to be changed by the specialist to a safer drug or dosage.

4. If a questionable substance is absorbed by the mother, close health care supervision is essential. If real potential for fetal or infant injury results, the parents need ongoing support as they endure the sometimes long wait for effects to be manifested. If birth defects or toxic effects are present or if invasive diagnostic tests or a therapeutic abortion is to be performed, objective psychologic intervention may help the parents endure this critical period.

## PEDIATRIC CLIENTS

### Neonates

Since newborns are small and immature, lacking many of the protective mechanisms that allow older children and adults to be relatively resistant to stressors of all kinds, they require special considerations. Their skin is thin and permeable, their stomachs lack acid, and their lungs lack much of the mucous barrier. Neonates regulate body temperature poorly and become dehydrated easily. Their liver and kidneys are immature and cannot manage foreign substances as well as older children and adults. Specific factors affecting medication use in neonates are covered in Table 8-2.

### Breast-Fed Infants

Almost *all* forms of drugs in maternal circulation can be readily transferred to the colostrum and breast milk. Since drugs or their biotransformed products are handled by different pathways in the infant and the fetus, the impact of maternal medications on the infant probably differs (is probably less) from that on the fetus. This difference can serve as a guide in prescribing for the breast-feeding mother. Typical nontherapeutic outcomes in the breast-fed infant are signs of the drug's usual side or toxic effects. Adverse effects may occur, such as gray-brown stains of the later-erupting teeth as a result of tetracycline therapy over 10 days in length or allergic sensitization to penicillin. Most drug products that reach the neonate via breast milk have undergone maternal biotransformation and are probably less than the original dose. However, immaturity of the neonate's liver and kidney systems limits its capacity for further metabolism and excretion.

Data about infants' capabilities for drug absorption, digestion, distribution, metabolism, and excretion are scant and conflicting. In general, the proved benefits of continuing breast-feeding must be weighed on an individual basis against the risks of maternal medication to the infant. Although the mammary glands are a relatively insignificant route for maternal drug excretion and the drug level in breast milk is usually less than the actual maternal dose, the infant's actual dose depends largely on the volume of milk consumed. Thus a single measurement of a drug in human milk will not accurately reflect the total dose the infant receives.

The concentration of the drug in maternal circulation depends on the relationship among several factors: dosing and route of administration, the drug's distribution, its protein binding, and maternal metabolism and excretion. The mammary alveolar epithelium presents to any potentially transferable substance a lipid barrier with water-filled pores. It is more permeable to drugs during the colostrum stage of milk production—during the first week of life. Drug factors that enhance drug excretion into milk are nonionization, low molecular weight, solubility in fat, and plasma binding versus milk-protein binding. Transfer of an active or passive form of a drug's metabolites into maternal plasma and then to milk depends mainly on passive diffusion. The absorptive processes of the infant's gastrointestinal tract and drug distribution are estimated to be similar to those in the adult, which means that lipid-soluble substances are well absorbed. The infant's age (thus the amount of drug-containing milk consumed) and the relative immaturity of the infant's important organs bear greatly on the outcome. If the drug is fat soluble, it may be more highly concentrated in breast milk at the end of feedings and at midday. Since the infant's total serum protein is lower in comparison to the adult's, more free drug is available to the circulation. Metabolic reactions in the infant's liver are slower than in the older child's; consequently, drug biotransformation may likewise be delayed. Other factors in the neonatal period may present risks: inadequate body temperature control, hypoxemia, or inadequate nutrition, for example. Drug excretion is delayed in the neonate because it is largely via the kidneys, where immature glomerular filtration rates and tubular functioning are maintained for several months. The extreme variability among drug effects and infants' capabilities makes it difficult to decide whether the mother should take a drug and whether or not she should breast-feed.

Human milk contains small, fixed amounts of many substances absorbed by the mother. Considerable evidence shows that certain other substances are incontrovertibly contraindicated unless necessary for survival and unless their effects are closely monitored. The usual recommendation

---

**DRUGS CONTRAINDICATED DURING BREAST-FEEDING**

The American Academy of Pediatrics committee on drugs has suggested the following drugs be avoided in the woman who is breast-feeding.

| | | |
|---|---|---|
| bromocriptine | cyclophosphamide | methimazole |
| cimetidine | ergotamine | methotrexate |
| clemastine | gold salts | phenindione |
| | | thiouracil |

---

is that breast-feeding be temporarily interrupted (usually for 24 to 72 hours) and the breasts pumped to remove drug-containing milk. Less often, it is advisable to cease breast-feeding altogether. Dosages and routes may also be changed. It is recommended that certain drugs be avoided while breast-feeding; see the box above.

Drug effects may be minimized by substituting formula for the midday breast-feeding, since that is the feeding highest in fat content and thus more likely to contain higher amounts of fat-soluble drug products. In addition, breast-feeding mothers who must be treated with medications can time their doses to be taken right *after* breast-feeding so as much time as possible elapses and the drug can reach a relatively low concentration before the next feeding (see Table 8-3).

With radioactive substances, therapy is of short duration; or if merely a diagnostic radioisotope test is to be done, breast-feeding must be interrupted until all radiation is absent from milk samples. Breast-feeding will probably be terminated when the drug is so potent that minute amounts may profoundly affect the infant, when the drug has high allergenic potential, when the mother exhibits evidence of decreased renal function (which augments drug excretion into breast milk), or when serious pathologic conditions require prolonged drug administration of high dosages.

Changes in the activity levels of the fetus or nursing infant signal dangerous effects resulting from drug administration; parents should be taught how to assess and report unusual fetal inactivity or infant apathy.

***Alternatives to drug therapy.*** Both health professionals and clients place high value on pharmaceutical solutions to health concerns. However, many illnesses are self-limited or cause only minor discomforts that end or decrease without medication or with non-drug alternatives, such as relaxation techniques rather than tranquilizers. The effect of any medication should be weighed against the mother and child's physical and psychologic stress of abrupt weaning.

Other considerations might be to delay the mother's pharmacologic therapy until the infant is weaned on his or her own or to select another drug to meet the therapeutic goal without interfering with breast-feeding. The age and ma-

**TABLE 8-3**   Some drugs considered relatively safe during breast-feeding

| Agents | Recommendations and precautions* | Agents | Recommendations and precautions* |
|---|---|---|---|
| ANALGESICS | | ANTICONVULSANTS | |
| acetaminophen<br>aspirin<br>mefenamic acid<br>propoxyphene<br>meperidine | Relatively safe | primidone<br>phenytoin | Relatively safe with close observation |
| | | BRONCHODILATORS | |
| ANTIINFECTIVES | | ephedrine<br>cromolyn sodium<br>theophylline | Safe; destroyed in infant's GI tract<br>Observe for infant irritability or in-<br>somnia |
| cephalexin<br>cephalothin<br>oxacillin | Safe; not found in breast milk | | |
| penicillin | Relatively safe after 1 mo, but may<br>sensitize the infant | PSYCHOTROPIC DRUGS | |
| | | chlorpromazine<br>phenothiazine<br>tricyclic antidepressants | Appear safe, although found in milk;<br>may cause drowsiness in baby |
| erythromycin<br>INH<br>ethambutol | Safe after 1 mo<br>Safe<br>Safe | | |
| | | ANTIDIABETICS | |
| CARDIOVASCULAR DRUGS | | insulin | Safe; destroyed in the GI tract |
| digoxin | Safe if maternal serum levels are<br>closely monitored | THYROID DRUGS | |
| guanethidine<br>methyldopa<br>propranolol | Safe in recommended dosages<br>Safe<br>Relatively safe at lowered maternal<br>dosages (higher drug levels in<br>breast milk than in maternal blood-<br>stream because of high lipid solu-<br>bility of drug) | thyroid hormones | Relatively safe if monitored for thy-<br>roid function and response |
| | | GASTROINTESTINAL DRUGS | |
| | | antacids<br>metoclopramide<br>laxatives (except cascara<br>and danthron) | Safe; electrolytes should be monitored |
| DIURETICS | | PESTICIDES | Under usual conditions found less in<br>human milk than in cow's milk |
| spironolactone<br>thiazides and<br>furosemide | Safe<br>May suppress lactation; avoid in first<br>month of lactation | AIR POLLUTANTS | Have not been found in human milk |
| SEDATIVE-HYPNOTICS | | VACCINES | |
| lorazepam<br>prazepam<br>oxazepam | Excreted in milk; no adverse effects<br>reported | RhoGAM | Considered safe |

*Over time, recommendations may change; therefore manufacturer's package inserts should always be consulted by pediatricians and nurses. Many substances should be avoided during the period of breastfeeding. (Details about specific drugs are located under relevant chapter headings in this text.) Consult bibliography for sources of information.

turity of the child must be considered also; as the infant develops physiologically the drug's ability to cause harmful effects will diminish. The frequency of feedings should also be considered. An infant dependent on breast milk for total nutrition will receive higher doses of drugs than an infant breast-feeding only once or twice a day and taking other forms of nourishment.

## Other Pediatric Clients

Drug administration to pediatric clients requires special knowledge and approaches. Physicians may prescribe the dosage of medication, but it is the nurse's responsibility to know the safe dosage range of any medication administered to children. A standard dosage of medication is nonexistent

in pediatrics; medications are usually ordered according to the weight or body surface area of the child. Some pharmaceutical companies continue to supply medications in a standard adult dosage strength, and the nurse must be able to evaluate the correct dosage before administering the medication.

***Weight as a basis.***   Following is a formula for calculating estimated safe dosages based on weight alone (Clark's rule). Because this is based on weight alone, it is a somewhat imprecise calculation for children.

$$\frac{\text{Average} \quad \text{Weight of}}{\text{adult dose} \times \text{child in pounds}}{150} = \text{Estimated safe dose}$$

Example: How much acetaminophen (Tylenol) should a 1-year-old child weighing 21 pounds receive if the average adult dose is 10 grains?

Answer: $\dfrac{10 \text{ (grains)} \times 21 \text{ (weight in pounds)}}{150} = \text{gr } 1^{2}/_{5}$

$= \text{gr } 1^{1}/_{2}$

A nurse preparing calculated dosages of digitalis, insulin, barbiturates, and narcotics should have the calculations as well as the prepared medication dosage checked by another nurse or pharmacist before the drug is administered. Pediatric dosages are often minute, and a slight mistake in calculating the amount of medication to be administered results in greater proportional error.

Pediatric dose calculation based on weight alone implies that the pediatric client is a small adult, which is not true. Physiologic differences in the infant when compared to an adult may definitely affect the amount of drug needed to produce a therapeutic effect. For example, infants have a body composition that is approximately 75% water (adults have 50% to 60%) and less fat content than the adult. Therefore, water-soluble drugs are generally administered in larger doses to infants/children per body weight than to an adult. A good example of this is the water-soluble drug gentamicin, an intravenous antibiotic. Recommended dosages from U.S.P.D.I., Volume 1, 1991 are: older neonates and infants, 2.5 mg/kg every 8 hours; children, 2.0-2.5 mg/kg every 8 hours; and adults, 1.0-1.7 mg/kg every 8 hours.

Rules based on weight, such as Clark's rule, are generally taught and used by students in clinical areas to assess pediatric dosages. While useful as a guide, their accuracy for a number of drugs is questionable. If the student is uncertain regarding dosage, the following sources are recommended: the drug monograph in a package insert, U.S.P.D.I., AHFS, pediatric drug handbooks, or a pharmacist.

***Body surface area as a basis.*** More than 100 years ago, Hufeland suggested that drug doses should be calculated on size or proportional amount of body surface area (BSA) to weight. Many physicians continue to use weight as the basis for calculating drug doses and body surface area for calculating fluid requirements. Most clinicians advocate using body surface area for determining drug dosage for adults as well as children. Physicians usually carry a simple slide rule or nomogram, such as the West nomogram (Figure 8-1) to make rapid BSA conversions from weight and height. It is believed that the larger amount of total body water (TBW) in children, as well as the percentage of water in body weight and the part of that percentage formed by extracellular water, accounts for the fact that children tolerate or require larger doses of some drugs on a mg/m² basis.

For the 75% of drugs that have no established pediatric dosage, calculating the child's dosage as a fraction of the average adult dose using Clark's rule is really too imprecise for most applications, yet it may be used (mg per kg) where

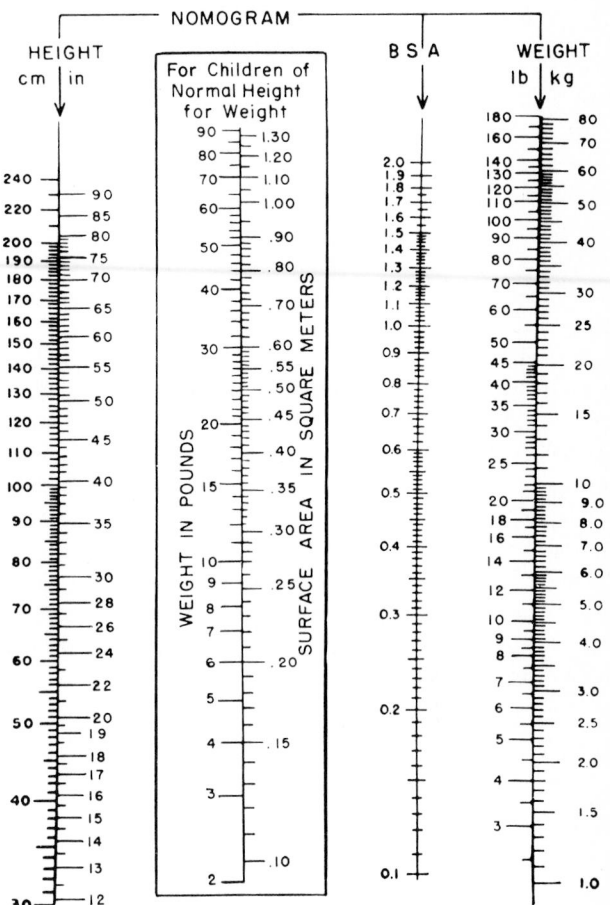

**FIGURE 8-1** BSA is indicated where straight line that connects height (on the left) and weight (on the right) levels intersects BSA column or, if client is about average size, from weight alone (enclosed area). *(Modified from data of E. Boyd by C.D. West.)*

the dosage according to body surface area has not been established. The surface area rule is the most accurate. As a relationship between height and weight, it can provide a more precise guide to the maturity of the child's organs and metabolic rate of functioning for effective pharmacokinetics. The dosage should be tailored to the individual child according to the amount of medication per square meter of body surface area. The BSA rule for children's dosages follows:

Child's approximate dose =

$\dfrac{\text{Child's BSA in square meters (from nomogram)} \times \text{Adult dose}}{1.73}$

For example, using Figure 8-1, a child with a height of 34 inches weighing 10 kg would be considered to have a body surface area (m²) of 0.5. The dosage calculation then would be:

$$\text{Child's approximate dose} = \frac{0.5 \times \text{Adult dose}}{1.73}$$

▷Nursing Management:
## Medication Administration in Pediatric Clients

Although these rules have been devised for relating adult doses to infants and children, it must be emphasized that *no rules or charts are adequate to guarantee safety of dosage at any age*, particularly in the neonate. No method takes into account all variables, particularly individual tolerance differences. Astute, accurate nursing observations of how individual children react to drugs can assist in choosing drugs and dosages.

The administration of medications to infants and children is both challenging and frustrating. Giving injections skillfully will enhance security and help to gain a child's cooperation. A sound knowledge of growth and development also provides the nurse with information about how a child might be approached, whether reasoning will help or hinder the process, and whether assistance will be needed. The principles of safe administration of medication apply to all age groups, but children differ from adults, and the nurse has added responsibilities. (See box below on pediatric drug administration guidelines.)

---

### PEDIATRIC DRUG ADMINISTRATION

1. Parents are frequently good sources of information about successful methods or vehicles of giving medications to their children.
2. Try to avoid using essential foods such as milk, cereal, or orange juice, since the child may refuse to accept that food in the future.
3. Never underestimate children's reactions. They may not require that the taste of medication be disguised.
4. A sip of cold fruit juice, ice chips, a frozen fruit-bar, or a mint-flavored substance before and after the administration of an unpalatable medicine may effectively dull its taste.
5. Sugarless vehicles such as those sweetened by saccharin should be used to disguise the taste of medications given to diabetic children or those on a ketogenic diet.
6. Honey and syrup are ideal for suspending drugs that do not dissolve easily in water.
7. Since fruit syrups are usually acid, they should not be used for medicines that react in an acid medium (e.g., sodium bicarbonate, soluble barbiturates, and penicillin).
8. Elixirs have an alcohol base that, when undiluted, may cause the child either to refuse them or to cough and choke; they may also cause a drug-drug interaction. Small amounts of water added to elixirs of phenobarbital or chloral hydrate occasionally help.
9. Nursing time can be saved by recording the most successful method of administering medications and pertinent nursing orders on the child's care plan. This notation also saves the child frustration, fear, and anxiety.

---

Ideally, a child will cooperate more readily with a nurse who has established a positive relationship. The child may also find it easier to accept the discomforts accompanying injections and some oral medications from the nurse who is associated with daily hygiene, feeding, holding, play, and happy times. In addition, the nurse will feel less guilty when the child associates the nurse with pleasure and comfort most of the time, and discomfort only when necessary to get well.

When a child is afraid or anxious, the natural response is to strike out at the frustration or avoid it. By accepting this behavior as a natural response, the nurse will be able to deal with it and be honest when a medication or procedure will be unpleasant or painful.

Truthful explanations to children are essential. Children have a right to some explanation of any procedure that concerns them. The timing and type of explanation should be geared to the child's ability to perceive and understand. For the child 2 years of age or younger very simple explanations such as "I have some medicine for you to drink" or "I have an injection to give you, and it will hurt a little" are sufficient. Long explanations to children through 5 years of age do little more than prolong the anticipation and increase anxiety or fear. Telling 4-year-olds to stop kicking, hitting, or other avoidance behavior only conveys to them that they are not understood and they will receive little or no help with their feelings of frustration about being medicated. Providing the preschool-age child opportunities at play (i.e., to give a doll an "injection" [empty syringe without a needle] or "drops") affords an important outlet and allows the child to work through the trauma of the experience.

Many children are courageous, or like to be considered so, and appealing to their courage is sometimes effective. Children 4 years old or over may choose to hold their own medicine cup, or drink unassisted, and to take pills from the container without any assistance from the nurse. Children of this age are motivated by social reinforcers, such as being praised for their cooperation, or "your job is to stay very still," which enhance their self-esteem and feelings of competence. Because of the sense of achievement that follows, they may want to save the medicine cups to show their parents.

***Oral medications.*** Success in administering oral medications usually requires a kind but firm approach with a positive attitude. No doubt that the child will take the medicine should be reflected in choice of words or tone of voice. The nurse might say, "Jimmy, it's time to take your yellow medicine" or "Do you want to take your pill now or with your Jell-O?" This indicates that Jimmy is expected to cooperate and to do it willingly. It also allows the child some control over the situation. An unwise approach that reveals doubt on the nurse's part might be: "I have your yellow pill, Jimmy. Will you take it for me, please?"

Nurses should try to be aware of how a medicine tastes

so that they can answer such questions as, "Does it taste bad? Will it burn my mouth?" A helpful reply would be, "It tastes like cherry to me. Tell me what it tastes like to you." Often the child will accept the suggestion to taste and find out. However, if the medication is bad tasting, attempting deceit or lying to the child is as futile and destructive as it is to an adult.

Disagreeable-tasting medications should be disguised if at all possible. Small amounts of honey, syrup, jam, fruit, and some fruit juices are suitable sweet vehicles for less palatable drugs. Some pills can be crushed and suspended in small amounts of these substances as long as the two are compatible. Infants and children swallow many liquid medications more readily if mixed with a sweet substance or diluted with a small amount of water. (If large amounts of water or other substances are used and the child refuses to take all of the mixture, estimating the amount of medication the child received is difficult.) Fortunately, many drugs are available in palatable syrups or suspension form well suited for administration to infants and children. Suspensions, however, should be thoroughly agitated to ensure that doses are not offered in unequal concentrations.

Caution must be exercised to prevent aspiration when giving oral medications to children. (See Special Situations later in this section for modifications as necessary.) Medications must be given to infants slowly and in small amounts to avoid choking. Liquid medications may be administered by nipple, plastic medicine cup, plastic dropper, or a plastic syringe without the needle. Water should be swished through the inside of these *first* to prevent medication from sticking, thereby undermedicating. Glass cups, droppers, or syringes should be avoided because of the obvious danger of breakage in the child's mouth. A dropper or syringe is best suited for placing a liquid medication along one side of the infant's tongue. Older infants and toddlers seem to prefer to take their medications from a plastic medicine cup. If children are held or placed in a sitting position, they are less likely to aspirate the medication than if lying on their backs. When administering a medication with a dropper or syringe, the nurse may purse the infant's lips with one hand to keep the medicine from running out of the mouth. Droppers and syringes used for medication should be kept clean, they should be reserved for only one client's use, and they should be rinsed or washed before being returned to the medication bottle.

If the child refuses to cooperate even after explanations and encouragement, the nurse may have to ask whether the child will take the medication alone or will need the nurse to give it. Physical coercion is seldom necessary, but if used, it should be mild and used with dispatch and firmness, since aspiration is a danger. The nurse must not combine force with anger or resort to force when one nurse has been unable to administer the medication. Careful consideration should be given to such factors as: Why does the child resist? Does the child disapprove only of one nurse? Have past experiences with medications given at home or in the hospital frightened the child? Will forcing a medication cause a struggle that will negate the effects of a drug given for sedation? If mild restraint is necessary, the nurse should explain to the child that this form of treatment is necessary. The child will not cooperate if force is seen as a punishment for inability to cooperate; often the child loses confidence in all personnel.

***Topical medications.*** Children have a large skin surface area in proportion to total body weight. Their skin, especially neonates', is particularly thin, permeable, and without much protective oil. Although adults absorb much more medication through intact skin than was previously believed, the child is at increased risk for systemic medication administration. The discovery that hexachlorophene can cause encephalopathy in newborns and that topically applied boric acid can cause systemic poisoning testifies to the hazard of applying drugs to children's skin, especially for prolonged contact or over broken skin areas. Plain soap and water may be preferred for abrasions or open lesions, replacing medicated dressings.

***Subcutaneous injections.*** There are wide swings in the amounts of subcutaneous fat during the childhood years. Neonates have proportionately smaller amounts; these increase slightly to 23% by 1 year of age. From 1 to 5 years of age they drop to between 8% to 12%. Then the amounts of bodily fat climb to about 20% when the child reaches the age of 10. Lipid-soluble drugs have an affinity for fat tissue; less subcutaneous fat means that lower dosages of drugs such as diazepam and barbiturates are necessary to maintain blood levels. In addition, less subcutaneous tissue for injections may be available. An alternate route may need to be selected—oral, intramuscular, or intravenous.

***Intramuscular injections.*** The principles and techniques of the administration of injections are similar to those for adults.

Most authorities believe that the risk of sciatic nerve injury is too great to warrant the use of the gluteal site of administration. The sciatic nerve is the largest nerve in the body; its normal pathway is the hollow midway between the ischial tuberosity and the greater trochanter, covered by the gluteus maximus muscle. This pathway, however, varies a great deal from individual to individual. In addition, the small size of the gluteal mass in the infant or neonate and the potential neurotoxicity of many drugs enhance the possibility of iatrogenic trauma secondary to IM injections. Trauma of this kind is the leading cause of sciatic neuropathy in infancy. A lesion at this height of the sciatic nerve is usually tragically associated with marked permanent disability.

The younger the child, the less muscle tissue may be available for IM injections anywhere on the body. If repeated injections are necessary, the available sites may become overused, inflamed, or dystrophic, requiring concerted efforts by the nurse to develop systematic plans for rotating

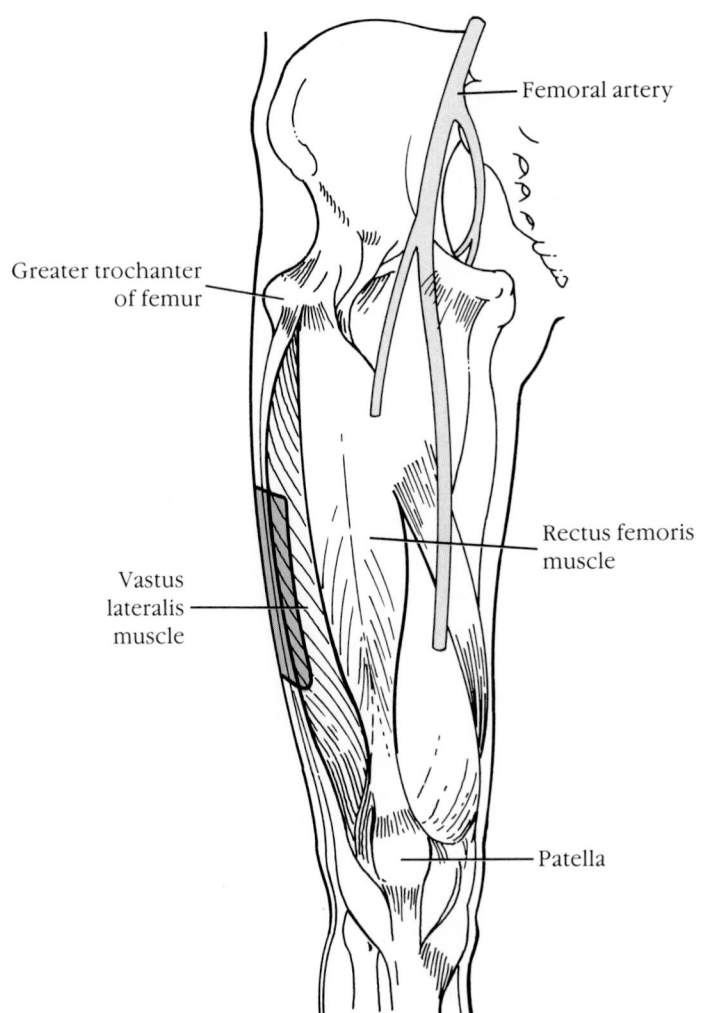

**FIGURE 8-2**   Vastus lateralis site for intramuscular injection. The vastus lateralis site is located on the medial outer aspect in the center third portion of the thigh in children. The belly of the muscle is one third the distance between the greater trochanter and the knee. It is the preferred site in children, since it is well developed at birth. It is also recommended for adults because the musle is large and can take up to 5 ml of medication per single injection. In the adult the site for injection is from one hand's breadth below the greater trochanter to a hand's breadth above the knee. The injection should be given at the right angle to the muscle or on an angle slightly toward the knee.

sites and communicating them to the rest of the staff. The vastus lateralis muscle is the site of choice for IM injections in children under 3 (Figure 8-2). The ventrogluteal site is preferred for the child over 3 years old who has been walking for a year or two (Figure 8-3). The dorsogluteal muscles should not be used for injections in the child under 4 to 6 years old if other IM sites are available. These muscles should not be used for injections at all until the younger child has been walking for at least 1 year.

For injection into the left gluteals, the thumb is placed on the trochanter and the middle finger on the iliac crest. The index finger placed midway between the thumb and middle finger will indicate a safe injection area. Infants should receive no more than 0.5 ml in each injection site.

Small children can tolerate a volume of up to 1 ml at each site. The deltoid muscle is likewise not used for children under 5 years of age because of its underdevelopment. Rather than the skin being held taut, as for adults, the muscle mass may instead be pinched up. The needle will thus avoid striking deeper-lying structures such as nerves, bones, or blood vessels. The IM injection is still made at a 90-degree angle to the top of the massed flesh. Preferred needle sizes for pediatric IM injections are 25- to 27-gauge and ½ to 1 inch in length. A 21- or 22-gauge needle may be preferred if a viscous medication such as procaine penicillin is to be given. In the interest of safety, the child should usually be restrained for an injection and the injection given rapidly. Two or more persons should be available for children over

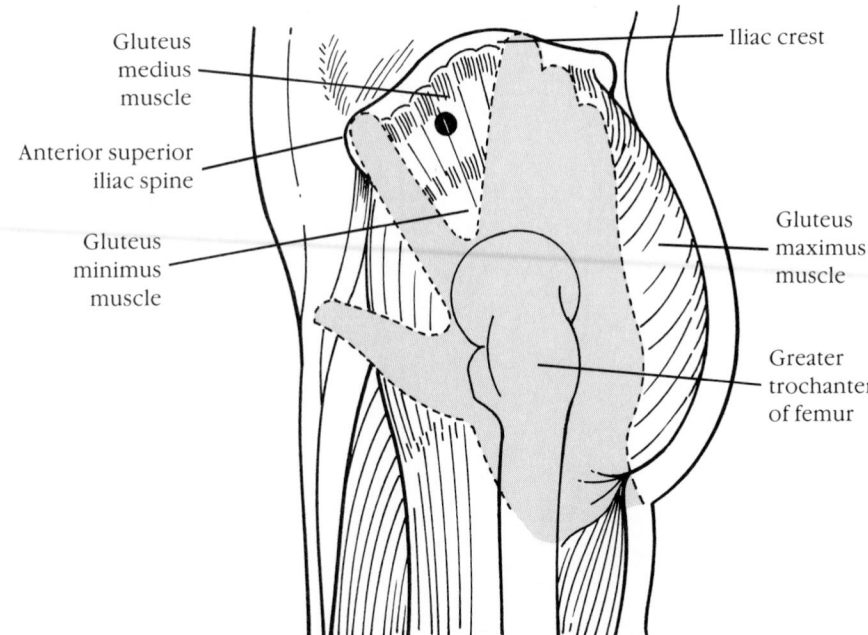

**FIGURE 8-3**   Ventrogluteal site for intramuscular injection. To locate this site, the nurse palpates the greater trochanter of the femur with the heel of the hand. The index and middle fingers are spread to form a V from the anterior superior iliac spine to just below the iliac crest. The triangle formed between the index finger, the middle finger, and the crest of the ilium is the injection site. The injection is made in the center area of the triangle with the needle directed slightly toward the iliac crest or at a right angle to the muscle. This site is relatively free from major nerves and vessels and has a larger muscle mass and less subcutaneous tissue than the dorsogluteal site. It is recommended for adults and children over 3 years of age who have been walking.

4 years of age despite promises that they will "hold still." An extra sterile needle may be carried in a pocket in case a needle becomes contaminated when a child moves unexpectedly. A child's attention may be distracted from the injection by asking the youngster to wiggle the toes. Since children enjoy trying out each other's beds, the identifying armband must be checked before giving each medication.

*Rectal administration.* When oral administration is difficult or contraindicated, the rectal route is often advised. Many children perceive use of the rectal route as an extreme invasion of their bodies or anticipate pain as a result. It may help to let them insert the suppository. Several drugs, such as sedatives, aspirin, and antiemetics, are available in suppository form. Suppositories made with a cocoa butter base will melt rapidly at normal body temperature, releasing the drug for absorption. After a suppository is inserted in an infant, the buttocks should be held or taped together for 5 to 10 minutes to relieve pressure on the anal sphincter and thereby help to ensure retention and absorption of the medication. Infants and children with diarrhea, however, may easily expel suppositories with explosive stools. Likewise, a suppository inserted into a child with a constipation problem or a rectum full of stool will be surrounded with stool and will have little chance for absorption of its contents.

Pharmacists and nurses often divide suppository doses by cutting them to obtain correct doses. This is a dangerous practice, since all the medication might be contained in one area of the suppository. If divided doses must be administered, the pharmacist should be contacted for alternate product advice and/or guidance.

*Nose drops, eardrops, and eyedrops.* Aqueous preparations of nose drops are the only safe preparations to use, if it is deemed necessary to use them at all, because of the danger of aspiration. Many nose drop preparations contain vasoconstrictors, and prolonged or excessive use may be harmful. Infants are nose breathers, and nasal congestion will inhibit their sucking. For this reason, nose drops, if necessary, should be instilled 20 minutes to ½ hour before feedings.

To instill *nose drops* (Figure 8-4):
1. Hold the infant in your arm, allowing the head to fall back over the edge of your arm, or place a small pillow under the shoulders and allow the head to fall back over the edge of the pillow.
2. Place your free arm so that the forearm is around the far side of the child's head, stabilizing the head between your forearm and your body. Use your hand to stabilize the arms and hands.

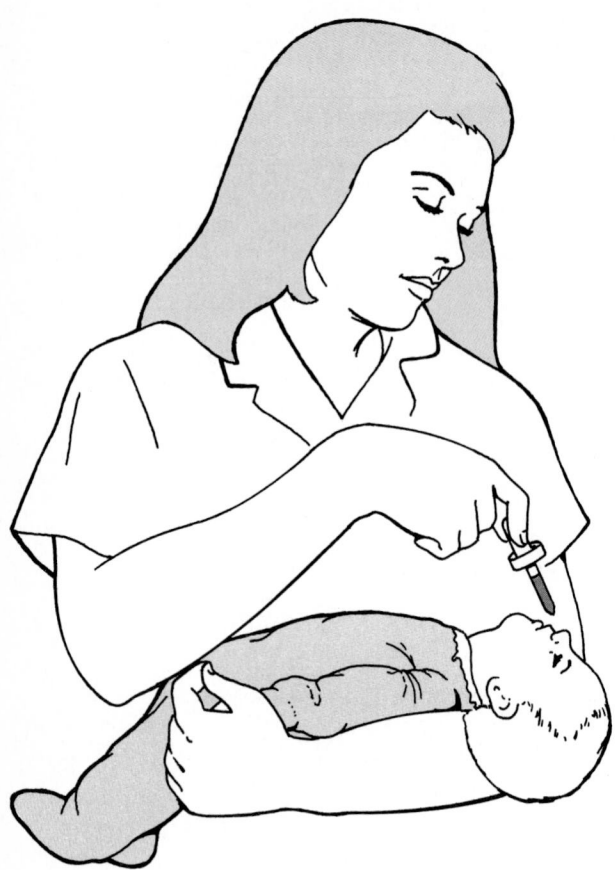

**FIGURE 8-4**  Administration of nose drops.

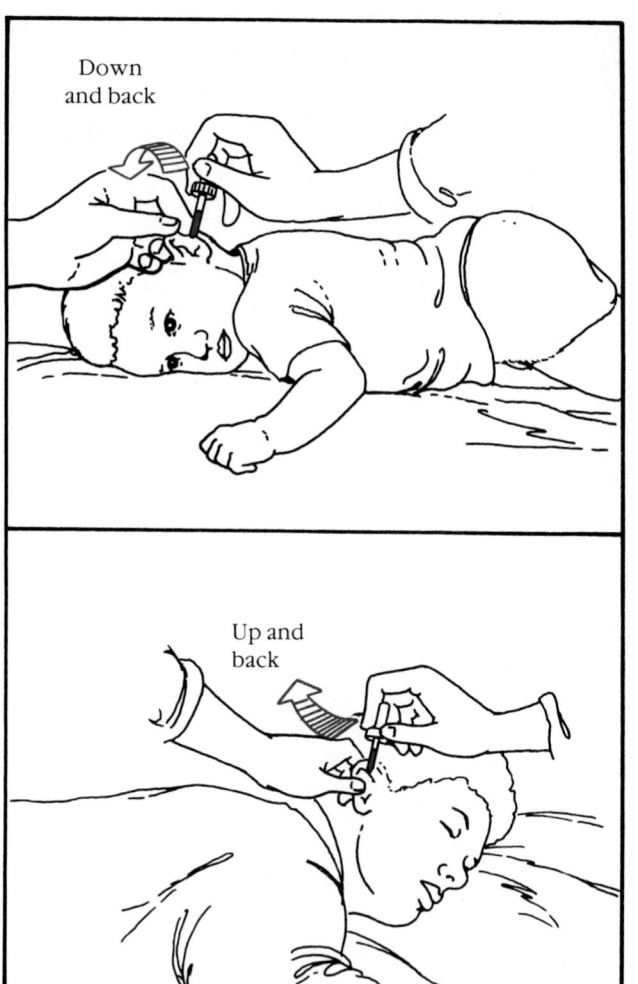

**FIGURE 8-5**  Administration of eardrops. The infant or child is positioned on the side of the unaffected ear. **A,** The nurse pulls the pinna down and back to administer eardrops to infants and children under 3 years of age. **B,** When administering eardrops to children older than 3 years and adults, the nurse gently pulls the pinna up and back. The nurse should stabilize his or her hand on the client's head for safety and instill the prescribed number of drops. The drops are directed toward the ear canal to avoid hitting the tympanic membrane, which can cause pain. The client should remain in the position for 5 to 10 minutes. Otic drops should be warmed before they are instilled to prevent nausea or vertigo.

3. With your free hand you can then instill the prescribed drops with minimum struggle and maximum accuracy.

The instillation of *eardrops* requires a knowledge of anatomic structure, since the shape of the auditory canal of a young child is different from that of an adult. Gentle massage of the area immediately anterior to the ear will facilitate the entry of the drops into the ear canal (Figure 8-5). Before the initial administration of a course of therapy with eardrops, the nurse should assess whether the child has excessive cerumen. If so, it may be necessary to consult with the physician about its removal with cerumen softeners and/or irrigation before instilling the eardrops.

*Eyedrop* instillation is done in the same way with children as with adults except that the head may be stabilized by an assistant. Many eyedrops cause a burning sensation for a few seconds, so if both eyes are to be medicated it is wise to do the second instillation quickly before the client begins to blink and tear as a reaction to the burning sensation occurring in the first eye medicated. Mild pressure for 30 seconds over the inner canthus next to the nose will prevent premature drainage of the medication away from the eye. (See Figure 8-6.)

Aqueous preparations of nose, ear, and eye drops may support the growth of bacteria and fungi. For this reason small volumes of such medications are ordered and should be used for only *one* individual (not shared by family members). The dropper (especially eye droppers) should not be permitted to become contaminated by touching anything but medication or rinsing water from the tap at any time. It should never be inverted so that medication or water runs into the rubber bulb to form a medium for microbiologic growth or to flavor the medication with a rubber taste. A dropper from one medication should usually not be used to measure and administer another type of medication because

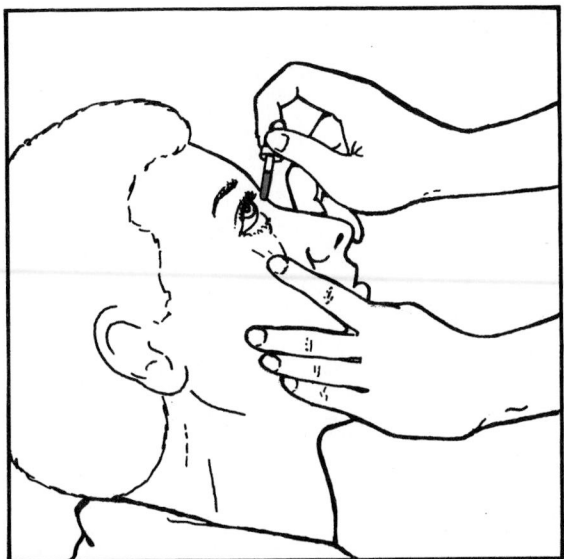

**FIGURE 8-6** Administration of eyedrops. The client should be asked to look up so that the cornea reflex is diminished, and the dropper should be introduced from the side. The lower lid is gently retracted, and the drops are instilled into the conjunctival sac. Drops should not be placed directly onto the cornea. After the drops are instilled, the lid is gently released.

droppers are not standardized—all droppers are not manufactured to deliver drops of the same volume. Viscosity of drugs also varies, affecting the drop size.

Eyedrops and eardrops are more comfortably tolerated if they are warmed (if not contraindicated) before instillation. Warming can be achieved by running warm water over the side of the bottle without the label or immersing the bottle in some warm water in a medicine cup. Even carrying the bottle in a pocket for half an hour or so will take the chill off the drops.

***Intravenous medications.*** The use of IV drug therapy is widespread on most pediatric services for several reasons. In children with vomiting and diarrhea, medications given by mouth may be vomited, losing precious time in drug management. These same children may have poor absorption of drugs and fluids as a result of dehydration or peripheral vascular collapse, so that drugs administered via the IM route may be equally ineffective. For premature or physiologically distressed neonates, it may be preferable to give certain high-osmolality drugs by IV rather than give the syrup or elixir forms by the oral route. These infants are prone to necrotizing enterocolitis (NEC) and death when administered feedings or oral drugs that have an osmolality greater than that of body fluids. Although elixirs of theophylline, phenobarbital, calcium, digoxin, and dexamethasone all have osmolalities 10 times greater than body fluids and have been implicated in causing NEC, analysis shows that the contained additives actually raise the medication's osmolality. Related studies continue.

---

### PEDIATRIC IV DRUG ADMINISTRATION

1. IV drug therapy should be used only if other channels of drug administration are impracticable. Pediatric nurses skilled in giving medications to children via other routes may be able to influence prescribers' decisions regarding successful routes of drug administration.
2. For small infants a scalp vein or a superficial vein of the wrist, hand, foot, or arm may be most convenient and most easily stabilized. Scalp veins have no valves, and thus infusions may be in either direction. They are the most frequent sites for infant infusions. Older children may receive infusions through any accessible vein.
3. A too-rapid IV infusion or injection may cause "speed shock": rapid fall in blood pressure, respiratory irregularity, blood incoagulability, and even death. Preventive measures include use of the minidropper (note that the milliliter per hour in the order translates to the drops per minute with this tubing), calibrated volume control chambers, and infusion pumps.
4. Total parenteral nutrition (TPN) solutions are usually infused into the vena cava or innominate or subclavian veins approached via the external or internal jugular veins. Occasionally, the inferior vena cava is entered via the femoral vein.
5. Once a drug is injected intravenously, the drug's action is relatively irreversible.
6. Drugs must be properly diluted. Too much emphasis cannot be placed on the caution: GIVE THE SMALLEST POSSIBLE DOSE AT THE SLOWEST POSSIBLE RATE.

---

The pediatric nurse responsible for the administration of IV drugs may find the suggestions in the box above helpful (see also Chapter 6). Most older children may be given fluids or drugs intravenously following the same principles and techniques used for adults. The younger and smaller the child, the greater the margin for error.

Neonates, infants, and children must be adequately restrained so as not to dislodge or pull out an infusion needle or catheter once it is in place. Some of the following may be helpful hints to the nurse caring for a client receiving IV therapy (see also Figure 8-7).

1. The needle or catheter should be fixed with plastic tape.
2. When a loop of tubing directly above the needle is secured to the tape, tension is relieved from the needle should it be pulled by sudden movement.
3. Since most children move about or are restless, it is necessary to support the limb with a padded arm board and immobilize the site of IV therapy. Support should extend to the joints above and below the site (with arm boards or IV boards).
4. If the infusion bottle is too high, the pressure in the

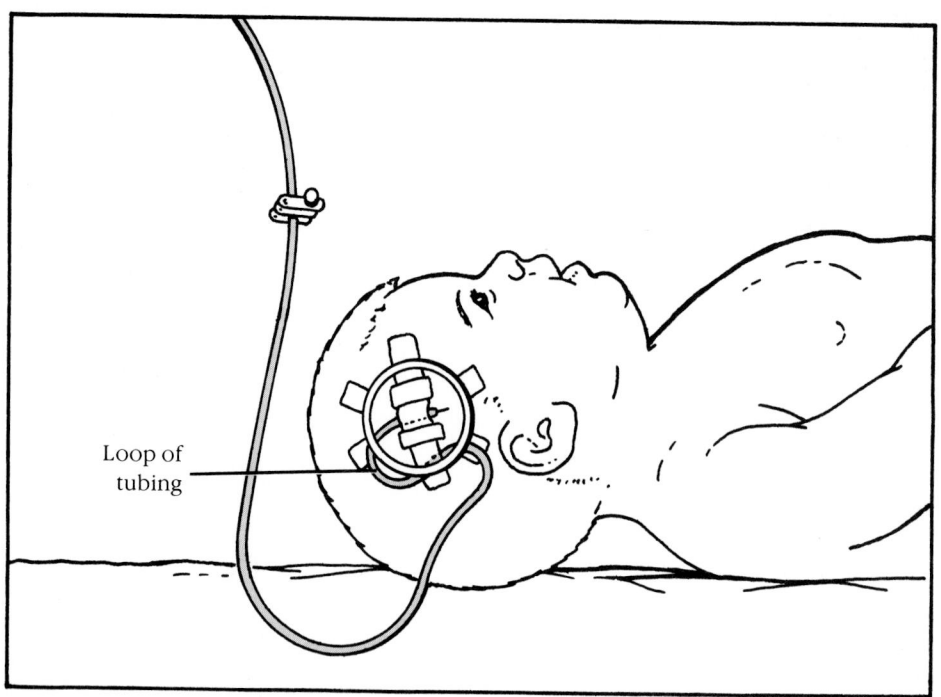

Loop of
tubing

**FIGURE 8-7** Securing a scalp vein infusion for infants.

vein will increase, causing fluid seepage into the surrounding tissues.

***Other factors influencing drug dosages.*** Again, the
dosage of most agents is related to the child's age, weight,
and height. A child's bodily systems grow and develop at
varying rates. This makes for unpredictable primary and
secondary effects in pediatric medication administration.
One example of secondary effects specific to children is
discoloration of teeth and depression of enamel growth in
the child under 8 years of age with administration of tetracycline liquid medications. (This adverse reaction is well-
documented, but many prescriptions for this drug are still
being written for this age group, according to the FDA.)
Skeletal growth of children receiving long-term adrenocortical steroids is similarly impaired.

Individual variations are noted in children's response to
digitalis, insulin, opiates, and oral enzyme products; dosages require careful titration. Paradoxical responses are
noted with a few drugs; responses may be directly opposite
that which could be expected in the adult. Excessive reactivity to atropine by infants may be related to immaturity
of the central nervous system. In addition, many drugs that
are safe and effective for adults have not been tested for
use with children, nor have dosages been established, because of the complex medicolegal issues involved in experimentation on children.

## GERIATRIC CLIENTS

Although individuals age 65 and over represent 12% of the
total population in the United States today, they use ap-

proximately 35% of all health care goods and services, 25%
to 30% of all prescribed drugs, and considerable quantities
of OTC, self-treatment medications. Today the elderly comprise one of every nine Americans, but in 50 years (or the
year 2040) it has been projected that one of every five
Americans will be 65 years or older (Lamy, 1988; Sloan,
1986).

At the turn of the century, only 1 person in 25 was over
65 years old. People died from parasitic and infectious diseases (pestilence and famine) then, while today the primary
causes of death result from degenerative, chronic diseases.
Three out of every four elderly deaths today are caused by
heart disease, cancer, or stroke.

The elderly are usually affected by age-related, altered
pharmacokinetics and pharmacodynamics and an increased
incidence of chronic diseases, which generally result in an
increase in physician's prescriptions and/or self-treatment
with various medications and home remedies. The age of
specialization has in some ways added to this problem, in
that, multiple physicians usually prescribe a variety of medications often without discontinuing any previous drugs the
client is taking. This practice, often referred to as *polypharmacy*, too often has a disastrous outcome.

The practice of polypharmacy has resulted in an increased
risk of inducing drug interactions, adverse reactions, and
the need for, or prolonging of, hospitalization. Pray (1989)
has reported that persons receiving two medications have a
5.6% potential for having a drug interaction, while clients
that receive five or eight different medications have a 50%
and 100% drug interaction risk, respectively. Dr. Robert
Kane (1989) reported that "adverse drug reactions in the

**Nursing Research:**
## DRUG-TAKING PRACTICES OF THE RURAL ELDERLY

A study to examine drug-taking practices of the noninstitutionalized rural elderly was conducted with 48 men and 52 women over the age of 65. Johnson and Moore* found that most subjects used both prescription and nonprescription medications daily. The majority of the study's participants combined medications without consulting a health care professional. Many ignored side effects and exceeded recommended dosages. Self-treatment of symptoms by the rural elderly may be the consequence of geographic and physical isolation, as well as many rural areas being medically underserved. However, the implications for nursing are that elderly clients, particularly those in rural areas, require additional education regarding responsible drug use and that nurses need to maintain an awareness that the elderly may be using multiple medications.

*Johnson JE and Moore J. (1988). The drug-taking practices of the rural elderly, Appl Nurs Res 1(3):128.

### ALTERED PHARMACOKINETICS IN THE ELDERLY

| | |
|---|---|
| Absorption | ↑ Gastric pH or acidity |
| | ↓ Intestinal blood flow |
| Distribution | ↓ Lean body mass |
| | ↑ Adipose (fat) stores |
| | ↓ Total body water |
| | ↓ Serum albumin |
| Metabolism | ↓ Liver size |
| | ↓ Liver blood flow |
| | ↓ Liver functions (microsomal enzyme activity) |
| Excretion | ↓ Kidney function |

elderly in 1985 were responsible for 243,000 hospitalizations; 32,000 hip fractures; 160,000 mental impairments, and 2,000,000 addictions." While the magnitude of problems with polypharmacy is enormous, it is frequently overlooked as the causative factor. It is important that health care providers realize that the vast majority of undesirable drug effects resulting from polypharmacy are preventable.

## Physiologic Changes

As people age they undergo a variety of physiologic changes that increase their sensitivity to drugs and drug-induced disease. General loss in body weight of many elderly clients may require reevaluation of dosages used for them; the criterion for dosage should be shifted from age to weight. Some older clients weigh no more than the average large child, and some weigh a lot less; yet they are prescribed the larger "adult" doses. In another case, stimulants are generally less effective in elderly individuals, and large doses are often necessary. However, CNS depressants produce intensified effects in the elderly. Sedatives and hypnotics can produce paradoxical side effects of irritability, incontinence, confusion, and disorientation.

Pharmacokinetics (see box) are altered in the aging client because of reduced gastric acid and slowed gastric motility, resulting in unpredictable rates of dissolution and absorption of drugs. Changes in absorption may occur when acid production decreases, altering the absorption of weakly acidic drugs such as barbiturates. However, few studies of drug absorption have shown clinically significant changes occurring with advanced age.

Changes in body composition, such as increased propor-

tion of body fat and decreased total body water, plasma volume, and extracellular fluid, have been noted in the elderly. The increased proportion of body fat increases the body's ability to store fat-soluble compounds such as phenothiazines and barbiturates, and thus increase the accumulation of those drugs. The reduced lean body mass affects drug distribution by decreasing the volume in which the drug circulates, thereby causing higher peak levels. The risk of toxicity with water-soluble drugs increases as total body water decreases. Decreased serum albumin for binding drugs leads to increased amounts of free drug in the circulation. Disorders common to the aging person such as congestive heart failure (CHF), which may impair liver function, influence biotransformation by decreasing the metabolism of drugs and increasing the risk of drug accumulation and toxicity. Renal function may be impaired because of loss of nephrons, decreased blood flow, and glomerular filtration rate. A reduction in renal function is also secondary to CHF. Decreased renal clearance may cause increased plasma drug concentrations and longer half-lives of drugs and active metabolites that the kidney usually excretes. Special precautions include careful monitoring of the elderly client for a safe drug regime.

## Problem Medications in the Elderly

The potent medications available to treat the diseases or illnesses of the elderly often have a narrow index between drug effectiveness and/or toxicity. The drug categories most commonly prescribed for the elderly are listed in the box on p. 142 (Lamy, 1988; Pulliam and Stewart, 1985). Therefore, it is not surprising that the top drugs or drug categories identified as problem causing in the elderly are primarily derived from this listing. See Table 8-3 for selected problem medications in the elderly (Stanaszek and Baker, 1983; Pulliam and Stewart, 1985).

***Responsibility of health care providers.*** The primary responsibility of a health care provider is to reduce or eliminate the potentially adverse risk factors associated with

**TABLE 8-4**  Selected problem medications in the elderly

| Medication | Elderly response |
|---|---|
| digoxin, digitalis preparations | Visual disorders, nausea, diarrhea, cardiac arrhythmias, hallucinations |
| anticholinergics (antispasmodics) | Blurred vision, dry mouth, constipation, confusion, urinary retention, tachycardia |
| phenothiazines | Hypotension, tremors, extrapyramidal side effects, restlessness |
| analgesics, opioid | Confusion, constipation, urinary retention, nausea, vomiting, respiratory depression, addiction |
| analgesics, non-narcotic (aspirin) | Tinnitus, gastric distress, GI bleeding |
| anticoagulant (heparin, warfarin) | Bleeding episodes, hemorrhage |
| thiazide diuretics | Electrolyte imbalance (hypokalemia), rashes, fatigue, leg cramps, dehydration |
| hypnotic-sedatives | Confusion, daytime sedation and ataxia, lethargy, increased forgetfulness |
| antihypertensives (e.g., methyldopa) | Nausea, hypotension, diarrhea, bradycardia, heart failure |
| antiarthritics (e.g., ibuprofen) | Edema, nausea, abdominal distress, gastric ulceration and/or bleeding |

---

### DRUG CATEGORIES MOST COMMONLY PRESCRIBED FOR THE ELDERLY

| | |
|---|---|
| antihypertensives | psychotropics |
| analgesics | hypnotic-sedatives |
| diuretics | antiarrhythmics |
| antispasmodics | anticoagulants |
| digitalis preparations | alpha/beta blockers |
| antiarthritics | |

---

various drug regimens. This can be accomplished by the following:

1. Identify the client at special risk, such as the elderly person with potential altered pharmacokinetics, multiple illnesses, or liver or kidney impairment. Other factors that may affect selected medications include a history of alcoholism, smoking, or specific dietary habits.
2. Take a complete medication history, preferably in the client's home. Note all medications on hand, ordering physician(s), expiration dates, and their storage. A thorough history should include prescribed drugs, OTC medications, and home remedies (e.g., herbal or health food store purchases), if used.
3. If unfamiliar with a drug, look it up for its primary and secondary effects. Also check recommended dosage, side and adverse effects, and contraindications.
4. Check all medications for possible drug interactions by using a current reference guide or by consulting a pharmacist.
5. Discuss drug regimen with the primary physician (or encourage the client to do so) if problem areas are identified (e.g., duplicate medications have been prescribed, possible drug interactions are present, or the client has had side effects that may be attributable to one or more of the medications).
6. Educate clients on their medications, safe storage, and proper method of disposing of discontinued medications.
7. Monitor therapy closely so that therapeutic response and/or development of side effects or adverse effects can be detected early in treatment.

Ideally the prescriber will individualize and simplify drug therapy for the client. Keeping medications to a minimum with the least frequent dosage administration necessary will help to reduce the potential for drug interactions and also improve client compliance with the drug regimen.

## Nursing Management of Medication Administration for Geriatric Clients

In view of the effects just outlined and the multiplicity of drugs prescribed for elderly clients, their occasionally unreliable memories and senses, inadequate financial status, and propensity for adverse secondary effects, nurses must make every attempt to simplify the geriatric drug therapy plan. Suspect medications as the cause whenever you note a change in an elderly client's behavior, particularly restlessness, irritability, and confusion. These alterations of thought processes may be the earliest signs of drug toxicity. Encourage nursing assistants to report to a nurse any changes they notice in the client's behavior. Often what passes for senility is drug-induced lethargy or confusion.

In the administration of medications, the geriatric client may have special needs. The elderly frequently have dry mucous membranes, which impede swallowing, so offer water before and after oral medications if the client's condition permits. Position the elderly client so that gravity will assist the drug through the esophagus and minimize the possibility of aspiration. Because of diminished sensation, the client may be unaware that the tablet is stuck between the lip and gum, so examine the client's mouth to ensure that the medication has been swallowed. Geriatric clients may have slowed reflexes and reduced understanding of treatment. It helps to organize the dispensing of medication so that enough time is allowed for clients who require a great deal of attention, possibly by medicating them last, and yet so that all clients will receive their medication on time. A nurse has roughly an hour's range in which to distribute all the medications during one administration period.

Diminished taste sensation usually keeps unpalatable drugs from being much of a problem, but many older individuals may have difficulty swallowing, especially if they have sustained a cerebrovascular accident (stroke). (See the discussion of special situations in Chapter 6.)

Selection of sites for injectable medications in elderly clients may present the nurse with a challenge. Since muscle mass declines with age, suitable sites for intramuscular injection may be fewer than in younger individuals and will require more skill and effort in palpating to detect muscles of adequate body and size. On the other hand, decreased sensory perception, including perception of pain, may make injections less painful.

Physical problems often interfere with the ability of the older client to comply with prescribed drug regimens. Some older clients may be unable to read labels or locate drugs because of failing eyesight; others, such as arthritic clients, may have difficulty opening bottles (particularly child-proof containers) or handling small pills, while the hard-of-hearing client may not hear all of the instructions. The logistics of obtaining drugs and the economic cost may be a deterrent to complying with therapy. Multiple drug therapy may simply be too complex for the client to manage without assistance. The nurse can simplify drug administration and scheduling as much as possible. Dosage schedules and calendars often help the forgetful client. Drug packaging that is easy to use and clearly labeled, as well as printed directions and drug information, help to ensure compliance in the older client.

The elderly client's functional capabilities must be assessed to determine the educational requirements for safe and accurate self-administration of medications in the home. The nurse's creativity and skill are essential in devising teaching plans to enhance client compliance with the home medication regimen (see Chapter 10, "Client Teaching for Self-Administration of Medications"). Discuss OTC medications with clients and their family and friends and have them describe in detail how and when they take all medications.

Probably the most important part of the nursing process for aging clients is the nurse's ability to communicate patience, warmth, and understanding and to treat the elderly as persons with dignity and with the ability to reason, to feel, and to contribute.

## SUMMARY

Nursing management of the administration of medications to clients of different age groups requires that the nurse be knowledgeable about the various effects of pharmaceutical agents in clients of different ages. Understanding the rationales behind these effects will help the nurse to administer medications safely and to evaluate client responses appropriately, regardless of the client's age. Childbearing clients, neonates, infants and children, and geriatric clients all have unique needs based on physiologic and psychosocial developmental needs.

## BIBLIOGRAPHY

Abramowicz M, editor. (1987). Safety of antimicrobial drugs in pregnancy, The Medical Letter 29(743):61.

American Hospital Formulary Service. (1990). ASHP drug information service. Bethesda, Md: American Society of Hospital Pharmacists, Inc.

Berlin CM Jr. (1987). The use of drugs during pregnancy and lactation, Public Health Rep, July-Aug, p 53.

Committee on Drugs, American Academy of Pediatrics. (1983). The transfer of drugs and other chemicals into human breast milk, Pediatr 72:375.

Erbe RW. (1983). Drugs and pregnancy: what are the dangers? Consultant 23(11):185.

Fanaroff AA and Martin RJ, editors. (1984). Behrman's neonatal-perinatal medicine: diseases of the fetus and infant. St Louis: The CV Mosby Co.

Fielo S and Rizzolo MA. (1985). The effects of age on pharmacokinetics, Geriatr Nurs 6(11/12):328.

Gilman JT. (1987). Pediatric considerations in drug therapy, Fla J Hosp Pharm 7:63.

Guyton G. (1989). Pharmacokinetic considerations in neonatal drug therapy, Neonat Netw 7(5):9.

Hall WC, Talbert RL, and Ereshefsky L. (1990). Cocaine abuse and its treatment, Pharmacotherapy 10(1):47-65.

Hurd PD and Butovich SL. (1986). Compliance problems and the older patient: assessing functional limitations, Drug Intell Clin Pharm 20(3):22.

Hussar DA. (1985). Drug interactions in the geriatric client. In American Association of Colleges of Pharmacy's Pharmacy practice for the geriatric patient. Carrboro, NC: Eli Lilly & Co.

Iafrate RP. (1987). Correct use of drugs in children, Am Druggist 195(6):82.

Kane R. (1989). Educate physicians on elderly needs, Am Pharm NS29(7):458.

Lamy PP. (1988). The elderly patient: health status and drug therapy, Pharm Times 54(8):31.

Noerr B. (1989). Neonates and drugs, Neonat Netw 7(5):36.

Oppeneer JE and Vervoren TM. (1983). Geronotological pharmacology: a resource for health practitioners. St Louis: The CV Mosby Co.

Parks BR Jr. (1988). Use of topical steroids in children, Pediatr Nurs 14(4):337.

Pray WS. (1989). Help your patient avoid drug interactions, US Pharmacist 14(7):19.

Pulliam CC and Stewart RB. (1985). Adverse drug reactions in the elderly. In American Association of Colleges of Pharmacy's Pharmacy practice for the geriatric patient. Carrboro, NC: Eli Lilly & Co.

Ramirez A. (1989). The neonate's response to drugs: unraveling the causes of drug iatrogenesis, Neonat Netw 7(5):45.

Ramsey R. (1988). Adjusting drug dosages for critically ill elderly patients, Nursing 18(7):47.

Riordan J and Riordan M. (1984). Drugs in breast milk. Am J Nurs 84:(3):328.

Roussea P. (1987). Pharmacologic alterations in the elderly: special considerations, Hosp Formul 22(6):543.

Sheahan SL et al. (1989). Drug misuse among the elderly: a covert problem, Health Values 13(3):22.

Shepard TH. (1982). Detection of human teratogenic agents, J Pediatr 101(5):810.

Sloan RW. (1986). Practical geriatric therapeutics, Oradell, NJ: Medical Economics Books.

Stanaszek WF and Baker D. (1983). Drug monitoring in the geriatric patient, Am Pharm ns23(7):32.

Todd B. (1986). When the risks outweigh the benefits, Geriatr Nurs 7(7/8):212.

United States Pharmacopeial Convention. (1989). Drug information for the health care provider, ed 11, Rockville, Md: US Pharmacopeial Convention.

Wade B and Bowling A. (1991). Appropriate use of drugs by elderly people, J Adv Nurs 11:47.

Young LY and Koda-Kimble MA. (1988). Applied therapeutics, ed 4, Vancouver, Wash: Applied Therapeutics, Inc.

# Case Study: Polypharmacy in the Elderly

Walter Smith is an 86-year-old, divorced man who lives alone in a public housing project for the elderly. He describes himself as a loner, loves to read, and expresses a great deal of pride at being independent for his entire life. He was admitted to the hospital following a fall from which he received scalp lacerations. He was alert but quite suspicious of the health care givers. He weighed 138 pounds and was 5' 10". He had very poor vision and hearing. He was diagnosed with hypertension, arteriosclerotic heart disease, atrial fibrillation, eczematous dermatitis of his legs, and a urinary tract infection. He spent 3 days in the hospital and was discharged on the following medications:

    betamethasone (Valisone) cream 0.1% to legs twice daily
    digoxin, 0.125 mg daily
    furosemide (Lasix), 20 mg daily
    methyldopa (Aldomet), 250 mg bid
    isosorbide dinitrate (isordil), 5 mg qid
    ferrous sulfate (Feosol spansule), 1 bid
    vitamin C, 1 capsule daily
    dicloxacillin, 500 mg qid for 10 days
    propoxyphene and acetaminophen (Darvocet-N), 100 mg qid as needed

Before this hospitalization, Mr. Smith had relied heavily on self-care and self-medication, which he resumed when discharged. He consumed large quantities of natural vitamin and mineral supplements. He used Corn Huskers Lotion on his legs. One week after discharge the visiting nurse found that Mr. Smith had fallen twice during the week but had sustained only minor bruises. He was weak and although he was oriented to place and person, he was uncertain as to time and showed memory loss and some incoherence in thought processes. He had trouble describing his medications but complained that they were expensive and caused him to experience incontinence. His blood pressure was 98/64.

The nurse convinced Mr. Smith to visit a physician he knew and liked. The physician was understanding of Mr. Smith's desire to remain in his home and of his health practices. Mr. Smith insisted on using the Corn Huskers Lotion instead of the "too expensive" cream. The physician agreed to this change and in addition was able to reduce Mr. Smith's medications to the following: digoxin, 0.125 mg daily; Isordil, 5 mg qid; and triamterene hydrochlorothiazide (Dyazide), 1 capsule daily. Mr. Smith agreed to take his heart medications and to use fewer of his nonprescription vitamins and minerals.

1. Why is polypharmacy a common problem with elderly clients?
2. What assessment data should the nurse obtain to understand the client's beliefs and practices regarding medications?
3. How might the following have contributed to the confusion Mr. Smith experienced?
   a. Effects of age-related changes in circulatory, renal, and hepatic function on the drugs taken.
   b. The specific actions or adverse effects of the following drugs:
      digoxin
      Lasix
      Aldomet
      Darvocet-N
4. What factors affected Mr. Smith's ability and willingness to carry out the medication regimen?

# Case Study: Pediatric Considerations

Timmy, a four-year-old child with reversible obstructive airway disease, is admitted to the emergency room with bilateral wheezing and moderate respiratory distress. He has received two aerosol treatments yet continues to be in moderate distress with continued wheezing. The physician has ordered an IV bolus of aminophylline to be followed by a continuous IV infusion of aminophylline.

1. What factors should be considered in selecting the intravenous route for drug administration in the child?
2. What measures should the nurse use to maintain the integrity of the intravenous infusion?
3. Timmy is to be discharged on oral theophylline. The appropriate dose of oral theophylline for a child Timmy's age is 16 mg/kg. Calculate the dose for Timmy, who weighs 42 pounds.
4. What should the nurse teach Timmy's parents about administering this oral medication?

# 9 Substance Misuse and Abuse

## INTRODUCTION

Although most drugs are prescribed and administered carefully, all drugs have the potential to be misused or abused. The prescribing of drugs without adequate exploration of the client's presenting complaint, for example, represents drug misuse by a physician. Prolonged and unsupervised administration of drugs for symptomatic relief is another example. In general, **drug misuse** refers to nonspecific or indiscriminate use of drugs, including alcohol. **Drug abuse**

---

## DRUG ABUSE TERMINOLOGY

**Drug Abuse Warning Network (DAWN)** federal agency that monitors data on medical and psychologic problems associated with drug abuse; it identifies currently abused drugs and patterns of drug abuse and monitors changing trends or new abuse substances; such data may be used to develop new drug controls or to reschedule drugs already on the market

**Hallucinogenic** tendency of a drug to produce auditory and/or visual hallucinations; hallucinogenic effects are not uniform, nor are they a primary property of all consciousness-altering drugs

**Psychotomimetic** ability of a drug to chemically induce symptoms of psychosis

**Psychedelic** mind-altering drug self-administered for its subjective effects of altering perception, thought, and feeling and for social-recreational purposes

**Psychic (psychologic) dependence** emotional reliance on a drug; manifestations range from a mild desire for a drug to a craving to repeated compulsive use for subjectively satisfying or pleasurable effects

**Physical (physiologic) dependence** adaptive physiologic state occurring after prolonged use of a drug; discontinuation causes intense physical disturbances (objective withdrawal symptoms) that are relieved by readministering the same drug or a pharmacologically related drug

**Tolerance** tendency to increase drug dosage to experience same effect formerly produced by a smaller dose

**Cross-dependent drugs** drugs capable of relieving withdrawal symptoms that result from withdrawal of another drug

---

refers to self-medication or self-administration of a drug in chronically excessive quantities, resulting in psychic and/or physical dependence, functional impairment, and deviation from approved social norms. See the box above on drug abuse terminology.

Drug abuse is neither a new nor a recent phenomenon. It has been known throughout history as one expression of an individual's search for relief of physical, psychological, social, and economic problems. Indeed, investigators suggest that epidemics of drug abuse have occurred throughout human history (Brecher, 1972). Contemporary drug abuse has attained prominence as an issue with moral, legal, religious, social, intrapsychic, and medical implications. Drug abuse is not a problem confined to any particular socioeconomic, cultural, or ethnic group. It is a major medical, social, and interpersonal problem affecting individuals from all economic backgrounds and across the life span.

Bissell and Haberman (1984) studied alcoholism and the use of other drugs with alcohol in U.S. professionals, including doctors, nurses, dentists, attorneys, social workers, and college women. They followed a group of approximately 400 professionals for 5 to 7 years after locating the

individuals from Alcoholics Anonymous programs. Nearly two thirds of the sample were graduated in the top third of their class.

Alcoholism or alcohol abuse with other drugs usually affected a professional in his or her first 15 years of practice. Drinking interfered with individual life-style at a median age of 28 for women and 30 for men. When asked reasons for seeking help from Alcoholics Anonymous, males reported family and economic pressures or difficulty with their profession, while women cited health problems, shame, or guilt as their primary reasons.

The combination of alcohol and other drugs was quite prevalent, especially with physicians and nurses. This group reported the greatest addiction to hard narcotics. Their narcotic of choice was meperidine (Demerol) because it was readily available in their settings and because it produced less pupillary constriction than the other opioids. Most physicians and nurses stated that they received their drugs through professional channels. Other professionals with combination drug abuse obtained their drugs from street sources.

When asked why they combined alcohol with other drugs, many professionals answered that they were not taught that alcohol can cause insomnia and aggravate agitation and depression. Therefore when such symptoms occurred, they had a tendency to blame other problems, such as stress, financial difficulties, marital problems, and fatigue for the symptoms. Medication was often prescribed for relief of these symptoms by attending physicians, while questioning regarding the use of alcohol was frequently overlooked.

Career pressures and accessibility of a supply of drugs place health care professionals at greater risk for drug abuse. Unfortunately, some impaired health professionals are in practice. They constitute a hazard to client well-being and to themselves, so they cannot be ignored, overlooked, or left unreported. It is vital that health agencies be alert to suspected drug abusers on their staffs. Many agencies and most states have active rehabilitation programs for impaired health professionals.

Drug and alcohol abuse in the workplace costs businesses an estimated $43 billion to $85 billion a year in the United States (Lawrence, 1983). Absenteeism, stealing, embezzlement, tardiness, and health care costs, which nationally are over $50 billion annually for the treatment of alcohol- and drug-related problems, are just a few of the cost factors related to substance abuse. Persons abusing alcohol and/or other substances will usually demonstrate a reduction in their job efficiency over time that is reflected by their attendance record, general behavior on the job, and job performance. (See Figure 9-1.)

A 1984 survey by the National Institute of Mental Health, considered one of the most comprehensive surveys of noninstitutionalized persons ever performed, indicated that drug abuse and drug dependence was the third most frequently reported psychiatric problem in men, ages 18 to 65

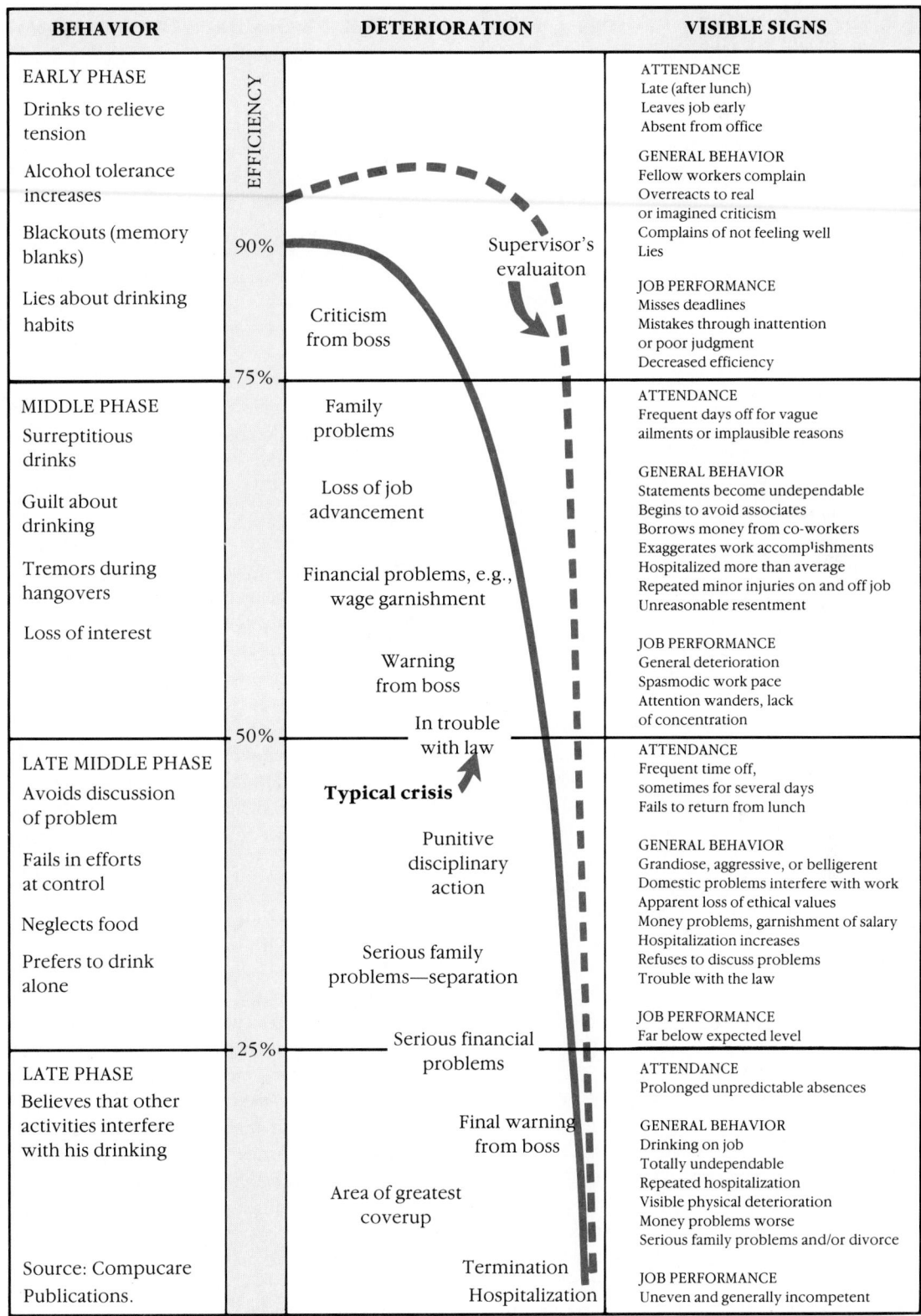

| BEHAVIOR | DETERIORATION | VISIBLE SIGNS |
|---|---|---|
| **EARLY PHASE**<br><br>Drinks to relieve tension<br><br>Alcohol tolerance increases<br><br>Blackouts (memory blanks)<br><br>Lies about drinking habits | *Supervisor's evaluaiton*<br><br>Criticism from boss | **ATTENDANCE**<br>Late (after lunch)<br>Leaves job early<br>Absent from office<br><br>**GENERAL BEHAVIOR**<br>Fellow workers complain<br>Overreacts to real<br>or imagined criticism<br>Complains of not feeling well<br>Lies<br><br>**JOB PERFORMANCE**<br>Misses deadlines<br>Mistakes through inattention<br>or poor judgment<br>Decreased efficiency |
| **MIDDLE PHASE**<br><br>Surreptitious drinks<br><br>Guilt about drinking<br><br>Tremors during hangovers<br><br>Loss of interest | Family problems<br><br>Loss of job advancement<br><br>Financial problems, e.g., wage garnishment<br><br>Warning from boss<br><br>In trouble with law | **ATTENDANCE**<br>Frequent days off for vague ailments or implausible reasons<br><br>**GENERAL BEHAVIOR**<br>Statements become undependable<br>Begins to avoid associates<br>Borrows money from co-workers<br>Exaggerates work accomplishments<br>Hospitalized more than average<br>Repeated minor injuries on and off job<br>Unreasonable resentment<br><br>**JOB PERFORMANCE**<br>General deterioration<br>Spasmodic work pace<br>Attention wanders, lack of concentration |
| **LATE MIDDLE PHASE**<br><br>Avoids discussion of problem<br><br>Fails in efforts at control<br><br>Neglects food<br><br>Prefers to drink alone | **Typical crisis**<br><br>Punitive disciplinary action<br><br>Serious family problems—separation<br><br>Serious financial problems | **ATTENDANCE**<br>Frequent time off, sometimes for several days<br>Fails to return from lunch<br><br>**GENERAL BEHAVIOR**<br>Grandiose, aggressive, or belligerent<br>Domestic problems interfere with work<br>Apparent loss of ethical values<br>Money problems, garnishment of salary<br>Hospitalization increases<br>Refuses to discuss problems<br>Trouble with the law<br><br>**JOB PERFORMANCE**<br>Far below expected level |
| **LATE PHASE**<br><br>Believes that other activities interfere with his drinking<br><br><br>Source: Compucare Publications. | Final warning from boss<br><br>Area of greatest coverup<br><br>Termination<br>Hospitalization | **ATTENDANCE**<br>Prolonged unpredictable absences<br><br>**GENERAL BEHAVIOR**<br>Drinking on job<br>Totally undependable<br>Repeated hospitalization<br>Visible physical deterioration<br>Money problems worse<br>Serious family problems and/or divorce<br><br>**JOB PERFORMANCE**<br>Uneven and generally incompetent |

EFFICIENCY: 90%, 75%, 50%, 25%

**FIGURE 9-1**   Relationship between alcohol abuse and employee behaviors. *(Redrawn from Lawrence C Jr. [1983]. As workers get high, so do prices, The Miami Herald, p C-1, Oct 24.)*

### DRUGS THAT MAY RESULT IN FALSE-POSITIVE RESULTS

| Testing for | False-Positives Reported in Presence of |
|---|---|
| amphetamines | diethylpropion (Tenuate) |
| | ephedrine (in Tedral, Quadrinal, Primatene) |
| | nylidrin (Arlidin) |
| | phenylpropanolamine (in Alka-Seltzer Plus Cold Medicine, Dexatrim) |
| barbiturates | phenytoin (Dilantin) |
| opiates | chlorpromazine (Thorazine) |
| | D-propoxyphene (Darvon) |
| | dextromethorphan (the DM in many cough-cold preparations) |
| phencyclidine (PCP) | chlorpromazine (Thorazine) |
| | dextromethorphan (see above) |
| | diphenhydramine (Benadryl) |
| | meperidine (Demerol) |
| | thioridazine (Mellaril) |

Data from Council on Scientific Affairs, 1987.

### TIME VERSUS DRUG DETECTION IN URINE

| Drug | Detection in Urine (Hours) |
|---|---|
| amphetamines | 48 |
| barbiturates | |
|    Short-acting | 24 |
|    Long-acting | 168 |
| cocaine | 48 to 72 |
| marijuana | |
|    One-time use | 72 |
|    Daily use | 240 |

Data from Council on Scientific Affairs, 1987.

(Braunwald, 1987). In women age 18 to 24, drug abuse was the second most common psychiatric disorder. Drug abuse is a major public health problem in America that affects nearly every aspect of the individual, i.e., life-style, relationships, health, finances, and the workplace.

In an effort to identify persons with alcohol- and drug-related problems, many businesses, government agencies, and health-related facilities are performing drug analysis or urine drug tests under specified conditions on their employees. Drug screens may also be part of a pre-employment physical examination. While a number of testing procedures are available, it is important to know the analytic techniques used and the purpose and the limitation of any tests performed. Such testing often affects the individual's reputation and employment, so knowing the sensitivity of the test is very important. Is the test being given to screen a population for drug use or is it specific for a particular drug substance? Generally, the screening method tests are very sensitive, although not always as specific as the confirming tests. Therefore, false-positive and false-negative results may occur. To ensure accuracy, a second test specific for the agent reported in the screening test is necessary. Physicians interpreting the tests should be familiar with drugs known to cross react or give a false-positive result with the test in use. If the individual reports taking such a medication, an alternate, more specific drug test could then be ordered. (See boxed material above.)

Urine testing for specific drugs may detect substances used days or even a week before testing. (See boxed material.) Such tests give evidence of use or prior exposure to a drug only; they do not indicate the individual's pattern of drug abuse of degree of drug dependency (Council on Scientific Affairs, 1987).

It is beyond the scope of this chapter to explore all aspects of drug abuse in depth, rather the focus is on drug actions and the treatment of drug abuse. However, the nurse is urged to investigate independently other aspects of the complex phenomenon of drug abuse to achieve a more holistic frame of reference.

## ETIOLOGIC FACTORS

A characteristic common to most drugs that cause dependence is that they are initially taken because the individual believes that a desirable pharmacologic effect will result. To cause dependence, then, a drug must produce favorable, pleasant, unusual, or desirable effects. The person who is dependent on a drug has found something that provides relief from problems, and the drug generally is used as an adjustive, coping mechanism. Since very few drugs or substances without CNS effects are abused, one of the predominant factors contributing to drug abuse appears to be intrapsychic—a desire to alter one's state of mind. This desire may arise from a number of factors, such as curiosity, boredom, peer pressure, multiple and diverse alienation, hedonism, affluence, and the attention paid to drug abuse by the mass media. All or any combination may lead to misuse of drugs and substances. More individual or subjective reasons are personal inadequacy or failure, conflicts terminating in tension, feelings of shame, and a predisposition to depression, which may lead to emotional and behavioral problems (see boxed material on p. 149).

Pleasure-seeking behavior (hedonism) often seems to be a factor in drug abuse. Among other goals, it may represent escape from inner tensions, a search for euphoria, an attempt to explore unknown aspects of cognitive function, or an attempt to discover one's self. More specifically, some psy-

---

### DRUG ABUSE CONSIDERATIONS

**Factors**

Abuse of drugs or substances that are dependence producing is a multifaceted complex including the influence of the following factors:

1. Social
2. Cultural
3. Economic
4. Political
5. Religious
6. Personal
7. Personality
8. Initial disease state
9. Pharmacologic profile of the drug or substance
10. Change in vogue, popularity, or access

**Characteristics**

The four characteristics of drugs of abuse are
1. Altered state of consciousness
2. Development of tolerance
3. Rapid onset of action of desired effects
4. Abstinence syndrome *may* appear if drug is discontinued abruptly after extended period of use

**Stages**

The four states of the seduction process* in the drug experience are
1. Experimentation (social recreational use)
2. Occasional use
3. Regular use
4. Dependence

---

*This seduction process ceases with dependence, when individual control is lost and the drugs themselves become the central theme in negotiating life.

cologic hypotheses have been advanced in relation to persons prone to use drugs as escape mechanisms. Persons with potentially drug-dependent predispositions are described as having strong psychologic dependence, low threshold of frustration, fear of failure, and feelings of inadequacy. Other authorities dispute the "addiction-prone" personality hypothesis, maintaining that everyone has the potential to become dependent on something.

### Types of Drugs and Substances Abused

All drugs have some abuse potential, and some sources indicate that drug abuse may be related to the personality characteristics of the user. Perhaps among the more frequently abused chemically active substances are the xanthines, found in coffee, tea, chocolate, and colas. Although these substances rarely are perceived as drugs by the lay public, they produce mild stimulant and euphoric effects, and their use may lead to psychic and physical dependence.

Nicotine and ethyl alcohol (ethanol) are the most frequently misused and abused drugs, with consequent physical and psychic dependence. Reserpine, anticholinergics, steroids, phencyclidine (PCP, angel dust), phenethylamines (e.g., amphetamines, epinephrine), pentazocine, cardiac glycosides, and L-dopa are examples of other drugs that may induce altered states of perception, thought, and feelings and drug-induced psychoses as a result of prolonged and concentrated therapeutic use or abuse. Few drugs without CNS effects are misused or abused.

The major categories of commonly abused drugs are opioids and related compounds, barbiturates and other sedative-hypnotics: antianxiety and antipsychotic agents; amphetamines, cocaine, and other CNS stimulants; cannabis drugs; other mind-altering drugs that have been variably classified as mood modifiers and include the psychotomimetic agents (hallucinogens); inhalants; and anabolic steroids. When used for prolonged periods, depressant drugs such as the opiates, cannabis drugs, barbiturates, and alcohol generally produce both physical and psychic dependence. Stimulant drugs such as the amphetamines and cocaine appear to produce psychic dependence and tolerance and may be associated with some physical dependence in increased dosages. See Table 9-1 for drugs commonly abused and symptoms of abuse. The other mind-altering drugs have variable and, at this time, questionable dependence-producing qualities, but it seems generally agreed upon that they all produce psychic dependence and have a rapid onset of action. See the box on p. 152 for the top 10 drugs misused or abused leading to emergency room visits or resulting in death (medical examiner's report).

Drug abuse may take several forms. (1) *Experimental abuse* occurs when individuals use drugs in an exploratory way and after which they accept or reject continuing use of the drugs. (2) *Social-recreational drug abuse* may occur only in social contexts; drugs that are frequently abused in social situations are alcohol, marijuana, cocaine, nicotine, and caffeine. (3) *Episodic drug abuse* refers to the periodic abuse of excessive amounts of a drug. (4) *Compulsive drug abuse* is characterized by irrational, irresistible, or compelling abuse of a drug. (5) *Ritualistic drug abuse* may be related to religious practices.

Polydrug or multiple drug abuse is common. Marijuana, alcohol, and other depressants frequently are used together and in conjunction with CNS stimulants. Heroin may be used with cocaine, pentazocine and tripelennamine, alcohol, or other depressants.

Patterns in use also develop regionally. The common use of LSD in the 1960s led to the use of amphetamines (speed) in the middle to late 1960s; in the early 1970s CNS depressants (downers) were used heavily. About the same time PCP use became common and remained so into the late 1970s. In the 1980s cocaine became popular again, and its abuse is seen more frequently but initially was somewhat

**TABLE 9-1**  Drugs commonly abused and symptoms of abuse

| Type of drug | Drug names | Street names | Methods of use | Symptoms of use | Hazards of use |
|---|---|---|---|---|---|
| MARIJUANA/ HASHISH | | Pot, Grass, Reefer, Weed, Columbian, Hash, Hash Oil, Sinsemilla, Joint | Most often smoked; can also be swallowed in solid form | Sweet, burnt odor Neglect of appearance Loss of interest, motivation Possible weight loss | Impaired memory, perception Interference with psychological maturation Possible damage to lungs, heart, and reproduction and immune systems Psychological dependence |
| ALCOHOL | | Booze, Hooch, Juice, Brew | Swallowed in liquid form | Impaired muscle coordination, judgment | Heart and liver damage Death from overdose Death from car accidents Addiction |
| STIMULANTS Drugs that stimulate the central nervous system | Amphetamines* Amphetamine Dextroamphetamine Methamphetamine | Speed, Uppers, Pep pills Bennies Dexies Moth, Crystal Black Beauties | Swallowed in pill or capsule form, or injected into veins | Excess activity Irritability; nervousness Mood swings Needle marks | Loss of appetite Hallucinations; paranoia Convulsions; coma Brain damage Death from overdose |
| | Cocaine | Coke, Snow, Toot, White lady | Most often inhaled (snorted); also injected or swallowed in powder form, smoked | Restlessness, anxiety Intense, short-term high followed by dysphoria | Intense psychological dependence Sleeplessness; anxiety Nasal passage damage Lung damage Death from overdose |
| | Nicotine | Coffin nail Butt, Smoke | Smoked in cigarettes, cigars and pipes, snuff, chewing tobacco | Smell of tobacco High carbon monoxide levels Stained teeth | Cancers of the lung, throat, mouth, esophagus Heart disease; emphysema |

| Category | Drug | Slang names | How taken | Effects | Dangers |
|---|---|---|---|---|---|
| **DEPRESSANTS** Drugs that depress the central nervous system | Barbiturates Pentobarbital Secobarbital Amobarbital | Barbs, Downers Yellow jackets Red devils Blue devils | Swallowed in pill form or injected into veins | Drowsiness Confusion Impaired judgment Slurred speech Needle marks Constricted pupils | Infection Addiction with severe withdrawal symptoms Loss of appetite Death from overdose Nausea |
| | Narcotics Dilaudid, Percodan Demerol, Methadone | | Swallowed in pill or liquid form, injected | Drowsiness Lethargy | Addiction with severe withdrawal symptoms Loss of appetite Death from overdose |
| | Morphine Heroin | Dreamer, Junk, Smack, Horse | Injected into veins, smoked | Needle marks | |
| | Codeine | School Boy | Swallowed in pill or liquid form | | |
| | Hypnotics Methaqualone | Quaaludes, Ludes Sopors | Swallowed in pill form | Impaired judgment and performance Drowsiness Slurred Speech | Death from overdose Injury or death from car accident; severe interaction with alcohol |
| **HALLUCINOGENS** Drugs that alter perceptions of reality | PCP (Phencyclidine) | Angel dust, Killer weed, Supergrass, Hog, PeaCe pill | Most often smoked; can also be inhaled (snorted), injected or swallowed in tablets | Slurred speech; blurred vision, uncoordination Confusion, agitation Aggression | Anxiety; depression Impaired memory, perception Death from accidents Death from overdose |
| | LSD | Acid, Cubes, Purple haze | Injected or swallowed in tablets | Dilated pupils Illusions; hallucinations Mood swings | Breaks from reality Emotional breakdown Flashback |
| | Mescaline | Mesc, Cactus | Usually ingested in their natural form | | |
| | Psilocybin | Magic mushrooms | | | |
| **INHALANTS** Substances abused by sniffing | Gasoline Airplane glue Paint thinner Dry cleaner solution | | Inhaled or sniffed, often with use of paper or plastic bag or rag | Poor motor coordination Impaired vision, memory and thought processes Abusive, violent behavior | High risk of sudden death Drastic weight loss Brain, liver, and bone marrow damage |
| | Nitrous oxide | Laughing gas, Whippets | Inhaled or sniffed by mask or cone | Lightheadedness | Death by anoxia |
| | Nitrites Amyl Butyl | Poppers, Locker room, Rush, Snappers | Inhaled or sniffed from gauze or ampules | Slowed thought Headache | Neuropathy, muscle weakness Anemia, death by anoxia |

From Blue Cross & Blue Shield Association, Chicago, Ill.

*Includes look-alike drugs resembling amphetamines that contain caffeine, phenylpropanolamine (PPA), and ephedrine

## LEADING 10 DRUGS ABUSED IN THE UNITED STATES*

### Emergency Room

*Males*
1. cocaine
2. alcohol in combination
3. heroin/morphine
4. marijuana/hashish
5. PCP/PCP combinations
6. diazepam
7. methamphetamine/speed
8. acetaminophen
9. aspirin
10. alprazolam

*Females*
1. cocaine
2. alcohol in combination
3. heroin/morphine
4. acetaminophen
5. aspirin
6. diazepam
7. marijuana/hashish
8. ibuprofen
9. alprazolam
10. PCP/PCP combinations

### Medical Examiners

*Males*
1. cocaine
2. alcohol in combination
3. heroin/morphine
4. codeine
5. methadone
6. diazepam
7. marijuana/hashish
8. amitriptyline
9. lidocaine
10. acetaminophen

*Females*
1. cocaine
2. alcohol in combination
3. heroin/morphine
4. amitriptyline
5. nortriptyline
6. codeine
7. diazepam
8. methadone
9. d-propoxyphene
10. acetaminophen

*As reported from 738 hospital emergency rooms located in 21 metropolitan areas and 87 medical examiners from 27 areas. Published in Data from Drug Abuse Warning Network (DAWN), Statistical Series (1989).

curtailed by its high cost. Since 1985 cocaine use has become extremely popular throughout the United States.

The 1980s have also documented the development of synthetic "designer drugs" produced by illegal laboratories or chemists. The molecular structure of a controlled substance is modified to produce a new variant that mimics the effects of the original drug. The types of drugs most commonly modified and sold are analogs of meperidine (Demerol), fentanyl (Sublimaze), and MDMA (3,4-methylenedioxymethamphetamine) from the illicit psychedelic agent MDA (methylenedioxyphenylethylamine). When "designer drugs" are identified, the Drug Enforcement Agency enacts regulations to ban them. Until it is banned, such a substance is legal to make, sell, or use. Once a substance is outlawed, the underground chemists will make a new, legal variation of the product; and it will be sold until a ban against it is established. Thus "designer drugs" are constantly changing and should be considered to be potentially dangerous substances. Contaminants have been identified in these products, and overdoses and deaths have been reported with their use.

## PHARMACOLOGIC BASIS OF DEPENDENCE AND TOLERANCE

Psychic and physical dependence on a drug can exist independently or simultaneously. Both types of dependence can potentially lead to compulsive patterns of drug use in which the user's life-style is focused on procurement and administration of the drug.

Several hypotheses attempt to explain the pharmacologic basis of the physiologic adaptation that occurs in tolerance and physical drug dependence.

Tolerance may exist with either psychologic or physical dependence and may be viewed in two ways. **Receptor site (tissue) tolerance** is a form of adaptation in which the effect produced depends both on the concentration of the drug and on the duration of the exposure. In this type of tolerance the clinical effect of the drug is reduced as the duration of exposure continues.

The second type of tolerance is **metabolic (pharmacologic) tolerance,** which refers to an aspect of drug disposition. Prolonged exposure to a drug can change the body's metabolic response to the drug, increasing drug clearance with repeated ingestion. For example, with prolonged exposure to barbiturates, the steady state blood concentrations will fall progressively with continued administration of the same dose. This may be attributed to the barbiturate's effect on hepatic microsomal enzymes to stimulate their own metabolism.

## PATHOPHYSIOLOGIC CHANGES

Physical and psychic dependence on drugs is frequently associated with debilitated physical states caused by the user's extensive involvement in procuring and using the drug. Malnutrition, dehydration, and hypovitaminosis often are evident. Respiratory complications such as pneumonia, pulmonary emboli, and abscesses frequently are associated with neglect, debilitation, and the respiratory depression produced by CNS depressants. The intravenous administration of illicit drugs often leads to a high incidence of sepsis, hepatitis, and AIDS as a result of the use of contaminated equipment. In addition, cellulitis, sclerosis of the veins, phlebitis, and skin abscesses may occur. Death from accidental overdose is common. Overdosage is a particularly significant potential danger because illegal drugs are notoriously unreliable in regard to the potency of their active ingredient. The drugs are frequently well adulterated with various substances by the time they reach the user (Table 9-2). If an individual who has been using cut drugs unknowingly receives pure or stronger drugs, the risk of toxicity and death exists. Overdosage also may occur when an individual who has been withdrawn from drugs for some time (thereby having lost accumulated tolerance) injects the previous usual dose, which now is in excess of the tolerance level.

As a consequence of all these factors, the life expectancy of persons who are physically dependent on drugs is gen-

**TABLE 9-2**  Illicit drug adulterants

| Illicit drug(s) | Adulterants | Diluents |
|---|---|---|
| cocaine | lidocaine, procaine, antipyrine, boric acid, ethyl aminobenzoate (Benzocaine), ephedrine, tetracine, phenylpropanolamine, barbiturates, amphetamines, CNS stimulants, caffeine, A.S.A., methapyrilene, PCP | Dextrose, quinine, inositol, mannitol, lactose, talcum powder |
| heroin | strychnine, tripelennamine, procaine, caffeine, barbiturates, PCP, methapyrilene, cocaine, scopolamine, pentazocine, propoxyphene, antihistamines, quinine, dyes, amphetamines, phenylpropanolamine, hashish, those adulterants listed under cocaine | Similar to those of cocaine |
| marijuana | PCP, hashish oil, organic solvents | |
| LSD | PCP, MDA, ethyl aminobenzoate, benzodiazepines, antihistamines | |
| amphetamines and their derivatives | caffeine, phenylpropanolamine | |

**TABLE 9-3**  Signs and symptoms of acute drug intoxication

| Drug(s) abused | Signs and symptoms |
|---|---|
| cannabis drugs | Tachycardia and postural hypotension, conjunctival vascular congestion, distortions of perception, dryness of mouth and throat, possible panic |
| opiates | Depressed blood pressure and respiration; fixed, pinpoint pupils; depressed sensorium; coma; pulmonary edema |
| barbiturates and other general CNS depressants | Depressed blood pressure and respirations, ataxia, slurred speech, confusion, depressed tendon reflexes, coma, shock |
| amphetamines | Elevated blood pressure, tachycardia, other cardiac dysrhythmias, hyperactive tendon reflexes, pupils dilated and reactive to light, hyperpyrexia, perspiration, shallow respirations, circulatory collapse, clear or confused sensorium, possible hallucinations, paranoid feelings |
| hallucinogenic agents | Elevated blood pressure, hyperactive tendon reflexes, pilorection, perspiration, pupils dilated and reactive to light, anxiety, distortion of body image and perception, delusions, hallucinations |

erally lower than that of nondependent individuals.

Table 9-3 presents common drug groups that are abused, along with signs and symptoms of acute intoxication. (The box on pp. 154 to 155 lists clinical signs and symptoms that may be found in a substance abuser and may be used as an aid to diagnosis of drug abuse.)

## CULTURAL ASPECTS OF DRUG ABUSE

Various societies accept certain drugs as legal and useful, while other drugs may be considered banned or illicit. For example, in the United States and parts of Western Europe, alcohol, caffeine, and nicotine are widely accepted and commonly used substances. In the Middle East cannabis is considered a legal drug while alcohol is usually forbidden. Specific Indian tribes in America use peyote (a hallucinogen) for religious services, but in general, such hallucinogens have no accepted therapeutic usage in the United States. Some research has been performed with such agents in clients with chronic cancer, but to date objective beneficial evidence is lacking.

In the high-altitude South American Andes and other mountainous areas (e.g., of Peru), cocaine is commonly consumed to decrease hunger and increase work performance. Thus the use and acceptance or rejection of a substance depend on the society and its subgroups. When drug substances are considered illicit or illegal and are in short supply, then certain elements within or from outside the society may be activated to produce and/or sell the banned substances. This activity is usually extremely profitable and thus attractive to the unethical or non–law-abiding persons.

## TYPES OF DRUGS MOST COMMONLY ABUSED

### Opioids

#### Opiates and Related Derivatives

Opioids are one of the most abused drug categories. Chronic use of a narcotic or opioid usually leads to a reduction in hunger, pain, aggressiveness, and sexual drive. The incidence of substance abuse and addiction is higher in males

## SUMMARY OF 1988 DAWN REPORT*

Cocaine was the top drug reported in both emergency rooms and from medical examiners' offices.

**DAWN Emergency Rooms:**

Over 160,000 drug abuse episodes reported; 56% were males and 43% females

Percentage of cases categorized by race: whites 41%; blacks, 39%; Hispanics 11%

Age group of the clients; 70% were between 20 to 39 years old

Drug dependence was motive in 41% of the episodes; 28% were suicide attempts; 17% were for psychic effects

Suicide attempts were reported in 43% of female clients and 17% of male clients

62% of clients age 10 to 17 reported suicide as primary reason

46% of all DAWN emergency room reports resulted from the use of two or more drugs

**DAWN Medical Examiners:**

Reported over 16,000 drug mentions involved with nearly 7000 drug abuse related deaths

73% of deaths were male

Of this population, whites totaled 46%, blacks 30%, and Hispanics 13%

Age group of the cases: 67% were between 18 to 39 years old

69% drug-induced deaths; 31% drug-related deaths.

21% of the deaths resulted from suicide

Cocaine reported in more black and Hispanic deaths (68% and 59%, respectively) than in white deaths (36%)

77% of the deaths involved more than one drug

*DAWN, *see* Drug Abuse Terminology. Data from Drug Abuse Warning Network (DAWN), Statistical Series, (1989).

## CLINICAL SIGNS AND SYMPTOMS OF DRUG ABUSE*

### Central Nervous System

*Coma:* amphetamines, antihistamines, atropine, barbiturates, chloral hydrate, diazepam, ethanol, glutethimide, meprobamate, methaqualone, narcotics, PCP, pentazocine, propoxyphene, quinine, scopolamine, sedative-hypnotics, toluene, tricyclic antidepressants

*Ataxia (incoordination):* atropine, barbiturates, cocaine, ethanol, glutethimide, hallucinogens, opiates, PCP, phenothiazines, propoxyphene, toluene, tricyclic antidepressants

*Tetanic rigidity:* caffeine, methaqualone, morphine, PCP, phenothiazines, scopolamine

*Convulsions:* amphetamines, antihistamines, atropine, barbiturates, benzodiazepines, caffeine, cocaine, ethanol, ethchlorvynol, glutethimide, meprobamate, methaqualone, methyprylone, opiates, PCP, propoxyphene, tricyclic antidepressants

*Muscle weakness or paralysis:* alcohol, hallucinogens, morphine, PCP, quinine

*Muscle spasm:* atropine, cocaine, methaqualone, phenothiazines

*Anesthesia:* barbiturates, benzene, cocaine, ethanol, ketamine, PCP

*Paresthesia:* barbiturates, benzene, cocaine, hallucinogens, morphine, psilocybin, quinine

*Muscle fasciculations (twitchings):* atropine, ethanol

*Hallucinations:* amphetamines, atropine, barbiturates, caffeine, cocaine, ethanol, ketamine, LSD, morphine, PCP, psilocybin

*Headaches:* atropine, barbiturates, benzene, caffeine, cocaine, ephedrine, ethanol, morphine, scopolamine, toluene, tricyclic antidepressants

### Respiratory System

*Rapid or deep breathing:* amphetamines, atropine, barbiturates, boric acid, caffeine, chloral hydrate, cocaine, ethanol, LSD, quinine

*Slow or labored breathing:* atropine, barbiturates, benzene, benzodiazepines, chloral hydrate, cocaine, ethanol, ethchlorvynol, glutethimide, heroin, methaqualone, methyprylon, morphine, narcotics, propoxyphene, quinine, tricyclic antidepressants

*Breath odor:* ethanol, fetid or pearlike with chloral hydrate, pungent with ethchlorvynol

*Respiratory paralysis:* barbiturates, ethanol, hypnotics, lidocaine, opiates, PCP, procaine, toluene

*Cough:* benzene, ethanol

### Digestive System

*Anorexia:* amphetamines, cocaine, codeine, ethanol, morphine

*Dysphagia:* atropine, cocaine, ephedrine, tricyclic antidepressants

*Thirst:* atropine, chloral hydrate, morphine

*Salivation:* cocaine, morphine, quinine

*Dry oral mucosa:* amphetamines, antihistamines, atropine, benzene, glutethimide, morphine, scopolamine, tricyclic antidepressants

*Nausea and vomiting:* antihistamines, atropine, benzene, benzodiazepines, boric acid, caffeine, cocaine, codeine, ephedrine, ethanol, lidocaine, LSD, marijuana, opiates, propoxyphene, quinine, toluene

*Colic:* morphine

*Diarrhea:* boric acid, chloral hydrate, cocaine, quinine

*Bloody stools:* morphine

*Constipation:* anticholinergics, barbiturates, codeine, ephedrine, glutethimide, morphine, tricyclic antidepressants

*From the Bio-Science Handbook of Clinical and Industrial Toxicology, ed 1. Van Nuys, Calif: Bio-Science Laboratories Main Laboratory, 1979.

CLINICAL SIGNS AND SYMPTOMS OF DRUG ABUSE—cont'd

## Cardiovascular System

*Circulatory collapse or shock:* amphetamines, antihistamines, barbiturates, benzodiazepines, boric acid, caffeine, chloral hydrate, cocaine, ephedrine, ethanol, methaqualone, opiate withdrawal, procainamide, procaine, propoxyphene, quinine

*Bradycardia:* codeine, ethchlorvynol, lidocaine, narcotics, quinine, sedative-hypnotics

*Tachycardia:* amphetamines, antihistamines, atropine, caffeine, cocaine, codeine, ephedrine, ethanol, glutethimide, methaqualone, methyprylon, PCP, quinine

*Hypertension:* amphetamines, ephedrine, glutethimide, methaqualone, PCP

*Hypotension:* barbiturates, benzodiazepines, caffeine, chloral hydrate, glutethimide, lidocaine, LSD, meprobamate, methyprylon, narcotics, propoxyphene, quinine

*Dysrhythmias:* amphetamines, meprobamate, propoxyphene, quinine, toluene, tricyclic antidepressants

*Vasoconstriction:* amphetamines, cocaine, ephedrine

*Hemorrhage, petechiae, purpura:* barbiturates, benzene, quinine

*Discoloration of skin*
Cyanosis: barbiturates, ethanol
Jaundice: benzene, chloral hydrate, nitrobenzene
Red: atropine, boric acid, scopolamine

*Bullae:* barbiturates, glutethimide

*Burns, irritation, corrosion, ulcers:* boric acid, cocaine, glutethimide, pentazocine

*Dermatitis inflammation:* amphetamines, atropine, barbiturates, benzene, boric acid, chloral hydrate, cocaine, codeine, ephedrine, morphine, quinine, toluene

*Alopecia:* boric acid, chloral hydrate, morphine

*Hirsutism:* antidepressants, barbiturates

*Exfoliation or desquamation:* boric acid

*Needle marks* (referred to as *tracks*): amphetamines, barbiturates, cocaine, narcotics, pentazocine, propoxyphene

## Urologic Disorders

*Glycosuria:* atropine, caffeine, morphine

*Hematuria:* benzene

*Oliguria:* atropine, morphine, quinine

*Polyuria:* atropine, benzene, caffeine, cocaine, ethanol, scopolamine

*Porphyrinuria:* benzene

*Proteinuria:* benzene, caffeine, ethanol, methaqualone, morphine, quinine, toluene

*Urobilinogenuria:* benzene, chloral hydrate, cocaine, quinine

## Hematologic Disorders

*Anemia:* barbiturates, benzene, ethanol, meprobamate, morphine, quinine

*Abdominal pain:* benzene, chloral hydrate, cocaine, codeine, morphine, procaine, quinine, tricyclic antidepressants

*Gastroenteritis:* atropine, benzene, chloral hydrate, codeine, ethanol, nonbarbiturates, sedative-hypnotics

## Skin and Mucous Membranes

*Pruritus:* atropine, boric acid, opiates, scopolamine

*Rash, urticaria:* barbiturates, gluthethimide, halogens, LSD, meprobamate, methaqualone, nonbarbiturates, procaine, quinine, sedative-hypnotics

*Dryness:* atropine, benzene, boric acid, ephedrine, ethanol, heroin, morphine, scopolamine

*Perspiration:* ethanol, tricyclic antidepressants

*Flush:* amphetamines, antihistamines, atropine, codeine, ephedrine, ethanol, morphine, scopolamine

*Pallor:* barbiturates, benzene, cocaine, ephedrine, heroin

*Hemolysis:* benzene, quinine

*Leukopenia:* benzene, meprobamate

*Polycythemia:* benzene

## Auditory, Personality, and Visual Disturbances

*Auditory disturbances*
Hearing impairment: atropine, benzene, cocaine, quinine
Tinnitus: benzene, codeine, morphine, quinine

*Personality alteration* (such as irritability, confusion, delirium, psychosis): amphetamines (psychosis), antihistamines, atropine, barbiturates, benzene, benzodiazepines, caffeine, cocaine, codeine, ephedrine, ethanol, ethchlorvynol, hallucinogens, LSD, marijuana, morphine, pentazocine, PCP, procaine, scopolamine, toluene

*Visual disturbances*
Blindness (partial or complete): ethanol, phenothiazines, quinine
Blurred vision: alcohol, atropine, barbiturates, benzodiazepines, CNS depressants, ephedrine, hallucinogens, lidocaine, morphine, quinine, scopolamine
Color distortions: ethanol, hallucinogens, LSD, quinine
Miosis (pinpoint pupil): benzodiazepines, caffeine, chloral hydrate, codeine, heroin, morphine, pentazocine, propoxyphene
Blank stare: PCP
Mydriasis: amphetamines, cocaine, glutethimide, hallucinogens, belladonna alkaloids (atropine)

than females and higher in the health professions and business segment than in the general population.

The pharmacologic types of drugs that cause opiate-like dependence include the opium alkaloids (heroin, morphine), the semisynthetic group (hydromorphone, oxymorphone), and the synthetic group (meperidine, levorphanol, methadone). Of the opiates, heroin, d-propoxyphene (Darvon), methadone, oxycodone (Percodan), and morphine are the most often abused; heroin (diacetylmorphine) is the most potent of the five.

**Mode of administration.** The opium derivatives generally can be administered percutaneously (absorbed through the mucous membranes) by sniffing, by subcutaneous injection (known as *skin popping*), or by direct IV injection *(mainlining)*. The rate of absorption is correspondingly increased, with mainlining producing almost immediate drug effects.

**Mechanism of action and effects.** The opium derivatives are CNS depressants that probably act on the sensory cortex, psychic or higher centers, and thalami. Because these drugs elevate mood; relieve tension, fear, and anxiety; and produce feelings of peace, euphoria, and tranquility; they are particularly likely to lead to physical and psychic dependence. Rapid intravenous injection of these drugs produces warm, flushing sensations described as being similar to sexual orgasm. This is followed by a soothing state that seems to be best characterized as a state of complete drive satiation. The individual "high" on opiates feels no need to satisfy drives for basic biologic needs and is often described as being "on the nod"—drowsy, content, and euphoric. The drugs do not produce hallucinogenic or psychotomimetic effects.

**Acute overdosage.** Acute overdosage of opiate-type substances may result in coma, pulmonary edema, and cessation of respiration. These outcomes are dose dependent and are related to the degree of individual tolerance. Symptoms occur rapidly in most clients. What constitutes a lethal dose depends on the individual's tolerance for the drug.

Opiate toxicity is manifested in various ways. Pupils are generally found to be pinpoint (miotic), but they may be dilated in mixed overdose conditions or severe acidosis. Thrombophlebitis, scarred veins, puckered scars from subcutaneous injections, severe acidosis, bradycardia, itching caused by histamine release, hypotension, hypoxia, muscle spasm, respiratory depression, and urinary retention also occur. There is rapid absorption of the opiates following either oral or intravenous administration. These drugs tend to delay motility and gastric emptying time, so that the revival of the client may increase peristalsis and thus further increase absorption of the drug, producing a coma cycle. Chronic abuse may result in abscesses, myelitis, anaphylaxis, dysrhythmias, cellulitis, endocarditis, fecal impaction, glomerulonephritis, hyperglycemia or hypoglycemia, myoglobinuria, osteomyelitis, encephalopathy, tetanus, and thrombophlebitis. These are caused by a spectrum of factors

ranging from injection technique to adulterants in the substance of abuse. An overdose with methadone may produce prolonged toxicity of 24 to 48 hours or longer, including respiratory depression.

The treatment of choice for acute overdosage is administration of an antagonist and respiratory support. Attention is focused on reversal of shock and treatment of apnea. The opiates depress brainstem sensitivity to carbon dioxide, and heavy dependence on a hypoxic respiratory drive device is paramount. When the triad of miotic pupils, coma or stupor, and bradypnea (respirations slowed to a rate of four to six per minute) appears, the administration of naloxone (Narcan) may differentiate narcotic poisoning from other conditions.

Naloxone is a pure narcotic antagonist and reverses the toxic effects of opiates and derivatives such as heroin, morphine, methadone, pentazocine, and propoxyphene. The usual adult dose is 0.4 to 0.8 mg intravenously. If a site for intravenous injection is not found because of abuse, the intramuscular (producing a longer lasting effect) or subcutaneous route may be used. Larger doses may be required to treat acute overdoses of buprenorphine, butorphanol, propoxyphene, and pentazocine. If a single dose fails, a dose of 2 mg or more may be used intravenously. Failure to respond to high doses of a narcotic antagonism may indicate a mixed substance overdose or involvement of a nonopiate substance.

Blood and urine samples should be examined with a multiple drug screen to aid in diagnosis. Heroin itself may not be detected in the urine because it appears as a derivative of morphine and may be detected from 12 to 24 hours after administration. It is necessary to support blood pressure and maintain respiration following response to naloxone. Pupils may be dilated if hypoxemia is severe or if the overdose is from meperidine; miosis is observed in barbiturate (dilated in severe toxicity), ethanol, and phenothiazine overdoses.

Children with a known or suspected narcotic overdose may receive 0.01 mg/kg as the first dose. Naloxone may be diluted with sterile water for injection. If the child is not responsive to the first dose, one or two additional intravenous doses may be given at 2-minute to 3-minute intervals.

Naloxone reverses apnea and coma within minutes. The naloxone must be titrated to the client's arousal with a respiratory rate in a range of 10 to 20 breaths per minute. Intravenous administration may be repeated to reverse narcotic respiratory depression in 2- to 3-minute intervals. Repeated doses may be required at 1- to 2-hour intervals, depending on the amount and type of drugs (short- or long-acting) and the interval since the last administration of the narcotic. Often a continuous intravenous infusion is implemented after an initial response is obtained. A positive response to naloxone is characterized by dilation of the pupils and an increase in respiratory function, blood pressure, and cardiac rate.

After satisfactory response is attained, the client is kept under observation; and naloxone doses are repeated as necessary, since the duration of action of some narcotics (morphine, heroin, methadone) exceeds that of naloxone (1½ to 2 hours).

***Physical dependence and acute abstinence syndrome.*** In a client physically dependent on opiates an abrupt and complete reversal of narcotic effects with naloxone may precipitate an acute abstinence syndrome. Although the opiate abstinence syndrome may be reversible by administration of opiates, the administration of narcotics to maintain a drug-dependent client is prohibited by law except if the person is an inpatient who was admitted for an emergency procedure or is being detoxified or maintained in an approved federal drug-treatment program. Methadone usually is considered the drug of choice in the treatment of this clinical condition.

Physical dependence on opiates usually is described in terms of the opium derivative heroin, since the other derivatives manifest similar symptoms. Physical dependence on heroin is evident in the withdrawal syndrome that develops if the drug is withheld and in the marked tolerance that develops with continued use of the drug. Also, because persons dependent on heroin so frequently feel satiated, physical, emotional, and social deterioration often occurs. The individuals may feel little need for food and become grossly malnourished and weak. Preoccupation with obtaining the drug makes participation in the usual social and vocational aspects of life difficult, if not impossible. As the drug craving grows, tolerance to the drug also increases; and eventually the motivation for using the drug becomes oriented more to the avoidance of withdrawal symptoms and less to the achievement of euphoria.

***Withdrawal symptoms.*** The initial withdrawal symptoms are related to the half-life of the narcotic being used. Symptoms of withdrawal from heroin are autonomic in origin and appear within 8 hours after the last dose in individuals who are physically dependent. These symptoms are less life-threatening than with other substances of abuse. They may originally be manifested as restlessness, chills and hot flashes, pilorection on the skin (which gives rise to the term "cold turkey"), rhinorrhea, drowsiness, lacrimation, mydriasis, sneezing, yawning, generalized anxiety, abdominal cramps, lower back pain, lower extremity cramps (which probably resulted in the phrase "kick the habit"), vomiting and diarrhea, anorexia, diaphoresis, muscular twitching, elevated pulse rate, blood pressure, and temperature, and a craving for the drug. Such symptoms usually are followed by a restless sleep for about 3 hours known as *yen,* from which the client may awaken irritable, weak, and depressed. Depending on the drug used, the abstinence syndrome develops within 2 to 48 hours and peaks at 72 hours.

Occasionally withdrawal symptoms are severe enough to result in cardiovascular collapse. If withdrawal is untreated, it may continue for up to 7 to 10 days, after which the physical dependence of the body on the presence of opiates is eventually lost. Psychic dependence continues for a longer period; some authorities claim it continues forever.

### Treatment of opiate dependence

*Withdrawal programs.* Generally, opiate withdrawal is difficult, and repeated relapses to drug abuse can be expected. Abrupt and complete withdrawal *(cold turkey)* can be accomplished but is generally avoided as a dangerous (especially in clients with a co-existing medical illness) and inhumane approach. Therapeutic withdrawal from an opiate may be somewhat more comfortably achieved by successively tapering the drug's dosage over a period of several days.

The choice of withdrawal program is partly influenced by the following factors: the client's physical condition, the duration of drug dependence, the type and amount of drug being taken, motivations for drug abuse and withdrawal, and whether the individual is also dependent on other drugs. In some instances, depending on these factors, opiate withdrawal may need to be accomplished within a hospital and with close medical supervision.

In identifying criteria for evaluating opiate withdrawal, one should note that recovery from morphine-type dependence is not equated with cure. Regardless of repeated relapses to drug abuse, therapeutic programs should continue. Progress in withdrawal may be indicated by progressively longer periods of abstinence from opiates without resort to the use of other psychoactive drugs and by the client's growing confidence in the ability to function effectively without drugs.

*Therapeutic community programs.* The ultimate goal of using any substance to treat dependency is to provide relief from the compulsive craving for the drug of abuse. To achieve rehabilitation, the abuser needs to turn to more than another substance. The individual also needs human dignity, sincerity, compassion, warmth, self-respect, and hope with positive reinforcement. To achieve independence and become a self-sustaining, productive member of the community, the abuser must be provided with emotional and social support. These human resources have not been effectively addressed by many treatment programs, and failures have resulted.

Because persons withdrawing from drugs frequently cannot make the transition easily, groups of persons who have decided to abstain from drug use can meet or live together in an attempt to support and guide one another. Such therapeutic community programs as Phoenix House and halfway houses have been established that include group psychotherapy and self-help approaches. Ultimately an individual should emerge from such a program with sufficient personal growth and appropriate support systems to be able to manage life satisfactorily without resorting to drug abuse.

*Methadone detoxification and withdrawal.* A currently preferred method of withdrawal is substitution of methadone hydrochloride, a program pioneered by Drs. Vincent Dole and Marie Nyswander. Methadone hydrochloride is a synthetic opiate analgesic that, by virtue of cross-tolerance, permits effective substitution of methadone dependence for heroin dependence. Its effectiveness against heroin dependence results from its ability to forestall the euphoriant effects of heroin and the craving for the drug without producing heroin's deleterious physical and mental effects. When properly administered, methadone allows the individual to function adequately, without intellectual or emotional impairment.

Methadone is taken orally, generally in daily doses of 10 to 20 mg and ranging up to 50 mg. Methadone is usually initiated in a 10 mg dose and titrated in 5 to 10 mg increments until symptoms are suppressed. Detoxification may be accomplished by 5 mg/day (to 25 mg), and then decreasing it by 2.5 mg/day. Methadone therapy is initiated empirically based on client symptoms. As a general guide, 1 mg methadone is substituted for 20 mg meperidine, 4 mg morphine, and 2 mg heroin.

For a review of recommended dosages and dosage adjustments, the reader is referred to current drug abuse references or the most recent edition of the American Hospital Formulary Service.

Regular administration results in the development of tolerance to methadone and cross-tolerance to heroin. The client will not experience the opiate-induced "rush" and euphoria unless higher doses than tolerance is exceeded. Because of this, the nurse should be aware that some clients might exaggerate their withdrawal symptoms to obtain more methadone. When the abuser is being treated with methadone, supportive psychologic or psychiatric counseling may relieve some of the burdens that led to drug dependence. During this phase the methadone may be gradually withdrawn, usually at a rate of 20% reduction or 5 mg in daily dosage. However, methadone substitution programs are controversial and are not always successful. Previous opiate abusers who are unable to negotiate life in a drug-free state may revert to their former dependence or alternative substance abuse or may return to the methadone therapy detoxification.

*Methadone maintenance.* In the U.S. methadone may be administered to opioid-dependent individuals for detoxification purposes. For outpatient or residential medication detoxification, methadone is given in decreasing doses on either a short-term basis (a period not exceeding 30 days) or a long-term basis (a period not in excess of 180 days). The methadone program includes psychologic, vocational, and/or rehabilitation services in addition to medical support.

Admittance to a methadone maintenance program usually requires evidence of current dependence on morphine-type drugs and at least a 2-year history of opioid dependence. Maintenance methadone treatment programs require both FDA and state licensing and/or approval. The ultimate goal of these programs is complete withdrawal from drug dependency for the participant, although some clients continue on methadone for extended time periods. Methadone maintenance programs assist clients to minimize opiate cravings and so provide the opportunity to lead functional productive life-styles rather than the chaotic, and perhaps criminal, life of the street addict.

Nurses should be aware that addicts hospitalized with medical conditions other than addiction may require pharmacologic support with methadone or opioids during their stay. Such individuals should be referred to an approved methadone maintenance program for follow-up care.

The nurse should also be aware that treatment centers may vary in their methods and/or drugs used for opioid withdrawal. Some treatment centers report having accomplished withdrawal from methadone through the use of clonidine (Reynolds, 1989), whereas others maintain that methadone is the drug of choice.

Methadone dependence does occur, but withdrawal symptoms are less severe although they last for a longer period. Methadone withdrawal programs generally include supplemental rehabilitation techniques such as vocational and social rehabilitation. After individuals have functioned free from heroin for a sufficient period, secured steady employment, and readjusted their life-style, theoretically they can be withdrawn from methadone maintenance.

*Heroin maintenance.* Heroin, a Schedule 1 drug (see Chapter 2), is a substance with no accepted medical use in the U.S. It was banned in 1924 because of its high potential for abuse and an increasing number of heroin addicts. Today it is still one of the top 10 drugs abused in the U.S. and often is used in combination with cocaine. Heroin is also a major public health problem in western Europe, especially in Italy, West Germany, and Great Britain (Hall, 1985).

While most countries have banned heroin use, it is a legal drug in Britain. Physicians are permitted to prescribe heroin and other opioids for persons who have a history of intractable dependence, thereby maintaining them and preventing withdrawal symptoms. Prescriptions currently are issued only through designated hospitals or clinics and the National Health Service.

*Clonidine treatment.* Clonidine (Catapres) is a sympatholytic antihypertensive; that is, it stimulates alpha receptors in the brain, resulting in a reduction in sympathetic outflow from the CNS, resulting in a decrease in peripheral resistance, heart rate, and blood pressure. It is also under investigation for relieving the symptoms of acute withdrawal in various opioid dependencies, such as with heroin and methadone. Opioid withdrawal symptoms may be caused by the hyperactivity of the locus ceruleus, a major nonadrenergic nucleus of the brain. Inhibitory receptors in the locus ceruleus are believed to be stimulated by opioids and by clonidine stimulation via the alpha-2 adrenergic receptors.

Clonidine transdermal skin patches (Catapres-TTS) have also been used to reduce or prevent opioid withdrawal effects. The nurse should be aware that it takes 2 to 3 days to reach a peak effect with the patches, which is often too late to treat the worse effects seen with opioid withdrawal. The tablet dosage form offers a quicker and a more easily titratable method of preventing or reducing unwanted effects (Tommasello, 1989).

A clonidine dosage of 5 μg/kg/day, increasing to 17 μg/kg/day, as necessary, has been used to prevent the withdrawal syndrome. The dose is dependent on the individual's tolerance and quantity and type of narcotic agonist used. The daily dosage is administered in equally divided doses over a 24-hour period for approximately 10 days. Then the dosage is gradually tapered by 0.1 or 0.2/mg daily at the end of the treatment to avoid emergence of the withdrawal syndrome and headaches. The clinical usefulness of clonidine is limited by the drug's sedative and hypotensive effects, and extremely close supervision of the client is necessary to monitor side effects, adverse effects, and any manipulation of the dose by the client. The nurse should hold the dose of clonidine and consult the physician if the blood pressure is less than 90 systolic or 60 diastolic. Physical dependence on opioids is eliminated by this detoxification process, and nonpharmacologic intervention can be used to address the remaining psychic dependence.

## Analgesics

### pentazocine (Talwin)

Pentazocine HCl (Talwin) 60 mg orally is considered approximately equivalent as an analgesic to 2.5 mg of hydromorphone or 66 mg of codeine. Sharp increases in the incidence of drug abuse involving pentazocine have led the Drug Enforcement Administration to place this drug in the controlled status (Class IV) under the Controlled Substances Act.

Pentazocine's potential for producing psychic and physical dependence is significant even in low doses, and infants born to pentazocine-dependent women experience withdrawal immediately postpartum. Pentazocine can cause psychotomimetic reactions such as visual hallucinations, feelings of depersonalization, and nightmares.

The CNS effects of pentazocine are similar to those of the opioids, including analgesia, sedation, and respiratory depression (reversed by naloxone). In high doses pentazocine causes increases in blood pressure and heart rate. Lung problems may be caused by the talc binders and other particulate matter from crushed tablets accumulating in the lungs. Other clinical effects include seizures and ulceration and severe sclerosis of the skin and subcutaneous tissue and muscles, caused by subcutaneous or intramuscular injections. These ulcerated areas may measure 8 × 5 cm, and extensive cellulitis is observable. Such areas often require debridement and grafting. The combination of pentazocine with other CNS depressants such as barbiturates and alcohol may be lethal.

Pentazocine and PBZ (tripelennamine) abuse first appeared in the late 1960s to the 1970s. Shortages or high cost of heroin in large metropolitan areas contributed to the substitution of pentazocine and tripelennamine, known as *T's and blues* (T for Talwin and *blue* for the color of the generic tablet of tripelennamine). T's and blues are oral tablets that are mixed together in solution and injected either through a cotton filter intravenously, like heroin, or subcutaneously, possibly resulting in abscess and necrotic tissues (many users require hospitalization and grafting). Drug abusers have indicated that tripelennamine is used to increase the onset of action and prolong the duration of the euphoria produced by pentazocine. Abusers report that when injected intravenously, T's and blues produce a rush "indistinguishable from a heroin rush."

To discourage abuse, the manufacturer sought alternate formulations of pentazocine to market. Other companies have had to take similar steps because of street abuse of their products (e.g., Darvon Compound to Darvocet-N). Eventually the manufacturer released a combination of pentazocine and naloxone (Talwin-Nx). The addition of naloxone nullifies or cancels the rush effect of the injected pentazocine-tripelennamine combination. Hopefully, this will reduce the abuse potential of pentazocine.

The treatment of pentazocine dependence is gradual reduction of the drug itself in a controlled environment. The psychotomimetic effects should be observed closely in a controlled environment and may persist for 5 to 7 days.

### propoxyphene (Darvon, Novopropoxyn ✳)

Use of propoxyphene products in excessive doses, either alone or in combination with other CNS depressants including alcohol, is a significant cause of drug-related deaths. In a survey of deaths reported from DAWN's medical examiners in 1988, propoxyphene was reported as the third most common narcotic analgesic identified. Since an overdose of propoxyphene may result in up to 5% fatalities within 15 minutes, many within an hour, intensive supportive and symptomatic therapy must be instituted immediately (AHFS, 1989).

Propoxyphene should not be taken in doses higher than those recommended by the physician, and clients should be so warned. The judicious prescribing of propoxyphene is essential for safe use of this drug. With clients who are depressed or suicidal, consideration should be given to the use of nonnarcotic analgesics.

Because of its added depressant effects, propoxyphene should be prescribed with caution for those individuals whose medical condition requires the concomitant administration of sedatives, tranquilizers, muscle relaxants, antidepressants, or other CNS depressant drugs. Clients should be cautioned against the concomitant use of propoxyphene products and alcohol because of potentially serious CNS additive effects of these agents. Many of the propoxyphene-related deaths have occurred in individuals with previous histories of emotional disturbances or suicidal ideation or attempts as well as histories of misuse of tranquilizers, alcohol, and other CNS active drugs. Some deaths have occurred as a consequence of the accidental ingestion of excessive quantities of propoxyphene alone or in combination with other drugs.

The clinical effects of overdose occur within ½ hour and include nausea, vomiting, and drowsiness followed by stupor and coma. Within ½ hour to 1 hour of an oral overdose, respiratory arrest, hypotension, and grand mal seizures often occur. Miotic pupils are frequently seen, and the individual may experience diabetes insipidus, pulmonary edema, cardiac dysrythmias requiring cardiopulmonary resuscitation, bundle branch block, nonspecific ST and T wave alterations, prolongation of the QRS complexes, and hypoglycemia.

This drug has also been abused by parenteral administration of the oral dosage form. The manufacturer recommends in all suspected overdose cases, a poison control center should be contacted for the most current treatment of the overdose.

The severe and sometimes unpredictable course of propoxyphene intoxication has stimulated an interest in its clinical kinetics. It is primarily metabolized in the hepatic microsomal enzyme system though the major metabolic pathway of demethylation to norpropoxyphene and is primarily eliminated by renal excretion. The most severely intoxicated individuals with the highest plasma levels also have metabolites with the longest half-life, which may indicate dose-dependent kinetics. Total urinary excretion of all metabolites is about 7 days. The systemic availability is reduced corresponding to extensive first pass metabolism of 30% to 70%, and the half-life is 8 to 24 hours for propoxyphene and 18 to 29 hours for the metabolite norpropoxyphene. The ranges indicate pronounced intraindividual dose-dependent variations in oral clearance. Transient changes in hepatic blood flow at the time the drug passes through the liver may influence kinetics of high-clearance drugs such as propoxyphene. This effect is further influenced by a high-affinity binding site in some tissues, which also occurs with tricyclic antidepressants.

Norpropoxyphene has less CNS depressant effect than propoxyphene but a greater anesthetic effect on the myocardium, similar to that of amitriptyline and antidysrhythmic drugs such as lidocaine and quinidine. Electrocardiographic monitoring is essential in management of overdosage.

Propoxyphene is pharmacologically related to the opioids; however, it may not elicit the narcotic response when naloxone is administered, and the client will need more protracted respiratory support measures. Overdose may be accompanied by seizures requiring anticonvulsants, and emergence from a coma may require restraints before administration of naloxone because of the client's disorientation, agitation, and confusion.

Clients need psychologic and emotional support during this time. A quiet, calm environment with reduced sensory stimulation may reduce the incidence of disorientation and

agitation. The nurse should use a simple, direct approach when communicating with reality orientation and reassurance.

The FDA Drug Bulletin has carried the warning that propoxyphene should not be taken during pregnancy. The warning against use during pregnancy is based on demonstrations of withdrawal symptoms in newborns from mothers taking the drug during pregnancy. The symptoms include tremors, irritability, high-pitched cry, diarrhea and weight loss with ravenous appetite, and infrequently, seizures.

## Sedative-Hypnotics

### Barbiturates

It is generally known by the lay public that barbiturates and some nonbarbiturate sedative-hypnotics can cause physical as well as psychic dependence. It appears that short-acting barbiturates, in addition to drugs such as glutethimide (Doriden), methaqualone, chloral hydrate, methyprylon (Noludar), and ethchlorvynol (Placidyl), are most likely to produce physical dependence, possibly because they produce sudden and forceful desired effects (rapid onset of action). The lipid solubility enables the drug to enter the central nervous system rapidly, with immediate appearance of effects.

Because these drugs are more extensively described in other chapters, mechanisms of action and effects are not explored here. Rather, this section focuses on acute intoxication and withdrawal syndromes resulting from dependence on these drugs.

Intoxication from barbiturates must be differentiated from other causes of intoxication. The client's breath odor is an indicator with alcohol, inhalants, and chloral hydrate, but not with the barbiturates. The effects of barbiturate intoxication resemble those of alcohol intoxication and include emotional lability, muscular incoordination, difficulty in cognitive processes, and sedation. Toxic doses lead to stupor and respiratory depression. The reasons for barbiturate abuse are similar to those for ethyl alcohol abuse: both drugs produce disinhibition and mild euphoria.

Specific and efficient antidotes to offset barbiturate/depressant drug overdoses are not available. Individuals dependent on the sedative-hypnotics should never be abruptly withdrawn because the withdrawal syndrome accompanying cessation of barbiturate administration is one of the most dangerous in the field of drug abuse. The withdrawal syndrome may begin with weakness, tremulousness, restlessness, anxiety, insomnia, gastrointestinal disturbances, and orthostatic hypotension that may last 3 to 14 days. The syndrome starts in the first 24 hours, possibly leaving the client too weak to get out of bed. Symptoms of psychoses may progress to confusion, delirium, and hallucinations. Major convulsive seizures are more common in barbiturate withdrawal than in alcohol withdrawal. Agitation and hyperthermia may lead to exhaustion, cardiovascular collapse, and death.

Coma and apnea from single high doses of mixed depressants may lead to high morbidity and mortality. If the withdrawal syndrome is untreated, it usually ends by the fourteenth day of drug abstinence, and its end generally is preceded by prolonged sleep. Clients experiencing barbiturate withdrawal must be hospitalized because even though the syndrome appears mild 24 hours after the last dose, convulsions and cardiovascular collapse may occur on the second or third day and last up to 2 weeks.

Treatment of barbiturate withdrawal generally consists of substitution of the drug with a longer-acting barbiturate such as phenobarbital. Dosage of the substitute is slowly tapered over a period of several weeks until it is completely withdrawn.

To establish a tolerance dose, investigators prefer a short-acting barbiturate, such as pentobarbital or secobarbital. A typical protocol used is the initial administration of 200 mg of either drug, then 100 mg hourly, until nystagmus or drowsiness is observed. When the total dose for tolerance is established, usually within a 6-hour period, the dose is converted to phenobarbital at a rate of 100 mg of secobarbital (or pentobarbital) to 30 mg phenobarbital, to determine the daily dose. For example, if the client is drowsy at 400 mg pentobarbital, then 120 mg per day—or 40 mg every 8 hours—is the conversion.

For safety purposes the nurse should carefully assess the client for signs of drug intoxication (nystagmus and ataxia) before starting the tolerance test. After the tolerance test is completed and the phenobarbital dose is calculated, a dose should be administered between 8 and 12 hours after completion of the tolerance test.

For detoxification the dosage reduction is greater, with 10 to 20 mg per day reductions in clients with high tolerance levels (such as 100 to 120 mg of phenobarbital per day) and lower, perhaps 5 to 10 mg reduction per day, in clients with low tolerance levels (10 to 50 mg). Phenobarbital permits safer withdrawal with fewer blood level fluctuations and less risk of overdose fatality in the sedative-hypnotic-dependent individual.

Some abusers inject the tablet or capsule oral forms of the barbiturates and sedative-hypnotics intravenously, which can result in serum hepatitis, septicemia, pulmonary emboli, papilloma, bacterial endocarditis, abscesses, tetanus, and various skin rashes. Because of the highly alkaline sclerosing of veins, phlebitis and extravascular abscesses occur with intravenous-injection abuse of barbiturates.

Long-acting barbiturates (phenobarbital, mephobarbital, metharbital, primidone [15% converted to phenobarbital]) are not generally the substances of abuse. Because of enzyme induction, long-term barbiturate use increases the metabolism of the barbiturate. Hepatic enzymes degrading barbiturates increase rapidly, metabolize the barbiturates, and reduce the barbiturate effect. Drug-dependent individuals have been known to take up to 1.5 g of barbiturate daily. The nurse should be aware that the chronic abuser will develop tolerance to the sedating effects of barbiturates while the lethal dose remains the same, thus they are high risk for accidental overdose. Doses in therapeutic ranges may achieve levels as high as 5 mg/100 ml; however, clients on long-term therapy or those who abuse the drug may sustain higher levels. In individuals who have not developed tolerance to barbiturates, a blood level of 3.5 mg/ml for the short-acting barbiturates or 8 mg/ml or more for the long-acting barbiturates can be fatal.

***Barbiturate dependence.*** Daily consumption of 400 mg of pentobarbital or secobarbital for approximately 3 months or 600 mg to 800 mg per day of amobarbital, butabarbital, pentobarbital, or secobarbital for 35 to 60 days will often result in some degree of physical dependence. Withdrawal symptoms begin in 8 to 12 hours after stopping the drug; tremors, anxiety, muscular weakness, anorexia, nausea, vomiting and hypotension. Seizures (clonic-tonic, or status epilepticus) may ensue 16 to 24 hours after the last drug dose or may have a delayed occurrence of up to 5 days.

Withdrawal may occur in neonates of mothers who receive barbiturates during the last trimester of pregnancy and may be seen soon after delivery or delayed up to 2 weeks. Hyperirritability, restlessness, and seizures may occur from 1 to 14 days after birth.

Treatment of an acute overdose is mainly supportive therapy. If activated charcoal is given within 30 minutes of the overdose, it can be very effective in adsorbing the drug. Some centers use multi-dose, activated charcoal via nasogastric administration for a phenobarbital overdose since it can increase drug elimination and reduce the duration of coma. In clients with normal renal function, forced alkaline diuresis can increase renal excretion of phenobarbital, aprobarbital, and mephobarbital. Hemodialysis or peritoneal dialysis has been useful for clients severely intoxicated or if the client is anuric or in shock.

## Nonbarbiturates
### ethchlorvynol (Placidyl)

Prolonged use of ethchlorvynol may result in tolerance, physical dependence, and psychic dependence. Dependence has been observed in individuals taking 1 g dosages over prolonged periods (4 to 5 months).

Some signs and symptoms of chronic intoxication are incoordination, tremors, ataxia, confusion, slurred speech, hyperreflexia, diplopia, and generalized muscle weakness. Some reversible symptoms are toxic amblyopia, nystagmus, and peripheral neuropathy. If the liquid in the capsule form is injected intravenously, pulmonary edema can result.

Severe withdrawal symptoms similar to those of barbiturate and alcohol withdrawal may occur as late as 9 days following abrupt cessation after prolonged use of this drug. Signs and symptoms of ethchlorvynol withdrawal are convulsions, delirium, schizoid reactions, perceptual distortions, retrograde amnesia, ataxia, insomnia, slurred speech, anxiety, irritability, agitation, tremors, anorexia, dizziness, nausea, vomiting, weakness, sweating, muscle twitching, and weight loss. Coma has been reported to last several days to weeks before recovery; a flat electroencephalogram may be seen during coma, but supportive care must be continued. Overdose-induced hypotension responds to fluids and vasopressor agents. A neonatal withdrawal syndrome has also been observed.

Respiratory depression necessitates artificial ventilation. Close nursing monitoring should include observations for bradycardia, pulmonary edema, peripheral neuropathy, cardiac arrest, respiratory arrest, and hypothermia. The half-life of the drug in an overdose may be more than four times that of the therapeutic half-life (25 hours).

The nurse should be alert for mixed ingestion, as in other cases of substance abuse. Alcohol potentiates this drug result so that lower levels of ethchlorvynol lead to a coma.

The client who manifests withdrawal symptoms is given either ethchlorvynol or phenobarbital (30 mg phenobarbital for each 350 mg ethchlorvynol abused) and the dosage tapered gradually over a period of days or weeks. The addition of a phenothiazine may be necessary for the client exhibiting psychotic withdrawal symptoms. Hospitalization in the withdrawal stage is absolutely necessary. A narrow margin exists between the toxic and therapeutic dose ranges for this drug, and dependency is produced even with lower doses. Overdose symptoms usually disappear in 1 to 2 weeks. It is recommended that ethchlorvynol be prescribed for only a 1-week time period. Prolonged drug administration may result in the development of tolerance or physical-psychic drug dependence.

## glutethimide (Doriden)

Glutethimide is a widely abused drug with a common street name of "goofers" or "goof balls". It is a CNS depressant that produces a dependence similar to the barbiturates. An overdose with glutethimide can result in a variety of complications, such as alternating periods of coma and wakefulness that may last for days, antimuscarinic effects that may result in a paralytic ileus and body storage of the drug in fat depots that can lead to irregular absorption of the drug.

Signs and symptoms of chronic intoxication include impairment of memory and ability to concentrate, impaired gait, ataxia, tremors, hyporeflexia, and slurring of speech. Withdrawal reactions ranging from nervousness and anxiety to grand mal seizures are seen upon abrupt cessation of the drug after prolonged use. Abdominal cramps, chills, numbness of extremities, and dysphagia are also found.

Acute overdosage is a life-threatening situation. Signs and symptoms of acute intoxication vary in severity with the ingested dose and are difficult to distinguish from barbiturate intoxication. Mild intoxication produces drowsiness and lethargy; and moderate to severe intoxication produces different degrees of coma, which may last as long as 4 or more days. The nurse should be alert for mixed drug inges-

tion (such as hypnotics, sedatives, alcohol, and illicit drugs) and suicide attempts.

Glutethimide produces significant anticholinergic effects, including adynamic ileus (diminished or absent peristalsis), urinary retention (atonic urinary bladder), dryness of the mouth, mydriasis, irritability, and convulsions. These effects are potentiated by a mixed drug ingestion involving, among other substances, alcohol. There is also depressed or absent response to painful stimuli, hypotension, and inadequate ventilation, sometimes with cyanosis. Sudden apnea may occur with manipulation such as gastric lavage or endotracheal intubation.

Cyclic coma (coma to wakefulness to coma) occurs because of the continued periodic absorption of the glutethimide from the gastrointestinal tract. The anticholinergic effects (cholinergic blockade) of glutethimide lower the motility of the gastrointestinal tract until the drug is metabolized, after which motility is resumed; following this, more glutethimide is absorbed, and the coma begins again. This pattern may be interrupted by increasing the emptying time of the gastrointestinal tract with a cathartic and charcoal to absorb the drug, and lavage or emesis. Prolonged coma may be caused by the accumulation in brain and plasma of the toxic active liver metabolite 4HG (4 hydroxy-2-ethyl-2-phenylglutarimide).

The anticholinergic effect and cyclic coma necessitate a period of observation to determine the toxicity of the ingestion. Death has occurred following ingestion of 5 g (10 tablets of 500 mg), and survival has been reported with ingestion of 35 g. The lethal dose is in a range of 10 to 20 g.

A phenobarbital equivalent dose of 30 mg is recommended for each 250 mg glutethimide abused in cases of withdrawal. Overdose is a potential problem, since the therapeutic-lethal range is narrow and active metabolites are present.

One gram of glutethimide combined with 240 mg of codeine is used as a substitute for heroin to produce heroine-like effects. This combination is called a "load." The codeine is obtained either from the Class V antitussives that contain 240 mg codeine in 120 ml of the product or from acetaminophen or aspirin products containing codeine. The Class V cough-suppressant product is referred to as "syrup." The nurse should be aware of the possibility of an overdose of both codeine and glutethimide in a client who admits to "loading."

## methaqualone

Methaqualone, a well-documented drug of abuse, was officially withdrawn from the U.S. market in 1984. While no longer legally available, methaqualone is still sold illegally (Dominquez, 1987). Analyzed samples of street "ludes" (methaqualone) have been found to contain methaqualone or diazepam.

Methaqualone, a hypnotic agent, was first released in

1965. Abuse of methaqualone can cause severe psychic and physical dependence. Abusers describe the effects produced by the drugs as sensual, euphoric, and similar to those of opiate drugs. Multiple drug abuse often occurs with methaqualone, and the concomitant abuse of alcohol may worsen the prognosis.

Acute overdose may result in delirium and coma, with restlessness, irritability, and hypertonia, progressing to convulsions. Spontaneous vomiting and increased secretions frequently occur and may lead to aspiration pneumonitis or respiratory obstruction. Large overdosages may result in cutaneous and pulmonary edema, hepatic damage, renal insufficiency, bleeding, shock, and respiratory arrest. Coma has been reported with doses of 2.4 g and death with a dose of 8 g, although individuals have survived doses of 22 g. Hyperexcitability and hyperreflexia are seen frequently in addition to myoclonic jerking, tetany, and tachycardia. Myocardial damage may result from use of this drug.

Withdrawal symptoms are familiar to those of barbiturate withdrawal, and there may be hallucinations, jitteriness, irritability, agitation, depression, and abdominal pain within 16 to 24 hours. Convulsions are experienced by 20% to 40% of individuals and can be controlled with intravenous administration of diazepam. The convulsions produced with this drug make overdose more dangerous than with other sedative-hypnotics that have a potential for causing dependence.

Because the drug is rapidly absorbed from the gastrointestinal tract, emesis or lavage is necessary in addition to cathartics and charcoal. Pulmonary edema is a contraindication to the use of forced diuresis. Hemodialysis is reserved for the person who is severely intoxicated with levels over 11 mg/100 ml.

Withdrawal is initiated with phenobarbital (30 mg phenobarbital for each 250 to 300 mg methaqualone abused). Phenobarbital is usually initiated with a dose not exceeding 180 mg daily in the adult, titrated to client comfort when symptoms of withdrawal subside for 1 or 2 days, and then gradually reduced. Continued absorption of the drug remaining in the gastrointestinal tract produces erratic peak plasma levels. Further, in abuse the continued exposure may be accounted for by differential metabolism of the drug. It is estimated that levels exceeding 2.5 mg/100 ml are intoxicating in most individuals.

### methyprylon (Noludar)

Methyprylon can cause dependence similar to that of barbiturates and alcohol in high dosages over extended periods. Symptoms reported in methyprylon intoxication are coma (lasting up to 30 hours), hypotension, respiratory depression, tachycardia, hypothermia, hyperthermia, somnolence, confusion, constricted pupils, and paradoxic excitability. The most dangerous complication is the hypotension.

The symptoms of withdrawal are restlessness, auditory and visual hallucinations, diaphoresis, polyuria, excitement, confusion, and convulsions on the abrupt cessation of the drug.

Methyprylon is water and lipid soluble, and most of the dose is excreted as a metabolite in the urine. Toxic blood levels are 3 to 5 mg/100 ml and 10 mg/100 ml is potentially lethal: therapeutic blood levels are less than 10 μg/ml (1 mg/100 ml).

Withdrawal syndrome is treated with phenobarbital. The dose used is 30 mg, equivalent to 300 mg methyprylon. The nurse should be alert for mixed substance abuse.

## Alcohols

Although there are many different kinds of alcohols, the term "alcohol" usually refers to ethyl alcohol. Methyl alcohol, propyl alcohol, butyl alcohol, and amyl alcohol are examples of other alcohols.

### ethyl alcohol

Ethyl alcohol has been known in an impure form since earliest times, and it is the only alcohol used extensively in medicine. Many of the OTC "nighttime" cough and cold remedies are abused because of their considerable sedative potential, since they contain 25% alcohol (50-proof) with antihistamines. Ethyl alcohol was formerly thought to be a remedy for almost any disease or disorder. It is a colorless liquid and lighter than water, with which it mixes readily. It lowers surface tension and acts as a good solvent for a number of substances. Ethyl alcohol, also referred to as ethanol or grain alcohol, is the product of the fermentation of a sugar by yeast.

***Mechanism of action.*** Ethyl alcohol may have either a local or a systemic action.

*Local.* Ethyl alcohol denatures proteins by precipitation and dehydration. This is said to be the basis for its germicidal, irritant, and astringent effects. It irritates denuded skin, mucous membranes, and subcutaneous tissue. Subcutaneous injection of alcohol may cause considerable pain and sloughing of the tissues. When it is injected into or near a nerve, alcohol may cause nerve degeneration and anesthesia. Alcohol evaporates readily from the skin, producing a cooling effect and reducing the temperature of the skin. When rubbed on the surface of the body, it acts as a mild counterirritant. It dries and hardens the epithelial layer of the skin and helps to prevent bed sores when used externally. However, its use on dry and irritated skin is usually contraindicated.

Solutions of ethyl alcohol that measure 70% by weight seem to exert the best bactericidal effects. High concentrations have a marked dehydrating effect but do not necessarily kill bacteria. Ethyl alcohol in proper concentrations is considered an effective germicide for a number of uses, but it does not kill spores.

*Systemic.* Modern scientific authorities do not consider alcohol to be a stimulant, popular ideas to the contrary.

**TABLE 9-4** Concentration of alcohol in blood/urine and clinical observations

| Stage | Blood alcohol (%) | Urine alcohol (%) | Clinical observations |
|---|---|---|---|
| Subclinical | up to 0.11 | up to 0.15 | Slight evidence of performance deterioration possible, such as motor function; coordination; personality or mood and mental acuity |
| Emotional instability | 0.09-0.21 | 0.13-0.29 | Decreased inhibitions; emotional instability; slight muscular incoordination; slowing of responses to stimuli |
| Confusion | 0.18-0.33 | 0.26-0.45 | Disturbance of sensation; decreased pain sense; staggering gait; slurred speech |
| Stupor | 0.27-0.43 | 0.36-0.58 | Marked decrease in response to stimuli; muscular incoordination approaching paralysis |
| Coma | 0.36-0.56 | 0.48-0.72 | Complete unconsciousness; depressed reflexes; subnormal temperature; anesthesia; impairment of circulation; possible death |
| Death (uncomplicated) | Over 0.44 | Over 0.60 | |

What sometimes appears to be stimulation results from the depression of the higher faculties of the brain and represents the loss of inhibitions acquired by socialization. Alcohol is thought to interfere with the transmission of nerve impulses at synaptic connections, but how this is accomplished is not known. It causes progressive and continuous depression of the central nervous system (cerebrum, cerebellum, spinal cord, and medulla). Its action is comparable to that of the general anesthetics. The excitement stage, however, is longer; and when the anesthetic stage is reached, definite toxic symptoms are present. The margin between the anesthetic stage and the fatal dose is a narrow one.

The action of alcohol varies with the individual, one's tolerance, the presence or absence of extraneous stimuli, the rate of ingestion, and gastric contents. Small or moderate quantities produce a feeling of well-being, talkativeness, greater vivacity, and increased confidence in one's mental and physical power. The personality becomes expansive, and there is a general loss of inhibitions. The finer powers of discrimination, concentration, insight, judgment, and memory are gradually dulled and lost. Large quantities may cause excitement, impulsive speech and behavior, laughter, hilarity, and in some cases, pugnaciousness in some persons, while others may become melancholy or unduly sentimental. The intoxicated individual usually becomes ataxic, mutters incoherently, has disturbance of the special senses, is often nauseated, may vomit, and eventually lapses into stupor or coma.

The respiratory center is not depressed except by large doses.

*Cardiovascular.* Alcohol depresses the vasomotor center in the medulla and causes dilation of the peripheral blood vessels, especially those of the skin. This causes a feeling of warmth. Heat is also lost from the interior, which accounts for the fact that an intoxicated person may freeze to death more quickly than a nonintoxicated person. Alcohol also depresses the heat-regulating mechanism; and before the advent of the modern antipyretics, it was used to reduce fever.

## CONTENT OF ETHANOL IN VARIOUS SOLUTIONS

| Beverages | Alcohol Content (%) | Alcohol Proof |
|---|---|---|
| Beer | 4 | 8 |
| Wine (red/white) | 12 | 24 |
| Brandy | 30-45 | 60-90 |
| Whiskey, vodka | 45 | 90 |
| Martini, Manhattan | 30 | 60 |
| Daiquiri, Alexander | 15 | 30 |
| **OTC Medicinals** | | |
| Formula 44-D | 20 | 40 |
| Prunicodeine | 25 | 50 |
| Nyquil | 25 | 50 |
| Elixir terpin hydrate with codeine (various) | 39-44 | 78-88 |

Data from Davidson, 1986; Hinds, 1985.

Small doses (10 to 25 ml) produce an insignificant increase in the pulse rate, caused mainly by the excitement and the reflex effect on the gastrointestinal tract. Larger doses (over 25 ml) produce the same effect but may be followed by lowered blood pressure caused by the effect on the vasoconstrictor center. Only high concentrations of alcohol depress the heart.

*Gastrointestinal.* The effect of alcohol on the function of the digestive organs depends on the presence or absence of gastrointestinal disease, the degree of alcohol tolerance, the concentration of the alcohol, and the type and amount of food present. Small doses of alcohol will stimulate the secretion of gastric juice rich in acid. Salivary secretion is also reflexly stimulated. Large and concentrated doses of alcohol tend to inhibit secretion and enzyme activity in the stomach, although the effect in the intestine seems to be negligible. However, when large quantities of alcohol are

**TABLE 9-5**   Selected significant alcohol-drug interactions

| Substances interacting with alcohol | Mechanism | Possible effect(s) |
|---|---|---|
| I. antihistamines<br>antidepressants<br>opioid analgesics<br>sedative-hypnotics<br>antianxiety agents<br>antipsychotic drugs | Additive | Enhanced CNS depressant effects |
| II. disulfiram (Antabuse)<br>chlorpropamide (Diabinese)<br>other oral antidiabetic agents<br>(to varying degrees)<br>metronidazole (Flagyl) | Inhibition of aldehyde dehydrogenase in metabolism of alcohol, leading to acetaldehyde accumulation (disulfiram or a "disulfiram-type reaction") | Most severe effects seen with disulfiram and alcohol: flushing, stomach pain, head throbbing, increased heart rate, hypotension, sweating, nausea, and vomiting. With antidiabetic agents: mild to severe hypoglycemia |
| III. phenytoin (Dilantin) | Increase or decrease in liver metabolism | In chronic alcohol abuse: possible decrease in anticonvulsant effect, due to increased metabolism<br>In acute alcohol use: a possible decrease in metabolism, causing increased serum level of phenytoin and toxicity |
| IV. salicylates | Additive | Increased gastrointestinal irritability and bleeding |
| V. nitrates<br>nitroglycerin | Additive | Vasodilation leading to hypotension, syncope |

taken over prolonged time periods, gastritis, nutritional deficiencies, and other untoward results have been observed.

***Pharmacokinetics.*** Alcohol does not require digestion before absorption. A small amount is absorbed in the stomach while most is absorbed in the small intestine. Approximately 90% of the alcohol is metabolized by alcohol dehydrogenase in the liver. In the presence of alcohol dehydrogenase, alcohol is oxidized to acetaldehyde; acetaldehyde oxidizes to acetic acid, which is buffered to an acetate that eventually oxidizes to carbon dioxide and water. The process of alcohol metabolism occurs at a fairly constant rate; a person weighing 70 kg usually metabolizes 20 to 30 ml of 90 proof spirits (45% alcohol) or 8 to 12 ounces of beer (4% alcohol) or 3 ounces of wine or champagne (12% alcohol) per hour.

Alcohol that escapes oxidation is excreted by way of the lungs and kidneys, and some is found in a number of excretions such as sweat.

Alcohol produces an increased flow of urine because of the increase in fluid intake. It has been suggested that alcohol may also act as a diuretic through CNS depression and inhibition of antidiuretic hormone (ADH) release. If the individual has preexisting renal disease, the kidney may be further damaged. Large and concentrated doses of alcohol are thought to injure the renal epithelium.

After absorption, alcohol is distributed in the tissues of the body in approximately the same ratio as their water content. Therefore a rough estimate of the quantity consumed may be obtained from an analysis of the blood and urine (Table 9-4).

At times alcohol is injected into a nerve to destroy sensory nerve fibers and relieve pain associated with a severe and protracted neuralgia, such as trifacial neuralgia (tic douloureux), or inoperable cancer. An injection of 80% ethyl alcohol is used. Effects may persist for 1 to 3 years, until regeneration of the peripheral nerve fibers takes place, or be permanent.

Alcohol is used to produce vasodilation in peripheral vascular disease. Concentrated solutions often produce greater peripheral vasodilation than any other drug. The pain of Buerger's disease may be relieved by oral ethyl alcohol. Alcohol may be prescribed to decrease the frequency of anginal attacks but effects are said to be unreliable. Benefits to the person with a cardiac condition, if they occur, are believed to result from the rest and relaxation that the alcohol produces.

Alcohol has been used as an appetite stimulant for clients with poor appetite during periods of convalescence and debility. Alcohol may be used as a hypnotic for older persons who do not tolerate other hypnotics.

***Dosage and administration.*** See box for various preparations of ethyl alcohol. Dosage varies with the purpose for which the alcohol is administered. When whiskey is prescribed as a vasodilator, 30 ml may be ordered to be given two or three times a day.

***Drug interactions.*** The most commonly used and abused drug in America is alcohol. It interacts with many prescription and OTC drugs, resulting in serious adverse effects leading to emergency room admissions or even death. The magnitude of this potential interaction is enormous. Most people, professionals and lay persons alike, are not fully cognizant of some of the most significant alcohol-drug interactions. (See Table 9-5.)

The National Safety Council regards concentration of alcohol in the blood up to 0.05% as evidence of unquestioned sobriety. Concentrations between 0.051% and 0.149% are regarded as grounds for suspicion and for use of performance tests, and anything more than 0.15% is evidence of unquestioned intoxication. The states differ as to what is accepted as a legal limit.

The effects of alcohol may become apparent when the individual attempts to operate machinery such as an automobile. Visual acuity (especially peripheral vision) is diminished, reaction time is slowed, judgment and self-control are impaired, and the individual tends to be complacent and pleased with himself. Many drivers will take chances when under the influence of alcohol that they would never take ordinarily. This leads to disaster, as accident statistics reveal.

**Indications.** Ethyl alcohol is used topically as an astringent and antiseptic. It is a popular disinfectant for the skin. Alcohol rubs are given to prevent decubiti on the back and buttocks. It is an excellent solvent and preservative for many medicines and medicinal mixtures (spirits, elixirs, fluid extracts). At times 80% ethyl alcohol is injected into a nerve to destroy sensory nerve fibers and relieve pain associated with a severe and protracted neuralgia, such as trifacial neuralgia (tic douloureux) or inoperable cancer.

## Toxic Alcohols

Isopropyl alcohol and methyl or wood alcohol are very toxic when taken internally. When some alcoholic individuals are unable to purchase ethanol (ethyl alcohol), they substitute agents such as isopropyl (rubbing) alcohol, methyl alcohol (antifreeze), or any available substance that might prevent alcohol withdrawal. This is a dangerous practice with serious systemic effects.

### isopropyl alcohol

Isopropyl alcohol is a clear, colorless liquid with a characteristic odor. It compares favorably with ethyl alcohol in its antiseptic action. It has been recommended for disinfection of the skin and for rubbing compounds and lotions to be used on the skin. Its bactericidal effects are said to increase as its concentration approaches 100%. Isopropyl alcohol is occasionally misused as a beverage. It can cause severe poisoning and death. The first symptoms are similar to intoxication from ethyl alcohol, but the symptoms progress to coma from which the client may not recover.

### methyl alcohol (wood alcohol, methanol)

Methyl alcohol is prepared on a large scale by the destructive distillation of wood. It is also prepared synthetically. It is important in medicine chiefly because of the cases of poisoning caused by its ingestion. The main effects are on the central nervous system. However, intoxication does not occur as readily as with ethyl alcohol unless large amounts are consumed. Methyl alcohol is oxidized in the tissues to formic acid, which is poorly metabolized. This is the basis for the development of a severe acidosis.

Symptoms of poisoning include nausea and vomiting, abdominal pain, headache, dyspnea, blurred vision, and cold clammy skin. Symptoms may progress to delirium, convulsions, coma, and death. In nonfatal cases the individual may become blind or suffer from impaired vision. Treatment is directed toward the relief of acidosis since this seems to be related to the severity of the visual symptoms. Large amounts of sodium bicarbonate may be needed to treat acidosis successfully. Obviously, methyl alcohol is much more toxic than ethyl alcohol. One dose of 60 ml has been known to cause permanent blindness. Fluids containing methyl alcohol usually bear a "Poison" label.

## Drugs Used in Treatment of Chronic Alcoholism (Alcoholism Deterrent)
### disulfiram (Antabuse)

Disulfiram is used to sensitize an individual to alcohol by bringing about an unpleasant alcohol-disulfiram reaction. This disulfiram reaction begins with flushing in the face and develops into intense vasodilation of the face, neck, and upper part of the body. Hyperventilation and increased pulse rate may occur. Nausea occurs in 30 to 60 minutes along with facial pallor, hypotension, and copious vomiting. There is usually an intense feeling of discomfort, pulsating headache, palpitations, dyspnea, syncope, and a constrictive feeling in the neck. The reaction lasts from 30 minutes to several hours, as long as alcohol is being metabolized; it is then followed by drowsiness and sleep. This experience is so unpleasant that use of alcohol tends to repel the individual.

**Mechanism of action.** In the body alcohol is oxidized to acetaldehyde. Disulfiram inhibits the enzyme aldehyde dehydrogenase, which converts acetaldehyde to acetate. This permits acetaldehyde to accumulate and cause unpleasant toxic effects. Disulfiram has few effects unless the person ingests alcohol.

**Pharmacokinetics.** Metabolism is hepatic and initial effect may be delayed up to 12 hours because of localization in adipose tissue; twenty percent of a dose remains in the body for 1 week or more. Renal excretion of metabolites occurs in addition to excretion of carbon disulfide via the lungs. Five to twenty percent of each dose is eliminated unchanged in the feces. Because of slow and incomplete absorption and eliminations, effects persist for up to 2 weeks after therapy is stopped. Clients should be warned not to ingest any alcohol-containing substance during this time.

Alcohol is available in prescription drugs, OTC drugs, liquid cough-cold analgesic products, foods, flavoring, mouthwashes, salad dressings, and the like, and the individual should be warned of possible interaction and the need to check all liquids for alcohol. Psychotherapy aimed at mental and social rehabilitation should accompany disulfiram therapy, and all clients should carry disulfiram treatment identification. Disulfiram is available in 250 and 500 mg tablets.

*Side effects/adverse reactions.* The most frequent side effect is sleepiness. Less frequent are headache, rash, stomach upset, increased tiredness, metallic taste, and decrease in sexual potency in males. If side effects continue, increase, or disturb the client, the physician must be informed. Adverse reactions are less frequent but include ocular pain or visual changes, psychosis, weakness, tingling sensation, pain or numbness in hands or feet, and jaundice. If adverse reactions occur, medical intervention may be necessary.

*Significant drug interactions.* When disulfiram is given with:

| Drug | Possible Effect and Management |
|---|---|
| anticoagulants | Increased anticoagulant effects; dosage adjustments may be necessary; monitor closely |
| phenytoin (hydantoins) | Increased serum levels of hydantoins; monitor serum levels before and during anticonvulsant therapy; dosage adjustments may be necessary |
| isoniazid (INH) | Increased CNS side effects (ataxia, inability to sleep, dizziness, increased irritability); disulfiram dosage may need to be reduced or stopped; monitor closely |
| metronidazole | Confusion and psychotic episodes; avoid this combination |
| paraldehyde | Increased serum levels of paraldehyde and acetaldehyde resulting from inhibition of acetaldehyde dehydrogenase; concurrent use not recommended |

*Dosage and administration.* Initial, up to 0.5 g orally daily for 7 to 14 days; maintenance, 250 mg orally daily

*Pregnancy safety.* FDA category undetermined

▷ **Nursing Management: Disulfiram Therapy**

*Assessment.* Ask if the client may be intolerant of other thiuram products, which are used in pesticides, fungicides, or the vulcanization of rubber.

Carefully consider the use of disulfiram if the client has a history of cardiovascular disorders, diabetes mellitus, cerebral damage or epilepsy, psychoses, eczema, hypothyroidism, and renal or hepatic impairment.

It must be ascertained that the client has not ingested alcohol in any form, i.e., beverages, sauces, OTC preparations, as well as liniments, colognes, and aftershave lotions, in the last 12 hours before beginning a disulfiram regimen.

Complete blood count (CBC), SMA-12, and liver function studies should be done as a baseline before therapy begins.

*Intervention.* If the client has impaired swallowing, the tablets may be crushed and mixed with a small amount of honey, gelatin, or ice cream.

Supportive measures will need to be instituted in instances of a severe alcohol-disulfiram reaction to restore the blood pressure and treat for shock.

Ensure safety precautions if the client has CNS effect of drowsiness, such as assistance with transferring and ambulation.

abstinence. Refer to an appropriate support group in planning for discharge.

*Education.* Caution the client that the ingestion of any form of alcohol while taking disulfiram, and for up to 14 days after the last dose, will cause a very unpleasant response—dizziness, syncope, nausea and vomiting, headache, chest pain, dyspnea, palpitations, tachycardia, profuse sweating, facial flushing, blurred vision; and if severe, seizures, unconsciousness, heart attack, and death. The extent of the reaction will depend on the dose of the drug and the amount of alcohol ingested. All foods and liquid medications should be checked for the presence of alcohol.

Encourage the client to wear a Medic Alert identification while taking the drug and to alert any health care providers with which he or she comes in contact.

Caution the client against driving or operating any hazardous equipment if drowsiness resulting from the drug occurs. A slight metallic taste may occur for the first few weeks of therapy.

The client should consult with the health care provider at six monthly intervals for blood studies or if any of the following occur: chest pain, respiratory difficulty, jaundice, and the ingestion of alcohol.

*Evaluation.* A transaminase test is recommended 10 to 14 days into disulfiram therapy and every 6 months during therapy, along with a CBC and SMA-12 to monitor for adverse effects of the drug. Clinically the client should be observed for visual disturbances and/or eye pain, which might indicate an optic neuritis. Peripheral neuritis may be developing if the client has tingling or numbness of the hands or feet. Jaundice may indicate a drug-induced hepatoxicity. Client success should include an awareness of the benefits of abstinence demonstrated by compliance with the disulfiram therapy and abstinence from alcohol use.

## Antianxiety and Antipsychotic Agents

In the late 1970s to 1980s, the number of prescriptions for antianxiety agents soared. Psychoactive agents were freely prescribed and taken. Women in particular were overmedicated, for reasons such as the following:

1. Women see physicians more often than men do. The National Center for Health statistics reports that approximately 60% of physician visits are with women. It has been said that men generally seek physicians' advice when they are ill, while women seek medical help when they are healthy (e.g., advice on birth control, prenatal care, birth of a child, routine Pap smears, and breast examinations).

2. Females are more vocal in reporting emotional problems or feelings than males. Physicians may not know how to appropriately respond to these "nonmedical" complaints, so they prescribe diazepam (Valium) or a similar benzodiazepine (Hughes and Brewin, 1979). The physician's prescriptions also meet the expectation of the client, that is, they are a confirmation of an ailment. In many instances, nonchemical approaches are not even considered.

---

## BENZODIAZEPINE CLASSIFICATIONS

**Short-Acting (Half-life less than 24 hours)**

alprazolam (Xanax)
lorazepam (Ativan, Apo-Lorazepam♣)
oxazepam (Serax, Ox-Pam♣)
temazepam (Restoril)
triazolam (Halcion)

**Long-Acting (Half-life longer than 24 hours)**

chloriazepoxide (Librium, Apo-Chlorax♣)
clorazepate (Tranexe)
diazepam (Valium, Apo-Diazepam♣)
flurazepam (Delmane, Novoflupam♣)
halazepam (Paxipam)
prazepam (Centrax)

---

3. Sexual bias among physicians has been asserted. When males and females visited the physician with the same complaints of emotional unhappiness (depression, crying periods, tension, worry, and anxiety), physicians prescribed tranquilizers for the females while ordering tests and therapies for male clients (Hughes & Brewin, 1979). This resulted in more prescriptions for psychoactive drugs for the women as compared to men.

The problem of overprescription of psychoactive drugs also affects elderly clients. In the United States, Canada, and the United Kingdom, prescriptions for psychotropic drugs increase proportionately with age (Hyams, 1984). A study of the Department of Health, Education, and Welfare reviewed the records of over 250,000 individuals living in nursing homes and discovered that nearly 47% of them were receiving psychotropic drugs. In Canada, a review of 1431 chronically ill elderly revealed that about 25% of them were receiving psychotropic medications. A different Canadian study of outpatient elderly reported similar percentages (26%) taking psychotropic drugs. This study also reported that in nearly 10% of these elderly the drugs were the cause of their symptoms (Hyams, 1984).

A study of the association between the risk of hip fractures in the elderly and the use of psychoactive drugs illustrates the potential dangers with these agents (Ray et al, 1987). A total of 1021 cases and 5606 controls were evaluated in this study. Forty-two percent of the studied population was over 85 years old, and 77% were women. Four categories of psychotropic medications were reviewed: (1) antianxiety or hypnotic drugs with short half-lives (less than 24 hours), (2) antianxiety or hypnotic agents with long half-lives (longer than 24 hours), (3) tricyclic antidepressants, and (4) antipsychotic agents. Categories 2, 3, and 4 were associated with increased risk and incidence of hip fractures.

Both the antianxiety and antipsychotic agents can lead to psychic and physical dependence. Abrupt withdrawal of phenothiazine-type drugs may result in anxiety, insomnia, gastrointestinal disturbances, and muscular discomfort. Abrupt discontinuance of benzodiazepines such as chlordiazepoxide (Librium), diazepam (Valium), and clorazepate (Tranxene) may produce withdrawal symptoms such as insomnia, increased irritability and nervousness, stomach pain, muscle cramping, nausea and vomiting, fear, tremors, sweating, headaches, decreased ability to concentrate, and increased tiredness. Such reactions have been reported even in clients abruptly stopping dosages of benzodiazepines within the usually recommended therapeutic range. The symptoms described occur more frequently and are more severe in individuals who suddenly withdraw from the short-acting benzodiazepines. (See boxed material.)

### Overdosage

*Benzodiazepines.* Benzodiazepine overdosage may cause sleepiness and minor extrapyramidal signs with some excitement. Because of the high probability of a mixed ingestion, one must watch for possible deep coma, marked hypotension, and respiratory depression. Other effects include dry mouth, tachycardia, dilated pupils, and absent bowel sounds. Abrupt cessation of a benzodiazepine may result in withdrawal symptoms if the drug has been taken daily for several months or years. Hallucinations, confusion, and seizures often are reported. These effects may be overcome by gradually withdrawing the drug. Flumazepil (Ro 15-1788) is a product marketed in Europe as a benzodiazepine receptor antagonist. While human studies are limited, the reports of the antagonist effects of this drug on benzodiazepine are quite impressive. Flumazepil is given intravenously and appears to have no pharmacologic effects of its own. This product has been given in both known and suspected cases of benzodiazepine toxicity and has also proved beneficial in clients that consumed benzodiazepines and other sedatives, such as alcohol. It has no effect on barbiturate or tricyclic antidepressant overdoses alone. It is currently only available in Switzerland and Great Britain (Drake, 1986; Reynolds, 1989).

*Phenothiazines.* Phenothiazine overdosage most often produces stiff neck, ataxia, protruding tongue, reduced activity and attentiveness, and psychomotor slowing. Initial symptoms may include agitation, hyperactivity, and seizures. Disturbance of the temperature-regulating processes by phenothiazines creates hyperthermia or hypothermia. The alpha-blocking and anticholinergic effects of phenothiazines frequently produce tachycardia, lethargy, and somnolence. The quinidine-like effect of the phenothiazines may produce a widening of the QRS complexes and ventricular tachycardia. The nurse should remember not to administer other sedatives, barbiturates, narcotics, or anesthetics concurrently with phenothiazines, since the potentiation of these depressant drugs may create respiratory depression and increased CNS effects.

## CNS Stimulants

### *Amphetamines*

Amphetamine was first synthesized in Germany during the 1930s. This stimulant soon became very popular worldwide. Some governments, including the Soviet Union, gave amphetamines to factory workers to increase their output. Although initially considered successful, in time these experiments were deemed to be unsuccessful. During World War II amphetamines were given to U.S. soldiers to help them improve their strength and reduce fatigue during battle.

In the 1950s and 1960s, tremendous amounts of amphetamines were produced and available both legally and illegally. Drug manufacturers were advising physicians to prescribe these products for the depressed housewife, for overweight persons, or to make someone happy and energetic (Weil and Rosen, 1983). Although Sweden classified amphetamines as "prescription only" in 1939, the United States did not institute this control until 1954. But even the prescription requirement did not curtail the abuse of amphetamines seen in many countries, including the United States, Sweden, and Japan (Brecher, 1972).

Abuse of oral amphetamines was reported as early as 1940. Intravenous use of amphetamines began in the 1950s and increased in popularity in the 1960s, when physicians in the San Francisco Bay area prescribed it for pain and as a treatment for heroin addiction.

In the 1960s new federal drug amendments were passed to control the manufacture and distribution of amphetamines; physicians, pharmacists, and others involved in illegal uses were arrested. Amphetamine abuse is still reported in the Drug Abuse Warning Network, but cocaine is clearly the leading CNS stimulant abused.

***Mechanism of action.*** The amphetamines are synthetic indirect sympathomimetic amines that are chemically and pharmacologically related to epinephrine and norepinephrine. The exact mechanism by which amphetamines act is unknown, but they cause CNS stimulation probably by releasing catecholamines (norepinephrine and dopamine) from sympathetic nerve terminals. Oral doses are absorbed from the GI tract and concentrated in the kidneys, lungs, and brain. Peak effects occur 15 minutes after intravenous administration. Approximately half the administered dose is excreted unchanged, with the balance being metabolized as deaminated metabolites. The half-life of the metabolites in the urine varies with changes in urine pH. Amphetamine is a basic drug with a **$pK_a$** level of 9.9 ($pK_a$ is the point at which half the amount in the body is ionized and half is nonionized). Its half-life in recipients with an acidic urine (pH less than 6.6) ranges from 7 to 14 hours. In recipients with alkaline urine (pH over 6.7, as from use of sodium bicarbonate), the half-life range is prolonged to 18 to 34 hours.

Deaths have occurred with doses of 5 mg/kg or more. Tolerance develops, and response is variable, since chronic abusers use from 5 to 8000 mg/day. The desired effects occur within 1 hour after ingestion. Because amphetamines and related derivatives possess a high $pK_a$, acid diuresis will enhance amphetamine excretion. The goal of acidification is to achieve a urine pH between 4.5 and 5.5.

***Effects.*** The amphetamines usually are abused because they produce an elevation of mood, a reduction of fatigue, a sense of increased alertness, and "invigorating aggressiveness." Amphetamines do not create extra physical or mental energy; rather, they promote expenditure of present resources, sometimes to the point of hazardous fatigue, which is often unrecognized. Intravenous injection results in marked euphoria, an orgasmic feeling known as the flash or **rush,** a sense of great physical strength and capacity, and a sense of crystal-clear thinking. The user feels little or no need for rest, sleep, or food and may continually engage in vigorous activity that may be perceived as exhilarating and creative. To an objective observer, however, inefficient, stereotyped, and repetitive behavior is common during an amphetamine high.

Depending on the dosage of the drug taken, the individual may experience a "run" of variable length, perhaps several days. Some amphetamine users force themselves to lie down and close their eyes for a few hours during such a run and also will force-feed themselves in an attempt to prolong the run. Termination of the drug's use may result from a variety of factors, such as exhaustion, fright, or inability to obtain more of the drug. Withdrawal of the drug is followed by long periods of sleep. On awakening, the individual often feels hungry, extremely lethargic, and profoundly depressed, a phenomenon known as **crashing**. The risk of suicide during this period must be considered.

The stimulant properties of amphetamines can cause dramatic cardiorespiratory effects, such as tachycardia, dyspnea, chest pain, and hypertension. Users of amphetamines may panic because these signs and symptoms are those of a myocardial infarction. To deal with these disturbing symptoms, amphetamine users often use depressants, or **downers**. Some drugs (such as dextroamphetamine sulfate and amobarbital) combine a CNS stimulant with CNS depressant in an attempt to minimize the overstimulation produced by the amphetamine ingredient.

Amphetamines are also said to be psychotomimetic. Although there is some conflicting evidence regarding the cause of amphetamine psychosis, it is claimed that heavy users may develop psychosis characterized by aggression, delusions of persecution, depression, paranoia, euphoria, and fully formed visual and auditory hallucinations. Some authorities suggest that these symptoms may be related to the insomnia produced by prolonged amphetamine abuse because sleep deprivation, in and of itself, leads to psychologic disturbance. Marked tolerance to amphetamines occurs.

Oral tablets are sometimes crushed for use in an intravenous solution. Although intravenous administration of amphetamine alone is not associated with pulmonary microemboli, tablet fillers such as magnesium silicate (talc) and cornstarch may produce pulmonary emboli, resulting in granuloma formation within the lung. Pulmonary emboli have also been observed following injection of methylphenidate tablets. Talc may also appear in the cornea of the eye after chronic parenteral administration of solutions made from oral tablets of methylphenidate. Because the lungs act as filters for these large talc particles, intravenous abusers who complain of nonspecific pulmonary symptoms should be examined for talc-containing microemboli; an eye examination may reveal the same source of talc.

**Withdrawal symptoms.**   Although amphetamines do not appear to lead to physical dependence, as identified by the criterion of a characteristic and reproducible withdrawal syndrome, most authorities maintain that the signs and symptoms characteristic of crashing constitute just such a syndrome.

**Preparations.**   Chemically, there are three types of amphetamines: salts of racemic amphetamines, dextroamphetamines, and methamphetamines, all of which vary in degree of potency and peripheral effects. Dextroamphetamine is said to have fewest peripheral effects, such as hypertension and tachycardia.

**Treatment of toxicity.**   No specific antidote is available to treat amphetamine overdose. Psychotic symptoms usually occur within 36 to 48 hours after a single, large overdose. This usually clears in approximately 1 week. Treatment is mainly supportive and symptomatic. If a sedative drug is necessary, a short-acting barbiturate is usually the drug of choice. To increase renal excretion of amphetamines, acidify the urine by administering ammonium chloride.

## Cocaine

Cocaine is classified as a narcotic but is an alkaloid, related to the belladonna alkaloids. A potent CNS stimulant, cocaine is used therapeutically mostly as a local anesthetic, since it is likely to cause toxic side effects when administered by other routes. Cocaine as a social-recreational drug of abuse is popular for its effects: elation and euphoria. It also produces increased energy, like the amphetamines, and may lead to a similar psychotic state with strong elements of paranoia.

The purity of the illicitly produced drug varies greatly (generally 5% to 10%). This short-lived CNS stimulant is often diluted or cut with agents such as amphetamines, boric acid, quinine, mannitol, procaine, and lidocaine. The vasoconstricting effect of cocaine may be responsible for limiting its own absorption. Abusers of this drug may mix it with alcohol, a concoction known as a "liquid lady."

Cocaine may be administered by sniffing (snorting) the white, fluffy crystalline powder (which resembles snow, hence the name), by direct intravenous injection, or by smoking (transalveolar route) the converted base form ("free

base"). It may be inhaled from a small spoon, rolled dollar bills, lengthened finger nail, or an inhalation device designed for cromolyn sodium. Sniffing causes vasoconstriction, which limits the amount of cocaine absorbed from the nasal mucosa into systemic circulation. Sometimes cocaine is mixed with heroin for heightened effects and to diminish dysphoria, a combination known as a **speedball**.

The cocaine hydrochloride salt is converted to the freebase form by the use of a solvent such as diethyl ether. The freebase form is heat resistant, lending itself to smoking in any form including "coke pipes." Smoking freebase cocaine produces a more intense effect and is dangerous because of the possibility of an excessive dose being administered. The freebase solvents are inflammable and may explode during the process, causing further harm to the user.

Freebase cocaine has largely been replaced by crack (rock) cocaine. Crack cocaine is also a freebase, but it is made without any volatile chemicals. It became popular because of its availability in smaller amounts at a much lower cost than freebase cocaine and because its use does not require any elaborate paraphernalia. The cocaine market has thus become affordable to all economic groups. (See boxed material for cocaine names and description.)

Cocaine is rapidly metabolized, and the abuser of cocaine may use the drug every half hour or less to maintain the high. Cocaine is metabolized in the liver by hepatic esterases, and plasma hydrolysis is the result of serum cholinesterase. It is absorbed from all mucous membranes. The serum levels are not proportional to the toxicity, and the elimination half-lives by oral, intranasal, and intravenous routes are similar (50, 80, and 60 minutes, respectively). Cocaine stimulation of the CNS initially affects the intellect (cognition) and behavior (affective domain).

At this time there is no absolute level known to be lethal. Toxic effects have been reported with a 20 mg dose and fatal outcomes with 1200 mg. The rapidity of the increase in blood level may be as important in determining fatal reactions as the peak blood concentration. Factors other than blood concentration of cocaine must be examined. These factors include tolerance, reverse tolerance, previous history of cocaine abuse, individual susceptibility, and presence of other drugs.

Initial symptoms of cocaine use are restlessness, mydriasis, hyperreflexia, vasoconstriction, tachycardia, hypertension, hallucinations, nausea, vomiting, and muscle spasms, which may be followed by respiratory failure, convulsions, coma, and circulatory collapse. In chronic abusers a toxic cocaine psychosis (similar to paranoid schizophrenia) is often found, characterized by hallucinations and paranoid delusions. Skin eruptions (with itching and compulsive scratching) caused by self-inflicted skin irritation are also frequently observed. The energetic client may be prone to outbursts of violent behavior. Blood in the nose and a perforated nasal septum are frequently seen in those who chronically snort cocaine. A large dose of cocaine has direct

---

### COCAINE NAMES AND DESCRIPTION

| | Street Names | Source/Comments |
|---|---|---|
| Freebase cocaine | Base, baseball, white tornado, snow toke | Purified base made by using volatile chemicals |
| Basuco cocaine | Coca paste, pasta | Crude form of cocaine; derived from coca leaves; mixed with tobacco or marijuana and smoked; cheapest form of cocaine and usually the most contaminated form |
| Crack cocaine | Rock, gravel | Base product; up to the early 1980s rock cocaine usually referred to chunks of pure cocaine hydrochloride; today the term usually refers to crack |

---

cardiotoxicity, but death from overdose may result from respiratory failure.

Physical dependence now appears to be an emerging characteristic of cocaine abuse. Strong psychologic dependence is also evident. (For discussion of drugs used to lessen the symptoms of cocaine withdrawal, see boxed material.)

## Cannabis Drugs (Marijuana)

The cannabis drugs are derived from the leaves, stems, fruiting tops, and resin of both female and male hemp plants, *Cannabis sativa.* The potency of the active ingredient, tetrahydrocannabinol ($\delta^9$-THC), is greatest in the flowering tops of the plant and seems to vary according to the climatic conditions under which the plant is grown. In the U.S. the plants grow wild or are illegally cultivated and thus potency varies. The only legal cultivation is that by the federal government for research purposes.

Both the availability of more potent species and varieties of marijuana and the alarming increase in use among young teenagers (12 to 14 years of age) require a new attitude of concern toward the substance. Imported marijuana and that grown under scientifically controlled conditions is often 10 times as potent as the domestic variety smoked in the past. Some of the marijuana from Central and South America has 4% to 6% THC compared with 0.2% to 4% in that grown in the U.S.

***Preparations.*** Marijuana and hashish are the most common forms of cannabis drugs used in the U.S. Hashish refers to the powdered form of the plant's resin, which is five to ten times as potent as some varieties of marijuana. Other forms of cannabis drugs, used in such countries as Jamaica, Mexico, Africa, India, and the Middle East, include *banji, ganja,* and *charas,* which correspond, respectively, to American marijuana, hashish, and unadulterated resin. In Morocco *kif* is used, whereas in South America a cannabis drug often used is called *dagga.*

***Mode of administration.*** Cannabis drugs may be absorbed when administered by oral, subcutaneous, or pulmonary routes, but they are most potent when inhaled. Ei-

---

### DRUGS TO REDUCE SYMPTOMS OF COCAINE WITHDRAWAL

Initial clinical studies with amantadine (Symmetrel) and bromocriptine (Parlodel) have reported promising results in reducing the craving for cocaine during cocaine abstinence. Additional studies on a longer term basis are currently being performed (El-Mourad, 1986; Tennant, 1987; Bohach, 1987). Cocaine acts to stimulate the release of dopamine in the brain initially, which provides the user with a feeling of pleasure. In chronic cocaine abuse, cocaine blocks the reuptake of dopamine resulting in dopamine depletion, depression, and anxiety. Thus the person has difficulty obtaining that initial high with continued drug use. The crash period, or low period, may result from a drop of dopamine level in the brain. This drop is believed to induce the craving for more cocaine and perhaps is responsible for the depression seen during this period. Because both amantadine and bromocriptine produce elevated levels of dopamine in the brain, their use may lessen the symptoms associated with cocaine withdrawal.

---

ther the pure resin or the dried leaves of the cannabis plant may be smoked in pipes or cigarettes. Because the smoke is acrid and irritating, some users prefer to smoke marijuana through a water pipe. The smoke is inhaled deeply and retained in the lungs as long as possible to achieve maximal saturation of the absorbing surface. Powdered hashish and marijuana may also be mixed with foods, a mode of administration that delays the drug's absorption. The sedative-hypnotic effects of smoking are rapid and generally last 2 to 3 hours, while the effects of the orally ingested drugs may not begin for several hours. Hashish oil injected intravenously has a high incidence of mortality.

Marijuana plants contain hundreds of different chemicals. Approximately 100 chemicals have been isolated and are generally termed cannabinoids. Of these, only THC (delta-9-tetrahydrocannabinol) and CBD (cannabidiol) have been studied in humans to identify their pharmacologic effects.

While many questions are still unanswered, it is believed the major psychoactive ingredient in cannabis is THC.

Marijuana cigarettes (joints) illicitly used in the U.S. generally have 1% to 2% THC and weigh approximately 500 mg, yielding from 5 to 10 mg THC. The effective dose may be reduced by half when the dose is smoked, yielding from 2.5 to 5 mg THC per 500 mg weight. Potency varies with plant strain and cultivation. Marijuana cigarettes usually produce moderate to intense psychopharmacologic effects, reaching a peak in 15 minutes and lasting 1 to 4 hours.

Marijuana cigarettes may be *dusted* (treated) or saturated with PCP (known as *super grass)*, which may cause PCP overdosage. Hashish oil is also used on marijuana cigarettes.

Dronabinol (Marinol or THC) and nabilone (Cesamet) are synthetic cannabinoids available for the treatment of nausea and vomiting induced by cancer chemotherapy that is not responsive to standard therapies. Both products have a high potential for abuse, so they are closely regulated under the Federal Control Substances Act (Schedule II).

***Mechanism of action.*** All the cannabis drugs seem to act as CNS depressants. They depress higher brain centers and consequently release lower centers from inhibitory influences. Although some controversy exists regarding their classification, the cannabis drugs are not narcotic derivatives but are legally classified as controlled substances. They are more frequently classified as sedative-hypnotic-anesthetics or psychedelic drugs. Like the sedative-hypnotics, they appear to depress the ascending reticular activating system. As their dosage increases, their effects proceed from relief of anxiety, disinhibition, and excitement to anesthesia. If dosage is high enough, respiratory and vasomotor depression and collapse may occur.

***Pharmacokinetics.*** Peak plasma levels of THC after smoking one marijuana cigarette are reported to be from 0.020 to 0.050 µg/ml. Within a few hours these values decrease to between 0.005 and 0.010 µg/ml. Only trace amounts of the unmetabolized THC are detected in the urine.

The liver is the primary site of metabolism, and the major route of elimination of THC is bile and feces. Prolonged enterohepatic circulation is reported with this lipophilic drug, and it is highly protein bound in the serum. Reports of death or overdose are rare. Between 10% and 20% of THC metabolites may be detected in the body 1 week after a single use or dose. When sensitive assays are used, the metabolites may be detected 30 days or even longer after the initial usage (Jones, 1987).

Marijuana may affect the metabolism of other drugs in the liver or compete with other drugs for protein-binding sites in the plasma. Ethyl alcohol, barbiturates, amphetamines, cocaine, opiates, and atropine are some of the reportedly affected drugs (Jones, 1987).

***Effects.*** The drug has intoxicating, mind-altering properties. It induces an anxiety-free state of relaxation characterized by a feeling of extreme well-being. Perceptions of time and space are distorted. Ideas flow freely and dis-

connectedly; interruptions in thought that are blanks or gaps similar to epileptic absence may occur. There may be states of inwardness and/or occasional excitement in the form of hilarity. Hallucinations can occur with high doses of the drug but are generally reported to be pleasant. Dissociative phenomena also are reported. Some controlled research has been done with this drug; some experiments suggest that impaired decision making and psychometric performance are related to the use of marijuana. The drug experience is highly subjective; the presence of an altered state of consciousness may not be perceived by the novice until he or she is sensitized to it by colleagues. Some factors that influence the psychologic and behavioral effects of marijuana are drug dose, user's personality, user's drug expectations, environment, social influences, and life experiences.

The incidence of adverse reactions to marijuana appears to be low. Minor side effects include immediate tachycardia and delayed bradycardia, delayed hypotension, conjunctival vascular congestion (red eyes), dryness of the mouth and throat, hyperphagia, delayed gastrointestinal disturbances, possible vasovagal syncope, and enhanced appetite and flavor appreciation. More serious side effects are psychologic and include fear, panic (especially among first-time or naive users), feelings of paranoia, disorientation, memory loss, confusion, and a variety of perceptual alterations. Marijuana has been known to precipitate acute psychotic reactions and toxic psychoses in poorly organized personalities. The incidence of adverse effects appears to be highest in novice users of the drug. However, these adverse effects generally appear to be short lived and self-limiting.

Apparently, psychic and physiologic dependence and tolerance to marijuana develop with long-term, regular use. The effects of prolonged abuse of marijuana have not yet been scientifically proved. However, there seems to be some indication that amotivational states, apathy, memory problems, and some loss of mental acuity may occur. Physiologically the possibility of chronic, long-term use of marijuana cigarettes leading to chronic bronchitis, emphysema, and lung cancer cannot be discounted.

Some question has also arisen regarding the use of marijuana leading to the use of opiates. This "stepping-stone" use is somewhat controversial, and some authorities state that any progression in drug use stems from personality and environmental factors rather than from the pharmacologic properties of marijuana. The multiple drug use theory lends support to this hypothesis, stating that a person predisposed to abuse one drug is also likely to abuse other, and perhaps stronger, drugs.

Treatment of the rare acute overdose is directed at the symptoms. If depressive, hallucinatory, or psychotic reactions occur, the client is taken to a quiet, nonthreatening area and given positive verbal reassurance. The psychologic effects are short lived, ranging from a few minutes to about 4 hours. If the client shows signs of excessive agitation, panic, or disorientation, an oral dose of 5 to 10 mg diazepam may be useful.

***Withdrawal symptoms.*** Physiologic withdrawal symptoms have been reported on discontinuance of marijuana. Minor discomfort may pass in several days but insomnia, anxiety, irritability, and restlessness may persist for weeks. Craving for the drug can recur intermittently for months after the drug is stopped. Generally nonpharmacologic interventions and an exercise program are preferred over substitution of another drug product.

## Psychedelic Drugs (Hallucinogens, Psychotomimetics, and Psychotogens)

Classifications of the most common hallucinogenic agents include (1) lysergic acid diethylamide (LSD) and its variants, dimethyltryptamine (DMT) and its analogs, and psilocybin, and (2) mescaline, DOM, and the anticholinergic hallucinogens. The phenylethylamine derivatives, such as mescaline, are structurally related to catecholamine, whereas LSD and DMT have structural relationships to serotonin that may involve the action of these agents as hallucinogens.

A number of psychoactive hallucinogenic drugs have been used as adjuncts to religious services or were used experimentally on college campuses in the 1960s. LSD, DMT, PCP (phencyclidine), mescaline, psilocybin, and MDMA (5-methoxy-3, 4-methylene dioxyamphetamine) (ecstasy) (see box above) are examples of the drugs that can produce distortions in perception or thinking at very low doses.

Fortunately the use of most of these drugs declined in the 1970s to 1980s, with the exception of PCP. Several drugs, such as LSD and MDMA, were said to expand the mind potential and help individuals to gain insight into their problems. Thus some therapists advocated their usage. But scientific studies have not supported these claims and such use in medical practice has been abandoned (Wyngaarden and Smith, 1988; Reynolds, 1989).

### LSD (lysergide)

LSD is a very potent hallucinogenic drug that illicitly is usually available in doses of approximately 200 μg. Following oral administration, it will cause a central sympathomimetic effect within 20 minutes: hypertension, dilated pupils, hyperthermia, tachycardia, and enhanced alertness. The psychoactive effects occur in about 1 to 2 hours and have been described as heightened perceptions, distortions of the body, and visual hallucinations. The effect on mood is unpredictable, ranging from euphoria to severe depression and panic.

However, unpleasant experiences with LSD are also rather frequent. Clinically, evidence of impaired judgment in the toxic state is frequent, and examples of such behavior are well known, as demonstrated, for example, by LSD users attempting to stop traffic with their bodies. Altered states of consciousness may cause psychosis to develop or trigger a latent psychosis into activity. The release of re-

---

> ### HALLUCINOGENS
>
> MDA—amphetamine type drug, similar in structure to MDMA. Destroys serotonin-producing neurons in the brain
>
> MDMA (ecstasy, Adam, XTC)—a stimulant-hallucinogenic used largely by college students. Evidence indicates it can destroy brain dopamine neurons. High dose or chronic use may lead to Parkinson's symptoms and eventually paralysis
>
> MPPP (meperidine analog)—synthesis usually produces a toxic byproduct, MPTP, which has caused permanent, irreversible Parkinson's disease in users (Hall, 1989)

---

pressed material may cause an acute panic psychosis. Feelings of acute panic and paranoia during a toxic LSD psychosis can result in homicidal thoughts and actions. Toxic delirium, with altering and alternating levels of consciousness, follows toxic psychosis, and the experience generally resolves in a stage of exhaustion in which the user feels "empty," unable to coordinate thoughts, and depressed. During this time suicide is a definite risk.

Significant unfavorable reactions induced by LSD include prolonged, delayed, and recurrent reactions such as depression and long-term schizophrenic or psychotic reactions. The recurrent reactions have been described as **flashback phenomena**, referring to the transient, spontaneous repetition of a previous LSD-induced experience that is unrelated to renewed administration of the drug. Moreover, a bad trip (anxiety or panic reaction) on LSD is likely to be a paranoid experience, and tendencies toward violence can be characteristic of LSD intoxication.

The chemical effects of LSD might be negated by administration of a tranquilizer, a barbiturate, or nicotinic acid. It is specifically recommended that chlorpromazine *not* be administered in LSD toxicity because chlorpromazine may accentuate anticholinergic-like drug effects and may, in high doses, lead to severe hypotension or confusion, further compounding the situation. In any case, the administration of medication is recommended only as an adjunct to crisis intervention psychotherapy. A "talk-down" approach in a quiet environment is often used. It consists of directing the person's attention away from perceptions that produce panic and providing reassurance that the experience will dissipate and that no permanent harm has been done. Hospital practices of administering massive doses of tranquilizers, applying restraints, and isolating such individuals are to be avoided. The client's dramatically heightened awareness of the environment and distorted perceptions may render these measures traumatic rather than therapeutic.

Pregnant women should be especially cautioned against taking LSD. Because lysergic acid is the base of all ergot alkaloids, it has uterine stimulant properties that can adversely affect a pregnancy. It may also have adverse cytogenetic effects.

Insofar as is known, no withdrawal symptoms follow discontinuation of long-term use. Tolerance develops in 3 to 7 days but disappears within 7 days of abstinence.

### mescaline

Mescaline is the chief alkaloid extracted from mescal buttons (flowering heads) of the peyote cactus, and it produces subjective hallucinogenic effects similar to those produced by LSD. Like the amphetamines, mescaline belongs to the phenylethylamine group, and its chemical structure distantly resembles that of norepinephrine. It is usually ingested in the form of a soluble crystalline powder that is either dissolved into teas or capsulated. The usual dose of mescaline is about 500 mg. Each button contains about 45 mg mescaline.

The effects of mescaline from a dose of 5 mg/kg (6 to 12 buttons) appear within 2 or 3 hours and may last 4 to 12 hours longer. Doses of up to 500 mg are characterized by prodromal abdominal pain, nausea, vomiting, and diarrhea, which are followed by vivid and colorful visual hallucinations. Mescaline is not a very potent psychotomimetic, and the oral dose of 5 mg/kg in adults is 4000 times larger than the equivalent milligram dose of LSD. After oral ingestion a syndrome of sympathomimetic effects of anxiety, hyperreflexia, static tremors, and psychic perturbations with vivid visual hallucinations is encountered. The half-life of mescaline is about 6 hours, and it is excreted in the urine.

Peyote cactus is used internally by Southwestern Plains Indians in religious practices.

### psilocybin

Psilocybin is a drug derived from Mexican mushrooms (*Psilocye mexicana*). It produces subjective hallucinogenic effects similar to those produced by mescaline but of shorter duration.

A phosphate ester of DMT, psilocybin is found in the Mexican mushroom at a concentration of about 0.3%. In vivo dephosphorylation by alkaline phosphatase converts psilocybin to psilocin, the most active psychotogen of the N-alkylated tryptamines. Since the molecule is less polar because of the loss of the phosphoric acid radical, psilocin is able to penetrate the blood-brain barrier more efficiently and therefore produce relatively greater hallucinogenic potency compared with psilocybin. Psilocin is not as potent as LSD (about 0.01% as active on a milligram-for-milligram basis) and creates a lesser psychedelic state, but when equivalent doses are used, the individual may be unable to differentiate between the two drugs.

The 5 hydroxy-DMT (bufotenine from the skin and parotid glands of the toad *Bufo marinus* and the cahobe bean) has less psychotomimetic activity than psilocin.

Within ½ to 1 hour after ingestion of 5 to 15 mg psilocybin a hallucinogenic dysphoric state begins. A dose of 20 to 60 mg may produce effects lasting 5 or 6 hours. The mood is pleasant to some users, and others experience apprehension. The user has poor critical judgment capacities and impaired performance ability. Also seen are hyperkinetic compulsive movements, laughter, mydriasis, vertigo, ataxia, paresthesias, muscle weakness, drowsiness, and sleep.

### PCP (phencyclidine)

PCP/PCP combinations led the DAWN list for hallucinogens in 1988. PCP has a history of leading to the most serious adverse effects; that is, more suicides, assaults, and murders appear to result from its usage. Prolonged periods of psychosis in even normal or healthy persons have been reported (Wyngaarden and Smith, 1988).

PCP was developed in the late 1950s as an anesthetic for dissociative anesthesia, a cataleptic state in which the person appears to be awake but is detached from the surroundings and unresponsive to pain. The drug is related chemically to ketamine (Ketaject, Ketalar), an anesthetic used primarily for children, and the analgesic meperidine (Demerol).

***Pharmacokinetics.*** PCP is rapidly metabolized in the liver to inactive metabolites, and ingestion of large amounts results in high concentrations of the unmetabolized drug in urine. PCP is lipophilic and has a half-life of ½ to 1 hour in small doses and from 1 to 4 days in larger doses. The $pK_a$ of the drug is 8.5. The "ion trapping" of the drug into extravascular areas, which are more acidic than the serum, is thought to be a major cause of prolonged toxicity. The recirculation of the drug secretion to the acidic gastric fluid and reabsorption in the small intestine may also account for the prolonged toxicity and offer a key to the management of the toxicity of overdosage. These observations have led to treatment using urine acidification with diuresis and continuous gastric drainage in severe intoxication to enhance elimination. Urinary excretion is enhanced when the urine is acidified to 5.5 pH or less with ascorbic acid. The fact that PCP may be found in adipose tissue may indicate that the long-term effects are related to its lipophilic nature. Possibly during a nutritional fast PCP is released and resulting symptoms are interpreted as a flashback.

***Effects.*** In humans common peripheral signs include flushing, profuse sweating, nystagmus, diplopia, ptosis, analgesia, and sedation. Other effects of PCP are as follows:

1. A state similar to alcohol intoxication with ataxia and generalized numbness of extremities
2. Psychologic effects that usually proceed in three stages:
   a. Change in body image and feelings of depersonalization
   b. Perceptual distortions (visual or auditory)
   c. Discomforting feelings of apathy, estrangement, or alienation
3. Disorganization of thought and derealization that is greater than with LSD

4. Impairment of attention span, motor skills, and sense of body boundaries, movement, and position
5. Hallucinations that can recur unpredictably for days, weeks, or months

PCP is similar to ketamine in producing stages of anesthesia. In addition, excitation, paranoid behavior, self-destructive acts (because sensation or feeling of pain is absent), horizontal and vertical nystagmus, tachycardia, hypertension, seizures, increased reflexes, muscle rigidity, respiratory depression, and coma with open eyes may ensue. PCP is a strong sympathomimetic and hallucinogenic dissociative anesthetic agent. Since the drug is now classified as a controlled substance (Class II), penalties for illegal manufacture have been enacted and enforced.

Effects of PCP are claimed by some investigators to mimic schizophrenia more accurately than those of other psychotomimetics or hallucinogenics. Like the symptoms of schizophrenia, the effects of PCP are reduced by sensory deprivation. Currently no chemical antidote exists for inhibiting the effects of PCP. Keeping the user quiet and away from sensory stimuli may decrease the intensity of some of the effects.

***Toxic effects.*** The pressor effects of PCP may cause hypertensive crisis, intracerebral hemorrhage, convulsions, coma, and death.

***Intoxication and treatment.*** The clinical symptoms and signs of PCP intoxication are dose related. The waxing and waning of the intoxicative signs may be related to the pharmacokinetics of enteric reabsorption for the alkalized (non-ionized) PCP with the recirculation and redistribution of the agent, as described earlier.

The nurse should be aware of these signs since this time period will constitute the greatest threat for both the client and health care provider. The client often has alternating periods of paranoia, assaultiveness, terror, and hyperactivity followed by a calm demeanor, blank stare, or withdrawn period. For the first 10 days after ingestion, the nurse should never assume that the calm states are permanent. During an acute intoxication phase the client is unable to process incoming sensory stimuli; therefore, the nurse should plan client interventions accordingly.

Treatment is primarily symptomatic. The client should be kept in a dark room with minimal sensory stimulation and protected from self-inflicted injury. The nurse should not attempt to talk down the PCP anxious individual as it may provoke more serious anxiety or agitation. Diazepam (Valium) or haloperidol (Haldol) have been used for their antianxiety and antipsychotic effects, respectively. Urine acidification will enhance the excretion rate of PCP. Cranberry juice is frequently used to acidify the urine for this purpose.

The use of PCP causes a wide range of subjective effects requiring careful observations of the overdosed client. The prolonged and severe behavioral disturbances may progress to respiratory and cardiovascular emergencies as serum levels of the drug change.

## Inhalants

Volatile hydrocarbons and aerosols are other substances of abuse. Representatives of this group are toluene, xylene, benzene, gasoline, paint thinner, typewriter correction fluid, lighter fluid, airplane glue, and nitrous oxide.

Volatile hydrocarbons are often used as propellants in aerosol products. When sniffed (inhaled), these agents may produce a rapid general CNS depression with marked inebriation, dizziness, floating sensations, exhilaration, and intense feelings of well-being that are at times seen as reckless abandonment, disinhibition, and feelings of increased power and aggressiveness similar to those seen with alcohol intoxication. Inhalation may result in bronchial and laryngeal irritation, transient euphoria, headache, giddiness, vertigo, ataxia, and renal tubular acidosis, especially with glue sniffing. At high doses confusion and coma occur with blood dyscrasia. Depression may follow these early excitatory effects. Chronic toluene abuse will lead to hepatic and renal toxicity, and death from cardiac dysrhythmia and respiratory failure has been reported. Recovery from lower doses may be seen in 15 minutes to a few hours. Inhalants are used mainly by young children and preteens (6- to 15-year-olds). The pediatric nurse may be the first health professional to become aware of a child's problem with inhalants.

Butyl nitrite is a clear, yellow liquid sold as a room deodorizer under trade names such as Rush, Bolt, and Bullet. The substance is sold in drug paraphernalia shops and adult book stores and by mail order. The opened container is placed under the nose; and the individual inhales in deep, nasal breaths and becomes dizzy, feels faint, and possibly loses consciousness. This rush lasts less than 1 minute and may include a headache, perspiration, and flushing, all caused by rapid vasodilation. It strongly resembles the effects achieved from amyl nitrite (a prescription smooth muscle relaxant and vasodilator). The FDA may change the status of butyl nitrite from a room odorizer or deodorizer because of its potential for abuse and for harmful effects. Amyl nitrite is sometimes abused to heighten a sexual orgasm in both partners. Both butyl nitrite and amyl nitrite lower blood pressure and reduce the heart's oxygen consumption.

Inhaled nitrite abuse has been implicated as being associated with or as being a contributory factor in the development of opportunistic infections and Kaposi's sarcoma in immunosuppressed homosexuals. In itself, nitrites are not considered a major risk factor; but as amyl nitrite (and other nitrite products) users tend to have more sexual partners, they could be at a higher risk of developing such infections (Reynolds, 1989).

The development of tolerance occurs with inhalants also,

---

### MAJOR ADVERSE EFFECTS OF ANABOLIC STEROIDS

**Females**

Oily skin; acne

Decrease in breast size, ovulation, lactation, or menstruation

Hoarse and deep voice tone (usually irreversible)

Clitoral enlargement

Unusual hair growth and/or male type baldness (usually irreversible)

**Males**

**Prepuberty**

Increased size of penis, number of erections, and secondary male characteristics

**Postpuberty**

Priapism (continuing erections), difficult/increased urination

Increase in breast size (gynecomastia)

Testicular atrophy, oligospermia, impotence

**Both Sexes**

Hypercalcemia

Edema of feet or legs

Jaundice, liver impairment

Liver carcinoma (rare)

Urinary calculi

Hypersensitivity

Insomnia

Iron deficiency anemia

Nausea, vomiting, anorexia, stomach pains

---

### MAJOR EFFECTS ASSOCIATED WITH ANABOLIC STEROIDS

**Androgen-Type Effects**

Increased growth and development of the seminal vesicles and prostate gland

Increased body and facial hair

Increased production of oil from the sebaceous glands

Deepening of the voice

Increased sexual interest and desire

Enhancement of abstract and spatial dimension thinking ability

Increase in different aspects of male behavior (e.g., aggressive behavior)

**Anabolic-Type Effects**

Increased organ and skeletal muscle mass

Increased calcium in bones

Increased retention of total body nitrogen

Increased hemoglobin concentration

Increased protein synthesis

Data from Duncan and Shaw, 1985.

---

for example, persons starting with one tube of sniffing glue per day, may eventually increase to three, four, or more tubes per day to maintain the effect. In low economic populations inhalants are often the first drug of abuse used.

## Anabolic Steroids

Anabolic steroids are synthetic formulations produced from testosterone, the male hormone. Young people are taking these agents to look good and to improve their chances of winning in sports and in athletic competitions. (See boxed material.) Lamb (1984) estimated that 80% to 100% of participants in weight lifting, discus throwing, and javelin throwing use anabolic steroid products. The abuse of these drugs is widespread and has been documented in young school-age students as well as in older persons and in both males and females.

Since 1984, many organizations have publicly denounced or banned the use of anabolic steroids, including the American College of Sports Medicine, the American Medical Association, the National Collegiate Athletic Association, the International Olympic Committee, and the U.S. Power-lifting Federation. Many states have also passed laws to ban or limit the selling of such products (Duncan and Shaw, 1985; Duda, 1986).

Nevertheless, the debate continues over the use of steroids. Many physicians have prescribed anabolic steroids, especially for underweight persons and/or for athletes seeking an edge in the competitive field. Many steroidal preparations are available and are used orally and parenterally. Many athletes do not follow these recommendations and use dosages far in excess of the stated dosages. While the dosage of methandrostenolone (Dianabol) was recommended at 5 mg/day, some athletes were taking 1000 to 1500 mg daily for extended periods. This misuse led to the withdrawal of this product from the market in 1982. "Stacking" of drugs or taking multiple anabolic steroids at one time is a practice employed by a number of athletes. This usually includes taking very large dosages of the steroids on an 8-week cycle schedule while following a regular strenuous exercise program (perhaps on isolated muscle groups) and consuming a high-protein diet. The long-term effects of such a schedule have not been studied, but documented short-term effects include increased aggressive behavior and some masculinization in the female.

The American College of Sports Medicine has released a position paper (Duncan and Shaw, 1985) that briefly states:

1. The use of anabolic steroids in individuals under 50 years old does not usually result in improved endurance, strength, lean body mass, or body weight.

2. Scientific documentation does not indicate that ex-

cessive doses of these drugs positively or negatively affect the performance of an athlete.

3. Continued use has resulted in reports of liver disease in some individuals; the disease process was reversible in some persons but irreversible in others.
4. Males taking anabolic steroids have had a decrease in testicular size and function and in sperm production. Whether these effects are reversible or irreversible is unknown.
5. Education is necessary to curb the misuse and abuse of these drugs.

This statement is directed to athletes, coaches, doctors, trainers, and physical education instructors. The general public should also be informed of the potential risks associated with short-term and long-term consumption of anabolic steroids.

## ▷NURSING MANAGEMENT: SUBSTANCE MISUSE AND ABUSE

Great diversity exists both among substances that may be abused and the manner of the abuse. The role of the nurse may involve prevention, detection, treatment, and rehabilitation. Preventive nursing roles both inside and outside the hospital environment include education regarding drugs of all types, particularly those prone to producing dependence. Promoting useful coping mechanisms and acceptable alternatives to drugs may prove beneficial.

Health care providers, including nurses, have a high rate of substance abuse and related problems. Nurses must be aware of the potential for drug or substance abuse among themselves and other health care providers and be alert to recognize and deal with this problem should it arise.

Each nurse must evaluate his or her own feelings and responses to drug abuse. Some nurses tend to react with disgust or disdain, behavior which often increases a client's low self-esteem and results in ineffective lectures and scare tactics. Another common response of the nurse is that of "enabler": someone who shields the client from the consequences of substance abuse or unintentionally encourages continued substance abuse. The most effective response is to recognize and confront the problem directly. Nurses must acknowledge that if left untreated, substance abuse often results in death. However, appropriate treatment can often help these individuals overcome their problems and restore them to productive lives without dependence on harmful substances or drugs.

Since substance abuse transcends the boundaries of economics, social class, race, and ethnic background, all clients have the potential to abuse substances or be affected by someone who does. The following discussion is focused on the client who is suspected or known to abuse substances or drugs.

*Assessment.* Assessment includes both physical and psychologic signs and symptoms of substance abuse. The nurse should closely observe both verbal and nonverbal responses to questions since an element of denial may often be ascertained in clients who abuse substances. The nonverbal response may provide additional information, contradict, or reinforce what is verbally stated.

Physical assessment includes vital signs, pupillary signs, and skin (especially for needle marks or "tracks" and abscesses that are often seen with injected drug abuse) and collecting data on nutrition, elimination, and sleep patterns. For clinical signs and symptoms of substances used, see the box on pp. 154 to 155. Diagnostic tests may be used to detect drugs or their metabolites in the blood or urine. The nurse should be aware of the possibility of falsely positive results (see box, p. 148).

Past medical history of the client may include prior treatment of drug abuse or history of drug-related illness such as hepatitis, abscesses, or bacterial endocarditis. A thorough drug history for current or past use of OTC, prescribed, or social/recreational drugs should be taken and should include the frequency, magnitude, and circumstances of drug use and abuse as well as the development of withdrawal symptoms if the drug was stopped.

*Intervention.* Interventions include monitoring of vital signs and administering medications (if prescribed for treatment of withdrawal). Clients abusing substances often have nutrition deficiencies as well as other health problems, which should be corrected.

The nurse should use a straightforward and receptive approach with clients abusing substances. Therapeutic communication should be focused on increasing self-esteem and confronting manipulative behavior while teaching effective coping mechanisms and problem solving. A client cannot restructure a manner of thinking, feeling, and acting until he or she achieves a new image. Many abusers suffer from deprivation of basic needs such as physical closeness and emotional openness, which may in part be caused by the dissolution of basic family relationships. Such deprivation affects individual needs and the expectations of what one is entitled to in these meaningful relationships. Lack of fulfillment of these needs leads to a pronounced disequilibrium.

A multidisciplinary approach often serves these clients best since they frequently have many health, personal, and social problems that must be addressed. Referral to appropriate agencies (i.e., Alcoholics Anonymous, Narcotics Anonymous, and Al-Anon) will assist in the follow-up care of these individuals and provide much needed support and encouragement.

*Education.* The nurse should assist the client to develop effective coping mechanisms and "non-drug strategies" to deal with stress. Education of the client and family should include drugs and abused substances, particularly those prone to producing dependence.

*Evaluation.* Evaluation is focused on how the client has tolerated the withdrawal period and developed new coping strategies. After the withdrawal period, the client must decide to remain drug free. Relapses may occur and should not be viewed as the nurse's failure, for the goal of treatment is longer and longer periods of sobriety/substance-free status and shorter and less frequent relapses. Ultimately the decision to use and abuse drugs remains with the client.

Referral to appropriate agencies (see Interventions) is beneficial. The long-term support is essential in helping these clients remain drug free.

• • •

Although the nurse plays an essential role in the prevention of drug abuse, her initial contact with the client may be in the acute setting during his/her acute drug intoxication and withdrawal.

Signs of acute intoxication differ according to the drug abused and may manifest themselves variably. Drug overdose and intoxication may be life threatening. Immediate goals are to stabilize and maintain vital functions and minimize damage. Supportive treatment is combined with specific treatment once the drug has been identified. This is a time of acute psychologic stress for the client, and the nurse must remember to treat the whole client, not just a physiologic system.

Physical and/or psychologic withdrawal symptoms may follow abrupt cessation of drug or substance use. Promotion of adequate nutrition, safety, rest, and orientation are areas of general nursing interventions during this time. Medications may be administered to reduce the withdrawal symptoms. Rehabilitation begins during the withdrawal period and is continued in an attempt to avoid relapse.

## SUMMARY

Although drug abuse is not a new phenomenon, the dimension of the problem for society is great. Substance abuse is a common denominator across cultural, ethnic, and socioeconomic populations and affects every aspect of the abuser's life. As a consequence the nurse needs to be familiar with drugs with the potential for abuse, not only in their therapeutic use but also in their street forms. This knowledge will enhance the nursing role for the prevention, detection, treatment, and rehabilitation of drug abuse.

The etiology of substance abuse for any given client may vary, but the drug must produce a desired effect for it to cause dependence. Currently the commonly abused drugs are opioids and related compounds; barbiturates and other sedative-hypnotics; antianxiety and antipsychotic agents; amphetamines, cocaine, and other CNS stimulants; cannabis; hallucinogens and other mood modifiers; inhalants; and anabolic steroids. In addition, multiple drug use is common, and psychic and physical dependence can exist independently or simultaneously.

Opioids are some of the most abused drugs. For that reason the nurse should be alert to opioid abuse in the general

population as well as the health professions. The "high" from opiates is characterized by complete drive satiation, so the client may exhibit malnutrition and other signs of neglect from ignoring basic biologic needs. Acute overdosage of opiates with miotic pupils, stupor, and respiratory depression is considered to be a medical emergency, but symptoms may be reversed by adequate amounts of naloxone, a narcotic antagonist. Treatment of opiate dependence may be withdrawal with supportive therapy, methadone detoxification and withdrawal, or clonidine treatment followed by either a methadone maintenance program and/or a therapeutic community program.

Other forms of analgesics such as pentazocine and propoxyphene tend to be abused based on access, fashion, and availability of other substances on the street.

Sedative-hypnotics, both barbiturates and nonbarbiturates, such as ethchlorvynol, glutethimide, and methaqualone, may cause severe psychic and physical dependence. The symptoms of withdrawal from these drugs are similar: hallucinations, irritability, agitation, depression, abdominal pain, and sometimes, convulsions.

Alcohol is the most common substance of abuse and the ingestion of alcohol does not carry with it the social stigma that the abuse of other drugs does. However, the chronic abuse of alcohol causes physiologic damage to every body system; its therapeutic use is quite limited. Disulfiram is used to sensitize the individual to alcohol by causing such an unpleasant response, nausea, headache, palpitations, dyspnea, and intense discomfort, that the use of alcohol is no longer desired.

Benzodiazepines and phenothiazines are the antianxiety and antipsychotic agents most abused, generally as the result of overprescription by physicians to women and the elderly.

Although amphetamines and cocaine are the most commonly abused CNS stimulants, the use of amphetamines peaked in the 1960s and the use of cocaine is much more prevalent today. Because cocaine is available as "crack" at a much lower cost than other drugs, it is becoming increasingly popular and much more of a health problem with its strong physical and psychologic dependence.

Cannabis drugs are increasingly used by young teenagers for recreation to produce an anxiety-free state of relaxation and sense of well-being. Studies indicate that impaired decision making, apathy, and memory loss are related to cannabis use. Psychic and physical dependence develop with chronic use.

Psychedelic drugs and inhalants are also substances for abuse for their mind-altering properties, whereas anabolic steroids are abused by individuals who want to improve their appearance or performance in sports.

The nurse has an important role in the prevention of drug abuse because of his or her knowledge and extent of contact with the public of all ages and circumstances. Assessment for the detection of drug abuse and intervening in an acute overdose or withdrawal situation is performed in a straightforward and receptive approach with the client abusing substances. Because of the multiplicity of the drug abuser's problems, the nurse may be part of a multidisciplinary team in the provision of support to these clients.

## BIBLIOGRAPHY

Adams FE. (1988). Drug dependency in hospital patients, Am J Nurs 88(4):477.

American Hospital Formulary Service. (1990). AHFS drug information. Bethesda, Md: American Society of Hospital Pharmacists, Inc.

Atkinson A. (1988). Addictive treatment . . . use methadone either as a maintenance or detoxification treatment, Nurs Times 84(17):42.

Bagnall G et al. (1987). Education on drugs and alcohol: past disappointments and future challenges, Health Educ Res 2(4):417.

Braunwald E et al, editors. (1987). Harrison's principles of internal medicine, ed 11. New York: McGraw-Hill, Inc.

Becker PH et al. (1988). Neonatal drug addiction: an analysis from two moral orientations, Holistic Nurs Pract 2(4):20.

Bennett G. (1988). Stress, social support, and self-esteem of young alcoholics in recovery, Issues Ment Health Nurs 9(2):151.

Bissell C and Haberman PW. (1984). Alcoholism in the professions. Oxford: Oxford University Press.

Bohach C. (1987). Combating cocaine dependence, amantadine tested as withdrawal aid, Street Pharmacol 2(1):1.

Booth PG. (1987). Managing alcohol and drug abuse in the nursing profession, J Adv Nurs 12(5):625.

Brecher EM. (1972). Licit and illicit drugs. Boston: Little, Brown & Co.

Chenitz WC et al. (1987). The nurse in a methadone maintenance clinic: revisited, J Psychosoc Nurs Ment Health Serv 25(11):13.

Compton P. (1989). Drug abuse: a self-care deficit, J Psychiatr Nurs Mental Health Serv 27(3):22.

Cook R et al. (1987). Drug abuse among working adults: prevalence rates and recommended strategies, Health Educ Res 2(4):353.

Council on Scientific Affairs. (1987). Scientific issues in drug testing: council report, JAMA 127(22):3110.

Creighton H. (1988). Legal implications of the impaired nurse, Nurs Manage 19(1):21.

Data from Drug Abuse Warning Network (DAWN). (1989). Statistical Series, Annual Data for 1988, Series 1(8), Rockville, MD: US Department of Health and Human Services.

Davidson DE, editor. (1986). Handbook of nonprescription drugs, ed 8. Washington, DC: American Pharmaceutical Association.

Davidson R. (1988). Prevention of drug misuse: a review of current policy with proposals for future development, Recent Adv Nurs (22):124.

Dominquez RA and Goldstein BJ. (1985). 25 years of benzodiazepine experience: clinical commentary on use, abuse, and withdrawal, Hosp Formul 20(9):1000.

Drake WC. (1986). Ro = 1788 (flumazepil): an antidote for benzodiazepine intoxication? Pharm Alert 16(3):1.

Drying out alcoholics: clonidine vs benzodiazepines. (1987). Emerg Med 19(18):40.

Duda M. (1986). Do anabolic steroids pose an ethical dilemma for US physicians?, Physician & Sports Med 14(11):173.

Duncan DF. (1987). Cocaine smoking and its implications for health and health education, Health Educ 18(4):24.

Duncan DJ and Shaw EB. (1985). Anabolic steroids: implications for the nurse practitioner, Nurse Pract 10(12):8.

El-Mourad R. (1986). Bromocriptine in the treatment of cocaine craving, Street Pharmacol 10(12):4.

Flandermeyer AA. (1987). A comparison of the effects of heroin and cocaine upon the neonate, Neonat Netw 6(3):42.

Foy A et al. (1988). Use of an objective clinical scale in the assessment and management of alcohol withdrawal in a large general hospital, Alcoholism 12(3):360.

Goodman AG et al, editor. (1990). Goodman & Gilman's the pharmacological basis of therapeutics, ed 8. New York: Macmillan, Inc.

Gorman E et al. (1987). The opioid-dependent patient with acute pain, Hosp Pract 22(11):113.

Green P. (1989). The chemically dependent nurse. Nurs Clin North Am 24(1):81.

Hall JN. (1989). US illicit drug production booming, Street Pharmacol 12:Spring:4.

Hall JN. (1985). Heroin 1985, Street Pharmacol, vol 8, no. 3.

Hamlin M et al. (1989). Drug withdrawal, Nurs Times 85(35):66.

Herfindal ET et al. (1988). Clinical pharmacy and therapeutics, ed 4. Baltimore: Williams & Wilkins.

Higgins R. (1989). Cocaine abuse: what every emergency nurse should know, J Emerg Nurs 15(4):318.

Hinds M, editor. (1985). How much blood alcohol content per drink? Informed families of Dade County 2(6):1.

Huckabee MC. (1988). Perioperative care of the active substance abuser, J Post Anesth Nurs 3(4):254.

Hughes R and Brewin G. (1979). The tranquilizing of America. New York: Warner Books.

Hughes TL. (1989). Models and perspectives of addiction: implications for treatment, Nurs Clin North Am 24(1):1.

Hyams DE. (1984). Central nervous system anxiolytics and hypnotics. In Brocklehut JC, editor: Geriatric pharmacology and therapeutics. Oxford: Blackwell Scientific Publications.

Izor-Povenmire K et al. (1989). Acute crack cocaine intoxication: a case study, Focus Crit Care 16(2):112.

Jack LW. (1989). Use of milieu as a problem-solving strategy in addiction treatment, Nurs Clin North Am 24(1):69.

Jones RT. (1987). Drug of abuse profile: cannabis, Clin Chem 33:11(B), 72B-81B.

Kirk E et al. (1987). Effects of alcohol on the central nervous system: implications for the neuroscience nurse, J Neurosci Nurs 19(6):326.

Knott DH et al. (1988). Acute withdrawal from alcohol: diagnosis and treatment, Emerg Med 20(5):217.

Lachman VD. (1988). The chemically dependent nurse, Holistic Nurs Pract 2(4):34.

LaSala C. (1988). Helping patients break free from cocaine, Nursing 18(11):32c.

Lamb D. (1984). Anabolic steroids in athletics: how well do they work and how dangerous are they? Am J Sports Med 12(1):31.

Lawrence C Jr. (1983). As workers get high, so do prices, The Miami Herald, p C1, Oct 24.

Levy DB. (1988). Narcotic review, Emergency 20(1):16.

Lewis KD et al. (1989). The care of infants menaced by cocaine abuse, MCN, no 5, p 324.

Long-term benzodiazepine use. (1988). Nurses' Drug Alert 12(3):22.

MacIsaac AM et al. (1989). Multiple medications: is your patient caught in the storm? Nursing 19(7):60.

Maternal substance use and neonatal drug withdrawal. (1988). J Perinat 8(4):387.

McCafferty M. (1989). Managing your patients' adverse reactions to narcotics, Nursing 19(10):166.

McCafferty M. (1988). When your patient is a drug user, Nursing 18(11):49.

Miller RW. (1987). Athletes and steroids: playing a deadly game, FDA Consumer 21(9):16.

Mullen G. (1988). Ecstasy, rhapsody or Mexican mud? A problem of recognition, J Emerg Med 13(11):62.

Murphy JF et al. (1987). Violations of the state's nurse practice act: how big is the problem? Nurs Manage 18(9):44.

Murphy SA. (1988). Addiction nursing: an agenda for the 1990's, Issues Ment Health Nurs 9(2):115.

Naigle MA. (1988). Theoretical perspectives on the etiology of substance abuse, Holistic Nurs Pract 2(4):1.

Nelson MA. (1989). Androgenic-anabolic steroid use in adolescents, J Pediatr Health Care 3(4):175.

Noyes RJ et al. (1988). Benzodiazepine withdrawal: a review of the evidence, J Clin Psychiatry 49(10):382.

Nuckols CC et al. (1989). Cocaine addiction: assessment and intervention, Nurs Clin North Am 24(1):33.

Oswald LM. (1989). Cocaine addiction: the hidden dimension, Arch Psychiatr Nurs 3(3):134.

Pearsall HR et al. (1987). Cocaine abuse, Hosp Med 23(10):126.

Pires M. (1989). Substance abuse: the silent sabateur in rehabilitation, Nurs Clin North Am 24(1):291.

Powell AH et al. (1988). Alcohol withdrawal syndrome, Am J Nurs 88(3):312.

Ray WA et al. (1987). Psychotropic drug use and the risk of hip fracture, N Eng J Med 316:363.

Reynolds JEF, editor. (1989). Martindale: the extra pharmacopoeia, ed 29. London: The Pharmaceutical Press.

Robinson DP et al. (1988). The adolescent alcohol and drug problem: a practical approach, Pediatr Nurs 14(4):305.

Rosen LF. (1987). Substance abuse: the nurse as user, Today's OR Nurse 9(9):32.

Salzman B et al. (1988). Use and abuse of opiates, Hosp Med 24(4):22.

Schneider JW et al. (1989). Infants exposed to cocaine in utero: implications for development assessment and intervention, Infants Young Child 2(1):25.

Sharon F et al. (1988). Drug screening in the workplace—scientific and legal issues, Nurs Pract 13(2):41.

Sheahan SL et al. (1989). Drug misuse among the elderly: a covert problem, Health Values 13(3):22.

Smart RG et al. (1988). Alcohol and drug use among the elderly: trends in use and characteristics of users, Can J Public Health 79(4):236.

Smith J. (1987). The dangers of prenatal cocaine use, MCN 13(3):174.

Stammer ME. (1988). Understanding alcoholism and drug dependency in nurses, QRB 14(3):75.

Swatek R. (1988). Urine testing for drug abuse, Phys Assist 12(2):107.

Taylor RF et al. (1989). Airway complications from free-basing cocaine, Chest 95(2):476.

Tennant FS and Sagherian AS. (1987). Double-blind comparison of amantadine and bromocriptine for ambulatory withdrawal from cocaine dependence, Arch Intern Med 147(1):109.

Tommasello T. (1989). Assessment and treatment of chemical dependence. II. PharmAlert, vol 18, no 4.

Twycross RG and Lacl SA. (1983). Symptom control in far advanced cancer: pain relief. London: Pitman.

United States Pharmacopeial Convention. (1990). Drug information for the health care provider, ed 10. Rockville, Md: US Pharmacopeia Convention.

Vandegaer F. (1989). Cocaine—the deadliest addiction, Nursing 19(2):72.

von Windeguth BJ et al. (1989). Cocaine-abusing mothers and their infants: a new morbidity brings challenges for nursing care, J Community Health Nurs 6(3):147.

Wade M. (1987). Meeting the challenge of alcohol and drug abuse in the older adult, Home Healthcare Nurse 5(5):19.

Weil A and Rosen W. (1983). Chocolate to morphine: understanding the mind-active drugs. Boston: Houghton Mifflin Co.

White GL et al. (1987). Preventing steroid abuse in youth: the health educator's role, Health Educ 18(4):32.

Williams E. (1989). Strategies for intervention, Nurs Clin North Am 24(1):95.

Yelverton GA. (1989). Anabolic steroids, Pediatr Nurs 15(1):63.

Young LY and Koda-Kimble MA. (1988). Applied therapeutics: the clinical use of drugs, ed 4. Vancouver: Applied Therapeutics, Inc.

Wyngaarden JB and Smith LH. (1988). Cecil's textbook of medicine, ed 18. Philadelphia: WB Saunders Co.

Zamula E. (1989). Drugs and pregnancy: often the two don't mix, FDA Consumer 23(5):7.

*Chapter*

# ≈10 Client Education for Self-Administration of Medication

## CHAPTER OBJECTIVES

*After studying this chapter, you should be able to meet the following objectives and define the key terms.*

1. Assess a client or his or her family regarding the need and readiness to self-administer medications.

2. Write measurable objectives for the client who is learning to self-administer medications.

3. Discuss at least three teaching techniques that may increase a client's knowledge of medications.

4. Identify four or more safety precautions necessary for clients in self-administering medications.

5. Document the client's/family's learning including the content, method, and progress toward learning goals.

6. Identify the nursing diagnoses of knowledge deficit and noncompliance relating to self-administration of medications.

7. Identify factors that affect client compliance in self-administration of medications.

## KEY TERMS

**compliance,** page 189

**knowledge deficit,** page 189

**locus of control,** page 183

**noncompliance,** page 189

**therapeutic seeding,** page 187

## INTRODUCTION

Nurses have been teaching their clients since the discipline had its beginnings. Within the last two decades, however, an increasing emphasis has been placed on the role of nurses for supporting clients' abilities for self-care, adaptation to illness, and high-level wellness. Various factors are responsible for this change in emphasis. A growing consumer awareness of health issues and services has made the client much more of a participant in his or her own health care than in the past. The client is more apt to request information; nurses have responded by promoting the client's active involvement in planning and implementing nursing care. The American Hospital Association published in 1972 "A Patient's Bill of Rights," which gave formal credence to the patient's right to know about his or her health status, treatments, alternative methods of treatment, and continuing care requirements. In addition, client education is being recognized as one way of enabling a shorter length of hospital stay. This is an important factor in the present economic climate since the development in 1983 by the U.S. Health Care Financing Administration of a prospective payment system for health care. Technology has extended life expectancy and increased the numbers of the chronically ill. Many of these elderly and/or debilitated clients require health teaching to enable them to remain independent. Since 1976, the Joint Commission for the Accreditation of Healthcare Organizations (JCAHO) has required that there be evidence in the client's clinical record of specific instructions provided to the client and his or her family regarding medications, diet, and follow-up care. Nurse practice acts have set guidelines and developed standards for the nurse's role in health education; on the other hand, there have been successful lawsuits alleging that nurses provided less than adequate health teaching (Barron, 1987). All of these factors have reinforced the nurse's participation in client education.

Client education, then, is a process assisting people to learn and incorporate health-related behaviors into everyday life (Smith, 1989). Because learning is defined as a change in behavior, nurses then assist individuals to change behavior. Nurses provide health-related information and teach in such a way as to ensure the client's compliance with a therapeutic regimen. Nowhere is that more important than in the area of client education for self-administration of prescription medications. Misuse and noncompliance with drug regimens have been well documented (Harris et al, 1989; Austin, 1989; Weed-Collins et al, 1989). Although a number of factors determine whether or not clients adhere to a medication regimen, they must be provided with accurate information upon which to base their behaviors.

The teaching-learning process may be structured along the lines of the nursing process with the first step being assessment, the gathering of facts and information that will assist the nurse to meet the client's/family's needs for learning. Planning, the next step in the process, begins as soon as a learning need has been identified with goals being written as outcomes for the client's learning. The implementation phase is the actual communication of information. And evaluation focuses on the client's behaviors and attitudes as a measure of whether the client has achieved the learning objectives.

## ASSESSMENT

A thorough assessment of the client is essential to the provision of health teaching about medications in the most efficient and effective way. The nurse should conduct a comprehensive assessment regarding the client's response to illness. A comprehensive assessment includes determining the client's competence in self-care and mobility, nutritional status, sleep patterns, and social support mechanisms. Data collected should describe factors influencing the client's ability, motivation, and interest in following health advice. The client's cultural perspectives, health beliefs, and attitudes need to be included in the assessment. All of these factors will influence the teaching-learning process for the self-administration of medications. Not all clients will need to know everything about their medications,

nor will all clients be ready to learn about them. Realistic goals for clients' medicating behaviors are the result of the nurse's accurate assessment.

Assessing learning needs means ascertaining what the client already knows. "What medications are you presently taking? What is each medication for? How often and how much of each medication should you be taking? What are the side effects of each drug? Which of these side effects should you report to your physician if it occurs?" (See Chapter 5 for a medication history form.) If the client knows the answers to these questions, the objective for learning may have been met.

The nurse also needs to determine a point of reference for learning by validating the client's present level of knowledge. New information is easier to absorb when it can be related to what the client already knows. For example, when teaching about nitroglycerin, the nurse might ask the client what he or she understands the diagnosis of angina to be. By using the words the client used to describe his or her condition, the nurse can discuss the therapeutic action of the nitroglycerin. In addition, a baseline of data must be determined to evaluate what knowledge the client has gained, by comparing what was known before and after the learning process.

The nurse needs to be aware of any incorrect knowledge or misunderstanding the client may have. The client's health information may be a collection of folklore, hearsay, handed-down family experience, advertising claims, and/or misconceptions. Incorrect information needs to be identified and dealt with before the teaching of the correct material can be initiated.

Sometimes because of the shortened length of stay, instruction has to be limited to survival content—only the most important information (Ruzicki et al, 1989). What will the client need to know about what to do when he or she returns home? What must the client learn to survive until additional information can be obtained? Does the client know whom to call if additional information is needed? Although many nurses would prefer to teach some pharmacokinetics of the client's drug as a foundation for the self-administration of medications, sometimes the client's anxiety and health status preclude that depth of explanation. A client can become easily overwhelmed by highly technical content and lose the essential information needed to take the drug safely and accurately. However, some may ask for additional technical information. Hospitalized patients tend to focus on issues related to hospitalization, such as how to administer the insulin injection, rather than long-term dietary management for their diabetes mellitus.

Not all clients are ready to learn. During an assessment, the nurse needs to consider the client's current emotional state, adaptation to the illness, level of maturity, and expectations. A client's emotional state influences his perspective on the world as well as readiness to learn. Smith et al (1987) found that clients' feelings of satisfaction not only correlated with current compliance but also predicted future compliance, indicating a readiness to participate in their own care. Mild anxiety may stimulate the client to learn, whereas severe anxiety may shorten the attention span so as to be incapacitating. A client goes through various stages in the adaptation to illness/injury, including developing awareness, reorganization, resolution, and identity change. During the assessment the nurse should be aware of the client's stage of adaptation. Understanding the client's coping strategies will keep the nurse from attempting to teach information that the client is not ready to learn. Anger, fear, and mistrust of health care personnel may also impede readiness for learning. Many factors affect the client's readiness to learn (see Table 10-1).

Attitude and the client's beliefs about himself and the illness often affect the level of adherence to a medication regimen. According to Becker (1979), a client is more apt to comply with the therapy when he believes the physician is correct, the illness can cause him harm, the prescribed treatment will reduce the risk of complication or death, or his health will improve. Individuals lacking functional literacy (that is, lacking the ability to read well enough to understand and use information as it was intended), as well as those with a language barrier, also are at risk for not following a medication regimen. In these instances the nurse may enlist the assistance of the client's support system, the individuals or group that provide him with comfort, aid, and information to help him cope with life—family, friends, and members of the community and church or religious groups.

In addition, Tripp-Reimer (1989) offers the following guidance for working with clients having a language barrier:

1. Speak slowly (plan the teaching session to last at least twice as long as a typical session).
2. Make the sentence structure simple (use active, not passive, voice; use a straightforward subject-verb pattern).
3. Avoid technical terms (for example, use "heart" rather than "cardiac"), professional jargon, and American idioms ("red tape").
4. Provide instructional material in the same sequence in which the patient should carry out the plan.
5. Do not assume you have been understood. Ask the patient to explain the protocol; optimally, if appropriate, obtain a return demonstration.

Although these guidelines are suggested for clients with a language barrier, they would hold true for most clients.

The manner in which a client perceives the ability to change or control his or her life has an impact on his or her willingness or ability to adhere to a medication regimen. **Locus of control** is the concept concerning how a client perceives his or her ability to influence or control his or her life along an internal-external continuum. At one end of the continuum, a client can be internally (self-) oriented and at the other end, externally (others or fate-) oriented about his

**TABLE 10-1**   Some factors affecting educational readiness

| | |
|---|---|
| Pathophysiologic | Severity of illness, pain, fatigue, sensory deprivation |
| Treatment-related | Complexity of regimen |
| Situational | Illiteracy, language differences, ineffective coping patterns, financial concerns, home environment |
| Maturational | Family roles and relationships, health maintenance practices |

or her health behaviors. Clients with an internal locus of control are more apt to be health-oriented and adhere to a medication regimen. The locus of control may be assessed by listening to the client making statements such as, "I forgot to take my medication" (internal locus) rather than, "My husband didn't remind me to take my medicine" (external locus). In one instance the client assumes the responsibility for the actions, and in the other the blame is placed elsewhere.

The nurse should assess the client's level of development since this will affect the ability to make decisions, assume the responsibility for the result of those decisions, and the ability to manage life. The physical, emotional, and psychologic stages of development and related developmental tasks have been described by Erickson (see box on p. 184). All individuals pass through the same predictable life stages; however, passage through these predictable stages occurs at different rates. Some are ready to accept adult responsibilities at age 18; others may be well past 35 before they are ready to accept responsibility for themselves and others. Although people move sequentially through the stages, they fluctuate among stages, often in response to stress. Stressors, such as illness and hospitalization, may cause the client to regress temporarily to an earlier stage. The client needs to be addressed at his or her current developmental stage, rather than the developmental stage that one would expect for the client's chronological age. If the client's developmental stage is not accurately assessed, the nurse may misdirect goals and inhibit client learning. (See box on educational strategies related to aging changes.) The aging changes are important in deciding whether the client can self-administer medications accurately.

The assessment phase can be used to establish rapport and gain the mutual respect of nurse and client necessary for the teaching-learning process. Because nurses are seen as having a position of power in relation to the client, they need to recognize the need to initiate the educational process. When the client perceives an attitude of sincerity, integrity, and warmth in the nurse, the milieu is set for the client to feel free to ask questions and to discuss all matters, regardless of how personal those issues may be.

The assessment for teaching-learning is similar to other

---

### ERICKSON'S STAGES OF DEVELOPMENT

**Infant** (birth to 1 year of age): Trust vs mistrust. Infant learns to trust himself, others, and the environment; learns to love and be loved.

**Toddler** (1 to 3 years of age): Autonomy vs shame and doubt. Toddler learns independence; learns to master the physical environment and maintain self-esteem.

**Preschooler** (3 to 6 years of age): Initiative vs guilt. Preschooler learns basic problem-solving; develops conscience and sexual identity; initiates activities as well as imitates.

**School-age child** (6 to 12 years of age): Industry vs inferiority. School-age child learns to do things well; develops a sense of self-worth.

**Adolescent** (12 to 18 years of age): Identity vs role confusion. Adolescent integrates many roles into self-identity through role models and peer pressure.

**Young adult** (18 to 45 years of age): Intimacy vs isolation. Young adult establishes deep and lasting relationships; learns to make commitment as spouse, parent, partner.

**Middle-aged adult** (45 to 65 years of age): Generativity vs stagnation. Adult learns commitment to community and world; is productive in career, family, civic interests.

**Older adult** (over 65 years of age): Integrity vs despair. Older adult appreciates life role and status; deals with loss and prepares for death.

---

### EXAMPLES OF MEASURABLE AND NONMEASURABLE VERBS

**Measurable Verbs**

| | | |
|---|---|---|
| describe | administer | stand |
| discuss | demonstrate | walk |
| identify | perform | has an increase in |
| list | self-administer | has a decrease in |
| relate | exercise | has an absence of |
| state | cough | |
| verbalize | sit | |

**Nonmeasurable Verbs**

| | | |
|---|---|---|
| accept | feel | think |
| appreciate | know | understand |

How will you know that the client understands? What behaviors need to be evident for you to observe that he or she appreciates (or accepts, etc.)?

---

types of nursing assessment in that it is continuous and involves observation, listening and questioning, and other communication skills.

## PLANNING

The next part of the teaching-learning process is planning, which begins once a learning need has been identified. The learning needs are discussed; and the planning of objectives is a mutual undertaking between the nurse, the client, and, where appropriate, the family. The learning objectives for the client's ability to self-medicate are goals or expected outcomes that should result from the teaching-learning interactions.

In order for objectives to clarify what is to be learned and how that learning will be evaluated, the objective should contain a verb that is measurable (see box). Although the nurse would like the client to "know" about his medications, "understand" how the medication relates to the illness, and "comprehend" what action to take if an adverse effect occurs, these verbs are not appropriate for writing goals, since they are neither easily interpreted nor measurable. On the other hand, terms such as "define," "list," "identify," and "state" are measurable, have fewer interpretations, and are

therefore more useful in evaluating achievement of goals for learning. The following are examples:

State the major action of digoxin.

Identify at least three adverse effects of digoxin that should be reported to the prescriber.

List the signs and symptoms of hypoglycemia, such as tachycardia; palpitations; cool, clammy skin; diaphoresis; irritability; tiredness; hunger; numbness; and blurred vision.

In addition, goals need to be realistic with regard to the client's achievements. Goals can only be determined by assessing with the client his or her ability to achieve the expected outcomes.

## IMPLEMENTATION

Once a learning need has been identified and the expected outcome agreed on by the client and the nurse, the most difficult steps of the teaching-learning process have been completed. The implementation phase consists of conveying the specific information required by the objectives.

Instructional sessions about medications should be integrated throughout the extent of nurse-client interactions and not saved for the day of discharge. Short encounters staggered over the course of the client's length of stay enhance learning because it takes place in small incremental steps, rather than one overwhelming session. For example, one of the most appropriate times to teach the client about medications is as they are being administered. This dialogue will assist the client to cue in specific medications at certain times of the day and at particular dosage intervals.

The practice of manual skills is rather straightforward,

---

## SELECTED AGING CHANGES AND EDUCATIONAL STRATEGIES APPROPRIATE TO PHARMACOLOGY CONTENT

| Changes Associated with Aging That May Influence Learning | Nursing Interventions |
| --- | --- |
| *Altered thought processes* | |
| Slowed cognitive functioning | Slow pace of presentation |
| Decreased short-term memory | Provide smaller amounts of information at one time |
| Decreased ability to think abstractly | Repeat information frequently |
| Decreased ability to concentrate | Use examples to illustrate information |
| Increased reaction time (slower to respond) | Decrease external stimuli as much as possible |
| | Allow more time for feedback from elderly learners |
| | Use a variety of methods—audiovisuals and practice sessions |
| | Provide written instructions for home use |
| *Altered sensory-perceptual status* | |
| Hearing | |
| Decreased ability to distinguish sounds, i.e., words beginning with S, Z, T, D, F, and G | Speak distinctly |
| | Sit on side of learner's "best" ear |
| Decreased conduction of sound | Do not shout; speak in a normal voice, but lower its pitch |
| Loss of ability to hear high frequency sounds | Face the client so that lip reading is possible |
| | Use visual aids to reinforce verbal instruction |
| | Reinforce teaching with easy-to-read materials |
| | Decrease extraneous noise |
| Vision | |
| Decreased visual acuity | Ensure glasses are clean and in place |
| Decreased ability to read fine detail | Use printed material with large print |
| Decreased ability to discriminate between blue, violet, and green; all colors tend to fade, with red fading the least | Use high-contrast materials, i.e., black on white |
| | Avoid use of blue, violet, and green in type or graphics; use red instead |
| Lens become thicker and yellower with decreased accomodation | Use nonglare lighting and avoid contrasts of light, i.e., darkened room with single light |
| Pupil smaller; decreased amount of light reaching retina | Adjust teaching to allow for the use of touch to gauge depth |
| Decreased depth perception | |
| Peripheral vision decreased | |
| Touch and vibration | |
| Sense of touch decreased | Increase time for the teaching of psychomotor skills, repetitions, and return demonstration |
| Decreased sense of vibration | Teach to palpate more prominent pulse sites, i.e., carotid and radial |

Adapted from Weinrich SP et al. (1989). Continuing strategies to teach the elderly, J Gerontol Nurs 15(11):17.

such as the manipulation of a syringe and vial to self-administer insulin. Nurses are familiar with the practices of demonstration and return demonstration, but variations exist that can conserve time. A nurse may draw up the insulin and ask the client to complete the injection, or the nurse may ask the client to direct her through the procedure, or the nurse may coach the client through the procedure. Equipment may be left with the client to allow for practice time without the nurse being present before a return demonstration is scheduled. Such equipment should be labeled as "practice equipment," and the client should be instructed that this material is contaminated and should not be used on himself or herself.

The communication of ideas is more complex, but just as necessary. Ideas are more easily understood if they are organized in a logical order and if they move from simple to complex. For example it is helpful for clients to know the therapeutic effect of a drug before learning about its side and adverse effects. Ideas need to be practiced, too. Application of information is important for clients. "What will you do if you take your pulse and the rate is below 60 beats per minute?" Knowing what to do is more helpful than reciting the symptoms of digoxin toxicity. Providing the client with scenarios in which decisions must be made regarding life-style and medications is beneficial. Asking a client who takes disulfiram (Antabuse), "Suppose you're

MEDICATION WARNINGS

☐ 1   Avoid alcoholic beverages while taking this medication.

☐ 2   Swallow these tablets. Do not chew them. Do not take if coating is cracked.

☐ 3   Do not drive a car or operate machinery if this medication makes you drowsy. If you have to drive home, wait until you get home to take your first dose.

☐ 4   Do not allow this medication to contact the skin, eyes, or clothing.

☐ 5   Take this medication on an empty stomach either 1 hour before meals or 2 hours after meals. You may drink water.

☐ 6   Do not take this medication with fruit juice.

☐ 7   Take this medication _____ hour(s) before meals.

☐ 8   Do not take this medication with milk or milk products. You may drink water or juice.

☐ 9   Take this medication with at least 8 ounces of water.

☐10   Take this medication immediately after meals.

☐ 11   This medication may discolor the urine or stools.

☐ 12   Do not take this medication with antacids.

☐ 13   Do not take aspirin with this medication.

☐ 14   Do not take mineral oil with this medication.

☐ 15   Take orange juice, bananas, and other foods high in potassium while taking this medication.

☐ 16   Avoid tyramine-rich foods such as cheese, pickled herring, and wine while taking this medication.

☐ 17   Count your pulse (by feeling at the wrist) each time before taking this medication. If it is less than 60 beats a minute, do not take the dose. Contact the prescriber.

☐ 18   Do not take this medication if pregnant or breast-feeding or if you have ever had an allergic reaction to it. Instead, contact prescriber for instructions.

☐ 19   Do not take this medication if you have the following medical problems or symptoms:

**FIGURE 10-1** Example of a medication instruction sheet for the client.

having dinner at a friend's home and you're asked to have a drink, how will you respond?" The client can demonstrate commitment if able to state to nurse and family how he or she intends to manage administration of a medication that needs to be taken four times a day within a schedule that includes home, office, and business travel. Gibson (1989) reported a self-medication program while the client is still in the hospital to be an approach to increase adherence to a medication regimen.

The client should be encouraged to plan for the administration of medications and the incorporation of this activity into his/her life-style. Written instructions are particularly helpful for the client to refer to once discharged from the health care setting. (See Figure 10-1 for an example of written instructions given to a client.) A medication calendar may be made by obtaining a calendar with space enough to write in the names of the drugs and the times of the day they should be taken. In this fashion they can be checked off when taken and the client will have a home medication record. This method is particularly helpful with clients who are concerned that they may forget or for those clients trying to establish a routine for taking their medications. Having an alarm clock next to the calendar so that the alarm may be reset for the next dose assists to decrease the anxiety related to forgetting a dose. Written information for each client should be available concerning the medication and including its name, purpose, appearance, directions for taking, time to take it, what action to take if a dose is missed, and any special precautions related to the drug. The side/adverse effects of the drug should also be written, along with those symptoms that should be reported and to whom they should be reported. In addition to information regarding

## CONSUMER EDUCATION TOPICS

1. Awareness that OTC medications are truly drugs, just as are prescription drugs, and deserve the same care in use.
2. Identification of some types of medications that are considered useful for home treatment (see Table 7-3).
3. Advising patient about safety precautions:
   a. Make sure all medications, including OTCs have clear and understandable labels.
   b. Heed instructions and explain warnings on labels—for example, "Do not drive or operate machinery while taking this medication" or "Discontinue use if rapid pulse, dizziness, or blurring of vision occurs" (see Figure 10-1).
   c. Take water, 1 to 2 ounces before taking solid dosage forms to hasten their movement to the stomach. Whenever possible, drink a full glass of water to assist in their dissolution.
   d. Check all medications periodically for expiration dates and for deterioration. Discard outdated or deteriorated medications.
   e. Discard unused portions of drugs and do not share these with friends or family even if they appear to have symptoms like your own. Do not even save them for yourself without asking a prescriber.
   f. Keep all medications out of children's reach, and never refer to medications as "candy" to induce children to take the medication.
   g. Do not take any medication in the dark.
   h. Do not mix medications in one container. Store drugs in the original container with the original label. Keep tightly capped.
   i. If you suspect a mistake or overdose, call your local Poison Control Center, prescriber, or pharmacist. Have the medication container at hand.
   j. Learn both the generic and brand or trade names of prescribed drugs. Learn the appearances of your drugs.
   k. Tell the prescriber and pharmacist about any allergies or other conditions you have as well as any previous unusual reactions, current pregnancy, or if you are breast-feeding.
   l. Take the medication precisely as directed and for the length of time prescribed. Ask the health practitioner or consult the U.S.P.D.I. about what to do if one dose of the medication is omitted. Do not just stop the medication on your own.
4. Instruction that nonprescription drugs do not usually cure a condition but rather just make the symptoms bearable. Treated conditions that persist, recur, or produce unusual reactions should be seen by a health care provider.
5. Counseling and instruction, when appropriate, about alternate nursing therapies or therapies that accompany drug taking (e.g., instruct about increasing fluids, activity, and roughage to reduce a laxative habit).
6. Warnings about certain drugs that can produce physical and psychological dependence (e.g., analgesics, stimulants, and laxatives).

the client's specific medication regimen, the nurse should take the opportunity to educate the client as a consumer of drugs. (See box, "Consumer Education Topics.")

The nurse should develop a repertoire of approaches and materials to be used for client teaching. A nurse who relies solely on the hearing of the client is not encouraging the optimal learning experience. The nurse should include as many of the client's senses in the learning experience as possible. For example, in teaching about medications while administering them within the hospital setting, the nurse allows the client to hear the reason the drug is indicated for the condition. The pill can also be seen and felt by the patient and tasted while taken. During recent years the amount of health teaching materials in a variety of media has proliferated. Audiovisual material such as pamphlets and videotapes can show the client settings and situations that are beyond the ability of the nurse to present at the bedside, in the clinic, or in the home setting. These are useful supplements and should be utilized by the nurse teacher to enhance the teaching process. With increasingly short lengths of stay or brief encounters in office, clinic, or home, these adjuncts become more important to include in the nurse's scope of teaching techniques. These materials should be selected as to the appropriateness of content, accuracy, simplicity, and appeal for the client. They should, however, never replace individualized instruction, since the client may overlook needed information or be overwhelmed by a comprehensive audiovisual presentation. These various media techniques should facilitate the nurse's role as teacher rather than act as substitutes.

Bille (1981) recommends the process of **therapeutic seeding** as a teaching approach when clients have not been able to express learning needs or concerns. This technique is one of mentioning ideas to clients, allowing time to pass so the client has a chance to think about the idea, then reintroducing the idea. On the second opportunity the client may more easily identify the concept and see it as a learning need. For example, if an older female client had been prescribed conjugated estrogens on a previous clinic visit, she may not have identified any drug-related learning needs at that time. The nurse on the next visit may use therapeutic seeding by a statement such as, "Ms. Ackerman, many women who take this medication have expressed concerns about its adverse effects. What concerns do you have about the medication?" If she states "I'm not concerned about that," she may be saying "I'm not ready to hear that infor-

---

### GENERAL CLIENT-TEACHING INFORMATION

- Antacids, milk of magnesia, bulk-forming laxatives (such as Metamucil), and antidiarrheal agents should always be spaced 1 to 2 hours apart from all medications unless specifically ordered for concurrent drug administration by the physician. Concurrent drug administration may result in a reduction in drug absorption.
- Bulk-forming laxatives should be mixed in a glass of water or juice immediately before administration. It is recommended that a full glass of fluid follow the previous glass, if not contraindicated by disease process. Reduced fluid intake can lead to GI blockade/impaction.
- Antacid tablets should be chewed thoroughly and taken with a glass of water. Reduced fluid intake can lead to GI blockade.
- Iron products (Fer-in-sol, Mol Iron, and others) should not be taken with antacids, eggs, milk or milk products, or fiber cereal. Concurrent administration may reduce iron absorption.

---

mation yet." Reference to the comment on the next visit may prepare the way for the nurse to discuss possible adverse effects and what symptoms should be reported to the prescriber if they occur. Therapeutic seeding allows the client more of an opportunity to negotiate the teaching-learning program.

Practical information about prescription drugs is available to consumers from the American Medical Association, package inserts produced by the pharmaceutical houses, some health care providers, or within the USPDI's *Advice for the Patient* volume. Most available printed information includes the drug's purpose, possible side and adverse effects, and the best way to take the drug. More than 1000 common drugs are listed annually in the *U.S. Pharmacopeia Dispensing Information,* which is geared partly to those who dispense or administer prescriptions and partly to those who take them. Section II, *Advice for the Patient,* offers jargon-free guidelines for safe and informed self-administration of prescription drugs by generic name. The USPDI is available to consumers by health practitioners or pharmacists who can reproduce for distribution a limited number of pages from the Advice section.* (See the box above for general client teaching information.)

The client and family need to be active members of the team, especially since much of the convalescent care is shifting from hospital to home. They need to be encouraged to participate when and wherever possible in all aspects of the client's care. Family members may be responsible for

---

*The USPDI is available for purchase from: Secretary of the USPC, Order Processing Department, 12601 Twinbrook Parkway, Rockville, MD 20852.

the changing of dressings, taking care of drains and intravenous lines, and running complex equipment, as well as the administration of intramuscular and intravenous medications. Their families may be of great support not only in providing assistance but also in easing the transition to home (Boyd, 1987).

The nurse needs to identify which family members are supportive and can assume the ongoing responsibility for care, including the administration of medications. In a crisis family members tend to gather around the client but may normally live at some distance or return to a daily work schedule when the client is ready to return home. The nurse must ensure that the appropriate family members are being the ones taught to provide the ongoing care. If the family will not be in attendance at home, it may be more appropriate to provide information to the client's friends or paid care providers regarding the medications.

Although there may be many opportunities to teach family members, the nurse may have to schedule an appointment with them to ensure that they are present to learn the medication regimen and other discharge instructions. The assistance of family members needs to be actively sought and encouraged since some may be hesitant because they are unsure of the part they are to play in the client's care.

In a review of successful teaching programs with clients and families about medications, Mullen and Green (1985) determined that five issues were necessary: (1) positive reinforcement or praise for desired behaviors; (2) feedback about progress towards goals; (3) individualization, where learning needs are determined for the specific client and the pace of teaching is mutually negotiated; (4) facilitation, in which the nurse assists the client to take action, such as making personalized medication schedules; and (5) relevance, making sure that the content and teaching-learning methods are meaningful for the client. The nurse should attempt to incorporate these issues into each of the teaching sessions.

There is no singular best way to educate clients to self-administer medications. Using the same approach each time does not take into account the data gathered from the client in the assessment phase of the teaching-learning process. The talent to assess each individual's learning needs and develop the best teaching approach determines the most effective use of nursing resources.

### EVALUATION

Evaluation of whether client education has taken place is essential. Some nurses may consider the process of teaching to be a brochure handed out or a videotape shown and consider the task of education to be complete. But the emphasis should be on the client's response—behavioral changes, knowledge, and skills gained as a result of the methodology and content of the teaching-learning process. The evaluation process should involve an assessment of the client's progress toward the specific goals for self-administration of medication as well as the response toward the teaching-learning process.

## DOCUMENTATION

Documentation is the final step in the process of client teaching for the self-administration of medications. Unfortunately the JCAHO has found that the lack of documentation of the client's and/or family's knowledge of self-care is one of the most commonly found nursing deficiencies during accreditation audits (Gilroth, 1985). Documentation relating to the teaching about medications should minimally contain three items: the specific content, the method of teaching, and the evaluation of learning (Barron, 1987).

Although the nursing care plan contains the specific learning goals agreed on by the nursing team and the client, the narrative documentation following the teaching-learning process should indicate the specific content that was covered. This information needs to be recorded in such a way that any other nurse will know enough about what was taught to be able to continue the teaching from that point. The following are appropriate examples: "the need for taking a pulse before a digoxin dose was discussed," "the client was cautioned not to take antacids with the tetracycline," or "the side effect of furosemide, low potassium, was discussed." A common error of documentation is the statement "medications taught," particularly in a setting where the client may have a polydrug regimen such as in home health care. The following questions are raised: What medications? What about them? What dosing schedule? What side/adverse effects? What special precautions?

Documenting the method of instruction allows the next nurse to know which teaching techniques were successful for the client's learning. Although "taught" is the most common verb used, it does not explain what or how the material was covered. More appropriate words are "discussed," "demonstrated," or "a specific piece of literature was reviewed and given to the client." These may also include the client's characteristics as a learner and any barriers to learning that the nurse may have determined. Recording the "teaching" part of the teaching-learning process leads then to the most important part, recording the "learning" of that process.

The recording of an evaluation of the client's and/or family's learning indicates the achievement of, or progress toward, the learning goals originally established by client and nurse. The evaluation documentation includes a description of what occurred; the client's response to the teaching-learning encounter, using his or her own words and behaviors; and the observable/measurable activities of the client/family, which would indicate the instructions were understood. Documentation, as the final step of the teaching-learning process, is essential to record the client's progress.

## NURSING DIAGNOSES RELATED TO SELF-ADMINISTRATION

Two of the most common nursing diagnoses determined in relation to clients and their medications are *knowledge deficit* and *noncompliance*. **Knowledge deficit** is the state in which the individual has a deficiency in cognitive knowledge or psychomotor skills regarding the condition or treatment plan, which is somewhat different from noncompliance. **Noncompliance** is the state in which an individual desires to comply but is prevented from doing so by factors that deter adherence to health-related advice given by health professionals (Carpenito, 1987). *All clients having drug therapy, whether administered by the client or a health care provider, should be assessed for the nursing diagnoses of potential knowledge deficit and potential noncompliance.* Because this is so, these two nursing diagnoses are not listed for each drug as it is discussed in the text.

Intervention to enhance compliance is focused on client concerns or health beliefs, such as concern over possible adverse effects or of the cost of the drug, and is distinctly different than teaching for knowledge deficit. Teaching for knowledge deficit is appropriate when the assessment clearly identifies that the client does not have sufficient or accurate information about the medication regimen and that the deficit is interfering with the client's ability to self-administer medications (Patsdaughter et al, 1988). Both diagnoses might present in the same fashion, that is, with the client's inability to administer medications safely and accurately; return of the client's symptoms or the occurrence of complications; or inappropriate behavior related to the therapeutic regimen. However, in the case of knowledge deficit, the client may request information, verbalize a misconception, or state the problem, "I don't understand . . ." With noncompliance, the client may also fail to keep appointments or evidence an inability to set or keep mutually agreed upon goals. The nurse may be aware of previous appropriate health education from the clinical record or may even have done the teaching and determine that the client did not seem to integrate the content into health-related behaviors. Then the issue is a matter of noncompliance rather than a lack of knowledge.

**Compliance** is the degree to which clients take medication instructions seriously, concur with them, and follow through. It is a term that can have an offensively controlling ring to it, implying that the prescriber directs the client who must follow those directions. Since compliance is the standard accepted term, it is used here; but "concurrence with therapy" and "adherence to instructions" are synonyms.

Why do clients seek medical care and then not follow through on the suggested medication plan at home? There are many reasons, some personal, some social, some psychological, some cultural. Everyone is a potentially noncompliant, whether intentionally or not. Studies show that 33% to 60% of prescription drugs purchased are never taken completely as directed. In addition, some clients never fill the prescription, most take them at unscheduled times, and many stop taking the medication early.

The consequences include inexplicable medication failures with continuing symptoms or overdoses. Medication not used may be kept and taken inappropriately later when its potency and chemical activities may have changed. Prescribers tend simply to increase the drug dosage or change medications when confronted with apparent medication failures instead of investigating for noncompliance with the therapeutic plan.

The following are examples of situations known to foster noncompliance.

1. The client is chronically ill or on prolonged therapy. The symptoms in chronic illness tend to grow worse, then improve in a cyclic fashion. Clients, therefore, do not often see any clear causal relationship between taking or not taking the prescribed medication methodically and the waxing and waning of symptoms. It has been shown that the routine action of reviewing medications with clients and inquiring how they are taken at home dramatically increases compliance. It should be stressed when appropriate that medication will have to be taken indefinitely and should not be precipitously discontinued.

2. The client is relatively asymptomatic or feels better. Reasons for needing to take the drug completely should be explained. Many people are not aware that organisms mutate, for example; and that to ensure their eradication in the first place, antibiotic medications should be completed as prescribed.

3. The medication is expensive or inconvenient to obtain. Prescription by generic name and explanations may be effective in remotivating this client.

4. The medication instructions are complex and not easily understood. "Take with meals" may mean twice a day to the person who always skips breakfast or before or after meals for others. Written instructions with a sample of the drug taped to them help as a reminder when the client is home and has forgotten what was heard in the office or in the hospital when being discharged.

5. The medication is unwieldy to take because the bottle cap is difficult for arthritic hands or there are complicated mixing or measuring directions. Measuring cups or droppers can be offered, and the client should be told that easy-to-remove caps can be requested when the medicine is purchased.

6. The medicine tastes unpleasant or must be taken at inconvenient times (during sleep hours, at work) or too many times a day to be feasible. Medication can be mixed with or taken with various liquids that are both pleasant and compatible. Medication prescriptions can often be changed after consultation with the prescriber to higher doses given less frequently or to a sustained-action form if available and if feasible.

7. The therapeutic plan contains many different medications, so the drug-taking schedule is complicated. Occasional systematic review of the medications by the prescriber and the nurse, especially in home health care, is necessary to see if the client still needs all of them and to simplify the care plan. Confrontation of the client's habits is necessary when medication containers remain full when they should be empty. Written schedules with sample drugs attached are helpful. Also, small medication boxes with separate compartments for each dosing time are available at pharmacies. The nurse may suggest that the client keep the medication near equipment used at a specific time each day (such as a coffee cup or the kitchen table) or associate medication taking with a specific routine activity, such as walking the dog or watching the television news.

8. Most people wait more than an hour in the physician's office. Waiting longer than this has been correlated with a distinct drop in following the prescriber's medication instructions. Often the wait is unavoidable, but the situation can be improved if the practitioner is empathic.

9. The client does not understand or accept the illness or disorder, or the explanation of the illness or treatment plan does not fit the client's concepts of illness, health care, or health. Typical of the factors that influence attitudes toward treatment are the extent to which clients believe (a) themselves to be susceptible to the illness, (b) the illness to be serious, and (c) that they will benefit from taking action. *Giving information, therefore, is not the entire answer.* It helps to seek active participation of the client in the health and nursing process and to show interest in and respect for client ideas, feelings, and beliefs.

10. The client and health care practitioners perceive the clients' problems or goals in divergent ways, yet do not effectively communicate this.

11. The medication is seen as an artificial additive or contaminant to the body or as a crutch on which dependence should be limited.

12. Side effects are severe or interfere with functioning in daily activities.

13. The client has problems with memory or confusion or is visually impaired.

## SUMMARY

Medications tend to be more effective when clients believe in their capacity to get well and in the drug itself. An accurate assessment of clients' past and present conditioning to drugs, illness, hospitals, nurses, and other health care personnel as well as their own health beliefs and practices all influence their response to drug therapy. This assessment is most important in order to plan and implement an effective care plan.

From the onset of drug therapy the client should be advised of the purpose of the medication and any possible side or adverse effects. All information should be presented in a nonthreatening and straightforward manner. It is important to listen to what the client has to say about the medication, the feelings associated with the drug and whether they are based on fear or anxiety, and the perception of the condition for which it has been prescribed.

Client education plays an important role when, at discharge, the individual needs to follow a prescribed medication plan. Routinely reviewing medications with clients and inquiring about how medications are taken at home have been shown to increase compliance in following a medication plan.

The nurse should make sure the client thoroughly understands the medication instructions. Written schedules and instructions will remind clients when they are at home and may have forgotten what they heard in the office or on discharge from the hospital.

Documentation of the teaching-learning process for self-administration of medications needs to include the content, method, and the client's/family's progress in relation to the planned objectives for learning.

Two of the most common nursing diagnoses related to the self-administration of medications are knowledge deficit and noncompliance. These need to be resolved so that the client may accurately and safely self-administer medications.

## BIBLIOGRAPHY

Armstrong ML. (1989). Orchestrating the process of patient education: methods and approaches. Nurs Clin North Am 24(3):597.

Armstrong N. (1987). Coping with diabetes mellitus: a full-time job, Nurs Clin North Am 22(3):559.

Austin JK. (1989). Predicting parent anticonvulsant medication compliance using the theory of reasoned action, J Pediatr Nurs 4(2):88.

Barron S. (1987). Documentation of patient education, Patient Educ Couns 9(1):81.

Becker M. (1979). Patient perceptions and compliance: recent studies for the health belief model. In Haynes R et al, editors: Compliance in health care. Baltimore: John Hopkins University Press.

Beeber LS. (1988). Medication refusal: what does it mean? J Psychosoc Nurs Ment Health Serv 26(12):31.

Bernal H. (1988). In-home medication checks with diabetes, Home Healthcare Nurse 6(5):14.

Bernstein SB. (1989). Breaking the vicious circle of noncompliance, Nursing 19(1):74.

Bille DA. (1987). Locus of decision making in patient and family education: its effect on promoting wellness, Nurs Adm Q 11(3):62.

Bille DA, editor. (1981). Practical approaches to patient teaching. Boston: Little, Brown & Co.

Billica K. (1989). To care or not to care for noncompliant patients: a discussion of ethical issues, Focus Crit Care 16(2):122.

Black HR. (1988). Hypertension therapy. Prescribing for compliance: the role of the fixed-dose combinations, Consultant 28(6):145.

Bond WS. (1990). Medication noncompliance, Facts & Comparisons Drug Newsletter 9(5):33.

Boyd CW. (1987). Patient education promotes transition from hospital to home, Patient Educ Couns 9(3):295.

Boyd MD. (1987). A guide to writing effective patient education materials, Nurs Manage 18(7):56.

Breeze W. (1987). Educational readiness in hospitalized adults, Today's OR Nurse 9(7):28.

Brim S. (1989). A quick guide for home use of inhalant medications, Pediatr Nurs 15(1):87.

Brown CS et al. (1987). Association between type of medication instruction and patient's knowledge, side effects, and compliance, Hosp Community Psychiatry 38(1):55.

Cameron K. (1987). Chronic illness and compliance, J Adv Nurs 12(6):671.

Carpenito LJ. (1987). Nursing diagnosis: application to clinical practice, ed 2. Philadelphia: JB Lippincott Co.

Cassino T et al. (1987). Invitation to compliance: the prolixin brunch, J Psychosoc Nurs Ment Health Serv 25(10):15.

Clark NM. (1989). Asthma self-management education: research and implications for clinical practice, Chest 95(5):110.

Comoss PM. (1988). Nursing strategies to improve compliance with life-style changes in a cardiac rehab population, J Cardiovasc Nurs 2(3):23.

Crist J. (1987). Successful client teaching—what makes the difference? Home Healthcare Nurse 5(1):45.

Crist J. (1987). Teaching time: the MI client's readiness to learn, Home Healthcare Nurse 5(3):56.

Davidhizer R et al. (1987). Patient medication education group, Hosp Topics 65(1):21.

Engelking C. (1987). Teaching, counseling, and caring, Am J Nurs 87(11):1439.

Fielo SB et al. (1988). Handle with caring: meeting elderly clients' special learning needs, Nurs Health Care 9(4):1097.

Forman H. (1986). Patient education and nonprescription drugs, Patient Educ Couns 8(4):415.

Fox B. (1988). Geriatric patient education: issues and answers, J Contin Educ Nurs 19(4):169.

Gibson J. (1989). A new approach to better medication compliance, Nursing 19(4):49.

Gilroth B. (1985). Incentives for planned patient education, Q Rev Bull 11:295.

Gorski LA. (1987). Effective teaching of home IV therapy, Home Healthcare Nurse 5(5):10.

Grady KE et al. (1988). The effect of reward on compliance with breast self-examination, J Behav Med 11(1):43.

Griesbach EH. (1985). Anxiety and the timing of diabetes teaching in the hospital: a literature review, Diabetes Educ 11(2):43.

Hahn K. (1988). About discharge medications, Nursing 18(11):89.

Harrigan JF et al. (1987). The application of locus of control to diabetes education in school-aged children, J Pediatr Nurs 2(4):236.

Harris M et al. (1989). 3 drug management problems: cost, confusion, and adverse reactions, Nursing 19(7):62.

Haynes RB et al. (1987). A critical review of interventions to improve compliance with prescribed medications, Patient Educ Couns 10(2):155.

Heringa P et al. (1987). The effect of a structured education program on knowledge and psychomotor skills of patients using beclomethasone depropionate aerosol for steroid dependent asthma, Health Educ Q 14(3):309.

Hurd PD and Butkovich SL. (1986). Compliance problems and the older patient: assessing functional limitations, Drug Intell Clin Pharm 20(3):228.

Hurxtal K. (1988). Quick! Teach this patient about insulin, Am J Nurs 88(8):1097.

Hussey LC et al. (1989). Compliance, low literacy, and locus of control, Nurs Clin North Am 24(3):605.

Johndrow PD et al. (1988). Making your patient and his family feel at home with TPN, Nursing 18(10):65.

Johnson EA et al. (1989). Teaching the home care client, Nurs Clin North Am 24(3):687.

Kick E. (1989). Patient teaching for elders, Nurs Clin North Am 24(3):681.

Kolton KA et al. (1988). Patient compliance: a challenge in practice, Nurse Pract 13(12):37.

Kontz MM. (1989). Compliance redefined and implications for home care, Holistic Nurs Pract 3(2):54.

Leventhal H et al. (1987). Behavioral theories and the problem of compliance, Patient Educ Couns 10(2):117.

Mann KV. (1988). Promoting adherence in hypertension: a framework for patient education. I. Can Bull Cardiovasc Nurse 12(3):4.

Markey BT et al. (1987). Medication discharge planning for the elderly, Patient Educ Couns 9(3):241.

McCord MA. (1988). Relating nursing diagnoses to drug therapy, Nursing 18(10):80.

Mikelo C. (1989). Patient education for enhancement of compliance, Gastroenterol Nurs 12(1):60.

Miller P. (1988). Influence of a nursing intervention on regimen adherence and societal adjustments postmyocardial infarction, Nurs Research 37(5):297.

Mooney MA. (1987). Uses of adult education principles in medication instruction . . . what do RNs know, J Cont Educ Nurs 18(3):89.

Mullen PD and Green LW. (1985). Meter-analysis points way toward more effective teaching, Health 6(6):8.

Niederpruem MS. (1989). Factors affecting compliance in the home IV antibiotic therapy client, J Intravenous Nurs 12(3):136.

Nieweg R et al. (1987). A patient education program for a continuous infusion regimen on an outpatient basis, Cancer Nurse 10(4):177.

Oberst MT. (1989). Perspectives on research in patient teaching, Nurs Clin North Am 24(3):621.

Padberg RM et al. (1987). Chemotherapy teaching and informed consent, Oncol Nurs Forum 14(14):91.

Patsdaughter CA et al. (1988). Medication regimens and the elderly home care client, J Gerontol Nurs 14(10):30.

Pavlish C. (1987). A model for situational patient teaching, J Contin Educ Nurs 18(5):63.

Rapoff MA et al. (1988). Educational and behavioral strategies for improving medication compliance in juvenile rheumatoid arthritis, Arch Phys Med Rehabil 69(6):439.

Regner MJ et al. (1987). Effectiveness of a printed leaflet for enabling patients to use digoxin side-effect information, Drug Intell Clin Pharm 21(2):200.

Rendon DC et al. (1986). The right to know: the right to be taught . . . the elderly client, J Gerontol Nurse 12(12):33.

Reville B et al. (1989). Continuous infusion chemotherapy in the ambulatory setting: the nurse's role in patient selection and education, Oncol Nurs Forum 16(4):529.

Rowland N et al. (1989). Alcohol education for patients; some nurses need persuading, Nurs Educ Today 9(2):100.

Ruzicki DA et al. (1986). Use of survey information to develop a hospital-based medication teaching program, Patient Educ Couns 8(4):407.

Ryan ER. (1987-88). Viewing health education within the framework of the consumer's personal value system, Nurs Forum 23(2):60.

Sanswero GE et al. (1989). Safe management of chemotherapy at home, Oncol Nurs Forum 16(5):711.

Smith CE. (1989). Overview of patient education: opportunities and challenges for the twenty-first century, Nurs Clin North Am 24(3):583.

Smith CE. (1987). Patient teaching: it's the law, Nursing 17(7):67.

Smith NA et al. (1987). Health beliefs, satisfaction, and compliance, Patient Educ Couns 10(3):279.

Stanton MP et al. (1988). Pointers for nurses on increasing patient compliance, Today's OR Nurse 10(7):34.

Swithers CM. (1988). Tools for teaching about anticoagulants, RN 51(1):57.

Tilley JD et al. (1987). The nurse's role in patient education: incongruent perceptions among nurses and patients, J Adv Nurs 12(3):291.

Tripp-Reimer T et al. (1989). Cross-cultural perspectives on patient teaching, Nurs Clin North Am 24(3):613.

Vallego BC. (1987). Is structured pre-surgical education more effective than non-structured education? Patient Educ Couns 9(3):283.

Wedman B et al. (1987). Diabetes graphic aids used in counseling improve patient compliance, J Amer Diet Assoc 87(12):1672.

Weed-Collins M et al. (1989). Knowledge and health beliefs regarding phosphate-binding medication in predicting compliance, AANA J 16(4):278.

Weinrich SP et al. (1989). Continuing education: adapting strategies to teach the elderly, J Gerontol Nurs 15(11):17.

Weintraub M. (1987). P & T policy issues: patients who refuse significant drugs, Hosp Formul 22(9):757.

Westberg J. (1986). Building a helpful relationship: the foundation of effective patient education, Diabetes Educ 12(4):374.

Westberg J. (1986). Gaining physician support for effective patient education, Patient Educ Couns 8(4):407.

Wilson-Barnett J. (1988). Patient teaching or patient counselling? J Adv Nurs 13(2):215.

# Part Two

## CLINICAL ASPECTS

# Drugs Affecting the Central Nervous System

*Chapter*

# ⟩11 Overview of the Central Nervous System

## CHAPTER OBJECTIVES

*After studying this chapter, you should be able to meet the following objectives and define the key terms.*

1. Identify the major components of the CNS.

2. Describe the functions of the components of the CNS.

3. Identify the structure and function of the blood-brain barrier.

4. Describe three major functional systems of the CNS.

5. List common neurotransmitter substances.

## KEY TERMS

# INTRODUCTION

The nervous system consists of the central nervous system (CNS) and the peripheral nervous system (PNS) (Figure 11-1). The PNS is discussed in Chapter 19. This chapter reviews the primary areas of the CNS, with focus on the specific areas affected by drug therapy.

The CNS, composed of the brain and spinal cord, essentially controls all functions in the body. The PNS is the network that transmits information to and from the CNS, thus alerting the CNS to internal and external changes, such as muscle tension, blood vessel alterations, pain, fever, sound, smell, taste, touch, and sight. This information is integrated, and instructions are then relayed to appropriate cells or tissues to produce the necessary actions and environmental adjustments. Information concerning these actions and adjustments is again fed back into the CNS. The constant feeding of information into the CNS permits continuous adjustment to be made in the instructions sent to various tissues to ensure effective control of body functions.

# BRAIN

The brain can be physically divided in various ways. A simplified developmental or embryonic approach is to divide it into the forebrain, brainstem, and cerebellum. The forebrain is made up of the **telencephalon** (which is located anterolaterally and includes the cerebrum) and the diencephalon (which arises from the midbrain but is considered part of the forebrain; it is located posteriorly and includes the thalamus and hypothalamus). The brainstem includes the midbrain, pons, and medulla oblongata. The cerebellum is attached to the cerebrum and brainstem in the occipital region of the head (Figure 11-2).

### Telencephalon

*Cerebrum.* The **cerebrum** is the highest functional area of the brain, where memory storage, sensory, integrative, emotional, language, and motor functions are controlled. The cerebrum consists of two hemispheres (right and left) connected by fibrous tracts. The outer surface of the cerebrum is called the cerebral cortex, or gray matter of the brain, and it covers the four lobes into which each hemisphere is divided. These lobes are named for the bones of the skull under which they lie—frontal, parietal, occipital, and temporal. The frontal lobe contains the motor and speech areas. The sensory cortex is located in the parietal lobe; the visual cortex, in the occipital lobe; and the auditory cortex, in the temporal lobe. Association areas lie near these lobes and act in conjunction with them. In addition, large parts of the cortex are concerned with higher mental activity—reasoning, creative thought, judgment, memory—those attributes that are unique to humans and separate them from other animals.

Drugs that depress cortical activity may decrease acuity of sensation and perception, inhibit motor activity, decrease alertness and concentration, and even promote drowsiness and sleep. Drugs that stimulate the cortical areas may cause more vivid impulses to be received and greater awareness of the surrounding environment. In addition, increased muscle activity and restlessness may occur. The specific response brought forth by a drug depends to a large extent on the personality of the individual, the emotional and physiologic state, the specific attributes of the drug, and a host of other factors.

*Diencephalon.* The **diencephalon** (between-brain) is composed of the thalamus, hypothalamus, and part of the third ventricle.

*Thalamus.* The **thalamus** is composed of sensory nuclei and serves as the major relay center for impulses to and from the cerebral cortex. It also registers such sensations as pain, temperature, touch, and many types of sensory impulses and relays this information to the cerebrum.

The thalamus enables the individual to have impressions of pleasantness or unpleasantness, and it also appears to play a part (with the reticular activating system) in arousal or alerting signals in the individual. (See Reticular Activating System later in this chapter for a further description.) Drugs that depress cells in the various portions of the thalamus may interrupt the free flow of impulses to the cerebral cortex. This is one way in which pain may be relieved.

*Hypothalamus.* The **hypothalamus** lies below the thalamus and is vital for maintaining vital functions and for the well-being of the individual. It is a major link between the mind and body, and it connects the nervous system to the endocrine gland mechanism. Functions of the hypothalamus include regulating body temperature, carbohydrate and fat metabolism, and water balance; the appetite center and pleasure or reward centers are also believed to be located here. There is evidence that a center for sleep and wakefulness also exists within the hypothalamus. Some of the sleep-producing drugs are thought to depress hypothalamic centers.

Neurons in the hypothalamus release hormones that affect the anterior pituitary gland. Growth hormone, hormones that affect sexual glands or functions, and thyroid and the adrenal cortex hormones are under the control of the hypothalamus. The hypothalamus, along with other specific areas of the brain, is also involved with the control of emotions. These functions of the hypothalamus may be affected by drugs. An example is the use of antidepressants to treat the symptoms of depression. The action of tricyclic antidepressants on the hypothalamus often reverses the symptoms of weight loss, anorexia, decreased libido, and insomnia associated with depression. Other psychotherapeutic agents may cause a number of hypothalamic side effects, including breast engorgement, lactation, amenorrhea, appetite stimulation, and alterations in temperature regulation.

*Brainstem.* The **brainstem** is composed of the midbrain, pons, and medulla oblongata and is the source of 10 of the 12 cranial nerves (see box on p. 199); the exceptions are

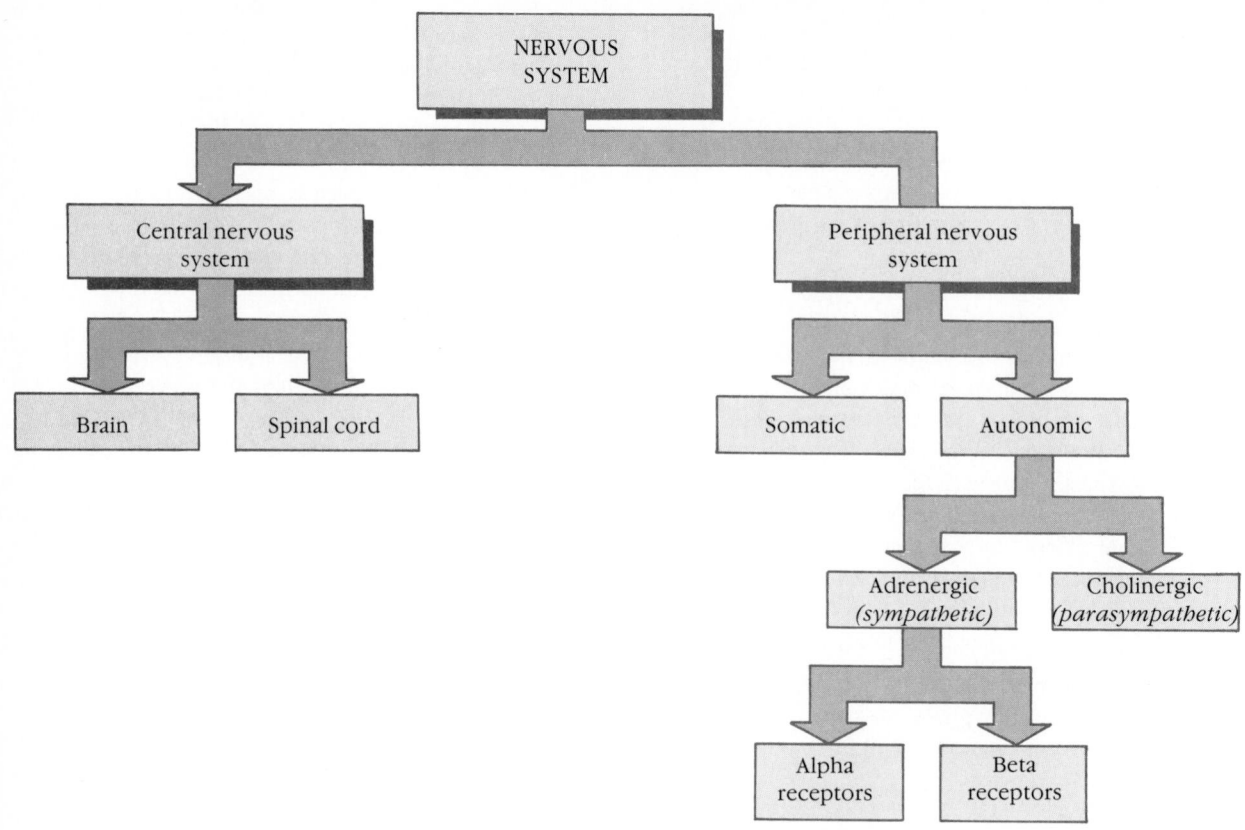

**FIGURE 11-1** Overview of the nervous system.

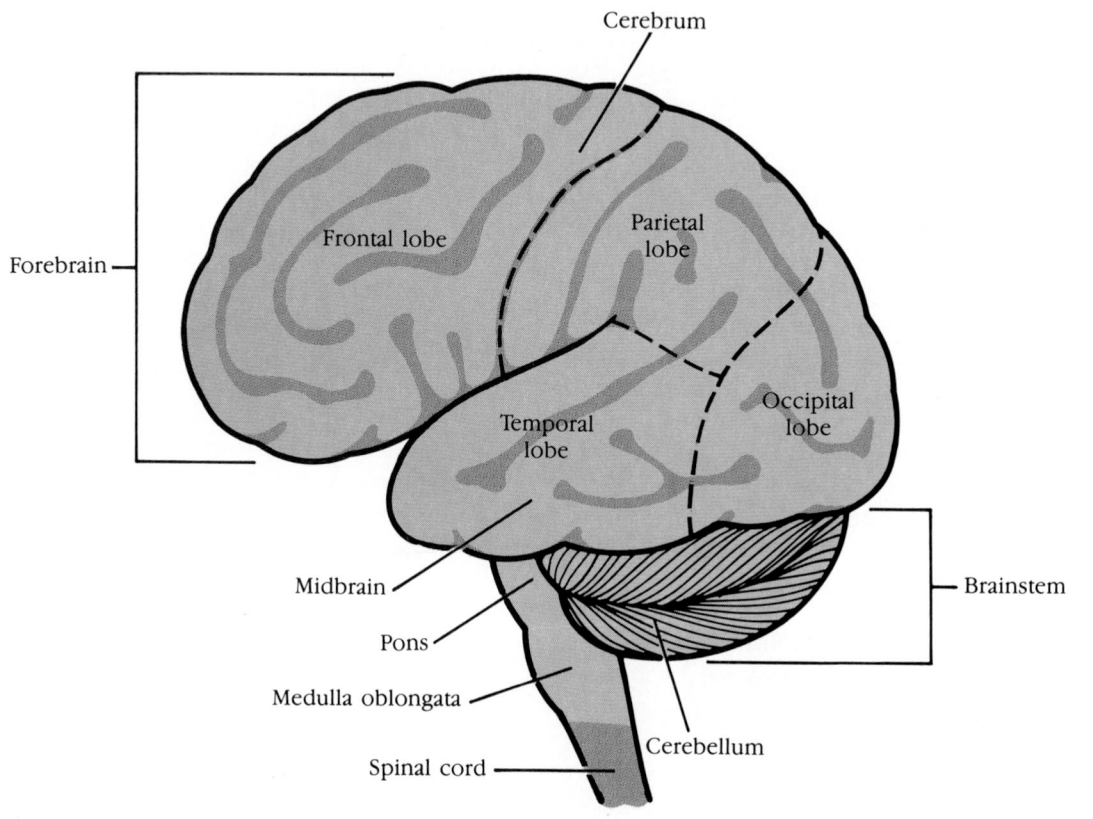

**FIGURE 11-2** The human brain.

## CRANIAL NERVES

| Cranial Nerve | Type of Nerve | Function |
|---|---|---|
| I Olfactory | Sensory | Smell |
| II Optic | Sensory | Sight |
| III Oculomotor | Motor | Movement of eye and eyelid muscles, pupillary constriction |
| IV Trochlear | Motor | Eye muscle for downward and inward motion of eye |
| V Trigeminal | Motor | Chewing, lateral jaw movement |
| | Sensory | Sensations of the face, scalp, oral cavity, teeth, and tongue |
| VI Abducens | Motor | Eye movements |
| VII Facial | Motor | Facial expressions |
| | Sensory | Taste |
| VIII Acoustic | Sensory | Hearing, equilibrium |
| IX Glossopharyngeal | Motor | Swallowing, salivation |
| | Sensory | Taste, throat sensations |
| X Vagus | Motor | Voice production, decrease in heartbeat, swallowing, increased peristalsis |
| | Sensory | Gag reflex; sensations of throat, larynx, and abdominal viscera |
| XI Spinal accessory | Motor | Head and shoulder movements |
| XII Hypoglossal | Motor | Tongue movements |

Drug effects, toxicity, or both have been reported to affect various cranial nerve functions. For example, ototoxicity, or eighth cranial nerve damage, has been reported with aminoglycoside antibiotics. Vincristine, an antineoplastic agent, may produce ptosis (cranial nerve III), trigeminal neuralgia (cranial nerve VII), facial palsy (cranial nerve V), and jaw pain. Since various medications have the potential for affecting the cranial nerves adversely, the student should be familiar with the functions of the cranial nerves.

the olfactory and optic nerves that originate in the diencephalon. The **midbrain** contains nerve tracts to and from the cerebrum. It is also the source of the third (oculomotor) and fourth (trochlear) cranial nerves; some optic fibers are also located here. The midbrain serves as a relay station from higher areas of the brain to lower centers. The source of the fifth, sixth, seventh, and eighth cranial nerves is the **pons.** It also contains a center that controls involuntary respiratory regulation. The midbrain and pons are affected by drugs as they stimulate or depress the reticular activating system. The medulla oblongata contains the vital centers: the respiratory, vasomotor, and cardiac centers. Such centers are referred to as vital because they are necessary for survival. Other essential functions also originate here, such as vomiting, hiccuping, sneezing, coughing, and swallowing reflexes.

If the respiratory center is stimulated by drugs, it will discharge an increased number of nerve impulses over nerve pathways to the muscles of respiration. If it is depressed, it will discharge fewer impulses, and respiration will be correspondingly affected. Other centers in the medulla that respond to certain drugs are the cough center and the vomiting center. The medulla, pons, and midbrain constitute the brainstem and contain many important correlation centers (gray matter) as well as ascending and descending pathways (white matter).

*Cerebellum.* The **cerebellum** contains centers for muscle coordination, equilibrium, and muscle tone. It receives afferent impulses from the vestibular nuclei, as well as the cerebrum, and plays an important role in the maintenance of posture. Drugs that disturb the cerebellum or vestibular branch of the eighth cranial nerve cause dizziness and loss of equilibrium.

## SPINAL CORD

The spinal cord, a center for reflex activity, also functions in the transmission of impulses to and from the higher centers in the brain and may be affected by the action of drugs. Ascending sensory tracts conduct up to the brain from peripheral nerves, and descending motor tracts conduct down from the brain to peripheral nerves.

A cross section of the spinal cord reveals an internal mass of gray matter enclosed by white matter (Figure 11-3). The butterfly-shaped gray matter is divided into horns; the **afferent** (sensory) **nerve fibers** are located in the dorsal or posterior section, whereas the **efferent** (motor) **nerve fibers** exit from the ventral or anterior horns. For example, when a pain impulse reaches the dorsal horn, the impulse will be transmitted along special tracts (lateral spinothalamic tract) to the thalamus, which then distributes the message to other areas of the brain. The brain responds by means of the descending efferent fiber pathways to inhibit or modify other incoming pain stimuli. (See the discussion of gate theory in Chapter 12.) Large doses of spinal stimulants may cause convulsions; smaller doses may increase reflex excitability.

When a drug is described as having a central action, it means that it has an action on the brain or the spinal cord.

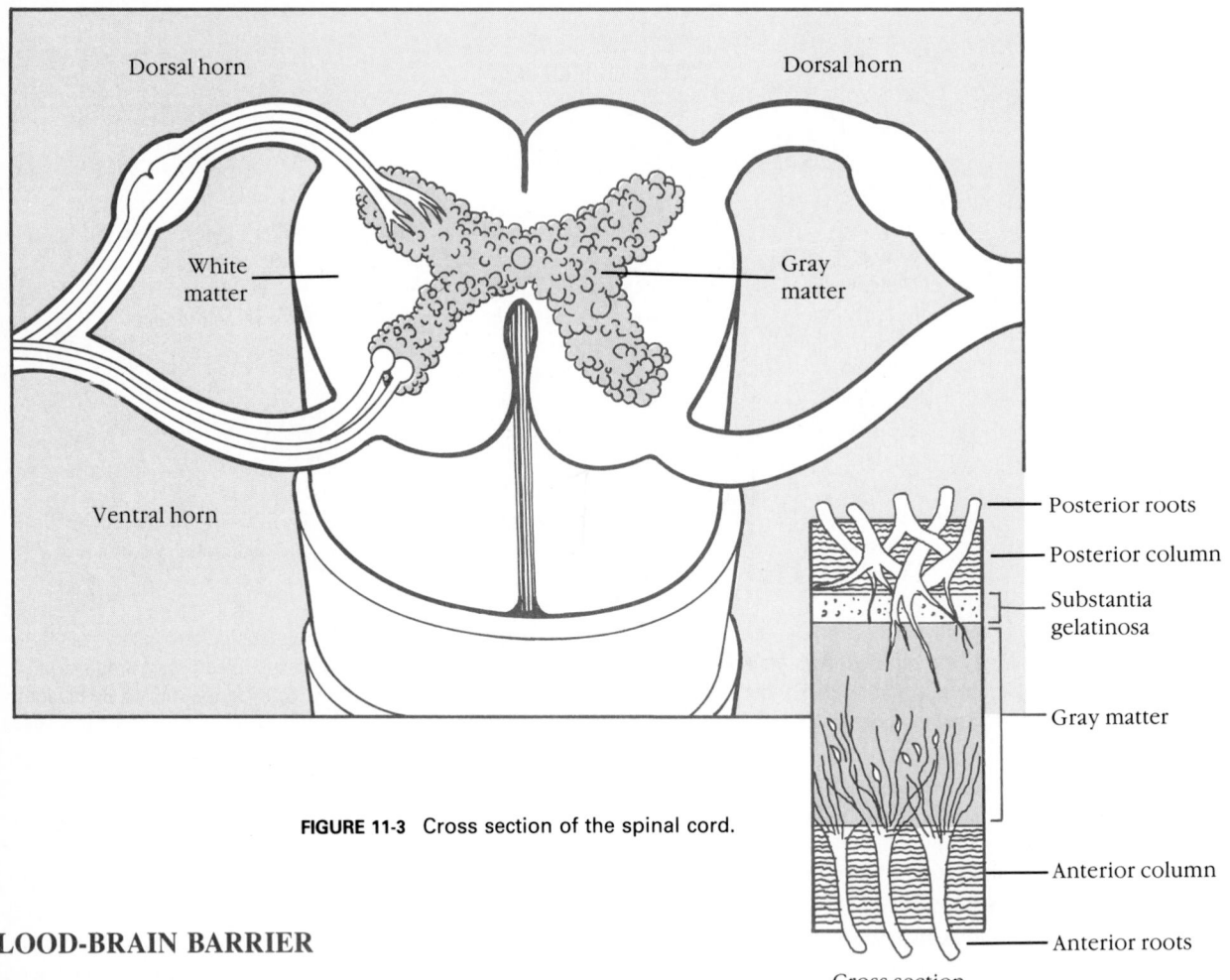

**FIGURE 11-3**    Cross section of the spinal cord.

## BLOOD-BRAIN BARRIER

The **blood-brain barrier** is actually a covering of nerve cells (astrocytes) that encircle the brain's capillary walls. This covering prevents the passage of many drugs or large molecules into the brain, but it will allow small molecules (such as water, alcohol, oxygen, and carbon dioxide), glucose, gases, and lipid-soluble substances to penetrate this barrier. Such selective processing allows the brain a degree of security against the toxic effects of some drugs on the CNS, but in large doses or in instances of meningeal inflammation the permeation of such substances across the blood-brain barrier would increase. Current research is studying methods to increase the permeability of the blood-brain barrier to specific therapeutic agents, such as antibiotics or antineoplastic agents, needed to treat a localized brain infection or brain tumors.

## CNS FUNCTIONAL SYSTEMS

The three major CNS functional systems affected by selected drug or chemical administration include (1) the reticular activating system, (2) the limbic system, and (3) the extrapyramidal system.

***Reticular activating system.*** The **reticular activating system** (RAS) is a diffuse system of nuclei in the brainstem

that permits a two-way communication between the RAS and the cerebral cortex. The primary functions of the RAS are as follows:

1. Consciousness and arousal effect
2. An alerting mechanism
3. A filter process that allows for concentration

When stimulated, the gray matter of the pons and the midbrain transmits impulses to the thalamus, which further transmits the impulse to various areas of the cerebral cortex. This results in consciousness or awakening and, possibly, an arousal effect. Arousal reactions require an external signal, such as a pain stimulus, an alarm clock, or bright lights. The cerebral cortex may signal the RAS or vice versa, but the end result is activation of both areas that may lead to additional transmission of impulses throughout the body (e.g., skeletal muscle activation). Inactivation of the RAS results in sleep, whereas injury or disease may produce a lack of consciousness or comatose state.

The alerting mechanism's primary function is self-preservation, for example, waking up at night because of a chilly sensation. Once awakened, the individual can assess the situation and discover the reason for awakening, perhaps

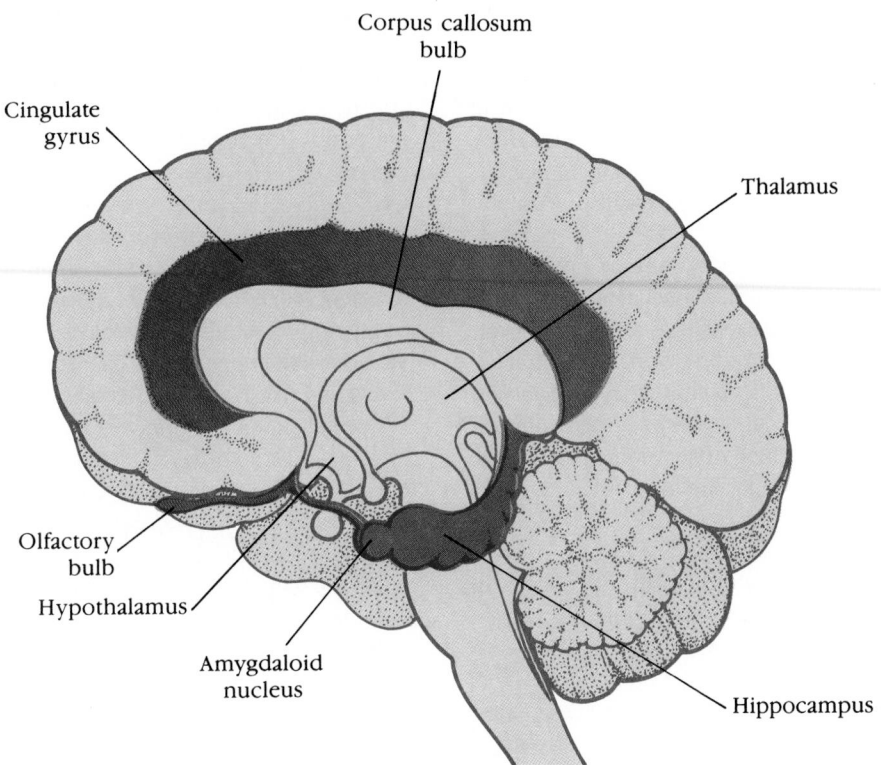

Corpus callosum
bulb

Cingulate
gyrus

Thalamus

Olfactory
bulb

Hypothalamus

Amygdaloid
nucleus

Hippocampus

**FIGURE 11-4**   The limbic system.

the blanket on the bed had fallen to the floor. The sensation of feeling chilly activated the RAS and caused the awakening, but the situation had to be assessed to determine why the chilliness had occurred.

The filter mechanism allows the individual to decrease the perception of monotonous stimuli that usually surround us. It permits us to concentrate on a specific at a given time. For example, imagine attending a large birthday party where nearly everyone is talking to someone at the same time. A functioning RAS will allow us to focus on the conversation or person we are interested in by filtering out all the other conversations. In other words, it permits us to have selective concentration.

Many drugs act on the RAS. Anesthetics dampen its activity and induce sleep, whereas amphetamines stimulate or activate the system. LSD and some of the other hallucinogenic agents may act on the RAS by interfering with its ability to filter out stimuli; therefore, the person taking this substance is bombarded by all kinds of wanted and sometimes unwanted stimuli. In contrast, it is a proposed theory that chlorpromazine stimulates the activity of the RAS and reinstitutes the activity of the filtering process, thus making it useful in reducing hallucinations in the psychotic patient and in patients experiencing an untoward reaction to LSD.

**Limbic system.** The **limbic system** is a border of subcortical structures that surround the corpus callosum (Figure 11-4). This system forms a ring around the top of the brain-

stem that consists of the portions of the brain remaining after the cerebral hemispheres and cerebellum have been removed.

The emotions of anger, fear, anxiety, sexual feelings, pleasure, and sorrow are related to this system. Learning and memory have been associated with the hippocampus.

The limbic system is extremely complex in its functioning. It may work with or inhibit other parts of the brain such as the cerebral cortex, brainstem, or hypothalamus to normalize expressions of emotions, influence their ultimate expression to other than normal, or affect the biologic rhythms, sexual behavior, and motivation of an individual.

Drugs that affect the limbic system are the benzodiazepines, meprobamate, and morphine. The benzodiazepines and meprobamate are believed to suppress the limbic system, preventing it from activating the reticular formation, thus resulting in drowsiness and sleep, especially in patients with anxiety. Morphine is thought to alter the subjective reactions of the patient to pain in addition to abolishing pain stimuli received by special areas within the limbic system.

*Extrapyramidal system.* The **extrapyramidal system** is a somatic motor pathway located in the CNS that affects skeletal muscles. This system is associated with coordination of muscle group movements and posture. Antipsychotic agents that block dopamine receptors may produce side effects or adverse effects related to this system. For further discussion of these effects see Chapter 17.

# SYNAPTIC TRANSMISSION IN THE CNS

The **synapse** is the junction point from one neuron to the next. There is evidence that transmission of impulses at synapses in the CNS is humoral (through a secretion). Many neurotransmitters are still to be identified. When released, they affect the postsynaptic neurons to stimulate or inhibit their activity.

Inhibition of motor neuron activity may be presynaptic or postsynaptic. Studies indicate that presynaptic inhibition occurs in the brain and is widespread at the spinal level, affecting transmission in afferent fibers from skin and muscle. The function of presynaptic inhibition is probably to suppress weak inputs that would otherwise cause unnecessary responses. This modulation of nerve impulses results in less transmitter substance being liberated. The net effect is a limiting or "inhibiting" of impulses to postsynaptic nerve fibers. Inhibition is important for orderly function.

Postsynaptic inhibition may be the result of changes in the membrane permeability of the postsynaptic cells caused by release of chemical transmitters from presynaptic nerve endings.

Upper motor neurons are scattered throughout the cerebral cortex; a number of them are located in the motor cortex. About three fourths of the nerve fibers from these motor neurons cross to the opposite side at the level of the medulla, descend to the spinal cord, and synapse with interneurons, which in turn synapse with the lower motor neurons. Almost all motor neurons of one side are controlled by the motor cortex of the other side. Therefore injury to the motor cortex of the right side causes paralysis on the left side of the body (hemiplegia). Systems other than the upper and lower motor neuron systems are concerned with voluntary movement, but lower motor neurons form the common final pathway for stimuli for voluntary movement.

Some of the neurotransmitters that will be discussed are acetylcholine, the catecholamines (dopamine, norepinephrine, and epinephrine), serotonin, and neuroactive peptides (enkephalins, endorphins, and dynorphins).

**Acetylcholine.** **Acetylcholine** is the best known chemical transmitter of nerve impulses. Not all parts of the CNS contain acetylcholine. Those areas that have high concentrations are the motor cortex, thalamus, hypothalamus, geniculate bodies, and anterior spinal roots; very low concentrations are found in the cerebellum, optic nerves, and dorsal roots of the spine. Acetylcholine can cause cardiac inhibition, vasodilation, gastrointestinal peristalsis, and other parasympathetic effects.

Lower motor neurons release acetylcholine at the neuromuscular junction, causing contraction in striated (voluntary) muscle. The concentration of acetylcholine must be high, since a large number of muscle fibers must respond synchronously for striated muscle contraction to occur and also because acetylcholine is very rapidly destroyed by the enzyme cholinesterase.

*Catecholamines and related substances.* **Catecholamines** (dopamine, norepinephrine, and epinephrine) and the amine serotonin (5-hydroxytryptamine) are synthesized, stored, and metabolized in the brain. These substances do not easily penetrate the blood-brain barrier, but their precursors do. The effect of injected catecholamines on the CNS is slight in comparison with the effect on the autonomic nervous system. However, an increase in catecholamines and serotonin causes cerebral stimulation. Drugs, such as reserpine, that release catecholamines and reduce amine concentration in the brain have a depressing or sedative action. Methyldopa lowers the serotonin and norepinephrine levels and this, too, has a cerebral depressing effect.

Special staining techniques indicate that there are adrenergic (sympathomimetic) and serotoninergic tracts within the CNS. Dopamine, a catecholamine, is especially concentrated in the basal ganglia. The low level of dopamine at this site in individuals suffering from Parkinson's disease led to the therapeutic approach of using its precursor L-dopa with good results in many cases.

*Neuroactive peptides.* Neuroactive peptides may be considered neuromodulators, neurohormones, or neurotransmitters. Studies indicate that a peptide may affect neuronal activity by increasing or decreasing the synthesis, release, or breakdown of neurotransmitters, neurohormones, or neuromodulators. Basically, little is known of the catabolism, conservation, storage, or synthesis of the neuroactive peptides. Our knowledge is only beginning to uncover the neuroreceptor mechanisms of these substances.

The parenteral or intracerebral injection of these components causes potent behavioral effects. A number of these peptides exist in tissues other than the CNS, primarily in the gastrointestinal tract cells (myenteric plexus). Studies are being done to provide more information about the functions, sites of activity, and mechanisms of action of these peptides. A continual search to find additional neuroactive peptides and other substances having a role in neurotransmission is in progress.

Enkephalins, endorphins, and dynorphins are three major polypeptides found in the brain that have opioid activity. Enkephalins may block opiate receptors in the dorsal horn of the spinal cord by blocking the release of substance P. Substance P, a transmitter of pain impulses in the nerve fibers, has been proposed to be transmitter for the primary afferent sensory fibers. Enkephalins behave as inhibitory neurotransmitters, decreasing the perception and emotional aspect of pain. Studies indicated that enkephalins may bind to the same neuroreceptor membranes as morphine, and the concept of internal opiates or natural pain killers developed. The enkephalins allow modification and control of the perception of pain.

**Endorphins** (from "endogenous morphine") is a general term that includes many peptides in the brain that suppress pain. These peptides are also found in the pituitary gland, intermediate lobe, and the corticotroph cells of the adenohypophysis. Subgroups of endorphins have been isolated and identified, including beta-endorphin, an analgesic substance that is much more potent than enkephalin.

Technology has shown that the brain, pituitary gland, and gastrointestinal tract each have enkephalins and beta-endorphins. These peptides are not found in the same cells. Further, the brain cells containing beta-endorphin are different from those that contain enkephalins.

Dynorphin is an endorphin found in the pituitary gland, hypothalamus, and spinal cord. This is the most potent pain-relieving substance discovered; dynorphin is 50 times more potent than beta-endorphin and 200 times more potent than morphine.

Naloxone, a potent opiate antagonist, reverses the analgesic effect of narcotics. Animal studies demonstrate that if naloxone is administered after enkephalins or endorphins are given, it will reverse the analgesic effect produced by the polypeptides. Endorphine release in the body is higher following acupuncture and transcutaneous electrical nerve stimulation, and both effects may be reversed by the use of naloxone. It has been proposed that the analgesic response associated with the use of a placebo may result from an increased release of endorphins in the body.

From peptide research may come pain relievers with fewer side effects and minimal to no addiction potential, and we may also gain increased understanding of mental disorders and addiction mechanisms.

Neurobiologists are only now beginning to understand what these and other yet to be discovered peptides are doing in the brain and spinal cord. Only basic research will provide the answers to the peptide cascade and an understanding of the functions in the nervous system.

## SUMMARY

The central nervous system (CNS) is composed of the brain and the spinal cord and essentially controls all of the functions of the body. The CNS integrates information received from the peripheral nervous system concerning the body's internal and external environment and then sends messages out again to produce the necessary adjustments to maintain homeostasis.

The brain is composed of the forebrain, which includes the telencephalon and the dicephalon; the brainstem, which includes the midbrain, pons, and medulla oblongata; and the cerebellum. The cerebrum is the highest functional area of the brain. Drugs that affect the cerebral cortex may decrease mental acuity, consciousness, and motor function by their depressive action or increase muscle activity and restlessness through their stimulating effects. The thalamus in the dicenphalon relays impulses to the cerebral cortex, as well as registering pain, temperature, touch, and other sensory impulses. Also in the dicenphalon is the hypothalamus, a major link between the nervous and the endocrine systems. The origins of ten of the twelve cranial nerves and the involuntary respiratory center are found in the brainstem. This respiratory center, as well as the centers for coughing and vomiting in the brainstem, are highly sensitive to drugs. Medications that disturb the cerebellum cause dizziness and loss of balance. The spinal cord, which transmits impulses to and from the brain, may also be affected by drugs. The passage of many drugs into the brain is prohibited by the blood-brain barrier.

The reticular activating system, the limbic system, and the extrapyramidal system are the three major CNS functional systems. They are responsible respectively for: consciousness, filtering, and alerting to stimuli; the emotions of anger, fear, anxiety, pleasure, and sorrow and learning and memory; and muscle coordination. All of these may be affected by medications.

Neurotransmitters affect the postsynaptic neurons to increase or decrease their activity. The most important of these are acetylcholine, the catecholamines, serotonin, and the neuroactive peptides. Currently neurobiologic research is demonstrating the increasing importance of understanding more about these substances and, in general, the central nervous system.

## BIBLIOGRAPHY

Anthony CP and Thibodeau GA. (1988). Textbook of anatomy and physiology, ed 12. St Louis: Times Mirror/Mosby College Publishing.

Beck EW et al. (1982). Mosby's atlas of functional human anatomy. St Louis: The CV Mosby Co.

Boss BJ and Stowe AC. (1986). Neuroanatomy, J Neurosurg Nurs 18(4):214.

Bullock BL and Rosendahl PP. (1988). Pathophysiology. Boston: Scott, Foresman & Co.

Carey KW. (1985). Pain (Nursing now series), Springhouse, PA: Springhouse Corp.

Conway-Rutkowski BL. (1982). Carini and Owens' neurological and neurosurgical nursing, ed 8. St Louis: The CV Mosby Co.

Dolphin NW. (1983). Neuroanatomy and neurophysiology of pain: nursing implications, Int J Nurs Stud 20(4):255.

Goth A and Vesell ES. (1984). Medical pharmacology principles and concepts, ed 11. St Louis: The CV Mosby Co.

Katcher BS et al. (1989). Applied therapeutics: the clinical use of drugs, ed 4. San Francisco: Applied Therapeutics, Inc.

Kerr FWL. (1981). The pain book. Englewood Cliffs, NJ: Prentice-Hall, Inc.

McClintic JR. (1983). Human anatomy. St Louis: The CV Mosby Co.

Mountcastle VB. (1979). Medical physiology, vols 1 and 2, ed 14. St Louis: The CV Mosby Co.

Price SA and Wilson LM. (1982). Pathophysiology: clinical concepts of disease processes. New York: McGraw-Hill Book Co.

Stewart D. (1980). Turning on the endorphins, Amer Pharm NS20(10):50.

West BA. (1981). Understanding endorphins: our natural pain relief system, Nursing '81 11(2):50.

*Chapter*

# 12 Analgesics and Antagonists

## CHAPTER OBJECTIVES

*After studying this chapter, you should be able to meet the following objectives and define the key terms.*

1. Describe the physiology, characteristics, and types of pain.

2. Explain the effect of opioid binding with the four major opioid receptors.

3. Name the three primary over-the-counter (OTC) analgesics and describe their mechanisms of action, indications, pharmacokinetics, side/ adverse effects, dosages, and implications for nursing interventions.

4. Discuss special considerations for use of CNS analgesics and antagonists in the very young or old client.

5. Describe the nurse's role in opioid therapy.

6. Differentiate among the opioid analgesics, opioid antagonist, and opioid agonist-antagonist agents.

7. Formulate an appropriate plan of care for individual clients who require the administration of CNS analgesics or antagonists.

## KEY TERMS

**abstinence syndrome,** page 227

**acute pain,** page 206

**analgesic,** page 205

**chronic pain,** page 206

**equivanalgesic,** page 227

**gate control theory,** page 206

**NSAIA,** page 210

**opioid,** page 214

**opioid agonist-antagonist,** page 230

**selective tolerance,** page 206

**somatic pain,** page 206

**step approach system,** page 214

**superficial pain,** page 206

**visceral pain,** page 206

## INTRODUCTION

Pain, an unpleasant sensation of physical discomfort, is one of the most common problems afflicting humans. It is the most distressing symptom of illness or trauma reported by clients. This is unfortunate since the potent analgesics currently available are both safe and effective when health care providers properly select the **analgesic**, or pain-killing medication, and apply pain management techniques based on the pharmacokinetics of the drug and the individual client's response. The greatest abuse with narcotic analgesics is not inducing addiction; rather it is using too little medication too infrequently to control pain.

Why do clients experience pain?

1. *Is it fear of tolerance or addiction on the part of the health care provider or client?* Study results indicate that health care providers are overly concerned about the danger of inducing addiction, or physiologic dependence on a drug (Marks and Sachar, 1973; Cohen, 1980; Cleeland, 1984; Foley, 1985). Porter and Jick (1980) reviewed nearly 40,000 hospital charts and reported that nearly 12,000 clients had received narcotic analgesics. Of this group only four cases of addiction were documented in clients with no previous history of drug abuse. Study results have indicated that the risk of addiction for hospitalized clients receiving narcotics at regular intervals, even for prolonged periods, is minimal.

   Tolerance, or the need to increase the dose of an analgesic to maintain the desired effect, is another concern in practice. Tolerance is not usually seen in clients who have severe acute or chronic pain for which there is a physical cause, such as trauma, tumor growth and invasion, and postsurgical pain. Clients in pain respond differently to an analgesic than individuals seeking euphoric effects from the drug. One must not confuse physical dependence with tolerance. Physical dependence is an altered physiologic condition in a long-term drug abuser who requires consistent use of the drug to avoid withdrawal symptoms. Clients with cancer may receive large amounts of narcotics to control the pain without producing the adverse effects of respiratory depression or excessive sedation. Pain specialists believe this is the result of **selective tolerance**, that is, tolerance to some of the effects of the drug without interfering with the drug's analgesic effect.

2. *Is it ignorance of basic pain management principles by the physician?* Bonica (1980, 1986) reviewed medical school curricula in the U.S. and found that very few schools include pain management techniques or even the basic pharmacology of narcotic drugs. Such information may or may not be acquired in the clinical setting of internship and residency, depending on the training of the senior physicians in the facility. Often, misconceptions or dealing with the problem of pain in an empirical manner takes precedence over basic pain management techniques. Bonica examined textbooks on oncology and reported that seven leading oncology texts contained nearly 5500 pages but devoted less than 20 pages to pain management: Thus he concluded that pain appears not to be an important topic to academicians and oncology clinicians.

3. *Is it failure on the part of the health care provider to listen to the client?* Published studies have indicated that approximately 75% of clients interviewed in hospital settings had moderate-to-severe pain even though analgesics were available and ordered for them. Chart re-

views substantiated the lack of administering prescribed analgesics by health care providers (Marks and Sachar, 1973; Cohen, 1980). A physician survey indicated that physicians tended to underestimate the effective dosage range of a drug and overestimate its length of action. Therefore many orders were insufficient for effective pain management, leading to undertreatment (Marks and Sachar, 1973).

## PAIN COMPONENTS AND CONCEPTS

Because of its highly subjective nature, pain is difficult to define. Pain can be viewed as having two components: the physical component, the sensation of pain, which involves the nerve pathways and the brain; and the psychologic component, the emotional response to pain, which is the product of such factors as the individual's anxiety level, previous pain experience, age, sex, and culture. Research has shown that a relatively constant pain threshold exists in all persons under normal circumstances. For example, heat applied to the skin at an intensity of 45° to 48° C will initiate the sensation of pain in almost all individuals. However, pain tolerance—the point beyond which pain becomes unbearable—varies widely among individuals and in one individual under different circumstances. Figure 12-1 shows factors affecting the pain threshold.

Pain can be classified in various ways. It may be acute or chronic. **Acute pain** has a sudden onset and usually subsides with treatment. Examples of acute pain include the pain of acute myocardial infarction, acute appendicitis, and kidney stones. **Chronic pain**, such as accompanies cancer and rheumatoid arthritis, is a persistent or recurring pain that can be difficult to treat (Table 12-1).

Pain may also be classified by its source as superficial, visceral, or somatic. **Superficial pain** arises from skin or mucous membranes. **Visceral pain** has its origin in the smooth musculature or organ systems. This pain is often difficult to localize since it is dull and aching. Visceral pain may also be referred, that is, felt at a site distant from its origin, such as the pain of a myocardial infarction that is experienced initially in the arm. **Somatic pain** arises from the skeletal muscles, facies, ligaments, vessels, or joints. Superficial and visceral pain may be relieved by narcotic analgesics; somatic pain may respond better to nonnarcotic analgesics.

Pain may also originate from psychogenic causes. Psychiatric illness, including anxiety and depression, has been known to cause severe pain. Obviously, in such a case drug therapy will not bring relief; rather, psychotherapy is indicated.

The great variation in the pain experience has prompted much research and led to the proposal of several theories of pain transmission and pain relief. The **gate control theory**, proposed by Melzack and Wall in 1965, attempts to explain the modulations in the pain experience (Figure

**TABLE 12-1**  Pain—acute vs chronic

|  | Acute pain | Chronic pain |
|---|---|---|
| Onset | Usually sudden | Usually of long duration |
| Characteristics | Generally sharp, localized, may radiate | Dull, aching, persistent, diffuse |
| Signs and symptoms | Physiologic response: increased blood pressure and heart rate, sweating, pallor | Physiologic response: often absent |
|  | Emotional response: increased anxiety and restlessness | Emotional response: client may be depressed, withdrawn, expressionless, and exhausted |
| Therapeutic goals | Relief of pain<br>    Sedation often desirable | Relief of pain<br>    Sedation *not* desirable |
| Drug administration |  |  |
|   Timing | As needed or upon request often adequate | Regular preventive schedule |
|   Dose | Standard dosages often adequate | Individualized according to client response |
|   Route | Parenteral | Oral |

Anxiety
Sleeplessness
Tiredness
Anger
Fear, fright
Depression
Discomfort
Pain
Isolation

Lower

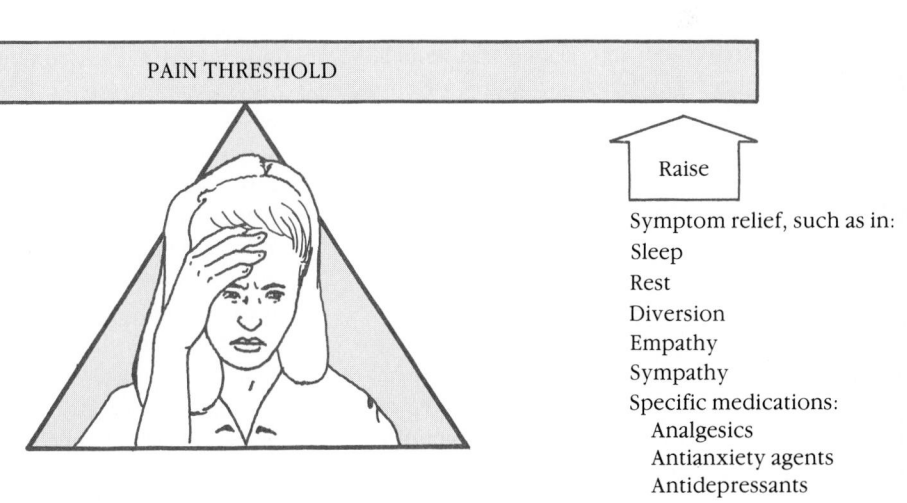

PAIN THRESHOLD

Raise

Symptom relief, such as in:
Sleep
Rest
Diversion
Empathy
Sympathy
Specific medications:
    Analgesics
    Antianxiety agents
    Antidepressants

**FIGURE 12-1**  Factors affecting pain threshold.

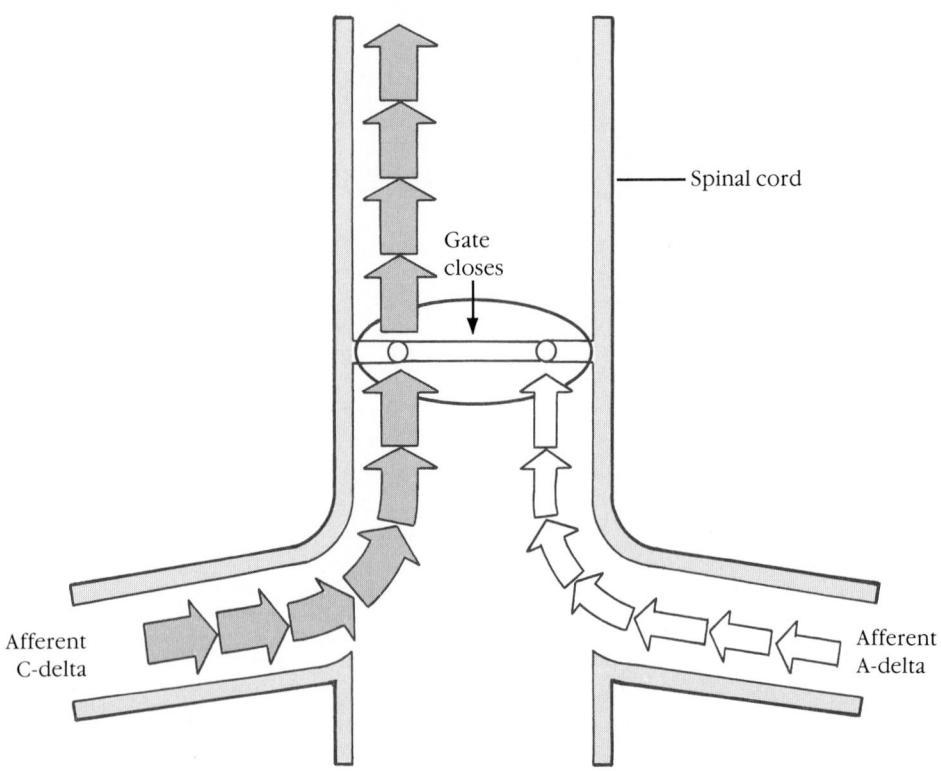

**FIGURE 12-2**   Gate control theory. Activity from A-delta (large afferent) fibers excites activity in the substantia gelatinosa, thus closing the gate to C-delta, pain-stimulating carrying fibers.

12-2). This theory proposes that a mechanism in the dorsal horn of the spinal cord (the "spinal gate") can alter the transmission of painful sensations from the peripheral nerve fibers to the brain. The "spinal gate" is closed by large-diameter afferent fibers (the fast-acting A-delta fibers) and opened by small-diameter afferent fibers (the slower-acting C-delta fibers). The "gate" is further influenced by descending control inhibition from the brain. Thus gentle stimulation of large-diameter fibers will "close the gate" to stop perception of slower-acting painful stimuli. It is on this theory that many nondrug regimens for pain relief are based, including massages or use of counterirritants. It is also a foundation of the Lamaze theory of "natural childbirth."

## ▷NURSING MANAGEMENT: PAIN THERAPY

Nurses must use all of their skills to successfully manage the care of clients who are experiencing pain. The nurse often instigates or coordinates the implementation of pain management.

***Assessment.***   Accurate assessment of pain relies on both subjective and objective information. While "pain" cannot be observed (pain is a perception, not an object), the physical and psychologic signs and symptoms of pain can be assessed. Each client perceives and reacts to pain differently based on physical, emotional, and/or cultural influences.

In particular, a client's cultural background affects the manner in which pain is communicated. Nurses should not assess pain by the presence or absence of any individual behavior such as crying or moaning but evaluate the totality of signs and symptoms that the client presents.

Assessment of pain includes both the quantity of pain (the duration and intensity [severity] of pain) and the quality of pain (sharp, dull, burning, radiating, stabbing, or cramping). The nurse should allow the clients, in their own words, to describe their pain and what seems to intensify or relieve it. The use of pain scales, asking the client to rate his pain on a scale of 0 (no pain) to 10 (unbearable pain), provides consistency for the assessment of the client's perceptions of his pain. In addition, having the client rate the pain at an appropriate time interval after the administration of an analgesic allows for evaluation of the effectiveness of the medication and titration of the dosage to achieve adequate pain relief without adverse effects.

Pain may bring forth many emotions from the client, such as fear, anger, or impatience. There are a number of physiologic responses, usually sympathetic in nature, to pain that include increased blood pressure, pulse, and/or respirations; sweating; pallor; restlessness and/or agitation.

***Intervention.***   All clients in pain should receive nursing care directed toward reducing the perception of, and reaction to, pain and to enhance the analgesic effect of medications. The nurse often has significant influence over pain medication through prn (when needed) prescribing of analgesic medications. As previously mentioned, the greatest abuse of analgesics is in the underutilization, which results in failure to adequately relieve or control pain. Analgesics should be used *before* the pain reaches peak intensity and painful events occur. A prn order can be used preventively if the nurse meticulously assesses the client's needs. If the order is for "q4h, prn" and the nurse determines that the pain will be fairly constant for the next 24 hours, the drug may be given at 4-hour intervals and documented in the medication record to be given every 4 hours around the clock. This regimen in no way exceeds what the physician has specified as long as the nurse monitors the client for signs that the frequency or the dose should be decreased. Because the blood levels of the analgesic remain steady, there should be no pain breakthrough. An alternate method of maintaining serum levels is the use of a patient-controlled analgesic (PCA) infusion pump. The client's anxiety should be reduced, knowing when the next dose is being administered. The consistent pain relief allows the client to participate more freely in his or her care, and hopefully, recover more quickly.

It is well known that anxiety exacerbates pain and causes muscle tension. Relaxation techniques can be effective in reducing the amount of pain experienced. Simple methods that promote comfort, a quiet, pleasant environment or proper body position may prove very effective. Rhythmic breathing, counting, and purposeful relaxation of muscle groups are among the techniques nurses can teach clients. More advanced methods include therapeutic touch, biofeedback, and hypnosis. An example of a highly successful relaxation technique for pain control is the psychoprophylactic or "Lamaze" method of rhythmical breathing and focusing to blunt the perception of pain during labor and delivery. The same techniques also are useful for the management of many other types of acute pain.

Transferring the client's focus of attention away from the painful stimulus is known as distraction. This technique greatly improves the client's ability to cope with chronic pain. Clients may even find that they have developed the ability to distract themselves without realizing it. Watching television, visiting with friends, walking, or working on a project can be effective distractions.

Stimulating the client's skin to relieve pain, or cutaneous stimulation, has been found to be very effective in pain management. Transcutaneous electrical nerve stimulation (TENS) is a method of applying a small electrical current to skin areas over nerves or around surgical incisions; it works very well in selected situations. TENS has been shown to cause both the release of natural analgesic substances (endorphins) and interference with pain impulse conduction (see gate control theory, p. 206). Nurses have used cutaneous stimulation for years in the form of massage, stroking, and application of heat and cold.

The nurse should always remember to question the clients

about pain relief methods they have used in the past. Reinforcing these methods and supplementing them with new techniques often lower the need for pain-relieving medications.

***Education.*** Instructing the clients in various self pain-relief techniques is an important part of pain therapy, especially in chronic pain. The nurse can provide the client with a method of dealing with pain. The nurse may know many techniques for dealing with painful situations that can be taught to the client, such as the technique of applying firm pressure to an abdominal incision with a pillow (splinting an incision) to reduce the discomfort of coughing. Clients given drugs for relief of pain should be informed of the medication's purpose. Analgesic effects may be enhanced by positive suggestion. Clients who self-administer pain-relieving medications should be taught adverse effects, proper dosage, drug or food interactions, correct administration, and safe storage of medications.

***Evaluation.*** Following the implementation of pain relief therapy, an evaluation of effectiveness must be made. Assessment once again evaluates the physiologic responses and the client's perception of pain. Rating the pain using a pain scale before and after treatment serves to document the response to treatment. In evaluation of analgesic drug therapy, the nurse also looks at several parameters. These areas include compliance with therapy and the development of addiction, dependence, tolerance, or adverse effects.

## NONPRESCRIPTION ANALGESIC-ANTIPYRETICS

Aspirin, acetaminophen, and ibuprofen are the most popular medications available for self-treatment of mild-to-moderate pain. These very effective over-the-counter (OTC) preparations are often used to treat muscle pain (myalgia), joint pain (arthralgia), and headaches and pain associated with the peripheral nerves (neuralgia).

Aspirin is available in a variety of dosage forms, including oral tablets, chewing gum, ointments, extended-release tablets, buffered formulations, combined with caffeine or various salts, and in rectal suppositories. The formulations include carbaspirin calcium, choline salicylate, magnesium salicylate, salsalate, salicylamide, and sodium salicylate. Carbaspirin calcium, a combination of urea and calcium acetylsalicylate, is reduced in the GI tract to aspirin, calcium, and urea. While it may be more rapidly absorbed, this product does not have a significant advantage over aspirin in producing an analgesic effect. It is a larger molecule than aspirin; therefore 414 mg of carbaspirin calcium is needed to produce an effect equivalent to 325 mg of aspirin. Choline salicylate is the only liquid salicylate available. It is absorbed faster from the GI tract and produces less adverse gastrointestinal effects when compared to aspirin. But it is also less potent than aspirin in that a 435 mg dose is considered equivalent to 325 mg of sodium salicylate. This form may be useful for clients experiencing difficulty in swallowing tablets. Magnesium salicylate and sodium salicylate are equivalent in potency. Magnesium may be absorbed, which may result in systemic toxicity in clients with renal impairment. Because of the possibility of sodium retention, sodium salicylate must be used cautiously in clients on sodium restricted diets.

Salsalate (salicylsalicylic acid) is converted to salicylate during absorption from the GI tract and in the liver. It produces less adverse gastrointestinal effects, and it does not affect platelet aggregation. Salsalate's analgesic effects are equivalent to aspirin. Salicylamide is not converted to salicylic acid in the body. Its pharmacologic effect depends on the salicylamide molecule itself. It is inferior to aspirin as an antipyretic, and doses greater than 600 mg are necessary to produce a therapeutic effect. The recommended analgesic dose is 500 to 1000 mg every 4 hours, not to exceed 6000 mg in 24 hours (Feldman et al, 1990). Persons allergic to aspirin generally will not have a cross-sensitivity to salicylamide. However, long-term studies of chronic drug administration and safety are unavailable at this time. Caffeine has been combined with aspirin in a number of oral preparations. Caffeine may provide a more rapid onset of aspirin action and an enhanced analgesic effect, thus allowing for lower doses of salicylates (USP-DI, 1991). In itself, caffeine also constricts cerebral blood vessels, which may help in headache relief. Buffered aspirin formulations have been promoted to produce a more rapid onset of effect with a decrease in the adverse gastrointestinal effects. Studies have indicated that buffering can enhance aspirin's dissolution and absorption rate, but there is no evidence to prove that buffered aspirin produces greater or faster pain relief than unbuffered aspirin (Feldman et al, 1991). With the exception of the effervescent buffered tablets, other buffered tablets were found to contain an insufficient amount of buffering agent to prevent gastric irritation (Lanza, 1980).

### Mechanisms of action

*Analgesic and anti-inflammatory.* Aspirin (acetylsalicylic acid), ibuprofen, and the nonsteroidal antiinflammatory agents (**NSAIAs**) primarily inhibit the synthesis and release of prostaglandins peripherally. This effect in inflamed tissue is believed to be responsible for their analgesic and antiinflammatory action. See Figure 62-1 for a diagram of prostaglandin synthesis and NSAIA effects in inflammation. While salicylates may also have a central analgesic action, this effect is considered secondary to their peripheral effects. The NSAIAs also inhibit leukocyte migration and the release of the lysosomal enzymes, which contributes to their antiinflammatory effect. Additional possible actions in the body have been postulated for several individual NSAIA agents. Acetaminophen appears to produce its predominant effect by inhibition of prostanglandin synthesis in the CNS, while its peripheral effect is considered secondary. It has minimal antiinflammatory effects.

*Antipyretic.* Antipyretic effect for the OTC analgesic drugs is mediated centrally via the hypothalamus. Fevers are reduced by a peripheral vasodilation effect, which results in an increased blood flow to the skin, sweating, and heat loss.

*Platelet aggregation inhibition.* Irreversible inhibition of platelet aggregation with aspirin is produced by its effects on the enzyme prostaglandin cyclooxygenase in platelets. This results in the prevention of the formation of thromboxane $A_2$. It may also inhibit the formation of platelet aggregation in the blood vessels by prostacyclin inhibition. This latter effect is considered reversible. Both effects are believed to be dose dependent.

***Indications.*** All three agents are effective analgesics for the treatment of mild-to-moderate pain. Aspirin and ibuprofen (NSAIAs) are used to treat rheumatic and nonrheumatic inflammation, that is, rheumatoid arthritis, osteoarthritis, juvenile arthritis, myalgia, tendonitis, musculoskeletal pain, and other symptoms of athletic injury. All effectively reduce fever while ibuprofen (and most of the NSAIAs) are used to treat the pain and symptoms of dysmenorrhea.

Aspirin (salicylates) is commonly used to treat the fever and joint inflammation associated with rheumatic fever. Prophylactically, because of its antiplatelet effect, aspirin is prescribed for males to reduce the risk of a recurrence of transient ischemic attacks (TIAs) and stroke. Large studies have reported that aspirin can significantly reduce the incidence of stroke and mortality in TIA clients. This potential benefit has been more difficult to document in women, although recent studies have reported significant beneficial effects in both men and women (Feldman et al, 1990; Chawluk, 1988). Similar studies advise it may also be used in both sexes to prevent a myocardial infarction, especially in clients with a history of myocardial infarctions or in persons with unstable angina pectoris (USP-DI, 1991).

### Pharmacokinetics

Salicylate tablets (aspirin and others) are rapidly absorbed, become highly protein bound, and have a half-life of 2 to 3 hours when administered in low doses or single doses. The half-life of antirheumatic aspirin doses is between 5 and 18 hours. Enteric-coated aspirin has a delayed absorption whereas aspirin chewing gum and rectal suppositories have a delayed and incomplete absorption. The time-to-peak plasma level with the tablet dosage form is usually within 1 to 2 hours while the buffered aspirin effervescent tablets are often more rapid. Therapeutic salicylate analgesic and antipyretic plasma levels are between 25 to 50 μg per ml. The antiinflammatory/antirheumatic desired plasma level is between 150 to 300 μg per ml. The time to reach a peak antirheumatic effect may require 2 to 3 weeks of chronic therapy. Excretion is primarily via the kidneys. Aspirin and salicylate salts are excreted as free salicylic acid and metabolites. Salicylates are excreted in breast milk in high levels, (173 to 483 μg/ml) even after

---

### ACETAMINOPHEN OVERDOSE

Early symptoms: sweating, anorexia, nausea or vomiting, abdominal pain or cramping and/or diarrhea. Usually occur in 6 to 14 hours after ingestion, lasting for approximately 24 hours

Late symptoms: abdominal area may exhibit swelling, tenderness, or pain in 2 to 4 days following ingestion (hepatotoxicity)

Treatment: gastric lavage or emesis. Determining acetaminophen serum levels at 4 hours or more, after ingestion. Hepatotoxicity is possible if serum acetaminophen is over 150 $\mu$/ml at 4 hours; 100 mcg/ml at 6 hours, 70 $\mu$/ml at 8 hours, 50 mcg/ml at 10 hours or 3.5 $\mu$/ml at 24 hours. Administer acetylcysteine orally as soon as possible, within 24 hours of ingestion. See USP-DI for dosage instructions.

---

### ASPIRIN OVERDOSE

Mild overdose (salicylate serum levels of 195-210 $\mu$g/ml): hearing loss, confusion, severe diarrhea, dizziness, sedation, tachypnea, severe headaches, sweating, severe nausea or vomiting, increased thirst, ringing in the ears, stomach pain, visual disturbances, and uncontrollable hand flapping, the latter especially in the elderly

Severe overdose (salicylate serum levels range >400 $\mu$g/ml): blood in urine, seizures, hallucinations, increased anxiety, severe confusion, respiratory difficulties, increased temperature. Children may present with severe sedation, rapid or deep breathing, and behavioral changes

Laboratory: alterations in acid-base balance, usually respiratory alkalosis and metabolic acidosis, hyperglycemia or hypoglycemia (especially in children), hyponatremia, hypokalemia, and proteinuria

Treatment: gastric lavage or emesis. Administration of activated charcoal, increasing salicylate excretion by a forced alkaline diuresis. (Usually acetazolamide is given concurrently with an alkaline IV solution containing sodium lactate or sodium bicarbonate.) Hemodialysis or peritoneal dialysis may be necessary in severe overdose. Close monitoring is necessary to institute appropriate nursing or medical interventions.

---

the consumption of a single 650 mg dose, maternally.

Acetaminophen is usually rapidly absorbed orally, has a half-life of 1 to 4 hours, and peak levels are reached in ½ to 2 hours while peak effect is seen within 1 to 3 hours. It is metabolized primarily by the liver and excreted by the kidneys, primarily as conjugate metabolites. In overdosage, an intermediate metabolite may accumulate leading to hepatoxicity and possibly, nephrotoxicity. Peak plasma level is 5 to 20 $\mu$g/ml following a 650 mg oral dose. It is transferred in breast milk with peak concentrations of 10 to 15 $\mu$g/ml reported after a single 650 mg dose maternally.

Ibuprofen is rapidly absorbed orally, is highly protein bound (99%), and reaches a peak plasma level in 1 to 2 hours. It is metabolized in the liver and excreted renally. Peak plasma levels vary with dosage administered, for example, 22 to 27 $\mu$/ml with a 200 mg dose, 23 to 45 $\mu$g/ml with a 400 mg dose. For side effects/adverse reactions, see Table 12-3.

#### Significant drug interactions

| Drug | Possible Effect and Management |
|---|---|
| adrenocorticoids, mineralocorticoids | If given chronically or in high doses with buffered aspirin or sodium salicylate, gastrointestinal ulceration, bleeding, and sodium and fluid retention may result. Monitor for abdominal pain or distress, black or blood tainted stools, vomiting of blood, etc. Always advise clients to take aspirin with a full glass of water. If stomach is upset, after meals administration may reduce GI irritation. Monitor for edema of the eyelids, fingers, sacrum, and lower extremities; and hypernatremia evidenced by elevated serum, sodium and dry mucous membranes, thirst, decreased reflexes, restlessness, and confusion |
| alcohol, especially chronic alcohol use, or with other hepatotoxic medications | Increased risk of inducing hepatotoxicity when given with acetaminophen. Avoid concurrent use if possible or, carefully monitor drug dosages and for signs and symptoms of liver toxicity |
| antacids (high dose, chronic use, and other urinary alkalizers, such as carbonic anhydrase inhibitors, citrates, sodium bicarbonate) | When coadministered with salicylates (aspirin, etc.), may result in an alkaline urine that leads to an increased excretion of salicylates. Buffered aspirin does not contain sufficient buffering to induce this effect, but the buffered effervescent aspirin tablets if used in large quantities may produce this effect. Avoid chronic high dose alkalizers whenever possible |
| antibiotics (such as cefamandole, cefoperazone, cefotetan, moxalactam, or plicamycin) | When coadministered with ibuprofen, these antibiotics may induce hypoprothrombinemia or platelet inhibition, which can result in an increased potential for bleeding episodes. Avoid concurrent drug administration |
| anticoagulants (coumarin or heparin or thrombolytic agents) | When given with ibuprofen, there is increased risk of bleeding caused by inhibition of platelet aggregation. Also increased potential for GI ulceration or hemorrhage. Avoid concurrent drug administration |
| diuretics, especially triamterene or antihypertensives | May result in a decrease in diuretic or antihypertensive effects when given with ibuprofen. Monitor closely for fluid retention, such as weight gain of 1 lb. +/daily and edema, or elevation of blood pressure |

**TABLE 12-2**   Dosage and administration of nonprescription analgesics-antipyretics

| Drug | Adults | Children |
|---|---|---|
| **Acetaminophen (Tylenol, others)** | | |
| Tablets, capsules, elixirs | 325 to 650 mg by mouth every 4 hr or 1 g every 4-6 hr to 4 times a day. Maximum dose in chronic therapy: 2.6 g daily | 1.5 g per square meter of body surface area daily in divided doses, or: Infants up to 3 mo: 40 mg orally (per dose); 4 mo-2 yr: 80-120 mg; 2-6 yr: 160-240 mg; 6-11 yr: 320-400 mg; 11-12 yr: 480 mg orally every 4-6 hr, when necessary. Children up to 12 yr: no more than 5 doses in 24-hr period for a maximum of 5 days |
| Suppositories, 325 mg, 650 mg | 325-650 mg rectally every 4 hr when needed | 1.5 g per square meter body area daily in divided doses. Dosage by age: see USP-DI |
| **Ibuprofen (Advil, Nuprin)** | | |
| Tablets, 200 mg | 200-400 mg every 4-6 hr; maximum 1200 mg per day | Not indicated for children under 12, unless ordered by a physician |
| **Salicylates (aspirin)** | | |
| Tablets/capsule/delayed release/ gum/suppository, 60, 120, 125, 130, 195, 200, 300, 325, 600, and 650 mg; 1.2 g | Analgesic, antipyretic, 325-650 mg orally or rectally or 454 mg gum every 4 hr when necessary | |
| Chewable tablets, 81 mg | | 1.5 g per square meter of body area daily in 4-6 divided doses, or check label or USP-DI for recommendations based on age |
| Suppositories | | Maximum daily dose is 2.5 g per square meter; give no more than 5 doses in a 24-hr period for a maximum of 5 days, unless otherwise ordered by a physician |

| | | | |
|---|---|---|---|
| lithium | May result in an increase in lithium serum levels when given with ibuprofen. Monitor lithium levels closely during concurrent drug administration and after ibuprofen is discontinued | salicylates, especially aspirin, plus ibuprofen | See comments below for nonsteroidal antiinflammatory agents |
| methotrexate | Given with ibuprofen, this drug may decrease methotrexate excretion leading to elevated methotrexate serum levels and toxicity. Avoid concurrent drug administration | vancomycin, aminoglycosides, bumentanide, furosemide, ethacrynic acid, or cisplatin | Increased risk for ototoxicity when given with salicylates. Furosemide with high doses of salicylates may also result in salicylate toxicity because of a competitive effect at excretion sites in the kidneys that result in increased salicylate serum levels. Avoid concurrent drug administration |
| nonsteroidal antiinflammatory analgesics (NSAIAs) | Increased risk when given with salicylates (aspirin, etc), for GI side effects such as bleeding and ulceration. Aspirin is also reported to decrease serum levels of diflunisal, fenoprofen, indomethacin, meclofenamate, piroxicam, and the active metabolite of sulindac. May also decrease protein binding resulting in elevated serum levels and possible toxicity of ketoprofen. Avoid concurrent drug administration | | |

Concurrent use of aspirin with NSAIAs may also increase potential of bleeding in areas other than the GI tract. This results from an additive inhibition of platelet aggregation. Avoid concurrent drug administration

| | |
|---|---|
| probenecid | May decrease ibuprofen excretion, which can result in an increase in serum levels and increased potential for toxicity. A dosage decrease in ibuprofen may be necessary |
| radiation therapy, bone marrow depressants, or drugs that cause blood dyscrasias | Concurrent administration with ibuprofen, may result in an increased potential of inducing hematological adverse effects. Avoid coadministration |

*Dosage and administration.* See Table 12-2.
*Side effects/adverse reactions.* See Table 12-3.
*Pregnancy safety.* Unclassified for acetaminophen, aspirin, and ibuprofen.

▷**NURSING MANAGEMENT: NONPRESCRIPTION ANALGESIC-ANTIPYRETIC THERAPY**

*Assessment.* The nurse should establish the client's allergies before administering these drugs. Those clients with aspirin intolerance or intolerance of any NSAIA described as a hypersensitivity or allergy manifested by asthmatic attack, bronchspastic activity, nasal polyps, or angioedema should not be administered aspirin or ibuprofen. Clients intolerant of tartrazine dye may also be intolerant of aspirin. Geriatric clients should be monitored more closely when taking ibuprofen since they are more likely to develop ad-

**TABLE 12-3**   Side effects/adverse reactions of nonprescription analgesics/antipyretics

| Drug | Side effects* | Adverse reactions† |
|---|---|---|
| acetaminophen (Tylenol, others) | | *Rare:* skin rash, hives, or pruritis, (allergy), increased weakness (anemia), jaundice of skin or eyes (hepatitis), decreased urine production and difficulty on urination, bloody/cloudy urine (reported in chronic, high-dose therapy in clients with impaired renal function caused by uremia, renal colic, or azotemia). See box on page p. 211 for acetaminophen overdosage |
| ibuprofen | *Most frequent:* stomach pain or cramps, indigestion, nausea, dizziness.<br>*Less frequent:* gas, vomiting, anorexia, constipation, headaches, increased nervousness | *Less frequent:* hives (allergic effect), edema, hypertension, ringing in the ears<br>*Rare:* GI bleeding, blood in urine, **SLE type syndrome,** visual disturbances, confusion, CHF, pruritis, mood changes |
| salicylates (aspirin)‡ | *Most frequent:* gas, indigestion | *Most frequent:* nausea, vomiting, stomach pain.<br>*Less frequent:* severe abdominal pain, red or black tarry stools, GI bleeding or ulceration, respiratory difficulties, increased weakness, skin rash, hives, or pruritis. For aspirin overdose, see box on page p. 211. |

*If side effects continue, increase, or disturb the client, inform the physician.

†If adverse effects occur, contact physician, since medical intervention may be necessary.

‡WARNINGS: Do not administer aspirin to children with viral symptoms (influenza or varicella or acute febrile conditions) without contacting a physician first. The development of Reye's syndrome has been associated with the use of aspirin in children. Pediatric clients are more susceptible to toxic side effects of aspirin, especially children with elevated temperature and dehydration.

 Selected nursing diagnoses related to administration of nonsteroidal antiinflammatory analgesics

| Nursing diagnosis | Outcome criteria | Nursing interventions |
|---|---|---|
| High risk for alteration in comfort related to CNS, GI, dermatological effects | Absence of dizziness and changes in sensorium<br>Absence of GI symptoms; nausea, and vomiting, abdominal pain or cramps, indigestion<br>Absence of rash, hives, pruritis, and SLE-type syndrome | Institute safety measures if CNS symptoms develop<br>Administer with food or after meals. Provide small, frequent meals. Caution against alcohol ingestion<br>Provide comfort measures to reduce pain, inflammation, and other dermatologic effects<br>Report adverse symptoms to the health care prescriber<br>Institute emergency procedures if severe adverse symptoms occur |
| High risk for injury related to CNS, GI, and sensitivity effects | No symptoms of injury occur | Assist to ambulate<br>Caution against driving and other hazardous activities. Advise against alcohol ingestion. Report sore throat, fever, rash, itching, sudden weight gain, edema of ankles and fingers, changes in vision, and black tarry stools |
| Knowledge deficit related to drug therapy | Self-administers drug with accuracy and safety<br>Relates signs and symptoms of side/adverse effects and those to report to prescriber | Instruct client in name and dosage of drug and its relationship to client's own condition. Avoid concurrent use of OTC medications and steroids. Teach signs and symptoms of side/adverse effects and how to prevent/minimize as in interventions above |

verse gastrointestinal, hepatic, or renal effects because of accumulation of the drug related to reduced renal function. It is recommended that geriatric clients be given half the usual adult dose initially. Careful consideration should also be taken before ibuprofen is administered to clients with anemia, fluid retention, bleeding disorders, hepatic impairment, and those with a history of or active peptic ulcer.

***Intervention.***   The doses may be taken 30 to 60 minutes before meals or 2 hours postprandially to reach a blood level more readily. Administration with a meal, however, will aid

in preventing gastric upset. Minimally, the tablets should be taken with a full glass of water and the client remain upright for 15 to 30 minutes after administration to reduce the risk of tablets lodging in the esophagus and causing esophageal irritation.

***Education.***   The nurse should discuss with the client the most common side effects and adverse effects, which are not always an indication of excessive dosage and should be reported to the physician. Clients should be told that if signs of an allergic reaction (shortness of breath, wheezing, skin

**TABLE 12-4**   Opioid receptor responses

| Receptor | Response |
| --- | --- |
| Mu | Supraspinal analgesia, respiratory depression, euphoria, and drug dependence |
| Kappa | Spinal analgesia, sedation, and pupillary constriction |
| Sigma | Anxiety, dysphoria, hallucinations, nightmares |
| Delta | Not identified |

rash, or itching); blood dyscrasia (unusual bleeding or bruising, tiredness, weakness, sore throat, and fever); or gastrointestinal irritation or bleeding (nausea and vomiting, stomach pain, black tarry stools) occur, they should immediately stop the medication and notify their physician. Dizziness, syncope, and drowsiness should be reported if the client is taking ibuprofen. Indications of hepatitis (yellow eyes or skin) should be observed for with the administration of acetaminophen.

Alcoholic beverages should be avoided since they increase the risk of gastric irritation with aspirin and ibuprofen, and liver toxicity with acetaminophen. Clients on sodium restricted diets should avoid buffered forms of these products. Oral tetracyclines are not to be taken within 1 to 2 hours of buffered forms of these products, since it results in decreased absorption of the antibiotic. If delayed release forms of these analgesics are being used, do not give antacids within 1 to 2 hours of administration, since they increase the pH level in the stomach and may cause premature absorption. Although not noted with therapeutic doses, the overuse or abuse of aspirin in the third trimester increases the risk of stillbirth and neonatal death. Aspirin taken in the last 2 weeks of pregnancy may increase the risk of fetal or neonatal hemorrhage. Aspirin should not be placed directly on a tooth or gum surface as it may result in tissue injury. Clients need to be instructed in the safe storage of these medications. Because they may be sweet and candy-flavored, they should be kept out of the reach of children. Aspirin should be kept in a tightly closed container and discarded if it has a vinegary odor, which indicates it has decomposed.

## OPIOID RECEPTORS

Research concerning the binding of opioid medications in the brain and other body organs has identified at least eight different opioid receptors. In the CNS, four major receptors have been identified: mu, kappa, delta, and sigma. Analgesia has been associated with the mu and kappa receptors, whereas the sigma receptors demonstrate dysphoric and psychotomimetic (inducing psychotic behavior) drug effects. Delta receptors appear to be involved with affective behavioral responses. (See Table 12-4 for receptor effects.) Naloxone, the narcotic antagonist, has an affinity for all the

---

**STEP SYSTEM APPROACH TO PAIN MANAGEMENT IN CANCER (WHO*)**

A three-step approach to pain management involves using the mild analgesics (nonopioid) first and progressing to stronger analgesics in the second and third steps.

Step 1: Mild pain
    Aspirin or acetaminophen, 650 mg every 4-6 hr
Step 2: Moderate pain
    Aspirin or acetaminophen with codeine, 60 mg every 4-6 hr
Step 3: Severe pain
    Morphine preparations (oral or rectal), individually dosed according to client response

In addition to the above progression, the following is recommended:

1. Administer medications on a *scheduled* basis to prevent pain.
2. Administer analgesics in adequate doses at appropriate intervals based on the drug's pharmacokinetics.
3. Evaluate frequently and add additional adjuvant medications as necessary (i.e., anticonvulsants, antianxiety agents, antidepressants, or steroids).

* World Health Organization guidelines for the use of oral agents to control cancer pain.

---

opioid receptors, but its affinity for the mu receptors is 10 times greater than for the other receptors sites. Morphine has an affinity for the mu and kappa receptors, whereas pentazocine and nalbuphine antagonize mu receptors but have a greater attraction for kappa and delta receptors (Gilman and others, 1990).

## OPIOID ANALGESICS-AGONISTS

Opium in the crude form was used until well into the nineteenth century, before the chief alkaloid, morphine, was isolated. The discovery of other alkaloids soon followed, and their use came to be preferred to that of the crude preparations. **Opiate** refers to drugs that contain or are extracted from opium, wheras **opioid** designates synthetic drugs that have pharmacologic properties similar to opium or morphine. Today *opioid* is a term used for both natural and synthetic products that have morphine-like effects. In a generic sense, the terms are considered interchangeable. Morphine is still obtained from opium because of the difficulty encountered in synthesizing it in the laboratory. Many analgesics are available now, but none has been proved to be clinically superior to morphine. All new analgesics are compared to morphine, which is the standard, in potency and in side or adverse effects. Over-the-counter (OTC) analgesics, are effective in mild-to-moderate pain situations and are included in the **step approach system** of pain management.

**TABLE 12-5**  Pharmacokinetics of morphine dosage forms

| Dosage form | Onset of action (min) | Peak effect (min) | Duration of action (hr) |
|---|---|---|---|
| Oral | | | |
|   Solution,* syrup,† tablets | 10-30 | 60-120 | 4-5 |
|   Extended release tablets‡ | — | — | 8-12 |
| IM | 10-30 | 30-60 | 4-5 |
| IV | | 20 | 4-5 |
| SC | 10-30 | 50-90 | 4-5 |
| Epidural§ | 15-60 | — | Up to 24 |
| Intrathecal§ | 15-60 | — | Up to 24 |
| Rectal‖ | 20-60 | — | 4-5 |

*Roxanol, M.O.S., and Morphitec (not commercially available in U.S.), MSIR.
†Morphite, and Morphitex-1, Morphitec-5 (not commercially available in U.S.).
‡M S Contin, Roxanol SR.
§Duramorph (preservative-free).
‖R.M.S. suppositories.

## morphine

***Mechanism of action.*** The active principles of opium are alkaloids, of which there are some 20 in number, although only three are used widely in the practice of medicine—morphine, codeine, and papaverine. Morphine and codeine act mainly on the CNS, where they produce a combination of depressing and stimulating effects. Both increase smooth muscle tone and promote contraction of smooth muscle; whereas papaverine has little effect on the nervous system but produces relaxation of certain smooth muscles in the body. As previously mentioned, morphine produces its potent analgesic effects by combining with receptor sites in the brain called opioid receptors. This interaction alters the client's pain perception and emotional response to the pain-provoking stimulus. Two receptors (mu and kappa) are involved with analgesia, and they are located in various areas of the CNS. Kappa receptors are mainly distributed in the cerebral cortex and spinal cord, whereas mu receptors are widely distributed in the CNS but are especially noted in the limbic system, thalamus, hypothalamus, and midbrain. Thus morphine's action on the limbic system reduces the unpleasant emotional response to pain that is typically evoked by a pain stimulus. Pain signals to the brain may be hindered or stopped by inhibitory impulses received at the dorsal horn neurons by descending neural-inhibiting responses. Therefore the perception of pain will also be reduced.

***Indications.*** The analgesic effect of morphine is indicated for the treatment of severe pain. Morphine may be administered by numerous routes, depending on the client's diagnosis, physical condition, and individual response. Generally, the oral step system is the preferred approach for terminally ill clients experiencing pain (see box, p. 214).

The drug is also used for diarrhea treatment. The gastrointestinal effects produced by morphine include a decrease in peristalsis and glandular secretions. Although this usually results in the side effect of constipation, this effect has been used therapeutically to treat diarrhea. Usually the less potent opioids such as codeine, paregoric, and opium tincture are used for this purpose. They are considered safer than morphine and are effective in the treatment of diarrhea.

Morphine is often used in the treatment of clients with lung cancer, pain aggravated by coughing, or an unproductive nagging cough. Small doses may cause depression of the cough center, and this secondary effect may be useful. However, in clients with a cough caused by a cold, less potent and potentially safer medications, such as codeine or the nonnarcotic antitussive, dextromethorphan, are usually preferred. Another indication for morphine therapy is the treatment of congestive heart failure and myocardial infarctions. In clients with congestive heart failure and pulmonary edema, morphine's peripheral vasodilation effect on veins and arteries can be very useful in aiding cardiac function and reducing the seepage of fluid into the lungs. Morphine is also used to treat clients with myocardial infarctions because (1) it does not produce significant changes in heart rate and blood pressure at the usual dosages ordered and (2) the calming effect it induces along with the peripheral vasodilation effect may result in a decreased work load on the heart rate that would be beneficial during an acute myocardial infarction.

***Pharmacokinetics.*** Morphine may be administered orally, intramuscularly, intravenously, subcutaneously, epidurally, intrathecally, and rectally. For onset, peak and duration of action, see Table 12-5. The drug is distributed widely in all body tissues, and metabolism is mainly in the liver. Excretion is primarily by the kidneys with between 7% and 10% excreted in the bile and feces.

***Side effects/adverse reactions.*** More frequently seen side effects include vertigo, faintness, lightheadedness,

**TABLE 12-6** Morphine analgesic dosage and administration

| Route | Adults | Children | Elderly |
|---|---|---|---|
| IV | 4-10 mg diluted in 4-5 ml sterile water administered slowly | 0.05-0.1 mg (50-100 μg)/kg body weight administered very slowly | Geriatric clients more suscepible to opioid drugs, especially respiratory depression effects; lower dosages than usually prescribed adult dose recommended |
| IM | 5-20 mg every 4 hr | | |
| SC | 5-20 mg every 4 hr | 0.1-0.2 mg (100-200 μg)/kg body weight every 4 hr; do not exceed 15 mg/dose | |
| Epidural (lumbar region) | 1-5 mg initially; assess in 1 hr; if inadequate for pain relief, 1-2 mg increments may be administered; 10 mg in 24 hr maximum | | |
| Intrathecal | 0.2-1 mg as single dose only; repeated dosage by this route not recommended | | |
| Oral (individualized) | Initially 10-30 mg every 4 hr for morphine sulfate syrup, oral solution, and tablets; may be increased according to pain severity, and client's response | Not established; must be individualized | |
| Preoperative | | 0.5-0.1 mg (50-100 μg)/kg body weight, IM; do not exceed 10 mg/dose | |
| Rectal suppositories | 20-30 mg rectally every 4-6 hr | Must be individualized | |

which occur most often in ambulatory clients. Fatigue, sleepiness, nausea and/or vomiting, increased sweating, constipation, and hypotension may also occur. Less frequently seen side effects include dry mouth, headache, anorexia, abdominal cramping, nervousness, increased anxiety, mental confusion, urinary retention or painful urination, visual disturbances, and nightmares.

Among the more serious adverse reactions reported are seizures (particularly with meperidine, propoxyphene), tinnitus, jaundice (hepatic toxicity), pruritus, skin rash or facial edema (allergic reaction), breathing difficulties, respiratory depression, excitability (paradoxic reaction seen mainly in children), confusion, and tachycardia.

***Significant drug interactions.*** When morphine is given with:

| Drug | Possible Effect and Management |
|---|---|
| alcohol or other CNS depressants | May result in enhanced CNS depression, respiratory depression, and hypotension. Reduce dosage of one or both drugs and monitor closely for decreased respiratory rate and blood pressure, slowed reflexes and drowsiness. |
| monamine oxidase (MAO) inhibitors | Test dose with $\frac{1}{4}$ of the dose of morphine (or any prescribed opioid analgesics) to ascertain compatibility of the medications. The possibility of inducing excitability, hypertension, or hypotension; increased sweating; convulsions; respiratory depression; fever; and cardiac dysfunctions exists. Therefore it is usually recommended that caution be |
| | taken and reduced dosages of opioids be prescribed for clients receiving MAO inhibitors. |
| naltrexone | Will produce withdrawal symptoms in clients dependent on opioid medications. Avoid concurrent administration in clients receiving opioids therapeutically. |

***Dosage and administration.*** See Table 12-6.
***Pregnancy safety.*** See the box on p. 217.

## Opioid Use in Children

Children are often untreated or inadequately treated for pain. The following are misconceptions that, unfortunately, persist in clinical areas today. Health care providers give numerous reasons for undertreatment including the following: infants lack the ability to communicate the site and intensity of pain, therefore they do not feel pain; children do not experience pain or interpret pain the way adults do; children will not remember pain; pain is a learned response; it is unsafe to give potent analgesics to young children because of the increased potential for inducing respiratory depression or addiction (Beyer and others, 1983; Burokas, 1985).

The pain for an injection is often believed to cause more pain for children than the underlying pain necessitating its administration. Young children are unable to make the connection between an immediate pain from the injection and the pain relief experienced later. Their reaction to the injection may interfere with nursing judgment, resulting in

## PREGNANCY SAFETY CLASSIFICATIONS

| Category | Drug |
|---|---|
| C | buprenorphine |
| | morphine |
| | codeine |
| | hydrocodone |
| | hydromorphone |
| | alphaprodine |
| | naltrexone |
| | pentazocine |
| B | nalaxone |
| Pregnancy safety not currently established by the FDA | meperidine |
| | methadone |
| | levorphanol |
| | oxycodone |
| | oxymorphone |
| | propoxyphene HCl |
| | butorphanol tartrate |
| | nalbuphine HCl |

## TIME REQUIRED TO PRODUCE MAXIMAL RESPIRATORY DEPRESSION EFFECTS WITH OPIOID ANALGESICS

| Approximate Times | Route of Administration |
|---|---|
| Within 7 minutes | IV |
| Within 30 minutes | IM |
| Within 90 minutes | SC |

nonmedication and unnecessary pain for the child.

The health care provider should consider medicating the pediatric client for pain in the same circumstances as the adult client would be given medication. In children under 2 years of age with observably increased irritability, anorexia, loss of interest in play, and in whom the assessment of whether the problem is "merely" irritability or pain is unclear, the decision to medicate appropriately is justified. Medicating in this instance should lead to a more comfortable, less anxiety-ridden child. In the child over 2, the health care provider should know how the child's age and stage of development will influence his or her ability to perceive and communicate the experience. The approach to the child should be individualized, using the child's words and gestures for communication. Figure drawings may be helpful for the child to point out "where it hurts." Other signs of discomfort, such as restlessness, decreased activity, anorexia, whining, and crying should be assessed. The child's parents are to be consulted regarding the child's pain status, since they are most familiar with the child.

As with adults, pain is best managed if the client is medicated early rather than when the pain becomes severe. To decrease the possibility of the child denying pain to avoid an injection, the nurse may administer analgesics by an alternative route. Children find suppositories, elixirs, and tablets crushed in applesauce more acceptable than injections. The nurse can assist the child in associating the medication with the relief from pain by indicating that it will make him or her "feel better." The nurse must check to see if the medication has been effective and remind the child that he or she probably "feels better" because of the medication.

Guidelines for administration of injections to the child are found in Chapter 8.

### Continuous Infusion of Opioids

Continuous infusion of opioids is used when traditional routes of administration are inappropriate or have failed to provide satisfactory pain relief, as with the client with intractable vomiting or severe local bruising following IM or SC injection, and/or the client with severe pain unrelieved by oral, rectal, or intermittent parenteral opioid dosing.

Before starting the infusion, the nurse should obtain a baseline blood pressure and respiratory rate and rhythm. All previous medication orders for pain are discontinued. The solution is administered using a microdrip infusion set and infusion control pump.

Figure 12-3, *A*, illustrates the CADD-PCA pump that may be programmed for continuous administration, client activated or clinician activated delivery. The pump also records all bolus attempts, successful and unsuccessful, made by the client. Thus the nurse and the physician are able to evaluate the appropriateness of the medication therapy and determine when the client is not receiving adequate medication. Because it is lightweight (about 15 ounces) and easily worn, ambulation by mobile clients is not impaired. Figure 12-3, *B,* is a portable wrist model of a PCA unit commonly used in a hospital setting, most often after surgery. This pump also allows the client to receive a predetermined IV bolus of an analgesic (usually morphine) by striking the syringe pump mechanism. Thus the client can control the administration of the analgesia. The physician orders the predetermined analgesic dose and a set lockout interval of 5 to 20 minutes. The pump then is calibrated to deliver the ordered dose whenever the client activates the button. The lockout mechanism prevents an inadvertent overdosage or excessive analgesic administration by the client. This pump can also record the number of times the button is struck and the total cumulative dose delivered.

The client's current pain treatment requirements and degree of pain control determine the initial infusion rate. Infusion rate adjustments thereafter are based on objective and subjective evidence of pain relief and side effects. The client

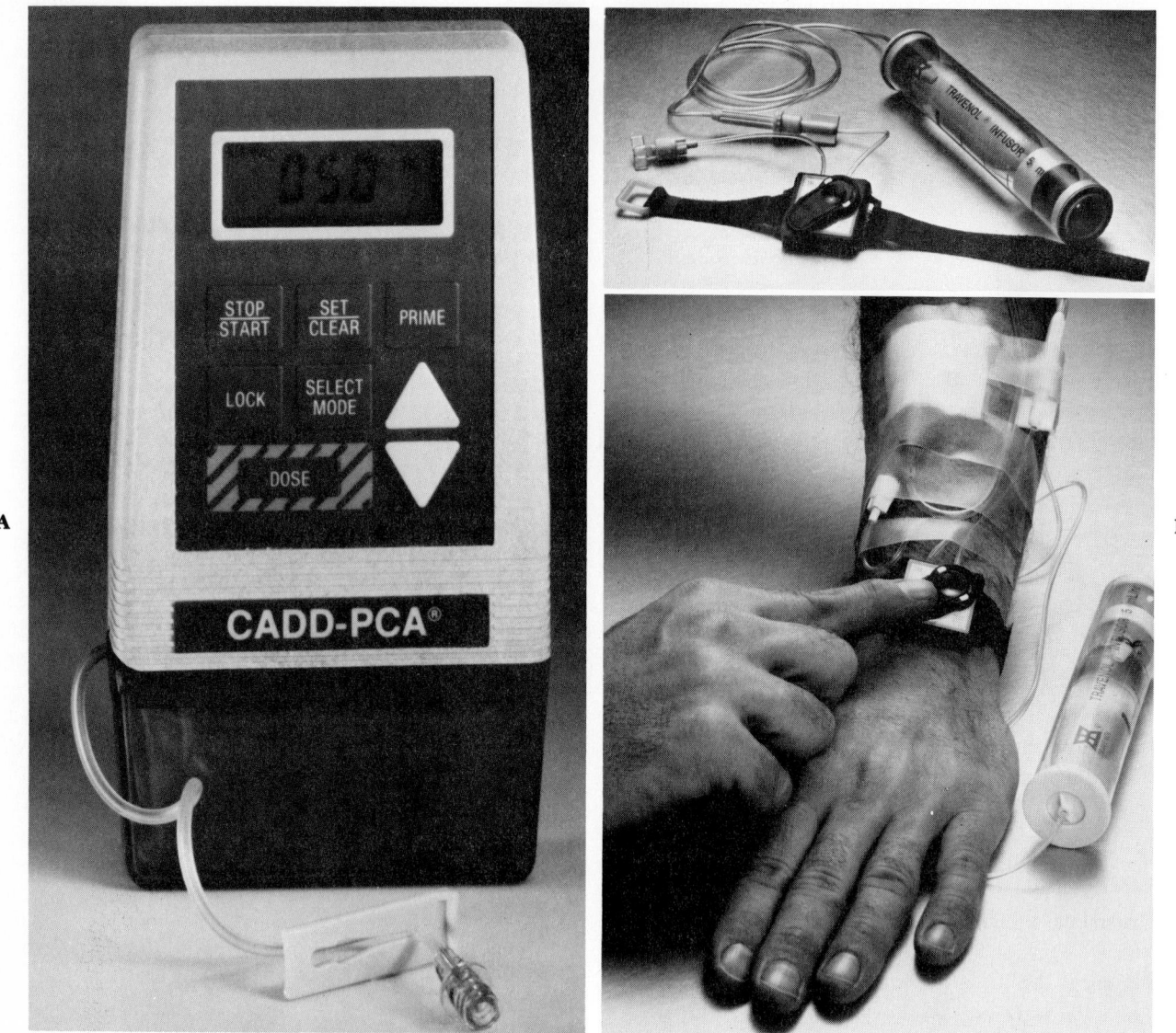

**FIGURE 12-3** Examples of continuous infusion pumps. **A,** Patient-controlled analgesia (PCA) pump (Model 5800 CADD-PCA) is designed for patient- or clinician-activated medication delivery. (Courtesy Pharmacia Deltec, Inc., St. Paul, Minn.) **B,** Portable wrist model. (Courtesy Baxter Healthcare Corporation, Deerfield, Ill.)

should be monitored for potential respiratory depression every hour for the first 4 hours and routinely thereafter. If the client's respiratory rate falls below the established limit, the nurse should reduce the rate of flow, notify the physician, and have naloxone ready to administer. Mechanical ventilation may be preferred to naloxone to relieve the respiratory depression, since naloxone will also diminish the client's pain relief.

The nurse should be aware of the potential side effects of the opioids, such as nausea, itching, sedation and respiratory depression. Duramorph, a morphine sulfate solution that is preservative free, is commonly prescribed for such units since it is used intravenously, epidurally, or intrathecally. Morphine's relatively poor lipid solubility delays the onset of analgesia when morphine is administered by epidural or intrathecal injection (see Table 12-5). The risk of inducing respiratory depression is reportedly greater by the intrathecal route than by epidural administration (PDR, 1990). The nurse should review the current package insert before using to be fully informed.

### Pregnancy, Labor, and Delivery

Teratogenic (tending to cause fetal malformation) defects have not been documented in humans with the use of morphine, codeine, hydrocodone, hydromorphone, or opium. However, animal studies report that very high doses of morphine, hydrocodone, and hydromorphone may produce teratogenic effects. Therefore the use of such potent analgesics during pregnancy should be carefully assessed (risk vs potential benefit) before use.

Opioid analgesics also cross the placenta, so that routine use of such drugs in the mother may lead to physical drug dependence in the fetus. After birth, severe withdrawal reactions may occur in the neonate. Pregnant women in methadone maintenance programs may demonstrate a fetal distress syndrome in utero and usually deliver an underweight baby at birth.

Since the opioid analgesics cross the placenta to enter fetal circulation, the potential for inducing respiratory depression in the fetus must be considered. If at all possible, such drugs should be avoided in the delivery of a premature infant because the respiratory depressant effect is enhanced. Because of its extended duration of action, methadone should not be used in obstetrics. Morphine, codeine, and, perhaps, other opioids reportedly prolong labor.

Several analgesics used when labor pain and contractions are regular include meperidine (intramuscularly or subcutaneously) 50 to 100 mg every 1 to 3 hours; or pentazocine lactate injection intramuscularly (30 mg) or intravenously (20 mg) on a 2- to 3-hour schedule when necessary for pain.

## Opioid Use in the Elderly

Analgesic dosing in the elderly usually requires dosage and dosing interval adjustments according to the client's therapeutic response and/or the development of undesirable side effects (confusion, excessive untoward CNS effects, respiratory depression). The height, weight, and body surface area are not accurate measures for dosing analgesics in the elderly.

Studies have reported that analgesia lasts longer in the geriatric client because of a decrease in drug clearance from the body (McCaffery, 1986). In the past, lower dosages of analgesics were often recommended for the aged, but this approach should generally not be the rule. Age is not a significant factor in determining analgesic dosage, but it is important in establishing the frequency of drug dosing. Liver or kidney impairment may reduce drug clearance, thus less frequent drug dosing may be necessary. Both dosage and drug frequency should be titrated to the individual's response to the analgesic medication. The presence of unwanted adverse effects would influence drug dosage and drug frequency.

The intramuscular and subcutaneous routes of analgesic administration may also be influenced by the aging process. The elderly may have a diminished circulatory process, which would result in slower absorption of drugs administered by these routes. Administering additional dosages in such a situation may result in unpredictable or increased drug absorption, which increases the potential for adverse side effects.

The elderly client may be less likely to ask for pain medication because of an acceptance of pain as a part of old age, not wanting to be a "bother," or denying discomfort as a cultural and ethnic issue. Nonverbal communication, such as irritability, anorexia, decreased activity, or gripping an object, should be carefully assessed. The decreased activity resulting from pain increases the risk of complications of immobility, especially in the elderly client. The stress of the pain experience leads to fatigue and anxiety, reducing the elderly client's diminished physical and psychologic resources. Because the elderly client may be taking many drugs concurrently, health care providers should be aware of specific drug interactions with analgesic therapy. Careful nursing care should be used in working with the elderly client experiencing pain.

## Adjuvant Medications

Adjuvant medications are commonly added to opioid analgesics to enhance pain control or relief in specific conditions. The nonsteroidal antiinflammatory analgesics (NSAIAs) have been found to be effective for the treatment of bone pain. Cancer metastasis to the bone results in increased production of prostaglandins, which in turn causes osteolysis and a lowered peripheral pain threshold. The NSAIAs include aspirin, diflunisal, ibuprofen, indomethacin, fenoprofen calcium, naproxen, piroxicam, and sulindac. They have antiinflammatory and analgesic properties that are associated with inhibition of prostaglandin synthesis. Such agents are also indicated for the treatment of pain and inflammation caused by rheumatoid arthritis, osteoarthritis, and various other acute and chronic musculoskeletal and soft tissue inflammations (see Chapter 61).

**Psychotropic** (drugs affecting mood) agents and corticosteroids have also been prescribed with systemic analgesics. Although selected phenothiazines are useful in treating nausea and vomiting induced by opioid analgesics, the routine use of antidepressants in clients with chronic intractable pain to potentiate analgesia is a debatable issue. Twycross and Lack (1984) have advocated the use of coanalgesia in clients exhibiting inadequate pain relief from opioids following large increases in dosage. Coanalgesia may include corticosteroids, NSAIAs, antianxiety and antidepressant medications, or nondrug measures such as nerve blocks or radiation therapy. Treating persistent pain with an antidepressant adjuvant medication is not uniformly accepted, but it is often used in practice. Low doses of doxepin, amitriptyline, or imipramine have been found effective in treating a variety of chronic pain syndromes both in the United States and in England (Black, 1989; Baines, 1987). Corticosteroids are beneficial in cancer pain that originates in a fairly restricted area, such as intracranially; alongside a nerve root; or in pelvic, neck, or hepatic areas. Dexamethasone is prescribed for an increase in intracranial pressure and for relief of pain caused by pressure on a nerve. Corticosteroids may also relieve pain by inhibiting the release of prostaglandins and thus improving the inflammatory process. Hypercalcemia tends to reduce the pain threshold, whereas this effect may be reversed by the increased ex-

Selected nursing diagnoses relating to opioid therapy

| Nursing diagnosis | Outcome criteria | Nursing interventions |
| --- | --- | --- |
| Ineffective airway clearance related to cough reflex suppression | Evidence of good pulmonary ventilation | Reposition the immobile client frequently. Teach turning, coughing, and deep breathing. |
| Ineffective breathing pattern: hypoventilation related to CNS depressant effects of drug | Respiratory rate 16-20/minute Absence of cyanosis | Assess respiratory rate before administering each dose; if below 12/minute, hold dose. Administer oxygen. Elevate head of bed. Have narcotic antagonist and respiratory support systems nearby during IV administration. |
| Altered comfort related to nausea and/or vomiting | Absence of and/or decrease in nausea and/or vomiting | Administer prescribed antiemetics. Administer oral analgesics with food. Reduce noxious environmental stimuli. Apply cool cloth to the face. Provide small, frequent meals. |
| Alteration in bowel elimination: constipation | Evidence of client's normal bowel patterns | Assess client's bowel status. Increase fluid consumption. Instruct in high-fiber diet. Encourage ambulation. Obtain an order for a stool softener and/or a bulk-forming laxative. Provide relaxed environment for elimination. |
| Alteration in patterns of urinary elimination related to urinary retention | Evidence of urinary status without urgency and/or retention | Increase fluid intake to about 2500 ml daily, unless contraindicated. Administer sitz bath. Provide relaxed environment for elimination. Suggest a dose reduction or switch to alternative therapy. |
| Injury related to sensory/perceptual alterations | Absence of injury | Assist to ambulate. Safeguard with side rails. Caution against driving and other hazardous activities. Caution against taking alcohol and other CNS depressants concurrently. |

cretion of calcium induced by corticosteroids. Additional steroid effects of appetite stimulation and elevation of mood have also been useful in selected cases.

## Treatment of Opioid Overdose

Naloxone hydrochloride (Narcan) should be available on every nursing unit where opioid medications are used. Naloxone is an opioid antagonist; that is, it can reverse opioid-induced respiratory depression and sedation by displacing the opioids at the receptor site. In opioid-dependent individuals, it can also induce acute drug withdrawal. The intravenous route of administration is the preferred method of administering naloxone. Its effects are seen within 2 minutes. It can also be given intramuscularly or subcutaneously but the onset of action is then seen within 2 to 5 minutes. Naloxone is shorter acting than most opioids; therefore, to prevent the recurrence of respiratory depression, it must be administered by a continuous infusion or by repeated injections (intramuscularly or subcutaneously). See drug monograph for additional information about naloxone.

## ▷ Nursing Management: Opioid Therapy

***Assessment.*** A thorough assessment of the client's pain as to location, severity, quality, and intensity needs to be accomplished to establish a baseline for management of the client's condition. It is necessary to individualize the drug dose and its frequency based on the potency and duration

of action of the specific drug used, severity of pain, using a pain scale, condition of the client, other medications that the client is receiving concurrently, and the client's response to the analgesic regimen. The nurse should observe the client's response to the analgesic and record the degree and duration of pain relief and any adverse effects that may occur.

Vital signs should be taken and recorded before morphine sulfate is given. Morphine can cause respiratory depression; if the client's respiratory rate is less than 12/min, the dose may need to be withheld or decreased. The nurse's assessment is important information required by the physician to determine the possibility of adverse drug effects on the client. Other signs of opioid overdose are cold and clammy skin, drowsiness, dizziness, restlessness and mental confusion, pinpoint pupils, and decreasing pulse rate and blood pressure. Oral and injectable opioid analgesics produce unacceptable or undesirable effects such as nausea and vomiting, constipation, urinary retention, cough reflex suppression, and CNS effects. In many instances, these effects may be overcome by appropriate nursing care (see nursing diagnosis table above).

Tolerance is another undesirable effect of narcotic analgesics. An increase in analgesic dosage may be needed to provide for the same degree of analgesic effectiveness. Lack of reliable data has led to many misconceptions about tolerance. Tolerance, for example, does not always occur. It is sporadic and unpredictable. One client may take the same dosage of the same opioid for years and never need an increase, whereas other clients with similar pain problems may require periodic increases. In the majority of clients with genuine pain who are receiving opioids in therapeutic doses, the dependence liability is relatively uncommon; and most do not report euphoria or psychologic dependence. Tolerance in clients needing pain relief (not tolerance in clients who take drugs for pleasure) is managed by gradually decreasing the dose when analgesic effect is achieved. Once pain is controlled (e.g., removal of a tumor that is causing the pain), a lower dose will maintain analgesic effects. The need for an increase in the analgesic dosage will usually be a result of the disease process or progression. The nurse should assess for pupillary constriction. As the drug is eliminated from the body, the pupils return to normal. Continued constriction of the pupils with early return of the symptoms for which the medication was administered may indicate a developing tolerance because the drug has not yet been eliminated from the body but has diminished effectiveness. Abstinence syndrome may occur after prolonged use of opioid analgesics. Gradually decreasing the dosage of the medication as the severity of the pain decreases may diminish the development of withdrawal symptoms.

**Intervention.** Preventive pain treatment with analgesics involves the frequent administration of analgesics on a regular fixed-time interval in anticipation of pain. Analgesics are to be given before the client's anticipation of the recurrence of pain or before it reaches an intensity that makes the client feel a loss of control. The client should actively participate in the pain treatment process with trust and confidence and be able to assist in planning a schedule of pain medication based on life-style. This fixed-schedule method of administration decreases suffering until the next scheduled dose because a blood level of the analgesic has been reached that controls the client's pain. If an order for the fixed-time schedule is unavailable, it is the nurse's responsibility to teach the client to request medication before the pain becomes severe. Oftentimes clients are unaware that they need to ask for pain medication, since none of their other medications may be on a demand schedule.

The nurse should encourage client and family willingness and belief to participate in the reinforcement of the pain-treatment process. Combinations of optimal doses of NSAIAs and narcotic agonists indicated for pain may permit lower doses of the opioid agonist. A stepped-care approach (see boxed material earlier in chapter) is the optimal plan to follow because it uses nonopioid analgesics progressing to other stronger analgesics to manage the client's pain with the most effective dosage.

After administering the medication, the nurse should provide comfort measures to allow the best effect: reduction of environmental stimuli, placing the client on bedrest, and back massage. Nonpharmacologic measures for pain such as these and others (relaxation techiques and cutaneous stimulation) may be used concurrently, as well as considered as substitutes for pharmacologic interventions with some clients.

---

### INTRASPINAL ANALGESIC INFUSION

An experimental type of analgesic therapy—continuous intraspinal morphine infusion—reduces the client's pain without diminishing CNS functioning. An implantable infusion device is connected to an implantable catheter placed in the epidural or intrathecal space. The system, which is refilled by injection through a septum into a central chamber of the device, administers the medication continuously. The client and family are taught how to care for the device and how to evaluate the response to the therapy. The device is usually refilled every 2 weeks by a home health care provider. Study is continuing with this unique method of pain control, which promises relief for clients with intractable pain while increasing the quality of life. See chapter 5 for additional information on intrathecal administration of drugs.

---

Injection sites should be rotated to prevent induration and abscess. If analgesic medication is required for more than 2 weeks, oral, intravenous, or other routes of administration should be considered. For prolonged pain relief, epidural or intrathecal administration may be considered (see box above for additional information). When a narcotic is administered intravenously, naloxone must be on hand because the risk of respiratory distress is markedly increased with this route of administration. Repeated intramuscular or subcutaneous administration of opioids to clients in shock, who may have impaired perfusion, may cause an overdose when the client's circulation is restored.

Morphine sulfate intensified oral solution (Roxanol, 20 mg/ml) comes with a specific calibrated dropper; no other dropper should be used for the medication, which is diluted in 30 ml or more of fluid or semisolid food. The nurse or client should make sure the entire dose is removed from the dropper.

When the physician is changing the client's medication from one route of administration to another, the nurse should check the dosage against the "Analgesic Equivalency Chart."

**Education.** Since orthostatic hypotension (a form of low blood pressure that occurs when a person stands) can occur in ambulatory clients, caution the client about rising quickly from a supine position. Opioids can impair the client's mental and/or physical abilities, so caution should be exercised when the drug is prescribed for ambulatory clients or for anyone who will be driving a car or operating any type of machinery. Clients should be instructed to call for assistance if they wish to smoke or to ambulate.

Roxanol is the most convenient method for receiving oral morphine but requires careful instruction of the client. Because it is a controlled substance, the client should be instructed to prevent theft by drug-dependent individuals.

**TABLE 12-7**   Dosage and administration for opium preparations

| | Adults | Children |
|---|---|---|
| opium tincture | 0.3-1 ml (usually 0.6 ml) four times daily orally; maximum 6 ml in 24 hr | Not established |
| camphorated tincture of opium (paregoric) | 5-10 ml orally one to four times a day; maximum 10 ml four times daily | 0.25-0.5 ml/kg body weight one to four times a day orally |
| opium alkaloid hydrochloride injection (Pantopon) | 5-20 mg every 4 or 5 hr when needed IM or SC | Not established |
| B & O Supprettes | One suppository rectally once or twice a day or as ordered by physician | Not established |

The dose may be altered by a physician if a client is receiving other opioid analgesics, CNS depressants, cyclic antidepressants, neuroleptics, anxiolytics, ethanol, or sedative-hypnotics. Since the combination of any of these can produce CNS depression, the client needs to be reminded that the combination of ethanol and their normal dosage of hydromorphone can render them incapable of normal functioning.

**Evaluation.** Because opioid analgesics are frequently used inappropriately, the nurse should be aware and report any instances of suspected abuse. Since some health professionals are not well versed in pain control, nurses should take the initiative in reversing the undertreatment of clients in pain. Educating others within the clinical setting is important to promote comfort for the client.

### opium preparations

Opium contains several alkaloids that include morphine and small amounts of codeine and papaverine. The effects of opium result from the presence of morphine in the preparations. The mechanism of action and pharmacokinetics are the same as or similar to morphine.

Opium tincture contains 10 mg morphine/ml and is used as an antidiarrheal agent and, when diluted, for the treatment of neonatal opioid dependence.

Camphorated tincture of opium (paregoric) contains 2 mg morphine/5ml. It is an antidiarrheal agent (an agent inhibiting diarrhea). In some instances, it has been used to treat neonatal opioid dependence, but the latter use is controversial. Paregoric contains camphor, which can cause serious toxicity including seizures and respiratory depression, and benzoic acid, which can displace bilirubin from albumin. Both substances may enhance the typical problems seen in such infants (such as convulsions and hyperbilirubinemia); therefore, many physicians seem to prefer the use of diluted opium tincture to paregoric.

Opium alkaloid hydrochloride injection (Pantopon) contains 10 mg morphine/ml. It is used as an analgesic for the relief of severe pain.

Opium and belladonna suppositories, No. 15A (B & O Supprettes) contain 30 mg powdered opium (10% morphine

and other alkaloids) and 16.2 mg powdered belladonna alkaloid (the principle alkaloids of belladonna are atropine and scopolamine). No. 16A contains 60 mg powdered opium and 16.2 mg belladonna extract. The preparations are used to relieve moderate to severe pain reported with ureteral spasms and have also been prescribed for breakthrough pain between injections of opioids. For side effects/adverse reactions see Table 12-6 (page 216). For significant drug interactions see morphine. Dosage and administration are discussed in Table 12-7.

### ▷ Nursing Management: Opium Preparation Therapy

Opium tincture may be diluted with water for administration; the solution will become milky. Other liquid forms of opioids may be given with fruit juice to increase their palatability. If rectal suppositories are being used to administer opioids, the rectum should be emptied first to enhance absorption of the drug.

### codeine (methylmorphine)

Codeine is available in sulfate and phosphate salts and marketed as oral tablets, oral solution, and injectable dosage forms. Codeine is absorbed well after either oral or parenteral administration and is excreted by means of the kidney, mainly as norcodeine and free and conjugated morphine. Oral administration is used for analgesic, antitussive (cough suppressant) and antidiarrheal effects. Codeine may also be injected for treatment of mild to moderate pain. See Table 12-8 for dosage forms and adult and pediatric dosages. Table 12-9 is a pharmacokinetic overview of selected opioid dosage forms.

### ▷ Nursing Management: Codeine Therapy

Oral codeine should be administered with milk or food to reduce any gastrointestinal distress. Codeine has been added to cough elixirs because it acts as a cough suppressant. The nurse should encourage fluid hydration, which will help to liquify sputum.

**TABLE 12-8**   Dosage and administration for selected opioid preparations

| Drug/preparation | Adults* | Children* |
|---|---|---|
| **Codeine tablets/solution** | | |
| Analgesic | 15-60 mg (most commonly 30 mg) orally every 3-6 hr as needed | Not recommended for premature infants; not established for newborns; infants and children, 0.5 mg/kg body weight or 15 mg/m² body surface orally every 4-6 hr as needed |
| Antidiarrheal | 30 mg orally one to four times a day | 0.5 mg/kg body weight up to four times a day |
| Antitussive | 10-20 mg orally every 4-6 hr; maximum 120 mg in 24 hr | Not established for children less than 2 yr old; 2-6 yr, 3-4.5 mg orally every 4-6 hr; 6-12 yr, 5-10 mg orally every 4-6 hr, maximum 60 mg/day |
| **Codeine injection** | 15-60 mg (most commonly 30 mg) IM, IV, or SC every 4-6 hr as needed | Not recommended for premature infants; not established for newborns; infants and children, 0.5 mg/kg body weight or 15 mg/m² body surface IM or SC every 4-6 hr as needed |
| **Hydrocodone bitartrate** | | |
| Antitussive | 5 mg tablet orally every 4-6 hr as needed | 0.15 mg/kg body weight orally every 6 hr as needed |
| Analgesic | 5-10 mg tablet orally every 4-6 hr as needed | |
| **Hydromorphone hydrochloride** | | |
| Analgesic tablets | 2 mg tablet orally every 3-6 hr as needed; may increase to 4 mg or more if necessary every 4-6 hr | Individualize according to age, size, and individual's response |
| Suppositories | 3 mg rectally every 4-8 hr as needed for pain | Not established |
| Injectable | 1-2 mg every 3-6 hr IM or SC; increase to 3 or 4 mg every 6 hr if necessary to control pain; 0.5-1 mg every 3 hr IV | Individualize according to age, size, and individual's response |
| **Meperidine*** | | |
| Analgesic | 50-150 mg every 3-4 hr as needed IM or SC; 15-35 mg hourly by IV infusion as needed using an infusion pump; dosage should be individualized | 1.1-1.76 mg/kg body weight IM or SC; do not exceed 100 mg every 3-4 hr as needed |
| Preoperatively | 50-100 mg IM or SC 30-90 min before anesthesia | 1-2.2 mg/kg body weight IM or SC; do not exceed 100 mg 30-90 min before anesthesia |
| Obstetric analgesia | 50-100 mg IM or SC when regular contractions are occurring; may be repeated every 1-3 hr as needed | |
| Intravenous infusion | Dilute to 1 mg/ml and titrate according to client's needs, anesthesia used, and type and length of operation | |
| **Methadone** | | |
| Analgesic | | |
| Oral solution | 5-20 mg every 4-8 hr; adjust dosage or dosing interval according to client's response | Individualize according to client's age, size, and response to medication |
| Oral tablet | 2.5-10 mg every 3-4 hr initially. In chronic dosing, adjust dosage and interval according to client's response | |
| Treatment of opioid abstinence syndrome | | |
| Detoxification | 15-40 mg orally or as solution (10 mg/ml) once daily or as necessary to control documented withdrawal symptoms. Reduce dosage at 1-2 day intervals based on client's response. Parenteral dosage form only indicated if client is unable to take oral medication | |
| Maintenance | Individualize according to client's response | |

*IM preferred route of administration for both adults and children.

**TABLE 12-9**   Pharmacokinetic overview of selected opioid dosage forms

| Drug/dosage form | Onset of action (min) | Peak effect (min) | Duration of action (hr) |
|---|---|---|---|
| codeine | | | |
| Oral | 30-45 | 60-120 | 4 |
| IM | 10-30 | 30-60 | 4 |
| SC | 10-30 | | 4 |
| hydrocodone bitartrate | | | |
| Oral | 10-30 | 30-60 | 4-6 |
| hydromorphone hydrochloride | | | |
| Oral | 30 | 90-120 | 4 |
| IM | 15 | 30-60 | 4 |
| IV | 10-15 | 15-30 | 2-3 |
| SC | 15 | 30-90 | 4 |
| Rectal | Not available | Not available | 6-8 |
| meperidine | | | |
| Oral | 15 | 60-90 | 2-4 (usually 3) |
| IM | 10-15 | 30-50 | 2-4 (usually 3) |
| IV | 1 | 5-7 | 2-4 (usually 3) |
| SC | 10-15 | 30-50 | 2-4 (usually 3) |
| methadone | | | |
| Oral | 30-60 | 90-120 | 4-6* |
| IM | 10-20 | 60-120 | 4-5* |
| IV | | 15-30 | 3-4 |
| levorphanol | | | |
| Oral | 10-60 | 90-120 | 4-5 |
| IM | Not available | 60 | 4-5 |
| IV | Not available | Within 20 | 4-5 |
| SC | Not available | 60-90 | 4-5 |
| oxycodone | | | |
| Oral | Not available | 60 | 3-4 |
| oxymorphone | | | |
| IM | 10-15 | 30-90 | 3-6 |
| IV | 5-10 | 15-30 | 3-4 |
| SC | 10-20 | Not available | 3-6 |
| Rectal | 15-30 | 2 | 3-6 |
| propoxyphene | | | |
| Oral | 15-60 | 120 | 4-6 |

*With active metabolites and continuous dosing, half-life and duration of action may increase to 22 to 48 hours.

## hydrocodone bitartrate (Dicodid, Vicodin, Hycodan, Robidone✦)

In the U.S. Hycodan is marketed as a combination including homatropine; in Canada Hycodan is hydrocodone bitartrate only. Although the product name is similar in both countries, the formulation is not identical. Hydrocodone bitartrate is used as an analgesic and antitussive. See Table 12-8 for dosage and administration.

## hydromorphone hydrochloride (Dilaudid, Dilaudid HP)

Hydromorphone is a semisynthetic opioid, used for its analgesic and antitussive effects, that has a faster onset of action but a shorter duration of action than morphine. See Table 12-8 for dosages.

## ▷ Nursing Management: Hydromorphone Therapy

Hydromorphone can produce a dose-related respiratory depression if the dosage exceeds what is normal for the client; signs of respiratory depression for which the nurse should observe are restlessness, disorientation, drowsiness, and tachycardia. This may not be a drug of choice for clients with chronic obstructive pulmonary disease because they have decreased respiratory rate and poor respiratory drive. In addition to its respiratory depressive capabilities, hydromorphone can exaggerate an already increased intracranial pressure. This drug may not be one of choice for clients with head injuries or increased intracranial pressure.

---

### ANALGESIC EQUIVALENCY CHART

All analgesics are compared to 10 mg (IM) morphine to determine an analgesic dosage equivalent. Such information is very useful for health care professionals assessing potency and considering drug alternatives.

| Analgesic | IM Dose (mg) | Oral Dose (mg) |
|---|---|---|
| morphine | 10 | 20–60* |
| hydromorphone | 1.5 | 7.5 |
| oxycodone | not available | 30 |
| levorphanol | 2 | 4 |
| methadone | 10 | 20 |
| meperidine | 75 | 300 |

**Suppository Dosage Form**

Hydromorphone, 3 mg, is approximately equivalent to 7.5 mg oral dosage and 1.5 mg IM dosage.

Morphine, 10-30 mg, is considered equivalent to the oral dosage. Individualize dosage according to client response.

Oxymorphone, 5-10 mg, is approximately equivalent to 1 mg of IM oxymorphone.

*For single dose or intermittent use. Chronic administration may decrease oral dose to 20 or 30 mg equivalent.

### meperidine (Demerol, Pethidine hydrochloride ✲)

Meperidine is one of the most commonly prescribed opioids in a hospital setting (McCaffery, 1986). Its pharmacologic profile is similar to morphine with several noted differences.

1. It is believed to interact more strongly with kappa receptors than morphine (Gilman and others, 1990).
2. Its duration of action is shorter than morphine. See Table 12-9 for onset, peak, and duration of effect.
3. Most equivalency charts (see Analgesic Equivalency Chart above) note oral meperidine as a 300 mg dosage equivalent to 10 mg intramuscular morphine. The manufacturers for meperidine market the oral preparation in 50 and 100 mg tablets. Therefore oral dosages of meperidine frequently prescribed are considered to be much less effective than the injectable form.
4. A major metabolite of meperidine produced in the liver is normeperidine. Normeperidine is further metabolized (partially) to the conjugated form and then excreted from the body. Prolonged administration and/or increasing the daily dosages of meperidine has produced significant mood changes (sadness, anger, restlessness, apprehension) and stimulation of the CNS (McCaffery, 1986; Gorman and Warfield, 1986). Increased serum levels of normeperidine are responsible

for the excitatory effects (i.e., quivering, tremors, and multifocal myoclonus [grand mal] seizures).

Although the use of meperidine for only a few days may generally result in mild and tolerable problems, meperidine should probably be avoided in clients requiring prolonged usage or high-dose continuous therapy and when renal or liver dysfunction is present. The nurse should be aware that naloxone (opioid antagonist) will antagonize meperidine but not normeperidine and may in some instances cause further CNS excitation and seizures. Management for normeperidine toxicity includes stopping the meperidine and substituting an alternate opioid, such as morphine. If seizures occur, an anticonvulsant (diazepam or others) may be used. Meperidine produces a vagolytic effect on the heart; therefore its use should probably be avoided or closely monitored in clients with dysrhythmias and/or myocardial infarction. In addition to drug interactions common to opioids, meperidine is contraindicated for clients receiving MAO-inhibiting agents currently or within the previous 2 weeks. Very severe, unpredictable reactions (severe respiratory depression, hypotension, hypertension, seizures, increased excitablity, hyperpyrexia or exceptionally high fever) and at times, death have resulted. This is a serious and avoidable drug interaction. For information on dosage and administration see Table 12-8. For pregnancy safety, see Table 12-8.

▷ **Nursing Management: Meperidine Therapy**

***Assessment.*** Vital signs should be monitored and recorded before and after administration of meperidine. It can cause tachycardia and hypotension.

Meperidine is contraindicated in severe dysfunction of the liver (since the drug is inactivated in the liver), in certain conditions involving the gallbladder and the bile ducts (since meperidine causes contraction of these structures), and in clients with head injury, increased intracranial pressure, increased CSF, respiratory depression, or shock. Respiratory depression occurs as with morphine but is of shorter duration. Meperidine causes CNS excitation ranging from irritability to seizures. When administered with a phenothiazine such as promethazine, which also lowers the seizure threshold, the client is at higher risk for seizures. Meperidine should be used with caution in clients who have atrial flutter and other supraventricular tachycardias, since meperidine may increase ventricular response through vagolytic action. Meperidine is not administered for chronic pain, because of its short duration of action. It may be given orally but is more effective intramuscularly.

Meperidine is contraindicated in clients receiving MAO inhibitor therapy or in those who have received it during the previous 14 days, since concurrent administration may produce coma, severe respiratory depression, and hypotension. In addition, meperidine potentiates CNS depressants.

Tissue irritation is common with the administration of intramuscular meperidine. Clients frequently experience muscle damage, poor absorption, and pain during injection. Common side effects with meperidine are dizziness, drowsiness, nausea and vomiting, constipation, increased sweating, and hypotension.

*Intervention.* Before mixing meperidine in solution with another medication, consult a specific reference, because it tends to be physically and chemically incompatible with a wide range of substances.

Meperidine is diluted for IV administration; however, it is not the recommended route of administration. It needs to be titrated for the client's response because of its respiratory depressant effects.

Meperidine dosage should be gradually tapered because abstinence symptoms, such as nausea, vomiting, and diarrhea, can occur. Such symptoms should be reported to the physician so that the dosage may be adjusted.

*Education.* The nurse should caution the client about rising too quickly because of the drug's hypotensive effects.

### methadone (Dolophine, Methadose)

Methadone was discovered by German chemists during World War II. It is an effective analgesic with properties similar to morphine with the exception of its extended half-life. The duration of action for methadone is usually listed at 4 to 6 hours, but with repeated oral dosing, the half-life may extend from 22 to 48 hours (perhaps even longer in the elderly and clients with renal dysfunction, etc.) This extended half-life is not related to its analgesic effect. To control pain methadone is administered every 3 to 4 hours or, with repeated dosing and dosing adjustments based on the individual's response, every 6 to 8 hours. See Table 12-8 for dosages. Because of its extended half-life, methadone is approved by the FDA for use in detoxification and maintenance treatment programs. Methadone dependence is substituted in individuals who are physiologically dependent on heroin, opium, or other opioids. See Chapter 9 for methadone treatment program. Mechanism of action is similar to that of morphine. It is indicated as an analgesic or for treatment of opioid abstinence syndrome. Pharmacokinetics are similar to morphine (see Table 12-9). Side effects/adverse reactions are also similar to those for morphine; the miotic and respiratory depressant effects may be present more than 24 hours. Excessive sedation is also reported in some clients following a regular dosing schedule. See morphine section for significant drug interactions and Table 12-8 for dosage and administration.

### ▷ Nursing Management: Methadone Therapy

*Assessment.* When the client is receiving methadone for treatment of heroin abuse, the nurse should be aware of possible outside sources of OTC drugs and alcohol, (such as liquid cough preparations with alcohol or alcohol beverages brought in by friends and family) which may potentiate the action of methadone. Although most adverse effects dissipate in the initial 3 weeks of therapy, constipation and diaphoresis may persist.

*Intervention.* Overdosage of this drug can cause extreme respiratory depression. Naloxone should be readily available for intravenous administration. The antagonist action is only 1 to 3 hours, and the action of methadone is 36 to 48 hours or more; thus repeated doses of nalozone for up to 8 to 24 hours may be required to treat respiratory depression.

When methadone is used for detoxification and maintenance therapy, it is administered as an oral liquid. If dispersable tablets are used, they are dissolved in 120 ml of water or citrus-flavored solution, such as Tang, Kool-Aid, or fruit juice. Dissolution takes a minute or so and may be enhanced by using cold and/or acidic solvents. If the concentrated oral solution is used, it should be diluted in at least 90 ml of solution to enable the complete dosage to be received. It has been used for the terminally ill, and each hospital may have a different formula for the "pain cocktails," which may contain different quantities and different ingredients, such as hydromorphone, cocaine, morphine, or methadone and hydroxyzine.

*Education.* Since methadone is commonly given on an outpatient basis for withdrawal from heroin or morphine-like drugs, the client should be cautioned about operating a car or other potentially dangerous equipment because mental and physical abilities may be impaired. Orthostatic hypotension is a common side effect, which can last for several weeks. Clients should be instructed to rise slowly from a recumbent position and to sit or lie down in the event of dizziness or faintness.

### levorphanol (Levo-Dromoran)

Levorphanol is an opioid analgesic used for moderate-to-severe pain, such as visceral pain associated with terminal cancer, renal and biliary colic, myocardial infarction, and trauma. It is also used as a preanesthetic narcotic as well as for the relief of postoperative pain. Adult dosages are 2 to 3 mg orally or subcutaneously, every 6 to 8 hours for analgesia. Dosage and time interval should be individualized according to severity of pain and the client's response to the medication. Levorphanol has also been given intravenously, as an adjunct to anesthesia, but optimal adult dosages are not established. Pediatric doses are individualized by physician according to the client's age, weight, and therapeutic response to the medication. For pregnancy safety see Table 12-8.

### ▷ Nursing Management: Levorphanol Therapy

The actions of levorphanol are identical to morphine, but the effective dose is one fourth that of morphine. Levorphanol should not be confused with levallorphan tartrate (Lorfan), which is used as a narcotic antagonist and sometimes as an antidote for levorphanol. If levallorphan is mistakenly given to a person who is chemically dependent on narcotics, it can cause an **abstinence syndrome** (a collection of symptoms that occur on withdrawal from a drug on which one is physically dependent). Although levallorphan tartrate has been discontinued by the U.S. manufacturer, it may continue to be available until existing supplies are depleted.

### oxycodone hydrochloride (Percodan, Tylox, Percocet, Supeudol ✱)

Oxycodone HC1 is approximately 10 times more potent than codeine and nearly equivalent in potency to morphine. It is available alone and in combination preparations, that is, with aspirin (Percodan) or acetaminophen (Tylox, Percocet). Adult doses are 5 mg orally 3 to 6 hours or, if combined with acetaminophen, every 4 to 6 hours as necessary for pain. Increase if required according to pain severity and the individual's response to medication. (Suppositories are not currently available in the United States, but they are available in Canada. Adult dosage is 10 to 40 mg rectally, three to four times daily.) Pediatric doses are individualized according to age and size.

### oxymorphone hydrochloride (Numorphan)

Oxymorphone is pharmacologically similar to morphine with the following exceptions. In equivanalgesic dosages, oxymorphone usually causes more nausea, vomiting, and psychic effects (euphoria) than morphine. It may also be less constipating and causes less suppression of the cough reflex than morphine. Oxymorphone is a potent analgesic used for: moderate-to-severe pain; preoperative medication; obstetric analgesia; or as adjunct therapy for the treatment of anxiety caused by dyspnea resulting from pulmonary edema associated with left ventricular failure. Adult doses are 1 to 1.5 mg IM or SC every 3 to 6 hours as needed for pain. IV dose is 0.5 mg. Dosages may be adjusted according to pain severity and client's response to the medication. Rectally: 5 mg every 4 to 6 hours as needed. Pediatric dosage has not been established.

### ▷ Nursing Management: Oxymorphone Therapy

Oxymorphone should be given with milk or meals to decrease the incidence of gastrointestinal distress. It tends to cause more nausea and vomiting than **equivanalgesic** (equal pain killing) doses of morphine sulfate.

### propoxyphene hydrochloride (Darvon, Novopropoxyn ✱) propoxyphene napsylate combinations (Darvocet-N)

Propoxyphene hydrochloride is a synthetic analgesic that is structurally related to methadone. Although indicated for the treatment of mild to perhaps moderate pain, it is generally considered to be a mild analgesic. Controlled studies

have reported that propoxyphene HC1, 65 mg, is equivalent or less effective than acetaminophen, 650 mg; aspirin, 650 mg; or codeine, 65 mg. When combined with aspirin or acetaminophen, propoxyphene combinations are generally as effective as codeine and aspirin. Propoxyphene binds to opioid receptors and produces an analgesic effect similar to codeine and the opioids. The hydrochloride dosage form is more rapidly absorbed than the water-insoluble napsylate formulation, although peak serum levels are approximately equivalent. The bioavailability of propoxyphene hydrochloride, 65 mg, is equivalent to that of propoxyphene napsylate, 100 mg. The half-life of propoxyphene is 6 to 12 hours. Propoxyphene crosses into the CNS and is believed to cross the placenta. (For pharmacokinetic overview, see Table 12-9.) Metabolism occurs mainly in the liver where approximately one fourth of the dose is metabolized to norpropoxyphene. Norproxyphene has less CNS-depressant effects than propoxyphene, but it has greater local anesthetic activity. Its half-life is 30 to 36 hours. Both propoxyphene and norpropoxyphene are excreted in the urine. Adult doses are propoxyphene HC1, 65 mg, or propoxyphene napsylate, 100 mg, every 4 hours as needed, but no more than 390 mg/day propoxyphene HC1 or 600 mg/day of propoxyphene napsylate.

### ▷ Nursing Management: Propoxyphene Therapy

Propoxyphene should be used with caution with clients who have a history of excessive alcohol intake and is contraindicated in those who are suicidal or addiction prone. Preparations containing propoxyphene taken in excessive doses, or in combination with alcohol or other CNS depressants, are a major cause of drug-related deaths. Ambulatory clients should be cautioned about driving a car or operating dangerous machinery, since their mental and physical judgment may be impaired.

## OPIOID ANTAGONISTS

The term "agonist" means "to do" and the term "antagonist" means "to block." Opioids or drugs that act to relieve pain are agonists, and drugs that block the effect of an agonist are the antagonists. In an opioid possessing both agonist and antagonist components, the antagonist portion acts to abate addiction and the agonist portion acts to relieve pain. Continuous contact with the receptor site is essential for addiction.

It has been theorized that a variety of subtypes of opioid receptors are located in the CNS. Each may represent a different therapeutic effect and/or side or adverse reaction relating to the opioid medication. Two receptors (mu and kappa) have been associated with analgesic effects and several specific side effects/adverse reactions. (See box on Opioid Receptor Response.) Sigma receptors mediate both the subjective and psychotomimetic effects of the opioids with a mixed activity, that is agonist and antagonist properties (pentazocine and others). Naloxone and naltrexone are opioid antagonists; that is, they competitively displace the opioid analgesics from their receptor sites, thus reversing their effects. The major difference is that naloxone must be administered parenterally, whereas naltrexone is available as an oral dosage formulation.

Antagonists block the subjective and objective effects of the opioids and will precipitate withdrawal symptoms in individuals physically dependent on opioids. Naloxone and naltrexone are opioid antagonists; therefore, they have been used to reverse the adverse or overdose effects of opioids (codeine, diphenoxylate, fentanyl, heroin, hydromorphone, levorphanol, meperidine, methadone, morphine, oxymorphone, opium derivatives, and propoxyphene) and of the partial agonists (agonist-antagonist drugs such as butorphanol, nalbuphine, and pentazocine). Respiratory depression induced by nonopioids (barbiturates, etc.), CNS depression, or a disease progression will not usually respond to antagonist drug therapy.

In an opioid analgesic overdosage, naloxone and naltrexone will reverse the respiratory depression, sedation, pupillary miosis (contraction), and euphoric effects; they may also reverse the psychotomimetic effects of the agonist-antagonists analgesics (pentazocine and others). Both drugs are believed to work at all three receptor sites, but their greatest activity is for the mu receptors.

Naltrexone (Trexan) 50 mg orally, will block the effects of 25 mg of intravenous heroin for approximately 24 hours; if the dose is doubled to 50 mg, the blockage is extended an additional 24 hours. Therefore, naltrexone is used for the maintenance of an opioid-free state in detoxified, formerly addicted opioid individuals. Other uses for naltrexone are under investigation and include sudden infant death syndrome, other pulmonary diseases, and the treatment of various forms of addiction including bulimia and compulsive gambling. Such indications have not been approved by the FDA (Weintraub & Evans, 1984).

▷ **Nursing Management:**
**Opioid Antagonist Therapy**

Nurses administer opioid antagonists in the emergency treatment of opioid overdose as well as in maintenance therapy of former opioid addicted individuals. The nurse must have an understanding of opioid analgesics as well as opioid antagonists to provide nursing care to these clients.

**Assessment.** Clients should be observed carefully; opioid antagonists should either not be administered or administered with extreme caution if the client is known or suspected to be physically dependent on opioids (including newborns of dependent mothers) because abrupt and complete reversal of opioid effects will produce an acute abstinence syndrome in the physically dependent client.

**Intervention.** To verify abstinence from opioids, as is frequently done before naltrexone therapy, a naloxone challenge test may be done. This test should not be done in the presence of withdrawal symptoms (body aches, diarrhea, gooseflesh, sneezing and runny nose, irritability, diaphoresis, trembling and weakness, abdominal cramping, tachycardia, nausea and vomiting) or opioids in the urine. If administered intravenously, an initial dose of 0.2 mg is given and the client is observed for 30 seconds for symptoms of withdrawal. If no symptoms occur, an additional 0.6 mg may be administered and the client is observed for 20 minutes. If administered subcutaneously, 0.8 mg is given, and the client is observed for 45 minutes. If withdrawal symptoms occur, the test should be repeated at an appropriate interval.

Continued nursing observation is necessary for the client who has responded to naloxone; and doses should be repeated as necessary, since the duration of action of some opioids exceeds the duration of action of naxolone. The intravenous infusion rate of administration should be titrated according to the client's response. An intensive care unit is probably the most appropriate place for this client until the effects of the drug have completely abated. Clients should be observed for a day or longer regardless of the apparent recovery.

It should be remembered that naloxone has no effect on respiratory depression caused by nonopiate drugs. If the client has taken multiple drugs, the naloxone will reverse only the opioids. In the reversal of opioid toxicity, the respiratory rate and volume will increase and the blood pressure will return to normal if it has been depressed.

Naloxone should be used with caution in clients with preexisting ventricular irritability because ventricular tachycardia and fibrillation may occur. It is recommended that naloxone not be mixed with other agents because it becomes unstable. After dilution, any unusual solution should be discarded after 24 hours. Additional resuscitative measures, such as oxygen and/or mechanical ventilation, should be available when necessary to counteract opioid overdosage.

The major indication for naltrexone is the treatment of opioid dependency and addiction, and it should be used as an adjunctive measure to a comprehensive drug rehabilitation program involving counseling and psychotherapy. Naltrexone therapy should not be instituted until the client has been completely detoxified as evidenced by being opioid free for 7 to 10 days, absence of withdrawal symptoms, and abstinence verification by a negative urinalysis for opioids and/or naloxone challenge test. If, in an emergency situation, an opioid analgesic is required for a client receiving naltrexone therapy, its administration should be accomplished in a hospital setting where careful monitoring is available. Because high doses of the analgesic will be required to overcome the effects of naltrexone, the client will be at high risk for prolonged respiratory depression and circulatory collapse.

**Education.** When opioid antagonists are used in emergency treatment, client education should be focused on assisting the client to cope with the immediate situation. Instructions should be given to keep the client informed of what is to occur and to help the client cooperate with treatment procedures, even when the client appears unresponsive. Discussion of the dangers of drug abuse or dependence may be appropriate at some time after emergency treatment. Compliance with naltrexone therapy is improved if someone other than the client (health care provider or family member) administers the naltrexone.

*Evaluation.* When opioid antagonists are used to counteract opioid overdose, close monitoring is essential. The danger exists that the duration of the antagonist action will be less than the duration of the opioid. In this case the symptoms of overdose may again manifest themselves. The nurse's close evaluation of therapy will identify the recur-

rence of opioid overdose and allow instigation of appropriate supportive therapy or repeat administration of antagonists, before the situation becomes life threatening. After administration of antagonists, evaluation takes place to help identify the development of opioid withdrawal syndrome in the possible opioid dependent patient. When naltrexone is used for maintenance of the opioid-free state in former opioid addicted individuals, follow-up evaluations are needed to reinforce and ensure compliance.

### naloxone hydrochloride (Narcan)

See general discussion of opioid antagonists for naloxone's mechanism of action. The drug is indicated to reverse respiratory depression induced by opioids, propoxyphene, and the partial agonists and it may be used as a diagnostic

**TABLE 12-10** Naloxone and naltrexone: side effects/adverse reactions

| Drugs | Side effects* | Adverse reactions† |
|---|---|---|
| naloxone | Nausea, vomiting, tremors, increased sweating, nervousness | Tachycardia, hypertension |
| naltrexone | Insomnia, nervousness; nausea, vomiting, abdominal distress; headaches, tiredness, generalized joint and muscle pain; chills; constipation, anorexia, diarrhea | Hallucinations, paranoia, confusion, severe depression; rash; stomach pain; earache; increased temperature; tinnitus; edema and phlebitis |

*If side effects continue, increase, or disturb the client, inform the physician.
†If adverse reactions occur, contact physician because medical intervention may be necessary.

**TABLE 12-11** Dosage and administration for naloxone hydrochloride

| | Adults | Children |
|---|---|---|
| Opioid antagonist | In emergencies, IV route preferred, although IM or SC may be used; 0.01 mg/kg body weight or 0.4 mg administered in single dose. If necessary, IV dose may be repeated at 2-3 min intervals. Dosage must be individualized according to response. Some clients require higher initial dosages (e.g., 0.8-1.2 mg); others, if physically addicted and not in danger, may receive lower doses initially (0.1-0.2 mg). Dosages may be repeated at 2-3 min intervals, if necessary. For long-acting effect, additional naloxone may be given by continuous IV infusion or by IM route | |
| Verification of abstinence from opioids | See "Nursing Management" | |
| Depression induced by opioids postoperatively | 0.1-0.2 mg IV every 2-3 min until adequate ventilation achieved and client recovery observed without presence of significant pain. Dosage may be repeated at 1-2 hr intervals. Carefully titrate dosage to avoid breakthrough of severe postoperative pain | |
| Depression induced by opioid analgesics | | Neonates: 0.01 mg/kg body weight IM or SC through umbilical vein. Dose may be repeated every 2-3 min until desired effect observed |
| Opioid overdose | | Children: substitute IV route for umbilical vein and proceed as above for neonate |

agent in cases of suspected opioid overdosage (see Nursing Management). Naloxone is inactivated orally, but it is very effective parenterally. Its onset of action is 1 to 2 minutes (IV); 2 to 5 minutes (IM or SC). Half-life is between 60 to 100 minutes; duration of action depends on the dose administered and the route of administration. Usually the IM dose results in a prolonged effect. Naloxone is widely distributed throughout the body; it also crosses the placenta. It is metabolized in the liver and excreted via the kidneys. For side effects / adverse reactions see Table 12-10. No significant drug interactions have been reported. For dosage and administration, see Table 12-11.

### naltrexone (Trexan)

See general discussion of opioid antagonists for naltrexone's mechanism of action. The drug is indicated for adjuvant treatment in the detoxified opioid-dependent person. Absorption is rapid, but it undergoes an extensive first-pass metabolism in the liver. About 5% of a dose reaches systemic circulation. A major metabolite formed in the liver is 6-beta-naltrexol, which also has opioid antagonist effects. Peak serum concentration for naltrexone and metabolite is reached in one hour; elimination half-life for naltrexone is 4 hours, metabolite half-life is approximately 13 hours. Duration of action is dose dependent; generally a single 5-mg dose of naltrexone blocks the effects of 25 mg IV heroin for up to 24 hours while a 100 to 150 mg dose will antagonize heroin effects for 48 to 72 hours, respectively. Excretion is via the kidneys. For side effects / adverse reactions, see Table 12-10. No significant drug interactions are reported. Treatment with naltrexone is started cautiously, generally adults are given 25 mg orally with close monitoring for withdrawal signs and symptoms for approximately 1 hour. If no withdrawal effects occur, give the balance of the daily dosage. Maintenance is usually 50 mg orally every 24 hours. Other dosage schedules have been advocated depending on the individual and client compliance. See current package insert. Dosage for children has not been established.

## OPIOID AGONIST-ANTAGONIST AGENTS

Although the exact mechanism of action of the **opioid agonist-antagonist agents** is unknown, these agents have both analgesic and opiate antagonist effects. It has been proposed that buprenorphine (Buprenex), nalbuphine (Nubain), and pentazocine (Talwin) produce agonist effects at the kappa and sigma receptors. Nalbuphine and pentazocine may displace agonists (opioids) from their receptor sites, thus inhibiting their effects. Butorphanol (Stadol) has minimal effects on the mu receptors. Morphine and opioid agonists produce their analgesic effects at the mu receptors. Buprenorphine has some agonist effect at the mu receptor sites (see box, "Opioid Receptor Responses"). Generally, these drugs have a lower dependency potential than opioids, and

withdrawal symptoms are not as severe as those reported with the opioid agonist medications. The opioid agonist-antagonist agents have pharmacokinetics, adverse effects, and significant drug interactions similar to morphine.

### butorphanol tartrate (Stadol)

Butorphanol tartrate is indicated for treatment of moderate-to-severe pain and as an anesthetic adjunct. It is administered parenterally (IM or SC); onset of action is 10 to 30 minutes (IM) and 2 to 3 minutes (IV); peak effect is in 30 minutes (IV) or between 30 to 60 minutes (IM). Duration of action is 3 to 4 hours (IM) and 2 to 4 hours (IV). Half-life is 2.5 to 4 hours. Butorphanol is metabolized in the liver; excretion is primarily in the kidneys with 72% excreted unchanged. More frequent side effects include sedation. Less frequent are difficulty in urination; increased weakness, dizziness; headaches, sweating, facial flushing; anorexia, nausea, and vomiting. Rare adverse effects include confusion, seizures, depression; tinnitus; tachycardia or bradycardia; skin rash, facial edema; hypertension; and respiratory difficulties.

***Significant drug interactions.*** When given concurrently with:

| Drug | Possible Effect and Management |
|---|---|
| alcohol or CNS depressants | May increase the potential for CNS depression, respiratory depression and hypotension. Monitor closely for adverse effects since one or both drugs may need to be reduced |
| buprenorphine | May reduce the therapeutic effects of butorphanol, nalbuphine, or pentazocine at the kappa receptors. May see increased respiratory depressant effects as buprenorphine is given with low doses of other mu receptor agonists or kappa receptor agonists. Avoid concurrent administration if possible; if not, monitor closely for increased adverse effects which might necessitate dosage decrease or medical intervention |
| monoamine oxidase (MAO) inhibitors | Use opioid analgesics (other than meperidine) cautiously in reduced dosages. For safety's sake, $\frac{1}{4}$ of the usual analgesic dose should be given to determine client's response to this combination |

***Dosage and administration.*** The adult dosage is 1 to 4 mg (usually 2 mg) intramuscularly every 3 to 4 hours as necessary or 0.5 to 2 mg (usually 1 mg) intravenously every 3 to 4 hours. Pediatric dosage has not been established.

### ▷ Nursing Management: Butorphanol Therapy

***Assessment.*** Use with caution as a preoperative medication with hypertensive clients because butorphanol may increase the blood pressure. It should not be administered to clients with coronary insufficiency, myocardial infarction, or ventricular dysfunction because its use has not been evaluated in these cases.

If the client is suspected of being physically dependent

**TABLE 12-12**   Pharmacokinetic overview of agonist-antagonist medications

| Drug/dosage form | Onset of action (min) | Peak effect (min) | Duration of action (hr) |
|---|---|---|---|
| nalbuphine HCl | | | |
|   IM | Within 15 | 60 | 3-6 |
|   IV | 2-3 | 30 | 3-4 |
|   SC | Within 15 | Not available | 3-6 |
| pentazocine | | | |
|   Oral | 15-30 | 60-90 | 3 |
|   IM | 15-20 | 30-60 | 2-3 |
|   IV | 2-3 | 15-30 | 2-3 |
|   SC | 15-20 | 30-60 | 2-3 |

**TABLE 12-13**   Dosage and administration for pentazocine

| | Adults | Children |
|---|---|---|
| analgesic (pentazocine HCl and naloxone HCl) | 50 mg pentazocine orally every 3-4 hr as necessary. If needed, single dose may be increased to 100 mg; maximum daily dosage is 600 mg | Not established |
| pentazocine lactate injection | | |
|   Analgesia | 30 mg IM, IV, or SC every 3-4 hr as necessary | |
|   Obstetric analgesia | 30 mg IM or 20 mg IV when contractions are regular. May be repeated two or three times at 2-3 hr intervals | |
|   Maximum | Equivalent of 360 mg/day. Single dose 30 mg IV or 60 mg IM pentazocine | |

on narcotics, butorphanol should not be given until the person is detoxified. Since butorphanol is a narcotic agonist-antagonist, it would only counteract the effects of the original narcotic, set up a need for an increase in the dosage, and precipitate an abstinence syndrome.

Butorphanol may elevate CSF pressure; therefore it should be used with caution in clients with head injuries or preexisting increased CSF pressure. Because butorphanol is metabolized in the liver, it should be given with caution to clients with compromised or impaired renal or hepatic function. Because of decreased metabolism of the drug in the liver, side effects and greater activity may result.

The safety of the use of butorphanol in pregnancy before the labor period has not been established, but the safety to the mother and fetus following the administration of butorphanol during labor has been established. Clients receiving butorphanol during labor have experienced no adverse effects other than those observed with commonly employed analgesics; however, this drug should be used with caution in women delivering premature infants.

Butorphanol tartrate can cause respiratory depression if the dose exceeds 4 mg as a single dose. If the usual intramuscular dose of 2 mg is insufficient to relieve the client's pain, the dose can be increased by 1 to 4 mg every 3 to 4 hours. It is important for the nurse to assess the client's response to this medication and to be aware of any signs of respiratory depression. These could be changes in rate, depth, or regularity of respiratory rate.

## pentazocine (Talwin)

Pentazocine is indicated for the treatment of moderate pain. It is not indicated for pain caused from an acute myocardial infarction because of its effects on cardiac function. It increases cardiac workload by increasing systemic and pulmonary arterial pressure, systemic vascular resistance, and left ventricular end-diastolic pressure. It also has a higher incidence of psychotomimetic side effects than the majority of other analgesics, thus limiting its usefulness, especially in terminally ill clients or those that are already anxious or fearful. Pentazocine HCl tablets (Talwin) are no longer available in the U.S. because of the incidence of pentazocine abuse; instead it has been reformulated to include naloxone in the oral preparation. Naloxone taken orally is not pharmacologically active, but if this combination formulation is injected, naloxone will block the effects of pentazocine. See Table 12-12 for pharmacokinetics. More frequent side effects are sedation, euphoria, nausea, or vomiting. Less frequent side effects include visual disturbances, constipation, urinary infrequency, or pain or difficulty in urination; increased tiredness, feeling faint or dizzy, hypotension; dry mouth, headaches, sweating, flushing of face; and increased anxiety. Less frequent adverse reactions include tachycardia; skin rash or facial edema (allergic reaction); tissue irritation, induration and nodules at injection sites; hypertension; and respiratory difficulties. Significant drug interactions are the same as butorphanol's. For dosage and administration, see Table 12-13.

### nalbuphine hydrochloride (Nubain)

Nalbuphine HCL is an analgesic for moderate-to-severe pain and is also used preoperatively as an adjunct to anesthesia and for obstetric analgesia. It is metabolized in the liver and primarily excreted via the kidneys. See Table 12-12 for pharmacokinetic overview. Significant side effects/adverse reactions are similar to butorphanol. Drug interactions are similar to pentazocine. The adult dosage is 10 mg (IM, IV, or SC) every 3 to 6 hours as needed. For a single dose, the maximum is 20 mg; the maximum total daily dosage is 160 mg. Pediatric dosage has not been established. See Nursing Management: Opioid Therapy for nursing considerations.

### buprenorphine (Buprenex)

Buprenorphine is the most recent analgesic agent released in the U.S. When compared to morphine, buprenorphine is more potent and has an extended duration of action. Administration is parenteral (IM, IV); the drug has a triphasic half-life with an average half-life elimination of 2 to 3 hours. Onset of action, IM, is approximately 15 minutes; IV onset is more rapid than that of IM dosage. Respiratory depressant effect occurs in 1 to 3 hours after IM injection. Time to peak effect, IM, is 1 hour; IV route's time to peak effect is less than when given IM. Duration of action is up to 6 hours in most clients. Buprenorphine is metabolized in the liver and excreted primarily in bile and feces.

More frequent side effects include sedation, faintness, and nausea in ambulatory clients. Less frequent are headache, sweating, vomiting, visual disturbances, euphoria, feelings of discomfort, tremors, and slurring of speech. More frequent adverse reactions include hypotension, slowed breathing (mild respiratory depression). Less frequent are confusion, severe respiratory depression, hallucinations, tachycardia or bradycardia, depression or mood changes, severe weakness, tinnitus, skin rash, pruritus, and paresthesia of extremities.

***Significant drug interactions.*** When buprenorphine is given with

| Drug | Possible Effect and Management |
|---|---|
| Other CNS depressants or MAO inhibitors | May result in increased CNS depressant effect, respiratory depression, and hypotension. Monitor closely since one or both drugs may need to be decreased by the physician. |
| Opioid analgesics | The therapeutic effects of the opioid may be reduced. In physically opioid-dependent clients, withdrawal symptoms may be precipitated by co-administration of buorenorphine. Avoid this combination. |

***Dosage and administration.*** Adult dose: 0.3 mg IM or IV (slowly) every 6 hours as needed. Adjust dosage and frequency by client's response. Pediatric dose has not been established. See Nursing Management: Opioid Therapy for nursing management.

## SUMMARY

Pain continues to be a worldwide health problem. It disables and distresses more people than any other symptom and is probably the most common reason a person seeks health care. Few things that a nurse does are more important than alleviating pain. The delicate task of balancing the therapeutic relief of analgesics against their toxicity continues to be a challenge for nurses. Attitudes, fears and biases of clients, families, and care givers contribute to the unnecessary undertreatment of pain. It requires skill and knowledge on the part of the nurse to assess accurately and intervene effectively for the relief of the pain of the clients in his or her care.

## *Case Study: Pain Management*

Daniel Watkins is a 53-year-old man who was admitted to the hospital for severe abdominal pain. A bowel resection was done to relieve an obstruction. By his fourth postoperative day he is ambulating and tolerating oral intake. He has been taking both injections and oral medication for pain. The following medications are currently ordered:

meperidine, 50-75 mg IM q4h prn for pain
Tylox, one or two capsules PO q4h prn for pain
Tylenol, 650 mg PO q4h prn for pain

Mr. Watkins is complaining of pain around his incision following a dressing change and removal of surgical drains. He is very anxious and upset. He is requesting pain medication. He had his last dose of meperidine 6 hours ago. He took one capsule of Tylox 2 hours ago for mild pain after ambulating.

1. What assessment data does the nurse need in order to decide how to intervene at this time?
2. The nurse decides to administer meperidine 50 mg IM. What assessment should be done to monitor for adverse reactions to the meperidine?
3. What should the nurse document in the client's chart about the pain management?
4. Mr. Watkins complains that the drugs don't always help when he has severe pain. What is the nurse's appropriate action for this situation?
5. What measures can the nurse teach Mr. Watkins to promote more effective pain management?
6. When Mr. Watkins complains of a headache, what medication would be most appropriate for the nurse to administer?

## BIBLIOGRAPHY

American Hospital Formulary Service. (1990). AHFS drug information 90. Bethesda, Md: American Society of Hospital Pharmacists, Inc.

Anthony CP and Thibodeau, GA. (1989). Textbook of anatomy and physiology, ed 13, St Louis: Time's Mirror/Mosby College Publishing.

Baines M. (1987). Drug control of common symptoms. Orpington, Kent, England: St Christopher's Hospice, AG Bishop & Sons, Ltd.

Beard K et al. (1987). Nonsteroidal anti-inflammatory drugs and hospitalization for gastroesophageal bleeding in the elderly, Arch Intern Med 147 (9):1621.

Beauclair TR and Stoner CP. (1986). Adherence to guidelines for continuous morphine sulphate solutions, Am J Hosp Pharm 43:671.

Beyer JE, DeGood DE, et al. (1983). Patterns of postoperative analgesic use with adults and children following cardiac surgery, Pain 17:71.

Beyer JE and Levin CR. (1987). Issues and advances in pain control in children, Nurs Clin North Am 22(3):661.

Black DJ. (1989). A rational approach to cancer pain management, J Fam Pract 28(3):267.

Bonica JJ. (1980). Cancer pain. In Bonica JJ, ed: Pain. New York: Raven Press.

Bonica JJ. (1987). Importance of effective pain control, Acta Anaesth Scand 31(suppl 85):1.

Bonica JJ and Benedetti C. (1986). Management of cancer pain. In Moossa Martin AR and others, eds: Oncology. Baltimore: Williams & Wilkins.

Burokas L. (1985). Factors affecting nurses' decisions to medicate pediatric patients after surgery, Heart Lung, 14(7):373.

Butler NC. (1987). The ethical issues involved in the practice of surgery on unanesthetized infants, AORN J 46(6):1136.

Carson JL et al. (1987). The relative gastrointestinal toxicity of the nonsteroidal antiinflammatory drugs, Arch Intern Med 147(6):1054.

Chawluk JB, Burg FD, et al. (1988). The aging patient: managing transient ischemic attacks, Drug Ther 13(8):75.

Cleeland CS. (1984). The impact of pain on the patient with cancer, Cancer 54 (11):2635.

Cohen FL. (1980). Postsurgical pain relief: patients' status and nurses' medication choices, Pain 9:265.

Coyle N. (1987). Analgesics and pain: current concepts, Nurs Clin North Am 22(3):727.

Feldman GG, et al, eds. (1990). Handbook of nonprescription drugs, ed 8. Washington, DC: American Pharmaceutical Association.

Eland JM. (1988). Pain management and comfort, J Geront Nurs 14(4):10.

Fitzgerald JJ and Shamy PG. (1987). Let your patient control his analgesia, Nursing '87 17(7):48.

Foley KM and Sundarescan N. (1985). Management in cancer pain. In DeVita VT Jr, Hellman S, and Rosenberg, SA: Cancer: principles and practice of oncology, ed 2. Philadelphia: JB Lippincott Co.

Gadish HS, Gonzales JL, and Hayes JS. (1988). Factors affecting nurses' decisions to administer pediatric pain medication postoperatively, J Pediatr Nurs 3(6):383.

Gedaly-Duff V. (1988). Pain theories and their relevance to nursing practices, Nurse Pract 13(10):66.

Gilman AG et al, eds. (1990). Goodman and Gilman's the pharmacological basis of therapeutics, ed 8. New York: MacMillan, Inc.

Gorman ES and Warfield CA. (1986). The use of opioids in the management of pain, Hosp Pract, vol 21, no 7.

Hanks GW. (1987). Opioid analgesics in the management of patients with cancer: a review, Palliative Med 1(1):1.

Harrison M and Cotanch PH. (1987). Pain: advances and issues in critical care, Nurs Clin North Am 22(3):691.

Henrikson ML and Wild LR. (1988). A nursing process approach to epidural analgesia, JOGNN, September/October, p 316.

Judson HF. (1974). Heroin addiction in Britain. New York: Harcourt Brace Jovanovich, Inc.

Kaiko RF. (1980). Age and morphine analgesia in cancer patients with postoperative pain, Clin Pharmacol Ther 28:823.

King KB, Norsen LH, Robertson RK, and Hicks, GL. (1987). Patient management of pain medication after cardiac surgery, Nurs Res 36(3):145.

Kleinman RL, Lipman AG, Hare BD, and MacDonald SD. (1987). PCA vs regular IM injections for severe postop pain, Am J Nurs 87(11):1491.

Kresl JS. (1988). Patient-controlled analgesia: a new system for pain management, AORN J 48(3):481.

Lanza FL, Royer GL, and Nelson RS. (1980). Endoscopic evaluation of the effects of aspirin, buffered aspirin and enteric-coated aspirin on gastric and duodenal mucosa, N Engl J Med 303(3):136.

Larrat EP and Mattea EJ. (1986). Pain cocktails: survey of formulations used in US hospitals, Hosp Formul 21:497.

*Lisson EL. (1987). Ethical issues related to pain control, Nurs Clin North Am 22(3):649.

*Lohrer JA. (1987). Intrathecal and epidural narcotics, J Am Assoc Nurse Anesth 55(4):381.

Macdonald N. (1989). Pain management, J Palliative Care 5(2):40.

Marks RM and Sachar EJ. (1973). Undertreatment of medical inpatients with narcotic analgesics, Ann Intern Med 78(2):173.

*Martinelli AM. (1987). Pain and ethnicity: how people of different cultures experience pain, AORN J 46(2):273.

McCaffery M. (1986). Narcotic analgesia for the elderly, Am J Nurs 85:296.

McCaffery M. (1987). Giving meperidine for pain: should it be so mechanical?, Am J Nurs 87(4):61.

McCaffery M. (1987). Patient-controlled analgesia: more than a machine, Nursing '87 17(11):62.

McCaffery M. (1987). A practical "postable" chart of equianalgesic doses, Nursing '87 17(8):56.

McCaffery M. (1988). When your patient is a drug abuser, Nursing '88 18(11):49.

McGuire DB. (1987). Advances in control of cancer pain, Nurs Clin North Am 22(3):677.

Olsson G and Parker G. (1987). A model approach to pain assessment, Nursing '87 17(5):52.

Paice JA. (1987). New delivery systems in pain management, Nurs Clin North Am 22(3):715.

Pain. (1988). Am J Nurs 88(6):816.

Physicians' desk reference (PDR). (1990). Oradell, NJ: Medical Economics Co.

Porter J and Jick H. (1980). Addiction rare in patients treated with narcotics, N Engl J Med 302:123.

Puntillo KA. (1988). The phenomenon of pain and critical care nursing, Heart Lung 17(3):262.

Radwin LE. (1987). Autonomous nursing interventions for treating the patient in acute pain: a standard, Heart Lung 16(3):258.

---

'Recommended for additional reading.

Schofferman J. (1988). Pain: diagnosis and management in the palliative care of AIDS, J Palliative Care 4(4):46.

Stevens B, Hunsberger M, and Browne G. (1987). Pain in children: theoretical, research, and practice dilemmas, J Pediatr Nurs 2(3):154.

Townsend A. (1988). Management of pain in patients with myocardial infarction, Intensive Care Nurs 4:18.

Twycross R and Lack S. (1984). Oral morphine in advanced cancer. Beaconsfield, England: Beaconsfield Publishers, Ltd.

United States Pharmacopeial Convention. (1991). Drug information for the health care provider, ed 11. Rockville, Md: United States Pharmacopeial Convention, Inc.

Warfield CA. (1986). Treating traumatic pain, Hosp Pract 21(3):48M.

Weinberg AD. (1988). The etiology, evaluation and treatment of head and facial pain in the elderly, J Pain Symptom Management 3(1):29.

Weintraub M and Evans P. (1984). Naltrexone: a potent oral narcotic antagonist for opiate addiction, Hosp Formul 19:449.

*Wright SM. (1987). The use of therapeutic touch in the management of pain, Nurs Clin North Am 22(3):705.

Young LY and Koda-Kimble MA. (1988). Applied therapeutics: the clinical value of drugs, ed 4, Vancouver, Wash: Applied Therapeutics, Inc.

# Chapter

## 13 Anesthetics

## INTRODUCTION

Anesthetic drugs are CNS depressants that possess two characterics: they have an affinity for nervous tissue and their action is reversible, with nerve cells returning to normal on elimination of the drug from the cells. There are three major categories of anesthesia: general, regional, and local. General anesthesia may be achieved by intravenous or inhalation routes of drug administration. Regional anesthesia is achieved by injecting a local anesthetic drug near a nerve trunk or into specific sites (spinal, caudal). Local anesthesia may be achieved topically or by setting up a field block in an area that encircles the operative field (infiltration anesthesia). Spinal, epidural, caudal, and nerve block anesthesia have been referred to as both regional and local anesthesia. The effect of application of regional anesthesia is related to the target nerve and its distribution in the body, whereas local anesthesia is generally a blockade of the nerves in the infiltrated tissues.

To simplify the anesthetic categories, this chapter will present two broad major classifications: general anesthetic agents and local anesthetic agents.

# General Anesthesia

**General anesthesia** is a drug-induced state in which the CNS is altered to produce varying degrees of analgesia, depression of consciousness, skeletal muscle relaxation, and reflex reduction. It is an important mode of therapy, especially for surgical procedures.

## MECHANISM OF ACTION

General anesthetics affect all excitable tissues of the body at concentrations that produce anesthesia. They vary widely in chemical structure, and the concentrations required of different anesthetics to produce a given state of anesthesia also differ greatly. Although many theories of anesthesia have been proposed, none satisfactorily explains the basic mechanisms of action. Indeed, different anesthetics may have different modes of action, and no single theory may suffice.

The **Overton-Meyer theory** stresses the relationship between the lipid solubility of an anesthetic agent and its potency; the greater the solubility in fat, the greater the effect. Since the nerve cell membrane has a high lipid content, the Overton-Meyer theory explains why anesthetics are preferentially taken up by the brain. However, not all lipid-soluble substances possess anesthetic activity.

When an anesthetic gas is first administered, the **concentration gradient** from alveolar air to blood is steep, and therefore absorption of the gas into the blood is rapid. With time the concentration of gas in alveolar air, blood, and tissues approaches equilibrium, and absorption of the gas slows. When the anesthetic is stopped, the reverse process occurs. Elimination is very rapid at first and then slower. Equilibrium of anesthetics in the fat depots of the body is more slowly reached than in other tissues, and anesthetic is more slowly eliminated. This effect probably is caused by the relatively small blood supply to the fat depots. Alveolar walls are highly permeable to anesthetics, and free diffusion occurs between the alveoli and the capillary membranes. Much investigational work is being done in this area, but regardless of the ultimate explanation, anesthesia is produced by progressively increasing the amount of the anesthetic agent, first in the blood and subsequently in the nervous system.

Unlike many other drugs, the anesthetics that can be given by inhalation were thought to be absorbed, transported, and excreted by the body without undergoing significant chemical change. There is evidence, however, for some quantitative hepatic metabolism of many anesthetics. They primarily are exhaled and excreted by the lungs, except for small amounts metabolized by the liver and excreted by the kidneys and the skin. Associations have been made between biotransformation of inhalation anesthetics and toxicity. The metabolic rate of inhaled anesthetics may be modified by the concentration being inhaled; for example, halothane metabolism is modified in a dose-dependent manner. An inhaled anesthetic may inhibit metabolism of other drugs. Anesthetics are relatively safe agents when used with skilled supervision, since their anesthetic effect can be rapidly reversed by elimination from the lungs, if respiration is maintained satisfactorily. This possibility of rapid removal by breathing permits the safe use of drugs when a surprisingly small difference exists between an anesthetic dose and a fatal dose.

The pattern of depression is similar for all anesthetics—irregular and descending. The medullary centers are depressed last. Fortunately, the medulla is spared temporarily, since it contains the vital centers concerned with heart action, blood pressure, and respiration. Initially, anesthesia produces a loss of the perception of sight, touch, taste, smell, awareness, and hearing. Usually unconsciousness is produced. The two classes of general anesthetics are inhalation anesthetics (gases or volatile liquids) and intravenous agents.

***Balanced anesthesia.*** A combination of drugs is necessary to produce all the desired effects sought with anesthesia. Analgesia, muscle relaxation, unconsciousness, and amnesic effects cannot be produced by a single anesthetic. The induction of anesthesia by using a combination of drugs, each for its specific effect, rather than by using a single drug with multiple effects, is termed **balanced anesthesia.** For example, anesthesia may be induced by premedicating with a short-acting barbiturate or a benzodiazepine and then an opioid analgesic and a skeletal muscle relaxant, followed by an anesthetic gas administered by the anesthetist. The specific drugs and dosages will depend on the procedure to be performed, the physical condition of the client, and the client's response to the medications. The advantage of balanced anesthesia is a lower reported incidence of postoperative nausea, vomiting, and pain.

## STAGES OF GENERAL ANESTHESIA

Anesthesia generally consists of four stages (Table 13-1). The stages of anesthesia vary with the choice of anesthetic, speed of induction, and skill of the anesthetist. The current practice of inducing anesthesia with an intravenously administered anesthetic before inhalation anesthesia promotes rapid transition from consciousness to surgical anesthesia, and the early stages of anesthesia are not seen. If the drug

**TABLE 13-1**  Stages of anesthesia

| CNS effects | Stage 1 | Stage 2 | Stage 3 planes 1 | 2 | 3 | 4 | Stage 4 |
|---|---|---|---|---|---|---|---|
| Consciousness | Maintained Analgesia Euphoria Some distortion of perceptions Variable amnesia | Lost | Absent | Absent | Absent | Absent | Absent |
| Respiration | No alteration, or increased rate with some irregularity | Rapid, irregular | Regular | Regular, but expirations longer than inspirations | Diaphragmatic | Thoracic ceased Diaphragmatic depressed | No respiratory movement Respiratory paralysis |
| Skeletal muscles | Normal tone | Tone increased | Small muscles relaxed | Large muscles relaxed | Complete relaxation | Complete relaxation | Diaphragm paralyzed |
| Eyes Pupils | Reaction to light | Dilated | Constricted | Mid-dilation | Increasing dilation | Dilated | Dilated |
| Movements | Unchanged | Increased | Increased | None | None | None | None |
| Tear secretion | | | | Decreased | Decreased | Absent | |
| Reflexes Lid | Present | Present | Absent | Absent | Absent | Absent | Absent |
| Corneal | Present | Present | Present | Absent | Absent | Absent | Absent |
| Pharyngeal or "gag" | | | Absent | | | | |
| Laryngeal | | | | Absent | | | |
| Cough | | | | | Absent in large bronchi | Absent in small bronchi | |
| Heart rate | | Increased | Decreased | | | | |
| Blood pressure | Unchanged | Increased | Normal | Normal | Decreased | Decreased | Decreased |
| Venous pressure | Unchanged | Increased | Unchanged | | | | Increased |

is given slowly enough, however, usually all stages can be observed. They are most easily seen when an anesthetic gas is used as the only anesthetic. Not all stages may be seen with all anesthetics.

**Stage 1: analgesia.** This stage begins with onset of anesthetic administration and lasts until loss of consciousness. Smell and pain are abolished before consciousness is lost. Vivid dreams and auditory or visual hallucinations may be experienced. Speech becomes difficult and indistinct. Numbness spreads gradually over the body. The body feels stiff and unmanageable. Hearing is the last sense lost.

The nurse should maintain a quiet and tranquil environment for the client because even low voices and equipment sounds may be interpreted as excessively loud and may be counterproductive to the anesthetic.

Before anesthesia is begun, restraining straps are placed on the client; and he or she is covered for warmth and modesty.

**Stage 2: excitement.** This stage varies greatly with individuals but begins with loss of consciousness. Reflexes are still present and may be exaggerated, particularly with sensory stimulation such as noise. The client may struggle, shout, laugh, swear, or sing. Autonomic activity, muscle tone, eye movement, and rapid and irregular breathing increase. Irregular respiration may cause uneven absorption of anesthetic; a period of apnea followed by a few deep breaths may produce a high concentration of anesthetic in the blood.

The variability in this stage results from (1) the amount and type of premedication, (2) the anesthetic agent used, and (3) the degree of external sensory stimuli. Since the advent of balanced anesthesia, excitement during induction is rare. However, this stage is important for classifying and analyzing drug effects in investigational studies.

Except to restrain for safety reasons, the client should not be touched during this stage.

Stages 1 and 2 constitute the *stage of induction.*

***Stage 3: surgical anesthesia.*** The third stage is divided into four planes of increasing depth of anesthesia. Which plane a client is in is determined by the character of the respirations, eyeball movement, pupil size, and degree to which reflexes are present. Most operations are done in plane 2 or in the upper part of plane 3 (see Table 13-1). As the client moves into plane 1, the respiratory irregularities of the second stage usually have disappeared and respiration becomes full and regular. As anesthesia deepens, respiration becomes more shallow and also more rapid. Paralysis of the intercostal muscles is followed by increased abdominal breathing; finally, only the diaphragm is active. The eyelid reflex is lost and the eyeballs, which exhibit a rolling movement at first, gradually move less and then cease to move. Normally, if the pupils were reflexly dilated in the second stage, they now constrict to about their size in natural sleep. The reaction to light becomes sluggish. The pupils dilate as plane 4 is approached.

The client's face is calm and expressionless and may be flushed or even cyanotic. The musculature becomes increasingly relaxed as reflexes are progressively abolished. Most abdominal surgery cannot be performed until the abdominal reflexes are absent and the abdominal wall is soft. The body temperature is lowered as the anesthetic state continues. The pulse remains full and strong. Blood pressure may be elevated slightly, but in plane 4 the blood pressure drops and the pulse becomes weak. The skin, which was warm, now becomes cold, wet, and pale.

The approval of the anesthetist should be obtained before preparing the skin and surgically draping the client.

***Stage 4: medullary paralysis (toxic stage).*** The fourth stage is characterized by respiratory arrest and vasomotor collapse. Respiration ceases before the heart action, so artificial respiration may lighten the anesthetic state (if a gaseous agent has been used) and save the client's life.

The nurse is part of the surgical team in providing resuscitative measures; the necessary drugs, equipment, supplies; and other assistance as necessary.

## SIGNIFICANT DRUG INTERACTIONS

Among the dangers facing a surgical client is an unexpected drug interaction occurring in preparation for or during anesthesia. Anesthetists must always be cognizant of the interactions between anesthetics and the maintenance drug therapies used in a wide range of illnesses. A serious drug interaction may be underway before surgery, and the surgical anesthesia may complicate the interaction. A critical analysis of the surgical candidate's drug regimen (prescribed and OTC) should be evaluated in relation to the anesthetic drugs and preanesthetic drugs to be used.

In obtaining a drug history, the nurse should ask the client to list all medications consumed in the 2- to 3-week preoperative period. Various pharmacologic classes of medication may result in adverse reactions in clients anesthetized for surgery. For example *anticoagulants,* such as heparin and coumadin, are usually discontinued 48 hours before surgery to reduce the increased risk of hemorrhage, while *CNS depressants* such as opioids and hypnotics may increase the risk of enhanced CNS depressant effects. *Antidysrhythmics* such as propranolol hydrochloride may induce a decreased cardiac output, decreased heart rate, and bronchospasms. Quinidine, procainamide, and lidocaine may reduce cardiac conduction, increase peripheral vasodilation, and potentiate neuromuscular blocking agents, such as tubocurarine.

Combining local anesthetic agents with *sympathomimetic or vasoconstrictive agents* (such as epinephrine, phenylephrine, or methoxamine) can cause ischemia, leading to sloughing of tissue or gangrene in fingers, toes, or areas that have end arteries. If combined with local anesthetics, these agents should be carefully dosed and closely monitored.

Selected *antihypertensive agents* such as guanethidine (Ismelin) and methyldopa (Aldomet) deplete the synthesis or storage of norepinephrine in the sympathetic (adrenergic) nerve endings and may result in severe hypotension when combined with anesthetics and analgesics. Physicians may consider reducing or stopping such medications before surgery.

When used as long-term chronic therapy, *corticosteroids* usually produce adrenal gland suppression, which may result in hypotension during surgery. Since the stress of anesthesia and surgery usually increases the need for and release of endogenous corticosteroids, it is recommended that corticosteroid dosages be increased in the perioperative period.

*Cholinesterase inhibitors* such as echothiophate iodide (Phospholine Iodide) and demecarium bromide (Humorsol), and exposure to organophosphate insecticides, may prolong succinylcholine blockade. Extended apnea and death have been reported with this combination. It is generally recommended that the eyedrops be stopped approximately 2 weeks before elective surgery.

*Antibiotics*—particularly aminoglycoside antibiotics (e.g., amikacin and gentamicin), clindamycin, tetracyclines, and polymixin antibiotics—may potentiate the neuromuscular blocking agent or cause neuromuscular blockade. A reduction in the dose of the neuromuscular blocking agent may be necessary, along with careful titration or careful dosing of the drug for the client, to response. Clients with myasthenia gravis, Parkinson's disease, or other neuromuscular disorders must be monitored carefully.

Many other drugs have the potential for inducing an unwanted effect intraoperatively or postoperatively. Concurrent administration of various drugs with anesthetic agents requires close supervision and monitoring of the surgical client. As a general guideline, if a drug is needed for treatment preoperatively, it should be continued through surgery. Unnecessary drugs should be discontinued, for a period at least fives times the half-life of the drug, prior to surgery. Drugs having significant interactions with anesthetic agents should be replaced, when possible, with an alternative medication prior to surgery. Notable exceptions are MAO inhibitors, anticoagulants (if surgical hemostasis is needed), and also dosage adjustments for insulin and corticosteroids.

## SPECIAL ANESTHESIA CONSIDERATIONS

Many disease states and risk factors can alter the individual's response to anesthesia.

*Alcoholism.* The alcoholic client may have a variety of associated disease states, including liver dysfunction, pancreatitis, gastritis, and esophageal varices. The anesthetic requirements for such a client may be increased owing to the increase in liver-metabolizing enzymes and the development of cross-tolerance. The alcoholic client should be monitored closely during the postanesthetic period for alcohol withdrawal syndrome, since diazepam or other pharmacologic agents may be required.

*Obesity.* Overweight or obese clients may have cardiac insufficiency, respiratory problems, atherosclerosis, hypertension, or an increased incidence of diabetes, liver disease, and thrombophlebitis. In such clients, obtaining the desired depth of anesthesia and muscle relaxation may be a problem. Generally, fat-soluble anesthetics, especially those with toxic metabolites such as methoxyflurane (Penthrane), should be avoided.

*Smoking.* Individuals who smoke usually have an increasingly rigid arterial vascular system, adrenal gland stimulation, and perhaps lung disease (bronchitis, emphysema, carcinoma, etc.). Therefore postoperative complications are six times more common in smokers than in nonsmokers. Smoking also increases the client's sensitivity to muscle relaxants.

*Young age.* The physical characteristics of a neonate may predispose the infant to upper airway obstruction or laryngospasms during resuscitation or anesthesia. A small mandible and neck, a narrow cricoid ring, and a large body water compartment with a high extracellular water turnover rate, immaturely functioning liver and kidneys, and a rapid metabolic rate all contribute to the need for careful considerations of the infant or pediatric client. Drug dosages and administered fluids must be carefully calculated using the body weight or the surface area of the child. Generally halothane and nitrous oxide are commonly used in pediatrics because the incidence of hepatitis (p. 243) in children is considered rare after halothane usage. Neonates are usually more sensitive to the nondepolarizing muscle relaxing agents (see Chapter 25).

*Advanced age.* Aging results in a generalized decline in organ function (approximately 1% per year after age 30), the existence of chronic disease processes, or both. As the number and complexity of illnesses increase with age, the complexity of drug treatment also increases, which results

---

## PREGNANCY SAFETY

FDA category B: etidocaine, lidocaine, prilocaine, methohexital

FDA category C: alfentanil, bupivacaine, chloroprocaine, dibucaine, etomidate, fentanyl, mepivacaine, procaine, sufentanil, tetracaine, thiopental

FDA category unclassified: droperidol, halothane, ketamine

---

in greater potential for drug interactions and side effects. Generally, an increased and prolonged drug effect is seen in the elderly. Mortality rates for the aged patient undergoing major surgery may be 4 to 8 times higher than for younger clients.

## ▷NURSING MANAGEMENT: GENERAL ANESTHETICS

Nursing during the perioperative period encompasses three distinct phases: preoperative, intraoperative, and postoperative. While these phases are connected, nursing care during each phase differs in its approach to the client and nursing care goals.

*Preoperative.* The night before surgery, sedatives or hypnotics may be administered to ensure a sound and restful sleep. The time of the administration of this medication provides an opportunity to assess the client's anxiety regarding the anticipated operative procedure. Many clients have anxieties regarding the experience of anesthesia, such as fear of not waking up, having pain during surgery, talking while they are anesthetized, or having nausea and vomiting after surgery. These anxieties can be minimized if the client and his or her family are well prepared about the anesthetic agents to be used. Questions about the rationale for a particular agent or method can best be answered by the surgeon or the anesthesiologist. Although very few clients talk while anesthetized, and those who do are generally unintelligible, clients do have other concerns that are valid regarding anesthesia and that need to be discussed to ensure that there is informed consent for the anesthesia. Clients can be reassured that they will have close surveillance throughout the surgical procedure and in the immediate postoperative period. Clients who persist in their fears regarding the anesthesia or the surgery need consultation with the surgeon and/or the anesthesiologist before final preparation for surgery is begun. Severe anxiety or fear, unless allayed, affects both the autonomic and central nervous systems and may cause reactions that are detrimental physiologically and psychologically. Anxious clients may resist relaxation and fight the anesthetic. A greater amount of anesthetic therefore is required, and toxic levels of drugs may be administered inadvertently. Preoperative teaching and counseling by the nurse assists in allaying the client's anxiety.

In addition to the preanesthetic medications, all of the preparation for surgical procedures should be carefully explained to clients. The necessity for postoperative coughing, deep breathing, frequent turning, and use of spirometers should be taught to the client preoperatively. These activities help to prevent the postoperative complications of general anesthetics such as hypostatic pneumonia and atelectasis. The preoperative teaching promotes cooperation when the client is asked to perform these activities that often cause discomfort after a surgical procedure.

Food is usually withheld after the evening meal, and standard procedure is to give the client nothing to eat or drink after midnight. This procedure helps prevent aspiration if vomiting occurs as a response to anesthesia.

Attention should be given to the client's drug history in preoperative preparation. Withholding maintenance medications while the client is NPO for surgery will have the physiologic impact of abrupt withdrawal. Specific orders should be obtained from the primary physician regarding rescheduling the time of administration, a change in the route of administration of the client's standing medications, or both. When a parenteral form of medication is not available, permission may sometimes be given for the client to take oral medications with a small amount of water (30 to 60 ml) while the client is held NPO before surgery.

In addition, some medications may remain in the client's system and interact to cause serious problems such as arterial hypotension and circulatory collapse or respiratory depression. See the discussion on p. 238 regarding these drugs and their interactions.

Premedication is used less commonly now than in the past. Drug choice takes into account the client's age, weight, physical condition, and level of anxiety, the anesthetic method selected, and the duration and type of surgery. Not including drugs in the preoperative preparation of some clients may be appropriate, while others may need aggressive pharmacologic intervention to produce the desired preoperative state. When prescribed, a combination of drugs, such as morphine or meperidine, hydroxyzine, and atropine, is generally used for the immediate preoperative preparation of the client for surgery. In this instance, atropine is used to block the action of acetylcholine at parasympathetic nerve endings, to overcome vagal effects of anesthesia, and to dry secretions. Atropine may cause tachycardia in addition to mild cerebral stimulation. A dose of 0.4 or 0.6 mg is most useful in adults, but as much as 2 mg is needed to produce palpitations and cardiac effects such as a rapid heart rate.

Narcotics, barbiturates, or anxiolytics administered before the client is taken to surgery promote serenity, amnesia, and smooth induction. It is important that the nurse administer the medications at the exact time that is ordered, since a narcotic given too close to the time of administration of the general anesthetic may achieve its full effect during anesthesia and cause severe respiratory depression.

The time it takes to complete specific surgical procedures is variable, and it becomes impossible for many preoperative medications, other than for the first cases of the day, to be ordered for a specific time. In these instances, the preoperative medication is ordered "on call" from the operating room.

All the physical tasks involved with the client's preparation for surgery (i.e., signing surgical permits, final voiding before surgery, taking vital signs) should be accomplished before the preoperative medication is administered. Once the medication is administered, the client should be placed on bed rest with the side rails up and the call light within reach. This decreases stimulation and favors the action of the medication. In addition, the consent for anesthesia, surgery, or both is not considered valid if the client has received sedation before signing.

***Intraoperative.*** The nurse has a highly specialized role within the operating room. The nursing responsibilities entail the maintenance of safety, physiologic monitoring, and psychologic support for the client, but the nurse's role in relation to the administration of anesthetic agents is that of a supportive one to the physician administering the anesthetic. The operating room nurse should monitor for factors that may precipitate hypotension, nerve injury, or malignant hyperthermia.

Hypotension may result from an excess of nonvolatile drugs that depress the vasomotor center. When narcotics are given, the client's pain must be assessed thoroughly and vital signs recorded. Narcotics should be avoided because they may increase hypotension. However, severe pain can also cause hypotension. In these cases a narcotic may both alleviate pain and increase blood pressure.

A second complication that the operating room nurse must be on the alert for is nerve injury, which may follow spinal anesthesia or malpositioning during general anesthesia. Brachial, radial, ulnar, and perineal nerves are most likely to be injured. The operating room nurse is responsible for taking appropriate measures to protect the client from nerve damage. A knowledge of proper positioning for the particular surgical procedure is essential.

A rare but very dangerous adverse effect of inhaled, fat-soluble anesthetics is **malignant hyperthermia.** This is an emergency situation, whereby the client's temperature suddenly escalates and if not treated appropriately and promptly the client may die. The use of neuromuscular blocking agents has also been associated with this adverse effect, especially when they are used in conjunction with the inhalation anesthetics. With concurrent use of succinylcholine, the onset may be more abrupt. The body temperature may increase as much as 1° C (1.8° F) every 5 minutes, reaching reported highs of 43° C (109.4° F). The operating room personnel should have a preplanned course of action, including the availability of dantrolene sodium, a complete change of anesthesia circuit, hyperventilation with 100%

oxygen, methods to lower body temperature rapidly, and other symptomatic treatment.

The clinical role of the nurse anesthetist, who assumes the direct responsibility for the administration of anesthetics, requires a formal certification program for advanced practice of that speciality.

*Postoperative.* The major objective of the immediate postoperative period is to assist the client in recovering from the effects of the anesthesia and the surgery safely, comfortably, and as quickly as possible. With general anesthesia, careful monitoring is required until the client is alert and oriented to time and place, with vital signs stabilized for at least 30 minutes. Since inhalation agents depress the hypothalamus and therefore can elevate or reduce body temperature, clients should be monitored for hypothermia or hyperthermia (subnormal temperature or high fever) during the recovery phase. If clients were febrile before surgery, their temperature should be monitored postoperatively.

After regional anesthesia, intensive monitoring should not cease before reflexes and sensation have returned to the affected area and the vital signs have returned to the client's preoperative norms.

A variety of signs and symptoms may be observed in the postoperative client. Nurses should be aware of the more common postoperative complications and the possible causative factors to enable them to determine effective modes of intervention.

*Nausea and vomiting,* for example, may be caused by stimulation of the vomiting center or by anoxia during anesthesia. Postoperatively the nurse can administer antiemetics and position the client on his or her side to prevent aspiration.

*Hypoventilation* may result from excess or cumulative effects of drugs administered during anesthesia. Neuromuscular blocking agents such as curare, anectine, and *d*-tubocurine can cause hypoventilation. Maintaining a patent airway until the client has fully responded is important in the postoperative period.

**Oliguria** (scanty urination) is very common after anesthesia, as are bladder *atony* and *urinary retention* after perineal and genital operations.

*Intestinal distention* and (at times) *paralytic ileus* may occur from the anesthetic agent, postoperative sedation, or a combination of both. Nursing measures to assess for distention include auscultation of the abdominal area for bowel sounds and frequent assessment of the client's nasogastric tube.

*Thrombosis* may result from the stasis of blood in the lower extremities. Nursing measures to prevent this include application of elastic stockings or Ace bandages, early ambulation, and frequent change of position for the client on bed rest.

Clients should be closely observed for signs and symptoms of *shock,* a not uncommon postoperative complication. Early detection of impending shock and institution of proper

---

### WASTE ANESTHETIC GASES AS OCCUPATIONAL HEALTH HAZARD

Chronic exposure of health care providers in the operating room to waste anesthetic gases may present a significant occupational health hazard. Studies have demonstrated an increased incidence of spontaneous abortions among women exposed to nitrous oxide, as well as among wives of men who are exposed. In addition, neurologic, hepatic, and renal disorders have been seen in the chronically exposed. Health care providers should protect themselves by avoiding the area within a foot of the client's mouth and nose where the breath contains exhaled anesthetic agents. Healthcare providers should be active in establishing exposure monitoring programs to detect unsafe levels caused by faulty equipment and unsafe practices.

---

therapy may prevent or at least modify its severity. Rate, volume, and rhythm of the pulse should be noted, as well as the client's color and skin temperature. A rapid, thready, weak pulse; cyanosis or extreme pallor; cold, clammy skin; and low blood pressure are characteristic signs of shock. Checking for bleeding at the operative site is important; if the client continues to lose blood postoperatively, hemorrhagic shock may occur. Postoperative shock also may result from extensive surgical trauma, prolonged operating time, prolonged deep anesthesia, or even inadequate anesthesia.

Finally, clients should be adequately ventilated postoperatively to prevent *atelectasis* (collapse of the lung). Nursing measures include encouraging clients to take deep breaths and cough every hour. Change of position to prevent pooling of pulmonary secretions also can help to improve ventilation.

With increasing numbers of surgeries being done at ambulatory surgical centers, the nurse should be concerned with client-family teaching for the client who is returning home, to help him or her recover more fully from the anesthesia and the surgery. In addition to specifics regarding the client's operative procedure and its relevant postoperative care, the nurse should prepare the client for some psychomotor impairment during the first 24 hours following anesthesia and caution against attempting tasks that require alertness and coordination, such as driving. The client should be instructed to avoid using alcohol or other CNS depressants within the first 24 hours unless prescribed by the physician.

## TYPES OF GENERAL ANESTHETICS

General anesthetics are usually divided into two groups: (1) the inhalation anesthetics, which include gases and volatile liquids, and (2) intravenous anesthetics, which include barbiturates and nonbarbiturates.

## Inhalation Anesthetics

Inhalation, or *volatile,* anesthetics are gases or liquids that can be administered by inhalation when mixed with oxygen. These can effect a concentration in the blood and brain to depress the CNS and cause anesthesia. They have the following characteristics:

1. They are complete anesthetics and thus can abolish superficial and deep reflexes.
2. They provide for controllable anesthesia, since depth of anesthesia is easily varied by changing the inhaled concentration.
3. Allergic reactions to these agents are uncommon.
4. Rapid recovery can occur as soon as administration ceases, since the anesthetic is excreted in expired air.

Malignant hyperthermia rarely may occur during the administration of inhaled, fat-soluble anesthetics. For treatment of malignant hyperthermia see nursing considerations for dantrolene in Chapter 22. Nitrous oxide, ether, and chloroform are three of the earliest used anesthetics (over 100 years). Ether and chloroform are generally considered obsolete anesthetic agents today. Ether has a wide safety margin and is an excellent muscle relaxant, but it is also inflammable and explosive; it has a slow, unpleasant induction; and the recovery phase is marked with nausea and vomiting. It also irritates the mucous membranes, with resulting increased mucous production, laryngeal spasms, and coughing episodes. Thus ether is rarely used today except in developing countries where resources are limited. Chloroform, a volatile liquid, is hepatotoxic and nephrotoxic, so its usage is also obsolete.

▷**Nursing Management:**
**Inhalation Anesthetic Agents**

The actual administration of general anesthesia is conducted by a physician or nurse who has specialized training in anesthetic management, which is beyond the scope of this textbook. General nursing measures discussed herein are focused on the care of the client after surgery has been completed.

*Assessment.* The vasodilating effect on smooth muscle may cause a drop in temperature and blood pressure; shivering and tremors may be observed postoperatively. Monitor the client's temperature and blood pressure closely during the immediate postoperative period. The recovery phase for volatile anesthetic agents is generally short, and they leave no analgesia residue; thus the postoperative analgesia phase will be short. Thoroughly assess the client for postoperative pain.

*Intervention.* Use caution when changing the client's position during the recovery phase. In addition to the vasodilation, compensatory vasoconstriction mechanisms are depressed, which may result in a significant drop in blood pressure with position changes (orthostatic hypotension). Oxygen is administered during the immediate recovery period to compensate for the respiratory depression from the anesthetic agents as well as the increased oxygen needs of the body from shivering. Pain relief medications will provide relief for immediate postoperative pain. The nurse should remember that any sedative or analgesic probably will need to be decreased one half to one fourth for the first dose after surgery. Measures to avoid heat loss from vasodilation include using warm blankets, covering the head with a blanket, and using a hyperthermic automatic blanket.

*Education.* To allay fears, explain preoperatively to these clients that they will receive oxygen during the recovery period and be closely monitored until the anesthetic effects have completely worn off.

### Gases

Two gases available for general inhalation anesthesia are cyclopropane and nitrous oxide. Cyclopropane is a flammable agent that is also explosive when combined with oxygen, whereas nitrous oxide is nonflammable. Therefore nitrous oxide is the most commonly used agent for dental surgery, minor surgery, and labor. It is often combined with other anesthetics to enhance its effects, so it is used extensively in major surgery.

#### cyclopropane

Cyclopropane, in addition to its use as an anesthetic, is commonly used as an obstetric analgesic. It is excreted mainly by the lungs.

Side effects include postanesthesia nausea, vomiting, headache, and slowing of heart rate. Adverse reactions include respiratory depression, hypotension, cardiac dysrhythmias, and postoperative delirium. The most significant drug interactions primarily involve aminoglycosides and sympathomimetics. (See previous drug interaction section.) Also, cyclopropane is explosive and flammable, so adequate antistatic safeguards should be implemented.

The gas is administered in a closed system with oxygen. Used for analgesia, it is administered at 3% to 5% continuous inhalation; for anesthesia, 25% to 50% for induction, and 10% to 20% for maintenance.

#### nitrous oxide

Nitrous oxide, like cyclopropane, is used in both anesthesia and obstetric analgesia. It is excreted 100% unchanged through the lungs. It has fewer side effects than cyclopropane, primarily consisting of postoperative nausea, vomiting, or delirium, and it has no known significant drug interactions.

For general anesthesia, the recommended dosage is 70% with 30% oxygen inhalation for induction; 30% to 70% with oxygen for maintenance. For analgesia the dosage is 20% to 40% with oxygen.

## ▷ Nursing Management: Nitrous Oxide

At the termination of nitrous oxide anesthesia, the rapid movement of large amounts of nitrous oxide from the circulation into the lungs may dilute the oxygen in the lungs, leading to a phenomenon known as diffusion hypoxia. To prevent this the anesthesiologist or anesthetist usually administers 100% oxygen to clear the nitrous oxide from the lungs. During recovery the client should be administered humidified oxygen by mask, and encouraged to breathe deeply to promote ventilation.

### Volatile Liquid Anesthetics

The volatile, nonflammable liquid anesthetics are commonly used anesthetic agents. The liquid is vaporized and usually combined with oxygen or nitrous oxide and administered by inhalation. The anesthetic is rapidly distributed by way of the blood flow to body tissues including the brain, liver, and kidneys. Excretion of inhaled volatile liquid anesthetics is mainly by the lungs. (For a discussion of anesthetic gases as an occupational health hazard, see the boxed materal.)

### halothane (Fluothane, Somnothane)

Halothane is used primarily as a general anesthetic. Pharmacokinetics are detailed in Table 13-2.

***Side effects/adverse reactions.*** A complete list of the drug's side effects/adverse reactions appears in Table 13-2. Halothane has been implicated as possibly causing liver damage, or *halothane hepatitis,* although this view is controversial. While the mechanism is not known, some experts believe the liver damage to be caused by a hypersensitive-type reaction to a metabolite of halothane. The diagnosis is made on the clinical findings of unexplained fever, eosinophilia, rashes, and abnormal liver function tests within 2 weeks of exposure, especially after a repeat exposure. The syndrome is more common in older and obese clients and is not seen in children. The National Halothane Study by the Committee on Anesthesia, National Academy of Sciences, National Research Council (1966), concluded that the occurrence of halothane-induced hepatic damage could not be ruled out, but was rare. Even though halothane is considered safe, its use is generally avoided in the presence of liver disease, as are repeat exposures within a short time interval.

***Significant drug interactions.*** Halothane sensitizes the myocardium to the effects of catecholamines (epinephrine, norepinephrine, or dopamine) or sympathomimetic agents (e.g., ephedrine, metaraminol). These agents may produce serious cardiac dysrhythmias in the presence of halothane. Levodopa, which pharmacologically increases the quantity of dopamine in the CNS, should be discontinued at least 6 to 8 hours before halothane is administered. Halothane is the only volatile anesthetic agent that sensitizes the myocardium.

Systemic aminoglycosides, lincomycins, polymyxins, and capreomycin when given concurrently with any of the volatile anesthetics may result in skeletal muscle weakness, respiratory depression, or **apnea** (absence of respiration). Patients usually require mechanical ventilation. If these medications are used, the dosage of the nondepolarizing neuromuscular blocking drugs should be decreased to one third or one half of the usually prescribed dosage.

***Dosage and administration.*** See Table 13-2.

### methoxyflurane (Penthrane)

Methoxyflurane is the only volatile anesthetic agent used for obstetric analgesia; it is given in concentrations of 0.3%-0.8%. It is highly metabolized; and a by-product of this metabolism is free fluoride, which is toxic to the kidney (nephrotoxic). Because of the potential for nephrotoxicity, it is rarely used except for obstetric analgesia. Its clinical effects, although similar to those of halothane, are more potent.

### enflurane (Ethrane)

Enflurane is only slightly metabolized in the body. Its clinical effects are similar to those of halothane, only it is less potent. Enflurane may cause seizures when given at high concentrations; therefore, it is not recommended for use in seizure-prone patients (epileptics, head injuries).

### isoforane (Forane)

Isoforane is the newest of the volatile anesthetic agents. It undergoes an extremely low degree of metabolism. Isoforane has a more rapid action than the other inhalation agents and causes less cardiovascular depression. It has not been associated with toxicity.

## Intravenous Anesthetics

Intravenous anesthetic agents are used for induction or maintenance of general anesthesia, to induce amnesia, and as an adjunct to inhalation-type anesthetics. The major groups include ultrashort-acting barbiturates, nonbarbiturates, dissociative anesthetics, and neuroleptanesthesia. Intravenous anesthetics are valuable to allay emotional distress, since many clients dread having a tight mask placed over the face while they are fully conscious. These anesthetics reduce the amount of an inhalation anesthetic required. The principal drug used for this purpose is thiopental sodium.

The intravenous anesthetics most commonly used are the ultrashort-acting barbiturates. These drugs are rapidly taken up by brain tissue because of their high oil-water solubility. For example, equilibrium between brain and blood occurs within 1 minute after injection of thiopental. Shortness of action results from the drug being quickly redistributed into the fat depots of the body. The amount of body fat affects drug action; the greater the amount of body fat, the briefer

**TABLE 13-2**    Volatile liquid anesthetic agents

| Agent | Pharmacokinetics | | | MAC $(O_2/N_2O)$* | Toxicity | Side effects/adverse reactions |
| | Absorption | Metabolism | Excretion | | | |
|---|---|---|---|---|---|---|
| halothane (Fluothane, Somnothane ✼) | By lungs | Up to 20% by liver | 60-80% unchanged by the lungs; remainder excreted or metabolized through kidneys | 0.75/0.29 | May cause "halothane hepatitis" (see p. 243) | Hypotension, cardiovascular depression, lowered body temperature, respiratory depression, malignant hyperthermia Emergence delirium— shivering and trembling, confusion, hallucinations, nervousness, increased excitability |
| methoxyflurane (Penthrane) | By lungs | About 50% by liver | 35% unchanged by lungs; remainder excreted as metabolites through kidneys | 0.16/0.07 | Dose-related nephrotoxicity (renal tube damage) from fluoride metabolite | See halothane |
| enflurane (Ethrane) | By lungs | About 2.5% by liver | 80% unchanged by lungs; remainder excreted as metabolites through kidneys | 1.68/0.57 | | See halothane |
| isoflurane (Forane) | By lungs | Less than 1% | Almost all through lungs: less than 1% as metabolites through kidneys | 1.15/0.5 | | See halothane |

*MAC, Minimum alveolar concentration that prevents movement in 50% of patients exposed to painful stimuli. May need higher concentrations in some patients; generally, highest in very young children, lowest with increasing age. pregnancy, hypotension, or concurrent CNS depressant use. $O_2/N_2O$, In oxygen (%); in 70% nitrous oxide (%).

the effect of a single intravenous dose. With prolonged administration or large doses, however, prolonged drug action results in delayed recovery; this is caused by saturation of fat depots and the slow rate of drug release (10% to 15% per hour).

## ▷Nursing Management: Intravenous Anesthetic Agents

Within this text, the nurse's role in intravenous general anesthetics does not include administration of the anesthetic. The focus of the role does include, however, client care during the recovery period that follows the anesthesia.

**Assessment.** The nurse should remember that the dose of any sedative or analgesic probably will need to be decreased by one third to one fourth for the first dose after surgery; thereafter the dose of the analgesic will be titrated according to the client's needs. Titration is not a nursing measure, but the nurse must assess the client's response to the analgesic and relay the information to ensure adequate medication dosage. Assessment of the client's cardiovascular and respiratory status should be done at frequent intervals.

**Intervention.** The nurse should note that intravenous anesthetics are seldom used alone for anesthesia, except for short procedures such as electroconvulsive therapy, cast application or removal, and hypnosis. When they are used, resuscitative equipment should be close to the client.

**Education.** Generally there is some impairment of psychomotor skills for 24 hours following the administration of these drugs. The client should be instructed not to engage in any activities requiring alertness and coordination, such as driving. Caution the client to avoid alcohol and CNS depressants for the first 24 hours after taking these drugs except as prescribed by the physician.

### Ultrashort-Acting Barbiturates

Ultrashort-acting barbiturates include thiopental sodium (Pentothal), thiamylal sodium (Surital), and methohexital sodium (Brevital sodium). These ultrashort-acting barbiturates are CNS depressants that produce hypnosis and anesthesia without analgesia. They frequently are combined with other drugs for muscle relaxation and analgesia in balanced anesthesia. Their exact mechanism of action for anesthesia, anticonvulsant effects, or the reduction of intracranial pressure (indication for thiopental) is unknown, although a variety of theories have been proposed. General anesthesia with ultrashort-acting barbiturates is believed to result from suppression of the reticular activating system.

The onset of action for these barbiturates is generally rapid—20 to 60 seconds—with an extremely short duration. They are distributed rapidly throughout the body with accumulation in the fatty tissues, followed by redistribution from brain to lean body mass in emergence. These drugs are metabolized in the liver and excreted through the kidneys.

---

### ADVANTAGES AND DISADVANTAGES OF INTRAVENOUS ANESTHETICS

*Disadvantages.* Swelling, pain, ulceration, tissue sloughing, and necrosis if drug infiltrates into tissue; thrombosis and gangrene if arterial injection occurs; and hypotension, laryngospasm, and respiratory failure from overdosage or prolonged administration. Muscle relaxation and analgesic effects are minimal.

*Advantages.* Rapidity with which unconsciousness is induced, amnesic effects, prompt recovery with minimal doses, and simplicity of administration. Intravenous anesthetics are nonirritating to mucous membranes, and use is not accompanied by the hazard of fire or explosion.

---

The most common side effects during the recovery period are shivering and trembling. Less frequently reported are nausea, vomiting, prolonged somnolence, and headache. Serious adverse reactions include emergence delirium (increased excitability, confusion, and hallucinations); cardiac dysrhythmias (tachycardia, bradycardia, or myocardial depression); hypersensitivity reaction (bronchospasm, rash, hives, edema of eyelids, lips, or face; and hypotension); respiratory depression; and thrombophlebitis.

Careful assessment and close monitoring are required when the intravenous barbiturates are used in combination with other CNS depressants (enhanced depression effects), diuretics, antihypertensive agents, and calcium-blocking drugs (hypotension may occur).

Dosages for induction of general anesthesia and resultant duration of action vary, with methohexital requiring 1 to 2 mg/kg for induction, with a duration of action of 5 to 7 minutes. Conversely, thiamylal and thiopental are both administered at 3 to 5 mg/kg and have a duration of action of 10 to 30 minutes.

### ▷Nursing Management: Ultrashort-Acting Barbiturates

Intravenous barbiturates must be administered by personnel trained in their use and in management of possible complications. Continuous monitoring is essential while these barbiturates are being administered. Barbiturates cause depression of respiratory and cardiovascular functions. Resuscitation equipment, a laryngoscope, an endotracheal tube, suction, and oxygen must be on hand when ultrashort-acting barbiturates are administered for anesthesia.

Ultrashort-acting barbiturates are very alkaline and therefore irritating to the tissues. Care should be taken to avoid extravasation of the drug into the tissues during intravenous injection; pain, swelling, ulceration, and necrosis may occur. Intraarterial injection may result in tissue necrosis and gangrene.

**TABLE 13-3**  Dosage and administration for nonbarbiturates

| Agent | Adults | Children |
|---|---|---|
| etomidate (Amidate) Anesthesia induction | 0.2-0.6 mg/kg body wieght | Children over 10 yr, 0.2-0.6 mg/kg body weight |
| fentanyl (Sublimaze) Adjunct to general anesthesia | | Children 2-12 yr, 2-3 µg (0.002-0.003 mg)/kg body weight IV |
| Minor surgery | 2 µg (0.002 mg)/kg body weight IV | Children less than 2 yr, no established dosage. Children 2-12, 2-3 µg (0.002-0.003 mg)/kg body weight |
| Major surgery | 2-20 µg (0.002-0.02 mg)/kg body weight IV. High doses are used for open-heart surgery, complicated neurosurgery, or orthopedic procedures, i.e., 20-50 µg (0.02-0.05 mg)/kg body weight IV | |
| Primary agent in major surgery | 50-100 µg (0.05-0.1 mg)/kg body weight IV given with oxygen, nitrous oxide, or both and neuromuscular blocking agent | |
| Presurgical or postoperative use | 0.07-1.4 µg (0.0007-0.0014 mg)/kg body weight IM | |
| sufentanil (Sufenta) Adjunct to general anesthesia | Low dosages, 0.5-1 µg (0.0005-0.001 mg)/kg body weight IV initially. Additional dosages of 10-25 µg may be given as needed. Moderate dosages, 2-8 µg/kg body weight IV initially. Additional dosages of 10-50 µg may be given as needed | |
| Primary agent in major surgery | 8-30 µg/kg body weight IV initially with oxygen. Additional dosages of 25-50 µg may be given as needed | Initially, 10-25 µg/kg body weight IV given with 100% oxygen. Maintenance, up to 25-50 µg IV |
| alfentanil (Alfenta) Adjunct to general anesthesia | 8-20 µg (0.008-0.02 mg)/kg body weight IV initially. Additional dosages of 3-5 µg/kg as needed for short duration (<1 hr). For induction anesthesia, may use initial dose of 130-245 µg (0.130-0.245 mg)/kg body weight. | Adjunct to anesthesia: IV 30-50 µg (0.03-0.05 mg)/kg body weight initially, then 0.5-1.5 µg/kg body weight by continuous infusion |

Intravenous barbiturates are incompatible with a wide range of solutions, including bacteriostatic diluents and lactated Ringer's solution. The nurse should consult the drug insert or specialized reference before mixing substances and should not administer them if they are cloudy or there is a precipitate. Thiamylal and thiopental solutions should be freshly prepared and used within 24 hours.

## Nonbarbiturates

Nonbarbiturate intravenous anesthetic agents include etomidate, a short-acting hypnotic; the opioids fentanyl, sufentanil, and alfentanil; and ketamine, which produces a dissociative anesthetic. Several drugs also may be combined to produce neuroleptanesthesia.

### etomidate (Amidate)

Etomidate is a short-acting, nonbarbiturate hypnotic used for the induction of general anesthesia. Etomidate is reported to decrease the activity of the reticular formation in the brainstem (in animals). Its cardiac and respiratory effects are minimal, so this product may be advantageous for the client with impaired cardiac functions, respiratory functions, or both. Etomidate is used intravenously in induction of general anesthesia and in concomitant anesthesia for supplementation of a subpotent anesthetic agent (nitrous oxide in oxygen). It is also used for maintenance of anesthesia for short procedures (dilation and curettage or cervical conization).

Etomidate (Amidate) induces hypnosis within 1 minute, with a duration of action between 3 and 5 minutes. To reduce recovery time in adults, a 0.1-mg IV dose of fentanyl is administered 1 or 2 minutes before anesthesia induction, thus reducing the amount of etomidate needed. Etomidate is metabolized in the liver and excreted by the kidneys.

The side effects most commonly reported during recovery period are nausea and vomiting; less often reported are hypotension, hypertension, dysrhythmias, and breathing difficulties. Involuntary muscle movements have been reported, especially when fentanyl is not given before induction with etomidate. Pain at the injection site is also reported. SPECIAL WARNING: Etomidate can suppress the adrenal gland production of steroid hormones (cortisol, etc.), which can result in a temporary gland failure. Electrolyte imbalance, hypotension, and shock may result. Seriously ill or postoperative patients may need adrenal cortex supplementation.

***Significant drug interactions.*** When etomidate is given with other CNS depressants, client should be monitored for enhanced CNS depression. For less significant but potential drug interactions, see the listing under IV barbiturates.

***Dosage and administration.*** See Table 13-3.

## ▷ Nursing Management:
### Etomidate

Since the recovery time for etomidate is short, the nurse should observe for any respiratory depression or hyperventilation. Blood pressure should be monitored for possible hypertension and hypotension. The nurse should monitor cardiac status for any dysrhythmias.

### fentanyl, sufentanil, and alfentanil

Adjunct medications for anesthesia include fentanyl (Sublimaze), sufentanil (Sufenta), and alfentanil (Alfenta). These agents have been theorized to produce their effects at the mu receptor. All three are opioid analgesics used for balanced anesthesia (see earlier section) and in combination with oxygen, nitrous oxide, or both for the induction and maintenance of anesthesia. When combined with a neuroleptic agent, such as droperidol, fentanyl, sufentanil, and alfentanil may be used for neuroleptanalgesia or neuroleptanesthesia (see p. 248).

The most commonly reported side effects/adverse reactions are drowsiness, hypotension, bradycardia, and respiratory depression (allergic reaction). Less frequent are chills, nausea, vomiting, increased weakness, dizziness, constipation, depression, pruritus, muscle spasms, and increased excitability (paradoxical reaction). Convulsions are reported with fentanyl; dysrhythmias are reported with sufentanil.

Concurrent usage of these drugs with CNS depressants may result in an enhanced CNS depressant effect, hypotension, and respiratory depression. Dosage adjustment and careful monitoring are required. When other opioid agonist analgesics are used during the recovery phase from fentanyl or sufentanil anesthesia, the dosage should be one fourth to one third the usually recommended dosage. Naltrexone blocks the effects of opioid analgesics. If an opioid is necessary for elective surgery, naltrexone should be stopped for several days before the scheduled operation.

Information on dosage and administration of these drugs appears in Table 13-3.

Fentanyl (Sublimaze), sufentanil (Sufenta) and alfentanil (Alfenta) all cross the blood-brain barrier and are rapidly distributed to various tissues. They are highly protein bound,

with a triphasic half-life—that is, distributive phase, redistributive phase, and elimination.

Fentanyl produces an analgesic effect in 7 to 15 minutes when given intramuscularly or 1 to 2 minutes when given intravenously. The rate of the loss of consciousness depends on the dose and the rate of administration (usually 4 to 5 minutes, rate of 0.4 mg/min IV). Its peak effect occurs at 3 to 5 minutes when given IV, and at 20 to 30 minutes when given IM. The duration of effect is 0.5 to 1 hour (IV), 1 to 2 hours (IM).

Sulfentanil has an immediate analgesic effect, with the time until loss of consciousness depending on dose and rate of administration (usually 1 to 1.6 minutes, rate of 0.3 mg/min). The duration of action is less than 1 hour.

Alfentanil has an immediate analgesic effect, producing a peak effect in 1 to 2 minutes. The duration of action is dose dependent but is usually less than 10 to 15 minutes.

All three drugs are metabolized in the liver, although sulfentanil may also have some intestinal metabolism. They are excreted by the kidneys.

## ▷ Nursing Management:
### Fentanyl, Sufentanil, Alfentanil

See also nursing management for opioid analgesics, Chapter 12.

Nurses should carefully monitor all clients receiving fentanyl during surgery, since respiratory depression is a side effect and all precautions need to be taken; an oral airway and oxygen should be readily available. CNS depressants can potentiate the respiratory and sedative effects of fentanyl, so the dosage of any sedative or analgesic should be reduced by one third to one fourth. The client should be made to lie down if he or she is experiencing nausea, vomiting, dizziness, or syncope.

### *Dissociative Anesthetic*
### ketamine hydrochloride (Ketalar)

Ketamine is a rapid-acting, nonbarbiturate, intravenous anesthetic. It is a derivative of the psychotomimetic drug of abuse phencyclidine. Ketamine acts on the midbrain within the reticular formation, as do the barbiturates. It produces analgesia and amnesia but not muscular relaxation. The mechanism of action is not fully known. It blocks afferent transmission of impulses associated with the affective-emotional aspect of pain perception. It may also suppress spinal cord activity. Ketamine has been called a **dissociative anesthetic;** that is, it produces a cataleptic state in which the client appears to be awake but detached from his or her environment and unresponsive to pain. The client's eyelids usually do not close, nystagmus (rapid, involuntary oscillation of the eyeballs) is common, and slight involuntary and purposeless movements may occur.

Ketamine increases secretions of salivary and bronchial glands; therefore the administration of an anticholinergic agent (such as atropine) may be necessary. Ketamine may increase blood pressure, muscle tone, and heart rate. Respir-

**TABLE 13-4**   Dosage and administration for Innovar

| Use | Adults | Children |
|---|---|---|
| Premedication for general anesthesia | 2.5-10 mg given ½-1 hr before surgery, IM or IV | Ages 2-12, 0.088-0.165 mg/kg IM or IV |
| General anesthesia adjunct Induction | 0.22-0.275 mg/kg administered slowly IV. Individualize dosage, since smaller dosages have been found adequate depending on client's response | |
| Without general anesthesia for diagnostic procedures | 2.5-10 mg IM approximately ½-1 hr before procedure | |

ation is usually not depressed. After recovery, the client has no recall of events while under the influence of ketamine.

Ketamine is best suited for short diagnostic or surgical procedures not requiring skeletal muscle relaxation. It is also used to induce anesthesia prior to administration of general anesthetics and as an adjunct to low-potency anesthetics, such as nitrous oxide.

When ketamine is given intravenously, the onset of anesthesia occurs within 30 seconds. When administered intramuscularly, the onset of action occurs within 3 to 4 minutes. The duration of action is 5 to 10 minutes for an IV dose of 2 mg/kg body weight or 12 to 25 minutes for an IM dose of 10 mg/kg.

Ketamine is metabolized in the liver. Termination of anesthetic action occurs with redistribution from the central nervous system and liver biotransformation. Ninety percent is excreted in the kidneys.

The most commonly reported side effects/adverse reactions of ketamine include hypertension and increased pulse rate and an emergence reaction, such as distortion in body image, delirium, explicit dreams, illusions, and dissociative-type experiences. In some clients, flashback of vivid dreams with or without illusions may occur weeks later. Less commonly reported side effects include hypotension, bradycardia, respiratory depression, and vomiting. No significant drug interactions have been reported.

The recommended adult dosage for anesthesia induction is 1 to 2 mg/kg body weight IV or 5 to 10 mg/kg body weight IM. The recommended rate for maintenance is 10 to 50 μg/kg body weight by infusion, at a rate of 1 to 2 μg/min. As with any anesthetic, the dosage needs to be carefully assessed and individualized.

▷**Nursing Management: Ketamine hydrochloride**

Observe ketamine-anesthetized clients for blood pressure elevation, tachycardia, bradycardia, dreaming, delirium, hallucinations, euphoria, and increased muscle tone. Ketamine is contraindicated in clients with hypertension, increased intracranial pressure, intracranial lesions, intracranial surgery, or a history of psychiatric problems or alcoholism.

Monitor cardiac status and observe for respiratory depression. Do not arouse these clients until they awake on their own, and warn these clients not to drive or engage in hazardous activities for 24 hours or more after recovery from ketamine.

When clients are given ketamine, protect them from visual, tactile, and auditory stimuli during emergence to decrease the possibility of psychic effects. Up to 50% of unpremedicated clients report dreams and hallucinations as the medication wears off. These dreams and hallucinations can occur up to 24 hours after administration of ketamine. Administer ketamine on an empty stomach, since it has a tendency to cause vomiting.

Ketamine produces a dissociative state; the client may not appear to be asleep but is dissociated from the environment.

## Neuroleptanesthesia

**Neuroleptanesthesia** is a general anesthesia produced by a combination of a neuroleptic (antipsychotic) such as droperidol, diazepam (Valium), or ketamine (Ketalar) and a narcotic analgesic, most commonly fentanyl but sometimes meperidine (Demerol), morphine, or pentazocine (Talwin). It is used primarily for procedures that require the client's cooperation.

An example of this classification is droperidol and fentanyl (Innovar injection). Innovar consists of 1 part fentanyl to 50 parts droperidol.

### droperidol and fentanyl (Innovar injection)

Innovar is used to produce neuroleptic anesthesia. Droperidol is a neuroleptic drug with prolonged action. This combination produces a state in which clients are neither asleep nor awake but in a state of profound analgesia and psychomotor sedation. This state permits the client to undergo short procedures requiring consciousness cooperation, such as bronchoscopy and cystoscopy without pain. Innovar is also used as a premedication for anesthesia and as an adjunct for induction and maintenance of anesthesia. Innovar has lost some of its earlier popularity, since clinical investigation has demonstrated that the depression of res-

**TABLE 13-5**  Preanesthetic agents

| Drug classification | Agent most frequently used | Desired effect |
|---|---|---|
| Narcotic analgesics | morphine<br>meperidine<br>(Demerol) | Sedation to decrease tension and anxiety, provide analgesia, and decrease amount of anesthetic used |
| Barbiturates | pentobarbital<br>(Nembutal) | Decreased apprehension |
| | secobarbital<br>(Seconal) | Sedation<br>Rapid induction |
| Phenothiazines | promethazine<br>(Phenergan) | Sedation<br>Antihistaminic<br>Antiemetic<br>Decreased motor activity |
| Anticholinergics | glycopyrrolate<br>(Robinol)<br>atropine | Inhibition of secretions, vomiting, and laryngospasms |
| | scopolamine | Sedation (with scopolamine) |
| Skeletal muscle relaxants | succinylcholine<br>(depolarizing)<br>(Anectine, Quelicin, Sucostrin) | Promotion of muscular relaxation |
| | *d*-tubocurarine<br>(nondepolarizing)<br>(Sux-cert) | |
| Intravenous barbiturate | thiopental (Pentothal) | Rapid induction |

piratory rate and alveolar ventilation may persist longer than the analgesic effect.

The onset of action for droperidol, when given either intravenously or intramuscularly, is between 3 and 10 minutes, with peak effect at 30 minutes. The duration of action is 2 to 4 hours; alteration of consciousness may persist up to 12 hours. Droperidol is metabolized in the liver and excreted in the kidneys.

The most commonly reported side effects/adverse reactions are hypotension, hypertension, dystonia, increased hyperexcitability, anxiety, and sweating. Less frequently reported effects include bronchospasm, emergence delirium (hallucinations), chills, shivering, depression, and nightmares. Respiratory depression has been reported when the drug is used in combination with an opioid analgesic; this can lead to respiratory arrest. Concurrent usage should be avoided, but if it is necessary, the dosage of the opioid should be reduced to one fourth to one third of the usual dosage. Other CNS depressants may result in enhanced CNS depressant effects.

See Table 13-4 for dosage and administration recommendations.

▷ **Nursing Management:**
**Innovar**

**Assessment.** Innovar produces neuroleptic analgesia; the client is usually free of pain, not necessarily asleep, easily aroused, able to cooperate, but psychologically indifferent to the environment, which is beneficial when the client must participate in breathing. Assess the client frequently for any signs of respiratory depression, because increased rigidity of the respiratory muscles may result in insufficient breathing. Innovar should be used with caution in clients with renal, respiratory, cardiovascular, or hepatic impairment.

**Intervention.** Postoperatively, the client may not complain of pain because droperidol alters *perception* of pain. In these clients pain may manifest itself as restlessness, agitation, or any number of other nonspecific complaints. If the client does experience pain, the normal dosage of analgesic may be decreased by one third to one fourth. Droperidol potentiates the actions of barbiturates and narcotics, so the analgesic dosage will be decreased until all the droperidol is eliminated. Some alteration of consciousness may last for 12 hours after the last dose.

Since droperidol has hypotensive effects, monitor blood pressure until the drug effects have dissipated completely. Orthostatic hypotension is possible. If given droperidol preoperatively, the client should be assisted if ambulation is necessary. If the hypotension is caused by hypovolemia, several approaches may need to be taken. Fluids may be ordered to treat hypotension, the client may be repositioned to improve venous return (supine with feet elevated), and a vasopressor may be given.

## PREANESTHETIC AGENTS

Various medications are used as preanesthetic agents to reduce undesirable effects produced by apprehension or by induction and maintenance of anesthesia. See Table 13-5 for a review of some of the common agents.

**TABLE 13-6**   Local anesthetics—administration and use

| Method | Tissue affected | Preparation used | Examples of drugs used | Therapeutic use |
|---|---|---|---|---|
| Topical | Sensory nerve endings in mucous membranes and dermis | Solution Ointment Cream Powder | cocaine benzocaine ethyl aminobenzoate lidocaine tetracaine bupivacaine | Relief of pain or itching Examination of conjunctiva |
| Infiltration | Sensory nerve endings in subcutaneous tissues or dermis | Injection | etidocaine procaine prilocaine lidocaine chloroprocaine mepivicaine | Minor surgery |
| Block | Nerve trunk | Injection | etidocaine procaine prilocaine lidocaine chloroprocaine mepivacaine | Dental and limb surgery Sympathetic block |
| Spinal (subarachnoid block) | Spinal roots | Injection | dibucaine procaine tetracaine lidocaine | Abdominal surgery Surgery of the lower extremities Muscle relaxation |

**TABLE 13-7**   Properties of commonly used local anesthetics

| | Cocaine | Procaine | Benzocaine |
|---|---|---|---|
| Trade names | — | Novocain | Americaine Hurricaine |
| Potency | 2-3 times that of procaine | | Very low |
| Onset of action | 1 min | 2-5 min | Immediate |
| Duration | ½-1 hr | ½-1 hr | During contact only |
| Dose | 1%-4% topically 5%-10% for anesthesia of nose and throat | 0.25%-2%, depending on method of administration 10% for spinal anesthesia Not used topically | Variable 5%-20% ointment topically |
| Toxicity | 4 times more toxic than procaine when injected subcutaneously | Least toxic of all local anesthetics | Relatively nontoxic |
| Precautions | Not recommended for infiltration, nerve block, or spinal anesthesia Repeated use causes psychic dependence Repeated use in eye may cause clouding, pitting, ulceration of cornea, and mydriasis | Overdose or rapid injection may cause stimulation | Suitable for topical use only Sensitization may develop |

# Local Anesthesia

**Local anesthesia** refers to the rendering of a portion of the body insensitive to pain. Unlike general anesthesia, consciousness is not depressed with local anesthesia. Local anesthetic agents may be applied to an area or injected into tissues, where they produce their effect in the immediate area only; hence the term local anesthesia. Local anesthetic drugs may also be injected around a nerve or nerve trunk (spinal, epidural) to produce anesthesia in a large region of the body. This is referred to as **regional anesthesia.**

## SURFACE OR TOPICAL ANESTHESIA

The use of surface, or topical, anesthesia is restricted to mucous membranes, damaged skin surfaces, wounds, and burns. The anesthetic is applied in the form of a solution, ointment, gel, cream, or powder to produce loss of sensation by paralyzing afferent nerve endings. Topical anesthetics do not penetrate unbroken skin. Topical anesthesia is used to relieve pain and itching and to anesthetize mucous membranes of the eye, nose, throat, or urethra for minor surgical procedures. Cocaine in a 4% to 10% solution continues to be one of the most widely used agents for topical anesthesia.

Local anesthesia may also be achieved by freezing. Low temperatures in living tissues produce diminished sensation. This form of anesthesia is sometimes employed for minor operative procedures. A caution is that tissues that are frozen too intensely for too long may be destroyed. Ethyl chloride is a local anesthetic that can be used to produce this effect, although it is not employed extensively.

## LOCAL ANESTHETICS

Local anesthetics are drugs used to abolish pain sensation in a particular part of the body (Tables 13-6 and 13-7). The basic mechanism of action of these drugs is unknown, but most act by stabilizing or elevating the threshold of excitation of the nerve cell membrane without affecting resting potential. This action is a result of reduction of membrane permeability to all ions; thus depolarization and transmission of nerve impulses are prevented.

Table 13-7 presents some commonly used local anesthetics and their properties. The alcohols (phenol, cresol, menthol, and benzyl alcohol) are seldom employed today. Benzyl alcohol, an aromatic alcohol of low potency, is used topically with procaine to extend procaine's duration of action. Examples of benzoic acid esters are proparacaine and cocaine. Examples of PABA esters are benzocaine, butamben, and tetracaine, which are all metabolized by plasma cholinesterase. Examples of the amides are dibucaine, etidocaine, lidocaine, prilocaine, mepivacaine, and bupivacaine, which are not metabolized by plasma cholinesterase but are excreted in the urine and metabolized in the liver (see Table 13-7). Vasoconstrictors (epinephrine) are used with the local anesthetic to decrease systemic absorption and prolong the anesthetic's duration of action. They are not used for nerve blocks in areas where there are end arteries (fingers, toes, ears, nose, penis) because ischemia may develop, resulting in gangrene.

The mechanism of action of local anesthetics is inhibition of the depolarization phase of the nerve cell membrane by means of diminishing sodium ion permeability. This leads

| Lidocaine | Tetracaine | Mepivacaine |
|---|---|---|
| Xylocaine | Pontocaine | Carbocaine |
| 2 times that of procaine | 10 times that of procaine | 2 times that of procaine |
| Immediate | 5-10 min | Less rapid than procaine |
| 1-1½ hr | 1½-2 hr | More prolonged than procaine or lidocaine (2-2½ hours) |
| 0.5%-4% for injection<br>2% and 5% topically | 1% topically<br>0.15%-0.25% for injection | 1%-2% solution |
| See procaine | More toxic than procaine, but toxic effects rare because of low dosage used | 2 times that of procaine; less than lidocaine |
| When administered rapidly or in large doses, may cause convulsions and hypotension | Has delayed onset of action, i.e., up to 15 min | Combined with vasoconstrictor to delay drug absorption and prolong duration |

to a failure in propagated action potential, causing blockade of conduction.

A number of local anesthetic agents cannot be injected. However, because they are absorbed slowly, they can be used safely on open wounds, ulcers, and mucous membranes. They occasionally cause dermatitis and allergic sensitization, which necessitate their discontinuance.

Topical anesthetics for skin disorders are used primarily to relieve pruritus, discomfort, pain, and soreness; indications for mucous membranes are similar. The anesthetics are poorly absorbed through the intact skin, but from mucous membranes and skin breaks and sores (abrasions, trauma, ulcers, and so on) absorption is increased, leading to the possibility of systemic involvement. When employed in the oral cavity (mouth and pharynx), interference with swallowing may occur. The nurse should be aware of this, since aspiration may occur if food is ingested within 1 hour after use of an oral topical anesthetic, particularly in children.

Local anesthetics are capable of abolishing all sensation, but pain fibers are affected first, probably because they are thinner, unmyelinated, and more easily penetrated by these drugs. Loss of pain is followed in sequence by loss of response to cold, warmth, touch, and pressure. Most motor fibers also can be anesthetized when an adequate concentration of the drug is present over sufficient time.

The parenteral local anesthetics have complete systemic absorption, which is decreased by the addition of a vasoconstrictor such as epinephrine. The amide type varies in protein-binding capacity. Bupivacaine and etidocaine are highly protein bound, whereas lidocaine and mepivacaine are moderately bound to protein. The amide type is hepatic, with only minor renal involvement, but the esters (PABA derivatives) are hydrolyzed primarily by plasma cholinesterases to PABA. The half-life of the ester types is as follows: bupivacaine, 3½ hours; etidocaine, 2¾ hours; lidocaine, 1½ hours; and mepivacaine, 2 hours. Onset of action is a function of the anesthetic technique employed, the type of block desired, dosage, and the $pK_a$ (negative logarithm of ionization constant) of each anesthetic. The time it takes for a drug to reach a peak concentration depends on the block type but ranges from 10 to 30 minutes.

## Reactions to Local Anesthetics

Local anesthetics produce vasodilation by direct action on blood vessels and by anesthetizing sympathetic vasoconstrictor fibers. This action can cause rapid absorption of the drug; when rate of absorption exceeds rate of elimination, toxic effects can occur. To decrease rate of absorption and incidence of toxic effects by allowing more time for metabolic degradation and to prolong local anesthetic effects, epinephrine or other vasoconstrictor drugs are used. Dosage of vasoconstrictors must be carefully determined to prevent ischemic necrosis at the injection site. Since local anesthetics are potentially toxic drugs, a client's age, weight, physical condition, and liver function must be taken into account in determining drug dosage. Caution is advised, with the use of amide anesthetics in clients with compromised livers, since the liver is the site of their metabolism.

Most reactions to local anesthetics result from overdosage, rapid absorption into systemic circulation, and individual hypersensitivity or allergic response.

*Central nervous system.* At first the CNS may be stimulated and cause anxiety, restlessness, confusion, dizziness, tremors, and even convulsions. Then depression may occur, and unconsciousness and death may ensue.

*Cardiovascular system.* Myocardial depression, bradycardia and hypotension can occur because of smooth muscle relaxation and inhibition of neuromuscular conduction. The client suddenly becomes pale, feels faint, and has a drop in blood pressure. Cardiac arrest can be the result of a cardiovascular reaction.

Anesthetics containing a vasoconstrictor are employed with caution in clients receiving drugs that may change blood pressure, such as monoamine oxidase inhibitors, phenothiazines, and tricyclic antidepressants. The combination may produce severe hypotension or hypertension. Cardiac dysrhythmias occur when catecholamine vasoconstrictors (e.g., epinephrine) are used with clients receiving cyclopropane, halothane, or trichloroethylene.

*Allergic reaction.* True allergic reactions are said to be uncommon. Sometimes a reaction is thought to be allergic when it is really caused by overdosage. However, allergic reactions can occur. They may be relatively mild (hives, itching, skin rash), or they may be acutely anaphylactic.

The allergic reactions are characteristically manifested by cutaneous lesions, urticaria, or edema. They may result from various factors, such as hypersensitivity, idiosyncrasy, or diminished tolerance. These rare hypersensitivity reactions are usually limited to the ester type of anesthetics. The most important risk of local anesthetics is a dose-related CNS toxicity, which may progress from sleepiness to convulsion. Clients from families that exhibit malignant hyperthermia (hyperpyrexia) should be administered only ester-type local anesthetics, since amide-type anesthetics are known for this reaction. Skin testing for sensitivity is of doubtful value. Allergy to PABA derivatives has not demonstrated a cross-sensitivity to the amide type (lidocaine).

Small test doses are frequently given by the physician to gauge the extent of the client's sensitivity to the anesthetic agent. The anesthetic agent chosen, its concentration, the rate of injection, and physical and emotional factors in the client all influence reactions to local anesthetics.

## ▷NURSING MANAGEMENT: LOCAL ANESTHETICS

Unlike general anesthetics, nurses often administer topical local anesthetic agents. Therefore, the nurse has a much broader role in relating to these agents.

***Assessment.*** Assess the client for previous response to local anesthetics and the existence of preexisting diseases or drug allergies. During and after administration of a local anesthetic, monitor the client for signs of toxicity, allergy, or other adverse reactions. It is especially important to monitor cardiac status for dysrhythmias and hypertension when a local anesthetic containing a vasoconstrictor such as epinephrine is administered.

***Intervention.*** Do not use the local anesthetic solution if it is cloudy, discolored, or contains crystals. Solutions that do not contain preservatives should be discarded after the vial has been opened. Resuscitative equipment must be available in case the client has an anaphylactic reaction.

If local anesthetics are used as ointments or creams, thoroughly cleanse and dry the area before applying. When the suppository form of the agent is used, chill in the refrigerator 30 minutes, remove wrapper, and moisten with water or lubricant to insert. Note that when local anesthetics are used topically in the nose or throat, they may cause paralysis of the upper respiratory tract, leading to possible aspiration. Measure the preparation accurately. Apply with a cotton swab; swishing should be used for mouth and gums and gargling for application to the throat. Do not allow the local anesthetic to be swallowed unless specifically cleared with the physician.

The client who has regional anesthesia needs to be protected from trauma to the anesthetized portion of the body, since the perception of pain and pressure, the body's normal protective mechanism, has been diminished or obliterated. Pressure from side rails and other objects normally perceived and avoided by the client may cause injury.

***Education (for local anesthetics that may be self-administered by the client).*** Instruct the client to use the preparation exactly as prescribed—not to use more, or more often, or for a longer period of time. Caution the client not to inhale while using the topical aerosol or spray dosage forms. Instruct the client in the use of the provided applicator for rectal aerosol foam preparation. Avoid using if bleeding hemorrhoids are present.

If local anesthetic preparations are used topically in the nose or throat, instruct the client not to eat for 1 hour after administration, since this may lead to aspiration. Because of the variability in response, each client must be able to swallow before food is offered. Advise the client not to chew gum while the anesthetic is in effect, since there is the risk of biting the tongue or buccal mucosa.

## ANESTHESIA BY INJECTION

Anesthesia by injection is accomplished by infiltration or by conduction, spinal, caudal, or saddle block.

**Infiltration anesthesia** is produced by injecting dilute solutions (0.1%) of the agent into the skin and then subcutaneously into the region to be anesthetized. Epinephrine often is added to the solution to intensify the anesthesia in a limited region and to prevent excessive bleeding and systemic effects. Repeated injection will prolong the anesthesia as long as needed. The sensory nerve endings are anesthetized. This method of administration is used for minor surgery such as incision and drainage or excision of a cyst (see Table 13-8).

**Conduction,** or **block, anesthesia** means that the anesthetic is injected into the vicinity of a nerve trunk that supplies the region of the operative site. The injection may be made at some distance from the surgical site. A single nerve may be blocked, or the anesthetic may be injected where several nerve trunks emerge from the spinal cord (paravertebral block). A more concentrated solution is required because of the thickness of nerve trunk fibers. This method of anesthesia is often used for foot and hand surgery.

**Spinal anesthesia** is a type of extensive nerve block sometimes called a subarachnoid block. The anesthetic solution is injected into the subarachnoid space and affects the lower part of the spinal cord and nerve roots (see next section).

For low spinal anesthesia, the client is placed in a flat or Fowler's position. A solution with a specific gravity greater than that of spinal fluid is used, since it tends to diffuse downward. For high spinal anesthesia, Trendelenburg's position with the head sharply flexed is used, along with an anesthetic solution of lower specific gravity than that of spinal fluid (which tends to diffuse upward) or a solution with the same specific gravity as spinal fluid (which may diffuse upward or downward, depending on position used). Solutions with the same specific gravity as spinal fluid act primarily at the site of injection.

Onset of anesthesia usually occurs within 1 to 2 minutes after injection. Duration of anesthesia is 1 to 3 hours, depending on the anesthetic used. Spinal anesthesia is used for surgical procedures on the lower abdomen, inguinal area, or lower extremities; it may be the method of choice for clients with severe respiratory problems or with liver, kidney, or metabolic disease. Marked hypotension, decreased cardiac output, and respiratory inadequacy tend to occur during anesthesia and are considered to be disadvantages of this method of anesthesia.

Postoperatively, headache is the most common complaint; this may be accompanied by difficulty in hearing or seeing. Headache may be postural and occur only in the head-up or sitting or standing position. This symptom is the result of the opening in the dura made by the large spinal needle, which may persist for days or weeks, permitting loss of cerebrospinal fluid. Headache and auditory and visual problems following lumbar puncture result from decreased intracranial pressure. These symptoms usually are alleviated when spinal fluid pressure returns to normal. Paresthesias such as numbness and tingling may occur after spinal anesthesia; they are usually limited to the lumbar or sacral areas and disappear within a relatively short time. The success and safety of spinal anesthesia depend primarily on the anesthetist's skill and knowledge.

**TABLE 13-8**   Pharmacokinetic overview of selected injected local anesthetic drugs

| Name | Metabolism | Use | Dosage and administration |
|---|---|---|---|
| **SHORT-ACTING (½-1 HR)** | | | |
| chloroprocaine (Nesacaine, Nesacaine-MPF, Nesacaine-CE✿) | Ester compound-metabolized by cholinesterases in plasma and liver to a PABA compound. Excretion: kidneys | Nesacaine—infiltration and regional anesthesia Nesacaine-CE—for caudal and epidural anesthesia | Usual adult dosage for infiltration nerve blocks: 30-800 mg as 1% or 2% solutions, depending on site and length of surgical procedure Caudal and epidural: 40-500 mg as 2% or 3% solution, without epinephrine Usual pediatric dosage for infiltration nerve blocks: up to 20 mg/kg body weight |
| procaine HCl (Novocain) | Ester compound—same as above | Infiltration, nerve block, spinal anesthesia, epidural block | Usual adult dosage for infiltration: 0.25%-0.5% solution, 350-600 mg, up to 1 g Peripheral nerve block: 500 mg as 0.5%, 1%, or 2% solution Spinal and epidural dosage, vary with individual client, procedure, and degree of anesthesia desired Pediatric dosage: not available |
| **INTERMEDIATE DURATION (1-3 HR)** | | | |
| lidocaine (Xylocaine, Xylocard✿) | Amide compound Metabolism: liver to active and toxic metabolites Excretion: kidneys | Infiltration, nerve block, spinal epidural | Usual adult dosage depends on site and length of surgical procedure Pediatric dosage: same as adult Lidocaine is available with and without epinephrine |
| mepivacaine HCl (Carbocaine HCl) | Amide compound—see above | Infiltration, nerve blocks, caudal, epidural | Available alone and with levonordefrin (vasoconstrictor). Dosage depends on site and length of surgical procedure Adult maximum dosage: Dental, up to 6.6 mg/kg body weight (300 mg maximum per appointment). Other usages, up to 7 mg/kg body weight. Pediatric, up to 5 or 6 mg/kg body weight |
| prilocaine HCl (Citanest, Citanest Forte, Xylonest✿) | Amide compound—see above | Infiltration, peripheral nerve blocks, caudal, epidural | Available alone or with epinephrine (vasoconstrictor). Although dosages vary with site and length of procedure, the adult maximum dosages are as follows: Dental, up to 400 mg as a 4% solution in 2-hr period. Other procedures, individualize Pediatric maximum: Dental, children up to 10 yr, 40 mg (4% solution) maximum. Other procedures, individualize |
| **LONG DURATION (3-10 HR)** | | | |
| bupivacaine (Marcaine, Sensorcaine, Carbostesin ✿) | Amide type—see above | Infiltration, caudal, epidural, peripheral nerve blocks | Available alone or with dextrose (Marcaine spinal) or with epinephrine. Dosages vary with site, additional drugs, and length of procedure |
| dibucaine HCl (Nupercaine) | Amide type—see above | Caudal, spinal | Available alone and with dextrose (heavy solution Nupercaine). Dosage varies with site of injection, additional drugs if ordered, and length of procedure |
| etidocaine (Duranest) | Amide type—see above | Infiltration; peripheral nerve blocks, caudal and epidural nerve blocks | Available alone and with epinephrine. Dosages vary with site and length of procedure |
| tetracaine HCl (Prontocaine HCl, Amethocaine HCl✿, Minims ✿) | Ester compound—see above | Saddle block (low spinal), up to costal margin, spinal anesthesia | Available alone and with dextrose. Dosages vary with site and length of procedure |

**Caudal anesthesia** is produced by injecting an anesthetic solution into the caudal canal, the sacral part of the vertebral canal containing the cauda equina, or the bundle of spinal nerves that innervates the pelvic viscera. It is used in obstetrics and for pelvic or genital surgery. Its advantage over spinal anesthesia is that the anesthetic does not have direct access to the spinal cord and medullary centers. Thus the respiratory muscles and blood pressure are not directly affected, and undesirable effects are less likely to occur.

**Saddle block** is sometimes used in obstetrics and for surgery involving the perineum, rectum, genitalia, and upper parts of the thighs. The client sits upright while the anesthetic is injected, following a lumbar puncture. The client remains upright for a short time, until the anesthetic has taken effect. The body parts that contact a saddle when riding become anesthetized; hence the name.

### Injectable Local Anesthetics

The short-, intermediate-, and long-acting local anesthetics for injection are listed in Table 13-8. Generally the onset of action for an anesthetic is the result of drug concentration and the targeted nerve-tissue area. Potency and duration of anesthetic action increase with drug lipid solubility. For more information on metabolism, indications, and pharmacokinetics, see Table 13-8.

*Side effects/adverse reactions.* The adverse reactions of injected local anesthetics generally require medical intervention.

Cyanosis caused by methemoglobinemia is one of the most common adverse reactions reported with an epidural block or high spinal injection. It has been reported with all local anesthetics but is most prevalent with prilocaine. Symptoms may include weakness, breathing difficulties, increased heart rate, dizziness, or collapse.

Other reactions reported with an epidural block or high spinal injection include diaphoresis, hypotension, bradycardia or irregular heart rate, pale skin color (cardiovascular depression), diplopia, seizures, tinnitus, increased excitability, shivering, involuntary shaking (due to stimulation of CNS), nausea, and vomiting.

Effects most commonly reported with ester compounds include skin rash and an allergic reaction manifested by edema of face, lip, mouth, or throat. Anaphylaxis and severe hypotension are reported rarely.

With central nerve block anesthesia, the most common adverse reactions are in the form of neuropathies or neurologic effects, including headaches. Other adverse reactions include paresthesia or paralysis of lower legs, breathing difficulties, severe hypotension, bradycardia, and backache. Some clients report a reduction or loss of sexual functions, bladder control, or bowel movements.

Meningitis-type effects are most often reported with spinal anesthesia. These include headaches, nausea, vomiting, and stiff or sore neck.

Allergic effects manifested by dental anesthesia are numbing or tingling of lips and mouth, as well as edema of lips or mouth, while sympathomimetic or adrenergic effects are reported with epinephrine or other vasoconstrictors. These most commonly include hypertension, shaking, increased anxiety or nervousness, tachycardia, headache, and chest pain.

*Significant drug interactions.* The significant drug interactions are limited, but this does not preclude a variety of unexpected responses, thus indicating the need for close observation.

Prior or concurrent administration of CNS depressant drugs may result in additive CNS depression effects. Adjust dosages and monitor closely.

Vasoconstrictor agents, such as epinephrine, norepinephrine, or phenylephrine, in combination with local anesthetics may cause impaired circulation of the area, resulting in sloughing of tissue. If vasoconstrictor agents are used for end arteries, such as toes or fingers, ischemia resulting in gangrene may develop. Extreme caution is advised.

*Dosage and administration.* See Table 13-8.

# Summary

Anesthetic agents are invaluable in the limiting of pain and suffering. By either altering consciousness or interfering with the conduction of impulses to the pain centers of the central nervous system, these agents allow surgical procedures and other painful therapies to be performed.

There are three major categories of anesthesia: general, regional, and local. General anesthesia may be achieved either intravenously or by inhalation; regional anesthesia is obtained by injecting an anesthetic drug near a nerve trunk or into a specific site; local anesthesia may be accomplished by topical application or by infiltration of the operative area. Because no anesthetic agent produces analgesia, muscle relaxation, unconsciousness, and amnesic effects with perfect safety, generally a combination of agents is used, each for its specific effect; this technique is called balanced anesthesia.

Although nurses do not administer general anesthetics unless they are certified nurse anesthetists, they may be called upon to assist the physician to a degree depending on the clinical setting. And it is necessary for the nurse to have an understanding of the effects of anesthetic agents in order to provide appropriate nursing care in the perioperative period. In the preoperative period, the emphasis of the nurse is on the thorough assessment and preparation of the client to alleviate anxiety and to minimize the potential for physiologic injury intraoperatively and in the postoperative period. Immediately after surgery, the need is to help the client to recover from the effects of the anesthetic safely, comfortably, and as quickly as possible. Common postoperative complications for which the nurse should be alert are hypotension, nausea and vomiting, hypoventilation, oliguria, nerve injury, paralytic ileus, thrombosis, shock, atelectasis, hypothermia/hyperthermia, and malignant hyperthermia.

Inhalation therapy can be administered by gases or volatile liquids. Cyclopropane and nitrous oxide (gases) and halothane (liquid) are most commonly used. Because these agents are primarily exhaled and excreted through the lungs, their anesthetic effect can be rapidly reversed, if respiration is maintained satisfactorily.

Intravenous anesthetic agents are used to induce amnesia, for induction and maintenance of general anesthesia, and as adjuncts to inhalation anesthetics. Because of the risk of respiratory and cardiovascular depression, the client's vital signs need to be closely monitored and resuscitation equipment must be at hand in the clinical setting where these agents are administered.

Neuroleptanesthesia is a general anesthesia that results from the combined use of a neuroleptic agent and a narcotic analgesic; and it is used for procedures in which the client's cooperation is desired. Although easily aroused, the client remains psychologically indifferent to events; however, hypotension and respiratory depression may still occur.

With local anesthesia consciousness is not depressed, but a portion of the body is rendered insensitive to pain. Because the perception of pain and pressure are protective mechanisms of the body, the observations of the nurse are important to ensure that the client does not aspirate (if topical anesthesia has been used in the nose and throat), or that tissue damage does not occur through trauma to anesthetized parts of the body.

The role of the nurse in the administration of anesthetics is generally not a direct one, but one in which assessment and the protection of the client take priority.

## BIBLIOGRAPHY

Ackerman J. (1985). Monitoring waste nitrous oxide: one medical center's experience, AORN J 41(5):895.

American Hospital Formulary Service. (1990). AHFS drug information '90. Betheseda, Md: American Society of Hospital Pharmacists, Inc.

Biddle C. (1988). Adverse reactions to drugs used in anesthesia, Curr Rev Nurse Anesth 10(25):195.

Biddle C et al. (1988). The cardiovascular and pulmonary effects of inhalation anesthetic agents, Curr Rev Nurse Anesth 10(21):163.

Boucher BA et al. (1986). The postoperative adverse effects of inhalation anesthetics Heart Lung 15(1):63.

Carter M. (1989). Effects of anesthesia on mental performance in the elderly, Nurs Times 85(1):40.

Catron D. (1978). The anesthesiologist's handbook, ed 2. Baltimore: University Park Press.

Civetta JM. (1988). Perioperative effects of anesthesia, Curr Rev Post Anesth Care Nurses 10(8):58.

Curran MA. (1988). Epidural anesthesia: practical considerations, Curr Rev Nurse Anesth 10(22):170.

Farrell RG (1988). Intravenous regional anesthesia for the emergency department: the mini dose Bier block, Top Emerg Med 10(1):53.

Feldman MEB. (1988). Inadvertent hypothermia: a threat to homeostasis in the post anesthetic patient, J Post Anesth Nurs 3(2):82.

Gilman AG et al, eds. (1990). Goodman and Gilman's the pharmacological basis of therapeutics, ed 8. New York: Macmillan, Inc.

Goodwin SR. (1989). Anesthesia and drug interactions, Curr Rev Nurse Anesth 11(17):130.

Gravenstein JS. (1988). The induction of general anesthesia, Curr Rev Nurse Anesth 11(2):11.

Haghenbeck K. (1989). Nursing care following spinal anesthesia, Crit Care Nurs 9(4):22.

Hemminki K et al. (1985). Spontaneous abortions and malformations in the offspring of nurses exposed to anaesthetic gases, cytostatic drugs, and other potential hazards in hospitals, based on registered information of outcome, J Epidemiol Community Health 39(2):141.

Houghton K. (1988). Local anesthesia, Nurs Times 84(41):63.

Kalbach LR. (1989). Spinal headache: cause and cure, Orthop Nurse 8(2):51.

Markowsky C. (1988). Spinal narcotics and the implications for nursing, Can Crit Care Nurs J 5(4):15.

Marshall MN. (1989). Demystifying general anesthesia, Can Crit Care Nurs J 6(1):13; 7(1):19.

McSwain NE Jr. (1989). Regional anesthesia procedures, Emerg Med 21(12):73.

McSwain NE Jr. (1989). Wrist block, Emerg Med 21(13):107.

Meagher TF. (1988). The incidence of emergence excitement: a descriptive study—restlessness following general anesthesia, J Post Anesth Nurs 3(4):247.

Miller ED Jr. (1988). What causes anesthetic deaths, Curr Rev Post Anesth Care Nurses 10(19):147.

Paris PM. (1986). No more pain, J Emerg Med 18(7):155.

Petrone S. (1989). Perioperative nurses must prepare themselves to monitor patients receiving local anesthetics, AORN J 50(2):442.

Pories WJ. (1986). Anesthesia, J Emerg Med 18(7):155.

Recommended practices: monitoring the patient receiving local anesthesia. (1989). AORN J 50(3):624.

Scott SL. (1988). Malignant hyperthermia: a review, Can Bull Cardiovasc Nurs 12(2):9.

Teeple E. (1987). Inhalation anesthetics for neuroanesthesia, Curr Rev Nurse Anesth 10(3):19.

Thomson DA. (1987). Anesthesia and the immune system, J Burn Care Rehabil 8(6):483.

Toledo LW et al. (1989). Stable and ready for transfer: nursing judgment of readiness for transfer from the PARU: post anesthesia recovery unit, J Post Anesth Nurs 4(4):247.

United States Pharmacopeial Convention. (1991). Drug information for the health care provider, ed 11. Rockville, Md: US Pharmacopeial Convention, Inc.

Vogelsang, J et al. (1989). Stadol attenuates postanesthesia shivering, J Post Anesth Nurs 4(4):247.

*Chapter*

# 14 Antianxiety, Sedative, and Hypnotic Drugs

## CHAPTER OBJECTIVES

*After studying this chapter, you should be able to meet the following objectives and define the key terms.*

1. Describe the physiology and stages of sleep.

2. Differentiate between antianxiety, sedative, and hypnotic drug effects.

3. Discuss the nursing management of sedative-hypnotic therapy.

4. Discuss specific nursing interventions for the use of antianxiety, sedative, and hypnotic agents in pediatric and geriatric clients.

5. Identify the characteristics of commonly used benzodiazepines and barbiturates.

6. Formulate an appropriate plan of care for individual clients who require the administration of antianxiety, sedative, or hypnotic agents.

## KEY TERMS

**amnesic effect,** page 262
**antianxiety agents,** page 257
**anxiety,** page 257
**anxiolytic,** p 257
**hypnotic,** page 258
**insomnia,** page 260
**monosynaptic reflex,** page 262
**non-REM sleep,** page 258
**polysynaptic reflex,** page 262
**REM sleep,** page 258
**sedative,** page 258
**Stevens-Johnson syndrome,** page 271

## INTRODUCTION

**Antianxiety**, or **anxiolytic**, **agents** are used to reduce feelings of **anxiety**, that is, apprehension, nervousness, worry, or fearfulness. Anxiety is usually a normal psychologic and physiologic response to a personally threatening situation. A threat to one's health, body, loved ones, job, or life-style may result in anxiety. Generally this anxiety stimulates the person to take a purposeful or deliberate action to counteract or offset the anxiety-producing state. When a person is unable to cope with a persistently stressful situation because excessive anxiety interferes with daily functioning, help is

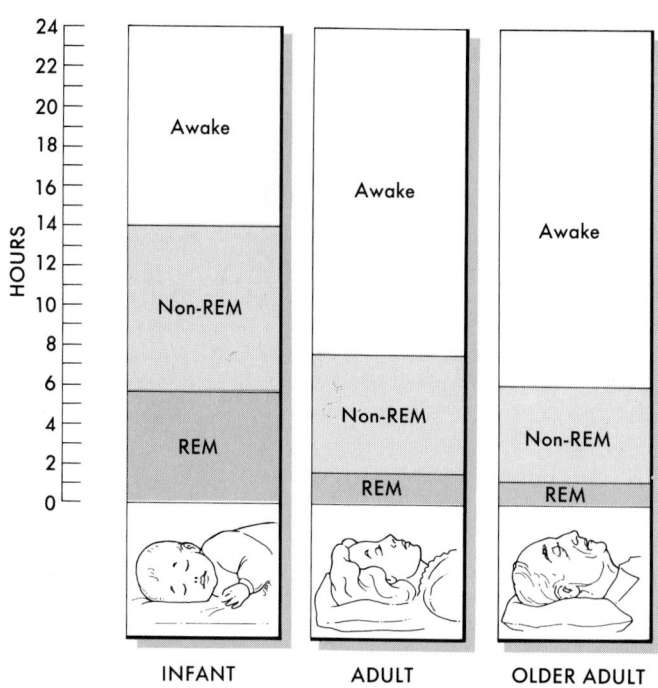

**FIGURE 14-1**   Sleep-wake cycles across the life span. Infants: approximately 40% of total sleep time is REM. Adults: 20% of total sleep time is REM. Older adults: total sleep time is slightly reduced; REM remains 20% of total. *(From Beare PB and Myers JL. [1990]. Principles and practice of adult health nursing. St. Louis: Mosby–Year Book, Inc.)*

necessary. Although many nonpharmacologic modalities are available, the antianxiety agents are most commonly prescribed for the treatment of anxiety. For proposed site of action for the benzodiazepines, see "Limbic System" in Chapter 11, "Overview of the Central Nervous System."

**Sedatives** and **hypnotics** are CNS depressant drugs. Although sedatives were commonly prescribed before the advent of the benzodiazepine family, their general use today has declined. Sedatives are chemical substances that reduce nervousness, excitability, or irritability by producing a calming or soothing effect. Hypnotics are used to induce sleep. The major difference between a sedative and a hypnotic is the degree of CNS depression induced. Small doses of a CNS-depressing agent may be used for a sedative effect, whereas larger dosages may be used for hypnotic effects. Barbiturates have been used extensively as sedative-hypnotic agents, but because of their low degree of selectivity and safety, they have been largely replaced by the safer benzodiazepines.

## PHYSIOLOGY OF SLEEP

Sleep can be defined as a recurrent, normal condition of inertia and unresponsiveness during which an individual's overt and covert responses to stimuli are markedly reduced. During sleep a person is no longer in sensory contact with the immediate environment, and stimuli that have bombarded the senses of sight, hearing, touch, smell, and taste

during waking hours no longer attract attention or exert a controlling influence over voluntary and involuntary movements or functions. It certainly is not difficult to understand that everyone needs to escape from constant stimuli.

Sleep research has shown that sleep is not one level of unconsciousness; it actually consists of two basic stages occurring cyclically:

1. Rapid eye movement (REM)
2. Non-rapid eye movement (non-REM)

During sleep, the individual moves through **REM sleep**, then through the four stages of **non-REM sleep**, with stage 4 considered the deepest level of non-REM sleep (see Figure 14-1). The stages of sleep are based on electrical activity that can be observed in the brain by means of an electro-encephalogram (EEG). The EEG provides graphic illustrations of brain waves, which are an indication of the electrical activity occurring in the brain. (See box for a description of the stages of sleep.)

From the standpoint of dreaming, sleep consists of two main functional states. One is called "slow-wave," non-dreaming, or non–rapid eye movement (non-REM) sleep. The other is referred to as "paradoxical," dreaming, or rapid-eye-movement (REM) sleep. It should be kept in mind that REM sleep is not synonymous with light sleep, since it takes a more powerful stimulus to arouse an animal or person from REM sleep than from synchronous slow-wave sleep.

Sleep research indicates that there are psychologic and physiologic reasons for the body to maintain an equilibrium

## STAGES OF SLEEP*

| Stage | Characteristics | Average Time (%) Spent in Stages in Young Adults |
|---|---|---|
| **Non-REM sleep** | | |
| Stage 1 | Dozing or feelings of drifting off to sleep. Person can be easily awakened. Insomniacs have longer stage 1 periods than normal. | 3%-6% |
| Stage 2 | Person is relaxed but can be easily awakened. Has occasional REM and also some slight eyeball movements. | 40%-52% |
| Stage 3 | Deep sleep, difficult to wake person up. Respirations, pulse, and blood pressure may decrease. | 5%-8% |
| Stage 4 | Sleepwalking or bedwetting may occur. Person very hard to wake up. If awakened, may be very groggy. Dreaming, especially about daily events. | 10%-19% |
| REM sleep | Rapid eye movements occur here. Vivid dreams occur during REM sleep. Respirations may be irregular. | 23%-34% |

* A complete cycle takes approximately 90 minutes.

between the various stages of sleep. Physiologic functions of the body tend to be depressed during nondreaming sleep. For example, it is known that:

1. Blood pressure falls (10 to 30 mm Hg)
2. Pulse rate is slowed
3. Metabolic rate is decreased
4. Gastrointestinal tract activity is slowed
5. Urine formation slows
6. Oxygen consumption and carbon dioxide production are lowered
7. Body temperature slightly decreases
8. Respirations are slower and more shallow
9. Body movement is minimal

Dreaming sleep tends to increase most of these parameters, and body movements are more noticeable—turning, jerking, arms and legs moving, talking, crying, or laughing—and, of course, eye movements can be seen under the closed lids. The dynamic physiologic equilibrium of the body continues to be maintained even during sleep. Depression of physiologic functions occurs during deep sleep, and an increase in functions occurs during dreaming. Repeated studies have shown that when individuals are deprived of deep sleep, they become physically uncomfortable, tend to withdraw from society and their friends, are less aggressive and outgoing, and manifest concern over vague physical complaints and changes in bodily feelings. The overall impression made by persons deprived of deep sleep is that of a depressive and hypochondriac reaction.

However, dreaming sleep is also important. From studies in which individuals were deprived of dreaming sleep (every time the subjects attempted to dream, as evidenced by rapid eye movements, they were awakened and not permitted to dream), the following results were observed. During their waking hours the individuals became less well integrated and less effective. They showed signs of confusion, suspicion, and withdrawal. They appeared anxious, insecure, and irritable; they had greater difficulty concentrating; they had a marked increase in appetite with a definite weight gain; and they were introspective and unable to derive support from other people.

Many psychologists and psychiatrists believe that wish fulfillment finds expression in dreams, and potentially harmful thoughts, feelings, and impulses are released through dreams so that there is no interference with the functioning of the personality during waking hours.

It is also known that in dream deprivation studies, the longer dream deprivation continues, the greater the increase in attempts to dream, until the individual begins to dream almost on falling asleep. When subjects are finally permitted to dream, a marked increase in dreaming is noted for the entire night, and as much as 75% of the night may be spent in dreaming. This amount diminishes for each succeeding recovery night until the individual has once again established his or her normal sleep pattern.

Research has shown that deep sleep takes priority over dreaming sleep when there has been prolonged sleep deprivation. In other words, deep sleep needs will be met first, after which dreaming sleep needs will be met. The body attempts to reestablish the normal equilibrium between the sleep stages.

Each individual establishes his or her own normal sleep pattern, which will vary somewhat from night to night and which is influenced by the individual's emotional and physical state. For most individuals, any alteration in sleeping habits will cause problems in falling asleep, staying asleep, or both. Since drugs affect an individual's physical and emotional states, they also influence his or her sleep pattern.

## PEDIATRIC DRUG USE

The use of antianxiety, sedative, or hypnotic agents in children is limited in practice. Childhood anxiety disorders usually respond better to counseling and psychotherapy than to medications (Anxiety, 1980). Also, young children are much more sensitive to the CNS-depressant effects of this classification of drugs. Paradoxical reactions, or reactions contrary to the expected reaction, have been reported with the use of barbiturates in both children and geriatric clients. These include increased excitability, hostility, confusion, hallucinations, and, perhaps, an acute elevation of body temperature. Sedation, though, may be indicated for particular situations if carefully selected (drug and dosage) for the individual child (e.g., the treatment of severe anxiety associated with an acute attack of asthma, as an adjunct preanesthetic agent, or in the treatment of convulsive disorders). But the use of such medications in children requires careful drug selection and dosage and close monitoring and assessment by the health care providers. (See box on pediatric implications.)

## GERIATRIC DRUG USE

Careful drug selection and dosage are necessary to avoid producing excessive CNS depression in the elderly. The aging process is usually associated with physiologic alterations including a decline in metabolism and in many organ functions, especially liver and kidney functions. Since drug half-lives may be extended, selecting agents with shorter half-lives and no active metabolites may be safer for the geriatric client. The elderly client should also be monitored for paradoxical reactions (i.e., increased excitability, rage, hostility, confusion, and hallucinations, which have been reported with both the benzodiazepines and the barbiturates). The appearance of such adverse reactions indicates immediate discontinuance of the medication and consultation with the prescribing physician.

The short-acting benzodiazepines are much safer than the barbiturates and are less effective anxiolytic and hypnotic agents. Oxazepam, lorazepam, temazepam, alprazolam, and triazolam have short to intermediate half-lives, and they are usually recommended for the elderly client requiring a benzodiazepine. Barbiturates should be avoided in the elderly because enhanced CNS depression, confusion, ataxia, and paradoxical reactions are commonly reported.

One of the most frequent complaints of the elderly is **insomnia** (difficulty falling asleep, or staying asleep, or waking up early in the morning). (See box for discussion.) Age-related physiologic changes may also contribute to the changes in sleep patterns reported. A recent study indicated that sleep problem complaints were more common with women than with men and generally were most common with subjects 80 years of age and older (Cornoni-Huntley et al, 1986). Chloral hydrate and benzodiazepines are usu-

---

### *Pediatric Implications:* ANTIANXIETY AGENTS AND SEDATIVES

Young children are more susceptible to the CNS-depressant effects of the benzodiazepines. In neonates, profound CNS depression may result because of the lower rate of drug metabolism by the immature liver.

Chronic use of clonazepam may result in impaired physical or mental functions in the developing child. This may not become apparent until years later.

Buspirone has not been studied in persons under 18 years; therefore it is not recommended for use in that age group.

Although diazepam (Valium) may be used in infants 6 months and over, this drug and other benzodiazepines should not be used to treat a hyperactive or psychotic child.

Methyprylon (Noludar) is not indicated for use in children under 12 years old.

To reduce or minimize potential adverse CNS-depressant effects, carefully follow the manufacturer's dosage instructions and, whenever possible, avoid concurrent administration of other CNS depressant types of drugs.

Monitor excessive sedation, lethargy, and lack of coordination; if any of these effects are present, dosage adjustments may be necessary.

Paradoxical reactions have been reported in both children and the elderly with the use of barbiturates. (See description under Pediatric Drug Use.

---

ally the agents of choice in treating insomnia in the elderly. When possible, physicians often suggest that the elderly limit their hypnotic dosages to three or four times a week, allowing clients to select the nights they need to take their medication. This schedule usually results in enhanced effectiveness, less daytime drowsiness or sedation, and a decreased potential for inducing tolerance to the medication. Regular and careful assessment, monitoring, and reevaluation of the need for hypnotics are highly recommended.

## ▷NURSING MANAGEMENT: SEDATIVE-HYPNOTIC THERAPY

***Assessment.*** The nurse should find out what a client's sleep habits are and how he or she ensures good sleep at home. A thorough sleep history is required before a regimen of medications is instituted. Such a history includes the following information:

* What does the client do about environmental control, which includes ventilation, lighting, and noise?
* What does the client do about physical care? Does he or she shower before retiring or go for a walk?
* What does the client do about food? Does he or she snack before retiring?

### *Geriatric Implications:*
## INSOMNIA AND HYPNOTICS

Studies indicate that in the elderly, sleep latency may increase, while REM and stage 4 sleep may be absent. The elderly often complain of sleep disturbances.

Evaluate the elderly for arthritic pain, hyperthyroidism, cardiac arrhythmias, and paroxysmal nocturnal dyspnea, since they may alter sleep patterns.

Reserve hypnotics for periods of acute insomnia only. They should not be used on a routine or long-term basis.

If a hypnotic drug is necessary, select one with a short half-life; it should be used for short time periods or intermittently.

Implement good sleep hygiene principles: Have a regular bedtime and a regular awakening time each day. Drink a hot milk beverage at bedtime. Do not eat or watch television in bed. Avoid caffeine-containing beverages or smoking cigarettes within 8 hours of bedtime. Avoid heavy meals before bedtime. Avoid daytime naps. In the evening engage in relaxing activities, such as reading, watching television, listening to relaxing music, taking a warm bath, or going for a pleasant walk. If you cannot fall asleep, get up and go into another room until sleepy. If nonprescription sleeping aids are used, limit to occasional usage at recommended doses.

Be aware that children, the elderly, and clients with CNS dysfunction may experience a paradoxical reaction (CNS stimulation) to hypnotics and antihistamines.

If longer-acting hypnotics are given to the elderly, daytime sedation, ataxia, and memory deficits may result.

Common side effects of antihistamine sleeping aids include dizziness, tinnitus, blurred or altered vision, gastrointestinal disturbance, and dry mouth.

## DRUGS ASSOCIATED WITH INDUCING INSOMNIA

**Chronic Use of Central Nervous System Stimulants**

caffeine (coffee, tea, colas, etc.)
amphetamines
methylphenidate (Ritalin)
nicotine
pemoline (Cylert)
protriptyline (Vivactil)
terbutaline
theophylline

**Withdrawal from CNS Depressants**

alcohol
barbiturates
tricyclic antidepressants, such as amitriptyline, imipramine, doxepin, and trimipramine
triazolam (Halcion)
hypnotic drugs

**Miscellaneous Drugs with Potential for Inducing Insomnia**

beta-blockers
contraceptives, oral
phenytoin
thyroid medications
corticosteroids
MAO inhibitors

---

• What does the client do about quiet recreation, such as reading, before sleep?

Various problems may cause the client to have insomnia. (see box above right). These include circadian rhythm irregularities, sleep apnea, restless leg syndrome, intake of alcohol or caffeine, various medications, and poor sleep hygiene, which is characterized by irregular bedtimes, daytime napping, and strenuous exercise or heavy eating just before bedtime.

When a client is admitted, a thorough drug history should be taken, including the use of both prescription and over-the-counter sleep preparations, and all medication brought from home should be removed for the client's safety.

***Intervention.*** Since nurses are in a strategic position to influence the client's sleep, it cannot be stressed enough that caution must be exercised when decisions are made about giving or repeating an hs or prn order for a sleeping medication. Immediately resorting to administering a sleep-ing medication when a client complains of being unable to sleep may be doing the client more harm than good. An assessment of the client and alternative methods of relaxing the client must be considered.

The nurse should try using supportive nursing measures (e.g., a back rub, reduction of environmental stimuli, relaxation therapy, or a warm drink) either alone, before a barbiturate is given, or in conjunction with the drug.

The nurse should prepare the client for sleep, raise the side rails on the bed, and caution the client to ambulate only with assistance. The normal adult dose may cause excitement, depression, or confusion.

Every effort should be made not to disrupt the sleeping client. If at all possible, medications are scheduled before sedatives or hypnotics are given. Vital signs are taken before the client falls asleep. Numerous interruptions for various aspects of care can do nothing but further alter the client's sleep pattern.

Since clients can become physically and psychologically dependent on these drugs, gradually taper off the medications to avoid an abstinence syndrome reaction.

***Education.*** The client should be cautioned against driving a car, operating machinery, or participating in any activity that may be dangerous while he or she is taking these drugs. Although the client may deny feeling sleepy the next day, his or her performance may show definable impairment because therapeutic levels of some of these drugs are retained.

Clients and their families need to be taught ways to promote good sleep without resorting to drugs, including OTC drugs (Sominex, NyTol, Sleep-eze, Unisom).

Stress to the client that sedative or hypnotic drugs should never be taken in combination with alcohol, antihistamines, antianxiety agents, antidepressants, or antipsychotic agents because they will produce an enhanced CNS-depressant effect.

**Evaluation.** Evaluation of compliance and effectiveness may be facilitated by use of a written "sleep diary." Among the information recorded in the diary are activities and eating before sleep, bedtimes, waking times, naps, and medication administration. Review of the diary will help identify success of therapy or areas of poor sleep hygiene. Indicators of effectiveness also include patient reports of feelings of rest and wakefulness without residual drowsiness or "drug hangover" during the daytime.

# BENZODIAZEPINES

Benzodiazepines are among the most widely prescribed drugs in clinical medicine. Their popularity probably results from their anxiolytic effects occurring at nontoxic doses. Drowsiness and undesirable CNS depression occur less frequently with benzodiazepine agents than with comparable doses of meprobamate or barbiturates.

**Mechanism of action.** Benzodiazepines do not exert a general CNS-depressant effect; instead a wide range of selectivity is seen with the various members of this class. Some of the general pharmacologic properties of this class include muscle relaxant, and antianxiety, anticonvulsant, and hypnotic effects. Although their exact mechanism of action is unknown, they appear to act at the limbic, thalamic, and hypothalamic areas of the CNS. Stimulation of the gamma-aminobutyric acid (GABA) receptors in the reticular activating system will block stimulation and arousal of the limbic and cortical areas, especially after stimulation of the brainstem reticular activating system. Presynaptic inhibition is enhanced, which may result in reduction of the spread of seizure activity, especially in the thalamus, cortex, and limbic areas of the CNS. The skeletal muscle relaxant effects are believed to be caused by blockade of the **monosynaptic and polysynaptic reflexes,** and these drugs also may directly decrease the motor nerve and muscle activity.

The limbic system, associated with the regulation of emotional behavior, contains a highly dense area of benzodiazepine receptors in the amygdala that may correspond to specific antianxiety action of certain drugs. These proposed benzodiazepine receptors may share some sites of action with other drugs (alcohol, meprobamate, barbiturates) and may further explain cross-tolerance to these drugs. The benzodiazepines' receptor concentration in the dorsal spinal cord may account for their muscle relaxant effect; an endogenous benzodiazepine-like substance also may exist. GABA, an inhibitory neurotransmitter, affects benzodiazepine receptors, and a benzodiazepine receptor may be a portion of a GABA receptor. Benzodiazepines enhance the action of GABA at its receptors. The identification of psychotropic drug receptors is leading to the discovery and understanding of the time and course of receptor site occupancy. This knowledge will allow more effective therapeutic use of the agents affecting mood and behavior and will further explain how the drugs exert their action in the neurotransmitter interaction within the CNS.

**Indications.** The most common indications for benzodiazepines include anxiety disorders, alcohol withdrawal, preoperative medication, sleep disorders, seizure disorders, and neuromuscular disease.

**Anxiety disorders.** Benzodiazepines, with the exception of clonazepam, flurazepam, temazepam, triazolam, and midazolam, are indicated for the treatment of anxiety. Several benzodiazepines (alprazolam, oral lorazepam, and oxazepam) are used as adjunct medications to treat anxiety associated with depression.

**Alcohol withdrawal.** The benzodiazepines most often used for treatment of alcohol withdrawal syndrome are chlordiazepoxide, clorazepate, diazepam, and oxazepam.

**Preoperative medication.** Parenteral chlordiazepoxide, diazepam, lorazepam, and midazolam are used preoperatively to reduce anxiety and to help induce general anesthesia; the last three drugs decrease the client's memory of the procedure. These three drugs are also used for endoscopic procedures to decrease anxiety and tension and to produce an anterograde **amnesic effect**.

**Sleep disorders.** Flurazepam, temazepam, and triazolam are usually prescribed for sleep disorders, such as insomnia, characterized by difficulty falling asleep or staying asleep or by early morning awakenings. Flurazepam is reported to be effective for up to 28 days, whereas temazepam's effectiveness may be demonstrated for up to 35 days of daily administration.

**Seizure disorders.** Clonazepam is available orally as an anticonvulsant. (See Chapter 15.) Also, parenteral diazepam is indicated for intractable, repetitive seizures, such as status epilepticus. Oral diazepam may be used for short-term adjunct therapy (1 to 2 weeks) with other anticonvulsants for the treatment of convulsions.

**Neuromuscular disease.** Benzodiazepines, especially diazepam, may be useful as adjunct medications for the treatment of skeletal muscle spasms caused by muscle or joint inflammation or spasticity resulting from upper motor neuron dysfunction, such as cerebral palsy and paraplegia.

**Pharmacokinetics.** Benzodiazepines are readily absorbed from the GI tract. Clorazepate and diazepam are the most rapidly absorbed drugs in this class, whereas oxazepam, prazepam, and temazepam are absorbed more slowly.

**TABLE 14-1**   Pharmacokinetic overview: benzodiazepines

| Name | Time to peak plasma concentration (hr) (oral) | Half-life (hr) | Active metabolites (half-life in hr) |
|---|---|---|---|
| alprazolam (Xanax) | 1-2 | 12-15 | alpha-hydroxy-alprazolam (12-15) |
| chlordiazepoxide (Librium, Libritab, Apo-Chlorax ♣, Medilium ♣) | 0.5-4 N/A* N/A | 5-30 | desmethylchloridazepoxide (18) demoxepam (14-95) desmethyldiazepam (30-100) oxazepam (5-15) |
| clonazepam (Klonopin, Rivotril ♣) | 1-2 (some patients from 4-8 hr) | 18-50 | none |
| clorazepate (Tranxene, Tranxene-SD, Novoclopate ♣) | 0.5-2 | Parent drug not active | desmethyldiazepam (30-100) oxazepam (5-15) |
| diazepam (Valium, Apo-Diazepam ♣, E-Pam ♣) | 0.5-2 0.5-2 N/A | 20-70 | desmethyldiazepam (30-100) temazepam (9.5-12.4) oxazepam (5-15) |
| flurazepam (Dalmane, Apo-Flurazepam ♣) | 0.5-1 | 2.3 | desalkylflurazepam (30-100) N-1-hydroxyethylflurazepam (2-4) |
| halazepam (Paxipam) | 1-3 | 14 | desmethyldiazepam (30-100) |
| prazepam (Centrax) | 2.5-6 hr for metabolite desmethyldiazepam (single dose) | Parent drug not active | desmethyldiazepam (30-100) oxazepam (5-15) |
| lorazepam (Ativan, Apo-Lorazepam ♣) | 1-6 | 10-20 | None |
| oxazepam (Serax, Ox-pam ♣, Zapex ♣) | 1-4 | 5-15 | None |
| midazolam HCl (Versed) | 0.5-1 | 1-5 | 1-hydroxymethyl and 4-hydroxy midazolam |
| temazepam (Restoril) | 2-3 | 9.5-12.4 | None |
| triazolam (Halcion) | within 2 | 1.6-5.4 | None |

*N/A, Information not available.

The more rapidly absorbed benzodiazepines produce a more prompt and intense onset of action.

After one dose, the benzodiazepines are dispersed rapidly to the body's fluids and tissues. This produces a rapid decrease in circulating drug, and the effects of a single dose end quickly. Lorazepam is not as extensively distributed and may have a longer duration of action, since effective blood concentrations may be more prolonged. After multiple doses, these drugs accumulate in the body's fluids and tissues. This saturation of storage sites allows for greater blood concentration and longer action. Accumulation in storage sites also accounts for the prolonged action of benzodiazepines after they have been discontinued.

The GI tract and the liver are the sites of metabolism for either the active drug forms or the inactive metabolites. The acid environment of the stomach is the site of conversion of clorazepate to its active form, desmethyldiazepam. Prazepam is transformed in the wall of the GI tract or during the first pass through the liver to desmethyldiazepam, but this process is not as rapid as clorazepate conversion.

These drugs are highly protein bound and lipid soluble and are excreted by the kidney. Protein binding is reduced in newborns, alcoholic clients, and those with cirrhosis or renal insufficiency. Because oxazepam and lorazepam are inactivated in one step by the liver, they may be preferred agents in elderly clients and those with liver disease.

The injectable benzodiazepines include chlordiazepoxide, diazepam, and lorazepam. The onset of action of these agents after intravenous administration is approximately 1 to 5 minutes. After intramuscular injection, the onset of action is approximately 15 to 30 minutes.

See Table 14-1 for a pharmacokinetic overview of selected benzodiazepam drugs.

***Side effects/adverse reactions.***   The most frequent side effects of benzodiazepines include drowsiness, hiccups (especially with midazolam), lassitude, and loss of dexterity. Less frequent side effects include dry mouth, nausea, vomiting, headaches, constipation, abdominal cramping, unsteadiness, dizziness, and blurred vision. If side effects continue, increase, or disturb the client, inform the physician.

Adverse reactions include increased behavioral problems, which are seen mostly with children (anger, decreased ability to concentrate). Neurologic reactions include insomnia, increased excitability, hallucinations, and apprehension (paradoxical reaction). In addition, the client may experience pruritus, skin rash, sore throat, elevated temperature, increased bruising or bleeding episodes, mental depression, hepatitis, confusion, mouth or throat sores, and muscle weakness. Finally, clients using midazolam have reported muscle tremors, tachycardia, shortness of breath, or breathing difficulties. If adverse reactions occur, contact the physician because medical intervention may be necessary.

***Significant drug interactions.*** Significant drug interactions may occur when benzodiazepines are used in combination with CNS depressants (such as alcohol), opioid analgesics, anesthetics, zidovudine (AZT), MAO inhibitors, and tricyclic antidepressants. Enhanced CNS-depressant effects have been reported. Monitor closely, since the dosage of one or both drugs may need to be adjusted. Doses of opioid analgesics should generally be reduced by one third when used in combination with benzodiazepines. Zidovudine metabolism may be inhibited, leading to an increased potential for toxicity. Avoid concurrent administration.

***Dosage and administration.*** For dosage and administration information, see Table 14-2.

## ▷NURSING MANAGEMENT: BENZODIAZEPINE THERAPY

***Assessment.*** Initially, it should be determined if the client has a hypersensitivity to any of the benzodiazepines, since there may be a cross-sensitivity to other benzodiazepines. Pregnant clients usually should avoid using benzodiazepines, since their use is associated with increased risk of congenital anomalies. Female clients of childbearing age should be advised that if they should become pregnant or intend to become pregnant during anxiolytic therapy, they should immediately notify the physician who prescribed the drugs about the advisability of conception. At that time a decision about discontinuing the drug must be made.

Nursing mothers should not be given benzodiazepines. Because of their molecular size, the benzodiazepines and their metabolites probably are excreted in breast milk.

For elderly or debilitated clients, the initial dose should be small and increments added gradually, based on the response of each client, to preclude ataxia or excessive sedation. Doses of benzodiazepines sufficient to control anxiety cause unwanted drowsiness less frequently than equivalent doses of barbiturates or meprobamate. The benzodiazepines have high therapeutic effectiveness and low addiction potential and lethality; they are generally desirable agents for anxious elderly clients. These drugs occasionally cause paradoxical reactions such as agitation and confusion, but these occur to a lesser degree than with barbiturates.

The nurse should remember that elderly clients are more vulnerable to the adverse effects of these drugs. Excretion is delayed in this population, and thus the half-life increases. This response may allow the client to attain therapeutic blood levels with a single dose rather than two or three doses per day. Daytime sedation can be reduced if the single daily dose is administered at bedtime. If the elderly client is continent, ambulatory, and alert, excessive doses of the benzodiazepines may produce an incontinent, nonambulatory, or confused client. Careful titration to individual needs is essential in elderly clients.

When depression accompanies the client's anxiety, the incidence of suicidal tendencies is significant. This may necessitate further protective measures to avoid self-destructive acts such as multidrug overdosage. As small an amount of the drug as possible should be available to such a client at any one time. This requires accurate medical office data about prescriptions and their refill dates and ensures greater control by the prescriber.

Because of their anticholinergic effects, benzodiazepines should be used with caution in clients with glaucoma. Their use may also precipitate ventilatory failure in clients with severe chronic obstructive pulmonary disease.

Clients receiving benzodiazepines for prolonged periods should have periodic blood counts to monitor for neutropenia, as well as liver function tests. Also, the usual precautions in treating clients with impaired renal or hepatic function should be observed. In animal studies hepatomegaly and cholestasis were observed.

Dosages should be carefully determined for clients with renal impairment, especially when chlordiazepoxide and diazepam are administered, since active metabolites may accumulate and produce toxicity. Flurazepam hydrochloride should be avoided, whereas other agents, such as clonazepam, lorazepam, oxazepam, and temazepam, seem to pose no risk of toxicity in renal impairment.

Multiple physical and psychiatric problems frequently occur together and may require treatment with several drugs. Multiple drug therapy is sometimes referred to as "polypharmacy." A client may benefit diagnostically and therapeutically from an evaluation made on the basis of a drug-free baseline.

Some clients abruptly withdrawn from high doses or therapeutic doses of benzodiazepines taken over prolonged periods exhibit symptoms of withdrawal. These may resemble the symptoms of anxiety for which the drug was originally prescribed. A mild withdrawal syndrome is characterized by feelings of tension or anxiety, anorexia, GI symptoms such as diarrhea, weakness, and lethargy, light-headedness, tremor, and mild numbness. Clients who exhibit moderately severe symptoms report anxiety, apprehension, restlessness, insomnia, increased frequency of dreaming, anorexia-induced weight loss, dysphoric moods, and palpitations. Rarely, clients exhibit seizures and delirium. Symptoms usually begin 24 to 72 hours after withdrawal. When the client is withdrawn from a short-acting benzodiazepine,

**TABLE 14-2**   Dosage and administration of selected benzodiazepines

| Adults | Elderly | Children |
|---|---|---|
| **ALPRAZOLAM** | | |
| Antianxiety, 0.25-0.5 mg orally 3 times daily. Dosage may be titrated if needed, up to a maximum of 4 mg/day | 0.25 mg orally 2-3 times daily. Increase dosage if necessary, according to client's requirements and individual response | Not established for children less than 18 yr |
| **CHLORDIAZEPOXIDE** | | |
| Antianxiety: 5-25 mg orally 3-4 times daily or 50-100 mg IM or IV initially; then 25-50 mg 3-4 times a day as needed<br>Sedative-hypnotic: 50-100 mg orally initially for acute withdrawal syndrome. Repeat when needed, up to 300 mg/day<br>Maintenance therapy usually requires a reduced dosage. Parenterally, 50-100 mg IM or IV initially; if necessary, dosage may be repeated in 2-4 hr | Antianxiety: 5 mg orally 2-4 times daily. If necessary, increase dose gradually according to client's requirements and individual response | Antianxiety: for children 6 yr and older, 5 mg orally 2-4 times daily, increased gradually according to child's requirements and response. Dosage not established for younger children. Parenterally, children 12 yr and older, 25-50 mg IM or IV. Dosage not established for younger children |
| **CLORAZEPATE** | | |
| Antianxiety: 7.5-15 mg orally, 2-4 times daily, or 15 mg at bedtime initially; then adjust dosage according to client's requirements and individual response | 3.75-15 mg orally initially; increase dosage gradually according to client's response and drug tolerance | |
| Sedative-hypnotic: for acute alcohol withdrawal syndrome, 30 mg orally initially, then 15 mg orally 2-4 times a day for the first 24 hr; 15 mg 3-6 times daily for the second day; 7.5-15 mg 3 times a day the third day; 7.5 mg 2-4 times daily the fourth day; and 3.75 mg 2-4 times a day thereafter | | |
| Anticonvulsant: up to 7.5 mg 3 times daily initially; then increase dose as necessary with the following limitations: limit increase to 7.5 mg/wk and daily dosage should not be more than 90 mg/day | | For children 9-12 yr, up to 7.5 mg orally initially, twice daily. Dosage may be increased by 7.5 mg increments weekly but should not exceed 60 mg daily. Dosage not established for children less than 9 yr |
| **DIAZEPAM** | | |
| Antianxiety: 2-10 mg orally in tablet form 2-4 times daily. Extended release capsules, 15-30 mg orally daily. Parenterally, preoperatively, individualize dosage; generally, 10 mg IM or IV given before surgery. For treatment of psychoneurosis, 2-10 mg IM or IV; may repeat in 3 or 4 hr if needed | 2-2.5 mg orally once or twice a day or titrated to the individual's requirements and tolerance. Use of the extended-release capsules is recommended only for persons maintained on a 5-mg tablet 3 times a day; then a 15-mg capsule daily may be substituted. Parenterally, 2-5 mg IM or IV initially. Titrate further dosage according to client's requirements and tolerance. | Children 6 mo and older, orally, 1-2.5 mg or 0.04-0.2 mg/kg body weight or 1.17-6 mg/m² body surface area given orally 3 or 4 times daily. Not recommended for infants less than 6 mo of age. Dosage increases should be gradual and carefully monitored. Parenterally, no established dosage for neonate less than 30 days old. Check current package insert or USP-DI for recommended parenteral dosing |
| Sedative-hypnotic: for acute alcohol withdrawal syndrome, 10 mg orally 3-4 times daily for the first 24 hr, then 5 mg 3-4 times daily thereafter as needed. Extended release capsules, 30 mg orally for the first 24 hr, then 15 mg daily if needed. Parenterally, 10 mg IM or IV initially, then 5-10 mg in 3 or 4 hr when necessary. | | |

**TABLE 14-2**   Dosage and administration of selected benzodiazepines—cont'd

| Adults | Elderly | Children |
|---|---|---|
| Anticonvulsant: 2-10 mg orally 2-4 times daily. Parenterally, status epilepticus or severe convulsive episodes (recurrent), 5-10 mg IM or IV initially; repeat dosage if needed at 10-15 min intervals. Maximum dosage, 30 mg. If required, the therapy may be repeated in 2-4 hr | | For infants more than 30 days old and less than 5 yr old, 0.2-0.5 mg IV (preferred) or IM, every 2-5 min up to maximum dosage of 5 mg. If repeated therapy is necessary, repeat in 2-4 hr. Children 5 yr and older, 1 mg every 2-5 min up to maximum dosage of 10 mg (IM or IV, latter is perferred). If necessary, dosage may be repeated in 2-4 hr |
| Skeletal muscle relaxant: 2-10 mg 3 or 4 times daily. Extended-release capsule, 15-30 mg daily. Parenterally, for muscle spasms, 5-10 mg IM or IV initially; repeat in 3-4 hr if needed. Tetanus requires larger dosages | | Tetanus: infants more than 30 days old and less than 5 yr, 1-2 mg IM or IV; may repeat every 3-4 hr if necessary. Children 5 yr and older, 5-10 mg IM or IV; repeat in 3-4 hr if necessary. NOTE: For IV dosages in infants and children, medication should be given over a 3-min period in a dose that does not surpass 0.25 mg/kg body weight. Wait 15-30 min before repeating dosage |
| Amnesic effect: for cardioversion, 5-15 mg IV, 5-10 min before performing procedure. Endoscopic, dosages up to 20 mg IV (which is the preferred route of administration); titrate dosage according to client's response. Administer just before performing this procedure. IM doses (5-10 mg) may be given half hour before procedure | | |
| FLURAZEPAM | | |
| Sedative-hypnotic, 15 or 30 mg orally | 15 mg orally to start. Increase dose if necessary and tolerated by client | Dosage not established in children less than 15 yr old |
| HALAZEPAM | | |
| Antianxiety, 20-40 mg orally, 3-4 times daily | 20 mg orally once or twice a day. Titrate dosage according to client's response and tolerance | Dosage not established for children less than 18 yr old |
| LORAZEPAM | | |
| Antianxiety, 1-3 mg orally 2-3 times daily. Sedative-hypnotic, 2-4 mg orally at bedtime. Parenterally, antianxiety, sedative-hypnotic, amnesic: 0.05 mg/kg body weight IM up to 4 mg maximum administered 2 hr before surgery to obtain greatest amnesic effect. IV, 0.044 mg/kg body weight or 2-mg dose, whichever is less. To produce amnesic action, doses up to 0.05 mg/kg body weight may be given (do not exceed 4 mg). This dose is given 15-20 min before surgery to obtain the greatest amnesic effect | 0.5-2 mg orally daily in divided doses. Titrate dosage according to client's response and tolerance | Dosage not established for children less than 12 yr old for oral dosage forms. For injectable, dosage not available for children less than 18 yr old |

**TABLE 14-2**  Dosage and administration of selected benzodiazepines—cont'd

| Adults | Elderly | Children |
|---|---|---|
| **MIDAZOLAM** | | |
| Sedation for presurgical and amnesic effects: 70-80 μg (or 0.07-0.08 mg of base)/kg body weight, usually administered IM 30-60 min before operation. It may be given with atropine and decreased dosages of narcotics. Sedation for endoscopic or cardiovascular scheduled procedures: if clients have been medicated with opioids, the dosage of midazolam should be reduced by 30%. If not premedicated, IV dose is 2.5 mg base given before the procedure. If additional dosages are needed, 25% of the initial dose (or increments of 25%) may be administered | Adjunct to general anesthesia: For clients more than 55 yr old, for healthy or good-risk clients, an initial 0.3 mg base/kg body weight IV given over 20-30 sec. For clients more than 55 yr old who have multiple or severe disease states, 0.15-0.25 mg base/kg body weight IV over 20-30 sec | Sedation for presurgical and amnesic effects: individualize dosage |
| Adjunct to general anesthesia: if not premedicated with opioids or other sedatives, for clients up to 55 yr old, 0.2-0.35 mg base/kg body weight IV given in 5-30 sec. For full effect to occur, wait at least 2 min. If clients are premedicated with sedatives or opioids and are 55 yr old or less, administer 0.15-0.25 mg base/kg body weight IV over 20-30 sec. For additional information, check current USP-DI | | |
| **OXAZEPAM** | | |
| Antianxiety, 10-30 mg orally, 3-4 times daily. Sedative-hypnotic, for acute alcohol withdrawal syndrome, 15 or 30 mg orally 3-4 times daily | 10 mg orally initially, 3 times daily. Titrate dosage to 15 mg orally 3 or 4 times daily, according to client's response and tolerance | Not recommended for children less than 6 yr. Dosages not available for children 6-12 yr old |
| **PRAZEPAM** | | |
| Antianxiety, 10 mg orally 3 times daily (20-60 mg/day as a range). Or an alternate dose is 20-40 mg at bedtime | 10-15 mg orally daily (in divided doses); titrate according to client's requirements and tolerance | Dosages not available for persons 18 yr and less |
| **TEMAZEPAM** | | |
| Sedative-hypnotic, 15 or 30 mg | 15 mg orally; titrate dosages according to client's requirements and tolerance | Not available for children up to 18 yr |
| **TRIAZOLAM** | | |
| Sedative-hypnotic, 0.25-0.5 mg orally | 0.125 mg initially; then titrate dosage according to client's requirements and tolerance | Not available for children up to 18 yr |

symptoms peak in about 5 to 7 days and subside after 7 to 10 days. The withdrawal syndrome of the long-acting benzodiazepines peaks at about 5 days but may last 2 to 4 weeks. Withdrawal symptoms can be relieved by administering a dose of the anxiolytic agent. The withdrawal syndrome can be avoided by gradually tapering the dose of the anxiolytic agent and supporting the client during this period with other anxiety-relieving techniques.

Because of the CNS effects of benzodiazepine therapy, clients are at risk for injury, alteration in sensory-perceptual function, alteration in self-concept, and a disturbance in sleep pattern. There may also be an alteration in bowel function as a result of the drug's gastrointestinal effects.

*Intervention.* Nonpharmacologic interventions for the reduction of anxiety related to the stress of everyday life should be encouraged, since the benzodiazepines are not indicated for the long-term management of this anxiety. Stress-reduction techniques such as self-coaching, thought stopping, guided imagery, and progressive relaxation exercises may be used as adjuncts to the benzodiazepines.

The nurse should avoid intramuscular administration because the preparations are highly alkaline and irritating to tissues. Absorption is also erratic by this route of administration.

Administer intravenous preparations slowly because apnea, hypotension, bradycardia, and cardiac arrest have been known to occur with rapid administration. Arteriospasm, with resultant gangrene, will be caused by accidental intra-arterial, rather than intravenous, administration. After receiving a parenteral dose of a benzodiazepine, the client needs close observation for at least 3 hours, preferably at bed rest.

Concern about overuse or overprescribing of benzodiazepines leading to tolerance, dependency, and withdrawal problems was discussed in Chapter 9. Several general guidelines are offered to reduce the potential for drug abuse with this drug classification.

First, benzodiazepines are antianxiety agents (i.e., they are used to control the symptoms of anxiety but are not curative agents).

Second, benzodiazepines are indicated for short-term therapy or on an as-needed only basis. The dosage should be the minimum necessary to produce the desired effect. The client should be re-evaluated every 2 weeks to ascertain the effectiveness of the medication, the need for continued therapy, or both.

Third, when a benzodiazepine is being discontinued, the dosage should be tapered over 2 weeks. In clients receiving the short-acting benzodiazepines (lorazepam, alprazolam), severe withdrawal symptoms have been reported if the medications have been abruptly stopped. Switching to a longer half-life benzodiazepine for a few weeks before instituting the tapering procedure has resulted in a reduction in the more serious withdrawal symptoms, such as tonic-clonic seizures.

Finally, concurrent consumption of two or more benzodiazepine agents even for daytime anxiety and bedtime insomnia is considered inappropriate therapy. Using one benzodiazepine to accomplish both purposes would be preferred, because (1) effectiveness is usually equivalent, (2) the drug will be better tolerated and controlled by the client, and (3) the therapy will be less expensive.

*Education.* The client should be instructed to avoid alcohol, sleep-inducing OTC medications, and other CNS depressants while taking benzodiazepines. The client should be cautioned not to take more than the prescribed dosage if the medication seems less effective, but to consult the prescriber. If on a scheduled dosing regimen (such as use as an anticonvulsant), the client should take a missed dose right away if the dose missed is remembered within 1 to 2 hours. If it is remembered much later, the client should not double the next dose, but should skip the missed dose and continue the regimen.

*Evaluation.* Reassessment of the medication's effectiveness as an antianxiety agent or as a sedative-hypnotic should be done periodically over the course of therapy. If a drug is being used for its antianxiety properties, the client should report an increase in psychologic and physiologic comfort and should appear to have relaxed facial expressions and body movements. Clients using a benzodiazepine for nighttime sedation should relate an increase in the amount and quality of sleep and daytime wakefulness, if the agent is effective.

## Selected Benzodiazepines

### alprazolam (Xanax)

Alprazolam is used as an antianxiety agent. Accumulation is minimal after multiple doses and elimination rapidly follows termination of therapy.

### chlordiazepoxide (Librium, Libritab, Medilium ✳)

In addition to its use as an antianxiety agent and a sedative-hypnotic, chlordiazepoxide is used as an antitremor and antipanic agent and for relief of acute alcohol withdrawal symptoms.

Intravenous administration is preferred because intramuscular absorption is slow and erratic. Intravenous administration should be slow, over a period of at least 1 minute. The nurse should be careful *not* to use the intramuscular diluent when preparing solution for intravenous administration, since it has a tendency to form air bubbles.

When preparing a chlordiazepoxide solution for intramuscular administration, use only the manufacturer's diluent and administer the drug deeply into the muscle. Mixing the drug with sodium chloride or sterile water for injection will cause pain on injection.

Solutions should be used immediately after reconstitution, and any unused solution should be discarded.

After receiving the drug parenterally, the client should be kept resting in bed and monitored carefully for up to 3 hours for decreases in respiratory rate, heart rate, and blood pressure.

Because of the long-acting metabolites that remain in the bloodstream for several days, the client should be monitored for accumulative effects of the drug.

### clonazepam (Klonopin)

Clonazepem is used as an anticonvulsant and in treatment of panic disorders. When used as an anticonvulsant, clients receiving long-term therapy should avoid abrupt withdrawal, since this may precipitate seizures.

### clorazepate (Tranxene, Novoclopate ✽)

Clorazepate is used as an antianxiety agent, sedative-hypnotic, and anticonvulsant, and for relief of acute alcohol withdrawal symptoms. When given orally, it is one of the most rapidly absorbed benzodiazepines. Accumulation of active metabolites may be significant with long-term therapy.

### diazepam (Valium, Valrelease, Apo-Diazepam ✽)

Diazepam is used as an antianxiety agent, sedative-hypnotic, anticonvulsant, and skeletal muscle relaxer. Parenteral diazepam is an amnesic and is used orally as an antitremor agent.

Intravenous administration should be accomplished slowly, at least 1 minute for each 5 mg of the drug, to prevent apnea, hypotension, bradycardia, or cardiac arrest. The client should be observed at bed rest for at least 3 hours after parenteral administration.

To minimize the occurrence of thrombophlebitis following intravenous administration of diazepam, the vein can be flushed with at least 1 ml of saline per milligram of diazepam. Injection should be made into a large vein, not small veins, such as found on the back of the hand and wrist.

Diazepam is not compatible with aqueous solutions. If direct intravenous injection is not possible, the drug should be slowly injected through an infusion tube as close to the point of needle insertion in the patient as possible.

Continuous intravenous infusion is not recommended, since diazepam may precipitate in the infusion bag and the medication may be absorbed by the plastic infusion bags and tubing.

When diazepam is used parenterally for peroral endoscopy, the use of a topical anesthetic is recommended. Increased coughing, decreased respirations, dyspnea, hyperventilation, and laryngospasm have been known to occur; measures to assist with respirations should be available.

See Chapter 15 for nursing considerations in regard to the use of diazepam as an anticonvulsant.

### flurazepam (Dalmane, Apo-Flurazepam ✽)

Flurazepam is indicated only for use as a sedative-hypnotic. The client should be instructed that 2 to 3 nights may be required before flurazepam becomes fully effective. Elimination is slow, since metabolites remain in the body several days. This may produce unwanted daytime carryover effects that result in poor coordination and drowsiness.

Overcome carryover effects by using lower doses and administering medication every other evening. The client must be warned of the sustained effect of the active metabolites.

### halazepam (Paxipam)

Halazepam is indicated for use only as an antianxiety agent. It has a long half-life and active metabolites, which may be significant when multiple doses are administered. Elimination may take several days or even weeks.

### lorazepam (Ativan, Alzapam, Novolorazem ✽)

Lorazepam is indicated for use as an antianxiety agent and sedative-hypnotic. Parenteral lorazepam is also indicated as an amnesic, anticonvulsant, antitremor agent, and skeletal muscle relaxant.

Lorazepam must be mixed with an equal amount of a compatible diluent immediately before intravenous use. It may be infused directly into a vein or through intravenous tubing. Infusion rates should not exceed 2 mg/min.

Intraarterial injection may cause arteriospasm and possible gangrene. Avoid using the drug intraarterially, if possible.

Intramuscular lorazepam is injected, undiluted, into deep muscle mass.

After receiving a parenteral dose of lorazepam, the client should be observed at bed rest for at least 1 hour for decreases in respiratory rate, heart rate, and blood pressure.

### midazolam (Versed)

Midazolam is used for its antianxiety, sedative-hypnotic, and amnesic effects, and as an adjunct to general anesthesia. Midazolam is only used in parenteral form. Unlike diazepam, it does not cause thrombophlebitis and irritation on injection.

Dosages should be individualized according to the health status of the client. The range between therapeutic dosage and unconsciousness or disorientation appears to be narrow, necessitating close monitoring of the client.

The client should be instructed not to engage in tasks requiring alertness, such as driving, until the effects of midazolam have abated or until the day after administration, whichever is longer.

Intravenous midazolam has been associated with severe respiratory depression and arrest, especially when given concurrently with an opioid analgesic or when administered too rapidly. A warning has been issued for the intravenous use of this drug: it should be employed only in a hospital or ambulatory care setting with continuous respiratory and cardiac monitoring and resuscitative drugs and equipment available.

As with diazepam, when midazolam is used for peroral endoscopic procedures, a topical anesthetic agent should also be used and measures to support respiration (oxygen, suction airway) should be available.

### oxazepam (Serax, Zapex♣)

Oxazepam is indicated as an antianxiety agent and for treatment of the symptoms of acute alcohol withdrawal. Accumulation is minimal during multiple-dose therapy, with rapid elimination following termination of therapy.

### prazepam (Centrax)

Prazepam is indicated only as an antianxiety agent. It is one of the least rapidly absorbed benzodiazepines after oral administration, and accumulation of active metabolites may be significant in long-term therapy.

### quazepam (Doral)

Quazepam is a benzodiazepine hypnotic, available in 7.5-mg and 15-mg tablets. Because of its extended drug half-life and active metabolites, daytime drowsiness is more common with quazepam than with most of the other benzodiazepamsines.

### temazepam (Restoril, Razepam)

Temazepam is indicated as a sedative-hypnotic. Only minimal accumulation occurs during multiple doses, and elimination is rapid when therapy is discontinued.

### triazolam (Halcion)

Triazolam is indicated only as a sedative-hypnotic. Anterograde amnesia has been reported more frequently with triazolam than with the other benzodiazepines. In several European countries, the 0.5-mg dose of triazolam was taken off the market because of the frequency of reports of amnesia and other adverse reactions (Abramowicz, 1988). A triazolam syndrome has been described in the elderly; it includes drug-induced behavioral side effects of confusion, disorientation, increased wandering, and verbal incoherence. Altered pharmacokinetics in the elderly may be responsible for these alterations (Patterson, 1987).

Overdosage of triazolam may occur with only a 2-mg dose, which is only four times the maximum recommended dose. The nurse should be especially alert for the signs and symptoms of adverse reactions and overdosage.

### New Benzodiazepines Not Available in the United States

Several benzodiazepines marketed in Canada and other countries are not currently available in the United States. Bromazepam (Lectopam♣) and ketazolam (Loftran♣) are marketed as antianxiety agents, while nitrazepam (Mogadon♣) is a hypnotic and anticonvulsant.

## BARBITURATES

The barbiturates were once the most commonly prescribed class of medications for hypnotic and sedative effects. With only a few exceptions, they have been largely replaced by the benzodiazepines.

*Classification.*   The barbiturates are classified according to the duration of their action as long-, intermediate-, short-, and ultrashort-acting drugs. The short-acting drugs produce an effect or onset in a relatively short time (10 to 15 minutes) and peak over a relatively short period (3 to 4 hours). Short-acting barbiturates are used for treating insomnia, for preanesthetic sedation, and in combination with other drugs for psychosomatic disorders. Long-acting barbiturates require over 60 minutes for onset and peak over a period of 10 to 12 hours. Long-acting barbiturates are used for treating epilepsy and other chronic neurologic disorders and for sedation in clients with high anxiety. Ultrashort-acting barbiturates are used as IV anesthetics. Thiopental sodium, which belongs to the ultrashort-acting group of barbiturates, acts rapidly and can produce a state of anesthesia in a few seconds. Intermediate-acting barbiturates have an onset of 45 to 60 minutes and a peak in 6 to 8 hours.

*Mechanism of action.*   Important actions of the barbiturates are those of sedation and hypnotic effect. Barbiturates have been shown to depress the neurons and synapses of the ascending reticular formation of the brainstem, and this effect may be responsible for the reduction in electrical activity of the cortex. Since the ascending reticular formation receives stimuli from all parts of the body and relays impulses to the cortex (thus promoting wakefulness and alertness), depression of the ascending reticular formation decreases cortical stimuli, reducing the need for wakefulness and alertness.

There is evidence that the barbiturates act at all levels of the CNS. The extent of effect varies from mild sedation to deep anesthesia, depending on the drug selected, the method of administration, the dosage, and the reaction of the individual's nervous system. The barbiturates are not usually regarded as analgesics and cannot be depended on to produce restful sleep when insomnia is caused by pain. However, when a barbiturate is combined with an analgesic the sedative action seems to reinforce the action of the analgesic and to alter the client's emotional reaction to pain.

All of the barbiturates used clinically depress the motor cortex of the brain in large doses, but phenobarbital, mephobarbital, and metharbital exert a selective action on the motor cortex, even in small doses. This explains their use as anticonvulsants.

Ordinary therapeutic doses have little or no effect on medullary centers, but large doses, especially when administered intravenously, depress the respiratory and vasomotor centers.

Smooth muscles of blood vessels and of the gastrointestinal organs are depressed after large amounts of barbiturates, but clinical doses do not usually produce untoward effects. Motility of the gastrointestinal organs may be reduced and emptying of the stomach delayed slightly, but there is apparently little interference with the ability to respond to normal stimuli. Uterine muscle is affected little by the hypnotic doses of barbiturates, and the force of uterine contractions at the time of childbirth is not diminished unless anesthesia has been produced by one of these drugs.

The effect of barbiturates (and also benzodiazepines) may result from their action on the inhibitory neurotransmitter GABA.

**Indications.** The most common current indications for these drugs include anesthesia, preanesthesia, and seizure disorders.

*Hypnotic.* Although barbiturates are indicated for the treatment of insomnia, they have generally been replaced by the benzodiazepine family of drugs. If barbiturates are used, they are only indicated for short-term use, since they tend to lose their effectiveness in 14 days or less.

*Antianxiety.* Barbiturates have been used for sedative effects in treating anxiety and nervousness. But for daytime use the benzodiazepines have largely replaced the barbiturates, primarily because they produce less drowsiness or ataxia.

*Anesthetic.* Short-acting barbiturate anesthetics, such as thiopental and methohexital, are used for selected surgical procedures, especially for surgery of short duration. These barbiturates were discussed more fully in Chapter 13.

*Preanesthetic.* The short-acting barbiturates, such as pentobarbital sodium, are selected for their preanesthetic effect. They are often ordered to be given the night before surgery to enable the client to sleep and may be ordered to be given the morning of the operation. Diazepam and other benzodiazepines are often used today for this purpose—that is, as a preanesthetic agent to help with anesthesia induction, to reduce anxiety, and to induce an amnesic effect.

*Anticonvulsant.* Barbiturates are also used to prevent or control convulsive seizures associated with tetanus, strychnine poisoning, meningitis, eclampsia, and epilepsy. They may be prescribed alone or in conjunction with other anticonvulsant drugs. Phenobarbital is used for epilepsy (generalized tonic-clonic) and for seizures induced by fever, whereas mephobarbital and metharbital, also long-acting barbiturates, are also useful for the symptomatic treatment of certain types of epilepsy.

*Narcoanalysis.* Intravenous amobarbital may be utilized in narcoanalysis, a form of psychotherapy that helps a client to talk about suppressed feelings and events.

*Hyperbilirubinemia.* Although not approved for treatment of hyperbilirubinemia, phenobarbital (oral and injectable) is often used to prevent or treat this condition in neonates and in clients with congenital nonhemolytic unconjugated hyperbilirubinemia.

**Pharmacokinetics.** Barbiturates are readily absorbed after oral, rectal, and parenteral administration. The most soluble sodium salts are absorbed faster than the free acids. Most of the barbiturates, with the exception of barbital, undergo change in the liver before they are excreted by the kidney. They are excreted in a partly altered form, a partly unchanged form, or a completely altered form. The longer-acting barbiturates are said to be metabolized or chemically altered more slowly than the rapidly acting barbiturates. The slower a barbiturate is altered or excreted, the more prolonged is its action. If excretion is slow and administration prolonged, cumulative effects will result.

**Side effects/adverse reactions.** The more frequent side effects of barbiturates include ataxia, drowsiness, dizziness, and hangover effect. Less frequent side effects are nausea, vomiting, insomnia, constipation, restlessness, faintness, headache, and night terrors. If side effects continue, increase, or disturb the client, inform the physician.

The most common adverse reactions to these drugs include a hypersensitivity reaction such as skin rash, exfoliative dermatitis, sore throat, fever, edema, serum sickness, apnea, bronchospasms, urticaria, and Stevens-Johnson syndrome. **Stevens-Johnson syndrome** is a severe, occasionally fatal inflammatory disease of children and young adults, characterized by fever, bullae of the skin, and ulcers of the mucous membranes of mouth, nose, eyes, and genitalia.

Clients of any age, but especially elderly or debilitated clients, may exhibit confusion, disorientation, and mental depression. In children and in elderly or debilitated clients, a paradoxical reaction (increased excitability) may occur.

Rarely reported effects include hallucinations and increased bleeding tendencies.

Chronic use may result in osteomalacia and rickets (bone pain or aching, anorexia, myalgia, loss of weight).

Finally, toxic signs include very severe confusion and persistent irritability. Acute toxic effects may include bradycardia, confusion, respiratory problems (apnea, laryngospasm), ataxia, extreme weakness, and visual disturbances.

If adverse reactions occur, contact a physician, since medical intervention may be necessary.

**Significant drug interactions.** The following effects may occur when barbiturates are given with the drugs listed below:

| Drug | Possible Effect and Management |
| --- | --- |
| alcohol and CNS depressants | Enhanced CNS-depressant effects may result. Monitor closely for respiratory pattern changes, and perhaps decrease the dosage of one or both drugs to reduce the possibility of inducing the effect. |
| anticoagulants (coumarin or indanedione types) | Decrease in anticoagulant effects caused by enhanced metabolism. Prothrombin time tests may be necessary to monitor therapeutic response and to determine dosage changes of the anticoagulant. |
| anticonvulsants (carbamazepine) | Monitor serum levels closely whenever carbamazepine or a succinimide is added or discontinued from a drug regimen. Increased anticonvulsant metabolism may occur, leading to a decrease in serum levels and therapeutic effects. |
| anticonvulsants (hydantoin) | Hydantoin metabolism may be affected by the addition of barbiturates. The effect on hydantoin is undependable and unpredictable; therefore serum levels of hydantoin should be closely monitored when combination therapy is used. |
| contraceptives (particularly oral estrogen) | Enhanced metabolism of estrogen may result in a decrease in contraceptive effects. The physician may need to consider a nonhormone birth control method or a progestin-only oral contraceptive. |

| | |
|---|---|
| corticosteroids (adreno-corticoids, glucocorti-coid, mineralocorti-coid, corticotropin) | When given with barbiturates (especially phenobarbital), corticosteroids may have enhanced metabolism and a decrease in therapeutic effects. Dosage adjustments may be necessary. Monitor closely for a lack of therapeutic corticosteroid response. |
| divalproex sodium or valproic acid | Monitor barbiturate serum levels closely, since the metabolism of barbiturates may decrease, leading to elevated levels and an increase in CNS depression and neurologic dysfunction. The half-life of valproic acid may also be reduced, which would also require monitoring of blood levels and dosage adjustments |

***Dosage and administration.*** See Table 14-3.

## ▷NURSING MANAGEMENT: BARBITURATE THERAPY

Barbiturates have proved to be useful drugs when used appropriately. Because of their potential for dependence, tolerance, abuse, or misuse, the role of the nurse is essential in providing safe and effective drug therapy.

***Assessment.*** The nurse should assess and note the sleeping pattern of the client. This observation can influence the physician's decision on the type of barbiturate to prescribe. Clients who become disoriented or confused by the barbiturate should not be restrained. Rather, the client should be reoriented and a calm environment promoted.

The nurse should avoid giving barbiturates to clients with hypersensitivity to them, respiratory conditions (involving dyspnea or obstruction), previous dependency on barbiturates, or porphyria, and to elderly persons and children with a history of paradoxical reactions.

Porphyria is a hereditary disease that involves errors in the formation or excretion of porphyrins (molecular components of hemoglobin, myoglobin, and various enzymes). Acute intermittent porphyria is characterized by irregular and unpredictable attacks, which may include abdominal distress, elevated blood pressure, psychotic episodes, and neuropathy. Acute intermittent porphyria may be aggravated through barbiturate inducement of the enzyme necessary for porphyrin synthesis.

If a client tells the nurse that he or she is hypersensitive to this group of drugs, the nurse should withhold the medication and then record the statement and inform the physician. Seriously impaired hepatic or renal function may also constitute a contraindication to the use of these drugs, although only the physician can decide whether the degree of damage warrants the use of a different type of drug.

Because of the CNS effects of barbiturate therapy, clients are at risk for injury, alteration in sensory-perceptual function, alteration in self-concept, and a disturbance in sleep pattern. There may also be an alteration in bowel function as a result of the drug's gastrointestinal effects. Respiratory problems may present as ineffective airway clearance and/or impaired gas exchange because of the respiratory depressant effects of barbiturates. (See general nursing management regarding sedatives and hypnotics.)

***Intervention.*** The nurse should be aware that barbiturates may be combined in the same capsule so that a long-acting and a short-acting or moderately long-acting preparation can be used to advantage for the client who has difficulty in both getting to sleep and remaining asleep for the desired number of hours.

To hasten the onset of sleep with oral administration, the rate of absorption may be increased by administering barbiturates well diluted or on an empty stomach.

When administering barbiturates intramuscularly, the nurse should not give more than 5 ml at any one site because the preparations are irritating to the tissue.

With the exception of anesthesia and control of status epilepticus, barbiturates are infrequently prescribed to be administered by the intravenous route. If the intravenous route has been prescribed, medication should be administered slowly and in diluted form, according to the directions. If the barbiturate is to be infused in an intravenous solution, monitor the infusion rate closely, since rapid injection can be dangerous. The airway should be patent and emergency resuscitative equipment should be available when the medication is given intravenously.

For intravenous injection, the nurse should use the larger veins to decrease the risk of irritation. The intravenous site should be assessed for any signs of thrombophlebitis or extravasation.

Barbiturates may be administered rectally if the oral or parenteral route is undesirable. A retention enema may be prepared from the soluble salt of the barbiturate if a rectal dosage form is not available.

***Education.*** Instruct the client to use the barbiturate only as directed. The client should not alter the dosage or take the drug more often or for a longer period than ordered. Barbiturates may impair mental and physical functioning. Caution must be exercised to avoid dangerous activities if the client is affected by barbiturates in this manner.

Barbiturates may affect the developing fetus. If a client is pregnant or may become pregnant during therapy, the client should discuss it with her doctor. Barbiturates will also pass into breast milk and may affect the nursing baby.

Barbiturates may cause mental or physical dependence or tolerance. Clients should consult their physicians if they experience the signs or symptoms of dependence or no longer receive the full effect of the drug.

If client is following a scheduled dosing regimen (as when a barbiturate is used as an anticonvulsant) and a dose is missed, he or she should take the dose immediately if remembered within 1 to 2 hours of the scheduled time; otherwise, the client should skip the dose and continue with the regimen.

Abrupt withdrawal may precipitate seizures in the epi-

**TABLE 14-3** Pharmacokinetic overview of selected barbiturate drugs

| Name | Half-life (hr) | | Indications/dosage |
|---|---|---|---|
| | Mean | Range | |
| **SHORT-ACTING** | | | |
| pentobarbital (Nembutal, Novopento-barb ✤) | * | 15-50 | *Oral dosage forms* Adult: sedation, 20 mg 3-4 times daily; hypnotic, 100 mg orally at bedtime Elderly and debilitated clients: lower doses usually required Pediatric: sedative, 2-6 mg/kg body weight daily; preoperative, 2-6 mg/kg body weight, maximum 100 mg/dose; hypnotic, dosage not established *Parenteral dosage form* Adult: sedative-hypnotic, 150-200 mg IM; IV, 100 mg initially, if necessary give additional small doses at 1-min intervals up to a maximum of 500 mg for hypnotic effect; anticonvulsant, IV, 100 mg initially, if necessary give additional small doses at 1 min intervals up to a maximum of 500 mg Elderly and debilitated clients: lower dosages are usually required Pediatric: hypnotic, 2-6 mg/kg body weight, maximum dose of 100 mg, administered IM; IV, 50 mg initially, if necessary give additional small doses at 1-min intervals until desired goal is reached. Sedative, preoperative, 2-6 mg/kg body weight to a maximum of 100 mg/dose, IV. Anticonvulsant, IM or IV, 50 mg initially; if necessary, give additional small doses at 1-min intervals *Rectal dosage form* Adult: sedative, 30 mg 2-4 times daily; hypnotic, 120-200 mg at bedtime; for elderly and debilitated clients, give lower doses and monitor closely Pediatric: hypnotic or preoperative, dosage not available for children less than 2 mo old; children 2-12 mo, 30 mg; children 1-4 yr old, 30 or 60 mg; children 5-12 yr old, 60 mg; children 12-14 yr old, 60 or 120 mg. Sedative, 2 mg/kg body weight or 60 mg/m² body surface 3 times a day |
| secobarbital (Seconal, Novosecobarb ✤) | 28 | 15-40 | *Oral dosage forms* Adult: hypnotic, 100 mg bedtime; sedative, 30-50 mg 3-4 times daily for daytime usage; preoperative, 200-300 mg, 1-2 hr before surgery. Elderly or debilitated clients: use lower doses Pediatric: sedative, 2 mg/kg body weight or 60 mg/m² body surface, 3 times daily; preoperative, 2-6 mg/kg body weight to a 100-mg dose maximum, 1-2 hr before surgery *Parenteral dosage form* Adult: hypnotic, 100-200 mg IM or 50-250 mg IV; sedative, 1.1-2.2 mg/kg body weight IV from 10-15 min before dental procedure, nerve block, 100-150 mg IV; anticonvulsant, tetany, 5.5 mg/kg body weight IM or IV, every 3-4 hr if needed Elderly or debilitated clients: lower doses usually required Pediatric: hypnotic, 3-5 mg/kg body wieght or 125 mg/m² body surface to a maximum of 100 mg IM; rectally, 1%-1.5% solution—administer 5 mg/kg body weight to children weighing up to 40 kg; children weighing 40 kg and over, give 4 mg/kg body weight; preoperative sedative, 4-5 mg/kg body weight; anticonvulsant (tetany), 3-5 mg/kg body weight or 125 mg/m² body surface per dose IM or IV |
| talbutal (Lotusate) | 15 | N/A | Adult: hypnotic, 120 mg 15-30 min prior to bedtime Pediatric: not established in children under 15 yr old |

*The mean half-life is dependent on the dose.

*Continued.*

**TABLE 14-3** Pharmacokinetic overview of selected barbiturate drugs—cont'd

| Name | Half-life (hr) | | Indications/dosage |
|---|---|---|---|
| | Mean | Range | |

**INTERMEDIATE-ACTING**

| | | | |
|---|---|---|---|
| amobarbital (Amytal) | 25 | 16-40 | *Oral dosage forms* <br> Adult: hypnotic, 65-200 mg at bedtime; sedative, 50-300 mg daily in divided doses; preoperative, 200-mg oral capsules, 1-2 hr before surgery; during labor, 200-400 mg oral capsules, may repeat in 1-3 hr if necessary to a 1-g maximum <br> Elderly or debilitated clients: lower doses may be necessary <br> Pediatric: hypnotic dosage not available; sedative, 2 mg/kg body weight or 60 gm/m² body surface 3 times daily; preoperative, 2-6 mg/kg body weight up 100-mg maximum dose <br> *Parenteral dosage forms* <br> Adult: hypnotic, 65-200 mg IM or IV; sedative, 30-50 mg IM or IV, 2 or 3 times a day; anticonvulsant, 65-500 mg IV <br> Elderly or debilitated clients: lower doses may be necessary <br> Pediatric: hypnotic, children up to 6 yr old, 2-3 mg/kg body weight per IM dose; children 6 yr old and older, 2-3 mg/kg body weight per IM dose; IV dose is 65-500 mg per dose; sedative, preoperative, 65-500 mg IV or 3-5 mg/kg body weight per dose; anticonvulsant, children up to 6 yr old, 3-5 mg/kg body weight or 125 mg/m² body surface per IM or IV dose; children 6 yr old and older, 65-500 mg/IV dose |
| aprobarbital (Alurate) | 24 | 14-34 | Adult: hypnotic, 40-160 mg orally at bedtime; sedative, 40 mg orally 3 times daily <br> Pediatric: dose not established |
| butabarbital (Butisol, Buticaps) | 100 | 66-140 | Adult: hypnotic, 50-100 mg orally at bedtime; sedative, 15-30 mg 3 or 4 times a day; preoperative, 50-100 mg orally 1 to 1½ hr before surgery <br> Pediatric: sedative, 2 mg/kg body weight orally 3 times daily; preoperative, 2 to 6 mg/kg orally up to a 100-mg dose maximum |

**LONG-ACTING**

| | | | |
|---|---|---|---|
| mephobarbital (Gemonil) | 34 | 11-67 | Adult: anticonvulsant, 200 mg orally at bedtime to 600 mg in divided doses daily; sedative, 32-100 mg 3 or 4 times daily <br> Pediatric: anticonvulsant in children up to 5 years old, 16-32 mg orally 3 or 4 times daily; 5 years and over, 32-64 mg 3 or 4 times daily |
| metharbital (Mebaral) | N/A | N/A | Adult: anticonvulsant, 100 mg orally 1 to 3 times daily; dose may be increased to 800 mg per day maximum <br> Pediatric: anticonvulsant, 50 mg orally 1 to 3 times daily |
| phenobarbital (Luminal) | 79 | 53-118 | *Oral dosage form* <br> Adult: elixir, capsule, oral solution, and tablets; hypnotic, 100-320 mg at bedtime; sedative, 30-120 mg in 2 or 3 divided doses; anticonvulsant, 60-250 mg daily in divided or single dose; antihyperbilirubinemic, 30-60 mg 3 times daily <br> Elderly or debilitated clients: lower doses may be necessary <br> Pediatric: hypnotic, dosage not established; sedative, 2 mg/kg body weight or 60 mg/m² body surface 3 times daily; preoperative, 1-3 mg/kg body weight; anticonvulsant, 1-6 mg/kg body weight in divided or single doses; antihyperbilirubinemic, neonates, 5-10 mg/kg body weight for a few days after birth; for children up to 12 yr old, 1-4 mg/kg body weight 3 times daily <br> *Parenteral dosage forms* <br> Adult: hypnotic, 100-325 mg IM or IV; sedative, 30-120 mg daily in 2 or 3 divided doses; preoperative, 130-200 mg 1 to 1½ hr before surgery; anticonvulsant, 100-320 mg IV, repeat if needed to a maximum of 600 mg in 24 hr; status epilepticus, 10-20 mg/kg body weight by slow IV; may repeat if needed <br> Elderly or debilitated clients: lower doses may be necessary <br> Pediatric: hypnotic, individualized; sedative, 1-3 mg/kg body weight IM or IV; preoperative, 1-3 mg/kg body weight IM or IV, 1-1.5 hr before surgery; anticonvulsant, 10-20 mg/kg body weight IV initially as a loading dose; then maintenance dosage is 1-6 mg/kg body weight daily; status epilepticus, 15-20 mg/kg body weight given IV over 10-15 min |

leptic patient. Abstinence syndromes (see Chapter 9) may be seen after abrupt withdrawal in any patient after long-term therapy.

Barbiturates interact with many other drugs and alcohol. Inform the client not to take any additional medications while taking a barbiturate unless they have been approved by the prescriber or pharmacist. Dangerous interactions may occur.

***Evaluation.*** Evaluation is focused on detection of adverse reactions or side effects, monitoring compliance, and monitoring effectiveness of the therapy. Indicators of effectiveness include sleep time, daytime wakefulness, and client reports on feelings of rest and wakefulness. Tolerance develops to all barbiturates during long-term therapy, but it develops at unpredictable rates. The development of tolerance, as well as possible dependence, should be closely evaluated. Monitoring for paradoxical reactions, allergic re-

actions, or drug interactions is also essential. The nurse should function as a client advocate when evaluation suggests that a change in drug therapy is needed.

## MISCELLANEOUS SEDATIVES AND HYPNOTICS

A number of sedatives and hypnotics do not fall into the previously discussed drug classes, but they will be discussed here because they are available for client use with prescription.

### chloral hydrate (Noctec, Novochlorhydrate ✤)

The CNS depressant effects produced are believed to be caused by the drug's active metabolite, trichloroethanol. The exact mechanism of action, though, is unknown. Chloral hydrate is indicated as a sedative and as a hypnotic.

**TABLE 14-4**   Side effects/adverse reactions of miscellaneous sedatives and hypnotics

| Drug | Side effects* | Adverse reactions† |
|---|---|---|
| chloral hydrate | More frequent: nausea, abdominal distress, vomiting<br>Less frequent: ataxia, dizziness, drowsiness | Skin rash or urticaria, confusion, increased excitability (paradoxical reaction), hallucinations |
| ethchlorvynol | More frequent: visual disturbances, nausea, vomiting, abdominal distress, increased weakness, facial numbness, dizziness<br>Less frequent: ataxia, confusion, daytime sedation or drowsiness | Skin rash or urticaria, increased excitability or nervousness (paradoxical reaction), jaundice, diplopia, trembling, slurred speech, weakness or numbness in the hands or feet |
| glutethimide | More frequent: daytime sedation or drowsiness<br>Less frequent: visual disturbances, ataxia, confusion, headaches, nausea, vomiting, dizziness | Skin rash, sore throat, fever, increased bleeding tendencies, severe weakness, confusion, trembling, CNS disturbances (memory recall problems, lack of concentrating ability) |
| meprobamate | More frequent: drowsiness or increased clumsiness<br>Less frequent: visual disturbances (blurred or changes in distant or near sight), diarrhea, dizziness, euphoria, headache, nausea or vomiting, increased weakness | Skin rash, urticaria, pruritus, slurred speech, increased confusion or persistant dizziness, ataxia, increased bleeding tendencies, sore throat, elevated temperature, increased excitability (paradoxical reaction), tachycardia, respiratory difficulties (wheezing, shortness of breath) |
| methyprylon | More frequent: daytime sedation, headache, dizziness<br>Less frequent: nausea, vomiting, diarrhea | Skin rash, increased excitability (paradoxical reaction), mouth sores, increased bleeding tendencies, respiratory difficulties, confusion, increased weakness |
| paraldehyde | More frequent: unpleasant mouth odor, drowsiness; nausea, vomiting, and abdominal distress reported with oral preparations<br>Less frequent: ataxia, dizziness, hangover-type effects | Skin rash, coughing (reported with IV use only), hepatitis, thrombophlebitis at injection site, tremors, confusion, increased nervousness or irritability (caused by metabolic acidosis from overdose), respiratory difficulties, increased weakness |
| propiomazine HCl | Most frequent: dry mouth, increase in daytime sedation, dizziness<br>Less frequent: confusion, diarrhea, nausea, vomiting, respiratory difficulties, skin rash, abdominal distress, tachycardia, increased restlessness | Thrombophlebitis or pain and swelling at injection site |

*If side effects continue, increase, or disturb the client, inform the physician.
†If adverse reactions occur, contact physician because medical intervention may be necessary.

Oral and rectal dosage forms are rapidly absorbed. Chloral hydrate is metabolized in liver and erythrocytes to its active metabolite, trichloroethanol; further liver metabolism is to inactive metabolites. Onset of action of a hypnotic dose (500 to 1000 mg) occurs within 30 minutes. The half-life is approximately 7 to 10 hours. The drug is excreted by the kidneys. Side effects/adverse reactions are listed in Table 14-4.

***Significant drug interactions.*** The following effects may occur when chloral hydrate is given with the drugs listed below:

| Drug | Possible Effect and Management |
|---|---|
| alcohol or other CNS depressants | Enhanced CNS depression effects may result. Monitor closely for respiratory depression and/or lethargy, and perhaps reduce the dosage of one or both drugs. |
| anticoagulants (coumarin or indanedione) | Within the first few weeks especially, the anticoagulant may be displaced from its protein binding, leading to an enhanced hypoprothrombinemic effect. Monitor closely for bleeding tendencies. |

***Dosage and administration.*** See Table 14-5.

▷**Nursing Management:**
**Chloral Hydrate Therapy**

Since the elixir has an unpleasant taste and odor, it may be difficult for clients, particularly children, to take. To make the elixir more palatable, the nurse should mix it with fruit juice or some type of chilled fluid (such as ginger ale). If the client is being given the elixir as a preoperative medication, flavored extract (e.g., peppermint extract, banana extract) should be added to make it more palatable.

Since the drug can cause gastric irritation, the nurse should administer it after meals with an 8-ounce glass of fluid, unless it is being administered as a preoperative medication. Use of the drug should be avoided in clients with esophagitis, gastritis, or gastric or duodenal ulcers.

Provision for client safety is essential. The client should be assisted with ambulation, side rails, and so on, if the client evidences somnambulism, confusion, or dizziness. In addition, the prescriber should be consulted for a dosage reduction or a change in medication for nighttime sedation.

Clients taking chloral hydrate concomitantly with oral anticoagulants should be monitored for hypoprothrombinemic effects, since chloral hydrate potentiates oral anticoagulants.

CNS depressants and alcohol given concurrently with chloral hydrate may increase the CNS depressant effects. Monitor closely for drowsiness and respiratory depression; dosage reduction in one or both drugs may be necessary if these symptoms occur.

Since chloral hydrate may interfere with urine glucose testing in diabetics, the nurse should instruct clients in the use of home blood glucose monitoring methods.

**ethchlorvynol (Placidyl)**

The CNS depressant effects are similar to those of chloral hydrate and barbiturates. The exact mechanism of action is unknown. Ethchlorvynol is indicated for use as a sedative-hypnotic. Absorption is good from the gastrointestinal tract. The drug's distribution is highly localized in lipid or fat tissues; the drug has also been located in cerebrospinal fluid, brain, bile, liver, kidneys, and spleen. Ethchlorvynol is 90% metabolized in the liver; some metabolism also occurs in the kidney. The drug has a half-life of approximately 10 to 20 hours, with onset of action occurring within 15 to 60 minutes and a duration of action of approximately 5 hours. Ethchlorvynol is excreted by the kidneys.

**TABLE 14-5** Chloral hydrate: dosage and administration

| | Adults | Children |
|---|---|---|
| **Oral** | | |
| Hypnotic | 500-1000 mg orally 15-30 min before bedtime | 50 mg/kg body weight or 1.5 g/m² body surface orally at bedtime; maximum single dose is 1 g |
| Sedative | 250 mg orally 3 times/day after meals | 8.3 mg/kg body weight or 250 mg/m² body surface to a maximum of 500 mg 3 times daily after meals |
| Preoperative | 500-1000 mg orally ½ hr before surgery | |
| Premedication (before electroencephalographic examination) | | 20-25 mg/kg body weight orally |
| **Suppositories** | | |
| Hypnotic | 500-1000 mg rectally at bedtime | 50 mg/kg body weight or 1.5 g/m² body surface area at bedtime, up to maximum of 1 g/single dose |
| Sedative | 325 mg 3 times a day; maximum adult dosage is 2 g daily | 8.3 mg/kg body weight or 250 mg/m² body surface rectally 3 times daily |

Table 14-4 provides side effects/adverse reactions, while the significant drug interactions are the same as those for chloral hydrate, discussed on p. 275.

When ethchlorvynol is administered to adults as a sedative-hypnotic, the recommended dose is 500 to 1000 mg orally at bedtime. Administration to the elderly may require decreased dosage because this group may be more sensitive to the drug. This drug is not available for use with children.

▷ **Nursing Management:
Ethchlorvynol Therapy**

The drug may produce transient giddiness and ataxia in some clients because it is absorbed rapidly. The symptoms should be lessened by administering the drug with milk or food. If the client awakens in the early morning hours after a bedtime dose of ethchlorvynol, a single additional dose of 100 to 200 mg may be administered. The nurse should check to see that the dosage for elderly, debilitated clients is reduced to the smallest effective amount. As with similar drugs, the nurse should inform the client that driving automobiles or operating any machinery that requires alertness should be avoided. The effects of the drug could last at least 5 hours. The client should be instructed to report any yellowing of the skin or eyes, which might be signs of cholestatic jaundice, rash, or excessive bruising, which might indicate thrombocytopenia. (See also nursing management for sedatives and hypnotics.)

**glutethimide (Doriden)**

Gluthethimide is a CNS depressant similar to the barbiturates. The mechanism of action is unknown. It is indicated as a sedative-hypnotic. Absorption is irregular from the gastrointestinal tract. Distribution takes place mostly in lipid or fat tissues, but the drug has also been detected in the brain, liver, bile, and kidneys. Gluthethimide is metabolized in the liver, with a half-life of approximately 10 to 12 hours. Onset of action occurs within ½ hour, with a duration of 4 to 8 hours. Gluthethimide is excreted by the kidneys.

For information on side effects/adverse reactions, see Table 14-4. Significant drug interactions are similar to those described for chloral hydrate on p. 275. The recommended dose for glutethimide in adults is 250 to 500 mg orally at bedtime to induce hypnotic effect. If necessary, the dose may be repeated but only if there are 4 hours or more until the client will arise. The elderly are usually more sensitive to this drug; therefore smaller doses initially (not exceeding 500 mg) at bedtime are usually prescribed. This drug is not available for children under 12 years old.

▷ **Nursing Management:
Glutethimide Therapy**

Gluthethimide can decrease bowel activity, so the nurse should take actions to help prevent constipation. Dependence on a laxative can lead to lazy bowel. Therefore the

nurse should encourage fluids, fruits, roughage, and exercise. (See nursing management of sedative-hypnotic drugs.)

**meprobamate (Equanil, Miltown, Meditran ✸)**

Meprobamate functions as a CNS depressant similar to the barbiturates. The exact mechanism of action is unknown. The drug appears to act at the hypothalamus, thalamus, limbic system, and spinal cord.

Meprobamate is indicated for use as an antianxiety agent. Absorption is good, and the drug is distributed throughout the body. Meprobamate is metabolized in the liver, with a half-life of approximately 10 hours. It is excreted by the kidneys.

For an examination of side effects/adverse reactions, see Table 14-4. Clients taking meprobamate concomitantly with alcohol or CNS depressants may experience increased alcohol and CNS-depressant effects (see data for chloral hydrate).

The recommended dosage for adults is 400 mg orally 3 or 4 times daily or 600 mg twice daily, up to a maximum of 2.4 g. Elderly clients may be more sensitive to this drug. Lower the dosage and/or monitor closely. Meprobamate is not recommended in children under 6 years old. For children 6 to 12 years old, give 100 to 200 mg orally 2 or 3 times daily.

▷ **Nursing Management:
Meprobamate Therapy**

See general nursing management for antianxiety, sedative, and hypnotic agents.

**methyprylon (Noludar)**

Methyprylon's mechanism of action is similar to that of barbiturates. The exact mechanism of action is unknown, but in animals an elevated threshold of arousal centers in the brainstem has been demonstrated. The drug is indicated as a sedative-hypnotic.

Absorption is good, but little information is available on distribution. The drug is metabolized in the liver, with a half-life of 3 to 6 hours. Onset of action occurs within 45 minutes; duration of action is 5 to 8 hours. Methyprylon is exceted by the kidneys.

Side effects/adverse reactions are listed in Table 14-4.

Significant drug reactions are related to alcohol and CNS depressants (see comments on chloral hydrate).

The recommended dosage for adults is 200-400 mg orally at bedtime. Elderly clients may have increased sensitivity to this drug. Monitor closely or use lower dosages. The drug is not recommended for children less than 12 years old. In children 12 years and over, individualize the dosage.

▷ **Nursing Management:
Methyprylon Therapy**

Methyprylon is similar to other agents. See the general discussion under sedatives and hypnotics.

## paraldehyde (Paral)

Paraldehyde's CNS-depressant effects are similar to those of alcohol, barbiturates, and chloral hydrate. The exact mechanism of action is unknown. Also the drug depresses the ascending reticular activating system. It is indicated as an anticonvulsant.

Absorption is good from the gastrointestinal tract and intramuscular sites; the drug appears in cerebrospinal fluid about 1/2 to 1 hour after administration, but levels are approximately 25% less than blood serum levels. Information on other tissue distribution is not available.

Paraldehyde is metabolized in the liver. When it is used as a hypnotic (an unapproved indication in the United States), onset of action occurs within 15 minutes, with a duration of action of 8 to 12 hours. Paraldehyde is excreted in the lungs, with only trace amounts excreted in urine.

For side effects/adverse reactions, see Table 14-4.

Significant drug interactions are seen when paraldehyde is used in combination with alcohol and CNS depressants, (see data on chloral hydrate). The drug also interacts with disulfiram; that is, disulfiram decreases paraldehyde metabolism, which may lead to increased blood levels of paraldehyde and acetaldehyde. Do not give disulfiram to clients receiving paraldehyde.

**Dosage and administration.** Anticonvulsant:

*Adults.* 10-20 ml rectally or up to 12 ml (diluted to a 10% solution) orally via gastric tube, as needed every 4 hours. IM dose is 5 to 10 ml. IV infusion: add 5 ml to 100 ml of sodium chloride (0.9%) solution; administer slowly, not faster than 1 ml/min.

*Children.* Orally or rectally: 0.3 ml/kg or 12 ml/m² body surface. IM: 0.15 ml/kg or 6 ml/m² body surface. IV: 0.1-0.15 ml/kg diluted in sodium chloride injection (0.9%); administer slowly.

▷ **Nursing Management: Paraldehyde Therapy**

**Assessment.** In addition to the other potential nursing diagnoses for sedatives and hypnotics, clients receiving paraldehyde parenterally may be at risk for an alteration in comfort (pain) related to the injection.

**Intervention.** To give this drug orally, the nurse should dilute it well in a suitable medium such as flavored syrup, iced fruit juice, or milk; the fluid should be chilled to minimize the odor and taste. Dilution also decreases gastric irritation. Administer in a glass container, since paraldehyde reacts with plastic. When given by the intramuscular or intravenous route, a glass syringe should be used. Paraldehyde will react with plastic syringes and cause a decomposition to toxic compounds.

When giving this drug by a parenteral route (rarely done), the nurse should have available resuscitative equipment in the event of a cardiorespiratory arrest. The client should be kept in the side-lying position to prevent aspiration of bronchial secretions, which are increased after administration of the drug.

Because the drug cannot be used after the container has been opened for longer than 24 hours, the container should be marked with the date and time it was opened. The nurse should not use the drug if it is colored or smells like acetic acid.

When giving this drug by the intramuscular route, the nurse should give no more than 5 ml per injection site and rotate the sites. Subcutaneous administration should be avoided because paraldehyde is irritating to the tissues.

The nurse should keep the client in a well-ventilated room, since the exhaled drug can be very pungent.

For rectal doses, paraldehyde should be diluted with 1 to 2 parts of olive oil, cottonseed oil, or normal saline solution to prevent rectal tissue irritation.

Because the solution is extremely volatile, the nurse should avoid contact with eyes, skin, and clothing. The solution and its fumes should be kept away from a heat source, open flame, or spark.

**Education.** The nurse should prepare the client for the strong unpleasant breath odor that results from administration of the drug and should instruct the client in oral hygiene. The client will need to be instructed to report yellowing of the skin or eyes, which might indicate hepatitis, and/or bloody stools, which might result from the irritation of the intestinal mucosa by paraldehyde. (See additional nursing management related to use in alcohol withdrawal syndrome, Chapter 9.)

## propiomazine hydrochloride (Largon)

Although the exact mechanism of action is unknown, propiomazine is a phenothiazine with sedative properties at therapeutic dosages.

Propiomazine is indicated as a sedative-hypnotic. It is well absorbed and is probably distributed widely throughout the body, similar to other phenothiazines. The mechanism of action is unknown but suspected to occur in the liver.

The time to peak effect is 40 to 60 minutes by the intramuscular route; 15 to 30 minutes by the intravenous route. The duration of action is approximately 3 to 6 hours. The route of excretion is unknown but may be kidneys and biliary tract, as occurs with other phenothiazines.

For side effects/adverse reactions see Table 14-4. Significant drug interactions occur when the drug is used with alcohol or CNS depressants (see chloral hydrate). Also, concurrent use with epinephrine may lead to severe hypotension. Monitor closely.

Dosage and administration for adults are as follows: preoperative, 20 to 40 mg IM or IV; local nerve block or spinal anesthesia adjunct, 10 to 20 mg IM or IV; obstetrics, 20 to 40 mg IM or IV, may repeat in 3 hours if needed. For sedation of children up to 27 kg (before surgery or anesthesia, or postoperatively), administer 0.55 to 1.1 mg/kg body weight IM or IV; in children 2 to 4 years, give 10 mg IM or IV; children 4 to 6 years should be given 15 mg IM or IV; and children 6 to 12 years are given 25 mg IM or IV.

## ▷ Nursing Management: Propiomazine Therapy

The nurse should inject only a clear solution and only into undamaged veins because this drug causes severe chemical irritation and thrombophlebitis. Intravenous injections are given slowly to prevent transient hypotension. Perivascular extravasation should be avoided because of chemical irritation.

When other sedatives are administered with this drug, the dosage should be reduced by one fourth to one half.

The nurse should relieve the side effect of **xerostomia**, (dry mouth) by providing mouth care, unless the client has received the medication preoperatively.

The nurse should monitor the client's vital signs, particularly blood pressure, for 5 hours after intramuscular or intravenous administration, because of the drug's hypotensive effect. If hypotension occurs, administration of the drug should be discontinued and the physician notified. If vasopressors are required, norepinephrine should be used rather than epinephrine. When epinephrine is used in combination with propiomazine, the vasopressor effect may be reduced or possibly reversed.

### buspirone hydrochloride (BuSpar)

Buspirone hydrochloride is a nonbenzodiazepine substance used for the management of anxiety disorders. It is equivalent in efficacy to the benzodiazepines but usually causes less sedation. The exact mechanism of action is unknown, but the drug has a high affinity for serotonin receptors and a moderate affinity for brain $D_2$-dopamine receptors. It does not affect gamma-aminobutyric acid (GABA), nor does it have any significant affinity for the benzodiazepine receptors. Absorption of the drug is very good, but it undergoes extensive first-pass metabolism in the liver. Protein binding is high (95%); onset of effect may take 1 to 2 weeks. The drug does not cause muscle relaxation or sedation, so clients may not notice any effects from the medication during this time. The half-life (elimination) is between 2 and 3 hours after a single 10 to 40-mg dose. Buspirone is metabolized in the liver; one of the metabolites is active. It is eliminated through the kidneys and feces.

The most common side effects include headache, nausea, increased nervousness, and faintness. Less frequent side effects include tinnitus, abdominal distress, insomnia, nightmares, increased weakness, dry mouth, blurred vision, muscle pain or spasms, and decreased ability to concentrate. Rarely are adverse reactions reported. They include chest pain, tachycardia, muscle weakness, paresthesias, sore throat, elevated temperature, depression, and confusion. If side effects continue, increase, or disturb the client, inform the physician. If adverse reactions occur, contact the physician, since medical intervention may be necessary.

Avoid concurrent administration with MAO inhibitors, since severe hypertension may occur.

The recommended dosage for adults is 5 mg orally 3 times daily. The dose may be increased by 5 mg per day, every 2 to 3 days, until the desired response is achieved, with a maximum dose of 60 mg per day. For persons under 18 years old, no dosage has been established.

## ▷ Nursing Management: Buspirone Hydrochloride Therapy

Contraindications to the use of buspirone therapy would be hepatic or renal impairment, since the drug is metabolized in the liver and excreted by the kidneys. It should be used with caution for clients who are also receiving digoxin therapy, since it displaces digoxin from the plasma protein binding sites and so increases the effects of the digoxin.

Clients may be instructed to use ice chips or sugarless candies to manage the side effect of dry mouth, if it occurs. Clients should be informed that 1 or 2 weeks of therapy may be necessary before the effects of buspirone therapy are evidenced. Chest pain, alterations in thought processes, palpitations, sensory or motor changes in the hands and feet, and fever or sore throat should be reported to the prescriber.

### hydroxyzine (Atarax, Vistaril)

The antianxiety effect of hydroxyzine may be due to hydroxyzine's suppression of activity in selected subcortical areas of the CNS. Its full mechanism of action is unknown, but it competes with histamine at $H_1$ receptor sites, which may be responsible for its antihistamine and sedative effects. The antiemetic effect may be due to its central anticholinergic effect. It decreases vestibular stimulation and labyrinthine function and may also have an effect on the chemoreceptive trigger zone.

Hydroxyzine, a piperazine antihistamine, is an antianxiety agent, sedative-hypnotic, antihistamine, and antiemetic (parenteral only).

Absorption of hydroxyzine is good. Onset of action occurs within 15 to 30 minutes after an oral dose. Duration of effect lasts 4 to 6 hours when the drug is given orally. It has a half-life of 2.5 to 3.4 hours. Hydroxyzine is metabolized in the liver and excreted by the kidneys.

The most common side effects include sedation, which usually disappears after a few days of therapy or when the dose is reduced. Less frequent and usually reported with high drug doses are anticholinergic side effects, such as dry mouth. Adverse reactions, rarely reported, include skin rash and trembling or seizures (in doses higher than recommended). When hydroxyzine is given concurrently with alcohol or CNS depressants, the CNS-depressant effects may be enhanced. It is recommended that the dose of CNS depressants be reduced by 50%.

The recommended adult dose when hydroxyzine is used as an antianxiety agent or sedative-hypnotic is 50 to 100 mg orally. As an antihistamine or antiemetic, the recommended dose is 25 to 100 mg orally 3 to 4 times daily as necessary. When the drug is administered to children as an antianxiety agent or sedative-hypnotic, the dosage is 0.6 mg/kg body weight orally. For antihistamine or antiemetic

## PREGNANCY SAFETY

FDA category B: methyprylon, buspirone

FDA category C: chloral hydrate, ethchlorvynol, glutethimide, paraldehyde

FDA category D: alprazolam, barbiturates, halazepam,
lorazepam (parenteral), midazolam (parenteral)

FDA category X: temazepam, triazolam, quazepam

FDA category unclassified: other benzodiazepines, meprobamate, propiomazine, hydroxyzine

effects, administer 0.5 mg/kg body weight orally every 6
hours when necessary. In parenteral therapy the adult dosage
is 25 to 100 mg IM, which may be repeated in 4 to 6 hours
if necessary. When used in children as an antiemetic or
adjunct to narcotic medication, hydroxyzine should be administered 1 mg/kg body weight IM.

▷**Nursing Management:
Hydroxyzine Therapy**

In addition to the nursing management of sedative and
hypnotic therapy, the nurse needs to be aware that because
of its antiemetic effects, hydroxyzine may mask symptoms
of serious conditions that might be evidenced by nausea and
vomiting, such as brain lesions, appendicitis, and other gastrointestinal disorders.

The drug is not to be administered subcutaneously, intravenously, or intraarterially, since significant tissue damage may occur. Hydroxyzine needs to be administered by
deep intramuscular injection.

Clients may be instructed to use ice chips and sugarless
candies to manage any symptoms of dry mouth that occur.
Involuntary motor activity, such as trembling and shaking,
should be reported to the prescriber for a change in medication dosage.

## SUMMARY

When a client is unable to cope with a persistently stressful
situation because excessive anxiety interferes with daily
functioning, an antianxiety agent may be prescribed. Benzodiazepines are the most commonly used drugs in this
group. Before their advent, sedatives were used to reduce
nervousness or irritability by producing a soothing effect.
Hypnotics are used to induce sleep. Sedatives and hypnotics
differ, primarily, only in the degree of CNS depression.
Benzodiazepines do not exert a general CNS-depressant effect, and their wide range of selectivity of action allows
their use for a variety of conditions—as anticonvulsants,
hypnotics, muscular relaxants, and antianxiety agents. Barbiturates, on the other hand, are used for mild sedation to

deep anesthesia. Although a barbiturate is not an analgesic,
when administered with an analgesic it reinforces analgesic
effects and alters the client's emotional response to pain.

Sleep is an important experience for humans, with both
REM sleep and non-REM sleep being essential for good
mental health. Drugs, in influencing an individual's physiologic state, also affect sleep patterns.

Both pediatric clients and geriatric clients are much more
sensitive to the CNS-depressant effects of these drugs. Children usually respond better to counseling and psychotherapy
than to antianxiety agents, and the elderly, because of a
decline in organ function, are better treated with shorter-
acting benzodiazepines. Both groups of clients are at greater
risk for paradoxical reactions than the general population.

The nurse's role in sedative-hypnotic therapy is to assess
the extent of the client's sleep pattern disturbance, its etiology, and the client's previous practices in coping with it.
Nonpharmacologic nursing interventions to induce sleep
should be utilized in place of or as adjuncts to medicating
the client with a sedative-hypnotic agent. Client education
should focus on safe self-administration, with cautions that
there may be performance impairments as blood levels of
some of these drugs are retained. Effectiveness will be indicated by the client reporting feelings of rest without residual drowsiness during the day.

Benzodiazepines are among the most frequently prescribed drugs today for a variety of disorders: anxiety
disorders, alcohol withdrawal, preoperative medication,
neuromuscular disease, and sleep and seizure disorders.
Barbiturates, once more widely used, have been largely
replaced by the benzodiazepines. However, they are still
indicated as hypnotic, antianxiety, anesthetic, preanesthetic,
anticonvulsant, antihyperbilirubinemic, and narcoanalytic
agents.

Although antianxiety, sedative, and hypnotic drugs create
many of the same responses within the client, it is necessary
for the nurse to become knowledgeable about the specific
agents used in his or her practice area. Because these agents
exert CNS effects, the nurse needs to be aware that the
client may be at risk for injury, alteration in sensory-
perceptual function, alteration in self-concept, and a further
disturbance of sleep pattern. The gastrointestinal effects of
many of these agents may result in an alteration of bowel
pattern. As with all agents, clients may also experience a
knowledge deficit related to their drug therapy.

## BIBLIOGRAPHY

Abramowicz M, ed. (1988). Choice of benzodiazepines, Medical
Letter 30(760):26.

American Hospital Formulary Service. (1990). AHPS drug information '90. Betheseda, Md: American Society of Hospital Pharmacists, Inc.

Anxiety. (1980). Fla Pharm J 64:22, March.

Armstrong P. (1987). Off the hook: Chemical addiction, Nursing
Times 83(45):34.

Betts TA and Birtle J. (1982). Effect of two hypnotic drugs on actual driving performance next morning, Br Med J 285:852.

Brocklehurst JC. (1984). Geriatric pharmacology and therapeutics. Oxford: Blackwell Scientific Publications.

Cornoni-Huntley J et al. (1986). Established population for epidemiolgic studies of the elderly, pub no 86-2443. Silver Springs, Md: National Institute on Aging, US Department of Health and Human Services.

Dominquez RA and Goldstein BJ. (1985). 25 years of benzodiazepine experience: clinical commentary on use, abuse, and withdrawal, Hosp Formul 20:1000.

Dommisse CF and Hayes PE. (1987). Current concepts in clinical therapeutics: anxiety disorders, part 2, Clin Pharm 6(3):196.

Dubovsky SL et al. (1987). Anxiolytics: when? why? which one? Patient Care 21(17):60.

Fagan DR and Illsley SS. (1985). Benzodiazepine hypnotics: a comparative review of recently approved agents, Hosp Formul 20:491.

Finlay S. (1989). Is Grandma drowsy, or is she drugged? . . . many nursing homes resorting to powerful sedatives to keep residents docile, US News World Report 106(23):68.

Finley R ed. (1985). Insomnia in the elderly: principles in management, Drug Ther Elderly 1(1):1.

Gilman AG et al. (1990). Goodman & Gilman's the pharmacological basis of therapeutics, ed 8. New York: MacMillan Publishing Co.

Hamlin M et al. (1989). Drug withdrawal, Nurs Times 85(35):66.

Johnson JE. (1988). Effect of benzodiazepines on older women, J Community Health Nursing 5(2):119.

Lyall J. (1989). The unknown addicts, Nurs Times 85(8):16.

Miller TW and Miller LLJ. (1986). Counseling patients with sleep disorders, Am Pharm NN26(12):26.

Miyagawa CI. (1987). Sedation of the mechanically ventilated patient in the intensive care unit, Respir Care 32(9):792.

Patterson JF. (1987). Triazolam syndrome in the elderly, South Med J 80(11):1425.

Ramsey R. (1986). The aging kidney: impact on drug therapy, Drug Ther Elderly 1(6):23.

Sussman N. (1985). The benzodiazepines: selection and use in treating anxiety, insomnia, and other disorders, Hosp Formul 20:298.

Tilley S and Weighill VE. (1986). How nurse therapists assess and contribute to the management of alcohol and sedative drug use among anxious patients, J Advanced Nurs 11:499.

Todd B. (1989). Disabling anxiety, Geriatr Nurs 10(3):152.

Trevelyan J. (1988). The forgotten addicts, Nurs Times 84(16):16.

United States Pharmacopeial Convention. (1991). Drug information for the health care provider, ed 11. Rockville, Md: US Pharmacopeial Convention.

Vollmer ME. (1988). Rational use of drugs in geriatric insomnia, Drug Ther 13(5):15.

Whaley LF and Wong DL. (1991). Nursing care of infants and children, ed 4. St. Louis: Mosby–Year Book, Inc.

Zarnow R et al. (1987). Use of night time sedations in the elderly at Calare Nusing Home, LAMP 44(10):10.

*Chapter*

# 🌀 *15* Anticonvulsants

---

## CHAPTER OBJECTIVES

*After studying this chapter, you should be able to meet the following objectives and define the key terms.*

1. Describe the international classification description of epileptic seizures.

2. Identify observations to be made about a client having a seizure.

3. Discuss the nursing management for anticonvulsant therapy.

4. Identify the major anticonvulsant drug classifications, including examples of drugs and their primary method of seizure control activity.

5. List the common side effects/adverse reactions of anticonvulsants.

6. Formulate an appropriate plan of care for the individual client receiving an anticonvulsant drug or drugs.

## KEY TERMS

## INTRODUCTION

Epilepsy occurs in approximately 0.5% to 1% of the population. In 50% of the cases, the cause of epilepsy is unknown; in this instance it is called **primary** or **idiopathic epilepsy**. **Secondary epilepsy** may be traced to trauma, infections, cerebrovascular disorder, or other illnesses that contribute to epilepsy. Detection of contributing factors has been advanced by computed tomography (CT scans) and nuclear brain scans.

**Epilepsy** is regarded as a symptom of disease or disorder of the brain rather than a disease in itself. It is associated with marked changes in the electric activity of the cerebral cortex, and these alterations are often detected in the electroencephalogram. Therefore the EEG is often a valuable aid to the physician in making a diagnosis. In addition to the EEG, other laboratory tests such as routine blood and urine series, calcium, blood sugar, electrolytes, phosphorus, and sometimes renal and hepatic function tests are done to assist in the determination of the diagnosis.

Epileptic seizures vary and have been traditionally classified according to grand mal seizures, petit mal seizures, jacksonian epilepsy, and psychomotor attacks. A new classification of seizures, however, has been implemented and is being more extensively used because it more adequately describes the seizure of the client. It is called the International Classification of Seizures. The box at right presents it with the traditional terms and characteristics. For the purpose of this text, both seizure classifications will be used.

## TYPES OF EPILEPSY

*Partial simple motor (jacksonian) epilepsy* is described by some as a type of **focal seizure;** it is associated with irritation of a specific part of the brain. A single part, such as a finger or an extremity, may jerk and such movements may end spontaneously or spread over the whole musculature. Consciousness may not be lost unless the seizure develops into a generalized convulsion.

*Partial complex (psychomotor) seizures* are characterized by brief alterations in consciousness, unusual stereotyped movements (such as chewing or swallowing movements) repeated over and over, temperamental changes, confusion, and feelings of unreality. These seizures are often associated with grand mal seizures and are likely to be resistant to therapy with drugs.

*Generalized absence, simple or complex (petit mal) seizures* are most often seen in childhood and consist of temporary lapses in consciousness that last for a few seconds. Clients appear to stare into space or daydream, are inattentive, and may exhibit a few rhythmic movements of the eyes (slight blinking), head, or hands. They do not convulse. They may have many attacks in a single day. EEG records a 3/second spike wave pattern. Sometimes an attack of generalized absence seizures is followed by a generalized tonic-clonic–type seizure; when the child reaches adulthood, other types of seizures may occur. Research is exploring the possibility of using drug combination therapies for childhood seizures as a prophylactic measure to avoid the development of other seizure patterns in adulthood.

**Tonic-clonic generalized (grand mal) epilepsy** is the type most commonly seen. Such attacks may be characterized by an aura and the sudden loss of consciousness. The aura is specific to the individual; it may consist of numbness, visual disturbance, or a particular form of dizziness that warns the client of an approaching seizure. The client falls forcefully and has a series of **tonic** (stiffening) and **clonic** (rapid, synchronous jerking) muscular contractions. The eyes roll upward, the arms flex, and the legs extend. The force of the muscular contractions causes air to be forced out of the lungs, which accounts for the cry that the client may make on falling. Respiration is suspended temporarily,

---

### INTERNATIONAL CLASSIFICATION OF SEIZURES

**Partial Seizures**

*Simple*

No impairment of consciousness

Motor symptoms (formerly called jacksonian)

Sensory (hallucinations of sight, hearing, or taste); somatosensory (tingling)

Autonomic—autonomic nervous system responses

Psychic (personality changes)

*Complex*

Impaired consciousness

Cognitive (memory impairment, confusion)

Affective (bizarre behavioral effects)

Psychosensory (automatisms—repetition, purposeless behaviors)

Psychomotor (complex symptoms that may include an aura, automatism [i.e., chewing, swallowing movements], unreal feelings, bizarre behaviors, and motor seizures)

Compound (tonic, clonic, or tonic-clonic seizures)

*Secondarily generalized*

**Generalized Seizures**

Widespread involvement of both cerebral hemispheres

Tonic-clonic seizures (formerly called grand mal)

Tonic (sustained contractions of large muscle groups)

Clonic (various dysrhythmic contractions in the body)

Myoclonic (unaltered consciousness, isolated clonic contractions)

Absence (formerly called petit mal—brief loss of consciousness for a few seconds, no confusion, EEG demonstrates 3/second spike wave patterns.

Atonic (head drop or falling down symptoms)

**Unclassified**

Available data incomplete, inadequate, or lacks classification status (such as neonatal seizures)

---

the skin becomes diaphoretic and cyanotic, perspiration and saliva flow, and the client may froth at the mouth and bite the tongue if it gets caught between the teeth. Incontinence may occur. When the seizure subsides, the client regains partial consciousness, may complain of aching, and then tends to fall into a deep sleep.

**Status epilepticus** is a recurrent seizure generally lasting 30 minutes or more without an intervening stay of consciousness. A 10% to 20% mortality rate results from anoxia in this medical emergency. *The major cause of status epilepticus is noncompliance with the drug regimen;* other causes include cerebral infarction, cerebral infection, or low blood concentration of calcium or glucose. The treatment of status epilepticus is discussed later in this chapter.

*Mixed seizures* are seen in some clients who have more than one type of seizure disorder. This is significant because different types of seizures respond specifically to certain anticonvulsant drugs. The aim of therapy is to find the drug or drugs that will effectively control the seizures with a minimum of undesirable side effects and restore physiologic homeostasis to arrest convulsive activity.

## RELATIONSHIP OF AGE TO SEIZURES

A relationship of age to onset of an epileptic seizure state exists. Most clients diagnosed as having epilepsy have their initial seizure before the age of 20; however, seizures may have an onset at any age in life. Idiopathic (undefined, unascertainable, or genetic in origin or cause) seizures are often diagnosed between the ages of 5 and 20. Onset before or after this age period is often from nonidiopathic (identifiable, ascertainable) causes and is termed symptomatic (acquired, organic) epilepsy.

**Neonates.** Neonatal seizures occur in newborn children less than 1 month old. Among the more common causes of neonatal seizures in this age group are the following: congenital defects or malformation of the brain, abnormality or infections (meningitis, encephalitis, abscess) within the CNS, hypoxia (in utero or during delivery), premature birth, and defects in metabolism. These epileptic seizures are also referred to as organic, symptomatic, or acquired because they may be caused by an identifiable preceding condition or cause.

**Infants.** In infants less than 2 years of age, the seizure types most frequently diagnosed include generalized tonic-clonic seizures and partial seizures. The atonic epileptic seizure seen in later development (ages 2 to 5 years) may be preceded by infantile spasms in those less than 2 years. The infantile spasm is not classified as a type of epileptic seizure itself. Among the more common causes of infant seizures are those causes as seen in the neonatal stage and additionally injury in the perinatal period, infection, exposure to toxins (in utero caused by maternal exposure or drug use, misuse, or abuse), maternal exposure to x-rays, and postnatal trauma.

**Children.** In children 2 to 5 years old, the seizure types that are frequently diagnosed include generalized tonic-clonic seizures and atonic seizures. The causes are similar to those mentioned in newborns and infants with the addition of chronic diseases involving the CNS. The parents of the child may wrongly believe the child has a behavioral disorder rather than a treatable seizure disorder.

In the age group 6 years and older, brain tumors and vascular disease may cause seizures. Sometimes the convulsive seizure is associated with a brain infection, head trauma, fever, growth of scar tissue, cerebrovascular disease, the presence of a toxin or a poison, or drug withdrawal.

In children 5 to 16 years old, the seizure types that emerge in diagnosis are absence seizures and generalized tonic-clonic seizures, which may be idiopathic in origin. Seizure types such as partial, myoclonic, and less commonly generalized tonic-clonic seizures may be caused by neurologic diseases, infection, postnatal trauma, or head trauma (accident or sport).

**Young adults.** Within the age group 16 to 25 years, the generalized seizures may be idiopathic in origin. The partial seizure and less commonly seen generalized seizures may result from the use of alcohol, social/recreational drug use, drug abuse or misuse, or head injury.

**Adults.** In clients over 20 years of age, the seizures emerging often are of the generalized type, which may be idiopathic. Also seen are partial seizures and less commonly generalized seizures, which may have been precipitated by trauma to the head or a tumor of the brain, or, in middle aged and elderly clients, a cerebrovascular disease.

## ANTICONVULSANT THERAPY

The effectiveness of anticonvulsant drugs is often measured by the amount of increased voltage necessary to provoke an electroconvulsion in an animal who has previously received the anticonvulsant to be tested or by the degree of their antagonism to chemical substances capable of producing convulsions. Pentylenetetrazol is a drug against which anticonvulsants are measured for effectiveness.

The anticonvulsants may be classified into the following groups:

Barbiturates—phenobarbital, mephobarbital, metharbital; amobarbital, pentobarbital, and secobarbital are for parenteral use only

Hydantoins—phenytoin, mephenytoin, ethotoin

Succinimides—ethosuximide, methsuximide, phensuximide

Oxazolidinediones—paramethadione, trimethadione

Benzodiazepines—clonazepam, diazepam, clorazepate, lorazepam

Miscellaneous—valproic acid, carbamazepine, divalproex, primidone, phenacemide, acetazolamide, magnesium sulfate

The exact mode and site of action of these drugs are still unknown at the molecular level. Stabilization of the cell membrane by altering cation transport (sodium, potassium, calcium) either by increasing sodium efflux or decreasing sodium influx is a proposed mechanism (AHFS, 1991). The main pharmacologic effects are (1) to increase motor cortex threshold to reduce its response to incoming electric or chemical stimulation, or (2) to depress or reduce the spread of a seizure discharge from its focus (origin) by depressing synaptic transport or decreasing nerve conduction. For example, hydantoins suppress the seizure by stabilizing cell membrane excitability, thus reducing the spread of seizure discharge, whereas barbiturates reduce neuron excitability

**TABLE 15-1**   Pharmacokinetic overview of selected anticonvulsant drugs

| Name | Fate | Therapeutic plasma levels in adults (µg/ml) | Serum half-life (hr) | Time to reach steady-state |
|---|---|---|---|---|
| carbamazepine (Tegretol, Mazepine ✻) | Absorption: slow and variable<br>Metabolism: liver<br>Excretion: urine, feces | 4-12 (in adults) | 1 dose: 26-65<br>Multidose:<br>  Adults 12-17 | 40 hr<br>  (range 8-55 hr) |
| clonazepam (Ionopin, Rivotril ✻) | Absorption: good<br>Metabolism: liver<br>Excretion: urine | 0.02-0.07 | 18-50 | 4-12 days |
| divalproex (Depakote, Epival ✻) | Absorption: 1-4 hr<br>Metabolism: liver<br>Excretion: urine, small amount from feces and lungs | 50-100 | 6-16 | 30-85 hr |
| ethosuximide (Zarontin, Petinimid ✻) | Absorption: good<br>Metabolism: liver<br>Excretion: urine | 40-100 | Adults: 56-60<br>Children: 30-36 | Adults: 12 days<br>Children: 6 days |
| methsuximide (Celontin, Petinutin ✻) | Absorption: good<br>Metabolism: liver<br>Excretion: urine | 10-40 | 1-3<br>Active metabolite:<br>  36-45 | 5-15 hr |
| phenobarbital (Luminal and others) | Absorption: good<br>Metabolism: liver<br>Excretion: urine | 10-40 | Adults: 53-118<br>Children: 40-70 | Adults: 10-25 days<br>Children: 8-15 days |
| phenytoin (Dilantin) | Absorption: orally, slow; poor in neonates<br>Metabolism: liver<br>Excretion: urine and feces | 10-20 | Adults: 22 (range 7-42) | 5-10 days |
| primidone (Mysoline, Sertan ✻) | Absorption: good<br>Metabolism: liver<br>Excretion: urine | 5-12 | primidone: 3-24<br>phenobarbital: 72-144<br>PEMA: 24-48 | |
| valproic acid (Depakene) | Absorption: complete and rapid<br>Metabolism: kidney<br>Excretion: urine; small amount from lungs and feces | 50-100 | Adults: 6-16 | Adults: 30-85 hr |

and increase the motor cortex threshold to electric stimulation.

Although there is no ideal anticonvulsant drug, if there were, a number of characteristics would be considered highly desirable:

1. The drug should be highly effective but exhibit a low incidence of toxicity.
2. The drug should be effective against more than one type of seizure and for mixed seizures.
3. The drug should be long acting and nonsedative so that the client is not incapacitated with sleep or excessive drowsiness.
4. The drug should be well tolerated by the client and inexpensive, since the client may have to take it for years or for the rest of his or her life.
5. Tolerance to the therapeutic effects of the drug should not develop.

6. The drug should control seizures and permit a client to function effectively in any environment.

The present-day drugs that are considered especially satisfactory and safe are phenobarbital and phenytoin sodium. The barbiturates have been discussed (see Chapter 14), but their use as anticonvulsants is emphasized again. They are an important group of drugs for this purpose, especially the longer-acting agents. Phenobarbital is effective against most types of epileptic seizures except certain absence types. It is considered one of the safest anticonvulsants. Its chief disadvantage is that it must often be given in doses that produce apathy and sleepiness.

See Table 15-1 for an examination of the pharmacokinetics of these drugs. Although anticonvulsant agents are usually given orally, there are a few parenteral forms. These are reserved for occasions when the parenteral form is the best choice of therapy. Table 15-2 lists these conditions or

**TABLE 15-2**   Indications for parenteral use of anticonvulsants

| Parenteral drug | Use |
| --- | --- |
| barbiturates, especially phenobarbital, also amobarbital, pentobarbital sodium, and secobarbital sodium | Eclampsia, status epilepticus, severe recurrent seizures, tetanus, convulsant drug toxicity, other convulsive states |
| phenytoin | Status epilepticus, seizure during neurosurgery |
| magnesium sulfate | Severe toxemias of pregnancy (preeclampsia and eclampsia) |
| paraldehyde injection | Status epilepticus, tetanus, eclampsia, convulsant drug toxicity |
| benzodiazepines: diazepam, lorazepam | Status epilepticus; severe, recurrent seizures |

### Investigational Drug Update:
### ANTICONVULSANTS

Progabide, a GABA agonist drug, has exhibited promise in the treatment of epilepsy, spasticity, and movement disorders.

Two other agents in the development stages with anticonvulsant activity are gabapentin and lamotrigine.

situations and the parenteral drugs indicated for the treatment of each.

Anticonvulsant drugs may exhibit varying blood levels in different clients after each client has received the same dose. This variation results from a complex of interrelated factors including individual client compliance; individual absorption, metabolism, distribution, and excretion, which may be caused by genetic and/or environmental factors; concomitant ailments, such as renal or hepatic dysfunctions; concurrent medication; diet; and physical status. Certain drugs require an adjusted dosage to obtain optimal therapeutic effects, and this dosage may have wide client variation.

Therapeutic dosage ranges are intended to serve merely as rough guides to therapy; they are not firm limits. The ranges provide a point from which the dosage of a drug may be individualized to account for the extremes in variation to response and adverse effects. The client beginning anticonvulsant therapy should have serum levels measured to establish his or her individual level/dose ratio. This level tends to be a constant measure for an individual, although it varies considerably among clients. The time required to reach a steady serum level is generally about four to five times the elimination half-life of a drug. A convenient time for serum level measurement is 1 month after initiating therapy, since levels measured much earlier may be lower than the steady-state level finally achieved.

The **serum half-life** of a drug (the time required for the serum level to drop 50% when no additional drug is administered) is a measure of its rate of excretion and depends on the client's age. As discussed in Chapter 4, the pharmacokinetics of a drug are affected by age. For example, drug metabolism is relatively slow in the neonate, but in infants and young children it is higher on a milligram per kilogram of body weight basis than it is for an adult. Usually the elderly, with a decrease in their metabolism, require a lower dosage schedule. (See Chapter 8.)

One of the characteristics of the anticonvulsant drugs is that either the parent drug or the active metabolite has a long serum half-life, so the exact daily medication schedule is seldom critical. Administration of these drugs may be one to three times daily.

The first serum concentration after the first intravenous dose is half the peak value attained during long-term administration. Therefore the client can attain steady-state serum concentration quickly if the first intravenous dose is twice the maintenance dose. In adults, for example, a loading (intravenous) dose of phenytoin (1000 mg or 13 to 14 mg/kg, which is twice the usual maintenance dose of 300 to 400 mg/half-life of about 24 hours) will produce a therapeutic serum concentration of 10 to 20 μg/ml. The intravenous route is necessary because phenytoin is absorbed very slowly and erratically by the intramuscular route because the water solubility of the drug decreases and phenytoin crystals precipitate in the muscle. A high degree of local irritation has also been reported with intramuscular injection.

## ▷NURSING MANAGEMENT: ANTICONVULSANT THERAPY

A client for whom anticonvulsants have been prescribed is treated most effectively with a holistic approach. This client has many special problems, including the fear of sudden loss of physical and emotional control and the stigma concerning seizures. In recent years, emphasis has been placed on public education regarding epilepsy to dispel the myths associated with it. This individual needs information about the seizure condition and its management, along with psychosocial support from the nurse. The client should understand that the condition can be controlled or modified with medication. The goal is to attain maximum seizure control with minimal medication side effects. The anticonvulsant or combination of such drugs prescribed depends on the type of seizure, whether the client is having more than one type of seizure, or whether the seizures are difficult to control. Finding the appropriate regimen for each client takes time.

Epilepsy may worsen during pregnancy, and status epilepticus increases in frequency during gestation and labor. Some of the anticonvulsants appear in breast milk. Emotional stress (psychologic, occupational, physiologic, marital, economic) may influence seizure frequency.

**Assessment.** Along with a general assessment and drug history, assessment of the client with a convulsive disorder includes data specific to the seizures. These data include the number of seizures within a specific time; precipitating events or activities; presence of sensations or perceptions that the client experiences before a seizure, called an aura; and the character of seizures.

The nurse should assess the presence or absence of an aura and its nature if present. It may also be helpful to evaluate the ability of the patient to describe it (somatic, visceral, psychic). It can also be useful to note the presence or absence of a cry. The onset of seizure should be assessed for site of initial body movements, deviation of head and eyes, chewing and salivation, posture of body, and sensory changes.

After onset of seizure, it is important to note characteristics of the tonic and clonic phases. Characteristics include movements of body as to progression; skin color and airway; pupillary changes; incontinence; and duration of each phase.

After the tonic and clonic phases, the nurse should try to assess duration of and behavior during the relaxation (sleep) phase. During the postictal phase, not only the duration should be noted but also general behavior; ability to remember anything about the seizure; orientation; pupillary changes; headache; and, finally, any injuries present. Finally, as accurate a picture as possible should be assessed of the duration of the entire seizure, level of consciousness, and length of unconsciousness if present.

Often the nurse will not be present when a seizure has occurred. In this situation family, friends, or other witnesses may provide valuable information about the seizure. The most common medical test to evaluate seizure activity is the electroencephalogram (EEG), a recording of electrical activity generated by the brain made by placing electrodes on the scalp. Subjective data to be obtained include the client's

 Selected nursing diagnoses for the client on anticonvulsive medications

| Nursing diagnosis | Outcome criteria | Nursing interventions |
| --- | --- | --- |
| Knowledge deficit related to newly prescribed or altered anticonvulsant drug therapy | The client will describe: the seizure condition; how the drug therapy relates to the condition; how and when to take the medications; common drug interactions; safety precautions; common side effects and which of these warrant reporting; storage requirements of the drugs; The client will: demonstrate less anxiety related to fear of the unknown, loss of control, and misconceptions | Assess learning needs and learning readiness<br>Plan with the client and family for the achievement of realistic goals<br>Provide information to meet outcome criteria |
| Noncompliance related to medication regimen | The client will: self-administer medications safely and accurately | Determine the client's reasons for noncompliance and take appropriate teaching/counseling interventions<br>Provide needed drug information concerning rationales for the specific client's seizure status<br>Discuss the increased possibility of seizures with noncompliance |
| High risk for injury related to effects of anticonvulsant drug therapy | The client will: maintain anticonvulsant drug therapy without untoward side effects, adverse reactions, and toxicity | Administer drug safely and accurately<br>Observe client for drowsiness, ataxia, behavioral changes, slurred speech, mental confusion, vertigo, and excessive sedation (see drug monographs for drug-specific side effects/adverse reactions)<br>Instruct client about symptoms to be reported<br>Explain the importance of Medic Alert card/tag<br>Discourage self-altering of medication regimen<br>Caution against activities requiring coordination and alertness until responses to drugs are known |

understanding and reaction to the convulsive disorder and drug therapy.

***Intervention.*** Anticonvulsant drugs should be administered intravenously in emergency situations (such as status epilepticus) because of the slow absorption from the intramuscular injection site and the low peak serum levels achieved. The anticonvulsant drugs should be administered using as long an interval between doses as possible, depending on their half-life. The anticonvulsant drugs that have an elimination half-life of 24 hours or more generally need to be administered only once a day to maintain a therapeutic serum concentration. The daily dose may be administered at bedtime to overcome the sedation seen with peak levels of anticonvulsant drugs. In a nonemergency situation it is best to make changes in drug therapy with one drug at a time. The nurse and the client must be aware that each time a new anticonvulsant drug is started or the dose of a drug is increased or decreased, it takes four to five elimination half-life intervals (so the concentration of the drug has dropped by 95%) to reach the new steady-state serum concentration and to achieve the total therapeutic effect of the new drug regimen.

Many of the anticonvulsants have known blood levels of an optimal therapeutic range, that is, the level of medication needed to control seizures (see Table 15-1). When serum levels of anticonvulsants are ordered, they should be scheduled for a time greater than 8 hours since the last dose of medication was given.

***Education.*** The client should be encouraged to use moderation in his or her life-style, follow an appropriate diet, and get sufficient rest and exercise. Stressful situations should be avoided; if this is not possible, the physician should be notified for dosage adjustment in ongoing stressful conditions. Drinking alcohol and taking OTC medications should be cautioned against (see specific drugs for interactions or effects). The client should understand that anticonvulsants take days or weeks to reach an effective level in the body. A missed dose may result in a seizure in a few days, and taking a dose will not prevent an impending seizure.

Although the client may be seizure free for some time and may perceive that a "cure" has occurred, the medication dose should not be decreased or stopped without consultation with the physician.

During initiation or change of therapy, the client should avoid activities that require coordination and alertness until response to the drug therapy has been determined.

Medications should be stored at home away from light and heat and out of the reach of children, since overdosage is especially dangerous in children. Outdated and discontinued medications should be flushed down the toilet.

The nurse should suggest that the family keep a daily record of the number and type of seizures that occur during drug therapy. This is one measure of the efficacy of the medication(s) and will help the physician determine if an increased dosage or an additional agent is needed.

The client and family should be taught seizure precautions, and the importance of wearing a Medic Alert tag/card (obtainable at local pharmacy) should be explained. A valuable resource for both the nurse and the client is the Epilepsy Foundation of America (located at 4351 Garden City Drive, Landover, Maryland 20785; phone (301) 459-3700).

---

 ***Geriatric Implications:***
**ANTICONVULSANTS**

The elderly tend to metabolize anticonvulsants more slowly; thus drug accumulation and toxicity may occur. Monitor closely as dosage adjustments (lower doses) may be necessary.

Serum albumin levels may be lower in geriatric clients, thus resulting in decreased protein binding of bound drugs, such as phenytoin and valproic acid. Monitor closely as lower drug doses may be necessary.

Administer intravenous doses at a rate slower than the recommended rate for an adult. Elderly rate of administration for phenytoin should be 5 to 10 mg/minute up to a maximum of 25 mg/minute.

---

 ***Pediatric Implications:***
**ANTICONVULSANTS**

The young client (under age 23) is more susceptible to gingival hyperplasia, especially with phenytoin or mephenytoin therapy. Gingivitis or gum inflammation usually starts during the first 6 months of drug therapy, although severe hyperplasia is unlikely in dosages under 500 mg/day. A dental program of teeth cleaning and plaque control started within 7 to 10 days of initiating drug therapy helps to reduce the rate and severity of this condition.

Coarse facial features and excessive body hair growth are more frequently reported in young patients.

Impaired school performance is reported with long-term, high-dose hydantoin therapy (especially at high or toxic serum levels).

Whenever possible, other anticonvulsants should be considered first as they are less apt to cause the adverse effects induced by the hydantoins.

Children receiving valproic acid, especially those up to 2 years old or those receiving multiple anticonvulsant drugs, are at a greater risk for developing serious hepatotoxicity. This risk decreases with advancing age.

*Evaluation.* Therapeutic alternatives are selected (monotherapy or polytherapy) that best control the client's seizure. Therapeutic drug monitoring includes interpreting results of serum concentrations with the client's clinical response. This monitoring has reduced the need of polydrug anticonvulsant therapy and added greater efficiency in drug selection for each client. A significant number of clients have seizure recurrences after treatment withdrawal. The withdrawal procedure should be initiated with close medical supervision (within a hospital), especially when polydrug anticonvulsant therapy is being adjusted or when inadequate seizure control is recognized. Seizures may occur even after long periods that were seizure free. Fewer seizures occur when the withdrawal is planned or gradual or when the dose is reduced to minimal maintenance therapy.

Increased anticonvulsant serum levels may signal impending toxic effects. Generally, adverse effects are more serious at higher serum levels. Maintaining a serum level within the therapeutic range is a challenge for some clients. The challenge surfaces when other drugs are added or deleted from the client's regimen, a client is noncompliant, there is an organ system dysfunction as seen in the hepatorenal systems, or undesirable drug effects cause the client to withdraw from drug therapy. When the client becomes fully informed about the drug therapy and need for serum concentrations within the therapeutic range, this may reduce therapeutic failures caused by noncompliance or adverse effects.

Check the chart of major side effects and adverse reactions (Table 15-3); it is divided according to frequency, impor-

tance, and recommendations regarding when to report such effects to the prescribing physician.

Evaluation of the client's progress on anticonvulsant therapy should be assessed in terms of achievement of the outcome criteria and the response to nursing interventions for the specific client. The nurse should also be aware of the behavioral and cognitive effects reported with the anticonvulsants (see Table 15-4).

## BARBITURATES

Barbiturates, especially phenobarbital, have been used for many years for the treatment of generalized tonic-clonic and partial seizures. This class of medications is relatively inexpensive, efficacious, and has a low incidence of side effects. Phenobarbital is one of two anticonvulsants most commonly prescribed in the United States; the other is phenytoin.

Mephobarbital (Mebaral) is converted by the liver-metabolizing enzymes to phenobarbital, whereas metharbital (Gemonil) is metabolized to barbital in the liver. All three barbiturates are long-acting compounds, but there is little or no advantage in using the latter two instead of phenobarbital, the most commonly prescribed barbiturate.

The parenteral dosage forms of amobarbital, pentobarbital, and secobarbital have been used in emergency treatment of seizures (Table 15-2). The oral dosage forms are generally not indicated for the treatment of seizure disorders because of their potent sedative-hypnotic effects. See Table 15-1 for a pharmacokinetic overview of selected anticonvulsant agents.

**TABLE 15-3** Anticonvulsants: side effects/adverse reactions

| Drug(s) | Side effects* | Adverse reactions† |
|---|---|---|
| barbiturates (phenobarbital, mephobarbital, metharbital) | More frequent: drowsiness, dizziness, tiredness, hangover-type effects<br>Less common: nausea, vomiting, constipation, headaches, insomnia, increased irritability, nervousness | Rashes; hives; fever; sore throat; sores on lips or in mouth; pain in chest, muscles, bones, or joints; confusion; depression or paradoxical excitement in children or elderly clients (exfoliative dermatitis; Stevens-Johnson syndrome; osteomalacia or rickets with chronic dosing) |
| hydantoins (phenytoin, ethotoin, mephenytoin) | More frequent: hirsutism (excessive hair growth seen primarily with phenytoin), constipation, nausea, vomiting, drowsiness, dizziness<br>Less common: headaches, insomnia, distortion of facial features (thick lips, broadening of nasal tip, jaw protuberance), diarrhea (mostly with ethotoin) | Gingival hyperplasia (bleeding, sensitive gum tissue, or overgrowth on gum tissue); rarely seen with ethotoin<br>Slurred speech, nystagmus, hand trembling, increased irritability or nervousness, skin rash, behavioral changes, ataxia, blood dyscrasias (thrombocytopenia), and skin rashes reported more often with mephenytoin |
| succinimides (ethosuximide, methsuximide, phensuximide) | More frequent: headaches, epigastric pain, anorexia, hiccups, nausea, vomiting<br>Less common: drowsiness, lethargy, irritability, dizziness | Rash, pruritus (possibly Stevens-Johnson syndrome), mood changes, sore throat and fever (agranulocytosis), increase in bleeding or bruising (thrombocytopenia) |

*If side effects continue, increase, or disturb the client, inform the physician.
†If adverse reactions occur, contact the physician, since medical intervention may be necessary.

**TABLE 15-3**  Anticonvulsants: side effects/adverse reactions—cont'd

| Drug(s) | Side effects* | Adverse reactions† |
|---|---|---|
| oxazolidinediones (para-methadione, trimetha-dione) | More frequent: headache, drowsiness, dizziness, photophobia<br>Less frequent: loss of appetite, weight loss, alopecia, pruritus, lethargy, nausea, vomiting | Visual changes, edema, rash, sore throat and fever, enlarged lymph glands, increased bleeding and bruising, and hepatitis |
| benzodiazepines (clonazepam, diazepam, clorazepate) | More frequent: drowsiness, ataxia, lethargy<br>Less frequent: blurred vision, diplopia, constipation, headache, nausea, vomiting, incontinence, slurred speech, dry mouth | Insomnia, hallucinations, confusion, excitability, paradoxical rage, depression, muscle weakness, vivid dreams, muscle weakness, sore throat, fever, increased bleeding or bruising, hepatic dysfunction |
| miscellaneous<br>valproic acid, divalproex | More frequent: tremors, mild gastric distress, diarrhea, weight gain, irregular menses<br>Less frequent: dizziness, drowsiness, alopecia (transient), headache, depression, constipation, hyperactivity, increased irritability | Hepatotoxicity (usually during first 6 months of therapy), abdominal cramps, nausea and vomiting, anorexia, ataxia, rash, increased bleeding or bruising, hepatitis, loss of seizure control |
| carbamazepine | More frequent: vertigo, drowsiness, nausea or vomiting, dizziness<br>Less frequent: dry mouth, headache, diarrhea, myalgia, arthralgia, leg cramps, photosensitivity, altered skin pigmentation, alopecia, anorexia, increased sweating | Increased release of antidiuretic hormone resulting in hyponatremia, activation of latent psychosis, blurred vision, diplopia, confusion, hives, pruritus, rash, oculomotor disturbances, nystagmus, visual hallucinations, lethargy, weakness, hostility, stupor, edema |
| primidone | More frequent: drowsiness, ataxia, dizziness<br>Less frequent: anorexia, headaches, impotence, nausea, or vomiting that usually decreases with continued drug usage | Rash, edema, swelling of eyelids, hives, unusual fatigue, confusion, restlessness, increased excitability (paradoxical reaction in children and elderly), difficult breathing |
| phenacemide | Anorexia, weight loss, drowsiness, tiredness, dizziness, insomnia, headache, muscle pain | An extremely toxic drug; has produced hepatitis, jaundice, fatal liver necrosis, severe bone marrow depression (aplastic anemia, agranulocytosis), acute psychoses, increase in suicide potential, nephritis |
| acetazolamide | More frequent: diarrhea, increased frequency of urination, anorexia, metallic taste, nausea, vomiting, weight loss, paresthesias<br>Less frequent: Drowsiness, nervousness, fatigue | Fever, sore throat, increased bleeding or bruising, rash, hives, confusion, depression, tinnitus, transient myopia, trembling, severe muscle weakness, shortness of breath, malaise |
| magnesium sulfate | | Reduced respiratory rate, depression of reflexes, flushing, hypotension, hypothermia, ECG changes (adverse effects require *immediate* notification of physician and treatment) |

**TABLE 15-4**  Central nervous system effects of selected anticonvulsants

| Drug | Behavioral alterations | Cognitive effects |
|---|---|---|
| Barbiturates, especially phenobarbital | May see paradoxical effect, especially in elderly, children or compromised clients (i.e., increased activity or excitement, irritability, altered sleep patterns, increased tiredness) | Impaired judgment, short-term memory impairment, decreased attention span |
| carbamazepine | Increased irritability, insomnia, behavioral changes especially in children, depression | Not significant |
| phenytoin | Fatigue, increased clumsiness, confusion, mood alterations | Decreased attention span, decreased ability to problem solve |

***Side effects/adverse reactions.*** See Table 15-3. Also, apnea, bronchospasm, and respiratory depression may occur following rapidly administered, intravenous injections of barbiturates. Severe symptoms of withdrawal may occur in individuals who have a barbiturate dependency from prolonged use at high dosages. Anxiety, trembling, nausea, vomiting, insomnia, orthostatic hypotension, seizures, hallucinations, and even death may result if the drug is withdrawn abruptly. Gradual withdrawal in a controlled setting is usually recommended for the treatment of dependence.

***Significant drug interactions.*** The following effects may occur when barbiturates, especially phenobarbital, is given with the drugs listed below:

| Drug | Possible Effect and Management |
|---|---|
| adrenocorticoids or corticosteroids (prednisone, etc.) | Effects may be decreased because of enhanced metabolism produced by barbiturates. Dosage adjustment may be necessary. |
| alcohol, anesthetics, CNS depressants (sedatives, hypnotics, narcotics) | Enhanced CNS depressant effects, respiratory depression; use extreme caution in combining such medications. Usually the dosage of one or both drugs should be reduced. |
| anticoagulants (coumarin or indandione types) | Effects may be decreased because of enhanced metabolism produced by barbiturates. Closely monitor prothrombin time. Dosage adjustment of anticoagulants may be necessary. |
| hydantoin anticonvulsants | Unpredictable effects on hydantoin metabolism may occur. Serum levels should be closely monitored when drugs are given concurrently. |
| divalproex sodium or valproic acid | Two effects may result from this combination: (1) valproic acid half-life may be decreased, which would require a dosage adjustment to maintain control; or (2) metabolism of barbiturates may be decreased, which can result in elevated barbiturate serum levels and toxicity. Monitor barbiturate levels, since a dosage adjustment may be necessary. |
| ascorbic acid, vitamin D | An increase in urinary excretion of ascorbic acid is reported. The increased metabolism of vitamin D may lead to a vitamin D deficiency in clients on long-term barbiturate therapy. Supplementation with vitamin D (to prevent osteomalacia) and ascorbic acid may be necessary. |

### amobarbital

Amobarbital is indicated for use as a sedative-hypnotic and anticonvulsant. Only the parenteral form is used as an anticonvulsant. Amobarbital should be administered deep intramuscularly to reduce the possibility of sterile abscesses and sloughing of tissue. When administered intravenously to an adult, the rate of injection should not exceed 100 mg/minute. Parenteral solutions should be clear and without precipitate when reconstituted. The solution should be used within 30 minutes of reconstitution, since it hydrolyzes easily.

### mephobarbital

Mephobarbital is a barbiturate indicated for use only as an anticonvulsant. Therapy is usually begun with small doses and increased over a period of 4 to 5 days until the optimal dosage has been established. Since mephobarbital is metabolized to phenobarbital, serum levels of phenobarbital may be monitored. Mephobarbital is available in oral dosage forms only.

### metharbital

Metharbital is used only as an anticonvulsant. It is metabolized to barbital, and serum barbital concentrations may be monitored. Metharbital is available in oral dosage forms only.

### phenobarbital

Phenobarbital is the prototype barbiturate to treat epilepsy. There are many dosage forms (tablets, elixers, solutions, and parenteral forms) and strengths available. The nurse must exercise special caution to ensure the proper dose is given as prescribed.

Several weeks of phenobarbital therapy may be necessary to achieve the maximum anticonvulsant effects. When administered intravenously, 15 to 30 minutes is required to reach the maximum anticonvulsant effect. It is important to wait for the anticonvulsant effect to develop before administering additional doses to avoid excessive barbiturate-induced depression. When administered intravenously, phenobarbital should be administered slowly to avoid respiratory depression; a rate of 60 mg/minute should not be exceeded. Resuscitative equipment should be readily available.

The optimal blood concentration of phenobarbital should be determined by seizure control and appearance of toxic effects. A serum concentration of 10 to 40 µg/ml is usually desired.

Dosage and administration of phenobarbital are addressed in Table 15-5.

## ▷NURSING MANAGEMENT: BARBITURATE THERAPY

***Assessment.*** Combination of these drugs with alcohol, antihistamines, antianxiety agents, antidepressants, or antipsychotic agents should be avoided because they may result in an enhanced CNS-depressant effect.

Pediatric and geriatric clients may be more sensitive to barbiturates and may respond to lower doses or may react with depression, confusion, or even excitement to the drug. These drugs should be used very cautiously in pregnant women because they can cause neonatal hemorrhage and an

**TABLE 15-5**   Phenobarbital: dosage and administration

| | Adults | Children |
|---|---|---|
| **Anticonvulsant** | | |
| Oral | 60-250 mg daily in single or divided doses | 1-6 mg/kg body weight daily in single or divided doses |
| Injectable | IV 100-320 mg, repeated if necessary to maximum of 600 mg in 24 hr | 10-20 mg/kg body weight as single loading dose; maintenance dose is 1-6 mg/kg/day IV |
| Status epilepticus | 10-20 mg/kg by slow IV injection; repeat if necessary | 15-20 mg/kg IV over 10-15 min |

increased incidence of teratogenic effects. If given throughout the third trimester, physical drug dependence and withdrawal reactions have been reported in the neonate from birth to approximately 2 weeks.

For clients receiving concurrent anticoagulant therapy, prothrombin times should be monitored carefully. Anticoagulant dose may need adjustment.

Barbiturates are to be used with caution if the following conditions are present: hypersensitivity to barbiturates; history of drug abuse, because the client is predisposed to dependence; hepatic impairment, which would interfere with barbiturate metabolism; respiratory disease, because of the risk of ventilatory depression; and pain, because symptoms of an underlying condition may be masked. Barbiturates are contraindicated for clients with porphyria or a history of the disease, because they may increase symptoms by stimulating enzymes for porphyrin synthesis.

*Intervention.* If barbiturates are administered intravenously, the nurse should ensure that the airway is patent and resuscitative equipment is readily available.

When drug therapy is initiated, the client may have some drowsiness and dizziness. Safety precautions should be taken when the client is ambulatory until the response to the medication has been ascertained.

Since the drug dosage schedule initially will be different until the correct dosage maintenance level is achieved, it is important that the nurse follow the dosage schedule accurately. The appearance of side effects or adverse reactions may require basic nursing measures such as reassurance, safety, or comfort, or it may indicate the need for further consultation (see Table 15-3).

If barbiturates are used during pregnancy, the nurse should consult with the client's physician to see if the client is to receive vitamin K in the last month of pregnancy to prevent hemorrhagic complications of delivery and in the newborn.

*Education.* Clients should be instructed to return to their physician routinely for CBC, blood chemistry studies, and drug blood level tests.

The client should be cautioned to avoid driving a car or operating potentially hazardous machinery until the response to drug therapy has been determined.

Self-alteration of prescribed medications or consumption of OTC drugs should be discouraged without consultation with the physician. OTC drugs may interfere with or enhance the drug's effectiveness. If used in combination with alcohol, CNS depression may occur. Abrupt withdrawal of the drug is contraindicated and could result in severe abstinence syndrome. Dosage should be tapered under a physician's supervision.

Clients taking oral estrogen-containing contraceptives should be aware that concurrent use of barbiturates may result in decreased contraceptive reliability, and they may wish to use a nonhormonal method of birth control or consult with their prescriber about a progestin-only oral contraceptive. Women using this drug therapy should be instructed to report to their physician if they become pregnant. Barbiturates have been shown to cause an increase in fetal abnormalities. Barbiturates are excreted in the breast milk and can cause CNS depression in the nursing infant.

*Evaluation.* In addition to the evaluation needed for anticonvulsant therapy in general, during prolonged barbiturate therapy, liver and renal function will be monitored (usually through blood and urine testing) at periodic intervals determined by the client's physician.

Determination of serum drug levels may be performed to monitor drug levels. The optimal blood levels are determined by response to seizure control and appearance of toxic effects.

## HYDANTOINS

The prototype hydantoin is phenytoin (Dilantin, Diphenylan), which was developed from a search for an anticonvulsant that would cause less sedation than the barbiturates. Phenytoin is a drug for primary treatment of all types of epilepsy except absence seizures. Two other hydantoin drugs are used for their anticonvulsant effects, ethotoin (Pegonone) and mephenytoin (Mesantoin). The use of ethotoin and mephenytoin is usually reserved for those clients whose symptoms could not be controlled with other drugs or those who had significant adverse effects from other anticonvulsants. In addition, both drugs are only available in the oral form, which limits their usefulness when a rapid response or parenteral route is needed.

Phenytoin and some other hydantoins appear to inhibit the spread of seizure activity by possibly promoting sodium efflux from neurons, and they tend to stabilize the threshold against hyperexcitability caused by excess stimulation or environmental changes capable of reducing membrane sodium gradient. This includes the reduction of post-tetanic potentiation at synapses. The loss of post-tetanic potentiation prevents cortical seizure foci from detonating adjacent cortical areas. The hydantoins as a group act to reduce the maximal activity of brain stem centers responsible for the tonic phase of grand mal seizures.

### phenytoin (Dilantin, various)
### phenytoin sodium extended (Dilantin)

For a description of phenytoin's mechanism of action, see general discussion of hydantoins. Phenytoin is used in the treatment of epilepsy. It is more effective for grand mal than petit mal seizures. It is also frequently prescribed in combination with phenobarbital, and it may be prescribed for clients following surgical operations on the brain, after head trauma, and for status epilepticus to prevent seizures. Table 15-1 examines the drug's pharmacokinetics.

***Side effects/adverse reactions.*** See Table 15-3. Signs of overdose or toxicity include blurred or double vision, nausea, vomiting, slurred speech, clumsiness, unsteadiness or staggering walk, dizziness, fatigue, confusion, and hallucinations. In addition, the diverse signs of toxicity seen with intravenous phenytoin are cardiovascular collapse, CNS depression, and hypotension (seen with rapid intravenous administration resulting from propylene glycol solvent). The rate of administration (not to exceed 50 mg over 1 minute) is important, since severe cardiotoxic reactions and fatal outcomes are reported in elderly or gravely ill patients.

***Significant drug interactions.*** A serious interaction between phenytoin and alcohol is the development of cross-tolerance to phenytoin in clients with epilepsy who are also heavy drinkers. Chronic alcohol use speeds up the metabolism of the drug apparently by enzyme induction and makes normal doses inadequate.

The following effects may occur when hydantoins are given with the drugs listed below:

| Drug | Possible Effect and Management |
|---|---|
| anticoagulants (coumarin or indandione type) | A decrease in metabolism may cause an increased serum level and/or toxicity of hydantions. Anticoagulant effect may be initially increased but will decrease with continuous combined usage. Monitor closely. |
| adrenocorticoids, corticosteroids, estrogens, or oral contraceptives | An increase in metabolism may decrease the therapeutic effects of these medications— monitor closely because a dosage adjustment may be necessary. |

| Drug | Possible Effect and Management |
|---|---|
| carbamazepine | A decrease in therapeutic effect may occur with one or both drugs. Serum drug levels should be closely monitored. |
| chloramphenicol, cimetidine, disulfiram, isoniazid, oxyphenbutazone, or sulfonamides | A decrease in metabolism may cause an increased serum level and/or toxicity of hydantoins. |
| CNS depressants | May result in enhanced CNS depression. Monitor closely for respiratory depression and drowsiness. |
| calcium | Calcium supplements or calcium sulfate may decrease phenytoin absorption by approximately 20%. Space medications apart by 1 to 3 hours. |
| diazoxide, oral | May decrease phenytoin effects and decrease the hyperglycemic action of diazoxide. This combination should be avoided. |
| folic acid | Hydantoins deplete folate from the body. Folic acid consumption may lower the serum hydantoin levels, leading to a possible loss of seizure control. |
| lidocaine, propranolol, and possible other beta-blocking agents | If given with IV phenytoin, additive cardiac depressant effects may occur. Hydantoins may also increase the metabolism of lidocaine. |
| methadone | Methadone metabolism may be increased by chronic dosing of phenytoin, which may precipitate an acute withdrawal reaction in clients being treated for narcotic dependence. Be aware that methadone dosages may need to be adjusted whenever phenytoin is started or discontinued. |
| trimethadione | Avoid concurrent use with mephenytoin because of the risk for aplastic anemia increases. |
| valproic acid | Monitor serum levels of phenytoin (preferably unbound phenytoin) closely, since variable responses have been reported. Adjustments of dosage may be necessary according to client's clinical response. |
| xanthines | Monitor serum concentrations of both drugs. If phenytoin plasma levels are in the therapeutic range, an increase in metabolism of xanthines (except for dyphylline) will occur. Also, if given with xanthines, a decrease in phenytoin absorption may result; monitor closely. |

***Dosage and administration.*** This information is presented in Table 15-6.

### ▷ Nursing Management: Phenytoin Therapy

***Assessment.*** Phenytoin is contraindicated in hypersensitivity, hepatic dysfunction, and hematologic disorders. There is an elevated incidence of birth defects in children born to mothers using anticonvulsants, although most de-

**TABLE 15-6**  Phenytoin: dosage and administration

| | Adults | Children |
|---|---|---|
| Oral | Anticonvulsant, 100 mg 3 times a day; dosage adjustments made at 7-10 day intervals as necessary. Loading dose method: 12-15 mg/kg body weight divided into 2 or 3 doses over 6 hr, then 1.5-2 mg/kg administered on subsequent days, 3 times daily. | Initially, 5 mg/kg body weight divided into 2 or 3 doses/day (maximum 300 mg/day). Maintenance, 4-8 mg/kg or 250 mg/m² body surface area daily (divided doses, 2 or 3 per day). |
| IV injection | Status epilepticus, 20 mg/kg IV at rate of up to 50 mg/min. Elderly, seriously ill, or debilitated clients or clients with liver dysfunction should receive smaller total dose given at slower IV rate (e.g., 50 mg over 2-3 min). | Status epilepticus, 15-20 mg/kg IV at a rate of 1 mg/kg/min. Do not exceed 50 mg/min. |
| IM injection | Not recommended if oral or IV routes are available; causes tissue irritation and delayed and erratic absorption. Should only be used as last choice for maximum of 1 wk. If IM administration required for client formerly stabilized on oral drug, compensating dosage adjustment needed to maintain therapeutic plasma levels. IM dose is 50% greater than oral dose to maintain these levels. When client returned to oral route, dose reduced by 50% of original oral dose for 7 days to compensate for excessive plasma levels resulting from sustained release from IM site of injection. | |

liver normal infants. Cautious administration is needed in clients with acute intermittent porphyria.

In addition to the nursing diagnoses related to anticonvulsant medications, clients receiving phenytoin should be assessed for altered comfort relating to the gastrointestinal and dermatologic effects of these drugs and a disturbance in self-concept if coarsening of the facial features, gum hyperplasia, or hirsutism occur with long-term therapy.

### Intervention

*Enteral administration.* When using the suspension dosage form, the nurse must shake the container vigorously before measuring out the dose in a graduated or exact measuring device (oral syringe). Clients with enteral tube feedings and pediatric clients have been undermedicated and, later, overmedicated because of improper shaking of the container.

Oral preparations should be given with meals to decrease gastric distress. The appearance of side effects or adverse reactions may require nursing intervention ranging from basic nursing skills to urgent consultation with the physician (see Table 15-3). Note that the 100-mg capsule of phenytoin sodium contains only 92% phenytoin and so is not equivalent to two 50-mg phenytoin chewable tablets that contain 100% phenytoin.

*Nasogastric tube administration.* Studies have reported that administration of phenytoin suspension without dilution or follow-up irrigation of the nasogastric tube after the phenytoin was given led to a significant decrease in plasma phenytoin concentrations (Cacek and others, 1986). When

phenytoin is administered to clients receiving enteral feedings, a significant decrease in absorption of oral phenytoin may occur. Until further research is performed, it is recommended that phenytoin suspension be diluted before administration and that the nasogastric tube be irrigated with 20 ml of fluid (D5W, normal saline). If the client is receiving an enteral feeding, the phenytoin should be administered intravenously; if this is not feasible, the serum concentrations of phenytoin should be monitored frequently (Yuen, 1984). Abrupt withdrawal may precipitate status epilepticus.

*Parenteral administration.* If the state of the client is such that immobilization of an extremity is impossible because of convulsions or inaccessible veins, then the intramuscular route may be useful. If the administration does not terminate the seizure, the nurse must consult with the prescriber to consider other anticonvulsants, intravenous barbiturates, general anesthesia, or other measures. The intramuscular route is not recommended for the treatment of status epilepticus, since the plasma levels of phenytoin in the therapeutic range cannot be readily achieved. Absorption is slow and erratic, and pain and necrosis may occur at the injection site.

The manufacturer supplies a special diluent for parenteral use. Because the preparation dissolves slowly, warming the vial in warm water after the diluent has been added is recommended to hasten dissolution. Only a clear solution is to be administered.

Because intravenous phenytoin is an irritant to the veins (and is incompatible with many solutions and medications), it is recommended that the intravenous line be flushed with normal saline (0.9% sodium chloride injection) before and after administration of this drug.

Some clients complain of burning and pain at the intravenous injection site. Because phenytoin is a highly alkaline solution, burning and pain raise suspicion that there may be a poorly seated needle, extravasation, or a fluid load that is being infused too quickly into a small vein. The nurse should restart the infusion into a large vein, using a larger gauge needle. Subcutaneous injection may cause inflammation and necrosis and should not be done.

The addition of phenytoin solution to an intravenous infusion is not recommended because of the lack of its solubility (the solution is made with propylene glycol 40%, alcohol 10%, water 50%, and pH adjusted with sodium hydroxide to 12) and the resultant precipitation.

The manufacturer does not recommend adding parenteral phenytoin sodium to intravenous solutions or mixing it with any other medications, since precipitation (even microcrystals) may occur. Since a number of physicians prescribe intermittent infusions of phenytoin, the USP-DI (1991) has stated that all the following criteria must be met in such situations:

1. Parenteral phenytoin sodium is mixed with sodium chloride 0.9% injection (normal saline) only and no more than 50 ml. The mixture is made immediately before administration of the infusion. The concentration of phenytoin in solution is between 1 and 10 mg/ml.
2. A 0.22 µ filter must be used in the administration of this solution and the infusion should be finished within 1 hour. The IV tubing should be flushed with 0.9% sodium chloride injection before and after the infusion.
3. The administration rate for the infusion should be a maximum of 50 mg/minute. Reduce to 25 mg/minute in clients that might develop hypotension, have cardiovascular disease, or are receiving sympathomimetic adjuvant medications. ECG monitoring is recommended during the infusion for these patients. Elderly, seriously ill, or debilitated clients or clients with liver function impairment should generally receive a lower dose at a much slower rate of administration.
4. Monitor blood pressure and cardiac function closely.
5. Carefully observe the admixture for crystals, cloudiness, or precipitation.

The nurse can readily determine that the rate and time for dilantinization is a function of the client's clinical situation. The dose-related side effects increase with the rapidity at which the client is dilantinized to the therapeutic range. Proceeding cautiously and slowly is clinically prudent. Nystagamus (bilateral and vertical) develops at levels of 10 to 20 µg/ml; ataxia, drowsiness, and diplopia are seen at levels about 30 µg/ml; and lethargy is seen at 40 µg/ml.

Parenteral phenytoin should be used with caution in clients with hypotension and severe myocardial insufficiency.

The effects of phenytoin on ventricular automaticity (fibrillation) prohibit its use in sinus bradycardia, sinoatrial block and second- and third-degree atrioventricular block and in clients with Adams-Stokes syndrome.

**Education.** One of the side effects of hydantoins is gum hyperplasia; it is therefore important that oral hygiene be emphasized. Clients should be encouraged to brush frequently, floss, and massage their gums. As the tissue overgrowth is usually greater and more apparent anteriorly than posteriorly, the client, particularly the adolescent, may have body image concerns. A program of professional dental prophylaxis and an aggressive program of plaque control by the client will minimize hyperplasia. Clients should be instructed to inform their dentists that they are taking hydantoins, so the dentist can observe and monitor for periodental problems.

Clients who have diabetes should be instructed to report any changes in blood or urine sugar concentrations. Hydantoins may affect blood sugar levels.

The client should be advised of possible skin changes. An erythematous-type rash with or without fever should be reported immediately to the physician. Hirsutism or excessive body and facial hair growth is reported in some clients. This side effect is particularly troublesome in young women. This alteration in body image will require supportive nursing care.

The client should be cautioned against exchanging brands since the bioavailability of phenytoin may vary. Generic phenytoin and Dilantin from Parke-Davis are not the same. Dilantin capsules are the only form of extended phenytoin sodium available; all the rest are prompt acting and are not intended for once-a-day dosage. The generic phenytoin capsules are a prompt-acting form of the drug. The chewable tablets are from Parke-Davis and are a prompt-acting form. The extended form can be used for once-a-day dosing and for those clients who are stabilized on a 300-mg divided dosage. It is important that the client and family have this information explained clearly.

When discussing the appropriate means of administration of the suspension dosage form, the nurse should stress that very vigorous shaking of the container is mandatory before measuring out the dose in a graduated or exact measuring device (oral syringe). Clients should be cautioned against unsupervised self-administration of other drugs while taking any of the hydantoins, since they interact with a variety of drugs.

Any patient with epilepsy should carry an identification card that indicates the medication he or she is taking.

**Evaluation.** When clients are taking phenytoin, serum levels should be monitored. It takes approximately 7 to 10 days before recommended serum levels are achieved. It is particularly important that serum levels be monitored closely in clients with renal and hepatic impairment. The client with impaired liver function, the elderly, or those who are very ill may demonstrate early toxic signs. A small percentage of persons metabolize the drug slowly because of limited enzyme availability that may be genetically determined. The metabolism of phenytoin is dose dependent at therapeutic doses.

The nurse should monitor closely for documented drug interactions that may alter the client's response to medications. Because some drugs can impair or enhance the effects of phenytoin, monitoring of drug serum levels will be important for accurate dosage administration and as a mechanism of determining compliance.

### mephenytoin (Mesantoin)

Mephenytoin is chemically similar in structure, activity, and pharmacokinetics to phenytoin, but it is less potent as an anticonvulsant. It produces more sedation than phenytoin, but this side effect is dose related. It also has a greater potential for producing blood dyscrasias and dermatologic effects than the other hydantoins. This product is usually reserved for clients whose seizures are not controlled with safer anticonvulsants.

The usual adult dose is 50 to 100 mg orally daily, increased weekly as necessary; for children, 25 to 50 mg daily.

### ethotoin (Peganone)

Ethotoin is similar to phenytoin but less effective and offers little advantage over phenytoin. Side effects of ataxia, hirsutism, and gum hyperplasia are rare, and ethotoin may be substituted for phenytoin to reduce these side effects. Ethotoin is available only for oral administration with dosage individualized according to response. Maintenance dosage (usually divided into four to six doses) of less than 2 g is usually not effective.

## SUCCINIMIDES

The succinimides include ethosuximide (Zarontin), methsuximide (Celontin), and phensuximide (Milontin).

These agents produce a variety of effects, such as increasing the seizure threshold and reducing the spike and wave pattern of absence seizures by decreasing nerve impulses and transmission in the motor cortex.

Ethosuximide and phensuximide are indicated for the treatment of absence seizures, whereas methsuximide is reserved for absence seizures that are nonresponsive to other medications.

Pharmacokinetics are discussed in Table 15-1; side effects/adverse reactions are presented in Table 15-3.

***Significant drug interactions.*** The following effects may occur when succinimides are given in combination with the drugs listed below:

| Drug | Possible Effect and Management |
|---|---|
| carbamazepine, phenobarbital, or phenytoin | Results in increased metabolism of succinimide anticonvulsants and decreased serum levels. Monitor serum levels especially when either drug is added, increased, decreased, or deleted from the drug regimen. |
| haloperidol | May change the pattern or frequency of seizures. Dosage adjustment of the anticonvulsant may be required. Also serum levels of haloperidol may be reduced, which may result in decreased effectiveness. |
| phenothiazines, thioxanthenes, antidepressants, loxapine, maprotiline, or CNS depressants | May result in a decrease in the effectiveness of the anticonvulsant, enhance CNS depression, and also may lower the seizure threshold. Monitor closely for respiratory depression and drowsiness because dosage modifications may be necessary. |

***Dosage and administration.*** See Table 15-7.

**TABLE 15-7**   Succinimide dosage and administration

| Drug | Adults | Children |
|---|---|---|
| ethosuximide (Zarontin) | Orally, initially 250 mg twice a day, increased as necessary at 4-7 day intervals; maximum total daily dose is 1.5 g. | Orally, for children 6 yr old and older, follow adult schedule. For children up to 6 yr, initial dose is 250 mg/day, increased by 250 mg at 4-7 day intervals. Maximum total daily dose is 1 g. |
| methsuximide (Celontin) | Orally, initial dose is 300 mg daily, increased as necessary by 300 mg increments at 1-wk intervals until seizures controlled or maximum daily dose of 1.2 g reached. | Dosage is individualized. 150 mg capsules available for pediatric dosage adjustments. |
| phensuximide (Milontin) | Orally, initial dose is 500 mg twice a day, increase by 500 mg increments at 1-wk intervals until seizures controlled or maximum daily dose of 3 g reached. | Pediatric dose similar to adult schedule. |

**TABLE 15-8**   Paramethadione and trimethadione: dosage and administration

| Drug | Adults | Children |
|---|---|---|
| paramethadione | Oral, 300 mg 3 or 4 times daily, increased at 1-wk intervals (300 mg/day increment) until seizures are controlled, toxic symptoms appear, or maximum limit of 2.4 g/day is reached. | Oral solution available; children up to 2 yr, 100 mg 3 times a day; children 2-6 yr, 200 mg 3 times a day; children more than 6 yr, 300 mg 3 times a day. |
| trimethadione | Oral, 300 mg 3 or 4 times daily, increase 300 mg/day at weekly intervals until seizures are controlled, toxic symptoms appear, or maximum limit of 2.4 g/day is reached. | Oral solution, 13 mg/kg body weight or 335 mg/m² body surface 3 times a day. |

## ▷NURSING MANAGEMENT: SUCCINIMIDE THERAPY

To decrease stomach distress, the succinimides may be taken with milk, food or antacids.

Liver, renal, and hematologic studies should be evaluated periodically because of the drug's possible effects on these systems. Report any signs of liver, kidney, or hematologic disorders to the physician.

Although their incidence is rare with the succinimides, the blood dyscrasia effects may result in gingival bleeding, delayed healing, and an increase in the number of infections for the client when they do occur. Dental work should be deferred until blood counts are within the normal range. Clients may have to modify their dental hygiene with cautious use of toothbrushes and dental floss. The client should alert other health care providers about his or her succinimide regimen if surgery, dental work, or emergency medical care is required.

The nurse should caution the client about drowsiness and other possible CNS disturbances. The other side effects and adverse reactions of the succinimides are listed in Table 15-4.

When dosage adjustments are made or medications added, serum drug levels may be ordered. The nurse should explain the importance of serum blood levels to the client who needs to have serum levels drawn frequently. The client should be cautioned that withdrawal of the succinimides may precipitate absence seizures. Adverse personality changes can occur while the client is taking this medication; the nurse should stress the importance of reporting any behavioral changes to the physician.

If the client is taking phensuximide, the nurse should caution him or her that the drug may change the color of the urine to pink, red, or red-brown; this is harmless.

## OXAZOLIDINEDIONES

The oxazolidinediones include paramethodione (Paradione) and trimethadione (Tridione). They appear to elevate the threshold for cortical seizures, decrease extension of focal discharges, and decrease the spike and wave patterns seen with absence seizures during an electroencephalogram. They are indicated for treatment of absence seizures that are nonresponsive to other medications. Oxazolidinediones are rapidly absorbed orally and are metabolized to active metabolites in the liver. Half-lives are as follows: paramethadione, 12-24 hours; trimethadione, 12-24 hours; active metabolite has 6- to 13-day half-life. These drugs are excreted by the kidneys. For side effects/adverse reactions, see Table 15-3. The FDA pregnancy safety category is D.

***Significant drug interactions.*** The following effects may occur when oxazolidinediones are given in combination with the drugs listed below:

| Drug | Possible Effect and Management |
|---|---|
| haloperidol, phenothiazines, antidepressants, thioxanthenes, loxapine, maprotiline, or CNS depressants | May result in a decrease in the effectiveness of the anticonvulsant and enhance CNS depression. Seizure threshold may also be lowered. Monitor closely for respiratory depression and drowsiness since dosage modifications may be necessary. |

***Dosage and administration.***   See Table 15-8.

## ▷NURSING MANAGEMENT: OXAZOLIDINEDIONE THERAPY

***Intervention.***   Paramethadione should be administered with food or milk to decrease gastric irritation. The tablets (trimethadione chewable tablets) may be crushed with a small amount of water for ease of administration, if necessary. Paramethadione capsules should not be chewed or crushed since they contain an oily liquid. A solution is available for clients unable to swallow tablets. Paramethadione oral solution has a high alcohol content (65%); therefore it is recommended the dose be diluted in 4 oz of water or juice before administration, especially to little children.

The drugs are not recommended for clients with hepatic or renal disease, disease of the optic nerve, or blood dyscrasias.

Careful medical supervision of the client receiving the medication is essential. It is advisable for the client to have periodic examinations of the blood to detect early signs of toxic effects, since rare instances of aplastic anemia have

**TABLE 15-9**   Benzodiazepine anticonvulsants: dosage and administration

| Drug | Adults | Children |
|---|---|---|
| clonazepam (Klonopin) | Orally, initially 0.5 mg three times daily with increases of 0.5-1 mg every third day until seizures are controlled, side effects occur, or the maximum of 20 mg/day is reached. | Orally (less than 10 years old or 30 kg body weight), initial 0.01-0.03/kg body weight in divided doses (three times a day); if necessary, increase by 0.25-0.5 mg every 3 days until seizures are controlled, side effects occur, or the maximum maintenance dose of 0.1-0.2 mg/kg body weight is reached. |
| diazepam (Valium) | 5-10 mg IM or IV (preferred method) initially; repeat at 10-15 min intervals if necessary to a maximum of 30 mg; inject slowly—at least 1 minute for each 5-mg dose administered intravenously.<br><br>Orally, 2-10 mg three to four times daily. | 1 mo to 5 yr of age, 0.2-0.5 mg IM or IV (preferred method) every 2-5 min to a maximum of 5 mg; this regimen may be repeated if necessary, in 2-4 hr.<br><br>5 yr or older, 1 mg every 2-5 min IM or IV (preferred method) to a maximum of 10 mg; this regimen may be repeated if necessary, in 2-4 hr. |
| clorazepate (Tranxene) | Orally, initially up to 7.5 mg three times daily; increase if necessary by 7.5 mg/wk to a maximum of 90 mg/day. | 9-12 yr old, orally, up to 7.5 mg twice daily; increase if necessary by 7.5 mg/wk to a maximum of 60 mg daily. |

been reported. Serum blood levels will be drawn frequently to control the level of the drug in relation to the seizure status of the client.

***Education.*** It may take from 1 to 4 weeks before the drug reaches its therapeutic levels, so clients may continue to have seizures. It is important that the client record the time, type, and length of seizure and report this to the physician.

One of the adverse reactions of the drugs is ophthalmic damage. The nurse should caution the client to report any visual disturbances, particularly day blindness. If vision blurs in the sunlight, the client should be advised to wear sunglasses and report the problem to the physician.

Since renal damage is a possibility, the client should be instructed to report edema, urinary frequency, burning on urination, and cloudy urine. Periodic urinalysis should be done.

These drugs tend to have more toxic effects than other drugs used to treat seizure activity. The client should be instructed to be observant for the toxic effects and report them to the physician.

## BENZODIAZEPINES

The benzodiazepines include clonazepam (Klonopin), diazepam (Valium), clorazepate (Tranxene), and lorazepam (Ativan). These drugs appear to suppress the propagation of seizure activity produced by foci in the cortex, thalamus, and limbic areas.

Clonazepam may be useful in tonic-clonic, simple partial, complex partial, absence, and various generalized seizures. It has been used alone, but more often it is prescribed as

an adjunct to other anticonvulsants to establish seizure control. Diazepam is used parenterally in status epilepticus or in severe recurrent convulsive seizures, but the oral dosage form is not an effective preventive for maintenance control. The oral diazepam dosage form has been used as an adjunctive medication for short-term treatment in convulsive disorders (such as 1 to 2 weeks of therapy.) Clorazepate has been prescribed as an adjunct medication for the treatment of simple partial seizures. Lorazepam parenteral is used for the treatment of status epilepticus.

See Table 15-2 and Chapter 14 for the pharmacokinetics of these drugs. See Table 15-3, as well as Chapter 14, for side effects/adverse reactions.

***Significant drug interactions.*** The following effects may occur when benzodiazepines are given in combination with the drugs listed below:

| Drug | Possible Effect and Management |
|---|---|
| CNS depressants, such as narcotic analgesics, alcohol, antidepressants, general anesthetics, hypnotics, sedatives | May result in additive or synergistic CNS-depressant effects. Generally, the dosage of one or both drugs should be reduced. Monitor closely. |
| zidovudine | May result in a decrease in the metabolism and excretion of zidovudine. Avoid concurrent administration. |

***Dosage and administration.*** See Table 15-9 for complete information. Dosages are usually individualized for each patient and are increased with caution to avoid adverse effects. Some patients may require higher doses than indicated. In elderly or debilitated persons and those taking other CNS-depressant–type medications, a lower dose with a slow increase is prudent.

▷NURSING MANAGEMENT:
BENZODIAZEPINE THERAPY

**Assessment.** Clients undergoing long-term benzodiazepine therapy can become physically dependent on the drug and show signs and symptoms of withdrawal when the drug is discontinued.

Baseline vital signs should be taken before parenteral forms of diazepam or lorazepam are given, and then the client should be observed at bed rest for at least 3 hours for diazepam and 8 hours for lorazepam for decreases in respiratory rate, heart rate, and blood pressure.

**Intervention.** Diazepam is insoluble in water; therefore each milliliter of the parenteral form contains 40% propylene glycol, 10% ethyl alcohol, 5% sodium benzoate and benzoic acid as buffers, and 1.5% benzyl alcohol as a preservative. If this ratio is altered, the diazepam is insoluble. If direct intravenous injection is not possible, diazepam may be injected through the infusion tubing as close to the insertion point as possible. Inject slowly, as least 1 minute for each 5 mg.

Lorazepam must be diluted with a compatible diluent immediately before intravenous use. It may be infused directly into a vein or through intravenous tubing. Infusion rates should not exceed 2 mg/minute.

Because of the short-lived effect of intravenous benzodiazepine administration, seizures, although brought under prompt control, may recur. The nurse should be ready to readminister the drug. Benzodiazepines are not for maintenance; once seizure control is achieved, agents useful in long-term seizure control should be considered. Tonic status epilepticus has been precipitated in some clients treated with intravenous diazepam for petit mal status or petit mal variant status. The nurse must exercise extreme care (monitor respirations every 5 to 15 minutes and before each intravenous dose) in administering benzodiazepines (especially by the intravenous route) to elderly or very ill clients or those with compromised pulmonary reserve because of the possibility of apnea and/or cardiac arrest.

Resuscitative equipment should be available because of the possible occurrence of hypotension, tachycardia, and respiratory depression.

In the neonate (age 30 days or less) the efficacy and safety of parenteral diazepam are not established. Prolonged CNS depression has been reported in the neonate, probably resulting from the inability to biotransform diazepam into the inactive metabolites. The benzoate in the injectable form has been reported to displace other drugs and bilirubin from the plasma protein binding sites, causing jaundice.

The combination of diazepam and cimetidine may cause drug accumulation and drug toxicity, since both of these drugs are metabolized by hepatic microsomal oxidases. It is therefore necessary to observe for adverse reactions elicited by either drug or a combination of the drugs. Adverse reactions from the combination may necessitate a reduction in dosage of either drug or both drugs.

To minimize the occurrence of thrombophlebitis following intravenous injection of diazepam, the vein can be flushed with 1 ml of saline per milligram of diazepam.

If benzodiazepines are intended to be given along with a narcotic, the dose of the narcotic should be reduced.

Diazepam is a drug that may be subject to abuse by medical and nursing professionals and clients. This is a controlled drug; therefore the nurse is responsible for proper documentation of the drug's distribution and use.

**Education.** When benzodiazepines are given for treating convulsive disorders, an abrupt withdrawal of the medication can cause an increase in frequency or severity of seizures. Clients should be instructed to take their medication as directed.

Diazepam does cross the placental barrier and has been associated with causing cleft lip in the infant. Risk/benefit ratio should be carefully considered in the client during pregnancy.

It is not advisable that alcohol or other CNS depressants be combined with benzodiazepines. Severe drowsiness, respiratory depression, and apnea may occur.

## Other Anticonvulsants

### valproic acid (Depakene) and divalproex sodium (Depakote)

The mechanism by which valproic acid exerts its anticonvulsant effects has not been fully established. It has been proposed that its activity is related to increased brain levels of the inhibitory neurotransmitter GABA. By competitive inhibition it prevents the reuptake of GABA by glial cells and axonal terminals. The drug has a marked effect on the generalized spike wave discharges (3/second) in the EEG.

Valproic acid and divalproex sodium are indicated for use as sole and adjunctive therapy in the treatment of simple and complex absence seizures, including petit mal, and as adjunctive therapy in clients with multiple seizure types including absence seizures.

See Table 15-1 for pharmacokinetic overview. Chemically, valproate sodium is converted in the stomach to valproic acid, which is rapidly absorbed from the gastrointestinal tract. Divalproex sodium is a prodrug, a combination of valproic acid and valproate sodium, in an enteric coated tablet. Divalproex dissociates into valproate, which is then absorbed in the small intestine. See Table 15-3 for side effects/adverse reactions.

**Significant drug interactions.** The following effects may occur when valproic acid and divalproex sodium (a drug that contains 50% valproic acid and sodium valproate) are given with the drugs listed below:

| Drug | Possible Effect and Management |
|---|---|
| alcohol, anesthetics (general), CNS-depressant–type drugs | May result in potentiated CNS-depressant effects. |

| Drug | Possible Effect and Management |
|------|-------------------------------|
| anticoagulants, coumarin, indandione types, heparin, or thrombolytic agents | Increased risk of bleeding and hemorrhage; monitor closely for early signs if given in combination. |
| aspirin, dipyridamole, or sulfinpyrazone | Increased risk of bleeding and hemorrhage; monitor closely and the physician might consider alternative therapeutic agents. |
| barbiturates or primidone | Phenobarbital and primidone serum levels may increase, resulting in increased depression and toxicity. Monitor since dosage adjustment by the physician may be necessary. |
| carbamazepine and phenytoin | Breakthrough seizures may occur because of decreased serum levels of carbamazepine or valproic acid. Phenytoin protein binding may be affected when combined with valproic acid. Therefore monitor closely using serum levels as a guide for physician dosing adjustments. |

***Dosage and administration.*** Adults and children, range of 15 to 60 mg/kg/day, starting at the lowest dose and increasing by 5 to 10 mg/kg at weekly intervals as needed. The dose may be given with or immediately after meals to decrease gastrointestinal upset. The dose should be the lowest consistent with seizure control.

▷ **Nursing Management: Valproic Acid Therapy**

***Intervention.*** The drug should be administered with or after meals to avoid gastric irritation. The client should avoid chewing or crushing the tablets and capsules; the nurse should avoid giving the tablet form with milk because of possible early dissolution and local irritation to the mouth and throat. Syrup is available for clients unable to swallow tablets or capsules. Divalproex sodium is prescribed for clients unable to tolerate the gastrointestinal irritation produced by valproic acid.

When other anticonvulsant drugs are used in combination, the dosage of valproic acid and/or the other anticonvulsants may need to be adjusted to maintain serum levels and seizure control.

***Education.*** The client should be instructed not to chew the tablet/or capsule, since it will irritate the mouth and throat. Combining this drug with alcohol or other CNS depressants can cause a potentiation of sedation. This drug can cause a false-positive urine ketone test in clients with diabetes mellitus; these clients should be instructed to consult their physicians about using some other form of diagnostic tool for ketones. The client should be instructed to be aware of signs of decreasing mental alertness, which can occur when valproic acid is given alone or in combination with other anticonvulsants.

The drug is excreted in breast milk and can cause CNS depression in the nursing infant. Birth defects (spina bifida) have occurred when this drug was taken during the first trimester of pregnancy. Clients taking this drug who are considering pregnancy may need to be given another anticonvulsant that has no documented risk of causing birth defects.

The client should be told to report to the physician if any of the following side effects occur: visual disturbances, rash, diarrhea, light-colored stools, jaundice, and protracted vomiting.

***Evaluation.*** Valproic acid has been shown to cause liver dysfunction; therefore the client should be instructed to report signs of liver dysfunction, such as spontaneous bleeding and/or bruising, immediately to the physician. The client should have liver function studies done at least every month during the first 6 months of therapy when heptotoxicity is most likely to occur.

## carbamazepine (Tegretol)

The exact mechanism of action is unknown, although this drug's effects are somewhat similar to those of phenytoin. Carbamazepine is indicated in the treatment of epilepsy for clients who are refractory or have not responded to phenytoin, phenobarbital, or primidone, for partial seizures with complex symptomatology, for generalized tonic-clonic seizures, for psychomotor seizures, and for mixed seizure patterns. This drug is also indicated in the treatment of pain associated with true trigeminal neuralgia.

See Table 15-1 for a pharmacokinetic overview. Autoinduction of metabolism occurs, and half-life decreases with repeated doses. Side effects/adverse reactions are listed in Table 15-3.

***Significant drug interactions.*** The following effects may occur when carbamazepine is given with the following drugs:

| Drug | Possible Effect and Management |
|------|-------------------------------|
| adrenocorticoids, glucocorticoids, or mineralocorticoids | Concurrent administration may decrease steroidal effect because of increase in hepatic metabolism. Monitor closely for lack of response to corticosteroid therapy as dosage adjustment may be necessary. |
| anticoagulants, oral (coumarin or indandiones) | Monitor for a decreased anticoagulant effect. Increased hepatic microsomal enzyme activity increases anticoagulant metabolism, resulting in a decreased half-life and effect. Dosage adjustments of anticoagulant may be necessary during and after treatment with carbamazepine. |
| anticonvulsants (hydantoin or succinimide): barbiturates; benzodiazepines metabolized by hepatic enzymes especially clonazepam, primidone, or valproic acid | Concurrent drug administration may result in increased drug metabolism and decreased serum levels and therapeutic effectiveness. Whenever any of these medications are added to or discontinued with carbamazepine, monitor blood levels and client closely for seizure activity; dosage adjustment may be necessary. |
| cimetidine, diltiazem, or varapamil | May increase plasma levels of carbamazepine, which can result in toxicity. Monitor closely. |

| Drug | Possible Effect and Management |
|------|-------------------------------|
| estrogen-containing contraceptives | Decrease in contraceptive reliability; clients should be advised to use a nonhormonal birth control method or to discuss the possibility of an oral progestin product with their physician. |
| loxapine, maprotiline, thioxanthenes, or tricyclic antidepressants | May reduce the convulsive threshold and/or enhance CNS depressant effects; dosage adjustment may be necessary to control seizures and reduce side effects. Monitor closely for seizure activity. |
| monoamine ozidase (MAO) inhibitors | Hypertensive crisis, elevated temperatures, severe convulsions, and even death have been reported with this combination. When switching from one therapy to another (MAO to carbamazepine or vice versa), at least a 14-day, drug-free interval is recommended. |
| quinidine | Due to increased metabolism, concurrent use may decrease quinidine's therapeutic effects. Monitor closely for cardiac arrhythmias; dosage adjustment may be necessary. |
| propoxyphene | May result in increased carbamazepine serum levels and toxicity. If an analgesic is necessary, it is recommended that another analgesic be selected. |

### Dosage and administration

*Adults.* In adults, carbamazepine should be given initially at 200 mg twice daily, increased by 200 mg/day weekly in divided doses until response is noted; maximum dose is 1200 mg/day, with a maintenance range of 800-1200 mg/day in divided doses.

*Children.* For children up to 6 years, initially give 10 to 20 mg/kg/day in divided doses; increase weekly if necessary to 100 mg/day. Maintenance usually requires between 250 and 300 mg/kg daily to maintain therapeutic serum level. The dose for children 6 to 12 years is initially 100 mg twice a day; increase by 100 mg/day weekly until desired response is obtained. Maintenance is weekly until desired response is obtained. Maintenance is usually between 400 and 800 mg/day in divided dosages.

## ▷ Nursing Management: Carbamazepine Therapy

Carbamazepine should be administered with meals to reduce gastrointestinal irritation. The importance of compliance with drug therapy should be stressed with all clients taking this drug.

Clients should report to the physician if they have any signs of hematologic dysfunction such as easy bruising, bleeding, sore throat or mouth, or malaise. It is not uncommon for the client to be drowsy during the initial therapy; clients should be cautioned about this so that they can avoid driving a car or operating hazardous equipment.

This drug is used specifically for the pain of trigeminal neuralgia. It should not be used as a routine analgesic.

Carbamazepine can cause breakthrough bleeding in women taking oral contraceptives. Women should be told that it may interfere with the effectivenss of the contraceptive, so other forms of birth control measures may need to be used.

Carbamazepine is excreted in breast milk, so it may not be recommended in nursing mothers. Abrupt withdrawal of the drug (in clients with epilepsy) can precipitate a seizure.

In middle-aged or elderly clients, carbamazepine may decrease salivary flow and contribute to the development of caries, periodontal disease, or discomfort. Ice chips, chewing gum, and sugarless candies may ease discomfort from the dry mouth.

Blood studies (CBC, liver function studies, BUN), urinalysis, physical examination, ophthalmic examinations, and ECG should be done before beginning carbamazepine therapy. Then the blood studies should be done every 2 weeks during the second and third months and then every month while the patient is taking this medication.

### primidone (Mysoline)

Primidone and its metabolites, phenobarbital and phenylethylmalonamide (PEMA), contribute to anticonvulsant activity. The mechanism of action is unknown, but primidone and its metabolites all appear to have active anticonvulsant effects. Primidone is used for control of generalized and complex seizures. For a pharmacokinetics overview, see Table 15-1; for side effects/adverse reactions, see Table 15-3.

*Significant drug interactions.* The following effects may occur when primidone is given with the drugs listed below:

| Drug | Possible Effect and Management |
|------|-------------------------------|
| adrenocorticoids, glucocorticoid, or corticotropin (ACTH) | Decreased therapeutic effects of these medications when used concurrently with primidone; monitor closely since physician may need to increase dosage during and after primidone. |
| CNS depressants | Enhanced CNS and respiratory depression reported. Monitor since physician may need to adjust dosages. |
| tricyclic antidepressants | May see enhanced CNS depression, decrease in convulsive threshold, and decrease in primidone effects. Physician may need to increase primidone to control seizures. |
| monoamine oxidase (MAO) inhibitors | May prolong the effects of primidone; dosage adjustments may be necessary. Monitor closely. |

### Dosage and administration

*Adults.* Administer oral primidone initially, 100-125 mg at bedtime for 3 days, increase by 100 or 125 mg twice a day for the fourth through the sixth day, then increase by 100-125 mg 3 times a day until the ninth day. On day 10 dosage of 250 mg three times a day is established and may be altered according to needs of client up to 2 g/day.

*Children.* For children up to 8 years initially give 50 mg

orally at bedtime for 3 days, increase to 50 mg twice a day through day 6, then increase to 100 mg twice daily through day 9. On day 10 maintenance dose of 125 or 250 mg 3 times a day may be given and adjusted according to client response.

▷ **Nursing Management:**
**Primidone Therapy**

See barbiturate discussion in this chapter. Clients with reported reactions to barbiturates may be intolerant of primidone. The nurse should shake oral suspension well for consistent dosing.

### acetazolamide (Diamox)

Acetazolamide is a carbonic anhydrase inhibitor usually prescribed for the treatment of open-angle glaucoma. It is used in combination with other anticonvulsant agents for the treatment of absence seizures, generalized tonic-clonic seizures, mixed seizures, and myoclonic seizure patterns. Acetazolamide's mechanism of action is unknown. It has been theorized that inhibiting carbonic anhydrase in the CNS may result in an increase in carbon dioxide that retards neuronal activity. Systemic metabolic acidosis may also play a part in its action.

See Chapter 43 for pharmacokinetics and side effects/adverse reactions.

***Significant drug interactions.*** The following effects may occur when acetazolamide is used with the drugs listed below:

| Drug | Possible Effect and Management |
|---|---|
| amphetamines, mecamylamine, or quinidine | Alkalinization of the urine may increase or prolong the effects and side effects of these drugs. Dosage alterations may be required, especially when a drug is added, increased, decreased, or deleted. Monitor closely. Mecamylamine should not be used in clients receiving acetazolamide because of the altered excretion. |
| methenamine | Effectiveness may be reduced because of the alkaline urine produced by acetazolamide. Do not use concurrently. |

***Dosage and administration.*** Adult, anticonvulsant, oral 8 to 30 mg (initial dose is usually 10 mg)/kg/day in four divided doses (usually 375 to 1000 mg/day). Pediatric dosage, see adult recommendations.

▷ **Nursing Management:**
**Acetazolamide Therapy**

The nurse should administer acetazolamide with food to decrease gastric irritation. Since bioequivalence problems have been reported, it is recommended that different generic brands not be used interchangeably for this product. Main-

tenance of an increased fluid intake is recommended, especially in clients with a history of gout or hypercalciuria. The nurse should closely monitor serum electrolytes and inform the physician if fever, sore throat, bleeding, hives, skin rash, difficult breathing, confusion, depression, or difficulty or pain on urination occurs.

The nurse should caution the client that drowsiness and dizziness may occur; therefore the client should avoid driving a car or operating potentially hazardous machinery until the response to this drug has been determined. Clients with diabetes mellitus should be informed that an increase in blood or urine glucose is usually reported with this medication. The nurse should advise the client on the signs of hypokalemia (dry mouth, muscle cramps, nausea, vomiting, tiredness, mood changes); if they occur, the client must be urged to report them to the physician. Discontinuance of acetazolamide should be under the physician's guidance.

### magnesium sulfate

Magnesium sulfate has a depressant effect on the CNS, which reduces striated muscle contractions. In addition, magnesium sulfate blocks peripheral neuromuscular transmission by reducing acetylcholine release at the myoneural junction, reducing the sensitivity of the motor endplate and lowering the excitability of the motor membrane.

The drug has three major indications. As an anticonvulsant, it is used in the prevention and control of seizures related to acute nephritis in children and seizures related to toxemias of pregnancy (see box). As a uterine relaxant, it

---

#### TOXEMIA OF PREGNANCY (PREECLAMPSIA AND ECLAMPSIA)

**Toxemia of pregnancy** is a syndrome of elevated blood pressure, edema, and proteinurea, which occurs in about 5% of all pregnancies in North America. The syndrome is described in clinical terms because its cause is unknown. Preeclampsia is another term for the syndrome. Depending on the severity of symptoms, preeclampsia may be classified as mild, which may be treated at home, or severe, which requires hospitalization for monitoring and treatment. If the disease progresses, convulsions will occur and the syndrome is classified as eclampsia, which is derived from a Greek word used to describe convulsions. Sensory changes that occur in severe preeclampsia and eclampsia include headache, epigastric pain, blurred vision, and hyperreflexia. Therapeutic goals for the treatment of toxemia of pregnancy are control of blood pressure, prevention of convulsions, maintenance of renal function and provision of optimal conditions for the fetus. Treatment is symptomatic since the only "cure" for toxemia is delivery of the baby. Convulsions may still occur up to 48 hours after delivery, necessitating continued therapy in the immediate postpartum period.

**TABLE 15-10**   Magnesium sulfate dosage and administration for seizure control

| Adults | Elderly | Children |
|---|---|---|
| IM: 1 to 5 g (8-40 mEq) as a 25%-50% solution up to 6 times/day in alternate buttocks | Often lower dosage is required because of reduced renal function | IM, 20 to 40 mg (0.16-0.32 mEq) kg of body weight as a 20% solution |
| IV: 1-4 g (8-32 mEq) as a 10%-20% solution, rate not to exceed 1.5 ml of 10% solution/min | | |
| IV infusion: 4 g (32 mEq) in 250 ml of D₅W or 0.9% NaCl. Administration rate not to exceed 4 ml/min | | |

is used in the treatment of uterine tetany and to inhibit contractions of premature labor. Finally, it is used as replacement therapy for magnesium deficiency.

About one third of dietary ingested magnesium is absorbed from the GI tract. With intravenous administration, onset of action is immediate with approximately 30 minutes duration of action; with intramuscular, onset is about 1 hour with a 3- to 4-hour duration of action. Magnesium undergoes no metabolism and is excreted by the kidneys.

Signs of hypermagnesemia, which may begin at a serum concentration at or above 4 mEq/L, include flushing, hypotension, sweating, depressed reflexes, reduced respiratory rate, hypothermia, flaccid paralysis, circulatory collapse, slowed heart rate, and CNS depression.

### Significant drug interactions

CNS depressants: When barbiturates, opiates, general anesthetics or other CNS depressants are used, dosage of these agents should be adjusted to avoid additive CNS depressant effects.

Neuromuscular blocking agents: Excessive neuromuscular blockade has occurred when these drugs are administered with magnesium sulfate.

Cardiac glycosides: Serious changes in cardiac function, including heart block, may occur if calcium is administered to counteract magnesium overdose.

### Dosage and administration.   See Table 15-10.

### Pregnancy safety.   Magnesium sulfate is administered in the treatment of toxemias of pregnancy. The drug crosses the placenta, with fetal blood levels approximately equal to maternal blood levels, and produces similar effects in the neonate as in the mother. Decreased reflexes, muscle tone, blood pressure, and respiratory depression may be seen if the mother received magnesium shortly before delivery. It is recommended that magnesium sulfate *not* be administered during the 2 hours before delivery, if possible.

▷ **Nursing Management:**
**Magnesium Sulfate Therapy**

Magnesium sulfate should not be used in the presence of heart block, significant heart damage, or renal failure. Caution must be exercised in the presence of renal function impairment or respiratory disease.

---

**PREGNANCY SAFETY**

FDA category C: carbamazepine
FDA category D: barbiturates, paramethadione, valproic acid, divalproex
FDA category unclassified: hydantoin, succinimides, trimethadione, primidone, acetazolamide, diazepam, clonazepam, clorazepate

---

Extreme care must be taken to avoid overdosage and toxic serum concentrations. Intravenous infusions should be administered with a regulating or controlling device.

The client must be closely monitored for the possible development of magnesium toxicity. ECG should be monitored continuously during intravenous administration. Serum magnesium determinations may be obtained as clinically indicated. Approximate serum concentrations (mEq/L) indicative of hypermagnesemia are as follows:

4-6: therapeutic range, mild depression of deep tendon reflexes

5-10: depression of deep tendon reflexes; prolonged PQ interval or widened QRS interval on ECG

10: loss of deep tendon reflexes

12-15: respiratory paralysis; complete heart block

25: cardiac arrest

The patellar reflex or knee jerk is an indication of CNS depression from magnesium. The patellar reflex should be checked before beginning therapy and before each dose. The disappearance of the reflex indicates excessive serum levels of magnesium. The respiratory rate should be at least 16/minute before administration of a parenteral dose.

Treatment of overdose includes the following:

Discontinue drug administration

Artificial respiration if necessary

Intravenous administration of 5-10 mEq of calcium (10-20 ml of 10% calcium gluconate) to reverse respiratory depression or heart block

Peritoneal or hemodialysis may be required if renal function is reduced

An intravenous calcium salt (calcium gluconate, calcium gluceptate, or calcium chloride) should be available when parenteral magnesium is administered.

### phenacemide (Phenurone)

Phenacemide is used for clients with severe epilepsy, especially partial seizures with complex symptoms that are refractory to other medications. This drug is extremely toxic and should be reserved for use *after* all available anticonvulsants have been proven ineffective. It may cause liver, blood, and psychologic problems, such as personality changes, bone marrow depression, and hepatitis. Deaths have been reported with its use so some physicians believe it is too toxic for routine use.

## SUMMARY

Epilepsy, a symptom of a disorder of the brain rather than a disease itself, occurs in only a small percentage of the population. Epileptic seizures have varied etiologies and so are classified by sympatology. The nurse needs to be particularly observant in the assessment and documentation of seizures. As with the etiologies, the drugs used for the treatment of seizures are varied: barbiturates, hydantoins, succinimides, oxazolidinediones, benzodiazepines, and others. Each client's therapy is individualized taking into account a complex of interrelated factors, such as the pharmacokinetics of the drug in an individual, concurrent ailments and medications, diet, physical status, and the client's compliance with the regimen. The nurse necessarily utilizes a holistic approach, not only to manage the client's physical symptoms but also dealing with psychosocial support. Moderation is the key for these clients, in rest, exercise, diet, and avoidance of stress. The most common nursing diagnoses for patients receiving anticonvulsant therapy are: knowledge deficit and noncompliance related to the medication regimen and high risk for injury related to the side effects/adverse reactions of these drugs. An important evaluation factor is the effectiveness of the regimen in controling and mimimizing seizures.

## BIBLIOGRAPHY

American Hosptial Formulary Service. (1991). AHFS drug information '91. Bethesda, Md: American Society of Hospital Pharmacists, Inc.

Austin JK. (1989). Predicting parental anticonvulsant medication compliance using the theory of reasoned action, J Pediatr Nurs 4(2):88.

Austin JK et al. (1988). Parental attitude and coping behaviors in families of children with epilepsy, J Neurosci Nurs 20(3):174.

Beniak J. (1982). Patient education in epilepsy, J Neurosci Nurs 14(1):19.

Burgess KE. (1985). Cerebral depressants: their effects and safe administration, Nursing 15(8):46.

Cacek TT et al. (1986). In vitro evaluation of nasogastric administration methods for phenytoin, Am J Hosp Pharm 43:689.

Carpenito LJ. (1987). Nursing diagnosis: application to clinical practice, ed 2. Philadelphia: JB Lippincott.

Cohen MR. (1983). Medication errors: don't mix Dilantin with dextrose solutions, Nursing 13(6):19.

Commission on Classification and Terminology of the International League against Epilepsy. (1981). Proposal for revised clinical and electroencephalographic classification of epileptic seizures, Epilepsia 22:489.

Conley NJ et al. (1987). Current controversies in pregnancy and epilepsy: a unique challenge to nursing, J Obstet Gynecol Neonatal Nurs 16(5):321.

Foxton W. (1988). Managing epilepsy, Nursing Standard 2(37):35.

Gever LN. (1984). Anticonvulsants, Nursing 14 (4):41.

Gilman AG et al, eds. (1990). Goodman and Gilman's the pharmacological basis of therapeutics, ed 8. New York: Macmillan Co.

Hartshorn JC et al. (1986). Nursing interventions for anticonvulsant drug interactions, J Neurosci Nurs 18(5):250.

Lesser RP and Pippenger CE. (1985). Choosing an antiepileptic drug: the care for individualized treatment, Postgrad Med 77(4):225.

McCormick KB. (1987). Pregnancy and epilepsy: nursing implications, J Neurosci Nurs 19(2):66.

Ozuna J and Friel P. (1984). Effect of enteral tube feeding on serum phenytoin levels, J Neurosci Nurs 16(6):1984.

Parrish MA. (1984). A comparison of behavioral side effects related to commonly used anticonvulsants, Pediatr Nurs 10(2):149.

Sasso SC. (1984). Phenobarbital for neonatal seizures, MCN 9(5):347.

Steinkruger M. (1985). Photosensitive epilepsy, J Neurosci Nurs 17(6):355.

United States Pharmacopeial Convention. (1991). Drug information for the health care professional, ed 11. Rockville, Md: The Convention.

Yuen GJ. (1984). Agents affecting phenytoin bioavailability, Drug Interactions Newsletter 4(10):37.

*Chapter*

# 16 Central Nervous System Stimulants

## INTRODUCTION

The CNS stimulants may produce dramatic effects, but their therapeutic usefulness is limited because of the multiplicity of their actions and side effects. Also, repeated administration and large doses tend to precipitate convulsive seizures, coma, and exhaustion. The number of drugs that stimulate the CNS is large, but the number actually used for this purpose is limited.

Stimulants are classified on the basis of where they exert their major effects in the nervous system—on the cerebrum, the medulla and brainstem, or the hypothalamic limbic regions. **Amphetamines** are mainly stimulants of the cerebral cortex; **analeptics** are mainly on the centers in the medulla and the brainstem; and **anorexiants** suppress the appetite, perhaps by a direct stimulant effect on the satiety center in the hypothalamic and limbic regions. These drugs may also affect other parts of the nervous system. The drugs that act primarily on the medullary centers are said to be the best analeptics.

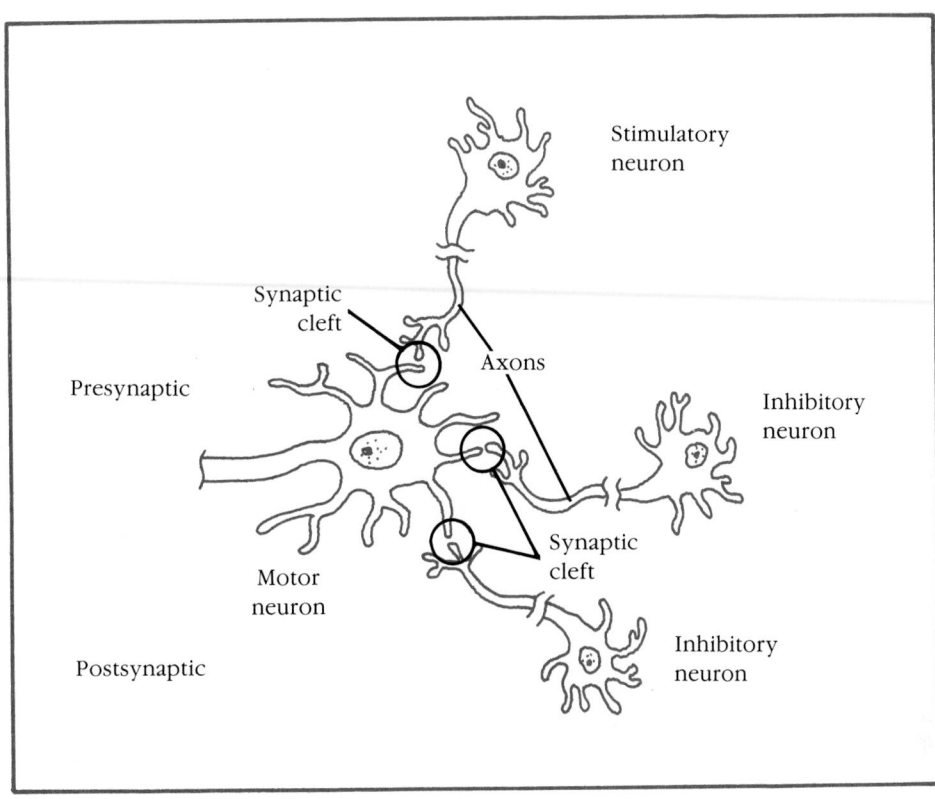

**FIGURE 16-1**  Neuron transmission.

Cerebral stimulants were commonly prescribed in the past for obesity and to counteract CNS-depressant overdosage, but such use today is considered obsolete. Although the CNS stimulants suppress appetite, tolerance develops to the anorexic effect usually before the weight reduction goal is reached. Treatment of severe CNS depression with stimulants is also discouraged, since close monitoring and supportive measures have been found to be quite successful without the production of undesirable adverse reactions. CNS stimulants, with their narrow therapeutic index between effectiveness and toxicity, may induce cardiac dysrhythmias, hypertension, convulsions, and/or violent behavior. Thus the CNS stimulants have limited use in practice today; that is, they are primarily used for the treatment of narcolepsy and **attention deficit disorder (ADD)** with hyperactivity.

ADD with hyperactivity is a syndrome characterized by distractibility, a short attention span, impulsive behavior, and hyperactivity. Stimulant medications tend to decrease the distractibility and hyperactivity, resulting in an increased attention span.

Studies indicate that about 80% of children with ADD no longer have problems after puberty. However, 20% continue to have ADD and need medication through adolescence. In either case, medication schedules are a challenge for the provider.

Although stimulant medications are available in short-acting (4-hour) and long-acting (8-10 hour) forms, it is general practice to establish a daily schedule using the short-acting form. The dosage required will be learned from empiric experience. For this reason, the prescriber needs to work closely with the client, the parents, and school personnel in evaluating results and planning dosages.

During school hours, management of the distractibility and hyperactivity is necessary. But it may be equally important to contain these symptoms at other times of the day to promote the child's psychosocial development by participating in club membership, religious activities, or social events. Rather than use a continuous approach to dosing, it is more helpful to consider the client's life in 4-hour units and provide a dosage appropriate to the needs of that time block. For example, the client might take 10 mg of a short-acting stimulant at 8 AM and again at noon on a school day but add another dose at 4 PM if a music lesson is planned for that evening.

**Narcolepsy** is characterized by excessive drowsiness and uncontrollable sleep attacks during the daytime. In addition, the client may exhibit a sleep paralysis (inability to move that occurs immediately on falling asleep or on awakening), **cataplexy** (stress-induced generalized muscle weakness), and **hypnagogic** illusions or hallucinations (vivid auditory or visual dreams occurring at onset of sleep). CNS stimulants are useful in controlling the daytime drowsiness and excessive sleep patterns, whereas tricyclic antidepressants are being tested in conjunction with the stimulants for cataplexy and sleep paralysis.

Cerebral stimulants can increase excitability by (1) blocking the activity of the inhibitory neurons or their respective neurotransmitters, or (2) enhancing the production or release of the excitatory neurotransmitters (see Figure 16-1). Neurons transmit messages by means of axons to neighboring neurons. When stimulatory neurons are activated (depolarized), a chemical neurotransmitter is released into the synaptic cleft located between neurons. The neurotransmitter may bind on the receptors and when sufficient quantities are attached, the postsynaptic neuron will be activated (depolarized). The two general groups of neurotransmitters are excitatory and inhibitory. Excitatory neurons may release either acetylcholine, norepinephrine, or dopamine (only one type of neurotransmitter per neuron), whereas inhibitory neurons release GABA and glycine, substances that stabilize the neuron to reduce its response to incoming stimuli. GABA is stored in the presynaptic inhibitory neuron, whereas glycine is located in the postsynaptic inhibitory neuron.

Strychnine, a toxic alkaloid used in pesticides, was previously a commonly used circulatory and respiratory stimulant. It was also available in many OTC preparations such as tonics, laxatives, and analgesics up to approximately 1970. It has no legitimate use in medicine today, but it is an important research product because it selectively blocks the postsynaptic inhibitory transmitter glycine. Picrotoxin, another powerful stimulant with limited use in therapeutics, blocks the presynaptic inhibitory transmitter GABA. Both block the receptors on their respective sites, thus reducing or antagonizing the inhibitory effects, which results in excessive muscle activity such as muscle spasms of the face and neck, lockjaw, nystagmus and generalized, violent spasms and convulsive episodes. Since the majority of CNS stimulants do not affect the inhibitory neurons, they are classified as analeptics, that is, drugs that enhance the production or release of the excitatory neurotransmitters. Amphetamines, anorexiant drugs, caffeine, doxapram, methylphenidate, and pemoline all have CNS stimulatory effects.

## ANOREXIANT DRUGS

Anorexiant or appetite suppressant drugs include a variety of medications that are used to treat exogenous obesity (see Table 16-1). Amphetamines affect the neurotransmitter norepinephrine, producing marked euphoria, stimulation, and abuse potential. The anorexiant drugs are lipid soluble and cross the blood-brain barrier.

Phenmetrazine affects norepinephrine and, like amphetamine, produces marked euphoria, stimulation, and abuse potential. Phentermine and diethylpropion affect norepinephrine and produce mild euphoria and mild to moderate stimulation with minimal abuse potential.

Mazindol affects dopamine and adrenergic receptors and has the same CNS effects as diethylpropion, with minimal abuse potential. Fenfluramine increases serotonin, which depresses the CNS while producing appetite suppression. It also increases glucose use and has minimal abuse potential. Fenfluramine would be the drug of choice for anxious individuals or for clients who should avoid the use of CNS-stimulant drugs (such as those with hyperthyroidism, agitation, and advanced arteriosclerosis).

Since anorexiants have a number of limitations, careful selection of the clinical choices is necessary to minimize the unwanted effects. As appetite suppressants, they are recommended as an adjunct to other regimens, such as physical exercise, behavior modification, and restriction of caloric intake, for a short period, usually 6 to 12 weeks. Tolerance to the anorectic effect usually occurs within 6 to 12 weeks.

*Side effects/adverse reactions.* Most frequently reported side effects include insomnia with all except fenfluramine; euphoria with all except fenfluramine and mazindol. Other side effects are as follows: increased nervousness and irritability with all except fenfluramine; diarrhea and increased daytime sedation reported mostly with fenfluramine; dry mouth with fenfluramine and mazindol.

Adverse reactions include CNS depression and confusion with diethylpropion and fenfluramine, allergic rashes or hives with fenfluramine, and hypertension (rare with fenfluramine).

*Significant drug interactions.* Concurrent use or use within 14 days of monamine oxidase inhibitors (MAO) with anorexiants should be avoided, since potentiated sympathomimetic effects, including hypertensive crisis, may result. Avoid administration of concurrent CNS-depressant drugs with fenfluramine because enhanced CNS depression may result.

## ▷ NURSING MANAGEMENT: ANOREXIANT THERAPY

*Assessment.* Anorexiant drugs are used to treat altered nutrition: more than body requirements. The nurse should work with the client to determine the causative factors for the obesity that results from the ingestion of calories in excess of metabolic need: sedentary life-style; lack of nutritional knowledge; or increased food intake related to stress, low self-esteem, or boredom. Nursing interventions can then be planned based on the specific etiologic factor to which the anorexiant drug therapy serves as a short-term adjunct. A realistic goal for weight loss should be 1 to 2 pounds a week, although the obese clients will tend to have a greater weight loss than this, at least initially.

Anorexiants are not to be administered during or within 14 days of an MAO inhibitor regimen. The interaction with these drugs may result in profound potentiation of the anorexiant effect and a hypertensive crisis may develop.

The use of fenfluramine is contraindicated in clients with alcoholism because depression and psychosis have occurred. It is also contraindicated in clients with a history of depres-

**TABLE 16-1**   Anorexiant medications

| Name | Pregnancy safety FDA category | Recommended dosages |
|---|---|---|
| benzphetamine (Didrex) | X | Adults, 25-50 mg orally, daily. Not recommended in children less than 12 yr old. |
| diethylpropion | B | |
|   Tablets (Tenuate, Tepanil) | | Adults, 25 mg 3 times daily, 1 hr before meals. Not recommended in children less than 12 yr old. |
|   Extended-release capsules (Nobesine ♣) | | Adults, 75 mg orally daily, at mid-morning. Not recommended in children less than 12 yr old. |
|   Extended-release tablets (Tenuate Dospan, Tepanil Ten-tab) | | Adults, 75 mg orally daily, at mid-morning. Not recommended in children less than 12 yr old. |
| fenfluramine | C | |
|   Tablets (Pondimin, Ponderal ♣ ) | | Adults, 20 mg initially orally, 3 times daily, ½-1 hr before meals. may increase by 20 mg daily at weekly intervals up to 40 mg 3 times a day. Not recommended in children less than 12 yr old. |
|   Extended-release capsules (Ponderal Pacaps ♣) | | Adults, 60 mg orally, initially, daily. May be increased to 120 mg daily if necessary. Not recommended in children less than 12 yr old. |
| mazindol (Mazanor, Sanorex) | C | Adults, 1 mg initially orally once a day before breakfast. Increase to 1 mg 3 times daily, an hour before meals or 2 mg daily, an hour before lunch. Not recommended in children less than 12 yr old. |
| phendimetrazine | Unclassified | |
|   Tablets (Adphen, Bontril PDM, and others) | | Adults, 17.5-35 mg orally, 2 or 3 times daily, an hour before meals. Not recommended in children less than 12 yr old. |
|   Capsules (Anorex) | | Capsules, same as tablet directions. |
|   Extended-release capsules (Adipost, Bontril Slow Release) | | Adults, 105 mg orally daily, ½-1 hour before breakfast. Not recommended in children less than 12 yr old. |
| phenmetrazine | Unclassified | |
|   Extended-release tablets (Preludin, Endurets) | | Adults, 75 mg orally daily. Not recommended in children less than 12 yr old. |
| phentermine | Unclassified | |
|   Tablets (Adipex-P, Phentrol) | | Adults, 8 mg orally ½ hour before meals or 15-37.5 mg daily before breakfast. Not recommended in children less than 12 yr old. |
|   Capsules (Fastin, Obephen) | | Adults, capsules same as above. |
|   Resin capsules (Ionamin) | | Adults, 15 or 30 mg orally daily before breakfast. Not recommended in children less than 12 yr old. |

sion, since they become depressed or more depressed following withdrawal of the drug. This is because fenfluramine is a CNS depressant, whereas the other anorexiants are CNS stimulants.

Anorexiants are, in general, contraindicated for clients with agitated states: arteriosclerotic disease; cardiovascular disease, particularly those with dysrhythmias; glaucoma; moderate to severe hypertension; uremia; hyperthyroidism; psychosis; and those with a history of drug abuse or dependence.

Once the client is started on anorexiant therapy, the nurse should be alert for other problems that may occur: distur-

bance in sleep pattern related to CNS effects; altered thought process related to CNS effects; altered cardiac output related to cardiovascular effects; altered comfort related to dry mouth, rash, headache, or gastrointestinal or urinary effects; and disturbance of self-concept related to changes in sexual desire or decreased sexual ability.

***Intervention.*** Because these drugs are to be used only for a short term, emphasis is on a total weight reduction program that includes a suitable diet, appropriate exercise regimen, and behavior modification related to the cause of the overeating.

Preparations that are administered on a daily basis should

be administered in the morning to decrease insomnia. Avoid administering anorexiant drugs within 6 hours of sleep times. These drugs should be administered with caution to clients with diabetes, since the need for insulin may be decreased as a result of the concomitant dietary regimen. Blood and urine glucose levels should be monitored closely. General anesthesia should be administered with caution.

**Education.** Clients should be cautioned not to self-regulate the dosage if the drug seems to be less effective but to consult the physician.

These drugs may impair the client's ability to perform tasks requiring physical coordination and alertness.

Clients should be instructed in ways to minimize unpleasant taste and dryness of mouth with mouth rinses, ice chips, chewing gum, and sugarless candies.

**Evaluation.** Adverse effects of these drugs, except for fenfluramine, usually relate to overstimulation, such as nervousness, restlessness, insomnia, and anxiety. Blood pressure and pulse should be monitored to assess whether response is adverse to the drug.

Tolerance is a frequent occurrence with anorexiants, and the client should be assessed for the possibility of habituation and addiction.

Fenfluramine is different from the other anorexiants because its adverse effects relate to drowsiness and depression. Diarrhea may be significant enough to decrease the dosage or end the course of fenfluramine.

## AMPHETAMINES

Although their exact mechanism of action is unknown, amphetamines increase the release of catecholamines (norepinephrine from stored sites in nerve terminals), block reuptake of dopamine and norepinephrine following release into the synapse, and inhibit the action of monoamine oxidase (MAO). The result is an increased stimulating effect on the cerebral cortex and reticular activating system, thus increasing alertness and response to incoming stimuli. Increased wakefulness, euphoria, or elation may be noted. Long-term amphetamine abuse can lead to chorea, which is mediated by alterations in the physiology of the basal ganglia; chorea is also seen with cocaine, which reduces dopamine levels.

Amphetamines used over long periods can produce psychologic and physical dependence. Prolonged use of amphetamines leads to the development of tolerance. Amphetamines are indicated for the treatment of ADD with hyperactivity and in the treatment of narcolepsy.

Amphetamines are well absorbed and are distributed to body tissues, with especially high concentrations in the brain and cerebrospinal fluid. The half-life depends on urinary pH. Generally they are as follows: amphetamine, 10 to 30 hours; dextroamphetamine, 10 to 12 hours for adults and 6 to 8 hours in children; methamphetamine, 4 to 5 hours. These drugs are metabolized in the liver and excreted by the kidneys. Excretion is pH dependent; it may be increased in an acidic urine and decreased in a more basic urine.

The most frequently reported side effects are euphoria, increased irritability, nervousness, insomnia, and restlessness. Less frequently reported are excessive sweating, dry mouth, abdominal cramps, impotency, alterations in sexual desire, diarrhea or constipation, dizziness, anorexia, nausea or vomiting, weight loss, and blurred vision. The most frequently reported adverse reactions include tachycardia or irregular heart rate. Less frequent are allergic reactions including urticaria, hives, angina or chest pain, tremors, hyperreactive reflexes, and dyskinesia. With high dosage or prolonged consumption, CNS mood changes including depression, increased agitation, and psychosis may occur. Drug dependency and tolerance may also develop.

**Significant drug interactions.** The following effects may occur when amphetamines are given with the drugs listed below:

| Drug | Possible Effect and Management |
|---|---|
| antidepressants, tricyclic | May result in adverse cardiovascular effects, such as arrhythmias, tachycardia, or severe hypertension. Monitor the pulse and blood pressure closely; dosage adjustments may be necessary. |
| beta adrenergic blocking drugs (systemic and ophthalmic) | May result in increased alpha adrenergic effects resulting in hypertension, bradycardia, and possible heart block. If necessary to use both classifications, labetalol, a beta-blocking agent that also has alpha-blocking effects, may reduce the risk of producing the above effects. Monitor closely for dysrhythmias. |
| CNS stimulants such as appetite suppressants, caffeine, methylphenidate, pemoline, sympathomimetics, theophylline, amantadine | May result in an increase in adverse cardiovascular effects, nervousness, insomnia, and convulsions. If necessary to use drugs concurrently, closely observe client for adverse reactions. |
| digitalis glycosides | May result in an increase in cardiac dysrhythmias. Avoid usage or, if necessary, monitor apical pulse very closely. |
| monoamine oxidase (MAO) inhibitors | Because of increased release of catecholamines, headaches; dysrhythmias; vomiting; sudden, severe hypertension; and possibly hyperthemia may result. |
| thyroid hormones | May result in enhanced effects of thyroid or amphetamines. If client has coronary artery disease, the potential of inducing coronary insufficiency is increased. If possible, avoid concurrent usage. |

**Dosage and administration.** See Table 16-2.

**Pregnancy safety.** Has been established at FDA Category C.

**TABLE 16-2**    Amphetamine dosage and administration

| | Adults | Children |
|---|---|---|
| amphetamine tablets | | |
| Narcolepsy | 5-20 mg 1-3 times daily | Children to 6 yr, dosage not determined; 6-12 yr, 2.5 mg orally twice daily; increase by 5 mg/day at 1-wk intervals until therapeutic effect or adult dosage achieved. Children 12 yr and older, 5 mg orally, increasing dose by 10 mg/day at weekly intervals until therapeutic effect or adult dosage achieved. |
| Attention deficit disorder | | Children up to 3 yr, not recommended. 3-6 yr, 2.5 mg orally; increase dosage by 2.5 mg/day at weekly intervals until desired therapeutic response achieved. 6 yr and older, 5 mg orally 1 or 2 times/day; increase by 5 mg/day at weekly intervals until desired therapeutic response achieved. |
| dextroamphetamine tablets, elixir | | |
| Narcolepsy | 5-20 mg orally 1-3 times daily | Children up to 6 yr, dosage not determined. 6-12 yr, 2.5 mg orally twice daily; increase by 5 mg/day at weekly intervals until therapeutic effect or adult dosage achieved. 12 yr and older, 5 mg orally twice daily; increase by 10 mg/day at weekly intervals until therapeutic effect or adult dosage achieved. |
| Attention deficit disorder | | Children up to 3 yr, not recommended. 3-6 yr, 2.5 mg orally daily; increase dosage by 2.5 mg/day at weekly intervals until therapeutic response achieved. 6 yr and older, 5 mg orally once or twice/day; increase dosage by 5 mg daily at weekly intervals until therapeutic response achieved. |
| dextroamphetamine sulfate extended-release capsules (use this dosage form after therapeutic dosage/day established): | | |
| Narcolepsy | 5-30 mg daily | Up to 6 yr, see above recommendations. 6-12 yr, 5-15 mg orally daily. 12 yr and older, 10 or 15 mg daily, orally. |
| Attention deficit disorder | | Children up to 6 yr, see above recommendations. 6 yr and older, 5-15 mg orally daily. |
| methamphetamine hydrochloride tablets (Desoxym), methamphetamine hydrochloride extended-release tablets (Desoxyn): | | |
| Attention deficit disorder | | Children up to 6 yr, not recommended. 6 yr and older, 5 mg orally 1 or 2 times daily; increase dosage by 5 mg/day at weekly intervals until therapeutic effect achieved (usually 20-25 mg/day). |

## ▷NURSING MANAGEMENT: AMPHETAMINE THERAPY

*Assessment.* As with other central nervous system stimulants, the nurse should be aware that amphetamines should be avoided by persons with hypertension and cardiovascular disease and by those who are unduly restless, anxious, agitated, and excited. Amphetamines should be used with caution in elderly and debilitated clients or those with a history of homicidal or suicidal tendencies.

*Intervention.* The last dose should be administered not later than 6 hours before the client's bedtime; if a sustained-release product is used, the last dose should be administered not less than 10 to 14 hours before bedtime to avoid insomnia.

The dose should be given 30 to 60 minutes before the client's meal. Dietary and behavior modification is essential if the drug is to be successful as an anorexiant. If weight loss is not desired, administer the drug with or after meals.

Help client overcome a dry mouth with sugarless candy, gum, or ice chips.

The dosage should be gradually reduced before discontinuing the drug following prolonged, high dosage to avoid withdrawal manifestations such as psychotic symptoms and lethargy.

Since fatigue occurs as the drug effects diminish, the nurse should be aware that the client will need more rest and sleep.

The nurse should know that some clients (e.g., those with bronchial asthma who are sensitive to tartrazine dye) should not use some of these dosage forms.

*Education.* The client should be instructed not to self-regulate the dose; the habit-forming potential should be stressed. If the effect of the drug seems to decrease, the nurse should caution the client not to increase the dosage but to consult the physician.

The nurse should inform the client of the CNS and cardiovascular side effects of the drug which need to be reported.

Clients should be cautioned that amphetamines may impair their functioning in the performance of tasks requiring mental alertness and physical coordination. These drugs are frequently abused by athletes, students, and drivers for the purpose of increasing alertness but may result in an impaired ability to function.

The client should be instructed to swallow the sustained-release tablet whole without breaking, chewing, or crushing.

The nurse should caution the client to keep the drug securely stored to avoid unintended use by another person.

*Evaluation.* Nurses should assess pulse and blood pressure of clients receiving amphetamines to monitor for adverse cardiovascular effects of the drug. Caution should be used and the possibility of psychologic dependence and addiction should be considered in clients with a history of addiction to alcohol or other drugs. The nurse should eval-uate for potential dependence in all clients receiving the drug.

Children receiving amphetamines for a prolonged period should have their growth carefully monitored, since the drug is thought to inhibit growth. These children should also be reevaluated periodically for the need for amphetamines to treat disorders of attention deficit by the interruption of the course of therapy and monitoring for the return of behavioral symptoms.

## OTHER CENTRAL NERVOUS SYSTEM STIMULANTS

### doxapram (Dopram)

Doxapram stimulates respiration by acting on the peripheral carotid chemoreceptors at low doses. At higher dosages, the medullary respiratory center is stimulated. This drug is used for the treatment of respiratory depression induced by a drug overdose, chronic obstructive pulmonary disease, or postanesthetic effects.

Doxapram is injectable and used for intravenous dosing. It has an onset of effect of 20 to 40 seconds and peak effect of 1 to 2 minutes. Doxapram's duration of action is 5 to 12 minutes. It is excreted by the kidneys.

Infrequent side effects include urination difficulties, headache, diarrhea, dizziness, cough, hiccups, confusion, warm or burning feeling, nausea or vomiting, sweating. Infrequent or rare adverse reactions include chest pains, tachycardia, extrasystoles, hemolysis, thrombophlebitis, dyspnea, tachypnea. Signs of overdosage are hypertension, convulsions, trembling, tachycardia, increased deep tendon reflexes.

Administration of doxapram with monoamine oxidase (MAO) inhibitors or vasopressors may result in increase in blood pressure or a hypertensive crisis. Monitor closely.

For dosage and administration, see Table 16-3.

### ▷Nursing Management: Doxapram Therapy

Before administering the drug to clients with respiratory depression, a patent airway should be established and an adequate oxygen supply ensured in an attempt to prevent aspiration. Because intravenous administration tends to cause hemolysis, only dilute solutions should be administered at a slow rate of infusion. To decrease local tissue reaction and thrombophlebitis, various injection sites should be used to avoid extravasation.

Doxapram hydrochloride has a narrow margin of safety. The nurse should observe for early signs of toxicity, such as increased blood pressure and pulse rate, dysrhythmias, dyspnea, and increased skeletal response with increased deep tendon reflexes and spasticity. The nurse should monitor pulse, blood pressure, and deep tendon reflexes frequently to avoid overdosage, and the rate of the infusion should be adjusted on the basis of these assessments.

Arterial blood gases should be analyzed before initiation

**TABLE 16-3** Doxapram: dosage and administration

| Indication | Adults | Children |
|---|---|---|
| Drug-induced CNS depression | 1-2 mg/kg body weight IV; may repeat in 5 min. Maintenance, 1-2 mg/kg body weight every 1-2 hr until desired therapeutic response achieved. Maximum, 3 g/day. Intermittent IV infusion, 1-3 mg/min until therapeutic response achieved or for 2-hr maximum time period. If needed, infusion can be repeated after ½-2 hr, with total dose maximum of 3 g. | Not recommended in children less than 12 yr old. |
| Chronic obstructive pulmonary disease with acute **hypercapnia** (excessive amounts of $CO_2$ in blood) | IV infusion, administer 1-2 mg/min; if necessary, administration rate may be increased to 3 mg/min. Maximum time for infusion with no additional infusions recommended, 2 hr. | |
| Postanesthesia respiratory depression | IV, 0.5-1 mg/kg body weight; do not exceed 1.5 mg/kg as single dose. If needed, dose may be repeated every 5 min up to maximum total dosage of 2 mg/kg body weight. | |

of therapy as a baseline and every 30 minutes thereafter to avoid the possibility of respiratory acidosis when used in chronic obstructive pulmonary disease.

Because narcosis may recur, close monitoring of the client is necessary until full alertness has been maintained for an hour. Doxapram is a *temporary* measure to correct acute respiratory insufficiency. Mechanical assistance with ventilation is safer, more reliable, and effective for long-term (over 2 hours) therapy.

### methylphenidate hydrochloride (Ritalin)

The mechanism of central action is unknown. Pharmacologic actions are similar to amphetamines, with CNS and respiratory stimulation; sympathomimetic activity is also reported. Sites of action are the cerebral cortex and subcortical areas. Methylphenidate also appears to block the reuptake of dopamine into the dopaminergic neurons. In ADD with hyperactivity, methylphenidate decreases motor activity and increases the attention span. In narcolepsy, it appears to stimulate the cortex and subcortex including the thalamic area to increase alertness, lift the spirits, and increase motor activity. The drug is indicated for treatment of ADD and narcolepsy. Methylphenidate is well absorbed. Peak serum concentration of tablets is 1.9 hours in children; the extended release tablets reach peak serum concentration in 4.7 hours in children. This drug is metabolized in the liver and excreted by the kidneys.

The more frequently reported side effects are anorexia, increased nervousness, and insomnia (usually more frequent in children). Less frequent side effects are headache, nausea, abdominal pain, drowsiness, and dizziness. The more frequent adverse reactions include hypertension and tachycardia. Less frequent are chest pain, trembling or uncontrolled movement of body, rash, fever of unknown origin, and increased bruising. Signs of overdosage may include confusion, delirium, dry mouth, euphoria, increased fever and sweating, severe headaches, hypertension, tremors, muscle twitching, irregular heartbeats, vomiting, convulsions, and possibly coma.

***Significant drug interactions.*** The following effects may occur when methylphenidate hydrochloride is given with the drugs listed below:

| Drug | Possible effect and management |
|---|---|
| other CNS stimulants | May result in additive CNS stimulation effects causing increased nervousness, irritability, insomnia, dysrhythmias, and convulsions. Monitor apical pulse and behaviors closely. |
| monoamine oxidase (MAO) inhibitors | May result in hypertensive crisis. Do not give drugs concurrently or within 14 days of administration of an MAO inhibitor. |
| pimozide | Should not be administered together. Withdraw client from methylphenidate before starting pimozide therapy. Concurrent use may mask reason for tic development because methylphenidate may also induce tics. Pimozide is indicated for the treatment of tics in clients with Gilles de la Tourette's syndrome. |

***Dosage and administration.*** See Table 16-4.

▷ **Nursing Management: Methylphenidate Therapy**

***Assessment.*** Methylphenidate must be used with caution in clients with epilepsy because the drug can lower the convulsive threshold. It also should be used with caution in clients with hypertension. Long-term therapy should be accompanied by repeated medical examinations, and tests for complete blood and platelet counts.

Use of methylphenidate in pregnant or lactating women

**TABLE 16-4**   Methylphenidate hydrochloride: dosage and administration

| Drug | Adults | Children |
|---|---|---|
| methylphenidate hydrochloride tablets (Ritalin) | 5-20 mg orally 2 or 3 times daily, 30-45 min before meals | For ADD with hyperactivity: children up to 6 yr, dosage not established; 6 yr and older, 5 mg orally twice daily before breakfast and lunch. Increase dosage by 5-10 mg weekly to maximum of 60 mg daily. Generally, if improvement not seen after dosage adjustments over 30 days; stop medication. |
| methylphenidate hydrochloride extended-release tablets (Ritalin-SR) | 20 mg orally 1-3 times daily every 8 hr on empty stomach | Children up to 6 yr, not established. 6 yr and older, 20 mg orally 1-3 times daily. |

is not recommended and is contraindicated in clients with glaucoma, agitation, depression and fatigue.

Once methylphenidate therapy has begun the client should be assessed for sleep pattern disturbance, altered thought processes, and high risk for injury related to its CNS effects; altered cardiac output related to its cardiovascular effects, and altered nutrition related to its anorexiant effects.

**Intervention.** Dosage should be calculated for each client based on the response to the drug. Extended-release forms of the drug should be used only after the initial therapy has established the apropriate dosage for the client.

The nurse should administer the last dose several hours before bedtime to avoid insomnia.

Sole dependence on methylphenidate for treatment of ADD is discouraged. Other therapies (psychologic, educational, social) should be used in conjunction with the drug therapy. When symptoms of ADD are improved, interruption of drug therapy during times of low stress may be possible. The client may be given medication-free weekends, holidays, or vacations.

**Education.** The client should be instructed to administer the medication on an empty stomach 30 to 45 minutes before eating. Extended-release forms should be swallowed whole, not crushed, broken, or chewed.

Do not increase the dose if the medication seems less effective.

Regular visits with the client's physician are needed to monitor progress of the drug therapy.

If the client takes large doses over an extended period, withdrawal must be gradual. Caution the clients that they should *not* stop taking the medication without checking with the prescribing physician.

**Evaluation.** Tolerance and psychologic dependence have occurred with long-term use, and abnormal behavior and psychotic episodes have been observed. When the drug is withdrawn, careful supervision is required since severe depression may result.

Clients should be monitored for weight loss from appetite suppression. Children, in particular, should be assessed on a regular basis for physical growth, since there may be

suppression of normal weight gain. Methylphenidate must be used cautiously in emotionally unstable persons and in those with a history of drug dependence or alcoholism. Drug abusers have used it as a substitute for amphetamines. The drug should be discontinued periodically to reassess therapeutic need as indicated by the return of symptoms.

### pemoline (Cylert)

The mechanism of central action is unknown. Pemoline may act by means of dopaminergic mechanisms. It is indicated for treatment of ADD with hyperactivity. Pemoline has good absorption and a half-life of 12 hours. Peak serum concentration occurs in 2 to 4 hours with peak effect reached in 3 to 4 weeks. Pemoline is partially metabolized in the liver and is excreted by the kidneys. More frequent side effects include anorexia, insomnia, and weight loss. Less frequent are dizziness, daytime sedation, irritability, depression, nausea, rash, and abdominal pain. A rare adverse reaction is jaundice.

Signs of overdosage include increased agitation, confusion, euphoria, hallucinations, severe headaches, hypertension, elevated temperatures, increased sweating, convulsions, fast heart rate, enlarged pupils, vomiting, and uncontrollable muscle movements of eyes. No significant drug interactions have been reported. Dosage is as follows: Children less than 6 years, not established; 6 years or older, 37.5 mg orally each morning. Dosage may be increased by 18.75 mg daily on weekly basis until therapeutic response noted or maximum of 112.5 mg day is reached.

Pemoline is classified as FDA Category B for pregnancy safety.

### ▷ Nursing Management: Pemoline Therapy

Pemoline should be administered in the morning to avoid insomnia at night. Pemoline must be used cautiously in emotionally labile clients and in clients with a history of drug dependence or alcoholism. The drug should be discontinued periodically to reassess the need for its administration as indicated by a return of symptoms. The nurse should caution the client that the most common side effects are insomnia and anorexia. These are dose related and may be decreased by a dosage adjustment by the physician.

The client should be prepared for an initial weight loss with a return to the normal weight in 3 to 6 months. Parents should be counseled that the beneficial effect of the medication may not be apparent for 3 to 4 weeks, but that it is important to the success of the regimen that the drug be administered as prescribed. Also see the discussion of nursing management of methylphenidate therapy.

### caffeine

Caffeine is a stimulant found in many beverages, foods, OTC drugs, and prescription drugs (see the box at right). In the United States, it has been estimated that 7 million kg of caffeine are consumed annually. Caffeine has been implicated in many controversial adverse health effects, such as cancer, fibrocystic breast disease, and birth defects.

***Short- and Long-Term Effects.***   Because caffeine has an effect on many body functions, both its short-term and possible long-term effects are of concern. Discussion of these effects, as they involve each body system, follows.

*CNS.* Although all levels of the CNS may be affected, regular doses of caffeine (100-150 mg) will stimulate the cortex to produce increased alertness and decreased motor reaction time to both visual and auditory events. Drowsiness and fatigue generally disappear. Larger dosages may affect the medullary, vagus, vasomotor, and respiratory centers, resulting in slowing of the heart rate, vasoconstriction, and increased respiratory rate. Studies attribute such effects to competitive blockade of adenosine receptors and accumulation of cyclic AMP. Thus caffeine is being investigated for the treatment of neonatal apnea, generally as an adjunct to nondrug measures and as an alternative to theophylline.

*Cardiac.* Caffeine stimulates the myocardium, bringing about both an increased heart rate and an increased cardiac output. This effect is antagonistic to that produced on the vagus center; consequently, a slight slowing of the heart may be observed in some individuals and an increased rate in others. The latter effect usually predominates after large doses. Overstimulation may cause tachycardia and cardiac irregularities.

*Vascular.* Caffeine constricts cerebral blood vessels, resulting in decreased cerebral blood flow and oxygen tension in the brain. Thus caffeine is used in analgesic products and in combination with ergotamine to enhance pain relief and, perhaps, to produce more rapid onset of action. When given with ergotamine, the enhanced effect is believed to be a result of better absorption of the ergotamine in the presence of caffeine.

Caffeine appears to dilate peripheral blood vessels, thereby decreasing peripheral vascular resistance. But this effect is usually offset by the increase in heart rate and cardiac output. Therefore the overall blood pressure re-

---

### CAFFEINE CONTENT IN DIETARY SOURCES

Chocolate, bittersweet—25 mg/ounce
Chocolate, milk—3 to 6 mg/ounce
Cocoa—6 to 42 mg/cup
Coffee, brewed—100 to 150 mg/cup
Coffee, decaffeinated—2 to 4 mg/cup
Coffee, instant—86 to 99 mg/cup
Cola drinks—40 to 72 mg/cup
Tea—60 to 75 mg/cup

From United States Pharmacopeial Convention. (1991). *Drug information for the health care professional;* ed 11. Rockville, Md: The Convention.

---

sponse will largely depend on the dosage and the effects that predominate in the individual.

*Skeletal muscles.* Caffeine affects voluntary skeletal muscles to increase the contractual force and decrease muscle fatigue.

*Gastrointestinal.* Caffeine increases secretion of pepsin and hydrochloric acid from the parietal cells. This is the reason coffee is restricted in clients who have a gastric or duodenal ulcer.

*Renal.* Caffeine produces a mild diuretic effect by increasing renal blood flow and glomerular filtration rate and by decreasing the reabsorption of sodium and water in the proximal tubules.

*Additional effects.* Caffeine also increases metabolic activity, inhibits uterine contractions, increases glucose levels by stimulating glycolysis, and increases catecholamine levels in plasma and urine.

***Mechanism of action.***   Multiple mechanisms of action for caffeine include an increase in calcium ion permeability within the sarcoplasmic reticulum; phosphodiesterase competitive inhibition, creating cyclic AMP accumulation; and competitive blocking of adenosine receptors.

***Indications and pharmacokinetics.***   Caffeine is used in the treatment of tiredness or drowsiness and as an adjunct to analgesics to enhance relief of pain. Its absorption is good, and it is distributed to all body compartments; it will cross and enter the CNS and readily crosses the placenta. Caffeine is metabolized in the liver. In adults caffeine is metabolized to theophylline and theobromine, whereas in the neonate only a small portion is metabolized to theophylline. Caffeine's plasma distribution half-life is 3.5 hours in adults, and 70 to 100 hours in neonates. Elimination half-life is 6 hours in adults, 36 to 144 hours in the neonate; between 4 and 6 months of age, the adult value will be achieved. Peak plasma level is achieved within 50 to 75 minutes, with therapeutic plasma levels at 6 to 13 $\mu$g/ml; adverse effects are reported in levels above 20 $\mu$g/ml. In adults, caffeine is excreted by the kidneys, with only 1% to 2% excreted unchanged; in neonates it is excreted by the kidneys, with approximately 85% excreted unchanged.

**TABLE 16-5** Caffeine: dosage and administration

| | Adults | Children |
|---|---|---|
| caffeine tablets (NoDoz, Quick Pep, Vivarin) | 100-200 mg orally, repeat in 3-4 hr if necessary. Maximum, 1000 mg in 24 hr. | Children less than 12 yr old, use not recommended. |
| caffeine extended-release capsules (Caffedrine, Dexitac) | 200-250 mg orally, repeat in 3-4 hr if necessary. Maximum, 1 g/day. | Children less than 12 yr old, use not recommended. |

***Side effects/adverse reactions.*** More frequent side effects include increased nervousness or jittery feelings and irritation of GI tract resulting in nausea.

More frequent adverse reactions in neonates include abdominal swelling or distension, vomiting, body tremors, tachycardia, jitters, or nervousness.

Signs of overdose are increased temperature, headache, increased irritability and sensitivity to pain or touch, increased urination, confusion, dehydration, abdominal pain, agitation, muscle twitching, nausea and vomiting, tinnitus, insomnia, and convulsions.

***Significant drug interactions.*** The following effects may occur when caffeine is given with the drugs listed below:

| Drug | Possible effect and management |
|---|---|
| other CNS-stimulating drugs, other caffeine-containing medications or drinks | May result in increased CNS stimulation and undesirable side effects, such as increased nervousness, irritability, insomnia, dysrhythmias, and seizures. Monitor client's apical pulse and behaviors closely. |
| monoamine oxidase (MAO) inhibitors | With large doses of caffeine, may produce hypertension or dangerous dysrhythmias. Monitor vital signs closely. |

***Dosage and administration.*** See Table 16-5.

***Pregnancy safety.*** Has not been established.

▷ **Nursing Management: Caffeine**

***Assessment.*** Assessment of caffeine intake should be a routine part of the nursing drug history. This includes caffeine intake from foods and beverages, as well as from medications.

Caffeine may exacerbate gastric ulceration in peptic ulcer disease and so should be used cautiously in clients with a history of peptic ulcer.

Because of its suspected potential for causing dysrhythmias, it is recommended that clients with symptomatic cardiac dysrhythmias or palpitations and clients in the recovery phase of acute myocardial infarctions avoid using caffeine.

The FDA has warned women to avoid or to decrease caffeine consumption during pregnancy. Although there is no direct link between human malformation and caffeine intake, a daily consumption of caffeine (600 mg or more) has been associated with human fetal death and birth defects.

Nurses in various settings should instruct pregnant and child-bearing-age women to avoid drugs and sodas containing caffeine. Women who continue to drink coffee during their pregnancy should be encouraged to drink decaffeinated or instant coffee and to limit their coffee intake to 2 to 3 cups a day. Those who drink tea should decrease the brewing time or select a decaffeinated brand or herb tea. The best solution would be to substitute fruit and vegetable juices or water for beverages that contain caffeine.

***Education.*** A client who is or may become pregnant should be advised to avoid or limit her consumption of caffeine-containing foods (e.g., coffee, tea, cola drinks, cocoa, and milk chocolate) and drugs (e.g., OTC stimulants, analgesic combinations, and cold preparations), because there is evidence that caffeine may be an animal teratogen. Further studies are needed to establish a relationship between caffeine and human birth defects.

Caffeine passes into breast milk and may accumulate in nursing infants. Research suggests that when nursing mothers consume large amounts of caffeine, their babies may appear jittery and have trouble sleeping.

When taken close to bedtime, medications and beverages containing caffeine may interfere with sleep. Caffeine is not intended to replace sleep and should not be used for that purpose.

Clients with a hypersensitivity to caffeine should be alerted to its combination with analgesics (acetaminophen, aspirin, and phenacetin) for the treatment of headache. Because the adverse CNS effects for the drug are increased in children, these same combination preparations should be avoided for pediatric use.

***Evaluation.*** The question is sometimes raised whether or not caffeine causes physical and psychologic dependence. Many persons note that if they do not have their usual cup or two of coffee in the morning, they feel irritable and nervous and develop a headache. This probably indicates psychologic and physical dependence. Such clients should be instructed to decrease their caffeine intake by gradually reducing the number of servings of coffee, cola, and tea or by mixing the amounts with decaffeinated preparations and gradually decreasing the proportion of the caffeinated form.

## SUMMARY

The CNS stimulants have limited use in practice today. Although used in the past for the treatment of obesity, their narrow therapeutic index and the rapid development of tolerance before significant weight reduction occurs has discouraged this use. Their prime indications are for attention deficit disorder and narcolepsy. When used for their anorexiant effect, they are an adjunct to a diet and exercise regimen. Because stimulation of the CNS occurs, clients may experience sleep pattern disturbance, altered thought processes, changes in sexual desire or ability, and altered comfort related to side effects such as dry mouth, headache, rash, gastrointestinal or urinary effects. Caffeine, although not often thought of as a drug, is also a CNS stimulant, and the nurse should take an active role in educating clients to the effects of its ingestion.

## BIBLIOGRAPHY

Aaronson LS et al. (1989). Tobacco, alcohol, and caffeine use during pregnancy, J Obstet Gynecol Neonatal Nurs 18(4):279.

American Hospital Formulary Service. (1991). AHFS drug information '91. Bethesda, Md: American Society of Hospital Pharmacists, Inc.

Brooten D et al. (1987). A survey of nutrition, caffeine, cigarette and alcohol intake in early pregnancy in an urban clinic population, J Nurse Midwifery 32(2):85.

Brown RT et al. (1984). How much stimulant medication is appropriate for hyperactive school children? J Sch Health 54(3):128.

Brugess KE. (1985). Nursing alert: understanding the spectrum of cerebral stimulants, Nursing 15(7):50.

Freeman DJ. (1986). The effectiveness of doxapram administration in hastening arousal following general anesthesia in outpatients, J Assoc Nurs Anesthetists 54(1):16.

Gilman AG et al, eds. (1990). Goodman and Gilman's the pharmacological basis of therapeutics, ed 8. New York: Macmillan Publishing Co.

Hall JN. (1987). Update on designer drugs, Street Pharmacologist 11(3):3.

Hallal JC. (1986). Are coffee, cold tablets, and chocolate innocuous or is caffeine hazardous to your patient's health? Am J Nurs 86(4):424.

Kunkel DB. (1985). The toxic emergency, Top Emerg Med 17(21):81.

Kurppa K et al. (1983). Coffee consumption during pregnancy and selected congenital malformations: a nationwide case-control study, Am J Public Health 73(12):1397.

Noerr B. (1989). Caffeine citrate: pointers in practical pharmacology, Neonatal Netw 7(6):86.

Raebel MA and Black J. (1984). The caffeine controversy: what are the facts? Hosp Formul 19(4):257.

Rossignol AM. (1985). Caffeine-containing beverages and premenstrual syndrome in young women, Am J Public Health 75(11):1335.

Schneider JR. (1988). Should patients with myocardial infarction receive caffeinated coffee? Focus Crit Care 15(1):52.

Schneider JR. (1987). Effects of caffeine ingestion on heart rate, blood pressure, myocardial oxygen consumption, and cardiac rhythm in acute myocardial infarction patients, Heart Lung 16(2):167.

Silver LB and Brunstetter RW. (1986). Attention deficit disorder in adolescents, Hosp Community Psychiatry 37(6):608.

Todd B. (1987). Drugs and the elderly: cigarettes and caffeine in drug interactions, Geriatr Nurs 8(2):97.

United States Pharmacopeial Convention. (1991). Drug information for the health care professional, ed 11. Rockville, Md: The Convention.

Wilson MC et al. (1986). Drug use in sports, Pediatr Nurs 12(6):452.

Worthington-Roberts B and Weigle A. (1983). Caffeine and pregnancy outcomes, J Obstet Gynecol Nurs 12(3):21.

*Chapter*

# 17 Psychotherapeutic Drugs

## CHAPTER OBJECTIVES

*After studying this chapter, you should be able to meet the following objectives and define the key terms.*

1. Discuss the use of drug therapy in psychiatry.

2. Identify the common psychotropic drugs.

3. Differentiate between phenothiazine derivatives, tricyclics, monoamine oxidase inhibitors, and lithium.

4. Discuss nursing management of the common side effects/adverse reactions of psychotherapeutic agents.

5. Identify common tyramine-containing substances and their interaction with MAO inhibitor drugs.

6. Formulate an appropriate plan of care for individual clients who require the administration of psychotherapeutic agents.

## KEY TERMS

**affective disorder,** page 337

**choreoathetoid motion,** page 326

**endogenous depression,** page 337

**exogenous depression,** page 337

**mania,** page 349

**neuroleptic malignant syndrome (NMS),** page 335

**neurotransmitter,** page 320

**tardive dyskinesia (TD),** page 326

**Tourette's syndrome,** page 333

**tranquilizer,** page 323

## INTRODUCTION

Medications discussed in this chapter include the antipsychotic agents, antidepressants, and lithium. Such drugs are used to treat psychoses and affective disorders, especially schizophrenia, depression, and mania. The student is referred to Chapter 11 for a review of the physiology and functions of the various components of the central nervous system (CNS). It is necessary to review the CNS functional systems (i.e., reticular activating system, limbic and extrapyramidal systems, plus acetylcholine and catecholamines) to enhance understanding of this chapter.

## ANATOMY AND PHYSIOLOGY OF EMOTIONS

To understand the action of drugs in alleviating the symptoms of mental illness, the health care provider must have knowledge of the functioning of the nervous system. The trend toward a holistic view of human beings and their phenomenologic experience no longer allows the practitioner to separate the functions of the mind from the body. Neurophysiologists traditionally have identified each part of the nervous system by a specific function or made tentative architectonic maps of the cerebral cortex, allocating specific functions to various areas of the brain. Research has indicated a change in this perspective. The brain is considered to be a single organ composed of various structures that produce a final, unified effect when they react with each other normally. The interrelationship of various structures is intricate, and allocating special functions to each structure is difficult.

Research has revealed methods for measuring certain types of brain activity, and such information has made it possible to speculate in some detail on the physiologic substrates of emotional activity. For purposes of clarity in the discussion of the neuroanatomic and neurophysiologic bases of emotions, the various aspects of the nervous system are discussed under the following headings:

1. Central nervous system
2. Autonomic regulation
3. Biochemical mechanisms

## Central Nervous System

The CNS functions in the coordination and direction of activities in the tissues and organs of the body. The various parts and levels of the CNS form a closely related and integrated series of mechanisms and systems through which the human being achieves adjustment and adaptation to the environment. The CNS is responsible for consciousness, behavior, memory, recognition, learning, and the more highly developed attributes such as imagination, abstract reasoning, and creative thought. In addition, it serves to coordinate such vital regulatory functions as blood pressure, heart rate, respiration, salivary and gastric secretions, muscular activity, and body temperature. Discussion is limited to consideration of CNS functions believed to affect the emotions and behavior.

The cerebrum, the largest part of the brain, is divided into two hemispheres. The outer surface of the cerebral hemispheres is composed of gray matter known as the cerebral cortex. It is believed to be the site of consciousness and is divided into sensory, motor, and association areas. These areas receive sensations from organs of special sense (sight, hearing, smell, taste), as well as from the skin, muscles, joints, and tendons (touch, pain, temperature). Large parts of the cortex now appear to function as a whole in providing the anatomic basis for such mental attributes as recognition, memory, intelligence, imagination, and creative thought.

Beneath the cortex are tracts of fibers comprising the white matter, which connect the lower centers of the brain, spinal cord, and associated areas of the cortex with each other. The basal ganglia (corpus striatum, claustrum, amygdaloid nucleus) are located near the lateral ventricle of the cerebrum. The hippocampus, a mass of gray matter lying close to the lateral ventricle, is connected by a tract of fibers (the fornix) to the mamillary bodies in the hypothalamus. The hippocampus, the fornix, the amygdaloid nucleus, the hippocampal gyrus, and the uncus are collectively referred to as the "limbic system." This system is believed to be concerned with the conscious experience of emotion.

The midbrain, pons, and medulla form the part of the brain below the cerebrum. The midbrain contains the nuclei of cranial nerves III and IV. The pons is mainly a pathway for ascending and descending tracts of the fibers. The medulla oblongata is continuous with the spinal cord. It contains vital groups of synapses that are concerned with the reflex control of blood pressure (vasomotor center), heart rate and force (cardiac center), respiration (respiratory center), and vomiting (vomiting center). The reticular formation consists of a complex network of cell bodies and interlacing fibers in the medulla, pons, midbrain, and diencephalon. The reticular activating system (Figure 17-1) is believed to function in alerting the cortex to sensory stimuli and in originating the emotional reactions associated with somatic sensory experiences (pain, touch, hearing, sight). Experimental stimulation of this system produces alertness in behavior, whereas a decrease in activity leads to relaxation and drowsiness. The reticular activating system has its upper end in the posterior hypothalamus and lower thalamus.

The cerebellum lies on the dorsal side of the pons and is attached to the brainstem. It functions as part of the feedback mechanisms concerned with subconscious control of equilibrium, posture, and movement.

The thalamus and hypothalamus are located in the region of the brain that is called the diencephalon (the "between-brain"). Most sensations are relayed through the thalamus to the cerebral cortex. The conscious appreciation of pain is said to be located in the thalamus. In recent years knowledge about the functions of the hypothalamus gradually has increased. Despite extensive research and experimentation, however, there still seems to be some question of its specific mode of function. It has been conjectured that the hypothalamus contains integrative mechanisms that, in addition to their effect on behavior patterns, also aid in regulating the basic human life functions (control of water excretion, appetite, sleep-wake mechanisms, temperature, blood pressure). The hypothalamus seems to function through its relationships with other parts of the nervous system and endocrine system. It is part of a system of complex circuits within the brain so strategically placed that its derangement may have profound effects.

These interrelationships among the various circuits in the brain produce patterns of behavior that can be modified by external situations or by internal autonomic adjustments. This allows the individual to adapt to changes in both external and internal environments.

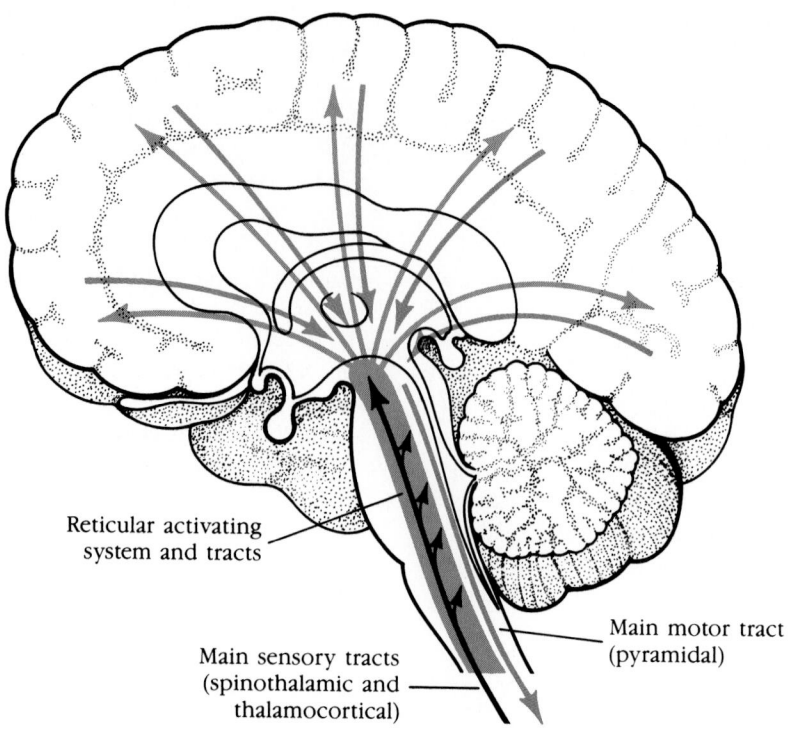

**FIGURE 17-1** Reticular activating system.

## Autonomic Regulation

The functions of the sympathetic and parasympathetic visceral nervous systems are discussed in Chapter 19. These systems play an important role in the production of behavior. An understanding of these mechanisms is the basis for learning the actions and side effects of the drugs affecting mood and behavior. The importance of these systems' reactions in the production of behavior is paramount in gaining an understanding of drug action or the behavioral manifestations of side effects from the use of drugs.

## Biochemical Mechanisms

The functions of the CNS depend on the actions of certain neurohormonal agents located in the brain and peripheral tissues. These neurohormones are stored in inactive forms; and at the right moment nerve impulses release their free forms, which then stimulate transmission of appropriate reactions.

Nerve impulses are conducted along the nerve cell by electric impulse and between nerve cells by chemical means. The **neurotransmitter** is the chemical substance that transmits an impulse or message from neuron to neuron; it is synthesized and stored in the presynaptic neuron. When the

presynaptic neuron is stimulated by an electric impulse, it releases the neurotransmitter into the synapse, allowing it to cross the synapse and come into contact with the postsynaptic site. This in turn is the stimulus to which the postsynaptic site responds.

The postsynaptic cell may be another nerve cell that responds by releasing a neurotransmitter, or it may be a muscle cell that responds by contracting or relaxing, as discussed earlier. In either case the neurotransmitter exerts its action by interacting with the receptor (a specialized protein), located on the outermost part of the postsynaptic cell. This produces both electric and biochemical change within the postsynaptic cell.

The postsynaptic cell can be made more or less sensitive to the neurotransmitter by various processes or chemicals. Desensitization, or reduced sensitivity of the postsynaptic cell, can be caused by tachyphylaxis or tolerance, which requires more neurotransmitter to produce a response in the postsynaptic cell. Supersensitivity, or increased sensitivity of the postsynaptic cell, can be caused by prolonged blockade with drugs called antagonists, which bind to the postsynaptic cell without activating it. In these cases the postsynaptic cell responds to less neurotransmitter substance.

Evidence shows that acetylcholine is released from central neural tissue, such as the surface of the cerebral cortex, into

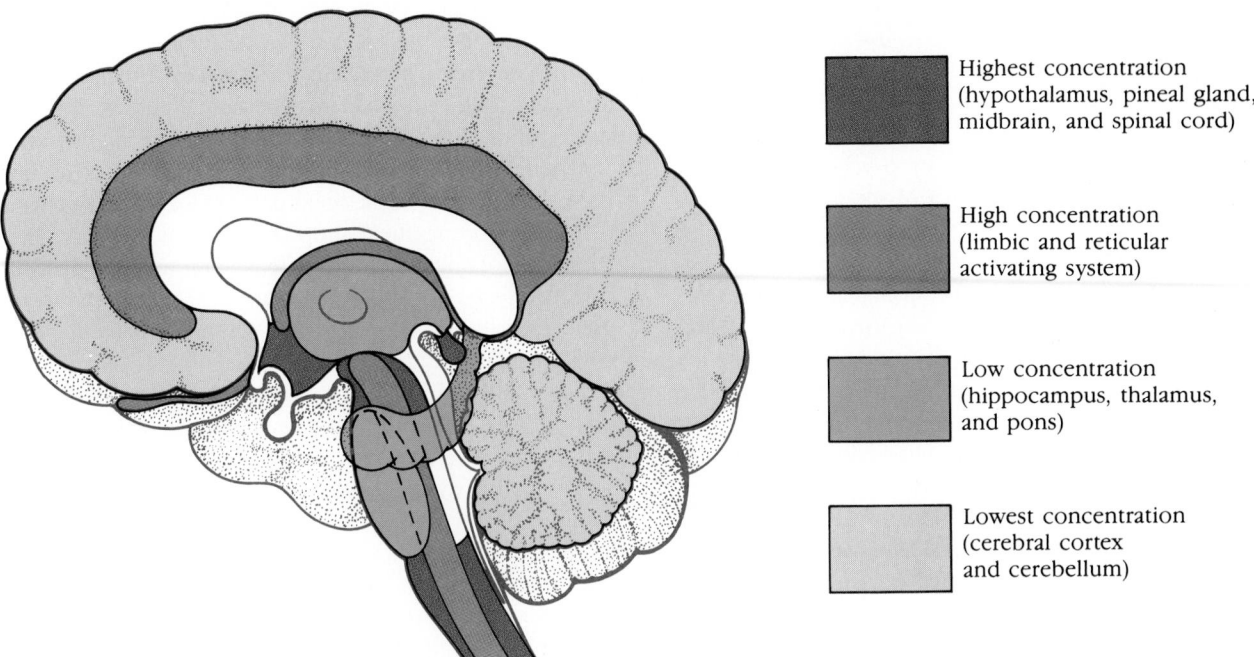

Highest concentration
(hypothalamus, pineal gland,
midbrain, and spinal cord)

High concentration
(limbic and reticular
activating system)

Low concentration
(hippocampus, thalamus,
and pons)

Lowest concentration
(cerebral cortex
and cerebellum)

**FIGURE 17-2** Comparative concentration of serotonin and norepinephrine in various parts of the brain.

the cerebrospinal fluid during activity. The rate of release is proportional to the level of activity, which is how it is known that some central synapses are cholinergic.

Norepinephrine also has been found in the CNS. Tyrosine and dopamine are normal constituents of the brain and known precursors of norepinephrine synthesis. High concentrations of norepinephrine are found in the hypothalamus, medulla, limbic system, and cranial nerve nuclei. Low concentrations are found in the striatum and caudate nucleus, where dopamine, the immediate precursor of norepinephrine, is found in high concentration (Figure 17-2). It is believed that both norepinephrine and dopamine function as transmitters. They have widespread inhibitory and excitatory effects on a wide variety of centrally mediated functions, such as sleep and arousal, affect, and memory. Thus some central synapses are adrenergic.

Serotonin is another transmitter substance found in the CNS. Areas rich in serotonin include the hypothalamus, pineal gland, midbrain, and spinal cord (see Figure 17-2). Serotonin is synthesized in the brain and stored in the subcellular particles. Alteration of the level of serotonin in the nervous system is associated with changes in behavior. Many drugs mimic or block the action of serotonin on peripheral tissues and produce changes in mood and behavior, which suggests that they interfere with the action of serotonin and norepinephrine in the brain.

Other proposed central neurotransmitters include histamine, amino acids (i.e., glutamate, glycine, excitatory transmitters, aspartate, and GABA, substance P (a polypeptide composed of 13 different amino acids), prostaglandins, and the endorphins.

The relationship of dopamine to major psychoses has received much attention. Drugs such as the phenothiazines block the effects of dopamine and function as antipsychotic agents.

## ROLE OF DRUG THERAPY IN PSYCHIATRY

Drugs play an important role in contemporary approaches of psychiatric care. The development of the tranquilizing drugs opened many avenues of treatment previously unavailable. Although many emphasize milieu factors in therapy, drug therapy is a valuable adjunct to providing comprehensive psychiatric care.

Drug therapy alleviates symptoms and allows the client an opportunity to participate more easily in other forms of treatment. Drugs temporarily modify behavior, whereas other therapies, such as psychotherapy, can shape behavior and produce a permanent change. Some drugs disrupt patterns of behavior or modify the electric patterns of fields within the brain that produce changes. However, any enduring effects on behavior are more likely to result from the individual's concurrent interaction with the environment. Since incoming information must be translated into biochemical changes before it can affect nervous system function, environmental transactions, as with drugs, may affect similar pathways before influencing behavior. Their effects can be additive, potentiating, or antagonistic, depending on their nature and direction. The milieu may potentiate the effectiveness of the drug or may detract from it.

In the past, physicians selected psychotherapeutic agents on the basis of the diagnostic category—schizophrenia, manic-depressive syndrome, or psychoneurosis. More recent proposals, however, have indicated a radical change in the physician's approach.

The pharmacologic treatment of psychiatric disorders would appear to be similar to that of somatic disorders—modifying the most disabling components of behavior so that the client may cope more effectively with the environment and take advantage of the therapeutic milieu available. The physician should try to match a particular drug's therapeutic advantages to the client's symptoms, assuming the person's diagnosis warrants the use of an antipsychotic agent. Since the introduction of the antipsychotic and other psychotropic agents, they have been widely prescribed, especially in the elderly. The National Nursing Home Survey (Burn, 1988) reported that only 45% of 212 psychotropic prescriptions for nursing home residents were appropriate, when compared with the individual diagnosis as documented in each client's chart. Beardsley (1989) and Jenike (1988) discuss how the inappropriate use of psychotropic agents is dangerous for the elderly since it exposes the older person to an increased risk of adverse or serious drug reactions that are often detrimental to cognitive and functional health status. This awareness has resulted in new regulations governing Medicare and Medicaid recipients in long-term care facilities that took effect in 1990.

For antipsychotic drugs to be prescribed, an appropriate specific condition must be documented, such as schizophrenia, schizo-affective disorder, delusional disorder, psychotic mood disorder, acute psychotic episode, brief reactive psychosis, schizophreniform disorder, atypical psychosis, Tourette's disorder, Huntington's disease, organic mental syndromes that have associated psychotic or agitation features. These features are defined as (1) specific behaviors that can be quantitatively and objectively documented (biting, kicking, scratching, etc.) that cause the client to present a danger to himself or others and actually interfere with the nursing staff's ability to provide care to the client; or (2) the presence of psychotic symptoms (delusions, hallucinations or paranoid behavior) that are not a result of a previously mentioned disorder but cause the resident extreme distress. To treat the symptoms of hiccups, nausea, vomiting, or pruritus, short-term therapy of a week is allowable.

The purpose of this regulation is to eliminate or reduce the inappropriate prescribing of such potent medications for behaviors that may be controlled by nonpharmacological approaches. For example, the presence of insomnia, pacing, wandering, restlessness, crying spells or screaming episodes, deficient memory, uncooperativeness, nervousness, or depression would not be acceptable reasons alone for the use of an antipsychotic agent. Such symptoms would have to be associated with an appropriate diagnosis as mentioned previously for an antipsychotic drug to be indicated.

Many other safeguards and issues are included in this regulation, such as drug holidays, medication errors, and drug regimen reviews. The student is referred to the current Medicare and Medicaid standards for further information and specifications for skilled and intermediate nursing facilities.

When the physician establishes the need for drug therapy, it must be decided what agent or combination of agents is best suited for the client's total health needs. This requires an intimate knowledge of the behavioral actions, pharmacologic effects, and potential adverse reactions of the agents used, as well as an awareness of the many individual and environmental factors present.

The additional effects or side effect profile of a drug is a useful tool in helping the physician select an appropriate antipsychotic agent (Table 17-1). If a drug with a strong sedation property is desired, chlorpromazine or thioridazine would probably be selected. If extrapyramidal side effects are particulary troublesome, the same two drugs have the least potential of inducing extrapyramidal side effects; thioridazine has the greatest anticholinergic effect, thus reducing its potential for this adverse effect.

If anticholinergic side effects such as dry mouth, blurred vision, constipation, and urinary retention continue and are disturbing to the client, the physician could select an agent with less potential of inducing such effects, such as fluphenazine (Prolixin, Permitil), thiothixene (Navane), or haloperidol (Haldol).

Continuous nursing and medical evaluation based on observation of the drug's effects is needed. An increase or reduction of dosage may be indicated to achieve the desired effects. Nurses play an important role in the evaluation and assessment of a client's response to drug therapy. They should be aware of the criteria the physician uses in selecting psychotherapeutic drugs and the expected effects so they can observe and report on the client's progress. This progress is evaluated by monitoring the client's behavioral and affective responses to the medications; the client's knowledge of the drug therapy; the presence and extent of expected side effects and adverse reactions and their response to dosage adjustment and supportive nursing interventions; and the potential for, or existence of, drug or food interactions. Knowledge of the action of drugs also assists health care providers in understanding the interpersonal responses that occur in the therapeutic client relationship with the client.

## ANTIPSYCHOTIC OR NEUROLEPTIC AGENTS
### Historical Background

Between 1900 and 1950 the population of the United States doubled, and the population in public mental hospitals quadrupled. The increase was from 130,000 to over a half million clients. During this time the average length of confinement was usually years, and the trend was definitely toward an

**TABLE 17-1**   Classification of selected antipsychotic agents and potential side effects

| Chemical class, generic name (trade name) | Potential frequency of side effects* | | | | |
| --- | --- | --- | --- | --- | --- |
| | **Sedation** | **Hypotension** | **Extrapyramidal** | **Anticholinergic** | **Antiemetic** |
| PHENOTHIAZINE, ALIPHATIC | | | | | |
| chlorpromazine (Thorazine, Largactil ♣ ) | 4 | 4 | 2 | 3 | 4 |
| PHENOTHIAZINE, PIPERIDINE | | | | | |
| thioridazine (Mellaril, Novoridazine ♣ ) | 3 | 3-4 | 1 | 3-4 | 1 |
| mesoridazine (Serentil) | 4 | 3-4 | 1 | 3-4 | 1 |
| PHENOTHIAZINE, PIPERAZINE | | | | | |
| trifluoperazine (Stelazine, Soloazine ♣ ) | 1-2 | 1 | 4 | 1 | 4 |
| fluphenazine (Permitil, Prolixin, Apo-Fluphenazine ♣ ) | 1 | 1 | 4 | 1 | 1 |
| perphenazine (Trilafon, Phenazine ♣ ) | 1-2 | 1 | 4 | 2-3 | 4 |
| prochlorperazine maleate (Compazine, Stemetil ♣ ) | 2-3 | 1 | 4 | 1 | 4 |
| BUTYROPHENONE | | | | | |
| haloperidol (Haldol, Novoperidol ♣ ) | 1-2 | 1 | 4 | 2-3 | 3 |
| THIOXANTHENE | | | | | |
| thiothixene (Navane) | 1-2 | 1 | 2 | 1 | † |
| DIHYDROINDOLONES | | | | | |
| molindone (Lidone, Moban) | 2-3 | 2-3 | 3-4 | 3-4 | † |
| DIBENZOXAZEPINES | | | | | |
| loxapine (Loxitane, Loxapac ♣ ) | 2-3 | 2-3 | 4 | 2-3 | † |
| clozapine‡ (Clozaril) | 3-4 | 1-2 | 1 | 1-2 | 1 |

*Potential frequencies are ranked from the least (1) to most frequent occurrence (4).

†Not documented or unknown.

‡Clozapine is only available in the US through a controlled management system. It has the potential of inducing a life-threatening agranulocytosis, thus it is reserved for clients that are nonresponsive to a minimum of two trials of different antipsychotic agents. Close monitoring with laboratory testing is required for usage of this drug product.

increase in clients admitted to such institutions yearly. Also, client and employee injuries caused by combative or abusive clients led to the use of physical restraints and client isolation.

For hundreds of years the treatment of mentally disturbed clients consisted of isolation (i.e., hidden in cellars or attics in their homes); if they came to the attention of local authorities, they were transferred to jails or homes for the insane. Actual therapies before the antipsychotic agents were limited to water or ice pack therapies, strait-jackets or the use of other physical restraints, shock therapy with insulin or electricity, lobotomy, and the use of a few drugs, such as paraldehyde, chloral hydrate, and the barbiturates.

Chlorpromazine (Thorazine) was the first **tranquilizer,** released in the early 1950s. However, the term "tranquilizer" had been used approximately 200 years ago by Dr. Benjamin Rush. Dr. Rush, an early pioneer in the mental health field and a signer of the Declaration of Independence, invented a restraining chair named the "tranquilizer chair" (Lyons and Petrucelli, 1978). This chair was modified by the addition of a pulley system, so that the extremely agitated client would be seated and restrained in the chair and the chair would be raised off the ground and rocked back and forth until the client was quieted (Figure 17-3). Thus the name tranquilizer chair. Neither the tranquilizer chair nor the tranquilizing agents cure mental illness. They have been and are used to control the symptoms associated with this disease state; the chair provides physical and eventually physiologic restraints, whereas the antipsychotic and tranquilizing agents constitute a chemical control of the symptoms.

The advent of antipsychotic drugs has proved to be a revolutionary force in the psychiatric field. Institutionalization time has decreased from years to months for many clients, and others live at home and are treated at community mental health centers. The reported incidences of injuries

**FIGURE 17-3** Tranquilizer or restraining chair used in the eighteenth century to "tranquilize" the agitated client.

have declined, along with the decrease in size or closing of many large public mental health facilities.

## Phenothiazine Derivatives

Discovery of the phenothiazine derivatives arose out of research in the area of the antihistamines. Chlorpromazine hydrochloride was introduced in 1951 and has found wide acceptance in the treatment of mental illness. Additional investigation of the action of chlorpromazine in producing undesirable side effects led to the development of numerous derivatives, which now comprise the largest group of psychotropic agents.

About two thirds of all antipsychotic drugs are phenothiazine derivatives. They are commonly divided chemically into the following three subgroups: (1) the aliphatic compounds (chlorpromazine, triflupromazine), (2) the piperidine compounds (mesoridazine, piperacetazine, thioridazine), and (3) the piperazine compounds (acetophenazine, carphenazine, fluphenazine, perphenazine, prochlorperazine, trifluoperazine). Although a close structural similarity exists, thioxanthene derivatives (thiothixene, chlorprothixene) are not phenothiazine derivatives. The chemical structure of these compounds and specific information regarding their action, effects, and adverse reactions are presented

separately after the general discussion of similarities. The type of action is essentially similar with all phenothiazine derivatives; individual compounds vary chiefly in their potency and in the nature and severity of their side effects.

*Mechanism of action.* Although the exact mechanism of action for the antipsychotic effects is unknown, a primary effect is the blockage of dopamine receptors in specific areas of the CNS. Dopamine is a major neurotransmitter in the mesolimbic (subcortical and basal ganglia) areas of the brain. These are the areas associated with emotions, cognitive functioning, and motor functions. Thus the major therapeutic effects and side affects are a result of the dopamine blockade in these areas.

In addition, phenothiazines may also produce an alpha-blocking effect (hypotension), depression of hormonal release from the hypothalamus and pituitary glands, inhibition or blockade of dopamine at the chemoreceptor trigger zone (CTZ) and peripherally, inhibition of the vagus nerve in the gastrointestinal tract (antiemetic effect). They produce an antianxiety effect by depression of the brainstem reticular system. Methotrimeprazine (Levoprome) is a phenothiazine with primarily analgesic and sedative effects. It is not usually used as an antipsychotic drug in the United States. Most phenothiazines and haloperidol increase prolactin release,

**FIGURE 17-4**  Persistent tardive dyskinesia. **A,** In-and-out movements of the tongue. **B,** Sucking and smacking of the lips. **C,** Lateral jaw movements. Lingual and facial hyperkinesias.

which infrequently results in swelling of the breast and milk secretion. Clozapine is not the typical antipsychotic drug because it has a greater effect in the limbic area than at the striatal dopamine receptors. Therefore it produces considerably less extrapyramidal side effects than the other antipsychotic agents. It also produces little, if any, prolactin secretion.

***Indications.***  Phenothiazine derivatives are used in the treatment of psychosis, nausea and vomiting (especially with prochlorperazine, chlorpromazine, perphenazine, and triflupromazine), pain and sedation (methotrimeprazine), adjunct to treatment of tetanus (chlorpromazine), acute intermittent porphyria (chlorpromazine), and intractable hiccups (chlorpromazine). Clozapine is only indicated for the treatment of severely ill schizophrenic clients who have failed to respond to other antipsychotic drug therapies. Haloperidol is also indicated for the treatment of Gilles de la Tourette's syndrome. Pimozide, an analog of butyrophe-

none, is indicated for the treatment of Tourette's syndrome in persons who cannot tolerate or have failed to respond to haloperidol therapy. See box and Figures 17-4 and 17-5 on tardive dysknesia.

***Pharmacokinetics.***  Phenothiazines are well absorbed when given orally. The onset of action when given orally occurs between ½ and 1 hour; when given IM it occurs within 30 minutes with exception of long-acting parenteral forms, i.e., fluphenazine, haloperidol decanoate, and fluphenazine enanthate. Duration of action for haloperidol averages 21 hours (range 13 to 35 hr); for loxapine, duration is up to 12 hours; for thiothexene, it lasts approximately 30 hours; for phenothiazines, 6 to 36 hours or more, depending on dosage and frequency of drug administration. Clozapine single dose has a half-life (elimination) of 8 hours, while the half-life at steady state increases to 12 hours (range 4 to 66 hr). Phenothiazines are metabolized in the liver and excreted primarily by the kidneys.

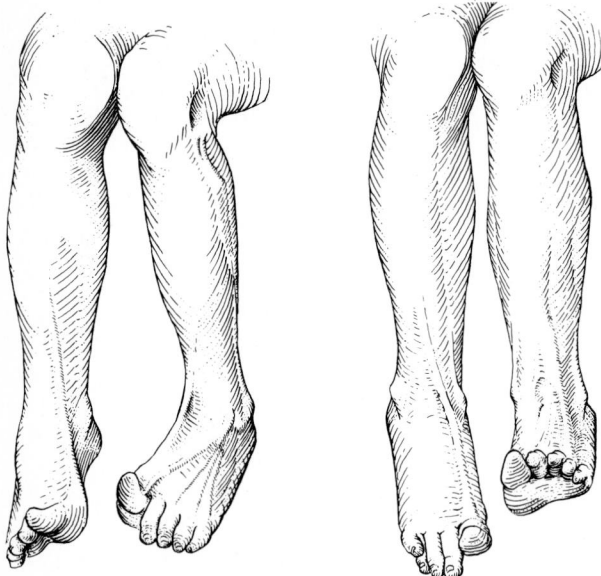

**FIGURE 17-5**  Abnormal (choreoathetoid) movements of extremities in persistent tardive dyskinesia. Complication of long-term therapy with antipsychotics (neuroleptics).

***Side effects/adverse reactions.*** See Table 17-2.

***Significant drug interactions.*** The following effects may occur when antipsychotic agents are given with the drugs listed below:

| Drug | Possible Effect and Management |
|---|---|
| alcohol, CNS depressants | May result in enhanced CNS depression, respiratory depression, and increased hypotensive effects. |
| | Reduce drug dosage to one fourth to one half usual dose. |
| | Concurrent alcohol use may increase the potential risk of inducing a heat stroke. Avoid concurrent drug administration. |
| | Barbiturates may decrease chlorpromazine serum levels through an increase in the liver metabolizing enzymes. Thioridazine may decrease serum phenobarbital serum levels. Monitor closely for loss of therapeutic effect since a dosage adjustment may be necessary. |
| anticholinergics | Concurrent drug usage with clozapine may result in an increase in anticholinergic side effects. |
| anticoagulant (warfarin) and digoxin | Clozapine is highly protein bound. Concurrent drug usage may increase the serum levels of warfarin, digoxin, or clozapine resulting in drug toxicity. Monitor closely as dosage adjustments may be necessary. |
| antihypertensive agents | Concurrent drug usage with clozapine may result in an increase in hypotensive side effects. |
| antithyroid medications | Increases the risk for agranulocytosis when phenothiazines are given concurrently. |

## TARDIVE DYSKINESIA

**Tardive dyskinesia** (TD) is a potentially irreversible neurologic disorder that primarily involves the buccolingual and masticatory muscles. This adverse effect to the antipsychotic agents may occur within a few months or years of treatment or after these agents have been discontinued. The risk of inducing TD increases with total dosage of the drug given and the length of the treatment period.

Incidence: Although 0.5% to 65% of the treated population may develop this syndrome, recent reports place the percentage of clients at risk as 10% to 20%.

Presenting features:

Facial: grimacing or scowl expression, facial tics, arching of the eyebrows

Ocular: blinking, eyelid spasms (blepharospasm)

Oral/buccal: lip smacking, lower lip thrusting, sucking, puffing of cheeks, chewing of the cheeks (the inside of the mouth should be checked for this)

Lingual/masticatory: lateral jaw movements, tongue protrusion or thrusting such as "fly catching movements," tongue in lip or cheek resulting in an observable bulge in the specific area (Figure 17-4).

Systemic effects: foot tapping; rocking from side to side; arms, hands, and fingers may display a jerking and/or a writhing motion (**choreoathetoid motion**) (Figure 17-5); pelvic thrusting motions.

Treatment: Prevention only. Early assessment and diagnosis is crucial in preventing the development of an irreversible disorder. Decreasing or discontinuing the antipsychotic agent if possible is the recommended procedure (Kalachnik, 1983, United States Pharmacopeial Convention, 1991). At present, there is no known effective treatment for TD.

Data from Kalachnik JE. (1983). Tardine dyskinesia, Minn Pharmacist 37(4):14.

| Drug | Possible Effect and Management |
|---|---|
| Bone marrow suppressing agents | Concurrent drug usage with clozapine may increase the potential of severe bone marrow suppression. Avoid concurrent use of any other drugs that suppress bone marrow function. |
| epinephrine | Antipsychotic agents may block alpha-adrenergic receptors, thus concurrent administration of epinephrine may result in severe lowering of the blood pressure (hypotension) and tachycardia. Avoid concurrent administration. |
| extrapyramidal inducing medications (such as amoxapine, droperidol, metoclopramide, reserpine, metyrosine, papaverine) | May result in increased frequency and severe extrapyramidal effects. |

**TABLE 17-2** Side effects/adverse reactions of antipsychotic medications

| Side effects* | Adverse reactions† |
|---|---|
| More frequent: sleepiness, dizziness, dry mouth, constipation, and nasal congestion reported with aliphatic and piperidine phenothiazines and thioxanthenes. Incidence is less with the piperazine phenothiazines with the exception of perphenazine. | Visual changes, hypotensive episodes (more common with aliphatic and piperidine phenothiazines, thioxanthenes, and possibly, molindone) |
| thioxanthenes: skin sensitivity to the sun | Dystonia and/or parkinson-type side effects including shuffle in walk, arm or leg stiffness, tremors, masklike facial expression, dysphagia, imbalance, muscle spasms or unusual twisting effects of face, neck, or back (more common with aliphatic and piperazine phenothiazines, thioxanthines, loxapine, molindone, and haloperidol) |
| loxapine: most often seen are blurred vision, confusion, dizziness, dry mouth, and increase in body weight | |
| haloperidol: usually blurred vision, constipation, dry mouth, and increase in body weight | Akathisia, increased pacing, restlessness, and insomnia (more often reported with haloperidol, loxapine, thioxanthene) |
| molindone: usually sedation, blurred vision, dry mouth, and constipation | Tardive dyskinesia, a very serious adverse reaction; although rare, neuroleptic malignant syndrome (NMS) may occur |
| clozapine: may cause sedation, dizziness, constipation, insomnia, headaches, tremor, and nausea | clozapine can cause agranulocytosis, hypotension, tachycardia, and seizures |

*If side effects continue, increase, or disturb the client, inform the physician.
†If adverse reactions occur, contact the physician, since medical intervention may be necessary.

| Drug | Possible Effect and Management |
|---|---|
| guanadrel or guanethidine | Concurrent use with antipsychotic agents, especially loxapine and thiothixenes, may reverse the hypotensive drug effectiveness. Closely monitor all clients receiving this drug combination. |
| levodopa | Concurrent use may render levodopa ineffective in controlling Parkinson's disease. |
| lithium | Phenothiazines may (1) decrease GI absorption of chlorpromazine by as much as 40%, (2) increase the rate of lithium excretion in the kidneys, (3) increase extrapyramidal symptoms, and (4) mask nausea and vomiting which are signs to monitor for lithium toxicity. With haloperidol, extrapyramidal side effects may be increased also. Although controversial, there are reports of irreversible neurologic and brain damage when both drugs are given for longer periods than the first couple weeks. If given concurrently, monitor clients closely since dosage reductions may be necessary. |
| metrizamide | When given concurrently with phenothiazines, may lower the seizure threshold. Discontinue phenothiazines at least 2 days before and also for 1 day after a myelogram. |
| quinidine | When given concurrently with the thioxanthenes (chlorprothixene, thiothixene), and increase in cardiac effects may occur. Avoid concurrent use if possible or monitor closely for adverse effects. |
| tricyclic antidepressants, MAO inhibitors, and procarbazine | Concurrent use may increase the duration and intensify the sedative and anticholinergic side effects of these medications. Metabolism of the phenothiazines and the antidepressants may be inhibited. May enhance the risk of inducing neuroleptic malignant syndrome (NMS)—hyperthermia, dehydration, cardiovascular instability, hypoxemia, and muscular rigidity. Avoid this combination if possible; if not, monitor closely. |

***Dosage and administration.*** See Tables 17-3 to 17-5.

Before beginning antipsychotic therapy, the client (most especially the geriatric client) should have a drug-free period to rule out drug-induced psychiatric illness. Visual and auditory hallucinations have been reported with anticonvulsants, baclofen, cimetidine, and levodopa, whereas anticholinergic-induced psychosis has been seen with amitriptyline (especially in children and the elderly) and other tricyclic antidepressants (Salerno, 1986).

The dosage of the antipsychotic agents may vary according to the individual, the reason for treatment, and client's response to the medication. It is best to titrate from a low dose, increasing when necessary to produce a therapeutic response, which usually occurs within days to a couple of months. Continue at this dosage for 14 days and then gradually decrease dosage to lowest amount that produces a therapeutic response.

When stopping antipsychotic therapy, gradually reduce the dosage over 2 or 3 weeks. When antipsychotic agents have been given to clients in high doses or for a long time and are suddenly discontinued, nausea, vomiting, dizziness, tremors, and dyskinesia have been reported.

Antipsychotic agents may cause a number of cardiovascular effects, including hypotension (caused by alpha-adrenergic blockade), tachycardia (anticholinergic effect), myocardial depressant effects, and electrocardiographic alterations affecting ST, T wave, and widening of QRS interval. The most cardiotoxic agents are chlorpromazine and thioridazine; and when possible, they should be avoided in clients with cardiac disease. The high-potency antipsychotics, such as haloperidol, have fewer cardiotoxic effects so they may be the preferred agents in such clients.

In the past, many clients said to be resistant to drug therapy were found to be noncompliant with the prescribed

**TABLE 17-3**   Aliphatic phenothiazine dosage and administration

| | Adults | Elderly | Children |
|---|---|---|---|
| chlorpromazine, oral | Psychosis: 10-25 mg 2 to 4 times daily. Increase dose by 20 to 50 mg daily, every 3 to 4 days, as necessary | | |
| | Nausea and vomiting: 10-25 mg every 4 hr; increase dose if necessary<br>Presurgery anxiety: 25 to 50 mg 2 to 3 hr before surgery<br>Hiccups or porphyria: 25-50 mg orally 3 or 4 times daily | | Nausea and vomiting: Infants less than 6 mo, not established. 6 mo and older, 0.55 mg/kg orally or 15 mg/m² body surface area, every 4-6 hr as needed |
| chlorpromazine, parenteral | Severe psychosis: 25-50 mg IM, repeat in 1 hr if needed, then every 3-12 hr as necessary<br>Nausea and vomiting: 25 mg IM, then 25-50 mg IM as necessary<br>Presurgery anxiety: 12.5-25 mg IM, 1 to 2 hr before surgery<br>Hiccups: 25-50 mg IM, 3 or 4 times daily<br>Porphyria: 25 mg IM every 6 or 8 hr until client can take oral medications<br>Tetanus: 25-50 mg IM 3 or 4 times daily. Increase dose as necessary. Or IV infusion 25-50 mg diluted to 1 mg/ml prior with 0.9% sodium chloride given at a 1 mg/min<br>Nausea and vomiting during surgery: 12.5 mg IM, may be repeated in ½ hr if needed. Or 25 mg by IV infusion. Dilute chlorpromazine to 1 mg/ml with 0.9% sodium chloride injection. Administer 2 mg/2 min | Should receive lower than adult dosages, increasing as necessary according to response and/or development of side effects | Nausea and vomiting: Infants less than 6 mo, not established. 6 mo or older, 0.55 mg/kg body weight IM every 6-8 hr, as needed<br>Nausea and vomiting during surgery: 0.275 mg/kg body weight diluted to 1 mg/ml with 0.9% sodium chloride injection administered at rate of 1 mg/2 min<br>Tetanus: 0.55 mg/kg body weight, diluted to 1 mg/ml with 0.9% sodium chloride injection, given at a rate of 1 mg/2 min. Maximum per day, 40 mg for children 6 mo to 5 years, up to 75 mg daily in children 5-12 years |
| chlorpromazine suppositories | Nausea and vomiting: 50-100 mg rectally 3 or 4 times daily as necessary | | Infants less than 6 mo, not established. 6 mo and older, 1 mg/kg body weight, rectally 3 or 4 times daily as necessary |

**TABLE 17-4**   Piperidine phenothiazine dosage and administration

| | Adults | Elderly | Children |
|---|---|---|---|
| thioridazine oral tablets/liquid | Treatment of psychosis: 25-100 mg 3 times daily as necessary. Maintenance, 10-200 mg 2-4 times daily. Maximum dosage is 800 mg daily | Should receive lower than adult dosages, increasing as necessary according to response and/or development of side effects | Children less than 2 yr, not established. Children 2-12 yr, 0.25-3 mg/kg body weight or 7.5 mg/m², orally 4 times daily or 10-25 mg 2 or 3 times daily |
| mesoridazine besylate oral tablet/liquid | 10-50 mg 2 or 3 times daily as necessary | Same as above | Children less than 12 yr, not established. Children 12 yr and older, same as adult dosage |
| mesoridazine besylate injection | 25 mg IM; may repeat in 30-60 min if necessary | Same as above | |

**TABLE 17-5**  Piperazine phenothiazine dosage and administration

| | Adults | Elderly | Children |
|---|---|---|---|
| trifluoperazine hydrochloride tablet/liquid | Treatment of psychosis: 2-5 mg twice daily initially, titrate dosage as necessary up to 40 mg daily | Should receive lower than adult dosage, increasing as necessary according to response and/or development of side effects | Children less than 6 yr, not established. 6 yr and older, 1 mg once or twice daily, titrate dosage as necessary |
| trifluoperazine hydrochloride injection | 1-2 mg IM every 4-6 hr as necessary. Maximum is 10 mg daily | Same as above | Children less than 6 yr, not established. 6 yr and older, 1 mg once or twice a day IM |
| fluphenazine hydrochloride tablet/liquid | 0.5-2.5 mg orally 1-4 times daily, adjust dosage as necessary | Same as above | 0.25-0.75 mg orally 1-4 times daily |
| fluphenazine decanoate injection (Prolixin decanoate, Modecate ♣) | 12.5-25 mg IM or SC; may repeat in 1-3 wk as necessary. Maximum, 100 mg/dose | | Children 5-12 years old; 3-12.5 mg IM or SC. Dose may be repeated in 1-3 weeks as necessary. Children 12 and over; 6.25-18.75 mg IM or SC initially, weekly. Dose may be increased to 12.5-25 mg every 1-3 weeks as necessary |
| fluphenazine enanthate injection (prolixin enanthate, Moditen ♣) | 25 mg IM or SC; repeat in 1-3 wk as necessary. Maximum, 100 mg | | Children less than 12 yr, not established. 12 yr and older, see adult dosage |
| fluphenazine hydrochloride injection | 1.25-2.5 mg IM every 6-8 hr as necessary. Maximum 10 mg daily | Same as above | Same as enanthate |
| perphenazine tablet/liquid | 4-16 mg orally, 2-4 times a day as necessary | Same as above | Same as enanthate |
| perphenazine injection | 5-10 mg IM every 6 hr as necessary. IV, dilute 5 mg with NaCl injection to 1 mg/ml and administer at rate of 1 mg/min. Maximum for ambulatory clients, 15 mg daily; for hospitalized clients, up to 30 mg daily | Same as above | Same as enanthate |
| prochlorperazine tablets/prochlorperazine syrup | Psychosis treatment: 5-10 mg orally 3-4 times daily as necessary up to 150 mg daily | Same as above | Children less than 2 yr or 9 kg, not established.<br>Psychosis treatment: children 2-12 years old, 2.5 mg 2-3 times daily. 12 yrs and older, see adult dosage<br>Antiemetic: children 9-13 kg, 2.5 mg once or twice a day; not to exceed 7.5 mg in 24 hr. Children 14-17 kg, 2.5 mg 2 or 3 times daily; not to exceed 10 mg in 24 hr. Children 18-39 kg, 2.5 mg 3 times daily or 5 mg twice a day; not to exceed 15 mg in 24 hr |
| prochlorperazine extended-release capsule | Psychosis treatment: 10-75 mg orally every 12 hr as necessary. Maximum, 150 mg daily<br>Nausea and vomiting: 15-30 mg daily in the morning or 10 mg every 12 hr. Maximum, 40 mg daily | Same as above | Not recommended |

*Continued.*

**TABLE 17-5**   Piperazine phenothiazine dosage and administration—cont'd

|  | Adults | Elderly | Children |
|---|---|---|---|
| prochlorperazine injection | Antiemetic 5-10 mg IM every 3 to 4 hr as necessary. Maximum, 40 mg/day. Antipsychotic: 10-20 mg IM every 4-6 hr as necessary. Maximum, 200 mg/day | Same as above | Children less than 2 yr or 9 kg, not established. Children 2-12 yr, 0.132 mg/kg body weight IM |
| prochlorperazine suppositories |  | Same as above | Nausea and vomiting: Children less than 2 yr or 9 kg, not established. Children 9-13 kg, 2.5 mg rectally once or twice daily; not to exceed 7.5 mg/24 hr. Children 14-17 kg, 2.5 mg 2 or 3 times daily; not to exceed 10 mg/24 hr. Children 18-39 kg, 2.5 mg rectally 3 times daily or 5 mg twice daily; not to exceed 15 mg/24 hr. See directions for further instructions |
| prochlorperazine suppositories | Psychosis: 10 mg rectally 3 or 4 times daily. Increase dose every 2-3 days by 5-10 mg, if necessary |  |  |
|  | Nausea and vomiting: 25 mg twice daily | Elderly usually require a lower dose initially. Increase dose as necessary and tolerated |  |

therapy. Many psychotic clients deny their illness or may see the consumption of medications as being associated with dependence or weakness. Clients refractory to antipsychotic medications should be reviewed for:

1. Compliance. The physician may order a plasma serum level of the medication, if such a test is available, to determine the reliability of the client; or the drug order may be switched to a liquid formulation to be administered in a supervised setting.
2. Inadequate dosage. The physician should adjust the dosage according to the individual needs of the client. Inadequate doses or the development of drug tolerance may result in an inadequate response to the medication.
3. Questionable oral bioavailability. Although this is not considered a common possibility, it is a variable to be considered. The physician may switch from an oral solid dosage form to a liquid formulation and also adjust the dosage as necessary, based on the individual's response or development of side effects. Switching to another antipsychotic agent may also be considered.

Rapid neuroleptization or high-dose therapy is appropriate in certain cases. For instance, aggressive treatment is used in clients with acute psychosis who may exhibit dangerous and/or destructive behaviors. Usually intramuscular therapy with a high-potency antipsychotic agent (such as haloperidol) is given, often on an hourly schedule, until the desired effects are achieved. If a client will take oral medication, then high-dose oral therapy may be substituted.

Once a client is stabilized on antipsychotic medications, the entire daily dosage may be prescribed to be given at bedtime. The long duration of action of these drugs makes a single bedtime dosage feasible. This dosage schedule has increased client compliance, lowered medication costs, decreased side effects, and decreased or eliminated the need for simultaneous hypnotic medication.

This dosage schedule would require both careful drug and client selection before implementation. Using a drug with a high anticholinergic potential in an elderly client or an individual with cardiovascular disease may result in an increased potential for cardiotoxic effects. In such cases, multiple (two or three times daily) daily dosages are indicated.

Long-acting injections are frequently useful in antipsychotic therapy. Depot fluphenazine enanthate, fluphenazine decanoate, and haloperidol decanoate are available for clients who are persistently noncompliant, do not understand the need for taking medications, or have a high frequency of relapses (psychotic episodes). Fluphenazine decanoate is often used in preference to the enanthate because the duration of action is approximately 2 weeks longer (an injection may last from 1 to 4 weeks). Clients receiving fluphenazine decanoate may exhibit a slight decrease in extrapyramidal side effects as compared with clients taking the enanthate formulation. Converting from an oral antip-

### Pediatric Implications
### PSYCHOTHERAPEUTIC AGENTS

Children are at a greater risk of developing neuromuscular or extrapyramidal side effects, especially dystonias. Monitor closely if antipsychotic agents are administered.

Pediatric clients with chickenpox, CNS infections, measles, dehydration, gastroenteritis or other acute illnesses will be at special risk of developing adverse reactions and possibly, Reye's syndrome. Avoid use of phenothiazine antiemetic therapy in such clients.

The tricyclic antidepressants are usually not recommended for the treatment of depression in children under 12 years old. Some agents though, such as amitriptyline, desipramine, and imipramine have been used in children over the age of 6 for major depressions. Several of these agents are also used in the treatment of enuresis and attention deficit disorder. Be aware though, that children are very sensitive to an acute overdose, which should always be considered very serious and potentially fatal. Adolescents often require a decreased dose because of their sensitivity to this drug category.

Adverse effects reported in children receiving the tricyclic antidepressants include changes in electrocardiogram patterns, increased nervousness, sleep disorders, complaints of tiredness, hypertension, and mild stomach distress.

Lithium may decrease the bone density or bone formation in children. If necessary to use, monitor closely serum levels and for signs of toxicity.

### Geriatric Implications:
### PSYCHOTHERAPEUTIC AGENTS

The elderly tend to have higher serum levels of the antipsychotic and antidepressant drugs because of changes in drug distribution resulting from a decrease in lean body mass, less total body water, less serum albumin, and usually an increase in body fat. Therefore, these clients require a lower drug dose and a more gradual drug dose titration than the adult client.

Geriatric clients are more prone to have orthostatic hypotension, anticholinergic side effects, extrapyramidal side effects, and sedation. They should be carefully evaluated before starting such potent medications; and if the antipsychotic agents are necessary, close supervision and the prescribing of the lowest dose possible is recommended.

The elderly client generally should receive half the recommended adult dose. The client with organic brain syndrome should only receive 33% to 50% of the usual adult dose with increases in dosage at 7- to 10-day periods. When clinical improvement is noted, attempts at tapering and discontinuing the drug should be instituted.

The tricyclic antidepressants may cause increased anxiety in the geriatric client. If the client has cardiovascular disease, the use of the tricyclic antidepressants increases the risk of inducing arrhythmias, tachycardia, stroke, congestive heart failure, and/or myocardial infarction.

Lithium is more toxic in the geriatric client; therefore, lower lithium dosages, a lower lithium serum level, and very close monitoring is critical in this age group. The elderly are more prone to develop CNS toxicity, lithium-induced goiter, and clinical hypothyroidism than the average adult. Generally, excessive thirst and elimination of large volumes of urine may be early side effects of lithium toxicity frequently seen in the elderly.

### ANTIPSYCHOTIC DRUG EQUIVALENCY DOSAGES

| Drug | Equivalent Dose (mg) |
|---|---|
| *Low potency* | |
| chlorpromazine | 100 |
| thioridazine | 100 |
| *Intermediate potency* | |
| molindone | 10 |
| loxapine | 15 |
| *High potency* | |
| trifluoperazine | 5 |
| perphenazine | 8 |
| thiothixene | 4 |
| haloperidol | 2 |
| fluphenazine | 2 |

Data from Knoben JE and Anderson PO. (1988). Handbook of clinical drug data, ed 6. Hamilton, Ill: Drug Intelligence Publications, Inc.

sychotic agent to fluphenazine decanoate requires various conversion considerations. The reader is referred to Young and Koda-Kimble (1988) for this information.

Clients being considered for haloperidol decanoate therapy should first receive oral haloperidol. Dosage and dosing interval adjustments should be carefully chosen and closely monitored. In some persons the effects of haloperidol decanoate may last up to 6 weeks.

Antipsychotic medications have been classified as low-potency, intermediate-potency, and high-potency drugs. The basis for the classification is the quantity of medication necessary to produce an equivalent effect when compared with other agents in the same category. For example, 50 mg of chlorpromazine is considered to be approximately equivalent to 25 mg of mesoridazine or 1 mg haloperidol. Thus chlorpromazine is a low-potency agent, mesoridazine an intermediate-potency agent, and haloperidol is a high-potency drug (see box at left). The student is cautioned not to confuse potency with effectiveness; potency refers to the quantity of a drug necessary to produce an equivalent effect as compared with another drug in the same classification. Effectiveness measures the therapeutic response to various agents and this may range from less effective, to equivalent in effectiveness, to greater in effectiveness, depending on the individual drugs being studied.

Acetophenazine (Tindal), promazine (Sparine), and triflupromazine (Vesprin) are available on the market, but they are not commonly used today.

## Tourette's Syndrome

**Tourette's Syndrome** (Gilles de la Tourette's syndrome) is a rare neurologic disease of unknown etiology that usually begins in childhood but often continues throughout the person's lifespan. It is more commonly seen in males and may present initially as tics (facial grimaces and blinking). Other symptoms include vocal tics or noises, such as grunting, barking, shouting, sniffing, compulsive swearing (coprolalia) and movement disorders (involuntary, purposeless movements). The individual's intellectual functions are normal. The symptoms may peak and wane throughout the person's life. While there is no cure for Tourette's syndrome, haloperidol and pimozide have produced dramatic improvement in some clients.

### pimozide (Orap)

Pimozide is a neuroleptic agent that blocks CNS dopamine receptors. It suppresses motor and phonic tics in Tourette's Syndrome. About 50% of the dose is absorbed. Peak serum levels occur within 6 to 8 hours and half-life (elimination), in about 55 hours. Pimozide is metabolized in the liver; two major metabolites have been identified. The drug is excreted in the kidneys.

Most frequent side effects include sedation, visual problems, constipation, dry mouth, hypotension, rash, swollen or painful breasts, with perhaps milk secretion.

Most frequent adverse effects include restlessness (akathisia), ventricular tachycardia/arrhythmias, drug-induced Parkinson's effects, and mood alterations. Less frequent reactions include intense, irregular muscle spasms, (dystonia), tardive dyskinesia, jaundice, neuroleptic malignant syndrome, and blood dyscrasias.

*Significant drug interactions.* The following effects may occur when pimozide is given with the drugs listed below:

| Drug | Possible Effect and Management |
|---|---|
| alcohol, CNS depressants | May enhance CNS depressant effects. Monitor closely. |
| amphetamines, methylphenidate or pemoline | These drugs may induce tics and mask the cause of them. Avoid concurrent drug administration. |
| anticholinergics | May result in increased anticholinergic side effects. |

| Drug | Possible Effect and Management |
|---|---|
| antidepressants, tricyclic, disopyramide, maprotiline, phenothiazines, procainamide, or quinidine | May enhance or potentiate cardiac arrhythmias. Avoid concurrent use if possible. |
| extrapyramidal-causing medications, including phenothiazines | May result in an increase in the extrapyramidal side effects of both medications. May also increase the anticholinergic and CNS depressant effects. |

*Dosage and administration.* In adults and children 12 and over, administer 1 to 2 mg orally in divided doses. Increase dose gradually every other day as necessary. For children under 12, dose has not been established.

### ▷Nursing Management: Phenothiazine Therapy

*Assessment.* The phenothiazines are contraindicated in clients with severe cardiovascular disease, severe CNS depression, or who are comatose. They are administered with caution for clients with active alcoholism, as they may potentiate CNS depression and liver impairment. Also, with decreased metabolism by the liver, there may be increased sensitivity to CNS effects, Reye's syndrome, and blood dyscrasias. Clients with the following disorders may find their symptoms increased: cardiovascular disease, glaucoma, Parkinson's disease, urinary retention, and chronic respiratory disorders. Phenothiazines should be used cautiously in clients with a history of convulsive disorders because of their action in reducing the convulsive threshold. Adequate anticonvulsant therapy needs to be maintained.

Once a client has started phenothiazine therapy, the nurse needs to assess for potential problems that may occur as the result of the drug's side effects and adverse reactions. See box for selected nursing diagnoses.

*Intervention.* Dosages of phenothiazines are individualized according to client response so that the lowest effective dose may be used. Dosages are increased more slowly and in smaller increments with elderly or debilitated clients.

Note that in institutional settings the severely agitated or combative client may be given larger intramuscular doses of the neuroleptics. Haloperidol and thiothixene have been given hourly to severely agitated clients to prevent them from hurting themselves or others. When symptoms are under control, the clients can be given the drug orally. Because of the half-life of the intramuscular doses, the first oral dose should be given 12 to 24 hours after the last intramuscular dose.

Note that in most cases concurrent treatment with more than one neuroleptic agent is not indicated. If the client does not respond to a particular drug, usually the dose of that drug should be increased or a different drug prescribed. Occasionally a client may respond best to a combination of two drugs from different classes. However, the potentiation

Selected nursing diagnoses related to antipsychotic medication administration

| Nursing diagnosis | Outcome criteria | Nursing interventions |
|---|---|---|
| Alteration in bowel elimination: constipation related to drug's anticholinergic effects | The client will maintain his/her usual bowel elimination pattern; select foods high in fiber from the daily menu; maintain a fluid intake of 2500 ml daily; increase activity as allowed | Assess client's usual bowel elimination pattern; monitor and record bowel movements<br>Instruct client to establish a routine for bowel elimination; select foods high in fiber; maintain fluid intake of 2500 ml/daily and perform isometric abdominal strengthening exercises, unless contraindicated; increase activity as allowed |
| Altered comfort related to dry mouth | The client will maintain a healthy oral cavity as evidenced by pink, moist, intact mucosa | Provide ice chips, sugarless candies, and frequent mouth hygiene if dry mouth occurs |
| High risk for injury related to increased sensitivity to the sun, visual effects, and the development of dizziness, hypotension and tardive dyskinesia | The client will not experience sunburn, falls, symptoms of tardive dyskinesia | Monitor blood pressure at appropriate intervals; keep client in recumbent position for 30 minutes after injection; provide assistance with ambulation if sedation, dizziness, orthostatic hypotension, or visual changes occur<br>Instruct client to change position from recumbent to upright slowly<br>Alert client to hypersensitivity to sun and the use of sunscreens and sunglasses<br>Monitor for and instruct client in the early signs of tardive dyskinesia (facial tics, grimacing, blinking, lip smacking, tongue protrusion, writhing motions of the arms, hands, and fingers). Report immediately |
| Knowledge deficit related to newly prescribed or altered psychotherapeutic agents | The client will describe his condition; how the drug therapy relates to the condition; how and when to take the medications; common drug interactions; common side effects and which of these warrant reporting; storage requirements of the drug; demonstrate less anxiety related to fear of the unknown, loss of control, and misconceptions | Assess learning needs and learning readiness<br>Plan with the client and family for the achievement of realistic goals<br>Provide information to meet outcome criteria |
| Noncompliance related to medication regimen | The client will self-administer medications safely and accurately | Determine the client's reasons for noncompliance and take appropriate teaching/counseling interventions<br>Discuss the increased possibility of the return of symptoms with noncompliance |

and a lowered margin of safety of such combinations require greater precautions for client safety.

Since administration of large doses over a prolonged time may lead to anticholinergic psychoses or tardive dyskinesia, adverse reactions may be prevented by providing periodic "drug-free holidays" during which the client does not receive phenothiazines to prevent these adverse reactions. Because of the long elimination half-life of these drugs, "holidays" should last several weeks.

Maintenance dosage should be periodically evaluated for a possible reduction in the dosage or cessation of drug therapy. Clients with preexisting renal or hepatic disease may require reduced dosage.

When preparing phenothiazines, the nurse should be aware that the injectable forms tend to be physically and/or chemically incompatible with a wide range of solutions. The nurse should check the package insert for compatibility information about the specific drugs being prepared. Avoid freezing phenothiazine solutions. Discolored solutions, slightly yellowed, may be used. However, if marked discoloration or a precipitate is apparent, the solution should not be used. Skin and eye contact with phenothiazine solutions should be avoided because it may cause contact dermatitis and irritation. Exposed areas should be washed immediately to minimize the effect.

Intramuscular injections of phenothiazines should be given slowly and deep into large muscle mass, such as the ventrogluteal or dorsogluteal site. Rotate and document the rotation of injection sites.

Oral forms of phenothiazines should be administered with food or a full glass of milk or water to decrease gastric irritation. Phenothiazines should not be administered concurrently with antacids or antidiarrheals; hours of administration should be altered to allow 2 hours between doses of these medications. Administration of the maintenance dosage at bedtime facilitates sleep and decreases drowsiness during the daytime.

Gradual reduction of the dosage over several weeks for clients on high or long-term dosages will help prevent withdrawal symptoms of nausea, vomiting, irritability, trembling, and transient dyskinetic signs. The only rationale for abrupt withdrawal is the occurrence of severe side effects/adverse reactions.

In pregnant women the risk of administration of these drugs should be weighed against the expected therapeutic outcome.

***Education.*** The nurse should caution clients against driving, operating dangerous machinery, or performing tasks that require absolute precision, motor coordination, and mental alertness.

The client should be instructed that the medication may take several weeks to treat the disorder effectively.

To prevent photosensitivity, the nurse should advise the client to stay out of the sun, use sunscreen lotion, or wear protective clothing to prevent solar erythema, or the nurse should assist clients by providing the necessary protective measures. A dark, purplish brown skin pigmentation induced by light (photosensitivity) has been reported in hospitalized psychiatric clients who were given large dosages of phenothiazines for 3 to 10 years.

The nurse should caution the client that dry mouth can be a bothersome adverse effect and contribute to the development of caries, gum disease, and oral candidiasis. The client should be instructed in the use of proper oral hygiene. Xerostomia may affect the fitting of full dentures; referral should be made for dental care for this and other dental problems.

Long-term therapy with phenothiazines necessitates dietary increases in riboflavin. Good dietary sources of vitamin $B_2$ are muscle meats, organ meats, milk, eggs, leafy and yellow vegetables, and enriched cereals and breads. However, if the client has altered nutrition, it may be ben-

eficial to use a vitamin supplement until adequate nutrition is assured.

Phenothiazines also affect regulation of body temperature; clients should be cautioned to avoid extremes of environmental temperature (i.e., swimming in cold water or walking in hot, humid weather), which could lead to hypothermia and respiratory distress or hyperthermia and heat prostration, respectively.

The client should be instructed to avoid alcohol and other CNS depressants, since they increase the CNS depressant effects of the phenothiazines. Using these drugs concurrently with extrapyramidal reaction-causing medications will increase the frequency and severity of extrapyramidal effects.

***Evaluation.*** If orthostatic (postural) hypotension occurs and causes severe difficulties or serious hazards, the nurse should alert the physician, who may institute one of the following remedial measures: (1) a change of medication to one of the phenothiazine derivatives that does not produce this side effect with such frequency, (2) reduction of dosage, or (3) discontinuation of medication for 24 hours with a gradual buildup of dosage as tolerated. The client who complains of dizziness, light-headedness, or palpitation may be experiencing orthostatic hypotension. This can easily be confirmed when the client's blood pressure is compared in the prone and standing positions. The client should be instructed to rise slowly from the recumbent position and to sit on the edge of the bed for a few minutes before attempting to stand. Support and reassurance may be necessary to allay the client's anxiety. Explaining orthostatic hypotension also may help him or her understand this experience and reduce anxiety. Clients should be encouraged to remain in a recumbent position for 1 hour after initial doses, parenterally administered doses, or large oral doses (rarely) of the phenothiazines to minimize hypotensive episodes.

The nurse should be alert to signs of agranulocytosis such as sore throat, fever, or weakness in clients taking these drugs; this usually occurs between weeks 4 and 10. When these symptoms appear, the drug is usually discontinued; the nurse should hold the dose and notify the physician as soon as possible. White blood cell and differential counts are required periodically.

Because of possible ocular changes, including particle deposition in the cornea and lens and pigmentary retinopathy (decreased vision, brownish coloring of vision, impaired night vision, and pigment deposits on the fundus), indicate on the client's record that the eye change may be related to dosage levels or therapy duration. The client on a long-term regimen or moderate-to-high dose therapy should have periodic ophthalmologic examinations. Exposure to light may increase the possibility of ocular changes; therefore, the client should be instructed to wear sunglasses.

The nurse should monitor the client closely for early signs of tardive dyskinesia, usually small, wormlike motions of the tongue. Since there is no known effective treatment for tardive dyskinesia, phenothiazines should be discontinued immediately and the prescriber notified.

These drugs should be administered cautiously to clients with heart disease since they may precipitate hypotension. If hypotension necessitating drug interaction occurs, norepinephrine or phenylephrine may be administered. Since phenothiazines tend to reverse epinephrine's vasopressor effects, epinephrine may not be effective in reversing hypotension.

The client should be monitored for signs and symptoms of urinary hesitancy or retention, prostatic hypertrophy, narrow angle glaucoma, or respiratory problems (e.g., intake and output for urinary retention and/or constipation).

Hepatic function tests, urine bilirubin, and bile examinations should be done weekly during the first month of therapy to assist in the detection of cholestatic jaundice. Clinically, the client should be observed for yellow skin, nausea, flulike symptoms, and rash. Phenothiazines are to be discontinued immediately.

The nurse should monitor the client for **neuroleptic malignant syndrome (NMS)** (hyperthermia, dehydration, cardiovascular instability, hypoxemia, and muscular rigidity). Therapy is essentially symptomatic and supportive with the phenothiazine being discontinued immediately.

Depression, especially if the client is not closely supervised, may account for the greater incidence of suicide in psychiatric clients undergoing drug therapy than in those receiving only institutional care.

## ▷Nursing Management: Selected Phenothiazine Derivatives

Each of the three subgroups of phenothiazine has unique considerations for the nurse.

*Aliphatic phenothiazines.* The aliphatic phenothiazine derivatives consist of chlorpromazine (Clorizine, Ormazine, Promaz, Thorazine), promazine (Prozine, Sparine), and triflupromazine (Vesprin) (see Table 17-3).

The oral route of administration is preferred unless the client is unable to take an oral dose. When given with at least 120 ml of fruit juice or other liquids or semi-soft foods, chlorpromazine becomes more palatable; however, the client should be informed that the medication is in the substance.

When given intramuscularly, it should be injected deeply and slowly in divided doses of not more than 1 ml per injection site. Irritation of the subcutaneous tissues can be reduced by diluting the drug with 0.9% sodium chloride injection and injecting the drug by the "Z track" technique. Massaging the client's injection site helps reduce local irritation. Some clients have been known to develop abscesses at the injection site, which are believed to result from large doses of this substance being administered in one area. Use of the intramuscular route when administering chlorpro-

mazine is usually indicated when the client refuses the tablet or concentrate form or when the most immediate effect of the drug is desired. If the client is severely agitated, combative, or struggling, the nurse should take care to follow safe administration technique. This technique usually requires enough well-trained personnel to restrain the client adequately while the medication is being given.

Intravenous administration of the undiluted drug should be avoided. If used for direct intravenous administration, chlorpromazine hydrochloride should be diluted to at least 1 mg/ml and administered at a rate of 1 mg/min for adults and 0.5 mg/min for children. For intravenous infusion, the drug should be added to 500 to 1000 ml of 0.9% sodium chloride solution and administered slowly. In both instances, the client should be kept recumbent to minimize hypotension.

*Piperidine phenothiazines.* The piperidine phenothiazine derivatives consist of mesoridazine (Serentil) and thioridazine (Mellaril-S, Apo-Thioridazine, Mellaril, Novoridazine, Thioridazine) (see Table 17-4). The oral concentrate solution should be diluted with a half glass (120 ml) of water, orange juice, or grape juice just before administration to make it more palatable. Contact with liquid forms of the drug should be avoided because contact dermatitis may result.

*Piperazine phenothiazines.* The piperazine phenothiazine derivatives consist of fluphenazine (Moditen, Prolixin, Permitil), perphenazine (Trilafon, Phenazine, Apo-Perphenazine), prochlorperazine (Compazine, Chlorazine, Stemetil), and trifluoperazine (Stelazine, Suprazine, Terfluzive, Novoflurazine) (see Table 17-5).

The fluphenazine hydrochloride oral concentrate solution should not be mixed with fluids containing caffeine (coffee, tea, cola), tannic acid (tea), or pectinates (apple juice) because a physical incompatibility may occur. As with fluphenazine, perphenazine oral concentrate should not be mixed with the preceding solutions. Instead, dilute with at least 60 ml of lemon-lime carbonated beverage or pineapple, orange, tomato, or grapefruit juice for each 5 ml of concentrate.

Decanoate and enthanthate, the long-acting forms of fluphenazine, are oil preparations; they may be given intramuscularly or subcutaneously using a 21-gauge or larger needle.

Intravenous administration of perphenazine is limited to recumbent hospitalized adult clients and requires the availability of resuscitative equipment and drugs for the treatment of severe hypotensive episodes or extrapyramidal responses in the client. If administered by fractional intravenous injection, the solution should be diluted to 0.5 mg/ml of 0.9% sodium chloride and administered slowly, 1 mg per injection at intervals of at least 1 to 2 minutes. Blood pressure and pulse should be assessed continuously during intravenous administration.

## Butyrophenone Derivatives
### haloperidol (Haldol)

The butyrophenones are structurally different from the phenothiazines and the thioxanthines but have similar properties in terms of antipsychotic efficacy. The receptor-blockade activity in the CNS may be at the level of the dopamine receptors. They have relatively less effect on the norepinephrine and epinephrine receptors and are probably more potent than most of the phenothiazine agents in their dopaminergic effects and possess a significant degree of extrapyramidal effects. The drug has both antiemetic and antipsychotic effects. Research conducted in Europe in the area of anesthesia brought this compound into view as a possible antipsychotic agent. Subsequent use indicated its effectiveness in the control of hyperactivity associated with the manic phase. For dosage and administration, see Table 17-6. For pregnancy safety, see box at left.

### ▷ Nursing Management: Haloperidol Therapy

In addition to the general nursing considerations for phenothiazines, the following points should be noted:

A special dropper should be used for oral liquid administration; if diluted with tea or coffee, a precipitate will form. Butyrophenone may be administered from a premeasured oral syringe without diluting if desired.

With the extended action injectable form of the drug, the effects may last up to 6 weeks; therefore, clients should be counseled that precautions and other side effect information will apply during this time.

The emotional status should be assessed carefully since there may be a rapid mood swing from mania to depression when haloperidol is administered to the client with a bipolar disorder.

---

### PREGNANCY SAFETY

FDA Category B: clozapine
FDA Category C: haloperidol, loxapine, pimozide
FDA Category unclassified: phenothiazines (although not recommended during pregnancy), thiothixene, molindone

---

**TABLE 17-6**   Haloperidol and thiothixene: dosage and administration

| | Adults | Elderly | Children |
|---|---|---|---|
| haloperidol tablet/liquid | 0.5-5 mg orally 2 or 3 times daily, adjust dosage as necessary. Maximum, 100 mg/day | 0.5-2 mg orally 2 or 3 times daily; increase as necessary | Children less than 3 yr, not established. Children 3-12 yr, 15-40 mg/kg body weight. Psychotic conditions, 0.05 mg/kg body weight orally, divided into 2 or 3 doses daily. Increase dose if necessary by 0.5 mg increments at 5-7 day intervals up to a total daily dose of 0.15 mg/kg body weight daily. Pediatric doses above 6 mg/day are usually unnecessary |
| nonpsychotic conditions and Tourette's syndrome | | | 0.05 mg/kg body weight orally divided into 2 or 3 doses daily. Increase dose if necessary by 0.5 mg increments at 5-7 day intervals up to a total daily dose of 0.075 mg/kg body weight daily |
| haloperidol injection | Acute psychosis: 2-5 mg IM, may repeat at 1-hr intervals or every 4-8 hr if client's symptoms are under control. Maximum dosage, 100 mg/day | | Not established |
| thiothixene capsules/liquid | 2 mg orally 3 times/day or 5 mg twice/day. Increase dosage as necessary to a maximum of 60 mg daily | Lower than adult dose, increasing as necessary according to response and/or development of side effects | Children less than 12 yr, not established |
| thiothixene hydrochloride injection | 4 mg IM 2-4 times daily. Adjust dosage as necessary to maximum of 30 mg daily | Same as above | Not established |

## thiothixene hydrochloride (Navane)

Thiothixene, a thioxanthene derivative, resembles the piperazine phenothiazines in its tranquilizing and antiemetic actions and to a lesser degree in its spasmolytic and hypotensive effects. Its indications for use, side effects, precautions, and drug interactions are the same as those for the phenothiazines. Extrapyramidal symptoms and insomnia occur frequently with this drug. For dosage and administration, see Table 17-6. See the general nursing management for phenothiazines.

## Dihydroindolone Derivative
### molindone (Moban)

Molindone is an antipsychotic agent; chemically it is an oxygenated indole (dihydroindolone) representing a new chemical class. In theory, molindone blocks dopamine receptors in the reticular activating and limbic systems, with activity similar to major tranquilizers such as phenothiazines. Molindone is administered orally. In adults, initial dose is 50 to 75 mg daily in divided doses. Dosages may increase to 100 mg daily in 3 or 4 days. Dosage must be individualized. Maximum, usually 225 mg/day. Dosage for the elderly is lower than adult dose, increasing as necessary according to response or development of side effects. Molindone is not recommended for children less than 12 years.

## ▷Nursing Management:
### Molindone Therapy

In addition to the general nursing management for phenothiazines, the following point should be noted. The tablet form contains calcium sulfate, which may impair the absorption of tetracycline and phenytoin. The client should be informed about this interaction.

## Dibenzoxapine Derivative
### Loxapine Succinate (Loxitane, Loxapac ✳)

Loxapine has structural similarity to the phenothiazines but is a member of a distinct chemical class of antipsychotic drugs, the dibenzoxapines. Loxapine HCl oral dose forms (liquid or capsule) are administered to adults at 10 mg orally twice daily, increased slowly during the first 7 to 10 days as necessary. Maintenance dose is 15 to 25 mg orally 2 to 4 times daily. Maximum dosage is 250 mg/day. Dosage for the elderly is 3 to 5 mg twice daily initially. Dosage for children less than 16 years old has not been established. Injection-form loxapine is administered to adults at 12.5-50 mg IM every 4 to 6 hours as necessary. Maximum, 250 mg/day. As in the oral form, injectable loxapine dosage for children less than 16 years old has not been established.

## ▷Nursing Management:
### Loxapine Succinate Therapy

In addition to the general nursing management for phenothiazines, the following points should be noted:

The nurse should administer the loxapine succinate oral concentrate with the calibrated dropper, which has 1 ml equal to 25 mg only. The drug should be mixed with orange or grapefruit juice shortly before administration.

Loxapine hydrochloride is to be administered only intramuscularly. The nurse should caution the client that temporary drowsiness may occur when initial therapy starts and when dosage is increased. Tolerance develops as therapy continues. It may require several weeks of therapy to obtain optimal effects. An ECG should be performed periodically and with dose adjustment, since the drug may potentiate cardiac dysrhythmias.

## ANTIDEPRESSANT THERAPY
## Affective Disorders

**Affective disorders,** or mood disturbances, include depression, which is the most common affective disorder, and mania or elation. Mania is discussed later in this chapter.

### Depression

Over the years many classifications of depression have been used, such as the time during life that depression occurred (childhood, adolescent, or senile depressions), or the reason for the depression, such as reactive (exogenous) depression or endogenous depression. Reactive depressions are often a person's response to a loss (loss of pleasure or interest in activities and everyday living caused perhaps by the loss of a loved one or the presence of a debilitating illness) or disappointment (from not meeting one's expectations or loss of a job, pet, friend, or lover). This is usually referred to as "the blues" or normal depression, which generally remits in several months without the use of antidepressant medications. The mobilization of support systems and, if necessary, psychotherapy are useful adjuncts in **exogenous depression.**

**Endogenous depressions** are characterized by the absence of external causes for depression. This type of depression may be caused by genetic determination and biochemical alterations (Csernansky and Hollister, 1982). Antidepressant medications are very useful in the treatment of this type of depression.

The current classification for depressive disorders (Andreason and others, 1980) has eliminated the use of the above terminology. Instead, major affective disorders are defined as bipolar disorders (mixed type and manic) and major depression (single episode or recurrent episodes), along with atypical affective disorders, which include depression. Psychiatrists have debated over whether the new classification was an improvement over the previous (endogenous, exogenous, or manic depression) types of classification, since it is important for the clinician to have a diagnostic framework from which to work.

The recognition of atypical depressions was considered a benefit (Csernansky and Hollister, 1982). Atypical depression usually does not meet the criteria for major depression or any other affective illness, thus it is characterized as atypical. Criteria for major depression include the presence of mood changes (sadness, despondency, anxiety, crying spells, guilt feelings, self-pity, pessimism, loss of interest in life and social activities), psychologic symptoms (low self-esteem, poor concentration, hopeless or helpless feelings, suicidal or increased focus on death), physiologic manifestations (sleep disturbances that may range from insomnia to hypersomnia, decreased interest in sex, complaints of fatigue, loss of energy, menstrual dysfunction, headaches, palpitations, constipation, loss of appetite, and weight loss or weight gain), and thinking alterations (a decrease in concentration or attention span, complaints of poor memory, confusion, delusions relating to health, persecution, or religion, and hallucinations if the client is also psychotic). Mood variations are usually diurnal and often worse in the morning.

Atypical depressions usually are of briefer duration and not as severe as a major depression. Often they are nonresponsive to the tricyclic antidepressants. Mood changes are usually worse in the evening; panic attacks, phobias such as agoraphobia, and physiologic complaints are often present. Csernansky and Hollister (1982) and Stimmel (1988) believe the MAO inhibitors are the drugs of choice for this type of depression.

Other measures to treat depression include electroshock therapy, psychotherapy, reduction of environmental stressors, and milieu therapy. In a number of cases, antidepressant drug therapy in combination with one or more adjunct measures is more effective than drug therapy alone.

### Phobia

Phobia and panic disorders affect at least 1% to 2% of American adults, but unfortunately only a small percentage of this population seeks or receives treatment. It has also been reported that physicians often fail to diagnose one or both of these conditions; thus it is important for health care professionals to recognize such symptoms in their clients. A person with phobia usually has an irrational fear of an object or situation. The fear is so prevalent and intense that the person will do anything possible to avoid the source of this distress. For example, agoraphobia (fear of open or crowded places) may upon exposure, result in a panic attack characterized by both physical and emotional responses. The individual that suffers from this problem may feel unsafe in a public setting or crowd, away from his or her home or familiar place. The reaction (panic attack) often includes a fear that he or she is dying of a heart attack, losing control over the situation, or perhaps, going crazy. The physical symptoms may include a feeling of choking, palpitations, lightheadedness and chest pain. Physical examinations and tests fail to uncover the cause of the reaction.

A panic disorder is usually diagnosed after a person has four or more similar attacks in a month that were not provoked by an actual fearful situation. Although effective

therapy is available for treatment, approximately 75% of the persons suffering from anxiety disorders are untreated. The medications most commonly used include the antidepressants (imipramine and phenelzine) and the antianxiety agent, alprazolam. Psychotherapy alone has not been very successful, but as an adjunct to drug treatment it can be very useful in helping the client identify and resolve internal conflicts (Phobia, 1989).

## Etiology of Affective Disorders

No single etiologic factor has been identified as the cause of affective disorders. Psychiatrists believing in psychosocial therapies will probe to identify stressful events or mental conflicts in one's life that preceded the onset of depression. Psychiatrists adhering to the biologic theory tend to explain affective disorders according to the monoamine theory (i.e., catecholamine [norepinephrine, dopamine, epinephrine] and indolamine [serotonin] levels in the CNS). Many practitioners today believe that both psychosocial and biologic factors lead to a common pathway that results in an affective disorder.

Many factors are involved with affective disorders, such as genetics, psychosocial events (divorce, death of a mate), physiologic stress (illness, infection, childbirth), and personality traits. Any combination of these factors may also affect the CNS's biochemical mechanisms leading again to the idea of the common pathway for affective disorders (Herfindal, 1988).

### Monoamine Theory in Affective Disorders

Centrally acting monoamines, especially norepinephrine and serotonin, have been theorized as the cause of depression and mania. A deficiency in central norepinephrine has

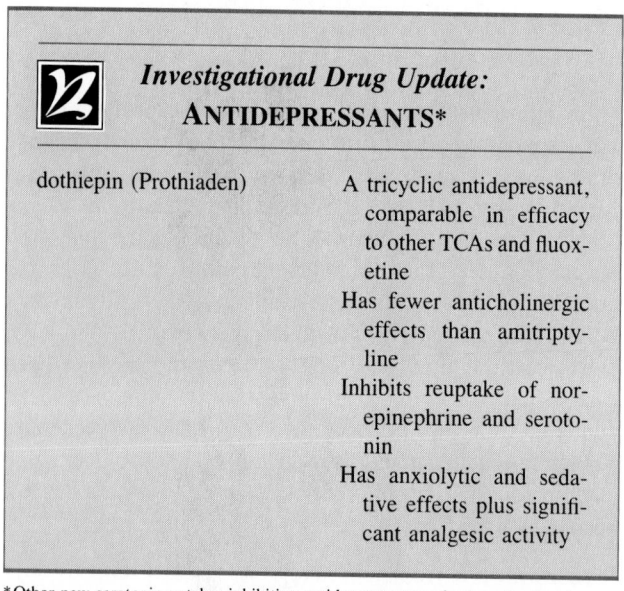

**Investigational Drug Update:
ANTIDEPRESSANTS***

| dothiepin (Prothiaden) | A tricyclic antidepressant, comparable in efficacy to other TCAs and fluoxetine |
| | Has fewer anticholinergic effects than amitriptyline |
| | Inhibits reuptake of norepinephrine and serotonin |
| | Has anxiolytic and sedative effects plus significant analgesic activity |

*Other new serotonin-uptake–inhibiting antidepressants under investigation include sertraline, paroxetine, fluvoxamine, and gepirone.

been associated with depression, whereas an excess of nor-epinephrine is believed to be related to mania. Both nor-epinephrine and serotonin may be important substances in regulating affective behaviors, and the most important receptors for them appear to be in the limbic system (Bachmann and Sherman, 1983).

The tricyclic antidepressants may block the reuptake of one or both monoamines into the adrenergic neuron. This blockade will lead to elevated levels of norepinephrine and serotonin in the synapse areas. MAO, an enzyme found in the mitochondria of nerve cells, is responsible for metabolizing norepinephrine within the nerve. MAO inhibitors block this enzyme, leading to increased levels of norepinephrine available for release to the synapse area. Although the mechanism of action of many antidepressants is inhibition of reuptake of norepinephrine or serotonin or inhibition of the MAO enzyme system, not all antidepressants have this effect. Therefore it is believed that the full range of antidepressant central activity of these medications is probably unknown (Figure 17-6).

## Selection of a Tricyclic Antidepressant

When drug therapy is indicated, the tricyclic antidepressants are usually the first drugs prescribed. No single agent is an ideal antidepressant because all of them may induce undesirable side or adverse effects; thus researchers are constantly searching for new antidepressant agents. See the box on page 338 for investigational antidepressant drugs according to chemical structures and comments.

Newer antidepressants include bupropion and fluoxetine, which are not chemically related to the other antidepressants. While bupropion's (Wellbutrin) mechanism of action is unknown, a major (although weak) effect noted is that it blocks reuptake of dopamine, serotonin, and norepinephrine. Bupropion is reserved for clients nonresponsive to the other tricyclic antidepressants; it is not usually an agent of first choice because of its seizure-producing potential. Fluoxetine (Prozac) is a potent antidepressant that primarily blocks reuptake of serotonin. Unlike the tricyclic agents that often cause weight gain in the individual, fluoxetine decreases appetite leading to weight loss. Clinical studies have reported weight reductions of 2 to 4 pounds in persons taking this product. Since its introduction in 1988, it has become one of the most widely prescribed antidepressants in the United States (Hussar, 1989).

Trazodone, with the least anticholinergic effect, has the greatest margin for safety in overdose when compared with the other antidepressants. It also does not affect cardiac conduction, so it may be a safer product for the client with heart disease.

Generally, physicians select sedating antidepressants (amitriptyline, doxepin, or fluoxetine) that are potent serotonin reuptake blocking agents for the agitated depressive client. The potent blockers of norepinephrine reuptake (desipramine, nortriptyline) are reserved for the withdrawn depres-

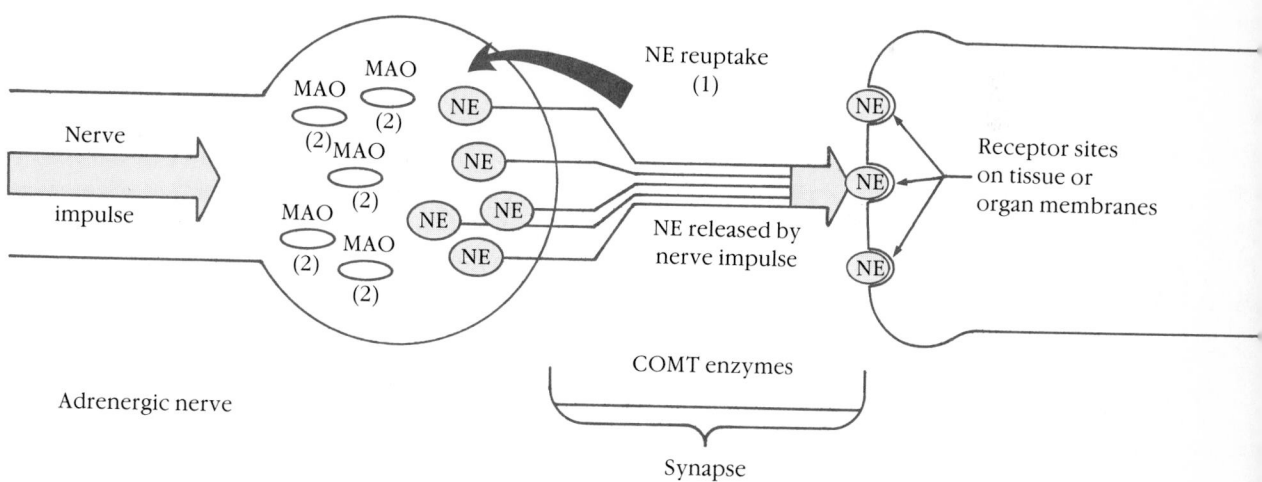

**FIGURE 17-6** Proposed action of antidepressant drug therapy. Normally norepinephrine (NE) is released from storage sites within the adrenergic nerve by the arrival of a nerve impulse. The released NE may be metabolized within the nerve by MAO enzyme or following the activity of NE at the receptor sites, by catechol-O-methyltransferase (COMT) enzymes located in the synaptic cleft. Most NE is taken back into the nerve and stored by way of the reuptake mechanism. Antidepressant drug therapy: (1) tricyclic antidepressants block the reuptake of released NE and prevent it from reentering the adrenergic nerve. (2) MAO inhibitors block MAO located on surface of the cell mitochondria. The result is more NE available for release or available in the synapse area. See text.

**TABLE 17-7**  Relationship between pharmacodynamic effects and side effects of selected antidepressants

| Name | Serum half-life (hr) | Blockade of reuptake of | | Sedative effects | Anticholinergic effects* | Orthostatic hypotension† |
|---|---|---|---|---|---|---|
| | | Norepinephrine | Serotonin | | | |
| amitriptyline (Elavil) | 8-93 | 2 | 4 | 4 | 4 | 4 |
| amoxapine (Asendin) | 8-30 | 3 | 2 | 1 | 3 | 2 |
| bupropion (Wellbutrin) | 9-21 | 1 | 1 | Unknown | 2 | 1 |
| desipramine (Pertofrane) | 12-24 | 4 | Unknown | 1 | 1 | 3 |
| doxepin (Sinequan) | 8-24 | 1 | 2 | 4 | 3 | 3 |
| fluoxetine (Prozac) | 48-216 | Unknown | 3 | 1 | 1 | 1 |
| imipramine (Tofranil) | 11-25 | 3 | 3 | 3 | 3 | 4 |
| maprotiline (Ludiomil) | 27-90 | 3 | 1 | 3 | 2 | 3 |
| nortriptyline (Aventyl) | 18-44 | 3 | 2 | 2 | 3 | 1 |
| protriptyline (Vivactil) | 67-89 | 3 | 2 | 1 | 3 | 2 |
| trazodone (Desyrel) | 3-9 | Unknown | 2 | 3 | 1 | 3 |
| trimipramine (Surmontil) | 9-11 | 1 | 1 | 4 | 4 | 3 |

Adapted from USP-DI (1991) and Young (1988). Activity potential 1 (low/slight) to 4 (high/greatest).
*Products block acetylcholine.
†Induced by drug and metabolites.

sive client. Selection of an antidepressant is empiric, taking into consideration the side effect potential of each antidepressant compared with the medical problems of the individual client.

For example, careful selection of an antidepressant is vital for the cardiac client. Many tricyclic antidepressants and the MAO inhibitors lower blood pressure, thus increasing the risk for orthostatic hypotension. Nortriptyline has been reported to be an alternative for the elderly client with preexisting left ventricular dysfunction or severe heart disease, since much less hypotension is reported with this drug. Desipramine and fluoxetine are other drugs with minimal potential for inducing hypotension.

Tachycardia, or increased heart rate, is reported with antidepressants having an anticholinergic effect. Amitriptyline and protriptyline will induce tachycardia more often than imipramine and desipramine. Also, fluoxetine tends to decrease instead of increase heart rate. Careful selection of an antidepressant is necessary for clients with a cardiac dysrhythmia, such as premature ventricular contractions (PVCs). Many antidepressants induce arrhythmias at toxic serum levels. At therapeutic or recommended dosages the tricyclic antidepressants possess antiarrhythmic effects. If the client is receiving quinidine-type medications, the tricyclic antidepressants should probably be avoided. Fluoxetine may be considered, since it does not appear to have this effect (Pary, 1989).

Plasma levels of the tricyclic antidepressants can vary widely between different individuals and often do not correlate with dose or therapeutic response. Physicians may order serum levels be monitored to help identify the noncompliant client. A low plasma level should initially indicate the need to interview the client for adherence to the pre-

scribed schedule. Seeking out reasons for noncompliance (side effects that are intolerable to client, misunderstanding of directions, lack of finances to purchase medications) can then be identified and perhaps resolved.

If compliance is verified and serum levels still remain low, dosage adjustments may be necessary or the physician might consider switching to a different tricyclic agent. If the client is nonresponsive to a predominantly norepinephrine-potentiating medication, a serotonin-potentiating agent might be indicated (see Table 17-7). Biochemical differences may be present in the individual that would indicate a trial with the opposite reuptake blocking agent.

The elderly often have reduced liver drug metabolizing enzymes, thus higher serum drug levels and a greater potential for side effects exist. Many physicians start geriatric clients at one third to one half the usual adult dosage, adjusting as necessary according to therapeutic response or presence of undesirable side effects.

The mechanisms of action of the tricyclic antidepressants are discussed in Etiology of Affective Disorders. These agents are indicated in the treatment of depression and enuresis (imipramine). They are well absorbed when given orally and are metabolized primarily in the liver. Active metabolites produced in the liver are as follows:

amitriptyline: nortriptyline
amoxapine: 7- and 8-hydroxyamoxapine
desipramine: 2 hydroxydesipramine
doxepin: desmethyldoxepin
imipramine: desipramine

Onset of antidepressant effect usually occurs within 2 to 3 weeks. (For half-life, serotonin- or norepinephrine-blocking potential, and sedative effects, see Table 17-7.) These drugs are excreted by the kidneys.

**TABLE 17-8**  Side effects/adverse reactions of tricyclic and tetracyclic antidepressants

| Drugs(s) | Side effects* | Adverse reactions† |
|---|---|---|
| **TRICYCLIC** | Most frequent: dizziness, dry mouth, headache, increased consumption of sweets, nausea, weakness, weight gain, unpleasant taste<br>Less frequent: sweating, diarrhea, gas, insomnia, vomiting | Most frequent: not reported<br>Less frequent: confusion, constipation (especially in geriatric clients), hypotension, dysrhythmia, nervousness, tremors, insomnia, tachycardia or bradycardia, visual pain or blurred vision |
| amoxapine only | | Less frequent: impairment of sexual functioning; extrapyramidal side effects (trouble speaking or swallowing, shuffle walk, slow movements, trembling, stiffness of arms and legs, loss of balance); tardive dyskinesia (abnormal chewing movements, lip smacking—see previous description on p. 326) |
| **TETRACYCLIC**<br>maprotiline | Most frequent: dizziness, blurred vision, dry mouth, pruritus, rash, insomnia, weakness, headache | Less frequent: severe constipation that may lead to impaction or paralytic ileus, nausea or vomiting, convulsions, tremors, increased excitement |
| **TRIAZOLOPYRIDINE**<br>trazodone | Most frequent: sedation, dry mouth, nausea, vomiting, headache, dizziness, blurred vision<br>Less frequent/rare: diarrhea, constipation, increased weakness, muscle pain or aches | Less frequent: muscle tremors, confusion<br>Rare: hypotension, bradycardia or tachycardia, painful delayed erection of the penis, rash, excitement |
| **BICYCLIC**<br>fluoxetine | Most frequent: anorexia, weight loss, nausea, increased nervousness, anxiety, insomnia, increased sweating<br>Less frequent: tremors, dry mouth, visual disturbance, cough, chest pain | Less frequent: fever, rash, respiratory difficulties, muscle aches<br>Rare: convulsions |
| **PHENYLAMINOKETONE**<br>bupropion | Most frequent: anorexia, dry mouth, lightheadedness, nausea, vomiting, tremors, constipation, weight loss<br><br>Less frequent: chills, fever, increased weakness, sedation, bad dreams, inability to concentrate | Most frequent: increased anxiety, agitation, confusion, tachycardia, headache, convulsions with high doses<br><br>Less frequent: rash |

*If side effects continue, increase, or disturb the client, inform the physician.
†If adverse reactions occur, contact physician, since medical intervention may be necessary.

For side effects/adverse reactions, see Table 17-8.

***Significant drug interactions.*** The following effects may occur when tricyclic antidepressants are given with the drugs listed below:

| Drug | Possible Effect and Management |
|---|---|
| alcohol or CNS depressants | May result in enhanced CNS depressant effects; avoid concurrent use if possible, or reduce dosage of one or both drugs and monitor closely. |
| antithyroid drugs | Increase risk of inducing agranulocytosis; avoid concurrent use if possible. |
| cimetidine, ranitidine | May inhibit metabolism of tricyclic agent leading to increased serum levels and toxicity; lower tricyclic dose by 20% to 30% and monitor closely. |

| Drug | Possible Effect and Management |
|---|---|
| clonidine, guanadrel, or guanethidine | May decrease the antihypertensive effects of these drugs; monitor closely since dosage changes or alternate antihypertensive agents may be necessary. Clonidine and tricyclic antidepressants may increase risk of CNS depression; monitor closely for lethargy, confusion and respiratory depression. |
| contraceptives, oral | May increase or decrease tricyclic serum levels; monitor closely for decreased therapeutic response or drug toxicity; dosage adjustments may be necessary. |
| extrapyramidal-inducing medications | Amoxapine and extrapyramidal-inducing drugs (phenothiazines, haloperidol, metoclopramide, reserpine, thioxanthenes) may increase risk and severity of extrapyramidal adverse effects. With phenothiazines, sedative and anticholinergic side effects may be enhanced; monitor closely. |

| Drug | Possible Effect and Management |
|---|---|
| metrizamide intrathecal | Concurrent use of tricyclic antidepressants increases risk of inducing seizures because of a lowered seizure threshold. Discontinue tricyclic agents for at least 2 days before and 1 day after a myelogram. |
| MAO inhibitors | Should be contraindicated in outpatient settings; hypertensive crises, severely elevated temperatures, convulsions, and death have been reported with concurrent administration of MAO inhibitors and tricyclic antidepressants. Before switching from one classification to the other, at least a 2-week drug-free period from either category should be instituted. If concurrent use is prescribed in an inpatient setting, it would require strict supervision and close monitoring because of the potentially serious adverse effects. See current USP-DI for dosing recommendations. |
| sympathomimetics | Increase possiblity of potentiating cardiovascular toxicities (severe hypertension, dysrhythmias, tachycardia) or severely elevated body temperatures. If this combination cannot be avoided, monitor very closely. If possible, avoid this combination. |

***Dosage and administration.*** See Table 17-9.

## clomipramine (Anafranil)

Clomipramine, a new tricyclic antidepressant, is an analogue of imipramine. It is a potent inhibitor of serotonin reuptake and its active metabolite (desmethylclomipramine) inhibits norepinephrine reuptake. It is indicated for the treatment of obsessive-compulsive disorders.

It is well absorbed orally, reaching the peak plasma level within 2 to 4 hours. It has a half-life of 19 to 37 hours and reaches steady state levels in 1 to 2 weeks. Metabolism is via the liver, and excretion is in the urine.

Side effects/adverse reactions and drug interactions are similar to the other tricyclic agents. The initial adult dose is 25 mg daily, gradually increasing the dose as necessary and tolerated, to about 100 mg during the first 14 days. Administer in divided doses to reduce the gastrointestinal side effects. After 2 weeks, the dose may be increased over several more weeks if necessary, to a maximum dose of 250 mg/day. After the dose is established, the total daily dose may be given at bedtime to reduce daytime sedation effects.

In children and adolescents, the initial dose is 25 mg a day increasing as necessary during the first 14 days, to a daily maximum of 3 mg/kg or 100 mg (or whichever is the smaller dose). Afterward, the dose may be increased to 3 mg/kg or 200 mg (whichever is smaller) as necessary. Once the titrated dose is established, the entire daily dose may be administered at bedtime.

See main discussion of nursing management of tricyclic antidepressant therapy.

## ▷Nursing Management: Tricyclic Antidepressant Therapy

***Assessment.*** Tricyclic antidepressants should not be administered to clients with increased intraocular pressure, history of urinary retention, or history of narrow-angle glaucoma, because these medications possess significant anticholinergic properties; hyperthyroid clients or those taking thyroid medication, because of the possibility of cardiovascular toxicity; individuals with a past history of seizure disorders, because this class of drugs has been demonstrated to lower the seizure threshold; or clients receiving guanethidine, methyldopa, clonidine, or similar agents, because the tricyclic antidepressants block the pharmacologic effects of these drugs. The following list summarizes the conditions that contraindicate administration of tricyclic antidepressants:

| | |
|---|---|
| Active alcoholism | Asthma |
| Glaucoma (narrow angle) | Angina pectoris |
| Kidney disease | Congestive heart failure |
| Pyloric stenosis | Paroxysmal tachycardia |
| Epilepsy | Benign prostatic hypertrophy |
| Overactivity, overstimulation, or agitation | Before surgery |
| Impaired liver function | Pregnancy (risks to fetus) |
| Myocardial infarction (recent) | Hyperthyroidism |
| | Blood disorders |

Clients must be closely assessed at the start of therapy and monitored closely throughout therapy for suicide potential. The risk of suicide increases as therapy improves the client's depressed state and energy levels increase.

***Intervention.*** The client's blood pressure and pulse should be monitored at appropriate intervals. Note that the possibility of suicide is inherent in any severely depressed client and persists until a significant remission occurs. The suicidal risks of tricyclic antidepressants are especially high, and suicide attempts with tricyclic antidepressants are frequently seen in many emergency departments. When a client has a serious overt suicidal potential and is not hospitalized, the quantity of the tricyclic antidepressant should not exceed 1 week's supply. In clients with schizophrenia, activation of the psychosis may occur, requiring reduction of the dosage or the addition of a major tranquilizer to the therapeutic regimen. Manic or hypomanic episodes may occur in individuals with the cyclic type of disorders. If this occurs, the tricyclic antidepressant should be discontinued until the episode is relieved and then may be reinstituted at a lowered dosage if still needed in the therapy.

Initial dosages in adolescent, elderly, and debilitated clients should be lower and increased gradually. The medication should not be withdrawn abruptly.

***Education.*** During initiation or change of therapy, the client should avoid activities that require coordination and alertness until response to the tricyclic antidepressant therapy has been determined.

**TABLE 17-9** Dosage and administration of tricyclic and tetracyclic antidepressants

| | Adults | Elderly | Children |
|---|---|---|---|
| amitriptyline tablets | 25 mg orally 2-4 times daily; adjust dosage as necessary Maximum daily dose, up to 150 mg if outpatient; up to 300 mg daily for hospitalized clients | 25 mg orally at bedtime. May increase dose as necessary up to 10 mg 3 times daily and 20 mg at bedtime. Maximum daily dose is 100 mg/day | Children 6-12 yrs old, 10-30 mg orally in two divided doses. Adolescents, 10 mg orally 3 times daily and 20 mg at bedtime initially. Dose may be increased as necessary up to a 100 mg/day maximum |
| amitriptyline HCl injection | 20-30 mg IM 4 times daily | | Children less than 12 yr, not established |
| amoxapine tablet | 50 mg orally 2-3 times daily. May increase dose to 100 mg 2 or 3 times daily during 1st week of therapy, if necessary. Do not increase over 300 mg/day until this dosage is determined to be ineffective, after a minimum 2-week trial. Maximum per day, institutionalized clients, up to 600 mg daily in divided dosages | 25 mg orally 3 times daily; if necessary, may increase to 50 mg 3 times a day, within first week | Children less than 16 yr, not established |
| desipramine tablet/capsule | 25-50 mg orally 3 times a day; increase dosage as necessary. Maximum daily dosage, adult up to 300 mg/day | 25-50 mg daily in divided dosages; increase if necessary; maximum, 150 mg/day | Children 6-12 yrs old, 10-30 mg orally in divided doses. Adolescents 25-50 mg orally in divided doses. Maximum, up to 100 mg/day |
| doxepin capsules/liquid | 25 mg orally 3 times daily; increase as necessary. Maximum daily dosage, up to 150 mg daily for outpatients; up to 300 mg daily for institutionalized clients | 25 to 50 mg orally daily. Increase dose slowly, as necessary | Children less than 12 yr, not established |
| imipramine tablet | 25-50 mg orally 3 or 4 times daily; adjust dosage as necessary Maximum daily dosages, up to 200 mg daily for outpatients; up to 300 mg/day for institutionalized clients | 25 mg orally at bedtime. Increase dose as necessary to maximum 100 mg/day | Antidepressant dosage: children less than 6 yr, not recommended; 6-12 yr, 10-30 mg orally in 2 divided doses. Adolescents, 25-50 mg orally in divided doses, adjust dose as necessary up to maximum of 100 mg/day Adolescents, same as elderly. Antienuretic: 25 mg orally daily 1 hr before sleep. If desired response is not achieved within 1 wk, increase to 50 mg at night for children under 12 and to 75 mg for children over 12. May give half dosage in midafternoon and one half at bedtime. This, at times, has proved more effective than single bedtime dosing |
| imipramine pamoate capsule | 75 mg orally at bedtime; increase dosage as necessary. Usually 150 mg at bedtime is optimum dosage. Maximum daily dosage, up to 200 mg daily for outpatients; up to 300 mg for institutionalized clients | | Children less than 12 yr, not established |
| imipramine hydrochloride injection | 25 mg IM 3 or 4 times daily. Maximum daily dosage, up to 300 mg/day | | Children less than 12 yr, not recommended |

**TABLE 17-9**    Dosage and administration of tricyclic and tetracyclic antidepressants—cont'd

| | Adults | Elderly | Children |
|---|---|---|---|
| nortriptyline capsule/liquid | 25 mg orally 3 or 4 times daily; adjust dosage as necessary up to 150 mg/day | 30-50 mg in divided dosages daily; adjust dosage as needed | Children 6-12 yr, 10-20 mg orally daily in divided doses. Adolescents, 25-50 mg/day orally in divided doses; adjust dosage as necessary |
| protriptyline tablets | 5-10 mg orally 3 or 4 times daily. Adjust dosage as necessary. Maximum daily dosage, up to 600 mg/day | 5 mg orally 3 times daily. Adjust dosage as necessary If daily dosage is above 20 mg/day for an elderly person, closely monitor for cardiovascular responses | Children less than 12 yr, not established. Adolescents, same as elderly |
| trimipramine maleate capsule | 25 mg orally 3 times daily; adjust dosage as needed Maximum daily dosages, up to 200 mg/day for outpatients, up to 300 mg/day for institutionalized clients | 25 mg orally twice daily; adjust dosage as necessary. Maximum daily dosage, up to 100 mg/day | Children less than 12 yr, not established. Adolescents, same as elderly |
| tetracyclic antidepressants maprotiline tablets | 25-75 mg orally in divided dosages daily for 2 wk; adjust dosage as necessary by 25 mg/day increments. Maintenance dose, usually 150 mg daily administered at bedtime | 25 mg daily initially; gradually increase dose as necessary; maintenance dosage, 50-75 mg daily | Children less than 18 yr, not established |
| **TRIAZOLOPYRIDINE** | | | |
| trazodone | 50 mg orally, 3 times a day. Dose may be increased by 50 mg/day, at 3-4 day intervals as necessary. Maximum for outpatients: 400 mg/day; for inpatients: 600 mg/day | 75 mg orally in divided doses; may increase dose slowly at 3- to 4-day intervals, as necessary | Children 6-18 yr, 1.5 to 2 mg/kg body weight in divided doses. Increased dosage as necessary, at 3- to 4-day intervals, up to maximum of 6 mg/kg/day |
| **BICYCLIC** | | | |
| fluoxetine | 20 mg orally in the morning for several weeks. If necessary, dose may be increased by 20 mg/day (morning and noon schedule). Maximum daily dose is 80 mg/day | Usually require lower dosages. Maximum, up to 60 mg/day | Not established |
| **PHENYLAMINOKETONE** | | | |
| bupropion | 100 mg orally twice daily. Increase dose at approximately every 3 days up to maximum of 450 mg/day | Not established | Not established |

Alert the client to report anticholinergic effects of the drugs, such as blurred vision, altered thought processes, constipation, difficulty starting urinary stream, and eye pain, which may be indicative of glaucoma. The client should be advised to schedule regular appointments with the health care professional for periodic blood cell counts, glaucoma tests, and hepatic and renal function studies.

Self-alteration of the prescribed medications or consumption of other medication including over-the-counter medications should not be done without consultation with the prescriber. Clients should be specifically instructed to avoid alcoholic beverages during the tricyclic antidepressant regimen since CNS depression may be heightened.

Orthostatic hypotension may occur. The nurse should instruct the client to come to a standing position slowly and carefully to avoid feeling faint.

Since dry mouth is a common side effect, the client should be taught appropriate oral hygiene to prevent caries and other dental problems. In addition, breath mints may be reassuring to the client in social situations. Ice chips and sugarless candies are also helpful in promoting comfort.

The nurse should caution the client that therapeutic response to tricyclic antidepressants is not immediate. It may be 10 to 14 days before there is demonstrative effect and 30 days for full effect.

Note that an emerging public health problem is tricyclic antidepressant poisoning or overdosage in children. Doses in excess of 10 mg/kg body weight are potentially dangerous. The incidents are characterized as accidental, since most occur when the drug is given to a household member for depression or to an enuretic child. Alert the adult family member to the possibility of accidental overdosage and the need for security and administrative responsibility over the medication.

*Evaluation.* In resistant cases of depression in adults, a dose of 2.5 mg/kg body weight/day or higher may have to be exceeded in the hospital. If such a dose or higher is necessary, maintain ECG monitoring during the initiation of therapy and at appropriate intervals during stabilization of the dose.

When tricyclic antidepressants are administered to pregnant clients, the potential benefits should be weighed against the potential fetal risks.

Employ extreme caution (monitoring, nursing observations) when the tricyclic antidepressants are administered to clients with any evidence of cardiovascular disease because of the possibility of conduction defects, dysrhythmias, myocardial infarction, cerebrovascular accidents, and tachycardia. The quinidine-like cardiac effects are well documented in the literature.

If the client is to be evaluated by plasma tricyclic determination because of a failure to respond to treatment, increased side effects, or a question of compliance, blood samples should be taken immediately before the first morning dose or at least 8 hours after a dose.

*Overdosage and treatment.* Nearly a half million cases of tricyclic antidepressant drug overdoses occur yearly in the United States. Therefore it is important that health care professionals know how to deal with tricyclic overdose.

The signs and symptoms of overdosage may vary in severity, depending on many factors, including but not limited to the amount of the tricyclic antidepressants ingested and absorbed, age of the individual, and interval between ingestion and initiation of treatment modality. Any acute overdosage or unwarranted ingestion (even in children) of any amount must be considered as serious and potentially fatal.

The CNS abnormalities caused by overdosage may be agitation, ataxia, choreoathetoid movements, coma, convulsions, drowsiness, hyperactive reflexes, muscle rigidity, restlessness, and stupor. Cardiac abnormalities may include the following: dysrhythmia, ECG evidence of impaired conduction, signs of congestive heart failure, and tachycardia. Quinidine-like effects are common in poisonings with tricyclic antidepressants.

These additional conditions may also be present: cyanosis, diaphoresis, hyperpyrexia, hypotension, mydriasis, respiratory shock, and vomiting. Renal failure is seen with amoxapine overdose.

Since no specific antidote is known, the treatment for tricyclic antidepressant overdose is supportive and symptomatic. It necessitates hospitalization and close medical attention for the CNS involvement, respiratory depression, and cardiac dysrhythmias of sudden onset. This is suggested at all times, even when the quantity ingested is alleged to be small or the initial degree of intoxication apparently is minor or moderate. Each client having ECG abnormalities must have continuous cardiac monitoring for at least 5 days, coupled with close observations until well after the cardiac status has returned to normal, since after the apparent recovery period a relapse may occur. Cardiac dysrhythmias have occurred up to 6 days after massive doses of tricyclic antidepressants and may be treated with lidocaine (phenytoin for dysrhythmias retractory to lidocaine). The reported greater sensitivity of children to acute tricyclic antidepressant overdosage necessitates hospital cardiac monitoring for at least 5 days or more.

If the client is not comatose and is alert, the stomach should be promptly emptied by inducing emesis followed by lavage. If the client is obtunded, the airway should be protected with a cuffed endotracheal tube before beginning the lavage; and emesis should be induced. The lavage is continued for at least 24 hours, based on the degree of intoxication. In children and adults the use of 0.9% or 0.45% saline solution avoids water intoxication. The use of activated charcoal instilled as a slurry may reduce absorption; however, this is done only after ipecac-induced emesis has occurred. If the activated charcoal and ipecac syrup are used concurrently, the charcoal will absorb the ipecac and therefore reduce substantially its emetic effect.

The use of physostigmine salicylate is directed at clients with life-threatening signs (coma with respiratory depression, severe hypertension, uncontrollable seizures). The adult dose should start with 1 to 3 mg (slow intravenous injection at 1 mg over 1 minute). This initial dose may be repeated in 10 to 15 minutes, not exceeding a total of 4 mg. In children the initial dose is 0.5 mg slowly and intravenously and repeated at 5-minute intervals to arrive at the minimal effective dose, which should not exceed 2 mg. The minimal effective dose may be repeated as necessary every 30 to 60 minutes because the duration of action of physostigmine is short. Slow intravenous use of physostigmine is mandatory because rapid injections may possibly cause physostigmine-induced convulsions. Physostigmine can increase conduction blocks, causing cardiac arrest, and can aggravate tricyclic antidepressant- or phenothiazine-induced conduction abnormalities. It may also cause bronchospasm, muscle weakness, an increase in respiratory secretions, and bradycardia.

Adequate respiratory exchanges must be maintained without the use of respiratory stimulants. Shock may be treated with supportive measures, such as intravenous fluids, oxygen, and corticosteroids. The use of digitalis may induce further conduction abnormalities and thus aggravate a previously sensitized myocardium. Extreme care must be exercised if rapid digitalization is required because of congestive heart failure.

The tendency to convulsions may be reduced by minimizing external stimulation. If anticonvulsants are necessary, diazepam, paraldehyde, or phenytoin may be useful. Hyperpyrexia may be controlled by ice packs, cooling sponge baths, and a cooling blanket.

Since the tricyclic antidepressants are rapidly fixed in the tissues, hemodialysis, peritoneal dialysis, exchange transfusions, and forced diuresis have been generally unsuccessful and ineffective. The level of tricyclic antidepressants in the blood and urine may not correlate with the degree of intoxication or reflect the severity of the poisoning and is thus an unreliable index in the clinical management of this tricyclic antidepressant-overdosage syndrome, but it does have diagnostic value.

## MAO Inhibitor Antidepressants

The monoamines (norepinephrine, dopamine, serotonin) are CNS transmitters. Norepinephrine is also a peripheral transmitter at the sympathetic neuroeffector junction. MAO is widely distributed throughout the body, with the highest concentrations in the brain, liver, and kidneys. It is located on the surface of the mitochondria of cells in the previously mentioned areas and also in the adrenergic nerve terminals. MAO regulates the metabolism of catecholamines and serotonin. In the liver it is an important substance because it inactivates monoamines such as tyramine, which are absorbed from the gut into the portal circulation.

Two types of MAO enzymes have been identified and named MAO-A and MAO-B. MAO-A appears to have a preference for serotonin and is located throughout the body, with high concentrations located in the human placenta. MAO-B is mainly contained in human platelets, but approximately equal amounts of both types are found in the liver and brain. The MAO inhibitor drugs currently in use are nonselective.

The MAO inhibitors (MAOIs) are capable of blocking or diminishing the activity of MAO. The result is a net increase in brain amine levels. MAOIs also block amine uptake. Current research indicates the MAOIs produce desensitization of the alpha-2 or beta and serotonin receptors (downregulation). During early clinical trials of MAOIs as antidepressants, orthostatic hypotension was encountered as a common but inconsistent side effect, and many MAOIs were then produced and studied specifically as antidepressant and antihypertensive agents.

MAOIs encompass a variety of activities: as an antidepressant, as an antineoplastic agent (procarbazine), as an antibiotic (furazolidone), and as an antihypertensive agent (pargyline hydrochloride). The MAOIs discussed in this section are the agents used as antidepressants: the hydrazines—isocarboxazid (Marplan) and phenelzine (Nardil),

and the nonhydrazine, tranylcypromine sulfate (Parnate). Evidence shows that the primary properties seem to have special relevance to their psychiatric or mood alteration activity, reserpine reversal (reserpine decreases the concentration of norepinephrine in the central and peripheral nervous system), and potentiation of indirect-acting pressor amines. The MAOIs are indicated primarily in resistant depressions (to tricyclic and tetracyclic antidepressants) and anxious and hostile depressions, especially those also involving panic attacks and/or phobic symptoms.

MAOIs can increase the concentration of all central amines, although different effects on the individual amines are possible. For example, some of the MAOIs may increase dopamine or norepinephrine concentrations to a more extensive degree than serotonin concentrations, whereas other MAOIs may raise the level of serotonins to a greater degree than those of norepinephrine and dopamine. The increase in amine concentration is associated with behavioral hyperactivity (amphetamine-like psychomotor stimulation with large doses) produced by the MAOIs and, in some cases, with the exacerbation of psychotic symptoms. In lower doses the antiphobic and antidepressant activities are seen. In general these compounds are most effective in reversing the dysphoric state and its attendant vegetative disturbances in clients with depressive syndromes.

The therapeutic doses of the MAOIs require days to weeks to attain a maximal therapeutic effect. MAOIs produce an irreversible inactivation of MAO by forming a stable complex with the enzyme; thus degradation of biologic amines by this route is prevented and as such does not inhibit MAO production. Recovery from the effect of MAOIs thus depends on enzyme regeneration, which may occur over several weeks. MAOIs inhibit enzymes other than MAO, such as dopamine-$\beta$-oxidase, diamine oxidase, amino acid decarboxylases, and choline dehydrogenase. Inhibition occurs only in very high doses and may be responsible for some of the toxic effects of MAOIs. The mechanism of action of MAOIs is discussed in the previous section. They are indicated in treatment of mental depression. See previous section. Absorption of MAOIs is very good from GI tract. They are metabolized in the liver. Onset of action in some individuals occurs from 7 to 10 days; full effect usually takes from 4 to 8 weeks of therapy. These agents irreversibly bind MAO activity; recovery may take 10 days to 2 weeks. MAOIs are excreted in the bile and kidneys. Side effects/adverse reactions are discussed in Table 17-10.

***Significant drug interactions.*** The following effects may occur when MAO inhibitors are given with the drugs listed below:

| Drug | Possible Effect and Management |
|---|---|
| alcohol or CNS depressants | May enhance CNS depressive effects. If alcohol contains tyramine, may result in severe hypertensive reaction. Avoid concurrent use. |

**TABLE 17-10**  Side effects/adverse reactions of MAOIs

| Side effects* | Adverse reactions† |
|---|---|
| More frequent: orthostatic hypotension, tremors, insomnia, headache, muscle twitching (during sleep), increased weakness, constipation, impaired sexual function, sleepiness, increased eating and weight gain, difficulty in urination | More frequent: orthostatic hypotension (dizziness when changing physical positions), fainting spells<br>Less frequent: diarrhea, edema of feet and legs, increased nervousness, tachycardia<br>Overdosage: increased anxiety, confusion, severe dizziness and drowsiness, elevated temperature, severe headache, hypotension or hypertension, irregular pulse, sweating, convulsions, severe insomnia, respiratory difficulties, hallucinations. Signs appear in 12 hr and reach maximum effect in 24-48 hr. Hospitalization and close monitoring are indicated since death has been reported |

*If side effects continue, increase, or disturb the client, inform the physician.
†If adverse reactions occur, contact physician, since medical intervention may be necessary.

| Drug | Possible Effect and Management |
|---|---|
| local anesthetics containing epinephrine or cocaine | May result in very severe hypertensive reaction. Avoid concurrent use. Cocaine should not be administered during or within 2 weeks after an MAO inhibitor. |
| anesthetics, spinal | Hypotensive response may be increased. If spinal anesthesia is planned, discontinue MAOIs at least 2 weeks before surgery. |
| antidepressants, tricyclic, carbamazepine, maprotiline, or other MAO inhibitors (furazolidone, pargyline, or procarbazine) | May result in severely elevated temperatures, hypertensive crises, severe seizures, and death. Before switching from one of these medications to an MAO inhibitor or vice versa, a 2-week drug-free period should be instituted. Several studies have used tricyclic antidepressants with an MAO inhibitor for refractory depression. See current USP-DI for explicit instructions on proper dosing and monitoring of this combination. |
| antidiabetic agents, oral, or insulin | Enhanced hypoglycemic effects reported. Reduction in oral hypoglycemic agent may be required during or even after concurrent drug therapy. |
| antihistamines or antimuscarinics (e.g., atropine) | May enhance CNS depressant effects of antihistamines. May increase anticholinergic effects that could lead to a paralytic ileus. Monitor clients closely receiving this combination. |
| buspirone | May cause hypertension. Avoid this combination. |
| caffeine (e.g., drug products, coffee, tea, chocolate, cola) | May result in severe cardiac dysrhythmias or hypertension. Avoid concurrent use. |
| carbamazepine, cyclobenzaprine, maprotiline, or other MAO inhibitors | May result in severe hypertensive crises, convulsions, and death. At least a 2-week drug-free interval is recommended to avoid this reaction. |
| dextromethorphan | May result in increased excitability, hyperpyrexia, and hypertension. Avoid concurrent use. |
| doxapram | Avoid concurrent use. Enhanced hypertensive effects may result. |
| fluoxetine | May result in agitation, restlessness, gastrointestinal distress, or seizures and hypertensive crises. For client safety, a minimum of a 2-week drug-free period should be instituted when switching from an MAO inhibitor to fluoxetine. When switching from fluoxetine to an MAO inhibitor, a 5-week drug-free period should be implemented. |
| guanadrel, guanethidine, or rauwolfia alkaloids | Severe hypertension may be produced. Withdraw MAOI at least 7 days before starting therapy with these agents. Rauwolfia alkaloid: if an MAOI is added to a medication schedule already containing a rauwolfia alkaloid, serious CNS depression may result. Or, if a rauwolfia alkaloid is added to a medication schedule already including an MAOI, hypertension and increased excitability may result. If at all possible, avoid concurrent use. |
| levodopa | *Avoid this combination.* Severe and sudden hypertensive crisis reported. Before starting levodopa therapy, the client should be withdrawn from MAOIs with at least 2- to 4-week drug-free period. |
| meperidine and maybe other opioid narcotics | Severe hypertension, increased excitability, sweating, and rigidity reported with concurrent use. Also in some individuals, hypotension, seizures, elevated temperature, respiratory depression, cardiovascular collapse, coma, and death reported, which may be caused by serotonin accumulation from the MAOI. To avoid this reaction, avoid the use of meperidine for at least 14 to 21 days after a MAOI is stopped. Morphine and other narcotics are not reported as causing such a severe reaction, but it is recommended that the opioid dosage be reduced to one fourth (test dose) the usual dosage. Monitor closely whenever opioids or anesthesia adjuncts (fentanyl, alpharprodine, or sufentanil) are given to clients who have received MAOIs in the previous 2 or 3 weeks. |
| methyldopa | Severe headache, hypertension, hallucinations, and increased excitability have been reported. Avoid concurrent use. |

T/

SUN

Emo
unifi
ulati
abili
junc
it is
for a
more
phar
for a

Si
stitu
only
sole
are r
resul

Pl
tipsy
the
thou
not k
met
areas
nothi
sym
deve
te
many
many
that
istrat
A
fecti
tidep
inhib
tryp
the d
no id
unde
teach
admi
unto

tyrar
so
an
bo

BIB

Abrar
tom
Amer
mat
ma
D
Andr
Pi
stat
Am
▷N
Bachi
M
mai
not
A
ma
clier
hype

# ❧ 18 Drugs for Specific CNS-Peripheral Dysfunctions

## CHAPTER OBJECTIVES

*After studying this chapter, you should be able to meet the following objectives and define the key terms.*

1. Explain the neurotransmitter balance theory in Parkinson's disease.

2. Name the two neurotransmitters that centrally affect motor function and balance.

3. Discuss medications used to treat Parkinson's disease.

4. Discuss medications used to treat myasthenia gravis.

5. Apply nursing measures to the treatment of Parkinson's disease, myasthenia gravis, dementia, and Alzheimer's disease.

## KEY TERMS

**akinesia,** page 355

**anticholinergic drugs,** page 355

**anticholinesterase agents,** page 364

**Alzheimer's disease,** page 368

**dementia,** page 367

**designer drugs,** page 359

**hyperorality,** page 368

**myasthenia gravis,** page 364

**on-off syndrome,** page 361

**Parkinson's disease,** page 354

## INTRODUCTION

Parkinson's disease, myasthenia gravis, dementia, and Alzheimer's disease are examples of the major CNS-neuromuscular disorders. Because each syndrome is essentially progressive and often incapacitating, appropriate assessment, intervention, and evaluation are important measures for nursing.

## PARKINSON'S DISEASE

**Parkinson's disease** is a progressively debilitating disorder of the CNS. The cause is unknown; however, genetic and viral causes have been suspected. The disease is caused by a degeneration of the dopamine-producing neurons of the substantia nigra, which produces a dopamine/acetylcholine imbalance. The correct balance of dopamine and acetylcholine is important in regulating posture, muscle tone, and voluntary movement (Figure 18-1). Drug therapy is aimed at correcting this imbalance by increasing dopamine levels and blocking acetylcholine levels. The classes of drugs used

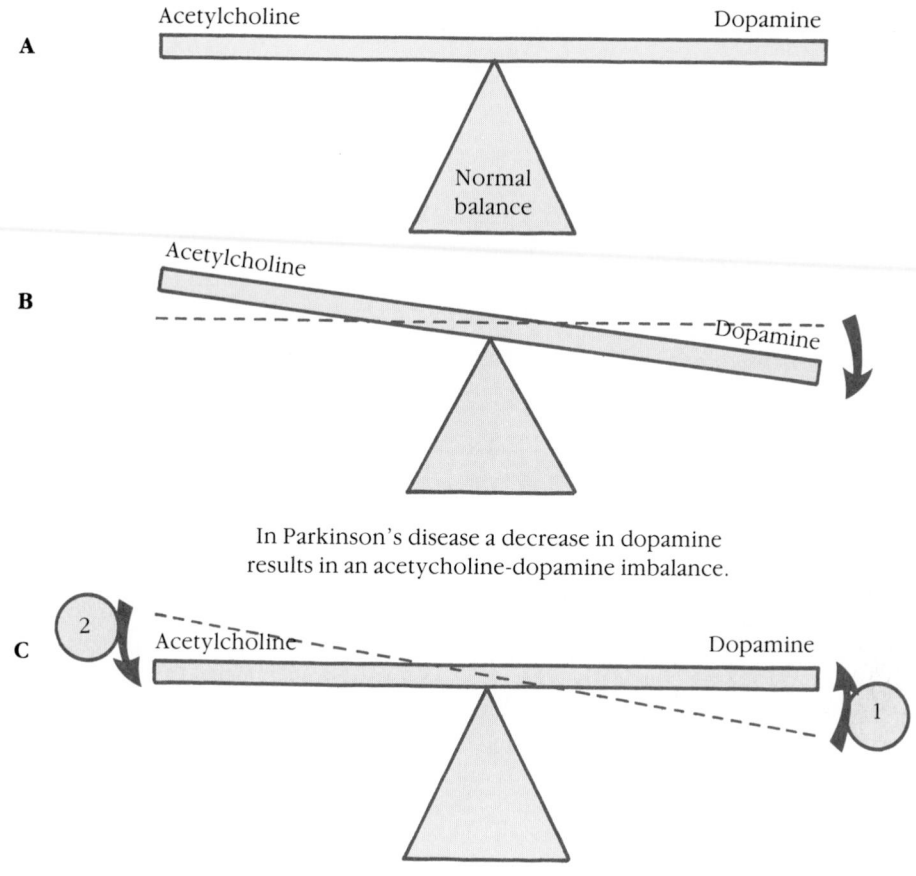

**FIGURE 18-1**  Central acetylcholine/dopamine balance. **A,** Normal "balance" of acetylcholine and dopamine. **B,** In Parkinson's disease, a *decrease* in dopamine results in an acetylcholine/dopamine imbalance. **C,** Drug therapy in Parkinson's disease aims at increasing the dopamine level, which restores the acetylcholine/dopamine balance toward normal by (1) increasing the supply of dopamine or (2) blocking or lowering acetylcholine levels.

in treatment are (1) drugs with central anticholinergic activity (anticholinergics and antihistamines) and (2) drugs that affect brain dopamine levels to enhance dopaminergic mechanisms.

## Drugs With Central Anticholinergic Activity

Symptoms of Parkinson's disease caused by an excess of cholinergic activity are muscle rigidity and muscle tremor. The muscle rigidity or increased tone appears as "ratchet resistance," or "cogwheel rigidity," wherein the affected muscle moves easily, then meets resistance or remains fixed in the new position. The muscle tremors appear to have a "to and fro" movement caused by the sequence of contractions of agonistic and antagonistic muscles involved. The tremors are usually worse at rest and are commonly manifested as "pill-rolling" motion of the hands and a bobbing of the head.

Various drugs with central anticholinergic activity are used to treat Parkinson's disease, such as anticholinergic agents, diphenhydramine, and ethopropazine, a phenothi-

azine. These agents are used in the treatment of mild Parkinson's disease and as an adjunct to dopamine replacement.

### Anticholinergic Agents

Drugs that inhibit or block the effects of acetylcholine are referred to as **anticholinergic drugs** (see Chapter 22 for a more complete discussion). The belladonna alkaloids, atropine and scopolamine, were the first centrally active (i.e., crossing the blood-brain barrier) anticholinergic agents used to treat parkinsonism and for many years were the only drugs available for such treatment. These drugs have been supplanted by synthetic anticholinergics, which were developed in an effort to produce drugs as effective as the belladonna drugs but with fewer side effects.

The anticholinergics that readily cross the blood-brain barrier can produce slight-to-moderate improvement in functional capacity. The usefulness of these drugs is limited due to their side effects and their tendency to be less effective with continued use. Some anticholinergics are also used to control the extrapyramidal reactions, such as rigidity, **akinesia** (difficulty in or lack of ability to initiate muscle move-

**TABLE 18-1**  Side effects/adverse reactions of anticholinergic drugs

| Side effects* | Adverse reactions† |
|---|---|
| More frequent: blurred vision, mydriasis, constipation, dry skin, anhidrosis, urinary hesitancy, pain on urination, nausea, vomiting, photophobia, drowsiness, xerostomia, dysphagia | Less common: confusion seen mostly in elderly receiving high doses, pain in eyes (result of increased intraocular pressure), and skin rash (face, upper trunk, urticaria, dermatitis) |
| Less frequent: orthostatic hypotension, euphoria (reported most often in elderly receiving high doses), headaches, abdominal pain, sore mouth and tongue, increased numbness in hands or feet, muscle cramping, nervousness | Overdosage: ataxia; dry mouth, nose, throat; difficulty breathing; tachycardia; flushed, red, dry skin; seizures; hallucinations; insomnia or severe CNS depression; mood changes |

*If side effects continue, increase, or disturb the client, the physician should be informed.
†If adverse reactions occur, the physician should be contacted because medical intervention may be necessary.

ment), tremor, and akathisia, caused by antipsychotic drugs such as the phenothiazines.

Anticholinergic drugs block central cholinergic excitatory pathways, returning the dopamine/acetylcholine balance in the brain (especially, the basal ganglia) to normal. The effects of the anticholinergic agents include decreased salivation and relaxation of smooth muscle with a decrease in tremors. Decreased rigidity and akinesia (in nearly 50% of the clients) are also reported. Some agents, such as procyclidine and trihexyphenidyl, may have a direct relaxing effect on smooth muscle.

Anticholinergic agents are indicated for use as antidyskinetics, for treatment of Parkinson's disease, and for treatment of drug-induced extrapyramidal reactions. These drugs are very well absorbed and the onset of action for specific drugs is as follows: benztropine oral, 1 to 2 hours; benztropine IM/IV, within minutes; ethopropazine, oral, 0.5 to 1 hour; and trihexyphenidyl oral, 1 hour. For onset of action for diphenhydramine, see antihistamines, Chapter 38. Duration of effect for specific agents is as follows: benztropine (oral, IM, or IV), 24 hours; ethopropazine, oral, 4 hours; procycline, oral, 4 hours; and trihexyphenidyl, oral, 6 to 12 hours. Metabolism of the anticholinergics is undetermined. They are most likely excreted in the kidneys.

For side effects/adverse reactions, see Table 18-1.

The following effects may occur when anticholinergics are given with the drugs listed below:

| Drug | Possible Effect and Management |
|---|---|
| alcohol and CNS depressant | May result in enhanced CNS depressant effects; monitor closely. |
| other antimuscarinic* or anticholinergic medications | May result in enhanced anticholinergic effects. Monitor for constipation because bowel impaction and/or paralytic ileus may be produced. Increased fluid intake, exercise, stool softeners, and/or laxatives may be necessary. |
| antacids | Concurrent administration may reduce absorption and therapeutic effects of anticholinergic agents. Separate antacids and anticholinergics by at least 1 to 2 hours. |

*Drugs that block cholinergic receptors at postganglionic parasympathetic synapses and a small number of postganglionic sympathetic synapses (atropine, scopolmine). See Chapter 22.

See Table 18-2 for dosage and administration.

▷**Nursing Management: Anticholinergic Therapy**

***Assessment.*** The nurse should note that clients who evidence an intolerance of one belladonna alkaloid or derivative may also respond similarly to other belladonna alkaloids or derivatives. Anticholinergics are contraindicated in breastfeeding clients since they inhibit lactation and also in children less than 3 years since they are very susceptible to the toxic effects of these drugs (see box). Elderly clients are also at risk for the development of health problems, such as dryness of the mouth, constipation, and urinary retention, particularly in males, due to the anticholinergic effects of these agents (see box). Geriatric clients may respond to usual doses with agitation, sleepiness, and altered thought processes. Because the anticholinergics block the actions of acetylcholine, which supports many functions of the brain including memory, elderly clients, particularly those with existing memory problems, may become more impaired with continued use of anticholinergics. Caution should be exercised with the use of anticholinergics in individuals over 40 years because of the possibility of precipitating undiagnosed glaucoma.

The anticholinergic activity that decreases tone and motility of the gastrointestinal tract necessitates caution for the use of these drugs in instances of reflux esophagitis, hiatal hernia, intestinal atony, paralytic ileus, pyloric obstruction, or ulcerative colitis. In addition, clients with or who have a predisposition to prostatic hypertrophy, urinary retention, or other obstructive uropathy may find the condition precipitated or exacerbated. Since the heart rate may be increased, it should be carefully considered before anticholinergics are administered to clients with preexisting tachycardia or other cardiac conditions such as arrhythmias, congestive heart failure, coronary heart disease, and mitral stenosis, in which such an increase would be undesirable. The mydriatic effect of these drugs increases intraocular pressure, which may precipitate an acute episode of angle-closure glaucoma or necessitate an adjustment in the therapy of clients with open-angle glaucoma.

**TABLE 18-2**   Dosage and administration of anticholinergic drugs

| | Adults | Elderly | Children |
|---|---|---|---|
| benztropine tablets (Apo-benztropine ✿, Cogentin) | Parkinson's disease: 1-2 mg orally daily. Dosage may be adjusted as necessary. Drug-induced extrapyramidal reactions: 1-4 mg once or twice daily or 1-2 mg 2 or 3 times a day. Maximum dosage, 6 mg/day | Lower dosages may be necessary, since elderly are more sensitive to these medications | Children less than 3 yr, not recommended. 3 yr and older, individualized dosage |
| benztropine mesylate injection (Cogentin) | Parkinsonism: 1-2 mg IM or IV daily; adjust dosage according to individual's need and response. Drug-induced extrapyramidal reactions: 1-4 IM or IV once or twice daily. Maximum dosage, 6 mg/day | See tablets | See tablets |
| biperiden tablet (Akineton) | Parkinson's disease: 2 mg orally 3-4 times daily. Adjust dose to individual's need and response. Drug-induced extrapyramidal reactions: 2 mg orally 1-3 times daily. Maximum dosage, 16 mg/day | Lower dosages may be necessary, since elderly are more sensitive to these medications | Not established |
| biperiden lactate injection (Akineton) | Drug-induced extrapyramidal reactions: 2 mg IM or slow IV. If necessary, may repeat at 30-minute intervals to maximum of 4 doses/day | See above | Drug-induced extrapyramidal reactions: 0.4 mg/kg body weight or 1.2 mg/m² body surface IM. If necessary, may repeat at 30-minute intervals up to maximum of 4 doses/day |
| ethopropazine hydrochloride tablet (Parsidal, Parsitan ✿) | Parkinson's disease: 50 mg orally once or twice daily. Adjust dosage as necessary and tolerated up to maximum of 600 mg/day divided into 3 or 4 doses/day | Same as above | Not established |
| procyclidine hydrochloride tablet (Kemadrin, Procyclid ✿) | Parkinson's disease: 2.5 mg orally 3 times daily after meals initially. Increase to 5 mg 3 times daily, and if needed 5 mg at bedtime may be ordered according to client's response and need. Drug-induced extrapyramidal reactions: 2.5 mg orally initially 3 times daily. Increase by 2.5 mg increments daily as needed and tolerated by client | See above | Not established |
| trihexyphenidyl hydrochloride tablets or elixir (Artane, Aparkane tablet ✿) | Parkinson's disease: 1-2 mg orally first day; increase by 2 mg at 3-5 day intervals until therapeutic response or maximum dose of 6-10 mg daily (divided in 3 or 4 doses) is reached. Drug-induced extrapyramidal reactions: 1 mg orally initially daily; increase dosage until therapeutic response or maximum dose of 5-15 mg/day is reached | Same as above | Not established |
| trihexyphenidyl hydrochloride extended-release capsule (Artane Sequels) | Parkinson's disease: 5 mg orally after breakfast. If necessary, additional 5 mg capsule may be taken 12 hr later. Maximum daily dosage, 15 mg | Same as above | Not established |

### Pediatric Implications:
## ANTICHOLINERGICS

Infants and young children are very susceptible to anticholinergic side/adverse effects.

Closely monitor pediatric clients with spastic paralysis or brain damage, since they generally have an increased reaction to these agents requiring a dosage reduction.

Anticholinergics, especially high doses, may cause a paradoxical type reaction of increased nervousness, confusion, and/or hyperexcitability.

Children receiving these agents where hot weather prevails or environmental temperatures are high, have an increased risk of developing a rapid body temperature increase (anticholinergic drugs suppress sweat gland activity).

Dosage adjustments are often necessary for infants, Down's syndrome clients, and blonds since they generally have an increased response to this drug category. Flushing, increased temperature, irritability, and increased pulse and respiratory rate may occur.

Start with low doses and increase gradually, as needed and tolerated.

### Geriatric Implications:
## ANTICHOLINERGICS

The elderly are highly susceptible to anticholinergic side effects especially constipation, dry mouth and urinary retention (usually in males).

Avoid use of these agents in clients with narrow-angle glaucoma or a history of urinary retention.

Memory impairment has been reported with continuous administration of these agents, especially in older clients.

When usual adult doses are administered, some elderly may have a paradoxical reaction; hyperexcitability, agitation, confusion and/or sedation.

Chronic use decreases or inhibits the flow of saliva, which may contribute to oral discomfort, periodontal disease, and/or candidiasis.

Overheating resulting in heat stroke has been reported during vigorous exercise or during periods of hot weather in persons receiving anticholinergic drugs.

Blurred vision and/or increased sensitivity to light may occur.

Anticholinergic dosing in the elderly should begin at the lowest dose with gradual increases, until maximum improvement is noted or intolerable side effects occur.

---

Once the client begins anticholinergic therapy, assessment should relate to the potential development of a number of nursing diagnoses related to the drug. There may be sensory-perceptual alterations related to the drug's effects on vision and somatosensory function, especially in the elderly. Geriatric clients are also more at risk for altered thought processes and at high risk for injury related to the CNS effects. There may be alteration in elimination patterns; bowel function because of the GI effects, and altered patterns of urinary elimination, primarily resulting from urinary retention. Comfort may be altered related to xerostomia, blurred vision, rash, and the GI and GU effects of anticholinergics.

**Intervention.** With beginning therapy, the dosages are low, increasing every 5 to 6 days until a therapeutic level can be obtained. When the drug is to be withdrawn, it is done so in the same fashion—gradually. Sudden withdrawal may cause vomiting, lassitude, and excessive sweating and salivation. Tolerance may develop if the therapy is prolonged, which may require an increase in dosage. If another antiparkinsonism agent is to be substituted for the initial drug, the dosage of the first drug should be gradually decreased, while the substitute is gradually increased.

Oral dosage forms of anticholinergics should be administered 30 minutes to 1 hour before meals to maximize absorption. If the client has gastrointestinal distress, it can be minimized by administering the drug with meals; however, absorption will be delayed. Antacids and antidiarrheal agents should not be administered within 1 hour of taking oral anticholinergics. With the parenteral administration of anticholinergics, the client may experience a temporary sensation of lightheadedness and the nurse should take precautions to meet the client's safety needs by having him rest in a sitting or preferably prone position for about 20 minutes. Local irritation may also occur with parenteral administration.

**Education.** The nurse should arrange for the client to check with a pharmacist, physician, or other prescriber for drug interactions before taking any other drugs, including OTC drugs.

The client should be cautioned that anticholinergics impair physical and mental functioning (i.e., drowsiness and blurred vision) and that care should be taken when driving or operating machinery.

The nurse should alert the client to the dangers of heat exhaustion and the avoidance of exercise during warm weather because of the decreased ability to perspire. This caution should also be of concern to clients with fever because hyperthermia may result.

The client should be instructed to avoid CNS depressants such as alcohol, barbiturates, and narcotics while taking the drugs.

---

## PARKINSON'S DISEASE INDUCED BY DESIGNER DRUGS

**Designer drugs,** or chemical variations of illegal or controlled substances, are an ever-increasing problem in the United States. Such products are usually not illegal but generally are produced to induce the psychoactive effects of selected illegal products. Often the user consumes an unknown substance that may or may not be the desired product. Reports indicate that MPTP, a chemical produced as an analog of meperidine in the clandestine laboratories, has been sold on the streets as heroin, cocaine, or a contaminant of other products.

MPTP has reportedly induced a degenerative CNS disorder characterized by tremors and muscle paralysis similar to the symptoms of Parkinson's disease. In a number of cases the paralysis reported has been permanent.

---

The client should also be instructed to change position slowly if orthostatic hypotension is a problem.

The nurse should advise the client to use hard candy, gum, mouthwash, or bits of ice to relieve dryness of the mouth.

The client should be counseled to have yearly ophthalmic examinations. The intraocular pressure determinations are of particular importance because increased ocular tension may occur with these anticholinergic agents.

***Evaluation.*** In clients with bladder neck obstruction, urinary retention may occur. Male clients, in particular, should be monitored for difficulty in starting their urinary stream.

Dysrhythmias have been noted as a result of these drugs, but they are dose-related. The vital signs should be monitored and changes in the cardiac status should be observed and reported.

The nurse should observe the client for symptoms of paralytic ileus and report symptoms of abdominal pain, distension, and constipation to the physician. Increasing dyspepsia in clients with hiatal hernias may indicate an aggravation of esophageal reflux because of gastric retention.

Because of the decrease in peristalsis, gastrointestinal transit is prolonged and the absorption of other drugs may be impaired. For this reason, these drugs are also contraindicated in clients with diarrhea. If the cause is infectious, the diarrheal symptoms will be prolonged by retention of bowel contents.

Caution should be taken with clients with chronic pulmonary disease because the resultant decrease in bronchial secretions may lead to bronchial mucus plugs.

Elderly clients are more sensitive to these drugs and require less than the usual adult dose. Monitor closely for agitation, sleepiness, and altered thought processes.

The nurse should observe the client for xerostomia, a reduction in the volume of saliva. This symptom is important

and should be reported, not only because the extreme dryness of the mouth usually is a discomfort to the client but also because xerostomia limits the amount of drug that can be administered. From this symptom, the progression of adverse effects is interference with visual accommodation and difficulty in urination.

## Drugs Affecting Brain Dopamine

Three classifications of drugs affect brain dopamine: those that release dopamine, those that increase brain levels of dopamine, and dopaminergic agonists. The drugs of choice in the treatment of Parkinson's disease are those that increase the brain levels of dopamine. The other two classifications are used as adjuncts or when therapy normally used is contraindicated.

The drugs affecting brain dopamine have their major effect on the akinesia seen in Parkinson's disease. Akinesia is a difficulty in or a lack of ability to initiate muscle movement caused in Parkinson's disease by decreased levels of brain dopamine. The client with akinesia exhibits a masklike facial expression, impairment of postural reflexes, and eventually an inability for self-care. Drugs affecting brain dopamine increase the level of brain dopamine, thus creating a balance between dopamine and acetylcholine in the brain, especially in the basal ganglia area.

### Drugs That Increase Brain Levels of Dopamine
#### levodopa (L-Dopa, Dopar, Larodopa)

A small percentage of levodopa crosses the blood-brain barrier intact. It is decarboxylated to dopamine, replacing the missing brain dopamine and balancing dopamine/acetylcholine concentrations. Levodopa is indicated for treatment of Parkinson's disease (idiopathic, postencephalitic, symptomatic, or parkinsonism associated with cerebral atherosclerosis).

Levodopa is absorbed by active transport; approximately 30% to 50% reaches systemic circulation. The drug is distributed to most body tissues; CNS receives less than 1% of the dose because of peripheral metabolism. The enzyme decarboxylase converts levodopa (95%) to dopamine in the stomach, intestines, and also the liver. Levodopa has a half-life of 1 to 3 hours. Usually improvement is seen within 2 to 3 weeks (although other clients may require levodopa for up to 6 months to obtain a therapeutic effect). Peak concentration is achieved in 1 to 3 hours. Duration of action lasts for up to 5 hours per dose. The drug is excreted by the kidneys.

More frequent side effects are increased anxiety, nervousness, and confusion (especially in the elderly), constipation, and nightmares. Less frequent side effects include diarrhea, headache, anorexia, tremors, insomnia, red flushing of skin, dry mouth, weakness; also darkening of the urine or sweat has been reported (insignificant).

More frequent adverse reactions include difficult urination, depression, orthostatic hypotension, mood changes, increased aggressiveness, irregular heart rate, severe nausea or vomiting, choreiform, and involuntary movements of body (face, arms, hands, tongue, head and upper body). Less frequently encountered are hypertension, abdominal pain (caused by development of duodenal ulcers), and increased weakness caused by hemolytic anemia.

**Significant drug interactions.** The following effects may occur when levodopa is given with the drugs listed below:

| Drug | Possible Effect and Management |
|---|---|
| anesthetics, hydrocarbon inhalation | May result in dysrhythmias. Discontinue levodopa 6 to 8 hours before hydrocarbon anesthetics, especially halothane. |
| anticonvulsants, haloperidol or phenothiazines | May result in decreased levodopa effects because hydantoin anticonvulsants increase levodopa metabolism and haloperidol and phenothiazines block dopamine receptors in the brain. When hydantoin and levodopa are given concurrently, monitor closely; increased doses of levodopa may be necessary. If at all possible, avoid the combination of haloperidol or phenothiazines with levodopa. |
| cocaine | May result in increased risk of arrhythmias. If medically necessary to give both drugs concurrently, reduce dosages and monitor closely with ECG monitoring. |
| monoamine oxidase (MAO) inhibitors | Not recommended. This combination may result in a hypertensive crisis. MAO inhibitors should be discontinued 2 to 4 weeks before starting levodopa therapy. |
| pyridoxine | Not recommended. Dosages of 10 mg or more may reverse the antiparkinsonian effect of levodopa. |

**Dosage and administration.** Levodopa capsules/tablets (Dopar, Larodopa) are administered to adults, 250 mg orally 2-4 times daily. Dosage may be increased by 100-750 mg/day at 3-7 day intervals until therapeutic response achieved. Maximum dose is 8 g/day. Elderly and postencephalitic clients may require lower dosages, since they are more sensitive to this medication. Dosage for children less than 12 yr has not been established. For children 12 yr and older, follow adult dosage.

▷ **Nursing Management:
Levodopa Therapy**

**Assessment.** Levodopa is not recommended for children less than 12 years old, pregnant women, or clients with undiagnosed skin lesions or a history of melanoma because these lesions may be activated. Levodopa may inhibit lactation in nursing mothers. Levodopa should be administered with great caution to clients with severe cardiovascular, pulmonary, renal, hepatic, or endocrine disease; peptic ulcer; narrow-angle glaucoma; diabetes; psychiatric distur-

bances; or a history of cardiac dysrhythmias. Levodopa may increase dsyrhythmias in predisposed clients. It may aggravate pulmonary conditions. Intraocular pressure may increase and precipitate an acute attack of glaucoma. There is increased risk of depression in clients with a psychiatric history. Upper gastrointestinal bleeding has been stimulated in clients with peptic ulcers. The administration of levodopa may precipitate or aggravate urinary retention, particularly in male clients.

**Intervention.** Levodopa should be administered before meals, since food impedes the drug's action. Nausea and vomiting occur in 80% of the clients in early levodopa therapy. However, tolerance develops with continued use of the drug.

For geriatric clients and individuals receiving other medications, the dosage of levodopa should be titrated to reach the client's therapeutic level with minimal side effects.

The client's vital signs should be monitored during periods of dosage regulation for the indication of hypotension and dysrhythmias.

**Education.** The client should be instructed to change to the upright position slowly if orthostatic hypotension is a problem. Hypotension can be minimized with the use of elastic stockings. In addition, elderly clients who respond to levodopa therapy, particularly those with osteoporosis, should be cautioned to resume higher activity levels gradually to minimize the risk of fractures.

Because levodopa has mydriatic effects, clients should be encouraged to have their intraocular pressure checked periodically for the detection of glaucoma.

The client should be instructed to call the physician if symptoms of overdosage develop (involuntary muscle twitching and involuntary winking). The nurse should caution the client receiving prolonged high-dosage therapy that the "on-off" syndrome may occur (see box on p. 361). The client should be advised that involuntary movement of the face, mouth, tongue, and head often develop with prolonged therapy and that the physician should be notified of these symptoms so that drug dosage can be adjusted.

Clients need to be alerted that the response to levodopa may not occur for several weeks after the treatment has begun. The urine and perspiration may be darkened, but this has no significance.

Clients with diabetes need to be aware that levodopa may interfere with urine tests for sugar and ketones.

Dietary counseling should be provided regarding protein and pyridoxine ($B_6$) ingestion. Proteins may be metabolized into the amino acids, which compete with levodopa for transport to the brain, making the response to levodopa unpredictable. Rather than restrict the client's protein intake, it should be divided in equal parts to be taken over the entire day. Vitamin compounds and foods high in pyridoxine, such as pork, beef, liver, bananas, ham, and egg yolks, may decrease the effects of levodopa and should be avoided. Dietary teaching should include the necessity of a

## ON-OFF SYNDROME OF PARKINSONISM

The **on-off syndrome** refers to a complication following prolonged levodopa therapy (2 years or more). The client will fluctuate from being symptom free ("on") to demonstrating full-blown Parkinson's symptoms ("off") any time during therapy. These effects may last for minutes to hours and are believed to be caused by altered sensitivity of the dopamine receptors or to serum level changes in levodopa.

Treatment may require more frequent administration of levodopa or levodopa-carbidopa and the addition of a direct-acting dopamine agonist, bromocriptine. Scheduling of meals and consumption of high-protein meals may also affect levodopa absorption. Perhaps taking levodopa 15 minutes before meals with a cracker (not milk since it may produce erratic drug absorption) and spacing protein equally over all meals may improve drug absorption and serum levels of levodopa.

Drug-free periods are also used to help reestablish receptor sensitivity to levodopa. Some medical centers advocate from 1 to 2 days to a 10- to 14-day "drug holiday" to permit resensitization of dopamine receptors. Following the latter regimen, most clients only need one third to one half their previous levodopa dosage. Such a program should be instituted under specific guidelines in a hospital setting so that close monitoring is available to reduce problems and avoid complications (Lannon et al, 1986).

high fiber and fluid intake to minimize the side effect of constipation with the drug, along with gradual increases in activity and the establishment of an elimination routine.

*Evaluation.* Periodic evaluations need to be done for hepatic, cardiovascular, and renal functioning, including hemoglobin determinations and complete blood count. Opthalmologic testing for glaucoma is especially important with the administration of levodopa.

Nightmares and mood changes, such as agitation, anxiety, and confusion are symptoms for which the client should be observed in addition to the side effects previously mentioned.

### levodopa-carbidopa (Sinemet)

Sinemet is the combination of levodopa with the dopa decarboxylase inhibitor, carbidopa. Carbidopa competes for the enzyme dopa decarboxylase, thus retarding the peripheral breakdown of levodopa. Carbidopa does not cross the blood-brain barrier as does levodopa and does not interfere with the intracerebral transformation of levodopa to dopamine. Because carbidopa prevents much of the peripheral conversion of levodopa to dopamine, the incidence of systemic side effects of levodopa, such as nausea, vomiting, and cardiac dysrhythmias, is decreased. The CNS effects of levodopa are a greater risk with this combination because more levodopa is reaching the brain to be converted to dopamine.

The addition of carbidopa to levodopa reduces the required dose of levodopa to 25% of the original levodopa dosage. The available levodopa-carbidopa combination dosage forms include 10/100 (10 mg of carbidopa and 100 mg of levodopa), 25/100 (25 mg of carbidopa and 100 mg levodopa), and 25/250 (25 mg of carbidopa and 250 mg of levodopa). To obtain the peripheral inhibitor effect of carbidopa, a minimum of 70 mg (range 70 to 100 mg) per day is necessary. Nausea and vomiting are reported in clients receiving dosages lower than 70 mg/day of carbidopa. Therefore three combination dosage forms are available to the physician to permit greater flexibility in prescribing sufficient amounts of both levodopa and carbidopa for the client. The manufacturer recommends that physicians not prescribe more than 200 mg of carbidopa per day. As with levodopa alone, the decarboxylation to dopamine replaces the missing brain dopamine and restores a balance to dopamine/acetylcholine concentrations.

Levodopa/carbidopa is indicated for the treatment of idiopathic, postencephalitic, and symptomatic Parkinson's disease. For levodopa's pharmacokinetics, see previous section. Between 40% and 70% of oral dose of carbidopa is absorbed. The drug is distributed widely to many body tissues with exception of CNS. The drug's metabolism is insignificant. It is excreted by the kidneys.

Side effects/adverse reactions are similar to those for levodopa. In addition, more frequently, choreiform and involuntary movements will be seen earlier in combination therapy than with levodopa alone. It is reported in 50% to 80% of clients and is dose-related. Eyelid spasms or closing may be an early sign of drug overdose. Mental or mood changes may also occur earlier and be dose-related.

See levodopa's drug interactions—all are noted, with exception of pyridoxine. Interaction between levodopa and pyridoxine does not occur in the presence of carbidopa.

For clients not previously on levodopa therapy, start oral dosage at 10/100 or 25/100 3 times daily. Increase dosage as needed every 1 or 2 days until desired response is obtained. For clients previously on levodopa therapy, discontinue levodopa at least 8 hr before instituting combination therapy then (1) if client is receiving less than 1.5 g levodopa daily, start with 10/100 or 25/100 of carbidopa/levodopa 3 or 4 times daily; increase at 1- or 2-day intervals until desired response obtained. (2) If client is receiving more than 1.5 g levodopa daily, then 25/250 carbidopa/levodopa orally 3 or 4 times daily, increasing if necessary at 1- or 2-day intervals until desired response obtained. Be aware that conversion from levodopa to combination levodopa-carbidopa requires only 25% of original dosage of levodopa initially. Maximum, up to 200 mg carbidopa and 2 g levodopa daily. If additional levodopa is necessary, give as single agent.

Geriatric and postencephalitic clients may require a lower

dose, since they are more sensitive to this combination. Dosage for children less than 18 yr is not established.

See nursing management for levodopa.

### Dopamine-Releasing Drug
#### amantadine hydrochloride (Symmetrel)

Amantadine hydrochloride is a synthetic antiviral compound. The exact mechanism of action is not completely known. It is postulated that amantadine releases dopamine and other catecholamines from neuronal storage sites. It also blocks the uptake of dopamine into presynaptic neurons, thus permitting peripheral and central accumulation of dopamine. Amantadine may also give the client a sense of well-being and elevation of mood. It is less effective than levodopa but produces more rapid clinical improvement and causes fewer untoward reactions.

Amantadine is indicated for use as an antidyskinetic (treatment of Parkinson's disease) and as an antiviral (systemic agent). Amantadine is well absorbed; it is not metabolized. The drug has a half-life of 11 to 15 hours with normal renal function. Onset of antidyskinetic action usually occurs within 48 hours. Peak serum levels are reached within 2 to 4 hours; level 0.3 μg/ml. Steady-state is reached within 2 to 3 days with daily drug administration. Steady-state level is from 0.2 to 0.9 μg/ml. Levels above 1.5 to 2 μg/ml are considered toxic. Amantadine is excreted by the kidneys.

More frequent side effects of amantadine include impaired concentration, dizziness, increased irritability, anorexia, nausea, nervousness, and purple-red skin spots (livedo reticularis usually seen with chronic therapy). Less frequent are blurred vision, constipation, headache, vomiting, and dryness of mouth, nose, and throat, also skin rashes and increased weakness. Less frequently observed adverse reactions include confusion, hallucinations, mental or mood variations, orthostatic hypotension, and difficult urination. Rarely reported are slurred speech, blurred vision, and oculogyric crisis. Symptoms of overdose include severe confusion, insomnia, nightmares, and seizures.

In long-term therapy, monitor for congestive heart failure, increased edema of feet and lower legs, difficulty in breathing, and rapid increase of body weight.

**Significant drug interactions.** The following effects may occur when amantadine is given with the drugs listed below.

| Drug | Possible Effect and Management |
|------|-------------------------------|
| alcohol | Not recommended. Increased CNS side effects, such as confusion, light-headedness, orthostatic hypotension, and fainting spells reported. Avoid concurrent use. |
| anticholinergics | May enhance anticholinergic side effects, such as inducing confusion, hallucinations, frightening dreams, etc. Dosage adjustments may be necessary. Also monitor for paralytic ileus. |
| CNS stimulants | Additive CNS stimulation reported; side effects include increased nervousness, irritability, difficulty sleeping, and at times, seizures and cardiac dysrhythmias. Closely monitor clients receiving concurrent stimulant therapy. |

**Dosage and administration.** Adult dosage when amantadine is used as an antidyskinetic is 100 mg orally once or twice daily. Maximum dosage is 400 mg/day. No specific recommendations apply to the drug's use as an antidyskinetic agent in children or the elderly.

### ▷ Nursing Management: Amantadine Therapy

**Assessment.** Use is contraindicated in pregnant women and will cause vomiting, urinary retention, and skin rash in the infant of the nursing mother to whom it is administered.

**Intervention.** Therapy should be discontinued gradually. Abrupt cessation of the drug may cause exacerbations of parkinsonism symptoms within 24 hours and onset of parkinsonian crisis within 3 days.

**Education.** The client should be informed that a reduction in benefits occurs after 4 to 12 weeks of therapy. Compliance with a full course of therapy is necessary.

The nurse should instruct the client not to drink alcohol while taking this drug because it may result in dizziness, fainting, and confusion.

See also general discussion of nursing management of anticholinergic therapy.

**Evaluation.** Dopamine-releasing drugs should be administered cautiously in the presence of impaired renal function, since the drug will accumulate and increase the risk of CNS toxicity. They should be used cautiously in elderly clients and in those with epilepsy, psychoses, and liver, cardiac, or cerebrovascular disease. The administration of urine-acidifying agents will increase the rate of excretion from the body.

### Dopaminergic Agonist
#### bromocriptine (Parlodel)

Bromocriptine is an ergot alkaloid derivative marketed as the first agonist of dopamine receptor activity. It activates postsynaptic dopamine receptors, stimulating the production of dopamine and correcting the brain dopamine/acetylcholine imbalance. The drug is indicated as an antidyskinetic, lactation inhibitor, growth hormone suppressant, and antihyperprolactinemic. Approximately 28% of a dose is absorbed, but only 6% reaches systemic circulation. Bromocriptine's half-life is biphasic: alpha, 4 to 4½ hours; beta, 15 hours.

Onset of activity from a single dose used for antiparkinsonism is ½ to 1½ hours, with a peak concentration of 1 to 3 hours. Peak effect occurs in 2 hours. The drug is metabolized in the liver. Metabolites of bromocriptine are excreted in bile (approximately 95%) and kidneys (2.5% to 5%).

The more frequently encountered side effects are drowsiness, headaches, nausea, and hypotension. Less frequent side effects include the following, usually after high-dose therapy: diarrhea or constipation, dry mouth, night time leg cramps, anorexia, depression, abdominal cramps, stuffy nose, vomiting, and tingling or pain in fingers or toes on exposure to cold. The less frequent adverse reactions seen with bromocriptine are confusion, hallucinations, and uncontrolled movements of body, face, tongue, arms, hands, and head. When bromocriptine is given with estrogens, progestins, or oral contraceptives, the hormones may cause amenorrhea and possibly galactorrhea, which counteracts the effects of bromocriptine. Do not give concurrently. Also, this drug may enhance alcohol side effects. See Table 18-1.

The adult dosage for bromocriptine mesylate as an antidyskinetic agent in tablet/capsules (Parlodel) is 1.25 to 2.5 mg orally daily. Increase dosage as necessary. Maintenance dosage is usually 2.5 to 100 mg daily in divided doses.

Dosage for children less than 15 years has not been established.

## ▷ Nursing Management: Bromocriptine Therapy

***Assessment.*** Bromocriptine should be used cautiously with clients receiving drugs known to have hypotensive action because there will be an additive effect. There is also an additive effect with other antiparkinsonism drugs.

Clients with an intolerance of ergot derivatives may also be intolerant of bromocriptine. It should not be administered to mothers expecting to breastfeed since the drug inhibits lactation. In addition, bromocriptine is contraindicated for clients with uncontrolled hypertension or the toxemia of pregnancy. Use with caution in clients with hepatic dysfunction since metabolism of the drug may be reduced. Clients with psychiatric disorders may have a worsening of symptoms with the administration of bromocriptine.

***Intervention.*** The nurse should administer with meals or milk to decrease the adverse effect of nausea. Bedtime administration may minimize the effects of dizziness and nausea for the client. Give the first dose at bedtime or with the client lying down, because the hypotensive effects of the drug are more likely to occur after the initial dose.

The dosage is initiated at a low level and gradually increased to the minimum effective dosage.

***Education.*** The nurse should caution clients to use a contraceptive measure, since this drug may result in a restoration of fertility. A mechanical barrier device, such as a diaphragm or condom, should be suggested rather than oral contraceptives, because oral estrogen contraceptives increase the risk of stimulating prolactin-secreting cells. Pregnancy tests should be performed every 4 weeks during therapy along with the use of contraceptive measures. A positive result of a pregnancy test should be reported to the physician immediately.

The nurse should caution clients that drugs may impair physical and mental functioning and that they should take care when driving or operating machinery.

The client should be instructed to limit alcohol consumption, since it increases CNS side effects.

The client should be taught to prevent or minimize constipation by increasing dietary fiber, increasing fluid intake

---

### TRANSPLANTATION RESEARCH

Research indicates that adrenal gland, fetal brain, or tissue from a human fetus may possibly be transplanted in persons with Parkinson's disease to replace the neurotransmitter deficit. While some transplants have been performed on humans, this is considered an investigational area needing both immediate and long-term analysis of potential therapeutic benefits (Williams, 1987).

---

to 3000 ml daily, performing moderate exercise daily, and establishing a regular time of day for bowel elimination.

The nurse should advise the client to limit exposure to the cold or to wear protective clothing to prevent discomfort of the fingers and toes.

The client should be cautioned to get up slowly from a sitting or supine position because of bromocriptine's hypotensive effects.

***Evaluation.*** If used with clients having a psychiatric history, the medication may exacerbate the condition.

Blood pressure should be monitored; 1% to 5% of the clients have symptomatic hypotension.

Other common effects include constipation, nausea, nasal congestion, and tingling or pain in the fingers and toes when exposed to the cold. These effects occur in 30% to 60% of the clients being treated for Parkinson's disease with this medication.

Regular dental examinations are advised since bromocriptine inhibits salivation and thereby increases the client's risk of discomfort, caries, and periodontal disorders.

See also the general discussion of nursing management related to anticholinergic therapy.

### pergolide (Permax)

Pergolide is a dopamine agonist, usually used in conjunction with levodopa or levodopa-carbidopa to treat the signs and symptoms of Parkinson's disease. This drug combination often results in the need for lowered doses of levodopa or levodopa-carbidopa. Ahlskog and Muenter (1988) reported the clinical fluctuations reported in clients receiving levodopa-carbidopa may be reduced by pergolide, that is, the "on" period was prolonged, while the "off" period was decreased in most of the clients studied.

Pergolide stimulates dopamine receptors in the nigrostriatal area but, unlike bromocriptine, its action is independent of dopamine synthesis or dopamine storage sites. It also inhibits prolactin secretion and in acromegaly, causes a decrease in growth hormone levels. Pergolide is indicated as an adjunct treatment for Parkinson's disease. It is well absorbed; serum protein binding is high (about 90%); the drug is excreted in the kidneys.

The most frequent side effects of pergolide include stomach distress/pain, constipation, lightheadedness, sedation, hypotension, cold-type symptoms, nausea, and lower back pain. Less frequent side effects are anorexia, facial edema, diarrhea, chills, dry mouth, and vomiting. The most frequent adverse reactions include confusion, dyskinesias such as uncontrollable body movements, and hallucinations. Less frequently encountered is hypertension; rare adverse reactions are cerebrovascular bleeding and myocardial infarction.

No significant drug interactions are reported to date, but the student should be aware that dopamine antagonists, such as the phenothiazines and haloperidol, may decrease the effects of this pergolide.

The recommended dosage for adults and elderly is 50 μg or (0.05 mg) given orally daily for 2 days, increased by 100 to 150 μg (0.1 to 0.15 mg) every 3 days over the next 12 days. The dose may then be increased by 250 μg (0.25 mg) every 3 days until maximum therapeutic effect is reached. Dosages should be divided and given 3 times daily. The maximum is 5 mg/day. Dosage for children has not been established.

## ▷ Nursing Management: Pergolide Therapy

**Assessment.** Individuals with a previous allergic experience with ergot alkaloids should not be administered pergolide. Clients with altered thought processes such as confusion or hallucinations may experience a worsening of these symptoms. The increased risk of atrial premature contractions and sinus tachycardia should be considered before pergolide is administered to clients with cardiac arrhythmias. The drug is contraindicated in mothers who anticipate breastfeeding since it inhibits lactation.

**Intervention.** The dosage of pergolide should be titrated so the client obtains the maximum therapeutic benefits and side effects are minimized. The client's blood pressure should be monitored on a regular basis, since blood pressure changes occur. Hypotension is more common than hypertension with pergolide.

Administer pergolide with meals to minimize nausea and vomiting, although these effects usually subside with continued therapy. Nausea and dizziness are not uncommon with the first dose. These effects can be mitigated by ad-

ministering the first dose at bedtime or while the client is lying down. Careful oral hygiene is required because of the reduced salivary flow.

**Education.** Encourage the client to seek regular appointments with the physician so that the client's progress may be monitored. Alert the client that possible sleepiness or dizziness may make it unsafe for him or her to drive or accomplish other tasks that require alertness. The client should be taught to slowly come to an upright position from a sitting or prone position because of the drug's hypotensive effects. Advise the client that sugarless candies or gum, ice chips, and saliva substitute may be used to minimize the possible dryness of the mouth.

**Evaluation.** The client should be observed for the advent of side effects, such as hypertension, myocardial infarction, urinary tract infection, cerebrovascular hemorrhage, and CNS effects—such as confusion, hallucinations, and uncontrolled movements of the face and head, hands and arms, and upper body.

## MYASTHENIA GRAVIS

**Myasthenia gravis** is a progressive and presently incurable disease characterized by the loss of, or decrease in, acetylcholine receptors caused by an autoimmune process resulting in skeletal muscle weakness and fatigue. Because of its involvement with the production of antibodies, the thymus gland is believed to have a role in the causation of myasthenia gravis. Nearly 15% of all myasthenia gravis clients have a thymoma, or tumor of the thymus gland.

Symptoms of myasthenia gravis usually become worse with exertion and are less noticeable with rest. Stress, infection, menses, surgery, and other factors may also increase the symptoms. The most common early reported symptoms are ptosis and diplopia. Dysarthria, dysphagia, and limb weakness, especially of the upper extremities, also occur in the advanced stages. The client may complain of shoulder fatigue after shaving or combing the hair or of hand weakness, that is, finding it difficult to open doors or kitchen jars or performing repetitive tasks, such as lawn work or playing the piano.

The most serious effects of myasthenia gravis are dysphagia and respiratory muscle weakness, since these may result in aspiration pneumonia or respiratory failure. Treatment of this disease state may include thymectomy, cholinesterase inhibitors, plasmapheresis, and, at times, corticosteroids. The mainstay though is cholinesterase-inhibitor drugs, such as anticholinesterase drugs.

### Anticholinesterase Agents

The **anticholinesterase agents** are drugs that enhance cholinergic action by blocking the effect of cholinesterase. These drugs act by inactivating or inhibiting cholinesterase at the sites of acetylcholine transmission, permitting the accumulation of acetycholine. Because of their ability to increase the amount of acetylcholine at the myoneural junction, the cholinesterase inhibitors are primarily used for the diagnosis and treatment of myasthenia gravis and for their local effects in the eye (see Chapter 43). These drugs are used also for urinary retention and paralytic ileus and as an antidote for the curariform effects of the nondepolarizing skeletal muscle relaxants, such as tubocurarine and pancuronium.

Antimyasthenics are cholinergic and act by inhibiting cholinesterase; acetylcholine released by the parasympathetic nerves accumulates in the synapse area to increase muscle strength and duration of action at the motor end plate. They are used in the treatment of myasthenia gravis, as antidotes for tubocurarine (nondepolarizing neuromuscular blocking agents) blockade, as diagnostic aids for myasthenia gravis, and are used postoperatively to prevent or relieve abdominal distention and urinary retention.

Orally, all are poorly absorbed from the gastrointestinal tract; IM neostigmine is rapidly absorbed. Onset of action of these drugs is as follows:

ambenonium: within 30 minutes

edrophonium: IM within 2 to 10 minutes; IV within 30 to 60 seconds

neostigmine: orally within 45 to 75 minutes; IM within 30 minutes; IV within 4 to 8 minutes

pyridostigmine: oral tablet/syrup, within 30 to 45 minutes; extended-release tablet, 30 to 60 minutes; IM within 15 minutes; IV within 2 to 5 minutes

Duration of effect of each is as listed below:

ambenonium: 3 to 8 hours

edrophonium: IM within 5 to 30 minutes; IV, approximately 10 minutes

neostigmine: oral and parenteral, 2 to 4 hours

pyridostigmine: oral syrup, tablets, 3 to 6 hours; extended release tablet, 6 to 12 hours; parenteral, 2 to 4 hours

These drugs (neostigmine, pyridostigmine) are metabolized mainly in the liver and are excreted in the kidneys.

*Side effects/adverse reactions.* More frequently reported side effects are nausea, vomiting, diarrhea, abdominal cramps, increased sweating, or drooling. Less frequent side effects are increased urge to urinate, pinpoint pupils, eye watering, increased bronchial secretions. A rare adverse effect is red swelling at site of injection (pyridostigmine only), or skin rash (caused by bromide ion of neostigmine or pyridostigmine). Overdose effects include blurred vision, severe diarrhea, increased salivation, increase in bronchial secretions, severe nausea or vomiting, respiratory difficulties, severe abdominal pain, bradycardia, increased weakness, ataxia, confusion, slurred speech, and muscle weakness (especially in arms, neck, shoulders, and tongue).

*Significant drug interactions.* The following effects may occur when cholinesterase inhibitors are given with the drugs listed below:

| Drug | Possible Effect and Management |
| --- | --- |
| other cholinesterase inhibitors (such as demecarium, echothiophate, and isofluorophate) | This combination of drugs is not recommended and should definitely be avoided, since serious additive toxicity may result. |
| guanadrel, guanethidine, mecamylamine, or trimethaphan | These are ganglionic blocking agents that may antagonize the action of the cholinesterase-inhibitor drugs, resulting in increased muscle weakness, respiratory muscle weakness, and difficulty in swallowing. Avoid concurrent drug therapy. |
| procainamide | The neuromuscular blocking action and, possibly, antimuscarinic effect of procainamide may antagonize the action of the cholinesterase inhibitor drugs. If used concurrently, monitor client closely. |

*Dosage and administration.* Ambenonium is a slowly reversible, cholinesterase inhibitor; therefore it may accumulate at cholinergic synapses and produce increased, prolonged effects. Because of the narrow margin between first appearance of side effects and serious toxicity, ambenonium is usually reserved for clients not responding adequately to neostigmine or pyridostigmine or for clients who are hypersensitive to the bromide component in both drugs.

Edrophonium chloride injection is used to diagnose myasthenia gravis. Because of its short duration of action, it is not indicated for the treatment of myasthenia gravis. See Table 18-3.

▷ **Nursing Management: Anticholinesterase Agents**

*Assessment.* Assess neuromuscular status (ptosis, diplopia, speed, ability to swallow, respiratory function, extremity strength) before administration of the drug. Caution should be used in clients with asthma, pneumonia, or atelectasis. An increase in bronchial secretions may aggravate these conditions. Antimyasthenics may cause an increase in dysrhythmias.

Clients who have a hypersensitivity to bromides, usually demonstrated by a rash, may also be sensitive to the bromide ion of neostigmine or pyridostigmine.

Anticholinesterase agents need to be considered carefully before they are administered during pregnancy. Muscular weakness has been demonstrated in some newborns whose mothers received these agents during pregnancy. In addition, anticholinesterase agents promote uterine irritability and may induce early labor in pregnant women near term.

Once the client begins antimyasthenic therapy, the nurse's assessment should focus on the potential development of nursing diagnoses related to the effects of the drugs. There may be alterations in the client's patterns of elimination; diarrhea related to the parasympathomimetic effects; and altered urinary patterns of urinary frequency, urgency, and incontinence. The increase in bronchial secretions may in-

**TABLE 18-3**   Dosage and administration of cholinesterase inhibitors

| | Adults | Children |
|---|---|---|
| ambenonium chloride tablets (Mytelase) | Antimyasthenic dosage: 5 mg orally 3 or 4 times a day. Adjust dosage every 24-48 hr as necessary | 0.3 mg/kg body weight or 10 mg/m² body surface divided in 3 or 4 doses/day orally. Increase dosage when necessary to 1.5 mg/kg body weight or 50 mg/m² |
| edrophonium chloride injection (Tensilon) | Diagnostic test: 10 mg IM. If cholinergic reaction results, repeat test in ½ hr using 2 mg dose to rule out possibility of false-negative effect. IV, 2 mg given over 15-30 sec. If no response after 45 sec, give 8 mg. NOTE: if a cholinergic effect results after a 2-mg dose, discontinue test and give atropine IV at dose of 0.4 mg. If necessary to repeat test, it may be done after 30 min has elapsed | |
| neostigmine bromide tablets (Prostigmin) | 15 mg orally every 3-4 hr. Adjust dosage as necessary. Maintenance, 150 mg over 24 hr orally. Selection of dosage times should be determined by client's response and need | 2 mg/kg body weight or 60 mg/m² divided into 6 or 8 doses |
| neostigmine methylsulfate injection (Prostigmin) | Antimyasthenic dosage: 0.5 mg IM or SC. Base additional doses on client's response. Diagnostic aid for myasthenia gravis: 1.5 mg given with 0.6 mg atropine IM or SC. If significant improvement in muscle weakness appears within few minutes to 1 hr, it is an indication of myasthenia gravis | Antimyasthenic: 0.01-0.04 mg/kg body weight IM or SC every 2-3 hr. (Dose of 0.01 mg/kg of atropine may be given with each dose or with alternate doses to offset muscarinic side effects.) Diagnostic aid for myasthenia gravis: 0.04 mg/kg body weight or 1 mg/m² body surface IM. IV, 0.02 mg/kg body weight or 0.5 mg/m² body surface |
| pyridostigmine bromide syrup/tablet (Mestinon) | Antimyasthenic: 60-120 mg orally every 3 or 4 hr. Adjust dosage as needed. Maintenance usually ranges from 60 mg to 1.5 g/day orally | 7 mg/kg body weight or 200 mg/m² body surface area divided into 5 or 6 doses orally daily |
| pyridostigmine bromide extended-release tablet (Mestinon Timespans) | Antimyasthenic: 180-540 mg once or twice daily; allow at least 6 hr between dosages | Not established |
| pyridostigmine bromide injection (Mestinon, Regonol) | Antimyasthenic: 2 mg every 2-3 hr IM or IV | Neonates of myasthenic mothers, 0.05-0.15 mg/kg body weight every 4-6 hr IM |

dicate ineffective airway clearance. A high risk for injury related to the visual and CNS effects exists, especially in the elderly client. The client's comfort may also be altered because of rash, GI effects, and muscle weakness.

**Intervention.** These drugs are initiated at a dosage less than that required to produce the client's maximum strength, and the dosage is gradually increased at intervals of 48 hours or more according to the severity of the disease and the response of the client. Oral dosage forms may take several days to produce any change. If the last dosage increment does not produce a corresponding increase in the client's muscle strength, the dose will need to be reduced to its previous level. Because it is essential that the smallest dose for maximum result be used, the nurse's assessment and documentation of the client's health status is critical.

The drugs administered for myasthenia gravis are best given with food or milk to decrease adverse muscarinic effects, such as abdominal cramping, nausea, and vomiting. However, if dysphagia is a problem, the medication should be administered 30 to 45 minutes before meals and a rest period from the time of medication until meal time should be provided to allow for peak muscle strength for eating. This may be enhanced by serving frequent, regular, soft foods and encouraging the client to take small bites of food with frequent rest intervals. The main meal should be served at the time of day when the client has the most strength.

The nurse should be prepared for crisis intervention with medications, (edrophonium and neostigmine) for myasthenic crisis and (atropine) for cholinergic crisis. Basic resuscitative equipment should be available: suction catheters, AMBU bag, oxygen, and intubation tray.

The drugs should be administered on time since they are rapidly metabolized. A delay of 15 to 20 minutes in administration may cause beginning impairment of the muscles involved in swallowing and respiration.

The nurse must be especially alert to the route of administration because the oral dosage is 30 times greater than parenteral doses.

It should be noted that atropine sulfate, 0.06 to 1.2 mg, may be administered before or concurrently with these drugs to prevent adverse effects such as excessive secretions or bradycardia.

When using these agents to counteract the neuromuscular blocking agents (e.g., tubocurarine), the nurse should administer them along with artificial ventilation and oxygen therapy. They should be used only when some definite sign of voluntary respiration can be observed.

The nurse should administer intravenous pyridostigmine bromide very slowly to prevent thrombophlebitis.

The syrup dosage form of pyridostigmine may be more easily tolerated by clients with impaired swallowing or when the client's condition warrants frequent fractional doses, less than 60 mg. Although there is an extended-release form of pyridostigmine, it is usually not recommended because it increases the risk of cholinergic crisis, may need to be supplemented temporarily with other oral dosage forms to control symptoms, or pass intact through the GI tract if the client has increased intestinal activity or diarrhea.

A client who has had prolonged drug therapy may become refractory to the drug. By decreasing the dosage or withdrawing the drug for a few days under medical supervision, responsiveness may be restored.

***Education.*** The client with myasthenia gravis should be instructed to take the medication as ordered, using an alarm clock for precise timing of doses if necessary. An adequate supply of medications should be kept on hand. The family should also be instructed about timing of doses.

The client and family should maintain a log of symptoms. This will assist them to be aware of what events, such as emotional stress, menstruation, or infection, worsen the symptoms and how they respond to medication. The client should be taught to observe for therapeutic effects of the drug: a decrease or absence of ptosis; improved chewing, swallowing, and speech; increased skeletal muscle strength, and less fatigue. Activities should be planned to take advantage of the drug's peak effectiveness.

When stabilized, the client can be taught to recognize muscarinic effects (diaphoresis, salivation, slowed heart rate, and decreased blood pressure) and modify the medication dosage or take atropine if needed. The greater the control the client has over the therapeutic regimen, the less the feeling of powerlessness the client will have in the face of a devastating debilitating disease.

The client should be cautioned to avoid alcoholic beverages for 1 hour after medications, since they hasten drug absorption. Tonic water should be avoided because it may contain quinine, which increases weakness.

***Evaluation.*** When treatment is initiated, the client should be observed closely for signs of toxic effects. Atro-

pine sulfate and equipment for respiratory support should be on hand. Observation for cholinergic effect should be ongoing when these drugs are used. The time of onset of weakness indicates whether the weakness is caused by overdosage or underdosage. If the weakness begins about 1 hour after administration of the drug, it would suggest overdosage. If it occurs after 3 or more hours, the weakness is usually caused by underdosage. The nurse should observe for subtle changes in the client's speech and facial expression. Ptosis increases and the ability to swallow decreases early since weakness increases with an increase in the nicotinic effects.

CNS effects are evidenced by altered thought processes (confusion, irritability), increasing unsteadiness, slurred speech, dyspnea, and seizures. Blurred vision, bradycardia, increasing bronchial secretions and salivation, severe vomiting, and diarrhea result from the muscarinic effects.

Blood pressure, pulse, respirations, movement of the respiratory muscles, respiratory rate, tidal volume, and inspiratory force should be monitored. The nurse should check vital capacity by asking the client to take a deep breath and count as high as possible without taking another breath; most people can count as high as 40 or 50. All these observations are important because symptoms usually seen in respiratory distress, such as nasal flaring and intercostal or suprasternal retractions, may not occur because of muscle weakness. Arterial blood gases should also be monitored. Dosage, route of administration, and frequency of the medication depend on the client's clinical response, the remissions and exacerbations of the disease, and the stresses experienced by the client.

These drugs should be used with extreme caution in clients with bronchial asthma. Note that these drugs are contraindicated in clients with intestinal or urinary obstruction, peritonitis, recent ileorectal anastomoses, or acute peptic ulcer. They should be avoided in clients with decreased gastrointestinal motility because the drug may accumulate and cause toxicity when gastrointestinal motility is restored.

## DEMENTIA

**Dementia,** or mental impairment, affects about 3 million elderly Americans. Although approximately 15% of the impaired may have an undetectable, reversible disorder; an additional 20% to 25% may have an undiagnosed contributing problem that is treatable by more than symptomatic treatments. Therefore, nearly 1 million Americans have an unrecognized but potentially treatable condition that may have directly, or perhaps indirectly, caused dementia. See the boxed material on p. 368 for selected potentially reversible causes of dementia.

Generally, most irreversible dementias are caused by Alzheimer's disease (50% to 60%) and multi-infarct dementia (approximately 35%). Multi-infarct dementia was formerly known as cerebrovascular arteriosclerosis and is

---

## POTENTIALLY REVERSIBLE CAUSES OF DEMENTIA

*D*rugs, chemicals, or toxins
  a. Bromides
  b. Mercury
  c. Drugs such as butyrophenones, phenothiazines, diuretics, sedatives
*E*motional problems
  a. Depression
  b. Chronic alcoholism
*M*etabolic disorders
  a. Hyperglycemia
  b. Hypothyroidism
  c. Hypopituitarism
*E*ye/ear deprivation
  a. Blindness
  b. Deafness
*N*utritional deficits
  a. Vitamin $B_{12}$ deficiency
  b. Folic acid deficiency
  c. Niacin deficiency
*T*umors/trauma, acute
  a. Subdural hematoma
  b. Brain metastasis
  c. Brain tumors
*I*nfections and/or fever
  a. Viral infections
  b. Bacterial (tuberculosis)
  c. Bacterial (endocarditis)
*A*rteriosclerotic events
  a. Vascular occlusion
  b. Stroke

Modified from Lamay PP (1980). Prescribing for the elderly, Littleton, Colo: PSG Publishing Co.

---

the result of localized infarcts of brain tissue. Other irreversible dementias include Huntington's chorea and Creutzfeldt-Jakob disease. Alzheimer's disease is discussed below.

The syndrome of dementia usually develops slowly. Early signs include depression; loss of ability to concentrate; and increased anxiety, irritability, and agitation. Intellectual ability is usually first to decline; then recent memory (such as names of acquaintances or recent events); followed by the loss of orientation as to time, place, and person. Personal habits will decline; the person may become loud or obscene, or some personality characteristics that were present might become magnified. Helplessness, total dependency, and loss of manual skills may occur next. In the final stages, the person may be bedridden with loss of sphincter control and eventually will die, usually of bronchopneumonia.

The physician should rule out all the possible reversible causes of dementia. Then treatment should be instituted to try to prevent or reduce the ongoing damage and to support the client and family in managing this disease process. Drug treatment is only indicated for symptom control, that is, the use of low dosage antipsychotic agents for treating severe agitation, delusions, and hallucinations, or antidepressants for severe depression. Supportive care should include proper nutrition, moderate exercise if permitted, vitamins if indicated, and the use of environmental aids in a consistent fashion, such as nightlights and daily calendar reminders.

## ALZHEIMER'S DISEASE

**Alzheimer's disease** is a slowly progressive, irreversible disease that is tragically incurable. It affects more than 1.5 million Americans and is considered to be the major underlying reason for over 50% of all nursing home admissions. Other names for this disease include presenile dementia for disease occurrences before the age of 65, and senile dementia for occurrences over age 65.

The first three problems identified in clients with Alzheimer's disease are usually memory loss, loss of logical thinking or judgment, and an increased tendency to wander as a result of progressive disorientation. Later stages may include development of a seizure disorder and incontinence. Clients may be unable to feed or groom themselves, speak, or recognize simple objects or familiar persons.

In the terminal or last phase, the client wants to touch or examine all objects with the mouth (**hyperorality**), exhibits a decrease or loss in emotions, may be bulimic, and may also have a compulsion to touch everything in sight. Insomnia, night time wandering, and restlessness have also been reported. The progressive deterioration of brain cells may lead to increased dependency for all needs, decreased mobility to the point of being bedridden, and eventually death.

Researchers are still searching for the cause of Alzheimer's disease. Currently the theories under study include (1) a deficiency in acetylcholine, a major neurotransmitter in the brain; (2) the outcome of a slow virus or infection that attacks selected brain cells; (3) genetic predisposition; (4) autoimmune theory, that is, the body fails to recognize host tissue and attacks itself, and (5) aluminum theory; autopsy studies have reported finding 10 to 30 times the normal amount of aluminum in the brain. Is aluminum the cause for Alzheimer's disease? Many questions remain to be answered about this disease state.

Unfortunately, no pharmacologic method is known to cure, treat, retard, or prevent Alzheimer's disease. Current prescribing is directed toward symptom control. Small dosages of antipsychotic agents, such as haloperidol, 0.5 to 5 mg/day, have been prescribed for delusions and hallucinations. Two precautions exist though: first, start with a low dosage and only gradually increase the dose, if necessary. Monitor closely for side effects. And second, be aware that antipsychotic agents, or any medications with a high anticholinergic potential, could worsen the cognitive functioning of the client.

To treat depression, antidepressants with a low anticholinergic profile, such as desipramine or trazodone, have been used. Start at one third to one half the usual adult dose for clients having Alzheimer's disease and increase slowly as necessary. The antianxiety agents, especially those with a short-to-intermediate half-life, such as lorazepam, oxazepam, or alprazolam, are generally selected for clients exhibiting severe anxiety. Be aware though that if such agents are used to treat agitation in clients with dementia (or specifically, Alzheimer's disease), the potential for inducing a paradoxical reaction is present. Such clients may respond with an increase in activity, restlessness, and agitation. So it is important for the physician to differentiate between agitation and anxiety. If the benzodiazepine antianxiety agents are used, they should be closely monitored because symptoms change with time. Short-term use or reevaluation at least every 3 to 6 months is necessary.

## ▷NURSING MANAGEMENT: DRUG THERAPY FOR ALZHEIMER'S DISEASE

In the pharmacologic management of clients with Alzheimer's disease, care needs to be taken to provide for their safety and comfort. With most of the medications prescribed for the treatment of the symptoms of Alzheimer's disease, the nurse should understand that the elderly excrete and metabolize these drugs less efficiently. Smaller dosages are required to produce the desired effect. The nurse's assessment of subtle changes in the client's health status and the documentation of them will allow prescribers to individualize medication dosages more closely. Drugs that have side effects of depression, confusion, alteration of sleep patterns, or those that compromise respiratory function should be avoided.

Alzheimer's disease remains, in many ways, a perplexing illness. Besides providing appropriate care, the nurse should keep abreast of medical and nursing research findings, be committed to conducting nursing studies regarding the care of Alzheimer's disease, and share ideas about effective nursing interventions with colleagues.

## SUMMARY

Examples of major CNS-neuromuscular disorders—Parkinson's disease, myasthenia gravis, dementia, and Alzheimer's disease—are progressive and often incapacitating syndromes. Pharmacologic therapy, then, is essential for symptom control, which allows the client to function as independently as possible for as long as possible.

Clients with Parkinson's disease require correction of the disorder's imbalance of dopamine/acetylcholine. For that reason, the client is treated with drugs that have central anticholinergic activity, anticholinergics and antihistamines, and drugs that affect dopamine levels to enhance dopaminergic mechanisms. Because the condition is debilitating and long term, the client and caregivers require support and education to maintain compliance with the medication regimen.

Myasthenia gravis, the diminishment of acetylcholine receptors caused by an autoimmune process, characterized by skeletal muscle weakness and fatigue, is also progressive and incurable. Central to the treatment of this disorder are the anticholinesterase drugs.

With dementia and Alzheimer's disease, the drug therapy is not as specific. Low dosages of antipsychotic drugs are used in both disorders to control severe agitation, delusions, and hallucinations.

An essential part of the nurse's role with such progressive illnesses is to identify the subtle changes in the client's health status, which enables the prescriber to individualize the medication regimen to sustain the highest quality of life for the client.

---

# *Case Study: Parkinson's Disease*

Mr. Edwards is a 64-year-old man who has been diagnosed with Parkinson's disease. He is to begin taking Sinemet-10/100 TID. After 3 days his dosage is increased by one tablet a day. His final dosage is now two tablets of Sinemet-10/100 TID.

1. How does levodopa contribute to the improved function of the client with Parkinson's disease?
2. Explain the rationale for giving carbidopa with the levodopa.
3. What points should the nurse include in teaching Mr. Edwards about his drug therapy?

After 2 years of therapy, Mr. Edwards' symptoms have improved, with adverse effects limited to occasional nausea, dry mouth, and anorexia. However, periodically he has increases in his disease symptoms even though he continues to take his medication. The physician has decided to add amantadine (Symmetrel) 100 mg daily to the drug treatment.

4. Why does Mr. Edwards experience an increase in his symptoms?
5. Symmetrel is pharmacologically classified as an antiviral agent. Explain its role in the treatment of Parkinson's disease.

Six months later Mr. Edwards comes to the clinic reporting that he has begun having episodes of confusion, insomnia, nightmares, and hallucinations. He has waited several months before discussing these episodes and expresses concern that he is "losing his mind." In addition the nurse notices while talking with him that he has developed some involuntary movements of his tongue and face.

6. How should the nurse respond to Mr. Edwards' concerns?
7. What is the significance of the involuntary movements noted in the nurse's assessment of the client?

After reviewing Mr. Edwards' case, the physician decides to discontinue the Symmetrel. Within 6 weeks Mr. Edwards reports that the nightmares and insomnia have stopped. He no longer experiences the hallucinations, and the confusion is minimal. The involuntary movements have decreased significantly.

## BIBLIOGRAPHY

Ahlskog JE and Muenter MD. (1988). Treatment of Parkinson's disease with pergolide: a double-blind study, Mayo Clin Proc 63(10):969.

American Hospital Formulary Service. (1990). AHFS drug information '90. Bethesda, Md: American Society of Hospital Pharmacists, Inc.

Bell JA. (1989). Understanding myasthenia gravis, Focus Crit Care 16(1):57.

Burns EM et al. (1988). Pathophysiology and etiology of Alzheimer's disease, Nurs Clin North Am 23(1):11.

Butler FR. (1987). Neuroleptics and behavior: a comparative study, J Gerontol Nurs 13(6):15.

Castro DT. (1987). Amantadine hydrochloride: an agent for the prevention and treatment of influenza, J Pediatr Health Care 1(1):51.

Crossfield T. (1989). Dementia: a topic of confusion, Nurs Standard 3(22):29.

Duffey BD. (1989). Demented, old and alone, Amer J Nurs 89(2):212.

Erwin WG and Turco TF. (1986). Current concepts in clinical therapeutics: Parkinson's disease, Clin Pharm 5(9):742.

Feldman RG. (1985). Parkinson's disease: individualizing therapy, Hosp Pract 20(1):80A.

Finley R. (1986). Dementia in the elderly: focus on Alzheimer's disease, Drug Ther Elderly 1(3):9.

Gelety JE, editor. (1988). When neurotransmitters fail . . . parkinsonism: present management and new horizons, CNS Newletters, Sept/Oct.

Hansen TE et al. (1988). Risk factors for drug-induced parkinsonism in tardive dyskinesia patients, J Clin Psychiatry 49(4):139.

Kess R. (1984). Suddenly in crisis: unpredictable myasthenia, Am J Nurs 84(8):994.

Lamy PP. (1980). Prescribing for the elderly, Littleton, Colo: PSG Publishing Co.

Lannon MC et al. (1986). Comprehensive care of the patient with Parkinson's disease, J Neurosci Nurs 18(3):121.

Mancoll EL. (1984). Therapy of neurologic disorders in the elderly, Hosp Pract 19(10):106E.

Mayer RF. (1986). Getting myasthenia patients through a crisis, Emer Med 98(5):110.

Noroian EL. (1986). Myasthenia gravis: a nursing perspective, J Neurosci Nurs 18(2):74.

Nutt JG. (1984). Turning off the "on-off" syndrome in parkinsonism, Emer Med 16(18):60.

Reisberg B. (1986). Dementia: a systematic approach to identifying reversible causes, Geriatrics 41(4):30.

Sargent SM et al. (1988). Autologous adrenal medulla transplant: investigational treatment for Parkinson's disease, AORN J 47(3):682.

Serby M. (1989). Psychopharmacology and Alzheimer's disease, J Adv Med Surg Nurs 1(2):32.

Seybold ME. (1986). Myasthenia gravis, Hosp Med 22(5):139.

Todd B. (1985). Therapy for Parkinson's disease, Geriatr Nurs 6(2):117.

United States Pharmacopeial Convention. (1991). Drug information for the health care professional, ed 11., Rockville, Md: The Convention.

Williams V. (1987). Parkinson's disease: auto transplantation of adrenal medulla to caudate nucleus of the brain, J Neurosci Nurs 19(3):174.

# Drugs Affecting the Autonomic Nervous System

*Chapter*

# 19 Overview of the Autonomic Nervous System

## CHAPTER OBJECTIVES

*After studying this chapter, you should be able to meet the following objectives and define the key terms.*

1. Describe the reflex control system.

2. Explain the major differences between the parasympathetic and sympathetic divisions of the autonomic nervous system.

3. Name the primary neurotransmitters for each system.

4. Relate the primary disposition of the neurotransmitters following release from their respective nerves.

5. Name the three basic characteristics of the autonomic nervous system.

## KEY TERMS

**adrenergic,** page 377

**autonomic nervous system,** page 372

**cholinergic,** page 380

**conduction,** page 377

**feedback control mechanism,** page 373

**muscarinic (M) receptors,** page 380

**neuroeffector junction,** page 377

**neurohumoral transmission,** page 377

**nicotinic (N) receptors,** page 380

**somatic nervous system,** page 374

**synaptic junction,** page 377

## INTRODUCTION

Autonomic means self-governing. The **autonomic nervous system (ANS)** functions primarily as a regulatory system for maintaining the internal environment of the body at an optimal level (homeostasis). This system automatically controls the function of smooth muscle, cardiac muscle, and glandular secretions, which interact in many vital physiologic tasks. Digestion of a meal, pressure of circulating blood, and many other processes are internally regulated by the ANS.

## REFLEX CONTROL SYSTEM

The nervous system in general is the important control and communication system of the body. It collects information about conditions inside and outside of the body. The simplest means by which the nervous system responds to environ-

**TABLE 19-1**   Schema of components of feedback control mechanisms

| | Sensory input | | CNS connection | | Motor output |
|---|---|---|---|---|---|
| 1. Reflex arc (anatomy) | Receptor ⟶ | Afferent neuron ⟶ | CNS† ⟶ | Efferent neuron ⟶ | Effector |
| 2. Reflex act (physiology) | Stimulus ⟶ | Sensory nerve impulse ⟶ | Integration Motor nerve impulse ⟶ | Motor response (motion) | |
| 3. Blood pressure regulation ↑ BP | Baroreceptor (anatomy) ⟶ | Afferent neuron ⟶ | Medulla ⟶ | Efferent neuron ⟶ | Arteriolar smooth muscle |
| | Stimulus (physiology) ⟶ | Afferent impulse ⟶ | VSMC ⟶ | Decrease in sympathetic nerve impulse ⟶ | Vasodilation (↓ PR + CO → ↓ BP) |
| 4. Visceral nervous system | Spontaneous digestive tract | | | | Muscle contraction |
| | Nervous system | Afferent | CNS | Efferent | Motor response |

†CNS, Central nervous system; BP, blood pressure; VSMC, vasomotor center; PR, peripheral resistance; CO, cardiac output; ANS, autonomic nervous system; ↑, Increase; ↓, decrease.

*The *sensory input* carries sensory information such as pain, temperature, or pressure *to the central nervous system*. The *motor output* conducts the altered impulse *from the central nervous system* to the effector and produces motor activity or motion such as muscle contraction or glandular secretion. NOTE: The visceral efferent system or autonomic nervous system performs motor activity.

mental change is through the action of the reflex arc. The term reflex arc is essentially anatomic; it is defined as the automatic motor response to sensory stimuli. The work it does is the reflex act. In any reflex a nerve fiber conducts a nerve impulse. These impulses are the basis of communication of information through the nervous system.

The reflex act consists of two major functional processes: the sensory input and the motor output. The first component of the reflex arc is the receptor, which detects environmental changes such as temperature, pressure in blood vessels, and distention in the viscera. These changes are responsible for producing a stimulus in the receptor. Information from the sensitized receptor is then transmitted as a nerve impulse along the afferent neuron to the central nervous system, the site of integration. The CNS then issues instructions as an altered motor nerve impulse along the efferent neuron to the effector, which produces the appropriate movements of muscles and glands (see *1* and *2* of Table 19-1).

The information carried *to* the central nervous system (sensory input) and instructions sent *from* the central nervous system (motor output) constitute a **feedback control mechanism.** That is, information fed back to the central nervous system from a receptor is modulated so that nerve impulses may vary in frequency and pattern according to the degree of activity required of the effector. The control of visceral function is involuntary, so the feedback mechanism must include all the components of a control system essential for performing the reflex act. Therefore reflex action functions as a feedback mechanism, operating from a

receptor to an effector. Its purpose is to prevent extreme changes in function that may create a disturbance in the internal environment.

A good example of feedback control is the blood pressure-regulating reflex. Again, the sequence of events follows the pattern of the reflex arc. The carotid sinus in the carotid artery and the aortic sinus in the aortic arch serve as pressure receptors (baroreceptors) that are highly sensitive to stretch, and the degree of wall stretching is determined by the amount of pressure within these vessels. Thus any increase in blood pressure stimulates the baroreceptors, and this information is conveyed as nerve impulses along the afferent neuron to the vasomotor center in the medulla. The medulla is the central nervous system site for integration of blood pressure. After the appropriate neuronal connections, a decrease in sympathetic discharge is conducted along the efferent neuron to the effectors and produces relaxation of arteriolar smooth muscles. This relaxation causes dilation of the arteries and a reduction in blood pressure (see *3* of Table 19-1). This is only a partial explanation of blood pressure regulation, since a decrease in arterial pressure produces the opposite response in the same neuronal pathway. In addition, this control mechanism operates in coordination with cardiac function.

## NERVOUS SYSTEM CLASSIFICATION

The nervous system is classified on the basis of the reflex arc (see *4* of Table 19-1). The two main divisions are (1)

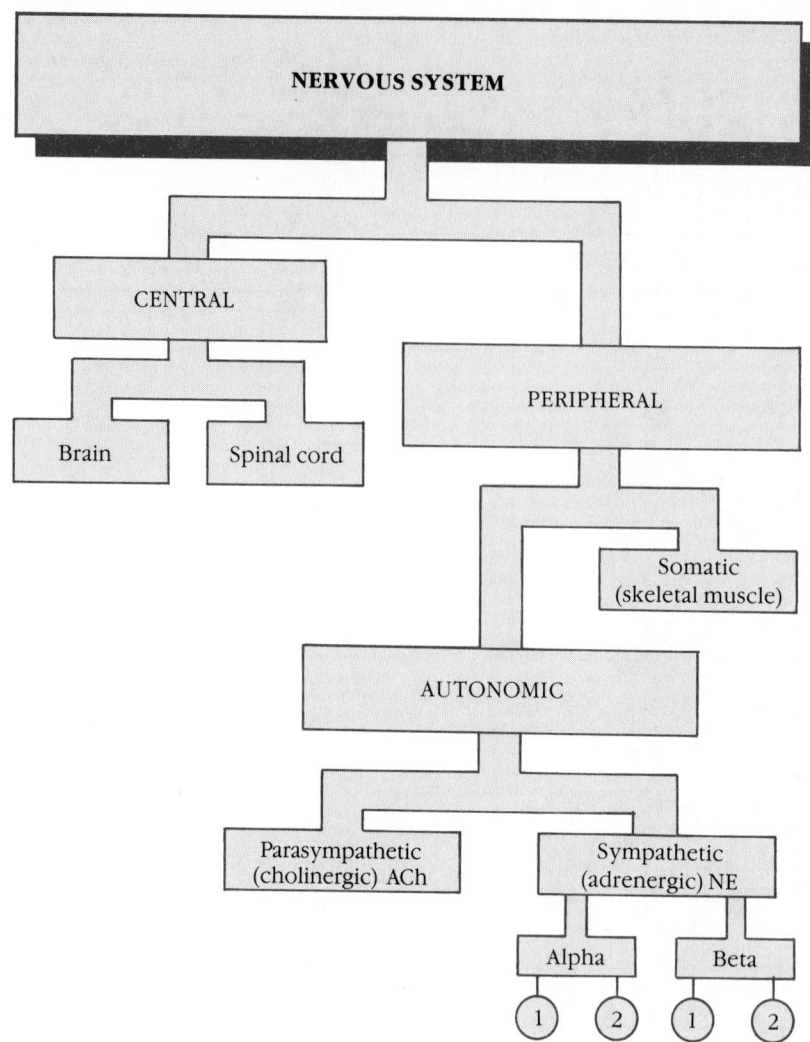

**FIGURE 19-1** Divisions of the nervous system.

the central nervous system and (2) the peripheral nervous system. The central nervous system consists of the brain and spinal cord and performs the important integrative functions from the peripheral sources. The peripheral system has two divisions: the **somatic nervous system,** which innervates voluntary or skeletal muscles, and the autonomic nervous system, which influences the involuntary activities of smooth muscles, cardiac muscles, and glands. The afferent fibers of both systems are the first link in the reflex arc by carrying sensory information to the central nervous system. Following integration at various levels in the brain, the motor outflow from the central nervous system is conducted along either the somatic efferent system or the visceral efferent system. Both of these systems constitute the final link in the reflex arc. (See Figure 19-1.)

Several centers in the central nervous system integrate all autonomic nervous system activities. There is evidence that the hypothalamus, in particular, performs such integrating activities. It contains centers that regulate body temperature, water balance, and carbohydrate and fat metabolism. It also

integrates mechanisms concerned with emotional behavior, the waking state, and sleep. The medulla oblongata integrates the control of blood pressure, respiration, and cardiac function. A series of "vital centers," including the vasomotor center, respiratory center, and cardiac center, respectively, coordinates these activities. The midbrain, limbic system, cerebellum, and cerebral cortex all are involved in the control of and in physiologic functions regulated by the autonomic nervous system. Remember, the autonomic nervous system is part of the central nervous system, not a distinct entity.

## DIFFERENCES BETWEEN THE PARASYMPATHETIC AND SYMPATHETIC SYSTEMS

The autonomic nervous system is organized into two subdivisions: (1) the parasympathetic system and (2) the sympathetic system (see box). The anatomic arrangement of each system consists of two motor nerves, a preganglionic

## ANS TERMINOLOGY

Over the years, various terminology has been used to describe the divisions of the autonomic nervous system. The anatomic names are sympathetic and parasympathetic, and the corresponding functional terms, which relate to the primary neurotransmitters for each system, are adrenergic and cholinergic, respectively. Generally, the terms are used interchangeably—that is, sympathetic or adrenergic and parasympathetic or cholinergic nervous systems. It is important to understand the terms parasympatho*mimetic* and sympatho*mimetic,* which means to mimic or produce an effect similar to activation of either system. Parasympatho*lytic* or sympatho*lytic* implies blocking the normal effects seen with activation of either system. Anticholinergic is synonymous with parasympatholytic.

| Anatomic | Functional | Primary Neurotransmitter |
|---|---|---|
| Sympathetic | Adrenergic | norepinephrine (NE) |
| Parasympathetic | Cholinergic | acetylcholine (ACh) |

nerve and a postganglionic nerve, with a ganglion (group of nerve cell bodies) connecting the two neurons (Figure 19-2).

***Physiologic differences.*** Since the parasympathetic system and the sympathetic system simultaneously innervate many of the same organs, the opposing actions of the two systems balance one another. The parasympathetic system functions mainly conserve energy and restore body resources of the organism, otherwise known as the system of rest and digestion. These include cardiac deceleration, a rise in gastrointestinal activity associated with increased digestion and absorption, and an increase in excretion. In contrast, the sympathetic system mobilizes the organism during emergency and stress situations, and so it is called the "fight or flight" system. These functions involve expenditure of energy, such as emotional stress, and increases in the blood sugar concentration, heart activity, and blood pressure (Table 19-2 presents effector organ responses).

***Anatomic and pharmacologic differences.*** The parasympathetic system's preganglionic fibers emerge with the cranial nerves III, VII, IX, and X and at the sacral spinal levels from about S3 through S4. The tenth cranial nerve or vagus nerve has extensive branches that supply fibers to

**TABLE 19-2**   Classification of the effector organ responses to autonomic nerve impulses

| Effector organs | Responses to parasympathetic (cholinergic) impulses | Response to sympathetic (adrenergic) impulses | |
|---|---|---|---|
| | | Receptor | Response |
| Cardiovascular system | | | |
| Heart | | | |
| Sinoatrial node | Decreased heart rate | Beta$_1$ | Increased heart rate |
| Atrioventricular node | Decreased conduction velocity | Beta$_1$ | Increased automaticity and conduction velocity |
| Ventricles | No innervation | Beta$_1$ | Increased force of contraction and conduction velocity |
| Arterioles (smooth muscle) | | | |
| Coronary | Dilation | Alpha, beta$_2$, dopaminergic | Constriction and dilation |
| Skin and mucosa | Dilation | Alpha | Constriction |
| Skeletal muscle | No innervation | Cholinergic | Dilation |
| Cerebral | Dilation | Alpha | Slight constriction |
| Mesenteric | None | Alpha, beta$_2$, dopaminergic | Constriction and dilation |
| Renal | None | Alpha, beta$_2$, dopaminergic | Constriction and dilation |
| Veins | None | Alpha, beta$_2$ | Constriction and dilation |
| Lung | | | |
| Bronchial muscle | Bronchoconstriction | Beta$_2$ | Relaxation (bronchodilation) |
| Bronchial glands | Stimulation | | Inhibition |
| Gastrointestinal tract | | | |
| Motility | Increased motility | Alpha, beta$_2$ | Relaxation (decreased motility) |
| Sphincters | Relaxation | Alpha | Contraction |
| Exocrine glands | Increased secretion | ? | Decreased secretion |
| Salivary glands | Dilation: copious, watery secretion | Alpha | Constriction: thick, viscous secretion |
| Gallbladder and ducts | Contraction | | Relaxation |
| Kidney | None | Beta$_2$ | Renin secretion |
| Urinary bladder | | | |
| Detrusor muscle | Contraction | Beta$_2$ | Relaxation |
| Sphincter | Relaxation | Alpha | Contraction |

*Continued.*

**TABLE 19-2**   Classification of the effector organ responses to autonomic nerve impulses—cont'd

| Effector organs | Responses to parasympathetic (cholinergic) impulses | Response to sympathetic (adrenergic) impulses | |
| --- | --- | --- | --- |
| | | Receptor | Response |
| Eye | | | |
| Radial muscle | Contraction of sphincter | Alpha | Contraction (mydriasis) |
| Iris | Muscle (miosis, pupillary constriction) | | |
| Ciliary muscle | Contraction | | No innervation |
| Liver | Glycogen synthesis | Beta | Glycogenolysis, gluconeogenesis |
| Pancreas | | | |
| Acini | Secretion | Alpha | Decreased secretion |
| Islets (beta cells) | None | Alpha | Decreased secretion |
| Skin | None | Beta$_2$ | Increased secretion |
| Sweat glands | No innervation | Cholinergic | Increased sweating |
| Pilomotor muscle | No innervation | | Contraction (gooseflesh) |
| Lacrimal glands | Increased secretion | | No innervation |
| Nasopharyngeal glands | Increased secretion | | No innervation |
| Male sex glands | Erection | | Ejaculation |

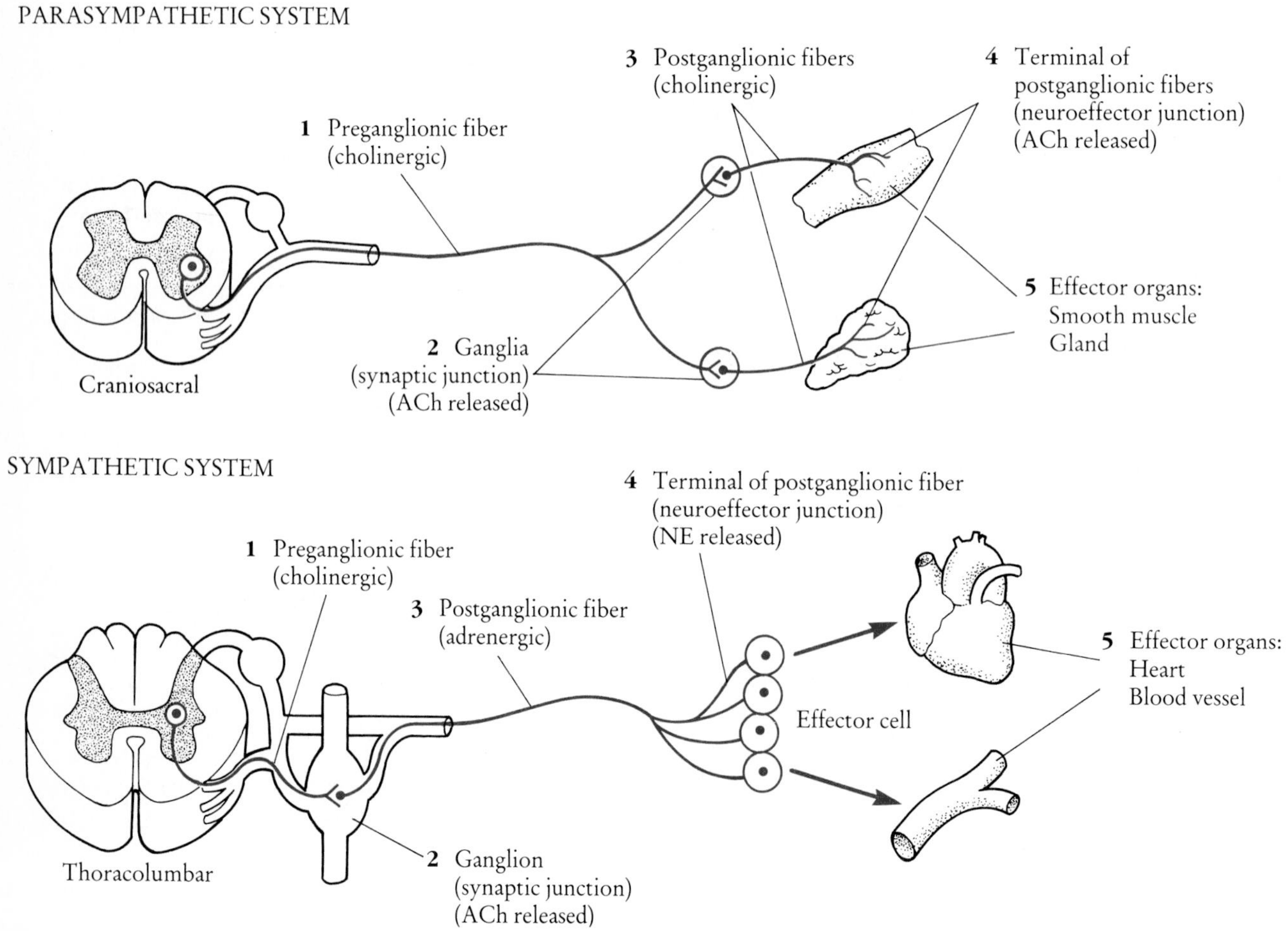

PARASYMPATHETIC SYSTEM

SYMPATHETIC SYSTEM

**FIGURE 19-2**  Preganglionic and postganglionic fibers and neurohormonal transmitters of the autonomic nervous system. The order in which the nerve impulse travels is numbered. Parasympathetic neuron releases acetylcholine, which acts on the ganglia and effector organs. Sympathetic neuron releases acetylcholine, which acts on the ganglion, and norepinephrine, which stimulates the effector organs.

**TABLE 19-3**  Differentiating characteristics between the parasympathetic and sympathetic nervous systems

| Characteristic | Parasympathetic nervous system | Sympathetic nervous system |
|---|---|---|
| Origin | Craniosacral | Thoracolumbar |
| Structure innervation | Cardiac muscle | Cardiac muscle |
| | Smooth muscle | Smooth muscle |
| | Glands | Glands |
| | Viscera | Viscera |
| Ganglia | Near the effector (vagus, atria of heart) | Near central nervous system |
| Length of fibers | Preganglionics (long) | Preganglionics (short) |
| | Postganglionics (short) | Postganglionics (long) |
| Ratio of preganglionics to postganglionics | Divergence in minimal (1:2), very discrete, fine responses | High degree of divergence (1:11, 1:17) |
| Response | Discrete | Diffuse |
| Ganglion transmitter | Acetylcholine | Acetylcholine |
| Transmitter substance (postganglionic nerve endings) | Acetylcholine | Norepinephrine (most cases); epinephrine and norepinephrine (adrenal medulla) |
| | | Acetylcholine for sweat glands and blood vessels of skeletal muscles |
| Blocking drugs (postganglionic nerve endings) | Cholinergic blocking agents (atropine) | Adrenergic blocking agents Alpha-phentolamine Beta-propranolol |

the heart, lungs, and almost all the abdominal organs. The parasympathetic system is also called the cholinergic system because the neurotransmitter released by its postganglionic fiber is acetylcholine (ACh).

The sympathetic system is also called the thoracolumbar system because its preganglionic fibers originate in the spinal cord from the thoracic segment T1 to the lumbar segment of L2 levels. Because the postganglionic fiber of this system releases the neurotransmitter norepinephrine or epinephrine from the adrenal medullary cells, the sympathetic system is also called the **adrenergic** system (Figure 19-2 and Table 19-3).

## NEUROHUMORAL TRANSMISSION

There is general agreement that information in the nervous system is transmitted both electrically and chemically. This phenomenon occurs because nerve cells have two special characteristics: (1) They can conduct electrical signals. The passage of a nerve impulse or an action potential along a nerve fiber or a muscle fiber is called **conduction.** (2) They have intercellular connections with other nerve cells and with innervated tissues such as muscles and glands. The presence of a specific chemical at these connections determines the type of information a neuron can receive and the range of responses it can yield in return. The passage of a nerve impulse across a synaptic or neuroeffector junction with the use of a chemical is called **neurohumoral transmission.**

Although each nerve fiber may conduct an impulse along the neuron, it is solely the chemical substance called the neurotransmitter or neurohormone that permits the action potential of a neuron to cross (1) the **synaptic junction** from one neuron to another neuron or (2) the **neuroeffector junction** from a neuron to an effector organ. In this mechanism the arrival of an action potential at a nerve terminal starts the release of the neurotransmitter. The hormone or mediator then acts as a messenger by which nerve cells communicate information to the structures they innervate. The neurotransmitter exerts its influence primarily at the junctional spaces, (synaptic junction or neuroeffector junction) to facilitate the transmission of impulses to their final destination, which is usually the transmitter. Many drugs also act selectively at these junctions (Figure 19-3).

### Types of Neurohumoral Transmission

The neurohormones acetylcholine and norepinephrine are responsible for neurohumoral transmission. Nerves that contain acetylcholine are called *cholinergic neurons,* and they are involved in cholinergic transmission. Nerves that contain norepinephrine or epinephrine (from adrenal medulla) are known as *adrenergic neurons,* and they are associated with adrenergic transmission.

In neurohumoral transmission the sequence of events includes (1) biosynthesis, (2) storage, (3) release, (4) action, and (5) inactivation of the mediator. Many autonomic drugs affect one of these individual events so it is essential to understand the basic mechanisms involved in this complicated process. These drugs have been useful in treating many patients afflicted with autonomic disorders.

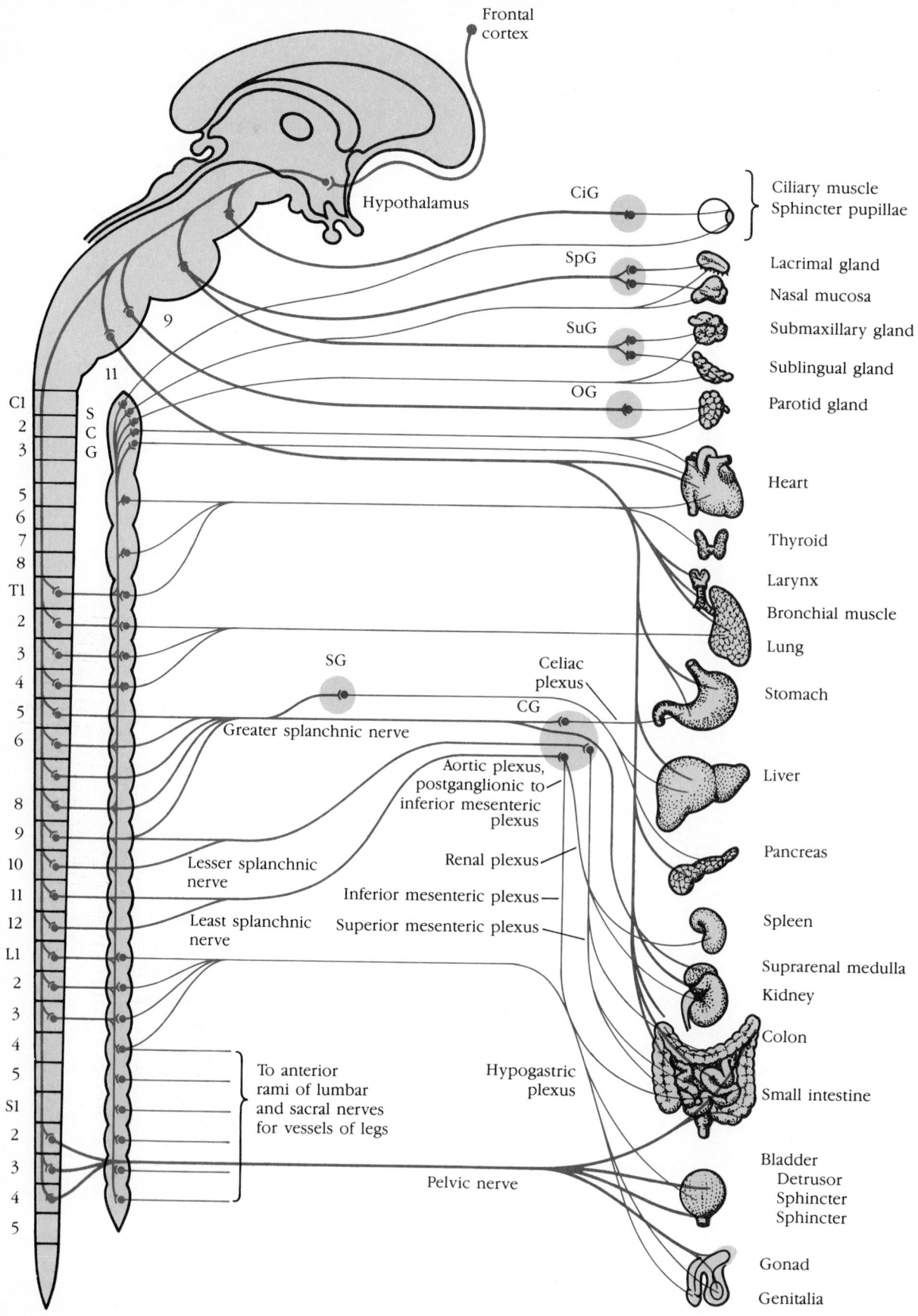

**FIGURE 19-3** Sympathetic division of the autonomic nervous system. *CiG,* Ciliary ganglion; *SpG,* sphenopalatine ganglion; *SuG,* submaxillary ganglion; *OG,* otic ganglion; *SG,* splanchnic ganglion; *CG,* celiac ganglion.

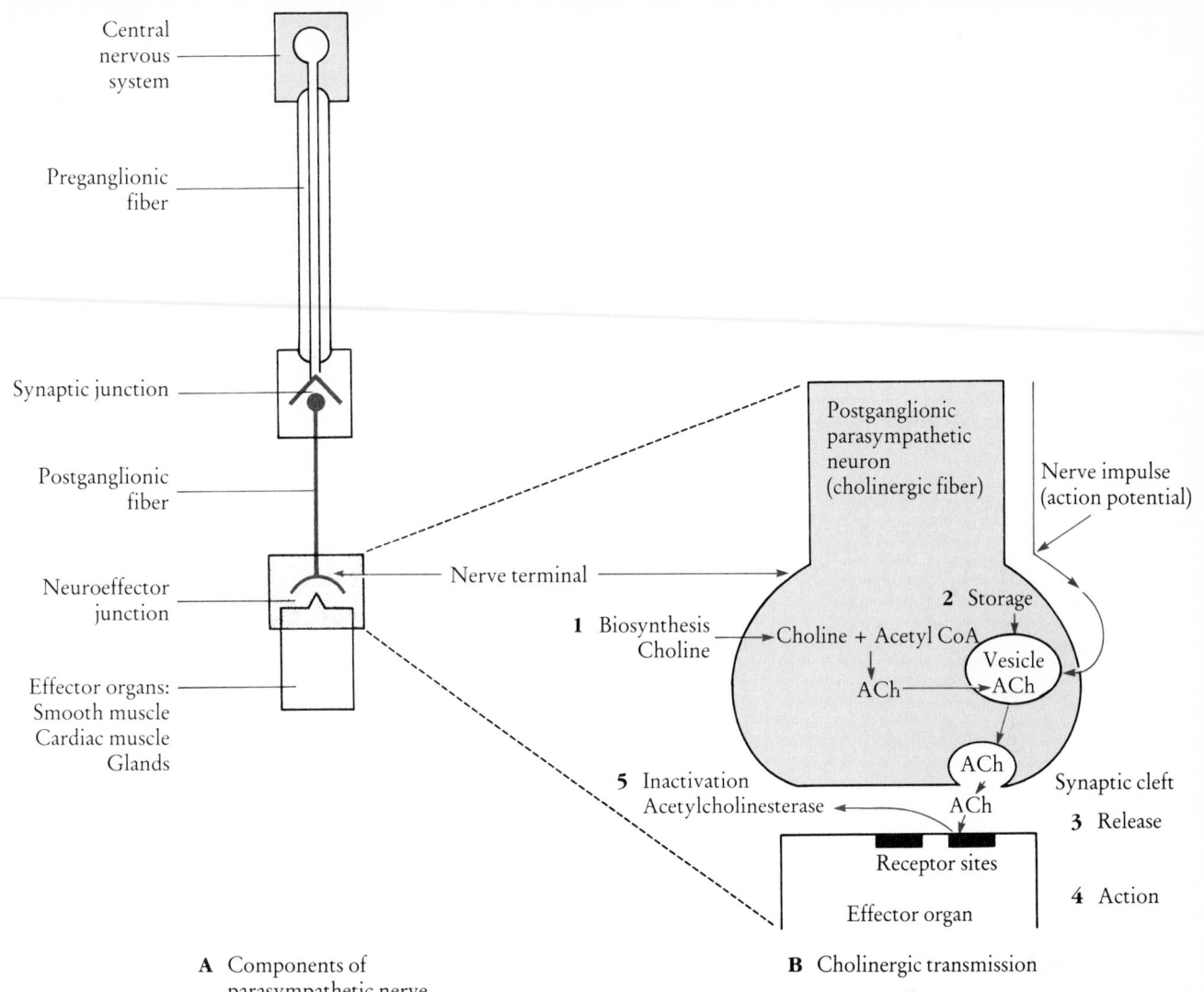

**A** Components of
parasympathetic nerve

**B** Cholinergic transmission

**FIGURE 19-4 A,** Schematic representation to show the relationship between a neuron in the central nervous system, a neuron in a peripheral ganglion, and an effector organ supplied by the parasympathetic nerve. **B,** Cholineric transmission. Schematic diagram of parasympathetic postganglionic neuron showing steps in cholinergic transmission at the neuroeffector junction. *1, Biosynthesis* of acetylcholine (ACh): Choline is taken up by the nerve terminal, and it interacts with acetyl coenzyme A to synthesize ACh. *2, Storage:* Following synthesis, ACh is stored in the vesicle until the arrival of a nerve impulse. *3, Release:* An action potential at the nerve terminal causes the vesicle to attach itself to the membrane and release ACh. The neurohormone then diffuses across the synaptic cleft and combines with the receptors on the effector cell. *4, Action:* The interaction of ACh with the receptor sites results in a motor response. *5, Inactivation* of ACh: At the synaptic cleft, ACh is hydrolyzed by the enzyme acetylcholinesterase.

## Cholinergic Transmission

***Synthesis and storage.*** Acetylcholine is synthesized in a reaction catalyzed by the enzyme choline acetylase (choline acetyltransferase) in the cytoplasm of the nerve terminal:

$$\text{Acetyl coenzyme A + Choline} \xrightleftharpoons[\text{Acetylcholinesterase}]{\text{Choline acetylase}} \text{Acetylcholine + Coenzyme A}$$

Once synthesized, the acetylcholine is stored in packets called synaptic vesicles or granules, which are located in the nerve terminal (see Figure 19-4, *B*).

***Release and action.*** The arrival of an action potential at the nerve ending causes the vesicle to approach the membrane and release the acetylcholine molecules into the synaptic cleft or space. Calcium ions must be present for an efficient release. Once free, the acetylcholine diffuses across the synaptic or junctional cleft and attaches itself to specialized receptors (postjunctional sites) on the membrane of the next neuron or neuroeffector. The binding of acetylcholine to the receptor increases the permeability of the membrane to sodium and potassium ions; thus a depolarizing action finally results in excitation or inhibition of neural, muscular, or glandular activity (see Figure 19-4, *A* and *B*).

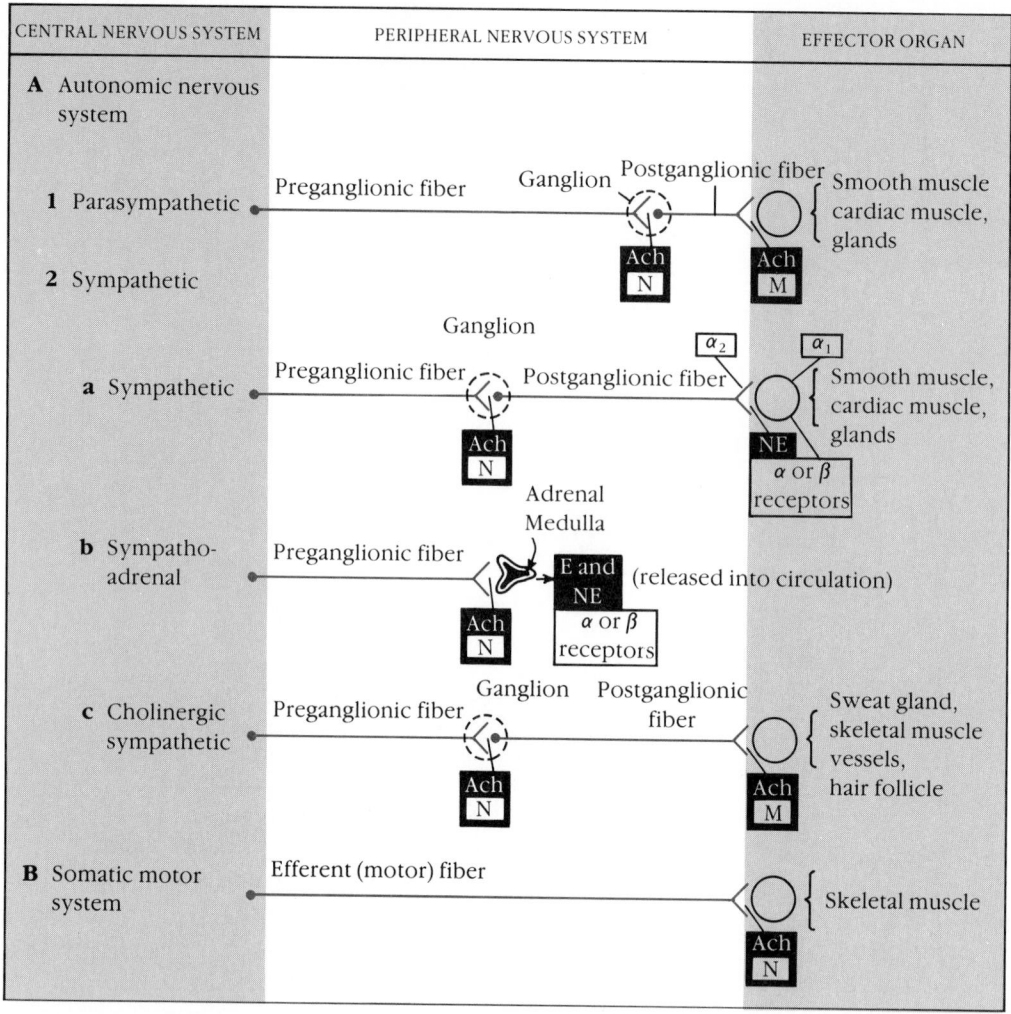

**FIGURE 19-5** Schema of receptor sites for neurohumoral transmission. **A,** Autonomic nervous system, where preganglionic fibers of both parasympathetic and sympathetic nerves synapse in the ganglia. **B,** Somatic motor nervous system. *N,* Nicotinic sites; *M,* muscarinic sites.

*Cholinergic receptors.* The cholinergic receptor sites that are stimulated by acetylcholine are either nicotinic or muscarinic. **Nicotinic (N) receptors** appear in the ganglia of both the parasympathetic and sympathetic fibers, the adrenal medulla, and the skeletal (striated) muscle that is supplied by the somatic motor system. **Muscarinic (M) receptors** are located in the smooth muscle, cardiac muscle, and glands of the parasympathetic fibers and the effector organs of the cholinergic sympathetic fibers. The N and M receptors are shown in Figure 19-5.

*Inactivation.* Once acetylcholine has exerted its effect on the postjunctional sites, the excess amount is inactivated rapidly by the enzyme acetylcholinesterase (AChE). The metabolites formed in this reaction are chemically inactive and are the same compounds from which acetylcholine is formed. Inactivation of this neurohormone is shown as a reverse action in the preceding formula (see Figure 19-4, *B*).

## Adrenergic Transmission

The term "catecholamine" refers to a group of chemically related compounds: norepinephrine (noradrenalin), epinephrine (adrenaline), and dopamine. They are all involved in some aspect of adrenergic transmission.

*Synthesis and storage.* The catecholamines produced by the sympathetic nervous system include norepinephrine and epinephrine. The complex pathway for synthesis of these neurotransmitters is mediated by different enzymes located in the postganglionic nerve terminals and in the chromaffin cells of the adrenal medullary glands. The production of norepinephrine and epinephrine proceeds through the following steps:

$$\text{Tyrosine} \xrightarrow[\text{hydroxylase}]{\text{Tyrosine}} \text{Dopa} \xrightarrow[\text{decarboxylase}]{\text{Dopa}}$$

$$\text{Dopamine} \xrightarrow[\text{β-hydroxylase}]{\text{Dopamine}} \text{Norepinephrine} \xrightarrow[\text{transferase}]{\text{Methyl}}$$

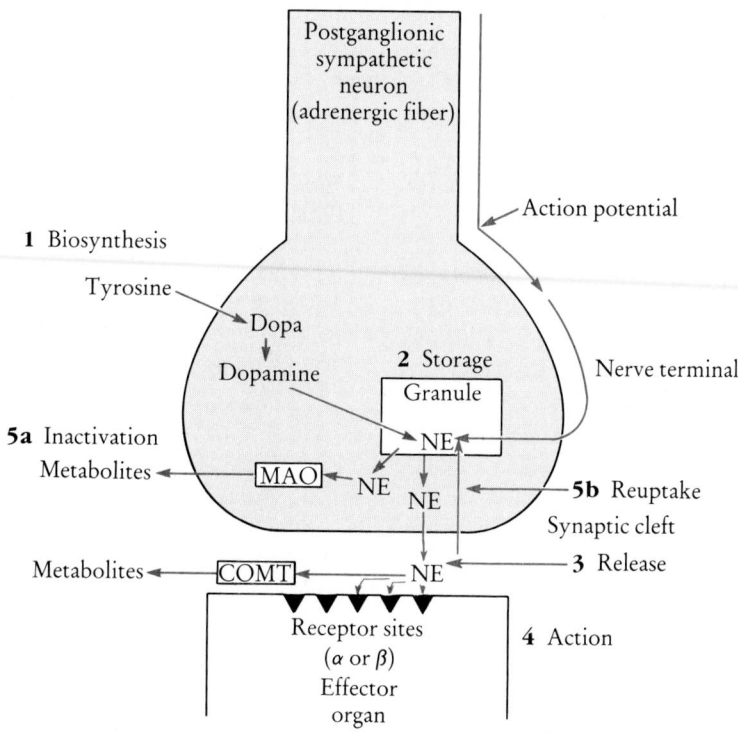

**FIGURE 19-6**  Adrenergic transmission at the neuroeffector junction.

The formation of norepinephrine is initiated by tyrosine, which is an amino acid derived from proteins in the diet. When tyrosine enters the cytoplasm of the nerve terminal, it is converted into dopa, which in turn is decarboxylated to dopamine. Dopamine is then taken up into the storage vesicles, or granules, where it is transformed into the neurotransmitter norepinephrine by the enzyme dopamine β-hydroxylase. Figure 19-6 shows the steps of the synthetic process. In the adrenal medullary gland, the enzyme methyl transferase converts norepinephrine to epinephrine. On stimulation, both epinephrine (E) and norepinephrine (NE) are released from the adrenal medulla and carried by the circulation to all parts of the body. The autonomic drugs may inhibit the rate of formation of norepinephrine.

**Release.**  The arrival of an action potential at the nerve terminal of the postganglionic fibers causes the vesicles to fuse with the cell membrane and release the stored supply of norepinephrine into the junctional cleft. Calcium ions must be present to enhance the release of norepinephrine from the vesicles. The free form of norepinephrine then diffuses across the cleft to the receptor sites on the postjunctional membrane of neuroeffector cells (smooth muscle, cardiac muscle, or glands). (See Figure 19-6.)

**Action.**  Once the norepinephrine combines with either the alpha or beta receptor sites on the membrane of the neuroeffector cells, a series of chemical and electrical events produces either an excitatory or an inhibitory effect. The alpha receptor activation is primarily responsible for excitatory response, although it results in intestinal relaxation.

By contrast, beta receptor activation is usually inhibitory except in the myocardial cells, where norepinephrine produces an excitatory effect.

**Adrenergic receptors.**  The adrenergic receptor sites that are stimulated by the endogenous catecholamines—norepinephrine, epinephrine, and dopamine—are classified as alpha and beta receptors. Both classes have two subtypes. The alpha receptors are identified by neuronal location: (1) alpha$_1$ sites are located on the postsynaptic effector cells and (2) alpha$_2$ sites appear on the presynaptic nerve terminals, controlling the amount of norepinephrine release that operates through a negative feedback mechanism. By contrast, the beta receptors are designated by organ location: (1) beta$_1$ receptors are located primarily in the heart and (2) beta$_2$ receptors appear in the smooth muscle of the bronchioles, arterioles, and various other visceral organs in the body. Dopaminergic receptors have been identified in the brain and on certain blood vessels (coronary, renal, and mesenteric vessels). (See Figure 19-5 and Table 19-2 for alpha and beta receptors.)

**Inactivation.**  Once norepinephrine has performed its adrenergic function, its action must be rapidly stopped to prevent prolongation of its effects, which could lead to a loss of regulatory control of visceral function. The inactivation of norepinephrine occurs by (1) enzymatic transformation, (2) reuptake into nerve terminals, and (3) diffusion.

Catecholamines are metabolized by two enzymes, monoamine oxidase (MAO) and catechol-*O*-methyltransferase (COMT). Free norepinephrine *within* the cytoplasm of the nerve terminal is metabolized by MAO, which is stored in the mitochondria of sympathetic neurons. COMT, which is located *outside* the neuron or at the synaptic cleft, participates in the inactivation or metabolism of norepinephrine outside the neuron.

The reuptake mechanism plays a more significant role than enzymatic transformation in catecholamine inactivation. In the reuptake process norepinephrine is removed by the active transport ("amine pump") from the junctional sites (synaptic and neuroeffector junctions) and is returned to the sympathetic nerve terminal and storage vesicles. Thus this mechanism provides a means other than the synthetic process for maintaining an adequate supply of norepinephrine.

Finally, a small portion of norepinephrine released at the synaptic cleft may be picked up by the circulation and metabolized elsewhere in the body. This is known as the diffusion process. Figure 19-6 portrays the steps in adrenergic transmission.

## General Actions of Autonomic Transmitters

In 1933 Dale and co-workers determined the chemical differences between fibers that release acetylcholine (**cholinergic** fibers) and those that release norepinephrine and epinephrine (adrenergic fibers). In the autonomic nervous system, all the preganglionic fibers originate in the central nervous system and synapse with the ganglia of the postganglionic fibers. The terminals of all the preganglionic fibers release acetylcholine and interact with nicotinic receptors in the membrane of the postganglionic fibers or the adrenal medulla.

In the parasympathetic system the terminals of the postganglionic fibers also release acetylcholine and interact with muscarinic receptors in the membrane of the smooth muscle, cardiac muscle, and glands.

In the sympathetic nervous system there are three different kinds of postganglionic neurons: (1) The sympathetic neuron, the major type, releases norepinephrine and activates either alpha or beta receptors in the membrane of the smooth muscle, cardiac muscle, and glands. (2) The sympathoadrenal neuron, in which the preganglionic fiber synapses with a modified sympathetic ganglion, the adrenal medulla, releases mostly epinephrine and a small amount of norepinephrine, which are secreted into the circulation and carried to all parts of the body. (3) The cholinergic sympathetic neuron releases acetylcholine and stimulates muscarinic receptor sites on the sweat glands to produce swelling and on the blood vessels in skeletal muscle to increase vasodilation and enhance blood flow.

In the somatic (sensory) nervous system a single neuron, the efferent (motor) fiber, releases acetylcholine and interacts with the nicotinic sites on the skeletal muscle membrane. The autonomic drugs play an important role by enhancing or inhibiting physiologic activity at these sites of neurohumoral transmission (see Figure 19-5 and Table 19-2).

## SUMMARY

The primary function of the autonomic nervous system is to control and integrate many physiologic tasks necessary to preserve internal homeostasis, emergency mechanisms, and repair. Its activities are integrated by a number of centers within the central nervous system: the hypothalamus, medulla oblongata, midbrain, limbic system, cerebellum, and cerebral cortex. The autonomic nervous system innervates the smooth muscles, cardiac muscles, and glands. It is composed of two divisions, the parasympathetic and the sympathetic; their actions oppose and balance each other.

1. Although both systems are present in the body, only one will predominate at any given time.
2. If a nervous system function is blocked, the opposite effect will take precedence.
3. Drugs are available to stimulate or block either system.

Functions stimulated by the parasympathetic system are chiefly those concerned with digestion, excretion, near vision, cardiac deceleration, and anabolism. Functions stimulated by the sympathetic system are primarily those concerned with the expenditure of energy and are called into play by physical or emotional stress.

Nerve impulse transmission is caused by the activity of chemical substances called neurotransmitters: acetylcholine and the catecholamines. Nerve fibers that synthesize and liberate acetylcholine are known as cholinergic fibers; those that synthesize and secrete norepinephrine and epinephrine are called adrenergic fibers.

For the nurse to achieve an understanding of the pharmacology of autonomic drugs a basic knowledge of the anatomy and physiology of the autonomic nervous system is essential. This information helps to predict the effects of drugs that stimulate or block autonomic function.

## BIBLIOGRAPHY

Avery GS, ed. (1987). Drug treatment: principles and practice of clinical pharmacology and therapeutics, ed 3. Sydney, Australia: Adis Press.

Bhagat BD. (1979). Mode of action of autonomic drugs. Flushing, NY: Graceway Publishing Co.

Gilman AG et al, eds. (1990). Goodman and Gilman's the pharmacological basis of therapeutics, ed 8. New York: Macmillan Publishing Co.

Guyton AC. 1990. Textbook of medical physiology, ed 8. Philadelphia: WB Saunders Co.

Milne, C. (1989). The autonomic nervous system, Nurs Standard 3(19):26.

Noback, C and Deramarest, R. (1986). The nervous system: introduction and review, ed 3. New York: McGraw-Hill Book Co.

Voke, J. (1986). The nervous system: reflex action, Nurs Times 82(40):52.

# Drugs Affecting the Parasympathetic Nervous System

## CHAPTER OBJECTIVES

*After studying this chapter, you should be able to meet the following objectives and define the key terms.*

1. Explain the difference between the muscarinic and nicotinic actions of acetylcholine.

2. Describe the side effects/adverse reactions of cholinergic, cholinergic blocking, and synthetic antispasmotic agents.

3. Describe the physiologic effects of the belladonna alkaloids.

4. List the physiologic effects of nicotine.

5. Describe the use of ganglionic blocking drugs.

6. Discuss nursing management of the care of clients receiving agents affecting the parasympathetic nervous system.

## KEY TERMS

**adrenergic,** page 384

**adrenergic blocking,** page 384

**antimuscarinic,** page 388

**antisialagogue,** page 393

**cholinergic,** page 383

**cholinergic blocking,** page 383

**curarization,** page 384

**muscarinic effect,** page 384

**muscarinic blocking,** page 388

**parasympatholytic,** page 388

**parasympathomimetic,** page 383

**sympatholytic,** page 384

**sympathomimetic,** page 384

## Autonomic Drugs

The autonomic drugs mimic, intensify, or block the effects of the parasympathetic and sympathetic divisions of the autonomic nervous system. They are divided into the following groups:

1. **Cholinergic (parasympathomimetic)** drugs, (e.g., bethanechol) act like mediators of the parasympathetic nervous system

2. **Cholinergic blocking** (anticholinergic) drugs (e.g., atropine) block the action of the parasympathetic nervous system

**TABLE 20-1**   Sites for muscarinic and nicotinic actions of acetylcholine

| Site | Muscarinic action* | Nicotinic actions |
|------|--------------------|--------------------|
| Cardiovascular | | |
|   Blood vessels | Dilation | Constriction ⎫ |
|   Heart rate | Slowed | Increased ⎬ With large doses after atropine |
|   Blood pressure | Decreased | Increased ⎭ |
| Gastrointestinal | | |
|   Tone | Increased | Increased |
|   Motility | Increased | Increased |
|   Sphincters | Relaxed | — |
| Glandular secretions | Increased salivary, lacrimal, intestinal, and sweat secretion | Initial stimulation, then inhibition of salivary and bronchial secretions |
| Skeletal muscle | — | Stimulated |
| Autonomic ganglia | — | Stimulated |
| Eye | Pupil constriction Decreased accommodation | — |
| Blocking agent | Atropine | Tubocurarine |
| **Remarks** | Above effects increase as dosage increases | Increased dosage inhibits effects and causes receptor blockade |

*Usual sites for therapeutic effects.

3. **Adrenergic (sympathomimetic)** drugs (e.g., norepinephrine) act like mediator of the sympathetic nervous system
4. **Adrenergic blocking (sympatholytic)** drugs (e.g., propranolol) block the action of the sympathetic nervous system

## CHOLINERGIC DRUGS

As previously mentioned, acetylcholine plays an important role in transmission of nerve impulses in both the parasympathetic and sympathetic divisions of the autonomic nervous system.

Acetylcholine has two major actions on the nervous system: (1) it has stimulant effects on the ganglia, adrenal medulla, and skeletal muscle, and (2) it has stimulant effects at postganglionic nerve endings in cardiac muscle, smooth muscle, and glands. The first action resembles the effects of nicotine and is referred to as the "nicotinic effect" of acetylcholine. The second action of acetylcholine at the postganglionic nerve endings is like that of muscarine (an alkaloid obtained from the toadstool *Amanita muscaria*) and is referred to as the **muscarinic effect** of acetylcholine. (See Table 20-1; Figure 19-5 shows nicotinic [N] and muscarinic [M] sites.)

Drugs that bring about effects in the body similar to those produced by acetylcholine are called cholinergic drugs. These agents are also called parasympathomimetics because they mimic the action produced by stimulation of the parasympathetic nervous system.

Cholinergic fibers are widespread: they are present in heart, spleen, uterus, vas deferens, colon, and the vessels of the skin and muscles. Cholinergic fibers probably are present in many more tissues of the body. In the gastrointestinal tract parasympathetic innervation predominates: it stimulates both motor and secretory action.

Although acetylcholine is important physiologically, it has no therapeutic value because (1) its actions are very brief owing to rapid hydrolysis by acetylcholinesterase and (2) no selective purpose can be achieved through its use, since it has several sites of action.

Cholinergic drugs may be obtained from plant sources or synthesized. The synthetic drugs are more stable and have a more selective action on particular organs. The two groups of cholinergic drugs available are (1) *direct acting* and (2) *indirect acting. Direct-acting drugs combine directly with the cholinergic receptors in postsynaptic membranes* innervated by parasympathetic neurons and evoke effects similar to those produced by acetylcholine. By contrast, instead of a direct effect on receptors, *indirect-acting drugs are primarily on the enzyme by inhibiting the action of cholinesterase (acetylcholinesterase)* that normally degrades acetylcholine. This results in an accumulation of acetylcholine at all the sites where it is liberated (see Figure 19-4, *B*). By rendering the enzymatic action ineffective, the anticholinesterase drugs cause a prolonged and intensified cholinergic response at the various effector sites.

Cholinergic drugs are used for the following purposes:
1. To stimulate the intestine and bladder postoperatively thus increasing peristalsis and urination
2. To lower intraocular pressure in clients with glaucoma
3. To promote salivation and sweating
4. To terminate **curarization** (reverse nondepolarizing, neuromuscular blockade)

**TABLE 20-2**   Cholinergic agents

| Generic name | Usual adult dose (24 hrs) | Usual route of administration |
|---|---|---|
| ambenonium* (Mytelase) | 5 mg tid to qid | Oral |
| bethanechol (Urecholine) | 10-50 mg tid to qid 5 mg tid or qid | Oral Subcutaneous |
| isoflurophate* (Floropryl) | Thin strip (0.5 cm) of 0.025%, variable instructions | Topical (eye) ointment |
| neostigmine bromide* (Prostigmin) | 15 mg q 3-4 hr | Oral |
| methylsulfate (Prostigmin) | 0.5 mg dose variable | Intramuscular or subcutaneous |
| physostigmine* (Eserine) | 1 drop, 0.25-0.5% bid or tid solution | Topical (eye) |
| physostigmine* (Antilirium) | 0.5 mg-2 mg (maximum) | IM or IV |
| pilocarpine | 1 drop, 0.5%-4% qid | Topical (eye) |
| pyridostigmine* (Mestinon) | Highly variable | Oral |

*Effects to be expected are similar to those that can be expected from stimulation of the parasympathetic nervous system (see Table 20-3). Drugs are listed in alphabetical order. The majority of drugs mentioned are administered in the form of their salts.

5. To treat myasthenia gravis symptomatically*

The therapeutic effectiveness of cholinergic drugs depends primarily on their muscarinic action, but some of them also possess nicotinic action. This nicotinic action usually requires doses much larger than those used therapeutically. However, some drugs may exhibit more nicotinic than muscarinic effects.

The ideal cholinergic or anticholinesterase drug would:
1. Mimic or inhibit the effect of acetylcholine on a particular structure or organ
2. Be effective when administered orally
3. Be more stable and less easily inactivated than the drugs now available
4. Produce a therapeutic effect with minimal side effects

Although these ideal drugs are not yet available, progress is being made in this direction.

Cholinergic drugs used primarily to lower intraocular pressure are discussed in Chapter 43. These include pilocarpine and carbachol. Table 20-2 lists the prominent cholinergic and anticholinesterase drugs.

## Direct-Acting Cholinergic Drugs (Choline Esters)

Drugs that are chemically similar to the neurotransmitter acetylcholine include bethanechol, carbachol, and methacholine. All compounds in this group are quarternary amines and so they are poorly absorbed orally. Their actions are comparable to those of the physiologic mediator acetylcho-

*Cholinergic but not parasympathomimetic action involves the somatic nervous system, innervating skeletal muscle.

line, but they are longer acting. The side effects of these drugs are a consequence of parasympathetic stimulation. They include bradycardia, hypotension, sweating, salivation, vomiting, diarrhea, and intestinal cramps.

### bethanechol chloride (Urecholine, Duvoid ✸)

Bethanechol is a synthetic choline ester with actions similar to those of acetylcholine. It produces the effects of stimulation of the parasympathetic nervous system. It has predominant muscarinic action with particular selectivity on the detrusor muscle of the urinary bladder and smooth muscle of the gastrointestinal tract. Hence contraction of the smooth muscle of the bladder is sufficiently strong to initiate micturition and empty the urinary bladder. Also, in the gastrointestinal tract, the drug stimulates gastric motility, increases gastric tone, and often restores impaired peristaltic activity of the esophagus, stomach, and intestine. It also promotes defecation. Unlike acetylcholine, bethanechol is not destroyed by cholinesterase, and therefore its effects are more prolonged than that of the natural neurotransmitter. Therapeutic test doses in normal human subjects have little effect on heart rate, blood pressure, or peripheral circulation.

Bethanechol chloride has been approved in the United States for the treatment of postoperative and postpartum nonobstructive urinary retention and for neurogenic atony of the urinary bladder associated with retention. Although not indicated on its U.S. product labeling, it is often used to relieve postoperative abdominal distention and gastric atony or stasis and reflux esophagitis associated with decreased pressure of lower esophageal sphincter.

Although it is poorly absorbed from the gastrointestinal tract, bethanechol chloride is effective orally. It is widely distributed to organs innervated by the parasympathetic nervous system. Onset of action is within 30 to 90 minutes after oral administration, peak effect within 1 hour, and duration of action up to 6 hours, depending on the dose administered. If administered subcutaneously, the onset of action is within 5 to 15 minutes, peak effect within 15 to 30 minutes, and duration of action approximately 2 hours. Route of excretion is currently unknown. For side effects/adverse reactions see Table 20-3.

**Significant drug interactions.** No significant drug interactions have been reported in the United States Pharmacopeia. However, the nurse should be aware of the following possibilities when bethanechol is given with the drugs listed below:

| Drug | Possible Effect and Management |
|---|---|
| other cholinergics or anticholinesterase medications | Enhances cholinergic effects and perhaps toxicity. Monitor closely for adverse effects or, if possible, avoid this combination of medications. (See Table 20-3.) |
| ganglionic blocking agents | May result in severe abdominal distress followed by a precipitous fall in blood pressure. Avoid this combination if possible. |
| procainamide or quinidine | Cholinergic effects may be antagonized. Monitor closely. |

### Dosage and administration
#### Oral
*Adults.* 10-50 mg orally, 3 to 4 times daily.

*Children.* 0.2 mg/kg body weight or 6.7 mg/m² of body surface, 3 times a day.

#### Parenteral
*Adults.* 5 mg *subcutaneously,* 3 or 4 times a day when needed.

*Children.* 0.15-0.2 mg/kg body weight or 5-6.7 mg/m² of body surface, 3 times a day. *(Subcutaneous use only.)*

### ▷ Nursing Management:
### Bethanechol Therapy

**Assessment.** Bethanechol should not be used after gastrointestinal anastomosis or bladder surgery until healing has occurred. It is contraindicated when peptic ulcer, peritonitis, or an inflammatory disease of the gastrointestinal tract is present. Its use is also contraindicated during pregnancy or in clients with coronary disease, hyperthyroidism, asthma, or gastrointestinal or urinary obstruction.

The client's vital signs should be taken as a baseline assessment before bethanechol therapy is initiated.

The client receiving bethanechol should be assessed for the following nursing diagnoses: ineffective airway clearance related to bronchoconstriction (shortness of breath, wheezing, tightness in chest); altered comfort related to belching or parasympathetic stimulation (headache, increased salivation or sweating, nausea or vomiting, flushing

---

> ## USE OF BETHANECHOL WITH CLIENTS HAVING NEUROGENIC BLADDER
>
> Bethanechol is frequently used as an adjunct therapy in clients with chronic neurogenic bladder. After several baseline measurements of residual urine volume, the adult client is administered 7.5 to 10 mg of bethanechol chloride subcutaneously every 4 hours. Twelve hours after the first dose of bethanechol, the client is asked to void, and a residual urine volume is measured. If the amount of residual urine is less than the baseline volume, the drug is continued for another 24 hours. At that time the drug's effectiveness is again evaluated by another residual urine volume measurement. If this, too, is below the baseline volume, the drug is continued for another 24 to 48 hours on the "every 4 hours" schedule. After that period, the dosage should be decreased to 5 to 7.5 mg every 4 hours. If measured residual urine volume continues to be below baseline amounts, the dosage is changed to an oral form, 50 to 100 mg every 4 hours. According to the client's response, the dosage interval may be gradually increased and the dosage decreased.

of the skin, and abdominal discomfort); altered bowel elimination pattern (diarrhea); altered urinary pattern (frequency); and high risk for injury related to blurred vision, change in near or distant vision, or orthostatic hypotension.

**Intervention.** Administer bethanechol on an empty stomach to minimize the possibility of nausea and vomiting. Bethanechol is to be parenterally administered only subcutaneously. Do not administer intramuscularly or intravenously because severe symptoms of cholinergic overstimulation (flushing of the skin, headache, severe hypotension, hypothermia, bradycardia, nausea and vomiting, abdominal cramps, bloody diarrhea, shock, or cardiac arrest) may occur.

**Education.** Instruct the client to move slowly from a lying to a sitting or standing position because orthostatic hypotension is a common effect of bethanechol.

**Evaluation.** Observe the client closely for side effects or adverse reactions, particularly with subcutaneous administration. Monitor vital signs and carefully check respiration for 30 to 60 minutes after injection. Keep available 0.6 mg atropine in a syringe to counteract severe side effects. Evaluate the effectiveness of the drug by monitoring intake and output, or residual urine volumes if applicable, when administering bethanechol for postoperative urinary retention. If the bladder sphincter fails to relax as the urinary bladder contracts in response to bethanechol administration, urine may be forced up the ureter into the kidney. If the client has bacteriuria, this reflux of urine into the kidney may cause a kidney infection. Intake and output must be carefully monitored in these clients.

**TABLE 20-3** Side effects/adverse reactions of drugs affecting the parasympathetic nervous system

| Drug(s) | Side effects* | Adverse reactions† |
|---|---|---|
| **CHOLINERGIC** | | |
| bethanechol chloride (Urecholine, Duvoid ✿) | More frequent with high dosages, unsteadiness; faintness; nausea or vomiting; headache; flushed skin; abdominal pains or upset; increased salivation and sweating<br><br>Less frequent: diarrhea; increased urination; blurred or disturbed vision; gas complaints | Rare and usually reported with subcutaneous injection: difficulty in breathing, shortness of breath, feeling of pressure in the chest<br>In overdosage or in patients hypersensitive to drug: hypotension; profuse and bloody diarrhea; shock; possibly sudden cardiac arrest |
| **CHOLINERGIC BLOCKING (PARASYMPATHOLYTIC)** | | |
| atropine | More frequent: inhibition of sweating; constipation; complaints of dry mouth, throat, and skin<br>Less frequent: abdominal distention; blurred vision; inhibition of lactation; urinary retention or dysuria; sedation; headache; photophobia; drowsiness; weakness; nausea or vomiting | Less frequent or rare: urticaria; dermatitis; eye pain from increased intraocular pressure<br>Overdosage/toxicity: blurred vision; ataxia; confusion; disorientation; severe dryness of mouth, throat, and nose area; hyperpyrexia; hallucinations; restlessness; delirium; tachycardia; difficulty in breathing |
| scopolamine | Same as atropine, plus euphoria; amnesia, insomnia or increased drowsiness reported more often with scopolamine | Dilated and fixed pupil on side where disk was applied have been reported with use of transdermal disk behind the ear. To avoid extensive neurologic exams, unconscious individuals appearing with above symptoms should be checked first for the use of a disk behind the ear. If the disk is removed, this syndrome usually abates within 2 weeks. To avoid misdiagnosis, drops of 1% pilocarpine solution may be instilled in the eye; this will reverse the nonneurogenic dilated pupil |
| **SYNTHETIC ANTISPASMODICS** | | |
| dicyclomine (Bentyl, Antispas) | More frequent: abdominal distention, headache, dizziness<br>Less frequent: nausea, vomiting, sedation, nervousness, decreased sexual ability, blurred or disturbed vision, confusion (especially in older clients)<br>Rare: inhibition of sweating, tachycardia, dry mouth | More frequent: usually constipation (especially in older clients)<br>Less frequent: dysuria<br>Rare: dermatitis |
| glycopyrrolate (Robinul) | More frequent: dry mouth, nose, throat, and skin<br>Less frequent/rare: the following may occur more often if high doses are given: abdominal distention, blurred vision, constipation, decreased lactation, inhibition of sweating, dysuria, sedation, headache, amnesia (especially in older clients), photophobia, nausea, vomiting, insomnia, weakness, decrease in sexual ability | Rarely reported: faintness, hypotension, dizziness, eye pain, dermatitis<br>Overdosage: respiratory difficulties; severe muscle weakness; extreme tiredness; drowsiness or a paradoxical effect of increased excitability; nervousness, restlessness; tachycardia; warm, dry, and red flushing of skin |

*If side effects continue, increase, or disturb the patient, the physician should be informed.

†If adverse reactions occur, the physician should be contacted because medical intervention may be necessary.

*Continued.*

**TABLE 20-3**   Side effects/adverse reactions of drugs affecting the parasympathetic nervous system—cont'd

| Drug(s) | Side effects* | Adverse reactions† |
|---|---|---|
| **SYNTHETIC ANTISPASMODICS** | | |
| clidinium (Quarzan) | More frequent: dry mouth, nose, throat and skin<br>Less frequent: abdominal distention, blurred vision, constipation, decreased lactation, insomnia, nausea, vomiting, increased weakness, headache, drowsiness, dysuria (especially in elderly men), inhibition of sweating, decrease in sexual ability | Rare: faintness, hypotension (especially in older clients); dermatitis<br>Overdosage: same as glycopyrrolate |
| **GANGLIONIC BLOCKING DRUGS** | | |
| trimethaphan camsylate (Arfonad) | Side effects are dose related: loss of appetite, nausea, vomiting, constipation, dilated pupil, dry mouth, impotency, pruritis, hives, hypotension, increased heart rate, urinary retention, and use may precipitate angina attack | Overdosage: severe hypotension, respiratory arrest |

## Indirect-Acting Cholinergic Drugs

The indirect-acting cholinergic drugs are called anticholinesterases or cholinesterase inhibitors because they inhibit the action of the enzyme cholinesterase, thereby prolonging the effect of acetylcholine. Anticholinesterase agents (e.g., neostigmine, physostigmine) exert their influence on both muscarinic and nicotinic sites. They are used in the treatment of myasthenia gravis and glaucoma. (See Chapters 18 and 43 respectively.) Certain compounds in this group are considered to be potent agents for chemical warfare. Physostigmine salicylate is used for overdosage and anticholinergic substance toxicity. See discussion about tricyclic antidepressant overdosage treatment in Chapter 17.

### Drugs Used to Treat Myasthenia Gravis

Myasthenia gravis is a condition characterized by weakness of the skeletal muscles innervated by the somatic efferent fibers. Since the disease affects cholinergic transmission, the anticholinesterase drugs are used because they elevate the concentration of acetylcholine at the myoneural junctions. The prolonged activity of the neurohormone at these sites results in a dramatic increase in muscle strength and function. There is a more extensive discussion of myasthenia gravis and its treatment in Chapter 18. (See also Figure 19-5, *B*, for site of action.)

## CHOLINERGIC BLOCKING DRUGS
## Muscarinic Cholinergic Blocking Drugs

The cholinergic blocking, or **parasympatholytic,** drugs have many important uses in medicine. More specifically, these agents are called **antimuscarinic** drugs because they block the muscarinic effects of acetylcholine. When the nerve fiber is stimulated, the acetylcholine liberated from the terminal is unable to bind to the receptor site and fails to produce a cholinergic effect. Thus these agents also are referred to as anticholinergic drugs. (See Figure 19-5, *A1,* for muscarinic [M] sites.)

### Belladonna Alkaloids

The best known muscarinic cholinergic blocking drugs are the belladonna alkaloids. The major drugs in this class are atropine and scopolamine. A number of plants belonging to the potato family *(Solanaceae)* contain similar alkaloids. *Atropa belladonna* (deadly nightshade), *Hyoscyamus niger* (henbane), *Datura stramonium* ( jimson weed or thorn apple), and several species of *Scopolia* also contain belladonna alkaloids. The principal alkaloids of these plants are atropine, scopolamine (hyoscine), and hyoscyamine. Atropine is the prototype of the antimuscarinic drugs. It has been in use for over half a century and continues to be a popular drug because of its therapeutic effectiveness.

#### atropine sulfate (Atropine, Isopto Atropine, Atropisol)

***Mechanism of action.*** As a competitive antagonist, atropine acts by occupying the muscarinic (M) receptor sites, thereby preventing or reducing the muscarinic response of acetylcholine (see Figure 19-5, *A1* and *2c*). The drug-receptor complex is formed at the neuroeffector junctions of smooth muscle, cardiac muscle, and exocrine glands.

Atropine has very little effect on the actions of acetylcholine at nicotinic receptor sites. So at autonomic ganglia, where transmission normally involves the action of acetylcholine, relatively high doses of atropine are required to produce even a partial block. At the neuromuscular junctions of the somatic nervous system, where the receptors are exclusively nicotinic, extremely high doses of atropine are required to produce any degree of block. See Figure 19-5, *A,* for nicotinic (N) sites on the ganglia or parasympathetic and sympathetic nerve divisions, and Figure 19-5, *B,* for N site on effector organ (skeletal muscle) of somatic motor system. Atropine can produce a wide range of pharmacologic effects because a vast distribution of parasympathetic cholinergic nerves normally exists in the body. Furthermore, drug activity is dose-dependent. Small doses depress salivary and bronchial secretions and sweating. Large doses dilate the pupils, inhibit accommodation of the eyes, and increase heart rate by blocking vagal effects of the heart. Larger doses inhibit micturition and decrease the tone and motility of the gut by inhibiting parasympathetic control of both the urinary bladder and the gastrointestinal tract. In addition, still larger doses are required to inhibit gastric secretion and motility.

### Pharmacologic properties

*Eye.* The pupil is dilated (mydriasis), and the ciliary muscle (muscle of accommodation) is relaxed (cycloplegia). The sphincter muscle of the iris and the ciliary muscle are both innervated by cholinergic nerve fibers and therefore are affected by atropine. Since the sphincter muscle is unable to contract normally, the radial muscle of the iris causes the pupil to dilate. *Pupil dilation may reduce outflow of aqueous humor, causing a rise in intraocular pressure. This is a hazardous situation for patients with glaucoma (angle closure).* These effects in the eye are brought about by both local and systemic administration of atropine, although the usual single therapeutic dose of atropine given orally or parenterally has little effect on the eye. After the pupil is dilated, photophobia occurs, and when the drug has reached its full effect, the usual reflexes to light and accommodation disappear.

Systemic absorption of ophthalmic medications resulting in undesirable side effects or adverse reactions has been reported with atropine and a number of other eye preparations. When the patient exhibits such effects, ophthalmic preparations should be included in the review of the patient's current medications; an ophthalmic preparation may be the offending agent (USP-DI, 1991).

*Skin and mucous membranes.* Since the sweat glands of the skin are supplied by sympathetic cholinergic nerves, atropine decreases or abolishes their activity. This causes the skin to become hot and dry. Further, since the flow of secretions from glands lining the respiratory tract is reduced, drying of the mucous membranes of the mouth, nose, pharynx, and bronchi occurs. Patients who have been given atropine, particularly for preoperative preparation, often complain of a dry mouth and thirst. Some of this discomfort may be relieved by frequent rinsing of the mouth.

*Respiratory system.* Secretions of the nose, pharynx, and bronchial tubes are decreased. The muscles of the bronchial tubes relax, and the airway widens to ease breathing.

**TABLE 20-4**  Selected anticholinergic agents containing specific alkaloids*

| Alkaloid formation† | Trade name |
| --- | --- |
| hyoscyamine | Cystospaz |
| | Cystospaz-M |
| | Levsinex Timecaps |
| | Levsin |
| | Anaspaz |
| hyoscyamine and scopolamine | Bellafoline |
| scopolamine | Triptone |
| | Transderm-Scop |
| | Transderm-V |
| atropine, hyoscyamine, scopolamine, and phenobarbital | Bellastal |
| | Donnatal |
| | Barbidonna |
| | Barophen |
| | Kinesed |
| | Donnatal Extentabs |
| atropine and phenobarbital | Antrocol |
| belladonna and butabarbital | Butibel |
| belladonna and phenobarbital | Belap |
| | Chardonna-2 |
| hyoscyamine and phenobarbital | Levsin-PB |
| | Anaspaz PB |
| hyoscyamine, scopolamine, and phenobarbital | Belledenal |
| | Belledenal-S |
| | Belladenal Spacetabs |

*Specific alkaloids include the active alkaloids of belladonna, such as hyoscyamine, atropine, and scopolamine.
†The alkaloid formulation lists the active ingredients as marketed under the various trade names. Individual salts, strengths, and dosing intervals may vary according to the manufacturer's instructions.

Atropine and scopolamine are less effective than epinephrine as bronchodilators and are seldom used for asthma.

*Cardiovascular system.* When low doses are given or an intravenous dose is administered slowly, the cardiac rate is temporarily and slightly slowed because of the central action of the drug on the cardiac center in the medulla (paradoxical bradycardia). Larger doses given rapidly intravenously will block the vagal effect on the SA and AV nodes and cause an increased heart rate.

In therapeutic doses atropine has little or no effect on blood pressure. This is expected because most vascular beds lack significant cholinergic innervation. However, large (and sometimes ordinary) doses cause vasodilation of vessels in the skin of the face and neck. This may result from a direct dilator action or from histamine release. Reddening of the face and neck is seen, especially after large or toxic doses.

*Gastrointestinal tract.* It appears that the amount and character of the gastric secretion are little affected by atropine given in ordinary therapeutic doses. The secretion of acid in the stomach is presumably less under vagal control than under hormonal or chemical control. The effect of atropine on the secretion of the pancreas and intestinal glands is not therapeutically significant. Atropine and other belladonna alkaloids decrease tone and peristalsis in the stomach and small and large intestine. Atropine does not affect the secretion of bile, but it exerts a mildly antispasmodic effect in the gallbladder and bile ducts.

*Urinary tract.* The drug relaxes the ureter, especially when it has been in a state of spasm. Therapeutic doses decrease the tone of the fundus of the urinary bladder. When the detrusor muscle is hypertonic, it is relaxed by atropine. Also, the constriction of the internal sphincter can produce urinary retention.

*Central nervous system.* Atropine has prominent effects on the central nervous system and in large doses causes excitement and maniacal behavior. These behavioral effects suggest the existence of important cholinergic pathways and receptors within the central nervous system.

Small or moderate doses of atropine have little or no cerebral effect. Large or toxic doses cause the patient to become restless, wakeful, and talkative. This condition may develop into delirium and finally stupor and coma. The exalted, excited stage has sometimes been called a "belladonna jag." A rise in temperature is sometimes seen, especially in infants and young children. This is probably the result of suppression of sweating rather than action on the heat-regulating center.

Atropine has been used to diminish tremor in Parkinson's disease. It probably reduces cholinergic synaptic transmission.

Therapeutic doses of atropine stimulate the respiratory center and make breathing faster and sometimes deeper. When respiration is seriously depressed, atropine is not always reliable as a stimulant; in fact, it may deepen the depression. Large doses stimulate respiration, but they can also cause respiratory failure and death.

Small doses stimulate the vagus center in the medulla, causing primary slowing of the heart. The vasoconstrictor center is stimulated briefly and then depressed. Because depression follows soon after stimulation, atropine has been called a borderline stimulant of the central nervous system.

*Topical effects.* There is a slight amount of absorption when atropine or belladonna is applied to the skin, especially if it is an alcoholic preparation or in the form of a plaster.

**Indications.** Atropine is indicated for the treatment of irritable bowel syndrome, spastic biliary tract disorders, genitourinary disorders; antidote for cholinergic toxicity from excessive amounts of cholinesterase inhibitors, muscarinics, or gamophosphate pesticide poisoning. Also used to treat sinus bradycardia and Parkinson's disease, to prevent excessive salivation and respiratory tract secretions (preanesthetic), and as an adjunctive medication for peptic ulcers and for gastrointestinal radiography.

**Pharmacokinetics.** Atropine is readily absorbed from oral and parenteral administration; it is also absorbed from mucous membranes.

After oral administration, the maximum effect is reached within 1 hour; duration of action is 4 to 6 hours. It is widely distributed in fluids of the body and easily passes the placental barrier to the blood of the fetus and the blood-brain barrier. Atropine is primarily in the liver, approximately 13% to 50% of atropine is excreted unchanged in the urine. It is excreted in the kidneys.

**Side effects/adverse reactions.** See Table 20-3.

**Significant drug interactions.** The following effects may occur when atropine (and other belladonna alkaloids) are given with the drugs listed below:

| Drug | Possible Effect and Management |
|---|---|
| antacids or antidiarrheal agents | May reduce absorption and therapeutic effectiveness of atropine. Space medications at least 1 hour apart. |
| other anticholinergics and monoamine oxidase (MAO) inhibitors | Increase in antimuscarinic effects reported. Monitor, because dosage adjustment may be necessary. |
| digitalis glycosides | The decrease in gastrointestinal tract motility may lead to an increased absorption of digoxin tablets, leading to increased serum level and toxicity. Monitor the client. |
| ketoconazole | Increase in gastrointestinal pH by atropine may result in reduced absorption of ketoconazole. Atropine should be administered preferably 2 hours after ketoconazole. |
| potassium chloride, especially wax matrix formulations | Increased contact with gastrointestinal tract may result in mucosal irritation and lesions. Liquid formulations of potassium should be considered a replacement for the wax matrix formulation in this situation. |

**Dosage and administration.** The oral anticholinergic adult dose for atropine sulfate for an is 0.3-1.2 mg PO, every 4 to 6 hours. The pediatric dose is 0.01 mg/kg, not exceeding 0.4 mg, every 4 to 6 hours. The adult oral dose to prevent excessive salivation and respiratory tract secretions during anesthesia is 2 mg. The dose should be titrated as necessary to client's response or to the appearance of side effects. The adult parenteral anticholinergic dose is 0.4-0.6 mg IM, IV, or SC every 4 to 6 hours. The pediatric anticholinergic dose is 0.01 mg/kg IM, IV, or SC, not exceeding 0.4 mg. The dose may be repeated every 4 to 6 hours if necessary. The adult parenteral dose to treat bradycardia (dysrhythmia) is 0.4-1 mg IV, every 1 to 2 hours, up to a maximum of 2 mg; the pediatric dysrhythmic dose is 0.01-0.03 mg/kg.

**Special considerations.** The use of atropine (or belladonna alkaloids) should be avoided in clients with a medical history of severe cardiac disease, reflux esophagitis, gastrointestinal tract obstructive disease states or intestinal atony, urinary retention, prostatic hypertrophy, or myasthenia gravis.

## ▷ Nursing Management:
### Atropine Therapy

See also Nursing Management: Anticholinergic Therapy (Chapter 18).

***Assessment.*** Use with caution in elderly clients and children under 6 years of age because they are more susceptible to adverse reactions, such as excitement, sleepiness, or confusion. Toxicity may occur in the elderly even when the drug is prescribed within the normal adult dosage range.

The use of anticholinergics in individuals over 40 years of age should be cautious because of the risk of precipitating undiagnosed glaucoma.

Do not use in patients with open-angle glaucoma, urinary and gastrointestinal obstruction, ulcerative colitis, asthma, renal or hepatic disease, or myasthenia gravis. Administer carefully in systemic forms to clients with chronic pulmonary disease because bronchial secretions may be sufficiently decreased to result in bronchial plugs. Use with caution in infants, blondes, clients with Down's syndrome, and pediatric clients with spastic paralysis and brain damage because they tend to be more sensitive to the drug's effects.

The client receiving atropine therapy is at risk for the following nursing diagnoses: hyperthermia related to the suppression of sweat gland activity; high risk for injury related to allergic reaction, blurred vision, dizziness or lightheadedness; altered thought processes (confusion); altered comfort related to dry mouth or increased sensitivity of eyes to light; urinary retention related to the drug's anticholinergic effects; and altered bowel elimination pattern (constipation) related to decreased motility of the gastrointestinal tract.

***Intervention.*** Administer oral preparations 30 to 60 minutes before meals. Administer antacids or antidiarrheal medications at least 1 hour after the administration of atropine.

***Education.*** Inform client of possible side effects, and warn against operating a car or other machinery; blurred vision or dizziness may occur. Advise the client about the use of sugarless gum and candy, ice, or saliva substitutes to relieve dry mouth. Instruct the client to avoid alcohol and other CNS depressants while taking atropine.

Inform client using ophthalmic preparation that his or her vision will be impaired for a few days. Client should protect eyes by wearing dark glasses. Also, client's ability to judge distance will be impaired; therefore client should avoid driving a car or operating machinery. Drug should be discontinued if signs of local irritation or follicular conjunctivitis occur. This may happen after prolonged periods of ophthalmic therapy.

Counsel the client involved in long-term use to follow a consistent dental hygiene program, including semiannual visits to the dentist because the decreased salivary flow promotes caries, buccal candidiasis, and peridontal disease.

Instruct the client to avoid exposure to high environmental temperatures, exercise in warm, humid weather, or prolonged hot baths. These activities may lead to heat prostration. The client should report any fever to the physician because the medication may have to be discontinued.

***Evaluation.*** Monitor pulse, which is a sensitive indicator of client's response to atropine. Also be alert to any change in blood pressure, temperature, and respiration, particularly after intravenous administration. Report any significant changes to physician. Monitor client for urinary output and bowel regularity. Notify physician of any significant changes.

Observe elderly clients for excitement, agitation, and delirium. Assess for constipation, dryness of mouth, and, in the elderly male client, urinary retention. Because of the mydriatic effects of atropine, intraocular pressure determinations should be done at regular intervals.

For additional atropine preparations see Chapters 40, 41, and 43.

### scopolamine (Transderm-Scop, Transderm-V)
### scopolamine hydrobromide

See the preceding discussion of atropine for mechanism of action. Its peripheral effects are similar to atropine, but it differs in its effects on the central nervous system. At therapeutic doses, it depresses the CNS and causes drowsiness, euphoria, memory loss, relaxation, sleep, and relief of fear. It does not increase blood pressure or respiration.

It is used in the treatment of irritable bowel syndrome; renal and ureteral colic; dysrhythmias induced during surgery owing to increased vagal stimulation; and postencephalitic parkinsonism and paralysis agitans. Because of its depressant action on vestibular function, it is used for motion sickness to prevent nausea and vomiting. It is used as a general anesthesia adjunct, as a preanesthetic medication, to check secretions, and to prevent laryngospasm, and for its sedative (twilight sleep) and amnesic effects. It has also been used, along with opioid analgesics, in cardiopulmonary bypass patients to avoid the risk of inducing severe hypotension or collapse with the use of deep and prolonged anesthesia.

Scopolamine's pharmacokinetics are the same as atropine. The transdermal dosage form produces its antiemetic effects for up to 72 hours. For side effects/adverse reactions see Table 20-3. Significant drug interactions are the same as atropine. In addition, concurrent use of scopolamine with other CNS depressants may result in increased CNS depression effects. Clients should be monitored closely.

An oral dosage form is not available in the United States. The parenteral dose in adults for use as an anticholinergic and an antiemetic is 0.3 to 0.6 mg as single dose. Used as an adjunct to anesthesia or for sedation-hypnosis, administer 0.6 mg IM, IV, or SC, 3 or 4 times daily. For amnesia give 0.32 to 0.6 mg IM, IV, or SC. The elderly are more sensitive to scopolamine. If used, lower doses than the adult ones are recommended. In children, when used as an antiemetic, give 6 μg (0.006 mg)/kg IM, IV, or SC as a single dose. To reduce excess salivation during anesthesia, various IM doses are recommended according to age. See current reference. When administering scopolamine transdermally as an adult antiemetic or antivertigo, apply patch (0.5 mg) behind ear for a period of 3 days. For antiemetic effect, apply 4 hours before desired effect is required. The elderly are more sensitive to this drug at adult dosage. Monitor closely. The drug is not recommended for children.

### ▷ Nursing Management: Scopolamine Therapy

For the transdermal application of scopolamine, instruct the client to wash and dry hands before and after application of the patch. It is to be applied to the hairless skin area behind the ear. It is not to be applied over abrasions or rashes. Alert the client that drowsiness and dilated pupils (photophobia and blurred vision) may occur, and if they occur, tasks such as driving or mowing the lawn may be hazardous.

If scopolamine has been administered as part of a preoperative medication for an outpatient or ambulatory procedure, caution the client before discharge about the effects on memory and motor tasks. These effects may persist for a few hours.

See the discussion of atropine sulfate.

## *Synthetic Substitutes for Atropine*

The usefulness of atropine is limited by the fact that it is a complex drug and produces effects in a number of organs or tissues simultaneously. When it is administered for its antispasmodic effects, it also produces prolonged effects in the eye, causing dilated pupils and blurred vision. It also causes dry mouth and possibly rapid heart rate. When the antispasmodic effect is desired, other effects become side effects, which may be distinctly undesirable.

A large number of drugs have been synthesized in an effort to capture the antispasmodic effect of atropine without its other effects. Drugs of this type are frequently used to relieve hypertonicity and hypersecretion in the stomach and to treat patients with gastric and duodenal ulcers.

Many products are marketed as antispasmodic and anticholinergic agents, but their formulations are either modifications of a belladonna alkaloid or include one or more of the natural alkaloids as their active ingredients. The pharmacologic properties are therefore similar to the previously reviewed substances and will not be repeated here (see Table 20-4). The more commonly used or newer systemic agents—dicylomine (Bentyl), a glycopyrrolate (Robinul), and clidinium bromide (Quarzan)—will be discussed.

### dicyclomine (Bentyl, Bentylol ✱, and others)

Mechanism of action is not known. It has been postulated that it produces both a local and direct effect on smooth muscle, resulting in a decreased tone and motility of the gastrointestinal tract. It only appears to produce the typical antimuscarinic effect when administered in large doses. Dicyclomine is indicated for the treatment of the irritable bowel syndrome.

Little has been determined about the pharmacokinetics of this product. It is rapidly absorbed after oral or parenteral administration, and about 50% of the dose is excreted by the kidneys and the other 50% in the feces. Half life is 1.8 hrs initially and 9 to 10 hrs for the second phase.

For side effects/adverse reactions, see Table 20-3.

***Significant drug interactions.*** The following effects may occur when dicyclomine is given with the drugs listed below:

| Drug | Possible Effect and Management |
|---|---|
| other anticholinergics or monoamine oxidase (MAO) inhibitors | Increased anticholinergic effects reported. Reduced dosage or discontinuance of one product may be necessary. |
| antacids or antidiarrheal preparations | Reduced absorption of dicyclomine. These drugs should be administered at least 1 to 2 hours apart. |
| cyclopropane | May induce ventricular arrhythmias if dicyclomine is given intravenously with cyclopropane. Dicyclomine should only be given IM. Monitor closely if given with this anesthetic. |
| ketoconazole | The increase in gastrointestinal pH produced by anticholinergics can result in a reduction in absorption of ketoconazole. Dose ketoconazole first, then 2 hours later administer the dicyclomine. |
| potassium chloride, especially wax matrix formulations | Increased gastrointestinal tract irritation and lesions may result. Liquid potassium preparations should be considered as an alternative. |

***Dosage and administration***

*Oral*

*Adults.* 10-20 mg orally 3 or 4 times daily. Dosage may be adjusted according to response, up to a maximum of 160 mg/day.

*Children*

Less than 6 months old, not recommended.

6 months to 2 years old, 5-10 mg orally (syrup available, 5 mg/tsp) 3 or 4 times daily; adjust as necessary.

2 years old and older, 10 mg orally 3 or 4 times daily; adjust as necessary.

*Parenteral*

*Adults.* 20 mg IM, every 4 to 6 hours. *Do not administer intravenously.*

*Children.* Not established.

### ▷ Nursing Management: Dicyclomine Therapy

Administer with food or milk to minimize gastric distress. Do not administer within 1 to 2 hours of antacids or antidiarrheal medications. The syrup form may be diluted with equal parts of water to make administration easier.

When administering the parenteral form, ensure that the client is lying or sitting down because he or she could experience some temporary lightheadedness. Alert the client that blurred vision may occur and should be reported to the prescriber.

For further discussion of nursing management, see discussion of atropine sulfate therapy.

### glycopyrrolate (Robinul, Robinul Forte)

This is a synthetic anticholinergic product with effects similar to atropine. Unlike atropine, it is unable to easily cross lipid membranes (such as blood-brain barrier) and therefore has minimal central nervous system side effects. It also appears to be less likely to produce pupillary or ocular eye effects.

The drug is indicated as an antimuscarinic to prevent or reduce hypersecretions and arrhythmias induced during anesthesia; to prevent or reduce toxicities induced by cholinesterase inhibitors (neostigmine or pyridostigmine). Glycopyrrolate is absorbed orally; about 10% to 25% of a dose is absorbed. Onset of action of intravenous dose occurs within 1 minute. For IM or SC route, onset of action is 15-30 minutes. Vagal blocking action lasts from 2 to 3 hours, while the **antisialagogue** effect, the inhibition of the flow of saliva, may last up to 7 hours. Glycopyrrolate is excreted in the kidneys.

For side effects/adverse reactions, see Table 20-3.

Significant drug interactions are the same as dicyclomine; see previous section. In addition, administering cyclopropane with glycopyrrolate IV may result in ventricular arrhythmias. To reduce this possibility, give smaller dosages of glycopyrrolate IV (0.1 mg or less) and monitor client closely.

#### Dosage and administration
##### Oral
*Adults.* For treatment of peptic ulcer, 1-2 mg orally 2 or 3 times daily and when necessary, 2 mg at bedtime; then reduce to 1 mg twice daily or adjust dosage according to client's response and tolerance. The elderly individual may be more sensitive to this dosage, so a lower dosage schedule should be considered.

*Children.* Not established.

##### Parenteral
*Adults.* Anticholinergic:.

For treatment of peptic ulcer, 0.1-0.2 mg IM or IV every 4 hr if necessary, up to a maximum of 4 doses per 24 hr.

To prevent or reduce excessive salivation and respiratory tract secretions or gastric hypersecretory situations during anesthesia, 4.4 μg/kg of body weight is given 30-60 min before anesthesia.

For dysrhythmias during anesthesia or in surgery, 0.1 mg IV is given at 2-3 min intervals, as necessary.

As a cholinergic adjunctive medication, 0.2 mg IV is given for each 1 mg of neostigmine or 5 mg of pyridostigmine. This may be given together in the same syringe.

##### Children
Peptic ulcer, not determined

To prevent or reduce excessive salivation and respiratory tract secretions or gastric hypersecretory situations during anesthesia, 4.4-8.8 μg/kg body weight IM is given 30-60 min before anesthesia.

For dysrhythmias during anesthesia or in surgery, 4.4 μg/kg of body weight IV given every 2 or 3 min, as necessary.

As a cholinergic adjunctive medication, 0.2 mg IV is given for each 1 mg of neostigmine or 5 mg of pyridostigmine. This may be given together in the same syringe.

### ▷ Nursing Management: Glycopyrrolate Therapy

Alert the client to have ophthalmic examinations for intraocular pressure periodically. Intraocular pressure may become elevated because of the mydriasis produced by the drug. If blurred vision occurs, it should be reported to the prescriber.

When contemplating mixing glycopyrrolate in a syringe with other drugs, consult the package insert, as the drug is unstable at a pH higher than 6.0 and will form a precipitate when combined with some other agents.

See atropine sulfate discussion for additional nursing management.

### clidinium (Quarzan)

Clidinium is a synthetic product related to the belladonna alkaloids, especially atropine. It competitively antagonizes acetylcholine at the postganglionic parasympathetic receptor sites in both smooth muscles and the secretory glands, thus reducing gastrointestinal motility and gastric acid secretion. Ganglionic blockade may be produced if high doses of clidinium are given. Unlike atropine, it produces few, if any, CNS side effects or alterations on the eye.

Clidinium is indicated as an adjunctive treatment for peptic ulcers. It is absorbed orally; about 10% to 25% of a dose is absorbed. Onset of action occurs within 1 hour; duration of action lasts up to 3 hours. Clidinium is metabolized in the liver and excreted through the kidneys primarily, some in feces.

For side effects/adverse reactions, see Table 20-3. Significant drug interactions are the same as for atropine. Oral dose for adults is 2.5-5 mg 3 or 4 times daily, before meals and at bedtime. Adjust dosage according to individual's response. Dosage for elderly is 2.5 mg orally 3 times a day, before meals. Children's dosage is not determined.

▷**Nursing Management:**
**Clidinium Therapy**

Administer ½ to 1 hour before meals to enhance absorption. The client should have intraocular pressure determinations done periodically, since intraocular pressure increases because of the drug's mydriatic effect. Blurred vision may occur and should be reported to the prescriber.

For further nursing management, see atropine sulfate discussion.

# Ganglionic Drugs

The major neurotransmitter of all autonomic ganglia is acetylcholine. This includes ganglionic synapses of both the parasympathetic and sympathetic nervous system. Acetylcholine activates the nicotinic receptor at the ganglionic sites, which is unlike that of the nicotinic receptors on the effector organ, the skeletal muscle. Thus stimulation of the preganglionic neuron results in the release of acetylcholine from its terminal. Acetylcholine then activates the nicotinic receptors on the ganglia of the postganglionic parasympathetic or sympathetic neurons, or adrenal medulla. This interaction ultimately generates a nerve impulse down the postganglionic fibers to produce specific effects on smooth muscle, cardiac muscle, and glands (see Figure 19-2). Ganglionic stimulation influences nerve impulse transmission to the entire autonomic nervous system, and because of such pervasive activity ganglionic drugs have limited therapeutic value.

The drugs that affect nicotinic or cholinergic receptor sites on autonomic ganglia are (1) ganglionic stimulating drugs and (2) ganglionic blocking drugs.

## GANGLIONIC STIMULATING DRUGS
### Nicotine

Nicotine is a liquid alkaloid, freely soluble in water. It turns brown on exposure to air and is the chief alkaloid in tobacco. Nicotine has no therapeutic use but is of great pharmacologic interest and toxicologic importance. Its use in experiments performed on animals has helped to increase understanding of the autonomic nervous system.

Nicotine is readily absorbed from the gastrointestinal tract, respiratory mucous membrane, and skin.

### Pharmacologic Effects

Nicotine may produce a variety of complex and often unpredictable effects in the body. Many actions are dose related, with generally small doses inducing activation or stimulation and larger doses producing a decreased or depressed response. Because nicotine acts on multiple systems within the body, the ultimate response may be the sum of the different stimulation and depressant actions of this chemical.

At the autonomic ganglia, nicotine temporarily stimulates all sympathetic and parasympathetic ganglia. This is followed by depression, which tends to last longer than the period of stimulation. Its effects on skeletal muscle are similar to its effects on the ganglia; that is, a depressant phase follows stimulation. During the depressant phase nicotine exerts a curare-like action on skeletal muscle.

Nicotine stimulates the central nervous system, especially the medullary centers (respiratory, emetic, and vasomotor). Large doses may cause tremor and convulsions. Stimulation is followed by depression. Death may result from respiratory failure, although it may be caused more by the curare-like action of nicotine on nerve endings in the diaphragm, rather than by action on the respiratory center.

The actions and effects of nicotine on the cardiovascular system are complex. The rate of the heart is frequently slowed at first, but later may be accelerated above normal. Various disturbances in rhythm have been observed. The small blood vessels in peripheral parts of the body constrict but may later dilate, and the blood pressure will fall; this occurs in nicotine poisoning. Nicotine also has an antidiuretic action. Repeated administration of nicotine causes development of tolerance to some of its effects.

### Toxicity

Nicotine has both short- and long-term toxic effects that are extremely important to the health care professional. Nicotine toxicity has resulted from misuse of insecticides containing nicotine, which at times has led to the death of the individual. And, because nicotine is a major ingredient in tobacco products, both acute toxicity (with ingestion of such products by small children) and chronic toxicity are well documented. See the box on p. 395 for acute symptoms of toxicity.

### Tobacco Smoking and Nicotine

Burning of tobacco can generate approximately 4000 compounds in a gaseous and a particulate or particle phase. Gas phase substances include carbon monoxide, carbon dioxide, hydrogen cyanide, ammonia, volatile nitrosamines, and many other substances. The particulate phase contains mainly nicotine, water, and tar. Known carcinogens have been identified as etiologic factors in a variety of neoplastic diseases, such as cancer of the bladder, lung, buccal cavity, esophagus, and pancreas. Other smoking-related illnesses include pulmonary emphysema, chronic bronchitis, coronary heart disease, and myocardial infarction. Chronic dyspepsia may develop in heavy smokers, and clients with gastric ulcer are usually advised to avoid overindulgence. Of considerable importance is the fact that smokers absorb sufficient nicotine to exert a variety of effects on the autonomic nervous system.

In individuals with peripheral vascular disease such as thromboangiitis obliterans (Buerger's disease), nicotine is

---

## ACUTE SYMPTOMS OF NICOTINE TOXICITY

Increased flow of saliva
Nausea and vomiting
Abdominal cramps
Diarrhea
Confusion
Cold sweat
Fainting
Hypotension
Tachycardia
Prostration and collapse
Convulsions may occur
Death results from respiratory failure

---

## NURSES AND SMOKING

Nurses, besides having the most prolonged contact with clients and their families, have the knowledge and skills to teach them about the hazards of smoking. Unfortunately, nurses continue to smoke at a frequency higher than other health professionals. In the United States, although 64% of physicians and 61% of dentists who have smoked in the past have stopped smoking, only 36% of nurses have stopped. This is particularly important because Dalton (1986) found that currently smoking nurses were less likely to agree that smoking was a major cause of cancer and other health problems and to counsel clients about those hazards. Nurses need to be role models and thus should decrease their smoking habits if they are to contribute to a change in the public's smoking behaviors.

An effective program of smoking cessation should incorporate acceptance, support, specific information, and regular opportunities for monitoring progress. Stretcher (1985) found that even a minimal-contact smoking cessation program, including a brief practitioner consultation with self-help manuals conducted in health care settings, produced significant reductions in cigarette smoking.

Besides educating and counseling clients and their families about the benefits of smoking cessation, nurses can participate in community antismoking activities. Such activities include supporting clean indoor air acts, supporting no-smoking areas on public transportation and teaching health education courses in schools.

---

generally believed to be a contributing factor in the disease and may cause spasms of the peripheral blood vessels and thus reduce the blood flow through the affected vessels. Vasospasm in the retinal blood vessels of the eye, associated with smoking of tobacco, is thought to cause serious disturbance of vision.

Passive smoking, the inhalation of cigarette smoke by nonsmokers, also has harmful effects. The fetus of a smoking mother may have a low birth weight and increased congenital abnormalities. Children of parents who smoke have an increased incidence of sudden infant death syndrome, an increased incidence of respiratory infections and allergic reactions, and an increased likelihood of becoming smokers. Nonsmoking adults exposed to smokers have increased symptoms as in those with chronic heart or lung disease, and higher rates of cancer are found in nonsmoking spouses.

The addictive component of tobacco is nicotine. Many drugs are reported to interact with nicotine and at least two, theophylline and propranolol, have very significant interactions requiring an increased dosage in smokers to produce their therapeutic effect. Referral may be made to the literature on smoking for additional information on both direct and indirect drug interactions with smoking and other related smoking issues.

### nicotine gum (Nicorette)

Nicotine is available in a resin for use in smoking cessation programs. The nicotine resin is in the form of chewing gum and provides a source of nicotine for the nicotine-dependent client who is undergoing acute cigarette withdrawal. When the client has a strong urge to smoke, he or she chews a stick of gum, which relieves the physical symptoms of nicotine withdrawal. The number of pieces of gum chewed is gradually reduced over a 2- to 3-month period. For mechanism of action, see the discussion of pharmacologic effects of nicotine. It is indicated for adjunct treatment

for nicotine dependence. It is absorbed through buccal mucosa, slower than if inhaled while smoking. It is metabolized primarily by the hepatic route, with small amounts in the kidney and lung. Half-life is 30 to 60 minutes. Elimination is primarily renal, 10% to 20% unchanged, the remainder as metabolites; the drug is excreted in breast milk.

More frequent side effects include belching, fast heart beat, mild headache, increased appetite, increased watering of mouth, and sore mouth or throat. Less frequently encountered are constipation, coughing, dizziness or light headedness, dry mouth, hiccups, hoarseness, laxative effect, loss of appetite, irritability, indigestion, and difficulty in sleeping.

More frequently encountered adverse reactions include injury to mouth, teeth, or dental work. A rare adverse reaction is irregular heartbeat. Early signs of overdose are nausea and vomiting, severe increased watering of the mouth, severe abdominal pain, diarrhea, cold sweat, severe headache, severe dizziness, disturbed hearing and vision, confusion, and severe weakness. Advanced signs of overdose are fainting, hypotension, difficulty breathing, fast, weak, or irregular pulse, and convulsions.

*Significant drug interactions.* The following effects may occur when nicotine is given with the drugs listed below:

| Drug | Possible Effect and Management |
|------|-------------------------------|
| insulin | May increase effect of insulin by increasing absorption; dosage reduction may be necessary. |
| propoxyphene, proprandol, possibly other beta-adrenergic blocking agents or xanthine bronchodilators | Smoking cessation may increase therapeutic effects by decreasing metabolism; dosage reduction may be necessary. |

*Dosage and administration.* Oral: 2 mg as a chewing gum, repeated as needed to curb the client's urge to smoke, up to 30 pieces of gum/day maximum. The gum should be chewed intermittently and very slowly when the client has the urge to smoke. Most clients require about 10 pieces of gum per day during the first month of treatment.

▷ **Nursing Management:**
**Nicotine Gum Therapy**

*Assessment.* It should be determined before the initiation of therapy with nicotine gum that the client does not have severe angina pectoris, severe cardiac arrhythmias, or a myocardial infarction as these will be worsened by the catecholaminic action on the heart (increased heart rate and blood pressure); or temporomandibular joint disorder, which might be aggravated by the chewing of gum. Other disorders that would require the cautious use of the gum would be insulin-dependent diabetes mellitus (increases serum concentrations of insulin); hypertension, hyperthyroidism, or vasospastic diseases (increased heart rate and blood pressure); dental problems; or esophagitis, inflammation of the mouth or peptic ulcer, which may be exacerbated.

The client participating in gum therapy is at high risk for the following nursing diagnoses: injury to mouth, teeth, or dental work; altered comfort related to headache, increased watering of the mouth, jaw muscle ache, fast heartbeat, sore throat or mouth; altered nutrition (more than body requirements) related to increased appetite; altered sleep pattern (insomnia); and altered thought processes (unusual irritability).

*Education.* The client is instructed that when the urge to smoke occurs, one piece of gum is chewed slowly for about 30 minutes. At that point, most of the nicotine will have been released. The amount of nicotine released depends on the rate of chewing and amount of time the saliva is in contact with the gum. Instruct the client not to chew more than 30 pieces in a day. The number of pieces of gum should be reduced each day over a 2- to 3-month period. The gum should be carried at all times during therapy. The use of the gum for more than 3 months is not advised and may indicate its use as a substitute for the maintenance of nicotine dependency. At 6 months of use a gradual withdrawal program should be instituted.

Because its viscosity is greater than regular gum, it may cause damage to dentures, inlays, fillings, and natural teeth. Excessive chewing may lead to some temporomandibular joint discomfort. Have the client use sugarless hard candies between doses of gum to meet the need for oral stimulation and relieve oral discomfort. Instruct the client to discontinue use and consult with physician or dentist if gum sticks to dental work.

The client should *not* smoke while being treated with nicotine gum.

Nicotine gum must be used under medical supervision and combined with a supervised program for smoking cessation including education, counseling, and psychological support.

*Evaluation.* Evaluation of the client's progress toward smoking cessation should occur at least monthly and determination of the efficacy of the gum in the therapy program made.

Women of child-bearing age should be advised to use effective birth control to avoid pregnancy because of nicotine's link with low birth weight infants and a decrease in fetal breathing movements, possibly the result of decreased placental perfusion.

Because an overdose of nicotine can be fatal, particularly in small children, the gum should be kept out of the reach of children. If many pieces are chewed at once or in rapid succession, an overdose may occur in an adult; however, the consequences of overdose may be mitigated by the early nausea and vomiting that generally occur with excessive nicotine intake.

## GANGLIONIC BLOCKING DRUGS

Ganglionic blocking drugs block transmission of both sympathetic and parasympathetic nerve impulses at the nicotinic receptors on the ganglia. The parent compound of this group of drugs is a quaternary ammonium compound called tetraethylammonium chloride. It is not good for treatment of hypertension because of its short duration of action, its ineffectiveness when given orally, and its distressing side effects.

In 1950 the methonium derivatives were introduced, and hexamethonium chloride became the drug of choice in managing severe and malignant hypertension. Despite the difficulties in managing individuals receiving hexamethonium because of its erratic absorption and action and severe side effects, its use demonstrated that severe hypertension could be controlled. Since 1961, the ganglionic blocking agents have been seldom used. Newer antihypertensive drugs that have more selective action and fewer severe side effects are preferred. However, the student should be aware of these products because some physicians may select trimethaphan as an alternative for clients resistant to the effects of sodium nitroprusside. Other physicians may use a ganglionic blocking agent such as trimethaphan for the treatment of a hypertensive crisis in individuals with an acute dissecting aortic aneurysm. The two ganglionic blocking agents available are mecamylamine hydrochloride (Inversine tablets) and trimethaphan camsylate (Arfonad injection). Since mecamylamine has many side effects and is not considered a first line drug in the treatment of hypertension, read the package insert or current USP-DI for additional information on this product.

### trimethaphan camsylate (Arfonad)

Ganglionic blocking agents lower arterial pressure by blocking the action of acetylcholine on the ganglion cells. This results in reduced transmission of impulses from preganglionic to postganglionic fibers in both sympathetic and parasympathetic nerves. Blocking transmission of impulses through the sympathetic ganglia abolishes vasoconstrictor tone; the blood vessels dilate and arterial pressure falls.

Trimethaphan camsylate is used in the treatment of hypertension and is administered by intravenous infusion. Onset of action is immediate; duration of effect is 10 to 15 minutes. Metabolism is probably by pseudocholinesterase. The drug is excreted in the kidneys (unchanged).

For side effects/adverse reactions, see Table 20-3.

***Significant drug interactions.*** The following effects may occur when trimethaphan is given with the drugs listed below:

| Drug | Possible Effect and Management |
|---|---|
| ambenonium or neostigmine or pyridostigmine | The antimyasthenic effects of these drugs will be blocked, leading to increased weakness and inability to swallow. Avoid concurrent administration of trimethaphan with these medications. |
| antibiotics and sulfonamides | Do not use ganglionic blockers in individuals with chronic pyelonephritis being treated with these medications. Trimethaphan may reduce renal blood flow and urine output or cause urinary retention. |

***Dosage and administration.*** Parenteral
*Adults*
Hypertensive emergency, initially, 0.5 mg to 1 mg/min by intravenous infusion. Adjust dosage according to client response. Maintenance dosage, 1 to 15 mg/min by intravenous infusion.
To control blood pressure during surgery: Initially, 3 to 4 mg/min, adjust as necessary. Maintenance dose is 0.2 to 6 mg/min by intravenous infusion.
*Elderly.* May be more sensitive to this drug so a lower dosage with close monitoring is indicated.
*Children.* Initially 0.1 mg/min, adjusted according to individual response, by intravenous infusion.

### ▷ Nursing Management:
### Trimethaphan Camsylate Therapy

***Assessment.*** Use with caution for children and elderly clients, who tend to be more sensitive to its hypotensive effects. Use with caution for clients with anemia, Addison's disease, diabetes, hepatic or renal disease, cardiovascular or cerebrovascular insufficiency, and for clients taking other antihypotensive or steroid medications.

The client receiving trimethaphan camsylate therapy should be assessed for the following nursing diagnoses: altered comfort related to nausea and vomiting, dry mouth, itching and anginal pain; altered bowel elimination pattern (constipation); high risk for injury related to blurred vision and orthostatic hypertension; and urinary retention.

***Intervention.*** Clients receiving trimethaphan camsylate should be in an intensive care setting for appropriate monitoring. Emergency equipment should be available in the event of respiratory arrest.

The solution should be diluted with dextrose 5% injection only and administered by infusion pump or micro-drip regulator to ensure a precise regulation of the flow rate. The prepared intravenous solution is stable at room temperature for 24 hours. The client should be in a supine position to avoid cerebral anoxia. Oral antihypertensive therapy should be started as soon as possible because a pseudotolerance to the drug may occur in some individuals.

If used for controlled hypotension during surgery, the drug should be discontinued before the wound is closed to allow the client's blood pressure to return to normal.

***Evaluation.*** Monitor the client's blood pressure and respiratory function frequently.

## Summary

Drugs that mimic, intensify, or inhibit the effects of the parasympathetic and sympathetic divisions of the autonomic nervous system are known as the autonomic drugs. They are grouped as cholinergic, cholinergic blocking, adrenergic, and adrenergic blocking drugs. The cholinergic (parasympathomimetic) drugs have nicotinic effects that stimulate the ganglia, adrenal medulae, and skeletal muscle, and muscarinic effects that stimulate the postganglionic nerve endings in glands, cardiac, and smooth muscle. They are used primarily to stimulate the intestine and bladder postoperatively, to terminate curarization, to lower intraocular pressure, to promote salivation and sweating, to dilate peripheral blood vessels, and to treat myasthenia gravis symptomatically. Anticholinergic (parasympatholytic) drugs block the muscarinic effects of acetylcholine, which can produce a wide range of pharmacologic effects. They are used to treat illnesses in which spasm is a component such as irritable bowel syndrome, spastic biliary disorders, and urinary disorders. Because anticholinergics decrease respiratory secretions, they are administered as a preanesthetic drug and to control the excessive salivation of some disorders, such as Parkinson's disease.

The ganglionic drugs are either ganglionic stimulating or ganglionic blocking drugs. Nicotine is a ganglionic stimulating drug. It has, however, no therapeutic use, but the nurse should be knowledgeable about its effects for health teaching purposes. In the 1950s, ganglionic blocking drugs were used for the management of severe and malignant hypertension, but since the 1960s the advent of more selective effective antihypertensive drugs has resulted in their limited use.

## BIBLIOGRAPHY

American Hospital Formulary Service. (1990). AHFS drug information '90. Bethesda, Md: American Society of Hospital Pharmacists.

Baucke SL. (1987). Seeing eye to eye on physostigmine, J Post Anesth Nurs 2(1):51.

Black T. (1985). Smoking in pregnancy revisited, Midwifery 1(3):135.

Booth K and Faulker A. (1986). Links between nurses and cigarette smoking? Nurse Educ Today 6(4):176.

Dalgas P. (1985). Understanding drugs that affect the autonomic nervous system, Nursing 15(10):58.

Dalton JA and Swenson I. (1986). Nurses and smoking: role modeling and counseling behaviors. Oncology Nurs Forum 13(2):45.

Fraulini KE and Gorski DW. (1983). Don't let perioperative medications put you in a spin, Nursing 13(12):26.

Gever LN. (1984). Anticholinergics . . . and what to teach your patient about them, Nursing 14(9):64.

Gever LN. (1984). Cholinergics: a concise review, Nursing 14(5):41.

Goodman AG et al, eds. (1990). Goodman and Gilman's the pharmacological basis of therapeutics, ed 8. New York: Macmillan Publishing Co.

Gray M et al. (1987). Urinary incontinence: pathophysiology and treatment, J Enterostomal Ther 14(4):152.

Miller K. (1986). Atropine, Emergency 18(4):12.

Reeder TM. (1986). Alzheimer's disease: using direct drug infusion to the central nervous system (bethanecol chloride), AORN J 44(2):222.

Rose DD. (1984). Review of anticholinergic drugs: their use and safe omittance in preoperative medications, AANA J 52(4):401.

Smith S. (1987). How drugs act: drugs and the parasympathetic nervous system, Nursing Times 83(24):36.

Strecher VJ et al. (1985). Evaluation of a minimal contact smoking cessation program in a health care setting, Patient Educ Couns 7(4):395.

Todd B. (1984). Central anticholinergic syndrome, Geriatr Nurs 5(2):117.

United States Pharmacopeial Convention. (1991). USP-DI: drug information for the health care professional. Bethesda, Md: United States Pharmacopeial Convention.

# Chapter

## 🌀 21 — Drugs Affecting the Sympathetic Nervous System

---

## CHAPTER OBJECTIVES

*After studying this chapter, you should be able to meet the following objectives and define the key terms.*

1. Discuss the three types of adrenergic drugs.

2. Differentiate between alpha$_1$, alpha$_2$, beta$_1$, and beta$_2$ adrenergic effects.

3. Describe the effects of the three naturally occurring catecholamines on the body.

4. List common adrenergic drugs and blocking agents, their effects and side effects/adverse reactions.

5. Describe nursing measures for adrenergic drugs and blocking agents.

---

## KEY TERMS

**alpha adrenergic blocking agents,** page 423

**beta adrenergic blocking agents,** page 429

**calorigenic effect,** page 402

**chronotropic effect,** page 402

**dromotropic effect,** page 402

**inotropic effect,** page 400

**sympathomimetic drugs,** page 399

## ADRENERGIC DRUGS

Agents that enhance the effects of sympathetic nervous system are called **sympathomimetic drugs** because they mimic the effects of sympathetic nerve stimulation. The drugs are designed to produce activities that are similar to those of the neurotransmitters. The sympathomimetic drugs are also called adrenergic drugs. There are three types of adrenergic drugs: (1) direct-acting, (2) indirect-acting, and (3) dual-acting (direct and indirect) agents.

### Direct-Acting Adrenergic Drugs

#### Catecholamines

The three naturally occurring catecholamines in the body—dopamine, norepinephrine, and epinephrine—are synthesized by the sympathetic nervous system. (For information on adrenergic transmission see Figure 19-6, and the discussion in Chapter 19.)

In the past there were confusing and conflicting reports that the effects of sympathetic nerve stimulation and the effects of epinephrine injection did not always correspond. In the mid-1940s it was shown that epinephrine had a twin, norepinephrine. The recognition that these were separate substances occurring naturally in the body helped clear up the confusion. With further research one more catecholamine has been positively identified—dopamine. Dopamine is a precursor of norepinephrine and epinephrine. However, dopamine has a transmitter role of its own in certain portions of the central nervous system. Epinephrine acts mainly as an emergency hormone; norepinephrine, on the other hand, is an important transmitter of nerve impulses. It is also an intermediary in epinephrine biosynthesis.

The catecholamines depend on their ability to interact *directly* with adrenergic receptors (alpha and beta) and are

**399**

called *direct-acting* drugs. Thus the response of these agents is mediated by directly stimulating the adrenergic receptors. In the sympathetic nervous system the adrenergic effector cells contained two distinct receptors, the alpha ($\alpha$) and beta ($\beta$) receptors.

There is evidence that the alpha receptors appear on two locations. The alpha$_2$ receptors are found on the presynaptic nerve endings or terminals and are called presynaptic (prejunctional) receptors. It has been suggested that the function of the presynaptic receptor is associated with the control of the amount of transmitter released per nerve impulse. The rate of transmitter synthesized can be regulated by a feedback mechanism. Thus when the concentration of transmitter released from the nerve terminal into the synaptic cleft reaches a high level, it can stimulate the presynaptic receptors and prevent the further release of the transmitter. This kind of feedback prevents excessive and prolonged stimulation of the postsynaptic cell. The postsynaptic receptors, which are located on the effector organs, are known as alpha$_1$ or alpha$_2$ (see Figure 19-6).

The beta receptors are subdivided on the basis of their responses to drugs. Beta$_1$ receptors are located mainly in the heart, and beta$_2$ receptors mediate the actions of catecholamines on bronchioles and arterial smooth muscles.

Norepinephrine acts mainly on alpha receptors and may cause pure vasoconstriction. Epinephrine acts on both alpha and beta receptors and produces a mixture of vasodilation and vasoconstriction. Isoproterenol, a synthetic catecholamine, acts only on beta receptors. For a discussion of receptor sensitivity see the box below.

The most important alpha adrenergic activities in humans are (1) vasoconstriction of arterioles in the skin and splanchnic area, resulting in a rise in blood pressure, (2) pupil dilation, and (3) relaxation of the gut. Beta adrenergic activity includes (1) cardiac acceleration and increased contractility, (2) vasodilation of arterioles supplying skeletal muscles, (3) bronchial relaxation, and (4) uterine relaxation.

---

### ADRENERGIC RECEPTOR SENSITIVITIES

| Receptor | Sensitivities |
|---|---|
| Alpha$_1$ ($\alpha_1$) | Epinephrine is equal to or more potent than norepinephrine, which is more potent than isoproterenol. |
| Alpha$_2$ ($\alpha_2$) | Epinephrine may be more or less potent than norepinephrine (depending on tissues involved). Isoproterenol is ineffective. |
| Beta$_1$ ($\beta_1$) | Isoproterenol is more potent than epinephrine. Epinephrine and norepinephrine are approximately equivalent in action. |
| Beta$_2$ ($\beta_2$) | Isoproterenol is equivalent to or more potent than epinephrine. Epinephrine is much more potent than norepinephrine. |

---

The effects of both alpha and beta stimulation result from a summation of action where they are interrelated. That is, a change in blood pressure will depend on the degree of vasoconstriction in the skin and splanchnic area *and* the extent of vasodilation in skeletal muscles, along with changes in heart rate. Large arteries and veins contain both alpha and beta receptors; the heart contains only beta receptors (Table 21-1).

Although there are specific drugs that stimulate the alpha or beta receptors, there are also drugs that selectively block alpha or beta receptors. These agents work at peripheral autonomic sites, which distinguishes them from ganglionic blocking agents that act at the ganglia. The adrenergic blocking agents include both alpha and beta blockers. In the United States in 1968 the first beta receptor blocking agent, propranolol, became available for clinical use.

As catecholamines, norepinephrine and epinephrine are important neurohormones in neural and endocrine integration. They are always present in arterial blood, although the amount varies widely during any one day. Certain physiologic stimuli such as stress and exercise significantly increase blood levels of catecholamine.

Studies indicate that the major sources of circulating norepinephrine are stimulated sympathetic nerve endings. Organs that receive a large fraction of blood and possess large numbers of sympathetic nerve endings contain the greatest amount of catecholamines. (Examples of such organs are the heart and blood vessels.) Thus the number of sympathetic nerve endings or adrenergic nerves to various organs determines the magnitude of response of these organs to increased levels or injections of catecholamines.

### Pharmacologic Effects

Catecholamines produce a variety of physiologic responses.

*Cardiac.* Epinephrine and norepinephrine produce almost the same cardiac responses when injected.

A marked increase in myocardial contraction (positive **inotropic effect**) is the result of increased influx of calcium into cardiac fibers. The strong myocardial contractions result in more complete emptying of the ventricles and an increase in cardiac work and oxygen consumption. The strong contractions brought about by isoproterenol and epinephrine also increase cardiac output, or volume. Norepinephrine, on the other hand, may not alter cardiac output and may even decrease it slightly. This effect of norepinephrine is believed to result from its potent vasoconstricting action, which increases resistance to ejection of blood from the heart. The increased work of the heart to move the blood against increased pressure is "pressure work" rather than "volume work."

It has been shown experimentally and clinically that 0.5 mg of epinephrine injected into arterial or venous blood and circulated by cardiac compression or massage may stimulate spontaneous and vigorous cardiac contractions. Even though

**TABLE 21-1**   Adrenergic receptor stimulation

| Effector organs | Receptor type | Adrenergic response |
|---|---|---|
| **HEART** | | |
| Cardiac muscle (atria, ventricles) | $\beta_1$ | Increased force of contraction |
| Sinoatrial node | $\beta_1$ | Increased heart rate |
| Atrioventricular node | $\beta_1$ | Increased conduction velocity; shortened refractory period |
| Conduction tissue | $\beta_1$ | |
| **BLOOD VESSELS** | | |
| Arterioles (smooth muscle) | | |
| Coronary | $\alpha$, $\beta_2$, dopaminergic | Constriction, dilation |
| Cerebral | $\alpha$ | Constriction |
| Pulmonary | $\alpha$, $\beta_2$ | Constriction, dilation |
| Mesenteric visceral | $\alpha$, $\beta_2$, dopaminergic | Constriction, dilation |
| Renal | $\alpha$, $\beta_2$, dopaminergic | Constriction, dilation |
| Skin, mucosa | $\alpha$ | Constriction |
| Skeletal muscle | $\alpha$, $\beta_2$ | Constriction, dilation |
| Veins | $\alpha_1$, $\beta_2$ | Constriction, dilation |
| **LUNG** | | |
| Bronchial smooth muscle | $\beta_2$ | Bronchodilation (relaxation) |
| Bronchial glands | $\alpha_1$, $\beta_2$ | Inhibition |
| **GASTROINTESTINAL TRACT** | | |
| Smooth muscle (motility, tone) | $\alpha_2$, $\beta_2$ | Decrease |
| Sphincter | $\alpha$ | Contraction |
| Secretion | ? | Inhibition |
| Gallbladder and ducts | — | Relaxation |
| **LIVER** | $\beta_2$ | Glycogenolysis, gluconeogenesis |
| **SPLEEN CAPSULE** | $\alpha$, $\beta_2$ | Contraction, relaxation |
| **PANCREAS: INSULIN SECRE-TION** | $\alpha$ | Decrease |
| **ADIPOSE TISSUE** | $\beta_1$ | Lipolysis |
| **URINARY BLADDER** | | |
| Detrusor muscle | $\beta_1$ | Relaxation |
| Sphincter | $\alpha$ | Contraction |
| **KIDNEY URETER** | $\alpha$ | Contraction |
| **KIDNEY SECRETION (RENIN)** | $\beta_2$ | Increase |
| **UTERUS** | | |
| Pregnant | $\alpha$ | Contraction |
| Nonpregnant | $\beta_2$ | Relaxation |
| **SEX ORGANS, male** | $\alpha$ | Ejaculation |
| **SKIN** | | |
| Pilomotor muscles | $\alpha$ | Contraction |
| Sweat glands | Cholinergic | Increased secretion |
| **EYE** | | |
| Radial muscle, iris (pupil size) | $\alpha_1$ | Contraction–pupil dilation (mydriasis) |
| Ciliary muscle | $\beta$ | Relaxation for far vision |

the heart is in ventricular fibrillation, epinephrine increases fibrillation vigor and frequently promotes successful electric defibrillation of the individual. In these situations the drug may be injected repeatedly. However, epinephrine cannot be used repeatedly to improve the function of a failing heart (congestive heart failure), since it increases oxygen consumption by cardiac muscle. It can also cause anginal pain in clients with angina pectoris because it increases cardiac oxygen demand. Therefore, although it increases coronary blood flow, its use is contraindicated for patients with angina. The production of strong contractions provides the rationale for the use of epinephrine in cardiac arrest.

A marked increase in cardiac rate (positive **chronotropic effect**) is the result of the increased rate of membrane depolarization in the pacemaker cells in the sinus node during diastole. Action potential threshold is reached sooner, pacemaker cells fire more often, and heart rate increases.

Norepinephrine, with its predominantly alpha adrenergic activity, may not produce as severe a tachycardia as epinephrine. The increased vasoconstriction and increased blood pressure may cause a reflex bradycardia. Isoproterenol usually produces a tachycardia, since its direct and reflex effects act in the same direction. Dosage and patient variables affect these responses.

An increase in atrioventricular conduction (positive **dromotropic effect**) is another physiologic response. Because epinephrine increases atrioventricular conduction, some cardiologists use it in the treatment of heart block.

Catecholamines may also produce spontaneous firing of Purkinje fibers, which may cause them to exhibit pacemaker activity. This effect may cause ventricular extrasystoles and increase the susceptibility of ventricular muscle to fibrillation. These effects are more likely to occur with epinephrine than norepinephrine.

**Vascular.**  Vascular effects of the catecholamines depend on the dose and the vascular bed affected. Low doses of epinephrine may decrease total peripheral vascular resistance and so decrease blood pressure. In large doses epinephrine activates alpha receptors in the greater peripheral vascular system, which increases resistance and increases blood pressure. Norepinephrine elevates blood pressure by increasing peripheral resistance and decreasing blood flow through skeletal muscles.

Norepinephrine is a vasoconstrictor and increases total peripheral resistance. Isoproterenol is not a vasoconstrictor but a pure vasodilator; epinephrine is both a vasoconstrictor and vasodilator, with vasodilation being greater in its overall net effects. For example, during great stress the release of epinephrine from the adrenal medulla constricts blood vessels in the skin and splanchnic areas but dilates those of skeletal muscles, thus shunting blood to the areas needed for "fight or flight" responses.

There is greater renal artery constriction and resistance with epinephrine than with norepinephrine. In large doses epinephrine may actually stop blood flow through some nephrons (up to 40%) and stimulate release of antidiuretic hormone (ADH), thereby reducing urinary excretion.

***Central nervous system.***  Epinephrine and isoproterenol in sufficient amounts can lead to alertness, tremulousness, respiratory stimulation, and anxiety. Norepinephrine is less likely to cause anxiety and tremulousness. Beneficial cerebral effects from epinephrine and norepinephrine in cases of hypotension are thought to be the result of increased systemic pressure with a resultant improvement in cerebral blood flow.

***Musculoskeletal.***  Generally, the catecholamines relax nonvascular smooth muscles. Smooth muscle of the gastrointestinal tract is relaxed, and amplitude and tone of intestinal peristalsis are reduced. This may retard propulsion of food and gastrointestinal emptying. However, with therapeutic doses this effect rarely occurs in humans.

The musculature of the splenic capsule is stimulated, causing increasing contractions of that organ. The increased contractions increase the number of circulating red cells and blood viscosity. This effect is not of great significance in humans.

In some situations smooth muscle of some organs reacts like vascular smooth muscle and contracts. For example, radial and sphincter muscles of the iris contract, and the smooth muscle that inserts into the lids may contract, giving rise to the widened, staring eyes seen in sympathetically stimulated individuals.

In the urinary bladder epinephrine causes trigone and sphincter contraction and detrusor relaxation with a delay in the desire to void.

***Respiratory.***  Catecholamines dilate bronchial smooth muscle. Isoproterenol is a more active bronchodilator than epinephrine, and epinephrine is a stronger bronchodilator than norepinephrine. Epinephrine also constricts bronchial vessels and inhibits bronchial secretions, which accounts for its time-honored use in the treatment of acute bronchial asthma.

***Glandular.***  Epinephrine may increase the amount of viscid saliva excreted, but as a rule sympathomimetics decrease secretion and produce a dry mouth. Catecholamines may produce local sweating on the palms of the hands and in the axillary and genital areas. The exact mechanism for these effects is not clear.

***Metabolic.***  Epinephrine inhibits insulin secretion. Catecholamines have antagonistic effects on gluconeogenesis, and they decrease liver and skeletal muscle glycogen and increase lipolysis in adipose tissue. The result of these effects is a rise in blood sugar and an increase in free fatty acids. Thus in response to stress ("fight or flight" response) there can be an abundant supply of fuel and energy.

Catecholamines also have a **calorigenic effect** (capable of generating heat, which increases oxygen consumption) resulting from the sum of the preceding effects. Norepinephrine's action in relation to these effects is weaker than that of epinephrine or isoproterenol.

***Other effects.*** Catecholamines cause a decrease in circulating eosinophils. The mechanism of this action is unknown.

### epinephrine (Adrenalin)

Epinephrine is available in solutions for inhalation or nebulization, parenteral and ophthalmic administration. Many bronchodilator aerosols are available over the counter in solutions containing up to 1% of the epinephrine base. For example:

epinephrine inhalation aerosol (Bronkaid Mist, Bronkaid Mistometer ✤ )

epinephrine bitartrate inhalation aerosol (AsthmaHaler, Medihaler-Epi)

racepinephrine inhalation solution (AsthmaNefrin, Vaponefrin)

Parenteral dosage forms and ophthalmic solutions are ordered by prescription only:

epinephrine injection (Adrenalin, EpiPen Auto-Injector)

sterile epinephrine suspension (Sus-Phrine)

Ophthalmic epinephrine is discussed in Chapter 43.

***Mechanism of action.*** Epinephrine is a direct-acting catecholamine that is naturally released from the adrenal medulla in response to sympathoadrenal stimulation. It also is prepared synthetically. Epinephrine stimulates alpha, beta$_1$, and beta$_2$ receptors. Its primary action is on the beta receptors of the heart, the smooth muscle of the bronchi, and the blood vessels. The beta$_1$ action stimulates the heart by in-

**TABLE 21-2** Direct adrenergic drug effects—catecholamine type

| | Epinephrine ($\alpha$, $\beta_1$, $\beta_2$) | Isoproterenol ($\beta_1$, $\beta_2$) | Norepinephrine ($\alpha$, $\beta_1$) |
|---|---|---|---|
| Trade names | Adrenalin | Isuprel | Noradrenalin<br>Levophed |
| Mode of action | | | |
| Alpha receptors | Stimulates | N.S.* | Stimulates |
| Beta receptors | Stimulates | Stimulates | Stimulates the heart |
| Effects | | | |
| Cardiovascular | | | |
| Myocardium | Increases strength of contractions<br>Increases cardiac output | Like epinephrine | Slows rate reflexly |
| Pacemaker cells | Increases heart rate<br>Increases irritability<br>May cause dysrhythmias | Like epinephrine | Stimulates—like epinephrine |
| Coronary vessels | Dilates—increases blood flow | Like epinephrine | Dilates |
| Blood pressure | Increases (depending on dose) | Decreases diastolic<br>Slightly increases systolic | Increases |
| Bronchi | Relaxes; dilates bronchi<br>Improves airway | Potent bronchodilator—more effective than epinephrine | Relaxes less than epinephrine |
| Blood vessels | | | |
| Skeletal muscle | Dilates—increases blood flow | Dilates—increases blood flow | — |
| Kidney | Constricts—decreases blood flow | N.S. | Constricts—decreases blood flow |
| Gastrointestinal tract | Relaxes smooth muscle<br>Inhibits peristalsis | N.S. | Like epinephrine |
| Metabolic | Increases oxygen consumption<br>Mobilizes glycogen<br>Causes hyperglycemia | N.S. | Increases metabolic rate but less than epinephrine |
| Remarks | Tolerance does not develop | Infiltration into tissues may cause necrosis and sloughing | Infiltration into tissues may cause necrosis and sloughing |
| Uses | Widely used for all allergic states and with local anesthetics<br>Given by injection or inhalation | Heart failure<br>Asthma | To elevate blood pressure, given by slow intravenous infusion |

*N.S., Not significant.

creasing heart rate, force of myocardial contraction, and cardiac output. The beta$_2$ action on the smooth muscle of the bronchioles produces bronchodilation, thereby increasing tidal volume and vital capacity of the lung. Stimulation of alpha receptors constricts arterioles of the bronchioles and inhibits histamine release, thus reducing nasal congestion and edema. In contrast, beta$_2$ adrenergic activity of the smooth muscle of arterioles causes vasodilation.

Another effect of epinephrine is alpha activity, which results in contraction of the radial muscle in the iris, causing dilation of the pupil (mydriasis). Constriction of the blood vessels in the skin also is activated by alpha activity. The detrusor muscle in the urinary bladder contains beta receptors and is relaxed by epinephrine. (See "epinephrine"—Table 21-2.)

### Indications

1. Used for symptomatic treatment of bronchial asthma and other obstructive pulmonary diseases, such as chronic bronchitis and emphysema that cause bronchospasm.
2. Used for symptomatic relief of acute hypersensitivity reactions. Indicated in the emergency treatment of acute anaphylactic shock and severe acute reactions to drugs, animal serums, insect stings, and other allergens to relieve bronchospasm, urticaria, hives, angioneurotic edema, and swelling of nasal mucosa. Pulmonary congestion is also alleviated by constriction of mucosal blood vessels.
3. Used as an adjunct with local anesthetics. Concurrent administration of epinephrine with local anesthetics reduces circulation to the site, which results in a slowing of vascular absorption. This promotes a local effect of the anesthetic and also prolongs its duration of action, thus reducing the risk of anesthetic toxicity.
4. Administered as a hemostatic agent to control superficial bleeding from arterioles and capillaries in the skin, mucous membranes, or other tissues.
5. Used in management of simple, open-angle glaucoma by reducing intraocular pressure; also indicated for relieving ocular congestion.
6. Used to treat cardiac arrest such as AV block with syncopal seizures. On occasion it may be given by intracardiac injection in acute attacks of ventricular standstill, after physical measures and electrical defibrillation have failed. Since epinephrine increases the amplitude of the fibrillatory waves, it may make the heart more responsive to the direct current (DC) shock. Therefore, after injection of epinephrine, the patient may again be given DC shock. The drug is not to be used in cardiac failure or in hemorrhagic, traumatic, or cardiogenic shock.

**Pharmacokinetics.** Epinephrine should not be given orally because it is rapidly metabolized in the mucosa of the gastrointestinal tract and liver, so serum levels acheived would be inadequate. Absorption from subcutaneous injec-

tion is also slow because of intense local vasoconstriction. (Heat and massage have been used to increase the rate of absorption from subcutaneous administration.) It is absorbed well from intramuscular administration.

Epinephrine has a rapid onset of action, from 3 to 5 minutes by inhalation or between 6 and 15 minutes when given subcutaneously. The duration of action of epinephrine is short, so, depending on the dose given and the indication, repeated doses may be scheduled for 5 to 10 minutes later (as in severe anaphylaxis, asthma, or cardiac arrest) or may be repeated in 20 minutes to 4 hours in more stabilized situations. Epinephrine is metabolized in the liver and excreted in the kidneys.

**Side effects/adverse reactions.** See Table 21-3.

**Significant drug interactions.** The following interactions may occur when epinephrine is given with the drugs listed below.

| Drug | Possible Effect and Management |
|---|---|
| anesthetics, such as cyclopropane, halothane and trichloroethylene | May sensitize the heart, increasing risk of severe dysrhythmias. Monitor closely because a reduction in epinephrine (sympathomimetics) is usually necessary. |
| local parenteral anesthetics | When used in end artery areas, such as fingers, toes, or penis, the reduced blood supply to the area may result in ischemia and gangrene. Use very cautiously in such areas and monitor closely. |
| beta-adrenergic receptor blocking agents, including ophthalmics | Therapeutic effects of both agents may be inhibited. With bronchodilators having both alpha and beta stimulating effects (epinephrine), with beta receptor blockade, stimulation of alpha receptors may result in hypertension, severe bradycardia with possibly heart block. If possible, avoid concurrent administration or if absolutely necessary, monitor closely. |
| digitalis glycosides | Digitalis sensitizes the myocardium to the effects of epinephrine; the additive effect of the catecholamine may precipitate ectopic pacemaker activity. |
| ergotamine or ergoloid mesylates | Concurrent use may produce severe hypertension, peripheral vascular ischemia, and gangrene. Avoid this combination. |
| maprotiline, tricyclic antidepressants, MAO inhibitor antidepressants, or cocaine | May cause dysrhythmias, tachycardia, and hypertension or hyperpyrexia. |

**Dosage and administration.** See Table 21-4.

▷ **Nursing Management: Epinephrine Therapy**

**Assessment.** This drug should not be used by individuals with narrow-angle glaucoma, coronary insufficiency, shock, organic brain damage, or by those who are receiving general anesthesia with cyclopropane or halothane.

Use with caution in elderly clients and those with car-

**TABLE 21-3**  Side effects/adverse reactions of adrenergic drugs

| Drug | Side effects* | Adverse reactions† |
|---|---|---|
| epinephrine (Adrenalin) | More frequent: Systemic reactions—increased nervousness, restlessness; insomnia<br>Less frequent: Elevation of blood pressure, tachycardia, tremors, sweating, nausea, vomiting, pallor, weakness<br>Inhalation reactions: Bronchial irritation and coughing (usually with high doses), dry mouth and throat, headaches, red or flushing face or skin | Chills, fever, dizziness, chest pain or pressure, severe headaches, severe hypertension, seizures, increased anxiety and nervousness, dilated pupils or blurred vision, respiratory difficulties (shortness of breath), severe tremors and pounding heart rate, either unusually fast or slow heartbeat, may result in cerebrovascular accident, tachyarrhythmias, or myocardial infarction (above are signs of overdosage) |
| isoproterenol (Isuprel) | Similar to epinephrine with the following exceptions: Inhalation and sublingual dosage forms may induce a pink to red discoloration of the saliva; this is an expected color alteration and it is not necessary to report it to physician | Dizziness, chest pain or pressure, severe headache, increased anxiety and nervousness, trembling, pallor, severe hypertension, rapid heart beat, dysrhythmias |
| norepinephrine (Levophed) | Less frequent: Increased nervousness or anxiety, dizziness, pallor, tremors, insomnia, headaches, pounding heart rate, swelling of thyroid gland in neck | Rare: Extravasation leading to severe vasoconstriction, ischemia and necrosis—this requires immediate therapeutic intervention to prevent sloughing of tissue and gangrene; cardiac dysrhythmias, bradycardia, and allergic reactions (usually to sodium bisulfite in preparation)<br>Overdosage: Severe hypertension and headaches, convulsions, vomiting, unusually slow heart rate |

*If side effects continue, increase, or disturb the client, inform the physician.
†If adverse reactions occur, contact physician, since medical intervention may be necessary.

**TABLE 21-4**  Dosage and administration of epinephrine

| Indication | Adults | Children |
|---|---|---|
| **PARENTERAL** | | |
| Bronchodilator | SC 0.2-0.5 mg every 20 min to 4 hr as needed, with dosage increase to max. 1 mg/dose if needed. | SC 0.01 mg/kg or 0.3 mg/m₂ every 15 min for 2 doses, every 4 hr if needed. Max. dose up to 0.5 mg/dose. |
| Anaphylaxis | IM/SC 0.2-0.5 mg repeated every 10-15 min as needed, with dosage increase to max. of 1 mg/dose if needed. | SC 0.01 mg/kg or 0.3 mg/m₂, repeated every 15 min for 2 doses, then every 4 hr as needed; severe cases: dosage may increase to 0.5 mg/dose. |
| Cardiac stimulant | IV or intracardiac injection 0.1-1 mg (base) diluted to 10 ml with sodium chloride injection given to restore myocardial contractility. After intracardiac administration, external cardiac massage should be applied to enhance drug entry into coronary circulation. May repeat every 5 min if needed. Endotracheal tube instillation dosage is 1 mg (base) for cardiac resuscitation. | IV or intracardiac, 0.005-0.01 mg/kg or 0.15-0.3 mg/m²; repeat every 5 min or follow with IV infusion at initial rate of 0.0001 mg/kg/min. May be increased in increments of 0.0001 mg/kg/min if necessary to max. of 0.0015 mg/kg/min. |
| Anesthetic (local) adjunct | Intraspinal 0.2-0.4 ml (0.2-0.4 mg) added to anesthetic spinal mixture. With local anesthetic: 0.1 to 0.2 mg in a 1:200,000 to 1:20,000 solution. | Intraspinal 0.2 0.4 ml (0.2-0.4 mg) added to anesthetic spinal mixture. |

*Continued.*

**TABLE 21-4**   Dosage and administration of epinephrine—cont'd

| Indication | Adults | Children |
|---|---|---|
| **PARENTERAL** | | |
| Auto-injection | | |
| Auto-injector for emergency self-treatment of anaphylaxis. (EpiPen Auto-Injector) | Available in 0.5 mg/ml and 1 mg/ml | |
| **SUSPENSION (SUS-PHRINE)** | | |
| Bronchodilator | SC 0.5 mg initially, followed by 0.5-1.5 mg every 6 hr as necessary. | SC 0.025 mg/kg or 0.625 mg/m². May be repeated in 6 hr. If child weighs 30 kg, max. single dose is 0.75 mg. |
| **INHALATION** | | |
| Bronchodilator 1:100 (1%) solution | Proper dose automatically dispensed by metered nebulizer. Allow 1-5 min between inhalations. Use fewest possible inhalations. | |
| **TOPICAL** | | |
| Nasal decongestant | 1-2 drops (0.1%) every 4-6 hr. | |
| Antihemorrhagic | 0.002%-0.1% (1:50,000 to 1:1000) solution of epinephrine applied locally. | |

diovascular disease, hypertension, hyperthyroidism, or psychosis. Pulmonary edema, which can be fatal, may occur because of peripheral constriction.

Use with caution in clients with bronchial asthma or emphysema who also have degenerative heart disease. Clients with coronary insufficiency may develop anginal pain.

Epinephrine should be administered to the pregnant client with great caution. It is known to cross the placenta, and although appropriate studies have not been conducted in humans to demonstrate the tetratogenic effects seen in rat studies, it may cause anoxia in the fetus. If administered during labor, it may delay the second stage because of the relaxation of uterine muscles. When epinephrine is given parenterally to maintain maternal blood pressure during delivery, it can cause acceleration of the fetal heart rate. It is contraindicated if the maternal blood pressure is greater than 130/80.

*Intervention.* Avoid overdosage, particularly inadvertent intravenous administration of the usual SC dosages, which may cause extreme hypertension. Cerebrovascular hemorrhage may result, particularly in the elderly client. Read labels very carefully; epinephrine ophthalmic, nasal, and topical solutions must not be injected.

Store medication in tight, light-resistant container at a temperature between 15° and 30° C (59° and 86° F). Do not use if solution is pink or brown in color or contains a precipitate. This color change is caused by oxidation of the drug; multiple-use vials in which air is injected to withdraw the solution are more prone to this change.

*Parenteral administration.* Carefully recheck solution strength, dosage, expiration date, and route of administration of drug. Avoid medication errors by not confusing the 1:100 solution with the 1:1000 solution. Overdosage has resulted in fatalities.

Use a small syringe (tuberculin syringe) to assure accuracy in measurement of parenteral injection. Aspirate syringe before parenteral injection (subcutaneous and intramuscular) to prevent intravenous injection that can result in sudden hypertension.

Intraarterial injection is contraindicated because the marked vasoconstriction that results may cause gangrene. Injection sites need to be rotated because repeated local injections may result in necrosis secondary to the vasoconstricting effects of the drug. Massage of the injection site will promote absorption of the drug. For the same reasons, epinephrine should not be administered intramuscularly into the buttocks. The presence of the anaerobic organism, *Clostridium welchii,* and reduced oxygen tension within the tissues as a result of the administration of epinephrine creates the potential for gas gangrene.

The use of sterile epinephrine in a suspension allows for the frequency of parenteral injection to be decreased to up to 10 hours; however, when administering the suspension, the solution should be injected promptly after it is withdrawn from the vial to prevent the solution from settling. 1:1000 solution must be diluted with 10-ml sodium chloride injection before intravenous or intracardiac administration.

In emergency situations, epinephrine may be administered intracardially, in which case it should be done by team members with experience in this technique. If the patient is intubated, the drug can be injected directly into the bronchial tree via the endotracheal tube at the same dosage as for intravenous administration.

*Inhalation.*   Epinephrine and other beta adrenergic agents may be used interchangeably; however, allow 4 hours between doses when changing from one to another. Do not administer concurrently.

*Nasal administration.*   To prevent drug from entering the throat, instill nose drops with head low in lateral position. Rinse nose dropper with hot water to prevent contamination of medication.

*Ophthalmic administration.*   Administer drug at bedtime or following a miotic to minimize discomfort, blurred vision, and sensitivity to light caused by mydriasis.

**Education.**   Caution the client against the repeated or prolonged use of epinephrine, which can cause *tolerance* or "epinephrine fastness." If the drug is withheld 12 hours to several days, its effectiveness usually returns.

*Emergency auto-injection.*   Remind the client that the medication requires a physician's prescription. Instruct client to consult physician or pharmacist before taking any over-the-counter drug concurrently with epinephrine.

Review with client in detail the operation of the EpiPen auto-injector. The package insert *must* be read carefully. Remind the client that the auto-injector contains the drug that the client injects intramuscularly in the anteriolateral region of the thigh or the deltoid part of the arm. Instruct client *not* to inject drug into buttock because of the increased risk of infection owing to fecal contaminants on the skin.

Emphasize importance of keeping the drug on hand in case of emergency and that the drug should be stored in a dark, cool place to prevent deterioration. Supplies should also be rotated so that the client uses the oldest supplies first. Caution client to check the auto-injector to make sure the solution is neither brown in color nor contains a precipitate. If so, the drug must be discarded.

*Inhalation.*   Teach the client how to use the metered dose nebulizer. (See box at right.)

Instruct client to take pulse rate before inhalation therapy. Allow 2 minutes between doses, and do not administer more frequently than required to relieve symptoms. Excessive repeated use may cause paradoxical bronchospasm.

To prevent drug tolerance, caution the client not to overuse the drug. Instruct the client to notify the physician if the symptoms are not relieved with the usual dosage, as this may be an indication of worsening of the bronchospasm requiring reassessment of therapy. The client may expect that the symptoms should be relieved in 20 minutes.

Instruct client to rinse mouth with water to prevent mucosal absorption of drug.

Teach client with history of allergic reaction or bronchial asthma how to self-inject epinephrine subcutaneously in case of emergency.

---

### METERED DOSE BRONCHODILATOR INHALATION TECHNIQUE

It is important that the client be instructed in the correct use of a metered dose nebulizer before it is needed to relieve an asthma attack. If used incorrectly, the dose may be dispersed into the air or even swallowed. Since only 10% of an inhaled dose reaches the lungs under the best of conditions, the ability to use the metered dose nebulizer appropriately is essential for the client.

A placebo nebulizer should be used for demonstration. This will enable the client to repeat the demonstration a number of times until the nebulizer can be easily and correctly used.

1. Shake the container for 2 to 5 seconds.
2. Hold the nebulizer with the drug container upside down.
3. Place the mouthpiece in the mouth, closing lips tightly around it.
4. Exhale steadily and completely through nose.
5. Inhale slowly and deeply, and at the same time press the container down on the mouthpiece.
6. Hold breath for as long as possible before exhaling.
7. Wait several seconds.
8. Repeat steps 1 through 6 above.
9. If no relief is achieved after 5 minutes and condition worsens, contact physician.

Advise client that rinsing the mouth after using the nebulizer prevents systemic absorption and minimizes dryness of the mouth. The mouthpiece should be rinsed at least once daily to avoid clogging. Stress the importance of keeping the equipment clean to prevent infection. If using a refillable nebulizer, do not place more than a day's supply of drug in nebulizer. Change solution daily.

Clients with asthma benefit greatly from the use of sympathomimetic inhalers; however, they should be discouraged from using over-the-counter inhalers because of the nonselective beta-agonist drug effect of the epinephrine base. The nurse needs to recognize the possibility of misuse and the consequences of abuse in order to successfully help the client with inhalant drug therapy.

---

*Nasal administration.*   Inform client that this route of application may produce a stinging sensation. Forewarn client that rebound congestion may occur with prolonged use, which may cause rhinitis. Nose drops should not be used for more than 3 to 5 days.

*Ophthalmic administration.*   Alert client that lightheadedness, increased perspiration and heart rate, trembling, and pallor are signs of systemic absorption. These symptoms may be avoided by limiting the amount of medication that enters the systemic circulation by proper instillation of eyedrops. Instruct the client to create a pocket for the solution by gently pinching the skin below the lower eyelid and pulling it away from the eye. Place a drop of the solution in the pocket and hold it open for 1 or 2 seconds to allow the solution to settle. Have the client look down and then gently release the lower eyelid. Press just under the inner corner of the eye for 1 minute. This obstructs the nasolacrimal duct and minimizes the absorption of the drug into the bloodstream.

Instruct client to discontinue drug and notify physician if signs of allergy develop (itching, edema of lids, discharge from lids).

Advise client that after initial administration, stinging of the eyes and headache may occur but, with continued drug use, these symptoms disappear. Notify physician if these symptoms, which may be controlled by lower dosage, persist. Recommend to the client that intraocular pressure determinations should be scheduled periodically.

The client should be alerted that after long-term use of epinephrine, brownish pigment deposits caused by oxidation of the drug may occur in the eyelids and conjunctiva or as large dark casts in the lacrimal sac or nasolacrimal duct. These may be mistaken as foreign objects in the eye. The casts may be removed by irrigation. Instruct client who wears soft contact lenses to consult with physician regarding concurrent use of ophthalmic epinephrine instillations because the medication may discolor lens.

**Evaluation.** Since epinephrine increases blood glucose levels, observe individuals with diabetes for loss of diabetic control. During intravenous administration, monitor blood pressure, observe electrocardiogram (ECG) results, and monitor pulse continuously until stabilized.

Because of the CNS effects of dizziness or lightheadedness, nervousness or restlessness, trembling, and insomnia, the client should be evaluated for the nursing diagnoses of altered comfort, sleep pattern disturbance, anxiety, altered thought processes, and high risk for injury. The cardiovascular effects, headache, hypertension, palpitations, tachycardia, flushing of the face, may indicate altered cardiac output and/or altered comfort for the client. There also may be altered comfort because of the drug's gastrointestinal, respiratory, and local effects.

### isoproterenol hydrochloride (Isuprel, Norisodrine)
### isoproterenol sulfate (Medihaler-Iso)

Isoproterenol, a synthetic catecholamine, is a nonselective beta adrenergic drug. This means that it stimulates beta$_1$ and beta$_2$ adrenergic receptors. The beta$_1$ receptor activity produces an increase in force of myocardial contraction and heart rate. The beta$_2$ receptor response of the smooth muscle of the bronchi, skeletal muscle, gastrointestinal tract, and blood vessels of the splanchnic bed causes a relaxation of these organs. More important, isoproterenol can greatly relax the smaller bronchi and may even dilate the trachea and main bronchi. This drug also stimulates insulin secretion and releases free fatty acid.

Hemodynamically, the beta$_1$ activity of the heart increases cardiac output and venous return to the heart. Moreover, peripheral vascular resistance is reduced and, in normal individuals, causes a significant drop in blood pressure with excessive dosage (see Table 21-2).

Isoproterenol is used as cardiac stimulant in cardiac arrest, Adams-Stokes syndrome, atrioventricular (AV) block, and carotid sinus hypersensitivity. It also may be used as adjunct therapy in treatment of cardiogenic shock, and it relieves bronchospasm associated with bronchial asthma, pulmonary emphysema, and bronchitis.

The drug is readily absorbed when given parenterally or as an aerosol. Absorption of sublingual isoproterenol is erratic and unreliable. It is rapidly absorbed following inhalation or parenteral administration and its duration of action is usually up to 2 hours after oral inhalation for bronchodilator effect. Duration of action is less than 1 hour after IV administration and up to 2 hours after subcutaneous or sublingual administration. Isoproterenol is metabolized in the gastrointestinal tract, liver, and lungs and is excreted in the urine. For side effects/adverse reactions, see Table 21-3.

With the exception of the local-parenteral anesthetic interactions, the drug interactions with isoproterenol are similar to those listed under epinephrine. In addition, avoid concurrent administration of epinephrine and isoproterenol due to the possibility of increased additive effects and cardiotoxicity. When the action of one medication is considered complete (usually 4 hours), the second one may be implemented.

### Dosage and administration

*Cardiac standstill and dysrhythmias.* Administer to adults IV, 0.02-0.06 mg initially, then 0.01-0.2 mg when necessary. Dosage via IV infusion is 5 $\mu$g/min (1.25 ml) of a diluted solution containing 2 mg in 500 ml of dextrose 5% in water. When administering IM, 0.2 mg initially, then 0.02-1 mg when necessary. Initial dosage SC is 0.2 mg followed by 0.15-0.2 mg as needed. Dosage in children has not been determined and is individualized by physician.

*Intracardiac.* Give adults 0.02 mg, and repeat as needed.

*Bronchodilator.* Sublingual dose for adults is 10-15 mg 3 to 4 times/day; for children it is 5-10 mg 3 times a day.

*Inhaler.* When administering isoproterenol hydrochloride inhalation aerosal/isoproterenol inhalation solution to adults, follow individual manufacturer's instructions carefully. Generally, a metered-dose nebulizer (120 or 131 $\mu$g/inhalation)—1 inhalation is administered, which may be repeated in 1 to 5 min if necessary, 4 to 6 times daily. In bronchospasm of chronic obstructive pulmonary disease (COPD), the second dose should be given 3-4 hr after the initial dose. When treating acute asthma in children, give oral inhalation of a 0.5% nebulized solution (5 to 15 deep inhalations). If necessary, repeat in 5-10 min. Dosage may be repeated up to 5 times daily.

▷ **Nursing Management:**
**Isoproterenol Therapy**

*Assessment.* Use with great caution in patients with cardiovascular disorders such as coronary insufficiency and hypertension, hyperthyroidism, pheochromocytoma, diabetes, or sensitivity to sympathomimetic amines. Excessive use may decrease effectiveness.

*Intervention.* Read labels carefully; solution for oral inhalation must not be administered intravenously.

*Intravenous administration.* Before therapy, hypovolemia should be corrected if possible. Plan nursing care so that the client is constantly attended while receiving the drug. Never leave the client unattended during the infusion.

Use a two-bottle setup so that an intravenous infusion can be kept running if this drug is discontinued. Use an infusion pump to precisely regulate infusion rate.

Record baseline blood pressure and pulse before starting therapy. During infusion, check blood pressure every 2 minutes until stabilized, then every 5 minutes during drug administration. Adjust the flow rate to maintain blood pressure, usually at systolic 80 to 100 mm Hg or in hypertensive clients, 30 to 40 mm Hg below preexisting blood pressure. Monitor ECG pattern and central venous pressure, as well as urine volume and blood gases for clients in shock. Follow physician's guidelines for titrating flow in relation to heart rate, central venous pressure, blood pressure, ECG changes, and volume of urine flow. If precordial pain occurs, stop drug.

If heart rate exceeds 110 beats/minute, physician usually will prescribe a slower infusion rate or temporarily discontinue drug. With doses that cause a heart rate of 130 beats/minute, anticipate the development of ventricular dysrhythmias. Intravenous isoproterenol frequently causes dysrhythmias in clients with heart disease. Have oxygen and other resuscitative equipment available. Monitor respiratory pattern and lung sounds during administration.

Barbiturates may be used for adjunct sedative therapy to manage the side effect of CNS stimulation.

*Education*

*Oral/sublingual administration.* Instruct patient to allow sublingual tablet to dissolve under tongue without swallowing saliva until tablet is completely dissolved. Swallowing drug with saliva causes epigastric pain. Instruct patient to rinse mouth thoroughly with water between sublingual doses. Prolonged use can cause tooth decay. Instruct patient to swallow sustained-release tablets whole and not chew.

*Oral inhalation.* Instruct the client to use oral inhalation correctly. (See box on p. 407.) The instructions for the metered powder nebulizer are the same as for metered dose nebulizer except that deep inhalation is not necessary.

The client should allow 1 to 5 minutes between first and second inhalations. Advise the client that there should be no more than six inhalations in an hour in any 24-hour period. If the client needs more than three aerosol treatments within a 24-hour period, the physician should be contacted.

If the client has 3 to 5 treatments in a 6- to 12-hour period with minimal or no relief, the therapeutic regimen needs to include other medications in addition to the aerosol.

Advise patient that drug may turn sputum and saliva pink. Warn patient of overuse since tolerance can develop and sudden deaths have been reported. Instruct patient to notify physician if prescribed doses are not producing desired relief or if there are adverse effects.

Store drug in tight light-resistant container. Do not use if precipitate or discoloration is present (solutions become pink or brownish pink on exposure to light, air, heat, or on contact with metal or alkali).

*Evaluation.* Assess the effectiveness of the sublingual dosage forms carefully because absorption of the drug may be erratic and unpredictable. Discontinue medication if severe paradoxical airway resistance develops; institute alternative therapy.

Isoproterenol may increase blood glucose levels. Observe individuals with diabetes for loss of diabetic control. Dosage of insulin or hypoglycemic agents may need to be increased. Evaluate the client's extremities for parathesias, color changes, and coldness. The client receiving isoproterenol may also experience altered comfort related to dryness of the mouth.

## norepinephrine bitartrate (Levophed Bitartrate)

Norepinephrine is a direct-acting sympathomimetic amine that is identical to the body catecholamine synthesized in the postganglionic nerve ending of the sympathetic nervous system. This agent has a high affinity for the alpha receptors. Since the blood vessels of the skin and mucous membrane contain only alpha receptors, norepinephrine produces a powerful constriction in these tissues. In addition, the blood vessels (both arteriolar and venous beds) in the visceral organs, including the kidneys, contain predominantly alpha receptors. Consequently, norepinephrine causes vasoconstriction and a reduced blood flow through the kidneys and other visceral organs. This agent also activates beta$_1$ receptors in the heart and exerts an increase in the force of myocardial contraction, resulting in an increase in cardiac output. The main therapeutic effect results from peripheral arteriolar vasoconstriction in all vascular beds. Both systolic and diastolic pressures are elevated, causing an increase in mean arterial pressure. Of importance during shock is constriction of the venous capacitance vessels, which reduces splanchnic and renal blood flow. This is brought about by severe restriction of tissue perfusion in these regions. In persistent hypotension after blood volume deficit has been corrected, norepinephrine helps to raise the blood pressure to an optimal level and establishes a more adequate circulation (see Table 21-2).

Norepinephrine is selectively employed for restoring blood pressure in certain acute hypotensive states such as sympathectomy, pheochromocytomectomy, myocardial infarction, and blood transfusion reaction. When this drug is used to treat hypotension associated with an acute myocardial infarction, an increase in cardiac output and oxygen demand plus the possibility of inducing dysrhythmias may offset the benefits of using the drug to increase blood pressure. This would have to be carefully considered when selecting norepinephrine for use in such conditions.

Norepinephrine is also used as adjunct therapy in cardiac arrest and profound hypotension. Since the advent of dopamine, the use of norepinephrine to treat shock has declined significantly. It is usually prescribed for patients whose shock produces severe hypotension and vasodilation of the peripheral blood vessels.

Oral norepinephrine is destroyed in the gastrointestinal tract, whereas subcutaneous norepinephrine is poorly absorbed. Therefore norepinephrine is only administered by intravenous infusion. Onset of action is immediate or rapid by intravenous infusion and distribution mainly concentrates in sympathetic tissues. The drug is metabolized in the liver, other tissues, and by reuptake into the sympathetic nerves. Its duration of action is approximately 1 to 2 minutes after an intravenous infusion is discontinued. The drug is excreted in the kidneys. For information on side effects/adverse reactions, see Table 21-3.

Norepinephrine's drug interactions with anesthetics, beta-adrenergic blocking agents, digitalis glycosides, tricyclic and MAO inhibitor antidepressants, maprotiline, cocaine, ergotamine, and ergoloid mesylates are the same as with epinephrine. In addition, when given concurrently with doxapram, an increase in central nervous system stimulation and blood pressure may occur. Monitor closely because dosage adjustments may be required. Also, when given

concurrently with methyldopa, the hypotensive effect of methyldopa is decreased while the hypertensive action of norepinephrine may be enhanced. If norepinephrine is given to individuals receiving methyldopa, initiate with very small doses with close monitoring.

The nurse should be aware that norepinephrine solutions are incompatible with iron salts, alkalies (sodium bicarbonate), and oxidizing agents. Also the use of sodium chloride solution alone is not recommended. If the solution turns brown or has a precipitate in it, do not use it.

When using norepinephrine in the treatment of hypotension, give adults IV infusion, initially 8 to 12 μg/min, adjusting dosage as necessary to raise and maintain the desired pressure. Maintenance dose is 2 to 4 μg/min, titrated according to patient's needs. When using this drug to treat children for acute hypotension, give by intravenous infusion at 2 μg/min or 2 mg/m²/min; adjust dosage as necessary to raise and maintain the desired pressure. In treating children for severe hypotension of cardiac arrest, give by intravenous infusion, initially 0.1 μg/kg/min; adjust dosage as necessary to raise and maintain blood pressure.

▷ **Nursing Management: Norepinephrine Therapy**

*Assessment.* Do not use in patients who are in hypovolemic states except as an emergency measure to maintain cerebral and coronary artery blood flow. Do not give to patients with mesenteric or peripheral vascular thrombosis because of risk of increasing ischemia and extending the thrombosis. Because of its vasoconstricting effects, norepinephrine should be used with caution for clients with occlusive vascular diseases, such as Buerger's disease or arteriosclerosis. Use with extreme caution in patients receiving monoamine oxidase inhibitors and tricyclic antidepressants because prolonged hypotension may result. Do not give during general anesthesia when halogenated hydrocarbons (halothane) are administered. It is also contraindicated in profound hypoxia or hypercapnia and pregnancy. Determine if the client is intolerant of sulfites as the injection dosage form of norepinephrine contains sodium bisulfite as a preservative. (See boxed material.)

*Intervention.* Be aware of the importance of maintaining adequate blood volume before administering norepinephrine. Blood should be administered separately. This is to prevent tissue ischemia that can result from the vasoconstrictive effect of the drug. Administer norepinephrine only intravenously; its vasoconstrictor effect prohibits intramuscular or subcutaneous administration. Anticipate that infusion will be administered through a plastic catheter deep into a large vein to minimize risk of extravasation. The veins of the leg are not recommended because of poor circulation, which can result in occlusive vascular disease.

During infusion, adjust dosage according to physician's guidelines. This includes the client's response, with partic-

---

### SULFITE SENSITIVITY

Sulfite is contained in the commercially available formulations of:
  amrinone
  dopamine
  meteraminol
  methoxamine
  norepinephrine
  phenylephrine
They should not be administered to individuals with a known sensitivity to sulfite agents (sulfur dioxide, potassium or sodium bisulfite, potassium or sodium metasulfite, sodium sulfite).
  Symptoms of sulfite sensitivity include:
  *Skin:* clamminess, flushed, pruritis, urticaria, cyanosis
  *Respiratory:* bronchospasm, shortness of breath, wheezing, laryngeal edema, respiratory arrest
  *Cardiovascular:* hypotension, syncope
  *CNS:* severe dizziness, loss of consciousness
  *Other:* anaphylaxis, death

ular attention to urinary output, respiration, blood pressure, pulse, and observation of extremities for color and temperature (for peripheral ischemia). These parameters must be accurately recorded to attain precise titration of drug. An intravenous pump flow regulator should be used for accuracy of the flow rate in drops per minute.

It is advised that the blood pressure be taken every 2 to 3 minutes during norepinephrine administration until the desired blood pressure is reached; then it should be measured every 5 minutes until the drug is discontinued. If the client were previously hypotensive, the desired systolic blood pressure range is 80-100 mm Hg; however, for those previously hypertensive, it should be maintained at 30-40 mm Hg below their preexisting systolic values.

If extravasation occurs, the area should be quickly infiltrated with 5 to 10 mg of phentolamine in 10 to 15 ml of sodium chloride with a fine-gauge needle to dilate blood vessels. Have phentolamine ready. To prevent sloughing of the skin secondary to extravasation, 5 to 10 mg of phentolamine may be added to every liter of norepinephrine solution. Norepinephrine should be diluted with 5% dextrose in distilled water or 5% dextrose in sodium chloride solution because the dextrose prevents a significant loss of potency by oxidation. Anticipate the addition of heparin to infusion solution to prevent thrombosis of infused vein in clients with severe hypotension following myocardial infarction.

Store medication by protecting it from light. The solution deteriorates after 24 hours; discard it after that time. Do not use solution if it is discolored or if precipitate is present.

**Evaluation.** Never leave client unattended during infusion. Inspect the infusion site for extravasation every 10 to 15 minutes. If extravasation occurs, notify the physician immediately. Observe client for blanching along route of infused vein and for cold, hard swelling around injection site. Have available phentolamine, which may be used at site of extravasation to dilate blood vessels.

Monitor by ECG; reduce or discontinue medication if cardiac dysrhythmia occurs.

Observe client for mentation (cerebral circulation), temperature of extremities, and color of earlobes, lips, and nail beds. Also monitor for paresthesias.

Monitor intake and output. After prolonged use of the drug a decrease in urinary output may indicate necrosis of the kidney.

Discontinue therapy gradually by slowing infusion rate, and continue to monitor patient and vital signs to ensure circulatory adequacy.

## Drugs Used for Circulatory Shock

In any instance of shock, treatment must be directed to the cause. A main concern is the need to improve circulation so that enough oxygen is available for tissue perfusion. Hypoxia that denotes impaired tissue perfusion may result from inadequate pumping action of the heart, decreased blood volume, decreased peripheral resistance of arterial vessels, or increased size of the venous bed.

During circulatory shock the autonomic nervous system plays an essential compensatory role in an attempt to restore normal circulation. Therefore many sympathomimetic drugs are used to manage this condition. Although there are other agents, the five drugs that are widely used for circulatory shock are dopamine, epinephrine, and norepinephrine, which are all vasopressors, and dobutamine and isoproterenol, which possess cardiogenic activity. Amrinone, which has positive inotropic and vasodilator effects, can also be used for clients with congestive heart failure who are not responsive to standard therapy. Milrinone, an analogue of amrinone, is under clinical investigation as possibly having fewer side effects than amrinone, as well as having both intravenous and oral administration activity. These are preliminary reports that will require extensive clinical trials and evaluation before the drug is marketed.

Vasopressors have strong alpha activity, and dopamine produces less vasoconstriction than epinephrine and norepinephrine. Dobutamine and isoproterenol are important for improving cardiac output because of their capability to stimulate beta$_1$ receptors in the heart. Most of the agents are nonselective beta acting drugs, but norepinephrine lacks beta$_2$ activity and amrinone does not appear to have beta agonist effects. Also, with the exception of isoproterenol and amrinone, all of them stimulate alpha receptors. (See drug monographs for epinephrine, norepinephrine, and isoproterenol.)

### amrinone (Inocor)

The mechanism of action has not been fully identified. It increases force and velocity of myocardial tissues, resulting in a positive inotropic effect. Experiments indicate that amrinone inhibits cyclic adenosine monophosphate (cAMP) phosphodiesterase activity, which in turn increases cellular cAMP concentration. The exact role of amrinone in producing the inotropic activity is not fully known. Amrinone appears to produce a direct relaxant effect on the vascular smooth muscle, resulting in vasodilation. It is used to treat congestive heart failure in individuals who do not respond to standard therapies, such as digitalis glycosides, diuretics, and vasodilators.

Administered intravenously, time to peak action is within 10 minutes. Duration of effect is dose-related. If 0.75 mg/kg is administered, duration of action is approximately 30 minutes. If 3 mg/kg is administered, duration is approximately 120 minutes. Half-life, by intravenous infusion, is nearly 5.8 hours; by intravenous injection, it is approximately 3.6 hours. The drug is metabolized in the liver and excreted via the kidneys primarily and some in the feces. For side effects/adverse reactions, see Table 21-5. Inotropic effects are additive to those of digitalis.

In administering amrinone to adults, give 0.75 mg/kg IV slowly over 2 to 3 minutes; if necessary, repeat in 30 min-

**TABLE 21-5**   Side effects/adverse reactions of cardiotonic and cardiac stimulant drugs

| Drug | Side effects* | Adverse reactions† |
|---|---|---|
| amrinone (Inocor) | Less frequent: Fever, nausea, vomiting, abdominal pain, decrease in taste perception | Less frequent: Dizziness (hypotension), dysrhythmias<br>Rare: Local pain at site of injection, angina or chest pain, unusual bruising or bleeding episodes (the thrombocytopenia that usually occurs after high dosages or chronic therapy is not usually symptomatic), jaundice |
| dobutamine (Dobutrex) | Less frequent: Nausea, headaches | Less frequent: Angina or chest pain, respiratory distress (shortness of breath), tachycardia, palpitation, increased heart rate and blood pressure, premature ventricular beats |
| dopamine HCl (Intropin) | More frequent: Headaches, nausea or vomiting<br>Less frequent: Increased anxiety, nervousness, or restlessness | More frequent: Angina or chest pain, respiratory difficulties, decreased blood pressure, irregular or ecotopic heart beats (usually with high doses), tachycardia, palpitations<br>Less frequent: Hypertension; decreased heart rate (unusually slow). Administration of chronic high dosages, or low doses in patients with peripheral vascular disease, may result in peripheral vasoconstriction, which may result in ischemia, necrosis, and gangrene; monitor for skin color changes in hands or feet, very cold hands or feet, complaints of numbness, tingling or pain in fingers or toes.<br>In sulfite-containing preparations, allergic reactions have been reported: flushing of skin; rash; hives; pruritus; edema of face, lips, or eyelids; respiratory difficulties; faintness. |

*If side effects continue, increase, or disturb the client, inform the physician.
†If adverse reactions occur, the physician should be contacted because medical intervention may be necessary.

utes. For maintenance by intravenous infusion, administer 5 to 10 μg/kg/minute, individualize dose according to clinical response. Maximum dosage is 10 mg/kg/day, but in several reports, dosages up to 18 mg/kg/day were given for short time periods. Dosage for children has not been established.

▷ **Nursing Management:
Amrinone Therapy**

**Assessment.** The nurse should ascertain the status of the client's sensitivity to sulfites since amrinone lactate injection contains sodium metabisulfite to which the client may be intolerant. Amrinone is not to be used with clients with severe aortic or pulmonic valvular disease. It is to be used with caution in clients with impaired hepatic or renal function; a dosage adjustment may be required because the elimination of the drug will be impaired. Amrinone may aggravate outflow obstruction in hypertrophic subaortic stenosis; use with caution.

**Intervention.** Examine the solution for color changes and/or precipitation. Amrinone is incompatible with dextrose because it loses its potency. Do not mix with furosemide or inject it into the same tubing because it precipitates.

For direct intravenous administration, it may be administered undiluted. Mix with sodium chloride solutions for continuous intravenous infusion. Use prepared solution within 24 hours. Administer slowly intravenous, over 2 to 3 minutes, to minimize pain and burning at the injection site. Avoid extravasation. Change infusion sites every 48 hours.

**Education.** Tell the client to move slowly from a sitting or lying position to a more upright position because of the drug's hypotensive effects.

**Evaluation.** Blood pressure and pulse should be monitored to assess hypotensive and dysrhythmic effects of the drug. The infusion rate should be slowed or stopped if the client becomes hypotensive. The appropriate range for blood pressure readings should be prescribed by the physician. In addition, assess cardiac index and pulmonary wedge pressure if warranted. Assess central venous pressure, urine output, body weight, and the status of any orthopnea, dyspnea, and fatigue to evaluate the drug's effectiveness and the client's progress.

Because of the resolution of the client's congestive heart failure, the risk for the nursing diagnoses of altered cardiac output, altered fluid volume, altered tissue perfusion, and altered urinary elimination pattern exists. The client is also at risk for altered cardiac output due to dysrhythmias and altered tissue perfusion due to hypotension while receiving amrinone.

Assess platelet counts before and frequently during therapy. Observe for unusual bleeding and bruising, which are clinical signs of thrombocytopenia. The drug may be discontinued if the platelet count falls below 150,000/mm.

Because physiologic injury related to hepatotoxicity is a possibility, liver function studies are usually done and the client is monitored for clinical signs of jaundice. These signs include yellowish skin or sclera, dark urine, and pruritis.

Report nausea and vomiting to the physician. It may be severe enough to require that the drug be discontinued.

If the drug is monitored through plasma concentrations, the therapeutic range is 0.5 to 7 $\mu$g/ml, but optimal level is about 3 $\mu$g/ml. Monitor for sulfite sensitivity (see box on p. 410). Monitor, too, for tachyphylaxis to the effects of amrinone, a common occurrence, usually taking place within the first 72 hours of therapy.

## dobutamine hydrochloride (Dobutrex)

Dobutamine is a synthetic catecholamine that acts directly on the heart muscle to increase the force of myocardial contraction. This response is attributed to the direct stimulation of the beta$_1$ adrenergic receptors of the heart. At the same time dobutamine produces comparatively little increase in heart rate or peripheral vascular resistance. By enhancing stroke volume, this agent is an effective positive inotropic drug. Because of its minimal influence on heart rate and blood pressure (both major determinants of myocardial oxygen demand), it is valuable for use in individuals with low cardiac output syndrome. In contrast to dopamine, which also is capable of increasing myocardial contractility, dobutamine does not produce renal vasodilation. In a comparative study of dobutamine and dopamine, the improvement in peripheral blood flow, urine flow, and sodium excretion noted with the use of dobutamine was probably caused by the elevation in cardiac output.

Dobutamine is administered intravenously in the *short-term* management of clients requiring inotropic support, as in congestive heart failure or following cardiac surgery. It is used to strengthen the decompensated heart in individuals with the low cardiac output syndrome. Its beneficial effects are a progressive increase in cardiac output and a decrease in pulmonary capillary wedge pressure, thereby improving ventricular contraction.

In a surgical procedure such as cardiopulmonary bypass, the concomitant use of sodium nitroprusside and dobutamine is often beneficial. It results in a higher cardiac output and a lower pulmonary capillary wedge pressure than when either drug is used alone. Because of the vasodilating effect of nitroprusside, the decrease in peripheral resistance lessens the workload on the heart. Absorption is via intravenous infusion. Onset of action occurs within 1 to 2 minutes. The plasma half life is 2 minutes. Dobutamine is rapidly metabolized by the liver and is excreted in the urine.

For side effects/adverse reactions, see Table 21-5. While no significant drug interactions are listed, the nurse should be aware that beta adrenergic blockers may cancel the beta$_1$ adrenergic effects of dobutamine; anesthetics such as cyclopropane and halothane may increase the risk for ventricular arrhythmias; reserpine or rauwolfia alkaloids may increase the duration of action of dobutamine and guanadrel or guanethidine's hypotensive effects may be decreased, which can result in hypertension and cardiac arrhythmias. Monitor for possible drug interactions whenever concurrent drug therapy is administered.

Adult dosage is by intravenous infusion, 2.5 to 15 $\mu$g/kg/minute. For children, dosage has not been determined.

## ▷ Nursing Management: Dobutamine Therapy

***Assessment.*** Use cautiously in clients with tachycardia and increased blood pressure because the drug may intensify both of these conditions. Safety of use of this drug is not established when used after myocardial infarction. There is concern that a drug which increases the force of myocardial contraction and heart rate may intensify the ischemia by increasing the size of the infarction. Note that dobutamine is contraindicated in idiopathic hypertrophic subaortic stenosis.

If the client is hypovolemic, this state should be corrected before dobutamine therapy is begun. Adequate fluid balance is required for the course of therapy.

***Intervention.*** Administer using an infusion pump or other device to control the rate of flow. Adjust dosage based on the clinical response of the client as for norepinephrine and isoproterenol. (See nursing management for intravenous administration of isoproterenol.) The concentration of dobutamine solution for administration should not exceed 5 mg of dobutamine per milliliter. Intravenous solution remains stable for 24 hours. A color change during this period indicates some oxidation, but there is no loss of potency during the first 24 hours.

Dobutamine is incompatible with alkaline solutions and should not be mixed with products such as 5% sodium bicarbonate injection. Check for drug incompatibilities when considering administration through an intravenous line with other drugs.

***Evaluation.*** During therapy, the electrocardiogram and blood pressure should be continuously monitored to ascertain any alteration in cardiac output. If possible, the pulmonary capillary wedge pressure and cardiac output also should be monitored to ensure safe infusion of the drug. If the client responds by an increase in the heart rate (30 beats/minute or more) and an increase in systolic blood pressure (50 mm Hg or greater) during the course of treatment, a reduction of dosage usually reverses these adverse effects because the drug is rapidly metabolized.

Monitor intake and output. Increased urine output indicates improved cardiac output and urinary perfusion. NOTE: Clients with atrial fibrillation and rapid ventricular response should be treated with a digitalis preparation before dobutamine therapy.

The client may also undergo an alteration in comfort related to the drug's tendency to cause nausea, headache, and cardiovascular effects such as angina, palpitation, and dysrhythmias.

Continue to observe client carefully after drug therapy is discontinued. The duration of action of the drug is brief, and the beneficial effects of the drug may be quickly terminated.

### dopamine hydrochloride (Intropin)

Dopamine is a catecholamine that occurs as an immediate precursor of norepinephrine (see Figure 19-6). It acts both directly and indirectly by releasing norepinephrine. It then stimulates dopaminergic receptors, beta$_1$ receptors, and, in high doses, alpha receptors. Actually, receptor activity depends on the amount of drug administered.

Unlike norepinephrine, in low doses (usually 0.5 to 2 $\mu$g/kg/minute) this drug is unique because it acts mainly on dopaminergic receptors to cause vasodilation of the renal and mesenteric arteries. Renal vasodilation increases renal blood flow with usually a greater amount of urine and sodium excretion. This prevents kidney failure secondary to shock.

In low to moderate doses (usually 2 to 10 $\mu$g/kg/minute), dopamine acts directly on the beta$_1$ receptors on the myocardium and indirectly by releasing norepinephrine from its neuronal storage sites in the sympathetic neuron. These actions increase myocardial contractility and stroke volume, thereby increasing cardiac output. Systolic blood pressure and pulse pressure may increase with either no effect or a slight elevation in diastolic blood pressure. Nevertheless, total peripheral resistance is usually unchanged. Coronary blood flow and myocardial oxygen consumption increase. However, heart rate increases only slightly at low doses.

In higher doses, alpha adrenergic receptors are stimulated, increasing peripheral resistance. Because of a rise in cardiac output, blood pressure increases. As a consequence, a high dose level may reduce urinary output, eliminating the benefit of vasodilation because the renal artery becomes constricted.

From the therapeutic standpoint, it is important to note that dopamine in low to moderate doses causes vasodilation in the renal, mesenteric, coronary, and cerebral blood vessels. These vasodilatory properties suggest that they may be attributed to the presence of specific dopamine receptors. Therefore, unlike norepinephrine, this agent helps alleviate inadequate tissue perfusion through the vital splanchnic organ systems. The combination of cardiac and circulatory effects has led to dopamine's successful use in the treatment of circulatory shock and refractory heart failure. Dopamine

is used to correct hemodynamic imbalances associated with shock syndrome caused by myocardial infarction, trauma, endotoxic septicemia, open heart surgery, renal failure, and chronic cardiac decompensation (as in congestive heart failure).

Administration must be by intravenous infusion. The drug has rapid onset of action (2 to 5 minutes) and a short duration of action (5 to 10 minutes). It is widely distributed in the body but does not cross the blood-brain barrier. Dopamine is rapidly metabolized by the liver, kidney, plasma, by monoamine oxidase and catechol-O-methyltransferase (COMT) to inactive substances. The drug is excreted in the urine.

For side effects/adverse reactions, see Table 21-5.

With the exception of local-parenteral anesthetics, significant drug interactions are similar to those for epinephrine. Also, if given concurrently with doxapram, blood pressure may increase. Coadministration with a monoamine oxidase (MAO) inhibitor may result in severe headaches, cardiac dysfunction, or a hypertensive and/or hyperpyretic crisis. Clients receiving an MAO inhibitor within several weeks of dopamine should have the initial dose of dopamine reduced to 10% of the usual adult dose. Monitor closely because dosage adjustments may be necessary.

For administration to adults, start intravenous infusion at 1 to 5 $\mu$g/kg/minute. Increase as necessary by 1 to 4 $\mu$g/kg/minute at 10 to 30 minute intervals. For chronic refractory CHF: administer IV infusion at 0.5 to 2 $\mu$g/kg/minute. If necessary, increase rate gradually until desired effects are achieved. In occlusive vascular disease administer, via IV infusion, at 1 $\mu$g/kg/minute; increase as necessary until desired effects are achieved. In seriously ill patients administer IV infusion at 5 $\mu$g/kg/minute, and increase in 5 to 10 $\mu$g/kg/minute increments (up to 20 to 50 $\mu$g/kg/minute) until desired response is achieved. Dosage in children has not been determined.

▷ **Nursing Management: Dopamine Therapy**

***Assessment.*** Use cautiously in individuals with occlusive vascular disease such as Buerger's or Raynaud's disease, atherosclerosis, diabetic endarteritis, and arterial embolism. Note that dopamine is contraindicated in pheochromocytoma, tachydysrhythmias, and ventricular fibrillation. See also nursing management for dobutamine.

***Intervention.*** Note that before dopamine therapy, hypovolemia should be corrected, if possible.

For precautions and care regarding extravasation, see norepinephrine nursing management. Have available a syringe with phentolamine mesylate (Regitine), 5 mg in 10 ml saline for use in extravasation (physician order).

Medication should be diluted immediately before administration. After dilution it is stable for 24 hours. Do not use the solution if it is darker than slightly yellow. However, dopamine is incompatible with sodium bicarbonate and other alkaline intravenous solutions; it will turn pink-violet.

Blood and additive medications should not be administered at the same time through the same infusion set as dopamine in dextrose injection because of possible incompatibilities.

Use an intravenous infusion device to regulate flow so that the dosage can be precisely titrated.

*Evaluation.* During infusion, adjust dosage according to physician's guidelines. Assess for altered cardiac output; this includes the client's response, with particular attention to urinary output, blood pressure, pulse, and observation of extremities for color and temperature (for peripheral ischemia). These parameters must be accurately recorded to attain precise titration of drug.

If a marked decrease in pulse pressure (disproportionate rise in diastolic pressure) is observed, decrease the infusion rate. Continue to observe patient for further evidence of vasoconstrictor activity. Decrease medication or stop temporarily and notify physician if the following occurs: reduced urine flow without hypotension, increasing tachycardia, dysrhythmia, and marked decrease in pulse pressure.

Monitor for sulfite sensitivity (see box on p. 410). When appropriate, decrease the dosage gradually to prevent severe hypotension.

Administering the dopamine and dextrose injection to a client with subclinical or overt diabetes may exacerbate the diabetic condition. The client may also be at risk of altered comfort because of dopamine's cardiac and gastrointestinal effects and its tendency to cause headaches.

## Indirect- and Dual-Acting Adrenergic Drugs

The direct-acting adrenergic drugs—the catecholamines—act directly on alpha and beta receptors to stimulate adrenergic response. The indirect-acting adrenergic drugs act indirectly on receptors by first triggering the release of the catecholamines norepinephrine and epinephrine from their storage sites; these neurotransmitters then activate the alpha and beta receptors. Finally, the *dual-acting* adrenergic drugs have both indirect and direct effects. These drugs have many and varied uses in medicine.

### ephedrine (Ephed II)

Ephedrine has both a direct and an indirect sympathomimetic action. It acts indirectly by stimulating release of norepinephrine from presynaptic nerve terminals. It acts directly on both alpha and beta receptors. Like epinephrine and norepinephrine, ephedrine has positive inotropic (myocardial stimulation) and chronotropic (increased heart rate) activities, but it is a less effective vasoconstrictor. However, it does raise the blood pressure and is used for this purpose during spinal anesthesia and to treat orthostatic hypotension.

Parenteral ephedrine has been used in hypotensive clients who do not respond to fluid replacement, position changes, and specific antidotes in the case of drug overdosage. Be aware though, if severe peripheral vasoconstriction is present; ephedrine may be ineffective and may actually worsen the situation. (See Table 21-6 for drug effects.)

Ephedrine is used to produce bronchodilation in the treatment of milder forms of bronchial asthma, since ephedrine is useful in preventing acute attacks. Epinephrine is preferable when attacks are acute because of its more rapid effect. It is also used to relieve nasal mucosal congestion. As an ingredient in nasal drops, jellies, and sprays, ephedrine relieves acute congestion of hay fever, sinusitis, head colds, and vasomotor rhinitis. Shrinkage of mucous membranes begins immediately and lasts for several hours. Vasodilation does not ordinarily follow vasoconstriction, as may occur after administration of epinephrine.

Ephedrine is also used as a pressor agent in hypotensive states during spinal anesthesia or after sympathectomy. Orally, ephedrine is also used to treat narcolepsy or mental depression.

Absorption of the drug is rapid after oral, IM, or SC administration. Onset of action for bronchodilation occurs within 15 to 60 minutes with oral dosage form; within 10 to 20 minutes with intramuscular dosage form. Duration of action is 3 to 5 hours following oral dosage form; 30 to 60 minutes following IM or SC injections of 25 to 50 mg doses. The pressor effects and cardiac responses following parenteral administration usually occur within 60 minutes. The drug is metabolized in the liver and excreted in the kidneys.

For side effects/adverse reactions, see Table 21-7.

*Significant drug interactions.* The following interactions may occur when ephedrine is given with the drugs listed below.

| Drug | Possible Effect and Management |
|---|---|
| adrenocorticoids, glucocorticoid, chronic therapy with corticotropin | Ephedrine may increase metabolism of glucocorticoids. Monitor closely because dosage adjustments may be necessary. |
| urinary alkalizers (antacids containing calcium and/or magnesium, citrates, sodium bicarbonate, and carbonic anhydrase inhibitors) | Alkalinization of the urine decreases excretion of ephedrine. An increase in duration of action and perhaps, ephedrine toxicity may occur. Monitor closely for increased nervousness, inability to sleep at night, and increased irritability or excitability because dosage adjustments may be necessary. |
| beta adrenergic blocking agents, including ophthalmic preparations | Therapeutic effects of both agents may decrease. An increase in alpha adrenergic activity may result in hypertension, increased bradycardia with the possibility of heart block. If possible, avoid concurrent administration of these drugs. If necessary, monitor closely because therapeutic interventions may be necessary. |
| cocaine, digitalis glycosides, and anesthetics, inhalation of hydrocarbons such as chloroform, enflurane, halothane and others | Increases risk of inducing serious cardiac dysrhythmias (such as severe ventricular dysrhythmias). If necessary to use concurrently, monitor closely with electrocardiographic readings because therapeutic interventions may be necessary. |
| ergotamine and ergoloid mesylates | Increased vasoconstriction, severe hypertension, and peripheral vascular ischemia and gangrene may occur. Avoid use of this combination. |

**TABLE 21-6**   Indirect- and dual-acting adrenergic drug effects

| Receptors, action sites | Ephedrine | Phenylephrine | Mephentermine | Metaraminol | Methoxamine |
|---|---|---|---|---|---|
| Trade names | Ephedrine Sulfate | Neo-Synephrine | Wyamine | Aramine Pressonex | Vasoxyl |
| Mode of action | | | | | |
| Alpha receptors | Stimulates | Stimulates | Stimulates | Stimulates | Stimulates |
| Beta receptors | Stimulates More prolonged but less intense action than epinephrine | N.S.* | | | |
| Effects | | | | | |
| Cardiovascular | | | | | |
| Myocardium | Variable | N.S. Bradycardia may occur reflexly | Increases contractility and rate May cause bradycardia | Some increase in contractility Bradycardia may occur | — Reflex bradycardia may occur |
| Pacemaker cells | N.S. | N.S. | N.S. | — | — |
| Coronary vessels | Dilates— increases blood flow | Dilates— increases blood flow | Dilates— increases blood flow | — | — |
| Blood pressure | Increases | Increases | Increases | Increases | Increases |
| Bronchi | Dilates | Dilates but less than epinephrine | Dilates but less than epinephrine | N.S. | |
| Cerebral effects | Stimulating action | N.S. | N.S. | — | — |
| Blood vessels Skeletal muscle | N.S. | —† | N.S. | N.S. | Decreases blood flow |
| Kidney | Constricts | Constricts | Constricts but less than ephedrine | Constricts— decreases blood flow | |
| Gastrointestinal tract | Decreases peristalsis | Decreases motility | Relaxes smooth muscle— inhibits | Some inhibition | Inhibits |
| Metabolic | Increases metabolic rate | Some increase in metabolic rate | N.S. | N.S. | N.S. |
| Remarks | Serious dysrhythmias may occur if used with digitalis  Can be given orally | | | Prolonged duration of action; cumulative effects may occur—give drug slowly May cause tissue sloughing— do not give subcutaneously | |
| Uses | Vasopressor Allergic states Nasal decongestant Enuresis Myasthenia gravis | Nasal decongestant Vasopressor Paroxysmal atrial tachycardia Mydriatic | Vasopressor | Vasopressor | Vasopressor Paroxysmal atrial tachycardia |

*N.S., Not significant.
†Effect is slight, nonexistent, or unknown in humans.

**TABLE 21-7**   Side effects/adverse reactions of indirect and dual-acting adrenergic drugs

| Drug | Side effects* | Adverse reactions† |
|---|---|---|
| ephedrine | Similar to epinephrine—ephedrine not available in aerosol dosage forms so coughing, respiratory difficulties from local irritation are not reported with ephedrine | Similar to epinephrine with addition of mood changes and hallucinations; pallor, pounding heart rate, and bradycardia have not been reported with ephedrine |
| phenylephrine (Neo-Synephrine Injection) | Less frequent: Anxiety, restlessness, dizziness, tremors, difficult breathing, pallor, increased weakness | Less frequent: Angina or chest pain, allergic reactions reported with preparations containing sulfites (see description under dopamine adverse reactions). <br> Overdosage: Persistent headache, decreased heart rate, hypertension, feeling of congestion in head, tachycardia, vomiting, tingling sensations in hands or feet |
| mephentermine sulfate (Wyamine sulfate) | Less frequent: Increased anxiety or nervousness, restlessness, tachycardia | Rare: Irregular heart rate, usually in patients with heart problems, convulsions <br> Overdosage: CNS adverse effects of visual hallucinations, paranoia, psychosis, severe headaches and hypertension also reported; vomiting. On discontinuance of drug, CNS adverse effects disappear. |
| metaraminol (Aramine) | None noted in USP-DI, but monitor for anxiety, restlessness, increased weakness, headaches, nausea and vomiting | Rapid administration may produce cardiac dysrhythmias, pulmonary edema, and cardiac arrest; follow dosage administration recommendations carefully. <br> Rare: Pallor and ischemia at injection site if extravasation occurs; abscess; pain, redness, and swelling at injection site. <br> Overdosage: Severe elevation of blood pressure; convulsions; dysrhythmias. <br> For preparations containing sulfites, allergic reactions may occur (see description under dopamine adverse effects). |
| methoxamine HCl (Vasoxyl) | Less frequent: Sweating and urinary urgency with high doses | Less frequent: Severe headaches, hypertension, persistent vomiting <br> High dosages: Bradycardia; for preparations containing sulfites, allergic reactions may occur (see description under dopamine adverse effects). |

*If side effects continue, increase, or disturb the client, the physician should be informed.
†If adverse reactions occur, the physician should be contacted because medical intervention may be necessary.

| Drug | Possible Effect and Management |
|---|---|
| maprotiline or tricyclic antidepressants | May decrease blood pressure response to ephedrine. Monitor closely or, if possible, another agent should be considered for administration. |
| monoamine oxidase (MAO) inhibitors | May result in a serious reaction because of the release of accumulated neurotransmitters into the synapse area, resulting in headaches, dysrhythmias, vomiting, severe hypertension and/or high fevers. Avoid concurrent administration of these drugs because ephedrine should not be given during or within 2 weeks after the administration of an MAO inhibitor. |

### Dosage and administration

*Bronchodilator, decongestant, or CNS stimulant.* Adults, oral (25-50 mg), SC, IM, or slow IV (12.5-25 mg) every 3 or 4 hours as needed. Children's dosage, oral, SC, or slow IV, is 3 mg/kg or 100 mg/m² a day divided into 4 to 6 doses.

*Vasopressor effects.* Adult dosage, IM or SC, is 25 to 50 mg. Repeat if necessary. Slow IV dose is 5 to 25 mg. This dose may be repeated if necessary in 5 to 10 minutes. Maximum dosage is 150 mg/24 hours.

*Intranasal.* For decongestion, several drops of a 0.5% to 1% solution may be applied topically and repeated every 4 hours if necessary.

▷**Nursing Management:**
**Ephedrine Therapy**

**Assessment.** Use with caution in clients with hypertension, hyperthyroidism, prostatic hypertrophy, and diabetes mellitus. Use ephedrine with caution in children under 6 years and with elderly clients.

Do not use in clients with severe hypertension, narrow-angle glaucoma, or history of hypersensitivity to sympathomimetic drugs or with those receiving digitalis or MAO inhibitor therapy.

**Intervention.** Administer only if the solution is clear; discard any unused portion. If possible, administer a few hours before bedtime and avoid administering at night to help prevent insomnia, altered sleep pattern.

**Education.** Advise client not to take over-the-counter drugs unless physician is consulted first. Caution client not to overuse drug because tolerance may develop. It may be necessary to withhold medication for several days to restore effectiveness. Instruct client to follow correct dosage and report any side effects or adverse reactions immediately to the physician. Also, advise client not to swallow nosedrops so as to avoid systemic effects.

**Evaluation.** During intravenous administration, closely monitor blood pressure repeatedly during first 5 minutes, then check every 3 to 5 minutes until it is stable. *Never leave client unattended during intravenous administration.*

If administered parenterally to maintain blood pressure in conjunction with low or spinal anesthesia during delivery, ephedrine may cause the fetal heart rate to accelerate and it should be discontinued when the maternal blood pressure reaches 130/80.

Monitor intake and output, and advise client to report any difficulty in urinating (particularly older male patients). Altered urinary output pattern may occur evidenced by sphincter spasm and retention caused by ephedrine's effects.

**phenylephrine systemic (Neo-Synephrine injection)**
**phenylephrine nasal (Neo-Synephrine, Alconefrin)**

Phenylephrine is also contained in many combination cough-cold, antihistamine and decongestant, and ophthalmic preparations. While phenylephrine is primarily a direct-acting agent, its main effects are stimulation of the alpha receptors, resulting in vasoconstriction, and an increase in both diastolic and systolic blood pressures. The drug has little effect on the beta$_1$ receptors of the heart. Its vasoconstricting action is more prolonged than that of epinephrine. For this reason it is often used to treat hypotension caused by myocardial infarction, orthostatic hypotension, and hypotension resulting from loss of vasomotor tone from spinal anesthesia. It is not effective in shock caused by loss of blood volume.

It is a synthetic adrenergic drug chemically related to epinephrine, norepinephrine, and ephedrine. Phenylephrine

hydrochloride is relatively nontoxic, exhibits fewer side effects than epinephrine, and has longer-lasting therapeutic effects. It has little or no effect on the central nervous system.

Phenylephrine has little inotropic or chronotropic effect. It does cause a reflex bradycardia as a result of its ability to elevate the blood pressure, which stimulates the baroreceptors and vagal activity. For this reason it had been used to treat paroxysmal supraventricular tachycardia, but today it has been replaced by more effective and safer drugs.

When applied topically to mucous membranes, it reduces swelling and congestion by constricting the small blood vessels. It is useful in the treatment of sinusitis, vasomotor rhinitis, and hay fever. It is sometimes combined with local anesthetics to retard their systemic absorption and to prolong their action.

Phenylephrine hydrochloride is used as a mydriatic for certain conditions in which dilation of the pupil is desired without cycloplegia (paralysis of the ciliary muscle). It is also used to prevent or treat acute hypotension induced during anesthesia, shock, or drug-induced hypotension. Phenylephrine is also used as vasoconstrictor in regional anesthesia, and it is applied intranasally for congestion caused by colds, hay fever, sinusitis, or allergies.

Phenylephrine is used as a mydriatic, as an ophthalmic decongestant, and for ophthalmoscopic examinations. It is also used to treat uveitis.

The drug, given orally, is irregularly absorbed. Nasal decongestion may result in 15 minutes, lasting 2 to 4 hours.

To produce vasopressor effects: IV, an immediate effect with a duration of action of 15 to 20 minutes; IM, effect occurs within 10 to 15 minutes and duration of effect is from ½ to 2 hours; SC, effect occurs within 10 to 15 minutes and duration of effect is from 50 to 60 minutes.

The drug is metabolized partially in gastrointestinal tract tissues and in the liver by the enzyme monoamine oxidase. The route of excretion is not identified. For side effects/adverse reactions, see Table 21-7.

**Significant drug interactions.** The following interactions may occur when phenylephrine is given with the drugs listed below:

| Drug | Possible Effect and Management |
|------|-------------------------------|
| alpha receptor-blocking agents | May reduce or block the vasopressor effect of phenylephrine, resulting in hypotension |
| anesthetics, inhalation of hydrocarbons such as chloroform, enflurane, halothane, and others, plus digitalis glycosides | Increases risk of inducing serious cardiac dysrhythmias. If necessary to use concurrently, monitor closely with electrocardiographic readings because therapeutic interventions may be necessary. |
| ergotamine and ergoloid mesylates | Increases vasoconstriction; severe hypertension and peripheral vascular ischemia and gangrene may occur. This combined use is not recommended. |
| doxapram | The vasopressor effects of either or both drugs may increase. Monitor closely since dosage adjustments may be necessary. |

| Drug | Possible Effect and Management |
|---|---|
| cocaine, maprotiline, or tricyclic antidepressants | May potentiate cardiovascular effects of phenylephrine, such as dysrhythmias, increase heart rate, and cause severe hypertension and elevated body temperature. Monitor closely. |
| methyldopa | May decrease hypotensive effects or increase vasopressor response to phenylephrine. If used concurrently smaller initial dosages of phenylephrine should be given with close monitoring. |
| monoamine oxidase (MAO) inhibitors | Release of accumulated neurotransmitters into the synapse area, may cause headaches, dysrhythmias, vomiting, severe hypertension, and/or high fevers. Avoid concurrent administration of these drugs because phenylephrine should not be given during or within 2 weeks after the administration of an MAO inhibitor. |

**Dosage and administration.** See Table 21-8.

▷ **Nursing Management:**
**Phenylephrine Therapy**

**Assessment.** Use with caution in individuals with hyperthyroidism, hypertension, diabetes mellitus, ischemic cardiac disease, cerebral arteriosclerosis, or with those undergoing MAO inhibitor therapy. Do not use in clients with narrow-angle glaucoma (ophthalmic preparations), severe coronary disease, severe hypertension, or ventricular tachycardia.

**Intervention.** After use, wash nasal tips and droppers with hot water to prevent contamination of solution; eye droppers should not touch the eye or any other surface.

Solutions lose potency with exposure to air, strong light, or heat. Keep container tightly sealed and away from light. Discard if solution is dark brown or contains a precipitate.

If nasal or ophthalmic preparations are administered to clients with hypertension, timing of the doses should not be at end of dosing periods of the antihypertensive drugs when therapeutic levels of antihypertensive medications are low.

**Nasal preparations.** Before administration of drug, instruct client to blow nose to clear nasal passages. Instill drops by having client tilt head back and remain in position a few minutes to permit medication to spread through nose. When administering a spray, have head upright, and squeeze bottle firmly and quickly to produce spray into each nostril; after 3 to 5 minutes blow nose and repeat.

**IV administration.** See nursing management under norepinephrine for intravenous administration. Have phentolamine available to treat hypertensive emergencies.

**Education.** Instruct client not to swallow topical solutions, in order to avoid systemic effects. Instruct the client to swallow the extended-release capsules whole.

Emphasize to client importance of adhering to drug regimen. Consult physician about any modification—dose, time interval, and others.

Alert client to the risk for injury, as dizziness and drows-

**TABLE 21-8** Dosage and administration of phenylephrine

| Dose/indication | Adults | Children |
|---|---|---|
| Hypotension | IM or SC: initially, 2-5 mg of 1% solution. Maximum is 5 mg. If necessary, may repeat every 10-15 minutes. IV: 0.2 mg from diluted solution (0.1%). Repeat in 15 minutes if necessary. IV infusion: Initial, 100-180 μg/min until blood pressure stabilizes. (Solution contains 10 mg phenylephrine to 500 ml 5% dextrose injection or 0.9% sodium chloride injection.) When client is stabilized, give 40-60 μg/min. | IM or SC, 0.1 mg/kg body weight or 3 mg/m² body surface. Repeat in 1-2 hr if necessary. For hypotension during spinal anesthesia, give 44-88 μg/kg body weight, IM or SC. |
| To prolong spinal anesthesia | Add 2-5 mg to anesthetic solution. | |
| Intranasal | | |
| Nasal solution or spray (0.25% to 0.5%) | 2 or 3 drops or 1 or 2 sprays in each nostril every 3 to 4 hr as necessary. | Children 6 to 12 yr (0.25%): 2 or 3 drops every 3-4 hr as necessary. Spray (0.25%): 1 or 2 sprays every 3-4 hr as necessary. Less than 6 yr (0.125%): 2 or 3 drops every 3-4 hr as necessary. |
| Nasal decongestant | Oral, 10 mg every 3-4 hr as necessary. | |
| Ophthalmic preparations | | |
| Ophthalmoscopy, 2.5% solution | 1 drop to conjunctiva. Repeat once in 15-30 min if necessary. | See adult dose. |
| Mydriasis and vasoconstriction | 1 drop topically to conjunctiva of a 2.5% to 10% solution. If necessary, may repeat in 1 hr. | 1 drop of a 2.5% solution topically to conjunctiva. If necessary, may repeat in 1 hr. |

iness are common side effects of the drug; activities should be modified to consider those effects. Advise client to avoid the ingestion of alcohol and other CNS depressants that would increase the severity of these effects. Notify the physician if insomnia, dizziness, or tremors occur.

Tell the client that phenylephrine inhibits salivation, and long-term use promotes caries, gum disease, and oral candidiasis. Regular dental checkups are advised.

*Ophthalmic preparations.* Instruct client to apply pressure to lacrimal sac during administration of eye drops and for 1 or 2 minutes after instillation.

Caution client about burning and stinging sensation after instillation of drops. Inform client that after instillation of drops, pupils will be dilated and may be sensitive to light. Notify physician if sensitivity persists beyond 12 hours after discontinuation of drug.

The client with contact lenses should consult the physician for specific instructions.

*Evaluation.* Monitor for sulfite sensitivity (see box on p. 410).

Pediatric clients are more likely to be sensitive to the vasopressor effects. Elderly clients may demonstrate confusion, sedation, hypotension, dryness of mouth, and urinary retention. The client's risk of altered comfort is related to phenylephrine's cardiovascular and neurologic effects as well as the local effects of topical preparations.

The blood pressure of clients with hypertension should be monitored carefully while they are receiving nasal or ophthalmic preparations of phenylephrine. Any signs of angina should be reported to the physician immediately. Altered cardiac output should be considered as a potential nursing diagnosis with the administration of phenylephrine related to its cardiovascular effects.

Observe client for rebound miosis (congestion) after topical administration.

### mephentermine sulfate (Wyamine sulfate)

Mephentermine's effects are similar to those of ephedrine, but it produces more cerebral stimulation. Mephentermine is a dual-acting (primarily) sympathomimetic. It releases catecholamines from storage sites in the heart and other tissues (indirect action). Therefore it tends to bring about both alpha and beta stimulating effects, including inotropic and chronotropic effects on the heart. Since mephentermine improves cardiac contraction and mobilizes blood from venous pools, thereby increasing cardiac output, it acts as a peripheral vasoconstrictor. (See Table 21-5.)

The drug is used as a pressor agent in the treatment of hypotension secondary to ganglionic blockade or spinal anesthesia.

Administered parenterally, IM, the drug's onset of action occurs within 5 to 15 minutes; duration of action is 1 to 4 hours. Administered IV, mephentermine is nearly immediate in action; duration of action is 15 to 30 minutes. The drug is metabolized in the liver and excreted in the kidneys.

For side effects/adverse reactions, see Table 21-6.

***Significant drug interactions.*** The following interactions may occur when mephentermine is given with the drugs listed below.

| Drug | Possible Effect and Management |
|---|---|
| anesthetics, inhalation of hydrocarbons such as chloroform, enflurane, halothane and others, cocaine and digitalis glycosides | Increase risk of inducing serious cardiac dysrhythmias. If used concurrently, monitor closely with electrocardiographic readings because therapeutic interventions may be necessary. |
| maprotiline or tricyclic antidepressants | May decrease blood pressure response to mephentermine. Monitor closely. |
| beta adrenergic blocking agents | May result in decreased therapeutic effects of both drugs. An increase in alpha adrenergic activity may result in hypertension, increased bradycardia, and the possibility of heart block. If possible, avoid concurrent drug administration. If necessary, monitor closely because therapeutic interventions may be necessary. |
| doxapram | The vasopressor effects of either or both drugs may increase. Also possible to increase CNS stimulation. Monitor closely because dosage adjustments may be necessary. |
| ergotamine and ergoloid mesylates | Increased vasoconstriction, severe hypertension and peripheral vascular ischemia and gangrene may occur. Combined use is not recommended. |
| monoamine oxidase (MAO) inhibitors | The release of accumulated neurotransmitters into synapse area may cause headaches, dysrhythmias, vomiting, severe hypertension and/or high fevers. Avoid concurrent administration of these drugs because mephentermine should not be given during or within 2 weeks after the administration of an MAO inhibitor. |
| sympathomimetics | When administered with other sympathomimetics, enhances CNS stimulation and possibly causes an increase in cardiovascular side effects. Monitor closely. |

***Dosage and administration.*** For hypotension:

Adult dosage is 30 to 45 mg IV in a single injection. Repeat doses of 30 mg as needed to maintain blood pressure. IV infusion, add 600 mg of mephentermine to 500 ml of 5% dextrose in water. Rate of administration is determined by physician according to individual's response to the infusion.

Dosage for children, IM or IV, is 0.4 mg/kg body weight or 12 mg/m² of body surface as a single dose. If necessary, it may be repeated. IV infusion, same as adult.

▷ **Nursing Management:**
**Mephentermine Therapy**

*Assessment.* Use cautiously in individuals with arteriosclerosis, hypertension, cardiovascular disease, hyperthyroidism, and chronically ill patients. Clients having hypoxia should have the condition corrected before the administration of mephentermine or the response to the drug may be decreased or the risk of adverse effects may be increased.

Drug may cause uterine contraction; therefore it should not be administered to pregnant women. The drug is contraindicated in individuals receiving MAO inhibitors, anesthetics (cyclopropane, halothane), or chlorpromazine.

**Intervention.** Administer using an infusion device to precisely regulate dosage according to the response of the client. Do not use if the solution is discolored or a precipitate has formed.

**Evaluation.** Monitor closely blood pressure, pulse, ECG, central venous pressure, and urinary output. The blood pressure and pulse should be checked every 2 minutes until stabilized, then every 5 to 15 minutes thereafter during therapy. The blood pressure should be maintained at slightly less than the client's normal blood pressure. In clients with hypertension, maintain at 30 to 40 mm Hg below usual blood pressure.

Observe client for possible development of tolerance if repeated injections are administered. Note that blood volume replacement must be instituted as soon as possible in treatment of secondary shock. The client may experience altered comfort related to mephentermine's neurologic and cardiovascular effects, such as increased anxiety, restlessness, dysrhythmias, and tachycardia.

### metaraminol (Aramine)

Metaraminol is a vasopressor agent with both direct (primarily) and indirect effects on the sympathetic system. It acts indirectly by releasing norepinephrine from tissues and storage sites and directly as a neurohormone. Metaraminol has positive inotropic effects. Since it constricts blood vessels, increases peripheral resistance, elevates both systolic and diastolic blood pressure, and improves cardiac contractility and cerebral, coronary, and renal blood flow, the drug is used for the treatment of shock.

Since metaraminol exhibits beta as well as alpha adrenergic activity, it is often effective in raising blood pressure when alpha adrenergic agents are ineffective. This may be because of its ability to bring about more effective venous flow. It does not appear to cause dysrhythmias. It generally lacks CNS stimulatory effects. (See Table 21-5.) Although similar to norepinephrine in action, it is generally considered a less potent drug.

Metaraminol is used for hypotensive states occurring with spinal anesthesia. It is also administered for the prevention and treatment of acute hypotension associated with surgery, drug-induced reactions, and shock.

The drug is administered parenterally only. When given IV, onset is within 1 to 2 minutes; duration of action is approximately 20 minutes. When given SC or IM, onset of action is 10 minutes (IM) or 5 to 20 minutes (SC). Duration of action is approximately 60 minutes (IM and SC). Metaraminol is metabolized in the liver and excreted in the bile and kidneys.

For side effects/adverse reactions, see Table 21-7.

**Significant drug interactions.** The following interactions may occur when metaraminol is given with the drugs listed below:

| Drug | Possible Effect and Management |
|---|---|
| anesthetics, inhalation of hydrocarbons such as chloroform, enflurane, halothane and others, cocaine and digitalis glycosides | Increases risk of inducing serious cardiac dysrhythmias. If necessary to use concurrently, monitor client closely with electrocardiographic readings because therapeutic interventions may be necessary. |
| alpha adrenergic blocking agents | May decrease the vasopressor effects of metaraminol. |
| beta adrenergic blocking agents | Therapeutic effects of both drugs may decrease. An increase in alpha adrenergic activity may result in hypertension and increase bradycardia with the possibility of heart block. If possible, avoid concurrent administration of these drugs. If necessary, monitor closely because therapeutic interventions may be necessary. |
| doxapram | The vasopressor effects of either or both drugs may increase. Monitor closely because dosage adjustments may be necessary. |
| ergotamine and ergoloid mesylates | Increased vasoconstriction, severe hypertension, and peripheral vascular ischemia and gangrene may occur. Combined use is not recommended. |
| maprotiline or tricyclic antidepressants | Cardiovascular side effects may occur, such as dysrhythmias, increased heart rate, and possibly severe hypertension or hyperpyrexia. |
| guanadrel or guanethidine | If given during or within 5 days of discontinuing guanethidine, hypertension may occur. The pressor effect of metaraminol is enhanced, but the antihypertensive effect of guanadrel or guanethidine is decreased. Hypertension and cardiac dysrhythmias may be induced. Monitor closely. |
| monoamine oxidase (MAO) inhibitors | The release of accumulated neurotransmitters into synapse area may result in headaches, dysrhythmias, vomiting, severe hypertension and/or high fevers. Avoid concurrent administration of these drugs because metaraminol should not be given during or within 2 weeks after the administration of an MAO inhibitor. |

**Dosage and administration.** Metaraminol is administered by parenteral route only.

*Adults.* Metaraminol is given SC, IM to prevent hypotension. Administer 2 to 10 mg. To avoid cumulative effects, wait 10 minutes before giving additional doses. When given via IV infusion, administer 15 to 100 mg in 500 ml of sodium chloride injection (0.9%) or 5% dextrose in water at rate determined by physician to maintain the desired blood pressure response. The drug is given by direct IV injection for severe shock, 0.5 to 5 mg followed by the infusion described above.

*Children.* Give SC, IM, 0.1 mg/kg body weight or 3 mg/m² of body surface. When given via IV infusion, give 0.4 mg/kg body weight or 12 mg/m² body surface. Dilution contains 1 mg in 25 ml of 0.9% sodium chloride solution or 5% dextrose in water. Administer at rate determined by physician to maintain the desired blood pressure response. When administering direct IV injection for severe shock, give 0.01 mg/kg body weight or 300 μg/m² body surface.

▷ **Nursing Management: Metaraminol Therapy**

*Assessment.* Use drug with caution in individuals with hypertension, peripheral vascular disease, thyroid disease, diabetes mellitus, cirrhosis of liver, and in individuals taking digitalis or MAO inhibitors. Clients with hypoxia should have this condition corrected before or concurrently with the administration of metaraminol or its effectiveness may be reduced or the risk of adverse effects may be increased. Do not use in individuals with cyclopropane or halothane anesthesia or with those hypersensitive to metaraminol.

*Intervention.* Subcutaneous injection is rarely given since it causes tissue necrosis. Moreover, avoid extravasation during intravenous infusion. Monitor closely to prevent injury to local tissue and necrosis. The use of larger veins may be helpful during infusion. Veins of the ankle and back of the hand should be avoided, particularly in clients with peripheral vascular disease and diabetes mellitus. Have on hand phentolamine (decreases pressor effect) and atropine (for bradycardia).

Metaraminol must be diluted before administration. Once diluted, it should be used within 24 hours. Because metaraminol is incompatible with many drugs, it should not be administered in a solution containing other medications.

*Evaluation.* Closely monitor blood pressure every 2 to 5 minutes during infusion (client must be constantly attended). Since the drug has a prolonged effect, adjust flow rate carefully to avoid a cumulative response. Before terminating infusion, reduce flow rate gradually to avoid abrupt withdrawal of drug, which otherwise may result in severe hypotension. If possible, correct plasma volume before starting therapy. Continue to monitor blood pressure closely after the drug has been discontinued. If severe hypotension occurs, the drug should be resumed quickly.

Monitor for cardiac arrhythmias. Monitor intake and output; also monitor sodium and potassium loss because clients with cirrhosis of liver may suffer from diuresis. Monitor for sulfite sensitivity (see box on p. 410).

### methoxamine hydrochloride (Vasoxyl)

Methoxamine is an alpha adrenergic stimulator that appears to be devoid of beta receptor activity. Therefore it is almost exclusively a vasoconstrictor. The direct-acting sympathomimetic agent is pharmacologically related to phenylephrine. Since it has no stimulating effect on the heart, the rise in blood pressure causes a reflex bradycardia. This effect makes it useful in treating paroxysmal supraventricular tachycardia and in restoring or maintaining blood pressure during anesthesia. (See Table 21-6.)

It is a parenteral drug. With IV administration, effects are immediate; duration of action as a vasopressor is 5 to 15 minutes. When the drug is given IM, effects are seen within 15 to 20 minutes; duration of effects is 60 to 90 minutes. Metabolism and excretion routes are unknown.

For side effects/adverse reactions, see Table 21-7.

*Significant drug interactions.* The following interactions may occur when methoxamine is given with the drugs listed below.

| Drug | Possible Effect and Management |
|---|---|
| alpha adrenergic blocking agents | May decrease the vasopressor effects of methoxamine. |
| anesthetics, parenteral or local | Avoid concurrent use. Methoxamine's prolonged effect may reduce circulation leading to tissue anoxia and necrosis. |
| maprotiline or tricyclic antidepressants | May increase cardiovascular adverse effects of methoxamine, resulting in dysrhythmias, increased heart rate, possibly severe hypertension or hyperpyrexia. Methoxamine should not be given concurrently or within 1 week of a tricyclic antidepressant. |
| digitalis glycoside | Increases risk of cardiac toxicity. Avoid if possible. If must be given, monitor closely with electrocardiographic monitoring. |
| ergoloid mesylate or ergotamine | Increased vasoconstriction, severe hypertension, and peripheral vascular ischemia and gangrene may occur. Combined use is not recommended. |
| doxapram | The vasopressor effects of either or both drugs may increase. Monitor closely because dosage adjustments may be necessary. |

*Dosage and administration.* As vasopressor, methoxamine is administered to adults 10 to 15 mg IM or 3 to 5 mg given slowly by direct IV. Maximum dose IM is 20 mg as a single injection up to a maximum of 60 mg in 24 hours; IV maximum is up to 10 mg as a single injection. Children's dosage is: IM, 0.25 mg/kg body weight or 7.5 mg/m² of body surface; IV, 0.08 mg/kg body weight or 2.5 mg/m² body surface.

▷ **Nursing Management: Methoxamine Therapy**

*Assessment.* Use cautiously in clients with acidosis, hyperthyroidism, pheochromocytoma, or hypertension and also following parenteral injection of ergot alkaloids. Clients with hypoxia should have this condition corrected before or concurrently with the administration of methoxamine, or its effectiveness may be reduced or the risk of adverse effects may be increased. Do not use in combination with local anesthetics to prolong their action and in clients with cardiovascular disease.

*Intervention.* Intramuscular doses may need to be repeated. If so, allow sufficient time for previous injection to have taken effect before considering administering another. Administer IV slowly if the systolic pressure falls below 60 or in another emergency.

***Evaluation.*** Monitor the blood pressure (BP) and pulse continuously during therapy and titrate the dose accordingly. The BP should be maintained at slightly less than the client's normal blood pressure. In clients with hypertension, maintain at 30 to 40 mm Hg below usual BP. Observe client for severe bradycardia with rhythm strips. Have atropine available if bradycardia occurs. Monitor intake and output because output increases when normal blood pressure levels occur (if the client is not hypovolemic). Observe client for sudden changes of blood pressure after the drug is terminated.

Monitor for sulfite sensitivity (see box on p. 410). In addition to altered cardiac output, the client may also experience altered comfort related to methoxamine's effects of headache, increased perspiration, and the sensation of urinary urgency.

## ADRENERGIC BLOCKING DRUGS
### Alpha Adrenergic Blocking Drugs

Most **alpha adrenergic blocking agents** are competitive blockers; that is, they compete with the catecholamines at receptor sites and inhibit adrenergic sympathetic stimulation. They are more effective against the action of circulating catecholamines than against catecholamines released from storage sites in the neurons. These drugs may be obtained

from natural sources, such as ergot and its derivatives, or they may be synthesized.

The alpha adrenergic blocking agents fall into three categories:

1. Noncompetitive, long-acting antagonists (e.g., phenoxybenzamine): action persists for several days or weeks because a stable bond is formed between a specific component of the drug and the alpha receptor site.
2. Competitive, short-acting antagonists (e.g., phentolamine, tolazoline): the blocking action is reversible and competitive at the alpha receptor site and the effects last only several hours.
3. Ergot alkaloids: usually act as partial alpha adrenergic antagonists. However, the drugs produce primarily a spasmogenic effect on smooth muscle of blood vessels, thereby causing vasoconstriction.

### *Noncompetitive, Long-Acting Antagonists*
### phenoxybenzamine (Dibenzyline)

Phenoxybenzamine is a long-acting alpha adrenergic blocking agent. The agent abolishes or decreases the receptiveness of alpha receptors to adrenergic stimuli. Its effects are mainly those of vasodilation and inhibition of vasospasm.

Since phenoxybenzamine competes with the catecholamines, it is also useful in decreasing the blood pressure of patients with pheochromocytoma. It does not block sym-

**TABLE 21-9**   Side effects/adverse reactions of adrenergic blocking drugs

| Drug | Side effects* | Adverse reactions† |
|---|---|---|
| **NONCOMPETITIVE** | | |
| phenoxybenzamine (Dibenzyline) | More frequent: Dizziness (postural hypotension), miosis, tachycardia, nasal congestion. <br> Less frequent: Lethargy, confusion, dry mouth, headache, weakness, inhibition of ejaculation | None noted in USP-DI but monitor closely, especially if patient is receiving large doses |
| **COMPETITIVE** | | |
| phentolamine HCl (Regitine, Rogitine ✦) | More frequent: Diarrhea, dizziness (postural hypotension), nausea, vomiting, abdominal pain <br> Less frequent: Nasal congestion, flushing | More frequent: Tachycardia <br> Less frequent: Increased weakness, fainting. <br> Rare (following parenteral): Angina or chest pain, respiratory distress, myocardial infarction, cerebrovascular accident (confusion, severe headache, loss of coordination, slurred speech) |
| tolazoline (Priscoline) | None noted in USP-DI (1990), monitor closely since most adverse effects are serious. | More frequent: Gastrointestinal bleeding, systemic alkalosis (hypochloremic), hypotension, thrombocytopenia, oliguria or acute renal failure <br> Less frequent: Nausea, vomiting or diarrhea, skin flushing, piloerection, tachycardia |

*If side effects continue, increase, or disturb the client, the physician should be informed.
†If adverse reactions occur, the physician should be contacted because medical intervention may be necessary.

pathetic impulses on the heart and therefore does not directly impair cardiac output.

Phenoxybenzamine is used in the management of pheochromocytoma: preoperative preparation of client for surgery, chronic treatment of individuals with malignant pheochromocytoma, and individuals for whom surgery of pheochromocytoma is contraindicated.

Oral absorption of the drug is variable. Onset of action occurs in 2 hours. The drug can persist for 3 or 4 days since it forms a stable bond with the receptor. The half-life is about 24 hours. Metabolism is in the liver; the drug is excreted in the kidney and bile.

For side effects/adverse reactions, see Table 21-9.

When phenoxybenzamine is given with other sympathomimetics, such as epinephrine, metaraminol, methoxamine, and phenylephrine, the results may be as follows:

1. Blocking of the alpha adrenergic receptor effects of epinephrine, which may result in severe hypotension and increased tachycardia
2. Decrease in the vasopressor effects of metaraminol
3. Blocking of the vasopressor effect of methoxamine, resulting in severe hypotension
4. Decrease in the vasopressor effect to phenylephrine

Avoid concurrent drug administration if at all possible.

Administer to adults, initially, 10 mg twice daily orally; dosage may increase by 10 mg every other day until the desired effect is noted. Maintenance dose is 20 to 40 mg two or three times daily. Administer to children, initially, 0.2 mg/kg body weight orally or 6 mg/m² body surface, up to a maximum of 10 mg, given once daily; dosage may be increased every 4 days until the desired effect is noted. Maintenance dose is 0.4 mg to 1.2 mg/kg body weight or 12 to 36 mg/m² body surface daily, given in 3 or 4 divided doses.

## ▷ Nursing Management: Phenoxybenzamine Therapy

**Assessment.** Use with caution in clients with renal insufficiency, marked cerebral or coronary arteriosclerosis, and respiratory infections or other pulmonary disease. Do not use in clients with compensated congestive failure because it will cause angina and congestive heart failure, or in conditions when a decrease in blood pressure might be dangerous, such as cerebrovascular insufficiency.

**Intervention.** Administer the oral drug with milk to reduce gastric irritation. The dosage should be adjusted according to the clinical response and level of urinary catecholamines. Dosage increases will be gradual from the lowest therapeutic dose, but the increments should be no more frequent than every 4 days.

Treat overdosage by intravenous infusion of norepinephrine. Do not use epinephrine since it will cause a further drop in blood pressure.

**Education.** Advise client to make position changes slowly (from recumbent to upright posture) to prevent orthostatic hypotension. Instruct client to dangle legs and exercise feet for a few minutes at the bedside before standing. If faintness or weakness occurs, a head-low position should be assumed or the person must lie down immediately. Physician may prescribe support stockings to help prevent orthostatic hypotension.

Advise the client to modify activities if dizziness and/or drowsiness occur, because of the risk for injury.

Advise the client that because the drug inhibits salivary flow and thus promotes the development of caries, periodontal disease, and buccal candidiasis, regular dental checkups are required. Dryness of the mouth can be relieved and the comfort of the client promoted by ice chips and sugarless gum.

Warn client against using any other drug, particularly over-the-counter sympathomimetics (such as cough, cold, or allergy preparations) without consulting the physician.

An effect of this drug can be inhibition of ejaculation, which should be reported to the physician.

Because of the risk of physiologic injury related to orthostatic hypotension, instruct the client not to drink alcohol, to avoid standing for long periods, and not to exercise during hot weather because the possibility of this effect would be increased.

**Evaluation.** Monitor blood pressure and pulse rate both in recumbent and standing positions during period of dosage adjustment, particularly when dosage is increased. Observe client for signs of hypotension and tachycardia. Inform client that these signs usually disappear with continued therapy. However, with the vasodilation associated with exercise, drinking alcohol, or eating a large meal, these signs may recur.

Clients with pheochromocytoma will note decreases in blood pressure, pulse, and sweating that are signs of therapeutic effectiveness.

## Competitive, Short-Acting Antagonists
### phentolamine mesylate (Regitine, Rogitine ✱)

Phentolamine is an alpha adrenergic blocking agent. It competitively blocks alpha₂ (presynaptic) and alpha₁ (postsynaptic) receptors. The action occurs at both arterial and venous vessels. This direct relaxation of vascular smooth muscle lowers total peripheral resistance. Accordingly, hypertension is inhibited when there are excessive levels of epinephrine and norepinephrine. It also decreases pulmonary vascular resistance. Phentolamine exerts a histamine-like action that enhances the secretion of hydrochloric acid and pepsin. It also stimulates beta receptors, which increases heart rate and cardiac output.

The drug is used to prevent or control hypertensive episodes in the patient with pheochromocytoma. It is also used to reverse the vasoconstrictive action of an overdose or excessive response to IV administration or extravasation of norepinephrine (Levophed) or dopamine. The subcutaneous injection of phentolamine following extravasation of intravenous norepinephrine or dopamine will prevent tissue necrosis if prompt action is taken.

Phentolamine is poorly absorbed; only approximately 20% of the drug is active following oral administration. Preferred method of administration is parenteral. When the drug is administered IV, half-life is approximately 19 minutes.

Metabolism and excretion sources are unknown; only about 13% of the drug is found in urine after parenteral administration. For side effects/adverse reactions, see Table 21-9. Significant drug interactions are the same as for phenoxybenzamine.

When phentolamine is used as an antiadrenergic preoperative, give 5 mg IV 1 to 2 hours before surgery; dosage may be repeated if needed; during surgery, give 5 mg IV or 0.5 mg-1 mg/minute by intravenous infusion. When using the drug as an antiadrenergic preoperative in children, give 1 mg or 0.1 mg/kg body weight or 3 mg/m² body surface area (IM or IV) 1 to 2 hours before surgery; dosage may be repeated if needed.

▷ **Nursing Management: Phentolamine Therapy**

*Assessment.* Use with caution in clients with coronary artery disease, myocardial infarction, gastritis, and peptic ulcer. Do not use in clients with hypersensitivity to phentolamine.

When administered intravenously as an antiadrenergic, the patient should be in a supine position as the drug may cause severe and prolonged hypotension with fainting, tachycardia and cardiac arrhythmias. Monitor blood pressure and pulse every 2 minutes until stabilized.

When phentolamine is used to prevent sloughing of tissue with administration of norepinephrine, 10 mg may be added to every liter of intravenous fluids containing norepinephrine without affecting its vasopressor effect. If extravasation has already occurred, 5 to 10 mg of phentolamine in 10 ml of 0.9% sodium chloride injection should be immediately infiltrated into the affected area. However, this treatment is ineffective if 12 or more hours have passed since the extravasation.

*Education.* After therapy, advise client to rise slowly from bed and remain in sitting position for a few minutes before standing upright, to prevent orthostatic hypotension. Clients receiving phentolamine should be evaluated for the potential for injury related to the drug's CNS and cardiovascular effects. Altered comfort may also be an issue for the patient if the adverse effects of syncope or nausea and vomiting occur.

**tolazoline (Priscoline)**

Like phentolamine, tolazoline produces a moderately effective competitive alpha adrenergic blocking action. However, tolazoline is considerably less potent. It acts as a vasodilator by a direct relaxant effect on vascular smooth muscle. It reduces pulmonary arterial pressure and peripheral vascular resistance.

The drug is used to treat persistent pulmonary hypertension in the newborn when systemic arterial levels of oxygen cannot be maintained by oxygen supplementation and/or mechanical ventilation machines.

When the drug is given by parenteral administration, onset of action is within ½ hour of initial dose. Half-life in neonates is 3 to 10 hours. Tolazine is excreted in the kidneys, mainly unchanged.

For side effects/adverse reactions, see Table 21-9.

Although the USP-DI (1991) does not list any significant drug interactions with tolazoline, the nurse should be aware that consumption of alcohol may potentiate the vasodilator effects of this drug. Also, if epinephrine or norepinephrine are used to treat a tolazoline overdose, a paradoxical hypotension effect followed by an exaggerated hypertensive response may occur. Avoid using epinephrine or norepinephrine with large amounts of tolazoline. Tolazoline may also reduce the pressor effects of ephedrine, metaraminol, and high doses of dopamine on peripheral vasoconstriction. Whenever concurrent drug therapy is administered, monitor the client closely for therapeutic response and/or side effects.

When the drug is given parenterally to children, administer 1 to 2 mg/kg body weight (IV) initially via a scalp vein over a 5 to 10 minute period. Maintenance dose is 1 to 2 mg/kg body weight by IV infusion per hour; when arterial blood gases appear to be remaining stable, the drug may be gradually withdrawn.

▷ **Nursing Management: Tolazoline Therapy**

*Assessment.* Tolazoline should not be used when systemic hypotension (systolic blood pressure less than 40 mm Hg) exists. Caution must be used when administering in the presence of acidosis or mitral stenosis.

*Intervention.* This drug is administered only in pediatric or neonatal intensive care units where respiratory support is immediately available. Use an infusion pump or micro drip regulator for administration to allow for precise flow regulation. Do not mix in a syringe or solution with other drugs. Pretreating the client with antacids may be necessary to prevent stress ulcers secondary to the increase in gastric secretion caused by the drug.

*Evaluation.* Monitor the client's response to the drug through ECG, blood gases, blood pressure, and pulse rates. Also observe serum electrolyte levels, particularly sodium and potassium levels. To monitor for gastrointestinal bleeding, perform a hematest of gastric aspirates.

Monitor for pain in upper abdominal area, increased pulse, and coffee-ground emesis.

Evaluate the client for the risk for physiological injury related to the tolazoline's cardiovascular and gastrointestinal effects. Altered comfort may occur due to the drug's adverse effects of diarrhea, nausea and vomiting, goose flesh, and flushing of the skin.

**ergot alkaloids:**
**dihydroergotamine mesylate (D.H.E. 45)**
**ergoloid mesylates (Hydergine, Hydergine LC)**
**ergotamine tartrate (Ergomar, Gynergen ✳ )**
**ergotamine tartrate and caffeine (Cafergot)**
**ergotamine tartrate inhalation (Medihaler Ergotamine)**
**ergotamine, belladonna alkaloids, and phenobarbital (Bellergal-S, Bellergal ✳ )**
**methysergide maleate (Sansert)**

For many years the ergot alkaloids were the only alpha adrenergic blocking agents available. Ergot is a fungus that grows on rye, and when it is hydrolyzed, many of its derivatives dissociate to yield lysergic acid diethylamide (LSD). These alkaloids have diverse and somewhat contradictory effects. The ergot alkaloids listed here are alpha adrenergic blockers; however not all ergot derivatives are alpha adrenergic blockers. With the exception of ergoloid mesylates, all of the ergot alkaloids may be used to treat or prevent migraine and other vascular headaches. The exact mechanism of action of ergoloid mesylates is unknown, but they may increase cerebral blood flow and metabolism in the brain, and so have been used to treat cerebrovascular insufficiency. This use is currently being questioned. The other ergot alkaloids stimulate smooth muscle, especially of the blood vessels and the uterus, so they decrease the cerebral blood supply.

The early phase of a migraine attack is associated with constriction of the cranial blood vessels. It is characterized by visual symptoms and malaise and appears as a warning or "aura" of an oncoming attack. This is followed by the painful phase of a migraine headache that results in cranial vasodilation. The increase in blood flow in the vessels produces pulsations that appear to be the source of the pain. The ergot alkaloids act as alpha adrenergic blocking agents and depress the central vasomotor center. They cause vasoconstriction of cranial blood vessels during the vasodilation phase, thereby reducing the pulsation thought to be responsible for the headache. The drugs also possess antiserotonin activity. Abnormalities in the metabolism of serotonin may play a role in the migraine syndrome. Serum levels of serotonin have been found to drop spontaneously just before a migraine attack. In addition, during the attack an increased quantity of serotonin metabolites is excreted in the urine. Evidence exists that the drugs that act favorably in alleviating migraine influence serotonin metabolism. Methysergide is a serotonin inhibitor and also acts as a potent vasoconstrictor. (See Chapter 38 for serotonin activity.) Ergotamine tartrate inhalation is used to abort or reduce a migraine attack, whereas ergotamine, belladonna alkaloids, and phenobarbital are used as a combination agent to prevent vascular headaches. Some of these drugs are used for treatment of vascular headaches, such as migraine and cluster headaches. The drug (dihydroergotamine mesylate and ergotamine tartrate) must be given early in the attack; it does not prevent migraine attacks.

Dihydroergotamine is administered parenterally. The ergoloid mesylates are slowly and erratically absorbed from the gastrointestinal tract. Ergotamine tartrate and ergotamine tartrate combinations, administered orally without caffeine, are absorbed slowly and erratically. Caffeine is said to aid oral absorption. Aerosol dosage form, like methysergide, is well absorbed.

Onset of action for dihydroergotamine mesylate IM is 15 to 30 minutes; for IV form, onset occurs within 5 minutes. In the ergoloid mesylates, response is usually seen within 3 to 4 weeks or longer. Ergotamine tartrate and ergotamine tartrate combinations have onset of action within 1 to 2 hours; for methysergide maleate, this occurs in 24 to 48 hours. Duration of action for dihydroergotamine mesylate IM is 3 to 4 hours; duration for methysergide maleate is within 24 to 48 hours. Half-life of dehydroergotamine mesylate is within 1.4-15 hours; half-life of ergoloid mesylates is 3.5 hours.

Ergotamine tartrate and ergotamine tartrate combinations each have a half-life of about 2 hours. The ergot alkaloids are metabolized in the liver. Dihydroergotamine mesylate and methysergide maleate are both excreted in the kidney. Ergotamine tartrate and ergotamine tartrate combinations are excreted in the bile.

For side effects/adverse reactions, see Table 21-10. When ergot alkaloids are given with other ergot alkaloids, vasopressors or vasoconstrictors, the combination may result in increased vasoconstriction, ischemia, and possibly gangrene. Avoid this drug combination. Vasospasms have been reported when oral contraceptives (estrogen and progestin) were given concurrently with ergotamine tartrate and dihydroergotamine. With chronic use of the latter product, breakthrough bleeding and a decrease in contraceptive effectiveness has also been reported. For information on dosage and administration, see Table 21-11.

▷ **Nursing Management:
Ergot Alkaloids**

**Assessment.** Do not use with clients with severe hypertension because it may be aggravated or those with recent or anticipated vascular surgery because of the risk of drug-induced ischemia. Caution should also be used if the client has cardiovascular or peripheral vascular disease, sepsis, or hepatic or renal disease. Elderly clients are also more at risk from the drug's vasospastic and hypothermic effects. Ergotamine is not recommended for use during pregnancy because of its oxytoxic effects. It is contraindicated in clients who are breastfeeding because it inhibits lactation and may cause peripheral ischemia or nausea and vomiting in the infant.

**TABLE 21-10**   Side effects/adverse reactions of ergot alkaloids

| Drug(s) | Side effects* | Adverse reactions† |
|---|---|---|
| dihydroergotamine (D.H.E. 45) | Less frequent: Nausea, vomiting, headache, dizziness | Less frequent: Pruritus, edema of lower extremities, leg weakness, headache<br>Rare: Red colored blisters on hands or feet might be the first indication of gangrene; bradycardia or tachycardia<br>Overdosage: Vasoconstriction leading to numbness, tingling and perhaps pain in the fingers, toes, arms, legs, face or back; cold hands and feet |
| ergoloid mesylates (Hydergine, Hydergine LC) | Less frequent: Dizziness (postural hypotension), sedation, bradycardia, rash; sublingual usage—soreness under tongue reported | Overdosage: Headaches, flushing, anorexia, nausea, vomiting, abdominal cramps, nasal congestion, impaired vision, dizziness, fainting |
| ergotamine tartrate (Ergomar, Gynergen ♣ )<br><br>ergotamine tartrate combinations (Cafergot, Bellergal-S) | More frequent: Diarrhea, nausea, vomiting, dizziness | More frequent: Edema of lower extremities (feet, lower legs)<br>Dose-related: Peripheral vasoconstriction or vasospasms (pruritus, cold hands or feet, leg weakness, pain in arms, legs or lower back)<br>Less frequent: Confusion, visual disturbances, angina or chest pain, red colored blisters on hands or feet might be early sign of gangrene; abdominal pain and gas<br>Acute overdosage: Bradycardia or tachycardia, increased weakness, confusion, abdominal pain, gas or bloating, shortness of breath<br>Chronic overdosage: Depression; headaches; nausea or vomiting that persists or is severe; pain in arms, legs, or lower back (severe); increased weakness; cold hands or feet |
| methysergide maleate (Sansert) | More frequent: Diarrhea, dizziness, (postural hypotension), sedation, nausea, vomiting or abdominal pain<br>Less frequent: Insomnia, gas, constipation | More frequent: Pruritus, leg weakness, feelings of numbness or tingling sensations in fingers, toes, or face, chest pain<br>Less frequent: Visual disturbances, increased excitability, distortions of body image, hallucinations, nightmares, difficulty in thinking, anxiety<br>Overdosage: Severe dizziness, unusual excitability, pale and cold extremities (hands or feet)<br>Monitor for signs of fibrosis, a rare but serious complication<br>Edema of hands or ankles, cold hands and feet, complaints of leg cramps or pain in lower back<br>Pleuropulmonary fibrosis: dyspnea, chest pain, fever<br>Retroperitoneal fibrosis: ureteral obstruction; fever, flank or groin pain, anorexia, weight loss, dysuria or painful urination |

*If side effects continue, increase, or disturb client, the physician should be informed.
†If adverse reactions occur, the physician should be contacted because medical intervention may be necessary.

**TABLE 21-11**   Dosage and administration of ergot alkaloids

| Alkaloid | Adults | Children |
|---|---|---|
| dihydroergotamine mesylate | IM: 1 mg at start of attack; repeat dosage of 1 mg every hr as needed up to 3 mg per migraine attack or 6 mg/week.<br>IV: 1 mg at start of attack; if needed give 1 mg in an hour up to 2 mg per migraine attack or 6 mg/week. | |
| ergoloid mesylates | 1 or 2 mg orally or sublingually, 3 times daily. | |
| ergotamine tartrate | Oral: 2 mg initially, may repeat in ½ hour if needed, maximum: 6 mg/day or 10 mg in 1 week.<br>Sublingual: 1 mg initially; may repeat in ½ to 1 hour if necessary. If repeat dose; necessary, at beginning of next attack, start with the larger dose; maximum for initial dose: 5 mg; maximum per week: 10 mg. | 10 years and older, sublingual: 1 mg dose; repeat in ½ hour if necessary. |
| ergotamine tartrate inhalation | Oral inhalation: 1 spray at beginning of attack, repeat every 5 minutes if necessary, to maximum of 6 sprays in 24 hours. | |
| ergotamine tartrate and caffeine | Oral: see sublingual dosage for ergotamine tartrate.<br>Suppositories: one rectally initially; if necessary, a second may be inserted in 1 hour; maximum: 2 suppositories per migraine attack, or 5 suppositories/1 week. | |
| ergotamine, belladonna alkaloids, phenobarbital | 1 tablet in the A.M. and at noon; 2 tablets at bedtime. Maximum: 6 tablets/day. When possible, physicians reduce dose weekly to lowest effective dose. | |
| methysergide maleate | 4-6 mg orally daily in divided doses, taken with milk or meals. | |

*Intervention.* Nonpharmacologic interventions for pain relief should be used to supplement the medication, such as a quiet environment, relaxation therapy, and other measures specific to the client. Because nausea and vomiting may be increased by the administration of ergotamine before relief of the headache occurs, phenothiazine antiemetics may be required to promote the comfort of the client. Safety measures should be taken to prevent injury to the client's extremities and they should be monitored for the ischemic effects of the drug.

*Education.* Tell client to take initial dose of drug during early part of migraine attack, during "aura" (visual field defects, scintillating scotomas, paresthesia, and nausea). The client then should lie down in a quiet, dark room for several hours. Assure the client that the quality of relief is related to the promptness with which the medication is started after the onset of symptoms.

Warn client to take drug exactly as prescribed. Prolonged use or overdose can cause circulatory impairment (ergot poisoning): numbness, tingling sensation, weakness, intermittent claudication, cyanosis of extremities, muscle pain and coldness of extremities. Report symptoms immediately to physician. If not corrected, gangrene may develop. Severe peripheral vasoconstriction may be treated by administering intravenous sodium nitroprusside. Discontinuing the drug for 2 to 3 days may relieve these symptoms.

Instruct the client to avoid alcohol ingestion because it aggravates the headache. Counseling should be provided for smoking cessation since nicotine increases the peripheral vasoconstriction effects of the drug. For the same reason, clients should be instructed to avoid exposure to cold.

Tell the client of the signs and symptoms of infection with the caution to report these to the physician as infection increases the sensitivity to the drug.

Warn female clients of childbearing age not to use ergot alkaloids because of potential oxytoxic effects during pregnancy.

Clients with migraine may require assistance to identify physical and emotional stresses that cause migraine attack. Relaxation techniques, adequate rest, and avoidance of stressful situations may alleviate the severity or frequency of attacks.

Instruct the client in the proper method of taking sublingual tablets, including the avoidance of eating, drinking, and smoking until the tablet is completely dissolved.

*Evaluation.* Examine extremities and palpate peripheral pulses at monthly intervals to detect ischemia as early as possible. In addition, the client should be evaluated for altered comfort secondary to the gastrointestinal and vasoconstricting effects of ergotamine. The potential for injury may occur if there is a decrease in peripheral sensation because of vasoconstriction.

### methysergide (Sansert)

Although methysergide is not as potent a vasoconstrictor as ergotamine, the preceding nursing measures should be observed.

Administer the oral dosage of methysergide with food to minimize gastrointestinal irritation.

Methysergide is not administered continuously for more than 6 months; a drug-free period of 3 to 4 weeks must occur before the drug is restarted. Advise client to withdraw drug gradually over 2- to 3-week period to prevent "headache rebound" resulting from abrupt drug withdrawal. If the drug does not provide a therapeutic response after a 3-week trial period, it is unlikely that longer administration will be of benefit.

Because there is a potential for serious side effects with methysergide, client should be advised to report dyspnea and chest or abdominal pain and to keep clinical appointments so that blood count, sedimentation rate, renal function, pulmonary function, and cardiac status may be assessed.

Regular examination must be performed by physician for possible development of fibrotic (formation of tissue) and vascular complications. Retroperitoneal fibrosis, as well as cardiac fibrosis, has been noted in a small number of patients. Often these conditions regress when the drug is discontinued.

Instruct client how to limit weight gain by checking for edema (daily weight) and by maintaining low salt intake and low caloric diet. Inform client of possible occurrence of postural hypotension. Position changes from recumbent to upright position should be made slowly to avoid dizziness or fainting. Alert the client to the possible need to modify activities if dizziness and drowsiness occur as side effects.

## Beta Adrenergic Blocking Agents

Beta blockers inhibit the beta receptors by competing with the catecholamines at the effector site. See the box above for a list of individual beta adrenergic blocking agents.

**Beta adrenergic blocking agents** are differentiated into two subclasses: beta$_1$ and beta$_2$ blockers. Drugs that selectively inhibit only one type of receptor—beta$_1$ or beta$_2$—are called either selective beta$_1$ or selective beta$_2$ blocking agents. Beta$_1$ selective antagonists are also frequently referred to as cardioselective blockers because these agents block the beta$_1$ receptors in the heart. Drugs that inhibit both types of receptors, beta$_1$ in the heart and beta$_2$ in the smooth muscle of the bronchioles and blood vessels, are referred to as nonselective beta adrenergic blocking agents.

The more important beta adrenergic blocking drugs found in each classification are:

1. Selective beta$_1$ adrenergic blocking agents (cardioselective), which include atenolol and metoprolol
2. Selective beta$_2$ adrenergic blocking agents (see Chapter 37)
3. Nonselective beta adrenergic blocking agents (beta$_1$ and beta$_2$ blockers), which are carteolol, nadolol, penbutolol, pindolol, propranolol, and timolol

*Mechanism of action.* Beta adrenergic blocking agents compete with beta adrenergic agonists (e.g., catecholamines) for available beta receptor sites that are located on the membrane of (1) cardiac muscle, (2) smooth muscle of bronchi, and (3) smooth muscle of blood vessels. As previously described, beta receptors appear to exist as two subclasses: beta$_1$ and beta$_2$. The cardiac muscle contains

---

### BETA ADRENERGIC BLOCKING AGENTS

acebutolol (Sectral)
atenolol (Tenormin)
carteolol (Cartrol)
esmolol HCl (Brevibloc)
labetalol (Normodyne, Trandate)
metoprolol (Lopressor, Apo-Metoprolol ✦ )
nadolol (Corgard)
penbutolol (Levatol)
pindolol (Visken)
propranolol (Inderal, Apo-Propranolol ✦ )
timolol (Blocadren)

---

beta$_1$ receptors, and the smooth muscle of the bronchi and blood vessels contain primarily beta$_2$ receptors. Pharmacologically, the beta$_1$ adrenergic blocking action in the heart decreases heart rate, conduction velocity, myocardial contractility, and cardiac output.

The antiangina effects produced by the beta blockers are primarily caused by their ability to lower the myocardial oxygen requirements. Their antihypertensive actions are not specifically identified, but these effects may result from a decrease in cardiac output, a diminished sympathetic outflow from the vasomotor center in the brain to the peripheral blood vessels, and an inhibition of renin release by the kidney (the latter with labetalol). The result is a decrease in peripheral vascular resistance that lowers blood pressure.

To prevent a recurrence of a mycardial infarction, beta blockers are used for their antidysrhythmic effect plus their ability to decrease the myocardial oxygen demands on the heart. The latter effect may reduce the progression of ischemia and its severity on the heart.

In regard to the prevention of vascular headaches, exact effects are unknown but it has been theorized that beta blocking agents, such as propranolol, act on the membrane of the smooth muscle of cerebral vessels, inhibiting vasodilation and arteriolar spasms.

Intrinsic sympathomimetic activity (ISA) is exhibited mainly by pindolol and also by acebutolol, penbutolol, and timolol. ISA or partial beta agonist (stimulation) activity along with beta blocking effects were initially believed to be advantageous when compared with agents that only possess beta blocking effects. It was projected that fewer serious side effects would occur with such agents, but clinically, the significance of this property has not been proved.

Propranolol is also capable of exerting a quinidine-like or anesthetic-like membrane function, which may affect cardiac action potential and depress cardiac function. This effect was once connected to the antidysrhythmic effect of these drugs but now is no longer considered important because very high dosages (in excess of therapeutic) are necessary to produce this activity.

Beta adrenergic blocking agents are effective antidysrhythmic agents, blocking stimulation activity at the cardiac pacemaker sites.

**Indications.** Used to treat chronic angina pectoris; to prevent and/or treat cardiac dysrhythmias; to treat hypertension; to prevent a second myocardial infarction; to prevent vascular headaches; as an adjunct to thyrotoxicosis and pheochromocytoma therapy. In addition, beta adrenergic blocking agents, especially propranolol, have been used to treat symptoms of hypertrophic cardiomyopathy, movement or essential tremors and anxiety (in specific stressful situations such as stagefright).

**Pharmacokinetics.** See Table 21-12.

**Side effects/adverse reactions.** See Table 21-13.

**Significant drug interactions.** The following interactions are possible when beta adrenergic blocking agents are given with the drugs listed below:

| Drug | Possible Effect and Management |
|---|---|
| oral hypoglycemic agents or insulin | May cause hyperglycemia or hypoglycemia. Symptoms of hypoglycemia, such as increased heart rate and decreased blood pressure, may be blocked, thus making it difficult to monitor. Monitoring of blood glucose levels and dosage adjustments of the hypoglycemic agent may be necessary. |
| calcium channel blocking agents, clonidine, or guanabenz | May result in potentiated antihypertensive effects; monitor closely. If therapy with a beta adrenergic blocking agent, clonidine, or guanabenz is to be discontinued, taper the dose of the beta blocker gradually over several days. When it is discontinued, the clonidine or guanabenz may then be tapered and discontinued also over several days. Closely monitor blood pressure throughout this procedure. |
| | Use caution when high doses of calcium blocking agents are given concurrently with a beta adrenergic blocking agent. Nifedipine may, in some instances, result in excessive hypotension in clients receiving concurrent therapy. |
| cocaine | May reduce or cancel the effects of the beta adrenergic blocking agents. Also, while beta blocking agents are used to treat symptoms induced by cocaine (i.e., increased heart rate, cardiac arrythmias, etc.), an increased risk of inducing hypertension, bradycardia, and heart block can occur. If necessary, labetalol may present less risk than the other beta adrenergic blocking agents (because of its alpha adrenergic blocking effect). |
| monoamine oxidase (MAO) inhibitors | Do not use this combination; severe hypertension may result, even up to 14 days after the MAO inhibitor is discontinued. |
| sympathomimetics | The effects of both drugs may be reduced or blocked (sympathomimetics with beta activity). In sympathomimetics with both alpha and beta activity, beta blockade may result in increased alpha effects; i.e., hypertension, severe bradycardia, and possibly heart block. Labetalol may be used if combination therapy is necessary because it has alpha blocking effects. In sympathomimetic drugs with beta ad- |

| Drug | Possible Effect and Management |
|---|---|
| | renergic activity, the beta blocking agent may cancel the beta$_1$ cardiac activity of dopamine or dobutamine; or the beta$_2$ bronchodilating effects of isoproterenol, metaproterenol. |
| xanthines (aminophylline or theophylline) | Therapeutic response of both drugs may be reduced or blocked. May also result in theophylline accumulation in the body. Monitor closely when this drug combination is prescribed. |

**Dosage and administration.** See Table 21-14.

**Precautions**

**Bronchospasm.** Blockade of the beta$_2$ receptors of the bronchial smooth muscle leads to bronchoconstriction. This effect is particularly hazardous for individuals with chronic obstructive pulmonary disease (asthma, bronchitis, and emphysema). There is less risk of inducing bronchospasm in these clients when a cardioselective beta blocker (beta$_1$ blocker) is used.

**Diabetes and hypoglycemia.** Beta$_2$ adrenergic blockade prevents the appearance of the warning signs and symptoms (sweating, increased heart rate, and anxiety) of acute hypoglycemia. Since these agents mask the appearance of the warning signs of hypoglycemia, they should be used with caution in diabetic individuals who take insulin or hypoglycemic drugs. Atenolol, a selective beta$_1$ adrenergic blocker, does not potentiate insulin-induced hypoglycemia.

**Thyrotoxicosis.** Since these drugs may mask clinical signs of hyperthyroidism (e.g., tachycardia), they give a false impression of improvement of hyperthyroidism. Abrupt withdrawal of the drug will exacerbate symptoms of hyperthyroidism, and therefore therapy should be discontinued gradually.

**Congestive heart failure.** The risk of decreasing myocardial contraction, thus increasing the risk of heart failure, must be considered when selecting a beta blocking agent. Long-term use of beta adrenergic blockers may aggravate congestive heart failure because of decreased cardiac output. If a beta blocking agent is necessary for a client with stabilized congestive heart failure, labetolol or drugs with ISA activity, such as pindolol, at low dosages may be the agents of choice. Monitor these clients closely.

**Mental depression.** Exacerbation of depression has been reported in clients with depression or with a history of depression; they should be closely monitored if taking a beta blocking agent.

▷ **Nursing Management:**
**Beta Adrenergic Blocking Agents**

**Assessment.** Clients with congestive heart failure may experience further depression of myocardial contraction. Clients with mental depression or a history of mental depression may have the condition exacerbated with the administration of beta adrenergic blocking agents.

Use with caution in clients with diabetes mellitus. By blocking adrenergic responses and thus preventing catecholamine-induced glycogenolysis, insulin can produce in-

**TABLE 21-12** Pharmacokinetic differences of beta-adrenergic blocking agents*

| Drug | Primary effect | Time to peak effect (hr) | Half-life (hr) | Metabolism | Excretion (% unchanged) |
|---|---|---|---|---|---|
| acebutolol | Beta$_1$† | 2.5 | 3-4 metabolite 8-13 | Liver | Bile/feces (50%-60%) Kidneys (30%-40%) |
| atenolol | Beta$_1$† | 2-4 | 6-7 (renal impairment 16-27 or more) | Liver (some) | Kidneys (85%-100%) |
| carteolol | Beta$_1$ Beta$_2$ | 1-3 | 6+ | Liver (some) | Kidneys (50%-70%) |
| esmolol | Beta$_1$† | Steady state 5 minutes with loading dose, 30 minutes with infusion) | 9 minutes | Esterases in red blood cells | Kidneys |
| labetalol | Beta$_1$ Beta$_2$ | oral, 2-4 IV, 5 minutes | Oral 6-8 IV approx 5 | Liver | Kidneys (55%-60%) |
| metoprolol | Beta$_1$† | oral, 1-2 IV, 20 minutes | 3-7 | Liver | Kidneys (3%-10%) |
| nadolol | Beta$_1$ Beta$_2$ | 4 | 10-24‡ | None | Kidneys (70%) |
| penbutolol | Beta$_1$ Beta$_2$ Beta$_2$ | 1.5-3 | 5+ | Liver | Kidneys (90%) |
| pindolol | Beta$_1$ Beta$_2$ | 1-2 | 3-4† (Liver impairment 2½-30 hr) (Renal impairment 3-11½ hr) (7-15 hr in elderly) | Liver | Kidneys (40%) |
| propranolol | Beta$_1$ Beta$_2$ | 1-1.5 | 3-5 | Liver | Kidneys (1%) |
| timolol | Beta$_1$ Beta$_2$ | 1-2 | 4 | Liver | Kidneys (20%) |

*Data from Frishman, WH, Kafka, KR, and Meltzer, AH: Antianginal agents. II β-Blockers, Hosp Formul 21(1):62, 1986.
†Selectivity for cardiac beta-$_1$ receptors decreases with increases in dosages.
‡Increased in renal failure.

**TABLE 21-13** Beta adrenergic blocking agents: side effects/adverse reactions

| Side effects* | Adverse reactions† |
|---|---|
| More frequent: decrease in sexual potency (possible with all drugs); increased anxiety (pindolol); diarrhea, paresthesia, nausea, vomiting, sedation (propranolol); dizziness, fatigue (metoprolol, pindolol, propranolol); insomnia (pindolol, propranolol)<br><br>Less frequent: increased nervousness and urination (acebutolol, carteolol); diarrhea reported with all except rare with nadolol; constipation (acebutolol, carteolol, nadolol, penbutolol, propranolol); dizziness, pruritus (labetalol, pindolol, timolol); nausea and vomiting (acebutolol, atenolol, carteolol, labetalol, penbutolol, pindolol) | More frequent: depression (metoprolol, propranolol); bradycardia (nadolol, propranolol)<br><br>Less frequent: respiratory difficulties (possible with all); CHF (possible with all except rare with nadolol and timolol); cold hands and feet due to reduced peripheral circulation (with all except labetalol); hallucinations (pindolol, propranolol); irregular heart rate (carteolol, labetalol, metoprolol, pindolol); skin rash (acebutolol, carteolol, nadolol, pindolol, propranolol)<br><br>OVERDOSAGE: bradycardia, severe dizziness, fainting, respiratory difficulties, blue coloration of nails or palms, convulsions, cardiac failure may occur. |

*If side effects continue, increase, or disturb the client, the physician should be informed.
†If adverse reactions occur, the physician should be contacted because medical intervention may be necessary.

**TABLE 21-14** Dosage and administration of beta adrenergic blockers

| Drug(s) | Adults | Elderly | Children |
|---|---|---|---|
| acebutolol (Sectral) | Antidysrhythmic: 200 mg orally twice daily or adjust according to client response. Antihypertensive: 400 mg orally daily as single dose or divided into 2 daily doses. Adjust as necessary. | Elderly persons may be more or less responsive to this medication. Monitor closely. Maximum: 800 mg/day. | Not determined. |
| atenolol (Tenormin) | Antianginic: 50 mg orally daily to start. If necessary, may be increased to 100 mg after 1 week of therapy. May require up to 200 mg/day to produce desired effect. Antihypertensive: 25-50 mg orally daily. If necessary, may be increased to 50-100 mg/day after 2 wks initial therapy. | Same as acebutolol. | Not determined. |
| carteolol (Cartrol) | Antihypertensive: 2.5 mg orally daily; adjust as needed to maximum of 10 mg daily. | Same as acebutolol. | Not determined. |
| esmolol HCl (Brevibloc) IV injection for infusion only | Begin with 500 μg/kg loading dose IV infused over 1 min; then 50 μg/kg/min for 4 minutes. If response inadequate, repeat loading dose and increase maintenance dose by 50 μg to 100 μg/kg/minute over 4 minutes. Repeat steps until desired effects. Close supervision and titration should follow manufacturer's recommendations. | | |
| labetalol (Normodyne, Trandate) | Antihypertensive: 100 mg orally twice daily. May be increased in 100 mg increments every 2 or 3 days until therapeutic response noted. Maintenance: 200-400 mg orally twice daily. (If side effects of nausea or dizziness occur, daily dose may be divided into three doses.) | Same as acebutolol. | Not determined. |
| metoprolol (Lopressor, Apo-Metoprolol ♣ ) | Antianginic or antihypertensive: 100 mg orally in single or divided dosage. May increase at weekly intervals up to maximum of 450 mg/day, if necessary. Prevention of second or recurrent myocardial infarction: 50 mg orally about 15 minutes after last IV dose or when clinical situation justifies change in dosage form. Continue dosage for 2 days (48 hours), then adjust to 100 mg orally twice daily for 3 months or up to 1-3 years. | Same as acebutolol. | Not determined. |
| metoprolol tartrate injection (Lopressor) | Prevention of recurrence of myocardial infarction. Treat early with 5 mg given rapid IV, every 2 min for 3 doses. | Same as acebutolol. | Not determined. |
| nadolol (Corgard) | Antianginic: 40 mg orally daily to start. Increase by 40 mg to 80 mg at 3- to 7-day periods as necessary. Maximum: 240 mg/day. Antihypertensive: 40 mg/day orally to start. Increase by 40 to 80 mg at 7-day periods as necessary. Maximum: 320 mg/day. | Same as acebutolol. | Not determined. |

**TABLE 21-14**   Dosage and administration of beta adrenergic blockers—cont'd

| Drug(s) | Adults | Elderly | Children |
|---|---|---|---|
| oxyprenolol ♣ (Trasicor ♣) Not available in U.S. | Antihypertensive: 20 mg orally 3 times daily. May be increased by 60 mg/day, every 1 to 2 weeks as necessary. Maximum: 480 mg/day. | Same as acebutolol. | Not determined. |
| penbutolol (Levatol) | Antihypertensive: 20 mg orally daily. | Same as acebutolol. | Not determined. |
| pindolol (Visken) | Antihypertensive: 5 mg orally twice a day to start. May be increased by 10 mg/day at 2- to 3-week intervals, if necessary. Once proper dosage is reached, once-a-day dosing may be instituted. Maximum: 60 mg/day. | Same as acebutolol. | Not determined. |
| propranolol (Inderal, Apo-Propranolol ♣) | Antianginic: 10-20 mg orally 3-4 times a day. May be increased slowly every 3 to 7 days to maximum of 320 mg/day, if necessary.<br>Antidysrhythmic: 10-30 mg orally, 3-4 times a day. Adjust as necessary.<br>Antihypertensive: 40 mg orally twice daily. Increase slowly as necessary to maximum of 640 mg/day.<br>Hypertrophic subaortic stenosis: Adjunctive therapy, 20-40 mg orally 3 to 4 times a day. Adjust as necessary.<br>Prevention of recurrence of myocardial infarction: 180-240 mg/day in divided dosages.<br>Pheochromocytoma therapy: adjunctive, 20 mg orally 3 times daily to 40 mg 3 to 4 times/day for 3 days before surgery. Administer alpha blocking agents before starting the beta adrenergic blockade. In cases of inoperable tumors, administer 30-160 mg in divided dosages, daily.<br>Prevention of vascular headaches: 20 mg orally 4 times/day to start. May be increased gradually up to maximum of 240 mg/day, if necessary. | Same as acebutolol. | Antiarrhythmic/antihypertensive: 0.5 mg to 1 mg/kg body weight orally in 2-4 divided doses to start. Adjust dosage according to individual response to treat hypertension or to prevent supraventricular tachycardia. Maintenance: 2-4 mg/kg/day orally in 2 divided dosages. |
| propranolol HCl injection (Inderal) | Antidysrhythmic. 1-3 mg IV given at rate of 1 mg/min. May be repeated after 2 minutes and, if necessary, again after 4 hours. In surgery, an IV dose of ⅒ the oral dose may be administered to temporarily replace PO dose. | Same as acebutolol. | Not determined. |
| timolol (Blocadren) | Antihypertensive: 10 mg orally twice a day to start. Increase at 7-day intervals as necessary. Maintenance: 20-80 mg orally in 2 to 4 divided doses.<br>Prevention of recurrence of myocardial infarction: 10 mg orally, twice daily. Start therapy 1-4 weeks after infarction. | Same as acebutolol. | Not determined. |

---

## WITHDRAWAL OF A BETA BLOCKING AGENT

Withdraw beta adrenergic blocking agents slowly by tapering or lowering the dose over 3 to 14 days. Withdrawl from nadolol usually requires 2 weeks because of its long half-life.

Advise client to avoid vigorous physical exercises or activity during this time to decrease the risk of a reinfarction or cardiac dysrhythmia.

If withdrawl signs occur (angina or chest pain, sweating, tachycardia, respiratory distress), temporarily reinstitute the beta blocking agent to stabilize the client, then slowly lower the dose with close supervision.

---

## PREGNANCY SAFETY

FDA category B: acebutolol, pindolol
FDA category C: epinephrine, isoproterenol, amrinone, dopamine, ephedrine, phenylephrine, metaraminol, methoxamine, atenolol, carteolol, labetalol, metoprolol, nadolol, penbutolol, propanolol, timolol
FDA category X: ergotamine tartrate
FDA category unclassified: norepinephrine, dobutamine, mephentermine, phenoxybenzamine, phentolamine, tolazoline, methysergide, dihydroergotamine*, ergoloid mesylates

*Not recommended.

---

sulin-induced hypoglycemia without the appearance of its signs and symptoms (diaphoresis, increased pulse rate, and blood pressure changes). Blood glucose levels will help determine adjustment of insulin dosage.

Use with caution in clients with nonallergic bronchospasm (emphysema, bronchitis), since the drug can block beta$_2$ receptors in bronchial smooth muscle and has the potential to precipitate bronchoconstriction.

Always check the apical pulse rate before administering the drug. If it is slower than 60 beats/minute or rate is irregular, hold drug and call physician immediately. Also check and report significant variations in blood pressure. Low parameters indicate overdosage.

**Intervention.** To minimize variations in absorption, be consistent in administering oral beta blocking agents with regard to taking them with food or on an empty stomach. Although the manufacturer recommends giving the drug before meals and at bedtime, there is disagreement about whether food enhances or delays bioavailability.

Notify anesthesiologist if client is scheduled for surgery and is receiving a beta blocker.

Note that the drug must be withdrawn slowly (see box above). Otherwise client will suffer from abrupt withdrawal syndrome: tremors, sweating, severe headache, malaise, palpitation, rebound hypertension, life-threatening dysrhythmias, myocardial infarction (in patients with cardiac problems and angina pectoris), and hyperthyroidism in patients with thyrotoxicosis. If drug is to be discontinued, reduce dosage over a 1- to 2-week period. It may be recommended that the drug be withdrawn well before surgery. In individuals with pheochromocytoma, the drug is usually not discontinued before surgery.

For administration of labetalol, the client should be in a supine position during injection and for 3 hours afterward. Increase client's activity and move client to an upright position gradually.

**Education.** Instruct client to take own pulse rate before each dose; also, withhold medication and inform physician if pulse rate drops below 60 beats/minute.

Counsel client not to alter established drug regimen prescribed by physician. The drug controls but does not cure, so lifetime compliance is necessary. Medication should be taken even if the client feels well, and the client should always have an adequate supply of drug available so that strict compliance is observed. Advise the client of the hazards of untreated hypertension. Emphasize the importance of keeping appointments for periodic laboratory tests.

Advise the client to carry medical identification to alert health professionals in an emergency situation that a beta blocker is being taken.

Caution the client not to take over-the-counter medications, especially decongestants and cough and cold medications, but to consult with the health care provider.

While the drug is being withdrawn, advise the client to avoid physical exertion to reduce the risk of myocardial infarction and/or dysrhythmias. Instruct client to restrict sodium intake to prevent unnecessary fluid retention. Caution client to avoid cold temperatures because he or she has an increased sensitivity to cold. Painful, cold, and tender hands and feet are a sign of impaired circulation. Take peripheral pulse to monitor decrease in peripheral circulation.

Advise hypertensive clients to make position changes slowly to prevent lightheadedness and dizziness. Alcohol ingestion, standing still for long periods, exercise, and hot weather enhance the orthostatic hypotensive effects of the drug. If the problem continues to exist, notify physician. Drowsiness and dizziness are common side effects, so caution client about operating a car or hazardous equipment.

In angina pectoris, exercise tolerance should increase and pain should be reduced with the drug. Caution client to avoid overexertion because there has been pain reduction. Instruct client to inform physician if adequate relief is not obtained from the drug.

Instruct client to monitor weight and to report to physician the possible signs of congestive heart failure: weight gain of 3 to 4 pounds a day, dyspnea, cough, fatigue, rapid pulse, and anxiety. (Weight gain of 1 pound represents approximately 500 ml of retained fluid; 4 pounds of weight gain represents about a half gallon of retained fluids.)

***Evaluation.*** Because of the potential for altered cardiac output and ineffective airway clearance related to the blockade of cardiac and bronchial beta adrenergic receptors, when these agents are administered intravenously, monitor ECG, blood pressure, and pulmonary wedge pressure. Have available atropine (for bradycardia), vasopressors (for hypotension), and bronchodilators (for bronchoconstriction). Institute oral therapy as soon as tolerated to reduce the risk of decreased cardiac output. Note if there is a considerable slowing of the pulse rate, however the drug is administered; notify the physician. Beta blocking action can result in cardiac standstill.

Monitor closely hypertensive individuals who have congestive heart failure that is controlled by digitalis and diuretics. The effects of digitalis and beta blockers are additive in depressing AV conduction. Discontinue therapy if cardiac failure continues with digitalis administration. Cardiac failure may be precipitated because of drug-depressed myocardial contractility. Evaluate the effectiveness of drug therapy by assessing the frequency of anginal attacks and activity tolerance. When the drug is used as an antihypertensive, a reduction in blood pressure will indicate effectiveness.

To monitor for potential/actual fluid volume excess, measure intake and output and weigh client daily. Fluid retention may cause dyspnea, orthopnea, nocturnal cough, pulmonary rales, distended neck veins, and edema, which are all signs of impending heart failure. Report weight gain and other such symptoms to the physician.

A common adverse effect of beta blocking agents is a disturbance in self-concept related to mental depression and/or impotence.

Observe client for possible signs of thyrotoxicosis, since the drug may mask clinical signs of hyperthyroidism. In individuals with renal and hepatic impairment, monitor for signs of excessive drug accumulation. The client may experience altered comfort related to the CNS, gastrointestinal, respiratory, and dermatologic effects of the drug and a risk for injury due to the possible CNS effects of drowsiness, dizziness, and light-headedness.

## SUMMARY

Because of the sympathetic nervous system's ability to produce generalized physiologic responses, drugs that act on the system may affect a wide range of body functions. These agents are described as either adrenergic (sympathomimetic) drugs—those that mimic the effects of sympathetic nerve stimulation—or adrenergic blocking (sympatholytic) drugs—those that compete with the catecholamines at receptor sites and inhibit adrenergic sympathetic stimulation. The adrenergic drugs may be direct-acting, indirect-acting, or dual-acting (direct and indirect) agents. Knowledge of these agents is essential, since many of them are used to

rectify life-threatening situations for clients when the nurse must act quickly to provide the necessary pharmacologic intervention. Other drugs that act on the sympathetic nervous system are used quite commonly in practice for a wide range of clients.

The adrenergic direct-acting drugs, catecholamines, interact with and stimulate adrenergic effector cells, which are alpha and beta receptors. Alpha adrenergic activities are vasoconstriction of arterioles in the skin and splanchnic area, which increases blood pressure; pupil dilation; and relaxation of the gut. Beta adrenergic activity includes cardiac acceleration and increased contractility; vasodilation of arterioles of skeletal muscles; bronchial relaxation; and uterine relaxation. Beta receptors are further defined into beta$_1$ receptors, located mainly in the heart, and beta$_2$ receptors within the bronchioles and arterial smooth muscle. Understanding the placement of these receptor cells assists the nurse in conceptualizing the activities of the various drugs that affect the sympathetic nervous system.

Epinephrine is a direct-acting catecholamine that stimulates alpha, beta$_1$, and beta$_2$ receptors. It is considered to be the classic or the standard drug of this classification because of its long history of use for symptomatic treatment of asthma, emergency treatment of anaphylactic shock and cardiac arrest, local hemostasis, and management of simple open-angle glaucoma. Isoproterenol is a nonselective beta adrenergic drug. Norepinephrine, on the other hand, has a high affinity for alpha receptors. Dobutamine is valuable for individuals with low cardiac output because it directly stimulates the beta$_1$ adrenergic receptors of the heart. Dopamine acts mainly to cause vasodilation of the renal and mesenteric arteries. All of these drugs are used for the treatment of circulatory shock.

The indirect-acting adrenergic agents act indirectly on receptors by triggering the release of epinephrine and norepinephrine from their storage sites, which then stimulate alpha and beta receptors. Dual-acting adrenergic agents have both indirect and direct effects. Ephedrine has both a direct and indirect sympathomimetic action and is used more commonly for bronchodilation for milder forms of asthma and as a nasal decongestant. Phenylephrine is also commonly found in many combination cough-cold, antihistamine and decongestant, and ophthalmic preparations. Mephentermine sulfate and metaraminol, as dual-acting adrenergic agents, are used primarily for their vasopressor effects with hypotensive clients.

The adrenergic blocking, or sympatholytic, drugs are also classified by alpha and beta receptors, and by their ability to inhibit adrenergic sympathetic nervous stimulation at these sites. There are noncompetitive, long-acting antagonists, such as phenoxybenzamine, which is used mainly for vasodilation and inhibition of vasospasm; competitive, short-acting antagonists, such as phentolamine, used locally to reverse the action of an extravasation of vasoconstricting drugs, and tolazine, which is indicated for pulmonary hypertension in the newborn; and the ergot alkaloids, which are used for the management of vascular headaches.

The beta adrenergic blocking agents are differentiated into selective beta$_1$ adrenergic blocking agents, such as atenolol and metoprolol, which decrease heart rate, conduction velocity, myocardial contractility, and cardiac output; selective beta$_2$ adrenergic blocking agents that are bronchodilators and will be discussed in Chapter 37; and the nonselective beta adrenergic agents such as carteolol, penbutolol, pindolol, propranolol, and timolol. The nonselective beta adrenergic agents affect cardiac muscle and smooth muscle of the bronchi and blood vessels but are used primarily to treat chronic angina, hypertension, and cardiac dysrhythmias and to prevent a second myocardial infarction, vascular headaches, and cardiac dysrhythmias.

Being knowledgeable about drugs affecting the sympathetic nervous system is essential for all areas of nursing practice.

## BIBLIOGRAPHY

American Society of Hospital Pharmacists. (1990). American hospital formulary service drug information '90. Betheseda, Md: American Society of Hospital Pharmacists, Inc.

Anderson, FD. (1988). Issues in the post-resuscitation period, Critical Care Nursing Quarterly 10(4):51.

Au BG et al. (1986). Drug therapy and dosage adjustment in asthma, Respir Care 31(5):415.

Brook U. (1989). The importance of inhalation of beta 2 sympathomimetic drugs in the home care treatment of asthma in children, Ann Allergy 63(1):37.

Cleary JD. (1988). Two inotropic agents: dopamine and dobutamine, Pediatric Nurs 14(5):414.

Crockett M et al. (1989). Dopamine and dobutamine: neonatal indications and implications, Neonatal Network 7(5):13.

Crowe DW. (1986). The beta and calcium channel blockers, Top Emerg Med 8(1):26.

Downie RL. (1986). Obstructive airway disease, Top Emerg Med 8(4):13.

Frishman WH et al. (1986). Antianginal agents II: β-blockers, Hosp Formul 21(1):62.

Gilman AG et al, eds. (1990). Goodman and Gilman's the pharmacologic basis of therapeutics, ed 8. New York: Macmillan Publishing Co.

Herlihy JT et al. (1986). Adrenergic receptors, Critical Care Nurse 6(2):16.

Hirsh AM. (1988). Type A behavior pattern and catecholamine excretion during cardiac catheterization, West J Nurs Research 10(3):307.

Jefferies PR et al. (1988). Cardiogenic shock: current management, Critical Care Nursing Quarterly 11(1);48.

Kochansky SW. (1986). Epinephrine: use, adverse effects, and dosage calculation, AORN J 43 (4):852.

Manzo M. (1989). Epinephrine in an emergency, Nursing 19(4):105.

McGraw JP. (1987). A graphic solution to the calculation of dopamine and other vasoactive drug dosages, J Emerg Nurs 13(3):172.

Miller K. (1986). Epinephrine, Emergency 18(6):10.

Moore J. (1988). Intravenous amrinone therapy at home for the patient with chronic congestive heart failure, Focus Crit Care 15(6):32.

Noerr B. (1988). Tolazine HCl (Priscoline), Neonatal Network 7(3):74.

Seligman M et al. (1987). Use of adrenergic agents in the critically ill patient, Hosp Formul 22(4):348.

Shapiro DB. (1987). Migraine prophylaxis: the effective role of β-blockers, Consultant 27(1):117.

Simkin P. (1986). Stress, pain and catecholamines in labor. I. A review, Birth 13(4):227.

Sodbinow E. (1988). AANA Journal course: advanced scientific concepts: update for nurse anesthetisis—pulmonary pharmacology: bronchodilators, AANA J 56(6):542.

Taylor RA et al. (1987). Reversible airway obstruction: inhaled β$_2$-bronchodilators as first-line therapy, Consultant 27(4);134.

Tucker SC. (1987). Dopamine use in neonates, Neonatal Network 6(2):21.

United States Pharmacopeial Convention. (1991). Drug information for the health care provider, ed 11. Rockville, Md: The Convention, Inc.

Vidt RG. (1987). β-blockers: choosing the best one for cardiac conditions and hypertension, Consultant 27(3):128.

Williams JR. (1989). Update on beta blockers, AANA J 57(1):29.

Wiltse O. (1987). For your logbook: dopamine, Emergency 19(3):19.

Wulf BG et al. (1986). Cardio-pulmonary arrest: asystole—a review of the medications used to restart the heart, Plast Surg Nurs 6(2):73.

*Chapter*

# 22 Skeletal Muscle Relaxants

## CHAPTER OBJECTIVES

*After studying this chapter, you should be able to meet the following objectives and define the key terms.*

1. Describe the physiology of muscle movement and motor nerve response.

2. Differentiate between muscle spasm and spasticity.

3. Compare the manifestations of the two primary types of muscle spasticity.

4. Compare the action of central-acting and direct-acting skeletal muscle relaxants.

5. Summarize the drug interactions associated with skeletal muscle relaxants.

6. Use nursing measures specific to skeletal muscle relaxants in planning care for clients receiving these agents.

## KEY TERMS

**cerebral spasticity,** page 438

**dystonia,** page 438

**spasms,** page 438

**spinal spasticity,** page 438

## INTRODUCTION

Skeletal muscles are affected by many different pharmacologic substances. Their effects may be at the neuromuscular junction or at different levels in the central nervous system, i.e., at the brain or spinal cord.

## NEUROMUSCULAR JUNCTION

Skeletal muscles are striated (striped) muscles attached to the skeleton. They are usually under voluntary control. These muscles produce body movements, maintain body position against the force of gravity, and counteract environmental stressors such as wind. A muscle is made of numerous muscle cells or muscle fibers. Each muscle cell is connected to only one motor nerve fiber, but each of the nerve fibers is connected to several muscle cells. Therefore stimulation of one nerve fiber will cause stimulation and activation of a group of muscle cells. The region where a motor nerve fiber makes functional contact with a skeletal muscle fiber (synaptic contact) is known as the neuromuscular junction.

## SKELETAL MUSCLE SPASM AND SPASTICITY

Skeletal muscle **spasms** result when there is an involuntary contraction of a muscle or group of muscles that is accompanied by pain or limited function. Most skeletal muscle spasms are caused by local injuries, but some may result from low calcium levels or epileptic myoclonic seizures. Each type of spasm is treated according to its etiology.

Skeletal muscle injuries are usually self-limiting and can be treated with rest; physical therapy; immobility by use of casts, neck collars, crutches, or arm slings; or whirlpool baths. With tissue damage and edema, however, antiinflammatory drugs may be used.

Central skeletal muscle relaxants are used mainly for conditions in which muscle spasms do not quickly respond to other forms of therapy. Such conditions include musculoskeletal strains and sprains, trauma, and cervical or lumbar radiculopathy as a result of degenerative osteoarthritis, herniated disk, spondylolysis, or laminectomy. Unlike diazepam, the centrally acting drug, baclofen, which is used for skeletal muscle spasticity, has not been found useful in the treatment of muscle spasms.

Skeletal muscle spasticity is characterized by skeletal muscle hyperactivity. Skeletal muscle spasticity happens when gamma motor neurons, which tonically control muscle spindle contractile activity, become hyperactive.

There are two primary types of muscle spasticity: spinal and cerebral. **Spinal spasticity** can be identified by a marked loss of inhibitory influences with hyperactive tendon stretch reflexes, clonus (alternate contraction and relaxation of muscles), primitive flexion withdrawal reflexes, and a flexed posture. Varying degrees of spasticity of the bladder and bowel can also be seen. **Cerebral spasticity** has less reflex excitability, increased muscle tone, and no primitive flexion withdrawal reflexes or flexed posture. **Dystonia** may also be present in such individuals with cerebral spasticity.

Muscle spasticity is most commonly seen in clients with central nervous system injuries and strokes. Moderate to severe spasticity can be seen in two thirds of clients with multiple sclerosis. Individuals with cerebral palsy and rare neurologic disorders can also have muscle spasticity, but it is seen less frequently in these instances.

Central-acting and direct-acting skeletal muscle relaxants are the drugs of choice in the treatment of muscle spasticity. These drugs include baclofen, diazepam, and dantrolene. They are more effective in the treatment of spinal spasticity than cerebral spasticity. However, optimal therapy cannot be achieved in the treatment of either unless physical therapy is given concurrently.

## CENTRAL-ACTING SKELETAL MUSCLE RELAXANTS

The exact mechanism of action of the central skeletal muscle relaxants is not known. Action results from CNS depression in the brain (brainstem, thalamus, and basal ganglia) and spinal cord. This CNS depression results in relaxation of striated muscle spasm. Removal of the central nervous depressive action from the skeletal muscle relaxation action of the central-acting skeletal muscle relaxants is not possible currently. As a result these drugs create the side effects of drowsiness, blurred vision, lightheadedness, headache, and feelings of weakness, lassitude, and lethargy that make their long-term use undesirable. The drugs used primarily as antispastic agents are baclofen, diazepam, and dantrolene. Dantrolene is a direct-acting skeletal muscle relaxant (peripheral action); it is discussed later in this chapter.

## ▷NURSING MANAGEMENT: CENTRAL-ACTING SKELETAL MUSCLE RELAXANT THERAPY

***Assessment.*** The client should be assessed for a history of allergic reaction to the specific agent. CNS depression may be exacerbated with the administration of central-acting muscle relaxants, so caution should be taken with these clients. The drugs should also be used cautiously in the presence of hepatic or renal dysfunction and in pregnant women. The FDA disapproves of prolonged administration of these drugs and discourages their use for periods longer than three weeks.

Once the client begins taking a central-acting skeletal muscle relaxant, the nurse's assessment should consider the potential development of a number of nursing diagnoses related to the effects of the drug. Because of the CNS effects of the drug, the client may experience altered thought processes, disturbed sleep pattern, and a risk for injury. Elimination patterns may be altered, such as with constipation and urinary frequency. Altered comfort may evidence as muscle weakness, nausea, headache, stomach discomfort, hiccoughs, and rash. Sensory-perceptual alterations may also occur.

***Intervention.*** For ease of administration, the tablets may be crushed and mixed with fluid, jelly, or other food. The drugs should be administered with meals or milk to prevent the side effects of nausea, vomiting, heartburn, and abdominal distress associated with large doses.

***Education.*** Inform individuals taking these agents to avoid activities that require mental alertness, judgment, and physical coordination, such as operating dangerous machinery or driving an automobile. Instruct the client that alcohol and other CNS depressants will increase the CNS effects of these drugs. Because many clients have postural hypotension with these medications, clients should be cautioned about standing suddenly and instructed to rise slowly, in keeping with individual physical limitations.

## baclofen (Lioresal)

Baclofen is an analogue of the inhibitory neurotransmitter gamma-aminobutyric acid (GABA). Baclofen acts at a spinal level, where it inhibits monosynaptic and polysynaptic transmission, although its exact mechanism of action is unknown. It is used in the treatment of spasticity resulting from multiple sclerosis or from injuries to the spinal cord. It has been used investigationally to treat trigeminal neuralgia. Absorption is generally good but may vary with different individuals. Reportedly, absorption decreased with an increase in dosage. Time to peak concentration is 2 to 3 hours. Variable effects may occur in hours or up to weeks. Baclofen has a half-life of 2.5 to 4 hours and a therapeutic serum level of 80 to 400 ng/ml. Baclofen is metabolized in the liver (15% only) and excreted in the kidneys (between 70% to 85% of a dose is excreted unchanged). For information regarding side effects/adverse reactions, see Table 22-1. The combination of baclofen and alcohol or other CNS depressants may result in enhanced CNS depressant effects and hypotension. Monitor closely because reduction in dosage of one or both drugs may be necessary. Administer 5 mg orally three times daily, increased by 5 mg per dose every three days, until desired response is achieved, not to exceed 80 mg/day. Dosage for children has not been determined.

## ▷ Nursing Management: Baclofen Therapy

In addition to the nursing management discussed as appropriate to central-acting skeletal muscle relaxant therapy in general, baclofen requires the following management.

***Intervention.*** The dosage should be increased gradually to therapeutic dosages to decrease the incidence of adverse effects. A gradual reduction in dosage over a period of 2 weeks is recommended, since abrupt withdrawal may cause hallucinations, paranoia, nightmares, confusion, and rebound spasticity.

***Education.*** Tell the client that maximum benefit of the medication may not be reached for 1 to 2 months.

If abrupt withdrawal is required, instruct the client that hallucinations and rebound spasticity may occur. Alert the client to possible side effects such as dermatitis, dark or bloody urine, CNS effects, chest pain, and syncope. If orthostatic hypotension is a concern, instruct the client to come to an upright position slowly and stay seated until the light-headedness dissipates.

***Evaluation.*** Administration of baclofen may increase the client's blood glucose levels, thus requiring an adjustment of the insulin dosage during therapy and when baclofen therapy is stopped. Geriatric clients are at risk for adverse CNS reactions. They should be assessed for the development of altered thought processes, such as hallucinations, depression, confusion, and excessive sedation. Observe for increased seizure activity in patients with epilepsy because the seizure threshold may be lowered. Monitor the client's clinical state and EEG results during therapy.

## diazepam (Valium, Apo-Diazepam ✱)

The mechanism of action is unknown. Diazepam appears to act primarily by inhibiting afferent monosynaptic and polysynaptic pathways. It may also directly suppress muscle function at the neuromuscular synapse. See Chapter 14 for a more complete description of indications. Diazepam is used in the treatment of skeletal muscle spasm caused by reflex spasm to local pathologic conditions, such as inflammation of muscle and joints or secondary to trauma. It is also used to treat spasticity caused by upper motor neuron disorders (cerebral palsy and paraplegia), athetosis, tetanus, and the stiff-man syndrome (to overcome the widespread chronic muscular rigidity, pain, and skeletal muscle spasms). For diazepam's pharmacokinetics, side effects/adverse reactions, and significant drug interactions, see Chapter 14. For dosage and administration, see Table 22-2.

**TABLE 22-1**  Side effects/adverse reactions of baclofen

| | Side effects* | Adverse reactions† |
|---|---|---|
| baclofen (Lioresal) | More frequent: Transient drowsiness, vertigo, confusion, sleepiness, increased weakness, muscle weakness, nausea<br>Less frequent: Diarrhea, stomach pain or upset, ataxia, headache, euphoria, insomnia, slurred speech, paresthesia, muscle stiffness, increased excitability, fatigue, constipation, dysuria, increased urgency to urinate, urinary incontinence, sexual difficulties in males, congested nasal passages, anorexia, edema of ankles, hypotension, tachycardia, weight gain | Rare: Fainting spells; chest pain; blood or dark coloration of urine; CNS alterations, such as hallucination (auditory and visual); depression; mood changes; tinnitus<br>Overdosage: Visual disturbances (e.g., blurred or double vision), convulsions, respiratory difficulties, severe muscle weakness, vomiting |

*If side effects continue, increase, or disturb the client, the physician should be informed.
†If adverse reactions occur, the physician should be contacted because medical intervention may be necessary.

**TABLE 22-2**   Dosage and administration of central-acting muscle relaxants

| Drug | Adults | Children |
| --- | --- | --- |
| baclofen (Lioresal) | 5 mg orally 2 to 3 times daily, increase by 5 mg/dose every 3 days until desired response is achieved | Not determined |
| carisoprodol (Rela, Soma) | 350 mg orally 4 times daily | Less than age 5, not determined; 5 to 12 years old, 6.25 mg/kg body weight orally, 4 times daily |
| chlorphenesin (Maolate) | Initially, 800 mg orally 3 times daily; may be later decreased to 400 mg 4 times daily (or less) to maintain desired effect | Not determined |
| chlorzoxazone (Paraflex) | 250 to 750 mg orally 3 or 4 times daily (usual initial dose is 500 mg 3 or 4 times daily); adjust according to individual response | 20 mg/kg body weight or 600 mg/m$^2$ body surface area, given in 3 or 4 divided doses daily |
| cyclobenzaprine (Flexeril) | 20 to 40 mg daily, in divided doses, orally (usual dose 10 mg 3 times daily) | Not determined |
| diazepam (Valium) | *Oral:* 2-10 mg 3 or 4 times daily<br>*Parenteral:* 5-10 mg IM or IV initially, repeated every 3-4 hr as necessary. For tetanus, larger doses may be required. | *Oral:* 1-2.5 mg 3 or 4 times daily (not for use in children less than 6 months of age)<br>*Parenteral:* check current package insert |
| metaxalone (Skelaxin) | 800 mg orally, 3 or 4 times daily | Not determined |
| methocarbamol (Robaxin, Marbaxin) | *Oral* initially: 1.5 g orally 4 times daily for 2-3 days; if condition is severe, may increase divided dosage to 8 g daily.<br>Maintenance therapy: 750 mg orally every 4 hr or 1 g 4 times daily or 1.5 g 3 times daily.<br>*Parenteral:* 1-3 g IM or IV daily for 3 days. After 2 drug-free days, the drug may be repeated, if necessary.<br>Adjunct therapy for tetanus, 1 or 2 g IV, an additional dose may be given by IV infusion. Total initial dose is up to 3 g. Dosage may be repeated every 6 hr as necessary.<br>Maximum dosage, do not exceed 3 g/day for more than 3 days except in the treatment of tetanus | Not determined<br><br>Not determined<br><br>Adjunct therapy for tetanus, 15 mg/kg body weight IV every 6 hr |
| orphenadrine (Disipal, Norflex) | *Oral:* 50 mg 3 times daily for plain tablets, 100 mg twice daily for extended-release dosage form, 250 mg/day maximum daily dose<br>*Parenteral:* 60 mg IM or IV every 12 hr, when necessary | Not determined<br><br>Not determined |

▷**Nursing Management:**
**Diazepam Therapy**

***Assessment.***  Baseline vital signs should be assessed before diazepam is given and then frequently after the injection.

***Intervention.***  Diazepam is insoluble in water, and so the parenteral form is prepared in a specific solvent. Do not mix or dilute parenteral dosages with other fluids or add to intravenous fluids. Administer intramuscular injections slowly and deeply into a large muscle to diminish local irritation.

Administer intravenous diazepam slowly, at least 1 minute for each 5 mg of the drug to prevent apnea, hypotension, bradycardia, or cardiac arrest. After receiving a parenteral dosage, the client should be observed and should stay in bed for at least 3 hours. Resuscitative equipment should be available. To avoid phlebitis and venous thrombosis, small veins on the back of the hand and wrist should not be used for intravenous administration. To minimize the occurrence of thrombophlebitis following intravenous administration of diazepam, flush the vein with a 1 ml of saline per 1 mg of diazepam.

Continuous intravenous infusion is not recommended because diazepam may precipitate in the infusion bag and the medication may be adsorbed to the plastic of infusion bags and tubing. If the drug cannot be administered by direct

**TABLE 22-3**   Pharmacokinetics of other central-acting skeletal muscle relaxants

| Drug | Onset of action | Time to peak concentration (hr)* | Peak serum concentration* | Duration of action (hrs) | Half-life (hrs) | Metabolism/ excretion |
|---|---|---|---|---|---|---|
| carisoprodol | ½ hr | 4 (350 mg) | 4-7 μg/ml | 4-6 | 8 | liver/kidneys |
| chlorphenesin | N/A | 1 to 3 | 3.8-17 μg/ml (800 mg) | N/A | 2.5-5 | liver/kidneys |
| chlorzoxazone | within 60 min | 1 to 2 | 10-30 μg/ml (750 mg) | 3-4 | 1-2 | liver/kidneys |
| cyclobenzaprine | within 60 min | 3 to 8 | 15-25 ng/ml (10 mg) | 12-24 | 24-72 | GI and liver/kidneys |
| metaxalone | 60 min | 2 (800 mg) | 295 μg/ml (800 mg) | N/A | 2-3 | liver/kidneys |
| methocarbamol | PO, within 30 minutes | 2 (2 g) | 16 μg/ml (2 g) | N/A | 0.9-2.2 | may be liver/kidneys and feces |
| | IV, immediate | nearly immediate | 19 μg/ml (1 g) | N/A | | |
| orphenadrine citrate extended release | within 60 min | 6 to 8 (100 mg) | 60-120 ng/ml (100 mg) | 12 | 14† | liver/kidneys and feces |
| IM | 5 min | ½ (60 mg) | | | | |
| IV | immediate | immediate | | | | |
| orphenadrine HCl | within 60 min | 3 (50 mg) | 110-210 ng/ml (100 mg) | 8 | 14† | liver/kidneys and feces |

*Single dose.
†Parent drug half-life. Metabolites may range between 2 and 25 hours.

intravenous infusion, it may be injected through the intravenous tubing, but the injection should be as close as possible to the insertion point.

***Education.*** Diazepam crosses the placental barrier and has been associated with causing cleft lip in infants. The risks versus the benefits should be considered in the pregnant client. It is also excreted in breast milk. See also general discussion of the nursing management of central-acting skeletal muscle relaxant therapy.

***Evaluation.*** Clients undergoing long-term therapy can become physically dependent on the drug and show signs and symptoms of withdrawal when the drug is discontinued. For additional nursing management, see Chapter 14.

**carisoprodol (Rela, Soma)**
**chlorphenesin carbamate (Maolate)**
**chlorzoxazone (Paraflex)**
**cyclobenzaprine (Flexeril)**
**metaxalone (Skelaxin)**
**methocarbamol (Robaxin, Marbaxin)**
**orphenadrine HCl (Disipal)**
**orphenadrine citrate extended-release (Norflex)**

Muscle spasms are treated with central-acting skeletal muscle relaxants that are analogs to various antianxiety medications. They include the drugs listed in the table above. The exact mechanism of action of these drugs has not been determined. All of the drugs have an action in the central nervous system. It is believed the muscle relaxant effects

of many of these drugs may be related to this CNS-depressant activity. These drugs are used in adjunct treatment for skeletal muscle spasms along with rest and physical therapy. For information on their pharmacokinetics, see Table 22-3. For information on their side effects/adverse reactions, see Table 22-4. When a skeletal muscle relaxant is given with alcohol, CNS depressants, or opioid analgesics, enhanced CNS depressant effects may occur. Monitor closely because the dosage of one or both drugs should be reduced. For an examination of the dosage and administration for these agents, see Table 22-2.

▷**Nursing Management:**

***carisoprodol (Rela, Soma).*** For all of the following drugs, see also the general discussion of the nursing management of central-acting skeletal muscle relaxant therapy. Carisoprodol is found in the milk of lactating mothers at levels two to four times the maternal plasma concentration, causing sedation and gastrointestinal distress in the infant. Risk and benefit should be considered before using this drug for a pregnant or lactating client. Carisoprodol is contraindicated in clients with acute intermittent porphyria. On occasion, an idiosyncratic reaction to carisoprodol has occurred within minutes or hours of the first dose. Symptoms may include disorientation, agitation, vision disturbances, impaired verbal communication, and extreme weakness. The symptoms are temporary, but supportive therapy may be needed and may require hospitalization. There have been

**TABLE 22-4**   Side effects/adverse reactions of other central-acting skeletal muscle relaxants

| Drug | Side effects* | Adverse reactions† |
|------|---------------|--------------------|
| carisoprodol | More frequent: Drowsiness<br>Less frequent: Hiccups, vomiting, stomach distress, ataxia, headache, tremors, insomnia, dizziness (postural hypotension), increased excitability, nervousness, or irritability. | Less frequent: Fainting spells, fever, allergic reaction (skin rash, pruritis, edema of face, lips or tongue, respiratory difficulties, or burning eyes), depression, tachycardia |
| chlorphenesin carbamate | Less frequent: Sleepiness, dizziness | Rare: Fever, skin rash, pruritus, sore throat, increased bleeding tendencies or bruising, fatigue |
| chlorzoxazone | More frequent: Sleepiness, dizziness<br>Less frequent: Abdominal distress, diarrhea, stomach gas, nausea, vomiting, constipation, headache, increased excitability, nervousness, restlessness | Rare: Dark or bloody stools; rash; pruritus; edema of face, lips, or tongue; sore throat; elevated temperature; increased bleeding tendencies; bruising; fatigue |
| cyclobenzaprine | More frequent: Dizziness, sleepiness, dry mouth<br>Less frequent: Blurred vision, headaches, nausea, paresthesias, difficulty speaking, insomnia, taste alterations, tremors, abdominal distress, constipation, uncommon fatigue, unusual pounding pulse, and muscle weakness | Rare: Ataxia, confusion, depression, tinnitus, dysuria, allergic reaction (rash, pruritus, edema of face, lips, or tongue), jaundice<br>Overdosage: Severe drowsiness, respiratory difficulties, dysrhythmias, hallucinations, altered body temperature, convulsions, muscle stiffness, vomiting, severe restlessness |
| metaxalone | More frequent: Abdominal distress, nausea or vomiting, dizziness, sleepiness, headaches, increased excitability, restlessness | Rare: Skin rash, pruritus, sore throat, fever, increased bleeding tendencies or bruising, unusual fatigue, jaundice |
| methocarbamol | More frequent: Visual disturbances (double, blurred vision), sleepiness, dizziness<br>Less frequent: Nausea, vomiting, ataxia, headaches, increased muscle weakness | Less frequent: Fever, rash, pruritus, nasal congestion, bloodshot eyes<br>If IV dosage form is administered too fast, bradycardia and unusual eye movements are seen. |
| orphenadrine | Less frequent: Abdominal distress, visual disturbances (blurred, double vision), disorientation, sleepiness, headaches, tremors, constipation, dizziness, increased excitability, nervousness | Less frequent: Fainting spells, tachycardia |

*If side effects continue, increase, or disturb the client, the physician should be informed.
†If adverse reactions occur, the physician should be contacted because medical intervention may be necessary.

rare reports of psychological dependence and abuse. Drowsiness is more frequent with carisoprodol than with most other muscle relaxants.

***chlorphenesin carbomate (Maolate).*** Watch for sensitivity reactions. Hold dose, and notify the physician if unusual reactions occur. Observe for unusual bleeding and indications of blood dyscrasias. Safety when used for longer than 8 weeks has not been determined.

***chlorzoxazone (Paraflex).*** Chlorzoxazone is contraindicated in individuals with hepatic disease. Liver function studies should be monitored closely during therapy because hepatotoxicity is a possible side effect. Tell the client that the drug may discolor the urine orange or purple-red. Drowsiness and/or dizziness is more common with chlorzoxazone than with most other muscle relaxants.

***diazepam (Valium).*** See previous section and Chapter 14.

***metaxalone (Skelaxin).*** Metaxalone is contraindicated in individuals with renal and hepatic disease. Monitor liver function studies. Monitor blood studies because hemolytic anemia may occur. Clinitest and Benedict's solution may give a false positive reading in urine tests of clients taking metaxalone. Use Clinistix, Diastix, or Testape instead. Caution client to notify prescriber if skin rash or yellowish discoloration of skin or eyes occurs (signs of liver-related jaundice). Gastrointestinal irritation with nausea, vomiting, and abdominal cramps is more common with metaxalone than with other muscle relaxants.

***methocarbamol (Robaxin, Marbaxin).*** Be aware that methocarbamol is not recommended for individuals receiving anticholinesterase agents or for those who have epilepsy or who are in renal failure (because this may increase preexisting acidosis and urea retention). Have epinephrine, injectable steroids, and/or injectable antihistamines available for intravenous injection to treat syncope should it occur. Anaphylactic reaction has occurred after intramuscular and intravenous administration. Have client recumbent during intravenous infusion and remain recumbent 10 to 15 minutes after infusion to decrease the incidence of adverse effects such as syncope, hypotension, and bradycardia.

Do not give subcutaneously. Administer deep (IM) injection to decrease local irritation. Avoid intravenous ex-

**TABLE 22-5**  Side effects/adverse reactions of direct-acting skeletal muscle relaxants

| Drug | Side effects* | Adverse reactions† |
|---|---|---|
| dantrolene (Dantrium) | More frequent: With short-term (1-3 days use) or chronic oral intake of dantrolene: mild diarrhea, dizziness, sleepiness, feelings of uncomfortableness or unusual fatigue, muscle weakness (not of respiratory muscles), nausea, or vomiting. Less frequent: Abdominal pain or discomfort With chronic oral drug only: visual disturbances, headache, slurred speech, insomnia, increased nervousness, chills, fever, mild constipation, dysphagia, increased urgency to urinate, urinary incontinence, anorexia, decrease in urinary output. | Less frequent: With short-term (1-3 days use) or chronic oral usage: severe diarrhea, respiratory difficulty, or depression With chronic oral use of drug only: Chest pain, severe constipation (may result in distention or appearance of bowel obstruction), dark or bloody urine, depression, disorientation, convulsions, dysuria, phlebitis of leg or foot, allergic skin reaction, and jaundice |

*If side effects continue, increase, or disturb the client, the physician should be informed.
†If adverse reactions occur, the physician should be contacted because medical intervention may be necessary.

travasation; thrombophlebitis, pain, and tissue sloughing may result. The intravenous infusion should not be refrigerated. In addition, its compatibility with other solutions is limited; see a specialized reference before mixing. It may be diluted in normal saline or 5% dextrose in water, but do not dilute to more than 10 ml (1 g) in 250 ml. If administering intravenous undiluted, inject at a rate not greater than 3 ml/minute. Note that tablets may be crushed and suspended in water or saline for administration via a nasogastric tube.

Advise client to notify the prescriber if skin rash, itching, fever, or nasal congestion occurs. Tell client that urine, if it is standing, may darken to green, black, or brown.

*orphenadrine (Disipal).* Use with caution in individuals with cardiac decompensation, coronary insufficiency, cardiac dysrhythmias, or tachycardia. Note that orphenadrine is contraindicated in clients with glaucoma, prostatic hypertrophy, obstruction of the neck of the bladder, and myasthenia gravis. Periodic blood, urine, and liver function studies should be done with prolonged therapy. Discuss side effects with the client.

## DIRECT-ACTING SKELETAL MUSCLE RELAXANT
### dantrolene (Dantrium)

Dantrolene is used in the treatment of malignant hyperthermia (see Chapter 13). Dantrolene acts directly on skeletal muscles to produce skeletal muscle relaxation by inhibiting the release of calcium from the sarcoplasmic reticulum to the myoplasm, resulting in decreased muscle response to the action potential and decreased muscle contraction. Used as an antispastic agent, dantrolene's direct effect on skeletal muscle dissociates the excitation-contraction coupling. This effect is probably induced by the interference with calcium ion release from the sarcoplasmic

reticulum. Dantrolene reduces both monosynaptic- and polysynaptic-induced muscle contractions.

The drug, then, is indicated for the prevention and treatment of malignant hyperthermia, and the treatment of spasticity, especially upper motor neuron disorders, such as multiple sclerosis, cerebral palsy, spinal cord insults, and cerebrovascular accident (CVA). Dantrolene is available orally and parenterally. The drug's oral absorption is fair; about 35% of dose is absorbed. Onset of action when dantrolene is used to treat the spasticity of upper motor neurons is 1 week or more. The drug has an oral half-life of 8.7 hours (100-mg dose); IV, 4-8 hours. Its time to peak concentration is 5 hours (oral dose), and it has a therapeutic serum level of 300 to 1100 ng/ml, variable with the individual. Dantrolene is metabolized in the liver and excreted in the kidneys. For side effects/adverse reactions, see Table 22-5.

*Significant drug interactions.* The following effects may occur when dantrolene is given with the drugs listed below.

1. When given for short-term use (1-3 days) or chronic use with alcohol or CNS depressants: enhanced CNS depression may occur. Dosage of one or both drugs may need to be decreased. Monitor closely.
2. When given for chronic use only with hepatotoxic drugs: the risk of inducing liver toxicity increases. Women over 35 years of age taking estrogen products are at particular risk for this toxicity.
3. IV dantrolene for malignant hyperthermia only, with calcium channel-blocking agents: avoid this combination while attempting management of a malignant hyperthermic emergency. In animals this combination has caused ventricular fibrillation, severe hypokalemia, and cardiovascular collapse. Although this interaction is not documented in humans, concurrent administration of this combination of drugs is not recommended.

**TABLE 22-6**   Dosage and administration of dantrolene

| Adults | Children |
|---|---|
| **FOR MUSCLE SPASTICITY:** | |
| Orally, 25 mg initially; increase by 25 mg/day every 4-7 days until therapeutic response is achieved or until the dosage of 100 mg 4 times a day is reached | 0.5 mg/kg body weight orally twice daily initially; increase by 0.5 mg/kg daily every 4-7 days until therapeutic response is achieved or until dosage of 3 mg/kg body weight 4 times/day is reached. Do not use dosages over 400 mg daily. |
| **ACUTE MALIGNANT HYPERTHERMIC REACTION (ADJUNCT):** | |
| IV push of a minimum of 1 mg/kg body weight; continue this dose until symptoms abate or until maximum cumulative dose of 10 mg/kg body weight is reached. If symptoms recur, dosage may be repeated. After IV therapy, usually 4-8 mg/kg body weight is administered orally in 4 divided doses daily for 24-72 hrs. | See usual adult dose |
| **AS PROPHYLAXIS FOR MALIGNANT HYPERTHERMIC CRISIS:** | |
| 4-8 mg/kg body weight given orally in 3 or 4 divided doses daily for 24-48 hr before surgery. Give last dose 3-4 hr before surgery with small amount of water. Intravenous infusion, 2.5 mg/kg over 1 hour before anesthesia. | Not available |

***Dosage and administration.*** See Table 22-6.

▷ **Nursing Management: Dantrolene Therapy**

***Assessment.*** Dantrolene should not be administered to clients with active hepatic disease. Use caution in clients with impaired cardiac, hepatic, or pulmonary function. The precautions do not apply to the short-term intravenous use of dantrolene to treat malignant hyperthermia. Lactose-intolerant clients may also react adversely to dantrolene capsules, which contain lactose. Careful assessment of the client is particularly important when dantrolene has been prescribed for spasticity. Because there is no way of knowing if a client will benefit without a clinical trial, the observations of the relief of spasticity are critical. The decision for long-term use of dantrolene depends on the balance between the drug-induced weakness and other adverse effects and the beneficial effects of the drug. Paraplegic clients may not consider the adverse effect of weakness as detrimental as spasticity. Ambulatory clients who use spasticity to remain upright or balance are not candidates for datrolene therapy.

***Intervention.*** The contents of the capsule may be mixed with fruit juice for oral administration to a client unable to swallow capsules. Administer immediately after mixing. When intravenous dantrolene is used to treat malignant hyperthermia, use of all anesthetic agents is discontinued, oxygen is administered, metabolic acidosis and fluid and electrolyte imbalances are corrected, and the client is cooled. Reconstitute intravenous dantrolene with 60 ml of sterile water for injection without a bacteriostatic agent and shake the mixture until it is clear. Use within 6 hours of preparation. Oral dantrolene may be given after the intra-

---

**PREGNANCY SAFETY**

The following drugs are unclassified by the FDA: baclofen, diazepam*, carisoprodol, chlorphenesin, chlorzoxazone, cyclobenzaprine, metaxalone, methocarbamol, orphenadrine, dantrolene

*To be avoided during pregnancy, especially during first trimester.

---

venous dose to prevent recurrence of symptoms. Avoid extravasation of intravenous dantrolene. It is painful and irritating to the tissue because of the high pH of the solution.

***Education.*** Caution clients that photosensitivity is possible with dantrolene, so they should avoid exposure to the sun. Instruct clients that the therapeutic effects may not become evident until a week after the usual initial oral dose. However, improvement should be seen within 45 days or the drug should be discontinued. Regular visits to the physician should be encouraged for assessment of progress and to monitor for side effects with blood studies. For other nursing considerations, see the nursing management of central-acting skeletal muscle relaxant therapy.

***Evaluation.*** When dantrolene has been administered to prevent malignant hyperthermia, carefully monitor the client postoperatively for possible delayed effects of the drug (Table 22-5). The client receiving long-term therapy should be monitored for blood cell counts and hepatic and renal functioning. The risk of hepatoxicity is greater in clients with previous liver disease, those taking 800 mg daily in the short-term therapy or 200 mg daily for longer than 2 months, and women over 35 concurrently receiving estrogen therapy. Hepatitis most frequently occurs between 3 and 12 months into therapy and is generally preceded by gastrointestinal symptoms such as anorexia, nausea, and vomiting. Side effects may be minimized by starting with low dosages and increasing them gradually. With short-term use, diarrhea may be a concern and may be severe enough to discontinue therapy. In chronic use, constipation may occur and health teaching should focus on its prevention.

## SUMMARY

Pharmacologic agents administered as skeletal muscle relaxants affect skeletal muscle at the neuromuscular junction or at different levels in the central nervous system, such as the spinal cord or brain. With central-acting skeletal muscle relaxants, the drugs' effects result from CNS depression in the brain and spinal cord. Direct-acting skeletal muscle relaxants affect striated muscle to dissociate the excitation-contraction coupling and so reduce monosynaptic and polysynaptic-induced muscle contractions. Although most skeletal muscle spasm is the result of local injury, other instances may be of a more systemic nature; but the treatment of each type of spasm is related to its etiology.

## BIBLIOGRAPHY

American Hospital Formulary Service. (1990). AHFS drug information '90. Bethesda, Md: American Society of Hospital Pharmacists, Inc.

Elenbaas JK. (1980). Centrally acting oral skeletal muscle relaxants, Am J Hosp Pharm 30(10):1313.

Gilman AG et al, eds. (1990). Goodman and Gilman's the pharmacological basis of therapeutics, ed 8. New York: Macmillan Publishing Co.

Glenn MB et al. (1986). Antispasticity medications in the patient with traumatic brain injury, J Head Trauma Rehabil 1(2):71.

Hildebrand RD. (1988). Muscle relaxants: a review, J Post Anesth Nurs 3(3):165.

Rice GPA. (1987). Pharmacotherapy of spasticity: some theoretical and practical considerations, Can J Neurol Sci 14(3):510.

United States Pharmacopeial Convention. (1991). Drug information for the health care provider, ed 11. Rockville, Md: United States Pharmacopeial Convention.

Wahlquist G. (1987) Evaluation and primary management of spasticity, Nurse Pract 12(3):27.

Young RR and Delwaide PJ. (1981). Drug therapy: spasticity, part 1, N Engl J Med 304(1):28.

Young RR and Delwaide PJ. (1981). Drug therapy: spasticity, part 2, N Engl J Med 304(2):96.

# Drugs Affecting the Cardiovascular System

# 23 Overview of the Cardiovascular System

## CHAPTER OBJECTIVES

*After studying this chapter, you should be able to meet the following objectives and define the key terms.*

1. Describe the anatomy and physiology of the heart.

2. Name the three major tissues of the heart.

3. Describe the role of electrical excitation in myocardial contraction.

4. Explain ion exchange during depolarization and repolarization of the myocardial cell.

5. Describe the events occurring in the cardiac cycles, that is, systole and diastole.

6. Describe the vagus nerve's effect on the heart.

7. Describe the energy balance between expenditure and restoration maintained by the coronary blood vessels.

## KEY TERMS

## INTRODUCTION

The development of microelectrode techniques and sophisticated recordings has resulted in new knowledge and greater understanding of cardiac activity. The resulting anatomic, electrophysiologic, and pharmacologic information has permitted greater precision in diagnosing and treating cardiac disease, particularly the dysrhythmias. Along with these advances has been the increased use of electrocardiographic

**TABLE 23-1** Effect of cardiac drug groups on cardiac tissues

| Cardiac tissue | Physiologic property | Drug group | Pharmacologic action |
|---|---|---|---|
| Cardiac muscle (myocardium) | Force of myocardial contraction (Frank-Starling's law) | Cardiac glycosides | Positive inotropic effect—increases cardiac output |
| Sarcomere (functional unit) | Contractility and conductivity | | |
| Cardiac conduction system | Automaticity (rhythm and rate) | Antidysrhythmic drugs | Converts to normal sinus rhythm or abolishes dysrhythmia |
| | Conductivity | Calcium channel blockers | |
| Coronary arteries | Nutritional blood flow to myocardium and other cardiac structures | Antianginal drugs Calcium channel blockers | Coronary vasodilation or lessens work of the heart |

monitoring of acutely ill patients and those with known or suspected cardiovascular disorders. In addition, the nurse's clinical role has expanded and now includes care of clients on many types of monitoring equipment. This requires the nurse to recognize and understand abnormal electrocardiographic patterns and in some cases to begin therapy, including pharmacologic therapy, to prevent serious complications and unnecessary deaths. Therefore nurses must understand the electrical and physiologic properties of the heart and the effects drugs have on cardiac activity to keep their knowledge current and their nursing care therapeutically effective.

Microelectrode techniques have grown increasingly sophisticated and helped provide greater understanding of the electrical properties of cardiac fibers and of what causes various cardiac disorders. Fortunately, these advances have led to the discovery of new drugs that are useful in treating cardiac conditions.

Cardiac drugs largely affect three major tissues of the heart: cardiac muscle (myocardium), conduction system, and coronary vessels. In this chapter the normal function of these structures is discussed. The physiologic properties of these structures and the drug groups used therapeutically are summarized in Table 23-1.

## THE HEART

The **heart** is a hollow muscular organ that consists of two main pumping chambers: the right ventricle, which is linked with the pulmonary circulation, and the left ventricle, which is connected to the systemic circulation. The cardiac muscle or myocardium is the largest and most important structure of the heart. As a contractile muscle, under normal conditions it can adapt its performance by adjusting the cardiac output according to the body's needs. However, when the heart cannot produce a variable output, the therapeutic use of digitalis or cardiac glycosides (i.e., the digitalis drugs) produces changes at the cellular level. A description of myocardial ultrastructure and the contractile process facilitates an understanding of the basic mechanisms in cardiac glycoside action.

## Cardiac Muscle

The pumping action of the heart depends on the ability of the cardiac muscle to contract. The **myocardium** is composed of many interconnected branching fibers or cells that form the walls of the two **atria** and two **ventricles** of the heart. Each individual myocardial fiber contains a nucleus in the middle and a plasma membrane (cell membrane), the sarcolemma (Figure 23-1, *1* and *2*). By joining end to end, the cells form a long fiber, with each cell separated from the other by a plasma membrane called the intercalated disk. This disk is believed to provide sites of low electrical resistance to permit the spread of exciting impulses throughout the cardiac muscle.

Each individual muscle fiber (cell) comprises a group of multiple parallel myofibrils, and each myofibril is arranged end to end in a series of repeating units called the **sarcomere.** By light microscope examination, the muscle fiber reveals its most characteristic feature, alternating light and dark bands. These bands result from crossing of the multiple parallel myofibrils, which are aligned in register with one another (Figure 23-1, *3*).

At the level known as the Z line, the sarcolemma of the muscle fiber interlocks (invaginates) at its end with the sarcomere to form the transverse sarcotubule or T system, which penetrates deeply into the cell. Furthermore, internal membranes form an extensive network called the sarcoplasmic reticulum. This structure encircles groups of myofibrils and makes contact with the sarcotubules. The tremendous energy requirements for cardiac muscle contraction may be seen by the great numbers of mitochondria lined up in long chains between the myofibrils (Figure 23-1, *3*). Figure 23-1, *4,* shows the sarcomere, which is the basic unit of contraction in the heart. It lies between two successive Z lines and in part of the myofibril. The sarcomere consists of dark bands called A bands and lighter I bands.

The end unit of the myofibril is the myofilament. The darkness of the A band results from the thicker myosin filaments, and the lightness of the I bands reflects the thinner actin filaments. Cross-bridges, which are small projections that extend from the sides of the myosin filament, appear along the entire length of the thick filament. The interaction

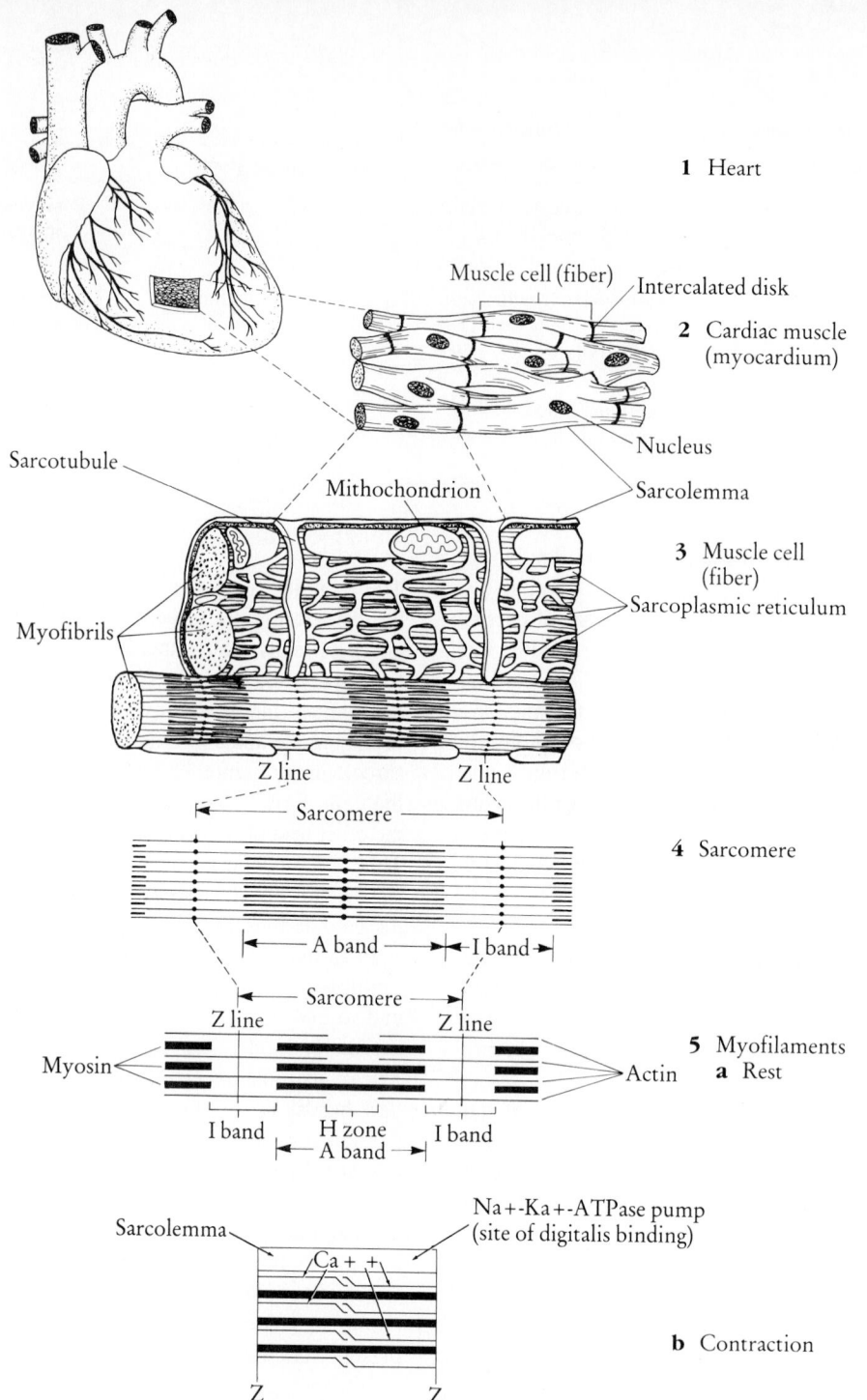

**1** Heart

Muscle cell (fiber) — Intercalated disk

**2** Cardiac muscle (myocardium)

Nucleus

Sarcotubule

Mithochondrion

Sarcolemma

Myofibrils

**3** Muscle cell (fiber)

Sarcoplasmic reticulum

Z line          Z line

Sarcomere

**4** Sarcomere

|← A band →|← I band →|

Sarcomere

Z line          Z line

Myosin          Actin

**5** Myofilaments

**a** Rest

I band   H zone   I band
A band

Sarcolemma          Na+-Ka+-ATPase pump (site of digitalis binding)

Ca + +

**b** Contraction

Z          Z

**FIGURE 23-1** Structure of heart and cardiac muscle cell fibers. The heart *(1)* is mainly a muscular organ. The enlargement of the square illustrates a portion of the cardiac muscle (myocardium) *(2)* that is composed of myocardial cells. Each cell contains a centrally located nucleus and a limiting plasma membrane (sarcolemma), which forms the intercalated disk at the termination of each cell. An individual muscle cell (fiber) *(3)* consists of multiple parallel myofibrils. Each myofibril is arranged longitudinally in a series of light and dark repeating units, and the content of a unit is called a sarcomere. At the Z line, the sarcolemma invaginates to form the transverse sarcotubules or T system. An extensive network, called the sarcoplasmic reticulum, encircles groups of myofibrils and makes contact with the sarcotubules. The sarcoplasmic reticulum contains a high concentration of calcium ions. The mitochondria appear in long chains between the myofibrils. The sarcomere *(4)* is the unit of muscle contraction. It is composed of two types of bands, the A band and the I band. The latter is divided by the Z line. Myofilaments *(5)* of the sarcomere include the thin filament, actin, and the thick filament, myosin. The dark appearance of the A band is caused by the myosin and the lighter appearance of the I band by the actin. Here, the sarcomere is at rest *(a)*. On contraction *(b)* the sarcomere shortens so that the thick filaments approach the Z line and the width of the H zone narrows between the thin filaments. Calcium ions are needed for systolic contractions.

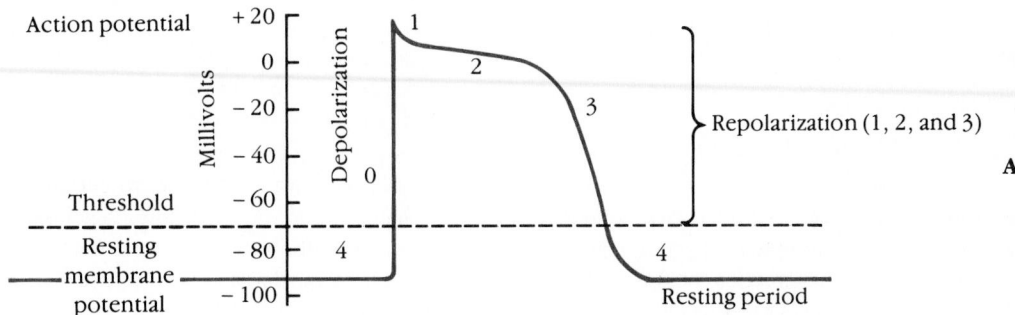

## Depolarization

Phase 0—membrane becomes permiable to $Na^+$,
   which rapidly flows into the cell

## Repolarization

Phase 1—membrane potential becomes slightly positive because of
   the rapid influx of $Na^+$

Phase 2—slow inward flow of $Ca^{++}$ and outward flow of $K^+$

Phase 3—rapid outward flow of $K^+$

## Resting period

Phase 4—cell membrane actively transports $Na^+$
   outside and $K^+$ inside, returning cell membrane
   to state of polarization

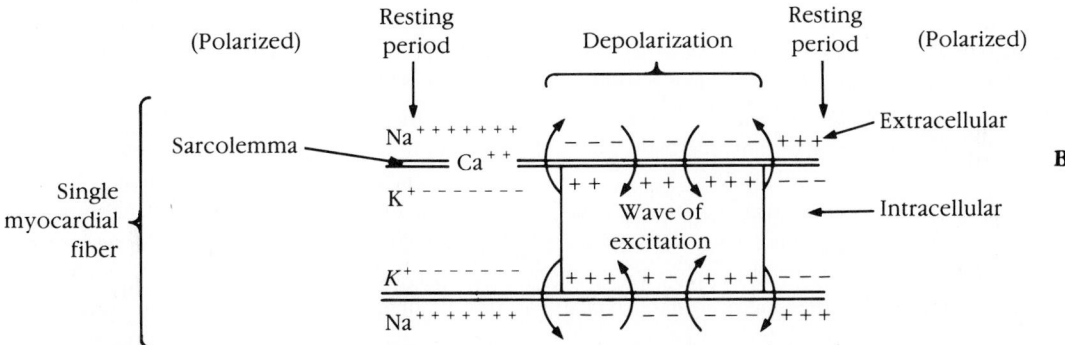

**FIGURE 23-2   A,** Action potential of a single myocardial fiber (cell). **B,** Ionic exchanges that occur across the cell membrane of a single myocardial fiber during an action potential.

between these crossbridges of myosin and the active sites of actin produces contraction. In the sarcomere the H zone represents the middle, less dense portion of the A band, and the myosin filament runs the entire length of this band. The I band, on the other hand, is divided by the Z line. The actin filament runs through the whole I band and termiates at the H zone. This arrangement is shown in Figure 23-1, 5.

## Myocardial Contraction

During the past decade our understanding of the fundamental mechanisms governing contraction of cardiac muscle in both normal and pathologic states has increased tremendously. Yet some aspects of this complicated process are still unknown. Cardiac muscle contraction begins with a rapid change in the cell membrane's electrical charge. This electrical current spreads to the interior of the cell where it causes release of calcium ions from the sarcoplasmic reticulum. The calcium ions then initiate the chemical events of contraction. The overall process for controlling cardiac muscle contraction, called excitation-contraction coupling, involves electrical excitation, mechanical activation, and contractile mechanisms.

**Electrical excitation.** Cardiac muscle contraction begins with electrical excitation or stimulus of the myocardial fiber. The source of electricity in the heart is found in the charges of ion concentration—mainly sodium, potassium, and calcium ions—across the cardiac cell membrane of the sarcolemma.

The **action potential,** or rapid change in membrane potential, which produces the ion changes, occurs in the membrane of the myocardial cell. The *resting state* of an inactive muscle cell in the ventricle is created by the difference in electrical charge across the sarcolemma. In this case the inside of the cell is negative with respect to the cell's outside, which is positively charged. Because the sarcolemma separates these opposite charges, the membrane in effect is polarized. At rest, the extracellular environment is rich in sodium ions ($Na^+$) and the intracellular environment in potassium ions ($K^+$), with calcium ion ($Ca^{++}$) concentration in the region of the sarcolemma and where it invaginates on the sarcotubule (see single myocardial fiber, Figure 23-2, *B*).

The cardiac action potential is divided into two stages: depolarization and repolarization. These stages are subdivided into five phases of ionic changes. The resting potential of an inactive myocardial cell is called phase 4; in this phase the membrane is polarized with a charge of approximately −90 millivolts (mv). At this voltage the interior of the cell is negative with respect to the cell's exterior. During this time the membrane cannot be penetrated by ions. However, any stimulus that changes the resting membrane potential to a critical value, called the threshold, can generate an action potential. (Follow Figure 23-2, *A,* for steps of the action potential.) Threshold is reached when the voltage becomes a fall in membrane potential. Thus the potential difference of the membrane is quickly lost and in fact results from the fast inward current of sodium ions (fast channel) and becomes positively charged to +20 mv. This sudden initial upstroke is depolarization and is designated as phase 0 of the action potential. Phase 0 in the ventricular muscle is the contraction phase and is represented by QRS on the surface electrocardiogram. Soon after, the repolarization period occurs, and this process has three phases. The beginning of phase 1 is the overshoot, and it makes a brief change toward repolarization. Phase 2 is a slow period that forms a plateau with a slow inward current of calcium ions (slow channel) and outward flow of potassium ion. Calcium ion entry into the cell is essential for the excitation-contraction coupling mechanism, which will be explained later. Phase 3 is accomplished by rapid potassium ion efflux from the cell. Following repolarization, phase 4 recovery or resting period ensues, whereby the cell membrane actively transports sodium ion outside and potassium ions inside, returning the cell membrane to a state of rest or polarization. These cation exchanges during recovery require the energy-utilizing transport mechanism of the $Na^+$-$K^+$-ATPase pump. The adenosine triphosphatase (ATPase) pump, which is powered by oxygen, is an enzyme that is located in the cell membrane or sarcolemma; it furnishes the energy needed for active transport to return sodium ions and potassium ions to their original resting positions at the membrane. Digitalis plays a key role at this site. By binding to the sarcolemma $Na^+$-$K^+$-ATPase pump, digitalis inhibits the return of sodium ions and potassium ions to their resting positions. Consequently, digitalis allows more sodium ions and calcium ions to enter the cell to strengthen myocardial contraction. However, it is also thought that if an excessive amount of these ions appears intracellularly, digitalis toxicity may occur (see Figure 23-2).

**Mechanical activation.** As previously stated, the unit that contracts is the sarcomere. It consists of two contractile proteins, actin and myosin. Myosin, the thicker filament, contains the ATPase enzyme system that is needed to hydrolyze ATP. Hydrolysis is required to provide the energy for contraction. ATP is synthesized in the mitochondria, which are normally abundant in cardiac muscle. Actin, the thin filament, is involved with calcium ion activity. These two filaments combine to help effect cardiac contraction.

Contraction is initiated when the nerve impulse reaches the myocardial cell and travels along the sarcolemma of the muscle fiber. As the depolarization wave spreads along the sarcotubules, it arrives at the sarcoplasmic reticulum, causing the release of its large quantities of calcium ions. These ions then bind to special receptors on the actin filaments. Hence the plateau, which is phase 2 of the action potential, is reached through the slow inward calcium current flow (slow channel). *Calcium ion movement is the chief component that links or couples electrical excitation of the sarcolemma with muscle activation of the myofilaments in the sarcomere.* Thus *mechanical activation* finally is accomplished when calcium ions bind to troponin, a regulator protein located on the actin filaments. This, in turn, then mediates the interaction of actin and myosin.

***Contractile mechanism.*** As soon as the actin filaments are activated by the calcium ions, the myosin filaments immediately become attracted to the active sites of the actin filament. This interaction pulls the actin along the immobile myosin filaments toward the center of the A band, thus shortening the sarcomere and producing muscle contraction. In this process the lengths of individual filaments remain unchanged. The I band narrows as the thick filaments approach the Z line, and the H zone narrows between the ends of the thin filaments when they meet at the center of the sarcomere (Figure 23-1, *5a* and *b*). The greater the quantity of calcium ions delivered to troponin, the faster the rate and numbers of interactions between actin and myosin. As a result of this response, the development of tension and contractility is increased.

When magnesium is present, ATP is cleaved by myosin ATPase. This reaction releases the energy needed to perform work. *The conversion of chemical energy to mechanical energy by ATP plays an essential role in energizing muscle shortening.* In other words, it provides the energy so the actin-myosin filaments move and produce muscle contraction. Although this is a somewhat simplified explanation of the contractile mechanism, it illustrates the important events pertinent to understanding cardiotonic drug action.

Finally, muscle relaxation depends on removing calcium ions from the sarcomere. The calcium pump ATPase (located in the walls of the sarcoplasmic reticulum) actively returns calcium ions to the sarcoplasmic reticulum and the sarcolemma, thereby allowing the actin-myosin filaments of the sarcomere to return to their resting positions.

In the normal heart Frank-Starling's law of the heart holds. This states that the longer the muscle fibers are at the end of diastole, the more forceful the contraction will be during systole. This law applies only when the muscle fiber is lengthened within physiologic limits. If a diseased heart is dilated and the fibers are stretched to a critical point beyond their limits of extensibility, the force of contraction and cardiac output are both diminished and ineffective. Thus the functional significance of Frank-Starling's law is that effective cardiac output can be brought about only by adequate relaxation and refilling of cardiac chambers after each myocardial contraction.

## Cardiac Conduction System

The effective pumping action of the heart depends on the regularity of events occurring in the cardiac cycle. Each cycle consists of a period of relaxation called **diastole** followed by a period of contraction known as **systole.** The rhythm and rate of the cardiac cycle are regulated by the conduction system, which has the ability to initiate and transmit the electrical impulses needed to stimulate contraction of the cardiac muscle.

The **conduction system** is made up of the following struc-

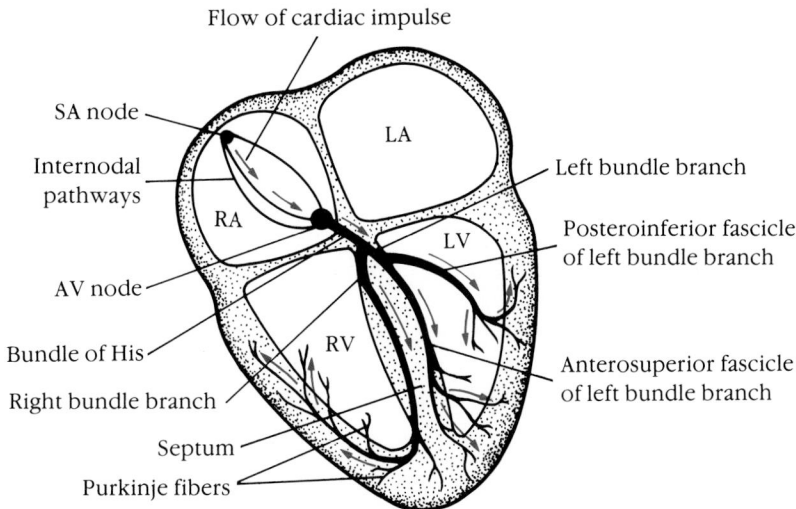

**FIGURE 23-3** Conduction system of the heart. The cardiac impulse is initiated at the SA node and is transmitted through the internodal pathways to the two atria, resulting in atrial contraction. At the AV node, the electrical impulse is delayed. Conduction then speeds up at the bundle of His, with the impulse traveling through the right bundle branch and the left bundle branch continuing through the posteroinferior fascicle and anterosuperior fascicle of the latter bundle branch. Finally, the arrival of impulses at the Purkinje fiber results in their distribution to all parts of both ventricles, where, upon excitation, ventricular contraction is produced. *RA,* Right atrium; *RV,* right ventricle; *LA,* left atrium; *LV,* left ventricle.

tures: (1) sinoatrial (SA) node, (2) internodal pathways, (3) atrioventricular (AV) node, (4) bundle of His, (5) right and left bundle branches, and (6) Purkinje fibers. The Purkinje fibers penetrate the endocardium and end in the myocardial cells. The AV node and the His area form the **AV junction,** which extends from the atrial fibers, through the AV node, to the bifurcation of the bundle of His. When referring to this region, the term "AV junction" is considered to be more accurate than "AV node" (Figure 23-3).

In the normal heart the SA node initiates the heartbeat. The impulses generated here are then conducted through the internodal pathways to the "working" fibers of the atrial myocardium, producing atrial contraction. When the impulses move through the AV node, electrical conduction is delayed. However, at the bundle of His, conduction speeds up and the impulses travel through the right bundle branch and the left bundle branch, then through the posteroinferior and anterosuperior fascicles of the left bundle branch. The transmission of impulses at the Purkinje fibers, which consist of tiny fibrils that spread around the ventricles and connect directly with the myocardial cells, is very rapid. Finally, the simultaneous depolarization of both ventricles produces ventricular contraction, whereupon the cardiac output propels a volume of blood through the pulmonary artery and aorta.

## Electrophysiologic Properties

The coordinated pumping action of the heart is initiated and regulated by the specialized fibers of the conduction system. The individual fibers of this system possess three basic **electrophysiologic properties:** (1) automaticity, (2) conductivity, and (3) refractoriness.

*Automaticity.* The specialized fibers of the conduction system have the inherent ability to spontaneously initiate an electrical impulse without any external stimuli. This is the most fundamental mechanism of impulse formation, and the cells that possess this property of **automaticity** or self-excitation are called pacemaker cells. They are found in specialized conducting tissues such as the SA node, the AV node, and the His-Purkinje system. Normally, the impulse of the heart is spontaneously and regularly initiated at the pacemaker cells of the SA node. During resting potential (phase 4), the membrane of the cell depolarizes itself—spontaneously and gradually—until it reaches threshold and an action potential occurs. The slow depolarization of the membrane in the resting state is called spontaneous diastolic depolarization, or phase 4 depolarization, and defines automaticity. Thus the membrane of pacemaker cells is never at rest, and this property is attributed to the continuous influx of sodium ions into the interior of the cells, which readily drives the membrane to threshold. The resting potential of automatic pacemaker cells differs from that of the nonautomatic myocardial cells. After full repolarization, the membrane of myocardial cells maintains a steady resting potential

until an external stimulus causes it to achieve threshold. To summarize, automaticity is a property of fibers of the conduction system that normally controls heart rhythm; it is not a feature of "working" muscle—atria and ventricles. However, under pathologic conditions, myocardial cells do have the potential to exhibit spontaneous depolarization.

The spontaneous excitation of pacemaker cells establishes the normal rhythm of the heart. The regularity of such pacemaking activity is termed **rhythmicity.** Under normal circumstances, only one functional pacemaker, the SA node, predominates because it has the highest frequency of depolarization. The normal rate of impulse formation is about 72 beats/minute. If the SA node decreases its rate of impulse formation to a level below the AV junction (40 to 60 beats/minute), then the AV junction becomes the primary pacemaker of the heart and will drive the heart at about 40 beats/minute.

*Conductivity.* **Conductivity** refers to the ability to transmit an action potential or nerve impulse from cell to cell. The property of conductivity therefore exists not only in the cells of the conduction system but also in the cardiac musculature. The speed of impulse conduction varies as it passes from one tissue to another in the heart. It is slowest in the AV node and fastest in the Purkinje fibers. The marked delay of conduction at the AV node allows more time for ventricular filling. On the other hand, the rapid depolarization of Purkinje fibers creates an instantaneous spread of impulses from the terminals to the ventricular muscles. Simultaneous activation of the musculature is essential for producing powerful ventricular contraction.

*Velocity of conduction.* The speed with which electrical activity is spread within the sinus node is quite slow, about 0.05 m/second. The impulse then spreads out rapidly over the atrial musculature at a rate of about 1.0 m/second. When the impulse reaches the AV node, a delay of about 0.05 m/second occurs and atrial systole takes place. The impulse then spreads rapidly, 2 to 4 m/second, along the right and left bundle branches and Purkinje fibers. Studies indicate that no more than 22 msec may elapse during this time. This rapid activation of contractile elements evokes a synchronous contraction of the ventricles.

The velocity of conduction is determined by the size of the resting potential of the cell membrane and the rate of rise of phase 0 of the action potential. This defines membrane responsiveness. Antidysrhythmic drugs may affect conduction by slowing phase 0 depolarization rate, thereby decreasing membrane responsiveness.

*Refractoriness.* Cardiac tissue is refractory to stimulation during the initial phase of systole (contraction). This is known as **refractoriness.** Throughout most of repolarization, the cell cannot respond to a stimulus. The effective refractory period represents that period in the cardiac cycle during which a stimulus, no matter how strong, fails to produce an action potential. Antidysrhythmic drugs can lengthen or shorten the refractory period of cardiac tissues by influencing the level of responsiveness of the cell membrane. Following the effective refractory period and as repolarization nears completion, a relative refractory period occurs. This is defined as that period during which a propagated action potential can be elicited, provided the stimulus is stronger than normally required in diastole. When this happens, the fiber is stimulated to contract prematurely.

## Autonomic Nervous System Control

Although the conduction system possesses the inherent ability for spontaneous, rhythmic initiation of the cardiac impulse, the autonomic nervous system has an important role in the regulation of the rate, rhythm, and force of myocardial contraction of the heart. The heart is innervated by both the parasympathetic and sympathetic nerves. Vagal nerve fibers of the parasympathetic branch are found primarily in the SA node, atrial muscles, and AV node, whereas the sympathetic fibers innervate the SA node, AV node, and the atrial and ventricular muscles.

Vagal stimulation to the heart is mediated by the release of the acetylcholine, a neurohormone that acts on the muscarinic receptors to decrease heart rate and is also believed to decrease ventricular contraction. The main effect of ace-

tylcholine on the AV node is to slow the rate of conduction and lengthen the refractory period. By contrast, sympathetic fiber stimulation is mediated by the release of norepinephrine, which acts specifically on the $beta_1$ receptors in the cardiac tissue. Circulating epinephrine from the adrenal medulla may also elicit cardiac responses. By acting on the beta adrenergic receptors, norepinephrine and epinephrine increase both heart rate and force of myocardial contraction. They also increase conduction velocity and shorten the refractory period of the AV node. Epinephrine has a very potent effect on the heart. In large doses its direct effect on the electrophysiologic properties of cardiac tissue can create cardiac dysrhythmias. Normally, the heartbeat is under the continuous influence of both parasympathetic and sympathetic control, so that the resting heart rate is the result of their opposing influences.

## Electrocardiograms

**Electrocardiograms** are graphic representations of the sequence of cardiac excitation. Nurses caring for patients on monitor equipment should be able to detect and interpret changes in the cardiac rate or rhythm or in the conduction of the wave of electric activity or excitation. The electro-

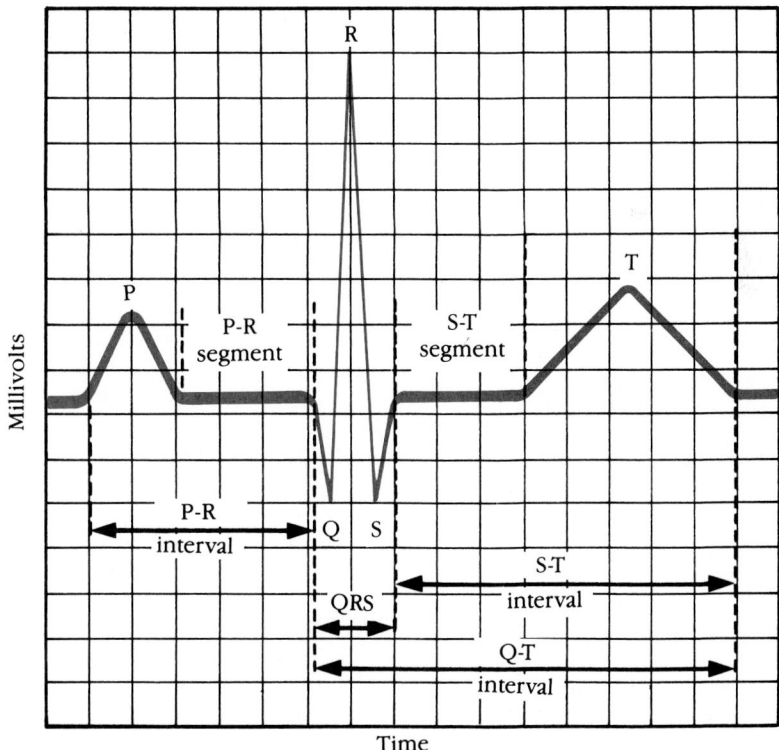

**FIGURE 23-4** Graphic representation of the normal electrocardiogram. Vertical lines represent time, each square represents 0.04 second, and every five squares (set off by heavy black lines) represents 0.20 second. The normal P-R interval is less than 0.20 second; the average is 0.16 second. The average P wave lasts 0.08 second; the QRS complex is 0.08 second; the S-T segment is 0.12 second; the T wave is 0.16 second; and the Q-T interval is 0.32 to 0.40 second if heart rate is 65 to 95 beats/minute. Each horizontal line represents voltage; every five squares equals 0.5 millivolt.

cardiogram (ECG) is a useful tool in determining the therapeutic effectiveness of certain drugs. Drugs used to treat cardiovascular disease may alter the electric activity of the heart. The ECG may provide the earliest objective evidence of a drug's effectiveness or its toxic manifestations. A knowledgeable and observant nurse can use the information obtained from the ECG to assess the effectiveness of drug therapy for cardiac dysrhythmias.

Electric activity always precedes mechanical contraction. Immediately after a wave of electric activity moves through atrial muscle, the muscle contracts and blood flows from the atria into the ventricles. (See Figure 23-4 for an illustration of the normal ECG.) The P wave is produced by a wave of excitation through the atria (atrial depolarization). The onset of the P wave follows the firing of the SA node. After the P wave, a short pause or interval (PR interval) occurs while the electric activity is transmitted to the AV node, conduction tissue, and ventricles. Repolarization, or recovery, of the ventricles is indicated by the T wave. Atrial recovery or repolarization does not show on the ECG because it is hidden in the QRS complex.

## Physiology of Fast and Slow Channels of Cardiovascular Fibers

To understand the clinical application of calcium channel blockers, one must review the normal physiology of the fast and slow channels that exist in the membrane of the cardiovascular fibers. The cell membrane is composed of two types of channels that are controlled by "gates." When opened, they allow the movement of an inward current of (1) sodium ions through the fast channels and (2) calcium ions through the slow channels into the cell, depending on the type of fibers involved. These channels appear in the cell membrane of three types of cardiovascular fibers. The heart contains two types: (1) fast-channel fibers, which appear in the myocardial cells of the atria and ventricles and the Purkinje fibers and (2) slow-channel fibers, which occur in the SA node and the AV node. Last, the third type, slow fibers, are present in the smooth muscle of the coronary and peripheral arterial vessels.

In this mechanism, the role of calcium ions is essential in affecting three physiologic processes:

1. Increasing the strength of myocardial contraction (fast fibers)
2. Enhancing automaticity and conduction speed (slow fibers)
3. Vasoconstriction of coronary arteries and peripheral arterioles (slow fibers)

As previously described, the action potential that generates excitation-contraction coupling in the fast fibers consists of five phases. Depolarization (phase 0) results from an electrical stimulus that produces a fast inward current of sodium ion (fast channel). This is then followed by repolarization, which begins with a short phase 1, but more

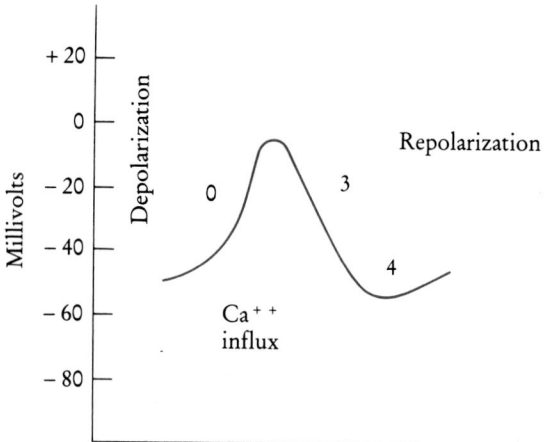

**FIGURE 23-5** Action potential of a slow channel fiber, the SA node. It consists of 3 phases. Unlike the fast fibers of myocardial cells, depolarization phase 0 is attributed primarily to $Ca^{++}$ inflow through slow channels of the cell membrane. Repolarization involves only phase 3, which is followed by phase 4.

---

### COMMON CARDIAC DYSRHYTHMIAS

Heart block—impaired impulse conduction through the heart; usually the impaired conduction occurs between atria and ventricles

    First-degree heart block—conduction time is prolonged but all impulses are conducted from atria to ventricles

    Second-degree heart block—some but not all atrial impulses are conducted to ventricles

    Third-degree heart block—no atrial impulses are conducted to ventricles

Ectopic beats—a contraction of the heart that originates some place other than the sinoatrial node

Extrasystole "premature beat"—a premature contraction of the heart that arises independent of the normal rhythm

Tachycardia—unusually rapid heart rate (usually over 100 beats/minute in adult)

Bradycardia—unusually slow heart rate (usually less than 60 beats/minute in adult)

Atrial flutter—extremely rapid rate of atrial contraction; may be 200 to 350 beats/minute

Atrial fibrillation—rapid and incoordinated contraction of the atria

Ventricular fibrillation—rapid and incoordinated contraction of the ventricles. Because of the incoordination of contractions, there is little or no effective pumping of blood; death will result if not immediately treated.

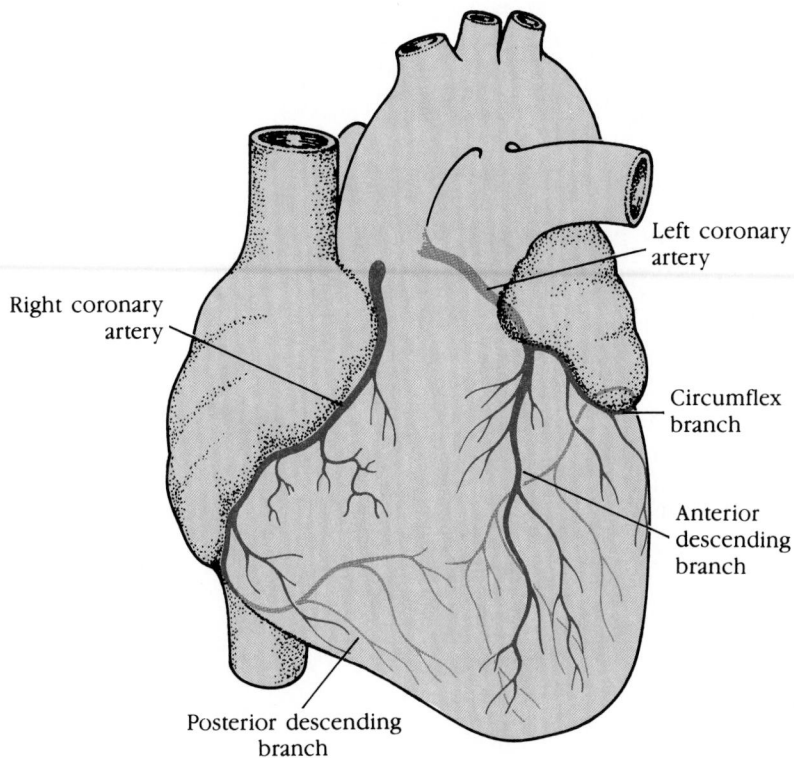

Right coronary
artery

Left coronary
artery

Circumflex
branch

Anterior
descending
branch

Posterior descending
branch

**FIGURE 23-6**  Coronary blood supply to the heart. Dark shaded vessels are those located on the external surface of the ventricles; light shaded vessels show penetration of arterial branches toward the endocardial surface.

importantly, phase 2, the plateau phase, produces a slow inward current of calcium ions into the cell (slow channel). The influx of calcium ions is responsible for linking electrical excitation to myocardial contraction (excitation-contraction coupling) required to promote the sliding of actin and myosin filaments for myocardial contraction (positive inotropic effect). Rapid repolarization occurs during phase 3, and finally, phase 4 reestablishes the resting state. (See configuration of action potential in Figure 23-2, *A*.)

In the slow fibers of the SA and AV nodes, the action potential consists of only three phases. The principal distinguishing feature of the pacemaker fiber resides in phase 4. A slow spontaneous depolarization occurs that requires no external stimulus and is termed "diastolic depolarization." This is responsible for automaticity. Also, unlike the fast fibers of the myocardium, depolarization (or phase 0) is achieved by the slower current carried by both calcium ions and sodium ions through the slow channels of nodal cells. Thus phase 0 results in a slower conduction velocity in nodal cells than in myocardial cells. Calcium channel blockers inhibit these slow channels. Repolarization is more gradual and involves only phase 3. The membrane then finally returns to phase 4. (See Figure 23-5.)

The smooth muscle of blood vessels depends primarily on the presence of calcium ions to initiate and sustain contraction. The main source of calcium ions in cardiac muscle cells is the sarcoplasmic reticulum. In the action potential for smooth muscle, it is believed that the onset of depolar-

ization (phase 0) is caused mainly by calcium ions rather than by sodium ions. Calcium ions enter the smooth muscle cell through slow channels, and it is the rise in free calcium ion concentration that is considered to be the primary event in excitation-contraction coupling that is responsible for increasing muscle tone and vasoconstriction. In addition, activation of smooth muscle can reduce the caliber of small vessels markedly as is apparent from the "spasm" that may occur in coronary vessels. The calcium channel blockers (specifically verapamil, nefidipine, and diltiazem) are capable of blocking the slow calcium ion influx in smooth muscle of blood vessels, thereby producing relaxation.

## CORONARY VASCULAR SUPPLY OF THE HEART

The entire blood supply to the myocardium is provided by the right and left coronary arteries, which arise from the base of the **aorta** (Figure 23-6). The right atrium and ventricle are supplied with blood from the right coronary artery. The left coronary artery divides into the anterior (descending) branch and the circumflex branch and supplies blood to the left atrium and ventricle. These main coronary vessels continue to divide, forming numerous branches. The result is a profuse network of coronary vessels. The major arterial vessels are located on the external surface of the ventricles. Arterial branches penetrate the myocardium toward the endocardial surface.

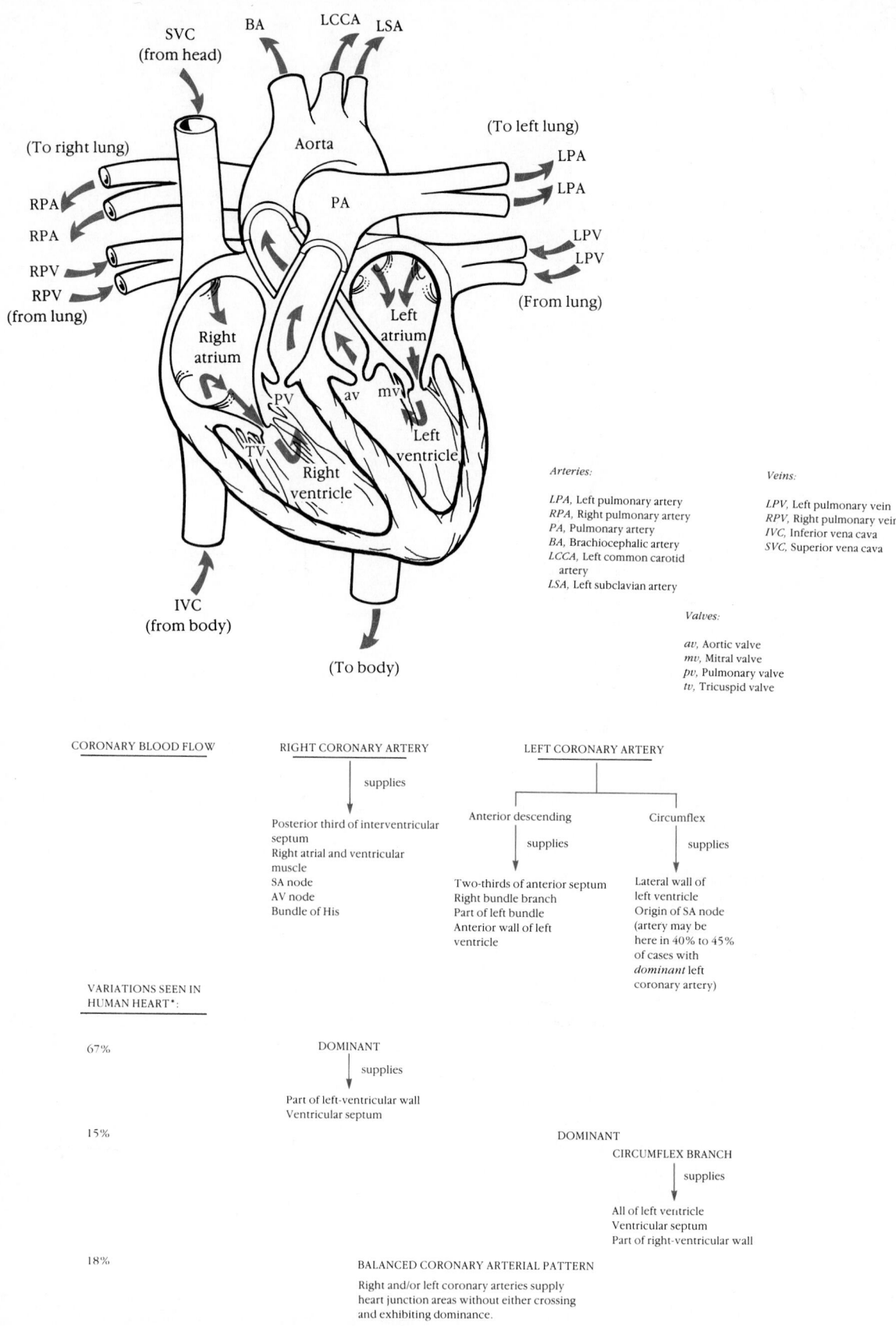

**SVC** (from head)

**BA**    **LCCA**    **LSA**

(To right lung)

Aorta

(To left lung)

**RPA**

**RPA**

**RPV**

**RPV** (from lung)

PA

**LPA**

**LPA**

**LPV**

**LPV**

(From lung)

Right atrium

Left atrium

PV    av    mv

TV

Right ventricle

Left ventricle

**IVC** (from body)

(To body)

Arteries:

LPA, Left pulmonary artery
RPA, Right pulmonary artery
PA, Pulmonary artery
BA, Brachiocephalic artery
LCCA, Left common carotid
   artery
LSA, Left subclavian artery

Veins:

LPV, Left pulmonary vein
RPV, Right pulmonary vein
IVC, Inferior vena cava
SVC, Superior vena cava

Valves:

av, Aortic valve
mv, Mitral valve
pv, Pulmonary valve
tv, Tricuspid valve

CORONARY BLOOD FLOW

RIGHT CORONARY ARTERY

| supplies

Posterior third of interventricular
septum
Right atrial and ventricular
muscle
SA node
AV node
Bundle of His

LEFT CORONARY ARTERY

Anterior descending    Circumflex

| supplies    | supplies

Two-thirds of anterior septum
Right bundle branch
Part of left bundle
Anterior wall of left
ventricle

Lateral wall of
left ventricle
Origin of SA node
(artery may be
here in 40% to 45%
of cases with
*dominant* left
coronary artery)

VARIATIONS SEEN IN
HUMAN HEART*:

67%

DOMINANT

| supplies

Part of left-ventricular wall
Ventricular septum

15%

DOMINANT

CIRCUMFLEX BRANCH

| supplies

All of left ventricle
Ventricular septum
Part of right-ventricular wall

18%

BALANCED CORONARY ARTERIAL PATTERN

Right and/or left coronary arteries supply
heart junction areas without either crossing
and exhibiting dominance.

*Percentages from Netter, F.: Heart: the Ciba collection of medical illustrations, volume 5, p 17, 1974.

**FIGURE 23-7** Overview of heart, blood vessels, blood flow, valves, and conduction system.

---

### CARDIOVASCULAR TERMINOLOGY

Automaticity—the ability to initiate an impulse

Cardiac output—the amount of blood pumped by the heart per minute (cardiac output = heart rate × stroke volume)

Conductivity—the ability to conduct or transmit the impulse

Depolarization—an electrical impulse that results in contraction of muscle (e.g., QRS interval represents the contraction of ventricular muscle)

Diastole—a period of heart relaxation

Electrocardiogram (ECG or EKG)—a graphic record of the electric currents produced by the heart

Excitability—the ability to respond to an impulse

Myocarditis—inflammation of heart muscle

Pericarditis—inflammation of thin membrane sac that surrounds the heart

Repolarization—the recovery phase following muscle contraction (e.g., T wave represents recovery of ventricle muscle)

Stenosis—the narrowing or stricture of an opening (e.g., valve stenosis)

Stroke volume—the amount of blood ejected with each contraction of the left ventricle

Systole—the period of contraction in the heart (e.g., atrial systole is contraction of the atria; ventricular systole is contraction of the ventricles)

Valvular insufficiency—valve does not close properly; permits flow of blood in the wrong direction

---

Increased oxygen delivery to the myocardium is supported almost exclusively by increased coronary blood flow. When there is increased demand for oxygen and nutrients by body tissues, the heart must increase its output. At the same time, the heart muscle itself must be supplied with enough oxygen and nutrients to replace the energy expended. In other words, a balance must be maintained between energy expenditure and energy restoration.

During systole the myocardial contraction compresses the coronary vascular bed. This restricts coronary inflow but increases coronary outflow. Coronary inflow in the left ventricle occurs primarily during diastole when the ventricles have relaxed and the coronary vessels are no longer compressed. Blood is driven through the coronary arteries by aortic pressure perfusing the myocardium.

A change in heart rate is accomplished by shortening or lengthening diastole. With tachycardia the increased number of systolic contractions per minute reduces the time available for diastole and coronary inflow. An increase also occurs in the metabolic needs of the rapidly beating heart. Normally, coronary dilation occurs in an attempt to meet increased metabolic demand and to overcome restricted blood inflow. With bradycardia, the decreased number of systolic contractions per minute prolongs the diastolic period. Resistance to coronary flow and metabolic requirements of the myocardium are reduced.

Whenever the delivery of oxygen to the myocardium is inadequate to meet the heart's oxygen consumption needs, myocardial ischemia occurs. One of the major causes of ischemia is coronary artery disease. See Figure 23-7 for an overview of heart, blood vessels, blood flow, valves, and conduction system.

## SUMMARY

Understanding the electrical and physiologic properties of the heart and the effects of drugs on cardiac activity is essential knowledge for nurses. The drugs used therapeutically effect the myocardium, the conduction system, and coronary vessels. The action of the myocardium to adjust cardiac output according to the body's needs is based on electrical excitation, mechanical activation, and the contractile mechanism of myocardial fiber. However, effective cardiac output can only be achieved with adequate relaxation and refilling of the cardiac chambers after each contraction. The cardiac conduction system initiates and transmits electrical impulses required for the contraction of the myocardium. Automaticity, conductivity, and refractoriness are the essential properties of the fibers of the conduction system. The sequence of cardiac excitation is graphically represented by electrocardiography. ECG is a useful tool for monitoring cardiac activity to assist nurses to evaluate the effectiveness of a number of drugs used to treat cardiovascular disease.

## BIBLIOGRAPHY

Anddreoli K et al. (1987). Comprehensive cardiac care: a text for nurses, physicians, and other health practitioners, ed 6. St Louis: The CV Mosby Co.

Anthony CP and Thibodeau, GA. (1987). Textbook of anatomy and physiology, ed 12. St Louis: Mosby Times Mirror/Mosby College Publishing.

Berne R and Levy M. (1986). Cardiovascular physiology, ed 5. St Louis: The CV Mosby Co.

Bowman W and Rand M. (1980). Textbook of pharmacology, ed 2, London: Blackwell Scientific Publications, Inc.

Braunwald E et al, eds. (1988). Harrison's principles of internal medicine, ed 11. New York: McGraw-Hill Book Co.

Goldberger E. (1982). Textbook of clinical cardiology. St Louis: The CV Mosby Co.

Gilman AG et al, eds. (1990). Goodman and Gilman's the pharmacological basis of therapeutics, ed 8. New York: Macmillan Publishing Co.

Guyton AC. (1987). Human physiology and the mechanism of disease, ed 4. Philadelphia: WB Saunders Co.

Netter, FF. (1983). Heart: the CIBA collection of medical illustrations. Rochester, NY: Case-Hoyt Co.

Viets JL et al. (1987). AANA Journal course. Advanced scientific concepts: update for nurse anesthetists. I. The cardiovascular system, AANA J 55(2):165.

## Chapter

# 24 Cardiac Glycosides

## INTRODUCTION

Drugs may change the force of myocardial contraction and the rate and rhythm of the heart. Pharmacologic terms that have specific meaning for the actions of drugs on the cardiovascular system include the following: "inotropic," "chronotropic," and "dromotropic" effects.

Drugs with an **inotropic** (Gr. *inos,* fiber; *tropikos,* a turning or influence) effect influence myocardial contractility. If the drug has a positive inotropic effect, it strengthens or increases the force of myocardial contraction (e.g., digitalis, dobutamine, dopamine, epinephrine, and isoproterenol). A drug with a negative inotropic effect weakens or decreases the force of myocardial contraction (e.g., lidocaine, quinidine, and propranolol).

Drugs with **chronotropic** (Gr. *chronos,* time) action affect the rate of the heart. If the drug accelerates the heart rate by increasing the rate of impulse formation in the sinoatrial (SA) node, it has a positive chronotropic effect (e.g., norepinephrine). A negative chronotropic drug has the opposite effect and slows the heart rate by decreasing impulse formation (e.g., acetylcholine).

When drugs have a **dromotropic** (Gr. *dromos,* a course) effect, they affect conduction velocity through the specialized conducting tissues. A drug having a positive dromotropic action speeds conduction (e.g., phenytoin). A drug with negative dromotropic action delays conduction (e.g., verapamil). Drugs in the digitalis group are among the oldest drugs known as therapeutic agents for treatment of heart failure. The effects of digitalis glycosides are twofold. They increase the strength of contraction (positive inotrope) and alter the electrophysiologic properties of the heart by slowing the heart rate and slowing conduction velocity. Other agents may produce varying effects with the same objective of treating heart failure. To better understand the beneficial and toxic effects of the digitalis glycosides and other agents, we will first outline the mechanisms of heart failure.

## HEART FAILURE

**Heart failure** or pump failure is a pathologic state in which the weakened myocardium is unable to pump sufficient blood from the ventricles (e.g., cardiac output) to sustain normal circulation required to meet the metabolic demands of the body organs. The etiologic factors of heart failure are listed in Table 24-1. Despite the etiology, depressed myocardial contractility is primarily the underlying cause of heart failure. Therefore, in heart failure, it is important to identify and remove the cause, correct problems, and then treat the heart failure state, as follows:

1. Remove excess water and salt in the body. Sodium restrictions, reduction of physical activity, and initiation of diuretic and/or digitalis glycoside therapy are the usual measures taken.
2. Enhance myocardial contraction. The positive inotropic effect of digitalis has been related to excitation-contraction coupling. (See Chapter 23 for explanation of this phenomenon.)

The nurse should be aware that drugs may exacerbate or precipitate congestive heart failure (see box, p. 462). Also, many drugs contain sodium; their use must be considered with a salt-restricted diet. (See Table 24-2.)

Heart failure appears to be associated with a defect in excitation-contraction coupling, and in some individuals dysfunction of *contractile proteins* may occur as an additional abnormality. Ineffective calcium pumping by the sarcoplasmic reticulum may alter the normal relaxation process. Furthermore, the mitochondria—*not* the sarcoplasmic reticulum—may act as the dominant calcium uptake storage site. If so, less calcium is available for release from the sarcoplasmic reticulum to activate contraction. Thus the amount of coupling is reduced, and depressed myocardial contractility ensues.

With regard to dysfunction of contractile proteins in heart failure, attention has been focused on abnormal energy utilization. Some workers have shown that the activity of myosin adenosine triphosphatase (ATPase) is decreased. When

**TABLE 24-1**  Etiology of heart failure

| Organic heart disorders | Other causes |
|---|---|
| Systemic hypertension | Anemia |
| Rheumatic fever | Liver disease |
| Infective endocarditis | Renal disease |
| Myocardial infarction | Hormonal disorders |
| Cardiac dysrhythmia | |
| Valvular disorders | |
| Pulmonary embolism | |

**TABLE 24-2**  Sodium content of selected prescription and over-the-counter medications

| Medications | Sodium/unit | Sodium/maximum daily dose (adult) |
|---|---|---|
| ANTIBIOTICS | | |
| carbenicillin disodium (Geopen, Pyopen) | 108-150 mg/g | 4.5 to 6 g/40 g |
| ticarcillin injection (Ticar) | 120-150 mg/g | 2.9 to 3.6 g/24 g |
| ampicillin sodium (Polycillin-N, Omnipen-N, and others) | 62-78 mg/g | 1 to 1.2 g/16 g |
| cephalosporins | | |
| cefamandole naftate (Mandol) | 77 mg/g | 0.9 g/12 g |
| ceftriaxone sodium (Rocephin) | 83 mg/g | 0.33 g/4 g |
| cephradine injection (Velosef) | 136 mg/g | 1 g/8 g |
| moxalactam disodium (Moxam, Oxalactam) | 88 mg/g | 0.53 g/6 g |
| OVER-THE-COUNTER MEDICATIONS | | |
| Alka-Seltzer Effervescent Pain Reliever and Antacid Tablets | 0.5 g/tablet | |
| Bromo-Seltzer powder | 0.76 g/capful | |
| Eno Powder | 0.8 g/tsp | |
| Rolaids | 53 mg/tablet | |
| Soda Mint Tablets | 90 mg/tablet | |

---

### DRUGS THAT MAY PRECIPITATE OR EXACERBATE HEART FAILURE

**Drugs that Cause Sodium and Water Retention**

corticosteroids (cortisone, hydrocortisone, fludrocortisone or Florinef, desoxycorticosterone)

androgens

estrogens

diazoxide (Proglycem, Hyperstat)

guanethidine (Ismelin)

methyldopa (Aldomet)

phenylbutazone (Butazolidin, Butazolidin-Alka)

**Drugs that Cause Osmotic Activity that may Result in Intravascular Volume Overload**

albumin

mannitol

urea

hypertonic glucose or saline

---

the activity of this enzyme is reduced in heart failure, the interaction between actin-myosin filaments is reduced in intensity, and thus the force of contractility is lowered.

An important consequence of inadequate performance of the myocardium is hemodynamic alterations. Then compensatory mechanisms are activated, and incomplete emptying of the heart during ventricular systole eventually allows blood to accumulate inside the heart chambers, causing dilation or enlargement of the heart. During this process, blood backs up into the atria. In the left atrium, this can lead to pulmonary congestion; in the right atrium, systemic congestion, including ascites, may occur. During the interim, the heart attempts to pump the blood forward in the circulation, but instead the increased fluid in the left ventricle produces stretching of the myocardial fibers and dilation of the ventricles.

Athletes commonly have cardiac hypertrophy, which is an enlargement of cardiac muscle and of the ventricular chambers. Thus the overall effectiveness of the heart as a pump is increased. Frank-Starling's law states that an increase in the length of the heart's muscle fibers results in increased contraction and cardiac output. This stretching of cardiac muscle results from increased preload, that is, an increased amount of blood returned to the heart and entering the heart chambers. Therefore the more the cardiac muscles are stretched during diastole, the greater the contraction in systole.

**Congestive heart failure** is a myocardial dysfunction resulting in a decreased cardiac output. Regardless of the primary cause, the result is that preload can increase until a massive overload results. The ventricles are unable to meet the needs for contraction or pumping. Mechanisms to com-

pensate, involving sympathoadrenergic stimulation, may occur as the body attempts to maintain an adequate cardiac output. But the increased heart rate and peripheral vascular resistance also elevate the heart's demand for oxygen, thus further contributing to myocardial dysfunction. The inability to obtain adequate cardiac output is referred to as myocardial insufficiency or cardiac decompensation. Furthermore, chronic progressive ventricular failure generally leads to congestive heart failure, which means that the heart's ability to contract decreases to the extent that the heart pumps out less blood than it receives. Subsequently, myocardial infarction produces circulatory failure.

A decrease in cardiac output means less blood is in the blood vessels, and the body's various organs are receiving less blood. The kidneys respond by retaining more water and electrolytes, producing fluid retention and electrolyte disturbances. This is called right-sided heart failure (or cor pulmonale), and the clinical signs include jugular vein distention, hepatomegaly, ascites, and peripheral edema. On the other hand, left-sided heart failure leads to fluid accumulation in the lungs—pulmonary edema—producing dyspnea, as well as interference with oxygen and carbon dioxide exchange. Failure of one side of the heart is usually followed by failure of the other side, which produces total heart failure. (See Figure 24-1.)

In summary, the failing heart may show increases in both preload (increased blood volume return to the heart chambers) and afterload (the increased pressure in the aorta that the ventricle muscles must overcome to open the aortic valve and push blood through). The decrease in renal perfusion just described may activate the renin-angiotensin-aldosterone (RAA) feedback mechanism. Then sodium and water are retained and intravascular volume and blood flow back to the heart increase. In less serious situations, this is usually enough to maintain arterial blood pressure, thus turning off the RAA system. But in individuals who have conditions bordering on heart failure, this can produce a frank decompensation or acute heart failure. The increase in circulatory blood volume increases the demands on the heart, which may result in acute pulmonary edema. Thus cardiotonic drugs such as digitalis glycosides (to increase contractility), diuretics (to reduce increased blood volume and edema), vasodilators (nitrates that pool blood in the extremities thus reducing blood return or preload, and arterial vasodilators that decrease arterial resistance, reducing afterload), and angiotensin II inhibitors (to decrease arterial resistance, afterload, and secretion of aldosterone) are all important drugs in the treatment of heart failure. In this chapter, the discussion will focus on digitalis glycosides and amrinone (Inocor).

## DIGITALIS GLYCOSIDES

The story of the origin of digitalis is interesting in that it demonstrates an herbal remedy that, although used for hun-

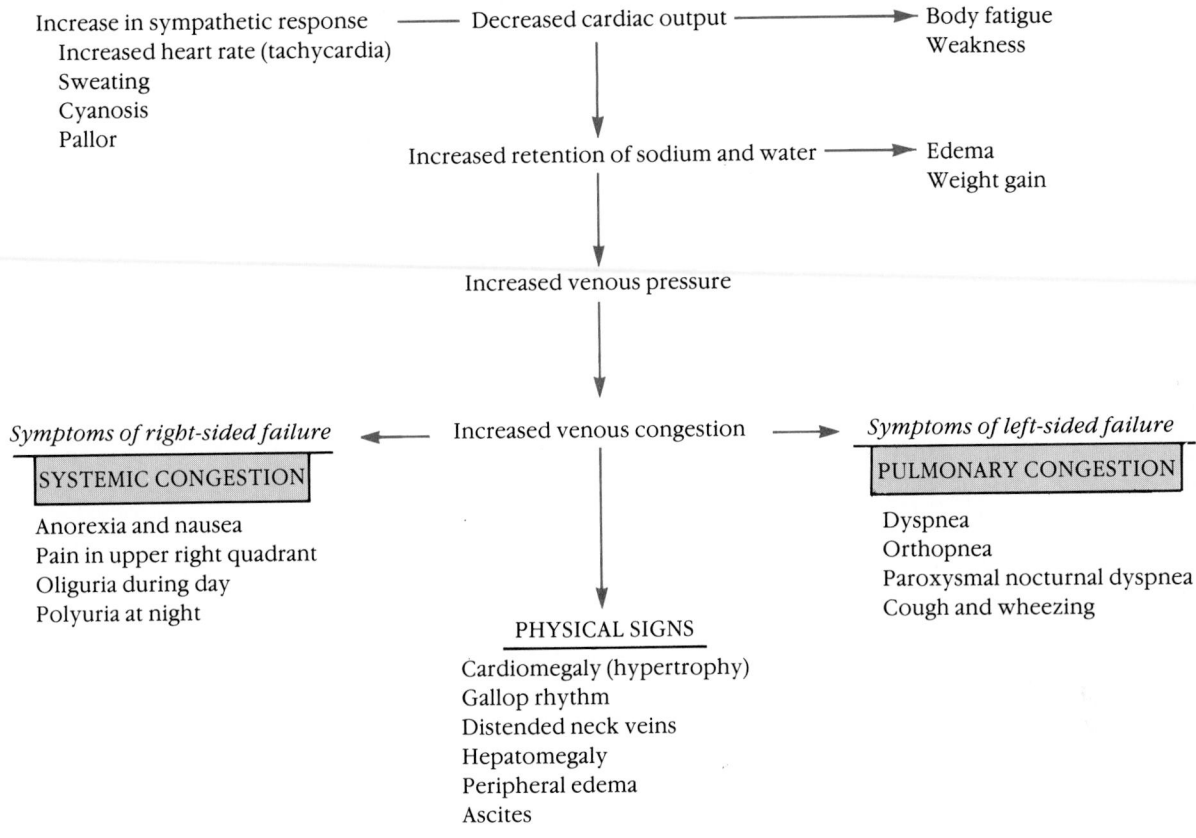

**FIGURE 24-1**  Signs and symptoms of heart failure.

dreds of years by common people, was shunned for many years by the medical profession as too toxic. Digitalis (the "housewife's recipe") was prepared by farmers and housewives for dropsy. Over 400 years ago, Dr. Leonhard Fuchs recommended that physicians use it "to scatter the dropsy, to relieve swelling of the liver, and even to bring on menstrual flow" (Silverman, 1942). Dr. Fuchs was a botanist-physician, and at that time, the medical profession paid little attention to a "mere flower picker."

Digitalis was finally admitted to the London Pharmacopeia in 1722. Foxglove (digitalis) was promoted by William Salmon as a miraculous cure for consumption (tuberculosis). Because it was difficult to differentiate between tuberculosis and dropsy (edema of the chest, heart failure), it is now believed that Salmon was actually treating dropsy instead of consumption.

In the mid-1700s, a female patient shared an old family recipe for curing dropsy with Dr. William Withering. This spurred Dr Withering to use digitalis with his dropsy patients and after spending 10 years studying digitalis, he published his conclusions, *An Account of the Foxglove*. This remarkable publication stressed instructions that are still valid today, that is, the necessity of individualizing dosage according to the patient's response.

The digitalis glycosides belong to many different botan-

ical families. The action of each is fundamentally the same, so that the description for digitalis, with minor differences, will apply to all. The principal forms will be discussed here.

### deslanoside (Cedilanid-D)
### digitoxin (Crystodigin)
### digoxin (Lanoxin, Novodigoxin ✿, Lanoxicaps)

Digitalis affects cardiac function through two important mechanisms:

1. Positive inotropic action. Influences the mechanical performance of the heart by increasing the strength of myocardial contraction.
2. Negative chronotropic and negative dromotropic actions. Involve alteration of electrophysiologic properties such as automaticity, conduction velocity, and refractory period.

***Positive inotropic action.***  The main function of digitalis is inotropic. The increased myocardial contractility is associated with more efficient use of available energy. If the failing heart is enlarged, the positive inotropic action of digitalis can cause the myocardium to beat more forcefully, thereby increasing cardiac output and decreasing oxygen use. Thus the improved pumping action of the heart in patients with congestive heart failure may reach levels that approach normal because the net effect is not only reduced

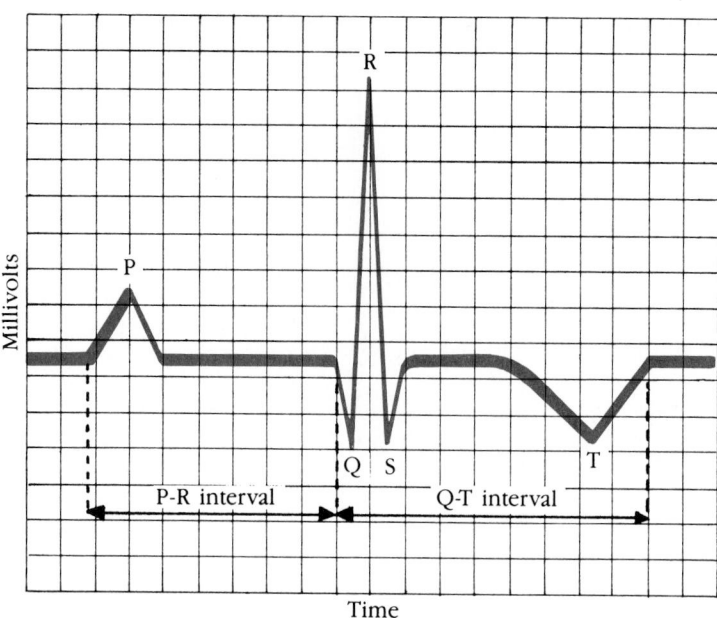

**FIGURE 24-2** Representation of typical effects of digitalization on the electric activity of the heart as shown on the electrocardiogram. Note the prolonged P-R interval, the shortened Q-T interval, and the T wave inversion.

heart size but also decreased venous pressure to relieve edema. The positive inotropic mechanism is not precisely known. However, one theory asserts that digitalis is bound to sites on the myocardial cell membrane (sarcolemma), where it inhibits the action of membrane-bound $Na^+-K^+-$ ATPase enzyme. Normally, this enzyme hydrolyzes ATP to provide the energy for the $Na^+-K^+$ pump needed to release $Na^+$ and transport $K^+$ into the cardiac cell during repolarization. By binding specifically to $Na^+-K^+-$ATPase, digitalis inhibits the active transport of $Na^+$ and $K^+$ (see Figure 23-1, 5b). Then intracellular $Na^+$ accumulates, which stimulates the release of large quantities of free calcium ion from the sarcoplasmic reticulum. The free calcium ion is essential for linking the electrical excitation of the cell membrane to the mechanical contraction of the myocardial cell, a mechanism known as excitation-contraction coupling. Thus, more free calcium ion produces a greater degree of coupling of actin and myosin to form actinomyosin, which results in more forceful myocardial contraction with a concomitant increase in cardiac output. Inhibition of $Na^+-K^+-$ATPase pump activity is projected to be the mechanism by which the cardiac glycosides increase myocardial contraction without causing increased oxygen consumption. (See "Myocardial Contraction" under "Cardiac Muscle" in Chapter 23).

**Negative chronotropic and negative dromotropic actions.** Digitalis has negative chronotropic (decreased heart rate) and negative dromotropic (slowed conduction velocity) effects because it can alter three electrophysiologic properties of cardiac tissues:

1. *Automaticity.* Cardiac tissue has the inherent ability to initiate and propagate an impulse without external stimulation. This property affects the rate and rhythm of the heart. Low to moderate doses of digitalis slow the heart rate because the SA node depolarizes less frequently. On the other hand, toxic concentrations of digitalis can directly increase automaticity. This increases the rate of both action potentials and spontaneous depolarization. This is one of the mechanisms responsible for digitalis-induced ectopic pacemakers. Toxic doses of digitalis may significantly increase impulse formation in latent or potential pacemaker tissue, causing dysrhythmia.

2. *Conduction velocity.* All concentrations of digitalis decrease conduction velocity. The AV conduction velocity is slowed both by the direct action of digitalis and by increased vagal action. The ECG shows a prolonged P-R interval, and in toxic doses the drug can lead to increased heart block. (See Figure 24-2.)

3. *The refractory period* effects of digitalis vary in different parts of the heart. If the refractory period in the ventricles is reduced, nearly toxic amounts of digitalis are required. A prolonged refractory period occurs in the AV conduction system, which is very sensitive to digitalis action. This action is partly direct and partly caused by increased vagal tone. Toxic doses of digitalis may prolong the refractory period and depress conduction in the AV conduction system until complete heart block may occur.

| Drug | Possible Effect and Management | Drug | Possible Effect and Management |
|------|-------------------------------|------|-------------------------------|
| antacids (especially aluminum and magnesium types) | May decrease digitalis glycoside absorption 25% to 35%. Space medications apart, preferably giving digitalis glycoside 1 to 2 hours before antacids. | magnesium sulfate injection | Use with extreme caution in individuals receiving digitalis. Alterations in cardiac conduction and heart block may result. Monitor closely. |
| antidysrhythmic agents, injectable calcium salts, cocaine, succinylcholine, or sympathomimetics | Concurrent administration may enhance risk of cardiac dysrhythmias. Avoid concurrent use whenever possible; if concurrent use is necessary, monitor closely with electrocardiographic monitoring. | potassium salts | Although potassium salts are commonly prescribed to treat hypokalemia, especially when clients are also taking a digitalis glycoside, potassium salts are not indicated in clients with severe heart block who are receiving digitalis. Hyperkalemia may be very dangerous in such individuals. |
| antidiarrheal adsorbents (kaolin, pectin, etc.), cholestyramine, colestipol, or large quantities of dietary fiber (bran) | May reduce absorption of digitalis glycosides resulting in a decreased therapeutic response. Dose medications 1 to 2 hours apart from digitalis products, preferably administering digitalis first. Then monitor closely. | quinidine | May result in an increased serum level of digoxin and digitoxin. Monitor serum levels and client's response closely; dosage adjustments may be necessary. |
| calcium channel-blocking agents (verapamil, diltiazem) | Concurrent use may cause severe bradycardia. Monitor closely since digitalis glycoside dosage may need to be reduced. | spironolactone | Concurrent administration may increase half-life of digoxin. Monitor closely; dosage reduction may be needed. |
| indomethacin | In premature neonate, the renal excretion of digitalis glycosides may be reduced, leading to increased serum levels and possibly toxicity. Reduce digitalis glycoside dosage by 50% when indomethacin is started. Monitor closely for both therapeutic and toxic effects and make dosage adjustments accordingly. | | |

Although glycoside serum levels are of limited value in establishing therapeutic serum levels, they are sometimes helpful as an indicator of toxicity.

***Dosage and administration.*** See Table 24-5. Also, the student should be aware of the following issues:

**TABLE 24-5**   Dosage and administration of cardiac glycosides

| | | Dosage range | |
|------|------|------|------|
| **Drug** | **Route** | **Digitalizing (loading)** | **Maintenance** |
| deslanoside (Cedilanid-D) | IV | *Adults:* 1.6 mg as single injection or 0.8 mg initially and repeated after 4 hours | |
| | IV/IM | *Children (over 3 yr):* 0.0225 mg/kg given in 2 or 3 divided doses at 3- or 4-hr intervals | |
| | IM | *Adults:* 0.8 mg given 2 times at 2 sites | |
| digitoxin (Crystodigin, Purodigin) | Oral | *Adults:* RAPID: 0.6 mg initially, followed in 4-6 hr by 0.4 mg and then 0.2 mg every 4-6 hr SLOW: 0.2 mg 2 times a day for 4 days *Children:* Not recommended | 0.05-0.3 mg/day (common dose 0.15 mg) |
| digoxin (Lanoxicaps, Lanoxin) | IV | *Adults:* 0.4-0.6 mg initially then 0.1-0.3 mg every 4-8 hr as needed | 0.125-0.5 mg daily as a single dose or in divided doses daily |
| | IV | *Children:* premature infant: RAPID: 15-25 μg/kg—give about ½ dose at once and remainder in fractional doses at 4-8 hr intervals | 20%-30% of loading dose daily in divided doses |
| | | Full-term infant: RAPID: 20-30 μg/kg—give about ½ dose at once and remainder in fractional doses at 4-8 hr intervals | 20%-35% of loading dose daily in divided doses |
| | | Infant (1-24 months): RAPID: 30-50 μg/kg—give about ½ dose at once and remainder in fractional doses at 4-8 hr intervals | 25%-35% of loading dose daily |

*Continued.*

**TABLE 24-5** Dosage and administration of cardiac glycosides—cont'd

| Drug | Route | Dosage range | |
|------|-------|--------------|---|
| | | Digitalizing (loading) | Maintenance |
| digoxin (Lanoxicaps, Lanoxin) | IV | *Children:*<br>2 to 5 yr—25-35 µg/kg<br>5 to 10 yr—15-30 µg/kg<br>Over 10 yr—8-12 µg/kg<br>Give about ½ dose at once and remainder in fractional doses at 4-8 hr intervals | 25%-35% of loading dose in divided doses 2 or 3 times a day<br>25%-35% of loading dose once a day |
| | tablet | *Adults:*<br>RAPID: 0.75-1.25 mg divided into 2 or more doses, each administered at 6-8 hr intervals<br>SLOW: 0.125-0.5 mg once a day for 7 days | 0.125-0.5 mg once a day |
| | | *Children:* 2 to 10 yr: 0.03-0.04 mg/kg in divided doses every 6-8 hr | 20%-30% of digitalizing dose daily |
| | capsule | *Adult:*<br>RAPID: 0.4-0.6 mg followed by 0.1-0.3 mg every 6-8 hr as necessary<br>SLOW: 0.05-0.35 mg daily in 2 divided doses; repeat dosage for 1-3 weeks to reach steady state serum levels<br>*Children:* See current literature as dosages vary according to age | 0.05-0.35 mg orally once or twice daily, as necessary |

*Bioavailability.* Bioavailability (discussed in more detail in Chapter 4) refers to the amount of the administered drug that is usable in the target tissue. Bioavailability must be considered when a client is transferred from a parenteral form to the oral form of a cardiac glycoside. Usually dosage adjustment is required to compensate for the pharmacokinetic differences of the drug. However, there is an exception: both digoxin injection and the liquid-filled, soft capsules of digoxin have the same bioavailability.

*Digitalization.* **Digitalization** is the saturation of body tissues with enough digitalis glycoside to cause the signs and symptoms of heart failure to disappear. Although nomograms and formula calculations are available to estimate digoxin dosage based on lean body weight and renal function, most physicians still prescribe digoxin according to body weight of the client. (See dosage chart, Table 24-5.) However, digitalis glycosides have a very narrow therapeutic index, i.e., the therapeutic dose is very close to the toxic dose. Many clients have digitalis toxicity, so it is vital for the nurse to monitor, and to teach the client to watch for, signs and symptoms of improvement and of drug toxicity. Drug serum levels should also be monitored. There are essentially two methods of digitalization: the rapid (fast) method, which requires hospitalization of the client, and the slow method, which is usually prescribed in an ambulatory setting.

The rapid digitalization method is reserved for the client in acute distress from heart failure. If the client has not previously received any digitalis glycoside, then intravenous digoxin or deslanoside is given in divided doses in a 24-hour period. The goal of treatment is to obtain the maximum therapeutic effect of the glycoside as rapidly as possible.

With this method, the drug toxicities will quickly become evident, while the client is in the controlled environment of the hospital unit. An advantage is that the toxicities can be easily correlated to a specific drug concentration. For example, the physician decides to digitalize an individual with a total dose of 1.0 mg digoxin intravenously. Digoxin may be prescribed as 0.5 mg IV now and 0.25 mg IV every 6 hours for two doses for a total of 1.0 mg. The nurse is expected to observe the client for signs of improvement. If the client demonstrates digitalis toxicity after the 1.0 mg dose, the physician would know that this person was not able to tolerate a 1.0 mg total dose and in the future would avoid any dosage regimen that might reach this level.

The slow method of digitalization is generally used in less acute situations in the ambulatory setting. The length of time before an individual is fully digitalized is much longer than with the rapid method. The physician may prescribe an oral maintenance dose of digitalis daily, and the client would not be fully digitalized until approximately the fifth half-life of the drug. Digoxin, which has a 36-hour half-life, would take 7½ days for digitalization, while digitoxin (with a half-life of 7½ days) would require over a month. The advantages of the slow method include (1) the individual may be treated on an outpatient basis, (2) it is a safer method, (3) close monitoring is not required, and (4) the doses may be taken orally. The disadvantages are (1) the extended length of time before the individual is digitalized and (2) the difficulty of determining when digitalis toxicity occurs since the onset of symptoms may be very gradual.

*Digitalis toxicity.* Almost every type of dysrhythmia can be produced by **digitalis toxicity.** The type of dysrhythmia

### Pediatric Implications: CARDIAC GLYCOSIDES

The digitalis glycosides are reported to be a leading cause of accidental toxicity in children (USP-DI, 1991). Individualized dosing with very close monitoring is necessary, especially in premature and immature infants.

Early signs of toxicity in infants and children may include a slow heart rate (less than 60 beats/minute) and irregular heart rhythms (Long, 1990).

### Geriatric Implications: CARDIAC GLYCOSIDES

The elderly often have a reduced tolerance for these drugs; lower doses of digitalis glycosides may be necessary to reduce the potential for drug toxicity.

Early toxic signs often include difficulty with reading (may also appear as visual alterations such as green and yellow vision, double vision, seeing spots or halos), headaches, dizziness, fatigue, weakness, confusion, increased nervousness, nausea, vomiting, diarrhea, or loss of appetite.

Decreased libido and impotence have been reported in approximately 35% of male users because of digoxin's estrogen-type effects. Also, male breast enlargement and/or breast tenderness have been reported (Long, 1990).

Advise client to avoid milk, cheeses, yogurt, and ice cream for at least 2 hours before and after taking digoxin because these foods reduce its absorption (Long, 1990).

produced varies with the age of the client and other factors. Premature ventricular contractions and bigeminal rhythm (two beats and a pause) are common signs of digitalis toxicity in adults, whereas children tend to develop ectopic nodal or atrial beats. Digitalis-induced dysrhythmias are caused by depression of the SA and AV nodes of the heart. This results in various conduction disturbances (first- or second-degree heart block or complete heart block). Digitalis may also cause increased myocardial automaticity, producing extrasystoles or tachycardias.

Nurses must be aware of the predisposing factors to digitalis toxicity. The presence of any of these factors in clients indicates the need for close observation for signs and symptoms of digitalis intoxication.

1. Potassium loss. Hypokalemia (low potassium levels) can increase digitalis cardiotoxicity. Since potassium inhibits the excitability of the heart, a depletion of body or myocardial potassium increases cardiac excitability. Low extracellular potassium is synergistic with digitalis and enhances ectopic pacemaker activity (dysrhythmias). The following are causes of potassium loss:

   a. Hypokalemia occurs if large amounts of body fluids are lost as a result of vomiting, diarrhea, gastric suctioning, or diuresis from administration of diuretics. The use of various diuretic agents (carbonic-anhydrase inhibitors, ammonium chloride, and thiazide preparations) induces potassium diuresis along with sodium and water diuresis.

   b. Poor dietary intake or severe dietary restrictions decreasing electrolyte intake can cause loss of potassium.

   c. Adrenal steroids cause potassium loss and sodium retention.

   d. Surgical procedures associated with severe electrolyte disturbances such as abdominoperineal resection, colostomy, ileostomy, colectomy, and ureterosigmoidostomy can cause loss of potassium.

   e. Use of potassium-free intravenous fluids can cause hypokalemia.

2. Hypercalcemia. Excess calcium in the presence of digitalis may cause sinus bradycardia, atrioventricular conduction block, and ectopic dysrhythmia.

3. Pathologic conditions. Kidney, liver, and severe heart disease are major factors in digitalis toxicity. Approximately 80% of digoxin is excreted by the kidneys, whereas approximately 90% of digitoxin is first metabolized by the liver. Therefore, in a clinical setting, the physician may choose digitoxin as the drug of choice for a client in renal failure, because of its mode of excretion, that is, liver metabolism. For a client with liver impairment, the physician may select digoxin as the drug of choice, mainly because it does not rely on the liver for metabolism before excretion. The long half-life of digitoxin is a disadvantage in treatment. If the client should develop digitalis toxicity, the half-life of digoxin may increase from 36 hours to 120 hours, whereas the half-life of digitoxin increases from 120 to 210 hours.

### Antidote for Digitalis Glycosides
**digoxin immune Fab(ovine) for injection (Digibind)**

This drug is an antidote for severe digitalis glycoside toxicity. Digoxin immune Fab(ovine) binds and makes complex molecules with digoxin or digitoxin in the serum. These molecules are then excreted by the kidneys. As more tissue digoxin is released into the serum to maintain an equilibrium, it will be bound and removed by this product, which results in lower levels of digoxin in serum and body tissues.

---

### FORMULAS FOR DIGOXIN IMMUNE FAB(OVINE)

For digoxin tablets, oral solution, or IM injection:

$$\text{Dose (mg)} = \frac{\text{dose ingested (mg)} \times 0.8}{0.6} \times 40$$

For digitoxin tablets, digoxin capsules, or IV digoxin or

$$\text{Dose (mg)} = \frac{\text{dose ingested (mg)}}{0.6} \times 40$$

When the amount of digitalis ingestion is unknown and the steady-state serum level is also not available, then 800 mg of digoxin immune Fab(ovine) is usually administered because it is reportedly sufficient to treat most life-threatening ingestions.

---

The drug is indicated for treatment of life-threatening digoxin or digitoxin overdose.

Onset of action takes place in less than 1 minute, with a half-life of 15 to 20 hours. Initial signs of improvement in digitalis toxicity can be seen in 15 to 30 minutes after administration but can take up to several hours. Arrhythmias and hyperkalemia are usually reversed first, whereas inotropic effect reversal may take several hours. The drug is excreted in the kidneys.

For side effects/adverse reactions see Table 24-5. No significant drug interactions have been reported.

Dosage in adults may be calculated on the amount of digoxin or digitoxin consumed or it may be based on steady-state serum levels. Usually a 40-mg dose of digoxin immune Fab(ovine) will bind approximately 0.6 mg of digoxin or digitoxin. The formulas in the box above may be applied to determine the dose of the antidote.

The pregnancy safety of this drug has been established by the FDA as category C.

## MISCELLANEOUS AGENT

### amrinone (Inocor)

Although its full mechanism is unknown, amrinone has positive inotropic effects and vasodilation activity. It does not inhibit $Na^+-K^+-ATPase$ activity, but it does appear to increase cellular concentrations of cyclic AMP. It reduces preload and afterload by its direct effect on vascular smooth muscle. Amrinone is used in the treatment of congestive heart failure, especially for individuals not responsive to digitalis glycosides, diuretics, or vasodilators.

With the parenteral dosage form, time to peak effect is approximately 10 minutes after intravenous injection. Du-

ration of action is dose related: 0.75 mg/kg, approximately ½ hour; 3 mg/kg, approximately 2 hours. Half-life when drug is administered by rapid intravenous injection is approximately 3.6 hours; by intravenous infusion, approximately 5.8 hours. Amrinone is metabolized in the liver and excreted by the kidneys (approximately 63%) and in the feces (18%).

For side effects/adverse reactions see Table 24-5. No significant drug interactions have been reported. In adults administer initially 0.75 mg/kg intravenously over 2 to 3 minutes. If necessary, dose may be repeated after 30 minutes. Maintenance dose is 0.005 to 0.01 mg/kg by intravenous infusion per minute. Dosage is adjusted according to therapeutic response. Dosage in children has not been established. Amrinone's safety level in pregnancy has been classified as FDA category C.

## ▷NURSING MANAGEMENT: CARDIAC GLYCOSIDE THERAPY

*Assessment.* Use drug cautiously when the following conditions are noted:

- Dysrhythmias. They may be caused by underlying heart disease or reflect digitalis intoxication; drug should be withheld if the latter occurs.
- Progression of AV block. Incomplete AV block may progress to advanced or complete heart block in digitalizing patients; this means that heart failure may need to be managed by other measures.
- Hypothyroidism, myocardial damage, renal disease, and severe respiratory disease. These clinical conditions may require lower doses of digitoxin because of its delayed excretion.
- Elderly clients. Because of their small body mass (i.e., lean body weight) and frequent renal impairments, elderly clients must be given the digoxin cautiously. Digitoxin is less affected by renal function impairment.
- Clients with electronic cardiac pacemakers. These clients require careful titration of their dosage because they may demonstrate symptoms of toxicity at dosages usually tolerated by other individuals.
- Electrolyte imbalances. Electrolyte imbalances require lower doses of digitalis glycoside. Potassium ion depletion increases risk of serious dysrhythmias and tends to diminish the positive inotropic effect of the drug. Potassium supplements are recommended. Also exercise great caution in giving drug to clients with hypercalcemia, to avoid dysrhythmia.

The use of digitalis glycosides is contraindicated in individuals with ventricular fibrillation, acute myocardial infarction, and hypersensitivity to any digitalis preparation. In addition, digitoxin is contraindicated in patients with heart disease secondary to beriberi.

*Intervention.* Rapid-acting digoxin is the most commonly prescribed form of a digitalis glycoside used in the coronary care unit (CCU). It may be given intravenously, intramuscularly, or orally.

Administer intravenously as an undiluted digoxin (0.25 mg/ml) slowly at 0.25 mg/minute. Avoid rapid administration to prevent pulmonary edema. The drug may be administered in diluted form. Administer intravenously with caution to clients with hypertension since it temporarily causes an increase in blood pressure. Make intramuscular injections deep into large muscle mass and follow with massage. This route is infrequently used because of erratic absorption and intense pain lasting for several days. Also, there is a potential for tissue necrosis to occur at the injection site.

The maintenance dose may be given orally if the client can tolerate food; otherwise intravenous injections are required. *Do not administer* oral preparation with meals having a high fiber content. Studies with digoxin show that the drug binds with the fiber, thereby reducing the amount of medication available for absorption from the gut. Advise the client to take drug after meals.

Be aware that digitoxin, though infrequently used, can be given undiluted intravenously (slowly) or orally to avoid pulmonary edema. Oral administration is more consistently absorbed and is safer for individuals with renal disease because the metabolites excreted in the urine are inactive and do not affect the half-life of a digitalis glycoside.

*Education.* Instruct client to take digitalis at the same time each day, precisely as prescribed. Do not skip or double a dose if missed. Also, do not change brand of drug when prescription is refilled. If using an elixir form of the drug, the dose should be determined using the special dropper that comes with the preparation. Caution client not to take other medications without prior approval of physician. Advise clients who are not hospitalized to report weight gain of 1 to 2 pounds a day. Caution clients to avoid licorice because it can induce sodium and water retention.

Advise the client to carry a medical identification and to alert health professionals unfamiliar with his or her drug regimen that the drug is being taken.

Teach the client how to take his or her pulse and recommend taking the pulse before each dose of the medication. The dose should be withheld and the physician notified if the pulse is below 60 and/or is erratic, or if the client suffers from anorexia, diarrhea, nausea, or vomiting. Visual disturbances, such as blurred vision or green or yellow halos around objects, should also be reported to the prescriber.

*Evaluation.* As altered cardiac output may occur related to the drug's positive inotropic effects, take the adult client's apical pulse for 1 minute before drug administration. Note rate, rhythm, and quality of pulse. If the pulse is 60 or below or a dysrhythmia that had not previously occurred is noted, withhold the drug and report immediately to the physician.

In children, also take the apical pulse 1 minute before administering the drug. Consult with the physician to determine the apical rate at which the drug should be withheld. Children's baseline rate usually is higher than adults.

Take apical and radial pulse for 1 minute to monitor for atrial fibrillation. In clients with atrial fibrillation, determine pulse deficit (apical pulse minus radial pulse).

Check the following parameters during digitalization:
* Observe the client for a positive response to digitalization. An increase in cardiac output reflects a more effective cardiac function, which includes improvement in rate and rhythm of heartbeat and in respiration, diuresis, reduction in weight (e.g., decrease in edema), and feeling of well-being.
* Know normal serum values of therapeutic digitalis levels and of potassium, calcium, and magnesium ion serum levels. (Low serum potassium level can potentiate digitalis intoxication; patients taking digitalis often receive potassium-depleting diuretics, which promote renal potassium excretion and lower serum potassium levels). Also monitor creatinine levels as evidence of renal function, especially in the elderly.
* Observe the rhythm strip for cardiac toxicity if the client is on ECG monitor.
* Discontinue drug if drug intoxication occurs. Blood digitalis level is ordered by physician if toxicity is suspected.

Observe client for symptoms of hypokalemia, such as unusual tiredness or weakness. Provide client taking potassium-depleting diuretics with foods that contain a high potassium content, such as bananas and orange juice if tolerated.

Be aware that the range of the therapeutic index of digitalis is extremely narrow. Observe client's food intake. Anorexia is an early sign of toxicity, as are nausea and vomiting and abdominal discomfort. In addition, these symptoms are indicators of altered comfort.

Draw blood samples before the regular daily dose of digitalis or 2 hours after an intravenous dose and 6 hours after an oral dose. Note that digitoxin has the greatest potential for toxicity because its slow elimination can produce cumulative effects in the body. However, digoxin may be preferred in individuals with impaired liver function because the drug does not require extensive hepatic metabolism.

Monitor intake and output. Delayed or diminished renal excretion of drug can lead to toxicity. Weigh client daily, preferably before breakfast to monitor for an alteration in fluid balance.

## SUMMARY

Cardiac glycosides increase the strength of cardiac contraction and alter the electrophysiologic properties of the heart by slowing conduction velocity, which accounts for their therapeutic properties for the treatment of heart failure. Clients may be hospitalized for rapid digitalization—which is the saturation of the body tissues with enough digitalis glycoside to cause the signs and symptoms of heart failure to disappear—or they may receive digitalization at a slower rate prescribed in an ambulatory setting.

In either case, because the therapeutic index of the drug is so narrow, the nurse has the responsibility to closely monitor the client for signs of toxicity, and to also teach the client about the drug's therapeutic and nontherapeutic effects. The nurse must be aware of the predisposing factors to digitalis toxicity and assist the client in also recognizing some of them. Potassium loss is the most common risk factor

for digitalis toxicity. It may be related to poor dietary intake; loss of large amounts of body fluids as with vomiting, diarrhea, or diuresis; the administration of adrenal steroids; surgical procedures that cause electrolyte loss such as ileostomy and colostomy; and the administration of potassium-free intravenous fluids. Digoxin immune Fab for injection is used as an antidote for severe digitalis glycoside toxicity.

The nurse has a major assessment and educational role with clients using cardiac glycosides since many clients take these drugs on a long-term basis. It is important not only that they take them accurately, but also that they are knowledgeable about the drugs to minimize the potential for injury inherent in their administration.

---

## Case Study: The Client with Cardiovascular Disease

Grace Markham is a 63-year-old widow who lives alone. She has a history of rheumatic heart disease manifested by moderate mitral valve stenosis with slight mitral insufficiency. She has been maintained on digoxin, 0.125 mg PO, daily for several years with few adverse effects. Compliance with therapy has generally been excellent. She understands the drug therapy and her 3-g sodium diet.

She was admitted to the hospital complaining of dyspnea on exertion, ankle edema, mild chest pain on exertion, and fatigue. The ECG shows no signs of infarction but does show atrial fibrillation with a ventricular response of 124 beats per minute. Her serum digoxin level was 0.9 ng/ml. A repeat cardiac catheterization showed no changes in the mitral valve but did indicate some early coronary artery narrowing. While she was in the hospital the following medications were ordered for Ms. Markham:

Digoxin, 0.25 mg PO, daily
Lasix, 20 mg PO, twice a day
K-Dur, 20 mEq PO, daily
Verapamil SR, 240 mg PO, daily
Isordil, 10 mg PO, three times a day

1. Describe the relationship between digoxin, Lasix, and K-Dur in the management of Ms. Markham's symptoms.
2. What additional data should be included in the assessment of the client related to the use of these three medications?
3. What is the significance of the serum digoxin level of 0.9 ng/ml?
4. How will the use of digoxin affect Ms. Markham's atrial fibrillation?

Several weeks later Ms. Markham comes to the clinic complaining of nausea, vomiting, and diarrhea. She reports having had these symptoms for several days. She has continued to take her medications except for the K-Dur, which she found increased the nausea.

5. What additional assessment data (subjective, objective, laboratory) do you want to gather related to these new symptoms?
6. A serum digoxin level for Ms. Markham was 2.5 ng/ml. Explain the significance of this change in relationship to the symptoms she was having.

# BIBLIOGRAPHY

American Hospital Formulary Service. (1990). AHFS drug information '90. Bethesda, Md: American Society of Hospital Pharmacists, Inc.

Anthony CP and Thibodeau GA. (1987). Textbook of anatomy and physiology, ed 12. St Louis: Times Mirror/Mosby College Publishing.

Barr S. (1985). Inocor (amrinone lactate), Crit Care Nurse 5(2):64.

Brown DD et al. (1987). PSVT: the problem is diagnosis, Patient Care 21(14):26.

Cooper JW. (1986). Digitalis drug interactions, Nurs Homes 35(3);14.

Curran CC et al. (1987). Use of cardiac glycosides in the critically ill, Critical Care Nurse 7(6):31.

Delafuente JC and Stewart RB. (1988). Therapeutics in the elderly. Baltimore: Williams & Wilkins.

Dunbar SB et al. (1988). Circadian rhythms and timing of digoxin administration, J Cardiovasc Nurs 2(4):1.

Few BJ. (1987). Digoxin immune fab, MCN 12(6):431.

Gilman AG et al, eds. (1990). Goodman and Gilman's the pharmacological basis of therapeutics, ed 8. New York: Macmillan Publishing Co.

Hartshorn EA et al. (1988). Factors affecting digoxin action and kinetics, J Cardiovasc Nurs 2(4):12.

Kastrup EK and Olin BR. (1987). Facts and comparisons, drug information. St Louis: JB Lippincott Co.

Kelleher RM. (1989). Cardiac drugs: new inotropes, Crit Care Nurs Clin North Am 1(2):391.

Long JW. (1990). The essential guide to prescription drugs. New York: Harper Collins.

Mercer ME. (1989). Myths and facts about cardiac drugs, Nursing 19(4):31.

Miller K. (1986). The use of digoxin in pre-hospital cardiac care, Emergency 18(9):6.

Molinari MA. (1988). Monitoring digoxin therapy in the elderly, RN 51(11):38.

Mooradian A and Wynn EM. (1987). Pharmacokinetic prediction of serum digoxin concentration in the elderly, Arch Intern Med 147(4):650.

Moore J. (1988). Intravenous amrinone therapy at home for the patient with chronic congestive heart failure, Focus Crit Care 15(6):32.

Norsen LH et al. (1985). Understanding cardiac output—and the drugs that affect it, Nursing 15(4):34.

Patterson JH and Pittman AW. (1985). Vasodilators: a review and outlook, US Pharmacist 10(8):H6.

Porterfield LM. (1988). Digitalis, AD Nurse 3(6):14.

Roberts R. (1988). Inotropic therapy for cardiac failure associated with acute myocardial infarction, Chest 93(1):22S.

Shinn AF, ed. (1985). Evaluations of drug interactions, ed 3. St Louis: The CV Mosby Co.

Silverman M. (1942). Magic in a bottle. New York: Macmillan Co.

United States Pharmacopeial Convention. (1991). Drug information for the health care provider, ed 11. Rockville, Md: The Convention.

White WB et al. (1988). The effects of cardiovascular drugs on exercise performance, J Cardiovasc Nurs 2(4):30.

Wilson DD. (1987). What's wrong with this patient? Nursing 17(11):70.

*Chapter*

# 25   Antidysrhythmics

## INTRODUCTION

A cardiac **dysrhythmia** may be defined as any deviation from the normal rhythm of the heartbeat. Dysrhythmia is caused by some disorder that modifies the electrophysiologic properties of the cells of the conduction system or cardiac muscle cells. For a review of the electrophysiologic events of a normal action potential, see Chapter 23, Overview of the cardiovascular system.

Antidysrhythmic drugs are used for the treatment and prevention of disorders of cardiac rhythm. Disturbances in cardiac rhythm result from some abnormality in the electrophysiologic properties of the cells of the specialized conduction system or the heart muscle. Dysrhythmias often develop in individuals about 4 to 72 hours after myocardial infarction ("heart attack"). In addition, abnormal rhythm may occur in those recovering from cardiac surgery or in clients with coronary artery disease. Also, individuals with extracardiac disorders, such as pheochromocytoma, electrolyte imbalance, or thyroid disease, generally have some abnormal cardiac rhythms.

# DISORDERS IN CARDIAC ELECTROPHYSIOLOGY

Disorders of cardiac rhythm arise as a result of (1) abnormality in spontaneous initiation of an impulse, or **automaticity,** or (2) abnormality in impulse conduction, or **conductivity.** In some conditions, a combination of both processes may occur.

*Abnormality in automaticity.* A disturbance in automaticity may alter the heart's rate, rhythm, or site of origin of impulse formation. When the rate of pacemaker activity is affected, a decrease in automaticity of the SA node produces **sinus bradycardia,** whereas an increase in automaticity of the SA node results in **sinus tachycardia.** On the other hand, a shift in the site of origin of impulse formation can generate an abnormal pacemaker or an ectopic focus. In an ectopic beat, the impulse originates from an abnormal focus or site, resulting in activation of some part of the heart other than the SA node. This is called an ectopic pacemaker. It may discharge at either a regular or an irregular rhythm. It occurs because the cardiac fibers depolarize more frequently than the SA node. Consequently, abnormal automaticity may develop in cells that usually do not initiate impulses, for example, atrial or ventricular cells. Clinical disorders such as hypoxia or ischemia can activate sympathetic receptors that in turn become centers to initiate impulses. In addition, ischemic sites can cause impulse disturbances in automaticity and also in conductivity, and both manifestations are responsible for ectopic beats. The ectopic beats are classified as escape beats, premature beats or extrasystoles, and ectopic tachydysrhythmia.

*Abnormality in conductivity.* Altered conduction of the cardiac impulse probably accounts for more dysrhythmias than a change in automaticity. A disturbance in conductivity may be caused by (1) delay or block of impulse conduction or (2) the reentry phenomenon.

*Delay or block of impulse conduction.* Normally, the SA and AV nodes are poor conductors of impulse transmission. Under abnormal circumstances, conduction of an atrial impulse to the ventricles may be delayed or blocked in the AV node or structures beyond this region in the conduction pathway. However, impaired impulse transmission generally appears in the AV node or junction and occurs in varying degrees of block. In the first-degree AV block the impulses from the SA node pass through to the ventricles very slowly, and this is noted by a prolonged P-R interval on the ECG. In the second-degree block some atrial beats fail to pass into the ventricles through the AV node. Finally, in the third-degree block or complete heart block, no impulses reach the ventricle, in which case the Purkinje fibers initiate their own spontaneous depolarization at a very slow rate. This results in independent ventricular and atrial rhythms referred to as ventricular "escape."

*Reentry phenomenon.* Reentry phenomenon is the mechanism responsible for initiating ectopic beats. A necessary condition for reentry is unidirectional block. Normally, when an impulse travels down the Purkinje fiber, it spreads along two branches. When it enters the connecting branch the impulses are extinguished at the point of collision in the center (Figure 25-1, *A*). At the same time, other impulses that begin laterally from the Purkinje fibers activate ventricular muscle tissue. In an abnormal situation the impulse descending from the central Purkinje fiber travels down the left branch normally but in the right branch encounters a block as a result of ischemia or injury (Figure 25-1, *B*). This is a unidirectional block, because the impulse is capable of passing in one direction but not in the other. As a result, in the right branch, where the impulse is blocked in the forward direction at the site of injury, a retrograde or reverse impulse from the ventricular tissue penetrates or reenters the depressed region from the other direction, provided that the pathway proximal to the block is no longer refractory. When the effective refractory period of the blocked area is over, reentry of the impulse from the ventricular muscle into this site causes the impulse to circulate or recycle repetitively through the loop, resulting in a circus-type movement that produces dysrhythmia.

As shown in Figure 25-1, *C*, reentry is abolished by certain drug groups such as I-A, IV, and possibly II, which are explained later in this chapter. *The drugs that decrease or slow conduction velocity can convert unidirectional block to a two-way or bidirectional block.* As the impulses traveling in the antegrade or forward direction and those appearing in a retrograde or reverse direction are blocked at the injured site, the reentry pathway is interrupted, thereby abolishing the ectopic beats. In Figure 25-1, *D*, the conditions required for preventing reentry by another mechanism are also illustrated. *The Group I-B drugs, which either increase or have no effect on conduction velocity, eliminate reentry by stopping unidirectional block entirely.* Consequently the normal impulse conduction along the right and left branches of the Purkinje fibers is again restored.

• • •

In recent years an increasing number of antidysrhythmic drugs have required classification into categories based on their fundamental mode of action on cardiac muscle (see box on p. 476). Such a grouping of antidysrhythmic mechanisms should prove of value in predicting the drug's therapeutic efficacy, as well as its potential toxic effects in a given clinical cardiac condition. Drugs belonging to a particular class do not necessarily possess actions that are identical in every respect. In some cases a given agent may have subsidiary properties (**extracardiac effects**) that alter the basic electrophysiologic actions on the cardiac muscle. The currently available antidysrhythmic drugs are classified into four categories according to their mechanisms of action (Table 25-1). However, these drugs have one major electrophysiologic property in common: they all have the ability to suppress automaticity. Group I compounds are subdivided

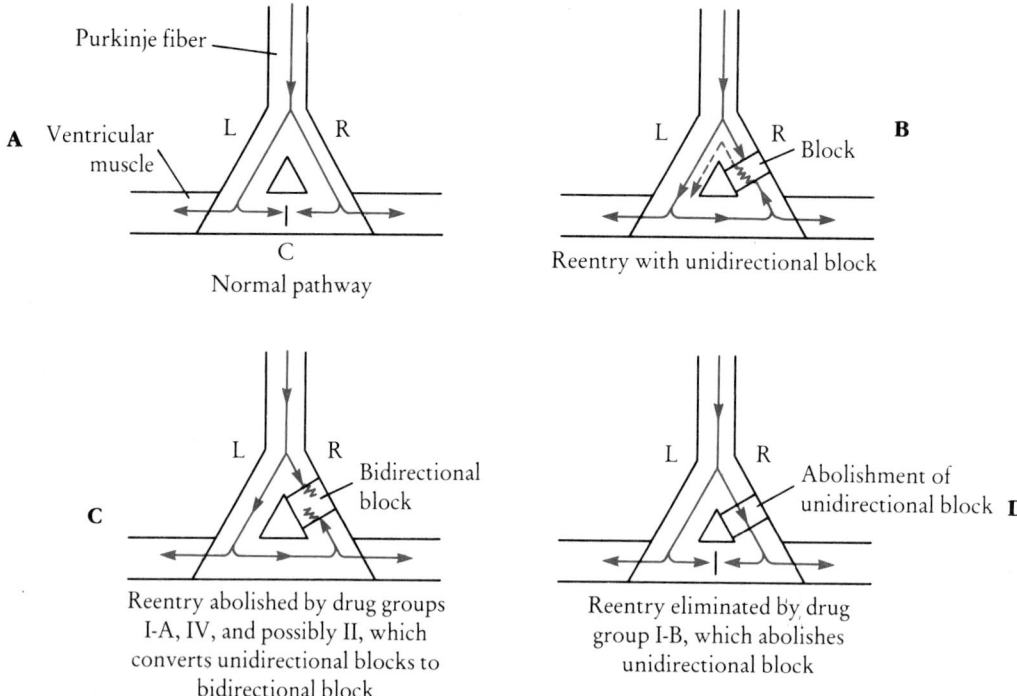

**FIGURE 25-1** Reentry phenomenon. Illustration of a branched Purkinje fiber that activates ventricular muscle. **L,** left branch; **R,** right branch.

---

### ANTIDYSRHYTHMIC CLASSIFICATIONS

Group I drugs—generally inhibit the fast sodium channel in cardiac muscle, resulting in an increased refractory period

(Subclasses I-A, I-B, and I-C further define the differences between the drugs. See Table 25-1.)

Group II drugs—beta adrenergic blocking agents that reduce adrenergic stimulation on the heart

Group III drugs—generally do not affect depolarization but work by prolonging cardiac repolarization

Group IV drugs—block the slow calcium channel, resulting in depression of myocardial and smooth muscle contraction, decreased automaticity, and, perhaps, decreased conduction velocity

---

into groups I-A, I-B, or I-C to reflect the similar electrophysiologic effects of each subgroup. Group I-A drugs include disopyramide, procainamide, and quinidine, all of which decrease conduction velocity and prolong the action potential. Group I-B drugs such as lidocaine, phenytoin, tocainide, and mexiletine either increase or have no effect on conduction velocity. Group I-C drugs include flecainide, encainide, and propafenone. These drugs, because of their prodysrhythmic effects in patients with poor left ventricular function, should be carefully selected and closely monitored

when prescribed. Propranolol, acebutolol, and esmolol are considered Group II drugs because of their beta-adrenergic blocking action.

The principal action of bretylium, a group III compound, is antiadrenergic. Unlike the other drug in this category, it has a decidedly positive inotropic action, and it prolongs repolarization. Amiodarone increases the refractory period and increases the P-R interval, QRS complex, and Q-T interval, contrary to the typical effects of bretylium. The last category, which is identified as group IV agents, is characterized by a selective calcium antagonistic action. For this reason, verapamil is classified independently of other conventional compounds and is discussed in Chapter 27. (See Table 25-1 for comparative electrophysiologic properties of antidysrhythmic drugs.)

### ▷NURSING MANAGEMENT: ANTIDYSRHYTHMIC THERAPY

***Assessment.*** Careful evaluation is necessary to determine the effect of a dysrhythmia for a specific client. Depending on the individual's health status and the degree of dysrhythmia, the effect may range from benign to life threatening. A thorough history, physical assessment, and an interpretation of the dysrhythmia are essential for formulating the possible nursing diagnoses. Possible nursing diagnoses that the client with a dysrhythmia might experience may include but are not limited to the following:

**TABLE 25-2**   Pharmacokinetics of selected antidysrhythmics

| Drug | Time to peak effect (hr) | Duration of action* (hr) | Therapeutic serum level (μ/ml) |
|---|---|---|---|
| GROUP I-A DRUGS | | | |
| disopyra-mide | 0.5-3 | 1.5-8.5 hr | 2-4 |
| procain-amide | 1-1.5 | 3 hr | 4-8 |
| quinidine | 1-4 | 6-8 hr | 3-6 |
| GROUP I-B DRUGS | | | |
| lidocaine | IV-1 min  IM-5-15 min | 10-20 min  60-90 min | 1.5-5 |
| tocainide | ½-2 | 8 hr | 3-10 |
| mexiletine | 2-3 | — | 0.5-2 |
| GROUP I-C DRUGS | | | |
| flecainide | 3 | — | 0.2-1 |
| encainide | 0.5-1.5 | — | — |
| propafenone | 3.5 | — | 0.2-1.5 |
| GROUP II DRUGS | | | |
| propranolol | 1-1.5 | 3-5 hr | 0.05-0.1 |
| GROUP III DRUGS | | | |
| bretylium | IM-1 (to control PVCs) | 6-24 hr | — |
| amiodarone | 3-7 | Variable | 1-2.5 |
| GROUP IV DRUGS | | | |
| Calcium antagonists—see Chapter 27 | | | |

*Metabolism/excretion is primarily via the liver/kidneys with the exception of amiodarone, which is mainly excreted via bile.

| Drug | Possible Effect and Management |
|---|---|
| antidysrhythmic agents, phe-nothiazines, alkaloids | May result in enhanced cardiac response. Monitor closely. |
| anticoagulants, such as cou-marin or indandione formu-lations | Monitor for signs of over-anticoagulation, hemorrhage. It may be necessary to adjust anticoagulant dosage both during therapy and after quinidine therapy is discontinued. |
| neuromuscular blocking agents | Monitor for increased or enhanced blocking effects, especially in the postsurgical client. |
| pimozide | Prolonged Q-T intervals and cardiac dysrhythmias may be reported with concurrent use. Monitor closely, preferably with an ECG, since intervention may be necessary. |
| urinary alkalizers, such as carbonic anhydrase inhibitors, citrus fruit juices in large amounts, antacids | May result in increased reabsorption of quinidine and elevated serum levels; dosage adjustments may be necessary. |

**Dosage and administration.** The quinidine salts have different percentages of active drug: quinidine gluconate, 62% active drug; quinidine polygalacturonate, 60% active drug; quinidine sulfate, 83% active drug. Because of this they are not interchangeable without appropriate dosage adjustment. For example, quinidine sulfate adult oral dosage for premature atrial and ventricular contractions is 200 to 300 mg 3 to 4 times daily. For children, the dose is 6 mg/kg body weight in 5 divided doses. Quinidine polygalacturonate adult dose is 275 mg to 825 mg every 3 to 4 hours for 3 or 4 doses; then increase dose by 127.5 to 275 mg every third or fourth dose until rhythm is restored or toxic effects occur. Maintenance dose is 275 mg 2 or 3 times daily. Children's dose is 8.25 mg/kg body weight, 5 times daily.

**Pregnancy safety.** FDA category C.

▷ **Nursing Management: Quinidine Therapy**

**Assessment.** Do not use in clients with atrioventricular block, AV conduction defects, congestive heart failure, hypotension, and myasthenia gravis (because of the drug's weak curare-like action). Quinidine should be used with

**TABLE 25-3**   Side effects/adverse reactions of antidysrhythmics*

| Drug | Side effects† | Adverse reactions‡ |
|---|---|---|
| **GROUP I-A DRUGS** | | |
| disopyramide, procainamide, quinidine | Most frequent: dry mouth and throat (disopyramide only), diarrhea, anorexia (procainamide, quinidine), bitter taste, nausea, vomiting, abdominal pain or cramps, flushing, rash (quinidine)<br>Less frequent: sexual impotency (disopyramide) dizziness, confusion | Most frequent: difficulty in urination (disopyramide only)<br>Less frequent: edema, brady or tachycardia, confusion, chest pain, weight gain (disopyramide), elevated temperature, chills, painful joints, rash (SLE-type reaction from procainamide), hypotension, confusion (all), visual changes, tinnitus, (quinidine) |
| **GROUP I-B DRUGS** | | |
| lidocaine, tocainide, mexiletine | Most frequent: dizziness anorexia, nausea, vomiting<br>Less frequent: paresthesia of fingers and toes, rash, (tocainide and mexiletine), increased sweating, (tocainide), pain at injection site (lidocaine) | Less frequent: tremors (to cainide) chest pain, breathing difficulties, tachycardia (mexiletine), agranulocytosis, pneumonitis (tocainide) |
| **GROUP I-C DRUGS** | | |
| flecainide, encainide, propafenone | Most frequent: blurred vision, (flecainide), dizziness (flecainide and propafenone), headaches, constipation, nausea, (propafenone)<br>Less frequent: headaches, nausea, increased weakness, (all 3 drugs) | Less frequent: chest pain, irregular heartbeats, arrhythmias (all of them) |
| **GROUP II DRUGS** | | |
| Beta adrenergic antagonists—see Chapter 21 | | |
| **GROUP III DRUGS** | | |
| bretylium tosylate, amiodarone | Most frequent: anorexia, headaches, nausea, vomiting, constipation, (amiodarone)<br>Less frequent: nausea, vomiting (bretylium), bitter taste in mouth, impotency, dizziness, flushing (amiodarone) | Most frequent: cough, breathing difficulties, temperature, paresthesia of fingers or toes hand tremors, extremity weakness, ataxia (amiodarone) |
| **GROUP IV DRUGS** | | |
| Calcium antagonists—see Chapter 27 | | |

*When drugs are specifically mentioned by name in the columns above, the side effect or adverse reaction listed applies to that drug(s) only.
†If side effects continue, increase, or disturb the client, inform the physician.
‡If adverse reactions occur, contact physician because medical intervention may be necessary.

caution with clients with a history of thrombocytopenia. Patients with hepatic and renal function impairment may require decreased dosages to avoid accumulation of the drug. Clients sensitive to quinine may also be sensitive to quinidine.

With the administration of quinidine, the client may possibly experience the following nursing diagnoses: altered comfort related to skin flushing, bitter taste, anorexia, nausea and vomiting, and abdominal cramping; potential for physiologic injury related to the development of allergic reaction (fever, rash, wheezing, dyspnea), cinchonism (blurred vision, dizziness, headache, altered hearing), hy-

potension (syncope), anemia (tiredness, weakness), tachycardia, thrombocytopenia (unusual bruising or bleeding); altered nutrition related to gastrointestinal effects; and altered thought processes (confusion).

*Intervention.* To determine if the client may have an idiosyncratic response or hypersensitivity to quinidine, give a test dose of 200 mg orally a few hours before the initiation of therapy. A parenteral dose of 200 mg is also administered before intramuscular or intravenous therapy if time permits. Observe the client for fever, acute asthma, angioedema, and anaphylactic shock. Cinchonism may also be manifested by headache, dizziness, fever, tinnitus, nausea, tremor, and visual disturbances. Administer oral preparation on an empty stomach 1 to 2 hours after meals with a full glass of water to promote absorption. However, quinidine may be given with food to decrease gastric distress if it occurs. Avoid administering with antacids because they may increase urinary pH and so increase the potential for quinidine toxicity.

*Education.* Instruct the client to report any symptoms of rash, ringing in the ears, or visual disturbances. Caution client to immediately report feeling of faintness (see "quinidine syncope" in a subsequent nursing management section). Also, examine buccal mucosa for petechial hemorrhage. If bleeding occurs, report immediately. The drug will be discontinued because of possible thrombocytopenic purpura.

Advise the client to have regular dental checkups and to practice good dental hygiene since the antimuscarinic effects of the drug inhibit salivary flow and so contribute to caries and gum disease, particularly in the elderly. Recommend that the client carry medical identification. Caution the client to alert health professionals, including dentists, that he or she is taking quinidine.

*Evaluation.* Use caution during intravenous administration because of possible vasodilation, depressed cardiac contraction, and cardiovascular collapse, which may lead to profound shock. NOTE: The intravenous route is seldom used. Continuously monitor both the ECG and the systemic arterial blood pressure during and immediately after parenteral administration. Toxic effects include widening of QRS complex in excess of 25%, abolition of P waves, and ventricular extrasystoles. Notify physician immediately when such effects occur.

Monitor intake and output, blood counts, serum electrolyte determinations, and kidney and liver function tests during prolonged therapy. The effect of quinidine is reduced if hypokalemia is present.

Use quinidine with caution in clients with atrial fibrillation or flutter. The vagal blocking effect of the drug may increase the number of atrial beats conducted across the AV junction, resulting in sudden acceleration in ventricular rate. *Prior administration of digitalis slows AV conduction and reduces the hazard of ventricular tachycardia.* Monitor ECG and blood serum levels of the two drugs to avoid toxicity. Reduction in digoxin dosage is suggested when quinidine is given simultaneously. Check plasma quinidine levels carefully. Be aware that concomitant administration with digitalis (digoxin) readily induces toxicity because the two drugs lead to an excessively high plasma concentration of digoxin (less digoxin is excreted by the kidney).

Be alert to premature ventricular contractions not noted before drug administration (appears as an ectopic foci by reentry phenomenon) because they may lead to ventricular tachycardia or fibrillation and subsequently to cardiac standstill (asystole).

Note that another form of ventricular disorder can cause "quinidine syncope." It produces ventricular tachycardia or fibrillation, causing a decrease in cardiac output and thereby diminishing blood flow to the brain. The symptoms are feeling of faintness, loss of consciousness, and ultimately sudden death.

### disopyramide phosphate (Norpace)
### disopyramide phosphate extended-release capsules (Norpace CR, Rythmodan ✱)

Mechanism of action includes both a direct effect and an indirect effect. The direct effect results in a decrease in excitability (by inhibition of cation exchange at the membrane site); a decrease in automaticity (decreases rate of diastolic depolarization or phase 4 and elevation of the threshold potential thus requiring more current to fire the cell) (see Figure 25-2). The result is a delay in the velocity of depolarization (phase 0), especially at the ectopic sites, which permits the SA node to reestablish control as the pacemaker in the heart. The direct effect also slows conduction velocity (velocity of depolarization or phase 0 is delayed) and the action potential duration is prolonged in myocardial tissue. The AV node is essentially unchanged. In addition to these effects, an effective refractory period is established. Reentrant dysrhythmias are abolished by converting a unidirectional block into a bidirectional block (see Figure 25-1).

The indirect effect involves an anticholinergic action, especially in the gastrointestinal and urogenital systems.

Disopyramide is indicated to treat premature (ectopic) ventricular contractions, ventricular arrhythmias, and episodic ventricular tachycardia. For pharmacokinetics and side effects/adverse reactions, see Tables 25-2 and 25-3.

*Significant drug interactions.* The following interactions may occur when disopyramide is given with the drugs listed below:

| Drug | Possible Effect and Management |
|---|---|
| Other antiarrhythmic agents, such as diltiazem, flecainide, lidocaine, procainamide, beta-adrenergic blocking agents, quinidine, tocainide, or verapamil | Monitor closely for prolonged electrophysiologic conduction and decreased cardiac output. Beta-adrenergic blocking agents may exacerbate heart failure, especially in individuals with compromised ventricular function. Do not administer disopyramide concurrently or within 48 hours before or 24 hours after verapamil, since fatalities have been reported. |
| pimozide | Concurrent therapy may reduce serum levels of disopyramide below therapeutic effectiveness range. Monitor therapeutic effects and serum levels closely. |

*Dosage and administration.* Dosage is individualized according to response and tolerance. Oral adult loading dose is 300 mg; then maintenance dose is 150 mg every 6 hours. For extended-release capsules dosage for adults is 300 mg every 12 hours given as maintenance dose. Do not use as initial dose. The elderly usually require a reduction in dosage, since they are more sensitive to the effects produced by the usual adult dosage. For children, the following total doses are divided by 4 and given orally, every 6 hours. Dosage for infants less than 1 year is 10-20 mg/kg; 1 to 4 years, 10-20 mg/kg; 4 to 12 years, 10-15 mg/kg and 12 to 18 years old, 6-15 mg/kg of body weight.

*Pregnancy safety.* FDA category B.

▷ **Nursing Management:**
**Disopyramide Phosphate Therapy**

*Assessment.* Despite the fact that little effect has been shown on the AV nodal conduction time, do not use this drug in clients with greater than first-degree block. Drug should be discontinued if second- or third-degree block occurs during therapy. The P-R interval will be prolonged. Do not use in clients with cardiogenic shock or known hypersensitivity to the drug. Disopyramide may cause hypoglycemia in clients with diabetes mellitus. Administer disopyramide phosphate cautiously in pregnant clients as it has been reported to produce uterine contractions in such clients.

The drug's anticholinergic properties may cause urinary retention in clients with prostatic enlargement or bladder neck obstruction or a myasthenic crisis if the client has myasthenia gravis. If administered to clients with either renal or hepatic function impairment, an accumulation of disopryamide may result; dosage reductions may be required. Administration to clients with cardiac conditions such as cardiac conduction abnormalies resulting in decreased conduction, congestive heart failure, and cardiomyopathies is not recommended. The client's serum potassium level must be within the normal range; if it is too high, then serious dysrhythmias may occur; if it is too low, the drug may not be effective.

A baseline assessment of the client should involve blood glucose determination, blood pressure status, ECG, serum potassium levels, intraocular pressure, and hepatic and renal function.

With the administration of disopyramide, the client has the potential for development of the following nursing diagnoses: urinary retention related to the drug's anticholinergic effects; altered comfort related to chest pain, dry mouth; altered thought processes (confusion, depression); altered cardiac output, decreased; excess fluid volume (swelling of the feet and lower legs, rapid weight gain, shortness of breath); potential for injury related to dizziness, syncope, and weakness, blurred vision, hypoglycemia, agranulocytosis (sore throat and fever); altered bowel elimination, constipation related to the anticholinergic effects; and altered self-concept related to decreased sexual ability.

*Intervention.* Administer on an empty stomach, either 1 hour before or 2 hours after meals. Clients with preexisting closed-angle glaucoma should receive disopyramide only if cholinergic eye drops are also administered to control the ocular anticholinergic effects of the drug. The drops should

be administered with caution to clients with a family history of angle closure glaucoma.

*Education.* Instruct client to make position changes slowly from recumbent posture if hypotension should occur. Advise client about possibility of dry mouth, which can be relieved by hard candy, gum, or frequent clear water rinses. Recommend regular dental checkups for the prevention of caries and periodontal disease. Also, avoid alcoholic beverages because of potential hypotensive effects.

Emphasize the importance of not skipping or stopping medication without consulting a physician since adverse cardiac effects may occur upon sudden withdrawal.

Instruct client to weigh daily to monitor fluid retention. Report to the physician a weight gain of 2 or more pounds. Observe for edema.

Caution the client about driving or other hazardous activities, since blurred vision and dizziness may occur. Alert clients about the hypoglycemic effects of the drug, particularly clients with diabetes. Teach signs and symptoms of hypoglycemia; if they occur, instruct the client to take a form of sugar and notify the physician. Caution the client that heat intolerance and reduced perspiration will occur and to avoid exertion and hot weather. Constipation may result from the anticholinergic effects of the drug. Instruct clients about high-fiber diet, increased fluid intake, moderate exercise, and regular bowel patterning.

*Evaluation.* Monitor blood pressure carefully; drug should be discontinued if hypotension, bradycardia, or congestive heart failure becomes worse. The symptoms of congestive heart failure are difficulty in breathing, shortness of breath, weight gain, distended neck veins, and pulmonary rales.

Monitor ECG intervals carefully to avoid cardiac toxicity. The following signs are indications to collaborate with the physician in planning for drug withdrawal:
* If QRS complex widens more than 25%
* If Q-T interval is prolonged more than 25% (use another antidysrhythmic agent)
* If P-R interval severely increases (dosage should be reduced)

ECG monitoring is essential for clients with severe cardiac disease, hypertension, or renal or hepatic impairment.

Monitor serum potassium level; it should be normal to achieve optimal effect. Toxic reactions are enhanced by excessive potassium levels. Measure intake and output, particularly in patients with impaired renal function or prostatic hypertrophy. Urinary retention may require stopping use of the drug. Observe clients with myasthenia gravis closely, since the drug's antimuscarinic properties may precipitate a myasthenic crisis.

**procainamide hydrochloride (Pronestyl, Pronestyl-SR)**

With the exception of slowing conduction in the bundle of His and prolonging of the refractory period in the atria, the direct electrophysiologic properties are the same as for disopyramide. In addition, contractility of the heart is usually not decreased unless myocardial damage exists. Also, alpha adrenergic blockade does not occur. (See Table 25-1.)

The primary indications for procainamide are to treat premature ventricular contractions, ventricular tachycardia, atrial fibrillation and paroxysmal atrial tachycardia. It is also used to treat cardiac dysrhythmias associated with anesthesia and surgery. For pharmacokinetics and side effects / adverse reactions, see Tables 25-2 and 25-3.

***Significant drug interactions.*** The following interactions may occur when procainamide is given with the drugs listed below.

| Drug | Possible Effect and Management |
|------|-------------------------------|
| other antiarrhythmic agents | Monitor for enhanced or additive cardiac effects. |
| antihypertensives | Increased hypotension has been reported, especially when parenteral (intravenous) procainamide is given with antihypertensive agents. Monitor closely, since dosage adjustments may be necessary. |
| antimyasthenia agents | The effect of antimyasthenic agents on skeletal muscle may be blocked by the antimuscarinic effects of procainamide. Monitor closely, since dosage adjustments of the antimyasthenic agent may be required. |
| neuromuscular blocking agents | Concurrent use may result in enhanced neuromuscular blockade. Monitor closely since reversal of blockade may be prolonged. |
| pimozide | Prolonged Q-T intervals and cardiac dysrhythmias may be reported with concurrent use. Monitor closely, preferably with an ECG, since intervention may be necessary. |

***Dosage and administration.*** Adult dosage for ventricular arrhythmias is 1 g orally initially, then 6.25 mg/kg body weight every 3 hours. In atrial dysrhythmias, the initial dose is 1.25 g followed by 0.75 g in 1 hour if needed, then 0.5 to 1 g every 2 hours. Maintenance dose is 500 to 1000 mg every 4 to 6 hours. The extended release dosage form is also used for maintenance therapy, i.e., 1 g every 6 hours for atrial dysrhythmias and 12.5 mg/kg every 6 hours for ventricular dysrhythmias. For current recommended dosing on the parenteral product, see current package insert or USP-DI.

***Pregnancy safety.*** FDA category C.

▷ **Nursing Management:**
**Procainamide Hydrochloride Therapy**

***Assessment.*** Procainamide is contraindicated for use in second- and third-degree block, complete heart block, myasthenia gravis, and hypersensitivity to the drug. Use with caution. In atrial fibrillation or flutter, the ventricular rate may increase suddenly since the atrial rate is slowed. Embolization may result from dislodgement of mural thrombi caused by forceful contraction of the atrium with conversion to sinus rhythm. Hepatic and renal impairment may cause drug accumulation, leading to toxicity.

Procainamide preparations contain sulfite and should not be used by clients with known sensitivity to sulfite agents. Symptoms of sulfite sensitivity include skin rash, itching, clamminess, shortness of breath, wheezing, cyanosis, hypotension, anaphylaxis, and respiratory arrest.

With the administration of procainamide, the client may experience the following nursing diagnoses: altered thought processes related to CNS effects (confusion, hallucinations, depression); potential for physiologic injury related to dizziness, allergic reaction, systemic lupus erythematosus-like syndrome (fever, chills, skin rash, arthralgia), leukopenia and agranulocytosis (fever, sore throat), thrombocytopenia (unusual bleeding and bruising); and altered bowel elimination, diarrhea.

***Intervention.*** To initiate intravenous therapy, the drug should be diluted in 5% dextrose to facilitate control of the dosage range; the dose should be administered at a rate not greater than 25 to 50 mg/minute by direct intravenous administration or infusion. Also, intravenous therapy is limited to use in hospitals where monitoring facilities are available.

Once prepared, the solution is stable for 24 hours at room temperature or 7 days if refrigerated. Procainamide is physically incompatible with many substances; check specific references when considering mixing with other drugs. The first oral dose should be administered at least 3 to 4 hours after the last intravenous dose. Administer oral dosage on an empty stomach with a full glass of water to promote absorption. To lessen gastrointestinal irritation, drug may be taken with or immediately after meals.

***Education.*** Urge client on long-term therapy to keep appointments for periodic laboratory work: lupus erythematosus (LE) test, antinuclear antibody (ANA) titers, blood counts, hepatic and renal function tests; and plasma procainamide and N-acetyprocainamide (NAPA) determinations. This is particularly important in clients with congestive heart failure, those with hepatic or renal function impairment, or those changing from regular oral to extended-release preparation of the drug. Symptoms of systemic lupus erythematosus (polyarthralgia, cough, fever, and pleuritic pain) should be reported to the prescriber so that the drug can be discontinued.

Counsel clients to report symptoms such as unusual bleeding and/or bruising; sore mouth, gums, or throat; fever; rash; or symptoms of an upper respiratory tract infection to the prescriber. These symptoms are more apt to occur with the extended-release dosage form.

The antimuscarinic effects may decrease salivary flow and lead to the development of caries and gum disease. Instruct clients in proper oral hygiene, including the use of toothbrushes and dental floss. Regular dental checkups are also advised.

Some clients, particularly elderly clients, may be prone to dizziness. Alert them that driving and operating other mechanical equipment might be hazardous.

Advise the client to continue to take the medication even though feeling well. Instruct the client that if a regular oral preparation dose is missed but remembered within 2 hours, to take it (within 4 hours for extended-release form), if a missed dose is remembered after this time it should *not be taken*. Instruct the client not to double up on doses. Alert the client not to discontinue the medication without consulting the physician, since a gradual withdrawal may be necessary to prevent worsening the condition.

Recommend that the client carry medical identification. The client should be instructed to alert health professionals, including dentists, that he or she is taking procainamide.

The oral forms of procainamide are hygroscopic (they will absorb moisture). Advise the client to keep them tightly closed in their original container and not to transfer them to other less tightly sealed containers or to leave them exposed to air.

Caution the client receiving the extended-release form of the medication that the dose is contained in a wax matrix that may be detected in the stools. This has no effect on the drug's absorption.

*Evaluation.* Monitor (qualified personnel only) intravenous administration constantly, and observe the following:

- Infusion pump: maintain desired flow rate. Keep patient in supine position. Avoid rapid administration to prevent "speed shock" (irregular pulse, tight feeling in chest, flushed face, headache, loss of consciousness, shock, cardiac arrest).
- ECG: discontinue therapy if QRS complex is widened greater than 50% and P-R interval is prolonged.
- Arterial blood pressure: during loading dose take every 5 minutes; if blood pressure drops more than 15 mm Hg, discontinue infusion. Have pressor solutions available: dopamine or norepinephrine to treat hypotension. Elderly clients are more apt to exhibit hypotension.

## GROUP I-B DRUGS

The Group I-B drugs (e.g., lidocaine and phenytoin) differ from Group I-A drugs in that they either increase or have no effect on conduction velocity. Lidocaine is particularly useful for acute ventricular dysrhythmias. It must be administered parenterally. Despite the fact that phenytoin is not approved by the FDA for this use, it is commonly used in the therapy of digitalis-induced dysrhythmias. Tocainide and mexiletine are also Group I-B drugs. They are therapeutically related to lidocaine and are used to treat some types of symptomatic ventricular dyrhythmias. Mexiletine is considered as effective as quinidine but its high incidence (40%) of side effects/adverse reactions has limited its use. Tocainide can cause the serious adverse reaction of agranulocytosis. Therefore it is usually reserved for clients that have not responded to other drug therapies.

### lidocaine hydrochloride (Xylocaine, Xylocard ✳ )

Lidocaine is better known and extensively used as a local and topical anesthetic agent. Systemically, it is now commonly used as an antidysrhythmic agent, especially for ventricular dysrhythmias seen after cardiac surgery or an acute myocardial infarction. Lidocaine exerts its most important cardiac effect by depressing excessive automaticity of ectopic pacemakers in the His-Purkinje fibers. Thus it is useful in suppressing premature ventricular contractions, a dysrhythmia that may be provoked by hypoxic or ischemic cells in myocardial infarction. Ischemia is a condition that favors the development of an ectopic pacemaker, discharging faster than the normal pacemaker in the SA node. In some cardiac disorders, premature ventricular contractions may eventually precipitate ventricular tachycardia or fibrillation. Therefore it is essential to provide effective treatment immediately.

In contrast to the findings with quinidine and procainamide, lidocaine has little, if any, effect on conduction velocity (phase 0) or on the effective refractory period in the AV node and the Purkinje fibers. The absence of these properties possibly prevents reentry types of dysrhythmia. For this reason the drug may play a part in improving AV conduction in the digitalis-intoxicated heart. Also, the potential for development of heart block, cardiac asystole, or ventricular ectopic rhythm is minimized with the use of lidocaine. On the ECG the P-R or Q-T intervals may not shorten, and the QRS is not prolonged. Unlike quinidine and procainamide, lidocaine has no vagolytic (resembling the effect produced by the interruption of impulses transmitted by the vagus nerve) properties nor does it influence cardiac output and arterial pressure. Also, it does not depress myocardial contractility and thereby provides no potential for the development of congestive heart failure. Since it exerts limited if any effect on the SA node and atrial myocardium, the drug has no use in the treatment of supraventricular tachycardias. Because electric activities are primarily limited to the ventricular cells, the major use of lidocaine is in abolishing ventricular dysrhythmias. (See Table 25-1 and Figure 25-1, *D*.)

Lidocaine is indicated for the treatment of ventricular arrhythmias. The pharmacokinetics and side effects/adverse reactions are in Tables 25-2 and 25-3. A significant drug interaction may occur when lidocaine is administered with phenytoin (hydantoin anticonvulsant), which may result in enhanced cardiac depressant effects. Also, the anticonvulsant may reduce lidocaine serum concentration by increasing the liver metabolism of lidocaine.

Lidocaine adult dose is by IV bolus, 1 mg/kg at a rate of 25 to 50 mg/minute. This dose may be repeated in 5 minutes if necessary, although the maximum dose per hour is 200 to 300 mg. Children may receive the same 1 mg/kg dose initially as a loading dose, but repeat dosages in 5 minutes should not exceed a total dose of 3 mg/kg. By IV infusion, the dose is usually 20 to 50 μg/kg/minute given at a rate of 1 to 4 mg/minute for both adults and children. The adult IM dose (not established for children) is 4.3 mg/kg or 300 mg for a 70 kg adult initially, which may be repeated in 1 to 1.5 hours if necessary. Pregnancy safety for lidocaine has been established at FDA category B.

## ▷ Nursing Management: Lidocaine Hydrochloride Therapy

*Assessment.* Do not administer lidocaine to clients with severe degrees of sinoatrial, atrioventricular, or intraventricular block, **Adams-Stokes syndrome** (sudden recurring episodes of loss of consciousness, caused by transient interruption of cardiac output by incomplete or complete heart block), **Wolff-Parkinson-White syndrome** (a supraventricular tachycardia), and known history of hypersensitivity to amide type of local anesthetics. Use with caution in individuals with hypovolemia, shock, and all forms of heart block. Use with caution and in lower doses in individuals with congestive heart failure or reduced cardiac output and in the elderly. To prevent toxicity in clients with impaired renal and hepatic function, employ caution with prolonged use since the drug is metabolized mainly in the liver and excreted by the kidney.

Its use in pregnancy is not established. Administer only when potential benefits outweigh potential hazards to the fetus. Not recommended for pediatric usage.

With the administration of lidocaine, the client should be assessed for the following nursing diagnoses: altered comfort related to the use of parenteral dosage forms (pain at the site of injection) and related to specific serum levels of the drug (nervousness, dizziness, drowsiness, and feelings of numbness, cold, and heat); decreased cardiac output related to cardiac conduction disturbances (hypotension, arrhythmias, heart block, and cardiac arrest); potential for physiologic injury related to allergic reaction (skin rash, urticaria, and dyspnea), and overdose (blurred vision, nausea, vomiting, tinnitus, tremors, dizziness, seizures, bradycardia).

*Intervention.* Recheck drug label; only lidocaine hydrochloride *without preservatives or epinephrine,* which specifically reads "IV use for cardiac dysrhythmias," should be administered. Preparations intended for use as an anesthetic contain epinephrine and *should not* be used for treating dysrhythmias. Intravenous infusions of lidocaine are usually prepared by adding 1 g of lidocaine to 1 L of 5% dextrose solution for a 1 mg/ml solution. Solution is stable for 24 hours. Do not add to blood transfusions.

For intravenous route, use a precision intravenous volume control set for continuous infusion. Monitor rate of flow prescribed by the physician, usually at no more than 4 mg/minute. Terminate intravenous infusion as soon as cardiac rhythm is stable or signs of toxicity develop. Have resuscitative equipment and drugs available to treat adverse reactions involving cardiovascular system, respiratory system, and CNS.

Note that intravenous infusions are rarely continued beyond 24 hours. The client is then given an oral antidysrhythmic agent for maintenance therapy.

When using bolus administration, if the loading dose does not provide the desired therapeutic effect within 5 minutes, administer a second dose one half to one third of the initial dose. However, give no more than 200 to 300 mg within a 1 hour period.

Use deltoid muscle for intramuscular site because therapeutic blood levels are reached faster than in gluteus or lateral thigh muscles. Aspirate to ensure that intravascular injection will be avoided. Intramuscular use may increase creatinine phosphokinase levels and interfere with diagnostic enzyme tests for myocardial infarction. Intramuscular administration is only for instances in which ECG is not available and the risk/benefit ratio has been considered by the physician. Following initial use, discard partially used solutions of lidocaine that contain no preservatives.

To avoid more serious ventricular dysrhythmias or complete heart block in patients with sinus bradycardia or incomplete heart block, anticipate administration of isoproterenol or electric pacing to accelerate heart rate before lidocaine administration.

In clients over 65 or in those with congestive heart failure or renal or hepatic function impairment, the dose and rate of infusion is generally reduced by one half and then adjusted in response to the client's condition.

Measure serum lidocaine levels to minimize the chance of toxicity if high-dose infusions are used or if the client is receiving other drugs that might affect lidocaine clearance.

*Education.* Instruct the client on the procedure for self-injection and have client state and demonstrate the procedure. The client should ensure that the medication is always readily available and that it is not out of date. If symptoms of heart attack occur, instruct the client to contact physician immediately. Client should not administer the medication unless instructed to do so by the physician. To administer, client removes safety cap, places black end of the cylinder on thickest part of thigh, and presses hard; client should feel a needle stick. The needle is held in place for a slow count of 10 and then area is massaged for a slow count of 10. Instruct the client not to drive after administering the drug unless there is no other alternative.

*Evaluation.* Constant ECG monitoring is essential for intravenous administration and recommended during intramuscular administration to observe for signs of toxicity. Monitor ECG and blood pressure to avoid potential overdosage and toxicity. If excessive cardiac depression occurs, such as prolongation of P-R interval, QRS complex, or aggravation of dysrhythmias, stop infusion immediately.

Serum electrolyte levels should be determined periodically during prolonged lidocaine infusions to correct imbalances.

Observe client for adverse effects of lidocaine (see box on p. 486).

---

**ADVERSE EFFECTS RELATED TO SERUM CONCENTRATIONS OF LIDOCAINE**

| 1.5-6 µg/ml | 6-8 µg/ml | >8 µg/ml |
|---|---|---|
| Anxiety, nervousness, drowsiness, dizziness, sensations of cold, heat, or numbness | Tremors, twitching, blurred or double vision, nausea, vomiting, tinnitus | Dyspnea, severe dizziness, loss of consciousness, bradycardia, convulsions |

---

If the intravenous administration should run for more than 24 hours, observe for local thrombophlebitis and assess the client for the risk of accumulation.

### phenytoin (Dilantin)

Phenytoin is not approved by the FDA as an antidysrhythmic agent Group I-B, but it is commonly used to treat digitalis-induced atrial and ventricular dysrhythmias. It has been found to be ineffective in dysrhythmias not produced by digitalis toxicity. This drug has been approved for use as an anticonvulsant (see Chapter 15).

Phenytoin may stabilize the sodium influx in Purkinje fibers of the heart, decrease abnormal ventricular automaticity, decrease the refractory period, and cause no change or an increase in the conduction rate through the atrioventricular tissues and Purkinje fibers. (See Table 25-1.)

Pharmacokinetics, side effects/adverse reactions, and significant drug interactions are noted in Chapter 15. Phenytoin is indicated for treatment of digitalis-induced dysrhythmias: usually 50 to 100 mg intravenously every 10 to 15 minutes as needed to stop the dysrhythmia or until toxicity appears. Do not exceed a dose of 15 mg/kg. Intravenous administration must be slow, usually at 25 to 50 mg/minute. For elderly patients, the dosage is reduced and the rate of intravenous injection should be 25 mg/minute (USP-DI, 1991).

### ▷ Nursing Management: Phenytoin Therapy

*Intervention.* Follow manufacturer's instructions for preparing drug for parenteral use (see dosage and administration, Chapter 15). Administer slowly intravenously to prevent toxicity. Do not exceed 50 mg/minute infusion rate. Consult laboratory reports for therapeutic serum levels and for blood sugar levels in clients with diabetes mellitus, since drug tends to cause hyperglycemia.

Since phenytoin is so highly alkaline, administer oral preparation with at least half a glass of milk or water or with meals to minimize gastric irritation.

Do not use in clients with hypersensitivity to phenytoin: skin rash may occur; seizures may be caused by hypoglycemia. Also, sinus bradycardia, incomplete heart block,

hepatic dysfunction, and hematologic disorders may result. (See Chapter 15 for additional information.)

*Evaluation.* Closely monitor blood pressure, respiration, and ECG during intravenous administration to avoid bradycardia and hypotension. Have appropriate antidotal medications and resuscitative equipment available. Observe client closely for drug toxicity, which may occur early in the elderly or in those with impaired liver function. Use caution in individuals with hepatic or renal dysfunction, hypotension, alcoholism, respiratory disorders, diabetes mellitus, and pancreatic adenoma. See also "Nursing management: hydantoin therapy," Chapter 15.

### tocainide (Tonocard)

Tocainide has been called an oral lidocaine as it is chemically and therapeutically related to lidocaine. Dysrhythmias responsive to parenteral lidocaine are usually responsive to tocainide. It is indicated for the treatment and/or prevention of ventricular arrhythmias. Pharmacokinetic and side effects/adverse reactions are in Tables 25-2 and 25-3. No significant drug interactions have been reported.

Adult dose is 400 mg orally every 8 hours. Maintenance dose is 1200 to 1800 mg orally daily, in three divided doses. The geriatric client should receive smaller doses since he or she may be more sensitive to this product. Adjust dose according to client's response and/or the development of side effects or toxicity. A dosage protocol has not been established for children. Pregnancy safety has been established as FDA Category C.

### ▷ Nursing Management: Tocainide Therapy

*Assessment.* Determine that client is not sensitive to amide-type anesthetics and has no AV block or preexisting second- or third-degree block without a ventricular pacemaker. Note whether client has congestive heart failure or renal or hepatic function impairment, since tocainide must be used cautiously, with intensive monitoring, in such clients.

With the administration of tocainide, the client should be assessed for the development of the following nursing diagnoses: altered comfort related to CNS effects (dizziness, headache, blurred vision, trembling, numbness or tingling of the fingers and toes), gastrointestinal effects (anorexia, nausea, vomiting); altered thought processes (confusion); potential for injury related to the development of leukopenia or agranulocytosis (fever, chills), thrombocytopenia (unusual bruising or bleeding), pneumonia, pulmonary fibrosis or edema (cough, dyspnea), premature ventricular contractions (irregular heart beat), and skin reactions (peeling, scaling, and blisters of skin).

**Intervention.** Administer with food or milk to reduce gastric distress. If the client has adverse reactions shortly after taking a dose of tocainide, lower each individual dose but administer with greater frequency. If the dysrhythmia returns before the next scheduled dose, a higher dosage or more frequent dosing should be considered.

**Education.** Instruct the client to take medication even though he or she feels well. Doses should not be missed and should be evenly spaced. If a forgotten dose is remembered within 4 hours, it should be taken. If a longer interval has passed, dose is not to be taken until the next scheduled time.

Advise the client to maintain regular visits to the physician to monitor progress. Recommend that a medical identification card be carried or a bracelet worn.

Alert the client that dizziness may occur and that caution should be taken when driving or operating other mechanical equipment. The elderly client might be at increased risk for falling. Instruct client to report signs and symptoms of leukopenia and thrombocytopenia (evidence of infection, delayed healing, fever, chills, sore throat, unusual bleeding, and/or bruising). If these symptoms occur, the client should postpone dental work and should be instructed to use toothbrushes, dental floss, and toothpicks cautiously.

**Evaluation.** Take blood counts and ECG before therapy and at periodic intervals, to detect bone marrow suppression and medication effectiveness. Chest x-ray examinations are required at the first sign of pulmonary complications, such as pneumonia, pulmonary edema, or pulmonary fibrosis. If the client evidences tremor, it may be an indication that the highest tolerable dose has been reached.

### mexiletine (Mexitil)

Mexiletine is similar to tocainide in mechanism of action and indications. Pharmacokinetics and side effects/adverse reactions are in Tables 25-2 and 25-3. No significant drug interactions are reported to date.

Mexiletine's adult dose is initially 200 mg orally every 8 hours. If necessary, dosage may be increased by 50 to 100 mg every 2 or 3 days. Maximum dose recommended is 1200 mg/day when administered at 400 mg/8 hours or, 900 mg/day if given at 450 mg per dose, every 12 hours. Children's dose is not established. Pregnancy safety has been established as FDA category C.

▷ **Nursing Management:**
**Mexiletine Therapy**

The nursing management of the client receiving mexiletine is much the same as for tocainide, except these clients may also experience altered bowel elimination related to the gastrointestinal effects of the drug, either constipation or diarrhea; and the potential for injury related to skin reactions is not quite so severe. Refer to the earlier discussion for tocainide for more detail.

## GROUP I-C DRUGS

The Group I-C drugs include flecainide (Tambocor), encainide (Enkaid), and propafenone (Rythmol), which are used to treat and/or prevent supraventricular tachydysrhythmias. These agents can cause sinus arrest, AV block and life-threatening ventricular arrhythmias. This prodysrhythmic effect is of special concern especially in clients with poor left ventricular function or sustained ventricular arrhythmias. The Group I-C drugs can also aggravate congestive heart failure.

### flecainide (Tambocor)

Flecainide depresses the rate of depolarization of the action potential (phase 0); decreases excitability, conduction velocity, and automaticity because of its effects on the atria, AV node, His-Purkinje fibers, and intraventricular conduction. It is indicated for the treatment of ventricular dysrhythmias, especially symptomatic, life-threatening dysrhythmias such as ventricular tachycardia and frequent premature ventricular contractions (PVCs).

The pharmacokinetics and side effects/adverse reactions are in Tables 25-2 and 25-3. If flecainide is administered with other antidysrhythmic agents, enhanced adverse cardiac effects may occur. In persons with hypotensive ventricular tachycardia, irreversible ventricular tachycardia or ventricular fibrillation has been reported. Avoid concurrent usage.

The adult dose is 100 mg orally initially every 12 hours. This dose may be increased by 50 mg twice a day, every 4 days, if necessary. Dose in children is not established. Pregnancy safety has been established as FDA category C.

▷ **Nursing Management:**
**Flecainide Therapy**

Nursing considerations are essentially the same as for tocainide, except pulmonary symptoms such as pneumonia and pulmonary fibrosis are not a concern with flecainide.

### encainide (Enkaid)

Encainide is similar to flecainide except the electrophysiologic effects appear to be greater in ischemia tissue than in normal cardiac tissue. It is indicated for treatment of ventricular arrhythmias. The pharmacokinetics and side effects/adverse reactions are in Tables 25-2 and 25-3. No significant drug interactions are reported with encainide.

The adult dose is initially 25 mg orally every 8 hours. This dose may be increased by 35 mg every 8 hours after 3 to 5 days of initial therapy. Maximum dose is 50 mg every 8 hours. Dose in children is not established. Pregnancy safety has been established as FDA category B.

▷ **Nursing Management: Encainide Therapy**

Assess for new or increasing arrhythmias. These usually occur within the first week of therapy, especially when the dosage exceeds 200 mg/day. Other nursing considerations are similar to those for flecainide.

### propafenone (Rythmol)

Propafenone is a Group I-C drug that also has some beta-adrenergic blocking effects and some Group III and IV antiarrhythmic-type properties. However, the latter properties may not contribute significantly to its therapeutic effect. It is indicated for the treatment of ventricular arrhythmias. The pharmacokinetics and side effects/adverse reactions are in Tables 25-2 and 25-3. A potentially significant drug interaction with concurrent administration of digoxin is reported; digoxin serum levels may increase from 35% to 85%, depending on the dose of propafenone consumed. Digoxin dose should be reduced when propafenone is started. Increased serum levels have also been reported with concurrent administration of beta-adrenergic blocking agents, such as propranolol and metoprolol. Monitor closely because dosage adjustments may be necessary.

Warfarin plasma concentrations also increase with concurrent administration, which leads to an increase in prothrombin times (25% increase). Monitor closely as warfarin dosage adjustments of warfarin are usually necessary. As propafenone appears to inhibit the hydroxylation metabolic pathway in the liver, the potential for drug interactions is present for any drugs that use this pathway. Monitor all concurrent drug therapy closely to detect early any undesirable adverse effects.

Dosage is individual, depending on client's response and side effect tolerance. Generally, 150 mg every 8 hours is prescribed with dosage adjustments at 3- to 4-day intervals, as necessary. The pregnancy safety has been established as FDA category C.

▷ **Nursing Management: Propafenone Therapy**

**Assessment.** The client's blood pressure and pulse should be known before propafenone is administered since it is contraindicated in marked hypotension and bradycardia. The drug is also contraindicated in severe congestive heart failure, cardiogenic shock, manifest electrolyte imbalance, and bronchospastic disease. The effective dose for the el-

derly client may be lower because of impaired hepatic or renal function in this age group.

Once propafenone has been administered to the client, the nurse should assess the client for the following potential nursing diagnoses due to the effects of the drug: altered comfort related to headache, nausea and vomiting, muscle cramps, hot flashes, flushing, pruritus, and dizziness; sensory-perceptual alterations related to CNS effects (vision disturbances, paresthesias, numbness, tinnitus, unusual taste or smell sensation); altered thought processes related to CNS effects (abnormal dreams, confusion, depression, memory loss, psychosis/mania); and risk for physiologic injury related to hematologic effects (anemia, agranulocytosis, granulocytopenia, leukopenia, and thrombocytopenia).

**Intervention.** The therapeutic response to the drug should be carefully recorded because the dosage of propafenone is titrated by the physician on the basis of the client's response and tolerance.

**Evaluation.** Vital signs are to be taken every 4 hours while the client is awake. An expected outcome would be that the client's dysrhythmia would diminish in severity.

## GROUP II DRUGS
### propranolol hydrochloride (Inderal)

Propranolol, a beta-adrenergic blocking agent; is used to control cardiac dysrhythmias caused by excessive sympathetic nerve activity. The principal action of propranolol is associated with its ability to inhibit adrenergic stimulation of the heart. Therefore dysrhythmias caused by increased sympathetic discharge (hyperthyroidism) are effectively blocked by the beta-adrenergic action of propranolol. (See drug monograph in Chapter 21 and Table 25-1.)

## GROUP III DRUGS

The electrophysiologic properties of drugs in this group differ markedly from the drugs previously discussed.

### bretylium tosylate (Bretylol, Bretylate ✷)

Unlike other antiarrhythmic agents, bretylium does not suppress automaticity. In addition, it has no effect on conduction velocity. The only direct electrophysiologic action on the heart appears to be prolongation of the action potential and a lengthening of the effective refractory period. It is believed that this mechanism helps to terminate dysrhythmias caused by the reentry phenomenon. As an antidysrhythmic agent, the significant effect of bretylium is related primarily to its adrenergic blocking action. The drug is taken up and concentrated in the adrenergic nerve terminals, where, after an initial release of norepinephrine, it prevents any further release. This sympatholytic action significantly increases the threshold, producing an antifibrillatory response in the ventricles. The drug exerts no influence on vagal reflexes. Furthermore, unlike other drugs in this category, bretylium produces a positive inotropic effect, increasing myocardial contractility. With long-term treatment, the drug shows increased responsiveness to circulating epinephrine and norepinephrine, which may account for the increased myocardial contractility. (See Table 25-1.)

The pharmacokinetics and side effects/adverse reactions are in Tables 25-2 and 25-3. Do not administer digitalis glycosides to clients receiving bretylium. The initial release of norepinephrine produced by bretylium may increase digitalis toxicity.

In the United States only the intravenous and intramuscular forms of bretylium are available. The adult dose for life-threatening ventricular fibrillation is initially 5 mg/kg of undiluted solution, then 10 mg/kg every 15 to 30 minutes if needed to a total of 30 mg/kg in 24 hours. The adult dose for unstable ventricular tachycardia intravenous infusion (diluted solution) is 5 to 10 mg/kg over 10 to 30 minutes. This may be repeated every 6 hours. A constant infusion may be administered at a rate of 1 to 2 mg/minute. Dosage for other ventricular arrhythmias is initially a diluted intravenous solution given at a rate of 5 to 10 mg/kg over 10 to 30 minutes. If necessary, this dose may be repeated in 1 to 2 hours. For maintenance, administer diluted intravenous solution at a rate of 5 to 10 mg/kg over 10 to 30 minutes. If necessary, repeat every 6 to 8 hours. Alternatively a constant infusion may be administered at a rate of 1 to 2 mg/minute.

For adult IM dose, give 5 to 10 mg/kg of undiluted bretylium. Repeat dose after 1 or 2 hours if needed. Maintenance dose is given every 6 to 8 hours.

The pregnancy safety has not been established.

## ▷ Nursing Management: Bretylium Therapy

**Assessment.** Bretylium should be administered with caution to clients with conditions involving reduced cardiac output, such as aortic stenosis and pulmonary hypertension, because severe hypotension may occur. Clients with renal function impairment require increased dosage intervals because elimination of the drug is reduced. With the administration of bretylium, the client may be assessed for the following nursing diagnoses: altered comfort related to angina (chest pain), gastrointestinal effects (nausea and vomiting); ineffective breathing pattern related to possible neuromuscular block (dyspnea, respiratory depression); and risk for injury related to postural hypotension (dizziness, syncope).

**Intervention.** Administer bretylium to clients in an area that is adequately staffed by qualified personnel and equipped with appropriate facilities for constant ECG monitoring and use of emergency equipment. Anticipate the possible development of transient hypertension and dys-

rhythmias during the early stage of therapy. This is caused by the initial release of norepinephrine from adrenergic nerve terminals.

Rotate intramuscular injection site. Do not administer more than 5 ml at one site. Necrosis, muscle atrophy, or fibrosis may occur if injection is repeatedly given at the same site. Note that intramuscular injection is rarely used. Administer slowly intravenously to prevent nausea and vomiting.

Bretylium is generally discontinued in 3 to 5 days and an alternate antidysrhythmic agent may be substituted if indicated. Do not administer digitalis glycosides simultaneously with bretylium because increased incidence of dysrhythmias may occur as a result of digitalis toxicity.

**Evaluation.** Closely monitor ECG and blood pressure. Keep client in supine position during therapy until tolerance to the hypotensive effect of the drug occurs. This may take a few days.

### amiodarone hydrochloride (Cordarone)

Amiodarone hydrochloride increases the refractory period in all cardiac tissues by a direct effect on the tissues. It decreases automaticity, prolongs AV conduction, and decreases the automaticity of fibers in the Purkinje system. It also causes adrenergic and calcium channel inhibition. It is indicated for prevention and treatment of ventricular dysrhythmias, especially unstable ventricular tachycardia or ventricular fibrillation.

For pharmacokinetics and side effects/adverse reactions, see Tables 25-2 and 25-3.

**Significant drug interactions.** The following drug interactions may occur when amiodarone is given with the drugs listed below.

| Drug | Possible Effect and Management |
|---|---|
| other antidysrhythmic agents | May increase cardiac effects and the risk of inducing tachyarrhythmias. It also increases serum levels of quinidine, procainamide, flecainide, and phenytoin. If amiodarone must be given with Group I antidysrhythmic agents, reduce the dose of the Group I antidysrhythmic drug by 30% to 50% several days after starting amiodarone and gradually withdraw the Group I drug. If additional treatment with amiodarone is necessary, start therapy at half the usual recommended dosage. |
| anticoagulants, coumarin | May increase anticoagulant effect. Dose of anticoagulant should be reduced by one third to one half of the dose when adding amiodarone to the client's drug regimen. Also, prothrombin times should be closely monitored. |
| digitalis glycosides | May increase the serum level of digoxin and other digitalis glycosides, resulting in toxicity. Digitalis glycosides should |

| Drug | Possible Effect and Management |
|------|-------------------------------|
| digitalis glycosides— cont'd | be stopped or the dose reduced to 50% whenever amiodarone is given. Monitor serum levels closely. May also see additive effects of both drugs on the SA and AV nodes. |
| phenytoin | May result in increased serum levels of phenytoin, possibly resulting in toxicity. Monitor serum levels of phenytoin. |

***Dosage and administration.***  Amiodarone has a delayed onset of action, a complex dosing schedule and some very serious adverse effects, so this drug is usually used only when other, safer agents are ineffective or they cannot be tolerated by the client.

*Adults.*  For ventricular dysrhythmias. Initially, a loading dose of 800 mg to 1.6 g orally daily for 1 to 3 weeks (sometimes longer), until a therapeutic response is noted or side effects appear. If stomach upset occurs or the dosage is greater than 1 g daily, the dose should be divided and given after meals. When therapeutic control of the dysrhythmia occurs or excessive side effects are noted, the dose should be reduced to 600 to 800 mg daily for 1 month. Afterward, decrease dosage to lowest effective dose. Maintenance: 400 mg orally daily; adjust dosage as necessary.

*Children.*  Initially, a loading dose of 10 mg/kg/day for 10 days, or until a therapeutic response is noted or side effects appear. Then decrease the dose to 5 mg/kg/day for several weeks and gradually taper the dose down to the lowest effective dose. Maintenance: 2.5 mg/kg/day orally.

***Pregnancy safety.***  FDA category C.

▷ **Nursing Management:**
**Amiodarone Therapy**

***Assessment.***  Determine that client does not have AV block, preexisting second- or third-degree block without a pacemaker, or syncope as a result of severe bradycardia unless controlled by a pacemaker. Use caution if the client has congestive heart failure or impaired hepatic or thyroid function. Hypokalemia should be corrected before the initiation of amiodarone therapy to ensure the drug's effectiveness.

With the administration of amiodarone, the client should be assessed for the development of the following nursing diagnoses: risk for injury related to neurotoxicity (ataxia, tremors of the hands, numbness and tingling of fingers and toes, weakness of the arms and legs), photosensitivity, pulmonary fibrosis or pneumonitis (cough, dyspnea, fever), new dysrhythmias, congestive heart failure (edema of feet and lower legs), hyperthyroidism (weight loss, insomnia, nervousness, sensitivity to heat), hypothyroidism (weight gain, tiredness, sensitivity to cold, dry skin), ocular toxicity (blurred vision), sinus bradycardia, allergic reaction (rash), and hepatitis (yellow skin and eyes); altered comfort related

### Investigational Drug Update: ANTIDYSRHYTHMICS

New investigational antidysrhythmic agents include acecainide (NAPA; Group III drug), cifenline (Cipralan; has properties of Groups I-A, III, and IV), and indecainide (Decabid; Group I-C). Cipralan is a unique antidysrhythmic drug that appears to be well tolerated.

to conditions above and noninfectious epididymitis (pain and swelling of the scrotum), dizziness, bitter taste, headache, nausea and vomiting; altered self-concept related to decreased libido, blue-gray coloring of the skin of the face, hands, and arms; and altered bowel elimination (constipation).

***Intervention.***  Begin the loading dose phase at the beginning of amiodarone therapy in the hospital, because of the difficulty in adjusting dosage and the potential for adverse effects, such as neurotoxicity and ocular, pulmonary, and thyroid toxicity.

Since gastrointestinal disturbances occur in 25% of clients during loading, take care to minimize these as much as possible. Instruct clients to eat a high-fiber diet and increase fluid intake, unless contraindicated, to prevent constipation. Administer with food or milk to decrease nausea. Make efforts to stimulate appetite to counteract anorexia.

***Education.***  Instruct client to continue the medication even if he or she is feeling well. If a dose is missed, the client should be advised not to take it at all, to avoid doubling up on doses. If two or three doses are missed, instruct the client to contact the physician.

Instruct client to maintain regular contact with the physician to monitor drug use. Advise the client to carry medical identification at all times. Instruct client to alert health professionals unfamiliar with the medication regimen to the amiodarone administration.

Photosensitivity is a potential adverse effect with this drug. Caution client to avoid exposure to the sun and to wear sun-protective clothing and sun-screening lotions. In addition, a blue-gray coloration of the skin occurs with long-term use (over 1 year) and affects sun-exposed parts of the body, such as face, neck, and arms, and those with fair skin.

Alert clients to report any of the following signs and symptoms to the physician: cough, dyspnea, fever (pulmonary toxicity); ataxia, numbness, tingling, weakness, or spasm of extremities (neurotoxicity); blurred vision or increased sensitivity of the eyes to light (ocular toxicity); unusual weight gain or loss, increased sensitivity to heat or cold (thyroid toxicity); pain and swelling of the scrotum;

### New Drug Release in 1990:
### MORICIZINE (ETHMOZINE)

Moricizine has both Group I-A and I-B properties. It is indicated for the treatment of life-threatening, sustained ventricular arrhythmias (ventricular tachycardia). Moricizine, similarly to other antiarrhythmic drugs, can induce new cardiac rhythmic disturbances or exaggerate an existing arrhythmia (proarrhythmic effect). It is recommended that treatment with this drug be initiated in a hospital setting. Multiple drug interactions and side/adverse effects are reported with moricizineil; therefore, the nurse is referred to a current package insert or USP-DI for additional information.

jaundice (hepatic toxicity); or swelling of the feet and lower legs (congestive heart failure).

*Evaluation.* Perform ECG, thyroid function studies, liver function studies (SGPT, SGOT, and serum alkaline phosphatase), chest x-ray examinations, and pulmonary studies before the initiation of therapy and periodically thereafter. Ophthalmologic examinations should be done initially, and if eye symptoms occur. Pulmonary fibrosis may occur in 10% to 30% of the clients receiving long-term amiodarone therapy. Because this is usually reversible if detected early enough, chest x-ray examinations every 3 months are recommended.

## SUMMARY

Antidysrhythmic agents are used for the treatment and prevention of disorders of cardiac rhythm that result from some abnormality in the electrophysiologic properties of the cells of the cardiac conduction system or cardiac muscle cells. Although all drugs in this grouping have the ability to suppress automaticity, it is subdivided into groups I-A, I-B, or I-C to reflect the similar electrophysiologic properties of each subgroup. Group I-A includes disopyramide, procainamide, and quinidine, all of which decrease conduction velocity and prolong the action potential. Group I-B drugs, lidocaine, phenytoin, tocainide, and mexiletine, either increase or have no effect on conduction velocity. Group I-C drugs, flecainide, encainide, and propafenone, are used to treat or prevent supraventricular tachydysrhythmias; however, they have prodysrhythmic effects that are of concern and require careful monitoring of the client. Group II drugs have beta-adrenergic blocking action and have been discussed in Chapter 21. The Group III agents, bretylium and amiodarone, are antiadrenergic. Group IV agents have selective calcium antagonistic action; verapamil will be discussed in Chapter 27.

Nursing management of cardiac dysrhythmias with the administration of antidysrhythmic agents should have the expected outcomes of having the client maintain cardiac output within normal limits, increase activity tolerance, experience less chest discomfort and associated symptoms, and evidence decreased or no dysrhythmias on ECG tracings. Client education is focused on the development of the client's knowledge of health status and medications, skill at pulse taking, and ability to recognize changes in health status that are reportable to enable the client to self-administer antidysrhythmic agents safely and accurately.

## BIBLIOGRAPHY

Abramowicz M, ed. (1989). Drugs for cardiac arrhythmias, Med Let Drugs & Therapeutics 31(790):35.

American Hospital Formulary Service. (1990). AHFS drug information '90. Bethesda, Md: American Society of Hospital Pharmacists, Inc.

Bachman J et al. (1989). The failing heart, Patient Care 23(1):132.

Benning CA et al. (1989). Tocainide in the cardiac ICU, Crit Care Nurse 9(2):45.

Carlstedt BC and Stanaszek WF. (1986). Cardiac arrhythmias, US Pharmacist 11(1):43.

Carr P. (1988). Cardiovascular drugs, Home Healthcare Nurse 6(5):37.

Catalano JT. (1986). Antiarrhythmic medications classified by their autonomic properties, Crit Care Nurse 6(3):44.

Frumin H et al. (1989). Classification of antiarrhythmic drugs, J Clin Pharmacol 29:387.

Gaining control of life-threatening arrhythmias, Emerg Med 20(2):45.

Gilman AG et al. (1990) Goodman and Gilman's the pharmacological basis of therapeutics, ed 8. New York: Macmillan Publishing Co.

Huang SK and Olin BR. (1987). Flecainide and encainide, Hosp Ther 12(8):33.

Kastrup EK and Olin BR. (1987). Facts and comparisons, drug information. St Louis: JB Lippincott Co.

Jones S et al. (1988). L-E-A-D drugs for cardiac arrest: lidocaine, epinephrine, atropine, and dopamine, Nursing 18(1):34.

Jost P. (1988). The role of antidysrhythmics in cardiac arrest, Crit Care Nurse 10(4):63.

Kowey PR et al. (1988). Safety and efficacy of amiodarone: the low dose perspective, Chest 93(1):54.

Krichbaum DW. (1988). Therapy review: combination drug therapy for ventricular arrhythmias, Clin Pharmacy 7(11):808.

Levy DB. (1988). Cardiac arrest medication, part 1, Emergency 20(7):18.

Levy DB. (1988). Update on lidocaine, Emergency 20(9):15.

Martin WJ et al. (1988). Amiodarone pulmonary toxicity: recognition and pathogenesis, part 1, Chest 93(5):1067.

McCollam PL et al. (1989). Proarrhythmia: a paradoxic response to antiarrhythmic agents, Pharmacotherapy 9(3):144.

Meola DR et al. (1987). Responding quickly to tachydysrhythmias, Nursing 17(11):34.

New anti-arrhythmics, part 1, Aust Nurses J 17(3):60.

New anti-arrhythmics, part 2, Aust Nurses J 17(4):66.

Pepper GA. (1986). New antiarrhythmic agents, Nurse Pract 11(7):62.

Robinson KC et al. (1987). Amiodarone: current perspectives from Europe, Heart Lung 16(6):636.

Rubin JN et al. (1988). Premature ventricular complexes: how to avoid the risks and maximize the benefits of therapy, Consultant 28(6):35.

Sargant RK. (1987). Advances in the treatment of ventricular dysrhythmias, Emerg Care Q 3(2):18.

Scordo K. (1986). Cardiac dysrhythmias: recognizing the ones that matter, Nursinglife 4(5):33.

Senoir S et al. (1988). Flecainide acetate: critical care administration guidelines, Heart Lung 17(1):76.

Shade BR. (1987). Lessons in lidocaine, Emergency 19(10):14.

Teplitz L. (1989). Clinical close up on lidocaine, Nursing 19(9):44.

The Formulary Drug Review. (1990). A review of propafenone, Hosp Pharmacy 25(2):177.

United States Pharmacopeial Convention. (1991). Drug information for the health care professional, ed 11. Rockville, Md: The Convention.

Wehmeyer AE et al. (1986). Encainide: a new antiarrhythmic agent, Drug Intell Clin Pharm 20(1):9.

Weiner B. (1989). Second generation antidysrhythmic agents, Crit Care Nurs Clin North Am 1(2):417.

Will surgery complicate your patient's drug therapy? Emerg Med 19(18):56.

Woosley RL and Funck-Brentano C. (1988). Overview of the clinical pharmacology of antiarrhythmic drugs, Am Cardiol 61:61A.

Zorb S. (1988). Care of the cardiac patient: assessment, evaluation, and nursing implications. I. ECG interpretation, nursing diagnosis, and cardiac medications, J Intravenous Nurs 11(1):26.

*Chapter*

# 26 Antihypertensives

## CHAPTER OBJECTIVES

*After studying this chapter, you should be able to meet the following objectives and define the key terms.*

1. Describe the physiologic control of blood pressure.

2. Define hypertension based on the criteria established by the National High Blood Pressure Coordinating Committee.

3. Describe the stepped-care regimen used in drug therapy for hypertension.

4. Describe the special considerations for antihypertensive drug therapy: sexual dysfunction; concerns with the pediatric, geriatric, pregnant, and surgical client.

5. Define the five major categories of antihypertensive drugs: diuretics, adrenergic inhibitors, vasodilators, angiotensin-converting enzyme (ACE) inhibitors, and calcium antagonists.

6. Identify commonly used antihypertensive drugs as to mechanisms of action, pharmacokinetics, side effects and adverse reactions, interactions, and dosages.

7. Identify nursing measures for individual clients with antihypertensive drug regimens.

## INTRODUCTION

**Hypertension** is a circulatory disease characterized by a sustained elevation of the systemic arterial pressure. It is the most common cardiovascular community health problem, affecting approximately 30 million Americans. Untreated hypertension or subtherapeutic treatment of hypertension increases the risk of stroke, cerebral hemorrhage, congestive heart failure, coronary heart disease, and renal failure, yet hypertension is rarely listed as the cause of death. Clients with elevated blood pressure are frequently asymptomatic. Because there is a potential for a steady progression of secondary organ damage that may become fatal, untreated hypertension is known as the "silent killer."

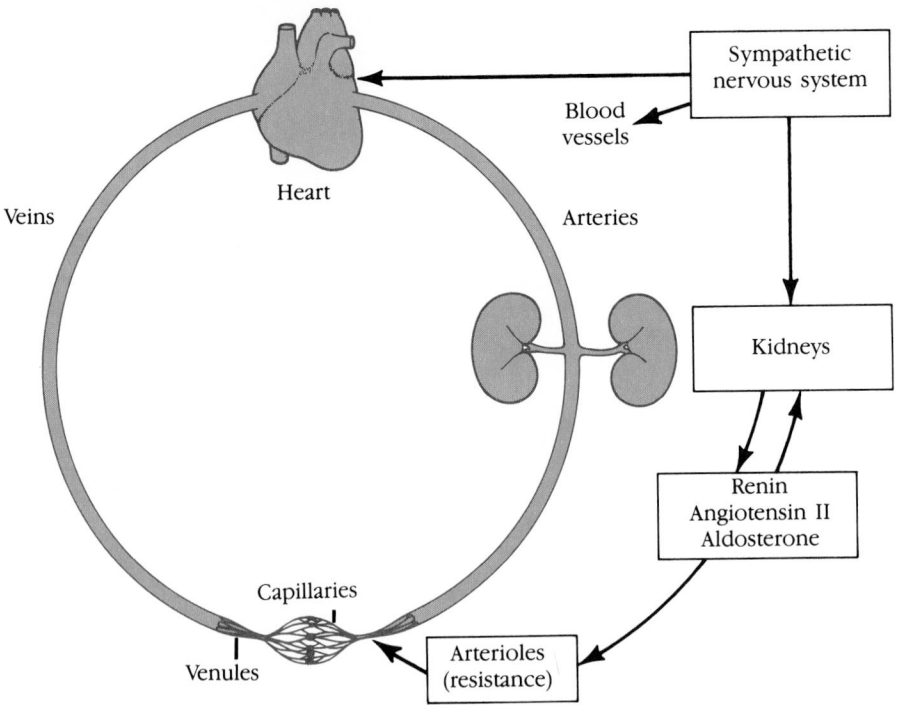

**FIGURE 26-1**  Sites of drug effects that can induce or exacerbate hypertension. Many drugs can do either. The sympathetic nervous system is affected by many drugs that can increase blood pressure by their action on the heart and blood vessels (i.e., sympathomimetics): cocaine, amphetamine, ergotamine, estrogen, MAO inhibitors, and NSAIDs. The kidneys are affected by NSAIDs, estrogens, corticosteroids, cocaine, and amphetamine. The renin–angiotensin II–aldosterone system is affected by estrogens, alcohol, and glycyrrhizic acid (licorice). Arterioles are affected by alcohol, sympathomimetics, cocaine, amphetamine, and ergotamine.

The diagnosis and treatment of hypertension have varied considerably over the years, which has resulted in a great deal of misunderstanding. The National High Blood Pressure Coordinating Committee, which is associated with the National Institutes of Health, is a leading group that reviews hypertension data and makes recommendations concerning diagnosis and treatment. **High blood pressure** is now defined as a systolic blood pressure over 140 mm Hg and/or a diastolic blood pressure greater than 90 mm Hg. An average of two or more diastolic or systolic blood pressures taken on at least two or more occasions is necessary to diagnose a patient as hypertensive. Persons with a blood pressure equivalent to or greater than 140/90 should be treated (nonpharmacologically and/or pharmacologically) to reduce the risk for premature death and disability.

Obtaining a careful and detailed drug history before diagnosis is very important, since many over-the-counter (OTC) and prescription medications may increase blood pressure or interfere with the effectiveness of the antihypertensive agent. Oral contraceptives (estrogen-containing agents), corticosteroids, nonsteroidal antiinflammatory agents, antidepressants, nasal decongestants, and appetite-suppressing agents are typical examples of interfering substances. See Figure 26-1 for sites of drug effects that can induce or exacerbate hypertension.

Controversy exists as to when the physician should start antihypertensive medications, especially in clients with a diastolic blood pressure between 90 and 94 mm Hg. In such cases, the long-term adverse effects of the medications are a particular concern. Clients at high risk for developing cardiovascular disease or who are 50 years and older with mild hypertension should receive the antihypertensive agents, since studies indicate a decrease in cardiovascular mortality and morbidity in this age group.

## CLASSIFICATION OF HYPERTENSION

In essential, **idiopathic,** or **primary hypertension** the specific cause of the hypertension is unknown. This group accounts for approximately 90% of cases. **Secondary hypertension,** affecting approximately 10% of cases, may be a symptom of pheochromocytoma, toxemia of pregnancy, or renal artery disease or may result from use of specific medications. If the cause of secondary hypertension is corrected, the blood pressure will usually return to normal.

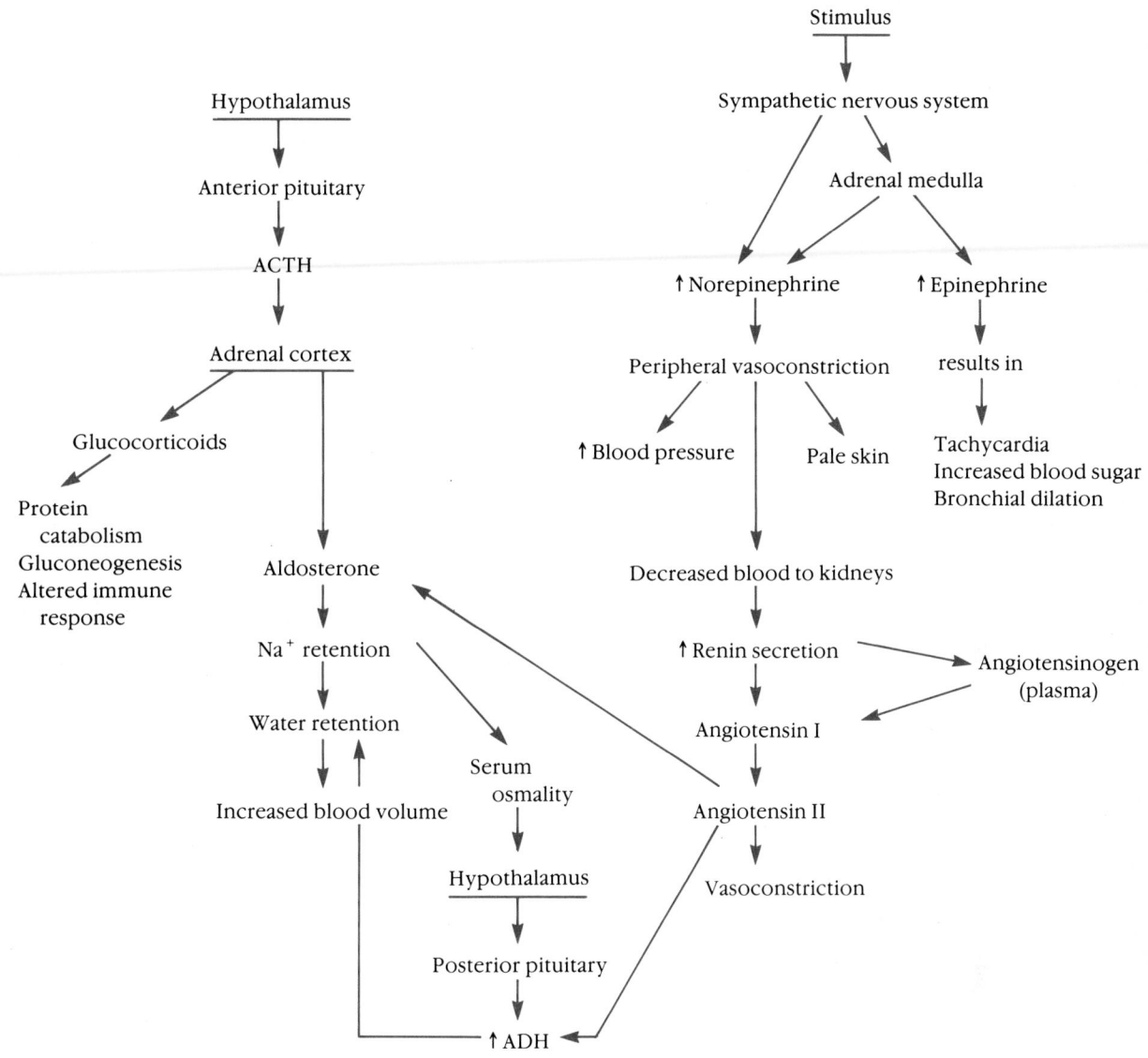

**FIGURE 26-2** Physiologic control of blood pressure. See also basic blood pressure equations (box on p. 497) for relationship to blood pressure.

## PHYSIOLOGIC CONTROL OF BLOOD PRESSURE

Control of blood pressure involves a complex interaction between the nervous, hormonal, and renal systems, since all play a part in regulating arterial blood pressure (see Figure 26-2).

The body has two primary mechanisms to control blood pressure:

1. Baroreceptor reflex—a rapid-acting system
2. Renin-angiotensin-aldosterone mechanism—a long-acting system

### Baroreceptor Reflex

The baroreceptors or pressoreceptors are spray-type nerve endings located in the walls of the internal carotid arteries and the aortic arch. Sensory receptors rapidly respond to changes in blood pressure. Any elevation in pressure stretches the receptors, which causes an impulse to be transmitted along the afferent neuron (vagus nerve) to the vasomotor center in the medulla of the brain. The vasomotor center responds to the impulse by causing (1) a decrease in heart rate and force of myocardial contraction, which lowers cardiac output, and (2) vasodilation of peripheral vessels, which decreases total peripheral resistance. The subsequent reduction in blood pressure is attributed to the reflex activity of the **baroreceptor reflex.**

This reflex functions as a rapidly acting system for short-term control of blood pressure. It has been demonstrated that over a prolonged period the rate of firing of the baroreceptors diminishes even if the blood pressure remains elevated. Therefore in hypertension it has been speculated that

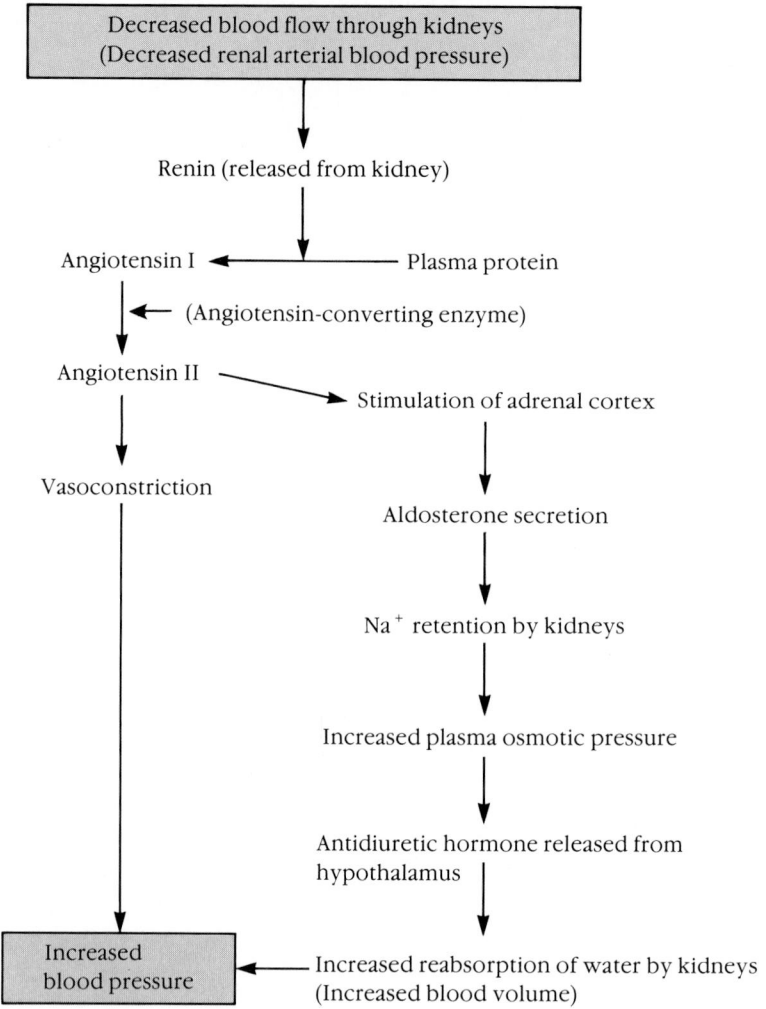

**FIGURE 26-3**   The renin-angiotensin-aldosterone system.

these receptors are "reset" to maintain a higher level of blood pressure.

***Sympathetic nervous system.*** The sympathetic nervous system is mediated by two hormones: norepinephrine and epinephrine. Stimulation of the postganglionic adrenergic nerve terminals causes the release of norepinephrine, while activation of the adrenal medulla results in secretion of mostly epinephrine and only a small amount of norepinephrine. Both of these adrenal medullary hormones influence the activity of the heart and blood vessels.

Norepinephrine acts mainly on alpha adrenergic receptors, and epinephrine acts on both alpha and beta adrenergic receptors. The alpha adrenergic receptors are located in most of the arterioles. The affinity of norepinephrine for these receptors produces vasoconstriction, with a resultant increase in blood pressure. The $beta_1$ adrenergic receptors prevalent in the heart are activated by norepinephrine. This response increases both the heart rate and the force of myocardial contraction, thereby indirectly causing an elevation in blood pressure.

On the other hand, because it produces dilation of blood vessels, epinephrine does not cause any increase in peripheral resistance. However, epinephrine does produce a considerable increase in heart rate and force of myocardial contraction, so the elevation in cardiac output indirectly raises the blood pressure. (See box for basic blood pressure equations.)

### Renin-Angiotensin-Aldosterone Mechanism

The **renin-angiotensin-aldosterone mechanism** (see Figure 26-3) regulates blood pressure by increasing or decreasing the blood volume through kidney function. The initiating factor is renin, an enzyme secreted by the juxtaglomerular cells located in the afferent arteriolar walls of the nephron. When blood flow through the kidneys is reduced, renal arterial pressure is reduced, which causes release of renin into the circulation. Here, renin catalyzes the cleavage of a plasma protein to form angiotensin I. Subsequently, in the

---

### BASIC BLOOD PRESSURE EQUATIONS

Blood pressure = Cardiac output × Peripheral resistance
Cardiac output = Stroke volume × Heart rate
Mean arterial pressure = Cardiac output × Peripheral resistance

---

### FRUITS AND VEGETABLES LOW IN SODIUM AND CALORIES AND HIGH IN POTASSIUM

| | |
|---|---|
| artichokes | oranges |
| bananas | orange juice |
| broccoli | peaches |
| brussel sprouts | potatoes |
| cantaloupe | strawberries |
| carrots | tomatoes |
| honeydew melon | |

---

### Investigational Drug Update: ANTIHYPERTENSIVES

The following drugs are currently under investigation for treatment of hypertension:
celiprolol (Selecor) and dilevalol (Unicard)—beta adrenergic blocking agents
cilazapril (Inhibrace)—ACE inhibitor
pinacidil (Pindac)—vasodilator

---

small vessels of the lung, angiotensin I is converted by angiotensin-converting enzyme (ACE) to angiotensin II.

Angiotensin II is one of the most potent vasoconstrictors known. It is particularly effective in constricting arterioles, which increases peripheral resistance and raises blood pressure. In addition, angiotensin II acts on the adrenal cortex to stimulate the secretion of aldosterone, a hormone that promotes reabsorption of sodium by the kidneys. The increased sodium elevates the osmotic pressure in the plasma, causing a release of antidiuretic hormone from the hypothalamus. Angiotensin II acts on the kidney tubules to promote reabsorption of water.

Excessive fluid retention is controlled by the negative-feedback mechanism operating within this system so that fluid balance is restored to a normal level. Thus the renin-angiotensin-aldosterone system involves slow adjustments to changes in fluid volume.

The kidneys are by far the most important organs in the body for long-term regulation of blood pressure. When the operation of the urinary system fails, increased peripheral resistance and retention of fluid volume produce a combination of hypertensive effects, which keep blood pressure constantly elevated. See the box above for antihypertensives currently under investigation.

## ANTIHYPERTENSIVE THERAPY

Client participation in antihypertensive therapy is essential for control of blood pressure. The client needs to understand that hypertension is usually asymptomatic and that therapy does not cure but only controls hypertension. Long-term therapy is necessary to prevent the morbidity and mortality secondary to hypertension. Compliance with an individualized antihypertensive regimen is associated with a good prognosis and normal life-style.

Nonpharmacologic approaches are legitimate interventions. They may be used independently in mild hypertension and always as an adjunct to drug therapy for clients with moderate to severe hypertension. Adherence by the client to a prescribed nonpharmacologic regimen may allow reduction of medication dosage and of subsequent side effects. These measures include weight control, sodium restriction (see box), elimination or limited consumption of alcohol and tobacco, reduction of dietary saturated fats, a regular exercise program, and behavior modification to promote relaxation.

Antihypertensive medications, like all medications, should be stored away from children, in a tightly closed container at room temperature (preferably between 15° and 30° C [59° and 86° F]) unless otherwise indicated by the manufacturer.

Careful use of antihypertensive drugs can effectively control the blood pressure in a majority of hypertensive individuals with less risk of serious complications and intolerable side effects. However, antihypertensive drug therapy remains empirical, since essential hypertension is a disease of unknown origin and the mechanism of action of many antihypertensive drugs also remains unknown. The ideal antihypertensive drug should maintain blood pressure within normal limits for various body positions and also maintain or improve blood flow, without compromising tissue perfusion or blood supply to the brain. It should also reduce the work load on the heart and have no undesirable side effects. Finally, the ideal antihypertensive should permit long-term administration without development of tolerance. See Table 26-1 for cardiovascular effects of existing antihypertensive agents.

***Stepped-care regimen.*** Medications used for the control of hypertension are generally prescribed on the basis of the stepped-care approach. The **stepped-care regimen** that has been suggested by the Joint National Committee on the Detection, Evaluation, and Treatment of High Blood Pressure follows a rational method of treatment. This plan is a

**TABLE 26-1**   Cardiovascular effects of antihypertensive agents

| Drug category | Cardiac output | | Total peripheral resistance | | Heart rate | | Renal blood flow |
|---|---|---|---|---|---|---|---|
| | E* | L* | E | L | E | L | |
| Diuretics | D† | N/C | N/C | D | N/C or I | N/C | D |
| Adrenergic inhibitors | | | | | | | |
| Central acting | N/C or D | | N/C or D | | D | D | N/C |
| Alpha blockers | N/C | N/C | D | D | N/C | N/C | N/C or I |
| Beta blockers (nonspecific) | D | D | I (slight) | | D | D | D |
| Beta blockers (cardioselective) | D | D | I | I | D | D | N/C |
| Vasodilators | I | I | D | D | I | I | I |
| ACE inhibitors | N/C | N/C | D | D | N/C | N/C | I |
| Calcium antagonists | N/C or D | | D | N/C or D | N/C or I | N/C or D | N/C or I |

*E, Early effect; L, late effect.
†I, Increase; D, decrease; N/C, no change.

progressive approach, which begins therapy with administration of a single drug, increases the dosage of that drug, and then, in sequential order, gradually adds more potent agents when the need for more intensive therapy is indicated (See Figure 26-4). Of importance is that the treatment be designed individually, which means that the medication is modified when necessary to achieve the maximal therapeutic response for the client. The stepped-care regimen is also applied to adolescents and children. The advantage of the stepped-care regimen is that it provides direction for treatment of clients with mild to severe hypertension. Nonpharmacologic approaches are beneficial for all clients with hypertension and should be included in the client's teaching plan.

Step 1 therapy, depending on the client and the medical history, permits the selection of a thiazide diuretic, beta blocking agent, calcium antagonist, or an ACE inhibitor. Usually a thiazide diuretic is preferred in elderly and black clients and in clients with asthma, peripheral vascular disease, or other chronic pulmonary disease states. Beta adrenergic blocking agents may provide initial therapy for the younger person with tachycardia and marked lability of blood pressure. Some elderly and black clients respond better to calcium antagonists or ACE inhibitors alone. The initial dosage is usually less than a full therapeutic dose, increasing to a full dose if necessary.

If control of blood pressure is not achieved, step 2 can be implemented. A drug from a different classification may be substituted or added to the drug regimen. If blood pressure control is not obtained, then step 3 and, if necessary, step 4 may be implemented.

---

## REBOUND HYPERTENSION

**Rebound hypertension,** discontinuation syndrome, or the withdrawal syndrome all refer to the problems associated with abrupt withdrawal or discontinuation of antihypertensive medications. The blood pressure usually returns to at least the pretreatment level or above, along with symptoms of sympathetic system hyperactivity (sweating, anxiety, tachycardia, insomnia, muscle pain).

---

*Pregnancy.* Hypertension during pregnancy is a serious condition that requires early detection and treatment. It has been estimated that annually 20% of maternal deaths and approximately 25,000 stillborn/neonatal deaths are caused by hypertension during pregnancy (Chobanian, 1982).

Hypertension during pregnancy may result from preeclampsia (a hypertension induced by pregnancy) or essential hypertension. Preeclampsia is usually treated empirically or with antihypertension therapy to reduce the possibility of eclampsia, a true hypertensive emergency characterized by convulsions and coma.

Although antihypertensive therapy has resulted in an increase in fetal survival, the therapies of choice are debatable and depend mainly on the prescribing physician. The 1988 Joint Committee on Hypertension recommended methyldopa and the beta adrenergic blocking agents during pregnancy but advised against using the angiotensin-converting enzyme (ACE) inhibitors because of an increase in fetal

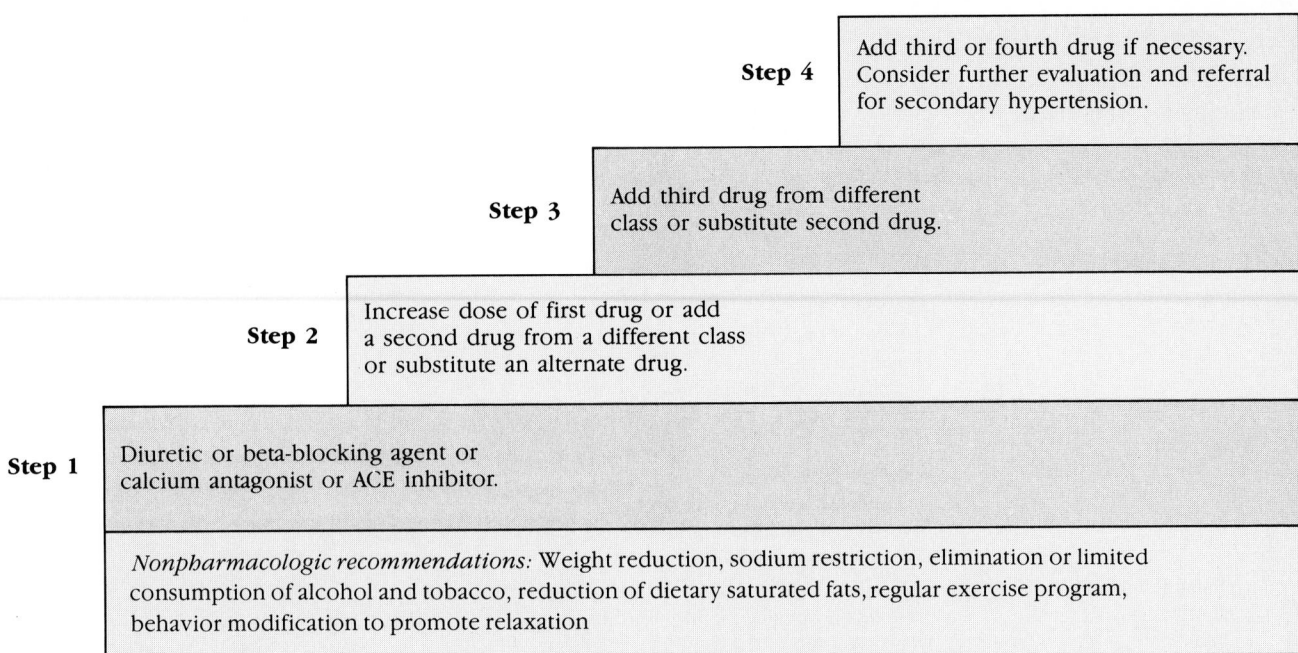

**FIGURE 26-4** Stepped-care regimen for hypertension.

mortality reported in pregnant animals. Chobanian (1982) suggests magnesium sulfate and hydralazine or diazoxide or methyldopa plus hydralazine for pregnancy-induced hypertension. Nitroprusside should be avoided since it may affect fetal thyroid function. Mothers receiving continuous antihypertensive therapy should be advised not to breast feed, since most of the agents are transferred to breast milk.

***Sexual dysfunction.*** Sexual dysfunction is a common complication of hypertensive medications and may be manifested in males as decreased libido, impotence, impaired or retrograde ejaculation, and gynecomastia and in females as decreased libido, decreased vaginal lubrication, and inability to achieve orgasm. Such symptoms may lead to the client's poor compliance with the drug regimen. The nature of the disorder and a knowledge of the effects associated with different antihypertensive agents (see Table 26-2) will assist in determining the cause of the symptoms. Frequently, a dosage reduction or the substitution of another drug will alleviate the problem.

***Surgical clients.*** Clients scheduled for elective surgery should receive their antihypertensive medications up to the time of surgery and as soon afterward as possible. Parenteral diuretics, adrenergic inhibitors, and vasodilators plus sublingual nifedipine or transdermal clonidine are available for clients unable to take oral medications. Such preparations should be used to prevent rebound hypertension, especially if the client was taking an adrenergic inhibitor before sugery.

The client's electrolyte status should be carefully checked before surgery. If hypokalemia is detected, it should be corrected before the scheduled operation. The anesthesiologist should always be completely informed about the client's medication regimen; this is vital information that may alter the medications or the monitoring methods used.

***Children.*** The goal of therapy for hypertensive children and adolescents is to reduce the blood pressure without adverse effects that limit compliance or interfere with normal growth and development. The type of intervention will be determined by the causative factors, the presence of complications, and the degree of hypertension. Nonpharmacologic measures (weight control, reduction of dietary sodium, exercise, avoidance of smoking and alcohol, and reduction of saturated fat) are strongly recommended. If children do not respond to nonpharmacologic measures or if their blood pressures place them at risk for organ damage, then pharmacologic therapy should be considered.

Pharmacologic interventions for children also follow the stepped approach, which includes diuretics, adrenergic inhibiting agents, and vasodilators. Continued assessment of the child and family is necessary to ensure satisfactory blood pressure control and compliance with the therapeutic program, whether pharmacologic or nonpharmacologic.

***Elderly clients.*** A significant proportion of those over 65 years of age have elevated systolic or diastolic blood pressure or both, which increases their risk of cardiovascular

**TABLE 26-2** Side effects/adverse reactions of antihypertensive agents

| Category/drugs | Side effects | Adverse reactions |
|---|---|---|
| **ADRENERGIC INHIBITORS** | | |
| Central acting clonidine, methyldopa, guanabenz | More frequent: methyldopa—drowsiness, dry mouth (clonidine, methyldopa), headaches; clonidine—constipation and increased weakness<br>Less frequent: clonidine, methyldopa—postural hypotension; all three drugs—impotency or decreased sexual drive; clonidine—insomnia, increased nervousness, eye irritation, anorexia, nausea and vomiting, dizziness | More frequent: methyldopa—edema of feet and legs; clonidine—pruritus<br>Less frequent: methyldopa—insomnia, depression, increased anxiety, vivid nightmares; clonidine—depression, edema of feet or lower legs |
| guanfacine | More frequent: constipation, dry mouth, sedation, lightheadedness.<br>Less frequent: headache, nausea, vomiting, insomnia, impotency, dry and/or itching eyes, increased weakness. | Less frequent: depression, constipation<br>Overdosage: respiratory difficulties, syncope, bradycardia, severe tiredness. |
| Peripheral acting guanethidine, guanadrel | More frequent: orthostatic hypotension, weakness, impaired ejaculation; guanethidine—diarrhea, bradycardia, stuffy nose<br>Less common: increased urination at night, muscle pain or tremors, dry mouth, headaches; guanethidine—alopecia, blurred vision, ptosis of eyelids, nausea, vomiting, rash | More frequent: edema<br>Less frequent: chest pain (angina), shortness of breath |
| *Rauwolfia* alkaloid reserpine | More frequent: nausea, vomiting, anorexia, diarrhea, dizziness, dry mouth, stuffy nose<br>Less common: fluid retention, especially of lower extremities; sexual dysfunctions: impotence | More frequent: lightheadedness<br>Less frequent: abdominal cramps, black stools or hematemesis (peptic ulcer reactivation); chest pain, bradycardia; headaches; bronchospasms (shortness of breath); weakness, drowsiness, lack of ability to concentrate, increased nervousness; nightmares, mental depression that may persist for months after drug is discontinued and has been reportedly severe enough to lead to suicide |
| Alpha blockers prazosin, terazosin | More frequent: terazosin—headaches, increased weakness<br>Less frequent: both drugs—nausea, vomiting, stuffy nose; terazosin—altered vision, joint and back pain | More frequent: terazosin—lightheadedness<br>Less frequent: orthostatic hypotension, chest pain (angina) edema of lower extremities, irregular heartbeat, syncope, shortness of breath |
| Beta blockers—see Chapter 21 | | |
| **VASODILATORS** | | |
| Arteriolar dilators diazoxide, hydralazine, minoxidil | More frequent: hydralazine—diarrhea, nausea, vomiting, tachycardia, anorexia, headache; minoxidil—excessive hair growth<br>Less frequent: diazoxide—anorexia, constipation, nausea and vomiting, abdominal cramps, changes in taste perception; hydralazine—dizziness, facial flushing, stuffy nose, constipation, eye irritation or watering; minoxidil—headaches | More frequent: diazoxide—edema; tachycardia, red flushing of skin (minoxidil)<br>Less frequent: hydralazine—angina, neuritis, skin blisters, sore throat, joint pain, fever (SLE-type syndrome), weakness, numbness of hands or feet, swelling of lymph nodes, edema; minoxidil—angina, pericarditis; diazoxide—tachycardia |

**TABLE 26-2**  Side effects/adverse reactions of antihypertensive agents—cont'd

| Category/drugs | Side effects | Adverse reactions |
| --- | --- | --- |
| Arteriolar and venous dilator<br>nitroprusside | | Excessive blood pressure—dizziness, excessive sweating, headaches, increased anxiety, abdominal cramps, tachycardia, twitching of muscles<br>Thiocyanate overdose: visual disturbances, dizziness, headache, unconsciousness, nausea, vomiting, tinnitus, respiratory difficulties, ataxia, delirium<br>Cyanide overdose: coma, absence of reflexes, severe hypotension, pink color, dilated pupils, shallow breathing |
| **ACE INHIBITORS**<br>captopril, enalapril, lisinopril | More frequent: dry cough<br>Less frequent: diarrhea, headache, loss of taste (which usually returns in several months, even if therapy continues), weakness, nausea | Less frequent: dizziness, hypotension, skin rash, increased temperature, joint aches |
| **CALCIUM-CHANNEL BLOCKERS**—see Chapter 27 | | |
| **GANGLIONIC BLOCKER**<br>trimethaphan | Dose-related effects: dry mouth, impotency, pruritus, postural hypotension, increased heart rate, anorexia, nausea, vomiting, constipation, dilated pupils, urinary retention | Overdosage: severe hypotension, respiratory arrest |

morbidity and mortality. Nonpharmacologic means of blood pressure reduction (weight reduction if necessary and dietary sodium restriction) are indicated.

Antihypertensive drugs should be started with smaller than usual doses, increased with smaller dosages, and scheduled at less frequent intervals with the elderly, since they are more sensitive to volume depletion and sympathetic inhibition than younger clients. They commonly have impaired cardiovascular reflexes, which make them more susceptible to hypotension.

In clients with isolated systolic hypertension who are treated with antihypertensive drugs, the systolic pressure should be cautiously decreased to 140 to 160 mm Hg. Only if this level is tolerated without side effects should consideration be given to further lowering the value.

The elderly client's response to both nonpharmacologic and pharmacologic therapies should be monitored closely.

***Clients with chronic illnesses.*** Careful selection and close monitoring of antihypertensive agents are necessary when used by clients with chronic illnesses, such as bronchial asthma, chronic obstructive pulmonary disease (COPD), diabetes mellitus, and hyperlipidemia. The beta adrenergic blocking agents can cause bronchospasms and therefore should be avoided in clients with a history of bronchial asthma or chronic obstructive pulmonary disease. The beta blocking agents may also reduce the client's control of diabetes mellitus by interfering with the individual's normal response to hypoglycemia. This may lead to prolonged hypoglycemia and severe hypertension. Although the beta blockers are not contraindicated for use in diabetic clients, individuals receiving such drugs should be educated about this potential problem and taught alternate methods for self-monitoring.

Several antihypertensive agents, such as the thiazide and loop diuretics and beta blockers, may increase serum lipid levels in some clients. Beta blockers with an intrinsic sympathomimetic effect or labetalol does not appear to have this effect on lipids. The ACE inhibitors and calcium antagonists also have no reported adverse effect on serum lipid levels. Therefore it is apparent that careful selection and monitoring of antihypertensive agents are necessary, especially in clients with coexisting chronic illnesses.

• • •

The antihypertensive drugs currently used to reduce blood pressure are classified into five major categories: diuretics,

Selected nursing diagnoses related to antihypertensive therapy

| Nursing diagnosis | Outcome criteria | Nursing interventions |
| --- | --- | --- |
| Knowledge deficit related to newly prescribed or altered antihypertensive drug therapy | Client will describe hypertension; how drug therapy relates to condition; how and when to take medications; common drug interactions; particularly with OTC drugs; safety precautions; common side effects and which are reportable; storage requirements of drugs; and will monitor effectiveness of drug therapy with sequential blood pressure readings. | Assess learning needs and learning readiness<br>Plan with client and family for achievement of realistic goals<br>Provide information to meet outcome criteria |
| Noncompliance with medication regimen | Client will self-administer medications safely and accurately. | Check refill frequency to determine compliance.<br>Explore with client reasons for noncompliance and take appropriate teaching/counseling interventions.<br>Provide needed drug information concerning rationales for specific client's hypertensive status.<br>Emphasize that drug therapy does not cure but controls hypertension and possible need for lifelong therapy.<br>Discuss possibility of rebound hypertension with noncompliance. |
| Sexual dysfunction related to antihypertensive drug therapy | Client will describe nature of dysfunction, consult with prescriber for dosage reduction or drug substitution, and resume sexual activity. | Assess for causative factors.<br>Encourage client to share concerns.<br>Provide health teaching and referral when needed.<br>Encourage return to sexual activity. |

adrenergic inhibitors, vasodilators, angiotensin converting enzyme (ACE) inhibitors, and calcium antagonists.

## DIURETIC DRUGS

Diuretic drugs play a vital role in lowering blood pressure. They are currently used as an initial drug in managing mild hypertension, or they may be administered in combination with other antihypertensive agents.

The use of **diuretics** results in a loss of excess salt and water from the body by renal excretion. The decrease in plasma and extracellular fluid volume subsequently depresses vascular reactivity to sympathetic stimulation. Thus volume depletion, plus a direct effect on the arterioles that produces vasodilation, results in lowering of the blood pressure. This response then causes an initial decline of cardiac output followed by a decrease in peripheral resistance and a lowering of blood pressure (See Figure 26-5).

The **thiazides** and related sulfonamide diuretics, such as chlorthalidone and metolazone, when used in maximum therapeutic doses, are moderately effective in decreasing blood pressure. Therefore they can be used alone for individuals with mild hypertension. By contrast, many of the other types of antihypertensive agents, when used alone, produce a gradual retention of sodium and water with resultant expansion of plasma fluid volume. This process then tends to diminish the effectiveness of the antihypertensive agent. For this reason thiazides are given concomitantly to prevent fluid retention.

**Loop diuretics,** such as furosemide and ethacrynic acid, are powerful drugs that cause excessive loss of potassium and water. Since these drugs produce fewer antihypertensive effects, they should be given to clients with complicated renal insufficiency or to individuals who cannot take other diuretics.

The **potassium-sparing agents,** such as spironolactone and triamterene, are useful in counteracting potassium loss induced by other diuretics. They promote sodium and water loss without accompanying loss of potassium. These drugs are indicated for management of hyperaldosteronism and renal vascular hypertension when the client's condition is resistant to other diuretics. See Chapter 33 for drug monographs of diuretic drugs. See box on p. 502 for examples of selected diuretic drugs for use with clients with hypertension.

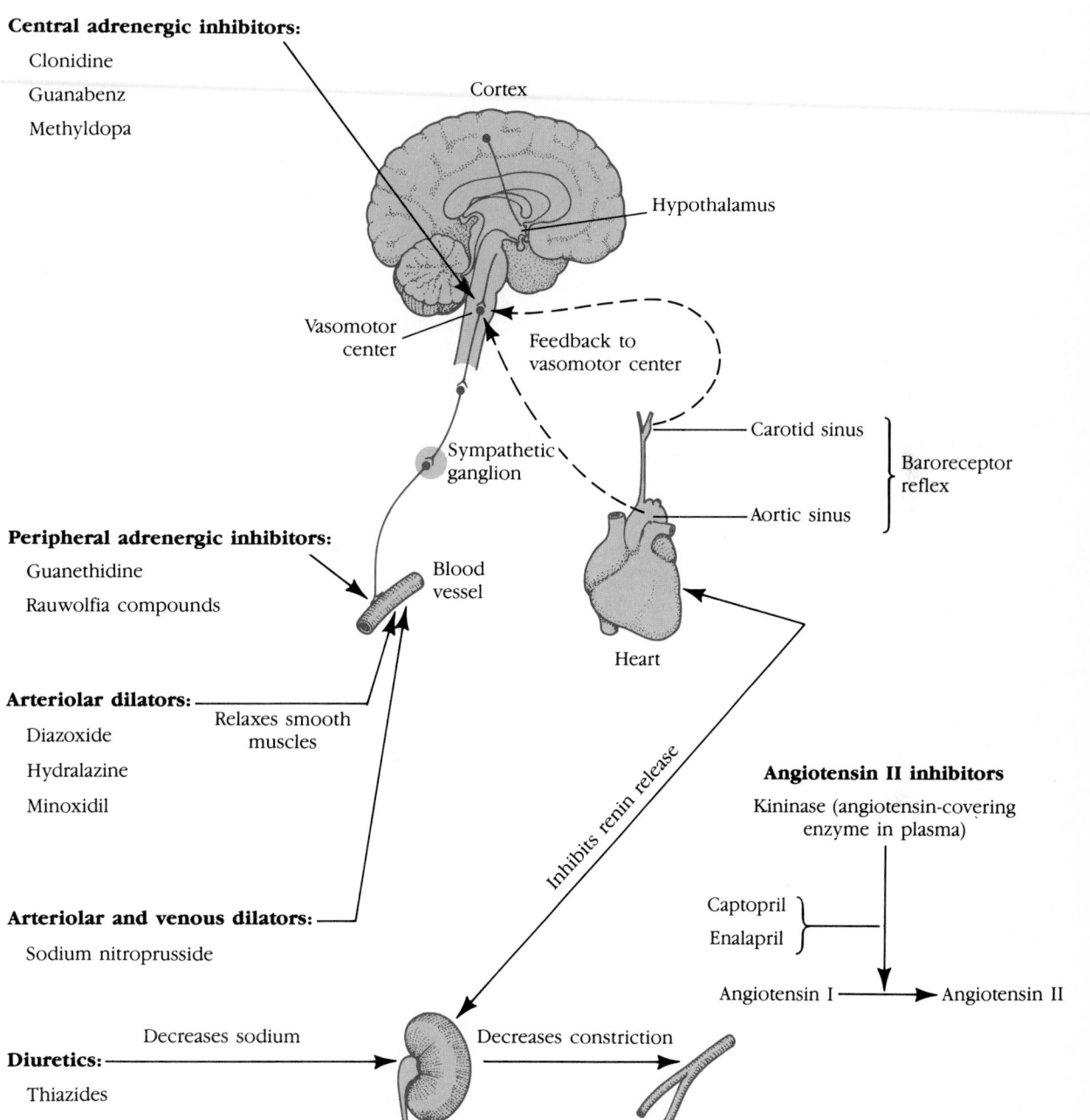

**Central adrenergic inhibitors:**

Clonidine

Guanabenz

Methyldopa

Cortex

Hypothalamus

Vasomotor center

Feedback to vasomotor center

Carotid sinus

Aortic sinus

Baroreceptor reflex

Sympathetic ganglion

**Peripheral adrenergic inhibitors:**

Guanethidine

Rauwolfia compounds

Blood vessel

Heart

**Arteriolar dilators:**

Diazoxide

Hydralazine

Minoxidil

Relaxes smooth muscles

Inhibits renin release

**Angiotensin II inhibitors**

Kininase (angiotensin-covering enzyme in plasma)

Captopril

Enalapril

**Arteriolar and venous dilators:**

Sodium nitroprusside

Angiotensin I ⟶ Angiotensin II

Decreases sodium

**Diuretics:**

Thiazides

Decreases constriction

**FIGURE 26-5**  Site and method of action of various antihypertensive drugs based on reported clinical and experimental evidence.

## SELECTED DIURETIC DRUGS FOR HYPERTENSION

| Generic Name | Trade Name |
|---|---|
| *Single agents* | |
| chlorothiazide | Diuril |
| hydrochlorothiazide | HydroDiuril |
| | Esidrex |
| chlorthalidone | Hygroton |
| | Apo-Clorthalidone ♣ |
| metolazone | Zaroxolyn |
| triamterene | Dyrenium |
| spironolactone | Aldactone |
| | Novospiroton ♣ |
| furosemide | Lasix |
| | Furoside ♣ |
| ethacrynic acid | Edecrin |
| *Hydrochlorothiazide (HCT) combination agents* | |
| HCT, 25 mg, plus spironolac-tone, 25 mg | Aldactazide |
| HCT, 25 mg, plus triamterene, 50 mg | Dyazide |
| HCT, 25 or 37.5 mg, plus triamterene, 50 or 75 mg | Maxzide |

## ADDITIONAL USES OF CLONIDINE

*Clonidine* has several additional uses that are not currently approved in the United States. It is being used as a prophylactic treatment of migraines, to treat dysmenorrhea, and to treat Tourette's syndrome and also to treat flushing that occurs during menopause. Another interesting use is during opiate and nicotine withdrawal. Clonidine reportedly reduces the symptoms of withdrawal during the detoxification process.

## ADRENERGIC INHIBITING (SYMPATHOLYTIC) AGENTS

**Adrenergic inhibitors,** the most effective antihypertensive drugs, modify the function of the sympathetic nervous system.

The heart, blood vessels, and kidneys influence arterial pressure through various reflex mechanisms. Sympathetic stimulation increases heart rate and force of myocardial contraction, constricts arterioles (resistance vessels) and venules (capacitance vessels), and releases renin from the kidney. These agents generally are effective in reducing blood pressure and preventing serious cardiovascular complications. The sites at which these drugs modify sympathetic nervous system activity vary widely and usually involve complex mechanisms.

Many of these drugs are believed to have multiple sites of action or have unknown mechanisms of action. For clarification, the drugs are characterized by their primary proposed site of action.

## Centrally Acting Adrenergic Inhibitors

The centrally acting agents clonidine, methyldopa, and guanabenz are effective step 2 antihypertensives, especially when combined with a diuretic. When given as a single agent, clonidine and methyldopa (guanabenz to a lesser extent) usually produce sodium and water retention. If they are combined with a diuretic, their antihypertensive effect is enhanced.

### clonidine hydrochloride (Catapres, Catapres-TTS)

Clonidine reduces systolic and diastolic blood pressure by suppressing sympathetic outflow from the brain. Stimulation of the alpha$_2$ receptors in the central nervous system (especially the medulla oblongata) decreases sympathetic outflow of norepinephrine from the brain to the heart, kidneys, and peripheral vascular system. This lowers blood pressure primarily by decreasing cardiac output rather than peripheral vascular resistance. The depressed cardiac output is the result of a reduction in both heart rate and stroke volume. Consequently, this action can cause bradycardia.

The decreased sympathetic outflow to the kidneys reduces renal vascular resistance and thus preserves renal blood flow. Hence, renin activity is suppressed. The decreased cardiac output, however, produces sodium retention and edema does occur. This, unfortunately, can reduce the antihypertensive effect of clonidine, and therefore a diuretic is needed to correct the extracellular fluid volume retention. See the box above for additional uses.

Clonidine oral has an onset of action within ½ to 1 hour and a peak effect in 2 to 4 hours, and its duration of effect is up to 8 hours. Serum half-life is between 12 and 16 hrs, whereas in clients with renal impairment, the half-life may be up to 41 hrs. It is metabolized in the liver and primarily excreted by the kidneys. Clonidine transdermal is best absorbed from the chest and upper arm. Onset of action and time to peak effect are 2 to 3 days, while duration of action is approximately a week if in continuous contact with body (about 8 hours if removed from the body). Metabolism and excretion are the same as for oral clonidine.

Side effects/adverse reactions are included in Table 26-2.

*Significant drug interactions.* The following interactions may occur when clonidine is given with the drugs listed below:

| Drug | Possible Effect and Management |
|------|-------------------------------|
| Beta adrenergic blocking agents | Concurrent administration with clonidine may lead to loss of blood pressure control. Additive bradycardia effects may also occur. Monitor closely. If the physician wants to discontinue both drugs in a client, the beta blocking agent should be stopped first. Discontinuing clonidine first may increase the risk of inducing a withdrawal hypertensive crisis. |
| Tricyclic antidepressants | The antihypertensive effectiveness of clonidine may be reduced. This usually occurs in the first or second week of therapy. Monitor closely since dosage adjustments and/or alternate hypotensive agents may need to be considered as alternative options by the physician. |

***Dosage and administration.*** Adult dose is 100 μg (0.1 mg) twice daily initially; increase every 2 to 4 days by 100 to 200 μg (0.1 or 0.2 mg) as necessary to control blood pressure. For maintenance, dose is 100 or 200 μg (0.1 or 0.2 mg) two to three times daily.

For a nonemergency, severe hypertensive episode, a loading dose method may be ordered. Initial dose is 200 μg (0.2 mg) orally followed by 100 μg (0.1 mg) hourly until the diastolic pressure is under control or a maximum of 800 μg (0.8 mg) has been given. Then a maintenance dosage schedule is begun. Dosage for children has not been established.

*Catapres-TTS.* (a clonidine transdermal therapeutic system). Clonidine is available in various strengths (0.1, 0.2, or 0.3 mg) programmed to deliver the specified strength daily for 1 week. The system is composed of four layers of film that contain a drug reservoir of clonidine, a membrane that controls the rate of drug delivery, an adhesive layer that also contains clonidine to initially saturate the skin site, and a top backing or cover layer. The system was formulated for the drug to flow from a higher concentration to the lower concentration in the body, which is limited by the rate-controlling membrane layer. It takes approximately 2 to 3 days to reach a therapeutic clonidine serum level on initial application, whereas replacing the system weekly at a new body site will maintain the therapeutic serum level.

▷ **Nursing Management: Clonidine Therapy**

***Assessment.*** Use with caution in clients with coronary insufficiency, recent myocardial infarction, cerebrovascular disease, chronic renal failure, Raynaud's disease, or history of mental depression. Elderly clients, too, are more sensitive to clonidine's hypotensive effects and are at risk of injury related to orthostatic hypotension. Dosage adjustments may be necessitated by age-related renal function impairment.

If the transdermal dosage form of clonidine is to be applied, the client's skin should be assessed for any irritation or abrasion so that they be avoided as absorption may be increased if the drug is applied to these areas. On the other hand, areas of skin involvement with disorders such as systemic lupus erythematosus or scleroderma might decrease drug absorption if the drug were applied to them, so avoid these areas.

***Intervention.*** Closely monitor blood pressure and pulse during initiation of therapy and continue to observe these parameters until dosage is properly titrated. Blood pressure should decrease within 30 to 60 minutes after administration and may persist for 8 hours.

Weigh client daily for 3 to 4 days after initiation of therapy, since fluid volume excess may occur because of sodium retention and edema. If fluid retention does not disappear, it may be necessary to add a diuretic to the regimen.

When applying clonidine using the transdermal system, select a hairless intact area of the patient's upper arm or torso. Do not trim the patch as it will alter the dosage. Reapply once every 7 days on a different skin site. If the system loosens, cover it with an adhesive overlay from the drug package to ensure good adhesion. It should remain in place while bathing or showering. Replace the patch if it falls off or becomes very loose. Discard used patches by folding in half with adhesive sides together.

Reduce dosages gradually over 2 to 4 days or preferably longer (1- to 2-week period) to prevent rebound hypertension.

With noncompliant clients, consultation with the prescribing physician may result in a change from oral to the transdermal therapeutic system or another antihypertensive drug because of the risk of rebound hypertension. When a client is being switched from an oral dosage form of clonidine to the transdermal form, the oral dose needs to be reduced over 2 to 3 days to avoid a withdrawal response because the transdermal dosage form's onset will take 2 to 3 days.

***Education.*** Emphasize the importance of periodic follow-up visits so that the clonidine level and blood pressure are closely monitored. Be explicit in instructions concerning the serious consequences of rebound hypertension caused by missing a dose or abrupt cessation of the drug. Clients with serious side effects should immediately report the problem to the physician so that the dosage may be adjusted or the drug may be withdrawn gradually over a period of 2 to 4 days. Abrupt withdrawal, including omission of sequential doses, can result in hypertensive crisis within 8 to 24 hours. The symptoms of hypertensive crisis are anxiety, sweating, tachycardia, insomnia, salivation, muscle pain, and stomach pain.

Instruct client to keep an adequate supply of the drug at all times, particularly during travel.

Instruct client to take last dose before bedtime to ensure continuous blood pressure control during the night and reduce daytime drowsiness, which occurs in about 33% of clients using oral dosage forms. Instruct client to make position changes slowly even though clonidine does not usually cause postural hypotension. Client should move slowly from recumbent to upright position and dangle feet from edge of bed to prevent dizziness and fainting. The client needs to be cautioned to avoid alcohol ingestion, prolonged standing and exercising, and exercising during hot weather because the potential for orthostatic hypotension is greatly increased. Altered comfort related to dry mouth may occur in 40% of the clients using oral dosage forms. Encourage the client to use sugarless candy or gum or ice to obtain relief. A saliva substitute such as Orex or Oralube may be used. If dry mouth persists longer than 2 weeks, the physician or dentist needs to be consulted because of the increased risk of caries and oral candidiasis.

Altered bowel function occurs as constipation in about 10% of the clients. Instruction should be provided to the client concerning adequate fluid and fiber intake, regular exercise, and establishing a regular bowel pattern to prevent or minimize constipation.

Advise client on long-term therapy to have a periodic eye examination (every 6 to 12 months) to avoid possible retinal degeneration. This has occurred in rats to which clonidine has been administered. Instruct client to carry medical identification card or Medic Alert. Warn client not to take OTC medication without consulting the physician. Caution client about the increased sedative effects of alcohol, barbiturates, and other CNS depressants during clonidine therapy particularly if the individual is operating a car or machinery.

*Evaluation.* Observe client for drug tolerance. Physician may increase dosage or add a diuretic to obtain the required antihypertensive response.

Blood pressure control may be impaired when taken concurrently with tricyclic antidepressants and beta adrenergic blocking agents. If taken concurrently, beta blockers should be discontinued before clonidine to decrease the risk of hypertensive crisis caused by clonidine withdrawal.

Closely monitor client with a history of mental depression because the drug may intensify this condition. Altered self-concept related to impotence may also occur.

## methyldopa (Aldomet)
## methyldopate injection (Parenteral Aldomet)

Although the exact hypotensive mechanism is unknown, the current theory is that methyldopa is converted to alpha methylnorepinephrine in centrally located adrenergic neurons. Alpha methylnorepinephrine lowers arterial blood pressure by stimulating the central alpha adrenergic inhibiting receptors. The result is a reduction in norepinephrine (sympathetic) outflow to the heart, kidneys, and peripheral vasculature. A reduction in total peripheral resistance and plasma renin levels may also contribute to the hypotensive effect.

Methyldopate hydrochloride is hydrolyzed to methyldopa in the body, which then must undergo the previous theoretical process to produce the hypotensive effect. The antihypertensive effect produced by the parenteral dosage form begins in approximately 4 to 6 hours, so it should not be used as the primary single agent in a hypertensive emergency. Faster acting agents such as nitroprusside or diazoxide are parenteral antihypertensive agents indicated for an emergency situation.

Methyldopa (Aldomet) is available orally and as methyldopate, parenterally. Time to peak effect is 4 to 6 hours after a single dose or in 48 to 72 hours with multiple dosing. Duration of action is 12 to 24 hrs (after oral single dose), 1 to 2 days (after multiple oral doses), or 10 to 16 hrs after IV. Serum half-life is from 1.7 (normal alpha) to 3.6 hours (anuric alpha). Methyldopa is metabolized centrally to alpha methylnorepinephrine, while methyldopate is converted to methyldopa. Excretion is primarily by the kidneys.

*Significant drug interactions.* The following interactions may occur when methyldopa is given with the drugs listed below:

| Drug | Possible Effect and Management |
|---|---|
| monoamine oxidase (MAO) inhibitors | Hyperexcitability, hallucinations, headache, and hypertension reported with this combination. If alternate therapies are unacceptable and this combination is prescribed, monitor very closely. |
| sympathomimetics (cocaine, norephinephrine, phenylephrine, and others) | A decrease in methyldopa's antihypertensive effect is reported. If necessary to use sympathomimetics, the physician should prescribe very small doses of the sympathomimetic agent. Monitor closely. |

*Dosage and administration.* Adult dose is 250 mg orally initially two to three times daily for 2 days. Dosage increases should be instituted after 2 days of therapy, according to the individual client's response. For maintenance, give 500 to 2000 mg/day, divided into two to four individual dosages. Maximum daily dosage is 3 g/day. In treating children, initially give orally 10 mg/kg body weight or 300 mg/m$^2$ of body surface in two to four divided doses. May be increased at 2-day intervals according to client's response, up to 65 mg/kg or 3 g/day, whichever is less.

In the administration of parenteral methyldopa, adult dose by intravenous infusion is 250 to 500 mg in dextrose 5% injection (100 ml) over a 30- to 60-minute period, every 6 hours as needed. Maximum dose is 1 g every 6 to 12 hours. Children's intravenous infusion dose is 5 to 10 mg/kg body weight in dextrose 5% injection over a 30- to 60-minute period every 6 hours, as needed, up to 65 mg/kg or 3 g/day, whichever is less.

## ▷ Nursing Management: Methyldopa Therapy

In addition to the nursing management previously indicated for oral clonidine, observe the following.

*Assessment.* Do not use in clients with active hepatic disease or hypersensitivity to methyldopa. Use with caution in clients with a history of mental depression or hemolytic anemia, pheochromocytoma, previous liver disease, or in those suffering from severe renal impairment. Risks and benefits must be considered in childbearing and lactating women.

*Intervention.* Take blood pressure and pulse as prescribed during initiation of therapy and continue until drug dosage is properly titrated. Take blood pressure at regular intervals with client in lying, sitting, and standing positions. Dosage increases should be initiated with the evening dose to minimize the effects of sedation. Monitor for fluid volume excess by measuring intake and output and weighing the client daily. Report fluid retention to the physician. Intramuscular or subcutaneous administration is not recommended because of unreliable absorption. When changing a client from intravenous to oral form once the blood pressure has stabilized, the same dosage is used. Administer intravenous infusion slowly over 30 to 60 minutes.

*Education.* Emphasize to the client the importance of keeping clinical laboratory visits for blood cell counts and hepatic function studies. Methyldopa hepatotoxicity (reversible) may occasionally develop 2 to 4 weeks after initiation of therapy. The flulike symptoms are chills, fever, headache, anorexia, fatigue, arthralgia, enlarged liver, and pruritus. If the liver function tests are positive, therapy will be discontinued. Instruct the client for the same precautions as for oral clonidine.

*Evaluation.* Observe client for drug tolerance, which may occur during the second or third month of therapy. Observe client for drug-induced depression and report symptom to physician. Observe client for side effects, especially unexplained fever, and immediately report any to the physician. If unexplained fever or rash occurs, obtain liver function studies (e.g., SGOT, bilirubin) especially during the first 2 or 3 months of therapy. If present, discontinue drug permanently to avoid drug-induced hepatitis. Hemolytic anemia may occur in 4% of clients with possible fatal complications. Before drug therapy, physician will prescribe a complete blood count and direct Coombs' test. These tests should be done periodically during treatment. Positive Coombs' test may or may not indicate hemolytic anemia. With prolonged use of methyldopa, 10% to 20% of patients develop a positive direct Coombs' test; this is not a contraindication to further use of the drug. With a positive Coombs' test with resultant hemolytic anemia, physician should discontinue therapy. If a blood transfusion is needed, both direct and indirect Coombs' test should be performed. Positive tests may interfere with the cross matching of blood. If reversible leukopenia occurs, drug therapy should be discontinued.

The refill frequency may be checked to determine the client's noncompliance to the antihypertensive regimen.

As with clonidine the client is at risk for altered bowel function, altered comfort, altered self-concept related to impotence and depression, and the potential for injury related to methyldopa's cardiovascular and CNS effects.

## guanabenz acetate (Wytensin)

The mechanism of action of guanabenz acetate is the same as clonidine; however, with guanabenz there is no fluid retention. In clinical trials of 6 to 30 months, hypertensive clients whose blood pressure was controlled with guanabenz actually lost 1 to 4 pounds. The mechanism of this weight loss is not known. In addition, plasma renin activity may be unchanged or decreased during long-term therapy. Cardiac output remains unchanged. The antihypertensive effect occurs without major changes in peripheral resistance. Nevertheless, peripheral resistance does eventually decrease with continued therapy. There is no evidence that tolerance develops to the hypotensive effect of this drug.

For side effects/adverse reactions, see Table 26-2. Guanabenz, when given concurrently with a beta adrenergic blocking agent or other hypotensive agents, may result in additive hypotensive effects. Monitor closely because dosage adjustments may be necessary. When discontinuing both drugs in a client, i.e., a beta blocking drug and guanabenz, taper the beta blocker first to prevent a withdrawal hypertensive reaction.

Guanabenz has onset of action within 1 hour (for single dose), peak effect within 2 to 4 hours, and duration of action is 12 hours. Serum half-life is 6 hours. It is metabolized in the liver and excretion is via the kidneys and feces. Initial dose for adults is 4 mg orally twice daily, increased if necessary every 1 to 2 weeks by increments of 4 to 8 mg/day, up to a maximum of 32 mg/day. Dosage for children is not established.

▷ **Nursing Management: Guanabenz Therapy**

*Assessment.* In addition to the nursing considerations discussed for oral clonidine, observe the following. Guanabenz should be used during pregnancy only if the benefits outweigh the potential risk of adverse effects to the fetus. In animal studies an increase in skeletal abnormalities has been observed, along with increased fetal loss and diminished body weight of the neonate. Always inquire if the female client is pregnant or plans to be. Do not use in clients who are hypersensitive to guanabenz. The drug should be used with caution for clients with cerebrovascular or cardiovascular disease and renal or hepatic impairment.

*Intervention.* The client's blood pressure should be monitored on a routine basis. The last dose of each day should be taken at bedtime to ensure overnight control of blood pressure. Guanabenz is usually not discontinued before surgery; however, the anesthesiologist must be aware that the client is receiving the drug.

*Education.* Emphasize the importance of periodic follow-up visits so that the guanabenz dosage and blood pressure are monitored. Some clients may be instructed to take their own blood pressure and report the readings at regular physician visits.

Caution client against abrupt withdrawal of drug. The

possibility of withdrawal syndrome should be considered, although rebound hypertension does not generally occur.

Inform client of the possible side effects, particularly dry mouth, and about the increased sedative effects of alcohol, barbiturates, and other central nervous system depressants, which require caution in operating a car or other machinery.

Instruct client to take last dose before bedtime to ensure continuous blood pressure control during the night.

Instruct client to carry medical identification card or Medic Alert. Warn client not to take OTC medication without consulting the physician.

*Evaluation.* Closely monitor blood pressure and pulse during the initiation of therapy and until the dosage is properly titrated. Closely observe clients with severe hepatic or renal failure, severe coronary insufficiency, recent myocardial infarction, or cerebrovascular disease.

As with other antihypertensive agents, the administration of guanabenz might be an indication for the following nursing diagnoses: altered comfort related to dizziness, drowsiness, weakness, headache, dry mouth, stomach cramps or chest pain; high risk for injury related to dizziness, syncope, or weakness; altered self-concept related to decreased sexual ability; and anxiety.

### guanfacine (Tenex)

Guanfacine (Tenex) is a centrally acting antihypertensive that appears to stimulate alpha$_2$ adrenergic receptors in the brain, which results in a decrease in sympathetic stimulation to the heart and blood vessels. Thus peripheral vascular resistance, heart rate, and blood pressure are lowered. It is indicated as an antihypertensive.

Guanfacine is well absorbed orally with peak effect in 8 to 12 hours (single dose) or 1 to 3 months (chronic dosing). Onset of effect occurs within 7 days of chronic dosing. Duration of effect is 1 day (single dose). Metabolism is in the liver, with excretion by the kidneys.

For significant side effects/adverse reactions, see Table 26-2. No significant drug interactions have been reported.

Administer guanfacine to adults, 1 mg orally daily at bedtime. Increase dose if needed, in 3 to 4 weeks (to 3 mg/day). If necessary, a third increase may be instituted in another 3 to 4 weeks. Children's dose has not been determined.

### ▷ Nursing Management: Guanfacine Therapy

Except for the precaution regarding the use of guanabenz during pregnancy, the nursing considerations for guanfacine are the same as for guanabenz. There is also the added concern that the client may experience depression with the use of guanfacine.

## Peripheral Adrenergic Inhibitors
### guanethidine sulfate (Ismelin)

Guanethidine sulfate is a powerful antihypertensive drug that acts as a postganglionic adrenergic neuron blocking agent. Guanethidine enters the storage vesicles of the adrenergic nerve terminal, where it gradually displaces the stored norepinephrine. The subsequent depletion of norepinephrine inhibits transmission of nerve impulses at the neuroeffector junction. Although there is no significant change in peripheral resistance, the drug reduces blood pressure by decreasing vascular tone, primarily at the venous side and secondarily at the arterial side of the circulatory system. This lowers venous return, which reduces cardiac output. Consequently, a proportional decrease in cerebral, splanchnic, and renal blood flow results.

The venous pooling of blood is responsible for orthostatic hypotension. The reduction in blood pressure is noticeably greater with the client in the standing position than in the recumbent position. The salt and water retention that increases plasma volume is probably caused by hemodynamic effects, such as reduced renal plasma flow and glomerular filtration rate. This is why tolerance to the drug may occur. The heart rate, however, is generally slowed. The adrenergic blocking action of guanethidine increases gastrointestinal motility, frequently causing diarrhea. It is speculated that this response may possibly be attributed to parasympathetic predominance. The drug does not affect the catecholamines in the adrenal medulla. In contrast, it may cause the release of catecholamines from a pheochromocytoma, thus producing a hypertensive crisis.

Guanethidine has a variable absorption orally (3% to 39% absorbed) with chronic dosing. Peak effect is within 8 hours (single dose) or 1 to 3 weeks (with chronic dosing). It has a biphasic half-life, i.e., alpha is 1 to 2 days, beta is between 5 and 10 days. Duration of effect when drug is stopped (with chronic dosing) is a gradual blood pressure increase to pretreatment levels within 1 to 3 weeks. It is metabolized in the liver and excreted by the kidneys.

For side effects/adverse reaction, see Table 26-2.

*Significant drug interactions.* The following interactions may occur when guanethidine is given with the drugs listed below:

| Drug | Possible Effect and Management |
|---|---|
| oral antidiabetic medications or insulin | May result in an increased hypoglycemic effect. Monitor closely and communicate with physician since dosage adjustments may be necessary. |
| minoxidil | Concurrent use with guanethidine is not recommended since antihypertensive effects may be potentiated. |
| monoamine oxidase (MAO) inhibitors | Severe hypertension may result. It is recommended that MAO inhibitors be discontinued for a minimum of 1 week before starting guanethidine. |
| metaraminol, norepinephrine, and possibly other sympathomimetics | The antihypertensive effectiveness of guanethidine may be reduced. Metaraminol and guanethidine concurrently may result in cardiac arrhythmias, severe prolonged hypertension, or a hypertensive crisis. If it is absolutely necessary to use this combination, the smallest dose possible should be pre- |

| Drug | Possible Effect and Management |
|------|-------------------------------|
|  | scribed with very close patient monitoring. |
| tricyclic antidepressants, loxapine, thioxanthenes, and possibly other psychotropic medications | May reduce the antihypertensive effect of guanethidine by blocking its access to the adrenergic nerve site. Monitor closely since dosage adjustments or alternate antidepressant medications on a trial basis may be ordered by the physician. |

***Dosage and administration.*** For adult ambulatory clients, the initial dose is 10 or 12.5 mg orally daily, increased by 10- or 12.5-mg increments at 5- to 7-day intervals, as necessary. Maintenance dose is 25 to 50 mg orally daily. For hospitalized clients, initial dose is 25 to 50 mg orally daily, increased by 25- to 50-mg increments at daily or every other day intervals, as necessary. Children's dosage is 200 μg (0.2 mg)/kg or 6 mg/m² body surface area orally daily. Increase by same amount daily at 7- to 10-day intervals, as necessary for blood pressure control.

▷ **Nursing Management: Guanethidine Therapy**

***Assessment.*** Anticipate that hospitalized clients will receive a higher initial dosage than ambulatory clients because they can be watched more carefully.

Use with caution in a client with a history of bronchial asthma, which may be precipitated because of hypersensitivity to catecholamine depletion. Use with caution in a client with peptic ulcer or colitis because depletion of norepinephrine may increase parasympathetic tone.

Do not use in clients who are hypersensitive to guanethidine or have pheochromocytoma or frank congestive heart failure not caused by hypertension. (See use of MAOI under drug interactions.)

Cautious use is indicated in a client with severe renal disease (nitrogen retention, increased BUN levels), coronary insufficiency, recent myocardial infarction, cerebrovascular disease, congestive heart failure, sinus bradycardia, impaired hepatic function, diabetes mellitus, or fever.

***Intervention.*** The most frequent problem with guanethidine is orthostatic hypotension. As a baseline for comparison, take blood pressure readings before initiation of drug therapy; continue to keep a record of client's blood pressures while in the supine and standing positions during therapy. The hypotensive effect of the drug is greater with the client in the upright position than in the supine position. Therefore dosage adjustment of guanethidine is determined by blood pressure taken first while the client is in the supine position, then again after the client has been standing for 10 minutes or performing mild exercise. If there is *no decrease* from the previous levels, an increase in dosage is indicated. Dosage should be reduced when the client has (1) normal supine blood pressure, (2) excessive fall in orthostatic pressure, or (3) severe diarrhea.

Note that guanethidine has a long duration of action as well as a prolonged half-life. Also, the full therapeutic benefits may not be noticed for 1 to 3 weeks. This means that dosage increase, when needed, is made at intervals of 5 to 7 days.

***Education.*** Forewarn client that orthostatic hypotension (dizziness, lightheadedness, or syncope) occurs frequently and is prominent when rising from sleep or making rapid position changes. Instruct client to change position gradually. Venous return to the heart can be increased by flexing arms and legs slowly before sitting or standing. Some physicians prescribe that the client don elastic stockings before getting out of bed. During dosage adjustment, the hospitalized client should receive help when getting out of bed. Inform client that orthostatic hypotension is aggravated by hot showers or baths, hot weather, prolonged standing, physical exercise, and alcohol ingestion. During an episode of orthostatic hypotension, caution client to sit or lie down at the first sign of dizziness or weakness.

Instruct client to report any signs of diarrhea. If it persists, physician may order an anticholinergic agent (atropine), paregoric, or a kaolin-pectin preparation. Guanethidine may be discontinued, or the dosage may be reduced. Note the state of hydration of the client, and check the level of electrolyte balance during this episode.

Alert client to inform surgeons, anesthesiologists, and dentists that he or she is taking guanethidine before any intrusive procedures are considered.

Emphasize the importance of drug compliance. Report side effects so that the physician can modify drug regimen without discontinuing medication. Also, advise client to avoid emotional encounters or any other form of stress.

Instruct client not to take any other medication or over-the-counter drugs, which may contain sympathomimetic agents, without consulting the physician.

Stress the importance of keeping follow-up appointments to the physician's office. Instruct client to carry medical identification card or Medic Alert.

***Evaluation.*** Closely monitor client receiving long-term therapy because the effects of guanethidine are cumulative. Periodic liver and kidney function tests and blood counts should be performed.

Monitor intake and output, observing for reduced urine volume, particularly in clients with limited cardiac or renal function. Weigh patient daily, and watch for signs of edema or fluid retention. Report increased weight (2 pounds or more) to physician.

Carefully monitor the client's pulse rate. If bradycardia occurs, report readings to physician.

Observe clients with diabetes receiving antidiabetic therapy since guanethidine may produce additive hypoglycemic effects.

With the administration of guanethidine, the client may experience the following nursing diagnoses: altered tissue perfusion: renal, cerebral, and/or cardiopulmonary related to the drug's ischemic effects secondary to hypotension; fluid volume excess; sexual dysfunction evidenced by ejaculation difficulties; altered comfort related to orthostatic hypotension (dizziness, fainting), headache, dry mouth, diarrhea; altered bowel elimination related to diarrhea; and high risk for injury related to the hypotensive effects of the drug.

### guanadrel sulfate (Hylorel)

Mechanism of action is the same as for guanethidine. Guanadrel has an onset of action within 2 hours; peak effect is usually between 4 to 6 hours (after single dose). Half-life can vary with individuals but generally it is about 10 hours. Its duration of effect is about 9 hours. It is metabolized by the liver and excreted by the kidneys.

See Table 26-2 for side effects/adverse reactions. Metaraminol and other sympathomimetics; monoamine oxidase inhibitors (MAOI); and tricyclic antidepressants, loxapine, thioxanthenes, and psychotropic agents may cause drug interactions; see under guanethidine. In addition, trimeprazine may reduce the antihypertensive effect of guanadrel by displacement and blocking guanadrel's access to the adrenergic neuron. Monitor closely.

Initial adult dosage is 5 mg orally twice daily. Dosage may be increased at daily, weekly, or monthly intervals, as necessary for blood pressure control. Maintenance dosage is 20 to 75 mg orally per day, in two to four divided doses. Children's dosage is not established.

For nursing management, see discussion of guanethidine.

## Rauwolfia Derivatives
### reserpine (Sandril, Serpasil, Rau-Sed, Reserpoid)

Rauwolfia derivatives are alkaloids obtained primarily from Rauwolfia serpentina, a shrub endemic to India and various tropical areas of the world. The major alkaloid reserpine was isolated in 1952, and it is still used for its antihypertensive effect. Other Rauwolfia alkaloids have different chemical structures, but in general they have similar actions, uses, and cautions. Since reserpine is the most commonly prescribed alkaloid, it will serve as the prototype for this category of drugs. Other available Rauwolfia derivatives include alseroxylon (Rauwiloid), deserpidine (Harmonyl), Rauwolfia serpentina (Raudixin, Rauverid, Wolfina), and rescinnamine (Moderil).

Blood pressure is lowered by reserpine (Rauwolfia alkaloids) by depleting the storage sites of norepinephrine in the peripheral postganglionic adrenergic neuron. Studies indicate that Rauwolfia compounds alter the ability of storage granules in nerve cells to take up and bind norepinephrine. Without adequate norepinephrine available for release, discharges of nerve impulses from the peripheral sympathetic neurons, which supply the smooth muscle of arterioles, produce little or no effect on these blood vessels. The resultant vascular relaxation decreases peripheral resistance, thereby reducing blood pressure. These compounds also decrease heart rate and thus lower cardiac output. In addition, they decrease plasma renin activity.

Depletion of brain norepinephrine and serotonin may account for the sedative action of reserpine. The antihypertensive effect, however, appears to be mainly caused by the peripheral adrenergic blockade, which results in peripheral pooling of blood and a reduction in cardiac output.

Although some CNS effects may be involved in the antihypertensive action, the central nervous system is not currently believed to be the major site of action for the Rauwolfia alkaloids.

Reserpine has an onset of action of days to 3 weeks with chronic dosing. Antihypertensive peak effect is seen within 3 to 6 weeks. Half-life is initially 4.5 hrs, but with chronic dosing, it is extended to 45 to 168 hours. Duration of effect is 1 to 6 weeks. It is metabolized in the liver and excreted mostly fecally.

See Table 26-2 for side effects/adverse reactions.

***Significant drug interactions.*** The following interactions may occur when reserpine is given with the drugs listed below:

| Drug | Possible Effect and Management |
|---|---|
| CNS depressants and/or alcohol | Enhanced CNS depressant effects. Monitor closely. |
| MAO inhibitors | May result in hyperpyrexia and hypertension (moderate to severe or even crisis level). Concurrent administration is not recommended. Patients receiving MAO inhibitors should be taken off this medication for at least 1 week before a Rauwolfia alkaloid is started. |

***Dosage and administration.*** Adult dose is 100 to 250 µg (0.1 to 0.25 mg) orally daily or 5 to 20 µg (0.005 to 0.02 mg)/kg in one or two divided daily doses. For administration of the less commonly used Rauwolfia alkaloid preparations, see package inserts.

## ▷ Nursing Management: Reserpine Therapy

***Assessment.*** Use with extreme caution in clients with history of mental depression. Discontinue therapy at the first sign of despondency; otherwise continued therapy could result in suicide.

Use cautiously in clients with a history of gallstones, to prevent biliary colic, or with a history of renal insufficiency (diuretic is usually required), to avoid difficulty in adjusting to lower blood pressure levels.

Use cautiously in clients with cerebral hemorrhage (severe hypotension may be precipitated with parenteral doses greater than 0.5 mg), epilepsy, cardiac damage, asthma, chronic sinusitis, parkinsonism, and pheochromocytoma. Do not use in clients with mental depression (particularly with suicidal tendencies), ulcerative colitis, and acute peptic ulcers or those who are hypersensitive to Rauwolfia derivatives.

With the administration of reserpine, the client may experience the following nursing diagnoses: high risk for injury related to cardiovascular and CNS effects (lightheadedness, dizziness, orthostatic hypotension) and GI effects (tarry stools, hematemesis, peptic ulcer); disturbance in self-esteem related to depression and sexual dysfunction; sexual dysfunction related to impotence or decreased sexual interest; altered comfort related to abdominal cramps, headache, chest pain; and anxiety.

***Intervention.*** Administer oral medication with meals or with milk or other food to minimize gastric irritation, since drug increases gastric secretions.

Note that the *Rauwolfia* derivatives have a slow onset of action and a long duration of action, so therapeutic benefits may take about 2 weeks to develop. This means that dosage adjustments should be made no more frequently than every 7 to 14 days so that the full effect of the previous dosage can be evaluated. Action may persist for approximately 1 month after discontinuation of therapy.

If client requires general anesthesia, including dental surgery, reserpine no longer needs to be withdrawn; however, the anesthesiologist must be aware of the therapy. It is recommended that reserpine be withdrawn 2 weeks before electroconvulsive therapy is instituted.

***Education.*** Although orthostatic hypotension does not usually occur, advise client to make position changes slowly to avoid potential dizziness and fainting. Because of the sedative effect of the drug, caution client about operating dangerous or hazardous machinery. Advise client not to take alcohol or other CNS depressants.

Teach the client or a responsible member of the family the possible side effects that may occur and that should be reported to the physician. Mental depression (anorexia, self-depreciation, detached attitude, and impotence) may lead to suicide. This usually occurs in clients who receive a high dosage.

If nasal stuffiness occurs, nasal decongestants or other OTC preparations containing sympathomimetics should not be used without first consulting the physician. Dry mouth may be relieved by rinsing with warm water, OTC saliva substitutes (Xero-Lube), sugarless gum, or sour hard candy. Consult physician before using any of these compounds.

Emphasize the importance of drug compliance even if the client is feeling well. Instruct client not to discontinue the drug suddenly but to report unpleasant side effects to the physician. Also stress the need for medical follow-up visits.

Instruct client to carry medical identification card or Medic Alert.

***Evaluation.*** Monitor the client's blood pressure and pulse rate frequently and compare with baseline readings, particularly before parenteral administration. A decrease in blood pressure may be a result of bradycardia. Weigh client daily. Excessive weight gain indicates fluid retention, which should be reported to the physician.

## Alpha Adrenergic Blocking Drugs

The alpha adrenergic blocking agents used in the management of hypertension include phenoxybenzamine, phentolamine, prazosin, and terazosin. Phenoxybenzamine and phentolamine are alpha blockers that are relatively nonselective because they antagonize responses mediated by both alpha$_1$ and alpha$_2$ receptors. Hence, they lower blood pressure by preventing norepinephrine from activating alpha$_1$ receptors on vascular smooth muscle to produce vasoconstriction. See Chapter 21 for monographs of phenoxybenzamine and phentolamine. Prazosin and terazosin are more selective in activity and are classed as alpha$_1$ adrenergic blocking agents.

### prazosin hydrochloride (Minipress)

Prazosin reduces blood pressure by decreasing peripheral vascular resistance. Although several mechanisms of action have been proposed, some aspects of how prazosin produces a hypotensive effect are still not completely understood. According to the current hypothesis, prazosin is an alpha$_2$ adrenergic blocking agent. By selectively blocking the postsynaptic alpha receptors on the vascular smooth muscle of both the arterioles and the veins, prazosin inhibits the action of norepinephrine when the sympathetic nerves are stimulated. This blocking action causes a decrease in peripheral vascular resistance, lowering blood pressure, especially diastolic blood pressure. Prazosin usually has little effect on cardiac output. In clients with congestive heart failure, prazosin may increase cardiac output by decreasing systemic and pulmonary venous pressure.

Prazosin has an onset of action within 2 hours, peak effect within 2 to 4 hours (single dose) or 3 to 4 weeks (with chronic dosing). In congestive heart failure, its effects are more rapidly seen; that is, onset of action is rapid and peak action is seen within 1 hour. Duration of effect in hypertension is up to 10 hours (single drug dose), whereas in CHF it is 6 hours. Metabolism is in the liver (it has 4 active metabolites). Excretion is mainly in bile and feces.

### terazosin (Hytrin)

Terazosin is a peripheral alpha$_1$ adrenergic blocking agent. It produces vasodilation and reduces peripheral resistance, but it has minimal effect on cardiac output or renal blood flow. It is indicated in the treatment of hypertension.

Terazosin is rapidly absorbed orally with onset of action within 15 minutes. Peak effect is seen within 1 hour; duration of action is approximately 1 day. Metabolism takes place in the liver (it has 4 identified metabolites, one of which is active); the drug is excreted in the feces primarily (60%) and in the kidneys (40%).

See Table 26-2 for side effects/adverse reactions. There are no known major drug interactions to date.

Adult dose is 1 mg orally daily at bedtime. Maintenance dose is between 1 and 5 mg daily, as necessary to control blood pressure. Maximum daily dose is 20 mg. Children's dose is not established.

### doxazosin (Cardura)

Doxazosin mesylate was released in 1991 for the treatment of hypertension. After administration it produces a maximum reduction in blood pressure in 2 to 6 hours, with a half-life of 22 hours. The most commonly reported side effects are dizziness (19%) and headaches (14%). The initial adult dose is 1 mg orally daily.

### ▷ Nursing Management: Alpha Adrenergic Blocking Agent Therapy

**Assessment.** For prazosin, use caution in clients with angina pectoris or severe cardiac disease. Clients with impaired renal function may require lower doses. With the administration of both prazosin and terazosin, elderly clients may be more sensitive to the effects of the drug.

Nursing diagnoses to be considered with both these agents might be the following: high risk for injury related to the cardiovascular and CNS effects, evidenced by drowsiness, dizziness, orthostatic hypotension, and sudden fainting; excess fluid volume evidenced by swelling of feet and lower legs, shortness of breath, and weight gain; altered comfort related to dry mouth, headache, chest pain, joint pain, and nausea and vomiting.

**Intervention.** Syncope along with dizziness, light-headedness, or sudden loss of consciousness may occur, generally within ½ to 1½ hours following an initial dose of prazosin "first-dose hypotensive reaction" or a rapid dose increase of the drug. These symptoms may also appear when other antihypertensive agents are added to the regimen. Occasionally, the syncopal episode is preceded by severe tachycardia (heart rate of 120 to 160 beats/minute). To minimize this reaction, limit initial dose to 1 mg, then increase dosage slowly. When adding a diuretic or other antihypertensive agent, reduce prazosin to 1 or 2 mg and then increase dosage as needed. It is recommended that the initial dose be administered at bedtime to minimize the "first-dose hypotensive reaction."

**Education.** Inform client of "first-dose hypotensive reaction."

Instruct client to avoid rapid postural changes, particularly from recumbent to upright positions. Also, if dizziness occurs, client should lie down. This effect tends to disappear with continued use of the drug or dosage reduction. Inform client not to drive or operate hazardous machinery during the early period of adjustment to drug therapy. Note that the full effect of the drug may not be achieved for 4 to 6 weeks.

Teach client to weigh daily and report any increase to the physician. These agents tend to increase fluid retention. Also, instruct client to minimize sodium intake.

Emphasize the importance of drug compliance and keeping physician's appointments. If tolerance to prazosin develops, ineffectiveness usually occurs within several months and the physician will need to alter the drug regimen. Inform client not to take any other drugs without first consulting the physician. This includes OTC medications that contain sympathomimetic agents used for a cold, cough, or allergic condition.

**Evaluation.** Monitor blood pressure and pulse rate frequently and observe for sudden drop in blood pressure and tachycardia.

## Beta Blocking Agents

Beta adrenergic blocking agents (see box below) have been successfully used to treat cardiovascular disorders, including hypertension. These drugs decrease cardiac output and inhibit renin secretion, which results in a lowering of blood pressure. Beta blocking drugs compete with epinephrine for available beta receptor sites, thus inhibiting typical organ or tissue response to beta stimulation.

For additional information about this category of drugs, see Chapter 21.

## VASODILATORS

**Vasodilators** exhibit a direct action on the smooth muscle walls of the arterioles and/or veins, thereby lowering peripheral resistance and blood pressure. Although various theories have been proposed, the mechanism of action, at least in part, involves the direct relaxation of vascular smooth muscle by stimulation of the calcium-binding process. The drop in blood pressure stimulates the sympathetic

---

### SELECTED BETA ADRENERGIC BLOCKING AGENTS

| Generic Name | Trade Name |
| --- | --- |
| **Beta₁ adrenergic (cardioselective) blocking agents** | |
| acebutolol | Sectral |
| atenolol | Tenormin |
| | Apo-Atenol ❧ |
| metoprolol | Lopressor |
| | Apo-Metoprolol ❧ |
| **Beta₁ and beta₂ adrenergic (nonselective) blocking agents** | |
| labetalol | Normodyne |
| | Trandate |
| nadolol | Corgard |
| pindolol | Visken |
| propranolol | Inderal |
| | Inderal LA |
| | Novopranol ❧ |
| timolol | Blocadren |
| | Apo-Timol ❧ |

nervous system and activates the baroreceptor reflexes, increasing heart rate and cardiac output. This also increases renin release. Therefore combined therapy is recommended. To inhibit sympathetic reflex response, use of a beta adrenergic blocker such as propranolol has been advocated, along with a diuretic to alleviate sodium and water retention that occurs during vasodilator therapy.

There are two types of vasodilators: (1) arteriolar dilators, such as diazoxide, hydralazine, and minoxidil, which exert a selective effect on arterioles, and (2) arteriolar and venous dilators, such as sodium nitroprusside, which lower blood pressure by acting on both arteriolar resistance vessels and venous capacitance vessels.

## Arteriolar Dilator Drugs
### diazoxide (Hyperstat IV)

The antihypertensive action results from direct relaxation of smooth muscles in the peripheral arterioles, which causes a decrease in peripheral resistance. The drug does not affect the venous capacitance vessels. As blood pressure is reduced, a reflex increase in heart rate and cardiac output occurs, with resultant maintenance of coronary and cerebral blood flow. This cardiovascular reflex mechanism also inhibits the development of orthostatic hypotension. Diazoxide also causes retention of sodium and water that produces increased plasma renin activity. Since tolerance usually develops, the drug is frequently given with a diuretic.

When administered intravenously, diazoxide is a potent antihypertensive agent. However, the oral form (Proglycem) produces only a slight decrease in blood pressure. Its main action is to stimulate hyperglycemia and decrease plasma insulin levels by suppressing insulin release. (See Chapter 50.)

Diazoxide is administered intravenously to reduce blood pressure promptly in *hypertensive emergencies* such as malignant hypertension, hypertensive encephalopathy, impaired renal function (acute or chronic glomerulonephritis), and eclampsia, when an urgent decrease in diastolic pressure is required. Drug is administered to hospitalized clients.

Intravenous diazoxide is ineffective in reducing elevated blood pressure in clients with MAO–induced hypertension or pheochromocytoma. Also, because of its adverse effects, the drug is not used for chronic treatment of hypertension.

Administered by IV push, onset of action is 1 minute; peak effect occurs within 2 to 5 minutes. Half-life is approximately 28 hours, whereas in clients with renal impairment, it is between 20 and 53 hours. Duration of effect is 2 to 12 hours. Diazoxide is metabolized in the liver and excreted by the kidneys.

For side effects/adverse reactions, see Table 26-2.

Diazoxide given concurrently with other antihypertensive medications or peripheral vasodilators may result in a severe hypotensive reaction. If concurrent use is necessary, smaller doses may be indicated. The client should be monitored closely for several hours for hypotension.

Adult dose is up to 150 mg (or 1 to 3 mg/kg of body weight) given intravenously within 10 to 30 seconds. Repeat dose in 5 to 15 minutes if necessary, up to a maximum of 1.2 g/day. Following the emergency period, give diazoxide for several days, until the ordered oral hypertensive agent is effective. Recommended dose is 1 to 3 mg/kg of body weight or 30 to 90 mg/m² body surface, given intravenously. Repeat dose if necessary in 5 to 15 minutes.

▷**Nursing Management:**
**Diazoxide Therapy**

***Assessment.*** Clients who are unable to tolerate thiazide diuretics or sulfonamide-type medications may also show intolerance to diazoxide. Do not use intravenous injection of diazoxide in the treatment of compensatory hypertension, such as aortic coarctation or anteriovenous shunt. Use with caution in clients with impaired cerebral or cardiac circulation since an abrupt drop in blood pressure may seriously reduce blood flow to these organs. With the administration of diazoxide, the client may be assessed for the following nursing diagnoses: altered tissue perfusion: cardiopulmonary, related to the ischemic effects of the drug (angina, myocardial infarction); high risk for injury related to hypotension, hyperglycemia, allergic reaction, and possible extravasation of intravenous preparation of diazoxide; altered comfort related to anorexia, nausea, vomiting, and abdominal distention; altered bowel elimination related to constipation; excess fluid volume related to sodium and water retention evidenced by edema of the lower extremities and pulmonary edema; and altered self-concept related to excessive hairiness with long-term use of the drug.

***Intervention.*** Intravenous diazoxide should be administered only in a peripheral vein through an established IV line to avoid cardiac dysrhythmias. Avoid extravasation, because the solution is alkaline and will cause pain and cellulitis of the tissue. If extravasation occurs, treat with cold packs.

Place client in recumbent position during therapy and keep in same position for at least 30 minutes after injection. If a diuretic such as furosemide (Lasix) is administered, the diuretic generally is given ½ to 1 hour before diazoxide. Have client remain supine for 8 to 10 hours because of additive hypotensive effect. The entire dose should be given by rapid intravenous injection (in less than 30 seconds). Slower administration may result in reduced effect or decreased duration of effect.

Notify physician of signs of abdominal distention, absence of bowel sounds, or constipation.

Simultaneous use of anticoagulants with diazoxide may require reduction in dosage of the former because of increased anticoagulant effects. Administer injection cautiously to clients who are treated concurrently with methyldopa, reserpine, or peripheral vasodilator agents, especially hydralazine, nitrites, and papaverine-like compounds.

*Evaluation.* Monitor blood pressure every 5 minutes until stable, then every hour during the duration of drug action. Before ending surveillance, take blood pressure with client standing. Take pulse before and during therapy. If tachycardia occurs with intravenous administration, report immediately to the physician.

Because of sodium and water retention, weigh client daily. Measure intake and output, and report weight gain to the physician because a diuretic may be indicated. After repeated injections, observe client closely for signs of congestive heart failure (edema, dyspnea, cough, pulmonary rales, distended neck veins, and fatigue).

Before intravenous diazoxide administration and during treatment, monitor blood and urinary glucose levels, serum electrolytes, and complete blood counts. (Hypokalemia potentiates hyperglycemia.) Overdosage of diazoxide requires that client with hyperglycemia be observed up to 7 days, until blood sugar level is stabilized. Hyperglycemia usually occurs in most clients, especially when injections are repeated; closely monitor blood glucose levels, particularly in individuals with diabetes mellitus. In some instances insulin may be indicated.

### hydralazine hydrochloride (Apresoline)

Hydralazine hydrochloride is thought to produce its hypotensive effects by direct relaxation of vascular smooth muscle, particularly the arteries and arterioles, with little effect on veins. Thus arteriolar vasodilation reduces peripheral resistance. Consequently, renal blood flow is increased, providing an advantage to clients with renal failure. Hydralazine also maintains cerebral blood flow and produces sodium and water retention. However, the resultant hypotension is thought to stimulate the baroreceptor reflex, causing an increase in heart rate and cardiac output. Unfortunately, this response offsets the antihypertensive effects of the drug.

This development of tolerance to the antihypertensive action may be offset by the addition of a diuretic to the drug regimen. The diuretic enhances the antihypertensive effect and reduces the potential for increased cardiac output and fluid retention. Hydralazine decreases diastolic pressure more than systolic. It also increases plasma renin activity.

Hydralazine has an onset of action in 45 minutes (oral dose) or 10 to 20 minutes (IV dose). Its peak effect is within 1 hour (orally) or 15 to 30 minutes (IV), while its half-life is between 0.44 and 0.47 hour (active metabolite half-life is 2 to 4 hrs). Duration of effect for both dosage forms is 3 to 8 hours. It is metabolized in the liver and excreted by the kidneys.

For side effects/adverse reactions, see Table 26-2. Hydralazine and diazoxide used concurrently may result in a severe hypotensive effect. If given together, monitor client for at least several hours for this effect.

For treatment of hypertension adult dose is 40 mg daily orally for 2 to 4 days, then 100 mg for the remainder of the first week. Give 200 mg orally daily thereafter in two to four divided doses. Once control is achieved, determine and use lowest effective dosage. Children receive 750 μg (0.75 mg)/kg body weight or 25 mg/m² body surface daily, divided into two to four doses. Increase the dosage slowly over 1 to 4 weeks as necessary, up to a maximum of 7.5 mg/kg or 300 mg/day. For parenteral administration for hypertension, adult dose is 10 to 40 mg given intramuscularly or intravenously. Repeat if necessary. Children's dose is 1.7 to 3.5 mg/kg or 50 to 100 mg/m² body surface daily, divided in four to six doses.

▷ **Nursing Management:**
**Hydralazine Hydrochloride Therapy**

*Assessment.* Tartrazine sensitivity may cause allergic-type reactions (bronchial asthma) in susceptible individuals who take apresoline 10 and 100 mg tablets that contain tartrazine (FD and C Yellow No. 5).

Hydralazine hydrochloride is administered with caution in coronary artery disease in which anginal attacks may be intensified, rheumatic mitral valvular disease that may precipitate congestive heart failure, and hypersensitivity to hydralazine. Clients with cerebrovascular disease may be at risk for increased cerebral ischemia, and those with advanced renal disease may need lower dosages with hydralazine.

Before initiation of hydralazine therapy, complete blood count, antinuclear antibody titer test, and lupus erythematosus (LE) cell preparation tests may be performed. Repeat these tests periodically if client is receiving prolonged therapy.

With the administration of hydralazine, the client may experience the following nursing diagnoses: high risk for injury related to the development of lupus erythematosus-like syndrome (malaise, sore throat, fever, arthalgia), peripheral neuritis (tingling, numbness, and weakness in hands or feet), hypotension (dizziness, lightheadedness); excess fluid volume related to sodium and water retention (swelling of feet or lower legs); altered comfort related to headache, nasal congestion, flushing of face, skin rash, anorexia, nausea, and vomiting; and altered bowel elimination (diarrhea or constipation).

*Intervention.* Use the parenteral form as quickly as possible after drawing through a needle. The drug changes color after contact with a metal filter. Most clients can be changed to oral dosage forms after 24 to 48 hours of parenteral therapy.

Administer drugs with meals or food; this minimizes first-pass metabolism of drug in the intestinal wall, thereby enhancing bioavailability.

*Education.* Teach client the importance of taking medication at the same time each day and to take it exactly as prescribed by the physician, even when feeling well. Inform client that drug should not be discontinued even if side effects occur; instead, the physician should be contacted.

This agent should be discontinued gradually; otherwise abrupt withdrawal will precipitate a sudden rise in blood pressure and heart failure.

Emphasize to the client the importance of keeping clinical appointments, including those involving laboratory studies. Following long-term administration of hydralazine, drug tolerance may develop, necessitating adjustment of the drug regimen.

Inform client that palpitations and headache may occur during the early stages of oral administration, but these symptoms usually subside with continued therapy. Usually, a beta blocker such as propranolol may be prescribed to prevent reflex tachycardia.

Instruct client to report any signs of peripheral neuritis (numbness, tingling, and paresthesias) so that pyridoxine (vitamin $B_6$) may be prescribed to combat the antipyridoxine response of hydralazine.

Since orthostatic hypotension may occur, advise client to make position changes slowly. Also, inform client to avoid standing still for long periods of time, taking hot baths or showers, and doing strenuous exercise.

Warn client against operating potentially hazardous machinery, since dizziness or faintness may occur.

Instruct client to carry medical identification card or Medic Alert.

*Evaluation.* Closely monitor blood pressure and pulse rate of clients receiving parenteral hydralazine. Measure every 5 minutes until stabilized; continue to check frequently (about every 10 to 15 minutes) during parenteral therapy. Monitor intake and output during parenteral therapy; output may be increased with improved renal blood flow.

Weigh client daily to check for edema. Report to physician any gain in weight. Also, advise client to reduce salt intake.

Observe mental status of client. Report to physician any signs of anxiety or mental depression; this condition may indicate cerebral ischemia.

Lupus erythematosus cell preparation tests are indicated if client develops fever, sore throat, arthralgia, chest pain, and chronic malaise. Systemic lupus erythematosis (SLE)-like syndrome may occur in clients receiving higher doses (more than 200 mg/day), in slow acetylators, and in patients with renal impairment. Discontinue drug if tests are positive.

To evaluate for blood dyscrasias obtain periodic blood counts during prolonged therapy; discontinue hydralazine if abnormalities develop.

With simultaneous use of parenteral diazoxide, observe client for several hours to assess for profound hypotension.

### minoxidil (Loniten)

Minoxidil (Loniten) is a potent and orally effective direct-acting peripheral vasodilator. It reduces elevated systolic and diastolic blood pressure by decreasing peripheral vascular resistance in the arteriolar vessels, with little effect on veins. This agent does not have any influence on vasomotor reflexes; therefore it does not cause orthostatic hypotension.

The vasodilator effect of minoxidil is considerably greater than that of hydralazine. Like other vasodilators, minoxidil causes a reflex increase in cardiac output, induces sodium retention, promotes development of edema, and increases plasma renin activity.

Minoxidil is used in *severe* hypertension that is refractory to the conventional antihypertensive agents. Thus it is not considered to be a primary drug for management of severe hypertension. Because of the serious adverse effects, minoxidil is indicated for use in severe hypertension associated with target organ damage such as chronic renal failure. Concomitant administration of a beta adrenergic blocking agent such as propranolol is necessary to prevent severe reflex tachycardia. Also, administration of a diuretic agent is essential to counteract sodium and water retention.

Minoxidil has an onset of action in 30 minutes, and a peak effect in 2 to 3 hours (after a single dose). Half-life of drug and metabolites is between 2.8 and 4.2 hours. Its duration of effect is between 1 and 2 days. It is metabolized by the liver and excreted mostly by the kidneys.

For side effects/adverse reactions, see Table 26-2.

*Significant drug interactions.* Interactions may occur when minoxidil is given with the following drugs:

| Drug | Possible Effect and Management |
|---|---|
| guanethidine | This combination is not recommended since antihypertensive effects may be potentiated. |
| diazoxide, nitrates, or nitroprusside | This combination may result in severe hypotensive reaction. Montior patient closely for several hours if given concurrently. |

*Dosage and administration.* Adult dose is 5 mg orally daily, increasing in 100% increments as necessary (10 mg, 20 mg, 40 mg, etc.). It is usually recommended that dosage increases be on a minimum 3-day schedule, but in selected cases increases can be made every 6 hours with close monitoring of the patient. For maintenance, 10 to 40 mg orally daily is administered in a single or in a divided dosage schedule. In children up to 12 years old, dose is 200 μg (0.2 mg)/kg body weight initially daily in a single dose. Increases may be made in increments of 100, 150, and 200 μg/kg, to a maximum of 50 mg/day. For maintenance, dose is 250 μg (0.25 mg) to 1 mg/kg daily in a single dose or divided dosage schedule. Maximum adult dosage is 100 mg/day.

### ▷ Nursing Management: Minoxidil Therapy

*Assessment.* Inquire if client is pregnant or has plans for pregnancy, since no adequate studies have been conducted to determine the risk to fetus. Do not use in clients with pheochromocytoma (minoxidil may stimulate catecholamine secretion from tumor). Use minoxidil cautiously in clients with recent myocardial infarction (of 1 month or less), since drug may further limit blood flow to myocardium. Report signs of chest, arm, or shoulder pain. Clients with renal function impairment may require lower dosages.

With the administration of minoxidil, the client may experience the following potential nursing diagnoses: excess fluid volume related to sodium and water retention; altered self-concept related to hypertrichosis; altered comfort related to headache, rash, itching, paresthesia, and chest pain.

*Education.*  Teach client to count radial pulse rate for 1 minute before taking minoxidil. Report to physician an increase of 20 or more beats/minute above normal.

Instruct client receiving combination therapy to take each medication at the proper time and not to mix them. A diuretic is given to reduce salt and fluid retention, and a beta blocker is given to control reflex tachycardia. Combined therapy is indicated to increase drug's effectiveness and to minimize side effects by lowering the dose of minoxidil.

Inform client that if a dose is missed, it may be taken a few hours later. However, a missed dose should not be made up the next day; instead the regular dosing schedule should be resumed. Consult the physician if there is a question.

Emphasize the importance of drug compliance despite uncomfortable side effects. Inform client that minoxidil is a powerful drug for reducing blood pressure and by relaxing small blood vessels, more blood flow protects vital organs (heart, kidney, and brain). Alert client not to discontinue drug without notifying the physician, since abrupt withdrawal will cause rebound hypertension.

Inform client that hypertrichosis will likely occur (incidence is 80%) 3 to 6 weeks after starting therapy. This involves elongation, thickening, and increased pigmentation of fine body hair over the temples, eyebrows, sideburns, malar area, shoulders, back, legs, and forearms. This side effect is particularly troublesome to women. Condition is reversible within 2 to 6 months following discontinuation of therapy. No endocrine abnormalities have been found to account for this distressing effect. Hair remover (depilatory creams) or shaving may be effective in removing unwanted hair.

Tell client that minoxidil may be taken with or without food. Advise client against increasing salt intake, and request that dietitian provide information regarding diet. Inform client that if difficulty in breathing occurs, especially when lying down, to notify the physician since this may mean impending congestive heart failure.

Advise client not to take other drugs including OTC agents without first consulting the physician. Instruct client to carry medical identification card or Medic Alert.

*Evaluation.*  When minoxidil is first administered, clients, particularly those who have been receiving guanethidine, should be monitored in a hospital setting to prevent too rapid a decrease in blood pressure. Take blood pressure and pulse rate before administering minoxidil and use these parameters as a guideline to determine progress. During therapy, monitor blood pressure and pulse rate regularly. Report to physician any sharp drop in blood pressure, which can precipitate cerebrovascular accident and myocardial infarction.

Monitor weight gain, intake and output, and edema. Inform physician of an increase in weight (3 or 4 pounds/day) so that fluid retention can be corrected. Client also should monitor weight at home.

Monitor electrolyte balance, especially potassium level if client is receiving a diuretic, which may produce an increase in serum potassium loss. Replacement therapy should be instituted.

Watch for pericardial effusion with or without tamponade, since this may occur in about 3% of clients not receiving dialysis. This requires more vigorous diuretic therapy, or if pericardiocentesis does not alleviate condition, discontinuation of minoxidil.

Observe for anginal symptoms or tachycardia, which can then be relieved by concomitant administration of a beta adrenergic blocker.

Closely supervise clients with renal failure or those receiving dialysis to prevent exacerbation of renal failure or precipitation of cardiac failure. Lower dose of minoxidil is indicated.

## Arterial and Venous Dilator Drugs
### sodium nitroprusside (Nipride, Nitropress)

Sodium nitroprusside is a potent direct-acting vasodilator agent that greatly reduces arterial blood pressure. This drug relaxes both arterial and venous smooth muscles. Because of the latter effect, more venous pooling of blood occurs when the client is upright. Consequently, there is no increase in venous return of blood to the heart. In addition, sodium nitroprusside produces a slight increase in heart rate and a mild decrease in cardiac output. It also enhances the secretion of renin.

Nitroprusside reduces cardiac load; that is, the decrease in systemic resistance results in a reduction in preload and afterload, thus improving cardiac output in the client with congestive heart failure. It is indicated for rapid reduction of blood pressure in hypertensive emergencies (see box on p. 517) and also, during surgery to reduce bleeding in the surgical field.

Sodium nitroprusside has an onset of action and peak effect almost immediately after administration by IV infusion. Half-life of thiocyanate (possible toxic metabolite) is 1 week. Duration of effect is between 1 and 10 minutes following the discontinuance of the infusion. Metabolism is by erythrocytes (to cyanide) and the liver (cyanide to thiocyanate). The drug is excreted by the kidneys.

See Table 26-2 for side effects/adverse reactions.

For adult dosage, mix contents of vial in dextrose 5% injection only. Administer by intravenous infusion, 0.5 $\mu$g (0.0005 mg)/kg/min. Slowly increase in increments of 0.5 $\mu$g according to patient response. Usual dose is 3 $\mu$g/kg/min, although dosage may range up to 10 $\mu$g/kg/min or a total dose of 3.5 mg/kg. Children's dose is 1.4 $\mu$g (0.0014 mg)/kg/min. Adjust dosage as needed.

---

**DRUGS INDICATED FOR HYPERTENSIVE EMERGENCIES**

---

diazoxide (Hyperstat)
nitroglycerin IV
nitroprusside (Nipride)
trimethaphan camsylate (Arfonad)

---

▷**Nursing Management:
Sodium Nitroprusside Therapy**

**Assessment.** Do not use drug in clients with inadequate cerebral circulation or compensatory hypertension (e.g., arteriovenous shunt or aortic coarctation). Sodium nitroprusside should be used cautiously with clients with renal or hepatic function impairment, vitamin $B_{12}$ deficiency, or tobacco amblyopia, because these conditions influence the metabolism and excretion of the drug.

With the administration of sodium nitroprusside, the client may experience the following nursing diagnoses: high risk for injury related to rebound hypertension upon abrupt withdrawal of the drug, hypotension (dizziness, restlessness, tachycardia); altered comfort related to headache; thiocyanate toxicity (ataxia, blurred vision, delirium, dizziness, nausea and vomiting, ringing of the ears); and cyanide toxicity (decreased consciousness progressing to coma).

**Intervention.** After preparing intravenous solution, promptly wrap container in aluminum foil or other opaque material to protect drug from light. Use fresh solution and do not keep longer than 24 hours. Freshly prepared solution has a faint brown tinge; discard if it is highly colored (e.g., blue, green, or dark red).

Administer infusion using a microdrip regulator or an automatic infusion pump. These devices must be available to allow precise measurement of the flow rate as prescribed by physician. Do not add other drugs to the nitroprusside infusion. Avoid extravasation as it results in tissue damage.

Raising the head of the client's bed will increase the hypotensive effect of the drug. Because sodium nitroprusside is converted to thiocyanate, monitor blood thiocyanate level when infusion is continued for more than 72 hours, especially in clients with renal dysfunction. If blood thiocyanate level exceeds 10 mg/dl, the infusion should be discontinued or decreased to prevent toxicity.

Be aware that client's therapy will be changed to oral antihypertensive agents as soon as response occurs. As oral therapy is instituted, the client will require lower doses of nitroprusside.

**Evaluation.** Monitor blood pressure every half minute when infusion is first started to avoid rapid hypotension. Later, check it every 5 minutes. Facilities and personnel must be adequate for this purpose; intensive care facilities are recommended. Observe client for precipitous drop in blood pressure, which may occur in large doses. Do not allow infusion rate to exceed 10 μg/kg/min. If adequate reduction in blood pressure does not occur in 10 minutes, the drug should be discontinued. Monitor intake and output.

Monitor client for thiocyanate toxicity (tinnitus, blurred vision, and delirium). With prolonged treatment and overdosage, a potential for cyanide intoxication exists. (Note that nitroprusside is metabolized first to cyanide, then to thiocyanate.) In the event of cyanide toxicity (coma, dilated pupils, pink color, shallow respirations, imperceptible pulse rate, distant heart sounds, hypotension, and absent reflexes), discontinue nitroprusside. The treatment for overdosage is as follows: administer amyl nitrite inhalations for 15 to 30 seconds each minute; inject sodium nitrite 3% solution intravenously at a rate not to exceed 2.5 to 5.0 ml/min up to a total dose of 10 to 15 ml; then administer sodium thiosulfate intravenously, 12.5 g/50 ml of 5% dextrose in water over a 10-minute period. If symptoms of overdosage reappear, repeat sodium nitrite and sodium thiosulfate injections at half the preceding doses. Continue to observe client for several hours to prevent the recurrence of signs of overdosage. Observe infusion site for swelling or pain. If extravasation occurs, readjust infusion as required.

## ANGIOTENSIN-CONVERTING ENZYME INHIBITORS

Angiotensin-converting enzyme (ACE) inhibitors—also called angiotensin II antagonists—inhibit the action of the renin-angiotensin-aldosterone system. The importance of this system in maintaining blood pressure and sodium and fluid balance is now well accepted. (see Figure 26-2 for normal activation of the renin-angiotensin-aldosterone system.)

It is apparent that a disturbance of the basic function of the renin-angiotensin-aldosterone system can cause hypertension. Further, a damaged kidney that cannot regulate its renin release through normal feedback mechanisms may easily cause an elevation in blood pressure in certain individuals. Fortunately, this evidence has given rise to a new concept in the pharmacologic treatment of hypertension. More importantly, it has led to the development of a new class of drugs, the angiotensin II inhibitors. Captopril, enalapril and Lisinopril are the currently marketed angiotensin-converting enzyme inhibitors in the United States.

### captopril (Capoten)

Captopril reduces blood pressure primarily through suppression of the renin-angiotensin-aldosterone system. By inhibiting the action of the angiotensin-converting enzyme (ACE), captopril prevents the conversion of angiotensin I to angiotensin II (see Figure 26-3). Angiotensin II is a powerful vasoconstrictor that raises blood pressure and also causes aldosterone release, which contributes to sodium and water retention. Thus, by inhibiting the action of ACE, captopril decreases the angiotensin II level, which in turn produces the following: (1) a decrease in vascular tone, thereby directly lowering blood pressure, (2) inhibition of aldosterone release, reducing sodium and water reabsorption; the resultant excretion of fluid is thought to cause only a secondary reduction in blood pressure (decrease in aldosterone secretion does lead to a slight elevation in serum potassium), and (3) an increase in plasma renin activity, caused by a loss of negative feedback on renin release.

Blood pressure is lowered to about the same extent in patients in supine and upright positions. Although orthostatic hypotension and tachycardia are uncommon, they may occur in volume-depleted individuals.

Long-term studies have shown that in clients with severe, treatment-resistant congestive heart failure, captopril enhances cardiac output by reducing ventricular afterload and possibly preload. Captopril is used as an antihypertensive and for the treatment of congestive heart failure (cardiac load-reducing agent).

Captopril has an onset of action between 15 and 60 minutes with a peak effect in 1 to 1.5 hours. Half-life is under 3 hours, and duration of effect is between 6 and 12 hours. It is metabolized in the liver and excreted by the kidneys. For side effects/adverse reactions, see Table 26-2.

**Significant drug interactions.**  Interactions may occur when captopril is given with the following drugs:

| Drug | Possible Effect and Management |
|---|---|
| alcohol or diuretics | If client receiving captopril is given alcohol or a diuretic, a very severe hypotensive episode may occur. To reduce this reaction either discontinue the diuretic 1 week before or increase the salt intake of the patient for 1 week before initiating the captopril. Generally, this reaction does not recur with continued dosing, and the diuretic may be given later, if necessary. |
| potassium-sparing diuretics, low-salt milk, potassium supplements, or potassium-containing medications and salt substitutes | Monitor for hyperkalemia. Frequently measure and closely monitor serum electrolytes, especially potassium. |

**Dosage and administration.**  When using captopril as an antihypertensive, initially give adult dose of 12.5 mg orally two or three times daily. Dose may be increased in 1 to 2 weeks to 25 mg three times daily. When treating congestive heart failure, initially give 12.5 mg orally three times daily; increase daily if necessary up to 50 mg three times daily. Increments higher than this should not be started for at least 2 weeks. (If patients have sodium and fluid depletion, reduce initial dose to 6.25 to 12.5 mg two or three times daily.) For maintenance give 25 to 100 mg orally, two or three times daily.

Captopril is used in children as an antihypertensive or to reduce cardiac load. Give initial dose of 300 µg (0.3 mg)/kg orally three times daily. If necessary to increase, add increments of 300 µg (0.3 mg)/kg after 8 to 24 hours until the minimum effective dose is reached. For newborns, initial dose is 10 mg (0.01 mg)/kg two or three times daily.

## ▷ Nursing Management: Captopril Therapy

**Assessment.**  Be aware that captopril is not used as a primary (first-line) drug because of its serious side effects. It is reserved for individuals who have not responded to "triple-drug antihypertensive therapy" (diuretic, beta blocker, and vasodilator) or who have developed serious side effects from this treatment. Clients with reduced renal function may require lower or less frequent doses or the risk of hyperkalemia is increased.

With the administration of captopril, clients may experience the following nursing diagnoses: altered nutrition, less than body requirements, related to taste impairment; high risk for injury related to hypotension, neutropenia, agranulocytosis (fever and chills) and hyperkalemia (confusion, weakness, cardiac arrhythmias); altered comfort related to nausea, headache, skin rash, joint pain, and chest pain; and altered tissue perfusion related to cardiovascular effects.

**Intervention.**  Whenever possible, before initiating therapy the current antihypertensive regimen should have been discontinued for at least 1 week. All other medications need physician approval.

Administer drug 1 hour before meals to enhance absorption.

Clients with renal disease, particularly those with renal artery stenosis, may have an increase in BUN and serum creatinine levels. Reduce dosage of captopril or discontinue diuretic therapy if necessary.

Neutropenia and agranulocytosis have also been observed. Some neutropenic clients develop systemic or oral cavity infections. Most appear to have complex medical histories such as advanced renal failure, systemic lupus erythematosus, or other autoimmune/collagen disorders. Therefore a few of these individuals may be receiving multiple concomitant drug therapy, including immunosuppressive therapy. An elevation in potassium level may occur because of depressed aldosterone levels. Monitor serum potassium level. Serum sodium levels should also be monitored.

During the first 4 weeks of therapy, skin rash occurs in approximately 10% of clients. Dosage reduction or cessation or administration of an antihistamine usually causes the rash to disappear.

**Education.**  Inform client that the full therapeutic benefits of the drug will not be noticed until several weeks of therapy. Therefore emphasize the importance of drug compliance. Report side effects so that physician can modify drug regimen without discontinuing medication. Also, advise client to avoid emotional encounters or any forms of stress.

Advise client that signs of infection (e.g., sore throat or fever) should be reported to the physician. Also, easy bruising or bleeding (possible agranulocytosis) should be reported. If taste impairment (dysgeusia) occurs, it generally disappears in 2 or 3 months, but it may cause weight loss. Provide the client with nutritional guidance.

Instruct client not to use potassium supplements or substances containing large amounts of potassium (i.e., salt substitutes or low-sodium milk, which may contain up to 60 mEq potassium/L) without physician approval.

Caution clients with heart failure to increase their physical activity slowly in response to decreased chest pain.

**Evaluation.** Before beginning therapy, obtain white blood cell and differential counts and continue every 2 weeks for first 3 months of therapy and periodically thereafter. Instruct client to report any sign of infection (e.g., sore throat, fever), which indicates possible neutropenia or edema associated with proteinuria and nephrotic syndrome.

Proteinuria associated with nephrotic syndrome may occur, particularly in clients with previous renal disease. Before beginning therapy, perform urinary protein determinations and continue at monthly intervals for the first 9 months, then monitor periodically thereafter. If proteinuria is greater than 1 g/day, drug should be discontinued unless benefits outweigh risks.

Monitor blood pressure closely because a precipitous fall can occur in 1 to 3 hours, particularly in clients who have been receiving salt-restricted diets, diuretics, or dialysis. Vomiting, diarrhea, and dehydration can intensify hypotension. The client is to discontinue salt-restricted diet. Monitor pulse rate. If bradycardia occurs, report readings to physician.

### enalapril (Vasotec)

The action of enalapril is due to an active metabolite, enalaprilat. Like captopril, enalapril inhibits angiotensin-converting enzyme activity. It is antihypertensive even in low-renin hypertension and is believed to reduce the breakdown of bradykinin (a potent vasodilator). It is used as an antihypertensive or vasodilator for treatment of CHF.

Enalapril is available orally and parenterally. Onset of action is within 1 hour (oral) or 15 minutes (IV), while peak effect is between 4 and 6 hours (oral) and 1 and 4 hours (IV). Half-life of enalaprilat (active metabolite) is 11 hours, and the duration of effect is 24 hours (oral) and 6 hours (IV). The oral dosage form is metabolized to enalaprilat, the active metabolite that is excreted mainly by the kidneys. The IV (enalaprilat) is excreted by the kidneys.

See Table 26-2 for side effects/adverse reactions. The drug interactions are the same as for captopril.

When using enalapril as an antihypertensive, initially the adult dose is 5 mg daily orally, increased if necessary. In patients who are salt and fluid depleted (because of diuretics or renal failure), the initial dose is reduced to 2.5 mg. For maintenance give 10 to 40 mg orally daily, in a single or twice daily dosage. In treatment of congestive heart failure, oral dose initially is 2.5 mg once or twice daily. Increase according to patient response. Maintenance dose is 5 to 20 mg orally, in a single or twice daily dosage. For children, initially give 100 μg (0.1 mg)/kg body weight orally daily. Adjust dose as necessary, up to a maximum of 500 μg (0.5 mg)/kg body weight daily. For enalapril injection, as an adult antihypertensive, administer 1.25 mg over 5 minutes IV, every 6 hours. Reduce to 0.625 mg initially in clients that are fluid and sodium depleted. Children's dosage is not established.

For nursing management, see discussion of captopril.

### lisinopril (Prinivil, Zestril)

Lisinopril has the advantage of being excreted unchanged in the kidneys. Therefore it may be of benefit to individuals with impaired liver function. Also, it has the longest half-life and peak time of the ACE inhibitors and thus may be prescribed once daily. Its pharmacologic profile is similar to the other ACE inhibitors.

Lisinopril has an onset of action within 1 hour and a peak effect in 6 hours. Its half-life is 12 hours and duration of effect is approximately 1 day. Lisinopril is excreted by the kidneys.

For side effects/adverse reactions: see Table 26-2. Significant drug interactions are the same as captopril's.

For adult dosage, give orally, 10 mg daily initially. Adjust dosage as necessary. Maintenance dose is 20 to 40 mg orally daily. (In fluid and sodium depleted persons, initial dose of 5 mg should be instituted.) Pediatric dose is not established.

For nursing management, see discussion of captopril.

### ramipril (Altace)

Ramipril is an ACE inhibitor released in 1991 for the treatment of hypertension alone or in combination with a thiazide diuretic. The recommended adult dose is 2.5 mg orally daily, adjusted as necessary., For nursing management, see discussion of captopril.

## CALCIUM CHANNEL BLOCKING AGENTS

Calcium channel blocking agents are a relatively new modality for the treatment of hypertension. They are reviewed in Chapter 27.

## GANGLIONIC BLOCKING DRUGS

The ganglionic blocking drug, trimethaphan camsylate (Arfonad), is available in the United States. Its use as an antihypertensive agent is limited because of its action in blocking both parasympathetic and sympathetic ganglia, which may result in many serious adverse effects (see Table 26-2). Whenever possible today, the newer, more selective, and safer agents have supplanted these drugs.

Their antihypertensive action depends on the sympathetic ganglia blockade, which results in a decrease in peripheral resistance, cardiac output, and stroke volume. Today some physicians use the ganglionic blocking agents as an alternative to sodium nitroprusside in clients who are resistant or nonresponsive to nitroprosside. They may also select the ganglionic blocking agents for use in hypertensive crisis in clients with an acute dissecting aortic aneurysm. (See Chapter 20 for more discussion of these drugs.)

### trimethaphan camsylate (Arfonad)

Trimethaphan's antihypertensive effect is due to a blockage of the autonomic nervous system transmission (both parasympathetic and sympathetic). It also produces a direct peripheral vasodilator effect. Trimethaphan is indicated for the treatment of hypertension and to control hypotension during surgery.

Trimethaphan (Arfonad Parenteral) has an immediate onset of action and a duration of effect of 10 to 15 minutes. It is possibly metabolized by pseudocholinesterase and excreted by the kidneys.

For side effects/adverse reactions, see Table 26-2. When trimethaphan is given concurrently with ambenonium, neostigmine, or pyridostigmine, a decrease in antimyasthenia effects is seen. Avoid concurrent administration. Also avoid administration concurrently with antibiotics and sulfonamides prescribed for the treatment of chronic pyelonephritis.

When giving parenteral adult dose for hypertensive crisis, administer 500 μg (0.5 mg) to 1 mg/minute by IV infusion; adjust as necessary to control pressure. For maintenance, give 1 to 15 mg/minute by IV infusion. To control hypotension during surgery, administer 3 to 4 mg/minute by IV infusion and adjust dose as necessary. Maintenance dose is 200 μg (0.2 mg) to 6 mg per minute. Children's dose is 100 μg (0.1 mg)/minute by IV infusion, adjusted as necessary.

### ▷ Nursing Management: Trimethaphan Therapy

**Assessment.** Use with caution for children and elderly clients, who tend to be more sensitive to its hypotensive effects. Use with caution for clients with anemia, Addison's disease, diabetes, hepatic or renal disease, cardiovascular or cerebrovascular insufficiency, and for clients taking other antihypotensive or steroid medications.

With the administration of trimethaphan, the client may have a potential for the following nursing diagnoses: altered comfort related to dry mouth, urticaria, anorexia, nausea and vomiting; altered tissue perfusion related to cardiovascular effects; high risk for injury related to orthostatic hypotension; and altered bowel elimination related to constipation.

**Intervention.** Clients receiving trimethaphan camsylate should be in an intensive care setting for appropriate monitoring. Emergency equipment should be available in the event of respiratory arrest.

The solution should be diluted with dextrose 5% injection only and administered by infusion pump to ensure a precise regulation of the flow rate. The prepared intravenous solution is stable at room temperature for 24 hours. The client should be in a supine position to avoid cerebral anoxia.

Oral antihypertensive therapy should be started as soon as possible because a pseudotolerance to the drug may occur in some individuals. If used for controlled hypotension during surgery, the drug should be discontinued before the wound is closed to allow the client's blood pressure to return to normal.

**Evaluation.** Monitor the client's blood pressure and respiratory function frequently.

## MONOAMINE OXIDASE INHIBITING DRUGS
### pargyline (Eutonyl)

The monoamine oxidase (MAO) inhibitors lower blood pressure by blocking the release of norepinephrine at the sympathetic junctions, thereby interfering with vasoconstriction. MAO is an enzyme active in the metabolic breakdown of catecholamines (norepinephrine, dopamine, and serotonin) within the adrenergic nerve terminals. By blocking the enzyme action, MAO inhibitors actually increase the amount of norepinephrine in the adrenergic nerve endings. Because these drugs interfere with the transmission of the sympathetic nerve impulse, they reduce peripheral resistance and decrease blood pressure.

With the many newer and safer medications available, there is little reason to use an MAO inhibiting agent to treat hypertension. The package insert and USP-DI (1991) lists numerous warnings, contraindications, interactions, and precautions associated with the use of this product. Pargyline may adversely interact with many OTC (cold-cough type) preparations, with numerous prescription drugs, and also with specific foods (aged cheese, alcoholic beverages, and many other foods and drinks containing tyramine). With the declining interest and/or use of this product today, a full drug review will not be presented in this text.

## SUMMARY

Hypertension is the most common cardiovascular health problem, affecting over 30 million Americans. Ninety percent of such cases are considered to be essential, idiopathic, or primary hypertension—i.e., the specific cause of the hypertension is not known. Because hypertensive individuals are at higher risk of cardiovascular injury, they are to be treated nonpharmacologically or pharmacologically to reduce their blood pressure and therefore reduce their risk of premature death and disability. Nonpharmacologically, clients are encouraged to modify their life-style to include weight reduction, sodium restriction, elimination or limited consumption of alcohol and tobacco, reduction of dietary saturated fats, regular exercise, and behavior modification

---

### PREGNANCY SAFETY

FDA category B: methyldopa, guanadrel, guanfacine, doxazosin

FDA category C: clonidine, guanabenz, guanethidine, reserpine, minoxidil, nitroprusside, captopril, enalapril, lisinopril, terazosin

FDA category unclassified: prazosin, diazoxide, hydralazine, trimethaphan*

---

*Not recommended during pregnancy.

to promote relaxation. Pharmacologically, a stepped-care regimen is recommended by the Joint Committee on the Detection, Evaluation, and Treatment of High Blood Pressure. This plan is a progressive approach, which begins therapy with the administration of a single drug, increases the dosage of that drug, and then, in sequential order, gradually adds more potent agents as the need for more intensive therapy is indicated.

Diuretic drugs play an important role in the management of hypertension. Their administration results in the loss of excess salt and water from the body by renal excretion. This volume depletion, plus a direct effect on the arterioles that produces vasodilation, results in a decrease in blood pressure. They are discussed primarily in Chapter 33.

Although adrenergic inhibiting agents were discussed in Chapter 21, as to their modification of the effects of the sympathetic nervous system, they are the most effective antihypertensive drugs. The centrally acting drugs clonidine, methyldopa, guanabenz, and guanfacine are effective as step 2 antihypertensives of the stepped-care regimen, especially when combined with a diuretic. The peripheral adrenergic inhibitors, guanethidine, guanadrel, and *Rauwolfia* derivatives, are also used an antihypertensives. Alpha adrenergic blocking agents such as prazosin and terazosin lower blood pressure by preventing norepinephrine from activating alpha$_1$ receptors on vascular smooth muscle to produce vasoconstriction. Beta adrenergic blocking agents are also used successfully in the treatment of hypertension (see Chapter 21).

Vasodilators act on the smooth muscle walls of the arterioles and/or veins, lowering peripheral resistance and blood pressure. Arteriolar dilator agents commonly administered for hypertension are diazoxide, hydralazine, and minoxidil. Sodium nitroprusside is a direct-acting vasodilator that relaxes both arteriolar and venous smooth muscle, which greatly reduce arterial blood pressure.

Captopril, enalapril, and doxazosin are angiotensin II antagonists that inhibit the action of the renin-angiotensin-aldosterone system, a disturbance of which may cause hypertension.

Although nurses have a major role in the administration of antihypertensive agents, the greatest contribution by far is that of client education to sustain adherence to the accurate and safe self-administration of antihypertensive agents, and to assist the client in changing his or her life-style to incorporate the modifications to promote a decrease in his hypertension and so a healthier life.

## Case Study: The Client with Hypertension

Ronald Sanford, age 37 years, is diagnosed with essential hypertension. His blood pressure has been ranging between 148 and 176 systolic and 90 and 110 diastolic. His average blood pressure is 150/94. There is a strong family history of hypertension and stroke on both sides of the family. Mr. Sanford is married with two school-aged children. He works full-time as a loading dock supervisor for a long-distance trucking company. His elevated blood pressure was found during a routine physical examination. He reports no other manifestations. At this time there is no evidence of renal insufficiency or retinopathy.

Mr. Sanford is to begin taking atenolol, 50 mg daily, and hydrochlorothiazide, 50 mg daily.

1. Atenolol is a beta adrenergic blocking agent. How will this drug contribute to the control of Mr. Sanford's blood pressure?
2. Describe the antihypertensive action of the hydrochlorothiazide.
3. What will Mr. Sanford need to know about taking his medications and avoiding adverse reactions?
4. In addition to drug therapy, what nonpharmacologic measures will you teach Mr. Sanford to help lower his blood pressure?
5. After 6 months on this drug therapy, Mr. Sanford's blood pressure is maintained at 124 to 138 systolic and 78 to 88 diastolic. However, he complains that he doesn't seem to have the energy he used to have and that he is having some decrease in sexual activity. What will you tell Mr. Sanford about these concerns and their relationship to the drug therapy?

Over the next 2 years, Mr. Sanford experiences a gradual increase in his blood pressure. Dosage adjustments in the atenolol and hydrochlorothiazide fail to effectively lower his blood pressure. Captopril, 25 mg three times a day, is added to his treatment program.

6. How does captopril lower blood pressure?
7. What does Mr. Sanford need to know about taking the captopril in order to achieve maximum therapeutic benefit?

# BIBLIOGRAPHY

ACE inhibitors. (1988). Aust Nurses J 18(2):27.

Alexander LM. (1988). Current controversies in antihypertensive therapies, J Am Acad Physician Assist 1(6):448.

American Hospital Formulary Service. (1991). AHFS drug information '91. Bethesda, Md: American Society of Hospital Pharmacists, Inc.

Bergman SM and Wallin JD. (1988). Effects of antihypertensive agents on renal function, Resident & Staff Physician 34(1):53.

Black HR et al. (1989). Antihypertensive treatment: monotherapy and beyond, Consultant 29(1):88.

Black HR. (1988). Hypertension therapy: prescribing for compliance—the role of fixed dose combinations, Consultant 28(6):145.

Brengman SL et al. (1988). Hypertensive crisis in labor and delivery, Am J Nurs 88(3):325.

Brest AV. (1988). Antihypertensive therapy: another look at the effects of cardioprotection, Consultant 28(5):46.

Chonbanian AV. (1988). The 1988 report of the Joint National Committee on Detection, Evaluation, and Treatment of High Blood Pressure, Arch Intern Med 148(5):1023.

Chobanian AV. (1982). Hypertension, Clin Symp 34(5):3.

Enalapril contained in new antihypertensive products. (1988). Nurse Pract 13(8):25.

Ferguson RK and Vlasses PH. (1986). The ACE inhibitors: clinical pharmacology of captopril and enalapril, Hosp Formul 21:46.

Fontana SA, (1988), Update on high blood pressure: highlights from the 1988 national report, Nurs Pract 13(12):8.

Gilman AG et al, eds. (1990). Goodman & Gilman's the pharmacological basis of therapeutics, ed 8. New York: Macmillan Publishing Company.

Gonzales DG et al. (1988). New approaches for the treatment of hypertensive urgencies and emergencies, Chest 93(1):193.

Goodman RP. (1987). Resistant hypertension: what to look for when a good regimen doesn't work, Consultant 27(9):65.

Gorkin JU. (1989). Managing the hypertensive crisis, Hospital Therapy 14(3):43.

Hahn K. (1988). Think twice about borderline hypertension, Nursing 18(4):90.

Halstenson CE. (1987). Terazocin HCL, Hosp Formul 22(11):946.

High blood pressure. (1988). AAOHN J 39(9):385.

Hypertension. (1988). Med Times 116(9):57.

Iron supplements interact with methyldopa. (1988). Nurses Drug Alert 12(7):51.

Jackson EA. (1988). Issues with hypertensive therapy: safety perspectives, Drug Intell & Clin Pharm 22(2):115.

Kirkendall WM et al. (1988). Which drug for the aging hypertensive? Patient Care 22(1):133.

Lipsitz LA. (1989). Hypertension in the elderly, Hosp Pract 24(4):119.

Maddens ME. (1989). Isolated systolic hypertension: the rationale for treating elderly patients, Consultant 29(4):125.

Mann KV. (1989). Promoting adherence in hypertension: a framework for patient education, Can J Cardiovascular Nurs 1(1):8.

Manzo M. (1987). Sodium nitroprusside for hypertensive crisis, Nursing 17(11):98.

McGarry-Myers RJ et al. (1988). The role of new antihypertensive drugs, Chest 93(4):868.

Messerli FH et al. (1988). Effects of calcium channel blockers on systemic hemodynamics in hypertension, Amer J Med 84(38):8.

Moser M. (1989). The new hypertension treatment guidelines, Med Times 117(6):51.

Nash DT. (1989). The new hypertension treatment guidelines: the pharmacist's role, Pharmacy Times 55(1):35.

Noel HC. (1988). Orthostatic hypotension occurring after discontinuation of long-term minoxidil therapy, Nurse Pract 13(8):25.

Ram CVS. (1987). Management of resistant hypertension, Chest 92(6):1096.

Second-stage antihypertensives in the elderly. (1988). Nurses Drug Alert 12(4):27.

Sternberg EB et al. (1984). Drugs that induce hypertension: a discussion of mechanisms, Dateline Hypertension 2(4):1.

Strong AG. (1988). Pharmacologic management of Black hypertensive patients, J Cardiovas Nurs 2(4):20.

Tideiksaar R. (1988). Hypertension in the elderly, Physician Assist 12(8):16.

Todd B. (1988). New antihypertensive drugs, Geriatric Nurs 9(3):187.

Trounson LW. (1988). Hypertensive crisis, J Post Anesth Nursing 3(2):102.

United States Pharmacopeial Convention. (1991). Drug information for the health care provider, ed 11. Rockville, Md: The Convention.

# Chapter

## 27 Calcium Channel Blockers

### CHAPTER OBJECTIVES

*After studying this chapter, you should be able to meet the following objectives and define the key terms.*

1. State the mechanism of action of calcium channel blockers on cardiac muscle, the cardiac conduction system, and the smooth muscle cells in the walls of blood vessels.

2. Compare and contrast the therapeutic effects of the calcium channel blockers diltiazem, nicardipine, nifedipine, nimodipine, and verapamil.

3. Describe specific nursing interventions that may inhibit side effects associated with calcium channel blockers.

4. Identify specific client education measures necessary when calcium channel blockers are prescribed.

### KEY TERMS

**automaticity,** page 524

**calcium channel blockers,** page 523

**cardiac afterload,** page 525

**coronary artery spasm,** page 525

**peripheral vascular resistance,** page 524

## INTRODUCTION

One of the newer subclassifications of cardiac drugs is the **calcium channel blockers,** discovered in 1969 by Flackenstein of West Germany. Although these compounds have diverse chemical structures, they all share a basic electrophysiologic property—they block the inward movement of calcium through the slow channels of the cell membranes of cardiac and smooth muscle cells. (See Chapter 23 for a discussion of the physiology of fast and slow channels of cardiovascular fibers.) This activity, however, varies according to the specific type of cardiovascular cells involved. The three types of tissues or cells are:

1. Cardiac muscle or myocardium
2. Cardiac conduction system—SA node and AV nodes
3. Vascular smooth muscle
   a. Coronary arteries and arterioles
   b. Peripheral arterioles

## ACTION

*Cardiac muscle or myocardium.* Calcium channel blockers decrease the force of myocardial contraction by blocking the inward flow of calcium ions through the slow channels of the cell membrane during phase 2 (or plateau phase) of the action potential. (See Figure 23-2 on p. 451.) The diminished entry of calcium ions into the cells thereby fails to trigger the release of large amounts of calcium from the sarcoplasmic reticulum within the cell. This free calcium is needed for excitation-contraction coupling, an event that activates contraction by allowing cross-bridges to form between the actin and myosin filaments. The force of the heart's contraction is determined by the number of actin and myosin crossbridges formed within the sarcomere. Decreasing the amount of calcium ion released from the sarcoplasmic reticulum causes fewer actin and myosin cross-

523

bridges to be formed, and the force of contraction then decreases, producing a negative inotropic effect.

*Cardiac conduction system (SA and AV nodes).* In these tissues calcium channel blockers decrease automaticity in the SA node and decrease conduction in the AV node. **Automaticity** means that a cell depolarizes spontaneously and initiates an action potential without an external stimulus. Automaticity is a normal characteristic of the SA nodal cells. Depolarization (or phase 0) of the action potential is normally generated by the inward calcium ion current through the slow channels. Thus the agents that can block the inward calcium ion current across the cell membrane of SA nodal tissue decrease the rate of depolarization and depress automaticity. The result is a decrease in heart rate (negative chronotropic effect). Similarly, an agent that decreases calcium ion influx across the cell membrane of the AV node slows AV nodal conduction (negative dromotropic effect) and prolongs AV refractoriness. When AV conduction is prolonged, fewer atrial impulses reach the ventricles. Diltiazem depresses SA nodal automaticity while verapamil slows AV conduction, so verapamil is used to treat supraventricular tachycardia.

*Vascular smooth muscle.* The smooth muscle of the coronary and peripheral vessels has a significant influence on the hemodynamics of circulation. Calcium channel blockers effectively inhibit calcium ion influx through the slow channels of the membrane of smooth muscle cells. They thereby depress interaction between actin and myosin, resulting in a decrease in force of smooth muscle contraction. As a consequence, coronary artery dilation occurs, which lowers coronary resistance and improves blood flow through collateral vessels, as well as oxygen delivery to ischemic areas of the heart. Hence drugs with these actions are useful in the treatment of angina pectoris. Calcium channel blockers also inhibit the contraction of smooth muscle of the peripheral arterioles. This results in widespread reduction in **peripheral vascular resistance** (resistance to blood flow through the body) and blood pressure. The hemodynamic change reduces afterload, which also decreases oxygen demands of the heart. This indirectly provides a beneficial effect in the management of angina.

•   •   •

The calcium channel blockers that have met with FDA approval include diltiazem, nicardipine, nifedipine, nimodipine, and verapamil. All five of these agents are effective in dilating coronary vessels. However, each drug has additional actions that make it different from the others. Verapamil has been shown to be effective as a dysrhythmic and an antianginal agent. It prolongs AV conduction time and depresses myocardial contraction. It can also lower blood pressure by dilating the systemic blood vessels and decreasing the oxygen demands of the heart. Because of its pronounced effect on the peripheral vascular bed, nifedipine causes the greatest fall in blood pressure. However, it exerts

minimal cardiac depressant action. The action of diltiazem is largely restricted to dilating the coronary blood vessels.

Nicardipine is a very potent peripheral vasodilator that does not affect the sinoatrial (SA) or atrioventricular (AV) nodes. Nimodipine is highly lipophilic; therefore it crosses the blood-brain barrier and has a greater effect on the cerebral arteries than other arteries in the body. It is indicated for the treatment of cerebral arterial spasm following subarachnoid hemorrhage. It also inhibits platelet aggregation.

The adult dose is 60 mg every 4 hours, starting within 96 hours after the subarachnoid hemorrhage and continuing for 3 weeks. Side/adverse effects (infrequent) reported include headaches, nausea, hypotension, skin rash, edema, and tachycardia. Be aware that beta adrenergic blocking agents, systemic and ophthalmic, when used concurrently with this product may result in excessive hypotension. Whenever possible, beta adrenergic blocking agents should be discontinued gradually before nimodipine is started.

Nitrendipine is a calcium antagonist that is under investigational study for the treatment of cardiovascular disorders (Hasegawa, 1988). See Table 27-1 for a comparison of the effects of calcium channel blockers.

The calcium antagonists have been approved for the treatment of angina pectoris and hypertension. Verapamil is indicated for the treatment of supraventricular tachyarrhythmias while nicardipine and nifedipine are used to treat Raynaud's phenomenon.

## ▷NURSING MANAGEMENT: CALCIUM CHANNEL BLOCKER THERAPY

*Assessment.* Do not use these drugs for individuals with severe hypotension (less than 90 mm Hg systolic). Calcium channel blockers should be administered with caution to clients with severe aortic stenosis, bradycardia, heart failure, cardiogenic shock, and mild to moderate hypotension because these conditions will be worsened. Clients with renal or hepatic function impairment will have reduced clearance of the drugs, and so the drugs will have prolonged half-life. Intolerance to the prescribed calcium channel blockers is also a contraindication for the drug. Ask the client if she is pregnant or plans to be. Tests in laboratory animals have resulted in teratogenic effects.

Elderly clients may require more caution in the dosage of calcium channel blockers because of age-related renal function impairment. The half-life of diltiazem, verapamil, and other calcium channel blockers may be increased because of decreased clearance, whereas in studies, nicardipine has shown no difference in the half-life in clients over 65 and young adults.

With the administration of calcium channel blockers, the client may be at risk for the following nursing diagnoses: altered self-concept related to gingival hyperplasia; altered comfort related to skin rash, flushing, dizziness, headache, and nausea; high risk for injury related to allergic reaction, congestive heart failure, and hypotension; fluid volume excess related to sodium and water retention evidenced by swelling of feet, ankles, and lower legs; altered cardiac output related to arrhythmias, and altered bowel elimination related to constipation.

***Intervention.*** Administer oral dosage on an empty stomach to promote rapid absorption. Take pulse before each dose; withhold dose and report to the physician if rate is 50 or below.

Instruct client to perform meticulous daily dental hygiene with regular dental examinations and cleaning, since this may reduce the incidence or severity of gingivitis and gingival hyperplasia (a rare side effect).

***Education.*** Since drug may be coadministered with sublingual nitroglycerin and other nitrates, instruct client to keep a record of nitroglycerin administration and anginal episodes and report promptly if changes occur in previous pattern (increased frequency, duration, and severity of anginal attacks). The symptoms may develop when starting calcium channel blockers or increasing dosages. (Nitroglycerin is used to abort acute angina attacks.)

Instruct the client to change from a sitting or lying position to a standing position cautiously to avoid orthostatic hypotension. Advise client to avoid alcohol to prevent dizziness and hypotension.

Emphasize the importance of regular visits to physician to check progress during therapy.

Teach client to take a pulse appropriately and report a heart rate less than 50. Instruct client to report headaches, rashes, nausea, and vomiting, as well as edema and weight gain (may indicate congestive heart failure).

If a dose is missed, advise the client to take it as soon as remembered, unless it is almost time for the next dose, in which case, it should be omitted.

If calcium channel blockers are taken as antihypertensives, instruct the client to take the medication even if feeling well, since lifelong therapy may be required. Compliance may be ascertained by monitoring refill frequency. Advise on the hazards of untreated hypertension and the need for decreased sodium intake and weight control. Caution the client to check with the physician before taking other medications, particularly OTC sympathomimetics, such as Neo-Synephrine nose drops.

***Evaluation.*** Monitor blood pressure and pulse rate, particularly if the drug is coadministered with a beta adrenergic blocking agent. Observe ECG for prolonged P-R interval, which is caused by slowing of AV conduction. Congestive heart failure may occasionally occur after initiation of calcium channel blocker therapy, particularly in those also receiving beta blocking agents. If beta blockers are withdrawn before calcium channel blocker therapy, taper dosage gradually. Abrupt withdrawal may provoke angina, especially when nifedipine is started. During long-term therapy with calcium channel blockers, hepatic and renal function studies may be required.

## SPECIFIC AGENTS
### diltiazem hydrochloride (Cardizem)

The therapeutic benefits of diltiazem are believed to be related to its ability to prevent the influx of calcium ions through the slow channels of the membrane of myocardial muscle and vascular smooth muscle during membrane depolarization. The slowed calcium ion influx reduces vascular tone and mildly decreases the force of myocardial contraction. Dilation of coronary arteries and arterioles is achieved, thereby improving oxygen supply to myocardial tissue and ultimately inhibiting **coronary artery spasm.** Further, dilation of peripheral arterioles reduces **cardiac afterload** (peripheral resistance), a hemodynamic function that also lessens oxygen requirements of the myocardial tissue. This property probably alleviates chronic stable angina. Diltiazem also decreases SA nodal function and AV nodal conduction because of inhibited influx of calcium ions to the SA and AV nodes. These inhibitory effects decrease heart rate and reduce myocardial contraction.

The indications for diltiazem are:

1. Treatment of coronary artery spasm (Prinzmetal's or variant angina).
2. Treatment of chronic stable angina (increases exercise tolerance).
3. Treatment of hypertension.

For pharmacokinetics, see Table 27-2. For side effects/adverse reactions, see Table 27-3.

**TABLE 27-1**   Comparison of effects of calcium channel blocking agents

| | Diltiazem | Nicardipine | Nifedipine | Verapamil |
|---|---|---|---|---|
| Heart rate | 0/—* | + | + | − / + |
| AV node conduction | — | 0/ + | 0/ − | — |
| Myocardial contractility | 0/ − | 0 | 0/ − | — |
| Myocardial oxygen demand | — | − | — | — |
| Cardiac output | 0/ + | + | + | − / + |
| Peripheral vascular resistance | − | − | − | — |

*−, decrease; +, increase; − / +, variable effect; 0, no effect.

**TABLE 27-2**   Pharmacokinetics of calcium channel blocking agents

| Drug | Onset of action (min) | Time to peak concentration (hr) | Therapeutic serum level (ng/ml*) | Half-life (hr) | Duration of action (hr) | Metabolism | Excretion |
|---|---|---|---|---|---|---|---|
| diltiazem (Cardizem) | 30 | 2-3 | 50-200 | Biphasic: Short phase: ½ Long phase: 3-5 | 4-8 | Liver—has active metabolite de-sacetyldilti-azem | Kidneys and bile |
| Extended-release | 30-60 | 6-11 | Same | 5-7 | 12 | Same | Same |
| nicardipine | — | 1 | 28-50 | Biphasic: Short: 2-4 Long: 8.6 | 8 | Liver | Kidneys |
| nifedipine (Procardia) | Oral: 20 (more rapid when given sublingually) | ½-1 | 25-100 | Biphasic: Short phase: 2½-3 Long phase: 5 | 4-8 | Liver | Kidneys (80%) feces (20%) |
| verapamil (Calan, Is-optin) | Oral: 60-120 IV: 1-5 | 1-2 | 80-300 | Oral, single dose: 2.8-7.4 Regular dose scheduling: 4½-12 IV: biphasic Short phase: 4 min Long phase: 2-5 | IV: 2 Oral regular: 8-10 Oral extended release: 24 | Liver—has active metabolite norverapamil | Kidneys and feces |

*Nanograms per milliliter.

**Significant drug interactions.** The following interactions may occur when diltiazem is given with the drugs listed below.

| Drug | Possible Effect and Management |
|---|---|
| alcohol, antihypertensives | May enhance hypotensive effects. Monitor closely. |
| beta adrenergic blocking agents, including ophthalmic preparations | Monitor closely for bradycardia, hypotension, and heart failure, which may be symptoms of prolonged AV conduction. In clients with impaired cardiac function, avoid concurrent use if possible; if a calcium antagonist is necessary, nifedipine would be the agent of choice. |
| carbamazepine, cyclosporine, quinidine, or theophylline | Metabolism of these drugs may be impaired by calcium channel blockers, leading to increased serum levels and possibly toxicity. Monitor serum levels closely. |
| digitalis glycosides | Increased serum levels of digitalis glycosides have been reported, so monitor digoxin serum levels closely whenever a calcium blocking agent is started or discontinued or when dosage is changed. Also, watch for prolonged AV conduction, increased |

| Drug | Possible Effect and Management |
|---|---|
| digitalis glycosides—cont'd | bradycardia, or AV blocks, especially during the initial week of therapy. A dosage decrease for digoxin may be necessary. |
| disopyramide | Use extreme caution when administering disopyramide with diltiazem or verapamil. It is recommended that disopyramide not be given 2 days before or 1 day after the administration of verapamil or diltiazem because of additive negative inotropic effects, which in some instances have caused fatalities. |

**Dosage and administration.** Give adults 30 mg orally three or four times daily for angina. Increase dosage at 1- to 2-day intervals until optimum response is obtained. Maximum daily dosage is 360 mg. Give extended-release capsules 60 to 120 mg orally twice daily. Dose may be adjusted after 2 weeks, as necessary. Elderly clients may be more sensitive to this drug, so monitor closely. Dosage for children is not established.

For nursing considerations, see the discussion under Nursing Management: Calcium Channel Blocker Therapy.

**TABLE 27-3**   Side effects/adverse reactions of calcium channel blocking agents

| | | |
|---|---|---|
| diltiazem (Cardizem) | Less frequent: dizziness, headaches, nausea, skin flushing or rash | Less frequent: edema of extremities, allergic skin reaction, shortness of breath or wheezing, severe hypotension, tachycardia |
| nicardipine (Cardene) | Less frequent: edema of lower extremities, tachycardia, chest pain | More frequent: feelings of warmth or flushing<br>Less frequent: dizziness, headache, nausea, increased weakness |
| nifedipine (Procardia) | More frequent: dizziness, headaches, nausea, feelings of warmth or flushing<br>Less frequent: constipation | Most frequent: edema of extremities<br>Less frequent: shortness of breath; tachycardia; hypotension; symptoms of CHF |
| verapamil (Calan, Isoptin) | Less frequent: constipation, dizziness, headache, nausea, increased weakness | Less frequent: shortness of breath, tachycardia, edema of extremities, bradycardia, hypotension, symptoms of CHF |

*If side effects continue, increase, or disturb the patient, inform the physician.
†If adverse reactions occur, contact physician, because medical intervention may be necessary.

## nicardipine (Cardene)

For mechanism of action, see previous section. Nicardipine is indicated for the treatment of angina pectoris and hypertension. For pharmacokinetics and side effects/adverse reactions, see Tables 27-2 and 27-3. Nicardipine's significant drug interactions are the same as diltiazem. Administer adults 20 mg orally three times a day. Adjust dose as needed. Children's dosage is not established. For nursing considerations, see the discussion under Nursing Management: Calcium Channel Blocker Therapy.

## nifedipine (Procardia)

The action of nifedipine is generally the same as that of diltiazem. One major difference is that nifedipine has a more powerful vasodilating effect on the coronary arteries and arterioles as well as on the peripheral arterioles. Thus, when arterial pressure is reduced, a reflex response is stimulated, causing a small increase in heart rate and a mild elevation in the force of myocardial contraction. Despite this response, the reduced total peripheral resistance (cardiac afterload) lessens the myocardial oxygen demand. This probably accounts for the drug's effectiveness in treating chronic stable angina and hypertension. In addition, unlike the other members of its class, nifedipine has no tendency to slow the SA nodal activity or prolong AV nodal conduction. The drug is indicated for the management of classic angina (chronic stable angina or effort angina), treatment of vasospastic angina (Prinzmetal's, variant or at-rest angina), and control of hypertension (investigational). For the drug's pharmacokinetics, see Table 27-2; for side effects/adverse reactions, see Table 27-3. For a discussion of significant drug interactions, see discussion of diltiazem. Also, closely monitor clients receiving phenytoin or cimetidine together with nifedipine; elevated levels of both phenytoin and nifedipine have been reported.

Administer to adults, initially, 10 mg orally, three times per day for angina. Dosage is gradually increased over 7 to 14 days as needed and tolerated. Elderly clients may be more sensitive to this drug, so monitor closely. Maximum daily dosage is 180 mg daily, although daily dosages greater than 120 mg are rarely necessary. Children's dosage is not established. In clients unable to swallow, the contents of a nifedipine capsule may be administered buccally or sublingually by piercing the capsule and squirting the medications under the tongue. This method of administration also produces a more rapid effect than oral administration. Dosage is equivalent to the oral dosage. For nursing considerations, see Nursing Management: Calcium Channel Blocker Therapy.

## verapamil hydrochloride (Calan, Isoptin)

See discussion of types of cardiac tissue for mechanism of action of verapamil. The drug is indicated for treatment of chronic stable angina and to relieve angina at rest. Parenteral verapamil is indicated for treatment of supraventricular tachyarrhythmias; it may also be used for temporary control of rapid ventricular rate in atrial flutter or atrial fibrillation. Verapamil is also used for control of hypertension. For pharmacokinetics, see Table 27-2; for side effects/adverse reactions, see Table 27-3. See discussion of diltiazem for significant drug interactions.

***Dosage and administration.***   When used for angina pectoris, supraventricular tachyarrhythmias, and hypertension, this drug should be administered to adults IV with an initial dose of 5 to 10 mg (0.075 to 0.15 mg/kg body weight) given as an IV bolus over a 2-minute period. Repeat dose is 10 mg (0.15 mg/kg body weight) 30 minutes following first dose, if the initial response is not adequate. In older patients, administer slowly (at least 3 minutes). In children up to 1 year, give 0.1 to 0.2 mg/kg body weight over 2 minutes. For children 1 to 15 years, give 0.1 to 0.3 mg/kg over period of 2 minutes. Repeat dose if necessary 30 minutes afterward. Maximum total dose is 10 mg. Give adults initial oral dose of 80 to 120 mg orally three times per day.

Increase dosage daily or weekly as needed and tolerated. The total daily required dosage usually ranges from 240 to 480 mg.

Elderly clients may be more sensitive to this drug, so monitor closely. Children's dosage is not established.

### ▷ Nursing Management: Verapamil Therapy

See also the discussion under Nursing Management: Calcium Channel Blocker Therapy.

***Assessment.*** Use drug with caution in clients with SA node dysfunction since verapamil depresses automaticity of the SA node. Do not use in individuals with ventricular tachycardia or second- or third-degree AV block unless a cardiac pacemaker is in place.

***Intervention.*** Inspect the parenteral drug preparation; discard if cloudy. Administer initial intravenous dosage in a treatment center with appropriate facilities for monitoring and resuscitation. Give slowly as a direct injection over at least 2 minutes (in the elderly, not less than 3 minutes). Monitor with ECG.

Avoid repeated doses in clients with hepatic or renal failure since intravenous dose may prolong duration of effects. If repeated injections are required, closely monitor blood pressure and P-R interval, and use smaller doses.

***Education.*** Instruct client to remain in recumbent position following IV bolus for at least 1 hour to diminish hypotensive effects. Instruct client receiving verapamil at home to take radial pulse before each dose and report an irregular pulse or one lower than 50. Warn client about signs of dizziness or light-headedness during early treatment period. Warn client to avoid driving or operating dangerous equipment. Instruct client to report edema and weight gain, since they may indicate congestive heart failure. If drug must be discontinued, withdraw gradually by decreasing dosage 25% each day.

### NEW AGENTS

Bepridil (Vascor) and isradipine (DynaCirc) were released in early 1991. Bipridil inhibits slow calcium and fast sodium channels; therefore, it is not similar to the other calcium channel blocking agents. It is indicated for the treatment of chronic stable angina. Its serious adverse effects (inducing ventricular arrhythmias and agranulocytosis) limit its use to clients who have not responded to other anti-angina agents. Isradipine has therapeutic properties similar to those of other calcium channel blocking agents, so it is indicated for the treatment of hypertension. It currently has few reported side effects. The initial adult dose is 2.5 mg twice a day.

### SUMMARY

Calcium channel blockers are one of the newest groupings of cardiac drugs. Their action is to block the inward move-

### *Geriatric Implications:* CALCIUM CHANNEL BLOCKERS

The elderly are more susceptible to these agents and the side effects of increased weakness, dizziness, fainting episodes, and falls.

While nitroglycerin (or other nitrates) may be taken concurrently with these agents, the client should be advised to report any increase in frequency or intensity of angina attacks to his or her physician.

Nicotine may reduce the effectiveness of these agents; thus reduction and/or avoidance of tobacco smoking is advisable (Long, 1990).

Alcohol consumption may result in hypotensive episodes in some clients. Whenever possible, the use of alcohol should be avoided.

These agents should not be discontinued abruptly, since severe rebound angina attacks may result (gradual drug withdrawal is recommended).

ment of calcium through the slow channels of the cell membranes of cardiac and smooth muscle cells. In cardiac muscle, this action decreases the force of myocardial contraction; in vascular smooth muscle, it decreases the force of the smooth muscle contraction and, in particular, inhibits the contraction of smooth muscle of the peripheral arterioles. Within the cardiac conduction system, calcium channel blockers decrease the automaticity in the SA node and decrease conduction in the AV node.

At present five calcium channel blockers have been approved by the FDA for the treatment of angina pectoris and hypertension. However, each has properties that make it distinct. Diltiazem is generally restricted to coronary blood vessel dilatation. Nicardipine and nifedipine are potent peripheral vasodilators, but do not affect the cadiac conduction system; this makes them effective as antihypertensive agents and in the treatment of Raynaud's phenomenon. Nimodipine has a greater effect on the cerebral arteries. Verapamil is also effective as an antidysrhythmic, as it prolongs AV conduction time and depresses contraction.

The goals for the administration and client teaching with calcium channel blockers would be for the client's frequency and intensity of the angina attacks to decrease; the blood pressure to be within the normal range; the tolerance for activity to increase; tissue perfusion to be increased, be it cerebral, cardiopulmonary, or peripheral; anxiety to decrease; and that the client would have sufficient understanding of his or her condition and medications for self-administration of medications with safety and accuracy.

# BIBLIOGRAPHY

American Hospital Formulary Service. (1991). AHFS drug information '91. Bethesda, Md: American Society of Hospital Pharmacists, Inc.

An antihypertensive role for nifedipine. (1987). Emerg Med 19(21):176.

Barner HB. (1986). Calcium-entry blockers in cardioplegia. Appl Cardiol 14(1):31.

Beare PG. (1989). Calcium channel blockers: nursing care for hypertension, Crit Care Nurse 9(2):37.

Brown DD. (1987). PSVT: the problem is diagnosis, Patient Care 21(14):26.

Cardin S. (1988). Cardiovascular pharmacology: nursing considerations in the administration of verapamil, J Cardiovascular Nurs 2(2):73.

Dix-Sheldon DK. (1989). Pharmacologic management of myocardial ischemia, J Cardiovascular Nurs 3(4):17.

Ehrenkranz RA et al. (1989). Nifedipine transfer into human milk, J Pediatr 114(3):478.

Fischer RG et al. (1986). Calcium channel blockers, Pediatr Nurs 12(5):379.

Frohlich ED. (1989). Calcium antagonists for initial therapy of hypertension, Heart Lung 18(4):370.

Hasegawa GR. (1988). Nicardipine, nitrendipine, and bepridil: new calcium antagonists for cardiovascular disorders, Am J Hosp Pharm 45(3):686.

Kastrup EK and Olin BR. (1991). Facts and comparisons: drug information. Philadelphia: JB Lippincott Co.

Kedas A et al. (1989). Nursing delivery of sublingual nifedipine, J Cardiovascular Nurs 3(4):31.

Lake CL. (1986). Calcium blockers and vasodilators, Curr Rev Recov Room Nurses 8(7):50.

Lam YWF et al. (1986). Calcium channel blockers and treatment of hypertension, Drug Intell Clin Pharmacol 20(3):187.

Levy DB. (1988). The nifedipine effect, Emergency 20(5):18.

Long JW. (1990). The essential guide to prescription drugs. New York: Harper & Row.

Meltzer AH et al. (1986). Antianginal agents: calcium-entry blockers, Hosp Formul 21(3):299.

Miller CL. (1988). Medications in angina, Focus Crit Care 15(4):23.

Misinski M. (1987). Role of conventional management and alternative therapies in limiting infarct size in acute myocardial infarction, Heart-Lung 16(6):746.

Nagelhout JJ. (1988). AANA Journal Course: advanced scientific concepts. Update for nurse anesthetists—cardiac pharmacology: calcium antagonists, AANA J 56(4):367.

Pierce CH. (1986). Heart drugs: how calcium antagonists interact with cardiac glycosides, Consultant 26(9):82.

Shapiro W. (1989). Calcium channel blockers: update on uses in ischemic heart disease, Consultant 29(8):132.

Shinn AF, ed. (1985). Evaluations of drug interactions. St Louis: The CV Mosby Co.

Stowe HO. (1986). Review of calcium-blockers, Nurse Pract 11(4):57.

United States Pharmacopeia Convention. (1991). Drug information for the health care professional, ed 11. Rockville, Md: The Convention.

Vertes V et al. (1988). Calcium channel blockers as antihypertensive agents, Physician Assist 12(2):15.

Weiner DA. (1988). Calcium channel blockers, Med Clin North Am 72(1):83.

Yusuf S. (1988). The use of beta-adrenergic blocking agents, intravenous nitrates and calcium channel blocking agents following acute myocardial infarction, Chest 93(1):255.

Zatuchni J. (1988). Bradycardia and hypertension after propranolol HCl and verapamil, Heart Lung 14(1):94.

*Chapter*

 *28* Vasodilators and Antihemorrheologic Agents

## CHAPTER OBJECTIVES

*After studying this chapter, you should be able to meet the following objectives and define the key terms.*

1. Identify the three therapeutic objectives for the use of antianginal agents.

2. Compare the effects of nitrates, beta blockers, and calcium blocking agents on the heart.

3. Discuss the mechanism of action, side effects/adverse reactions, significant drug interactions, and dosages for nitrates.

4. Explain the transdermal system for the administration of nitroglycerin.

5. Discuss cyclandelate, isoxsuprine, and nylidrin as agents used in the treatment of peripheral vascular disease.

6. Implement nursing management in the administration of vasodilators.

7. Define the science of hemorrheology.

8. Apply nursing management to the client receiving pentoxifylline.

## KEY TERMS

**angina pectoris,** page 531

**carboxyhemoglobin,** page 531

**classic angina,** page 531

**hemorrheology,** page 537

**nitrates,** page 530

**unstable angina,** page 531

**variant angina,** page 531

## INTRODUCTION

The drugs reviewed in this chapter, vasodilators and antihemorrheologic agents, are used for the treatment of vascular disorders, including peripheral vascular conditions. Vasodilators produce peripheral vasodilation by relaxing smooth muscle in the blood vessel walls, whereas the antihemorrheologic agents improve microcirculatory blood flow to ischemic tissues.

## VASODILATORS

The classic vasodilators are the **nitrates.** Nitrates are effective for treatment of angina pectoris because of their effect on the veins (capacitance blood vessels) and arteries (resistance blood vessels). The pooling of blood in the veins decreases the amount of blood returned to the heart (preload), which reduces left ventricular end-diastolic volume. This decrease in blood return may help reduce the myocardial oxygen demand. Chest pain induced by angina pectoris largely results from an inadequate supply of oxygen to the heart (see box).

---

## TYPES OF ANGINA PECTORIS

**Classic Angina (Stable or Effort)**

Pain usually associated with coronary arteriosclerosis. The attack can be precipitated by exertion or stress (e.g., cold, fear, emotion) and by eating. The pain lasts about 15 minutes and disappears with rest or nitrates.

**Unstable Angina (Crescendo or Preinfarction)**

A progressive form of angina whereby pain occurs more frequently and becomes more severe in time. The attack may appear during rest and may last longer, with less relief with antianginal drugs. These individuals eventually show signs and symptoms of impending myocardial infarction or coronary failure.

**Variant Angina (Prinzmetal's or Vasospastic)**

Pain that may be associated with spasms of the coronary arteries and that usually occurs in the presence of coronary stenosis. The pain often happens during rest without any cause. Its occurrence follows a regular pattern (e.g., it appears at the same time during the night). Dysrhythmias often accompany the attack, and the ECG shows an elevation in the S-T segment during the anginal episode.

---

The miscellaneous vasodilators used for peripheral occlusive arterial disease have generally been very discouraging. Many of the drugs discussed in this section have been awarded the possibly effective rating by the U.S. Food and Drug Administration. Substantial evidence of effectiveness would need to be submitted in order to upgrade this rating to effective.

## Antianginal Drugs

Antianginal drugs are used to treat the pathologic condition known as angina pectoris. The term **angina pectoris** refers to temporary interference with the flow of blood, oxygen, and nutrients to heart muscle, or intermittent myocardial ischemia. Angina is characterized by pain below the sternum. The pain usually occurs with exercise or stress and is relieved by rest (see box). Angina pectoris occurs when the work load on the heart is too great and oxygen delivery is inadequate. Coronary flow is very responsive to oxygen requirements of the heart. Inadequate oxygenation of the heart implies that coronary blood flow is less than the amount actually needed. Therefore angina pectoris is usually associated with myocardial ischemia. When coronary blood flow is inadequate, hypoxia causes an accumulation of pain-producing substances such as lactic acid (anaerobic metabolite) and other chemical irritants such as potassium ions, kinins, and prostaglandins. These products then stimulate the cardiac sensory nerve endings, which transmit impulses to the central nervous system to produce the typical anginal pain response.

Inadequate oxygenation may be caused by coronary atherosclerosis or vasomotor spasm of the coronary vessels. Other causes of anginal pain may be pulmonary hypertension and valvular heart disease. Individuals with severe anemia, even with minimal coronary artery disease, may suffer from anginal attacks because of inadequate oxygen supply. The presence of carbon monoxide hemoglobin (**carboxyhemoglobin**) in smokers, who have reduced amounts of available blood oxygen, is another factor in causing angina pectoris.

Drug therapy of angina pectoris is based on the belief that relaxation of coronary smooth muscle will bring about coronary vasodilation, which in turn will improve blood flow to the heart. However, coronary arteries narrowed by disorders such as sclerosis and calcification cannot respond to any coronary vasodilator.

There are three therapeutic objectives for the use of antianginal agents: (1) to decrease the duration and intensity of pain during an attack; (2) to prophylactically decrease frequency of attacks and improve work capacity even though angina may occur; and (3) to prevent or delay the onset of myocardial infarction.

Although evidence exists that the first objective may be achieved, less evidence exists that the second objective can be attained, and no real proof exists that the third objective is attainable. The ideal antianginal drug would (1) establish a balance between coronary blood flow and the metabolic demands of the heart; (2) have a local rather than a systemic effect (it would act directly on coronary vessels to promote coronary vasodilation with no effects on other organ systems). It would also (3) promote oxygen extraction by the heart from arterial flow; (4) be effective when taken orally, and have sustained action. Finally, the ideal antianginal drug would (5) have absence of tolerance.

Currently, no drug meets these criteria. Drugs presently available provide only temporary relief. Evidence is increasing that the nitrates exert their effect not so much by coronary vasodilation but by lowering blood pressure and decreasing venous return and cardiac work.

See the box on p. 532 for a comparison of the effects of nitrates, beta blockers, and calcium blocking agents.

### Nitrates

The nitrate drug category contains a variety of drug entities and dosage forms, such as amyl nitrite inhalant; erythrityl tetranitrate (Cardilate); isosorbide dinitrate (Isordil, Sorbitrate); nitroglycerin (NTG) sublingual tablet (Nitrostat); NTG extended-release buccal tablet (Nitrogard); NTG lingual aerosol (Nitrolingual); NTG oral, extended-release capsules (Nitro-Bid; NTG parenteral injection (Nitro-Bid, Nitrol); NTG ointment (Nitro-Bid, Nitrostat): NTG transdermal topical systems (Nitrodisc); pentaerythritol tetrani-

## COMPARISON OF EFFECTS OF NITRATES, BETA BLOCKERS, AND CALCIUM BLOCKING AGENTS

| | Nitrates | Beta Blockers | Calcium Blocking Agents |
|---|---|---|---|
| Systolic blood pressure | (−) | (−) | (−) |
| Ventricular volume | (−) | (+) | (−) or (0) |
| Heart rate | (+) | (−) | (−), (+), or (0) |
| Myocardial contractility | (0) | (−) | (−) |
| Coronary blood flow | (+) | (+) or (0) | (+) |
| Coronary vessel resistance | (−) | (+) or (0) | (−) |
| Coronary spasms | (−) | (+) or (0) | (−) |
| Collateral flow of blood | (+) | (0) | (−) |

(−), decreased; (+), increased; (0), no change.

**TABLE 28-1**   Pharmacokinetics of nitrates

| Drug | Onset of action (min) | Duration of action (hr) | Metabolism | Excretion |
|---|---|---|---|---|
| erythrityl tetranitrate | | | | |
|   Oral tablet | 15-30 | Up to 6 | Liver | Kidneys |
|   Sublingual tablet | 5 | 2-3 | | |
| isosorbide dinitrate | | | | |
|   Oral tablet/capsule | 15-40 | 4-6 | Liver | Kidneys |
|   Chewable tablet | 2-5 | 1-2 | | |
|   Extended release | 30 | 12 | | |
|   Sublingual | 2-5 | 1-2 | | |
| nitroglycerin | | | | |
|   Sublingual | 1-3 | ½-1 | Liver | Kidneys |
|   Extended release (buccal) | 3 | 5 | | |
|   Lingual aerosol | 2-4 | — | | |
|   IV infusion | Immediate | Several minutes | | |
|   Ointment | 30 | 4-8 | | |
|   Transdermal | 30 | 8-24 | | |
|   Extended release tablet/capsule | — | 8-12 | | |
| pentaerythritol tetranitrate | | | | |
|   Tablet | 30 | 4-5 | Liver | Kidneys |
|   Extended release tablet and capsule | Slow | 12 | | |

trate tablet (Peritrate); pentaerythritol tetranitrate extended-release capsules (Duotrate), and others.

Nitrates reduce myocardial oxygen demand by causing peripheral vasodilation. They especially dilate venous capacitance and arterial resistance vessels. The arterial dilation results in a more efficient distribution of blood in the myocardium. The antihypertensive effect of nitrates also is a result of peripheral vasodilation.

Amyl nitrite has been used to treat acute angina attacks, but it has been replaced by the other, safer nitrate dosage forms. Although not approved by FDA labeling in the United States, amyl nitrite has been used as an antidote for cyanide poisoning and in cardiac function tests to assess reserve cardiac function. It has also been abused and used as a sexual stimulant or euphoric agent, but it is very toxic and should not be used for these purposes.

Nitrates are used to reduce pain of angina (isosorbide

## NITROGLYCERIN CONTENT DELIVERED IN 24 HOURS

| Dosage Form | mg/24 hr |
|---|---|
| Nitro-Dur 2.5 | 2.5 |
| Nitro-Dur 5 | 5 |
| Nitro-Dur 7.5 | 7.5 |
| Nitro-Dur 10 | 10 |
| Nitrodisc 5 | 5 |
| Nitrodisc 10 | 10 |
| Transderm-Nitro 5 | 5 |
| Transderm-Nitro 10 | 10 |

**TABLE 28-2**   Dosage and administration of nitrates

| Drug | Adults | Children |
|---|---|---|
| erythrityl tetranitrate | *Tablets:* 5-10 mg orally, sublingually, or buccally, three or four times daily. Adjust dosage as necessary, to a maximum of 100 mg/day. | Not established |
| isosorbide dinitrate | *Capsules and tablets:* 5-20 mg orally every 6 hr. Adjust dosage as necessary. (Range is usually 5-40 mg four times daily.)<br>*Chewable tablets:* 5 mg, chewed well and swallowed, every 2 or 3 hr. Adjust dosage as necessary. Hold chewed tablet in mouth 1-2 min before swallowing.<br>*Sublingual tablets:* 2.5-5 mg sublingually or buccally, every 2 or 3 hr as needed.<br>*Extended-release tablets or capsules:* 40-80 mg orally every 8-12 hr. | Not established |
| nitroglycerin | *Sublingual tablet:* 150-600 µg (0.15-0.6 mg) sublingually or buccally, repeated at 5-min intervals if necessary. If relief is not obtained following three tablets (or 15 min), immediately contact physician or transport individual to a hospital. Maximum dose is 10 mg/day.<br>*Extended-release buccal tablet:* 1 mg dissolved bucally every 5 hr during waking hours. Adjust dosage as necessary.<br>*Lingual aerosol:* Apply one or two metered doses on or under tongue. Dose may be repeated at 5-min intervals up to a total of three doses. If relief is not obtained, contact a physician or transport individual to a hospital. Maximum daily dose is 1.2 mg. Each metered dose is equivalent to 400 µg (0.4 mg).<br>*Oral, extended-release capsules:* 2.5, 6.5, or 9 mg orally every 12 hr. Dosage may be increased to every 8 hr, if necessary.<br>*Oral, extended-release tablets:* 1.3, 2.6, or 6.5 mg every 12 hr. Dosage may be increased to every 8 hr if necessary.<br>*Parenteral injection:* Intravenous infusion—initial 5 µg/min increased in increments of 5 µg/min at 3- or 5-min intervals until desired effect is obtained. If no response is seen at 20 µg/min, increase by 10 µg/min and then 20 µg/min. When partial blood pressure response is observed, reduce size of dosage increments and lengthen interval between increases. (This preparation is not for direct injection. Follow manufacturer's instructions carefully.)<br>*Ointment:* Apply 1-2 inches (15-30 mg) to skin every 8 hours and at bedtime. If angina occurs before 8 hr elapse, drug may be applied every 6 hr. Maximum is 5 inches (75 mg) per application.<br>*Transdermal topical system:* Apply a transdermal unit to intact skin every 24 hr. Dosage adjustments are instituted by changing the dose to the next larger dose or by using a combination of the units. Many dosages are available. See the package insert for additional information. | |
| pentaerythritol tetranitrate | *Tablet:* 10-20 mg orally, four times daily. Increase dosage as necessary to a maximum of 160 mg/day.<br>*Extended-release capsules/tablets:* 30-80 mg orally twice daily. Increase dosage as necessary to a maximum of 160 mg/day. | Not established |

dinitrate, nitroglycerin); to prevent angina attacks (nitroglycerin, erythrityl tetranitrate and isosorbide dinitrate); as antihypertensives (nitroglycerin injection); as cardiac load-reducing agents (nitroglycerin); and to treat congestive heart failure associated with myocardial infarction (nitroglycerin).

Pharmacokinetics are listed in Table 28-1. Side effects include dizziness, headaches, nausea or vomiting, agitation, facial flushing, and an increased pulse rate. Adverse reactions are rare or infrequent; they include dry mouth, rash, prolonged headaches, and blurred vision.

Administration of nitrates with alcohol, antihypertensives, or other vasodilators may result in enhanced hypo-

tensive effects. Avoid concurrent use if possible; if not, monitor closely since dosage reductions may be necessary. For dosage and administration, see Table 28-2 and box at left and on p. 535. Pregnancy safety is FDA category C.

▷ *Nursing Management:*
  *Nitrate Therapy*

***Assessment.***   Although it is rare, clients intolerant of one nitrate may show intolerance to other nitrates. Nitroglycerin injection is not considered appropriate for use for patients with cerebral hemorrhage or other head injury because of its tendency to increase cerebrospinal fluid pressure. In addition, caution should be used in administering nitrates to clients with recent myocardial infarction, glaucoma, severe anemia, or hyperthyroidism. Patients with hypovolemia should have it corrected before the administration of nitroglycerin by injection because it may precipitate severe hypotension and shock.

With the administration of nitrates, the client may experience the following nursing diagnoses: altered comfort related to dry mouth, flushing, headache, rash, dizziness, nausea and vomiting; high risk for injury related to syncope, blurred vision; and impaired skin integrity related to the application of topical dosage forms.

*Intervention.* Dosage must be adjusted by the prescriber to needs and tolerance of the individual client. Following long-term or high-dose administration, dosage should be reduced gradually to prevent possible withdrawal rebound angina.

Store stock supply of drug in original container that is tightly closed with tight metal screw cap. Federal regulation requires that the sublingual form of nitroglycerin be dispensed in the original unopened manufacturer's container. Check expiration date on container.

*Intravenous infusion.* Use special nitroglycerin disposable infusion sets provided by manufacturer. They are made of non–polyvinyl chloride plastic to minimize the loss of nitroglycerin. Polyvinyl chloride (PVC) plastic may adsorb up to 40% to 80% of the nitroglycerin from a diluted solution of infusion. Therefore use glass intravenous bottles or manufacturer's administration set provided. Observe aseptic technique during procedure.

The drug is not to be used with a direct intravenous infusion. Dilute with 5% dextrose injection USP or 0.9% sodium chloride injection USP before infusion. Since the concentration and/or volume of the drug varies, carefully follow the dosage instructions of the manufacturer. Be aware that switching from a standard (PVC) set to a special (non-PVC) set is likely to affect the dosage—the PVC set requires a higher dosage, which would be excessive if changed to a non-PVC set. In addition, *do not mix nitroglycerin with other medications.*

To titrate dosage for desired hemodynamic function, monitor blood pressure, heart rate, and pulmonary capillary wedge pressure continuously until the correct dose is obtained. Clients with normal or low capillary wedge pressure are likely to be sensitive to hypotensive effects of intravenous nitroglycerin.

*Ointment.* Take baseline blood pressure and heart rate with the client in a sitting position, after having been at rest for 10 minutes. Repeat the vital signs 1 hour after drug administration and report them to physician. An appropriate dosage produces a 10 mm Hg fall in blood pressure or 10-beat rise in heart rate with the patient in a resting position. Squeeze prescribed dose onto a specially designed dose-measuring applicator supplied with the package. *Avoid use of fingers* to spread ointment. Apply in a thin, uniform layer to premarked 6-square-inch surface on clean, dry, nonhairy

skin area of chest, abdomen, anterior aspect of thigh, or forearm. Rotate sites to prevent inflammation. Also, wash off last application. Do not massage or rub in ointment because rapid absorption will interfere with the drug's sustained action. Last, cover area with a transparent wrap and secure with tape.

If medication is to be terminated, dosage and frequency of application are reduced gradually over a 4- to 6-week period to avoid withdrawal responses (pain or severe myocardial ischemia).

*Education.* Instruct client to avoid alcoholic beverages while taking nitrates because of a shocklike syndrome (flushing, weakness, pallor, hypotension, and syncope) that may occur.

Inform client about the importance of learning to identify stressful situations that precipitate anginal attacks. These include emotional stress, overeating, smoking, temperature extremes, and sudden increase in physical activity. The client should receive support to modify behaviors that precipitate anginal attacks.

When nitrates are used to prevent angina in the buccal, lingual, sublingual, and chewable oral forms, instruct the client to take the drug 5 to 10 minutes before the occurrence of the anticipated stressor.

Dizziness, lightheadedness, and slight headache may occur. Have client sit and rest until symptoms pass. However, instruct client to report to physician if blurring of vision, dry mouth, or severe headaches occur. These are signs of overdosage that require immediate attention.

Inform client about the inactivation of nitroglycerin by exposure to air, heat, and moisture. It is generally recommended that unused tablets be discarded 6 months after the bottle is opened. The length of time of potency appears to vary with the manufacturer. Read drug insert and check expiration date. After the bottle is opened, do not leave cotton or package insert in container; these articles may absorb some of the drug, which results in less potent tablets.

Be sure hands are dry, since moisture hastens deterioration of the drug. Nitroglycerin is affected by cold and heat. Do not store in refrigerator or in bathroom medicine cabinet. Also, the drug should not be carried close to the body; carry it in jacket pocket or handbag.

Usually potency of drug is indicated by a burning or stinging sensation under the tongue. However, the newer, more stable preparations may not produce this effect.

*Sublingual tablets.* Instruct the client to sit or lie down and take the medication on the first indication of an oncoming anginal attack. This prevents postural hypotension that results from the drug. The signs and symptoms include dizziness, syncope, and weakness.

Explain to the client that the tablet should be placed under the tongue or in the buccal pouch and allowed to dissolve; tablet is not to be swallowed. Avoid eating, drinking, smoking while the drug dissolves.

Dosage may be repeated at 5-minute intervals for three doses if necessary. If pain is not relieved in 15 minutes, the physician should be notified. For a hospitalized individual, the physician usually prescribes that a specific number of tablets (about 25) be placed at the bedside in an appropriate container and properly labeled for the client's use.

Instruct client to keep a record of frequency of anginal attacks, precipitating factors, number of tablets used, and occurrence of side effects.

Warn client of transient headaches, which usually last 5 to 20 minutes following sublingual administration. Report to physician if the headache persists. Headache occurrences may disappear within several days to weeks if the drug is continued. The headache may be relieved by aspirin or acetaminophen or a temporary reduction of the nitrate dosage.

*Buccal extended-release tablets.* Instruct the client to place the tablet between the upper lip and gum to dissolve, above the incisors if food or drink is to be taken within 3 to 5 hours. Caution against using at bedtime since aspiration is a risk. The tablet may be replaced if it is accidentally swallowed.

*Chewable tablets.* Instruct the client to chew the tablet well and to hold it in the mouth for 2 minutes before swallowing.

*Oral sustained-release tablets or capsules.* Administer on an empty stomach (1 hour before or 2 hours after meals) with a full glass of water and swallow medication whole. Alert the client to notify the physician if undigested tablets are found in stools.

*Lingual aerosol.* When administering, do not shake the can. Hold the can vertically and spray it onto or under the client's tongue. Instruct the client not to inhale the spray and not to swallow immediately.

*Ointment.* Instruct the client in the application of ointment as described previously. Have the client store nitroglycerin ointment in a cool place and in the original container with the tube tightly capped.

Instruct the client not to change dosage or medication without consulting the physician and to report to the physician regularly for cardiac function monitoring.

*Transdermal system.* Remove the old system and apply the new one at the same time each day. The system should be applied to clean, dry, and hairless skin areas of the chest, shoulder, or inside of the upper arm. Avoid skin folds, areas distal to the knee or elbow, and irritated or excessively scarred areas. Rotate application sites to prevent irritation. Apply a new system if the current one becomes loosened. Do not trim the units, since this will alter the dosage. (See box.)

*Evaluation.* Tolerance has been reported and is manifested by a lack of pain relief following the usual dose. Nitrates may be discontinued for several days until tolerance is lost and then the drug is reinstated.

The client should be able to identify events that may precipitate attacks of angina and be able to safely and accurately self-administer nitrates to reduce the number and severity of those episodes.

## Drugs for Peripheral Occlusive Arterial Disease

The use of vasodilators in chronic occlusive arterial disease or peripheral vascular disease has been discouraging. Adrenergic blocking agents are frequently used to treat peripheral vascular diseases. Because several drugs that are not adrenergic blocking agents have had some success in treating these disorders, they are also included. The FDA rating for these drugs is only possibly effective for the treatment of peripheral vascular diseases.

### cyclandelate (Cyclospasmol)

Cyclandelate produces a direct relaxation effect on the smooth muscles of peripheral arterial walls. It increases

---

### TRANSDERMAL NITROGLYCERIN SYSTEMS

Since the transdermal nitroglycerin delivery systems are quite popular, the nurse should be familiar with several issues and concerns associated with these products. Three systems are currently available, and the actual amount of nitroglycerin delivered by each system can vary, depending on the system and the individual client's skin absorption of the nitroglycerin.

Each system has a different mechanism of drug delivery. For example, Nitrodisc contains nitroglycerin mixed in a solid polymer similar to silicone. The drug is absorbed through the skin from this polymer, which also contains a cosolvent to enhance skin penetration.

Nitro-Dur contains a gel-like matrix surrounded by fluid. Nitroglycerin moves from the matrix to the fluid to the skin.

Transderm-Nitro contains a semipermeable membrane between the drug supply and the skin. The membrane is actually the controlling factor for the drug delivery. (See Figure 28-1.)

Drug absorption in all systems is by passive diffusion and is based on processes relating to heat transfer (or Fick's law of diffusion).

The three systems are not interchangeable, since the patch size, nitroglycerin content, and average amount of nitroglycerin delivered in 24 hours can differ (see box on p. 532). Although many individuals are reportedly controlled or have responded to this dosage form, other clients do not achieve adequate therapeutic blood levels or a clinically significant therapeutic response. Some researchers believe maintaining stable nitroglycerin serum levels over 24 hours is not always desirable, since tolerance to the drug and the need to increase dosages would occur. Parker (1988) has suggested that intermittent use of transdermal products, such as application for 12 to 16 hours and then removal for the night, would result in prolonged clinical results without the development of significant drug tolerance.

Research and studies are ongoing in this area, and manufacturers are continuing their search for better methods of delivering their drug products.

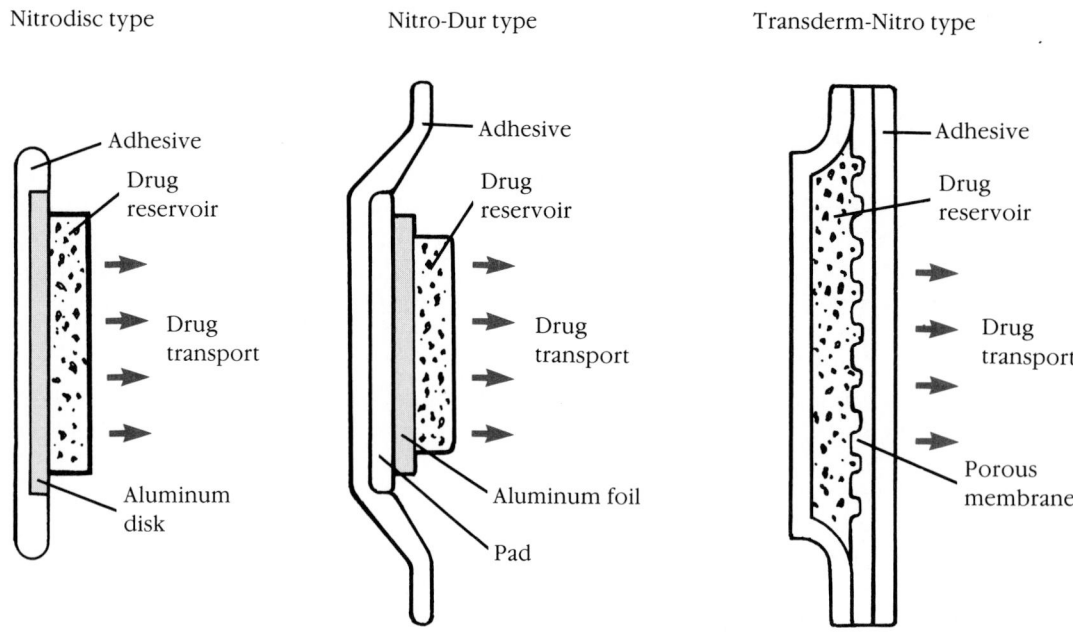

**FIGURE 28-1** Transdermal systems.

peripheral circulation of the extremities and digits and elevates skin temperature of the extremities.

The drug possibly may be effective for treatment of peripheral vascular disease or cerebrovascular insufficiency. It is indicated as adjunctive therapy in Raynaud's disease, thrombophlebitis, intermittent claudication, and arteriosclerosis obliterans. Cyclandelate is well absorbed orally. Peak effect after single dose occurs within 1½ hours. Therapeutic improvement occurs slowly, over a period of several weeks. Side effects include gas, heartburn, nausea or abdominal pain; dizziness; facial flushing; headaches; rapid heart rate; paresthesia of fingers, toes, or face; increased weakness; and unusual sweating. If these effects continue, increase, or disturb the client, inform the physician. No significant drug interactions have been reported.

Adult dose is 1.2 to 1.6 g orally in divided doses, given before meals and at bedtime. When clinical effects are noted, reduce dosage by 200 mg amounts until a maintenance dose of 400 to 800 mg orally, in two to four divided doses, is achieved. Children's dosage is not established. Pregnancy safety has not been established.

▷ **Nursing Management:**
**Cyclandelate Therapy**

*Assessment.* Before administration of cyclandelate, it should be ascertained that client does not have severe cerebrovascular disease and has not recently had a myocardial infarction or severe coronary artery disease. Because it has a greater vasodilating effect on peripheral vessels than those of coronary or cerebral areas, cyclandelate may reduce blood flow and so increase ischemia in those areas. With the administration of cyclandelate, the client should be assessed for the potential occurrence of the following nursing diag-

noses: altered comfort related to gastrointestinal effects such as belching, heartburn, nausea; also, effect of flushing of face, headache, and tingling of fingers and toes; and high risk for injury related to dizziness and weakness.

*Intervention.* Administer with milk, food, or antacids to prevent gastrointestinal distress.

*Education.* Alert the client that symptoms such as flushing of the face, dizziness, weakness, headache, and rapid heart rate usually disappear after a few weeks of taking the medication. Instruct the client to move slowly upright from a sitting or lying position because of the drug's hypotensive effects.

Advise clients to avoid smoking, since nicotine's vasoconstrictive properties are counterproductive to the use of cyclandelate.

*Evaluation.* Monitor blood pressure in lying, sitting, and standing positions to detect hypotension. Monitor peripheral pulses during drug administration to evaluate its effectiveness.

**isoxsuprine hydrochloride (Vasodilan, Vasoprine)**

Isoxsuprine produces a direct relaxation effect on the smooth muscles of peripheral arterial walls located within skeletal muscle, It has little effect on cutaneous flow of blood. It also stimulates the heart and relaxes the uterus. Heart rate and peripheral vascular resistance decrease while cardiac output increases. Isoxsuprine is possibly effective for the treatment of peripheral vascular disease or cerebrovascular insufficiency and may relieve symptoms of Raynaud's disease, arteriosclerosis obliterans, and thromboangitis obliterans (Buerger's disease).

Isoxsuprine is well absorbed from the gastrointestinal tract and has an onset of action of 10 minutes when given intravenously or 1 hour when administered orally. In neonates, its duration of action is from 1.5 to 3 hours for near-term babies to 6 to 8 hours for less mature infants. It is partially metabolized in the blood and excreted via the kidneys. Side effects include nausea or vomiting, or rarely, chest pain, rash and respiratory difficulties. No significant drug interactions are reported with isoxsuprine. It is administered in 10- to 20-mg tablets orally, three or four times a day. Pregnancy safety has not been established.

For nursing management, see discussion under cyclandelate.

### nylidrin hydrochloride (Arlidin, PMS Nylidrin ✲)

Nylidrin may have both a direct effect and a beta adrenergic stimulation effect on skeletal arteries and arterioles, resulting in vasodilation.

Nylidrin is possibly effective for the treatment of peripheral vascular disease or cerebrovascular insufficiency. It is also used for treatment of frostbite, thrombophlebitis, diabetic vascular disease, night leg cramps, Raynaud's disease, arteriosclerosis obliterans, thromboangiitis obliterans, and circulatory problems of the inner ear.

Nylidrin has an onset of action in 10 minutes and reaches a peak effect within 30 minutes. Its action lasts 2 hours. Side effects include facial flushing, complaints of feeling chilly, headache, nausea and vomiting, anxiety and tremors. Notify the physician if the following adverse reactions occur: dizziness; a rapid, irregular heart rate; and increased weakness. No significant drug interactions have been reported with nylidrin. Adult dosage is 3 to 12 mg orally, 3 or 4 times daily. Pregnancy safety has not been established.

Time doses so that the last dose is not at bedtime. On occasion, palpitations may cause insomnia. See discussion of cyclandelate for further nursing considerations.

### papaverine hydrochloride (Cerebid, Pavabid)

Papaverine is an old drug that was exempted from the FDA's review on drug effectiveness. However, the advisory committee of the FDA, the Peripheral and Central Nervous System Drug Review Committee, concluded after reviewing studies and open hearings that papaverine has vasodilator effects but was not proved to be effective for its claimed indications, namely, smooth muscle relaxation.

If information is required on this drug, please see a package insert or recent reference book.

### Other Vasodilating Agents

Sodium nitroprusside, hydralazine, and minoxidil are other potent vasodilators. They exhibit their effects primarily by direct relaxation of vascular smooth muscle, particularly the arteries and arterioles. Hydralazine and minoxidil have little effect on veins. These three agents are used primarily for their hypotensive effects and are discussed in detail in Chapter 26.

## HEMORRHEOLOGY

**Hemorrheology** is a science that deals with the deformation and flow properties of blood under physiologic and pathophysiologic conditions. Because arteriosclerosis reduces blood flow to tissues distal to the obstruction, blood viscosity is elevated, thereby diminishing the flow of blood still further. In addition, the impaired blood flow at the microcirculatory level affects the normal capacity of the red blood cells to flex as they enter the narrowed capillary lumen, which has a mean diameter smaller than the erythrocytes. A major function of red blood cells is to transport hemoglobin that carries oxygen, which during the metabolic process is converted to energy for muscle movement such as walking. Accordingly, the decreased flexibility of the red blood cells and the elevated blood viscosity are responsible for diminishing tissue oxygenation. Hence, during exercise the demand for an increase in blood flow and tissue oxygenation may result in claudication, thereby limiting the distance a person can walk.

Intermittent claudication is a syndrome that results from an insufficient blood supply to skeletal muscles in the legs. Reduced microcirculatory blood flow causes ischemia and pain. This syndrome is a common complication of atherosclerosis and is characteristic of Buerger's disease. While walking, these individuals have first pain, and then cramps and weakness in muscles.

### Antihemorrheologic Agent
### pentoxifylline (Trental)

Pentoxifylline represents an important concept in the therapy of peripheral vascular disorders because the ability of vasodilators to improve blood flow by dilation of rigid, arteriosclerotic blood vessels is somewhat limited. Further, because capillary walls lack smooth muscle, dilation by this group of drugs is often unlikely to occur.

Pentoxifylline improves hemorrheologic disorders in the microcirculation, which involves the flow of blood through the fine vessels (arterioles, capillaries, and venules). Although the mechanism of action of pentoxifylline is not completely clear, current evidence shows that the drug possesses several properties to improve microcirculatory blood flow to ischemic tissues:

1. It restores red blood cell flexibility, probably by its inhibition of phosphodiesterase, which results in an increase in cyclic AMP in red blood cells.
2. It lowers blood viscosity by decreasing fibrinogen concentrations and inhibiting aggregation of red blood cells and platelets.

The result is increased microcirculatory blood flow and oxygenation of tissues.

Pentoxifylline is indicated as an adjunct to surgery for

the treatment of peripheral vascular disease, the intermittent claudication caused by occlusive arterial disease of the limbs.

It is administered orally and on absorption is bound to the erthyrocyte membranes. It has a half-life of 0.4 to 0.8 hours for the primary drug, 1 to 1.6 hours for the metabolites. Peak concentration in the blood occurs in 2 to 4 hours, and the onset of action with chronic dosing is between 2 and 4 weeks. It is metabolized by red blood cells and in the liver and is excreted via the kidneys and feces.

The less frequent side effects reported are dizziness, headaches, abdominal distress, nausea, and vomiting. Rare adverse reactions are chest pain and an irregular heart rate. With an overdose the client experiences increased sedation, flushing of skin, feeling of faintness, increased excitability, or convulsions. No significant drug interactions have been reported to date with this drug.

For adult dosage give 400 mg orally three times daily with meals. If undesirable side effects occur, such as gastrointestinal upset or CNS disturbances, the dosage should be decreased to 400 mg twice daily. Pregnancy safety for pentoxifylline has been established as FDA category C.

▷ **Nursing Management: Pentoxifylline Therapy**

**Assessment.** Since pentoxifylline is a xanthine derivative, do not administer to clients with an intolerance to other xanthine derivatives such as caffeine, theophylline, or theobromine. With the administration of pentoxifylline, the client may be at risk for altered comfort related to gastrointestinal effects such as nausea, vomiting, and abdominal cramping; CNS effects, dizziness, drowsiness and headache; and palpitations and chest pain.

**Intervention.** Administer with food, milk, or antacids to decrease gastrointestinal distress. If gastrointestinal side effects persist, notify the physician to consider a reduction in the dosage.

**Education.** Instruct client to swallow extended-release tablets whole without crushing or chewing. Instruct the client that improvement in the clinical status may not occur before 8 weeks of therapy and that it is essential for the medication to be taken as prescribed until discontinued by the physician.

Advise smoking cessation since nicotine constricts the blood vessels and defeats the purpose of the medication. The client should receive support in smoking avoidance through group or individual counseling.

**Evaluation.** Monitor blood pressure periodically in clients receiving concurrent antihypertensive therapy. Small decreases in blood pressure have been noted in clients receiving pentoxifylline alone, so a reduction of the hypotensive agent might be indicated.

Monitor the client with peripheral vascular disease for an improvement in walking distance and duration. Monitor pulses, color, and temperature of affected extremities. Assess the client with cerebrovascular disease for memory loss, disorientation, motor impairment, dizziness, and frequency of transient ischemic attacks.

## SUMMARY

Vasodilators and antihemorrheologics are both used in the treatment of vascular disorders. Vasodilators produce vasodilation by relaxing smooth muscle in the blood vessel walls, whereas antihemorrheologic agents improve microcirculatory blood flow to ischemic tissues by lowering blood viscosity and increasing cyclic AMP in red blood cells. Vasodilators have been more effective in the treatment of angina, intermittent myocardial ischemia, than they have been for peripheral vascular disease.

The goals of therapy with nitrates, the classic antianginal agents, are to decrease the duration and intensity of pain during an attack, decrease the frequency of attacks, and improve work capacity even though angina may occur. Nursing management of the client taking nitrates is to assist, through medication administration and evaluation, in the determination of the appropriate dosages for the client based on symptom control. The nurse also prepares the client for safe and accurate self-administration of nitrates.

Chronic occlusive arterial disease has been less successfully treated with vasodilating agents. The FDA has indicated that vasodilators are only possibly effective in the treatment of peripheral vascular disease because dilation of rigid, arteriosclerotic blood vessels is limited and capillaries lack smooth muscle. The antihemorrheologic agent, pentoxifylline, increases microcirculatory blood flow and thereby oxygenation of the tissues. It is a valuable new adjunct in the treatment of occlusive arterial disease of the limbs, such as Buerger's disease.

## BIBLIOGRAPHY

Abrams J. (1988). Nitrates, Med Clin North Am 72(1):1.

American Hospital Formulary Service. (1991). AHFS drug information '91. Bethesda, Md: American Society of Hospital Pharmacists, Inc.

Ashby D. (1988). Vasoactive drugs in the PACU, J Post Anesth Nurs 3(3):196.

Bailie GR et al. (1988). Patient's knowledge of sublingual glyceryl trinitrate, British Med J 297(6640):32.

Baker DE et al. (1985). Pentoxifylline: a new agent for intermittent claudication, Drug Intell Clin Pharm 19(5):345.

Bartz C. (1988). Pharmacologic augmentation of cardiac output following cardiac arrest, Crit Care Nurse Q 10(4):43.

Bernhard R. (1988). Heart failure: can earlier diagnosis and vasodilators boost survival? Emerg Med 20(5):2.

Coffman JD. (1988). New drug therapy for peripheral vascular disease, Med Clin North Am 72(1):259.

Cooke DH. (1988). When angina destabilizes, Emerg Med 20(9):142.

Conant CC. (1988). Plasma nitroglycerin levels, blood pressure and apical heart rate variations to site of application of nitroglycerin ointment, Nurse Pract 13(10):56.

Deans KW et al. (1986). Nitrates in the treatment of coronary artery disease, J Cardiovasc Nurs 1(1):81.

Doyle JE. (1986). Treatment modalities in peripheral vascular disease, Nurs Clin North Am 21(2):241.

Eberts MA. (1986). Advances of pharmacologic management of angina pectoris, J Cardiovasc Nurs 1(1):15.

Elizardi DJ. (1988). Angina pectoris: special considerations in treating elderly patients, Consultant 28(1):115.

Gunner RM. (1988). Beta blockers and nitrates in myocardial infarction, Patient Care 22(4):88.

Hancock BG et al. (1988). The pharmacologic management of shock, Crit Care Nurse Q 11(1):19.

Kastrup EK and Olin BR. (1991). Facts and comparisons, drug information. Philadelphia: JB Lippincott Co.

Kelleher RM. (1989). Cardiac drugs: new inotropes, Crit Care Nurs Clin North Am 1(2):391.

Manzo M. (1988). Newer uses for nitroglycerin, Nursing 18(4):124.

Miller CL. (1988). Medications in angina, Focus Crit Care 15(4):23.

Miller K. (1986). Nitroglycerin, Emergency 18(7):14.

Parker JO. (1988). Pharmacologic treatment of angina: nitrate tolerance, Hosp Pract 23(11):63.

Pepper GA. (1985). New drug for intermittent claudication . . . pentoxifylline (Trental), Nurse Pract 10(5):54.

Poirer T. (1988). An evaluation of patients' subjective responses to two transdermal nitroglycerin delivery systems, Hosp Formul 23(9):739.

Riegel B et al. (1988). Effect of nitroglycerin ointment placement on the severity of headache and flushing in patients with cardiac disease, Heart Lung 17(4):426.

Todd B. (1986). Transdermal nitroglycerin ointment and patches, Geriatr Nurs 7(3):152.

United States Pharmacopeial Convention. (1991). Drug information for the health care professional, ed 11, Rockville, Md: The Convention.

Yusuf S. (1988). The use of beta-adrenergic blocking agents, intravenous nitrates and calcium channel blocking agents following acute myocardial infarction, Chest 93(1):255.

*Unit 7*

# Drugs Affecting the Blood

# 29 Overview of the Blood

## CHAPTER OBJECTIVES

*After studying this chapter, you should be able to meet the following objectives and define the key terms.*

1. Describe the functions of blood in the body.

2. List the three types of blood cells and their function.

3. Compare and contrast the five types of white blood cells.

4. Describe the role of platelets in blood clotting in the body.

5. Name the three major blood proteins and their function.

## KEY TERMS

## INTRODUCTION

Blood is the major transport system in the body. It is also vitally important for the proper functioning and regulation of a human body. Pumped by the heart, blood carries nutrients and oxygen from the digestive and respiratory systems to cells throughout the entire body. In addition, it picks up waste products from body cells and delivers them to the proper system for excretion, usually the liver, kidneys, and lungs. Hormones, enzymes, buffers, and many other biochemical substances are also transported by the blood from one site in the body to the receptors or target cells.

Blood also helps regulate body heat by absorbing and transporting heat from the body core where it can be more easily dispersed.

## BLOOD VOLUME

Blood is composed of billions of cells and a fluid portion called **plasma.** While blood volume can vary from person to person, the average blood volume in a normal adult is approximately 5000 ml (5 L). Of this volume, 3000 ml is usually plasma, and the remainder is red blood cells.

**Hematocrit** is the percent of cells in the blood, or the blood viscosity. For example, if a person has a hematocrit of 40, then 40% of the blood volume is cells, with the remainder being plasma. Hematocrit is measured by a laboratory test performed on a blood sample. The higher the hematocrit, the greater the blood viscosity. For example, persons with polycythemia may have a hematocrit of 60 or 70, because of an excessive number of red blood corpuscles. Increased blood viscosity can retard blood flow through blood vessels, resulting in headaches, fatigue, weakness, dyspnea, and perhaps an enlarged spleen and increased basal metabolism.

## BLOOD COMPOSITION

Blood is composed of three types of blood cells: (1) red blood cells, or **erythrocytes,** which transport oxygen and carbon dioxide; (2) **leukocytes,** or white blood cells, which defend the body against bacteria and infections; and (3) **platelets,** or **thrombocytes,** which are necessary for blood coagulation. Proteins such as serum albumin, globulins, and fibrinogen are also present in the blood.

Plasma may contain thousands of other substances, such as glucose, electrolytes, vitamins, hormones, and waste products. This discussion on blood, however, is limited to blood cells, blood proteins, and blood groups, or types.

### Blood Cells

*Red blood cells.* Red blood cells (RBCs, erythrocytes) are small and disk shaped. They are the cells present in the largest quantities in the bloodstream. Their life span is approximately 120 days. The major function of red blood cells is to carry **hemogloblin** within the cell. Each hemogloblin molecule contains four iron atoms, which combine with four oxygen molecules to transport oxygen from the lungs to the tissues. Hemoglobin can also combine with carbon dioxide and carry it from the cells to the lungs for excretion. It also serves as an acid-base buffering system in whole blood.

After birth, red blood cells are produced by the bone marrow. They are manufactured by most bones in early life, but after 20 years of age most red blood cells are produced

in the bone marrow of the vertebrae, sternum, ribs, and ilia.

Males have more hemoglobin in their blood than females do. Generally, most normal men have between 14 and 16 g/dl, while women have a range of 12 to 14 g/dl. A person with a hemoglobin below 10 is usually diagnosed as having **anemia.** Anemias are classified according to both the size and the number of functional red blood cells in the blood.

Red blood cells are rapidly formed and destroyed in the body. It has been estimated that over 100 million red blood cells are produced every minute during adulthood. The normal healthy adult has between 4.5 and 5.5 million cells/mm$^3$ of blood. The body balances production versus destruction of these cells to maintain a relatively constant body level of red blood cells. The exact body mechanism for this is unknown.

It is known that the rate of red blood cell production can be increased if a considerable decrease in red blood cells occurs or tissue hypoxia develops. Then the kidneys will be stimulated to increase secretion of **erythropoietin,** a hormone. Erythropoietin increases red cell production by stimulating the bone marrow. With maximum bone marrow stimulation, red blood cell production can be increased nearly seven times over normal.

The bone marrow needs adequate supplies of vitamin $B_{12}$, iron, and other substances to make new red blood cells. A deficiency in absorption of vitamin $B_{12}$ from the gastric tract, caused by a lack of intrinsic factor (see Chapter 40), can lead to pernicious anemia.

Anemias can also be induced by increased red cell destruction, such as occurs in infections and cancer (malignancies) or from bone marrow suppression caused by radiation therapy and many cancer chemotherapeutic agents. (See box on p. 544 for a selected list of drugs that cause bone marrow depression.)

*Leukocytes.* There are five types of leukocytes (white blood cells) found in the blood. They are classified according to the presence or absence of granules in the cell cytoplasm. The granular leukocytes are neutrophils, eosinophils, and basophils, while the nongranular leukocytes are lymphocytes and monocytes. The granular leukocytes have two or more nuclear lobes, so they are referred to as polymorphonuclear leukocytes or "polys."

Blood in the normal person usually contains between 5000 and 9000 leukocytes per cubic milliliter. (See box on p. 544 for approximate percentages for each type.) A differential count may be ordered by the physician to aid in diagnosis. For example, in acute appendicitis, the percentage of neutrophils increases, as does the total leukocyte count.

Leukocytes are produced primarily in the bone marrow. Lymphocytes are produced mainly in lymph tissues and organs, such as the spleen, thymus, tonsils, and various other lymphoid tissue in the bone marrow, gastrointestinal tract, and elsewhere.

Several terms are important to understand. **Leukopenia** refers to a decrease in the number of leukocytes present,

## DRUGS THAT CAUSE BONE MARROW DEPRESSION

amphotericin B, systemic (Fungizone)
antithyroid medications
azathioprine (Imuran)
busulfan (Myleran)
carmustine (BCNU; BiCNU)
chlorambucil (Leukeran)
chloramphenicol (Chloromycetin)
cisplatin (Platinol, Platinol-AQ ♣)
colchicine
cyclophosphamide (Cytoxan, Procytox ♣)
cytarabine (Ara-C, Cytosar ♣)
dacarbazine (DTIC ♣, DTIC-Dome)
dactinomycin (Actinomycin-D, Cosmegen)
daunorubicin (Cerubidine)
doxorubicin (Adriamycin RDF)
etoposide (VePesid, VP-16)
floxuridine (FUDR)
flucytosine (Ancobon, 5-FC, Ancotil ♣)
fluorouracil, systemic (5-FU, Adrucil)
hydroxyurea (Hydrea)
interferon (Roferon-A, Intron A)
lomustine (CCNU, CeeNU)
mechlorethamine, systemic (Mustargen, nitrogen mustard)
melphalan (Alkeran, L-PAM)
mercaptopurine (Purinethol)
methotrexate (Mexate)
mitomycin (Mutamycin)
pentamidine (Pentam)
plicamycin (Mithracin, mithramycin)
procarbazine (Matulane, Natulan ♣)
sodium iodide I 131 (Iodotope)
sodium phosphate P 32
streptozocin (Zanosar)
thioguanine (Lanvis ♣)
thiotepa
uracil mustard
vinblastine (Velban, Velbe ♣)
vincristine (Oncovin)
zidovudine (Retrovir)

## DIFFERENTIAL NORMAL LEUKOCYTE COUNT

| | |
|---|---|
| Neutrophils, polymorphonuclear | 62% |
| Eosinophils, polymorphonuclear | 2.3% |
| Basophils, polymorphonuclear | 0.4% |
| Monocytes | 5.3% |
| Lymphocytes | 30% |

Data from Guyton, AC: Textbook of medical physiology, ed 7, Philadelphia, 1986, WB Saunders Co.

The life span of granulocytes is estimated to be 4 to 8 hours in the bloodstream and 3 to 5 days in body tissues. If involved in ingestion of invading organisms, this life span can be reduced to only a few hours, because during this process they are also destroyed. Monocytes also have a short life span in blood, but in the body tissues, they can live for months or even years if not destroyed by phagocytosis. Monocytes in the tissues often increase in size to become tissue macrophages, so they often provide a first line of defense against tissue infections.

**Platelets.** Platelets (thrombocytes) are small, round, or oval, colorless cells produced by the bone marrow. They have a life span of 5 to 8 days. A normal platelet level in the blood is between 150,000 and 350,000/mm³.

Platelets are key substances for blood clotting in the body. If a blood vessel is injured and blood is escaping, platelets will quickly congregate at the site and clump together to form a plug to stop the bleeding. If the wound is large, platelets will set off a series of chemical reactions within the body to form a clot and seal the injury. (See Chapter 30 for detailed information on the clotting mechanisms.)

Persons with a low quantity of platelets have **thrombocytopenia.** Such persons tend to bleed, and their skin usually displays small purple spots, hence the name thrombocytopenia purpura. Bleeding problems usually do not occur until the platelets are below 50,000/mm³. Thrombocytopenia is often induced by irradiation injury to the bone marrow or from aplasia of the bone marrow induced by specific drugs.

while **leukocytosis** is an increased number of leukocytes.

Neutrophils, monocytes, lymphocytes, and basophils are very mobile. They can leave the capillaries and migrate to organisms or foreign particles that have entered the body. The neutrophils and monocytes will ingest and destroy the invaders through a process known as **phagocytosis.** Lymphocytes defend the body against bacteria, fungus, and viruses by forming B-lymphocytes or T-lymphocytes. (See Chapter 64 for an overview of the immune system.)

Eosinophils are considered weak phagocytes and have limited mobility. An increased level is usually seen with allergic reactions or a cell injury caused by parasites (e.g., hookworm).

## Blood Proteins

The blood contains three major proteins: **albumin, globulins,** and **fibrinogen.** Albumin is responsible for the osmotic pressure gradient produced at the capillary membrane. This prevents plasma fluid from leaving the capillaries to enter the interstitial spaces.

Globulins are divided into alpha, beta, and gamma globulins. Gamma globulin and perhaps beta globulin (to a lesser extent) help to protect the body against infections. Gamma globulin is involved with humoral immunity.

Alpha and beta globulins are also believed to perform other functions, such as transportation of certain substances in the blood by reversibly combining with them. They may also be a substrate to form other substances.

Fibrinogen is necessary for coagulation.

# COAGULATION

## Hemostatic Mechanism

**Hemostasis** is a process that spontaneously stops blood loss from damaged blood vessels. Blood is normally fluid while circulating in the vessels, but with vessel injury, it rapidly clots at the site of injury.

After any injury to a blood vessel, hemostasis is achieved by three sequential steps: (1) blood vessels constrict to retard blood flow from the injured area, (2) platelet plugs form to temporarily seal the leaking small arteries and veins, and (3) blood coagulates to plug openings within the damaged vessels and wounds to prevent further bleeding.

*Blood vessel constriction.* Immediately after a blood vessel is injured, vascular constriction occurs as a reflex response. This response instantly slows the flow of blood from the ruptured vessel.

*Platelet plug formation.* Following injury to a blood vessel, interruption of the continuity of its endothelial lining exposes the collagen (a fibrous protein) in the underlying connective tissue. Immediately, platelets adhere to the exposed collagen to form a dense aggregate, a process known as platelet adhesion. This attachment triggers the release of adenosine diphosphate (ADP), which causes the outer surface of the platelets to become extremely sticky so that other adjacent platelets adhere to one another at the damaged site (platelet aggregation). This process eventually forms the platelet plug. Because this plug is relatively unstable, it can stop bleeding quickly as long as the damage to the vessel is minute. However, for long-term effectiveness, the platelet plus must be reinforced with fibrin. This involves a chemical mechanism called blood coagulation.

*Blood coagulation.* Blood coagulation is the final stage of a complex series of events in hemostasis. The process ultimately results in the formation of a stable fibrin clot, which is composed of a meshwork of fibrin threads that entraps platelets, blood cells, and plasma. Thus the physical formation of a blood clot or thrombus plays a key role in hemostasis by permanently closing the hole in the injured vessel to prevent further bleeding.

The chemical events in the blood coagulation mechanism involve two distinct pathways: the intrinsic pathway and the extrinsic pathway.

*Intrinsic pathway.* Because all the chemical substances involved in coagulation are normally found in the circulating blood, this pathway is referred to as the intrinsic system of coagulation. In this pathway, activation of specific blood coagulation factors is initiated by injury to the endothelial lining of the blood vessel wall. When blood contacts the exposed underlying collagen, this activates the Hageman factor (factor XII) by enzymatically converting it to the active form (factor XIIa). The simultaneous damage of

**TABLE 29-1**   Blood coagulation factors and synonyms

| Factor | Name or synonym |
| --- | --- |
| I | Fibrinogen |
| II | Prothrombin |
| III | Tissue thromboplastin |
| IV | Calcium |
| V | Proaccelerin (labile factor, accelerator globulin) |
| VII | Proconvertin (stable factor, serum prothrombin conversion accelerator [SPCA]) |
| VIII | Antihemophilic factor (AHF) |
| IX | Plasma thromboplastin component, Christmas factor |
| X | Stuart-Power factor |
| XI | Plasma thromboplastin antecedent (PTA) |
| XII | Hageman factor |
| XIII | Fibrin stabilizing factor |

platelets also causes the release of platelet phospholipid (platelet factor 3), which is required later in the coagulation process. Factor XIIa then activates factor XI to XIa. The reaction of factor XIa with factor IX requires calcium ions to form activated factor IX. In the presence of calcium ions and platelet phospholipid, factor IXa interacts with factor VIII and thrombin to form a complex. This combination then speeds up the activation of factor X. Factor Xa combines with factor V, calcium ions, and platelet phospholipid to form a complex known as the prothrombin activator (factor IIa). Factor IIa initiates the cleavage of prothrombin to form thrombin, which then enzymatically converts fibrinogen into fibrin, forming an unstable clot. The final step involves the action of factor XIII (a fibrin-stabilizing factor), thrombin, and calcium ions, which catalyze the formation of a stronger, stable fibrin clot. Figure 29-1 summarizes the main events of the intrinsic pathway.

*Extrinsic pathway.* The extrinsic pathway is activated by trauma to the vascular wall or to the tissues outside the blood vessels. In this pathway, clotting occurs when products of tissue damage gain access to the blood. The tissue factor thromboplastin is released and becomes part of a complex with factor VII and calcium ions. This combination of components activates factor X, which is the step at which the extrinsic pathway converges with the intrinsic pathway; coagulation then continues through a common route with the resultant formation of a final stable clot. (See Figure 29-1 for the extrinsic pathway and Table 29-1 for a listing of blood coagulation factors.)

The final pathway common to both the intrinsic and the extrinsic coagulation systems begins with the activation of factor X and ends in the formation of fibrin. Both systems function simultaneously in the body. The lack of a normal factor in either system will usually result in a blood disorder.

## Blood Coagulation Abnormalities

Diseases associated with abnormal clotting vessels cause many deaths. It is estimated that over a million persons

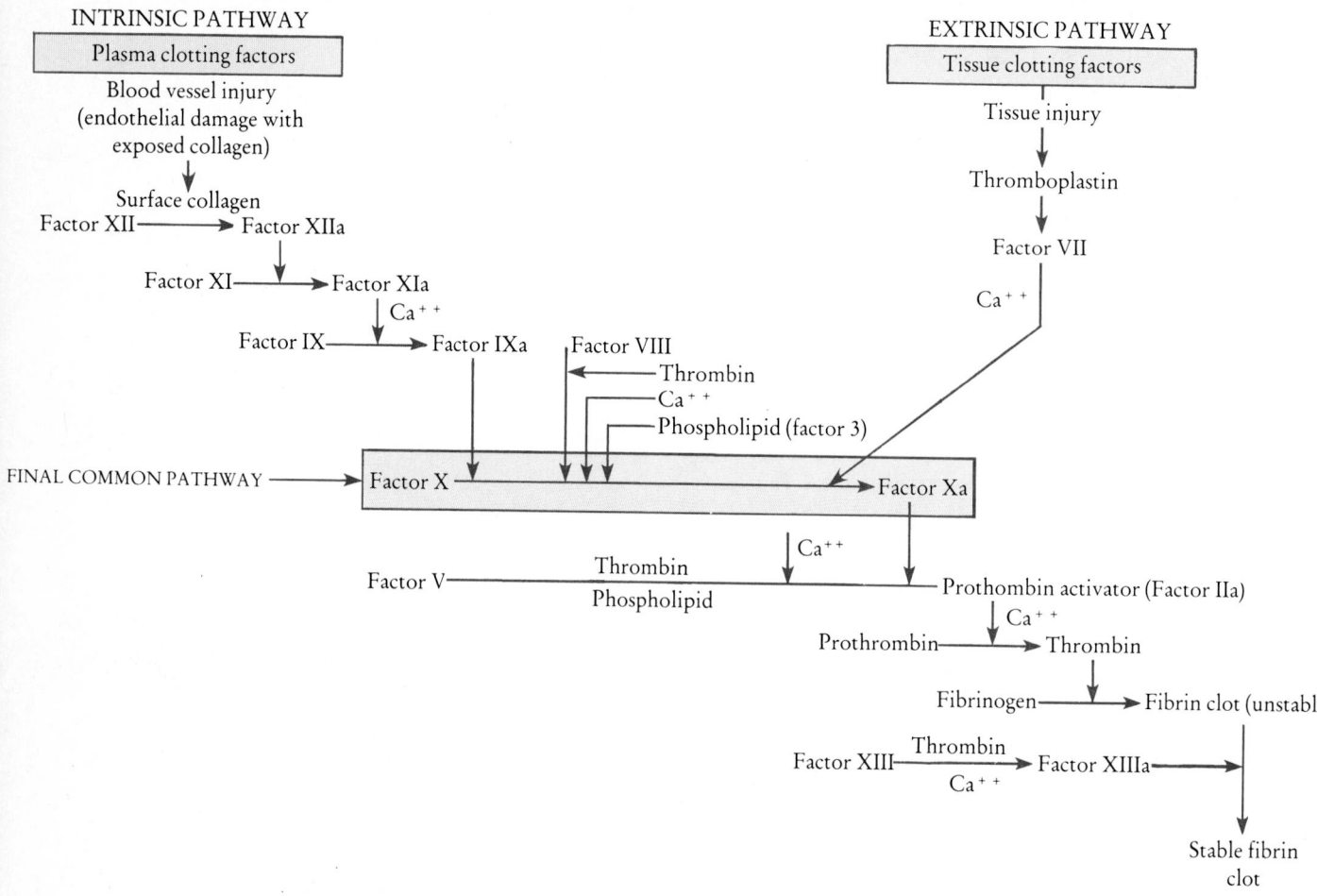

**FIGURE 29-1** Coagulation mechanism for intrinsic and extrinsic pathways for blood clotting. Final common pathway (activation of factor X) is common to both the intrinsic and extrinsic coagulation systems.

suffer from thrombosis or embolism in the United States each year. Diseases caused by intravascular clotting include some of the major causes of death from cardiovascular sources—coronary occlusion and cerebrovascular accidents. Drugs that inhibit clotting are therefore important.

Local trauma, vascular stasis, and systemic alterations in coagulability of blood are considered the main factors in the initiation of thrombosis. Basically, coagulation mechanisms are responsible for forming two kinds of thrombi: arterial thrombi and venous thrombi. Arterial thrombi are most frequently associated with atherosclerotic plaques, high blood pressure, and turbulent blood flow that damages the endothelial lining of the blood vessel and causes platelets to stick and aggregate in the arterial system. Arterial thrombi are mostly platelets, and their formation is associated with the intrinsic pathway of the coagulation mechanism.

Venous thrombi occur most often in areas where blood flow is reduced or static. This appears to initiate clotting and produces a thrombus in the venous system. Its formation involves the extrinsic pathway of the coagulation mechanism. Current anticoagulants are more effective in preventing venous rather than arterial thrombi.

## BLOOD TYPES

Blood type refers to the type of antigen located on red blood cell membranes. Although many antigens have been identified, antigens A, B, and Rh are the most important blood antigens involved with blood transfusions and newborn survival. Every person belongs to one of the four blood groups and, in addition, is also Rh positive or Rh negative. The ABO blood groups are:

Type A: A antigen on red blood cells (while the plasma has antibody B)

Type B: B antigen on red blood cells (while the plasma has antibody A)

Type AB: A antigen and B antigen on red blood cells (no antibodies)

Type O: neither A nor B antigens on red blood cells (plasma contains A and B antibodies)

Persons with type A blood can safely receive blood from A and O donors. Persons with type B blood can safely receive blood from type B and O donors. People with AB blood are known as the universal recipients, because their blood is compatible with types AB, A, B, and O. Before transfusion, however, cross matching of the blood is necessary since other agglutinins may be present. Type O persons can only receive type O blood, but they are called the universal donors since they can donate blood to anyone. (See Chapter 30 for additional information on blood transfusion.)

A person who is Rh positive carries Rh antigen on the red blood cells. One who is Rh negative does not have any Rh antigens on the red blood cells. Approximately 85% of the population is Rh positive. Rh factor is particularly important when an Rh-negative woman is impregnated by an Rh-positive man. The mother may have antibodies against the Rh antigen that can cross the placenta and attack the fetus should its blood be Rh positive. If this occurs, the infant may develop jaundice or be dead on delivery.

An Rh-negative woman could acquire Rh antibodies via blood transfusions. It is also possible for her to develop them if fetal blood enters her bloodstream during childbirth or miscarriage. Regardless, the first pregnancy usually has less risk associated with it than subsequent pregnancies. Physicians can reduce this danger by administering an anti-Rh antibody (Gamulin Rh, RhoGAM, HypRho-D) to Rh-negative women after each pregnancy. This will prevent their systems from making antibodies to Rh-positive blood. Rh-negative women who have a spontaneous or induced abortion or a termination of an ectopic pregnancy of up to and including 12 weeks gestation are given a micro dose of immune globulin (MICRhoGAM, Mini-Gamulin Rh) if the father is Rh positive.

## SUMMARY

The role of blood is to transport cellular requirements and products from one part of the body to another. The continuous exchange between the interstitial fluid and the blood serves to maintain a cellular environment that fluctuates only within narrow limits. An appreciation of the role of blood in the body's homeostasis is essential.

## BIBLIOGRAPHY

Guyton AC. (1986). *Textbook of medical physiology*, ed 7. Philadelphia: WB Saunders Co.

Guyton AC. (1987). *Human physiology and the mechanism of disease*, ed 4. Philadelphia: WB Saunders Co.

Kastrop EK, ed. (1991). *Facts and comparisons*. Philadelphia: JB Lippincott Co.

Milne C. (1988). Blood groups, *Nursing standard* 3(6):26.

Thibodeau G. (1988). *Anatomy and physiology*. St Louis: Times Mirror/Mosby College Publishing.

United States Pharmacopeial Convention. (1991). *Drug information for the health care provider*, ed 11. Rockville, Md: The Convention.

*Chapter*

# 30 Anticoagulants, Thrombolytics, and Blood Components

## CHAPTER OBJECTIVES

*After studying this chapter, the student will be able to meet the following objectives and define the key terms.*

1. Identify the disease processes that require the administration of drugs to inhibit clotting.

2. Differentiate between the mechanisms of action of parenteral and oral anticoagulant agents.

3. Discuss the nursing management concerned with the administration of anticoagulants.

4. Discuss the use of protamine sulfate and vitamin K as anticoagulant antagonists.

5. Differentiate between the actions of thrombolytic and anticoagulant drugs on blood clots.

6. Discuss drugs that may be successfully used in treating hemophilia.

7. Discuss the appropriate nursing assessment and interventions needed before, during, and after the administration of blood components.

## KEY TERMS

## INTRODUCTION

This chapter concerns drugs and substances that affect blood clotting, preformed thrombi, and blood administration.

Normally, blood clotting functions as a defense mechanism that is constantly available for protection against excessive hemorrhage. However, the development of a **thrombus** (clot) in a blood vessel can obstruct blood flow and cause an infarction with resultant tissue necrosis. An **embolus,** a mass of undissolved matter that breaks off from the thrombus, can travel in the blood vessel and lodge in areas of the body; this can cause death. By contrast, a defect in the blood clotting mechanism may lead to excessive bleeding or hemorrhage, even after a minor injury.

Both thrombotic and hemorrhagic disorders can be treated with drugs. The following discussion describes the rationale for use of various groups of therapeutic agents.

## ANTICOAGULANT DRUGS

Anticoagulant therapy is primarily prophylactic. These agents act by preventing (1) fibrin deposits, (2) extension of a thrombus, and (3) thromboembolic complications. Long-term anticoagulant therapy remains controversial. Nevertheless, there is evidence that anticoagulant therapy reduces the incidence of thrombosis and therefore prolongs life.

Anticoagulation therapy is directed toward preventing intravascular thrombosis by decreasing blood coagulability. This therapy has no direct effect on a blood clot that has already formed or on ischemic tissue injured by an inadequate blood supply because of the clot.

There are two main groups of anticoagulant drugs: (1) parenteral anticoagulant drugs and (2) oral anticoagulant drugs. For effective anticoagulant therapy with both types, the manner of use is important. They can be used to complement each other. In some instances the administration of both parenteral (heparin) and one of the synthetic oral anticoagulants is started simultaneously. The heparin is discontinued as soon as the prothrombin time has been sufficiently reduced and the oral compound is producing a full therapeutic effect. Heparin is needed when a rapid anticoagulant effect is required or when adequate facilities for determining the prothrombin time are unavailable (this prevents the use of one of the synthetic anticoagulants). Heparin is usually given in a hospital setting. Oral anticoagulants are given inside and outside hospital settings.

## ▷NURSING MANAGEMENT: ANTICOAGULANT THERAPY

*Assessment.* The role of the nurse with the client receiving anticoagulant therapy is primarily one of assessing the client for altered protection related to the increased tendency for bleeding and educating the client for the safe and accurate self-administration of the particular anticoagulant agent. The skin should be assessed for signs of bleeding such as ecchymosis, petechiae, and hematomas. The client's urine and stool should be checked periodically for blood. Laboratory values should be monitored before the drug is administered to ensure that the patient's values are in the therapeutic, not dangerous, range.

*Education.* Clients need to recognize and report signs of bleeding: excessive bruising, bleeding gums, nosebleeds, cuts that do not stop bleeding, red or brown urine, and red or black bowel movements. Instruct the client to use a soft toothbrush for oral hygiene and an electric razor to shave and to avoid activities with a potential for injury. Caution female clients with heavy menstrual flow, although treatment is not contraindicated unless bleeding is excessive. Advise the client to alert any other health care providers, such as dentists, that the drug is being taken. A medical alert bracelet or card should be carried. Medications containing ibuprofen, aspirin, and other salicylates are not to be administered while the client is receiving anticoagulant therapy. Instruct client how to read labels for OTC drugs that may contain these products. In addition, nonpharmacologic measures such as the following should be reinforced

with the client: avoiding constrictive clothing, crossing legs at knees, sitting or standing for long periods of time, and pressure on ischemic areas; smoking cessation; regular exercise; good nutrition; and prevention of injury.

## Parenteral Anticoagulant Drugs
### heparin sodium (Liquaemin, Hepalean ✷ )
### heparin calcium (Calciparine, Calcilean ✷ )

Heparin was found first in the liver and subsequently in the lungs and intestinal mucosa. It is formed in especially large amounts in the mast cells of these tissues. It has also been found in the tunica intima of blood vessels. Heparin for injection is obtained from beef lung and the mucosal lining of pig intestine or from other domestic mammals.

Heparin produces its anticoagulant effect by combining with antithrombin III (heparin cofactor), a naturally occurring anticlotting factor in the plasma. This compound is unrelated to factor III (tissue thromboplastin), which is involved in blood coagulation. The binding of heparin with antithrombin III forms a complex that acts at multiple sites in the normal coagulation system. It inactivates factors IXa, Xa, XIa, and XIIa. Inactivation of factor Xa of the intrinsic and extrinsic pathways prevents the conversion of prothrombin to thrombin, thereby inhibiting the formation of fibrin from fibrinogen. Furthermore, by preventing the activation of factor XIII (fibrin stabilizing factor), heparin also prevents the formation of a stable fibrin clot. The drug does not have **fibrinolytic activity.** This means that it will not dissolve existing clots but can prevent the extension of existing clots.

The normal function of antithrombin III is to maintain intravascular fluidity of the blood. Thromboembolism frequently occurs in individuals with acquired or congenital deficiency of this plasma protein. Therefore, in the absence of antithrombin III, heparin is unable to perform its anticoagulating effect.

Heparin is used to prevent and treat all types of thromboses and emboli. It is used prophylactically to prevent blood clotting in surgery of the heart or blood vessels, during blood transfusion, in clients with disseminated intravascular coagulation (DIC), and in the hemodialysis process. It is considered the drug of choice for sudden arterial occlusion, since its action is immediate and can be readily reversed, if surgery is necessary.

Heparin is superior to the coumarin drugs in preventing pulmonary complications in cases of thrombophlebitis. It is also preferred for the treatment of thrombophlebitis during pregnancy, since it does not cross the placental barrier and is not excreted in breast milk. When rapid anticoagulation is necessary, it is used before the oral anticoagulants. (See Table 30-1.)

It is administered via the parenteral route of administration because its large molecular size and polarity prevent any gastrointestinal absorption. By intravenous injection its onset of action is immediate. Subcutaneous injection usually

**TABLE 30-1**  Comparison of characteristics of anticoagulant drugs

| | | |
|---|---|---|
| Onset of action | Immediate | Slow (24 to 48 hours) |
| Route of administration | Parenteral | Oral |
| Duration of action | Short (less than 4 hours) | Long (approximately 2 to 5 days) |
| Laboratory test for dosage control | APTT,* clotting time | Prothrombin time |
| Antidote | Protamine sulfate | Vitamin K, whole blood, or plasma |
| Cost | Expensive | Inexpensive |

*APTT, activated partial thromboplastin time.

results in an onset of action within 20 to 60 minutes. The half-life is dose dependent but averages 1.5 hours (range is 1 to 6 hours). It is highly protein bound, metabolized in the liver, and excreted via the kidneys. For side effects/adverse reactions, see Table 30-2.

### Significant drug interactions

| Drug | Possible Effect and Management |
|---|---|
| aspirin, sulfinpyrazone, or NSAIDs | Increased risk of bleeding because of platelet inhibition by these drugs. Also, large doses of aspirin may produce hypoprothrombinemia. All drugs increase the risk of toxicity due to their potential of producing gastrointestinal ulceration and bleeding. If possible, avoid this combination therapy. If necessary to give concurrently, monitor closely. |
| azlocillin, parenteral carbenicillin, dextran, dipyridamole, divalproex, mezlocillin piperacillin, ticarcillin, or valproic acid | Increased risk of bleeding tendencies due to platelet inhibition induced by any of these drugs. Avoid concurrent therapy if possible. If necessary to give concurrently, monitor closely. |
| cefamandole, cefoperazone, moxalactam, or plicamycin | Increased risk of bleeding and hemorrhage possible with these drugs. These agents can cause hypoprothrombinemia and platelet inhibition, and moxalactam reportedly causes irreversible platelet damage. Avoid concurrent therapy if possible. If necessary to give concurrently, monitor closely. |
| methimazole or propylthiouracil | May produce a hypoprothrombinemic effect that can increase the anticoagulant effect of heparin. If necessary to give concurrently, monitor closely. |
| probenecid | May prolong and enhance heparin's anticoagulant effects. If necessary to give concurrently, monitor closely. |
| thrombolytics, such as alteplase, streptokinase or urokinase | Increased risk of bleeding and hemorrhage possible with this combination. Avoid concurrent usage. Some studies indicate that heparin may be given with low doses of thrombolytic agents via the intracoronary route of administration. Also, heparin may be administered before or after thrombolytic therapy. |

**Dosage and administration.** Dosage is expressed in USP heparin units in the United States. In Canada, dosage

may be expressed in USP units or in International Units (IU).* The following recommended dosages will be given in USP units. Also, 1 mg of sodium heparin is no longer equivalent to 100 USP units. The strength of sodium heparin is labeled in USP units/ml.

Heparin sodium adult dose is 10,000 to 20,000 USP units subcutaneously or, 10,000 USP units intravenously initially, followed by 8,000 to 10,000 units subcutaneously every 12 hours or 5,000 to 10,000 units intravenously every 4 to 6 hours. If administered by intravenous infusion, an intravenous dose of 5,000 USP units usually precedes the infusion of 20,000 to 40,000 USP units in 1000 ml of normal saline, which is administered over 24 hours. Pediatric dose is usually 50 USP units/kg initially, followed by 50 to 100 units/kg every 4 hours.

Heparin dosage is closely monitored with coagulation tests such as the activated partial thromboplastin time (APTT), the activated clotting time (ACT), or other tests as ordered. For consistency, it is recommended that a single laboratory be used to monitor a client on heparin therapy.

**Pregnancy safety.** Established at FDA Category C.

### ▷ Nursing Management: Heparin Therapy

**Assessment.** The client should be assessed to determine that heparin is not contraindicated by preexisting conditions such as:

- Blood dyscrasias, liver disease (with hypoprothrombinemia), kidney disease, peptic ulcer, chronic ulcerative colitis, and active bleeding.
- Individuals undergoing eye, spinal cord, or brain surgery, since even minor bleeding may cause serious consequences.
- Individuals with continuous drainage of the stomach or small intestine, threatened abortion, subacute endocarditis, severe hypertension, or hypersensitivity to the drug.

---

*USP heparin units are not equivalent to International Units. Since the potency may vary between USP and IU, the student should review the current package insert for dosage instructions whenever packages are labeled in International Units.

**TABLE 30-2**    Anticoagulant agents: side effects/adverse reactions

| Drug | Side effects* | Adverse reactions† |
|---|---|---|
| heparin | | Less frequent or rare: chest pain, chills, elevated temperature, respiratory difficulties, wheezing, rash, pruritus, hives, increase in nasal secretions (allergic reaction), anaphylaxis, paresthesis of hands or feet, blue tinge on arms or legs, increased or persistent erections<br>Early signs of overdosage: increased bruising, nosebleeds, excessive bleeding from minor cuts, wounds, brushing of teeth, or menstrual period<br>Internal bleeding signs: stomach pain or swelling, backaches, bloody urine, bloody or black stools, dizziness, severe persistent headaches, swollen, stiff, or painful vomiting or coughing up of blood<br>Following 6 months or more of therapy: rib or back pain, height decrease (osteoporosis), alopecia<br>At site of injection: hematoma or blood accumulation under the skin, pain, local skin reaction such as irritation, peeling, or sloughing |
| anisindione | | The following effects, though not yet reported with this drug, were reported with phenindione, another indanedione derivative, and may also be seen with this product: edema of face or lower extremities, unexpected weight gain, leukopenia, agranulocytosis, liver toxicity, diarrhea, nausea, vomiting, severe abdominal distress |
| dicumarol | More frequent: stomach gas<br>Less frequent: anorexia, alopecia | More frequent: diarrhea<br>Less frequent or rare: leukopenia, liver toxicity, nausea, vomiting, mouth sores, agranulocytosis |
| warfarin | Less frequent: alopecia | Less frequent or rare: leukopenia, nausea, vomiting, abdominal cramps or distress |

*If side effects continue, increase, or disturb the patient, inform the physician.
†If adverse reactions occur, contact the physician, as medical intervention may be necessary.

Caution must be used in administering heparin to clients with any condition in which hemorrhage is possible. Clients over the age of 60, especially women, are more susceptible to the hemorrhagic effects of heparin. Use cautiously in individuals with mild hepatic or renal disease or in cases of alcoholism.

A baseline assessment should consist of an activated partial thromboplastin time (APTT), a platelet count, and a hematocrit evaluation. Anticipate that each dose of heparin will be individualized after the physician has evaluated the APTT. Check to be sure that these tests are performed as ordered (before each IV or SC injection) and the results are reported promptly.

With the administration of heparin, clients are at risk for the following nursing diagnoses: high risk for injury related to increased bleeding tendencies, allergic reaction, and osteoporosis (long-term therapy); altered comfort such as irritation, pain, redness, or ulceration at the injection site related to parenteral administration; and altered self-concept related to unusual hair loss (long-term therapy).

**Intervention.** Heparin comes in many concentrations: carefully check the vial and the physician's order. Be alert that the heparin-lock flush solution maintains patency of the indwelling venipuncture unit and that it is not used for systemic anticoagulation.

For subcutaneous administration, use a small-gauge (25 to 27) ⅜ to ⅝ inch needle. Use a "bunching" technique (pulling the fatty layer away from the underlying tissue) or Z-tract method. Inject the heparin deep into the fatty tissue above the iliac crest or into the abdominal fat layer. Avoid the umbilical veins by avoiding a 2-inch radius around the umbilicus. This distance should also be maintained from scars and lesions. Do not aspirate and *do not massage the injection site.* Hold the needle in place for 10 seconds after administration and withdraw gently to minimize bruising. Apply direct pressure for 1 to 2 minutes if needed. Rotate sites to prevent the formation of hematomas. Document the location of injection sites graphically. Intramuscular injection is not recommended because it causes hematomas, irritation, and pain at the injection site and because it causes erratic absorption.

A loading dose usually precedes a continuous infusion. This IV dose may be given undiluted over at least a minute. For continuous IV infusion of heparin, use an infusion pump or a volume control unit so that the flow rate and fluid volume of the drug can be precisely controlled. Check the system frequently to prevent overdosage or underdosage. Never piggyback other drugs into an intravenous line containing heparin, as many other drugs inactivate heparin.

For clients receiving intermittent heparin dosage, sub-

Selected nursing diagnoses for clients receiving anticoagulant therapy

| Nursing diagnosis | Outcome criteria | Nursing interventions |
| --- | --- | --- |
| Tissue perfusion, alteration in: reduced blood flow (prevention and treatment of thromboembolic disorders) | Clotting studies are maintained within therapeutic range; PTT is prolonged to 1.5-2 times the control (heparin). PT is prolonged to 1.5-2 times the control (warfarin). Extension of the thrombus or embolization of thrombi does not occur. | Monitor clotting studies as ordered. Administer anticoagulant therapy and assess effectiveness. Monitor vital signs and blood pressure every 4 hours. Report immediately any change in vital signs or decrease in blood pressure. Auscultate breath sounds every 4 hours. Report the development of rales. Assess for other developments of pulmonary emboli, in addition to above, such as dyspnea, cough, or hemoptysis. Apply antiembolism stockings as ordered. Measure calf dimension, bilaterally; compare and record every 8 hours. |
| Injury, high risk for hemorrhage | No signs of hemorrhage occur. | Administer heparin SC rather than IM to prevent hematoma formation. Inject into lower abdomen using a small-gauge needle (25-27); do not massage injection sites. Rotate sites. All personnel should be alerted that the client is on anticoagulant therapy. Venipunctures and injections should be kept to a minimum and pressure applied to prevent bleeding when they are done. Observe client for excessive bruising, bleeding gums, nosebleed, blood in urine and/or secretions, and report. |
| Knowledge deficit related to medication regime | Client will describe underlying condition and how the drug relates to the condition, how and when to take the medication, common drug interactions, safety precautions, common side effects, and which of these warrant reporting. Self-administer warfarin safely and accurately. | Assess learning needs and learning readiness. Plan with client for the achievement of realistic goals. Provide information to meet outcome criteria. Caution the client to use a soft toothbrush and an electric razor. Recommend to client that all health care personnel be informed of anticoagulant therapy before treatment. Advise on the importance of having blood studies done as ordered. Instruct client on the need to report any signs of bleeding. |

cutaneously or by heparin lock, the blood samples for the APTT should be drawn ½ hour before the next dose to avoid a falsely high APTT. This false reading can also be avoided for the client with a continuous heparin infusion by drawing the sample from the arm opposite the infusion.

Although controversy exists on whether normal saline or diluted heparin solutions (10 to 100 units of heparin sodium per milliliter) should be used to irrigate and maintain patency of an indwelling venipuncture device, the nurse should be aware that the purpose of the device is to maintain an open intravenous line so that ordered intermittent drugs, intravenous solutions, or both may be administered through this line. Therefore, within each clinical practice setting, obtain information about the accepted (usually medically approved) practices or policies concerning the solution to be used and how often the device should be flushed if not in frequent use; then closely monitor the unit for patency.

If heparin solution is being used to maintain the patency of an indwelling peripheral venipuncture device, usually 1 ml of heparin lock flush solution will be effective for 4 to 8 hours. If the device is being used to administer a drug that is incompatible with heparin, the device should be flushed with sterile water or 0.9% sodium chloride for injection before and after the drug is given. Inject the heparin-lock flush solution after the second flush. If the device is being used to obtain blood samples for laboratory analysis and heparin might alter the results of the test, the heparin solution should be cleared from the device by aspirating and discarding 1 ml of solution from the device before the blood sample is taken. After the blood sample is drawn, the device is again filled with 1 ml of heparin-lock flush solution.

Heparin is to be stopped immediately if the client complains of a chill, low back pain (sign of abdominal bleeding), or spontaneous bleeding. Notify the physician and have on hand protamine sulfate. In some cases it may be necessary to give whole blood or plasma.

Alert other staff that the client is receiving heparin (i.e., sign over the client's bed). Pressure should be applied to venipuncture and injection sites to minimize bruising. These invasive procedures should be avoided if at all possible. Consult with the physician regarding a change from intramuscular administration of other drugs to other routes of administration while the client is receiving heparin.

***Education.*** In addition to the client education information discussed in "Nursing Management: Anticoagulant Therapy," inform the client of the potential for diuresis beginning 36 to 48 hours after initial dose of heparin and lasting 36 to 48 hours following termination of therapy.

Advise client that alopecia may occur several months following heparin therapy and that the condition is reversible on discontinuation of drug.

***Evaluation.*** Adjust heparin dosage to maintain the APTT between one and one-half and two and one-half times normal control level and WBCT between two and one-half and three times the control value, with client remaining free of signs of hemorrhage. Any value under or over this range should be reported to the physician immediately.

Test stools for occult blood daily to determine hidden bleeding. Monitor platelet count and examine patient for possible thrombocytopenia, which may be associated with arterial thrombosis or "white clot" syndrome. Perform hematocrit tests frequently.

Be aware of the possibility of "heparin resistance" in conditions associated with infection, thrombophlebitis, fever, pleurisy, cancer, myocardial infarction, and extensive surgery.

Be aware that abrupt withdrawal of heparin may precipitate an increase in coagulability; usually a full dose of heparin is followed by oral anticoagulants for prophylaxis. Thus there generally is an overlap of both drugs for 3 to 5 days while heparin is being tapered off.

## Parenteral Anticoagulant Antagonist
### protamine sulfate (Heparin Antidote)

Protamine sulfate is protein-like substance derived from the sperm and mature testes of the salmon and other fish. Protamine alone is a very weak anticoagulant but will prolong clotting time; it is an antithromboplastin but is not as active as heparin. When protamine is given in conjunction with heparin, they form a combination that dissociates the heparin–antithrombin III complex, thus reducing the anticoagulant action of heparin. Because protamine is a basic protein (many free amino groups), it is able to combine with the sulfuric acids of heparin and inactivate them.

Protamine is indicated for the treatment of a severe heparin overdose that has resulted in hemorrhaging. Blood transfusions may also be necessary. It is also used to neutralize the effects of heparin administered during dialysis or cardiac or arterial surgery. It is administered intravenously

and has an onset of action within 30 to 60 seconds; the duration of effect is usually 2 hours.

When protamine is administered too rapidly, respiratory difficulties, bradycardia, and a sudden hypotensive effect may result. Less often reported are bleeding problems and rarely, coughing spells, facial edema, or a rash. These are adverse effects that should be reported to the physician immediately. Less frequent and usually less troublesome side effects include sensations of heat, flushing, nausea, vomiting, or feelings of increased weakness. No significant drug interactions have been reported with protamine.

Protamine is administered by slow intravenous injection, over 1 to 3 minutes. One milligram of protamine is necessary to neutralize approximately 100 USP units of heparin. It is recommended that not more than 50 mg of protamine be given in any 10-minute period nor more than 100 mg be administered over a 2-hour period. Close monitoring with blood coagulation tests is required. Pregnancy safety for protamine has been established as FDA Category C.

▷ **Nursing Management: Protamine Sulfate Therapy**

***Intervention.*** Protamine sulfate is to be administered by a physician. The drug should be administered slowly intravenously—over 1 to 3 minutes—not more than 50 mg in any 10-minute period. Too rapid administration may potentially cause injury, dyspnea and shock. Emergency equipment should be available.

***Evaluation.*** Observe client for spontaneous bleeding or heparin "rebound" (the effects of heparin last longer than the effects of protamine) following procedures involving extracorporeal circulation such as cardiac or arterial surgery or dialysis. This may occur as long as 18 hours after the initial neutralization of the heparin. Monitor APTT to determine protamine efficacy and dosage.

## Oral Anticoagulant Drugs

There are two major types of oral anticoagulant drugs: coumarins and indanediones.

*Coumarins*
   **dicumoral (Dicumoral)**
   **warfarin sodium (Coumadin, Marevan ✳)**
*Indanediones*
   **anisindione (Miradon)**

Both the coumarin and the indanedione derivatives interfere with liver synthesis of the vitamin K–dependent clotting factors. Thus they depress the synthesis of factors X, IX, VII, and II (prothrombin). Factor VII is depleted quickly; the sequential depletion of factors IX, X, and II follows. These agents do not affect established clots but do prevent further extension of formed clots, thereby diminishing the potential for secondary thromboembolic complications.

**TABLE 30-3**   Pharmacokinetics and dosage and administration of oral anticoagulants

| Generic/trade name | Onset of action (days) | Duration of action (days) | Half-life (days) | Dosage and administration |
|---|---|---|---|---|
| **COUMARIN** | | | | |
| dicumarol (Dicumarol)* | 1-5 | 2-10 | 1-4 (dose dependent) | Adult: 25-200 mg daily orally, as indicated by prothrombin time<br>Children: not established |
| warfarin sodium (Coumadin) | ½-3 | 2-5 | 1.5-2.5 | Adult: 10-15 mg orally for 2-4 days; then 2-10 mg daily, as indicated by prothrombin time<br>Children: not established<br>Injectable dosage form: same dosage as oral |
| **INDANEDIONES** | | | | |
| anisindione (Miradon) | 2-3 | 1-3 | 3-5 | Adult: 25-250 mg orally daily, as indicated by prothrombin time<br>Children: not established |

*Dicumarol activity is variable.

The oral anticoagulant drugs are used for the prophylaxis and treatment of deep venous thrombosis and pulmonary thromboembolism. They are also used for the prophylaxis of thromboembolisms associated with chronic atrial fibrillation or myocardial infarction. The major advantages of these drugs are the facts that they are effective orally and that they need to be given only once daily, when the maintenance dose has been established. (See Table 30-3.)

With the exception of dicumarol, all the oral anticoagulants are well absorbed from the gastrointestinal tract. The absorption of dicumarol is slow, incomplete, and erratic from the gastrointestinal tract. Oral anticoagulants are highly protein bound (99%), metabolized in the liver, and excreted via the kidneys.

For side effects/adverse reactions, pharmocokinetics, and dosage and administration, see Tables 30-2 and 30-3. Significant drug interactions can be found in the box on p. 555. Pregnancy safety has not been established, but both coumarin and anisindione cross the placenta and should not be used during pregnancy. Fetal abnormalities and facial anomalies have been reported. If an anticoagulant is necessary during pregnancy, heparin is usually the drug of choice since it does not cross the placenta.

▷**Nursing Management: Oral Anticoagulant Therapy**

**Assessment.**  Use cautiously in individuals with allergic disorders, hazardous occupations, conditions that may increase prothrombin time (collagen diseases, disorders of the pancreas, alcoholism, hepatic and renal insufficiency), and conditions that may decrease prothrombin time (hypothyroidism, diabetes mellitus, hyperlipidemia, and hypercholesterolemia).

Contraindications include hemorrhagic tendencies, aneurysm, hemophilia, open ulcerative or visceral carcinoma, colitis, diarrhea, severe hypertension, recent surgery of spi-

nal cord, brain, or eye, suspicion of cerebrovascular hemorrhage, subacute bacterial endocarditis, regional block anesthesia, and vitamin C deficiency. Before therapy, inquire if client is pregnant and inform her of the potential risk of congenital malformations.

With the administration of oral anticoagulant therapy, clients are at risk for the following nursing diagnoses: high risk for injury related to increased bleeding tendencies, acute adrenal insufficiency (diarrhea, nausea with or without vomiting, abdominal cramps), agranulocytosis or leukopenia (chills, fever, sore throat, excessive tiredness), and hepatotoxicity (dark urine, yellow sclera and skin); altered comfort with irritation, pain, redness, or ulceration at the injection site related to parenteral administration or allergic dermatitis; altered bowel elimination related to gastrointestinal effects (diarrhea); and altered self-concept related to unusual hair loss (long-term therapy).

**Intervention.**  Be aware that the onset of action of oral anticoagulants is slow; therefore heparin sodium is usually given during the first few days of treatment. Blood for prothrombin time should be drawn within 5 hours of intravenous heparin administration.

Terminate therapy gradually over a 3- or 4-week period to prevent rebound thromboembolic complications.

**Education.**  Once maintenance therapy is established and client is discharged, stress the importance of adherence to schedule of laboratory procedures and physician's appointments. Prothrombin time should be performed from intervals of 1 to 4 weeks, depending on dosage. Also, periodic urinalysis, blood counts, stool guaiac, and liver function tests should be performed.

In addition to the points discussed in "Nursing Management: Anticoagulant Therapy," instruct client to carry an identification card that lists the client's and physician's names and phone numbers and the name and dosage of the oral anticoagulant drug.

Emphasize the importance of not taking any other med-

---

### SIGNIFICANT DRUG INTERACTIONS OF ORAL ANTICOAGULANTS

The oral anticoagulants have a great potential for causing drug interactions; therefore clients must be cautioned against taking any drug and/or making significant dietary changes, without prior consultation with their physician. Check a current USP-DI for major drug interactions.

| Agents that may increase the anticoagulant effect, often necessitating a dosage reduction | | | Agents that may decrease the anticoagulant effect, often necessitating an increase in anticoagulant dosage |
| --- | --- | --- | --- |
| allopurinol | dextrothyroxine | nalidixic acid | oral antidiabetic agents§ |
| amiodarone | diflunisal | phenytoin‡ | barbiturates |
| anabolic steroids | dipyridamole† | piperacillin | carbamazepine |
| androgens | disulfiram | plicamycin | cholestyramine |
| aspirin | erythromycins | propylthiouracil | colestipol |
| azlocillin | fenoprofen | quinidine | contraceptives, oral |
| cefamandole | gemfibrozil | salicylates | estramustine |
| cefoperazone | indomethacin | sulfinpyrazone | estrogens |
| chloral hydrate* | mefenamic acid | sulfonamides | ethchlorvynol |
| chloramphenicol | meperidine | sulindac | glutethimide |
| cimetidine | mezlocillin | ticarcillin | griseofulvin |
| clofibrate | methimazole | thyroid hormone | primidone |
| danazol | metronidazole | urokinase | rifampin |
| dextran | moxalactam | | vitamin K |

*Usually occurs during first 2 weeks of therapy. With chronic concurrent therapy, the anticoagulant effect may return to normal or be decreased.

†With doses of dipyridamole over 400 mg/day.

‡Increased anticoagulant effect occurs initially. With chronic concurrent therapy decreased activity may occur. May also see a decrease in metabolism of phenytoin, possibly leading to increased serum levels and toxicity.

§May initially increase anticoagulant effects, but with long-term concurrent therapy, such effects may decrease. Also, the decrease in metabolism of the antidiabetic agent may increase serum levels and cause prolonged half-life, hypoglycemia, and toxicity.

---

ication, especially ibuprofen, aspirin, and other salicylates, without checking with the physician, since so many drugs interact with anticoagulant agents. Also, alcoholic individuals should be closely monitored because of potential for noncompliance to drug regimen.

Vitamin K$_1$ (phytonadione) should be readily accessible if bleeding occurs. Outpatients should carry vitamin K$_1$ with them and, after first consulting with the physician, take 1 to 10 mg at once if bleeding occurs. Statistics show that bleeding occurs in approximately 10% of all patients on long-term anticoagulant therapy; however, fatalities are rare.

Advise client of proper diet because prothrombin time is shortened by a high-fat diet or vitamin K–rich foods such as broccoli, asparagus, cabbage, cauliflower, lettuce, turnip greens, spinach, fish, liver, green tea, or coffee.

Instruct client not to cross legs or wear garments (girdles, knee-high stockings, or garters) that would promote venous stasis in persons with potential venous thrombosis or thrombophlebitis.

***Evaluation.*** Anticipate that dosage is based on prothrombin time. Check to be sure that this test is performed as ordered, and report results to the physician immediately. The therapeutic aim for clients undergoing anticoagulant therapy is to produce a prolongation of the prothrombin time within one and one-half to two times the control.

### Oral Anticoagulant Antagonist

*Vitamin K*

**menadiol sodium diphosphate (Synkayvite)**
**phytonadione (Mephyton, AquaMephyton)**

Vitamin K is essential to the hepatic synthesis of prothrombin (factor II) and factors VII, IX, and X. It contributes to the activation of an enzyme necessary to the formation of prothrombin. Deficiency of vitamin K leads to hypoprothrombinemia and hemorrhage.

Vitamin K is used to prevent and treat hypoprothrombinemia. Prothrombin deficiency may occur because of inadequate absorption of vitamin K from the intestine (usually caused by biliary disease in which bile fails to enter the intestine) or because of destruction of intestinal organisms, which may occur with antibiotic therapy. It is also seen in the newborn, in which case it is probably caused by the fact that the intestinal organisms have not yet become established. It may result from therapy with certain anticoagulants.

### Geriatric Implications:
### ANTICOAGULANTS

The elderly may be more susceptible to the effects of anticoagulants, such as warfarin (Coumadin) and dicumarol, thus a lower maintenance dose is usually recommended for the geriatric client along with very close supervision and monitoring.

The primary adverse effects of excessive drug usage are prolonged bleeding from gums when brushing teeth or from small shaving cuts, excessive or easy skin bruising, blood in urine or stools, and unexplained nosebleeds. These may be early signs of overdose that indicate the need for medical intervention.

Caution clients to carry an identification card indicating the use of an anticoagulant. Also, remind client to always consult his or her physician before starting any new drug, including OTC medications and vitamins, or if changing a medication dose or when any drug product is discontinued. Many medications can change the effects of an anticoagulant in the body.

Be aware that administration of concurrent drug therapy that may induce gastric irritation, increases the risk for gastrointestinal bleeding. Drugs such as the nonsteroidal antiinflammatory agents (NSAIDs such as ibuprofen, indomethacin) that are commonly prescribed for the elderly client often cause gastrointestinal effects.

Alcohol consumption can alter the effect of this medication in the body. Clients should be instructed to avoid or, at the least, limit their daily alcohol intake to one alcoholic drink a day. Alcohol may cause liver damage, which increases the individual's sensitivity to anticoagulants. (USP-DI)

---

Vitamin K is useful only in conditions in which the prolonged bleeding time is caused by a low concentration of prothrombin in the blood and not by damaged liver cells. Vitamin K is routinely administered to newborns to help prevent hemorrhage. Although prothrombin levels may be normal at birth, they decline until about the sixth day, when the liver is able to form prothrombin. Vitamin K may be given to the mother before delivery.

Vitamin K is also indicated in the preoperative preparation of individuals with deficient prothrombin, particularly those with obstructive jaundice. In addition, it is given as an antidote for overdosage of oral anticoagulants. It is important to measure prothrombin activity of the blood frequently when the client is receiving a preparation of vitamin K. Parenteral preparations should be administered if for some reason the intestinal absorption is impaired.

Natural vitamin K is normally synthesized by the intestinal flora. When synthetic forms of vitamin K are administered, the absorption is good, but phytonadione requires

the presence of bile salts. The onset of action for menadiol sodium diphosphate injection is 8 to 24 hours; for oral phytonadione it is 6 to 12 hours, whereas for the injectable form it is 1 to 2 hours. Vitamin K is metabolized in the liver and excreted via the kidneys and in the bile. Infrequent side effects reported are facial flushing, taste alterations, and redness or pain at the injection site.

When vitamin K is given concurrently with the oral anticoagulants, a decrease in anticoagulation effect is reported. The dose of menadiol (vitamin K) as a nutritional supplement for hypoprothrombinemia is 5 mg/day orally, or 5 to 15 mg once or twice daily intramuscularly or subcutaneously. As an antidote for drug-induced hypoprothrombinemia, the oral dose is 5 to 10 mg daily and the intramuscular or subcutaneous dose is 5 to 15 mg once or twice daily. The pediatric dose for both nutritional and antidote indications is 5 to 10 mg orally, or 5 to 10 mg once or twice daily given intramuscularly or subcutaneously.

### ▷Nursing Management: Vitamin K Therapy

**Assessment.** Monitor prothrombin time as a baseline measurement and throughout vitamin K therapy to evaluate response. Administration of vitamin K may place the client at high risk for altered comfort related to facial flushing, unusual taste, and discomfort and redness at the injection site and high risk for injury related to hemolytic anemia or a rare hypersensitivity-like reaction.

**Intervention.** Because vitamin K has a delayed onset, the administration of plasma or fresh whole blood may be necessary with severe bleeding. Administer by slow intravenous infusion, over 2 to 3 hours. Protect the infusion container from light by wrapping it in aluminum foil.

**Education.** Generally, dietary supplements for vitamin K are not necessary, as normal diet and intestinal bacterial synthesis supply sufficient amounts. However, green leafy vegetables, meats, and dairy products are the best sources of vitamin K with little nutritional loss of the vitamin during ordinary cooking. The client's intake of dietary vitamin K should be considered in determining therapeutic dosages for long-term use.

**Evaluation.** During intravenous infusion, observe for signs of side effects such as flushing, weakness, and hypotension, and report them to the physician.

## THROMBOLYTIC AGENTS

**Thrombolytic** (fibrinolytic) **drugs** are used to treat acute thromboembolic disorders. They dissolve clots and are used in a hospital setting only by physicians who are experienced in the management of diseases caused by thrombosis. The thrombolytic drugs dissolve thrombi after their formation, unlike the coagulants, which prevent their extension. Thrombolytic enzyme therapy alters the hemostatic capability of the client more profoundly than does anticoagulant therapy. Consequently, when bleeding ocurs, it is more severe and very difficult to control.

## alteplase (Activase)
## anistreplase (Eminase)
## streptokinase (Streptase, Kabikinase)
## urokinase (Abbokinase, Ukidan ✿)

These agents dissolve clots via the endogenous fibrinolytic system. All four drugs have similar biochemical mechanisms of action on the endogenous fibrinolytic system—that is, converting plasminogen in the blood to plasmin. Plasmin is, a fibrinolytic enzyme that digests or dissolves fibrin clots wherever they exist and can be reached by plasmin. Streptokinase and urokinase are indicated for the treatment of acute pulmonary thromboembolism, while only streptokinase currently (USP-DI, 1991) is indicated for lysis

of an acute, deep venous thrombosis. All four drugs can be used to treat an acute coronary arterial thrombosis associated with an acute myocardial infarction.

These agents are administered intravenously and/or intra-arterially. Alteplase has a half-life of 35 minutes, while streptokinase and urokinase half-lives are approximately 23 minutes and up to 20 minutes, respectively. Anistreplase, which is an acylated complex of streptokinase and human plasminogen, has a long half-life of approximately 105 minutes. Plasma clearance of anistreplase is 1½ hours, while streptokinase and urokinase are cleared in 15 to 20 minutes and alteplase is cleared in 9 minutes. Therefore anistreplase can be administered over 4 to 5 minutes, whereas the other drugs need to be administered by infusion for longer periods of time, usually an hour or more. See Tables 30-4 and 30-5 for side effects/adverse reactions and significant drug interactions.

**TABLE 30-4**  Thrombolytic agents: side effects/adverse reactions

| Drug | Side effects/adverse reactions* |
| --- | --- |
| alteplase | More frequent: bleeding episodes (cuts, wounds, gums); elevated temperature<br>Less frequent: allergic reactions of facial flushing, headache, arthralgia, nausea, rash, pruritus, and respiratory difficulties; easy bruising |
| anistreplase | More frequent: bleeding episodes; hypotension; arrhythmias; allergic reactions of rash, pruritus, and facial flushing<br>Less frequent: chills, fever, headaches, nausea, vomiting, tremors, paresthesia, irritability, and respiratory difficulties |
| streptokinase and urokinase | Most frequent: stomach pain or swelling; backache; bloody urine; bloody or black stools; constipation; coughing up of blood; severe headaches; dizziness; swollen stiff, or painful joints; painful or stiff muscles; nosebleeds; excessive bleeding from vagina; vomiting of blood or substances that look like coffee grounds; tachycardia; bradycardia; oozing of blood from cuts or scratches. Elevated temperature is more frequent with streptokinase than urokinase.<br>Less frequent with streptokinase but rare with urokinase are flushed red skin, mild headaches or muscle pain, nausea, rash, pruritus, hives, respiratory difficulties.<br>Rare: for streptokinase only: severe and/or sudden hypotension; shortness of breath; chest tightness; severe wheezing; or edema of eyes, face, lips, or tongue (anaphylaxis or a severe allergic reaction) |

*If adverse reactions occur, contact physician because medical intervention may be necessary.

**TABLE 30-5**  Thrombolytic agents: drug interactions

| Drug | Possible effect and management |
| --- | --- |
| aminocaproic acid or other antifibrinolytic drugs | May inhibit effectiveness of thrombolytic agents. Reserve such drugs to treat severe bleeding induced by the thrombolytic agents. |
| anticoagulants, oral or heparin | Increased risk of bleeding and hemorrhage. Heparin has been administered with thrombolytic agents to treat an acute coronary arterial occlusion. Monitor closely when concurrent therapy is prescribed. |
| antiinflammatory agents, nonsteroidal, aspirin,* or sulfinpyrazone | Inhibition of platelet aggregation may increase potential for gastrointestinal ulceration and bleeding. Avoid concurrent drug administration. |
| carbenicillin, dextran, dipyridamole, divalproex, ticarcillin, valproic acid | These drugs inhibit platelet aggregation; if used concurrently with the thrombolytic agents, they may increase the risk of severe bleeding and hemorrhage. Avoid concurrent drug administration. |
| cefamandole, cefoperazone, moxalactam, or plicamycin | May cause hypoprothrombinemia and inhibit platelet aggregation. Moxalactam can also cause irreversible platelet damage. Use of these drugs is not recommended because of increased risk of hemorrhage. |

*Low doses of aspirin have been given concurrently with thrombolytic therapy, especially with streptokinase. This combination is reported to decrease the risk of reocclusion, stroke, and death more significantly than streptokinase alone (USP-DI, 1991).

In an acute coronary artery thrombosis evolving into a transmural myocardial infarction, thrombolytic therapy is most effective when started within 3 to 4 hours after the onset of symptoms. Usually alteplase is given at 1.25 mg/kg intravenously in divided doses over 3 hours for clients weighing less than 65 kg or 100 mg intravenously for clients 65 kg or over (in divided doses over 3 hours). See current literature for recommended dosages over each of the 3 hours. The dose of anistreplase is 30 units in solution administered by intravenous injection over 2 to 5 minutes. For streptokinase, the dose is 1,500,000 IU intravenously administered in an hour. Smaller doses of 20,000 IU initially followed by an additional 2,000 IU/minute are used for intraarterial administration. Urokinase 6000 IU/minute is administered intraarterially until the artery is opened. For other indications, refer to a current package insert or USP-DI for dosing information. Pediatric dosages are not established. See Tables 30-4 and 30-5 for side effects/adverse reactions and drug interactions. Pregnancy safety for alteplase, anistreplase, and streptokinase is established as FDA Category C; for urokinase it is FDA Category B.

## ▷NURSING MANAGEMENT: THROMBOLYTIC THERAPY

**Assessment.** Note that thrombolytic therapy is contraindicated in individuals with recent (past 2 months) cerebrovascular accident or intracranial or intraspinal surgery, active internal bleeding, and intracranial neoplasm. Use with caution in high-risk clients with recent (within past 10 days) surgery, obstetric delivery, serious gastrointestinal bleeding, organ biopsy, previous puncture of noncompressible vessels, recent trauma including cardiopulmonary resuscitation, severe, uncontrolled hypertension, suspected left heart thrombus involving mitral stenosis with atrial fibrillation, subacute bacterial endocarditis, hemostatic defects including secondary to severe hepatic and renal disease, pregnancy, diabetic hemorrhagic retinopathy, evidence of cerebrovascular disease, other conditions in which bleeding causes a significant hazard or would be difficult to control because of its location, septic thrombosis, or serious infection at the site of occluded antrioventricular cannula.

If the client has been treated previously with streptokinase, the formation of antibodies to the drug may either cause a resistance to the therapeutic effects of the drug or a severe allergic reaction.

Before thrombolytic therapy, thrombin time (TT), activated partial thromboplastin time (APTT), prothrombin time (PT), and hematocrit and platelet count must be performed. With the administration of thrombolytic agents, the client is at risk for the following nursing diagnoses: high risk for injury related to increased bleeding tendencies and embolism, and hyperthermia. In addition, with streptokinase the client is at risk from injury related to an allergic reaction.

**Intervention.** Thrombolytic therapy is administered only by a physician who is experienced in management of thrombotic diseases and where skilled personnel and laboratory resources are available. Also, typed and cross-matched whole blood and packed red cells should be available in case of hemorrhage.

Follow manufacturer's instructions when reconstituting and diluting drug to minimize fibrin formation:

- *alteplase.* Reconstitute using the diluent supplied with the drug (sterile water for injection). It may be used as is or diluted further. If it is diluted further, use only 0.9% sodium chloride solution or 5% dextrose injection without preservatives. Mix gently to prevent foaming. Leave the solution undisturbed for a few minutes and any bubbles created will dissipate. Do not add any other medication to the container of alteplase solution or administer other medications through the same intravenous line.
- *streptokinase.* Slowly add 5 ml of sodium chloride injection or 5% dextrose injection, directing the stream toward the side of the vial rather than into the powder. Do not shake the vial but gently roll and tilt it for reconstitution (i.e., returning a substance altered for storage nearly to its original state). Note that shaking may cause foaming and increase flocculation. Then slowly dilute the entire contents of the vial to a total of 45 ml or, if necessary, up to 500 ml in 45 ml increments. If solution is not used soon after reconstitution, store at 2° to 4° C, and use within 24 hours. Note that a patient with a recent streptococcal infection may require a higher loading dose because of higher resistance levels.
- *urokinase.* Add 5.2 ml of sterile water (not bacteriostatic water) for injection immediately before use. Then for intravenous infusion, dilute reconstituted powder with 0.9% sodium chloride injection to a total volume of 195 ml. Discard the unused portion of the reconstituted material.

Do not administer by intramuscular injection because of the danger of hematoma. In addition, use venipuncture sites as seldom as possible, and perform this procedure with care. Maintain pressure dressings at the site for at least 30 minutes, and check frequently for bleeding.

Start streptokinase therapy as soon as possible after the thrombotic event, preferably within 7 days. If after 4 hours of therapy, thrombin time is less than one and one-half times the normal control value, discontinue therapy. Administer using a constant infusion pump. For arteriovenous cannula occlusion, administer heparinized saline solution to clear the cannula. If adequate flow is not reestablished, use streptokinase.

To prevent bruising during therapy, avoid unnecessary handling of patient. The side rails of the client's bed should be padded.

Following completion of thrombolytic therapy, begin continuous intravenous infusion of heparin (without a loading dose) when thrombin time has decreased to less than twice the normal control value (usually within 4 hours after completion of the infusion). Use an infusion pump for heparin. Later give the client oral anticoagulant therapy, a procedure that prevents the recurrence of thrombosis.

*Evaluation.* Observe client carefully during early phase of therapy for allergic reactions. With urokinase, relatively mild reactions (e.g., bronchospasm, skin rash) are reported. Streptokinase may produce more serious reactions and possibly anaphylaxis. (See allergic effects under side effects/adverse reactions.) If allergic manifestations occur, discontinue infusion and treat with epinephrine, antihistamines, and corticosteroids. If fever occurs, treat symptomatically with acetaminophen.

Monitor vital signs frequently (i.e., pulse rate, temperature, respiratory rate, and blood pressure), at least every 4 hours. To avoid possible dislodgment of deep vein thrombi, do not take blood pressure in the lower extremities. Monitor client carefully for bleeding: every 15 minutes for the first hour, every 30 minutes for the next 8 hours, and every 4 hours until therapy is discontinued. The physician should be notified immediately if bleeding occurs. Therapy should be discontinued if bleeding occurs that is not controlled by local pressure.

In addition to observing for overt bleeding, observe client for internal bleeding—bloody sputum, hematuria, hematemesis, dark stools (i.e., guaiac positive), flank and abdominal pain, and neurologic changes. For uncontrollable bleeding, stop treatment and administer whole blood (fresh blood if available), packed red cells, cryoprecipitate or fresh-frozen plasma, and aminocaproic acid.

Observe extremities and palpate pulses of affected extremities every hour. The physician should be notified immediately if there are signs of circulatory impairment.

Observe client carefully for dysrhythmias during and after intracoronary infusion of streptokinase. Rapid lysis of coronary thrombi has caused atrial and ventricular dysrhythmias.

Continue to observe client for bleeding during and after treatment. Because the thrombolytic effects of the drug last for several hours, the sites of invasive devices are common areas for hematoma formation.

Following therapy, monitor fibrinogen levels—which are decreased by thrombolytic agents—until they return to normal.

## ANTIHEMOPHILIC AGENTS

**Hemophilia** is a hereditary disorder caused by a deficiency of one or more plasma protein clotting factors. This condition usually leads to persistent and uncontrollable hemorrhage after even minor injury. The symptoms include excessive bleeding from wounds and hemorrhage into joints, urinary tract, and on occasion the central nervous system. There are two types of hemophilia: hemophilia A, the classic type, in which factor VIII activity is deficient, and hemophilia B, or Christmas disease, in which factor IX complex activity is deficient. In recent years a correct diagnosis of the coagulation disorder has led to specific factor replacement therapy, and this medical advance has resulted in effective management of the client at home.

### factor VIII (Factorate, Koāte)

In the intrinsic pathway of the coagulation mechanism, antihemophilic factor (AHF), or factor VIII, is required for the transformation of prothrombin to thrombin. In the treatment of hemophilia A administration of factor VIII is based on replacement of this missing plasma clotting factor. Thus AHF specifically corrects or prevents bleeding episodes in individuals with only hemophilia A.

When administered intravenously, factor VIII is rapidly cleared from the plasma. It has an average half-life of 4 hours. Mild allergic reactions, such as bronchospasm, elevated temperature, chills, or rash, may occur. More serious adverse effects—which may be related to the rate of infusion—include headache, increased heart rate, tingling of fingers, fainting, lethargy, sedation, hypotension, back pain, nausea or vomiting, visual disturbances, and chest constriction. No significant drug interactions are reported with factor VIII.

Dosage of factor VIII must be individualized according to the individual's weight, severity of the deficiency, and the amount of hemorrhage loss. During hemorrhage, the dosage is adjusted so that a level of at least 40% of normal levels of factor VIII can produce hemostasis. Clients who develop inhibitors to factor VIII may not respond to factor VIII therapy. After careful evaluation of the client, the administration of antiinhibitor coagulant complex, which reduces factor VIII inhibitors, may be indicated to correct this condition.

### ▷ Nursing Management: Factor VIII Therapy

*Assessment.* Weigh the benefits of antihemophilic factor against the risk of hepatitis associated with its administration. Obtain baseline values of coagulation studies and vital signs before administering antihemophilic factor. If the pulse increases significantly, reduce the rate of the administration or stop the drug.

*Intervention.* Vaccinate the client against hepatitis B, as ordered, using hepatitis B vaccine inactivated. Since factor VIII is prepared from human plasma, the risk of transmitting hepatitis exists.

Refrigerate the concentrate, but do not freeze it until ready for use. Do not refrigerate after reconstitution, as the active ingredient may precipitate. Warm the concentrate and diluent to room temperature before reconstitution. Gently rotate (do not shake) vial containing the concentrate and diluent until it is completely dissolved. This may take as long as 5 to 10 minutes. Since the antihemophilic factor is filtered before administration, the active components would be filtered out if it is not fully dissolved. Although antihemophilic factor remains stable for 24 hours at room temperature after reconstitution, it should be used within 3 hours. Do not mix with other medications.

Antihemophilic factor is for intravenous infusion only. Use only plastic syringes to prepare for administration, since the solution adheres to the ground surfaces of glass syringes.

*Evaluation.* Monitor vital signs over the course of the drug's administration. Adverse effects are related to the rate of administration. Slow the rate of flow or stop the infusion until the symptoms of flushing, headache, and alterations of blood pressure and pulse disappear. Periodic coagulation studies will determine the efficacy of the drug with each client.

### antiinhibitor coagulant complex (Autoplex, Feiba VH Immuno)

Antiinhibitor coagulant complex is made from pooled human plasma. It contains variable quantities of clotting factors and kinin system factors and has been standardized to help correct clotting time in factor VIII–deficient individuals or to treat factor VIII–deficient individuals who have plasma-containing inhibitors to factor VIII.

Antiinhibitor coagulant complex is indicated for clients with factor VIII inhibitors who are bleeding or if they are being prepared for surgery. Approximately 10% of factor VIII–deficient individuals have inhibitors to factor VIII present. Generally clients with factor VIII inhibitor levels greater than 10 Bethesda units are treated with this product.

Allergic reactions and hypersensitivity (fever, chills, rash, hypotension) reactions have been reported. If administered too rapidly, the recipient may experience flushing, headache, and changes in blood pressure and heart rate. These are indications to slow the rate of flow or stop the infusion until the symptoms disappear. Concurrent administration with epsilon-aminocaproic acid or tranexamic acid is not recommended.

Antiinhibitor coagulant complex is administered only by intravenous infusion. The recommended dose varies from 25 to 100 units/kg depending on site and severity of the hemorrhage. Check current package insert or USP-DI for specific recommendations. Pregnancy safety for this product is FDA Category C.

For nursing management, see factor VIII discussion.

### factor IX complex (Konȳne HT Proplex T)

Factor IX complex is a purified plasma fraction prepared from pooled units of plasma. It contains factors II, VII, IX, and X, which are known as the vitamin K coagulation factors. This agent is used for therapy in individuals with a deficiency of these factors during hemorrhage or before surgery. It is also indicated for hemophilia B in which factor IX is deficient. Factor IX complex is used to prevent or control bleeding in individuals with factor IX deficiency. It is also used to treat clients with bleeding problems who have

inhibitors to Factor VIII and will reverse hemorrhage induced by coumarin anticoagulants.

Factor IX has a half-life of approximately 24 hours. Chills and fever have been reported, especially when large doses are given. Also, if the intravenous infusion is given too rapidly, headache, flushing, rash, nausea, vomiting, sedation, lethargy, elevated temperature, and tingling have been reported. The infusion should be stopped and in most clients it can be resumed at a much slower rate.

**Thrombosis** or disseminated intravascular coagulation (DIC) has occurred as a result of the administration of factor IX. It should not be used in individuals undergoing elective surgery, since they are at a greater risk for thrombosis. No significant drug interactions have been reported to date. It is administered slowly by intravenous injection or by intravenous infusion. The dosage is individualized according to the client's coagulation assay, which is performed before treatment. Check current references for specific dosing recommedations. Pregnancy safety for factor IX is FDA Category C.

### ▷ Nursing Management: Factor IX Therapy

The considerations are as for factor VIII, except for instructions for preparation.

Factor IX is administered intravenously or by intravenous infusion only, at a rate not to exceed 3 ml/min. Warm diluent to room temperature before reconstitution. Gently rotate mixture in vial until it is completely dissolved, or the active components will be filtered out when it is administered through the filter needle. Although stable for 12 hours at room temperature, it should be used within 3 hours of reconstitution. Do not refrigerate reconstituted preparation, since the active ingredients may precipitate.

## HEMOSTATIC AGENTS

Hemostatic agents are compounds used to hasten clot formation to reduce bleeding. The purpose of these agents is to control rapid loss of blood.

### Systemic Hemostatics

#### aminocaproic acid (Amicar, Epsikapron ✷)

Aminocaproic acid is a synthetic compound that inhibits fibrinolysis when excessive bleeding occurs. This drug acts as a competitive antagonist of plasminogen, preventing the generation of plasmin and thereby inhibiting the dissolution of clots. To a lesser degree, it may inhibit plasmin (fibrinolysin) by noncompetitive mechanisms.

It is used in the treatment of fibrinolysis-induced hemorrhage such as fibrinolytic bleeding following heart surgery, prostatectomy, nephrectomy, and hematologic disorders such as aplastic anemia, hepatic cirrhosis, and neoplastic disease states. It has also been used as a specific antidote for an overdose of thrombolytic drugs such as streptokinase and urokinase, even though this use is not approved.

Aminocaproic acid is absorbed orally and reaches a peak concentration within 2 hours. The therapeutic serum concentration is 130 μg/ml to inhibit systemic hyperfibrinolysis. It is excreted mainly by the kidneys. Side effects reported with this drug include nausea, diarrhea, menstrual difficulties, and increased weakness. Adverse reactions include weakness or severe muscle pain; a decrease in urination; edema of face, feet, or lower legs; unusual weight gain; slow or irregular heart rate; abdominal pain; rash; stuffy nose; tinnitus; bloodshot eyes; and thrombosis. No significant drug interactions are reported with aminocaproic acid.

Adult dose is 5 g orally initially followed by 1 or 1.25 g hourly for up to 8 hours or until the desired response is achieved. Maximum dose is 30 g/24 hours. Pediatric dose is 100 mg/kg body weight the first hour, followed by 33.3 mg/kg hourly up to 18 grams/m²/24 hours. Parenteral adult dose is 4 or 5 g by intravenous infusion initially during the first hour, then 1 g/hour up to 8 hours or until the desired response is achieved. Pediatric dose by intravenous infusion is the same as the oral dose.

▷ **Nursing Management:**
**Aminocaproic Acid Therapy**

*Assessment.* Aminocaproic acid is contraindicated for use in clients with active intravascular clotting. It is used cautiously in individuals with cardiac, hepatic, or renal disease or those with a predisposition to thrombosis. With the administration of aminocaproic acid, the client is at risk for the development of the following nursing diagnoses: altered comfort related to headache, myopathy, tinnitus, rash, nausea, abdominal cramping, diarrhea, or unusual menstrual cramping; high risk for injury related to renal failure or thromboembolism; altered bowel elimination (diarrhea); and altered urinary pattern related to bladder obstruction caused by blood clot formation.

Assess baseline vital signs and coagulation studies initially and periodically during administration.

*Intervention.* Dilute before administering intravenously. Administer slowly, since too rapid infusion may result in hypotension or bradycardia. Take care with insertion and positioning of the infusion needle to minimize thrombophlebitis.

*Evaluation.* Monitor client for signs of thromboembolic complications such as thrombophlebitis, pulmonary embolus, myocardial infarction, and cerebrovascular accident. Aminocaproic acid therapy is generally discontinued when there is cessation of bleeding or when laboratory values for fibrinolysis are normal.

### tranexamic acid (Cyklocapron)

Tranexamic acid is a competitive inhibitor of plasminogen activation; at high doses, it is a noncompetitive inhibitor of plasmin. Its effects are similar to aminocaproic acid but it

is appoximately 5 to 10 times more potent in vitro. It is used after dental surgery in clients with hemophilia to reduce or prevent bleeding episodes. Peak plasma level is reached 3 hours after oral administration; peak plasma level is 8 μg/ml after a 1-g dose. Duration of action in serum is 7 to 8 hours, and excretion is by the kidneys.

Nausea, vomiting, or diarrhea are side effects that may occur, but they usually disappear if the dosage is reduced. Giddiness or dizziness is reported infrequently. With intravenous injection, hypotension may be observed if the injection is given too rapidly. No significant drug interactions have been reported.

The oral adult and adolescent dose preceding dental surgery in hemophiliacs is 25 mg/kg three or four times daily, starting a day before the planned dental procedure. Postsurgically, the dose is 25 mg/kg orally three or four times daily for 2 to 8 days. By injection the dose is 10 mg/kg before surgery and 10 mg/kg postsurgically three or four times daily for 2 to 8 days. The parenteral postsurgical dose is only used in clients that cannot take the oral product. Pregnancy safety for tranexamic acid is FDA Category B.

▷ **Nursing Management:**
**Tranexamic Acid Therapy**

See nursing management of aminocaproic acid. In addition to those nursing measures, tranexamic acid places the client at risk for visual disturbances. For this reason ophthalmologic examinations (visual acuity, color vision, eyegrounds, and visual fields) are suggested before and periodically during therapy. It is recommended that administration of the drug be discontinued if visual changes occur or if thromboembolic complications occur.

Tranexamic acid, as an intravenous medication, should not be administered at a rate greater than 100 mg/minute, or the client may experience hypotension.

## Topical Hemostatics

### absorbable gelatin sponge (Gelfoam)

Absorbable gelatin sponge is a specially prepared form of nonantigenic gelatin that is capable of holding many times its weight in whole blood. It is used in thin strips to control capillary bleeding and may be left in place in a surgical wound. It is completely absorbed in 4 to 6 weeks. It should be well moistened with isotonic saline solution or thrombin solution before it is applied to a bleeding surface. Its presence does not induce excessive scar formation. Sterile technique must be used to avoid infection.

When inserted into cavities or tissue spaces, the gelatin sponge reduces bleeding by acting as a tampon. The contact with the sponge damages platelets, liberating thromboplastin that is needed for clot formation. This product completely dissolves within 2 to 5 days when applied to bleeding areas on skin or in nose, rectum, or vagina.

It is indicated in surgical procedures as an adjunct to hemostasis when bleeding is not controlled by ligature or when such methods are impractical. It is also used by dentists to aid in hemostasis. Insertion of the gelatin sponge in the prostatic cavity promotes hemostasis in open prostatic surgery. The gelatin sponge may provide a site for infection. Monitor the surgical incision/implantation site closely for redness, swelling, or discomfort, as well as for signs of recurrent bleeding. No significant drug interactions have been reported. This product is available in different sizes and diameters. Application instructions and size depend on the area to be treated.

### absorbable gelatin film (Gelfilm)

A sterile absorbable gelatin film (Gelfilm) is also available for specific indications, as in neurosurgery, thoracic, or ocular surgery. When implanted in tissues, the rate of absorption could range from 1 to 6 months, depending on the site of implantation and the size of the film implanted. This product is useful as a dural substitute (neurosurgery) or to repair pleural defects during thoracic surgery.

### absorbable gelatin powder (Gelfoam)

A sterile absorbable gelatin powder (Gelfoam) is also available to promote hemostasis. This powder can be made into a paste to control bleeding from bone areas when standard procedures such as ligatures are ineffective or not practical. It is also used to treat chronic leg ulcers and decubitus ulcers.

### oxidized cellulose (Novocell, Oxycel, Surgicel)

Oxidized cellulose is a specially treated form of surgical gauze or cotton that exerts a hemostatic effect but is absorbable when buried in the tissues. The hemostatic action is caused by the formation of an artificial clot by cellulosic acid. Absorption of oxidized cellulose occurs between the second and the seventh days following implantation, although absorption of large amounts of blood-soaked material may take 6 weeks or longer. Oxidized cellulose is valuable in controlling bleeding in surgery of organs such as the liver, pancreas, spleen, kidney, thyroid, and prostate. Its hemostatic action is not increased by the addition of other hemostatic agents. It should not be used as a surface dressing except for the control of bleeding, because cellulosic acid inhibits the growth of epithelial tissue. Since it interferes with bone regeneration, it should not be implanted in fractures.

No significant drug interactions are reported. Use sterile techniques in applying or inserting the cellulose. Do not moisten it. Serious adverse reactions are related to site of application, amount used, and pressure applied to blood vessel or specific area. Careful application and monitoring are necessary to reduce complications such as obstruction, necrosis, and stenosis. When used following nasal polyp removal or hemorroidectomy, a burning sensation has been reported. Headache, stinging, and sneezing may also occur.

### microfibrillar collagen hemostat (Avitene)

This is an absorbable topical hemostatic substance that, when placed on a bleeding surface, will attract platelets and platelet aggregation in the area, forming thrombi. It is used as an adjunct to hemostasis during surgery when ligature or standard procedures are not effective or impractical.

Adhesions, allergic or foreign body reactions, hematomas, or infections such as abscesses may occur. Monitor closely, as these conditions may cause serious problems. No significant drug interactions are reported.

Generally it is applied directly on the source of bleeding in a dry form. Do not moisten or wet this substance, and do not resterilize it. Apply pressure over the area with a dry sponge for a minute or more. Use dry forceps to handle, as it will adhere to wet gloves or instruments. Do not use gloved fingers to apply the necessary pressure.

### thrombin (Thrombinar, Thrombostat)

Thrombin is a hemostatic agent prepared as a sterile powder obtained from bovine prothrombin that has been treated with thromboplastin in the presence of calcium. Thrombin catalyzes the conversion of fibrinogen to fibrin. It has several additional mechanisms, which may include stimulating the release reaction and aggregation of platelets. It is used topically to treat capillary bleeding. It has also been used during various surgeries with absorbable gelatin sponge for hemostasis.

Usually 2 US units are needed to clot 1 ml of oxalated human plasma.*

Some febrile reactions and an allergic type reaction when used for epistaxis have been reported. No significant drug interactions are reported.

Thrombin may be applied topically as a powder or solution. Concentration of the preparation varies with its use. See package insert.

▷ **Nursing Management:
Thrombin Therapy**

***Assessment.*** Ascertain whether the client is sensitive to bovine products.

***Intervention.*** Do not inject thrombin into large blood vessels, since extensive intravascular clotting and even death may result. Sponge—do not wipe—all blood from recipient surface before applying the thrombin as a powder or a solution. If applied as a powder, it may need to be pulverized with a sterile instrument before use. Do not sponge once the thrombin is applied to avoid disturbing the clotting. Thrombin may be used in association with absorbable gelatin foam. In this case, the saturated sponge is applied to the bleeding area for 10 to 15 seconds to promote hemostasis.

---

*One US unit is equivalent to 1 National Institutes of Health (NIH) unit.

Following reconstitution, use solution within a few hours or freeze and use within 48 hours.

**Evaluation.** Monitor client for recurrent bleeding, infection, and allergic reaction.

## BLOOD AND BLOOD COMPONENTS

The bloodstream is the main mode of transport and distribution in the body. As such, it functions to deliver vital nutrients, water, and oxygen from the digestive and respiratory systems to all body parts. Wastes are retrieved for excretion by the bloodstream. In the kidneys, the bloodstream provides the hydrostatic pressure necessary to create urine as an excretory vehicle for those waste products. It conveys hormones from endocrine glands and enzymes, vitamins, buffers, and other biochemical substances to target areas. The bloodstream buffers and regulates the body's heat-exchange processes by absorbing and transferring core body heat to the surface for dissipation, and it buffers the body's acid-base balance. The bloodstream also carries components such as platelets, blood cells, and antibodies to sites where a sudden need for these exists, as in hemorrhage, inflammation, or infection. It creates oncotic or colloid osmotic pressure to regulate the volume of interstitial fluids. It also transports therapeutic additives such as medications, fluids, electrolytes, and nutrients to their respective sites of action.

### Abnormal States of Blood Components

Normally, a thrifty bodily balance is maintained between the production and loss, attrition, or excretion of all components that comprise the bloodstream. Pathologic conditions result from a disturbance in production or an excessive loss or excretion of one or more components. Hemorrhage results in a generally impoverished bloodstream and may significantly alter many body functions. Impaired production or increased destruction of any one component may impinge on one or more functions. All this is a matter of degree. If the impairment is minor or is detected early, correction of the cause and replenishment by natural or therapeutic means may restore functioning. Naturally harmful or foreign substances also may build up in the bloodstream when excretory systems fail (e.g., renal failure) or when metabolizing capabilities fail (e.g., liver failure). Some examples follow.

Depending on the individual's size and preexisting blood integrity, acute whole blood loss of more than 500 ml is manifested by signs of anemia. Chronic, gradual, unnoticed blood loss from gastrointestinal tract malignancy, ulcers, or hemorrhoids may be compensated for naturally, or iron deficiency anemia may develop. Signs of anemia usually reflect the true importance of red blood cell loss. Deficiencies in intake or functioning of certain essential nutritional elements may result in iron deficiency anemia or one of the megaloblastic anemias, which usually are caused by deficiencies in vitamin $B_{12}$ or folic acid. A pathologic overabundance of erythrocytes can be compensation for long-standing hypoxia from pulmonary or cardiac disease, certain tumors, or polycythemia vera. Delayed or disordered production of erythrocytes (aplastic anemia) may result from disorders of the reticuloendothelial system, primarily the bone marrow, which is responsible for their systematic production. The bone marrow is particularly vulnerable to certain drugs, poisons, and antineoplastic agents. On the other hand, too-rapid destruction of erythrocytes can lead to hemolytic anemia.

Leukocytes also are lost in hemorrhage, but reductions in their numbers most often are associated with certain specific conditions. Each of the five types of white blood cells—neutrophils, eosinophils, basophils, lymphocytes, and monocytes—is associated with different disorders. For example, abnormally low neutrophil counts are associated with certain aplastic diseases, as well as with acute reactions to such drugs as sulfonamides, propylthioracil, and chloramphenicol. Excessively high neutrophil counts primarily are found with bacterial infections, as well as with some inflammatory disorders, leukemia, and hyperplastic disorders.

Thrombocytes also may be present in inadequate numbers because of their rapid destruction, typically caused by idiopathic thromboyctopenia purpura. Conversely, excessive platelet counts are associated most often with hyperplastic disorders, iron deficiency anemia, splenectomy, and chronic inflammatory conditions such as tuberculosis. Other factors crucial to the clotting process may be absent in hemophilia and similar disorders.

Losses of the liquid portion of the blood can create dehydration problems, impede metabolic processes that function only through use of hydrogen or oxygen molecules, or subvert hydrodynamic and hydraulic processes.

In addition to hemorrhage, plasma proteins may be lost through burn wounds or wound drainage or may be insufficient because adequate available substrates such as amino acids are lacking. The results vary, depending on the type of plasma protein, and may include deficiencies in immune status, blood viscosity, or colloid osmotic pressure (oncotic pressure).

### Replacement Therapies

Therapy to replace all or certain components of the bloodstream is a common practice in most health facilities. Since blood is considered a tissue, transfusions are technically tissue transplants. The usual treatment of choice is replacement of the sole blood component that is deficient rather than whole blood, since the body is better able to replace intravascular fluids than formed elements of the blood. Transfusing only the depleted blood fraction serves two

**TABLE 30-6**   Indications for common blood component therapies

| Component | Indications |
|---|---|
| Whole blood | Hemorrhage, hypovolemic shock |
| Fresh whole blood | Multiple transfusions, exchange transfusions; priming agent for hemodialysis machines (normal saline also may be used) |
| Packed red blood cells | Transfused when whole blood could result in circulatory overload |
| Deglycerolized or washed red cells | Transfused when hypersensitivity reactions are likely; as in immunosuppressed clients and those with history of reactions or extreme hypersensitivity |
| Fresh-frozen plasma (FFP) | Clotting deficiencies, especially factors V and VII; blood volume expansion in burns, shock, or protein deficiencies (believed to be overused for these deficiencies) |
| Plasma exchange (plasmapheresis): blood drawn off, cleansed, and components returned | Immune-related disorders: multiple myeloma, glomerulonephritis, systemic lupus erythematosus, rheumatoid arthritis, myasthenia gravis |
| Plasma expanders (Dextran—large polysaccharide polymer) | Temporary volume expansion in hemorrhagic shock states (sole use for Dextran 70 or 75); not a substitute for blood or plasma |
| Granulocytes | Granulocyte counts below 500 |
| Platelets | Platelet counts at or below 20,000/mm³ |
| Cryoprecipitate (fresh-frozen plasma precipitate; contains factors I and VIII) | Hemophilia, fibrinogen deficiency, von Willebrand's disease |
| Antihemophilic factor (AHF) concentrate Factor VII | Treatment of hemophilia; preferred over FFP |
| Factor IX complex | Hemophilia B; deficiencies of clotting factors II, VII, X; coumarin overdose |
| Plasma protein fraction (PPF) | Hypovolemic shock; protein replacement; burns; adult respiratory distress syndrome, dehydration, and hypoalbuminemia; as additive to complement packed cells when necessary |
| Fibrinogen | When fibrinogen levels insufficient for adequate control of bleeding |
| Albumin | Blood volume expansion by oncotic pressure; prevention and treatment of cerebral edema |
| Gamma globulins | Exposure to hepatitis; to prevent complications of mumps |

other purposes: (1) it prevents the fluid overload in high-risk individuals such as the elderly and those with cardiovascular or renal disease, and (2) it more efficiently uses the remaining blood fractions for other clients needs. Table 30-6 outlines indications for this therapy. When a client is to receive blood, the nurse is largely responsible for its safe administration.

▷ **Nursing Management:**
**Blood and Blood Component**
**Replacement Therapies**

**Assessment.** Take client history regarding previous transfusions and the client's response to them. Report any history of an adverse reaction to the physician and the blood bank. Gather baseline data about the client's blood studies and vital signs before administration and observe the general appearance and demeanor of the client.

**Intervention.** Administer blood components promptly to ensure that the transfused product is fresh, uncoagulated, and without toxic breakdown products. Before administration, the product should remain out of the blood bank's refrigerator and untransfused for no longer than 30 minutes.

Refrigeration in the standard hospital units or home refrigerator will not prevent deterioration. Blood and blood components must not lie unused at the nursing station but must be returned to the blood bank refrigerator if not administered within half an hour. A unit of whole blood or packed RBCs cannot be returned to a blood bank if it has been out of a monitored environment (1° to 6° C) for more than 30 minutes. Whole blood or packed red blood cells should be transfused within 2 hours, 4 hours at the most.

Since incompatibility is a possibility, especially after multiple doses of these products, take such precautions as scrupulously comparing the product ordered and the label on the product before administration. Often the worst adverse reactions to blood transfusions result from misidentification of the blood or client. Although procedures of various institutions vary, at least two persons, often two registered nurses, must verify the identification of blood product and client. Client identification must match, as well as the prescriber's name, blood type, Rh factor, and unit number. Note Venereal Disease Research Laboratories' (VDRL) information and expiration date. Compare the client's identifying armband or tag to the label on the container.

Nurses should be aware of transfusion hazards in certain blood-type combinations. Careful typing and crossmatching help to prevent serious complications. ABO antigen-antibody reactions result from the following and must be avoided:

| Recipient's Blood Type | Should Not Receive |
|---|---|
| A | Type B or AB |
| B | Type A or AB |
| O | Any except type O |

| Recipient's Blood Type | Reactions with Multiple Transfusions |
|---|---|
| A | Type O |
| B | Type O |
| AB | Type A, B, or O |

Immediately report to the blood bank any discrepancies between the information on the compatibility tag, the unit of blood, and the physician's order on the clinical record; blood that is past its expiration date; or any signs of contamination.

Hypersensitivity is also common, since most of these products are essentially foreign proteins. Exceptions include autologous transfusions collected previously from the patient's own blood or transfusions of inert, synthetic products. Twenty-five milligrams of diphenhydramine injected into blood transfusion tubing before the transfusion or taken orally is recommended to prevent allergic reactions.

Return the product to the blood bank or laboratory if the contents appear unusual because of discoloration, gas bubbles, or an overfull (gaseous) appearance. Mix the contents by gently upending the container once or twice, taking care not to bruise or damage blood cells or other fragile components by squeezing or agitating the bag carelessly.

Note that many of these agents require the concomitant use of a 170 µg filter incorporated into the transfusion tubing to remove the debris and tiny clots found in the blood. Check the filter often to ensure that it is not clogged and slowing the transfusion. If the rate of transfusion is too slow, it may be necessary to use a filter with a larger surface area. This may also be necessary when administering packed RBCs because of the viscosity of the product. Access to the vein should be provided by a needle no smaller than 19 gauge and fresh tubing. For adults with small veins and for children, a 22- or 23-gauge needle is recommended. A normal saline solution should be hung in tandem with the blood product using a Y-set multiple lead tubing. Use the saline solution to flush the tubing before connecting it to the insertion site. Using straight tubing limits the possibility of stopping the transfusion while keeping the vein open if the client has an untoward response to the blood. Piggybacking on an established intravenous line increases the risk of contamination, especially with the administration of multiple units of blood. Do not tranfuse more than 2 units per administration set.

Infuse appoximately 60 ml of saline through the tubing before and after the transfusion. Do not use dextrose and other solutions with red blood cell products, since they may react with the product in the tubing to clump cells and cause hemolysis.

When inserting the spike of the administration set into the port of the blood bag, guide it straight into the container to avoid puncturing the side of the bag. Note that infusion pumps specifically for maintaining transfusion rates are safe and reliable when used with appropriate tubing and filters. Raising the height of the container or applying a pressure sleeve to the bag (at pressures up to 300 mm Hg) is also useful to maintain transfusion flows at prescribed rates. Higher pressures may burst the bag.

To maintain the prescribed infusion rate, agitate the blood by inverting the bag frequently during administration. If a rapid transfusion is to be made through a CVP line, a blood-warming device (up to 37° C or 98.6° F) will be necessary.

Do not administer any medications through the same tubing while any blood products are infusing.

Documentation should include the client's baseline vital signs before the transfusion was started; the signatures of the two persons who identified the client and the blood product; the blood product administered; the time the transfusion was started and completed; the total volume of fluid transfused, listing the starter solution separately; the client's response to the transfusion; and any nursing intervention taken in response to an adverse response to the blood.

Be aware that the risks of nursing personnel contracting diseases such as or hepatitis when accidentally injected with pooled blood, especially repeatedly, are not entirely known. Therefore take care when manipulating these products and their equipment.

**Education.** Explain the transfusion procedure to the client, especially the reason it has been ordered. Many elderly clients associate blood transfusion with being critically ill and may be upset about the need for a blood transfusion. Ensure that a consent form for the procedure has been signed.

Instruct the client to report any symptoms of an adverse reaction, such as nausea, chills, burning sensations, or headache.

**Evaluation.** As administration begins, observe the client closely for reactions for 15 minutes or more while the flow rate is kept at 20 to 30 drops/minute. Assess and record vital signs several times during the first 15 minutes. If reactions occur, stop the transfusion and administer prescribed corrective measures. Observe the client for the development of the following:

- Apprehension; restlessness; flushed skin; increased pulse and respiratory rates; burning sensations; fever; chills; dyspnea; chest, head or back pain; shock—hemolysis (possible blood type incompatibility)
- Rash; swellings of the skin, face, or throat; pruritus; shock—allergic reaction

- Fever and chills starting 1 hour after administration and lasting up to 10 hours—febrile reaction
- Nausea, weakness, jaundice considerably later—possible viral hepatitis
- Fever and chills, hypotension, vomiting, abdominal pain, bloody diarrhea—bacterial contamination
- Dyspnea, tight chest, cough with basilar rales, pulmonary edema—circulatory overload
- Cyanosis, dyspnea, abrupt onset of localized pain, shock—air embolism
- Frequent assessment of the needle insertion site is essential, since absorption of infiltrated blood is very slow.

If no symptoms of reactions appear after the first 15 minutes, the flow rate may be calculated and set so that therapy is concluded in 1½ to 2 hours (volumes usually are between 250 and 500 ml). Continue monitoring vital signs and observing for symptoms throughout administration.

One unit of whole blood typically raises the average adult's hemoglobin level by 1 to 1.5 g/dl and the hematocrit by 2% to 3%.

## SUMMARY

This chapter reviewed substances that concern anticoagulant therapy, thrombolytic therapy, and blood and blood component administration.

Anticoagulant therapy is primarily prophylactic; it acts to prevent fibrin deposits, thrombus extension, and thromboembolic complications by decreasing blood coagulability. Anticoagulants may be administered parenterally or orally. Heparin (the parenteral drug) acts immediately but has a short duration of action (less than four hours). Coumarin and the indanedione derivatives are administered orally; the onset of action is slow (24 to 48 hours) and the duration is long (2 to 5 days). This allows heparin and coumarin to be used in a complementary fashion. They may be started simultaneously, heparin being used when an immediate an-

ticoagulant effect is needed, with its dosage being tapered off as the oral agent is producing its full therapeutic effect. In the administration of both types of anticoagulants, the client has potential for injury related to increased bleeding tendencies, so nursing care focuses on observation, protection, and education of the client to prevent injury. There are specific antidotes for both parenteral and oral anticoagulants: protamine sulfate is the antidote for heparin, and vitamin K for the oral anticoagulants.

Whereas anticoagulants are used prophylactically, thrombolytic agents are used to dissolve clots in the treatment of acute thromboembolic disorders. Thrombolytic enzyme therapy with streptokinase, urokinase, alteplase, or anistreplase alters the hemostatic capability of the client to a greater extent than anticoagulant therapy; therefore when bleeding does occur, it is more severe and more difficult to control. Hemostatic agents are compounds used to hasten clot formation to reduce bleeding and therefore control rapid blood loss. Aminocaproic acid, a hemostatic agent, has been used as an antidote for the thrombolytic agents, but this use is not approved.

The antihemophilic agents are specific factors within the clotting process that can be used in replacement therapy for clients who have a hemophilia, a deficiency of one or more plasma protein clotting factors. With accurate diagnosis of the specific missing factor, this replacement therapy has allowed for successful management of these clients at home.

Blood and blood components may need to be replaced as the result of impaired production, excessive loss, or increased destruction of any of the components. Since blood is considered a tissue, transfusions are essentially tissue transplants. The preferred therapy is replacement of the sole blood component that is deficient rather than whole blood. However, the nurse needs to be alert to the many responses that clients may have to such transfusions. Careful typing and crossmatching helps to prevent many serious complications, but careful observation of the client is essential during transfusion of blood and blood components.

## Case Study: The Client with Deep-Vein Thrombosis

John Tucker, a 53-year-old construction worker, has been admitted to the hospital with a diagnosis of deep-vein thrombosis of the right leg. Mr. Tucker has had increasing pain and swelling of the right leg over several days. He has received an intravenous bolus of 5000 units of heparin followed by a continuous infusion of heparin (25,000 units in 1000 ml of 0.9% sodium chloride).

1. What measures should the nurse implement to ensure accurate administration of the continuous heparin infusion?

2. What data are used by the nurse to evaluate the client's response to the heparin therapy?

3. In preparation for discharge in 4 days, Mr. Tucker is started on warfarin sodium (Coumadin) while he is still receiving the intravenous heparin. What is the reason for administering two anticoagulants?

4. The nurse carefully questions Mr. Tucker about his use of OTC medications. He admits to using aspirin for headaches and assorted muscle aches from his job. He also takes a multiple vitamin daily. How should the nurse respond to this information?

5. What additional information does the client need to promote safety during anticoagulant therapy?

# BIBLIOGRAPHY

American Hospital Formulary Service. (1991). AFHS drug information '91. Bethesda, Md: American Society of Hospital Pharmacists, Inc.

Anistreplase (Eminase by Beecham)—a thrombolytic agent. (1990). Hosp Pharmacy 25(2):199.

Ansari A et al. (1987). Sudden abdominal pain during antiplatelet and anticoagulant therapy, Physician Assist 11(8):53.

Are you overdoing anticoagulant therapy? Emerg Med 21(11):173.

Bagnall HA et al. (1989). Continuous infusion of low dose urokinase in the treatment of central venous catheterization thrombosis in infants and children, Pediatrics 83(6):963.

Birdsall C et al. (1988). How is auto transfusion done? Amer J Nurs 88(1):108.

Blood transfusion: the state of the art. (1988). Emerg Med 20(20):180.

Brewer-Senerchia C. (1989). Thrombolytic therapy: a review of the literature on streptokinase and tissue plasmogen activator with implications for practice, Crit Care Nurs Clin North Amer 1(2):359.

Brewer-Senerchia C. (1988). The thrombolysis in myocardial infarction (TIMI) trial phase I and phase IIa pilot results: implications for nursing, Prog Cardiovascul Nur 3(4):128.

Brooks-Brunn JA. (1988). Thrombolytic intervention and its effect on mortality in acute myocardial infarction: review of clinical trials, Heart Lung 17(6):756.

Cunliffe MT et al. (1986). How to clear catheter clots with urokinase, Nursing 16(12):40.

Cygenski JM et al. (1987). The case for heparin flush, Am J Nurs 87(6):796.

Davis KG. (1986). The blood story. IV. Adverse reactions to blood transfusion, Aust Nurs J 15(6):40.

Devine P et al. (1988). Quality assurance of hospital transfusion practices: the role of nursing staff, QRB 14(8):250.

Elguidi AS et al. (1986). Embolex: to prevent a double post-op danger . . . DVT and pulmonary embolism, Nursing 16(5):73.

Gilman AG et al, eds. (1990). Goodman and Gilman's the pharmacological basis of therapeutics. ed 8. New York: Macmillan Publishing Co.

Ginsberg JS et al. (1989). Use of coagulants during pregnancy, Chest 95(2):1565.

Gold HK. (1988). Heart attacks: the first few hours, Harv Med Sch Health Lett 13(11):5.

Hall MA et al. (1987). The routine use of vitamin K in the newborn, Midwifery 3(4):170.

Hanson MJS. (1987). Hematoma associated with subcutaneous heparin administration, Focus Crit Care 14(6):62.

Hematuria during anticoagulant therapy deserves workup. (1987). Nurses Drug Alert 11(10):77.

Henderson E. (1989). Clinical experience with thrombolytic agents, J Emerg Nurs 15(2):174.

Herfindal ET et al. (1988). Clinical pharmacy and therapeutics, ed 4. Baltimore: Williams & Wilkins.

Hirsh J et al. (1989). Optimal therapeutic range for oral anticoagulants, Chest 95(2):55.

Hirsh J et al. (1986). Treatment of venous thromboembolism, Chest 89(5):426S.

Hull RD et al. (1986). Prophylaxis of venous thromboembolism: an overview, Chest 89(5):374S.

Hyers TM et al. (1989). Antithrombolic therapy for venous thromboembolic disease, Chest 95(2):37S.

Jowett NI et al. (1986). Do indwelling cannulae on coronary units need a heparin flush? Intensive Care Nurs 2(6):16.

Kennedy JW. (1987). Thrombolytic therapy for acute myocardial infarction: a brief review. Heart Lung 16(6):740.

Kleven MR. (1988). Comparison of the agents: mechanism of action, efficacy and safety, Heart Lung 17(6):750.

Kline E. (1988). Management of bleeding in the patient receiving thrombolytic therapy for acute myocardial infarction: a nursing perspective, Heart Lung 17(6):771.

Korsmeyer C et al. (1987). The nurse's role in thrombolytic therapy for acute myocardial infarction, Crit Care Nurse 7(6):22.

Krokosky NJ et al. (1989). Running an anticoagulant clinic, Am J Nurs 89(10):1304.

Lancier WC et al. (1987). How to administer blood components to children, MCN 12(3):178.

Lichtor JL. (1989). Transfusion reaction, part 1, Curr Rev Post Anesth Nurs 11(6):42.

Litwach K. (1987). Practical points for transfusion therapy, J Post Anesth Nurs 2(4):257.

Miller JA. (1989). Transfusion of blood and and blood products, Prof Nurse 4(11):560.

Olson AR. (1987). What you should know about thrombolytic therapy, Nursing 17(12):52.

Niemyski P et al. (1989). Patient selection and management in thrombolytic therapy: nursing implication, Crit Care Nurs Q 12(2):18.

Pariser R. (1987). Thrombolytic therapy in acute myocardial infarction, Emerg Care Q 3(2):86.

Peck NL. (1987). Action STAT! Blood transfusion reaction, Nursing 17(1):33.

Phillips A. (1987). Are blood transfusions really safe? Nursing 17(6):63.

Ramsden CS. (1988). Treatment strategies after successful thrombolysis in acute myocardial infarction, Heart Lung 17(6):777.

Reidy SJ et al. (1989). Streptokinase use in children undergoing cardiac catheterization, J Cardiovas Nurs 4(1):46.

Smith Kline Beecham Laboratories & The Upjohn Co. (1990). Eminase (anistreplase, 30u) Information Letter, January 1990.

Study suggests added benefit from combined aspirin-streptokinase therapy after myocardial infarction. (1988). Clinical Pharmacy 7(11):785.

Todd B. (1987). Use heparin safely, Geriatr Nurse 8(4):48.

Topol EJ. (1987). Clinical use of streptokinase and urokinase therapy for acute myocardial infarction, Heart Lung 16(6):760.

United States Pharmacopeial Convention. (1991). Drug information for the health care professional, ed 11. Rockville, Md: The Convention.

Vitello-Ciccini J. (1987). Thrombolytic therapy-urokinase, J Cardiovascul Nurs 1(2):59.

Weinstein SM. (1986). Thrombolytic therapy, NITA 9(1):31.

Wilson JM. (1988). Avoiding errors in intravenous heparin therapy, AD Nurse 3(3):31.

# Chapter

## 🌿 31     Antihyperlipidemic Drugs

---

## CHAPTER OBJECTIVES

*After studying this chapter, you should be able to meet the following objectives and define the key terms.*

1. Define hyperlipidemia and describe the pathophysiology of this condition.

2. Identify the four types of lipoproteins and differentiate according to their lipid content.

3. Discuss the importance of combining dietary modifications with drug therapy to treat hyperlipidemia.

4. Utilize the appropriate nursing management with clients receiving antihyperlipidemic agents.

## KEY TERMS

**atherosclerosis,** page 568

**chylomicrons,** page 569

**high-density lipoproteins (HDLs),** page 569

**hyperlipidemia,** page 568

**lipoproteins,** page 569

**low-density lipoproteins (LDLs),** page 569

**very low-density lipoproteins (VDLs),** page 569

## INTRODUCTION

Antihyperlipidemic or antilipemic drugs are used along with dietary modifications to modify a condition known as **hyperlipidemia.** This is a metabolic disorder characterized by increased concentrations of cholesterol and triglycerides, two of the major serum lipids in the body. Both clinical and experimental studies offer evidence that an important relationship exists between **atherosclerosis** and high levels of circulating triglycerides and cholesterol. Atherosclerosis is a disorder involving the large- and medium-sized arteries. Lipids are deposited in the lining of these blood vessels, eventually producing degenerative changes and obstructing blood flow. Atherosclerosis is a causative factor in coronary artery disease and myocardial infarction, in cerebral arterial disease that results in senility or cerebrovascular accidents, in peripheral arterial occlusive disease (which may cause gangrene and loss of limb), and in renal arterial insufficiency. It is also a factor in hypertension. Therefore there is intensive research to develop more effective and safer antihyperlipidemic drugs. If serum lipid or blood lipid levels could be controlled within normal limits, the development and progression of atherosclerosis might be inhibited or prevented.

That a positive relationship exists between high serum lipid levels and atherosclerosis is controversial. Some individuals with high serum lipid levels have no objective evidence of atherosclerosis, whereas others with marked atherosclerotic signs and symptoms have normal serum lipid levels. However, more persons with high blood lipid levels have atherosclerosis than those with so-called normal blood lipid levels. Consequently, some researchers and clinicians believe that if lipid levels can be controlled, so can the atherosclerotic process. At the present time the available antihyperlipidemic drugs are also controversial, and their place in drug therapy requires more long-term critical studies. None of the antihyperlipidemic or antilipemic drugs is thought to have any effect on reversing the atherosclerotic process once it has begun. Means of preventing atherosclerosis remain obscure. Multicausative factors are undoubtedly involved and include dietary saturated fats, faulty fat metabolism, genetic influence, and other factors as yet unknown.

## HYPERLIPIDEMIC DISORDERS

Lipid compounds do not circulate freely in the bloodstream but rather are bound to plasma proteins (albumin, globulin), which act as carriers. These complexes are called **lipoproteins.** Hyperlipoproteinemia is always associated with an increased concentration of one or more lipoproteins, particularly cholesterol.

*Classification of lipoproteins.* Lipoprotein complexes are classified according to their densities and electrophoretic mobilities. Paper electrophoresis is a process by which the blood lipid fraction is separated and identified; it includes alpha (most mobile of the moving particles), beta, and prebeta (least mobile of the moving particles) lipoproteins. The density of lipoproteins varies with the proportion of lipid to protein. The larger the size of the particle, the lower the density.

The major groups of lipoproteins are classified into four types and are listed according to their lipid composition:

1. **Chylomicrons.** The chylomicrons are the largest particles and the least dense of the lipoproteins. They consist of 85% to 95% triglycerides and 3% to 5% cholesterol. In a normal person they are produced in the small intestine during absorption of a fatty meal and are cleared from the bloodstream by the enzyme lipoprotein lipase after 12 to 14 hours. A deficiency of the enzyme is rare, but when present, it results in increased levels of chylomicrons, causing a disease called exogenous hyperlipoproteinemia. This condition is usually found in children, but it may also be induced by alcoholism. Therapy is aimed at keeping the diet low in fat. Chylomicrons lack electrophoretic mobility.

2. **Very low-density lipoproteins (VLDLs).** VLDLs or prebeta lipoproteins, contain a large amount of triglycerides (64% to 80%) and 7% to 14% cholesterol, which is formed in the liver from endogenous fat sources.

3. **Low-density lipoproteins (LDLs).** LDLs, or beta lipoproteins, contain the major portion of cholesterol in blood and may be considered the most harmful. They consist of 40% to 50% cholesterol and 7% to 10% triglycerides. An elevation of LDL levels suggests that an individual has a high potential risk for developing atherosclerosis.

4. **High-density lipoproteins (HDLs).** HDLs, or alpha lipoproteins, which are the smallest and most dense of lipoproteins, contain about 17% to 20% cholesterol and 1% to 7% triglycerides. HDL appears to be beneficial. The higher the HDL levels, the lower the potential risk for developing cardiovascular disease. HDL is protective because it picks up cholesterol and triglycerides from the body cells of membranes and carries them back to the liver, where they are metabolized and then excreted. This transport mechanism prevents the accumulation of lipids in the arterial walls, thereby providing protection against the development of coronary artery disease. It has now been found that physical exercise is beneficial because it elevates the HDL levels.

*Lipid production and hyperlipidemias.* The body has two lipid transport mechanisms; that is, exogenously, dietary fats and cholesterol are orally consumed and transported into the system by bile acids while, endogenously, the liver converts excess calories from carbohydrates and fatty acids into triglycerides (see Figure 31-1). The liver ultimately produces both HDL (high-density lipoprotein, or the good cholesterol) and LDL (low-density lipoprotein, or the bad cholesterol). The function of HDL is to carry about 25% of blood cholesterol to the liver where it is processed into bile acids. Thus the cholesterol it carries is for ultimate excretion. LDL carries over 50% by weight of cholesterol and this LDL-cholesterol combination can penetrate arterial walls resulting in atherosclerotic plaques. Therefore, in excess, it is referred to as the bad cholesterol.

The intermediate steps to producing LDL in the liver are as follows: the liver produces very low-density lipoprotein (VLDL), which consists mainly of triglycerides and a small amount of cholesterol (about 12%). It carries liver fats to peripheral tissues in the presence of lipase and insulin. Eventually it is broken down into intermediate density lipoprotein (IDL), which contains 50% each of cholesterol and triglycerides. It is this substance, about 50% of it, that is converted to the cholesterol-rich lipoprotein, or LDL.

Usually the plasma lipoproteins are in a state of dynamic equilibrium, for LDL is needed to transport fats such as fatty acids and cholesterol throughout the body. When cells outside the liver need cholesterol, they produce LDL receptors on their surfaces (see Figure 31-1). These receptors are necessary for LDL to enter the cell where it is broken down into amino acids and free cholesterol. When the cellular need for cholesterol is met, the production of LDL receptors stops and the excess cholesterol is discarded into the plasma. LDL receptors are also located in the liver where they function to monitor the plasma levels and LDL; and when the appropriate level of LDL is present in the plasma, the liver will suppress its production. This is essentially a feedback system that functions like a thermostat in the home; it maintains adequate plasma levels of LDL in order to provide cholesterol to body cells on demand.

Thus the hyperlipidemias result from one of three types of defects: (1) an overproduction of VLDL leading to an

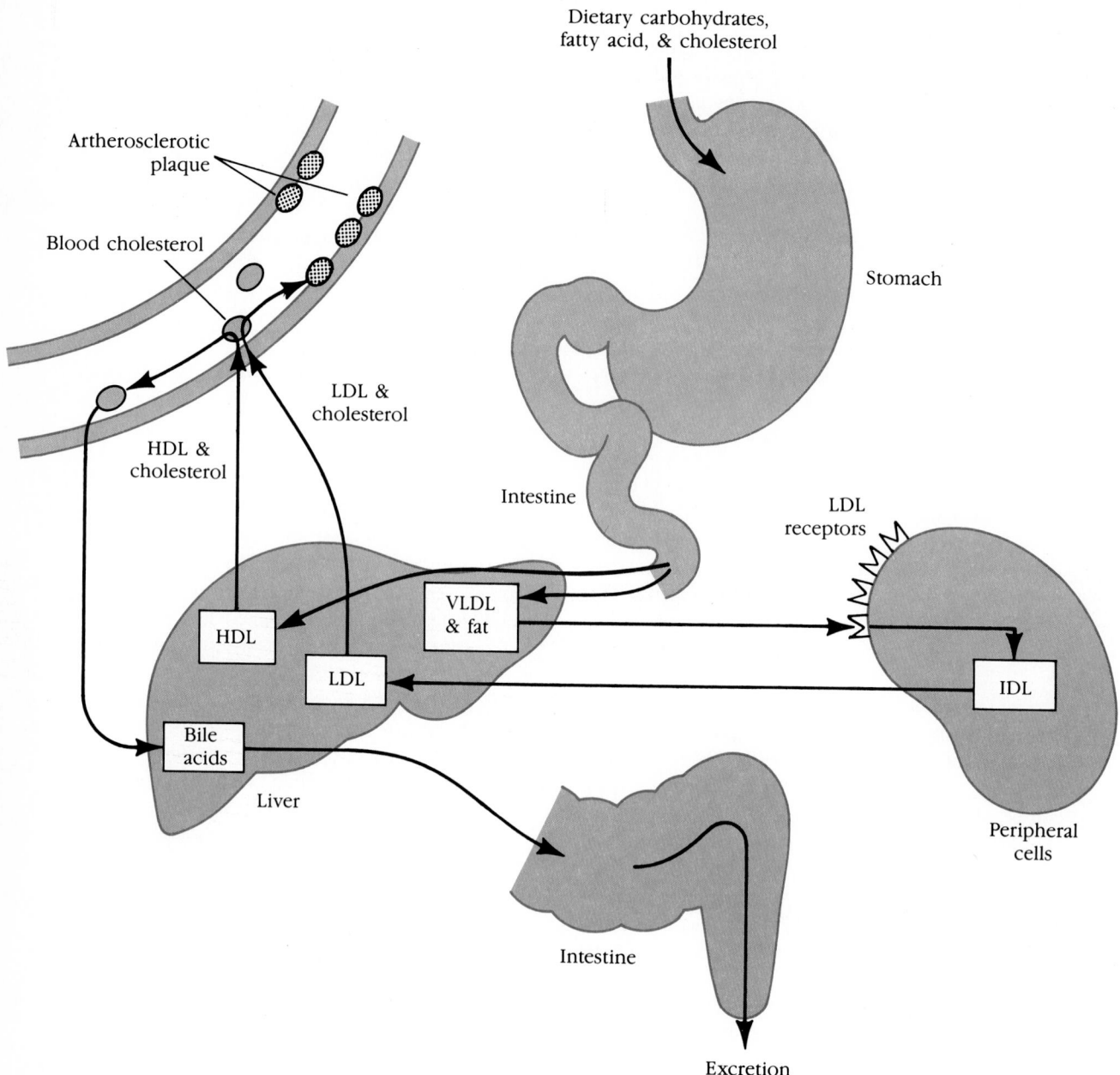

**FIGURE 31-1** Dietary carbohydrates, fatty acids, and cholesterol conversion sites/process.

excess in LDL production; (2) a decrease in lipolysis of the triglycerides lipoproteins or (3) a decrease in excretion or clearance of LDL. Thus a typical dietary management plan consists of limiting total fat intake to less than 30% of total calories, saturated fat consumption to less than 10% of the calories and cholesterol intake to less than 300 mg/day. Dietary failure to decrease hyperlipidemia may indicate a genetic cause, which usually requires drug treatment. Dietary noncompliance may also require pharmacologic intervention.

At present the lipid disorders are classified into six types, each of which may be identified by a generic name (Table 31-1). Table 31-1 also lists the elevation of the lipoprotein pattern and the treatment of each type. Although the incidence is rare, it is important to describe briefly the existence of intermediate-density lipoproteins (IDLs) or broad-beta lipoproteins. As VLDL loses its triglycerides, it is converted into IDL and then into LDL, with a resultant chemical composition between the two lipoproteins. IDL consists of an elevation of endogenous triglycerides and carries about 30% cholesterol. Like VLDL, it tends to be atherogenic. Normally, IDL is not found in plasma in significant amounts.

Many drugs may affect serum levels of LDL cholesterol, HDL cholesterol, and triglycerides; Table 31-2 contains a listing.

**TABLE 31-1** Classification and treatment of hyperlipidemic disorders

| Type | Generic name | Elevated lipoprotein pattern | Elevated Cholesterol | Elevated Triglycides | Incidence | Treatment Diet | Treatment Drugs |
|------|-------------|------------------------------|------------|-------------|-----------|------|-------|
| I | Exogenous hyperlipemia | Chylomicrons | ↑ | ↑↑ | Rare | Very low fat: 25-35 g/day; high carbohydrate | None |
| IIa | Familial hypercholesterolemia | LDL (beta lipoproteins) | ↑↑ | | Common | Low cholesterol (300 mg/day); low saturated fat; high unsaturated fat | cholestyramine, colestipol, cholestyramine, nicotinic acid, probucol |
| IIb | Combined hyperlipoproteinemia | LDL + VLDL | ↑↑ | ↑ | Common | Low cholesterol; high unsaturated fat; reduce obesity | nicotinic acid, probucol, colestipol, lovastatin, gemfibrozil, cholestyramine |
| III | Broad-beta hyperlipidemia (familial dysbeta-lipoproteinemia) | IDL (broad-beta lipoproteins) | ↑↑ | ↑↑ | Rare | See IIb | clofibrate, nicotinic acid, gemfibrozil |
| IV | Endogenous hyperlipemia | VLDL (pre-beta lipoproteins) | ↑ | ↑↑ | Common | Low carbohydrate; high unsaturated fat; low cholesterol and alcohol; reduce obesity | clofibrate, gemfibrozil, nicotinic acid |
| V | Mixed hyperlipemia | VLDL + chylomicrons | ↑ | ↑↑ | Rare | Low fat and carbohydrate; high protein; low alcohol | clofibrate, nicotinic acid, gemfibrozil |

***Government review and guidelines.*** In the early 1980s, a random sample survey of physicians was conducted by the National Heart, Lung and Blood Institute. The survey revealed that 50% to 75% of physicians surveyed failed to provide diet instructions or prescribe drugs for clients with high serum cholesterol levels, persons at high risk for coronary artery disease (CAD) or stroke. This indicated clearly the need for more definitive educational programs for both health care professionals and the general public.

Then in 1985, the National Institutes of Health organized the National Cholesterol Education Program. A primary goal of this program was to have all Americans 20 years old or older tested for total cholesterol levels. Those found to be at high risk for CAD would be advised to obtain medical help. Guidelines were developed and criteria for identification, treatment, and monitoring of individuals were issued in 1987 (See box on p. 572 for NIH adult recommendations of risk classification and cholesterol levels).

Treatment recommendations are based on the client's cholesterol level and the presence of CAD or two other risk factors, such as smoking, hypertension, family history of CAD, male sex, obesity, and lack of exercise. Borderline individuals with CAD or at least two other risk factors pres-

**TABLE 31-2** Drugs and serum lipids

| Drug(s) | LDL cholesterol | HDL cholesterol | Triglycerides |
|---------|-----------------|-----------------|---------------|
| barbiturates | +* | + | |
| beta blocking agents (with exception of labetalol) | | − | + |
| corticosteroids | + | | + |
| oral contraceptives | + | | − |
| phenytoin | | + | |
| phenothiazines | + | | |
| thiazide diuretics | + | | + |

\*+, Increase; −, decrease.

ent were advised to have an IDL cholesterol level performed. The primary goals are as follows. First, individuals with borderline total cholesterol (200 to 239 mg/dl) with no CAD or less than two risk factors should receive dietary instructions and be reevaluated in 1 year. The minimum goal is to lower their LDL cholesterol to below 160 mg/dl. A second goal is that individuals with borderline cholesterol results

## RECOMMENDED CHOLESTEROL LEVELS

| Risk | Total Cholesterol (mg/dl) | LDL Cholesterol (mg/dl) |
|---|---|---|
| Desirable | Below 200 | Below 130 |
| Borderline/high risk | 200-239 | 130-159 |
| High risk | 240 or greater | 160 or greater |

and CAD or two or more risk factors, with an LDL cholesterol up to 160 mg/dl, should be given dietary instructions and additional advice if necessary for risk factors that are present. Their goal is to lower the LDL cholesterol to less than 130 mg/dl by diet. A final goal is that individuals at high risk should have an LDL cholesterol level performed. If CAD or at least two other risk factors are present and their LDL cholesterol level is up to 190 mg/dl, then medication is indicated to lower the LDL cholesterol level to less than 130 mg/dl. If the individual did not have CAD or less than two risk factors, then the goal is to lower the LDL cholesterol level to less than 160 mg/dl.

The student is referred to the reference by Naito (1987) for a detailed review of drug application, current drug application, and management.

Antihyperlipidemic agents offer the client a pharmacologic method for reducing serum lipid levels and ideally reducing the risk of atherosclerosis with its many complications. Use of antihyperlipidemic agents is reserved for clients who have specifically been identified at significant increased risk (see box above) and are unable to satisfactorily lower their serum lipid levels through exercise, diet, and other nondrug methods. Drug therapy for these clients augments their therapy aimed at lowering serum lipids and cardiovascular risk.

## BILE ACID SEQUESTERING AGENTS
### cholestyramine (Questran)
### colestipol hydrochloride (Colestid)

Cholestyramine and colestipol are nonabsorbable anion-exchange resins. They are also called bile acid sequestrants. These drugs are used for their cholesterol-lowering effects. Cholesterol is the major precursor of bile acids that normally are secreted from the gallbladder and liver into the small intestine. Here, the bile acids perform two functions: (1) they emulsify fat present in food to facilitate chemical digestion and (2) they are required for absorption of lipids (including fat-soluble vitamins, A, D, E, and K). After their physiologic performance, the major portion of the bile acids is returned to the liver.

 ### Geriatric Implications: ANTIHYPERLIPIDEMIC DRUGS

Geriatric clients may be taking other medications in addition to the antihyperlidemia medications; therefore the nurse should be aware that diuretics such as hydrochlorothiazide and chlorthalidone can increase cholesterol levels by 10%; that beta blockers such as propranolol and estrogen may increase triglyceride serum levels by 25% to 50%. It is important to assess and evaluate the total drug regimen when monitoring drug therapy (Raasch, RH, 1988).

Dietary modifications and/or recommendations are vital to a successful lipid reduction program. When goals are not obtainable by diet alone, drug therapy may be prescribed.

A common side effect, constipation (sometimes severe), has been reported in geriatric clients taking cholestyramine and colestipol. Encourage client to increase daily fluid intake to help reduce the constipating effects of this drug.

Be aware that long-term use of cholestyramine or colestipol may lead to vitamins A, D, E, K, folic acid, and calcium deficiencies. Additional nutritional supplementation may be necessary and prescribed by the physician (Long, 1990).

Administer the antihyperlipidemic drugs before or with meals (follow manufacturer's instructions) because the drugs are generally not effective if not administered with food. Lovastatin is often given with supper to obtain its maximum beneficial effects, as the highest rate of cholesterol production occurs from midnight to 5 AM (Long, 1990).

As anion-exchange resins, these drugs combine with bile acids in the intestine, thus preventing their absorption and producing an insoluble complex that is excreted in the feces. To compensate for the loss of bile acids removed by the drugs, the liver increases the rate of oxidation of cholesterol by converting more sterol to bile acids. Subsequently, the long-term fecal loss of bile acids causes a reduction of serum cholesterol levels and low-density (beta) lipoprotein.

In individuals with partial biliary obstruction, excess bile acids may be deposited in the dermal tissues, resulting in pruritus. Since cholestyramine increases fecal bile acid excretion, it can alleviate this condition.

Both cholestyramine and colestipol are used in the treatment of hyperlipidemia of the primary hypercholesterolemia type (type IIa). Cholestyramine is also indicated as an antidiarrheal agent for diarrhea caused by bile acids (not for common diarrhea), an antipruritic (for pruritus caused by cholestasis), and an antidote for negatively charged and other medications (e.g., digoxin, oral penicillins, tetracyclines, and thyroid medication).

Plasma cholesterol levels usually decrease within 1 to 2 days after initiation of therapy. With cholestyramine, plasma

**TABLE 31-3** Antihyperlipidemic agents: side effects/adverse reactions

| Drug | Side effects* | Adverse reactions† |
|------|---------------|--------------------|
| cholestyramine | Most frequent: gas or indigestion, nausea or vomiting, abdominal pain<br>Less frequent: diarrhea, bloated or distended stomach | Most frequent: constipation<br>Rare: severe abdominal pain with nausea and vomiting (gallstones, pancreatitis), increased weight loss, black stools (gastrointestinal bleeding or peptic ulcers) |
| clofibrate | Most frequent: diarrhea, nausea<br>Less frequent and rare: tenderness or muscle pain, muscle cramping, increased fatigue, impotence, headache, increased appetite or weight gain, abdominal pain or gas, vomiting, mouth and lip sores | Rare: edema of lower extremities; decreased, painful, or bloody urination; chest pain; respiratory difficulties; increased temperature; chills; sore throat; irregular heart rate; severe abdominal pain with nausea and vomiting |
| colestipol | Less frequent: distended stomach, gas, diarrhea, nausea or vomiting, abdominal pain | Most frequent: constipation<br>Rare: same as cholestyramine |
| dextrothyroxine | Rare: nausea, vomiting | Rare: chest pain; increased, very fast, or irregular heart rate; abdominal pain with nausea and vomiting<br>Drug overdose: appetite changes, altered menstrual cycle, diarrhea, increased temperature, hand tremors, headache, increased heat sensitivity, increased anxiety, leg cramps, shortness of breath, rash, pruritus, insomnia, tachycardia, increased sweating, flushing, vomiting, weight loss, increased urination |
| gemfibrozil | Less frequent: muscle ache and cramping, nausea or vomiting, rash, diarrhea, abdominal gas, pain or distress | Rare: increased temperature, chills, sore throat, severe abdominal pain with nausea and vomiting (gallstones) |
| niacin (nicotinic acid) | Less frequent: increased feelings of warmth, flushing or red skin on face and neck, headache<br>With high doses: diarrhea, dizziness, dry skin, nausea or vomiting, abdominal pain | Rare: skin rash, pruritus, wheezing (seen mostly after intravenous administration—anaphylactic reaction)<br>High doses may be associated with: elevated serum glucose levels, hyperuricemia, dysrhythmias, liver toxicity |
| probucol | Most frequent: increased gas production, diarrhea, nausea and vomiting, abdominal pain or distress<br>Less frequent: dizziness; headache; paresthesia of fingers, toes, or face | Rare: edema of face, hands, feet, or mouth (angioneurotic edema) |
| lovastatin | Most frequent: increased gas, stomach pain or cramps, rash, constipation or diarrhea, nausea, headaches | Need to monitor its usage to determine additional side effects or adverse reactions |

*If side effects continue, increase, or disturb the client, inform the physician.
†If adverse reactions occur, contact physician, since medical intervention may be necessary.

cholesterol levels may continue to fall for up to a year. After the initial decrease, plasma cholesterol levels in some individuals may increase to previous levels or even exceed these levels with continued therapy. Close monitoring for effectiveness is necessary. Diarrhea induced by increased bile acids will respond to cholestyramine within 24 hours, whereas pruritus caused by cholestasis usually takes 1 to 3 weeks of therapy before a response is noted.

Colestipol's peak effect is noted within 1 month. After the initial decrease in cholesterol, some clients may exhibit an increased cholesterol level that equals or surpasses the previous level.

After withdrawal of colestipol and cholestyramine, plasma cholesterol levels will increase in about 2 to 4 weeks. Pruritus will return in about 1 to 2 weeks after discontinuance of the medication.

Side effects/adverse reactions are noted in Table 31-3.

### Significant drug interactions

| Drug | Possible Effect and Management |
|------|-------------------------------|
| oral anticoagulants, coumarins or indanediones | Concurrent usage significantly decreases absorption of oral anticoagulants and vitamin K, thus anticoagulant effect may be increased or decreased. It is suggested that oral anticoagulants |

| Drug | Possible Effect and Management |
|---|---|
| | be given 6 hours before these drugs. Also monitor prothrombin times closely as dosage adjustments may be necessary. |
| digitalis glyco-sides, especially digitoxin | Half-life of digitalis glycosides, as well as gastrointestinal absorption, may be reduced. It is recommended that cholestyramine or colestipol be administered at least 8 hours after digoxin to reduce the potential for interactions. Also, if cholestyramine or colestipol is discontinued with a client also taking a digitalis product, monitor the individual closely for digitalis toxicity. |
| oral penicillin G, oral tetracyclines, or oral vancomycin | Decreased absorption of antibiotics has been reported. Give such medications several hours before or after cholestyramine or colestipol. Whenever possible, give antibiotics first. |
| thyroid hormones | Decreased absorption of thyroid products is reported. Give thyroid first on the medication administration schedule, then give cholestyramine or colestipol several hours later. |

**Dosage and administration.** Cholestyramine is available as a powder for oral suspension and a chewable bar. Adult dose is 4 g one to six times daily before meals, adjusted according to the individual's response. For children under 6 years old, dose is not established. For ages 6 to 12 years, the dose is 80 mg/kg orally, three times daily. Children over 12 should use the adult schedule. Colestipol is given at 15 to 30 g orally before meals in two to four divided dosages. Pediatric dosage has not been established.

▷ **Nursing Management:**
**Cholestyramine and Colestipol Therapy**

**Assessment.** Ascertain whether client has a preexisting condition for which the drug would be used with great caution or contraindicated. Use with caution in clients with gastrointestinal disorders (peptic ulcer and constipation), especially in individuals with clinically symptomatic coronary artery disease, bleeding disorders, steatorrhea, hemorrhoids, and impaired renal function and with the elderly. These drugs are contraindicated for use in clients who have an allergy to bile acid sequestrants and complete biliary obstruction. Safe use by pregnant women and lactating mothers is not established.

Be aware that clients receiving cholestyramine and colestipol are at risk for the following nursing diagnoses: altered bowel elimination (constipation in about 10% to 50% of clients, mild to severe and possible fecal impaction); altered comfort related to belching, bloating, heartburn, nausea or vomiting, and abdominal discomfort; and high risk for injury related to gallstones, pancreatitis, peptic ulcer, or malabsorption syndrome.

Determine baseline serum cholesterol and triglyceride levels before drug therapy, and continue to monitor them periodically at regular intervals.

**Intervention.** Administer the drug before meals. Mix powder by sprinkling it on the surface of 2 to 6 ounces of a preferred liquid or semiliquid, such as cold beverages, hot cereals, thin soups (tomato, chicken noodle), pulpy fruit (fruit cocktail, pears, peaches, or pineapple), to increase palatability of the drug. Allow drug to sit on the surface of the liquid for 1 to 2 minutes before stirring to prevent lumpiness. Be sure the drug is thoroughly mixed, since it does not dissolve. Incomplete mixing of the dry form may result in mucosal irritation and esophageal impaction, or it may be accidentally inhaled.

Rinse the glass or cup with a small amount of liquid and have the client drink it to ensure the complete dose is taken.

Because resins interfere with absorption of other drugs when taken concurrently, administer the other drugs 1 hour before or 4 to 6 hours following cholestyramine or colestipol.

**Education.** Instruct client in preparation of medication for administration as discussed above. Warn client that sudden withdrawal of resins could lead to uninhibited absorption of other drugs taken concomitantly, resulting in overdosage or toxicity.

Usually, supplemental parenteral or water-miscible vitamins A, D, E, and K and also folic acid are prescribed to avoid vitamin deficiencies in clients receiving long-term therapy. Instruct individual to report immediately early symptoms of bleeding: petechiae, ecchymoses, bleeding from mucous membranes of gums or nose, or tarry stools (which indicate hypoprothrombinemia). Administration of vitamin $K_1$ (parenteral) and vitamin $K_2$ (oral) may be necessary.

Encourage client to observe bowel habit and to adhere to a high-bulk diet (e.g., grains, fruits, raw vegetables) and an increased fluid intake as adjunctive therapy to the drug. If constipation occurs, dosage may be lowered to prevent fecal impaction, or a stool softener or laxative may be prescribed. Instruct individual to report gastrointestinal symptoms to the physician: gastric distress, nausea and vomiting (pancreatitis), and unusual weight loss (steatorrhea).

**Evaluation.** Monitor serum cholesterol and triglycerides at regular intervals. Drug is withdrawn if response is unsatisfactory after 3 months of therapy. Monitor cardiac glycoside levels in clients receiving both drugs simultaneously. To avoid toxicity, adjust dosage of cardiotonic glycoside before discontinuing anion-exchange resin.

## ADDITIONAL ANTIHYPERLIPEDEMIC AGENTS

### clofibrate (Atromid-S, Claripex ✽)

Clofibrate is more effective in reducing very low-density lipoproteins (VLDLs) rich in triglycerides than in lowering low-density lipoproteins (LDLs) high in cholesterol. The exact mode of action of the drug is unknown, but it appears to block synthesis of triglycerides in the liver by increasing catabolism of VLDLs to LDLs. In addition, the drug inhibits early cholesterol formation in the liver and promotes fecal excretion of the neutral sterols. Clofibrate also possesses platelet-inhibiting effect (e.g., decreases platelet adhesiveness), but this action is not significant enough to warrant its use as an antiplatelet drug.

Clofibrate is indicated for the treatment of hyperlipidemia type III. It is slowly but completely absorbed from the intestines, is highly protein bound (96%), and reaches peak plasma levels in 2 to 6 hours after a dose. Peak effect with continued therapy is seen in approximately 3 weeks. A reduction in plasma VLDL concentrations is seen within 2 to 5 days. The half-life of this drug ranges from 6 to 25 hours for a single dose or 54 hours at steady state in normal healthy individuals. It is metabolized in the liver and gastrointestinal tract and excreted by the kidneys. For side effects/adverse reactions, see Table 31-3.

When clofibrate is given with oral anticoagulants, coumarin or indanedione-type, an increased anticoagulant effect is reported. Monitor prothrombin times closely, since the anticoagulant dosage may need to be decreased significantly. Adult dose is 1.5 to 2 g orally daily in two to four divided doses with maximum daily dose at 2 g. A pediatric dose has not been established. Although clofibrate has not been rated by the FDA pregnancy scale, it is not recommended for use in pregnant women.

## ▷ Nursing Management: Clofibrate Therapy

**Assessment.** Perform appropriate laboratory studies, and obtain personal family and complete health history. Because of genetic tendency of the disease, children and other family members should be screened for abnormal lipid levels.

Inquire if client is pregnant. Strict birth control measures must be observed to prevent damage to the fetus. Drug must be withdrawn at least 2 months before conception.

Use with caution in clients with peptic ulcer because the drug may reactivate a previous ulcer.

Do not use in clients who are pregnant and in lactating women, in individuals with clinically significant hepatic or renal dysfunction, and in individuals with primary biliary cirrhosis because drug may raise the already elevated cholesterol level. Diabetes mellitus and hypothyroidism should be controlled if present.

While taking clofibrate, the client has the potential for the development of the following nursing diagnoses: altered comfort related to nausea, vomiting, diarrhea, flu-like syndrome, headache, heartburn and abdominal discomfort; altered mucous membranes (stomatitis); high risk for injury related to angina, cardiac arrhythmias, anemia or leucopenia, pancreatitis, gallstones, and renal toxicity; and altered self-concept related to decreased libido.

**Intervention.** Administer drug with meals to prevent gastric distress.

**Education.** Before initiating clofibrate therapy, advise client to adhere to diet prescribed by physician. The diet is usually low in fats, cholesterol, and/or sugars. Encourage weight reduction and physical exercise.

During the first and second months of therapy, a decrease in serum lipid levels indicates a therapeutic response. Warn client that a paradoxic rise may occur in 2 or 3 months, but afterward a further decrease is customary.

Instruct client to keep clinical appointments. If serum cholesterol and triglyceride levels are not lowered within 3 months, discontinue drug therapy. Initially, these levels are performed every 2 weeks for the first few months and then at monthly intervals.

Advise client to report flu-like symptoms (muscular aching, soreness, cramping). This condition may be remedied by dosage reduction. Instruct individual to check with physician about alcohol intake since its use may be restricted to prevent hypertriglyceridemia.

The client should be aware that there is no substantial evidence that the drug reduces the incidence of coronary artery disease or fatal myocardial infarction. Further, an increased incidence of cardiac dysrhythmias, thromboembolism, intermittent claudication, and angina has been reported in clients treated with clofibrate.

**Evaluation.** Since clofibrate may increase the risk of biliary diseases such as cholelithiasis and cholecystitis, appropriate diagnostic tests should be performed if signs and symptoms of biliary disease occur.

Evaluate both liver and renal function tests, complete blood counts to detect anemia or leukopenia (fever, chills, sore throat), and blood sugar tests. In diabetic individuals, drug may produce hyperglycemia and glycosuria. Consult with the prescriber to withdraw drug if any of the test results are abnormal.

Use with caution in clients with a history of jaundice or hepatic disease since the drug may cause hepatic impairment. An elevation of serum transaminase levels and abnormal results of other liver function tests require withdrawal of the drug.

### dextrothyroxine (Choloxin)

Dextrothyroxine's mechanism of action as an antihyperlipidemic agent is not fully understood. Dextrothyroxine appears to act in the liver to increase function of LDL and, to a greater extent, to increase the breakdown of LDL. The result is an increased excretion of cholesterol and bile acids via bile into the feces, which results in a decrease in serum cholesterol and LDL.

A definite relationship exists between thyroid function and serum cholesterol levels. Hypothyroidism is associated with high serum cholesterol levels, and administration of thyroid hormones lowers serum cholesterol. Dextrothyroxine apparently stimulates the liver to increase the rate of oxidation of cholesterol, and it promotes biliary excretion of cholesterol and its byproducts.

Dextrothyroxine is used for hyperlipidemia (type IIa) in conjunction with other medications. Dextrothyroxine is approximately 25% absorbed from the gastrointestinal tract. It is highly protein bound, has a half-life of 18 hours, and reaches its peak effect as an antihyperlipidemic agent in 1 to 2 months. Duration of action after the drug is withdrawn is 6 weeks to 3 months. It is metabolized in the liver and excreted by the kidneys and in feces. For side effects/adverse reactions see Table 31-3.

When dextrothyroxine is given with oral anticoagulants (coumarin or indanediones), depending on the thyroid status of the client, the anticoagulant effects may be increased or decreased. Monitor prothrombin times closely as oral anticoagulant dosage may need to be adjusted. If given concurrently with cholestyramine or colestipol, dextrothyroxine absorption is reduced. Dextrothyroxine should be taken approximately 4 to 5 hours before or after these drugs.

Adult dose for antihyperlpidemia effect is 1 to 2 mg daily orally. Increase by 1 to 2 mg increments per month to achieve the minimum effective dose. The maximum dosage recommended is 8 mg/day. For children, give 0.05 mg/kg orally and increase by 0.05 mg/kg increments at monthly intervals up to the minimum effective dose. Maximum dose recommended is 4 mg/day. Use caution in dosages for elderly persons, since they are much more sensitive to thyroid hormones. Monitor therapy closely.

▷ **Nursing Management: Dextrothyroxine Therapy**

**Assessment.** Perform appropriate laboratory studies, and obtain personal family and complete health history. Because of genetic tendency of the disease, children and other family members should be screened for abnormal lipid levels. Inquire if client is pregnant. Strict birth control measures must be observed to prevent damage to the fetus. Drug must be withdrawn at least 2 months before conception.

Do not administer drug to clients with organic disease (e.g., angina pectoris, history of myocardial infarction, cardiac dysrhythmias, congestive heart failure, rheumatic heart disease), hypertensive states (other than mild, labile systolic hypertension), liver or kidney disease, or history of iodism. Also, do not give to pregnant women, lactating mothers, or as treatment for obesity (i.e., the large doses that are required may produce life-threatening toxicity). Use with caution with elderly clients, who may be more sensitive to thyroid hormones.

Clients receiving dextrothyroxine have the potential for injury related to myocardial infarction, angina, gallstones, and hyperthyroidism.

**Intervention.** Dextrothyroxine should be discontinued at least 2 weeks before surgery to reduce the potential for precipitating cardiac dysrhythmias during operative procedure. In clients receiving digitalis, do not give more than 4 mg/day of dextrothyroxine to prevent danger of increasing myocardial oxygen requirement. Also, closely monitor effects of both drugs. Diabetes mellitus and hypothyroidism should be controlled if present.

**Education.** Before initiating dextrothyroxine therapy, advise client to adhere to diet prescribed by physician. The diet is usually low in fats, cholesterol, and/or sugars. Encourage weight reduction and physical exercise.

Instruct the client to keep clinical appointments so that physician can check progress. Also, laboratory values will show that a decrease in cholesterol levels may not occur until 2 to 4 weeks after initiation of drug therapy; maximum decrease occurs about 2 or 3 months later. During therapy, determine serum lipid values at monthly intervals. If response is inadequate after 3 months of therapy, discontinue drug.

Advise client to immediately report the following side effects: chest pain, palpitation, headache, sweating, diarrhea, nocturnal coughing, and dyspnea. Also, report promptly signs of iodism: stomatitis, bronchitis, laryngitis, coryza, brassy taste, conjunctivitis, acneiform rash, and pruritus. Side effects may not occur for 6 weeks.

**Evaluation.** With pediatric clients receiving long-term therapy, measurements of bone age, growth, and psychomotor development should be monitored periodically. Evaluation of the drug's efficacy is assessed by periodic serum cholesterol and triglyceride determinations. The drug may increase blood sugar levels and therefore in diabetic individuals, an increase in antidiabetic drugs or a decrease in dextrothyroxine may be required. Loss of diabetic control is noted by the following symptoms: glycosuria, polydipsia, and polyuria.

### gemfibrozil (Lopid)

Gemfibrozil is a lipid-lowering agent that primarily decreases serum triglycerides found in very low–density lipoprotein (VLDL). It also variably lowers total serum cholesterol that occurs in low-density lipoprotein (LDL) fractions. In the process, the drug provides a beneficial effect by increasing high-density lipoprotein (HDL) concentrations that may inhibit the progression of atherosclerosis. The mechanism of this complicated action has not been established. It may involve an inhibition of peripheral lipolysis and a decrease in hepatic extraction of free fatty acids, which result in reduction of triglyceride production. In addition, the drug may accelerate turnover and removal of cholesterol from the liver, which is ultimately excreted in the feces.

Gemfibrozil is indicated for the treatment of hyperlipidemia type IV. Orally it is well absorbed from the gastrointestinal tract and reaches peak levels in 1 to 2 hours. The onset of action in reducing serum VLDL levels is within 2 to 5 days, while the peak effect is seen in 4 weeks. A greater decrease in VLDL may be seen over the next few months. It is metabolized in the liver and excreted by the kidneys and with the feces. For side effects/adverse reactions see Table 31-3. When gemfibrozil is given with oral anticoagulants, coumarin or indanedione-type, an increased anticoagulant effect is reported. Monitor prothrombin times closely, since the anticoagulant dose may need to be decreased significantly.

The adult dose is 1.2 g daily in two divided doses, preferably before breakfast and supper. Pediatric dosages have not been established. Pregnancy safety for gemfibrozil is FDA Category B.

Gemfibrozil has chemical, pharmacologic, and clinical effects that are similar to those of clofibrate. See discussion of clofibrate for nursing management.

### niacin (nicotinic acid, Nicobid)

Niacin is a water-soluble vitamin that can lower serum cholesterol and triglyceride levels. It is used as an adjunct to other therapies only, because its vasodilating and other side effects limit its usefulness. Niacin interferes with triglyceride synthesis, which ultimately lowers hepatic secretion of VLDL. The decrease in VLDL concentration subsequently leads to a reduction in circulating levels of LDL, with a resultant lowering of cholesterol concentration. In fact, plasma triglyceride levels decrease within a few hours following the administration of nicotinic acid, and a reduction of cholesterol levels occurs several days after drug therapy. Since nicotinic acid inhibits lipolysis in adipose tissue, it lowers the plasma concentration of free fatty acids, which usually is the main source of synthesis of triglycerides in the liver.

Niacin is used as adjunctive therapy in the treatment of both hypertriglyceridemias and hypercholesterolemia (types IIa, IIb, III, IV, or V). It is also used to prevent and treat niacin (vitamin $B_3$) deficiency.

It is well absorbed orally and has a half-life of approximately 45 minutes. It reduces cholesterol levels several days after therapy is started while reduction in triglyceride levels occurs within several hours after oral doses are begun. Metabolism occurs in the liver and it is excreted via the kidneys. For side effects/adverse reactions see Table 31-3. No significant drug interactions have been reported to date.

The adult dose for antihyperlipidemic effect is 1 g orally three times daily. Dosage may be increased to 500 mg/day, every 2 to 4 weeks as necessary. Maximum dose is 6 g per day. Pregnancy safety for niacin is FDA Category C.

### ▷ Nursing Management: Niacin Therapy

***Assessment.*** The drug should be used cautiously in individuals with allergies and peptic ulcers, since nicotinic acid causes a release of histamine and stimulates hydrochloric acid secretion. The drug is contraindicated for use in individuals with hepatic dysfunction, active peptic ulcer, hemorrhagic diathesis, glaucoma, diabetes mellitus, and gout.

With the administration of niacin, the client may experience altered comfort related to flushing of the skin of the head and neck and headaches, dizziness, nausea and vomiting; and risk for injury related to the development of peptic ulcer.

***Intervention.*** Giving the drug with meals or with antacids may reduce the incidence and severity of side effects.

Prolonged treatment with niacin has resulted in hepatic disease.

***Education.*** Instruct client to swallow the extended-release form whole, without chewing or crushing. The powder within the capsule may be mixed with jam or applesauce for ease of administration. Advise the client to adhere to dietary regimen—low cholesterol and low saturated fats.

Instruct client to maintain clinical appointments so that serum cholesterol and triglycerides may be monitored on a periodic basis.

Alert the client that numerous and often disagreeable side effects may occur from nicotinic acid. Common side effects include severe gastrointestinal upset, flushing, pruritus, nervousness, and urticaria.

### probucol (Lorelco)

Probucol appears to be effective in reducing cholesterol levels in individuals with elevated concentrations of low-density lipoproteins (LDLs). The drug is believed to act by inhibiting the earlier stages of cholesterol synthesis, but it does not affect the latter stages of its production. In addition, probucol enhances excretion of bile acids in feces and slightly inhibits absorption of dietary cholesterol. It is indicated for the treatment of hyperlipidemia type IIa. Probucol is administered orally and it has a variable, limited absorption pattern. It tends to accumulate in fatty tissues with chronic therapy. Peak serum levels occur after 3 or 4 months of treatment, while the peak effect usually occurs in 20 to 50 days after initiation of the drug. Half-life ranges from 12 to 500 hours, and it is excreted as bile in the feces. For side effects/adverse reactions, see Table 31-3. It has no reported significant drug interactions.

The adult dose is 500 mg orally twice daily with breakfast and supper. A pediatric dose has not been established. Pregnancy safety has been established at FDA Category B.

### ▷ Nursing Management: Probucol Therapy

***Assessment.*** Administer drug to individuals who do not respond adequately to dietary management and weight reduction. Do not give probucol to clients with evidence of myocardial damage, unresponsive congestive heart failure, or any indication of ventricular dysrhythmias or to those with primary biliary cirrhosis since probucol increases cholesterol concentrations. With the administration of probucol, the client may experience altered comfort related to gastrointestinal irritation (bloating, nausea, vomiting, abdominal discomfort), dizziness, headache, and tingling of the fingers and toes.

***Education.*** If medication is given, adherence to a low-cholesterol and low-fat diet and physical exercise should continue. Instruct individual to take drug with food to minimize gastric irritation.

***Evaluation.*** Determine cholesterol levels before therapy; reduction in level should occur 2 to 3 months following drug

**TABLE 31-4**   Summary of comparison of antihyperlipidemic effects

| Drug | Effect on lipids | | Effect on lipoproteins | | | Typical response | Indications with diet control |
|------|------|------|------|------|------|------|------|
| | Cholesterol | Triglycerides | VLDL | LDL | HDL | | |
| cholestyramine | −* | 0 or slight + | 0 or + | − | 0 or + | Decreases cholesterol 20%-40% | Type IIa |
| colestipol | − | 0 or slight + | + | − | 0 or + | Decreases cholesterol 20%-40% | Type IIa |
| clofibrate | − | − (greatest effect) | − | 0 or − | 0 or + | Lowers triglycerides; only slight decrease in cholesterol | Type III |
| dextrothyroxine | − | 0 | 0 or − | − | 0 | | Type IIa |
| gemfibrozil | − | − | − | 0 or − | + | Decreases triglycerides; only slight decrease in cholesterol; increases HDL | Type IV |
| niacin | − | − | − | − | + | Decreases triglycerides and cholesterol 10%-20% | Types II, III, IV, and V |
| probucol | − | 0 or + | + or − | − | − | Decreases cholesterol 12%-25%; also decreases HDL | Type IIa |
| lovastatin | − | − | − | − | + | LDL cholesterol levels reduced 19%-39%, total cholesterol levels reduced 18%-34% | Types IIa and IIb |

*+, Increased; −, decreased; 0, no change. Typical response was approximated with individual taking drug while concurrently on specified diet.

administration. Also, perform serum triglyceride levels during therapy. Change medication if serum cholesterol and triglyceride levels are not reduced within the first 3 to 4 months.

Animal studies have shown that a marked prolongation of the Q-T interval and syncope can occur. Perform ECG before drug therapy, then periodically thereafter (e.g., 6 months, then after 1 year). If prolongation of Q-T interval is not corrected, change to another drug.

## ENZYME INHIBITOR
### lovastatin (Mevacor)

Lovastatin is a recently released agent that is highly effective in lowering serum cholesterol levels. Lovastatin inhibits liver synthesis of cholesterol and has been effective in lowering both normal and increased LDL cholesterol serum concentrations. Lovastatin is used as an adjunct to dietary measures for clients with primary hypercholesterolemia (types IIa and IIb), especially when dietary measures and other nonpharmacologic methods are unsuccessful.

Lovastatin is given orally and is highly protein bound. Peak serum levels for the drug and its active metabolites are reached within 2 to 4 hours. Its onset of action is within 2 weeks, while its peak effect is achieved in 4 to 6 weeks. It is excreted in the feces and a lesser amount, by the kidneys. For side effects/adverse reactions, see Table 31-3. It has no reported significant drug interactions to date.

The adult dose is 20 mg daily with the evening meal. Increase dosage as necessary according to client's response to therapy, up to a maximum of 80 mg/day. Dosage adjustments should be instituted at monthly intervals. Pregnancy safety for lovastatin is established at FDA Category X.

▷ **Nursing Management:**
**Lovastatin Therapy**

As with other antihyperlipidemic medications, an appropriate diet, exercise, and weight reduction in obese clients should be instituted along with drug therapy.

Lovastatin may elevate creatine phosphokinase and transaminase levels. Do not administer to clients with active liver disease or unexplained persistent elevations of serum transaminases.

## SUMMARY

Along with dietary modifications, antihyperlipidemic agents are used to treat hyperlipidemia, a metabolic disorder characterized by increased serum concentrations of cholesterol and triglycerides. High levels of these serum lipids have been associated with atherosclerosis in which lipids are deposited in the linings of medium and large size arteries. Atherosclerosis is a causative factor in hypertension, coronary artery disease, cerebral artery disease, peripheral artery occlusive disease, and renal arterial insufficiency. Although atherosclerosis has many causes, such as dietary saturated fats, faulty fat metabolism, genetic influences and others, some clinicians believe that if serum lipid levels can be controlled, the progression of atherosclerosis can also be controlled. At the present time, however, the available antihyperlipidemic agents remain controversial.

The bile acid sequestering agents, cholestyramine and colestipol hydrochloride, combine with bile acids in the intestine, preventing their absorption and promoting their loss from the body in feces. To compensate for their loss, the liver increases its rate of oxidation of cholesterol to replace the bile acids, which causes a reduction of serum cholesterol levels. Clofibrate is more effective in lowering serum triglyceride levels; it appears to block the synthesis of triglycerides in the liver. Dextrothyoxine and probucol enhance the excretion of cholesterol. Gemfibrozil and niacin lower both triglyceride and cholesterol levels. As an enzyme inhibitor, lovastatin inhibits liver synthesis of cholesterol and so is effective for clients with primary hypercholesterolemia. Each agent is indicated for specific instances of hyperlipidemia (see Table 31-4).

Nursing management focuses on client education for compliance for life-style changes, particularly adherence to a low fat dietary regimen as a long-term commitment, and in the short term for most clients, adherence to the prescribed medication regimen until the hyperlipidemia is resolved.

## BIBLIOGRAPHY

American Hospital Formulary Service. (1991). AHFS drug information '91. Bethesda. Md: American Society of Hospital Pharmacists, Inc.

Cholesterol guidelines issued by expert panel. (1987). Pharmacy Weekly 26(40):161.

Gilman AG et al, eds. (1990). Goodman and Gilman's the pharmacological basis of therapeutics, ed 8. New York: Macmillan Publishing Co.

Ginsberg HN et al. (1986). Treatment of common lipoprotein disorders, Physician Asst 10(4):122.

Goldwater SH. (1988). Drug therapy for hyperlipidemia, Amer Pharmacy NS28(3):91.

Hartshorn JC et al. (1987). Treatment of hyperlipidemia with gemfibrozil, J Cardiovasc Nurs 1(4):76.

Hoeg JM et al. (1986). An approach to the management of hyperlipoproteinemia, JAMA 255(4):512.

Lamy PP. (1989). Cholesterol: the beginning of a crusade, Eldercare, The Center for the Study of Pharmacy and Therapeutics for the Elderly. Baltimore: University of Maryland School of Pharmacy.

Long JW. (1990). The essential guide to prescription drugs, New York, Harper-Collins.

Naito HK. (1987). Reducing cardiac deaths with hypolipidemic drugs, Postgrad Med 82(6):102.

Raasch RH. (1988). Hyperlipidemias. In Young LY and Koda-Kimble MA. Applied therapeutics: the clinical use of drugs, ed 4. Vancouver: Applied Therapeutics, Inc.

United States Pharmacopeial Convention. (1991). Drug information for the health care professional, ed 11. Rockville, Md: The Convention.

# Unit 8

# Drugs Affecting the Urinary System

# ✑*32*  Overview of the Urinary System

## CHAPTER OBJECTIVES

*After studying this chapter, you should be able to meet the following objectives and define the key terms.*

1. Describe the anatomy and physiology of the urinary system.

2. Identify the functions of the various segments of the nephron.

3. Describe the major functions of the kidneys.

4. Describe the site and primary effects of antidiuretic hormone and aldosterone on the nephrons.

## KEY TERMS

**electromagnetic gradient,** page 583

**glomerular filtration,** page 582

**glomerulus,** page 582

**hypertonic,** page 584

**hypotonic,** page 584

**isotonic,** page 584

**osmotic gradient,** page 583

**threshold concentration,** page 583

**tubular transport maximum,** page 583

## INTRODUCTION

The urinary system is composed of organs that manufacture and excrete urine from the body: two kidneys, two ureters, the bladder, and the urethra (see Figure 32-1). Urine formed in the kidneys flows through the ureters to the bladder, where it is stored. When approximately 250 ml of urine is collected, the bladder expansion will result in a feeling of distention and a desire to void. The urine flows from the bladder into the urethra to be expelled from the body.

In the male the urethra is surrounded by the prostate gland; it then passes through fibrous tissue connected to the pubic bones and terminates at the urinary meatus, or tip of the penis (see Figure 32-2). The male urethra serves a dual purpose, that is, the elimination of urine from the body and semen transport. In the female the urethra is the final vehicle for urination (see Figure 32-3).

The kidneys regulate homeostasis in the body; that is, they are responsible for the maintenance of body fluids, electrolytes, and acid-base balance in addition to elimination of body waste, urea, and urine. The primary focus of this chapter will be the kidneys.

## ANATOMY AND PHYSIOLOGY OF THE KIDNEY

The kidney is composed of millions of individual units called nephrons. Each nephron consists of a glomerulus and a tubular system. The volume and composition of urine as a result of concentration and dilution depend on three major processes in the kidney: glomerular filtration, tubular reabsorption, and tubular secretion.

***Glomerular filtration.*** **Glomerular filtration** occurs as a result of plasma flowing across a capillary bed called the **glomerulus.** The heart works to create pressure in the blood vessels, which in turn provides the force necessary to ac-

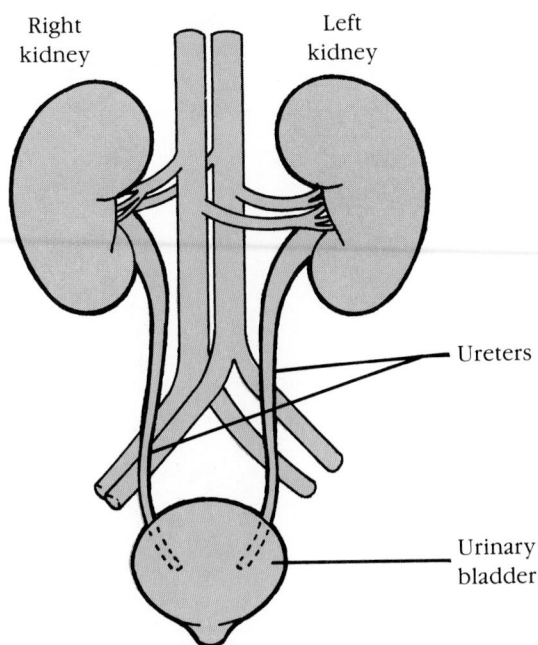

**FIGURE 32-1**   Urinary system.

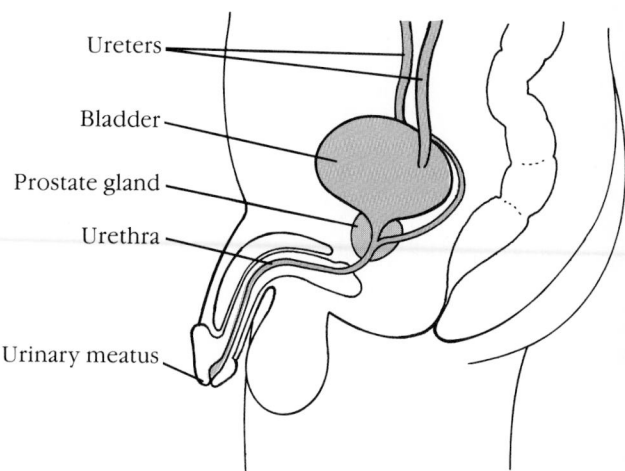

**FIGURE 32-2**   Male urethra.

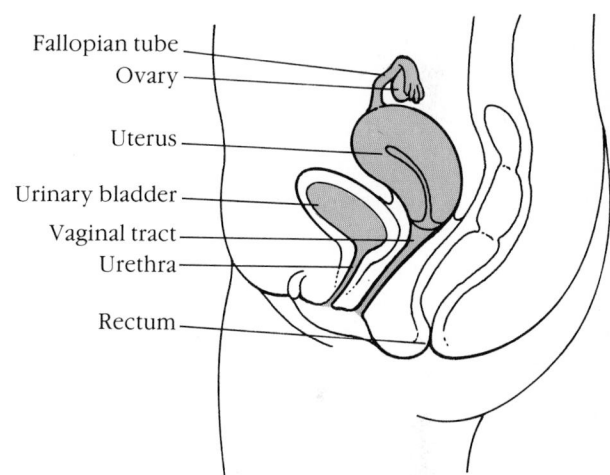

**FIGURE 32-3**   Female urethra.

complish glomerular filtration. Blood flow to the kidney is 1200 ml/min, which is 20% to 25% of cardiac output. The blood pressure within the glomerular capillaries is about 60% of arterial pressure. Systemic blood pressure has to be significantly reduced before glomerular filtration is greatly altered. Usually some degree of filtration will exist if the mean blood pressure remains above 50 mm Hg. Maintenance of glomerular hydrostatic pressure is aided by the ability of the afferent and efferent arterioles to effectively alter vessel resistance. In the absence of disease the glomerular membrane does not filter plasma proteins greater than 100 angstroms (Å), such as hemoglobin and albumin and the small amount of protein-bound substances. The glomerular filtrate is otherwise almost identical to plasma. The rate of filtration in an average adult is approximately 125 ml/minute; 99% of this tubular filtrate is ultimately reabsorbed throughout the tubule.

**Tubular reabsorption.** Tubular reabsorption involves both active and passive transport of substances into the tubular epithelial cell and into the extracellular fluid compartment. Passive transport or diffusion through the tubular membrane occurs because of a difference in concentration of particles (**osmotic gradient**) or electrical charge (**electromagnetic gradient**).

In the proximal tubule, sodium is *actively* transported across the tubular cell membrane from tubule filtrate. Chloride follows passively because of an electromagnetic gradient. Water, in turn, follows passively in response to an osmotic gradient established by sodium chloride solute. Then diffusion of 60% of urea content occurs to maintain a chemical gradient. Depending on the amount of a drug in

ionized or nonionized form and the pH of the tubular fluid, weak acids and weak bases may be reabsorbed by diffusion.

For almost every substance that is actively transported across the membrane, there is a maximum rate at which the transport mechanism can function. This is called the **tubular transport maximum.** For example, the tubular transport maximum for glucose averages 320 mg/minute for most adults. If the tubular load becomes greater than 320 mg/min, then the excess will not be reabsorbed but will appear in the urine. Every substance that has a tubular transport maximum also has a **threshold concentration** that is the plasma concentration below which none of the substance appears in the urine and above which progressively larger quantities appear.

**Tubular secretion.** Tubular secretion affects the composition of urine by allowing compounds such as penicillin, probenecid, methotrexate, and thiazides to enter into tubular fluid from peritubular or interstitial capillaries. This is ac-

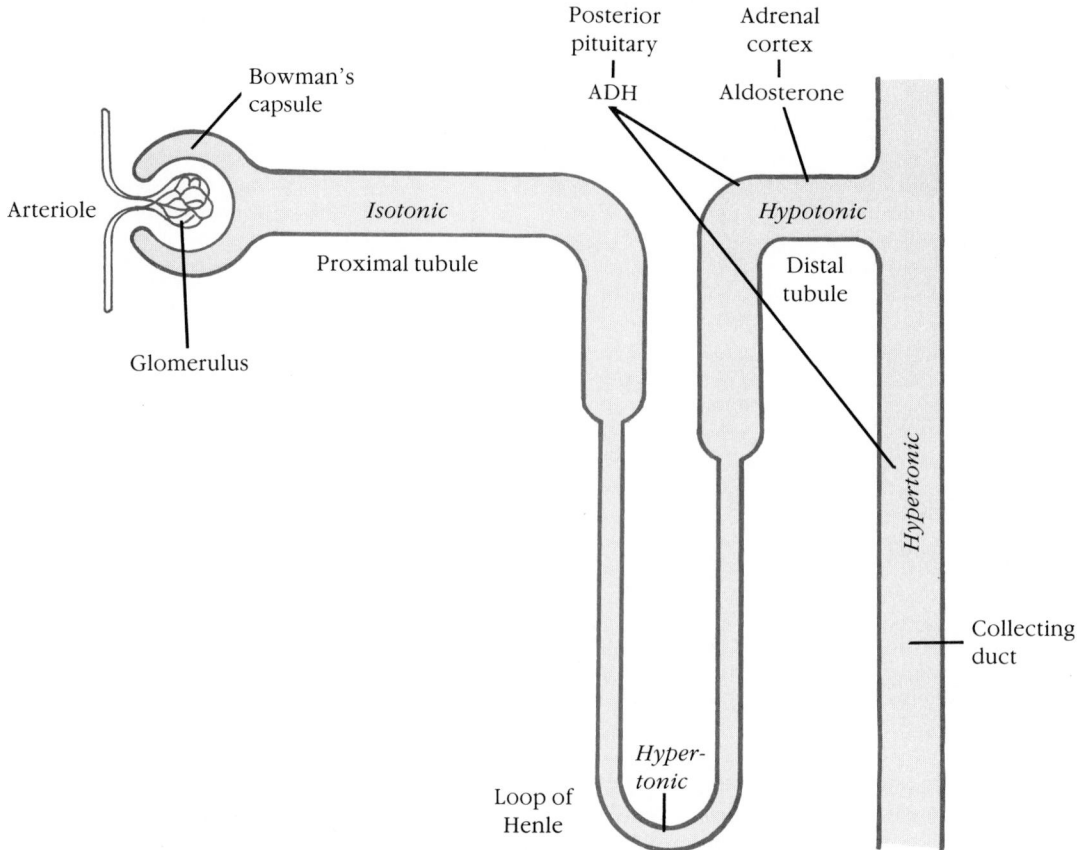

**FIGURE 32-4**  The functioning of the nephron.

complished via specific transport mechanisms for secretion of organic acids, organic bases, and ethylenediaminetetra-acetic acid (EDTA) in the proximal tubule. Other very important examples of tubular secretion include that of the hydrogen ion, ammonia, and potassium.

***Proximal tubule.*** Most of the glomerular filtrate is reabsorbed in the proximal tubule and returned to the bloodstream. Approximately 60% to 70% of salt and water is reabsorbed rapidly, maintaining nearly the same osmolality between tubular fluid and interstitial fluid at the end of the proximal tubule **(isotonic).** The general mechanism for sodium, chloride, water, and urea reabsorption is under tubular reabsorption with respect to gradient transport. There are *no* dilutional or concentration changes of these ions in the proximal tubule.

Other substances reabsorbed in the proximal tubule include glucose, amino acids, phosphate, uric acid, and a major portion of potassium. Nearly 90% of bicarbonate in tubular filtrate is reabsorbed as carbon dioxide if hydrogen ion is secreted in the tubular lumen. Plasma carbon dioxide is hydrolyzed in the tubular cell to form carbonic acid, which dissociates to give bicarbonate and hydrogen ion. This reversible reaction is catalyzed by carbonic anhydrase. The hydrogen ion secreted into the lumen combines with bicar-

bonate of the glomerular filtrate to form carbonic acid in the lumen. This again dissociates to give water and carbon dioxide, which are reabsorbed. This reaction is again catalyzed at both steps by carbonic anhydrase. Proximal tubule reabsorption is usually constant in spite of moderate changes in glomerular filtration rate.

***Descending loop of Henle.*** This portion of the nephron is permeable to water; water is passively taken up to equilibrate medullary interstitial osmolality. This produces a **hypertonic** (more concentrated) filtrate at the tip of the loop of Henle, the papilla. There is very low sodium and urea permeability in this segment.

***Ascending loop of Henle.*** Water permeability is almost nil in the ascending limb of the loop of Henle, whereas sodium and chloride permeability is high. Approximately 20% to 25% of sodium load in glomerular filtrate is reabsorbed and sodium *passively* follows. Consequently, two very important situations occur. The concentration of tubular filtrates becomes very dilute, or **hypotonic;** this is often termed "free water production." Meanwhile, the medullary interstitium becomes hypertonic, which is necessary to the concentration capacity of the countercurrent multiplier. The concentration gradient established across the tubular epithelium becomes multiplied in a longitudinal direction, re-

---

### NEPHRON FUNCTIONS

| Site | Major Functions |
|------|-----------------|
| Glomerulus | Filtration |
| Proximal tubule | Reabsorption of glucose, potassium, sodium, amino acids, water, and nutrients; remaining fluid isotonic |
| Loop of Henle | Sodium and chloride reabsorbed in ascending loop. Countercurrent mechanism produces decrease in osmolality of filtrate in ascending loop of Henle; i.e., sodium chloride is transported into the body but not water. Filtrate leaves loop of Henle as hypotonic urine. |
| Distal tubule | Sodium and bicarbonate reabsorbed. Potassium, hydrogen, and ammonia may be secreted. ADH necessary to reabsorb water at this site. Filtrate leaves distal tubule as hypotonic urine. |
| Collecting duct | ADH, if present, will reabsorb water at this site. Urine may be hypertonic. If ADH is unavailable or not functioning, dilute urine (hypotonic) may be excreted. |

---

sulting in a large osmotic gradient between the isosmotic renal cortex and the hyperosmotic medulla and papilla. The ascending limb of the loop of Henle is not responsive to any hormones as are other segments.

***Distal convoluted tubule.*** Between 5% and 10% of sodium reabsorption *actively* takes place in the distal tubule. This uptake is largely determined by the presence of a hormone called aldosterone. When the extracellular fluid volume is decreased, the renin-angiotensin system is involved, stimulating the release of aldosterone. Increased levels of aldosterone act to increase the active reabsorption of sodium. Although an increase in potassium secretion is seen, a simple sodium-potassium exchange pump is no longer recognized.

***Collecting duct.*** The hypotonic fluid entering the collecting duct may be altered in the medullary portion by the presence of antidiuretic hormone (ADH). Fluid is lost because of the osmotic gradient set up by hypertonic medullary interstitium. Thus the collecting duct is responsible for urine concentration.

## SUMMARY

The kidneys excrete metabolic by-products of the body, especially nitrogenous-type substances such as urea.

The kidneys maintain electrolyte homeostasis (sodium,

potassium, chloride, etc.) and body fluids. Sodium is actively reabsorbed in the proximal tubules (approximately 65%) and ascending loop of Henle (27%). Approximately 8% sodium reaches the distal tubules, and the rate of reabsorption here depends on the presence of aldosterone. If large quantities of aldosterone are present, sodium is reabsorbed. A lack of aldosterone will result in elimination of sodium in the urine. Generally, healthy kidneys excrete the daily sodium intake. See Figure 32-4 and box for nephron functions. Potassium is also reabsorbed from the proximal tubules and loop of Henle in percentages equivalent to sodium. Thus approximately 8% of the filtered potassium reaches the distal tubules. Aldosterone controls potassium secretion; that is, in its presence, sodium is reabsorbed and potassium is secreted in the distal tubules. The daily potassium intake is generally excreted daily in the kidneys.

ADH (vasopressin), synthesized in the hypothalamus and stored in the posterior pituitary gland, is a water-conserving hormone. When plasma osmolarity increases as a result of dehydration or water deprivation, osmoreceptors in the supraoptic area of the hypothalamus will stimulate the release of ADH. The released ADH will act at the distal tubule and collecting duct to reabsorb water to increase plasma volume, thus lowering plasma osmolality. Urine output is more concentrated and also decreased.

Acid-base control is in the kidneys. The kidneys are one of three pH control mechanisms in the body; the others are blood buffering and the respiratory adjustment mechanism. As the blood pH becomes more acidic, the kidneys will respond by increasing the renal tubule excretion of hydrogen and ammonia, which results in an increase in blood bicarbonate and an increase in pH (toward normal). This is an effective method of adjusting hydrogen ions within the system.

The hormone erythropoietin is synthesized in the kidneys. A decrease in red blood cells below normal, or tissue hypoxia, will stimulate an increased release of erythropoietin from the kidneys. The increased serum concentration of erythropoietin will stimulate the bone marrow to increase its production of red blood cells, so that the red blood cell average is restored to normal.

## BIBLIOGRAPHY

Braunwalk E et al. (1987). Harrison's principles of internal medicine, ed 11. New York: McGraw-Hill Co.

Guyton AC. (1987). Human physiology and mechanisms of disease, ed 4. Philadelphia: WB Saunders Co.

Thibodeau GA. (1990). Textbook of anatomy and physiology, ed 13. St Louis: Times Mirror/Mosby College Publishing.

# Chapter

## 33 Diuretics

## KEY TERMS

## INTRODUCTION

Diuretics are among the most commonly used medications. They represent the mainstay in the treatment of hypertension (see also Chapter 26) and are an integral part of drug therapies in edematous conditions such as cirrhosis, nephrotic syndrome, and congestive heart failure. **Diuretics** induce diuresis, or loss of body water by urination. They influence water and electrolyte balance, particularly sodium, in the body. This action is exerted on tubular function of the kidney rather than on glomerular filtration. It generally involves the inhibition of solute reabsorption and thus water reabsorption, since water passively diffuses across the tubular membrane when sodium transport occurs. Diuretics have their primary effect on tubular function in the nephron. Understanding their action requires knowledge of the events that take place along each of the tubular segments. (See Chapter 32.)

Therapeutically, drug selection is best understood if each diuretic is presented according to the major site of action. This approach does not preclude drug effect at other sites in the nephron. Figure 33-1 shows the various sites of action of diuretic groups by means of water and electrolyte transport system in a kidney nephron.

### PROXIMAL TUBULE DIURETICS
### Carbonic Anhydrase Inhibitors
#### acetazolamide (Diamox, Acetazolam ✳)

Acetazolamide is the prototype of the **proximal tubule agents** that are sulfonamides. These drugs act primarily to reduce the volume of sequestered fluids, especially of the aqueous humor.

Acetazolamide inhibits the action of the enzyme **carbonic anhydrase,** which in turn prevents the reabsorption of bicarbonate ions from the proximal tubules. These bicarbonate ions then act to increase tubular osmotic pressure, causing osmotic diuresis. With long-term use, however, the diuretic

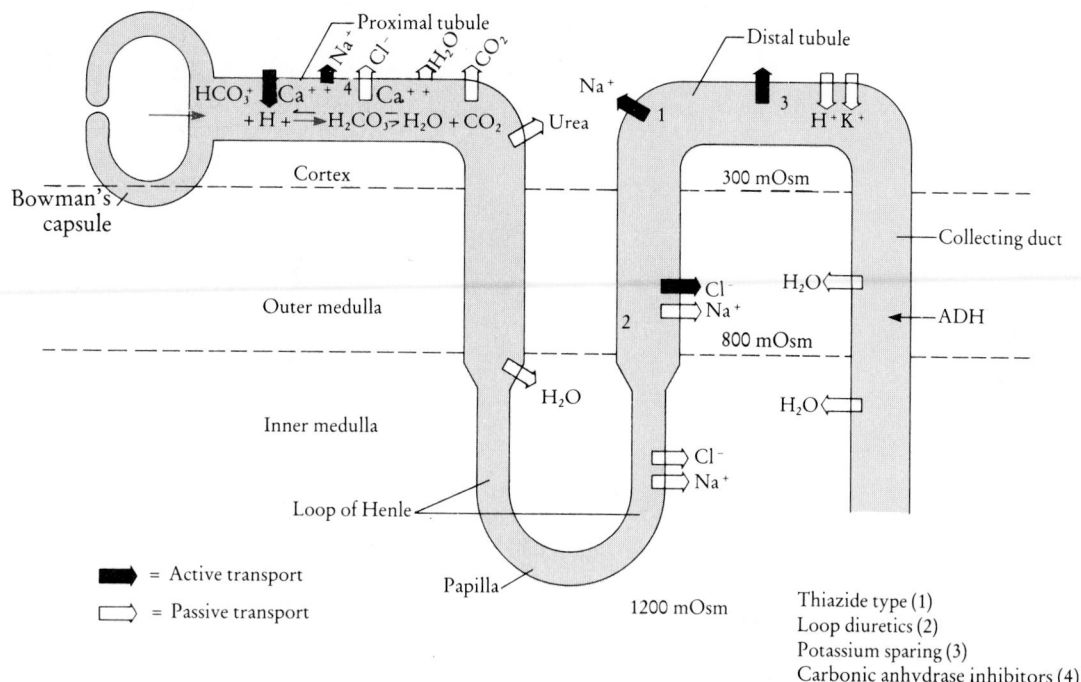

**FIGURE 33-1**  Diuretics. Site of action by means of water and electrolyte transport.

effect of these drugs is lost. Therefore acetazolamide is used primarily to produce an alkaline urine, which helps increase excretion of weakly acidic drugs in cases of drug overdose.

Acetazolamide is widely used as an antiglaucoma agent because it lowers intraocular pressure by decreasing production of aqueous humor by over 50%. This will be discussed in Chapter 43. Acetazolamide is indicated for the treatment of open-angle glaucoma and is also used as adjunct treatment with anticonvulsants to manage absence seizures (petit mal), generalized tonic-clonic seizures (grand mal), mixed seizure patterns, and myoclonic seizures. It has been found especially useful for women who experience an increase in seizures during their menstrual periods. It is also used to treat altitude sickness. Orally, it has been found to decrease the incidence and severity of symptoms of altitude sickness in mountain climbers.

Acetazolamide is well absorbed orally, reaches a peak level in 2 to 4 hours after a 500 mg dose or a 8- to 12-hour range after a 500-mg extended-release capsule. Its half-life is 10 to 15 hours and excretion is mainly by the kidneys. For reported side effects/adverse reactions see Table 33-1.

***Significant drug interactions.*** The following interactions may occur when acetazolamide is given with the drugs listed below.

| Drug | Possible Effect and Management |
|---|---|
| amphetamines, mecamylamine, or quinidine | Because of alkalinization of urine, the excretion of these drugs is decreased. Therefore increased serum levels and toxicity may be seen. Avoid concurrent drug administration with mecamylamine. Dosage adjustments may be necessary |

| Drug | Possible Effect and Management |
|---|---|
| | with the other two drugs whenever a carbonic anhydrase inhibitor is started, dosage is changed, or medication is discontinued. |
| methenamine | Alkaline urine will reduce the effectiveness of methenamine. Avoid concurrent usage. |

***Dosage and administration.*** Adult dose of acetazolamide for glaucoma is 250 mg orally, one to four times daily. As an anticonvulsant, 4 to 30 mg orally/kg divided into four doses per day. For altitude sickness the dose is 250 mg orally, two to four times daily. The pediatric dose for glaucoma is 8 to 30 mg/kg orally per day in divided doses. Acetazolamide is also available in extended-release capsules dosed 500 mg twice a day and a parenteral injection for intravenous or intramuscular use. See current package insert for dosing instructions.

***Pregnancy safety.*** Has not been established.

▷ **Nursing Management:**
**Acetazolamide Therapy**

***Assessment.*** Ascertain whether the client has diabetes or a familial history of diabetes because acetazolamide has caused elevations of blood glucose and glycosuria in these clients. Do not give acetazolamide to clients allergic to sulfonamides. Because they are more susceptible to electrolyte imbalances, clients with adrencortical insufficiency, hepatic or renal function impairment, or those with a preexisting electrolyte imbalance should receive acetazolamide with caution. Clients with a history of calcium containing renal stones may have a recurrence of calculi.

**TABLE 33-1**   Side effects/adverse reactions of diuretics

| Drug | Side effects* | Adverse reactions† |
|---|---|---|
| Proximal tubule diuretics: acetazolamide (Diamox, etc.) | Most frequent: moderate headaches<br>Less frequent/rare: alopecia, rash on arms and face | Most frequent: increased nervousness, anorexia, nausea or vomiting, depression, tremors<br>Less frequent/rare: severe or sudden headaches; sudden ataxia; pain in chest, groin, calves, or legs; slurred speech; visual disturbances; respiratory difficulties |
| Diluting segment diuretics: thiazide and thiazide-type drugs (see Table 33-3) | Less frequent: impotence, diarrhea, postural hypotension, skin photosensitivity, anorexia, abdominal distress | Most frequent: dry mouth; increased thirst; mood or mental alterations; pain or cramping in muscles; increased weakness, nausea, or vomiting; dysrhythmias or weak pulse (electrolyte imbalance)<br>Rare: abdominal or joint pain, sore throat, and elevated temperature, jaundice, increased bleeding tendencies |
| Loop diuretics: bumetanide ethacrynic acid furosemide | Most frequent: postural hypotension<br>  ethacrynic acid only: diarrhea, anorexia (dose-related effects)<br>Less frequent: blurred vision, headaches, abdominal cramping or pain<br>  bumetanide: chest pain, diarrhea, anorexia, premature ejaculation<br>  ethacrynic acid: confusion, anxiety<br>  furosemide: diarrhea, skin photosensitivity, anorexia | Less frequent: weak pulse<br>Rare: abdominal or joint pain, hives or allergic reaction, sore throat, elevated temperature, nausea, vomiting, increased bleeding episodes, jaundice, tinnitus or loss of hearing<br>  ethacrynic acid: bloody urine or black stools associated with injection |
| Distal tubule diuretics/potassium-sparing diuretics: amiloride spironolactone triamterene | Most frequent (spironolactone): nausea, vomiting, abdominal cramps, diarrhea<br>Less frequent: dizziness, dry mouth, sedation, increased thirst, loss of energy, (caused by hyponatremia), headache<br>  amiloride: constipation, muscle cramps, abdominal distress, decreased sexual activity<br>  triamterene: skin photosensitivity, abdominal distress<br>  spironolactone: gynecomastia (dose related), clumsiness, decreased sexual activity | Most frequent: signs of hyperkalemia—increased weakness; heavy feeling in legs; increased anxiety; respiratory difficulties; paresthesias of hands, feet, or lips; dysrhythmias<br>Rare: rash, pruritus, shortness of breath<br>  triamterene: red tongue (patient may complain of burning sensation), cracks at corners of mouth; increased weakness; flank pain; sore throat, elevated temperature, increased bleeding episodes |
| Osmotic diuretics:<br>Parenteral: mannitol urea | Most frequent<br>  mannitol: headache, increased urination, nausea, vomiting, dry mouth<br>  urea: nausea or vomiting<br>Less frequent<br>  mannitol: visual disturbances, dizziness, rash<br>  urea: headaches | Less frequent (urea): inadvertent intravascular or intraperitoneal administration may result in abdominal pain, weakness, myometrial necrosis, and dehydration<br>Rare: confusion, muscle cramping or pain, paresthesias in hands or feet, increased weakness, legs feel heavy and weak, dysrhythmias<br>  mannitol: chest pain; chills; elevated temperature; confusion; tachycardia; dysrhythmias; pain or cramping of muscles; paresthesias, pain, or weakness in hands and feet; convulsions; tremors; increased weakness; legs feel heavy and weak; respiratory difficulties; dysuria; redness, pain, or swelling at injection site; edema of lower extremities |
| Oral: glycerin | Most frequent: headache, nausea or vomiting<br>Less frequent: dry mouth, increased thirst, diarrhea, dizziness | Less frequent: confusion<br>Rare: dysrhythmias |
| isosorbide | Nausea, vomiting, abdominal distress, hiccoughs, rash, dizziness, lethargy, increased irritability | Disorientation, syncope |

*If side effects continue, increase, or disturb the client, inform the physician.
†If adverse reactions occur, contact the physician, since medical intervention may be necessary.

Note that elderly clients are especially susceptible to excessive diuresis and may be unable to tolerate the usual adult doses.

With the administration of acetazolamide, clients are at risk for the following nursing diagnoses: altered comfort related to dry mouth, bitter taste, nausea, vomiting, and numbness or tingling of fingers, toes, lips, or tongue; altered urinary elimination pattern with an increase and frequency of urination; altered bowel elimination (diarrhea or constipation); altered self-concept (depression); altered thought processes (confusion); electrolyte imbalances; and potential for physiologic injury related to renal calculi or nephrotoxicity, blood dyscrasias (fever, sore throat, unusual bleeding or bruising).

***Intervention.*** Reconstituting acetazolamide with at least 5 ml sterile water is necessary before parenteral use. Discard it after 24 hours of reconstitution since it contains no preservatives.

Administer the oral forms of acetazolamide with meals or with antacids such as Maalox to decrease gastrointestinal distress. For clients unable to tolerate tablets for oral administration, crush acetazolamide tablets and mix with a flavored syrup such as chocolate or cherry. Although up to 500 mg may be prepared in 5 ml syrup, it is more palatable if only 250 mg/5 ml is used. Refrigeration also increases palatability but not stability of the preparation; use within a week of preparation. Mixing the drug with fruit juices and elixirs is not as satisfactory.

Planning a high fluid intake for the client with gout or hypercalciuria (excessive calcium in the urine) is necessary because of the risk of renal calculi. Establish dosing schedules that minimize the inconvenience of diuresis for the client because of altered urinary elimination patterns. When this drug is used in diuretic therapy, consult the physician and dietitian to provide a high-potassium diet.

Acetazolamide is used to prevent or minimize high altitude sickness, but it is not a substitute for rapid descent if the climber manifests signs of pulmonary or cerebral edema.

***Education.*** Oral and intravenous routes of administration are preferred, but if the drug is to be given intramuscularly, alert the client that the injection will be painful because of the drug's alkalinity.

Alert the client that constipation is common with diuretic therapy and may be prevented or minimized by adequate fluid intake, high-fiber diet, and moderate exercise if these are not contraindicated by the client's health status. High fluid intake, 2500 to 3000 ml/day, is necessary to reduce the risk of renal calculi.

Instruct the client to move gradually from a sitting or lying position to a more upright one to prevent lightheadedness caused by orthostatic hypotension. Caution the client that the ability to accomplish tasks requiring mental alertness and physical coordination may be impaired.

Advise the client that dryness of the mouth may occur, but its discomfort may be minimized by the use of sugarless hard candies and frequent mouth rinses. Advise the client to get regular dental checkups to monitor caries and gum disease development that may occur as the result of xerostomia.

Although the sensation of "not feeling well" is common with the drug, malaise should be reported to the physician so that monitoring for acidosis, blood dyscrasias, or hypokalemia may be done. Advise the client to notify the physician if paresthesias (numbness, tingling, or burning) of the mouth, fingers, and toes occur.

Instruct the client and the family member who shops for and prepares the food about a high-potassium diet in keeping with the client's usual dietary patterns.

Advise the client to consult the physician before switching brands or using a generic formulation of acetazolamide because bioequivalence problems have been noted.

***Evaluation.*** Observe the client for signs of allergic reaction and photosensitivity. Weigh the client daily. A rapid loss of body water (which may cause hypotension) will be reflected in a rapid weight loss. Monitor intake and output and electrolytes, especially serum potassium levels. Do complete blood cell counts periodically to monitor for blood dyscrasias. Monitor blood and urine sugar levels for clients with diabetes or those at risk for diabetes.

Since acetazolamide is indicated primarily to reduce intraocular pressure in glaucoma, as an adjunct in anticonvulsant therapy, and for altitude illness, depending on the indication for a specific client, it would be an expected outcome to observe a reduction in the client's symptoms related to that condition.

## DILUTING SEGMENT DIURETICS
### Thiazide and Thiazide-Type Drugs
#### chlorothiazide (Diuril), hydrochlorothiazide (Hydro-Diuril, Esidrix, Oretic), metolazone (Zaroxolyn)

The thiazides, the major diuretics active within the diluting segments of the kidney, are synthetic drugs chemically related to the sulfonamides.

Hydrochlorothiazide is one of the most commonly used thiazides. Since quinethazone, metolazone, and chlorthalidone—other common diluting segment diuretics—are pharmacologically and structurally similar to the thiazides, all of the diluting segment diuretics will be described collectively as the **thiazide-type diuretics.** Important differences will be mentioned later. Table 33-2 presents these selected diuretics and their dosages.

The primary action and site of action appear to be inhibition of sodium reabsorption at the cortical diluting segment of the nephron, including portions of the thick ascending loop of Henle and the distal convoluted tubule. The role of these drugs in carbonic anhydrase inhibition is minor. They are less potent than the loop diuretics, since the maximum portion of the sodium load they can affect at the distal tubule

**TABLE 33-2** Examples of diuretic dosages and administration

| Generic/trade name | Age | Usual daily dosage |
|---|---|---|
| **THIAZIDE AND THIAZIDE-TYPE DIURETICS** | | |
| chlorothiazide (Diuril) | Adults | Diuretic, 250 mg orally, every 6-12 hr; injectable form is same. Antihypertensive, 250 mg to 1 g daily, as single or divided doses; adjust dosage according to response. Injectable form; 500 mg to 1 g IV daily as a single dose or in 2 divided doses. Elderly may be more sensitive to adult dosages, so monitor closely. |
| | Children | Up to 6 mo old, 10-30 mg/kg orally as single dose or in 2 divided doses daily; adjust dose as necessary. 6 mo and older, 10-20 mg/kg orally daily as a single dose or in two divided doses daily; adjust dose as necessary. Injectable form not recommended. |
| chlorthalidone (Apo-Chlorthalidone ✿, Hygroton) | Adults | Diuretic, 25-100 mg orally daily; or 100-200 mg once every other day, or once daily for 3 days/wk. Antihypertensive, 25-100 mg orally daily; adjust dosage as necessary. Elderly may be more sensitive to adult dosages, so monitor closely. |
| | Children | 2 mg/kg or 60 mg/m² orally once daily for 3 days/wk. Adjust dosage as necessary. |
| hydrochlorothiazide (Esidrix, Hydro-Diuril, Nefrol ✿) | Adults | Diuretic, 25-100 mg orally once or twice daily. Antihypertensive, 25-100 mg daily in 1 or 2 divided doses; adjust dosage as necessary. Elderly may be more sensitive to adult dosages, so monitor closely. |
| **LOOP DIURETICS** | | |
| bumetanide (Bumex) | Adults | 0.5-2 mg orally daily; adjust dosage as necessary by adding a second or third dose, every 4-5 hr. An alternative schedule of dosing on alternate days may also be used. Maximum is 10 mg daily. Injectable form; 0.5-1 mg IV or IM, may repeat at 2-3 hr intervals, if necessary, up to 10 mg daily. Elderly may be more sensitive to adult dosages, so monitor closely. |
| | Children | Not established |
| ethacrynic acid (Edecrin) | Adult | Diuretic, 50-100 mg orally daily in single or divided doses; may increase by 25-50 mg daily, as needed up to 400 mg maximum/day; maintenance, usually 50-200 mg daily. Injectable form; diuretic, 50 mg IV; may repeat in 2-4 hr if needed; if client is responsive, dosage may be repeated every 4-6 hr thereafter; in emergencies, dosage may be repeated every hour; maximum dosage is 100 mg daily. Elderly may be more sensitive to adult dosages, so monitor closely. |
| | Children | Diuretic, 25 mg orally daily; adjust dosage by 25 mg/day as necessary; do not use in infants. Injectable form; 1 mg/kg IV. |
| furosemide (Lasix, Furoside ✿) | Adults | Diuretic, 20-80 mg orally initially. Increase dosage by 20-40 mg at 6-8 hr intervals if necessary. Maintenance dose as determined by adjustments. Antihypertensive, 40 mg orally initially twice daily. Increase dosage as necessary to achieve desired results. maximum daily dosage is 600 mg. Elderly may be more sensitive to adult dosages, so monitor closely. (Note that in chronic renal failure doses have been increased up to 4 g daily to achieve desired results.) |
| | Children | Diuretic, 2 mg/kg orally as a single dose. Increase dose by 1-2 mg/kg every 6-8 hr until desired results are achieved. Although dosages as large as 5 mg/kg have been used in children with nephrotic syndrome, dosages above 6 mg/kg daily are not recommended. |

**TABLE 33-2**   Examples of diuretic dosages and administration—cont'd

| Generic/trade name | Age | Usual daily dosage |
|---|---|---|
| **DISTAL TUBULE DIURETICS/POTASSIUM-SPARING DIURETICS** | | |
| spironolactone (Aldactone, Novospiroton ❋) | Adults | Diuretic for edema as a result of congestive heart failure, cirrhosis, or nephrotic syndrome, 25-200 mg orally in 2-4 divided doses for at least 5 days. Maintenance, 75-400 mg daily orally in 2-4 divided doses.<br>Antihypertensive, 50-100 mg orally initially as a single dose or in 2-4 divided doses for approximately 14 days. Then gradually adjust dosage as necessary up to 200 mg daily.<br>For primary hyperaldosteronism, 100-400 mg orally daily in 2-4 divided doses before surgery. For individuals unable to undergo surgery, lower dosages are used for longer-term maintenance.<br>Also used as a diagnostic tool for primary hyperaldosteronism<br>For hypokalemia caused by diuretics, 25-100 mg daily as single dose or divided into 2-4 doses.<br>Elderly may be more sensitive to adult dosages, so monitor closely. Maximum daily dosage is 400 mg. |
| | Children | Diuretic or antihypertensive, 1-3 mg/kg orally as single dose or in 2-4 divided doses; adjust dosage as necessary after 5 days. Dosage increments may be increased up to 3 times the starting initial dose. |
| triamterene (Dyrenium) | Adults | Diuretic, 25-100 mg orally daily; adult dosage as necessary to achieve desired results. Maximum is 300 mg daily. Elderly may be more sensitive to adult dosages, so monitor closely. |
| | Children | Diuretic, 2-4 mg/kg orally daily or on alternative days in divided doses. Maintenance, increase to 6 mg/kg orally daily or adjust according to the individual's response to a maximum of 300 mg/day in divided dosages. |
| **OSMOTIC DIURETICS** | | |
| Parenteral preparations mannitol (Osmitrol ❋) | Adults | Diuretic, IV infusion 50-100 g (as 5%-25% solution), given at a rate to establish a urine flow of approximately 30-50 ml/hr.<br>Cerebral edema or increased intracranial pressure or glaucoma, 1.5-2 g/kg in a 15%-25% solution given as an IV infusion over ½-1 hr. (If client is small or debilitated, a dose of 500 mg/kg may be adequate.)<br>Adjunct to remove toxic substances, IV infusion of 50-200 g (as 5%-25% solution) given to establish and maintain a urine flow of 100-500 ml/hr.<br>Antihemolytic, 2.5% bladder-irrigating solution during transurethral prostatic resection.<br>Maximum dosage daily is 6 g/kg. |
| | Children | Diuretic, IV infusion, 2 g/kg as a 15%-20% solution, given over 2-6 hr.<br>Cerebral edema, increased intracranial pressure, or glaucoma, IV, 1-2 g/kg or 30-60 g/m² as a 15%-20% solution, given over ½-1 hr. In small or debilitated clients, a dose of 500 mg/kg may be adequate.<br>Adjunct to remove toxic substances, up to 2 g/kg as a 5%-10% solution given as IV infusion. |
| urea | Adults | Diuretic or antiglaucoma agent, 500 mg-1.5 g/kg as 30% solution in 5% or 10% dextrose injection administered as an IV infusion at a rate of 60 drops (4-6 ml)/min over ½-2 hr. Maximum dose is up to 2 g/kg in 24 hr. |
| | Children | If 2 yr or older, see adult dosage. For 2 yr and younger, 100 mg to 1.5 g/kg as a 30% solution in 5% or 10% dextrose injectable, administered as IV infusion at a rate of 60 drops (4-6 ml)/min over ½-2 hr. |
| **ORAL PREPARATIONS** | | |
| glycerin | Adults | 1-1.5 g/kg orally as single dose. Additional doses of 500 mg/kg may be given every 6 hr if necessary. |
| | Children | 1-1.5 g/kg orally as a single dose. May be repeated in 4-8 hr if necessary. |

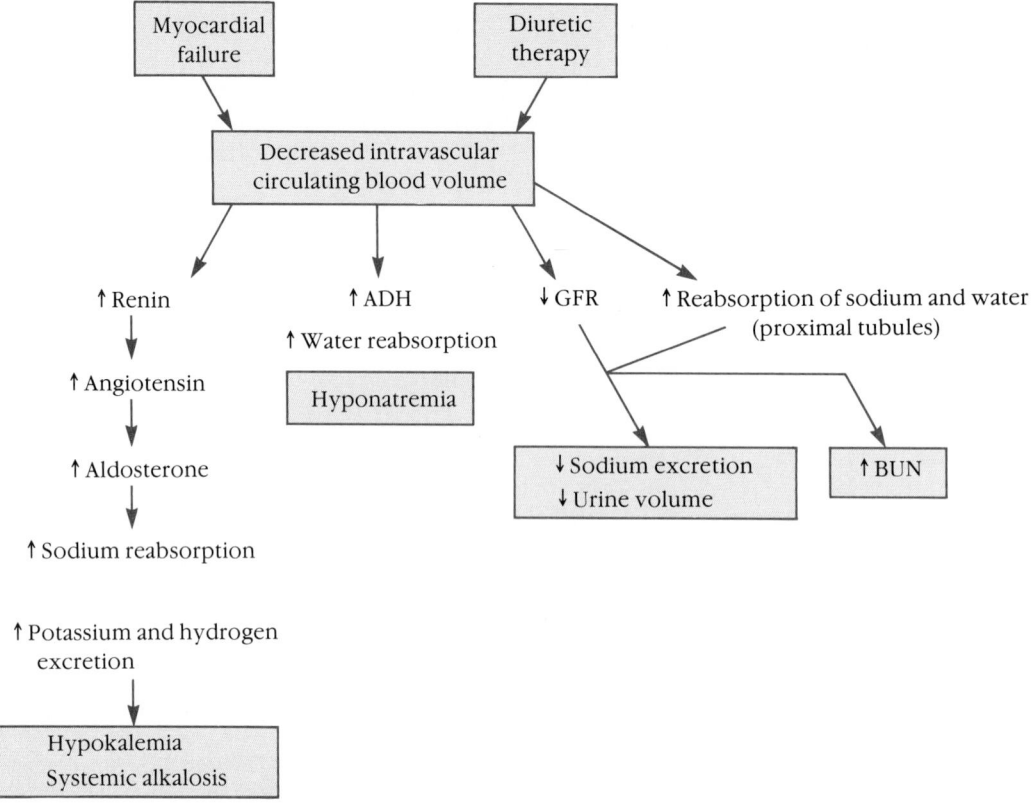

**FIGURE 33-2**   Body adaptation to extracellular volume depletion.

is less than 10% of the glomerular filtrate. The thiazide-type diuretics therefore primarily promote the excretion of sodium, chloride, and water. Especially important is their ability to impair free water clearance with no effect on concentration ability. The initial natriuretic effect lasts for about 1 week and then resets at a lower level. This diuretic tolerance occurs because of increased aldosterone levels and a decreased sodium load at the distal tubule. The mechanisms of antihypertensive action are unknown, but they are believed to be of both extrarenal and renal origins and perhaps an altered sodium balance in the body.

When an increased sodium load is presented to the distal tubule, there is a corresponding increase in potassium secretion. In addition, as the extracellular fluid volume decreases, plasma renin activity and aldosterone levels increase, with resulting potassium loss. See Figure 33-2 for the body's adaptation to extracellular volume depletion. Potassium is one of the most common electrolytes lost, with loss occurring in up to 40% of clients. This loss is dose related; that is, it occurs more frequently with the larger diuretic doses, with the long-acting type of diuretics (e.g., chlorthalidone), and in individuals with a high sodium intake (Herfindal, 1988). However, in many cases, the loss is intermittent and neither harmful nor clinically observable. Potassium loss may be a serious threat in those who are taking digitalis preparations, since it can precipitate serious

dysrhythmias as a result of digitalis toxicity. Hypokalemia may predispose the client with cirrhosis to hepatic encephalopathy and coma.

Usually health care providers caution clients with prescribed thiazide therapy to increase their dietary intake of potassium (see box for foods high in potassium). If hypokalemia occurs, the physician may prescribe oral potassium preparations or, if urgent replacement is necessary, intravenous potassium chloride administration. Potassium loss may also be reversed by the addition of a potassium-sparing diuretic that acts to inhibit potassium loss at the distal tubule. However, potassium replacement is usually not necessary in 80% to 90% of individuals taking the thiazide diuretics, particularly in the treatment of nonedematous states. It should be remembered that potassium replacement may be dangerous in the elderly, in renal dysfunction, and when used in combination with potassium-sparing diuretics, since dangerously high serum potassium levels may occur.

The thiazide-type diuretics are noted to increase serum uric acid in 40% of men (less often in women). The 1 to 2 mg/dl increase in serum uric acid is persistent and probably results from inhibition of tubular secretion of uric acid. However, this effect is reversible when the drugs are discontinued. In the absence of gout or genetic predisposition the hyperuricemia is usually no problem and requires no treatment. However, in a client with a history of gout the

**TABLE 33-3**   Diuretic pharmacokinetics

| Drug | Onset of action (hr) | Peak effect (hr) | Duration of action (hr) |
|---|---|---|---|
| **THIAZIDE AND THIAZIDE-TYPE DIURETICS** | | | |
| chlorothiazide (Diuril, SK-Chlorothiazide) | 2 | 4 | 6-12 |
| chlorthalidone (Apo-Chlorthalidone ♣, Hygroton) | 2 | N/A* | 24-72 |
| hydrochlorothiazide (Esidrix, HydroDiuril, Oreton) | 2 | 4 | 6-12 |
| **LOOP DIURETICS** | | | |
| bumetanide (Bumex) | ½-1 within minutes (IV) | 1-2 ¼-½ (IV) | 4 (usual dosages) 4-6 (higher dosages) 3½-4 (IV dose) |
| ethacrynic acid (Edecrin) | ½ (PO); 5 min (IV) | 2 (PO); ¼-½ (IV) | 6-8 (PO) 2 (IV) |
| furosemide (Lasix, Furoside ♣) | ½-1 (PO); 5 min (IV) | 1-2 (PO);' ⅓-1 (IV) | 6-8 (PO) 2 (IV) |
| **DISTAL TUBULE DIURETICS OR POTASSIUM-SPARING DIURETICS** | | | |
| spironolactone (Aldactone, Novospiroton ♣) | N/A* | 48-72 | 48-72 |
| triamterene (Dyrenium) | 2-4 | multiple dosing, 24 or more | 7-9 (single dose) |

*N/A, Not available.

use of allopurinol or probenecid is suggested to counteract any elevation of serum uric acid.

Hyperglycemia or impaired glucose tolerance has been reported with the thiazide-type and loop diuretics. This effect is reported most often in the elderly, and the thiazides can precipitate diabetes in individuals with overt and subclinical disease patterns. The thiazide diuretics are not contraindicated in diabetic clients because if hyperglycemia is noted, it can usually be controlled by diet alterations or increasing the insulin dose. When hyperglycemia does occur in the nondiabetic client, many physicians prefer to try another type of diuretic such as furosemide to see if the problem can be reduced or alleviated.

The thiazide diuretics and perhaps furosemide have been associated with increasing serum levels of cholesterol and triglycerides. Since elevated serum lipids are associated with an increase in coronary heart disease, it is important that serum lipids be monitored and perhaps a specific dietary approach or weight loss program be implemented if necessary.

The indications for the thiazide diuretics include treating hypertension, edema associated with congestive heart failure, cirrhosis with ascites, and some types of renal impairment, such as nephrotic syndrome, acute glomerulonephritis, and chronic renal failure. These agents are well absorbed orally and are usually excreted by the kidneys. For a review

of side effects/adverse reactions, selected dosage and administration, and pharmacokinetics, see Tables 33-1, 33-2 and 33-3, respectively.

***Significant drug interactions.*** The following interactions may occur when thiazide and thiazide-type diuretics are given with the drugs listed below.

| Drug | Possible Effect and Management |
|---|---|
| adrenocorticoids, glucocorticoid, mineralocorticoid, corticotropin (ACTH) | Electrolyte disturbances such as hypokalemia and sodium retention may occur. Diuretic effects may also be decreased. Monitor closely if concurrent therapy is necessary. Frequent electrolyte serum levels should be done, since potassium supplements may be necessary. |
| digitalis glycosides | Increased risk of digitalis toxicity in presence of hypokalemia. Monitor closely. |
| lithium | Not recommended. Increased risk of lithium toxicity possible because of decreased lithium excretion. Also, lithium has potential for nephrotoxic side effects. Avoid this combination. |
| methenamine | Thiazides may cause an alkaline urine that would decrease the effectiveness of methenamine. Avoid this combination. |

***Pregnancy safety.*** Established at FDA Category B for benzthiazide, chlorothiazide, chlorthalidone, hydrochlorothiazide, metolazone, and trichlormethiazide; at FDA Category C for cyclothiazide and methyclothiazide; and at FDA Category D for hydroflumethiazide.

## ▷Nursing Management: Thiazide and Thiazide-Type Diuretic Therapy

**Assessment.** Do not give thiazide and thiazide-type diuretics to individuals who are allergic to sulfonamides, since there may be a cross-sensitivity. Thiazide diuretics are given with caution to clients with severe renal impairment, hepatic impairment in which they might precipitate hepatic coma, diabetes mellitus (because the dosages of hypoglycemic agents may need to be altered), and electrolyte imbalances (because they may be exacerbated). They are contraindicated or given carefully to pregnant women, since they cross the placental barrier. Check creatinine clearance for elderly clients before administering thiazide-type diuretics to ensure adequate renal function.

Clients receiving thiazide and thiazide-like diuretics are at risk for the following nursing diagnoses: electrolyte imbalances (hypokalemia, hyponatremia, and hypocholoremic alkalosis); altered comfort related to nausea; altered self-concept related to decreased libido; altered urinary elimination pattern (frequency and amount); altered bowel elimination (diarrhea or constipation); and high risk for physiologic injury related to orthostatic hypotension, allergic reaction, agranulocytosis (fever, lower back pain, dysuria), gout, hepatoxicity, and thrombocytopenia (unusual bleeding and bruising, petechiae, and blood in urine or stools).

**Intervention.** To reverse hypokalemia, add foods rich in potassium to the diet (see below). Liquid potassium for oral use, although unpleasant tasting, may be disguised in cold

### FOODS RICH IN POTASSIUM

| Food | Amount | Potassium (mg) | Food | Amount | Potassium (mg) |
|---|---|---|---|---|---|
| Apricots | | | Prunes | | |
| Fresh | 1 | 105 | Dried | 1 cup | 1200 |
| Canned in water | 1 cup | 465 | Juice, canned or bottled | 1 cup | 706 |
| Dried, uncooked | 1 cup | 1791 | | | |
| Avocado | 1 | 1369 | Raisins | 1 cup | 1089 |
| Banana | 1 | 471 | Lima beans, frozen, cooked | 1 cup | 694 |
| Figs | | | | | |
| Fresh | 1 | 116 | Beets, sliced, cooked | 1 cup | 532 |
| Canned in heavy syrup | 1 cup | 258 | | | |
| Dried, uncooked | 1 cup | 1418 | Brussels sprouts, cooked | 1 cup | 494 |
| Grapefruit | | | Peanuts roasted in oil | 1 ounce | 200 |
| Canned in water | 1 cup | 322 | | | |
| Fresh | ½ | 312 | Potato | | |
| Juice, canned, unsweetened | 1 cup | 378 | Baked | 1 | 610 |
| | | | Boiled | 1 | 515 |
| Melon, fresh cantaloupe | 1 cup | 494 | Spinach | | |
| Orange | | | Cooked, fresh | 1 cup | 838 |
| Fresh | 1 | 237 | Canned | 1 cup | 709 |
| Juice, frozen, diluted | 1 cup | 474 | From frozen | 1 cup | 566 |
| Peaches | | | Squash | | |
| Fresh | 1 | 171 | Acorn, baked | 1 cup | 896 |
| Canned in water | 1 cup | 241 | Hubbard, mashed | 1 cup | 504 |
| Dried | 1 cup | 1594 | Winter, mashed | 1 cup | 895 |
| | | | Zucchini, canned | 1 cup | 622 |
| Pears | | | Sweet potato, baked | 1 | 397 |
| Fresh | 1 | 208 | Tomato | 1 | 297 |
| Canned in juice | 1 cup | 238 | Tomato juice, canned | 1 cup | 535 |
| Dried | 1 cup | 959 | | | |

From Burtis, G, Davis, J, and Martin, S: Applied nutrition and diet therapy, Philadelphia, 1988, WB Saunders Co.

juices and taken with food. Tomato juice is not recommended for this purpose because its sodium content is high. Enteric-coated potassium tablets should be avoided because they have been implicated in ulcerations of the gastrointestinal tract lining.

Discontinue thiazides before parathyroid function tests are performed, since they may alter serum calcium concentrations.

As with other diuretics, plan dosing schedules to minimize the inconvenience of diuresis for the client.

*Education.* Teach clients that thiazides may make them feel unusually tired. Because of the potential for digitalis toxicity while taking these drugs in combination with digitalis, they also need to know how to take their pulse rate before taking digitalis medications. If the pulse rate is less than 60 beats/minute or is irregular, digitalis medications should be discontinued and the physician notified. Nausea, vomiting, and anorexia are even earlier signs of digitalis toxicity that nurses and clients should recognize.

Clients should understand that diuretic drugs, if prescribed for a chronic condition, need to be taken as an integral part of their life-style. Compliance may be enhanced when nurses closely observe client's self-medicating habits and verbally reinforce them.

As with acetazolamide, the client should receive instruc-

tion related to the prevention and minimization of the effects of xerostomia, constipation, and orthostatic hypotension. Signs and symptoms of electrolyte imbalances and blood dyscrasias should be taught with proper referral to the physician.

Instruct clients to eat foods rich in potassium if a supplement is not prescribed (see p. 594).

*Evaluation.* Take the client's blood pressure before administering the diuretic to ensure the client is not hypotensive. Daily weight and fluid balance monitoring will assist in determining the progress of the diuretic therapy. Since hypokalemia is possible, monitor laboratory reports of serum potassium levels. Monitoring is particularly important when digitalis compounds are part of the regimen, since hypokalemia primes clients taking digitalis preparations for toxic cardiac effects of the digitalis, such as bradycardia or ventricular irritability. Latent diabetes or gout may occasionally occur; laboratory reports should be monitored for hyperglycemia or hyperuricemia.

Observe the client for signs and symptoms of fluid and electrolyte imbalances: hypovolemia, hyponatremia, hypokalemia, hypocalcemia, hypochloremia, and hypomagnesemia (see box at left). As these diuretics are indicated for hypertension and fluid volume excess, it would be an expected outcome that the client's blood pressure would decrease or be within normal limits and that, if evident, the client's edema would resolve.

## LOOP DIURETICS
### bumetanide (Bumex), ethacrynic acid (Edecrin), furosemide (Lasix, Furoside ✽, Apo-Furosemide ✽)

Bumetanide, furosemide, and ethacrynic acid are the classic examples of the **loop diuretics,** so called because they exert their action in the loop of Henle. These drugs for the most part are very similar to the thiazide-type diuretics in pharmacology and in the side effects they produce. Furosemide and ethacrynic acid exhibit their major effect by inhibiting active chloride transport in the thick portion of the ascending limb of the loop of Henle. The resulting passive sodium transport is also inhibited. The maximal effect of the loop diuretics is their indirect influence on urine concentration rather than on urine dilution. Furosemide and ethacrynic acid are more potent diuretics than the thiazides because they have the potential for altering 20% to 25% of the filtered sodium load, which is presented to the ascending limb of the loop of Henle. The loop diuretics do not inhibit carbonic anhydrase, except when furosemide is administered in very high doses. Carbohydrate intolerance, an increase in blood glucose levels, may occur but is less frequent. Rather than the hypocalciuric effect of the thiazides, the loop diuretics (particularly furosemide) promote calcium excretion. Furosemide in combination with normal saline infusion is the treatment of choice in hypercalcemia. Eth-

---

### SIGNS AND SYMPTOMS OF FLUID AND ELECTROLYTE IMBALANCES ASSOCIATED WITH DIURETIC THERAPY

*Hypovolemia:* hypotension, weak pulse, tachycardia, clammy skin, rapid respirations, and reduced urinary output

*Hyponatremia:* low serum sodium levels (normal range 135 to 145 mEq/L), lethargy, disorientation, muscle tenseness, seizures, and coma

*Hypokalemia:* low serum potassium levels (normal range 3.5 to 5.0 mEq/L), weakness, abnormal ECG, postural hypotension, and flaccid paralysis

*Hypocalcemia:* low serum calcium levels (normal range 8.4 to 10.2 mg/dl), irritability, vomiting, diarrhea, twitching, hyperactive reflexes, cardiac dysrhythmias, tetany, and seizures

*Hypochloremia:* low blood chloride levels (normal range 100 to 110 mEq/L)

*Hypomagnesemia:* low serum magnesium levels (normal range 1.3 to 2.1 mEq/L), nausea and vomiting, lethargy, muscle weakness, tremors, and tetany

**With potassium-sparing diuretics, be alert for:**

*Hyperkalemia:* above-normal values for potassium serum levels, nausea, diarrhea, muscle weakness, postural hypotension, and ECG changes acrynic acid has little or no direct effect on glomerular filtration rate, whereas furosemide exhibits a renal vasodilator effect, resulting in less vascular resistance and increased renal blood flow. Furosemide is therefore useful in renal failure, although it is contraindicated in anuria. Bumetanide inhibits sodium reabsorption in the ascending limb of the loop of Henle, as shown by marked reduction of free-water clearance during hydration and tubular free-water reabsorption during dehydration. Reabsorption of chloride in the ascending loop is also blocked by bumetanide, which may have an additional action in the proximal tubule. Since phosphate reabsorption takes place largely in the proximal tubule, phosphaturia during bumetanide-induced diuresis indicates this additional action. This proximal tubular activity does not seem to be related to an inhibition of carbonic anhydrase. Bumetanide does not appear to have a noticeable action on the distal tubule. It decreases uric acid excretion and increases serum uric acid.

The loop diuretics also differ from the thiazides in that they have an infinite dose-response curve. Increasing the dose continues to produce greater responses; hence they are referred to as "high-ceiling" diuretics.

The indications for the loop diuretics include treatment of edema associated with congestive heart failure, cirrhosis, and renal disease. Furosemide is also used to treat hypertension. These agents are also used as adjunct therapy in clients with acute pulmonary edema and in clients who are refractory to the other diuretics. The loop diuretics have fair to good absorption orally, are highly protein bound, are metabolized in the liver, and are excreted by the kidneys and in the bile. Side effects/adverse reactions, dosage and administration, and pharmacokinetics information is listed in Tables 33-1, 33-2, and 33-3, respectively.

**Significant drug interactions.** The following interactions may occur when loop diuretics are given with the drugs listed below.

| Drug | Possible Effect and Management |
|------|-------------------------------|
| adrenocorticoids, amphotericin B injectable | See thiazide drug interactions. Avoid concurrent therapy. Increases risk for ototoxicity, nephrotoxicity, and electrolyte imbalance (especially hypokalemia). If given concurrently, monitor serum electrolytes frequently. |
| anticoagulants, oral coumarin, indandione-type or heparin | Anticoagulant effects may be decreased with concurrent therapy. With ethacrynic acid, the anticoagulant effects may be enhanced due to displacement of the anticoagulant from its protein binding sites. Gastrointestinal ulcers or bleeding is a possible adverse reaction to ethcrynic acid, which with anticoagulant therapy, may increase the risk for hemorrhage. When possible, avoid giving ethacrynic acid to clients receiving anticoagulants. If loop diuretics are given concurrently, monitor clients closely for increased or decreased anticoagulant effectiveness. |
| lithium | See discussion of thiazide drug interactions. |

| Drug | Possible Effect and Management |
|------|-------------------------------|
| nephrotoxic medications or other ototoxic medications | Increases risks for ototoxicity and nephrotoxicity (especially in clients with renal impairment). Avoid concurrent and even sequential drug administration. |

**Pregnancy safety.** Has been established at FDA Category C for bumetanide and furosemide; none has been established for ethacrynic acid, although it is generally not recommended in pregnancy.

## ▷NURSING MANAGEMENT: LOOP DIURETIC THERAPY

**Assessment.** The use of loop diuretics is not recommended in the presence of anuria and liver dysfunction. With bumetanide and furosemide, there may be cross hypersensitivity to sulfonamides. Note precautions if the client is also receiving the following medications:
- Aminoglycoside antibiotics: watch for tinnitus, vertigo, or hearing difficulties.
- Digitalis compounds, amphotericin B, corticosteroids, or corticotropin: review serum electrolyte reports closely.
- Cephalothin, cephaloridine, or lithium: watch for diminished urinary output and other signs of nephrotoxicity.

Clients receiving thiazide and thiazide-like diuretics should be assessed for the development of the following nursing diagnoses: altered comfort related to headache, local irritation at site of injection, and abdominal cramping; altered urinary elimination pattern (frequency and amount); altered bowel elimination (diarrhea or constipation); altered self-concept related to impotency; sensory-perceptual alterations (visual—blurred vision, auditory—tinnitus, deafness); and high risk for injury related to orthostatic hypotension, allergic reaction, gout, hepatotoxicity, pancreatitis, thrombocytopenia, and a granulocytosis or leucopenia.

**Intervention.** Use of the intramuscular route can produce temporary pain at the site, so oral or intravenous routes are preferable. Administer these drugs so that onset and peak of action will coincide with access to toilet facilities. Administer with food if gastrointestinal upset occurs with oral forms. When administering oral solutions, use the calibrated dropper provided by the manufacturer for accurate dosages.

For bumetanide and furosemide, administer intravenous injection slowly over 2 minutes. Administer ethacrynic acid intravenously at a controlled rate over 30 minutes.

Because many glass ampules are required to be broken to prepare large dosages of furosemide intravenous infusions, there is the possibility of glass fragments occurring in the solution. Use filter to remove these particles while drawing the drug into the syringe and also during intravenous administration.

**Education.** Caution the client to move carefully from sitting or lying positions to upright ones because of positional hypotension. Alcohol ingestion, hot weather, and standing or lying for long periods also increase the risk of orthostatic hypotension. Instruct the client in the symptoms of electrolyte imbalances (see box on p. 595), particularly hypokalemia. Provide dietary counseling so the client will know which foods are rich in potassium.

Checking refills of the medication prescription provides a basis for client counseling for compliance with the regimen and also provides the opportunity for appropriate feedback.

Photosensitivity is a problem for some clients taking furosemide; caution them to avoid prolonged exposure to the sun or sunlamps. Encourage clients to use sunblocking lotion and cover themselves with clothing.

Weigh the client at the initiation of therapy and periodically thereafter to monitor fluid loss. When these diuretics are administered for acute excess fluid volume, it may be necessary to weigh the client on a daily basis. Weigh the client at the same time each day, preferably before breakfast, in similar clothes, and on the same scale for the most accurate readings. Weight loss and reduction in the extent of the edema would indicate effectiveness of the drug. A reduction in blood pressure to values within normal limits is also sought.

***Evaluation.*** Closely monitor clients, especially the elderly, for blood pressure changes; postural hypotension; dehydration (e.g., body weight loss of more than 2 pounds/day); allergic reactions (rashes); nausea, vomiting, and diarrhea; ototoxicity (tinnitus, hearing loss), and serum potassium deficiency.

Monitor carefully clients who may be experiencing potassium loss through other causes, such as vomiting, diarrhea, diaphoresis, gastrointestinal drainage, or paracentesis for signs and symptoms of hypokalemia.

Be aware that hyperuricemia may occur; reversible elevation of BUN and creatinine levels may occur, especially in association with dehydration and particularly in clients with renal insufficiency.

Check reports of serum electrolytes, uric acid, blood and urine glucose tests, and BUN levels for abnormalities. Excessive doses or too frequent administration can lead to prolonged water loss, electrolyte depletion, dehydration, reduction in blood volume, and circulatory collapse, with the possibility of vascular thrombosis and embolism, especially in elderly clients.

Be aware that hypokalemia can occur. Prevention of hypokalemia requires particular attention to the following conditions: individuals receiving digitalis and diuretics for congestive heart failure, hepatic cirrhosis and ascites; states of aldosterone excess with normal renal function; potassium-losing nephropathy; and certain diarrheal states. Measure serum potassium levels periodically and add potassium supplements or potassium-sparing diuretics if necessary. Periodic determination of other electrolytes is advised in clients with high doses for prolonged periods, particularly in those on low-salt diets.

Periodically determine blood sugar, particularly in clients with diabetes or suspected latent diabetes.

## DISTAL TUBULE DIURETICS/POTASSIUM-SPARING DIURETICS
### amiloride (Midamor), spironolactone (Aldactone), triamterene (Dyrenium)

The **potassium-sparing diuretics** will be considered together because many of their actions are similar. Important differences among them will be noted. They are generally considered weak diuretics that act at the distal renal tubules, but they are primarily considered useful when combined with other potassium-losing diuretics. Amiloride is a salt of a moderately strong base; spironolactone is an aldosterone antagonist; and triamterene directly inhibits reabsorption of sodium and water and yet retains potassium at the distal tubule. Any of the three agents may be used when it is necessary to restore or preserve the normal serum potassium level if other concurrent diuretic therapy challenges it and when potassium supplementation by medication or diet is inappropriate. They are highly effective for this purpose. Thus these drugs are usually administered as an adjunct to diuretic therapy. If prescribed singly, however, their efficacy may actually result in an undesirable and rapidly developing hyperkalemia.

Amiloride is not an aldosterone antagonist, and it is chemically unrelated to any other diuretic in use. It acts to block sodium-potassium exchange in the distal renal tubule with resultant increases in sodium and chloride excretion and with decreased potassium and hydrogen excretion. Its action leaves glomerular filtration rate and renal blood flow unchanged.

Spironolactone is a synthetic steroidal compound used to antagonize the effect of aldosterone by competitively binding to the protein that permits potassium secretion at the distal tubule. This response is directly related to the amount of circulating aldosterone in the serum. Spironolactone produces a very mild diuresis of sodium and water at the distal tubule by means of this mechanism. It does not interfere with renal tubule transport of sodium and chloride and does not inhibit carbonic anhydrase.

Triamterene directly depresses the renal tubular transport of sodium in the distal tubule independent of the presence of aldosterone. Excretion of sodium, chloride, bicarbonate, magnesium, and calcium is increased. The increased loss of bicarbonate, which may slightly alkalinize the urine, is not a result of carbonic anhydrase inhibition. The decreased serum bicarbonate levels can produce metabolic acidosis. More important is the ability of triamterene to decrease the secretion of potassium at the distal tubule. Unlike the thiazide-type diuretics, triamterene does not inhibit uric acid excretion, although elevated serum levels have been reported, particularly in clients with a history of gout. Cardiac output is decreased, as is the glomerular filtration rate, which may result in an increased BUN level and a decreased creatinine clearance rate.

The potassium-sparing diuretics are indicated for the prevention and treatment of hypokalemia. They are also used as adjunct therapy in the treatment of edema and hypertension, and spironolactone is indicated in the diagnosis and treatment of primary hyperaldosteronism. These agents have low (amiloride), moderate (triamterene), and good (spironolactone) absorption from the gastrointestinal tract. Spironolactone and triamterene are metabolized in the liver, and amiloride and spironolactone are excreted mainly by the kidneys. Triamterene is excreted primarily in bile. For side effects/adverse reactions, dosage and administration, and pharmacokinetics, see Tables 33-1, 33-2, and 33-3, respectively.

*Significant drug interactions.* The following interactions may occur when potassium-sparing diuretics are given with the drugs listed below.

| Drug | Possible Effect and Management |
|------|-------------------------------|
| lithium | See discussion of thiazide drug interactions. |
| blood from blood bank; captopril, cyclosporine, or other potassium-sparing diuretics; enalapril; low-salt milk; potassium-containing medications; or potassium supplements. | May increase potassium levels and result in hyperkalemia. Monitor closely. |

*Pregnancy safety.* Has been established at FDA Category B for amiloride and triamterene; FDA category has not been established for spironolactone.

▷ **Nursing Management:**
**Distal Tubule and Potassium-Sparing Diuretic Therapy**

*Assessment.* Before giving these compounds, ascertain that the client has no related drug history of allergy or hyperkalemia. For clients at risk for the development of hyperkalemia because of preexisting conditions such as impaired renal or hepatic function or diabetes mellitus, for severely ill patients, and for those with decreased urine volumes, which might aggravate electrolyte imbalances, greater caution is required in the administration of these diuretics.

With the administration of distal tubule and potassium-sparing diuretics, the client should be assessed for the following nursing diagnoses: altered comfort related to muscle cramps, headache, dizziness, and gastrointestinal effects (nausea, vomiting, and abdominal cramping); altered bowel elimination (constipation or diarrhea); altered self-concept related to decreased libido, gynecomastia in males, and hirsutism in females; and high risk for physiologic injury

related to the development of hyperkalemia, allergic reaction, nephrolithiasis, agranulocytosis, and thrombocytopenia.

*Intervention.* Administering these drugs with food or milk may allay some gastrointestinal symptoms and possibly enhance bioavailability. Deal with discomforting side effects such as dry mouth, thirst, or drowsiness if they arise.

Plan nursing measures common to diuretic agents, for example, measurements of fluid intake and output, daily weight changes, vital signs and heart rhythm, assessment of postural hypotension, weakness, or confusion. Monitor closely for hyperkalemia when transfusing blood. Whole blood may contain up to 30 mEq of potassium per liter; this may be doubled if blood has been stored more than 10 days.

*Education.* The client should be counseled to avoid excessively stringent low-salt diets and relatively concentrated potassium intake in the form of citrus juices, cola beverages, low-sodium milk, some salt substitutes, and other potassium supplements.

*Evaluation.* Monitor blood pressure, weight loss, and fluid balance to evaluate effectiveness of diuretic. Evaluate compliance with the client frequently. Especially at first, be alert to an irregular heartbeat (often the first clinical sign of hyperkalemia) or peaked T waves on ECG. Other warning signs of hyperkalemia are confusion, tingling in the extremities, difficulty in breathing, unexplained anxiety, fatigue, and physical weakness. Serum electrolyte determinations and an ECG are probably indicated if these occur.

Check laboratory reports closely, especially if the client is taking other similar drugs or potassium-rich foods. Rapidly increased serum potassium levels may occur. Act immediately to reverse hyperkalemia if serum potassium level exceeds 6 to 6.5 mEq/L and anticipate treatment with sodium bicarbonate, with glucose and regular insulin preparations, or with other therapy.

If the client is receiving spironolactone, remain sensitive to cues that he or she may be concerned about body image changes that may threaten sexual identity.

Note that when triamterene is being given, a complete blood count is probably indicated if the client has an unexplained sore throat, mouth ulcerations, or fever, indications of a possible blood dyscrasia.

## OSMOTIC DIURETICS
### mannitol (Osmitrol ✳ ), urea (Ureaphil), glycerin (Glyrol, Osmoglyn)

**Osmotic diuretics** include mannitol and urea parenterally and glycerin orally. The two parenteral agents cause diuresis by adding to the solutes already present in the tubular fluid; they are particularly effective in increasing osmotic pressure there because they are not reabsorbed by the tubules. Thus more water is pulled into tubular fluid, and less sodium, chloride, and water are reabsorbed by the kidneys in an effort to equalize the higher solute content. These excesses are then excreted in the urine. The oral agents are primarily used to reduce intraocular pressure before and after intra-ocular surgery or to interrupt an acute attack of glaucoma.

For indications for oral agents, see previous section. Parenteral agents are used to treat cerebral edema and secondary glaucoma when other methods have been unsuccessful. Mannitol has also been used to increase urinary excretion of toxic substances (salicylates, barbiturates, lithium, bromides), as an irrigating preparation to prevent hemolysis and hemoglobin accumulation during transurethral prostatic resection, and as an adjunct to other therapies in the treatment of edema in acute renal failure.

Very little if any mannitol is metabolized in the liver. Urea is partially metabolized in the gastrointestinal tract to ammonia and carbon dioxide, which may be resynthesized into urea.

Mannitol has a half-life of approximately 100 minutes (up to 36 hours in acute renal failure). Urea has a half-life of approximately 1.17 hours. Mannitol's diuresis effect takes place in 1 to 3 hours; lowering of cerebrospinal and intraocular fluid pressure occurs within 15 minutes. Lowering of intracranial and intraocular pressure with urea occurs within 10 minutes. The peak effect for mannitol in lowering intraocular pressure occurs ½ to 1 hour after administration. For urea it occurs in 1 to 2 hours.

Mannitol lowers cerebrospinal fluid for 3 to 8 hours after the injection is stopped; it lowers intraocular pressure for 4 to 8 hours. Urea promotes diuresis for 3 to 10 hours after the infusion is stopped; it lowers cerebrospinal fluid pressure for 3 to 10 hours after stopping the infusion; and it lowers intraocular pressure for 5 to 6 hours.

Both mannitol and urea are excreted by the kidneys.

Glycerin is well absorbed orally, has an onset of action within 10 minutes and a peak effect in lowering intraocular pressure within 1 to 1.5 hours, respectively. Glycerin's effect lasts approximately 5 hours. It is metabolized in the liver and excreted by the kidneys. Pregnancy safety has been established as FDA Category C for mannitol, urea, and glycerin.

## ▷ Nursing Management: Osmotic Diuretic Therapy

***Assessment.*** Ascertain that the client does not have preexisting congestive heart failure, severe dehydration, or pulmonary or renal disease for which osmotic diuretics are contraindicated. Intracranial bleeding, except during craniotomy, would negate the use for mannitol and urea.

Recommend that baseline serum electrolyte and renal function determinations be performed if they have not been done, and monitor the results.

Mannitol is different from the drug mannitol hexanitrate. Do not confuse them.

Clients receiving osmotic diuretics should be assessed for the following nursing diagnoses: altered comfort related to dry mouth, nausea, vomiting, headache, dizziness, rash, chest pain, and blurred vision; hyperthermia; altered urinary elimination pattern (frequency and amount); altered bowel elimination (constipation); and high risk for injury related to electrolyte imbalance and thrombophlebitis.

***Intervention.*** If the adequacy of renal function is suspect before the administration of mannitol, a test dose is usually ordered by the physician. It is given as an intravenous infusion over 3 to 5 minutes. Urine flow should increase to at least 30 to 50 ml/hr for 2 to 3 hours after this or a second test dose. If it does not, mannitol should be withheld and the client reevaluated.

Infuse mannitol and urea separately from other drugs and blood. Crystalization in solution is common; it may be countered by warming the solution until crystals are invisible and by inserting a filter in the line any time this drug is infused.

Avoid extravasation of urea and mannitol; observe the intravenous site periodically for tissue inflammation, irritation, and necrosis.

With urea, use large veins for infusion. With both urea and mannitol, avoid using lower extremity intravenous sites since phlebitis and thrombosis may occur, particularly in the elderly.

Do not infuse urea more rapidly than 4 ml/minute because hemolysis and cerebral vasomotor symptoms may occur.

To assist in the prevention and relief of headache caused by cerebral dehydration, have the client lie down during and after the administration of these drugs.

Use an indwelling catheter with comatose clients to ensure urinary drainage. The use of a urometer that allows for precise measurement of output is important because the therapy is based on evaluation of accurate intake and output.

When these drugs are administered preoperatively, the dosing schedule should be: glycerin, isosorbide, and mannitol, 1 to 1½ hours before surgery; and urea, 1 hour before surgery if for the reduction of intraocular pressure or at the time of scalp incision during intracranial surgery.

Glycerin and isosorbide may be mixed with iced unsweetened fruit juice and sipped through a straw to increase palatability.

With repeated doses of these drugs, maintain adequate fluid and electrolyte balance.

***Education.*** Prepare the client for the diuresis that will occur with these drugs. Provide for the convenience, comfort, and privacy of the client.

Advise client taking glycerin and isosorbide for the reduction of intraocular pressure to visit the physician regularly for intraocular pressure monitoring.

***Evaluation.*** Since these are potent osmotic drugs, alertness to rapidly changing client conditions is essential: frequent assessment of urinary output and vital signs for changing intravascular volume, pulmonary edema, or hemoconcentration. Monitor fluid and electrolyte balance, particularly serum and urine potassium and sodium levels.

## Geriatric Implications:
### DIURETICS

Elderly are more susceptible to the development of the adverse reactions of hypotension (orthostatic), impaired mentation, hypokalemia (with exception of potassium-sparing diuretics), and increased glucose serum levels. Other signs and symptoms of toxicity that should be reported to the physician include anorexia, nausea, vomiting, confusion, increased weakness, and paresthesia of the extremities.

Lower doses are advised in the elderly with dosage increases based on the client's individual, therapeutic response and/or the development of adverse reactions. The smallest effective dose should be used.

When a diuretic is to be discontinued, it is recommended that the drug be reduced gradually to avoid the development of serious fluid retention (edema).

### EXAMPLES OF FIXED-DOSE DIURETIC COMBINATIONS

| Trade Name | Contents |
| --- | --- |
| Moduretic | amiloride HCl, 5 mg; hydrochlorthiazide, 50 mg |
| Aldactazide 25/25 | spironolactone, 25 mg; hydrochlorothiazide, 25 mg |
| Aldactazide 50/50 | spironolactone, 50 mg; hydrochlorothiazide, 50 mg |
| Dyazide | triamterene, 50 mg; hydrochlorothiazide, 25 mg |
| Maxzide | triamterene, 75 mg; hydrochlorothiazide, 50 mg |
| Maxzide-25 | triamterene, 37.5 mg; hydrochlorothiazide, 25 mg |

When urea is administered, BUN determinations should be done before and frequently during intravenous administration. If the BUN exceeds 75 mg/dl or if there is no diuresis within 1 to 2 hours, slow or stop the infusion and have the client reevaluated.

If the osmotic diuretics are administered for reduction of intraocular pressure, monitor the pressure closely.

## DIURETIC COMBINATIONS

As mentioned previously, a thiazide diuretic may be combined with a potassium-sparing diuretic. Fixed-dose combinations, which are commercially available (see box above), may provide additional diuretic activity and decrease the potassium depletion characteristic of the thiazide diuretics.

## SUMMARY

Diuretics are valuable assets to the therapeutic regimen for the treatment of hypertension and other conditions in which fluid volume excess is an issue, such as congestive heart failure, cirrhosis, and nephrotic syndrome. The action of these drugs is exerted on the tubular function of the kidneys and involves the inhibition of solute reabsorption, thus involving water reabsorption because water diffuses passively across the tubular membrane when sodium transport occurs. Diuretics are therefore generally grouped by the major site of their action along the tubule: proximal tubule diuretics, diluting segment diuretics, loop diuretics, and distal tubule diuretics. Osmotic diuretics act by adding to the solutes already present in tubular fluid; since they are not reabsorbed, more water is pulled into tubular fluid and less

sodium, chloride, and water are reabsorbed by the kidneys in an effort to equalize the higher solute volume that is excreted in the urine.

Nursing management focuses on the education of the client for safe and accurate self-administration of diuretics, particularly in the early recognition of adverse reactions. Hypokalemia, except for clients taking potassium-sparing diuretics, is common, and clients should understand the importance of potassium-rich foods in their diet if a potassium supplement has not been prescribed. Evaluation of the effectiveness of the therapeutic regimen through the accurate measurement of the client's blood pressure, fluid balance, and weight is essential.

## BIBLIOGRAPHY

American Hospital Formulary Service. (1991). AHFS drug information '91. Bethesda, Md: American Society of Hospital Pharmacists, Inc.

Burtis G et al. (1988). Applied nutrition and diet therapy. Philadelphia: WB Saunders Co.

Cohen MR. (1988). Medication errors, Nursing 18(12):8.

DiPiro JT et al. (1989). Pharmacotherapy: a pathophysiological approach. New York: Elsevier.

Franciosa JA et al. (1987). Intervening effectively in early CHF, Patient Care 21(2):39.

Gever LN. (1987). Bumetanide: the latest loop diuretic, Nursing 17(4):115.

Guyton AC. (1986). Textbook of medical physiology, ed 7. Philadelphia: WB Saunders Co.

Herfindal ET et al. (1988). Clinical pharmacy and therapeutics, ed 4. Baltimore: Williams & Wilkins.

Hill MN. (1987). Diuretics for mild hypertension: still the best choice? Nursing 17(9):62.

Hutcheon DE and Martinez JC. (1986). A decade of developments in diuretic drug therapy, J Clin Pharmacol 26(8):567.

Kastrup EK and Olin BR. (1991). Facts and comparisons: drug information. Philadelphia: JB Lippincott Co.

McConnell EA et al. (1988). An almost-tragedy of errors, Nursing 18(4):76.

Melmon KL. (1986). Getting the most out of antihypertensives, Emerg Med 18(2):80.

Mende CW. (1990). Current issues in diuretic therapy, Hosp Pract 25(1)15.

Miller K. (1986). Mannitol conscious, Emergency 18(10):17.

Paige DM. (1987). Manual of clinical nutrition. ed 2. St Louis: The CV Mosby Co.

Pennington AT and Church HN, eds. (1985). Bowes & Church's food values of portions commonly used, ed 14. Philadelphia: JB Lippincott Co.

Porterfield LM. (1989). Diuretics, AD Nurse 4(2):46.

United States Pharmacopeial Convention. (1991). Drug information for the health care professional, ed 11. Rockville, Md: The Convention, Inc.

Young LY and Koda-Kimble MA. (1988). Applied therapeutics: the clinical use of drugs, ed 4. Vancouver: Applied Therapeutics, Inc.

# 34 Antimicrobials for Urinary Tract Infections

## CHAPTER OBJECTIVES

*After studying this chapter, you should be able to meet the following objectives and define the key terms.*

1. Discuss the prevalence and risk factors associated with urinary tract infections.

2. Describe the principles of preventive therapy for urinary tract infections.

3. Describe nursing interventions in antimicrobial therapy related to urinary tract infections.

4. Discuss the role of antibiotics, sulfonamides, urinary antiseptics, and urinary tract analgesics in urinary tract infections.

5. Describe the mechanism of action, indications, pharmacokinetics, dosages, and side effects/adverse reactions of common agents used in the treatment of urinary tract infections.

6. Discuss appropriate nursing management for clients receiving drug therapy for urinary tract infections.

## KEY TERMS

**bactericidal,** page 604

**bacteriostatic,** page 604

**bacteriuria,** page 602

**nosocomial infection,** page 602

**prostatitis,** page 602

**Stevens-Johnson syndrome,** page 607

**urinary tract infections,** page 602

## INTRODUCTION

**Urinary tract infections (UTIs)** include a variety of clinical conditions, such as cystitis, pyelonephritis, prostatitis, urethritis, and catheter-related bacteriuria. The incidence of UTIs increases with age and results in nearly 6 million physician office visits annually and approximately 20% of all prescribed antibiotics. Nearly 40% of UTIs are caused by **nosocomial infection,** that is, acquired in an institutional setting such as a hospital or nursing home, with such infections often resulting in or harboring resistant organisms. The incidence of **bacteriuria** (the presence of bacteria in the urine) in women between the ages of 20 and 50 years increases with advancing age more so than with men. Usually in men, UTI is associated with inflammation of the prostate gland **(prostatitis),** prostate hypertrophy leading to urinary retention, or use of urinary tract instrumentation.

Important predisposing risk factors for UTIs need to be assessed in clients (see box). UTIs occur in approximately 25% of individuals who have an indwelling urethral catheter. It has been stated that the risk of a catheterized client developing a UTI is nearly 5% per day (Stamm and Turck, 1987). In the past it was believed that chronic renal failure was the result of UTIs. It was also thought that if UTI occurred during pregnancy, it may have resulted in low birth weight and infants with congenital defects. These beliefs have been discounted by many researchers (Critchley and Robson, 1987), but one must be aware that there is an increased risk of developing acute pyelonephritis in untreated, asymptomatic UTIs (30%). Also, infants and young children with intrarenal reflux and adults with abnormal kidneys or urinary tracts are definitely at risk for developing renal failure from untreated UTIs. Because of the risks from UTIs it is recommended that all clients with symptomatic or asymptomatic UTI be treated with the appropriate antimicrobial medication.

Many oral and parenteral antimicrobial agents are commonly used to treat UTIs. Before selecting an agent, the physician should try to identify the microorganism and determine its antimicrobial sensitivity. The most common bacteria causing UTI include *Escherichia coli*, *Klebsiella* species, *Proteus* species, *Pseudomonas* species, and other gram-negative organisms. The goal is to eliminate the causative agent with an appropriate drug regimen. To do this, short-term treatment (3 to 7 days) is usually prescribed for the client with an acute UTI, whereas clients with recurrent UTIs are often treated with low-dose, long-term drug therapy. The primary agents used are penicillins, cephalosporins, sulfonamides, urinary tract antiseptics (nitrofurantoin, methenamine mandelate, nalidixic acid, and cinoxacin), aztreonam, and norfloxacin. For simplification, this chapter divides the agents into antibiotics, antiseptics, monobactams and fluoroquinolones, and analgesics. See also the box on an investigational drug (p. 608).

## NURSING MANAGEMENT: ANTIMICROBIAL THERAPY

***Assessment.*** Initial assessment of the client provides baseline information and includes history of past UTIs and the signs and symptoms of the current UTI. Drug allergies, concurrent drug therapy, and altered function of any body system may affect the drug therapy. Specific considerations are discussed for each class of antimicrobial drug later in the chapter and in Chapter 61.

***Intervention.*** Nursing interventions relative to antimicrobial drug therapy are discussed in greater detail in Chapter 61. Generally, these interventions relate to (1) assistance in the identification of the infecting organism, (2) actual administration of the drug, (3) assessment of the client's response to the drug, (4) client education, and (5) prevention and treatment of adverse responses, including pharmacologic and chemical drug-drug interactions. Obtaining urine specimens to determine the causative organism for UTI is frequently the nurse's responsibility. Through client education, most clients can obtain a clean-catch urine sample

---

### PREDISPOSING RISK FACTORS FOR UTIS

| Risk Factors | Frequency |
| --- | --- |
| Diabetes | 20% |
| Indwelling catheter (closed system) | 37%-50% |
| Condom catheter | 50% |
| Urologic disease (congenital) | 57% |
| Nephrolithiasis | 85% |
| Indwelling catheter (open system) | 98% |

Data from Goldstein EJC. (1987). Consultant Pharmacist 2(suppl A):3-7.

---

of appropriate quantity and quality for laboratory testing. The physician will specify whether a midstream clean-catch or catheterized specimen is required. In either case it is essential that the procedure be done appropriately to ensure the most accurate results. A basic nursing text should be consulted for these procedures. Specimens for culture should be taken directly to the laboratory to prevent death of the suspect organisms and to prevent the growth of contaminating ones.

If an antimicrobial agent is ordered before the infecting organism has been identified, it is important that the urine sample for initial culture be obtained before the administration of the first dose of the drug. With subsequent specimens for culture, it is important to describe the client's antimicrobial regimen for the laboratory, since the selection and interpretation of laboratory tests often depend on this information. Because around-the-clock administration of antimicrobial drugs at prescribed dosage intervals is required for maintaining therapeutic blood levels of these drugs, it is the nurse's responsibility to see that this is accomplished. This is done by providing the necessary client education, which may entail awakening sleeping clients and ensuring that tests or therapies do not interrupt the dosage.

***Education.*** Clients should be taught the principles of antimicrobial therapy so that these drugs can be self-administered safely. The necessity of adherence to an inconvenient around-the-clock schedule may require special counseling. Compliance for the full course of therapy is essential to prevent the possible development of resistant strains of microorganisms. "Leftover" antimicrobial medications should not be used for new bouts of infection; rather, medical attention should be sought. For specific instructions for each drug, refer to the text.

Instruct the client to avoid coffee, tea, juices with high citric acid content, cola, alcohol, chocolate, and spices, which often irritate a sensitive bladder. Daily fluid intake for a client with a UTI should be at least 3000 ml to help cleanse the urinary tract of organisms. The client should be

---

**CLIENT EDUCATION TO REDUCE OCCURRENCE OF UTIS**

UTIs frequently occur as a result of contamination of the lower urinary tract with perineal bacteria. Preventive measures attempt to reduce perineal bacteria and prevent bacteria from entering the lower urinary tract. Client education should focus on these two measures and include the following instructions:

1. Good perineal hygiene helps reduce bacterial growth.
2. Female clients should always wipe from the front to the back to prevent contamination of the urinary tract with fecal bacteria.
3. Emptying the bladder soon after intercourse helps wash out bacteria that may have entered the urethra.
4. Cotton undergarments (or synthetics with a cotton crotch) that "breathe" are preferred to synthetics that foster bacterial growth.
5. Drinking six to eight glasses of fluids per day and urinating often help to cleanse the urinary tract of bacteria.

---

**THE ROLE OF CRANBERRY JUICE IN UTIS**

Although cranberry juice has traditionally been recommended to help prevent and treat UTIs, its role in the treatment of UTIs remains controversial. It has been felt that cranberry juice served to acidify the urine, which created a less favorable environment for bacterial growth. However, very large quantities of juice must be consumed to adequately lower the urine pH (Kinney and Blount, 1979). Cranberry juice has also been shown to reduce bacterial adherence to mucosal surfaces (Sobota, 1984), an important prerequisite for UTI, which may explain its efficacy in treatment. Cranberry juice should not be taken during sulfonamide therapy since the sulfonamide drugs require an alkaline urine to achieve maximum effectiveness.

---

taught health practices that may reduce the chance of developing another UTI (see box above).

***Evaluation.*** Evaluation of the client for therapeutic responses to antimicrobial agents is a primary nursing responsibility. A decrease in the severity or a disappearance of the clinical and laboratory manifestations of the UTI indicates a positive response to antimicrobial therapy. Documentation should include the client's health status relating to fever, chills, flank pain, and nausea and vomiting; frequency and urgency of urination; dysuria; costovertebral tenderness; gross hematuria and pyuria; and general well-being. Urinalysis should be monitored for WBCs, RBCs, casts, protein, crystals, and bacteria. Urine culture and sensitivity examinations should indicate the drug's efficacy. CBCs should also be monitored. Serum antibiotic concentrations can be monitored through the course of therapy to assess for therapeutic and toxic levels of specific antimicrobials. In addition to monitoring the therapeutic effects of these antimicrobials, the nurse must assess the client for the development of common side effects/adverse reactions of individual drugs. (See discussions of specific drugs for these effects.)

## ANTIBIOTICS

The primary antibiotics used to treat UTIs include ampicillin, amoxicillin, and the cephalosporins (reviewed in Chapter 61) and sulfonamides. They are used to treat microorganisms such as *E. coli* that are sensitive to their antibacterial action. Ampicillin causes a maculopapular rash in approximately 10% to 15% of the clients; therefore amox-

icillin combined with potassium clavulanate (a beta lactamase inhibitor) appears to have an advantage over ampicillin. That is, the incidence of rash is less, and the presence of potassium clavulanate has reduced the development of resistant organisms. Thus the effectiveness of this product is reportedly equivalent to or better than the sulfonamides. Many cephalosporins are also effective in treating UTIs (see Chapter 61).

### sulfonamides

Sulfonamides are among the most widely used antibacterial agents in the world, particularly for UTI. All the sulfonamides used therapeutically are synthetically produced and contain the para-aminobenzene-sulfonamide group, which gives them their common characteristics. See Table 34-1 for a list of sulfonamides in current clinical practice. The sulfonamides are primarily **bacteriostatic** (that is, they inhibit bacterial growth) in concentrations that are normally useful in controlling infections in the human being rather than **bactericidal** (that is, causing cell death). They are structurally similar to para-aminobenzoic acid (PABA), and they inhibit a bacterial enzyme (dihydropteroate synthetase) that is necessary to incorporate PABA into dihydrofolic acid. By blocking the synthesis of dihydrofolic acid, a decrease in tetrahydrofolic acid results, which interferes with the synthesis of purines, thymidine, and DNA in the microorganism. Therefore, the bacteria most sensitive to sulfonamides are those that synthesize their own folic acid. The presence of pus, necrotic tissue, and serum interferes with the activities of the sulfonamides, since PABA is present in such materials. Among the microorganisms highly susceptible to sulfonamides are group A beta hemolytic streptococci, pneumococci, *Neisseria meningitidis, N. gonorrhoeae, E. coli, Pasteurella pestis, Bacillus anthracis, Shigella* species, *Haemophilus influenzae,* and *Pneumocystis carinii.*

**TABLE 34-1**   Sulfonamides: dosage and administration

| Generic/trade name | Dosage | |
| --- | --- | --- |
| | Adults | Children |
| sulfacytine (Renoquid) | 500 mg initially, then 250 mg every 6 hr for 10 days; maximum daily dose is 2 g | Not recommended children older than 14 yr—see adult dose |
| sulfamethoxazole (Gantanol) | 2-3 g daily | Infants less than 1 mo, do not use; 1 mo and older, 50-60 mg/kg (maximum is 2 g) initially, then 25-30 mg/kg every 12 hr (maximum is 75 mg/kg daily) |
| sulfamethoxazole and tri-methoprim (Bactrim, Septra, Protrin ✦) | 800 mg sulfamethoxazole, 160 mg trimeth-oprim every 12 hr | Children: up to 40 mg/kg body weight; 20 mg sulfamethoxazole and 4 mg trimethoprim/kg every 12 hr<br>Children 40 kg and over: adult dose |
| Injectable dosage form | IV infusion, 10-12.5 mg sulfamethoxazole and 2-2.5 mg trimethoprim/kg every 6 hr, or 20-25 mg of sulfamethoxazole and 4-5 mg trimethoprim/kg every 12 hr | Not for use in infants under 1 mo old; otherwise, adult dosage |
| sulfisoxazole (Gantrisin, Novosoxazole ✦) | 2-4 g orally initially, then 750 mg to 1.5 g every 4 hr or 1-2 g every 6 hr; maximum daily dose is 12 g day | Not for use in infants less than 1 mo old; infants 1 mo old and older; orally, 75 mg/kg or 2 g/m² initially, then 25 mg/kg or 667 mg/m² every 4 hr; maximum daily dose should not exceed 6 g |

Sulfonamides are indicated for the treatment of bacterial sensitive UTIs, otitis media caused by *H. influenzae,* bronchitis caused by *H. influenzae* or *Streptococcus* pneumonia, enteritis caused by *Shigella flexneria* and *S. somnei,* pneumonia caused by *P. carinii* in immunocompromised clients and other sulfonamide-sensitive bacterial infections. The absorption of sulfonamides is good with a time interval for peak urine concentration at 30 minutes and the time interval for peak serum levels between 2 to 4 hours for sulfamethoxazole and sulfisoxazole. The half-life of sulfacytine is 4 hours; sulfamethoxazole, 6 to 12 hours, and sulfisoxazole, 3 to 7 hours with half-lifes extended in end-stage renal disease. Acetylation is the major process by which the sulfonamides are metabolically inactivated. This change is probably caused by the action of the liver. Acetylation is important to the physician when choosing a drug: the acetylated forms are believed to be nontherapeutic, and they may produce toxic symptoms.

Excretion of the sulfonamides occurs chiefly by way of the kidney, where both the free and the acetylated forms of the drug are filtered through the glomerulus. Most sulfonamides are reabsorbed to some extent in the kidney. Some of the sulfonamides, and especially their acetyl derivatives, are relatively insoluble in neutral or acid media; so as the kidney concentrates the urine, which becomes more acid, there is some danger that sulfonamide will precipitate, causing crystalluria, hematuria, and even renal shutdown. The forcing of fluids to keep the urine dilute helps to keep a number of the sulfonamides from precipitating in the urine. However, sulfonamide precipitation is no longer a great clinical problem. Newer sulfonamides, such as sulfisoxazole and sulfacetamide, are quite soluble even in acid urine. The problem of solubility in the urine can also be dealt with by administration of combinations of small doses of two or three different sulfonamides. In this way the saturation point of each is not reached, and each drug remains in solution. The "insoluble" sulfonamides are poorly absorbed from the gastrointestinal tract and are excreted largely in the feces. Their action is mainly on intestinal flora; they are used to inhibit bacterial growth in the colon. For side effects/adverse reactions, see Table 34-2.

### Significant drug interactions

| Drug | Possible Effect and Management |
| --- | --- |
| para-aminobenzoic acid (PABA) | Bacteria absorb PABA, antagonizing therapeutic effects of sulfonamides. Avoid concurrent administration. |
| anticoagulants, such as coumarin or indane-dione derivatives; anticonvulsants (hydantoin); oral antidiabetic agents, or methotrexate | These agents are highly protein bound; concurrent drug administration may displace them from their protein-binding sites, resulting in increased serum levels and possible toxicity. Metabolism of these agents may also be inhibited by sulfonamides. Monitor closely for signs of toxicity, indicating need for dosage adjustments. |
| bone marrow suppressants | Increased potential for toxicity. If concurrent therapy is necessary, monitor closely. |
| hemolytics, other | Increased potential for toxicity. Monitor closely. |
| hepatotoxic medications | Increased risk of inducing liver toxicity. Closely monitor for signs of liver toxicity. |

**TABLE 34-2**    Agents for UTIs: side effects/adverse reactions

| Drug | Side effects* | Adverse reactions† |
|---|---|---|
| **SULFONAMIDES** | | |
| sulfacytine (Renoquid)<br>sulfamethoxazole (Gantanol),<br>  with trimethoprim (Bactrim,<br>  Septra, Protrin ✿)<br>sulfisoxazole (Gantrisin, Novos-<br>  oxazole ✿) | Most frequent: diarrhea, anorexia,<br>  headaches, dizziness, nausea, or<br>  vomiting | Most frequent: pruritus, rash<br>Less frequent: muscle and joint pain; in-<br>  creased temperature; sore throat; in-<br>  creased bleeding tendencies; pallor; red,<br>  blistering, or peeling skin (Stevens-<br>  Johnson syndrome); weakness, jaundice<br>Rare: bloody urine, pain on urination, low<br>  back pain, swelling or edema in neck<br>  (thyroid dysfunction) |
| **URINARY TRACT ANTISEPTICS** | | |
| cinoxacin (Cinobac, Cinobac-<br>  tin ✿) | Less frequent/rare: nausea, rash,<br>  pruritus, swelling, diarrhea, an-<br>  orexia, abdominal distress, vom-<br>  iting | Less frequent/rare: photosensitivity (eye),<br>  tinnitus, insomnia, headache, dizziness |
| methenamine mandelate (Man-<br>  delamine), methenamine<br>  hippurate (Hiprex, Urex,<br>  Hip-Rex ✿) | Less frequent: nausea, rash, ab-<br>  dominal distress | Less frequent: bloody urine, low back<br>  pain, painful urination |
| nalidixic acid (NegGram) | Most frequent: diarrhea, nausea or<br>  vomiting, rash, pruritus, head-<br>  ache<br>Less frequent: dizziness, sedation,<br>  skin photosensitivity | Most frequent: visual disturbances,<br>  (changes in color vision or double vi-<br>  sion, halos encircling lights, etc.)<br>Rare: jaundice, severe abdominal distress,<br>  light-colored stools, dark urine (chole-<br>  static jaundice); mental alterations, hal-<br>  lucinations, convulsions, (CNS toxicity<br>  usually with very high doses); sore<br>  throat, elevated temperature, increased<br>  bleeding tendencies, increased weak-<br>  ness, pale skin (blood dyscrasias) |
| nitrofurantoin (Furadantin,<br>  Macrodantin, Novofuran ✿) | Most frequent: abdominal distress,<br>  diarrhea, anorexia, nausea, or<br>  vomiting<br>Less frequent: rash, itching | Most frequent: chest pain, chills, increased<br>  temperature, respiratory difficulties,<br>  cough (pneumonitis)<br>Less frequent: dizziness, sedation, head-<br>  ache, pale skin, increased weakness,<br>  paresthesias<br>Rare: jaundice |
| **MONOBACTAMS AND FLUOROQUINOLONES** | | |
| aztreonam (Azactam) | Less frequent/rare: stomach dis-<br>  tress, dizziness, nausea or vomit-<br>  ing, diarrhea, double vision, vag-<br>  inal itching, tinnitus | Less frequent: rash, pruritus<br>Rare: convulsions, confusion, jaundice of<br>  skin or eyes |
| norfloxacin (Noroxin) | Most frequent: drowsiness, an-<br>  orexia, nausea, or vomiting<br>Less frequent/rare: abdominal dis-<br>  tress; bloody urine; low back<br>  pain; painful urination (crystallu-<br>  ria); diarrhea; constipation; dry<br>  mouth; skin rash; swollen, pain-<br>  ful joints; insomnia | Most frequent: dizziness, headache (CNS<br>  toxicity)<br>Less frequent: depression<br>Rare: visual disturbances, eye photosensi-<br>  tivity |
| **URINARY TRACT ANALGESIC** | | |
| phenazopyridine (Phenazo ✿,<br>  Pyridium) | Client complains of dizziness,<br>  headache, abdominal pain,<br>  cramps, or gas | Skin discoloration (blue to purple tint on<br>  skin caused by methemoglobinemia),<br>  rash, increased weakness (hemolytic<br>  anemia), jaundice |

*If side effects continue, increase, or disturb the client, inform the physician.
†If adverse reactions occur, contact physician, since medical intervention may be necessary.

| Drug | Possible Effect and Management |
|------|-------------------------------|
| methenamine | Methenamine requires an acid urine to be active and effective. It may precipitate if given with a sulfonamide and result in crystalluria. Do not administer concurrently. |

***Dosage and administration.*** See Table 34-1.

## ▷ Nursing Management: Sulfonamide Therapy

***Assessment.*** In addition to instituting the nursing management common to all types of antimicrobial therapy for UTIs, the nurse should observe these considerations for individuals receiving sulfonamides.

***Assessment.*** Although cross-sensitization is not as severe as among penicillins, it is safer to avoid all sulfonamides in clients who develop hypersensitivity to any one agent. Cross-sensitivity also exists with some diuretics, such as actazolamide and the thiazides, and with sulfonylurea antidiabetic agents, so the nurse should obtain an accurate history of the client's sensitivities. Avoid sulfonamides in clients with hepatic and renal dysfunction, blood dyscrasias, allergies, and porphyria. Administration of sulfonamides is contraindicated during the last trimester of pregnancy, in nursing mothers, and in infants. Clients receiving sulfonamides should be assessed for the development of the following nursing diagnoses: altered comfort related to dizziness, headache, and gastrointestinal distress (anorexia, nausea, vomiting, and diarrhea); high risk for injury related to hypersensitivity (rash, fever), photosensitivity, blood dyscrasias (unusual bruising or bleeding, sore throat, fever), hepatitis, Lyell's syndrome (difficulty in swallowing, blistering of skin), **Stevens-Johnson syndrome** (aching joints and muscles, weakness, skin changes), hematuria, or crystalluria.

***Intervention.*** Administer sulfonamides on an empty stomach with a full glass of water to enhance absorption. However, if the common adverse reaction of nausea and vomiting occurs, administer with food to decrease gastrointestinal distress. Do not administer sulfonamides with antacids because the latter inhibit their action by decreasing absorption.

***Education.*** Inform the client of the importance of completing a full course of drug therapy, even though he or she may feel better after several days of therapy. Instruct the client to observe for and report any dermatologic reactions after initiation of the sulfonamide. Fever may occur after 7 to 10 days of therapy, indicating a serum-sickness-like reaction. It may be accompanied by joint pain, urticaria, and leukopenia. All these responses are indications for discontinuation of the drug and physician referral. Advise the client to avoid exposure to the sun and sunlamps because skin photosensitivity may be present. Alert clients with diabetes that sulfonamides may cause false urine sugar and urine ketone test results.

***Evaluation.*** Because renal toxicity may present a potentially serious problem, monitor the hospitalized client's urinary output and ensure that it amounts to at least 1500 ml in 24 hours. Maintenance of urinary output at this level decreases the tendency for crystals to form. Individuals who are not hospitalized should be instructed to drink at least 3 quarts of fluids per day. Liquids and vitamins that produce acid urine should be avoided. The urine should be visually examined for the presence of crystals, and in long-term sulfonamide therapy periodic urinalysis should be done to determine if crystals are present. Monitor urinalysis to determine status of UTI and early detection of crystalluria. Carefully observe the client for toxic effects, such as rash, sore throat, or purpura. Instruct nonhospitalized individuals to report these symptoms to their physicians and to discontinue taking the drug. In prolonged sulfonamide therapy, refer to the periodic blood counts usually performed to assess the occurrence of hematologic side effects (anemia, granulocytopenia, and thrombocytopenia).

## URINARY TRACT ANTISEPTICS

Cinoxacin, nitrofurantoin, nalidixic acid, and methenamine mandelate are the primary urinary tract antiseptics. Urinary tract antiseptics, although given simultaneously, are drugs that exert antibacterial activity in the urine but have little or no systemic antibacterial effects. Their usefulness is limited to the treatment of UTIs. Table 34-2 lists the urinary tract antiseptics that are currently used in medical practice.

### cinoxacin (Cinobac)

Cinoxacin inhibits replication of bacterial DNA and has bactericidal urinary effects.

It is absorbed well orally; its serum levels are usually low while its urinary levels are high. This product does cross the placenta. The time to peak serum levels is between 2 to 3 hours. Cinoxacin is metabolized in the liver and excreted by the kidneys. For side effects/adverse reactions, see Table 34-2. There are no reported significant drug interactions with this drug. For children 12 years and older and adults the dose is 250 mg orally every 6 hours or 500 mg every 12 hours for 1 to 2 weeks. This dose should be reduced for clients with impaired renal function. It is not recommended for use in children less than 12 years old.

### methanamine mandelate (Mandelamine) methenamine hippurate (Hiprex, Urex, Hip-Rex ✳)

Methenamine, which is used to treat UTIs, combines the action of methenamine and mandelic acid or hippurate acid salts. Its effectiveness depends on the release of formaldehyde, which requires an acid medium. Acids released from the mandelate or hippurate salts contribute to this acidity. Formaldehyde may be bactericidal or bacteriostatic, and its effects are believed to be the result of denaturation of bacteria protein. It is ineffective if the urine is alkaline. Because of its fairly wide bacterial spectrum, low toxicity, and a low incidence of resistance, methenamine has often been the drug of choice in long-term suppression of infections. Methenamine is indicated for the treatment or prevention of bacterial UTIs. Orally its absorption is good since it takes ½ to 1.5 hours peak urinary formaldehyde levels at a urinary pH of 5.6. For methenamine hippurate, peak urinary levels are reached in 2 hours; enteric-coated methenamine mandelate reaches its urinary peak in 3 to 8 hours. Excretion is via the kidneys. For side effects/adverse reactions and dosage instructions see Table 34-2.

### Significant drug interactions

| Drug | Possible Effect and Management |
|---|---|
| urinary alkalizers, such as antacids (calcium and/ or magnesium), carbonic anhydrase inhibitors, citrates, sodium bicarbonate, or thiazide diuretics | May result in an alkaline urine, thus inhibiting methenamine's conversion to formaldehyde and rendering it ineffective. Avoid concurrent drug administration. |
| sulfonamides | In acid urine, the formaldehyde produced may precipitate with certain sulfonamides, which increases the potential for crystalluria. Avoid concurrent drug administration. |

**Dosage and administration.** The adult dose for methenamine mandelate is 1 g four times daily, after meals and at bedtime. The maximum daily dose is 12 g per day. For children less than 6 years, 18.3 mg/kg every 6 hours; 6 to 12 years, 500 mg every 6 hours; and 12 years and older, see adult dosing schedule. For methenamine hippurate tablets the dose is 1 g every 12 hours up to a maximum of 4 g daily. Children 6 to 12 years old, the dose is 0.5 to 1 g every 12 hours; for children 12 years and older, see adult dosing schedule.

### nalidixic acid (NegGram)

Nalidixic acid is believed to inhibit bacterial DNA synthesis by interfering with polymerization of DNA. Resistance usually develops rapidly during treatment with this drug. It is indicated for the treatment of UTIs caused by the *Proteus, Klebsiella,* and *Enterobacter,* and *E. coli* species. Nalidixic acid is well absorbed orally, reaches peak serum levels in 1 to 2 hours and peak urine levels in 3 to 4 hours. Its serum half-life with normal renal function is 1.1 to 2.5 hours, with renal impairment it is extended up to 21 hours. Nalidixic acid is metabolized in the liver with approximately 30% converted to the active metabolite, hydroxynalidixic acid, while excretion is via the kidneys. For side effects/adverse reactions, see Table 34-2.

Nalidixic acid when given with oral anticoagulants (e.g., coumarin, dicumarol) may displace the anticoagulants from their protein binding sites, resulting in enhanced anticoagulant action. Dosage adjustments may be necessary, so monitor the client's potential for physiological injury related to

### *Investigational Drug Update:* ENOXACIN

Enoxacin (Comprecin) is an investigational drug that combines nalidixic acid and norfloxacin, biochemically. It inhibits bacterial RNA and DNA and is effective against gram-negative bacteria including in-vitro *Pseudomonas aeruginosa.* Both oral and intravenous dosage forms are under investigation.

an increase in bleeding tendency if concurrent therapy is necessary. Adult dose is 1 g orally every 6 hours for 7 to 14 days. The maintenance dose is 500 mg every 6 hours with a daily maximum dose of 4 g. Its use is not recommended for infants and children.

### nitrofurantoin (Furadantin, Macrodantin, Novofuran ✲)

Nitrofurantoin's mechanism of action is unknown, but it is believed to interfere with bacterial enzymes. Depending on urine concentration, nitrofurantoin may be bacteriostatic or bactericidal. It is indicated for the treatment of urinary tract infections with organisms such as *E. coli, S. aureus, Klebsiella* species, *Enterobacter* species, and *Proteus* species. Following oral administration, it is completely absorbed and has a half-life of 20 to 60 minutes. It is metabolized in body tissues (50% to 70%) and excreted by the kidneys (30% to 40%). For side effects/adverse reactions, see Table 34-2.

### Significant drug interactions

| Drug | Possible Effect and Management |
|---|---|
| other hemolytic agents | Increased possiblity of toxic side effects. Monitor blood counts for anemia closely if concurrent therapy is necessary. |
| neurotoxic medications | Increased risk of inducing neurotoxicity. Monitor closely for dizziness, drowsiness, or headache if concurrent therapy is necessary. |
| probenecid or sulfinpyrazone | Tubular secretion of nitrofurantoin will be inhibited, leading to increased serum levels and possibly toxicity. A decrease in urinary concentrations and effectiveness may also result. Dosage adjustment of probenecid may be required. |

**Dosage and administration.** The recommended adult dose for nitrofurantoin is 50 to 100 mg every 6 hours with a maximum dose of 600 mg daily. For infants 1 month and older, the recommended dose is 1.25 to 1.75 mg/kg every 6 hours. It is not recommended for infants less than 1 month old.

Selected nursing diagnoses related to administration of urinary tract antiinfectives

| Nursing diagnosis | Outcome criteria | Nursing interventions |
|---|---|---|
| Infection, high risk for | Prevention of infection or resolution of symptoms of infection:<br>Temperature remains within the normal range.<br>WBC remains within the normal range.<br>Urine cultures demonstrate no pathogens.<br>Urine is clear and odorless.<br><br>Fluid intake of 3000 ml/24 hr. | Monitor and record temperature at least every 4 hours. Report elevations.<br>Monitor WBCs. Report significant changes.<br>Culture urine as ordered and monitor results.<br>Use strict aseptic technique when inserting urinary catheters.<br>Encourage a fluid intake of at least 3000 ml daily. |
| Knowledge deficit related to medication regimen | Client will describe underlying conditions and how the drug relates to the condition, how and when to take the medication, common drug interactions, safety precautions, common side effects/adverse reactions, and which of these warrant reporting.<br><br><br>Self-administer medication safely and accurately. | Assess learning needs and learning readiness.<br>Plan with client for the achievement of realistic goals.<br>Provide information to meet outcome criteria.<br>Administer medication with food or milk to decrease GI distress.<br>Alert client that medication may cause a discoloration of the urine.<br>Instruct client to take medication as ordered and to consult with the physician if no improvement is seen within a few days. |

## ▷NURSING MANAGEMENT: URINARY ANTISEPTIC THERAPY

The following nursing measures include both general ones for all urinary antiseptics and specific ones for particular antiseptics. Refer to "Nursing Management: Antimicrobial Therapy" (p. 603) for general nursing care for these clients.

***Assessment.*** The nurse should ascertain whether the client has preexisting hepatic or renal function impairment because urinary antiseptics are used cautiously in such instances.

Photophobia may occur during cinoxacin use. The client should be advised to avoid bright sunlight and to wear sunglasses. A possibility of photosensitivity exists with nalidixic acid during therapy and for up to 3 months after it is discontinued. The client should be cautioned to avoid exposure to sunlight and sunlamps.

Clients with diabetes should use Clinistix, Diastix, or TesTape to test for glucosuria because nitrofurantoin and nalidixic acid may produce a false-positive result with Clinitest. The client taking nitrofurantoin should be told that urine may have a brown color. Nitrofurantoin is discolored by alkalies and strong light. The client should also avoid metal pill boxes unless they are stainless steel or aluminum because the drug decomposes on contact with other metals. The client should be assessed for an intolerance to either nalidixic acid or cinoxacin since cross-sensitivity may occur.

***Intervention.*** Acidification of the urine inhibits the growth of many urinary tract microorganisms and thereby enhances the effects of several urinary antiseptics. Thus, when encouraging clients with UTIs to consume large volumes of fluids, the selection of fluids should be those that increase urine acidity, such as cranberry juice (see box, p. 604) or prune juice. Vitamin C will also acidify the urine and can enhance antiinfective therapy. Methenamine is most effective when the urine pH is 5.5 or less. Urine pH is easily monitored at the bedside by commercially available test strips.

Urinary antiseptics may be administered on an empty stomach or, if gastric distress is a concern, with food or just after meals. If oral solutions are used, the nurse should ensure that they are shaken well and administered with the calibrated device provided by the manufacturer.

***Education.*** The client should be instructed to complete a full course of therapy even if marked improvement occurs within a few days. If no such improvement occurs, the physician should be notified. Compliance can be increased by suggesting cranberry sauce if the client considers cranberry juice unpalatable. Most fruits, particularly citrus fruits and juices, milk and other dairy products, and other alkalinizing foods should be avoided. Alka-seltzer and sodium bicarbonate, which alkalinize the urine, should be avoided.

The client should be told that dizziness and drowsiness may occur with these drugs and that these symptoms should be reported to the physician. Driving and other activities requiring alertness should be avoided until there is resolution of symptoms. With nalidixic acid, caution the client to report any visual disturbances to the health care provider.

*Evaluation.* The client's progress should be monitored periodically by urinalysis and objective and subjective signs and symptoms.

## MONOBACTAMS AND FLUOROQUINOLONES

New classes of antibiotics, the monobactams (aztreonam) and fluoroquinolones (norfloxacin), are potent drugs that were released in 1987 for the treatment of UTIs. Aztreonam is effective against many gram-negative bacteria and appears to be a safer agent than aminoglycoside therapy in the seriously ill. At present, it is only available in an injectable form. Norfloxacin is an oral antibiotic that has a broad spectrum of action against both gram-positive and gram-negative bacteria, including *Pseudomonas aeruginosa* and many drug-resistant bacteria species.

### aztreonam (Azactam)

Aztreonam inhibits bacterial cell wall synthesis, which usually results in lysis of the bacterial cell and death. Stable in the presence of bacterial beta lactamases, it is effective in treating infections caused by drug-resistant or virulent pathogens. Its activity is mainly against aerobic-type gram-negative bacteria. It is indicated as a secondary agent in the treatment of moderately severe systemic infections and UTIs.

When aztreonam is administered intramuscularly, it reaches peak serum levels between 0.6 to 1.3 hours; intravenously, peak bile concentration is reached in approximately 2.4 hours. Intramuscular peak serum levels of 20 to 25 μg/ml and 40 to 45 μg/ml are reached after an intramuscular dose of 500 mg and 1 g, respectively. Intravenous peak serum levels of 40 to 60 μg/ml, 100 to 125 μg/ml, and 240 μg/ml are reached 5 minutes after intravenous injection of 500 mg, 1 g, and 2 g, respectively. Following a 30-minute intravenous infusion, peak serum levels of 55 to 65 μg/ml, 90 to 165 μg/ml, and 205 to 255 μg/ml after half administration of an intravenous infusion of 500 mg, 1 g, and 2 g, respectively. Peak bile concentration is approximately 43 μg/ml after a 1-g intravenous dose. Urine concentration is approximately 500 mg/ml and 1200 μg/ml about 2 hours after an intramuscular dose of 500 mg and 1 g, respectively. Urine concentration is approximately 1100 μg/ml, 3500 μg/ml, and 6600 μg/ml about 2 hours after a 30-minute intravenous infusion of 500 mg, 1 g, and 2 g, respectively. Only 6% to 16% of astreonam is metabolized since most is excreted unchanged by the kidneys. For side effects/adverse reactions, see Table 34-2. Aztreonam has no significant drug interactions reported to date.

The recommended adult dose for systemic, moderately severe infections is 1 to 2 g every 8 to 12 hours. For life-threatening, severe systemic infections, administer 2 g every 6 to 8 hours. For UTIs, the dose is 0.5 to 1 g IM or IV, every 8 to 12 hours. The maximum dose daily is 8 g. A dosage has not been established for children.

### ▷ Nursing Management: Aztreonam Therapy

The following nursing considerations are in addition to the general nursing management for urinary tract antimicrobial therapy. Use with caution in clients with cirrhosis or renal function impairment. When administering aztreonam intravenously, the nurse should give the bolus over 3 to 5 minutes, or, as an intermittent infusion, in 50-100 ml of fluid over 20 to 60 minutes. The nurse should observe the intravenous site for the development of phlebitis.

When giving aztreonam intramuscularly, use large muscle masses rather than the deltoid muscle. Observe the intramuscular sites for pain and swelling. Aztreonam is incompatible with a number of other substances; consult drug insert before mixing with other drugs.

### norfloxacin (Noroxin)

Norfloxacin's mechanism of action is unknown. It is believed to inhibit DNA coiling reaction; it inhibits relaxation of supercoiled DNA; and it promotes the breakage of DNA double strands in bacteria. At low concentrations it is bacteriostatic; at high concentrations it is bactericidal. It is used to treat urinary tract infections. Norfloxacin is incompletely absorbed orally (30% to 40%) and reaches a peak serum level in 1 to 2 hours. The peak serum concentration is approximately 1.4 to 1.6 μg/ml 1 to 2 hours after a single 400-mg dose; approximately 2.5 μg/ml 1 to 2 hours after a single 800-mg dose.

In individuals with normal renal function, urine concentration is 98 to 200 μg/ml or more, 2 to 3 hours after a single 400-mg dose. The urine levels will remain above 30 μg/ml for at least 12 hours. In individuals with impaired renal function, described as a glomerular filtration rate of less than 10 ml/min, norfloxacin urine concentration will be approximately 20 to 25 μg/ml after a 400-mg dose. Its half-life in normal renal function is 3 to 4 hours. For those with impaired renal function or a creatinine clearance equal to or less than 30 ml/min, it is between 6.5 and 8.3 hours. This drug is metabolized in the liver and excreted by the kidneys (40% to 50%) and bile/feces (about 30%).

For side effects/adverse reactions, see Table 34-2. A significant drug interaction, a reduction in absorption of norfloxacin, may occur when norfloxacin is given with antacids. Administer antacids at least 2 hours after or 1 hour before norfloxacin.

The norfloxacin adult dose in uncomplicated UTIs is 400 mg orally every 12 hours for 72 hours. In complicated UTIs, the dose is 400 mg every 12 hours for 10 to 21 days. For clients with impaired renal function, reduce the dose to 400 mg daily for 7 to 10 days (uncomplicated cases) or 21 days (complicated cases). It is not recommended for administration for children.

## ▷ Nursing Management: Norfloxacin Therapy

The following nursing considerations are in addition to the general nursing measures for urinary tract antimicrobial therapy. Determine whether the client has a sensitivity to nalidixic acid or cinoxacin because of the possibility of cross-sensitivity with this drug. Dizziness may occur with norfloxacin. The client should be told to modify activities that require alertness and coordination, such as driving. Dry mouth may cause oral mucosa discomfort and lead to oral candidiasis; recommend dental care as necessary. Instruct the client to avoid taking antacids at the same time as norfloxacin or within 2 hours of norfloxacin.

## URINARY TRACT ANALGESIC
### phenazopyridine (Azo-Standard, Pyridium, Pyronium ✲)

Phenazopyridine's mechanism of action is unknown, but it appears to provide a topical analgesic or local anesthetic effect on the mucosa of the urinary tract. Phenazopyridine is used for urinary tract irritation, such as pain on urination, urinary frequency, and burning on urination. It is only indicated for short-term use because the underlying reason for the irritation should be determined and treated appropriately. Phenazopyridine is metabolized by the liver and other body tissues and is excreted by the kidneys. Nearly 90% of an oral dose is excreted renally in 24 hours. For side effects/adverse reactions see Table 34-2. No significant drug interactions have been reported with this drug. The usual adult dose is 200 mg orally, three times a day after meals. Children are given 4 mg/kg orally, three times daily with food.

## ▷ Nursing Management: Phenazopyridine Therapy

***Assessment.*** Phenazopyridine is contraindicated in clients with impaired renal and hepatic function.

***Intervention.*** Phenazopyridine is usually prescribed in conjunction with an antimicrobial or urinary antiseptic to treat the underlying cause of the irritation. Administer with food to decrease gastrointestinal distress.

***Education.*** The client should be told that the urine will become reddish orange and may stain clothing. The client should be instructed to observe for yellow color of the skin and sclera. This may indicate an accumulation of the drug owing to renal impairment. Discontinue drug and notify the physician. Clients with diabetes should use Clinistix, Diastix, or TesTape to test for glucosuria because Clinitest may give a false-positive result with this drug.

***Evaluation.*** Phenazopyridine may be discontinued after 2 days if the client no longer has discomfort.

---

| PREGNANCY SAFETY |
| --- |
| FDA category B: aztreonam, phenazopyridine |
| FDA category C: cinoxacin, methenamine, sulfisoxazole and trimethoprim, norfloxacin (norfloxacin should not be used in children or pregnant women) |
| FDA category unclassified: nalidixic acid, nitrofurantoin (nitrofurantoin is contraindicated in pregnant women during labor and delivery) |

## SUMMARY

Urinary tract infections are a common reason for seeking medical care in the community as well as a major result of nosocomial infections in institutions; and their incidence increases with age. Because of the risk of developing acute pyelonephritis, even in asymptomatic individuals, UTIs require treatment with appropriate antimicrobial medication.

Before therapy begins, a urine specimen should be obtained so that the organism and its antimicrobial sensitivity can be determined the most appropriate agent selected. Clients with acute UTIs usually manage with short-term treatment (3 to 7 days), but clients with recurrent UTIs are often treated with low-dose long-term therapy. Client education for adherence to long-term therapy is important.

Antimicrobial therapy for UTIs includes antibiotics (sulfonamides), urinary tract antiseptics, monobactams and fluoroquinolones, and urinary tract analgesics. With all of these medications, client education needs to stress good perineal hygiene and adequate fluid intake as adjuncts to therapy and also to prevent future urinary tract infections.

## BIBLIOGRAPHY

American Hospital Formulary Service. (1991). AHFS drug information '91, Bethesda, Md: American Society of Hospital Pharmacists, Inc.

Burgener S. (1987). Justification of closed intermittent urinary catheter irrigation/instillation: a review of current research and practice, J Adv Nurs 12(2):229.

Conti MT et al. (1987). Preventing UTIs: what works? Amer J Nurs 87(3):307.

Critchley JA and Robson JS. (1987). Renal diseases in TM Speight's Avery's drug treatment, ed 3. Baltimore: Adis Press.

Eggleston M et al. (1987). Review of the 4-quinolones, Inf Control 8(3):119.

Glenister H. (1987). The journal of infection control nursing: the passage of infection, Nursing Times 83(22):68.

Goldstein EJC. (1987). Urinary tract infections in the elderly patient: an overview, Consultant Pharmacist 2(suppl A):3.

Hawley JM. (1987). Evaluation of a diagnostic category: potential for infection in renal failure, ANAA J 14(5):331.

Hooton T et al. (1987). Up-to-date advice on managing urethritis, Patient Care 21(3):93.

Latham RH. (1986). Acute lower urinary tract infection in women, Hosp Med 22(8):77.

Lowthian P. (1988). Steps to combat infection, Nursing Times 84(12):64.

Millette-Petit JM. (1988). Urinary tract infection in older adults, Nurse Pract 13(12):21.

Pritchard V. (1988). Geriatric infections: the urinary tract, RN 51(5):36.

Roe BH et al. (1988). Comparison of four urine drainage systems, J Adv Nurs 13(3):374.

Ruge CA. (1987). Catheter-related urinary tract infections: what's the way to prevent them? Nursing 17(12):50.

Sawyer DL. (1989). Potential for infection: a nursing diagnosis for the patient with an indwelling catheter, Focus Crit Care 16(1):46.

Simpson RA. (1986). Systemic and local antimicrobial agents in the prevention of catheter-associated bacteriuria and its consequences, Infect Control (Suppl) 7(2):100.

Stamm WE and Turck M. (1987). Urinary tract infection, pyelonephritis and related conditions. In Braunwald E et al, editors. Harrison's principles of internal medicine, ed 11, New York: McGraw-Hill Book Co.

Stein G. (1987). New antimicrobial therapy for treatment of urinary tract infections in the elderly, Consultant Pharmacist 2(suppl 2):12.

Tideksaar R. (1987). Infections in the elderly: diagnosis and treatment, part I, Physician Assist 11(2):17.

United States Pharmacopeial Convention. (1991). Drug information for the health care professional. Rockville, Md: The Convention.

Wilson D. (1989). Urinary tract infections in pediatric patients, Nurse Pract 14(7):38.

*Chapter*

# ℘35 Drug Therapy for Renal System Dysfunction

## CHAPTER OBJECTIVES

*After studying this chapter, you should be able to meet the following objectives and define the key terms.*

1. Differentiate between acute renal failure and chronic renal failure.

2. Describe two laboratory tests used to evaluate renal impairment.

3. Explain why dietary protein, fluid intake, potassium, magnesium, and phosphorus are restricted in chronic renal failure.

4. Describe the differences between and advantages of the drug dosage reduction method and the interval extension method of treatment.

5. Apply nursing management of drug therapy for the client with renal system dysfunction.

## KEY TERMS

**acute renal failure,** page 613

**azotemia,** page 614

**chronic renal failure,** page 613

**end-stage renal disease,** page 615

**hemodialysis,** page 613

**peritoneal dialysis,** page 613

## INTRODUCTION

Many potentially toxic drugs are excreted by the kidneys unchanged or as active metabolites of the parent drug. If individuals with impaired renal function receive standard drug dosages on standard schedules, the drugs may accumulate in the system because of reduced excretion, resulting in elevated serum levels, extended drug half-life, and toxicity. Therefore it is important for the health care provider to evaluate and monitor clients with impaired renal function because drug dosages or time intervals frequently need to be adjusted.

## ACUTE VERSUS CHRONIC RENAL FAILURE

**Acute renal failure,** or a rapid decline in renal function, occurs in approximately 5% of all hospitalized individuals. Primary causes include trauma, pregnancy, renal ischemia as a result of surgery, severe hemorrhage, severe volume depletion, and shock. In some instances, nephrotoxic agents such as heavy metals and aminoglycosides may also induce acute renal failure. If recognized early and treated promptly, acute renal failure may be reversed before acute tubular necrosis or permanent damage occurs.

On the other hand, **chronic renal failure** (CRF) is usually the result of an irreversible kidney injury that results in permanent nephron or renal mass loss. The most common causes of CRF are glomerulonephritis, diabetes mellitus, hypertension, polycystic kidney disease, and other diseases that may lead to destruction or impaired functioning of the kidneys. Individuals with CRF may be treated conservatively initially, but eventually **hemodialysis, peritoneal dialysis,** or organ transplantation may be necessary. Since the focus of this book is pharmacology, this chapter concentrates on the therapeutic regimen and recommendations for drug dosage adjustments in clients with impaired renal function.

## SIGNS AND SYMPTOMS OF RENAL FAILURE OR INSUFFICIENCY

One of the more common signs of acute renal failure is a marked alteration in the expected urine output, usually a significant reduction (<400 ml/day). Signs of acute renal failure, in the presence of reduced urine production, are usually the result of fluid overload: edema, weight gain, weakness, hypertension, and tachycardia.

The most common complaints with CRF are increasing weakness, fatigue, and lethargy. Gastrointestinal signs include anorexia, gastrointestinal distress, nausea, vomiting, thirst, and weight loss. Paresthesias, peripheral neuropathy, convulsions, and neuromuscular irritability may also occur. On examination, the client may appear pale and dehydrated and have an increased respiratory rate and uremic breath. Hypertension with retinopathy, cardiac hypertrophy, pulmonary edema, or pericarditis may often be present.

A detailed client history, thorough physical examination, urinalysis, and blood chemistry levels are important for assessment, diagnosis, and determination of an appropriate treatment plan. The degree of renal impairment is usually estimated by reviewing the serum creatinine and blood urea nitrogen (BUN) levels. Elevated levels indicate a decrease in renal clearance, which, of course, predisposes the individual to drug toxicity.

## MEASUREMENT OF RENAL FUNCTION

Many formulas and nomograms are available to determine the client's approximate creatinine clearance and the appropriate dosage adjustment necessary to minimize the possibility of toxicity. Although BUN levels (normal 5 to 25 mg/dl) and creatinine serum levels (normal 0.5 to 1.2 mg/dl) are usually ordered, the BUN is directly related to protein metabolism and thus is a nonspecific test for renal function. The creatinine level, which is related to muscle mass, is independent of protein consumption and is a more accurate measure of renal function than is the BUN. A review of the formulas and nomograms is not within the purview of this chapter; therefore the interested reader is referred to the bibliography for further study.

## SPECIAL NEEDS OF THE CRF CLIENT

The individual in CRF has special dietary, electrolyte, and fluid requirements. In general, dietary protein is usually restricted to 0.5 to 1 g/kg of lean body weight daily. This limitation will reduce the incidence of **azotemia** (buildup of urea in the blood), hyperkalemia, and acidosis. Fluid intake is based on daily losses and metabolic needs. Dietary sodium is restricted to approximately 4 g/day. Potassium,

magnesium, and phosphorus are also restricted. Often, an aluminum hydroxide gel is prescribed to decrease phosphate absorption from the gastrointestinal tract. The reduced excretion of phosphates, magnesium, and potassium from the kidneys in chronic renal failure can lead to elevated serum levels or hypermagnesemia, hyperkalemia, and hyperphosphatemia, which in turn lead to hypocalcemia and osteodystrophy. Thus dietary restrictions are absolutely necessary. Calcium supplements and vitamin D are often prescribed for these clients to reduce or prevent hyperparathyroidism and bone disease. Magnesium levels are kept somewhat in check by client avoidance of magnesium-containing antacids and laxatives.

Production of red blood cells (erythropoiesis), which is usually decreased in CRF, leads to anemia, weakness, and fatigue. Iron therapy may be prescribed for those clients with iron deficiency anemia resulting from chronic blood loss; folic acid, vitamin C, and soluble B-complex vitamins are often given to replace substances usually lost during dialysis. Therefore it is not unusual to care for CRF clients with many dietary and fluid restrictions, as well as prescriptions for vitamins, calcium, specific antacids, and additional drugs as necessary. A drug specifically used to stimulate erythropoiesis in CRF is epoetin alfa.

### Epoetin alfa, recombinant (Epogen)

Epoetin alfa is a glycoprotein that is chemically identical to human erythropoietin. It is indicated for the treatment of anemia associated with renal failure but should not be considered a substitute for blood or blood transfusions. An unapproved indication is the use of epoetin for severe anemia in AIDS clients or in persons receiving zidovudine therapy for AIDS.

Epoetin alfa has the same biologic action as the endogenous hormone; that is, it stimulates erythropoiesis in the bone marrow and also induces the release of reticulocytes from bone marrow. Since endogenous erythropoietin is manufactured mainly in the kidneys, anemia resulting from chronic renal failure is caused by an inadequate production of the hormone. With the use of epoetin, the initial increase in reticulocytes is seen within 7 to 10 days while an increase in red cell count, hematocrit, and hemoglobin occurs within 2 to 6 weeks. This product reaches peak serum level within 15 minutes after intravenous administration and within 5 to 24 hours following a subcutaneous dose. Half-life is between 4 to 13 hours after intravenous or subcutaneous administration. When therapy is discontinued, the hematocrit decreases in approximately 2 weeks (duration of action).

The most common adverse effects include clotting of the arteriovenous (AV) shunt and/or dialyzer, hypertension, and polycythemia. No significant drug interactions have been reported.

The initial adult dose (IV, SC) is 50 to 100 units/kg three times a week. If hematocrit has not increased after 2 months of therapy by at least 5 to 6 points and the client is still below the desired range of 30% to 33%, then dosage increments of 25 units/kg may be instituted. For maintenance, decrease the dose gradually by 25 units/kg monthly to the lowest dose that maintains hematocrit at the desired level. Dosage has not been determined for children below 12 years of age. Pregnancy safety has been established at FDA category C.

▷**Nursing Management:**
  **Epoietin Alfa Therapy**

*Assessment.* The client with hypertension is at risk with the administration of epoetin alfa because its resultant increase in hematocrit increases blood viscosity and peripheral vascular resistance, leading to a rise in blood pressure. Clients with poorly controlled hypertension should have epoetin alfa therapy delayed until it is controlled. Even then, the client's (and the previously normotensive client's) blood pressure should be monitored closely because of the increased risk of hypertension, which may lead to hypertensive encephalopathy. The drug should not be used if the client is hypersensitive to human albumin or to mammalian cell-derived products, such as beef and pork insulin. CBCs, as ordered by the physician, should be monitored for change. Hematocrit values are particularly important with baseline and twice weekly frequencies being recommended as a guide for dosage and efficacy. A rise in the hematocrit of more than four points in a 2-week period or a value over 36%, which is considered the safety limit for the prevention of adverse effects, should be brought to the physician's attention.

It is recommended that the client's iron status be monitored to determine the need and the amount of iron supplementation for the client. Since iron is incorporated into hemoglobin as a result of the drug's effectiveness, the client's iron stores may be depleted causing a decrease in the epoetin alfa's efficacy.

Neurologic assessments for premonitory signs for the risk of seizures should be done periodically, particularly during the first 90 days of therapy and at times when the hematocrit rises rapidly. Renal function studies should be monitored since the need to begin or increase dialysis may occur with the administration of epoetin alfa. Daily weights should be taken and the client's fluid balance monitored by intake and output measurements.

Clients receiving epoetin alfa may be at risk for the following nursing diagnoses: altered comfort related to arthalgias, headache, chest pain, nausea, and flu-like syndrome; fatigue; fluid volume excess (swelling of face, fingers, feet, and ankles; weight gain); impaired skin integrity (skin reaction at administration site); altered protection related to polycythemia (increased clotting tendency), and potential for injury related to seizures.

*Intervention.* Each vial of epoetin alfa should be used to administer one dose only because the injection contains no preservative. Discard any unused portion of the drug.

Do not shake the vial; shaking may denature the substance and render it biologically inactive. Do not mix with other medications.

*Education.* Alert the client to avoid activities that may be hazardous if seizures would occur, especially during the first 90 days of therapy.

The client should be instructed in dietary sources of iron, folic acid, and B$_{12}$ as an adjunct to iron and other vitamin supplementation. Dietary restrictions as part of the anti-hypertensive regimen and those pertinent to clients with chronic renal failure should be reviewed with the client. The correction of the anemia may result in an increased appetite, making it more difficult for the client to maintain compliance with the dietary restrictions required. Keeping physician and dialysis appointments should be encouraged.

*Evaluation.* A clinically significant increase in the red cell count, hematocrit, and hemoglobin should be seen in 2 to 6 weeks of initiation of epoetin alfa therapy. The hematocrit should stabilize in the 30% to 33% range. With the correction of the client's anemia, the nurse should evaluate for an improved activity tolerance; decreased fatigue; improved appetite, sleep pattern, and cognitive function; and an improved sense of well-being.

## SELECTED DRUG MODIFICATIONS IN RENAL FAILURE

As previously mentioned, BUN and serum creatinine are waste products excreted by the kidneys. Serum levels of these substances are used to measure renal function. Unfortunately, neither test is useful in discovering early renal impairment because abnormal levels do not appear until 50% or more of renal function is impaired. Fortunately, our kidneys are functional even if 90% of the glomerular filtration rate is lost. However, the continuing progressive loss may result in **end-stage renal disease,** which then leads to the need for hemodialysis, peritoneal dialysis, or even organ transplantation.

Normal values may vary from laboratory to laboratory, but in general a normal BUN ranges between 5 and 25 mg/dl, while the range of serum creatinine, which varies with age, is usually between 0.5 and 1.2 mg/dl. The most reliable test is the creatinine clearance test; but since accurate collection of all urine excreted for a 24-hour period is difficult, many clinicians use a formula to estimate creatinine clearance whereas others may prefer to use a nomogram. The formulas most commonly used are noted in the box on the next page. The mean endogenous creatinine clearance in an adult is usually between 90 and 130 ml/min/1.73 m$^2$ body surface per 24 hours. Therefore reductions in this quantity signify impairment of renal function. (See box for usual ranges for grading renal impairment.)

Another important factor in evaluating drug blood levels in clients with renal failure or renal impairment is an assessment of serum albumin and total protein for the client.

---

## ESTIMATING CREATININE CLEARANCE*

$$\text{Men: } \left[ \frac{145 - \text{age}}{\text{Serum creatinine}} \right] - 3$$

Values for women are 85% of the above predicted value, or the following formula may be used:

$$\text{Women: } 0.85 \left[ \frac{145 - \text{age}}{\text{Serum creatinine}} \right] - 3$$

---

*Values obtained are in ml/min/70 kg.

---

## TYPICAL GRADING FOR RENAL IMPAIRMENT USING CREATININE CLEARANCE

| Degree of Renal Failure | Creatinine Clearance |
|---|---|
| Normal | Men: 90-139 ml/min |
| | Women: 80-125 ml/min |
| Mild impairment | 50-80 ml/min |
| Moderate impairment | 10-50 ml/min |
| Severe impairment | <10 ml/min |

Data from Bennett WM and others (1983). Am J Kidney Dis 3(3):155.

---

Serum protein is decreased in individuals with renal insufficiency, which can alter the interpretation of serum levels of drugs that are protein bound (90% or more) in the normal person. Individuals with a lower albumin or protein value may have a drug concentration in the low range that appears to be therapeutic. This is possible if the laboratory does not differentiate between the bound and unbound drug in their testing. Lower protein levels may lead to a higher unbound concentration of the drug (the active form), thus producing an adequate therapeutic response.

## DOSING METHODS

In individuals with renal insufficiency or impairment, the drug dosage may be decreased (dosage reduction method) while maintaining the usual interval, or the dosage may be the usually prescribed dose, but the interval between doses is lengthened (interval extension method). Usually the dosage reduction method is preferred for drugs that require a constant blood theapeutic level. For most clients receiving a loading dose, the dose is similar to the dose given to a client without renal impairment. This permits a therapeutically desirable blood level that is then maintained by one of the above dosing methods. Table 35-1 gives typical dosing recommendations for selected medications along with a list of drugs that may or may not be removed by hemodi-

alysis or peritoneal dialysis. The reader is referred to the current package inserts or renal failure dosing guides for specific data. Table 35-2 lists the medications that are most commonly associated with inducing renal dysfunction.

## ▷NURSING MANAGEMENT: PHARMACOLOGIC THERAPIES FOR CLIENTS WITH RENAL SYSTEM DYSFUNCTION

*Assessment.* The initial assessment should include a history of recent weight changes, edema, malaise, increasing irritability or mental changes, metallic taste in the mouth, polyuria and nocturia (caused by reduced ability to concentrate urine), headache, dizziness, gastrointestinal disturbances, and hypertension. Because other body systems may be affected by renal dysfunction, a thorough multisystem assessment should be conducted.

*Intervention.* Fluid intake may be restricted. If so, fluid allotments should be planned with the client as to the type of fluids and time of intake to enhance the regimen's acceptability by the client and to maintain the client's feeling of control. Dietary sodium is usually restricted, and intake will need to be planned with the client, based on degree of restriction.

Drug therapy is based on each client's particular form of dysfunction and its cause. Because of the many body systems that are affected by renal dysfunction, several medications may be used. The more common agents are diuretics for control of fluid balance, edema, and hypertension and antibiotics to treat infection. Because altered renal function also alters pharmacokinetics of many drugs, dosages and dose intervals are adjusted based on the drug and degree of renal system dysfunction.

*Education.* As with any condition, particularly those with multisystem consequences, knowledge deficit may be likely. The client should be instructed in the purpose of the medications, such as antihypertensives, diuretics, calcium supplements, vitamin D, and phosphate binders. In addition, the client should be told of the side effects and adverse reactions of any medications being taken because with increasing renal insufficiency the margin of safety with any medication is diminished. Multiple drug therapy increases the chance of a drug interaction. The stressors placed on the client with increasing renal insufficiency are multiple. Changes in life-style, body image, and the impact of the disease on the client require the nurse to exercise skill in the roles of support and education for the client and family to minimize the potential for ineffective coping.

*Evaluation.* Daily weights should be taken at the same time of day, with the same amount of clothing, and with the same scale. The client at home may be better able to establish a routine by weighing first thing in the morning after the first voiding and before dressing or eating. The daily weight can be evaluated in light of the 24-hour intake and output balance for determination of fluid volume excess or fluid volume deficit.

**TABLE 35-1** Selected medications and dosing recommendations in renal insufficiency

| Medication | Dosage recommendation based on creatinine clearance (glomerular filtration rate [ml/min])* | | | Drug removal by (H) hemodialysis or (P) peritoneal dialysis† |
|---|---|---|---|---|
| | >50 | 10-50 | <10 | |
| AMINOGLYCOSIDE ANTIBIOTICS | | | | |
| amikacin (Amikin) | 60-90 (q12h) | 30-70 (q12h) | 20-30 (q24h) | Yes (H,P) |
| gentamicin (Garamycin) | 60-90 (q8-12h) | 30-70 (q12h) | 20-30 (q24h) | Yes (H,P) |
| tobramycin (Nebcin) | 60-90 (q8-12h) | 30-70 (q12h) | 20-30 (q24h) | Yes (H,P) |
| CEPHALOSPORIN ANTIBIOTICS | | | | |
| cefaclor (Ceclor) | 100 | 50-100 | 33 | Yes (H) |
| ceftriaxine (Rocephin) | 45-100 | 10-45 | 5-10 | Unknown |
| cephradine (Anspor, Velosef) | 100 | 50 | 25 | Yes (H,P) |
| CARDIOVASCULAR DRUGS | | | | |
| digoxin (Lanoxin) | 100 | 25-75 | 10-25 | No (H,P) |
| OTHER DRUGS | | | | |
| cimetidine (Tagamet) | 100 | 75 | 50 | No (H,P) |
| metoclopramide (Reglan) | 100 | 75 | 50 | Unknown |

*Dosing schedule may use percent of dosage and/or extension of time interval. When an extended interval is recommended along with a dosage adjustment, it is so noted. Yes/no refers to need for dose supplement following the procedure. For additional drugs based on time extension intervals, the reader is referred to Bennett WM and others (1983).

**TABLE 35-2** Medications associated with renal toxicity or dysfunction

| Medications | Possible toxicity or dysfunction |
|---|---|
| kanamycin, colistin, amikacin (rare), tobramycin (rare), gentamicin (rare), cephalothin, cephaloridine, lithium, amphotericin B, cisplatin | Damage and/or necrosis to renal tubules |
| penicillins, methoxyflurane, cephalothin, sulfonamides, nonsteroidal antiinflammatory drugs, allopurinol | Acute interstitial nephritis, vasculitis, etc. |
| trimethadione, paramethadione, gold, probenecid, lithium, heroin | Glomerular damage |
| Injectable antihypertensive drugs given to elderly, excessive dosages of low molecular weight dextran, diuretics, opioid medications | May induce acute ischemic renal failure |

From Speight TM (1987). Avery's drug treatment, principles and practice of clinical pharmacology and therapeutics, ed 3, Baltimore: The Williams & Wilkins Co.

The fluid intake and output of the client should be accurately recorded on a 24-hour basis. The 24-hour balance should be calculated by subtracting the output from the intake. The balance, whether positive or negative, should relate to weight loss or gain at approximately 500 ml to the pound. Serum BUN and creatinine levels should be monitored to ascertain the client's end-stage renal disease and to anticipate clinical signs and symptoms of physiologic injury that would require nursing intervention and client education.

Serum potassium levels should be monitored daily. When the level exceeds 6 mEq/L, cardiovascular monitoring should become more intense. In addition to blood pressure and apical heart rate determinations, assessment by cardiac monitor is required.

Serum levels of calcium and phosphate should be monitored every 3 to 4 days, and the client should be clinically assessed for hypocalcemia and hyperphosphatemia as evidenced by irritability, muscular twitching, and tetany.

The client's arterial blood gases should be monitored. Clinically, the client should be observed for increased respiratory rate and depth and changes in mental status that would indicate impending metabolic acidosis. CBCs should be taken periodically, and the client should be assessed for signs and symptoms of anemia that might necessitate interventions such as iron supplements and anabolic steroids or, in the extreme, transfusion of packed or frozen RBCs.

## SUMMARY

In summary, renal system dysfunction may be a source of tremendous stress for the client and family, and it also presents a challenge for the nurse. Therapy is complicated by multiple drug therapy and altered pharmacokinetics. Drug interactions or adverse reactions may appear at any time and make close monitoring of drug effects and renal function by the nurse essential. In addition, nondrug therapy, such as diet modification and fluid restriction, and involvement of other body systems present additional areas for nursing intervention.

## BIBLIOGRAPHY

Allaire M. (1986). Implications of administering drugs in renal insufficiency, Focus Crit Care 13(1):46.

Banerjee AK et al. (1986). The management of acute renal failure in intensive care units, Intensive Care Nurs 2(2):84.

Bennett W. (1986). Update on drugs in renal failure, Adv Nephrol 15:379.

Bennett WM et al. (1983). Drug prescribing in renal failure: dosing guidelines for adults, Amer J Kidney Dis 3(3):155.

Betts DK et al. (1988). Response to illness and compliance of long-term hemodialysis patients. ANNA J 15(2):96.

Braunwald E et al, editors. (1987). Harrison's principles of internal medicine, ed 11. New York: McGraw-Hill Book Co.

Brennan DT. (1987). Outcome criteria and nursing diagnosis in ESRD patient care planning. Section I: conservative management, ANNA J 14(1):36.

Butler B (1986). Protein restriction in renal disease: how much is enough? J Nephrol Nurs 3(1):27.

Chambers JK. (1987). Fluid and electrolyte problems in renal and urologic disorders, Nurs Clin North Amer 22(4):815.

Coco P. (1988). When kidneys fail—nursing management of acute renal failure, AD Nurse 3(4):16.

Cunha BA et al. (1988). Antibiotic dosing in patients with renal insufficiency or receiving dialysis, Heart Lung 17(6 Pt 1):612.

Gurklis JA et al. (1988). Identification of stressors and use of coping methods in chronic hemodialysis patients, Nurs Res 37(4):236.

Hahn K. (1987). The many signs of renal failure, Nursing 17(8):34.

Herfindal ET et al. (1988). Clinical pharmacy and therapeutics, ed 4. Baltimore: Williams & Wilkins.

Knoben JE and Anderson PO. (1986). Handbook of clinical drug data, ed 5. Hamilton, Ill: Drug Intelligence Publications.

Krupp MA et al, editors. (1987). Current medical diagnosis and treatment. Norwalk, Conn: Appleton & Lange.

Mann HJ et al. (1986). Acute renal failure, Drug Intell Clin Pharmacol 20(6):421.

Miller CA et al. (1987). CNS manifestations of acute renal failure, Crit Care Nurse 7(3):94.

Myers AR. (1986). Medicine, Media, PA: Harwal Publishing Co.

Nitz J et al. (1986). A model for patient education, ANNA J 13(5):253.

Nova G. (1987). Dialyzable drugs, Amer J Nurs 87(7):933.

O'Brien ME et al. (1986). Therapeutic options in end stage renal disease: a preliminary report, ANNA J 13(6):313.

Plawecki HM et al. (1987). Chronic renal failure, J Gerontol Nurs 13(12):14.

Speight TM. (1987). Avery's drug treatment: principles and practice of clinical pharmacology and therapeutics, ed 3. Baltimore: Williams & Wilkins.

Spiegel DM et al. (1987). Acute renal failure, Postgrad Med 82(4):96.

Srivastava RH. (1986). Fatigue in the renal patient. ANNA J 13(5):246.

Wallach J. (1986). Interpretation of diagnostic tests. Boston: Little, Brown & Co.

Young LE and Koda-Kimble MA. (1988). Applied therapeutics, ed 4. Vancouver: Applied Therapeutics.

*Unit 9*

# Drugs Affecting the Respiratory System

*Chapter*

# 36 Overview of the Respiratory System

## KEY TERMS

## INTRODUCTION

The respiratory system includes all structures involved in the exchange of oxygen and carbon dioxide—such as the airway passages, the lungs, nasal cavities, pharynx, larynx, trachea, bronchi, bronchioles, pulmonary lobules with their alveoli, the diaphragm, and all muscles concerned with respiration itself.

The most urgent and critical need for maintaining life is a continued, uninterrupted supply of oxygen. Oxygen is supplied to the body through the process of respiration. **Respiration** is a term loosely used to describe three distinct but interrelated processes.

1. **Pulmonary ventilation,** which involves the movement of air into and out of the lungs

2. **Gas transport,** which involves the exchange of gases between the air in the lungs, the blood, and the cell

3. **Cellular respiration,** which involves the utilization of oxygen in the catabolism of energy-yielding substances for the production of energy

Respiration, one of the body's regulating systems, helps maintain physiologic dynamic equilibrium. It also compensates for rapid adjustment to changes in metabolic states.

The air passages permit air to flow from the external environment to pulmonary blood and modify the air taken in by warming and moistening it and removing noxious substances. Airway efficiency is determined by the following factors:

1. Shape and size of each portion of the respiratory tract (nasal cavity, pharynx, larynx, trachea, bronchi, bronchioles, alveolar sacs)

2. Presence of a ciliated, mucus-secreting, epithelial lining throughout most of the respiratory tract

3. Character and thickness of respiratory tract secretions

4. Compliance of the cartilaginous and bony supports

5. Pressure gradients
6. Traction on airway walls
7. Absence of foreign substances in the lumen of the respiratory tract

Any alteration of any of these factors will affect the ease with which air flows through the air passages. Congenital anomalies, injuries, allergies, or disease will cause air flow resistance if these factors are abnormally affected. Resistance occurs, for example, if there is stenosis or narrowing of any portion of the respiratory tract, loss of cilia that ordinarily sweep out foreign substances, any thick or tenacious secretions, loss of elasticity, or presence of foreign objects.

## RESPIRATORY TRACT SECRETIONS

The tracheobronchial tree, made up of repeated branching tubes, is a tubular airway that serves as a conduit for passage of air from the external environment to the alveolar-capillary exchange unit. The inner surface of the tracheobronchial tree is lined with ciliated columnar epithelium interspersed with **goblet cells.** The gelatinous mucus (gel layer) produced by goblet cells is normally discharged into the tubular lumen. In some obstructive pulmonary diseases, mucus secretion is greatly increased, thus making it difficult for the cilia to transport secretions along the airway (see Figure 36-1).

The **bronchial glands,** which are located in the submucosa of the tracheobronchial tree, secrete a relatively watery fluid (sol layer) through ducts leading to the surface of the ciliated epithelium. Under vagal (parasympathetic) control, the glands can be stimulated by irritant agents or aerosol drugs to release their contents into the lumen of the airway (see Figure 36-1, *B*).

The products of these two sources—goblet cells and bronchial glands—form the sol-gel film that makes up the mucociliary blanket. This protective blanket of fluid bathes the ciliated epithelium of the tracheobronchial tree. In addition, the cilia continuously propel the sol-gel film toward the larynx along the respiratory tree. The normal adult produces approximately 100 ml of respiratory secretions per day, and swallows this material without being aware of it. The process of moving mucus along the tracheobronchial tree is called **mucokinesis.** The mucociliary blanket is a basic concern in most chronic obstructive pulmonary disease. The cilia must sustain appropriate function; a dry atmosphere causes the respiratory secretions to become thick and tenacious, which tends to interfere with ciliary movements. Thus adequate humidity should be maintained to prevent the change in the normal consistency of the respiratory secretions.

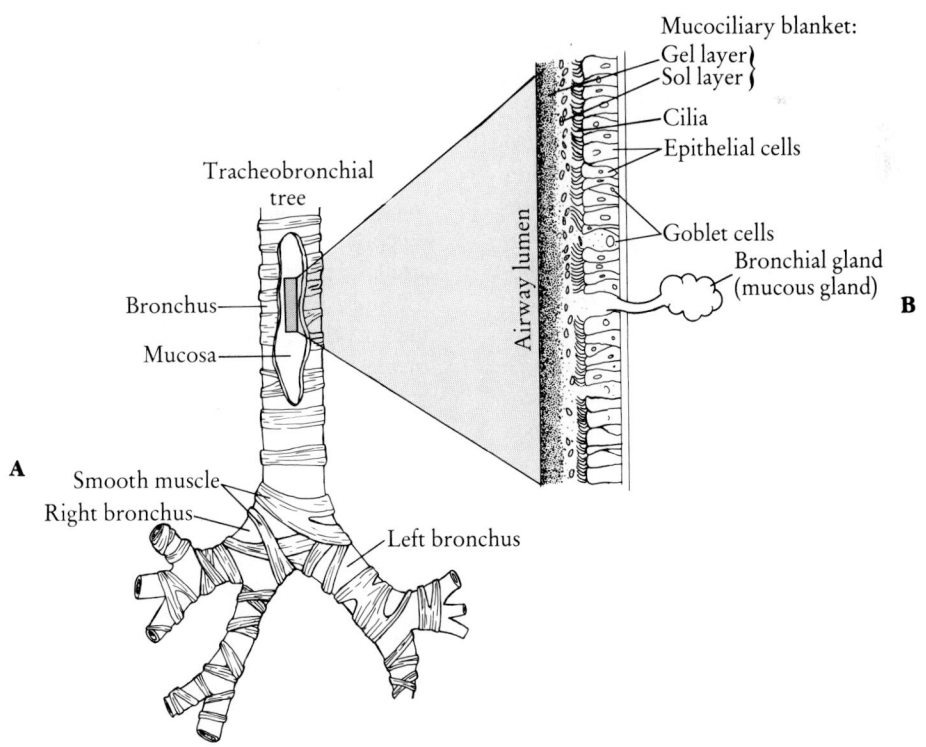

**FIGURE 36-1** Tracheobronchial tree and bronchial smooth muscle. **A,** Diagram of tracheobronchial tree. **B,** Cut-out section of inner lining of bronchus.

## BRONCHIAL SMOOTH MUSCLE

*Smooth muscle arrangement.* An important structure of the tracheobronchial tree is the smooth muscle. The mass of muscle fibers along the bronchi progressively increases as it extends down toward the distal bronchioles. Isolated muscle fibers may be found as far down as the alveolar ducts. The smooth muscle fibers are arranged along the length of the tubular tree in a double helical or spiral pattern, and this formation profoundly influences the diameter or the lumen of the airways. Because of this structural feature, the effect of muscle contraction reduces both the caliber and the length of the bronchus (see Figure 36-1, *A*).

*Nerve supply.* The airway or tracheobronchial tree is innervated by the autonomic nervous system. The bronchial smooth muscle tone is influenced by the balance maintained between parasympathetic and sympathetic stimuli during rest. Activation of the parasympathetic fiber (vagus nerve) releases acetylcoline, which results in **bronchoconstriction** and narrowing of the airway. By contrast, the stimulation of the sympathetic fiber and the sympathoadrenal system releases epinephrine and norepinephrine from the adrenal medulla into circulation. Their action on the beta$_2$ receptor sites in the bronchial smooth muscle produces **bronchodilation** by means of smooth muscle relaxation.

*Receptors.* Several kinds of receptors are found along the bronchial airway. The release of acetylcholine activates muscarinic receptors during stimulation of the parasympathetic system, whereas the sympathetic system affects adrenergic receptors. Most of the adrenergic receptors present in the bronchial smooth muscle are beta$_2$ receptors that are stimulated mainly by epinephrine released from the adrenal medulla. Beta$_1$ receptors are also found, although the ratio of beta$_2$ to beta$_1$ receptors is approximately 3:1. Thus bronchial smooth muscle is supplied primarily by beta$_2$ receptors. The sympathomimetic drugs used principally as bronchodilators stimulate the beta$_2$ receptors. Because many of these agents are not purely selective in their pharmacologic effect, they also stimulate the beta$_1$ receptors in the heart, as well as alpha receptors in the lungs and peripheral arterioles. The side effects on the heart are increased cardiac output, tachycardia, and dysrhythmia. The presence of alpha receptors on the bronchial smooth muscle is relatively scarce, and their stimulation results in only mild bronchoconstriction.

*Bronchodilation.* The beta$_2$ adrenergic receptors mediate bronchodilation. This mechanism presumably is initiated by epineprhine released from the adrenal medulla and norepinephrine released from the peripheral sympathetic nerves. Also located in the cell membrane is an enzyme system known as adenyl cyclase. In the presence of magnesium ions, adenyl cyclase catalyzes the action of adenosine triphosphate (ATP) in the cytoplasm of the cell to produce cyclic 3'5' adenosine-monophosphate (cyclic 3'5' AMP or c3'5' AMP). Cyclic AMP then performs its important function, that is, inducing relaxation of bronchial smooth muscle or bronchodilation. The hormone epinephrine is designated as the "first messenger" and cyclic 3'5' AMP as the "second messenger." As a final action, cyclic 3'5' AMP is inactivated by an enzyme, phosphodiesterase, which catalyzes it to the inactive 5' AMP. This results in a fall in the cyclic 3'5' AMP level. The action of phosphodiesterase may be inhibited by a xanthine drug such as theophylline. As a consequence, the cyclic 3'5' AMP level remains elevated, thereby affecting smooth muscle dilation.

Circulating catecholamines can exert their effects on beta$_1$, beta$_2$, and alpha receptors. Clients with asthma may have a normal reaction to both alpha and beta stimulation through a reduced cyclic AMP response, by an abnormally sensitive response to alpha stimulation, and by an exaggerated response to the muscarinic agonists via the vagal pathways. This exaggerated airway response may result from the effects of a decrease in cyclic AMP, histamine effects on smooth muscle, the vagal reflex pathway, an increase in cyclic guanylic acid secondary to calcium influx, and histamine-induced release of the contents of mast cells. Bronchodilation is induced by circulating catecholamines or administration of a sympathomimetic agent.

Circulating catecholamines reach the lung via circulation and interact with the beta$_2$ adrenergic receptors in the cell membrane of the bronchial smooth muscle cell.

*Bronchoconstriction.* The bronchial smooth muscle is innervated by the parasympathetic fibers from the vagus nerve. Acetylcholine released from the terminal interacts with the muscarinic receptors on the membrane of the cell. Stimulation of the muscarinic receptor increases the activity of the enzyme guanylate cyclase in the membrane, thereby promoting the rate of formation of cyclic 3'5' guanosine monophosphase (cyclic 3'5'GMP) from guanosine triphosphate (GTP). The cyclic GMP level affects the bronchial muscle by producing bronchoconstriction. In addition, alpha receptors found on the bronchial smooth muscle have a similar involvement with this mechanism. On activation, the alpha receptors also increase the cyclic GMP level. Further, cyclic 3'5'GMP stimulates the release of chemical mediators from the mast cell during an asthmatic attack, and these mediators are responsible for causing bronchoconstriction.

## CONTROL OF RESPIRATION

*Central control.* The basic rhythm for respiration is initiated and maintained in the medullary rhythmicity area located beneath the lower part of the floor of the fourth ventricle in the medial half of the medulla. Neurons that control inspiration and expiration intermingle and discharge, or fire impulses alternately. However, signals from the spinal cord, the cerebral cortex and midbrain, the apneustic area of the pons, and the pneumotaxic area of the upper pons can enter the medullary rhythmicity area, modify the rhythm of respiration, and contribute to the normal pattern of respiration.

Normally, the human organism is unaware of the respiratory process. However, voluntary influence and control of breathing are possible. This is important when a client must learn to voluntarily control breathing patterns.

*Peripheral control.* The medullary rhythmicity area is also influenced by various sensory and peripheral stimuli, the vasomotor center, reflex mechanisms (e.g., the Hering-Breuer reflex), the chemoreceptors in the carotid and aortic bodies, and the baroreceptors in the carotid sinus and aortic arch. Fear, pain, stress, blood pressure, body temperature, and blood levels of oxygen and carbon dioxide can all modify the activity of the respiratory centers.

Humoral regulation of respiration is achieved primarily through changes in the concentrations of oxygen, carbon dioxide, or hydrogen ions in body fluids. In a healthy individual, carbon dioxide is the chief respiratory stimulant. An increase in the carbon dioxide tension of the blood directly stimulates the inspiratory and expiratory centers, which increases both the rate and depth of breathing. This results in a blowing off of carbon dioxide to keep the carbon dioxide tension of the blood constant. The pH of the blood is determined by the ratio of bicarbonate ion ($HCO_3$) to carbon dioxide. When the carbon dioxide content of the blood is increased, there is a subsequent increase in the formation of carbonic acid in the blood. This alters the bicarbonate/carbonic acid ratio from the normal value of 20:1 and results in acidosis. Conversely, a decrease in the carbon dioxide content of the blood results in alkalosis. Therefore respiration is important for regulating the pH of the blood by controlling the carbon dioxide tension of the blood.

Basically, changes in arterial oxygen concentration have little, if any, direct effect on the respiratory center. However, if the arterial oxygen concentration falls below normal, the chemoreceptors in the carotid and aortic bodies are stimulated and in turn stimulate the respiratory center to increase alveolar ventilation. This mechanism operates primarily under abnormal conditions such as chronic obstructive pulmonary disease.

## SUMMARY

The highest priority for the survival of the human organism is an adequate, uninterrupted supply of oxygen. Oxygen is supplied to the various body tissues by the processes of pulmonary ventilation, gas transport, and cellular respiration. Although it is possible to influence and control respiratory pattern voluntarily, the rhythm and depth of pulmonary ventilation is generally initiated and maintained centrally in the medulla and influenced peripherally by reflex mechanisms, chemoreceptors, and baroreceptors.

Nurses have a role in the administration of medications by aerosol therapy, which is sometimes shared with respiratory therapists. This form of topical treatment allows for bronchodilation and pulmonary decongestion; loosening of secretions; application of steroids; and humidification, cooling, or heating of air. Because of the effectiveness of this route of drug administration, it is an important mode of therapy to be used by nurses.

## BIBLIOGRAPHY

Bogatz LJ. (1983). Control of respiration: a review and update, Curr Rev Respir Ther 5(21):167.

Boushey EJ et al. (1984). The role of the parasympathetic system in the regulation of bronchial smooth muscle, Respir Dis 65(S135):80.

Bullock BL and Rosendahl PP. (1988). Pathophysiology: adaptations and alterations in function, ed 2. Boston: Little, Brown & Co.

Chatbum RL et al. (1987). A rational basis for humidity therapy, Respir Care 32(4):249.

Guyton AC. (1990). Textbook of medical physiology, ed 8. Philadelphia: WB Saunders, Co.

Harper RW. (1981). A guide to respiratory care: physiology and clinical application. Philadelphia: JB Lippincott Co.

Hedemark LL et al. (1982). Chemical regulation of respiration, Chest 82(4):488.

Holland MS et al. (1987). AANA Journal course: advanced scientific concepts: update for nurse anesthetists, part III. The respiratory system, AANA J 55(4):346.

Knepil J. (1983). The control of breathing . . . the neuronal and chemical control of breathing, Nursing Mirror 156(19):44.

Lehnert BE and Schachter EN. (1980). The pharmacology of respiratory care. St. Louis: The CV Mosby Co.

Mecca R. (1983). The physiology and physics of ventilation II, Curr Rev Recov Room Nurses 5(12):99.

Moser KM and Spragg RG, editors. (1982). Respiratory emergencies, ed 2. St Louis: The CV Mosby Co.

Newhouse M. (1984). Aersol therapy in adult lung disease, Respir Technol 20(4):11.

Shapiro BA et al. (1985). Clinical applications of respiratory care, ed 3. Chicago: Year Book Medical Publishers, Inc.

Whaley LF and Wong DL. (1991). Nursing Care of infants and children, ed 4. St. Louis: Mosby–Year Book, Inc.

West JB. (1987). Pulmonary pathophysiology: the essentials, ed 3. Baltimore: The Williams & Wilkins Co.

# ☙37 Mucokinetic and Bronchodilator Drugs

## CHAPTER OBJECTIVES

*After studying this chapter, you should be able to meet the following objectives and define the key terms.*

1. Define mucokinetic agent.

2. Compare the advantages and disadvantages of water and saline as diluents.

3. State the purpose of administering mucolytic agents and appropriate nursing considerations.

4. Discuss the therapeutic goals of bronchodilator drugs.

5. Compare and contrast the sympathomimetic bronchodilator drugs.

6. Name drugs and beverages in the xanthine group.

7. Discuss the use of the xanthine derivatives in the treatment of asthma and appropriate client education.

8. Discuss the use of corticosteroid drugs in the treatment of asthma.

## KEY TERMS

**aerosol therapy,** page 625

**expectorants,** page 626

**mucokinetic agent,** page 624

**mucolytics,** page 626

**mucus,** page 625

**nebulizer,** page 625

**sputum,** page 624

**xanthine derivatives,** page 637

## INTRODUCTION

Mucokinetic drugs concerned with expectoration and bronchodilator drugs that maintain patency of the respiratory tract are the two main groups discussed in this chapter.

## Mucokinetic Drugs

A **mucokinetic agent** is a compound that promotes the removal of abnormal or excessive respiratory tract secretions by thinning hyperviscous secretions, therefore allowing more effective ciliary action. These agents prevent sputum retention, which may result from abnormal ciliary activity, defects in airflow, or modification in cough effectiveness. **Sputum** (or phlegm) may be defined as an abnormal, viscous secretion that is an excretory product of the lower respiratory tree. It consists mainly of **mucus,** a proteinaceous material having a mucopolysaccharide as its major component. In addition, sputum contains deoxyribonucleic acid (DNA) molecules, which are derived from the breakdown of mucosal cells, leukocytes, and bacteria. These products are responsible for the characteristic heavy quality and yellow color of the sputum. The terms "sputum" and "mucus" should not be used interchangeably. Sputum is an abnormal secretion originating in the lower respiratory tract, whereas mucus is a normal secretion produced by the surface cells in the mucous membrane.

Individuals with respiratory disorders such as chronic bronchitis develop disturbances of the mucociliary blanket, which results in a significant impairment of the mucus clearance process. (See Chapter 36, Figure 37-1, *B*.) Consequently, mucus plugging and pathogenic colonization of microorganisms occur in the lower respiratory tract. These changes then lead to overproduction of thick, tenacious sputum. Thus the advantage provided by the mucokinetic drugs is that they alter the consistency of the sputum, thereby promoting the eventual expulsion of these secretions.

## DILUENTS
### Water

Water is the most commonly used diluent of respiratory secretions. Clients with chronic obstructive pulmonary disease frequently suffer from dehydration, thus respiratory secretions are retained. These secretions then become highly viscous in consistency and lead to widespread plug formation in the respiratory tree. Water may be administered by ultrasonic nebulizer. Small amounts of water deposited on the gel layer of the respiratory tree appear to reduce the adhesive characteristics and general viscosity of the gelatinous substances found in this layer. Care is needed with clients receiving restricted fluid intake, since water can be absorbed through the inhalation route. (If fluid intake is being measured, water absorbed through the inhalation route must be added to the client's intake record.) If a client's fluid intake is not restricted, large amounts of water are usually encouraged to liquefy the respiratory secretions.

### Saline Solutions

Normal saline (0.9% sodium chloride) is physiologic salt solution or isotonic solution that exerts the same osmotic pressure as plasma fluids. Therapy by nebulization is well tolerated, resulting in hydration of respiratory secretions. Hypotonic solution (0.45% sodium chloride) is thought to provide deeper penetration into the more distal airways or in the alveoli via the inhalation route, whereas inhalation or hypertonic solution (1.8% sodium chloride) stimulates a productive cough since the particles deposited on the respiratory mucosa are irritating. Hypertonic solution osmotically attracts fluid out of the mucosa and into the respiratory secretions, thereby promoting their excretion.

## AEROSOL THERAPY

**Aerosol therapy** is a form of topical pulmonary treatment. An aerosol is a suspension of fine liquid or solid particles dispersed in a gas or in solution. Dry powder inhalers are also available. Liquid or solid particles range in size from about 0.005 to 50 μm in diameter. **Nebulizers** are designed to deliver a maximum number of particles of a desired size. Thus aerosol therapy is delivered through nebulization. The terms "aerosol therapy" and "nebulization therapy" are often used interchangeably. Aerosol medication is inhaled as a fine mist deposited on the respiratory tract. This form of therapy promotes the following:

1. Bronchodilation and pulmonary decongestion
2. Loosening of secretions
3. Topical application of steroids
4. Moistening, cooling, or heating of inspired air

The effectiveness of nebulization therapy depends on the number of droplets that can be suspended in an inhaled aerosol. The number that can be suspended is directly related to the size of the droplets. Small droplets can be suspended in greater numbers than large droplets. Smaller droplets (about 2 to 4 μm in diameter) are more likely to reach the periphery of the lungs—the alveolar ducts and sacs. Currently in many institutions ultrasonic nebulizers are used to treat bronchial constriction and pulmonary congestion. Larger droplets (8 to 15 μm in diameter) will be deposited primarily in the bronchioles and bronchi. Droplets of more than 40 μm will be deposited primarily in the upper airway (mouth, pharynx, trachea, and main bronchi).

Rate and depth of breathing are other factors that determine effectiveness of nebulization therapy. Rapid or shallow breathing decreases the number, as well as the retention, of droplets reaching the periphery of the lungs. Rapid breathing permits escape of significant amounts of fine droplets during expirations, although few droplets will escape if the breath is held long enough after deep inspiration to permit droplet deposit in the lung periphery. Small droplets are more effective for absorption of bronchodilators.

Almost all large droplets will be retained somewhere in the air passage. Large droplets are used for keeping large airways (nose, trachea) moist and for loosening secretions. Slow and deep breathing is required for proper lung aeration and penetration of the mist into peripheral lung areas. The breath should be held for a few seconds after a full inspiration.

Droplet size can be controlled by the amount of pressure used to force oxygen or room air through the solution to produce a mist. The tubing used, its length, and its number of bends affect turbulent flow and mist temperature. With most nebulizers maximum density of the inhaled mist is achieved by making the flow of mist as smooth and direct as possible. Nebulizers commonly used in hospitals produce similar mists. *A note of precaution:* drug reconcentration can occur with both jet and ultrasonic nebulizers if a humidity deficit occurs. Evaporation of water molecules causes a gradual increase in drug concentration in the droplets being returned to the fluid reservoir, thus increasing the risk of drug toxicity. Control of temperature and humidity can prevent this.

The main groups of drugs conventionally administered by aerosol include bronchodilators, cromolyn sodium, and steroid preparations. It is important to remember that the lung is an absorptive organ and thus is a route of access for drugs to enter the systemic circulation. For example, after inhalation anesthetic agents enter the blood, they exert their main effect on the central nervous system. Aerosol therapy, when used as a method of administering drugs, is supposed to minimize their side effects. Yet certain bronchodilator aerosols do produce cardiovascular effects simply because the drug may possess a property that adversely influences cardiac action after it is *absorbed* into the bloodstream.

When combination inhalation aerosols are prescribed for a client without specific physician instructions on order of administration, the nurse should be aware of the proper recommendations for drug administration. For example, if adrenocorticoids (Beclovent, Vanceril) or cromolym (Intal) is prescribed to be administered with ipratropium (Atrovent), the ipratropium should be administered 5 minutes before either of the other drugs. Whenever a beta agonist (Alupent, Proventil, etc.) is prescribed with ipratropium (Atrovent), the beta agonist is always administered first with a 5-minute wait before administration of the second drug. Do not administer both aerosols in rapid sequence, because of the possibility of inducing fluorocarbon toxicity; also, this procedure decreases drug effectiveness.

## MUCOLYTIC DRUGS

**Mucolytics** are drugs that exert a disintegrating effect on mucus. These agents, also called **expectorants,** promote coughing or spitting and thereby the removal of mucus or other exudates from the lung, bronchi, or trachea. One of the more commonly used mucolytics is acetylcysteine.

### acetylcysteine (Mucomyst, Airbron✻)

Acetylcysteine reduces the thickness and stickiness of purulent and nonpurulent pulmonary secretions by breaking up the linkages or bonds of mucoprotein molecules of the respiratory secretions into smaller, more soluble, and less viscous strands. In addition to altering the molecular composition of the mucopolysaccharides, this drug also affects similar changes in the DNA molecule and cellular debris. The decrease in viscosity of bronchial secretions aids their removal by coughing, postural drainage, or suctioning. Acetylcysteine reduces the extent of liver injury following acetaminophen overdose. This protective effect is thought to occur as a result of altered hepatic metabolism by acetylcysteine. This mucolytic agent is used as an adjunct treatment for thick, viscid, or abnormal mucous secretions in

person with bronchopulmonary disease, cystic fibrosis, or atelectasis caused by a mucus obstruction. It is also used as a diagnostic aid in a variety of bronchial studies, such as bronchospirometry and bronchograms. When administered systemically, it is a specific antidote for an acetaminophen overdose.

Although some acetylcysteine is absorbed from the pulmonary epithelium, its primary effects are local, on the mucus in the lungs. By inhalation it produces an effect within 1 minute, although direct instillation via an intratracheal catheter produces an immediate effect. The peak response from inhalation occurs within 5 to 10 minutes and metabolism is in the liver. Less frequently reported side effects of acetylcysteine include an elevated temperature, nausea, vomiting, runny nose, throat or lung irritation, clammy skin or sore mouth. Its less frequent adverse reactions include hemoptysis and respiratory difficulties. No significant drug interactions have been reported with acetylcysteine.

The usual adult and pediatric dose by nebulization using a face mask, mouthpiece, or tracheostomy is 3 to 5 ml of a 20% solution or 6 to 10 ml of a 10% solution given three or four times daily. As a diagnostic aid, 1 to 2 ml of a 20% solution or 2 to 4 ml of a 10% solution is instilled by intratracheal or inhalation for two or three doses before a procedure. To treat an acetaminophen overdose, it is administered orally in a dose of 140 mg/kg initially, then 70 mg/kg every 4 hours for 17 doses.

Pregnancy safety has been established as FDA category B.

▷ **Nursing Management:**
**Acetylcysteine Therapy**

*Assessment.* Use acetylcysteine with caution in the elderly and debilitated and those with asthma or severe respiratory insufficiency, because it may increase airway obstruction; bronchospasm may occur in susceptible clients.

With the administration of acetylcysteine, the client has the potential for the following nursing diagnoses: altered comfort related to the drug's unpleasant odor during administration or facial stickiness after nebulization by face mask, nausea or vomiting, rash, rhinorrhea, and throat irritation; hyperthermia; altered mucous membranes (stomatitis); ineffective airway clearance; and physiologic injury related to hemoptysis.

*Intervention.* Ultrasonic nebulizers are recommended for administration of the drug. Hand nebulizers are discouraged because the output is too small and the fluid particles too large. The nebulized drug may be inhaled either directly or by the use of a plastic face mask, face tent, mouthpiece, or oxygen tent. The nebulizer may be used with an intermittent positive pressure breathing (IPPB) apparatus. When the drug is nebulized using a dry gas, it may become concentrated because of evaporation of the solution. The last remaining quarter of the drug can be diluted with an equal part of sterile water for injection to continue nebulization so the client is ensured the appropriate dosage. After nebulization, the face should be washed with water to remove the sticky coating left by the drug.

The equipment should be cleaned immediately after use to prevent blockage of the fine parts and corrosion of the metal ones. Some clients may develop nausea and vomiting, but this may be from the disagreeable odor of the nebulized drug and quantity of respiratory secretions eliminated. With the aid of these agents and postural drainage, most individuals can expectorate pulmonary secretions without further assistance; however, in the elderly or debilitated, suctioning may be indicated. Because of release of hydrogen sulfide, solutions of acetylcysteine will harden rubber and become discolored on contact with certain metals. Acetylcysteine solutions should be used with equipment made of glass, plastic, or stainless steel. If the vacuum seal has been broken on the bottle, the solution should be refrigerated to retard oxidation and then used within 48 hours. When acetylcysteine is administered orally, it may be diluted in soft drinks or citrus juices. The diluted solution should be used within the hour.

*Education.* The client should clear the airway by coughing before the drug is administered by aerosol. Instruction should be given on the correct use of the nebulizer.

*Evaluation.* The frequency of the client's cough and its character should be monitored and documented. The character and quantity of expectorated material should be observed. Percussion and auscultation of the chest should be accomplished on a periodic basis.

*Antidotal use.* When acetylcysteine is administered as an antidote for acetaminophen overdose, it is of most benefit when started within 10 to 12 hours after the ingestion of the overdose; but it is still beneficial if started within the first 24 hours. The client should be supported through gastric lavage or induced emesis and other appropriate therapies. The greatest risk is of hepatotoxicity, the potential for which can be assessed from plasma acetaminophen concentrations, so monitoring these and liver function studies are essential. Nursing care is provided for the client with a potential for self-harm.

### Other Expectorants

Over the years, many other products have been used as expectorants in both prescription and over-the-counter medications. Until 1989, the FDA advisory review panel on nonprescription products did not find any marketed expectorant to be effective. Although this area is still controversial, guaifenesin has been reclassified by the FDA as the only expectorant in Category I (safe and effective). This reassignment was based on several subjective studies that reported that guaifenesin decreased cough frequency plus reduced the thickness and quantity of sputum (Feldmann, 1990).

---

| EXPECTORANTS IN CATEGORY III* |
| --- |
| ammonium chloride |
| beechwood creosote |
| potassium guaiacolsulfonate |
| syrup of ipecac |
| terpin hydrate |

*Safe but not proven to be effective. Recommended dosages and additional information available (Feldman and Davidson, 1986).

## DRUGS THAT ANTAGONIZE BRONCHIAL SECRETIONS

Atropine, although not used as an expectorant, may be given cautiously to decrease secretions and excessive expectoration in certain forms of bronchitis. Many remedies used to treat colds contain atropine. Morphine, codeine, and papaverine not only act as sedatives but also tend to dry the mucous membranes. In many cases the best treatment of a cold or inflammation of the respiratory mucous membranes is extra rest, forcing fluids, and eating simple but nutritious food.

# Bronchodilator Drugs

Bronchodilator drugs are primarily used to treat chronic pulmonary diseases such as asthma, chronic bronchitis, and emphysema. Major causes of ineffective airway clearance include (1) bronchial smooth muscle contraction (asthma), (2) mucus hypersecretion (chronic bronchitis), and (3) mucosal edema or inflammation (chronic bronchitis). Bronchial asthma may present with some or all of these symptoms. See Figure 37-1.

Traditionally asthma was classified on the basis of the stimuli that may induce an attack; thus intrinsic asthma might be caused by emotional factors or exercise, for example, while extrinsic asthma was induced by pollens, molds, dust, or animal hair. As many asthmatics have a combination type asthma, this type of classification is not considered useful. Instead clients are now classified according to the frequency and severity of their asthma attacks as this information is the most useful when considering pharmacologic interventions. See Figure 37-2 for an overview of the effects of antiasthmatic medications.

The major drugs used in treatment of asthma include sympathomimetic drugs, theophylline, cromolyn sodium, and the corticosteroids. Figure 37-3 illustrates major sites of action for these drugs. The principal agents used in the treatment of airway obstruction include sympathomimetic drugs and xanthine derivatives. Prophylactic antiasthmatic agents also prevent airway obstruction in individuals with

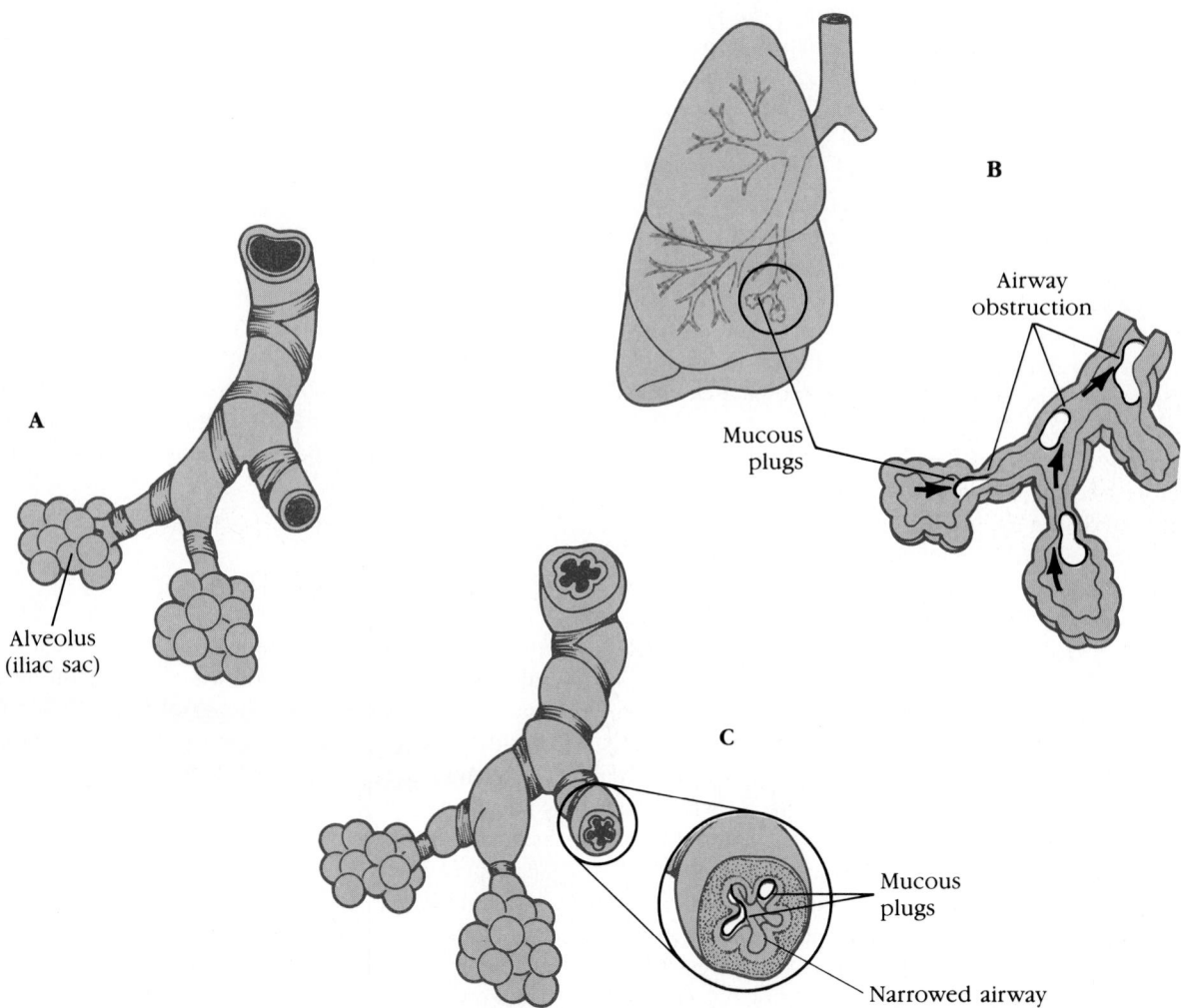

**FIGURE 37-1** Bronchiole in, **A,** normal state and, **B,** during an asthma attack. An asthmatic attack is illustrated by bronchial muscle spasms, inflammation, excessive mucus resulting in mucus plugs, edema and trapped air in the air sacs (alveoli), resulting in airway obstruction, **C.** Total amount of air inhaled and exhaled is decreased because of air trapped in the lungs after expiration.

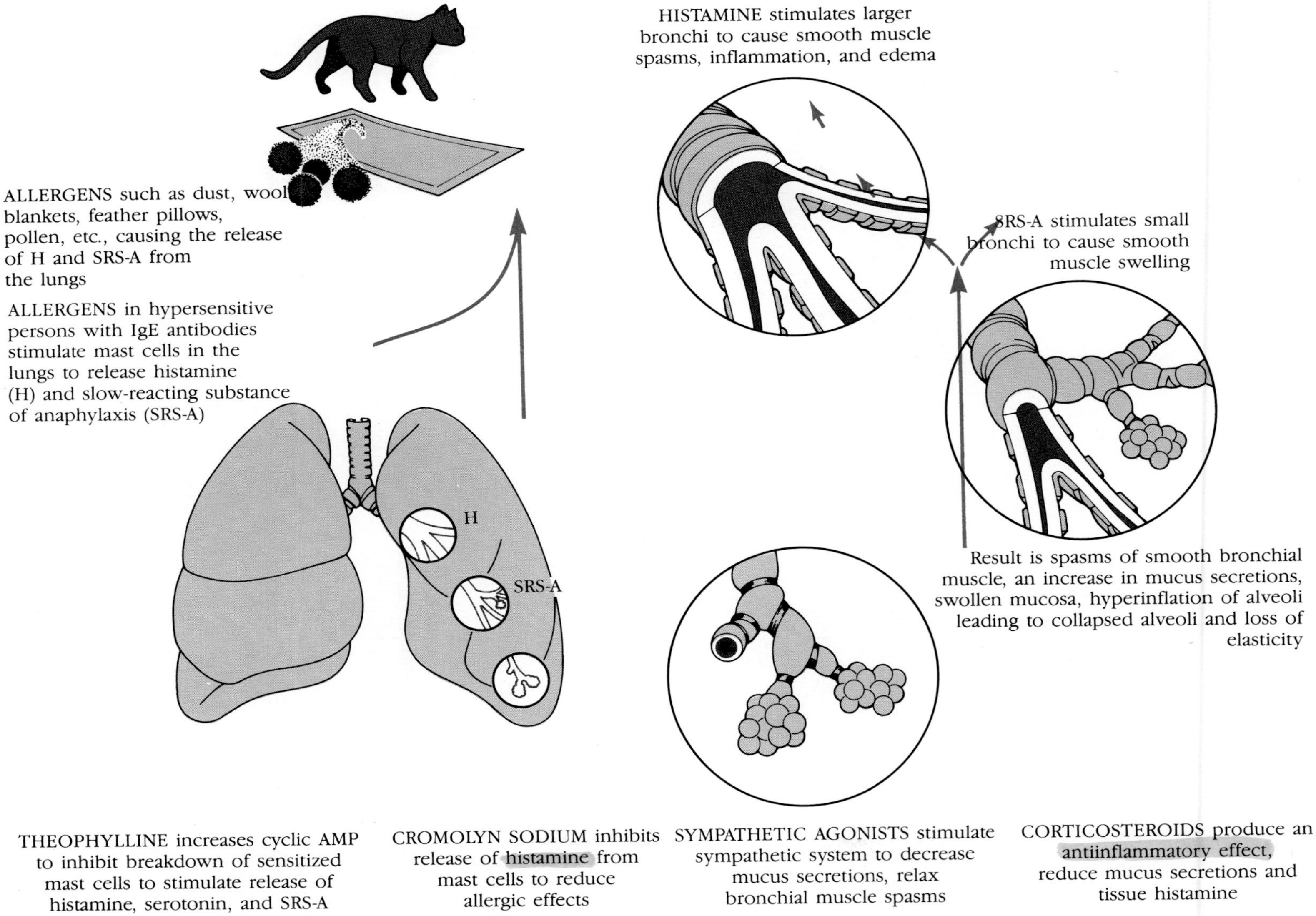

HISTAMINE stimulates larger bronchi to cause smooth muscle spasms, inflammation, and edema

SRS-A stimulates small bronchi to cause smooth muscle swelling

Result is spasms of smooth bronchial muscle, an increase in mucus secretions, swollen mucosa, hyperinflation of alveoli leading to collapsed alveoli and loss of elasticity

CORTICOSTEROIDS produce an antiinflammatory effect, reduce mucus secretions and tissue histamine

SYMPATHETIC AGONISTS stimulate sympathetic system to decrease mucus secretions, relax bronchial muscle spasms

ALLERGENS such as dust, wool blankets, feather pillows, pollen, etc., causing the release of H and SRS-A from the lungs

ALLERGENS in hypersensitive persons with IgE antibodies stimulate mast cells in the lungs to release histamine (H) and slow-reacting substance of anaphylaxis (SRS-A)

THEOPHYLLINE increases cyclic AMP to inhibit breakdown of sensitized mast cells to stimulate release of histamine, serotonin, and SRS-A

CROMOLYN SODIUM inhibits release of histamine from mast cells to reduce allergic effects

**FIGURE 37-2**  Overview of the effects of various antiasthmatic medications.

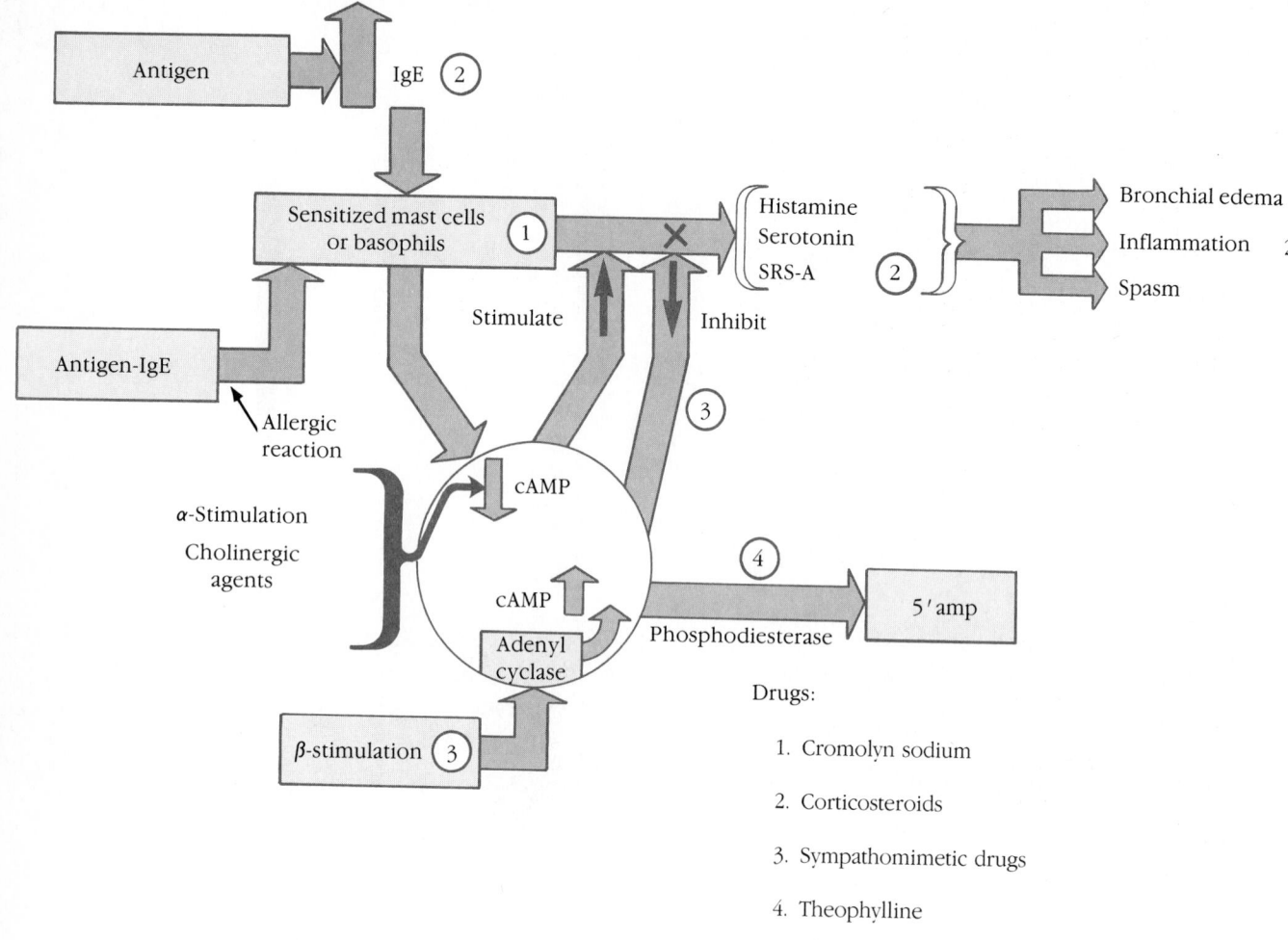

**FIGURE 37-3** Major sites of medication action of drugs used to treat asthma.

certain types of asthma. Most of these drugs enhance the production of cyclic 3'5' AMP in bronchial smooth muscle cells to affect bronchodilation. (See Figure 37-4.)

In the management of constricted airways the use of bronchodilator drugs includes the following therapeutic goals:

1. Maximal bronchial smooth muscle relaxation
2. Prolonged activity of the drug
3. Prevention of tachyphylaxis or development of tolerance to the beta-adrenergic agonsits
4. Production of minimal adverse adrenergic (sympathomimetic stimulation) effects or theophylline toxicity; close monitoring and supervision of client dosing should reduce this potential for adverse effects

## ▷NURSING MANAGEMENT: BRONCHODILATOR DRUG THERAPY

Bronchodilators are primarily indicated for the treatment of chronic pulmonary conditions, such as asthma, chronic bronchitis, and emphysema. As these diseases interfere with the basic human need for air, expect the client to exhibit

anxiety, not only during acute episodes but also in anticipation of such events. Besides providing supportive nursing care to bring respiration within the normal range for rate, depth, and effort during acute episodes, an important aspect of nursing management is to provide the clients information that enables them to maintain some measure of the control over what is happening to them and so decrease their anxiety. Education for clients receiving bronchodilators should be an integral part of their care and include instruction so that they will be able to state factors that tend to precipitate an acute episode; maintain a diary of symptoms and the time and dose of medications during attacks; explain their medication program; demonstrate how to take inhaled medications; describe what measures to take when an attack occurs; and state those signs and symptoms that need to be reported to the health care provider.

## SYMPATHOMIMETIC DRUGS

Based on their receptor action, three groups of sympathomimetic drugs are recognized: (1) nonselective adrenergic

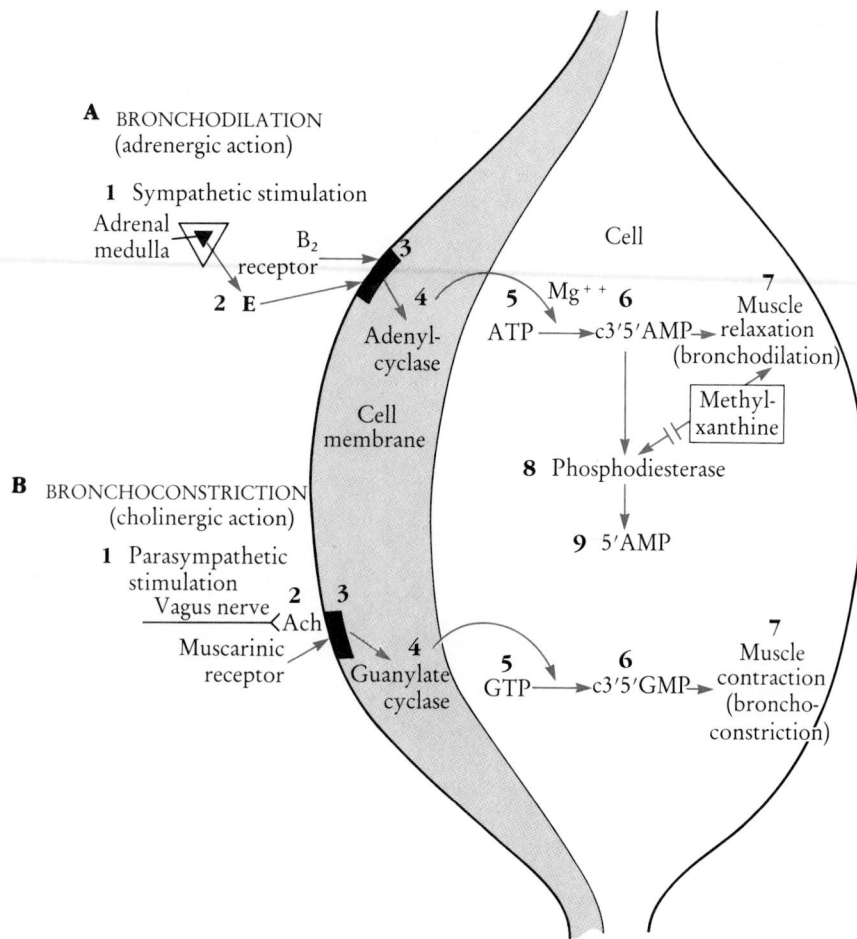

**FIGURE 37-4** Mechanism of bronchial smooth muscle action. **A,** Bronchodilation pathway. **B,** Bronchoconstriction pathway.

drugs that have alpha, beta$_1$ (cardiac), and beta$_2$ (respiratory) activities (e.g., epinephrine); (2) nonselective beta adrenergic drugs with both beta$_1$ and beta$_2$ effects (e.g., isoproterenol); and (3) selective beta$_2$ agents (e.g., albuterol) that act primarily on beta$_2$ receptors in the lungs (bronchial smooth muscle).

## Nonselective Adrenergic Drugs

Nonselective adrenergic drugs such as epinephrine, ephedrine, and others possess both alpha- and beta-receptor stimulating properties. Alpha activity appears to mediate vasoconstriction to reduce mucosal edema, while beta$_2$ stimulation increases the level of cyclic 3'5' AMP, producing bronchodilation and vasodilation. In contrast, beta$_1$ receptor action causes unwanted cardiac side effects such as increases in heart rate and force of myocardial contraction. Undesirable effects on beta$_2$ receptors include muscle tremors, glycogenolysis, and gluconeogenesis. These products may also cause an increase in CNS stimulation.

### epinephrine

For the various forms of epinephrine available, see the box on p. 632. Epinephrine acts as a bronchodilator that stimulates beta$_2$ receptors in the lungs, resulting in relaxation of bronchial smooth muscle and alleviates bronchospasm, increases vital capacity and reduces airway resistance. It also inhibits the release of histamine and slow-reacting substances released during anaphylaxis. Also the bronchial vasoconstrictor effects of histamine are antagonized.

Epinephrine is indicated for the treatment of bronchial asthma, bronchitis, and other pulmonary disease states and the prevention of bronchospasm and bronchial asthma. By inhalation, only slight absorption occurs; but if large doses of epinephrine are administered, systemic absorption can increase. Absorption is rapid by intramuscular or subcutaneous administration. The onset of action is within 3 to 5 minutes by inhalation, between 6 and 15 minutes by subcutaneous injection, and variable with an intramuscular injection. The duration of action is between 1 and 3 hours by inhalation or 1 and 4 hours by the parenteral routes. It is

Selected nursing diagnoses related to bronchodilators

| Nursing diagnosis | Outcome criteria | Nursing interventions |
|---|---|---|
| Airway clearance, ineffective, related to reversible airway obstruction | Coughs effectively and expectorates sputum<br>Absence of abnormal breath sounds<br><br>Normal sputum production<br><br>Fluid intake of at least 3000 ml/24 hours | Assess respiratory status every 4 hours<br>Assist client to turn, cough, and deep breathe as necessary<br>Provide adequate humidification as ordered<br>Monitor characteristics of sputum every 8 hours and record<br>Encourage fluids to at least 3000 ml daily |
| Activity intolerance related to reversible airway obstruction | Increasing level of activity<br>Pulse, respiration, and blood pressure remain within acceptable limits during activity | Plan with client for increasing levels of activity including activities that have priority for client<br>Identify and limit the factors that decrease the client's tolerance for activity<br>Monitor pulse rate, respiration, and blood pressure while increasing the level of activity |
| Knowledge deficit related to medication regimen | Client will describe underlying condition and how the drug relates to the condition, how and when to take the medication, common drug interactions, safety precautions, common side/adverse effects and which of those warrant reporting<br>Self-administer medication safely and accurately | Administer oral forms with food to minimize gastrointestinal distress<br>Emphasize the need for drug to be taken as prescribed around the clock<br>Caution the client not to self-administer any over-the-counter drugs without physician consultation<br>Advise the client to notify the physician if the usual dose fails to be therapeutic or if condition worsens after treatment<br>Instruct the client to minimize ingestion of foods and beverages containing xanthine (coffee, chocolate, colas)<br>Emphasize the need for ongoing contact with the physician for serum levels and evaluation |

---

### EPINEPHRINE: AVAILABLE FORMS

| Form | Trade name |
|---|---|
| epinephrine inhalation aerosol | Bronkaid Mist<br>Dysne-Inhal |
| epinephrine inhalation solution | Adrenalin |
| epinephrine bitartrate inhalation aerosol | AsthmaHaler<br>Bronkaid Mist Suspension |
| racepinephrine inhalation solution | AsthmaNefrin<br>Vaponefrin |

---

metabolized in the liver and at sympathetic nerve endings with a small amount of excretion in the kidneys.

Side effects most frequently reported are nervousness, insomnia, and tachycardia. The less frequently reported side effects include dizziness, headaches, hypotension, anorexia, nausea, a pounding tachycardia, sweating, vomiting, dry mouth and throat (especially with inhalation), and difficulty in urination. Rare adverse reactions observed are breathing difficulties and chest pain. In overdose, the following reactions may occur: blue discoloration of skin, chest pressure or pain, chills, elevated temperature, severe dizziness, hallucinations, severe hypertension, irregular heart rate, mood changes, severe headaches, convulsions, respiratory difficulties, tremors, increased anxiety, restlessness, visual changes, unusually fast or slow heart rate and increased weakness.

Many drug interactions have been reported with epinephrine. For example, when it is given concurrently with a corticosteroid (or other) inhaler that also contains a fluorocarbon propellant, fluorocarbon toxicity may result. Teach the client to allow at least a 5-minute interval between the use of such inhalants. Also alpha-adrenergic blocking agents (e.g., prazosin, tolazoline) or other medications with alpha-blocking properties (e.g., phenothiazines, haloperidol) or the fast-acting vasodilators (nitrites), may block the alpha-stimulating effects of epinephrine, which may result in severe hypotension and tachycardia. Monitor closely as medical interventions may be necessary. The vasodilator effects of nitrites may also be decreased with concurrent drug administration.

Concurrent use of epinephrine with anesthetics, such as chloroform, cyclopropane, and halothane, may increase the risk for severe arrhythmias. When used with local parenteral anesthetics for end artery extremities (such as fingers or toes), ischemia leading to gangrene may occur. If possible, avoid this usage. Tricyclic antidepressants or cocaine and epinephrine may increase the risk for cardiac arrhythmias, tachycardia, hypertension, and hyperpyrexia. It is suggested such combinations be avoided.

Beta-adrenergic blocking agents (oral, parenteral, and ophthalmic) may reduce the therapeutic effects of both agents. In addition the cardiovascular side effects (hypertension, bradycardia, and heart block) may be enhanced. Whenever possible, avoid concurrent administration. With the digitalis glycosides (digoxin, digitoxin), an increase in the risk for cardiac arrhythmias may occur. If concurrent therapy is necessary, monitor with an electrocardiogram. Ergotamine and the ergoloid mesylates may result in peripheral vascular ischemia, gangrene, or with ergotamine, severe hypertension. This drug combination should be avoided.

By inhalation, the adult dose is usually 10 drops of a 1% solution or a diluted racepinephrine solution (2.25%) in a nebulizer. Generally one inhalation of the former or 2 or 3 inhalations of the latter preparation is administered. Doses may be repeated at sufficient intervals as stated in the current package inserts or USP-DI. With the aerosol preparations, one inhalation is administered which, if necessary, may be repeated in 1 to 2 minutes. Subsequent doses, if necessary, are usually administered in 3 hours. Pediatric doses are individualized according to response, by the physician.

Pregnancy safety has been established at FDA category C.

Many other adrenergic bronchodilators are available, which include isoproterenol, isoetharine, albuterol, metaproterenol and terbutaline. In choosing a beta-receptor agonist, the beta$_2$ selectivity, potency, and duration of action of the drug are considered. The high incidence of undesirable cardiotoxic effects caused by the beta$_1$ property of sympathomimetic agents (nonselective agents) led to the search for a more specific beta$_2$ receptor agonist such as isoetharine and the noncatecholamine beta$_2$ receptor agonists, albuterol, metaproterenol, and terbutaline.

▷ **Nursing Management:**
  **Epinephrine Therapy**

The nursing management of clients receiving epinephrine is discussed in detail in Chapter 21, p. 404. This section should be consulted because the drug has far-reaching systemic effects. However, some interventions relate specifically to its administration by inhalation. Epinephrine and other beta adrenergic agents may be used interchangeably during inhalation therapy; allow 4 hours between doses when changing from one to another. Do not administer concurrently. Instruct the client in the use of the metered dose nebulizer (see box on p. 635). Teach the client to take pulse rate before inhalation therapy. Allow 2 minutes between doses, and do not administer more frequently than required to relieve symptoms, for excessive use may cause paradoxical bronchospasm. Symptoms should be relieved within 20 minutes. The prescriber should be notified if symptoms are not relieved with the usual dosage, since this may indicate a worsening of bronchospasm requiring reassessment of therapy. Advise the client to rinse mouth with

water to prevent mucosal absorption of the drug. In case of emergency the client should be taught to self-inject epinephrine subcutaneously.

## Nonselective Beta Adrenergic Drugs

Nonselective beta adrenergic drugs exhibit both beta$_1$ and beta$_2$ agonist activity. Their main action is on the bronchial smooth muscle, as well as the heart. Isoproterenol is the prototype example for this drug category.

### isoproterenol solution (Vapo-Iso,Isuprel) isoproterenol inhalation aerosol (Isuprel Mistometer)

Isoproterenol is indicated for the treatment of bronchial asthma, bronchitis, and other pulmonary disease states. By inhalation it has an onset of action within 2 to 5 minutes, sublingually within 15 to 30 minutes, and by intravenous injection, an immediate effect. Its duration of action is 0.5 to 2 hours by inhalation, 1 to 2 hours sublingually, and less than 1 hour by intravenous injection. It is metabolized in the liver, lungs, and other body tissues and excreted by the kidneys, the quantity depending on the route of administration. For example, about 40% to 50% is renally excreted if administered by IV; however, only 5% to 15% has renal excretion by inhalation.

The most frequently reported side effects are increased restlessness or anxiety, insomnia, pink or red colored saliva, and a dry mouth or throat after inhalation usage. Less frequent side effects are dizziness, flushing of the skin, headache, tremors, palpitations, sweating, tachycardia, weakness, vomiting, hyper- or hypotension.

Adverse reactions rarely seen include chest pain and an irregular heart rate. In overdose, the adverse effects are similar to epinephrine with the exception of a blue discoloration of the skin, hallucinations, mood changes, respiratory difficulties, visual disturbances, bradycardia, and pallor.

Significant drug interactions are similar to those of epinephrine, except for the interactions noted with parenteral local anesthetics, alpha-blocking agents, and the ergoloid mesylates or ergotamine, since isoproterenol does not have alpha effects.

Adult bronchodilator dose for the inhalation solution is 6 to 12 inhalations of a 0.25% nebulized solution that may be repeated at 15-minute intervals, if needed, for three doses. The maximum number of treatments recommended in a 24-hour period is eight. In an acute asthmatic attack, 5 to 15 deep inhalations of a 0.5% nebulized solution or three to seven inhalations of 1% nebulized solution are administered. It may be repeated once after 5 to 10 minutes, if needed. Up to 5 subsequent doses per day may be administered, if necessary. For bronchospasm in chronic obstructive lung disease (COPD), a nebulizer of IPPB drug administration may be used. Pediatric dose recommendations are similar to an adult with the exception of using the 1% solution. It is recommended that one inhalation of iso-proterenol aerosol may be repeated in 2 to 5 minutes if necessary, up to four to six times per day.

Isoproterenol injection is used intravenously as a bron-chodilator for bronchospasm during anesthesia at a dose of 10 to 20 μg. If necessary, the dose may be repeated. It is also used intracardially, intramuscularly, intravenously, sub-cutaneously, and by intravenous infusion for the treatment of cardiac arrhythmias and cardiac standstill. It is also in-dicated for shock syndrome (hyperperfusion syndrome), ad-ministered in an intravenous infusion. For exact dosage rec-ommendations, check a current package insert or USP-DI.

Pregnancy safety has been established at FDA category C.

▷ **Nursing Management:**
**Isoproterenol Therapy**

The nursing management of clients receiving isoproter-enol is discussed in detail in Chapter 21, p. 409. This section should be consulted because the drug has both bronchodi-lating and cardiotonic effects. However, some interventions relate specifically to its administration by inhalation. Instruct the client to use the nebulizer correctly (see box on p. 635). The instructions for the metered powder nebulizer are the same as for the metered dose nebulizer except that deep inhalation is not necessary. The client should allow 1 to 5 minutes between first and second inhalations. Advise the client that there should be no more than 6 inhalations in any 24-hour period. If three are needed within a 24-hour period, the prescriber should be notified. This may indicate that other medications may need to be added to the therapeutic regimen. Advise the client that sputum and saliva may turn pink with use of the drug. Isoproterenol needs to be stored in a tight, light-resistant container and is not to be used if a precipitate or discoloration occurs.

## Selective Beta₂ Receptor Drugs

*Catecholamine Beta₂ Receptor Agents*
  **isoetharine inhalation solution (Bronkosol,**
  **Disorine)**
  **isoetharine mesylate inhalation aerosol**
  **(Bronkometer)**

Isoetharine is a direct-acting sympathomimetic catechol-amine that selectively stimulates beta₂ receptors. Since it possesses a weak beta₁ response, less risk of cardiotonic side effects exists than is experienced with epinephrine and isoproterenol. Its beta₂ adrenergic-receptor activity relaxes bronchial smooth muscle, thereby relieving bronchospasm, increasing vital capacity, and decreasing resistance of bron-chial airways. It may also inhibit antigen-induced release of histamine by stimulating the production of cyclic 3'5' AMP, which stabilizes the mast cell.

Isoetharine has the same indications as epinephrine. This drug has an onset of action with 1 to 6 minutes and a peak effect between 15 to 60 minutes. Its duration of action is 1 to 4 hours. It is metabolized in the liver, lungs, gastroin-testinal tract and other body tissues and is excreted by the kidneys. The less frequent side effects reported with iso-etharine include dizziness, headaches, dry mouth, and a bad taste in the mouth or throat following the inhalation product. Also nausea, increased anxiety, palpitations, tremors, in-somnia, tachycardia, weakness, and vomiting have been reported. Adverse reactions such as breathing difficulties are rare. Overdose effects are the same as isoproterenol with the exception of an irregular heart rate. For significant drug interactions see isoproterenol.

Adult bronchodilator dose with a hand nebulizer is four inhalations of an undiluted 0.5% or 1% solution, usually administered every 4 hours. For intermittent positive pres-sure breathing (IPPB) or oxygen aerosolization dosage, see current package insert or USP-DI. Dosage in children has not been established.

Pregnancy safety has been established at FDA category C.

▷ **Nursing Management:**
**Isoetharine Therapy**

***Assessment.*** Determine initially if the client has a preexisting condition in which the drug is used with caution: cardiovascular disease, such as hypertension, coronary ar-tery disease, limited cardiac reserve; hyperthryoidism; or pheochromocytoma.

With the administration of isoetharine, the following nursing diagnoses should be considered for the client: altered comfort related to dryness of the mouth and throat, head-ache, nausea, nervousness, trembling, and palpitations; al-tered sleep pattern (insomnia); and ineffective airway clear-ance related to paradoxical bronchospasm (increase in wheezing and difficulty breathing).

***Intervention.*** Isoetharine may be administered by hand nebulizer, IPPB, and oxygen aerosolization. The use of IPPB is currently limited as a method of aerosol deposition. However, it is a convenient procedure for helping clients with airway obstruction to breathe deeply. The disadvantage is that the amount of drug lost in the room air and the apparatus is approximately 40% to 65%, and the amount of drug deposited in the lower airways is about 5% to 15%. IPPB is generally administered by the respiratory therapist.

***Education.*** Instruct client in the use of the nebulizer. See client education box on p. 635. Warn client to avoid contact of spray with eyes and to rinse mouth after therapy to prevent dryness and throat irritation.

Advise client to use inhalation therapy as prescribed since rapid relief encourages overuse. Thus tolerance to a bron-chodilator agent may occur, with a potential for causing cumulative drug toxicity (e.g., palpitations, tachycardia, headache, dizziness, and nausea). Repeated use may cause paradoxical airway resistance, which produces sudden dys-

## CLIENT EDUCATION: USING AN INHALER

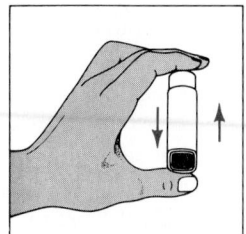

1. Instruct the client to fully insert canister into the plastic shell, remove cap from the mouthpiece, and shake unit as illustrated.

4. Hold breath and inhale as long as possible for the spray to penetrate deeply in the lungs.

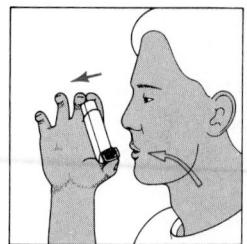

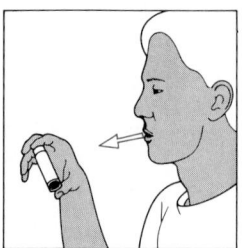

2. Client must exhale fully (until no more air can be expelled).

5. Release pressure on top of canister, remove inhaler, and breathe slowly. Wait at least 1 full minute before administering the second puff. Repeat previous instructions.

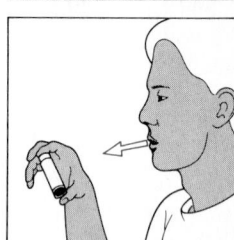

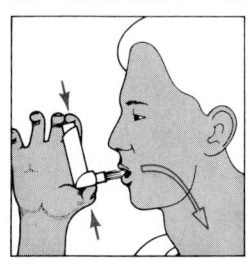

3. The mouthpiece of the unit must be placed over the tongue in the mouth. The client should be instructed to close his or her lips tightly around the mouthpiece, then to press the top of the canister firmly (note position of forefinger and thumb), and, at the same time, inhale deeply through the mouth.

---

pnea. To relieve possible bronchospasm, the physician may discontinue therapy and have epinephrine available. Instruct client to take no more than two inhalations at a time and to allow 1 to 2 minutes between inhalations. Also, encourage client to increase fluid intake to aid in liquefying bronchial secretions. Inform client that sputum may be rust-colored because of oxidation of medication.

### Noncatecholamine Beta₂ Receptor Drugs

Noncatecholamine drugs have two advantages when compared to the catecholamine type agents: they are longer acting and they have fewer cardiovascular side effects.

#### albuterol inhalation aerosol, syrup, tablets (Proventil, Ventolin, Novosalmol ✲) albuterol inhalation solution (Ventolin)

Albuterol is a sympathomimetic bronchodilator. It possesses a relatively selective specificity for beta₂ adrenergic receptors in the lungs and therefore is less likely to cause unwanted cardiovascular effects. Its interaction with the beta₂ receptor in the cell membrane of the bronchial smooth muscle stimulates the enzyme adenyl cyclase, which is also located in the membrane, to produce cyclic 3′5′ AMP. The cyclic AMP thus formed mediates a response that is capable of relaxing the smooth muscle of the bronchi (see Figure 37-4), thus relieving bronchospasms and decreasing airway resistance. In addition, this mechanism causes relaxation of the smooth muscle of the uterus and blood vessels of the skeletal muscle. However, it has been reported that high doses of the drug administered intravenously would be required to inhibit uterine contractions to delay premature labor. This drug has the same indications as epinephrine.

By inhalation, albuterol has an onset of action between 5 and 15 minutes, peak effect in 1 to 1 ½ hours after two inhalations, and a duration of action of 3 to 6 hours. Orally, its onset of action is between 15 and 30 minutes, peak effect in 2 to 3 hours, and duration of action of 8 hours or more (12 hours for the sustained-release dosage form.) The drug is metabolized in the liver and excreted by the kidneys and in feces.

The most frequently reported side effects are nausea, increased anxiety, pounding heart rate, tremors, and tachycardia. Less frequently seen effects include sedation, difficulty in urination, dizziness, headaches, heartburn, cramping of muscles, insomnia, increased sweating, vomiting, increased weakness, hypotension or hypertension, and an unusual taste in the mouth. Rarely reported adverse effects are breathing difficulties and chest pain. Overdose reactions are similar to those of isoproterenol, with the exception of an irregular heart rate and weakness.

Significant drug interactions are similar to those of iso-proterenol, except for the interactions noted with alpha adrenergic blocking agents, ergoloid mesylate, and ergotamine. Albuterol also has a significant drug interaction with MAO inhibitors, that is, the effects of albuterol on the vascular system may be enhanced.

The adult bronchodilator dose for inhalation is 200 to 400 µg every 4 to 6 hours. Tablet dosage is 2 to 6 mg orally, three or four times daily. Dose may be increased up to 8 mg four times daily, if necessary. Extended-release tablets are dosed at 4 or 8 mg orally, every 12 hours. The pediatric doses for inhalation and extended-release tablets have not been established for children under 12 years old. See package insert for children's dosing schedule. Pregnancy safety has been established at FDA category C.

▷ **Nursing Management:
Albuterol Therapy**

***Assessment.*** Initially clients should be assessed for a previous intolerance to other sympathomimetic agents, since this may indicate an intolerance to albuterol. Albuterol should be used with caution in clients having coronary insufficiency, hypertension, or pheochromocytoma. Clients with diabetes mellitus may need an increased dosage of insulin when receiving albuterol. Clients with hyperthyroidism may have an exaggerated response to albuterol. Elderly clients are more susceptible to the drug's effects and usually require lower dosages.

With the administration of albuterol, the client should be assessed for the following nursing diagnoses: altered comfort related to dryness of the mouth and throat, coughing, flushing of the face and increased sweating, nausea and vomiting, heartburn, headache, weakness, muscle cramps, nervousness, trembling, and palpitations; altered sleep patterns (drowsiness or insomnia); and the risk for paradoxical bronchospasm.

***Intervention.*** A mouthpiece or a face mask may be used to administer the inhalation solution through a nebulizer. The nebulizer may be used with compressed air or oxygen, 6 to 10 liters per minute. An average treatment lasts about 10 minutes.

***Education.*** The client should be taught the correct use of the inhaler. Inform client that after long-term use, drug may have a shorter duration of action (1 to 2 hours). Report to physician failure to respond to usual dose, which may mean the development of drug tolerance. This may stimulate adverse effects such as cardiac arrest. Advise client to rinse mouth after inhalation therapy to prevent dryness, throat irritation, and systemic absorption. If a bad taste occurs, it will gradually disappear with repeated usage.

Warn client that excessive use of aerosol may be harmful, causing paradoxical (rebound) bronchospasm, which means that the effects of the drug are no longer therapeutic. Stress the importance of not changing dosage or frequency without consulting physician. Chest pain, extreme dizziness and lightheadedness, severe headache, palpitations, continuing tachycardia, dysrhythmias and hypertensive episodes should be reported to the physician.

***Evaluation.*** Signs of the client's anxiety should decrease as breathing becomes more effective. Wheezing, if present, should also decrease. Signs of respiratory distress such as increased effort to breathe, increased use of accessory muscles, contraction of the abdominal muscles on expiration, and diaphoresis will decrease as the medication becomes effective. The client will respond subjectively if relief from the respiratory distress is felt.

### metaproterenol inhalation aerosol, solution, syrup, and tablets (Alupent, Metaprel)

The mechanism of action for metaproterenol is the same as for albuterol, while its indications are the same as epinephrine's. Metaproterenol by inhalation has an onset of action within 1 minute, a peak effect in 1 hour, and a duration of action of 1 to 5 hours after a single dose. Orally its onset of action is within 15 to 30 minutes, its peak effect occurs in an hour, and duration of action is up to 4 hours. It is metabolized in the liver and excreted in the kidneys.

The most frequent side effects associated with its usage are increased anxiety and restlessness. Less frequently reported are dizziness, headaches, hypertension, muscle cramps, nausea, vomiting, palpitations, tremors, sweating, tachycardia, and weakness. Respiratory difficulties are a rare adverse reaction seen with this drug. Overdose adverse reactions are the same as for isoproterenol.

Significant drug interactions are similar to those of albuterol, with the exception of the tricyclic antidepressants and MAO inhibitors. Adult bronchodilator dose by inhalation is 1.3 to 2.25 mg (two or three inhalations) every 3 to 4 hours. Do not exceed 9 mg (12 inhalations) in 24 hours. The oral dose is 20 mg three or four times daily. For children under 6 years, dosage is not established. Children 6 to 9 years old that weigh up to 27 kg, the oral dose is 10 mg three or four times daily. Children over 9 years old or weighing 27 kg and over, apply the adult dosage scale.

Pregnancy has been established at FDA Category C.

For nursing management, see discussion under albuterol, this page.

### terbutaline inhalation aerosol (Brethaire)
### terbutaline tablets and injection (Brethine, Bricanyl)

Mechanism of action is similar to albuterol and indications are the same as epinephrine. Its onset of action by inhalation is within 5 to 30 minutes, peak effect in 1 to 2 hours, and duration of action in 3 to 6 hours. Orally its onset of action is within 1 to 2 hours, peak effect in 2 to 3 hours, and duration of action in 4 to 8 hours. Parenterally, its onset of action is within 15 minutes, peak effect in 0.5 to 1 hour, and duration of action in 1.5 to 4 hours. It is metabolized in the liver and excreted in the kidneys.

The most frequently reported side effects are tremors and increased anxiety or restlessness. Less frequently seen are dizziness, sedation, headaches, hypertension, muscle cramps, nausea, vomiting, palpitations, insomnia, sweating, tachycardia, increased weakness, dry mouth or throat, and an unusual taste in the mouth. Rare adverse reactions include chest pain and an increase in respiratory difficulties. Overdose effects are the same as isoetharine with the addition of severe nausea or vomiting.

Adult bronchodilator dose is one to two inhalations (200-500 μg), the second inhalation separated by at least 1 minute, every 4 to 6 hours. Orally a 2.5 to 5 mg tablet three times daily at 6-hour intervals is recommended. For children 12 to 15 years, 2.5 mg orally 3 times a day. Parenterally, a 250 μg subcutaneous dose is administered, which may be repeated in 15 to 30 minutes. A total dose of 500 μg is maximum in a 4-hour period.

Pregnancy safety is established at FDA Category B.

For nursing management information, see discussion under albuterol, p. 636.

## XANTHINE DERIVATIVES

The xanthine group of drugs includes caffeine, theophylline, and theobromine. Beverages from the extracts of plants containing these alkaloids have been used by humans since ancient times. **Xanthine derivatives** relax smooth muscle, particularly bronchial muscle, stimulate cardiac muscle and the central nervous system, and also produce diuresis, probably through a combined action of increased renal perfusion and increased sodium and chloride ion excretion.

The drugs in this category are methylated forms of xanthines and referred to as methylxanthines. The effectiveness of these preparations as bronchodilators depends on their conversion to theophylline, which is the active constituent. Therefore with the exception of dyphylline, the action of xanthine depends on the content of theophylline. Xanthines inhibit mast cell degranulation and the release of histamine and other mediators that are responsible for bronchoconstriction. Because they impede enzymatic action, the methylxanthines are also called phosphodiesterase inhibitors (see Figure 37-2).

Combinations of theophylline with iodides (Elixophyllin KI and others) and with ephedrine (Tedral and others) are not considered rational formulations (Hendeles and Weinberger, 1982), since the reported increase in toxicity is not balanced or offset by an increased therapeutic effect. Therefore, these products should be avoided because they do not offer an increase in beneficial effects.

Theophylline products, especially slow-release products, can vary in their rate of absorption and therapeutic effects. Some states, such as Florida, do not permit generic substitution for theophylline products.

Theophylline toxicity at levels above 20 μg/ml presents with different signs and symptoms. See Table 37-1 for reported side effects and adverse reactions. Also, dosage ad-

---

### FACTORS AFFECTING THEOPHYLLINE'S THERAPEUTIC EFFECTS

**May be Increased by:**

*Age:* elderly and newborn
*Drugs:* erythromycin, cimetidine, and oral contraceptives
*Disease states:* cirrhosis, pulmonary edema, congestive heart failure, and severe COPD
*Diet:* high carbohydrate

**May be Decreased by:**

*Substances:* tobacco, marijuana
*Drugs:* corticosteroids (inconclusive data), phenobarbital
*Diet:* high protein
*Age:* adolescence

---

justment with theophylline is necessary under certain conditions. The box lists some of the factors affecting theophylline's therapeutic effects.

**aminophylline (Aminophyllin, Palaron ✱)**
**dyphylline (Dilor, Lufyllin, Protophylline ✱)**
**oxtriphylline (Choledyl, Apo-Oxtriphylline ✱)**
**theophylline (Bronkodyl, Elixophyllin, and others)**

Theophylline is the prototype of the xanthine derivatives. It competitively inhibits the action of phosphodiesterase, the enzyme that degrades cyclic 3'5' AMP to the inactive form 5' AMP. Thus the resulting inhibition increases the level of intracellular cyclic 3'5' AMP, which mediates pharmacologic action such as relaxation of smooth muscle of bronchial airways and pulmonary blood vessels. This produces a reversal of bronchospasm and increases respiratory flow rates and vital capacity. (See Figure 37-4.)

These drugs are used for the treatment and prevention of bronchial asthma; treatment of bronchitis, pulmonary emphysema, and other chronic obstructive pulmonary diseases.

Orally liquids and uncoated tablets of aminophylline, oxtriphylline, and theophylline are rapidly absorbed while enteric-coated tablets have a delayed and, at times, an unreliable absorption pattern. Extended-release dosage forms are slowly absorbed with some forms having complete absorption while others are unreliable. The retention enema is rapidly absorbed, whereas rectal suppositories are slow and unreliable. Dyphylline has good oral absorption. The time to peak levels with aminophylline, oxtriphylline, and theophylline is 1 hour with the oral solution, 2 hours with the uncoated tablets, 1 to 1.5 hours with chewable tablets, 5 hours with enteric coated tablets, 4 to 7 hours for extended-release capsules/ tablets, and 1 to 2 hours for the retention enema. Dyphylline reaches peak levels within 1 hour.

The half-life of aminophylline, oxtriphylline, and the-

**TABLE 37-1**  Side effects/adverse reactions of mucokinetic and bronchodilator drugs

| Drug(s) | Side effects* | Adverse reactions† |
|---|---|---|
| xanthine derivatives (aminophylline, dyphylline, and theophylline) | Most frequent: nausea, increased anxiety or restlessness<br>Less frequent: rectal irritation with rectal dosage form only | Less frequent: gastric upset, vomiting<br>Rare: rash or hives that usually occur 12 to 24 hours after administration of aminophylline (thought to be a result of ethylenediamine in aminophylline)<br>Injectable aminophylline or theophylline, if given too fast IV: dizziness, tension, red skin or flushing, headaches, pounding heart rate, chest pain, and rapid breathing<br>Overdosage or toxicity: levels above 20 $\mu$g/ml usually result in behavior changes, insomnia, headaches, flushing, dizziness, increased irritability, anorexia, severe nausea or vomiting, convulsions, abdominal cramping or pain, fast breathing, irregular heart rate, increased weakness, black stools or blood in stools or vomiting of dark material (dry blood) or blood, increased urgency for urination |
| cromolyn sodium (Intal, Fivent ✿) | Most frequent: hoarseness, cough<br>Less frequent: dry mouth or throat, nasal congestion, sneezing, irritated throat, eye watering, bad taste in mouth from inhalation device | Less frequent: pain on urination, difficulty urinating, dizziness, severe headache, increased wheezing, pain or weak muscles or joints, nausea or vomiting, rash, hives, edema of lips and eyes, chest pressure, breathing difficulties, difficulty in swallowing |
| beclomethasone dipropionate (Vanceril, Beclovent) and other corticosteroids: dexamethasone, flunisolide, and triamcinolone | Most frequent: flunisolide: tachycardia, gastrointestinal distress, anorexia, cough without infection, dizziness, headaches, unpleasant taste in mouth; dexamethasone: gastrointestinal distress<br>Less frequent/rare: cough without infection, dry nose or oral cavity, hoarseness; dexamethasone: insomnia, increased anxiety, increased appetite, and euphoria or false sense of well-being; flunisolide: feeling ill, shaky, or faint, increased appetite, and insomnia | Most frequent: oral fungal infection (candidiasis); dexamethasone and flunisolide: increased potential for developing infections<br>Reported with flunisolide: development of respiratory tract infections, pruritis, rash, nausea, vomiting, respiratory difficulties, menstrual irregularities |

*If side effects continue, increase, or disturb the client, inform the physician.
†If adverse reactions occur, contact physician since medical intervention may be necessary.

ophylline in newborns up to 6 months old is greater than 24 hours; children over 6 months, 2.6 to 4.8 hours; an adult nonsmoker with uncomplicated asthma, 6.5 to 10.9 hours. In smokers of one to two packs of cigarettes per day, the half-life is shorter—4 to 5 hours. If the client stops smoking, the normal pharmacokinetics for theophylline may not appear for 3 months to 24 months. In elderly clients with chronic obstructive pulmonary disease, cor pulmonale, or other forms of heart failure and liver dysfunction, the half-life is in excess of 24 hours. With dyphylline the half-life is 2 to 2.5 hours.

Aminophylline, oxtriphylline, and theophylline salts all release free theophylline in vivo. Theophylline is metabolized by the liver to caffeine. Caffeine concentrations may average about 30% of the theophylline concentration, but in neonates it may be much greater than that. Caffeine does not accumulate in adults. Dyphylline is not metabolized.

The therapeutic serum levels for bronchodilator effects with theophylline are usually stated to be between 10 and 20 $\mu$g/ml. Some studies, though, have indicated that therapeutic response may be seen at the 5 to 10 $\mu$g serum level while in some clients, toxicity is noted in the 15 to 20 $\mu$g/ml range. Therefore close supervision with dosage adjustments according to client's therapeutic response or the presence of toxic effects, is necessary. Dyphylline serum level is not established. As a respiratory stimulant, theophylline serum level is between 5 and 10 $\mu$g/ml. Excretion is via the kidneys. For side effects/adverse reactions, see Table 37-1.

***Significant drug interactions.***  When xanthine products are given with phenytoin, primidone, or rifampin, increased metabolism of xanthines occurs. Decreased absorption of phenytoin, leading to low serum levels, may be seen with concurrent administration. Serum levels of both drugs

**TABLE 37-2** Dosage and administration of xanthine derivatives

| Drug | Dosage |
|---|---|
| aminophylline injection | Adult dose in an acute attack for persons not receiving theophylline: IV infusion of the equivalent of 5 mg of anhydrous theophylline/kg administered over 20 min. If person was receiving theophylline, then obtain a serum level and dose according to theophylline instructions below. For specific instructions on maintenance, children's doses, etc., see a current package insert |
| theophylline oral, (tablets, liquids) | Adult dosing in an acute attack for persons not receiving theophylline: 5 to 6 mg/kg. If client is receiving a theophylline product, obtain a theophylline serum level and dose appropriately. (Each 0.5 mg of theophylline/kg of lean body weight will produce a 1 μg/ml increase [range 0.5 to 1.6 μg] in serum theophylline.) If unable to wait for the results of a serum theophylline level because of the client's urgent need for therapy, 2.5 mg/kg of anhydrous theophylline may be administered if no symptoms of theophylline toxicity are present. Additional dosages are given according to serum theophylline level reports<br>Maintenance in an acute attack:<br>  Smokers, young adults—4 mg/kg of anhydrous theophylline every 6 hr<br>  Elderly individuals, clients with cor pulmonale, congestive heart failure, or liver impairment—2 mg/kg anhydrous theophylline every 12 hr; not to exceed 400 mg anhydrous theophylline every 24 hr<br>  Healthy, nonsmoking adults—3 mg/kg anhydrous theophylline every 8 hr<br>Long-term therapy: 6 to 8 mg/kg of anhydrous theophylline up to a 400 mg/day maximum, given in three or four divided doses. Increase the dose 25% every two or three days up to a maximum dose of 13 mg/kg or 900 mg daily. If the maximum dosage is to be continued or exceeded, monitor closely with serum theophylline levels<br>*Children*<br>Acute attack, loading dose for children (up to 16 years old) not receiving theophylline: give 5 to 6 mg/kg of anhydrous theophylline orally. If child is receiving theophylline, then follow theophylline instructions for an adult<br>For maintenance in an acute attack and chronic therapy, refer to current package insert or USP-DI |
| dyphylline elixir, oral solution, and tablets | 15 mg/kg orally every 6 hr, up to four times daily<br>Children—must be individualized by physician |
| dyphylline extended-release tablets | 400 mg orally every 8 hr<br>Children—not established |
| dyphylline injection | 500 mg IM initially, followed by 250 to 500 mg every 2 to 6 hr as indicated; maximum is 15 mg/kg every 6 hr<br>Children—must be individualized by physician |
| oxtriphylline elixir, syrup, tablet | See theophylline |

should be closely monitored, since dosage adjustments may be necessary.

When these products are given with beta-adrenergic blocking agents, therapeutic effects of both drugs may be inhibited. Concurrent use may also decrease theophylline excretion. Monitor closely as dosage adjustments may be necessary.

When these agents are given with cimetidine, ranitidine, erythromycin, or troleandomycin, they may decrease theophylline metabolism resulting in elevated serum levels of theophylline and possible toxicity. Monitor closely as dosage adjustments may be necessary.

When xanthine products are given to clients who smoke tobacco or marijuana, the metabolism of theophylline may increase, which may result in low serum theophylline levels. Dosage adjustments of 50% to 100% greater dosage has been required in smokers.

***Dosage and administration.*** The dosage for clients receiving theophylline preparations must be tailored to the medical circumstances in each case and in selected individuals must be monitored by measurement of serum theophylline concentration. *The usual efficacy of a theophylline preparation depends on the attainment of a serum concentration of 10 to 20 μg/ml* (see previous comments on serum levels). The rapid intravenous administration of theophylline and its derivatives has caused severe and even fatal acute circulatory failure; therefore the drug should be administered slowly. (See Table 37-2 for the individual preparations and dosages of the various xanthine derivatives.) Since theophylline has a low therapeutic index, using caution when determining the dosage is essential. Also, specific dyphylline serum levels may be used to maintain therapy because serum theophylline levels will *not* measure dyphylline.

Hemoperfusion with resin or activated charcoal is now

used in the treatment of theophylline overdosage. It is indicated for individuals who develop a plasma theophylline level greater than 60 $\mu$g/ml within 4 hours following drug administration. In addition, it may be used for individuals with such risk factors as age (60 years or older), congestive heart failure, liver disease, theophylline half-life value of 24 hours, and a plasma theophylline concentration range of 30 to 50 $\mu$g/ml. Since these high-risk clients tend to clear the drug slowly from the body, they require immediate hemoperfusion before any seizures develop. The bronchodilator effect of the xanthines depends on the theophylline concentration. The various xanthine preparations contain the following:

| Drug | Percent of Anhydrous Theophylline Present |
| --- | --- |
| aminophylline anhydrous | 86 |
| aminophylline dihydrate | 79 |
| oxtriphylline | 64 |
| theophylline monohydrate | 91 |
| theophylline sodium glycinate | 49 |
| dyphylline | 0 |

**Pregnancy safety.** Aminophylline, oxtriphylline, theophylline, and dyphylline—FDA category C.

## ▷NURSING MANAGEMENT: XANTHINE DERIVATIVE THERAPY

**Assessment.** Use with caution in individuals with a history of peptic ulcers, since theophylline products may cause local gastrointestinal irritation. This condition can be aggravated when the serum theophylline level exceeds 20 $\mu$g/ml. Exercise great caution in clients with severe cardiac disease, acute myocardial injury, cardiac dysrhythmias, congestive heart failure, or cor pulmonale, since circulatory impairment may cause very slow serum theophylline clearance. Also, individuals with severe hypoxemia, hypertension, hyperthyroidism, prostatic hypertrophy, diabetes mellitus, and renal and hepatic disease require cautious use of xanthines. In addition, use caution with young children and the elderly.

During pregnancy theophylline crosses the placenta; since teratogenic effects have been demonstrated in mice, the risk benefit to the fetus and mother must be considered. Also, dangerous levels of caffeine concentration in the neonate may occur, since the newborn is unable to metabolize this compound. The xanthines are excreted in breast milk, and toxicity may be exhibited by the neonate: tachycardia, jitteriness, irritability, gagging, and vomiting.

Smoking 1 to 2 packs a day decreases the serum half-life of theophylline and, consequently, smokers require larger doses of xanthines than nonsmokers. This effect may persist for months to years, even after the person has stopped smoking.

Xanthines are contraindicated in individuals with hypersensitivity to any of its components.

With the administration of the xanthine derivatives, the client should be assessed for the following nursing diagnoses: high risk for aspiration related to the drug's ability to induce gastroesophageal reflux in those clients who may have impaired gag reflex, infants under 2, and elderly, debilitated, or stuporous clients; altered comfort related to flushing of the face, headache, nausea, nervousness, and palpitations; high risk for injury related to allergic reaction and drug toxicity; and altered mucous membranes (rectal irritation with rectal dosage forms of the drug).

**Intervention.** Be aware of the following intravenous admixture incompatibilities:
- Do not mix theophylline in a syringe with other drugs; add it separately to the intravenous solution.
- When administering "piggyback," turn off the other intravenous solution already in place while giving drug.
- Do not mix with alkali-labile drugs such as epinephrine, norepinephrine, isoproterenol, or penicillin G.

Administer oral dosage on an empty stomach to promote faster absorption; to lessen local gastrointestinal irritation, give the drug with food. For chewable tablet form, client should chew tablets before swallowing; for enteric-coated tablet form, client should swallow tablet whole without crushing, breaking, or chewing; for extended-release form, client should swallow tablet or capsule whole without breaking, crushing, or chewing. Also, contents of capsule may be mixed with 1 teaspoon of jelly, jam, or applesauce if too large to swallow.

To enhance absorption, schedule administration of rectal preparations when rectum is free of feces. Have client remain in recumbent position for 15 to 20 minutes. Administer before meal to enhance retention. Rectal suppositories are irritating to tissues, and absorption is unreliable. Although rectal retention enema provides rapid and more reliable absorption, it should be used only if client is unable to take oral preparations. Rectal preparations are also contraindicated if irritation or infection of the rectum or lower colon is present. If enemas are used, they should not be administered for more than 24 to 36 hours because of the irritating effect of the alkaline solution on the bowel wall.

Store medication in a tightly closed container at room temperature. Also follow manufacturer's directions regarding storage of suppositories, since some are stored at room temperature and others refrigerated.

**Education.** Caution client not to take over-the-counter remedies that contain ephedrine or other sympathomimetics for treatment of asthma or cough. Instruct individual to limit intake of xanthine-containing beverages, namely, coffee, tea, cocoa, and cola beverages. Also inform client to limit charcoal-broiled foods because charcoal increases theophylline elimination.

Warn elderly clients of possible dizziness during therapy and to take necessary precautions for safety.

If the client is taking the extended-release form of the drug, advise against changing brands unless prescribed by the physician, since the various brands may not be bioequivalent.

The client should notify the physician of any fever, flu-like symptoms, or diarrhea as the prescribed dosage may need to be changed. Advise client to keep physician and laboratory appointments to check progress of therapy.

*Evaluation.* Anticipate adverse effects if serum theophylline level exceeds the normal serum therapeutic range of 10 to 20 µg/ml. Because of the variation in the metabolism of xanthines, constant monitoring of serum theophylline concentration and client response will prevent toxicity.

Be sure that intravenous administration is given slowly with volumeter infusion pump. Monitor vital signs and observe client for signs of toxicity such as hypotension, tachycardia, ventricular dysrhythmias, or convulsions. There may not be early, less severe signs of toxicity. Have available oxygen, respirator, and IV diazepam (for convulsions). Maintain airway, hydration, and normal temperature by tepid water sponges or hypothermic blanket for hyperpyrexia. Unconscious client may require gastric lavage. Serum levels taken immediately before the next dose (trough concentrations) tend to be more consistent than peak serum levels. Accomplish pulmonary studies to assess the client's progress on the drug. Intake and output should also be monitored.

Observe children closely because they are more susceptible than adults to CNS effects (nervousness, restlessness, insomnia, hyperactive reflexes, twitching, and convulsions).

Monitor client during a change from one route of administration to another until dosage is regulated. Wait 4 to 6 hours after changing from intravenous to oral therapy and 12 hours when changing from rectal administration, since its absorption tends to be less consistent.

If client with status asthmaticus does not respond quickly to bronchodilating agents, additional medication such as corticosteroids will be required. Note positive responses to the medication, such as increased ease of respiration, decreased wheezing, and a decrease in the client's anxiety regarding the dyspnea.

## PROPHYLACTIC ASTHMATIC DRUGS
### cromolyn sodium (Intal, Fivent ✱)

Cromolyn is a mast cell stabilizing agent that inhibits the release of histamine, leukotrienes, especially SRS-A, and other agents from the mast cell that causes hypersensitivity reactions. This may be mediated through an interference with calcium transport across the membrane of the mast cell. Cromolyn also provides a local protectant action on the gastrointestinal mucosa, thus aiding in preventing gastrointestinal allergies and perhaps, stopping the absorption of the allergic antigen.

Cromolyn is indicated to prevent bronchospasms and bronchial asthmatic attacks. It has no bronchodilator effects. It is administered by oral inhalation with approximately 8% to 10% absorbed in the lungs. It has a half-life of 80 minutes and is excreted in the kidneys and bile.

By inhalation, the adult dose to prevent bronchial asthma is two inhalations (1.6 mg) orally, four times daily. To prevent exercise-induced or allergen-induced bronchospasms, the dose is two inhalations orally approximately 10 to 15 minutes before exposure. A dose is not established for children under 5 years old. For 5 years and older, see adult dose. Pregnancy safety is established at FDA category B.

▷ **Nursing Management:**
**Cromolyn Therapy**

*Assessment.* Determine that the client does not have an intolerance to lactose, milk, or milk products, since this would prohibit the use of the inhalation capsule form of cromolyn, which contains a lactose base. The inhalation aerosol may be contraindicated in clients with a history of cardiac dysrhythmias or coronary artery disease because of the propellants in the aerosol. Clients with preexisting hepatic or renal impairment may require a reduction in dosage.

With the administration of cromolyn, the client has the potential for the following nursing diagnoses: altered comfort related to unpleasant taste (aerosol inhalation), dryness of mouth and throat, sneezing and watering of eyes, dizziness, nausea, headache, and rash; altered urinary elimination patterns (urgency and frequency); and physiologic injury related to eosinophilic pneumonia.

*Intervention.* Cromolyn helps prevent but does not relieve asthma or bronchospasm attacks. If used during an acute attack, it may actually worsen the client's symptoms. If the client is also using a bronchodilator inhaler, it should be used 15 minutes before the cromolyn inhalation.

*Education.* The client should be taught to rinse the mouth and gargle after an inhalation treatment to relieve the dryness of the mouth and throat and the bad aftertaste.

If the client is using the aerosol, capsule, or solution dosage form for inhalation, the individual should be aware that instructions come with each preparation. The nurse should make sure the client can administer the drug correctly. Demonstration kits are available for the inhalation capsule dosage form. Caution clients using the aerosol form to avoid medication contact with the eyes. Inhalation capsules are to be used with a special inhaler; they are not effective if swallowed. The inhalation solution is to be used with a power-operated nebulizer, since the hand-held nebulizers do not provide sufficient force to administer the medication.

The client should be advised that it may be as long as 4 weeks before the drug is fully beneficial. Compliance with the regimen is necessary to achieve these results. It is also important to maintain any concurrent therapies, such as adrenocorticoids, until discontinued by the physician. If the client's condition does not improve or becomes worse, the physician should be notified.

*Evaluation.* A satisfactory response to cromolyn therapy is indicated by a reduction in the number of attacks, reduced cough, decreased sputum production, and/or a decreased need for other antiasthma drugs. Some clients show improvement in pulmonary function. These responses occur in 4 weeks of treatment. Only those clients showing improvement should continue to receive cromolyn.

## Corticosteroid Drugs

Corticosteroid drugs are used in chronic asthma to decrease airway obstruction. As antiinflammatory agents, they stabilize the membranes of lysosomes, thus preventing the release of hydrolytic enzymes that produce the inflammatory process in the tissues. The exact mechanism in asthma is still poorly understood, but it does involve suppression of antibody formation that is responsible for provoking the asthmatic attack. In addition, corticosteroids potentiate an increase in cyclic AMP, a compound needed to promote bronchodilation. At the same time it is thought that they prevent the formation of cyclic GMP, which induces bronchial constriction.

Corticosteroids are used in conjunction with other drugs, in clients with asthma to treat **status asthmaticus,** which is life-threatening exacerbation of asthma associated with bronchospasm. Individuals with this condition are usually unresponsive to nonsteroid bronchodilators. Corticosteroids are also indicated for clients with severe chronic asthma when relief is difficult to obtain from other bronchodilating agents.

Steroids should not be used when other measures are available. Although maintenance programs of steroid therapy decrease the frequency of severe asthmatic attacks, they do not prevent all asthmatic episodes. Furthermore, it is not known whether all episodes of asthma could be prevented by continuous administration of large doses of these drugs. Actually, prolonged administration of large doses is associated with severe adverse effects that are permanent— osteoporosis, subcapsular cataracts, and stunting of growth in children. Other adverse effects caused by this group of drugs are usually reversible.

Daily administration of systemic corticosteroid therapy provides great therapeutic benefits, but the high incidence of adverse effects has led to the use of the alternate-day schedule of treatment. This regimen provides the best benefit/risk ratio for prolonged therapy beause it minimizes the likelihood of unwanted side effects. The corticosteroids generally used have an intermediate-acting duration of action. These corticosteroids include prednisone, prednisolone, and methylprednisone (see Chapter 49 for details of these drugs).

Recently, the use of steroid aerosols has become increasingly popular. Topical corticosteroid therapy offers the possibility of limiting action at the site of application and thereby avoiding systemic effects. By chemically modifying the structural arrangement of the steroid molecule, several compounds were developed to diminish systemic absorption from the respiratory tract. One such topical agent is beclomethasone dipropionate (Vanceril), which offers the ad-

vantage of producing few systemic adverse effects, including that of limited or no adrenal suppression.

### beclomethasone diproprionate (Vanceril Inhaler, Beclovent)

Beclomethasone, a synthetic corticosteroid chemically related to prednisolone, has high antiinflammatory activity. It is indicated only for clients who require chronic treatment with corticosteroids for control of bronchial asthma in conjunction with other therapy. It may be used after bronchodilator or cromolyn failure when long-term steroid control is considered or when oral steroids are producing undesirable side effects.

Beclomethasone is used in clients not receiving systemic steroids (withheld because of concern of potential adverse reactions). It is also administered when nonsteroid measures inadequately control the disease; improvement in pulmonary function appears in 1 to 4 weeks.

When stable asthmatic clients who are dependent on systemic steroids take beclomethasone, management is difficult because of the slow recovery from impaired adrenal function. Suppression of adrenal function may last up to 1 year. Beclomethasone may be effective in managing these clients and may permit significant reduction in the oral corticosteroid dosage. The slow rate of withdrawal is emphasized. During withdrawal from sytemic steroids some individuals exhibit symptoms of systemically active steroid withdrawal (e.g., joint and muscle pain, lassitude, and depression).

Because beclomethasone is an inhalational agent, only a limited amount of systemic absorption occurs from respiratory and gastrointestinal tissues, with excretion in the feces and urine (less than 10%).

For side effects/adverse reactions see Table 37-1. Beclomethasone has no known drug interactions.

For adults, administer two inhalations orally, three or four times daily. For severe asthma, 12 to 16 sprays initially a day, then decrease dosage according to client response. Maximum is 840 μg (or 20 metered sprays daily.)

For children under 6 years old, a dosage is not established; for 6 to 12 years old, administer one or two metered sprays three or four times daily to a maximum of ten sprays daily.

Pregnancy safety has not been established for this drug.

### ▷ Nursing Management: Beclomethasone Therapy

***Assessment.*** Beclomethasone is contraindicated in clients with status asthmaticus or nonasthmatic bronchial conditions. Its use is not appropriate for asthma controlled by other medications, such as bronchodilators or other noncorticosteroids. Do not use for acute attack. With the administration of beclomethasone by inhalation the client is at risk for the following nursing diagnoses: altered comfort related to dry/irritated mouth and throat, and cough and hoarseness without signs of infection; and high risk for injury related to oral candidiasis (creamy, white patches within the mouth), monilial esophagitis (difficulty in swallowing), bronchospasm, and allergic reaction.

*Intervention.* If the client also uses a bronchodilator, it should be used 15 minutes before the beclomethasone inhalation.

*Education.* The client should hold the inhaled drug for a few seconds and allow a minute to elapse between each inhalation to increase its effectiveness. The nurse should ensure that the client is able to self-administer the inhaler. The client should be told that fungal infections of the mouth may occur with inhalation of this drug. The mouth should be thoroughly examined daily for the presence of infection. In addition, tell the client that rinsing the mouth after each treatment and washing and drying the inhaler thoroughly after use will help prevent infection.

*Evaluation.* If the client's response to the drug begins to diminish, the physician should be notified so that the dosage can be adjusted.

### dexamethasone sodium phosphate (Decadron Phosphate)

Dexamethasone is used for allergic or inflammatory nasal conditions and nasal polyps (excluding polyps originating within the sinuses). Adults should receive two sprays in each nostril two or three times a day; children should receive one or two sprays in each nostril two times a day, depending on age. Maximum daily dosage is 12 sprays per day for adults and 8 sprays per day for children.

The nurse should review with the client the instructions for use of the Decadron Turbinaire for nasal use. Immediately before using the spray, the client should be reminded to blow accumulated mucus and secretions from the nose and, while holding the breath, to press the cartridge to release one measured dose of medication. The client should not inhale but should hold the breath (to avoid systemic absorption by the lungs) for several seconds after applying the medication for its full nasal topical effectiveness. The client should be told not to blow the nose immediately after applying the medication. Each cartridge delivers 170 metered nasal sprays; 12 sprays deliver about 1 mg of dexamethasone.

The most common side effects are nasal irritation and dryness. Headache, light-headedness, urticaria, nausea, epistaxis, rebound congestion, bronchial asthma, perforation of the nasal septum, and loss of the sense of smell have occurred. Signs of adrenal hypercorticism may occur, especially with overdose. (See drug monograph in Chapter 49.)

### ipratropium (Atrovent)

Ipratropium is an anticholinergic drug that produces a local bronchodilation after inhalation. It is indicated for maintenance (not for acute episodes) therapy in clients with chronic obstructive pulmonary disease, chronic bronchitis, or emphysema. After administration, onset of action is between 5 and 15 minutes, and peak effect is in 1 to 2 hours, with duration of action between 3 and 6 hours.

More frequently reported side effects include dry mouth or throat, coughing, headache, anxiety, and abdominal upset. Although rare, the following adverse effects should be reported immediately to the physician: hives, skin rash, or stomatitis.

The usual adolescent or adult dose is 1 or 2 inhalations (18 to 40 μg), three or four times daily, administered every 4 hours. Shake unit well before using.

## Summary

In clients with ineffective airway clearance, both mucokinetic and bronchodilator drugs might be prescribed by the physician as adjuncts to nursing interventions taken with the client. Mucokinetic agents promote the removal of abnormal or excessive respiratory tract secretions by thinning hyperviscous secretions, thereby enhancing the ciliary action of the respiratory tract. Bronchodilators diminish airway obstruction by bronchial smooth muscle relaxation.

Mucokinetic agents can either be diluents of respiratory secretion or actually mucolytic by dissolving linkages of mucoprotein molecules of the respiratory secretions. Bronchodilators may be sympathomimetic drugs, either nonselective adrenergic, nonselective beta adrenergic, or selective beta$_2$ agents. Use of the nonselective adrenergic drugs, e.g., epinephrine, not only results in bronchodilation and vasodilation but also in unwanted side effects such as increased heart rate, muscle tremors, CNS stimulation, glycogenolysis, and gluconeogenesis. The nonselective beta adrenergic agents, e.g., isoproterenol, act upon bronchial smooth muscle, as well as the heart, whereas the selective beta$_2$ receptor agents, e.g., isoetharine and albuterol, have less cardiotonic effect and act primarily to relieve bronchospasm. Xanthine derivatives are also used as bronchodilators. Cromolyn is used as a prophylactic asthmatic agent.

Nursing management of the care of the client receiving these drugs is focused on the client experiencing increased ease of respiration, decreased wheezing, and a decrease in medications as a part of an overall self-management regimen.

## Case Study: The Client With Asthma

Christine Newman is a 32-year-old woman with a long history of bronchial asthma. She is currently being maintained on Theo-Dur, 200 mg once a day. When respiratory wheezing increases, she uses a Proventil inhaler, two puffs, every 4 hours, until her breathing improves. In spite of her history of asthma, Christine continues to smoke at least half a pack of cigarettes a day. She is making an effort to quit smoking but finds it is hard to stop.

Oxygen must be continuously supplied to tissue cells, since no fiber or cell can remain without oxygen, or hypoxic, for very long and survive. The adult human brain consumes from 40 to 50 ml oxygen/minute. The cortex consumes more than the centers in the medulla or spinal cord. Cerebral oxygen consumption proceeds without pausing, and the replenishment of oxygen by the blood must be maintained continuously. Whenever any circulatory stress exists, cerebral blood flow tends to be preserved at the expense of other less vital organs. Of all the tissues affected by hypoxia, the brain is most susceptible to disruption of normal function and irreversible damage. An acute reduction of the $Po_2$ to 50 mm Hg decreases mental functioning, emotional stability, and finer muscular coordination. Further reduction of the $Po_2$ to 40 mm Hg produces impaired judgment, decreased pain perception, and impairment of muscular coordination. When the $Po_2$ is reduced to 32 mm Hg or less, unconsciousness and a progressive descending depression of the central nervous system ensue.

The kidneys are vital organs in which there must be considerable constancy of blood flow and oxygen supply. Oxygen consumption is greater in the renal cortex; renal medullary tissue has an oxygen consumption that is 15% less than that of the renal cortex. This difference is related to the variation in pressure gradient and to the fact that cortical flow is rapid while the medullary flow is slower. The renal cortex is highly dependent on oxygen, whereas the renal medulla can function relatively independently of the oxygen supply.

The rate of oxygen consumption by the kidneys is approximately 0.06 ml/g/minute, more than most other tissues. For each 100 ml of blood entering the kidney, 1.4 ml of oxygen is consumed. The oxygen consumed by the kidneys is primarily used for sodium reabsorption. When the renal arterial content falls to less than 55% of normal, renal vasoconstriction occurs. This response is believed to be mediated by chemoreceptors, which stimulate the vasomotor center to produce renal vasoconstriction. Renal vasoconstriction also occurs as a result of the action of either, barbiturates, and other anesthetics. Renal blood flow is also decreased during periods of exercise. It is important to note that autoregulation of renal perfusion does occur.

In skeletal muscles oxygen consumption is related to blood flow. Oxygen consumption and blood flow are decreased when muscle is at rest and significantly increased during exercise.

Reduction of oxygen supply to the intestinal tract is regarded by some investigators as a key factor for inadequate splanchnic vasoconstriction during hypotension. Inadequate oxygen supply impairs myocardial metabolism and function.

Arterial blood pressure determinations, when used alone, are unreliable indicators of the adequacy of tissue perfusion. Therefore arterial blood gas determinations should be obtained, since these results provide a more accurate and reliable indication of shifts in the partial pressures of oxygen and carbon dioxide. Severe hypoxia may produce changes in the ST segment and T wave of the ECG, dysrhythmias, ectopic beats, and myocardial infarction.

**Indications.** Oxygen is used chiefly to treat **hypoxia** (oxygen lack) and **hypoxemia** (diminished oxygen tension in the blood). Basically, the four types of hypoxia are the following:

1. Hypoxic hypoxia—produced by any condition causing a decrease in $Po_2$
2. Ischemic hypoxia—inadequate blood flow to an organ or tissue in the presence of a normal $Po_2$ and hemoglobin content
3. Anemic hypoxia—inadequate hemoglobin to carry $O_2$ in the presence of a normal $Po_2$
4. Histotoxic hypoxia—adequate $Po_2$ and hemoglobin, but inability of tissues to use oxygen delivered because of a toxic agent

Clinically, hypoxic hypoxia is the most common form of hypoxia. A variety of pathologic conditions result in hypoxic hypoxia, which makes the use of oxygen treatment necessary. Some of these conditions are hypoventilation, increased airway resistance, pneumothorax, respiratory center depression, abnormal ventilation perfusion ratio, congenital cyanotic heart disease, decreased pulmonary compliance, and breathing oxygen-poor air. The use of oxygen is also indicated in (1) cardiac failure or decompensation and coronary occlusion and (2) anesthesia administration (to increase the safety of general anesthesia).

**Administration.** Oxygen is administered by inhalation. Various methods are used, each having advantages and disadvantages (Figure 38-1).

A *nasal catheter* is made of soft plastic. When used, it should be lubricated with water-soluble K-Y Jelly and passed through the nose until the tip is just above the epiglottis. This distance is usually the same as the distance from an individual's external nares to the tragus of the ear, minus 1 cm. The catheter should not be inserted so far that the client swallows oxygen, since this will cause stomach distention and abdominal discomfort. The catheter is fastened with tape to the forehead and/or nose. Flow rate varies according to individual need, but 4 to 8 L oxygen/minute of a 25% to 40% concentration of oxygen is commonly used. Since this form of therapy is very drying to the mucous membrane, the oxygen should be humidified. In addition, nasal and oral hygiene is important to maintain cleanliness and intact mucous membrane and to prevent infection and discomfort. Most clients receiving oxygen therapy are mouth breathers, and frequent mouth care is required to prevent sores. Nasal catheters become obstructed with encrusted secretions and must be removed and cleaned or replaced several times a day.

A *nasal cannula* is much more comfortable for the client than is a catheter. Cannulas have either single or double short prongs that are inserted into the lower part of the nostrils. They are less likely to become obstructed with secretions. Nasal and oral mucosa still require frequent attention. A flow of 1 to 6 L/minute of a 23% to 40% con-

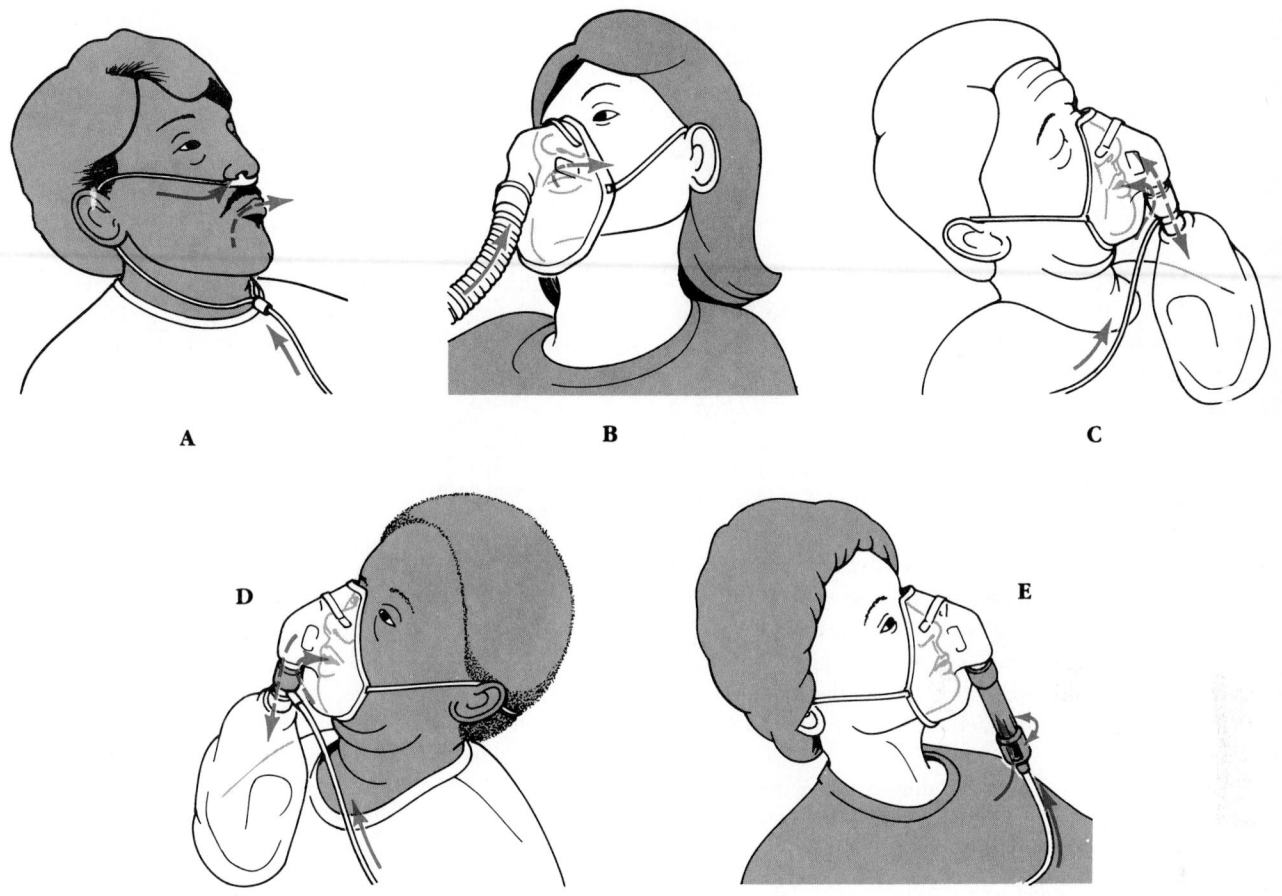

**FIGURE 38-1**   Various oxygen delivery systems. **A,** Nasal cannula. **B,** Simple face mask. **C,** Partial rebreathing mask. **D,** Nonrebreathing mask. **E,** Venturi mask.

centration of oxygen is adequate for many clients.

An *oxygen mask* is the most effective means of delivering needed oxygen. Oxygen concentrations up to 90% can be administered by mask. To be effective, the mask must fit well over the nose and mouth; high flow rates can compensate to some extent for a poor fit. Masks are better tolerated when used intermittently or when disposable plastic masks are used. Only absolutely clean and uncontaminated rubber masks should be used, since they can be a source of nosocomial infection. There are two main types of oxygen masks: (1) those that deliver low concentrations of oxygen and (2) those that deliver high concentrations of oxygen.

A *simple face mask,* which is lightweight and disposable, is useful for short-term therapy of oxygen administration, such as in the early postoperative period or when intermittent oxygen therapy is required. The flow rate is only 6 to 10 L/minute at a low oxygen concentration of 35% to 60%. Since the mask is loose-fitting and can leak, simple face masks are suitable for individuals with carbon dioxide retention.

A *partial rebreathing mask* is a disposable, light-weight plastic face mask consisting of a reservoir bag and a partial rebreathing valve. It is commonly used by individuals who

require oxygen. On expiration, only a portion of the exhaled air enters the reservoir. Accordingly, to prevent the rebreathing of carbon dioxide, the reservoir bag should deflate only slightly on inhalation. By this method a concentration of 60% to 90% of oxygen can be delivered at a flow rate of 10 L/minute.

A *nonrebreathing mask* is designed to fit tightly over the face and is usually made of rubber with a reservoir bag and a nonbreathing valve. On inhalation, oxygen flows into the bag and mask, and the one-way valve prevents exhaled air from flowing back into the bag. The expired air instead escapes through the one-way flap valve in the mask. The concentration of oxygen is 95%, which is high, and the flow is adjusted to keep the reservoir bag fully inflated. This type of mask is used for short-term therapy such as counteracting smoke inhalation. The rubber can become hot and sticky so that prolonged use can cause discomfort.

An *oxygen tent* is of limited value, particularly when it is necessary to open the canopy for monitoring vital signs and administering care to the client. The rate of flow is 20 L/minute at an oxygen concentration of 60%. Obviously, the oxygen concentration falls, making the flow difficult to control each time the tent is opened. Consequently, oxygen tents are now used less frequently.

The *Ventimask (Mix-O-Mask)* is a recent development originating from the Venturi mask. It is used for clients with chronic alveolar hypoventilation and carbon dioxide retention. Exact low-flow concentrations of oxygen are delivered to the individual. The Ventimask provides an air-oxygen mixture with the desired oxygen concentration. The size of the orifice to the mask determines the concentration of oxygen—24%, 28%, 35%, and 40% with flow rates of 4, 6, 8, and 10 L/minute, respectively. A thin elastic band holds the Ventimask in position and tends to cut into the skin behind the ears. A gauze padding under each side of the elastic band will alleviate this discomfort. The device must be removed when the client eats and may give the client a feeling of being smothered.

Most of the oxygen administered in hospitals for therapy is provided from a central source where it is stored as a gas or liquid oxygen. The gas is piped into a client's room at a standard pressure of 50 pounds per square inch (psi) at the gauge. Compressed oxygen is marketed in steel cylinders that are fitted with reducing valves for the delivery of the gas. The cylinders are usually color coded; green is used in the United States. Since the gas is under considerable pressure, the tanks must be handled carefully to prevent falling or jarring.

The effectiveness of oxygen administration depends on the carbon dioxide content of the blood. Individuals with chronic obstructive pulmonary disease (COPD) have difficulty with carbon dioxide and oxygen exchange and are subject to **hypercapnia** (high carbon dioxide content in the blood). Because of chronic hypercapnia, the medullary center of these individuals is relatively insensitive to stimulation of carbon dioxide; rather, a low $PaO_2$ serves as a stimulant to respiration. Nursing care should be used to prevent a greater accumulation of carbon dioxide by encouraging the improvement of gas exchange. This involves having the client turn, deep breathe, and use pursed lip breathing periodically. Toxic carbon dioxide levels may result in further depression of respiration and respiratory acidosis. The nurse should be alert to neurologic symptoms that indicate an accumulation of carbon dioxide. Symptoms may include drowsiness, mental confusion, paresthesias, and visual disturbances. The occurrence of carbon dioxide narcosis may be prevented by gradually increasing the concentration of oxygen administered.

**Oxygen administration in the premature infant.** Nurses caring for premature infants in incubators must be constantly aware of the danger of retrolental fibroplasia. This is a vascular proliferative disease of the retina that occurs in some premature infants who have had high concentrations of oxygen at birth.* The oxygen concentration should be

---

*Excessive oxygen constricts the developing retinal vessels of the eye. Consequently, normal vascularization is suppressed; since the endothelial cells become disorganized, they cause destruction of the immature retina. The result is blindness.

---

## PULSE OXIMETRY

A recent advance in monitoring for tissue hypoxia is the development of **pulse oximetry.** It has been called one of the most significant technologic advances ever made in monitoring the respiratory function of clients. Simply explained, pulse oximetry works by passing light of differing wavelengths through living tissue and analyzing the differences in absorption. Oxygenated hemoglobin absorbs light differently, and these variations in absorption serve as the basis of calculations that determine the presence and amount of oxygenated hemoglobin compared to nonoxygenated hemoglobin. This provides a continuous reading of arterial blood oxygen saturation. A saturation of 90 percent or greater is desired for clients. (This correlates with a $PaO_2$ of 60).

Current pulse oximeters work with a small probe (light source and detector), which may be placed on a client's ear, finger, toe, bridge of the nose, nasal septum, or temple. Pulse oximetry monitors are relatively inexpensive, noninvasive, safe, extremely accurate, require no calibration, and provide almost instantaneous results. While initially used with clients during anesthesia, recovery, and critical care, the use of pulse oximetry is rapidly expanding as an immediate and safe method of determining tissue oxygenation in any client having respiratory difficulties.

---

kept between 30% and 40%. Higher concentrations can be administered to cyanotic infants without increasing the danger of retrolental fibroplasia because it is $PaO_2$, not inspired $PO_2$, that is implicated in this disease. Therefore careful monitoring of arterial blood gases is essential. Some incubators are equipped with a safety valve that automatically releases any excess oxygen outside the chamber. When orders for an infant include oxygen prn, the nurse must make certain that it is administered only as needed and at low concentrations rather than continuously. Frequently, the removal of a very small plug of mucus can clear the airway, thus enabling the infant to breathe oxygen without assistance.

**Hyperbaric oxygen.** In recent years hyperbaric oxygen has been used in the treatment of various conditions. In the treatment of infections caused by *Clostridium welchii*, the anaerobic bacillus producing gas gangrene, the intermittent use of hyperbaric oxygen has been valuable. It is believed that an increased oxygen pressure in the tissue may exert an inhibitory effect on enzyme systems of these bacteria. This same inhibitory effect may be implicated in the use of hyperbaric oxygen on other anaerobic microorganisms. Hyperbaric oxygen has been used in the treatment of tetanus, but the results are less satisfactory than those obtained in the treatment of gas gangrene. Hyperbaric oxygen has also been used in certain circulatory disturbances. In shock, in which there is a generalized circulatory deficit, hyperbaric

---

### NORMAL VALUES FOR ARTERIAL BLOOD GASES

| | |
|---|---|
| pH | 7.36-7.44 |
| $PaCO_2$ | 36-44 mm Hg |
| $PaO_2$ | 80-100 mm Hg |
| $O_2$ saturation | 95% or above |
| $HCO_3$ | 22-26 mEq/L |

---

oxygen may be of some value. It has also been used in certain local circulatory disturbances such as various peripheral vascular diseases.

***Helium-oxygen mixtures.*** Helium-oxygen mixtures have been used to treat obstructive types of dyspnea. Helium is an inert gas and so light that a mixture of 80% helium and 20% oxygen is only one third as heavy as air. Helium is only slightly soluble in body fluids and has a high rate of diffusion. Because of its low specific gravity, mixtures of this gas with oxygen can be breathed with less effort than either oxygen or air alone when air passages are obstructed. These mixtures are recommended for individuals with status asthmaticus, bronchiectasis, and emphysema, as well as during anesthesia for a client with respiratory tract obstruction.

***Oxygen toxicity.*** Exposure to 100% oxygen for a period of 6 hours causes an inflammatory response with subsequent destruction of the alveolocapillary membrane of the respiratory tract. Toxicity is often difficult to recognize, but the most common symptoms are substernal distress (ache or burning sensation behind the sternum), increase in respiratory distress, nausea, vomiting, restlessness, tremors, twitching, paresthesias, convulsions, and a dry, hacking cough.

▷**Nursing Management: Oxygen Therapy**

***Assessment.*** **Dyspnea** or increased respiratory rate, may indicate the need for oxygen therapy. The best means of gauging the need for oxygen or the effectiveness of oxygen therapy is via arterial blood gas evaluations or pulse oximetry (see box) before and during therapy. The nurse should know normal blood gas values (see box) and recognize deviations. The goal of oxygen therapy is to achieve a $PO_2$ range between 60 to 80 mm Hg or oxygen saturation greater than 90%. In chronic carbon dioxide retention, the $PO_2$ may range between 55 to 60 mm Hg. Arterial blood gas analysis is required 30 minutes after the oxygen dosage is changed unless the oxygen saturation is being monitored.

Oxygen should be given with extreme caution to some clients. The client with COPD maintains respiratory drive by low oxygen tension. A high oxygen concentration in the blood causes the client to have reduced ventilation and result

in acute acidosis and carbon dioxide narcosis. Arterial blood gas evaluations should be checked frequently with clients with COPD.

***Intervention.*** To prevent dryness of nose and throat and respiratory complications, add sterile, distilled water to the humidifying device, and administer oxygen concentration and liter flow as prescribed. Because oxygen is a dry gas, adequate humidification is essential to the client and must be monitored frequently.

Since oxygen supports combustion and combustible materials (linens, wooden furniture, plastic articles) burn with greater ease and intensity, smoking and using matches, woolen blankets, clothing, or electric equipment (radios, electric razors, hair dryers) that may cause sparks are strictly forbidden in rooms where oxygen is being administered. Also, post NO SMOKING signs on the individual's door and above the bed.

Because oxygen therapy is frequently administered to debilitated clients, take special care to prevent contamination of the equipment used in the administration of oxygen to prevent nosocomial infection. Nasal cannulas, Venti-masks, other masks, tubing, nebulizers, and other equipment exposed to moisture need to be changed daily. Nasal catheters should be changed every 8 to 12 hours. Remove an oxygen mask periodically, if the client's condition permits, to dry, powder, and massage the skin around the mask.

***Education.*** The equipment for oxygen administration should be shown to the client and family. Explain the procedure and the benefits of oxygen therapy. Point out the importance of not smoking in the client's room to the client and visitors. (Since oxygen supports combustion, the possibility of fire always exists.)

***Homecare.*** For home use of oxygen, instruct the client and family to ensure that the oxygen tank is stable and placed in a safe, out-of-the-way location. They should be able to read and adjust the oxygen flowmeter and be able to determine the amount of oxygen available in the tank to meet the client's needs. The supplier's name and phone number need to be in a handy place for reordering or in case of emergency. Fire hazards should be prevented by instructing the client and family not to smoke or use an open flame in the room where and when the oxygen is on. Electrical appliances, such as razors and electric blankets, should not be used in the vicinity of the administration of the oxygen. No oils (vaseline, hair oils, body oils), wool blankets, or flammable liquids (alcohol) should be used in the area. "No smoking" signs should be posted as reminders. The local fire department should be alerted to the presence of oxygen tanks in the house.

***Evaluation.*** Monitor the client's vital signs—pulse rate, blood pressure, and respiratory rate and pattern. Also, observe level of consciousness, skin temperature, and color. Report any abnormal findings to the physician. Examine the client and the equipment frequently to see if skin and mucous membrane in contact with the equipment are intact and without irritation; the equipment is patent, without leaks, and properly positioned; the flow rate is at the prescribed level; the humidifier contains solution; and, if an oxygen cylinder is being used, that it is stablilized and contains enough oxygen.

### carbon dioxide

Carbon dioxide is a colorless, odorless gas that is heavier than air. Carbon dioxide used as a pharmacologic agent affects respiration, circulation, and the central nervous system. Inhalation of carbon dioxide for a short period of time increases both rate and depth of respiration unless the respiratory center is depressed by narcotics or disease.

Carbon dioxide stimulates cells of the sympathetic nervous system, the respiratory center, and the peripheral chemoreceptors. Carbon dioxide also depresses the cerebral cortex, myocardium, and smooth muscle of the peripheral blood vessels. Carbon dioxide may also interfere with nerve conduction and transmission. When carbon dioxide increases the rate and force of respiration, venous return to the heart is usually enhanced as a result of decreased peripheral resistance; there is improved rate and force of myocardial contraction and less likelihood of myocardial irritability and dysrhythmias.

Too much carbon dioxide has a depressant effect and results in acidosis and unresponsiveness of the respiratory center to the gas. Therefore it is important that carbon dioxide be administered with caution.

*Indications.* The following are indications for use of carbon dioxide.

*Carbon monoxide poisoning.* A 5% to 7% concentration of carbon dioxide in oxygen is sometimes used in the treatment of carbon monoxide poisoning. Physiologically, carbon dioxide increases the rate of separation of carbon monoxide from carboxyhemoglobin.

*General anesthesia.* Most general anesthetics cause a reduction in response to carbon dioxide, which is reflected in central nervous system depression. The degree of depression is directly related to the depth of anesthesia. The more deeply the individual is anesthetized, the greater the depression of the central nervous system. Carbon dioxide initially speeds up anesthesia by increasing pulmonary ventilation. By lessening the sense of asphyxiation, it reduces struggling. In the postanesthesia period, it hastens the elimination of many anesthetics. Inhalation of 5% to 7% carbon dioxide increases cerebral blood flow by approximately 75%, primarily by dilation of cerebral vessels.

*Respiratory depression.* The use of carbon dioxide as a respiratory stimulant in the presence of depressed respiration is limited. When used, close monitoring of pulse oximetry and $PaO_2$ is important; if desired results are not obtained, it should be discontinued. Mechanical assistance to respiration and oxygen administration is the usual treatment in cases of respiratory depression.

*Postoperative use.* Occasionally, carbon dioxide is used

postoperatively to increase ventilation and prevent atelectasis. Most investigators think the use of deep breathing exercises, coughing, frequent turning, tracheal suction, and intermittent positive pressure breathing produces better results. Carbon dioxide administration has also been used in the treatment of postoperative hiccups. Relief of hiccups is apparently accomplished by stimulating the respiratory center, causing large excursions of the diaphragm that suppress spasmodic contractions of that muscle, thereby promoting regular contractions.

*Administration.* Carbon dioxide is kept in metal cylinders and vaporizes as it is delivered from the cylinder. When carbon dioxide is used for medical purposes, it is administered in combination with oxygen. A 5% to 10% concentration of carbon dioxide delivered through a tight-fitting face mask is inhaled by the client until the depth of respiration is definitely increased, which usually occurs within 3 minutes. For the postoperative individual, the procedure would be repeated every hour or two for the first 48 hours, and then several times a day for several days.

Another way of administering carbon dioxide is to allow the client to hyperventilate with a paper bag held over the face. Reinhaling expired air causes the carbon dioxide content to be continually increased.

Signs of carbon dioxide overdosage are dyspnea, breathholding, markedly increased chest and abdominal movements, nausea, and increased systolic blood pressure. Administration of the gas should be discontinued when these symptoms appear. The administration of 5% carbon dioxide may produce severe mental depression if given over an hour, and a 10% concentration can lead to loss of consciousness within 10 minutes. The administration should be stopped as soon as the desired effects on the client's respiration have been obtained.

## Direct Respiratory Stimulants

Direct respiratory stimulants come under a broader classification of central nervous system stimulants and are often referred to as **analeptics.** These drugs act directly on the medullary center to increase respiratory rate and tidal exchange. Although these drugs are available for stimulating depth of respiration and rate of respiration, airway management and support of ventilation are more effective in the treatment of respiratory depression. The mechanical support of ventilation is often superior to the use of drugs, since respiratory stimulants in large doses can cause convulsions.

Respiratory stimulants (analeptics) have in the past been advocated in the treatment of drug-induced respiratory depression; but since these drugs are not specific antagonists to sedatives or narcotics, their use in drug-induced respiratory depression is now considered obsolete. Indeed, repeated doses of an analeptic may potentiate the depressant effects of central nervous system depressants.

Analeptics have also been used to counteract respiratory

depression caused by anesthetics or to shorten postanesthetic recovery time. However, these methods of therapy are not recommended, since decreasing the concentration of the anesthetic agent in the blood is accomplished more effectively with mechanical ventilatory measures.

### doxapram hydrochloride (Dopram)

Doxapram is a short-acting drug that stimulates all levels of the central nervous system. It stimulates the respiratory center in the medulla and the peripheral carotid chemoreceptors and the ventilatory response increases both tidal volume and oxygen uptake. Doxapram is indicated for the treatment of respiratory depression induced by anesthesia, muscle relaxant medications, drug overdoses, and in individuals with acute respiratory insufficiency, such as COPD. The latter use is temporary and used generally with mechanical ventilation. It is administered by intravenous push or by intravenous infusion and has an onset of action between 20 to 40 seconds, peak effect of 1 to 2 minutes and duration of action between 5 and 12 minutes. It is primarily excreted in the feces.

Infrequently reported side effects include coughing, diarrhea, dizziness, confusion, headache, nausea, vomiting, sensations of warmth, sweating, and urinary difficulties. Rare or infrequent adverse reactions include feelings of heaviness or pain in chest, fast or irregular heart rate, redness or swelling at site of injection, fast irregular breathing, wheezing, and hemolysis of blood cells. In overdosage, adverse reactions such as convulsions, hypertension, an increase in deep tendon reflexes, tremors, and tachycardia may result. When doxapram is given with monoamine oxidase inhibitors, such as procarbazine, furazolidone and pargyline or vasopressor agents, an increase in pressor effects is reported. Avoid concurrent use or, if necessary, monitor closely as dosage adjustments may be necessary.

The adult dose for postanesthesia respiratory depression is 0.5 mg to 1 mg/kg IV, not to exceed 1.5 mg/kg. If necessary, dosage may be repeated in 5-minute intervals up to a maximum total dosage of 2 mg/kg body weight. By intravenous infusion, a rate of 5 mg/minute is administered initially until the desired response is noted, then decrease to 1 to 3 mg/minute. The maximum total dose is 4 mg/kg without exceeding 300 mg per dose.

For drug-induced CNS depression, administer 1 to 2 mg/kg IV as a single dose, initially. This dose may be repeated in 5 minutes. Maintenance dose is 1 to 2 mg/kg IV every 60 to 120 minutes until desired response is achieved, up to a maximum total dose of 3 g per day. Before a second regimen is given, 24 hours from the initial dose should have elapsed. The intermittent IV infusion dose is 1 to 3 mg/minute until desired effect is achieved. If necessary, the infusion may be repeated after 30 to 120 minutes. Maximum infusion time is 2 hours while maximum daily dose is 3 g.

For acute respiratory insufficiency in COPD, administer 1 to 2 mg/minute up to 3 mg/minute as needed, given by intravenous infusion. Maximum infusion time is 2 hours. Additional infusions are not suggested. This drug is not recommended for children under 12 years old.

Pregnancy safety is established at FDA category B.

### ▷ Nursing Management: Doxapram Therapy

***Assessment.*** Do not use in individuals with known hypersensitivity to doxapram or in those with convulsive disorders, head injury, coronary artery disease, cerebrovascular accident, pulmonary embolism, severe hypertension, or pneumothorax. Administer cautiously in clients with cerebral edema, dysrhythmias, bronchial asthma, hyperthyroidism, or peptic ulcer. In children under 12 years and in pregnant women, safe use has not been established.

With the administration of doxapram, the client should be assessed for the development of the following nursing diagnoses: altered comfort related to nausea or vomiting, headache, dizziness, and coughing; altered thought processes (confusion); altered bowel elimination (diarrhea); and risk for injury related to cardiovascular effects (chest pain, arrhythmia), hemolysis, thrombophlebitis, and dyspnea.

Check the patent airway before drug administration.

***Intervention.*** Mix drug with normal saline solution or dextrose in water; do not mix with alkaline solution such as 2.5% sodium thiopental or bicarbonate, since precipitate will result. Have available intravenous short-acting barbiturates, oxygen, and resuscitative equipment in case of overdosage. Too rapid a rate of infusion may result in hemolysis. Avoid extravasation or use of a single injection site for prolonged periods, since thrombophlebitis may result.

***Evaluation.*** Carefully monitor blood pressure, pulse rate, and deep tendon reflexes to avoid overdose. Observe client continuously during therapy. Maintain vigilance for at least 1 hour until client is alert and pharyngeal and laryngeal reflexes are completely restored.

Although doxapram may be considered safer than other agents in this category, it is not without side effects. Be alert for early signs of toxicity such as tachycardia, muscle tremor, or spasticity. Notify physician immediately if any of these occur. Drug should be discontinued if sudden hypotension or dyspnea develops. Determination of arterial blood gases is essential before doxapram infusion in clients with COPD. During infusion, monitor at least every half hour.

## Reflex Respiratory Stimulants

Ammonia is the only drug given by inhalation for its action as a reflex respiratory stimulant. In cases of fainting, aromatic spirits of ammonia is administered by inhaling the vapor. When given orally, 2 ml of aromatic ammonia spirits is diluted with at least 1 fluid ounce of water. Reflex stimulation of the medullary center occurs through peripheral irritation of sensory nerve receptors in the pharynx, esophagus, and stomach. The rate and depth of respiration are then increased through afferent messages to the respiratory control centers. Reflex stimulation of the vasomotor center results in a rise in blood pressure.

## Respiratory Depressants

The most important respiratory depressants are the central depressants of the opium group and those of the barbiturate group of drugs. These agents depress the respiratory center, thereby making breathing slower and more shallow and lessening the irritability of the respiratory center. Respiratory depression, however, is seldom desirable or necessary, although it is sometimes unavoidable. It is frequently a side effect of otherwise very useful drugs. Occasionally, an opiate, such as codeine, is administered to inhibit the rate and depth of respiration for a painful or harmful cough. Too-high concentrations of carbon dioxide in inhalation mixtures may paradoxically act to depress respiration.

## COUGH SUPPRESSANTS

Coughing is a protective reflex for clearing the respiratory tract of environmental irritants, foreign bodies, or accumulated secretions and thus should not be depressed indiscriminately. The afferent impulses that arise from irritated pharyngeal and laryngeal tissues initiate the cough reflex. Drugs act either by suppressing the cough center in the medulla oblongata or peripherally by lessening irritation of the respiratory tract. A **productive cough** is when irritants or secretions are removed from the respiratory tract; a **nonproductive cough** is dry and irritating. Frequent and prolonged coughing should be diminished since it can be exhausting, painful, and taxing to the circulatory system and the elastic tissue of the respiratory system, particularly in the elderly and in young children. Some coughs occur primarily at night or when the individual is recumbent because of the accumulation of secretions, and some coughs occur in the morning on arising as a result of the gravitational movement of secretions. Coughing is under some voluntary control; a person can cough at will and at times can suppress coughing. However, coughing is usually initiated by a respiratory tract reflex, which, on irritation, sends an impulse to the cough center in the brain. Intake of fluids and inhalation of fully water-saturated vapors (steam) should be stressed as one of the most important means of producing increased amounts of mucus and thinning such secretions.

Treatment of the cough is secondary to treatment of the underlying disorder. Antitussives should not be given in situations in which retention of respiratory secretions or exudates may be harmful. The therapeutic objective is to decrease the intensity and frequency of the cough yet permit adequate elimination of tracheobronchial secretions and ex-

udates. Medications that may be used to relieve the cough include narcotic and nonnarcotic antitussive agents.

## Opioid Antitussive Drugs

Opioids such as morphine and hydromorphone are potent suppressants of the cough reflex, but their clinical usefulness is limited by side effects. They inhibit the ciliary activity of the respiratory mucous membrane, depress respiration, and may cause bronchial constriction in allergic or asthmatic patients. In addition, they can cause drug dependence. Codeine and hydrocodone exhibit less pronounced antitussive effects, but they also have fewer side effects. They are widely used. (See Chapter 12 for narcotic agents.)

## Nonopioid Antitussive Drugs

The instillation of a local anesthetic agent before various diagnostic techniques such as bronchoscopy has proved effective in suppressing the cough reflex. This has led to the investigation of other agents that exert a similar action. The clinical effectiveness of these drugs against pathologic cough still remains to be established. Newer nonnarcotic drugs in this group have fewer gastrointestinal side effects than do codeine and related compounds. The medicating effect of these drugs is local; therefore, they should not be followed by liquids of any sort for 30 to 35 minutes or the effect will be washed away.

### benzonatate (Tessalon)

Benzonatate is chemically related to the local anesthetic tetracaine. It relieves coughing through a peripheral action involving selective anesthesia of stretch receptors in the lungs.

Benzonatate is indicated for the symptomatic treatment of nonproductive cough. After oral administration, the onset of action is within 15 to 20 minutes with duration of action between 3 to 8 hours.

Side effects reported include drowsiness, headaches, dizziness, tightness or numbness in chest, nausea, constipation, abdominal upset, skin eruptions, nasal congestion and a vague sensation of chill. No significant drug interactions have been reported with this drug.

Dosage for adults and children over 10 years old is 100 mg three times a day; maximum daily dose is 600 mg. Warn client not to chew capsules; doing so may produce a temporary mouth anesthesia.

Pregnancy safety has not been established.

▷ **Nursing Management:
Benzonatate Therapy**

***Assessment.*** Assess from the client's history that there is no known hypersensitivity to the drug to be administered. Also determine cause of cough, since cough could indicate congestive heart failure or other disease. With the administration of benzonatate, the client should be assessed for the following nursing diagnoses: altered comfort related to the gastrointestinal effects (nausea, heartburn) and nasal congestion; altered skin integrity related to the occurrence of rash; and risk for injury related to CNS effects (sedation, dizziness) and allergic reaction.

*Intervention.* Nursing actions supportive of antitussives are deep breathing exercises, postural drainage, frequent change of position, limitation or cessation of smoking, maintenance of adequate humidity in the environment, and adequate hydration. The nurse should attempt to pinpoint the cause of the cough and then direct nursing measures toward the cause. Infections should be treated with pulmonary hygiene (e.g., cough, deep breathing, as discussed above). If a specific stimulus for the cough can be identified, such as dust, smoking, or pollen, then attempts should be made to minimize exposure to these substances.

*Education.* The capsule should be swallowed whole. If it is chewed or dissolved in the mouth, temporary local anesthesia of the oral mucosa would result. Caution client about operating a car or other machinery, since drug may cause drowsiness or dizziness.

*Evaluation.* Clients should be observed for drowsiness and dizziness, nausea, gastrointestinal distress, constipation, and rash. Assess the client's cough as to whether it is productive or nonproductive. Chest pain associated with the cough should be noted. The intensity and frequency of the client's cough should diminish with the administration of the antitussive.

### diphenhydramine hydrochloride (Benylin, Benadryl, and others)

Diphenhydramine depresses the cough center in the medulla of the brain (antitussive effect). It also has antihistamine effects (blocks $H_1$ receptors) and central antimuscarinic effects (antiparkinson action). In addition to the previous effects, it also has sedative-hypnotic effects and is used to prevent or treat nausea and vomiting associated with motion sickness.

It is well absorbed with an onset of action within 15 to 60 minutes after oral administration or between 20 to 30 minutes following an intramuscular dose. Peak concentration following an oral dose is within 1 to 4 hours while duration of action is between 6 to 8 hours. Diphenhydramine is metabolized in the liver and excreted by the kidneys.

The most frequently reported side effects with diphenhydramine and other antihistamines include constipation, a decrease in sweating, difficulty in initiating urinary stream in elderly males, sedation, visual disturbances, dry mouth, nose or throat, photosensitivity, and nausea or vomiting. Less often reported effects are orthostatic hypotension, euphoria (especially with high doses in the elderly), headaches, anxiety, weak hands or feet, sore mouth and tongue,

abdominal pain or upset, increased excitability, and muscle cramps.

Rarely reported adverse effects include glaucoma or eye pain in susceptible persons (individuals with predispostion to angle closure glaucoma), skin rash, and confusion, especially in elderly receiving high doses. Signs of overdosage may include ataxia; severe dry mouth, nose, or throat; respiratory difficulty; tachycardia; red, dry, flushing skin; severe CNS depression; mood swings; toxic psychosis; hallucinations; convulsions; and insomnia.

Reported withdrawal symptoms include increased nervousness, loss of balance, dysphagia, muscle spasms (especially face, neck, and back), increased excitability, and stiff feeling in arms or legs. Also reported are tremors and shaking of hands and fingers, extrapyramidal-type side effects, postural hypotension, insomnia, and tachycardia.

For significant drug interactions, see the antihistamine section in this chapter. Adult dose for antitussive effect (syrup) is 25 mg orally, every 4 to 6 hours; antihistamine dose is 25 to 50 mg orally every 4 to 6 hours when necessary and as a sedative-hypnotic, the dose is 50 mg given 20 to 30 minutes before bedtime. Antidyskinetic or antiparkinson effect dosage is 50 to 150 mg orally daily, in divided doses. For antiemetic or antivertigo effects, the dose is 25 to 50 mg orally 30 minutes before traveling and before each meal, as necessary. The elderly may be more sensitive to the effects of this drug; therefore, lower adult doses should be prescribed with close monitoring for any adverse effects.

The maximum daily dose recommended for all indications except antitussive syrup effect is 300 mg daily, in divided dosages. For the syrup, the maximum antitussive daily dose is 100 mg per day, in divided dosages.

For children, the antihistamine dose is 1.25 mg/kg orally every 4 to 6 hours. Maximum daily dose is 300 mg, or for children weighing up to 9.1 kg, 6.25 to 12.5 mg orally, every 4 to 6 hours. For children 9.1 kg and over, give 12.5 to 25 mg orally every 4 to 6 hours. The antiemetic or antivertigo dose is 1 to 1.5 mg/kg orally every 4 to 6 hours as necessary. Maximum dose is 300 mg per day. Do not use diphenhydramine in premature or full-term neonates.

Syrup dosage for antitussive effect in children under 2 years old is individualized by the physician. From 2 to 6 years old, give 6.25 mg orally every 4 to 6 hours with a maximum dose of 25 mg in 24 hours while in 6- to 12-year-old children the dose is 12.5 mg orally every 4 to 6 hours with a maximum of 50 mg in 24 hours.

The adult dose of diphenhydramine injection used as an antihistamine or antidyskinetic is 10 to 50 mg IM or IV, every 2 to 3 hours. As an antiemetic or antivertigo agent, the dose is 10 mg initially IM or IV, which may be increased to 20 to 50 mg every 2 or 3 hours. In children the antihistamine or antidyskinetic dose is 1.25 mg/kg IM four times daily, up to a 300 mg per day maximum. For an antiemetic or antivertigo effect, the dose is 1 to 1.5 mg/kg IM every

6 hours, up to 300 mg maximum daily. Do not use in premature or full-term neonates.

For a discussion of nursing management, see benzonatate (p. 652).

### dextromethorphan (Mediquell, Sucrets Cough Control)
### dextromethorphan in combination with cough syrups, antihistamines, expectorants, and benzocaine (Pertussin, Benylin DM, and others)

Dextromethorphan causes depression of the cough center in the medulla, when used as an antitussive; 15 to 30 mg of dextromethorphan is considered equivalent in effect to 8 to 15 mg of codeine. Dextromethorphan is an antitussive used to control nonproductive coughs. It is well absorbed orally from the gastrointestinal tract with an onset of action between 15 to 30 minutes and a duration of activity between 3 to 6 hours.

In usually recommended doses, side effects are minimal. Nausea and some dizziness have been reported. In over-dosage in children, nausea, vomiting, blurred vision, ataxia, psychosis including hallucinations, insomnia, hysteria, edema and coma have been recorded. Thus far, no fatalities have been reported. It is recommended to use caution when administering dextromethorphan with MAO inhibitors.

The dosage for adults and children 12 years and over is 10 to 20 mg orally every 4 hours or, 30 mg every 6 to 8 hours, up to a maximum of 120 mg per day. For children 6 to 11 years, the recommended dosage is 5 to 10 mg every 4 hours or 7.5 mg every 6 to 8 hours up to a maximum of 30 mg per day. In children under 2 years old, dosage is individualized by the physician.

Pregnancy safety is not established.

### ▷ Nursing Management: Dextromethorphan Therapy

As with other nonnarcotic antitussives, advise the client not to drink fluids for 30 to 35 minutes after taking the lozenge or chewable tablet or the effect will be washed away. Advise the client also to consult with the physician if the cough persists for 7 days, or if other symptoms occur with the cough such as fever, rash, or continuing headache. Many other products have been used as antitussive agents in various preparations, but the FDA advisory review panel on nonprescription cold, cough, allergy, bronchodilator, and antiasthmatic products has placed most of them in Category III; that is, more evidence is needed to prove their effectiveness. (Some of the products in this category include nonscapine, beechwood creosote, elm bark, cod liver oil, horehound, and others.)

## NASAL DECONGESTANTS

Vasoconstricting drugs are most commonly used for their capacity to shrink the engorged nasal mucous membranes in mild upper respiratory infections. Many drugs are used exclusively as nasal vasoconstrictors. Because of their wide popular use and lack of serious hazard (when used topically), a large number of preparations have been provided by the pharmaceutical industry for direct sale to the public.

**TABLE 38-1** Dosage of topical and oral nasal decongestants

| Drug/strength | Adults | Children (6 to 12 years old) |
|---|---|---|
| ephedrine, 0.5% (in Va-Tro-Nol nose drops and others) | 2-3 drops every 4 hours | 1-2 drops every 4 hours |
| naphazoline (Privine and other combinations) | | |
| 0.05% | 1-2 drops/spray, every 6 hours | Not recommended |
| 0.025% | — | 1-2 drops every 6 hours |
| oxymetazoline (Afrin, Allerest, Dristan Long-Lasting Nasal Spray and others) | | |
| 0.05% | 2-3 drops twice daily | Not recommended |
| phenylephrine (Neo-Synephrine and others) | — | 2-3 drops twice daily |
| 1% | 2-3 drops/spray every 4 hours | Not recommended |
| 0.25% | Same as 1% | 2-3 drops/spray every 4 hours |
| xylometazoline (Neo-Synephrine II and others) | | |
| 0.1% | 2-3 drops/spray every 8-10 hours | Not recommended |
| 0.05% | Same as 0.1% | 2-3 drops/spray every 8-10 hours |
| ORAL NASAL DECONGESTANTS (USUALLY COMBINED WITH OTHER DRUG PRODUCTS) | | |
| phenylephrine | 10 mg every 4 hours | 5 mg every 4 hours |
| phenylpropanolamine | 25 mg every 4 hours | 12.5 mg every 4 hours |
| pseudoephedrine | 60 mg every 6 hours | 30 mg every 6 hours |

The FDA advisory review panel recommended the following products as safe and effective topical nasal decongestant products: ephedrine (0.5%), naphazoline hydrochloride (0.05%, 0.025%) (Privine), oxymetazoline hydrochloride (0.05%, 0.025%) (Afrin, Dristan Nasal Spray), phenylephrine hydrochloride (0.125%, 0.25%, 1%) (Neo-Synephrine), and xylometazoline hydrochloride (0.1%, 0.05%) (Otrivin). The oral decongestant products found safe and effective include phenylephrine (in Dristan), phenylpropanolamine (component in many products, such as Sinarest, Sine-Off, Sinutab, Comtrex), and pseudoephedrine (component in Ambenyl-D Cosanyl, Fedahist, and others). See Table 38-1 for recommended dosages for topical nasal decongestant products and oral decongestant products. These drugs are adrenergic agents that act on alpha receptors of blood vessels in the nasal mucosa to produce mucosal constriction. Some nasal decongestant products (those containing ephedrine, epinephrine, metaproterenol, and others) also possess beta-stimulating effects, which may cause nervousness, restlessness, insomnia, irregular heart rate, and perhaps the adverse effect of vasodilation following vasoconstriction.

Nasal decongestant drugs are used to shrink engorged mucous membranes of the nose and to relieve nasal stuffiness. However, there is a tendency on the part of the public to misuse them by taking too large an amount and too frequently. Excessive use may result in "rebound" engorgement or swelling of the mucous membranes, a paradoxical bronchospasm. Preservatives, antihistamins, detergents, and antibiotics are sometimes added to the preparation of the decongestant. In some cases, reactions are believed to be caused by the additive rather than by the decongestant. Frequent interference with the vasomotor mechanism in the nose may do more harm than good, and there is always the possibility of spreading the infection deeper into the sinuses or to the middle ear. Sprays and nose drops are beneficial when used judiciously under the advice of a physician.

## HISTAMINE
### Distribution

Histamine is a chemical mediator that occurs naturally in almost all body tissues. It is present in highest concentration in the skin, lung, and gastrointestinal tract. These structures are frequently exposed to environmental assaults and require protection against damage. When liberated from its cells, the free form of histamine plays an early transient role in the inflammatory process that defends the exposed tissues against injury.

In many tissues the chief site of production and storage of histamine occurs in the cytoplasmic granules of the mast cell or, in the case of blood, the basophil, which closely resembles the mast cell in function. The mast cells are small, ovoid-shaped structures widely distributed in the loose connective tissue. They are especially abundant along small blood vessels and along the bronchial smooth muscle cell, which appears to have the highest concentration of mast cells of any organ in the body. Both the mast cells and basophils make up the mast-cell histamine pool. A second major site of histamine production is known as the nonmast pool where the amine is stored in the cells of the epidermis, gastrointestinal mucosa, and the central nervous system. Although histamine is present in various foods and is synthesized by intestinal flora, the amount absorbed does not contribute to the body's stores of this amine.

### Pharmacologic Actions

The reactions mediated by histamine are attributed to receptor activity, which involves two distinct populations of receptors called $H_1$ and $H_2$ receptors. The principal actions of histamine include vascular effects mediated by $H_1$ and $H_2$ receptors of both arterioles and capillaries, smooth muscle effects of the bronchioles and the gastrointestinal tract as a result of activation of the $H_2$ receptors, and secretory glandular effects caused by $H_2$-receptor stimulation of the gastric mucosa (see Table 38-2).

***Vascular effects.*** In the microcirculatory component of the cardiovascular system (arterioles, capillaries, venules) the liberation of histamine has been shown to involve both the $H_1$ and $H_2$ receptors. Stimulation of these receptors dilates the capillaries and venules, producing an increased localized blood flow, and promotes capillary permeability, allowing the escape of plasma protein and fluids through

**TABLE 38-2**   Receptor-mediating effects of histamine

| Structure | Histamine receptors | Pharmacologic effects |
|---|---|---|
| Vascular system | | |
| Capillary (Microcirculation) | $H_1$ and $H_2$ | Dilation<br>Increased permeability |
| Arteriole (Smooth muscle) | $H_1$ and $H_2$ | Dilation |
| Smooth muscle | | |
| Bronchial, bronchiolar | $H_1$ | Contraction |
| Gastrointestinal | $H_1$ | Contraction |
| Exocrine glands | | |
| Gastric | $H_2$ | Gastric acid secretion (HCl) |
| Epidermis | $H_1$ | Triple response (flush, flare, wheal) |
| Adrenal medulla | — | Epinephrine and norepinephrine release |
| Central nervous system | $H_1$ | Motion sickness |

the capillary wall into the interstitial space. These are localized responses that result in erythema and swelling of the tissues. By activating the $H_1$ and $H_2$ receptors on the smooth muscles of the arterioles, histamine is also capable of eliciting a systemic response. In certain conditions it causes massive vasodilation of the arterioles, which can result in profound fall in blood pressure.

*Smooth muscle effects.* Although histamine exerts a powerful relaxing effect on the smooth muscle of the arterioles, it produces a contractile action on smooth muscles of many nonvascular organs, such as the bronchi and gastrointestinal tract. In sensitized individuals activation of the $H_1$ receptors of the lungs can cause marked bronchial muscle contraction that often progresses to dyspnea and leads to airway obstruction.

*Exocrine glandular effects.* Histamine stimulates the gastric, salivary, pancreatic, and lacrimal glands. The chief effect on human beings, however, is seen in the gastric glands. Stimulation of $H_2$ receptors in the exocrine glands of the stomach increases production of gastric acid secretions. Its high hydrochloric acid concentration is attributed to the activity of the parietal cells of the stomach and is implicated in the development of peptic ulcers.

*Central nervous system effect.* Histamine is also known to be present throughout the tissues of the brain. Its effects seem to involve both $H_1$- and $H_2$-receptor mediation. The activation of $H_1$ receptors of the semicircular canals is associated with motion sickness.

*Triple response.* An intradermal injection of histamine causes a series of reactions called the "triple response." This is characterized as a local action resulting from stimulation of $H_1$ receptors in the skin. Blood vessels (capillaries) immediately affected by the histamine dilate and produce a flush, or redness. Surrounding blood vessels then dilate to produce a flare, or diffuse redness. This reaction is probably the result of a neural mechanism—axon reflexes stimulate sensory nerves and their branches to produce dilation of blood vessels. Widely dilated blood vessels have increased permeability. There is an increase in tissue fluid or local edema, termed a wheal. Any chemical or mechanical injury to the skin can cause this triple response of flush, flare, and wheal. Therefore it is believed that histamine is released from injured skin. The triple response is believed to be one of the body's protective mechanisms, since increased permeability of blood vessels permits the passage of plasma proteins and white cells into the tissues.

## Pathologic Effects

Histamine as a chemical mediator is implicated in many pathologic disorders. Conditions for which drugs are used to counteract this compound are concerned with the hypersensitivity response known as the allergic reaction. Although four different types of hypersensitivity responses to immunologic injury exist, the type I-anaphylactic reaction

is the one associated with the disorders caused by histamine release.

Individuals with type-I-mediated hypersensitivity develop allergies as a result of sensitization to a foreign agent that may be ingested, inhaled, or injected. An incalculable number of these agents acting as antigens exist. They vary widely in that seasonal exposure to pollens, grasses, and weeds or nonseasonal agents such as house dust, feathers, molds, and other similar substances can develop different forms of allergic reactivity. Hypersensitivity to a variety of foods such as shellfish or strawberries requires ingestion of the antigen. Insects such as bees or wasps and even drugs, particularly penicillin, also possess allergic properties that may induce a severe response in hypersensitive individuals. Thus type I-anaphylactic hypersensitivity accounts for a substantial number of allergic disorders, and it involves a complex series of anomalies that range from mild urticaria to anaphylactic shock.

The mechanism of type I-anaphylactic reaction involves the attachment of an antigen (Ag) to an antibody (Ab), specifically immunoglobulin E (IgE), and this complex in turn becomes fixed to the mast cell. The pathologic manifestations of Ag-IgE interaction are caused by mast cell degranulation, resulting in the release of histamine and other mediators responsible for producing the allergic symptoms. The type I-anaphylactic reaction is responsible for various disorders, such as urticaria, atopy (allergic rhinitis, hay fever), food allergies, bronchial asthma, and systemic anaphylaxis.

*Urticaria.* Urticaria is a vascular reaction of the skin characterized by immediate formation of a wheal and flare accompanied by severe itching. Contact with an external irritant such as drugs or foods produces the Ag-IgE mediated response with resultant release of histamine from the mast cell into the skin. The local vasodilation produces the red flare, and the increased permeability of the capillaries leads to tissue swelling. These swellings are called "hives," and when giant hives occur, they are known as angioneurotic edema. Antihistaminic drugs administered before exposure to the antigen will prevent this response.

*Atopy.* Atopy occurs in genetically susceptible individuals and is usually caused by seasonal pollen. This condition is manifested as an upper respiratory tract disorder known as **allergic rhinitis** (hay fever) (see box). Following the interaction of Ag-IgE antibody on the surface of the bronchial mast cells, histamine is released, producing local vascular dilation and increased capillary permeability. This change produces a rapid fluid leakage into the tissues of the nose, resulting in swelling of the nasal linings. In certain individuals antihistaminic therapy can prevent the edematous reaction if the drug is administered before antigenic exposure.

*Food allergies.* Food allergies involve intestinal immunoglobulin E (IgE)—mast cell responses to ingested antigens. If the upper gastrointestinal tract is affected, vomiting results; if the lower gastrointestinal tract is invaded, cramps and diarrhea occur. This condition also has been known to produce systemic anaphylaxis following ingestion of a large amount of antigen.

***Bronchial asthma.*** When the inhaled antigen combines with the IgE antibody, stimulation of the mast cells triggers the release of mediators in the lower respiratory tract, usually in the bronchi and bronchioles. Histamine plays a minor role in this response because the slow-reacting substance of anaphylaxis (SRS-A) is a more potent mediator, causing long-term contraction of the bronchiolar smooth muscle. The difficulty in breathing may be relieved by a bronchodilator such as epinephrine. The administration of antihistaminic drugs actually has no value in relieving this condition, since more potent chemical mediators than histamine are responsible for causing the reaction.

***Systemic anaphylaxis.*** Systemic anaphylaxis is a generalized reaction manifested as a life-threatening systemic condition. The Ag-IgE mediator response involves the basophils of the blood and the mast cells in the connective tissue. The most common precipitating causes of this response are drugs, particularly penicillin; insect stings (wasps and bees); and occasionally certain foods. The release of massive amounts of histamine into the circulation causes widespread vasodilation, resulting in a profound fall in blood pressure. The excessive dilation also allows plasma to leave the capillaries, and a loss of circulatory volume ensues. When the reaction is fatal, death is usually caused not only by shock but also by laryngeal edema. The symptoms of the latter condition include smooth muscle contraction of the bronchi and pharyngeal edema, which usually leads to asphyxiation. Since the mediator, SRS-A, also is released from the cells, spasm of the smooth muscle of the bronchioles elicits the asthmalike attack.

Antihistaminic drugs are less effective against systemic anaphylaxis because these agents do not antagonize the SRS-A mediator that causes the severe bronchoconstriction. Accordingly, a drug such as epinephrine, a bronchodilator, is indicated for this life-threatening situation. The relief produced by this drug results from the beta$_2$-receptor action that relaxes bronchial smooth muscles.

---

### SIGNS OR SYMPTOMS OF COLDS, ALLERGIC RHINITIS, AND INFLUENZA

| Signs or Symptoms | Common Cold | Allergic Rhinitis | Influenza |
|---|---|---|---|
| Fever | Rare | Absent | Common—sudden onset, may range 102-104° F |
| Aches and pains | Slight | Absent | May be severe |
| Sneezing | Usual | Common | Infrequent |
| Pruritus | Absent or rare | Common | Absent |
| Cough | Mild-moderate | Uncommon | Common |
| Headaches | Rare | Can occur | Prominent |
| Causative | Usually viruses | Usually allergans | Usually viruses |
| Occurrence | Anytime | Usually seasonal | Anytime |
| Complications | Sinus congestion, earache | Uncommon | Bronchitis, pneumonia |

---

**TABLE 38-3**  Common manifestations of drug-induced allergic reactions

| Tissue or organ | Symptom | Hapten commonly involved |
|---|---|---|
| Skin | Hives (urticuria) and generalized itching | penicillin, aspirin |
| | Rashes | barbiturates, sulfonamides, streptomycin |
| | Exfoliative dermatitis (loss of superficial skin layers) | tetracycline, streptomycin, phenobarbital |
| Mucous membranes (particularly of nose and eye) | Inflammation, swelling, and excessive secretions | sulfonamides, barbiturates |
| Respiratory tract | Difficulty in breathing | penicillin, local anesthetics, aspirin, heroin |
| Vascular system | Fall in blood pressure | penicillin, aspirin |
| Blood and blood-forming tissues* | Reduction in the number of one or more types of circulating blood cells | aminopyrine (Pyramidon) quinidine |

From Levine R. (1978). Pharmacology: drug actions and reactions, ed 2, Little, Brown & Co. Used with the permission of Little, Brown & Co.
*The presence of an antibody that reacts specifically with the sensitizing drug has been demonstrated in the case of each of the drugs cited as well as for a number of other drugs. Such demonstrations provide proof that drug allergy can account for some disorders of blood and the blood-forming tissues.

Drug allergies frequently develop in susceptible individuals who show no adverse effects following the first dose of drug administration. However, a second or subsequent reexposure to even a minute amount of this same antigen may elicit an exaggerated IgE response either locally or systemically. Individuals who exhibit such reactions are said to be allergic to the drug. The IgE-mediated response, particularly with penicillin, may occur either in the skin, producing severe urticaria, or in the respiratory tract, causing bronchial asthma. On the other hand, even limited contact in certain sensitized individuals can produce a fatal systemic anaphylaxis. Some of the drugs that elicit an allergic response include penicillin, chloramphenicol, streptomycin, sulfonamides, aspirin, and phenacetin. Allergic reactions to penicillin account for nearly 100 deaths per year in the United States. Therefore, if an individual exhibits even the mildest sign of an allergic response, such as a slight skin rash, this symptom should be reported immediately to the physician. In all probability the drug will be discontinued to avoid the possibility of an exaggerated type I hypersensitivity reaction. See Table 38-3 for symptoms of drug allergies involving various organ systems.

## Histamine Dosage and Administration for Testing

**Gastric function testing.** Client should fast for a minimum of 12 hours and be at rest under basal conditions. Use a nasogastric tube to empty the stomach contents before the examination and to obtain specimens during the exam. Client may swallow 300 ml of water; then the histamine dose of 0.01 mg/kg (equal to histamine phosphate 0.0275 mg/kg) is given subcutaneously. Monitor pulse rate and blood pressure closely. Prevent the client from swallowing saliva; its alkalinity may interfere with test results. Obtain four samples for volume and acidity of gastric contents, 15 minutes apart for analysis. The maximum effect from the histamine is usually seen in about ½ hour.

**Test for pheochromocytoma.** Before giving histamine, withdraw all antihypertensive drugs, sympathomimetics, sedatives and opioids for at least 24 hours—preferably for 3 days. Food is given routinely. The individual should be at rest in a supine position so that the blood pressure stabilizes. Then a cold pressure test* is performed; 30 minutes afterward, a slow intravenous infusion of 5% dextrose injection or normal saline is started. When blood pressure is stablized, a 2-hour collection of urine is obtained to test for catecholamines. Then histamine is given through the intravenous infusion and another 2-hour collection of urine is obtained for testing. Initial dose of histamine is 0.01 mg. Monitor blood pressure and pulse rate every 30 seconds for

*Cold pressure test is immersing one hand in cold water for 60 seconds and then measuring the rise in blood pressure. The increase in blood pressure after histamine is compared to the cold pressure test; it must exceed the water test to be indicative of pheochromocytoma.

15 minutes. If no response is noted, give a second dose of 0.05 mg.

Nearly all individuals will experience flushing, headache, and a decrease in blood pressure after the administration of the histamine. Within a couple of minutes, the blood pressure will increase. The package insert has further information on this test.

•   •   •

*Both of these tests should be performed by or under the direction of a physician.*

## ▷ Nursing Management: Histamine Testing

**Assessment.** Histamine should be used cautiously in individuals with any cardiac abnormality. The gastric histamine test is contraindicated in clients with a history of hypersensitivity to the drug, bronchial asthma, vasomotor instability, urticaria, or severe cardiac, pulmonary, or renal disease.

For the gastric histamine test, the drug is administered subcutaneously. Before the medication is injected, the plunger of the syringe should be drawn back to ensure that the needle is not in a blood vessel. Epinephrine should be available in case of inadvertent injection into a vessel.

The procedure and any anticipated effects of the histamine test should be explained to the client.

## ANTIHISTAMINES

Antihistamines are drugs that compete with histamine for its receptor sites. With the discovery of two histamine receptors, $H_1$ and $H_2$, the antihistamines should be divided into the $H_1$-receptor antagonists and the $H_2$-receptor antagonists. The $H_2$-receptor blocking agents, which include cimetidine (Tagamet), ranitidine (Zantac), and famotidine (Pepcid), are discussed in Chapter 40. These are valuable agents with a variety of indications, especially in the treatment or prevention of peptic ulcers (see Chapter 40).

## $H_1$ Receptor Antagonists

Antihistamines prevent the physiologic action of histamine. It is postulated that the antihistamines act by preventing histamine from reaching its site of action, by competing for the receptors. The antihistamines of the $H_1$ type have the greatest therapeutic effect on nasal allergies, particularly on seasonal hay fever. They relieve symptoms better at the beginning of the hay fever season than during its height but fail to relieve the asthma that frequently accompanies hay fever. These preparations are palliative and do not immunize the individual or protect him over time against allergic reactions. Their benefits are therefore comparatively short-lived and provide only symptomatic relief. They must be regarded only as adjuncts to more specific methods of treat-

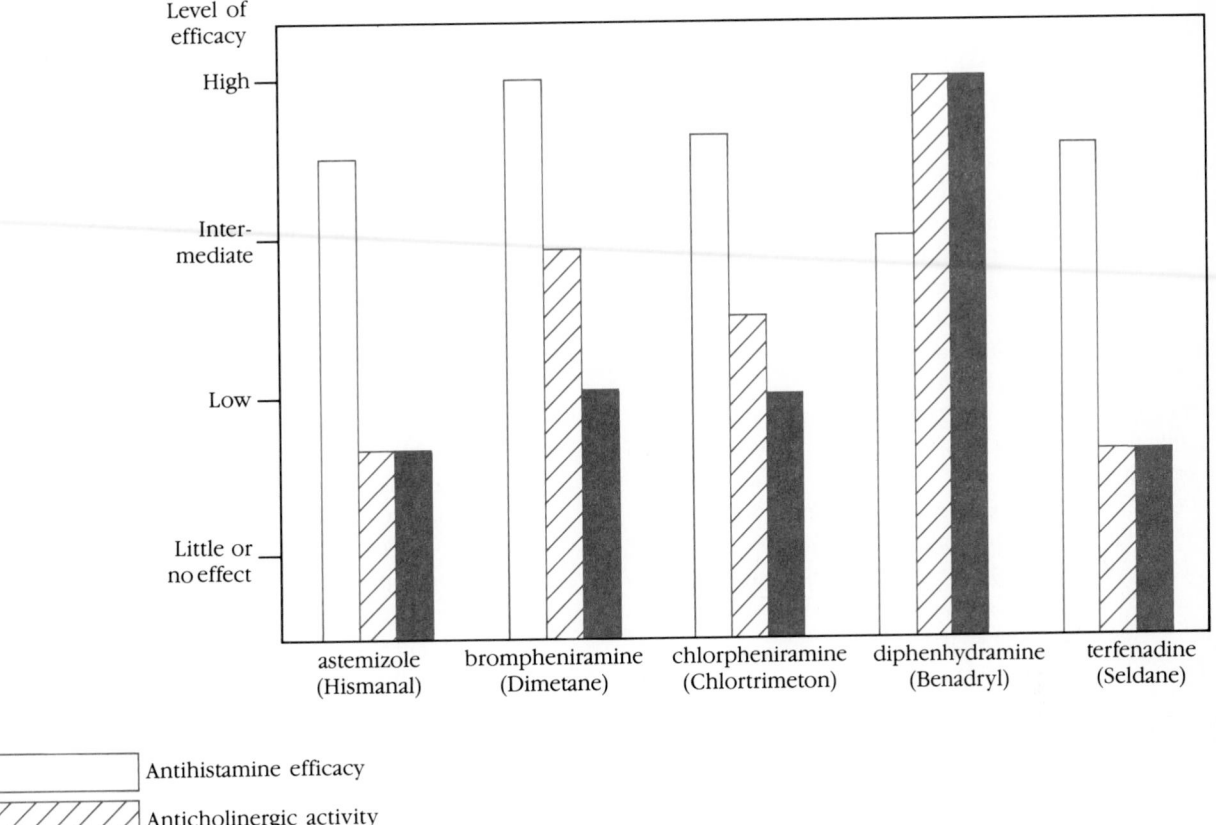

**FIGURE 38-2**  Comparison of selected antihistamine efficacy and side effects.

ment. They do not begin to replace such remedies as epinephrine, ephedrine, and aminophylline. In acute asthmatic reactions the antihistamine drugs serve only as supplements to these remedies. Also, relief of various symptoms of allergy is obtained only while the drug is being taken. Antihistamines do not appear to have a cumulative action and can therefore be taken over a period of time.

Dozens of antihistamine drugs are available and generally differ from each other by potency, duration of action, and incidence of side effects, particularly sedation. It is often necessary to try different types of antihistamines to determine the appropriate one for a client. Many OTC preparations also contain antihistamines; some contain two or more different ones. Antihistamines are used in antitussive preparations, cough-cold products, nighttime sedation or OTC sleeping products, oral analgesic products, menstrual tablets, and many other products. The nurse and consumer should check ingredients of all medications they buy, recommend, consume, or administer. Often individuals have unwanted side effects or are accidently overdosed since the same product may be available in several different medications they are consuming. Unfortunately this is frequently overlooked in a clinical setting.

Antihistamines compete with histamine for $H_1$ receptors on various effector structures, such as smooth muscle of vascular system and bronchioles, lacrimal, salivary, and respiratory mucosal glands. They do not inhibit histamine already attached to receptors. Thus these drugs are more effective if given before histamine is released.

Antihistamines are indicated for the treatment of allergies, vertigo, motion sickness, antitussive effect (diphenhydramine), and sedative and local anesthetic effects in dentistry. Generally, their oral absorption pattern is good and onset of action is within 15 to 60 minutes. Dimenhydrinate rectally has an onset of action within 30 to 45 minutes. The most highly protein bound antihistamines, 90% or greater, include astemizole, diphenhydramine, and terfenadine.

The time to peak effect can vary with each individual preparation. For example, bromphiramine has a peak effect in 3 to 9 hours, chlorpheniramine within 6 hours, terfenadine within 3 to 4 hours, and triprolidine within 2 to 3 hours. Duration of action is also variable with dimenhydrinate between 3 to 6 hours, pyrilamine at 8 hours, azatadine and diphenylpyraline at 12 hours, and astemizole possibly lasting several weeks after stopping the drug. These agents are primarily metabolized in the liver and excreted in the kidneys with the exception of astemizole and terfenadine, which are mainly excreted fecally.

For side effects/adverse reactions, see previous section for diphenhydramine.

When antihistamines are given with alcohol and CNS depressants, enhanced CNS depressant effects may be noted. If CNS depressant also has anticholinergic side effects, enhanced anticholinergic side effects may be seen. Monitor closely since interventions may be necessary. When antihistamines are given with anticholinergic medications, psychotropics, and others, an enhanced CNS depressant effect may be noted. When they are given with monoamine oxidase (MAO) inhibitors, prolonged anticholinergic and CNS depression effects may result. Avoid concurrent drug administration.

The antihistamine dosage varies with each drug's chemical classification and pharmacokinetic profile. The newer agents released generally are longer-acting drugs with less sedative side effects, such as astemizole (Hismanal), which is dosed once a day and has little, if any, sedative and anticholinergic side effects. The older agents that usually exhibit these side effects carry warnings about the drug use in the elderly; the geriatric client is usually more sensitive to the effects of these drugs and may require a reduction in dosage. Drugs that issue this warning include azatadine, brompheniramine, carbinoxamine, chlorpheniramine, clemastine, cyproheptadine, dexchlorpheniramine, dimenhydrinate, diphenhydramine, diphenylpyraline, doxylamine, phenindamine, pyrilamine, tripelennamine, and triprolidine.

The adult and children's dosages are noted in Table 38-4.

## ▷Nursing Management: Antihistamine Therapy

Take client medication history to determine if there is a previous intolerance to antihistamines. Use antihistamines with caution in clients with: asthma, since the drying effect may thicken secretions and diminish expectoration; prostatic hypertrophy or predisposition to urinary retention, because the urinary retention may be aggravated; or a predisposition to narrow-angle glaucoma, since the drug may precipitate an acute episode.

With the administration of antihistamines, the client should be assessed for the following nursing diagnoses: altered sleep pattern (drowsiness); altered comfort related to dryness of mouth and throat, rash, and/or tinnitis; risk for injury related to blurred vision, blood dyscrasias (unusual bleeding or bruising, sore throat, fever), paradoxical reaction (excitement), and hypotension (fainting); altered thought processes (confusion); and altered urinary elimination pattern (difficult or painful urination).

*Intervention.* In the administration of the parenteral form of brompheniramine, the concentrated solution (100

mg/dl) is not recommended for intravenous use. Do not break, crush, or chew sustained-release capsules or long-acting tablets.

*Education.* Advise the client who will be using antihistamines on a long-term basis to maintain dental hygiene by brushing and flossing because the diminished salivary flow resulting from antihistamines will contribute to caries and gum disease. Regular dental checkups should also be advised. The discomfort of the dryness of the mouth may be minimized by using ice, sugarless gum, or hard candy.

Drowsiness is a common effect of antihistamines. Caution the client about driving or using other hazardous equipment until the response to the drug has been ascertained. When the effect is known, then the client may modify life-style accordingly. Also, if the drowsiness is severe, another antihistamine may be prescribed.

Alert the client to the symptoms of blood dyscrasias, such as sore throat, fever, unusual bruising and bleeding, and tiredness, since these should be reported to the physician. Caution the client about ingesting alcohol or CNS depressants because the effects of the drugs will be potentiated.

Inform the client that antihistamines may be taken with food or milk to minimize gastric distress.

If the client is taking antihistamines as prophylaxis of motion sickness, the dose should be taken 30 minutes to 1 to 2 hours before its effect is needed. The client taking antihistamines should alert the allergist if scheduled for allergy skin tests because these drugs interfere with the results.

*Evaluation.* Clients on long-term antihistamine therapy should have periodic blood counts to monitor for the development of blood dyscrasias. Tolerance to some antihistamines may occur. If a tolerance develops, another antihistamine may be prescribed.

In the older child a paradoxical response to the drug may occur and the child may exhibit hyperexcitability rather than the drowsiness that is usually seen. With the elderly client, sedation and hypotension are more likely to occur, as well as the antimuscarinic effects of the drug, resulting in dryness of the mouth or urinary retention, particularly in the male. Closely monitor individuals with hypertension or cardiac or renal disease who are taking antihistamines.

## Inhibitor of Histamine Release

See cromolyn sodium in previous chapter. Cromolyn sodium provides a local protective effect in the mucosal airways by inhibiting the granulation of pulmonary mast cells and thereby preventing the release of histamine and SRS-A.

## SEROTONIN

Over a century ago scientists found that serum from coagulated blood contained a vasoconstrictor substance. During experiments involving the perfusion of isolated organs in blood, this substance appeared as an unwanted compound

**TABLE 38-4**   Recommended dosages for antihistamines

| Antihistamine | Adult dosage | Children's dosage |
|---|---|---|
| astemizole (Hismanal) | 10 mg daily | 6-12 yr, 5 mg/day |
| azatadine (Optimine) | 1-2 mg every 8-12 hr | 12 yr and over, 0.5-1 mg twice daily |
| brompheniramine (Dimetane) | 4 mg every 4-6 hr up to maximum of 24 mg/day<br>Extended release form:<br>  8 mg every 8-12 hr or 12 mg every 12 hr as necessary<br>Parenteral IM, IV, or SC: 10 mg every 8-12 hr as necessary | 0.5 mg/kg in three or four divided doses<br><br>6 yr and over, 8 or 12 mg every 12 hr as necessary<br>12 yr and under, 0.125 mg/kg three or four times daily as needed |
| carbinoxamine (Clistin) | 4-8 mg every 6-8 hr as needed | 1-3 yr, 2 mg every 6-8 hr; 3-6 yr, 2 to 4 mg every 6-8 hr; 6 yr and over, 4-6 mg every 6-8 hr as needed |
| chlorpheniramine (Chlortrimeton and others) | 4 mg every 4-6 hr as needed<br><br>Parenteral IM, IV, SC: 5-40 mg as single dose as necessary | 6-12 yr, 2 mg three or four times a day as needed<br>SC: 87.5 µg/kg every 6 hr as needed |
| clemastine (Tavist) | 1.34 mg twice daily or 2.68 mg one to three times a day, as needed | 6-12 yr, 670 µg to 2.68 mg twice a day, as necessary |
| cyproheptadine (Periactin) | 4 mg every 8 hr, increase as necessary (range 4 to 20 mg/day) | 0.125 mg/kg every 8-12 hr as needed |
| dexchlorpheniramine (Polaramine) | 2 mg every 4-6 hr as needed<br>Extended release:<br>  4 or 6 mg every 8-12 hr as needed | 150 µg/kg in four divided doses<br><br>Not recommended |
| dimenhydrinate (Dramamine) | 50-100 mg every 4 hr as necessary<br>Parenteral, IM, IV:<br>  50 mg IM or 50 mg in 10 ml normal saline for IV, every 4 hr (administer IV slowly) | 5 mg/kg in four divided doses<br><br>1.25 mg/kg IM or IV, every 6 hr as necessary (maximum 300 mg/day) |
| diphenhydramine | See previous section | |
| diphenylpyraline (Hispril) | 5 mg every 12 hr as necessary | 6 yr and over, 5 mg daily, as needed |
| doxylamine (Unisom) | 12.5-25 mg every 4-6 hr as necessary | 6-12 yr old, 6.25-12.5 mg every 4 to 6 hr as necessary |
| phenindamine (Nolahist) | 25 mg every 4-6 hr as necessary | 6-12 yr 12.5 mg every 4-6 hr as necessary |
| pyrilamine | 25-50 mg every 8 hr as necessary | 6 yr and older, 12.5 to 25 mg every 8 hr as necessary |
| terfenadine (Seldane) | 60 mg every 8-12 hr as necessary | Dosage not established |
| tripelennamine (Pyribenzamine) | 25-50 mg every 4-6 hr, as necessary<br><br>Extended-release:<br>  100 mg every 8-12 hr as necessary | 1.25 mg/kg every 6 hr as needed (maximum 300 mg/day)<br><br>Not recommended |
| triprolidine (Actidil) | 2.5 mg every 4-6 hr as necessary | 4 to 24 mo, 312 µg every 6-8 hr; 2-4 yr, 625 µg every 6-8 hr; 4 to 6 yr, 937 µg every 6-8 hr; 6 to 12 yr, 1.25 mg every 6-8 hr as needed |

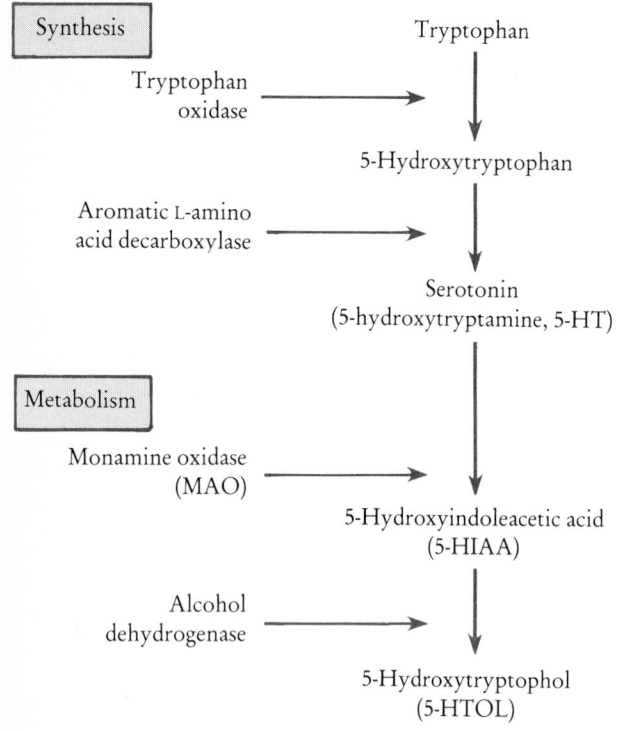

**FIGURE 38-3**  Synthesis and metabolism of serotonin.

that had to be eliminated to obtain accurate laboratory results. In 1948 researchers at the Cleveland Clinic finally isolated the vasoconstrictor material and named it serotonin. One year later the active moiety of this complex was identified as 5-hydroxytryptamine (5-HT).

As with histamine, serotonin has no therapeutic application; however, its importance is related to the action of other drugs and several disease states.

Serotonin is widely distributed in nature, occurring in both plants and animals. It appears in fruits such as pineapples, bananas, strawberries, and tomatoes, as well as in various nuts. In human beings, serotonin occurs in various body tissues. The sites of endogenous serotonin are discussed in the next section.

## Chemistry

*Synthesis.*  In human beings, the synthesis of serotonin begins with the essential dietary amino acid, tryptophan. Only two enzymatic steps are required to form serotonin in the tissues (Figure 38-3).

*Metabolism.*  The inactivation of serotonin is not complex. The principal enzyme concerned with this process is monamine oxidase, which forms 5-hydroxyindoleacetic acid (5-HIAA). The compound is then excreted in the urine along with a much smaller amount of another metabolite, 5-hydroxytryptophol (5-HTOL). Normal excretion of 5-HIAA is 2 to 9 mg a day.

*Distribution.*  Serotonin appears primarily in three types of tissues in the body: (1) the largest fraction (90%) is synthesized and stored in the enterochromaffin cells of the gastrointestinal tract mucosa, particularly in the pylorus of the stomach and in the upper region of the small intenstine; (2) a much smaller fraction is stored but not synthesized in platelets; on disintegration this fraction is released in serum and in the spleen; and (3) in the CNS the greatest concentration occurs in the hypothalmus, midbrain, reticular formation, raphe (midline) regions of medulla and pons, and pineal gland. A neuron that releases serotonin is termed a serotoninergic or tryptaminergic fiber. Finally, only a very low concentration of serotonin appears in cells.

## Pharmacologic Actions

Serotonin appears to possess multiple pharmacologic actions, but because of discrepant experimental findings, this variability has caused much controversy. Despite the need for additional experimental analysis, it is now known that the primary function of serotonin is exerted on various smooth muscles and nerves. As previously stated, serotonin is not a therapeutic agent, but its more prominent effects are associated with its influence on other drugs and some disease states.

*Gastrointestinal tract.*  Among the columnar epithelial cells of the stomach and intestine are located specialized cells called argentaffin or enterochromaffin cells. The serotonin secreted by these cells is responsible for contraction of the gastrointestinal smooth muscle, thereby producing the peristaltic response.

Carcinoid syndrome is a condition that elicits a complex array of signs and symptoms mediated by humoral compounds released from malignant carcinoid tumors. Carcinoid tumors are best described as slowly growing neoplasms of enterochromaffin cells of the stomach, intestine, or bronchial trees. The overproduction of serotonin is an important biochemical reaction caused by these tumors; bradykinin and histamine also may be elaborated. Serotonin is responsible for causing this syndrome, which is characterized by paroxysmal flushing, hyperperistalsis, diarrhea, bronchoconstriction, and cardiac valvular lesions. The diagnosis of carcinoid syndrome is confirmed by the presence of excess 5-HT, which eventually is excreted in the urine as 5-HIAA. The normal daily urinary excretion is 2 to 9 mg in adults. Obviously this amount is greatly increased in the presence of carcinoid tumor.

*Blood platelets.*  Serotonin is released from platelets during their breakdown within the circulation. This compound then activates receptors on the surface of other blood platelets, thereby promoting platelet aggregation. It has been suggested that through this mechanism the discharge of serotonin from platelets may contribute to the formation of pulmonary embolism.

*Central nervous system.*  Serotonin is manufactured and stored in the neurons in the brain. The central action of the neuronal system appears to elicit primarily in inhibitory response from the specific nuclei of the brain. Researchers now postulate that altered function of serotoninergic pathways is a factor in various CNS dysfunctions. Serotonin synthesized in the pineal gland serves as a precursor for the synthesis of melatonin, a hormone that functions as a potent lightening agent in animals. Melatonin does not affect human skin and pigment.

***Sleep.*** Serotonin-synthesizing cells are required for the induction of non-rapid-eye-movement (NREM) sleep (quiet brain, potentially excitable muscles) and the onset of REM sleep (active brain, rapid-eye movements, dreams, atonic muscles). Normal sleep depends on serotonin along with the combined functions of norepinephrine and cholinergic systems. The basic sleep pattern consists of four to six cycles that alternate between NREM and REM sleep. Destruction of the raphe nuclei results in insomnia. Other disorders of sleep are quite common; for example, narcolepsy is characterized by a sudden change from wakefulness dirctly to REM sleep.

Sleep hypnotics such as barbiturates tend to decrease REM sleep, which is an essential component of restful sleep. Also, the drug *p*-chlorophenylalanine inhibits formation of serotonin, and this depletion can cause prolonged wakefulness when administered to animals.

***Pain perception.*** The serotoninergic neurons located in the raphe nuclei of the brainstem have axons that project to the spinal cord and forebrain. One important system related to the brain involves a substance called beta-endorphin, which is associated with neurons that interconnect various neclei in the hypothalamus, limbic system, and thalamus. The beta-endorphin neurons mediate euphoric and emotional behavior. The thalamic nuclei mediates poorly localized deep pain, which is best influenced by opiates. The density of opiate receptors in the brain appears to be much greater in the medial and lateral thalamus. Many receptors are required to determine how addiction and withdrawal can be influenced.

Serotonin also is implicated in the action of morphine. Studies suggest that as tolerance develops toward this narcotic, the synthesis but not the accumulation of serotonin doubles. In addition, a decrease in brain serotonin level increases a person's sensitivity to painful stimuli, thus decreasing the analgesic effect of morphine.

***Mental illness.*** CNS depression correlates with low levels of total brain serotonin. The enzyme monoamine oxidase metabolizes serotonin, resulting in a lower level of the transmitter (see Figure 38-3). Accordingly, a monoamine oxidase inhibitor (MAOI) blocks the degradation of serotonin and thereby increases the concentration level of the neurotransmitter in the brain. The antidepressant effects of MAOI drugs are discussed in Chapter 17. The tricyclic compounds also act as antidepressants, blocking the reuptake of serotonin and norepinephrine at the membrane of the neuron and thereby potentiating the action of the synapse. Reserpine, formerly an antipsychotic drug, is now used as an antihypertensive agent. Because it causes a prolonged depletion of serotonin and norepinephrine in the

---

**PREGNANCY SAFETY**

FDA category B: azatadine, brompheniramine, cyproheptadine, dexchlorpheniramine, dimenhydrinate, triprolidine

FDA category C: astemizole, carbinoxamine, terfenadine

FDA category unclassified: doxylamine

---

brain, reserpine is responsible for producing a tranquilizing effect (see Chapter 22).

## ANTISEROTONINS

Antiserotonins, or serotonin antagonists, are considered complex compounds because they posses varying degrees of specificity, and thus the exact mechanism of action is unknown. In addition to performing serotonin-blocking activity, many other pharmacologic actions are involved in inhibiting responses to serotonin.

### cyproheptadine (Periactin)

Cyproheptadine blocks serotonin activity in smooth muscle of blood vessels and the intestine and also has antihistaminic and possibly anticholinergic properties. It may produce weight gain in children because of stimulation of appetite through action in the hypothalamus. It is administered primarily for allergic disorders. (See "antihistamines" and Figure 38-3.)

### lysergic acid diethylamide (LSD)

The basic mechanism underlying LSD's hallucinogenic properties is not known. Experts agree, however, that its profound effects on behavior are mediated through the central neurotransmitter, serotonin. Studies in the 1970s have suggested that the more powerful hallucinogenic drugs exert a dual function in the brain: they inhibit the action of serotonin and stimulate the norepinephrine system (see Chapter 9).

### methysergide maleate (Sansert)

Although its mechanism of action is unknown, methysergide is both a potent antiserotonin and a vasoconstrictor agent. These properties apparently help to relieve migraine and other vascular headaches (see Chapter 21).

## INVESTIGATIONAL ANTIHISTAMINE DRUGS

Some agents that may be released in the near future include cetirizine, an hydroxyzine derivative that has low sedation properties; acrivastine, a peripheral $H_1$ receptor antagonist that is nonsedating; and ketotifen fumarate, a mast cell stabilizer, $H_1$ receptor antagonist, and phosphodiesterase inhibitor. Ketotifen, which has sedating side effects, will probably be indicated for the treatment of asthma and rhinitis.

## SUMMARY

The drugs in this chapter cover a wide range of therapeutic effects on the respiratory system. Oxygen, a therapeutic gas, is essential to sustain life, and its administration is required for many clients. Although most acute care facilities have a respiratory therapy department, the nurse is responsible for evaluating the client's response to oxygen and, in some circumstances, initiating oxygen therapy. Doxapram, a respiratory stimulant, has been used in the treatment of drug-induced respiratory depression, but mechanical support of respirations is considered more effective.

Cough suppressants are generally used for nonproductive coughs in which prolonged coughing is annoying, exhausting, and painful. Opioid antitussive drugs are discussed in Chapter 12. However, nonnarcotic antitussive drugs may be effective and have fewer gastrointestinal side effects. Because their action is local, liquids should be withheld for 30 minutes after dosing or their effect will be washed away.

Nasal decongestants are agents which cause vasoconstriction of the engorged nasal mucous membranes and so relieve nasal stuffiness. However, overuse will lead to "rebound" swelling of the mucous membranes.

Histamine is a chemical mediator naturally occurring in most body tissues and has been implicated in a number of pathologic conditions, such as urticaria, atopy, food allergies, bronchial asthma, and systemic anaphylaxis. This makes antihistamines, which compete at receptor sites with histamines to prevent their physiologic actions, invaluable as medications. Antihistamines are contained in numerous antitussive preparations, cold-cough products, OTC sleeping compounds, and oral analgesic products.

Serotonin is also a naturally occurring substance with no therapeutic application. However, it is related to the action of other drugs, such as the opiates. CNS depression also correlates with low levels of total brain serotonin. The antiserotonin methysergide maleate may be used to relieve vascular headaches.

## BIBLIOGRAPHY

Ahrens TS. (1987). Concepts in the assessment of oxygenation, Focus Crit Care 14(1):36.

American Hospital Formulary Service.(1991): AHFS drug information '91. American Society of Hospital Pharmacists, Inc.

Anderson KL. (1989). Long-term oxygen therapy: indications and guidelines for use, Home Health Nurse 7(3):40.

Bower KJ. (1986). Oxygen transport, Crit Care Nurs 6(6):10.

Braunwald E et al, editors. (1987). Harrison's principles of internal medicine, ed 11. New York: McGraw-Hill Book Co.

Ehrenwerth J et al. (1987). Pulse oximetry in the postanesthesia unit, J Post Anesth Nurs 11(1):9.

Feldman EG and Davison DE. (1986). Handbook of nonprescription drugs, ed 8. Washington, DC: American Pharmaceutical Association and The National Professional Society of Pharmacists.

Gilboy NS et al. (1989). Noninvasive monitoring of oxygenation with pulse oximetry, JEN 15(1):26.

Gilman AG et al, editors. (1990). Goodman & Gilman's the pharmacological basis of therapeutics, ed 8. New York: Macmillan Publishing Co.

Gossel TA. (1987). The common cold: new defenses against an old enemy, U S Pharmacist 12(1):35.

Gossel TA. (1986). Counseling consumers on OTC antihistamines, U S Pharmacist 11(6):37.

Kastrup EK and Olin BR. (1991). Facts and comparisons: drug information. St Louis: JB Lippincott Co.

Krupp MA et al, editors. (1987). Current medical diagnosis and treatment. Norwalk, Conn: Appleton & Lange.

Mathewson HS. (1988). Tissue oxygenation in the critically ill, AANA J 56(5):419.

Mims BC. (1987). The risks of oxygen therapy, RN 50(7):20.

Openbrier DR et al. (1988). Home oxygen therapy: evaluation and prescription, Amer J Nurs 88(2):192.

Pepper GA. (1987). OTCs vs. Rx for allergic rhinitis, Nurse Pract 12(6):58.

Pepper GA. (1986). OTCs vs. Rx for coughs and colds, Nurse Pract 11(10):66.

Rogge JA et al. (1989). Effectiveness of oxygen concentrations of less than 100% before and after endotracheal suction in patients with chronic obstructive pulmonary disease, Heart Lung 18(1):64.

Toleda LW. (1987). Pulse oximetry: clinical implications in the PACU, J Post Anesth Nurs 11(1):12.

United States Pharmacopeial Convention. (1991). Drug information for the health care professional, ed 11. Rockville, Md: The Convention.

Weil EK and Rosenberg JM. (1989). Antihistamine agents in the pipeline, Hosp Phar 24(10):864.

Whitney JD. (1989). Physiologic effects of tissue oxygenation on wound healing, Heart Lung 18(5):466.

*Unit 10*

# Drugs Affecting the Gastrointestinal System

*Chapter*

# 39 Overview of the Gastrointestinal Tract

## CHAPTER OBJECTIVES

*After studying this chapter, you should be able to meet the following objectives and define the key terms.*

1. Identify the major parts of the gastrointestinal tract.

2. Describe the functions of individual components of the gastrointestinal tract.

3. List the effects of parasympathetic and sympathetic enervation on the gastrointestinal tract.

4. Describe common disorders affecting the gastrointestinal tract.

## KEY TERMS

**alimentary canal,** page 666
**acute gastritis,** page 669
**cholecystitis,** page 669
**cholelithiasis,** page 669
**chronic gastritis,** page 669
**defecation,** page 670
**deglutition,** page 668
**digestion,** page 666
**dysphagia,** page 668
**hemorrhoids,** page 670
**peptic ulcer disease,** page 669
**peristaltic process,** page 668

## INTRODUCTION

Gastrointestinal disorders are the most common of human problems. Since the cause of many gastrointestinal diseases remains unclear, pharmacologic management is often directed at relieving symptoms rather than at control or cure.

The gastrointestinal system itself (see Figure 39-1) is made up of the alimentary canal or digestive tract, the biliary system, and the pancreas.

The **alimentary canal** extends from the mouth to the anus. Food substances entering the canal undergo mechanical and chemical changes called **digestion.** These changes permit nutrients to be absorbed and undigestible materials to be excreted by the body. Absorbed nutrients may be used

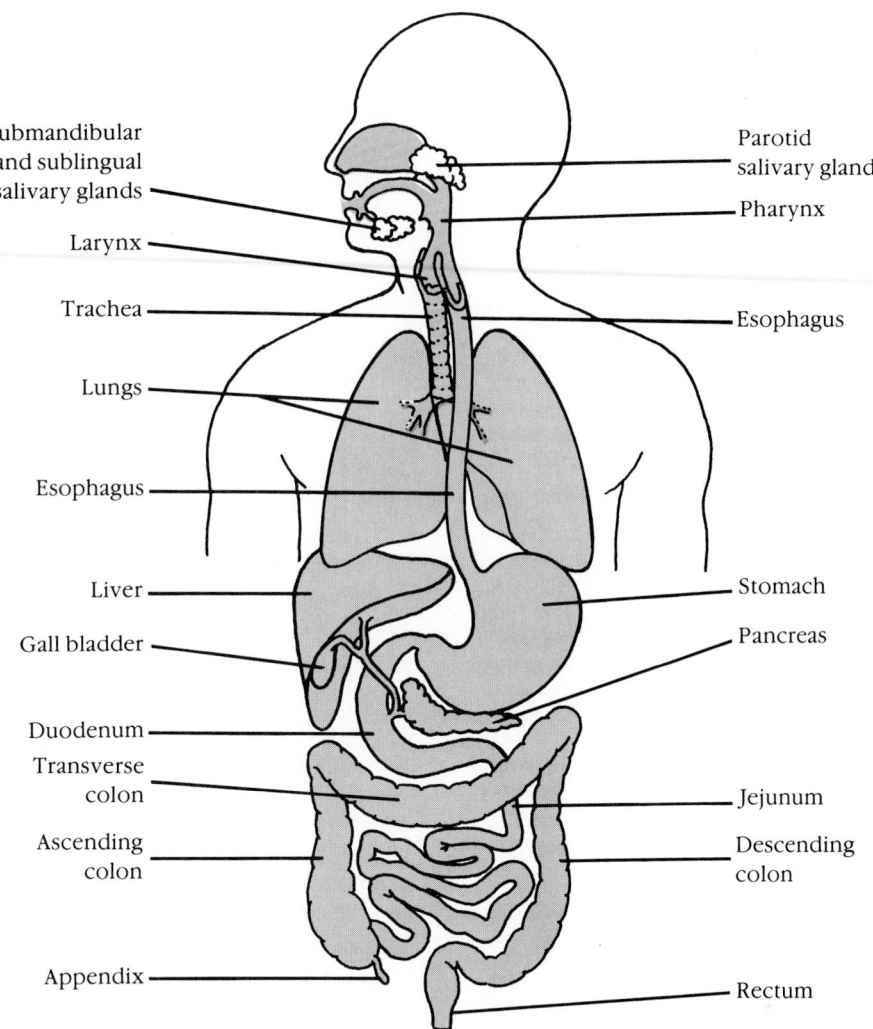

Submandibular and sublingual salivary glands

Larynx

Trachea

Lungs

Esophagus

Liver

Gall bladder

Duodenum

Transverse colon

Ascending colon

Appendix

Parotid salivary gland

Pharynx

Esophagus

Stomach

Pancreas

Jejunum

Descending colon

Rectum

**FIGURE 39-1**  Gastrointestinal system.

as an energy source or stored (glycogen for glucose or fat for carbohydrate). Movements by the smooth muscle fibers surrounding the canal (1) mix the contents by segmental contractions and (2) move the mass through the tract by peristalsis.

The secretory and muscular activities of the gastrointestinal system are regulated by neural mechanisms. An interconnecting network of neurons is located in smooth muscle and secretory cells. This system is self-regulating; it is capable of controlling exocrine gland secretions and muscular contractions without any external influence.

By contrast, the external innervation of the gastrointestinal system is supplied by the divisions of the autonomic nervous system. Their major function is to correlate activities between different regions of the gastrointestinal system and also between this system and other parts of the body.

The influence of the parasympathetic division is mediated by two branches of the vagus nerve. This division exerts an excitatory action, which increases digestive secretions and muscular activity. By contrast, the splanchnic nerves

of the sympathetic division are primarily inhibitory, depressing digestive secretions and muscular activity. Under normal conditions, the two divisions of the autonomic nervous system maintain a delicate balance of control of functions.

Drugs affecting the gastrointestinal tract exert their action mainly on muscular and glandular tissues. The action may be directly on the smooth muscle and gland cells or indirectly on the autonomic nervous system. Drugs also may cause increased or decreased function, tone, emptying time, or peristaltic action of the stomach or bowel. In addition, they may be used to relieve enzyme deficiency, to counteract excess acidity or gas formation, to produce or prevent vomiting, or as diagnostic aids.

## MOUTH (ORAL CAVITY)

The mouth, or oral cavity, is composed of the lips, cheeks, tongue, and hard and soft palates. The mouth functions as the starting point of the digestive process. Food is taken in, cut and ground between the teeth, and mixed with saliva. Saliva contains the enzyme amylase (ptyalin), which begins the process of chemical digestion.

Three pairs of salivary glands secrete saliva into ducts emptying into the mouth. The sublingual and submandibular salivary glands are located beneath the tongue; the largest pair, the parotid glands, are found in front of and slightly below the ears.

When the food bolus has been chewed and so mechanically reduced in the mouth, it is swallowed. Swallowing (**deglutition**) is a complex process that begins as a voluntary movement but is continued as an involuntary muscular reflex as the food is propelled through the gastrointestinal tract.

***Disorders affecting the mouth.*** Systemic diseases, nutritional deficiencies, and mechanical trauma can cause irritation or inflammation of buccal structures. Dental disorders (e.g., caries, gingivitis, and pyorrhea) and bacterial, viral, or fungal infections (e.g., candidiasis or herpes simplex) can affect the structures of the oral cavity, causing such symptoms as mouth blistering or other lesions, swelling, pain, and inflammation.

Agents acting on the oral cavity are discussed in Chapter 40.

## PHARYNX

The pharynx (throat) is a tubelike passageway connecting the mouth and the esophagus. It is important in swallowing. Food and fluid pass through the pharynx into the esophagus. During this passage the trachea is closed to prevent aspiration into the lungs.

***Disorders affecting the pharynx.*** Like the mouth, the pharynx can be affected by various systemic diseases. It can become irritated and inflamed (e.g., from sinusitis or the "common cold") and treated symptomatically with an antiinflammatory agent. It can also become a locus of infection (e.g., with strep throat), requiring systemic antibiotic therapy.

## ESOPHAGUS

The esophagus is a pliable muscular structure approximately 25 cm long that extends from the pharynx to the cardiac end of the stomach. It extends through the diaphragm as it drops from the thoracic cavity into the abdominal cavity.

The esophagus is considered the beginning of the digestive system proper, since the rest of the gastrointestinal tract organs function only in digestion and/or excretion.

The esophagus continues the process of swallowing and begins the **peristaltic process,** or the squeezing of the food bolus down the gastrointestinal tract by band contraction. The peristaltic band wave stimulates the lower esophageal sphincter, which closes to prevent gastroesophageal reflux and then returns the esophagus to its normal resting state.

***Disorders affecting the esophagus.*** Esophageal disorders are characterized by retrosternal pain (heartburn) and difficulty in swallowing (**dysphagia**). The sources of the pain are numerous; some potential causes include diffuse esophageal spasm, achalasia, pyloric or duodenal ulcers, scleroderma, postural changes (bending forward), excessive alcohol ingestion, and nonspecific dysmotility.

However, heartburn commonly results from reflux esophagitis, in which the incompetent lower esophageal sphincter permits gastric contents to flow back into the esophagus, or from hiatal hernia, in which a part of the stomach protrudes into the diaphragm. One type of hiatal hernia, paraesophageal hernia, may be associated with esophageal obstruction and strangulation.

Difficulty in swallowing can be a symptom of esophageal obstruction, mechanical interference with or paralysis of the muscles of deglutition, neuromuscular incoordination, achalasia, carcinoma of the esophagus, anxiety states, hysteria, or schizophrenic hallucinations.

Inflammation of the esophagus can have many causes: reflux esophagitis associated with hiatal hernia, irritant ingestion, infection, peptic ulceration, prolonged gastric intubation, and uremia.

## STOMACH

The stomach is a pouchlike structure lying below the diaphragm. It has three divisions: the fundus, the body, and the pylorus. Two sphincter muscles—the cardiac sphincter and the pyloric sphincter—regulate the stomach opening. Gastric glands secrete mucus and gastric juice, which is composed of enzymes and hydrochloric acid. They also produce intrinsic factor, a protein essential for absorption of vitamin $B_{12}$. Vitamin $B_{12}$ in turn is needed for erythropoiesis (red blood cell formation).

The stomach functions as a temporary storage site for food as it is being digested. It also manufactures gastrin, a hormone that regulates enzyme production to facilitate digestion.

The stomachs of men and women differ, both in food storage capacity and size. Females have smaller and more slender stomachs. The stomach is capable of holding 1500 to 2000 ml. It distends after eating and gradually collapses as the food bolus moves out into the small intestine. Its churning action further breaks down the food bolus and mixes it with gastric juice to continue chemical digestion. A limited amount of nutrient and drug absorption takes place in the stomach.

The time required for digestion in the stomach depends on the amount of food eaten. Normal emptying time is 2 to 6 hours. However, the gastric emptying time may be affected by drug administration, physical activity of the individual, and body position during digestion. Gastric emptying time is a factor to consider in the timing of drug administration, since the presence of food may block the absorption of some drugs.

***Disorders affecting the stomach.*  Acute gastritis** is an inflammatory response of the stomach lining to ingestion of irritants, such as ethanol or nonsteroidal antiinflammatory agents, including aspirin. Symptoms include epigastric discomfort, nausea, abdominal tenderness, and gastrointestinal hemorrhage. Treatment consists of life-style modifications and drugs such as antacids, antiemetic agents, anticholinergics, and antihistamines (see Chapter 40).

**Chronic gastritis** is a degeneration of the gastric mucosa, but its causes are not well established. It is more common in women, and the incidence increases with age and excessive smoking and ethanol use. Symptoms are nonspecific but may include flatulence, epigastric fullness after meals, diarrhea, and bleeding. Treatment is the same as for acute gastritis.

Iron deficiency anemia and pernicious anemia may result from chronic gastritis. Treatment of symptoms with antacids, anticholinergics, and sedatives, as well as vitamin $B_{12}$ if pernicious anemia is present, and elimination of possible causative or aggravating factors (e.g., aspirin use) comprise the usual therapeutic regimen.

**Peptic ulcer disease** is a broad term encompassing both gastric and duodenal ulcers. Although both types of ulcers produce a "break" in the gastric mucosa, the causes differ. With gastric ulcers, the ability of the gastric mucosa to protect and repair itself seems to be defective; in duodenal ulcers hypersecretion of gastric acid is responsible for the erosion of the gastric mucosa.

Duodenal ulcers are more common than gastric ulcers, accounting for nearly 80% of all peptic ulcers. Duodenal ulcers usually occur more frequently in younger persons. Overall, the reported incidence of peptic ulcers is much lower in females.

Pharmacologic treatment of peptic ulcer disease involves use of antacids, histamine-2 receptor antagonists, and sucralfate. However, nondrug treatment (diet and life-style modifications) are equally important. (See "Nursing Management" in Chapter 40.) Hereditary factors, use of some drugs (e.g., aspirin and corticosteroids), psychic factors, stress, and diet have been implicated in the development of peptic ulcer disease.

## LIVER

Immediately under the diaphragm and above the stomach is the largest gland in the body, the liver. It weighs approximately 1.5 kg. It is an extremely active and important organ that performs over 100 different functions.

The liver consists of two lobes composed of multitudes of lobules that function to remove toxins from the bloodstream, store nutrients such as iron and some vitamins, and secrete bile. Bile is transported, via the hepatic ducts, to the gallbladder for storage. In the intestine, bile aids in digestion, emulsification, and absorption of fat. Because it is normally alkaline, bile also functions to neutralize gastric acid in the duodenum.

Venous blood goes directly to the liver from the intestinal tract, so nutrients and absorbed drugs pass through the liver before reaching the systemic circulation. Thus the liver plays an active role in absorbing and metabolizing fats, carbohydrates, and proteins. It also stores vitamins A, $B_{12}$, and D and iron.

Some drugs are taken up by the liver, released into the bile, and then excreted in the feces. Other drugs move from the bile into the small intestine, where they are reabsorbed and recirculated. Still other drugs are transformed by the liver and excreted in the urine. In all of these cases the liver metabolizes the drug to make it more water soluble. This biotransformation changes the parent compound to a metabolite that may have greater, lesser, or equal activity. Cytochrome P-450 in the liver is responsible for biotransformation. There are also drugs that pass through the body and are secreted unchanged in the urine.

***Disorders affecting the liver.*** Viral hepatitis, Laënnec's and postnecrotic cirrhosis, carcinoma, or chronic alcoholism causes damage to the liver and liver cell dysfunction.

## GALLBLADDER

Lying on the undersurface of the liver is the gallbladder, a pear-shaped organ 7 to 10 cm long and 2.5 to 3.5 cm wide. The gallbladder can hold 30 to 50 ml of bile. It concentrates the bile and stores it until it is needed for digestion in the stomach and small intestine.

***Disorders affecting the gallbladder.*  Cholecystitis,** inflammation of the gallbladder, is often associated with the presence of gallstones **(cholelithiasis).** The stones lodge in the gallbladder neck or ducts, causing congestion and edema as bile builds up. This may be an acute or a chronic condition. Treatment of cholecystitis and cholelithiasis includes administration of analgesics, antispasmodics, and chenodeoxycholic acid.

Malignant tumors of the gallbladder are infrequent.

## PANCREAS

The pancreas is a gland about 15 to 20 cm long and 5 cm wide. It weighs approximately 75 g. The gland has three major segments: the head (found in the curve of the duodenum), the body, and the tail (which touches or nearly touches the spleen). The role of the pancreas is twofold: the exocrine cells secrete the digestive enzymes found in pancreatic juice, and the endocrine cells help control carbohydrate metabolism with their production of glucagon and insulin.

***Disorders affecting the pancreas.*** With the exception of diabetes mellitus, many pancreatic diseases have symptoms that are not readily diagnosed. Inflammation of the pancreas may be acute or chronic. Among the many causes are blockage of the pancreatic ducts, trauma to the pancreas, alcohol consumption, drug use, and tumors, cysts, or abscesses. Symptoms are nonspecific but ultimately include severe pain. Carcinoma of the pancreas is as difficult to diagnose as other pancreatic disorders.

## SMALL INTESTINE

The small intestine is a coiled tube approximately 21 feet long. It consists of the duodenum, jejunum, and ileum. Within the small intestine the food bolus is thoroughly mixed with the digestive juices to complete the "breakdown" process. The intestinal mucosa then absorbs nutrients and drugs, which are filtered through the liver before entering the circulatory and lymphatic systems.

***Disorders affecting the small intestine.*** Two disorders affecting the entire lower gastrointestinal tract are diarrhea and constipation. These are discussed in Chapter 41 along with the drugs used in their treatment.

Other disorders affecting the small intestine include obstruction, malabsorption syndrome, and blind loop syndrome. Symptomatic treatment is customary while the underlying causative factors are investigated.

## LARGE INTESTINE

The cecum, colon, and rectum make up the large intestine. The distal 2.5 cm of the rectum is known as the anal canal. The large intestine is approximately 5 feet long. It completes the digestive and absorptive processes. The large intestine is involved mainly with water absorption (from 1800 to 3000 ml/day) and synthesis of vitamin K. The lining of the large intestine secretes mucus to coat the undigested residue and protect the bowel lining. The undigestible residue is expelled through the reflex action known as **defecation.**

***Disorders affecting the large intestine.*** Diarrhea and constipation, mentioned earlier and in Chapter 41 also affect the large intestine. Other disorders include diverticular disease, which has no specific therapy; ulcerative colitis, treated with life-style modifications, antidiarrheals, and steroids, carcinoma; and irritable bowel syndrome.

**Hemorrhoids** (varicosities of the external or internal hemorrhoidal veins) are common, with many kinds of drugs used in treatment (see Chapter 41).

## SUMMARY

Food sustains life and determines nutritional status, which contributes to an individual's state of health, levels of achievement, and resistance to and ability to handle disease. The primary function of the gastrointestinal tract is to provide the body cells with nutrients, electrolytes, and water through the processes of ingestion, digestion, and absorption of food and fluid and elimination of waste products and residue. Drugs affect the gastrointestinal tract by acting primarily on muscular and glandular tissue. Although some drugs are prescribed primarily for their effect on the gastrointestinal tract, the nurse needs to be aware that most drugs prescribed for other reasons also have gastrointestinal side effects and/or adverse reactions.

## BIBLIOGRAPHY

Age-related changes in the gastrointestinal tract. (1988). Geriatr Nurs 9(5):22.

Bullock BL and Rosendahl PP. (1988). Pathophysiology: adaptations and alterations in function, ed 2, Boston: Little, Brown & Co.

Gitnick G, editor. (1988). Current gastroenterology. New York: John Wiley & Sons, Inc.

Price SA and Wilson LM. (1982). Pathophysiology, ed 2, New York: McGraw-Hill Book Co.

Sleisenger MH and Fordtran JS. (1988). Gastrointestinal disease: pathophysiology, diagnosis, and management. Philadelphia: WB Saunders Co.

Smith CE. (1988). Assessing bowel sounds: more than just listening, Nursing 18(2):42.

Test your knowledge of adult health care: gastrointestinal disorders. (1988). Nursing 18(4):106.

*Chapter*

# 40 Drugs Affecting the Upper Gastrointestinal Tract

## CHAPTER OBJECTIVES

*After studying this chapter, you should be able to meet the following objectives and define the key terms.*

1. Discuss the use and side effects of antacids.

2. List four drugs administered to promote digestion.

3. Describe the vomiting reflex.

4. Differentiate the five classes of antiemetic medications and their sites of action.

5. Describe two emetic agents and their use.

6. Discuss the effect of $H_2$ receptor antagonists on gastric acid secretion.

7. Use nursing measures in planning care for clients who are receiving agents affecting the upper gastrointestinal tract.

## KEY TERMS

## AGENTS THAT AFFECT THE MOUTH

In general, drugs have little effect on the mouth. Good oral hygiene, which includes brushing properly after meals and at bedtime, flossing, and gum stimulation, has more influence on the tissues of the mouth than most medicines. Some clients may require more than two visits per year to their dentists for professional plaque removal. Many other mouth and throat preparations are available containing steroids, anesthetics, and antiseptics for various disorders of the oral cavity, including chapped lips, sun and fever blisters, inflammatory lesions, ulcerative lesions secondary to trauma, gingival lesions, teething pain, toothache, irritation caused by orthodontic appliances or dentures, and oral cavity abrasions.

### Mouthwashes and Gargles

It has been estimated that Americans spend approximately $500 million annually for mouthwashes and gargles, and this figure may be increasing as a result of the introduction of products promoted to control plaque and reduce periodontal or gum disease. Mouthwashes and gargles are dilute aromatic solutions that contain a sweetener and an artificial coloring agent. They may also contain an antiseptic (alcohol, cetylpyridinium chloride, phenol, povidone-iodine, carbamate peroxide), anesthetic (eugenol, clove oil), astringent (zinc chloride), and anticaries agent (sodium fluoride). Although several products claim to contain ingredients that reduce plaque formation, clinical trials have demonstrated success only with volatile oils and cetylpyridinium chloride alone or in combination with domiphene bromide. Commercial products that contain at least one of these active ingredients include Cepacol (cetylpyridinium chloride), Listerine (volatile oils), and Scope (cetylphyridinium chloride and domiphene bromide). Also, an oral rinse containing

0.12% chlorhexidine gluconate (Peridex) was the first product approved for prevention of gingivitis. It has received the American Dental Association Council of Therapeutics' seal of acceptance for control of plaque and gingivitis (FDC Report, 1986).

Mouthwashes are often used for **halitosis,** or "bad breath," or as gargles to treat colds or sore throats. They are generally not effective for such problems. Mouthwashes may improve mouth odor briefly, but if such a problem persists, the underlying cause needs to be identified and treated. For example, poor dental hygiene, various gum diseases, consumption of odorous products such as onions and garlic, postnasal drip, infections, tumors, diabetes, and many other disease states may produce bad breath.

Sore throats are usually caused by infection, most often viral rather than bacterial. Gargling cannot reach the site of infection, which is usually deep in the throat tissues. The FDA has prohibited manufacturers from claiming that their OTC products will prevent colds and sore throats or that the products will stop bad breath, because these are considered false claims (Cornacchia and Barrett, 1985). Sodium chloride solution (½ tsp of salt to an 8-oz glass of warm water) has been recommended for use as a gargle and mouthwash. It is probably as effective, if not more effective, than some of the remedies sold today.

## Oxygen-Releasing Agents

Hydrogen peroxide is a weak antibacterial agent used to clean wounds topically and orally. The antibacterial effect depends on the liberation of oxygen, which occurs when the peroxide comes in contact with the tissue enzyme catalase. The resulting effervescence (bubbling action) loosens pus and tissue debris, which helps reduce bacterial content. Hydrogen peroxide is usually used in a 1.5% to 3% solution for cleaning wounds or as a mouthwash. As a gargle, the 3% solution should be diluted with an equal amount of water before use.

A number of other oxygen-releasing products are commercially available. Gly-oxide peroxide (Carbamide Peroxide) in a 10% solution is used for treatment of canker sores, denture irritation, and irritation following orthodontic intervention. This preparation is applied directly to the affected area for a few minutes, and then the solution is expectorated. Hydrogen peroxide gel (Peroxyl) is also available for minor mouth irritation and is applied and expectorated after use.

## Fluoridated Mouthwash

A number of fluoride-containing preparations, including mouthwash (Fluorigard), toothpaste, tablets, and solutions, are available for use as anticaries agents. The exact mechanism of action of fluoride in preventing caries is not fully understood; however, fluoride ions appear to exchange for hydroxyl or citrate (anion) ions and then settle in the anionic

---

### ALCOHOLIC MOUTHWASH WARNINGS

**Pediatric Alert**

The leading mouthwashes usually contain from 14% to 25% alcohol. Safety closures are not generally used with mouthwashes, so parents of young children should be cautioned to store such products in a safe area, preferably a locked cabinet. Young children appear to be extremely sensitive to alcohol-induced hypoglycemic effects; hypoglycemia requiring hospitalization has been reported after the consumption of only ½ to 1 oz of an alcoholic mouthwash in a 2-year-old (D'Arcy, 1985). The use of mouthwash in young children is not recommended since children often swallow the mouthwash rather than expectorate it.

**Adult Use**

It is reported that 10% to 15% of alcoholics in detoxification units use nonbeverage alcohol (mouthwashes, hair tonics, and aftershave lotions with high alcohol contents) as a substitute for alcohol. Such products are easily accessible. Be alert for ingestion abuse of alcohol-containing external products (Egbert and others, 1985).

---

space in the surface of the enamel (Gilman et al, 1990). This results in a harder outer layer of tooth enamel that is more resistant to demineralization.

Mouthwashes are generally used once a day (rinsed for a minute and expectorated), usually after brushing and flossing. Fluoridated mouthwashes have been used in communities with both limited fluoridated and unfluoridated water supplies, and their use has been associated with a significant decrease in tooth decay. Such products are generally approved by the Council on Dental Therapeutics of the American Dental Association, and the packages bear its seal of approval.

## Antiseptic Mouthwash

Chloraseptic mouthwash contains phenol and sodium phenolate, which act as antimicrobial and anesthetic agents. In spray form it is reported effective for treatment of sore throat (Gossel, 1986). It provides surface anesthesia when this is indicated for oropharyngeal discomfort, and it maintains oral hygiene. It is diluted with equal parts of water or sprayed full strength.

## Dentifrices

A **dentifrice** is a substance used to aid in cleaning teeth. Ordinary dentifrice contains one or more mild abrasives, a foaming agent, and flavoring materials made into a powder or paste (toothpaste) to be used as an aid in the mechanical cleansing of accessible parts of the teeth.

The following ingredients, alone or mixed, are found in a number of dentifrices:

| | |
|---|---|
| Glycerin | Pumice (flour) |
| Alcohol | Stannous fluoride |
| Sweetening agents | Soap |
| Propylene glycol | Sodium borate |
| Precipitated calcium carbonate | Milk of magnesia |

The essential requirement of a toothpaste or cleaner is that it not injure the teeth or surrounding tissues. If toothpaste is not available, the patient can use a toothbrush and proper flossing techniques, since thorough mechanical cleansing of bacterial plaques and food debris is the primary objective. Fluoride (stannous fluoride and sodium monofluorophosphate) dentifrices are effective anticaries agents. These products carry the American Dental Association Council on Dental Therapeutics seal to indicate its endorsement. See box on fluoride toxicity.

Dentifrices are also available for the treatment of hypersensitive teeth. Such products contain strontium chloride (Sensodyne, Thermodent) or potassium nitrate (Promise, Denquel). These products are not generally accepted as effective by the American Dental Association. Others are said to remove or reduce the formation of tartar (calculus or plaque). Studies have not yet proven their effectiveness.

## Oral Antifungal Agents
### clotrimazole (Mycelex)
### ketoconazole (Nizoral)
### nystatin (Mycostatin, Nilstat)

Clotrimazole, ketoconazole, and nystatin are believed to attach to sterols in the fungal wall, increasing permeability of the cell membrane and resulting in loss of important cellular contents. Ketoconazole and clotrimazole also inhibit

oxidative enzyme activity, which may increase intracellular hydrogen peroxide to toxic levels and thus contribute to the destruction of the fungal cells and their contents. In addition, they inhibit fungal synthesis of triglycerides and phospholipids. They are indicated for the treatment of candidiasis or fungal infections caused by Candida species.

Ketoconazole requires acidity to be dissolved and absorbed in the gastrointestinal tract. It is highly protein bound and widely distributed in the body. Peak serum level is reached in 1 to 4 hours, metabolism is by the liver and excretion is primarily in bile. Nystatin is not absorbed from the gastrointestinal tract, thus its effects are produced by local interaction with the fungus sites. It is excreted fecally. Clotrimazole is also primarily a topical agent with minimal systemic absorption. The absorbed drug is metabolized in the liver. Duration of action for clotrimazole is up to 3 hours with primary elimination in the feces.

The most commonly reported side effects of clotrimazole and nystatin are nausea, vomiting, abdominal pain, and diarrhea. Ketoconazole's most frequent side effects include nausea or vomiting. Less often reported are diarrhea, sedation, headaches, skin rash, pruritus, insomnia, photophobia, and dizziness. A rare adverse reaction reported is hepatitis, which presents as abdominal pain, yellowing of skin or eyes, anorexia, dark urine, and pale stools.

***Significant drug interactions.*** While no significant drug interactions are reported with clotrimazole or nystatin and other drugs, ketoconazole has the following important drug interactions.

| Drug | Possible Effect and Management |
|---|---|
| antacids and H₂ receptor antagonists (e.g., cimetidine, famotidine, nizatidine, ranitidine) | Increased gastrointestinal PH, which may result in reduction in dissolution and absorption of ketoconazole. Advise client to separate such medications by at least 2 to 3 hours, preferably consuming ketoconazole first. |
| cyclosporine | Cyclosporine serum levels increase in the presence of ketoconazole, which increases the risk for nephrotoxicity. Extreme caution and close monitoring are required when this combination is administered. |
| isoniazid, rifampin | Coadministration with ketoconazole may reduce serum concentrations of ketoconazole or rifampin. Monitor concurrent therapy closely since some reports state that serum levels, when all three drugs are taken concurrently, are nearly nonexistent. |
| other hepatotoxic drugs or alcohol | Increased risk of inducting liver toxicity. Whenever possible, such substances should be avoided. |

***Dosage and administration.*** See Table 40-1.

▷ **Nursing Management:
Oral Antifungal Agent Therapy**

***Assessment.*** Improperly fitting dentures can be a source of inflammation.

**TABLE 40-1** Dosage and administration of selected oral antifungal agents

| Drug | Adults | Children |
|------|--------|----------|
| clotrimazole troches | Dissolve one 10 mg lozenge slowly orally five times daily for approximately 2 weeks<br>Immunosuppressed individuals: Can be administered for longer periods | Dissolve one 10 mg lozenge slowly orally five times daily for approximately 2 weeks<br>Immunosuppressed individuals: Can be administered for longer periods |
| ketoconazole | 200 mg to 400 mg daily for 5 days | Children over 2 yr: 5 to 10 mg/kg orally daily for 5 days |
| nystatin<br>  tablets | 500,000 to 1 million units orally three times daily | Children 5 yr and older: 500,000 units four times daily |
|   suspension | 500,000 units four times daily | Premature/low birth weight infants: 100,000 units four times daily<br>Older infants: 200,000 units four times daily<br>Older children: see adult dose |

Patients who have cancer or are taking immunosuppressive drugs, such as steroids, are particularly at risk for oral candidiasis.

Clients receiving oral antifungal agents for candidiasis may experience altered comfort related to gastrointestinal disturbances with nausea or vomiting, diarrhea, and, perhaps, abdominal cramping.

**Intervention.** Brush teeth or have client brush teeth carefully before each dose is administered. For infants and dependent patients, gently swab the medication on the oral mucosa.

When administering the oral suspension, shake well to ensure consistency in dosing. Protect the suspension from freezing. When preparing the oral suspension from powder, shake well and use immediately, since it contains no preservatives.

To improve retention within the mouth, nystatin can be administered in the form of flavored frozen water on a stick.

The nystatin vaginal tablet may also be used as a lozenge since its slow rate of dissolution prolongs contact with the oral mucosa.

**Education.** Instruct the client in good oral hygiene techniques. Inform the client that a yearly dental examination is recommended.

When using the suspension forms of nystatin, instruct the client to swish the medication around in the mouth and maintain contact with the mucosa for several minutes before swallowing. The client may also gargle the solution.

Provide a careful explanation to the client using the troche form (clotrimazole) that it is to be dissolved slowly (15 to 30 minutes) in the mouth. It is not to be chewed or swallowed whole. The client is to swallow the saliva. The troche may be cut in half to facilitate administration. Instruct the client to continue the medicine for the full time of prescription and report to the prescriber if symptoms persist.

Before an initial course of antineoplastic chemotherapy, instruct the client to consult a dentist to complete any care needed, to avoid oral complications.

**Evaluation.** Instruct the client to continue therapy for 48 hours after symptoms have disappeared to prevent relapse. Assess and document daily the size and condition of the affected areas of the mouth, using a tongue blade and flashlight.

## Saliva Substitutes

Saliva substitutes (Orex, Xero-Lube, Moi-stir, Salivart) are used to overcome dry mouth and throat. They are available as solutions in squirt bottles and as pump or aerosol sprays. They contain electrolytes (potassium phosphate, magnesium chloride, potassium chloride, calcium, and sodium), sodium fluoride, sorbitol, and carboxymethylcellulose as the base.

## Drugs Used to Treat Mouth Blistering

Acute and chronic diseases contribute to mouth blistering and erosions. Acute viral diseases such as herpes simplex, herpes zoster, herpangina, and varicella have previously been treated only symptomatically. With the advent of acyclovir (Zovirax), a new era began with an antiviral agent that is effective against herpes simplex virus and varicella zoster virus, the viruses associated with skin manifestations. Acyclovir is available in topical, oral, and parenteral dosage forms and is covered in Chapter 60.

Skin blistering may also be caused by drug therapy (fixed or acute erythema multiforme types); in these cases treatment is directed at the underlying cause.

Mouth lesions or blistering (acute or chronic) may be caused by local irritation, medications, radiation, dental manipulations, or systemic disease. To properly treat, one must first identify the causative factor and then institute appropriate treatment.

## DRUGS THAT AFFECT THE STOMACH

Conditions of the stomach requiring drug therapy include hyperacidity, hypoacidity, ulcer disease, nausea, vomiting, and hypermotility. Some of the drugs used for these con-

**TABLE 40-2**   Antacid side effects/adverse reactions

| Name | Side effects/adverse reactions |
|---|---|
| Aluminum<br>   aluminum carbonate (Basaljel)<br>   aluminum hydroxide (Alterna-<br>      GEL, Alu-Cap, Amphojel)<br><br>   aluminum phosphate (Phos-<br>      phaljel)<br>   aluminum/magnesium com-<br>      pounds (Aludrox, Gaviscon,<br>      Maalox, Mylanta) | Constipation (combination products with magnesium reduce this)<br>Phosphate depletion via feces (including weakness, apnea, hemolytic anemia, tetany)<br>Delay in gastric emptying<br>Concretions (intestinal and renal)<br>Encephalopathy from aluminum intoxication<br>Impaired absorption of drugs such as digitalis, isoniazid, tetracycline<br>Dialysis "dementia" (from CNS accumulation)<br>Bone demineralization (osteomalacia, osteoporosis) |
| Bicarbonate<br>   sodium bicarbonate (Alka-Seltzer,<br>      Instant Metamucil) | Systemic alkalosis or sodium overload (elevated plasma pH and carbon dioxide,<br>   anorexia, mental confusion)<br>Gastric acid hypersecretion ("acid rebound")<br>Enhanced effects of amphetamines, quinidine, quinine |
| Calcium<br>   calcium carbonate (Tums) | Milk-alkali syndrome (including metabolic alkalosis, anorexia, nausea, vomiting,<br>   confusion, hypercalcemia, possibly renal impairment)<br>Increased potential for calcium stone formation<br>Nephrocalcinosis<br>Gastric acid hypersecretion ("acid rebound")<br>Antagonism of digitalis preparations<br>Elevated serum and urine calcium levels<br>Kidney failure<br>Constipation<br>Decreased phosphate levels (if dietary phosphate intake low) |
| Magnesium<br>   magnesium hydroxide (Milk of<br>      Magnesia)<br>   magnesium trisilicate | Diarrhea (combination products with aluminum reduce this)<br>Decreased potassium levels (hypokalemia)<br>Increased magnesium levels (hypermagnesemia) in clients with renal failure or severe<br>   kidney impairment (causing low blood pressure, nausea, vomiting, respiratory<br>   depression, CNS depression, coma) |
| Sodium<br>   sodium bicarbonate | Sodium overload or systemic alkalosis<br>Salt and water retention (causing edema, ascites, effusion, hypertension)<br>Metabolic alkalosis<br>Milk-alkali syndrome (see under calcium)<br>Gastric acid hypersecretion ("acid rebound") |

ditions are not unique in their treatment of gastric dysfunction but are members of other major groups of drugs, such an anticholinergic preparations, antihistamines, and antidepressants.

## Drugs Used to Treat Gastric Hyperacidity
### Antacids

Antacids are chemical compounds that buffer or neutralize hydrochloric acid in the stomach and thereby increase the gastric pH. The major ingredients in antacids include aluminum salts, calcium carbonate, magnesium salts, and sodium bicarbonate, alone or in combination.

Traditionally, the antacids have been termed nonsystemic or systemic. Nonsystemic indicates the almost negligible amount of drug absorbed into the circulation; activity occurs only locally within the gastrointestinal tract. The nonsystemic metal ion, however, is absorbed to some degree. The aluminum ion is absorbed the most and magnesium the least; calcium is absorbed slightly more than magnesium. Increased adverse effects from metal ion absorption occur in the presence of impaired renal function and long-term excessive use of calcium carbonate and magnesium hydroxide.

Antacids are indicated for the relief of symptoms associated with hyperacidity related to the diagnosis of peptic ulcer, gastritis, peptic esophagitis, gastric hyperacidity, heartburn, or hiatal hernia. The selection of an antacid is usually based on the following:

1. It must be an effective neutralizer of hydrochloric acid.
2. It should be relatively harmless to the client.
3. It should not produce diarrhea or constipation.
4. It should be economical and palatable, to improve client compliance.

Antacids generally have a rapid onset of action. Their effects usually last 30 to 60 minutes, although magnesium compounds may have a prolonged effect. Only a small amount of the metal compound is absorbed (15% to 30%). The remainder is broken down via the digestive process and excreted via the feces.

For side effects/adverse reactions, see Table 40-2.

***Significant drug interactions.*** The following interactions may occur when antacids are given with the drugs listed below.

| Drug | Possible Effect and Management |
| --- | --- |
| ketoconazole | Increased gastric pH may decrease absorption of ketoconazole. Advise patients to take antacids at least several hours after ketaconazole. |
| mecamylamine | Effects of mecamylamine may be prolonged because an alkaline urine decreases its excretion. Concurrent administration should be avoided. |
| methenamine | An alkaline urine may decrease methenamine's effectiveness by prohibiting its conversion to formaldehyde. Concurrent administration is not recommended. |
| tetracyclines, oral | Antacids may complex with tetracyclines, decreasing their absorption in the gastointestinal tract. Advise patients to take antacids at least 1 to 2 hours before or after tetracycline. |
| digitalis preparations | Antacids may decrease absorption of digitalis preparations, resulting in a decrease in serum concentration of digitalis. Space medications by at least 1 to 2 hours. |
| ion-exchange resin (e.g., sodium polystyrene sulfonate) | When calcium- or magnesium-containing antacids are given concurrently with this agent, neutralization of gastric acid may be impaired. The binding of the calcium and magnesium may result in anion absorption and systemic alkalosis. Avoid oral administration of this combination. |
| phenothiazine | Magnesium trisilicate, aluminum hydroxide, and magnesium hydroxide gel anacids decrease plasma phenothiazine levels (especially chlorpromazine) by decreasing absorption. |
| isoniazid | Aluminum antacids interfere with the absorption of isoniazid. Separate the administration of these drugs over 1 hour or administer a non aluminum-containing antacid to prevent this interaction. |

Additional interactions reported are hypernatremia with the combination use of sodium bicarbonate and corticosteroids; reduction of the therapeutic effectiveness of the cellulose product in preventing hypercalciuria with cellulose sodium phosphate (Calcibind) and calcium antacids; and the reduction of antacid effectiveness of magnesium containing antacids as the magnesium may bind to the cellulose. Advise clients to separate administration of magnesium-containing antacids from the cellulose sodium phosphate by at least 1 hour.

***Altered drug solubility, stability, and absorption.*** Many drugs are either weak acids or weak bases, and the pH of the stomach is an important factor in their absorption. Drugs that are weak acids are nonionized in the acidic environment of the stomach. These are lipid soluble and are absorbed by simple diffusion across the gastric mucosal cells. The administration of an antacid either with a weak acidic drug or shortly before or after its administration will raise the pH of the stomach contents, causing the formation of a more ionized drug that will not be absorbed to the degree the nonionized, lipid-soluble form was absorbed. A weakly basic drug is absorbed in a more alkaline medium. Changes in pH will modify drug solubility and stability, which also affect absorption.

As the pH of the gastric contents increases, alterations of absorption of weak acids and bases occur as a result of altering the degree of ionization in the following manner: for basic drugs absorption increases because as the pH increases as a result of antacid administration there is an increase in the nonionized concentration of basic drugs; for acidic drugs absorption decreases because as the pH increases there is a decrease in the nonionized concentration of acidic drugs.

Drugs that are weak bases include morphine sulfate, quinine, pseudoephedrine, antihistamines, amphetamines, theophylline, tricyclic antidepressants, and quinidine. Examples of weak acids are isoniazid, barbiturates, nalidixic acid, nonsteroidal antiinflammatory agents, sulfonamides, salicylates, nitrofurantoin, and coumarins.

***Additional drug interactions.*** Because antacids change the pH of the stomach, they cause the medication in enteric-coated tablets to be released into the stomach instead of the alkaline duodenum.

Generally, large doses of antacids must be administered on a chronic basis to induce such alterations in absorption. However, the antacid-enteric–coated drug interaction can result from single, high doses of antacids given concurrently with the long-acting product. Thus the nurse should administer antacids separately from other drugs whenever antacids lack specific instructions for administration with a particular drug product. Close monitoring for both therapeutic response and possible side effects is also recommended.

***Dosage and administration.*** The amount of antacid necessary to neutralize hydrochloric acid depends on the individual, the condition being treated, and the buffering capability of the preparation used. The acid-neutralizing property of antacids varies, so the physician must select the proper dosage for the individual client.

The liquid and powder dosage forms have been found to be much more effective antacids than the tablet dosage formulations. Most tablets require chewing before swallowing to be effective.

Most major antacids contain 10 mg or less of sodium per recommended adult dose. Examples of antacids containing more than 10 mg per recommended adult dose include:

| | |
| --- | --- |
| Alka-Seltzer Effervescent Pain Reliever & Antacid | 551 mg sodium/tablet |
| Alka-Seltzer Effervescent Antacid | 296 mg sodium/tablet |
| Bisodol Antacid Powder | 157 mg sodium/tsp |
| Gaviscon Oral Suspension | 12.9 mg sodium/5 ml |
| Gaviscon Chewable Tablets | 19 mg sodium/tablet |
| Gaviscon-2 Chewable Tablets | 36.8 mg sodium/tablet |
| Rolaids | 53 mg sodium/tablet |

**TABLE 40-3**   Acid-neutralizing capacity of antacids

| Antacids | Ingredients | Acid-neutralizing capacity | Dose to neutralize 80 mEq HCl |
|---|---|---|---|
| **LIQUID PREPARATIONS** | | *mEq/ml* | *ml needed* |
| Aludrox | AlOH, MgOH | 2.8 | 28 |
| Amphojel | AlOH | 2 | 40 |
| Gelusil | | 2.4 | 33 |
| Gelusil-II | AlOH, MgOH, simethicone | 4.8 | 16.6 |
| Gelusil-M | | 3 | 26.6 |
| Maalox | | 2.7 | 29.6 |
| Maalox Plus | AlOH, MgOH (plus: simethicone) | 2.7 | 29.6 |
| Maalox TC | | 5.7 | 14 |
| Mylanta | | 2.5 | 32 |
| Mylanta-II | AlOH, MgOH, simethicone | 5.1 | 15.6 |
| Phosphalgel | AlPO₄ | 0.4 | 200 |
| **TABLET PREPARATIONS** | | *mEq per tablet* | *Tablets needed* |
| Gelusil Chewable | | 11 | 7.3 |
| Gelusil-II Chewable | AlOH, MgOH, simethicone | 21 | 3.8 |
| Maalox No. 1 Chewable | | 8.5 | 9.4 |
| Maalox No. 2 Chewable | AlOH, MgOH | 18 | 4.4 |
| Maalox Plus Chewable | | 11.4 | 7 |
| Mylanta Chewable | AlOH, MgOH, simethicone | 11.5 | 7 |
| Mylanta II Chewable | | 23 | 3.5 |
| Riopan Tablet | | 13.5 | 5.9 |
| Riopan Chewable Tablet | magaldrate (plus: simethicone) | 13.5 | 5.9 |
| Riopan Plus Chewable Tablet | | 13.5 | 5.9 |
| Rolaids | Dihydroxyaluminum sodium carbonate | 8 | 10 |
| Titralac Tablet | Calcium carbonate, glycine | 7.5 | 10.7 |

Adapted from Zaenger P. (1981). Fl J Hosp Pharm 1(1):1; and Kutsop JJ. (1984). Am Pharmacy N524(12):778, USP-DI, 1990.

Antacids given before meals have a duration of action of approximately 30 minutes (range 20 to 60 minutes). If the antacid is given after meals the duration may be prolonged up to 3 hours.

Duodenal ulcers require 75 to 150 mg of acid-neutralizing effect; gastric ulcers usually require 40 to 80 mEq (see Table 40-3; Zaenger, 1981).

The FDA has set a limit of 8 g/day as a recommended maximum dose for calcium carbonate, for a maximum period of 2 weeks. This is equivalent to 16 Tums tablets per day or approximately 10 Tums Extra Strength per day. Since Tums are frequently used for calcium supplementation as well as for an antacid, it is believed that many people exceed the FDA's recommendations, thus increasing the potential for producing many of the side effects or adverse reactions discussed.

**Pregnancy safety.** Antacids are generally considered safe for use in pregnancy if prolonged or high doses are avoided. FDA category is not established.

▷ *Nursing Management:*
*Antacid Therapy*

**Assessment.** Do not give magnesium salts to clients in renal failure without careful assessment; if given, use low doses (50 mEq magnesium/day) under close monitoring and physician's supervision.

With the administration of antacids, the client may experience altered comfort related to their chalky taste. Other concerns for the client are related to the type of antacid administered. With aluminum- or calcium-containing antacids, constipation may be the alteration of bowel function, whereas diarrhea may result from magnesium-containing antacids. Excessive use of calcium- and sodium bicarbonate-containing antacids may place the client at risk for metabolic alkalosis.

**Intervention.** The scheduling of dosing of antacid therapy is important. Antacids given immediately after meals will delay gastric emptying and the buffering effect. When given at 1 and 3 hours after meals and at bedtime, the gastric pH remains at about 3 throughout the day. Because of their ability to interact with numerous medications, scheduling in relation to other medications should be considered. Administer antacids 1 hour before or 2 hours after digoxin, tetracyclines, phenothiazines, and all enteric-coated medications. However, antacids combined with ibuprofen, indomethacin, phenylbutazone, potassium chloride supplements, reserpine, sulindac, and tolmetin can help to reduce the gastric distress that these drugs can cause.

Shake liquid preparations vigorously before administration to achieve a uniform suspension. When administering antacids via a nasogastric tube, assess the placement and patency of the tube before giving the medication and follow the dose with sufficient water to clear the tube.

Refrigerate antacids to make them more palatable. (Do not freeze.)

Do not administer calcium carbonate antacids with milk, milk products, or other foods or vitamin supplements high in vitamin D, since milk-alkali syndrome may occur.

**Education.** Discuss the sodium content and side effects of various antacids with the client (see Table 40-2). Inform clients that antacids differ in their sodium content, which can be significant for clients who are on low-sodium diets or who take antihypertensive drugs or diuretics. Instruct clients with hypertensive, cardiac, or renal disease to avoid antacids containing sodium, particularly if antacids are used frequently.

Inform clients that liquid antacids have superior neutralizing properties compared with tablets. However, clients who must frequently take liquid antacids may lose their desire for food or drink. For this reason chewable tablets followed by adequate water may be of value.

Instruct clients taking chewable antacid tablets to chew or pulverize the tablets thoroughly. The tablets will not mix well with water. A sip of water or milk will facilitate swallowing of tablets.

Stress compliance to antacid therapy schedules. Allow clients to take their own antacids while they are hospitalized to encourage compliance.

Caution clients about side effects, and instruct them to consult their physician if these occur.

Teach clients to check the expiration dates of the antacids, since the effectiveness of antacids decreases with age.

Teach clients to carefully check the name when purchasing OTC antacids. Names may be similar (Mylanta versus Mylanta II, Gelusil versus Gelusil II), but dosage requirements will differ.

Advise clients who self-medicate with antacids for recurring gastrointestinal symptoms to seek medical care, since they are treating the symptoms rather than the cause of the problem. Since antacids are all OTC drugs and there is no medically supervised restriction, clients may abuse or misuse antacids through self-medication.

Help clients to identify the source of gastric discomfort, such as overeating, tension, anxiety, or other emotional stress, since this may teach them to avoid the causes of discomfort and eliminate the need for antacid therapy.

**Evaluation.** Note the frequency and consistency of stools. If diarrhea occurs, it may be advantageous to change to another antacid, such as magnesium hydroxide with magnesium trisilicate or aluminum hydroxide. If constipation occurs, a magnesium hydroxide antacid or an increase in the intake of bran and roughage in the diet may be instituted.

Assess epigastric discomfort at the time of each dose and record the client's progress. Evaluation of antacid therapy is important. The client's subjective response to antacid therapy and the nurse's objective observations (e.g., frequency with which the client takes the antacid) can help determine the effectiveness of therapy. Monitor clients undergoing long-term aluminum antacid therapy regularly for serum phosphate levels, as phosphate depletion may result in osteoporosis.

### Antacid Combinations

There are many antacid combinations; however, the antacid combination Gaviscon deserves particular attention because of its uniqueness and widespread use.

#### gaviscon

Gaviscon forms a viscous cohesive foam that floats on the surface of the stomach contents, neutralizing stomach acid. This helps protect the sensitive mucosa from irritation, because the foam precedes the stomach contents into the lower esophagus when reflux occurs. The foam is caused by the alginic acid contained in the product. The other ingredients are aluminum hydroxide, magnesium trisilicate, and sodium bicarbonate. Gaviscon is available in two tablet strengths and a liquid suspension.

### Antiflatulents
#### simethicone (Mylicon, Silain, Orol ✦)

Simethicone acts in the stomach and intestines. This defoaming agent relieves flatulence by dispersing and preventing the formation of mucus-surrounded gas pockets in the gastrointestinal tract.

The approved clinical use is for relief of painful symptoms of gas in the gastrointestinal tract. Gas retention is a problem in conditions such as air swallowing, diverticulitis, functional dyspepsia, peptic ulcer, postoperative gaseous distention, and spastic or irritable colon.

The tablets are chewed thoroughly four times daily, after meals and at bedtime, and as needed for flatulence. Several antacid combination products contain simethicone.

### Digestants

Digestants are drugs that promote the process of digestion in the gastrointestinal tract. Problems with digestion may be caused by a deficiency of hydrochloric acid, digestive substances, enzymes, or bile salts; organic disease states (stomach cancer, pernicious anemia, cholecystectomy); or possibly a reaction to emotional situations or stress.

Dilute hydrochloric acid (10% solution) was formerly used as a digestant but is rarely prescribed today. Instead betaine hydrochloride or glutamic acid hydrochloride (Acidulin) may be ordered. These preparations, available as tablets or capsules, usually release only a small amount of free hydrochloric acid in the stomach, but this is usually sufficient to treat many cases of gastric **achlorhydria** (the absence of hydrochloric acid). They must be given with a full glass of water.

Digestive enzymes are secreted by the mouth, stomach,

small intestine, pancreas, and liver. They are necessary to process the digestion of food.

**Pepsin** is the stomach enzyme that reduces protein to smaller particles. It can be given alone or in combination with a hydrochloric acid source in hypochlorhydric or achlorhydric clients. Hydrochloric acid keeps the gastric pH below 4 and protects the proteolytic activity of pepsin. A pH of 1.5 to 2.5 is usually the optimal range. Pepsin is not considered a critical enzyme, because proteolytic enzymes released from the pancreas and intestine cause the same effects.

### pancreatin

Pancreatin is a powdered substance obtained from the pancreas of the hog or ox. It contains principally pancreatic amylase, trypsin, and pancreatic lipase. Acid chyme entering the duodenum and vagal stimulation regulate pancreatic secretion, so that replacement therapy may be necessary for clients who have had vagal fibers surgically severed or surgical procedures that cause food to bypass the duodenum. Pancreatin and pancrelipase aid in the digestion and absorption of fats, carbohydrates, and triglycerides. In addition, replacement therapy is usually necessary in exocrine pancreatic enzyme deficiency states, chronic pancreatitis, cystic fibrosis, pancreatic tumors, pancreatic obstruction, and pancreatectomy. The drug is available in enteric-coated capsules to avoid destruction in the stomach.

The dosage for adults is 325 mg to 1 g daily in divided doses before meals, during meals, or within 1 hour after meals, with an extra dose taken with any food eaten between meals. In high doses this drug may cause nausea, diarrhea, hyperuricosuria, and hyperuricemia. To avoid temporary indigestion the client must maintain a dietary balance of fat, protein, and starch.

### pancrelipase (Pancrease, Viokase)

Pancrelipase is similar to other pancreatic enzyme preparations, but its lipase activity is greater and it can be given in lower doses to control steatorrhea (fatty stools). It is a concentrate of pancreatic enzymes from hogs. The dosage for adults is one to three capsules or tablets or one or two packets before or with meals or snacks. In extreme deficiency the dosage interval may be changed to hourly if no nausea or diarrhea develops. Because of its enteric-coated microsphere formulation, Pancrease resists gastric inactivation, so enzymes reach the duodenum to hydrolyze fats into glycerol and fatty acids, proteins into proteases, and starch into dextrins and sugars.

Pancrelipase is indicated for use in clients with deficient secretion of exocrine pancreatic enzymes and for use as an enzyme replacement in cystic fibrosis, chronic pancreatitis, postpancreatectomy, pancreatic duct obstructions secondary to pancreatic carcinoma, and pancreatic insufficiency. Pancrelipase is also indicated for the steatorrhea or malabsorption syndrome and following gastrectomy.

The side effects/adverse reactions reported include nausea, abdominal cramps, and loose stool. The most significant drug interaction occurs when calcium and magnesium antacids negate pancrelipase enzyme action. Serum iron response to oral iron therapy is decreased by pancreatic extracts.

The dose is one to three capsules or tablets given before or with meals and snacks. Dose may be increased to 8 in cases of severe deficiency if no nausea, cramps, or diarrhea results. With the powder form 0.7 g is given with meals.

Pregnancy safety has been established at FDA category C.

▷ **Nursing Management:**
**Digestant Therapy**

Instruct the client to swallow enteric-coated tablets whole; do not crush or allow them to be chewed or irritation of the mouth may occur.

Because pancretin is inactivated by gastric pepsin and acid pH, cimetidine or antacids (except for those containing calcium and magnesium) may be prescribed to be taken with it.

For children or adults who cannot swallow the capsules or tablets, sprinkle the powder from the opened capsule or the powdered form on food.

Instruct the client on the rationale for taking the pancreatic enzyme preparations. Also instruct client not to stop taking the medication without physician approval. Urge the client to adhere to the prescribed diet, since the dosage for pancrelipase is individualized and determined by the client's maldigestion and malabsorption and the fat content of the diet.

If capsules need to be opened to be administered, advise client to be careful not to spill the contents on hands or to inhale them, since this substance is very irritating to nasal membranes, respiratory tract, and skin. If side effects such as nausea, abdominal cramping, and diarrhea occur, have the client contact the physician.

## Antiemetics

**Antiemetics** are drugs given to relieve nausea and vomiting. Control of vomiting is important and often difficult. Numerous preparations have been used, but effective treatment usually depends on treating the cause. Vomiting may result from very different causes, including strong emotion, severe pain, increased intracranial pressure, and labyrinthine disturbances. Other causes include motion sickness, endocrine disturbances, toxic reaction to drugs, gastrointestinal disease, roentgenographic treatments, and chemotherapy.

Antiemetics may exert their effects on the vomiting center, the cerebral cortex, the chemoreceptor trigger zone, or the aural vestibular apparatus.

The following drugs are used as antiemetics:

1. Anticholinergics, such as scopolamine, reduce the ex-

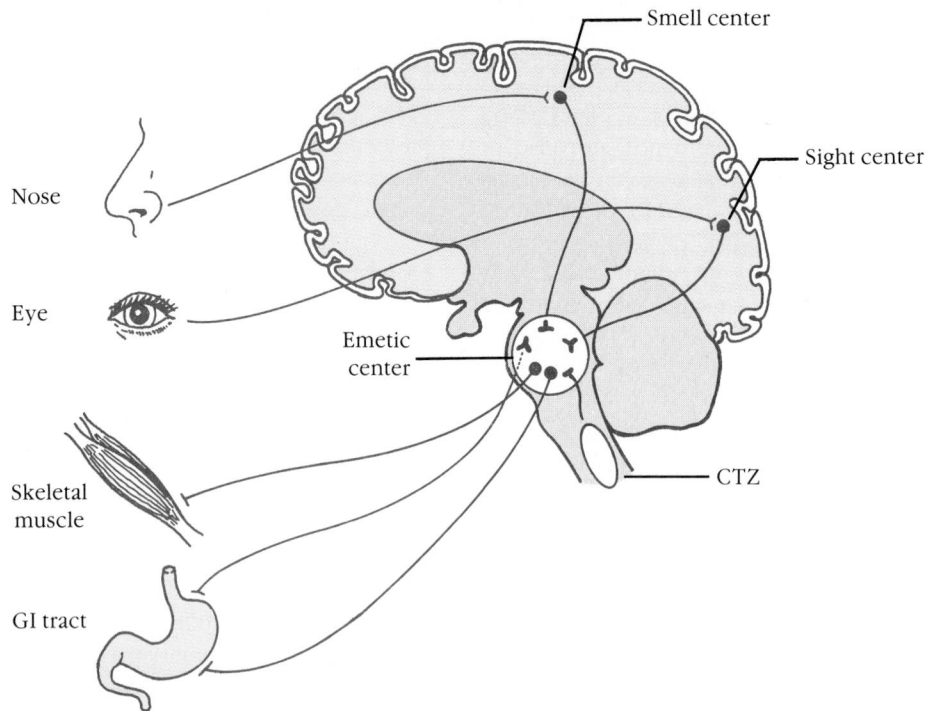

**FIGURE 40-1** Sites activating the emetic center. *CTZ,* Chemoreceptor trigger zone.

citability of labyrinth receptors, depress conduction in the vestibular cerebellar pathways, or prevent impulses from stimulating the chemoreceptor trigger zone.

2. Antihistamines $H_1$ affect neural labyrinth pathways. Examples include cyclizine (Marezine), dimenhydrinate (Dramamine), and diphenhydramine (Benadryl).
3. Phenothiazines, such as chlorpromazine (Thorazine) and promethazine (Phenergan) and metoclopramide (Reglan) are dopamine antagonists. They act on the chemoreceptor trigger zone and on the vomiting center. These are the most effective antiemetics and often the drugs of choice.
4. Antacids relieve gastric irritation.
5. Miscellaneous drugs include diphenidol (Vontrol), which acts on the aural vestibular apparatus, and benzquinamide (Emete-Con), which acts on the chemoreceptor trigger zone. Steroids (dexamethasone, methylprednisolone) and cannabinoids (nabilone, THC) are also used.

Most of the drugs are discussed elsewhere in the text (see Index).

*Emetic (Vomiting) Reflex*

The **emetic center** is located in the medulla oblongata. Smells, various sights, and psychologically based responses from the cerebral cortex may all stimulate the emetic center. Disturbances of the stomach and of the vestibular apparatus can also activate the emetic center (see Figure 40-1). These stimuli involve vagal and/or sympathetic afferent nerve transmission. Dopamine is a primary neurotransmitter.

A **chemoreceptor trigger zone** is a relay station that can send messages to the emetic center. The chemoreceptor trigger zone detects irritating chemicals in the blood or cerebrospinal fluid. In itself, the chemoreceptor trigger zone is not able to induce vomiting.

Since the chemoreceptor trigger zone is located close to the respiratory center in the brain, it is difficult to completely control vomiting initiated from this site without affecting respiration. Various neurotransmitters are involved in this area. The cerebral cortex area is involved in anticipatory nausea and vomiting, a conditioned response caused by a stimulus connected with a previous unpleasant experience. For example, a client receiving cancer chemotherapy that has resulted in vomiting might vomit at the sight of the hospital, even before treatment is given (Bergmann, 1986).

If the emetic center is activated by any of the stimuli mentioned, it sends impulses (via efferent nerves) to the diaphragm, stomach muscles, esophagus, and salivary glands, resulting in vomiting.

The proposed sites of action for antiemetics are reported in the box (Bergmann, 1986).

*Cancer Chemotherapy–Induced Vomiting*

Vomiting from cancer chemotherapy can be serious enough to limit the dosages of chemotherapeutic agents given to a client. Since antiemetics are usually more effective in preventing vomiting than they are in treating it, they should be administered prophylactically, before the chemotherapy administration. Also, chemotherapy-induced vomiting often requires several antiemetic agents with different sites of

---

### PROPOSED SITES OF ACTION FOR ANTIEMETIC DRUGS

| Proposed Sites | Drugs |
|---|---|
| Emetic center | anticholinergic<br>antihistamines<br>thiethylperazine maleate* |
| Chemoreceptor trigger zone | benzquinamide hydrochloride<br>butyrophenones<br>diphenidol hydrochloride*<br>metoclopramide*<br>phenothiazine<br>thiethylperazine maleate*<br>trimethobenzamide HCl |
| Cerebral cortex | cannabinoids (THC), nabilone (Cesamet ✦), dronabinol (Marinol)<br>diazepam, lorazepam<br>scopolamine*<br>antihistamines |
| Peripheral | diphenidol hydrochloride*<br>metoclopramide*<br>scopolamine* |
| Unknown | corticosteroids |

*Dual action.

action for effectiveness—for example, metoclopramide (Reglan) and lorazepam (Ativan) metoclopramide and dexamethasone; or prochlorperazine (Compazine) and dexamethasone (Bergmann, 1986). Combinations of rectal antiemetic suppositories are also under investigation.

### ▷ Nursing Management: Antiemetic Therapy

**Assessment.** Do not give antiemetics until the underlying cause of nausea has been established. For example, overdosage of drugs or increased intracranial pressure may cause nausea.

If antiemetic therapy is unavailable or cannot be given, or to support the administration of antiemetics, provide a quiet environment, make the client comfortable, and give ice chips, a carbonated beverage, or, if allowed, hot tea to drink.

**Intervention.** Give antiemetics, such as prochlorperazine maleate (Compazine), thiethylperazine maleate (Torecan), trimethobenzamide (Tigan), and metoclopramide (Reglan), before the administration of chemotherapeutic agents. The time of administration of the antiemetic agent will depend on the chemotherapeutic regimen prescribed.

**Education.** Instruct the client that any hypersensitivity to these drugs necessitates discontinuance of the drug and reporting the effects to the physician.

Most antiemetics cause drowsiness as a side effect. Caution clients against performing hazardous tasks until the effects of the drug have subsided.

Caution clients against combining antiemetics with alcohol or any CNS depressants. The CNS depressant effects of the drug can be potentiated when these drugs are combined.

Vomiting during pregnancy or as the result of cancer chemotherapeutic agents can cause serious electrolyte imbalance and a nutritional deficit. Instruct the pregnant client to take small frequent meals or small nutritional snacks between meals.

### metoclopramide (Reglan, Maxeran ✦)

Metoclopramide is structurally similar to procaine and procainamide but without significant anesthetic or cardiac effects. The central action of metoclopramide in preventing or relieving nausea and emesis is by blockade of dopamine receptors in the chemoreceptor trigger zone. The peripheral mechanism is by improvement of orthograde motility of the upper gastrointestinal tract, increase of stomach peristaltic action, and overcoming the immobility, dilation, and reverse motility occurring with the vomiting reflex.

Metoclopramide is indicated as an adjunct for gastrointestinal radiologic examination. Parenteral metoclopramide facilitates small bowel intubation. It also hastens barium's transit through the upper gastrointestinal tract by its stimulation of gastric emptying and acceleration of intestinal transit. It is also used for diabetic gastroparesis, gastroesophageal reflux, and, parenterally, for prevention of nausea and vomiting secondary to emetogenic cancer chemotherapeutic agents.

The onset of action is ½ to 1 hour after administration of an oral dose, 10 to 15 minutes after an intramuscular dose, and within 3 minutes after an intravenous dose. Effects last up to 2 hours after an intravenous dose and 2 to 3 hours following oral administration. The half-life is 4 to 6 hours. The drug is moderately bound to protein.

For side effects/adverse reactions, see Table 40-4.

**Significant drug interactions.** The following interactions may occur when metoclopramide is given with the drugs listed below.

| Drug | Possible Effect and Management |
|---|---|
| acetaminophen | Coadministration may increase the absorption of this drug. |
| alcohol | Coadministration may increase the absorption of this drug. |
| anticholinergic agents and narcotic analgesics | Coadministration of these agents may antagonize motility effects of metoclopramide. |
| aspirin | Coadministration may increase the absorption of this drug. |
| diazepam | Coadministration may increase the absorption of this drug. |
| digoxin | Digoxin tablets, other than Lanoxin, may have decreased absorption. |
| extrapyramidal effect-producing agents | Extrapyramidal reactions have been reported more often in children and young adults taking metoclopramide, but high doses or com- |

**TABLE 40-4**    Selected antiemetics: side effects and adverse reactions

| Drug | Side effects* | Adverse reactions† |
|---|---|---|
| metoclopramide (Reglan, Maxeran ♣) | More frequent: loose stools, dizziness (orthostatic hypotension), sleepiness, nausea, vomiting, abdominal pain<br>Less common: depression, insomnia, poor physical coordination | Anorexia, weight loss, difficulty in urination, hyperthermia, difficult breathing, chest pain, pruritus, leg weakness, paresthesia, hallucinations, visual disturbances, disassociation, change in cardiac rate, nightmares |
| diphenidol hydrochloride (Vontrol) | More frequent: sleepiness<br>Less common: dry mouth, headache, insomnia, weakness, rash, dizziness, indigestion | Disorientation, delusion, hallucinations |
| thiethylperazine maleate (Torecan, Toresten ♣) | More frequent: sleepiness, dry mouth<br>Less common: hyperthermia, ringing of the ears, blurred vision, headache, edema of extremities and face | Extrapyramidal side effects, convulsions, orthostatic hypotension (usually after first intramuscular injection) |
| trimethobenzamide hydrochloride (Tigan) | More frequent: sleepiness<br>Less common: headache, loose stools, dizziness, muscle cramps, blurred vision | Seizures or severe vomiting, depression, tremors, weakness, sore throat, jaundice, back muscle pain |
| benzquinamide hydrochloride (Emete-Con) | More frequent: sleepiness, agitation, inability to sleep, headache<br>Less common: dry mouth, increased sweating, increased salivation, hiccups, blurred vision | Extrapyramidal side effects (usually from large doses of the drug), hypotension or hypertension, dysrhythmias (especially with intravenous administration) |
| scopolamine transdermal (Transderm-Scop) | More frequent: constipation, dry skin, dry mucous membranes<br>Less common: flatulence, blurred vision, dysphagia, photophobia, difficulty in urination, sleepiness, insomnia (paradoxic reaction with large doses) | Allergic reaction (rash, hives), glaucoma or eye pain caused by increased intraocular pressure |

*If side effects continue, increase, or disturb the client, inform the physician.
†If adverse reactions occur, contact physician, since medical intervention may be necessary.

| Drug | Possible Effect and Management |
|---|---|
| extrapyramidal effects-producing agents. | bination therapy with other drugs that cause extrapyramidal effects may increase the frequency and seriousness of this reaction. Metoclopramide is contraindicated for use in in clients receiving other medications that produce extrapyramidal side effects. |
| insulin | Insulin dosing or time of administration may have to be adjusted to reflect metoclopramide's influence on food delivery to the intestine and the increased rate of its absorption. Monitor closely. |
| L-dopa | Coadministration may increase the absorption of this drug. |
| lithium | Coadministration may increase the absorption of this drug. |
| tetracycline | Coadministration may increase the absorption of this drug. |

### Dosage and administration

*Adults.* With diabetic gastroparesis or gastroesophageal reflux, oral dose is 10 mg 30 minutes before each meal and at bedtime (up to four times daily). Check package insert for further instructions.

Intravenously, 10 mg is given to facilitate small bowel intubation if the biopsy tube has not passed the pylorus in 10 minutes. When using metoclopromide as an antiemetic (chemotherapy-induced emesis), give 2 mg/kg IV 30 minutes before chemotherapy; dose may be repeated every 2 to 3 hours as necessary.

*Children.* Intravenous dose is 0.1 mg/kg in children under 6 years and 2.5 to 5 mg/kg in children 6 to 14 years old.

*Pregnancy safety.* Has been established at FDA category B, although metoclopramide is excreted in breast milk and is usually avoided in women who are breast-feeding

### ▷ Nursing Management: Metoclopramide Therapy

*Assessment.* Do not give metoclopramide to clients with epilepsy or pheochromocytoma, or those in whom stimulation of gastrointestinal motility is hazardous (e.g., those with gastrointestinal hemorrhage, perforation, or mechanical obstruction). Clients with an intolerance to procaine and procainamide may experience cross-sensitivity. Metoclopramide crosses the blood-brain and placental barriers.

With the administration of metoclopramide, the client may experience altered sleep patterns (drowsiness); altered comfort related to headache, dryness of the mouth, breast tenderness and swelling, and dizziness; altered thought processes (confusion, depression); and altered bowel function (constipation or diarrhea).

*Intervention.* Administer oral preparations 30 minutes before meals and at bedtime.

Administer intravenous injections slowly over 1 to 2 minutes. If metoclopramide is administered more rapidly, a brief episode of anxiety and restlessness will occur followed by drowsiness. Infusions should not be for a period of less than 15 minutes.

Keep solutions of the parenteral dosage for 48 hours after dilution; protect from light; discard unused portions after 48 hours. Do not give in combination with drugs having extrapyramidal side effects (e.g., phenothiazines, butyrophenones).

Be aware that extrapyramidal side effects may be seen at therapeutic doses and more likely to occur in children and young adults.

*Education.* Because this drug can cause drowsiness, caution client against operating any potentially hazardous equipment. Caution client against using alcohol or other CNS depressants with this drug.

*Evaluation.* Approximately 20% to 30% of clients experience mild and reversible side effects after the drug is withdrawn. If the drug therapy has been successful, the client should report that nausea is relieved and there are no vomiting episodes.

### diphenidol hydrochloride (Vontrol)

Diphenidol controls nausea and vomiting by inhibiting the medullary chemoreceptor trigger zone. It controls vertigo by a specific antivertigo effect on the vestibular apparatus. It is recommended for the prevention and control of nausea and vomiting, the vertigo of Ménière's disease, labyrinthitis following middle or inner ear surgery, and motion sickness. It is also used to control drug-induced vomiting and vomiting after surgery or because of radiation therapy.

Diphenidol is well absorbed after oral administration. It reaches peak serum levels in 1.5 to 3 hours, has a half-life of 4 hours, and is excreted by the kidneys. For side effects/adverse reactions, see Table 40-4. When diphenidol is given with alcohol or other CNS depressants, the effects of either drug may be potentiated. One must monitor closely for enhanced CNS depressant effects. Adult dosage for antiemesis and antivertigo is 25 to 50 mg orally, every 4 hours as needed. Pregnancy safety has not been established.

### ▷ Nursing Management: Diphenidol Therapy

*Assessment.* Use diphenidol cautiously in clients with glaucoma or gastrointestinal or urinary obstruction. Clients with hypotension may have an additional decrease in blood pressure. Do not use diphenidol in the presence of renal failure.

Diphenidol contains tartrazine, which may cause allergic reactions in sensitive clients. An increased frequency of tartrazine sensitivity occurs among aspirin-sensitive individuals.

Because diphenidol may cause hallucinations, disorientation, and confusion within the first 3 days of administra-

tion, its administration should be limited to clients within the hospital setting. Assess the client's mental status before and during therapy.

*Intervention.* Administer diphenidol with food, water, or milk to decrease gastric irritation. Do not administer concurrently with CNS depressants.

*Education.* Caution the client to consult physician if drowsiness or blurred vision occurs.

*Evaluation.* The antiemetic effect may mask symptoms of an underlying disorder such as intestinal obstruction, brain tumor, or drug overdose. If diphenol therapy is successful, the client should state that nausea is relieved and there should be no vomiting episodes.

### thiethylperazine maleate (Torecan)

Thiethylperazine is a phenothiazine derivative with activity as an antiemetic and antinauseant on the chemoreceptor trigger zone and vomiting center. Studies indicate that this drug is a more effective antiemetic than other phenothiazines. It is used for the prevention of nausea and vomiting caused by anesthetics, radiation therapy, and chemotherapy. For pharmacokinetics see discussion of phenothiazines in Chapter 17. For side effects/adverse reactions see Table 40-4.

*Significant drug interactions.* The following interactions may occur when thiethylperazine is given with the drugs listed below.

| Drug | Possible Effect and Management |
| --- | --- |
| epinephrine | Avoid use of epinephrine to treat hypotension induced by thiethylperazine. Norepinephrine and phenylephrine are drugs of choice for this purpose. |
| phenothiazines | Monitor for increased potential for extra-pyramidal reactions. |

*Dosage and administration.* Thiethylperazine is given to adults in a 10-mg dose one to three times daily orally, intramuscularly, or rectally. Thiethylperazine is not recommended for children. This product also contains tartrazine; see previous warning.

*Pregnancy safety.* Has not been established.

### ▷ Nursing Management: Thiethylperazine Therapy

Do not administer thiethylperazine intravenously since this may cause severe hypotension. (See additional considerations for phenothiazine drugs in Chapter 17.)

### trimethobenzamide hydrochloride (Tigan)

Trimethobenzamide is believed to depress the chemoreceptor trigger zone in the medulla rather than the vomiting center directly. It is indicated for the prevention or relief of nausea and vomiting caused by radiation sickness, infection, and operative procedures and also, for the relief of nausea and vomiting caused by a number of other conditions. Trimethobenzamide is metabolized in the liver and excreted in the urine. For side effects/adverse reactions, see Table 40-4.

*Significant drug interactions.* The following interactions may occur when trimethobezamide is given with the drugs listed below.

| Drug | Possible Effect and Management |
|------|-------------------------------|
| alcohol, CNS depressants | May potentiate effects of either medication. Monitor closely. Avoid use of alcohol. |
| phenothiazines, barbiturates, belladonna | Has resulted in extrapyramidal reactions, opisthotonos, seizures, and coma. Closely supervise client and take appropriate actions if adverse reactions occur. |

*Dosage and administration.* Oral adult dose of trimethobenzamide is 250 mg three or four times per day. Rectally or intramuscularly, 200 mg is given three or four times per day. For children 15 mg/kg is given orally per day, divided into three or four doses. For children weighing 15 to 45 kg, administer 100 to 200 mg orally or rectally three to four times per day. IM route is not recommended.

*Pregnancy safety.*   Has not been established

## ▷ Nursing Management: Trimethobenzamide

Trimethobenzamide is not recommended for use in children with viral illness, since it may contribute to development of Reye's syndrome, an acute encephalopathy.

Inject the drug deeply into the upper outer quadrant of the gluteal area to minimize injection site irritation. Hypotension can occur in the surgical client when trimethobezamide is administered parenterally. Assess blood pressure before administering the medication and frequently after it has been given. Caution the client against using alcohol or other CNS depressants with this drug. Suppositories contain 2% benzocaine (use caution in allergic clients). Administration of trimethobenzamide may mask symptoms of appendicitis or signs of ototoxicity (tinnitus, dizziness) secondary to large doses of salicylates.

## benzquinamide hydrochloride (Emete-Con)

Benzquinamide is believed to depress the chemoreceptor trigger zone to produce its antiemetic effects. It is indicated for prevention and treatment of nausea and vomiting associated with anesthetics and surgery in those clients in whom emesis would endanger the results of surgery or be harmful. Benzquinamide is metabolized in the liver and excreted in the urine. Half-life is about 40 minutes in plasma.

For side effects/adverse reactions, see Table 40-4. No major interactions have been noted. For adult dose by deep intramuscular administration, give 50 mg initially and repeat in 1 hour with subsequent doses every 3 to 4 hours as necessary. By intravenous administration, a single dose of 25 mg is given slowly (1 ml over 30 seconds to 1 minute) in clients without cardiac disease. Pregnancy safety has not been established.

## ▷ Nursing Management: Benzquinamide Therapy

Do not give benzquinamide intravenously to clients with cardiovascular disease or to those who demonstrate hypersensitivity (fever, urticaria). Use with caution in the elderly. Medication may cause a dry mouth. For best effect the anesthesiologist or anesthetist should give the drug about 15 minutes before expected emergence from anesthesia. Reconstituted solutions remain potent for 14 days and need not be refrigerated.

## scopolamine transdermal (Transderm-Scop)

Scopolamine acts either on the cortex or peripherally on maculae of the utriculus and saccule to decrease labyrinthine receptor excitability and depress the vestibular cerebellar pathway conduction. It is indicated for the prevention of motion sickness. Scopolamine is metabolized in the liver and excreted by the kidneys. For side effects/adverse reactions, see Table 40-4.

Drug interactions may result from the decreased gastrointestinal tract motility, and delay of gastric emptying time may decrease the absorption of other medications. Also, anticholinergic/antimuscarinic drugs or CNS depressants may be potentiated.

Monoamine oxidase (MAO) inhibitors may increase antimuscarinic effects. They may also potentiate the effects of scopolamine by preventing its detoxification in the body (United States Pharmacopeial Convention, 1991).

Scopolamine transdermal is used in adults only. A four-layered film, 2.5 cm$^2$, contains 1.5 mg scopolamine that is released gradually from the adhesive matrix after application on the skin behind the ear. A priming dose is released to saturate the dermal binding site for scopolamine, thus bringing the plasma concentration to a steady-state level. The rate-controlling membrane of the matrix provides controlled release that maintains a constant plasma drug level. This film will deliver 0.5 mg of scopolamine over a 3-day period.

Pregnancy safety has been established at FDA category C.

## ▷ Nursing Management: Scopolamine Transdermal Therapy

*Assessment.* Take precautions when clients have asthma, narrow-angle glaucoma, pyloric or intestinal obstruction, urinary tract obstruction, or diminished renal or hepatic function. Elderly clients are more susceptible to scopolamine's effects.

Do not use in children because of adverse effects.

Use cautiously, if at all, during pregnancy or for women who are breast-feeding.

*Intervention.* Apply the system at least 4 hours before the antiemetic effect is desired.

Wash and dry the hands thoroughly before and after application of the system.

Apply to intact skin in the hairless area behind the ear.

Amnesic effects can occur with this drug. Protect the elderly client by raising the bedrails after the drug has been given.

***Education.*** Warn client that operating machinery or driving a motorized vehicle is hazardous because of drowsiness, disorientation, confusion, and blurred vision.

***Evaluation.*** Scopolamine may cause delirium, excitement, and disorientation before sedative effects occur. Consider client safety when this drug is given.

Be aware that clients can develop tolerance to the drug after prolonged use.

## Cannabinoids

Delta-9-tetrahydrocannabinol (THC), an active ingredient of marijuana, has been used as an investigational drug in many studies involving cancer chemotherapy–induced vomiting. Clinical studies on the effectiveness of THC have been conflicting. It was found to be more effective than placebos and at least as effective as prochlorperazine in some studies. Other studies reported that certain chemotherapeutic agents (cisplatin, mechlorethamine, and nitrosoureas) often produced a refractory nausea and vomiting that did not respond to THC or many other agents.

Significant CNS side effects including hallucinations, grand mal convulsions, and psychosis have also been reported. Teenagers and young adults seem to tolerate this drug much better than older adults (Frytak and Moertel, 1981). Absorption problems and lack of flexibility in the dosage schedule may be contributing factors to the large variable response in clients (Anderson and McGuire, 1981).

### dronabinol (Marinol)

Dronabinol is the synthetic derivative of delta-9-tetrahydrocannabinol approved by the FDA in 1985 for the treatment of nausea and vomiting related to cancer chemotherapy. Since this drug is listed in the Controlled Substances Act, each individual state legislature must approve its use before it can be prescribed in that state.

Dronabinol is indicated as a second line agent to prevent nausea and vomiting associated with chemotherapy when other antiemetics are ineffective. It reaches peak serum levels in 2 to 3 hours, is metabolized in the liver, and excreted mainly in the feces.

Side effects reported most often include dizziness, sedation, impaired mentation, and ataxia. Less frequent or rare effects are visual changes, dry mouth, restlessness, and hypotension. Adverse reactions reported are tachycardia or bradycardia and CNS side effects, such as confusion, delusions, hallucinations, depression, and anxiety. The elderly are particularly prone to the CNS adverse reactions.

The adult dosage is 5 mg/m² by mouth 1 to 3 hours before chemotherapy, then every 2 to 4 hours afterward for 4 to 6 doses daily. The maximum daily dose is 14 mg/m². Pediatric dosage is similar to adult dose.

Pregnancy safety is FDA category B.

### nabilone (Cesamet)

Nabilone is a synthetic derivative of cannabinoid (not THC) that was tested as an antiemetic in clients receiving cancer chemotherapy. It is reportedly more effective than placebos and prochlorperazine. It has an onset of action within ½ to 1 hour after an oral dose (2 mg). It peaks in 2 hours, and its effects last about 8 hours. Adverse effects include somnolence, dry mouth, dizziness, and a mild euphoric effect (Weintraub and Standish, 1983). Nabilone received FDA approval in the United States in December 1985. It has been available for use in the United Kingdom and Canada since the early 1980s. Pregnancy safety has been established at FDA category B.

## ▷*Nursing Management: Cannabinoid Therapy*

Assess the client's mental status before and during therapy. Some clients report feelings of well-being and euphoria, others have transient psychoses characterized by hallucinations and depersonalization.

Before giving dronabinol, assess the client's intolerance to sesame oil since the gelatin capsule dosage form of dronabinol contains this substance.

Caution the client about performing tasks that require alertness, since sleepiness and dizziness are common adverse reactions.

Instruct the client to make position changes slowly, particularly from the recumbent to upright position, and to dangle feet from the edge of the bed to prevent dizziness and fainting, symptoms of orthostatic hypotension.

Instruct the client to avoid alcoholic beverages and other CNS depressants while taking cannabinoids.

Administer 1 to 3 hours before chemotherapy.

## Corticosteroids

Corticosteroids have been reported to be effective for chemotherapy-induced nausea and vomiting when used in combination with other antiemetics. The mechanism of action is unknown, but it has been proposed that these drugs may inhibit prostaglandin synthesis, which may be involved in cancer chemotherapy–induced vomiting. Research has indicated that certain prostaglandins (especially the PGE series) can induce nausea and vomiting.

Many studies with corticosteroids have involved the use of dexamethasone or methylprednisolone. Antiemetic use is not yet an FDA-approved indication for the drugs. Their possible effectiveness as antiemetics was a serendipitous discovery—clients receiving various chemotherapeutic regimens had less nausea and vomiting when prednisone was one of the agents administered. Corticosteroids are not approved or generally recommended for common use. Further trials in clients not responding to all other available antiemetic agents might be warranted with this class of medications (Ryan, 1983).

## Emetic Agents

Emetic drugs exert their effects on the same centers as antiemetic drugs but with the opposite effect. They are used to induce vomiting as part of the treatment for certain drug overdoses and poisonings.

### apomorphine

Apomorphine, a product formulated by mixing morphine with dilute hydrochloric acid, is an agent with enhanced emetic effects and greatly reduced analgesic properties. Apomorphine is given parenterally as a single dose only. It directly stimulates the chemoreceptor trigger zone and may affect the vestibular centers, since client movement increases the individual's response to this product. It also stimulates dopamine receptors. Apomorphine may cause respiratory depression, increased salivation, hypotension, and sedation.

Subcutaneous administration produces vomiting in 90% of clients within 15 minutes (usually within 5 minutes). Sedative effects also occur within a few minutes and may last for several hours. When used early in treatment of an acute oral drug overdose, apomorphine produces emesis in 80% to 100% of clients with a recovery of gastrointestinal contents in the range of 3% to 92% (mean 31%). For client safety other measures—including gastric lavage, activated charcoal, and supportive measures—should also be instituted, since some toxic substances may remain in the gastrointestinal tract.

A glassful of water (approximately 240 ml) should be given with apomorphine to facilitate its action (young children should have less water).

The adult dose is 5 to 6 mg (range 2 to 10 mg) subcutaneously. Give children 0.07 to 1.0 mg/kg subcutaneously as a single dose.

Pregnancy safety has been established at FDA category C.

### ipecac syrup

Ipecac syrup is an over-the-counter drug for home emergency treatment. Its major alkaloids are emetine and cephaeline, which stimulate the chemoreceptor trigger zone and irritate the gastric mucosa.

Approximately 90% of patients vomit within a half hour following oral drug administration; the average time for vomiting is 20 minutes. Although this product is generally given in the home, a poison control center or medical personnel should be called for advice before administration. However, if medical help is not available, one should still use this product. See precautionary box.

---

**IPECAC SYRUP PRECAUTION**

Ipecac syrup is the only product to be used as an emetic. *Do not use ipecac fluidextract;* it is 14 times more concentrated than the syrup, and its use has resulted in serious injury and sometimes death. Although the fluidextract is no longer commercially produced in the United States, this product may still be on the shelves of some older pharmacies.

---

Vomiting induced by ipecac syrup occurs in 80% to 99% of clients, and gastrointestinal contents recovered may range from up to 78% (mean 28%). Therefore clients need further monitoring and/or treatment, since not all the toxic substances are recovered from the gastrointestinal tract.

Although apomorphine is faster acting, ipecac syrup has the advantage of oral administration. Ipecac does not produce the CNS effects or respiratory depression reported with apomorphine.

Active alkaloids of ipecac include emetine, a cardiotoxic substance. Although administation of a single dose does not usually lead to major problems, serious complications including fatalities have resulted from chronic use of this product by persons with an eating disorder, such as anorexia or bulimia. Emetine is excreted very slowly so with repeated doses, ipecac accumulates in the body. It may produce systemic effects for months, even after the drug is discontinued.

Myopathy or muscle aching and weakness, especially in muscles of the neck and extremities, hyporeflexia, slurred speech, and dysphagia have been reported. Cardiotoxicity has caused some fatalities. The cardiac alterations include premature ventricular contraction, supraventricular tachycardia, inverted T waves, prolonged QT and PR intervals, QRS complex alterations, ventricular tachycardia and fibrillation, and cardiac arrest. Signs and symptoms may include procardial chest pain, hypotension, congestive heart failure, pericardial effusion, pulmonary edema, and dyspnea.

Adults and children over 12 years are given 15 to 30 ml (1 oz) orally. Children 1 to 12 years are given 15 ml orally. Follow dose by 8 oz (240 ml) of water. If vomiting does not occur in 20 minutes, a second dose may be given. If vomiting does not occur then, gastric lavage should be implemented.

Pregnancy safety has been established at FDA category C.

### ▷ Nursing Management: Ipecac Therapy

Following administration of ipecac syrup, give a glassful (approximately 240 ml) of water. Less water or clear liquid should be given to younger children. Sometimes giving the

## Geriatric Implications:
## ANTI-ULCER THERAPIES

Gastrointestinal complaints are very common in elderly clients. Every complaint should be properly evaluated before instituting drug therapy.

Pain is less frequently the initial complaint while melena (black stool that contains digested blood) is the more frequent presentation and indication of ulcer disease in the elderly (Achkar, 1985).

Acid secretion reaches its peak during sleep, between the hours of 10 PM and 2 AM (Nix, 1986). Therefore, H$_2$ receptor antagonists prescribed as a daily dose should be administered at bedtime.

Cigarette smoking, which increases the amount of acid produced in the stomach, may decrease the effect of H$_2$-blockers. Clients should be advised to stop smoking if possible, or at least, not to smoke after the last daily dose of medication is taken (USP-DI, 1991).

With the routine administration of H$_2$ blockers, confusion and dizziness are more commonly reported by the elderly than in younger adults (USP-DI, 1991). With cimetidine (Tagamet), mental status changes have been reported, especially in elderly persons that have impaired liver or renal function or are severely ill. Acute mental changes in the elderly may indicate the need for lowering the drug dose or discontinuing the medication (Delafuente JC, 1988).

Decreased sexual function has been reported with cimetidine, such as decreased libido (at doses of 600 mg daily); impaired erection, impotency and male breast enlargement (1000 mg/day); and decreased male fertility (1200 mg/day) (Long, 1990).

Antacids effectively neutralize gastric acid while food also serves as a buffer for gastric acid. Thus antacids are most beneficial if administered between meals and at bedtime.

When H$_2$ receptor antagonists are prescribed with antacids, schedule medications at least 1 hour apart, administering antacid first.

---

water before the medication is more helpful in young or frightened children. If a child will not drink water, dilute, clear juice (apple) may be substituted. Do not give milk, since it will delay the emetic effect of the drug.

If the client is conscious, drug-induced vomiting is usually preferable to gastric lavage, particularly in children, since aspiration of vomitus is less likely to occur. Nurses should employ the necessary measures to reduce the likelihood of aspiration of vomitus (e.g., proper positioning of client). Occasionally, induction of vomiting may be faciliated by stimulating the pharynx, but time should not be wasted in repeated futile attempts.

CAUTION: Vomiting should never be induced in the client who is unconscious, has swallowed corrosive substances, or who has depressed gag or cough reflexes. Vomiting may result in aspiration of gastric contents into the lungs, which may be fatal.

## Drugs Used to Treat Peptic Ulcers

Treatment of peptic ulcer disease includes the following drugs, antacids, anticolinergics, antidepressants, H$_2$ receptor antagonists, and cytoprotective agents (substances that protect cells from damage) such as sucralfate. In addition, use of anxiolytics and avoidance of smoking, ethyl alcohol, and other ulcerogenic substances are suggested.

### Cytoprotective Agents
#### sucralfate (Carafate, Sulcrate ✱)

The aluminum complex of sucrose sulfate is believed to act as a locally active topical agent that hastens healing of the peptic ulcer by protecting the mucosa. The mechanism of action is thought to involve the formation of an ulcer-adherent complex with the fibrinogen in the ulcer crater that produces a protective, acid-resistant barrier. It is indicated for short-term (up to 8 weeks) duodenal ulcer treatment.

Only 3% to 5% of sucrose sulfate is absorbed from the gastrointestinal tract. Excretion is primarily by the fecal route, with minute amounts secreted in the urine. The duration of action is about 5 hours.

The most common side effect is constipation. Other reported effects include diarrhea, nausea, gastric discomfort, indigestion, dry mouth, dizziness, drowsiness, back pain, rash, and itching. Antacids may interfere within the sucralfate binding; therefore they should be given either 30 minutes before or 1 hour after sucralfate administration. Sucralfate interferes with absorption of fat-soluble vitamins which makes vitamin depletion possible with long-term use.

For adults, give 1 g four times daily on empty stomach 1 hour before each meal and at bedtime. Therapy should continue for 4 to 8 weeks until healing is documented.

Pregnancy safety has been established at FDA category B.

### ▷ Nursing Management:
### Sucralfate Therapy

Administer to client with water on an empty stomach, 1 hour before meals and at bedtime. Instruct client not to chew the tablet. If the client's regimen also includes antacids, they may be administered ½ hour before or 1 hour after the sucralfate.

Encourage compliance with the regimen for at least 4 to 8 weeks, until healing has been documented by x-ray or endoscopic examination. Sucralfate therapy is not recommended for longer than 8 weeks.

#### misprostol (Cytotec)

Misoprostol (a prostaglandin analog) is a gastric mucosa protectant agent indicated for the prevention of gastric ulcers associated with the use of nonsteroidal antiinflammatory agents, especially in clients at increased risk of developing complications from gastric ulcers. It produces its effects by increasing gastric mucus and the mucosal secretion of bicarbonate. It also inhibits basal and nocturnal gastric acid secretion by its action on the parietal cells.

It is rapidly absorbed orally reaching a peak serum level in approximately 15 minutes with a duration of action of 3 to 6 hours. It is metabolized to an active metabolite that is later metabolized to inactive metabolites in various body tissues. It is primarily excreted by the kidneys. The most frequent side effects associated with its use are stomach distress and diarrhea, which are dose-related. Less frequent side effects include constipation, gas, headache, nausea, or vomiting. At the present time, no significant drug interactions have been noted with misoprostol.

The adult dose is 0.2 mg four times daily during or after meals and at bedtime or 0.4 mg twice daily, taking the last dose at bedtime. Pediatric dosage has not been established. Pregnancy safety has been established at FDA Category X, because an increase in uterine contractions, uterine bleeding, and miscarriages may result if used during pregnancy.

## ▷ Nursing Management: Misoprostol Therapy

Administer to client with or after meals. The course of therapy should be started at the same time as the NSAIAs. Misoprostol may be administered with antacid, but magnesium-containing antacids are not recommended because they may aggravate any misoprostol-induced diarrhea. Alert the client to report any diarrhea episode lasting more than 1 week to the prescriber. Misoprostol is not to be taken longer than 4 weeks unless otherwise prescribed.

### omeprazole (Prilosec)

Omeprazole is an inhibitor of the gastric acid pump, thus it is indicated for short-term periods to treat severe erosive esophagitis that occurs with gastroesophageal reflux; or the long-term treatment of hypersecretory gastric conditions, Zollinger-Ellison syndrome, mastocytosis and multiple endocrine adenoma. It binds irreversibly to the hydrogen/potassium ATPase enzyme system, thus inhibiting the transport of hydrogen ions into the gastric lumen.

The most frequent side effect reported is stomach colic or pain. Less often reported are increased weakness, muscle aches, dizziness, headache, sedation, chest pain, heartburn, constipation or diarrhea, gas, nausea, vomiting, or skin rash. Rare adverse reactions include hematologic alterations, such as anemia, neutropenia, pancytopenia, or thrombocytopenia. Urinary problems possible include blood or protein in the urine or urinary infections. A physician should be contacted when any signs or symptoms of adverse reactions occur.

Omeprazole may interact and cause an inhibition of the liver-metabolizing enzyme system (P-450), thus decreasing the metabolism of the coumarin and indandione anticoagulants, diazepam, or phenytoin. Serum levels of these agents can rise resulting in toxicity. Monitor concurrent therapy closely.

For gastroesophageal reflux, the adult oral dosage is 20 mg daily for 1 to 2 months. For the gastric hypersecretory conditions, the oral dose is 60 mg daily, adjusting dose as necessary. For elderly clients the dosage should not exceed 20 mg per day. Children's dosage has not been established.

Pregnancy safety has been established at FDA category C.

## H₂ Receptor Antagonists

Histamine is found in the mucosal cells of the gastrointestinal tract, extending from the stomach to the colon. The action of histamine is mediated through $H_2$ receptors and has been associated with gastric acid secretion. The major components of the gastric acid secretion. The major components of the gastric secretion of the stomach include hydrochloric acid (HCl) and intrinsic factor (IF), produced by the parietal (acid-forming) cells; pepsinogen, synthesized by the chief cells; and mucus. The principal function of mucus is to protect the epithelial cells of the gastrointestinal tract from attack by pepsin and irritation by the HCl secreted by the stomach. Pepsinogen, an enzyme, is the precursor of pepsin; HCl catalyzes the cleavage of pepsinogen to active pepsin by providing a low pH environment in which pepsin can initiate the digestion of proteins.

Gastric secretion is regulated by a neural mechanism, parasympathetic (vagus) fibers, and a hormonal mechanism, gastrin. Activation of the vagus nerve causes secretion of vast quantities of pepsinogen and HCl. In contrast, the hormonal mechanism involves the actual presence of food, which distends the stomach and stimulates the antral mucosa to release gastrin. This hormone is then absorbed into the blood and carried to the parietal cells and chief cells secreting HCl and pepsinogen, respectively. Histamine is believed to activate the gastric mucosa much the same as gastrin does. In addition, caffeine and alcohol are potent stimuli for gastrin release. When the acidity of the gastric juice is increased to a pH of 2, a negative feedback mechanism helps to block production of gastric secretion from the parietal and chief cells. Thus inhibition of gastric gland secretion plays an essential role in protecting the stomach against excessively acidic secretions, which are responsible for causing peptic ulcerations.

Normally the mucosal surface of the stomach and upper duodenum is protected from the irritation of gastric acid by a layer of mucus. If a circumscribed area of the mucosal surface is damaged and fails to repair rapidly, it may become eroded, forming an ulcer at one of these sites. When gastric acid comes in contact with this inflammatory region, pain may result. Moreover, clinical studies have suggested that esophageal, gastric, and duodenal ulcers (peptic ulcers) are associated with the excessive production of gastric acid.

Clinical evidence has shown that histamine released by severe injuries, particularly burns, may lead to the formation of peptic ulcers.

The H$_2$ receptor blocking agents include cimetidine (Tagamet), ranitidine (Zantac), famotidine (Pepcid), and nizatidine (Axid). They act to prevent histamine from stimulating the H$_2$ receptors located on the gastric parietal cells, thus resulting in a reduction in the volume of gastric acid secretion (from stimuli such as food, pentagastrin, histamine, caffeine, and insulin) and the concentration (acid content) of the secretions. All four drugs are presently considered to be equally potent and effective, although pharmacokinetics, side effects/adverse reactions, and drug interactions may differ.

### cimetidine (Tagamet)
### ranitidine (Zantac)
### famotidine (Pepcid)
### nizatidine (Axid)

These agents are used to treat and prevent gastric ulcer, duodenal ulcer, gastroesophageal reflux (ranitidine), and hypersecretory gastric states. For pharmacokinetics, see Table 40-5; for side effects/adverse reactions, see Table 40-6.

***Significant drug interactions.*** Since cimetidine, unlike the other H$_2$ receptor antagonists, inhibits the liver drug metabolism systems, the major drug interactions noted are with cimetidine. All of the H$_2$ receptor antagonists may exhibit a similar effect with ketoconazole and antacids.

| Drug | Possible Effect and Management |
|---|---|
| anticoagulants (coumarin, indanedione) metoprolol, phenytoin, propranolol, or xanthines (exception: dyphylline) | May result in decreased metabolism and excretion of these medications. Since dosage adjustments may be necessary, blood concentration (for phenytoin and xanthines), prothrombin time (for anticoagulants), and blood pressure monitoring (for metoprolol and propranolol) are indicated. |
| antidepressants, tricyclic | May decrease metabolism of tricyclic antidepressant, causing an increased serum level and toxicity. Assess the client for signs of toxicity, and monitor for serum levels. |
| antacids | Concurrent use is often prescribed by physicians, but if the H$_2$ receptor antagonist is given concurrently with an antacid, absorption of the antagonist may be decreased. Give antacids at least 1 hour apart from these medications. |
| ketoconazole | An increase in gastrointestinal pH induced by the H$_2$ receptor antagonists may result in a reduced absorption of ketoconazole. Advise clients to take the H$_2$ receptor antagonist at least 2 hours after ketoconazole. |

**TABLE 40-5**   Pharmacokinetics of H$_2$ receptor antagonist

| Drug | Absorption | Time to peak plasma level | Plasma half-life (hr) | Duration of action (hr) | Metabolism/excretion |
|---|---|---|---|---|---|
| cimetidine (Tagamet) | Very good orally, 60%-70% | 45-90 min after oral dose | 2-3 | 4-5 basal 6-8 nocturnal | Liver/kidneys |
| famotidine (Pepcid) | Fair orally, 40%-45% | 1-3 hr after oral dose | 2.5-3.5 | 10-12 | Liver/kidneys |
| nizatidine (Axid) | Very good orally, 90% | 0.5-3 hr after oral dose | 1-2 | Up to 8 basal Up to 12 nocturnal | Liver (has active metabolite)/kidneys |
| ranitidine (Zantac) | Good orally, 50% | 1-3 hr after oral dose | 2.5-3 | Up to 4 hr (basal and stimulated); up to 13 hr (nocturnal) | Liver/kidneys |

**TABLE 40-6**   H$_2$ receptor antagonist: side effects/adverse reactions

| Drug(s) | Side effects | Adverse reactions |
|---|---|---|
| cimetidine (Tagamet) famotidine (Pepcid) nizatidine (Axid) ranitidine (Zantac) | Less frequent: rash, diarrhea, constipation, dizziness, headaches, muscle pain (cimetidine, famotidine), stomach cramps or pain<br>Cimetidine only: breast swelling or pain in males and females (with chronic therapy)<br>Famotidine only: dry mouth or skin, anorexia, depression, nausea or vomiting, temporary loss of hair, taste alterations, decrease in libido | Rare: confusion, sore throat, elevated temperature, bruising (blood disorder), increased weakness, altered heart rate (slow, fast, irregular), chest pain (famotidine), eyelid edema (allergic reaction—famotidine) |

**TABLE 40-7**   Receptor antagonists: dosage and administration

| Drug | Dosage recommendations |
| --- | --- |
| cimetidine (Tagamet) | Adult dose for duodenal and benign active gastric ulcer is 300 mg orally, 4 times daily, with meals and at bedtime; or 800 mg at bedtime. Preventive therapy is 400 mg at bedtime. For gastric hypersecretory states, increase dose as necessary. Maximum daily dose is usually 2.4 g but in some hypersecretory states up to 12 g per day may be necessary. In clients with renal impairment, start with 300 mg every 12 hr, increasing dose as necessary and as tolerated by client. Children are dosed at 20 to 40 mg/kg in divided doses, four times daily. |
| parenteral | Adult dose by IM, IV, or IV infusion solution is 300 mg every 6 to 8 hr. The IV dose should be administered over 2 min or more while the IV infusion is mixed in a compatible solution and given over 15 to 20 min. Clients with renal impairment receive 300 mg IV every 12 hr, adjusting dose and interval as necessary and tolerated. Maximum daily dose is up to 2.4 g. Children's IM, IV, or IV infusion dosage is 5 to 10 mg/kg every 6 to 8 hr. |
| famotidine (Pepcid) oral | Adult dosage for duodenal and benign active gastric ulcer is 40 mg daily at bedtime. For gastric hypersecretory states, administer 20 mg every 6 hr, adjusting dose as necessary. In severe renal impairment (creatinine clearance less than 10 ml/min), the dose is 20 mg at bedtime. Adjust dose interval as needed since it may need to be increased to every 36 to 48 hr. Pediatric dosage is not established. |
| parenteral | Adult dose is 20 mg IV or IV infusion every 12 hr. Dilute preparation and administer according to package insert instructions. Pediatric dosage not established. |
| nizatidine (Axid) | Adult oral dosage for duodenal ulcer is 300 mg daily at bedtime or 150 mg twice daily. Preventive therapy is 150 mg at bedtime. Pediatric dose is not established. |
| ranitidine (Zantac) oral | Adult oral dosage for duodenal, benign active gastic ulcer and gastroesophageal reflux, is 150 mg twice daily or 300 mg at bedtime. Preventive therapy is 150 mg at bedtime. To treat gastric hypersecretion, start with 150 mg twice daily and adjust dose as necessary, up to a maximum of 6 g per day. Pediatric dosage has not been established. |
| parenteral | Adult dose by IM, IV, or IV infusion is 50 mg every 6 to 8 hr. See current literature for dilution instructions and administration times. Maximum daily dose is up to 400 mg. Pediatric dosage has not been established. |

High dosages of ranitidine may also interact with coumarin or indandione anticoagulants, metoprolol and phenytoin and produce the same results as cimetidine.

**Dosage and administration.** See Table 40-7.

**Pregnancy safety.** Has been established at FDA Category B for cimetidine, famotidine and ranitidine and at FDA Category C for nizatidine

▷ *Nursing Management:*
*H₂ Receptor Antagonist Therapy*

**Assessment.** Note that clients with impaired renal function require a reduction in dosage of cimetidine, famotidine, or ranitidine because of delayed excretion. The recommended dosage of cimetidine is 300 mg every 12 hours orally or parenterally. In clients with impaired liver function, a further reduction in dosage may be necessary. For clients undergoing hemodialysis, adjust the time of dosage so that the medication is administered at the end of the procedure, thus preventing a decrease in blood level of the drug. These agents are dialyzable.

Do not use the drugs for minor digestive complaints. Before administering, rule out the potential existence of malignant gastrointestinal neoplasm. Do not administer to nursing mothers, pregnant women, women of childbearing potential, and children under 16 years of age.

With the administration of H₂-receptor antagonists, the client may experience altered comfort related to headache, nausea or vomiting, and dizziness; altered bowel function (constipation or diarrhea); altered sleep pattern (drowsiness); altered thought processes (confusion); hyperthermia; and risk of injury related to allergic reaction, bradycardia or tachycardia, or neutropenia or other blood dyscrasias (sore throat, fever, unusual bleeding or bruising).

**Intervention.** Administer drug with meals, since food slows gastric emptying and prolongs the drug's effect. If prescribed, a bedtime dose protects the stomach from nocturnal hypersecretion of gastric acid. Give concomitant antacids to relieve acute ulcer pain 1 hour *before* or *after* administration of H₂ antagonist, to prevent drug interaction.

Note that the parenteral form of the drug is stable for 48 hours at room temperature. The intravenous solutions in which cimetidine and famotidine are compatible for dilution are 0.9% sodium chloride, dextrose (5%, 10%), lactated Ringer's, and 5% sodium bicarbonate.

Warn client that intramuscular administration may be painful.

Rapid intravenous bolus administration (less than 2 minutes) may result in cardiac dysrhythmias and hypotension.

**Education.** Instruct client to keep clinical and laboratory appointments as scheduled. Periodic evaluation of blood counts and renal and hepatic function tests are required during therapy.

Encourage the client with peptic ulcer disease to discontinue smoking or at least to discontinue smoking after the last dose of the day, since the effectiveness of H$_2$ antagonists to inhibit nocturnal gastric acid secretions is diminished by smoking.

*Evaluation.* Be aware that following long-term treatment (1 month or more), mild bilateral gynecomastia in males and galactorrhea in females have been observed in some clients taking cimetidine. This drug also may cause a reversible decline in sperm count or impotence. No such problems have been reported with ranitidine.

The use of ranitidine, which is metabolized in the liver, may cause elevated hepatic enzyme levels, especially serum glutamic-pyruvic transaminase (SGPT) level. Since ranitidine is potentially hepatotoxic, perform periodic hepatic studies. It is not advisable to prolong therapy; most clients with active duodenal ulcers heal within 8 weeks, and the usefulness of further treatment is unknown.

# DRUGS THAT AFFECT THE GALLBLADDER
## chenodiol (Chenix, Chendol ✶)

Chenodiol (chenodeoxycholic acid) is a normal bile acid synthesized in the liver. Cholesterol is broken down by bile acids and lecithin, so when the amount of cholesterol exceeds the capacity of bile acids and lecithin to perform this effect, crystallization and gallstones may result. Chenodiol blocks liver synthesis of cholesterol, thus reducing biliary cholesterol levels and leading to gradual dissolving of floating, radiolucent cholesterol gallstones.

Chenodiol is indicated for the patient with radiolucent stones who has a well-opacified, functioning gallbladder, but who is at increased surgical risk for elective surgery because of systemic disease, age, or cardiovascular, renal, or respiratory disease.

Chenodiol is absorbed in the small intestine, metabolized by the liver, and excreted in feces.

Dose-related diarrhea has been reported in 30% to 40% of patients taking chenodiol. It may occur with initial therapy or any time during the treatment period. Most cases of diarrhea are mild and tolerated, so they do not interfere with therapy. In 10% to 15% of clients, a dosage decrease and/or antidiarrheal agent may be required.

Other side effects of chenodiol include fecal urgency, cramps, heartburn, constipation, nausea, vomiting, anorexia, flatulence, and nonspecific abdominal pain.

Cholestyramine and colestipol sequester bile acids, reducing the absorption of chenodiol. Products that adsorb bile acids (e.g., aluminum-based antacids) will also reduce absorption.

Estrogen therapy, oral contraceptives, and clofibrate may increase biliary cholesterol secretion, counteracting the effectiveness of this drug.

Adult dose is 13 to 16 mg/kg/day in two divided doses orally morning and night, beginning with 250 mg twice daily for 2 weeks and increasing by 250 mg/day each week thereafter until either maximum tolerated dose or recommended dose is attained.

Pregnancy safety has been established at FDA category X.

## ▷ Nursing Management:
## Chenodiol Therapy

*Assessment.* Ultrasonography is a screening procedure for gallstone detection, but initiation and continuation of therapy are based on the results of oral cholecystograms.

Determine serum aminotransferase levels each month for 3 months and every 3 months thereafter (discontinue monitoring if over three times normal upper limits). Oral cholecystograms or ultrasonograms are needed at 6- and 9-month intervals to monitor response. The response to therapy may be noted on a cholecystogram or ultrasonogram taken 1 month after therapy is begun. Success usually occurs within 12 to 18 months. If no therapeutic response is achieved by 18 months the drug is discontinued; use beyond 24 months is not recommended. Stones recur within 5 years in about 50% of patients. Radiolucency and gallbladder function must be established before intiating another course of treatment.

*Intervention.* Administer with food or milk, since the presence of bile and pancreatic juice in the intestine enhances dissolution.

*Education.* Instruct the client about a high-fiber, low-fat diet and a weight reduction program if necessary.

Because therapy is long term, compliance may be a problem. Encourage the client through a relationship of trust and confidence.

## ursodiol (Actigall)

Ursodiol is an oral product used to dissolve cholesterol gallstones (anticholelithic agent) in clients that have uncomplicated gallstone disease. It is more effective against small, floatable stones (<20 mm) and is not indicated for the treatment of calcified cholesterol stones, radiopaque (calcium containing) stones, radiolucent bile pigment type stones or when surgery is clearly necessary.

While its exact mechanism of action is unknown, ursodiol inhibits intestinal absorption of cholesterol and also decreases cholesterol synthesis and secretion in the liver. A reduction in cholesterol saturation allows the gradual dissolution of cholesterol from the gallstones. Ursodiol also increases bile flow in the body. Be aware, though, that gallstone dissolution may necessitate 6 to 24 months of oral therapy, depending on the composition and size of the stone. This therapy is monitored by performing ultrasonograms at 6 month intervals during the first year. If partial effectiveness is not recorded after one year of treatment, then ursodiol is usually determined to be ineffective and drug therapy is discontinued. If successful, ursodiol is recommended for at least 3 months after complete dissolution of the stones to

for routine bowel function. Instruct the client not to take laxatives unnecessarily. For example, some individuals believe that laxatives are to be taken to "clean out" the system, as a tonic, in the case of colds, or at the change of seasons.

*Evaluation.*   Determine that the client has returned to his or her normal, adequate bowel pattern.

## Saline Laxatives

The saline laxatives are soluble salts that are only slightly absorbed from the alimentary canal. Because of their osmotic effect in the small intestine, these salts retain water and increase the water content of feces.

An isotonic saline solution inhibits absorption of water from the bowel and therefore increases the total fluid bulk. Peristalsis is increased, and several liquid or semiliquid stools result. A hypertonic saline solution causes diffusion of fluid from the blood in the wall (semipermeable membrane) of the bowel (small intestine) and into the lumen of the organ until the solution becomes isotonic.

The water in the intestinal lumen produces fluid accumulation and distention, leading to peristalsis and eventual evacuation of bowel contents. The laxative effect may be enhanced by the intestinal release of cholecystokinin (CCK). Diarrhea is created in the small intestine to overcome constipation in the colon. Laxation results in 30 minutes to 3 hours.

The saline laxatives are the laxative of choice for securing a stool specimen for examination, for fecal impactions, for use with certain anthelmintics, and in some cases of food and drug poisoning. Phosphate enemas are useful as preparations for a barium enema. When the object is merely to empty the intestine, magnesium sulfate, sodium phosphate, or milk of magnesia is effective. Milk of magnesia (magnesium hydroxide) is the mildest of the salines and is often the cathartic of choice for children. The sodium salts are contraindicated in cardiac clients or those on a low-sodium diet. The magnesium and potassium salts are contraindicated in clients with renal disease.

The intestinal membrane is not entirely impermeable to the passage of saline laxatives. Electrolyte disturbances have been reported with their long-term daily use. Some saline laxatives find their way into the general circulation only to be excreted by the kidney, in which case they act as saline diuretics. Hypertonic saline solutions in the bowel may result in so much fluid loss that little or no diuretic effect will be possible. Some saline laxatives contain up to 1 g or more of sodium per dose. Some ions may have a toxic effect in impaired renal function if they accumulate in the blood in sufficient quantity. This may occur with magnesium ions if a solution is retained in the intestine for a long time or if the client suffers from renal impairment. It may also occur when large doses of the salt are given intravenously. Magnesium acts as a depressant of the central nervous system and neuromuscular activity.

*Dosage and administration.*   The following salts, when given for their laxative effect, are usually given orally. Certain of them may be given rectally as an enema. The salts tend to have a rapid action, especially if orally administered before breakfast. They may be taken at bedtime with food for early morning evacuation (food delays the effect). Clients sometimes complain of gaseous distention after taking saline laxatives. All preparations should be dissolved and accompanied by a liberal (8-oz) intake of water, since the salts do not readily leave the stomach and may cause vomiting unless well diluted.

When a salt such as magnesium sulfate is given, it should not only be dissolved in an adequate amount of water on an empty stomach but it should also be disguised in fruit juice, plain water (chilled), citrus-flavored carbonate beverage, or chipped ice.

*magnesium sulfate (Epsom salt).*   Magnesium sulfate occurs as glassy, needlelike crystals or as a white powder. It is readily soluble in water. It has a bitter saline taste. The usual dose for laxative effect is 10 to 15 g in 8 ounces of water. Children over 6 are given 5 to 10 g in 8 ounces of water.

*milk of magnesia; magnesium hydroxide mixture.*  Milk of magnesia (MOM) is also used as an antacid. In the stomach the magnesium hydroxide reacts with the hydrochloric acid to form magnesium chloride, which is responsible for the laxative effect. The usual dose for adults is 15 ml (½ fluid ounce) with additional liquids, although the range of dosage is 5 to 60 ml. Children are given one-fourth to one-half the adult dose, depending on the child's age.

*magnesium citrate solution.*   Magnesium citrate solution is not very soluble, hence the need for a relatively large dose. It is not unpleasant to take because it is carbonated and flavored. The usual adult dose is 240 ml, and the usual dose for children 6 to 12 years old is 50 to 100 ml. Results occur in 30 minutes to 3 hours.

*effervescent sodium phosphate.*   Effervescent sodium phosphate is made effervescent by the addition of sodium bicarbonate and citric and tartaric acids. The usual dose is 10 g.

A concentrated aqueous solution of sodium biphosphate and sodium phosphate is available under the name of Fleet Phospho-Soda. The usual adult dose as a laxative is 10 to 40 ml mixed with ½ glass of cold water. Children 6 to 10 years old are given 2.5 to 5 ml. It is also marketed in a disposable enema unit. It should be used cautiously in clients on low-sodium diets.

## ▷Nursing Management: Saline Laxative Therapy

Dosing may be made more palatable by following the dose with fruit juice or citrus-flavored soda.

If mixed from a solid, thoroughly dissolve the preparation before it is administered.

**TABLE 41-2**  Oral stimulant laxatives

| Name | Therapeutic effect (hrs) | Stool consistency | Remarks |
|---|---|---|---|
| bisacodyl<br>Dulcolax | 6-10 | Soft | Not to be taken within 1 hr after ingestion of milk or antacids to prevent premature dissolving of enteric coating and gastrointestinal irritation |
| castor oil<br>Neoloid emulsion,<br>Castor Oil | 2-6 | Watery | Chilling, mixing with fruit juice or carbonated drinks increases palatability |
| cascara sagrada<br>Cascara sagrada | 6-10 | Soft, formed | Gives a yellowish brown color to acid urine; reddish color to alkaline urine |
| phenolphthalein<br>Ex-Lax, Feen-A-Mint,<br>Phenolax, Doxidan | 6-10 | Semifluid | Gives pink color to alkaline urine or feces; action may persist for 3-4 days; may cause skin eruptions as dermatitis |
| senna<br>X-prep, Senokot | 6-12 | Soft | Crude senna may cause urine discoloration like cascara |

These laxatives have a quicker effect when taken on an empty stomach with a full glass of water. Since results occur within ½ to 3 hours, do not administer late in the day.

Use preparations that contain added sugar or sodium with caution in clients on sodium-restricted diets or with diabetes.

## Stimulant Laxatives

The principal members of the stimulant group of laxatives are botanical glycoside drugs obtained from the bark, seed pods, leaves, and roots of a number of plants. Cascara, senna, rhubarb, and aloe yield anthraquinones in the alkaline portion of the small intestine. These are absorbed and later secreted to produce irritation in the large intestine. These compounds are partially absorbed from the intestine.

The anthracene laxatives act in 6 to 24 hours. They exert their main action on the small and large intestines, which explains their tendency to produce cramping. Aloe and rhubarb are almost obsolete because of their irritating properties.

Stimulant laxatives are used in preparation for barium enemas, in some cases of acute constipation, and before a proctologic examination.

The side effects and adverse reactions of stimulant laxative abuse include hypokalemia, enteric loss of protein, and malabsorption. Senna, cascara sagrada, danthron, and aloe are passed through the breast milk, initiating laxation in the nursing infant. Their occasional use should be restricted to 1 week, since long-term abuse may lead to a poorly functioning large intestine. The stimulant laxatives may lead to mucus secretion and fluid evacuation. Table 41-2 compares the stimulant laxatives in use today. They may cause discoloration of the urine (yellow-brown in acid urine, pink to red in alkaline urine). Laxatives are habit forming; they should be used judiciously.

### cascara sagrada

Cascara sagrada is obtained from the bark of the *Rhamnus purshiana*, a shrub or small tree, and was one of the most extensively used laxatives. Its action is mainly on the small and large bowel. Although its effects are comparatively mild, it does act by irritation. It is less likely to cause gripping than some of the other laxatives belonging to this group of compounds. The active ingredients reach the large bowel by way of the bloodstream, after absorption in the small bowel, as well as by passage along the alimentary tract. Bowel evacuation occurs in about 8 hours. Prolonged use leads to melanotic pigmentation in rectal mucosa, which is reversible 4 to 12 months after discontinuation of the drug.

Aromatic cascara fluid-extract is prepared using magnesium oxide as a debitterizing agent to make it more palatable. Flavoring agents, sweeteners, and alcohol (18%) are also added. Each milliliter represents 1 g cascara sagrada. The presence of magnesium oxide decreases some bitter irritating substances and the laxative action, requiring a higher dose than the other preparations. The usual dose is 5 ml (range 5 to 15 ml). For infants up to 2 years the dose is 1 to 2 ml. Cascara is also available in 325-mg tablets. The average adult dose is 325 (gr 5) to 650 mg.

### senna

Senna is obtained from the dried leaves of the *Cassia acutifolia* plant. It produces a thorough bowel evacuation in 6 to 12 hours and is likely to be accompanied by abdominal pain or gripping. It may cause hemorrhagic gastritis and nephritis. Senna resembles cascara but is more powerful. It is found in the proprietary remedies Fletcher's Castoria and Black Draught.

Senna tea is an infusion of senna leaves made from a teaspoonful of leaves to a cup of hot water.

A powdered concentrate of senna (X-prep), obtained from

increased in 5- and 10-ml increments to 60 ml daily following breakfast. Severe constipation and treatment with other laxatives plus enemas and suppositories may require an initial dose of 30 ml.

To reduce blood ammonia levels in portal systemic encephalopathy the initial dose is 30 to 45 ml, three to four times daily, adjusted to produce a fecal pH of 5 to 5.5 and two to three soft, formed stools daily.

## ▷ Nursing Management: Lactulose Therapy

To make lactulose more palatable, mix it in water, juice, or milk.

Results may take 24 to 36 hours after administration of lactulose.

Use of lactulose during pregnancy has not been evaluated; therefore another type of laxative may be given under the physician's direction.

Lactulose use in diabetic clients may cause elevations in blood glucose levels; another type of laxative without galactose or lactose may be better.

Elderly and debilitated clients receiving lactulose for 6 months or more should have serum electrolytes (potassium, chloride, and carbon dioxide) periodically evaluated.

Since lactulose contains galactose (less than 2.2 g/15 ml), it is contraindicated in low-galactose diets.

The solution may darken on exposure to high temperature, but this will not change its therapeutic effect. Freezing does not alter the therapeutic effect.

## ANTIDIARRHEALS

The term **diarrhea** describes the abnormal passage of stools with increased frequency, increased fluidity, or increased weight and increase in stool water excretion. Diarrhea is acute when it is of sudden onset in a previously healthy individual, lasts about 3 days to 3 weeks, is self-limiting, and resolves without sequelae. Morbid and mortal consequences are seen in malnourished populations, the elderly, infants, and debilitated persons. Chronic diarrhea lasts for over 3 to 4 weeks, with the recurring passage of diarrheal stools, fever, anorexia, nausea, vomiting, weight reduction, and chronic weakness. It is the result of multiple causative factors, as seen in the box on p. 707. Chronic diarrhea necessitates definitive treatment directed to the organic cause or causes. The causes vary from psychogenic to neoplastic origins.

The objectives of treatment are to (1) replenish fluid and electrolyte loss, (2) ascertain, if possible, the cause or causes of diarrhea, (3) reduce the frequency of evacuation, (4) absorb toxins, (5) restore the intestinal flora, and (6) treat the underlying cause or causes.

Nonspecific treatment is directed at the increased stool frequency, which burdens daily life-style; the alleviation of abdominal cramps; the prevention of dehydration and metabolic acidosis from fluid and electrolyte loss; and the minimization of weight loss and nutritional deficits resulting from malabsorption. Specific treatment is directed at the cause or condition creating the diarrhea, as demonstrated by the sample nursing diagnoses on p. 705.

Ideally, the nursing process lends itself to ascertaining the type or cause of diarrhea to be treated through careful individual client evaluation. Such evaluative questions for discovering the cause or causes may be used in assessing the following criteria:

Age of the client
Occupation
Duration of diarrhea (precipitating factors tantamount to onset)
Stool description (frequency of evacuation, rectal bleeding or black stool appearance, foul-smelling odor, light color, or greasy consistency)
Medication profile (prescribed and self-administered as OTC drugs)
Presence or absence of anorexia, weight reduction (involuntary), fever, abdominal tenderness, dehydration
Ingestion of foods, toxic substances, milk intake, alcohol use
Travel outside the United States or Canada
Symptom description (location)
Relief obtained, if any, and treatment modality
Chronic diseases, presence of acute or concurrent illness, emotional or behavioral problems

Fluid and electrolyte loss may cause tachycardia, postural hypotension, elevated hematocrit or blood urea nitrogen, and poor skin turgor. The stool specimen may reveal occult blood (gastrointestinal bleeding), fecal leukocytes, parasites, or fat. Endocrine diseases such as diabetes mellitus and hyperthyroidism should be considered. Hospitalization is needed for dehydration that would compromise a client with congestive heart failure or chronic renal disease, since this complicates fluid replacement efforts. If any child or infant is unable to consume oral replacement fluid, hospitalization is needed to replace fluids and maintain urine flow. Bed rest alone may reduce stool frequency. In addition to the child or infant, the elderly client with a poor medical history, a client with chronic illness (heart disease, asthma), and pregnant women are at risk from acute or chronic diarrhea.

Maintenance of fluid and electrolyte balance is the most important goal of supportive therapy in acute diarrhea. If left untreated, a loss of anions (bicarbonate, organic anions as short-chain fatty acids) will create a gain of hydrogen ions, resulting in metabolic acidosis. This gain will be exacerbated by the (often) concomitant ketoacidosis of starvation and acidosis of prerenal azotemia. As volume increases in diarrhea, a rise in sodium and chloride develops with a decrease in potassium concentration. The decreased contact time of the luminal contents with the mucosal surface decreases the passive secretion of potassium. The electrolyte composition of stool water will then be close to that of plasma. The electrolyte loss of sodium, potassium, chloride, and bicarbonate is the basis of therapy.

## ▷ Nursing Management:
## Bisacodyl Therapy

Because bisacodyl tablets are enteric coated, instruct clients not to chew them, or administer them chipped. Instruct clients to swallow bisacodyl tablets whole no sooner than 1 hour before or after ingestion of dairy products or antacids. Milk or antacids can break down the enteric coating, which can lead to gastric irritation, cramping, and vomiting.

## Bulk-Forming Laxatives

The laxatives comprising this group are polycarbophil (Mitrolan) and other natural or semisynthetic cellulose derivatives made from agar, plantago seed, kelp, and plant gums. Often these products are combined with fecal softeners (Dialose) or stimulant laxatives (Dialose Plus). They may also be emulsified with liquid petrolatum (Petrogalar, Agoral), cascara, phenolphthalein, or milk of magnesia.

The mineral oil and agar emulsions are widely advertised but are of little value because the agar content is so small (2% to 6%). The laxative effect of these emulsions is usually caused by the addition of some other ingredient.

Hydrophilic colloids stimulate peristalsis by increasing bulk and so modifying the consistency of the stool. This mechanism of laxative action is normal stimulus and is one of the least harmful. These drugs do not interfere with absorption of food, but they can cause fecal impaction and obstruction, so it is important to administer them with adequate daily fluids (8 ounces per dose). The effect of these laxatives may not be apparent for 12 to 24 hours, and their full effect may not be achieved until the second or third day after administration. Some physicians maintain that bran and dried fruits (e.g., prunes and figs) exert the same effect, and they prefer to advise these foods rather than the bulk-forming laxatives. When moistened, they swell, forming a mass of material that passes through the intestine without being affected by the digestive juices. By their blandness and bulk they make the stool large and soft so that it is easily moved along the colon and into the rectum.

The bulk-forming or bulk-producing laxatives are often the first choice for constipation. They are also used in irritable bowel syndrome, diverticular disease, postpartum constipation, and in the elderly.

The primary side effects/adverse reactions reported are flatulence and bulky stools.

The bulk-forming laxatives interact with salicylates, digitalis drugs, and other drugs by inhibiting their absorption from the gastrointestinal tract.

## ▷ Nursing Management:
## Bulk-Forming Laxative Therapy

Because there is a possibility of impaction or obstruction if fluid intake is not substantial, avoid use of bulk-forming laxatives in clients with stenosis, adhesions, or dysphagia.

Administer with a full glass of liquid (240 ml) plus additional liquid every day to avoid intestinal impaction.

Results may not occur for 12 to 72 hours.

Some preparations contain sugar and sodium and so may not be used with clients for whom these substances are restricted.

### polycarbophil calcium (Mitrolan)

Polycarbophil is used to normalize stools both in diarrhea and in constipation by restoring the normal moisture level and providing bulk in the intestinal tract. In diarrheal conditions the intestinal mucosa is unable to absorb the excess fecal water. This agent absorbs the water (up to 60 times its weight) by forming a gel in the intestinal lumen, thus creating formed stools. In constipation the agent retains water in the lumen.

Polycarbophil has a low sodium content, and each tablet contains 150 mg calcium. The maximum dosage of calcium recommended by the FDA is much higher than the 1800 mg a patient would receive by taking the maximum dosage of 12 tablets per day. Nevertheless, clients with hypercalcemia or those susceptible to hypercalcemia should not take this product without prior consultation with their physician.

Decreased absorption of tetracyclines may occur if they are given concurrently with polycarbophil. The client should be counseled about this possibility.

## ▷ Nursing Management:
## Polycarbophil Calcium Therapy

Instruct the client to follow each dose of polycarbophil calcium for constipation with at least 8 ounces of water or other liquid. Also, instruct the client to thoroughly chew polycarbophil tablets before swallowing.

### plantago seed (psyllium seed)

Plantago seed is the dried ripe seed of the *Plantago psyllium, Plantago indica*, or *Plantago ovata*. The small brown or blond seeds contain a mucilaginous material that swells in the presence of moisture to form a jellylike indigestible mass. Although the seeds swell, their ends remain sharp and may be the cause of irritation in the alimentary tract. At present, only the preparations of the extracted gums are available, and these have the advantage of causing less mechanical irritation.

Psyllium hydrophilic mucilloid (Metamucil, Karacil ✿) is a white- to cream-colored powder containing about 50% powdered mucilaginous portion (outer epidermis) of blond psyllium seeds and about 50% dextrose or sucrose. This mixture is used to treat constipation because it promotes the formation of a soft, water-retaining gelatinous residue in the lower bowel within 12 to 72 hours. In addition, it has a demulcent effect on inflamed mucosa. The dosage is 4 to 7 g, administered one to three times daily.

Sugar-free Metamucil contains aspartame (Nutra-Sweet).

Products containing aspartame should not be given to clients on a phenylalanine-restricted diet.

### methylcellulose (Cologel)

Methylcellulose is a synthetic hydrophilic colloid. It is a grayish white, fibrous powder that, in the presence of water, swells and produces a viscous, colloidal solution in the upper part of the alimentary tract.

Methylcellulose is available in liquid, tablets, capsules, and powder dosage forms. Whichever form is used, it is recommended that a full glass of water be given. Defecation usually occurs within 12 to 72 hours.

## Lubricant Laxatives
### mineral oil

Mineral oil (liquid petrolatum, MO) is a mixture of liquid hydrocarbons obtained from petroleum. The oil is not digested, and absorption is minimal. Mineral oil softens the fecal mass and prevents excessive absorption of water.

Mineral oil is especially useful when it is desirable to keep feces soft and when straining at stool must be reduced, as after abdominal surgery, rectal operations, prevention of hemorrhoidal tearing, repair of hernias, cerebrovascular or spinal cord accidents, aneurysm, or myocardial infarction. It is also useful for clients who have chronic constipation because of prolonged inactivity, as in the case of clients with orthopedic conditions.

Some physicians object to the use of mineral oil on the basis that it dissolves (acts as a lipid solvent) certain of the fat-soluble vitamins (A, D, E, and K), food, and bile salts and inhibits their absorption. Others maintain that only the precursor to vitamin A (carotene) is so affected and that natural vitamin A is absorbed from the intestine in the presence of mineral oil. Another objection to its use is that in large doses it tends to leak or seep from the rectum, which may cause pruritus ani and interfere with healing of postoperative wounds in the region of the anus and perineum. Although absorption of mineral oil is limited, it is said to cause a chronic inflammatory reaction in tissues where it is found after absorption. Indiscriminate use by elderly or weak individuals should be discouraged. Mineral oil may also produce a lipid pneumonia if drops coating the pharynx enter the trachea.

Concurrent use with fecal moistening agents should be avoided, since they increase absorption of mineral oil.

The adult dose ranges from 15 to 45 ml. For children over 6 years, doses range from 10 to 15 ml.

Mineral oil should not be given immediately after meals, since it may delay the passage of food from the stomach.

### ▷ Nursing Management: Mineral Oil Therapy

Mineral oil is not recommended for children or the elderly, because they are more at risk for aspiration of droplets, which may result in lipid pneumonia.

Administer at bedtime for results in 6 to 8 hours.

Protect client's clothing, since there may be leakage of oil from the rectum.

Do not give mineral oil routinely to pregnant women, since it decreases vitamin K availability to the fetus, resulting in hypoprothrombinemia and hemorrhagic disease.

Do not give mineral oil within 2 hours of meals or for prolonged periods, because it interferes with the absorption of dietary nutrients, particularly with the fat-soluble vitamins A, D, E, and K.

## Emollient or Fecal Moistening Agents

Emollient or fecal moistening agents include stool softeners, surfactants, and wetting solutions. They are constantly being improved and are commonly used for treatment of hard or dry stools.

The stool softener/surfactant or wetting agent type of laxative has its site of action within the colonic epithelium. In this area, alterations in colonic transport produce increased mucosal secretion. There are several mechanisms that decrease colonic absorption, increase secretion, or both. These mechanisms are stimulation of adenyl cyclase, inhibition of sodium absorption, mucosal alterations or permeability, and stimulation of prostaglandin E.

### docusate or dioctyl sodium sulfosuccinate (Colace, D-S-S, Doxinate)

Docusate acts like a detergent. It permits water and fatty substances to penetrate and to be well mixed with the fecal material. Thus this agent promotes the formation of soft-formed stool (occasionally diarrhea) and is useful in the treatment of constipation. Formed stools are usually excreted in 1 to 3 days. Docusate is available in three different salt formulations: calcium (Surfak, D-C-S), potassium (Dialose, Diocto-K), and sodium (Colace, Regulex, DSS, Modane Soft).

These agents are indicated for clients with rectal impaction, hemorrhoids, chronic constipation, postpartum constipation, and painful conditions of the rectum and anus.

They are also used in treatment of clients who should avoid straining (e.g., with rectal surgery or myocardial infarction) at the time of defecation. Docusate may be useful for bedridden clients, especially children. It is said to have a wide margin of safety and some potential negligible adverse reactions.

Concurrent use with mineral oil may promote absorption of the oil.

All of the following dosages should be given with a full glass of water.

*sodium docusate:* For adults and children over 12 years, give 50 to 500 mg daily orally. Children 6 to 12 years, give 40 to 120 mg daily.

*calcium docusate (Surfak):* For adults, one capsule daily (50 to 240 mg daily orally); children over 6 years, give 50 to 150 mg daily.

*Dialose or Kasof:* For adults, 100 to 300 mg daily with a glass of water; children over 6 years, give 100 mg at bedtime.

### hyperosmotic suppository

Glycerin suppositories are available in adult, child, and infant sizes. They promote peristalsis through local irritation of the mucous membrane of the rectum. The adult dose is 3 g; for children under 6 years of age the dose is 1 to 1.5 g held high in the rectum for 15 minutes. The effects are achieved in 15 minutes to 1 hour.

## Bowel Evacuant
### PEG electrolyte gastrointestinal lavage solution (GoLYTELY)

This powder consists of polyethlylene glycol and sodium salts (sulfate, bicarbonate, and chloride) with potassium chloride, which are dissolved in 4 L of water. Bowel movement occurs within 1 hour after oral administration, with bowel cleansing taking approximately 4 hours. The drug acts as an osmotic agent. Less stool is retained after its use, but the water or electrolyte balance does not change.

GoLYTELY is used for bowel cleansing before colonoscopy and before barium enema for radiologic examination.

There is a low incidence of nausea, vomiting, bloating, cramps, and abdominal fullness with GoLYTELY.

GoLYTELY is given orally, 4 L at a rate of 240 ml every 10 min (rapidly swallowed). Fasting 3 to 4 hours before use is necessary. Generally a midmorning examination permits 3 hours for consumption, followed by a 1-hour period for bowel movement. Only clear liquids are permitted following administration and before examination. Refrigeration of dissolved powder before use (up to 48 hours) is necessary.

Pregnancy safety is established at FDA category C.

### lactulose syrup (Chronulac, Cephulac, Duphalac ✱)

The normal colonic bacteria (*Lactobacillus* and *Bacteroides; Escherichia coli; Streptococcus faecalis*) metabolize lactulose syrup to organic acids, primarily lactic acid, plus small amounts of carbon dioxide, acetic acid, and formic acid. This produces a drop in pH (7 to 5) of the contents of the ascending colon and softening of the feces. There is also an increase in the number of osmotically active molecules because of the formation of low-molecular weight acids.

The drop in pH and the increased osmotic action combine to stimulate the colon's own propulsive activity. A stool of increased weight, volume, and moisture content results. This unique colon-specific laxative does not cause net secretion of water and electrolytes in the small intestine and does not inhibit absorption in the small bowel.

After oral administration only small amounts reach the blood. Urinary excretion is less than 3% and is complete in

24 hours. The drug works on the colon where transit time is slow. The laxative effect occurs 24 to 48 hours after administration.

Lactulose syrup is used in clients with history of chronic constipation. It increases the number of bowel movements daily and the number of days on which bowel movements occur.

Dose-related flatulence and intestinal cramps, gas, belching, and extension (transient) are seen. Excessive doses may produce some diarrhea (hypokalemic) and nausea (caused by the sweet taste).

The effectiveness of lactulose may be reduced if it is used concomitantly with an antibiotic that destroys the normal colonic bacteria. A nonabsorbed antibiotic such as neomycin destroys enough luminal colonic bacteria to interfere with lactulose. Most systemic, highly absorbable antibiotics do not affect the colonic bacteria in the lumen.

For adults give 1 to 2 tablespoons (15 to 30 ml) daily,

---

 *Geriatric Implications:*
## LAXATIVES, NONPHARMACOLOGIC

Elderly clients often frequently use and/or abuse laxatives even though studies have indicated that 80% to 90% of persons over 60 years old have at least one bowel movement daily (Delafuente, 1988).

To reduce the potential for chronic laxative use and/or dependency, the client should be taught nonpharmacologic measures, such as encouraging an increase in fluid intake to 6 to 8 glasses of water/day if permitted and tolerated. Also recommended is a regular exercise routine, such as a daily walk or active and passive exercise for bedridden clients.

The nurse should obtain a dietary and laxative history from the client. Consistent intake of low fiber diets or a regular intake of foods that tends to harden stools, such as processed cheese, hard-boiled eggs, liver, cottage cheese, high sugar content foods and rice, may result in constipation.

High-fiber or high-residue diets along with adequate fluid intake serves to accelerate food transport time in the gastrointestinal tract and exert a mild laxative effect. Obesity is reportedly rare in countries in which the customary diet is rich in fiber since fiber increases the feelings of satiety and generally reduces caloric intake (Gossel, 1987).

High-fiber foods include orange juice with pulp or a fresh orange, bran or whole grain cereals, whole grain or bran breads, leafy vegetables, and fresh fruits. While prunes, bananas, figs, and dates are high in dietary fiber, prunes also contain a laxative substance that stimulates intestinal motility pharmacologically.

Several geriatric facilities are supplementing dietary fiber with crude bran or bran cookies to reduce the use of laxatives in their institutions. Significant cost savings have been reported (Delafuente, 1988).

increased in 5- and 10-ml increments to 60 ml daily following breakfast. Severe constipation and treatment with other laxatives plus enemas and suppositories may require an initial dose of 30 ml.

To reduce blood ammonia levels in portal systemic encephalopathy the initial dose is 30 to 45 ml, three to four times daily, adjusted to produce a fecal pH of 5 to 5.5 and two to three soft, formed stools daily.

### ▷ Nursing Management: Lactulose Therapy

To make lactulose more palatable, mix it in water, juice, or milk.

Results may take 24 to 36 hours after administration of lactulose.

Use of lactulose during pregnancy has not been evaluated; therefore another type of laxative may be given under the physician's direction.

Lactulose use in diabetic clients may cause elevations in blood glucose levels; another type of laxative without galactose or lactose may be better.

Elderly and debilitated clients receiving lactulose for 6 months or more should have serum electrolytes (potassium, chloride, and carbon dioxide) periodically evaluated.

Since lactulose contains galactose (less than 2.2 g / 15 ml), it is contraindicated in low-galactose diets.

The solution may darken on exposure to high temperature, but this will not change its therapeutic effect. Freezing does not alter the therapeutic effect.

## ANTIDIARRHEALS

The term **diarrhea** describes the abnormal passage of stools with increased frequency, increased fluidity, or increased weight and increase in stool water excretion. Diarrhea is acute when it is of sudden onset in a previously healthy individual, lasts about 3 days to 3 weeks, is self-limiting, and resolves without sequelae. Morbid and mortal consequences are seen in malnourished populations, the elderly, infants, and debilitated persons. Chronic diarrhea lasts for over 3 to 4 weeks, with the recurring passage of diarrheal stools, fever, anorexia, nausea, vomiting, weight reduction, and chronic weakness. It is the result of multiple causative factors, as seen in the box on p. 707. Chronic diarrhea necessitates definitive treatment directed to the organic cause or causes. The causes vary from psychogenic to neoplastic origins.

The objectives of treatment are to (1) replenish fluid and electrolyte loss, (2) ascertain, if possible, the cause or causes of diarrhea, (3) reduce the frequency of evacuation, (4) absorb toxins, (5) restore the intestinal flora, and (6) treat the underlying cause or causes.

Nonspecific treatment is directed at the increased stool frequency, which burdens daily life-style; the alleviation of abdominal cramps; the prevention of dehydration and metabolic acidosis from fluid and electrolyte loss; and the minimization of weight loss and nutritional deficits resulting from malabsorption. Specific treatment is directed at the cause or condition creating the diarrhea, as demonstrated by the sample nursing diagnoses on p. 705.

Ideally, the nursing process lends itself to ascertaining the type or cause of diarrhea to be treated through careful individual client evaluation. Such evaluative questions for discovering the cause or causes may be used in assessing the following criteria:

Age of the client
Occupation
Duration of diarrhea (precipitating factors tantamount to onset)
Stool description (frequency of evacuation, rectal bleeding or black stool appearance, foul-smelling odor, light color, or greasy consistency)
Medication profile (prescribed and self-administered as OTC drugs)
Presence or absence of anorexia, weight reduction (involuntary), fever, abdominal tenderness, dehydration
Ingestion of foods, toxic substances, milk intake, alcohol use
Travel outside the United States or Canada
Symptom description (location)
Relief obtained, if any, and treatment modality
Chronic diseases, presence of acute or concurrent illness, emotional or behavioral problems

Fluid and electrolyte loss may cause tachycardia, postural hypotension, elevated hematocrit or blood urea nitrogen, and poor skin turgor. The stool specimen may reveal occult blood (gastrointestinal bleeding), fecal leukocytes, parasites, or fat. Endocrine diseases such as diabetes mellitus and hyperthyroidism should be considered. Hospitalization is needed for dehydration that would compromise a client with congestive heart failure or chronic renal disease, since this complicates fluid replacement efforts. If any child or infant is unable to consume oral replacement fluid, hospitalization is needed to replace fluids and maintain urine flow. Bed rest alone may reduce stool frequency. In addition to the child or infant, the elderly client with a poor medical history, a client with chronic illness (heart disease, asthma), and pregnant women are at risk from acute or chronic diarrhea.

Maintenance of fluid and electrolyte balance is the most important goal of supportive therapy in acute diarrhea. If left untreated, a loss of anions (bicarbonate, organic anions as short-chain fatty acids) will create a gain of hydrogen ions, resulting in metabolic acidosis. This gain will be exacerbated by the (often) concomitant ketoacidosis of starvation and acidosis of prerenal azotemia. As volume increases in diarrhea, a rise in sodium and chloride develops with a decrease in potassium concentration. The decreased contact time of the luminal contents with the mucosal surface decreases the passive secretion of potassium. The electrolyte composition of stool water will then be close to that of plasma. The electrolyte loss of sodium, potassium, chloride, and bicarbonate is the basis of therapy.

Selected Nursing Diagnoses Related to Administration of Antidiarrheal Medications

| Nursing diagnosis | Outcome criteria | Nursing interventions |
|---|---|---|
| Altered bowel elimination related to diarrhea | Decrease in number of stools to less than three per day<br>Formed stools | Record frequency, number, consistency of stools<br>Encourage bland diet and liquids<br>Administer antidiarrheal agents as prescribed |
| High risk for fluid volume depletion related to diarrhea | The client will:<br>Maintain electrolytes within normal limits<br>Maintain normal fluid balance<br>Experience less diarrhea<br>Maintain normal body weight | Monitor client's intake and output<br>Monitor bowel movements, recording diarrhea as output<br>Weigh client daily<br>Administer antidiarrheal agents as prescribed<br>Assess client for signs of dehydration<br>Encourage high fluid intake |
| High risk alteration in comfort related to abdominal cramping and diarrhea | The client will:<br>Verbalize comfort or pain relief<br>Maintain ADL without disruption because of discomfort | Assess comfort status of client<br>Instruct client in appropriate diet to minimize intestinal cramping<br>Provide suggestions for nondrug pain management (positioning, activities, distraction)<br>Administer antidiarrheal medications as prescribed<br>Consult physician if additional pain relief is needed |

It is recommended that clear liquids (noncarbonated soft drinks, fruit juice, diluted and flavored gelatin, and apple juice) and a bland diet be continued for 1 to 2 days. According to the cause of the diarrhea, several different medications can be given along with bed rest. These include:

Activated attapulgite
Activated charcoal
Adsorbents
Aluminum hydroxide
Antibiotics (some)
Anticholinergic activity drugs
Antiemetics
Aspirin
Astringents
Belladonna alkaloids
Bismuth salts
Bulk-forming products (including polycarbophil)
Cholestyramine
Colestipol
Digestive enzymes
Electrolyte replacement
Kaolin and pectin
*Lactobacillus* cultures (intestinal flora modification)
Metronidazole
Narcotic derivations
Quinacrine
Sedatives
Smooth muscle relaxants
Steroids
Sulfasalazine
Tranquilizers (anxiolytics and cyclic antidepressants)

This section focuses on the drugs with a direct pharmacologic effect on the gastrointestinal tract. The drugs providing symptomatic therapy do not alter the pathophysiology of diarrhea and do not prevent electrolyte and fluid loss. The antidiarrheal agents diminish stool water by inhibiting intestinal fluid secretion or by increasing intestinal fluid absorption. Although these drugs decrease the number, consistency, and fluidity of the stool, there is no absolute clinical evidence that an effective antidiarrheal therapeutic benefit accrues to the client. However, there is a relief of the bothersome symptoms that interrupt daily routines.

Over-the-counter antidiarrheals may contain the following ingredients: limited amounts of opiates; adsorbents, such as bismuth salts, aluminum salts, kaolin, pectin, activated charcoal, activated and colloidal attapulgite, carageenan enzymes, belladonna alkaloids (hyoscyamine, hyoscine [scopolamine], atropine); homatropine; intestinal flora modifiers, carboxymethylcellulose, phenyl salicylates, zinc sulfocarbonate, calcium salts (carbonate and hydroxide), salicylates. Inactive ingredients vary, but the nurse should be aware of the alcohol content variation (1.5% to 18%).

These antidiarrheal products have a warning not to use beyond 2 days, not to use if a fever is present, and not to use in infants or children under 3 years of age. The physician may modify these instructions.

The intractable diarrhea of infancy is traditionally treated with clear liquids and gradual reintroduction of milk or formula with the addition of oral elemental diets or total parenteral nutrition. The infant syndrome is described as loose stools, resulting in dehydration and a failure to thrive.

Since newborn's total body weight is usually 75% water, a 10% or greater weight loss may occur if the infant has severe diarrhea. If an infant has eight to ten bowel movements in a 24-hour period, the fluid loss may cause circulatory collapse and renal impairment. Diarrhea in infants should be considered serious enough to refer the client to a physician for evaluation.

Persistent diarrhea in the elderly can result in fluid and electrolyte loss, dehydration, and perhaps more serious medical complications. Such clients should be referred to a physcian.

## Adsorbents

**Adsorbents** act by coating the walls of the gastrointestinal tract, adsorbing the bacteria or toxins causing the diarrhea and passing them out with the stools. Examples of drugs in this class not requiring a presciption are activated charcoal, aluminum hydroxide, bismuth salts, kaolin, pectin, and activated attapulgite. Colestipol and cholestyramine are anion exchange resins requiring a prescription.

Kaolin is a natural hydrated aluminum silicate that is relatively inert but carries the danger of obstruction; stools appear to be more formed with this agent. The adsorbents kaolin, pectin, activated charcoal, and attapulgite are recognized as safe in therapeutic doses. Pectin causes a decrease in the intestinal pH, which destroys bacterial growth because of the unfavorable acid medium. The anion exchange resins (colestipol and cholestyramine) have adsorbent affinity directed at acidic materials (e.g., bile acids). The bismuth salts are used as adsorbents, astringents, and protectives.

Generally the adsorbent preparations are taken after each loose bowel movement until the diarrhea has been controlled. Constipation may develop because of the large amounts of the adsorbent products that must be used.

A caution with all the adsorbents is the interference with absorption of medications given concurrently (e.g., digoxin, clindamycin, lincomycin, and quinidine). The interactions are a function of their adsorbent properties. The drugs and nutrients adsorbed include a wide range of ingested substances. These may be decreased by administering the adsorbent 2 hours or more before or after a drug (except when used to inactivate a drug or desired poison for overdose therapy).

### bismuth subsalicylate (Pepto-Bismol)

Bismuth subsalicylate is available in suspension and chewable tablets. The adult dosage is 30 ml or two tablets chewed or dissolved every 30 to 60 minutes up to eight doses. A dose of 2 ounces can be given every 6 hours to prevent pathogens from attaching themselves to the intestinal wall. This impedes their replication in the gut and inhibits intestinal secretion of fluids and electrolytes (see Chapter 40).

Since bismuth subsalicylate is a salicylate and may be taken in large amounts to control the diarrhea, it will enhance the effects of oral anticoagulants (i.e., increased bleeding time, bruising). Methotrexate may be displaced from its protein binding sites, thus causing toxicity. Probenecid, an antigout agent, promotes the renal excretion of uric acid. When combined with bismuth subsalicylate the uricosuric effects of probenecid can be inhibited by the salicylate.

The salicylate may antagonize the effects of hypoglycemic agents. It could require a change in the dosage of the hypoglycemic agent. Be aware of possible salicylate toxicity when given in large doses to persons taking large amounts of aspirin daily.

### ▷ Nursing Management: Bismuth Subsalicylate Therapy

Exercise caution when giving bismuth subsalicylate to a client taking any of the following medications: oral anticoagulants, methotrexate, probenecid, nonsteroidal antiinflammatory agents, and hypoglycemic agents.

Do not give bismuth subsalicylate to those allergic to salicylates.

Warn clients that bismuth subsalicylate may cause their stools to become black.

### activated charcoal (Charcocaps, Charcodote ✱, charcoal)

Activated charcoal is indicated for the prevention and relief of intestinal gas and diarrhea and gastrointestinal distress associated with indigestion. It acts as an adsorbent and detoxicant of irritants. It may also adsorb medication, nutrients, and enzymes.

The activated vegetable charcoal is administered as two capsules repeated every 30 to 60 minutes as needed up to eight doses (16 Charcocaps) for treatment of diarrhea symptoms. Tablets may be chewed or dissolved in the mouth and followed by water.

### kaolin with pectin (Kaopectate)

Kaolin with pectin is a suspension with 6 g kaolin and 130 mg pectin/30 ml; the dosage is 60 to 120 ml after each loose bowel movement.

Kaopectate concentrate is a peppermint-flavored liquid with 8.7 g kaolin and 190 mg pectin/30 ml; the dosage is 45 to 90 ml after each loose bowel movement. Kaopectate tablets contain 600 mg attapulgite per tablet; the dose is two tablets after each bowel movement.

### cholestyramine (Questran)

Cholestyramine has a direct absorbent affinity for acidic materials (e.g., bile acids). It is indicated as adjunctive therapy to diet in the treatment of hypercholesterolemia. It has also been used for diarrhea, but this is not an FDA-approved indication for this drug.

## CAUSES OF ACUTE AND CHRONIC DIARRHEA

**Causes of Acute Diarrhea**

A. Bacterial
  1. Invasive organisms
    a. *Campylobacter fetus (jejuni)*
    b. *Clostridium difficile*
    c. *Escherichia coli* (enteropathogenic)
    d. *Salmonella*
    e. *Shigella dysenteriae*
    f. Staphylococci
  2. Noninvasive toxigenic organisms
    a. Cholera *(Vibrio cholerae)* enterotxin
    b. *Escherichia coli* (enterotoxigenic) toxin
  3. Food poisoning as toxin mediated
    a. *Bacillius cereus*
    b. *Clostridium perfringens*
    c. *Salmonella*
    d. *Staphylococcus aureus*
B. Viral
  1. Adenoviruses
  2. Coxsackievirus
  3. Coronaviruses
  4. Echoviruses
  5. Norwalk agent
  6. Rotavirus
C. Protozoal
  1. Amebic dysentery *(Entamoeba histolytica)*, amebiasis
  2. Giardiasis *(Giardia lamblia)*
D. Drug induced
  1. Antacids (magnesium containing)
  2. Antiadrenergic antihypertensive
    a. Guanethidine
    b. Methyldopa
    c. Reserpine
  3. Antibiotics
    a. Ampicillin
    b. Cephalosporins
    c. Clindamycin (clindamycin colitis associated with toxin-producing *Clostridium difficile)*
    d. Chloramphenicol
    e. Erythromycin
    f. Lincomycin
    g. Metronidazole
    h. Neomycin
    i. Penicillin G
    j. Sulfonamides
    k. Tetracyclines
    l. Trimethoprim-sulfamethoxazole
  4. Antineoplastics
  5. Antitubercular agents
  6. Chenodeoxycholic acid—chenodiol
  7. Cholinergic agents
  8. Colchicine
  9. Digitalis
  10. Ethanol
  11. Ferrous sulfate
  12. Laxatives
  13. Nitrofurantoin
  14. Other osmotic agents
  15. Parasympathomimetic (alpha agonist) drugs
  16. Prostaglandin E
  17. Quinidine
  18. Sorbital
E. Nutritional
  1. Allergy
  2. Ingestion without discretion (spices, fats, roughage, seeds, preformed toxin)
F. Other
  1. Bile acids
  2. Carcinoma
  3. Diverticulitis
  4. Fatty acids
  5. Neurogenic
  6. Psychogenic
  7. Radiation therapy
  8. Regional and ulcerative colitis
  9. Stress

**Causes of Chronic Diarrhea**

A. Addison's disease
B. Diabetic enteropathy/neuropathy
C. Iatrogenic
  1. Bacterial overgrowth
  2. Postsurgical
D. Inflammatory bowel disease
  1. Chronic ulcerative and granulomatous colitis
  2. Crohn's enteritis
E. Irritable bowel syndrome
F. Malabsorption syndrome
G. Pancreatic adenoma—non-gastrin secreting, such as syndrome of watery diarrhea-hypokalemia-achlorhydria (WDHA)
H. Pancreatic insufficiency
I. Thyroid—hyperthyroidism
J. Tumors
  1. Carcinoma of colon and rectum
  2. Intestinal
  3. Lymphoma
  4. Polyposis
  5. Villous adenoma
K. Other
  1. Blind loops, ileostomy, colostomy
  2. Carcinoid syndrome
  3. Enteritis
  4. Gardner's syndrome
  5. Gastrointestinal hormones
  6. Gluten enteropathy
  7. Zollinger-Ellison Syndrome
  8. Many other conditions

## ▷Nursing Management:
## Cholestyramine Therapy

Dissolve cholestyramine well in water or fruit juice before administration. Cholestyramine may be difficult for the client to drink because of its unpleasant taste. It is best poured on the surface of the liquid and allowed to sit a few minutes to prevent lumps. It should be drunk immediately after mixing. Water should be added to residue to ensure that the full dose is taken. It may be given with soups or applesauce.

The client's CBC, serum cholesterol, triglycerides, electrolytes, and glucose level should be monitored while the client is taking this medication.

Elderly clients are more likely to experience gastrointestinal side effects, such as heartburn, nausea, and vomiting.

Clients often complain of constipation while taking cholestyramine. This can be averted by increasing the fluid intake, adding more roughage to the diet, or taking a stool softener. Often a stool softener is ordered when this drug is started.

This drug may decrease the levels of vitamins A, D, and K. Supplemental vitamins should be added to the diet.

## Anticholinergics

The belladona alkaloids—atropine, hyoscyamine and hyoscine, and homatropine methylbromide—are found in antidiarrheal products often with the absorbents and other antidiarrheal agents as opium extracts. These are effective agents in treating diarrhea, but the recommended doses found in nonprescription products are somewhat ineffective. The higher effective doses have a narrow margin of safety in both children and adults.

The belladonna alkaloids, however, offer effectiveness in the treatment of diarrhea by causing a decrease in intestinal tone and peristalsis at doses of 0.6 to 1 mg of atropine sulfate, thus decreasing intestinal cramps and pain. The "cotton mouth" or "dry mouth" effect usually indicates therapeutically effective drug levels when these doses are administered. This dose of atropine, however, requires a prescription.

The following warnings on these products should be heeded by the nurse: not to be used by persons having glaucoma or excessive pressure within the eye; not to be used by children under 6 years of age; discontinue use if blurring of vision, rapid pulse, or dizziness occurs; a dry mouth may occur, necessitating a lower dosage. These anticholinergics are also contraindicated in clients with urinary retention. They may precipitate ileus and the toxic megacolon of ulcerative colitis.

The following toxic effects of belladonna alkaloids are dose related: an increase in viscosity of bronchial mucus; bradycardia and tachycardia; obstructive uropathy. They are contraindicated in clients with heart disease, hypertension, hyperthyroidism, and prostatic hypertrophy.

### Donnagel

Donnagel is a suspension of kaolin and pectin, with 0.105 mg hyoscyamine sulfate, 0.018 mg atropine sulfate, and 0.0060 mg hyoscine hydrobromide in each 30 ml. The dosage is 30 ml immediately and then 15 to 30 ml after each loose bowel movement.

## Opiates

The opiates (codeine and paregoric—Rx C-III) act by virtue of their constipative and sedative action. They lower the propulsive motility of the bowel, reduce pain, and relieve **tenesmus** (rectal spasms). The delay in transit time of food permits contact time of intestinal contents with the absorptive surface of the bowel, which increases the reabsorption of water and electrolytes and reduces stool frequency and net volume.

The anticholinergics and opium derivatives decrease the motility of the bowel. They should not be used when the cause of diarrhea is an invading organism (as toxigenic bacteria or pseudomembranous enterocolitis), because these drugs permit epithelial penetration and multiplication of the organism by decreasing the intestinal motility with the subsequent lowered excretion of the organisms and their toxins.

Codeine and paregoric cause depression and sedation. This factor must be considered if the client is taking other CNS depressant drugs because of the additive effects. The opiates are short acting; frequent administration (4- to 6-hour intervals) is needed to control the gastrointestinal smooth muscle function.

### combination products

Parepectolin suspension contains 15 mg opium, equivalent to 3.7 ml paregoric/30 ml, with kaolin and pectin and 0.69% alcohol. The dosage is 15 to 30 ml after each loose bowel movement. This class V drug may not require a prescription.

Parelixir is a liquid containing 0.2 ml tincture of opium/30 ml with pectin in an 18% alcohol elixir with fruit flavor. The dosage is 15 to 30 ml, administered three to four times daily. This class V drug may not require a prescription.

Dia-Quel liquid has 18 mg opium (4.5 ml paregoric)/30 ml homatropine and pectin in a 10% alcohol base. The dosage is 15 to 30 ml, administered three to four times daily. This class V drug may not require a prescription.

Donnagel-PG suspension contains 24 mg powdered opium/30 ml with kaolin, pectin, hyoscyamine, atropine, hyoscine (scopolamine) and a 5% alcohol base. The dosage is 30 ml immediately and then 15 ml every 3 hours as needed for loose stools.

### opium tincture, deodorized

Tincture of opium, a hydroalcoholic (19% alcohol) solution, contains 10% opium with an average dose of 0.6 ml four times daily. This is a class II prescription under the Controlled Substances Act.

## paregoric

Paregoric (camphorated opium tincture) requires a prescription. It is a class III drug that is equivalent to 2 mg of morphine per 5 ml. It is important that the nurse not confuse opium tincture, deodorized (10 mg morphine equivalent/1 ml), and camphorated opium tincture (0.4 mg morphine equivalent/1 ml), because opium tincture, deodorized, has 25 times more of the morphine equivalent than camphorated opium tincture. Addiction liability has been reported with these preparations. When paregoric is combined with another product, it becomes a class V product when the combination contains no more than 100 mg of opium or 25 ml of paregoric/100 ml of the mixture. The adult dosage is 5 to 10 ml, one to four times daily. For children the dose is 0.25 to 0.5 ml/kg one to four times daily.

## codeine

Codeine, a class II product, when administered at a dosage of 15 mg four times daily, has shown effective antidiarrheal properties, although a range of up to 120 mg daily is suggested.

## Intestinal Flora Modifiers

Intestinal flora modifiers are bacterial cultures that consist of viable *Lactobacillus* organisms. They suppress the growth of diarrhea-causing pathogens and reestablish the normal intestinal flora.

*Lactobacillus acidophilus* produces lactic acid in the gastrointestinal tract. This alteration creates an unfavorable environment for the overgrowth of pathogens, especially bacteria and fungi. The acidic media also aid in the development of favorable bacteria in the gastrointestinal tract.

The modifiers may be useful in the treatment of uncomplicated diarrhea (including that caused by antibiotic therapy) and acute fever blisters and canker sores. The nurse may consider the use of a diet rich in milk or buttermilk and yogurt and high lactose or dextrose, since this is equally effective in colonizing the intestine. Patients with milk allergies should not take any of these dairy products or intestinal flora modifiers.

## Lactinex

Lactinex (*Lactobacillus acidophilus* and *Lactobacillus bulgaricus*) is available in tablets and granules. Both need to be refrigerated. The dosage for gastrointestinal disturbances is one packet of granules (or four tablets) added to or taken with cereal, food, milk, fruit juice, or water three or four times daily.

## Bacid

Bacid capsules are *Lactobacillus acidophilus* in sodium carboxymethylcellulose. They should be administered with milk. The dosage is two capsules two to four times daily. A fruity odor may be apparent in the stools because of these drugs.

## Other Antidiarrheal Agents
### diphenoxylate hydrochloride (with added atropine sulfate) (Lomotil, Diarsed ✶)

Diphenoxylate, a class V product, is a narcotic chemical analog of meperidine. It does not have analgesic effects. It inhibits intestinal propulsive motility by acting directly on intestinal smooth muscles and thus decreases transit time.

The half-life of this product is about 2.5 hours (range 1.9 to 3.1 hours). Because of its short duration of action (3 to 4 hours), it is administered four times or more daily. Peak plasma concentrations are reached in 2 hours.

Diphenoxylate is used for effective adjunctive treatment of diarrhea.

Side effects include drowsiness, dizziness, tachycardia, dry mouth, hyperthermia, abdominal distress, rash, and agitation.

Significant drug interactions include:
1. The CNS depressant effects are potentiated by alcohol and other CNS depressant drugs.
2. Concurrent use with monoamine oxidase inhibitors (MAOIs) may precipitate hypertensive crisis because of the chemical similarity to meperidine.
3. Additive effects are seen with drugs that have anticholinergic/antimuscarinic effects because of the atropine present.

For adults, give one to two tablets (5 to 10 ml) three or four times daily until control is achieved; then reduce dosage.

In children, use liquid dosage form only with the calibrated dropper. Use of tablets in children under 12 years is not recommended. The oral solution is not recommended for children under 2 years old. Older children usually are given 0.3 to 0.4 mg/kg or diphenoxylate daily, in divided doses. When used in children, monitor closely since atropine side effects may occur even at recommended doses.

Pregnancy safety has been established at FDA Category C.

## ▷Nursing Management:
## Diphenoxylate Therapy

Pediatric and geriatric clients are more susceptible to the respiratory depressant effects of diphenoxylate.

Children with Down's syndrome are reported to be more susceptible to the toxic effects of atropine.

Monitor hepatic function in the client receiving long-term therapy.

Dehydration in clients may cause a variability in the response to diphenoxylate. Clients can have a delayed toxic response. In hospitalized clients electrolytes must be monitored and dehydration corrected. If the client is not hospitalized, fluid intake should be increased to prevent dehydration.

Diphenoxylate should not be given to clients with ulcerative colitis, because toxic megacolon can occur. If abdominal distention occurs, discontinue the drug. Also, diphenoxylate use should be carefully monitored to observe if constipation, a potential side effect, occurs.

Caution clients about taking alcohol and CNS depressants with the drug. Instruct about its habit-forming potential.

Dizziness and drowsiness are common side effects. Caution the client regarding tasks that involve alertness.

Refer the client to a physician if diarrhea increases or fever develops.

### loperamide hydrochloride (Imodium)

Loperamide is a synthetic oral antidiarrheal similar to diphenoxylate. It inhibits peristalsis in the intestinal wall, improving both stool frequency and consistency. The slowing of intestinal motility acts directly on the neuronal pathways of the intestinal wall. Loperamide also may inhibit intestinal secretion, producing a decrease in stool water excretion.

Peak plasma levels of this highly protein-bound drug are highest within 5 hours after administration. Plasma half-life ranges from 7 to 15 hours, with elimination half-life up to 15 hours (11-hour average). One hour following an oral dose, 85% of loperamide is found in the gastrointestinal tract; 25% of a 4-mg dose is excreted in the feces within 3 days, while 1.3% is found in the urine as free drug and a glucuronide metabolite.

Indications include symptomatic control of acute and chronic diarrhea (as in inflammatory bowel disease) and in ileostomy clients to decrease the volume of intestinal discharge resulting from the intestinal resection. The results are prolonged intestinal transit time, increase in density and viscosity of discharge, and normalization of diarrheal-induced loss of fluid and electrolytes. It may be used in diarrhea secondary to radiation therapy of diarrhea following gastrointestinal surgery.

CNS fatigue and dizziness are side effects seen only when therapeutic doses are greatly exceeded. Drug-induced gastrointestinal side effects are difficult to separate from those of diarrhea itself (epigastric pain, abdominal cramps, nausea, dry mouth, vomiting, anorexia). Skin rash hypersensitivity has been reported. Overdose symptoms include CNS depression, constipation, gastrointestinal irritation, nausea, and vomiting. Naloxone may reverse the CNS depression, but the long duration of action of loperamide requires that the nurse monitor vital signs for at least 24 hours and repeat naloxone (because of naloxone's short duration of action) when necessary for recurring symptoms. Fluid and electrolyte levels must also be carefully watched.

For acute diarrhea in adults, 4 mg is given orally, then 2 mg after each loose stool, usually not exceeding 16 mg daily. For chronic diarrhea, the dose begins as in acute diarrhea and is then titrated to individual client needs. The dosage is administered in divided doses. Average daily maintenance dose is 4 to 8 mg, not exceeding 16 mg daily.

The following are recommended dosages for children for the first day of treatment:

2 to 5 years: 1 mg three times daily
5 to 8 years: 2 mg twice daily
8 to 12 years: 2 mg three times daily

After the first day, children should receive 0.1 mg/kg following each unformed stool. Dosage should not exceed the dosage recommended for the first day of therapy. Pregnancy safety has been established as FDA category B.

### ▷Nursing Management: Loperamide Therapy

**Assessment.** Do not give antidiarrheal agents (e.g., diphenoxylate, loperamide, or narcotics) for acute diarrhea or traveler's diarrhea caused by bacteria (enterotoxin-producing strains of *Escherichia coli, Campylobacter jejuni, Salmonella,* or *Shigella*), parasites *(Giardia lamblia),* and viruses (parvovirus or rotavirus), because these penetrate the intestinal wall if retained in the intestine and must be eliminated in the feces.

Do not use these agents in clients with antibiotic-induced pseudomembranous colitis (*Clostridium difficile* toxin).

If after 48 to 72 hours of therapy the symptoms of acute diarrhea have not clinically improved, if fever persists, or if blood or mucus appears in the stool, discontinue these agents and notify the physician.

Loperamide hydrochloride may be used to reduce the volume of ileostomy discharge and so decrease fluid and electrolyte loss.

CNS side effects are not as pronounced as with diphenoxylate hydrochloride.

Dryness of the mouth can be relieved by increasing the fluid intake or rinsing the mouth frequently.

This drug is classified as a class V controlled drug. It can cause physical dependence if taken in high doses.

Since it can cause drowsiness, caution the client against operating any hazardous equipment or driving a car.

## SUMMARY

Drugs affecting the lower gastrointestinal tract are either laxatives or antidiarrheal agents. Laxatives are given to relieve or prevent constipation, to expel parasites or poisonous substances, to obtain a specimen, or to cleanse the bowel for diagnostic examination. They are usually classified by their mechanism of action: saline, stimulant, bulk-forming, emollient or lubricant laxatives, or bowel evacuants. The goal is to return the client to a normal, adequate bowel pattern.

The antidiarrheals are administered to reduce the frequency of evacuations. This is only part of a treatment plan that should also include replenishment of fluid and electrolyte loss, diagnosis and treatment of the underlying cause, and restoration of the intestinal flora. Again the goal of treatment is to return the client to a normal, adequate bowel pattern.

# Case Study: Drug Therapy for Bowel Elimination

Margaret Gordon, a 73-year-old widow, is recovering at home from an internal fixation of a fractured left hip. Mrs. Gordon is recovering well from the surgery. She continues with physical therapy, but she does not go out much and spends most of the day sitting in a chair watching television. Her primary meal of the day is delivered to her home by a voluntary agency. The remainder of her food intake includes snack foods and, occasionally, soup and crackers.

The medications for Mrs. Gordon include the following:
Colace, 100 mg orally at bedtime as needed
Milk of Magnesia, 1 tbsp at bedtime as needed
Metamucil, 2 tsp daily
Kaopectate, 2 tbsp after each loose stool

A review of the client's history by the community health nurse reveals that Mrs. Gordon takes the Colace daily. When questioned, she reports that this is the same way it was given to her in the hospital. Her physician routinely orders Colace for all clients who have orthopedic surgery. If she goes more than one day without a bowel movement, she takes the Milk of Magnesia as she has done for years. She has been taking Metamucil daily for several years. When she returned home from the hospital she began using the Metamucil again. Several weeks later she developed diarrhea. She began taking the Kaopectate without consulting her physician.

Mrs. Gordon readily admits that she believes "normal" bowel habits are essential to her health. She thinks that one well-formed stool daily is her normal pattern. Any deviation from this pattern she calls diarrhea or constipation and promptly treats the problem with any or all of the above medications, which she purchases over the counter. The physician's office renews the prescription for Colace at her request.

1. What factors during Mrs. Gordon's postoperative recovery may have contributed to the present situation?
2. What affect does each medication have on Mrs. Gordon's bowel elimination?

3. Why did Mrs. Gordon have diarrhea after she returned home and began taking the Metamucil and Milk of Magnesia?
4. What key points should the nurse include in teaching Mrs. Gordon about her bowel elimination habits?

## BIBLIOGRAPHY

American Hospital Formulary Service. (1991). AHFS drug information '91. Bethesda, Md: American Society of Pharmacists, Inc.

American Pharmaceutical Association. (1990). Handbook of non-prescription drugs, ed 9. Washington, DC: The Association.

Anderson BJ. (1986). Tube feeding: is diarrhea inevitable? Amer J Nurs 86:704.

Basch A. (1987). Symptom distress: changes in elimination, Semin Oncol Nurs 3(4):287.

Brady M et al. (1989). Chronic diarrhea: management in pediatrics, J Pediatr Health Care 3(3):163.

Brunton LL. (1990). Laxatives. In Gilman AG et al, editors. Goodman and Gilman's the pharmacological basis of therapeutics, ed 8. New York: Macmillan Publishing Co.

Delafuente JC and Stewart RB. (1988). Therapeutics in the elderly. Baltimore: Williams & Wilkins.

Gossel TA. (1987). High-fiber diet products, US Pharmacist 12(7):42.

Hahn K. (1987). Think twice about diarrhea, Nursing 17(9):78.

Joubert DW. (1987). Use of emetic, adsorbent, and cathartic agents in acute drug overdose, JEN 13(1):49.

Osis M. (1987). Laxatives: are we making the best choices, Gerition 2(3):5.

Sadler C. (1988). The power of purgatives, Community Outlook 8:11.

United States Pharmacopeial Convention. (1991). Drug information for the health care professional, ed 11. Rockville, Md: The Convention.

Woodward WE and Woodward TE. (1986). Management of dehydrating diarrhea, Hosp Pract 21(3):60.

# Drugs Affecting the Visual and Auditory Systems

*Chapter*

# 42 Overview of the Eye

## CHAPTER OBJECTIVES

*After reading this chapter, you should be able to meet the following objectives and define the key terms.*

1. Describe the anatomy and physiology of the eye.

2. Identify the muscles involved with miosis and mydriasis and explain their functions.

3. Define accommodation and cycloplegia.

4. Name four protective mechanisms associated with the eye.

## KEY TERMS

**accommodation,** page 716

**cataract,** page 716

**cornea,** page 714

**cycloplegia,** page 716

**miosis,** page 714

**mydriasis,** page 714

The eye is the receptor organ for one of the most delicate and valuable senses—vision. Figure 42-1 shows the parts of the eye.

The eyeball has three layers or coats: the protective external layer (cornea and sclera), the middle layer (which contains choroid, iris, and ciliary body), and the light-sensitive retina.

The eyeball is protected in a deep depression of the skull called the orbit. It is moved in the orbit by six small extraocular muscles.

The anterior covering of the eye is the **cornea.** The cornea is normally transparent, so it allows light to enter the eye. The cornea has no blood vessels and receives its nutrition from the aqueous humor and its oxygen supply by diffusion from the air and surrounding structures. The corneal surface consists of a thin layer of epithelial cells, which are quite resistant to infection. However, an abraded cornea is very susceptible to infection. The cornea is also supplied with 60 to 80 sensory fibers that elicit pain whenever the corneal epithelium is damaged. Seriously injured corneal tissue is replaced by scar tissue, which is usually not transparent. Increased intraocular pressure results in loss of transparency.

The sclera, which is continuous with the cornea, is nontransparent; it is the white fibrous envelope of the eye.

The conjunctiva is the mucous membrane lining the anterior part of the sclera and the inner surfaces of each eyelid.

The iris gives the eye its brown, blue, gray, green, or hazel color. It surrounds the pupil; the sphincter and dilator muscles in the iris alter pupil size. The sphincter muscle, which encircles the pupil, is parasympathetically innervated; the dilator muscle, which runs radially from the pupil to the iris periphery, is sympathetically innervated. Contraction of the sphincter muscle, either alone or with relaxation of the dilator muscle, causes constriction of the pupil, or **miosis.** Contraction of the dilator muscle and relaxation of the sphincter muscle causes dilation of the pupil, or **mydriasis.** (See Figure 42-2.)

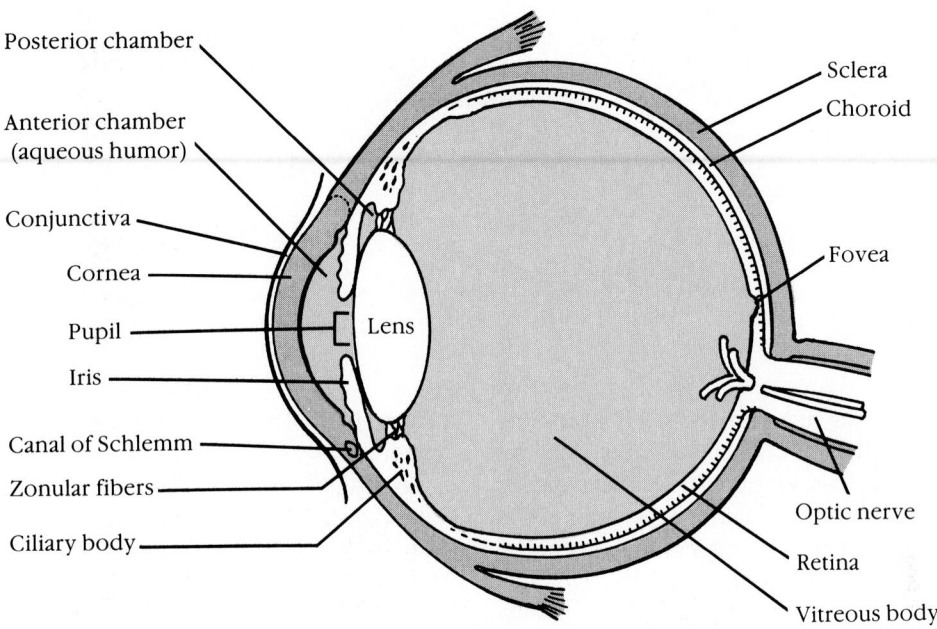

**FIGURE 42-1**  Parts of the eye.

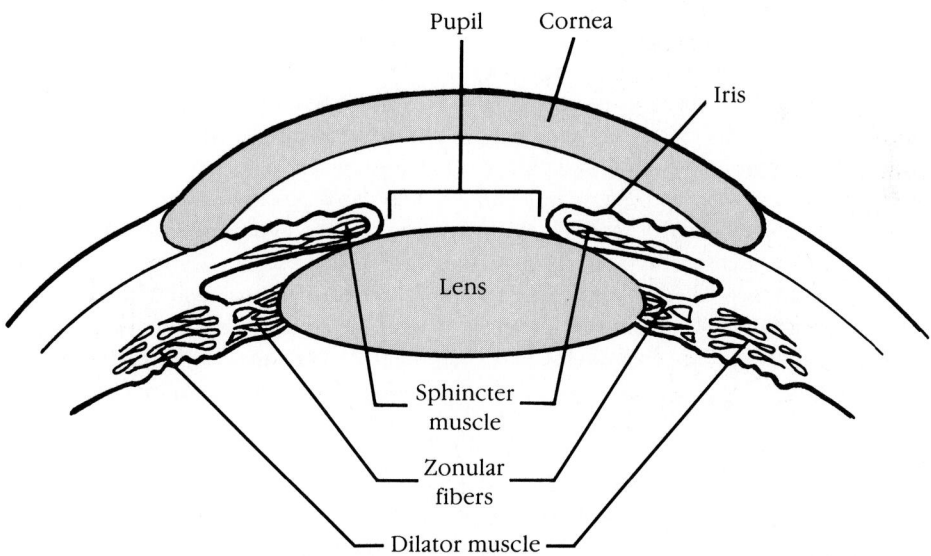

**FIGURE 42-2**  Accommodation and pupillary alterations. When zonular fibers contract, the pupil dilates, resulting in sharp distant vision and blurred near vision (unaccommodated eye). Parasympathetic stimulation accommodates the eye for near vision; the pupil constricts in response to contraction of the sphincter muscle. The zonular fibers are relaxed. *Pupillary diameter.* Constriction (miosis): contraction of sphincter muscle (parasympathetic stimulation) alone or with relaxation of dilator muscle. Dilation (mydriasis): contraction of dilator muscle (sympathetic stimulation) alone or with relaxation of dilator muscle.

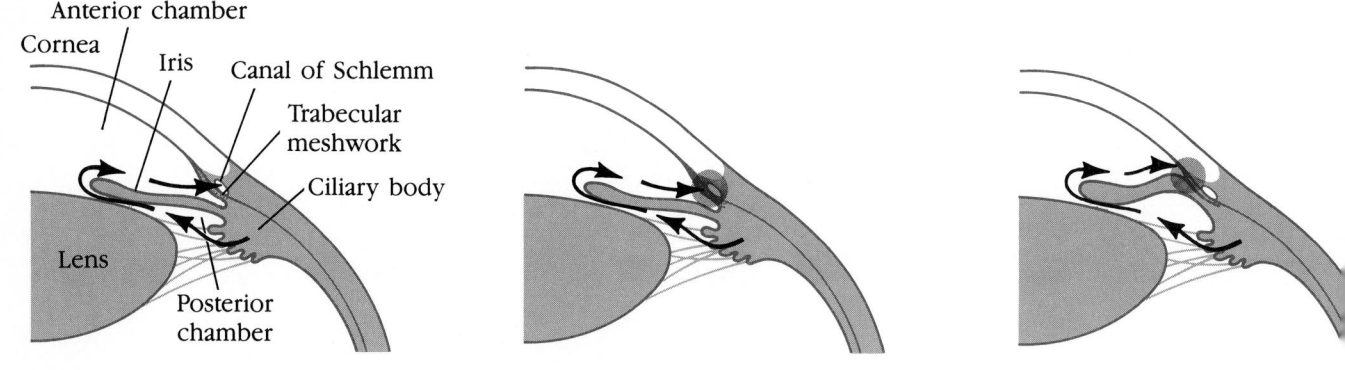

**FIGURE 42-3**   Main structures of the eye and an enlargement of the canal of Schlemm showing aqueous flow.

Drugs producing miosis (miotics) act by (1) interfering with cholinesterase activity or (2) acting like acetylcholine at receptor sites in the sphincter muscle. Drugs producing mydriasis (mydriatics) act by (1) interfering with the action of acetylcholine or (2) stimulating sympathetic or adrenergic receptors. Pupil constriction normally occurs in bright light or when the eye is focusing on nearby objects. Pupil dilation normally occurs in dim light or when the eye is focusing on distant objects.

The lens is situated behind the iris. It is a transparent mass of uniformly arranged fibers encased in a thin elastic capsule. Its protein concentration is higher than that of any other tissue of the body.

The function of the lens is to ensure that the image on the retina is in sharp focus. The lens does this by changing shape (**accommodation**). This occurs readily in young persons, but with age the lens becomes more rigid. The ability to focus on close objects is then lost, and the *near point* (the closest point that can be seen clearly) recedes. With age the lens may also lose its transparency and become opaque. This is known as a **cataract.** Unless it can be treated or removed surgically, blindness can occur. However, if the opaque (cataract) portion is located peripherally in the lens, vision is not compromised.

The lens has suspensory ligaments called zonular fibers around its edge, which connect with the ciliary body. Their tension helps to change the shape of the lens. In the unaccommodated eye, the ciliary muscle is relaxed and the zonular fibers are taut. When zonular fibers contract, the pupil dilates, resulting in sharp distant vision and blurred near vision (unaccommodated eye). Parasympathetic stimulation accommodates the eye for near vision; the pupil constricts in response to contraction of the sphincter muscle. The zonular fibers are relaxed.

Accommodation depends on two factors: (1) ciliary muscle contraction and (2) the ability of the lens to assume a more biconvex shape when tension on the ligaments is relaxed. The ciliary muscle is innervated by parasympa-

thetic fibers. Paralysis of the ciliary muscle is termed **cycloplegia.**

Aqueous humor is formed by the ciliary body. It bathes and feeds the lens, iris, and posterior surface of the cornea. After it is formed, it flows forward between the lens and the iris into the anterior chamber. It drains out of the eye through drainage channels located near the junction of the cornea and sclera. A trabecular meshwork called the canals of Schlemm drains the aqueous humor into the venous system of the eye. (See Figure 42-3.)

The retina contains nerve endings plus the rods and cones that function as visual sensory receptors. It is connected to the brain by the optic nerve, which leaves the orbit through a bony canal in the posterior wall.

Eyelashes, eyelids, blinking, and tears all serve to protect the eye. Each eye has about 200 eyelashes. A blink reflex occurs whenever a foreign body touches the eyelashes. The lids close quickly to prevent the foreign substance from entering the eye. Blinking, which is bilateral, occurs every few seconds during waking hours. It keeps the corneal surface free of mucus and spreads the lacrimal fluid evenly over the cornea. Tears are secreted by lacrimal glands and contain lysozyme, a mucolytic enzyme with bactericidal action. Tears provide lubrication for lid movements. They wash away noxious agents. By forming a thin film over the cornea, tears provide it with a good optical surface. Tear fluid is lost by evaporation and by draining into two small ducts (the lacrimal canaliculi) at the inner corners of the upper and lower eyelids.

## BIBLIOGRAPHY

Thibodeau GA. (1990). Textbook of anatomy and physiology, ed 13. St Louis: Times Mirror/Mosby College Publishing.

Gittinger JW. (1984). Opthalmology: a clinical introduction. Boston: Little, Brown & Co.

Guyton AC. (1987). Human physiology and mechanism of disease, ed 4. Philadelphia: WB Saunders Co.

# 43  Ophthalmic Drugs

## KEY TERMS

**blepharitis,** page 731

**chalazion,** page 731

**conjunctivitis,** page 730

**cycloplegia,** page 727

**endophthalmitis,** page 731

**glaucoma,** page 720

**hordeolum,** page 731

**keratitis,** page 731

**miotics,** page 720

**mydriasis,** page 727

**uveitis,** page 731

## INTRODUCTION

Drugs used to treat eye disorders can be divided into three major groups: the antiglaucoma agents, the mydriatics and cycloplegics, and the antiinfective/antiinflammatory agents. Those groups of agents most likely to be encountered by the nurse in clinical practice are outlined in the box on p. 718. There are many other eye preparations, including ophthalmic diagnostic products, enzymes, irrigating solutions, eye washes, and hyperosmolar preparations. This chapter discusses the major groups and these other eye preparations, along with their major dosage and administration and other nursing considerations.

## ▷NURSING MANAGEMENT: DRUGS AFFECTING THE EYE

*Assessment.* Monitor the affected eye(s) on a daily basis for improvement in the condition for which the medication was prescribed. Assess for redness, itching, swelling, and burning sensation that was not present before therapy started, and so might be indicative of a hypersensitivity. Systemic absorption may occur with eye drops and cause adverse systemic reactions, which are discussed in Table 43-7. Assess the client for ocular side effects/adverse reactions related to administration of systemic medications as outlined in Table 43-6.

*Intervention.* In addition to developing a working knowledge of the ophthalmic agents available, the nurse must be especially aware of the special considerations in administering these drugs.

Ocular drugs are administered by topical application of a solution or ointment (see box, p. 718). Ocular solutions are sterile, easily administered, and usually do not interfere with vision. Their main disadvantage is the short time the drug is in contact with the eye. Ocular ointments have the

---

### MAJOR CATEGORIES OF OPHTHALMIC AGENTS

Antiglaucoma agents
    Direct-acting miotics
    Indirect-acting miotics
    (Anticholinesterase inhibitors)
    Sympathomimetics
    Beta adrenergic blocking agents
    Carbonic anhydrase inhibitor agents
    Osmotic agents
Mydriatic and cycloplegic agents
Antiinfective/antiinflammatory agents
    Antibacterial
        Antibiotics
        Sulfonamides
    Antifungal
    Antiviral
    Antiseptics
    Corticosteroids
Anesthetics
Artificial tear solutions/lubricants
Antiallergic agents
Diagnostic aids
Enzyme preparations
Hyperosmolar preparation
Nonsteroidal antiinflammatory agents
Ophthalmic surgery aids
Irrigating solutions
Contact lens products

---

### GUIDELINES FOR INSTALLATION OF EYEDROPS AND OINTMENTS

**To Instill Eyedrops**

Wash your hands.

Gently cleanse exudate from the eye, if necessary.

Ask the client to tilt the head toward the side of the affected eye.

Gently pull the lower eyelid down and ask the client to look up.

Instill the correct number of drops in the sac formed by the lower eyelid (see Figure 43-1).

Gently apply pressure for 30 seconds to 1 minute over the inner canthus next to the nose to prevent absorption through the tear duct and premature drainage of the medication away from the eye.

Ask the client to gently close the eye, which distributes the solution. Warn against squeezing the eye tightly, which will force out the medication.

Wipe away any excess medication.

If both eyes are to be medicated, do the second instillation quickly before the patient begins to blink and tear as a reaction to the burning sensation occurring in the first eye medicated.

**To Instill Eye Ointment**

The procedure is the same except the ointment is expressed directly onto the exposed conjunctiva from inner to outer canthus with a small individual tube and closed eye; gently massage to distribute the medication.

---

advantages of being quite comfortable on instillation and keeping the drug in longer contact with the eye for more prolonged effects. However, ointments form a film or haze over the eye that interferes with vision and causes a higher incidence of contact dermatitis than solutions. In addition, most ointments are not sterile.

Packs may also be used to apply drugs to the eye. These are cotton pledgets saturated with an ophthalmic solution and inserted into the inferior or superior cul-de-sac. Ocular drugs may also be administered by iontophoresis, subconjunctival (sub-Tenon's) injection, retrobulbar injection, and injection directly into the vitreous or anterior chamber of the eye.

Ocular gel formulations and Ocuserts provide new delivery systems for pilocarpine and perhaps other medications as well. The newer systems were developed to overcome some of the problems with conventional eye drops or ointments. Their longer duration of action improves client compliance and convenience and avoids the peak and valley response found with the previous solutions and ointments. It has been theorized that maintaining a steady pilocarpine release or range should reduce drug-induced adverse reactions and improve treatment outcome (Weintraub, 1985).

*Education.* Instruct the client and/or home care giver in proper administration of eye medications (see box above).

Caution the client to always check the bottle label for correct medication and concentration, such as 0.1% or 1%. This is an increasing concern, since many substances such as beauty aids and home products (glues) are now packaged in similar containers. Discard solutions that have become cloudy or darkened.

Store medications as directed on the label; some may need refrigeration. Once opened, most medications have a limited life (3 months or the end of the current illness). If stored longer, the medication is more likely to become contaminated. To avoid such contamination from the outset, the sterility of the preparation and/or dropper must be maintained. Do not allow the tube tip or dropper to touch anything, including the skin. Hold the dropper with the tip down. Never allow medication into the bulb of the dropper. Keep the container closed when not in use. If two or more family members are using eye medications, each should have a separate vial to prevent cross-contamination.

Inform the client of signs of side effects/adverse reactions, as well as signs of progress. Advise client when to contact or return to the prescriber for assessment.

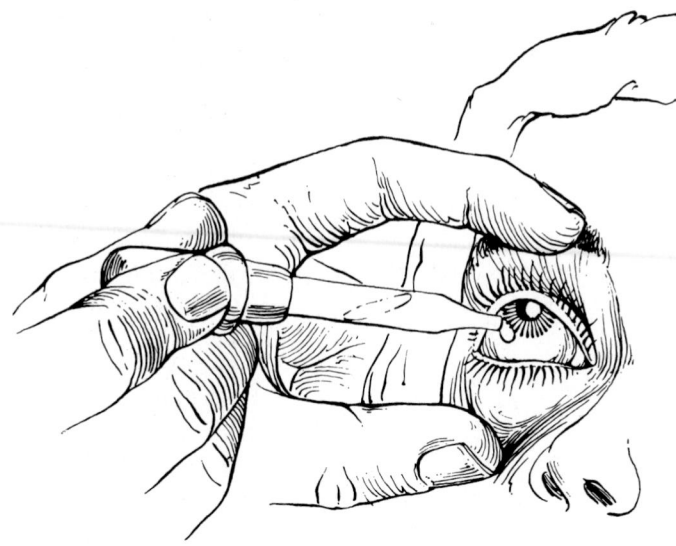

**FIGURE 43-1** Instillation of drops onto the conjuctiva of the lower lid of the eye.

 Selected nursing diagnoses related to ophthalmic drugs

| Nursing diagnosis | Outcome criteria | Interventions |
|---|---|---|
| Knowledge deficit related to new ophthalmic drug regimen | Client will:<br>Express understanding of purpose, function, side effects/adverse reactions<br>Demonstrate proper handling and administration<br>Discuss possible drug interactions | Assess client's level of understanding.<br>Determine educational needs of client.<br>Instruct client in:<br>Purpose and function of medicine<br>Side effects/adverse reactions that may occur and appropriate response<br>Proper storage and handling<br>Correct method of administration<br>Systemic reactions that may occur with topically applied eye prepartions<br>Provide client with a list of possible drug interactions. |
| Anxiety related to possible decrease in or loss of vision | Client will:<br>Verbalize fears and concerns | Assess client for perceptions and fears related to eye disorder.<br>Encourage open communication about fears.<br>Provide emotional support.<br>Provide information related to effectiveness of drug therapy.<br>Allay unwarranted fears. |
| Alteration in comfort related to ophthalmic disorder | Client will:<br>Express a decrease in discomfort | Closely assess the client's symptoms and level of comfort.<br>Provide rest and limiting of eye activity (reading, etc.).<br>Provide emotional support and encouragement. |
| High risk for injury related to impaired vision | Client will:<br>Maintain activity appropriate for level of vision without injury<br>Discuss necessary life-style adjustments | Assess level of vision impairment.<br>Provide safety measures as needed.<br>Encourage client to adjust activities in accordance with client's level of vision. |

*Evaluation.* Once clients have begun a course of therapy with ophthalmic preparations, they should be evaluated for the following possible nursing diagnoses: knowledge deficit related to the self-administration of the medication and condition for which it is administered; risk for the development of hypersensitivity, superinfections, and systemic effects of the drug; and risk for injury related to blurred vision as the result of the instillation of drops or ointment into the eye. For other selected nursing diagnoses for clients with ophthalmic conditions to be considered, see the box on p. 719.

## ANTIGLAUCOMA AGENTS

**Glaucoma** is an eye disease characterized chiefly by abnormally elevated intraocular pressure (IOP). This may result from excessive production of aqueous humor or from diminished ocular fluid outflow. Increased pressure, if sufficiently high and persistent, may lead to irreversible blindness.

There are three major types of glaucoma—primary, secondary, and congenital. Primary glaucoma includes narrow-angle (acute congestive) glaucoma and wide-angle (chronic simple) glaucoma. Clients with narrow-angle glaucoma have a shallow anterior chamber that may be a physiologic/anatomic predisposition. Drugs are needed to control the acute attack associated with narrow-angle glaucoma, followed usually by surgery (such as iridectomy or laser surgery). Wide-angle glaucoma has a gradual insidious onset, and its control depends on permanent drug therapy. Secondary glaucoma may result from previous eye disease or may follow cataract extraction. Therapy for secondary glaucoma is usually with drugs for an indefinite period. Congenital glaucoma requires surgical treatment.

Cholinergic and anticholinesterase drugs are used to treat glaucoma; selection of a drug is determined largely by the requirements of the individual.

### Miotic Agents

**Miotics,** so called because they cause pupillary constriction, are topically applied agents useful in treating glaucoma and accommodative estropia (crossed eyes). the parasympathomimetic miotic agents are cholinergic (minimizing the effects of acetylcholine at autonomic synapses or the neuroeffector junction of the parasympathetic nervous system) or anticholinesterase (inactivating the enzyme cholinesterase by preventing hydrolysis of acetylcholine and thus prolonging the effect of acetylcholine). (See Table 43-1 for the pharmacokinetics of miotic agents.)

### Side Effects/Adverse Reactions

The disadvantages to instillation of cholinergic and anticholinesterase drugs into the eye include the following.

1. Visual blurring, myopia, ciliary spasm, brow pain, and headache result from stimulation of accommodative ancillary muscles.
2. Miosis makes it difficult to adjust quickly to changes in illumination. This may be serious in elderly persons, since their light adaptation and visual acuity are often reduced. Nighttime is particularly hazardous for these individuals.
3. These drugs may cause irritation, conjunctivitis, blepharitis, dermatitis, and so on.
4. Cysts of the iris, synechiae, retinal detachments, obstruction of tear drainage, and even cataracts may develop with prolonged usage, especially with the long-acting anticholinesterases.
5. Tolerance and resistance may develop with any of the miotics.
6. Instillation must be frequent with the liquid and ointment forms.
7. Systemic side effects include salivation, nausea, vomiting, diarrhea, precipitation of asthmatic attack, fall in blood pressure, and other symptoms of parasympathetic stimulation (see Chapter 20).
8. Anticholinesterase drugs may cause spasm of the wink reflex, which is annoying to the individual.
9. Anticholinesterase agents (including those used to treat myasthenia gravis) lower plasma pseudocholinesterase activity. If an adjunctive skeletal muscle relaxant such as succinylcholine (a neuromuscular blocking agent) is used during surgery, respiratory and cardiovascular collapse will result. Because of their long duration of effects, the eye drops must be discontinued several weeks before surgery or electroshock therapy. Another depolarizing neuromuscular blocking agent is decamethonium bromide. Some nondepolarizing agents are metocurine iodide, tubocurarine, gallamine, and pancuronium bromide.
10. Cholinesterase inhibitors also interact with carbamate and organophosphate pesticides, causing additive systemic effects from absorption through the respiratory tract or skin. Nursing intervention includes advising clients of the need for respiratory mask and frequent bathing and changes of clothing if these substances are encountered in the house, garden, or working/living environment or in treatment of head lice (malathion).

Two antidotes are available for overcoming effects caused by cholinergic stimulation—atropine and pralidoxime. Pralidoxime chloride (Protopam) is effective only against anticholinesterases that phosphorylate the enzyme. Given early enough, it reactivates the enzyme.

### Cholinergic Miotics

Cholinergic miotics (direct acting) are chemically related to acetylcholine, the neurotransmitter that mediates nerve impulse transmission at all cholinergic or parasympathetic nerve sites. Applied topically to the eye, cholinergic drugs

**TABLE 43-1**  Pharmacokinetics of miotic agents

| | | | | |
|---|---|---|---|---|
| **DIRECT-ACTING** | | | | |
| carbachol (Isopto Carbachol, 0.75%, 1.5%, 2.25%, 3%) | Open-angle glaucoma | M, 2-5 min IOP, 4 hr | 4-8 hr 8 hr | 1 drop 1 to 3 times daily |
| pilocarpine HCL solution (Pilocar, Miocarpine) | Open- and closed-angle glaucoma; secondary glaucoma; during and after iridectomy; to neutralize mydriatics during eye examinations | M, solution 10-30 min IOP, peak action: Ocusert 1½-2 hr; solution usually within 75 min | 4-8 hr  1 wk 4-14 hr | † |
| **INDIRECT ACTING** | | | | |
| (anticholinesterases) demecarium (Humorsol, 0.125%, 0.25%) | Open- and closed-angle glaucoma; after iridectomy; to diagnose and treat accommodative esotropia | M, 15-60 min IOP, within 1 day (peak) | 3-10 days 9 days or more | For glaucoma, 1 drop one or twice daily. |
| echothiophate iodide (Phospholine Iodide, 0.03%, 0.06%, 0.125%, 0.25%) | Same as demecarium; in addition, used to treat secondary glaucoma | M, 10-30 min IOP, 1 day | 7-28 days up to 28 days | For glaucoma, 1 drop of 0.03% to 0.25% to conjunctiva, once or twice daily. |
| isoflurophate ophthalmic ointment (Floropryl, 0.025%) | Same as demecarium; in addition, used to treat secondary glaucoma | M, 10-30 min IOP, 1 day | 7-28 days 1 week | Apply thin strip from once every 3 days up to three times daily |
| physostigmine salicylate ophthalmic solution (Eserine, Isopto Eser- | Open-angle glaucoma | M, 10-30 min | 12-48 hr | Apply 1 cm ointment or 1 drop solution up to 3 times daily |

*M, miotic effect; IOP, to reduce intraocular pressure.
†Dosage in acute glaucoma, 1 drop of 1% or 2% solution every 5 to 10 minutes for 6 doses, then 1 drop every 1 to 3 hours until pressure is reduced. Chronic (open-angle) glaucoma: 1 drop of 0.5% to 4% solution up to four times daily. Ocusert system: apply topically to conjunctiva once weekly. System delivers between 20 and 40 µg of pilocarpine per hour. Ophthalmic gel: apply approximately ½ inch strip of 4% gel topically to conjunctiva at bedtime.

(1) cause contraction of the sphincter muscle of the iris, resulting in pupil constriction (miosis), (2) cause spasms of the ciliary muscle and deepening of the anterior chamber, and (3) cause vasodilation of intraocular vessels (such as those in the iris) or where intraocular fluids leave the eye, leading to an increase in aqueous humor outflow. The ciliary muscle effect leaves the eye in accommodation of near vision.

The cholinergic agents have a duration of miotic action of approximately 4 to 8 hours (pilocarpine drops) or 2 to 8 hours (carbachol). These agents are very effective in many cases of chronic glaucoma. Their side effects are less severe and occur less frequently than those caused by anticholinesterase agents.

The cholinergic drugs are used to lower intraocular pressure in glaucoma and in accommodative esotropia. Unless the elevated pressure is lowered, the result is an impaired blood supply to the optic nerve, with eventual atrophy of the nerve and visual field loss. Contraction of the ciliary

muscles and constriction of the pupil may widen the filtration angle and permit increased outflow of aqueous humor. Increased outflow may also result from dilation of collector channels and veins peripheral to the canal of Schlemm.

Clinical toxicity from overdosage or unusual sensitivity to these drugs is manifested by headache, salivation, sweating, abdominal discomfort, diarrhea, asthmatic attacks, and a fall in blood pressure.

### Anticholinesterase Miotics

Anticholinesterase drugs (indirect acting) inhibit the enzymatic destruction of acetylcholine by inactivating cholinesterase. This permits acetylcholine to act on the iris sphincter and ciliary muscles, producing pupil constriction (miosis) and ciliary muscle contraction (accommodation).

Physostigmine and demecarium act on true cholinesterase. Echothiophate and isoflurophate depress both plasma (true cholinesterase) and erythrocyte cholinesterase.

The irreversible anticholinesterase drugs (echothiophate,

**TABLE 43-2**   Drug effects on aqueous humor

| Drug | Decreases aqueous humor production | Increases aqueous humor drainage or outflow |
|---|---|---|
| **SYMPATHOMIMETICS** | | |
| epinephrine | + + + | + + |
| dipivefrin | + + + | + + |
| **BETA-BLOCKERS** | | |
| betaxolol | + + + | U |
| levobunolol | + + + | U |
| timolol | + + + | + |
| **DIRECT MIOTICS** | | |
| acetylcholine | + | + + + |
| carbachol | + | + + + |
| pilocarpine | + | + + + |
| **INDIRECT MIOTICS** | | |
| physostigmine | U | + + + |
| demecarium | U | + + + |
| echothiophate | U | + + + |
| isoflurophate | U | + + + |
| **CARBONIC ANHYDRASE INHIBITORS** | | |
| acetazolamide | + + + | U |

+, low potential; + + +, greatest potential; U, unknown

isoflurophate) form stable complexes with cholinesterase and thus irreversibly impair the destructive function of the enzyme. Destruction of acetycholine then depends on synthesis of new enzymes.

Demecarium is more toxic than the other agents in this category, so it is not as commonly used. Although it is a reversible inhibitor, its prolonged action has results similar to the irreversible inhibitors. Isoflurophate is available only in an ointment formulation.

## Sympathomimetic Agents

The primary sympathomimetic agents are dipivefrin and epinephrine. The mechanism by which the topically applied adrenergic epinephrine acts is by contraction of the dilator muscle of the pupil. Mydriasis (pupillary dilation) is achieved within minutes following ophthalmic instillation and has a duration of action of several hours, during which time it lowers the intraocular pressure.

Sympathomimetic ophthalmic effects are pupil dilation, alpha adrenergic agonist effects (vasoconstriction, decreased aqueous humor production, and increased aqueous humor outflow), and beta adrenergic agonist effects (ciliary muscle relaxation and decreased aqueous humor formation). The effects on aqueous humor are outlined in Table 43-2.

### dipivefrin hydrochloride ophthalmic solution (Propine 0.1%)

Dipivefrin is a prodrug of epinephrine. Enzymes in the eye will convert dipivefrin to epinephrine, which acts as an adrenergic agonist. The chemical modification creates a more lipophilic compound that facilitates absorption and penetration through the cornea into the anterior chamber of the eye. The penetration and absorption of dipivefrin are about 17 times greater than those of epinephrine. It decreases the intraocular pressure by reducing aqueous humor production and enhancing aqueous outflow.

Dipivefrin is indicated for the treatment of open-angle glaucoma. It has an onset of action within ½ hour, peak effect in 1 hour, and a duration of action of up to 12 hours. The most frequently reported side effect is burning or stinging sensation in the eye that is rarely troublesome. If the drug is absorbed, systemic effects of tachycardia, dysrhythmias, and hypertension may occur. No significant drug interactions have been reported to date with dipivefrin. The child and adult dose is 1 drop topically to the conjuctiva every 12 hours. Pregnancy safety has been established at FDA Category B.

▷ **Nursing Management: Dipivefrin Therapy**

*Assessment.* Dipivefrin is contraindicated in clients with narrow-angle glaucoma because pupil dilation may aggravate the condition. In aphakic clients (those devoid of a crystalline lens), depivefrin or epinephrine may cause macular edema.

*Intervention.* If dipivefrin is administered with other antiglaucoma ophthalmic solutions, review the regimen carefully. When dipivefrin is to replace epinephrine, the epinephrine should be discontinued when the dipivefrin is started. If the antiglaucoma agent to be replaced is something other than epinephrine, that agent should be discontinued on the second day of dipivefrin administration. If administered in addition to other antiglaucoma agents, dipivefrin is given at the usual adult dose.

**Education.** Review with the client the safe and accurate techniques for the self-administration of ophthalmic agents. See "Nursing management: drugs affecting the eye," p. 717.

**Evaluation.** The client's condition should be evaluated periodically by the physician throughout therapy by fundus and intraocular pressure examinations to ensure the effectiveness of dipivefrin. In addition, clients receiving these ophthalmic solutions may be at risk for altered comfort related to possible photophobia and burning, stinging, and other eye irritations.

### epinephrine ophthalmic solution (Epifrin, Glaucon in 0.1%, 0.25%, 0.5%, 1%, and 2%) epinephrine bitartrate ophthalmic solution (Epitrate, 1% and 2%)

A direct-acting sympathomimetic agent, epinephrine decreases production of aqueous humor and increases its outflow. Epinephrine is also used as a surgical agent or antihemorrhagic mydriatic. It stimulates alpha adrenergic receptors in the conjunctiva, producing vasoconstriction and hemostasis of the small blood vessels. It contracts the dilator muscle of the pupil (alpha stimulating effect), which produces pupillary dilation.

Epinephrine is indicated to treat open-angle glaucoma and topical hemorrhage in ocular surgery or to induce a mydriatic effect. It produces a vasoconstriction effect within 5 minutes and reduces intraocular pressure within 1 hour of administration. The time until peak reduction of intraocular pressure is between 4 and 8 hours. The duration of action for reduction of intraocular pressure is up to 24 hours. Vasoconstrictor effects usually last less than 60 minutes.

Most frequently reported side effects (rarely troublesome) are headaches, pain in brow, stinging or burning sensation in the eye, or watering of the eye. Less often reported is eye pain. The following adverse effects require a physician's attention: signs and symptoms of systemic absorption, such as tachycardia, palpitations, increased sweating, tremors, and lightheadedness. Visual disturbance such as blurred vision may indicate maculopathy (edema) in eyes without the crystalline lens (aphakia).

**Significant drug interactions.** The following interactions may occur when epinephrine is given with drugs listed below:

| Drug | Possible Effect and Management |
|---|---|
| guanethidine | Potentiate the pressor response of epinephrine. |
| H₁ antihistimines | Potentiate the pressor response of epinephrine. |
| halothane | Myocardial sensitization may occur with ophthalmic use of epinephrine before halothane general anesthesia. |

| Drug | Possible Effect and Management |
|---|---|
| monoamine oxidase inhibitors | May exaggerate sympathomimetic effects. |
| tricyclic antidepressants | Potentiate the pressor response of epinephrine. |

**Dosage and administration.** For glaucoma, instill 1 drop of Epitrate 1% or 2% solution, Epinal 0.5% to 1% solution, Epifrin 0.5% to 2% solution to conjunctiva twice daily.

As a surgical agent or for antihemorrhagic and/or mydriatic effect, instill 1 drop of 0.1% epinephrine ophthalmic solution only to conjunctiva for up to three doses or as needed to produce the specific effects.

**Pregnancy safety.** Has been established at FDA category C.

### ▷Nursing Management: Epinephrine Therapy

**Assessment.** Watch for systemic effects such as tachycardia and elevated blood pressure, which may occasionally occur with its use. Other possible side effects may include altered comfort with eye pain, ocular irritation, and tearing. There have also been reports of epinephrine causing macular edema.

**Intervention.** Discoloration or precipitation of epinephrine indicates oxidation to inactive products, and the solution should be discarded.

**Education.** Warn client not to use the OTC sympathomimetic drugs such as phenylephrine (an alpha agonist vasoconstrictor) with timolol ophthalmic drops (a beta blocker). The beta blocker eye drops may prevent the vasodilation, which opposes the alpha adrenergic vasoconstriction. Further, epinephrine or phenylephrine may be absorbed systemically to interact with beta blockers and MAO inhibitors.

**Evaluation.** Monitor the affected eye(s) on a daily basis for improvement.

## Beta Adrenergic Blocking Agents

The beta blocking agents include betaxolol, levobunolol, and timolol. Betaxolol is a cardioselective (beta₁) blocking agent, whereas levobunolol and timolol are noncardioselective, that is, they can block both beta₁ and beta₂ adrenergic receptors. These agents reduce intraocular pressure in clients with or without glaucoma. The precise mechanism of action is not understood, but the effect may be related to the reduction of aqueous humor formation and to a minimal increase in outflow (reported with timolol).

### betaxolol hydrochloride ophthalmic solution (Betoptic 0.5%)

Betaxolol is indicated for the treatment of open-angle glaucoma and ocular hypertension; it may be a drug of choice for clients with pulmonary disease because of its selective beta$_1$ blocking effects, although the nurse should still monitor for respiratory difficulties.

It has an onset of effect within 30 minutes and peak action within 2 hours. Following a single dose of medication, the drug has a duration of action of 12 hours.

The most often reported side effect is a stinging sensation in the eye. Less often reported is photosensitivity or eye irritation. Discontinue drug and contact the physician immediately if severe irritation or inflammation occurs in the eye. If drug is systemically absorbed, depression, confusion, bradycardia, insomnia, increased weakness, wheezing, or respiratory difficulties may be seen. No significant drug interactions have been reported to date.

The dose is 1 drop of a 0.5% solution to conjunctiva, twice daily.

Pregnancy safety has been established at FDA category C.

### levobunolol hydrochloride ophthalmic solution (Betagan 0.5%)

Levobunolol is indicated for the treatment of open-angle glaucoma and ocular hypertension. Its onset of action is within 60 minutes, peak effect occurs within 2 to 6 hours, and duration of action in lowering intraocular pressure is up to 24 hours after a single-dose administration.

Burning or stinging sensation in the eye is an infrequently reported and rarely troublesome side effect. The following adverse reactions require medical attention and intervention if they occur. Rare adverse reactions include severe eye inflammation or irritation, visual disturbances, rash, pruritus, or allergic reaction. Signs and symptoms of systemic absorption may include chest pain; ataxia; depression; confusion; lightheadedness; headaches; bradycardia or tachycardia; nausea; vomiting; edema of feet, ankles, or lower extremities; increased weakness; and wheezing or respiratory difficulties.

No significant drug interactions have been reported. The usual dose is 1 drop to the conjunctiva once or twice daily.

Pregnancy safety has been established at FDA category C.

### timolol ophthalmic solution (Timoptic 0.25%, 0.5%)

Timolol is indicated for the treatment of open-angle glaucoma, ocular hypertension, secondary glaucoma, and glaucoma in aphakic eyes. It has an onset of action within 30 minutes, peak effect between 1 and 2 hours, and duration of effect up to 24 hours after a single dose.

Timolol's side effects/adverse reactions are similar to those of levobunolol. In addition, the following systemic effects have been reported: increased anxiety, decreased libido, diarrhea, hallucinations, abdominal distress, and pain.

The usual dose is 1 drop to the conjunctiva, once or twice daily.

Pregnancy safety has been established at FDA category C.

## ▷Nursing Management: Beta Adrenergic Blocking Agent Therapy

Usually these agents are well tolerated with occasional signs of mild ocular irritation. Local hypersensitivity (rash) occurs rarely. A slight reduction of resting heart rate may occur, and acute bronchospasm in clients with bronchospastic disease has been reported.

There is sufficient absorption from the conjunctiva and nasopharynx to produce systemic nonselective beta adrenergic (beta$_1$ and beta$_2$) effects such as cardiopulmonary complications and exacerbation of asthma. Use caution in administering beta adrenergic blocking agents to clients who have bronchial asthma, heart disease, sinus bradycardia or greater than first-degree heart block, cardiogenic shock, right ventricular failure caused by pulmonary hypertension, or congestive heart failure. Also see nursing management of beta adrenergic blocking agents in Chapter 21.

## Carbonic Anhydrase Inhibitor Agents

The three carbonic anhydrase inhibitors include acetazolamide, dichlorphenamide, and methazolamide. Acetazolamide, the most widely used drug of this class, is the focus of this discussion.

The carbonic anhydrase inhibitors are sulfonamides (nonbacteriostatic). The mechanism of action is not completely understood, but they appear to lower intraocular pressure by decreasing the aqueous production to half of its baseline measurement.

These drugs are indicated for the treatment of open-angle, secondary, and angle-closure glaucoma. For pharmacokinetics of the three agents, see Table 43-3.

**TABLE 43-3** Pharmacokinetics of carbonic anhydrase inhibitors

| | acetazolamide | dichlor-phenamide | mehtazola-mide |
|---|---|---|---|
| Peak effects | Tablet: 2-4 hr Sustained-released capsule: 8-12 hr | 2-4 hr | 6-8 hr |
| Onset of action | Tablet 1-1½ hr Sustained released capsule: 2 hr | 30-60 min | 2-4 hr |
| Duration of action | Tablet: 8-12 hr Sustained release capsule: 18-24 hr | 6-12 hr | 10-18 hr |

Side effects include diarrhea, feeling of discomfort, diuresis, anorexia, metallic taste in mouth, nausea, vomiting, tingling or numbness (paresthesia) of fingers, hands, toes, feet, mouth, or anus, and weight loss. Physician intervention is necessary if client has the signs and symptoms of acidosis, blood dyscrasias, or hypokalemia.

***Significant drug interactions.*** The following interactions may occur when carbonic anhydrase inhibitors are given with the drugs listed below.

| Drug | Possible Effect and Management |
| --- | --- |
| amphetamines, quinidine, mecamylamine | Carbonic anhydrase inhibitors decrease excretion of these drugs because of alkalinization of the urine, and they may increase their side effects and prolong their duration of effect. Avoid concurrent use of mecamylamine. Monitor closely, since dosage adjustments are usually necessary with other medications. |
| methenamine | Carbonic anhydrase inhibitors reduce the effectiveness of methenamine because of alkalinization of urine, which prevents conversion of methanamine to formaldehyde. Concurrent drug administration is not recommended. |

***Dosage and administration.*** The adult dose of acetazolamide (Diamox) for open-angle glaucoma is 250 mg orally up to four times daily. Maintenance dose is titrated according to the client's response. Pediatric dosage is 8 to 30 mg/kg (usually 10 to 15 mg/kg) orally daily, in divided doses. For recommended dosages of dichlorphenamide (Daranide) and metazolamide (Neptazame), refer to a current reference source, such as the package insert or the USP-DI.

***Pregnancy safety.*** Has not been established for the carbonic anhydrase inhibitors.

▷**Nursing Management:**
**Carbonic Anhydrase Inhibitor Therapy**

***Assessment.*** Recall that these drugs cause some decrease in renal blood flow and glomerular filtration rate, which produces an increased excretion of sodium, potassium, bicarbonate, and water alkaline diuresis. Monitor appropriate serum concentrations for electrolyte imbalances.

Reactions to sulfonamide agents (thiazide diuretic, oral sulfonylureas), will raise an index of suspicion for cross allergenicity and hypersensitivity. Contraindications include clients with decreased sodium/potassium serum levels and hepatic and renal dysfunction (potential for renal calculi formation).

***Education.*** Consider use of potassium supplements by client or suggest dietary sources of potassium for client.

***Evaluation.*** Monitor the affected eye(s) on a daily basis for improvement.

The client is at risk for altered comfort in a variety of ways, including metallic taste; anorexia; nausea and vomiting; numbness or tingling of the fingers, toes, mouth, and tongue; and feelings of malaise. In addition, the client may experience altered patterns of bowel elimination, such as diarrhea, and altered urinary elimination pattern, or polyuria. The client's feelings of malaise should be carefully assessed, as the client may also be at risk for physiologic injury related to the development of hypokalemia, blood dyscrasias, and acidosis.

## Osmotic Agents

Osmotic agents are given intravenously or orally to reduce the intraocular pressure. These agents generally do not cross the blood aqueous barrier into the anterior chamber of the eye and are rarely found in ocular humor.

The osmotherapeutic agents (glycerin and mannitol) create ocular hypotension by producing an osmotic gradient (making the blood hypertonic relative to the intraocular fluids). This gradient forces the water from the aqueous and vitreous humors into the bloodstream. The effect on the eye is reduction of volume of intraocular fluid, producing a decrease in intraocular pressure.

### glycerin oral solution (Glyrol, Osmoglyn)
### glycerin ophthalmic solution (Ophthalgan)

Glycerin is given orally before iridectomy to reduce intraocular pressure in individuals with acute narrow-angle glaucoma. It is used preoperatively and postoperatively in conditions such as congenital glaucoma, retinal detachment, cataract extraction, and keratoplasty (corneal transplant). It may also be used in some secondary glaucomas.

A local anesthetic (1 to 2 drops) is administered before use of glycerin ophthalmic solution because of pain and irritation from glycerin instillation.

Glucose (Glucose-40 Ophthalmic ointment) is indicated for topical osmotherapy to reduce corneal edema. This 40% ointment is used two to six times daily.

The onset of effect with oral glycerin in reducing intraocular pressure is within 10 minutes. The time to peak effect is 1 to 1.5 hours and duration of action is 5 hours. Metabolism is in the liver with excretion by the kidneys.

Reported side effects (rarely troublesome) include headaches, nausea, vomiting, diarrhea, dry mouth, increased thirst, and lightheadedness. Notify the physician as medical intervention is necessary for confusion or irregular heart rate. No significant drug interactions have been reported.

The oral dose is 1 to 1.5 g/kg before surgery for adults and children. Additional doses of 500 mg/kg (children) up to 1.5 g/kg (adults) may be administered in 4 to 8 hours, if necessary.

Ophthalmic glycerin may be instilled (1 or 2 drops) before examination to reduce edema, clear the cornea, and improve visualization for ophthalmoscopic gonioscopic examination.

▷**Nursing Management:**
**Glycerin Therapy**

**Assessment.** Use glycerin cautiously in clients with cardiac, renal, or hepatic disease. The shift in body water may cause pulmonary edema or congestive heart failure. Elderly clients may be subject to dehydration because of a mild diuretic action. Diabetic individuals receiving glycerin should be carefully observed for symptoms of acidosis, since the metabolism of glycerin to carbohydrates may cause transient hyperglycemia and glycosuria.

**Intervention.** Flavor glycerin with lemon or lime juice, pour over cracked ice, and have the client sip it through a straw to decrease the incidence of nausea and vomiting.

**Education.** Headache is the result of cerebral dehydration. To relieve the symptoms of headache, nausea and vomiting, have the client lie flat during and after oral administration of glycerin.

**Evaluation.** Monitor the affected eye(s) by intraocular pressure determinations on a daily basis for improvement.

### isosorbide (Ismotic 45% Solution)

Isosorbide is an oral osmotic agent used for emergency treatment of acute angle-closure glaucoma.

Isosorbide has an onset of action between 10 and 30 minutes, peak effect in 1 to 1.5 hours, and duration of action of 5 to 6 hours. Side effects associated with its use include nausea, vomiting, headaches, confusion, and disorientation. No significant drug interactions have been reported with its use.

The initial dose is usually 1.5 g/kg (with a dosage range of 1 to 3 g/kg) given 2 to 4 times daily.

Pregnancy safety has been established at FDA category B.

▷**Nursing Management:**
**Isosorbide Therapy**

Prepare as for oral glycerin to increase palatability. Isosorbide is contraindicated in clients with dehydration, pulmonary edema, hemorrhagic glaucoma, and anuria caused by kidney disease.

### mannitol (Osmitrol✱)

Mannitol injection has osmotic and diuretic properties. It is available in 5%, 10%, 15%, 20%, and 25% solutions. For mechanism of action, see discussion for osmotic agents.

Mannitol is indicated for the treatment of ocular hypertension, edema, and cerebral edema and for the promotion of urinary excretion of selected toxic substances, such as salicylates, barbiturates, and bromides.

Mannitol's diuretic effect occurs in 1 to 3 hours; a reduction of intraocular fluid pressure or cerebrospinal pressure is seen within 15 minutes. The time to peak reduction in intraocular pressure is ½ to 1 hour after starting the infusion. The reduction in intraocular pressure lasts from 4 to 8 hours, whereas reduction in cerebrospinal fluid pressure is between 3 and 8 hours after the infusion is stopped. Both pressures will increase in about 12 hours after a mannitol infusion is discontinued. Mannitol is partially metabolized in the liver and excreted by the kidneys.

The following side effects are rarely troublesome: dry mouth, thirst, headache, nausea, vomiting, increased frequency of urination, lightheadedness, rash, and blurred vision. Notify the physician if client has chest pain, tachycardia, elevated temperature, chills, confusion, irregular heart rate, muscle cramping or pain, paresthesia in hands or feet, convulsions, tremors, increased weakness, pulmonary congestion, difficulty urinating, or edema of lower extremities.

When mannitol is given concurrently with digitalis glycosides, an increase in digitalis toxicity may result. Monitor concurrent therapy closely.

The adult dose to treat cerebral edema, elevated intracranial pressure, or glaucoma is 1.5 to 2 g/kg by intravenous infusion given over ½ to 1 hour (usually a 15% to 25% solution is used). Small clients or very debilitated persons may require only a 500 mg/kg dosage. Maximum daily dose is 6 g/kg.

In children, give 1 to 2 g/kg by intravenous infusion or 30 to 60 g/m² (15% to 20% preparation) given over ½ to 1 hour.

Pregnancy safety has been established as FDA category B or C.

▷**Nursing Management:**
**Mannitol Therapy**

**Assessment.** Mannitol should be carefully considered for clients with marked oliguria or possible inadequate renal function. A test dose is recommended to ensure sufficient renal function to prevent an overexpansion of extracellular fluid and circulatory overload. The drug is contraindicated in clients with anuria, intracranial bleeding, severe dehydration, or pulmonary congestion.

**Intervention.** If the solution has crystallized, warming will return the crystals to solution. Care should be taken in the selection and care of the intravenous site as extravasation of mannitol may cause edema and skin necrosis.

**Evaluation.** Carefully monitor clients for fluid and electrolyte balance with serum electrolyte studies, vital signs, and urinary output determinations, since mannitol produces more diuresis than urea. Clients may also have altered comfort related to increased thirst, dry mouth, headache, diuresis, nausea, and vomiting.

### urea, sterile (Ureaphil)

For mechanism of action of urea, see osmotic agent section. Urea is used in the treatment of cerebral edema, secondary glaucoma, and malignant glaucoma. Following the start of a urea infusion, intraocular and intracranial pressure is reduced within 10 minutes with a peak effect reported between 1 to 2 hours. The diuretic effect has a duration of effect of 3 to 10 hours, while the reduction in intraocular pressure lasts 5 to 6 hours after an infusion is discontinued. A rebound effect or increase in intraocular pressure may occur in approximately 12 hours after urea is stopped. The half-life of urea is 1.17 hours, and it is partially metabolized in the gastrointestinal tract and excreted by the kidneys.

Side effects (rarely troublesome) include dry mouth, increased thirst, headache, nausea, vomiting, lightheadedness, and skin blemishes. Notify the physician if the client has visual disturbances, severe headaches, confusion, tachycardia, elevated temperature, increased anxiety, irregular heart rate, muscle cramping, paresthesia of hands or feet, convulsions, tremors, increased weakness, or redness or swelling at injection site. No significant drug interactions are reported with urea.

The adult dose as a diuretic or to treat glaucoma is 500 mg to 1.5 g/kg by intravenous infusion (a 30% solution in 5% or 10% dextrose injection), given at a rate of 60 drops (4 to 6 ml) per minute over ½ to 2 hours. Maximum daily dose is 2 g/kg/day.

In children 2 years and older, see adult dose. Less than 2 years old, administer 100 mg to 1.5 g/kg. Preparation of solution and administration are the same as for adults.

Pregnancy safety has been established at FDA category C.

▷ **Nursing Management:**
**Urea Therapy**

***Assessment.*** Urea is contraindicated in clients with severe dehydration, active intracranial bleeding (except during craniotomy), and hepatic and renal impairment.

Assess BUN before and frequently during intravenous administration. If it becomes elevated to 75 to 100 mg/100 ml, slow infusion rate and notify the physician to possibly discontinue infusion.

Monitor blood pressure and fluid intake and output, and evaluate serum electrolyte concentrations, especially sodium and potassium, and renal function studies.

***Intervention.*** Preparation for administration varies from product to product depending on the manufacturer. Consult package insert.

Do not infuse at a rate greater than 4 ml/minute, since it may result in hemolysis and cerebral vasomotor symptoms. During intracranial surgery, the dose is started at the time of the scalp incision to produce the maximum reduction of pressure.

Use urea as soon as it is reconstituted. Discard any unused solution.

Do not infuse into veins of lower extremities, since phlebitis and thrombosis may occur, especially in the elderly. To prevent tissue irritation and necrosis at the injection site, avoid extravasation. The risk of thrombosis is greater with the use of hypothermia while urea is being infused.

If the client has difficulty urinating or is comatose, an indwelling urethral catheter should be inserted. Finally, if there is a need to concurrently administer urea and blood, do not administer through the same intravenous administration set.

***Education.*** Prepare the client for the anticipated diuresis. Explain to the client that urea is usually administered 60 minutes before ocular surgery to reduce intraocular pressure.

***Evaluation.*** The client should be evaluated for degree of diuresis and for improvement in the reduction of intraocular or intracranial pressure. Clients may have altered comfort with increased thirst, dryness of mouth, headache, nausea, and vomiting. In addition, the risk exists for altered thought processes (confusion), hyperthermia, and physiologic injury from thrombosis, extravasation, electrolyte imbalances, and subdural or subarachnoid hemorrhage.

## MYDRIATIC AND CYCLOPLEGIC AGENTS

These topically applied autonomic drugs can cause dilation of pupils (**mydriasis**) and paralysis of accommodation (**cycloplegia**). Both sympathomimetic and parasympatholytic agents can cause mydriasis, by different mechanisms of action. The effects of these agents depend on the client's age, race, and color of iris. Mydriatic agents evoke less of a response in persons with heavily pigmented (dark) irides than in those with lighter pigmented (blue) irides. Thus blacks tend to respond less to the agents than whites.

### Anticholinergic (Parasympatholytic) Agents

Anticholinergic agents block acetylcholine stimulation of the sphincter muscle of the iris and the accommodative muscle of the ciliary body. They are indicated for the treatment of inflammations such as uveitis and keratitis to relieve ocular pain by relaxing inflamed intraocular muscles by putting the eye at rest. They are also used for relaxation of ciliary muscle for accurate measurement of refractive errors, which permits proper lens determination for eyeglasses, and

---

### ANTICHOLINERGIC EFFECT ON THE EYE

The circular smooth muscles of the iris, which constrict the pupil, are innervated by parasympathetic fibers from the oculomotor (third cranial) nerve. Anticholinergics (parasympatholytics) block the effects of the neurohormonal mediator, acetylcholine. This leaves the pupil (radial fibers of the iris) under the unopposed influence of its sympathetic, or adrenergic, nerve supply, and pupil dilation occurs. The oculomotor nerve also supplies the ciliary muscle. Contraction of this muscle slackens the suspensory ligament of the lens and allows the lens to become more convex. Accommodation for near vision depends on the ciliary muscle's ability to contract.

**TABLE 43-4**   Anticholinergic agents (mydriatics): approximate maximum range of effects

| | Maximal mydriasis | Usual recovery time | Maximal cycloplegia | Usual recovery time |
|---|---|---|---|---|
| atropine | 30-40 min | 7-12 days | Several hr | 6 or more days |
| cyclopentolate | 30-60 min | 1 day | 25-75 min | ¼-1 day |
| homatropine | 40-60 min | 1-3 days | 30-60 min | 1-3 days |
| scopolamine | 15-30 min | 3-7 days | 30-60 min | 3-7 days |
| tropicamide | 20-40 min | 6 hr | 20-35 min | 6 hr |

for preoperative and postoperative use in intraocular surgery.

For pharmacokinetics, see Table 43-4. Local side effects/adverse reactions reported with their use include stinging or an increase in intraocular pressure. With chronic use, allergic lid reactions, red eye, and various eye irritation injuries may be induced.

If absorbed systemically, mild to serious adverse reactions may result, such as dryness of the mouth, inhibition of sweating, flushing, tachycardia, ataxia, hallucinations, psychiatric and behavioral problems, fever, delirium, convulsions, respiratory depression, and coma. Deaths have been recorded in children after systemic absorption.

Pupillary dilation from either local or systemic administration can precipitate acute glaucoma in predisposed persons. If unrecognized or untreated, this can result in blindness. No significant drug interactions have been reported.

#### atropine sulfate ophthalmic solution

The dose of atropine sulfate ophthalmic solution in adults is, as a mydriatic, preoperatively 1 drop of 1% solution along with 1 drop of a 2.5% or 10% phenylephrine solution. Postoperatively, instill 1 drop (1% or 2% solution) to conjunctiva one to three times daily. For uveitis, instill 1 drop (1% solution) to conjunctiva up to three times daily.

For use in children for cycloplegic refraction, instill 1 drop of the following concentrations two times daily for 1 to 3 days before scheduled refraction. Select solution according to age and eye color:

Less than 12 months old, 0.125% solution
1 to 5 years old, 0.25% solution
5 years and older with blue irides, 0.25% solution
5 years and older with dark irides, 0.5% to 1% solution

For use in children with uveitis, instill 1 drop (0.125% to 1% solution) to conjunctiva one to three times daily. For treatment of postoperative mydriasis, instill 1 drop (0.5% solution) to conjunctiva one to three times daily.

Pregnancy safety has been established at FDA category C.

▷**Nursing Management:
Atropine Ophthalmic Therapy**

***Assessment.*** Atropine is contraindicated in clients with glaucoma. Dilation of the pupil causes a narrowing of the iridocorneal angle where the canal of Schlemm is located. This restricts drainage of intraocular fluids, although secre-

tion continues and intraocular pressure rises. This may precipitate an attack of acute glaucoma.

***Education.*** Instruct clients that the next instillation should be omitted if side effects (dryness of mouth, tachycardia) are present. Alert client that during therapy he may be unable to focus (blurred vision) on nearby objects and will be unusually sensitive to light. Dark glasses should be worn to decrease this photophobia. The eye will be accommodated for distant vision.

Since atropine is highly toxic, store it in a safe place out of the reach of children.

***Evaluation.*** The potential for systemic side effects is more pronounced in infants, young children, children with blond hair or blue eyes, clients with Down's syndrome, children with brain damage, and the elderly. Monitor these clients for fast irregular pulse, skin dryness, confusion, slurred speech, dry mouth, fever, and unusual drowsiness or weakness.

#### cyclopentolate hydrochloride ophthalmic solution (Cyclogyl, Minims Cyclopentolate ✦)

For treatment of cycloplegic refraction: for adults instill 1 drop (0.5% to 2% solution) to conjunctiva. Repeat in 5 minutes. Schedule refraction for approximately 40 to 50 minutes following the second dose. Cyclopentolate is also used in children for cycloplegic refraction; for premature and small infants, instill 1 drop (0.5% solution) to conjunctiva as single dose. For use in other children, instill 1 drop (0.5% to 2% solution) to conjunctiva. Repeat in 5 minutes, and schedule examination for 40 to 50 minutes after the second dose. For ophthalmoscopic examination, instill 1 drop (0.5% or 1% solution) to conjunctiva. In neonates, do not use concentrations above 0.5%.

Pregnancy safety has not been established.

#### homatropine ophthalmic solution (Isopto Homatropine, Minims Homatropine ✦)

The dose for homatropine ophthalmic solution in adults for cycloplegic refraction is 1 drop (2% or 5% solution) to conjunctiva every 5 to 10 minutes for two to five doses before refraction. For uveitis, instill 1 drop (2% or 5% solution) to conjunctiva two or three times daily. In children, for cycloplegic refraction, instill 1 drop (1% or 2% solution) every 10 minutes for two or three doses before refraction. In uveitis, instill 1 drop (1% or 2% solution) to conjunctiva two or three times daily.

**TABLE 43-5** Ophthalmic mydriatic-vasoconstrictor drugs

| Name | Duration of action (hours) | Availability | Strength (% solution) | Dosage and administration |
|---|---|---|---|---|
| epinephrine | 1-3 | Prescription | 0.1 | 1 or 2 drops into eye, repeat once if necessary |
| naphazoline (Allerest, Clear Eyes, others) | 2-3 | Over-the-counter | 0.012<br>0.02<br>0.03<br>0.05 | 1 or 2 drops into conjunctival sac |
| oxymetazoline (Ocu Clear) | <6 | Prescription<br>Over-the-counter | 0.1<br>0.025 | 1 or 2 drops into affected eye every 6 hours |
| phenylephrine (Neo-Synephrine, others) | 0.5-1.5<br>5-7 | Over-the-counter<br>Prescription | 0.12<br>2.5<br>10.0 | 1 or 2 drops (only 1 drop for 10% solution) into eye |
| tetrahydrozoline (Visine, Murine Plus, others) | 2-3 | Over-the-counter | 0.05 | 1 or 2 drops 2 to 4 times a day |

Pregnancy safety has not been established.

## scopolamine ophthalmic solution (Isopto Hyoscine)

The dose for scopolamine ophthalmic solution in adults for mydriasis for diagnostic procedures is 1 drop (0.25% solution) to conjunctiva as necessary. For uveitis, instill 1 drop (0.25% solution) to conjunctiva up to three times daily. In posterior synechiae, instill 1 drop (0.25% solution) to conjunctiva every minute for five doses. If necessary to enhance the mydriatic effect of this drug, instill 1 drop of 2.5% or 10% phenylephrine solution every minute for three doses. In preoperative and postoperative iridocyclitis, instill 1 drop (0.25% solution) to conjunctiva one to four times daily as necessary.

In children, for cycloplegic refraction, instill 1 drop (0.25% solution) to conjunctiva twice daily for 2 days before refraction. In children with uveitis, instill 1 drop (0.25% solution) to conjunctiva one to three times daily. Scopolamine is also used for treatment of preoperative and postoperative iridocyclitis and mydriasis in diagnostic procedures. See adult doses.

Pregnancy safety has not been established.

The adult dose for tropicamide ophthalmic solution (Mydriacyl) for cycloplegic refraction is to instill 1 drop (1% solution) to conjunctiva; repeat in 5 minutes. For fundus eye examination, instill 1 drop (0.5% solution) to conjunctiva approximately 15 to 20 minutes before examination. In children, for cycloplegic refraction, instill 1 drop (0.5% or 1% solution) to conjunctiva; repeat in 5 minutes. For fundus eye examination, see adult dose recommendations.

Pregnancy safety has not been established.

## Adrenergic (Sympathomimetic) Agents

Adrenergic agents mimic (direct acting) or potentiate (indirect acting) the action of epinephrine on the dilator muscle of the iris. Mydriasis and decreased congestion of conjunctival blood vessels are produced when these drugs are applied topically to the eye. Six adrenergic drugs are used in ophthalmology—epinephrine (see p. 723), phenylephrine, oxymetazoline, hydroxyamphetamine, naphazoline, and tetrahydrozoline.

Adrenergic drugs applied topically to the eye elicit the following sympathetic responses:

1. Mydriasis brought about by contraction of the radial or dilator muscle of the eye
2. Constriction of conjunctival blood vessels
3. Slight relaxation of the ciliary muscle
4. Decreased formation of aqueous humor and increased outflow with a resultant drop in intraocular pressure

Exactly how these effects are produced remains uncertain, but there is some evidence that alpha adrenergic receptors are present in the outflow mechanism of the eye. When stimulated, they increase outflow of aqueous humor. It has also been shown experimentally that vasoconstriction decreases the rate of aqueous humor formation.

Adrenergic drugs are used to treat wide-angle glaucoma and glaucoma secondary to uveitis, to produce mydriasis for ocular examination, and to relieve congestion and hyperemia. Adrenergic drugs are contraindicated in the treatment of narrow-angle glaucoma or abraded cornea since dilation of the pupil will further restrict ocular fluid outflow and this may cause an acute attack of glaucoma.

See discussion of pharmacokinetics of adrenergic agents in Chapter 21.

Serious systemic side effects from these drugs are unusual, but care must be taken in clients with cardiovascular disease, since tachycardia and elevated blood pressure can occur with these agents.

As with other sympathomimetic amines, the potential exists for drug interactions between these adrenergic drugs and monoamine oxidase inhibitors, creating exaggerated adrenergic effects. The potentiation of adrenergic pressor effects is increased with the use of the tricyclic antidepressants.

See Table 43-5 for trade names, duration of action, market availability, and strength and for dosage and administration.

Pregnancy safety for epinephrine, phenylephrine, and naphazoline is FDA category C; for others it is not established.

## ANTIINFECTIVE/ANTIINFLAMMATORY AGENTS

In treatment of ocular infections, the drug of choice and the dose required should be determined by laboratory isolation of the offending organism. The initial culture from the infected area is obtained before any antiinfective/antiinflammatory agent is applied. However, treatment is not withheld if the time required to make these determinations may cause increased severity of infection and if the type of infection (for example, most cases of conjunctivitis, which tend to be self-limiting) does not warrant the expense of laboratory analysis. Prophylactic use of antiinfective/antiinflammatory agents in general is useless, wasteful, and potentially dangerous. A large proportion of the inflammatory diseases seen in ophthalmology are caused by viruses or other agents that are not susceptible to any currently available antiinfective agents. Obviously, the use of these agents in such situations is unwarranted. Systemic medications that can induce ocular side effects need to be considered before introducing an antiinfective or antiinflammatory agent. Drugs that induce ocular side effects are listed in Table 43-6.

Most antiinfective agents do not readily penetrate the eye when applied. However, some drugs will penetrate the inflamed eye when the blood-aqueous barrier is decreased by injury or inflammation. Topically applied antiinfective agents can cause sensitivity reactions (stinging, itching, angioneurotic edema, urticaria, dermatitis). Individuals sensitized to one drug may show cross reactions to chemically related drugs. Topical application of antiinfective agents also interferes with the normal flora of the eye, which may encourage growth of other organisms.

Eye infections require prompt treatment to help prevent spread of infection. Severe infections may damage the eye and impair vision. Solutions are preferred for treatment of eye infections, since ointment bases often tend to interfere with healing.

### Antibacterials

#### Antibiotics

All systemic antibiotics are used at indicated times to treat external ocular and intraocular infections. To avoid possible sensitization to common systemic antiinfective drugs and to discourage development of resistant strains of offending organisms, the antibiotic of choice is not given systemically. Rather, these agents are administered topically, subconjunctivally, intrauveally, or intravenously.

Selection of an antibiotic for ocular infection is based on (1) clinical experience, (2) nature and sensitivity of the organisms most commonly causing the condition, (3) the disease itself, (4) sensitivity and response of the client, and (5) laboratory results.

Some of the common ocular infections treated with antibiotics include the following:

**conjunctivitis**—Acute inflammation of the conjunctiva (the mucous membrane lining the back of the lids and the front of the eye, except for the cornea) resulting from bacterial invasion or viral infection. It is a common sign in severe colds. "Pink eye" is the acute contagious epidemic form of conjunctivitis usually caused by *Haemo-*

**TABLE 43-6**   Ocular side effects induced by systemic medications

| Drug | Possible ocular side effect induced |
|---|---|
| allopurinol | Retinal hemorrhage, exudative lesions |
| aspirin | Allergic dermatitis including keratitis and conjunctivitis |
| barbiturates | Nystagmus |
| busulfan | Cataracts |
| cannabis, marijuana | Nystagmus, conjunctivitis, double vision |
| chloral hydrate | Eyelid edema, conjunctivitis, miosis |
| chloroquine | Lenticular and corneal opacity, retinopathy |
| clomiphene citrate | Blurred vision, light flashes |
| clinidine | Miosis |
| corticosteroids | Cataracts, increased intraocular pressure, papilledema |
| diazoxide | Oculogyric crisis |
| digitalis glycosides | Scotomas, optic neuritis |
| ethyl alcohol | Nystagmus |
| guanethidine | Miosis, ptosis, blurred vision |
| hydralazine | Lacrimation, blurred vision |
| ibuprofen | Altered color vision, blurred vision |
| indomethacin | Mydriasis, retinopathy |
| isoniazid | Optic neuritis |
| lithium carbonate | Exophthalmos |
| nitroglycerin | Transient elevations in intraocular pressure |
| opiates | Niosis, nystagmus |
| phenothiazines | Corneal and conjunctival deposits, cataracts, retinopathy, oculogyric crisis |
| phenytoin | Nystagmus |
| quinine | blurring of vision, optic neuritis, blindness (reversible) |
| thiazide diuretics | Acute transient myopia, yellow coloring of vision |
| vincristine | Ptosis, paresis of extraocular muscles |
| vitamin A overdose or toxicity | Papilledema, increased intraocular pressure |
| vitamin D toxicity | Calcium deposits in cornea |

*philus* organisms. Symptoms include redness and burning of the eye, lacrimation, itching, and at times photophobia. Conjunctivitis is usually self-limiting. The eye should be protected from light.

**hordeolum** (sty)—An acute localized infection of the eyelash follicles and the glands of the anterior lid margin, resulting in the formation of a small abscess or cyst.

**chalazion**—Infection of the meibomian (sebaceous) glands of the eyelids. A hard cyst may form from blockage of the ducts.

**blepharitis**—Inflammation of the margins of the eyelid resulting from bacterial infection or allergy. Symptoms are crusting, irritation of the eye, and red and edematous lid margins.

**keratitis**—Corneal inflammation caused by bacterial infection; herpes simplex keratitis is caused by viral infection.

**uveitis**—Infection of the uveal tract, or the vascular layer of the eye, which includes the iris, ciliary body, and choroid.

**endophthalmitis**—Inner eye structure inflammation caused by bacteria.

### bacitracin ophthalmic ointment (Baciguent)

Bacitracin is rarely used systemically because of its nephrotoxic effects. It is particularly useful in treating surface superficial infections caused by gram-positive bacteria (it inhibits protein synthesis). Bacitracin does penetrate the conjunctiva or the cornea slightly, but in therapeutic amounts it is nonirritating to the eye, is excreted in the nasolacrimal system, and produces no systemic effects.

A broader spectrum of antimicrobial activity is produced when bacitracin is used in combination with gramicidin, neomycin, and polymyxin (Neosporin, Neo-polycin) than when it is used alone. Bacitracin is preferable to neomycin for topical use, since fewer organisms are resistant to it, allergic reactions occur less frequently, and sensitization is avoided. It may impede corneal wound healing, and the ointment form will cause a temporary clouding or haze. Prolonged use may lead to overgrowth of nonsusceptible microorganisms.

Thimerosal and silver nitrate (both of which are heavy metals) will inactivate bacitracin; therefore concurrent use is not advisable. Ophthalmic bacitracin is available as an ointment containing 500 units/g of suitable base and as a powder containing 10,000 and 50,000 units for making solutions for topical use. Ointment is instilled into the lower conjunctival sac of the affected eye one to three times daily or more often. Ointment preparations are stable for about 1 year at room temperature.

### chloramphenicol ophthalmic solution/ointment (Chloroptic, Isopto Fenicol ✱)

A bacteriostatic, chloramphenicol prevents peptide bond formation and protein synthesis in a wide variety of gram-positive and gram-negative organisms. Thus it is an ex-

tremely useful drug for superficial intraocular infections.

Side effects are usually rare. Burning and stinging on instillation have been reported. Irreversible aplastic anemia has not been reported with this dosage form of chloramphenicol, although it would be prudent to monitor for blood dyscrasias. One must observe for symptoms of sore throat, elevated temperature, increased bleeding episodes, increased weakness, and indicative changes in the complete blood count.

When treating adults, apply a thin strip of ointment (1% solution) to the conjunctiva every 3 hours, or more often if necessary. Solution dose in adults is 1 drop into conjunctiva every 1 to 4 hours. Children's dosage is similar to that for adults.

Pregnancy safety has not been established.

▷**Nursing Management:**
**Chloramphenicol Ophthalmic Therapy**

Avoid prolonged (over 3 days) or frequent use. Chloramphenicol has been implicated in the development of aplas-

**TABLE 43-7**  Adverse systemic effects from ophthalmic drugs

| Ophthalmic drug | Reported adverse effect |
| --- | --- |
| **ANTIMICROBIAL AGENTS** | |
| chloramphenicol eye drops | Aplastic anemia |
| sulfacetamide eye drops | Stevens-Johnson syndrome, systemic lupus erythematosus |
| **ANTICHOLINERGIC DRUGS** | |
| atropine eye drops | Tachycardia, elevated temperature, fever, delirium |
| cyclopentolate | Convulsions, hallucinations |
| scopolamine eye drops | Acute psychosis |
| **ANTIGLAUCOMA MEDICATIONS** | |
| beta blocking agents (timolol) | Bradycardia, syncope, low blood pressure, asthmatic attack, congestive heart failure, hallucinations, loss of appetite, headaches, nausea, weakness, depression |
| anticholinesterase (echothiophate) | Asthmatic attack, systemic cholinergic effects |
| parasympathomimetic (pilocarpine) | Nausea, stomach pain, increased sweating, salivation, tremors, bradycardia, lightheadness |
| **SYMPATHOMIMETIC MEDICATIONS** | |
| phenylephrine (10%) | Severe hypertension, cerebral hemorrhage, dysrhythmias, myocardial infarction |
| epinephrine eyedrops | Tremors increased sweating, headaches, hypertension |

tic anemia after prolonged use; monitor CBCs. Monitor the client for pallor, sore throat and fever, unusual bleeding or bruising, and unusual tiredness, which may indicate irreversible bone marrow depression, associated with aplastic anemia. See Table 43-7 for systemic effects from a variety of ophthalmic agents.

### erythromycin ophthalmic ointment (Ilotycin)

Erythromycin ophthalmic ointment is a bacteriostatic agent, but in high concentrations against very susceptible organisms it may be bactericidal. It is indicated for the treatment of neonatal conjunctivitis caused by *Chlamydia trachomatis;* prevention of ophthalmia neonatorum (against *Neisseria gonorrhoeae* or *C. trachomatis*) and other ocular infections caused by susceptible organisms.

Eye irritation not present before therapy is the only rare, adverse reaction reported with this drug. The dose in adults and children for ocular infections is to apply a thin ointment strip to conjunctiva daily or more often, if necessary. The same dose is also used topically after cesarean or vaginal delivery for neonatal conjunctivitis or ophthalmia neonatorum.

Pregnancy safety has not been established.

### neomycin, polymyxin B sulfate, and bacitracin ophthalmic ointment (Mycitracin, Neosporin)

While all three agents have been or are available as single ophthalmic drugs, reports of sensitization to the individual drug have somewhat limited their usefulness. The combination dosage form provides a bactericidal effect against many gram-positive and gram-negative organisms. It is indicated for the treatment of superficial ocular infections caused by susceptible organisms. A small amount (cm) of ointment is usually applied to the conjunctiva every 3 to 4 hours.

### tetracycline hydrochloride ophthalmic ointment and suspension (Achromycin)
### chlortetracycline hydrochloride ophthalmic ointment (Aureomycin)

The tetracyclines are used topically to treat superficial infections of the cornea and conjunctiva. Generally they are bacteriostatic rather than bactericidal; they have a broad antimicrobial spectrum. Organisms resistant to one tetracycline are usually resistant to the others. Trachoma may be treated with both topical and oral tetracycline therapy for 60 days or more. The tetracyclines have been recommended for prophylaxis of gonorrheal ophthalmia neonatorum, since they produce a lower incidence of conjunctivitis and less irritation of the eye than does silver nitrate. Topical tetracyclines rarely cause adverse reactions.

### *Aminoglycosides*
### gentamicin sulfate (Garamycin, Genoptic)

Gentamicin is effective against a wide variety of gram-negative and gram-positive organisms. It is particularly use-

ful against *Pseudomonas, Proteus,* and *Klebsiella* organisms and *Escherichia coli,* as well as staphylococci and streptococci that have developed resistance to other antibiotics. It is applied as an ointment two or three times daily, or 1 drop of solution is applied every 4 to 8 hours.

### tobramycin (Tobrex)

This water-soluble aminoglycoside is used topically on a wide variety of culture-verified gram-positive and gram-negative external ophthalmic pathogens. It is particularly valuable for treating gentamicin-resistant infections. Among the pathogens affected by the aminoglycoside are the staphylococci, streptococci, *Pseudomonas, Escherichia coli, Klebsiella, Enterobacter, Proteus, Haemophilus influenzae, Moraxella, Acinetobacter,* and some *Neisseria.* Adverse reactions include ocular toxicity and hypersensitivity including lid itching, swelling, and conjunctival erythema. When topical aminoglycosides are used concurrently with systemic aminoglycosides, the total serum concentration will be affected and should be monitored. Systemic toxicity from absorption may occur from excessive use.

The dose for mild to moderate infection is 2 drops in the affected eye every 4 hours. For severe infections 2 drops are instilled hourly in the eye until improvement is seen, and then the dose is reduced before the drops are discontinued.

### *Sulfonamides*
### sulfacetamide sodium ophthalmic ointment/ solution (Bleph-10, Sulamyd)
### sulfisoxazole ophthalmic ointment and solution (Gantrisin)

These bacteriostatic antiinfective agents block the synthesis of folic acid in susceptible bacterial organisms. Their effectiveness is antagonized by the presence of para-aminobenzoic acid (PABA) or its derivatives procaine and tetracaine.

The presence of purulent drainage or exudate interferes with the action of the sulfonamides, since the purulent matter contains para-aminobenzoic acid. Any lid exudate should be removed before instillation of the drugs.

Since the activity of sulfacetamide may be inhibited by concurrent administration of ophthalmic anesthetics, the drugs are applied 30 to 60 minutes apart. They are physically incompatible with thimerosal and silver preparations.

Before administration the client should check to see that the solution has not darkened in color; if so, discard it. Solutions are instilled 1 drop every 1 or 2 hours initially, with increased time intervals based on response. Instillation of the drops may cause some mild pain and discomfort. The ointments are applied one to three times a day and at bedtime.

Sulfisoxazole is available in 4% ophthalmic solution and a 4% ophthalmic ointment. It is applied topically to the conjunctiva three or more times daily.

Sulfacetamide is available as a 10% ointment or a 10%,

15%, or 30% solution. It is preferred over other sulfa drugs used systemically. It may cause local irritation. Intraocular penetration is variable.

## Antifungal Agents

### natamycin ophthalmic suspension (Natacyn)

Natamycin is used in treatment of fungal blepharitis, fungal conjunctivitis, and fungal keratitis. By binding to steroids in the cell membrane of the fungus, natamycin produces an altered membrane permeability and causes loss of the cellular constituents. It is mainly retained in the conjunctival area; significant drug levels in the ocular fluids are not usually achieved. It is not systemically absorbed. Natamycin may cause irritation of the eye. One drop of the 5% solution is instilled into the conjunctiva every 1 to 2 hours initially. The dose is gradually tapered to 1 drop every 3 or 4 hours after the first 3 to 4 days of therapy.

## Antiviral Agents

Three antiviral ophthalmic preparations are on the market: idoxuridine, trifluridine, and vidarabine.

### idoxuridine ophthalmic ointment/solution (Stoxil, Herplex)

Idoxuridine resembles thymidine, a substance necessary for viral DNA; thus it replaces it and inhibits the replication of the viral DNA. It is indicated for the treatment of herpes simplex virus keratitis. These preparations may increase flow of tears from the eye. Notify the physician if client reports photosensitivity, blurred vision or visual disturbances, or eye irritations that were not present before therapy.

Adult dose of idoxuridine solution for treatment of herpes simplex virus keratitis is 1 drop hourly during waking hours and every 2 hours during the night or 1 drop every minute for five doses. Repeat this dosage schedule every 4 hours day and night. When improvement is seen, dosage may be decreased to 1 drop every 2 hours during waking hours and every 4 hours during the night. For ointment, apply a thin strip every 4 hours (five times daily) during waking hours. For children, see adult dosage.

Pregnancy safety has not been established.

### trifluridine ophthalmic solution (Viroptic)

For mechanism of action and indications, see idoxuridine. In addition, it is used to treat herpes simplex virus keratoconjunctivitis.

Frequent but usually not troublesome side effects include burning or stinging of the eyes. Refer to a physician if these rare symptoms occur: hypersensitivity reaction, evidenced by redness, swelling, or eye irritation not present before therapy.

When using trifluridine in adults, instill 1 drop (1% solution) into conjunctiva every 2 hours during waking hours.

Maximum daily dose is 9 drops. Continue therapy until cornea has recovered. Then reduce dosage to 1 drop every 4 hours during waking hours (minimum of 5 drops per day) for 1 week.

Pregnancy safety has not been established.

### vidarabine ophthalmic ointment (Vira-A)

The antiviral mechanism of action is not established for this agent, but it appears to interfere with early steps of viral DNA synthesis. Activity is directed against herpes simplex (types 1 and 2), varicella-zoster, and vaccinia viruses. An epithelial defect in the cornea permits trace amounts of the parent and metabolite to be found in the aqueous humor. Generally, systemic absorption is not expected after ocular administration. It is indicated for the treatment of herpes simplex virus keratitis and keratoconjunctivitis.

Increased tear flow and a sensation of something being in the eye have been reported as side effects. Notify the physician if client has photosensitivity, redness, eye swelling, or increased eye irritation not present before treatment.

Apply a thin ointment strip to conjunctiva every 3 hours five times daily when treating adults. Continue therapy until cornea is completely reepithelialized. Then decrease dosage to twice daily for 7 to 10 days.

Pregnancy safety has been established at FDA category C.

## Antiseptics

Many antiseptics used to treat surface infections of the eye before the advent of antibiotics are now obsolete. Not only were many of these drugs relatively ineffective, they also delayed healing and in some cases caused permanent damage to the eye. Antiseptic solutions are employed in ophthalmology for irrigation, dissolution of secretions, and precipitation of mucus and in certain instances in which specific antimicrobial agents cannot be used. A 2.2% boric acid solution is used as an irrigant; this concentration is thought to be isotonic with tear fluid.

Inorganic mercuric salts such as yellow mercuric oxide ophthalmic ointment (1% to 2%), thimerosal (Merthiolate), and ammoniated mercury formerly served as bacteriostatic agents. Today they are seldom used, since they do not completely sterilize, spores are resistant to them, and they are irritating to the eye.

### silver nitrate

Two drops of a solution of 1% silver nitrate in each eye is routinely employed immediately after birth as a prophylaxis against gonorrheal ophthalmia neonatorum. In many states this is required by law. The gonococci are particularly susceptible to silver salts. Liberated silver ions precipitate bacterial proteins. Silver nitrate is preferred to effective antibiotic agents, since these may sensitize the client and silver nitrate has stood the test of time. Inactivation by bacitracin can occur. Silver nitrate ophthalmic solution is available in collapsible capsules containing about 5 drops of a 1% solution. The solution should be in contact with the conjunctival sac for not less than 30 seconds to produce a mild chemical conjunctivitis. Irrigation following use is not recommended.

## Corticosteroids

Many corticosteroids are available for ophthalmic use as topical solutions, suspensions, or ointments. They include betamethasone (Betnesol), dexamethasone (Maxidex, Decadron), fluorometholone (FML S.O.P., FML), hydrocortisone (Cortamed), medrysone (HMS Liquifilm), and prednisolone (Pred-Forte, Predair-A). These are available in varying strengths and in combination with various antibiotics or mydriatics. They are indicated for the treatment of allergic and inflammatory ophthalmic disorders of the conjunctiva, cornea, and anterior segment of the eye.

Burning or eye watering rarely occurs and is not generally bothersome. Physician intervention is usually necessary when blurred vision or visual disturbances, eye pain, headaches, ptosis, or enlarged pupils occur. For dosage and administration, see USP-DI or current package inserts for dosing information.

Pregnancy safety for prednisolone, fluorometholone, and medrysone has been established as FDA category C; for others, pregnancy safety has not been established.

▷Nursing Management:
**Ophthalmic Corticosteroid Therapy**

*Assessment.* Ophthalmic corticosteroid therapy is not used for pyogenic (pus-producing) inflammations of the eye, since corticosteroids decrease defense mechanisms and reduce resistance to pathogenic organisms.

Corticosteroid therapy is not recommended for minor corneal abrasions. Steroids may actually increase ocular susceptibility to fungal infection. When steroids are used for various eye conditions, they should be used for a limited time only and the eye should be checked for increased intraocular pressure.

Corticosteroids may diminish the resistance to infection and may also mask the allergic reactions or hypersensitivity reactions to other drugs.

*Intervention.* The glucocorticoids used in ophthalmology may be applied topically, injected into the conjunctiva, or given systemically to diminish leukocyte infiltration where inflammation exists.

*Education.* Instruct the client to shake the ophthalmic suspensions well before use for adequate dispersion of the active ingredients. The use of contact lenses should be avoided during and for some time after corticosteroid therapy because of the risk of infection. Caution the client not to stop the medication without consulting the physician.

Inflammation recrudescence secondary to abrupt cessation of ophthalmic steroid administration may be overcome by dose frequency reduction (from every 3 hours, to every 6 hours, to 3 times daily, to twice daily, to once daily, and to every other day) or by decreasing the percentage strengths and using the above schedule.

*Evaluation.* Periodic examination by a physician by tonometry and slit-lamp examination should be performed to monitor client progress.

## TOPICAL ANESTHETIC AGENTS

Local anesthetics stabilize neuronal membranes so that they become less permeable to ions; this prevents initiation and transmission of nerve impulses. It is theorized that sodium ion permeability is limited by these agents.

Local anesthetics are used to prevent pain (deep anesthesia) during surgical procedures (removal of sutures and foreign bodies) and tonometry examinations. The local anesthetics have rapid onset (within 20 seconds) and last for 15 to 20 minutes.

### proparacaine hydrochloride (Ophthaine, Ophthetic)

Proparacaine is similar to tetracaine. A 0.5% solution is administered by topical instillation. Anesthesia is produced within 20 seconds and lasts for 15 minutes. It is relatively free from the burning and discomfort of other anesthetics, but it is highly toxic if it enters the systemic circulation. Allergic contact dermatitis, softening and erosion of corneal epithelium, pupillary dilation, cycloplegia, conjunctival congestion and hemorrhage, and stromal edema have been reported.

### tetracaine hydrochloride (Pontocaine)

Tetracaine is used topically in a 0.5% ointment and solution for rapid, brief, superficial anesthesia. It is a widely used local ocular anesthetic. One to two drops of a 0.5% solution of tetracaine will produce anesthesia within 30 seconds; the client may feel a burning or stinging sensation. The anesthetic effect lasts for 10 to 25 minutes. Tetracaine can cause epithelial damage and systemic toxicity; therefore it is not recommended for prolonged home use by clients. It is physically incompatible with the mercury or silver salts often found in ophthalmic products.

▷NURSING MANAGEMENT:
**TOPICAL ANESTHETIC AGENTS**

The practice of repeatedly applying such an anesthetic to an eye after removal of a foreign body is to be condemned. Besides delaying wound healing, this can produce sensitivity, permanent corneal opacification, visual loss, or perforation of the cornea.

Question the client about past experiences with anesthetics to determine if a hypersensitivity reaction occurred. Those local anesthetics that produce systemic toxicity are manifested as central nervous system excitation followed by CNS and cardiovascular depression. Patching the anesthetized eye is prudent, since the blink reflex is lost and protection of the cornea from debris and irritants is then needed. The client should be instructed not to touch or rub the eye until the anesthesia has worn off to prevent damage to the eye.

## OTHER OPHTHALMIC PREPARATIONS
### Artificial Tear Solutions and Lubricants

Lubricants or artificial tears are used to provide moisture and lubrication in diseases in which tear production is deficient, to lubricate artificial eyes and moisten contact lenses, to remove debris, and to protect the cornea during procedures on the eye. These agents are also incorporated into ophthalmic preparations to prolong the contact time of topically applied drugs.

Such products have a balanced salt solution (equivalent to 0.9% sodium chloride), buffers to adjust pH, highly viscous agents (methylcellulose, propylene glycol, gelatin, dextran, and others) to extend eye contact time, and preservatives to maintain sterility. These products are usually administered three or four times a day.

An artificial tear insert (Lacrisert) was devised to extend the effect of the preparation. It is usually inserted daily or at most twice a day for selected clients.

Ointment preparations are also used as ocular lubricants. They will help protect the eye (such as during and following eye surgery) and lubricate the eye. They are particularly valuable for clients with an impaired blink reflex and nighttime use. Examples include Lacri-Lube, Duratears, and Hypo Tears.

### Antiallergic Agents
#### cromolyn sodium (Opticrom)

Cromolyn sodium inhibits degranulation of sensitized mast cells occurring after exposure to a specific antigen. This mast cell release inhibition prevents the mediators of inflammation (histamine and slow-releasing substance of anaphylaxis) from producing their characteristic effects. The drug is used for allergic eye disorders (vernal and allergic keratoconjunctivitis, papillary conjunctivitis, keratitis) that have symptoms of itching, tearing, redness, and discharge. Absorption is 0.03% from the eye.

Stinging and burning of eyes may occur as a side effect. Concomitant corticosteroids may be necessary.

In adults and children (over 4 years old), instill 1 drop in each affected eye four to six times a day at regular intervals.

Pregnancy safety has been established at FDA category B.

### ▷ Nursing Management:
### Cromolyn Sodium Therapy

Assess the client for itching, tearing, redness, and discharge from eyes.

Refrigerate drug, keep out of direct sunlight, and discard unused portion after 4 weeks. Remind client to remove soft contact lenses before the first instillation of drops and resume wearing them only after drug discontinuation. Note that signs and symptoms of relief will appear within days but that treatment at regular intervals for as long as 6 weeks may be required.

### Diagnostic Aids
#### fluorescein sodium (AK-Fluor, Fluorescite, Ful-Glo, Fluor-I-Strip, etc.)

Fluorescein is a nontoxic water-soluble dye that is used as a diagnostic aid. When applied to the cornea, it stains corneal lesions or ulcers a bright green; foreign bodies appear surrounded by a green ring. These effects permit detection of corneal epithelial defects caused by injury or infection and location of foreign bodies in the eye. The dye is also used in fitting hard contact lenses. Areas that lack fluorescein-stained tears will appear black under ultraviolet light, indicating the contact lens is touching the cornea at those areas. Fluorescein is used in retinal photography to determine retinal vascular status and to identify defects in the retinal pigment epithelium. In addition, it may be used to test lacrimal apparatus patency; if after the dye is instilled into the eye it appears in the nasal secretions, the nasolacrimal drainage system is open.

Injection is used in ophthalmic angiography to examine the fundus, vasculature of the iris, and aqueous flow, to make differential diagnosis of cancerous and noncancerous tumors, and to determine time for circulation in the eye.

Nausea, headache, abdominal distress, vomiting, hypotension, hypersensitivity reactions, and anaphylaxis have been reported following injection.

Topical solution is used to detect foreign bodies and corneal abrasions; instill 1 or 2 drops of 2% solution. For strip application and injection, check a current drug reference for instructions.

### Enzyme Preparation
#### chymotrypsin (Alpha Chymar, Catarase)

This proteolytic enzyme is used in selected cases to facilitate cataract extraction. It is injected behind the iris into the posterior chamber where it dissolves the filaments or zonules that hold the lens, thereby facilitating intracapsular lens extraction. This effect is usually obtained in 1 to 2 minutes with 0.2 to 0.5 ml of a freshly prepared 1:5000 solution. Chymotrypsin may cause a transient postoperative glaucoma lasting about 1 week, which can be relieved by the use of pilocarpine. Acids, alcohol, alkalies, antiseptics, blood, detergents, and serum inactivate this enzyme. It is inhibited by chloramphenicol and isoflurophate. Epinephrine inactivates it in 1 hour.

It is available in ampules containing 150, 300, or 750 units (proteolytic activity) in lyophilized enzyme dissolved in 2 to 10 ml of diluent.

### Hyperosmolar Preparation
**sodium chloride ointment (Muro-128) and solution (Adsorbonac)**

This 5% ointment and 2% or 5% solution are used to reduce the corneal edema that occurs in certain corneal dystrophies and after cataract extraction. It is also used as an aid in **gonioscopy** (examination of the angle of the anterior chamber of the eye), funduscopy, and biomicroscopy. The dose is 1 to 2 drops in affected eye(s) every 3 to 4 hours as directed. The ointment is applied once a day.

### Nonsteroidal Antiinflammatory Agent
**flurbiprofen sodium (Ocufen)**

Fluribiprofen is a topical nonsteroidal antiinflammatory agent used to inhibit intraoperative miosis. Minor symptoms of transient burning and stinging may occur on instillation into the eye. Systemic absorption is possible, so the nurse should monitor for increased bleeding tendencies. Concurrent administration of acetylcholine and carbachol is avoided, since both drugs may be ineffective if used in clients receiving flurbiprofen. One drop (0.03% solution) is instilled every 30 minutes starting 2 hours before surgery. Maximum dosage is 4 drops.

Pregnancy safety has been established at FDA category C.

### Ophthalmic Surgery Aids
**sodium hyaluronate (Healon, Amuisc)**

Sodium hyaluronate, a purified viscoelastic gel, is used during anterior segment and vitreous procedures in cataract surgery (intracapsular and extracapsular). During intraocular lens implantation it is used to coat the instruments and the lens before insertion. A dose of 0.5 ml in the anterior chamber before insertion of the new lens delivery protects the corneal endothelium from damage when a cataractous lens is being removed. Other indications include glaucoma filtration surgery and corneal transplant surgery. Sodium hyaluronate is also used as a vitreous replacement after retinal detachment surgery and vitrectomy.

### Irrigating Solutions

The sterile isotonic external irrigating solutions are used in tonometry, fluorescein procedures, and removal of foreign material, and to cleanse and soothe eyes of patients wearing hard contact lenses. These external products do not require a prescription and are available in drops, irrigations, and eyewashes. Examples of irrigating solutions include BSS Plus, Surgisol, and Lavoptik Eye Wash.

## SUMMARY

Although there are myriad ophthalmic preparations, the drugs to treat eye disorders can be divided into three major groups: the antiglaucoma agents, the mydriatics and cycloplegics, and the antiinfective/antiinflammatory agents. Antiglaucoma agents may be miotics. These cause pupillary constriction by direct action (cholinergic) to minimize the effects of acetylcholine at autonomic synapses or the neuroeffector junction of the parasympathetic nervous system, or by indirect action (anticholinesterase), inactivating the enzyme cholinesterase by preventing hydrolysis of acetylcholine. Antiglaucoma drugs may also be sympathomimetic agents that decrease aqueous humor production (beta adrenergic effect) and increase its outflow (alpha adrenergic effect). Beta adrenergic blocking agents, carbonic anhydrase inhibitor agents, and osmotic agents are also used in the treatment of glaucoma.

Mydriatic and cycloplegic agents used for ophthalmic disorders are topically applied autonomic drugs that cause dilation of the pupils (mydriasis) and paralysis of accommodation (cycloplegia). In addition to being used for specific treatment of ophthalmic disorders, they are also used during eye examinations and in preparation of the client for intraocular surgery.

Antiinfective/antiinflammatory agents used in the treatment of ocular infections may be antibacterial, antifungal, and antiviral agents, as well as corticosteroids.

The role of the nurse in the clinical management of the client receiving ophthalmic drugs focuses on the safe administration and the preparation of the client for self-administration of such drugs.

## BIBLIOGRAPHY

Abramowicz M, ed. (1982). Adverse systemic effects from ophthalmic drugs, Med Lett 24(610):53.

Cascella PJ. (1987). Topical administration of eye medications, US Pharmacist 12(3):54.

Donnelly D. (1987). Instilling eyedrops: difficulties experienced by patients following cataract surgery, J Adv Nurs 12(2):235.

Goldstein J. (1987). Pharmacology of ophthalmic drugs, Part II: antiinflammatory and antiinfective agents, J Ophth Nurs Technol 6(5):193.

Goldstein J. (1987). Pharmacology of ophthalmic drugs, Part III: ocular decongestants, ocular lubricants and miscellaneous agent, J Ophth Nurs Technol 6(6):238.

Hahn K. (1989). Administering eye medications, Nursing 19(9):80.

Kastrup EK, ed. (1991). Facts and comparisons. St Louis: JB Lippincott Co.

Osis M. (1987). Drugs and vision: unexplained symptoms—are they due to eye medications? Gerontion 2(1):14.

Smith S. (1987). How drugs act: drugs and the eye, Gerontion 2(1):14.

United States Pharmacopeial Convention. (1991). Drug information for the health care professional, ed 11. Rockville, Md: The Convention.

Weintraub M and Evans P. (1985). Pilocarpine: the method is the message, Hosp Formul 20(2):177.

Wuest JR. (1987). Advising consumers on eye preparations, Part II: OTC drugs for use in the eye, Fla Pharm J 51(11):10.

# Chapter

 *44* Overview of the Ear

## CHAPTER OBJECTIVES

*After studying this chapter, you should be able to meet the following objectives and define the key terms.*

1. Differentiate between the external, middle, and inner ear.

2. Name the three bones of the inner ear.

3. Describe the function of the eustachian tube.

4. List common ear disorders.

## KEY TERMS

**auditory ossicles,** page 738

**cochlea,** page 738

**eustachian tube,** page 738

**external ear,** page 738

**inner ear,** page 738

**middle ear,** page 738

**otitis media,** page 739

**tympanic membrane,** page 738

## ANATOMY AND PHYSIOLOGY

The ear consists of three sections or parts: external ear, middle ear, and inner ear (see Figure 44-1).

The **external ear** has two divisions, the outer ear, or pinna, and the external auditory canal. The external auditory canal leads to the eardrum, or **tympanic membrane,** a thin transparent partition of tissue between the canal and the middle ear. The function of the external ear is to receive and transmit auditory sounds to the eardrum. The eardrum protects the middle ear from foreign substances and transmits sound to the bones of the middle ear.

The **middle ear** is an air-filled cavity that contains three small bones called the **auditory ossicles.** The ossicles are the malleus (hammer), incus (anvil), and stapes (stirrup). The tip of the malleus is attached to the surface of the tympanic membrane. Its head is attached to the incus, which in turn is attached to the stapes. The ossicles amplify and transmit sound waves to the inner ear. The middle ear is also directly connected to the nasopharynx by the **eustachian** (auditory) **tube.** The eustachian tube is usually collapsed except when the individual swallows, chews, yawns, or moves the jaw. This tube equalizes air pressure on both sides of the eardrum, to prevent the eardrum from rupturing. On airline flights pressure changes are relieved by action of the eustachian tube when the individual chews gum, yawns, or swallows deliberately.

The **inner ear,** also referred to as the labyrinth because of its series of canals, has two main divisions. The bony labyrinth consists of the vestibule, cochlea, and semicircular canals, and the membranous labyrinth consists of a series of sacs and tubes within the bony labyrinth. The **cochlea** is the primary organ of hearing, and the vestibular apparatus is necessary to maintain equilibrium and balance. (See Figure 44-1.)

738

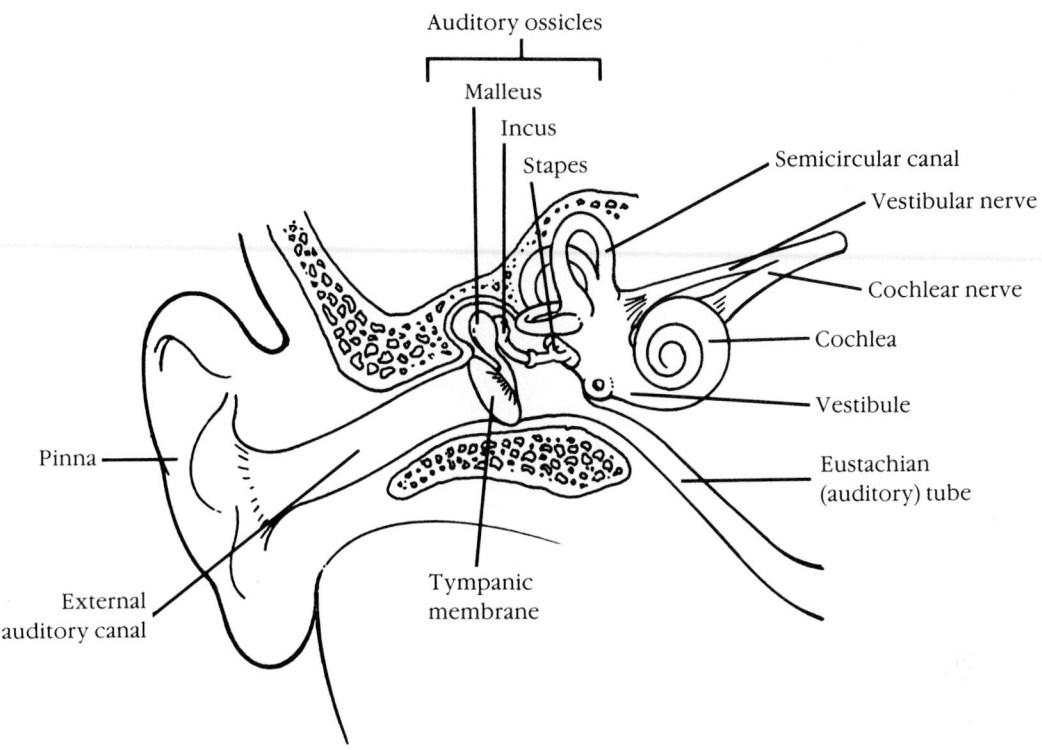

**FIGURE 44-1** Anatomy of the ear.

## COMMON EAR DISORDERS

The most common ear disorders include infections of the ear (bacterial or fungal), earwax accumulation, and various other painful or distressing conditions. Many ear disorders are minor and easily treated or are self-limiting. Persistent pain or ear problems should be professionally evaluated since some untreated disorders can lead to hearing loss.

External ear disorders usually include trauma, such as lacerations or scrapes to the skin. These are often minor and heal with time. If the injury results in bleeding and perhaps a hematoma, a physician referral is necessary. Localized infections of the hair follicles resulting in boils may occur. Clients with recurring boils and small boils that do not respond to good hygiene and topical compresses should be referred to a physician for evaluation and possibly systemic antibiotics.

Dermatitis of the ear, itching, local redness, weeping, or drainage are also reported. Such conditions must be individually evaluated, since the causes can vary from inflammation induced by seborrhea, psoriasis, or contact dermatitis to head trauma producing ear discharge. Self-medication should be discouraged when infection is suspected or in the presence of known injuries of the ear or whenever drainage, pain, and dizziness are present.

Middle ear disorders are never treated with OTC medications. Most commonly reported problems are infections of the middle ear, such as **otitis media.** This most often occurs in children, although with adults chronic otitis media may be caused by a nasopharyngeal tumor. Pain, fever, malaise, pressure, a sensation of fullness in the ear and hearing loss are common symptoms. Clients with such conditions should be treated promptly by a physician. Acute tympanic membrane perforation from foreign objects or from water sports (such as diving or water skiing) will result in a multitude of symptoms, if untreated. Pain at the time of injury that subsides, a diminished hearing acuity, tinnitus, nausea, vertigo, and otitis media or mastoiditis may be noted. A physician's examination is vital when a perforated tympanic membrane is suspected.

Loss of hearing, especially unilateral hearing loss, may result from viral infection of the inner ear. Hearing deficits may be caused by genetic diseases or slowly progressive diseases such as otosclerosis or Meniere's disease. Untreated external and middle ear infections may also affect hearing and the functioning of the inner ear.

## BIBLIOGRAPHY

Anthony CP and Thibodeau GA. (1990). Textbook of anatomy and physiology, ed 13. St Louis: Times Mirror/Mosby College Publishing.

Guyton AC. (1987). Human physiology and mechanisms of disease, ed 4. Philadelphia: WB Saunders Co.

*Chapter*

# 45 Auditory Drugs

## CHAPTER OBJECTIVES

*After studying this chapter, you should be able to meet the following objectives and define the key terms.*

1. List drugs commonly used to treat ear infections.

2. Discuss the various preparations used to treat ear ailments.

3. List five drugs reported to cause ototoxicity.

4. Apply appropriate nursing management for the care of the client receiving drugs affecting the ear.

## KEY TERMS

**ototoxicity,** page 743

**tinnitus,** page 743

**vertigo,** page 743

## INTRODUCTION

Drugs used to treat ear ailments or infections include antibiotic solutions, steroid and antibiotic combinations, and miscellaneous preparations such as wax emulsifiers, antibacterials, antifungals, local anesthetics, antiinflammatory and local analgesic-type preparations. Such preparations are useful for minor problems with the external ear canal. The potent systemic medications that may adversely affect the client's hearing and/or balance are also reviewed.

## ANTIBIOTIC EAR PREPARATIONS

Chloramphenicol (Chloromycetin Otic, Pentamycetin ✿) is a broad-spectrum antibiotic (bacteriostatic) solution used to treat infections of the external auditory canal surface. Organisms susceptible to chloramphenicol usually include *Staphylococcus aureus, Escherichia coli, Pseudomonas aeruginosa, Enterobacter aerogenes, Haemophilus influenzae,* and others. However, if the client has an inner ear infection, systemic antibiotics would be indicated.

The possible side effects produced by chloramphenicol are burning, redness, rash, swelling, or other signs of topical irritation that were not present before the start of therapy. These would indicate a hypersensitivity reaction. Usual dosage for adults and children is 2 or 3 drops inserted in the ear canal every 6 to 8 hours.

Gentamicin sulfate otic solution (Geramycin) is a bactericidal antibiotic, another antibiotic that is not presently available in the otic preparation in the United States. Although not FDA approved, physicians sometimes use the ophthalmic preparation marketed in the United States for otic infections.

## STEROID AND ANTIBIOTIC COMBINATIONS

The steroid hydrocortisone is most commonly combined with antibiotics, such as neomycin sulfate and polymyxin

740

B sulfate, for treatment of superficial bacterial infections in the external auditory canal. Hydrocortisone is included for its antiinflammatory, antipruritic, and antiallergic effects. The antibiotics are used primarily for their antibacterial action. These products also may be used to treat mastoidectomy cavity infections caused by susceptible organisms, including *S. aureus, P. aeruginosa, E. coli, Klebsiella* species, and others. See Table 45-1 for examples of steroid and antibiotic combinations.

## MISCELLANEOUS PREPARATIONS

A wide variety of both single and combination products is used to treat ear wax, inflammation, bacterial or fungal infections, ear pain, and other minor or superficial problems associated primarily with the external ear canal. More serious problems such as an earache secondary to an upper respiratory tract infection, ear discharge or drainage, persistent or recurrent otitis, or ear pain caused by recent injury or head trauma require a physician's thorough evaluation and intervention to prevent complications. In such cases systemic medications with or without ear preparations are usually necessary.

Although most OTC otic preparations are considered safe and effective, health care professionals should advise clients to see a physician if symptoms do not improve within several days of using these preparations or if an adverse reaction occurs. Tables 45-2 and 45-3 demonstrate common uses.

**TABLE 45-1** Steroid and antibiotic otic preparations

| Ingredients | Trade name |
| --- | --- |
| Solution of hydrocortisone 1%, 5 mg neomycin sulfate, and 10,000 units of polymyxin B sulfate/ml | Cortisporin Otic Otocort |
| Solution of hydrocortisone 0.5% and 10,000 units of polymyxin B sulfate/ml | Otobiotic Otic Pyocidin Otic |
| Suspension of hydrocortisone 1%, 5 mg neomycin sulfate, and 10,000 units of polymyxin B sulfate/ml | Cortisporin Otic Otocort |
| Suspension of hydrocortisone acetate 1%, 3.3 mg neomycin, and 3 mg colistin/ml | Coly-Mycin S Otic |

**TABLE 45-2** Over-the-counter ear preparations

| Ingredients | Use |
| --- | --- |
| boric acid 2.75% in isopropyl alcohol (Aurocaine 2, Ear Dry, Swim Ear) | Antibacterial preparation, commonly used after bathing or swimming to prevent excessive water accumulation and infection |
| chloroxylenol and acetic acid with benzalkonium chloride and glycerin (Aurinol Ear Drops, Benzodyne Drops, Halogen Ear Drops) | Antibacterial, antifungal, in an acid medium. Increasing acidity of external auditory canal results in an undesirable site for bacteria growth, especially *Pseudomonas* |
| solution of 10% triethanolamine with 0.5% chlorobutanol in propylene glycol Cerumenex Drops | Agent to emulsify and aid in removal of ear wax |
| solution of 2% acetic acid in aluminum acetate solution (Borofair Otic, BurOtic, Otic Domeboro) | Antibacterial or antifungal in acid medium |

**TABLE 45-3** Miscellaneous prescription otic preparations

| Ingredients | Use |
| --- | --- |
| Solution of 1% hydrocortisone, 1% pramoxine, and 0.1% chloroxylenol; also propylene glycol, acetic acid, and benzalkonium (Ear-Eze, Otic-HC Ear Drops, Tega-Otic) | Antibacterial, antifungal, local anesthetic, antiinflammatory products |
| Solution of 1% hydrocortisone, 2% acetic acid, 3% propylene glycol diacetate, and 0.02% benzethonium chloride (VoSol HC Otic) | Antiinflammatory, antibacterial, or antifungal in an acid medium |
| Solution of 1.4% benzocaine, 5.4% antipyrine, glycerin, and oxyquinoline sulfate (Allergen Ear Drops, Auralgan Otic, Auromid) | Local anesthetic, analgesic, emollient |
| 6.5% carbamine peroxide in glycerin and/or propylene glycol (Debrox Drops, Murine Ear Drops, Auro Ear Drops) | Treatment of ear wax |

## ▷NURSING MANAGEMENT: DRUGS AFFECTING THE EAR

*Assessment.* Before initiation of therapy, assess hearing and extent of symptoms (earache, pain, erythema, vertigo, drainage, and others) that may be present. Before the instillation of ear drops, assess that the ear canal is clear and not impacted with cerumen.

To identify areas for education, assess client for improper hygiene or health practices that may contribute to the development of infections.

*Intervention.* Ear drops are more comfortably tolerated if they are warmed (if not contraindicated) before instillation. This can be achieved by running warm water over the side of the bottle without the label or immersing the bottle in warm water in a medicine cup. Even carrying the bottle in a pocket for half an hour or so will take the chill off the drops.

To prepare for the instillation of ear drops cleanse any drainage present from the ear and position the client so that the ear to be medicated is facing upward.

The instillation of ear drops requires a knowledge of anatomic structure across the life span, since the shape of the auditory canal of a young child is different from that of an adult. In children 3 years of age or younger, gently pull the pinna of the ear slightly down and back to instill eardrops. In older children and adults, hold the pinna up and back. Gentle massage of the area immediately anterior to the ear will facilitate the entry of the drops into the ear canal. See Chapter 6 for illustration.

*Education.* Instruct the client to remain on his side for 5 minutes. A small cotton pledget may be gently inserted into the ear canal, if desired. Alert the client to the hazard

**TABLE 45-4** Potential ototoxic effects of aminoglycoside

| Drug | Cochlear | Vestibular |
|------|----------|------------|
| amikacin | + + | + |
| gentamicin | + | + + |
| kanamycin | + + + | + |
| neomycin | + + + + | + |
| netilmicin | + | + + |
| sisomicin | + | + |
| streptomycin | + | + + + |

From Knoben JE and Anderson PO: Handbook of clinical drug data, ed 6, Hamilton, Ill, 1988, Drug Intelligence Publications, Inc.
+ , low potential; + + + + , greatest potential

**TABLE 45-5** Selected drugs reported to cause ototoxicity

| Drug | Comments |
|------|----------|
| **Antibiotics** | |
| aminoglycosides | See Table 48-4 |
| erythromycin lactobionate IV | When administered in high doses (4 g/day), hearing loss (usually reversible) has been reported. |
| minocycline (Minocin) | Vestibular toxicity including dizziness, lightheadedness, and ataxia reported. Studies indicate that women are more susceptible than men. Toxicity is reversible if drug is stopped. |
| vanomycin (Vancocin) | Tinnitus usually precedes hearing loss, which may be either transient or permanent. This drug appears to affect the auditory portion of the eighth cranial nerve. It should not be given concurrently with other known ototoxic medications. |
| **Diuretics** | |
| ethacrynic acid (Edecrin) and furosemide (Lasix) | Both transient and permanent hearing loss have been reported with high-dose, parenteral administration. Concurrent administration with other ototoxic drugs may increase the potential for hearing loss. |
| **Cardiac drugs** | |
| quinidine | Tinnitus, vertigo, and transient hearing loss have been reported with this drug. Irreversible hearing loss is rare. |
| **Analgesics** | |
| NSAIDs, aspirin | Salicylates, especially in high doses, can cause tinnitus, vertigo, and hearing loss. Generally it is considered reversible if drug is reduced or discontinued, although some cases of irreversible hearing loss are documented. |
| indomethacin (Indocin), ibuprofen (Motrin), others | NSAIDs have reportedly caused tinnitus, vertigo, and transient hearing loss. |
| **Antineoplastic agents** | |
| bleomycin, cisplatin, dactinomycin, mechlorethamine | Ototoxicity is reported when these drugs are given in high dosages, especially in persons with renal impairment or those receiving other ototoxic drugs. Tinnitus, vertigo, and transient high tone deafness have been documented. These effects may be reversible or irreversible. |

of impaired hearing related to the drops, the cotton pledget, or the ear ailment itself. Instruct the client and/or family member in the appropriate ear drop instillation method based on the client's age.

*Evaluation.* Monitor the client's affected ear(s) for improvement of the condition for which the ear drops are being administered. Monitor for possible hypersensitivity to the ear drops, evidenced by burning, redness, and swelling. If hypersensitivity occurs, discontinue drops and notify the prescriber.

## DRUG-INDUCED OTOTOXICITY

Many medications have reportedly caused **ototoxicity** in humans. The ototoxicity may affect the person's hearing (auditory or cochlear function), balance (vestibular function), or both. The most common symptom reported is **tinnitus,** a ringing or buzzing sound in the ears.

Cochlear ototoxicity causes a progressive or continuing hearing loss. Loss of the highest tones occurs first, then progresses to affect the lowest tones. Because of this slow progression, most clients are not aware that it is occurring. Vestibular damage may be indicated by dizziness, ataxia, and difficulty with equilibrium. The person may feel as though the room is in motion (**vertigo**). Ototoxicity is usually bilateral and may be reversible, but it can become irreversible if not recognized early enough to stop the offending medications. Most drug-induced ototoxicity is associated with the use of aminoglycosides. Table 45-4 notes the potential ototoxic effects of selected aminoglycosides. Table 45-5 lists other drugs reported to induce ototoxicity.

## ▷NURSING MANAGEMENT: DRUGS THAT INDUCE OTOTOXICITY

*Assessment.* Assess hearing function before starting therapy with an ototoxic drug. Concurrent administration of more than one ototoxic drug may increase the potential for hearing loss. Use caution when administering ototoxic drugs in clients with any condition that may increase their risk of adverse reaction from auditory drugs. An example is the client with renal failure, which alters the elimination of aminoglycosides and may result in ototoxic serum levels.

*Intervention.* Serum levels of some drugs may be monitored to help detect the development of dangerously high blood levels. When given intravenously, aminoglycosides should be administered over 30 to 60 minutes to avoid high peak levels.

*Education.* Instruct clients to report tinnitus or any other hearing impairment immediately. Auditory damage is usually reversible if the causative drug is discontinued.

*Evaluation.* Monitor the client's ability to hear by observing for cues indicative of increasing hearing loss (inappropriate responses to others' conversation, speaking loudly, moving closer to others when they speak) and noting client's comments of not being able to hear or understand what others are saying. Report indications of increased hearing loss to the prescriber.

## SUMMARY

Drugs that affect the ear may relate to the treatment of inflammation, excess cerumen, bacterial or fungal infection, or ear discomfort; or they may cause ototoxicity as an adverse effect of being administered for some other condition. In both instances, the nurse needs to be concerned for the client's comfort, auditory perception, and the risk for injury from the adverse effects of the drugs or as an extension of the client's symptoms.

## BIBLIOGRAPHY

Davidson DE. (1990). Handbook of nonprescription drugs, ed 9. Washington, DC: American Pharmaceutical Association and The National Professional Society of Pharmacists.

Fischer RG. (1985). Drug management of otitis media, Pediatr Nurs 11(6):474.

Kastrup EK, ed. (1991). Facts and comparisons: drug information. St Louis: JB Lippincott Co.

Knoben JE and Anderson PO. (1986). Handbook of clinical drug data, ed 5. Hamilton, Ill: Drug Intelligence Publications, Inc.

Richman E. (1987). Swimmer's ear: timely management tips, Patient Care 21(10):28.

Sloan RW. (1986). Practical geriatric therapeutics. Oradell, NJ: Medical Economics Inc.

United States Pharmacopeial Convention. (1991). Drug information for the health care provider, ed 11. Rockville, Md: The Convention.

# ✺46 Overview of the Endocrine System

## HORMONES

The **hormones** are natural chemical substances that act after being secreted into the bloodstream from the endocrine glands. They have specific, well-defined physiologic effects on metabolism. The list of major hormones includes the products of the secretions from the anterior and posterior pituitary glands, the thyroid hormones, parathyroid hormone, insulin and glucagon from the pancreas, epinephrine and norepinephrine from the adrenal medulla, several potent steroids from the adrenal cortex, and the gonadal hormones of both sexes.

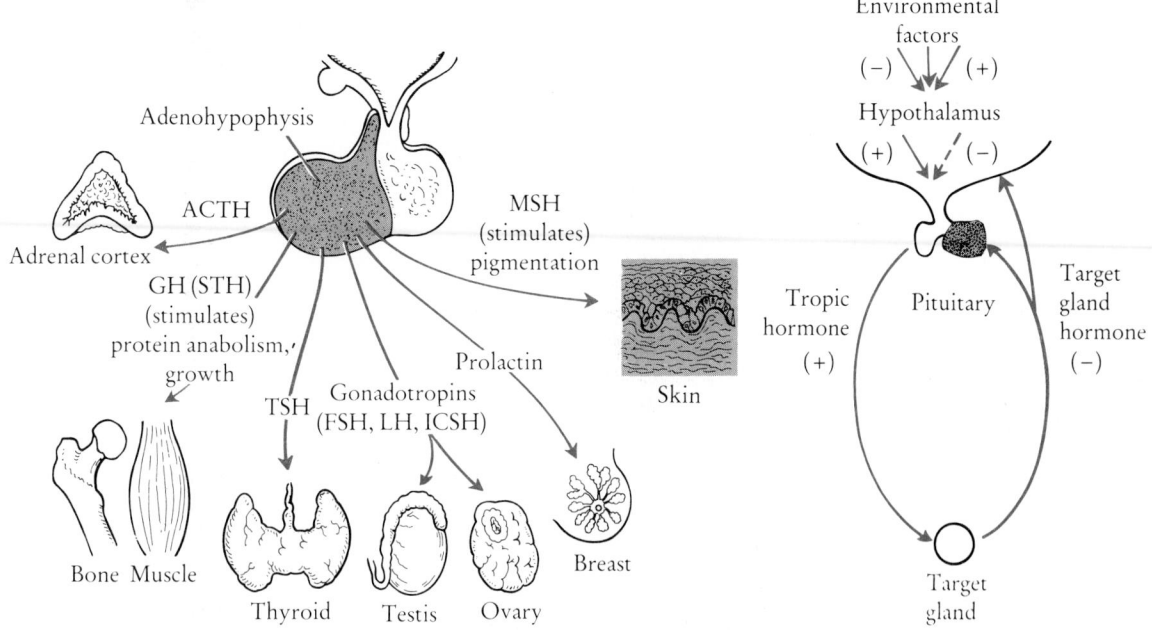

**FIGURE 46-1** Various internal and external environmental factors may inhibit or stimulate the hypothalamus to secrete inhibitory (−) or releasing (+) factors to control output of hormones from anterior pituitary and ultimate hormone release from target glands.

The major types of hormones are the steroid hormones and the amino acid-derived hormones. Steroid hormones are those substances secreted by the adrenal gland and the sex glands. They are found in the plasma to transport proteins. Their physiologic effect begins when the steroid enters the cell, with subsequent binding to the specific cytosol or nusclear protein receptor.

Hormones from the various endocrine glands work together to regulate vital processes, including the following:
1. Secretory and motor activities of the digestive tract
2. Energy production
3. Composition and volume of extracellular fluid
4. Adaptation, such as acclimatization and immunity
5. Growth and development
6. Reproduction and lactation

Hormones may exert their effects by controlling the formation or destruction of an intracellular regulator such as cyclic 3'5' adenosine monophosphate (cyclic AMP), controlling protein synthesis, or controlling membrane permeability and the movement of ions and other substances. The effect of a hormone depends on its interaction with a receptor and is determined by the level of the circulating active hormone.

To maintain the internal environment, hormone secretion must be controlled. This is achieved by a self-regulating series of events known as "negative feedback"; that is, a hormone produces a physiologic effect that, when it is strong enough, inhibits further secretion of that hormone, thereby inhibiting the physiologic effect. Increased hormonal secretions may be evoked in response to stimuli from the external environment; cessation of external stimuli ends the internal secretion response (Figure 46-1).

Hormones are not "used up" in exerting their physiologic effects but must be inactivated or excreted if the internal environment is to remain stable. Inactivation occurs enzymatically in the blood or intercellular spaces, in the liver or kidney, or in the target tissues. Excretion of hormones is primarily via the urine and to a lesser extent the bile.

Most hormones are destroyed rapidly, having a half-life in blood of 10 to 30 minutes. However, some, such as the catecholamines, have a half-life of seconds, and thyroid hormones have a half-life measured in days. Some hormones exert their physiologic effects immediately; others require minutes or hours before their effects occur. In addition, some effects end immediately when the hormone disappears from the circulation. Other responses may persist for hours after hormone concentrations have returned to basal levels. The exposure of a tissue to an active hormone also is controlled by that hormone's pathway for metabolism, including molecular alterations, consumption at the site of action, and hepatorenal excretion. This wide range of onset and duration of hormonal activity contributes to the flexibility of the endocrine system.

One of the major developments of this century in the fields of biology and medicine has been the recognition and isolation, purification, and chemical and cellular understanding of most known hormones. In addition, once their chemical structure is known, duplicating hormones by chemical synthesis becomes theoretically possible. This had been accomplished for some but not all hormones.

In medicine, hormones generally are used in three ways: (1) for replacement therapy, exemplified by use of insulin for diabetes or adrenal steroids in Addison's disease; (2) for pharmacologic effects beyond replacement, as in the use of larger than endogenous doses of adrenal steroids for their antiinflammatory effects; and (3) for endocrine diagnostic testing.

Research in endocrinology has advanced the concept of specific receptors within or on the surface of cells. This has led to knowledge of hormone specificity and the essential cellular mechanisms involved in the hormone-receptor complex. The recognition and activation properties found in the hormone-receptor complex come from different receptor molecular sites. Only specific receptor material binds a hormone and begins its activity; the hormone has no effect on other tissues that do not carry specific receptors. Alterations in either hormone secretion or hormone receptor responses may culminate in endocrine disease states. Certain cell surface receptors may become antigenic and develop antibodies that accelerate receptor destruction, block receptor function, or mimic the action of the target tissue. Among the receptor-like disorders, referred to as antireceptor autoimmune diseases, are myasthenia gravis, Graves' disease, insulin-resistant diabetes mellitus, and bronchial asthma.

## PITUITARY GLAND

The hormones of the pituitary gland exert an important effect in regulating the secretion of other hormones. The pituitary body is about the size of a pea and occupies a niche in the sella turcica of the sphenoid bone. It consists of an anterior lobe (adenohypophysis), a posterior lobe (neurohypophysis), and a smaller pars intermedia composed of secreting cells. The anterior lobe is particularly important in sustaining life. The function of the pars intermedia is not well known.

### Regulation of Anterior Pituitary Function

The pituitary and target glands have a negative feedback relationship. A tropic hormone from the pituitary stimulates the target gland to secrete a hormone that inhibits further secretion of the tropic hormone by the pituitary. When the serum concentration of the target gland hormone falls below a certain level, the pituitary again secretes the tropic hormone until the target gland produces enough hormone to inhibit the pituitary secretion. However, the negative feedback concept alone is not enough to account for changes in serum levels of target gland hormones, especially those caused by changes in the external environment. Thus the central nervous system is believed to play a decisive role in regulating pituitary function to meet environmental demands.

The discovery of various hypothalamic-releasing factors is of great research interest. These factors cause the release of inhibition of the various hormones from the anterior pituitary. Among these releasing factors are thyroid-stimulating hormone releasing factor, corticotropin-releasing factor, growth hormone releasing hormone, growth hormone inhibitory hormone (somatostatin), luteinizing hormone releasing hormone and prolactin inhibitory factor.

### Anterior Pituitary Hormones

The number of hormones secreted by the anterior pituitary gland is unknown, but at least seven extracts have been prepared in a relatively pure state, and they have definite specific action.

1. A growth factor influences the development of the body. It promotes skeletal, visceral, and general growth. Acromegaly, gigantism, and dwarfism are associated with pathologic conditions of the anterior lobe of the pituitary gland.

   Growth hormone (GH) (somatotropin, somatropin, somatotropic hormone, STH) has been obtained as a small crystalline protein, but thus far the growth hormone has found no established place in medicine except in documented clinical and laboratory evidence of growth hormone deficiency. Its use in various clinical conditions is largely experimental. It tends to increase the blood sugar and antagonize insulin, and it may be the "diabetogenic" hormone postulated in the past.

2. Follicle-stimulating hormone (FSH) stimulates the growth and maturation of the ovarian follicle, which in turn brings on the characteristic changes of estrus (menstruation in women). This hormone also stimulates spermatogenesis in the male. FSH appears to be a protein or is associated with a protein, but this human pituitary gonadotropin has not yet been obtained in a highly purified form.

3. Luteinizing hormone (LH), also known as the interstitial cell-stimulating hormone (ICSH), together with FSH (Pergonal), causes maturation of the graafian follicles, ovulation, and the secretion of estrogen in the female. It causes spermatogenesis, androgen formation, and growth of interstitial tissue in the male. Luteinizing hormone also promotes the formation of the corpus luteum in the female.

4. Thyrotropic hormone (TSH) is necessary for normal development and function of the thyroid gland. If too much is present, it is known to produce hyperthyroidism and increase the size of the gland in laboratory animals.

5. A lactogenic factor (prolactin or mammotropin) plays a part in proliferation and secretion of the mammary glands of mammals. This may be identical to the hormone responsible for the development of the corpus luteum. In its absence the corpus luteum fails to produce progesterone.

6. Adrenocorticotropic hormone (corticotropin or ACTH) stimulates the cortex of the adrenal gland.
7. Melanocyte-stimulating hormone (intermedin or MSH) is probably produced in the intermediate lobe. Its physiologic role is unknown, but when injected in human beings, it will darken the skin.

The hormones produced by the anterior lobe of the pituitary gland are important physiologically, but only recently have purified preparations been available, at least for clinical study; and such preparations are both expensive and limited in supply. They may become useful in combating certain disorders in the future, however, as chemically defined preparations become available.

## Posterior Pituitary Hormones

Two hormones obtained from the posterior lobe of the pituitary gland have been identified and chemically analyzed. These compounds, **oxytocin** and **vasopressin** (antidiuretic hormone), are both peptides, and each contains eight amino acids. It has proved possible to synthesize them chemically. Availability of these hormones in pure form has clarified their mechanism of action and has allowed better control of their therapeutic use. For example, a certain overlap of pharmacologic action exists even in the pure preparation; pure oxytocin has some vasopressor activity, and vice versa. The antidiuretic potency of vasopressin is much greater than its pressor potency. While vasopressin is available in a natural state, synthetic formulations, such as lypressin and desmopressin have been developed; and they act primarily as ADH. They have very little, if any, pressor or oxytoxic activity.

Oxytocin is discussed in Chapter 53.

## THYROID GLAND

The thyroid gland, one of the most richly vascularized tissues of the body, secretes three hormones essential for proper regulation of metabolism: thyroxine ($T_4$), triiodothyronine ($T_3$), and calcitonin. Because of its role in calcium metabolism, calcitonin is discussed later with the parathyroid gland hormones. (See Chapter 48).

The thyroid gland is composed of at least two types of cells: follicular, which produce $T_3$ and $T_4$; and parafollicular, the source of calcitonin.

## Thyroid Hormones

The large amount of iodine in thyroid hormones and the availability of radioactive iodine have led to detailed knowledge about thyroid physiology and its role in metabolism. Iodine is essential for thyroid hormone synthesis. About 1 mg of iodine per week is required, most of which is ingested in food, water, and iodized table salt. About two thirds of this iodine is reduced in the gastrointestinal tract,

enters the circulation as iodide, and is excreted into the urine. The remaining third is taken up by the thyroid gland for hormone synthesis. This process is aided by the "iodide pump," which takes up the iodide from the extracellular fluid, traps it, and concentrates it to many times that found in plasma. The ratio of iodide in the thyroid gland to that in the serum is expressed as the T/S ratio; normally this ratio is 20:1. In hypoactivity the ratio may be 10:1; in hyperactivity it may be as great as 250:1.

Thyroglobulin is synthesized first. It contains thyrosine, an amino acid that reacts with iodine to form thyroid hormones. The thyroglobulin-thyroid hormone complex is stored in the follicles of the thyroid gland and is called "colloid." About 30% of the thyroid mass is stored thyroglobulin, which contains enough thyroid hormone to meet normal requirements for 2 to 3 months without any further synthesis.

Normally, thyroglobulin is not released into the circulation but undergoes proteolytic digestion (a coupling reaction), which releases the active thyroid hormones $T_3$ and $T_4$. Hormone synthesis—iodine trapping, iodination and proteolysis of thyroglobulin, and hormone release—is controlled by the thyroid-stimulating hormone (thyrotropin, TSH) from the beta cells of the anterior pituitary gland. Thyroid secretion is maintained by this TSH secretion. Decreased serum levels of $T_3$ and $T_4$ stimulate thyrotropin-releasing hormone (TRH) from the hypothalamus, which stimulates the pituitary gland to secrete TSH, which in turn stimulates release of thyroxin from thyroglobulin.

TSH secretion is negatively regulated by $T_3$ and $T_4$, which directly inhibit the pituitary gland's thyrotopic cells. An increase in free, unbound thyroid hormone causes a decrease in TSH secretion and inhibits TRH production, and a decrease in the free unbound hormone causes an increase in TSH secretion and stimulates TRH production—a negative feedback mechanism.

### Physiologic Effects of Thyroid Hormones

The precise physiologic role of the thyroid hormones is not yet known, although several hormonal actions have been identified and studied. Three generalizations can be made about thyroid hormones:

1. They have a diffuse effect and do not seem to have any specific target organ effect; no special cells or tissues appear to be particularly affected by the thyroid hormones.
2. Their long delay in onset of action and their prolonged action rule them out as minute-to-minute regulators of physiologic function. Instead, their role is more likely to be that of establishing and maintaining long-term functions such as growth, maturation, and adaptation.
3. They are not necessary for survival, although reduced levels can affect quality of life.

Thyroxine and triiodothyronine appear to have the same

physiologic actions, although $T_3$ is far more potent than $T_4$.

***Growth and maturation.*** A normal, functioning thyroid is essential for normal growth. Thyroid hormones stimulate production of messenger ribonucleic acid (RNA) molecules, which are involved in the synthesis of various proteins, thus facilitating growth and development. The hormones must be present in the right amounts for growth to occur at the normal rate. In children who are hypothyroid, rate of growth is retarded, which may lead to shortness of stature. Conversely, children who are hyperthyroid may have excessive skeletal growth and become taller than they otherwise would. If there is premature closing of the epiphyses because of accelerated bone maturation, however, stunting of growth results. In the adult, excess thyroid hormone causes increased demineralization of bone and increased loss of calcium and phosphate.

Cells in the interstitial tissue between follicles of the thyroid gland produce calcitonin; the effect of this hormone is to reduce the blood calcium ion concentration, the exact opposite effect of parathyroid hormone. Calcitonin is essential for bone formation in children, since it promotes deposition of calcium. In the adult, calcitonin has a very weak effect on plasma concentration, since absorption and deposition of calcium are slow in the adult and calcitonin effects are rapidly overridden by parathyroid hormone.

***Central nervous system function.*** At time of birth through the first year of life, thyroid hormone must be present for normal development of the cerebrum; if the hormone is not present, irreversible mental retardation occurs. In the adult, hypothyroidism causes listlessness, a general dulling of mental capacity, decreased sensory capacity, slow speech, impaired memory, and somnolence. Hyperthyroidism in the adult results in hyperexcitability, irritability, restlessness, exaggerated responses to environmental stimuli, and emotional instability. Psychosis can occur in either hypo- or hyperthyroidism.

***Basal metabolic rate.*** Thyroid hormones increase oxygen consumption in most cells of the body with the exception of the lungs, spleen, gastric smooth muscle, the gonads, and accessory sex organs. In hypothyroidism the basal metabolic rate is subnormal; in hyperthyroidism it may be 40% to 60% above normal.

***Carbohydrate and lipid metabolism.*** Thyroid hormones accelerate glucose catabolism, increase cholesterol synthesis, and enhance the liver's ability to excrete cholesterol in the bile. Since the effect on cholesterol excretion is greater than that on cholesterol synthesis, the result is a decrease in plasma cholesterol level. The hormones also stimulate the mobilization of fatty acids from adipose tissue. The hypothyroid individual will have an elevated serum cholesterol level and increased blood levels of phospholipids and triglycerides.

***Protein metabolism.*** Thyroid hormones are essential for the development of protein mass. In hypothyroidism both the synthesis and the breakdown of protein are diminished, but the effect on protein synthesis is more profound. In addition, deposition of mucoproteins occurs in subcutaneous spaces, which osmotically attracts water, causing "puffiness." In hyperthyroidism increased catabolism of protein, or breakdown of muscle mass, and increased nitrogen excretion occur.

***Gastrointestinal function.*** Thyroid hormones increase gastrointestinal motility, absorption of food, and secretion of digestive juices. Hypothyroidism decreases both intestinal absorption and secretion of pancreatic enzymes. Constipation also may occur.

***Water and electrolyte balance.*** In thyroid hormone deficiency, water and electrolytes accumulate in subcutaneous spaces; administering a thyroid hormone results in diuresis and a loss of fluid and electrolytes from the subcutaneous spaces.

***Cardiovascular function.*** Since the thyroid hormones increase metabolism, the tissues have an increased need for oxygen and nutrients, which in turn demands increased blood flow. In hyperthyroidism these effects cause increased cardiac output, increased pulse pressure, and tachycardia. If these effects are prolonged, cardiac hypertrophy and even high-output myocardial failure may occur. Opposite effects occur in hypothyroidism.

***Muscle function.*** Moderate increases in thyroid hormone makes muscle react with vigor; large increases result in muscle weakness because of excess protein catabolism. A characteristic sign of hyperthyroidism is a fine muscle tremor. Hypothyroidism causes the muscles to be sluggish.

***Temperature regulation.*** Thyroid hormones must be present for an increase in heat production or a decrease in heat loss to occur. Although the hormones do not initiate the physiologic response to cold, they appear to magnify the body's response to catecholamine effects, which innervate the sympathetic system during cold exposure. Hypothyroidism causes decreased tolerance to cold.

***Lactation.*** Thyroid hormone is necessary for normal milk production; without thyroid hormone, fat content of milk and total milk production are greatly reduced.

***Reproduction.*** Thyroid hormone is required for normal rhythmicity in the reproductive cycle.

## Thyroid Gland Disorders
### Goiter

The synthesis of the thyroid hormones and their maintenance in the blood in adequate amounts depend largely on an adequate intake of iodine. Iodine ingested by way of food or water is changed into iodide and is stored in the thyroid gland before reaching the circulation. Prolonged iodine deficiency in the diet results in enlargement of the thyroid gland, known as a simple **goiter.** When thyroid hormones fail to be synthesized because of a lack of iodine, the anterior lobe of the pituitary is stimulated to increase the secretion of thyrotropic hormone, which in turn causes hypertrophy and hyperplasia of the gland. The enlarged thyroid then removes residual traces of iodine from the blood. This type of goiter (simple or nontoxic) can be prevented by providing an adequate supply of iodine for young persons. Iodine is not abundant in most foods except fish and seafoods, and iodized salt is frequently the primary source for iodine in areas where seafood is expensive or not readily available.

## Hypothyroidism

Clients with primary hypothyroidism have decreased $T_3$ and $T_4$ levels and an elevated TSH level. Those with pituitary (secondary) hypothyroidism have decreased levels of $T_3$, $T_4$, and TSH but normal levels of TRH, whereas those with hypothalamic (tertiary) hypothyroidism have decreased levels of $T_3$, $T_4$, and TSH and normal levels of TRH.

The TSH test, the most sensitive index of hypothyroidism, is elevated in primary hypothyroidism and depressed in secondary hypothyroidism. The free thyroxine index (FTI $= TT_4 \times RT_3U$) is depressed in clients with both primary and secondary hypothyroidism but elevated in clients with hyperthyroidism. The $T_3$ resin uptake ($RT_3U$) is depressed in pregnancy and in clients with primary and secondary hypothyroidism but elevated in clients with hyperthyroidism. The serum $T_3$ level is depressed in both secondary and primary hypothyroidism but elevated in hyperthyroid states and $T_3$ thyrotoxicosis. The total $T_4$ ($TT_4$ Murphy-Pattee) is elevated in pregnancy and hyperthyroidism but depressed in both primary and secondary hypothyroidism. The free $T_4$ (unbound) is depressed in both primary and secondary hypothyroid states but is elevated in hyperthyroid states.

In children, normal skeletal growth is evidence of adequate therapy; an increase in serum alkaline phosphatase indicates that growth will occur. In cretinism (see below), thyroid hormone levels equal to or above those required for the adult must be established immediately after birth to prevent permanent mental and physical retardation. Treatment of the older cretin will not reverse the mental retardation that has already occurred. Clients with hypothyroidism need to be informed of their lifelong need for replacement therapy.

Hypothyroidism in the young child is known as **cretinism** and is characterized by cessation of physical and mental development, which leads to dwarfism and idiocy. Clients with cretinism usually have thick, coarse skin; a thick tongue; gaping mouth; protruding abdomen; thick, short legs, poorly developed hands and feet; and weak musculature. This condition may result from faulty development or atrophy of the thyroid gland during fetal life. Failure of development of the gland may be caused by lack of iodine in the mother.

Severe hypothyroidism in the adult is called **myxedema** (acid mucopolysaccharide accumulation). When it is the last stage of a long-standing, inadequately treated or untreated hypothyroidism, coma appears, accompanied by hypotension, hypoventilation, hypothermia, bradycardia, hypona-

tremia, and hypoglycemia. The development of myxedema is usually insidious and causes gradual retardation of physical and mental functions. There is gradual infiltration of the skin and loss of facial lines and facial expression (a puffy, expressionless face). The formation of subcutaneous connective tissue causes the hands and face to appear puffy and swollen. The basal metabolic rate becomes subnormal, the skin is cold and dry, the hair becomes scanty and coarse, movements become sluggish, cardiac output is reduced, and the patient becomes hypersensitive to cold.

## Hyperthyroidism (Thyrotoxicosis)

Excessive formation of the thyroid hormones and their escape into the circulation result in a toxic state called **thyrotoxicosis.** This occurs in the condition known as diffuse toxic goiter, or exophthalmic goiter (Graves' disease), or in some forms of adenomatous goiters.

Primary hyperthyroidism is characterized by elevated levels of $T_3$ and $T_4$ and decreased level of TSH. In pituitary (secondary) hyperthyroidism levels of $T_3$, $T_4$, and TSH increase.

Hyperthyroidism leads to symptoms quite different from those seen in myxedema. The metabolic rate is increased, sometimes as much as $+60$ or more. The body temperature frequently is above normal, the pulse rate is fast, and the client complains of feeling too warm. Other symptoms include restlessness, anxiety, emotional instability, muscle tremor and weakness, sweating, and exophthalmos. The increased thyroxine levels may cause cardiomegaly, tachycardia, congestive heart failure, hepatic alterations (necrosis, dysfunction, fatty changes), lymphoid hyperplasia, osteoporosis, pretibial myxedema, and neurologic irritability. In thyroid storm sudden onset of hyperthyroid symptoms occurs, especially those affecting the nervous and cardiovascular systems, because of elevated thyroxine levels.

Before the advent of antithyroid drugs, treatment was limited to a subtotal resection of the hyperactive gland. Propylthiouracil is the most commonly used antithyroid medication. However, antithyroid drugs provide less rapid control of hyperthyroidism than do surgical measures. Radioactive therapy is used primarily in treatment of middle-age and elderly clients.

## PARATHYROID GLANDS

Lying just above and behind the thyroid gland are bean-shaped glands known as the parathyroids. Humans have two pairs. The adult glands consist of encapsulated masses of cells, between which are abundant adipocytes and vascular channels. The primary function of the parathyroids is to maintain adequate levels of calcium in the extracellular fluid. Parathyroid hormone has multiple effects, ultimately culminating in mobilization of calcium from bone. It also reduces phosphate concentration, permitting more calcium to be mobilized.

## Parathyroid Hormones

Parathyroid hormone (PTH) is a polypeptide. The active component has a half-life of 30 minutes; the inactive component, 7 to 10 days. PTH circulates in elevated concentrations in clients with hyperplastic parathyroid glands as a result of diminished calcium levels, as found in persons with impaired renal function or intestinal malabsorption. These elevated PTH levels may cause metabolic bone disease, including osteoporosis and osteomalacia.

The mechanism of PTH action in the bone or kidney is incompletely understood. Some researchers suggest that PTH receptor-binding and adenylate cyclase activity are coupled events subject to down regulation of the receptors. Patients with hyperparathyroidism may be resistant to PTH action on kidney and bone. The decreased number of these receptors, not their altered affinity, produces a reduction in PTH-stimulated adenylate cyclase activity.

Cholesterol-derived provitamin D is converted to vitamin $D_3$ by action of sunlight on the skin. The vitamin is also present as a milk additive. Along with PTH, vitamin $D_3$ is converted to its active form in the kidney. It is involved in calcium, phosphate, and magnesium metabolism in bone and the gastrointestinal tract.

Primary hyperparathyroidism is the most common parathyroid disorder. Generally it is caused by adenomas, chief cell hyperplasia, or hypertrophy. PTH elevations produce altered function of renal tubular cells, bone cells, and gastrointestinal tract mucosa. Elevated levels of calcium and increased bone resorption with the development of renal calculi occurs, generally, in hyperparathyroidism. In secondary hyperparathyroidism, an overactive parathyroid gland causes increased calcium excretion and possibly kidney stones, but generally, serum calcium levels remain stable due to an effective feedback mechanism.

Hypoparathyroidism leads to manifestations of hypocalcemia and tetany, the symptoms of which include muscle spasms, convulsions, gradual paralysis with dyspnea, and death from exhaustion. Before death, gastrointestinal hemorrhages and hematemesis frequently occur. At death the intestinal mucosa is congested, and the calcium content of the heart, kidney, and other tissues is increased.

The symptoms of tetany are relieved by administration of calcium salts. Large doses of vitamin D also help to relieve tetany and to restore the normal calcium level in the blood. The client is hospitalized, since frequent assessment of blood calcium and phosphate levels is essential.

## ADRENAL GLANDS

The adrenal glands are located just above the kidneys. They consist of two parts, the inner medulla and the outer cortex.

The adrenal cortex synthesizes three important classes of hormones: the **glucocorticoids** (cortisol), **mineralo-corti-coids** (primarily aldosterone), and **androgens** (primarily de-

hydroepiandrosterone). The glucocorticoids are synthesized primarily in the zona fasciculata and are under the control of ACTH from the pituitary gland. Although the basal production rate averages 30 mg every 24 hours, under stressful conditions (trauma, major surgery, infection) there is a reserve capacity production of up to 300 mg daily. Increases in glucocorticoid production may be related to proportional increases in release of ACTH by the pituitary.

The mineralocorticoids are synthesized specifically in the zona glomerulosa. Production is primarily under the control of both the renin-angiotensin axis system (discussed later) and the blood potassium level. The production of aldosterone is stimulated by salt depletion and causes sodium retention in the kidney at the distal convoluted tubule to preserve the extracellular fluid volume.

The androgens are synthesized in the zona fasciculata and the zona reticularis and essentially control growth of the hair follicles in the skin.

Normally a reaction to serious stress causes a prompt and noticeable increase in cortisol and aldosterone production; these hormones operate together to maintain the cardiovascular tone essential for survival. A client under stress who has impaired ability to produce these hormones incurs the risk of developing acute adrenal crisis. The production of cortisol is under the control of a continous feedback mechanism involving the pituitary and ACTH production, which is in turn inhibited by the circulating cortisol levels. Stress is a stimulus to override this inhibition and initiates secretion of corticotropin-releasing factor, which culminates in ACTH release and activation of the adrenal cortex, leading to an increased production of cortisol.

## Mineralocorticoids: Aldosterone

**Aldosterone** is the primary mineralocorticoid in humans. It is synthesized in the adrenal zona glomerulosa, which is the outer edge of the adrenocortical tissue below the adrenal capsule. Aldosterone production is maintained primarily by the renin-angiotensin system and the concentration of circulating serum potassium. A drop in the circulating arterial volume stimulates volume receptors in the juxtaglomerular apparatus. As a result, renin (a proteolytic enzyme) is produced and acts on angiotensinogen, which is synthesized by the liver to form angiotensin I. When the angiotensin I passes through the pulmonary circulation, two amino acids are cleared from it to form angiotensin. Angiotensin II stimulates the adrenal zona glomerulosa to produce aldosterone. Aldosterone promotes sodium reabsorption in the kidney at the distal convoluted tubule to preserve extracellular fluid volume. In the normal client, aldosterone secretion is stimulated by a decrease in circulating volume (loss of blood, excessive diuresis, low salt intake, etc.) and increased potassium levels. Aldosterone secretion is suppressed by an elevation of sodium levels in the blood (e.g., by excessive dietary salt intake). It restricts the loss of sodium and its accompanying anions, chloride and bicarbonate, and thereby helps maintain extracellular fluid volume. It also maintains acid-base and potassium balance.

In adrenal insufficiency, aldosterone deficit occurs, sodium reabsorption is inhibited, and potassium excretion decreases. Hyperkalemia and mild acidosis occur. In adrenalectomy the loss of aldosterone leads to an overall reduction of sodium reabsorption and a powerful and uncontrolled loss of extracellular fluid. Plasma volume drops, and a state of hypovolemic shock may ensue. This may cause death unless a mineralocorticoid, salt, and water are administered. In excessive doses, aldosterone increases potassium excretion, and unless dietary intake compensates for the loss, hypokalemia results. Acidification of the urine then occurs, leading to metabolic alkalosis.

Aldosterone is much more potent in its electrolyte effects than desoxycorticosterone, though it has not yet established a therapeutic status comparable to that of desoxycorticosterone. Its use has been limited because of its cost and relative unavailability and because it must be administered intramuscularly.

The amount of aldosterone secreted by the adrenal cortex apparently is affected by the concentration of sodium in body fluids rather than by the stimulation of the adrenal cortex by ACTH.

## PANCREAS

The pancreas is a gland that lies transversely across the posterior wall of the abdomen. It secretes a limpid, colorless fluid that digests proteins, fats, and carbohydrates. It also produces internal secretions—insulin and glucagon—that affect blood sugar levels.

**Insulin** is a hormone secreted by the beta cells of the islets of Langerhans in the pancreas. On hydrolysis, this hormone yields several amino acids. In its crystalline state it appears to be chemically linked with certain metals (zinc, nickel, cadmium, or cobalt). Normal pancreatic tissue is rich in zinc, which may be significant to the natural storage of the hormone. Insulin consists of two polypeptide chains and contains 48 amino acids, the exact sequence of which is known. Insulin is stored in the beta cells as a larger protein known as proinsulin.

Since relatively small amounts of insulin are necessary in the body tissues, it is thought that insulin acts as a catalyst in cellular metabolism.

Carbohydrate metabolism is controlled by a finely balanced interaction of several endocrine factors (adrenal, anterior pituitary, thyroid, insulin), but the particular phase of carbohydrate metabolism that is affected by insulin is not entirely known. When insulin is injected subcutaneously, however, it produces a rapid lowering of the blood sugar. This effect is produced in both diabetic and nondiabetic persons. Moderate amounts of insulin in the diabetic animal promote the storage of carbohydrate in the liver and also in

the muscle cells, particularly after the feeding of carbohydrate. In the normal animal the deposit of muscle glycogen also increases, but apparently the level of liver glycogen does not. In both diabetic and nondiabetic persons the oxygen consumption increases and the respiratory quotient rises.

**Glucagon,** like insulin, is a pancreatic extract and is thought to oppose the action of insulin. Glucagon is a product of the alpha cells of the islets of Langerhans. Glucagon acts primarily by mobilizing hepatic glycogen and converting it to glucose, which produces an elevation of the concentration of glucose in the blood.

### Diabetes Mellitus

**Diabetes mellitus** is a heterogenous metabolic disease characterized particularly by an inability to use carbohydrate. Insulin action is ineffective at the tissue site, or not enough insulin is available. Obesity, certain drugs, viruses, autoimmune phenomena, genetic predisposition, and age may have roles in its development. The blood sugar becomes elevated, and when it exceeds a certain amount, the excess is secreted by the kidney (glycosuria). Symptoms include increased appetite (polyphagia), thirst (polydipsia), weight loss, increased urine output (polyuria), weakness (fatigue), and itching such as pruritus vulvae.

In diabetes mellitus, glycogen fails to store in the liver, although the conversion of glycogen back to glucose or the formation of glucose from other substances (gluconeogenesis) is not necessarily impaired. As a result, the level of blood sugar rapidly rises. This derangement of carbohydrate metabolism results in an abnormally high metabolism of proteins and fats. The ketone bodies, which result from oxidation of fatty acids, accumulate faster than the muscle cells can oxidize them, resulting in ketosis and acidosis. The course of untreated diabetes mellitus is progressive. The symptoms of diabetic coma and acidosis are directly or indirectly the result of the accumulation of acetone, beta-hydroxybutyric acid, and diacetic acid. Respirations become rapid and deep, the breath has an odor of acetone, the blood sugar is elevated, the client becomes dehydrated, and stupor and coma develop unless treatment is started promptly.

The long-term complications of diabetes mellitus can lead to an increase in morbidity and mortality. Some of the most commonly associated problems are peripheral atherosclerosis, which may result in coronary artery disease, infections, gangrene, or strokes; diabetic retinopathy which can include vitreal hemorrhage, retinal detachment, and blindness; renal disease, peripheral sensory neuropathy, and cardiomyopathy leading to heart failure are also reported.

Diabetes mellitus usually is treated with exogenous insulin, diet, and exercise. Glucose and insulin promote the formation and retention of glycogen in the liver, and the oxidation of fat in the liver is arrested. Therefore the rate of formation of acetone bodies is slowed and the acidosis is checked. Other supportive measures, such as restoring the fluid and electrolyte balance of the body, are very important in its treatment.

Diabetic therapy includes (1) the synthesis of human insulin by bacteria genetically altered by recombinant DNA technology, (2) islet-cell and/or pancreas transplantation, and (3) external and implanted continuous insulin infusion pumps.

## SUMMARY

The endocrine system carries out integrative and regulatory functions within the body through the actions of hormones. Hormones regulate mechanisms that allow the body as a whole to meet needs. The endocrine system consists of specialized glands and their hormones, which act on specific target cells and stimulate various responses. The overproduction or underproduction of hormones results in pathologic conditions for man. Hormonal replacement therapy is the major concern in the underproduction of hormones by the endocrine system.

## BIBLIOGRAPHY

Brewer J. (1986). The anatomy and physiology of the pancreas, SGA J 8(£):38.

Groer MW and Shekleton ME. (1989). Basic pathophysiology: a holistic approach, ed 2. St Louis: The CV Mosby Co.

Guyton AC. (1987). Human physiology and mechanisms of disease, ed 4. Philadelphia: WB Saunders Co.

Hobbie WL et al. (1989). Endocrine late effects among survivors of cancer, Semin Oncol Nurs 5(1):14.

Kupperman HS. (1986). Hypothyroidism, Physician Assist 10(3):60.

Lancaster LE. (1987). Renal and endocrine regulation of water and electrolyte balance, Nurs Clin North Amer 22(4):761.

Mathewson MK. (1987). Thyroid disorder, Crit Care Nurse 7(1):74.

Mathewson MK. (1986). Antidiuretic hormone, Crit Care Nurse 6(5):88.

Miller SM. (1986). Action and assessment of parathyrin, a calcium regulating hormone, J Med Technol 3(6):335.

Palmieri MJ. (1987). Pathophysiology of the pancreas . . . certification review, SGA J 9(3):134.

Schoeff L. (1986). Antidiuretic hormone and water regulation, J Med Technol 3(6):342.

Taylor DL. (1987). Hypoglycemia: physiology, signs and symptoms, Nursinglife 7(1):36.

Thibodeau GA. (1990). Textbook of anatomy and physiology, ed 13. St Louis: Times-Mirror/Mosby College Publishing.

Chapter

# 47  Drugs Affecting the Pituitary

## CHAPTER OBJECTIVES

*After studying this chapter, you should be able to meet the following objectives and define the key terms.*

1. Describe the primary functions of the anterior and posterior pituitary hormones.

2. Describe the effects of somatrem and somatropin.

3. List the effects of vasopressin.

4. Discuss nursing management of the care of the client receiving drugs affecting the pituitary.

## KEY TERMS

Creutzfeldt-Jakob disease, page 756

diabetes insipidus, page 757

dwarfism, page 756

gigantism, page 756

growth hormone-inhibiting hormone (somatostatin), page 756

growth hormone-releasing hormone (GHRH), page 755

somatomedins, page 756

## INTRODUCTION

There are a variety of preparations available that affect the pituitary gland. They are generally used as replacement therapy for hormone deficiency; drug therapy for specific disorders, using such preparations to produce a therapeutic hormonal response; and diagnostic aids to determine hypofunctional or hyperfunctional hormone states.

A number of hormones have been identified, and many have been synthesized, including the following: growth hormone–releasing hormone (GRH), growth hormone–inhibiting hormone (Somatostatin), thyrotropin-releasing hormone (TRH), corticotropin-releasing hormone (CRH), gonadotropin-releasing hormone (GnRH), and prolactin-inhibiting hormone (PIH or dopamine). Also, six anterior pituitary hormones and two posterior pituitary hormones have been identified. The anterior pituitary hormones include growth hormone (GH), thyrotropin (TSH), adrenocorticotropin (ACTH), follicle-stimulating hormone (FSH), luteinizing hormone (LH) and prolactin. The posterior pituitary hormones are vasopressin and oxytocin.

This chapter covers specific agents affecting the pituitary. It does not discuss formulations that directly affect or involve the pancreas, thyroid, parathyroid, and adrenal cortex. These latter formulations are discussed in the chapters devoted to these areas.

Of the above-mentioned hormones, gonadotropin-releasing hormone (gonadorelin) is discussed in Chapter 52 while thyrotropin-releasing hormone (TRH) and corticotropic-releasing hormone (CRH) are discussed in Chapters 48 and 49. While a true hormone with prolactin-inhibiting effects has not been identified, the substance is believed to be dopamine. Bromocriptine, a drug with dopamine-agonist properties, is reviewed in Chapters 18 and 53.

Of the remaining two substances, the **growth hormone-releasing hormone (GHRH)** has been identified in vivo

755

but is still under investigation. This substance has been found to stimulate the release of growth hormone after intranasal application. If it is marketed, it will be used to test clients with growth hormone deficiency, thus testing the responsiveness of the anterior pituitary gland.

The **growth hormone–inhibiting hormone (somatostatin)** was obtained from human cadaver pituitaries, but its distribution in the United States was stopped in 1985. **Creutzfeldt-Jakob disease** (a neurotropic virus) that is very rare in young people, was diagnosed in some clients and resulted in the death of several clients 5 to 7 years after receiving this product. Therefore human-derived preparations are now replaced by a biosynthetic hormone grown through recombinant DNA technology. This product (somatrem) is considered equivalent to the pituitary human growth hormone in effectiveness.

## ANTERIOR PITUITARY HORMONES
### somatrem (Protropin)

Somatrem contains the identical sequence of the pituitary-derived human growth hormone plus one additional amino acid, methionine. In tests it has been demonstrated to be therapeutically equivalent to somatrotropin, or the human growth hormone from the pituitary.

*Mechanism of action.* Somatrem stimulates the release of **somatomedins** (hormones that are synthesized in the liver and elsewhere), in response to the growth hormone. It is believed most of the actions of somatrem are related to the effects of the somatomedins, which include stimulation of growth by their effect on organ size and growth of long bones and by an increase in the number and size of muscle tissue cells. Therefore a major pharmacologic consequence of somatrem use is an increase in longitudinal growth, whereas a deficiency in growth hormone usually results in **dwarfism.**

Somatrem also has metabolic effects—it impairs glucose uptake, and antagonizes the effects of insulin; increases lipolysis; promotes cellular growth by retaining phosphorus and potassium and enhances protein synthesis by increased nitrogen retention.

*Indications.* For the treatment of growth failure in children caused by a pituitary growth hormone deficiency.

*Pharmacokinetics*
*Parenteral (IM or SC)*

While the half-life of somatrem is 20 to 30 minutes, the distribution and effects of this product are longer lasting. It is metabolized in the liver, and less than 1% (approximately 0.1% of a dose) is excreted by the kidneys.

*Side effects/adverse reactions.* Antibodies to somatrem have been reported in 30% to 40% of treated clients during the first 3 to 6 months of therapy, but only 5% of the clients develop neutralizing antibodies. It is rare that a client does not respond to therapy. However, pain and edema have been reported at the site of injection.

Excessive doses may produce **gigantism** in children, so before the drug is used, growth failure must be carefully documented and dosages and individual responses closely monitored. Hypothyroidism has been rarely reported.

*Significant drug interactions.* When somatrem is given concurrently with adrenocorticoids, glucocorticoids, or corticotropin (ACTH), the growth response effects of somatrem may be impaired. ACTH should not be given concurrently and if it is necessary to treat with an adrenocorticoid agent, the daily dosages should be limited. For example, the total daily dose per square meter of body area should not be greater than the following: cortisone (12.5 to 18.8 mg); hydrocortisone (10 to 15 mg); methylprednisolone (2 to 3 mg); prednisone or prednisolone (2.5 to 3.75 mg); betamethasone (300 to 450 μg) and dexamethasone (375 to 563 μg)

*Dosage and administration*
*somatrem for injection (Protropin)*

For children, give 0.05 to 0.1 IU/kg intramuscularly every other day or three times weekly. (A minimum of 48 hours between doses is recommended.) Monitor growth rate response in 6 months to determine if dosage adjustment is necessary.

*Pregnancy safety.* Has not been established.

▷ **Nursing Management:**
**Somatrem Therapy**

*Assessment.* It should be ascertained that the client does not have a malignancy, especially an intracranial tumor. Somatrem is also contraindicated in clients with closed epiphyses or those with a known sensitivity to benzyl alcohol such as neonates. Use with caution in clients with diabetes mellitus or untreated hypothyroidism.

Obtain baseline data from bone age determinations, thyroid function studies, and blood glucose determinations. Monitor these data periodically during therapy.

*Intervention.* Prepare the drug for parenteral use by diluting with 1 to 5 ml of the diluent provided by the manufacturer. Do not shake the vial; rotate it gently between the palms of the hands until the solution is clear. Store in the refrigerator.

*Education.* Advise the client of the importance of regular visits to the pediatric endocrinologist for the monitoring of blood and urine studies, thyroid function studies, and growth rate and bone age determinations.

*Evaluation.* Increases in the growth pattern should occur by which to evaluate the efficacy of the therapy.

Pain and swelling has occurred at the site of injection. After several months of therapy, antibodies to somatrem may be formed in some clients. These rarely reduce the response to therapy.

Monitor for signs of hypothyroidism such as lethargy, intolerance to cold, weight gain, dry skin, and brittle, lackluster hair, which have been reported in less than 5% of clients with hypopituitarism receiving somatrem therapy.

**TABLE 47-1**  Side effects/adverse reactions of vasopressin (Pitressin)

| Drug | Side effects* | Adverse reactions† |
|---|---|---|
| vasopressin (Pitressin) | Most frequent: pain at injection site (usually with tannate dosage form)<br>Less frequent: stomach gas and pain, diarrhea, dizziness, increased pressure for bowel evacuation, nausea, vomiting, tremors, sweating, pallor | Rare: chest pain due to angina or myocardial infarction, increased or continuing headaches, confusion, coma, convulsions, weight gain, drowsiness, urinary difficulties (usually due to water retention or intoxication, occurs more with tannate dosage form). Allergic type reactions include elevated temperature; rash; pruritus; hives; edema of face, hands, feet or mouth; wheezing or respiratory difficulties. |

*If side effects continue, increase, or disturb the patient, inform the physician.
†If adverse reactions occur, contact physician as medical intervention may be necessary.

## somatropin (Humatrope)

Somatropin is a DNA recombinant product that is identical to the amino acid sequence of human growth hormone. It is used to stimulate linear growth in clients that lack sufficient endogenous growth hormone thus resulting in increased skeletal growth (an increased length of the epiphyseal plates of long bones reported). The number and size of muscle cells, organs and red cell mass are also increased. A increase in cellular protein synthesis and lipid mobilization resulting in a decrease in body fat stores is also reported.

The mechanism of action, indications and other properties of somatropin are similar to somatrem. The recommended dosage is individualized up to 0.06 mg/kg (0.16 IU/kg) SC or IM, three times weekly.

## POSTERIOR PITUITARY HORMONES

The two hormones from the posterior lobe of the pituitary gland are oxytocin and vasopressin (ADH, or antidiuretic hormone). Oxytocin will be discussed in Chapter 53; only vasopressin is discussed in this chapter.

### vasopressin (Pitressin)

***Mechanism of action.*** Antidiuretic hormone effect includes increasing water reabsorption in the collecting ducts of the nephron, resulting in a decreased urine volume with a higher osmolarity. Vasopressin stimulates peristalsis through a direct effect on gastrointestinal motility. Thus it has been used for abdominal distention due to bowel gas. It also increases secretion of corticotropin, growth hormone, and follicle-stimulating hormone. At larger doses, it causes vasoconstriction.

***Indications.*** Vasopressin is used to treat insufficient antidiuretic hormone release centrally, in other words, to treat the symptoms of **diabetes insipidus** resulting from true deficiency of ADH. It is not effective for polyuria induced by renal impairment, nephrogenic diabetes insipidus, psychogenic diabetes insipidus, or drug-induced (lithium or demeclocycline) diabetes insipidus.

Vasopressin is also used to treat abdominal distention or gas, especially before abdominal x-rays or postoperatively.

***Pharmacokinetics.*** Vasopressin's intramuscular absorption may be erratic; its intranasal absorption is poor. While usually given subcutaneously, it may be administered intravenously or intraarterially. The vasopressin tannate oil suspension dosage form should only be administered intramuscularly. Vasopressin has a half-life of 10 to 20 minutes. Duration of action with vasopressin aqueous is 2 to 8 hours; vasopressin tannate in oil—between 1 and 3 days. Vasopressin is metabolized in the liver and kidneys and excreted by the kidneys.

***Side effects/adverse reactions.*** See Table 47-1.

***Significant drug interactions.*** None are reported.

***Dosage and administration***

*Vasopressin injection, aqueous (Pitressin)*

The adult dosage is 5 to 10 units intramuscularly or subcutaneously two or three times a day when needed to treat central diabetes insipidus. For abdominal gas and distention: 5 units intramuscularly initially. If necessary, the next dose may be increased to 10 units. The dose may be repeated every 3 to 4 hours as necessary. Prior to abdominal roentgenography (x-rays): 10 units intramuscularly or subcutaneously approximately 2½ hours before the planned x-rays.

In children the dose for treatment of central diabetes insipidus is 2.5 to 10 units intramuscularly or subcutaneously, three or four times daily. Use as a peristaltic stimulant must be individualized by the prescribing physician.

*Sterile vasopressin tannate oil suspension (Pitressin)*

Adult dosage is 1.5 to 5 units intramuscularly every 1 to 3 days for central diabetes insipidus; in children 1.25 to 2.5 units, every 1 to 3 days for central diabetes insipidus.

***Pregnancy safety.*** Has not been established.

▷**Nursing Management: Vasopressin Therapy**

***Assessment.*** Use with caution in clients with angina, myocardial infarction, inadequate coronary circulation, and hypertension as vasopressin may increase blood pressure and precipitate anginal pain.

Use with caution in elderly clients because of the risk of water intoxication and hyponatremia. Its use should be avoided if at all possible in clients with chronic nephritis with nitrogen retention.

Obtain a baseline ECG. Assess the client for altered cardiac output related to increased fluid volume and the drug's vasopressor effect.

*Intervention.* Note that the spontaneous disappearance of side effects such as skin blanching, abdominal cramps, and nausea may be hastened by concomitant administration of 1 or 2 glasses of water.

Be aware that vasopressin tannate cannot be given intravenously. Prolonged rotation and shaking of the vial and warming it in hands is necessary so that all of the particles are included in the suspension. Failure to shake the ampule thoroughly can result in inaccurate dosage and inadequate therapeutic response. Tannate injection is indicated only for treatment of diabetes insipidus.

To allow for a precise intravenous or intraarterial flow rate, administer the vasopressin aqueous injection by an infusion pump. Avoid extravasation because tissue necrosis and gangrene may result.

If the drug is administered to relieve the client's abdominal distention due to flatus, use a rectal tube following the injection to enhance the action of the drug.

*Education.* Warn the client that the side effects of paleness, nausea, abdominal or stomach cramps, or vomiting may occur. Drinking one or two glasses of water at the time of drug administration may help reduce the occurrence of the side effects. If they do occur, they are not serious and generally will disappear within minutes.

*Evaluation.* Obtain fluid and electrolyte determinations periodically during therapy. Monitor the specific gravity of the client's urine as well as the intake and output and daily weights to evaluate the drug's effectiveness. Monitor blood pressure; hypertension may occur, or in the case of nonresponse to the drug, hypotension.

Be alert for early signs of water toxicity such as confusion, headache, drowsiness, weight gain and seizures. Withdraw drug and restrict fluid intake until specific gravity of urine is at least 1.015 and polyuria occurs. Notify the physician immediately.

Assess whether the client has obtained relief from abdominal distention, e.g. the passage of flatus and stool, as a result of the drug. There should be a diminished urinary output.

## SUMMARY

Drugs affecting the pituitary are generally used as replacement therapy for hormone deficiency, drug therapy for a specific disorder, or diagnostic aids to diagnose hypofunc-

tional or hyperfunctional hormone states. Somatrem is therapeutically equivalent to somatropin, or the human growth hormone from the anterior pituitary, and is used for the treatment of growth failure in children caused by a deficiency of that hormone. The two posterior pituitary hormones are oxytocin and vasopressin. Oxytocin is discussed in the chapter on labor and delivery. Vasopressin is used for the treatment of diabetes insipidus, which results from a deficiency of ADH and for abdominal distention or gas. The pituitary gland serves a major role in the regulation of the endocrine system.

## BIBLIOGRAPHY

Achauer BM et al. (1989). Burn excision with intraoperative vasopressin, J Burn Care Rehabil 10(4):375.

American Hospital Formulary Service. (1991). AHFS drug information '91. Bethesda, Md: American Society of Hospital Pharmacists, Inc.

German K. (1987). Fluid and electrolyte problems associated with diabetes insipidus and syndrome of inappropriate antidiuretic hormone, Nurs Clinics North Amer 22(4):785.

Harbison G. (1990). A chance to be taller: growth hormone provides hope — and the potential for abuse, Time 135(2):70.

Hartshorn J. (1988). Pharmacology update: vasopressin in the treatment of diabetes insipidus, J Neurosci Nurs 20(1):58.

Hobbie WL et al. (1989). Endocrine late effects among survivors of cancer, Semin Oncol Nurs 5(1):14.

Horn LJ. (1988). Pharmacologic interventions in neuroendocrine disorders following traumatic brain injury, part 2, J Head Trauma Rehabil 3(3):86.

Jacoby AG et al. (1990). Cardiovascular complications of intravenous vasopressin therapy, Focus Crit Care 17(1):63.

Kastrup EK, ed. (1991). Facts and comparisons. St Louis: JB Lippincott Co.

Lippe BM. (1987). Short stature in children: evaluation and management, J Pediatr Health Care 1(6):313.

Littlefield LC. (1988). Interaction of drugs and antidiuretic hormone, J Pediatr Health Care 2(6):325.

Moshang T Jr et al. (1988). Late effects: disorders of growth and sexual maturation associated with the treatment of childhood cancer, J Assoc Pediatr Oncol Nurses 5(4):14.

Patterson LM et al. (1989). Diabetes insipidus versus syndrome of inappropriate antidiuretic hormone, DCCN 8(4):226.

Schultz PN. (1989). Hypopituitarism in patients with a history of irradiation to the head and neck area: diagnoses and implications for nursing, Oncol Nurs Forum 16(6):823.

Stachura ME. (1987). Human growth hormone: use and potential abuse, Hosp Formul 22(1):48.

United States Pharmacopeial Convention. (1991). Drug information for the health care professional, ed 11. Rockville, Md: The Convention.

# Drugs Affecting the Parathyroid and Thyroid

## CHAPTER OBJECTIVES

*After studying this chapter, you should be able to meet the following objectives and define the key terms.*

1. Describe the clinical complications associated with hypothyroidism, hyperthyroidism, hypoparathyroidism, and hyperparathyroidism.

2. Describe the dose and action of calcium and vitamin $D_2$ products in the treatment of hypoparathyroidism.

3. Describe the primary therapy and the agents available to treat hypothyroidism.

4. Name two diagnostic agents used to assess thyroid function.

5. Describe the actions of iodine (iodide ion), radioactive iodine, and thioamide drugs in treating hyperthyroidism.

6. Discuss nursing measures for the client receiving drugs affecting the parathyroid or thyroid gland.

## KEY TERMS

**adenomas,** page 760

**desiccated thyroid,** page 760

**iodine,** page 765

**myxedema,** page 761

**primary hyperparathyroidism,** page 759

## INTRODUCTION

A number of medications are available to treat the various conditions of the thyroid and parathyroid glands.

## PARATHYROID

With hypoparathyroidism (idiopathic), serum calcium levels are decreased while serum phosphate levels are increased. Usually vitamin D levels are low. The administration of vitamin D (25,000 units or more, three times weekly) and calcium supplements (see box on p. 760) usually will restore the calcium and phosphorus levels to normal. Calcitriol (Rocaltrol) is an active metabolite form of vitamin D that is also used to elevate serum calcium levels. See Table 48-1 for drugs used to treat hypoparathyroidism.

**Primary hyperparathyroidism** causes excessive serum and urinary levels of calcium. While the urine phosphate is

---

### CALCIUM SUPPLEMENTS

The activity of calcium depends on calcium ion (elemental) content. The following calcium salts are listed by milligrams per gram, milliequivalents per gram, and percent of calcium in the preparation.

| Preparation | Calcium mg/g | Calcium mEq/g | Percent of Calcium |
|---|---|---|---|
| calcium carbonate | 400 | 20.0 | 40 |
| calcium chloride | 272 | 13.6 | 27.2 |
| calcium citrate | 211 | 10.5 | 21.1 |
| calcium gluceptate | 82 | 4.1 | 8.2 |
| calcium gluconate | 90 | 4.5 | 9 |
| calcium lactate | 130 | 6.5 | 13 |
| calcium phosphate | | | |
| dibasic | 230 | 11.5 | 23 |
| tribasic | 380 | 19 | 38 |

When low-percentage preparations are used, larger quantities of the drug are necessary to provide adequate calcium supplementation. For example, if the physician desired 1 g of elemental calcium from either calcium carbonate or calcium lactate preparations, it would require 2.5 g of calcium carbonate or nearly 7 g of calcium lactate to provide the calcium ordered. Other considerations would indicate client acceptance—that is, taste, tolerance, side effects, and other factors.

---

**TABLE 48-1** Drugs used to treat hypoparathyroidism

| Drug(s) | Purpose/dose |
|---|---|
| PTH (oral) | Not available<br>Severe hypocalcemia—calcium gluconate 10%, intravenously until symptoms of tetany are relieved or serum calcium levels are above 7.5 mg/dl. Start oral calcium supplements as soon as possible.<br>Mild to moderate hypocalcemia—restrict phosphate absorption with aluminum hydroxide-binding preparations. A 1-to-2 oral intake of calcium (elemental) is usually sufficient. If calcium serum level is below 7.5 mg/dl, then administer vitamin D to maintain an adequate serum calcium level. See box for comparisons for calcium preparations. |
| vitamin $D_2$ (ergocalciferol) | Inactive. It requires activation by liver 25-hydroxylation and by kidneys 1-alpha hydroxylase. Also need bile salts for improved absorption in the gut. Usual dose is 50,000 to 100,000 units daily. This is least expensive formulation, but its onset of action is slow (2 weeks or more) and duration of action is long (16-18 weeks after it is discontinued). |
| dihydrotachysterol (DHT) (Hytakerol) capsules | Needs only liver 25-hydroxylation to activate. While more expensive than vitamin $D_2$, it has a rapid onset of action (within 2 hours); duration is 7 to 15 days. Dose is 0.2-2.5 mg/day (average dose is 0.5 mg). May be preferred for postoperative hypocalcemic tetany. |
| calcitriol (Rocaltrol) | Active drug. Rapid onset, 1 to 3 days duration. More expensive. Dose 0.25 μg initially (range 0.5 to 1 μg), increased in 2- to 4-week periods. |
| calcediol (Calderol) | Active drug. Has a metabolite with a long half-life of 16 days. Onset of action is faster than vitamin $D_2$ but slower than DHT. Dose is 50 to 100 μg/day. |

---

high, the serum level is low to normal. This can lead to renal stones, bone pain with skeletal lesions, and possibly pathologic fractures. Since **adenomas** or tumors may be causing this syndrome, usually surgery is the primary treatment. In clients with mild hypercalcemia or mild hyperparathyroidism, a thorough examination by a physician would determine whether or not surgery is indicated. High serum levels of calcium may require immediate treatment. See Table 48-2 for typical recommendations for treatment of hypercalcemia.

# THYROID
## Thyroid Preparations

Practitioners have agreed that individuals with hypothyroidism need thyroid replacement therapy. However, there is disagreement about which preparation is best for substitution therapy (see box on available preparations). For many years, natural or **desiccated thyroid** has served admirably for replacement therapy, and it is still considered to be satisfactory for many clients. A major problem with desic-

**TABLE 48-2**   Recommendations for treatment of hypercalcemia

| Methods | Special comments |
|---|---|
| **INHIBITION OF BONE RESORPTION** | |
| mithramycin | Lowers serum calcium within 1 to 2 days after single dose of 25 to 50 $\mu$g/kg injection. Maximum effect seen within 2 to 5 days. This is a toxic drug that is usually reserved for use when other therapies have been unsuccessful. |
| calcitonin | Usual dosages of 4 MRC units/kg may induce serum calcium decreases of 1 to 2 mg/dl. Produces maximum effect in 6 to 9 hours. Used to treat Paget's disease. |
| **INCREASE IN CALCIUM EXCRETION** | |
| hydration | Hydrate client with normal saline. This can reduce serum calcium by 2 to 3 mg/dl. Monitor for fluid overload and electrolyte disturbances. (Not therapy of choice for client with heart failure or compromised cardiac function.) |
| furosemide diuretic | Used with administration of large quantities of normal saline hydration, usual dose is 100 mg every 2 hours. Monitor electrolytes closely because replacement electrolytes may be necessary. |
| **DECREASE CALCIUM ABSORPTION** | |
| oral phosphates | 250 mg every 6 hours orally if phosphorous level is low. Correcting hypophosphatemia usually lowers calcium serum levels. May cause diarrhea and compromise renal function. Monitor closely. |
| **OTHER MECHANISMS** | |
| glucocorticoids, such as prednisone or hydrocortisone | They decrease calcium absorption, increase calcium excretion, and inhibit the effects of vitamin D. |

---

## THYROID PREPARATIONS

thyroid tablets (various manufacturers)
levothyroxine tablets (Synthroid, Eltroxin ♣)
liothyronine sodium tablets (Cytomel)
liotrix tablets (Euthroid, Thyrolar)
thyroglobulin tablets (Proloid)

---

**TABLE 48-3**   Dose equivalents of selected thyroid products

| Product | Dosage |
|---|---|
| thyroid, USP | 60 mg |
| thyroglobulin | 60 mg |
| levothyroxine | 100 $\mu$g (0.1 mg) or less |
| liothyronine | 25 $\mu$g (0.025) mg) |
| liotrix—levothyrtoxine (T$_4$) and liothyronine (T$_3$), 4:1 ratio | |
| T$_3$ | 12.5 to 15 $\mu$g |
| T$_4$ | 50 to 60 $\mu$g |

cated thyroid is that its potency varies among different brands of the preparation. The rate at which it loses its potency also varies. No requirement for metabolic potency exists, and preparations may not contain enough metabolically active substance to produce the desired therapeutic effect, even though the drug meets USP requirements. This has led to a decline in use of natural thyroid products.

Thyroid USP is mainly derived from hog thyroid glands, although cattle and sheep thyroid glands have also been used. Thyroglobulin (Proloid) is an extract of hog thyroid gland, whereas levothyroxine sodium, liothyronine, and liotrix are synthetic thyroid replacement products. The question as to which preparation is superior has not yet been fully answered, but the synthetic preparations have a higher standardization in potency. See Table 48-3 for dose equivalents of selected thyroid products.

In the plasma, about 95% of the hormone is thyroxine, and the remainder is liothyronine. Approximately 99% of the hormones are protein bound (thyroxine-binding globulin, TBG) and may be expressed as iodide; thus the term protein-bound iodide (PBI). The normal PBI concentration is 4 to 8 $\mu$g/dl plasma. T$_4$ is bound more firmly than T$_3$; this permits a more rapid entry of T$_3$ into the cells.

The goal of treatment of clients with hypothyroidism or **myxedema** is to eliminate their symptoms (see box on p. 762 for clinical features of hyperthyroidism versus hypothyroidism) and to restore them to a normal emotional and physical state. Clinical response is more important than blood hormone level. However, laboratory assessments of T$_3$, T$_4$, serum cholesterol, and TSH levels are used as criteria for adequacy of therapy.

*Mechanism of action.* While not completely understood, thyroid hormones have both anabolic and catabolic effects; therefore they are involved in metabolism, growth, and development (especially development of the central nervous system in infants).

---

### CLINICAL FEATURES OF HYPERTHYROIDISM VERSUS HYPOTHYROIDISM

| | Hyperthyroidism | Hypothyroidism |
|---|---|---|
| Eyes | Prominent | Eyelids edematous, ptosis |
| Hair | Thin, fine texture | Dry, brittle, thin |
| Temperature | Intolerance to heat | Intolerance to cold |
| Weight | Appetite increases, weight loss | Appetite decreases, weight gain |
| Emotional | Increased nervousness, irritability, insomnia | Lethargic, depressed, increase in sleeping needs |
| Gastrointestinal | Diarrhea | Constipation |
| Neuromuscular | Fast deep-tendon reflexes | Slow or delayed deep-tendon reflexes |
| Extremities | Hot, moist skin | Cold, dry skin |

---

Thyroid hormone concentrations are regulated by the hypothalamic-anterior pituitary and thyroid body feedback mechanism.

**Indications.** Thyroid supplements are indicated for the treatment of hypothyroidism; treatment and prevention of goiter; treatment and prevention of thyroid carcinoma; and thyroid function diagnostic tests.

Thyroid, thyroglobulin, and levothyroxine are incompletely and/or erratically absorbed from the gastrointestinal tract, whereas liothyronine is completely absorbed. They are highly protein bound with time to peak effect of 3 to 4 weeks with thyroid, thyroglobulin, and levothryroxine and 1 to 3 days with liothyronine. Thyroid, thyroglobulin, and levothyroxine have a duration of effect after withdrawal of long-term therapy of 1 to 3 weeks while liothyronine has up to 3 days. These agents are metabolized the same as endogenous thyroid hormone, that is, some in peripheral tissues, smaller amounts metabolized in the liver and excreted in bile.

**Side effects/adverse reactions.** Side effects are dose related and may occur more rapidly with liothyronine than with the other products mainly because it has a faster onset of action. The general signs of underdosing or hypothyroidism are dysmenorrhea, ataxia, coldness, dry skin, constipation, lethargy, headaches, drowsiness, tiredness, weight gain, and muscle aching.

Rare adverse reactions include severe headaches and an allergic skin rash. Overdose with thyroid products results in hyperthyroidism—alterations in appetite and menstrual periods, elevated temperature, diarrhea, hand tremors, increased irritability, leg cramps, increased nervousness, tachycardia, irregular heart rate, increased sensitivity to heat, chest pain, respiratory difficulties, increased sweating, vomiting, weight loss, and drowsiness.

**Significant drug interactions.** When thyroid hormone preparations are given concurrently with the following drugs, a significant drug interaction may occur:

| Drug | Possible Effect and Management |
|---|---|
| anticoagulants, oral (coumarin or indandione) | May alter the therapeutic effects of the oral anticoagulant. An increase in thyroid hormone may require a decrease in anticoagulant oral dosage. Monitor coagulation time closely, utilizing the prothrombin time (PT) test. |
| cholestyramine or colestipol | May bind thyroid hormones, delaying or decreasing their absorption from the gastrointestinal tract. A 4- to 5-hour interval is recommended between administration of these drugs. |
| sympathomimetics | The effects of one or both medications may be increased. May result in an increased risk of coronary insufficiency if individual has coronary artery disease, or, if a thyroid preparation is given with tricyclic antidepressants, an increase in cardiac arrhythmias may result. Monitor closely, since dosage adjustments may be necessary. |

**Dosage and administration.** Levothyroxine adult oral dose for hypothyroidism is 50 μg initially, increasing every 2 to 3 weeks by 25 μg as necessary. The initial dose is reduced to 25 μg in clients with longstanding hypothyroidism. Maintenance dose is usually 75 to 125 μg daily. With elderly persons or individuals with cardiovascular disease, the initial dose is 12.5 to 25 μg with dosage increases at 3- to 4-week intervals. As pediatric dosages vary according to age or weight, the nurse is referred to a current package insert or USP-DI for individual recommended dosages.

Levothyroxine sodium for injection dose for hypothyroidism in adults is 50 to 100 μg IM or IV daily. For myxedema stupor or coma, the dose is 200 to 500 μg initially intravenously, even in geriatric clients. If improvement is not noted by second day, an additional 100 to 200 μg (0.1 to 0.3 mg) may be given. Continuous daily administration would depend on client's response and tolerance for the medication. Switch to oral dosage form as soon as possible. Clients with cardiovascular disease may require smaller dosages.

### Geriatric Implications
## THYROID HORMONES

Since the elderly are usually more sensitive to and experience more adverse reactions to thyroid hormones than other age groups, it is recommended that thyroid replacement doses be individualized. In some clients, the dose should be 25% lower than the usual adult dose.

Hypothyroidism, the second most common endocrine disease in the elderly, is often misdiagnosed. Only one third of the geriatric clients exhibit the typical signs and symptoms of cold intolerance and weight gain. Most often the symptoms are nonspecific, such as failing to thrive, stumbling and falling episodes, weight loss, incontinence, and, if neurologic involvement has occurred, the client may be misdiagnosed as having dementia, depression, or a psychotic episode (USP-DI, 1991; Delafuente, 1988).

Laboratory tests for serum T₄ and TSH are used to confirm hypothyroidism.

Levothyroxine (Synthroid, others) is usually the drug of choice for thyroid replacement.

---

The pediatric dose is approximately 75% of the usual oral pediatric dose, IV or IM.

Liothyronine oral adult dose is 25 μg initially, with daily increases every 7 to 14 days by 12.5 to 25 μg increments as necessary. The maintenance daily dose is between 25 and 50 μg. For myxedema and simple, nontoxic goiter, the initial dose is 2.5 to 5 μg daily, increasing at 5- to 10-μg increments every 7 to 14 days, as necessary. The maintenance dose for myxedema is usually 25 to 50 μg orally a day, whereas for simple goiter, it is 50 to 100 μg orally.

In elderly persons and individuals with cardiovascular disease, the initial dose is 5 μg daily, increasing by 5-μg increments every 14 days. This product is not recommended for use in children.

The adult oral dose for Liotrix for hypothyroidism without myxedema is 50 to 60 μg of levothyroxine and 12.5 to 15 μg of liothyronine daily. Increase by similar amounts on a monthly basis, if necessary. For myxedema or hypothyroidism with cardiovascular disease present, reduce dose to 12.5 μg of levothyroxine and 3.1 μg of liothyronine daily. Maintenance dose is 50 to 100 μg of levothyroxine and 12.5 to 25 μg of liothyronine daily.

In geriatric clients, the initial dose is from 25% to 50% of the usual adult dose. This dose may be doubled at 6- to 8-week intervals, if necessary. For pediatric dosages, see current package insert or USP-DI.

Thyroglobulin adult oral dose for hypothyroidism without myxedema is 32 mg daily initially, increase as necessary, every 7 to 14 days. For myxedema or hypothyroidism with

cardiovascular disease present, the initial dose is 16 to 32 mg daily, increasing every 2 weeks, if necessary. Maintenance dose is 65 to 160 mg daily. For children with cretinism or severe hypothyroidism, see adult dose for myxedema. For children with hypothyroidism, see adult dose for hypothyroidism without myxedema.

Thyroid adult oral dose for hypothyroidism without myxedema is 60 mg initially daily, increasing by 30 mg increments monthly if necessary. Maintenance dose is 60 to 120 mg daily. For myxedema or hypothyroidism with cardiovascular disease present, the initial dose is 15 mg daily, which may be increased to 30 mg daily after 14 days and 60 mg daily after another 2 weeks. Maintenance dose is 60 to 120 mg daily. Geriatric clients should start with a 7.5 to 15 mg daily dose. This dose may be doubled every 6 to 8 weeks, if necessary.

For pediatric dose for cretinism or severe hypothyroidism, see the adult dose for myxedema. For pediatric hypothyroidism, see adult dose for hypothyroidism without myxedema.

***Pregnancy safety.*** For all thyroid products, pregnancy safety has been established at FDA category A.

## ▷Nursing Management:
## Thyroid Preparation Therapy

***Assessment.*** Use with care in elderly clients, because they are more sensitive to the effects of thyroid hormones. A 25% reduction in the dose of the thyroid hormone replacement may be required for clients over 60 years of age (see box above).

The use of thyroid hormonal therapy is carefully considered if the client has preexisting adrenocortical or pituitary insufficiency (thyroid hormonal replacement increases physiologic need for adrenocortical hormone), cardiovascular disease (too rapid thyroid hormonal replacement increases metabolic demand), history of hyperthyroidism, or thyrotoxicosis. In cases of chronic hypothyroidism or myxedema, an increased sensitivity may exist. The client is started on the lowest possible dosage, with increases in the dosage titrated in accordance with the client's clinical response and laboratory data.

***Intervention.*** Since hypothyroid clients respond rapidly to replacement doses, therapy is begun with a small dose and gradually increased over several weeks until the optimal clinical response is obtained. Once the maintenance dose has been established, it is taken or given daily, preferably before breakfast.

It is recommended that levothyroxine be taken on an empty stomach. In its parenteral form, levothyroxine sodium is reconstituted with 5 ml of sodium chloride injection (without preservative) to a solution of 100 μg (0.1 mg)/ml. It should be reconstituted immediately before use.

***Education.*** Lifelong therapy is a possibi'    ᵛith thyroid

Selected nursing diagnoses related to thyroid therapy

| Nursing diagnosis | Outcome criteria | Nursing interventions |
|---|---|---|
| Knowledge deficit related to thyroid dysfunction | Client will:<br>Express understanding of normal thyroid function and the effects of altered thyroid function | Assess client's level of understanding.<br>Determine educational needs of client and family.<br>Instruct client in function of the thyroid gland and thyroid hormones.<br>Instruct client in specific effects related to client's alteration in thyroid function.<br>Provide opportunity for client to ask questions and verbalize concerns. |
| Knowledge deficit related to drug regimen (thyroid drug) | Client will:<br>Understand the purpose of drug therapy and recognize side effects/adverse reactions of the medication | Teach the client:<br>Purpose and action of the drug<br>Proper administration<br>The need for continued therapy throughout lifetime, even after euthyroid state is obtained<br>Signs and symptoms of hypothyroidism and hyperthyroidism<br>Side effects/adverse reactions<br>Provide the client with a list of drugs or conditions that interact with or alter the drug requirements.<br>Explain the benefit of wearing or carrying a medical identification tag, bracelet, or card. |
| Alteration in body image related to thyroid dysfunction | Client and family will:<br>Express concerns regarding body image changes<br>Understand basis for body changes related to thyroid function and recognize the benefit of drug therapy | Assess the client and family for perceptions and concerns related to body image.<br>Encourage open communication and talking about perceived body image.<br>Encourage adequate rest periods.<br>Adjust adequate rest periods.<br>Adjust calorie intake and diet to changing client needs.<br>Encourage a high-bulk diet, fluids, and exercise to prevent or limit constipation.<br>Encourage good grooming and attractive dress to promote self-confidence and positive self-image.<br>Administer thyroid drugs as prescribed. |
| Altered nutrition related to altered metabolic needs | Client will:<br>Maintain a stable body weight<br>Show evidence of maintaining a well-balanced diet | Assess normal dietary patterns.<br>Instruct client to monitor his or her weight weekly.<br>Instruct client to adjust diet to match caloric needs.<br>Assist client in planning meals and dietary modifications. |
| Potential for impaired skin integrity related to altered thyroid function | Client will:<br>Maintain intact skin<br>Demonstrate proper skin care | Assess skin for dryness, itching, or altered integrity.<br>Monitor client for development of skin disruption.<br>Keep skin clean and well lubricated.<br>Apply moisturizer as needed.<br>Use skin massage and position changes.<br>Instruct client in proper skin care. |

hormonal replacement. Counsel the client accordingly. This means regular consultations with the physician to monitor effectiveness of the therapy, as well as compliance with the prescribed regimen. To simulate the natural process of the body, the client should take the dosage at the same time every day. Morning administration will help to prevent insomnia.

Inform the client that if a dose is missed, it is to be taken as soon as possible. If it is close to the next day's dose, caution the client not to take the dose, since this will have the effect of doubling doses. Contact the physician if two or more consecutive doses are missed.

Tell the client to alert other health care providers as to the thyroid hormonal replacement—particularly if any kind of surgery is required, including dental surgery. A medical

identification should be worn. Advise the client to consult with the physician before taking other medications concurrently with thyroid replacement.

Advise the client to inform the physician if the pulse rate increases or if palpitations or chest pain occur. Irritability, nervousness, heat intolerance, and excessive sweating may indicate a need for a reduction in dosage; however, insomnia is usually the earliest sign. If such symptoms occur, withdrawal of the drug may be indicated for a few days before it is resumed at a lower dose.

Alert parents of a pediatric client that partial hair loss sometimes occurs during the first few months of therapy with children, but it is temporary and the hair will usually return, even if hormonal replacement is continued.

Advise the client not to change brands of thyroid replace-

**TABLE 48-4**   Diagnostic testing for hypothyroidism

| Origin of deficiency | Level of TSH | TSH levels following TRH testing |
|---|---|---|
| Thyroid gland | Increased | Very increased |
| Pituitary gland | Decreased | No response |
| Hypothalamus | Increased | Slow response |
| Hyperthyroid | Decreased | No response |

ment therapy, since different brands of the drug are not bioequivalent.

***Evaluation.*** Assess the client for a decrease in the symptoms of hypothyroidism: weight loss, loss of constipation, and increased activity levels, appetite, sense of well-being, and pulse rate should be seen. Laboratory reports should indicate normal $T_3$ and $T_4$ levels.

Monitor thyroid function studies before and throughout therapy. Such studies may include free $T_4$ index determinations, TSH determinations, $T_3$ or $T_4$ resin uptake determinations, and total serum $T_3$ and $T_4$ determinations. Assess pediatric clients periodically for growth, bone age, and psychomotor development.

Monitor baseline apical pulse and blood pressure before and periodically during therapy. Clients are at risk for altered cardiac output related to the thyroid's cardiovascular effects. If the resting pulse is over 100, hold the dose and notify the physician. For clients with preexisting cardiovascular disease, observe closely for ischemia and tachyarrhythmias.

## Diagnostic Testing for Hypothyroidism

Protirelin (Thypinone, Relefact TRH) and thyrotropin (thyroid-stimulating hormone, TSH) are diagnostic agents used to assess thyroid function. See Table 48-4 for a comparison of the tests. The thyroid-stimulating hormone (TSH) test is a very sensitive test used to diagnose hypothyroidism. The thyroid-releasing hormone (TRH) test measures the pituitary's response to TRH. For example, in hypothalamic hypothyroidism, the pituitary responds slowly to exogenous TRH and produces a slow but rising TSH. In clients with primary hypothyroidism, TSH basal levels are increased, and the pituitary is hyperreactive to TRH stimulation. If the client has hypothyroidism resulting from hypopituitarism, no response to TRH is expected. Therefore the TRH test can differentiate a primary from a secondary hypothyroidism and also differentiate hypopituitary from hypothalamic hypothryroidism. (See box for physiology of thyroid gland and its hormones.)

## Antithyroid Agents

An antithyroid drug is a chemical agent that lowers the basal metabolic rate by interfering with the formation, release, or action of the hormones made by the thyroid gland. Those

---

### PHYSIOLOGY OF INFLUENCES ON THE THYROID GLAND: A FEEDBACK MECHANISM

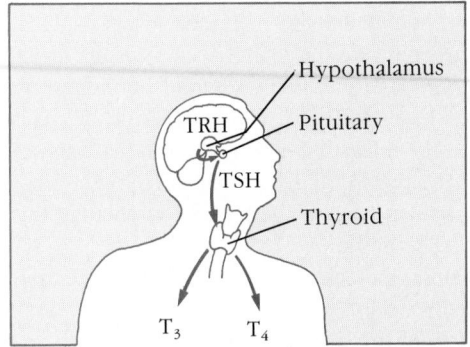

When serum levels of $T_3$ and $T_4$ are increased, the release of TRH from the hypothalamus and TSH from the anterior pituitary gland is reduced, thus inhibiting their effects on the thyroid gland.

When serum levels of $T_3$ and $T_4$ are decreased, TRH release triggers the release of TSH from the pituitary. TSH effects on the thyroid are an increase in the size and number of follicular cells in the thyroid, thus increasing their ability to absorb iodide, and an increase in thyroglobulin breakdown, which releases $T_3$ and $T_4$ hormones from the thyroid gland into the bloodstream, thus increasing blood levels of the thyroid hormones.

---

that interfere with the synthesis of the thyroid hormones are known as goitrogens. A variety of compounds are included in this category of antithyroid drugs, but only iodine (iodide ion), radioactive iodine, and thioamide derivatives are discussed here.

### Iodine, Iodides

**Iodine** is the oldest of the antithyroid drugs. Although a small amount of iodine is necessary for normal thyroid function and to synthesize thyroid hormones, the response of the client with thyrotoxicosis is prompt inhibition of thyroid release from the hyperfunctioning thyroid gland.

### Thyroid-Iodide Pump

Iodide enters the body from the diet and is rapidly absorbed into the bloodstream. Approximately one third of it is removed from the blood by the iodide pump in the thyroid. The initial iodide removed from the blood is usually sodium or potassium iodide. The enzyme perioxidase converts the iodides to iodine, which is then used to form monoiodotyrosine (MIT) and diiodotyrosine (DIT), which are the components of $T_3$ and $T_4$. The synthesized hormones ($T_3$, $T_4$) are stored within thyroglobulin until they are released into the blood circulation. These activities involve a complex negative feedback mechanism between the thyroid gland and the hypothalmus-pituitary gland. Low levels of circulating thyroid hormone increase the release of thyroid-stimulating hormone (TSH) from the pituitary and appear to influence the secretion of thyrotropin-releasing factor (TRF) from the hypothalamus. Increased levels of TSH increase iodide trapping by the gland, which results in an increase in synthesis and circulating thyroid hormones. As thyroid hormone levels increase, the hypothalmic and pituitary centers stop the release of TRF and TSH. This process will be repeated if the thyroid hormone levels decrease again, in response to the declining levels of circulating thyroid hormones. (See box on p. 765)

Although iodides are used to synthesize thyroid hormones, an excess of iodides, as previously used to treat hyperthyroidism since the 1940s, will block thyroid hormone synthesis and release and will also decrease the vascularity of the thyroid gland. Although the mechanism of effect is unknown, the inhibition of thyroid hormone release for several weeks will lead to an increase in TSH secretion that can overcome this blockade. Thus, large doses of iodides are generally used for 7 to 14 days before thyroid surgery in order to decrease the thyroid's size and vascu-larity, resulting in diminished blood loss and a less complicated surgical procedure.

Radioactive iodine (RAI) is preferred for clients who are poor surgical risks, such as debilitated clients, those with advanced cardiac disease, and elderly clients. It is also used for clients who have not responded adequately to drug therapy or who have had recurrent hyperthyroidism after surgery. The primary disadvantage of using surgery or RAI therapy, in addition to the risk involved with surgery and postsurgical complications, is the induction of hypothyroidism.

### Iodine Products
**strong iodine solution (Lugol's solution)**
**sodium iodide**
**potassium iodide**

For iodine's mechanism of action, see previous section. Iodine is indicated to protect the thyroid gland from radiation before and after the administration of radioactive isotopes of iodine or in radiation emergencies and may be used with an antithyroid drug in clients with hyperthyroidism in preparation for thyroidectomy. Therapeutic effects may be noted within 24 to 48 hours with maximum effects achieved within 10 to 14 days of continuous therapy. For side effects / adverse reactions, see Table 48-5.

**TABLE 48-5**    Antithyroid agents: significant side effects and adverse reactions

| Drug(s) | Side effects* | Adverse reactions† |
|---|---|---|
| iodine or iodide products | Diarrhea, nausea, vomiting, abdominal pain | Most frequent: skin rash, swelling or tenderness of the salivary gland<br>Rare: bloody or black colored stools (due to GI bleeding), irregular heart rate, paresthesias of hands or feet, increased tiredness, leg weakness, confusion (due to potassium toxicity), increased temperature (hypersensitivity), edema of neck or throat<br>With prolonged usage: severe headaches, sore gums or teeth, increased salivation, burning in mouth or throat, metallic taste in mouth |
| sodium iodide I 131 (Iodotope) | Less frequent: sore throat, neck swelling or pain, loss of taste (temporary), nausea, vomiting, painful salivary glands | After treatment for hyperthyroidism: increased or unusual irritability or tiredness<br>After treatment of thyroid carcinoma: fever, sore throat, and chills (due to leukopenia), increased bleeding episodes (due to thrombocytopenia)<br>Signs of hypothyroidism may follow treatment, including changes in menstrual cycle, increased clumsiness, cold feelings, sedation, dry, puffy skin, headaches, muscle aching, temporary dryness or thinning of hair, increased weakness, and unusual weight gain. |
| thioamide derivatives: methimazole tablets, propylthiouracil tablets | Most frequent (3% to 5%): rash or pruritus<br>Less frequent: dizziness, loss of taste, nausea, vomiting, paresthesias, abdominal pain | Less frequent: elevated temperature, chills or sore throat, overall feelings of discomfort or weakness (may be agranulocytosis, leukopenia, or lupus-like syndrome), jaundice of skin and eyes (due to cholestatic hepatitis)<br>Rare: edema of feet or lower legs, backache, unusual increases or decreases in urination (nephritis), joint pain, swollen lymph nodes, increased bleeding tendencies or bruising<br>Signs of overdosage or hypothyroidism: see above<br>Signs of thyrotoxicosis or subtherapeutic therapy: fever, diarrhea, increased irritability, weakness, tachycardia, vomiting |

*If side effects continue, increase, or disturb the patient, inform the physician.
†If adverse reactions occur, contact physician since medical intervention may be necessary.

***Significant drug interactions.*** When iodide products are given concurrently with the following drugs, the noted significant drug interactions may occur:

| Drug | Possible Effect and Management |
|---|---|
| antithyroid drugs | May increase the hypothyroid and goitrogenic effects of the drugs. Monitor closely. |
| diuretics, potassium-conserving type | If these diuretics are used concurrently with potassium iodide, increased levels of potassium may result in hyperkalemia, cardiac arrhythmias, or cardiac arrest. Monitor serum potassium levels closely. |
| lithium | The hypothyroid and goitrogenic effects of both drugs may be potentiated. Obtain and monitor baseline thyroid status periodically to plan appropriate interventions. |

***Dosage and administration.*** Strong iodine solution and sodium iodide injection are not listed in the USP-DI. For information on dosage and administration of these products, refer to a current package insert or reference source (Kastrup, 1991).

Potassium iodide liquid or tablets are also commonly known as KI or SSKI. The adult oral dose to protect the thyroid gland from radiation is 100 to 150 mg 24 hours before radiation, then daily for 3 to 10 days afterward. The maximum daily dose is up to 12 g. In infants up to a year old, 65 mg orally is given for 10 days after exposure to radioactive isotopes of iodine. Children 1 year and older are given a 130 mg oral dose daily for 10 days following exposure to radioactive iodine.

***Pregnancy safety.*** While unclassified regarding pregnancy safety, potassium iodide does cross the placenta and may produce abnormal thyroid function in infants.

▷ **Nursing Management:**
**Iodine Product Therapy**

***Assessment.*** Thyroid function studies should be monitored before and periodically during therapy.

Be aware that iodine products are contraindicated in hyperkalemic states and in clients receiving lithium therapy, since lithium has synergistic hypothyroid and goitrogenic activity, resulting in hypothyroidism. Checking serum potassium levels is advisable before administering iodine products. Pulmonary edema and pulmonary tuberculosis are also contraindications to the use of iodines.

Iodine therapy during pregnancy can cause abnormal thyroid function or goiter in the newborn.

Iodine products are contraindicated in clients sensitive to them. Initial assessment should determine if the client is allergic to seafood, since this may be indicative of a cross-sensitivity to iodine. Skin testing is recommended before administering parenteral doses. The earliest symptoms of the hypersensitivity are irritation and swelling of the eyelids.

***Intervention.*** Dilute Lugol's solution and saturated solutions of sodium or potassium in one-third to one-half glass of fruit juice, carbonated beverage, or another substance to improve taste. Administer after meals to minimize gastric irritation.

Dilute the liquid dose of SSKI with fruit juice, water, or milk. Since the medication evaporates rapidly, do not leave open to air for long periods before administration. Do not use if the solution has turned brownish yellow.

Administer iodides through a straw to prevent discoloration of the teeth.

***Education.*** Instruct the client to discontinue use and notify the physician if any of the following occur: fever, skin rash, metallic brassy taste, swelling of the neck and throat, burning soreness of gums and teeth, head cold symptoms, or severe gastrointestinal distress. These symptoms are characteristic of chronic iodide poisoning.

Instruct the client to consult with the physician regarding the use of iodized salt and seafood in the diet. Iodine-rich foods, such as soybeans, cabbage, kale, and other green leafy vegetables may need to be restricted.

Caution the client to maintain the prescribed dosage. Missing doses may precipitate a thyroid storm. Instruct the client to consult with the prescriber before taking OTC cold remedies, because some contain iodides.

***Evaluation.*** A decrease in the symptoms of hyperthyroidism should occur. For clients receiving the drug as part of a preoperative course of therapy, there should be a decrease in the size and vascularity of the thyroid. Assess the client for altered comfort related to the gastrointestinal and dermatologic effects of iodine.

### sodium iodide I 131 (Iodotope)

Sodium iodide I 131 (Iodotope) is a radioactive isotope of iodine. It will accumulate in thyroid tissue and selectively damage or destroy it. It is indicated for the treatment of hyperthyroidism and thyroid carcinoma and for testing of thyroid function.

It is administered orally, and the onset of thrapeutic effect is within 2 to 4 weeks. The peak therapeutic effect occurs between 2 and 4 months, whereas the peak diagnostic effect is within 4 to 24 hours. It is mainly excreted by the kidneys with 65% to 90% eliminated within 24 hours. Up to 20% of the dose may appear in breast milk within 24 hours. It has a half-life of approximately 8 days; the principal types of radiation are beta (90%) and gamma rays. For side effects/adverse reactions, see Table 48-5.

While no significant drug interactions are noted with this product, many drugs are capable of interfering with test results. Refer to a current USP-DI for possible drug interferences and also for current dosage recommendations. Although pregnancy safety is unclassified, this product crosses the placenta and can cause severe hypothyroidism in newborns; therefore it is not recommended for use during pregnancy.

▷ **Nursing Management:**
**Sodium Iodide I 131 Therapy**

*Assessment.* Thyroid function studies should be performed before and after therapy. Do not give radioactive iodine to pregnant women or nursing mothers. In a patient with childbearing potential, therapy begins the first few days after the onset of menses.

*Intervention.* The client should take nothing by mouth after midnight before a morning dose, because food slows the absorption of the drug.

To avoid exposure to the radioactive products of the iodine, wear rubber gloves when giving I 131 to clients and when disposing of their excreta.

If the dose is administered for hyperthyroidism, institute full radiation precautions for 24 hours. If the dose is for cancer of the thyroid, isolate the client for 3 days. Check the institution's protocol for radiation precautions. Pregnant women, be they personnel or visitors, should not have contact with the client. Use disposable utensils with the client. Increase the fluid intake of the client to 2500 ml/daily to enhance excretion of the isotope. Consult with nuclear medicine personnel about limitations for individual staff contact with the client.

*Education.* To prevent radiation contamination of others and the environment, instruct the client in appropriate methods for disposal of urine and feces, such as double-flushing toilet and washing hands after using toilet, until radiation precautions are no longer needed.

If the client is discharged but radiation precautions are still necessary, ensure that the client receives specific instructions for visitor contact and disposal of utensils and excreta from the personnel in the nuclear medicine department.

If the client received dosage of I 131 for the treatment of hyperthyroidism or thyroid carcinoma, these 48- to 72-hour precautions may include the following: avoiding close contact with others, especially children; not kissing anyone or sharing other persons' eating or drinking utensils; not engaging in sexual activities; sleeping alone; washing sink and tub after use; and, using and washing clothes, towels and linens separately.

*Evaluation.* Assess post-therapy thyroid function with serum thyroxine examinations. The client may experience temprary altered comfort following a course of I 131 therapy, evidenced by loss of taste, nausea and vomiting, and tenderness of the salivary glands. In addition, with therapeutic dosages there is physiologic injury, resulting in hypothyroidism, the incidence of which should be 100% if the regimen has been successful. Other reactions may include leukopenia, evidenced by fever, chills and sore throat, and thrombocytopenia, evidenced by unusual bleeding or bruising.

*Thioamide Derivatives*

**methimazole (thiamazole) tablets (Tapazole)**
**propylthiouracil tablets (Propyl-Thyracil ✦)**

Thioamide derivatives, or antithyroid agents, inhibit the synthesis of thyroid hormone by inhibition of iodide into tyrosine and the coupling of iodotyrosines. They do not affect exogenous thyroid hormones. Propylthiouracil (not methimazole) also inhibits the conversion of thyroxine ($T_4$) to triiodothyronine ($T_3$), which may make it more effective for treatment of a thyroid crisis or storm. They are indicated for the treatment of hyperthyroidism, prior to surgery or radiotherapy, or as adjunct therapy for treatment of thyrotoxicosis or thyroid storm (propylthiouracil preferred for latter indication).

Propylthiouracil has a half-life of 1 to 2 hours, and methimazole has a variable half-life of 4 to 14 hours. Both drugs have an onset of action within 10 to 20 days and a peak effect within 2 to 10 weeks. They are metabolized in the liver and excreted by the kidneys. For side effects/adverse reactions, see Table 48-5.

A potentiation of hypothyroid and goitrogenic effects may result if methimazole or propylthiouracil is given with iodinated glycerol, lithium, or potassium iodide.

The oral adult dose of methimazole is 15 mg (mild), 30 to 40 mg (moderate to severe), or 60 mg (severe) for hyperthyroidism, divided into three doses given at 8-hour intervals for 6 to 8 weeks. The maintenance dose is 5 to 30 mg daily in 2 to 3 divided doses. To treat thyrotoxic crisis, the dose is 15 to 29 mg every 4 hours for 24 hours used as an adjunct to other therapies. Pediatric dose for hyperthyroidism is 0.4 mg/kg daily; maintenance dose is 0.2 mg/kg daily.

The oral adult dose of propylthiouracil for hyperthyroidism is 300 to 900 mg daily in divided doses. Maintenance dose is 50 to 600 mg daily; the dose for thyrotoxic crisis is 200 to 400 mg every 4 hours for 24 hours (as adjunct therapy), decreasing the dose thereafter as necessary. Children between 6 and 10 years old receive 50 to 150 mg daily, while children over 10 years old receive 50 to 300 mg daily. For neonatal thyrotoxicosis, the dose is 10 mg/kg daily in divided doses. Pregnancy safety has been established at FDA Category D; both drugs cross the placenta and can cause fetal hypothyroidism and goiter.

▷ **Nursing Management:**
**Thioamide Derivative Therapy**

*Assessment.* Monitor thyroid function studies before and periodically during therapy.

Concomitant thyroid administration during thioamide therapy in the hyperthyroid pregnant woman may avert hypothyroidism in the mother and fetus.

*Intervention.* Administer with meals to minimize gastric irritation.

Use the smallest effective dose (less than 300 mg daily) for pregnant clients. Propylthiouracil crosses the placental barrier; therefore large doses can cause goiter in the newborn or cretinism in the fetus.

Because therapy to obtain a prolonged remission may last from 6 months to several years, client adherence may become an issue. To be most effective the doses should be divided into evenly spaced intervals throughout the day.

However, to improve compliance and decrease the incidence of side effects, a once- or twice-a-day dosage schedule may be used, although it is less effective. Propylthiouracil needs to be taken at the same time every day in relation to meals, because food may alter the response to the drug by affecting its absorption.

Because of the risk of thyroid storm, the client should consult with the physician if his or her health status changes from infection, injury, or other illness, or if surgery, dental surgery, or emergency treatment is required.

*Education.* Instruct clients that if they develop sore throat, a head cold, skin eruptions, or malaise, they should report these symptoms immediately to their physicians, since these symptoms signal the onset of agranulocytosis. It may occur too quickly to be determined by periodic blood testing.

Instruct the client to consult with the prescriber about the restriction of iodized salt and seafood. Caution against taking OTC medications because many contain iodine preparations.

Advise breast-feeding mothers not to take this drug, since it is excreted in the milk.

*Evaluation.* Take a complete blood count periodically during therapy to detect blood dyscrasias such as agranulocytosis, leukopenia, or thrombocytopenia. Propylthiouracil may reduce thrombin and result in bleeding; monitor prothrombin time during therapy.

The client should be assessed for the effectiveness of the therapeutic regimen. Signs of thyrotoxicosis, such as fever, tachycardia, irritability, weakness, diarrhea, and vomiting indicate inadequate therapy; signs of hypothyroidism, such as intolerance to cold, constipation, lethargy, and weight gain indicate overdosage.

## SUMMARY

As with other of the endocrine glands, the parathyroid and thyroid functioning may be increased or decreased resulting in pathological conditions for the client. With hypoparathyroidism, the administration of vitamin D and calcium supplements will usually restore the calcium and phosphorus levels to normal. However, with hyperparathyroidism, surgery is usually the primary treatment. In hypothyroidism, the clinical goal is to eliminate the client's symptoms by thyroid replacement therapy, for which a number of preparations are available. Hyperthyroidism is managed by either large doses of iodides, which inhibit thyroid hormone release and decreases the thyroid's size; by thioamide derivatives which inhibit the synthesis of thyroid hormone; by radioactive iodine; or by surgery.

Through all the therapies associated with hormonal replacement or inhibition, the client requires support and ex-

planation to understand the many changes of body and mood that may occur with these therapies. Because clinical manifestations of the therapies are as important as the laboratory studies in determining the efficacy of treatment, ongoing skilled assessment of the client's health status is essential.

## BIBLIOGRAPHY

Avioli LV. (1987). Primary hyperparathyroidism: recognition and management, Hosp Pract 22(9):69.

Braunwald E et al, eds. (1987). Harrison's principles of internal medicine, ed 11. New York: McGraw-Hill Book Co.

Bullock BL and Rosendahl PP. (1988). Pathophysiology, ed 2. Glenview, Ill: Scott, Foresman & Co.

Bybee DE. (1987). Saving lives in parathyroid crisis, Emerg Med 19(15):62.

Bybee DE. (1987). Saving lives in thyroid crisis, Emerg Med 19(16):20.

Dong BJ. (1988). Thyroid and parathyroid disorders. In Herfindal ET et al, eds. Clinical pharmacy and therapeutics, ed 4. Baltimore: Williams & Wilkins.

Francis B. (1990). Hypothyroidism, Adv Clin Care 5(2):29.

Goldberger J et al. (1989). Iatrogenic thyroid dysfunction, Hosp Pract 24(9):30.

Hobbie WL et al. (1989). Endocrine late effects among survivors of cancer, Semin Oncol Nurs 5(1):14.

Huff BB, ed. (1990). Physician's desk reference, ed 44. Oradell, NJ: Medical Economics Co., Inc.

Hypothyroidism on the horizon. (1987). Emerg Med 19(21):47.

Kastrup EK, ed. (1991). Facts and comparisons. St. Louis: JB Lippincott Co.

Katzung BG. (1987). Basic and clinical pharmacology, ed 3. Norwalk, Conn: Appleton & Lange.

Kerlikowski K et al. (1987). Euthyroid sick or "hyperthyroid" sick? Hosp Pract 22(10):113.

Krupp MM et al, eds. (1987). Current medical diagnosis and treatment. Norwalk, Conn: Appleton & Lange.

Mathewson MK. (1987). Thyroid disorder, Crit Care Nurse 7(1):74.

Mcmillan JY. (1988). Preventing myxedema coma in the hypothyroid patient, DCCN 7(3):136.

O'Neill JR. (1987). Action STAT! Thyroid crisis, Nursing 17(11):33.

Schneeberg NG. (1989). Incurable hyperthyroidism? Consultant 29(4):89.

Sherwood LM. (1987). Diagnosis and management of primary hyperparathyroidism, Hosp Pract 23(3):9.

Thyroxine therapy and bone loss. (1988). Nurses Drug Alert 12(9):70.

Tucker SM et al. (1989). Hyperthyroidism: thyroid crisis, J Emerg Nurs 15(4):352.

United States Pharmacopeial Convention. (1991). Drug information for the health care professional, ed 11. Rockville, Md: The Convention.

*Chapter*

# 49 Drugs Affecting the Adrenal Cortex

## CHAPTER OBJECTIVES

*After studying this chapter, you should be able to meet the following objectives and define the key terms.*

1. Compare and contrast glucocorticoids and mineralocorticoids.

2. Describe the major pharmacologic effects of the corticosteroids.

3. Describe five significant drug interactions of the glucocorticoids.

4. Describe the advantages for an alternate-day regimen schedule.

5. Describe a recommended method for corticosteroid drug withdrawal.

6. Name four major adverse reactions associated with the use of adrenocorticoids.

7. Discuss nursing management of drug therapy for the care of clients receiving agents affecting the adrenal cortex.

## KEY TERMS

**circadian rhythm,** page 771

**corticosteroids,** page 770

**fight-or-flight phenomenon,** page 771

**glucocorticoids,** page 770

**mineralocorticoids,** page 770

**septic shock,** page 776

**ultradian rhythms,** page 771

## INTRODUCTION

All the adrenocortical hormones, and the synthetic analogs of even higher potency, are commercially available. The generic name for these hormones and analogs is **corticosteroids.** Some corticosteroids, such as cortisol, have a profound effect on carbohydrate metabolism, whereas aldosterone primarily affects mineral (or electrolyte) and water metabolism. Therefore corticosteroids are divided into two classes, **glucocorticoids** and **mineralocorticoids** (halogenated glucocorticoids).

*Biosynthesis of corticosteroids.* Cholesterol, which is used for the biosynthesis of corticosteroids, is synthesized and stored in the adrenal cortex. The adrenal cortex also obtains cholesterol from the blood. This cholesterol may be from dietary sources or synthesized by the liver.

Synthesis of corticosteroids depends on the ACTH secreted by the pituitary. The predominant action of ACTH on the adrenal cortex is synthesis of corticosteroids and secretion of glucocorticoids. The exact mechanism for these events is not known.

The release of ACTH by the pituitary is believed to be stimulated by the corticotropin-releasing hormone (CRH) from the hypothalamus, although CRH has not yet been chemically identified. Some evidence suggests that the corticosteroids can inhibit the adrenal glucocorticoid system by inhibiting the release of CRH from the hypothalamus and by inhibiting the release of ACTH from the pituitary.

## GLUCOCORTICOIDS

***Glucocorticoid rhythms.*** Two rhythms appear to influence glucocorticoid function: circadian (daily) rhythm and ultradian rhythm. **Circadian rhythm** appears to be controlled by the dark/light and sleep/wakefulness cycles. Normal persons sleeping in the dark at night will have increased plasma cortisol levels in the early morning hours that reach a peak after they are awake. These levels then slowly fall to very low levels in the evening and during the early phase of sleep. The importance of this rhythm is emphasized by the finding that corticosteroid therapy is more potent when given at midnight than when given at noon.

**Ultradian rhythms** are periodic or intermittent functions with frequencies higher than once every 24 hours. In human beings, four to eight adrenal glucocorticoid bursts occur each 24 hours, which may follow bursts in CRH and ACTH releases. These bursts are clustered close together and are very pronounced during the circadian rise in plasma glucocorticoid levels in the early hours of the morning. At other times they may be so widely spaced that adrenal secretion is zero. Consequently the adrenal cortex secretes glucocorticoids only about 25% of the time in unstressed individuals.

***Pharmacologic actions.*** Glucocorticoids have the following pharmacologic actions:

1. *Antiinflammatory action.* Glucocorticoids, especially cortisol in larger than normal dosages, can stabilize lysosomal membranes and prevent release of proteolytic enzymes during inflammation. They can also potentiate vasoconstrictor effects.
2. *Maintenance of normal blood pressure.* Glucocorticoids potentiate the vasoconstrictor action of norepinephrine. When glucocorticoids are absent, the vasoconstricting action of the catecholamines is diminished, and blood pressure falls.
3. *Carbohydrate and protein metabolism.* Glucocorticoids help to maintain the blood sugar level and liver and muscle glycogen content. They facilitate breakdown of protein in muscle and extrahepatic tissues, which leads to increased plasma amino acid levels. Glucocorticoids increase the trapping of amino acids by the liver and stimulate the deamination of amino acids. They also increase the activity of enzymes important to gluconeogenesis and inhibit glycolytic enzymes. This can produce hyperglycemia and glycos-

uria. They are diabetogenic. These effects can aggravate diabetes, bring on latent diabetes, and cause insulin resistance. Inhibition of protein synthesis can delay wound healing and cause muscle wasting and osteoporosis. In young persons these effects can inhibit growth.

4. *Fat metabolism.* Glucocorticoids promote mobilization of fatty acids from adipose tissue. This increases the concentration of fatty acids in the plasma and their use for energy. Despite this effect, clients taking glucocorticoids may accumulate fat stores (rounded face, buffalo hump). The effect of glucocorticoids on fat metabolism is complex and little known.
5. *Thymolytic, lympholytic, and eosinopenic actions.* Glucocorticoids can cause atrophy of the thymus and decrease the number of lymphocytes, plasma cells, and eosinophils in blood. They also decrease the rate of conversion of lymphocytes into antibodies. These effects ultimately can interfere with the immune and allergic responses. This, along with their antiinflammatory action, makes them useful immunosuppressants for delaying rejection in clients with organ or tissue transplants, as well as useful antiallergenics for the treatment of acute allergic reactions such as urticaria, bronchial asthma, and anaphylactic shock. However, steroids can be a source of danger in infections by limiting useful protective inflammation. These hormones also inhibit activity of the lymphatic system, causing lymphopenia and reduction in size of enlarged lymph nodes.
6. *Stress effects.* During stressful situations, corticosteroids are suddenly released, which is believed to be a protective mechanism. The corticosteroids support blood pressure and increase blood sugar to provide energy for emergency actions such as running. This is known as the **fight-or-flight phenomenon.** Clients with decreased adrenal function require increased amounts of steroids during stressful periods such as surgery. Without steroid administration, hypotension and shock tend to occur. (See Figure 49-1.)

During stress, epinephrine and norepinephrine also are released from the adrenal medulla, and these catecholamines have a synergistic action with the corticosteroids. However, there is disagreement about the physiologic usefulness of the steroids during stress.

***Mechanism of action.*** ACTH, or corticotropin, stimulates the synthesis of adrenal steroids by combining with a receptor in the adrenal cell plasma membrane in clients with a normal adrenal cortex function or in clients with a adrenocortical insufficiency secondary to corticotropin deficiency.

The released adrenocorticoids can cross cell membranes and combine with specific receptors in the cytoplasm. The complexes may then enter the cell nucleus, bind to DNA, and ultimately affect protein synthesis.

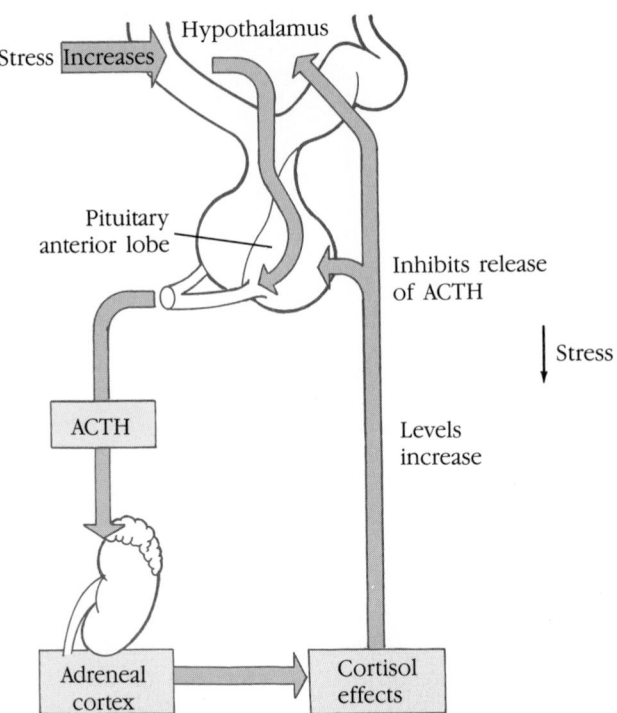

**FIGURE 49-1**    Glucocorticord secretion.

***Indications.*** They are used in replacement therapy for adrenocortical insufficiency and also to treat severe allergic reactions; anaphylactic reactions not responsive to other therapies; collagen disorders such as systemic lupus erythematosus, carditis, and systemic dermatomyositis (polymyositis); treatment of dermatologic conditions, gastrointestinal disorders, hematologic disorders, treatment of hypercalcemia associated with neoplasms, adjunct treatment for neoplastic disease, nephrotic syndrome, neurologic disease, ophthalmic disorders, respiratory disorders, rheumatic disorders, and treatment of shock.

***Pharmacokinetics.*** The glucocorticoids are well absorbed orally; parenterally (IM) the soluble esters (sodium phosphate, sodium succinate) are rapidly absorbed while the less soluble derivatives (acetate, acetonide, diacetate) are slowly but completely absorbed. Topically, the soluble esters are less rapidly absorbed while the less soluble derivatives are slowly but completely absorbed. Rectally about 20% of the drug is absorbed normally, but if the rectum is inflamed, absorption may increase up to 50%.

These agents are mainly metabolized in the liver but may also be somewhat metabolized in tissues and kidneys. Cortisone and prednisone need to be metabolized to their active metabolites, which are hydrocortisone and prednisolone, respectively. The fluorinated adrenocorticoids are more slowly metabolized than the other drugs.

For onset of action, peak effect, and duration of action, see Table 49-1. For the relative potency of the major short-acting, intermediate-acting, and long-acting adrenocorticoids, see Table 49-2.

***Side effects/adverse reactions.*** See Table 49-3.
***Significant drug interactions.*** The following interactions may occur when corticosteroids are given concurrently with the drugs listed below.

| Drug | Possible Effect and Management |
|---|---|
| aminoglutethimide | Aminoglutethimide suppresses adrenal function, therefore do not administer corticotropin concurrently. When aminoglutethimide is given, glucocorticoid supplements are often prescribed. Be aware that aminoglutethimide can increase the metabolism of dexamethasone, reducing its half-life significantly. Hydrocortisone is recommended though, because its metabolism does not appear to be affected by aminoglutethimide. |
| amphotericin B parenteral | May result in severe hypokalemia. If given concurrently, monitor serum potassium levels closely.<br>May also decrease the adrenal gland response to corticotropin. |
| antacids | When given concurrently with prednisone or dexamethasone, a decrease in steroid absorption may result. Monitor closely; dosage adjustments may be necessary. |
| antidiabetic drugs (oral) or insulin | Glucocorticoids may elevate serum glucose levels (both during therapy and after, if the glucocorticoid is stopped); therefore a dosage adjustment of one or both drugs may be necessary. |
| digitalis products | May result in increased potential for toxicity (dysrhythmias) associated with hypokalemia. |

**TABLE 49-1**  Pharmacology of adrenocorticoids/corticotropin

| Drug (route) | Onset of action | Peak effect | Duration of action |
|---|---|---|---|
| betamethasone (PO) | — | 1-2 hr | 3.25 days |
| sodium phosphate (IM, IV) | Rapid | — | — |
| acetate/sodium phosphate (IM) | 1-3 hr | — | 7 days |
| (IA) (IS) | — | — | 7-14 days |
| (IL) (ST) | — | — | 7 days |
| corticotropin repository (IM) | — | — | 12-24 hours |
| zinc hydroxide (IM) | — | — | 2 days |
| cortisone acetate (PO) | Rapid | 2 hr | 30-36 hours |
| (IM) | Slower | 20-48 hr | — |
| dexamethasone (PO) | — | 1-2 hr | 66 hours |
| acetate (IM) | — | 8 hr | 6 days |
| (IA) (ST) (IL) | — | — | 1-3 weeks |
| sodium phosphate (IV) (IM) | Rapid | — | 72 hr-3 wk |
| (IA) (IS) (IL) (ST) | — | — | 30-36 hr |
| hydrocortisone (PO) | — | 1 hr | — |
| (IM) | — | 4-8 hr | — |
| rectal enema (retention) | 3-5 days | — | 3-28 days |
| acetate (IA) (IS) (IB) (IL) (ST) | — | 1-2 days | — |
| rectal foam | 5-7 days | — | — |
| cypionate (PO) | Slow | 1-2 hr | — |
| sodium phosphate (IV) | Rapid | — | Varies |
| (IM) | Rapid | 1 hr | — |
| sodium succinate (IV) | Rapid | — | Varies |
| (IM) | Rapid | 1 hr | 30-36 hr |
| methylprednisolone (PO) | — | 1-2 hr | 1-4 wk |
| acetate (IM) | 6-48 hr | 4-8 days | 1-5 wk |
| (IA) (IL) (ST) | Very slow | 7 days | — |
| sodium succinate (IV) | Rapid | — | — |
| (IM) | Rapid | — | 2 days |
| paramethasone acetate (PO) | — | 1-2 hr | 30-36 hr |
| prednisolone (PO) | — | 1-2 hr | — |
| acetate (IM) | Slow | — | Up to 4 wk |
| acetate/sodium phosphate (IM) | — | — | 3-28 days |
| (IB) (IS) (IA) (ST) | — | — | — |
| sodium phosphate (IV) (IM) | Rapid | 1 hr | 3-21 days |
| (IA) (IL) (ST) | — | — | 7-21 days |
| tebutate (IA) (IL) (ST) | 1-2 days | — | 30-36 hr |
| prednisone (PO) | — | 1-2 hr | 52 hr |
| triamcinolone (PO) | — | 1-2 hr | 1-6 wk |
| acetonide (IM) | 1-2 days | — | Several weeks |
| (IB) (IA) (IL) (ST) | — | — | — |
| diacetate (PO) | — | 1-2 hr | 4-28 days |
| (IM) | Slow | — | 1-2 wk |
| (IL) | — | — | 1-8 wk |
| (IA) (IS) (ST) | — | — | 3-4 wk |
| hexacetonide (IA) (IL) | — | — | — |

Abbreviations: —, specific times not listed in USP-DI (1990); *PO*, orally; *IA*, intraarticularly; *IB*, intrabursal; *IL*, intralesion; *IM*, intramuscularly; *IS*, intrasynovial; *ST*, in soft tissue.

---

## SEPTIC SHOCK

**Septic shock** usually results from a gram-negative bacteremia that leads to circulatory insufficiency. The inadequate tissue perfusion generally results in hypotension, oliguria, tachycardia, elevated temperature, and tachypnea.

### Mechanism

Septic shock may be caused by bacterial substances that interact with body cell membranes and systems, especially coagulation and the complement system, resulting in injury to cells and alterations in blood flow in the body.

### Treatment

Treatment may consist of volume replacement, antibiotics, surgery (if client has an abscessed or necrotic bowel or organs/tissues), vasoconstricting agents (dopamine, norepinephrine, or levarterenol), diuretics, and glucocorticoids (steroids). Use of steroids is somewhat controversial, but several published studies have reported a benefit with their use if used early in the treatment of shock.

### Steroid Beneficial Effects

Beneficial effects of steroids include protecting cellular membranes from injury, decreasing platelet aggregation, reducing extracellular release of leukocyte enzymes, and preventing the formation of vasoactive substances in the body.

---

or subcutaneous, 1.6 USP units/kg or 50 USP units/m² daily is given in 3 or 4 divided doses.

For repository corticotropin injection in adults, therapeutic dose is, intramuscular (preferred) or subcutaneous, 40 to 80 USP units every 24 to 72 hours. To treat multiple sclerosis (acute exacerbation) give 80 to 120 USP units daily for 14 to 21 days.

For children, the therapeutic dose is intramuscular (preferred) or subcutaneous, 0.8 USP units/kg or 25 USP units/m² daily, given as a single dose or divided into two.

### cortisone tablets (Cortone)

The adult dose is 25 to 300 mg daily. Pediatric dose for adrenocortical insufficiency is 0.7 mg/kg orally daily, in divided doses. For other indications the dose is 2.5 to 10 mg/kg orally.

### dexamethasone liquids/tablets (Decadron, Hexadrol, and others)

The adult dose is 0.5 to 8 mg daily. The dexamethasone suppression test for Cushing's syndrome is 1 mg orally at 11 PM or 0.5 mg every 6 hours for 2 days. Then appropriate blood or urine tests are performed to determine levels of cortisol or metabolites present. To distinguish between

Cushing's syndrome due to pituitary ACTH excess and Cushing's syndrome due to other causes, a 2-mg dose of dexamethasone every 6 hours for 2 days of testing is used.

Dexamethasone has also been used as a diagnostic aid for depression, but the accuracy of this test is considered questionable. It is often used to treat cerebral edema in recurrent or inoperable brain tumors at doses of 2 mg orally, two or three times daily following the use of the injectable dexamethasone.

For children, the dose for adrenocortical insufficiency is 23.3 µg/kg daily in three divided doses. For other indications the dose is 83.3 to 333.3 µg/kg daily in three or four divided doses.

The long-acting preparation is dexamethasone acetate suspension (Dalalone LA or DP, Decadron LA) is used for intraarticular or soft tissue injection. The adult dose is 4 to 16 mg that may be repeated at 1- to 3-week intervals. If dosed intramuscularly, the dose is 8 to 16 mg at 1- to 3-week intervals. Dosage for children has not been established.

Dexamethasone is also available in the faster acting, more soluble sodium phosphate injection. This formulation may be administered IM, IV, intraarticular, intralesional, or by soft-tissue injection. Intravenously it is used to treat cerebral edema and shock. As dosage schedule recommendations may vary, refer to a current package insert or USP-DI for indication-related instructions.

### hydrocortisone (Cortef, Hydrocortone)

Hydrocortisone is available in oral, injectable, and rectal dosage forms. The recommended adult and child dose varies according to the specific indication and the dosage formulation. Usually the adult oral and intramuscular dose is 15 or 20 mg up to 240 mg daily, according to the individual's response to the medication. For further dosing instructions, refer to a current reference source, such as a package insert or the USP-DI.

### methylprednisolone (Medrol, Depo-Medrol, Solu-Medrol)

Methylprednisolone's adult dose is 4 to 48 mg orally daily, as a single dose or in divided doses. In multiple sclerosis, administer 160 mg orally daily for 7 days, then 64 mg every other day for 30 days. For children with adrenocortical insufficiency, the dose is 117 µg/kg daily in three divided doses. For other indications, the dose is 417 µg to 1.67 mg/kg in three or four divided doses.

Methylprednisolone is also available in a long-acting suspension (Depo-Medrol), a short- or fast-acting dosage form, or sodium succinate (Solu-Medrol), and as a rectal enema (Medrol Enpak). The sodium succinate dosage form is given intramuscularly or intravenously, whereas the suspension form is for intraarticular, intralesional, or soft tissue injections. For specific dosing instructions, refer to a current reference source.

## prednisolone (Delta-Cortef and others)

Prednisolone is an active adrenocorticoid, but prednisone is considered an inactive substance because it has to be metabolized in the liver to prednisolone to produce a therapeutic effect. The adult dose is usually 5 to 60 mg orally daily with a maximum limit of 250 mg/day. To treat an acute episode of multiple sclerosis, the dose is 200 mg daily for 7 days, then 80 mg daily every other day for 1 month. In children with adrenocortical insufficiency, the oral dose is 140 μg/kg daily in three divided doses.

For intraarticular, intralesional, or soft tissue injection in adults, the dose of prednisolone acetate suspension may range from 4 to 100 mg. The intramuscular dose is 4 to 60 mg daily. For children with adrenocortical insufficiency, the intramuscular dose is 140 μg/kg in 3 divided doses every third day. The adult dose for the longer acting formulations, that is, prednisolone tebutate suspension (4 to 40 mg every 2 to 3 weeks), prednisolone sodium phosphate injection (2 to 30 mg at 3-day to 3-week intervals), or the combination of prednisolone acetate and prednisolone sodium phosphate suspension is 20 to 80 mg and 5 to 20 mg, respectively, at 3-day to 4-week intervals, as necessary. For more specific information and current recommended dosing schedules, refer to a current reference source.

The adult oral dose for prednisone tablet/liquid (Deltasone and others) is 5 to 60 mg daily. To treat an acute episode of multiple sclerosis, the recommended oral dose is the same as for prednisolone. In children, the dose varies according to indication and age. It is currently indicated for the treatment of nephrosis, rheumatic carditis, leukemia, tumors, tuberculosis (if given along with antitubercular drugs), and for adrenogenital syndrome. For the appropriate dose, see a current reference source such as a package insert or the USP-DI.

## triamcinolone

This synthetic glucocorticoid is available in tablet, liquid, and parenteral dosage forms (Aristocort, Kenalog, and others). The adult oral dose for adrenocortical insufficiency is 4 to 12 mg daily although for other indications the necessary dose may be considerably higher (4 to 48 mg/day or more in selected cases). The pediatric dose for adrenocortical insufficiency is 117 μg/kg daily. Other indications may require a dosage range of 416 μg to 1.7 mg/kg daily.

For parenteral use, triamcinolone acetonide suspension is administered intraarticularly, intrabursally, or via the tendon sheath in a dose of 2.5 to 15 mg for the acetonide suspension. A 1-mg dose per intradermal or intralesional site may also be administered at 7-day intervals, if necessary. Intramuscularly, 40 to 80 mg is injected on monthly intervals. The longer acting dosage forms of triamcinolone include diacetate suspension and hexacetonide suspension. The diacetate dose intraarticular, intrasynovial, intralesional, sublesional or into soft tissues is 3 to 48 mg; this may be repeated at 1- to 8-week intervals. The intramuscular dose is 40 mg

weekly for adults and children 6 to 12 years old. It is not recommended for children under 6 years old. The hexacetonide suspension dose is 2 to 20 mg intraarticularly at 3- to 4-week intervals. Up to 0.5 mg/square inch of affected skin may be injected intralesionally or sublesionally. This product does not have an established dose for children.

## ▷NURSING MANAGEMENT: GLUCOCORTICOID THERAPY

***Assessment.*** Use glucocorticoids cautiously in individuals with psychosis, peptic ulcer, tuberculosis, acute glomerulonephritis, vaccinia or varicella, herpes simplex of the eye, and infections uncontrolled by antibiotics.

Note that myasthenic crisis may be induced if these drugs are administered to clients with myasthenia gravis. Use cautiously in pregnant women also, since adrenal insufficiency in both mother and child is possible at delivery. Fetal abnormalities also can occur.

Carefully assess for severe fluid and electrolyte imbalances when hypertension is present, as well as with congestive heart failure, diabetes mellitus, thrombophlebitis, renal insufficiency, and osteoporosis.

Do not give glucocorticoids to clients with systemic fungal and amebiasis infections. These drugs can exacerbate the disease state.

Because these clients are at risk for altered cardiac output related to sodium and fluid retention, obtain baseline weight before therapy. Weigh daily; report any sudden increases, which would indicate fluid retention, to the prescriber. Monitor intake and output daily. Correlate with physical findings of edema. Also obtain baseline data for hematologic values, serum electrolytes, and serum and urine glucose. Check stool for occult blood. These determinations should be monitored during therapy.

Assess children for growth before and periodically during therapy as there is a risk for altered growth and development with glucocorticoid therapy.

***Intervention.*** Note that an alternate-day regimen may be valuable when considering the long-term use of glucocorticoids in less severe disease processes, especially when an intermediate range–acting agent (methylprednisolone, prednisolone, prednisone) is used, since it diminishes hypothalamic-pituitary-adrenal (HPA) axis suppression. The alternate-day dose given every other morning before 9 AM is at least twice the daily dose equivalent. This therapy requires that a client possess a responsive pituitary axis and be stabilized initially on the alternate-day schedule.

Give glucocorticoids as a single daily dose in the morning before 9 AM if possible, with food or milk. They suppress adrenal activity the least when it is at its peak, which is early morning.

Administer IM injections of suspensions deep in the gluteal muscle to avert local tissue atrophy at the injection sites. Note that injections into the deltoid muscle can cause atrophy.

---

**ALTERATIONS IN BODY IMAGE WITH GLUCOCORTICOID THERAPY**

Alterations in body image may be a major concern in clients receiving glucocorticoid therapy. Among these body changes that may occur are the following:

Abdominal distention
Acneiform eruptions
Fat deposits on upper back ("buffalo hump")
Fluid retention
Hirsutism
Hyperpigmentation
Loss of muscle mass
Lupus erythematosus-like lesions
Round face ("moon face")
Petechiae and ecchymosis
Purpura
Straie
Thin fragile skin
Thinning of extremities, thickening of torso
Weight gain

---

Note that clients taking cortisone who require surgery should receive a preoperative dose of a rapid-acting corticosteroid. The drug is continued postoperatively in decreasing doses for several days. Clients with atrophy of the adrenal gland may be unable to cope with the stress of surgery if cortisone treatment is interrupted.

Be prepared to do an HPA axis suppression test following high doses or long-term therapy to determine level of suppression.

Know that withdrawal should be carried out slowly and under close supervision to avoid adrenal insufficiency. Note that the usual rate of withdrawal of systemic corticosteroids is the steroid equivalent of 2.5 mg prednisone every 4 days, when the client is under close and continuous medical supervision. When this is not possible, withdrawal of systemic corticosteroids is slower, approximately 2.5 mg prednisone (or equivalent corticosteroid dosage) every 10 days. When withdrawal symptoms such as weakness, lethargy, hypoglycemia, depression, anorexia, and nausea appear, the previous dose may be resumed for 7 days before continuing the decrease.

When the drug is to be discontinued, be aware that it usually is withdrawn gradually. If a medical-surgical emergency or stressful event occurs, the drug is given again to prevent the possibility of acute adrenal insufficiency.

**Education.** After intraarticular injection, instruct the client not to overuse the injected joint. Weight-bearing joints should be rested 24 to 48 hours after injection.

Instruct clients to report any signs of infections, such as sore throat, fever, and poor wound healing. Corticosteroids can mask infection and increase its spread. The client should avoid individuals with known contagious illnesses. Also tell clients to avoid any immunizations while taking glucocorticoids, since they impair the antibody response.

Instruct clients to report any visual disturbances. Long-term glucocorticoid therapy can cause cataracts, glaucoma, or optic nerve damage.

Since these drugs can cause gastric distress, instruct clients to report any persistent symptoms and instruct them to take the drug with meals or milk in the morning. Antacids may be necessary to prevent or relieve gastric irritation.

Warn the client and family that disturbances in self-concept may occur as the result of changes in appearance (see box at left). The nurse should assist the client and family in dealing with the changes that occur, as well as reassure them that they will disappear when the drug is stopped.

Most clients receiving glucocorticoids should be on a high potassium, low sodium diet to counter the potassium-depleting and sodium-retaining effects of the drug. Clients should limit alcohol, caffeine, aspirin, and other gastric irritants to minimize peptic ulceration. Long-term therapy may require increased protein intake to decrease the effects of protein catabolism.

Inform female clients that they may experience menstrual irregularities while taking glucocorticoids and that the following drugs are unsafe to take during pregnancy because of their effects on the fetus: cortisone, dexamethasone, hydrocortisone, methylprednisolone, and prednisolone.

Have clients carry a card describing their medical condition and drug therapy.

Remember that any client who has received a significant amount of cortisone or related glucocorticoids is likely to have some atrophy of the adrenal cortex. The amount of hormone that will produce atrophy is unknown, as is how long the atrophy will persist, but acute adrenal insufficiency may result from too rapid withdrawal of therapy. Instruct the client to report withdrawal symptoms including weakness, lethargy, malaise, restlessness, hypoglycemia, psychologic despondency, anorexia, and nausea.

Because altered thought processes may occur, have the client report changes in mental status (euphoria, mood swings, depression, insomnia) to the prescriber. Also caution the client to report to the physician any symptoms of abdominal pain, bone pain, tiredness, bruising, or tarry stools.

**Evaluation.** Assess for the following when excessive doses are given: CNS symptoms (anxiety, depression/stimulation), hyperglycemia, glycosuria, elevated blood pressure, and Cushing's syndrome.

Remember that not only the total daily dose, but also frequent individual doses during the day must be adjusted to meet the client's needs. Notify the physician of the client's varying responses to the drugs.

Closely monitor the blood sugar of clients taking glucocorticoids, since these drugs can cause hyperglycemia. Diabetic clients may need changes in diet or insulin dosage to maintain blood sugar control.

In addition, clients have the potential for impaired physical mobility related to the musculoskeletal effects of long-term use of corticosteroids; sleep pattern disturbance due to drug-induced insomnia; and physiologic injury related to the previously mentioned complications of the drug therapy.

## MINERALOCORTICOIDS

The primary agents with mineralocorticoid effects are desoxycorticosterone and fludrocortisone. Desoxycorticosterone has mainly mineralocorticoid activity with no glucocorticoid effects, whereas fludrocortisone has high levels of mineralocorticoid activity with some moderate glucocorticoid effects. However, the latter is still used primarily for its mineralocorticoid effects.

These agents act on the renal distal tubule to reabsorb sodium and enhance excretion of potassium and hydrogen. They are indicated for the treatment of Addison's disease (chronic primary adrenocortical insufficiency) and adrenogenital syndrome.

Desoxycorticosterone is administered parenterally. Fludrocortisone is available in oral dosage form, as it has good oral absorption, a half-life of about 3.5 hours in the plasma with a biological half-life of activity in the body of 18 to 26 hours. The duration of action for both drugs is 24 to 48 hours. They are metabolized in the liver and kidneys and excreted mainly by the kidneys.

The less frequent or rare adverse reactions reported with their use include severe or persistent headaches, hypertension, dizziness, edema of lower extremities, joint pain, hypokalemia, increased weakness, and tingling or numbness in legs that may progress to arms, trunk, and face, congestive heart failure and anaphylaxis. Such adverse reactions should be reported immediately to the physician. Pregnancy safety for both drugs has been established at FDA category C.

**Significant drug interactions.** The following significant drug interactions may occur when mineralocorticoids are given concurrently with the drugs listed below:

| Drug | Possible Effect and Management |
|---|---|
| digitalis glycosides | Hypokalemic effect may potentiate the risk for cardiac dysrhythmias or digitalis toxicity. Monitor closely. |
| diuretics | Effectiveness of diuretics may be decreased with these medications. Concurrent use of potassium-depleting diuretics or hypokalemic-inducing medications may produce severe hypokalemia. Monitor serum potassium levels closely. |
| liver enzyme inducers | Increased metabolism of mineralocorticoids may result in a decrease in the effectiveness of these drugs. |
| potassium supplements | May decrease effectiveness of these drugs. Monitor serum potassium levels frequently. |

| Drug | Possible Effect and Management |
|---|---|
| sodium in food or medications | In type IV renal tubular acidosis, concurrent use of sodium with fludrocortisone may result in hypertension, hypernatremia, and edema. Monitor sodium intake closely and advise clients on safe consumption of foods and medications to avoid hypernatremia. Instruct clients to read labels on both foods and medication. |

**Dosage and administration.** The adult dose of desoxycorticosterone acetate injection (DOCA) for adrenocortical insufficiency is 1 to 5 mg IM daily (DOCA) or 25 mg for each 1 mg of the acetate injection, which is usually 25 to 100 mg IM monthly for the desoxycorticosterone pivalate suspension (Percorten). The pediatric dose for the acetate dosage form is also 1 to 5 mg daily by intramuscular injection; the conversion to the pivalate suspension is the same as for an adult.

The adult and adolescent fludrocortisone oral dose (Florinef) is 0.1 mg daily. The usual pediatric dose is 50 to 100 μg daily.

## ▷NURSING MANAGEMENT: MINERALOCORTICOID THERAPY

**Assessment.** Determine that the client does not have hypertension, congestive heart failure, or cardiac disease for which these drugs are contraindicated.

Because these clients are at risk for altered cardiac output related to sodium and fluid retention, establish the client's baseline weight and blood pressure and report weight increases to the physician. Periodically assess the client's blood pressure and check for evidence of edema. Monitor intake and output.

**Intervention.** Desoxycorticosterone comes as a sesame oil solution injection; it is not for intravenous use. Administer by deep intramuscular injection. Withdraw medication from the vial with a 19-gauge needle and administer with a 23-gauge needle.

**Education.** Advise the client to arrange periodic checking of the serum electrolyte levels, especially during prolonged therapy, and to implement dietary salt restrictions. Use of a potassium supplement may be necessary.

Instruct the client to take daily weight measurements and to report a sudden weight gain to the prescriber. Consult with the physician for specific weight-gain limitations for each individual client.

**Evaluation.** Monitor blood pressure, and if hypertension develops, adjust the dosage of the steroid and the salt intake.

As there is a potential for hypokalemia, be aware that excessive loss of potassium can cause dysrhythmias and sudden weakness, palpitations, paresthesia, or nausea.

In addition, clients have the potential for impaired physical mobility related to the musculoskeletal effects of long-term use of mineralocorticoids; disturbance in self-concept

**TABLE 49-4**   Side effects/adverse reactions of antiadrenal drugs

| Drug | Side effects* | Adverse reactions† |
|------|---------------|--------------------|
| aminoglutethimide (Cytadren) | Most frequent: Ataxia, dizziness, sedation, loss of energy, uncontrolled eye movements (CNS effects are usually dose-related; effects may decline in 2-6 weeks of continuous therapy but if severe, drug may need to be stopped); anorexia, nausea, vomiting, measle-like rash on face and/or palms of hands<br>Rare: Dark skin, depression, dizziness, headaches, pain in muscles | Rare: Increased temperature, chills, sore throat (caused by leukopenia or agranulocytosis), fever or jaundice of eyes and skin (hypersensitivity), increased bleeding episodes or unusual bruising (thrombocytopenia) |
| trilostane (Modrastane) | Most frequent: Diarrhea, abdominal distress<br>Less frequent: Muscle aches, headache, increased temperature, flushing, increased salivation, nausea, dizziness, gas, burning sensation in mouth or nose, watery eyes | Rare: Dark skin, sedation, anorexia, vomiting, rash, depression |

*If side effects continue, increase, or disturb the patient, the physician should be informed.
†If adverse reactions occur, contact the physician, since medical intervention may be necessary.

due to weight gain; and altered comfort related to irritation at injection site and headaches.

## ANTIADRENALS (ADRENAL STEROID INHIBITORS)

Aminoglutethimide, metyrapone, and trilostane are antiadrenals or adrenal steroid inhibitors. They inhibit or suppress adrenal cortex function.

### aminoglutethimide (Cytadren)

Aminoglutethimide inhibits the enzyme conversion of cholesterol to pregnenolone, thereby blocking the synthesis of adrenal steroids. It also may have other suppression effects in the synthesis and metabolism of the steroids.

By blocking the aromatase enzyme in the peripheral tissues, it inhibits estrogen production from androgens. It is indicated for the treatment of Cushing's syndrome associated with adrenal carcinoma, ectopic adrenocorticotropic hormone tumors, or adrenal gland hyperplasia.

Aminoglutethimide is absorbed orally and has a half-life of 13 hours. After prolonged therapy of 2 to 32 weeks, the half-life decreases to 7 hours because of the increase in liver enzymes induced by aminoglutethimide. Time to peak concentration is 1.5 hours. Adrenal function suppression occurs within 3 to 5 days of therapy.

Aminoglutethimide is metabolized in the liver and excreted by the kidneys. For side effects/adverse reactions see Table 49-4. The only significant drug interaction reported in the USP-DI (1991) is with dexamethasone. Aminoglutethimide increases the metabolism of dexamethasone, thus reducing its effectiveness. If a glucocorticoid is necessary for a client receiving aminoglutethimide, hydrocortisone is usually the drug of choice.

The adult oral dose for antiadrenal effect is 250 mg two or three times daily for approximately 14 days. Then the maintenance dose is 250 mg every 6 hours, four times daily. A pediatric dose has not been established. Pregnancy safety has been established at FDA category D.

▷ **Nursing Management: Aminoglutethimide Therapy**

***Assessment.*** Because of the cortical hypofunction, use antiadrenals cautiously in clients undergoing stress such as surgery, infection, trauma, and acute illness.

Do not give to pregnant women, since aminoglutethimide may harm the fetus.

Obtain baseline thyroid function studies. Monitor periodically during therapy.

Since this drug can cause blood dyscrasias and liver and electrolyte abnormalities, routinely monitor serum electrolytes and hematologic and liver function studies.

Since hypotension (weakness, dizziness) is caused by aldosterone suppression, monitor blood pressure.

***Education.*** Because the client may experience orthostatic hypotension, advise the client to change position or to stand slowly to minimize this effect.

Alert the client to avoid activities that require alertness until response to the drug has been determined.

Instruct the client to alert other health care providers that the drug is being taken and to carry a medical identification card indicating such. The prescriber should be notified if injury, infection, or illness occurs because a steroid supplement may be needed.

***Evaluation.*** The client is at risk for the following nursing diagnoses: physiologic injury related to the development of hypersensitivity, thrombocytopenia, leukopenia, or agranulocytosis; injury related to the CNS effects of hypotension, drowsiness, dizziness, and clumsiness; altered nutrition related to gastrointestinal effects evidenced by anorexia, nausea, and vomiting; and altered comfort related to dermatologic effects (measles-like rash), headache, and muscle pain.

### metyrapone (Metopirone)

Metyrapone inhibits the synthesis of cortisol and corticosterone by inhibiting the 11 B-hydroxylation reaction that occurs in the adrenal cortex. This normally leads to an increase in ACTH production and secretion from the pituitary, which in turn produces an increase in the precursors of the adrenal glucocorticoids. The result is an increase in the steroids 11-deoxycortisol and desoxycorticosterone in the plasma and of their metabolites in the urine. Metyrapone may also decrease the synthesis of aldosterone in the body. It is indicated to test the hypothalamic-pituitary ACTH function.

Metyrapone is administered orally, and plasma concentration during treatment is usually 0.5 to 1 µg/ml. Peak steroid excretion is within 24 hours of drug administration in normal individuals. See dosage and administration for test interpretation. It has a half-life of 1 to 2.5 hours and is metabolized in the liver and excreted by the kidneys. Its major side effects include nausea, stomach distress, dizziness, headache, drowsiness, and rash.

A significant drug interaction may occur in individuals who are taking or have taken either cyproheptadine or phenytoin within the previous 2-week period; test results may be affected. Phenytoin accelerates the metabolism of metyrapone. Estrogens have also repeatedly led to a subtherapeutic response with metyrapone.

***Dosage and administration.*** All corticosteroid drugs should be discontinued before and during testing with this drug.

First day—Collect 24-hour urine to measure 17-hydroxycorticosteroids (17-OHCS) or 17-ketogenic steroids (17-KGS).

Second day—Administer ACTH test, that is, give 50 units of ACTH by intravenous infusion over 8 hours and measure the 24-hour steroids in the urine. If results are within normal limits, continue with test. (The normal 24-hour urinary excretion of 17-OHCS is 3 to 12 mg. After ACTH, this will increase to 15 to 45 mg/24 hours.)

Third and fourth day—Rest day

Fifth day—Administer the metyrapone. Adults: 750 mg orally, every 4 hours for 6 doses. Children: 15 mg/kg every 4 hours for 6 doses; minimum dose is 250 mg.

Sixth day—Collect and determine the 24-hour steroids in the urine. If the client has a normally functioning pituitary, metyrapone will increase the 17-OHCS by twofold to fourfold or double the 17-KGS excretion.

A subnormal response indicates the possibility of an impaired pituitary function in patients with sufficient adrenal function (panhypopituitarism or partial hypopituitarism). The student is referred to the package insert or a suitable reference source for other interpretations of this test.

***Pregnancy safety.*** Has been established at FDA category C

### ▷ Nursing Management: Metyrapone Therapy

The ability of the adrenal gland to respond to exogenous ACTH should be determined before the test, since acute adrenal insufficiency is precipitated in clients with reduced adrenal secretory capacity. Note that metyrapone testing requires that all corticosteroid therapy be stopped before and during testing. Explain to the client the purpose of and procedures for this test.

### trilostane (Modrastane)

Trilostane suppresses synthesis of adrenal steroids by inhibiting enzyme in the adrenal cortex. It is indicated for the treatment of Cushing's syndrome.

Trilostane has a half-life of 8 hours and is metabolized by the liver. For side effects/adverse reactions, see Table 49-4. It has no significant drug interactions.

The adult dose initially is 30 mg orally, four times daily. Provider may gradually increase the dosage every 3 or 4 days until the desired effect is noted. Maintenance dose is usually less than 360 mg in 24 hours orally daily, given in four divided doses. Maximum is 480 mg/day. Pediatric dosage has not been established. Pregnancy safety is established at FDA category X.

### ▷ Nursing Management: Trilostane Therapy

Trilostane is contraindicated in clients with adrenal insufficiency, severe renal disease, or hepatic disease. Because trilostane may prevent physiologic responses to stress, it may be discontinued briefly before surgery or in times of physiologic stress, such as trauma, infection, or shock.

Because orthostatic hypotension may occur with the drug, alert the client to change positions or come to a standing position slowly.

Monitor the blood pressure periodically and alert the prescriber if hypotension becomes a concern for the client.

Clients are at risk for altered comfort related to abdominal cramping, headache, nausea, and flushing; and injury related to adrenal insufficiency evidenced by anorexia, tiredness, nausea, vomiting, rash, depression, and darkening of the skin.

## SUMMARY

Drugs affecting the adrenal cortex—corticosteroids—are divided into glucocorticoids and mineralocorticoids. Glucocorticoids have many pharmacologic actions: antiinflammatory action; maintenance of blood pressure; fat, carbohydrate, and protein metabolism; thymolytic, lympholytic, and eosinopenic actions; and stress effects. Mineralocorticoids act on the renal distal tubules to reabsorb sodium and enhance the excretion of potassium and hydrogen. Because the actions of both of these groups of agents affect all aspects of the body's physiology, evaluation of the client for therapeutic and adverse effects of their administration is particularly important.

Of the antiadrenals or adrenal steroid inhibitors, aminoglutethimide and trilostane are used for the treatment of Cushing's syndrome, whereas metyrapone is used as an agent to test hypothalamic-pituitary ACTH function.

## BIBLIOGRAPHY

American Hospital Formulary Service. (1991). AHFS drug information '91. Bethesda, Md: American Society of Hospital Pharmacists, Inc.

Anderson MR. (1989). The pharmacology of intervention for respiratory emergencies, Emerg Care Q 5(1):23.

Brassell MP. (1988). Pharmacologic management of rheumatic diseases, Orthop Nurs 7(2):43.

Braunwald E et al, eds. (1987). Harrison's principles of internal medicine, ed 11. New York: McGraw-Hill Book Co.

Brown SM et al. (1989). Drug protocols (dexamethasone), Neonat Netw 7(5):63.

Chang JC. (1988). Neoplastic fever: naproxen or corticosteroids? Amer J Nurs 88(9):1255.

Dacre JE et al. (1989). Injections and physiotherapy for the painful stiff shoulder, Ann Rheum Dis 48(4):322.

Dexamethasone for bacterial meningitis. (1989). Nurses Drug Alert 13(2):10.

Ettinger AB et al. (1988). The use of corticosteroids in the treatment of symptoms associated with cancer, part 3, J Pain Symptom Manage 3(2):99.

Few BJ. (1988). Corticosteroids and respiratory distress, MCN 13(1):17.

Harper J. (1988). Use of steroids in cerebral edema: therapeutic implications, Heart Lung 17(1):70.

Heller MB. (1987). Local injection therapy: techniques that work in tendinitis/bursitis syndrome, Consultant 27(12):107.

Ho E. (1988). Prenatal corticosteroid in preventing respiratory distress syndrome, Midwifery 4(1):24.

Kastrup EK, ed. (1991). Facts and comparisons. St Louis: JB Lippincott.

Katzung BG. (1987). Basic and clinical pharmacology, ed 3. Norwalk, Conn: Appleton & Lange.

Krohmer JR. (1988). Asthma out of control, Emerg Med 20(9):96.

Linck CA. (1987). The effectiveness of epidural steroid injections for the treatment of back pain, J Post Anesth Nurs 2(4):249.

McPherson ML. (1990). Pharmacotherapy for chronic obstructive pulmonary disease, J Home Health Care Pract 2(2):61.

Molitor RE et al. (1988). Home intravenous administration of adrenocorticotropic hormone in patients with multiple sclerosis, J Intravenous Nurs 11(4):249.

Nicholson DP. (1988). Steroid therapy in sepsis-related adult respiratory distress syndrome, Respir Care 33(1):38.

Otwell JA et al. (1988). Teaching renal transplant patients with steroid-induced diabetes mellitus, ANNA J 15(5):295.

Parks BR Jr. (1988). Use of topical steroids in children, Pediatr Nurs 14(4):337.

Schira MG. (1987) Steroid-dependent states and adrenal insufficiency: fluid and electrolyte disturbances, Nurs Clin North Am 22(4):837.

Single-dose dexamethasone in severe croup. (1990). Nurses Drug Alert 14(1):3.

The risks of treating COPD . . . chronic obstructive pulmonary disease. (1989). Emerg Med 21(17):114.

United States Pharmacopeial Convention. (1991). Drug information for the health care professional, ed 11. Rockville, Md: The Convention.

Will surgery complicate your patient's drug therapy? (1987). Emerg Med 19(18):56.

Wyngaarden JB and Smith LH. (1988). Cecil textbook of medicine, ed 18. Philadelphia: WB Saunders Co.

# 50 Drugs Affecting the Pancreas

## KEY TERMS

## INTRODUCTION

Insulin and glucagon are the two primary hormones released by the pancreas. When serum blood glucose declines, glucagon is released from the pancreas. Glucagon, which is synthesized in the A cells of the pancreatic islets, facilitates the catabolism of stored glycogen in the liver. The result is an increase in blood glucose, or **gluconeogenesis.** The release of glucagon stimulates insulin secretion, which then inhibits the release of glucagon.

The most important disease involving the endocrine pancreas is diabetes mellitus. Diabetes mellitus is primarily a disorder of carbohydrate metabolism that involves an insulin deficiency or an insulin resistance or both. All causes of diabetes will lead to hyperglycemia (see Chapter 46, "Overview of the Endocrine System").

## HYPERGLYCEMIA

The two general classifications for diabetes mellitus are **insulin dependent diabetes mellitus** (IDDM or type I) and **non–insulin dependent diabetes mellitus** (NIDDM or type II). Clients with type I diabetes have very little or no endogenous insulin capacity. This type of diabetes usually occurs before early adulthood and so was previously called juvenile onset diabetes. The client with type I diabetes is ketosis prone and requires exogenous insulin therapy for survival.

Type II diabetes was previously known as maturity onset diabetes. Generally, clients with this type of diabetes have some insulin function, so they are not fully dependent on insulin for survival. At times insulin treatment may be necessary to control type II diabetes, but usually weight reduction through dietary treatment will help reduce the hyperglycemia in clients with type II diabetes. The vast majority of individuals with type II diabetes are obese, and ketosis is rare. Although insulin resistance may occasionally occur with type I diabetes, it is believed to be more common in type II diabetes because of receptor and postreceptor defects. See the box below for a comparison of the primary features of both types of diabetes. See Figure 50-1 for possible causes of type II diabetes.

## INSULIN PREPARATIONS

**Insulin,** which is normally secreted by the beta cells of the pancreas, is composed of two amino acid chains, A (acidic) and B (basic). These chains are joined together by disulfide linkages. Insulin preparations are derived from animals (extracted from cattle or pig pancreas) or synthesized in the laboratory from either an alteration of pork insulin or recombinant DNA with strains of *E. coli* to form human insulin (a biosynthetic human insulin). The difference between the sources is that the beef insulin differs from human insulin by three amino acids, whereas the pork insulin differs from human insulin by only a single amino acid. The human insulin is identical to the insulin produced by the pancreas.

Usually, the beef-pork combination insulins are suitable for most clients. If the client has not developed insulin resistance, insulin allergies, or lipoatrophy at the insulin injection sites, the combination product is usually sufficient and also less expensive. The beef-only insulins are indicated mainly for clients who are allergic to pork or for use in clients who must avoid the use of pork for religious reasons. Pork insulin has been found to be useful for clients who have local or systemic allergies, insulin resistance, or lipoatrophy or for clients who have a short-term need for insulin. The pure pork insulin is closer to human insulin, and in many instances, its use has resulted in reduction of the insulin dose (in insulin resistance) and in the improvement of local allergy in approximately 80% of the clients with insulin allergies.

Human insulin can be substituted for the same reasons as pork insulin, and it has been used instead of pork insulin in clients who are allergic to pork. Human insulin is much less antigenic than the animal-based insulin. The physician will make the decision about which type of insulin is best for a specific client.

Insulin controls the storage and metabolism of carbohydrate, protein, and fat by attaching insulin molecules to receptor sites on cellular plasma membranes, especially in the liver, muscle, and adipose tissues.

While insulin's exact molecular mechanism of action is still being investigated, it is known that insulin influences cell membrane transport, cell growth, enzyme activation and inhibition, and the metabolism of protein and fats.

Insulin is indicated for:

1. Treatment of diabetes mellitus, insulin dependent (Type I, IDDM)
2. Treatment of non–insulin dependent diabetes mellitus during emergencies or in specific situatons, such as when needed as a supplement to the low physiologic endogenous insulin in an individual, during high fevers, severe infection, ketoacidosis or significant ketosis, severe burns, after major surgery, following severe trauma or during pregnancy.

For pharmacokinetics and side effects/adverse reactions, see Tables 50-1 and 50-2, respectively.

***Significant drug interactions.*** The following significant drug interactions may occur when insulin is given concurrently with the drugs listed below. In addition, many commonly abused substances can be very problematic in the client with diabetes. See the box on page 786. Also the boxes on pages 786-787 evaluate drugs commonly reported to cause hyperglycemia and list sugar-free drugs available to such clients.

---

### FEATURES OF INSULIN DEPENDENT (IDDM) AND NON–INSULIN DEPENDENT (NIDDM) DIABETES

|  | IDDM | NIDDM |
|---|---|---|
| Synonym | Type I | Type II |
| Age of onset | Usually <30 | Usually >40 |
| Onset of symptoms | Sudden (symptomatic) | Gradual (usually asymptomatic) |
| Body weight | Usually nonobese | Obese (80%) |
| Incidence | 10% | 90% |
| Insulin dependent | Yes | Usually not required |
| Insulin resistance | No | Yes |
| Receptors | Normal | Usually decreased or defective |
| Plasma insulin | Decreased | Normal or increased |
| Complications | Frequent | Frequent |
| Ketoacidosis | Prone to | Usually resistant |
| Diet | Mandatory | Mandatory |

| Drug | Possible Effect and Management |
|---|---|
| adrenocorticoids, glucocorticoids | Adrenocorticoids and glucocorticoids may increase blood glucose levels. A dosage adjustment of one or both drugs may be necessary. Monitor closely. |
| alcohol | May increase the hypoglycemic effect of insulin. Monitor closely, since dosage adjustments may be necessary. If possible, avoid the concurrent use of alcohol. |
| antidiabetic agents | These agents enhance hypoglycemic effects. Although a small number of carefully selected individuals may find the combination therapy more effective than single therapy, this type of treatment is not generally advocated. |
| beta adrenergic blocking agents (including eye preparations) | These agents may mask symptoms of hypoglycemia, such as increased pulse rate and decreased blood pressure. May also prolong hypoglycemia by blocking gluconeogenesis. Dosage adjustments of insulin may be necessary. Selective beta blockers in low dosages, such as metoprolol and atenolol, cause fewer problems than the other beta adrenergic blocking agents. Propranolol may cause hyperglycemia or hypoglycemia when given concurrently with insulin. Periodic blood glucose tests are recommended to monitor the combined effects and allow for adjustment of insulin dose, if necessary. |

***Dosage and administration.*** There is no average dose of insulin for the diabetic person; each client's needs must be determined individually. These needs are frequently determined by blood glucose monitoring, which has been simplified by the availability of both visual test strips and strips used in blood glucose meters or instruments. Such devices have allowed clients to monitor their diabetes and make the necessary adjustments with medication, diet, or exercise, as instructed by their physician or health care provider. The visual glucose testing strips are less expensive than the testing instruments, but the meter readings are much more precise (assuming they are properly calibrated). Thus clients with visual problems or a need for a more accurate blood glucose reading will benefit from using a blood glucose meter instrument.

Insulin dosage is expressed in units rather than in milliliters or minims. Insulin injection is standardized so that each milliliter contains 40 or 100 USP units. Insulin is classified according to its duration of action (short- or rapid-acting, intermediate-acting, and long-acting). Generally meals should occur at the same time that administered insulin reaches its peak effect. Insulin requirements can vary widely among individuals, so dosages must be adjusted to an individual's needs.

**TABLE 50-1**   Characteristics of insulin preparations after subcutaneous administration

| Insulins* | Onset (hours) | Peak effect (hours) | Duration of action (hours) |
|---|---|---|---|
| **RAPID ACTING** | | | |
| insulin injection (Regular Insulin)† | ½-1 | 2-4 | 5-7 |
| prompt insulin zinc suspension (Semilente) | 1 | 2-6 | 12-16 |
| **INTERMEDIATE ACTING** | | | |
| insulin zinc suspension (Lente Insulin) | 1-3 | 8-12 | 18-28 |
| isophane insulin suspension (NPH Insulin) | 3-4 | 6-12 | 18-28 |
| isophane insulin suspension (70%) plus insulin injection (30%) (Mixtard, Novolin 70/30) | ½ | 4-8 | 24 |
| **LONG ACTING** | | | |
| extended insulin zinc suspension (Ultralente) | 4-6 | 18-24 | 36 |
| protamine zinc insulin suspension (PZI) | 4-6 | 14-24 | 36 |

*All above insulins, with the exception of Mixtard, Novolin combinations, are available in 40 unit and 100 unit strengths. Beef, pork, beef-pork, and human insulins are available in rapid-acting insulins and the three insulins listed under intermediate acting. The others are animal sources only.
†This is the only insulin for intravenous use. Intravenously, the onset of action is within ⅙ to ½ hour, peak effect within ¼ to ½ hour, and duration of action within ½ to 1 hour.

**TABLE 50-2**   Symptoms of hypoglycemia and hyperglycemia

Persons administering insulin should be aware of the symptoms of hypoglycemia and hyperglycemia and know what action to take if they occur.

**Hypoglycemia:** Increased anxiety, blurred vision, chilly sensation, cold sweating, pallor, confusion, difficulty in concentrating, drowsiness, headache, nausea, increased pulse rate, shakiness, increased weakness, increased appetite

**Hyperglycemia:** Drowsiness; red, dry skin; fruity breath odor; anorexia; abdominal pain; nausea, vomiting; dry mouth; increased urination; rapid, deep breathing; unusual thirst; rapid weight loss

## EFFECTS OF COMMONLY ABUSED DRUGS ON DIABETIC MANAGEMENT

Many drugs can increase or decrease blood glucose levels, but rarely are the commonly abused drugs reviewed in relation to diabetes. Because substance abuse by the client with diabetes can be very problematic, the most commonly abused drugs are reviewed here.

### Alcohol

Alcohol promotes hypoglycemia; blocks the formation, storage, and release of glycogen. It also may interact with many other drugs, including oral hypoglycemic agents such as chlorpropamide. In alcoholics who have decreased their food intake, alcohol can cause a serious drop in blood glucose levels, leading to a need for acute intervention.

### CNS Stimulants

Amphetamines, sympathomimetics, anorexics, cocaine, psychedelic drugs, and others may result in hyperglycemia and an increase in liver glycogen breakdown. Large amounts of caffeine in products such as coffee, tea, and cola drinks can also increase blood glucose levels.

### Marijuana

Marijuana may increase appetite and food consumption. Heavy use may produce a glucose intolerance leading to hyperglycemia.

### Cigarettes

Nicotine in cigarettes is a potent vasoconstrictor. It can decrease the absorption of subcutaneous insulin or increase the person's insulin requirements by 15% to 20%. Cigarette smoking can cause a drop of 1 to 2 degrees in skin temperature. It also is a risk factor for the development of diabetic nephropathy.

### Abuse of CNS-Acting Drugs

CNS-acting drugs (such as stimulants, depressants, sedative-hypnotics, opiates, marijuana, alcohol) can impair judgment and alter perceptions (time, place) and thus interfere with the individual's control of the diabetic state.

## SUGAR-FREE PRESCRIPTION AND OVER-THE-COUNTER MEDICATIONS

Advise clients to always read the labels or check with their pharmacists before purchasing medications. The sugar contents of both prescription and over-the-counter medications are changed often by the manufacturer, so the best advice is to check the list of contents every time medication is purchased. The following is a selected listing of medications that are currently sugar-free:

### Antacids, Antiflatulents

| | | |
|---|---|---|
| Di-Gel Liquid | Alka-Seltzer | Maalox |
| Riopan-Plus | Maalox | Suspension |
| Pepto-Bismol | Therapeutic | Concentrate |
| Silain-Gel Liquid | Gelusil Liquid | Mylanta Liquid |
| | WinGel Liquid | Titralac |

### Antidepressants, Antipsychotics

| | |
|---|---|
| Aventyl HCl Liquid | Lithium Citrate Syrup |
| Sinequan Oral Concentrate | Mellaril Concentrate |
| Serentil Concentrate | Thorazine Concentrate |

### Antihistamines, Decongestants

| | |
|---|---|
| Bayhistine Elixir | Dimetapp Elixir |
| Bromophen Elixir | Novahistine Elixir |

### Cough Medicines

| | |
|---|---|
| Cerose DM Expectorant | Codimal DM Syrup |
| Conar Suspension | Hycomine Syrup |
| Tuss-Ornade Liquid | Tricodene Liquid |

Clients with diabetes who become hyperglycemic, perhaps because of hospitalization or an infection (at home or in the hospital), may need insulin coverage in addition to their regular insulin. This is often referred to as sliding-scale insulin. The amount of insulin given will vary with the blood values or (in some instances) with the glucose in the urine, which roughly approximates blood glucose levels. The latter method may be used in some areas, but it is generally a poor way to monitor blood glucose. If at all possible, urine glucose tests should not be used to determine insulin dosages. There may be some variation between urine glucose tests; therefore they should not be used interchangeably for urine glucose monitoring. (See box on urine tests.)

Dietary intake, physical activity, and the client's glucose tolerance are all taken into consideration when insulin doses are established. Insulin dosages should not be considered to be a fixed regimen; the dosage may need to be adjusted as a result of physical growth (child growing into adulthood), illness, stress, the development of antiinsulin antibodies, concomitant administration of certain medications, or changes in exercise and diet. Treatment programs need to be reviewed and adjusted as necessary, with the physician, nurse, and client working closely to manage the hyperglycemia and if possible, avoid its complications.

Insulin is given subcutaneously (or intravenously for regular insulin only). It cannot be given by mouth because it is destroyed by digestive enzymes. Regular insulin is usually given about 15 to 30 minutes before meals.

*Insulin pumps and new devices.* Portable insulin pumps have improved the metabolic state of some type I clients who did not have adequate diabetic control after intensive dietary restrictions and multiple daily injections of insulin.

---

### DRUGS COMMONLY REPORTED TO CAUSE HYPERGLYCEMIA

chlorthalidone (Hygroton)
corticosteroids
diazoxide (Proglycem, Hyperstat)
furosemide (Lasix)
estrogens (birth control tablets, estrogen replacement)
epinephrine-type drugs (sympathomimetics or decongestants in cold preparations, diet pills)
nicotinic acid (in large doses)
phenytoin (Dilantin)
thyroid preparations
thiazide diuretics
caffeine (large quantities)
cyclophosphamide (Cytoxan)
ethacrynic acid (Edecrin)
asparaginase (Elspar)
morphine
nicotine (smoking)
lithium (Lithane)

---

The insulin pump is a battery-operated pump connected to a small computer that is programmed to give small amounts of insulin per hour. It does not analyze the blood glucose level; however, it is programmed based on the individual's daily insulin needs, diet, and physical exercise. The client can also push a button that releases a bolus dose to cover each meal consumed. Although the pumps are effective and useful in clients who are properly trained, health care professionals need to be aware of several problems associated with them. Malfunction of the infusion of insulin may occur because of battery failure, and defects in the tubing may cause leakage of insulin solution or may block the infusion tubing. Therefore it is vitally important to teach the client to change the infusion set and battery. Clients must be highly motivated and educated in the handling of insulin pumps. The client should be capable of keeping records and following specific procedures, and should be willing to perform blood tests daily or more often. Also, these pumps are very expensive. Therefore insulin pumps currently are not recommended for every type I diabetic.

Needleless injectors, such as the Vitajet, Medi-jector, and Precijet 50 are also available. These devices are expensive

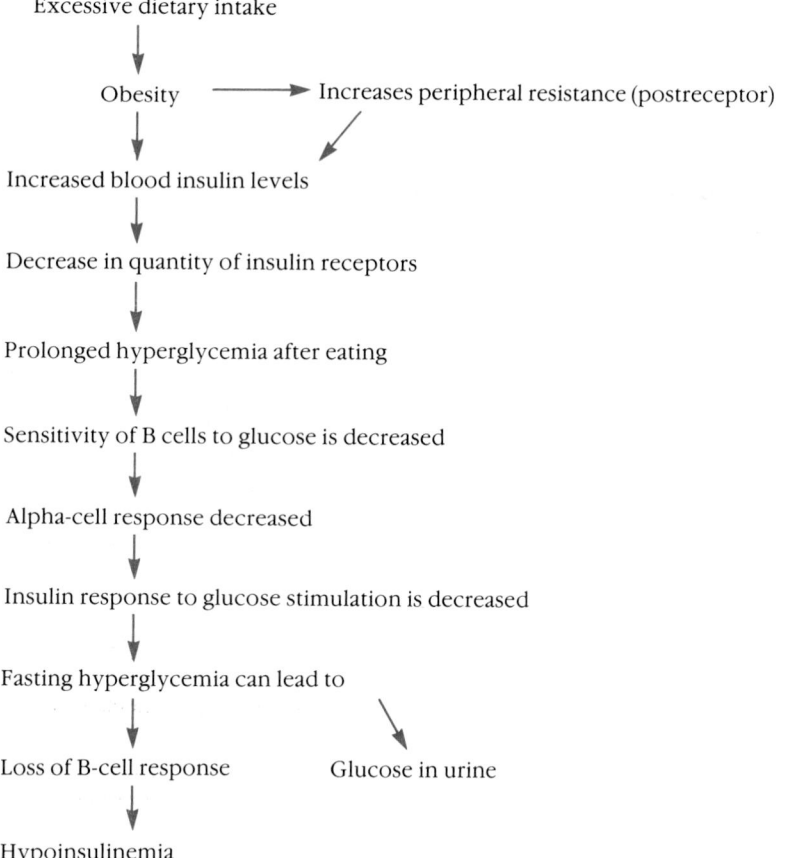

Excessive dietary intake
   ↓
Obesity ──────→ Increases peripheral resistance (postreceptor)
   ↓
Increased blood insulin levels
   ↓
Decrease in quantity of insulin receptors
   ↓
Prolonged hyperglycemia after eating
   ↓
Sensitivity of B cells to glucose is decreased
   ↓
Alpha-cell response decreased
   ↓
Insulin response to glucose stimulation is decreased
   ↓
Fasting hyperglycemia can lead to
   ↓                              ↘
Loss of B-cell response        Glucose in urine
   ↓
Hypoinsulinemia

**FIGURE 50-1** Possible etiology of type II (non–insulin dependent) diabetes. Beta cells secrete insulin, while alpha cells secrete glucagon.

and appear to have limited usefulness in practice. Many devices are also available for the visually impaired or blind client with diabetes. Information on injection aids for the blind may be obtained from state and national associations for the blind, such as the American Foundation for the Blind and the American Diabetic Association.

Aldose reductase inhibitors, such as Sorbinil and Tolrestat, are currently being investigated because they have been proven to reduce or reverse sorbitol and fructose accumulation in animals, thus preventing long-term diabetic complications affecting the eyes, nerves, and kidneys. One of the most serious ocular complications is diabetic retinopathy, the leading cause of blindness in the United States. In hyperglycemia, aldose reductase will convert glucose to sorbitol, which will then be converted to fructose. The accumulation of sorbitol in the eyes leads to lens swelling and diabetic cataracts. It may also effect retinal capillaries leading to diabetic retinopathy. Clinical trials in humans are limited and have reported conflicting results. Larger controlled studies with humans will be necessary to evaluate the real potential of these agents in preventing the complications of diabetes (Bond, 1988; White and Martin, 1988).

The future may hold some exciting new methods of insulin administration. Research is underway for a nasal spray insulin, insulin in a transdermal patch, and transplantation of the beta cells of the pancreas. Although periodic releases of information are available from time to time, these areas of exploration should be closely monitored.

*Pregnancy safety.* FDA category has not been established. Insulin is the drug of choice for control of diabetes in pregnancy. Insulin requirements may drop for 24 to 72 hours following delivery and slowly return to prepregnancy levels in about 6 weeks.

## ▷NURSING MANAGEMENT: INSULIN THERAPY

*Assessment.* A comprehensive nursing history is necessary for the nurse to help the client manage his or her diabetic state. This is as essential for the newly diagnosed client with diabetes as it is for the client who is seeking reassurance that they are managing their diabetes appropriately or for readjustment of the therapeutic regimen because of stress, illness, change of life-style, or noncompliance.

Determine the client's daily exercise, dietary management and preferences, and understanding of diabetes and its control. Also note any physical impairments, such as decreased manual dexterity and limitations of vision, that would impede the self-administration of insulin. Because the cost of insulin, injection equipment, and blood and urine testing equipment can be considerable, assess the client's financial status and health insurance coverage and locate alternative resources if necessary. Clients with certain religious affiliations (such as Jewish or Islamic clients) prefer not to use pork insulin because their dietary codes involve the avoidance of pork.

*Intervention.* See nursing diagnoses box, p. 789.

Note that all insulin preparations are stable as long as the vials are protected from heat or cold. Vials of insoluble preparations (all except regular insulin) should be rotated between the hands and inverted end-to-end several times before a dose is withdrawn. A vial should not be shaken vigorously or the suspension made to foam.

Use a properly calibrated syringe for insulin. For doses of less than 50 units of U-100, use a low-dose syringe (50 units of U-100/0.5 ml). The decreased diameter of the barrel of the syringe results in the calibrations being further apart, which enhances accuracy of measurement. Avoid bubbles in the solution because the displacement of a few units of insulin, particularly with U-100 insulin, can alter the actual dose that the client receives.

Administer the insulin subcutaneously, using a 25- or 26-gauge needle, with the length of the needle determined by the client's size. A ⅜ to ⅝ inch needle is usually used, and the injection is administered at a 90 degree angle in a large fold of skin that has been gently pinched up. Alternately, the injection may be inserted at a 30 to 45 degree angle at the base of the fold of skin.

Understand that only the regular form of insulin may be injected by the intravenous route. Insulin adsorption onto plastic intravenous infusion administration sites removes up to 80% of an insulin dose; most often not less than 20% to 50% of a dose is removed by adsorption. The adsorption on the tubing surface occurs within 1 hour and requires individual client monitoring of insulin needs. Saturation of the adsorption sites on the tubing requires special care when changing the tubing for reexposure to the insulin and further monitoring of client needs. When insulin is administered as an infusion, use an intravenous pump for accurate administration.

*Education.* Teach clients about insulin administration and instruct them in urine and blood glucose monitoring so they can adjust insulin doses when their urine or blood levels are above normal limits. Instruct the client in the administration of insulin, including the type of insulin, the proper storage of insulin, the disposal of syringes, and rotation of the injection site.

Unopened vials of insulin should be stored under refrigeration. When a client is using a vial of insulin it is *not* necessary to store it in the refrigerator.

Be sure the patient understands that frequent serum glucose monitoring and urine testing are necessary to achieve insulin control. Stress compliance with the understanding that insulin helps to control hyperglycemia but is not a cure for diabetes.

Instruct clients about signs and symptoms of hypoglycemia that can occur secondary to insulin dosage. Dosage adjustment may be necessary to compensate for the hypoglycemia. The hypoglycemic individual should have a carbohydrate with a high sugar content (such as fruit juice) promptly, and the physician should be notified. If the patient is conscious, orange juice, candy, or a lump of sugar can

Selected nursing diagnoses for clients receiving insulin

| Nursing diagnosis | Outcome criteria | Nursing interventions |
| --- | --- | --- |
| Knowledge deficit related to newly diagnosed diabetes | Client and family will:<br>Demonstrate an understanding of diabetes, its therapy and complications, and measures to minimize or prevent complications | Assess the understanding and level of intelligence of client and family.<br>Determine educational needs and desires.<br>Provide information regarding the pathophysiology of diabetes and the function of insulin.<br>Explain methods and goals of diet and drug therapy.<br>Explain function and purpose of tests.<br>Answer questions and clarify misconceptions.<br>Provide resources for further learning and support (American Diabetics Association [ADA], Juvenile Diabetics Foundation [JDF], and others). |
| Knowledge deficit related to newly prescribed diabetic medication (insulin) | Client and family will:<br>Demonstrate correctly appropriate storage, handling, and administration of insulin<br>Be familiar with the signs and symptoms of insulin reaction/hypoglycemia reaction and appropriate response<br>State the different insulin preparations and appropriate adjustment of drug therapy<br>Be aware of possible side effects or adverse reactions to insulin | Administer insulin as prescribed.<br>Teach the client and family:<br>The function and importance of therapy; name and dosage of insulin<br>Technique of blood (or urine) glucose monitoring and adjusting insulin appropriately<br>Proper technique of administration<br>Need for lifelong dietary and drug management<br>The differences between the three forms of insulin<br>How to correctly calculate dosages<br>Proper storage and handling of insulin<br>Importance of rotating sites to minimize adverse local reactions<br>Signs and symptoms of insulin/hypoglycemic reaction and appropriate management<br>Help client establish and maintain a monitoring record of blood (or urine) glucose and insulin administration.<br>Advise client to wear or carry a medical identification tag, bracelet, or card.<br>Provide client with a list of drugs and conditions that may alter insulin requirements. |
| Altered nutrition related to hyperglycemia or hypoglycemia or insulin administration | Client will:<br>Achieve control of blood glucose and maintain desired nutritional intake<br>Client and family will:<br>Demonstrate knowledge of appropriate diabetic diet and modifications of dietary practices | Administer insulin as prescribed<br>Teach client and family:<br>Correct method of blood (or urine) glucose monitoring<br>Signs, symptoms, and treatment for hyperglycemia and hypoglycemia<br>Importance of balanced diabetic diet to control diabetes |

Selected nursing diagnoses for clients receiving insulin—cont'd

| Nursing diagnosis | Outcome criteria | Nursing interventions |
|---|---|---|
| | | Provide dietary instruction and counseling in appropriate diet/refer to dietitian.<br>Assist client and family in planning a sample diet. |
| Alteration in body image related to insulin dependence | Client and family will:<br>Verbalize feelings and concerns<br>Understand disease and measures of control<br>Client will:<br>Maintain, as much as possible, prediagnosis activities | Encourage client and family to express feelings and concerns.<br>Determine assets and strengths.<br>Determine, with client and family, strategies for managing areas of difficulty or concern.<br>Provide resources for further learning and support (ADA, JDF, others).<br>Be alert for signs of nonacceptance or difficulties such as noncompliance or denial. |
| Feelings of powerlessness related to perceived lack of personal control | Client and family will:<br>Identify those areas of diabetes that are possible to control and participate in decision making related to diabetic management | Assess client and family coping patterns and support mechanisms.<br>Assess client and family perceptions related to diagnosis.<br>Allow and encourage expression of concerns and fears.<br>Encourage client and family participation in therapy planning and implementation. |

be given. Early symptoms of hypoglycemia are fatigue, headache, drowsiness, lassitude, tremulousness, or nausea. Late symptoms are weakness, sweating, tremors, or nervousness. Observe the client at night for excessive restlessness and profuse sweating.

Teach clients to assess for signs of hyperglycemia: thirst, polyuria, drowsiness, flushed skin, fruity odor to breath, and unconsciousness. Instruct the family to have insulin available for administration and to observe the client closely after insulin has been given.

Discuss the following with the client and family to prevent recurrences of ketoacidosis:
- Use a regimented pattern of diabetic control.
- Never omit antidiabetic drugs, particularly when a secondary illness is manifested.
- Consume clear liquids and eat smaller meals when illness occurs.
- When ill, frequently test urine for ketones and sugar.
- Notify the physician of secondary illness, nausea and vomiting, fever, inability to eat, or inability to control blood glucose levels. Inform the family and client that the following factors may lead to diabetic ketoacidosis: insulin dependent diabetes mellitus, omission of insulin, infections, cerebrovascular accidents (stroke), myocardial infarction, pregnancy, trauma, surgery, and stress (especially emotional).

Teach the client the following about combining insulins and preparing syringes. When mixing insulins, draw regular insulin into the syringe first to avoid contamination of the regular insulin vial with the other insulin admixture. The interaction of regular and NPH insulin occurs within 15 minutes after mixing and then will remain at this stability for 30 days at room temperature and 90 days if refrigerated. Regular and lente mixtures require up to 24 hours for the interaction to reach a stable level of consistent response; if premixed in the same syringe, their activity is also 30 days at room temperature and 90 days under refrigeration. Clients stabilized on this premixed insulin will have a different response if they inject the insulin separately from each component. Dosage errors are avoided by not changing the injection order of mixing insulins or changing the model of needles, brands of syringes, or sources of insulins.

Instruct the client in the planned rotation of injection sites. Observe for **lipodystrophies,** abnormal accumulations of fat, and avoid such skin lesions.

Note that the abdomen is the area of rapid subcutaneous absorption pattern for insulin, following by the upper arm, with intermediate absorption rate; the slowest rate is in the thigh. Physical activity in the client accelerates absorption, especially in the injected limb; alert joggers and walkers.

Teach the client that alternating the insulin injection sites from the leg to the abdomen or arm has the effect of ac-

## GLUCOSE URINE TESTING

| Name of Test | Procedure | Color Range | Results |
|---|---|---|---|
| Chemstrip uG | Dip strip in urine, compare color to chart at 2 minutes. | Buff, green to dark blue | 0, 1/10%, 1/4%, 1/2%, 1%, 2%, 3%, 5% |
| Clinistix | Dip strip in urine, compare color at 10 seconds. | Buff to dark purple | 0, light (0.1%), medium, dark |
| Clinitest 2-Drop method | Add 2 drops of urine to 10 drops water in a test tube. Add a Clinitest tablet and watch reaction. Wait 15 seconds after boiling stops, shake tube and compare color to chart. | Blue, green, brown to orange | 0, 1/2%, 1%, 2%, 3%, 5% |
| Clinitest 5-Drop method | Add 5 drops of urine to 10 drops of water in test tube. Add Clinitest tablet and watch reaction. Wait 15 seconds after boiling stops, shake tube and compare color to chart. | Blue, green, brown to orange | 0, 1/4%, 1/2%, 3/4%, 1%, 2% |
| Diastix | Dip strip in urine, wait 60 seconds and compare color to chart. | Light blue, green to brown | 0, 1/10%, 1/4%, 1/2%, 1%, 2% |
| Tes-Tape | Dip strip in urine, wait 60 seconds and compare color to chart. | Yellow to green | 0, 1/10%, 1/4%, 1/2%, 2% |

The urine glucose percentages are generally equivalent to the following: 1/10% = 100 mg/dl; 1/4% = 150 mg/dl; 1/2% = 500 mg/dl; 3/4% = 750 mg/dl; 1% = 1000 mg/dl; 2% = 2000 mg/dl; 3% = 3000 mg/dl; 5% = 5000 mg/dl.

Note that the above tests do not always report the same ranges of urinary glucose. For example, only Chemstrip uG and Clinitest 5-Drop report 3% and 5%, whereas Tes-Tape does not report 3/4% or 1% values. The only product that reports the 3/4% value is Clinitest-5 Drop. The nurse is therefore cautioned about substituting one test for another without being aware of the test limitations.

Urinary ketones (acetone, acetoacetic acid, and beta-hydroxybutyric acid) are found in the urine when fats are not properly metabolized in the body. Their presence is indicative of poorly controlled diabetes, ketonemia and diabetic acidosis (ketoacidosis) caused by a lack of available insulin. This is seen primarily in individuals with insulin dependent diabetes. The tests for urinary ketones include Acetest Tablets, Chemstrip K or uGK, Ketostix, and Keto-Diastix. Chemstrip uGK and Keto-Diastix measure both glucose and ketones by means of separate areas on the same strip.

Many drugs can cause urine discoloration thus interfering with the reading of the urine tests. Phenytoin (Dilantin), phenazopyridine (Pyridium), metronidazole (Flagyl), methyldopa (Aldomet), rifampin (Rifadin), and riboflavin are a few of the drugs that may cause test interference. Clients taking these medications will need to resort to blood testing as an alternative.

celerating the absorption of insulin and diminishing the postprandial rise in plasma glucose. Varying the insulin injection sites within the same anatomic region rather than between different regions may diminish daily fluctuations or variations in insulin absorption and in metabolic control in insulin-dependent diabetic patients.

Inform the client that an important part of insulin control is diet therapy. The dietitian and the meal preparer must be included in the total care of the client with diabetes. Before clients are discharged, they must be able to verbalize an understanding of their diet therapy and be willing to participate in meal planning.

Caution clients against the ingestion of alcohol, since hypoglycemia could result. If alcohol is consumed, their insulin dosage may be reduced, since alcohol potentiates the hypoglycemic effect of insulin.

If the client is using urine testing, emphasize that it is important in determining correct insulin dosage. Whichever method is used, the client should test the second voided specimen. Urine should be tested before each meal.

At all times the client should carry a medical identification that describes the therapeutic regimen.

For other aspects of client education for the client with diabetes not directly related to insulin therapy, such as skin care, foot care, stress reduction, and dietary regimen, the reader is referred to a nursing text.

***Evaluation.*** Monitor blood glucose levels frequently in the client with diabetes. Recently developed products, such as Chemstrip and Dextrostix, allow for blood glucose monitoring at home. The home glucose-monitoring devices are for clients with diabetes. They are much more reliable than urine glucose tests and facilitate tighter control of blood sugar levels.

Urine glucose testing is a much more commonly done assessment, although it is an indirect measurement of the client's glycemic status because of individual differences in

**TABLE 50-3**   Hypoglycemic agents

| Drug | Remarks |
|---|---|
| **FIRST GENERATION SULFONYLUREAS** | |
| acetohexamide (Dymelor, Dimelor ✿) | Intermediate-acting drug. Metabolized to active metabolite (hydroxyhexamide) in liver; a potent hypoglycemic agent. Use with caution in renal insufficiency. |
| chlorpropamide (Diabinese) | Longest acting oral hypoglycemic. Generally more potent and more toxic than other drugs. Also used in treatment of polyuria of diabetes insipidus; may enhance effects of ADH. Usually given as single morning dose with food. |
| tolazamide (Tolinase) | Intermediate-acting drug. Alternative drug for persons who do not respond to other sulfonylureas. |
| tolbutamide (Orinase, Mobenol ✿) | Short-acting drug. It is rapidly metabolized to inactive metabolites. Useful in clients with kidney disease. |
| **SECOND GENERATION SULFONUREAS** | |
| glipizide (Glucotrol) | Highly protein bound. Metabolized by liver to inactive metabolites. |
| glyburide (DiaBeta, Micronase) | Highly protein bound (99%). Produces less active metabolites that are excreted by kidneys. |

**APPROXIMATELY EQUIVALENT THERAPEUTIC DOSES**

acetohexamide, 500 mg
chlorpropamide, 250 mg
glipizide, 5-10 mg
glyburide, 5 mg
tolazamide, 250 mg
tolbutamide, 1000 mg

the renal threshold for glucose. Usually glucose spillage into the urine occurs at blood levels of 160 to 180 mg/100 ml, but it may be higher in elderly clients or lower in children and pregnant women. Therefore it may not correlate well with serum glucose levels. See the box on p. 791 for various agents used for the testing of urine glucose levels. The maintenance of euglycemia (70 to 140 mg/100 ml) indicates the appropriate dosage of insulin for the client.

## ORAL HYPOGLYCEMIC AGENTS

In the early days of insulin therapy, many attempts were made to obtain a preparation of insulin that remained active after oral administration. None were successful, and it is unlikely that any can be, since both polypeptides and proteins (which compose insulin) are susceptible to destruction in the gastrointestinal tract and are poorly absorbed in an intact state.

However, certain drugs have been found to have blood glucose-lowering or "insulin-like" action when given by mouth. They are principally the group of sulfonylureas. These compounds were originally discovered after the observation that some of the antibacterial sulfonamides had hypoglycemic effects. Although these drugs are sometimes called "oral insulins," this definitely is incorrect, since chemically they are completely different from insulin. They also differ from insulin in origin and mode of action. Table 50-3 lists the agents that are available for clinical practice.

They enhance the release of insulin from the beta cells in the pancreas, decrease liver glycogenolysis and gluconeogenesis, and increase the sensitivity to insulin in body tissues. Therefore they reduce blood glucose concentration in persons with a functioning pancreas. (See Figure 50-2.) Antidiuretic effect—chlorpropamide increases the effect of low levels of antidiuretic hormone present in persons with central diabetes insipidus.

Oral hypoglycemic agents are indicated for the treatment of uncomplicated non–insulin dependent diabetes mellitus (type II) in persons whose diabetes cannot be controlled by diet only.

For pharmacokinetics and side effects/adverse reactions see Tables 50-4 and 50-5, respectively.

***Significant drug interactions.*** The following interactions may occur when the oral hypoglycemic agents are given with the drugs listed below:

| Drug | Possible Effect and Management |
|---|---|
| alcohol | May result in disulfiram (Antabuse)-type reaction, especially with chlorpropamide (Diabinese). The reaction may include stomach pain, nausea, vomiting, flushing, lowered blood glucose levels, and headaches. Avoid concurrent administration if possible. This problem is reported less often with glipizide and glyburide. |
| anticoagulants, oral, coumarin or indandione | Initially increased serum levels of both drugs may be seen but with chronic therapy, a reduction in plasma levels and effectiveness of the anticoagulant is reported. An increased serum level of the oral hypoglycemic agent may result in increased effects and toxicity because of a decrease in liver metabolism. Monitor closely because one or both drugs may require a dosage adjustment. |

**TABLE 50-4**   Pharmacokinetics of oral hypoglycemic agents

| Drug | Absorption orally | Half-life (hours) | Time to peak effect (hours) | Duration of action (hours) | Metabolism (in liver) | Excretion |
|------|-------------------|-------------------|------------------------------|-----------------------------|------------------------|-----------|
| acetohexamide | Good | 6-8 (metabolite) | 1-3 | 12-24 | To active metabolite | Kidneys bile |
| chlorpropamide | Good | 36 | 2-4 | 24-48 or more | 80% activity or metabolites unknown | Kidneys |
| glipizide | Good | 2-4 | 1-3 | 12-24 | To inactive metabolites | Kidneys |
| glyburide | Good | 10 | 4 | 24 | To inactive metabolites | Kidneys bile |
| tolazamide | Fair (slow) | 7 | 3-4 | 10 | To slightly active metabolites | Kidneys |
| tolbutamide | Good | 5 | 3-4 | 6-12 | To inactive metabolite | Kidneys Bile |

**TABLE 50-5**   Hypoglycemic oral agents: side effects/adverse reactions

| Side effects* | Adverse reactions† |
|---------------|---------------------|
| Most frequent: Diarrhea or constipation, dizziness, gas, anorexia, headache, nausea, vomiting, abdominal distress | Less frequent: Chlorpropamide only—respiratory difficulties (CHF in persons with cardiac problems). Sedation; cramping of muscles; convulsions; edema of face, hands, or ankles; comatose, increased weakness (antidiuretic effect). |
| Less frequent/rare: Photosensitivity, rash | Rare: Pruritus, jaundice, light colored stools, dark urine (impairment of liver function). Increased fatigue, sore throat, increased temperature, increased bleeding or bruising (blood dyscrasias). Overdosage: Symptoms of hypoglycemia (see insulin side effects/adverse reactions). |

*If side effects continue, increase, or disturb the client, the physician should be informed.

†If adverse reactions occur, contact the physician because medical intervention may be necessary.

| Drug | Possible Effect and Management |
|------|-------------------------------|
| chloramphenicol (Chloromycetin), guanethidine (Ismelin), insulin, monoamine oxidase (MAO) inhibitors, salicylates or sulfonamides | May result in an increase in hypoglycemic effect. Monitor closely, since dosage adjustments may be necessary. |
| beta adrenergic blocking agents (including ophthalmics) | Increases risk of hyperglycemia or hypoglycemia. See drug interaction for insulin for further information. |
| insulin | Enhanced hypoglycemic effect. |

**Pregnancy safety.**   Has been established at FDA category B for glyburide, FDA category C for all other agents.

### acetohexamide tablets (Dymelor)

The adult dose initially is 250 mg orally daily. Adjust dosage gradually until desired effect is achieved. Maximum daily dose is 1.5 g. (In persons requiring doses of 1 g or more, divided doses are recommended.) Usually, it is administered before breakfast and evening meals. Elderly, undernourished, or debilitated clients or persons with impaired renal or liver function require a lower initial dose, such as 125 to 250 mg daily. The drug is not effective for treatment of insulin dependent diabetes in children.

### chlorpropamide tablets (Diabinese)

Adult dose is initially 250 mg orally, once a day. It may be increased gradually by 50 to 125 mg every 3 to 5 days until diabetes is under control or the total daily dose reaches 750 mg. In the higher dosage range, divided doses (before breakfast and the evening meal) are recommended. In the elderly, the initial oral dose is 100 to 125 mg daily, increased if necessary, by 50 to 125 mg every 3 to 5 days. For use in children, see comment under acetohexamide.

### glipizide tablets (Glucotrol)

Adult dose initially is 5 mg orally daily. The dosage may be increased at 2.5 to 5 mg doses every 7 days until diabetic control is achieved, or the maximum total dose of 40 mg is reached. Elderly persons or those with kidney or liver impairment should be started on a daily dose of 2.5 mg. Persons receiving 15 mg daily or more should have the dosage divided into two, with administration before breakfast and evening meals. For use in children, see comment under acetohexamide.

### glyburide tablets (DiaBeta, Micronase)

Adult dose initially is 2.5 to 5 mg orally daily. Increase dosage gradually at no more than 2.5 mg at 7-day intervals until diabetes is under control or the total daily dose reaches 20 mg.

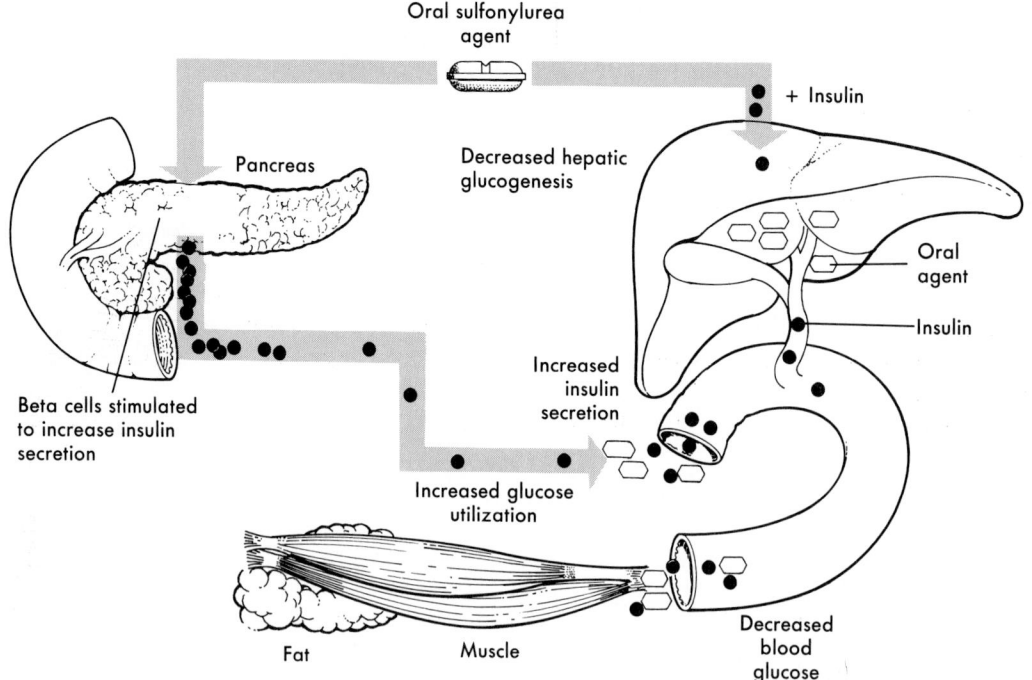

**FIGURE 50-2**   Mechanism of action of oral sulfonylurea agents. *(From Beare PG and Myers JL. [1990]. Principles and practice of adult health nursing. St. Louis: Mosby–Year Book, Inc.)*

**TABLE 50-6**   Administration of oral hypoglycemic agents

| Drug | Usual adult dose per day | Recommended administration times |
| --- | --- | --- |
| acetohexamide | 250 mg 1-2 times daily | Before breakfast and evening meal* |
| chlorpropamide | 250 mg daily | With breakfast |
| glipizide | 10-15 mg 1-2 times daily | 30 minutes before meals* |
| glyburide | 2.5-5 mg 1-2 times daily | With or 30 minutes before breakfast or 1st main meal† |
| tolazamide | 100-1000 mg 1-2 times daily | With breakfast or 1st main meal* |
| tolbutamide | 1000-2000 mg 2-3 times daily | Before (USP-DI, 1991) or after meals |

*If dosed twice daily, second dose is before, with, or after supper or evening meal.
†Studies with glyburide indicate divided doses provide better blood glucose control if given 30 minutes before a meal (American Hospital Formulary Service, 1991).

Elderly clients or persons with kidney or liver impairment should start at 1.25 mg daily. Persons receiving 10 mg or more per day should receive a divided dosage, that is, before breakfast and evening meals. For use in children, see comment under acetohexamide.

### tolazamide tablets (Tolinase)

Adult dose initially is 100 to 250 mg orally daily in the morning. Dosage may be increased gradually until diabetes is under control or the total maximum daily dose of 1 g is reached. (When more than 500 mg/day is necessary, divide dose and administer before breakfast and evening meals.)

Elderly initial dose is 100 mg daily, adjusting dose gradually according to the individual's response. For use in children, see comment under acetohexamide.

### tolbutamide tablets (Orinase)

Adult dose initially is 500 mg to 2 g daily, in divided doses administered before breakfast and evening meals. Maximum daily dose is 3 g. Elderly generally require lower initial doses and gradual dosage adjustment. For use in children, see comment under acetohexamide; for the best time to administer these agents, see Table 50-6.

## ▷NURSING MANAGEMENT: ORAL HYPOGLYCEMIC AGENT THERAPY

***Assessment.*** The client's level of knowledge for health maintenance related to diabetes mellitus and the prescribed oral hypoglycemic agent should be assessed. Information is to be provided or reinforced related to compliance with the appropriate ADA diet, weight monitoring, activity program, stress management, and adverse signs and symptoms to report to the health care provider. In addition, clients receiving oral hypoglycemic agents may experience altered bowel patterns of either diarrhea or constipation; altered comfort such as headache, heartburn, nausea, vomiting, abdominal discomfort, rash, and photosensitivity; and physiologic injury related to the development of agranulocytosis, aplastic or hemolytic anemia, eosinophilia, hepatitis, and thrombocytopenia.

With chlorpropamide only, the client is at risk for fluid volume excess and altered cardiac output related to the drug's antidiuretic effect, evidenced by weight gain, difficulty in breathing, oliguria, and edema of the face, hands, and feet.

These agents are not substituted for insulin in clients with diabetic coma, ketoacidosis, significant ketosis or acidosis, severe burns, infection, or trauma or those undergoing major surgery. They are to be used with caution with clients with adrenal or pituitary insufficiency or renal or hepatic impairment. Consideration should be given to use of oral hypoglycemic agents other than chlorpropamide with clients with cardiac impairment because of chlorpropamide's antidiuretic effects.

*Intervention.* Remember that the client with diabetes requires close supervision, especially when an oral hypoglycemic agent is tried for the first time.

When converting from insulin to an oral hypoglycemic agent for control of the diabetic status, monitor the client's blood for glucose three times a day before meals. No transition period is usually required when changing from one hypoglycemic agent to another one, except with chlorpropamide. In the case of chlorpropamide caution should be exercised in the first week because of its prolonged half life, 25 to 60 hours.

*Education.* Recognize that the need for instruction stressing dietary restriction is even greater for clients receiving oral hypoglycemic agents than for those taking insulin. Clients weighing more than 20% over their ideal weight may not respond to oral hypoglycemic agents. The client should weigh in once a week at the same time using the same scale and keep a weight record. Remember that these clients should be taught testing for blood glucose levels, skin care, and signs and symptoms of hypoglycemia and hyperglycemia.

Caution clients about excessive alcohol intake (and medications containing alcohol) when oral sulfonylurea therapy is begun. Alcohol can increase the rate of metabolism of these drugs when there is long-term consumption of these drugs when there is long-term consumption of excessive quantities.

When clients are switched from insulin to oral sulfonylureas, advise them to perform blood testing frequently during this period.

Teach clients to carry or have access to forms of glucose at all times.

Have the client administer the initial dosage in the morning to decrease nocturnal hypoglycemia. Drugs given with food will decrease any gastric upset.

If the client is taking divided doses of oral sulfonylureas and omits a dose, advise him/her that it should be taken as soon as it is remembered. The missed dose should be administered near the time for the next dose, but they should not be taken together. Administration before meals will maximize postprandial insulin release.

Make the client aware that the administration of these agents has been associated with increased incidence of death from cardiovascular disease compared with treatment with diet alone or diet plus insulin.

*Evaluation.* Elderly persons tend to be more sensitive to the effects of the oral hypoglycemic agents. Because hypoglycemia may be more difficult to recognize in these clients, they require lower dosages and closer monitoring.

Observe for hypoglycemia in the client who has irregular meal patterns, exercises more than usual, or ingests significant amounts of alcohol; hypoglycemia is more likely in these clients. A moderate life-style is essential to diabetes management. Periods of physiologic or psychologic stress may necessitate a temporary use of insulin.

## HYPERGLYCEMIC AGENTS
### glucagon

Glucagon (for injection) is a polypeptide hormone secreted by the pancreatic islet alpha cells. Hepatic glycogenolysis is accelerated by glucagon through stimulation of synthesis of cyclic AMP (cAMP) and increasing phosphorylase kinase activity. The resulting blood glucose elevations are caused by both increased breakdown of glycogen to glucose and glycogen synthesis inhibition. Glucagon stimulates liver gluconeogenesis through promotion of amino acid uptake and then conversion of the amino acids to precursors of glucose. Hepatic and adipose tissue lipolysis is enhanced by activation of adenyl cyclase, producing free fatty acids and glycerol, which stimulate ketogenesis and gluconeogenesis.

It is indicated for the treatment of hypoglycemia in clients with diabetes or during insulin shock therapy. It is effective only if liver glycogen is available; thus it is ineffective in chronic states of hypoglycemia or starvation and adrenal insufficiency.

Used as an adjunct to barium in gastrointestinal radiography. It produces relaxation of the esophagus, stomach, duodenum, small bowel, and colon (hypotonicity).

Parenterally administered (intramuscular, intravenous, or subcutaneous), it has a half-life of 3 to 6 minutes and an onset of action as a diagnostic aid as follows, according to route of administration: intravenous, 0.25 to 2 USP units, within 1 minute; intramuscular, 1 USP unit, within 8 to 10 minutes; 2 USP units, within 4 to 7 minutes. The drug's duration of effect as a diagnostic aid is as follows, according to route: intravenous, 0.25 to 0.5 USP units, 9 to 17 minutes; 2 USP units, between 22 and 25 minutes; intramuscular, 1 USP unit, between 12 and 27 minutes; 2 USP units, within 21 to 32 minutes. It is metabolized in the liver and excreted by the kidneys.

Side effects/adverse reactions are not usually severe. Less frequent include rash, dizziness, respiratory distress (allergic reaction), nausea, or vomiting. No significant drug interactions have been reported.

When using this drug in adults for antihypoglycemic effects, administer 0.5 to 1 USP units (0.5 to 1 mg) of glucagon, intramuscular, intravenous, or subcutaneous. Repeat in 20 minutes if necessary. As a diagnostic aid, give 0.25 to 2 USP units (0.25 to 2 mg) of glucagon intramuscularly or intravenously. Dosage depends on area to be examined, desired onset of action, and duration of effect. For example, to examine the colon, it is recommended that 2 USP units be given intramuscularly approximately 10 minutes before the procedure.

When using the drug in children for antihypoglycemic effect, administer 0.025 USP unit (0.025 mg)/kg up to a maximum dose of 1 USP unit (1 mg), intramuscularly, intravenously, or subcutaneously; dose may be repeated in 20 minutes if needed.

Pregnancy safety has been established as FDA category B.

▷ **Nursing Management:**
**Glucagon Therapy**

**Assessment.** It is important for the nurse to recognize the symptoms of hypoglycemia: anxiousness, irritability, altered mood, nervousness, weakness, shakiness, inability to concentrate; perspiring, cool, pale skin; hunger, nausea, headache; and unconsciousness.

**Intervention.** Glucagon is administered for hypoglycemia in the unconscious client as directed by the physician. After administering, turn the individual on one side to prevent choking and/or aspiration. Inform the physician of the client's status. If the client has not regained consciousness in 5 to 20 minutes, give a second dose and transport the client to the hospital. Intravenous glucose will need to be started if the individual does not respond to the second dose of glucagon. Glucagon and glucose may be given at the same time.

If the client does regain consciousness and can swallow, offer some oral form of sugar followed by a more complex carbohydrate, such as crackers and cheese or a glass of milk. This will help prevent a recurrence of the hypoglycemia before the next meal. If the client is experiencing nausea and vomiting that prevent food intake for more than an hour after the administration of the glucagon, seek medical assistance.

Replace the client's supply of glucagon as soon as possible.

**Education.** Teach the family and the client how to mix the drug and how to inject properly before the need arises to use glucagon. A standard insulin syringe may be used for injection unless the dose is greater than the capacity of the syringe. However, the injection should be made at a 90 degree angle instead of the usual subcutaneous approach. Advise the client and family to keep supplies on hand and check the expiration dates frequently.

Instruct the client and family about the symptoms of hypoglycemia and the importance of ingesting some form of sugar, such as orange juice, honey, syrup, hard candy, sugar cubes, or milk, when symptoms first occur.

### diazoxide (Proglycem)

Diazoxide administered orally produces a prompt, dose-related increase in blood glucose levels primarily by inhibition of insulin release from the pancreas and an extrapancreatic effect. It is indicated for the treatment of hypoglycemia caused by hyperinsulinism, which is caused by an inoperable islet cell adenoma or carcinoma, an extrapancreatic malignancy, or an islet cell hyperplasia. It is not indicated for treatment in functional hypoglycemia.

Diazoxide is rapidly absorbed orally, has an onset of action within 1 hour, duration of effect not longer than 8 hours, and a half-life of between 20 to 36 hours in normal individuals. It is highly protein bound (more than 90% bound to albumin), metabolized in the liver, and excreted by the kidneys.

Side effects reported less frequently include taste alterations, constipation, anorexia, nausea, vomiting, and abdominal pain. With chronic use it may cause increased hair growth on arms, legs, back, and forehead (**hypertrichosis**). Most frequently reported adverse reactions include a decrease in urine output resulting in edema of hands, feet, or lower extremities, weight gain, and possibly congestive heart failure in susceptible individuals. Less often reported is a fast or irregular heart rate. Hyperglycemia or ketoacidosis are the typical symptoms reported with a diazoxide overdose.

**Significant drug interactions.** The following significant drug interactions may occur when diazoxide is given with the drugs listed below:

| Drug | Possible Effect and Management |
|---|---|
| Anticonvulsants, hydantoin (phenytoin) | May decrease or nullify the action of both drugs. Avoid concurrent drug administration. |
| Medications that induce hypotension (alcohol, diuretics, calcium channel blocking agents, beta adrenergic blocking drugs) and peripheral vasodilators | Concurrent use may cause enhanced severe, hypotensive effect. Monitor closely, since dosage adjustments may be necessary. |

***Dosage and administration.*** The adult dose of diazoxide initially is 1 mg/kg every 8 hours; adjust dosage as necessary. Maintenance dose is 3 to 8 mg/kg orally daily; divide into 2 or 3 equal doses and administer every 12 or 8 hours, as indicated. Maximum dose in usually 15 mg/kg/day. The antihypoglycemic dose in neonates and infants is initially 3.3 mg/kg orally every 8 hours; adjust dosage according to therapeutic response. Maintenance dose is 8 to 15 mg/kg orally daily; divide total dose into 2 or 3 equal doses and administer every 12 or 8 hours, as indicated. For children, see usual adult dosage.

***Pregnancy safety.*** Has been established at FDA category C.

## ▷ Nursing Management: Diazoxide Therapy

***Assessment.*** Determine whether the client has a sensitivity to thiazide diuretics or other sulfonamide medication because he or she may also be sensitive to diazoxide.

Carefully consider the use of diazoxide in clients with cardiac problems, because of the potential for fluid volume excess resulting from the drug's tendency to increase water and sodium retention. Observe clients for swelling of the feet and lower legs, increased weight gain, and decrease in urinary output as signs of fluid retention. Diuretics are sometimes given concurrently to avert these side effects.

***Intervention.*** Since pain may occur at the site of injections, it is recommended that diazoxide be administered intravenously and then only into a peripheral vein by an established intravenous line. Avoid extravasation because it results in cellulitis and pain. Treat conservatively with cold packs if extravasation does occur. Keep the client recumbent during and at least 30 minutes after injection.

Dosage forms vary in their ability to produce blood concentrations of diazoxide. The oral suspension dosage form produces higher concentrations than those of the capsule form. Caution needs to be taken in changing the client from one to the other.

***Education.*** Instruct clients in the importance of diet, testing of blood for glucose, regular visits to the physician, symptoms of hypoglycemia and hyperglycemia, and of not taking other medications unless discussed with the physician.

Clients receiving diazoxide may experience the following nursing diagnoses: altered comfort related to changes in taste, nausea, vomiting, and abdominal pain; altered bowel pattern: constipation; altered self-concept related to hypertrichosis; impaired physical mobility related to the drug's extrapyramidal effects, evidenced by stiffness of limbs, and trembling and shaking of fingers and hands; the risk of physiologic injury related to allergic reaction, angina pectoris, myocardial ischemia or infarction, thrombocytopenia, and transient cerebral ischemic attacks.

### glucose (Glutose, Insta-Glucose)

Glucose is a monosaccharide that is absorbed from the intestine and then used, distributed in the body, or stored in the tissues. It is indicated to treat or manage hypoglycemia. It is absorbed from the gastrointestinal tract and distributed readily to tissues. Glucose provides 4 calories per gram. The only side effects have been some reports of nausea. No significant drug interactions have been reported.

In adults approximately 10 to 20 g are administered orally; repeat in 10 minutes if necessary. Glucose must be swallowed to produce an effect. It is not absorbed from the buccal cavity. Administer to children only under instructions of the physician.

## SUMMARY

The two primary hormones released by the pancreas are insulin and glucagon. When the blood glucose falls, glucagon is released, facilitating the catabolism of glycogen stored in the liver, which increases blood glucose. The release of glucagon stimulates the secretion of insulin, inhibiting the release of glucagon, maintaining homeostasis of carbohydrate metabolism. Diabetes mellitus is a disorder of carbohydrate metabolism that is the result of an insulin deficiency or resistance or both. Diabetes mellitus is classified as insulin dependent diabetes mellitus (type I), previously called juvenile onset diabetes, and non–insulin dependent diabetes mellitus (type II), maturity onset diabetes. Although type II may require insulin at some time, it is usually managed by dietary treatment, weight reduction of the client, and, if necessary, oral hypoglycemic agents.

Insulin may be rapid, intermediate, and long acting. Therapeutic dosages are not fixed, but are set considering the client's dietary intake, physical activity, and glucose tolerance. The requirement for client education is essential for the client to participate in ascertaining the insulin dosage needed through blood testing and to self-administer insulin safely and accurately. See the selected nursing diagnoses for clients receiving insulin on pages 789-790.

Oral hypoglycemic agents encourage the release of insulin from the pancreas, decrease glycogenolysis and gluconeogenesis, increase the sensitivity of body tissues to insulin, and are used for type II diabetes mellitus.

Hyperglycemic agents are used in the treatment of hypoglycemia in which the client is unable to ingest sufficient amounts of glucose to meet body requirements.

# Case Study: The Client with Diabetes Mellitus

Edward Milton is 25 years old. He was recently diagnosed with insulin dependent diabetes mellitus. In addition to a 2300 calorie ADA diet, Mr. Milton was started on an insulin administration program that includes 25 units of NPH insulin each morning. He is also instructed in the procedure for self-monitoring blood glucose. Mr. Milton is advised to check his blood sugar in the morning before his insulin dose and in the late afternoon before supper.

One month after beginning treatment, he came to the emergency room at 6:00 in the evening with profuse sweating, tremors, headache, and an elevated blood pressure. His blood sugar by fingerstick was 45 mg/dl. A serum blood sample confirmed the diagnosis of hypoglycemia. Mr. Milton was given an intravenous bolus of 50 cc of 50% dextrose. In interviewing Mr. Milton before he was released from the ER, you discover that he had not eaten his usual meals that day because of vague feeling of nausea, anorexia, and mild diarrhea. He also admits that he has not been testing his blood sugar at home because he is too rushed in the morning. He frequently eats out in the evening with friends and is too embarrassed to test his blood sugar "in front of my friends." Mr. Milton says he does follow his diet and finds no problems in balancing his food intake.

1. What is the significance of the time of day that Mr. Milton experienced his hypoglycemia?
2. Outline the instructions you will give Mr. Milton about managing his diabetes on days when he is sick.
3. Explain the importance of self-monitoring of blood glucose for diabetes management.

After his first hypoglycemic episode, Mr. Milton began monitoring his blood glucose twice a day as he had been instructed. One year later he reports that his sugars have been increasing both in the morning and the afternoon. He denies any change in food intake or activity. He says he follows his diet faithfully. His insulin regimen is changed to add 10 units of regular insulin to the morning dose of NPH. He is also to take 10 units of NPH and 5 units of regular insulin in the evening, before supper. Although Mr. Milton agrees to the twice a day insulin injections, he asks why he can't take pills for diabetes the way his grandfather did for his diabetes.

4. How will you respond to Mr. Milton's questions about taking pills for his diabetes?
5. What are the differences between NPH and regular insulin that Mr. Milton needs to learn?
6. List the steps you will teach Mr. Milton about preparing the two insulins for injection.

7. What additional points will you review with Mr. Milton regarding his insulin administration techniques?

## BIBLIOGRAPHY

American Diabetic Association. (1990). Clinical practice recommendations: insulin administration 1989-1990, Diabetes Care 13(Suppl 1):28.

American Diabetic Association. (1990). Clinical practice recommendations: continuous subcutaneous insulin infusion 1989-1990, Diabetes Care 13(Suppl 1):32.

American Diabetic Association. (1990). Clinical practice recommendations: jet injectors 1989-1990, Diabetes Care 13(Suppl 1):39.

American Hospital Formulary Service. (1991). AHFS drug information '91. Bethesda, Md: American Society of Hospital Pharmacists, Inc.

Ammon JR. (1989). Perioperative management of the diabetic patient, Curr Rev Nurse Anesth 12(2):10.

Baccus H. (1989). Heading off a diabetic crisis, Emerg Med 21(20):20.

Beaulieu JA. (1989). Nursing diagnoses co-occurring in adults with insulin-dependent diabetes mellitus, Classif Nurs Diagn, Proc Eighth Conf p 199.

Blackshear PJ et al. (1989). Basal-rate intravenous insulin infusion compared to conventional insulin treatment patients with type II diabetes: a prospective crossover trial, Diabetes Care 12(7):455.

Bond WS. (1988). Aldose reductase-related complications in diabetes and efficacy of aldose reductase inhibitors, Facts & Comparisons Drug Newsletter 7(6):41.

Braunwald E et al, eds. (1987). Harrison's principles of internal medicine, ed 11. New York: McGraw-Hill Book Co.

Campbell RK. (1987). Insulin: buying guide, Diabetes Forecast 40(10):38.

Danish M. (1988). When should oral hypoglycemic agents be taken in relation to meals? US Pharmacist 13(3):38.

Davis RE. (1989). Equipment guide for administering insulin, Prof Nurse 5(2):91.

Dellasega C. (1990). Self-care for the elderly diabetic, J Gerontol Nurs 16(1):16.

Field JB. (1990). Insulin dosage and the ripple effect, Patient Care 24(1):209.

Geffner ME et al. (1989). Bittle diabetes: strategies for achieving glycemic stability, part 2, Consultant 29(9):37.

Glyburide vs insulin in non-insulin-dependent diabetes. (1988). Nurses Drug Alert 12(8):59.

Graber AL. (1987). When you trade pills for insulin, Diabetes Forecast 40(1):40.

Guthrie D. (1988). What's wrong with this patient? Nursing 18(4):84.

Hahn K. (1990). Teaching patients to administer insulin, Nursing 20(4):70.

Hahn K. (1989). Think twice . . . about insulin administration, Nursing 19(4):66.

Hernandez CMG. (1987). Surgery and diabetes: minimizing the risks, Amer J Nurs 87(6):788.

High-fiber diet in poorly controlled Type II diabetics. (1988). Nurses Drug Alert 12(12):94.

Hurxthal K. (1988). Quick! Teach this patient about insulin, Amer J Nurs 88(8):1097.

Huzar JG. (1989). Diabetes now: preventing acute complications RN 52(8):34.

Huzar JG et al. (1989). Diabetes now: the role of diet and drugs, RN 52(4):46.

Implantable insulin pumps. (1989). Nurses Drug Alert 13(1):7.

Kastrup EK, ed. (1991). Facts and comparisons. St Louis: JB Lippincott Co.

Katzung BG. (1987). Basic and clinical pharmacology, ed 3. Norwalk, Conn: Appleton & Lange.

Kitabchi AE et al. (1987). Hypoglycemia: pathophysiology and diagnosis, Hosp Pract 22(11):45.

Krosnick A. (1987). Diabetes treatment update: switching to biosynthetic human insulin, Consultant 27(7):78.

Lumley WA. (1989). Recognizing and reversing insulin shock, Nursing 19(9):34.

Mackowiak L et al. (1989). Managing diabetes on "sick days," Amer J Nurs 89(7):950.

Nath C et al. (1988). Lessons in living with type II diabetes mellitus, Nursing 18(8):44.

Price JP et al. (1989). Evaluation of the insulin jet injector as a potential source of infection, Am J Infect Control 17(5):258.

Robertson C. (1989). The new challenges of insulin therapy, RN 52(5):34.

Rubin RR et al. (1989). Effect of diabetes on self-care, metabolic control, and emotional well-being, Diabetes Care 12(10):673.

Shannon LF. (1988). Insulin usage in the neonate, Neonatal Network 6(5):31.

Solomons HC. (1989). Adaptive responses to diabetes mellitus, West J Nurs Res 11(3):276.

Skelly AH et al. (1987). Insulin allergy in clinical practice, Nurse Pract 12(4):16.

Trevelyan J. (1990). A view from the inside . . . diabetes can affect mental ability and personality, Community Outlook, March, p 12.

United States Pharmacopeial Convention. (1991). Drug information for the health care professional, ed 11. Rockville, Md: The Convention.

van Faassen I et al. (1989). Carriage of Staphylococcus aureus and inflamed infusion sites with insulin-pump therapy, Diabetes Care 12(2):153.

Vasser AP et al. (1989). Benefits of intensive treatment of insulin-dependent diabetes patients: the importance of patient education, Patient Educ Couns 14(1):21.

White LK and Martin DB. (1988). Aldose reductase inhibitors: a possible therapeutic role in diabetes? Hosp Therapy 13(10):63.

Will surgery complicate your patient's drug therapy? (1987). Emerg Med 19(18):56.

Wilson M et al. (1988). A contract for change in diabetes self-management: case report, Diabetes Educ 14(1):37.

Wozniak L. (1988). Your teaching plan: the key to controlling type II diabetes, RN 51(8):29.

Young LY and Koda-Kimble MA. (1988). Applied therapeutics: the clinical use of drugs, ed 4. Vancouver, Wash: Applied Therapeutics, Inc.

# Overview of the Female and Male Reproductive Systems

## CHAPTER OBJECTIVES

*After studying this chapter, you should be able to meet the following objectives and define the key terms.*

1. Identify the anterior pituitary gland hormones that influence the female and male reproductive systems.

2. Describe hormonal influences on uterine function during the menstrual cycle.

3. Identify the primary male and female hormones.

4. Describe the effects of estrogen during the proliferative stage.

5. Trace the transport of sperm in the male body, from production to ejaculation.

6. Discuss the role that vas deferens ducts play in male sterility.

## KEY TERMS

**androgens,** page 802

**ejaculation,** page 808

**endometrium,** page 804

**estrogens,** page 802

**follicle-stimulating hormone (FSH),** page 802

**gonads,** page 803

**luteinizing hormone (LH),** page 802

**ovulation,** page 804

**progestogens,** page 802

**semen,** page 808

**testosterone,** page 807

## INTRODUCTION

Reproduction is the sum of genetic and hormonal influences originating from the sexes of a species to perpetuate the species. In human beings, the reproductive process in both sexes is highly complex, involving **follicle-stimulating hormone (FSH)** and **luteinizing hormone (LH)** from the anterior pituitary gland, as well as the hormones from the reproductive systems of the male **(androgens)** and the female **(estrogens** and **progestogens).**

## ENDOCRINE GLANDS

The reproductive system of the human female consists of the ovaries, fallopian tubes, uterus, and vagina. The male reproductive system consists of the testes, seminal vesicles, prostate gland, bulbourethral glands, and penis. The reproductive organs of both male and female are mainly under the control of the endocrine glands. The ovaries and testes, known as **gonads,** not only produce ova and sperm cells but also form endocrine secretions that initiate and maintain the secondary sexual characteristics in men and women. The structure and physiologic functions of the pituitary gland are reviewed in Chapter 47; the discussion of the pituitary gland in this chapter is limited to its effect on the female and male reproductive systems.

## PITUITARY GONADOTROPIC HORMONES

The gonadotropins or pituitary hormones responsible for the development and maintenance of sexual gland functions are the following:

1. FSH, which stimulates the development of the ovarian (graafian) follicles up to the point of ovulation in the female; in the male FSH stimulates the development of the seminiferous tubules and promotes spermatogenesis.

2. LH or interstitial cell-stimulating hormone (ICSH), which acts in the female to promote the growth of the interstitial cells in the follicle and the formation of the corpus luteum; in the male, ICSH stimulates the growth of interstitial cells in the testes and promotes the formation of the hormone androgen, testosterone.

3. Luteotropic hormone (LTH) or luteotropin, which is identical with the lactogenic hormone, or prolactin.

In the female, FSH initiates the cycle of events in the ovary. Under the influence of both FSH and LH the graafian follicle grows, matures, secretes estrogen, ovulates, and forms the corpus luteum. LTH promotes the secretory activity of the corpus luteum and the formation of progesterone. In the absence of LTH the corpus luteum undergoes regressive changes and fails to make progesterone.

## FEMALE REPRODUCTIVE SYSTEM

Figure 51-1 illustrates the effects of the pituitary hormones, ovarian hormones, and uterine functions during the menstrual cycle. Body temperature fluctuations are also included with this diagram.

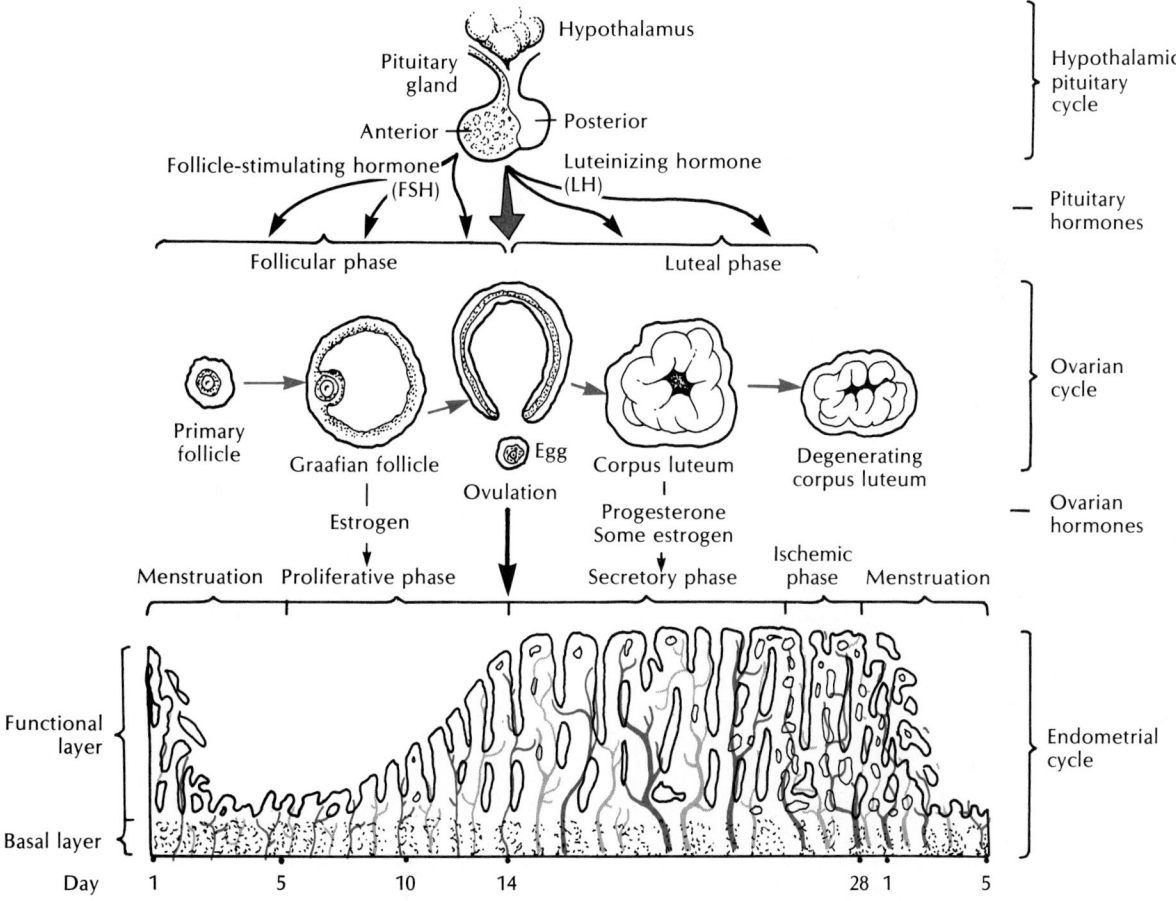

**FIGURE 51-1** Menstrual cycle. *(From Bobak I et al. [1989]. Maternity and gynecological care, ed 4. St Louis: The CV Mosby Co.)*

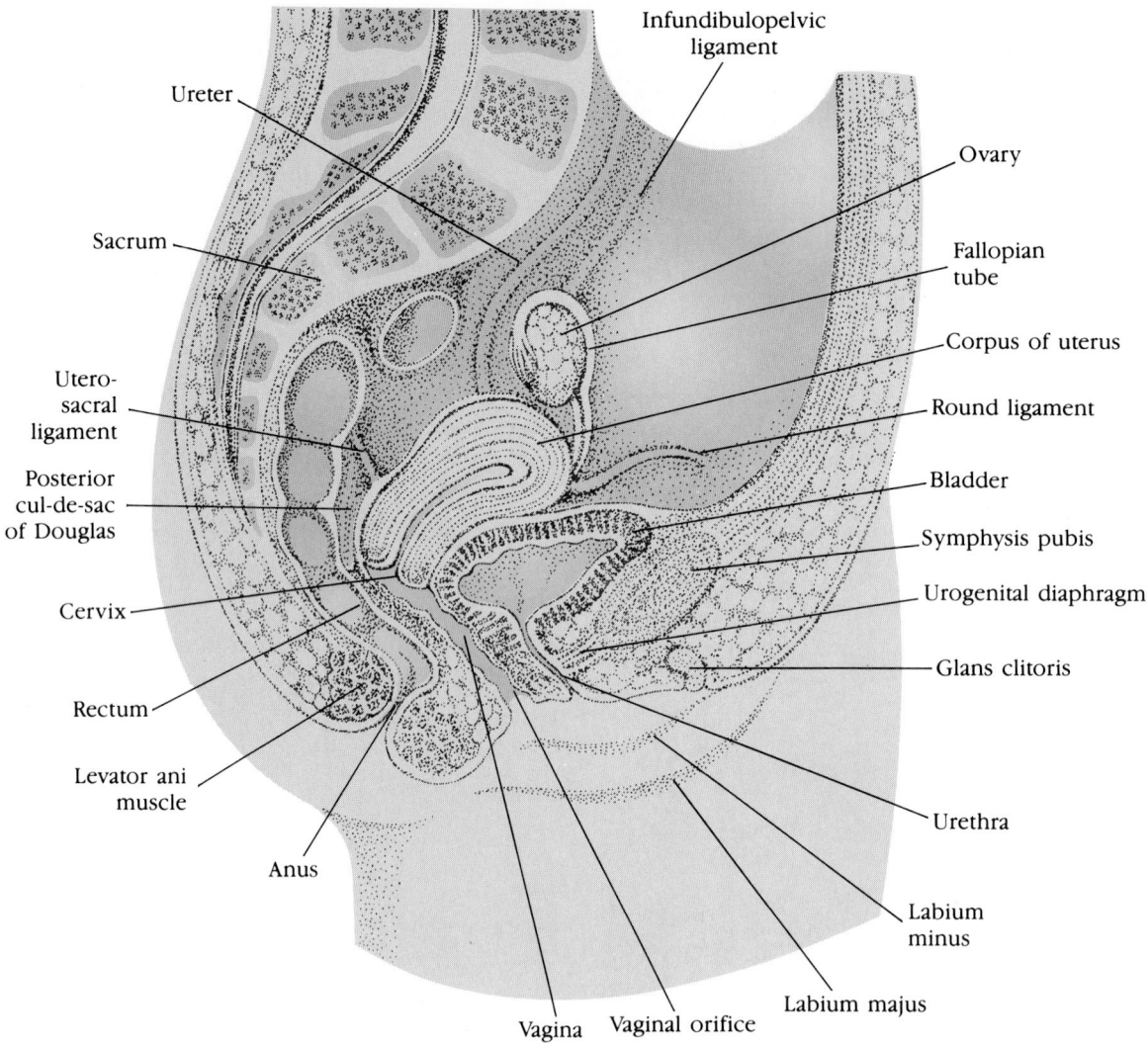

**FIGURE 51-2**  Female reproductive system.

Day 1 of the menstrual cycle is the onset of menses, and Day 5 usually signifies the end of menstruation. During this time, FSH is stimulating follicular growth in the ovary and also stimulating the ovary to produce estrogen, which is low at the beginning of the cycle. As estrogen levels increase, FSH levels decrease. The rising estrogen levels are preparing the uterus for a fertilized ovum, which is known as the proliferative stage of the uterus and results in the following:

1. Estrogen stimulates the growth of glandular surface of the **endometrium,** or inner lining of the uterus.
2. Estrogen affects the mucus glands of the cervix to produce a more plentiful, viscous mucus that contains nutrients that can be used by the sperm.

The increasing levels of estrogen also stimulate the pituitary gland to release LH. As FSH is decreasing, LH is increasing. At this time (day 14), **ovulation** occurs when the mature follicle ruptures and releases its ovum. The ovum travels through the fallopian tube to the uterus. Female pelvic organs are shown in Figure 51-2.

The increasing levels of LH will affect the ruptured follicle by changing the follicle capsule into the corpus luteum. Under the influence of LH, the corpus luteum releases estrogen and progesterone. In the second phase, or secretory phase, both uterine hormones increase secretion of the glands of the endometrium. If the ovum is fertilized and reaches this area on approximately the eighteenth day of the cycle, it will be able to thrive on the nutrient secretions of the endometrium.

Progesterone has an additional effect: it inhibits the flow of cervical mucus and reduces the thickness of the vaginal lining. But if fertilization does not occur, the pituitary will respond to the increased levels of estrogen and progesterone by shutting off the release of FSH and LH. Without the central stimulation, the corpus luteum cannot produce estrogen or progesterone, so the surface layer of the endometrium will slough off, resulting in menstruation. Figure 51-3 depicts the feedback mechanism of FSH and LH and their main effects on the ovaries.

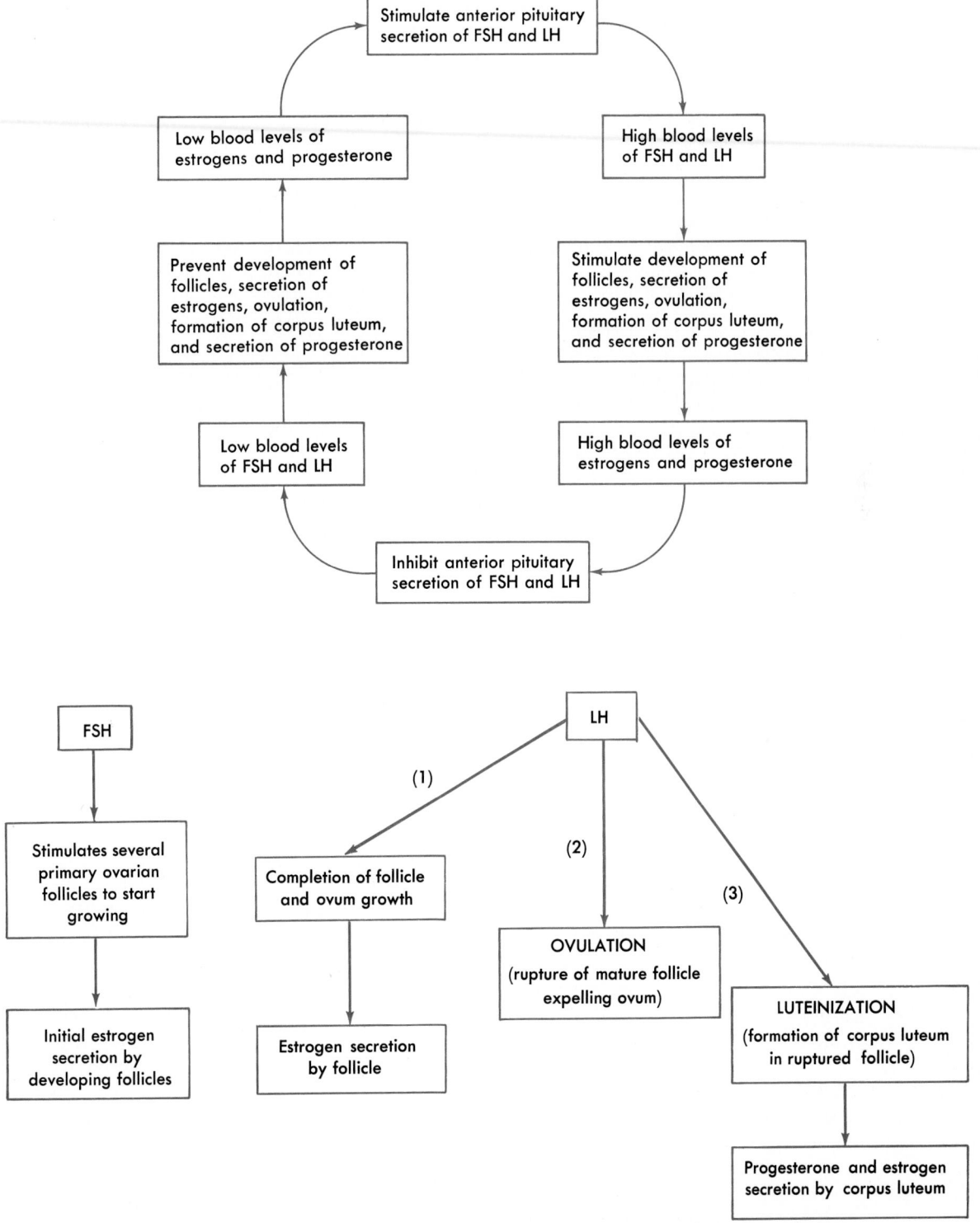

**FIGURE 51-3** Feedback mechanism of follicle-stimulating hormone (FSH) and luteinizing hormone (LH) and their main effects on the ovaries. *(From Anthony C and Thibodeau G. [1987]. Textbook of anatomy and physiology, ed 12. St Louis: Times Mirror/Mosby College Publishing.)*

Most women demonstrate month-to-month variations in their menstrual cycles; therefore ovulation is not always predictable. The previous description of the menstrual cycle is based on a 28-day cycle, but ovulation varies and occurs on different days in different length cycles. Physiologically, this is the primary reason for the unreliability of the rhythm method of contraception, which depends on predicting the day of ovulation based on previous menstrual cycles.

## Female Sexual Response

For both males and females, psychic stimulation and local sexual stimulation are necessary for a satisfactory sexual experience. Psychic stimulation may be aided by an individual's erotic thoughts, although sexual desire is also affected by increasing levels of estrogen secretion, especially during the preovulatory period.

Local sexual stimulation causes similar responses in both sexes; that is, massage, increasing stimulation or irritation of the perineal region or sexual organs can result in an enhancement of sexual sensations. In the female, the clitoris is very sensitive, and its stimulation can initiate a sexual sensation. Erectile tissue is located in the introitus (vaginal opening) and clitoris areas. This tissue is under parasympathetic nerve control; therefore in early stimulation, the parasympathetic nerves dilate the arteries located in the erectile tissues. Blood collects in the erectile tissue in the area so that the introitus will tighten around the penis, which aids male satisfaction for sexual stimulation, thus leading to ejaculation.

The parasympathetic nerves also signal the Bartholin's glands situated near the labia minora resulting in an increase in mucus secretion inside the introitus. This secretion, in addition to mucus from the vaginal epithelium, serves as a lubricant during sexual intercourse.

The female climax, or orgasm, is reached when the local

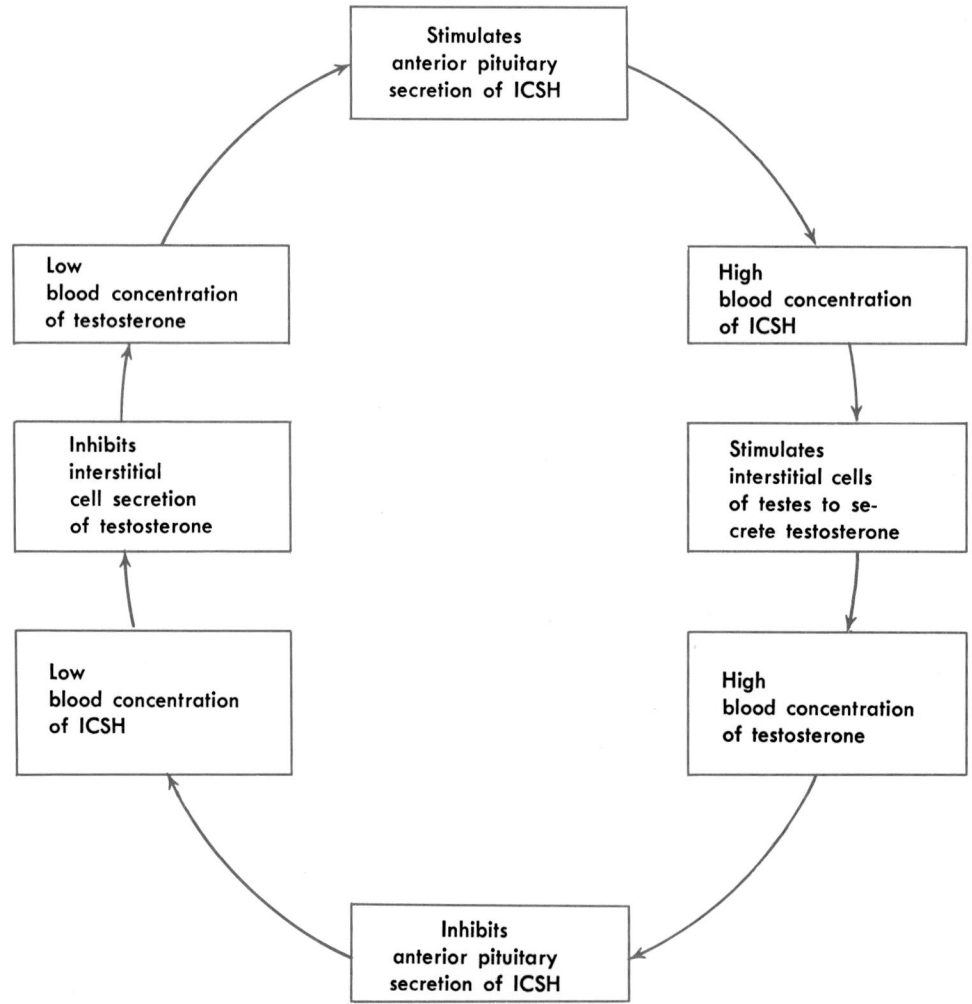

**FIGURE 51-4** Effect of interstitial cell–stimulating hormone (ICSH) on testosterone. *(From Anthony C and Thibodeau G. [1987]. Textbook of anatomy and physiology, ed 12. St Louis: Times Mirror/Mosby College Publishing.)*

sexual stimulation reaches the maximum sensation or intensity. It is considered similar to emission and ejaculation in the male and may also help to promote fertilization of the ovum. It has been theorized that orgasm produces a rhythm in the female tract from spinal cord reflexes that increase both uterine and fallopian tube motility and may result in cervical canal dilation for up to 30 minutes. This will allow for easy sperm transport in the female.

The intense sexual sensations that develop during orgasms also result in an increase in muscle tension throughout the body. After the sexual act, this tension subsides into relaxation or feelings of satisfaction, sometimes referred to as resolution.

## MALE REPRODUCTIVE SYSTEM

The effects of FSH and LH or ICSH in the male were described in the section on pituitary gonadotropic hormones. The effects of ICSH on secretion of testosterone are seen in Figure 51-4. **Testosterone,** an androgen, performs numerous functions, which are described below. FSH from the anterior pituitary gland stimulates the seminiferous tubules to increase production of spermatozoa, while ICSH stimulates the interstitial cells to increase secretion of testosterone. A high level of testosterone will inhibit the pituitary's release of FSH and ICSH.

Testosterone has many functions in the male. It aids in developing and maintaining the male secondary sex characteristics and male accessory organs, such as prostate, seminal vesicles, and bulbourethral glands. Testosterone promotes adult male sexual behavior, as well as regulating metabolism and protein anabolism, that is, growth of bone and skeletal muscles. This hormone affects fluid and electrolyte metabolism, by reabsorbing sodium and water and increasing excretion of potassium. FSH and ICSH secretion is also inhibited from the anterior pituitary by testosterone.

### Transport of Sperm in the Male

Sperm produced in the testes mature by spending 1 to 3 weeks in the epididymis in the male. The sperm, or seminal fluid, then travels through the epididymis (ducts that lie around the top of the testes) to the vas deferens. The vas deferens, a duct extension of the epididymis, extends over the bladder surface (posteriorly) to the ampulla to form the ejaculatory duct. Sperm can be stored in the vas deferens in excess of one month without loss of fertility depending on sexual activity. Thus a vasectomy, or severing of the vas deferens will make a man sterile primarily because it interrupts the journey of sperm to the ejaculatory duct and urethra. Male pelvic organs and the anatomy of the ejaculatory ducts are shown in Figure 51-5.

### Male Sexual Response

Penile erection is a parasympathetic response that consists of dilation of the arteries and arterioles in the penis, which compresses the veins in this area. Thus more blood enters

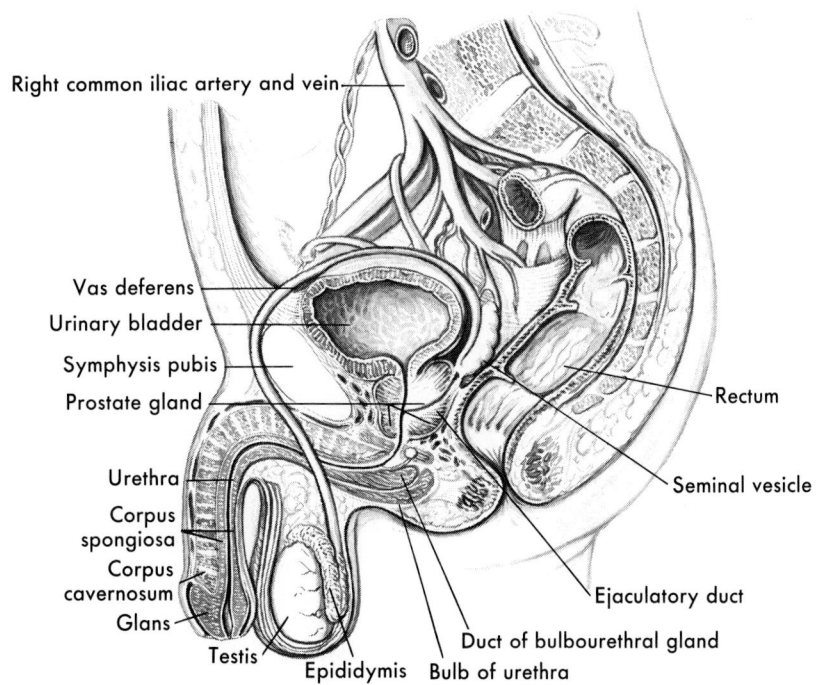

**FIGURE 51-5**  Male reproductive system. *(From Anthony C and Thibodeau G. [1987]. Textbook of anatomy and physiology, ed 12. St Louis: Times Mirror/Mosby College Publishing.)*

the penis than leaves, it becomes larger, and erection occurs. Emission and **ejaculation** of the sperm or semen is a reflex response. The stimulus that initiated erection will also help to move the sperm and secretions **(semen)** from the genital ducts to the prostatic urethra. Orgasm, the climax of the sexual act, moves the semen through the ejaculatory ducts. During coitus, the sperm can be transferred from male to female.

Later in life gonadal function ceases. Women undergo menopause or cessation of menses, and men have a decrease in sex hormone production, which is sometimes called the male climacteric.

## SUMMARY

Disorders of the reproductive system of men and women result in acute and chronic physical and emotional stress. The nurse requires a sound knowledge of the anatomy and physiology of the reproductive system to assess clients for health adaptations and alterations in this domain.

## BIBLIOGRAPHY

Guyton AC. (1990). Textbook of medical physiology, ed 8, Philadelphia: WB Saunders Co.

Thibodeau GA. (1990). Textbook of anatomy and physiology, ed 13. St Louis: Times Mirror/Mosby College Publishing.

# 52 Drugs Affecting the Female Reproductive System

## CHAPTER OBJECTIVES

*After studying this chapter, you should be able to meet the following objectives and define the key terms.*

1. List drugs affecting the female reproductive system.

2. Describe the source and action of chorionic gonadotropin.

3. Describe the function of the primary female sex hormones.

4. Describe side effects / adverse reactions of estrogens and progestins.

5. Compare and contrast monophasic, biphasic, and triphasic oral contraceptives.

6. Discuss nursing management of drugs affecting the female reproductive system.

## KEY TERMS

**anovulation,** page 822

**biphasic,** page 818

**estrogens,** page 813

**monophasic,** page 818

**oral contraception,** page 817

**progestogens,** page 813

**triphasic,** page 818

## INTRODUCTION

Drugs affecting the female reproductive system include synthetic and natural substances, such as gonadotropin-releasing hormone, nonpituitary chorionic gonadotropin, menotropins, female sex hormones, oral contraceptives, ovulatory stimulants, and drugs used for infertility.

## GONADOTROPIN-RELEASING HORMONE

Gonadotropin-releasing hormone or gonadorelin is a synthetic hormone used to diagnose hypogonadism in males and females. It is under investigation for use in the treatment of delayed puberty, amenorrhea, and infertility, alone and with other medications.

### gonadorelin (Factrel)

Gonadorelin is a synthetic hormone with an effect similar to endogenous gonadotropin-releasing hormone; it stimulates the release of luteinizing hormone (LH) and follicle-stimulating hormone (FSH) from the anterior pituitary. Therefore it is indicated in the evaluation and treatment of infertility due to primary hypothalamic amenorrhea, due to defective gonadotropin-releasing hormone stimulation from the hypothalamus. It is used to induce ovulation in women with this condition.

Intravenously it has an initial half-life of 2 to 10 minutes followed by a terminal half-life of 10 to 40 minutes. It is metabolized rapidly in the body and excreted by the kidneys. Avoid the coadministration of an ovulator-stimulating drug with gonadorelin acetate. For side effects / adverse reactions, see Table 52-1.

Dosage for the treatment of primary hypothalamic amenorrhea is at 5 μg (range is 1 to 20 μg) every 1.5 hours, delivered by a Lutrepulse pump. The treatment intervals are every 3 weeks. The nurse is referred to a current package

**TABLE 52-1**   Side effects/adverse reactions of female hormones/drugs

| Drug(s) | Side effects* | Adverse reactions† |
|---|---|---|
| gonadorelin (Factrel) | | Anaphylaxis, inflammation or mild phlebitis at the catheter site (when administered via the pump); multiple pregnancies also reported |
| nafarelin acetate (Synarel) | Most frequent: hot flashes, decreased libido, vaginal dryness, headaches, insomnia<br>Less frequent: oily skin, acne, muscle pain, edema, weight gain, hirsutism, nasal irritation | Less frequent/rare: Hypersensitivity, paresthesia |
| gonodotropin, chorionic (A.P.L., Pregnyl) | Less frequent: headaches, increased anxiety, depression, breast enlargement, increased weakness<br>(Warning: may also see an increase in multiple births and, possibly, arterial thrombolism) | More frequent: abdominal bloating, pain<br>Less frequent in boys only: oily skin or acne, penis and testes enlargement, increase in height and growth of pubic hair |
| menotropins (Pergonal) | Less frequent for males: breast enlargement; for females, fever<br>(Warning: same as above) | More frequent for females only: abdominal bloating or pain |
| estrogens (various manufacturers) | Most frequent: red or irritated skin with transdermal product<br>Most frequent but can be reduced with continuous therapy: stomach cramps or gas, anorexia, nausea<br>Less frequent: chloasma, mild diarrhea, dizziness, increase in headaches, decreased tolerance to contact lenses, vomiting, decrease in male sexual drive, increase in female libido | In males, the large doses used to treat cancer increase risk for a myocardial infarction, pulmonary embolism, and/or thrombophlebitis. Severe hypercalcemia reported in cancer patients with bone metastases treated with estrogens.<br>Most frequent: edema of lower extremities, breast pain and enlargement<br>Less frequent/rare: change in menstrual bleeding, spotting, breakthrough bleeding, excessive bleeding, and complete termination of bleeding have been reported; sudden ataxia, headaches (which may be severe), chest, groin or leg pain, sudden respiratory difficulties, slurred speech, visual changes, increased weakness in arms or legs |
| contraceptives, oral | Most frequent (may decrease with chronic therapy): stomach cramps or gas, oily skin (acne) during first 3 months of therapy; anorexia, nausea, edema of lower extremities, weight gain, increased weakness<br>Less frequent/rare: brown spots on skin, mild diarrhea, dizziness, increase in headaches or migraines, increase in hair on face and body, photosensitivity, unable to tolerate contact lenses, increased irritability, alopecia (some), significant increase or decline in sexual desire, vomiting | *Need immediate medical attention:* hemoptysis (coughing up blood); sudden, severe headaches or ataxia, sudden loss of breath, slurred speech or visual changes; pain in leg, chest, or groin, weakness or pain in extremities<br>Less frequent/rare: visual changes (double vision, bulging eyes, visual loss), changes in menstrual bleeding patterns, faintness, increased frequency or painful urination, hypertension, lactation or breast lumps, depression, pain in abdomen or side, jaundice, rash, increased tenderness, swelling or pain in upper abdominal section (hepatoma), development of dark colored moles (malignant melanoma), increase in vaginal discharge (candidiasis) |
| clomiphene citrate (Clomid) | Most frequent: hot flashes<br>Less frequent/rare: dizziness; headaches; nausea; vomiting, depression; increased anxiety; restlessness, weakness; breast feels uncomfortable in female, enlarged in males | Most frequent: abdominal pain or gas, visual disturbances (blurred vision)<br>Rare: visual disturbances, eyes sensitive to light, double vision, decline in vision (see light flashes), jaundice of eyes and skin |

*If side effects continue, increase, or disturb the patient, the physician should be informed.
†If adverse reactions occur, contact the physician because medical intervention may be necessary.

**TABLE 52-1**   Side effects/adverse reactions of female hormones/drugs—cont'd

| Drug(s) | Side effects* | Adverse reactions† |
|---|---|---|
| progesterone progestins (various manufacturers) | Most frequent: weight and appetite changes; redness or pain at site if injection; edema of lower extremities, increased weakness Less frequent/rare: oily skin (acne), brown skin spots (chloasma), increase in body hair including facial hair, nausea, alopecia (some), increase in breast tenderness | Most frequent: changes in menstrual bleeding patterns Less frequent/rare: visual changes (double vision, bulging eyes, visual loss); sudden headaches or ataxia, severe headaches; pain in chest, leg (calf), or groin, slurred speech; depression; increased weakness or pain in extremities (blood clot); loss of breath, jaundice; lactation; rash; pruritus, abdominal or side pain |

insert or USP-DI for dilution instructions and additional information concerning this drug.

Pregnancy safety has been established at FDA Category B.

▷ **Nursing Management:**
**Gonadorelin Therapy**

*Assessment.* Before the initiation of gonadorelin therapy, it should be determined that the client is in good general health. Once therapy has begun, the client should be assessed for the following nursing diagnoses: potential for infection at the infusion site; electrolyte imbalance; fluid volume excess related to ovarian overstimulation (ascites and pleural effusion); impaired gas exchange related to pleural effusion; altered protection related to hemoconcentration; and altered comfort, abdominal pain related to ovarian hyperstimulation (ovarian cyst rupture).

*Intervention.* A presterilized reservoir with the infusion catheter set supplied with the kit is filled with the reconstituted gonadorelin solution and administered intravenously using the Lutrepulse pump. The pump will be set by the physician to deliver the medication dosage over approximately 7 consecutive days.

*Education.* Instruct the client and provide written instructions regarding the infusion pump, care of the infusion site, and potential sepsis to minimize the frequency of pump malfunction and inflammation at the catheter site. The client should report signs and symptoms of inflammation, infection, phlebitis, or hematoma at the catheter site. She should weigh daily and report any sudden increase in weight, change in abdominal girth, abdominal discomfort, or respiratory symptoms that might be indicative of fluid volume excess related to ovarian stimulation. The client should be alerted to the possibility of multiple pregnancy if the drug is successful.

*Evaluation.* The client's infusion site should be monitored at every visit for inflammation, phlebitis, or trauma. The client's health status should be monitored by physical examination including a pelvic examination. Ovarian ultra-

sounds are usually done for baseline measurement and at day 7 and day 14. Mid-luteal phase serum progesterone is also monitored.

## GONADOTROPIN-RELEASING HORMONE AGONIST
### nafarelin acetate (Synarel)

Nafarelin acetate is a potent agonist of gonadotropin-releasing hormone that initially stimulates the release of LH and FSH but, with continued dosing, results in a decreased secretion of the gonadotropins in about 1 month. It is indicated for the treatment or management of endometriosis.

This product is administered nasally with maximum serum levels reported in 10 to 40 minutes and a half-life of 3 hours. There are no recorded significant drug interactions with its usage. For side effects/adverse reactions, see Table 52-1.

Nafarelin therapy usually begins between days 2 and 4 of the menstrual cycle. The dose is one nasal spray of 200 μg in one nostril in the morning and one spray in the other nostril at night. It is usually administered for a period of 6 months.

Pregnancy safety has been established at FDA category X.

▷ **Nursing Management:**
**Nafarelin Therapy**

*Assessment.* It should be determined before therapy that the client is not pregnant, breastfeeding, or experiencing any undiagnosed abnormal vaginal bleeding. Because some bone density loss has been demonstrated with use of the drug, caution should be used if more than one 6-month course is considered for women who are at high risk for osteoporosis (women with a strong family history of osteoporosis, chronic alcohol or tobacco use, or chronic use of drugs that can reduce bone mass [anticonvulsants or corticosteroids]). The client should be assessed for the development of the following nursing diagnoses related to the adverse reactions of nafarelin: altered comfort (hot flashes, headaches, and nasal irritation); altered sexuality related to libido increase or decrease, and vaginal dryness; altered sleep patterns (insomnia); ineffective individual coping related to emotional lability or depression; and altered self-image related to acne, weight gain or loss, and hirsutism.

*Intervention.* Treatment is initiated between days 2 and 4 of the menstrual cycle. One spray of nafarelin is administered into one nostril in the morning and one spray into the other nostril in the evening.

*Education.* The client should be alerted that menstruation will cease with effective nafarelin therapy, so if regular menstruation continues the physician needs to be notified. If the client develops rhinitis during therapy, the physician may also prescribe a nasal decongestant. In that case, the client should be instructed to use the decongestant at least 30 minutes after the nafarelin spray to minimize the possibility of decreasing drug absorption. If therapy is successful, the client will have pain relief and reduction of her endometrial lesions.

## NONPITUITARY CHORIONIC GONADOTROPIN

Certain gonadotropic substances formed by the placenta during pregnancy are extracted from the urine of pregnant women. The action of human chorionic gonadotropin is nearly equivalent to the pituitary's luteinizing hormone (LH) with little or no follicle-stimulating effects. Although there is therapeutic use in both sexes, the discussion of nonpituitary chorionic gonadotropin and menotropins is in this chapter.

### gonadotropin, chorionic (A.P.L, Pregnyl, Antuitrin ✳)

This drug is administered to make up for a deficiency in luteinizing hormone. Chorionic gonadotropin is indicated for

1. Prepubertal cryptorchidism and hypogonadotropic hypogonadism: stimulates androgen production in the testes, which may enhance the descent of the testes and increase development of the secondary sex characteristics in the male
2. Diagnostic aid for hypogonadism
3. Corpus luteum insufficiency: stimulates progesterone production by the ovaries to promote the development and maintenance of the corpus luteum
4. Female infertility: substitute for LH in individuals with insufficient gonadotropin levels to cause ovulation in ovarian follicles that were prepared by FSH

Administered intramuscularly, it has a biphasic half-life of between 5.6 and 24 hours, and in females, ovulation usually occurs within 18 hours of administration. Approx-

imately 10% to 12% is excreted by the kidneys within 24 hours. It has no significant drug interactions; for side effects/adverse reactions, see Table 52-1.

The adult dose for hypogonadotropic hypogonadism in males is 1000 to 4000 U intramuscularly two to three times a week for several weeks to months. In some cases, it is administered indefinitely if a response occurs. For induction of ovulation, give 5000 to 10,000 U intramuscularly following last dose of menotropins or from 5 to 7 days after the last dose of clomiphene.

In treating children for prepubertal cryptorchidism, administer 1000 to 5000 U intramuscularly two to three times a week for up to several weeks (discontinued when desired response is achieved). Treatment for longer than 2 months is not recommended.

Pregnancy safety has been established at FDA category C.

### ▷ Nursing Management: Chorionic Gonadotropin Therapy

*Assessment.* It should be determined whether the client has a preexisting pituitary hypertrophy or tumor, because the medication will stimulate growth of the tumor. The drug should not be used with individuals with precocious puberty, prostatic cancer, abnormal vaginal bleeding, fibroids, ovarian cysts, or thrombophlebitis.

The drug should be used with careful monitoring in clients with asthma, cardiac disease, epilepsy, migraine headaches, and renal dysfunction, because of the potential for fluid volume excess due to fluid retention.

The following nursing diagnoses may occur with the client receiving chorionic gonadotropin: altered comfort related to nausea, abdominal discomfort, and distention, headache, or pain at the injection site; disturbance in self-concept related to physical changes in the secondary sexual characteristics of young male clients, and infertility in females; altered thought processes related to depression or irritability; excess fluid volume evidenced by oliguria, rapid weight gain, shortness of breath, swelling of feet and lower legs; and altered bowel patterns, diarrhea.

*Intervention.* Reconstitute with the 10 ml of sodium chloride provided by the manufacturer.

*Education.* When used to treat infertility, provide support for the client and spouse throughout their attempt to achieve fertility. Societal and familial pressures create stress for them as a couple and individually. They should be advised that gonadotropin-induced ovulation is expensive and may result in multiple births. Since success is difficult to achieve, the couple should be counseled on alternatives such as adoption.

If the physician has requested daily recording of the woman's temperature, inform the client about the relationship of temperature to ovulation and its importance for the appropriate timing of intercourse to enhance the chance of pregnancy. Daily intercourse from the day before chorionic gonadotropin is given until ovulation occurs is advised. Ovulation usually occurs 18 hours after the medication is given.

In treating prepubertal cryptorchidism, prepubertal males receiving chorionic gonadotropin should be prepared for an acceleration in sexual development and supported through self-image changes.

**Evaluation.** The client's progress should be assessed periodically. Although the regimen is lengthy and time consuming, the client should be supported and encouraged to cooperate.

To monitor the female client receiving the drug for induction of ovulation, an estrogen excretion determination should be done 1 week after the initiation of each course of the drug. Examinations of the cervical mucus will determine if there has been follicular maturation or ovulation.

Hyperstimulation of the ovaries may be indicated by abdominal or pelvic pain and should be reported to the physician immediately. A pelvic examination may be done to evaluate ovarian size.

To monitor the male client for hypogonadism, serum testosterones may be measured periodically to assess progress. Sperm counts and determinations of sperm mobility should also be done.

## MENOTROPINS

Menotropin is a human pituitary gonadotropin, a purified preparation of follicle-stimulating hormone (FSH) and luteinizing hormone (LH) obtained from the urine of postmenopausal women.

### menotropins (Pergonal)

The mechanism of action is equivalent to effects produced by FSH and LH. Menotropin stimulates the development of the ovarian follicle, causes ovulation, and may stimulate corpus luteum development. In males, it stimulates sperm production.

Menotropin is indicated in the treatment of the following conditions:

1. Female infertility, usually used in combination with chorionic gonadotropin. This is usually reserved for individuals that have not responded to other treatment modalities, such as clomiphene or bromocriptine.
2. Male infertility, used in combination with chorionic gonadotropin to stimulate spermatogenesis in primary or secondary hypogonadotropic hypogonadism.

Menotropins are administered intramuscularly with ovulation usually occurring 18 hours after administration. Excretion is by the kidneys. It has no reported significant drug interactions; for side effects/adverse reactions, see Table 52-1.

The adult dose for menotropins for injection for induction

of ovulation is 1 ampule (75 units of FSH and LH activity) intramuscularly daily for 9 to 12 days. If necessary, dosage may be increased by 1 or 2 ampules every 4 to 5 days, up to a maximum of 6 ampules. When estrogen activity is equal to or greater than that of a normal individual, chorionic gonadotropin is administered a day after the last dose of menotropins. For treatment of hypogonadotropic hypogonadism in males, administer 1 ampule intramuscularly three times weekly (in addition to chorionic gonadotropin twice a week) for a minimum of 4 months, following pretreatment with chorionic gonadotropin for 4 to 6 months. An increase in dose may be necessary if an increase in spermatogenesis does not occur within 4 months.

Pregnancy safety has not been established for this product.

## ▷ Nursing Management: Menotropin Therapy

Nursing management is similar to that for chorionic gonadotropin, except that the preparation is diluted with only the 2 ml of sodium chloride provided by the manufacturer.

## FEMALE SEX HORMONES

The ovaries, in addition to providing ova, manufacture and secrete steroid female hormones that control secondary sex characteristics, the reproductive cycle, and the growth and development of the accessory reproductive organs in the female. Two main types of hormones are secreted by the ovary: (1) the follicular or estrogenic hormones (**estrogens**) produced by the cells of the developing graafian follicle and (2) the luteal or progestational hormones (**progestogens**) derived from the corpus luteum that is formed in the ovary from the ruptured follicle. The periodic cycling of the female sex hormones depends on an interaction between FSH and LH with the ovarian hormones estrogen and progesterone. This results in a menstrual cycle that normally continues throughout life, except for pregnancy, until menopause. While estrogens are primarily secreted by the ovarian follicles, some may also be secreted by the adrenals, corpus luteum, placenta, and testes.

### Estrogens

Estrogens are available from natural sources (the urine of pregnant mares) and in conjugated dosage forms and have been synthetically formulated. Examples of natural steroidal estrogens include estradiol, estrone, and estriol; nonsteroidal estrogens include diethylstilbestrol (DES), dienestrol, and chlorotrianisene.

### estrogen (various manufacturers)

Estrogen increases the synthesis of DNA, RNA, and protein in estrogen-responsive tissues. Elevated estrogen serum levels will inhibit the secretion of FSH and LH from the pituitary. This results in inhibition of lactation, ovulation, and the development of a proliferative endometrium.

Estrogen is indicated for the following conditions:

1. Treatment of estrogen deficiency: estrogen replacement is recommended for atrophic vaginitis, female hypogonadism, insufficient primary ovarian function, abnormal uterine bleeding, and severe vasomotor symptoms in menopause.
2. Treatment of breast carcinoma: used in metastatic breast carcinomas in postmenopausal women with tumor estrogen-negative receptors; also in selected male breast carcinomas.
3. Treatment of advanced prostatic carcinomas.
4. Prophylaxis of osteoporosis in postmenopausal women: may be effective in reducing or preventing bone mass loss and fractures in estrogen insufficiency.

Estrogen is protein bound, metabolized in the liver, and excreted by the kidneys. For side effects/adverse reactions, see Table 52-1.

***Significant drug interactions.*** The following significant drug interactions may occur when estrogens are given with the drugs listed below.

| Drug | Possible Effect and Management |
|---|---|
| anticoagulants, oral | A decrease in anticoagulant effect reported especially with ethinyl estradiol. Monitor closely. |
| bromocriptine | Estrogens may result in amenorrhea, interfering with bromocriptine's therapeutic effect. Concurrent use is not recommended. |
| cyclosporine | Cyclosporine metabolism is inhibited, which may result in increased cyclosporine plasma levels and increased risk of hepatotoxicity and nephrotoxicity. Use concurrently only with very close monitoring of cyclosporine serum levels and liver and kidney function. |
| hepatotoxic drugs, especially dantrolene | Estrogens increase risk of inducing hepatotoxicity; females over 35 years old are at increased risk. Avoid concurrent drug administration if at all possible. |
| smoking tobacco | Tobacco smoking increases the risk of serious cardiac adverse reactions, such as cerebrovascular accident (CVA), transient ischemic attacks (TIAs), thrombophlebitis, and pulmonary embolism. The risk is higher in women over 35 years old who smoke; therefore they should be advised against smoking while undergoing estrogen therapy. |

### Precautions

1. The risk of endometrial cancer increases with prolonged use of estrogens in postmenopausal women. However, low-dose estrogen given cyclically or the use of a progestin (concurrently or sequentially) may reduce the risk of inducing endometrial cancer.
2. Estrogens should not be administered during pregnancy because studies indicate an increased risk of congenital malformations, especially with DES (FDA category X).
3. Estrogens are excreted in breast milk and will also inhibit lactation; therefore administration of estrogens to nursing women is not recommended.

### Dosage and administration

1. The lowest effective dose of estrogens should be administered for the shortest time period to reduce the possibility of serious adverse effects. When continuous therapy is required, the physician should reevaluate the client at least every 6 months.
2. To avoid overstimulation of estrogen-sensitive tissues, a cyclic dosing schedule of 3 weeks of estrogen administration and 1 week off or of adding progestin for the last 10 to 13 days of the cycle will most closely approximate the natural hormonal cycle. This is not the schedule for oophorectomized individuals or clients with cancer who are receiving hormonal therapy.
3. Estradiol and estrone are naturally occurring steroidal estrogens that are principal endogenous estrogens. Estradiol is available alone or synthetically as estradiol cypionate, estradiol valerate, ethinyl estradiol, and polyestradiol phosphate. The primary pharmacologic effects of all the estrogens are similar.
4. Conjugated estrogens are a mixture of estrogenic substances, especially estrone and equilin. They are available in oral tablet, parenteral, and vaginal cream dosage formulations. Dosage must be individualized according to the diagnosis and the client's therapeutic response, for example, vasomotor symptoms associated with menopause. The usual oral adult dose is 0.3 to 1.25 mg daily for 21 days, followed by 7 days without estrogen. Some women may even require higher doses to achieve an adequate therapeutic response.
5. Diethylstilbestrol (DES) is a synthetic nonsteroidal estrogen that has the same indications primarily as the other estrogens. In addition, it has been used as a postcoital contraceptive after rape or incest to prevent pregnancy, although this use has not been approved in the United States. DES should not be administered to pregnant women since it will not terminate pregnancy but it can cause very serious fetal toxicities. Congenital defects plus an increased risk of developing a rare vaginal or cervical cancer in later life has been reported in females exposed in utero to DES. A higher incidence of genital tract abnormalities has also been reported in males exposed in utero to DES.
6. Transdermal estradiol (Estraderm) is also available in the United States. It is usually used to supply estrogen in conditions of estrogen deficiency. Applied topically to intact skin, 50 μg (0.05 mg) or 100 μg (0.1 mg) daily is released from the transdermal patch. It should

be replaced twice weekly and is usually worn continuously.

## ▷ Nursing Management: Estrogen Therapy

**Assessment.** The drug is contraindicated if breast cancer is known or suspected or if the client has abnormal or undiagnosed vaginal bleeding.

Estrogens are to be used with caution with the client who has hypercalcemia, endometriosis, active thrombophlebitis, or a history of thrombophlebitis secondary to estrogen use.

Clients receiving estrogen therapy may experience the following nursing diagnoses: altered comfort related to anorexia, nausea, vomiting, abdominal cramping, headaches, or skin irritation (transdermal patches); impaired skin integrity related to the development of acne; impaired vision related to a steepening of the corneal curvature contributing to an intolerance of contact lenses; fluid volume excess; risk for physiologic injury related to thrombophlebitis, thromboembolism, hepatitis, hypercalcemia, chorea, erythema multiforme, erythema nodosum, irregular menses, breast tumors, and disturbance in self-concept related to melasma (brown, blotchy skin changes), gynecomastia (men), increased libido (women), or decreased libido (men).

**Intervention.** Estrogens are usually administered on a cycle of 3 weeks on and 1 week off the medication, except for males.

Administer the intramuscular forms slowly to minimize client discomfort. Large muscles, such as gluteus maximus, should be used to maximize absorption. For oil-based preparations use at least a 21-gauge needle and a dry syringe.

Administer intravenous estrogens slowly; vaginal burning occurs if administered too rapidly.

Vaginal forms should be administered at bedtime to enhance absorption. Sanitary napkins or panty shields may be used to protect clothing from stains.

**Education.** Assist the client in exploring her concerns about the risks of taking estrogens. Provide her with information regarding the occurrence of cardiovascular disease and cancer in relationship to her age, smoking habits, and other health characteristics. Encourage the client to read the patient package insert carefully and then discuss any concerns she might have.

Advise the client to have regular physical examinations, which should include a pelvic and breast examination and a Pap smear, every 6 to 12 months during treatment.

The client should be advised to stop the medication immediately and contact her physician if she suspects she is pregnant.

Caution the client that smoking increases the incidence of serious side effects of the drug, particularly in women over 35.

Instruct the client to notify her health provider in the instance of severe headache, blurred or lost vision (which may signal possible stroke), or symptoms of chest pain, shortness of breath, or leg pain, which may indicate thromboembolism elsewhere in the body. The physician should also be informed of severe abdominal pain or mass, jaundice, severe mental depression, or unusual bleeding. Instructions should be provided for monthly self-examination of the breasts and any lumps found should be reported to the physician. Mammograms should be done annually.

Nausea, frequently occurring at the beginning of therapy, usually ceases after 1 or 2 weeks. Seldom severe, it can be controlled by taking the medication with meals.

Advise the client to weigh one or two times weekly and report a sharp increase in weight or other signs of fluid retention, such as swollen ankles, puffy eyelids, and "tight" rings. A low-sodium diet and diuretic may be prescribed to control these symptoms.

Encourage the client to maintain a program of good oral hygiene, including teeth cleaning by a professional and thorough brushing and plaque control by the client to minimize any gingival hyperplasia that may occur during estrogen therapy.

Warn the client that exposure to the sun or tanning devices may result in brown, blotchy discoloration of skin.

Bleeding after estrogen withdrawal is expected. Explain to postmenopausal women that such bleeding does not indicate that a state of fertility has returned.

Instruct users with diabetes to report positive urine or blood sugar tests so the dosage of their antidiabetic medications can be adjusted.

Forewarn male clients of estrogen-induced feminization and impotence, which will disappear when therapy terminates. Advise clients of the increased risk of myocardial infarction, pulmonary embolism, and thrombophlebitis while undergoing estrogen therapy.

Instruct clients taking prescribed conjugated estrogens and esterified estrogens for osteoporosis prophylaxis to increase their intake of calcium and vitamin D and to engage in regular weight-bearing exercise such as walking.

When applying the transdermal form of the drug, the client should wash her hands before and after application of the patch. It should be applied to the abdomen on clean, dry, intact skin without hair. The sites on the abdomen should be rotated to prevent application to any site more frequently than every 7 days. The patch should not be applied to the breasts or to the waistline where clothing might cause the patch to become loose. The patch should be pressed into place for 10 seconds and then examined to ensure all the edges are tight. If the patch becomes loose, it may be reapplied or a new one may be applied.

**Evaluation.** Blood pressure should be monitored weekly. Hepatic function studies should be done every 6 to 12 months. Males treated with estrogens should be checked regularly for the development of breast carcinomas.

## Progesterone and Progestins

Progesterone is a naturally occurring progestin secreted from the corpus luteum mainly during the latter half of the menstrual cycle. The pituitary luteinizing hormone stimulates the synthesizing and secretion of progesterone from the corpus luteum. Progesterone may also be formed from steroid precursors available in the ovaries, testes, adrenal cortex, and placenta.

Progesterone and synthetic progestins have similar pharmacologic effects in the body. Progestins were developed because progesterone was not always satisfactory in therapeutic application. It often had to be administered in large oral dosages, and its injections were often painful and caused local reactions. The progestins provided many advantages for the client, as well as the physician. Their greater potency lowered the dose of progestins necessary to produce an equivalent response to progesterone; there is a longer duration of action and, with some products, an effective oral/sublingual dosage form.

### progesterone/progestins (various manufacturers)

Progesterone and progestins cause induction of biochemical changes in the endometrium to prepare for the implantation and nourishment of the embryo. They supplement the action of estrogen in its effects on the uterus and mammary glands. They cause suppression of ovulation during pregnancy and relaxation of the uterine smooth muscles. They also increase the synthesis of DNA and RNA; large doses will inhibit the secretion of luteinizing hormone (LH) from the anterior pituitary.

Progesterone/progestins are indicated for the following conditions:

1. Treatment of female hormonal imbalance of amenorrhea and dysmenorrhea
2. Treatment of endometriosis
3. Diagnosis for endogenous estrogen deficiency
4. Treatment of specific carcinomas
5. Prevention of pregnancy

They are metabolized primarily in the liver and excreted by the kidneys. For side effects/adverse reactions, see Table 52-1.

Progestins may cause amenorrhea and/or excessive lactation, which will interfere with bromocriptine's therapeutic effect. Concurrent use is not recommended.

Congenital anomalies have been reported with the use of progestins during the first 4 months of pregnancy. They should not be used as diagnostic tests for pregnancy. See Pregnancy Safety box. Progestins are also excreted in breast milk; therefore they are not recommended for use by nursing women either.

***Dosage and administration.*** Because dosage and method of administration for progestins can vary according

---

### PREGNANCY SAFETY FOR PROGESTINS

FDA category D: progesterone
FDA category X: norethindrone, norgestrel
FDA category unclassified: medroxyprogesterone, megestrol

---

to indications and current standards of practice, the student is referred to a current package insert or USP-DI for the most recent recommendations. The following are examples of selected progestins and dosing regimens.

*Hydroxyprogesterone injection (Delalutin).* This progestin is used for the treatment of hormone imbalance, primary or secondary amenorrhea, or functional bleeding of the uterus; administer 375 mg intramuscularly during the menstrual cycle. After 4 days of bleeding or, if no bleeding, 3 weeks (21 days) after the injection, start the cyclic therapy schedule. This cyclic schedule should be repeated every 28 days for four cycles with close monitoring of the client. Cyclic schedule is 20 mg IM estradiol valerate on first day of cycle, then 250 mg hydroxyprogesterone caproate injection and 5 mg estradiol valerate IM on day 15 of the cycle.

*Megestrol (Megace).* Megestrol is used to treat breast and endometrial cancers. The dose to treat breast cancer is 40 mg orally, four times daily; dosage to treat endometrial cancer is 10 to 80 mg orally four times daily. Allow 2 months of therapy with megestrol before evaluating its effectiveness. Maximum daily dosage is 800 mg daily.

*Norethindrone (Norlutin).* Norethindrone is used to treat female hormone imbalance and endometriosis and as a contraceptive. The dose to treat amenorrhea or functional bleeding of the uterus caused by a female hormone imbalance is 5 to 20 mg orally from day 5 through day 25 of the menstrual cycle. The dose used to treat endometriosis is 10 mg orally daily for 14 days; then the daily dosage may be increased by 5 mg daily (every 2 weeks) up to a maximum of 30 mg/day. Continue this dosage for 6 to 9 months. When used as a contraceptive give 350 μg (0.35 mg) orally daily, starting on the first day of the menstrual cycle.

*Norgestrel tablet (Ovrette).* This is primarily used as a contraceptive. The dose is 75 μg (0.75 mg) orally daily starting first day of menstrual cycle and continued daily thereafter.

*Progesterone injection (Femotrone).* When used to treat amenorrhea caused by female hormone imbalance, progesterone injection is given as a single dose of 50 to 100 mg IM or 5 to 10 mg IM daily for 6 to 8 days, usually starting 8 to 10 days before menses. Bleeding will usually occur within 2 to 3 days following the last injection; normal menstrual cycles may then follow. Discontinue injections if menstrual bleeding occurs during the series of injections.

## ▷ Nursing Management:
### Progesterone/Progestin Therapy

***Assessment.*** It should be determined that the client does not have preexisting cancer of the breast or reproductive tract, suspected pregnancy, abnormal and undiagnosed vaginal bleeding, a history of active thrombophlebitis, or hepatic dysfunction or conditions for which progestins are contraindicated.

Because of the tendency of progestins to cause fluid retention that might aggravate these conditions, these drugs should be used cautiously in clients with asthma, a history of active depression, epilepsy, cardiac insufficiency, or renal dysfunction. Clients with a history of ectopic pregnancy or diabetes should also be monitored carefully for any unusual symptoms.

Clients on progestin therapy are at risk for the following nursing diagnoses: altered comfort related to headache, nausea, breast tenderness, or irritation at injection site; fluid volume excess; sleep pattern disturbance (insomnia); disturbance in self-concept related to increased facial and body hair, weight gain, or melasma; impaired skin integrity related to acne; potential for physiologic injury related to changes in vaginal bleeding pattern, hepatitis, thrombophlebitis, retinal thrombosis, or thromboembolism; and visual disturbances (double vision or loss of vision).

***Intervention.*** Give oil preparations deep intramuscularly.

A low-sodium diet and diuretic may be prescribed to control symptoms of fluid retention, such as swollen ankles and puffy eyelids.

***Education.*** Encourage the client to read the package insert carefully and then discuss with her health care provider any concerns she might have. Advise the client to have regular physical examinations, which should include a pelvic and breast examination and a Pap smear, every 6 to 12 months during treatment.

Instruct client to notify her health provider in the instance of severe headache, blurred or lost vision (which may possibly signal stroke), and symptoms of chest pain, shortness of breath, or leg pain, which may indicate thromboembolism elsewhere in the body. The physician should also be informed of severe abdominal pain or mass, jaundice, severe mental depression, or unusual bleeding. Instructions should be provided for monthly self-examination of the breasts, and any lumps found should be reported to the physician.

Instruct users with diabetes to report positive urine tests so that the dosage of their antidiabetic medications can be adjusted.

If progestins are used for contraceptive purposes, instruct the client to take the drug at same time of the day, every day of the year. The tablets need to be kept in their original containers. It is best to keep an extra month's supply, replacing it with the new container of tablets purchased each month. This will always ensure a fresh supply.

The client should be advised to discontinue the medication immediately and notify the physician if she suspects she is pregnant. Pregnancy should be avoided during the first month of administration of progestins and for at least 3 months after they have been discontinued. Contraceptives should be used during this time.

***Evaluation.*** Since progestins may cause glucose intolerance, diabetic clients may need an adjustment in insulin or oral hypoglycemic dosage.

Undesirable effects are usually mild or absent during short-term use. However, as the duration of progestin therapy increases, the number and severity of adverse reactions also increase. Evaluation for these effects must continue as long as therapy continues.

## ORAL CONTRACEPTIVES

**Oral contraception** is the most effective form of birth control presently available. "The pill" is a fixed combination of estrogen and progestin that was approved for marketing by the FDA in 1960. Since then millions of women have used oral contraceptives, and through experience an enormous amount of information about effectiveness, estrogen-progestin combination, the relationship of risk factors to major side effects, and mortality have been collected. Performing a thorough history and physical examination, selecting an appropriate contraceptive method with the individual/couple, and instituting a client teaching and monitoring program are basic for the development of a good family planning program.

### estrogens and progestins (oral contraceptives) (various manufacturers)

The mechanism of action is that increased serum levels of estrogens and progestins inhibit the secretion of FSH and LH from the pituitary, resulting in suppression of ovulation. Changes in the endometrium result in failure of implantation of the ova, plus an increase in cervical mucus impedes sperm ingress.

Estrogens and progestins are indicated for the prevention of pregnancy and for treatment of hypermenorrhea, endometriosis, and female hypogonadism.

The oral contraceptives are protein bound, metabolized mainly in the liver, and excreted primarily by the kidneys.

***Side effects/adverse reactions.*** Hormone-related side effects are caused by an excess or a deficiency in estrogen or progestin or by an androgen excess. Androgen effects are more common with norgestrel and levonorgestrel than with the other progestins. Reporting side effects to the physician is useful as it then allows the choice of a more appropriate oral contraceptive for the individual.

Estrogen excess side effects include nausea, dizziness, abdominal bloating, leg pain, chloasma, hypertension, cyclic weight gain, hypertension, breast tenderness, and an increase in size of breast. A deficiency in estrogen may produce an increase in anxiety, hot flashes, midcycle spotting, decrease in menstrual flow and a possible decrease in libido. An excess in progestins may result in alopecia, oily skin (acne) and scalp, increased fatigue, increased appetite and weight gain that is noncyclic, decrease in length of menstrual flow, breast tenderness, and increased breast size.

A progestin deficiency may manifest itself as dysmenorrhea, heavy menstrual flow, weight loss, and/or a delayed onset of menses. An androgen excess may result in hirsutism, oily skin or skin rash, acne, pruritus, increased appetite and weight gain (noncyclic), and cholestatic jaundice (Dickey, 1984).

***Significant drug interactions.***  The following significant drug interactions may occur when oral contraceptives are given with the following drugs:

| Drug | Possible Effect and Management |
|---|---|
| inducers of hepatic enzymes | Barbiturates, anticonvulsants, griseofulvin, and rifampin are inducers of hepatic enzymes. Concurrent use with oral contraceptives may decrease the effectiveness of contraception. |
| anticoagulants, oral coumarin or indandione | Both increased and decreased anticoagulant effects have been reported. Monitor closely. |
| antidepressants, tricyclic | Antidepressant toxicity or a reduction in antidepressant therapeutic effects may be seen. These effects are probably dose-related. Low estrogen dosages have less effect on enzyme inhibition than larger dosages. Dosage adjustment of the antidepressant may be necessary; monitor closely for unusual effects. |
| bromocriptine | Concurrent use is not recommended. Oral contraceptives may cause amenorrhea and/or galactorrhea. Such effects interfere with the action of bromocriptine. |
| other hepatotoxic drugs, especially dantrolene | The risk of inducing hepatotoxicity is increased. Females over 35 years old are especially at risk. Avoid concurrent drug administration if possible; if not, monitor closely for hepatotoxicity. |
| smoking tobacco | Not recommended. An increase in cardiovascular risk such as CVA, transient ischemic attacks (TIAs), pulmonary embolism, and thrombophlebitis may result, especially in women over the age of 35. Avoid smoking if taking oral contraceptives. |

***Dosage and administration***

1. Although the use of exogenous estrogenic substances alone will inhibit ovulation, undesirable bleeding frequently occurs during the latter phase of the cycle. If estrogen levels are increased to prevent this, severe nausea and breast tenderness occur. It is for these reasons that estrogens are combined with progestins in oral contraceptives.

2. Since naturally occurring progesterone is inactivated or extremely weak in its effect when taken orally and must be given by injection to be effective, the progestins (steroidal compounds related to progesterone) have been developed. The majority of the oral contraceptives contain a synthetic progestin, usually norethynodrel, norethindrone, or norgestrel.

3. Norethynodrel is a basic progestin, norethindrone is a more androgenic progestin, norgestrel is a synthetic progestogen similar to norethindrone. Norethindrone is sometimes recommended for patients having excess side effects from estrogen, such as greater weight gain and amenorrhea. Norethynodrel is good for patients with oily skin, acne, hirsutism, and breakthrough bleeding.

4. Three methods of oral contraception are avialable: combination estrogen and progestin, low-dosage progestogens (minipill), and postcoital contraception with diethylstilbestrol. Table 52-2 lists the composition, doses, and brand names or oral contraceptives used in these three methods.

5. Combination estrogen and progestin contraceptives are divided into three types:
   a. **Monophasic** oral contraception is a fixed ratio of estrogen and progestin that is taken for 21 days of the normal menstrual cycle. Originally these preparations contained high doses of hormones and had increased reports of adverse side effects. Most of these preparations have been reformulated into lower dosage hormones, but the biphasic and triphasic oral contraceptives are more commonly used today.
   b. **Biphasic** oral contraception supplies various amounts of hormone during the first and second halves of the menstrual cycle—that is, low levels of hormones in the follicular phase, which is increased during the luteal phase of the menstrual cycle.
   c. **Triphasic** oral contraception is the newest form of oral contraception; it most closely simulates the normal estrogen and progesterone levels during the menstrual cycle. The dose of estrogen is kept at a low and constant level during the 21-day dosing period while the progestin is progressively increased to mimic the natural release of hormones in the female. Because the lowest dosages of hormones possible are used in this formulation, the incidence and severity of adverse reactions reported are considerably lower than with the monophasic or biphasic formulations.

6. Low-dosage progestogens (minipill) oral contraceptives do not contain any estrogen hormone. They are generally prescribed for 28 days of the menstrual cycle. These preparations are usually less effective than

**TABLE 52-2**   Oral contraceptives

| Estrogen | Progestin | Trade name |
|---|---|---|
| **MONOPHASIC** | | |
| 0.035 mg ethinyl estradiol | 0.4 mg norethindrone | Brevicon 21-Day |
| 0.035 mg ethinyl estradiol | 0.5 mg norethindrone | Brevicon 28-Day (21 tablets active ingredients plus 7 tablets inert ingredients) |
| 0.035 mg ethinyl estradiol | 1 mg norethindrone | Norinyl 1 + 35 Tablet (21 tablets) |
| 0.035 mg ethinyl estradiol | 1 mg norethindrone | Norinyl 1 + 35 Tablet (28 tablets plus 7 tablets inert ingredients) |
| 0.05 mg mestranol | 1 mg norethindrone | Norinyl 1 + 50 Tablet (21 tablets) |
| 0.05 mg mestranol | 1 mg norethindrone | Norinyl 1 + 50 Tablet (28 tablets plus 7 tablets inert ingredients) |
| 0.08 mg mestranol | 1 mg norethindrone | Norinyl 1 + 80 Tablet (21 tablets) |
| 0.08 mg mestranol | 1 mg norethindrone | Norinyl 1 + 80 Tablet (28 tablets plus 7 tablets inert ingredients) |
| 0.1 mg mestranol | 2 mg norethindrone | Norinyl 2 mg Tablets |
| 0.020 mg ethinyl estradiol | 1 mg norethindrone | Loestrin 1/20 Tablets (21 tablets) |
| 0.020 mg ethinyl estradiol | 1 mg norethindrone | Loestrin FE 1/20 (contains 21 oral contraceptive tablets plus 7 tablets of ferrous fumarate [75 mg]) |
| 0.030 mg ethinyl estradiol | 1.5 mg norethindrone | Loestrin FE 1.5/30 (contains 21 oral contraceptive tablets plus 7 tablets of ferrous fumarate [75 mg]) |
| 0.030 mg ethinyl estradiol | 0.15 mg levonorgestrel | Nordette-21 |
| 0.030 mg ethinyl estradiol | 0.15 mg levonorgestrel | Nordette-28 (21 tablets, plus 7 tablets inert ingredients) |
| 0.030 mg ethinyl estradiol | 0.3 mg norgestrel | Lo/Orval (21 tablets) |
| 0.030 mg ethinyl estradiol | 0.3 mg norgestrel | Lo/Ovral-28 (21 tablets plus 7 tablets inert ingredients) |
| 0.035 mg ethinyl estradiol | 0.4 mg norethindrone | Ovcon-35 (21 tablets) |
| 0.050 mg ethinyl estradiol | 1 mg norethindrone | Norlestrin 21 1/50 (21 tablets) |
| **BIPHASIC** | | |
| 0.035 mg ethinyl estradiol | 0.5 mg norethindrone (10 tablets)<br>1 mg norethindrone (11 tablets) | Ortho-Novum 10/11-21 (21 tablets) |
| **TRIPHASIC** | | |
| 0.030 mg ethinyl estradiol | 0.05 mg levonorgestrel (6 tablets) | Triphasil 21 (21 tablets) |
| 0.040 mg ethinyl estradiol | 0.075 mg levonorgestrel (5 tablets) | Triphasil 28 (21 tablets plus 7 tablets inert ingredients) |
| 0.030 mg ethinyl estradiol | 0.125 mg levonorgestrel | |
| 0.035 mg ethinyl estradiol | 0.5 mg norethindrone (7 tablets) | Ortho-Novum 7/7/7-21 (21 tablets) |
| 0.035 mg ethinyl estradiol | 0.75 mg norethindrone (7 tablets) | Ortho-Novum 7/7/7-28 (21 tablets plus 7 tablets inert ingredients) |
| 0.035 mg ethinyl estradiol | 1 mg norethindrone (7 tablets) | |

the combination products (approximately 97% protection from pregnancy), and they reportedly have a higher incidence of spotting and breakthrough bleeding. An advantage is that they generally do not cause the more serious adverse reactions associated with estrogen therapy.

7. For postcoital contraception with diethylstilbestrol, see the section on diethylstilbestrol on p. 814.

(See Table 52-3 for recommendations for selection of an oral contraceptive.)

***Pregnancy safety.*** Has been established at FDA category X.

▷ **Nursing Management:**
**Oral Contraceptive Therapy**

***Assessment.*** See assessment in previous sections on estrogens and progestins.

***Education.*** Instruct the client to take the medications as prescribed by the physician. The tablets should be taken at the same time each day, preferably in association with another daily routine, i.e., brushing of teeth, cleansing of face in the morning or at night. Nighttime administration may be preferable to decrease nausea. Nausea occurs in some clients during the first cycle but tends to subside after the

**TABLE 52-3**   Recommendations for selection of an oral contraceptive

| Conditions | Contraceptive management |
| --- | --- |
| AGE | |
| Sexually active teenagers | Low estrogen (30-35 μg)/low progestin |
| 20-30 yr | Low estrogen (30-35 μg)/low progestin |
| 30-35 yr | Low estrogen (30-35 μg)/low progestin (discourage smoking) |
| over 35 yr | Low estrogen (30-35 μg)/low progestin for nonsmokers. Switch to other methods of contraception may be recommended if smoker is 35 and over or, if nonsmoker is over 40 years old. |
| CONCURRENT DISEASE STATES | |
| Cancer | Generally, not contraindicated; the risk of endometrial and ovarian cancer is decreased with oral contraceptives. |
| Estrogen-dependent cancer (breast or liver cancers) | Oral contraceptives contraindicated. |
| Gallbladder disease | Requires individual evaluation. If oral contraceptives are used, use lowest possible dose. |
| Uterine fibroids | Not a contraindication for use of oral contraceptives. |
| Hypertension | If blood pressure is under control and diastolic pressure is 90 or less, low dose oral contraceptives may be used with close monitoring. When diastolic is over 90, these agents are not recommended. |
| CVA, thromboembolism, or cardio-vascular disease | Oral contraceptives are contraindicated. |
| SIDE EFFECT MANAGEMENT | |
| Breakthrough bleeding | If client started with 30-35 μg estrogen/low progestin regimen, increase estrogen dose (usually by 20 μg of ethinyl estradiol) and administer with the oral contraceptive for two cycles; then resume previous drug regimen. |
| Acne | Lower progestin dose. |
| Hirsutism | Lower progestin dose. |
| Withdrawal bleeding absent | Physician must first rule out pregnancy. If not pregnant, then an oral contraceptive with a lower progestin dose may be prescribed. |

third or fourth month. It may be prevented or reduced by taking the medication with food.

Caution clients never to let their tablet supply run out and to keep an extra month's supply on hand. The packages should be rotated by using the extra package after the pills currently being used and replacing the extra supply each month on a regular basis.

Instruct the client to use the pills in the same sequence that they appear in the container.

Instruct client beginning to use oral contraceptives to use a second method of birth control for the first cycle until the body adjusts to the medication. If she misses a dose of the medicine for 1 day of the 21-day schedule, she should take it as soon as she remembers. If she does not remember until the next day, tell her to take the missed tablet and the regularly scheduled one together. If she does not remember a dose for 2 days in a row, she should take 2 tablets a day for each of the next 2 days. In addition she should use a second method of birth control for full protection. If she misses 3 doses or more in a row, then she should stop taking the medicine and use another method of birth control until

she menstruates or until it is determined she is not pregnant. Then she may restart the medication with the appropriate cycle.

If the client is using a 28-day schedule and misses any of the first 21 tablets, instruct her to follow the preceding instructions. If she misses any of the last 7 tablets, which are inactive, there is no hazard of pregnancy; however, the first tablet of the next month's series must be taken on the regularly scheduled day. Be sure to review the literature provided with the medication with the client to ensure understanding.

Assist the client in exploring her concerns about the risks of taking oral contraceptives. Provide her with information regarding the occurrence of cardiovascular disease and cancer in relationship to her age, smoking habits, and other health characteristics. Encourage the client to read the patient package insert carefully and then to discuss with her health care provider any concerns she might have.

Advise the client to have physical examinations, which should include a pelvic and breast examination and a Pap smear, every 6 to 12 months during the treatment.

Nursing diagnoses related to hormone therapy and oral contraceptive use

| Nursing diagnosis | Outcome criteria | Nursing interventions |
| --- | --- | --- |
| Potential knowledge deficit related to female hormone therapy | Client will be able to verbalize action, use, dose, and side effects/adverse reactions of hormonal therapy.<br><br>Client will demonstrate a reduction in symptoms without side effects/adverse reactions. | Instruct client to take medication as prescribed.<br>Advise client taking dosage in vaginal cream form to administer at bedtime to increase absorption. Use a sanitary napkin, not tampons, to protect clothing.<br>Advise client that the medication may be taken with food to minimize or prevent nausea.<br>Alert client to stop taking her medication and consult with the physician if she suspects she is pregnant.<br>Advise client to report to the prescriber any symptoms of thromboembolism (sudden, severe headache, sudden change in vision, sudden pain, weakness, or numbness); liver impairment (yellow eyes or skin, dark urine, pale stools); or mental depression. Alert client that cigarette smoking while on this medication increases the risk of thromboembolism (deep-vein thrombosis, pulmonary embolism, heart attack, stroke), particularly after age 35.<br>Stress the importance of regular visits to the physician for follow-up care every 6-12 months. |
| Potential knowledge deficit related to oral contraceptive regimen | Client will demonstrate compliance with medication regimen (oral contraception) without side effects/adverse reactions | Instruct client to take medication as prescribed.<br>Advise client to use an additional method of birth control during the 3 weeks of the initial cycle.<br>Encourage client to take the medication at the same time each day, not more than 24 hours apart.<br>Alert client that although nausea may occur in the first few weeks of therapy, it is usually temporary and may be minimized by taking the dose with food.<br>Advise client to always keep a month's supply on hand. Replace the extra supply each month.<br>Provide specific information regarding appropriate action to be taken by the client when "missed" doses occur.<br>Stress the importance of regular visits to the physician for follow-up care every 6 to 12 months.<br>Advise client to alert other health care providers that she is taking oral contraceptives, since they may cause serious symptoms and interact with other drugs to lessen contraceptive effectiveness.<br>Alert client to stop taking her medication and consult with the physician if she suspects she is pregnant.<br>Advise client to report to the prescriber any symptoms of thromboembolism (sudden severe headache, sudden change in vision, sudden pain, weakness, or numbness); liver impairment (yellow eyes or skin, dark urine, pale stools); or mental depression.<br>Alert client that cigarette smoking while on this medication increases the risk of thromboembolism (deep-vein thrombosis, pulmonary embolism, heart attack, stroke), particularly after age 35. |

Instruct the client to notify her health care provider immediately in the instance of severe headache, blurred or lost vision (which may signal possible stroke), and symptoms of chest pain, shortness of breath, or leg pain, which may indicate thromboembolism elsewhere in the body. The health care provider should also be informed of severe abdominal pain or mass, jaundice, severe mental depression, or unusual bleeding. Instructions should be provided for monthly self-examination of the breasts, and any lumps found should be reported to the physician.

Medical intervention is necessary for various changes in menstrual bleeding pattern, increased and painful urination, jaundice, abdominal cramping, ocular changes (double vi-

sion, partial or complete loss of vision, bulging eyes), increased blood pressure, breast alterations (lumps, secretions), depression, pain or numbness in fingers or toes.

***Evaluation.*** Clients should be monitored for the development of side effects or adverse reactions. Among the more commonly seen reactions are salt and water retention, breakthrough bleeding, thromboembolic disorders, hypertension, and nausea (see Table 52-1 for a more complete listing). If significant adverse reactions occur, a different birth control pill formula or alternate birth control method should be used.

Compliance with therapy is especially important if oral contraceptives are to be effective. Periodically review with the client the appropriate use and importance of taking the drug on a daily schedule. Ensure that the client knows the proper procedure to follow should one or more doses be missed.

## OVULATORY STIMULANTS AND DRUGS USED FOR INFERTILITY

**Anovulation,** the absence of ovulation, is physiologic in women who are pregnant, breast feeding, or postmenopausal. It becomes a suspected pathologic condition in individuals with abnormal bleeding or infertility. The incidence of anovulation is unknown and cannot be ascertained, but diagnostic tests may determine its presence. Methods of ovulation induction include use of gonadotropins, thyroid preparations, cortisone preparations, estrogens, and synthetic agents.

### clomiphene citrate (Clomid, Serophene)

Clomiphene has estrogen and antiestrogenic properties. Although its exact mechanism of action is unknown, it has been postulated that its competition with estrogen for receptor sites in the hypothalamus causes an increased secretion of FSH and LH. The result is ovarian stimulation, maturation of the ovarian follicle, and development of the corpus luteum.

Clomiphene is indicated for the treatment of female infertility. It is freely absorbed from the gastrointestinal tract. It is also recirculated in the enterohepatic system, which may account for its prolonged duration of action in the body.

It has a half-life of 5 to 7 days in the plasma. Ovulation usually occurs between 4 to 10 days after the first day of treatment. Clomiphene is metabolized in the liver and excreted in the feces (biliary) for up to 6 weeks. It has no known significant drug interactions; for side effects/adverse reactions, see Table 52-1.

The adult dose for female infertility is 50 mg orally daily for 5 days, on the fifth day of the menstrual cycle if bleeding occurs or at any time in women who have no recent uterine bleeding. This cycle is repeated until conception occurs, up to three or four cycles. If ovulation does not occur, the dose is increased to 100 mg a day for 5 days, which may be repeated if necessary. Some clients may need larger doses to induce ovulation (up to 250 mg/day), but higher dosages are associated with a higher incidence of side effects. Pregnancy safety has not been established.

### ▷ Nursing Management: Clomiphene Therapy

*Assessment.* It should be determined whether the client has preexisting conditions for which clomiphene is contraindicated, such as abnormal and undiagnosed vaginal bleeding, endometriosis, fibroid tumors, mental depression, active or a history of hepatic dysfunction, or thrombophlebitis. If the client has ovarian cysts, clomiphene may cause enlargement of them.

Clients receiving clomiphene therapy are at risk for the following nursing diagnoses: altered comfort related to premenstrual syndrome (over 5%), hot flashes, headache, breast tenderness, nausea and vomiting; sleep pattern disturbance (insomnia); visual disturbances (blurred vision, after images, diplopia, floaters, or photophobia); altered thought processes (depression); and the potential for physiologic injury related to the development or enlargement of ovarian cysts, enlargement of uterine fibroids, hepatatoxicity, or thromboembolism.

*Education.* Instruct the client to take basal body temperature daily and record on flow chart. This determines when ovulation occurs and assists in properly timing coitus so as to enhance fertilization. Easy-to-read oral thermometers are available that register 96° to 100° F; however, some physicians prefer rectal temperatures for accuracy. The temperature is taken from day 1 of the menstrual period and every morning upon awakening and before the client engages in any activity, such as drinking coffee, brushing teeth, smoking, or intercourse. The body temperature is low (approximately 97.5° F) and stable for 2 weeks after menstruation. At ovulation there is a slight decrease, followed the next day by an increase (approximately 98.5° F), which continues if progesterone levels are normal. The temperature decreases again just before menstruation. If this decrease does not occur, the client may be pregnant; the next series of the drug should be delayed until it is determined she is not pregnant, since clomiphene may have teratogenic effects. Coitus should occur every other day for 3 to 4 days before ovulation and for 2 to 3 days after ovulation to enhance fertilization.

Advise the client that taking the medication at the same time every day maintains drug levels and helps her remember the daily dose.

If the medication is to start on day 5, count the first day of the menstrual period as day 1.

If a dose is missed, advise client to take it as soon as possible. If the dose is not remembered until time for the next dose, both should be taken together. If more than one dose is missed, the physician should be consulted.

Inform the client and her spouse of the posssibility of multiple births with this drug.

Advise the client that abdominal pain is an indication for immediate medical attention, since this may be symptomatic of ovarian cyst or enlargement.

Counsel the client to report visual disturbances to the physician at once.

Advise the client to be cautious with tasks that require alertness, since clomiphene may cause visual disturbances, vertigo, and light headedness.

*Evaluation.* If pregnancy does not occur, review the course of therapy with the client and her spouse to ensure understanding.

A pelvic examination to assess ovarian size should be completed before each course of the drug.

# SUMMARY

Drugs used for diagnostic purposes, to treat disorders, or to alter the normal functioning of the female reproductive system include many substances such as gonadotropin-releasing hormone, nonpituitary chorionic gonadotropin, menotropins, female sex hormones, oral contraceptives, ovulatory stimulants, and drugs used for infertility. Gonadotropin-releasing hormone, or gonadorelin, is used for the diagnosis of hypogonadism in both males and females and, investigationally, for the treatment of primary hypothalamic amenorrhea. The gonadotropin-releasing hormone agonist, nafarelin, is used in the management of endometriosis. A deficiency in luteinizing hormone is the indication for chorionic gonadotropin. Menotropins are used in the treatment of both male and female infertility.

Estrogens, progesterone, and progestins are the more commonly used drugs in this group. Estrogen is used for hormonal replacement therapy, the treatment of breast and prostatic carcinomas, and prevention of osteoporosis in postmenopausal women. Progesterone/progestins are indicated for hormonal replacement, the treatment of endometriosis and specific carcinomas, and the prevention of pregnancy.

Oral contraception with combinations of estrogen and progestin is the most effective form of birth control currently available. Because these drugs are primarily for self-administration, the emphasis for the nurse is on client education for accurate and safe administration and for early recognition of adverse reactions, particularly thromboembolism. Clomiphene, on the other hand, is indicated for the treatment of infertility.

Since all of these drugs affect sexual identity, the nurse must be sensitive to the client's needs as a sexual being and alert to cues that reflect problems such as a disturbance of self-concept.

---

# Case Study: The Client Taking Oral Contraceptives

Linda Cosgrove is a 35-year-old woman who has been taking oral contraceptives for 5 years. She is currently using Ortho-Novum 7/7/7-28. On a recent routine physical examination the nurse noted that Ms. Cosgrove's blood pressure had increased to 154/90 from a previous range of 122/70 to 134/80. She has also had a recent 10-pound weight gain without a change in eating habits or activity.

1. Why might these symptoms be significant for this client?
2. What additional assessment data does the nurse need to gather from this client related to her drug therapy and her current status?

3. What elements of the physical examination are important for this client?
4. What information should the nurse provide this client about adverse reactions to oral contraceptives and her options for contraception?

## BIBLIOGRAPHY

American Hospital Formulary Service. (1991). AHFS drug information '91. Bethesda, Md: American Society of Hospital Pharmacists, Inc.
Barrett-Connor E. (1986). Postmenopausal estrogen, cancer and other considerations, Women Health 11(3/4):179.
Bush T et al. (1989). How ERT affects heart disease, Patient Care 23(10):67.
Carlone JP et al. (1989). Oral contraceptive use in women with chronic medical conditions, Nurse Pract 14(9):9.
Clark PI et al. (1988). Relation of results of exercise stress tests in young women to phases of the menstrual cycle, Am J Cardiol 61(1):197.
Cobb JO. (1987). Demystifying menopause, Can Nurse 83(7):16.
Collins J. Overview of commonly-practiced birth control methods, Imprint 36(4):63.
Cook RJ. (1989). Antiprogestin drugs: medical and legal issues, Fam Plann Perspect 21(6):267.
Curran DL et al. (1987). Contraception update: improvements in safety, convenience, and benefits, Consultant 27(11):23.
Dickey RP. (1984). Managing contraceptive pill patients. ed 4. Durant, Okla: Creative Informatics, Inc.
Duchin SE et al. (1989). OCs: risks, benefits, guidelines, Patient Care 23(6):89.
Engel NS. (1990). Update on cancer risk and oral contraception, MCN 15(1):37.
Ettinger B. (1987). Estrogen and postmenopausal osteoporosis, AAOHN J 35(12):543.
Flowers DS. (1987). Estraderm (Ciba-Geigy): a review of transdermal estrogen, Fla Pharm J 51(8):14.
Frazier J. (1987). The dilemma of the perimenopausal female: a sexual/physical health issue, Holistic Nurs Pract 1(4):67.
Gambrell RD Jr. (1990). Estrogen-progestogen replacement and cancer risk, Hosp Pract 25(3):81.
Gilman AG et al, eds. (1990). Goodman & Gilman's the pharmacological basis of therapeutics, ed 8. New York: Macmillan Publishing Co.
Goldzieher JW et al. (1987). Medical aspects of contraception, Hosp Pract 22(3):93.
Harvey SM et al. (1989). Factors associated with use of the contraceptive sponge, Fam Plann Perspect 21(4):179.
Lindsey AM et al. (1987). Endocrine mechanisms and obesity: influences in breast cancer, Oncol Nurs Forum 14(2):47.
Luy M. (1987). Primary osteoporosis: new thinking on an old problem, AD Nurse 2(3):15.
McKeon VA. (1989). Cruel myths and clinical facts about menopause, RN 52(6):52.
Mishell DR Jr, ed. (1987). Dialogues in contraception 6. University of Southern California School of Medicine: Health Learning Systems, Inc.
Monier M et al. (1989). Contraceptives: a look at the future, Amer J Nurs 89(4):496.

Orshan SA. (1988). The pill, the patient, and you, RN 51(7):49.

Rowlands S. (1987). Pill-taking routine, Midwife Health Visit Community Nurse 23(12):531.

Sawyer RG et al. (1989). Oral contraceptives: a survey of college women's concerns and experience, Health Educ 20(3):17.

Shapero GH. (1988). Current choices in contraception, J Am Acad Physician Assist 1(1):19.

Shimp LA et al. (1988). Relationship between drug use and urinary incontinence in elderly women, Drug Intell Clin Pharm 22(10):786.

Sobel S. (1987) Osteoporosis: regulatory view, Public Health Rep (Suppl) Jul-Aug: 136.

Tyrer LB. (1989). Oral contraceptives: counseling for selection and use, Physician Assist 13(1):46.

United States Pharmacopeial Convention. (1991). Drug information for the health care professional, ed 11. Rockville, Md: The Convention.

Utian WH. (1989). Oral contraceptives: safe after 40? Patient Care 23(6):115.

Walter RM Jr. (1987). Osteoporosis: therapy that can make a difference, Consultant 27(3):115.

White JE. (1987). Influence of parents, peers, and problem-solving on contraceptive use, Pediatr Nurs 13(5):317.

Witwer M. (1989). Oral contraceptive use linked to chiamydial, gonococcal infections, Fam Plann Perspect 21(4):190.

Younglin EQ et al. (1987). The triphasics: insights for effective clinical use, Nurse Pract 12(2):17.

# Chapter

# ℘53 Drugs for Labor and Delivery

## CHAPTER OBJECTIVES

*After studying this chapter, you should be able to meet the following objectives and define the key terms.*

1. Describe the altered pharmacokinetic pattern of drugs during labor and delivery.

2. Discuss the pharmacologic action of oxytocics on the uterus.

3. Identify the three primary indications of oxytocin.

4. Explain the two primary actions of ergonovine.

5. Discuss the mechanism of action and use of ritodrine.

6. Explain the action of the two lactation inhibitors.

## KEY TERMS

**multiparity,** page 826

**oxytocics,** page 826

**preterm labor,** page 828

## INTRODUCTION

Since many drugs are available for use during labor and delivery, it is important to consider the benefit versus risk to the fetus. The pharmacokinetics of drugs may be altered during labor and delivery. For example, during labor, gastric emptying is delayed and vomiting may result, which would alter drug absorption. Also, vomiting is often exacerbated by the use of opioid analgesics. Thus, because oral drug absorption is unpredictable at this time, parenteral routes should be used. Drug metabolism and excretion may be altered and prolonged during labor; and although clinical data are currently sparse, the potential for inducing adverse or undesirable effects is always a concern. If a drug, such as potent analgesics (opioid) and sedatives, may be potentially harmful to the fetus, then the smallest possible dose should be used if alternate methods are not available.

Complications in pregnancy may also dictate the use of additional medications, such as those to treat diabetes, hypertension, pre-eclampsia, eclampsia, and systemic infections. The medications and proper use of them are covered under the appropriate pharmacologic sections in this book. In this chapter, the discussion is limited to the drugs used to induce labor (oxytocics), inhibit preterm labor (tocolytics), and suppress lactation.

## DRUGS AFFECTING THE UTERUS

The uterus is a highly muscular organ that exhibits a number of characteristic properties and activities. The smooth muscle fibers extend longitudinally, circularly, and obliquely in the organ. The uterus has a rich blood supply; but when the uterine muscle contracts, blood flow is diminished. Profound changes occur in the uterus during pregnancy: it increases in weight from about 50 g to approximately 1000 g, its capacity increases tenfold in length, and new muscle fibers may be formed. These changes are accompanied by changes in response to drugs.

Drugs that act on the uterus include (1) those that increase the contractility of the uterus and (2) those that decrease uterine contractility.

## Oxytocics

**Oxytocics** are drugs that exert a selective action on the smooth muscle of the uterus. The most commonly used oxytocics are alkaloids of synthetic oxytocin and ergot, although many other drugs may exhibit some effect on uterine contractility.

Oxytocin is one of two hormones secreted by the posterior pituitary; the other hormone is vasopressin, or antidiuretic hormone (ADH). Oxytocin means "rapid birth," a term derived from its ability to contract the pregnant uterus. It also facilitates milk ejection during lactation.

The nonpregnant uterus is relatively insensitive to oxytocin, but during pregnancy uterine sensitivity to oxytocin gradually increases, with the uterus being most sensitive at the term. Oxytocin secretion may precede and possibly trigger delivery of the fetus. Large amounts of oxytocin have been detected in the blood during the expulsive phase of delivery. It is believed oxytocin is released in response to stretching of the uterine cervix and vagina. A positive feedback mechanism may be operant; that is, more forceful contractions of uterine muscle and greater stretching of the cervix and vagina result in more oxytocin release. Oxytocin acts directly on the myometrium, having a stronger effect on the fundus than on the cervix.

### oxytocin (Pitocin, Syntocinon)

Oxytocin stimulates uterine smooth muscle contractions indirectly, which simulates normal contractions of a spontaneous labor and transiently reduces uterine blood flow. It also stimulates the mammary gland to increase milk excretion from the breast. (It does not increase the production of milk.)

Oxytocin is indicated for induction of labor, to stimulate or reinforce labor when contractions are dysfunctional or irregular, for control of postpartum hemorrhage, and for stimulation of lactation. For side effects/adverse reactions, see Table 53-1. Oxytocin is administered in nasal and parenteral dosage forms. Though rapidly absorbed nasally, absorption may be erratic by this route; therefore, it is primarily recommended before nursing or pumping of the breasts.

Oxytocin has a half-life of 1 to 6 minutes and an onset of action as follows: nasal—within a couple of minutes, intramuscular—within 3 to 5 minutes, intravenous—immediate, although the uterine contractions will increase gradually over 15 to 60 minutes before it stabilizes. Duration of action is as follows: nasal—20 minutes, intramuscular—30 to 60 minutes, intravenous—20 minutes after the infusion is stopped.

Oxytocin is metabolized in the liver and kidneys and excreted via the kidneys. It has no significant drug interactions.

The dosage to stimulate or induce labor is 1 to 2 mU (0.001 to 0.002 units) per minute by intravenous infusion. The dose may be gradually increased by 1 to 2 mU per minute every 15 to 30 minutes until a contraction pattern is established that simulates normal labor (up to a maximum of 20 mU per minute).

Control of postpartum uterine bleeding: 10 units at a rate of 20 to 40 mU in a nonhydrating diluent infused intravenously, following birth of the infant. Nasal solution: 1 spray or 3 drops in one or both nostrils 2 or 3 minutes before nursing or pumping of breasts.

## ▷ Nursing Management: Oxytocin Therapy

**Assessment.** It should be ascertained that the client in labor does not have cord presentation or prolapse, placenta previa or vasa previa, fetal distress, hypertonic uterine patterns or uterine inertia, pre-eclampsia or severe toxemia, or an obstetrical emergency requiring surgery before the administration of oxytocin.

Oxytocin should be used cautiously if the client in labor exhibits grand **multiparity** (several prior births), overdistention of the uterus, past history of trauma or major surgery on the cervix or uterus, invasive cervical carcinoma, partial placenta previa, prematurity of the fetus, or an unfavorable fetal position. Caution is also reccommended in women over 35 years of age or those having an abortion using hypertonic saline.

It should be determined that there is pelvic adequacy of the client in labor and that there is fetal maturity.

Clients receiving oxytocin are at risk for the following nursing diagnoses: fluid volume excess related to the drug's antidiuretic effect; altered comfort with nasal use related to nasal irritation and tearing of the eyes; and the potential for injury related to anaphylaxis and other allergic reactions, cardiac dysrhythmias, postpartum hemorrhage, or water intoxication. The fetus may also be at risk because of the potential for injury related to fetal bradycardia and neonatal jaundice.

Before administering the drug, record a baseline of data, including blood pressure and other vital signs, characteristics, frequency and duration of contractions, and fetal heart rate. During the infusion, assess the client for blood pressure and pulse and the fetal heart rate at least every 15 minutes. Assess the myometrium for tonus during and between contractions and report hypertonic uterine contractions or a period of uterine relaxation. Discontinue oxytocin at the first sign of uterine hyperactivity or fetal distress.

**Intervention.** Administration should be only in a hospital setting and under the supervision of a physician.

Accurate administration by infusion pump is mandatory, as is using a Y connection so that the oxytocin solution may be discontinued while the vein is kept open. When preparing

**TABLE 53-1**   Side effects/adverse reactions of labor and delivery drugs

| Drug | Side effects* | Adverse reactions† |
|---|---|---|
| **OXYTOCICS** | | |
| oxytocin (Pitocin) | Rare or infrequent: With parenteral use only—nausea, vomiting, tachycardia, irregular heart rate | May occasionally cause nausea, vomiting, premature ventricular contractions, fetal bradycardia, dysrhythmias, neonatal jaundice, postpartum excessive bleeding<br>Rarely: Hematoma in the pelvic area, increased loss of blood, and afibrinogenemia<br>Allergic and anaphylactic reactions have also occurred<br>Prolonged therapy may result in water intoxication and possible maternal death because of its slight antidiuretic effects. Monitor clients closely during prolonged use, since hypertensive episodes and subarachnoid hemorrhage may result<br>When given in excessive dosages to hypersensitive clients, uterine spasms and tetanic contractions can occur, which may lead to uterine rupture, abruptio placentae, reduction in blood flow to the uterus, amniotic fluid embolism, and trauma to the fetus (resulting in dysrhythmias, intracranial hemorrhage, and asphyxia) |
| ergonovine (Ergotrate) | Most frequent: Nausea or vomiting, seen mostly after IV administration<br>Less frequent: Diarrhea, dizziness, tinnitus, increased sweating, confusion<br>Dose-related effect: Abdominal cramping | Less frequent: Coronary vessel spasms resulting in chest pain<br>Rare: Respiratory difficulties (allergic effect); hypertensive episode (client complains of sudden, very severe headache); pruritus; pain in arms, legs, or lower back; cold hands or feet; leg weakness |
| methylergonovine maleate (Methergine) | Same as ergonovine | Same as ergonovine |
| **PREMATURE LABOR INHIBITOR** | | |
| ritodrine (Yutopar) | With IV dosage form, nearly 80% to 100% of the clients have increased maternal heart rate and increased systolic and decreased diastolic maternal blood pressure. Oral dosage forms may cause small increases in maternal heart rate but do not affect maternal blood pressure or fetal heart rate. | |
| | Most frequent:<br>  Orally—trembling or tremors;<br>  IV—trembling or tremors, red colored skin, nausea, vomiting, headaches<br>Less frequent:<br>  IV—increased anxiety or nervousness and restlessness;<br>  Orally—rash, jitteriness | Most frequent (10% to 15% with oral dosage forms, 35% with IV administration): Tachycardia, irregular heart rate<br>Rare (1% to 2% after IV use): Chest pain, respiratory difficulties<br>Signs of excessive dosing: Severe nausea, vomiting, nervousness, trembling, shortness of breath, tachycardia or irregular heart rate<br>With IV, monitor closely as some cases of maternal pulmonary edema resulting in death have occurred. Cause is unknown but contributing factors include concurrent corticosteroids, hypokalemia, twin gestations, a sustained rapid heartbeat of over 140 beats/minute and perhaps undiagnosed cardiac disease |

*If side effects continue, increase, or disturb the client, the physician should be informed.
†If adverse reactions occur, contact the physician because medical intervention may be necessary.

an infusion with oxytocin, distribute the drug throughout the solution by gently rotating the bottle.

When administered by nasal spray, instruct the client to clear nasal passages. Then, holding the client's head vertically and the bottle upright, spray the solution into nostril.

Do not administer by more than one route simultaneously.

***Evaluation.*** The maternal blood pressure and pulse should be monitored frequently, along with the frequency, duration, and force of the contractions. Continuous fetal monitoring should be done while the client is receiving oxytocin. Fluid intake and output determinations and as-

sessment of breath sounds are needed since the drug has a slight antidiuretic effect, which, with prolonged intravenous infusion, could result in severe water intoxication. Hypochloremia and hyponatremia may occur in the client because of water intoxication. Hyperbilirubinemia may oc-

### ergonovine (Ergotrate)

The mechanism of action is direct stimulation of the smooth muscle of the uterine wall. The drug also has antiserotonin effects on the CNS and has been used as a diagnostic agent for coronary vasospasm (because it vasoconstricts the coronary arteries). Ergonovine is indicated to prevent and treat postpartum hemorrhage.

It is administered orally or parenterally and has an onset of action in stimulating uterine contractions as follows: orally, within 6 to 15 minutes; intramuscularly, within 2 to 5 minutes; intravenously, 1 minute. Duration of uterine contraction action is as follows: orally, about 3 hours; intramuscularly, approximately 3 hours; intravenously, about 45 minutes but rhythmic contractions can persist for up to 3 hours. The drug is mainly excreted via the kidneys.

Ergonovine has no significant drug interactions; for side effects/adverse reactions, see Table 53-1.

Orally the dosage for ergonovine maleate tablets is 0.2 to 0.4 mg two to four times a day (on a schedule of every 6 to 12 hours) until the dangers associated with uterine atony and hemorrhage are over. The usual course is 48 hours. Parenterally, 0.2 mg is administered intramuscularly or intravenously and repeated in 2 to 4 hours if necessary, for up to five doses for use as a uterine stimulant. The intravenous route is usually only recommended in emergencies or when excessive uterine bleeding is present.

▷ **Nursing Management:**
**Ergonovine Therapy**

*Assessment.* If the client does not tolerate other ergot derivatives, she may not tolerate ergonovine.

Ergonovine should be used with caution in clients with coronary artery disease because it causes coronary vasospasm. It may also increase blood pressure, thus its use should be limited in clients with hypertension, as well as those with pre-eclampsia. As with most drugs, it is to be administered with care to clients with hepatic or renal function impairment. Septic clients may have an increased sensitivity to the drug.

Ergonovine is contraindicated before delivery of the placenta, since it may result in the entrapment of the placenta. It is not to be used for the induction of labor or in cases of threatened spontaneous abortion.

A baseline standard should be obtained for the pulse and blood pressure.

Clients receiving ergonovine are at risk for the following nursing diagnoses: altered comfort related to severe uterine cramping, dizziness, nausea and vomiting; altered bowel pattern (diarrhea); perceptual disturbances (ringing in the ears); and the potential for injury related to severe hypertension, coronary vasospasm, ergotism, peripheral vasospasm, allergic reaction, and overdose (severe headache, diarrhea, nausea and vomiting, respiratory depression, seizures).

*Intervention.* When given intravenously, the drug should be administered slowly over a minimum of 1 minute.

*Education.* Clients should be instructed to avoid smoking, because the action of the drug is enhanced as nicotine constricts the blood vessels. Caution the client about ex-

posure to cold because the body's ability to respond may be diminished. The client should be alerted that the drug may cause discomfort from uterine contractions and instructed in methods to alleviate the discomfort.

*Evaluation.* Blood pressure and pulse should be monitored, as well as fundal tone and placement; the character and amount of vaginal bleeding should also be assessed. If the client has chest pain, the physician should be notified immediately and an ECG obtained.

If the client does not respond to the drug, tests to determine serum calcium levels should be done. Correction of hypocalcemia with intravenous calcium salts will restore the oxytoxic action of the drug.

The client should be observed for signs of ergotism, such as headache, nausea and vomiting, peripheral ischemia, and paresthesia.

### methylergonovine maleate (Methergine)

The mechanism of action is direct stimulation of the smooth muscle of the uterine wall, which results in hemostasis. This drug has an antiserotonin effect in CNS.

Methylergonovine is indicated to prevent and treat postpartum hemorrhage. It may be administered orally, intramuscularly, or intravenously, with a postpartum uterine contraction effect noted within 3 to 10 minutes, 2 to 5 minutes, or immediate effect, respectively. Duration of action orally and intramuscularly is approximately 3 hours, while intravenously the effect lasts about 45 minutes. The drug is metabolized in the liver, and less than 5% is excreted by the kidneys. It has no reported significant drug interactions; for side effects/adverse reactions, see Table 53-1.

The oral dose is 200 to 400 μg (0.2 to 0.4 mg) orally two to four times daily (spaced every 6 to 12 hours) until uterine bleeding and atony is under control. Usually oral dosing follows the administration of an initial parenteral dose. See discussion of nursing management for ergonovine therapy.

## Premature Labor Inhibitors

**Preterm labor,** or labor that occurs before the thirty-seventh week of pregnancy, is a major problem in obstetrics. It occurs in approximately 10% to 15% of all pregnancies. Premature birth increases the possibility of neonatal morbidity and mortality.

### ritodrine (Yutopar)

Ritodrine's mechanism of action is as a beta$_2$ adrenergic stimulant that relaxes the uterine muscle by inhibiting uterine contractions. It is indicated to prevent and treat premature labor in pregnancies of 20 or more weeks' gestation.

Following oral administration, the drug has an onset of action within ½ to 1 hour; intravenously, within 5 minutes. The time to peak serum concentration orally and intravenously is within 1 hour. Peak serum levels orally are 5 to

15 nanograms/ml (following a 10 mg dose). Intravenous peak serum levels are 42 to 52 nanograms/ml (following an infusion of 9 mg over 1 hour). Half-life orally is biphasic, 1.3 and 12 hours. Intravenously half-life has three phases: 6 to 9 minutes, 1.7 to 2.6 hours, and 15 to 17 hours. The drug is metabolized in the liver and excreted by the kidneys. For side effects/adverse reactions, see Table 53-1.

*Significant drug interactions.* The following significant drug interactions may occur when ritodrine is given with the drugs listed below.

| Drug | Possible Effect and Management |
|---|---|
| corticosteroids, long acting (betamethasone, dexamethasone, paramethasone) | Pulmonary edema and death have been reported in pregnant women. If concurrent drug administration is absolutely necessary, monitor closely and discontinue both drugs at first sign of pulmonary edema. |
| beta adrenergic blocking agents (labetalol, nadolol, propranolol, and others) | Usage is not recommended because the two drugs are antagonistic toward each other. Drugs with greater beta₁ selectivity may be less antagonistic. |

### Dosage and administration

*Tablets.* 10 mg orally initially ½ hour before the intravenous infusion is stopped; then 10 mg every 2 hours for 24 hours. Maintenance—10 to 20 mg orally every 4 to 6 hours until birth or as directed by the physician. Maximum recommended daily dosage is 120 mg.

*Injectable.* 50 to 100 µg (0.05 to 0.1 mg) intravenous/minute, increase every 10 minutes if necessary by increments of 50 µg (0.05 mg) to an effective dosage. Maintenance—150 to 350 µg (0.15 to 0.35 mg) intravenous/minute. Continue intravenous infusion for 12 to 24 hours after labor contractions have stopped, then institute oral therapy as described above.

*Pregnancy safety.* Has been established at FDA category B.

### ▷ Nursing Management: Ritodrine Therapy

*Assessment.* Length of gestation should be determined, since ritodrine is not recommended for use before the twentieth week of pregnancy. Preterm labor should not have progressed more than 4 cm of cervical dilation or 80% effacement or the drug may not be effective.

Ritodrine is contraindicated when the client has cardiac disorders, hyperthyroidism, eclampsia, pulmonary hypertension, or intrauterine infection, hemorrhage, or intrauterine fetal death. Caution is indicated if the client has diabetes or pre-eclampsia.

Clients receiving ritodrine are at risk for the following nursing diagnoses: fluid volume excess (pulmonary edema); altered comfort related to possible undiagnosed cardiac problem (angina), headache, or nausea and vomiting; anxiety (restlessness, nervousness, emotional labile); and phys-

iological injury related to the development of hepatitis.

*Intervention.* A controlled infusion device should be used when administering ritodrine intravenously to better enable dosage titration. Avoid the use of sodium chloride for infusion because of the risk of pulmonary edema. The client is placed on her left side to reduce blood pressure changes. Intravenous administration is usually continued for 12 to 24 hours after contractions stop, and then followed by oral dosage.

*Education.* The client should be cautioned to notify the physician if her water breaks or if her contractions begin again. If the client's contractions do not recur, she may gradually resume ambulation and other activities of daily living after 36 to 48 hours.

*Evaluation.* The client's blood pressure, heart rate, and uterine activity should be monitored periodically, as well as the fetal heart rate. Increases in maternal heart rate and systolic blood pressure are common with intravenous ritodrine. Oral dosages do not affect maternal blood pressure.

For those clients receiving prolonged intravenous therapy, blood glucose level, lung sounds, and fluid and electrolyte balance should be monitored. Closely monitor fluids to prevent circulatory overload. Tachycardia and dyspnea may indicate impending pulmonary edema. Other side effects for which to observe are headache, nausea and vomiting, erythema, and trembling.

## LACTATION INHIBITORS

Estrogens such as chlorotrianisene (Tace) and bromocriptine (Parlodel) have been used to treat postpartum breast engorgement and inhibition of lactation, respectively. The use of estrogens for breast engorgement has declined over the years, mainly because the incidence of painful engorgement is considered low and studies have indicated that analgesics or other supportive therapies are quite effective. Also, the physician must weigh the benefit of using estrogens for this purpose against the risk, especially the risk of possibly inducing a thromboembolism.

Bromocriptine directly inhibits the release of prolactin from the anterior pituitary gland, resulting in suppression of lactation. For further information on bromocriptine, see the drug monograph for dopamine agonist in Chapter 18.

## SUMMARY

Although many drugs are available for use during the labor and delivery process, it is essential to consider possible alteration of drug pharmacokinetics during labor and to weigh the risks and benefits to the fetus. The drugs discussed in this chapter focus directly on uterine contractility. This contractility controls the labor process. Therefore, drugs that increase or decrease the contractility of the uterus also enhance or inhibit labor.

Oxytocics are drugs that increase uterine motility to induce labor, augment labor, control postpartum hemorrhage, and facilitate milk ejection during lactation. The most commonly used oxytocics are oxytocin, ergonovine, and methylergonovine. When oxytocics are used to induce or augment labor, the nurse should perform a baseline assessment of fetal heart tones, uterine status, and maternal vital signs from which to evaluate the client's status. These indicators should be monitored every 15 to 30 minutes during the administration of these drugs.

Preterm labor, occurring before the thirty-seventh week of pregnancy, increases the possibility of neonatal morbidity and mortality. Once a determination is made that it is in the mother's and baby's best interest to halt the labor process, the physician may prescribe ritodrine. Ritodrine, a beta$_2$ adrenergic stimulant that relaxes uterine muscle and inhibits uterine contractions, is used to prevent and treat premature labor in pregnancies of 20 weeks or more gestation.

The role of the nurse in the administration of these drugs is to facilitate healthy outcomes for both the fetus and the mother.

## BIBLIOGRAPHY

American Hospital Formulary Service. (1991). AHFS drug information '91. Bethesda, Md: American Society of Hospital Pharmacists, Inc.

Few BJ. (1988). Indomethacin for treatment of premature labor, MCN 13(2):93.

Gill P et al. (1989). Terbutaline by pump to prevent recurrent preterm labor, MCN 14(3):163.

Givens SR. (1988). Update on tocolytic therapy in the management of preterm labor, J Perinat Neonat Nurs 2(1):21.

Gupta RC et al. (1989). Acute pulmonary edema associated with the use of oral ritodrine for premature labor, Chest 95(2):479.

Harding JE et al. (1989). Views of mothers and midwives participating in the Bristol randomized, controlled trial of active management of the third stage of labor, Birth 16(1):1.

Huston CJ. (1987). Action STAT, preterm labor, Nursing 17(3):33.

MacKenzie IZ. (1987). Prostaglandins and the induction of labour: aspects of medicine, Midwife Health Visit Comm Nurse 23(1):12.

Roberts J et al. (1989). Use of prostaglandins in nurse-midwifery practice, J Nurse Midwife 34(3):137.

Saunders NJ et al. (1989). Oxytoxin infusion during second stage of labour in primiparous women using epidural analgesia: a randomised double blind placebo controlled trial, Br Med J 299(6713):1423.

United States Pharmacopeial Convention. (1991). Drug information for the health care professional, ed 11, Rockville, Md: The Convention.

Weiner CP et al. (1988). The therapeutic efficacy and cost-effectiveness of aggressive tocolysis for premature labor associated with premature rupture of the membranes, Am J Obstet Gynecol 159(1):216.

## *Case Study: The Client in Labor*

Karen Evans has spent 12 hours in labor with her first pregnancy and has made little progress. She is becoming exhausted, and the uterine contractions have decreased in strength. Oxytocin is being considered as an alternative to improve the progress of labor.

1. How might the oxytocin be administered?
2. What are the associated risks of the drug for both the mother and the fetus?
3. What physiologic signs and symptoms should be monitored in this client?
4. How should the nurse describe the drug therapy to this client?

*Chapter*

# 54  Drugs Affecting the Male Reproductive System

## CHAPTER OBJECTIVES

*After studying this chapter, you should be able to meet the following objectives and define the key terms.*

1. Compare the pharmacokinetics of the three androgens.

2. Discuss the approved indications for androgen therapy.

3. List the side effects/adverse reactions of androgen therapy.

4. Discuss appropriate nursing management in the care of clients undergoing androgen therapy.

## KEY TERMS

**anabolic agents,** page 831

**androgens,** page 831

**priapism,** page 832

**testosterone,** page 831

## INTRODUCTION

Normal development and maintenance of male sex characteristics depend on adequate amounts of the male sex hormones, the **androgens.** Testosterone and its derivatives plus synthetic agents are commonly used as replacement therapy for males who lack the hormone. In hypogonadism and eunuchoidism, the androgens produce marked changes in growth of the male sex organs, body contour, voice, and other secondary sex characteristics.

## TESTOSTERONES

**Testosterone,** the natural hormone, is available in combination with esters to prolong the medication's duration of action. For example, testosterone propionate is formulated in an oily solution that produces hormonal effects for 2 or 3 days, whereas testosterone cypionate and testosterone enanthate in oil are much longer acting. They are usually administered once every 2 to 4 weeks. Testosterone pellets are available for subcutaneous implantation. This form will also provide an extended duration of action; depending on the number of pellets used, it may extend from 2 to 6 months before replacement pellets are necessary.

Oral testosterone is absorbed but is mainly destroyed by the liver before it reaches systemic circulation. Administering methyltestosterone by the buccal route of administration increases its serum level and effectiveness. Fluoxymesterone is a synthetic androgen that is effective orally in tablet form.

***Mechanism of action.*** As a natural hormone in normal males, testosterone stimulates the synthesis and activity of RNA, which results in an increased protein production. Androgens are also potent **anabolic agents;** they stimulate the formation and maintenance of muscular and skeletal protein. They bring about retention of nitrogen (essential to the formation of protein in the body) and enhance storage of inorganic phosphorus, sulfate, sodium, and potassium. Athletes have used androgens to increase weight, musculature, and muscle strength. Weight gains may be caused by fluid retention, a side effect of androgen therapy. The potential risk of developing the major serious adverse reactions from androgens far outweighs the advantages to be gained in athletic events. Many major sporting events disqualify athletes whose use of such products is documented. Chapter 9, on substance abuse, has additional information on the abuse of androgens.

*Indications.* Testosterones are indicated for the following:

1. Treatment of androgen deficiency, such as testicular failure caused by cryptorchidism, orchitis, orchidectomy, or pituitary-hypothalamic insufficiency
2. Treatment of delayed male puberty when not induced by a pathologic condition
3. Treatment of breast carcinoma: palliative or secondary treatment for inoperable metastatic breast cancer in postmenopausal women, although newer agents are generally available for this indication. Androgens have also been used in premenopausal women with breast cancer in association with an oophorectomy, if such tumors are believed to be responsive to the hormone
4. Anemia: androgens stimulate erythropoiesis in males and females

*Pharmacokinetics.* The half-life of testosterone is between 10 and 100 minutes; fluoxymesterone: dose related— that is, a 2 mg dose is 13.7 hours, whereas a 10 mg dose is approximately 10 hours; methyltestosterone; between 2.5 and 3.5 hours.

The time to peak concentration: Methyltestosterone, buccal tablet—within 1 hour; oral tablet—2 hours.

Duration of action: depends on the dose and the ester formulation administered. The longest duration of testosterone preparations is with enanthate, then cypionate, with the propionate form being the shortest.

Testosterone is metabolized in the liver and excreted by the kidneys.

*Side effects/adverse reactions.* In females the most frequent adverse reactions are an increase in oily skin or acne, deepening of the voice, increased hair growth or alopecia, enlarged clitoris, and irregular menses. The deep voice or hoarseness may not be reversed, even when medication is stopped. The most frequent adverse reactions reported in males are urinary urgency, breast swelling or tenderness, and frequent or continuous erections. Less frequent side effects occurring in both sexes include abdominal pain, insomnia, diarrhea or constipation, dizziness, increased weakness, red skin or changes in skin color, redness at the site of injection, mouth soreness, frequent headaches, confusion, respiratory difficulties, depression, nausea, vomit-

ing, pruritus, edema of lower extremities, jaundice, an increase in bleeding episodes, and an unusual increase or decrease in libido.

*Significant drug interactions.* Significant drug interactions are reported when testosterone is given concurrently with oral anticoagulants (coumarin or indandione) or with other hepatotoxic medications. In the former, the anticoagulant effects may be enhanced or increased; in the latter, the risk of inducing hepatotoxicity is increased.

*Dosage and administration*

1. Choice of dosage and length of therapy depend on the diagnosis, the client's age and sex, and the intensity of the side effects/adverse reactions.
2. Usually in delayed puberty and hypogonadal males, dosage regiments are started in the lower ranges and gradually increased according to the individual's needs and response. In delayed puberty, after 4 to 6 months of therapy, the androgens are discontinued for 1 to 3 months while x-ray examinations are evaluated to determine the drug's effect on bone growth. The hypogonadal male will receive the androgens through puberty with dosage adjustments as required. Usually lower maintenance dosages are used after puberty.
3. Androgen antineoplastic therapy usually requires a 3-month period to evaluate effectiveness.
4. Temporary withdrawal of the drug is required if the male experiences **priapism** (persistent, abnormal penis erection). This is an indication of excessive dosing of the androgen.
5. Women with metastatic breast cancer should receive a shorter-acting androgen, especially during the initial therapies. It has been reported that androgens occasionally increase the extension of breast cancer.

*Sterile testosterone suspension*

*Adults (intramuscular).* Androgen replacement therapy: 25 to 50 mg two or three times a week. Antineoplastic therapy for metastatic breast carcinoma in females: 100 mg three times a week.

*Children (intramuscular).* Delayed puberty in males: 12.5 to 25 mg intramuscularly two or three times a week for approximately 4 to 6 months.

*Testosterone enanthate injection*

*Adults (intramuscular).* Androgen replacement therapy: 50 to 400 mg every 2 to 4 weeks. Antineoplastic therapy for inoperable breast cancer in females: 200 to 400 mg every 2 to 4 weeks.

*Children (intramuscular).* Delayed puberty in males: 50 to 200 mg every 2 to 4 weeks for approximately 4 to 6 months.

*Methyltestosterone capsules (Metandren)*

*Adults.* Oral dosage for replacement therapy (hypogonadism, climacteric, or impotence): 10 to 50 mg daily. For treatment of postpubertal cryptorchidism: oral dosage is 10 mg three times a day. Antineoplastic therapy for metastatic breast carcinoma in females: 50 mg one to four times a day.

*Children.* Oral dosage for treatment of delayed puberty in males: 5 to 25 mg per day for approximately 4 to 6 months.

### Methyltestosterone buccal tablets (Metandren)

*Adults.* Dosage (buccal) for replacement therapy (hypogonadism, impotence, or climacteric): 5 to 25 mg daily. For postpubertal cryptorchidism: 5 mg three times a day. Antineoplastic therapy for metastatic breast carcinoma in females: 25 mg one to four times daily.

*Children.* Buccal dosage for treatment of delayed puberty in males is 2.5 to 12.5 mg daily for approximately 4 to 6 months.

### Fluoxymesterone tablets (Halotestin)

*Adults.* Oral dose for replacement therapy: 5 mg one to four times a day. Dosage for antineoplastic therapy for metastatic breast carcinoma in females: 20 to 50 mg daily for 2 to 6 months.

*Children.* Dosage for treatment of delayed puberty in males: 2.5 to 10 mg daily for approximately 4 to 6 months.

***Pregnancy safety.*** Has been established at FDA category X.

## ▷NURSING MANAGEMENT: TESTOSTERONE THERAPY

***Assessment.*** Assess whether the male client has breast cancer or known or suspected prostatic cancer, since androgens are contraindicated in both conditions.

The drugs should be used with caution in clients with severe cardiorenal disease, prostatic hypertrophy, hepatic failure, hypercalcemia, and, because of their hypercholesterolemic effects, those with a history of myocardial infarction and coronary artery disease.

The client receiving androgen therapy is at risk for the following nursing diagnoses: disturbance in self-concept related to virilism in female clients, gynecomastia and priapism in male clients, increased or decreased libido in both sexes; fluid volume excess (rapid weight gain, edema of feet and lower legs, shortness of breath); altered comfort related to nausea, vomiting, and abdominal pain; altered sleep pattern; and the risk for physiologic injury related to the development of erythrocytosis, hepatic impairment, hypercalcemia, and polycythemia.

***Intervention.*** Administer the oral preparations with food to minimize gastric distress. Administer intramuscular testosterone deep within the gluteal muscle. The nurse should be aware that testosterone cypionate and testosterone enanthate are not interchangeable with testosterone propionate and suspension forms of the drug because of the difference in duration and action. With testosterone cypionate, the preparation may be warmed and shaken to dissolve the crystals. It may also turn cloudy if a wet needle or syringe is used, but this does not affect its potency.

The nurse should be sensitive to the emotional responses of clients taking androgens. Female clients may have changes in secondary sex characteristics such as unnatural hair growth or heightened libido, which will subside with the cessation of the drug. Other changes that may occur, such as enlarged clitoris or hoarseness or deepening of the voice, may not be reversible. Male clients may need support to deal with deepening of the voice and rapid changes in height, size of sex organs, and hair growth patterns. Frequent or continuing erection may be a concern.

***Education.*** Work with the client and/or responsible family member to develop a diet high in protein, calories, vitamins, and minerals that is individualized to the client's food preferences.

Monitor the client with diabetes closely. Antidiabetic agents may require dosage adjustment with concurrent administration of androgens.

Instruct the client to weigh daily to monitor for fluid retention. Sodium restriction and/or diuretics may be required if edema occurs.

Advise the client to maintain regular visits to the physician for monitoring progress.

***Evaluation.*** Monitor the client's serum calcium carefully. Promptly report indications of hypercalcemia: nausea and vomiting, lethargy, loss of muscle tone, polyuria, increased urine and serum calcium levels. Hypercalcemia in clients with metastic breast cancer usually indicates bone metastasis. The client should be encouraged to drink 3 to 4 L or more of fluids to ensure adequate urinary output to prevent urinary calculi. Active clients should be encouraged to include weight-bearing exercise, i.e., walking daily. Clients confined to bed should have range of motion exercises at least daily. This exercise inhibits mobilization of calcium from bone.

Serum cholesterol levels should be monitored to ascertain the client's risk of cardiovascular disease as the result of androgen administration.

Hepatic function should also be monitored; hemoglobin and hematocrit should be evaluated for polycythemia.

Bone age determinations should be done every 6 months to assess the rate of bone maturation in children and adolescents.

Tumor growth should be monitored by radiography.

Elderly men should be observed for increasing difficulty or frequency of urination, which may indicate enlargement of the prostate secondary to the drug.

## SUMMARY

Androgens, the male sex hormones, are responsible for the normal development and maintenance of male sex characteristics. Testosterone is most commonly used for hormonal replacement therapy in males, as well as being indicated for the treatment of breast carcinoma and anemia. Clients receiving androgen therapy require additional support for their risk of experiencing a disturbance in self-concept because of the drug's effects upon secondary sex character-

**TABLE 55-1**   Drug effects on human sexual behavior*

| Drug or drug category | Principal effect | Probable action |
| --- | --- | --- |
| ANTIDEPRESSANTS | | |
| amitriptyline (Elavil)<br>desipramine (Norpramin, Pertofrane)<br>imipramine (Tofranil) | Adverse | Central depression; peripheral blockade of nervous innervation of sex glands |
| lithium<br>nortriptyline (Aventyl)<br>pargyline (Eutonyl)<br>phenelzine sulfate (Nardil)<br>protriptyline (Vivactil)<br>tranylcypromine sulfate (Parnate) | Adverse | Impotence |
| ANTIHISTAMINES | Adverse | Blockade of parasympathetic nervous innervation of sex glands |
| chlorpheniramine (Chlor-Trimeton)<br>diphenhydramine (Benadryl)<br>promethazine (Phenergan) | | |
| ANTIHYPERTENSIVES | Adverse | Peripheral blockade of nervous innervation of sex glands |
| guanethidine (Ismelin)<br>mecamylamine (Inversine)<br>methyldopa (Aldomet) | Adverse | Depression, decreased libido, breast enlargement, gynecomastia, galactorrhea, amenorrhea, impotence, failure to ejaculate |
| pargyline (Eutonyl) | Adverse | Impotence, delayed ejaculation |
| *Rauwolfia* alkaloids | Adverse | Decreased libido, impotence, breast engorgement, pseudolactation, gynecomastia |
| reserpine (Serpasil)<br>spironolactone (Aldactone)<br>trimethaphan (Arfonad) | | |
| ANTISPASMODICS | Adverse | Ganglionic blockage of nervous innervation of sex glands |
| atropine (Lomotil)<br>glycopyrrolate (Robinul)<br>hexocyclium (Tral)<br>methantheline (Banthine) | Adverse | Impotence |
| BARBITURATES | Adverse | Central depression; suppression of motor activity; hypnosis |
| DIURETICS | | |
| chlorothiazide (Diuril)<br>hydrochlorothiazide (HydroDIURIL) | Adverse | General fatigue; rarely, impotence |
| OPIOIDS AND PSYCHOACTIVE DRUGS | Eventually adverse | Central depression; decreased libido and impaired potency |
| amphetamines | Questionable | Release of inhibitions; increased suggestibility; relaxation |
| anorectic agents | Transiently positive | Impotence, gynecomastic, menstrual disorders |
| cocaine<br>heroin<br>LSD<br>marijuana<br>methadone<br>morphine | Adverse | Suppression of secondary sex organ function in male, reduction of libido, impotence |
| NICOTINE | Adverse | Vasoconstriction may impair erection and lubrication |
| SEDATIVES AND TRANQUILIZERS | Adverse | Central sedation; blockade of autonomic innervation of sex glands; suppression of hypothalamic and pituitary function |
| haloperidol<br>chlordiazepoxide (Librium)<br>chlorpromazine (Thorazine)<br>chlorprothixene (Taractan) | | |
| diazepam (Valium) | Transiently positive | Tranquilization and relaxation |

Modified from Woods JS: Drug effects on human sexual behavior. In Woods NF. (1984). Human sexuality in health and illness, ed 3, St Louis, Mosby–Year Book.

*Many effects are dosage-dependent and reversible on discontinuance of drug.

**TABLE 55-1**   Drug effects on human sexual behavior—cont'd

| Drug or drug category | Principal effect | Probable action |
|---|---|---|
| haloperidol (Haldol)<br>mesoridazine (Serentil)<br>phenoxybenzamine (Dibenzyline)<br>prochlorperazine (Compazine)<br>thioridazine (Mellaril) | Generally adverse | Impotence, gynecomastia, breast engorgement, lactation, menstrual irregularities |
| ETHYL ALCOHOL | Progressively adverse | Central depression; suppression of motor activity; diuresis; decreased testosterone |
| STEROID HORMONES AND DERIVATIVES | Adverse | Antiandrogenic effects on sexual function; loss of libido; decreased potency |
| cortisone<br>cyproterone acetate<br>methandrostenolone (Dianabol) | Adverse | Menstrual disorders, decreased libido caused by antiandrogenic effect |
| methyltestosterone<br>nandrolone phenpropionate (Durabolin) | Mixed effects | Phallic enlargement, prolonged penile erections, testicular atrophy, impotence, decreased ejaculatory volume, oligospermia; menstrual disorders, hirsutism, clitoral enlargement, male pattern baldness |
| MISCELLANEOUS | | |
| progesterone or estrogen | Adverse | Depression, decreased libido, breast tenderness, testicular atrophy |
| amyl nitrite | Questionable | Vasodilation of genitourinary tract; smooth muscle relaxation |
| cantharis (Spanish fly) | Adverse | Irritation and inflammation of genitourinary tract, systemic poisoning |
| L-dopa and *p*-chlorophenylalanine (PCPA) | Questionable | Improved feeling of well-being |
| histamine $H_2$ antagonist (cimetidine) | Adverse | Impotence, gynecomastia, alopecia, or galactorrhea |
| vitamin E | Questionable | Supports fertility in laboratory animals |
| yohimbine | Questionable | Stimulation of lower spinal nerve centers |

the genital protruberance appears identical in both sexes. The embryo is characteristically female initially and does not differentiate until fetal androgens begin to masculinize tissues (seventh to twelfth weeks of pregnancy). Thus it is not surprising that the mature analogous organs function similarly.

In the male, sympathetic (adrenergic) impulses produce ejaculation by causing contraction of the prostate and seminal vesicles along with effects on the bulbocavernous and ischiocavernous muscles. Drugs that block adrenergic impulses may affect ejaculatory function through sympathetic blockade. Parasympathetic (cholinergic) stimulation controls penile erection. This response results from congestion of the vascular sinuses in the penile corpora caused by parasympathetic nerve action in the venous channels. Drugs that interfere with parasympathetic nerve transmitters (cholinergic nerves) can cause defects in erection. In addition, ganglionic blocking agents, which may block both sympathetic and parasympathetic nerve transmission, can cause complete impotence and impaired sexual functioning.

In the female, parasympathetic (cholinergic) impulses cause arterial dilation and venoconstriction, which produce clitoral erection and vasocongestion of the vulva, **transudation** (oozing of a fluid through pores) of lubricating secretions from the vaginal walls, and swelling of the **introitus** (vaginal opening). Continued stimulation of the clitoris and/or the Graefenberg spot, which is located on the anterior wall of the vagina, may then produce orgasm and, for some, a miniature facsimile of ejaculation from glands that surround the female urethra.

See Table 55-1 for drug effects on human sexual behavior.

## DRUGS THAT IMPAIR LIBIDO AND SEXUAL GRATIFICATION
### Antihypertensives

Certain drugs successfully used to treat high blood pressure produce vasodilation through blockade of the sympathetic nervous system. This interferes with the response to sympathetic nervous stimulation. Such adrenergic inhibition, however, occasionally results in **impotence,** inability of a man to achieve or maintain an erection, and decreased sexual function. Guanethidine (Ismelin) and reserpine (Serpasil), which act partly by depleting the postganglionic adrenergic nerve transmitter norepinephrine (originating from nerve endings), or by blocking release of this transmitter from the nerve terminal, may produce impotence by inactivating the nervous mechanisms responsible for sexual function. Experiments with guanethidine have shown that erectile potency, ability to ejaculate, and intensity of climax are all reduced significantly during use of this drug. Similar observations have been made with reserpine, which also has central nervous system effects that decrease libido and lead to male impotence. In women reserpine blocks ovulation, causes infertility and pseudopregnancy, and induces lactation. These actions can affect sexual function and behavior profoundly.

Anticholinergic drugs and especially those with ganglionic blocking activity may also produce impotence and other untoward effects on sexual function. Guanethidine falls into this category. Other agents include mecamylamine (Inversine) and trimethaphan (Arfonad), which are used as antihypertensive agents. Since these drugs may both block sympathetic and parasympathetic innervation of the sex organs, both erectile capability and ejaculatory function may be affected during their use.

Another drug used in treating hypertension is spironolactone (Aldactone), a diuretic. This drug displaces aldosterone in the kidneys, thus interfering with the normal resorption of sodium ions. Resultant sexual dysfunction in both men and women has been reported. Amenorrhea was observed in six women who took spironolactone for 9 months, with normal menses returning within 2 months after drug therapy was discontinued. Gynecomastia and impotence in men have also been observed during spironolactone therapy.

### Antihistamines

Histamine is a naturally occurring substance that possesses various physiologic properties, including smooth muscle stimulation, mediation of the inflammatory response, and cardiovascular effects. Antihistaminic drugs act as competitive inhibitors of histamine at physiologic receptor sites and prevent its action. Well-known examples of such drugs include diphenhydramine (Benadryl), promethazine (Phenergan), and chlorpheniramine (Chlor-Trimeton). These drugs are consumed by millions as antiemetics, as mild sedatives, and for the control of allergy symptoms. Most antihistamines display anticholinergic effects such as dryness of the mouth, urinary retention, and constipation. Continuous use of these drugs may interfere with sexual activity. This effect is presumably mediated by the blockade of parasympathetic nerve impulses to the sex glands and organs.

### Antispasmodics

Most antispasmodic drugs are quaternary ammonium compounds. Their primary effect is relaxation of the smooth muscle of the gastrointestinal tract, bilary tract, ureter, and uterus. Because these drugs may act as ganglionic blocking agents, postural hypotension and impotence can result from their use. Drugs in this category include glycopyrrolate (Robinul) and hexocyclium (Tral).

### Sedatives and Tranquilizers

Many of the wide variety of sedatives and tranquilizers available in recent years affect sexual interest and capability both directly and indirectly. Two of the most frequently used classes of tranquilizers are the phenothiazines and the benzodiazepine compounds. Several minor categories of sedative drugs also affect sexual function.

Phenothiazines comprise one of the most widely used classes of drugs in medical practice today. More than 30 phenothiazines with a broad spectrum of action are currently available. Known as the major tranquilizers, phenothiazines are used primarily in the treatment of psychosis, but they are also used as antiemetics and analgesics. Examples are chlorpromazine (Thorazine), prochlorperazine (Compazine), thioridazine (Mellaril), and mesoridazine (Serentil). Although the precise workings of their sedative effect are not fully understood, these drugs are thought to modify sensory input into the reticular formation of the brainstem. The sedative effect may partly account for decreased sexual interest of persons undergoing phenothiazine therapy.

In addition to their central nervous system effects, the peripheral effects of these drugs may contribute to inhibition of sexual function. Phenothiazines decrease skeletal muscle tone and block cholinergic synapses at both muscarinic and nicotinic receptors. Various adrenergic impulses may be inhibited as well. Impotence, decreased libido, ejaculation disorders, and prolonged amenorrhea have been reported in individuals taking phenothiazines. Failure to ejaculate has been reported in men treated with thioridazine, although erection and orgasm do not appear to be affected. Ejaculation problems have also been reported with the use of chlorprothixene (Taractan) and mesoridazine (Serentil).

Chlorpromazine may also influence sexual function by affecting the endocrine glands, possibly through acting on the hypothalamus. In animal studies phenothiazine derivatives have suppressed hypothalamic and pituitary function, resulting in decreased hormone secretion and affecting sex organ function in both males and females. Chlorpromazine has been shown to be spermicidal in dogs and to reduce the copulation rate of male rats. Regressive and atrophic changes in the testes of experimental animals receiving phenothiazines have also been reported. Chlorpromazine can reduce urinary levels of gonadotropins, as well as estrogens and progestins. Like reserpine, chlorpromazine blocks ovulation, suppressed estrus in animals, induces lactation, and maintains a decidual reaction. The release of pituitary gonadotropins by relatively small doses of chlorpromazine delays ovulation and menstruation in female clients.

Benzodiazepine compounds are the second most widely used class of tranquilizing drugs. The best known is diazepam (Valium). As a mild tranquilizer, this drug is used for treating anxiety and alcholism and as a skeletal muscle relaxant. Sexual impairment has been associated with diazepam's effects on both cholinergic and adrenergic facets of the autonomic nervous system. The sedative and relaxing effects of this drug may account for the decreased interest in sexual activity also noted. Alternatively, the judicious use of these tranquilizers has been considered of value in the treatment of sexual impotence and other problems involving sexual performance when excessive anxiety was a factor in decreased sexual performance.

Several other types of drugs used in the treatment of psychologic problems depress sexual activity in human beings. Haloperidol, an antipsychotic, can adversely affect the libido in men. Failure to ejaculate without concomitant alteration of erection or orgasm has been reported in individuals treated with phenoxybenzamine (Dibenzyline), an alpha adrenergic blocking agent once used to supplement psychiatric therapy. Its potent adrenergic blocking effects have been advanced to account for the adverse reactions on sexual function. Lithium carbonate has also been associated with disturbed sexual function in clients treated for mania with this drug.

## Antidepressants

Contemporary life, often fast paced and frustrating, is increasingly associated with psychologic depression. Diminished sexual interest, drive, and activity are characteristic of such depression. (See also Chapter 17.) The drugs used to treat this depression compound the negative effects on sexual function.

While antidepressants generally elevate mood and thus increase sexuality, they can cause impotence and influence sexual behavior adversely. Two groups of drugs commonly used as antidepressants are the tricyclic compounds and the monoamine oxidase (MAO) inhibitors. Adverse reactions on sexuality of the first group may be related to peripheral anticholinergic effects, such as those produced by some antihypertensives. Examples of these drugs include imipramine (Tofranil) and amitriptyline (Elavil). Although MAO inhibitors may be used as antihypertensives and antidepressants, the impotence that can result may be caused by their tendency to block peripheral ganglionic nerve transmission.

## Ethyl Alcohol

Ethyl alcohol is considered for its effects on human sexual function and behavior as a drug of individual and unique notoriety. Revered for centuries as a sexual stimulant and cure of all ills, alcohol is in fact a depressant and is recognized today to have far greater social than therapeutic value. Although a sedative, alcohol in moderate amounts may enhance sexual activity by relieving anxieties and loosening the inhibitions that often shroud sexual behavior. Beyond a certain limit, however, neither desire nor potency will overcome the depressed physical capability that occurs under its influence.

Studies on the pharmacologic action of alcohol show that the central nervous system is more affected by alcohol than any other system of the body. Electrophysiologic studies suggest that alcohol first depresses the part of the brain responsible for integrating the various activities of the nervous system. The result is that various processes related to thought and motor activities become disrupted. The first mental processes affected are related to sobriety and self-restraint, producing a less inhibited and less restrained approach to sexual behavior and other activities normally inhibited by previous training or experience. With continued consumption of alcohol, however, the brain becomes narcotized, reflexes become slowed, blood vessels are dilated, and the capacity for sexual function is diminished. In addition, alcohol produces a severe diuretic effect, which may also interfere with sexual function.

Alcohol overindulgence by males is a frequent cause of forcible sexual assault on females. One study assessed various types of sexual offenders for frequency of offense; drunk persons constituted 12% to 16% of reported incidents. Alcohol consumption had not reached the point of physical incapacitation but rather a stage of confusion, belligerence, and misinterpretation, resulting in violent antisocial acts. Thus, although it first lowers inhibitions, alcohol eventually decreases physical capability and enjoyment of sexual activities.

Typically, the male alcoholic experiences delayed ejaculation during intoxication and impotence after years of chronic alcoholism. Vascular changes, peripheral neuropathy, and lowered testosterone levels because of liver damages are thought to cause the impotence. Body image changes such as testicular atrophy and gynecomastia compound the problem. However, occasionally favorable effects have been reported after sex therapy, despite alcohol-induced organ damage. These effects may result from resolution of negative, sexually repressive feelings. Much remains to be learned about the effects of alcohol on sexuality.

Of the 10 million people who have a drinking problem, 2 million are women, many of them elderly. The effects on women are also mixed. But most women alcoholics lose interest in sex generally, and alcoholism adversely affects their sexual interactions.

## Barbiturates

Barbiturates, such as amobarbital (Amytal), pentobarbital (Nembutal), secobarbital (Seconal), and thiopental (Pentothal), are sedative-hypnotic drugs that have general depressant effects on all nervous tissues. As with alcohol, these drugs in prescribed dosage produce relaxation, hypnosis, and sleep with depression of various body functions, including sexual performance and ability. With prolonged use or overdose barbiturates can cause respiratory failure and death. Withdrawal after long-term heavy consumption of barbiturates may result in convulsions. There is no rationale for their use in altering sexual behavior in human beings.

## Steroid Hormones and Derivatives

Sex hormones act on the central nervous system and other body organs to influence sexual and aggressive behavior, as well as mood and emotional outlook. Thus variations in female hormones may produce the anxiety, irritability, and depression associated with **premenstrual syndrome (PMS),** whereas male hormones are associated with aggression and increased sexual interest. Evidence indicates that sexual drives may be influenced by sex hormone treatment.

Synthetic sex hormone preparations have also been shown to influence sexual behavior. The antiandrogen steroid cyproterone acetate decreases libido and potency and is used successfully in the treatment of male **hypersexuality** and investigatively in female polycystic ovary syndrome. Synthetic estrogens and progesterones are widely accepted as oral contraceptive agents. Another class of synthetic sex hormones are the anabolic steroids, derived from the male sex hormone testosterone. These drugs, which include methandrostenolne (Dianabol) and nandrolone phenpropionate (Durabolin), are used to promote nitrogen retention and weight gain in elderly or undernourished clients. The substances have also been the source of controversy over their use and misuse by athletes and other postpubertal persons to promote muscle growth and endurance. When used by normally developed, well-nourished individuals, the effects of these drugs on strength and development are questionable. Considerable evidence shows that sexual activity may be adversely affected because of the effects these drugs have on gonadal function.

## Methadone

Methadone, a drug widely used in treating the symptoms of heroin withdrawal and in narcotics maintenance programs, produces both serious fertility problems and impaired sexual performance in male users. Fertility changes are associated with greatly reduced size and secretory activity of the secondary sex organs, resulting in extremely low ejaculate volume and low sperm motility. Whether this condition is reversible after the drug is withdrawn is not known; animal studies suggest that normal secondary sex organ function returns after discontinuing methadone treatment.

## DRUGS THAT ENHANCE LIBIDO AND SEXUAL GRATIFICATION

Substances to increase sexual potency or drive have been sought throughout history. Inscriptions in the ruins of an-

cient cultures have described the preparation of "erotic potions," and an endless number of "aphrodisiacs" have been described since then. In contemporary society many drugs and chemicals that modify mood and behavior are claimed to have aphrodisiac properties.

In reality, no known drugs specifically increase libido or sexual performance, and chemicals taken for this purpose without medical advice and especially in combination with other drugs pose the danger of drug interaction or overdose. However, many pharmacologically active agents temporarily modify both physiologic responsiveness and subjective perception to enhance the enjoyment, if not the fulfillment, of the sex act. Some of these agents are considered in this section.

### cantharis

Cantharis (cantharidin, Spanish fly), a legendary sexual stimulant, is a powerful irritant and potent systemic poison. It is not an effective sexual stimulant. A powder made from dried beetles *(Cantharis vesicatoria)* found in southern Europe, cantharis can produce severe illness characterized by vomiting, diarrhea, abdominal pain, and shock. When taken internally, it causes irritation and inflammation of the genitourinary tract and dilation of the blood vessels of the penis and clitoris, sometimes producing prolonged erections (priapism) or engorgement, usually without increased sexual desire. Deaths have been reported from the promiscuous use of cantharis as an aphrodisiac. It is currently recognized that cantharis is not an effective sexual stimulant, and it is seldom used in modern medical practice.

### yohimbine

Another natural substance with purported aphrodisiac properties is yohimbine, an alkaloid derived from the west African tree *Corynanthe yohimbe.* Yohimbine produces a competitive alpha adrenergic block of limited duration and antidiuresis, probably from the release of antidiuretic hormone. Although yohimbine stimulates the lower spinal nerve centers controlling erection, there is no convincing evidence that it acts as a sexual stimulant. It currently has no therapeutic uses.

### opioids and psychoactive agents

The use of drugs such as morphine, heroin, cocaine, marijuana, LSD, and amphetamines as aphrodisiacs has become widespread in contemporary society. These agents can, under certain circumstances, enhance the enjoyment of the sexual experience for some. More commonly, however, sexual behavior decreases. Responsiveness varies because these agents have no particular properties that specifically increase sexual potency, but rather they tend to affect the user according to expectations. Thus the user's state of mind and the amount consumed contribute considerably to the effect achieved. Like alcohol, these drugs act on the central nervous system to weaken inhibitions, which are often the cause of problems involving sexual behavior.

Taken in excess or too often, however, these drugs have the opposite effect and inhibit sexual drive and function. Because of these variations, researchers are skeptical of their value.

Recent studies have shown that both morphine and heroin in sufficient doses produce markedly reduced sexual activity in men and women. In men nonemissive erections and impotence can result. Assessment of impotence among narcotics users is complicated by the multiplicity of drugs taken concurrently, the unknown composition and actual dosage strength of street drugs, and the addictive potential of narcotics.

Marijuana (cannabis), an extract of the *Cannabis sativa* plant, is considered by many to be a sexual stimulant. However, like alcohol, its effect results indirectly from relaxation and release of inhibitions surrounding sexual activity. The active ingredient in marijuana is tetrahydrocannabinol. The pharmacologic effects resulting from smoking marijuana depend on the expectations and personality of the user, the dose, and the prevailing circumstances. Usually the effects of marijuana are time distortion and enhanced suggestibility, producing the illusion that sexual climax is somewhat prolonged. Thus the expectation that marijuana is an aphrodisiac may enhance enjoyment of the sex act. Studies on the properties of marijuana for a specific effect on sexual behavior, however, have shown that it has no such properties. On the contrary, there is evidence that marijuana smokers have a higher incidence of decreased libido and impaired potency than nonusers. In addition, chronic intensive use of marijuana depresses plasma testosterone levels in healthy males and produces gynecomastia in some users. Chromosomal breaks have also occurred.

Lysergic acid diethylamide (LSD) is another drug that, although considered an aphrodisiac by some, has potentially untoward effects on sexual function and behavior. Like marijuana, any alteration of sexual performance produced by LSD is principally subjective. This drug acts almost entirely on the central nervous system. Little response, if any, has been noted in other organ systems that can be attributed to direct effect of LSD, and no biochemical or pharmacologic evidence supports the contention that LSD or similar drugs contain any sex-stimulating properties. On the other hand, the repeated use of LSD may produce serious psychologic problems, which could overall adversely affect sexual interest or activity. Users of LSD during pregnancy may have a higher rate of malformed babies or stillbirths than nonusers.

Amphetamines, such as Dexedrine, have also been used to stimulate sexual function. These drugs have a powerful central stimulant action, in addition to peripheral alpha and beta sympathomimetic effects. The main results of an oral dose of 10 to 30 mg are wakefulness and alertness, mood elevation, increased motor and speech activity, and often elation and euphoria. Physical performance is usually improved, and fatigue can be prevented or reversed. The effects of amphetamines on sexual performance, however, are in-

consistent. At moderate dosage levels there is seldom any effect on sexual behavior, aside from the accompanying mood elevation or reversal of fatigue. Doses in the range of 20 to 50 mg can alter sensations to enhance the orgasmic feeling. However, higher doses, such as 1 g taken intravenously, produce loss of interest and withdrawal from sexual activity.

Amphetamines, along with other psychoactive agents, do little to promote the enjoyment of sexual activity and over time may produce adverse psychologic and physical effects that reduce sexual interest and capability.

## Drugs That Stimulate Sexual Behavior

Various clinically used or experimental drugs enhance sexual interest or potency as a side effect in both humans and laboratory animals.

### L-dopa

Levodihydroxyphenylalanine (L-dopa) is a natural intermediate in the biosynthesis of catecholamines in the brain and peripheral adrenergic nerve terminals. In the biologic sequence of events it is converted to dopamine, which in turn serves as a substrate of the neurotransmitter norepinephrine. L-dopa is used successfully in the treatment of Parkinson's syndrome, a disease characterized by dopamine deficiency. When L-dopa is administered to an individual with this syndrome, the symptoms are ameliorated, presumably because the drug is converted to dopamine, thereby counteracting the deficiency. Recently clients being treated with L-dopa, especially elderly men, have been observed to have a sexual rejuvenation. This effect has led to the belief that L-dopa stimulates sexual powers. Consequently, studies with younger men complaining of decreased erectile ability have shown that L-dopa increases libido and incidence of penile erections. Overall, however, these effects have been short-lived and do not reflect continued satisfactory sexual function and potency. Thus L-dopa is not a true aphrodisiac, but the increased sexual activity experienced by parkinsonian clients treated with L-dopa reflects improved well-being and partial recovery of normal sexual functions impaired by Parkinson's disease.

### p-chlorophenylalanine (PCPA)

PCPA, a drug chemically related to L-dopa, has been claimed to have potent aphrodisiac properties in laboratory animals. Considerable controversy characterizes the potential sex-stimulating powers of this drug, which is used experimentally as a selective blocker of serotonin biosynthesis in the brain. In one report PCPA, when used with the monoamine oxidase inhibitor phenelzine, significantly increased male sexual activity. The sexual improvement paralleled the amelioration of headaches and mood. Since PCPA has not yet come into clinical use, its direct effects on human libido or sexual ability are unknown.

## amyl nitrite

Amyl nitrite, a drug used in the past to treat angina pectoris, is alleged to enhance sexual activity in humans. As a vasodilator and smooth muscle stimulant, amyl nitrite has been reported to intensify the orgasmic experience for men if inhaled at the moment of orgasm. This effect is probably the result of relaxation of smooth muscles and consequent vasodilation of the genitourinary tract. No effects of amyl nitrite on libido have been reported, but loss of erection or delayed ejaculation may result. Women generally experience negative effects on orgasm when taking this drug.

## vitamin E

Much has been said about the positive effects of vitamin E (alpha-tocopherol) on sexual performance and ability in human beings. Unfortunately, little scientific rationale substantiates such claims. The primary reasons for attributing a positive role in sexual performance to vitamin E come from experiments on vitamin E deficiency in laboratory animals. In such experiments the principal manifestation of this deficiency is infertility, although the reasons for this condition differ in males and females. In female rats there is no loss in ability to produce apparently healthy ova or any defect in the placenta or uterus. However, fetal death occurs shortly after the first week of embryonic life, and fetuses are reabsorbed. This situation can be prevented if vitamin E is administered any time up to the fifth or sixth day of embryonic life. In the male rat the earliest observable effect of vitamin E deficiency is immobility of spermatozoa, with subsequent degeneration of the germinal epithelium. However, secondary sex organs are not altered and sexual vigor is not diminished, although vigor may decrease if the deficiency continues. Because of experimental results such as these, vitamin E has been conjectured to restore potency, or preserve fertility, sexual interest, and endurance in humans. No evidence supports these contentions, but since sexual performance is often influenced by mental attitude, a person who believes vitamin E may improve sexual prowess may actually find improvement. The only established therapeutic use for vitamin E is for the prevention or treatment of vitamin E deficiency, a condition that is rare in humans.

## THE NURSE'S ROLE IN HUMAN SEXUALITY

An appreciation of the serious effects of sexual dysfunction on people's lives can produce a special sensitivity to clients' concerns. People often find it easier to confide in and discuss such important personal information with a nurse, male or female, than with anyone else.

High-quality professional nursing therefore should be directed toward achieving the following goals:
- Gaining understanding and acceptance of feelings about one's own sexuality. It takes time and effort to be comfortable enough to be therapeutic with others who are having sexual problems.
- Being open to clients' discussions about sexual concerns.
- Allowing clients to hold any belief or sexual practice they choose that is not overtly harmful.
- Recognizing that it is probably impossible to be truly comfortable with all clients or all related topics. It may be necessary to refer some clients with questions to more adequately prepared personnel. This might be a clinical nurse specialist or a social worker with expertise in dealing with sexual issues.
- Keeping current with the constantly changing data about drugs with potential for causing sexual dysfunction. This becomes more complex with the discovery, for example, that certain drugs in combination elicit unusual sexual responses. Currently, some that are suspect include antihypertensives, antidepressants, antihistamines, antispasmodics, sedatives and tranquilizers, ethyl alcohol, barbiturates, steroid hormones and derivatives, narcotics and psychoactive drugs, and certain natural substances.
- Being able to identify and interpret client cues about problems dealing with sexuality, such as unexplained noncompliance with medication instructions, certain subjective data from the nursing history, avoidance of the topic, or other subtle hints.
- Discussing clients' medication with them (casual use of drugs and over-the-counter and prescribed drugs), including information about potential adverse reactions.
- Consulting with the prescriber when adverse reactions do appear and suggesting that alternate forms or dosages of drug therapy be sought, if feasible. Such changes may be the route to enhanced compliance.
- Listening with sensitivity to expressed feelings of frustration, anger, anxiety, or fear that may attend body image changes or perceptions of aging and waning sexual attractiveness, which may actually result from drug effects.

## SUMMARY

Because drug therapy has many dimensions that affect sexuality and sexual behavior, nurses must be sensitive in their assessment of clients' needs as sexual beings and be able to intervene to promote health in this area.

## BIBLIOGRAPHY

Caruso D. (1987). Helping your patients enjoy sex again, RN 50(5):69.

Chapman J et al. (1987). A model for sexual assessment and intervention, Health Care Women Int 8(1):87.

Durie B. (1987). Drugs and sexual function, Nurs Times 83(32):34.

Melman A. (1986). Male sexual dysfunction. I. Office evaluation that identifies the problem's source, Consultant 26(12):72.

Melman A. (1986). Male sexual dysfunction. II. Office management that leads to restored function, Consultant 27(1):56.

Osis M. (1986). Sexuality: an interactional perspective . . . drugs and healthy aging, Gerontion 1(1):6.

Steele D. (1989). Drugs causing sexual dysfunction and their alternatives: a reference tool, Urol Nurs 9(6):10.

Sullivan EJ. (1988). Associations between chemical dependency and sexual problems in nurses, J Interpers Violence 3(3):326.

Webb C et al. (1987). Nurses' knowledge and attitudes about sexuality in health care: a review of the literature, Nurse Educ Today 7(2):75.

Woods NF. (1984). Human sexuality in health and illness, ed 3, St Louis: The CV Mosby Co.

# Drugs Used in Neoplastic Diseases

# 56 Antineoplastic Chemotherapy

## CHAPTER OBJECTIVES

*After studying this chapter, you should be able to meet the following objectives and define the key terms.*

1. Identify four major developmental stages of normal and malignant cells.

2. List common antineoplastic drugs and their effects on the cell cycle.

3. Describe the major principles of chemotherapy.

4. Describe the common toxicities of antineoplastic chemotherapy.

5. Discuss age-related considerations for cancer in the elderly and in the child.

6. Describe nursing management common to all antineoplastic drug therapy.

## KEY TERMS

## INTRODUCTION

**Cancer** is a generic term that includes over 300 defined disease states. An estimated 25% of Americans face a cancer diagnosis during their lifetimes. Many people fear cancer, since it is difficult to accept that a small lump or mole that has the potential for rapid growth may lead to serious illness or death. Therefore education and early treatment are imperative to win the battle against cancer, which is second to cardiovascular disease as a cause of death.

Statistically, the chances of developing cancer and dying from cancer are greater now than ever before. However, more persons are cured of cancer today than ever before. In 1971 approximately 535,000 new cases of cancer were detected. In 1989, the number of new cases of cancer was estimated to be 1,010,000 persons. This is an increase of nearly 90% in the reported incidence of cancer. In 1971, 337,398 Americans died from cancer, whereas 1989 cancer-related deaths were estimated at 502,000 (Silverberg, 1989). While the figures are still staggering, the fact that the rise in cancer deaths has not paralleled the rise in cancer incidence indicates that we have made some progress in the war against cancer.

This chapter discusses the principles of antineoplastic chemotherapy and the use of chemotherapeutic drugs in the treatment of cancer. However, to better understand the mechanisms and sites of action of the cancer chemotherapeutic agents, it is important to understand the kinetics of both normal cells and cancer cells.

## CELL KINETICS

The reproductive cycles of normal and cancer cells are essentially the same (see Figure 56-1). In the pre-synthesis phase ($G_1$), RNA and protein synthesis may occur. Also during this phase the decision for cell replication or cell differentiation is determined. The cell progresses to the synthesis phase (S), which is the replication phase; that is,

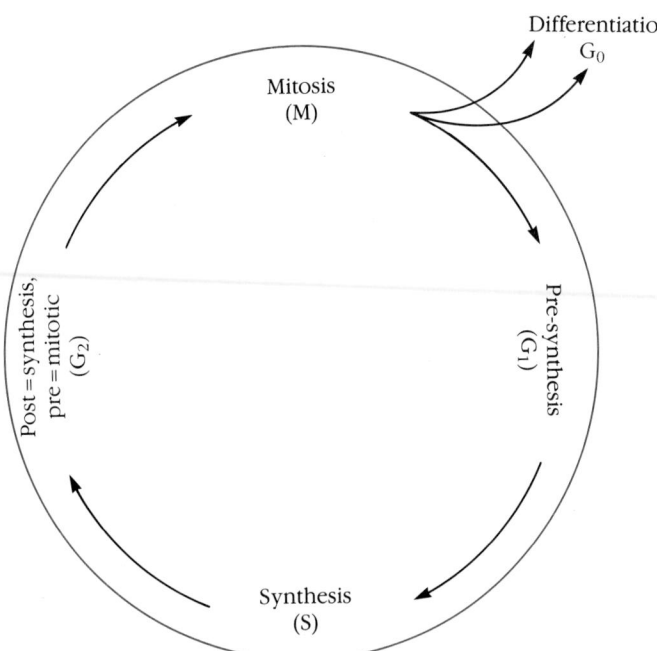

**FIGURE 56-1** Phases of a cell cycle.

DNA doubles in preparation for cell division. During the post-synthesis or pre-mitotic phase (G₂), DNA synthesis ceases but RNA and protein synthesis continues in order to prepare the cell for **mitosis** (M), or spindle formation. During the M-phase, cells divide into two completely new cells that may leave the cell cycle to: (1) develop into differentiated cells that perform a specialized function (such as neuron, epithelium, etc.); these cells can no longer undergo cell division; (2) become either temporarily or permanently non-proliferative (G₀ phase). Cells in the G₀ (or resting) phase may remain in this phase, or may reenter the cell cycle in time, or may mature and die.

The anticancer agents have different sites of action on the dividing cell cycle. Agents that are most effective in one specific phase are referred to as cell cycle-specific agents. For example, methotrexate is more active in the S-phase of the cell cycle, so it is considered an S-phase cell cycle-specific agent. Antineoplastic agents that are active against both proliferating and resting cells are called cell cycle-nonspecific agents. An example of this group is the alkylating agents (see Table 57-1 p. 856). Antineoplastic classifications are an important consideration in selecting the appropriate drug(s) for the specific cancerous state. Methotrexate, an agent active predominantly in the S-phase of the cell cycle, would be much less effective in treating large tumor masses, which generally have slowly dividing cancer cells.

Normal cells grow and divide in an orderly fashion. The body process of cell adhesion inhibits the movement of the newly formed cells, and the body's homeostatic mechanisms control the entire cell growth process. Cancer cells may evolve from a hereditary or genetic predisposition plus contact with certain environmental conditions. Generally such neoplastic cells lack the cellular differentiation of the tissues in which they originate and therefore are unable to function like the normal cells around them. Cancer growth is enhanced by an increased rate of cell proliferation that lacks the normal body control system on cellular growth patterns. The cancer cells, because of the genetic differences, lack the cell adhesive property of normal cells, which may lead to **metastasis,** or spread of the cancer.

The growth of a cancer is usually rapid in the early stages; but as the tumor enlarges in size, it nearly outgrows its blood and nutrient supply, and the growth rate pattern decreases or reaches the plateau phase for the tumor. This is referred to as **Gompertzian growth** kinetics (see box on p. 848). A cell burden of 10⁹ is usually the smallest tumor burden (quantitative size) that is physically detectable (palpated). At this point the client has approximately 1 billion cancer cells, which is equal to a tumor about the size of a small grape and weighing 1 g. This is the point at which clinical symptoms usually first appear.

The Papanicolaou, or **PAP, smear** is a cytologic test capable of detecting carcinoma of the cervix and endometrium in the subclinical stages (10² to 10⁶ cells). Early detection and treatment of small cancer lesions that are not detectable by visual examination have dramatically reduced the mortality of cancer of the cervix in the United States.

Animal studies have shown that chemotherapeutic drugs given in adequate doses for the host will kill a constant fraction of the cancer cells. For example, a drug or drug combination capable of killing 99.9% of the cells would only reduce a $10^{10}$ cell burden to $10^{7}$ cancer cells. Each course of chemotherapy may reduce cancer cells to eventual levels that may be controlled by the client's immune system (see Figure 56-2). This reduction may produce a remission; but if further therapies are not instituted or the immune system is inadequate, the remaining cells may grow into another detectable tumor.

## PRINCIPLES OF CHEMOTHERAPY

To obtain the maximal therapeutic effects with an antineoplastic agent or with combination cancer chemotherapies, the following principles should be considered:

1. Cancer chemotherapy is most effective against small tumors because they usually have an efficient blood supply and therefore drug delivery is increased. Also,

small tumors generally have a higher percentage of proliferating cells so that a higher cell-kill factor is possible.

2. The removal of large, localized tumors by surgery reduces the tumor cell burden and thus contributes to the success of the adjuvant chemotherapy. The major use of adjuvant chemotherapy is to help eradicate the **micrometastases** (some cancer cells may migrate via the bloodstream or lymphatic system and grow in organs, bone, or tissues, far from the primary site) of cancer after surgery or radiation.

3. In general, combination cancer chemotherapeutic agents have a higher cancer cell-kill than treatment with a single drug agent.

## COMBINATION CHEMOTHERAPY

In the 1960s combination chemotherapy was initiated for the treatment of acute lymphoblastic leukemia and Hodgkin's disease. When the complete response rates for single agents were compared with the response rates for combination drugs, the results were enlightening. The response rates for the **MOPP treatment** of advanced Hodgkin's disease are as follows:

|   | Drug | Complete Response Rates |
|---|------|-------------------------|
| **M** | mustine (Mustargen) | 20% |
| **O** | vincristine (Oncovin) | <10% |
| **P** | procarbazine | <10% |
| **P** | prednisone | <5% |
|   | MOPP combination | 80% |

The following considerations are used to select the drugs for combination chemotherapy:

1. Each drug when used alone should be active against the specific cancer.
2. Each drug should have a different site of action and act at a different point of the cell cycle (specificity).
3. Each drug should have a different organ toxicity or,

---

**CANCER CELL GROWTH (GOMPERTZIAN)**

Number of
cells present

| | | |
|------|--------------------|---|
| $10^{0}$ | 1 | |
| $10^{1}$ | 10 | |
| $10^{2}$ | 100 | |
| $10^{3}$ | 1000 | Subclinical disease (undetectable by physical examination) |
| $10^{4}$ | 10,000 | |
| $10^{5}$ | 100,000 | |
| $10^{6}$ | 1,000,000 | |
| $10^{7}$ | 10,000,000 | |
| $10^{8}$ | 100,000,000 | |
| $10^{9}$ | 1,000,000,000 | (1 g) Clinical symptoms appear |
| $10^{10}$ | 10,000,000,000 | Regional spread |
| $10^{11}$ | 100,000,000,000 | Metastases (regional-advanced) |
| $10^{12}$ | 1,000,000,000,000 | |
| | | Possible lethal number of cancer cells |
| $10^{13}$ | 10,000,000,000,000 | |

---

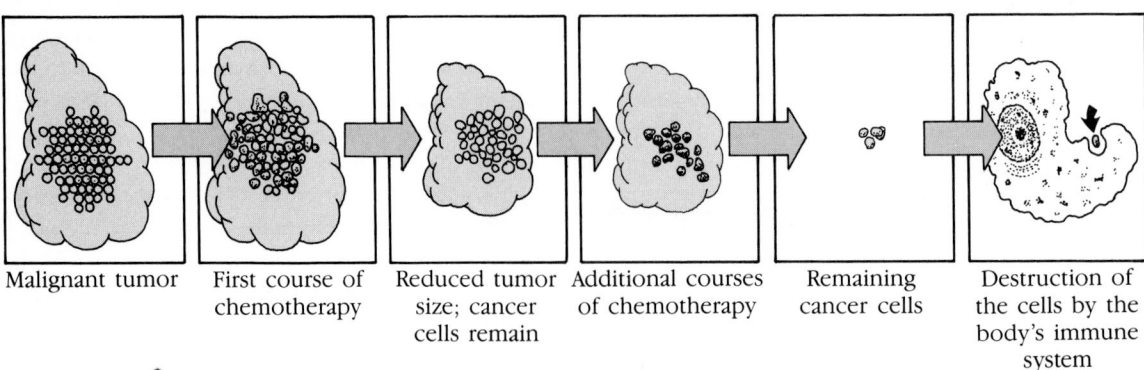

| Malignant tumor | First course of chemotherapy | Reduced tumor size; cancer cells remain | Additional courses of chemotherapy | Remaining cancer cells | Destruction of the cells by the body's immune system |

**FIGURE 56-2** Cancer cell response to chemotherapy. (From Beare PG and Myers JL. [1990]. Principles and practice of adult health nursing. St Louis, Mosby–Year Book, Inc.)

if the toxic effect is similar, it should occur at different times after drug administration.

When the preceding principles are applied to the MOPP drug therapy, the concept of combination chemotherapy can be understood. First, the previous list illustrates the effectiveness of each of the drugs against Hodgkin's disease. Second, the sites of major activity for each antineoplastic agent are believed to be different.

1. Mustine (Mustargen) is an alkylating agent that can interfere with the replication, transcription, and translation of DNA.
2. Vincristine (Oncovin) inhibits mitosis by interfering with the mitotic spindle.
3. Procarbazine is a weak monoamine oxidase (MAO) inhibitor, and its antineoplastic action is believed to occur during the S-phase. It inhibits the synthesis of DNA, RNA, and protein.
4. Prednisone has lympholytic properties and may produce an antifibrotic effect that would be useful in treating cancer metastases surrounded by fibrous materials. It also improves appetite and general feelings of well-being.

The third principle, that of different organ toxicity or toxicities that occur at different times, has also been substantiated for the MOPP combination. The dose-limiting toxicity of bone marrow suppression is a property of both mustine and procarbazine, but the nadir, or the lowest depression point for this effect, occurs approximately 10 days after drug administration for mustine and 21 days after for procarbazine. Thus additive myelosuppressive effects from this combination are essentially avoided. Vincristine does not have bone marrow suppression effects but does exhibit a dose-limiting neurotoxicity. Prednisone does not demonstrate bone marrow suppression or neurotoxicity. Therefore the third principle of combination drug therapy is fulfilled.

Frequently the oncologist uses combination therapy in antineoplastic treatment. For other commonly prescribed drug combinations, see Table 56-1.

## TOXIC EFFECTS

Most of the currently available antineoplastic agents appear to act on similar metabolic pathways in both normal and malignant cells. A major limitation of cancer drugs is their lack of tumor specificity. Drug toxicities or side effects may be divided into (1) common side effects, (2) adverse reactions, and (3) specific dose-limiting drug effects.

### Side Effects/Adverse Reactions

The most common side effects are **alopecia** (hair loss), nausea, vomiting, anorexia, diarrhea, and **stomatitis** (inflammation of the mouth). Cancer chemotherapy is most active or effective against dividing cells, but they are not capable of differentiating between cancer cells and normal dividing body cells. Therefore, the most rapidly dividing cells in the body are in the bone marrow, hair follicles, and gastrointestinal tract; thus these areas are generally the most affected by the toxicity of the anticancer drugs.

The most common adverse reactions that can lead to serious and even life-threatening infections are leukopenia, thrombocytopenia, and anemia.

Bone marrow suppression is the major dose-limiting property most frequently encountered in cancer chemotherapy. Nursing assessment and monitoring are critical to improving client care and are reviewed in the nursing management section.

Specific dose-limiting effects are adverse reactions that occur only with certain drugs. For example, drugs that can produce liver disease include methotrexate, mercaptopurine, lomustine, dacarbazine, doxorubicin, and carmustine. Cyclophosphamide is associated with hemorrhagic cystitis.

**TABLE 56-1**   Combination chemotherapeutic therapies

| Cancer | Therapy | Drugs included* |
|---|---|---|
| Breast | CMF | cyclophosphamide (Cytoxan, Procytox ♣) methotrexate 5-fluorouracil |
| | Cooper's regimen (CVFMP) | cyclophosphamide (Cytoxan, Procytox ♣) vincristine (Oncovin) 5-fluorouracil methotrexate prednisone |
| Hodgkin's disease | ABVD | doxorubicin (Adriamycin) bleomycin (Blenoxane) vinblastine (Velban, Velbe ♣) dacarbazine (DTIC) |
| | MOPP | mechlorethamine (Mustargen) vincristine (Oncovin) procarbazine (Matulane, Natulan ♣) prednisone |
| Acute lymphocytic leukemia (ALL) | VP | vincristine (Oncovin) prednisone |
| | OAP | vincristine (Oncovin) cytarabine (Ara C, Cytosar ♣) prednisone |
| Acute myelocytic leukemia (AML) | DA | daunorubicin (Cerubidine) cytarabine (Ara C, Cytosar ♣) |

*The underlined letters refer to the letters used in the combination therapy.

(Since dehydration increases the risk factor, adequate fluid intake is important when this agent is administered.) Methotrexate is associated with tubular necrosis, which can be prevented by prehydrating with normal saline and alkalinizing the urine to increase the elimination of the drug. Cisplatin is associated with tubular necrosis. Prehydration with 1 to 2 L of intravenous fluid and adequate fluids after drug administration help to reduce this adverse reaction. Nephrotoxicity, ototoxicity, and peripheral neuropathy have been reported with cisplatin.

Cardiac toxicity is reported with both doxorubicin and daunorubicin. **Cardiotoxicity** increases in clients who receive more than 550 mg/m$^2$ of body surface (total accumulated dosage given throughout therapy). Toxicity is also greater in geriatric clients and children under 2 years of age. Since this effect is cumulative if either drug is given, the amount of one drug already received by the client must be considered when planning therapy with the other drug.

Neurologic toxicity may range from tingling of the hands and feet and loss of deep tendon reflexes to ataxia, footdrop, confusion, and personality changes. Drugs reported to produce neurologic effects include vincristine, vinblastine, and methotrexate.

## AGE-RELATED CONSIDERATIONS
### Cancer in the Elderly

Cancer is one of the most serious diseases of the elderly population, and its incidence increases sharply with age. Fifty percent of all cases of cancer in the United States occur in the oldest one eighth of the population. Sixty percent of all cancer deaths occur among persons 65 years of age or older. Compared with younger cancer victims, the elderly have more concurrent illnesses, which may decrease their ability to withstand the effects of cancer or the antineoplastic therapies. In addition, decreased pulmonary and renal function and decreased bone marrow cellularity may interfere with treatment. Other factors to be considered when managing regimens for elderly persons are the possibility of reduced income and loss of loved ones and family support. Often compromises in treatment are made because of a person's advanced age; however, data suggest that a dosage reduction of chemotherapy based on age alone is not indicated in clients with solid tumors. Clinical trials are needed to further examine the relationship between responsiveness to chemotherapy and the person's age.

### Cancer in Children

Cancer in children is relatively uncommon. In the United States only about 6000 pediatric cases are diagnosed annually; children represent approximately 3% of all cancer patients. Carcinomas are rare in children, with nearly 50% of pediatric carcinomas being leukemias and lymphomas and 20% nonepithelial tumors of the CNS. Since tumors in children grow rapidly, childhood cancer is generally more responsive to chemotherapy than is cancer in an adult. Children also tend to tolerate the acute side effects of chemotherapy better than adults. Fifty percent of children with cancer are long-term survivors or are actually cured.

## ▷NURSING MANAGEMENT: ANTINEOPLASTIC CHEMOTHERAPY

*Assessment.* Nursing care for clients receiving drug therapy with antineoplastic agents is complex and inseparable from nursing care of the family. The client may be in any state of the disease process and may be facing impending death. In the assessment of the client and family, special considerations should be given to their coping abilities. The approach taken by the nurse should be sensitive and appropriate to the individual needs of the client and family. The client's degree of acceptance of chemotherapy should be assessed, and the nurse may need to help the client deal with mixed emotions about the chemotherapy. The client's and family's knowledge of the chemotherapy and their expectations should also be assessed. For specific nursing diagnoses related to the use of antineoplastic agents, see p. 851.

*Intervention.* The nurse has many responsibilities in dealing with the inevitable side effects of antineoplastic drugs. The potential for infection is increased because of bone marrow depression. Strict aseptic technique should be used during contact with the hospitalized client, who should also be protected from persons harboring harmful microorganisms. Frequent blood counts are necessary, and the nurse is often responsible for ensuring that they are taken and the results monitored for early signs of bone marrow depression. A client with an absolute granulocyte count below 100 cells/mm$^3$ is in danger of infection. Clients with granulocytopenia should maintain scrupulous oral hygiene and receive topical antibiotics for abrasions and scratches. Clients should be instructed to report to the physician any signs of infection, such as elevated temperature, sore throat, cough, mouth ulcerations, or burning on urination.

The risk for physical injury exists for clients with thrombocytopenia when platelet levels fall below 50,000 cells/mm$^3$. The nurse should avoid taking rectal temperatures and administering suppositories to such a client. Protective care for these clients might include the administration of stool softeners and the use of soft-bristled toothbrushes and electric razors. Soft tissue injury should be avoided, and the use of side rails on beds should be considered. Oral preparations of analgesics and other medications should be used to avoid the tissue damage resulting from intramuscular injections. Venipunctures should be done carefully by experienced personnel using strict sterile technique. The client should be instructed to report signs that indicate decreased platelets, such as petechiae, easy bruising, hemorrhage, bleeding from the gums, epistaxis, and blood in the stool and urine.

Selected nursing diagnoses relating to antineoplastic agents

| Nursing diagnosis | Outcome criteria | Nursing interventions |
|---|---|---|
| Potential alteration in oral mucous membrane related to stomatitis | Client will:<br>Demonstrate knowledge of oral hygiene<br>Maintain adequate nutrition and hydration<br>Maintain normal oral mucosa or have decreasing inflammation and/or ulceration | Instruct client to complete all dental work before beginning chemotherapy.<br>Teach optimal oral hygiene to prevent stomatitis.<br>Inspect oral cavity with a tongue blade and light twice daily and before each administration of the antineoplastic drug.<br>Implement appropriate mouth care if inflammation is present.<br>Encourage soothing foods: bland foods, cool liquids, cool foods (popsicles).<br>Instruct client to avoid spicy or acidic foods, extremes in food temperature, and abrasive foods or those difficult to chew.<br>Consult with physician if oral pain relief solution is needed.<br>Instruct client to report any ulcers in or around the mouth. |
| Potential for infection related to bone marrow depression | Client will:<br>Remain free of infection | Instruct client in reading a thermometer. Teach client to take temperature daily in the afternoon and report any elevation over 101° F.<br>Teach client to avoid being immunized with live virus vaccines and having contact with people with infections.<br>Instruct client to report any signs of infection, such as cough, sore throat, and burning on urination. |
| Potential for injury related to bone marrow depression | Client will:<br>Exhibit no signs of bleeding or excessive bruising | Avoid performing invasive procedures such as intramuscular injections and rectal temperatures.<br>Inspect intravenous sites, skin, and mucous membranes for signs of bleeding and bruising.<br>Instruct client to report easy bruising, bloody urine, and bleeding from nose or gums.<br>Test urine, emesis, and stool for occult blood.<br>Instruct client to exercise care in oral hygiene and in using safety razors and nail clippers.<br>Teach client to avoid constipation.<br>Encourage the use of caution to prevent falls. |
| Potential for alterations in bowel elimination, diarrhea, or constipation | Client will:<br>Maintain a normal bowel pattern<br>Have less constipation or diarrhea | Assess client's normal bowel pattern as baseline. If client is constipated, increase fluid intake and roughage in diet. If client has diarrhea, decrease roughage, increase fluids, and give small feedings. Consult with physician if stool softener, laxative, or antidiarrheal is needed.<br>Assess client for fluid and eletrolyte status.<br>Monitor bowel movements; record diarrhea as output.<br>Clean and dry the perianal area after each bowel movement. |
| Disturbance in self-concept related to alopecia | Client will:<br>Demonstrate progress toward coping with altered body image | Allow client to express apprehensions related to alopecia.<br>Encourage client to obtain cap or hairpiece before treatment begins.<br>Reassure client that hair growth should begin 8 weeks after therapy, but the new growth may be of a different color and texture. |

The kidneys are at risk of injury because of the effectiveness of the antineoplastic agents. Purines are released through cell destruction and converted to uric acid. The possibility of renal failure may result from the precipitation of uric acid crystals in the kidneys. The nurse should monitor the client's intake and output and serum uric acid and creatinine levels. Fluid intake should be 3 L daily. Cold, clear liquids, such as tea, unsweetened apple juice or other juices, and soft drinks or carbonated beverages such as ginger ale may be well tolerated. Freezing a favorite beverage into ice cubes or popsicles is also recommended.

The client's body image may be disturbed as a result of alopecia. This side effect is extremely distressing to women, even when they have been prepared for it, have cosmetic aids available, and are aware that it is reversible. Clients, even those who have only thinning of the hair, need assurance that the hair will begin to grow back in about 6 to 8 weeks, although it may be a different texture or color. Treatment with hormones may necessitate support for the client in the event of such effects as masculinization in a female client or feminization in a male client. These clients need assistance in coping with body image problems.

Some clients lose their appetite or complain of a bitter or metallic taste in the mouth. Their desire for red meat or other protein foods may be reduced, since these foods are the most commonly perceived as bitter tasting. Because protein is essential for good nutrition, alternative methods of serving proteins should be pursued. Cold cooked turkey, fish, eggs, and dairy products may be suitable substitutes. The biggest meal of the day should be planned for the time the client is usually hungriest, even if that time is early morning or midnight.

Nausea and vomiting that accompany the use of antineoplastic drugs can be relieved by (1) the administration of an antiemetic drug 1 to 3 hours before administration of the antineoplastic drugs or (2) the administration of the antineoplastic drug at night with an antiemetic and a hypnotic, so that the client sleeps all night and experiences fewer side effects. The antiemetic can then be continued afterward as necessary. Speeding the passage of food through the stomach is sometimes the solution to the problem of nausea, vomiting, and feelings of fullness. Some quantities of carbohydrates eaten at frequent intervals help achieve this effect. Liquids should not be drunk at mealtime but instead should be taken frequently throughout the day, up to 30 to 60 minutes before eating. Since hot foods have been reported to contribute to nausea, foods should be served at room temperature or cooler. Resting for 1 to 2 hours after eating is advised because activity can slow the digestive process.

Stomatitis, oral ulcerations, **xerostomia** (dryness of the mouth), and other oral changes are common side effects of the potent antineoplastic agents and may interfere with the client's nutrition. Good oral hygiene is important to maintain a proper nutritional intake and decrease the possibility of oral infections becoming systemic. The kind of mouthwash solutions used depends on the status of the client's lesions. Small, frequent servings of cold or room-temperature, bland, nonirritating foods are best tolerated by the client. This type of diet also decreases the diarrhea that is a common side effect of cancer chemotherapy.

Diarrhea, as a side effect of antineoplastic drugs, results from the death of the rapidly dividing cells of the bowel mucosa. The nurse should assess the client's bowel status, hydration, and electrolyte levels and record diarrhea as output. Fluid intake should be encouraged between meals, although intravenous therapy may be needed to replace lost fluids if the diarrhea is severe. Because of the client's frequent defecation, special attention should be given to skin care in the perianal area. Modification of the diet will prevent or decrease diarrhea. The client should be instructed to avoid foods that may cause gas and cramping, such as cabbage, beans, and highly spiced foods. Hot food should be avoided because it increases peristalsis that reduces nutrition absorption and may cause diarrhea. Reducing high-fiber foods in the diet, such as raw fruits and vegetables, bran, and whole grain cereals and bread, may help to control diarrhea. Foods that are high in potassium (to replace potassium loss through diarrhea) and that usually do not worsen diarrhea include bananas, apricot or pear nectar, red meat, saltwater fish, boiled or mashed potatoes, and orange juice.

Constipation may also be a problem with some clients. This may be an early symptom of CNS toxicity from the drug therapy or may result from eating mostly soft and liquid foods. High-fiber foods and prune juice have a laxative effect; 1 or 2 tablespoons of bran may be added to cooked cereals, casseroles, and homemade baked goods. The client should be encouraged to drink plenty of fluids, preferably 8 to 10 glasses daily. Hot lemon water in the morning usually stimulates bowel activity. The physician may order a laxative or stool softener as needed.

Pain commonly occurs in clients receiving antineoplastic drugs. The treatment of pain associated with cancer, especially chronic pain, requires a careful assessment of the client, consideration of appropriate nursing interventions, and skillful application of pharmacologic agents. Nonpharmacological techniques for pain relief may assist the client, such as relaxation therapy, guided imagery, aromatherapy, and diversional activities. Chronic pain may progress in a cycle to anxiety or depression, insomnia, fatigue, and increased pain. The factors in the box above modify the pain threshold. (Analgesics are discussed in Chapter 12.)

Nursing interventions may include physical activity to help prevent further deterioration resulting from inactivity. Deep breathing, turning the client, and skin care are some of the actions that reduce complications. In addition to physical and pharmacologic interventions, the client may need psychosocial, intellectual, and spiritual support. The holistic approach of carefully assessing the client's current needs and anticipating and planning for continued care is important in the care of many illnesses but is crucial for a client dying of a progressive illness. A variety of home-care programs are available. In addition, hospice programs have been developed through the United States to help provide the supportive and palliative services necessary for clients with life-threatening illness and their families. The American Cancer Society offers a variety of resources for the client with cancer and the family.

It must be remembered that anticancer drugs are potent drugs that are mutagenic and carcinogenic in animals and may be carcinogenic in humans. Nurses and pharmacists who prepare antineoplastic drugs should institute safety measures such as using proper technique; wearing gloves,

## FACTORS THAT AFFECT PAIN

| Lower Threshold | Raise Threshold |
| --- | --- |
| Anger | Symptom relief |
| Fear | Adequate relief from pain |
| Discomfort | Rest |
| Fatigue | Diversion |
| Anxiety | Elevation of mood |
| Sadness | Understanding |
| Loneliness | Sympathy |
| Depression | |
| Isolation | |

mask, and protective clothing; and whenever possible, preparing the solutions in a vertical laminar flow, biologically safe hood. All unused solutions, vials, needles, syringes, gloves, and materials used to clean up spills should be processed as hazardous materials; that is, the waste should be properly incinerated.

Although the development of cancer in professionals has not yet been directly related to handling of materials, a relationship between fetal loss and occupational exposure to antineoplastic drugs in nurses has been reported (Selevan 1988). Governmental regulatory agencies have indicated that it is unacceptable to allow exposure to potential carcinogens to continue until cancer actually occurs. Regulatory agencies should not wait for epidemiologic evidence before taking action to limit exposure to chemicals considered to be carcinogenic.

*Education.* Teaching the client about drug administration and drug effects may help to ease his or her anxiety. An assessment should reveal the expectations of the client and the family; they may need assistance in accepting a realistic view of the results of chemotherapy. Expectations of total cure may be unrealistic and should not be reinforced, whereas expectations of remission are often appropriate. One of the most important nursing interventions is emotional support to a client who is receiving physically and psychologically distressing therapy. The long periods of therapy, with frequent interruptions and sporadic progress, may compound the client's anxieties.

A client receiving cancer chemotherapy should be cautioned *not* to take any over-the-counter medication before checking with the oncologist. Many over-the-counter preparations contain aspirin, alcohol, or other substances that could interfere with the antineoplastic agents or increase the risk for toxicity.

See the box on p. 851 for specific areas of client instruction related to nursing diagnosis.

*Evaluation.* Evaluation of drug effects is an integral nursing function in antineoplastic chemotherapy. Often no dosage schedule for antineoplastic agents is universally therapeutic, and the dosage is changed according to the client's response and the toxic effects of the drug. Thus the nurse's evaluation of progress toward therapy goals and communication of both drug toxicity and client response are essential. In evaluating toxic effects, the nurse should be vigilant for early signs, since progression of toxic effects may have severe and irreversible consequences.

## SUMMARY

Cancer is a major health issue today. Although many people fear cancer, more people are cured of cancer then ever before. Education for cancer prevention, early detection, and early treatment are essential to combating this disease. For the nurse a knowledge of cell kinetics is essential to understand the mechanisms and sites of action of the cancer chemotherapeutic agents and to appropriately manage the nursing care of clients receiving such agents.

## BIBLIOGRAPHY

A critical look at the new chemotherapy recommendations. (1988). Healthfacts 13(11):1.

Almadrones L et al. (1990). Problems associated with the administration of intraperitoneal therapy using the Port-A-Cath system, Oncol Nurs Forum 17(1):75.

Benhamou S et al. (1988). Sister chromatid exchanges and chromosomal aberrations in lymphocytes of nurses handling cytostatic agents, Int J Cancer 41(3):350.

Betcher D. (1987). Local toxicities of chemotherapy, J Assoc Pediatr Oncol Nurses 4(1):56.

Birdsall C et al. (1988). How do you manage chemotherapy extravasation? Am J Nurs 88(2):228.

Blecke C. (1989). Home chemotherapy safety procedures, Oncol Nurs Forum 16(7):719.

Blesch KS. (1988). The normal physiological changes of aging and their impact on the response to cancer treatment, Semin Oncol Nurs 4(3):178.

Brixey MT. (1988). Chemotherapeutic agents: intravesical instillation, Urol Nurs 9(2):4.

Bulcavage LM et al. (1987). Safety issues in handling of chemotherapeutic agents, Emphasis Nurs 2(2):75.

Byram DA. (1989). Future expectations for critical care nurses: competence in immunotherapy, Crit Care Nurs Clin North Am 1(4):797.

Camp-Sorrell D. (1990). Intra-arterial chemotherapy infusion, Oncol Nurs Forum 17(1):103.

Caudell KA et al. (1988). Quantification of urinary mutagens in nurses during potential antineoplastic agent exposure: a pilot study with concurrent environmental and dietary control, Cancer Nurs 11(1):41.

Chang JC. (1988). Antipyretic effect of naproxen and corticosteroids on neoplastic fever, J Pain Symptom Manage 3(3):141.

Cohen DG. (1987). Emergencies in the pediatric oncology patient, J Assoc Pediatr Oncol Nurses 4(3/4):5.

Dillman JB. (1989). New antineoplastic therapies and inherent risks: monoclonal antibodies, biologic response modifiers and interleukin-2, J Intravenous Nurs 12(2):103.

Dodd MJ. (1988). Efficacy of proactive information on self-care in chemotherapy patients, Patient Educ Couns 11(3):215.

Dunne CF. (1989). Safe handling of antineoplastic agents: self-learning module, Cancer Nurs 12(2):120.

Eilers J et al. (1988). Development, testing, and application of the Oral Assessment Guide . . . high-dose radiation and/or chemotherapy, Oncol Nurs Forum 15(3):325.

Frick SB et al. (1988). Chemotherapy-associated nausea and vomiting in pediatric oncology patients, Cancer Nurs 11(2):118.

Gard D et al. (1988). Sensitizing effects of pretreatment measures on cancer chemotherapy nausea and vomiting, J Consult Clin Psych 56(1):80.

Gullo SM. (1988). Safe handling of antineoplastic drugs: translating the recommendations into practice, Oncol Nurs Forum 15(5):595.

Herfindal ET et al. (1988). Clinical pharmacy and therapeutics, ed 4, Baltimore: Williams & Wilkins.

**TABLE 57-2**   Side effects/adverse reactions of antineoplastic agents

| Drug(s) | Side effects* | Adverse reactions† |
|---|---|---|
| fluorouracil (Adrucil, 5-FU) | More frequent: Anorexia, alopecia, nausea, vomiting, rash, pruritus, lethargy | Diarrhea, chills, elevated temperature, sore throat, stomatitis, heartburn, abdominal distress, dark stools, increased frequency of bleeding and bruising |
| methotrexate (Mexate, Folex) | More frequent: Anorexia, nausea, vomiting<br>Less frequent: Alopecia, pale skin, rash, pruritus, acne, boils<br>High-dose therapy: Erythematous (red) skin | Black stools, diarrhea, abdominal distress, blood in vomitus, elevated temperature, chills, sores throat, stomatitis, increased frequency of bleeding and bruising<br>Intrathecal: Seizures, headaches, lethargy, visual disturbances, dizziness, disorientation |
| mechlorethamine (Mustargen) | More frequent: Nausea and vomiting<br>Less frequent: Anorexia, diarrhea, headache, alopecia, metallic taste in mouth, drowsiness | Elevated temperature, chills or sore throat, increased bleeding or bruising, painful rash, amenorrhea, abdominal distress, joint pain, edema of lower extremities<br>With high-dose therapy or regional perfusion: Tinnitus, hearing loss, and dizziness |
| leucovorin (folonic acid, Wellcovorin) | None reported | Allergic reaction: Rash, hives, pruritus, or difficulty in breathing |
| cyclophosphamide (Cytoxan) | More frequent: Dark discoloration of skin and fingernails, alopecia, anorexia, nausea, vomiting<br>Less frequent: Facial flushing, headache, rash, pruritus, increased perspiration, swollen lips | Elevated temperature, chills, sore throat, irregular menstrual cycle, increased bleeding<br>High dose or long-term therapy: Lethargy, disorientation, blood in urine, pain on urination, cough, shortness of breath, tachycardia, edema of lower extremities, painful joints, abdominal distress |
| cisplatin (Platinol) | More frequent: Nausea, vomiting<br>Less frequent: Anorexia | Tinnitus, impaired hearing, elevated temperature, chills, sore throat, increased bleeding episodes, anemia, abdominal distress, painful joints, edema of lower extremities, impairment of taste perception, blurred vision, peripheral neuropathy, facial edema, difficulty in breathing |
| doxorubicin (Adriamycin) | More frequent: Alopecia, nausea, vomiting<br>Less frequent: Diarrhea, dark discoloration of soles, palms, or nails, which is reported most often in blacks and children | Elevated temperature, chills, sore throat, stomatitis, inflammation of esophageal lining, red skin rash, abdominal distress, painful joints, edema of lower extremities, tachycardia, difficulty in breathing, increased bleeding or bruising |
| vinca alkaloids<br>vincristine<br>(Oncovin) | More frequent: Alopecia<br>Less frequent: Nausea, vomiting, rash, weight loss, gas | Neurotoxicity that includes diplopia or blurred vision, paresthesias of hands and feet, ataxia, loss of deep tendon reflexes, ptosis, headache, jaw pain, abdominal distress, constipation, edema of lower extremities, disorientation, seizures, depression, insomnia |
| vinblastine (Velban, Velbe ♣) | More frequent: Alopecia<br>Less frequent: Nausea, vomiting, muscular pains | Elevated temperature, chills, sore throat, abdominal distress, edema of lower extremities, increased bleeding or bruising; neurotoxic side effects are considered rare |

*If side effects continue, increase, or disturb the client, the physician should be informed.
†If adverse reactions occur, contact the physician because medical intervention may be necessary.

tissues to active metabolite floxuridine monophospate. Final metabolic degradation occurs in the liver. The drug is distributed throughout the body and also crosses the blood-brain barrier; half-life for alpha phase is 10 to 20 minutes; beta phase is prolonged because of the tissue storage of metabolities, possibly extending to 20 hours.

Excretion depends on catabolic degradation to inactive metabolities in the liver; primary excretion route is respiratory as carbon dioxide (60% to 80%); balance is excreted by way of the kidneys (up to 15% unchanged). For side effects/adverse reactions, see Table 57-2.

When fluorouracil is given with other bone marrow depressant drugs or radiation, increased bone marrow depression may occur. A decrease in drug dosage is usually indicated.

The administration of any live virus vaccine concurrently with fluorouracil should only be performed with very close supervision of the oncologist. Fluorouracil will suppress the client's normal defense mechanisms and thus may increase the virus' replication and adverse effects. It is usually recommended that live virus vaccines not be administered until months after chemotherapy has been discontinued. Persons in close contact with the client should not receive immunization with the oral poliovirus vaccine because the live virus is excreted by the person receiving it and can be transmitted to the immunocompromised individual.

### Dosage and administration

*Intravenous injection.* 7 to 12 mg/kg body weight per day for 4 days; if no toxicity occurs during the following 3 days, a dose of 7 to 10 mg/kg body weight is then administered every 3 to 4 days for a total course of 2 weeks, or 12 mg/kg body weight daily for 4 days. If no toxicity occurs after another day, 6 mg/kg body weight is administered on alternate days for an additional four or five doses over a two-week total period.

*Maintenance dosage.* 7 to 12 mg/kg body weight intravenously every 7 to 10 days or 300 to 500 mg/m² body surface daily for 4 or 5 days, repeated on a monthly cycle. Maximum dosage for adults is 800 mg/day or 400 mg/day for the high-risk client. Investigational protocols may employ higher dosages than stated in the product's package insert. Review Chapter 2 for legal implications.

*Topical.* For treatment of skin cancer (basal cell carcinomas) and precancerous skin lesions.

*Pregnancy safety.* Has been established at FDA category D.

### ▷ Nursing Management: Fluorouracil Therapy

*Assessment.* Carefully consider use of fluorouracil when the client is pregnant or breastfeeding or has renal or hepatic function impairment, infection, bone marrow depression, or tumor cell infiltration of the bone marrow.

Fluorouracil is contraindicated if the client presently has or recently has had chickenpox or herpes zoster, because of the risk of occurrence or exacerbation of these diseases. This contraindication applies to those who have had recent exposure to chickenpox or herpes zoster.

Clients receiving fluorouracil are at risk for the following nursing diagnoses: risk for infection related to the drug's immunosuppression action; altered oral mucous membranes related to stomatitis; altered comfort related to anorexia, heartburn, nausea and vomiting, rash or chest pain related to myocardial ischemia; altered bowel elimination pattern (diarrhea); altered protection related to increased tendency for bleeding; or disturbance in self-concept related to alopecia.

*Intervention.* Dosages are determined by the client's weight. In obese clients or those with edema or ascites, estimated lean body mass is used. Administer antiemetics to reduce nausea and vomiting.

Fluorouracil may be administered intraarterially by an infusion pump to ensure a consistent rate of infusion. The nurse should be knowledgeable about and skillful with the specific equipment being used.

In addition to other probable nursing diagnoses associated with the drug, the client is also at risk for injury related to the prolonged use of an arterial catheter to administer the drug, such as thrombosis, embolism, thrombophlebitis, abscesses, and bleeding, leakage, or infection at the catheter site.

Toxicity appears to be reduced by slow intravenous infusion (over 2 to 24 hours); however, bolus injections (over 1 to 2 minutes) may be more effective. Because of the hazards in preparing the dosages, consult your institution's guidelines for the handling of antineoplastic agents.

Take precautions against intravenous infiltration. If extravasation occurs, administration should be stopped immediately and the remaining dose injected into another vein. Cold compresses may reduce local tissue damage.

Safety precautions should be taken if the platelet count is low. Platelet transfusions may be required. The precautions include avoidance of invasive procedures or use of extreme care in such procedures; regular examination of skin, mucous membranes, and injection sites for bruising or bleeding; testing of emesis, urine, and stool for signs of occult bleeding; care in the use of grooming implements, toothbrushes, toothpicks, razors, and nail clippers; prevention of constipation; and prevention of physical injury. Protective isolation should be instituted if WBC falls below 3500/mm³. Broad-spectrum antibiotics may be administered pending appropriate cultures.

The client's mouth should be examined for ulcerations before each dose is administered, since stomatitis is a sign of toxicity. Therapy should be discontinued but may be reinstated at a lower dosage when the side effects have subsided.

Gastrointestinal disturbances usually occur about the fourth day of therapy and subside 2 or 3 days after the medication is withdrawn. Weakness occurs immediately af-

## PRECAUTIONS FOR HANDLING ANTINEOPLASTIC AGENTS

All persons handling cytotoxic (hazardous) drugs, such as antineoplastic agents, should be properly trained in safety procedures and have access to policies and procedures that follow current government and professional practice standards.

### Drug Preparation and Administration

Wash hands thoroughly then wear a disposable gown, surgical latex gloves, and eye protection when preparing or administering cytotoxic drugs.

Whenever possible, it is highly recommended that preparation of injectable antineoplastic agents be performed in the clean-air work station (Hepa filter in BSC or biohazard cabinet).

Use areas for the preparation of drugs only for that purpose. Limit access to that area.

Remove only the required amount of the drug into the syringe. If more is withdrawn accidently, inject the excess back into the vial and dispose of it properly.

Vent vials with a 20-gauge needle to avoid the creation of aerosol particles.

Nurses should not prepare or administer intravenous chemotherapy if they are pregnant because of suspected risk to the fetus from these agents.

### Disposal of Antineoplastic Drugs and Equipment

All antineoplastic drugs and all vials, needles, syringes, tubing, and equipment used in their administration need to be discarded with caution. Special leak-proof, puncture-proof, double bagged containers should be used and labeled BIOHAZARD for disposal by incineration.

Needles and syringes should not be broken and/or separated before disposal because leakage of the medication may occur.

### Spillage or Antineoplastic Drug Contact with Nurse or Client
*Spillage*

Wear two pairs of gloves when cleaning up an antineoplastic drug spill. Wash hands before and after.

Wear a mask and eye protection if the medication is powdered.

Place the spilled substance in a plastic bag. Wipe up the remainder with a damp cloth and also place in the plastic bag.

Seal the bag and place it inside of a second bag, and seal the second bag. Label it BIOHAZARD and send it for disposal by incineration.

*Drug contact with nurse or client*

Thoroughly wash the affected area with soap and water. If clothing was contaminated, remove clothing immediately.

If eye contact was made, flush the eyes with copious amounts of water, holding the eyelids open during flushing.

### Disposal of Client Excreta

Urine, vomitus, and other body fluids from clients receiving antineoplastic drugs should be handled with caution. Flush excreta down the toilet; wear gloves to avoid contact. Wash containers thoroughly.

---

ter the dose is administered and lasts for 12 to 36 hours or longer.

Watch for signs of toxicity and indications for discontinuing the drug, including intractable vomiting, diarrhea, severe stomatitis, WBC below 3500/mm³, thrombocytopenia (below 10,000/mm³), and gastrointestinal bleeding.

The leukopenia and thrombocytopenia associated with the drug's pharmacologic action are used as measures for the titration of each client's dosage.

See also the box above on precautions for handling antineoplastic agents.

***Education.*** Be aware that skin and ocular sensitivity to the sun may occur. Sunglasses and sun-blocking lotions may be advised.

Clients should be instructed to avoid excessive alcohol and any aspirin intake because of the risk of gastrointestinal bleeding.

The client should be cautioned against being immunized with live virus vaccines during fluorouracil therapy, since it may cause rather than prevent the disease. Vaccination is also contraindicated in family members and other persons

in close contact with the client. The client should avoid being exposed to infections.

Inform the client that alopecia may occur but is reversible. Instruct client on safety precautions previously mentioned.

***Evaluation.*** Monitor CBC and hematocrit and watch client for signs of bruising and bleeding, particularly gastrointestinal bleeding. Lowest levels of leukocyte and platelet counts generally occur 9 to 14 days after the first day of fluorouracil therapy and recover by 30 days.

Monitor BUN, creatinine clearance, and serum uric acid levels. A decrease in creatinine clearance and an increase in the other test values may indicate nephrotoxicity. Fluid intake should be 3000 ml daily.

Monitor temperature and observe for signs of infection, fever, chills, sore throat, low back pain, or painful urination.

### methotrexate (Mexate, Folex)

Methotrexate is an antimetabolite that is cell cycle–specific for the S-phase. To synthesize DNA, folic acid must be reduced to tetrahydrofolic acid by the enzyme folic acid reductase. Methotrexate binds with folic acid reductase, thus inhibiting the synthesis of DNA and RNA. Since malignant cellular growth is usually greater than cell growth of normal tissues, cancer growth may be impaired by methotrexate.

It is indicated for the treatment of the following:

1. Breast, head and neck, and lung cancers; also acute lymphocytic leukemia and non-Hodgkin's lymphomas and for the prevention and treatment of meningeal leukemia

2. Advanced cases of mycosis fungoides, osteosarcoma, and severe psoriasis that is unresponsive to standard therapies

It is administered orally, intramuscularly, intravenously, and intrathecally.

Oral formulation is usually rapidly absorbed with peak serum levels reached in 1 to 2 hours. Oral doses below 30 mg are completely absorbed, whereas doses above 30 mg are only partially absorbed.

Limited amounts of methotrexate can cross the blood-brain barrier, but significant quantities pass into the systemic circulation following intrathecal drug administration. Systemically, approximately 50% of the drug is protein bound. It is metabolized intracellularly and in the liver. Unchanged drug is primarily excreted renally with a small percentage excreted in the bile (feces). Individuals vary in their excretion of this drug. Small amounts have remained in body tissues for periods of weeks to months. For side effects/adverse reactions, see Table 57-2.

***Significant drug interactions.*** The following interactions may occur when methotrexate is given with the drugs listed below.

| Drug | Possible Effect and Management |
| --- | --- |
| alcohol and hepatotoxic drugs | Increases risk of hepatotoxicity. Avoid combination; or if absolutely necessary, monitor closely. |
| acyclovir injection | Neurologic complications may occur with use of intrathecal methotrexate. |
| asparaginase | Cell replication is inhibited by asparaginase, thus impairing the therapeutic effects of methotrexate. If asparaginase is administered 9 to 10 days before or within 24 hours after methotrexate, this effect is not reported. The major side effects of methotrexate—gastrointestinal and hematologic (blood components suppression)—are usually reduced with this drug administration schedule. |
| bone marrow depressants or radiation | Bone marrow depressant effects increase. A decrease in drug dosage is usually indicated. |
| NSAIAs (nonsteroidal antiinflammatory agents) | Concurrent administration may result in severe methotrexate toxicity. Refer to manufacturer's recommendations on individual NSAIAs to reduce this possibility. |
| probenecid or salicylates | May interfere with excretion of methotrexate, which results in elevated serum levels. Salicylates may also displace methotrexate from its protein-binding sites, also resulting in increased, and possibly toxic, serum |

| Drug | Possible Effect and Management |
| --- | --- |
| | levels. If necessary to use in combination, monitor serum methotrexate levels closely. Methotrexate dosage level should be decreased and the client closely monitored for signs of toxicity. |
| vaccines, live oral | May result in a decrease in antibody response along with an increase in side effects/adverse reactions. Avoid if possible, or, if necessary, monitor closely for adverse effects and client response. |

***Dosage and administration.*** Methotrexate adult and pediatric dosage varies according to indication and course of treatment. Generally, the antineoplastic adult dose orally is 15 to 30 mg daily for 5 days, repeating the course of therapy between three to five times with a 7- to 14-day interval between each course. The pediatric oral dose is 20 to 40 mg/m² once a week. The antineoplastic adult dose for methotrexate sodium for injection is 15 to 30 mg IM daily for 5 days; repeat the regimen between three to five times with a 7- to 14-day interval between each course. The pediatric oral antineoplastic dose is 20 to 40 mg/m² IM weekly. For other indications, refer to a current package insert or USP-DI for dosing instructions.

***Pregnancy safety.*** Has been established at FDA category X.

▷ **Nursing Management: Methotrexate Therapy**

***Assessment.*** Carefully consider use of methotrexate when the client is pregnant or breastfeeding or has ascites, pleural effusion, bone marrow depression, infection, oral mucositis, peptic ulcer, renal function impairment, ulcerative colitis, or a history of gout, urate renal stones, or previous cytotoxic drug therapy or radiation therapy. Caution should be used with debilitated, very young, or elderly clients.

Clients receiving methotrexate should be assessed for the possibility of the following nursing diagnoses: altered protection related to increased tendency to bleed as the result of the drug's thrombocytopenic effects; risk for injury related to its dermatologic effects (cutaneous vasculitis or photosensitivity, or related to nephrotoxicity or hepatotoxicity; altered protection related to its immunosuppressive effects; altered mucous membrane related to stomatitis; altered comfort related to headache, back pain, dizziness, anorexia, nausea and vomiting; altered thought processes (confusion); visual disturbances; and altered sleep patterns (drowsiness).

***Intervention.*** Administer leucovorin calcium within the first 36 to 42 hours of starting methotrexate (or earlier) to block the systemic toxic effects of high-dosage methotrexate (known as "leucovorin rescue"). Leucovorin should be immediately available for administration or high-dosage methotrexate administration should not be initiated.

Reconstitute with sterile, preservative-free sodium chloride for injection for intrathecal use.

Safety precautions should be taken if the platelet count is low. Precautions include avoidance of invasive procedures or use of extreme care in such procedures; regular examination of skin, mucous membranes, and injection sites for bruising or bleeding; testing of emesis, urine, and stool for signs of occult bleeding; care in the use of grooming implements, toothbrushes, toothpicks, razors, and nail clippers; prevention of constipation; and prevention of physical injury.

The client should be maintained on an adequate fluid intake to ensure an increase in urinary output to prevent nephrotoxicity.

*Education.* Caution the client against being immunized with live virus vaccines during methotrexate therapy, since it may cause the disease rather than prevent it. It is also contraindicated in family members and other persons in close contact with the client. The client should avoid being exposed to infections.

Instruct the client in the importance of continuing the medication despite gastric distress.

Alcohol ingestion should be avoided, since it increases the hepatotoxicity associated with the drug.

The client should be aware that skin sensitivity and photophobia may occur. Sun-blocking lotions and sunglasses may be advised.

Inform the client that alopecia may occur but is reversible.

*Evaluation.* Because of the risk of injury related to nephrotoxicity, monitor serum uric acid levels and intake and output to ensure that the client is adequately hydrated to prevent hyperuricemia and uric acid nephropathy. Alkalinization of urine will also help prevent renal toxicity.

Monitor SGOT and SGPT and observe the client for signs of hepatotoxicity (yellowing of eyes and skin and dark urine).

Monitor CBC and watch for signs of brusing and bleeding, particularly gastrointestinal bleeding. The nadir of the platelet count occurs after 7 to 10 days, with recovery about 7 days later.

Because of the risk for infection related to immunosuppression, monitor temperature and observe for signs of infection, fever, chills, or sore throat. The nadir of the leucocyte count occurs after 7 to 10 days, with recovery about 7 days later.

The client's mouth should be examined for altered mucous membranes before the administration of each dose, since stomatitis is a sign of toxicity. Therapy should be discontinued, but may be reinstated at a lower dosage when the side effects have subsided.

### leucovorin (folinic acid, Wellcovorin)

Leucovorin, or folinic acid, is a form of folic acid that does not require dihydrofolate reductase to produce folic acid. Therefore it is used to prevent or treat toxicity induced by folic acid antagonists. It is indicated for the following:

1. Use as an antidote for folic acid antagonists, such as methotrexate, pyrimethamine, and trimethoprim. **Leucovorin rescue** is a term used to describe high-dose methotrexate treatments that use leucovorin to reduce the time that sensitive (normal) cells are exposed to the toxic effects of methotrexate. It has been useful in the treatment of osteogenic sarcoma, carcinomas of the head and neck, refractory acute leukemia, and lung carcinomas.

2. The treatment of megaloblastic anemia caused by nutritional deficiencies, sprue, in infants and whenever oral folic acid therapy is not appropriate.

Leucovorin is rapidly absorbed orally and converted by the intestinal mucous membrane and liver to 5-methyltetrahydrofolate, an active metabolite. The onset of action orally is between 20 to 30 minutes; intramuscularly, 10 to 20 minutes and intravenously, in less than 5 minutes. Duration of action by all routes is betwen 3 to 6 hours. It is mainly excreted by the kidneys (80% to 90%) and feces (5% to 8%). For side effects/adverse reactions, see Table 57-2. No significant drug interactions are reported with leucovorin.

As an antidote to the toxic effect of folic acid antagonists, the adult oral dose is 10 mg/m$^2$ of body surface every 6 hours, until methotrexate blood levels fall to less than 5 × 10$^{-8}$ M. As an antidote for pyrimethamine or trimethoprim, the oral adult dose is 0.4 to 5 mg with each dose of folic acid antagonist. For pediatric dosage, see adult dosage. Pregnancy safety has been established at FDA category C.

▷ **Nursing Management: Leucovorin Therapy**

Leucovorin is administered after methotrexate rather than simultaneously with methotrexate. The first dose is usually administered within 24 to 42 hours of beginning high-dose methotrexate therapy. Such high-dose therapy should not be initiated unless leucovorin is immediately available for administration, since rescue is critical. All nursing management measures for methotrexate administration should be observed.

## ALKYLATING DRUGS

Alkylating drugs are frequently used as anticancer agents and are believed to be the first class of medications applied clinically in the modern era of antineoplastic drug therapy. Although research was conducted during World War I with sulfur and nitrogen mustards, this information was kept classified because mustard gas was used by the military. Not until 1942 was nitrogen mustard used to treat a lymphosarcoma client who had become resistant to radiation therapy. Since then a variety of alkylating agents have been tested and used in the treatment of various cancerous states.

Three alkylating-type drugs are reviewed in this chapter: mechlorethamine (Mustargen), cyclophosphamide (Cytoxan), and cisplatin (Platinol). Several other alkylating drugs have special properties that the reader should know about. For example, from the nitrosourea category, carmustine and lomustine cross the blood-brain barrier and so are useful in the treatment of primary brain tumors. They are also used to treat Hodgkin's disease, while carmustine is also indicated for non-Hodgkin's lymphomas and multiple myeloma. Bone marrow suppression is the most severe adverse effect of the nitrosoureas. This toxicity is cumulative; thus drug dosage is adjusted regularly, based on the nadir blood count from the previous dose administered. Because of the seriousness of this effect, blood counts are performed weekly for at least 6 weeks following a drug dose. Current reference sources should be reviewed when monitoring a client receiving these agents. Pregnancy safety has been established at FDA category D for carmustine and lomustine. See also the box on double syringe method of administration.

Streptozocin (Zanosar) is indicated for the treatment of pancreatic cancer. It causes irreversible damage to the islet beta cells that may produce a sudden release of insulin initially (hypoglycemia) that eventually results in a diabetogenic effect because of the loss of insulin secretion. In addition to producing bone marrow suppression, it frequently causes renal toxicity. Thus the use of this drug requires very close monitoring by the health care professionals caring for the client. Pregnancy safety has been established at FDA category C.

### mechlorethamine (Mustargen)

Mechlorethamine is an alkylating agent capable of cross-linking DNA and interfering with DNA and RNA, thus preventing cell division and protein synthesis. It is cell cycle–nonspecific. It is indicated by intravenous or by intracavitary route (such as intrapleurally or intraperitoneally) for the treatment of Hodgkin's disease, lymphomas, chronic leukemia, malignant effusions, mycosis fungoides, lymphosarcoma, metastatic carcinomas, and polycythemia vera.

When administered intravenously, it is rapidly converted to reactive ions that usually are not detectable in the blood after approximately 10 minutes; it is rapidly inactivated in body fluids. Excretion is believed to be via the kidneys. For side effects/adverse reactions, see Table 57-2.

***Significant drug interactions.*** The following significant drug interactions may occur when mechlorethamine is given with the drugs listed below.

| Drug | Possible Effect and Management |
|---|---|
| bone marrow depressants or radiation | Increased bone marrow depression may occur. A decrease in drug dosage is usually indicated. |
| probenecid or sulfinpyrazone | Hyperuricemia and gout may occur. The physician may adjust the antigout medications or prescribe allopurinol. The latter is often preferred to prevent drug-induced hyperuricemia. |
| vaccines, live viral | See methotrexate drug interactions. |

---

## DOUBLE SYRINGE METHOD

Some antineoplastic agents have **vesicant** properties (causing blisters) and require careful handling. The following are common vesicant agents:

| | |
|---|---|
| dactinomycin | mithramycin |
| carmustine (BiCNU) | mitomycin C |
| daunorubicin | vinblastine |
| doxorubicin | vincristine |
| mechlorethamine | |

These agents should be administered by the double-syringe technique as follows:

1. Select site for administration according to following order of preference: forearm, dorsum of hand, wrist, or antecubital fossa.
2. Use 20- or 21-gauge "butterfly" needle for drug administration. Administer 5 ml normal saline solution and withdraw small amount of blood into tubing to test vein patency. If blood return is poor, select site other than distal location.
3. Administer vesicant agent for at least 3 minutes, drawing blood back into tubing after every 2 to 3 ml solution.
4. Flush with 3 to 5 ml saline solution after administration.
5. If client has pain at site of injection or an unusual sensation during drug administration, extravasation may have occurred, and a new site for drug injection should be selected.

---

### Dosage and administration

*Adults.* Intravenously, total dosage of 0.4 mg/kg ideal body weight in divided doses two to four daily doses) or in a single dose. If clients have previously received drug chemotherapy or radiation, this dosage should not exceed 0.2 to 0.3 mg/kg body weight. Intracavitary, 0.4 mg/kg of body weight. Intrapericardial, 0.2 mg/kg of body weight. Topically, for mycosis fungoides, available in ointment (0.01% to 0.04%) and topical solution (approximately 10 mg/50 ml). Medication is applied topically to skin surface daily until a complete response is achieved. With ointment and solution dosage forms, maintenance usually requires application one or more times per week for approximately 3 years.

*Children.* See recommended adult dosages.

***Pregnancy safety.*** Has been established at FDA category D.

▷ **Nursing Management:**
**Mechlorethamine Therapy**

***Assessment.*** Carefully consider use of mechlorethamine when the client is pregnant or breastfeeding or has bone marrow depression, infection, or a history of gout, urate renal stones, or previous cytotoxic drug therapy or radiation therapy.

Over the course of mechlorethamine therapy, the client should be assessed for the occurrence of the following nursing diagnoses: sensory-perceptual alterations related to the drug's ototoxic effects evidenced by hearing loss and tinnitus; altered protection related to increased bleeding tendency (thrombocytopenic effect), and leukopenic effects; altered comfort related to headache, rash, pain/redness at injection site, metallic taste, anorexia, nausea and vomiting; risk for physiologic injury related to peripheral neuropathy, allergic reaction, or nephrotoxocity; altered mucous membranes related to stomatitis; altered bowel elimination pattern (diarrhea); altered sleep pattern (drowsiness); disturbance of self-concept related to alopecia or menstrual irregularities; and altered thought processes (confusion).

**Intervention.** Do not use if droplets of water appear in the vial before reconstitution. Reconstitute with sterile water for injection or sodium chloride injection fluid only.

Reconstitute immediately before or less than 15 minutes before each dose. Discard any unused solution after neutralizing.

Avoid contact with the solution by wearing gloves while preparing and administering it. If contact with the skin, mucous membranes, or eye occurs, irrigate the affected area immediately with large amounts of water for 15 minutes; follow with 2% thiosulfate solution. Neutralize all equipment used in the administration of the drug by soaking for 45 minutes in a solution of equal parts of 5% sodium thiosulfate and 5% sodium bicarbonate.

When mechlorethamine is given by the intracavitary route, change the client's position (prone to supine to right side to left side) every 10 minutes for an hour to distribute the drug. Administer analgesics before intracavitary administration of mechlorethamine to minimize the discomfort of the therapy. Removal of fluid before intracavitary administration of mechlorethamine improves contact of the medication with the cavity lining. Fluid is usually removed from the cavity again 24 to 36 hours after therapy.

Caution should be taken against intravenous infiltration. If extravasation occurs, promptly infiltrate the area with sterile isotonic sodium thiosulfate or 1% lidocaine and apply ice compresses for 6 to 12 hours.

When applying mechlorethamine topically, follow the specific instructions for application for that client. Usually the client showers, rinses, and dries thoroughly before each treatment and does not shower until treatment the next day. Use plastic gloves to apply mechlorethamine, avoiding contact with the eyes, nose, and mouth. The treatment may be continued for months or even years.

Safety precautions should be taken regarding invasive procedures and infection avoidance as mentioned previously with antimetabolite drugs.

Nausea and vomiting occur in about 90% of clients, generally within 1 to 3 hours of the dose. Although the vomiting usually lasts only 8 hours, nausea may persist 24 hours. These symptoms may be decreased by the administration of antiemetics before mechlorethamine dosing. However, if the use of sedatives is also required to control the nausea and vomiting, the mechlorethamine may be administered at night for the convenience of the client.

Avoid invasive procedures such as intramuscular injections when the platelet count is low. The nadir of thrombocytopenia usually occurs within 6 to 8 days, with recovery in 10 days to 3 weeks.

**Education.** The client should be instructed not to be immunized with live virus vaccines during mechlorethamine therapy and to avoid contact with others receiving immunization during that time.

The female client should be alerted that menstrual periods may become irregular.

Hair loss may occur in clients but they should be told that this effect is usually temporary.

The client should be instructed in the importance of adequate hydration in the prevention of complications.

Alert the client to the frequency of nausea and vomiting with the administration of this drug, but stress the importance of continuing the medication despite these symptoms.

For clients receiving high doses, instruction should be provided to report auditory disturbances to their prescriber and/or receive audiometric testing at periodic intervals.

**Evaluation.** Monitor serum uric acid and BUN levels. Adequate hydration will help prevent renal complications, although alkalinization of the urine may be necessary if serum uric acid levels begin to increase.

Monitor the client's CBC and monitor for the presence of fever, chills, and sore throat. Within 24 hours of the first dose, lymphocytopenia occurs. Granulocytopenia occurs 6 to 8 days after the dose and lasts 10 days to 3 weeks.

### cyclophosphamide (Cytoxan, Procytox ✷)

Cyclophosphamide is a cell cycle–nonspecific agent that cross links DNA and RNA strands and also inhibits the synthesis of protein. It is indicated for:

1. Acute and chronic leukemias, carcinomas of the ovary and breast, neuroblastomas, retinoblastomas, Hodgkin's and non-Hodgkin's lymphomas, multiple myeloma, sarcomas, and mycosis fungoides

2. As an immunosuppressant in drug-resistant nephrotic syndrome, rheumatoid arthritis, and other autoimmune disease states

The drug is well absorbed from the gastrointestinal tract with distribution across the blood-brain barrier. Cyclophosphamide undergoes hepatic metabolism to active and inactive metabolites. There is little binding, but active metabolites are approximately 50% protein bound. Serum half-life is approximately 4 to 6½ hours, but drug or drug metabolites have been detected for up to 72 hours in the plasma.

Excretion is primarily by way of the kidneys. For side effects/adverse reactions, see Table 57-2.

**Significant drug interactions.** The following interactions may occur when cyclophosphamide is given with the drugs listed below.

| Drug | Possible Effect and Management |
|---|---|
| bone marrow depressants or radiation | Increased bone marrow depression may occur. A decrease in drug dosage is usually indicated. |
| probenecid or sulfinpyrazone | Hyperuricemia and gout may occur. The physician may adjust the antigout medications. Allopurinol is not indicated, since it may increase the bone marrow toxicity of cyclophosphamide. If drugs are given concurrently, monitor closely for toxicity. |
| immunosuppressant agents including adrenocorticoids, azathioprine, chlorambucil, cyclosporine, and mercaptopurine | Increased risk of infections and further development of neoplasms. |
| vaccines, live viral | See methotrexate drug interactions. |

**Dosage and administration.** Adult antineoplastic dose is 1 to 4 mg/kg orally daily. Pediatric oral dose for induction is 2 to 8 mg/kg in divided doses for 6 or more days. Maintenance dose is 2 to 5 mg/kg orally, twice weekly. The intravenous dose for adults is 40 to 50 mg/kg in divided doses over 2 to 5 days. Pediatric intravenous dose is 2 to 8 mg/kg in divided doses for 6 or more days. Maintenance intravenous dose is 10 to 15 mg/kg every week to 10 days, at 21- to 30-day intervals following bone marrow recovery.

**Pregnancy safety.** Has been established at FDA category D.

▷ **Nursing Management:**
**Cyclophosphamide Therapy**

**Assessment.** Carefully consider use of cyclophosphamide when the client is pregnant or breastfeeding or has renal or hepatic function impairment, infection, bone marrow depression, tumor cell infiltration of the bone marrow, or previous cytotoxic drug or radiation therapy. It is not to be used if the client at present has, has recently had, or has been exposed to chickenpox or has herpes zoster because of the risk of exacerbation or increased severity of the disease.

The nurse should assess the client receiving cyclophosphamide therapy for the following nursing diagnoses related to the drug's effects: altered protection related to leukopenia and an increased tendency for bleeding related to thrombocytopenia; disturbance of self-concept related to gonadal suppression, darkening of skin and nails, or alopecia; altered cardiac output related to cardiotoxicity; high risk for injury related to the drug's metabolite excretion evidenced by hemorrhagic cystitis, nephrotoxicity as a result of hyperuricemia

from rapid cell breakdown; high risk for alteration in respiratory function related to the development of pneumonitis or interstitial pulmonary fibrosis; activity intolerance related to anemia; altered comfort related to headache, rash, anorexia, nausea, and vomiting; altered bowel elimination pattern (diarrhea); and altered mucous membranes related to stomatitis.

**Intervention.** Reconstituted solutions may be stored for 24 hours at room temperature or 6 days if refrigerated. Antiemetics may be administered concurrently to reduce nausea and vomiting.

Maintain the client's fluid intake at 3000 ml daily, unless contraindicated, before treatment and for 72 hours following treatment to ensure frequent voiding, including at least once during the night, thereby minimizing the risk of hemorrhagic cystitis and promoting the excretion of uric acid. Administration of cyclophosphamide is best accomplished early in the day so that most of the drug's metabolites have been excreted before bedtime, preventing continued contact of the metabolites with the bladder mucosa. The drug should be discontinued at the first sign of hemorrhagic cystitis; symptomatic treatment may be instituted through such routes as blood replacement, cryosurgery, or formaldehyde bladder instillations.

**Education.** Alopecia may occur but is reversible; however, the new hair may be different in color and texture.

As with antineoplastic agents, previously discussed, instruct the client not to be immunized with live virus vaccines during the course of therapy. Advise client of the safety precautions mentioned with previous antineoplastic agents.

Advise the client that nausea and vomiting frequently occur with cyclophosphamide therapy, but stress that the medication needs to be taken despite these symptoms.

**Evaluation.** Monitor BUN, creatinine clearance, and serum uric acid level determinations. A decrease in creatinine clearance and an increase in the other test values may indicate nephrotoxicity. Intake should be 3000 ml daily for adequate hydration to prevent uric acid nephropathy. Alkalinization of urine or allopurinol administration may also be used to prevent uric acid nephropathy.

Observe the client for reduced urinary output, weight gain over several days, edema of the feet and lower legs, flank pain, pruritus, urine odor on breath, anorexia, nausea, and vomiting.

Monitor for myelosuppression as evidenced by anemia and leukopenia. Monitor hematocrit, platelet count, and total and differential leukocyte counts. Lowest levels of leukopenia generally occur 7 to 12 days after the first dose. The leukocyte count recovers 17 to 21 days after the last dose. Observe the client for fever of unknown origin, chills, sore throat, unusual bleeding, or bruising.

Monitor urinalysis for microscopic hematuria and the client for painful urination as indications of hemorrhagic cystitis.

## ALKYLATOR-LIKE DRUGS
### cisplatin (Platinol)

The mechanism of action of cisplatin is unknown, but it is believed to be a cell cycle–nonspecific agent that has an action similar to the alkylating agents.

It is indicated for the treatment of bladder, testicular, and ovarian carinomas. When cisplatin is administered intravenously, it locates in the liver, small and large intestines, and kidney, but it does not significantly cross the blood-brain barrier. Half-life is biphasic; alpha or initial half-life is 25 to 49 minutes, and beta or later phase is 58 to 73 hours. It is metabolized to inactive metabolites that are highly protein bound (greater than 90%); partially renally excreted (27% to 43%) after 5 days, although platinum has been detected in body tissues for 4 months or longer. For side effects/adverse reactions, see Table 57-2.

**Significant drug interactions.** The following interactions may occur when cisplatin is given with the drugs listed below.

| Drug | Possible Effect and Management |
| --- | --- |
| bone marrow depressants or radiation | Increased bone marrow depression may occur. A decrease in drug dosage is usually indicated. |
| probenecid or sulfinpyrazone | Hyperuricemia and gout may occur. The physician may adjust the antigout medications or prescribe allopurinol. The latter is often preferred to prevent drug-induced hyperuricemia. |
| nephrotoxic or ototoxic drugs | Concurrent or sequential administration is not recommended. The risk for nephrotoxicity and ototoxicity is increased, especially in clients with renal impairment. |
| vaccines, live viral | See methotrexate drug interactions. |

**Dosage and administration (adults only).** Dosage varies according to site of cancerous growth; for example, for advanced bladder cancer intravenous dosage is 50 to 70 mg/m$^2$ of body surface area every 3 to 4 weeks. For metastatic ovarian tumors or testicular tumors, cisplatin and other antineoplastic agents are given in combination or by sequential drug administration. Recommended dosages vary according to protocol and also whether therapy is initial or maintenance. Current recommendations should be reviewed to determine indications, dosages, dosage schedules, or different drug combinations for specific cancers.

**Pregnancy safety.** Has not been established.

▷ **Nursing Management:**
**Cisplatin Therapy**

**Assessment.** Carefully consider use of cisplatin when the client is pregnant or breastfeeding or has renal function impairment, infection, healing impairment, bone marrow depression, or a history of gout, urate renal stones, or previous cytotoxic drug or radiation therapy. Observe cautions for chickenpox and shingles as with other antineoplastic agents.

Clients receiving cisplatin therapy are at risk for the following nursing diagnoses: activity intolerance related to anemia due to myelosuppression; altered protection related to leukopenia; an increased bleeding tendency due to thrombocytopenia; physiologic injury related to nephrotoxicity, or related to neurotoxicity (loss of reflexes, numbness of fingers and toes, ataxia, seizures); sensory-perceptual alteration related to ototoxicity (hearing loss, tinnitus) or visual disturbances due to optic neuritis or papilledema; altered mucous membranes related to stomatitis; and altered comfort related to pain/redness at injection site, anorexia, nausea, or vomiting.

**Intervention.** Hydrate client with 1 to 2 L of intravenous infusion fluid, and dilute cisplatin in 2 L of 5% dextrose in one-half or one-third normal saline containing 37.5 g of mannitol. This infusion should be administered over 6 to 8 hours. To reduce nephrotoxicity, adequate hydration of 3000 ml daily should be maintained. Urinary output should be closely monitored. Alkalinization of urine and allopurinol administration may also be used to prevent uric acid nephropathy.

Reduce nausea and vomiting by administering a parenteral antiemetic ½ hour before cisplatin is given. These symptoms usually begin 1 to 4 hours after a dose. Therefore the antiemetic therapy is continued on a schedule as long as necessary. If the nausea and vomiting are severe, cisplatin may be discontinued.

As with antineoplastic agents discussed in Chapter 56, observe safety precautions regarding invasive procedures.

Do not use aluminum needles or other equipment containing aluminum. Cisplatin is incompatible with aluminum, which causes a black precipitate and a potency loss.

**Education.** As with other antineoplastic agents previously discussed, caution the client against being immunized with live virus vaccines and signs and symptoms to report to the prescriber.

**Evaluation.** Evaluate for nephrotoxicity, hyperuricemia, and uric acid nephropathy. Nephrotoxicity is cumulative, and the effects may be irreversible with repeated or high dosages. Symptoms are reduced urinary output, weight gain over several days, edema of the feet and lower legs, flank pain, pruritus, urine odor on breath, anorexia, nausea, and vomiting. Metoclopramide is indicated for cisplatin-induced emesis.

Monitor BUN, creatinine clearance, and serum uric acid level. A decrease in creatinine clearance and an increase in the other test values may indicate nephrotoxicity.

Test hearing status before the initial dose and each subsequent dose. Ringing in the ears and difficulty in hearing high frequencies may indicate ototoxicity. Hearing loss is cumulative and may be unilateral.

Monitor for myelosuppression as evidenced by anemia, leukopenia, and thrombocytopenia. Hematocrit, platelet count, and total and differential leukocyte counts should also be monitored. The lowest leukocyte and platelet counts generally occur 18 to 23 days after a dose and recover by

39 days. The client should be observed for fever of unknown origin, chills, sore throat, unusual bleeding, or bruising.

Discontinue administration of cisplatin at the first indication of peripheral neuropathy because it may be irreversible. Symptoms to watch for are numbness or tingling in the fingers, toes, or face and loss of taste.

Do not administer subsequent doses of cisplatin until platelet levels are over 100,000 cells/mm$^3$, WBC is over 4000 cells/mm$^3$, creatinine clearance is greater than 90 ml/minute, serum creatinine is less than 1.3 mg/100 ml, or BUN is under 20 mg/100 ml.

## ANTIBIOTIC ANTITUMOR DRUGS
### doxorubicin (Adriamycin)

Doxorubicin is an antineoplastic and antibiotic agent that is specific for the S-phase of cell division. It binds DNA and inhibits RNA synthesis. It is a cell cycle–nonspecific agent. It is indicated for the treatment of acute leukemia, Wilms' tumor, neuroblastoma, soft tissue and bone sarcomas, Hodgkins' disease, lymphomas, and breast and various other carcinomas.

Doxorubicin is administered intravenously. While it does not cross the blood-brain barrier, it is rapidly cleared from the blood and is highly tissue bound. It is metabolized in the liver to produce the active metabolite, adriamycinol. The half-life of doxorubicin is biphasic, 0.6 hours and 16.7 hours. The active metabolite has a half-life of 3.3 hours and 31.7 hours. Further metabolism is by the liver, and excretion is primarily biliary (50% unchanged; 23% as adriamycinol). For side effects/adverse reactions, see Table 57-2.

Significant drug interactions are reported with other bone marrow depressant drugs or radiation, probenecid or sulfinpyrazone, and with live virus vaccines; see prvious comments regarding mechlorethamine drug interactions. Use of doxorubicin in clients who have received daunorubicin (Cerubidine) increases the risk of inducing cardiotoxicity. Both drugs have cumulative maximum dosing limits that must be followed; a total dose of 550 mg/m$^2$ from either drug alone or both drugs together. If the client has received previous chest radiation or other cardiotoxic drugs, the maximum dose is reduced to 400 mg/m$^2$.

Antineoplastic adult dosage is 60 to 75 mg/m$^2$ of body surface intravenously, repeated every 3 weeks. The pediatric dosage is 30 mg/m$^2$ of body surface daily on 3 consecutive days, every month.

Pregnancy safety has not been established; it is generally recommended to avoid the use of doxorubicin during the first trimester of pregnancy.

▷ **Nursing Management:**
**Doxorubicin Therapy**

***Assessment.*** Carefully consider use of doxorubicin when the client is pregnant or breastfeeding or has bone marrow depression, heart disease, hepatic function impairment, or a history of gout, urate kidney stones, or cytotoxic drug or radiation therapy. Caution should be used with elderly clients because of their decreased bone marrow reserves. Observe cautions for chickenpox and shingles as with other antineoplastic agents.

Assess the client receiving doxorubicin for the possibility of the following nursing diagnoses: altered mucous membranes related to stomatitis; altered protection related to an increased tendency to bleed due to thrombocytopenia and immunosuppression; altered cardiac output related to cardiotoxicity; physiologic injury related to extravasation or cellulitis at the injection site, related to nephrotoxicity, or related to allergic response; altered comfort related to anorexia, nausea, and vomiting; and disturbance of self-concept related to loss of hair or darkening of skin.

***Intervention.*** Reconstitute with sterile sodium chloride for injection. Use reconstituted solutions within 24 hours if stored at room temperature or within 48 hours if stored between 2° and 8° C (36° and 46° F) and protected from light.

Avoid contact with the solution by wearing gloves while preparing and administering it. If contact with the skin or mucous membranes occurs, wash thoroughly with soap and water. See institutional guidelines for the safe handling of antineoplastic agents.

Take precautions against intravenous extravasation. Administer doxorubicin slowly into a freely running IV infusion of 0.9% sodium chloride injection or 5% dextrose injection over not less than 3 to 5 minutes.

If extravasation occurs, the intravenous line should be moved to another site for completion of the dose. Ice packs should be applied and the extremity should be elevated to minimize injury. If inflammation is extensive, surgical excision of the area may be required. Do not give intramuscularly or subcutaneously because it will cause tissue necrosis.

As with other antineoplastic agents discussed in Chapter 56, observe safety precautions for invasive procedures.

***Education.*** The client's urine may become reddish for 1 or 2 days after administration of doxorubicin, but it generally clears in 48 hours.

As with previously discussed antineoplastic agents, discuss with the client the importance of adequate hydration, the possibility of alopecia, the contraindication of being immunized with live virus vaccines during therapy, and the importance of taking medications despite gastric distress.

***Evaluation.*** Monitor serum uric acid levels and intake and output to ensure that the client is adequately hydrated to prevent hyperuricemia. Allopurinol administration and alkalinization of urine may be used to decrease serum uric acid levels.

Monitor CBC and watch the client for signs of bruising and bleeding, particularly gastrointestinal bleeding.

Monitor the elecrocardiogram and observe the client for swelling of the feet and lower legs and shortness of breath, which indicate cardiotoxicity. Cardiotoxicity is more common in elderly persons over 70 years of age and in children under 2 years of age. It usually occurs within 1 to 6 months after therapy has begun. Cardiotoxicity may develop suddenly and may be irreversible; it is critical that cardiotoxicity be detected early, when it usually responds to therapy.

Monitor temperature and observe for signs of infection, fever, chills, or sore throat. The lowest leukocyte count usually occurs 10 to 14 days after dosage and recovers within 21 days.

Examine the client's mouth for ulcerations before the administration of each dose since stomatitis is a sign of toxicity.

## MITOTIC INHIBITORS

### vincristine (Oncovin)

Vincristine is a cell cycle–specific agent that inhibits mitosis during M-phase. It is used to treat acute lymphoblastic leukemia, Hodgkin's disease, lymphosarcoma, rhabdomyosarcoma, neuroblastoma, Wilms' tumor, and carcinomas of lung and breast.

Vincristine is administered intravenously. It does not cross the blood-brain barrier and is highly tissue bound with a triphasic half-life, 0.07 hour, 2.27 hours, and 85 hours. It is metabolized in the liver and excreted via the bile. For side effects/adverse reactions, see Table 57-2. Neurotoxicity is the major dose-limiting side effect.

***Significant drug interactions.*** The following interactions may occur when vincristine is given with:

| Drug | Possible Effect and Management |
|---|---|
| probenecid or sulfinpyrazone | Hyperuricemia and gout may occur. The physician may adjust the antigout medications or prescribe allopurinol. The latter is often preferred to prevent drug-induced hyperuricemia. |
| asparaginase | When given concurrently with vincristine, an increase in neurotoxocity may result. To reduce the possibility of this interaction, asparaginase should be given only after vincristine is administered, not concurrently or before vincristine. |
| doxorubicin | If administered with vincristine and prednisone, an increase in bone marrow depressant effects may occur. This combination should be avoided. |
| vaccines, live viral | See methotrexate drug interactions. |

***Dosage and administration.*** The adult antineoplastic dosage is 0.01 to 0.03 mg/kg body weight as a single dose, weekly. The pediatric dose is 1.5 to 2 mg/kg body weight as a single dose, weekly. Combination therapies may employ various dosage regimens according to the client's condition and the cancer under treatment.

***Pregnancy safety.*** Has been established at FDA category D.

▷ **Nursing Management: Vincristine Therapy**

***Assessment.*** Carefully consider use of vincristine when the client is pregnant or breastfeeding or has hepatic function impairment, infection, leukopenia, neuromuscular disease or a history of gout, urate kidney stones, or cytotoxic drug or radiation therapy. Observe for contraindications for chickenpox and shingles as with other antineoplastic agents.

Vincristine therapy places the client at risk for the possibility of the following nursing diagnoses: altered urinary elimination pattern related to autonomic toxicity evidenced by bed-wetting, increased or decreased urination, painful or difficult urination; physiologic injury related to nephrotoxicity, neurotoxicity (numbness in fingers and toes, blurred vision); altered comfort related to headache, extravasation at injection site, rash, bloating, anorexia, nausea, and vomiting; altered mucous membranes related to stomatitis; altered bowel elimination pattern, either diarrhea or constipation; and disturbance of self-concept related to alopecia.

***Intervention.*** Reconstitute with bacteriostatic sodium chloride injection provided by the manufacturer, sterile water for injection, or sodium chloride injection. Store reconstituted solutions up to 14 days if refrigerated.

Take precautions against intravenous infiltration. If extravasation occurs, stop administration immediately, and inject remaining dose into another vein. To alleviate discomfort and inflammation, inject hyaluronidase locally and apply heat or cold compresses.

Administer by intravenous push or inject into the tubing of a running intravenous infusion for 1 minute. Administer only intravenously; intramuscular or subcutaneous administration will cause tissue necrosis; intrathecal administration will cause death.

As with other antineoplastic agents discussed in Chapter 56, observe safety precautions for invasive procedures and avoidance of infections.

***Education.*** Stress the importance of adequate hydration, the possibility of alopecia, the contraindication of being immunized with live virus vaccines during therapy, and the importance of taking medications despite gastric distress. See Chapter 56.

***Evaluation.*** Monitor the client's bowel status for early signs of autonomic toxicity, such as constipation. Use of a laxative or stool softener will help prevent upper colon impaction.

Monitor serum uric acid levels and the client's intake and output to ensure adequate hydration for the prevention of uric acid nephropathy. Intake should be 3000 ml daily. Urine may be alkalinized if serum uric acid levels increase.

Monitor CBC and observe client for fever, chills, sore throat, bleeding, and bruising to assess risk for infection or physical injury. The lowest level of leukocytes occurs 5 to 10 days after the last day of administration, and recovery occurs within another 7 to 14 days.

Monitor the client's neuromuscular status. Watch for ataxia, numbness, tingling or pain in the fingers or toes, headache, double vision, and other early signs of neurotoxicity.

### etoposide

Etoposide (VePesid, VP-16) is a semisynthetic podophyllin derivative used in combination with other antineoplastics to treat refractory testicular and small cell lung cancer. It appears to act at the premitotic phase with maximum effects on the S and $G_2$ phases of cell division. It is administered by intravenous infusion and is highly protein bound with a half-life of approximately 7 hours. Metabolism may be by the liver with excretion primarily in the kidneys.

Significant drug interactions reported are with other bone marrow depressants (additive effect) and with live virus vaccines (potentiation of virus may result). The most frequent side effects reported are anorexia, nausea, and vomiting. The most frequent adverse effects include leukopenia and thrombocytopenia.

The adult dose for testicular cancer is 50 to 100 mg/m² body surface daily by intravenous infusion on days 1 to 5. This regimen is usually repeated every 3 to 4 weeks. The pediatric dose has not been established.

Pregnancy safety has been established at FDA category D.

### ▷ Nursing Management: Etoposide Therapy

Care of the client receiving etoposide is essentially the same as with vincristine, except this drug lacks vincristine's nephrotoxicity and autonomic toxicity. Etoposide is to be diluted for intravenous administration with either 5% dextrose injection or 0.9% sodium chloride injection to produce a solution containing 400 µg or less per ml. It is to be administered slowly over 30 to 60 minutes to minimize the drug's hypotensive effects.

## ADDITIONAL ANTINEOPLASTIC AGENTS

Prednisone and dexamethasone are corticosteroids that are often prescribed for clients with cancer. Prednisone has demonstrated a lympholytic and antiinflammatory effect that is useful in the treatment of leukemias, lymphomas, and breast carcinomas. Steroids, especially dexamethasone, are useful in reducing cerebral edema induced by the increasing growth of a brain tumor or from radiation therapy.

Mitotane (Lysodren) is a cytotoxic agent with a high affinity for the adrenal cortex. It is indicated for inoperable adrenal cortex carcinomas. Side effects include adrenal gland insufficiency, skin rash or darkening of the skin, depression, and lethargy.

Vinblastine (Velban, Velbe ♣) is a vinca alkaloid. Although similar to vincristine in mechanism of action and metabolism, it differs in its tumor specificity and toxic ef-

fects. It is indicated for the treatment of Kaposi's sarcoma, carcinoma of the breast and testes, and choriocarcinoma. Its major undesirable effect is bone marrow suppression.

Extramustine phosphate (Emcyt) is indicated for the palliative treatment of prostatic carcinoma, especially in clients resistant to estrogen. This product combines nitrogen mustard with estradiol; thus cytotoxic effects are combined with hormonal therapy.

The estrogen is a carrier to transport the nitrogen mustard into estrogen receptor positive cells; thus the action of nitrogen mustard is increased in these cells. The main precautions in monitoring estramustine are:

1. An increased risk of inducing thrombosis, especially in clients with a history of thrombophlebitis or thromboembolic disease
2. A decreased tolerance to glucose, so diabetics must be carefully monitored
3. Possible increase in blood pressure

Estramustine is taken orally (14 mg/kg per day in divided doses), preferably an hour before meals with water. Avoid concurrent consumption of milk, milk products, or any calcium-containing products.

Tamoxifen (Nolvadex, Nolvadex-D ♣) is a synthetic (nonsteroidal) antiestrogen agent indicated for the treatment of metastatic breast cancer in women. Studies have indicated its use in postmenopausal women delays recurrence of breast cancer, following a total mastectomy and axillary dissection. It is also used in premenopausal women as an alternate therapy for oophorectomy or ovarian radiation therapy. It blocks the uptake of estradiol, thus it is effective for tumors that contain high concentrations of estrogen receptors. (Also see box on progesterone receptors in breast cancer.) Common side effects include nausea, vomiting, weight gain, and

---

### PROGESTERONE RECEPTORS IN BREAST CANCER

Progesterone receptors (PR) are important factors in predicting client response and length of survival in both newly diagnosed and advanced stage breast cancer patients. Estrogen receptors (ER)-positive women generally are reported to have significantly longer survival times than ER-negative clients. The risk of earlier recurrence of cancer is also more prevalent in the ER-negative client. It is predicted that PR analysis will be an important biologic variable that can provide quantative assay data that are more significant for survival prognosis than the presence of estrogen receptors. The further development of this test will allow for improved treatment planning for the client with breast cancer (McGuire, 1986).

hot flashes. A flare-up of bone pain or erythema is sometimes reported by clients, but such effects are usually transient and unrelated to the disease process. Some physicians believe such effects are positive indicators of client response to the drug. Tamoxifen is given orally, usually 10 to 20 mg twice daily (morning and evening).

Interferon alfa-2a, recombinant (Roferon-A), and interferon alfa-2b, recombinant (Intron A), were approved in 1986 for the treatment of hairy cell leukemia. Since then, they have also received approval for the treatment of condylomata acuminata (genital warts) and AIDS-related Kaposi's sarcoma. Investigationally, they are under study for the treatment of chronic myelocytic leukemia, renal and bladder cancers, multiple myeloma, and a number of other cancerous conditions. Both interferon products induce partial or complete remissions in larger numbers of hairy cell leukemia cases than reported with previous therapies. Interferons are natural body proteins formed in response to viral infections and stimulation of the immune system and by certain chemical substances.

Interferons have antiviral (inhibit virus replication), antiproliferative (decrease cell proliferation), and immunomodulatory properties (enhance phagocyte activity and assist the cytotoxicity properties of lymphocytes for target cells). Their mechanism of action as an antineoplastic agent is unknown but may be the result of one or more of the three properties identified. For example, in some types of cancer, interferon appears to have a dual effect of both cytotoxic and immune stimulation. Some clients demonstrate an increase in the hematologic factors, granulocytes, platelets, and hemoglobin serum levels. Toxicities reported include a flulike syndrome that includes fever, chills, muscle pain, loss of appetite, and lethargy. At higher doses, myelosuppression, nausea, vomiting, neurotoxicity (changes in personality, disorientation, paranoid behavior), and various cardiotoxic signs may occur.

Flutamide (Eulexin) is the first oral antiandrogen product on the market. It is used in combination with leuprolide (a luteinizing hormone-releasing hormone agonist) to treat metastatic prostate carcinomas. This combination has been reported to prolong survival by at least 25% more when compared to leuprolide therapy alone.

A new combination antineoplastic therapy is the use of ifosfamide (Iflex) with mesna (Mesnex). Ifosfamide, an alkylating agent, has been studied since the early 1970s but its adverse effect of urotoxicity has limited its usefulness. Mesna has been discovered to be a specific antidote for this type toxicity, thus using both drugs in combination allows for a more aggressive therapy, while reducing the potential of ifosfamide-induced hematuria and cystitis. Ifosfamide is indicated in combination with other agents for the treatment of testicular tumors. It is also being investigated for use in pancreatic and lung cancers.

Ifosfamide must be metabolized in the liver before it can exert its alkylating effects. Two metabolic substances of ifosfamide, 4-hydroxyifosfamide and acrolein, are responsible for the toxic effects of this drug on the kidneys. Mesna will bind and detoxify these metabolites, thus reducing their urotoxic effects in the kidney. It does not interfere with the antineoplastic properties of ifosfamide, because in the blood it is in an oxidized form or dimesna, which is too hydrophilic to penetrate any cell membranes or inactivate ifosfamide at the cellular sites. In the kidneys it is converted ($\frac{1}{3}$) to mesna, which then detoxifies the metabolites of ifosfamide responsible for urotoxicity.

Ifosfamide is administered intravenously in an infusion (over a minimum of 30 minutes) at a dosage of 1.2 gm per meter of squared body surface daily for 5 days. This dose is repeated approximately every 3 weeks. Mesna is given by rapid IV injection in a dose equal to 20% of the ifosfamide dose at the same time as ifosfamide, plus 4 hours and 8 hours after each dose. Therefore, the total daily dose of mesna is 60% of the ifosfamide dose, given each day that ifosfamide is administered.

Carboplatin (Paraplatin) is a newly released drug that is chemically related to cisplatin for the palliative treatment of clients with recurrent ovarian cancer. Its mechanism of action is believed to be similar to cisplatin. It has been used in women with persistent ovarian cancer, including those that were treated with cisplatin. It is reported that carboplatin has produced complete or partial remissions in 15% to 35% of clients (Abramowicz, 1989). This product is believed to be equally effective with less side effects than cisplatin.

Goserelin acetate (Zoladex) is a palliative agent used in the treatment of advanced carcinoma of the prostate. It is a potent inhibitor of pituitary gonadotropins; that is, with long-term administration, the serum levels of testosterone usually drop to the range seen in surgically castrated men within 2 to 4 weeks after initiation of drug therapy. A 3.6 mg dose is implanted subcutaneously in the upper abdominal wall every 28 days. Adverse effects reported are generally related to the lowered testosterone levels and may include hot flashes, sexual dysfunction, and decreased erections. For additional side/adverse effects, see current package insert or USP DI.

## CANCER CHEMOTHERAPY RESEARCH

Cancer chemotherapy research is a priority area of study in the United States. Many new drugs are being studied with the hope of improving the treatment and survival of cancer and AIDS-induced cancer clients. (AIDS is reviewed in Chapter 66.) The reader is encouraged to monitor professional literature for the release of new drugs for the treatment of cancer.

Granulocyte macrophage-colony stimulating factor (GM-CSF) is an immunomodulator agent under investigation as an adjunct treatment to chemotherapy, especially for the treatment of AIDS clients. Another promising area of study is liposomes. Liposomes provide a new delivery system that

## Investigational Drug Classifications

Investigational drugs are agents that have not been released for marketing by the Food and Drug Administration. While responsibility for regulating drugs rests with the FDA, the National Cancer Institute (NCI) is the largest developer of antineoplastic agents in the United States. The NCI has established stringent regulations to monitor the receipt, use, and disposal of investigational drugs. It also requires that investigators report adverse reactions on an established time schedule. For example, anaphylactic reactions to an investigational drug must be reported by phoning a specific branch office that is available on a 24-hour basis. This call must be followed up with a written report within 10 working days.

Investigational drugs are divided into three groups:

| | Drug Group | Purpose |
|---|---|---|
| Phase I | A | To determine maximum tolerated dosage |
| | | To detect toxicities associated with various dosage schedules |
| | | To determine pharmacokinetics and optimum dosing schedule |
| Phase II | B | To identify antineoplastic activity in specific cancers affecting humans |
| | | To determine client's response to various drug dosages and schedules |
| Phase III | C | New agent now compared with previously marketed drugs to ascertain effectiveness, effect on quality of life, mortality, and morbidity |

is composed of one or more lipid membranes which hold lipid-soluble drugs) encapsulating a discrete aqueous compartment capable of holding water-soluble drugs. Drugs that are encapsulated in a liposome capsule can be distributed differently in the body than free drugs.

Liposomes accumulate at sites of inflammation and infection, as well as in some solid tumors. Thus they are under study for the treatment of systemic fungal infections (with amphotericin B) and for the treatment of specific cancers. Doxorubicin, cisplatin, and methotrexate are just several of the antineoplastic agents currently undergoing clinical testing. Doxorubicin in liposome administration has been reported to deliver the drug more directly to the site of action, which results in less cardiac adverse effects and less nausea, vomiting, and alopecia. Cisplatin in liposomes has been reported to cause much less kidney damage than cisplatin alone. If studies of liposome drug therapy continue to report that, in addition to a decrease in side/adverse

effects, therapeutic outcome is also efficacious, then liposomes will have the potential of opening an exciting new avenue of drug delivery in the last decade of the twentieth century.

Other new cancer products that are in Phase III or clinical trials include toremifene, A.P.D., difluorodeoxycytidine, fenretinide for the treatment of breast cancers; gamma interferon and tauromustine for colon cancer; and buserelin for prostate cancer. (See box: Investigational Drug Classifications.)

## SUMMARY

The antineoplastic agents act by interfering with cell reproduction or replication at some point in the cell cycle. They are classified into various groupings based on their probable mechanisms of action: antimetabolites, alkylating agents, antibiotic antitumor agents, hormones, and miscellaneous agents. Because the drugs are nonselective and affect all cells in the body as they replicate, there is always some degree of injury to normal cells. Particularly susceptible are those with a high rate of growth, such as bone marrow, gastrointestinal epithelium, and hair follicles. Bone marrow suppression with the resultant anemia, leukocytopenia, and thrombocytopenia is unavoidable, and so the laboratory values for blood counts are used to titrate the individual client's dosage and to determine when the client is most susceptible to infection and hemorrhage. Much of the nursing management of antineoplastic therapy is to prevent injury and infection; promote comfort; provide care for the gastrointestinal effects of stomatitis, nausea and vomiting, and changes in bowel elimination; assess for the development of nephrotoxicity, neurotoxicity, cardiotoxicity, pulmonary toxicity, and dermatologic effects of these drugs. Although there is short-term toxicity and side effects, the potential for cure or reduction of symptoms is a benefit that most often outweighs the risk and discomfort of the administration.

## Case Study: The Client with Hodgkin's Disease

Matthew Bennett is a 32-year-old, married salesperson who has been referred to an oncology clinic after a diagnosis of stage III-A Hodgkin's disease was confirmed by his primary physician. Mr. Bennett first went to his physician after finding a lump in his right axilla that persisted for several months. The oncologist has recommended a program of chemotherapy to include the following drugs:

  mechlorethamine (Mustargen)
  vincristine (Oncovin)
  prednisone (Deltasone)
  procarbazine (Matulane)

1. How is each drug classified as a chemotherapeutic agent and what is its effect on the cell cycle?
2. Why is prednisone used as part of the chemotherapy regimen?
3. What measures should the nurse implement before administration of mechlorethamine to reduce nausea and vomiting?
4. What should the nurse do if the intravenous infusion infiltrates during administration of mustargen or vincristine?
5. During the course of therapy with vincristine, Mr. Bennett complains of numbness and tingling in his hands and feet. What is the significance of these symptoms?
6. What precautions should the nurse take when handling the equipment used for drug administration and body fluids?

## BIBLIOGRAPHY

A critical look at the new chemotherapy recommendations. (1988). Healthfacts 13(11):1.

Abramowicz M, editor. (1989). Carboplatin, The Medical Letter, 31(800):83.84.

Almadrones L et al. (1990). Problems associated with the administration of intraperitoneal therapy using the Port-A-Cath system, Oncol Nurs Forum 17(1):75.

American Hospital Formulary Service. (1991). AHFS drug information '91. Bethesda, MD: American Society of Hospital Pharmacists, Inc.

Benhamou S et al. (1988). Sister chromatid exchanges and chromosomal aberrations in lymphocytes of nurses handling cytostatic agents, Int J Cancer 41(3):350.

Betcher DL. (1988). Pharmacology: carboplatin, J Assoc Pediatr Nurses 9(2):29.

Betcher D. (1987). Local toxicities of chemotherapy, J Assoc Pediatr Oncol Nurses 4(1):56.

Birdsall C et al. (1988). How do you manage chemotherapy extravasation? Am J Nurs 88(2):228.

Brixey MT. (1988). Chemotherapeutic agents: intravesical instillation, Urol Nurs 9(2):4.

Bulcavage LM et al. (1987). Safety issues in handling of chemotherapeutic agents, Emphasis Nurs 2(2):75.

Burnham N et al. (1987). Ifosfamide, J Assoc Pediatr Oncol Nurses 4(3):4.

Camp-Sorrell D. (1990). Intra-arterial chemotherapy infusion, Oncol Nurs Forum 17(1):103.

Caudell KA et al. (1988). Quantification of urinary mutagens in nurses during potential antineoplastic agent exposure: a pilot study with concurrent environmental and dietary control, Cancer Nurs 11(1):41.

Chang JC. (1988). Antipyretic effect of naproxen and corticosteroids on neoplastic fever, J Pain Symptom Manage 3(3):141.

Cohen DG. (1987). Emergencies in the pediatric oncology patient, J Assoc Pediatr Oncol Nurses 4(3/4):5.

Cunningham M. (1990). Nonhematologic toxicities of selected chemotherapic agents used in the treatment of adult leukemia, Semin Oncol Nurs 6(1):67.

Curran CF et al. (1989). Accidental acute exposure to doxorubicin, Cancer Nurs 12(6):329.

Dillman JB. (1989). New antineoplastic therapies and inherent risks: monoclonal antibodies, biologic response modifiers and interleukin-2, J Intravenous Nurs 12(2):103.

Doig B. (1988). Adjuvant chemotherapy in breast cancer, Cancer Nurs 11(2):91.

Dunne CF. (1989). Safe handling of antineoplastic agents: self-learning module, Cancer Nurs 12(2):120.

Eilers J et al. (1988). Development, testing, and application of the Oral Assessment Guide. . . high-dose radiation and/or chemotherapy, Oncol Nurs Forum 15(3):325.

Engelking C. (1987). Lung cancer: chemotherapy, Am J Nurs 87(11):1438.

FDA approves marketing of Flutamide for prostate cancer indication. (1989). Clin Phar 8(5):240-241.

Fraser MC et al. (1988). Late effects of cancer therapy: chemotherapy-related malignancies, Oncol Nurs Forum 15(1):67.

Harris LL et al. (1989). Chemotherapy in head and neck cancer, Semin Oncol Nurs 5(3):174.

Herfindal ET et al. (1988). Clinical pharmacy and therapeutics, ed 4. Baltimore: Williams & Wilkins.

Horoszewicz JS et al. (1987). Interferon: a review of its development and potential clinical applications, Hosp Formul 22(9):776.

In development, new medicines for older Americans. (1988). Pharmaceutical Manufacturers Association in cooperation with the American Cancer Society.

Jordan LN. (1989). Effects of fluid manipulation on the incidence of vomiting during outpatient cisplatin infusion, Oncol Nurs Forum 16(2):213.

Kastrup EK, editor. (1991). Facts and comparisons, St Louis, JB Lippincott Co.

Keller JF et al. (1988). Nursing issues and management in chemotherapy-induced alopecia, Oncol Nurs Forum 15(5):603.

Lange BJ et al. (1988). Home care involving methotrexate infusions for children with acute lymphoblastic leukemia, J Pediatr 112(3):492.

Lasater S. (1988). Testicular cancer: a nursing perspective of diagnosis and treatment, J Urol Nurs 7(1):329.

Lydon J. (1989). Assessment of renal function in the patient receiving chemotherapy, Cancer Nurs 12(3):133.

Masoorli ST et al. (1988). Putting some comfort in chemotherapy, RN 51(8):73.

Mayer DK. (1989). Dimensions in biological response modifiers, Dimens Oncol Nurs 3(3):6.

McGuire WL and Clark GM. Role of progesterone receptors in breast cancer, CA 36(5):302, 1986.

Meadows AT. (1989). Second malignant neoplasms in childhood cancer survivors, J Assoc Pediatr Oncol Nurses 6(1):7.

Methotrexate therapy and arthritic joint degeneration. (1988). Nurses Drug Alert 12(3):21.

Ostchega Y et al. (1988). High-dose cisplatin-related peripheral neuropathy, Cancer Nurs 11(1):23.

Ostro MJ and Cullis PR. (1989). Use of liposomes as injectable-drug delivery systems, Am J Hosp Pharm 46(8):1576.

Parkinson DR. (1989). The role of interleukin-2 in the biotherapy of cancer, Oncol Nurs Forum (Suppl) 16(6):16.

Power LA, senior consultant. (1990). ASHP technical assistance bulletin on handling cytotoxic and hazardous drugs, J Hosp Pharm 47(5):1033.

Power LA, Anderson RW, et al. (1990). Update on safe handling of hazardous drugs: the advice of experts, Am J Hosp Pharm 47(5):1050.

Ranade VV. (1989). Drug delivery systems. I. Site-specific drug delivery using liposomes as carriers, J Clin Pharmacol 29:685.

Robinson ME et al. (1989). A chemotherapy self-learning package: a cost-effective method, J Nurs Staff Dev 5(3):144.

Rogers B et al. (1987). Handling antineoplastic agents: urine mutagenicity in nurses, Image J Nurs Sch 19(3):108.

Schoenike SE and Dana WR. (1990). Ifosfamide and Mesna, Clin Phar 9(5):170.

Simonson GM. (1988). Caring for patients with acute myelocytic leukemia, Am J Nurs 88(3):304.

Smith DB. (1988). Chemotherapy: its effects on a stoma, J Enterostom Ther 15(3):138.

Stam HJ et al. (1988). Rating the toxicities of cancer drugs, Am J Nurs 88(10:1362.

Studies of adjuvant therapy for node-negative breast cancer are published; disagreement on indications for treatment continues. (1989). Clin Phar 8(5):312.

Turcillo P. (1988). Treatment of testicular cancer: a historical review and current update, AUAA J 8(3):19.

Valanis BG et al. (1987). Antineoplastic drugs: handle with care, AAOHN J 35(11):487.

Vizcarra C. (1988). Intraperitoneal chemotherapy: IV team responsibility, J Intravenous Nurs 11(3):184.

Wadler S et al. (1989). Clinical toxicities of the combination of 5-fluorouracil and recombinant interferon alfa-2a: an unusual toxicity profile, Oncol Nurs Forum (Suppl) 16(6):12.

Walker ED. (1988). Hyperglycemia: a complication of chemotherapy in children, Cancer Nurs 11(1):18.

Walters P. (1990). Chemo: a nurse's guide to action, administration, and side effects, RN 53(2):52.

Weeks DD et al. (1988). When leukemia complicates pregnancy, MCN 13(1):28.

Williamson KM et al. (1988). Occupational health hazards for nurses, part 2, Image J Nurs Sch 20(3):162.

*Chapter*

58 Overview of Infections, Inflammation, and Fever

## CHAPTER OBJECTIVES

*After studying this chapter, you should be able to meet the following objectives and define the key terms.*

1. Describe the mediators of the inflammatory system.

2. Identify different types of fever.

3. Explain the body's set point temperature mechanism.

4. Describe the goal and mechanisms of action of antimicrobial therapy.

5. Identify the general adverse reactions to antimicrobial drugs.

6. Discuss general guidelines for the optimal use of antimicrobial agents.

7. Describe nursing management of antimicrobial therapy.

## KEY TERMS

**bacteremia,** page 878

**bactericidal agents,** page 881

**bacteriostatic agents,** page 881

**colonization,** page 878

**fever,** page 879

**hypersensitivity,** page 882

**infection,** page 876

**inflammation,** page 878

**pyrogens,** page 879

**sepsis,** page 878

**septicemia,** page 878

**Stevens-Johnson syndrome,** page 882

**superinfection,** page 882

## INFECTIONS

Infectious diseases comprise a wide spectrum of illnesses caused by pathogenic microorganisms. Some common pathogens and their most likely sites of infection in the body are listed in Table 58-1. These pathogens cause pneumonia, urinary tract infections, upper respiratory tract infections, venereal disease, vaginitis, tuberculosis, and candidiasis.

**Infection,** the invasion and multiplication of microorganisms in body tissues, is classified primarily as either local or systemic. A localized infection, which may involve

**TABLE 58-1** Primary organisms and common sites of infection

| Organism | Infection site |
|---|---|
| **GRAM-POSITIVE COCCI** | |
| *Staphylococcus aureus* | Burns, skin infections, decubital and surgical wounds, paranasal |
|   Non-penicillinase producing |   and middle ear (chronic sinusitis and otitis), lungs, lung ab- |
|   Penicillinase producing |   scess, pleura, endocardium, bone (osteomyelitis), and joints |
| *Staphylococcus epidermidis* | |
|   Non-penicillinase producing | |
|   Penicillinase producing | |
|   Methicillin resistant | |
| *Streptococcus pneumoniae* | Paranasal and middle ear, lungs, pleura |
| *Streptococcus pyogenes* (group A β-hemolytic) | Burns, skin infections, decubitus and surgical wounds, paranasal and middle ear, throat, bone (osteomyelitis), and joints |
| *Streptococcus,* viridans group | Endocardium |
| **GRAM-POSITIVE BACILLI** | |
| *Clostridium tetani* (anaerobe) | Puncture wounds, lacerations, and crush injuries; toxins affecting nervous system |
| *Corynebacterium diphtheriae* | Throat, upper part of the respiratory tract |
| **GRAM-NEGATIVE COCCI** | |
| *Neisseria gonorrhoeae* | Urethra, prostate, epididymis and testes, joints |
| *Neisseria meningitidis* | Meninges |
| **ENTERIC GRAM-NEGATIVE BACILLI** | |
| As a group (*Bacteroides, Enterobacter, Escherichia coli, Klebsiella pneumoniae, Proteus mirabilis, other Proteus, Salmonella, Serratia, Shigella*) | Peritoneum, biliary tract, kidney and bladder, prostate, decubital and surgical wounds, bone |
| *Bacteroides* | Brain abscess, lung abscess, throat, peritoneum |
| *Enterobacter* | Peritoneum, biliary tract, kidney and bladder, endocardium |
| *Escherichia coli* | Peritoneum, biliary tract, kidney and bladder |
| *Klebsiella pneumoniae* | Lungs, lung abscess |
| **OTHER GRAM-NEGATIVE BACILLI** | |
| *Haemophilus influenzae* | Meninges, paranasal and middle ear, lungs, pleura |
| *Pseudomonas aeruginosa* | Burns, paranasal and middle ear (chronic otitis media), decubital and surgical wounds, lungs, joints |
| **ACID-FAST BACILLI** | |
| *Mycobacterium tuberculosis* | Lungs, pleura, peritoneum, meninges, kidney and bladder, |
| *Mycobacterium avium* | testes, bone, joints |
| **MYCOPLASMAS** | |
| *Mycoplasma pneumoniae* | Lungs |
| **SPIROCHETES** | |
| *Treponema pallidum* (syphilis) | Any tissue or vascular organ of the body |
| **FUNGI** | |
| *Aspergillus* | Paranasal and middle ear, lungs |
| *Candida* species | Skin infections, throat, lungs, endocardium, kidney and bladder, |
| *Cryptococcus* | vagina |
| **VIRUSES** | |
| Herpes virus or varicella-zoster virus | Skin infections (herpes simplex or zoster) |
| Enterovirus, mumps virus, and others | Meninges, epididymis, and testes |
| Respiratory viruses (including Epstein-Barr virus) | Throat, lungs |
| **ANAEROBES** | |
| Gram-positive | Deep wounds |
|   *Clostridium difficile* | |
|   *Clostridium perfringens* | |
|   *Peptococcus* species | |
|   *Peptostreptococcus* species | |
| Gram-negative | |
|   *Bacteroides fragilis* | |
|   *Fusobacterium* species | |

the skin or internal organs, may progress to a systemic infection. A systemic infection involves the whole body rather than a localized area of the body. Several terms describe the degree of local or systemic infection. **Colonization** is the localized presence of microorganisms in body tissues or organs. These microorganisms can be pathogenic or part of the normal flora. Colonization alone does not denote infection but rather signifies the potential for infection resulting from the multiplication of the resident organisms or the alteration in host defense mechanisms of the individual. When flora at its normal colonization site is altered (e.g., by the administration of an antibiotic that affects pathogens and some but not all normal microorganisms), unaffected microorganisms within that environment may grow uninhibited and cause a secondary infection.

**Inflammation** is a defense mechanism of body tissues in response to invasion or toxins produced by colonizing microorganisms. This reaction consists of cytologic and histologic tissue responses for the localization of phagocytic activity and destruction or removal of injurious material leading to repair and healing. **Bacteremia** is the presence of viable bacteria in the circulatory system. **Septicemia** refers to a systemic infection caused by the multiplication of microorganisms in the circulation. Although bacteremia may lead to septicemia in the immunocompromised host, it is (depending on the pathogen) usually a short-lived, self-limited process. In the immunocompromised host, bacteremia may rapidly produce an overwhelming systemic disease. **Sepsis** is a syndrome involving multiple system organ involvement that is a result of microorganisms or their toxins circulating in the blood.

For nonpathogenic organisms colonizing humans or causing transient bacteremias without tissue invasion, antibiotic therapy is rarely required in the immunocompetent host, whereas prophylactic antibiotic therapy may be required in immunocompromised hosts. In most cases of localized inflammation, such as wound infections, pneumonia, or urinary tract infections, antimicrobials reduce the number of viable pathogens. This permits the immune system to eliminate microorganisms. Antimicrobials are also an essential part of the treatment of septicemia and sepsis.

Microorganisms are divided into several groups: bacteria, mycoplasmas, spirochetes, fungi, and viruses. Bacteria are classified according to their shape, such as bacilli, spirilla, and cocci, and their capacity to be stained. Specific identification of bacteria requires a Gram stain and culture with chemical testing. Gram stain is a sequential procedure that involves crystal violet and iodine solutions followed by alcohol. Gram stain allows the rapid identification of organisms into groups, such as gram-positive or gram-negative rods or cocci. The culture procedures identify specific organisms, but they require 24 to 48 hours for completion. Often the initial or empiric antibiotic selection is based on the physician's clinical impression plus the Gram-stain pro-cedure; the antibiotic may be changed once culture and sensitivity results are available.

## INFLAMMATION

Inflammation is the reaction of body tissues to injury, such as physical trauma, foreign bodies, chemical substances, surgery, radiation, and electricity. The area affected will undergo a series of changes as the body processes attempt to wall off, heal, and/or replace the injured tissue. For example, after an injury occurs, the body will release chemical substances into the tissue that form a wall (called a chemotactic gradient). Fluids and cells will begin to move toward this area.

Blood vessels dilate within 30 minutes of the insult. This will provide for increases in blood flow and in exudation of fluid from the blood vessels into the injured tissues. The exudate includes protein-rich fluids high in fibrinogen that will attract other substances to the area, such as complement, antibodies, and leukocytes. Fluids collecting in this area will result in edema or swelling. Generally, this occurs within 4 hours of the injury.

During the cellular phase, granulocytes will migrate to the area from the dilated blood vessels at the site. The granulocytes will migrate toward the chemotactic site and accumulate in the area of injury. If the injury is a foreign substance or bacteria, they will engulf and destroy the foreign material (phagocytosis). Neutrophils, monocytes (macrophages), and lymphocytes (which arrive later) are the granulocytes that affect the injured area. The phagocytosis process tends to localize or wall off the foreign material, to prevent its spread through the tissues. Large numbers of phagocytes lead to pus accumulation and the eventual destruction and removal of the foreign material.

Some pathogens are resistant to destruction and are only walled off, such as tuberculosis bacilli. Thus they can live for many years within the confined cells in the body. Others may transform from a local infection into a systemic infection, thus requiring antimicrobial or antibiotic treatment.

***Mediators of the inflammatory system.*** The complement system is composed of complement components (18 distinct proteins and their cleavage products) present in the blood in the form of inactive proteins called zymogens. Complement is essential in reacting to an acute inflammatory reaction caused by bacteria, some viruses, and immune complex diseases. Complement enhances chemotaxis, increases blood vessel permeability, and eventually causes cell lysis.

Histamine, prostaglandins, arachidonic acid, and leukotrienes are other mediators capable of producing local reactions, smooth muscle contraction, increased chemotaxis, blood vessel vasodilation, and other inflammatory effects. When the foreign agent is destroyed, the resulting debris will be removed by the macrophages and neutrophils, thus resolving the inflammatory reaction.

# FEVER

**Fever,** or elevated body temperature, is a sign of inflammation. It may be caused by the release of endogenous pyrogens from the macrophages. These **pyrogens,** or fever-producing substances, will interfere with the temperature-regulating centers located in the hypothalamus, raising the thermostat set point. The body may respond to the pyrogens by releasing arachidonic acid and prostaglandin (PGE1) that also affect the central control, further increasing the hypothalamic set point. The body will react by conserving heat through vasoconstriction, piloerection (goose flesh), and shivering—all factors that increase the body temperature.

The normal body temperature is 98.6° F (37° C), and the normal range is 97° F to approximately 99° F when measured orally. Rectally, a person's body temperature is 1° F higher than oral. Hyperthermia occurs when the body's temperature rises above normal. When the body temperature reaches 106° F, convulsions may result. If the body's thermoregulatory mechanisms have trouble returning the body temperature to a normal setting, body metabolism may increase so rapidly that the body cannot regulate its own heat production. At 108° F tissue damage occurs and cells begin to die, resulting in irreversible brain damage.

Several types of fever are known. For example, a constant fever that rises or falls only a few degrees above or below a specified point is seen with typhoid fever. An intermittent fever may return to normal once or several times in 24 hours. This type of fever is associated with pyogenic infections, abscesses, lymphomas, tuberculosis, and drug reactions. A remittent fever fluctuates but does not usually return to normal; this occurs in many viral and bacterial infections. Relapsing fever consists of afebrile episodes of 1 or more days between fevers, such as in malaria and Hodgkin's disease. Fever of unknown origin (FUO) has been described as a temperature greater than 103° F recorded daily for more than 2 weeks in a client with an uncertain diagnosis, following a week's evaluation in a hospital setting. Most clients with FUO are later found to have an infection, neoplasm, or connective tissue disease.

Body temperature is regulated by nervous system feedback mechanisms through a temperature-regulating center in the hypothalamus. When the hypothalamus is no longer in contact with the pyrogens, it will reset the temperature to the normal set point. Experimental studies indicate that prostaglandins of the E series are produced in response to endogenous pyrogens. The E prostaglandins act on the anterior hypothalamus to increase the set point, thus resulting in fever. Drugs that inhibit the synthesis of E prostaglandins have antipyretic activity (acetaminophen, salicylates). For example, salicylates reduce raised body temperatures by causing the hypothalmic center to reestablish a normal set point. Heat production will not be inhibited, although heat

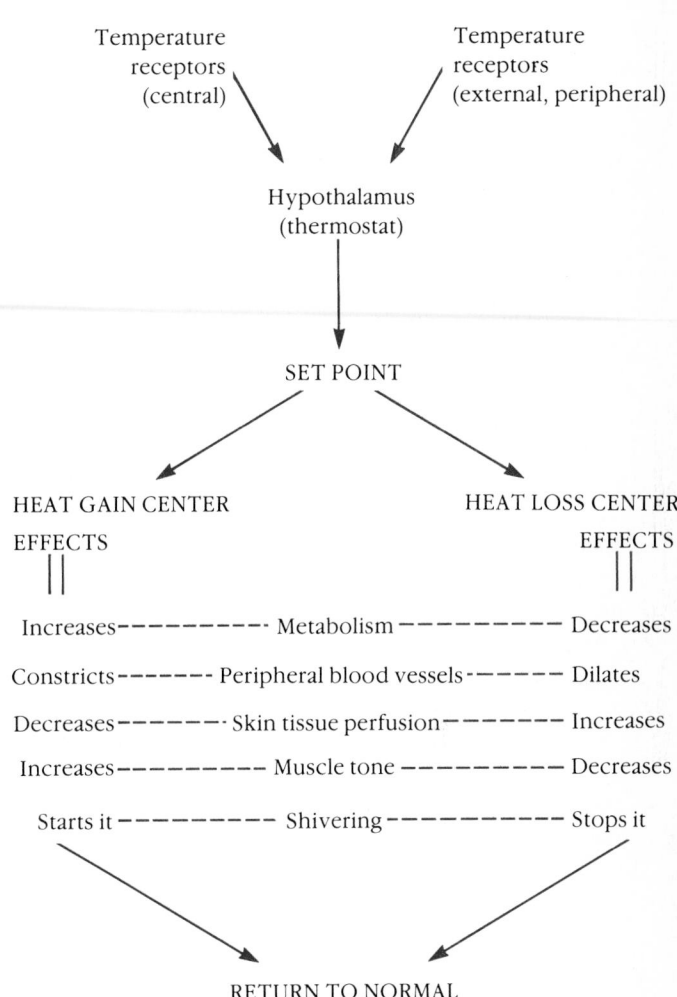

**FIGURE 58-1**  Set point temperature mechanism.

loss will be increased by an increase in cutaneous blood flow and sweating, caused by the lowered thermostat (see Figure 58-1). Antibiotics indirectly reduce temperature by destroying the bacteria causing the fever.

## ANTIMICROBIAL THERAPY

The treatment of an infectious disease caused by a microorganism depends on the group to which the microorganism belongs; different groups of antimicrobial agents are used for treating different groups of microorganisms. Table 58-2 lists some antimicrobial agents used in the treatment of infectious diseases. Antimicrobial drugs can help cure or control most infections caused by microorganisms. However, antimicrobials alone do not necessarily produce the cure. They are adjuncts to methods, such as surgical incision and drainage, pulmonary toilet, and wound debridement for removal of nonviable, infected tissue.

The first major antimicrobial agents were the sulfon-

**TABLE 58-2** Antimicrobial drugs of choice

| Organism | Drug(s) |
|---|---|
| **GRAM-POSITIVE COCCI** | |
| *Staphylococcus aureus* | |
|   Non-penicillinase producing | penicillin G or V, first generation cephalosporins, vancomycin |
|   Penicillinase producing | first generation cephalosporins, cloxacillin, dicloxacillin, methicillin |
|   Methicillin resistant | ciprofloxacin, vancomycin |
| *Streptococcus pneumoniae* | penicillin G or V |
| *Streptococcus pyogenes* (group A) | penicillin G or V |
| *Streptococcus* (group B) | penicillin G or V, ampicillin, amoxicillin |
| *Streptococcus viridans* | penicillin G or V |
| **GRAM-POSITIVE BACILLI** | |
| *Bacillus anthracis* | penicillin G or V |
| *Corynebacterium diphtheriae* | erythromycin |
| *Corynebacterium,* JK strain | erythromycin, vancomycin |
| *Listeria monocytogenes* | amikacin, gentamicin, tobramycin, netilmicin |
| **GRAM-NEGATIVE COCCI** | |
| *Neisseria gonorrhoeae* | penicillin G or V, ampicillin, amoxacillin, azlocillin, piperacillin, cefoxitin, and most third generation cephalosporins |
| *Neisseria meningitidis* | penicillin G or V |
| **GRAM-NEGATIVE ENTERIC BACILLI** | |
| *Escherichia coli* | amikacin, gentamicin, tobramycin, cefamandole, cefotetan, third generation cephalosporins, ciprofloxacin |
| *Klebsiella pneumoniae* | same as for *E. coli* |
| *Proteus mirabilis* | same as for *E. coli* |
| *Salmonella* sp | ampicillin, amoxocillin, ciprofloxacin |
| **OTHER BACILLI** | |
| *Pseudomonas aeruginosa* | azlocillin, amikacin, gentamicin, piperacillin, ceftazidime, ciprofloxacin |
| **ANAEROBES** | |
| Gram-positive | |
|   *Clostridium difficile* | tetracyclines |
|   *Clostridium perfringens* | penicillin G or V |
|   *Clostridium tetani* | penicillin G or V |
|   *Peptococcus* sp | penicillin G or V |
| *Peptostreptococcus* sp | penicillin G or V |
| Gram-negative | |
|   *Bacteroides fragilis* | clindamycin, metronidazole |
| **MYCOPLASMAS** | |
| *Mycoplasma pneumoniae* | clindamycin, erythromycin, tetracyclines |
| **SPIROCHETES** | |
| *Treponema pallidum* (syphilis) | penicillin G or V |
| **FUNGI** | |
| *Asperigillus, candida* sp | amphotericin B |
| **VIRUSES** | |
| Herpes simplex | vidarabine, acyclovir |

amides. The second group of antimicrobials were the true antibiotics, such as penicillin. They were substances derived from certain organisms used against infections caused by other organisms. As a result of research, there are now many synthetic and semisynthetic antibiotics. Other antimicrobial agents include the urinary tract antiseptics and the anti-mycobacterial, antifungal, and antiviral agents.

*Mechanism of action.*  The goal of antimicrobial therapy is to destroy or to suppress the growth of infecting micro-organisms so that normal host defense and other supporting mechanisms can control the infection, resulting in its cure. To exert their effects, antimicrobial agents must first gain access to target sites. Usually this can be accomplished by absorption and distribution of the drug into and by way of the circulatory system. More specific antibiotics or anti-microbial agents are capable of penetrating to the site and having an affinity for the bacterial target proteins. Some-times, as in the case of infections of the skin and eyes, local application to the infected area may be necessary. Once the drug has reached its site of action, it can have bactericidal or bacteriostatic effects, depending on its mechanisms of action.

**Bacteriostatic agents** inhibit bacterial growth, allowing host defense mechanisms additional time to remove the in-vading microorganisms. **Bactericidal agents,** on the other hand, cause bacterial cell death and lysis, superimposing the killing effect of the drug on the effects of host defenses. Antimicrobial agents may be divided into bacteriostatic and bactericidal categories, with the sulfonamides as an example of the former and the penicillins exemplifying the latter. Such categorization is not always valid or reliable, however, because the same antimicrobial agent may have either effect depending on the dose administered and the concentration achieved at its site of action. Tetracycline, for example, is generally bacteriostatic but may be bactericidal in high con-centrations. Chloramphenicol, which is often listed as a bacteriostatic drug, has bactericidal effects against *S. pneu-moniae* and *H. influenzae* in the cerebrospinal fluid.

Antimicrobial agents may exert their bacteriostatic or bac-tericidal effects in one of four major ways:
1. Inhibition of cell wall synthesis in bacteria. Unlike host cells, bacteria are not isotonic with body fluids. Their contents are under high osmotic pressure and their viability depends on the integrity of the cell walls. Any compound that inhibits any step in the synthesis of this cell wall causes it to be weakened and the cell to lyse. Antimicrobial agents having this mechanism of action are bactericidal.
2. Disruption or alteration of membrane permeability, resulting in leakage of essential bacterial metabolic substrates. Agents causing the effects can be either bacteriostatic or bactericidal.
3. Inhibition of protein synthesis. Antimicrobial agents may induce the formation of defective protein mole-cules; such agents are bactericidal in their action. An-

> ### CLASSIFICATION OF ANTIMICROBIALS BY MECHANISM OF ACTION
>
> **Inhibit Cell Wall Synthesis**
>
> penicillins
> cephalosporins
> vancomycin
> bacitracin
> cycloserine
> ristocetin
>
> **Alter Membrane Permeability**
>
> amphotericin B
> nystatin
> polymyxin
> colistin
>
> **Inhibit Protein Synthesis**
> *Impede replication of genetic information*
> nalidixic acid
> griseofulvin
> novobiocin
> rifampin
> pyrimethamine
> *Impair translation of genetic information*
> chloramphenicol
> tetracycline
> erythromycin
> aminoglycosides
> lincomycins
>
> **Antimetabolites**
>
> sulfonamides
> sulfones
> PAS
> INH
> ethambutol

timicrobial agents that inhibit specific steps in protein synthesis are bacteriostatic.
4. Inhibition of synthesis of essential metabolites. An-timicrobial agents that work in this manner structurally resemble physiologic compounds and act as compet-itive inhibitors in a metabolic pathway. Generally, they are bacteriostatic agents. (See the box above.)

*Side effects/adverse reactions.*  Although the devel-opment of antimicrobial agents represents one of the most important advances in drug therapy, these drugs can have adverse and toxic effects. The list of side effects and toxic effects of each specific drug group is long and varied. Table 58-3 identifies some of the major allergic and toxic effects of a few antimicrobial agents. All antimicrobial agents, however, are capable of producing two general types of adverse reactions of which the nurse must be aware.

**TABLE 58-3** Selected allergic and toxic effects of antimicrobial drugs

| Effect | Drug |
|---|---|
| Anaphylaxis | penicillin |
| Hematologic effects | chloramphenicol (low incidence but high mortality) |
| | sulfonamides (low incidence) |
| Nephrotoxicity | polymyxins |
| | aminoglycosides |
| | sulfonamides (low incidence with newer drugs) |
| Potential for neuro-muscular block-ade | polymyxins |
| | aminoglycosides |
| Injury to eighth cranial nerve | aminoglycosides |

*Allergic or hypersensitivity reactions.* Allergic or hypersensitivity reactions occur in response to all available antimicrobial agents. **Hypersensitivity** is a state of altered reactivity in which the body reacts with an exaggerated immune response. Such responses include rash, fever, urticaria with pruritus, chills, a generalized erythema, anaphylaxis, and the Stevens-Johnson syndrome. **Stevens-Johnson syndrome** is a form of toxic epidermal necrolysis in which the epidermis separates from the dermis, leaving the client with a skin loss similar to a second degree burn.

A minor rash may be easily tolerated, but an individual with a generalized rash or erythema accompanied by chills and fever needs medical intervention. For example, an allergic response to a rapid infusion of vancomycin can result in a generalized red skin reaction, fever and chills; to mitigate this reaction, antihistamines would need to be given. Some rashes fade with continued treatment, as with some individuals receiving ampicillin; whereas other symptoms may become more severe, necessitating discontinuing the medication. Respiratory distress (wheezing) or anaphylaxis is a medical emergency requiring immediate attention to prevent a fatal outcome.

Sensitization has occurred through indirect exposure to a drug, such as drinking milk from cows treated with antibiotics or eating poultry or beef from livestock treated with antimicrobials. Also, previous topical application of antimicrobials may cause sensitization.

Treatment of allergic reactions includes the use of antihistamines and epinephrine, which block or counteract the effects of the vasoactive mediators of allergy, and the use of corticosteroids, which may reduce tissue injury and edema in the inflammatory response. The use of steroids is controversial in the face of systemic infection because of their prolonged inhibition of normal host defense responses.

*Superinfection.* **Superinfection** is an infection that occurs during the course of antimicrobial therapy delivered for either therapeutic or prophylactic reasons. Most antibiotics reduce or eradicate the normal microbial flora of the body, which is then replaced by resistant exogeneous or endogenous bacteria. If the number of these replacement organisms is large and the host conditions favorable, clinical superinfection can occur. Approximately 2% of persons treated with antibiotics get superinfections. The risk is greater when large doses of antibiotics are used, when more than one antibiotic is administered concurrently, and when broad-spectrum drugs are employed. The administration of some specific antimicrobials are more commonly associated with superinfection than others. For example, *Pseudomonas* organisms frequently colonize in and infect individuals taking cephalosporins. In a similar manner, clients taking tetracyclines may become infected with *Candida albicans*. Generally, superinfections are caused by microorganisms that are resistant to the drug the client is receiving. In the past penicillinase-producing staphylococci were the most common cause of superinfection. *S. aureus* and *S. epidermidis* superinfections, especially with methicillin-resistant strains, are again on the rise. Also, gram-negative enteric bacilli and fungi are the most common offenders. The proper management of superinfections includes (1) discontinuation of the drug being given or replacement of it by another drug to which the organism is sensitive, (2) culture of the suspected infected area, and (3) possible administration of an antimicrobial agent effective against the new offending organism.

*General guidelines for use.* Several important principles guide the judicious and optimal use of the antimicrobial agents. Causes of adverse reactions to antimicrobial agents and therapeutic failures are often related to lack of adherence to the following principles of antimicrobial therapy.

*Identification of infecting organism.* Because most antimicrobial agents have a specific effect on a limited range of microorganisms, the physician must formulate a specific diagnosis about the potential pathogens or organisms most likely causing a given infectious process. The drug most likely to be specifically effective against the suspected microorganism can then be selected. This objective is most validly and reliably accomplished by obtaining specimens from the infected area if possible (e.g., urine, sputum, wound drainage) or by obtaining venous blood specimens and sending them to the laboratory for culture and identification of the causative organism. The recovery of a specific microorganism from appropriate specimens is a significant factor in the determination of antimicrobial therapy. When a significant microorganism has been isolated, laboratory tests for antimicrobial susceptibility (sensitivity) to various antimicrobial agents are completed.

It is desirable to receive culture and sensitivity reports before initiating antimicrobial therapy. In some situations, however, it is not practical to wait for these laboratory results. For example, antimicrobial therapy must be initiated without delay in acute, life-threatening situations, such as peritonitis, septicemia, or pneumonia. In such situations the choice of antimicrobial agent for initial use must be based on tentative identification of the pathogen and Gram stain. It is known, for example, that microorganisms commonly isolated in acute adult infections of the lung include pneumococci, Haemophilus strain streptococci, and staphylococci. Antimicrobial agents specifically toxic to those organisms may be administered temporarily. The drugs can then be changed, if necessary, after laboratory reports have been received. When even tentative identification is difficult, either *broad-spectrum* antibiotics, which are effective against a wide range of microorganisms, can be prescribed or several antimicrobial agents may be prescribed for simultaneous administration.

Some infections are most effectively treated with the use of only one antibiotic. In other situations *combined antimicrobial drug therapy* may be indicated. Indications for the simultaneous use of two or more antimicrobial agents include (1) treatment of mixed infections, in which each drug may act on a separate portion of a complex microbial flora; (2) need to delay the rapid emergence of bacteria resistant to one drug; and (3) need to reduce the incidence or intensity of adverse reactions by decreasing the dose of a potentially toxic drug. Indiscriminate use of combined antimicrobial drug therapy should be avoided because of expense, toxicity, and higher incidence of superinfections and resistance.

*Sensitivity and resistance of microorganisms.* Sensitivity testing measures the ability of a specific antibiotic to limit the growth or kill microorganisms in vitro. Two accepted methods of testing sensitivity of microorganisms to selected antibiotics are the disk method and the tube dilution method. The disk method, which is rapid and inexpensive, gives an index to microbial susceptibility. Tube dilution testing is required when bactericidal activity is essential, as in bacterial endocarditis. By this method the minimum inhibitory concentration (MIC) and the minimum bactericidal concentration (MBC) of an antibiotic agent against a particular organism are measured.

Frequently, a discrepancy exists between the in vitro testing and the activity of the drug within the body. This depends on a number of variables such as affinity for antibiotic active sites and penetration into the bacteria, pH, temperature, and ability of the drug to reach the site of an infection. For example, in the case of meningitis it would be inappropriate to use a drug that does not cross the blood-brain barrier even though the organism tested may be sensitive to the drug.

Resistance refers to the ability of a particular microorganism to resist the effects of a specific antibiotic. Resistance occurs in one of three ways: (1) the antibiotic is unable to reach the potential target site of its action—some organisms, such as *Pseudomonas,* elaborate a protective membrane (a glycocalyx or slime) that prevents the antibiotic from reaching the cell wall; (2) the microorganism may produce an enzyme that acts to reduce or eliminate the toxic effect of the antibiotic to the cell wall. Examples of these enzymes are the beta lactamases that cleave the beta-lactam ring on penicillins and cephalosporins, forming inactive compounds; acylases that acetylate chloramphenicol to yield inactive derivatives and enzymes that inactivate aminoglycosides by phosphorylation, adenylation, and acetylation; and (3) the microorganism may also be altered in the individual through several biochemical changes. The changes occur in such a way that the target site for the antibiotic no longer accommodates the drug. In this case a specific organism is said to have "become resistant" to a previously susceptible antibiotic. As a rule, microorganisms resistant to a certain drug will tend to be resistant to other chemically related antimicrobial agents, a phenomenon known as *cross-resistance*. For example, bacteria unresponsive to tetracycline will also be resistant to oxytetracycline and chlortetracycline.

*Role of host defense mechanisms.* No antimicrobial agent will affect the cure of an infectious process if host defense mechanisms are inadequate. Such drugs act only on the causative organisms of infectious disease and have no effect on the defense mechanisms of the body, which need to be assessed and supported. Many infections do not require drug therapy and are adequately combated by individual defense mechanisms, including antibody production, phagocytosis, interferon production, fibrosis, or gastrointestinal rejection (vomiting, diarrhea). However, host defense mechanisms may be diminished, as in, for example, diabetes mellitus, neoplastic disease, and immunologic suppression. In addition, the very ill client may require supportive care to ensure adequate oxygenation, fluid and electrolyte balance, and optimal nutrition for antimicrobial therapy to be effective. In some situations surgical intervention is also necessary. In general, in the presence of a substantial amount of pus, necrotic tissue, or a foreign body, the most effective treatment is a combination of an antimicrobial agent and an appropriate surgical procedure.

The status of the host's defense mechanisms will also influence choice of therapy, route of administration, and dosage. If an infection is fulminating, for example, parenteral (preferably intravenous) administration of a bactericidal drug will be selected rather than oral administration of a bacteriostatic drug. Large "loading" doses of antimicrobial agents are often administered at the beginning of treatment of severe infections, to achieve maximum blood concentrations rapidly. However, factors influencing drug dosage are also related to the status of a client's renal function. Because many antimicrobial agents are metabolized and/or excreted by the kidneys, a major management problem exists in regard to individuals with compromised renal function. Drug doses are then generally reduced in parallel with the client's creatinine clearance levels. Hemodialysis may further alter the therapeutic regimen. In some disease states (such as burns) antibiotic dosage may need to be increased to achieve therapeutic levels.

In short, the administration of an antimicrobial agent specifically toxic to the isolated microorganism is not the only important measure in antimicrobial therapy. An additional and very important determinant of the effectiveness of an antimicrobial agent is the functional state of the host's defense mechanisms.

*Dosage and duration of therapy.* Administering antimicrobial drugs for therapeutic purposes in adequate dosage and for long enough periods of time is an important principle of infectious disease therapy. Fortunately, serum levels of some of the more potent antibiotics can be monitored to avoid or reduce the potential for toxicity, for example, aminoglycosides. The nurse should assess for alterations in renal and hepatic functions, since they both can affect drug dosage, dosing interval, and/or drug toxicity.

Failures in antimicrobial therapy are frequently the result of drug doses being too small or being given for too short a period of time. Generally, antimicrobial therapy should not be discontinued until the client has been afebrile and clinically well for 48 to 72 hours. Follow-up cultures should be obtained to assess the effectiveness of therapy.

Inadequate drug therapy may lead to remissions and exacerbations of the infectious process and may contribute to the development of resistance. When antibiotics are used prophylactically, they usually are given for short periods of time to enhance host defense mechanisms. For example, with perioperative antibiotics a loading dose is given immediately before surgery and continued for 48 hours following surgery.

Antimicrobial agents currently being used are discussed as chemically related groups of drugs. The nurse should be familiar with the general characteristics of each drug group or category and with one or two prototype drugs in each group. Because the dosage for any given antibiotic varies with the type of infection, the site of infection, and the age of the client, only general dosages are given in this text. It is recommended that the manufacturer's package insert or a formulary be consulted for specific dosages.

## ▷NURSING MANAGEMENT: ANTIMICROBIAL THERAPY

Antimicrobial agents destroy or inhibit the growth of microorganisms. Some of these agents are derived from living organisms; others are synthetic and semisynthetic chemical compounds. The goal of antimicrobial therapy for infectious diseases is to destroy or suppress the growth of infecting microorganisms so that normal host defense mechanisms can gain control and eliminate the infecting organisms. Among the microorganisms that can be controlled by these drugs today are most bacteria, many fungi, and a few viruses. For the nurse to safely and effectively manage clients taking antimicrobials, knowledge of host defenses and antimicrobial drugs is necessary.

The primary defense mechanisms against infection in the body are intact skin and mucous membranes, the chemical composition and pH of specific body secretions, phagocytic cells, mechanical movements of certain cells or tissues such as cilia action, coughing, peristalsis, and the inflammatory process. Many factors can impair host defenses and thereby increase the risk for the development of infection by virulent organisms.

Any disruption in the integrity of skin or mucous membranes becomes a portal of entry for disease-producing organisms. In very ill, hospitalized clients or in those who are immunoincompetent (e.g., individuals with acquired immune deficiency syndrome [AIDS] or receiving immunosuppressive therapies), relatively minor breaks in the skin or mucosa can lead to fatal infections. Vigorous teeth cleaning, tube insertions, and injections should be avoided, if possible. Environmental hazards such as furniture obstructions, wet flooring, or the presence of irritating agents should be corrected so that injury is prevented. An impairment of blood supply to body tissues will also reduce host defenses by reducing the overall resistance of the tissues to injury and by preventing the migration of inflammatory cells to the area of injury. Other factors that impair the body's defenses against infection include neutropenia, anemia, protein malnutrition, and autoimmune and antiinflammatory agents such as antineoplastic agents and corticosteroids. Persons with chronic preexisting cardiopulmonary, renal, or metabolic disease and those at the extremes of age are now susceptible to the development of infection because of altered organ function. Poor personal hygiene and the suppression of the normal bacterial flora by antibiotics create conditions whereby normal defenses are overwhelmed, resulting in pathogen overgrowth (superinfection).

To exert their effects, antimicrobial agents must first gain access to target sites, usually by absorption of the drug into and distribution through the circulatory system. Then they have bacteriostatic or bactericidal effects, depending on the mechanisms of action. Bacteriostatic agents such as sulfonamides inhibit bacterial growth, allowing host defense mechanisms additional time to remove the invading microorganisms. Bactericidal agents, such as the penicillins, cause bacterial cell death and lysis, superimposing this effect on the effects of host defenses. Antimicrobial agents may exert their bacteriostatic or bactericidal effects by inhibition of cell wall synthesis in bacteria, disruption or alteration of membrane permeability, or inhibition of protein synthesis or synthesis of essential metabolites.

Hundreds of antimicrobial agents are marketed currently, and it is impossible for the nurse to be infinitely knowledgeable about each drug. However, in spite of the numerous and varied drugs available, there are still only a few drug categories to remember. Knowledge of general characteristics of each drug category and of general principles of antimicrobial drug therapy should enable the nurse to function effectively.

In addition to the antibiotics, which include penicillins, cephalosporins, macrolides, lincomycins, vancomycin, aminoglycosides, tetracyclines, chloramphenicol, and polymyxins, major groups of antiinfective drugs include sulfonamides, urinary tract antiseptics, and antimycobacterial, antifungal, and antiviral agents. Table 58-3 (page 882) gives a brief summary of some major allergic and toxic effects of antimicrobial agents.

Nursing interventions in antimicrobial drug therapy generally relate to (1) assisting in the identification of the infecting organism, (2) actual administration of the drug, (3) assessment of the client's response to the drug, (4) client education, and (5) prevention and treatment of adverse reactions, including pharmacologic and chemical drug interactions.

**Assessment.** Obtaining cultures to determine the source and type of infection is frequently the nurse's responsibility. In the event that orders for an antimicrobial agent are given before establishment of an infective source, the nurse should obtain cultures before administering the first dose of the drug ordered. Specimens obtained for culture should be taken directly to the laboratory and not allowed to stand. Delay may cause the death of fastidious organisms and allow contaminating organisms to overgrow the pathogen. Subsequent culture specimens obtained while the client is receiving antimicrobials should be sent to the laboratory with information regarding the drug(s) being administered. The appropriate selection of laboratory tests for the identification of offending organisms often depends on this knowledge.

**Intervention.** Because the constant and consistent administration of an antimicrobial drug at prescribed dosage intervals is necessary for maintaining therapeutic blood levels of the drug, the nurse should administer such a drug according to prescribed times as accurately as possible. This may mean awakening sleeping clients and ensuring that tests or therapies do not interrupt this schedule.

When antimicrobial agents are administered intravenously, the nurse must observe additional precautions: (1) the drugs should be diluted in neutral solutions (pH 7.0 to 7.2) of isotonic sodium chloride (0.9%) or 5% dextrose in water; (2) the drugs should be administered without the admixture of any other drug, to avoid chemical or physical incompatibilities; (3) the drugs should be administered by intermittent intravenous infusions to avoid inactivation (e.g., by temperature) and prolonged vein irritation from high drug concentration; (4) the infusion site must be changed every 48 hours to reduce the risk of chemical phlebitis; and (5) intramuscular antimicrobials should be injected deeply into large muscle masses (such as gluteal), and injection sites should be rotated to prevent tissue irritation.

**Education.** Clients should be taught principles of antimicrobial therapy clearly enough to understand that these drugs should never be taken without medical supervision and should be taken in strict accordance with physicians' prescriptions. This is especially important because many individuals receiving antimicrobial drugs are not hospitalized and are responsible for self-medication. Clients should be taught, for example, not to take "leftover" antimicrobial drugs for new illnesses, even if symptoms appear similar; not to stop taking these drugs as soon as symptoms abate; and not to share these drugs with family and friends. Clients who are allergic to an antimicrobial agent should be taught how to protect themselves from future treatment with the drug in question such as by medical alert wallet cards or tags.

Expected effects, side effects, and adverse reactions of individual antimicrobials could be appropriately described on "drug sheets" for clients to refer to at home while taking antimicrobial therapy. A telephone number to call when questions arise could also be written on the drug sheets and would convey the message that it was expected and desirable for clients to discuss their concerns about their medications with health care workers.

Occasionally antimicrobials will interfere with the results of home laboratory testing kits, and clients using these must be cautioned. For example, the cephalosporins may produce a false positive reading when individuals with diabetes use commercial chemical testing strips to monitor their urine glucose.

**Evaluation.** A decrease in the severity or a disappearance of the clinical and laboratory manifestations of infection indicates a positive response to antimicrobial therapy. With local infections redness, heat, edema, and pain should decrease. In the case of a systemic infection, temperature, heart rate, respiratory rate, and white blood cell count should return to normal, and appetite and a sense of well-being should improve. Purulent drainage, if present, should decrease in amount and change to a more normal appearance and consistency. In clients who are seriously ill, an improvement in organ function should accompany other signs of resolution of infection. Serum antibiotic concentrations can be monitored through the course of therapy to assess for therapeutic and toxic levels of individual antimicrobials.

In addition to monitoring therapeutic effects of antimicrobials, nurses must monitor the client for the development of common side effects of individual drugs. Fluid and electrolyte imbalances can occur during the course of administering many antibiotics, either from the drug itself, the mode of administration, or side effects such as diarrhea. For example, extracellular volume excess may result from administering multiple intravenous drugs, each of which is diluted in 100 ml of saline. Edema, pulmonary congestion with subsequent shortness of breath, and an increase in body weight all indicate the presence of an extracellular volume excess. Hypokalemia, resulting from severe diarrhea or the administration of antibiotic containing large quantities of sodium, produces no obvious clinical signs or symptoms until the potassium deficit is significant. At this point, widespread muscular weakness and cardiac conduction abnormalities appear. In the client whose cardiac function is being monitored, the appearance of U waves may be an earlier indication of low serum potassium. Laboratory demonstration of hypokalemia is frequently the only way to detect this disorder. Hypernatremia, another commonly seen disorder in clients receiving antimicrobial therapy, is also associated with few early clinical signs or symptoms, with the exception of a high serum sodium value, which occurs frequently because many antimicrobials have a sodium base. In general, when individuals must take prolonged courses of antimicrobials that can cause fluid and electrolyte imbalances, it may be necessary to obtain serum electrolyte studies periodically.

### Prevention and management of adverse responses

*Allergic response.* Assessment of a client's previous reactions to drugs and to antimicrobial agents in particular is especially important in avoiding allergic reactions to drugs. Careful questioning of the individual regarding drugs previously taken and exact clinical responses to them is an important part of the client's history. Some clients equate common side effects such as nausea and diarrhea with drug allergy. Although these drug responses are important, knowledge of their appearance may not be as sufficient a reason to withhold a specific antibiotic as would a true allergy. Once drug allergy is known, warnings should be prominently displayed on the client's record or hospital chart. As additional precautions, the nurse should (1) ask the client if he or she has drug allergies before administering any medications; (2) tell the client what drug he is receiving; (3) observe the client for at least half an hour after administration of the drug (penicillin in particular), especially if it is administered parenterally and the client has never taken the drug previously; and (4) knows what drugs are used for the treatment of allergic responses and where they are kept.

*Anaphylaxis.* The most serious allergic reaction to antimicrobials is an acute anaphylaxis. This reaction can occur anywhere from a few seconds to 30 minutes after an antibiotic injection. The syndrome associated with this reaction usually begins with diffuse flushing, itching, and a feeling of warmth. Hives may appear on the client's face, neck, and chest. As the syndrome progresses, generalized body edema develops. Massive facial edema signals the possibility of upper airway edema, with impending obstruction and respiratory difficulty from pulmonary involvement. These problems are manifested as a choking sensation, stridor, chest tightness and pain, wheezing, shortness of breath, and restlessness.

The initial step in the emergent management of anaphylaxis is to immediately stop the antibiotic if it is still being infused. If the individual is not in a medical facility, immediate transport to one should be arranged, preferably by a vehicle staffed by paramedics who could establish an artificial airway in the event the client's airway becomes totally obstructed. Reversal of anaphylaxis is accomplished by drug therapy. The antihistamine diphenhydramine HCl (Benadryl) is administered parenterally or orally. Epinephrine 1:1000 can be injected subcutaneously and will reverse the vascular effects of anaphylaxis. Aminophylline or theophylline is administered if bronchospasm persists. If the individual is in anaphylactic shock, vasopressors may be necessary concomitantly with the administration of intravenous fluids for short-term management of hypotension. Corticosteroids (methylprednisolone) may be administered for prevention of protracted symptoms in severe reactions.

*Superinfection.* The emergence of superinfection may be suspected in the presence of diarrhea or recurrent fever in the client taking antimicrobial drugs. Stomatitis is indicated by the presence of a sore mouth or white patches on the oral mucosa. Monilial vaginitis may produce a vaginal discharge or perineal rash. Localized superinfections may be heralded by increasing redness, heat, edema, pain, and possibly drainage. Children, elderly persons, and others whose normal host defense mechanisms may be weakened should be especially observed for signs of superinfection. In the course of prolonged antimicrobial drug therapy, periodic cultures of the upper respiratory tract and of feces may be indicated to determine changes in bacterial flora that subsequently may be responsible for secondary infection. The nurse should be careful not to introduce new microorganisms and should emphasize asepsis in contacts with clients receiving antimicrobial therapy.

*Stop and renewal orders.* The establishment of automatic stop and renewal orders in many hospitals is another precaution against adverse reactions. Such orders restrict the administration of a prescribed antimicrobial agent to a definite time period (e.g., 7 days); its continued use past that time requires a new prescription from the physician.

*Drug interactions.* Because the administration of more than one drug to a client is the rule rather than the exception in current hospital practice, the possibility of drug interactions must be taken into account if antimicrobial therapy is to be optimally effective. The nurse should be alert to drugs that interact biologically with antimicrobial agents, as well as chemical incompatibilities between antimicrobial drugs and other agents when they are mixed for intravenous administration. The hospital formulary on each unit provides accurate and current information about these interactions.

## SUMMARY

Infectious disease has been a major health concern of man even before recorded history and comprises a variety of illnesses caused by pathogenic microorganisms, bacteria, fungi, and viruses. Inflammation is a reaction of the body tissues, not only to infection but also to physical, chemical, and thermal injuries. Fever is a sign of inflammation. All present challenges for nursing care and for antimicrobial therapy.

Antimicrobial agents may be bacteriostatic (inhibiting bacterial growth) or bactericidal (causing bacterial cell death and lysis), or both depending on the concentration at the site of action. These agents are effective by either inhibiting the bacterial cell wall synthesis, altering the membrane permeability, inhibiting protein synthesis, or inhibiting the synthesis of essential metabolites. In general antimicrobials are well tolerated by man; however, common to all antimicrobials there may be an allergic or hypersensitive response or a superinfection, an infection that occurs during the course of antimicrobial therapy because of reduction in the normal microbial flora of the body.

The following are guidelines for the use of antimicrobials: identification of the infecting organism, which allows for the selection of the most effective antimicrobial for the specific infecting organism; determination of the ability of a specific antimicrobial to limit the growth or kill microorganisms in vitro; supportive therapy for the host defense mechanisms; and administration of the agent in an adequate dosage and for long enough periods of time to be effective. Nursing management of antimicrobial therapy includes the assessment of the individual's ability to deal with the stressor of infection, the administration of antimicrobial drugs safely and accurately, the education of the client to do the same with regard to self-administration of the drug, the prevention and management of adverse responses, and the evaluation of the client's response to the drug and progress toward the goal of resolution of the infection.

## BIBLIOGRAPHY

Alexander JW et al. (1989). Which antibiotics before surgery? Patient Care 23(6):126.

Braunwald E et al. (1987). Harrison's principles of medicine, ed 11 New York: McGraw-Hill Book Co.

Bryant-Armstrong TB. (1988). The pathophysiology of human immunodeficiency virus infections, J Adv Med Surg Nurs 1(1):9.

Bullock BL and Rosendahl PP. (1988). Pathophysiology, adaptations, and alterations in function, ed 2 Glenview, Ill: Scott, Foresman and Co.

Cerase PA. (1989). Neonatal sepsis, J Perinat Neonat Nurs 3(2):48.

Craig WA. (1988). Do antibiotic combinations prevent the emergence of resistant organisms? Infect Control Hosp Epidemiol 9(9):417.

Engel NS. (1989). Multiple drug therapy for pediatric tuberculosis, MCN 14(3):169.

Fekety R et al. (1989). Does antibiotic prophylaxis help? Patient Care 23(9):76.

Grady C. (1988). Host defense mechanisms: an overview, Semin Oncol Nurs 4(2):86.

Griswold JA et al. (1989). Determinants of donor site infections in small burn grafts, J Burn Care Rehab 10(6):531.

Hamby S. (1989). Not in vein . . . I.V. drug administration, J Urol Nurs 8(3):697.

Jeter KF et al. (1988). Principles of wound cleansing and wound care, J Home Health Pract 1(1):43.

Meijer K et al. (1990). Infection control in patients undergoing mechanical ventilation: traditional approach versus a new development—selective decontamination of the digestive tract, Heart Lung 19(1):11.

Musher DM. (1988). The gram-positive cocci. II. Resistance to antibiotics, Hosp Pract 23(5):105.

Oniboni AC. (1990). Infection in the neutropenic patient, Semin Oncol Nurs 6(1):60.

Penicillin-resistant enterococci. (1989). Emerg Med 21(16):59.

Rowland MA. (1989). When drug therapy causes diarrhea, RN 52(12):32.

Sanford JP. (1990). Humans and animals: increasing contacts, increasing infections, Hosp Pract 25(2):123.

Steiner JF et al. (1989). Review and update of antibiotic therapy in ambulatory pediatrics, J Am Acad Physician Asst 2(5):399.

Wahdan MH. (1989). Communicable diseases, World Health, July, p 20.

Walters J. (1989). How antibiotics work: the cell membrane, Prof Nurse 10(4):508.

Willis RE et al. (1990). Action of antimicrobial agents on the bacterial cell wall, Surg Technol 22(1):10.

Wright RA. (1989). Outpatient intravenous antibiotics: a cost-effective approach to managing infectious disease, Consultant 29(5):143.

Wyngaarden JB and Smith LH. (1988). Cecil textbook of medicine, ed 18 Philadelphia: WB Saunders Co.

## Chapter

# 59  Antibiotics

## INTRODUCTION

**Antibiotics** are chemical substances that kill or suppress the growth of microorganisms. The four major classifications of antibiotics are penicillins, cephalosporins, macrolide antibiotics, and quinolones. The many available antibiotics vary in antibacterial spectrum, mechanism of action, potency, toxicity, and pharmacokinetic properties. An understanding of the general principles of antibiotic therapy, as discussed in Chapter 58, is essential for the nurse. In addition, before administering antibiotics, nurses must familiarize themselves with particular drugs and their actions and effects.

### ▷NURSING MANAGEMENT: ANTIBIOTIC THERAPY

*Assessment.* When an infection is suspected, the nursing assessment is particularly important. Detailed information regarding the client's general health, as well as symptoms indicating an infection, such as elevated temperature, chills, sweats, redness, pain or swelling in an area previously unaffected, fatigue, anorexia, weight loss, cough, change in character or amount of sputum, increased white blood cell count, amount and quality of pus or drainage, should be obtained.

Whenever possible, the infecting organism should be identified before drug therapy begins. The collection of specimens (blood, urine, sputum, wound drainage and discharge) and cultures should be completed before antibiotic therapy starts. Specimens should be carefully obtained following institutional and agency guidelines to ensure test accuracy and to protect personnel from exposure to infectious organisms. Prompt treatment is imperative in serious infections, and antimicrobial drugs should not be withheld pending laboratory study and culture results.

Selected nursing diagnoses related to antibiotic therapy

| Nursing diagnosis | Outcome criteria | Nursing interventions |
|---|---|---|
| Knowledge deficit related to anti-microbial drug therapy | Client will:<br>Express understanding of the purpose, function, and side effects/adverse reactions of drug therapy<br>Demonstrate understanding of proper handling and administration | Assess client's level of knowledge and understanding.<br>Determine education needs of client.<br>Provide information related to:<br>  Specific problem being treated with the antimicrobial agent<br>  Purpose and function of drug therapy<br>  Side effects/adverse reactions of the drug<br>  Methods of reducing side effects<br>  Answer questions and clarify misconceptions.<br>If drug is to be self-administered, instruct the client in:<br>  Proper route and method for administration<br>  Proper storage and handling<br>  Importance of taking all of the prescribed drug<br>Alert client to possible drug interactions.<br>Instruct the client not to take additional medications without first checking with the prescriber. |
| Altered nutrition related to gastro-intestinal effects of antimicrobial drugs | Client will maintain desired nutritional status | Assess client's normal dietary patterns and intake.<br>Assess normal pattern of bowel function.<br>Emphasize the importance of adequate nutrition.<br>Instruct client to report any gastrointestinal changes (nausea, vomiting, cramping, gas, diarrhea, constipation).<br>Administer in relation to meals and food to minimize side effects (with meals, before or after, depending on specific drug) yet maintain effectiveness of therapy.<br>Encourage intake of yogurt, buttermilk, or lactin to maintain or restore intestinal flora.<br>Report adverse effects to prescriber. |

Antibiotics, particularly penicillins, have been associated with serious hypersensitivity and allergic reactions. A complete drug history of the client and family helps identify possible hypersensitivity or cross-sensitivity administration of the drugs. Cross-sensitivity often exists between drugs of the same class (e.g., penicillins). Clients intolerant of one antibiotic may be intolerant of similar antibiotics. Information regarding possible contraindications, cautions, potential drug interactions and drug-taking patterns is also obtained.

***Intervention.*** Dosage and routes of administration are highly individualized and are based on the organism or infection being treated, as well as a variety of individual client factors such as age, weight, general health, and preexisting diseases or organ or system dysfunction. Antibiotics are available in various dosage forms for topical, oral, or parenteral use. Dosage adjustments between different forms or routes of administration are necessary because of differences in absorption, distribution, metabolism, or excretion. For example, an oral dose of penicillin G requires five times the parenteral dose to achieve the same serum levels of the drug.

Special attention must be paid to interactions of oral antibiotics with food or other drugs. Some antibiotics should not be administered with food. For example, tetracycline forms a nonabsorbable complex with dairy products, whereas other antibiotics are administered with food to minimize gastric irritation.

The time of antibiotic administration should be spaced as evenly as possible over a 24-hour period to ensure stable and consistent serum levels. Antibiotics ordered four times a day (q.i.d.) should be administered every 6 hours. Three times a day (t.i.d.) means every 8 hours. It is important to administer antibiotics at the scheduled time to maintain a consistent blood level. Allowable variation differs with specific drugs and institutional policy. As a general rule, antibiotics should be administered within 15 minutes of the scheduled time.

Serum levels of many antibiotics are monitored to determine if the concentration is at the correct, (therapeutic) level, high (toxic) level, or low (subtherapeutic) level. Timing of serum determinations is also important. To determine the lowest, or trough, level, the blood is drawn immediately before administering a dose. Mean serum levels are determined at some point between doses, and the highest serum level, or peak level, is determined shortly after dose administration. The desired serum concentration may vary with different drugs and the infecting organism. The exact timing of peak, mean, or trough serum level determinations is determined by each particular drug and route of administration.

***Education.*** Clients should be fully informed about the nature of their condition and the treatment plan. They should understand the medication regimen, including the name of medication (generic as well as trade name), general action, its purpose, proper handling, dosage, and correct administration. Provide the client with a list of adverse drug effects, drug-drug interactions, and food-drug interactions, and advise the client of the proper response if these interactions occur.

Clients should be instructed to take the medication exactly as prescribed, at evenly spaced intervals, for the full length of time prescribed or until all the drug is gone. Even if the client feels well, the infection may return if the full course of therapy is not completed. Any leftover medication should be appropriately discarded.

A rash, itching, hives, fever, chills, joint pain or swelling, difficulty breathing, or wheezing are signs of an adverse reaction. The drug should be stopped and the health care provider contacted immediately.

***Evaluation.*** When an antibiotic is administered for prophylaxis, the client should be monitored for signs indicating the absence or development of infection. When a specific infection is treated, a therapeutic response will be indicated by a decrease in specific signs of infection identified in the initial assessment (fever, malaise, elevated WBC count, redness, inflammation, pain, positive cultures). Evaluation of the therapeutic responses is important, since antibiotic therapy may be ineffective for several reasons, including incorrect route of administration, inadequate drainage of abscesses, poor antibiotic penetration of infected tissues, subtherapeutic serum levels, or bacterial resistance to the antibiotic.

Reducing or eliminating normal flora by antibiotic therapy provides an environment conducive to growth of undesirable bacteria, fungus, or yeasts, a condition known as **superinfection.** Examples commonly seen include diarrhea from altered intestinal flora or vaginal yeast infections resulting from a reduction in normal vaginal flora, which suppresses yeast growth.

Adverse effects vary widely, depending on drug, dose, route of administration, and client-related factors. Refer to

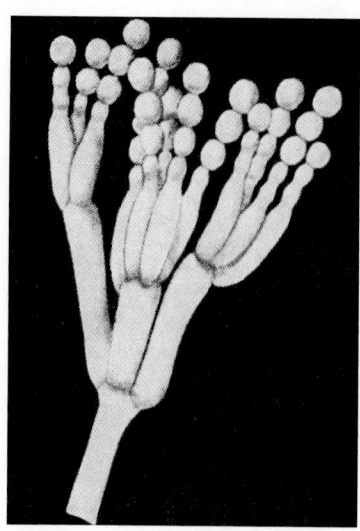

**FIGURE 59-1**   Typical penicillus of *Penicillium notatum;* Fleming's strain. *(From Raper KB and Alexander DF (1945). J. Elisha Mitchell Sc. Soc. 61:74.)*

nursing management for specific antibiotics for side effects or adverse reactions and specific nursing evaluation related to those drugs.

Allergic reactions are always possible following the first or successive doses. In general it is important to monitor for allergic reactions such as anaphylaxis, skin rashes, urticaria, and bronchospasm. Administration should immediately stop at the first sign of an allergic reaction, and the prescriber should be notified.

## PENICILLINS

**Penicillins** are antibiotics derived from a number of strains of *Penicillium notatum* and *P. chrysogenum,* common molds often seen on bread or fruit (Figure 59-1). Introduced into clinical practice in 1941, penicillins constitute a large group of antimicrobial agents that remain the most effective and least toxic of all available antimicrobial drugs. Penicillins encompass true antibiotics, as well as many newer, semisynthetic compounds that share a common structural nucleus and a common mechanism of action.

***Mechanism of action.*** The penicillins specifically inhibit synthesis of bacterial cell walls, probably by interfering with the biosynthesis of mucopeptides and preventing linkage of structural components of the cell wall. They are bactericidal for a wide variety of gram-positive and some gram-negative organisms. Bacterial species considered highly susceptible to the penicillins include *Streptococcus pneumoniae,* group A beta hemolytic streptococci, *Neisseria meningitidis, N. gonorrhoeae,* non-penicillinase–producing *Staphylococcus aureus, Clostridium tetani, Clostridium perfringens, Corynebacterium diphtheriae, Actinomyces,* and *Treponema pallidum* and other spirochetes. Most penicillins are much more active against gram-positive than gram-negative bacteria. There are exceptions, however.

**TABLE 59-1**   Pharmacokinetics of penicillins

| Drugs | Oral absorption (%) | Time to peak serum levels (hr) | Half-life (hr) Normal renal function | Neonate | Liver metabolism (%) | Kidney excretion (% unchanged) |
|---|---|---|---|---|---|---|
| amdinocillin | None | IM, ½ | 0.9 | — | Very low | 70 in 6 hr |
| amoxicillin | 75-90 | PO, 2 | 1-1.3 | — | 28-50 | 68 |
| amoxicillin and clavulanate | Very good | PO, 1-2 | 1.3 (amoxicillin) 1 (clavulanate) | — | 28-50 (amoxicillin) | 50-70 (amoxicillin) |
| ampicillin | 35-50 | PO, 1.5-2 IM, 1 | 1-1.5 | 1.7-4 | 12-50 | 25-60 (PO) 50-85 (IM) |
| azlocillin | — | — | 1 | — | <10 | 50-70 in 24 hr |
| bacampicillin | Very good (98) | PO, ½-1 (young children) PO, 0.9-1 (adults) | 0.7-1.1 | — | Mostly liver | 75 within 8 hr |
| carbenicillin disodium | None | IM, 1 | 1-1.5 | 2.7-4 | 2 | 60-90 |
| carbenicillin indanyl sodium | 30-50 | PO, 1-3 | 1-1.5 | 2.7-4 | 2 | 60-90 |
| cloxacillin | 50 | PO, 1-2 | 0.5-1.1 | — | 9-22 | 30-45 |
| cyclacillin | Very good | PO, 0.5-1 | 0.5-0.7 | — | 15-17 | 85 |
| dicloxacillin | 37-50 | PO, 0.5-1 | 0.5-1 | Not recommended | 9-10 | 60 |
| methicillin | None | IM, 0.5-1 | 0.4-0.8 | — | 8 | 80 |
| mezlocillin | Very little | IM, 0.75 | 0.8-1 | 1.8-2.1 | 45 | 55-60 in 6 hr |
| nafcillin | Poor to variable | PO, 1-2 IM, 1-2 | 0.5-1 | — | 60 | 10-30 |
| oxacillin | 30-33 | PO, 0.5-1 | 0.5-0.7 | 1.2-1.6 | 49 | 40 |
| penicillin G | Poor to variable (15-30) | IM, 0.5 PO, 1-2 | 0.5-0.7 | 1.4-3 | 19 | 20 (PO) |
| benzathine | Poor | IM, 24 | — | — | | |
| potassium | 30 | IM, 0.25-0.5 | — | — | | 60 (pen GK) |
| procaine | — | IM, 1-4 | — | — | | 60-90 (pen G procaine) |
| penicillin V | 60 | PO, 0.5-1 | 1 | — | 56 | 20-40 |
| piperacillin | None | IM, 0.5 | 0.6-1.2 | — | None | 60-90 in 24 hr |
| ticarcillin | None | IM, 0.5-1 | 1-1.2 | 5 | Minimal | 86 |
| ticarcillin and clavulanate | None | — | 1-1.2 (ticarcillin) | — | Minimal | 60-70 (ticarcillin) |

Gram-negative gonococci, for example, are penicillin susceptible. Generally, gram-negative bacteria have thinner cell walls and a lipopolysaccharide coat; *Neisseria* and *Haemophilus* species have much thicker cell walls and more permeable lipopolysaccharide coats than other gram-negative pathogens and thus are more penicillin sensitive.

***Indications.*** Antibacterial agents are used to treat microorganisms or infections that are susceptible to their individual effects. The penicillins are not useful in the presence of bacteria-producing enzymes capable of destroying penicillins, such as penicillinase-producing strains of the beta-lactamase enzymes produced by these strains (via chromosomal and plasmid-mediated enzymes) with strains of *S. aureus, E. coli,* indole-positive *Proteus* or *P. aeruginosa.* However, in some instances, synthetic penicillins are effective in treating infections caused by these organisms.

Studies of the prophylactic use of penicillin have shown it to be of value in (1) treating persons exposed to group A *S. pyrogenes,* (2) preventing rheumatic fever recurrences, (3) treating persons exposed to gonorrhea and syphilis, and (4) preventing subacute bacterial endocarditis in clients with valvular heart disease who must undergo surgical or dental procedures.

***Pharmacokinetics.*** See Table 59-1.

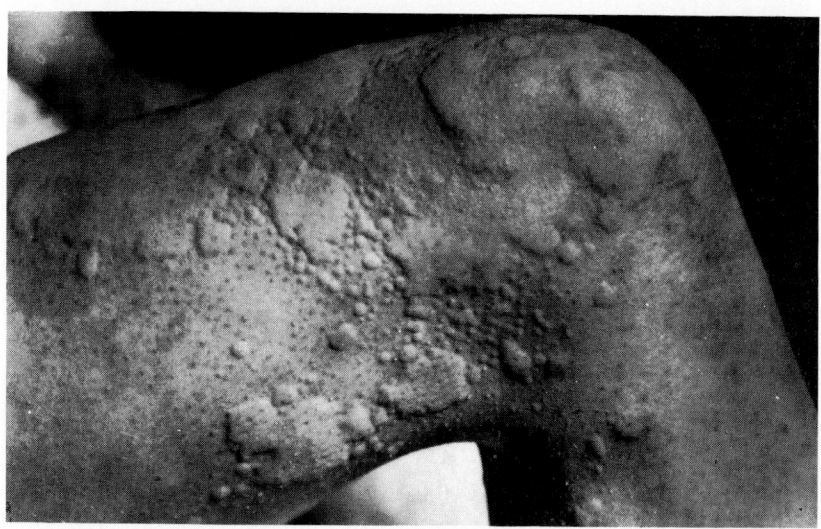

**FIGURE 59-2** Uticaria such as those seen in individuals sensitive to penicillin.

***Side effects/adverse reactions.*** Most often reported side effects are mild diarrhea; taste alterations (carbenicillin); nausea or vomiting; sore mouth; and dark, discolored, or sore tongue. The adverse reactions most frequently reported are pseudomembranous colitis with symptoms of stomach pain, gas, severe diarrhea, fever, increased thirst, weight loss, nausea or vomiting, and increased weakness (amoxicillin, ampicillin, bacampicillin); bloody urine, face and ankle edema, respiratory difficulties due to interstitial nephritis (parenteral methicillin); convulsions with high injectable doses, especially in renal impairment (penicillin G); rash, hives, pruritis, wheezing, hypersensitivity reaction (see Figure 59-2); increased bleeding episodes and bruising. When adverse reactions occur, contact a physician since medical intervention may be necessary. All penicillins except amdinocillin can cause pseudomembranous colitis after the medication is discontinued.

***Significant drug interactions.*** When penicillins are given with the following drugs, the following significant drug interactions may occur:

| Drug | Possible Effect and Management |
|---|---|
| anticoagulants, oral coumarin or indandione, heparin or thrombolytic agents | Increased risk of bleeding when given with high doses of parenteral carbenicillin or ticarcillin; these drugs inhibit platelet aggregation. Monitor closely for signs of bleeding. Concurrent use of these penicillins with thrombolytic agents also increases the risk for severe bleeding; thus, concurrent drug administration is not recommended. |
| antiinflammatory nonsteroidal analgesics, platelet aggregation inhibitors (such as salicylates, dextran, dipyridamole, valproic acid) and sulfinpyrazone | With high dosages of carbenicillin or ticarcillin (parenteral dosage forms), an increased risk for bleeding or hemorrhage exists. These drugs inhibit platelet function and large doses of salicylates may induce hy- |

| Drug | Possible Effect and Management |
|---|---|
| | poprothrombinemia and also gastrointestinal ulcers (from NSAIDs, salicylates, or sulfinpyrazone), all adding to the potential risk of hemorrhage. |
| captopril, potassium-sparing diuretics, Enalapril, Lisinopril, potassium-containing drugs, or potassium supplements | If given concurrently with parenteral penicillin G potassium, serum potassium levels may increase, causing hyperkalemia. Monitor closely, as dosage adjustments may be necessary. |
| cholestyramine or colestipol | May decrease absorption of oral penicillin G if given concurrently. Advise clients to take antibiotic first and other medications 3 hours later. |
| probenecid | Decreases renal tubular secretion of penicillins, resulting in elevated serum levels and an increase in half-life. It may also increase toxicity. Several combinations of penicillin and probenecid are marketed to take advantage of this effect. |
| estrogen-containing contraceptives | When used concurrently with ampicillin, bacampicillin, or penicillin V, the effectiveness of the oral contraceptives may be decreased because of increase in estrogen metabolism or reduction in enterohepatic circulation of estrogens. Advise clients to use an alternate method of contraception while taking these antibiotics. |

***Dosage and administration.*** See Table 59-2.

***Drug combinations.*** Amoxicillin and ticarcillin have been combined with a beta-lactamase inhibitor, clavulanic acid, and marketed as Augmentin and Timentin, respectively. In recent years, the usefulness of ampicillin has been limited because of an increase in bacterial resistance resulting mainly from the enzymatic inactivation of ampicillin

**TABLE 59-2**   Dosage and administration of penicillin preparations

| Drug | Adults | Children |
|---|---|---|
| amdinocillin (Coactin) | IM, IV, 10 mg/kg every 4 hr | Under 12 yr, not established; over 12, adult dose |
| amoxicillin (Amoxil) | PO, 250-500 mg every 8 hr | Infants to 6 kg, 25-50 mg PO every 8 hr. Infants 6 to 8 kg, 50-100 kg every 8 hr |
| amoxicillin and clavulanate (Augmentin) | PO, 250-500 mg amoxicillin plus 125 mg clavulanic acid every 8 hr | Infants/children to 40 kg, 6.7-13.3 mg/kg body weight of amoxicillin every 8 hr |
| ampicillin (Amcill) | PO, 250-500 mg every 6 hr. Gonorrhea: 3.5 g ampicillin plus 1 g probenecid in single dose<br>IM, IV, 250-500 mg every 6 hr | Infants/children to 20 kg, 12.5-25 mg/kg body weight every 6 hr<br>IM, IV, infants to 20 kg, 6.25-25 mg/kg every 6 hr |
| ampicillin and sulbactam (Unasyn) | IM, IV, 1.5-3 g every 6 hr. (Each 1.5 g = 1 g ampicillin and 500 mg sulbactam) | Up to 12 yr, dose not established |
| azlocillin (Azlin) | IV, 33.3-50 mg/kg body weight every 4 hr | Children with acute pulmonary exacerbation of cystic fibrosis, IV, 75 mg/kg body weight every 4 hr |
| bacampicillin (Spectrobid) | PO, 400-800 mg every 12 hr. Gonorrhea: 1.6 g plus 1 g probenecid as single dose | Infants/children to 25 kg, 12.5-25 mg/kg body weight, every 12 hr |
| carbenicillin indanyl sodium (Geocillin) | PO, 382-764 mg every 6 hr | Pediatric dose not established |
| carbenicillin disodium (Geopen) | IM, IV, 50-83.3 mg/kg every 4 hr. UTI, IM/IV 1-2 g every 6 hr. Gonorrhea: IM 4 g divided and administered at two sites with 1 g probenecid given orally 30 minutes before carbenicillin. | Neonates to 2 kg, IM, IV, 100 mg/kg initially, then 75 mg every 8 hr for 1 week<br>Neonates 2 kg and over, 100 mg/kg initially, then 75 mg/kg every 6 hr for 3 days, then 100 mg/kg every 6 hr |
| cloxacillin (Tegopen) | PO, 250-500 mg every 6 hr | PO, infants/children to 20 kg, 6.25-12.5 mg/kg every 6 hr |
| cyclacillin (Cyclapen-W) | PO, 250-500 mg every 6 hr | Not recommended for infants under 2 months. Acute otitis media, 16.7-33.3 mg/kg PO every 8 hr. Other infections, 12.5-25 mg/kg every 6 hr |
| dicloxacillin (Dynapen) | PO, 125-250 mg every 6 hr | Infants/children to 40 kg, PO 3.125-6.25 mg/kg every 6 hr |
| methicillin (Staphcillin) | IM, 1 g every 4 to 6 hours. IV, 1-2 g every 4 hr | IM, 25 mg/kg every 6 hr<br>IV, 16.7-33.3 mg/kg every 4 hr |
| mezlocillin (Mezlin) | IM, IV, 33.3-58.3 mg/kg every 4 hr | Infants up to 7 days, 75 mg/kg every 12 hr<br>Infants 8 to 30 days, 75 mg/kg every 6 to 8 hr<br>Infants 30 days to 12 yr, 50 mg/kg every 4 hr |
| nafcillin (Unipen) | PO, 250 mg to 1 g every 4 to 6 hr<br><br>IM, 500 mg every 4 to 6 hr<br>IV, 500 mg-1.5 g every 4 hr | Neonates 10/kg PO every 6 to 8 hr. Older infants/children, 6.25-12.5 mg/kg every 6 hr<br>Neonates, IM, 10-20 mg/kg every 12 hr. IV, 10-20 mg/kg every 4 hr. Older infants/children, IM, 25 mg/kg every 12 hr. IV, 10-20 mg/kg every 4 hr. |
| oxacillin (Bactrocill) | PO, 500 mg-1 g every 4 to 6 hr<br><br>IM, IV, 1-2 g every 4 hr | Children to 40 kg, 12.5-25 mg/kg every 6 hr<br>Over 40 kg, see adult dose<br>(same dose as PO) |

*Continued.*

**TABLE 59-2**  Dosage and administration of penicillin preparations—cont'd

| Drug | Adults | Children |
|---|---|---|
| penicillin GK (Pentids) | PO, 200,000-500,000 units every 6 to 8 hr | Infants/children to 12 yr, PO, 4167-15,000 units/kg every 4 hr. Children 12 yr and over, see adult dose |
| penicillin G benzathine (Bicillin L-A) | IM, 1.2 million units monthly for prophylaxis of streptococcal infections in clients with history of rheumatic heart disease | Group A streptococcal pharyngitis in infants/children up to 27.3 kg, IM, 300,000-600,000 units |
| penicillin GK for injection (Pfizerpen) | IM, IV, 1-5 million units every 4 to 6 hr | Premature and full-term neonates, IM, IV, 30,000 units/kg every 12 hr. Older infants/children, up to 400,000 units/kg daily in divided doses |
| penicillin G procaine (Crysticillin) | IM, 600,000-1.2 million units daily | Congenital syphilis, infants/children to 32 kg, IM, 50,000 units/kg daily for 10 days |
| penicillin V potassium (Pen Vee K) | PO, 125-500 mg every 6 to 8 hr | Infants/children to 12 yr, 2.5-9.3 mg/kg every 4 hr. Children 12 yr and over, see adult dose |
| pipercillin (Pipracil) | IM, IV, 3-4 g every 4-6 hr | Infants/children under 12 yr, dose not established |
| ticarcillin (Ticar) | IV infusion, 3 g every 3 to 6 hr | Since infant and child doses can vary according to diagnosis, see current package insert for dosing instructions |
| ticarcillin and clavulanate (Timentin) | Adults under 60 kg, 50-75 mg/kg ticarcillin IV every 6 hr<br>Adults 60 kg and over, 3 g ticarcillin IV every 4 to 6 hr | Infants/children to 12 yr, dose not established |

by bacteria beta-lactamases. In 1987 the third combination of a beta-lactam antibiotic and beta-lactamase inhibitor was released: ampicillin and sulbactam (Unasyn). The sulbactam binds with beta-lactamase–producing bacteria, thus preventing the inactivation of ampicillin.

The pharmacokinetics of ampicillin are not affected by the concurrent administration of sulbactam (see pharmacokinetics of ampicillin). The antibacterial in vitro activity of ampicillin has been extended to include bacterial strains that produce beta-lactamase, such as *Proteus*, *Klebsiella*, *E. coli*, *H. influenza*, *Staphylococcus aureus*, and many anaerobes. Therefore this combination may be effective in urinary tract, skin, intraabdominal, and gynecologic infections that usually have a mixture of aerobic and anaerobic organisms.

The side effects and adverse reactions are similar to those of ampicillin alone. Unasyn should be avoided in individuals with mononucleosis, since a high incidence of skin rash is reported with its usage. Several other concerns include the following:

1. The drug may produce a false-positive reaction for glucose with Clinitest; therefore diabetics should use Clinistix or Ketodiastix for monitoring when using this drug.

2. The sodium content of Unasyn is 5 mEq/1.5 g. At the maximum dosage of 12 g/day, over 900 mg of sodium will be administered. Clients with cardiac disease on sodium-restricted diets should be monitored.

3. Dosage is by the intravenous or intramuscular route. The usual dose is 1.5 g (1 g of ampicillin/0.5 g sulbactam) to 3 g (2 g ampicillin/1 g sulbactam) every 6 hours. In clients with impaired renal function, check package insert or current USP-DI for dosing instructions.

▷ **Nursing Management:**
**Penicillin Therapy**

**Assessment.** Obtain cultures to assess sensitivity before administering the first dose of penicillin, but begin therapy before obtaining the results. Ascertain sensitivity history to penicillins. Because allergic reactions are a significant problem in the use of penicillins, the nurse must meticulously assess the client's previous drug experiences with special attention to the development of prior drug-related rashes. For infants less than 3 months old, a history of penicillin allergy in the mother should be sought. If at all possible, no penicillin preparation of any kind should be prescribed for or administered to an individual with a history of allergic

tuna
of b
Pl
for c
react
divid
cillin
Ce
and
ceph

**TABl**

cel

cel

cef

cef

cefi
(
cefi
(
cefe
I
I
cefe
Il
I'

cefe
Il
I'

cefe
I!
I'

cefe
Il
I'

cefo
Il
I'

cefta
Il
I'

cefti
Il
I'

---

### Pediatric Implications: ANTIBIOTIC THERAPY

To assess the appropriateness of antibiotic therapy in children, the following criteria are generally accepted:

1. In choosing empiric therapy, the selected antimicrobial should have documentation of both adequate penetration at the site and proven effectiveness against the common organisms usually isolated from that specific site.
2. If a broad range of possible microorganisms is suspected or if multiple organisms have been isolated from an infection site, then multiple drug therapy may be indicated. Whenever possible though, the minimal number of drugs necessary to treat the infection should be used.
3. If no contraindication is present, the drug of first choice should be selected. The drug dosage regimen should be within the accepted range of current usage for the individual client, taking into account the client's body surface area (height, weight), organ function, and concurrent disease processes.
4. Unless the benefit far outweighs the risks, no antibiotic should be used in clients with prior documentation of an allergic or adverse reaction to the specific medication.
5. Clients receiving potent and potentially dangerous drugs, such as gentamicin, amikacin, tobramycin, or vancomycin, for more than 2 days, should have steady-state drug serum concentrations drawn at the appropriate times for evaluation.
6. Whenever possible, cultures should be drawn before initiation of antibiotic therapy. Usual sites cultured include sputum, urine, blood, wound, or non-healing topical sites.
7. Duration of antibiotic therapy should be continued until infection is no longer present. Time periods, though, should not exceed the usual treatment time established for the suspected infection. Prophylactic antibiotic therapy given after uncomplicated surgery is usually discontinued within 48 hours with few exceptions, such as cardiac surgery.

---

### PENICILLINS: FDA PREGNANCY SAFETY CATEGORIES

| Category B | amdinocillin |
| | amoxicillin |
| | amoxicillin and clavulanate |
| | ampicillin and sulbactam |
| | azlocillin |
| | bacampicillin |
| | mezlocillin |
| | piperacillin |
| | ticarcillin and clavulanate |
| Not established | all others |

---

### EFFECT OF FOOD ON ORAL PENICILLIN ABSORPTION*

| Drug | Food Effect |
|------|-------------|
| amoxicillin | None |
| amoxicillin and clavulanate | None |
| ampicillin | Decreased slightly |
| bacampicillin | None |
| carbenicillin indanyl sodium | Increased |
| cloxacillin | Decreased |
| dicloxacillin | Decreased |
| nafcillin | Decreased |
| oxacillin | Decreased |
| penicillin G benzathine | Decreased very slightly |
| penicillin V potassium | Decreased very slightly |

*Penicillins whose absorption decreases after food intake are generally acid labile; therefore, administer with a full glass of water on an empty stomach 1 hour before or 2 hours after meals.

---

reaction to the drug. Because of possible cross-sensitization, it also seems wise to avoid the use of cephalosporins in clients with severe or immediate allergic reactions to penicillins. See also pediatric implications box on assessing the appropriate antibiotic therapy in children.

Clients receiving penicillin therapy are at risk for the possibility of the following nursing diagnoses: physiologic injury related to allergic response, or a cross-sensitivity to cephalosporins, cephamycins, griseofulvin, or penicillamine; superinfection related to reduction in normal flora evidenced by darkened tongue (fungal superinfection), white oral plaques and creamy vaginal discharge (Candida superinfection); altered bowel elimination pattern related to the development of antibiotic-associated pseudomembranous colitis evidenced by watery and severe diarrhea; and altered comfort related to nausea and vomiting.

***Intervention.*** In addition to performing nursing measures common to all types of antibiotic drug therapy, as discussed previously in the chapter, the nurse must be especially cognizant of several factors when penicillins are prescribed.

In administering penicillins, the nurse should remember that oral penicillins are bound to food and are poorly absorbed in acid media. Their administration, therefore, should not be preceded or followed by food for at least 1 hour, to minimize binding. Penicillins should not be taken with acidic fruit juices, since juices may facilitate decomposition of penicillins. See box on effect of food on oral penicillin absorption.

*The perc

**TABLE 59-4** Pharmacokinetics of the cephalosporins—cont'd

| Drug | Absorption | Half-life (hr) | Time to peak level (hr) | Peak serum level μg/ml | Peak serum level Dose | Peak urine level μg/ml | Peak urine level Dose | Liver and kidney metabolism of the drug | Kidney excretion* (%/hr) |
|---|---|---|---|---|---|---|---|---|---|
| ceftriaxone | | | | | | | | No | 33-67/? |
| IM | | 5.8-8.7 | 2 | 43 | 500 mg | 425 | 500 mg | | |
| IV | | 4.3-4.6 | 0.5 | 80 | 500 mg | 525 | 500 mg | | |
| cefuroxime | | 1-3 | | | | | | No | 90/8 |
| IM | | | 0.75 | 27 | 750 | 1300 | 750 mg | | 90/8 |
| IV | | | 0.25 | 50 | 750 mg | 1150 | 750 mg | | |
| PO | (After meals-52%) | | 2 | 43 | 500 mg | 425 | 500 mg | | 50/12 |
| cephalexin | | | | | | | | No | 80/6 |
| PO | | 0.9-1.2 | 1 | 9 | 250 mg | 1000 | 250 mg | | |
| cephalothin | | 0.5-1 | | | | | | Yes (33%) | 60-70/6 |
| IM | | | 0.5 | 10 | 500 mg | 800 | 500 mg | | |
| IV | | | 0.25-0.5 | 30 | 1 g | | | | |
| cephapirin | | 0.5-0.8 | | | | | | Yes (40%) | 50-70/6 |
| IM | | | 0.5-1 | 9 | 500 mg | 900 | 500 mg | | |
| IM | | | | | | | | | |
| IV | | | 0.1 | 35 | 500 mg | | | | |
| cephradine | | 0.8-1.3 | | | | | | No | 60-90/6 |
| PO | Very good | | 1 | 9 | 250 | 1600 | 250 mg | | |
| IM | | | 0.8-2 | 6 | 500 mg | | | | |
| IV | | | 0.1 | 86 | 1 g | | | | |
| moxalactam | | | | | | | | No | 55-65/24 |
| IM | | 2.1-2.3 | 1-2 | 10 | 250 mg | | | | |
| IV | | 1.7-3.5 | At end of infusion | 50 | 500 mg | 170 | 250 mg | | |

reported are stomach pain, gas, distress, severe watery diarrhea, bloody diarrhea, elevated temperature, thirst, nausea or vomiting, increased weakness, weight loss (pseudomembranous colitis). An increase in bleeding episodes and bruising due to hypothrombinemia is reported with cefamandole, cefoperazone, cefotetan, and moxalactam. Convulsions have been noted with high doses of moxalactam in clients with renal impairment.

***Significant drug interactions.*** When cephaloporins are given with the following drugs, these significant drug interactions may occur:

| Drug | Possible Effect and Management |
|---|---|
| alcohol | Not recommended with cefamandole, cefoperazone, cefotetan, or moxalactam. An increase in acetaldehyde in the blood may result, producing a disulfiram (Antabuse)-type reaction such as stomach pain, nausea, vomiting, headaches, low blood pressure, tachycardia, respiratory difficulties, increased sweating, or flushing of the face. Clients should avoid drinking alcohol-containing beverages, medications containing alcohol, or using intravenous alcohol solutions during the administration of these drugs and for 3 days afterward. |

| Drug | Possible Effect and Management |
|---|---|
| anticoagulants, coumarin or indandione, heparin, or thrombolytic agents | Increased risk of bleeding and hemorrhage when given concurrently with cefamandole, cefoperazone, cefotetan or moxalactam. These cephalosporins interfere with vitamin K metabolism in the liver, resulting in hypoprothrombinemia. Also, moxalactam causes irreversible platelet damage. Dosage adjustments of the anticoagulants may be necessary during and after administration of these drugs. Avoid concurrent use of these drugs with thrombolytic agents because of the increased risk of serious bleeding and hemorrhage. |
| nonsteroidal antiinflammatory drugs (NSAIDs), especially aspirin, platelet aggregation inhibitors, and sulfinpyrazone | When given with high doses of moxalactam or, less commonly, with cefamandole, cefoperazone, or cefotetan, an increased risk of hemorrhage exists because of the additive effect on platelet inhibition. Also, high dosages of salicylates and/or the specified antibiotics may induce hypoprothrombinemia, and the GI potential for ulcers or hemorrhage with NSAIDs, salicylates, or sulfinpyrazone may increase when used with the previously mentioned cephalosporins. Monitor closely. |

| Drug | Possible Effect and Management |
|------|-------------------------------|
| probenecid | Probenecid decreases renal tubular secretion of the cephalosporins that are excreted by this mechanism, which can result in increased serum levels, extended half-life, and increased potential for toxicity. Probenecid does not affect the secretion of cefonranide, ceftazidime, or ceftriaxone. Cephalosporins and probenecid are also used concurrently to treat specific infections such as sexually transmitted diseases, in which a high serum level and prolonged effect is desirable. |

***Dosage and administration.*** See Table 59-5.

## ▷ Nursing Management: Cephalosporin Therapy

***Assessment.*** Determine whether the client is hypersensitive to other cephalosporins. In some clients the use of cephalosporins is contraindicated. If the client has a history of sensitivity to penicillin, cephalosporins should be used with caution, since cross-sensitivity is possible.

Cultures for sensitivity of the organism should be obtained before the first dose of cephalosporin is administered; however, therapy should begin before the results are obtained.

Clients receiving cephalosporins should be assessed for the possibility of the following nursing diagnoses: altered bowel elimination pattern related to antibiotic-associated pseudomembranous colitis; risk for injury related to hypersensitivity or seizures (high doses or with renal impairment); altered comfort related to nausea and vomiting or to serum sickness-like reaction (cefaclor only) evidenced by joint pain, rash, and fever; and risk for infection related to fungal overgrowth evidenced by sore mouth or tongue or by itching of the genital area.

***Intervention.*** In addition to performing nursing measures common to all types of antimicrobial drug therapy as discussed in the previous chapter, the nurse must be aware of other factors when cephalosporins are prescribed.

Intramuscular cephalosporins, because they are irritating to tissues and can cause pain, induration, and sterile abscesses following injection, should be given deeply into a large muscle mass.

***Education.*** Instruct client to take the full course of medication, even though he or she may feel better and be symptom free. Stress the importance of taking evenly spaced doses to maintain therapeutic blood levels. Cephalosporins

**TABLE 59-5** Cephalosporins: dosage and administration

| Drug | Adults | Children |
|------|--------|----------|
| cefaclor (Ceclor) | PO, 250-500 mg every 8 hr | Infants 1 month and over, 6.7-13.4 mg/kg body weight every 8 hr |
| cefadroxil (Duricef) | PO, 500 mg to 1 g daily | 15 mg/kg body weight every 12 hr |
| cefamandole (Mandol) | IM, IV, 500 mg every 6 hr | Infants 1 month and over, 8.3-16.7 mg/kg every 4 hr |
| cefazolin (Ancef) | IM, IV, 250 mg-1.5 g every 6 to 8 hr | Infants 1 month and over, 6.25-25 mg/kg body weight every 6 hr |
| cefixime (Suprax) | PO, 400 mg daily | PO, 8 mg/kg body weight daily |
| cefmetazole (Zefazone) | IV, 2 g every 6 to 12 hr for 5-14 days | Not established |
| cefonicid (Monocid) | IM, IV, 500 mg to 1 g every 24 hr | Not established |
| cefoperazone (Cefobid) | IM, IV, 1-2 g every 12 hr | Not established |
| ceforanide (Precef) | IM, IV, 500 mg-1 g every 12 hr | Children 1 year and older, 10 to 20 mg/kg body weight every 12 hr |
| cefotaxime (Claforan) | IV infusion, 1-2 g every 4 to 12 hr | Neonates 1-4 wk, 50 mg/kg every 8 hr. Infants and children up to 50 kg, IM or IV, 8.3-30 mg/kg every 4 hr |
| cefotetan (Cefotan) | IM, IV, 1-2 g every 12 hr for 5-10 days | Not established |
| cefoxitin (Mefoxin) | IV, IM, 1 g every 6-8 hr | Infants and children 3 months and over, IV, 13.3-26.7 mg/kg body weight every 4 hr |
| ceftazidime (Fortaz) | IV infusion, 500 mg-2 g every 8-12 hr | Neonates to 1 month, 30-50 mg/kg body weight by IV infusion every 12 hr. One month to 12 yr, 30-50 mg/kg body weight every 8 hr |
| ceftazidime for injection (Tazicef) | IM, IV, 500 mg-2 g every 8-12 hr | Same as above |
| ceftizoxime (Cefizox) | IV, 1 g every 8-12 hr | Children 6 months and older, IV, 50 mg/kg body weight every 6-8 hr |

*Continued.*

**TABLE 59-5** Cephalosporins: dosage and administration—cont'd

| Drug | Adults | Children |
|------|--------|----------|
| ceftriaxone (Rocephin) | IV, 1-2 g every 12 hr | IV, 25-37.5 mg/kg body weight every 12 hr |
| cefuroxime (Zinacef) | PO, 250-500 mg every 12 hr | Children up to 12 yr, 125 mg orally, every 12 hr |
| | IM, IV, 750 mg-1.5 g every 6 hr | Neonates, IM, IV, 10-33.3 mg/kg every 8 hr. Infants and children 3 months and over, IM, IV, 25-40 mg/kg body weight every 8 hr |
| cephalexin (Keflex) | PO, 250-500 mg every 6 hr | Orally, 6.25-25 mg/kg every 6 hr |
| cephalothin (Keflin) | IV infusion, 500 mg-2 g every 4-6 hr, or IM, IV, 500 mg-2 g every 4-6 hr | IV infusion, 13.3-26.6 mg/kg every 4 hr |
| cephapirin (Cefadyl) | IM, IV, 500 mg-1 g every 4-6 hr | Infants and children 3 months and over, IM, IV, 10-20 mg/kg every 6 hr |
| cephadrine (Velosef, Anspor) | PO, 250-500 mg every 6 hr<br>IM, IV, 500 mg-1 g every 6 hr | PO 6.25-25 mg/kg body weight every 6 hr<br>IM, IV, infants and children 1 yr and over, 12.5-25 mg/kg body weight every 6 hr |
| moxalactam (Moxam) | IM, IV, 667 mg-1.33 g every 8 hr | IM, IV 50 mg/kg body weight every 6-12 hr according to age |

---

**CEPHALOSPORINS: FDA PREGNANCY SAFETY CATEGORIES**

| | | |
|--|--|--|
| Category B | cefadroxil | ceftazidime |
| | cefamandole | ceftizoxime |
| | cefazolin | ceftriaxone |
| | cefonicid | cefuroxime |
| | ceforanide | cephalexin |
| | cefotaxime | cephalothin |
| | cefotetan | cephapirin |
| | cefoxitin | |
| | cephradine | |
| Category C | moxalactam | |
| Not established | all others | |

---

may be taken with food if gastric irritation develops.

Clients with diabetes mellitus who are using copper sulfate urine glucose tests (Clinitest) may have false-positive results while taking cephalosporins. Have the client use glucose-enzymatic tests such as Clinistix or Ketodiastix.

The client should be cautioned not to drink alcoholic beverages or to take alcohol-containing medications because abdominal cramps, nausea, and vomiting; hypotension, tachycardia, and shortness of breath; and sweating and facial flushing may occur.

Instruct clients to read labels, because many cough remedies contain alcohol.

**Evaluation.** Because of the possibility of superinfection, observe clients, particularly the elderly and debilitated, for symptoms of bacterial and fungal overgrowth.

Precautions with cephalosporins should include monitoring those drugs that increase the effects of cephalosporins (loop diuretics, gentamicin, and probenecid) and those that

decrease the effects (tetracyclines). Loop diuretics and aminoglycosides can lead to acute renal failure, which subsequently impairs renal excretion of the cephalosporins. Probenecid decreases renal excretion of the cephalosporins and thereby increases blood levels. Tetracyclines slow the rate of bacterial reproduction; thus when given concurrently with the cephalosporins, which act against rapidly multiplying bacteria, tetracyclines inhibit the effectivensss of the cephalosporins.

For clients taking cefamandole, cefoperazone, cefotetan, and moxalactam, bleeding time and prothrombin time should be monitored, since hypoprothrombinemia has occurred with these drugs.

## MACROLIDE ANTIBIOTICS

The **macroliide antibiotics** constitute a large group of substances that were introduced in the early 1950s. They are bacteriostatic, since they inhibit protein synthesis; but in high concentrations with selected organisms, they may also be bactericidal. The most important macrolide antimicrobial agent is erythromycin.

**erythromycin delayed-release capsules (Eryc, Eryc Sprinkle ✱)**
**erythromycin delayed-release tablets (E-Mycin)**
**erythromycin estolate (Ilosone, Novorythro ✱)**
**erythromycin ethylsuccinate (E.E.S., Pediamycin)**
**erythromycin stearate (Erypar, Novorythro ✱)**
**sterile erythromycin gluceptate (Ilotycin)**
**erythromycin lactobionate for injection (Erythrocin)**

Erythromycin inhibits protein synthesis by penetrating the bacterial cell membrane and binding ribosomes of susceptible bacteria.

Indications for erythromycin are as follows:

Treatment of susceptible bacterial infections such as chlamydial conjunctivitis, genitourinary tract and systemic infections caused by *Chlamydia trachomatis, Corynebacterium diphtheriae, Neisseria gonorrhoeae,* Legionnaires' disease, *Listeria monocytogenes, Haemophilus influenzae, Bordetella pertussis, Streptococcus epidemicus, Staphulococcus aureus,* and others.

Prevention of bacterial endocarditis in individuals who are allergic to penicillin.

The absorption of oral erythromycin on an empty stomach is very good. If taken with food, the absorption of the base tablets and stearate dosage form is decreased. Erythromycin is distributed to most fluids in the body with the exception of cerebrospinal fluid. Highest levels are noted in the liver, bile, and spleen. It is highly protein bound and is partially metabolized in the liver. Erythromycin ethylsuccinate is hydrolyzed to free drug in the gastrointestinal tract and the blood. Erythromycin stearate is reduced to free drug in the gastrointestinal tract. Erythromycin estolate is reduced to propanoate ester in the gastrointestinal tract, absorbed, and then hydrolyzed to free drug in the blood.

Erythromycin has a half-life between 1.4 and 2 hours, with a peak effect between 1 to 4 hours. Excretion is via the liver and bile.

***Side effects/adverse reactions.*** See Table 59-6.

**TABLE 59-6**  Antibiotics: side effects and adverse reactions

| Drug(s) | Side effects* | Adverse reactions† |
|---|---|---|
| erythromycin | Less frequent: diarrhea, nausea or vomiting, soreness of tongue and mouth, abdominal distress | Rare (except for erythromycin estolate—more frequent): yellow eyes or skin, severe abdominal pain, increased weakness, pale stools, or dark, orange urine (resulting from cholestatic jaundice); if clients have renal impairment and receive high drug doses, hearing loss may occur but is usually reversible |
| lincomycins (clindamycin and lincomycin) | Most frequent: mild diarrhea, skin rash<br>Less frequent: pruritus of skin, rectum, or genital areas (resulting from fungal infection) | Most frequent: severe abdominal cramps, pain or gas; severe watery and perhaps bloody diarrhea; increased temperature; thirst; weight loss, increased weakness (from pseudomembranous colitis)<br>The above symptoms may occur after drug is discontinued |
| vancomycin | Oral dosage form, most frequent: nausea or vomiting or taste alterations<br>Parenteral: none | Parenteral:<br>Less frequent: hearing loss, ringing or buzzing in ears (ototoxicity), respiratory difficulties, hematuria, sedation, increased frequency of urination, thirst, anorexia, nausea, vomiting, weakness (nephrotoxicity)<br>Rare (usually with bolus or rapid injection of drug): "red-neck syndrome"—chills; fever; tachycardia; pruritus; nausea; vomiting; rash or red face; rash of neck, upper body, back, and arms; paresthesia (resulting from histamine release)<br>Ototoxicity and nephrotoxicity may occur after the medication is stopped. Medical attention is necessary |
| aminoglycosides (amikacin, gentamicin, kanamycin, neomycin, netilmicin, streptomycin, tobramycin) | | Most frequent: hearing loss, ringing or buzzing in ears (ototoxicity); bloody urine, thirst, anorexia, increased or decreased urination (nephrotoxicity); ataxia, dizziness (ototoxicity, vestibular); nausea, vomiting, paresthesias (usually only from streptomycin); numbness, tingling, muscle twitching, convulsions (neurotoxicity)<br>Less frequent: visual loss, skin rash, pruritus, edema (hypersensitivity with gentamicin or streptomycin, less often with others) |

*If side effects continue, increase, or disturb the client, inform the physician.

†If adverse reactions occur, contact physician, as medical intervention may be necessary.

*Continued.*

**TABLE 59-6**   Antibiotics: side effects and adverse reactions—cont'd

| Drug(s) | Side effects* | Adverse reactions† |
|---|---|---|
| aminoglycosides (amikacin, gentamicin, kanamycin, neomycin, netilmicin, streptomycin, tobramycin)—cont'd | | Rare: respiratory difficulties, weakness, sedation (neuromuscular blocking effects, nephrotoxicity)<br><br>If signs and symptoms of ototoxicity or nephrotoxicity occur after drug is discontinued, contact physician. Also, after local irrigation or topical application of aminoglycosides during surgery, neuromuscular blockade, respiratory paralysis, ototoxicity and nephrotoxicity have been reported<br><br>With aminoglycosides given concurrently by parenteral and intrathecal routes, leg cramps, skin rash, elevated temperature, and convulsions have been reported |
| tetracyclines | Most frequent: stomach cramps, diarrhea, pruritus of rectum or genitals, sore mouth or tongue (fungal overgrowth), nausea, vomiting<br><br>Photosensitivity to sunlight reported with all tetracyclines except minocycline (rare)<br><br>Ataxia, dizziness, or CNS toxicity reported with minocycline only | Most frequent: discoloration of teeth in infants and children<br><br>Low frequency: demeclocycline may increase thirst, frequency of urination, or weakness (nephrogenic diabetes insipidus); minocycline may cause skin and mucous membrane discoloration (pigmentation) |
| chloramphenicol (Chloromycetin, Mychel, Novochlorocap ✿) | Less frequent: diarrhea, nausea, or vomiting | Less frequent: pale skin, elevated temperature, sore throat, increase in bleeding episodes or bruises, increased weakness (blood dyscrasias)<br><br>Rare: gas, bloated stomach, sedation, gray skin, hypothermia, respiratory difficulties (gary syndrome)<br><br>Visual disturbances or loss (optic neuritis); numbness, burning sensation, tingling or weakness in hands or feet (peripheral neuritis)<br><br>Bone marrow depression can occur during or after the drug is discontinued; if sore throat, fever, unusual bleeding episodes, or tiredness occurs, contact a physician immediately |
| quinolones (ciprofloxacin, norfloxacin) | Most frequent: nausea, diarrhea, vomiting, headache, skin rash, stomach upset, restlessness | Rare: nephritis, increased urination, urinary retention, impaired renal function, seizures, depersonalization, cardiac toxicity (atrial flutter, ventricular ectopy, angina pectoris, syncope); most of these effects occur with ciprofloxacin |
| metronidazole (flagyl, flagyl I.V., Neo-Metric ✿) | Most frequent: diarrhea, dizziness, headache, anorexia, nausea, vomiting, abdominal pain, or cramping<br><br>Less frequent/rare: constipation, taste alterations, dry mouth, metallic taste in mouth, increased weakness<br><br>Dark urine reported—no need for medical intervention | Most frequent: hand or feet pain, tingling, weakness or numbness (peripheral neuropathy)<br><br>Less frequent: vaginal discharge or irritation (treatment failure or fungus infection); rash, hives, pruritus, sore throat, elevated temperature. CNS effects—ataxia, mood changes, convulsions (with high doses) |

***Significant drug interactions.*** When erythromycin is given with the following drugs, the following interactions may occur.

| Drug | Possible Effect and Management |
|---|---|
| alfentanil (Alfenta) | May increase plasma levels and action of alfentanil. Monitor closely if given in combination. |
| carbamazepine (Tegretol) | Carbamazepine metabolism may be inhibited, leading to elevated serum levels and, possibly, toxicity. This is reported more often with troleandomycin that erythromycin, but similar precautions and monitoring are indicated for both drugs. |
| chloramphenicol or lincomycins | May antagonize the therapeutic effects of chloramphenicol and lincomycin. Avoid concurrent administration. |
| cyclosporine | Concurrent administration with erythromycin may increase cyclosporine serum levels and increase risk for nephrotoxicity. Monitor closely if given concurrently. |
| hepatotoxic medications | Increased possibility for liver toxicity; monitor closely if given concurrently. |
| warfarin (coumarin, coumadin) | May result in decreased warfarin metabolism and excretion leading to an increased risk of bleeding or hemorrhage. Dosage adjustments of coumarin may be necessary during and after treatment with erythromycin. Monitor prothrombin times closely. |
| xanthines, such as aminophylline, caffeine, oxtriphylline, and theophylline (exception dyphylline) | An increase in theophylline levels and/or toxicity is reported with this combination of drugs. This effect is usually seen at approximately the sixth day of erythromycin therapy, since it appears to be related to the peak erythromycin serum level. Monitor closely, since dosage adjustments of the xanthines may be necessary during and after erythromycin therapy. |

***Dosage and administration.*** The oral adult dose of erythromycin is 250 mg every 6 hours. For endocarditis prophylaxis in clients with congenital heart disease or history of rheumatic fever before surgical procedure of upper respiratory tract or dental procedures is 1 g orally, 1 hour before the procedure and 500 mg administered 6 hours afterward. Children's dose is 7.5 to 12.5 mg/kg body weight every 6 hours.

Erythromycin ethylsuccinate adult oral dose is 400 mg every 6 hours. Pediatric dose is 7.5 to 12.5 mg/kg body weight every 6 hours. Parenteral erythromycin gluceptate or erythromycin lactobionate adult dose is 250 to 500 mg by intravenous infusion, every 6 hours. Maximum dose is 4 g per day. Pediatric dose is 3.75 to 5.0 mg/kg by intravenous infusion every 6 hours.

***Pregnancy safety.*** Has been established at FDA category C.

▷ **Nursing Management:**
**Erythromycin Therapy**

***Assessment.*** If the client has hepatic impairment, use erythromycin with caution. Periodic hepatic function studies

may be required for those clients receiving high-dose or prolonged intravenous erythromycin gluceptate therapy.

The client receiving erythromycin should be assessed for the possibility of the following nursing diagnoses: altered bowel elimination pattern (diarrhea); risk for physiologic injury related to hypersensitivity and the development of cholestatic jaundice evidenced by dark urine, pale stools, tiredness and yellowing of sclera and skin; altered comfort related to pain and inflammation at injection site, and nausea and vomiting; sensory-perceptual disturbance related to hearing loss; and risk for infection related to fungal overgrowth evidenced by sore mouth or tongue or by itching of the genital area.

***Intervention.*** General nursing management related to antimicrobial therapy discussed earlier also applies to the client receiving erythromycin.

Erythromycins should be administered with a full glass of water on an empty stomach (1 hour before or 2 hours after meals) to obtain maximum effect. Enteric-coated tablets, delayed-release capsules, and estolate and ethylsuccinate preparations may be taken with meals and may be used with clients who have a gastrointestinal intolerance to other forms of oral erythromycin. When administering oral suspensions, ensure that they have been refrigerated, shaken well, and that the calibrated liquid-measuring device has been used for accurate dosing.

Continuous infusion is preferable to intermittent; however, if intermittent infusion is considered, it should be diluted in 100 to 250 ml of 0.9% sodium chloride injection or 5% dextrose injection and administered over 20 to 60 minutes.

***Education.*** The importance of complying with a full course of therapy, even though the client feels better or is symptom free, should be stressed. This course of therapy should continue at least 10 days in group A beta-hemolytic streptococcal infections to prevent the occurrence of acute rheumatic fever.

***Evaluation.*** Observe the client for symptoms of superinfection.

## LINCOMYCINS
### clindamycin hydrochloride (Cleocin, Dalacin C ✳)
### lincomycin hydrochloride (Lincocin)

Lincomycin is primarily bacteriostatic, although it may be bactericidal in high doses with selected organisms. Clindamycin, which is a semisynthetic derivative of lincomycin, is more effective and causes fewer untoward effects.

Clindamycin and lincomycin are effective against most aerobic gram-positive cocci, including staphylococci, streptococci, and pneumococci. Both antibiotics are also active against several anaerobic and microaerophilic gram-negative and gram-positive organisms.

Because clindamycin is more effective in general than lincomycin, most clinicians believe that there are no recommended uses for lincomycin. Therefore lincomycin is not being reviewed in this section. Clindamycin has also been used in combination with aminoglycosides to treat mixed aerobic-anaerobic bacterial infections. Clindamycin inhibits protein synthesis in bacteria by binding ribosomes of susceptible bacteria.

**Indications.** Treatment of chronic bone infections, genitourinary tract infections, intraabdominal infections, anaerobic pneumonia, septicemia caused by streptococci and staphylococci, and serious skin and soft tissue infections when caused by susceptible bacteria.

**Pharmacokinetics.** Orally clindamycin is well absorbed (90%) if administered before meals. Absorption is decreased if the drug is given with meals. It is rapidly distributed to most body fluids and tissues with the exception of cerebrospinal fluid. The highest concentrations are noted in bone, bile, and urine. Clindamycin has a half-life between 2 to 3 hours and reaches peak blood levels within ¾ to 1 hour following oral administration, 1 hour in children, and 3 hours in adults by intramuscular injection and by the end of the infusion by intravenous injection. It is metabolized in the liver and excreted by the kidneys, bile, and intestines.

**Side effects/adverse reactions.** See Table 59-6.

**Significant drug interactions.** When clindamycin is administered with the following drugs the following interactions may occur:

| Drug | Possible Effect and Management |
|---|---|
| anesthetics, such as chloroform, cyclopropane, enflurane, halothane, isoflurane, methoxyflurane, trichloroethylene, or the neuromuscular blocking agents | May result in enhanced neuromuscular blockade, skeletal muscle weakness, respiratory depression, or paralysis. Use extreme caution if this combination is used during or immediately after surgery. Monitor closely and, if necessary, treat with calcium salts or anticholinesterase agents if blockade occurs. |
| antidiarrheals, adsorbent type (kaolins, attapulgite) | Decreases absorption of oral lincomycins. Avoid concurrent usage or advise client to take the antidiarrheal 2 hours before or 3 to 4 hours after the oral lincomycins. |
| chloramphenicol or erythromycins | May antagonize the therapeutic effect of lincomycins. Avoid concurrent administration. |

**Dosage and administration.** Clindamycin oral adult dose is 150 to 450 mg every 6 hours. In infants 1 month and over, the oral dose is 2 to 5 mg/kg body weight every 6 hours. Clindamycin IM or IV adult dosage is 300 to 600 mg every 6 to 8 hours. Infants up to 1 month old, IM/IV 3.75 to 5.0 mg/kg every 6 hours. One month and over, IM/IV, 3.75 to 10 mg/kg body weight every 6 hours.

**Pregnancy safety.** Has not been established.

▷**Nursing Management:**
**Clindamycin Therapy**

**Assessment.** Determine whether the client has a history of gastrointestinal disease, particularly colitis or enteritis, because pseudomembranous colitis may occur with linco-

mycin therapy as well as hepatic function impairment.

The client receiving clindamycin therapy should be assessed for the possibility of the following nursing diagnoses: altered bowel elimination pattern related to the development of antibiotic-associated pseudomembranous colitis; risk for physiologic injury related to hypersensitivity; altered comfort related to pain and inflammation at injection site, abdominal cramping and bloating, and nausea and vomiting; and risk for infection related to fungal overgrowth evidenced by sore mouth or tongue or by itching of the genital area.

**Intervention.** Administer clindamycin capsules with a full glass of water or with meals to prevent esophageal ulceration.

**Education.** Stress the importance of complying with a full course of the medication, even though the client feels well and is symptom free. Ten days is considered a minimal course of therapy for streptococcal infections. Instruct the client to take the medication at evenly spaced times to ensure maintenance of serum levels.

**Evaluation.** During therapy, observe the client for abdominal cramps, diarrhea, weight loss, or weakness, which might be indications of pseudomembranous colitis.

### vancomycin

Vancomycin is derived from *Streptomyces orientalis* cultures. It is bactericidal for many organisms and bacteriostatic for enterococci. It inhibits bacterial cell walls, resulting in lysis by a mechanism that differs from that in penicillin or cephalosporins. The drug also inhibits RNA synthesis. Vancomycin is indicated for the treatment of antibiotic-induced pseudomembranous colitis (*Clostridium difficile*) and the treatment of staphylococcal enterocolitis.

Vancomycin's absorption from the intestinal tract is poor. It is effective for intestinal infections caused by susceptible organisms, such as *Clostridium difficile*. It is excreted mainly in the feces. For side effects/adverse reactions, see Table 59-6.

**Significant drug interactions.** When vancomycin is given with the following drugs, the following interactions may occur:

| Drug | Possible Effect and Management |
|---|---|
| aminoglycosides, amphotericin B parenteral, aspirin, bacitracin parenteral, bumetanide parenteral, capreomycin, cisplatin, cyclosporine, ethacrynic acid parenteral, furosemide parenteral, paromomycin, polymyxins, or streptozocin | Increases potential for ototoxicity and/or nephrotoxicity. In clients with pseudomembranous colitis or severe kidney impairment, the serum levels of vancomycin may be increased, thus leading to an increased potential for toxicity. Monitor closely. |
| cholestyramine or colestipol | When given concurrently, a reduction in vancomycin antibacterial activity is reported. Avoid this combination if possible. If not, give oral vancomycin several hours apart from the other medications. |

***Dosage and administration.*** The oral adult dose of vancomycin for the treatment of antibiotic-induced pseudomembranous colitis, (*C. difficile* or enterocolitis), is 125 to 500 mg every 6 hours, which may be repeated if necessary. In children the dose is 11 mg/kg body weight every 6 hours for 5 to 10 days. It also may be repeated if necessary. Vancomycin parenteral is administered by intravenous infusion for the prophylaxis of endocarditis in penicillin-allergic clients with prosthetic heart valves or valvular heart disease who are undergoing upper respiratory tract or dental surgery: 1 g 1 hour before the procedure, repeated 8 hours afterward. For recommended doses for gastrointestinal and genitourinary tract procedures, enteric infections, etc., see current package insert. For children the prophylactic dose is 20 mg/kg body weight 1 hour before and 8 hours after the procedure.

***Pregnancy safety.*** The oral dosage form is FDA category C. Pregnancy safety has not been established for the parenteral dosage form, although it is reported vancomycin crosses the placenta and has caused eighth cranial nerve damage in the fetus. Therefore, risk to benefit must be carefully reviewed before use in pregnant women.

▷ **Nursing Management:**
**Vancomycin Therapy**

***Assessment.*** Assess the client for hearing loss, since vancomycin has ototoxic properties. Assess elderly clients for hearing loss over the course of therapy, since they excrete vancomycin more slowly.

Clients receiving vancomycin therapy should be assessed for the possibility of the following nursing diagnoses: risk for injury related to hypersensitivity; altered comfort related to pain and inflammation at injection site, nausea and vomiting, and "red-neck syndrome" due to histamine release common with bolus or rapid injection evidenced by tachycardia, redness of face and upper body; risk for physiologic injury related to the development of nephrotoxicity evidenced by blood in urine, greatly increased or decreased frequency of urination and amount of urine; and sensory-perceptual disturbance related to ototoxicity evidenced by loss of hearing and tinnitus.

***Intervention.*** The general nursing management for the administration of antimicrobial therapy should be applied to vancomycin administration.

Administer the oral liquid using the calibrated liquid-measuring device provided by the manufacturer. If the intravenous form is used for oral administration, each vial should be dissolved in 30 ml of water or juice. It may be administered straight or through a nasogastric tube to minimize the unpleasant taste.

Parenteral vancomycin is only to be administered intravenously because it is so irritating to the tissues. Care must be taken to avoid extravasation. To avoid side effects such as hypotension, thrombophlebitis, and "red-neck syndrome," do not administer as a bolus injection. Vancomycin may be administered intermittently in at least 100 ml of 0.9% sodium chloride injection or 5% dextrose injection over 60 minutes. Rotation of the venous sites will help prevent local irritation.

***Education.*** Alert the client to possible side effects or adverse reactions. Instruct the client to take the medication as prescribed and for the full course of therapy.

***Evaluation.*** Urinalysis and renal function studies may be needed before and periodically during high-dose or prolonged therapy. Vancomycin serum concentration determinations may be necessary in clients with renal impairment or in clients over 60.

## AMINOGLYCOSIDES

Aminoglycosides are potent bactericidal antibiotics that are usually reserved for serious or life-threatening infections. They are very effective against many bacteria (gram-positive and gram-negative) but are generally reserved for gram-negative infections. Safer and less toxic agents are available to treat the majority of gram-positive infections. See box below for generic and trade names of various aminoglycosides.

Their mechanism of action is to irreversibly bind ribosomes of susceptible bacteria, thus inhibiting protein synthesis leading to eventual cell death (bactericidal). They are indicated for the treatment of serious or life-threatening infections when other agents are ineffective or contraindicated. They are used with penicillins, cephalosporins, or vancomycin for their synergistic effects. They are especially useful for the treatment of gram-negative infections such as those caused by *Pseudomonas* spp., *E. coli, Proteus* spp., *Klebsiella* spp., *Serratia* spp., and others.

Aminoglycosides are poorly absorbed from an intact intestinal tract, but they are rapidly absorbed intramuscularly. Local topical application or irrigation may lead to absorption from most areas of the body with the exception of the urinary bladder.

Distribution of aminoglycosides is as follows:
amikacin: Mainly in extracellular fluid. The cerebrospinal fluid of normal infants is approximately 10% to 20%

---

**AMINOGLYCOSIDES**

amikacin sulfate (Amikin)
gentamicin sulfate (Cidomycin ♣, Garamycin)
kanamycin sulfate (Kantrex, Klebcil)
neomycin sulfate (Neo-IM, Mycifradin ♣)*
netilmicin sulfate (Netromycin)
streptomycin sulfate
tobramycin sulfate (Nebcin)

---

*Safer drugs are available; therefore the systemic use of this drug is not recommended.

of the plasma drug level; but if the meninges are inflamed, these levels may increase to 50% of the blood concentration. High and therapeutic concentrations are also reached in the synovial fluid and the urine.

gentamicin: Mainly in extracellular fluid. High concentrations are reported in the urine.

kanamycin: Mainly in extracellular fluid. The cerebrospinal fluid of normal infants is approximately 10% to 20% of the plasma drug level; but if the meninges are inflamed, these levels may increase to 50% of the blood concentration. High concentrations also reported in urine and synovial fluids.

netilmicin: Rapidly distributed to body tissues (liver, gallbladder, stomach, appendix, renal cortex) and body fluids (urine, blood, bile, sputum, peritoneal, synovial, pleural, pericardial, and blister fluids).

streptomycin: Mainly in extracellular fluids; to most body tissues except the brain. High levels found in urine. Also found in pleural, bile, and ascitic fluids and tuberculous tissues and/or abscesses.

tobramycin: Mainly in extracellular fluid. High concentrations in urine and synovial fluids.

Peak serum levels with amikacin are 12 μg/ml in 1 hour after a dose of 250 mg. Intravenously, peak serum levels of 38 μg/ml are noted at the end of a 30-minute IV infusion of 500 mg. Gentamicin IV peak serum level is 4 to 6 μg/ml in ½ to 1 hour after the infusion. Kanamycin's peak level is 22 μg/ml following a 7.5 mg/kg IM or IV dose. Streptomycin's IM peak serum level is 25 to 50 μg/ml after an IM dose of 1 g while tobramycin's peak serum level is 4 μg/ml after an IM dose of 1 mg/kg. In clients with serious burns or fever, all drugs may have decreased serum concentrations. For peak urine and bile concentration times, see current package insert or USP-DI. For side effects/adverse reactions see Table 59-6.

**Significant drug interactions.** When aminoglycosides are given concurrently with the following drugs, the following interactions may occur.

| Drug | Possible Effect and Management |
|---|---|
| other aminoglycosides (two or more concurrently) or capreomycin | Potential for ototoxicity, nephrotoxicity, and neuromuscular blockade is enhanced. Hearing loss may progress to deafness even after the drug is stopped. In some cases, hearing loss may be reversed.<br>Administration of two or more aminoglycosides may reduce uptake of both drugs, possibly resulting in reduced effectiveness.<br>An increased potential for neuromuscular blockade. Treat with an anticholinesterase agent or calcium salts to prevent or reverse this effect.<br>The administration of topical and systemic aminoglycosides is not recommended. Hypersensitivity effects are |

| Drug | Possible Effect and Management |
|---|---|
| | reported more frequently with this combination. |
| amphotericin B, parenteral; aspirin; bacitracin, parenteral; bumetanide, parenteral; cephalothin; cisplatin; cyclosporine; ethacrynic acid, parenteral; furosemide, parenteral; paromomycin; streptozocin or vancomycin | Increased potential for ototoxicity and/or nephrotoxicity. Hearing loss may be permanent. If drugs are given concurrently, serial audiometric hearing determinations are suggested.<br>Vancomycin and aminoglycosides may be ordered to prevent bacterial endocarditis or to treat specific infections such as endocarditis caused by organisms such as streptococci and corynebacteria. In such instances, frequent determinations of drug serum levels and renal function are recommended, since dosage adjustments or other interventions may be necessary. |
| anesthetics (halogenated hydrocarbon) or citrate-anticoagulated blood by massive transfusions or neuromuscular blocking agents | May increase neuromuscular blockade. Monitor closely as interventions may be necessary. |
| indomethacin, intravenous | May reduce excretion of aminoglycosides, leading to elevated serum levels and possible aminoglycoside toxicity. Monitor closely, since dosage adjustments may be indicated. Aminoglycoside toxicity is usually reported in the premature neonate, but it may also occur in the adult. |
| methoxyflurane or polymyxins, parenteral | Increased possibility for nephrotoxicity and/or neuromuscular blockade. If used concurrently, monitor closely. |

**Dosage and administration.** The usual adult dose of amikacin IM/IV is 5 mg/kg every 8 hours. Neonates are administered 10 mg/kg IM/IV dose initially followed by 7.5 mg/kg every 12 hours. Gentamicin adult dose is 1 to 1.7 mg/kg IM or by IV infusion every 8 hours, while pediatric dose is usually 2.5 mg/kg every 12 hours (premature neonates up to 1 week old), and every 8 hours (older neonates, infants, and children). Kanamycin adult and pediatric dose is 3.75 mg/kg IM every 6 hours or 5 mg/kg every 8 hours by IV infusion.

Netilmicin adult dose is 1.3 to 2.2 mg/kg IM/IV every 8 hours. Neonates up to 6 weeks old receive 2 to 3.25 mg/kg every 12 hours for 1 to 2 weeks. Infants and children 6 weeks to 12 years old are given 1.83 to 2.67 mg/kg every 8 hours. Streptomycin tuberculosis adult dose is 1 g IM daily given in combination with other antimycobacterials. This dose is reduced as soon as possible to 1 g two or three times a week. Pediatric dose is 20 mg/kg IM daily, not to exceed 1 g daily. Tobramycin's adult dose is 0.75 mg to 1.25 mg/kg IM or IV infusion every 6 hours. Premature or full-term neonates up to 1 week old receive up to 2 mg/kg every 12 hours. Older infants and children's dose is 1.5 to 1.9 mg/kg every 6 hours.

**Pregnancy safety.** Category for amikacin and gentamicin is C; category for kanamycin, netilmicin, and to-bramicin is D.

## ▷ Nursing Management: Aminoglycoside Therapy

***Assessment.*** Clients receiving aminoglycoside therapy should be assessed for the possibility of the following nursing diagnoses: risk for injury related to hypersensitivity; altered comfort related to anorexia, nausea and vomiting; risk for physiologic injury related to the development of nephrotoxicity evidenced by blood in urine, greatly increased or decreased frequency of urination and amount of urine, or to neurotoxicity evidenced by muscle twitching, numbness or seizures; and sensory-perceptual disturbance related to auditory ototoxicity evidenced by loss of hearing and tinnitus, vestibular ototoxicity evidenced by dizziness and loss of balance, or optical neuritis (streptomycin only) evidenced by any loss of vision. Elderly clients are at greater risk of nephrotoxicity and ototoxicity because of reduced renal function, and they generally require smaller daily doses. Loss of hearing however, may occur in clients with normal renal function. Audiograms, renal function studies, and vestibular function studies should be done before and periodically during high-dose therapy or therapy over 10 days.

***Intervention.*** For intravenous administration, dilute appropriately and administer slowly over a 30- to 60-minute period to prevent neuromuscular blockade for toxic serum levels.

Clients should be well hydrated while taking these medications to minimize chemical irritation of the urinary tubules. Intake and output should be monitored. Daily urinalysis may be required during therapy for signs of renal irritation.

***Education.*** Instruct the client to report any loss of hearing or any ringing or buzzing in the ears that would indicate ototoxicity; any change in urinary pattern or blood in the urine that would indicate nephrotoxicity; dizziness that would indicate vestibular toxicity; or numbness, tingling, or twitching that would indicate neurotoxicity.

Stress the importance of taking the full course of medication as prescribed.

***Evaluation.*** Monitor peak and trough drug levels routinely, since evidence suggests that the incidence of ototoxicity and nephrotoxicity with aminoglycosides correlates with slight elevations of either drug level but particularly with trough levels. The trough concentration is believed to be a more sensitive indicator of renal function than the serum creatinine.

## TETRACYCLINES

**Tetracyclines,** the first broad-spectrum antibiotics, were introduced in 1948. They include a large group of drugs that have a common basic structure and similar chemical activity.

**demeclocycline (Declomycin)**
**doxycycline (Doxychel, Vibramycin)**
**methacycline (Rondomycin)**
**minocycline (Minocin)**
**oxytetracycline (Terramycin)**
**tetracycline (Achromycin V, Novotetra ✳)**

Tetracyclines block the binding of transfer RNA complex to the ribosome. No amino acid is available to the messenger RNA to produce polypeptides; therefore protein synthesis is prevented. These agents are bacteriostatic for many gram-negative and gram-positive organisms. The tetracyclines exhibit cross-sensitivity and cross-resistance.

These agents are indicated for the treatment of acne vulgaris, actinomycosis, anthrax, bacterial urinary tract infections, and systemic bacterial infections sensitive to the tetracyclines.

Tetracyclines are fairly well absorbed orally and distributed to most body fluids, although cerebrospinal fluid levels vary and can range from 10% to 25% of the plasma drug concentration following parenteral administration. Tetracyclines localize in teeth, liver, spleen, tumors, and bone. Doxycycline can reach clinical concentrations in the eye and prostate.

Doxycycline and minocycline are inactivated in the liver, but most tetracyclines are excreted via the kidneys. For half-life of tetracyclines, see box. For side effects/adverse reactions see Table 59-6.

***Significant drug interactions.*** When tetracyclines are given concurrently with the following drugs, the following interactions may occur:

| Drug | Possible Effect and Management |
|---|---|
| antacids; calcium supplements (such as calcium lactate, calcium gluconate); choline and magnesium salicylates; iron supplements; magnesium salicylate or magnesium-containing laxatives; foods containing milk and milk products | May result in nonabsorbable complex, thus reducing the absorption and serum levels of the antibiotic. Also, antacids may increase gastric pH, which decreases the absorption of tetracyclines. If given concurrently, advise clients to separate medications by 1 to 3 hours from the oral tetracycline. |

---

### TETRACYCLINE HALF-LIVES

| Drug | Half-Life (hr) |
|---|---|
| demeclocycline (Declomycin) | 10-17 |
| doxycycline (Vibramycin, others) | 12-22 |
| methacycline (Rondomycin) | 14-17 |
| minocycline (Minocin) | 11-23 |
| oxytetracycline (Terramycin) | 6-10 |
| tetracycline | 6-11 |

| Drug | Possible Effect and Management |
|------|-------------------------------|
| colestipol, cholestyramine | Decreases absorption to tetracyclines. Avoid concurrent usage. |
| estrogen-containing oral contraceptives | Concurrent long-term therapy may reduce contraceptive effectiveness; also may result in breakthrough bleeding |

***Dosage and administration.*** The adult dose of deme-clocycline and methacycline is 150 mg every 6 hours. For children 8 years and older, the oral dose is 1.65 to 3.3 mg/kg every 6 hours. Doxycycline adult dose is 100 mg every 12 hours on the first day, then 100 to 200 mg daily. For pediatric dose check a current package insert. Minocycline's adult oral dose is 200 mg to start, then 100 mg every 12 hours. Dose for children 8 years and over is 4 mg/kg orally initially, then 2 mg/kg every 12 hours.

Oxytetracycline's and tetracycline's oral adult dose is 250 to 500 mg every 6 hours; the pediatric dose is 6.25 to 12.5 mg/kg orally every 6 hours. Tetracycline is available parenterally for IM and IV usage, usually 100 mg IM every 8 hours or 250 to 500 mg IV every 12 hours. Dose for children 8 years and over is 5.0 to 8.3 mg/kg IM every 8 hours or 5 to 10 mg/kg IV every 12 hours.

***Pregnancy safety.*** Since tetracyclines cross the placenta and are excreted in breast milk, their usage is not recommended, especially during the last half of pregnancy or during breast-feeding.

▷ **Nursing Management: Tetracycline Therapy**

In addition to nursing management common to all types of antimicrobial drug therapy, the nurse should observe the following measures when clients are receiving drugs of the tetracycline family.

***Assessment.*** Tetracyclines are contraindicated in pregnant women and children under 8 years of age because they cause permanent mottling and discoloration of the teeth and a decrease in linear skeletal growth rate.

Clients with a hypersensitivity to one tetracycline may be hypersensitive to the others as well. In addition, clients with hypersensitivities to "caine-type" drugs, such as lidocaine or procaine, may be intolerant of the lidocaine in oxytet-racycline injection or the procaine in the tetracycline intramuscular injection.

Use of tetracyclines in clients with renal impairment is not recommended (except for doxycycline and minocy-cline).

Clients receiving aminoglycoside therapy should be assessed for the possibility of the following nursing diagnoses: risk for injury related to hypersensitivity; altered comfort related to anorexia, abdominal cramping, nausea and vomiting; risk for physiologic injury related to the development of nephrogenic diabetes insipidus evidenced by greatly increased or decreased frequency of urination and amount of urine or to increased sensitivity of the skin to sunlight; altered bowel elimination (diarrhea); and risk for infection related to fungal overgrowth evidenced by sore mouth or tongue or itching of the genital area.

***Intervention.*** Tetracyclines should be taken with a full glass of water to prevent esophageal erosion and gastrointestinal irritation. Except for doxycycline and minocycline, they should be taken on an empty stomach (1 hour before or 2 hours after meals) for maximum effectiveness. Avoid administering antacids and laxatives containing aluminum, calcium, or magnesium; iron products; and food, milk, or other dairy products for 1 hour before and 2 hours after tetracycline administration, as they form nonabsorbable complexes with tetracyclines. Administer the oral suspension using the calibrated liquid-measuring device provided by the manufacturer.

***Education.*** Stress the importance of taking the full course of the medication in evenly spaced doses to maintain serum levels. Photosensitivity may occur and persist for some time after discontinuance of the drug. Instruct the client to avoid direct sunlight and ultraviolet light. If exposure is unavoidable, a sun screen may help prevent a reaction. Instruct the client to discard outdated tetracyclines (show client where date is found), since they become toxic as they decompose.

***Evaluation.*** Because the risk for superinfection is greater in tetracycline therapy than in therapy with other antimicrobial agents, observe clients carefully for signs and symptoms of secondary infections, especially *Candida* infections. Meticulous oral and perineal hygiene is helpful in preventing *Candida* superinfections.

## CHLORAMPHENICOL (CHLOROMYCETIN)

Chloramphenicol, discovered in 1949, is a potent inhibitor of protein synthesis. It is a bacteriostatic agent for a wide variety of gram-negative and gram-positive organisms; but because it is potentially seriously toxic to bone marrow (aplasia leading to aplastic anemia and possibly death), its approved indications are limited.

Chloramphenicol is usually bacteriostatic, but in high doses with highly susceptible organisms, it may be bactericidal. It penetrates bacteria cell membranes and reversibly prevents peptide bond formation, thus inhibiting protein synthesis.

It is indicated for the treatment of meningitis *(Haemophilus influenzae)*, paratyphoid fever, Q fever, rickett-sialpox, Rocky Mountain spotted fever, typhoid fever *(Salmonella typhi)*, typhus infections, and bacterial septicemia.

Chloramphenicol has good oral and intravenous bioavailability with highest concentrations reported in the liver and kidneys. Concentrations of up to 50% of serum levels have been noted in cerebrospinal fluid. Chloramphenicol is metabolized in the liver to the inactive glucuronide, while the palmitate and sodium succinate forms of chloramphenicol are hydrolyzed to free drug in the intestinal tract or the plasma, liver, lungs, and kidneys respectively. In utero and in neonates an immature liver cannot conjugate chloramphenicol, which may result in toxic levels of active drug accumulation (gray syndrome).

Half-life of chloramphenicol in an adult is 1.5 to 3.5 hours; in infants it is 1 to 2 days or more. In infants 10 to 16 days old it is 10 days. Peak serum levels are reached in 1 to 1.5 hours via the intravenous route or 1 to 3 hours after an oral dose. Chloramphenicol is excreted mainly by the kidneys. For side effects/adverse reactions, see Table 59-6.

***Significant drug interactions.*** When chloramphenicol is given concurrently with the following drugs, the following interactions may occur:

| Drug | Possible Effect and Management |
|---|---|
| alfentanil | May result in increased alfentanil blood levels, prolonging its effect. Monitor closely. |
| anticonvulsants, hydantoin, bone marrow depressants, radiation therapy | May result in enhanced bone marrow depressant effects. Dosage reduction may be necessary. Decreased hydantoin metabolism may result in increased serum levels and toxicity. Monitor closely, as dosage adjustments may be needed. |
| antidiabetic oral agents | May displace the antidiabetic drug from protein binding, leading to hypoglycemia. Dosage adjustment may be necessary. Monitor closely. |
| erythromycins or lincomycins | Therapeutic action of chloramphenicol and these drugs may be antagonized. Avoid this drug combination. |

***Dosage and administration.*** The oral/intravenous adult dose is 12.5 mg/kg every 6 hours. Pediatric oral/intravenous dose for premature and full-term infants up to 2 weeks old is 6.25 mg/kg every 6 hours. Infants 2 weeks old and over, 12.5 mg/kg every 6 hours. Chloramphenicol is not recommended for use during pregnancy nor during breast-feeding.

▷ **Nursing Management: Chloramphenicol Therapy**

***Assessment.*** Consider carefully before using chloramphenicol in clients with bone marrow depression, hepatic or renal impairment, or clients who have had previous cytotoxic drug or radiation therapy.

Clients receiving chloramphenicol therapy should be assessed for the possibility of the following nursing diagnoses: risk for injury related to hypersensitivity; altered comfort related to headache, anorexia, nausea and vomiting; risk for physiologic injury related to the development of blood dyscrasias evidenced by unusual bruising or bleeding, tiredness, sore throat and fever; altered bowel elimination (diarrhea); altered thought processes (confusion, delirium) related to neurotoxic reactions; and sensory-perceptual disturbances related to optic neuritis evidenced by blurred vision and to peripheral neuritis evidenced by tingling, numbness, and burning pain of the hands and feet.

***Intervention.*** Administer chloramphenicol with a full glass of water on an empty stomach (1 hour before meals or 2 hours after) to maximize effectiveness. When administering the oral suspension, use the calibrated liquid-measuring device provided by the manufacturer. If administered intravenously, the drug should be infused over at least a 1-minute period. Check the intravenous site daily for local irritation.

***Education.*** Because the bone marrow depressant effects of chloramphenicol may increase gingival bleeding and delay healing, instruct the client to delay dental work until blood counts return to normal. Instruct all clients in proper oral hygiene, with cautious use of toothbrushes, dental floss, and toothpicks.

Advise the client to report to the physician immediately any symptoms of blood dyscrasias, such as sore throat, fever, extreme fatigue, or unusual bleeding or bruising.

Caution clients who test their urine with copper sulfate glucose tests (Clinitest tablets) that they may get false-positive reactions. For the course of the antibiotic therapy, recommend the use of Clinistix or Keto-diastix.

***Evaluation.*** Perform complete blood counts periodically to monitor for dose-related reversible bone marrow depression.

## QUINOLONES

**Quinolones** (also referred to as 4-quinolone or fluoroquinolone), are recent synthetic chemical additions to the antimicrobial classification. Two members of this class, ciprofloxacin and norfloxacin, are reviewed.

### ciprofloxacin (Cipro)

Ciprofloxacin alters bacterial DNA by interfering with DNA gyrase and possibly by direct interaction with DNA itself. It may also inhibit bacterial RNA synthesis, especially at high concentrations. It is bactericidal.

It is indicated for the treatment of susceptible strains of bacteria (gram-negative and gram-positive) affecting the lower respiratory tract, bone and joint infections, infectious diarrhea, urinary tract infections, and skin infections.

Ciprofloxacin has good oral absorption (70%), especially in the fasting state. It is widely distributed throughout the body and reaches peak serum levels within 1 to 2 hours. Half-life is in approximately 4 hours. It is metabolized in the liver to less active metabolites and excreted via the kidneys. For side effects/adverse reactions, see Table 59-6.

***Significant drug interactions.*** When ciprofloxacin is given concurrently with the following drugs, the following interactions may occur:

| Drug | Possible Effect and Management |
|---|---|
| antacids, especially magnesium hydroxide or aluminum hydroxide | May decrease absorption of cipro-floxacin, reducing drug effective-ness. Avoid concurrent drug ad-ministration. |
| probenecid | Blocks renal tubular secretion of cip-rofloxacin, resulting in elevated se-rum levels. |
| theophylline | May result in increased plasma levels of theophylline and increased risk of toxicity. Monitor plasma levels closely, as dosage adjustments may be necessary. Monitor closely. |

***Dosage and administration.*** The adult oral dose is 500 to 750 mg every 12 hours for 1 to 2 weeks. It is not recommended for use in infants, children, or adolescents.

***Pregnancy safety.*** Has been established at FDA category C.

### norfloxacin (Noroxin)

Norfloxacin inhibits bacterial DNA synthesis and is bactericidal. It is indicated for the treatment of urinary tract infections (complicated or uncomplicated) caused by susceptible strains of bacteria such as *E. coli, K. pneumoniae, Enterobacter cloacae, Proteus mirabilis, Pseudomonas aeruginosa, Stapholococcus aureus,* group D streptococci, and others. It is effective against many gram-negative and gram-positive organisms.

It is incompletely absorbed orally (30% to 40%) but is widely distributed to most body fluids, organs, and tissues. Time to peak serum levels is between 1 to 2 hours; half-life is 3 to 4 hours. Norfloxacin is metabolized in the liver and excreted in the kidneys. Urine concentration is between 98 to 200 $\mu$g/ml for 2 to 3 hours, then it remains above 30 $\mu$g/ml for at least 12 hours, after a single 400-mg dose. For side effects/adverse reactions, see Table 59-6.

When norfloxacin is given with probenecid, a decrease in urinary excretion of norfloxacin may result. Monitor closely to avoid toxicity. Antacids may decrease absorption of norfloxacin; therefore, avoid concurrent administration. If antacids are ordered, administer them at least 2 hours after norfloxacin.

Pregnancy safety has been established at FDA category C.

### ▷ Nursing Management: Quinolone Therapy

***Assessment.*** Clients with hepatic or renal impairment may require reduced dosages. Since norfloxacin administration may result in CNS toxicity, another drug should be used if possible for clients with a history of seizures.

Clients receiving quinolone therapy should be assessed for the possibility of the following nursing diagnoses: risk for injury related to hypersensitivity; altered comfort related to anorexia, nausea and vomiting; risk for physiologic injury related to the development of crystalluria evidenced by blood in the urine and lower back pain and to photosensitivity; altered bowel elimination (diarrhea); and sensory-perceptual disturbances related to visual disturbances; and altered sleep patterns related to CNS stimulation evidenced by insomnia and restlessness.

***Intervention.*** Administer with a full glass of water on an empty stomach.

Hydrate the client to maintain a urinary output of at least 1200 to 1500 ml daily for adults, since crystalluria has been reported.

***Education.*** Stress the importance of taking a full course of therapy, taking all doses as prescribed at evenly spaced intervals to maintain therapeutic serum levels.

Caution the client that the drug may decrease salivation and that dry mouth may result. This may be relieved by sugar-free candies or gum, ice cubes, or frequent mouth rinses. If the therapy is long-term, caries and gum disease may result; the client should be advised to have regular dental checkups.

Advise the client to report dizziness, lightheadedness, or depression, since these signs indicate CNS toxicity. Visual disturbances such as blurred or double vision and increased light sensitivity should be reported for the same reason.

Avoid taking antacids and norfloxacin within 2 hours of each other.

Advise the client that photophobia is a possible effect of this drug. Avoiding bright lights and wearing sunglasses may assist the client with this symptom.

Because visual disturbances, dizziness, lightheadedness, or drowsiness may occur, advise the client to limit activities that require alertness and dexterity until the response to the drug has been determined.

## MISCELLANEOUS ANTIBIOTICS

Except for metronidagole hydrochloride and spectinomycin, the other antibiotics in current use are topical agents and are discussed in Chapter 68.

### metronidazole hydrochloride (Flagyl, Flagyl I.V.)

Metronidazole is reduced intracellularly to a short-acting, cytotoxic agent that interacts with DNA, thus inhibiting bacteria synthesis and resulting in cell death (microbicidal). It is active against many anaerobic bacteria and protozoa.

It is indicated for the treatment of amebiasis (intestinal and extraintestinal), bone infections, brain abscesses, CNS infections, bacterial endocarditis, genitourinary tract infections, liver abscess (amebic), septicemia, trichomoniasis, *Bacteroides* pneumonia, and other infections due to organisms susceptible to metronidazole's action.

Metronidazole is well absorbed orally and well distributed throughout the body. It has a half-life of 8 hours and reaches peak serum levels within 1 to 2 hours. It is metabolized in the liver and primarily excreted in the kidneys. For side effects/adverse reactions, see Table 59-6.

***Significant drug interactions.*** When metronidazole is given concurrently with the following drugs, the following interactions may occur:

| Drug | Possible Effect and Management |
|---|---|
| alcohol | Metronidazole interferes with the metabolism of alcohol, leading to an accumulation of acetaldehyde. This may result in disulfiram-type effects: flushing, headaches, nausea, vomiting, and abdominal distress. Avoid concurrent drug administration. |
| anticoagulants (coumarin or indandione) | May enhance anticoagulant effects by inhibiting their metabolism. Monitor closely with prothrombin tests if given concurrently. Dosage adjustments may be necessary. |
| disulfiram | Avoid concurrent administration with metronidazole. Adverse effects, including confusion and psychosis, have been reported. |

***Dosage and administration.*** The adult oral dose is usually 500 mg three or four times daily. Maximum daily dose is 4 g. Pediatric dose depends on type of protozoal infection present. See current package insert for dosing recommendations.

***Pregnancy safety.*** Has been established at FDA category B.

▷ **Nursing Management: Metronidazole Therapy**

***Assessment.*** Because metronidazole may cause CNS toxicity, any individual with preexisting CNS disease should be carefully evaluated before treatment with the drug.

The client receiving metronidazole should be assessed for the possibility of the following nursing diagnoses: risk for injury related to hypersensitivity and seizures related to CNS effects; altered comfort related to headache, change in taste, anorexia, nausea and vomiting; risk for physiologic injury related to the development of thrombophlebitis (IV administration only); altered bowel elimination (constipation); risk for infection related to leukopenia and fungal overgrowth due to reduction of normal flora evidenced by vaginal irritation not present before therapy; and sensory-perceptual disturbances related to peripheral neuropathy evidenced by numbness, tingling, and pain in the hands and feet; and altered thought processes related to CNS effects evidenced by mood changes.

***Intervention.*** Administer oral forms with meals to minimize gastrointestinal irritation. Parenteral metronidazole is to be administered by slow intravenous infusion. It may be administered continuously or intermittently over 1-hour period. The sodium content of the parenteral forms of the drug should be considered in the sodium intake for clients on sodium restriction.

***Education.*** Advise the client that the drug may cause an unpleasant taste in the mouth, diminished taste sensation,

and a dry mouth. The use of sugar-free candies, ice cubes, and frequent mouth rinses may bring some relief to the client. If therapy is long-term, dry mouth may contribute to dental caries and gum disease, and the client should receive regular dental checkups.

Stress the importance of completing a full course of therapy, even though the client may be feeling well and be symptom free. The doses should be evenly spaced to ensure therapeutic serum levels are maintained.

Advise the client not to ingest alcoholic beverages while taking metronidazole, because a disulfiramlike effect may result (flushing, nausea and vomiting, and abdominal cramping).

If metronidazole is being prescribed for trichomoniasis, the client will need to prevent reinfection from her male partner. He will need concurrent drug therapy and to use a condom until the infection is resolved in both partners.

Advise the client that the urine may turn a darker color, but this change is not medically significant.

***Evaluation.*** Assess clients periodically for symptoms of peripheral neuropathy such as numbness and tingling of the hands or feet. Mood changes and irritability also indicate of CNS toxicity.

Monitor complete blood counts frequently for blood dyscrasias and instruct the client to report immediately to the physician any symptoms of sore throat, unusual tiredness or weakness, or unusual bleeding or bruising.

If metronidazole is administered for giardiasis, three stool examinations taken several days apart, beginning 1 to 2 weeks after treatment, should be accomplished to determine the success of therapy. Additional specimens may be required if symptoms persist.

**spectinomycin (Trobicin)**

Spectinomycin was marketed in 1971, but its sole therapeutic indication is the treatment of infections caused by *Neisseria gonorrhoeae*. It inhibits protein synthesis in the bacteria cell. It is for intramuscular use only and generally is recommended for individuals with gonorrhea who are allergic to penicillin, cephalosporins, or probenecid and who cannot tolerate tetracyclines. It also has been recommended for gonorrhea treatment in geographic locations where high antibiotic resistance has been reported. It is not effective for treating syphilis and should not be used for mixed infections (gonorrhea and syphilis), since it can mask the symptoms of syphilis.

## SUMMARY

Antibiotics are chemical substances that kill or suppress the growth of microorganisms. Once the nurse has acquired an understanding of the principles of antibiotic therapy, the particular drugs may be classified by groups, actions, and effects for familiarization. They are generally classified as follows. Penicillins are derived from molds and inhibit the synthesis of bacterial cell walls; they are bactericidal for a wide range of gram-positive and some gram-negative organisms. Cephalosporins, now in their third generation, are chemical modifications of the penicillin structure and are bactericidal by inhibiting cell wall synthesis. Macrolide antibiotics, the most important of which is erythromycin, are bacteriostatic by inhibiting protein synthesis and bactericidal in higher concentrations with selected organisms. Lincomycins, which inhibit protein synthesis in bacteria by binding ribosomes of susceptible organisms, are primarily bacteriostatic, except in higher concentrations with selected organisms, in which case they are bactericidal. Vancomycin is bactericidal for many organisms and bacteriostatic for enterococci by inhibiting RNA synthesis and bacterial cell walls causing lysis. Aminoglycosides are potent bactericidal antibiotics that are usually held in reserve for serious or life-threatening infections. Tetracyclines block the binding of transfer RNA complex to the ribosome and so are bacteriostatic for a wide range of gram-positive and gram-negative organisms. Chloramphenicol inhibits protein synthesis and is bacteriostatic for a wide range of organisms; however, because of its toxicity for bone marrow, its use is limited. Quinolones inhibit bacterial RNA synthesis and are bactericidal. Metronidazole, a short-acting cytotoxic agent that interacts with DNA, is effective against anaerobic bacteria and protozoa.

Although a repertoire of antibiotics can be used in the treatment of infections, we cannot become complacent in their use. With the emergence of newly recognized pathogens and drug resistance in known strains of organisms, the use of immunosuppressive agents, and the increase in invasive procedures for diagnosis and treatment, the risk of infection in certain populations has increased.

---

## Case Study: The Client with a Bacterial Infection

Gloria Lawton, a 42-year-old secretary, has come to the clinic complaining of a fever, sore throat, and cough for the past 24 hours. Her posterior pharynx is reddened with patches of purulent exudate. She complains of pain with swallowing. Her cervical lymph nodes are enlarged and tender to touch. Based on the client's symptom history and physical examination, the physician suspects a streptococcal infection. After a throat culture is taken, Ms. Lawton is started on amoxicillin 500 mg PO every 8 hours for 10 days.

1. Explain the rationale for getting a throat culture before the first dose of amoxicillin is administered.
2. Before administering the first dose of amoxicillin, what additional assessment data does the nurse need to collect from the client?

3. What should the nurse teach Ms. Lawton about taking the amoxicillin?
4. After the completion of the 10 days of drug therapy Ms. Lawton's upper respiratory symptoms have resolved. However, she is now complaining of intense perineal itching and a vaginal discharge. How should the nurse respond to Ms. Lawton's questions about these symptoms?

## BIBLIOGRAPHY

A case of ciprofloxin-related vasculitis. (1989). NDA 13(4):30.

Alexander JW et al. (1989). Which antibiotics before surgery? Patient Care 23(6):126.

American Hospital Formulary Service. AHFS drug information '91. Bethesda, Md: American Society of Hospital Pharmacists, Inc.

An antibiotic gonococci can't resist. (1989). Emerg Med 21(11):81.

A single antibiotic for the biliary tract. (1988). Emerg Med 20(6):56.

Braunwald E et al, editors. (1987). Harrison's principles of internal medicine, ed 11. New York: McGraw-Hill Book Co.

Brown SM et al. (1989). Drug protocols (cephalosporins), Neonat Netw 7(5):63.

Brubakker KM. (1989). Preoperative antibiotic administration: a case for interdisciplinary monitoring, J Nurs Qual Assur 3(2):69.

Bryan CS. (1989). Serious infections in the elderly: choosing from among old and new antimicrobial agents, Consultant 29(11):56.

Cefotetan-induced anaphylaxis. (1988). NDA 12(12):92.

Cephalosporins for pneumonia. (1988). Emerg Med 20(5):94.

Craig WA. (1988). Do antibiotic combinations prevent the emergence of resistant organisms? Infect Control Hosp Epidemiol 9(9):417.

Cunha BA. (1990). Oral cephalosporins for common infections, Emerg Med 22(5):89.

Czachor JS et al. (1989). Using the oral cephalosporins, Patient Care 23(11):142.

Dangers of nonprescribed antibiotics. (1988). Emerg Med 20(10):51.

Davidson DE. (1986). Handbook of nonprescription drugs. Washington, DC: American Pharmaceutical Association and The National Professional Society of Pharmacists.

Erythromycin for impetigo. (1989). NDA 13(1):8.

Failure of once daily penicillin V. (1989). NDA 13(7):50.

Gantz NM et al. (1989). Quinolones: their current role, Patient Care 23(11):241.

Gastrointestinal side effects from oral erythromycin. (1987). NDA 11(12):89.

Gilman AG et al. (1990). Goodman and Gilman's the pharmacological basis of therapeutics, ed 8. New York: Macmillan Publishing Co.

Green GR et al. (1988). Circumventing penicillin allergy, Patient Care 22(8):43.

Hagerty JW. (1989). The amino-glycosides, Focus Crit Care 16(2):104.

Herfindal ET et al. (1988). Clinical pharmacy and therapeutics, ed 4. Baltimore: Williams & Wilkins.

Howrie DL et al. (1987). Antibiotic restriction programs and cephalosporin use in pediatrics: a survey on infectious disease specialists, Hosp Formul 22(9):797.

Hoffman SA et al. (1987) Antibiotic resistance in the hospital setting: extent of the problem and possible solutions, Hosp Formul 22(10):852.

Hussar DA. (1988). New drugs update 88, Nursing 18(5):33.

Jewell M et al. (1988). Infection following coronary artery surgery: comparison of two antibiotic prophylaxis regimens, Chest 93(4):712.

Karb VB. (1988). Two new fluoroquinolones: ciprofloxacin and norfloxacin, J Neurosci Nurs 20(5):327.

Kastrup EK, editor. (1991). Facts and comparisons. St Louis: JB Lippincott Co.

Katzung BG. (1987). Basic and clinical pharmacology, ed 3. Norwalk, Conn: Appleton & Lange.

Kuhar MB et al. (1988). Evaluation of selected new drugs, AAOHN J 36(10):425.

Lopez AM et al. (1989). A reliable and cost-effective neonatal aminoglycoside administration system, Neonat Netw 7(4):7.

Martin ME. (1989). Oral antibiotics for treatment of patients with chronic osteomyelitis, Orthop Nurs 8(3):35.

McCue JD. (1988). Outpatient IV antibiotic therapy: practical and ethical considerations, Hosp Pract 23(3):208.

Minocycline-related tooth discoloration. (1990). NDA 14(2):11.

Munster AM et al. (1989). Control of endtoxemia in burn patients by use of polymyxin B, J Burn Care Rehabil 10(4):327.

Mupirocin vs erythromycin for impetigo. (1990). NDA 14(1):5.

Musher DM. (1988). The gram-positive cocci. III. Resistance to antibiotics, Hosp Pract 23(5):105.

Neiderman MS. (1989). Pneumonia: the ongoing challenge, Emerg Med 21(7):77.

Peacock JE et al. (1988). Nosocomial respiratory tract colonization and infection with aminoglycoside-resistant acinetobacter calcoaceticus var anitratus: epidemiologic characteristics and clinical significance, Infect Control Hosp Epidemiol 9(7):302.

Penicillin-resistant enterococci. (1989). Emerg Med 21(16):59.

Porterfield LM. (1989). Tetracyclines, Adv Clin Care 4(3):46.

Questions and answers about penicillin. (1988). Patient Care 22(8):132.

Rolston K et al. (1987). Managing infections in the neutropenic patient: antimicrobial therapy reviewed, Hosp Formul 22(8):710.

Salamone FR. (1988). Clinical pharmacology of antibiotics: sulbactam/ampicillin, Infect Control Hosp Epidemiol 9(7):323.

Septic shock: a threat to the threatened. (1987). Emerg Med 19(18):24.

Smith KS et al. (1988). Multidisciplinary program for promoting single prophylactic doses of cefazolin in obstetrical and gynecological procedures, Am J Hosp Pharm 45(6):1338.

Steiner JF et al. (1989). Review and update of antibiotic therapy in ambulatory pediatrics, J Am Acad Physician Assist 2(5):399.

Todd B. (1990). Treating UTIs, Geriatr Nurs 11(2):95.

United States Pharmacopeial Convention. (1991). Drug information for the health care provider, ed 11. Rockville, Md: The Convention.

Vancomycin: current perspectives and guidelines for use in the NICU, Neonat Netw 7(5):31.

Vancomycin in pregnancy. (1990). NDA 14(3):23.

Washington TG et al. (1988). The use of intraperitoneal antibiotics to treat dialysis-associated peritonitis, Infect Control Hosp Epidemiol 9(1):37.

Wright RA. (1989). Outpatient intravenous antibiotics: a cost-effective approach to managing infectious disease, Consultant 29(5):143.

Wyngaarden JB and Smith LH. (1988). Cecil's textbook of medicine, ed 18. Philadelphia: WB Saunders Co.

Zinacef: new prescribing information. (1989). NDA 5(1):22.

*Chapter*

# 60 Antifungal and Antiviral Drugs

## CHAPTER OBJECTIVES

*After studying this chapter, you should be able to meet the following objectives and define the key terms.*

1. List commonly used antifungal agents.

2. Describe the side effects/adverse reactions of antifungal agents.

3. Discuss nursing management of the client receiving antifungal agents.

4. Give two reasons why effective antiviral drug therapy is more limited than antibacterial and antifungal therapy.

5. List commonly used systemic antiviral agents.

6. Discuss nursing management of antiviral therapy.

## KEY TERMS

**candidiasis,** page 914

**chemoprophylactic,** page 921

**fungi,** page 914

**mycoses,** page 914

## ANTIFUNGAL DRUGS

Infection of humans by **fungi** (plantlike, parasitic microorganisms) can be caused by any of about 50 species. These infections, termed **mycoses,** can range from mild and superficial to severe and life threatening. Infecting organisms can be ingested orally or become implanted under the skin after injury; air-borne fungal spores can be inhaled. One species of fungi, *Candida albicans,* is usually part of the normal flora of the skin, mouth, intestines, and vagina. Overgrowth and systemic infection from *C. albicans* can occur with antibiotic, antineoplastic, and corticosteroid drug therapy. Oral **candidiasis** (thrush) is common in newborn infants, whereas vaginal candidiasis is common in pregnant women with diabetes mellitus or in women who take oral contraceptives.

Antifungal chemotherapy has not developed to the same degree as antibacterial chemotherapy. Most fungi are completely resistant to the action of chemicals at concentrations that can be tolerated by the human host, and only a few antifungal compounds are available for use internally. As a result most antifungal drugs are used topically. Table 60-1 lists the antifungal agents most commonly used in clinical medicine. All topical preparations will be discussed in Chapter 68. The following discussions include only those agents that are taken by oral or parenteral routes.

### amphotericin B (Fungizone)

Amphotericin B can be fungistatic or fungicidal, depending on the concentrations achieved clinically. It does not affect bacteria or viruses. It is believed to bind to sterols in the fungus cell membrane, thereby increasing permeability and removing potassium and other elements from the cell.

Amphotericin B is effective for treating aspergillosis; blastomycosis; candidiasis (moniliasis); coccidioidomyco-

914

sis; cryptococcosis; histoplasmosis; leishmaniasis; and American mucocutaneous, disseminated sporotrichosis.

Administered parenterally, amphotericin B is distributed to lungs, liver, kidneys, adrenal glands, muscle, spleen and to other body tissues. Half-life initially is 24 to 48 hours while terminal or elimination half-life is approximately 15 days. Peak plasma level is between 2 and 4 µg/ml after an initial infusion of 1 to 5 mg daily. The site of metabolism is unknown, but excretion is via the kidneys. About 40% of the drug is excreted over 7 days, but it has still been detected in the urine for at least 7 weeks after the drug was discontinued. For side effects/adverse reactions, see Table 60-2.

***Significant drug interactions.*** When amphotericin B is given concurrently with the following drugs, the following interactions may occur.

| Drug | Possible Effect and Management |
|---|---|
| adrenocorticoids, glucocorticoids, mineralocorticoids, corticotropin (ACTH) | May result in severe hypokalemia; if given concurrently, frequent serum potassium determinations should be performed. |
|  | May decrease adrenal cortex response to corticotropin (ACTH). |

| Drug | Possible Effect and Management |
|---|---|
| bone marrow depressants, radiation therapy | May produce increased bone marrow depressant effects; monitor closely, as dosage adjustments may be necessary. |
|  | If given with flucytosine, the antifungal effects of both drugs may be increased. Also, amphotericin B may increase the uptake of flucytosine into cells and impair |

**TABLE 60-1**   Systemic antifungal agents

| Drug | Trade names |
|---|---|
| amphotericin B | Fungizone |
| fluconazole | Diflucan |
| flucytosine | Ancobon, Ancotil ✦ |
| griseofulvin | Grisactin |
| griseofulvin (microsize) | Grifulvin V, Grisovin-FP ✦ |
| griseofulvin (ultramicrosize) | Fulvicin P/G, Grisactin Ultra |
| ketoconazole | Nizoral |
| miconazole | Monistat IV |
| nystatin | Mycostatin |

**TABLE 60-2**   Antifungal drugs: side effects/adverse reactions

| Drug | Side effects* | Adverse reactions† |
|---|---|---|
| amphotericin B | *With IV infusion.* Most frequent: weight loss, headaches, nausea, vomiting, diarrhea, gas, anorexia<br>*With intrathecal injection.* Pain in back, leg, or stomach; dizziness; headache; nausea; or vomiting | With IV infusion: Most frequent: chills, fever, muscle pain, increased weakness, irregular heart rate (hypokalemia)<br>Less frequent/rare: visual disturbances, increased or decreased urination, tinnitus, convulsions, hand or feet numbness, pain, respiratory difficulties, skin rash, (hypersensitivity), sore throat, fever (leukopenia), bleeding episodes (thrombocytopenia)<br>With intrathecal injection: Less frequent: hands or feet numbness, tingling, weakness or pain; urinary difficulties<br>Rare: visual disturbances |
| fluconazole (Diflucan) | More frequent: nausea, vomiting, stomach pain, diarrhea | Rare: hepatotoxicity, exfoliative skin reaction |
| flucytosine | Most frequent: diarrhea, nausea, or vomiting<br>Less frequent: headache, sluggishness, dizziness | Most frequent: rash, sore throat, elevated temperature, increased bleeding episodes, increased weakness<br>Less frequent: confusion, hallucinations |
| griseofulvin | Most frequent: headaches<br>Less frequent: diarrhea, dizziness, nausea or vomiting, abdominal pain, insomnia, increased weakness | Less frequent: confusion, photosensitivity, rash, hives, pruritus, sore mouth or tongue<br>Rare (occurs more often with chronic use and/or high dosages): hands or feet numbness, pain, tingling, or weakness; sore throat and elevated temperature |
| ketoconazole | Most frequent: nausea or vomiting<br>Less frequent: rash, pruritus, insomnia, diarrhea, dizziness, sluggishness, photosensitivity, sexual impairment in males | Rare: dark urine, pale stools, abdominal pain, increased weakness, jaundice of eyes or skin; in males, breast enlargement (gynecomastia) |
| miconazole | Most frequent: nausea or vomiting<br>Less frequent: diarrhea, sluggishness, red flushing of skin (face), anorexia | Most frequent: chills, elevated temperature, pain at injection site, rash, pruritus<br>Less frequent: increase in bleeding episodes, increased weakness, respiratory difficulties |

*If side effects continue, increase, or disturb the client, inform the physician.
†If adverse reactions occur, contact physician because medical intervention may be necessary.

| Drug | Possible Effect and Management |
|------|-------------------------------|
| | its renal excretion, thus possibly increasing toxicity with flucytosine. |
| digitalis glycosides | Amphotericin B-induced hypokalemia may increase the potential for digitalis toxicity. Monitor closely for arrhythmias, anorexia, nausea, vomiting or other indications of possible toxicity. |
| nephrotoxic medications | Increase potential for nephrotoxicity; monitor closely, since dosage adjustments may be necessary. |

***Dosage and administration.*** Adult dose for systemic fungus infections, 25 to 100 µg (0.025 to 0.1 mg) initially every 48 to 72 hours; increase the dose gradually to 500 µg (0.5 mg), as tolerated by the individual, up to a maximum of 15 mg.

Intravenous infusion: initially, test dose 1 mg in 5% dextrose injection given over 2 to 4 hours. Dose may then be increased by 5- to 10-mg increments or more, depending on individual tolerance and the severity of the infection. Maximum dose is 50 mg daily.

The pediatric dose for systemic fungus infections: initially administer by intravenous infusion, 250 µg (0.25 mg)/kg daily in 5% dextrose injection over a 6-hour period. Gradually increase the dose (usually by 250 µg/kg increments every other day), depending on individual tolerance, up to a maximum of 1 mg/kg or 30 mg/m$^2$.

***Pregnancy safety.*** Has been established at FDA category B.

## ▷ Nursing Management: Amphotericin B Therapy

***Assessment.*** The renal function status of the client should be ascertained and amphotericin B used with caution if renal impairment exists. Clients receiving amphotericin B are at risk for the following nursing diagnoses: altered comfort related to pain at infusion site, headache, abdominal cramping, anorexia, nausea and vomiting; hyperthermia; activity intolerance related to anemia or hypokalemia; risk for physiologic injury related to hypersensitivity or increased tendency to bleed related to thrombocytopenia; risk for infection related to leukopenia; and sensory-perceptual disturbances related to polyneuropathy (numbness, tingling, or burning in hands and feet), hearing loss or change in vision.

***Intervention.*** Amphotericin B should not be used if there is any evidence of precipitate or foreign matter in the vial. The package inserts should be read before administration of the drug for major points of safe delivery. It should not be mixed with any other drug unless absolutely necessary.

Reconstitute only with the diluents recommended; others will cause the drug to precipitate. If in-line intravenous filters are used, they should have at least a 1-µm mean pore diameter, or they may filter out clinically significant amounts of the drug. Gloves should be worn while preparing the drug. Every half hour during administration, shake the hanging solution to keep it in suspension.

Administering the drug on alternate days and over a 6-hour period may reduce the incidence of side effects. If therapy is interrupted for more than 7 days, the dosage should be restarted at the lowest level and increased to the appropriate therapeutic level. The duration of the course of amphotericin B should be sufficient to prevent a relapse.

Febrile reactions to drug administration may be minimized if the physician orders a small dose of intravenous adrenocorticoid to be given just before the infusion of amphotericin B. Nephrotoxicity may also be minimized by sodium bicarbonate diuresis or salt loading just before administration of amphotericin B.

Heparin may be added to the intravenous infusion of amphotericin B to help prevent thrombophlebitis at the intravenous site. Sites should be changed with each dose to minimize thrombophlebitis.

If the client has gastrointestinal symptoms with the administration of amphotericin B, a pleasant and relaxed atmosphere for mealtimes should be provided, small, frequent feedings of high-protein, high-calorie foods of the client's choice should be encouraged, and good oral hygiene maintained. Palliative medication may be necessary if the client is experiencing indigestion, vomiting, or diarrhea.

***Education.*** The client should be advised to complete essential dental work before starting therapy with amphotericin B or to delay it until completing the course of the drug because the bone marrow depressant effects may cause gingival bleeding and delay healing. Appropriate oral hygiene should be taught, including gentle use of toothbrushes and floss and avoidance of toothpicks. Advise the client to alert the nursing staff at the first indication of pain at the intravenous site.

***Evaluation.*** Blood urea nitrogen (BUN) and serum creatinine values should be determined every other day as the dosage is increased to optimal level, and then weekly until the drug is discontinued. If BUN levels exceed 40 mg/dl or serum creatinine increases to 3 mg/ml, dosage should be decreased or discontinued until renal function improves. Serum potassium levels should be monitored twice a week. Blood counts should be monitored in anticipation of bone marrow depression.

Monitor vital signs and observe the client carefully during the test dose (1 mg in 50 to 150 ml of dextrose 5% in water and administered over 20 to 30 minutes) and the first 1 to 2 hours of each dose for shortness of breath, fever, chills, nausea, and vomiting. Febrile response usually lasts for less than 4 hours after the end of the infusion.

Pain at the site of infusion may indicate extravasation. Be cautious, since the drug causes local tissue irritation and thrombophlebitis.

Clients receiving the drug intravenously should be assessed for gastrointestinal disturbances such as anorexia, indigestion, nausea and vomiting, and diarrhea. Daily monitoring of weights will determine if these symptoms are associated with weight loss.

Monitor fluid intake and output to determine renal status. Observe for signs of hypokalemia such as muscle cramps, irregular pulse, and weakness or lethargy. Monitor for symptoms of bone marrow depression (fever, sore throat, and unusual bleeding or bruising) and report them to the physician.

### fluconazole (Diflucan)

Fluconazole is a synthetic antifungal agent that was marketed in 1990. It is indicated for the treatment of cryptococcal meningitis, oropharyngeal and esophageal candidiasis, and serious systemic candidal infections. It is available in both oral and intravenous formulations.

Mechanism of action has been postulated to be prevention of the synthesis of ergosterol in the fungal cell membranes by inhibition of the cytochrome P-450 enzymes, especially in fungal cells. This disruption results in an accumulation of phospholipids and unsaturated fatty acids in the fungus cells. Other mechanisms may also be involved, which would also result in the degeneration of the cellular structure. For side effects/adverse reactions, see Table 60-2.

While significant drug interactions are currently not reported, any substance that interacts with the cytochrome P-450 system has the potential of interfering with the metabolism of other drugs. With more prevalent use of a drug, more side effects/adverse reactions and potential drug interactions will be identified. Therefore the student is urged to monitor closely all drug therapy when clients are receiving this product.

For the treatment of systemic candidiasis or cryptococcal meningitis, the adult dose is 400 mg the first day, followed by 200 mg daily. Treatment for systemic candidiasis is usually 1 month with at least 2 weeks' therapy after symptoms have resolved. For cryptococcal meningitis, treatment is continued for 10 to 12 weeks after cerebrospinal fluid cultures are negative. Usually a 200 mg daily dose is recommended in clients with AIDS to prevent relapse of meningitis. Additional studies are underway with this drug and with other antifungal agents; therefore treatment protocols and recommendations may change in the future. The student is encouraged to review current literature and references for the most current information on antifungal therapy.

### flucytosine capsules (Ancobon, Ancotil ✳)

Flucytosine enters fungus cells, where it is converted to fluorouracil, an antimetabolite. It interferes with pyrimidine metabolism, thus preventing nucleic acid and protein synthesis. It has selective toxicity against susceptible strains of fungi because the body cells do not convert significant quantities of this drug into fluorouracil.

Flucytosine is indicated for the treatment of fungal endocarditis caused by *Candida* species, fungal meningitis (by *Cryptococcus* species), fungal pneumonia, fungal septicemia or urinary fungal infections caused by *Candida* or *Cryptococcus* species. It is absorbed orally and is widely distributed in the body. Even cerebrospinal fluid (CSF) concentrations are approximately 60% to 90% of serum concentrations. Flucytosine, with a half-life of 2.5 to 6 hours is not significantly metabolized but is excreted via the kidneys, mostly as unchanged drug. For side effects/adverse reactions, see Table 60-2. Administration of flucytosine concurrently with bone marrow depressants or radiation therapy may enhance bone marrow suppressant effects; monitor closely, since dosage adjustments may be necessary.

The adult and pediatric oral dose is 12.5 to 37.5 mg/kg body weight every 6 hours. Pregnancy safety has been established at FDA category C.

### ▷ Nursing Management: Flucytosine Therapy

***Assessment.*** Use with caution if a client has preexisting bone marrow depression, on clients who have had cytotoxic drug or radiation therapy, or hepatic or renal function impairment. Renal impairment necessitates a dosage adjustment.

Clients receiving flucytosine should be assessed for the possibility of the following nursing diagnoses: altered comfort related to headache, abdominal cramping, anorexia, nausea and vomiting; activity intolerance related to anemia; risk for physiologic injury related to hypersensitivity, increased tendency to bleed related to thrombocytopenia or the development of hepatitis; risk for infection related to leukopenia; and altered thought processes (confusion, hallucinations) related to CNS effects.

Perform blood counts and renal function studies before and frequently during the course of therapy. Periodically perform hepatic studies such as SGOT, SGPT, and serum alkaline phosphatase during therapy.

***Intervention.*** As with antibiotics, obtain specimens for culture and sensitivity before starting therapy. However, the initial dose is administered as soon as adequate specimens are obtained.

Administer multiple-dosage units, prescribed as a single dose, over 15 minutes to help prevent nausea and vomiting. Treat palliatively with antiemetics if these symptoms occur.

***Education.*** Encourage the client to comply with the full course of therapy, even if feeling better. Progress should be monitored by regular visits to the health care provider. Advise the client to report any syncope, dizziness, or drowsiness to the physician.

As with amphotericin B, advise the client to complete dental work before, or delay it until after, a course of flucytosine. Recommend the gentle use of toothbrushes and dental floss and avoiding toothpicks because of the risk of gingival bleeding.

***Evaluation.*** The serum level of flucytosine may be measured to ascertain whether it is being maintained in the therapeutic range, 25 to 120 μg/ml. Monitor the client for signs of bone marrow depression such as sore throat and fever and signs of unusual bleeding, bruising, weakness, or tiredness.

**griseofulvin capsules (Grisactin)**
**griseofulvin oral suspension, microsize (Grifulvin V)**
**griseofulvin microsize (Fulvicin-U/F, Grisovin-FP✴)**
**griseofulvin tablets, ultramicrosize (Fulvicin P/G)**

Griseofulvin inhibits fungus cell mitosis during metaphase. It is also deposited in the keratin precursor cells in skin, hair, and nails, thus inhibiting fungal invasion of the keratin. When infested keratin is shed, healthy keratin will replace it.

Griseofulvin is indicated for the treatment of strains of organisms susceptible to griseofulvin; onychomycosis, tinea barbae, tinea capitis, tinea corporis, tinea cruris, and tinea pedis.

Griseofulvin microsize oral absorption varies from 25% to 70%, whereas the ultramicrosize is nearly completely absorbed. If griseofulvin is administered with or after a fatty meal, absorption is significantly enhanced. Griseofulvin is distributed in keratin layers in the skin, hair, and nails. Very little of the drug is distributed in body tissues and fluids. It has a half-life of 24 hours and reaches peak serum levels in about 24 hours after a single dose of 250 mg ultramicrosize or 500 mg microsize dosage form. Metabolism is in the liver with excretion via the kidneys. For side effects/adverse reactions, see Table 60-2.

***Significant drug interactions.*** When griseofulvin is given concurrently with the following drugs, the following interactions may occur.

| Drug | Possible Effect and Management |
| --- | --- |
| anticoagulants, oral: coumarin or indandione | Decreased anticoagulant effect may be noted; monitor prothrombin times closely until a stable serum level is achieved. Dosage adjustments may be required during and after griseofulvin administration. |
| contraceptives, estrogen-containing oral | Chronic, long-term use of griseofulvin may decrease the effectiveness of oral contraceptives. May see intercycle menstrual bleeding, amenorrhea, or pregnancy. Advise client to use an alternate method of contraception when taking griseofulvin. |
| Other hepatic-enzyme–inducing agents | May increase potential for toxicity; monitor closely. |

***Dosage and administration.*** The adult microsize dose to treat tinea corporis, tinea cruris, or tinea capitis: 500 mg orally daily as single dose or in two divided doses. To treat tinea pedis or onychomycosis: 1 g orally in two divided doses.

The pediatric dose is 5 mg/kg body weight daily.

***Pregnancy safety.*** Has not been established, although it is recommended not to take this drug during pregnancy because of reported teratogenic effects.

▷ **Nursing Management:**
   **Griseofulvin Therapy**

***Assessment.*** If the client has preexisting porphyria, lupus erythematosus, or hepatic function impairment, administer the drug with caution.

The client receiving flucytosine should be assessed for the possibility of the following nursing diagnoses: altered comfort related to headache, abdominal cramping, anorexia, nausea and vomiting; risk for physiologic injury related to hypersensitivity, photosensitivity, or the development of hepatitis; risk for infection related to leukopenia and a reduction of normal flora; altered sleep pattern (insomnia) related to CNS effects; sensory-perceptual disturbances related to peripheral neuritis evidenced by numbness and tingling of the hands and feet; and altered thought processes (confusion) related to CNS effects.

***Intervention.*** Administer with meals to help prevent gastrointestinal distress and to enhance absorption. Therapy is even more effective if the meal is fatty. If the client is on a low-fat diet, consult the physician.

Administer the oral suspension using the calibrated measuring device provided by the manufacturer.

***Education.*** Encourage the client to comply with the full course of therapy, even if feeling better. Regular visits to the physician are necessary to check progress.

Frequent shampoos and clipping of the hair and nails will support the therapeutic effect of the drug, as will keeping affected skin areas clean and dry.

Advise the client that skin may be more sensitive to sunlight and recommend avoiding direct sunlight and using sun screens.

Advise the client to report any symptoms of fever and sore throat to the health care provider, since they may indicate blood dyscrasias.

Because the drug may cause dizziness, the client should avoid tasks that require mental alertness until the response to the drug can be ascertained.

Instruct the client about good oral hygiene and to report any soreness or irritation of the mouth, which might indicate a fungal overgrowth, oral thrush.

Instruct female clients taking estrogen-containing oral contraceptives to use an alternative or additional form of contraception while taking griseofulvin.

Advise the client not to ingest alcoholic beverages while taking griseofulvin, because it may potentiate the effects of alcohol, causing tachycardia and flushing.

***Evaluation.*** Monitor blood counts and hepatic and renal function studies periodically during therapy. Therapy is continued until a clinical or laboratory examination indicates the causative organism is eradicated.

## ketoconazole (Nizoral)

Depending on concentration, ketoconazole may be fungistatic or fungicidal. It alters the biosynthesis of fungal cell wall sterols, thus altering cell permeability and causing loss of essential intracellular substances. It also inhibits the synthesis of triglycerides and phospholipids by fungus and inhibits oxidative and peroxidative enzyme activity, which leads to an intracellular accumulation of toxic concentrations of hydrogen peroxide, which subsequently causes cellular deterioration and death. In *Candida albicans,* it interferes with the conversion of blastospores into the invasive mycelial form.

Ketoconazole is indicated for treatment of blastomycosis, disseminated candidiasis, mucocutaneous candidiasis, oropharyngeal candidiasis, candiduria, chromomycosis, coccidioidomycosis, histoplasmosis, paracoccidioidomycosis, and tinea corporis, tinea cruris, tinea pedis, and tinea versicolor by strains of organisms susceptible to this drug.

Ketoconazole requires an acid medium for dissolution and absorption. It is widely distributed in humans to inflamed joint fluids, saliva, bile, urine, sebum, feces, tendons, skin or soft tissues. Highly protein bound to albumin, it has a biphasic half-life of between 1.4 to 3.3 hours during the first 10 hours (alpha phase), then 8 hours afterward (beta phase). Peak serum levels are reached between 1 to 4 hours; metabolism is by the liver with primary excretion via bile. For side effects/adverse reactions, see Table 60-2.

***Significant drug interactions.*** When ketoconazole is given concurrently with the following drugs, the following interactions may occur.

| Drug | Possible Effect and Management |
|---|---|
| alcohol or other hepatotoxic drugs | Increases risk for hepatotoxicity. If possible, avoid other hepatotoxic medications. Monitor closely. |
| cyclosporine | May increase serum levels of cyclosporine and increase potential for nephrotoxicity. If given together, monitor closely. Serum levels of cyclosporine should be obtained and monitored. |
| histamine H₂-receptor blocking agents (cimetidine, famotidine, ranitidine) | Usually increases GI pH, which can reduce absorption of ketoconazole. Advise clients to take these drugs approximately 2 hours after ketoconazole. |
| isoniazid or rifampin | When both isoniazid and rifampin are given with ketoconazole, a decrease in serum levels of ketoconazole or rifampin is noted. In some cases, serum levels are not detectable. If necessary to use this combination, monitor very closely. |

***Dosage and administration.*** For systemic antifungal effects, 200 to 400 mg orally daily. Tinea versicolor, 200 mg orally once daily for 5 to 10 days. Maximum daily dose is 1 g.

For systemic antifungal effects in infants and children up to 2 years old, not established. For children 2 years and older, 5-10 mg/kg orally, once daily for 5 days.

***Pregnancy safety.*** Has been established at FDA category C.

## ▷ Nursing Management: Ketoconazole Therapy

***Assessment.*** Ascertain whether the client has a history of alcoholism or liver function impairment. If so, ketoconazole should be used with caution, since the drug is hepatotoxic.

The client receiving ketoconazole therapy should be assessed for the occurrence of the following nursing diagnoses: altered comfort related to headache, nausea and vomiting; risk for physiologic injury related to hypersensitivity, photophobia, or the development of hepatitis; altered sleep pattern (insomnia) related to CNS effects; altered bowel elimination pattern (diarrhea); and disturbance of self-concept in male clients related to gynecomastia or impotence.

***Intervention.*** Take culture specimens before beginning drug therapy. Once adequate specimens are obtained, therapy should not be delayed.

For clients with achlorhydria, absorption may decrease. To minimize this effect, dissolve each tablet in 4 ml of 0.2N hydrochloric acid. The solution may be further diluted with a small amount of water and administered through a plastic or glass straw to prevent contact with the teeth. Have the client rinse his or her mouth with water and swallow the solution. If antacids, anticholinergics, or H₂ blockers are needed, give at least 2 hours after administering ketoconazole, since these drugs may decrease absorption.

***Education.*** Recommend that the client take ketoconazole with meals or food to decrease the risk of gastrointestinal distress. Therapy is usually long term; at times it lasts months or years. Encourage the client to continue to take the medication for the full course of therapy even if feeling better. Taking the drug at the same time every day increases compliance.

Advise the client to visit the health care provider regularly to monitor progress. Infected areas should be evaluated periodically.

Caution the client to avoid alcoholic beverages while on this course of therapy.

Advise the client to avoid exposure to bright light or to wear sunglasses because of the drug's photophobic effects.

Because ketoconazole causes drowsiness, caution the client to avoid activities that require mental alertness until the response to the drug has been determined.

***Evaluation.*** Perform hepatic function studies before and periodically during the course of therapy. Observe the client for clinical symptoms such as nausea, lethargy, yellowing of the eyes or skin, skin rash, dark urine, or clay-colored stools.

Men may experience enlargement of the breasts and decreased sexual ability because the drug decreases testosterone and adrenal steroid levels.

### miconazole injection (Monistat IV)

Depending on its concentration, miconazole may be fungistatic or fungicidal. It alters the biosynthesis of fungal cell wall sterols, thus altering cell permeability, which results in the loss of essential intracellular substances. It also inhibits the synthesis of triglycerides and phospholipids by fungus; inhibits oxidative and peroxidative enzyme activity, which leads to an intracellular accumulation of toxic concentrations of hydrogen peroxide and subsequent cellular deterioration and death. In *Candida albicans,* it interferes with the conversion of blastospores into invasive mycelial form.

Miconazole is indicated for the treatment of susceptible strains of fungus in disseminated candidasis, mucocutaneous (chronic) candidiasis, coccidioidomycosis, cryptococcosis, fungal meningitis, paracoccidioidomycosis, petriellidiosis, and fungal urinary bladder infections. This drug is reserved as a second-line drug (after systemic amphotericin B and ketoconazole) for the treatment of severe systemic fungal infections. It is more toxic and often not as effective as the previously mentioned drugs.

For side effects/adverse reactions, see Table 60-2. When miconazole is given concurrently with isoniazid (INH) or rifampin, decreased serum levels of ketoconazole (chemically similar to miconazole), or rifampin may result. If both INH and rifampin are given concurrently with ketoconazole, serum levels of ketoconazole and rifampin are reportedly undetectable. Avoid concurrent administration of either ketoconazole or miconazole with these drugs.

Miconazole parenteral is administered by intravenous infusion, 200 mg to 1.2 g daily in adults. See current package insert or USP-DI for specific dosage recommendations. In children 1 year and older, the dose by infusion is usually 20 to 40 mg/kg body weight daily, not to exceed 15 mg/kg.

Pregnancy safety has not been established.

▷ **Nursing Management:**
   **Miconazole Therapy**

*Assessment.* As with other antifungal agents, obtain culture specimens before beginning drug therapy. However, start therapy as soon as adequate specimens are obtained rather than waiting for the culture results.

The client receiving ketoconazole therapy is at risk for the following nursing diagnoses: altered comfort related to pain at infusion site, flushing of the face, rash, anorexia, nausea and vomiting; hyperthermia; risk for physiologic injury related to hypersensitivity, or increased tendency to bleeding related to thrombocytopenia; activity intolerance related to anemia; and altered bowel elimination pattern (diarrhea).

The first dose of miconazole should be a test dose of 200 mg administered by intravenous infusion to determine whether the client is hypersensitive to the drug.

*Intervention.* Administer intravenous infusions of miconazole over 30 to 60 minutes to prevent dysrhythmias or increases in heart rate that may result from rapid administration. Minimize nausea and vomiting secondary to the administration of miconazole by reducing the dosage, slowing the infusion rate, or administering an antiemetic before beginning the infusion. Infusions of the drug should not be administered at mealtimes to help prevent gastrointestinal effects.

Intravenous administration of miconazole must be supplemented by intrathecal administration of the drug in the case of fungal meningitis and by bladder irrigation with miconazole solution in mycoses of the bladder.

Dilute each dose of miconazole in at least 200 ml of 0.9% sodium chloride solution or 5% dextrose injection for intravenous infusion. This solution will be stable at room temperature for 24 hours. If the solution darkens, it should be discarded because it has deteriorated. Do not mix with other medications.

*Education.* Instruct the client to alert the nurse if he or she has trouble breathing, skin rash, or fever and chills, which are signs of hypersensitivity.

*Evaluation.* Monitor the client's infection throughout the course of therapy. The intravenous site should be monitored periodically for pain and inflammation, which would indicate phlebitis. Monitor hematocrit and hemoglobin values for adverse effects of anemia. Serum electrolytes and lipids should be monitored periodically.

### nystatin lozenges (Mycostatin)
### nystatin oral suspension (Mycostatin, Nadostine✱)
### nystatin tablets (Mycostatin, Nadostine✱, Nilstat)

Nystatin, an antibiotic obtained from *Streptomyces noursei,* is primarily used to treat oropharyngeal infections caused by the monilial organism *Candida albicans.* Although not an approved indication, oropharyngeal candidiasis is often treated with nystatin vaginal tablets in lozenge form, mainly because they dissolve slowly. Nystatin adheres to sterols in the fungal cell membrane, leading to a loss of essential intercellular contents.

Nystatin is an antifungal agent indicated for the treatment of oropharyngeal candidiasis. It is not absorbed from the gastrointestinal tract as it produces a local antifungal effect. It is excreted in the feces. Side effects are generally rare; in high doses, it may cause diarrhea, nausea, vomiting, or abdominal distress. No significant drug interactions have been reported with nystatin.

In children over 5 years old and in adults, the dose for nystatin lozenges is 200,000 to 400,000 units dissolved completely in the mouth, four or five times daily, for up to 2 weeks. Nystatin oral suspension for adults is dosed at 400,000 to 600,000 units four times daily, while the tablet dosage form is dosed at 500,000 to 1,000,000 units three times a day. For specific recommendations for children, see a current package insert or USP-DI.

Pregnancy safety has not been established.

▷ **Nursing Management:**
**Nystatin Therapy**

*Assessment.* The client receiving nystatin should be assessed for the possibility of the following nursing diagnoses: altered comfort related to anorexia, nausea and vomiting; and altered bowel elimination pattern (diarrhea).

*Intervention.* Shake oral suspensions thoroughly before measuring dosages. With the prepared oral suspension, use the calibrated dosage-measuring device provided by the manufacturer. When mixing dry powdered nystatin, add the dose to 120 to 240 ml of water; administer immediately since it contains no preservatives. Vaginal tablets may be used as lozenges to treat oral candidiasis because they are slow to dissolve and are in contact longer with the buccal mucous membrane.

*Education.* Instruct the client to perform oral hygiene before taking each dose of nystatin. Half the dosage is placed in each side of the mouth. The medication is swished and then held in the mouth for as long as possible. Vaginal tablets are to be dissolved slowly in the mouth as with throat lozenges.

Caution the client to complete the full course of therapy even if feeling better. It should be continued for at least 48 hours after normal culture results are obtained and symptoms have disappeared.

Alert the client to report to the health care provider symptoms of nausea, vomiting, diarrhea, or increased irritation at the site of infection.

*Evaluation.* Nystatin is virtually nontoxic and well tolerated by all age groups. Monitor the client's infection throughout the course of therapy.

## ANTIVIRAL DRUGS

Chemotherapy for viral diseases has been more limited than chemotherapy for bacterial diseases because development and clinical application of antiviral drugs are difficult. In many viral infections, the replication of the virus in the body reaches its peak before any clinical symptoms appear. By the time signs and symptoms of illness appear, the multiplication of the virus is ending, and the subsequent course of the illness has been determined. To be clinically effective, therefore, antiviral drugs must be administered in a **chemoprophylactic** manner—that is, before disease appears. A second factor limiting the development of antiviral drugs is that viruses are true parasites; they replicate within the mammalian cell and utilize the host cells' enzyme systems. Thus drugs that would inhibit virus replication would also disturb the host cells and therefore would be too toxic for use. Table 60-3 lists common systemic antiviral agents.

### acyclovir capsules/tablets (Zovirax)

Acyclovir is selectively taken up by herpes simplex virus (HSV)-infected cells and converted to an active triphosphate form, which is then incorporated into growing DNA chains produced by the virus, thus terminating chain development.

Acyclovir is indicated for the treatment of herpes genitalis infections; the oral form is used to treat and manage herpes genitalis infections in immunocompromised and uncompromised clients. Injectable acyclovir is used to treat severe initial herpes genitalis and herpes simplex infections in non-immunocompromised clients.

The oral dosage form is poorly (15% to 30%) absorbed, but serum levels achieved are therapeutic. It is widely disseminated to various body fluids and tissues such as brain, kidneys, lungs, muscle, spleen, uterus, vaginal mucosa and secretions, cerebrospinal fluid (CSF), and herpetic vesicular fluid. CSF levels are approximately 50% of the serum concentration.

The half-life is approximately 2.5 hours, while the mean peak serum level is about 0.6 µg/ml after an oral dose of 200 mg every 4 hours for 5 days; or 10 µg/ml after a parenteral dose of 5 mg/kg every 8 hours, administered over an hour. Acyclovir is metabolized by the liver and excreted in the urine. For side effects/adverse reactions, see Table 60-4.

*Significant drug interactions.* When acyclovir is given concurrently with the following drugs, the following interactions may occur.

| Drug | Possible Effect and Management |
|---|---|
| Interferon or methotrexate, intrathecal | When given with parenteral acyclovir, monitor closely for neurologic abnormalities, such as lethargy, obtundation, tremors, confusion, hallucinations, agitation, seizures, or coma. |
| other nephrotoxic drugs | May increase the potential for nephrotoxicity, especially if client already has renal impairment. Monitor renal function closely. |

*Dosage and administration.* Adult dose for herpes genitalis infections: initially, 200 mg orally every 4 hours during waking hours (five times daily) for 10 days. Intermittent therapy, 200 mg orally every 4 hours during waking hours (five times daily) for 5 days. As a chronic suppressant agent for recurrent infections, 200 mg orally every 8 hours for up

**TABLE 60-3**   Systemic antiviral agents

| Drug | Trade names |
|---|---|
| acyclovir | Zovirax |
| amantadine HCl | Symadine, Symmetrel |
| ribavirin | Virazole, Vilona ♣ |
| vidarabine | Vira-A |
| zidovudine | Retrovir |

**TABLE 60-4**    Antiviral drugs: side effects/adverse reactions

| Drug | Side effects* | Adverse reactions† |
|---|---|---|
| acyclovir | *Oral* Most frequent with chronic usage: diarrhea, dizziness, headache, pain in joints, nausea or vomiting<br>Less frequent with chronic use: acne, anorexia, insomnia<br>*Injectable form* Dizziness<br>Less frequent: headache, sweating | *Oral* Less frequent with chronic usage: menstrual irregularities, rash<br>*Injectable form* More frequent: rash or hives<br>Less frequent: bloody urine, confusion, hallucinations, tremors. Rare (usually with bolus injection): stomach pain, respiratory difficulties, decreased urination, thirst, anorexia, nausea or vomiting, increased weakness, convulsions |
| amantadine | Most frequent: anorexia, nausea, anxiety, red-purple skin spots, increased irritability, dizziness, insomnia, difficulty concentrating, nightmares<br>Less frequent/rare: visual disturbances; dry mouth, nose, and throat; headache; rash; vomiting; constipation; increased weakness | Most frequent: mood changes, hallucinations, confusion (especially in elderly)<br>Less frequent: difficulty in urination, hypotension<br>Rare: slurred speech, oculogyric crisis, sore throat, fever<br>With chronic dosing: edema of feet or lower legs, shortness of breath, weight gain<br>Overdosage: severe confusion, serious mood alterations, convulsions, severe insomnia or nightmares |
| ribavirin | Less frequent: dizziness, blurred vision, increased weakness, lightheadedness (hypotensive effect), visual alterations (feeling of particles in eye; photosensitivity, edema, pruritus, or red eyes) | None reported |
| vidarabine | Frequency not reported: increased lacrimation, feeling of particles in eye | Frequency not reported: photosensitivity, eye irritation (pruritus, redness, edema, pain, burning)<br>*Parenterally,* monitor for leukopenia, thrombocytopenia, megaloblastic anemia, and a drug-induced, parkinsonian type reaction |
| zidovudine | Most frequent: taste alterations, nervousness, diarrhea, dizziness, headaches, anorexia, nausea, rash<br>Less frequent: stomach distress or pain, pruritus, mouth sores, edema of lips or tongue, insomnia, vomiting, faintness, confusion, anxiety, agitation | Most frequent: chills, sore throat, elevated temperature, pale skin, increase in bleeding tendencies, increased weakness<br>Bone marrow depression may occur when drug is stopped: pale skin, chills, sore throat, elevated temperature, increase in bleeding episodes, increased weakness (agranulocytopenia and anemia) |

to 6 months. (If necessary, may be increased up to 200 mg five times daily for up to 6 months.)

The pediatric dose is not established.

The parenteral dose for serious herpes genitalis infections in an adult is 5 mg/kg body weight every 8 hours for 5 days. For herpes simplex (HSV-1 and HSV-2) mucocutaneous infections in immunocompromised individuals; 5 to 10 mg/kg by intravenous infusion every 8 hours for 7 to 10 days. Infusions should be administered over a minimum of 1 hour. Maximum daily dose is up to 30 mg/kg of body weight. For serious herpes genitalis infections in infants and children up to 12 years old, 250 mg per meter squared body surface every 8 hours for 5 days.

***Pregnancy safety.*** Has been established at FDA category C

▷ **Nursing Management:**
**Acyclovir Therapy**

***Assessment.*** If the client has preexisting dehydration or renal function impairment, use acyclovir with caution, since these clients are at greater risk for nephrotoxicity. A history of neurologic abnormalities or a previous neurologic reaction to cytotoxic agents may indicate a tendency for such responses to acyclovir.

Assess lesions before administering the drug and daily throughout therapy.

The client receiving acyclovir therapy should be assessed for the possibility of the following nursing diagnoses: altered comfort related to pain at injection site, joint pain, rash, headache, anorexia, nausea and vomiting; altered sleep pattern (insomnia); disturbance in self-concept related to the development of acne; risk for physiologic injury related to the development of acute renal failure or hypotension; and altered bowel elimination pattern (diarrhea).

***Intervention.*** The capsules may be administered with meals to minimize gastrointestinal distress. Intravenous acyclovir should be administered via infusion pump at a constant rate for at least 1 hour to prevent precipitation of drug crystals in the renal tubules. The client should also be hydrated during the infusion and for 2 hours afterward to prevent this effect. Avoid rapid or bolus injection of the drug. Rotate infusion sites to prevent phlebitis. The intravenous solution is not to be used topically, orally, or administered intramuscularly or subcutaneously.

***Education.*** The client will need accurate information about herpes. Because herpes genitalis is sexually transmitted, misinformation about it abounds. The client should avoid sexual activity if either or any participant has symptoms of herpes. Condom use may help prevent the spread of the infection, but spermicidal jellies or diaphragms probably will not. Acyclovir will not prevent the transmission of the disease or cure it.

The full course of therapy should be taken; however, caution the client not to take the drug longer than prescribed. Six months is generally the limit of long-term therapy. Report to the health care provider if symptoms do not ease.

Medication should be initiated as soon as possible after symptoms appear. The client should be instructed to begin the medication as soon as itching, tingling, or pain develop at the site to minimize the episode of herpes.

Instruct the client regarding comfort measures such as wearing loose-fitting clothing to minimize irritation of the lesions. The infected areas should be kept clean and dry.

Caution female clients to obtain a Pap smear at least annually, since women with genital herpes are at higher risk for cervical cancer than women without genital herpes.

As dizziness is an adverse effect of this agent, the client should be cautioned against performing tasks that require mental alertness, such as driving, until the response to the drug has been ascertained.

The client should be encouraged to maintain good dental hygiene and visit the dentist regularly for teeth cleaning and to monitor for the development of gingival hyperplasia.

***Evaluation.*** Renal function studies, BUN levels, and serum creatinine concentrations should be done before and during therapy to monitor for the drug's nephrotoxic effects. Fluid intake and output should be monitored, particularly if the client is receiving bolus injections of acyclovir.

### amantadine hydrochloride (Symadine, Symmetrel)

Although its mechanism of action is not fully understood, amantadine is believed to prevent influenza A virus from penetrating respiratory epithelial cells, to uncoat the virus, and thus release viral nucleic acid into host cells. It is indicated for the prevention and treatment of influenza A and for the treatment of drug-induced, extrapyramidal reactions and Parkinson's disease.

Amantadine is rapidly absorbed orally and distributed to saliva and nasal secretions. It has a half-life of 11 to 15 hours and reaches peak serum level within 2 to 4 hours. Its onset of action as an antidyskinetic is usually within 2 days. It is excreted mostly unchanged by the kidneys. For side effects/adverse reactions, see Table 60-4.

***Significant drug interactions.*** When amantadine is given concurrently with the following drugs, the following interactions may occur.

| Drug | Possible Effect and Management |
|---|---|
| alcohol | Not recommended; increased risk for CNS side effects such as dizziness, fainting episodes, confusion, or circulatory problems reported. |
| anticholinergics | May result in an increase in anticholinergic side effects, such as hallucinations, dry mouth, blurred vision, confusion, and nightmares. Monitor closely since dosage adjustment of amantadine may be required. |
| CNS-stimulating agents | May cause increased CNS stimulation, resulting in insomnia, increased irritability and nervousness. Cardiac arrhythmias and convulsions may also occur. Avoid if possible. If given concurrently, be sure to monitor closely. |

### Dosage and administration

***Adults.*** As antiviral agent: 200 mg orally daily or 100 mg every 12 hours. Antidyskinetic: 100 mg orally once or twice a day. Clients with renal impairment should check the current PDR or USP-DI for dosing instructions. Maximum daily dosage: antiviral, 200 mg/day; antidyskinetic, 400 mg/day.

***Children.*** Neonates and infants up to a year old, not established; children 1 to 9 years old, 1.5 to 3 mg/kg orally every 8 hours maximum dose is 200 mg daily; children 9 to 12 years old, 100 mg orally every 12 hours; children 12 years old and older, see adult dosage.

***Pregnancy safety.*** Has been established at FDA category C

### ▷ Nursing Management: Amantadine Therapy

***Assessment.*** When the client's health assessment is done before drug therapy, the following health problems should indicate cautious use of amantadine: congestive heart failure and/or peripheral edema, since the drug may worsen the condition; epilepsy, since the drug may increase seizure activity; and renal impairment, since accumulation of the drug increases CNS adverse effects.

Elderly clients are more prone to have confusion and difficulty in urination as frequent effects of amantadine because of its antimuscarinic activity.

The client receiving amantadine should be assessed for the possibility of the following nursing diagnoses: altered comfort related to rash, headache, dry mouth, anorexia, nausea and vomiting; altered sleep pattern (insomnia); risk for injury related to the development of orthostatic hypotension, seizures, and congestive heart failure; risk for infection related to leukopenia; altered thought processes (confusion, hallucinations, severe mental or mood changes) related to CNS toxicity; impaired verbal communication related to CNS effects; and altered bowel elimination pattern (constipation).

***Intervention.*** Syncope, insomnia, and nausea may be

minimized by changing from a once-daily dosage to a twice-daily schedule. Administering the last daily dose several hours before bedtime helps to minimize insomnia.

When administering the syrup form of the drug, use the calibrated measuring device provided by the manufacturer.

**Education.** Caution the client to avoid alcoholic beverages while taking amantadine, since alcohol increases the risk of CNS effects such as dizziness, syncope, and confusion.

If the client is taking amantadine as an antiviral medication, its course should be started before, or as soon as possible after, exposure. Client should complete the full course of therapy and should notify the health care provider if symptoms do not decrease within a few days.

Clients taking the drug as an antidyskinetic medication should complete the course of therapy as prescribed and not take more than the prescribed dosage. The client should be advised that it may require 2 or more weeks to obtain full benefit from the drug. Counsel the client to gradually resume physical activities. The drug dosage should be discontinued gradually.

Mental confusion, hallucinations, and difficulty sleeping are indications of CNS toxicity and should be reported to the physician promptly.

Advise clients to change positions from lying to sitting or standing and from sitting to standing with caution because of the orthostatic effects of amantadine.

Clients may decrease the discomfort of mouth dryness with ice, sugarless gum, or candy. Encourage oral hygiene to prevent caries and oral candidiasis.

Alert the client to the possible occurrence of a purplish, red rash, which disappears 2 to 12 weeks after the medication is discontinued.

Because amantadine may cause drowsiness or dizziness, caution the client to avoid tasks such as driving until the response to the drug has been determined.

**Evaluation.** Closely monitor clients receiving dosages over 200 mg/day for side effects or adverse reactions. Blood pressure and TPR monitoring is indicated, particularly for the first few days after a dosage increase.

If the client is taking amantadine for parkinsonism, dyskinetic symptoms such as tremors, rigidity, and disturbances of gait should be monitored throughout the course of therapy.

### ribavirin for inhalation aerosol (Virazole, Vilona✤)

Mechanism of action is unknown. The drug is believed to reduce intracellular guanosine triphosphate (GTP) storage and impair viral RNA and protein synthesis, thus inhibiting viral duplication, spread to other cells, or both. It is indicated for serious viral pneumonia caused by respiratory syncytial virus (RSV).

Following oral inhalation, it is well absorbed and rapidly distributed to plasma, respiratory tract secretions and erythrocytes. Half-life is 9.5 hours after oral inhalation and approximately 40 days in erythrocytes. Time to peak serum level is within 1 to 1.5 hours. Ribavirin is metabolized in the liver and excreted by the kidneys. For side effects/adverse reactions, see Table 60-4. No significant drug interactions have been reported.

The adult dose for ribavirin for inhalation aerosol has not been established. For viral pneumonia in children, administer by oral inhalation via a Viratek small-particle aerosol generator, using a 20-mg/ml ribavirin concentration in the reservoir. Administer over 12 to 18 hr/day for 3 to 7 days.

Pregnancy safety has been established at FDA category X.

▷ **Nursing Management: Ribavirin Therapy**

**Assessment.** The client receiving ribavirin is at risk for altered comfort related to direct contact chemical irritation evidenced by conjunctivitis; and altered cardiac output related to hypotension evidenced by faintness, lightheadedness, or weakness.

**Intervention.** Therapy with ribavirin may begin before the diagnosis is determined by diagnostic tests; however, treatment should not continue if the presence of the respiratory syncytial virus (RSV) is not confirmed.

Ribavirin aerosol is to be administered only with the Viratek SPAG Model SPAG-2. See the SPAG-2 manual for exceptions.

To prepare the solution for inhalation, add a measured quantity of sterile water for injection or for inhalation, which is adequate to dissolve the drug, to each 6-g vial. Do not use bacteriostatic water. Transfer the solution to a clean, sterilized SPAG-2 reservoir. Dilute the solution with sterile water to a total volume of 300 ml. Ensure that the final solution is free of particulate matter. Always discard the remaining solution as its level gets low and add freshly reconstituted solution to the reservoir. The solution retains its potency at room temperature for 24 hours. Do not administer concurrently with any other medication by aerosolization.

**Evaluation.** If administered to clients receiving ventilation assistance, observe for increased positive-end expiratory pressure and increased positive inspiratory pressure, which occur if ribavirin precipitates within the ventilator apparatus. The equipment should be checked at least every half hour to prevent fluid accumulation in the tubing.

### vidarabine (Adenine Arabinoside, Ara-A)

Mechanism of action is unknown although in cells it is converted to a triphosphate that is a selective competitive inhibitor of DNA polymerase. It may also penetrate the viral DNA molecule at different positions, thus terminating the chain. It is indicated for the treatment of herpes simplex virus encephalitis.

Available parenterally, it is administered by slow intravenous infusion only. It is well distributed to body tissues where it is converted to Ara-Hx, which has about 10% of the antiviral activity of vidarabine. Half-life for Ara-A is 1 hour, for Ara-Hx is 3.3 hours. Excretion is via the kidneys. For side effects/adverse reactions, see Table 60-4. While no significant drug interactions have been reported, monitor clients receiving allopurinol since it may interfere with vidarabine metabolism.

The adult dose by slow intravenous infusion is 15 mg/kg day for 10 days. Infuse total daily dose slowly over 12 to 24 hours. Follow manufacturer's instructions closely when administering this drug. Pregnancy safety has been established at FDA category C.

## ▷ Nursing Management:
### Vidarabine Therapy

*Assessment.* The client receiving vidarabine is at risk for altered comfort related to rash, pain at injection site, anorexia, nausea and vomiting; altered thought processes (confusion); activity intolerance related to anemia; and altered bowel elimination (diarrhea).

*Intervention.* Parenteral vidarabine is for intravenous use only. It is poorly absorbed from intramuscular or subcutaneous sites. For intravenous administration, dilute to a concentration of less than 0.5 mg/ml with any intravenous solution except for blood products or protein solutions. For ease of dissolution, warm the intravenous solution to 35° to 40° C (95° to 100° F). Shake until the solution is completely clear. Administer using an in-line filter (0.45-μm pore size or smaller). Use an infusion pump for accurate rate flow.

*Evaluation.* When vidarabine is administered for herpes simplex virus (HSV) encephalitis, monitor the level of consciousness and neurologic status throughout therapy.

Monitor blood studies, including hemoglobin, hematocrit, and blood cell counts, periodically during therapy.

### zidovudine (Retrovir)

The mechanism of action for zidovudine is possibly virostatic. It is converted in the virus to triphosphate, which competes with natural thymidine triphosphate for incorporation in growing chains of viral DNA. Once in the DNA chain, it inhibits viral replication. It has a greater affinity for retroviral reverse transcriptase than for the human alpha-DNA polymerase; thus it selectively inhibits viral replication.

Zidovudine is indicated for the treatment of acquired immunodeficiency syndrome (AIDS) and acquired immunodeficiency syndrome-related complex (ARC). Administered orally, it is rapidly absorbed; but it has a first-pass metabolism in the liver that reduces the average bioavailability to approximately 65%. It is distributed to plasma and cerebrospinal fluid, reaches a peak serum level in 0.5 to 1.5 hours, and has a half-life of approximately 1 hour. Its major active metabolite GAZT also has a half-life of about 1 hour. Zidovudine is metabolized in the liver and excreted by the kidneys. For side effects/adverse reactions, see Table 60-4.

*Significant drug interactions.* When zidovudine is given concurrently with the following drugs, the following interactions may occur.

| Drug | Possible Effects and Management |
|---|---|
| acetaminophen, aspirin, benzodiazepines, cimetidine, indomethacin, morphine, or sulfonamides | May inhibit hepatic metabolism and decrease excretion of zidovudine. Avoid concurrent usage to avoid toxicity. |
| bone marrow depressants, radiation therapy | May exacerbate bone marrow depression and toxicity. Dosage reductions may be necessary. Monitor closely. |

*Dosage and administration.* Adult oral dose is 200 mg every 4 hours around the clock. After a month, the dose may be reduced to 100 mg every 4 hours. For asymptomatic HIV infections, the dose is 100 mg every 4 hours while awake or 500 mg daily. Maximum daily dose is up to 60 mg/kg. Pediatric dose has not been established. Parenteral dose is 1 to 2 mg/kg intravenously infused over one hour, every 4 hours around the clock. See current package insert or reference sources for up-to-date dosing instructions.

*Pregnancy safety.* Has been established at FDA category C

## ▷ Nursing Management:
### Zidovudine Therapy

*Assessment.* Assess the client's health before initiating zidovudine therapy. The following health problems indicate that the drug is to be used with caution: bone marrow depression, which may result in blood dyscrasias; hepatic and renal function impairment, which may affect elimination of the drug and cause toxicity; and folic acid or vitamin B$_{12}$ deficiency, which may result in increased sensitivity to hematotoxicity.

The client receiving zidovudine is at risk for altered comfort related to rash, change in taste, anorexia, nausea and vomiting; altered thought processes (confusion); activity intolerance related to anemia; injury related to increased tendency to bleed due to bone marrow depression; anxiety; and altered bowel elimination (diarrhea).

*Intervention.* The client may experience changes in taste, swelling of the lips and tongue, and mouth ulcers. These symptoms may affect the client's desire or ability to eat. The client must receive good oral hygiene to prevent infection and promote comfort. Food and fluid intake should be monitored to ensure adequate nutrition. Encourage the client to take small but frequent high-protein meals. Serve meals attractively and cater to the client's food preferences. Bland and smooth textured foods may be better tolerated.

*Education.* Advise the client to take the medication exactly as prescribed and not to take more in the hope that it will be more effective or to discontinue the medication without medical advice in despair that it is not effective. Other medications should not be taken concurrently without the approval of the physician. The client should take the medication every 4 hours around the clock. Setting an alarm clock to interrupt sleep and maintain this schedule can ensure therapeutic blood levels.

The client should be advised of the importance of regular supervision by the health care provider to check blood counts.

Alert the client that dizziness and syncope are effects of zidovudine and that hazardous activities requiring mental alertness should be avoided until the response to the drug has been determined.

Advise the client to avoid sexual contact, to use condoms to prevent transmission of the AIDS virus to sexual partners, and not to share needles with others.

Advise the client to complete essential dental work before starting therapy with zidovudine or to delay it until completing the course of the drug because bone marrow depressant effects may result in gingival bleeding and delayed healing. Teach appropriate oral hygiene, including gentle use of toothbrushes and floss, and avoidance of toothpicks.

*Evaluation.* Perform CBCs at least every 2 weeks during therapy. Observe the client for fever, sore throat, unusual bleeding or bruising, or unusual tiredness, all of which are symptoms of bone marrow depression. These symptoms may occur even after the medication is discontinued and should be reported to the health care provider.

## SUMMARY

Mycoses, infections of humans by fungi, range from the very mild to the life threatening, some even the result of overgrowth during antibiotic, antineoplastic, or corticosteroid therapy. Unfortunately, antifungal therapy is not as developed as antibacterial chemotherapy. Most are quite toxic to humans in concentrations that would be effective against most fungi, so most preparations are topical. However, amphotericin B, fluconazole, flucytosine, griseofulvin, ketoconazole, miconazole, and nystatin are effective systemic fungistatic and fungicidal agents used for the treatment of a wide variety of mycotic infections.

Antiviral chemotherapy is even more difficult because by the time symptoms of the illness appear, the multiplication of the virus is ending and the course of the illness is set. Antiviral agents would need to be administered prophylactically to be most effective. In addition, viruses are true parasites and use the host cells' enzyme systems, so any effective therapy would also injure the host and thereby be too toxic for use. Antiviral agents in use are acyclovir, amantadine, ribavirin, vidarabine, and zidovudine. Prevention and management of adverse effects are a major nursing responsibility for both antiviral and antifungal agents.

## BIBLIOGRAPHY

Acyclovir tried in the chronic fatigue syndrome. (1989). NDA 13(4):26.

American Hospital Formulary Service. (1991). AHFS drug information '91. Bethesda, Md: American Society of Hospital Pharmacists, Inc.

Bailey EM et al. (1990). The triazole antifungal agents: a review of intraconazole and fluconazole, Pharmacotherapy 10(2):146.

Bennett J. (1988). NIH-sponsored clinical trials begin for antiviral drug AL721, Am J Nurs 88(4):432.

Braunwald E et al, editors. (1988). Harrison's principles of internal medicine, ed 11 New York: McGraw-Hill Book Co.

Brunetta L. (1989). Fluconazole: new hope against cryptococcus, AIDS Patient Care 3(2):22.

Byron PR et al. (1988). Ribavirin administration by inhalation: aerosol-generation factors controlling drug delivery to the lung, Respir Care 33(11):1011.

Casto DT. (1987). Amantadine hydrochloride: an agent for the prevention and treatment of influenza A infection, J Pediatr Health Care 1(1):51.

Eggleston M. (1987). Therapy of ocular herpes simplex infections, Infect Control 8(7):294.

Engel NS. (1989). AZT for children with AIDS, MCN 14(2):121.

Fletcher A. (1989). Amphotericin B — antifungal agent, Aust Nurses J 19(5):28.

Fluconazole certain to win FDA approval researchers say, Aids Alert 4(5):88.

Gee G et al. (1989). Current treatment strategies for HIV infection, Semin Oncol Nurs 5(4):249.

Hall JE et al. (1987). Amphotericin B dosage for disseminated candidiasis in premature infants, J Perinat 7(3):195.

Hamby S. (1989). Not in vein . . . IV drug administration, J Urol Nurs 8(3):697.

Hayden FG. (1988). An office guide to antiviral therapy, Emerg Med 20(5):155.

Kastrup EK, editor. (1991). Facts and comparisons. St Louis: JB Lippincott Co.

Lamb C. (1987). Fungal infections from head to toe, Patient Care 21(11):62.

LePage ME et al. (1988). Patint acceptance of prefilled disposable vaginal applicator, Am J Obstet Gynecol 158(4):1006.

Liss HP et al. (1988). Ribavirin aerosol in the elderly, Chest 93(6):1239.

Lynn MM et al. (1989). Current HIV therapy: an update on zidovudine, Nurse Pract 14(11):52.

Mack JE. (1988). Ribavirin: an antiviral agent with promise, Pediatr Nurs 14(3):220.

Mahon SM. (1988). Taking the terror out of amphotericin B, Am J Nurs 88(7):960.

Manser A. (1989). Zidovudine — AZT, Aust Nurses J 18(9):37.

Masur H. (1987). Fungal infections in AIDS patients: optimal treatment regimens, Hosp Ther 12(9):47.

More hospitals using zidovudine prophylaxis for HCWs, Hosp Employee Health 8(11):137.

Mossinghoff GJ. (1989). AIDS medicines in development: a 2-year review shows 9 treatments approved, AIDS Patient Care 3(5)4.

Mostow SR et al. (1988). Today's antiviral armamentarium, Patient Care 22(13):162.

Nederhand KC et al. (1989). Respiratory syncytial virus: a nursing perspective, Pediatr Nurs 15(4):342.

Occupational exposure to ribavirin aerosols. (1988). Lancet 2(8617):976.

Podrasky DL. (1989). Amphotericin B: the nurse's role in controlling adverse reactions, Focus Crit Care 16(3):194.

Prows CA. (1989). Ribavirin's risks in reproduction — how great are they? MCN 14(6):400.

Public Health Service statement on management of occupational exposure to human immunodeficiency virus, including considerations regarding zidovudine postexposure use, MMWR 39(RR-1):1.

Rashotte J. (1989). The seasonal invader . . . respiratory syncytial virus, Can Nurse 85(10):28.

Robertson S. (1989). Drugs that keep AIDS patients alive, RN 52(2):35.

Rosen T. (1989). Cutaneous fungal infections. I. Dermatophytosis: practical tips for avoiding common mistakes, Consultant 29(8):29.

Rosen T. (1989). Cutaneous fungal infections. II. Tinea versicolor and candidiasis: practical tips for avoiding common mistakes, Consultant 29(8):46.

Saag MS et al. (1988). Treatment of histoplasmosis and blastomycosis . . . amphotericin B . . . ketoconazole, Chest 93(4):848.

Should health care workers use zidovudine prophylaxis? AIDS Alert 5(2):21.

Sipes C. (1988). Giving amphotericin B in the home, Am J Nurs 88(7):965.

Staver S. (1988). Zidovudine trail to focus on health workers, Am Med News 31(29):1.

Stone B. (1987). Fast-tracking the first AIDS drug, FDA Consum 21(8):13.

Systemic antifungal agent fluconazole receives marketing approval. (1990). Clin Pharm 9(4):231.

Taravella S. (1989). AIDS drug found to slow development of disease, Mod Healthc 19(34):6.

United States Pharmacopeial Convention. (1991). Drug information for the health care provider, ed 11. Rockville, Md: The Convention.

Zidovudine breakthroughs expected to overwhelm system. (1989). AIDS Alert 4(10):161.

Zoler ML. (1989). Needlestick response is a riddle, Med World News 30(19):48.

*Chapter*

# 61 Other Antimicrobial Drugs and Antiparasitic Drugs

## INTRODUCTION

Antimicrobial and antiparasitic agents include antimalarial, antituberculous, amebicidal, anthelmintic, and leprostatic medications. Sulfonamides are reviewed in Chapter 34, "Antimicrobials for Urinary Tract Infections."

## MALARIA

**Malaria** is a prevalent disease in spite of efforts to control the causative parasite and insect vector. Malaria is generally limited to the tropics and subtropic areas, but cases are also imported into the United States and Canada. Four species

**TABLE 61-1**   Clinical differences among species causing malaria

| Species | Presentation | Asexual cycle | Relapse |
|---|---|---|---|
| *P. falciparum* | Parasitemia (elevated), anemia (severe), renal impairment, possible brain tissue infestation, pulmonary edema, death | 2 days | No; usually resistant to chloroquine |
| *P. vivax* | Rupture of spleen, anemia | 2 days | Yes |
| *P. ovale* | — | 2 days | Yes |
| *P. malariae* | Infection of red blood cells that persists for years; nephritis | 3 days | No |

of the genus *Plasmodium* are responsible for human malaria: *Plasmodium vivax, P. malariae, P. ovale,* and *P. falciparum. P. ovale,* which is found in West Africa, is considered rare. *P. falciparum* malaria is the most lethal form of malaria and is usually resistant to chloroquine.

Malaria is transmitted to humans by the bite of an infected female *Anopheles* mosquito, as well as by blood transfusions, congenitally, or contaminated needles commonly used by drug abusers. For clinical differences among the four species of malaria, see Table 61-1.

## Life Cycle of the Malarial Parasite

To understand the chemotherapy of malaria, it is essential to review the life cycle of the malarial parasite, the plasmodium. Figure 61-1 presents the cycle in seven basic steps.

Plasmodia have two interdependent life cycles: the sexual cycle, which takes place in the mosquito, and the asexual cycle, which occurs in the human body.

**Sexual cycle.** The sexual cycle is noted in step 7 of Figure 61-1. The female *Anopheles* mosquito becomes the carrier of the parasite by drawing blood containing male and female forms from an infected person. These sexual forms of the parasite are known as gametocytes. In the stomach of the mosquito the female gametocytes are fertilized by the males; zygotes form, which result in numerous cell divisions that develop into sporozoites. The formation of sporozoites in the mosquito completes the sexual cycle. Sporozoites then migrate to the salivary glands of the infected mosquito and are injected into the bloodstream of the human by the bite of the female insect (step 1, Figure 61-1).

**Asexual cycle.** In the human the asexual cycle of the plasmodium consists of the exoerythrocytic phase and the erythrocytic phase.

*Exoerythrocytic phase.* Shortly after the introduction of the sporozoites into the circulation of the human, they leave the blood and enter fixed tissue cells (reticuloendothelial cells) of the liver, where multiplication and maturation take place (step 2). For a period of time (8 to 42 days), which varies with different plasmodia, the individual exhibits no symptoms, no parasites are found in erythrocytes, and the blood is noninfective. This phase is known as the preerythrocytic stage. The parasites are called primary tissue schizonts, or preerythrocytic forms. After the preerythrocytic

stage, the young parasites burst from the liver cells as merozoites.

*Erythrocytic phase.* When merozoites enter the bloodstream, they penetrate the erythrocytes and begin the erythrocytic phase of their existence (step 3a). In the case of *P. vivax* (but not *P. falciparum*) some of the merozoites invade other tissue cells to form secondary exoerythrocytic forms (step 3b). The relapses in vivax and other forms of malaria are believed to be caused by the successive formations of merozoites producted by various secondary exoerythrocytic forms of the parasite. Drugs affecting malarial parasites in the bloodstream do not always destroy those in the exoerythrocytic, or tissue, stage.

After the merozoites bore into the red blood cells, they again multiply, but this time asexually, and erythrocytic schizonts are formed. The erythrocytic phase is completed when the parasitized red blood cells rupture, setting free many more merozoites that are formed from the schizonts. Pyrogenic substances are also liberated, causing a rapid rise in body temperature (step 4). Some of the merozoites may be destroyed in the plasma of the blood by leukocytes and other agents, but some enter other erythrocytes to repeat the cycle (step 5). The recurring chills, fever, and prostration that are prominent clinical symptoms of malaria occur when the red blood cells rupture and release the young parasites with foreign protein and cell products. The erythrocytic phase lasts 48 to 72 hours, depending on the plasmodium involved. After a few cycles, some of the asexual forms of the malarial parasites develop into sexual forms called gametocytes (step 6). When the mosquito bites a person infected with malarial parasites and ingests the sexual forms, the cycle begins again.

Persons who harbor the sexual forms of plasmodia are called carriers, since it is from carriers that mosquitoes receive the forms of the parasite that perpetuate the disease. The asexual forms cause the clinical symptoms of malaria. Carriers should avoid giving blood, since it is possible that the recipient of this blood will contract malaria or become a carrier. An increasing number of malaria cases (some fatal) have occurred from transfusions of infected blood. Some of these infected individuals who donated blood may have once lived in a malarious area. Any person who has had malaria or has been exposed to the disease by visiting a region where it is prevalent must be disqualified as a blood donor.

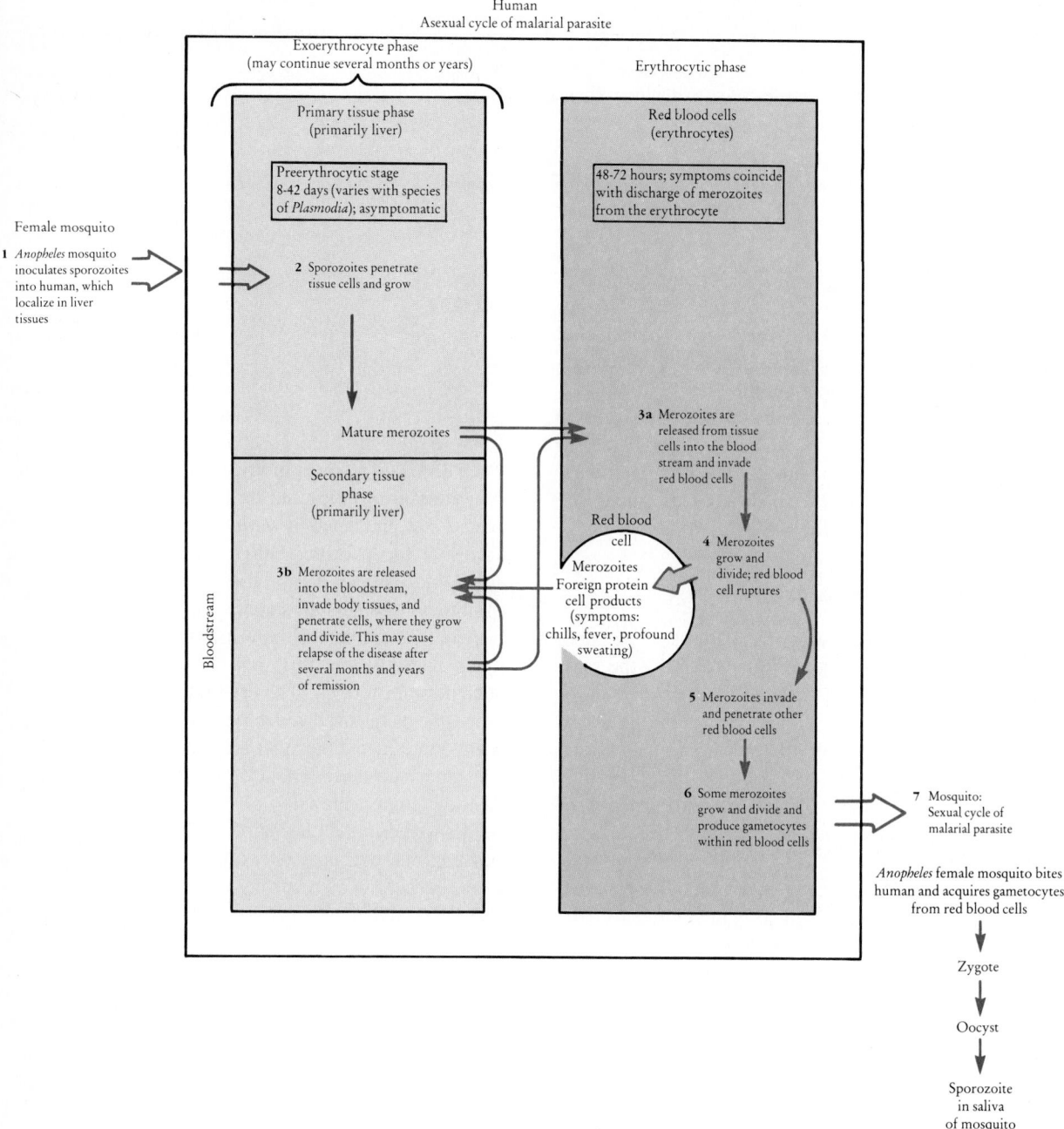

**FIGURE 61-1**  Life cycle of the malarial parasite.

## Antimalarial Medications

The choice of a drug for treatment of malaria is based on the particular malarial strain involved and the stage of the *Plasmodium* life cycle. The drugs, therefore, are classified according to the type of therapy they provide, which is as follows:

1. Prophylaxis is achieved in the preerythrocytic stage with drugs that are called primary tissue schizonticides. They destroy erythrocytic forms of the parasite, thereby preventing invasion of red blood cells. As a consequence, the drug prevents a malarial infection after the host is bitten by an infected mosquito. Pyrimethamine exerts an effective prophylactic effect on *P. falciparum*. However, these drugs are usually so toxic that their prophylactic use is avoided.

2. Suppressive treatment of clinical symptoms involves drugs that inhibit the erythrocytic stage of parasite development. Thus the infected individual is free of the clinical symptoms manifested by the disease. However, the exoerythrocytic forms continue to exist in the liver. The drugs administered for suppressive treatment are chloroquine, hydroxychloroquine, and pyrimeth-

amine. *P. falciparum* infection is usually cured by this treatment. In other forms of malaria, relapses occur when therapy is discontinued.

3. Clinical cure of an acute attack occurs when multiplication of the parasites within the erythrocyte is interrupted, thereby terminating the malarial symptoms of the attack. These drugs are called blood schizonticides and include the 4-aminoquinolines. Pyrimethamine is also used but has a slower action than the other drugs. Infections with *P. vivas* and *P. falciparum* respond well. If relapse occurs, therapy should be repeated with other agents such as quinine as combination therapy.

4. Radical cure requires drugs (secondary tissue schizonticides) that destroy both the exoerythrocytic and erythrocytic parasites to prevent relapsing malaria. This is generally reserved for individuals with vivax malaria. The only drug available is primaquine. It is usually given with chloroquine, which suppresses the erythrocytic cycle to effect a radical cure.

The emergence of drug-resistant strains of malaria, particularly that caused by *P. falciparum*, poses a major public health problem throughout the world. Despite the combined efforts of many countries to eradicate malaria, it remains the most devastating infectious disease in the world because of the many lives lost and the economic burdens it imposes. Fortunately, in the United States, endemic malaria has been completely eradicated.

It is essential that travelers contemplating a trip to malarious areas of the world be aware of the need to obtain information from their physician about measures for reducing exposure to the disease. Malaria exists in Haiti, Mexico, Central America, South America, the Middle East, India, Africa, Southeast Asia, Korea, and Indonesia. To reduce exposure to mosquitoes, the individual should stay indoors in well-screened areas after sundown, sleep under mosquito netting, wear adequate clothing, and use mosquito repellents over exposed areas of the body.

Antimalarial products include quinine sulfate, quinacrine HCl, 4-aminoquinoline compounds (chloroquine phosphate, chloroquine HCl, and hydroxychloroquine sulfate), 8-aminoquinoline compounds (primaquine phosphate), folic acid antagonist (pyrimethamine), and combinations (chloroquine phosphate with primaquine phosphate; sulfadoxine and pyrimethamine).

### quinine sulfate (Quinamm, Quinite)

As an antiprotozoal the mechanism of action is unknown, but it is believed to bind to and alter DNA properties. Action is schizonticidal. Drug concentrates in parasitized erythrocytes, which may be why it has selective toxicity during the erythrocytic stages of plasmodial infections. As an antimyotonic it increases refractory period of skeletal muscle and decreases the excitability of the motor end-plate, thus reducing response to nerve stimulation.

Quinine sulfate is indicated for the treatment of malaria, especially chloroquine-resistant malaria, by *P. falciparum* and the prevention and treatment of leg muscle cramps.

Quinine is absorbed orally and is highly protein bound with a half-life of 8.5 hours. After a single oral dose, the time to peak serum level is between 1 and 3 hours. Quinine is metabolized in the liver and excreted by the kidneys. For side effects/adverse reactions, see Table 61-2. When quinine is given with alfentanil, an increased accumulation and duration of action of alfentanil may occur. Monitor closely if drugs are given concurrently.

The adult oral dose for malaria is 200 mg to 1 g orally, three times daily for 3 to 10 days. A 200- to 300-mg dose at bedtime may also be prescribed for night-time leg cramps. The pediatric dose for chloroquine-resistant *P. falciparum* malaria is 8.3 mg/kg orally every 8 hours for 3 to 7 days. Pregnancy safety has been established at FDA category X; in humans, quinine has been reported to cause congenital malformations and stillbirths. Avoid using quinine in pregnant women.

▷ **Nursing Management:**
**Quinine Sulfate Therapy**

***Assessment.*** Quinine is to be administered with caution in clients with glucose-6-phosphate dehydrogenase (G-6-PD) deficiency, tinnitus, optic neuritis, myasthenia gravis, and pregnancy. Use with caution in patients with cardiac disease, particularly cardiac dysrhythmia that is treated with quinidine. Note quinine has quinidinelike activity.

The client receiving quinine should be assessed for the possibility of the following nursing diagnoses: altered comfort related to headache, rash, abdominal cramping, anorexia, nausea and vomiting; risk for physiologic injury related to hypersensitivity and increased tendency for bleeding related to blood dyscrasias; risk for infection related to leukopenia; activity intolerance related to anemia; sensory-perceptual disturbances related to cinchonism evidenced by blurred vision, double vision, color vision disturbance, tinnitis, or hearing loss.

***Intervention.*** Since quinine irritates the gastrointestinal mucosa, the capsule should be administered intact with food. Except for its use in chloroquine-resistant falciparum malaria, quinine, which has been the traditional antimalarial remedy, has been replaced by more effective and less toxic drugs.

***Education.*** Instruct the client to remain compliant to the antimalarial medication regimen for the full course of the prescription. Instruct client to report to the physician if any side effects/adverse reactions appear.

***Evaluation.*** Observe for symptoms of cinchonism (tinnitus, dizziness, altered auditory acuity, visual disturbances, headache, gastrointestinal distress, nausea, and diarrhea). These symptoms disappear when the drug is discontinued.

If quinine is administered for nocturnal recumbency leg cramps, it may be discontinued after several consecutive symptom-free nights, to determine if therapy is still required.

**TABLE 61-2**   Antimalarial drugs: side effects/adverse reactions

| Drug | Side effects* | Adverse reactions† |
|---|---|---|
| quinine sulfate | Most frequent: diarrhea, nausea, vomiting, abdominal pain or discomfort | Most frequent: visual disturbances, dizziness, severe headaches, tinnitus, hearing loss<br>Less frequent: rash, pruritus, hives, respiratory difficulties, wheezing |
| quinacrine HCl | Most frequent: transient headaches, dizziness, GI distress, diarrhea, nausea; temporary yellow skin and urine coloration—not jaundice | Chronic therapy; hepatitis, skin eruptions, aplastic anemia, visual disturbances, seizures (after high doses), psychosis.<br>Less frequent: anxiety, mood changes, nightmares |
| 4-aminoquinolines: chloroquine, hydroxychloroquine | Most frequent: diarrhea, headaches, anorexia, nausea, vomiting, abdominal distress<br>Less frequent: alopecia or bleaching of hair; dark discoloration of skin, nails, or inside of mouth; dizziness, increased anxiety, rash, pruritus | Less frequent: visual disturbances<br>Rare: mood alterations, tinnitus, convulsions, sore throat, fever, increased bleeding episodes<br>Overdosage: sedation, lightheadedness, severe respiratory difficulties |
| 8-aminoquinoiline: primaquine phosphate | Most frequent: nausea, vomiting, abdominal distress<br>Less frequent: headaches, pruritus | Most frequent: dark discoloration of urine (hemolytic anemia due to G-6-PD deficiency)<br>Less frequent: dizziness, respiratory difficulties, increased weakness<br>Rare: sore throat, elevated temperature |
| folic acid antagonist: pyrimethamine | Most frequent with high dosages: anorexia, vomiting | Most frequent with high dosages: taste alterations; sore, red, swelling or burning of tongue; diarrhea; throat pain; swallowing difficulties; sores, ulceration or white spots in mouth; sore throat; fever; increased bleeding; increased weakness<br>Rare: rash<br>Overdose: ataxia, tremors, convulsions |

*If side effects continue, increase, or disturb the client, inform the physician.
†If adverse reactions occur, contact physician because medical intervention may be necessary.

### quinacrine hydrochloride (Atabrine)

Quinacrine combines with DNA, interfering with its ability to replicate or even to serve in transcription of RNA; therefore protein synthesis decreases. It suppresses and destroys erythrocytic asexual forms of *P. falciparum* and *P. vivax* and sexual forms (gametocytes) of *P. vivax*. It is not effective against *P. falciparum* gametocytes and sporozoites of all species of malaria-causing pathogens.

Although the mechanism of action for giardiasis is unknown, it is primarily indicated for the treatment of giardiasis caused by *Giardia lamblia*. It is rarely used to treat malaria as safer and more effective agents are available.

Administered orally, quinacrine is rapidly absorbed from the intestinal tract and widely distributed in tissues and the liver. It is mainly excreted by the kidneys and in feces. For side effects/adverse reactions, see Table 61-2. When quinacrine is given with primaquine, the metabolism of primaquine may be inhibited leading to increased quinacrine serum levels and toxicity. Concurrent drug administration is not recommended.

The adult oral dose for giardiasis is 100 mg three times daily for 5 days. Pediatric dose is 2 mg/kg three times daily for 5 days. Maximum dose in children is 300 mg/day. Pregnancy safety has not been established.

### ▷ Nursing Management: Quinacrine Therapy

***Assessment.*** Use caution in the administration of quinacrine to clients with psychosis, glucose-6-phosphate dehydrogenase (G-6-PD) deficiency, renal or cardiac disease, hepatic disease, and alcoholism. Cautious use is also indicated in pregnant women, children, and individuals over age 60. Use in patients with porphyria or psoriasis may exacerbate these conditions; therefore the benefit must outweigh the risk.

The client receiving quinacrine should be assessed for the possibility of the following nursing diagnoses: altered comfort related to dizziness, headache, rash, abdominal cramping, anorexia, nausea and vomiting; altered bowel elimination pattern (diarrhea); self-concept disturbance related to acridine dye coloration evidenced by yellow discoloration of eyes and skin; and altered thought processes related to the development of toxic psychosis evidenced by hallucinations, mood and mental changes, irritability, nightmares.

***Intervention.*** Administer drug after meals with a large glass of water or other fluid (tea or fruit juice) to minimize gastric irritation. The bitter taste may be masked by jam or honey.

When quinacrine is given as an anthelmintic agent, the

client generally requires hospitalization. Give a bland, semi-solid, nonfat diet for 1 to 2 days before drug therapy. Individual should fast after evening meal the night before and on morning of drug therapy.

Give a saline or cleansing enema in the evening and 1 or 2 hours before medication. This will decrease the amount of stool required to examine for scoleces after the drug is given. Repeat saline enema 1 or 2 hours after quinacrine is administered to dispel worms. Sodium bicarbonate is given concurrently with the drug to prevent nausea and vomiting. Vomiting may cause the worms to move toward the stomach, where the ova can pass through the stomach wall and cause cycticercosis, or invasion of tissue. Vomiting is also prevented by administering the drug through a duodenal tube, particularly for treatment of pork tapeworm.

***Education.*** Advise client that the drug imparts a reversible yellow coloration to urine and skin (not jaundice). It also causes a cyanotic coloration (gray-blue tinge) to fingernail beds, ears, and nasal cartilage.

Instruct client to report to the physician any skin eruptions, psychotic behavior (may last up to 2 weeks after discontinuation of drug), or visual disturbances (blurred vision, halos of light, or difficulty in focusing).

***Evaluation.*** Perform compete blood counts and ophthalmoscopic examinations periodically, particularly in clients on prolonged therapy. Drug may need to be discontinued if there are significant abnormalities.

If quinacrine is given as an anthelmintic agent, collect entire stool specimen after treatment (usually for 48 hours); do not put toilet paper in bedpan. The search for scoleces in the laboratory is done by using ultraviolet light: the worm fluoresces on absorption of quinacrine. Scoleces must be found to be certain of a cure; otherwise the tapeworm will grow again.

If quinacrine is administered for giardiasis, evaluation of the success of therapy is based upon three stool examinations, taken several days apart, beginning 1 to 2 weeks following treatment. Finding the organism means continued therapy is necessary.

## 4-Aminoquinoline Compounds
### chloroquine (Aralen)
### hydroxychloroquine (Plaquenil)

The mechanism of action as an antiprotozoal to treat malaria is unknown but may be a result of its ability to bind or alter DNA properties. During suppressive therapy, they inhibit the erythrocytic stage of development of plasmodia. In acute malarial attacks, they interfere with erythrocytic schizogony of parasites. These drugs selectively accumulate in parasitized erythrocytes, which may be the reason for their selective toxicity in the erythrocytic stages of plasmodial infestation.

These agents are indicated for the prevention and treatment of malaria and also for the treatment of extraintestinal amebiasis, rheumatoid arthritis, and systemic lupus erythematosus. They are well absorbed orally, widely distributed in body tissues, at peak serum levels in 1 to 2 hours, metabolized in the liver, and excreted by the kidneys. For side effects/adverse reactions, see Table 61-2. When the 4-aminoquinolines are given concurrently with alcohol or other hepatotoxic agents, the potential for inducing hepatotoxicity increases. Monitor very closely.

Chloroquine oral adult dose to suppress malaria is 500 mg daily every 7 days. Pediatric dose is 8.3 mg/kg orally daily (not exceeding adult dose), once every 7 days. The parenteral dosage form for adult administration is 200 to 250 mg IM initially, repeated in 6 hours if needed. Do not exceed 1000 mg in the first day. Pediatric parenteral dose is 6.25 mg/kg IM or SC, repeated in 6 hours if needed. Do not exceed a total 24-hour dose of 12.5 mg/kg in 24 hours.

Hydroxychloroquine adult oral dose to suppress malaria is 400 mg daily, every 7 days. The pediatric dose is 6.4 mg/kg orally daily, repeated weekly. Pregnancy safety has not been established.

▷ **Nursing Management:**
**4-Aminoquinoline Compound Therapy**

***Assessment.*** These drugs are used with caution in the presence of hypersensitivity to 4-aminoquinolines, retinal or visual field changes, and pregnancy (to prevent retinal damage in the fetus). Long-term therapy in children is also contraindicated.

Also use with caution in individuals with liver disease or alcoholism, individuals with G-6-PD deficiency, and hematologic disorders.

Perform baseline ophthalmoscopic and audiometric examinations.

The client receiving therapy with a 4-aminoquinolone compound should be assessed for the possibility of the following nursing diagnoses: altered comfort related to dizziness, headache, rash, itching, abdominal cramping, anorexia, nausea and vomiting; altered bowel elimination pattern (diarrhea); risk for injury related to the development of seizures or blood dyscrasias; self-concept disturbance related to blue-black discoloration of the skin and fingernails or alopecia; sensory-perceptual disturbances related to ototoxicity evidenced by tinnitus and hearing loss, or to the development of retinopathy, keratopathy, or cataracts evidenced by blurred vision; and altered throught processes related to the development of psychosis evidenced by mood and mental changes.

***Intervention.*** Administer oral drugs with milk or meals to minimize gastric irritation. If client is on parenteral therapy, substitute oral administration as soon as possible.

Hydroxychloroquine tablets may be crushed and placed in gelatin capsules or mixed with jam or jello to make them easier to swallow.

Initiate suppressive therapy 2 weeks before exposure and continue medication while staying in malarious area. Maintain drug regimen for 6 to 8 weeks after leaving the region.

*Education.* Instruct client to take drug for the full course of treatment even if feeling better. This will ensure that the infection is completely eradicated and that the symptoms will not return. To obtain the full effect of the drug, inform the client to follow a regular schedule by taking it the same day each week. Keep drug out of reach of children. Fatalities in children have occurred following ingestion of three or four tablets.

Instruct the client to keep regularly scheduled visits for ophthalmoscopic and audiometric examinations and report to the physician any signs of visual and auditory disturbances. This is to prevent irreversible retinopathy, which may occur even after discontinuation of therapy.

Explain to client that the drug may cause a red or brown discoloration of the urine.

When drug is administered for rheumatoid arthritis, inform the client that therapeutic benefits usually do not occur until 6 to 12 months after therapy has been initiated.

Caution the client to avoid alcoholic beverages while taking this drug.

In addition to taking this medication to avoid contracting malaria, the client should also be instructed to sleep under mosquito netting at night, to wear trousers and long-sleeved shirts, and to use mosquito repellent on exposed skin surfaces.

Since the medication may cause dizziness, advise the client to avoid tasks that require mental alertness until the response to the medication has been determined.

*Evaluation.* Obtain a baseline and periodic CBC and test for glucose-6-phosphate dehydrogenase (G-6-PD) deficiency to avoid the occurrence of hemolytic anemia. Signs of blood dyscrasia are fever, sore throat, fatigue, and easy bruising.

Perform periodic tests of muscle strength and reflexes, particularly in patients on long-term therapy. Discontinue therapy if positive signs occur.

Observe client for drug resistance to 4-aminoquinolines. Failure to prevent or cure clinical malaria may require treatment with quinine if the person is infected with a resistant strain of the parasite. Avoid the use of these drugs in individuals with psoriasis or porphyria, since these conditions may become exacerbated. Discontinue drugs at first sign of retinal changes and/or visual disturbances and continue to observe client for possible progression even after therapy has been discontinued.

### 8-Aminoquinoline Compound
#### primaquine phosphate

Primaquine's mechanism of action is unknown, but it has the ability to bind and alter DNA. It is very effective in the exoerythrocytic stages of *P. vivax* and *P. ovale* malaria and against the primary phase (exoerythrocytic stage) of *P. falciparum* malaria. It is also effective against the sexual forms (gametocytes) of plasmodia (especially *P. falciparum*). It is indicated for the treatment of malaria and prevention of relapses of malaria caused by *P. vivax* and *P. ovale;* also effective against gametocytes of *P. falciparum.*

Primaquine is absorbed orally and reaches peak level within 2 to 3 hours. With a half-life of approximately 7 hours it is rapidly metabolized in an unspecified site and excreted via the kidneys. For side effects/adverse reactions, see Table 61-2.

When primaquine is given concurrently with the following drugs, the following significant drug interactions may occur:

| Drug | Possible Effect and Management |
|---|---|
| other hemolytic agents | May increase risk for toxicity; monitor closely. |
| quinacrine | Not recommended; an increase in primaquine toxicity is reported. |

The adult oral dose is 26.3 mg daily for 2 weeks. Pediatric dose is 680 μg (0.68 mg)/kg daily for 2 weeks.

Primaquine is not recommended for use during pregnancy.

### ▷ Nursing Management: Primaquine Therapy

*Assessment.* Persons with active forms of rheumatoid arthritis or lupus erythematosus have a tendency to develop granulocytopenia. Avoid the use of primaquine in these individuals. The client receiving primaquine should be assessed for the possibility of the following nursing diagnoses: altered comfort related to headache, itching, abdominal cramping, anorexia, nausea and vomiting; risk for physiologic injury related to the development of blood dyscrasias; and activity intolerance related to the development of hemolytic anemia or methemoglobinemia.

*Intervention.* Gastric irritation can be minimized by administering drug with meals or antacids.

*Education.* Encourage the client to comply with the full course of medication.

*Evaluation.* Emphasize the importance of periodic complete blood counts and hemoglobin determinations to the client. The signs of hemolytic anemia are fever, chills, precordial pain, darkened urine, and a sudden decrease in hemoglobin.

Discontinue medication if a sudden decrease in hemoglobin concentration, erythrocyte count, or leukocyte count occurs.

The more serious adverse effects of primaquine involve individuals with a genetically determined glucose-6-phosphate dehydrogenase (G-6-PD) deficiency, which can cause a lethal hemolysis of red blood cells. This disorder occurs in about 8% of black males and other dark-skinned individuals such as Asians and some Mediterranean peoples. However, there is evidence that the enzyme G-6-PD in the red blood cells is essential for metabolism in the plasmodia; hence persons with a genetic deficiency of G-6-PD in their red blood cells are believed to have some natural immunity to malaria.

## *Folic Acid Antagonist*
### pyrimethamine tablets (Daraprim)

Pyrimethamine blocks the protozoal enzyme dihydrofolate reductase, thus inhibiting the conversion of dihydrofolic acid to tetrahydrofolic acid. The depletion of folate reduces protozoal nucleic acid and protein production. It is effective against asexual erythrocytic forms of malaria, and it has a lesser effect against the tissue forms of *P. falciparum*. It arrests sporogony in the mosquito but it does not destroy gametocytes.

Pyrimethamine is indicated for preventing and treating malaria caused by *Plasmodium* spp. and is used in combination with sulfadoxine to suppress chloroquine-resistant, *P. falciparum* malaria. It is also combined with quinine and a sulfapyrimidine sulfonamide (sulfadiazine, trisulfapyrimidines) to treat uncomplicated attacks of chloroquine-resistant *P. falciparum* malaria. For treating toxoplasmosis, the drug is combined with a sulfapyrimidine sulfonamide to treat toxoplasmosis caused by *Toxoplasma gondii*.

Pyrimethamine is absorbed orally and widely distributed in the body, although it concentrates mainly in red and white blood cells, kidneys, liver, lungs, and spleen. It is highly protein bound with a half-life of approximately 110 hours. It reaches peak serum levels in 2 to 4 hours, is metabolized in the liver, and is excreted via the kidneys. For side effects/adverse reactions, see Table 61-2. No significant drug interactions have been reported with its use.

The adult oral dose for an acute attack in chloroquine-resistant *P. falciparum* malaria is 25 mg twice a day for 3 days. For prophylaxis, the dose is 25 mg of pyrimethamine with 500 mg of sulfadoxine daily, every 7 days. The pediatric dose in an acute attack of chloroquine-resistant *P. falciparum* malaria is 300 μg (0.3 mg) pyrimethamine/kg given with a sulfonamide three times daily for 3 days. As the dose for prophylaxis varies with age, the student is referred to a current package insert or USP-DI for dosing instructions. Pregnancy safety has not been established, although it is generally not recommended because animal studies report birth defects.

▷ **Nursing Management:**
**Pyrimethamine Therapy**

**Assessment.** Since the drug crosses the placenta, its use is not recommended in pregnancy. In animal studies defects have occurred in the fetus. Moreover, risk-benefit must be considered in nursing mothers because pyrimethamine may disrupt the folic acid metabolism in the nursing infant. The drug also can cause hemolytic anemia in glucose-6-phosphate dehydrogenase (G-6PD)-deficient infant.

To prevent possible central nervous system toxicity in individuals with convulsive disorders, use a small initial dose for treatment of toxoplasmosis. Use pyrimethamine with caution for clients with preexisting blood dyscrasias. Do not use for treatment of resistant form of parasite.

The client receiving pyrimethamine should be assessed for the possibility of the following nursing diagnoses: altered comfort related to rash, change of taste, sore tongue (folic acid deficiency), anorexia, nausea and vomiting; risk for physiologic injury related to the development of blood dyscrasias; altered oral mucous membranes related to folic acid deficiency evidenced by ulcers, or white spots, in the mouth; altered bowel elimination pattern (diarrhea) related to folic acid deficiency; and activity intolerance related to the development of anemia.

**Intervention.** Administer medication with milk or food to minimize gastric irritation. For children, tablets may be crushed to prepare 1% solution in normal saline. Use within 24 hours at room temperature. If mixed with cherry syrup NF, use immediately after preparation.

If taken to prevent malaria, the medication should be taken 2 weeks before entering a malarious area and be continued for 6 weeks after leaving it. Besides building tissue stores of the drug, early administration will allow assessment of the client's tolerance of the drug.

**Education.** Advise the client to have weekly blood counts and platelet counts during therapy if on high dosage therapy.

If taken as a malaria suppressant, instruct the client to follow the dosage schedule as prescribed by taking the drug the same day each week.

Advise the individual to sleep under mosquito netting to avoid being bitten by malaria-carrying mosquitoes while in the endemic areas. Advise the wearing of proper clothing so that arms and legs are covered, especially at dawn and during evening hours, when mosquitoes are out. The use of mosquito repellent on uncovered areas of the skin may help to protect the individual from the bites of infected mosquitoes.

Instruct the client to report to physician any signs of possible blood dyscrasia (fever, sore throat, unusual bleeding or bruising, extreme weakness and fatigue).

Fansidar (pyrimethamine with sulfadoxine) should only be used when the traveler is going to areas where chloroquine-resistant malaria is prevalent and is planning to stay longer than 3 weeks because of the risk of severe skin reactions. The drug should be discontinued and a health care provider notified at the first sign of a rash.

**Evaluation.** The high dosage required for treating toxoplasmosis could approach the toxic level. If folic acid deficiency develops, dosage may be reduced. Clinical symptoms of folic acid deficiency are soreness, redness, or burning of the tongue; pharyngitis; ulcers in the mouth; or diarrhea. Folinic acid (leucovorin) restores the depressed platelet or white blood counts to normal levels.

### *Combination Therapy for Malaria*

Chloroquine phosphate with primaquine phosphate tablets is used for malaria prophylaxis in all areas where the disease is prevalent, regardless of the causative organism. The tablets are available as 500 mg of chloroquine phosphate (300 mg of base) and 79 mg primaquine phosphate (45 mg base). Adult dose is one tablet before entering the area, then one tablet weekly on the same day each week. Continue this dosage for 2 months after leaving the endemic area. For further information on this product, see previous section describing the individual drugs.

Sulfadoxine and pyrimethamine tablets (Fansidar) are used to treat *P. falciparum* malaria in travelers in areas where this malaria strain is prevalent. For additional information on the ingredients in this product, see previous section and sulfonamides in Chapter 37. Refer to a current package insert or a current *Facts and Comparisons Drug Information* (Kastrup, E.K., ed.) reference for detailed dosing and additional information on this product.

## TUBERCULOSIS

**Tuberculosis** (TB) in native-born Americans increased in 1986 for the first time since 1953. Nationwide, nearly 23,000 cases of TB were reported in 1986 (Hayden, 1987). Between 10 and 15 million asymptomatic Americans are infected with this disease (Visconti, 1990), and nearly 10% will develop tuberculosis. This increase is largely attributed to the increasing numbers of individuals with AIDS, to street living or homelessness, drug abusers, undernourished or malnourished persons, or those taking immunosuppressant drugs or suffering from cancer.

Tuberculosis also occurs much more frequently in older persons than in young people and has been found to be quite prevalent in elderly nursing home patients. Approximately one in four of all newly reported cases of tuberculosis in the United States is in persons 65 years of age or older (Nagami, 1983). There are also reports that undetected tuberculosis in a nursing home patient tremendously increases the risk and spread of this disease in this population (Stead, 1985).

With the antituberculosis chemotherapy and chemoprophylaxis available today, great progress has been made in treating this disease state.

*Mycobacterium tuberculosis* is the bacteria that causes tuberculosis. The most common infection site is the lungs, but other body areas can also be infected, such as bones, joints, skin, meninges, or genitourinary tract. This bacteria is an aerobic bacillus that needs a highly oxygenated organ site for growth; thus the lungs, growing ends of bones, and cerebral cortex are ideal sites. Tubercle bacilli may be transmitted by airborne droplets but cannot be transmitted on objects such as dishes, clothing, or sheets and bedding. Sharing an enclosed environment with an infected person creates a high risk of developing this infection (Health Information for International Travelers, 1988).

Fortunately, though, the transmission of the bacilli is blocked by good room ventilation, ultraviolet light, and specific chemotherapy. Many clients are treated as outpa-

tients, assuming they are not public health hazards (that is, highly infectious) and do not have severe symptoms of disease. Usually after 2 weeks of appropriate chemotherapy, most clients are no longer infectious to their family or contacts (Herfindal and others, 1988). When sputum cultures are negative, many persons return to their work setting.

### Pathogenesis

Tubercle bacilli droplets are transmitted by coughing or sneezing by an infected person. Persons producing sputum generally have many bacilli and are more infectious than the infected person that does not cough. Nevertheless, an uninfected person must be exposed to an infectious case of tuberculosis for many weeks before the infection can be transferred (Glassroth, 1981). Three types of tubercle bacilli are pathogenic to humans: human to human, bovine to human, and avian to human. Avian TB is rare in the United States and with the pasteurization of milk and testing of cows, bovine TB is much less prevalent. Thus the primary source of transmission is human to human.

When the tubercle bacilli enter the lungs, infection can spread from there to other body organs through the blood and lymphatic system. Usually, however, the infection becomes dormant and is walled off by calcified and fibrous tissues. The bacilli become inactive, perhaps for the lifetime of the host. If host defenses break down, however, or if the host receives an immunosuppressive drug, the bacilli may be reactivated. The ensuing disease may be chronic tuberculosis or miliary tuberculosis. Chronic tuberculosis may occur in any body organ but, as previously stated, it occurs most frequently in areas with the greatest oxygen tension. Miliary tuberculosis refers to the spread of many bacilli in the body; it is most often seen in children under 4 years old and can rapidly lead to death of the individual (Herfindal and others, 1988).

### Drug Treatment Regimens

Effective drug regimens are available to treat tuberculosis. Drug selection is based on toxicity and also on the development of drug-resistant organisms. General guidelines include:

1. For clients with tuberculosis, administer two or more sensitive drugs for the specific TB bacilli. One drug alone will increase the risk of organisms developing drug resistance. Isoniazid is recommended for newly infected persons without existing disease, which is determined by the individual's delayed hypersensitivity reaction to an intradermal injection of purified protein derivative (PPD).

2. Two or more drugs are combined to treat the disease because they will provide additive antituberculous action and also because one drug will help to prevent or delay the development of resistance to the other drug.

3. Avoid combinations with additive toxicities, such as nephrotoxic or ototoxic effects.
4. Monitor the prescribed therapy regimen closely to avoid client noncompliance, to detect side effects or adverse reactions, and to register progress of the treatment program (Roffman, 1981).

Although in the past tuberculosis treatment required 1 to 2 years of therapy, today 9 to 12 months of combined isoniazid and rifampin therapy is reported to be effective. Short-course drug regimens are also used, especially in areas where client noncompliance has led to the development of drug-resistant organisms. Various drug protocols range from daily drug administration to twice-weekly administration (Braunwald and others, 1987). See Table 61-3 for typical drug treatment regimens for tuberculosis.

## ▷Nursing Management: Antituberculous Therapy

These general nursing managements for antituberculous agents are supplemented by specific considerations for each agent.

**Assessment.** Cultures for *Mycobacterium* and tests for the organism's susceptibility to the antitubercular drugs should be obtained before and periodically during the course of drug therapy.

**Intervention.** The nurse should attempt to administer these drugs with consideration for the client's comfort. For example, gastrointestinal disturbances following administration can be reduced by concurrent administration of food or antacids.

**Education.** The client must take prescribed medications regularly and without interruption for maximum therapeutic effectiveness. A person who is responsible for self-medication should be instructed about the necessity of taking these drugs, two or more concurrently, according to the prescribed regimen and not to discontinue them when feeling better.

Instruct clients responsible for self-medication about the necessity for periodic medical evaluations to evaluate the effectivness of therapy.

Because of the long-term nature of drug therapy in tuberculosis, clients may need support in maintaining the therapeutic regimen and in managing side effects of the tuberculosis drugs.

When peripheral neuritis appears as a side effect of the antitubercular drugs, teach clients precautionary strategies to avoid injury from burning agents and sharp objects until the alteration in sensation is remedied.

Teach clients measures that minimize disease transmission, such as covering the mouth when coughing and sneezing. The disease may also be transmitted through unpasteurized milk or milk products.

**Evaluation.** Monitor the client for symptoms that indicate resolution of the infection: diminished cough and spu-

**TABLE 61-3**   Drug regimens for tuberculosis

| Drug regimen (adult dosage) | Comments |
|---|---|
| isoniazid (INH) (300 mg) and rifampin 600 mg daily for 9 to 12 months | Common regimen for initial treatment of TB; if drug resistance is possible, ethambutol 15 mg/kg is added |
| INH 300 mg and ethambutol (15 mg/kg) daily for 12 to 18 months | Least toxic protocol; used for individuals with minimal disease state; also used for pregnant women |
| INH (300 mg), rifampin (600 mg), pyrazinamide (2 g), and streptomycin (1 g) or ethambutol (15 mg/kg) daily for 2 months, followed by one of the following regimens:<br>1. INH, 300 mg, and rifampin, 600 mg, daily for 4 months<br>2. INH, 300 mg, rifampin, 600 mg, and streptomycin, 1 g, twice weekly for 6 months | Typical short, intensive course of therapy; these regimens need close client supervision; the regimens have been reported to be effective |

tum production; decreased fever and night sweats; reduction of cavitation on x-ray; reduction of anorexia with concomitant weight gain; and decreased acid-fast bacteria (AFB) in sputum specimens. If the drug is taken to prevent tuberculosis, the absence of the disease demonstrates its effectiveness.

## Antituberculous Agents
### aminosalicylates, systemic
### aminosalicylate sodium (Nemasol ✱, PAS, Tubasal)

These bacteriostatic agents inhibit bacterial resistance to streptomycin and isoniazid. They are closely related to aminobenzoic acid (PABA) and competitively inhibit folic acid formation in tuberculosis, thus suppressing growth and reproduction.

These agents are indicated for the treatment of tuberculosis, pulmonary and extrapulmonary, caused by *M. tuberculosis*.

Aminosalicylates are well absorbed orally, especially the sodium dosage forms. They are distributed to various body fluids with high levels accumulating in pleural fluids, kidney, lungs, and liver tissues. Half-life is between 45 and 60 minutes, although clients with impaired renal function may have a half-life of up to 23 hours. Peak serum level is reached within 1 to 2 hours. This drug is metabolized in the liver and excreted by the kidneys. For significant side effects/adverse reactions, see Table 61-4. When aminosalicylates are given concurrently with aminobenzoates, the bacteriostatic effect of aminosalicylates may be antagonized. Avoid concurrent drug administration.

The adult oral dose given in combination with other antimycobacterials is 3.3 to 4 g every 8 hours. Maximum daily dose is 20 g. The pediatric dose in combination with other

antimycobacterials is 50 to 75 mg/kg orally, every 6 hours. Pregnancy safety has not been established.

▷ **Nursing Management:**
**Aminosalicylate Therapy**

***Assessment.*** Aminosalicylates should be used with caution if the client has the following preexisting conditions: gastric ulcer, as gastric irritation may increase; G-6-PD de-

**TABLE 61-4**   Antituberculosis agents: side effects/adverse reactions

| Drug | Side effects* | Adverse reactions† |
|---|---|---|
| aminosalicylates | Most frequent: diarrhea, abdominal distress | Most frequent: chills, rash, sore throat, increased temperature, increased weakness, confusion, constipation, sedation, increased thirst and frequency of urination, anorexia, depression, nausea, vomiting, pruritus, low back pain, pain on urination<br>Less frequent: bloody urine, menstrual changes, decreased libido, dry skin, weight gain, edema in throat (goiter), headaches, photosensitivity, jaundice of eyes/skin |
| capreomycin | Less frequent: rash, pruritus, swelling, increased temperature, pain, bleeding, hardness at site of injection | Most frequent: bloody urine, increased thirst and frequency of urination, anorexia (hypokalemia)<br>Less frequent: hearing loss, tinnitus, ataxia, dizziness, increased weakness, irregular heart rate, mood alterations, muscle pain or cramps, abdominal distress, weak pulse, nausea, vomiting |
| cycloserine | Most frequent: headaches<br>Less frequent: pale skin, more frequent bleeding episodes, weakness | Most frequent: increased anxiety, confusion, dizziness, sedation, increased irritability, restlessness, depression, muscle tremors, nightmares, mood alterations, speech difficulties, suicidal tendencies<br>Less frequent: visual disturbances, photosensitivity, tingling, pain, numbness in hands or feet, jaundice of eyes or skin<br>Rare: convulsions |
| ethambutol | Less frequent: lightheadedness, abdominal distress, rash, pruritus | Less frequent: chills; joint pain or swelling, (especially big toe, ankle, or knee); hot skin over affected joints<br>Rare: visual disturbances; pain, burning, tingling, or numbness of hands or feet |
| ethionamide | Most frequent: diarrhea, drooling, anorexia, metal mouth taste, nausea, vomiting, mouth soreness, abdominal distress, hypotension, sedation, tiredness<br>Less frequent/rare: acne, breast enlargement in men, alopecia, photosensitivity, rash | Most frequent: depression<br>Less frequent: ataxia, confusion, mood alterations, jaundice of eyes or skin<br>Rare: menstrual irregularities, decreased libido, dry skin, goiter, joint swelling and pain |
| isoniazid (INH) | Most frequent: lightheadedness, abdominal distress, tingling<br>Less frequent: breast enlargement in males | Most frequent: hands and feet pain, burning dark urine, jaundice of eyes or skin, anorexia, nausea, increased weakness<br>Rare: visual disturbances |
| pyrazinamide | Less frequent: nausea, vomiting, urination difficulties<br>Rare: pruritus, rash, photosensitivity | Most frequent: anorexia, increased temperature, increased weakness, jaundice of eyes or skin<br>Less frequent: joint pain and swelling, especially of big toe, ankle, and knee; feeling of heat over affected joint |
| rifampin | Most frequent: anorexia, discoloration of body fluids (urine, saliva, feces, tears, sweat—red orange to brown), abdominal distress<br>Less frequent: pruritus, rash, mouth or tongue soreness | Less frquent: chills, respiratory difficulties, lightheadedness, shivers, increased temperature, headaches, fever, bone and muscle pain<br>Rare: bloody urine, decreased urination, anorexia, nausea, vomiting, increased weakness, sore throat, increased bleeding episodes, jaundice of eyes or skin |

*If side effects continue, increase, or disturb the client, inform the physician.
†If adverse reactions occur, contact physician because medical intervention may be necessary.

ficiency because there is a risk of hemolytic anemia; severe renal or hepatic function impairment. Avoid the administration of aminosalicylate calcium in conditions in which there might be increased calcium levels, such as adrenal insufficiency, hyperparathyroidism, and carcinoma. Congestive heart failure should preclude the use of aminosalicylate sodium because of the risk of fluid accumulation. A history of allergic reaction to other salicylates and sulfonamides may indicate a cross-intolerance for aminosalicylates.

The client receiving aminosalicylates should be assessed for the possibility of the following nursing diagnoses: altered comfort related to stomach pain, or back pain and pain on urination related to crystalluria; risk for physiologic injury related to the development of hepatitis; altered bowel elimination pattern (diarrhea); and activity intolerance related to the development of anemia, myxedema, or an infectious mononucleosis-like syndrome.

***Intervention.*** Administer with meals or antacids to minimize gastrointestinal distress. When administering the dry powder form of the drug, mix thoroughly with diluent and ensure that the client takes all of liquid to obtain the full dose.

Do not administer aminosalicylates within 6 hours of rifampin or aminosalicylate calcium within 2 or 3 hours of oral tetracyclines.

The client should have a fluid intake of 3000 ml daily to minimize crystalluria.

***Education.*** Clients with diabetes who test their urine with copper sulfate urine glucose tests may have false-positive test results. Clients should instead use Clinistix or Ketodiastix.

***Evaluation.*** Serum electrolytes and urinalyses should be monitored periodically during drug therapy.

### capreomycin sulfate, sterile (Capastat)

Mechanism of action is unknown. Capreomycin sulfate is indicated for the treatment of pulmonary tuberculosis caused by *M. tuberculosis* after primary medications (streptomycin, isoniazid, rifampin, and ethambutol) fail or when these medications cannot be used because of resistant bacilli or drug toxicity.

Administered parenterally, capreomycin achieves high concentrations in the urine. Half-life is 3 to 6 hours and time to peak serum level is 1 to 2 hours after IM administration. It is excreted by the kidneys (50% to 60%), primarily unchanged. For side effects/adverse reactions, see Table 61-4.

When capreomycin is given concurrently with the following drugs, the following interactions may occur:

| Drug | Possible Effect and Management |
|---|---|
| aminoglycosides | Avoid concurrent drug administration. The risk for developing ototoxicity, nephrotoxicity and neuromuscular blockade is increased. Hearing loss may progress to |

| Drug | Possible Effect and Management |
|---|---|
| | deafness, even after the drug is stopped. This can be a very dangerous combination. *Avoid.* |
| amphotericin B, parenteral; bacitracin, parenteral; bumetanide, parenteral; cisplatin, cyclosporine, ethacrynic acid, or furosemide, parenteral; paromomycin, streptomycin; or vancomycin | Concurrent or even sequential use of capreomycin with any of these drugs can increase the risk for ototoxicity and/or neephrotoxicity. Hearing loss may occur and progress to deafness—even if drugs are stopped. *Avoid if at all possible.* |
| anesthetics, halogenated hydrocarbon inhalation, or citrate anticoagulated blood in massive transfusions or neuromuscular blocking agents | May result in increased neuromuscular blocking effects, resulting in respiratory depression or paralysis. Monitor closely, especially during surgery or in the postoperative period. If possible, avoid this combination. If not, closely monitor and keep anticholinesterase agents or calcium salts on hand to reverse the blockade. |
| methoxyflurane or polymyxins, parenteral | *Avoid concurrent or sequential drug administration.* The potential for nephrotoxicity and/or neuromuscular blockade is increased, which may lead to respiratory depression or paralysis. |

The adult intramuscular dose given in combination with other antitubercular agents is 1 g daily for 2 to 4 months followed by 1 g two or three times weekly. The pediatric dose has not been established.

Pregnancy safety has not been established.

▷ **Nursing Management: Capreomycin Therapy**

***Assessment.*** The health assessment should determine if the client has the following preexisting conditions: dehydration, which increases the risk of toxicity due to increased serum levels of the drug; myasthenia gravis and parkinsonism, in which the neuromuscular deficits may increase; impairment of the eighth cranial nerve, because the drug may cause increased auditory and vestibular toxicity; and renal impairment, which may increase because of the nephrotoxic effects of the drug.

Because of these effects, audiograms and vestibular and renal function determinations should be monitored before and periodically during therapy. If the BUN is above 30 mg/dl, the medication should be stopped. Fluid intake and output should be monitored throughout therapy. In addition, liver function studies should be done periodically, as well as serum potassium levels.

The client receiving capreomycin should be assessed for the possibility of the following nursing diagnoses: altered comfort related to pain at the injection site, or anorexia, nausea, and vomiting related to nephrotoxicity or hypokalemia; risk for injury related to hypersensitivity; altered urinary elimination pattern (increased or decreased frequency of urination or amount of urine) related to nephrotoxicity;

risk for (super)infection related to the reduction of normal flora; activity intolerance related to hypokalemia or the development of neuromuscular blockade; sensory-perceptual disturbances related to auditory ototoxicity evidenced by tinnitus or hearing loss, or to vestibular ototoxicity evidenced by dizziness or unsteadiness.

**Intervention.** To prepare for intramuscular administration, add 2 ml of 0.9% sodium chloride injection or sterile water for injection to the vial. Allow 2 to 3 minutes for dissolution to occur. Reconstituted solutions may darken, but this does not affect their potency. They are stable for 48 hours at room temperature or 14 days if refrigerated.

Administer intramuscularly deep into a large muscle mass to minimize pain and the risk of sterile abscesses.

**Education.** The client should maintain regular contact with the health care provider to monitor his or her condition. Symptoms of tinnitis, hearing deficit, and/or vertigo should be reported to the physician.

**Evaluation.** With prolonged therapy, the client should be monitored for an overgrowth of nonsusceptible organisms.

### cycloserine (Seromycin)

This is a broad-spectrum antibiotic that can be bacteriostatic or bactericidal, depending on drug concentration at infection site and organism susceptibility. It interferes with bacterial cell wall synthesis.

It is indicated for the treatment of active pulmonary and extrapulmonary tuberculosis after failure of the primary antitubercular medications and for the treatment of urinary tract infections.

Cycloserine is well absorbed orally, is widely distributed to body tissues and fluids and results in high urine concentrations. The time to peak serum level is between 3 to 4 hours, with a half-life of 10 hours. About 35% of cycloserine is metabolized with excretion via the kidneys. For side effects/adverse reactions, see Table 61-4. When cycloserine is given concurrently with the following drugs, the following interactions may occur:

| Drug | Possible Effect and Management |
|------|-------------------------------|
| alcohol | In chronic alcohol abusers, it may increase the risk of seizures. *Avoid concurrent usage.* |
| ethionamide | May increase CNS side effects such as seizures. Monitor closely, as dosage adjustments may be necessary. |

The adult oral dose used in combination with other drugs to treat tuberculosis is 250 mg every 12 hours for 1 to 2 weeks, then dose is increased as necessary up to 250 mg every 6 to 8 hours. Maximum daily dose is 1 g. Pediatric dose is 5 to 20 mg/kg daily, in divided doses.

Pregnancy safety has been established at FDA category C.

### ▷ Nursing Management: Cycloserine Therapy

**Assessment.** Cycloserine should be used with caution if the client has the following preexisting conditions: severe renal impairment, alcoholism, and seizure disorders, as the risk of seizures is greater.

The client receiving cycloserine is at risk for the following nursing diagnoses: altered comfort related to numbness and pain of the hands and feet related to peripheral neuropathy and headache; risk for injury related to hypersensitivity and seizures; activity intolerance related to anemia; altered thought processes related to the development of CNS toxicity evidenced by confusion, mood and mental changes, nightmares, depression, and thoughts of suicide; and sensory-perceptual disturbances related to optic neuritis evidenced by blurred vision or vision loss.

**Education.** Caution the client to avoid alcohol while taking this medication, as it increases risks of CNS toxicity such as dizziness, mental disturbances, and seizures. If the client experiences gastrointestinal irritation, recommend taking cycloserine after meals.

Advise the client to report immediately to the physician any signs of dizziness, drowsiness, vision disturbances, or thoughts of suicide.

### ethambutol hydrochloride (Etibi ✤, Myambutol)

This bacteriostatic agent is believed to diffuse into the mycobacteria bacilli and suppress RNA synthesis. It is effective only against actively dividing mycobacteria. It is indicated for the treatment of tuberculosis. Ethambutol is absorbed orally and distributed to most body tissues and fluids with the exception of cerebrospinal fluid. High concentrations are found in the kidneys, lungs, saliva, urine, and erythrocytes. The time to peak serum level is 2 to 4 hours, half-life is between 3 to 4 hours. Ethambutol is metabolized in the liver and excreted by the kidneys. For side effects/adverse reactions, see Table 61-4. Ethambutol has no reported significant drug interactions.

The adult oral dose to treat tuberculosis in combination with other agents is 15 mg/kg daily initially. If client requires retreatment, the dose is 25 mg/kg daily for 2 months, then 15 mg/kg daily. Dosage has not been established for children under the age of 13 years.

Pregnancy safety has not been established.

### ▷ Nursing Management: Ethambutol Therapy

**Assessment.** When the client has preexisting optic neuritis and/or renal impairment, use ethambutol with caution. It may also increase uric acid concentrations, so care must be taken with clients with gout. Uric acid determinations are required periodically during the course of therapy.

The client receiving ethambutol is at risk for the following nursing diagnoses: altered comfort related to rash, numbness and pain of the hands and feet related to peripheral neuritis or painful and swollen joints related to the development of gout; and sensory-perceptual disturbances related to optic neuritis evidenced by red-green color blindness, blurred vision or vision loss.

**Intervention.** Administer with food to minimize gastrointestinal distress. Administer ethambutol in a single daily dose, as divided doses may not result in therapeutic serum levels. It is administered concurrently with other antitubercular agents because of the tendency for bacterial resistance to occur when it is used alone.

*Education.* Encourage the client to visit the health care provider regularly to monitor progress. If no improvement occurs in 2 to 3 weeks, this should be reported to the physician.

Report promptly signs of optic neuritis (blurred vision, any loss of vision or red-green perception, or eye pain) or peripheral neuritis (numbness, tingling, or weakness in the hands and feet).

*Evaluation.* Ethambutol is known to decrease visual acuity and the ability to see red and green. This presents a safety hazard, especially in driving motor vehicles, and clients should be tested for these visual disturbances frequently during drug therapy. Discontinuation of the drug is usually indicated when visual acuity is disturbed.

### ethionamide (Trecator-SC)

Mechanism of action is unknown, but it is believed to inhibit peptide synthesis. Depending on concentration at site of infection and susceptibility of the organism, ethionamide may be bacteriostatic or bactericidal. It is indicated for the treatment of tuberculosis after failure of the primary antitubercular agents (streptomycin, isoniazid, rifampin, and ethambutol).

Ethionamide is well absorbed orally and distributed to most body tissues and fluids, including cerebrospinal fluid. With a half-life of 3 hours, it is probably metabolized in liver and excreted by the kidneys. For side effects/adverse reactions, see Table 61-4. When ethionamide is given with cycloserine, an increase in CNS side effects, especially convulsions, may result. Monitor closely because dosage adjustments may be necessary.

To treat tuberculosis, the adult oral dose used in combination with other agents is 250 mg every 8 to 12 hours. The pediatric dose is 4 to 5 mg/kg orally every 8 hours. Pregnancy safety has not been established.

### ▷ Nursing Management: Ethionamide Therapy

*Assessment.* The physician should carefully weigh risks and benefits for clients with diabetes mellitus or severe hepatic dysfunction before a course of ethionamide. Clients with an intolerance for niacin, isoniazide, and pyrazinamide may also be intolerant of ethionamide.

Cultures and sensitivity testing should be done before and periodically throughout therapy to monitor progress.

The client receiving ethionamide is at risk for the following nursing diagnoses: altered comfort related to rash, painful joints, photosensitivity, metallic taste, anorexia, nausea and vomiting, or numbness and tingling of the hands and feet related to peripheral neuritis; activity intolerance related to the development of CNS toxicity (weakness), hypothy-roidism (lethargy), hepatitis (lethargy) or orthostatic hypotension (dizziness); altered thought processes related to CNS toxicity evidenced by confusion, depression, mood and mental changes; self-concept disturbance related to changes in appearance such as acne, gynecomastia in males, hair loss, goiter, and weight gain (hypothyroidism); and sensory-perceptual disturbances related to optic neuritis evidenced by blurred vision or vision loss.

*Intervention.* Administer with meals to minimize gastrointestinal distress. If gastrointestinal upset occurs, it may be minimized by a divided dosage schedule or by administration with a rectal suppository. In both cases, however, serum concentrations may not be adequate. Pyridoxine may be prescribed concurrently to prevent peripheral neuritis.

*Education.* Advise the client about the importance of complying with the medication regimen, particularly when such a course may be continued for 1 or 2 years of more. Regular visits to the physician are necessary to monitor progress and for periodic eye exams. Any symptoms related to changes in vision should be promptly reported to the physician.

Advise the client that because ethionamide may cause dizziness, drowsiness, or weakness, hazardous activities requiring mental alertness such as driving should be avoided until the response to the medication has been ascertained. Alert the client to other potential side effects, such as mental depression or mood changes.

*Evaluation.* Although its incidence is rare, optic neuritis (blurred vision, vision loss, and/or eye pain) does occur. The client should have a thorough ophthalmologic examination before starting the drug and at the first indication of symptoms related to vision changes. Symptoms of CNS toxicity such as mental depression, mood changes, and weakness may be observed.

To monitor for hepatotoxic effects, AST (SGOT) and ALT (SGPT) should be done before and at least monthly during the course of therapy. Observe the client for jaundice.

### isoniazid (Izonid, Nydrazid, INH)

Isoniazid is a bactericidal agent that affects mycobacteria in the division phase. Exact mechanism of action is unknown but is believed to inhibit mycolic acid synthesis and cause cell wall disruption in susceptible organisms. Isoniazid is indicated for the treatment and prevention of tuberculosis.

It is well absorbed orally and is widely distributed throughout the body. The time to peak serum level is 1 to 2 hours for fast drug acetylators (metabolism) or 4 to 6 hours for slow drug acetylators. Half-life in fast acetylators is 0.5 to 1.6 hours, and slow acetylators' half-life is 2 to 5 hours. Isoniazid is metabolized in the liver, primarily by acetylation to inactive metabolites, some of which may be hepatotoxic. The rate of acetylation by the liver is genetically determined; slow acetylators have a decrease in hepatic N-acetyltransferase. Excretion is via the kidneys. For side effects/adverse reactions, see Table 61-4.

*Significant drug interactions.* When isoniazid is given concurrently with the following drugs, the following interactions may occur:

| Drug | Possible Effect and Management |
|------|-------------------------------|
| alcohol | Daily use of alcohol may result in increased isoniazid metabolism and increased risk of hepatotoxicity. Monitor clients as adjustment may be necessary. |
| alfentanil | Isoniazid inhibits liver metabolism. This effect may decrease the metabolism of alfentanil, leading to increased serum levels and duration of action. Monitor closely. |
| disulfiram | May increase incidence of CNS side effects such as ataxia, irritability, dizziness, or insomnia. Monitor closely, as dosage reduction or even discontinuation of disulfiram may be required. |
| hepatotoxic drugs | May increase potential for hepatotoxicity. Avoid concurrent drug administration. |
| ketoconazole, miconazole (parenteral), or rifampin | Isoniazid increase with ketoconazole may increase serum levels of ketoconazole; if both isoniazid and rifampin are given with ketoconazole, the serum levels of ketoconazole or rifampin have been reported to be undetectable. Therefore combining isoniazid or rifampin together or singly with ketoconazole or parenteral miconazole is not recommended. Rifampin with isoniazid may increase the potential for hepatotoxicity, especially in clients with liver impairment and/or in fast acetylators of isoniazid. Monitor closely for hepatotoxicity, especially during the first 90 days of therapy. |
| phenytoin | May result in impaired phenytoin metabolism, leading to increased serum levels and toxicity. Phenytoin dose may need to be adjusted. Monitor closely. |

*Dosage and administration.* The adult oral and parenteral (IM) prophylactic dose is 300 mg daily. The parenteral (IM) treatment dose when administered in combination with other agents is 5 mg/kg up to 300 mg, once daily. The oral treatment dose when given in combination with other agents to treat tuberculosis is 300 mg daily. The pediatric dose for prophylaxis orally and parenterally (IM) is 10 mg/kg, up to 300 mg daily. Treatment dose in combination with other agents is 10 to 20 mg/kg, up to 300 mg daily.

*Pregnancy safety.* Has not been established.

▷ **Nursing Management:**
**Isoniazid Therapy**

*Assessment.* Mycobacterial cultures and sensitivities should be done before and periodically throughout therapy to monitor progress.

As isoniazid is metabolized in the liver, this drug should be administered cautiously to clients with a history of alcoholism and/or hepatic function impairment.

The client receiving isoniazid should be assessed for the following nursing diagnoses: altered comfort related to rash (hypersensitivity), stomach pain, anorexia, nausea and vomiting, or numbness and tingling of the hands and feet related to peripheral neuritis; activity intolerance related to the development of hepatitis (weakness, lethargy); self-concept disturbance related to gynecomastia in males; and sensory-perceptual disturbances related to optic neuritis evidenced by blurred vision or vision loss.

*Intervention.* Administer with meals to minimize gastrointestinal distress. If antacids are required, administer at least 1 hour after isoniazid is given.

Pyridoxine may be prescribed concurrently to prevent peripheral neuritis. This may not be required for children if their dietary intake of vitamins is adequate.

*Education.* Encourage the client's compliance with the full course of isoniazid therapy.

Regular visits to the physician are necessary to monitor progress and for periodic eye examinations. Any symptoms related to changes in vision should be promptly reported to the physician.

Since alcohol and oral antacids decrease the effects of isoniazid, they should not be used in combination with it. Alcohol increases isoniazid metabolism, and antacids decrease its absorption from the gastrointestinal tract.

Clients with diabetes who test their urine with copper sulfate tests (Clinitest) may obtain false-positive test results. Other tests (Clinistix, Tes-Tape) for urine glucose are unaffected.

*Evaluation.* To monitor for hepatotoxic effects, AST (SGOT) and ALT (SGPT) should be done before and at least monthly during the course of therapy. The client should be observed for symptoms of jaundice. Clients over 50 years of age are more prone to the development of hepatitis. At the first signs of hepatotoxicity, isoniazid should be discontinued.

Although its incidence is rare, optic neuritis (blurred vision, vision loss, and/or eye pain) does occur. The client should have an ophthalmologic examination before and at the first indication of symptoms related to vision changes.

### pyrazinamide (PMS Pyrazinamide ✿, Tebrazid ✿)

The mechanism of action is unknown. Depending on concentration at site of action and susceptibility of the mycobacteria, it can be bacteriostatic or bactericidal. It is indicated in combination with other agents in the treatment of tuberculosis after failure with the primary drugs, such as streptomycin, isoniazid, rifampin, and ethambutol.

Pyrazinamide is well absorbed orally and is widely distributed in the body. The time to peak serum level is 2 hours, half-life is 9 to 10 hours. Pyrazinamide is primarily metabolized in the liver and excreted by the kidneys. For side effects/adverse reactions, see Table 61-4. It has no reported significant drug interactions.

The adult oral dose when given in combination with other agents in the treatment of tuberculosis is 5 to 8.75 mg/kg every 6 hours, up to a maximum dose of 3 g daily. It is not recommended for use in children.

Pregnancy safety has not been established.

## ▷Nursing Management: Pyrazinamide Therapy

**Assessment.** Mycobacterial cultures and sensitivity testing should be done before and periodically throughout therapy to monitor progress. Clients with impaired hepatic function should not receive pyrazinamide unless absolutely essential. It should be ascertained if the client has an intolerance for ethionamide, niacin, or isoniazid because there may be a cross-intolerance with pyrazinamide.

The client receiving pyrazinamide should be assessed for the following nursing diagnoses: altered comfort related to rash, photosensitivity, pain and swelling of the joints, especially the big toe, ankle and knee (gouty arthralgia), nausea and vomiting; and activity intolerance related to hepatotoxicity evidenced by unusual tiredness and weakness.

**Intervention.** Reduced dosages may be required for clients with impaired renal function.

**Education.** Encourage the client to remain compliant with the full course of therapy, which may take years. Regular visits to the health care provider are essential for monitoring progress.

Clients testing their urine with sodium nitroprusside urine ketone tests may have color interference and should use another test for urine ketones.

Teach clients measures to prevent gout, such as maintaining a fluid intake of 2500 ml daily, adjusting to optimum weight, and limiting intake of alcohol and foods high in purines, such as organ meats (liver, kidneys, hearts, sweetbreads), shellfish, and sardines.

**Evaluation.** In addition to the hepatic function studies required before and intermittently during therapy with other antitubercular drugs, serum uric acid determinations should be monitored to ensure that an acute episode of gout may be prevented. Observe clients for jaundice and symptoms of acute gouty arthralgia (pain and swelling of joints such as the big toe, knee, and ankle).

### rifampin (Rifadin, Rofact)

Rifampin is a broad-spectrum bactericidal antibiotic that blocks RNA transcription. It is indicated for the treatment of tuberculosis and for asymptomatic meningococcal carriers of Neisseria meningitidis. It is well absorbed orally and widely distributed in the body. Rifampin is lipid soluble, thus it may reach and kill intracellular and extracellular susceptible bacteria. Time to reach peak serum level is 1.5 to 4 hours, half-life is up to 5 hours. It is metabolized in the liver and excreted primarily in the feces. For side effects/adverse reactions, see Table 61-4.

**Significant drug interactions.** When rifampin is given concurrently with the following drugs, the following interactions may occur:

| Drug | Possible Effect and Management |
|---|---|
| alcohol | Daily usage of alcohol may increase the risk of rifampin-induced hepatotoxicity and increase rate of rifampin metabolism. Monitor closely, as dosage adjustments may be necessary. |
| adrenocorticoids, glucocorticoids, and mineralocorticoids, anticoagulants, oral coumarin or indandione, corticotropin, digitalis glycosides, disopyramide, or quinidine | Rifampin increases levels of liver-metabolizing enzymes and therefore may decrease the effectiveness of these medications, which are metabolized by liver. Monitor closely, as dosage adjustments may be needed. (Except for digoxin—a cardiac glycoside—because liver plays small role in its metabolism.) |
| estrogen-containing oral contraceptives, estramustine, or estrogens | Decreases effectiveness due to increased liver metabolism of estrogen. May result in menstrual irregularities, spotting, and unplanned pregnancies. Advise clients of the possible effects when these drugs are combined and advise alternative contraception. |
| isoniazid or ketoconazole (oral) or miconazole (parenteral) | Increased risk for hepatotoxicity. See comments under isoniazid. |
| methadone | May decrease the effectiveness of methadone, which may induce methadone withdrawal in dependent clients. Monitor closely, as dosage adjustments may be necessary during and after rifampin therapy. |

**Dosage and administration.** The adult oral dose in combination with other agents to treat tuberculosis is 600 mg daily. To treat asymptomatic *Neisseria meningitidis* carriers, the dose is 600 mg orally daily for 4 days. For children 5 years and over, the dose is 10 to 20 mg/kg daily. For asymptomatic *Neisseria meningitidis* carriers, the dose is 10 mg/kg orally every 12 hours for four doses.

**Pregnancy safety.** Has not been established.

### ▷Nursing Management: Rifampin Therapy

**Assessment.** Mycobacterial cultures and sensitivity testing should be done before and periodically throughout therapy to monitor progress. Clients with impaired hepatic function should not receive rifampin unless absolutely essential.

The client receiving rifampin should be assessed for the following nursing diagnoses: altered comfort related to rash (hypersensitivity), "flu-like" syndrome, nausea and vomiting; altered bowel elimination (diarrhea); risk for infection related to fungal overgrowth evidenced by sore mouth and tongue; risk for physiologic injury related to hepatitis and blood dyscrasias; and altered urinary elimination related to interstitial nephritis evidenced by greatly decreased frequency of urination and amount of urine.

**Intervention.** Reduced dosages may be required for clients with impaired renal function.

**Education.** Encourage the client to complete the full course of therapy, which may take years.

There may be a reddish brown discoloration of urine, feces, saliva, sputum, sweat, and tears. Clients should be reassured that this effect is not hazardous. However, clients that wear soft contact lens should be alerted that this same effect may permanently color the lens.

Women taking oral contraceptives who are also receiving rifampin should be cautioned to use an alternate form of contracption.

Clients should be advised to avoid alcoholic beverages while taking rifampin because it increases the risk of hepatotoxicity. Rifampin is to be taken with a full glass of water to minimize gastrointestinal irritation.

Caution the client, too, that rifampin may cause drowsiness and to avoid hazardous tasks involving mental alertness until the response to the drug has been ascertained.

*Evaluation.* In addition to the hepatic function studies required before and intermittently during therapy with other antitubercular drugs, serum uric acid determinations should be monitored to ensure that an acute episode of gout may be prevented. Clients should be observed for jaundice as well as symptoms of acute gouty arthralgia (pain and swelling of joints such as the big toe, knee, and ankle).

Regular visits to the health care provider are essential for monitoring progress.

### streptomycin sulfate injection

Streptomycin is a aminoglycoside antibiotic that is poorly absorbed from the gastrointestinal tract; therefore it is given intramuscularly. It was one of the first effective agents used in the late 1940s to treat tuberculosis, and it still is an important agent in managing severe tuberculosis. Like the other aminoglycosides, its major toxicities include ototoxicity and nephrotoxicity, especially when given to clients with impaired renal function or with other medications with the same toxicities. See Chapter 59 for detailed information on the aminoglycosides.

The adult dose for streptomycin when given with other antitubercular agents is 1 g IM daily. As soon as possible, reduce dose to 1 g, two or three times weekly. For geriatric clients, the dose is 500 to 750 mg daily, in combination with other antitubercular agents. For children, the dose is 20 mg/kg daily, in combination with other antitubercular agents. Maximum daily dose is 1 g. If used during pregnancy, monitor closely because irreversible deafness in children has been reported.

## AMEBIASIS

**Amebiasis** is an infection of the large intestine produced by a protozoan parasite, *Entamoeba histolytica*. This infestation is found worldwide but is prevalent and severe in tropical areas. It also has been detected in poorly sanitized areas, including some rural communities, Indian reservations, and migrant farm camps. Transmission is usually through ingestion of cysts (fecal to oral route) from contaminated food or water or from person-to-person contact. Poor personal hygiene can increase the spread of this parasite.

### Life Cycle of Ameba

The protozoan has two stages in its life cycle: (1) the trophozoite (vegetative ameba), which is the active, motile form, and (2) the cyst, or inactive, drug-resistant form that appears in intestinal excretion. The *trophozoite stage* is capable of ameboid motion and sexual activity. Because of its susceptibility to injury, it generally succumbs to an unfavorable environment. However, under certain circumstances, the trophozoite protects itself by entering the *cystic stage*. During this phase the protozoan becomes inactive by surrounding itself with a resistant cell wall within which it can survive for a long time, even in an unsuitable environment.

The complete life cycle of the ameba occurs in humans, the main host. It begins by ingestion of cysts that are present on hands, food, or water contaminated by feces. On reaching the stomach the hydrochloric acid does not destroy the swallowed cysts, but instead they pass unharmed into the small intestine. The digestive juices penetrate the cystic walls, and the trophozoites are released. The motile amebae later pass into the colon, where they live and multiply for a time, feeding on the bacterial flora of the gut. The presence of bacteria is essential for their survival. Finally, before excretion, the trophozoites move toward the terminal end of the bowel and again become encysted. After the cysts are eliminated in the feces, they remain viable and infective. Unfortunately, the cycle may begin again when the cysts appearing in fecal excretion are ingested through contamination of food or water.

The parasite causing amebiasis replicates in three major locations: (1) the lumen of the bowel, (2) the intestinal mucosa, and (3) extraintestinal sites. Thus amebiasis is classified according to its primary site of action: intestinal amebiasis, where amebic activity is restricted to the bowel lumen or intestinal mucosa, or extraintestinal amebiasis, where parasitic invasion occurs outside the intestine.

*Intestinal amebiasis.* Intestinal amebiasis may be manifested as an asymptomatic intestinal infection or a symptomatic intestinal infection that may be mild, moderate, or severe.

*Asymptomatic intestinal amebiasis.* In asymptomatic intestinal amebiasis the action of the parasite is restricted to the lumen of the bowel. The individual is asymptomatic but becomes a carrier of the disease by passing mature cysts of the parasite in formed stools. Outside the body the cysts can live for several weeks, surviving dry, freezing, or high temperature conditions. By this means the infection is transmitted from person to person by flies or contaminated food or water. Ordinary concentrations of chlorine in water purification do not destroy the cysts. If the carrier fails to follow any drug treatment, serious gastrointestinal pathologic problems eventually develop. Occasionally mild symptoms exist; they include vague abdominal pain, nausea, flatulence, fatigue, and nervousness.

*Symptomatic intestinal amebiasis.* Symptomatic amebiasis occurs when the trophozoites in the lumen of the
bowel penetrate the mucosal lining of the colon. After they
multiply and thrive on bacterial flora, a large infestation
occurs, producing diarrhea and abdominal pain. The increased loss of fluid may cause prostration. In addition,
ulcerative colitis may result. This state of the disease is
called intestinal amebiasis and is usually diagnosed as mild,
moderate, or severe according to the intensity of the symptoms and the extent of the disease.

*Extraintestinal amebiasis.* The term "extraintestinal
amebiasis" means that the parasites have migrated to other
parts of the body, such as the liver or occasionally the spleen,
lungs, or brain. When the parasites are in the liver, necrotic
foci develop because of the parasites' destructive effect on
tissues. When there is liver involvement, the terms "liver
abscess" and "hepatic amebiasis" are usually used.

## Antiamebiasis Agents

Drugs for the treatment of amebiasis are classified according
to the site of the previously described amebic action. Luminal amebicides act primarily in the bowel lumen and are
generally ineffective against parasites in the bowel wall or
tissues. Tissue amebicides are drugs that act primarily in
the bowel wall, liver, and other extraintestinal tissues. No
single drug is effective for both types of amebiasis; therefore
a luminal and extraluminal (tissue) amebicide or combination therapy is often prescribed.

### emetine hydrochloride

Emetine is a potent amebicide that is highly effective
against the trophozoites (vegetative) forms of *Entamoeba
histolytica*. Emetine blocks protein synthesis by inhibiting
attachment of RNA to the ribosomes. The drug acts primarily on the intestinal and extraintestinal parasites.

It is indicated for the treatment of acute amebic dysentery
or acute intestinal amebiasis and the treatment of extraintestinal amebiasis, amebic abscesses, and amebic hepatitis.

Emetine is administered parenterally (IM, SC) and is
distributed to the liver, lungs, spleen, and kidney. High
concentrations in the liver with insignificant levels in the
intestinal tract may account for the greater success in treating
hepatic than in intestinal amebiasis. Some of the drug is
excreted in the urine in 20 to 40 minutes; the remainder is
eliminated very slowly, with some remaining in the tissues
for 40 to 60 days after administration. For this reason, the
potential for cumulative toxic reactions is a constant danger.
This drug is a potentially dangerous drug that requires strict
medical supervision and close monitoring. The reader
should refer to a current reference source or package insert
for complete information before using this medication.

For side effects/adverse reactions, see Table 61-5. No
significant drug interactions have been reported with emetine.

Deep subcutaneous injection is the preferred method of
administration although it may also be given intramuscularly. Some authorities recommend a dose of 1 mg/kg/day,
not to exceed 65 mg/day or 10 days of therapy (total dose
of 650 mg). If therapy needs to be repeated, wait at least
6 weeks before starting another course of therapy.

In *children*, use *only* in very severe dysentery that cannot

---

**AMEBICIDE INDICATIONS**

**Intestinal Amebiasis**

emetine HCl
iodoquinol
metronidazole
paromomycin

**Extraintestinal Amebiasis**

chloroquine
emetine HCl
metronidazole

---

**TABLE 61-5**   Amebicides: side effects/adverse reactions

| Drug | Side effect* | Adverse reactions† |
|------|-------------|-------------------|
| emetine | Muscle aching, stiffness, nausea, vomiting, headache, diarrhea, dizziness | Toxic reactions may occur at any dose. Cardiotoxic effects, increased heart rate, precordial pain, ECG disturbances, congestive heart failure, gallop rhythm, severe hypotension, extreme weakness |
| iodoquinol | Most frequent: diarrhea, nausea, vomiting, abdominal pain<br>Less frequent: dizziness, headaches, pruritus of rectum | Less frequent: chills, increased temperature, rash, hives, pruritus, neck swelling<br>Chronic use of high doses: visual disturbances, ataxia, increased tiredness, muscle pain<br>Children with chronic, high-dose therapy: eye pain, decreased visual acuity; pain, tingling, or weakness in hands or feet |
| paromomycin | Nausea, vomiting, diarrhea | Stomach cramps, hearing loss, dizziness, tinnitus |

*If side effects continue, increase, or disturb the client, inform the physician.
†If adverse reactions occur, contact physicians because medical intervention may be necessary.

be controlled by other amebicides. Under 8 years old, do not exceed 10 mg/day; over 8 years old, do not exceed 20 mg/day. For amebic hepatitis or abscesses, administer for 10 days.

*Do not give this drug intravenously, as this route is dangerous and contraindicated.*

Pregnancy safety has been established at FDA category X.

▷ **Nursing Management:**
**Emetine Hydrochloride Therapy**

***Assessment.*** Emetine is contraindicated in individuals with cardiac or renal disease, except those with amebic hepatitis or abscess not controlled by chloroquine. It should not be used during pregnancy or in children except those with severe dysentery not responsive to other amebicidal agents. Do not repeat therapy in clients who have received a course of treatment less than 6 to 8 weeks previously.

Use emetine with caution in elderly or debilitated clients. Discontinue medication if tachycardia, hypotension, muscular weakness, or dyspnea occurs.

The client receiving emetine should be assessed for the following nursing diagnoses: altered comfort related to pain at injection site, headache, muscle aching and stiffness, nausea and vomiting; altered bowel elimination (diarrhea); activity intolerance related to hypotension; and decreased cardiac output related to cardiotoxic effects evidenced by increased heart rate, gallop rhythm, ECG disturbances, and precordial pain.

***Intervention.*** Emetine is administered in a hospital, and bed rest is indicated for the course of therapy and for several days after emetine is discontinued. Treatment is usually limited to 10 days. If necessary, a course of therapy may be repeated only after a 6- to 8-week rest period.

Administer medication by deep subcutaneous or intramuscular injection. Aspirate syringe before injecting drug to avoid inadvertent intravenous administration, which can result in dangerous toxic effects. Rotate injection site to prevent local irritation and swelling.

When preparing emetine for parenteral use, avoid contact with eyes or mucous membranes, as the drug is irritating.

Monitor pulse and blood pressure several times a day. Perform ECG before administering emetine to use as a baseline; repeat after the fifth dose, on completion of therapy, and 1 week later. ECG pattern resembles that of myocardial infarction (e.g., ST elevation, T-wave inversion, Q-T interval prolongation). These changes occur about 7 days following drug administration and are reversible, with complete return to normal in about 6 weeks. If tachycardia occurs, anticipate the appearance of ECG abnormalities.

***Education.*** Because the drug is cardiotoxic, advise client to avoid strenuous exercise for several weeks following termination of therapy. Teach client meticulous personal hygiene to avoid reinfection. Stress the importance of handwashing and of sanitary disposal of feces. Family members should also observe proper hygiene.

***Evaluation.*** Observe client for unusual symptoms such as muscle stiffness, restlessness, fatigue, or pain in the neck or upper extremities. Report these signs to the physician, for the drug may need to be discontinued.

Monitor intake and output. Report oliguria or any other change in renal function. Keep a record of the character of stools: number, consistency, unusual odor, presence of mucus or other abnormal matter.

Deliver still-warm stool specimen to the laboratory so that ameba can be identified. Inform client that stool specimens must be examined periodically for up to 3 months following therapy to ensure continued elimination of ameba. Because clients with acute amebic dysentery frequently become asymptomatic carriers, it is essential to check family members and other contacts.

**iodoquinol (Diquinol, Yodoxin)**

Iodoquinol's mechanism of action is unknown. It is an amebicidal agent that is poorly absorbed from the intestinal tract; thus it produces its effect against the trophozoites of *E. histolytica* at the site of intestinal infestation. It is indicated for the treatment of intestinal amebiasis in asymptomatic carriers of *E. histolytica*.

Following administration and local effect, it is excreted in the feces. For side effects/adverse reactions, see Table 61-5. No significant drug interactions have been reported with its use.

The adult oral dose is 630 or 650 mg three times a day, after meals for 20 days. The pediatric dose is 13.3 mg/kg orally three times daily after meals for 20 days. Pregnancy safety has not been established.

▷ **Nursing Management:**
**Iodoquinol Therapy**

***Assessment.*** Iodoquinol should be used with caution if the client has the following preexisting conditions: intolerance to iodine, pentaquine, or primaquin; optic neuripathy; thyroid, hepatic, or renal disease.

Intake and output should be documented, as well as frequency and character of stools. Fresh, warm stools should be monitored for the presence of amebae. Diarrhea may occur the first few days of therapy with iodoquinol. Alert the physician if it continues for more than 3 days.

Clients should have an ophthalmologic examination before and periodically during therapy.

The client receiving iodoquinol should be assessed for the following nursing diagnoses: altered comfort related to rash (hypersensitivity), headache, nausea and vomiting, or numbness and tingling of the hands and feet related to the development of peripheral neuropathy; altered bowel elimination (diarrhea); activity intolerance related to light-headedness and dizziness; and visual disturbances related to optic atrophy, optic neuritis, or subacute myelooptic neuropathy.

***Intervention.*** Administer drug with meals to minimize gastrointestinal irritation. The course of therapy may be repeated if necessary only after a 2- to 3-week rest period.

For ease of administration to children and for clients that may have difficulty swallowing, tablets may be crushed and mixed with applesauce, gelatin dessert, or ice cream.

*Education.* Clients should be instructed in proper hygiene to prevent reinfection. Inform the client that any results of thyroid function studies completed within 6 months of the discontinuance of iodoquinol may be distorted.

*Evaluation.* The development of a neurologic disorder such as myelooptic neuropathy has been implicated in treatment with prolonged high doses. This is characterized by the presence of blurred vision, optic atrophy, optic neuritis, and peripheral neuropathy (numbness, pain, or weakness in hands or feet).

Iodoquinol can cause thyroid enlargement, and it interferes with certain thyroid function tests by increasing protein-bound serum iodine levels. The drug contains approximately 64% iodine.

In children, the administration of iodoquinol for chronic diarrhea has been responsible for causing optic atrophy and permanent loss of vision. Thus administration of this drug is not advocated for treatment or prophylaxis of "traveler's diarrhea" or for use in chronic nonspecific diarrhea.

The drug is contraindicated for use in clients who have liver disease or who are hypersensitive to iodine.

### paromomycin (Humatin)

Paromomycin is both an amebicidal and an antibacterial agent. The drug is a broad-spectrum aminoglycoside antibiotic that is produced from cultures of *Streptomyces rimosus*. Its antibacterial properties are similar to those of kanamycin and neomycin. Paromomycin acts directly on intestinal amebae and on bacteria such as *Salmonella* and *Shigella*. Because the drug is poorly absorbed from the gastrointestinal tract, it exerts no effect on systemic infections such as extraintestinal amebiasis.

It is indicated for the treatment of acute and chronic intestinal amebiasis and for adjunct therapy in management of hepatic coma.

Paromomycin is poorly absorbed from the intestinal tract; thus most of the drug is excreted in the feces. For side effects/adverse reactions, see Table 61-5. Paromomycin is an aminoglycoside; therefore the drug interactions possible with this family of medications may also occur with paromomycin. See aminoglycosides (antibiotic) in Chapter 59.

The adult and pediatric dose to treat intestinal amebiasis is 25 to 35 mg/kg daily, in three divided doses given with meals for 5 to 10 days. To manage hepatic coma, the adult dose is 4 g daily in divided doses at regular intervals for 5 or 6 days. Pregnancy safety has not been established.

### ▷ Nursing Management: Paromomycin Therapy

*Assessment.* Paromomycin is contraindicated for use in intestinal obstruction and in ulcerative bowel lesions because of possible systemic absorption. Notify the physician if ringing of the ears or dizziness occurs.

The client receiving paromomycin should be assessed for the following nursing diagnoses: altered comfort related to nausea and vomiting; altered bowel elimination (diarrhea); activity intolerance related to lightheadedness and dizziness; and auditory disturbances related to tinnitus and hearing loss.

*Intervention.* Administer after meals to minimize gastrointestinal distress.

*Education.* Teach the client proper personal hygiene to prevent reinfection.

*Evaluation.* Examine fresh, warm stools for the presence of amebae at weekly intervals for 6 weeks after the end of therapy and monthly for 2 years to indicate that the client is not harboring the parasite.

### Other Drugs

Metronidazole is an antibacterial, antiprotozoal, and anthelmintic agent. When used in the treatment of invasive amebiasis, it is recommended that it be administered with a lumenal amebicide, such as iodoquinol or paromomycin. Mechanism of action is unknown, but it appears to be due to a direct effect on the amebicides. For additional drug information, see the antibiotic chapter.

Chloroquine phosphate and chloroquine hydrochloride are also used to treat extraintestinal amebiasis. See drug monograph for further information on these drugs. Dehydroemetine (Mebadin) and diloxanide furoate (Furamide) are also antiinfective agents used to treat amebiasis but are only available from the Centers for Disease Control (Parasitic Disease Drug Service, Division of Host Factors, Center for Infectious Disease, Atlanta, GA 30333), as they are considered investigational agents.

## OTHER PROTOZOAN DISEASES

Several other protozoan diseases are widespread throughout the world and may be encountered in medical practice in the United States. In this section each disease and the primary antiprotozoan agent used in its treatment will be described.

### Balantidiasis

*Balantidium coli,* which causes **balantidiasis,** is the largest of the protozoa that infest the lumen of the large intestine. The organism performs ciliated movement and reproduces asexually and sexually. It feeds on intestinal bacteria and can also invade the intestinal wall by penetrating the mucosa. The organism is capable of producing lesions similar to those caused by *E. histolytica.* The symptoms are nausea, vomiting, abdominal pain, and diarrhea. The organism also forms cysts, which are eliminated with the feces. Some individuals become asymptomatic carriers. The pharmacologic treatment of the disease is emetine and iodoquinol.

## Giardiasis

The distribution of **giardiasis,** caused by *Giardia lamblia,* is worldwide. The parasite is similar to *E. hisolytica* in that it appears in two forms. The motile trophozoites exist and multiply in the upper small intestine, the duodenum, jejunum, and occasionally the biliary tract of the human. The cysts develop in the gastrointestinal tract and are usually expelled with the feces.

*G. lamblia* is transmitted by ingesting water or food contaminated with fecal matter that contains cysts. The incubation period is 1 month. Symptoms include anorexia, nausea, diarrhea, and foul-smelling, bulky stools. However, the disease is not life-threatening. Sporadic outbreaks of the disease have developed in various parts of the United States. Old, overworked filtration systems allow the organisms to enter the water supply. Giardiasis is treated with metronidazole.

## Pneumocystosis

**Pneumocystosis** is a disease found commonly in individuals who have impaired immune systems caused by malignancies, collagen vascular diseases, AIDS, or immunosuppressive therapy. It is caused by the parasite *Pneumocystis carinii.* Characteristically the disease's symptoms initially are vague and generalized and include a dry cough, dyspnea or tachypnea or both, chest discomfort, and marked pallor. Cyanosis is the most common and consistent finding. If untreated, the disease progresses into interstitial plasma cell pneumonia, where its infiltration into the lungs and lung tissue causes a honeycombed appearance. Fatality is 50% or more of individuals who do not receive treatment at this advanced stage of the disease. Children are more susceptible to pneumocystosis than are adults. The drug of choice for treatment is trimethoprim/sulfamethoxazole. Clients who do not respond to this drug or who have a severe adverse reaction to it are often given pentamidine. See Chapter 66, which deals with immunosuppressants and immunomodulators.

## Trypanosomiasis

**Trypanosomiasis** is not commonly found in the United States but is found extensively in other parts of the world. There are two types of trypanosomiasis, the African variety and the South American variety.

African trypanosomiasis (sleeping sickness) is caused by *Trypanosoma gambiense* or *T. rhodesiense.* These protozoans are transmitted from host to host by the bite of the tsetse fly. The organism then invades the lymphatic system and causes intermittent attacks of fever, lymphadenopathy, hepatosplenomegaly, dyspnea, and tachycardia. This is called the hemolytic stage of the disease and is treated with suramin sodium, the drug of choice.

As the disease progresses into the central nervous system, the victim experiences headaches, disturbances in coordination, mental dullness, apathy, and eventually constant sleep, resulting in emaciation and death. This latter state, with involvement of the central nervous system, has been treated effectively with melarsoprol, an investigational drug available from the Centers for Disease Control.

The South American variety of trypanosomiasis is often referred to as Chagas' disease. It is caused by the protozoan *T. cruzi* and is transmitted by the bite of reduviid bugs infected with these parasites. The disease may be asymptomatic or symptomatic, varying from region to region. Early symptoms may be local swelling (chagoma) at the site of the insect bite, rash, fever, and edema of eyelids and face. The chronic form of the disease may result in visceromegaly, cardiopathy, or meningoencephalitis resulting in death, or the individual may remain asymptomatic. *T. cruzi* seems to have an affinity for cardiac parenchymal cells and nerve cells in the mesenteric plexus.

Chagas' disease is resistant to most forms of therapy. The drug nifurtimox has shown activity against both extracellular and intracellular parasites that no other drug has demonstrated.

All the agents now used in treating both African and South American trypanosomiasis are severely toxic. As a result, their usefulness in treating these diseases has been limited. All three agents used in treating trypanosomiasis are available from the Centers for Disease Control.

## Toxoplasmosis

**Toxoplasmosis** is caused by an intracellular parasite, *Toxoplasma gondii.* This parasite is found worldwide and infests a variety of animals, including humans. It is often harbored in the host with no evidence of the disease. Toxoplasmosis is contracted by ingesting cysts found in inadequately cooked raw meat or by accidentally ingesting cysts from cat feces.

The most common form of the disease in the United States is usually subclinical. Symptomatically the individual may experience lymphadenopathy, fever, and occasionally a rash on the palms and soles. The most serious complication of toxoplasmosis is meningoencephalitis. Toxoplasmosis is treated with a combination of sulfadiazine and pyrimethamine, both of which alter the folic acid cycle of the *Toxoplasma* organism, resulting in its death. The oral dosage of pyrimethamine is 25 mg/day for 3 to 4 weeks; the dosage of sulfadiazine is 4 g/day for 3 to 4 weeks.

## Trichomoniasis

**Trichomoniasis** is a disease of the vagina caused by *Trichomonas vaginalis.* Its characteristic presentation consists of a wet, inflamed vagina, a "strawberry" cervix, and a thin, yellow, frothy malodorous discharge. Usually both sexual partners are infected by this organism, which can be identified microscopically from semen, prostatic fluid, or exudate from the vagina. Infections often recur, which indicates that the protozoans persist in extravaginal foci, male urethra, or the periurethral glands and ducts of both sexes. Metronidazole is the drug of choice, and treatment must be given simultaneously to both partners involved for cure. Two other agents—tinidazole and nimorazole—are being used successfully in its treatment in other countries.

## HELMINTHIASIS

The disease-producing **helminths** are classified as metazoa, or multicellular animal parasites. Unlike the protozoa, they are large organisms that have a complex cellular structure and that feed on host tissue. They may be present in the gastrointestinal tract, but several types also penetrate the tissues, and some undergo developmental changes during which they wander extensively in the host. Because most anthelmintics used today are highly effective against specific parasites, the organism must be accurately identified before treatment is started, usually by finding the parasite ova or

larvae in the feces, urine, blood sputum, or tissues of the host.

Parasitic infestations do not necessarily cause clinical manifestations, although they may be injurious for a number of reasons.

1. Worms may cause mechanical injury to the tissues and organs. Roundworms in large numbers may cause obstruction in the intestine; filariae may block lymphatic channels and cause massive edema; and hookworms often cause extensive damage to the wall of the intestine and considerable loss of blood.
2. Toxic substances produced by the parasite may be absorbed by the host.
3. The tissues of the host may be traumatized by the presence of the parasite and made more susceptible to bacterial infections.
4. Heavy infestation with worms will rob the host of food. This is particularly significant in children.

Helminths that are parasitic to humans are classified as (1) Platyhelminthes (flatworms), which include two subclasses: cestodes (tapeworms) and trematodes (flukes), and (2) Nematoda (roundworms). See Table 61-6.

**TABLE 61-6**   Drugs used in treatment of helminthiasis

| Disease | Organism | Drug of choice | Alternate choice |
|---|---|---|---|
| CESTODES (TAPEWORMS) | | | |
| Diphyllobothriasis | *Diphyllobothrium latum* (fish tapeworm) | Niclosamide* | Paromomycin |
| Hymenolepiasis | *Hymenolepis nana* (dwarf tapeworm) | Niclosamide* | Paromomycin |
| Taeniasis | *Taenia saginata* (beef tapeworm) | Niclosamide* | Paromomycin |
| Taeniasis | *Taenia solium* (pork tapeworm) | Niclosamide,* Quinacrine | Paromomycin |
| TREMATODES (FLUKES) | | | |
| Fascioliasis | *Fasciola hepatica* (liver fluke) | Bithionol* | None |
| Fasciolopsiasis | *Fasciolopsis buski* (intestinal fluke) | Hexylresorcinol† | None |
| Paragonimiasis | *Paragonimus westermani* (lung fluke) | Bithionol* | None |
| Schistosomiasis *(Bilharziasis):* | *Schistosoma* (blood fluke): | | |
| Urinary *Bilharziasis* | S. *haematobium* | Metrifonate* | Niridazole* |
| Oriental schiztosomiasis | S. *japonicum* | Niridazole* | Antimony sodium dimercapto-succinate* |
| Intestinal or hepatosplenic *Bilharziasis* | S. *mansoni* | Niridazole* or oxamniquine | Antimony sodium dimercapto-succinate* |
| NEMATODES (ROUNDWORMS) | Intestinal roundworms: | | |
| Ascariasis | *Ascaris lumbricoides* (giant roundworm) | Pyrantel pamoate or Mebendazole | Piperazine citrate |

*Available only from the Parasitic Disease Service, Centers for Disease Control, Atlanta, GA 30333.
†Not available in the United States.

*Continued.*

**TABLE 61-6**   Drugs used in treatment of helminthiasis—cont'd

| Disease | Organism | Drug of choice | Alternate choice |
|---|---|---|---|
| NEMATODES (ROUNDWORMS)—cont'd | | | |
| Enterobiasis | *Enterobius vermicularis* (pinworm) | Pyrantel pamoate or Mebendazole | Piperazine citrate |
| Uncinariasis | *Necator americanus* (hookworm) | Pyrantel pamoate or Mebendazole | Thiabendazole |
| Strongyloidiasis | *Strongyloides stercolaris* (threadworm) | Thiabendazole | |
| Trichuriasis | *Trichuris trichiura* (whipworm) | Mebendazole | None |
| TISSUE ROUNDWORMS | | | |
| Cutaneous larva migrans (creeping eruptions) | *Ancylostoma braziliense* | Thiabendazole | |
| Dracunculoida | *Dracunculus medinensis* (guinea worm) | Niridazole* | Metronidazole |
| FILARIAL NEMATODES | | | |
| Filariasis | *Brugia (W.) malayi* | Diethylcarbamazine | None |
| No common name | *Dipetalonema perstans* | Diethylcarbamazine | |
| Loiasis | *Loa loa* | Diethylcarbamazine | |
| Filariasis | *Wuchereria bancrofti* | Diethylcarbamazine | |
| Tropical eosinophilia | Tropical pulmonary eosinophilia | Diethylcarbamazine | |
| Onchocerciasis | *Onchocerca volvulus* | Diethylcarbamazine plus Suramin* | |
| Trichinosis | *Trichinella spiralis* (pork roundworm) | Thiabendazole plus steroids for severe symptoms | Mebendazole |

## Platyhelminths (Flatworms)

**Cestodes.** Cestodes are tapeworms, of which there are four varieties: (1) *Taenia saginata* (beef tapeworm), (2) *T. solium* (pork tapeworm), (3) *Diphyllobothrium latum* (fish tapeworm), and (4) *Hymenolepis nana* (dwarf tapeworm). As indicated by the name of the worm, the parasite enters the intestine by way of improperly cooked beef, pork, or fish or from contaminated food, as in the case of the dwarf tapeworm.

The cestodes are segmented flatworms with a head or scolex, which has hooks or suckers that are used to attach to tissues, and a number of segments, or proglottids, which in some cases may extend for 20 to 30 feet in the bowel. Drugs affecting the scolex allow expulsion of the organisms from the intestine. Each of the proglottids contains both male and female reproductive units. When filled with fertilized eggs, they are expelled from the worm into the environment. Upon ingestion, the infected larvae develop into adults in the small intestine of the human. The larvae may travel to extraintestinal sites and enter other tissues such as the liver, muscle, and eye. The tapeworms, with the exception of the dwarf tapeworm, spend part of their life cycle in a host other than humans—pigs, fish, or cattle. The dwarf tapeworm does not require an intermediate host.

The tapeworm has no digestive tract and, therefore, it depends on the nutrients that are intended for the host. Subsequently, the victim suffers by eventually developing nutritional deficiency.

**Trematodes.** Trematodes, or flukes, are flat, nonsegmented parasites with suckers that attach to and feed on host tissue. The life cycle begins with the egg, which is passed into fresh water following fecal excretion from the body of the human host. The egg containing the embryo forms into a ciliated organism, the *miracidium*. In the presence of water the miracidium escapes from the egg and enters the intermediate host, the freshwater snail, which exists extensively in rice paddies and irrigation ditches. After entry, the fluke forms a cyst in the lungs of the snail. In the cyst, many organisms develop. They can penetrate other parts of the snail and grow into worms called *cercariae*. Eventually, the cercariae are released from the snail into the water, attaching themselves to blades of grass to encyst. A human, the final host, then becomes infected by the parasite.

When encysted organisms in snails or even fish and crabs are swallowed by humans, they develop into adult flukes in different structures of the body. The flukes therefore are classified according to the type of tissues they invade. Following ingestion, the eggs of *Schistosoma haematobium* appear in the urinary bladder and cause inflammation of the urogenital system. This can result in chronic cystitis and hematuria. Infestations with *S. japonicum* and *S. mansoni* produce intestinal disturbance with resultant ulceration and necrosis of the rectum. *S. japonicum* is more concentrated in the veins of the small intestine. If the liver and spleen become infected, the disease is usually fatal. *S. mansoni* prefers the portal veins that drain the large intestine, particularly the sigmoid colon and rectum. Unlike the other parasites, the cercariae of *S. mansoni* are not ingested but burrow through the skin, especially between the toes of the human host who is standing in contaminated water. They then make their way to the portal system, where they mature into adult flukes.

Schistosomiasis (bilharziasis) occurs endemically in Africa, Asia, South America, and the Caribbean islands. The disease can be controlled largely by eliminating the intermediate host, the snail. Travelers to these areas must avoid contact with contaminated water for drinking, bathing, or swimming. Unfortunately, the disease has been introduced in the United States by immigrants or individuals who have traveled to the endemic areas.

## Nematoda (Roundworms)

Nematoda are nonsegmented, cylindrical worms that consist of a mouth and complete digestive tract. The adults reside in the human intestinal tract; there is no intermediate host. Two types of nematode infection exist in the human: the egg form and the larval form.

***Egg infective form.*** *Ascaris lumbricoides* is a large nematode (about 30 cm in length) and is known as the "roundworm of humans." The adult *Ascaris* usually resides in the upper end of the small intestine of the human, where it feeds on semidigested foods. The fertilized egg, when excreted with feces, can survive in the soil for a long time. When inadvertently ingested by another host, the embryos escape from the eggs and mature into adults in the host. To prevent the disease, proper sanitary conditions and meticulous personal habits must be observed.

Infection with *Enterobius vermicularis*, or pinworm, is highly prevalent among children and adults in the U.S. Adult pinworms reside in the large intestine. However, the female migrates to the anus, depositing her eggs around the skin of the anal region. This causes intense itching and can be noted especially in children. Diagnosis is made with the Graham sticky tape method. Ingestion of excreted eggs can infect an individual. In addition, eggs that contaminate clothing, bedding, furniture, and other items may be responsible for continuing the reinfection of an individual and initiating the infection of others.

***Larval infective form.*** *Necator americanus* (New World) or *Ancylostoma duodenale* (Old World) hookworms are somewhat similar in action. They reside in the small intestine of humans. When the eggs are excreted in the feces, the larvae hatch in the soil. The larvae can penetrate the skin of humans, particularly through the soles of the feet, producing dermatitis (ground itch). On entry into the small intestine, they develop into adult worms. During the process they extravasate blood from the intestinal vessels and cause a profound anemia in the victim. The presence of eggs in the feces indicates a positive test for hookworm disease. This infection can be avoided by wearing shoes.

*Trichinella spiralis* is a small pork roundworm that causes trichinosis. In humans the disease begins by ingestion of insufficiently cooked pork or bear meat. On entry of encysted meat into the small intestine, the larvae are released from the cysts. Following maturation, the females develop eggs that later form into larvae. They then migrate by the bloodstream and the lymphatic system to the skeletal muscles and encyst. Encapsulation and eventually calcification of the cysts occur. Diagnosis of trichinosis is made by muscle biopsy, whereby microscopic examination reveals the presence of larvae. The disease is prevented by thoroughly cooking pork and bear meat before eating.

## Anthelmintic Agents

Anthelmintic drugs are used to rid the body of worms (helminths). Anthelmintics (*anti*, against; Gr. *helmins*, worm) are among the most primitive types of chemotherapy. It has been estimated that one third of the world's population is infested with these parasites.

### diethylcarbamazine (Hetrazan)

Diethylcarbamazine has a microfilaricidal effect; it increases the loss of microfilariae and inhibits the rate of embryogenesis from nematodes. It has no sterilizing effect on adult worms. It is indicated for the treatment of Bancroft's filariasis, loiasis, onchocerciasis and tropical eosinophilia.

It is absorbed after oral administration and is distributed to nonfatty tissues. Excretion is via the kidneys. The most frequently reported side effects include joint pains, increased weakness, headache, and dizziness. Less often reported are the symptoms of nausea and vomiting. The most frequently reported adverse reactions are facial swelling, especially around the eyes, and pruritis. Less often reported are elevated temperature, rash and painful, tender glands especially in the neck, armpits, or groin area. No significant drug interactions have been reported.

The adult dose for all indications except tropical eosinophilia is 2 to 3 mg/kg orally three times daily. For tropical eosinophilia, the dose is 6 mg/kg orally daily for 4 to 7 days. No dose has been established for use in children.

While pregnancy safety has not been established, it is generally not recommended for use during pregnancy as fetal damage in laboratory animals has been demonstrated.

▷ **Nursing Management: Diethylcarbamazine Therapy**

**Assessment.** Use with caution in children under 2 years of age.

The client receiving diethylcarbamazine should be assessed for the following nursing diagnoses: altered comfort related to headache, itching, and swelling of face, rash, and nausea and vomiting; altered bowel elimination (diarrhea); activity intolerance related to lightheadedness and dizziness; and visual disturbances related to night blindness, tunnel vision, and vision loss.

**Intervention.** For ease of administration, the tablet may be chewed, swallowed whole, or crushed and mixed with food. No dietary restrictions, laxatives, or posttreatment purging are required. A second course of therapy will be required if the client is not cured in 3 weeks.

Anticipate expulsion of roundworms in 1 to 2 days following initial therapy.

An individual with a recent history of malaria should be given an antimalarial agent before initiating diethylcarbamazine therapy. This prevents recurrence of a malarial attack.

In pinworm infestation, treat all family members because it is readily transmitted from person to person.

Collect stool specimen in clean, dry, and properly labeled container and send to laboratory. Do not contaminate specimen with water, urine, or chemicals because parasite may be destroyed. Collect pinworm specimen: wrap a transparent strip of cellophane (sticky side out) around a tongue blade and press against perianal area. Then place sticky side of tape on a glass slide and send to laboratory. Female worm emerges from the rectum during the night to lay eggs in the perianal area. This causes the client to become restless during sleep. The emerging worms can be seen at night with a flashlight.

**Education.** Emphasize the importance of following meticulous hygiene: washing hands before eating and after going to toilet; keeping hands or objects from mouth. Avoid walking barefoot to prevent hookworm. The larvae hatch in the soil and penetrate through the skin. Instruct client to take frequent showers rather than baths, to change underclothes, nightclothes, bedclothes, and towels daily, and to disinfect toilet facilities daily.

For treatment of filiaris, stress the importance of remaining under physician's care. Failure to follow drug regimen eventually can obstruct lymph flow, thereby producing hydrocele, elephantiasis of limbs, enlarged scrotum or breasts, and chyluria (milk-like urine).

**Evaluation.** If allergic reactions occur (swelling and itching of skin, fine papular rash, tenderness of lymph nodes,

headache, fever, tachycardia, conjunctivitis, uveitus), report to physician. Antihistamine therapy or corticosteroids are usually prescribed to relieve these symptoms. Ophthalmoscopic examinations are performed on clients treated for onchocerciasis. Report immediately any signs of itching or swelling of eyes. Corticosteroid eye drops may be administered for treatment of this condition.

### mebendazole (Vermox)

Mebendazole is a vermicidal and may also be ovicidal for most helminths. It causes degeneration of a parasite's cytoplasmic microtubules, which results in blocking glucose uptake in the helminth, leading to death of the helminth. It is indicated for the treatment of *Trichuris trichiura* (whipworm), *Enterobius vermicularis* (pinworm), *Ascaris lumbricoides* (roundworm), *Ancylostoma duodenale* (common hookworm), or *Necator americanus* (American hookworm), singly or in mixed infestations.

Mebendazole is poorly absorbed orally (5% to 10%) and is distributed to serum, cyst fluid, liver, hepatic cysts, and muscle tissues. It is highly protein bound with a half-life of 2.5 to 5.5 hours and is metabolized in the liver and excreted primarily in feces. The less frequent side effects reported include stomach pain or upset, diarrhea, nausea, and vomiting. In high doses neutropenia has been reported. No significant drug interactions have been reported.

The adult and pediatric dose (children 2 years and over) is 100 mg orally twice daily for 3 days. If necessary, this dose may be repeated in 2 to 3 weeks.

Pregnancy safety has been established at FDA category C.

▷ **Nursing Management: Mebendazole Therapy**

**Assessment.** The client receiving mebendazole should be assessed for the following nursing diagnoses: altered comfort related to headache, rash (hypersensitivity), nausea and vomiting; altered bowel elimination (diarrhea); and activity intolerance related to lightheadedness and dizziness.

**Intervention.** For ease of administration, tablets may be crushed and mixed with applesauce or other food. No dietary restrictions, laxatives, or posttreatment enemas are necessary.

**Education.** Stress the importance of handwashing and of sanitary disposal of feces. Instruct the client to wash the perianal area daily to prevent reinfestation. Underwear and bed linens should be changed daily. All family members should be treated at the same time.

### niclosamide (Niclocide)

Niclosamide affects the mitochondria of the cestode, inhibiting aerobic metabolism. It also impedes anaerobic metabolism, on which many cestodes depend for survival. Contact with the drug results in destruction of the scolex and proximal segments of the organism, the proglottids. The scolex, when loosened from the intestinal wall, is usually digested in the intestine. Consequently, identification of the worm in the feces cannot be made.

Niclosamide is indicated for the treatment of *Taenia saginata* (beef tapeworm), *Diphyllobothrium latum* (fish tapeworm), and *Hymenolepis nana* (dwarf tapeworm) infestations.

Niclosamide is poorly absorbed from the intestinal tract; thus the drug can exert its effect on intestinal helminths, the site of its action. Excretion is in the feces. The most frequently reported adverse reactions are stomach pain or distress, anorexia, nausea, and vomiting. Less frequent or rare adverse reactions include diarrhea, dizziness, sedation, pruritus of the rectum, rash, and a bad taste in the mouth. No significant drug interactions have been reported.

Niclosamide tablets should be thoroughly chewed and taken with water. The adult dose for *T. saginata* and *D. latum* (beef and fish tapeworms) is four tablets (2 g) as single dose; for *H. nana* (dwarf tapeworm), four tablets (2 g) daily for 1 week.

For young children, tablets may be crushed to a fine powder and a paste made with water. Take after a light meal such as breakfast.

For *T. saginata* and *D. latum* (beef and fish tapeworms) the dose for a child over 75 pounds is three tablets (1.5 g) as single dose; a child from 25 to 75 pounds, two tablets (1 g) as single dose.

For *Hymenolepis nana* (dwarf tapeworm) the dose for a child over 75 pounds is three tablets (1.5 g) on first day, then two tablets (1 g) daily for 6 days; between 25 and 75 pounds, two tablets (1 g) the first day, then one tablet (0.5 g) daily for next 6 days.

Pregnancy safety has been established at FDA category B.

▷ **Nursing Management:**
**Niclosamide Therapy**

*Assessment.* The safety for use in pregnancy has not been established. The drug should be used only if the potential benefit outweighs the risk to the fetus. It is not known whether niclosamide is excreted in breast milk. Since it is not absorbed in significant amounts from the gastrointestinal tract, the drug is unlikely to be excreted through this route.

Niclosamide should not be administered to clients who are hypersensitive to the drug.

The client receiving niclosamide should be assessed for the following nursing diagnoses: altered comfort related to headache, rash, nausea, and vomiting; altered bowel elimination (diarrhea); altered sleep pattern (drowsiness); and activity intolerance evidenced by lightheadedness and dizziness.

*Intervention.* Treatment may be administered on an outpatient basis.

Administer the drug after a light meal such as breakfast. No dietary restrictions are required before or after treatment.

Instruct client to chew tablet thoroughly and swallow with a small amount of water. For children crush the tablet to a fine powder and mix with a small amount of water to form paste. If the client is constipated, a mild laxative should be prescribed to ensure a normal bowel movement.

*Education.* Advise client to take the drug for the full course of therapy to prevent return of infection. Stress the importance of reporting progress to the physician. If there is no improvement, a second course of therapy may be required. Niclosamide destroys the tapeworm on contact while in the intestine. The killed worms (including the scolex) are passed in the stool and may not be seen. In the treatment of *T. solium* (pork tapeworm), a saline purge such as magnesium sulfate should be given 1 or 2 hours after the administration of niclosamide to prevent the development of cysticercosis in the intestinal tract. Moreover, the procedure provides a good possibility of expulsion of an intact scolex. Note that niclosamide has no effect on cysticercosis.

Because the drug may cause dizziness, warn individual about driving a motor vehicle or operating dangerous machinery.

Instruct client to observe strict hygiene (both personal and environmental) to prevent reinfection. This observance applies particularly to *H. nana* (dwarf tapeworm).

*Evaluation.* Stress the importance of followup studies; the client is considered cured only if stool examination results are negative for a minimum of 3 months. Stool examination is required 1 month and 3 months following drug regimen.

### oxamniquine (Vansil)

Oxamniquine is schistosomicidal against both immature and mature worms. It produces its effect by causing worms to shift from the mesenteric veins to the liver where they are then destroyed. Male schistosomes appear to be more susceptible to this drug than females, but after a successful treatment with this agent, the female schistosomes stops laying eggs. Oxaminiquine is indicated for the treatment of schistosomiasis.

It is well absorbed orally with a time to peak serum level of 1 to 1.5 hours. It is metabolized in the liver and excreted by the kidneys. It is usually well tolerated. Reported side effects include transitory dizziness, sedation, nausea, vomiting, stomach pain, anorexia, and headaches. No significant drug interactions are reported.

The adult oral dose is usually 15 mg/kg twice a day for 1 or 2 days, depending on the strain of organism. The pediatric dose is 10 to 15 mg/kg twice daily for 1 to 3 days, depending on the identified strain of schistosomiasis.

Pregnancy safety has been established at FDA category C.

▷ **Nursing Management:**
**Oxamniquine Therapy**

*Assessment.* Use oxamniquine with caution in individuals with a history of convulsive disorders.

The client receiving oxamniquine should be assessed for the following nursing diagnoses: altered comfort related to headache, rash, nausea, and vomiting; altered bowel elimination (diarrhea); altered sleep pattern related to drowsiness; hyperthermia; risk for injury related to seizures; altered thought processes related to hallucinations; and activity intolerance evidenced by lightheadedness and dizziness.

***Intervention.*** Administer after meals to minimize side effects such as dizziness, drowsiness, and gastrointestinal distress. Oxamniquine therapy does not require special preparation such as fasting, dietary restrictions, or enemas.

***Education.*** Caution the client to avoid hazardous tasks requiring mental alertness, such as driving, until the response to the drug has been ascertained.

Advise the client that oxamniquine causes a reddish orange discoloration of the urine that is harmless.

Encourage the client to complete the full course of therapy and to check with the health care provider if there is no improvement after completing a full course of therapy.

### piperazine (Vermizine)

Piperazine affects the musculature of the helminth, possibly by blocking the stimulating effects of acetylcholine at the myoneural junction. Accordingly, muscle paralysis of the roundworms makes them unable to maintain their position in the host. The paralyzed worms are then dislodged and expelled as a result of normal peristalsis.

Piperazine is indicated for treatment of enterobiasis (pinworms) and ascariasis (roundworm). It is absorbed orally, with some metabolism in the liver and excretion by the kidneys. The major side effects reported are gastrointestinal (nausea, vomiting, stomach cramps, diarrhea); central nervous system (headaches, dizziness, ataxia, trembling, muscle weakness, paresthesia, convulsions, memory defect); ocular (blurred vision, nystagmus, and other visual disturbances); hypersensitivity (rash, hives, fever, cough, bronchospasm, lacrimation). If gastrointestinal or hypersensitivity responses are severe, the drug should be discontinued.

When piperazine is given with chlorpromazine, the extrapyramidal side effects of chlorpromazine may be increased. Also, fatal seizures have been reported. Avoid concurrent administration.

The adult dose for ascariasis (roundworm) is 3.5 g orally daily for 2 days. For children, the dose is 75 mg/kg (up to 3.5 g) daily for 2 days. For adults and children, the dose for enterobiasis (pinworm) is a single daily dose of 65 mg/kg (maximum daily dose is 2.5 g) for 7 consecutive days. For severe infections, the dose may be repeated after a 1-week interval.

Pregnancy safety has not been established.

### ▷ Nursing Management: Piperazine Therapy

***Assessment.*** Observe individuals with renal insufficiency for signs of neurologic symptoms. The drug is contraindicated for use in renal or hepatic impairment and in convulsive disorders.

The client receiving piperazine should be assessed for the following nursing diagnoses: altered comfort related to headache, rash (hypersensitivity), and nausea and vomiting; altered bowel elimination (diarrhea); altered sleep pattern related to drowsiness; hyperthermia (hypersensitivity); risk for injury related to seizures; altered thought processes evidenced by memory defect; and activity intolerance evidenced by lightheadedness and dizziness.

***Intervention.*** The drug may be taken with food. Some physicians prefer single-dose therapy with mebendazole or pyrantel pamoate. No dietary restrictions, laxatives, or enemas are required with piperazine.

***Education.*** Stress the importance of handwashing and of sanitary disposal of feces. Instruct the client to wash the perianal area daily to prevent reinfection. Underwear and bed linens should be changed daily to prevent reinfection. All family members should be treated at the same time.

### praziquantel (Biltricide)

Praziquantel penetrates cell membranes and increases cell permeability in susceptible worms This results in an increased loss of intracellular calcium, contractions, and muscle paralysis of the worm. Drug also disintegrates the schistosome tegument (covering). Subsequently, phagocytes are attracted to the worm and kill it.

Praziquantel is indicated for the treatment of *Schistosoma mekongi, S. japonicum, S. mansoni,* and *S. haematobium* infestations.

Praziquantel is absorbed orally and reaches peak serum level in 1 to 3 hours. Half-life is 0.8 to 1.5 hours for praziquantel, 4 to 5 hours for its metabolites. It is excreted by the kidneys and is generally well tolerated.

Side effects are mild, transient, and are only more severe in clients with a large worm infestation. They include headache, lightheadedness, stomach distress, weakness, fever, rash. No significant drug interactions have been reported.

The adult or pediatric dosage is 20 mg/kg three times a day for 1 day. The doses should be spaced apart by 4 to 6 hours.

Pregnancy safety has been established at FDA category B.

### ▷ Nursing Management: Praziquantel Therapy

***Assessment.*** Praziquantel is contraindicated in clients with ocular cysticercosis, as destruction of the parasites in the eye by the medication may cause severe ocular damage.

The client receiving praziquantel should be assessed for the following nursing diagnoses: altered comfort related to headache, rash (hypersensitivity), and nausea and vomiting; altered bowel elimination (diarrhea); hyperthermia (hypersensitivity); and activity intolerance evidenced by lightheadedness and weakness.

*Intervention.* No special preparations such as fasting, dietary restrictions, or laxatives are necessary for the administration of praziquantel. However, the tablets should be taken with meals and swallowed whole with a small amount of fluid to avoid the extremely bitter taste. Chewing the tablets may cause gagging and vomiting.

*Education.* The client should be encouraged to comply with the medication regimen and to visit the health care provider regularly to monitor progress. Because of praziquantel's side effects of dizziness and drowsiness, caution the client to avoid hazardous activities such as driving until the response to the medication has been ascertained.

*Evaluation.* To monitor the effectiveness of praziquantel, stool examinations are completed at specific intervals, depending on the parasite:

* Intestinal, liver, and blood flukes: 1 week and 1, 6, and 12 months following treatment
* Lung flukes: 1 month following treatment.
* Tapeworms: 1 and 3 months following treatment

For *Schistosoma haematobium* and *S. mekongi*, urine examinations are required at 1, 3, and 6 months to determine proof of cure. A client is not considered cured unless examination results have been negative for several months.

### pyrantel (Antiminth, Helmex ✷)

Pyrantel is a depolarizing neuromuscular blocking agent; it causes contraction and then paralysis of the helminth muscles. The helminths are dislodged and then expelled from the body by peristalsis. Pyrantel is indicated for the treatment of ascariasis, enterobiasis, and helminth infestations.

This product is poorly absorbed from the gastrointestinal tract. It reaches peak serum level in 1 to 3 hours and is excreted in the feces. The less frequent side effects reported include stomach cramps, diarrhea, dizziness, sedation, headaches, insomnia, anorexia, nausea, and vomiting. Skin rash is an infrequently reported adverse reaction. When pyrantel is given concurrently with piperazine, it may reduce or antagonize pyrantel's antihelmintic action. Avoid concurrent drug administration.

The adult and children's (2 years and over) dose for ascariasis and enterobiasis is 11 mg/kg orally as a single dose. If necessary, it may be repeated in 2 to 3 weeks.

Pregnancy safety has not been established.

### ▷ Nursing Management: Pyrantel Therapy

*Assessment.* Use cautiously in individuals with hepatic impairment.

The client receiving pyrantel should be assessed for the following nursing diagnoses: altered comfort related to headache, rash (hypersensitivity), anorexia, and nausea and vomiting; altered bowel elimination (diarrhea); and activity intolerance related to CNS effects evidenced by drowsiness, lightheadedness, and dizziness.

*Intervention.* The administration of pyrantel does not require special preparation such as fasting, dietary restrictions, laxatives, or enemas. It may be taken with or without food or at any time of day. Shake well and use the calibrated measuring device provided to accurately measure the dosage.

*Education.* Encourage the client to take the full course of therapy and visit the health care provider on a regular basis to monitor progress.

Alert the client to avoid hazardous tasks requiring mental alertness such as driving until the response has been determined.

For pinworm infestation, it is important to wash, without shaking, all the bed linens and nightclothes to prevent reinfestation. All household members should be treated simultaneously.

Stress proper hygiene, both personal and environmental, with the client.

*Evaluation.* For pinworms, perianal examinations using cellophane tape swabs should be completed before and 1 week following pyrantel therapy. Negative examination results for 7 consecutive days indicate cure. Swab tests are taken in the morning before bathing or defecation. For roundworms, stool examination results should be negative for ova, larvae, or worms 2 to 3 weeks after completion of therapy.

### thiabendazole (Mintezol, Foldan ✷)

Thiabendazole's mechanism of action is unknown but it has been demonstrated to inhibit specific enzymes (fumarate reductase) in the helminth. It is vermicidal. Thiabendazole is indicated for the treatment of cutaneous larva migrans (creeping eruption) strongyloidiasis, toxocariasis, and trichinosis. It is rapidly absorbed orally reaching a peak serum level in 1 to 2 hours. Half-life ranges from 0.9 to 2 hours, with metabolism in the liver and excretion via the kidneys. Most frequently reported side effects include lightheadedness, anorexia, and nausea or vomiting. Less frequently reported effects are diarrhea, sedation, headache, bed-wetting, lower back pain, pain on urination, and abdominal distress.

Infrequently reported adverse reactions include chills; elevated temperature; muscle or joint aches; rash; pruritus; red, blistering, or peeling skin; edema; and increased weakness. No significant drug interactions are reported.

The adult and pediatric (30 pounds and over), dose for cutaneous larva migrans is 25 mg/kg orally twice a day for 2 to 5 days. If lesions are still present, the dose may be repeated 2 days after the completion of the initial treatment. For dosages for other indications, refer to a current package insert or USP-DI.

Pregnancy safety has been established at FDA category C.

### ▷ Nursing Management: Thiabendazole Therapy

*Assessment.* The drug should be used with caution in patients with hepatic or renal dysfunction.

The client receiving thiabendazole should be assessed for the following nursing diagnoses: altered comfort related to headache (CNS toxicity), low back pain or pain on urination (crystalluria), numbness and tingling of the hands and feet (CNS toxicity), rash, anorexia, nausea and vomiting; altered bowel elimination (diarrhea); altered urinary elimination pattern (bed-wetting); auditory disturbances related to CNS toxicity evidenced by tinnitus; and activity intolerance related to Stevens-Johnson syndrome evidenced by extreme tiredness and weakness.

**Intervention.** Thiabendazole should be administered after meals; no dietary restrictions, laxatives, or enemas are required with this drug.

For the oral suspension form, shake well and use the calibrated measuring device provided to ensure accurate dosage. Chew or crush tablet form before swallowing.

**Education.** Encourage the client to comply with the full course of treatment and to visit the health care provider to monitor progress.

Because of the side effects of dizziness and drowsiness, caution the client to avoid hazardous activities such as driving that require alertness.

Teach proper hygiene, personal and environmental.

**Evaluation.** Observe client for hypersensitivity reaction to detect severe erythema multiforme (Stevens-Johnson syndrome).

Sputum and stool examinations are required to monitor progress of the roundworm infection.

## LEPROSY

Leprosy, or **Hansen's disease,** is caused by *Mycobacterium leprae* in humans. Although estimates indicate that nearly 15 million people have leprosy worldwide, in the United States it is more frequently found in Hawaii and areas of Texas, Louisiana, and Florida. Leprosy has also been seen in foreign-born clients, especially those from the Philippines, Mexico, and Vietnam.

Although the precise mode of transmission is unknown, the incubation period for leprosy is a few months to decades. Large numbers of leprosy bacilli are generally shed from skin ulcers, nasal secretions, the gastrointestinal tract and, perhaps, biting insects. It is more prevalent in males than females (3 to 1) in some areas.

*M. leprae* is a bacillus that in humans first presents as a skin lesion—a large plaque or macule that is erythematous or hypopigmented in the center. More numerous lesions, peripheral nerve trunk involvement, and the common complications of plantar ulceration of the feet, footdrop, loss of hand function, and corneal abrasions may follow.

Most cases can be arrested, if not cured, by appropriate therapy and management. The drugs of choice are dapsone, rifampin, and clofazimine.

### dapsone (DDS, Avlosulfon ✳)

Dapsone is a bacteriostatic agent with an action similar to that of the sulfonamides. It may also be a dihydrofolate reductase inhibitor. Dapsone is effective against *M. leprae,* the cause of leprosy. Thus it is indicated for the treatment of all types of leprosy and for dermatitis herpetiformis.

Dapsone is absorbed orally, distributed throughout the body, and found in body fluids and in all body tissues. Half-life is approximately 28 hours, and a time to peak serum level of 1 to 3 hours. It is acetylated by N-acetyltransferase in the liver; thus slow acetylators are more apt to develop higher serum levels and adverse reactions than fast acetylators. Excretion is via the kidneys. For side effects/adverse reactions, see Table 61-7.

When dapsone is given concurrently with the following drugs, the following interactions may occur:

| Drug | Possible Effect and Management |
|---|---|
| aminobenzoic acid (PABA) | May reduce effect of dapsone by interfering with its mechanism of action. Avoid concurrent usage. |
| hemolytic agents | Increase the potential for serious adverse effects; avoid if possible. |

**TABLE 61-7**   Leprostatic agents: side effects/adverse reactions

| Drug | Side effects* | Adverse reactions† |
|---|---|---|
| dapsone | Rare: dizziness, headaches, nausea, vomiting | Most frequent: pain in abdomen, legs, or back; anorexia; pale skin, elevated temperature; rash; increased weakness<br>Rare: jaundice; sore throat; hand or feet pain; tingling, or burning sensations; blue nails, lips, or skin; respiratory difficulties; pruritus; dry, red, or scaling of skin; alopecia; mood alterations<br>In high doses, more peripheral motor (muscle) weakness is seen |
| clofazimine | Most frequent: dry, scaly skin<br>Less frequent/rare: anorexia, rash, taste alterations, dizziness, sedation, dryness, burning, irritation, itching, or photosensitivity of eyes | Most frequent: stomach colic or pain, diarrhea, nausea, vomiting, red to brown or black skin discoloration<br>Rare: visual loss, jaundice, depression, red or black tarry stools (GI bleeding) |

*If side effects continue, increase, or disturb client, inform the physician.
†If adverse effects occur, contact physician because medical intervention may be necessary.

The adult dose as an antileprosy agent is 100 mg orally daily. As a suppressant for dermatitis herpetiformis, the adult and pediatric dose is 50 mg orally daily initially, increased as necessary until symptoms are controlled. The dose for children as an antileprosy agent is 1.4 mg/kg orally daily.

Pregnancy safety has been established at FDA category C.

▷ **Nursing Management:**
**Dapsone Therapy**

*Assessment.* Administer dapsone cautiously in clients with anemia, deficiencies of G-6-PD and methemoglobin reductase, or hepatic or renal impairment.

CBC should be completed prior to dapsone therapy for a baseline assessment.

The client receiving dapsone should be assessed for the following nursing diagnoses: altered comfort related to headache, exfoliative dermatitis, numbness and tingling of the hands and feet (peripheral neuritis), rash (hypersensitivity), anorexia, nausea and vomiting; altered thought processes related to mood and mental changes; self-concept disturbance related to methemoglobinemia (bluish discoloration of the skin and lips); and activity intolerance related to hemolytic anemia.

*Education.* Encourage the client to comply with the dapsone regimen and stress that use of the drug is long-term or indefinite. Taking the medication at the same time each day will assist compliance.

Stress the importance of regular visits to the health care provider to monitor progress.

Caution the client that dapsone may cause dizziness and drowsiness; hazardous activities requiring mental alertness such as driving should be avoided until the response to the drug has been determined.

*Evaluation.* Once therapy has started, a complete blood count should be determined weekly for the first month, monthly 6 months, and then semiannually for the remainder of dapsone therapy. The dosage may be reduced or suspended if CBC values are diminished: RBCs, below 2.5 million/mm$^3$; hemoglobin, below 9 g/dl; WBCs, below 5000/mm$^3$. In addition, the client should be observed for the development of hemolytic anemia; symptoms are pale skin, fever, and unusual tiredness and weakness.

Hepatic function studies should be done if the client develops anorexia, nausea, vomiting, or jaundice.

Peripheral neuritis (numbness and tingling of the hands and feet) and exfoliative dermatitis (itching and scaling of the skin and loss of hair) are also indications for dosage interruption.

### clofazimine (Lamprene)

Clofazimine's mechanism of action is unknown. It may have a slow bactericidal effect on *M. leprae*. Clofazimine inhibits the growth and tends to bind preferentially to my-cobacterial DNA. It is indicated as a secondary drug for the treatment of leprosy, especially in the dapsone-resistant type of leprosy. Investigationally, it is also used with other antimycobacterial agents to treat clients with atypical mycobacterial infections, as seen in individuals with acquired immunodeficiency syndrome (AIDS).

Clofazimine has a variable oral absorption (45% to 62%) and is distributed primarily in fatty tissues and cells. Macrophages take up this drug and further distribute it throughout the body. Half-life is about 70 days with chronic therapy. It is excreted primarily in feces. For side effects/adverse reactions, see Table 61-7. No significant drug interactions have been reported.

The adult dose in dapsone-resistant leprosy, in combination with one or more other agents, is 50 to 100 mg orally daily. The pediatric dosage has not been established.

Pregnancy safety has been established at FDA category C.

▷ **Nursing Management:**
**Clofazimine Therapy**

The client receiving clofazimine should be assessed for the following nursing diagnoses: altered comfort related to photosensitivity, rash and itching, change in taste, anorexia, nausea and vomiting; altered thought processes related to mood and mental changes, especially depression and suicidal thoughts related to skin discoloration; self-concept disturbance related to pink, red, or brownish-black discoloration of the skin and lips; and activity intolerance evidenced by dizziness and drowsiness. See discussion of dapsone.

### Alternate Drug Therapy

Rifampin has been used investigationally in the treatment of leprosy, but leprosy is not yet an approved indication for this drug. In the treatment of multibacillary leprosy, the World Health Organization (WHO) has recommended a three-drug combination of dapsone, clofazimine, and rifampin. (For further information on dosing schedules and alternate treatment modalities, see Wyngaarden and Smith, 1988.)

## SUMMARY

Malaria is still a prevalent disease despite the World Health Organization's attempts to eradicate it by controlling the insect vector and the causative parasite. Although it is essentially considered a tropical disease, nurses in the United States and Canada may come into contact with imported cases as both countries have populations that travel extensively and provide havens for refugees and immigrants from areas in which the disease is endemic. Quinine sulfate, quinacrine, 4-aminoquinoline compounds, 8-aminoquinolone compounds, and pyrimethamine are commonly used agents for the prevention and treatment of malaria.

The incidence of tuberculosis is increasing because of the

increasing numbers of persons with AIDS, street living or homelessness, drug abusers, malnourished individuals, or those taking immunosuppressant drugs. Generally two or more antituberculous agents are administered concurrently for their additive effect and to minimize the risk of the organism becoming drug resistant. Aminosalicylates, capreomycin, cycloserine, ethambutol, ethionamide, isoniazid, pyrazinamide, rifampin, and streptomycin are commonly used antituberculous agents.

Amebiasis, an infection of the large intestine by *Entamoeba histolytica,* is prevalent in tropical areas, again imported by travel, but it is also found in poorly sanitized areas of Canada and the United States. Transmission is fecal to oral transmission through the ingestion of cysts from contaminated food and water. Antiamebiasis agents in current use are emetine HCl, iodoquinol, and paromomycin. Other protozoan diseases of concern are balantidiasis, giardiasis, pneumocystosis, trypanosomiasis, toxoplasmosis, and trichomoniasis.

Helminthiasis, worms parasitic to man, may be flatworms (platyhelminthes), of which there are two types, tapeworms (cestodes) and flukes (trematodes), or roundworms (nematodes). They cause injury to the host in a variety of ways: by causing damage to and loss of blood from the intestinal wall, producing toxic substances absorbed by the host, traumatizing the host's tissues and making the host more susceptible to infection, and by competing with the host for sustenance within the bowel. Anthelmintic agents most commonly used are diethycarbamazine, mebendazole, niclosamide, oxamniquine, piperazine, praziquantel, pyrantel, quinacrine, and thiabendazole.

Leprosy, or Hansen's disease, caused by *Mycobacterium leprae,* is treated with dapsone and clofazimine.

All of these diseases and the therapeutic agents used in their prevention and treatment are not commonly dealt with by most nurses; however, familiarity with them is necessary to appropriately manage them when they do occur.

## BIBLIOGRAPHY

Baciewicz AM et al. (1987). Update on rifampin drug interactions, Arch Intern Med 147(3):565.

Beausoleil EG. (1986). Malaria and drug resistance—chloroquine, World Health, Aug/Sept:7.

Beers LM et al. (1989). Shigellosis occurring in newborn nursery staff, Infect Control Hosp Epidemiol 10(4):147.

Berkey P et al. (1988). Rifampin-resistant meningococcal infection in a patient given rifampin chemoprophylaxis, Am J Infect Control 16(6):250.

Braunwald E et al, eds. (1987). Harrison's principles of internal medicine, ed 11. New York: McGraw-Hill Book Co.

Cohn JP. (1989). Leprosy: out of the dark ages, FDA Consum 23(7):24.

Eggelston NSM. (1989). Metronidazole: direct therapy for pediatric tuberculosis, MCN 14(3):169.

Fekety R et al. (1989). Prophylaxis for children and travelers, Patient Care 23(9):104.

Gilman AG et al, eds. (1990). Goodman & Gilman's the pharmacological basis of therapeutics, ed 8. New York: Macmillan Publishing Co.

Glassroth J. (1981). Tuberculosis: a review for clinicians. In Clinical notes on respiratory diseases, American Thoracic Society 20:25.

Gold R. (1989). Shigellosis in the nursery, Infect Control Hosp Epidemiol 10(4):145.

Grossman RJ et al. (1989). PCP and other protozoal infections, Patient Care 23(17):89.

Hayden C. (1987). Tuberculosis surveillance officer, Centers for Disease Control, Atlanta, Ga. The Miami Herald, March 25, p 12A.

Health information for international travelers. (1988). Washington, DC: US Department of Health and Human Services.

Herfindal ET et al. (1988). Clinical pharmacy and therapeutics, ed 4. Baltimore: Williams & Wilkins.

Hood L et al. (1989). Caring for the patient with TB, Adv Clin Care 4(4):14.

Jong EC. (1988). Infectious disease problems during international travel, Emerg Care Q 4(3):47.

Just a viral syndrome? . . . Ruling out drug-related problems, Emerg Med 21(11):67.

Kastrup EK, ed. (1991). Facts and comparisons. St Louis: JB Lippincott Co.

Katzman EM. (1989). What's the most common helminth infection in the U.S.? MCN 14(3):193.

Krupp MA et al. (1987). Current medical diagnosis and treatment. Norwalk, Conn: Appleton & Lange.

Loken S. (1986). Giardiasis: diagnosis and treatment, Nurse Pract 11(12):20.

Madsen LA. (1990). Tuberculosis today, RN 53(3):44.

Malaria: the unwelcome immigrant, Emerg Med 21(13):128.

McEvoy GK ed. (1990). AHFS drug information '90. Bethesda, Md: American Society of Hospital Pharmacists.

Nagami PH and Yoshikawa TT. (1983). Tuberculosis in the geriatric patient, J Am Geriatr Soc 31:356.

Overturf GD. (1989). Bacterial and rickettsial zoonosis associated with tick and flea bites, Top Emerg Med 10(4):67.

Roccoforte JS et al. (1988). Attempts to eridicate methicillin-resistant *Staphylococcus aureus* colonization with the use of trimethoprim-sulfamethoxazole, rifampin, and bacitracin, Am J Infect Control 16(4):141.

Roffman DS. (1981). Tuberculosis: differential insights. Bristol Lab 2(5):2.

Sanford JP. (1987). Guide to antimicrobial therapy. West Bethesda, Md: Merck Sharp & Dohme.

Sheahan SL et al. (1987). Management of common parasitic infections encountered in primary care, Nurse Pract 12(8):19.

Shoop NM. (1990). Prepare for the 1990s: update: tuberculosis, hepatitis and acquired immunodeficiency syndrome, part 1, Gastroenterol Nurs 12(3):200.

Spencer L. (1989). What do you know about Hansen's disease? J Enterostom Ther 16(1):34.

Stead WW et al. (1985). Tuberculosis as an endemic and nosocomial infection among the elderly in nursing homes, N Eng J Med 312:1483.

United States Pharmacopeial Convention. (1991). Drug information for the health care provider. ed 11. Rockville Md: The Convention.

Uzodinma MS et al. (1989). Chiamydia and trichomoniasis in pregnancy: nurse-midwifery management, J Nurse Midwife 34(1):31.

Visconti JA. (1990). Drug information for tuberculosis infection, The White Sheet 6(7-8):3.

Wyngaarden JB and Smith LH. (1988). Cecil's textbook of medicine, ed 18. Philadelphia: WB Saunders.

*Chapter*

62 # Nonsteroidal Antiinflammatory Drugs

## INTRODUCTION

Aspirin and other selected agents are used to treat the signs and symptoms of inflammation, fever, and pain. The gastric irritation and undesirable side effects induced by moderate to large doses of aspirin led to a search for alternate medications. With the discovery of ibuprofen in the mid-1970s, the era of aspirin-like drugs or **nonsteroidal antiinflammatory drugs (NSAIDs)** was introduced. Although aspirin is also a NSAID, this term most commonly refers to the newer aspirin substitutes on the market. (Aspirin is reviewed in Chapter 12, Analgesics and Antagonists.)

All of these products have antipyretic, analgesic, and antiinflammatory effects, but the indications for the individual products may vary according to specific testing and clinical data submitted to the FDA for approval. In this chapter the specific drugs are divided by their chemical groups: fenamates, indoles, oxicams, and derivatives of propionic acid, pyrroleacetic acid, and salicylic acid.

*Mechanism of action.* Although the exact mechanism of action is unknown, the inhibition of the biosynthesis of **prostaglandin** may be responsible for the therapeutic effects and some of the adverse effects of this drug classification. See Figure 62-1 for an illustration of the inhibition of prostaglandin production and the mechanism of action of NSAIDs.

The analgesic and antiinflammatory activity of NSAIDs is primarily due to inhibition of **arachidonic acid** metabolism. An inflammatory process may be stimulated by heat or cold, foreign substances (organisms, drugs, and others) or by trauma. In response to stimuli, arachidonic acid is released from the membrane phospholipids and is metabolized by either of two major pathways, the leukotriene pathway or the prostaglandin pathway. Both routes will

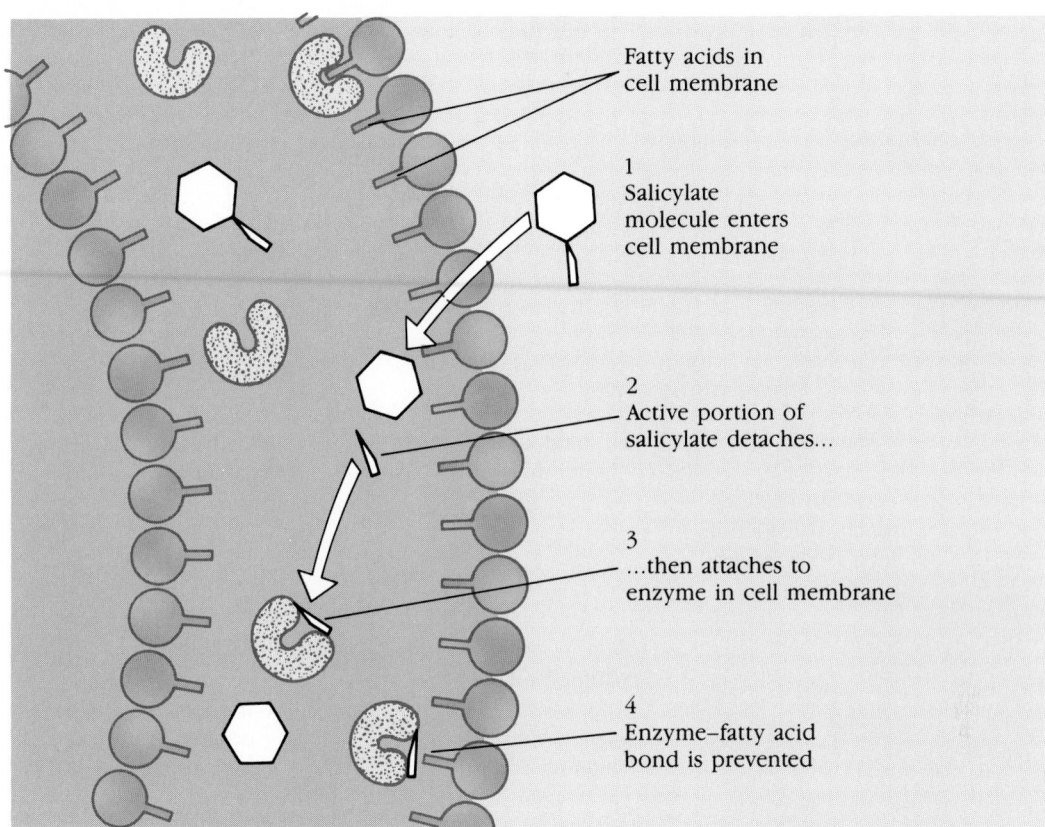

Fatty acids in
cell membrane

1
Salicylate
molecule enters
cell membrane

2
Active portion of
salicylate detaches...

3
...then attaches to
enzyme in cell membrane

4
Enzyme–fatty acid
bond is prevented

**FIGURE 62-1** Inhibition of prostaglandin production. Inflammatory diseases and local injuries often lead to a increased production of prostaglandins. Nonsteroidal antiinflammatory drugs (NSAIDs) act peripherally by entering the cell membrane (1), the active portion (salicylate) detaches (2), and attaches to the enzyme (cyclooxygenase) in the cell membrane (3). This new complex (4) cannot react with fatty acids to induce prostaglandin synthesis, thus reducing inflammation and pain in the affected area.

result in an inflammatory process, and both may also be blocked by the NSAIDs. The leukotriene pathway may result in vasoconstriction, bronchoconstriction, and increased vascular permeability, whereas the prostaglandin pathway utilizes cyclooxygenase to convert arachidonic acid to prostacyclin ($PGI_2$) and thromboxane ($TXA_2$). See Figure 62-2 for effects reported for each substance. The nurse should be aware, though, that the inflammatory process has a purpose in the body; that is, it attempts to neutralize, destroy, or try to prevent the dissemination of the toxic or foreign substances. The cardinal signs of inflammation that result may include swelling, pain, redness, and heat at the site. By interfering with prostaglandin synthesis, the NSAIDs tend to reduce the inflammatory process and ultimately provide pain relief.

It is quite possible that other actions (currently unknown) may also contribute to the therapeutic effects of these medications. Possible effects include the following:

1. Analgesic effect—decreases the biosynthesis of prostaglandins peripherally, and the generation of pain impulses may be blocked. It is also possible that the

synthesis of other substances is also reduced, such as substances (mechanical or chemical) that generally sensitize the pain receptors to stimulation.

2. Antigout effect—may be due to the analgesic and antiinflammatory effects of the agents. They do not affect hyperuricemia. (See Chapter 63, Uricosuric Drugs.)

3. Antiinflammatory effect—not fully understood. It has been hypothesized that NSAIDs act in peripheral, inflamed areas by inhibiting the synthesis and perhaps reducing the action of prostaglandins in the area. They may also affect the synthesis and/or effects of other local inflammatory substances. They also inhibit leukocyte migration and lysosomal enzyme release and activity and, perhaps, provide additional inhibition effects on both cellular and connective tissues.

4. Antipyretic effect—may reduce prostaglandin effects centrally in the hypothalamus, resulting in peripheral vasodilation, an increase in blood flow through the skin, and an increase in sweating and heat loss.

5. Antidysmenorrheal effect—prevents the synthesis and

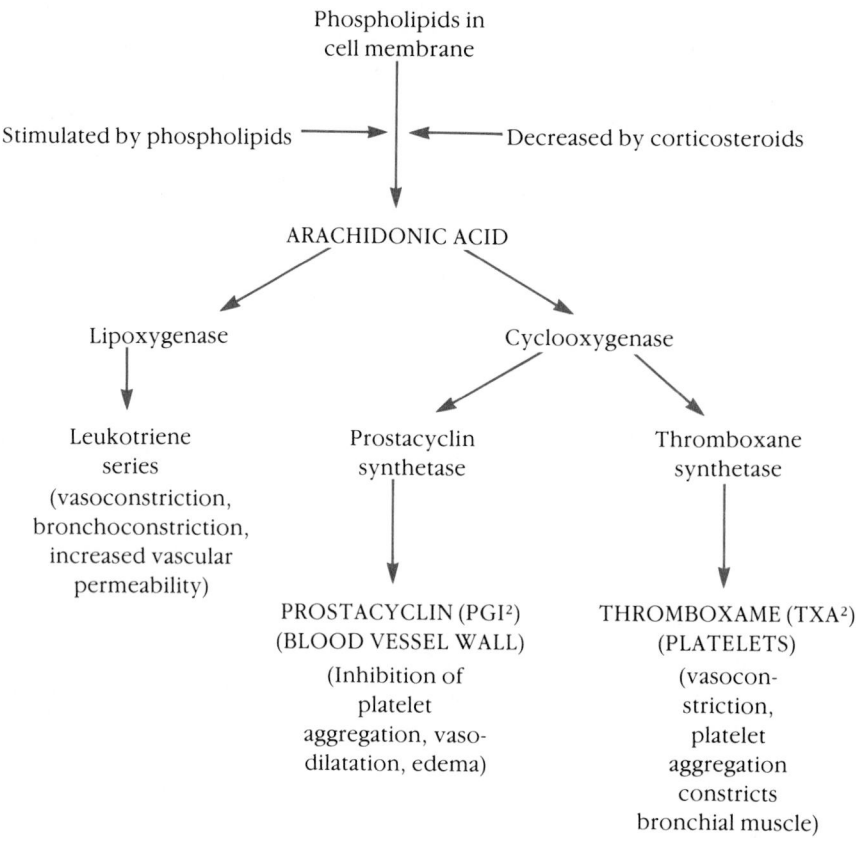

**FIGURE 62-2** Prostaglandin synthesis and NSAID effects in inflammation.

action of intrauterine prostaglandins, which may be responsible for the pain and symptoms of primary dysmenorrhea. NSAIDs may also decrease uterine contractions and increase blood perfusion to the uterus, which relieves ischemia and spasmodic pains.

6. Vascular headaches—may be prevented. Specific types of headaches that are believed to be caused by prostaglandin-induced dilation or constriction of cerebral blood vessels may be suppressed. The action may be caused by the reduction of prostaglandin activity or by a direct effect centrally.

7. Platelet inhibition—exerted by NSAIDs but to a lesser degree than by aspirin. The usual doses of meclofenamate or mefenamic acid do not usually significantly alter platelet aggregation. Additional information on platelet inhibition, gastrointestinal side effects, and renal toxicity will be noted in the section on side effects/adverse reactions.

***Indications.*** The NSAIDs are indicated for the following:

The treatment of acute or chronic rheumatoid arthritis, osteoarthritis, ankylosing spondylitis, and other rheumatic diseases as listed in the package inserts of the individual drugs.

The treatment of mild to moderate pain, especially when the antiinflammatory effect is also desirable (such as after dental procedures, obstetric and orthopedic surgery, and soft tissue athletic injuries).

The treatment of gouty arthritis (naproxen, sulindac), fever (ibuprofen), nonrheumatic inflammation (naproxen, sulindac), and dysmenorrhea (ibuprofen, mefenamic acid, naproxen). The reader is referred to a current package insert or USP-DI for a listing of approved and investigational NSAIDs use.

***Pharmacokinetics.*** The following are general pharmacokinetics; pharmacokinetics for specific other drugs are noted later.

Absorption of these drugs is very good orally. Although food may delay absorption, it has not been proven to significantly change the total amount absorbed. To decrease

**TABLE 62-1**   NSAIDs: side effects/adverse reactions

| Drug(s) | Side effects* | Adverse reactions† |
|---|---|---|
| diflunisal, fenoprofen, ibuprofen, meclofenamate, mefenamic acid, naproxen, piroxicam, sulindac, tolmetin | Most frequent: stomach distress (all except fenoprofen); constipation (fenoprofen, naproxen, sulindac); diarrhea (diflunisal, meclofenamate, mefenamic acid, sulindac, tolmetin); dizzy spells (all except diflunisal and piroxicam); sedation (fenoprofen, mefenamic acid, naproxen); headaches (all except diflunisal, fenoprofen, piroxicam); nausea or vomiting (all); anxiety, (fenoprofen); tachycardia (fenoprofen).<br><br>Less frequent: gas or mild stomach distress (diflunisal, fenoprofen, ibuprofen, piroxicam, sulindac); constipation (diflunisal, ibuprofen, meclofenamate, piroxicam, tolmetin); anorexia (fenoprofen, ibuprofen, sulindac, piroxicam, meclofenamate; diarrhea (fenoprofen, ibuprofen, naproxen, piroxicam); dizziness (diflunisal, piroxicam); sedation (diflunisal, piroxicam, tolmetin); increased sweating (fenoprofen, naproxen); sore, dry mouth (fenoprofen, meclofenamate, naproxen); tremors (fenoprofen); insomnia (diflunisal, fenoprofen, tolmetin); nervousness (ibuprofen, sulindac, tolmetin). | Most frequent: itching (ibuprofen, naproxen); edema and increased blood pressure (naproxen, tolmetin); tinnitus (naproxen); respiratory difficulties (naproxen); allergic skin rash (all); sedation (diflunisal, ibuprofen, meclofenamate, sulindac); increased bleeding episodes (naproxen); weakness (fenoprofen, tolmetin).<br><br>Less frequent: weakness (diflunisal) (piroxicamanexmia); increased thirst (naproxen); edema (ibuprofen, meclofenamate, piroxicam); white areas or sores in mouth (meclofenamate, naproxen, piroxicam); skin rash (fenoprofen, mefenamic acid, naproxen, piroxicam, tolmetin); tinnitus (diflunisal, fenoprofen, ibuprofen, tolmetin, sulindac, meclofenamate, piroxicam); elevated blood pressure (ibuprofen, meclofenamate, piroxicam, sulindac); pruritis (ibuprofen, meclofenamate, piroxicam, sulindac, tolmetin); hives (fenoprofen, meclofenamate); visual changes (fenoprofen, tolmetin); gastrointestinal ulcers or perforation (meclofenamate, tolmetin). |
| indomethacin | Incidence of 3% to 9%—stomach distress, dizzy spells, gas, nausea or vomiting. Between 1% and 3%—constipation, diarrhea, sedation, ill feeling. | Greater than 10%—morning headaches.<br>About 1%—black or bloody stools; mental disturbances; memory lapses; depression; tinnitus; edema of face, feet, or lower extremities; weight gain.<br>Incidence of approximately 1%—severe stomach pain or cramps; severe and, perhaps, bloody diarrhea; vomiting of blood; bleeding sores on lips; blood in urine; pain in chest; seizures; hearing loss; elevated blood pressure; hallucinations; fainting episodes; muscle weakness; skin peeling; respiratory difficulties; allergic skin reaction; white mouth sores; sore throat, fever, chills; decreased urine output; nosebleeds; unexplained vaginal bleeding; jaundice. |
| ketoprofen | Greater than 3% incidence—gas, indigestion, nausea, abdominal distress, pain, itching in rectum, constipation, diarrhea, headache, anxiety, insomnia. Between 1% and 3% incidence—dizzy spells, anorexia, vomiting, ill feeling. About 1%—decreased libido; dry nose or throat; tachycardia; photosensitivity; sore tongue, gums, or mouth; paresthesia of hands/feet; alopecia; increased thirst. | Greater than 3% incidence—rectal bleeding from suppository form; edema in feet or lower legs; weight gain. Between 1% and 3% incidence—severe stomach pain, visual disturbances, urinary problems, increased urinary frequency, depression, tinnitus, mouth sores or ulcers, allergic skin reaction.<br>About 1% incidence—black or bloody stools, vomiting of blood, blood in urine, decreased urine output, edema of face, hives, chills, itching skin, runny nose, memory loss, confusion, hearing loss, red eyes, fever, severe headaches, loose fingernails, red and scaly skin, respiratory difficulties, sore throat and fever, weakness, nosebleeds, jaundice. |

*If side effects continue, increase, or disturb the client, the physician should be informed.

†If adverse reactions occur, the physician should be contacted, since medical intervention may be necessary.

the gastrointestinal side effects, it is recommended that indomethacin, sulindac, and mefenamic acid be administered with antacids or meals. Protein binding is very high (greater than 90%).

Sulindac is an inactive substance (pro-drug) that is converted by the liver to an active sulfide metabolite. Most of the agents are metabolized by the liver and excreted by the kidneys.

***Side effects/adverse reactions.*** See Table 62-1.

***Significant drug interactions.*** The following interactions may occur when NSAIDs are given concurrently with the drugs listed below.

| Drug | Possible Effect and Management |
|---|---|
| anticoagulants, oral (coumarin or indanedione, heparin, streptokinase, or urokinase) | May increase the risk of gastrointestinal ulcers or hemorrhage. Monitor closely for signs of these effects.<br>Coumarin or indanedione anticoagulants may be displaced from protein-binding sites, resulting in an increased risk of bleeding episodes. Monitor closely with laboratory coagulation test.<br>Platelet inhibition by fenoprofen, ibuprofen, naproxen, piroxicam, sulindac, tolmetin, or diflunisal (in higher than recommended dosages) may be dangerous for the individual receiving anticoagulant or thrombolytic agents. Avoid concurrent drug administration if possible. If not, monitor closely for potential serious side effects. |
| antihyptertensives, diuretics (especially triamterene) | Indomethacin, ibuprofen, naproxen, and piroxicam may reduce the effectiveness of antihypertensive agents. Monitor closely as medical intervention may be necessary.<br>Concurrent use of NSAID and a diuretic may result in a decrease in diuretic, natriuretic, and antihypertensive diuretic effect. Diflunisal has not been reported to decrease furosemides's effectiveness, although it increases the serum level of hydrochlorothiazide and decreases the hyperuricemic response to hydrochlorothiazide or furosemide.<br>May increase the risk of inducing a renal failure in some clients. Triamterene and indomethacin reportedly cause acute renal failure or renal function impairment; therefore avoid this drug combination whenever possible. |
| administration of two NSAIDs concurrently, especially diflunisal and indomethacin or aspirin | May increase the risk of gastrointestinal side effects, such as duodenal ulcers or hemorrhage. These combinations should be avoided. |
| bone marrow depressants, radiation therapy, or administration of any drug that causes blood dyscrasias | Concurrent use with phenylbutazone may increase the risk of inducing agranulocytosis or other serious hemotologic abnormalities. Concurrent use of NSAIDs with radiation or bone marrow depressants may also increase the potential of inducing serious hematologic alter |

| Drug | Possible Effect and Management |
|---|---|
| | ations. Concurrent use is not recommended. |
| cefamandole, cefoperazone, cefotetan, moxalactam, or plicamycin | These drugs may cause a decrease in prothrombin blood levels, an inhibition of platelet aggregation, and with moxalactam, irreversible platelet damage. Concurrent administration with a NSAID may increase the risk for bleeding episodes, gastrointestinal ulceration, and hemorrhage. Avoid concurrent administration if possible. If not, monitor closely for side effects. |
| hydantoin anticonvulsants (especially phenytoin) | Phenylbutazone may displace protein-bound phenytoin and also inhibit its metabolism, thus increasing the potential for increased serum levels and toxicity. Monitor serum levels and for signs of toxicity as phenytoin dosage may require an adjustment. |
| indomethacin | When given with diflunisal, the renal excretion of indomethacin is decreased, which may result in increased serum levels, increased risk of toxicity, and even fatal gastrointestinal hemorrhage. Avoid concurrent drug administration. |
| lithium | Indomethacin may decrease excretion of lithium, which may result in an increased lithium serum level and toxicity. Be aware that diclofenac, naproxen, and piroxicam have also been reported to cause this effect. Thus the possibility of inducing this effect with the other NSAIDs exists. Monitor for signs of lithium toxicity and also lithium serum levels, both during concurrent therapy and afterward, if the NSAID is discontinued. |
| methotrexate | Concurrent use of methotrexate with low to moderate doses of a NSAID may result in methotrexate toxicity. Adjust methotrexate as necessary according to methotrexate serum levels and the client's renal function. This reaction can be severe and even fatal; thus close monitoring is necessary. |
| penicillamine | When phenylbutazone is given concurrently with penicillamine, serious adverse effects such as hematologic or renal toxicity may result. Monitor closely if concurrent therapy is necessary. |
| probenecid | May result in an increase in serum levels of the NSAIDs and an increased risk of toxicity. Monitor closely, since a decrease in NSAID dosage may be indicated. |
| zidovudine | When given concurrently with indomethacin, a decrease in the metabolism of zidovudine may result, leading to increased serum levels and toxicity. It is also possible that an increase in indomethacin serum levels and toxicity may occur. Avoid concurrent use of these medications. |

## ▷NURSING MANAGEMENT: NSAID THERAPY

***Assessment.*** The nurse should establish the client's allergies before administering these drugs. In individuals with a documented history of allergy or hypersensitivity to aspirin, the anaphylactoid reaction is life threatening. Clients with the triad of aspirin allergy, nasal polyps, and bronchospastic disease experience bronchospasm leading to respiratory failure with the use of the NSAIDs. The NSAIDs are contraindicated in these individuals when the drugs have caused asthmatic symptoms, rhinitis, urticaria, nasal polyps, angioedema, or bronchospastic events.

NSAIDs are to be used with caution in elderly clients, who are more prone to upper gastrointestinal, hepatic, or renal effects of these agents.

These drugs should be used cautiously in individuals with preexisting hepatic impairment. Prudent long-term management for clients should include liver enzyme monitoring and determinations of the baseline level. Cautious use in individuals with impaired renal function is required; creatinine clearance should be closely monitored in these clients. A reduced dosage should be employed in clients with diminished renal function to prevent drug accumulation.

Clients receiving NSAID therapy are at risk for the following nursing diagnoses: altered bowel elimination pattern (constipation or diarrhea); altered comfort related to gas or mild stomach distress or skin rash; sensory-perceptual alterations evidenced by visual changes, tinnitus, or dizziness; and altered health maintenance related to insufficient knowledge of contraindications, potential hazards, or signs and symptoms of bleeding. The potential complications of hemorrhage and gastroinestinal ulcers and perforation exist with the administration of NSAIDs.

***Intervention.*** The doses may be taken 30 to 60 minutes before meals or 2 hours postprandially to reach a blood level more readily. Administration with a meal, however, followed by a full glass of water, will aid in preventing gastric upset.

***Education.*** The women who is pregnant or intends to become pregnant while using a NSAID should notify her physician, since these drugs may interfere with maternal and infant blood clotting and prolong the duration of pregnancy and parturition. There is an increase in the incidence of stillbirths and neonatal deaths in humans. If the mother intends to breastfeed, she should be made aware of the fact that salicylates are detected in the breast milk and are cleared from the body more slowly by infants.

The client with a clinical problem such as errosive gastritis, ulcers, bleeding disorders, mild diabetes, or gout or those individuals receiving anticoagulant drugs should be warned to discuss this new change with their physician before commencing therapy again with a NSAID. Large doses of salicylates are to be avoided in clients with carditis.

The effect of edema caused by these agents should be considered in individuals with diseases such as congestive heart failure and hypertension.

To reduce the risk of esophageal irritation caused by tablets lodging against the lining of the esophagus, the client should be instructed to take the medication with a full glass of water and to remain upright for 15 to 30 minutes after taking the medication.

---

### *Geriatric Implications:* NSAIDS

The incidence of perforated peptic ulcers and/or bleeding is more common in the elderly taking a NSAID than in younger adults. Serious consequences more often occur in this age group.

Clients with renal impairment may be at increased risk for NSAID-induced liver or renal toxicity and often require a dosage reduction to prevent drug accumulation.

Clinicians have recommended that clients 70 years or older be started at one-half the usual adult dose with close monitoring and careful dosage increases. A dosage increase would be based on the client's therapeutic response and lack of signs and symptoms of toxicity. Specific drug warnings include:

1. Flurbiprofen (Ansaid) may result in increased peak serum levels in females between 74 and 94 years old. This serum level has not been documented in elderly male clients (USP-DI, 1991). Therefore elderly females may need a lower dose to produce a therapeutic response.
2. Indomethacin (Indocin) is responsible for a higher incidence of CNS side effects, especially confusion in the elderly.
3. Naproxen (Naprosyn) administration in the elderly results in a higher proportion of unbound (free) naproxen, which may not be reflected by the total serum level. The steady state concentration of unbound naproxen may be nearly double that of a younger adult, which may result in an increase in side/adverse/toxic effects, even with a normal serum level range. The nurse should be aware of this potential because the physician may need to be notified about the possible need for a dosage reduction (USP-DI, 1991).
4. Phenylbutazone (Butazolidin) has the potential of inducing very severe side effects, including agranulocytosis and aplastic anemia, especially in the elderly. Its use should be avoided whenever possible or at least restricted to only very severe arthritic (or other severe inflammatory disease) states after less toxic medications have been found to be ineffective. If prescribed, it should be limited to very short time periods; that is, whenever possible, do not exceed 1 week of therapy.

The client who omits a scheduled dose should not double the next dose but resume the usual dosing interval.

Alcoholic beverages produce a synergistic effect with the NSAID and aspirin in causing gastrointestinal bleeding. Aspirin used chronically has caused iron deficiency anemia.

The nurse should discuss with the client the most common side effects and adverse reactions, which, however, are not always an indication of excessive dosage and should be reported to the physician. Clients should be told that if a skin rash, itching, visual disturbances, edema, persistent headache, or dark stools occur, they should immediately notify their prescribing physician, and a therapeutic alternative may be reevaluated.

Some individuals have drowsiness and dizziness and should be cautioned about performing tasks with which the drug would interfere. The problem of morning stiffness in affected joints may be overcome by taking the last dose as late as possible in the evening.

The client should be cautioned not to use any OTC analgesics concurrently with the NSAID unless the physician specifically prescribes them.

*Evaluation.* Clients should be made aware of the need for periodic determinations of WBCs, hemoglobin, and/or hematocrit. They require close prothrombin time monitoring in clients receiving concomitant anticoagulant therapy and those with other intrinsic hemostatic coagulation defects.

Precipitation of acute renal failure may occur in clients with preexisting diminished sodium excretion, congestive heart failure, cirrhosis, hypertension, or renal disease.

The surfacing of eye problems during therapy should be handled by an ophthalmologic examination and the drug therapy should be discontinued until evaluation has ruled out the drug therapy as a causal agent.

## FENAMATES
### meclofenamate capsules (Meclomen)

The adult dose for meclofenamate is 200 mg orally daily, in 3 or 4 divided doses. This drug is not recommended for children under 14 years old.

▷ **Nursing Management:**
**Meclofenamate Therapy**

In addition to the following points, see the general nursing management for NSAIDs on p. 965.

Improvement in the client's condition may occur within a few days; however, 2 to 3 weeks may be necessary for maximum effect.

A client with a history of upper gastrointestinal tract disease requires close supervision, since peptic ulceration and sometimes severe gastrointestinal bleeding are reported to have occurred with this drug.

If the client is undergoing long-term meclofenamate therapy, CBC and renal and hepatic functions should be evaluated periodically. Decreases in hemoglobin and/or hematocrit levels may occur, and these values need determination if anemia is suspected.

If gastrointestinal side effects occur with meclofenamate, it may be necessary to reduce the dose or discontinue the drug.

### mefenamic capsule (Ponstel)

The adult dose of mefenamic is 500 mg initially, then 250 mg every 6 hours, as necessary. This medication is not recommended for children under 14 years old.

▷ **Nursing Management:**
**Mefenamic Therapy**

In addition to the following points, see the section on nursing management for NSAIDs on p. 965.

Use with caution in individuals with a history of renal disease, hepatic dysfunction, blood dyscrasias, or asthma and in those with diabetes or gastrointestinal disorders.

Monitor the client for diarrhea or skin rash. Both are indications to discontinue the drug immediately. If diarrhea develops, the client will be unable to tolerate mefenamic acid in the future. Mefenamic acid is not administered for more than 7 days.

Mefenamic acid is more likely to cause gastrointestinal symptoms, dizziness, and drowsiness than other NSAIDs.

Caution client to avoid driving or operating machinery in early stages of therapy because of drowsiness and dizziness.

## INDOLES

Indomethacin is an indoleacetic acid derivative. Sulindac and tolmetin are chemically related to indomethacin, but since they are pyrroleacetic acid derivatives, they will be listed in that section.

### indomethacin capsule (Indocin, Indocid✦)

The adult indomethacin dose is 25 or 50 mg 2 to 4 times daily. If necessary and the drug is tolerated, it may be increased by 25 or 50 mg weekly until a therapeutic response is achieved, up to a maximum dose of 200 mg/day. The pediatric dose is 1.5 to 2.5 mg/kg/day, administered in 3 or 4 divided doses up to a maximum dose of 4 mg/kg/day.

▷ **Nursing Management:**
**Indomethacin Therapy**

In addition to the following points, see the section on nursing management for NSAIDs on p. 965.

Indomethacin should be used with caution in individuals with mental depression or other psychiatric problems. Evaluate the client periodically for confusion, mood changes, and hallucinations.

Although the capsules may be taken with antacids or after meals to minimize gastrointestinal distress, the oral suspension should not be mixed with antacids or other liquids for administration.

When administering the suppository form of the drug, ensure that it remains in the rectum for at least 1 hour to maximize effectiveness.

Administer sterile indomethacin sodium intravenously for 5 to 10 seconds. Avoid extravasation because the drug is irritating to the tissues. Fluid restriction usually accompanies intravenous use of the drug.

Dosages in the elderly may begin as low as half the usual adult dose.

Encourage long-term compliance because it may take 2 weeks for a noticeable effect or up to a month for maximum effectiveness.

## OXICAMS
### piroxicam capsule (Feldene)

The piroxicam adult dose is 20 mg daily. The pediatric dose has not been established. For nursing management, in addition to those considerations listed under sulindac, see the general nursing considerations for NSAIDs on p. 965.

### sulindac tablet (Clinoril)

The adult sulindac dose is 150 or 200 mg twice daily. The dose for children has not been established.

▷ **Nursing Management:**
**Sulindac Therapy**

In addition to the following points, see the section on nursing management for NSAIDs on p. 965.

Advise the client with arthritis that although improvement may be felt within a week of the initiation of sulindac therapy, continuous use for 2 to 3 weeks may be necessary before the maximum effect occurs.

### tolmetin (Tolectin)

The adult tolmetin dose is 400 mg orally three times a day. Maximum daily dose is 2 g. For children 2 years and over, give 20 mg/kg/day in divided doses initially, followed by 15 to 30 mg/kg/day in divided doses.

▷ **Nursing Management:**
**Tolmetin Therapy**

In addition to the following points, see the section on nursing management for NSAIDs on p. 965.

Tolmetin is not to be used in individuals with a history of upper gastrointestinal tract disease unless there is close supervision for signs of ulcer perforation or severe gastrointestinal bleeding.

Advise the client that although improvement of the condition occurs within the first days, the maximum effect of tolmetin may not occur until 1 to 2 weeks after the initiation of therapy.

Monitor the fluid intake and output because of the fluid-retaining properties of tolmetin. Observe the client for increase in weight, increase in blood pressure, and headache.

## PROPIONIC ACID DERIVATIVES

Propionic acid derivatives include fenoprofen, ibuprofen, ketoprofen, and naproxen derivatives.

### fenoprofen capsule (Nalfon)

The adult fenoprofen dose is 300 to 600 mg 3 or 4 times daily. Maximum daily dose is 3.2 g. The dosage for children has not been established.

▷ **Nursing Management:**
**Fenoprofen Therapy**

In addition to the following points, see the section on nursing management for NSAIDs on p. 965.

The nurse should be aware that headache and drowsiness occur in about 15% of individuals taking fenoprofen.

Advise the client with arthritis that although improvement may be noticeable in a few days, maximum effectiveness may not occur until fenoprofen has been taken regularly for 2 to 3 weeks.

### flurbiprofen tablet (Ansaid)

The adult flurbiprofen dose is 200 or 300 mg in 2 to 4 divided doses. The maximum single dose is 100 mg, while the total daily dose maximum is up to 300 mg. The pediatric dose has not been established. For nursing management, see the discussion about fenoprofen on p. 965.

### ibuprofen (Motrin, Advil)

The adult ibuprofen dose is 1.2 to 3.2 g daily in 3 or 4 divided doses. For children under 12 years old, dose should be determined by physician. For children 12 years and over, for OTC use (nonprescription), give 200 to 400 mg every 4 to 6 hours for pain, fever, or dysmenorrhea. Maximum daily dose is 1.2 g.

▷ **Nursing Management:**
**Ibuprofen Therapy**

In addition to the following considerations, see the section on nursing management for NSAIDs on p. 965.

Gastrointestinal side effects and dizziness are more common with ibuprofen than with other NSAIDs.

Advise the client with arthritis that although improvement may be noticeable in the first few days of ibuprofen therapy, it may be 1 to 2 weeks before maximum effectiveness is reached.

Because photosensitivity occurs with ibuprofen, advise the client to avoid the use of sun lamps and prolonged exposure to the sunlight.

Ibuprofen is available without prescription in the 200 mg

strength for self-medication. Clients using ibuprofen as an OTC medication should be instructed to report to their health care provider if their symptoms do not improve, if fever persists for more than 3 days, or if swelling or redness occurs in the painful area.

### ketoprofen (Orudis)

The adult ketoprofen dose is 150 or 300 mg daily in 3 or 4 divided doses. The dosage for children has not been established.

▷ **Nursing Management: Ketoprofen Therapy**

In addition to the following points, see the section on nursing management for NSAIDs on p. 965.

Advise the client that the maximum effectiveness of ketoprofen therapy may not occur for 2 to 4 weeks.

Use caution in elderly clients or in clients with impaired renal function.

### naproxen (Naprosyn)

The adult naproxen dose is 250, 375, or 500 mg twice a day. The maximum daily dose is 1.25 g/day. The pediatric dose is 10 mg/kg/day administered in 2 divided doses.

▷ **Nursing Management: Naproxen Therapy**

In addition to the following considerations, see the general nursing management for NSAIDs on p. 965.

Caution should be used in elderly clients and those with hepatic and renal impairment.

Monitor fluid intake and output because of the fluid-retaining effects of naproxen. Observe the client for clinical signs of fluid retention (unusual weight gain; swelling of the face, feet, and lower extremities; and shortness of breath).

Advise the client that it may be as long as 2 to 4 weeks before the maximum therapeutic effect of naproxen is achieved.

## PHENYLACETIC ACIDS
### diclofenac (Voltaren)

The adult diclofenac dose is 100 mg daily. The dosage for children has not been determined. For nursing management, see the general nursing management for NSAIDs on p. 965.

## SALICYLIC ACID DERIVATIVES

Aspirin, salicylates, and diflunisal are the only medications listed under this category. Since aspirin and salicylates have been discussed previously, this section will be devoted to diflunisal. Diflunisal is a salicylic acid derivative that chemically differs from aspirin and is not metabolized to salicylic acid in the body. It is a prostaglandin synthetase inhibitor; therefore it is a nonsteroidal agent with antiinflammatory and antipyretic effects.

### diflunisal tablets (Dolobid)

The adult diflunisal dose is 250 to 500 mg twice a day. Maximum daily dose is 1.5 g. The pediatric dose has not been determined.

▷ **Nursing Management: Diflunisal Therapy**

In addition to the ones listed below, see the general nursing management for NSAIDs on p. 965.

Tablets are to be swallowed whole and not crushed.

Administration of a loading dose is recommended to initiate diflunisal therapy. Otherwise, a delay of 2 to 3 days may occur in reaching a therapeutic level and in evaluating alterations of the medication regimen.

Because of the possibility of photosensitivity with diflunisal, alert the client to avoid the use of sunlamps and prolonged exposure to sunlight.

## PROSTACYCLIN (PGI₂) AND THROMBOXANE (TXA₂)

Thromboxane $A_2$ is a potent vasoconstrictor that stimulates additional platelet aggregation. Therefore inhibiting the formation of thromboxane $A_2$ will decrease platelet aggregation. NSAIDs inhibit synthetase, thereby preventing prostaglandin formation. Aspirin irreversibly blocks prostaglandin synthetase, whereas the other NSAIDs are primarily reversible inhibitors.

Prostacyclin is a vasodilator and an inhibitor of platelet aggregation; therefore inhibiting its effects might increase the potential of a thrombus formation. Studies have indicated that very high blood levels of aspirin (perhaps equivalent to 100 mg to 200 mg/kg dosage) are needed to inhibit prostacyclin, resulting in these effects. Studies of individuals with rheumatoid arthritis receiving high doses of aspirin did not reveal an increased risk of atherosclerotic thrombotic episodes. Thus this is a potential problem that is not frequently detected clinically (Quandt and others, 1987).

## OTHER DRUGS

Several other products, such as the antimalarial agents (Chapter 61), gold salts, and penicillamine, are also used to treat inflammation in clients who have not responded to or cannot tolerate salicylates or other NSAIDs.

Although in use for over 50 years in the treatment of rheumatoid arthritis, gold compounds are generally much slower acting and more toxic than the other products. Therefore they are reserved for individuals who demonstrate continued or increased disease activity while receiving conservative therapy.

### auranofin capsules (Ridaura)
### aurothioglucose suspension, sterile (Solganal)
### gold sodium thiomalate injection (Myochrysine)

The mechanism of action is unknown, but they appear to suppress the synovitis of the acute stage of rheumatoid disease. Proposed mechanisms of action include inhibition of prostaglandin synthesis, inhibition of various enzyme systems; suppression of phagocytic action of macrophages and leukocytes; and alteration of immune response.

Gold products are indicated for the treatment of rheumatoid arthritis, auranofin in also used to treat juvenile arthritis. About 25% of an oral dose is absorbed, whereas auranofin is moderately protein bound (60%); aurothioglucose and gold sodium thiomalate are highly protein bound. Half-life of gold administered orally is 21 to 31 days in the blood, 42 to 128 days in body tissues. The time to reach onset of action with oral gold is between 3 and 4 months whereas the parenteral dosage form takes at least 6 to 8 weeks. Auranofin is rapidly metabolized, but the metabolism of aurothioglucose and gold sodium thiomalate is un-

known. Excretion is primarily by the kidneys. For side effects/adverse reactions, see Table 62-2.

When gold compounds are given concurrently with penicillamine, the risk for very serious kidney or blood adverse reactions is increased. Avoid administration of this combination.

***Dosage and administration.*** The adult dose for auranofin is 6 mg daily. Maximum daily dose is 9 mg/day. The pediatric dose has not been determined. The adult dose for aurothioglucose suspension is 10 mg IM the first week, 25 mg the second and third weeks, then 25 to 50 mg weekly until the total dose of 800 mg to 1 g has been reached. Maintenance dose is 25 to 50 mg IM every 2 weeks for 2 to 20 weeks; then extend the dose to every 3 to 4 weeks. In children 6 to 12 years old, the dose is 2.5 mg IM the first week, 6.25 mg IM the second and third weeks, then 12.5 mg weekly until the total dose of 200 to 250 mg has been reached. Maintenance dose is 6.25 to 12.5 mg IM every 3 to 4 weeks.

The adult dose for gold sodium thiomalate injection is 10 mg IM the first week, 25 mg IM the second week, then 25 to 50 mg weekly until the desired effect is achieved, up to a total dose of 1 g. Maintenance dose is 25 to 50 mg IM every 2 weeks for 2 to 20 weeks, then 25 to 50 mg every 3 or 4 weeks. The pediatric dose is 10 mg IM the first week,

**TABLE 62-2**  Side effects/adverse reactions of gold and penicillamine

| Drug(s) | Side effects* | Adverse reactions† |
|---|---|---|
| gold products:<br>auranofin<br>aurothioglucose<br>gold sodium<br>thiomalate | Most frequent: abdominal distress or pain, gas, diarrhea, nausea, vomiting. (GI irritation is a delayed effect occurring with all 3 drugs.) Anorexia (auranofin).<br>Less frequent: usually occurs after injection. Hypotension, faintness, red face, nausea, vomiting, tiredness (not reported with auranofin). Constipation and taste alterations reported (auranofin). | Most frequent: sore, irritated tongue or gums (all but auranofin); allergic skin reaction or pruritis; mouth ulcers or fungus in mouth (all three drugs). Metallic taste in mouth (all but auranofin); protein in urine (auranofin); eye redness (auranofin).<br>Less frequent: blood in urine; hives, glossitis, increase in bleeding tendencies (auranofin). Protein in urine reported with all drugs except auranofin. |
| penicillamine | Most frequent: diarrhea, decrease in taste, anorexia, nausea, vomiting, mild abdominal distress. | Most frequent: elevated temperature, rash, hives, pruritis, joint pain, swollen lymph glands, mouth ulcers or white spots.<br>Less frequent: blood in urine; edema of face, feet, or lower extremities; weight gain, sore throat, chills, fever, increased bleeding episodes, weakness.<br>Rare: stomach pain (severe because of peptic ulcer reactivation), skin blisters, chest pain, dark urine, pruritis, jaundice or pale stools, respiratory difficulties, increased weakness, difficulty talking or swallowing, diplopia, muscle weakness, visual disturbances, red or irritated skin or eyes, tinnitus. |

*If side effects continue, increase, or disturb the client, the physician should be informed.
†If adverse reactions occur, the physician should be contacted, since medical intervention may be necessary.

then 1 mg/kg (up to 50 mg per dose) following the adult recommendations for weekly intervals.

## ▷ Nursing Management: Gold Therapy

**Assessment.** Clients should be assessed for a sensitivity to gold and other heavy metals, since they may also be intolerant to gold salts. Gold therapy is contraindicated in renal or hepatic dysfunctions, uncontrolled severe diabetes, debilitation, marked hypertension, congestive heart failure, systemic lupus erythematosus, urticaria, eczema, colitis, hematologic disorders, and following radiation therapy.

Assessment of the client receiving gold compounds should include consideration of the following nursing diagnoses: altered comfort related to numbness and tingling of the hands and feet (peripheral neuritis), rash and itching (hypersensitivity), exfoliative dermatitis, conjunctivitis, metallic taste, anorexia, nausea and vomiting; risk for injury related to allergic reaction, increased tendency to bleed (thrombocytopenia), or seizures; altered oral mucous membranes related to glossitis, gingivitis, or stomatitis; hyperthermia; activity intolerance related to anemia or hepatitis; potential for infection related to leukopenia; altered thought processes related to CNS effects evidenced by confusion and hallucinations; visual disturbances related to iritis or corneal ulcers; and altered urinary elimination pattern related to renal effects evidenced by decreased urinary output.

**Intervention.** To administer the intramuscular injection, the nurse must first shake the vial vigorously and warm it to body temperature to ease drawing the suspension into the syringe. An 18-gauge, 1½-inch needle should be used to deposit the gold deep into the muscular tissue of the upper quandrant of the gluteal region. A 2-inch needle may be used for obese patients.

Adverse responses such as anaphylaxis, angioedema, and syncope may result after an injection. Have emergency equipment available.

**Education.** Advise clients that dental work should not be undertaken if the administration of gold compounds has had a leukopenic and/or thrombocytopenic effect. In addition, instruction should be provided by the nurse regarding appropriate oral hygiene, including gentle toothbrushing and flossing and the avoidance of the use of toothpicks.

Caution the client that exposure to sunlight may aggravate gold-induced dermatitis and/or cause a rash.

Encourage compliance; relief from symptoms may not occur for 3 to 6 months. Regular visits to the health care provider are necessary to monitor progress.

With parenteral forms of the medication, there is the possibility of a nitritoid reaction following the injection and joint pain for 1 to 2 days following an injection.

Alert the client that side effects may occur even after the discontinuation of gold compounds.

**Evaluation.** Platelet counts, WBCs and urinalyses

should be completed before and periodically during therapy (urinalysis before every injection and platelets and WBCs before every second injection). All three should be accomplished monthly with auranofin therapy. Also with auranofin therapy, renal and hepatic function studies are required before and periodically during the course of therapy.

Glossitis, gingivitis, and stomatitis may result from gold compound therapy. Since these conditions may cause a lack of appetite, monitor the client's food intake.

Skin symptoms such as itching and rash are quite common with auranofin. Gastrointestinal symptoms such as abdominal cramps and diarrhea are quite common. Both should be reported promptly to the physician.

### ketorolac (Toradol)

Ketorolac is the first injectable analgesic NSAID that is stated to be comparable to morphine and meperidine in efficacy without the undesirable side effects/adverse reactions. It has no respiratory depression effects and produces far fewer CNS side effects as compared to the opioids. At this time it is reported to have little or no potential for abuse or addiction so it has no special handling procedures required by the federal government.

Ketorolac is chemically related to indomethacin and tolmetin. It inhibits cyclooxygenase, which decreases prostaglandin synthesis and activity peripherally. It may also inhibit the effects or synthesis of other substances that sensitize pain receptors, thus contributing to its analgesic effect. At this time the specific substances have not been identified. Ketorolac has antiinflammatory and antipyretic effects; it also inhibits platelet aggregation. It is indicated for the short-term management of pain but should not be used as an obstetrical preoperative medication or for obstetrical analgesia.

Ketorolac is completely absorbed after an intramuscular injection, and has an onset of action within 10 minutes. The peak effect is reached in 75 to 150 minutes. Its half-life is 4.5 hours in normal adults (7 hours in healthy geriatric clients), and ketorolac is metabolized in the liver (less than 50%) and primarily excreted by the kidneys. The more frequent side effects reported include stomach pain, sedation, indigestion and bruising at the injection site. Less frequently seen are headache, sweating, diarrhea, lightheadedness and pain at the injection site.

The less frequent and rare adverse reactions include edema (swelling of face, fingers, and lower extremities and unusual weight gain), visual disturbance, respiratory difficulty such as wheezing, shortness of breath, blood in stools, depression, increased frequency of urination or oliguria, peptic ulcers, rectal bleeding and/or stomatitis.

The adult analgesic dose is 60 mg IM initially, followed by 30 mg every 6 hours. If client's weight is under 50 kg, if the client has impaired renal function or in an elderly client, a dose of 30 mg IM initially, followed by 15 mg every 6 hours is recommended. The maximum daily dose recommended is 150 mg the first day, then 120 mg/day thereafter. Pediatric dose has not been established.

### penicillamine (Cuprimine, Depen)

Penicillamine is a *chelating agent* for heavy metals, such as mercury, lead, copper, and iron. The metals are made more soluble so that they can be readily excreted by the kidneys. The mechanism of action as an antirheumatic agent is unknown.

It has been proposed that penicillamine may improve lymphocyte function. This product also reduces IgM rheumatoid factor and immune complexes located in the serum and synovial fluids, but overall it does not significantly decrease the absolute levels of serum immunoglobulins. The relationship of these effects to rheumatoid arthritis is unknown.

Penicillamine is indicated for the prophylaxis and treatment of Wilson's disease and the treatment of rheumatoid arthritis, especially for individuals with severe arthritis who have not responded to other therapies. Another use is to prevent cystine renal calculi and in the treatment of cystinuria. For side effects/adverse reactions, see Table 62-2. See the section on gold compounds for significant drug interactions with penicillamine.

The adult dose of penicillamine as a chelating agent is 250 mg orally, four times daily. As an antirheumatic agent, 125 or 250 mg orally daily is administered initially; then increases, if needed, are made at 125- or 250-mg doses at 2- to 3-month intervals. The maximum daily dose is 1.5 g. The dose as an antiurolithic agent is 500 mg orally, 4 times daily. For infants over 6 months and young children, the chelating dose is 250 mg daily, administered in fruit juice. While the dose as an antirheumatic has not been determined, the dose as an antiurolithic agent is 7.5 mg/kg orally four times daily.

### ▷ Nursing Management: Penicillamine Therapy

In addition to the following discussion, see the general nursing management for NSAIDs on p. 965.

**Assessment.** Use with caution in clients with hepatic or renal dysfunctions.

Twenty-four-hour urinary copper analyses are recommended for clients with Wilson's disease to determine optimum penicillamine dosages.

**Intervention.** Administer drug on empty stomach at least 1 hour apart from any other drug, food, antacid, or milk.

If the course of therapy is interrupted, it needs to be restarted at a low dosage and gradually increased to the appropriate dosage.

Penicillamine dosage should be reduced to 250 mg if the client is going to have surgery because of the drug's effects on collagen and elastin, which results in increased skin friability. Return to the usual dosage should be delayed until wound healing is complete.

---

**PREGNANCY SAFETY**

FDA category B: ketoprofen, naproxen, diclofenac, ketorolac

FDA category C: mefenamic, ibuprofen, tolmetin diflunisal, auranofin, aurothioglucose, gold sodium thiomalate

FDA category unclassified: meclofenamate, indomethacin, fenoprofen, piroxicam, sulindac, flurbiprofen, penicillamine

---

If administered for cystinuria, the client should be on high fluid intake, especially at night when the urine is more acidic and concentrated; 500 ml at bedtime and 500 ml once in the middle of the night is adequate. The greater the fluid intake, the lower the therapeutic dose of penicillamine.

**Education.** The client should be encouraged to comply with the medication regimen, since an interruption in the medication for even a few days may cause a sensitivity reaction when it is restarted. Long-term compliance may be especially difficult for clients with rheumatoid arthritis because an improvement in the status of their illness may require 2 to 3 months of therapy.

If administered for Wilson's disease, the dosage is calculated on the basis of the urinary copper excretion; the objective is to maintain a negative copper balance. The client should be advised that a low copper diet may be necessary. This means omitting mushrooms, chocolate, nuts, shellfish, liver, molasses, and broccoli.

Alert the client that taste may be impaired. The ability to taste may be enhanced by administering 5 to 10 mg of copper daily, except for individuals with Wilson's disease in which copper intake is restricted.

**Evaluation.** Take urinalyses and complete blood and platelet counts twice a month for the first 6 months and each month thereafter to monitor for toxicity.

Hepatic function studies should be completed every 6 months for the first 18 months of therapy to monitor for toxic hepatitis.

For clients with cystinuria, x-ray examinations for renal calculi should be done on an annual basis.

### SUMMARY

Nonsteroidal antiinflammatory drugs (NSAIDs) are used to treat the signs and symptoms of inflammation, fever, and pain. Since the mid-1970s, these aspirin substitutes have become quite popular for the treatment of mild to moderate pain and for the antiinflammatory treatment of arthritis. Although widely available, these agents are not without adverse gastrointestinal, hepatic, and renal effects. Gold compounds, also used in the treatment of arthritis, are much slower acting and much more toxic than the rest of the NSAIDs.

## BIBLIOGRAPHY

Arnold W et al. (1988). When NSAIDs are the right choice, Patient Care 22(12):190.

Arzeno S. (1990). Toradol product monograph. Syntex Laboratories, 9019-17.

Beard K et al. (1987). Nonsteroidal antiinflammatory drugs and hospitalization for gastroesophageal bleeding in the elderly, Arch Intern Med 147(9):1621.

Braunwald E et al, eds. (1987). Harrison's principles of internal medicine, ed 11. New York: McGraw-Hill Book Co.

Carson JL et al. (1987). The relative gastrointestinal toxicity of the nonsteroidal antiinflammatory drugs, Arch Intern Med 147(6):1054.

Foley JJ et al. (1987). Selecting an appropriate NSAID, Hosp Pract 22(4):54.

Hochberg MC. (1989). NSAIDs: patterns of usage and side effects, Hosp Pract 24(5):167.

Kaplan H et al. (1989). Advances in arthritis drug therapy, Patient Care 23(12):31.

Kastrup EK, ed. (1991). Facts and comparisons. St. Louis: J.B. Lippincott.

Katzung BG. (1987). Basic and clinical pharamacology, ed 3. Norwalk, Conn: Appleton & Lange.

Nonsteroidals in the GI tract. (1987). Emerg Med 19(9):55.

Quandt CM et al. (1987). Current concepts in clinical therapeutics: ischemic cerebrovascular disease, Clin Pharm 6(4):292.

Portenoy RK. (1988). Practical aspects of pain control in the patient with cancer, CA 38(6):327.

United States Pharmacopeial Convention. (1991). Drug information for the health care provider, ed 11. Rockville, Md: The Convention.

Wyngaarden, JB and Smith LH. (1988). Cecil's textbook of medicine, ed 18. Philadelphia: WB Saunders Co.

# Chapter

## 63 Uricosuric Drugs

## INTRODUCTION

Hyperuricemia and gout occur in persons with an abnormality in uric acid production and/or excretion.

## GOUT

**Gout** is a metabolic disease of unknown origin. Heredity may have a bearing on the incidence of this disease, since it occurs more often in relatives of persons with gout than in the general population. The hallmark of gout is **hyperuricemia**, or high levels of uric acid in the blood.

Countries with an increase in protein consumption appear to have the highest reported incidences of gout. For example, gout previously was rare in Japan, but it is much more common now because of the increase in protein consumption in that country (Wyngaarden, 1988).

Gout occurs most often in adult men, with only about 5% of the diagnosed cases occurring in women. It is characterized by a defective purine metabolism and manifests itself by attacks of acute pain, swelling, and tenderness of joints, such as those of the big toe, ankle, instep, knee, and elbow. The amount of uric acid in the blood becomes elevated, and **tophi**, which are deposits of uric acid or urates, form in the cartilage of various parts of the body. These deposits tend to increase in size. They are seen most often along the edge of the ear. Chronic arthritis, nephritis, and premature sclerosis of blood vessels may develop if gout is uncontrolled.

Treatment goals for gout are: (1) to end the acute gouty attack as soon as possible, (2) to prevent a recurrence of acute gouty arthritis, (3) to prevent the formation of uric acid stones in the kidneys, and (4) to reduce or prevent disease complications that result from sodium urate deposits in joints and kidneys.

The drugs used to treat an acute gout attack include col-

**TABLE 63-1** Medications affecting serum uric acid levels

| Increase levels | Decrease levels |
| --- | --- |
| alcohol | acetohexamide |
| cancer chemotherapeutic agents | ACTH hormone |
| | allopurinol |
| diuretics, (thiazides, furosemide) | glyceryl guaiacolate |
| | mannitol |
| levodopa | tetracycline (outdated) |
| ethambutol | probenecid |
| salicylates (less than 2 g/day) | radiopaque dyes |
| epinephrine (adrenalin) | salicylates (more than 3 g/day) |
| norepinephrine | |

chicine, nonsteroidal antiinflammatory drugs (NSAIDs), and corticosteroids. Colchicine, specifically used to treat gout, will be reviewed in this chapter. To treat chronic gouty arthritis or to prevent gout attacks, allopurinol, probenecid, sulfinpyrazone, and salicylates have all been used. Salicylates require very high daily dosages, such as 4 to 6 g/day. Since few individuals can tolerate this high dose on a long-term basis, it is not commonly prescribed for gout. The nurse should be aware that low doses of aspirin can interfere with uric acid excretion, resulting in exacerbation of gout.

The reader should be aware that a secondary hyperuricemia may occur from neoplastic diseases or cancer, psoriasis, Paget's disease, and other common and rare disease states. Many drugs have also been reported to cause an increase or a decrease in uric acid levels (see Table 63-1). It is preferable for the physician to identify the cause of the hyperuricemia and then to make the decision whether or not to treat it. Asymptomatic hyperuricemia in an elderly person may or may not be drug induced and often is not treated by the physician because of the adverse reactions and the cost of the medications. But if symptoms are present or a treatable disease state is identified, then specific treatments would be indicated.

### colchicine tablets/injection

The mechanism of action for antigout activity is unknown. It has been reported to decrease phagocytosis and the motility of leukocytes, as well as the production of lactic acid, which results in a decrease in deposits of urate crystals and the inflammatory reaction. This drug does not affect levels of uric acid in the circulatory system.

Colchicine also constricts blood vessels and effects central vasomotor stimulation (resulting in hypertension), depresses the respiratory center, and causes a decline in body temperature.

Colchicine is used in the treatment and prophylaxis of acute gouty arthritis and the treatment of chronic gouty arthritis. In acute gouty arthritis, it has an onset of action within 12 hours after oral administration and between 6 and 12 hours by intravenous injection. The peak effect for relief of pain and inflammation is reached in 1 to 2 days, but reduction of swelling may require 3 days or more. It is metabolized in the liver and excreted mainly in bile. For side effects/adverse reactions, see Table 63-2.

When colchicine is given concurrently with radiation therapy or drugs that induce blood dyscrasia or bone marrow depression (such as phenylbutazone, chloramphenicol, antineoplastics, and others; see current USP-DI), the risk of inducing bone marrow depression or other serious, toxic, hematologic effects may be increased.

The adult antigout dose for prophylaxis is 0.5 to 0.65 mg orally, one to three times daily. The dose for acute gouty attacks is 0.5 mg to 1.3 mg orally initially, then 0.5 to 0.65 mg every 1 to 2 hours until pain is relieved, or until nausea, vomiting, or diarrhea side effects have occurred, or until the 10-mg maximum dose has been reached. Pediatric dose has not been established. The adult intravenous dose for prophylaxis is 0.5 mg to 1 mg once or twice daily. For use in acute gouty attacks, the dose is 2 mg initially followed by 0.5 mg every 6 hours until desired effect is achieved.

Pregnancy safety has been established at FDA category D.

### ▷ Nursing Management: Colchicine Therapy

**Assessment.** Caution should be used when this drug is given to elderly persons and to those with cardiac, renal, or gastrointestinal disease.

Assessment of the client receiving colchicine should include consideration of the following nursing diagnoses: altered comfort related to numbness and tingling of the hands and feet (peripheral neuritis), pain at injection site (thrombophlebitis), rash, stomach pain, anorexia, nausea and vomiting; risk for injury related to increased tendency to bleed (thrombocytopenia) or seizures; hyperthermia; activity intolerance related to aplastic anemia, respiratory depression, or pulmonary edema; risk for infection related to leukopenia; altered thought processes related to mood and mental changes; disturbance of self-concept related to hair loss; and altered urinary elimination pattern related to renal effects evidenced by decreased urinary output.

**Intervention.** Oral colchicine may be administered with food to prevent gastrointestinal distress.

The drug should not be administered for 3 days after the dosage for the acute episode to avoid toxic effects from accumulation.

Colchicine cannot be given subcutaneously or intramuscularly because it is highly irritating and will cause tissue necrosis. When given intravenously, extravasation must be avoided. Change the needle before administration. Administer the intravenous injection over an interval of 2 to 5 minutes.

**TABLE 63-2**   Side effects/adverse reactions of uricosuric drugs

| Drug | Side effects* | Adverse reactions† |
|---|---|---|
| colchicine | Most frequent (with oral administration): diarrhea, nausea, vomiting, abdominal pain.<br>Less frequent: anorexia.<br>With chronic therapy or after a serious toxicity: alopecia. | Rare: redness, edema, or pain at site of injection.<br>With chronic drug administration: pain, tingling, feelings of numbness or weakness in hands or feet, skin rash, sore throat, elevated temperature, chills, increased bleeding episodes, weakness.<br>Serious overdose may occur 24 to 72 hours after administration: blood in urine; decreased urine output; seizures; severe or bloody diarrhea; mood alterations; severe muscle weakness; respiratory difficulties; burning sensations in stomach, throat, or on skin; severe vomiting (which can lead to profound dehydration and hypotension). |
| allopurinol | Less frequent/rare: diarrhea, sedation, abdominal pain, gas, headaches, nausea, vomiting, alopecia. | Most frequent: rash, hives, pruritis, allergic-type reaction.<br>Rare: bloody urine or bleeding from sores on the lips; painful urination; pain in lower back area; chills; elevated temperature; sore throat; muscle pain or muscle aches; nausea; vomiting; decrease in quantity of urine; edema of face or lower extremities; nosebleed; jaundice; red, itching, or peeling skin; red eyes; scaly skin; mouth or lip sores; ulcers or white spots; increased weakness. |
| probenecid | Most frequent: headaches, anorexia, mild nausea or vomiting.<br>Less frequent: lightheadedness, red face, increased need to urinate, sore gums. | Less frequent: blood in urine, lower back pain, pain on urination.<br>Rare: respiratory difficulties, elevated temperature, pruritus, rash, allergic reaction, increased bleeding episodes, weakness, decrease in urine output, weight gain, edema of face or lower extremities, jaundice.<br>Acute overdose: seizures, CNS stimulation, serious vomiting. |
| sulfinpyrazone | Most frequent: nausea, vomiting, abdominal pain. | Less frequent: rash or allergic reaction.<br>Rare: black or bloody stools, blood in urine, lower back pain, elevated temperature, sore throat, increased bleeding episodes, weakness, difficulty or pain on urination.<br>Overdose: ataxia, seizures, diarrhea; severe, persistent nausea or vomiting; abdominal pain; respiratory difficulties. |

*If side effects continue, increase, or disturb the client, the physician should be informed.
†If adverse reactions occur, the physician should be contacted because medical intervention may be necessary.

To be effective, colchicine must be given properly at the first indication of an oncoming attack, and dosage must be adequate. Once the dose that will cause diarrhea has been determined, it is often possible to reduce subsequent doses to prevent diarrhea and still achieve satisfactory relief of pain.

Colchicine is incompatible with and will precipitate if mixed with or injected into intravenous tubing containing 5% dextrose solution, solutions which contain a bacteriostatic agent, or any solution that would change the pH of the colchicine solution. To dilute, use 0.9% sodium chloride injection or sterile water for injection.

Fluid intake needs to be encouraged to ensure a urinary output of at least 2000 ml daily.

**Education.** Advise the client to maintain regular visits to the health care provider to monitor progress.

Caution the client not to drink alcoholic beverages while taking colchicine, since it increases the risk of gastrointestinal toxicity and decreases the effectiveness of the medication by increasing uric acid levels. With clients who are chronic alcoholics, the intravenous route of administration may be preferred to avoid the risk of gastrointestinal symptoms.

Since colchicine has such a narrow margin of safety, alert the client to report to the physician as soon as possible any signs of nausea, vomiting, diarrhea, sore throat, unusual bleeding or bruising, or unusual tiredness.

Caution the client to tell any health care providers that colchicine is being taken before any surgery or dental procedures are done.

**Evaluation.** The nurse should monitor the client's involved joints for range of motion, pain, and swelling. The drug should be discontinued as soon as the pain of the acute gout episode is relieved, if gastrointestinal symptoms occur, or if the maximum dosage is reached.

Monitor fluid intake and output to assess adequacy of urinary output.

CBCs should be monitored for clients on long-term therapy because the drug's effects on bone marrow may result in blood dyscrasias.

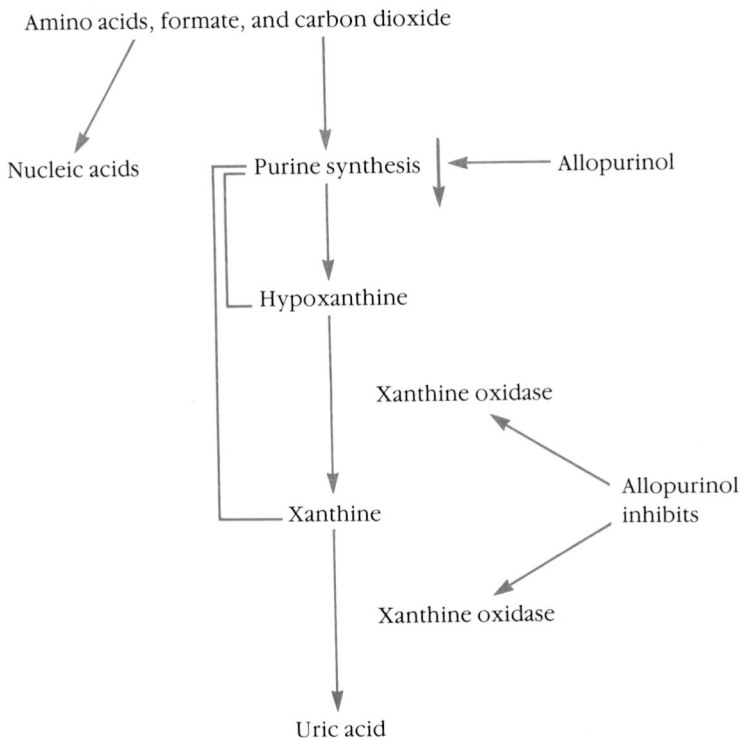

Amino acids, formate, and carbon dioxide

**FIGURE 63-1**  Uric acid production and allopurinol effects in the body.

### allopurinol tablets (Zyloprim, Alloprin ✽)

Allopurinol decreases the production of uric acid by inhibiting **xanthine oxidase**, the enzyme necessary to convert hypoxanthine to xanthine and xanthine to uric acid (see Figure 63-1). It also increases the reutilization of both hypoxanthine and xanthine for nucleic acid synthesis, thus resulting in a feedback inhibition of de novo purine synthesis. The result is a decrease of uric acid in both the serum and urine.

This decrease of uric acid will prevent or decrease urate deposits, thus avoiding or reducing both gouty arthritis and **urate nephropathy**. The reduction in urinary urate levels prevents the formation of uric acid or calcium oxalate calculi in the kidneys.

Allopurinol is indicated for the treatment of chronic gouty arthritis and for the prophylaxis and treatment of hyperuricemia, uric acid nephropathy, and renal calculi. It is well absorbed orally, with an onset of action in reducing serum uric acid in 2 to 3 days. Approximately 70% of a dose is metabolized in the liver to an active metabolite, oxipurinol. Reduction of uric acid to a normal range occurs in 1 to 3 weeks, whereas a decrease in frequency of acute gout attacks may require several months of drug therapy. Excretion is via the kidneys. For side effects/adverse reactions, see Table 63-2.

***Significant drug interactions.***  The following significant drug interactions may occur when allopurinol is given concurrently with the drugs listed below:

| Drug | Possible Effect and Management |
|---|---|
| anticoagulants, oral (coumarin or indanedione) | Allopurinol may inhibit metabolism of the oral anticoagulant resulting in an increase in serum levels, activity and, perhaps, toxicity. Monitor prothrombin levels closely, since dosage adjustment may be necessary. |
| azathioprine or mercaptopurine | Allopurinol's effect of inhibiting xanthene oxidase may result in decreased metabolism of these medications, leading to an increased potential for therapeutic and/or toxic effects (especially bone marrow depression). Monitor closely since interventions or dosage adjustments may be necessary. |

***Dosage and administration.***  The adult antihyperuricemic dose is 100 mg daily initially, increased by 100 mg/day at 7-day intervals if necessary. Maximum daily dose should not exceed 800 mg/day. Maintenance is 100 to 200 mg two to three times daily or 300 mg once daily. For treatment of hyperuricemia resulting from antineoplastic therapy, administer initially, 600 to 800 mg orally daily,

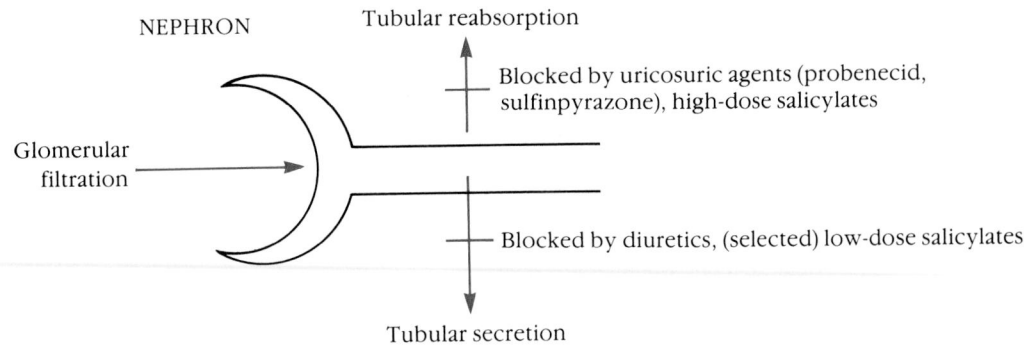

**FIGURE 63-2**  Drug effects on uric acid excretion in the kidney.

beginning 2 to 3 days before beginning of chemotherapy or radiation therapy. For maintenance therapy, adjust dosage according to serum uric acid levels that are analyzed about 2 days after the initiation of allopurinol and periodically thereafter. Discontinue the allopurinol during the period of tumor regression.

To treat uric acid calculi **(antiurolithic),** give 100 to 200 mg orally one to four times daily or 300 mg daily as a single dose.

For pediatric dose as an antihyperuricemic agent in antineoplastic therapy, see a current package insert or USP-DI.

***Pregnancy safety.***  This has been established at FDA category C.

▷**Nursing Management:**
**Allopurinol Therapy**

***Assessment.***  If the client has impaired renal function, a reduction in dosage and monitoring of renal function may be necessary.

Assessment of the client receiving allopurinol should include consideration of the following nursing diagnoses: altered comfort related to numbness and tingling of the hands and feet (peripheral neuritis), allergic dermatitis, exfoliative dermatitis, headache, stomach pain, anorexia, nausea and vomiting; risk for injury related to thrombocytopenia (increased tendency to bleed); altered bowel elimination (diarrhea); activity intolerance related to hepatitis; disturbance of self-concept related to hair loss; and altered urinary elimination related to renal effects evidenced by decreased urinary output.

***Intervention.***  Administer with food to minimize gastrointestinal distress. For ease of administration for clients with difficulty swallowing, the tablets may be crushed and mixed with a small amount of applesauce or jelly.

A high fluid intake (80 to 96 ounces daily to produce 2 L of urine) and alkalinization of the urine are necessary to lessen the risk of stone formation and sludging of the tubules with urates.

Any single dose of allopurinol should not exceed 300 mg; it may be given in divided doses.

***Education.***  Encourage the client to comply with the medication regimen. The client should be advised that allopurinol helps prevent, but does not relieve, acute gout episodes.

Regular visits to the physician are necessary to monitor progress through periodic blood testing and assessment for side effects/adverse reactions.

Caution the client not to drink alcoholic beverages because alcohol increases uric acid concentrations.

Alert the client that drowsiness may occur and that hazardous activities requiring mental alertness, such as driving, need to be avoided until the response to the medication has been determined.

Stress the importance of the large amount of fluid intake necessary to ensure adequacy of fluid output.

To minimize the formation of calcium oxalate stones, the client should maintain a diet that enhances the alkalinity of the urine, such as milk, fruits (except plums, prunes, and cranberries), carbonated beverages, vegetables (except corn and lentils), molasses, and baking soda and baking powder. Large doses of vitamin C should be avoided.

The client should be advised to report to the physician immediately any signs of a skin rash or other adverse reactions. Skin rash usually precedes severe hypersensitivity reactions.

***Evaluation.***  For proper dosing, serum uric acid levels should be monitored. CBCs and renal and hepatic function studies are recommended at periodic intervals during therapy, particularly in the first few months.

Monitor fluid intake and output to ensure the adequacy of fluid intake.

**probenecid tablets (Benemid, Benuryl ✹)**

Used in the treatment of hyperuricemia or to prevent gout, probenecid competitively inhibits the reabsorption of urate at the proximal renal tubule, thus increasing the urinary excretion of uric acid, which effectively lowers the serum urate levels (uricosuric effect). It has no antiinflammatory action or analgesic effects.

As an adjunct to antibiotic therapy, probenecid competitively inhibits the secretion of weak organic acids, such as penicillin and some of the cephalosporins, at both the proximal and distal renal tubules in the kidneys. The result is an increase in blood concentrations and duration of action of these antibiotics.

Probenecid is indicated for the treatment of chronic gouty arthritis and hyperuricemia; it is also adjunct therapy with selected antibiotics such as penicillins and some cephalosporins used for the treatment of sexually transmitted diseases (e.g., gonorrhea, acute pelvic inflammatory disease [PID], and neurosyphilis). It is well absorbed orally and is highly bound to plasma proteins, especially to albumin. The therapeutic serum level for uricosuric effect is 100 to 200 μg/ml; for suppression of penicillin excretion, 40 to 60 μg/ml. Peak uricosuric effect is reached within 30 minutes, while peak suppression of penicillin excretion is noted in 2 hours. After a single dose of probenecid, penicillin serum levels will be elevated for an extended period of time. Probenecid is metabolized in the liver and excreted by the kidneys. For side effects/adverse reactions, see Table 63-2.

**Significant drug interactions.** The following interactions may occur when probenecid is given concurrently with the drugs listed below:

| Drug | Possible Effect and Management |
|---|---|
| indomethacin, ketoprofen, and other NSAIDs | Probenecid decreases the renal excretion of ketoprofen by 66%, protein binding by 28%, and the formation of ketoprofen conjugates. This leads to an increase in ketoprofen serum levels and, possibly, toxicity. Avoid this combination.<br><br>Probenecid may also decrease excretion of indomethacin and possibly other NSAIDs from the body, thus leading to increased serum levels, extended half-life, and an increased potential for NSAID toxicity. Monitor closely as the physician may need to lower the NSAID daily dose if adverse effects are reported. |
| antineoplastic drugs, rapidly cytolytic | Do not administer with probenecid because of potential toxicity of uric acid nephropathy. Also, the rapidly acting antineoplastic drugs may increase plasma uric acid levels and interfere with any control of the previous hyperuricemia and gout. |
| aspirin or salicylates | Not recommended because salicylates in moderate to high doses given chronically will inhibit the effectiveness of probenecid. Also, if high doses of salicylates are being given for their uricosuric effects, probenecid may lower the excretion of salicylates, which may result in elevated serum salicylate levels and toxicity. |

| Drug | Possible Effect and Management |
|---|---|
| cephalosporins, penicillins | Probenecid decreases the renal tubular secretion of penicillin and selected cephalosporins, which may result in an increased serum level and prolonged duration of action of the antibiotic. An increased risk of toxicity may also be present. Monitor serum levels closely if given concurrently. Two cephalosporins not affected by probenecid are ceforanide and ceftazidime. |
| heparin | The anticoagulant effects of heparin may be enhanced and prolonged. Avoid concurrent administration if possible; if not, monitor laboratory tests closely. |
| methotrexate | Probenecid may decrease the renal excretion of methotrexate, which may increase the risk of serious toxicity with methotrexate. If used concurrently, administer a lower dose of methotrexate and monitor closely for toxicity or monitor methotrexate serum levels. |
| nitrofurantoin | Probenecid may decrease the renal tubular secretion of nitrofurantoin, resulting in an increase in serum levels and, possibly, toxicity. This may reduce the urinary levels and effectiveness of nitrofurantoin. A reduction in probenecid dosage may be necessary to use nitrofurantoin in urinary tract infections. Monitor effectiveness closely. |

**Dosage and administration.** The antihyperuricemic adult dose is 250 mg twice daily for 7 days then increased to 500 mg twice a day. As an adjunct to penicillin/cephalosporin drug therapy, the dose is 500 mg four times daily. Pediatric dose as an antihyperuricemic agent is not established.

**Pregnancy safety.** Has not been established.

▷ **Nursing Management: Probenecid Therapy**

**Assessment.** Probenecid is well tolerated by most patients (except those with peptic ulcer disease, glucose-6-phosphate dehydrogenase deficiency, acute intermittent porphyria, blood dyscrasias, and a history of uric acid kidney stones).

Assessment of the client receiving probenecid should include consideration of the following nursing diagnoses: altered comfort related to allergic dermatitis, low back pain (uric acid renal calculi), headache, stomach pain, anorexia, nausea and vomiting; risk for injury related to thrombocytopenia (increased tendency to bleed); hyperthermia; activity intolerance related to anemia; disturbance of self-concept related to hair loss; and altered urinary elimination related to renal effects evidenced by decreased urinary output.

**Intervention.** Probenecid may be administered with an antacid or food to minimize gastrointestinal distress.

A high fluid intake (2500 ml of water daily) to produce copious volumes of urine is recommended to minimize formation of uric acid stones and occurrence of renal colic and hematuria.

Alkalinization of the urine may be required to minimize the formation of kidney stones. Sodium bicarbonate, potassium citrate, and acetazolamide are agents recommended for the alkalinization of urine. Diet therapy is also recommended as with allopurinol therapy.

**Education.** Encourage the client to comply with the medication regimen. Variations in the dosages may precipitate an acute episode of gout. It is important for the client to understand that this drug is to help prevent attacks, but it does not relieve acute gout episodes. Regular visits to the physician are necessary to monitor progress.

Stress the importance of maintaining adequate fluid intake.

Alert clients with diabetes who test urine for glucose with copper sulfate tests (Clinitest) that a false positive result may result while taking this medication. Enzymatic tests (Ketodiastix, Tes-Tape) should be used to assess urine glucose levels.

Caution the client not to drink alcohol because it increases uric acid levels. Aspirin and other salicylates should be avoided because they decrease the effectiveness of probenecid and may precipitate a gout attack. Advise client to read the labels of OTC medications carefully because aspirin and other salicylates are found as common ingredients of OTCs.

The client should be cautioned to report to the physician any symptoms of hypersensitivity (skin rash), renal stones (hematuria, dysuria, low back pain), or blood dyscrasias (sore throat, fever, unusual bleeding or bruising, unusual fatigue).

**Evaluation.** The nurse should monitor the client's involved joints for range of motion, pain, and swelling during the course of medication.

Fluid intake and output are monitored to ensure adequacy of urinary output (2000 to 3000 ml daily) to minimize urate stone formation.

CBCs, uric acid determinations, and renal function studies should be evaluated periodically during probenecid therapy.

### sulfinpyrazone (Anturane, Antazone ✳)

The mechanism of action is similar to probenecid. It is indicated for the treatment of chronic gouty arthritis and hyperuricemia. Sulfinpyrazone is well absorbed orally and is highly bound to plasma proteins. It is metabolized in the liver into various metabolites; two of these have therapeutic effects. Parahydroxy-sulfinpyrazone produces about 50% of the uricosuric effect of sulfinpyrazone, whereas a sulfide metabolite has approximately 10 times the antiplatelet action when compared to sulfinpyrazone. The duration of effect for the uricosuric effect is 4 to 6 hours. Sulfinpyrazone is excreted by the kidneys. For side effects/adverse reactions, see Table 63-2.

**Significant drug interactions.** The following interactions may occur when sulfinpyrazone is given concurrently with the drugs listed below:

| Drug | Possible Effect and Management |
|---|---|
| Anticoagulants, (coumarin or indanedione, heparin, or thrombolytics; streptokinase or urokinase) | Sulfinpyrazone may increase the anticoagulant effect by displacing coumarin or indanedione from their protein-binding sites and by inhibiting their metabolism. Monitor prothrombin time closely, since dosage adjustments may be necessary. |
| | An increase in bleeding episodes or hemorrhage may result from concurrent administration of sulfinpyrazone and anticoagulant or thrombolytic therapy. The potential for this reaction is caused by the inhibitory effect of sulfinpyrazone on platelet aggregation and its possibility of causing gastrointestinal ulceration or hemorrhage. |
| azlocillin; carbenicillin, parenteral; dextran; dipyridamole; divalproex; mezlocillin; piperacillin; ticarcillin or valproic acid | These drugs inhibit platelet aggregation; therfore concurrent drug administration may increase the potential of bleeding episodes. Monitor closely. |
| antineoplastic agents, rapidly cytolytic | Do not give concurrently with sulfinpyrazone. Increased risk of inducing uric acid nephropathy or losing control of uric acid serum levels (preexisting levels) and gout is possible. |
| aspirin or salicylates | Concurrent use is not recommended. When salicylates are given long term in moderate to high doses, the uricosuric effect of sulfinpyrazone may be inhibited. See comments about probenecid. |
| cefotetan, cefamandole, cefoperazone, moxalactam, or plicamycin | These drugs can cause platelet function inhibition and hypoprothrombinemia. (Moxalactam can cause irreversible platelet damage.) Monitor closely. |
| nitrofurantoin | Sulfinpyrazone may decrease kidney excretion of nitrofurantoin, which may increase the risk of nitrofurantoin toxicity and reduce the effectiveness of nitrofurantoin as a urinary tract antiinfective agent. Avoid this combination. |

**Dosage and administration.** When administered to adults, for antigout effect, initially give 100 to 200 mg orally twice daily. Increase dosage gradually, if needed, over a 1-week period to a dosage sufficient to control the elevated serum uric acid levels (usually 400 to 800 mg/day).

Maintenance dose is 100 to 400 mg orally twice daily. Pediatric dose is not established.

**Pregnancy safety.** Has not been established.

### ▷ Nursing Management: Sulfinpyrazone Therapy

**Assessment.** Sulfinpyrazone is used with caution in clients with a history of blood dyscrasias, peptic ulcer, renal stones, or renal function impairment.

Assessment of the client receiving sulfinpyrazone should include consideration of the following nursing diagnoses:

altered comfort related to allergic dermatitis, low back pain (uric acid renal calculi), stomach pain, anorexia, nausea and vomiting; risk for injury related to thrombocytopenia (increased tendency to bleed); hyperthermia (allergic reaction); activity intolerance related to anemia; altered bowel elimination (diarrhea); and altered urinary elimination related to renal effects evidenced by decreased urinary output.

**Intervention.** Sulfinpyrazone may be administered with an antacid or food to minimize gastrointestinal distress. Clients should maintain adequate fluid intake (8 ounces 10 to 12 times daily) and urinary alkalinization if necessary, since sulfinpyrazone is a potent uricosuric agent that may cause urolithiasis and renal colic, especially in the initial stages of therapy.

**Education.** Encourage the client to comply with therapy. This is essential since optimal effectiveness of the drug may not be reached for several months. Advise the client that sulfinpyrazone helps prevent gout attacks but does not relieve an acute episode. Regular visits to the health care provider should be maintained to monitor progress.

Stress the importance of adequate fluid intake in the prevention of the formation of stones.

Caution the client not to use alcohol because it increases uric acid levels. Aspirin and other salicylates should be avoided because they decrease the effectiveness of sulfinpyrazone and may precipitate a gout attack.

**Evaluation.** CBCs, uric acid determinations, and renal function studies should be completed at intervals during therapy.

Monitor fluid intake and output to ensure that intake is adequate for sufficient urinary output (2 to 3 L/day) to help prevent urinary stones.

• • •

The nonsteroidal, antiinflammatory agents naproxen, phenylbutazone, and sulindac are also used in the treatment of acute gouty arthritis. For information on these drugs, see Chapter 62.

## SUMMARY

Gout is a metabolic disorder characterized by hyperuricemia. The aims of therapy for gout are to end the acute attack quickly, to prevent a recurrence, to prevent uric acid renal calculi, and to prevent or minimize complications of sodium urate deposits in the joints. Agents used for these purposes are colchicine, allopurinol, probenecid, and sulfinpyrazone.

## BIBLIOGRAPHY

A toxic effect of colchicine. (1988). Emerg Med 20(6):51.

Brassell MP. (1988). Pharmacologic management of rheumatic diseases, Orthop Nurs 7(2):43.

Braunwald E et al. (1987). Harrison's principles of internal medicine, ed 11. New York: McGraw-Hill Book Co.

Kastrup EK, ed. (1991). Facts and comparisons. St. Louis: JB Lippincott Co.

Luciani I. (1989). Fatal IV colchicine in a 60 year old woman, J Emerg Nurs 15(2):80.

United States Pharmacopeial Convention. (1991). Drug information for the health care provider. ed 11. Rockville, Md: The Convention.

Wyngaarden JB and Smith LH. (1988). Cecil's textbook of medicine, ed 18. Philadelphia: WB Saunders Co.

# Unit 16

## Drugs Affecting the Immunologic System

# Overview of the Immunologic System

## CHAPTER OBJECTIVES

*After studying this chapter, you should be able to meet the following objectives and define the key terms.*

1. Identify the lymphoid organs of the immune system.

2. Describe the role of each of the lymphoid organs in the defense of the body against foreign biologic and/or chemical substances.

3. Identify the immunocompetent cells involved in the immune response.

4. Compare and contrast the function of the three major groups of T cells.

5. Describe the action of B cells in response to foreign antigens.

6. Identify the five classes of antibodies and their function.

7. Compare and contrast humoral and cell-mediated immunity.

8. Describe the various types of immunity.

## KEY TERMS

**acquired immunity,** page 981

**antibodies,** page 985

**B lymphocytes (B cells),** page 984

**complement system,** page 987

**immunity,** page 986

**immunocompetent cells,** page 984

**lymphokines,** page 984

**natural resistance,** page 987

**passive immunity,** page 987

**T lymphocytes (T cells)** page 984

### INTRODUCTION

The immunologic system is composed of cells and organs that defend the body against invasion of foreign biologic and/or chemical substances. The immunocompetent cells in the body have an inherent ability to identify foreign protein substances from their own body cells. This chapter will review the organs and tissues of the immune system, the immunocompetent cells, and the types of immunity.

### THE IMMUNE SYSTEM

The spleen, tonsils, lymph nodes, and thymus are the lymphoid organs located in the body. The lymphoid tissues are mainly lymphocytes and plasma cells, which travel freely

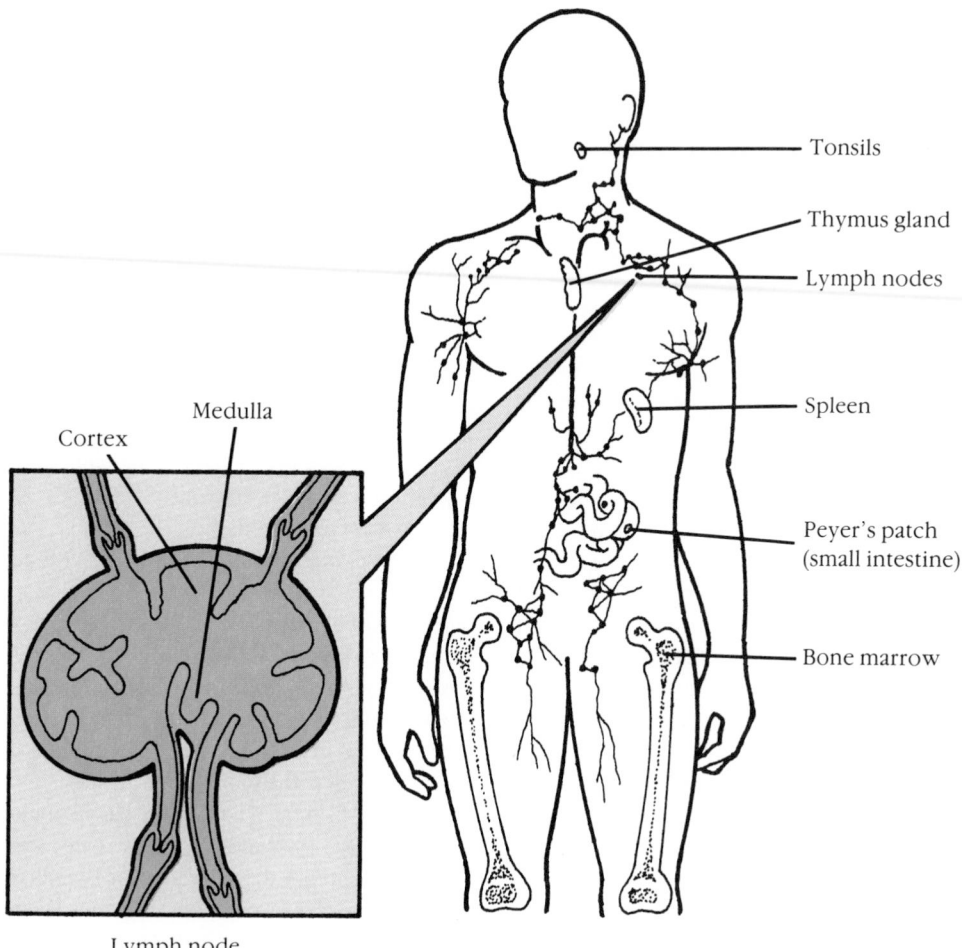

**FIGURE 64-1**  Location of organs and tissues of the immune system; insert shows cross-section of lymph node.

throughout the human system. The two major classes of lymphocytes are T cell and B cell lymphocytes, which are discussed in the section "Immunocompetent Cells." Figure 64-1 identifies the organs and tissues of the immune system.

## Spleen

The spleen, the largest lymphatic organ in the body, performs two main functions: (1) a storage site or reservoir for blood and (2) a processing station for red blood cells (i.e., the RBCs near the end of their life cycle will break down in the spleen).

Macrophages lining the pulp and sinuses of the spleen remove cellular debris and process hemoglobin in the red pulp area of the spleen.

The white pulp area of the spleen contains lymphocytes and plasma cells that are involved in the immune process. The spleen intercepts foreign matter or antigens that have reached the bloodstream.

## Tonsils

The tonsils are an accumulation of lymphoid tissue, named according to their location; lingual, palatine, and pharyngeal tonsils. They intercept foreign bodies or antigens that enter the body by way of the respiratory tract. Similar lymphoid tissue is located in the submucosal areas of the gastrointestinal tract (Peyer's patches) to intercept antigens (bacteria and viruses) entering from the gut. Other lymphoid tissues are located in the bone marrow (help intercept antigens in the blood) and in the lymph nodes.

## Lymph Nodes

The lymph nodes are capsulated organs located throughout the body that are involved with lymph circulation. The outer portion of the lymph node is the cortex, and the inner portion is the medulla. The thymus-dependent zone exists in the deep area or middle cortex. This area contains mainly T lymphocytes, lymphocytes formed or seeded from the thymus gland.

Lymph nodes are essentially a row of in-line filters that screen the lymph flowing through it. Many lymphocytes and macrophages are located throughout the lymph nodes, especially in the cortical, paracortical, and medullary areas. T lymphocytes are located mainly in the paracortical region, whereas plasma cells are found in the medullary sinuses.

## Thymus Gland

The thymus gland is located in the mediastinal area. It processes lymphocytes, and in the early years up to puberty, it rapidly produces lymphocytes. The immune system is developed when immature lymphocytes from the bone marrow are processed in the thymus gland and then sent to the spleen, the lymphatic system, and other tissues and organs in the body to mature. The lymphocytes are active against some bacteria and viruses, allergens, fungus infections, and foreign tissue.

At birth, the thymus gland is larger than in an adult. By the time a person reaches puberty, the thymus has grown to nearly six times its original size. After puberty, this gland undergoes involution, and in the elderly, it is usually a small mass of reticular fibers with some lymphocytes and connective tissue. Although its importance was largely discounted over the years, today it is one of the most important areas for medical research. Scientists are searching for answers to the many questions about the thymus gland and its relationship to the other tissues and organs in the immune system.

## IMMUNOCOMPETENT CELLS

Mononuclear T and B cells and the polymorphonuclear leukocytes (PMLs) are involved in the immune response, although only the mononuclear T cells and B cells are **immunocompetent cells.** The PMLs are nonspecific cells that interact with lymphocytes to produce an inflammatory response, whereas the B cells and T cells are capable of recognizing specific antigens and initiating the immune response.

In humans, stem cells from the bone marrow are transformed to T cells or **T lymphocytes** in the thymus gland and B cells or **B lymphocytes** elsewhere in the body. The T lymphocytes then migrate to lymphoid tissue and organs as reviewed in the previous section. When in contact with an antigen, T lymphocytes will form specialized cells to provide cellular immunity. The B lymphocytes form antibodies to provide humoral immunity.

## T Lymphocytes (T Cells)

T cells are generally long-lived. When they are not in their special areas, they circulate continuously through the body by way of the bloodstream and lymphatic system. They are involved with the B lymphocytes (B cells) in that they can cooperate with them (helper T cells) or inhibit them (suppressor T cells). The B cells do not interact with the thymus. Clones are groups of lymphocytes capable of forming one specific antibody (B cell or T cell) to respond to a specific type of antigen. Only the specific antigen can activate the specialized clones.

When the T cells first contact an antigen, the lymphocytes that recognize the foreign substance will proliferate, thus giving rise to larger numbers of cells that have the capacity to recognize and respond to this antigen. Some of the cells will go on to produce antibody or cell-mediated immune-type responses, whereas others will increase the population of antigen-sensitive memory cells. This is called acquired immunity. The second exposure to this antigen will provoke a more powerful response by the specific T cells.

Three major groups of T cells have been identified in the past few years: (1) cytotoxic T cells, (2) helper T cells, and (3) suppressor T cells.

*Cytotoxic T cells.* This type of cell can bind tightly to organisms or cells that contain their binding-specific antigen. Then the T cells release cytotoxic (probably lysosomal) enzymes directly into the cell. Cytotoxic T cells are capable of killing microorganisms, cancer cells, viruses, heart transplant cells, and other cells that are foreign to the person's body. Body tissue that contains viruses or foreign cells may also be attacked by the killer cells.

*Helper T cells.* These compose the majority of the T cells and help the immune system in many ways.

They increase the activation of B cells, cytotoxic T cells, and suppressor T cells by antigens. Helper T cells clones are activated by very small amounts of antigens, quantities that may not activate the previously mentioned three cells. Once the helper T cells are activated, they secrete **lymphokines** that will increase the response of the three lymphoid cells to the antigen.

Helper T cells may also secrete interleukin-2 (a lymphokine), that is capable of stimulating the action of other T cells (cytotoxic T cells, some suppressor T cells).

Helper T cells also secrete macrophage migration inhibition factor, another lymphokine. This slows or stops the migration of macrophages into the affected area and will also activate the macrophages present to be more effective phagocytotic agents. The activated macrophages can attack and destroy a vastly increased number of the invading organisms.

Acquired immunodeficiency syndrome (AIDS) is the final outcome of an infection with the human immunodeficiency virus (HIV). This virus binds to protein on the cell membranes of the helper T lymphocytes (T4 cells), monocytes, macrophages and colorectal. The helper T cells are destroyed by the virus, which leads to the immunodeficiency known as AIDS. See additional information on this disease state and treatment in Chapter 66.

*Suppressor T cells.* Less is known about these cells than the others, but it is known that they can suppress the function of both cytotoxic and helper T cells. This suppression may be useful in preventing excessive immune reactions that can cause severe body damage. These cells are often called the regulatory T cells.

## B Lymphocytes (B Cells)

B lymphocyte clones are dormant in lymphoid tissue until a foreign antigen appears. The macrophages in the lymphoid tissue phagocytize the foreign substance and the adjacent B lymphocytes and perhaps the T cells are activated. B cells specific for the antigen will enlarge, and some will differentiate to form plasmablasts, a plasma cell precursor, and memory cells. The plasmablasts proliferate and divide, so that in 4 days, approximately 500 plasma cells will be present for each original plasmablast. The plasma cells rapidly produce gamma globulin antibodies that are secreted into the lymph and transported by the blood.

Cells similar to those in the original clone are called memory cells. A second exposure to the same antigen will cause a more rapid and potent antibody response. The first response to an antigen may be slow, weak, and of short duration. The second response will be much more rapid, far more potent and prolonged, and antibodies will be formed for months rather than only for a few weeks. This is the reason why vaccination using several doses given at periods of weeks or months apart is so effective.

## ANTIBODIES

**Antibodies** are gamma globulins (a type of protein), called immunoglobulins, that are specific for particular antigens. At the present time, five classes of antibodies have been identified: IgG, IgM, IgA, IgD, and IgE. (The "Ig" stands for immunoglobulin, and the other letters designate the classes.)

IgG is the major immunoglobulin in the blood (about 75% to 80% of the total antibodies in the normal person) and is

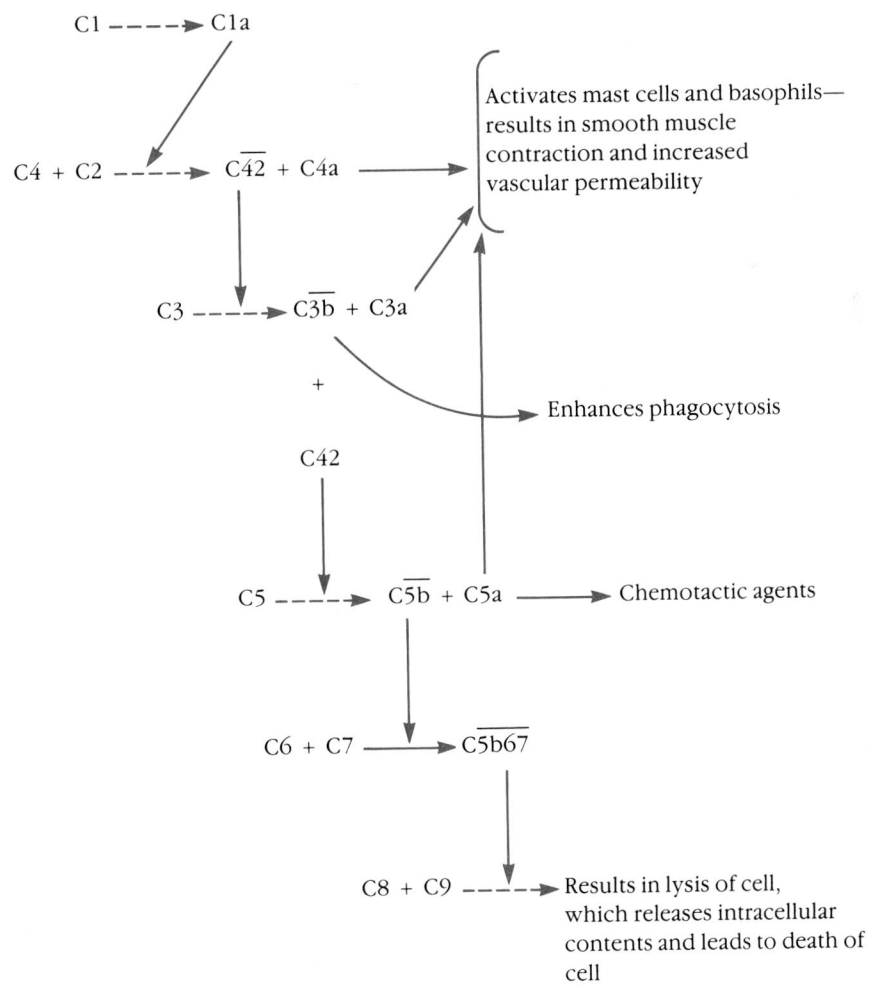

**FIGURE 64-2** Complement system or cascade.

capable of entering tissue spaces, coating microorganisms, activating the complement system and thus accelerating phagocytosis. It is the only immunoglobulin capable of crossing the placenta to provide the fetus with passive immunity until the infant can produce its own immune defense system.

IgM is the first immunoglobulin produced during an immune response. It is located primarily in the bloodstream and develops in response to an invasion of bacteria or viruses. IgM activates complement and can destroy foreign invaders during the initial antigen exposure. Its level decreases in approximately 1 week, while IgG levels are progressively increasing.

IgA is located primarily in external body secretions— that is, saliva, sweat, tears, mucus, bile, and colostrum— and it is found in respiratory tract mucosa and in plasma. It helps to provide a defense against antigens on exposed surfaces and antigens that enter the respiratory and gastrointestinal tracts. The plasma cells in the intestinal area secrete IgA and secretory component to defend the body against bacteria and viruses.

The function of IgD is unknown. It is in the plasma and has been located on lymphocyte surfaces together with IgM, so it may be associated with binding antigens to the cell surface. Although levels of IgD are increased in chronic infections, IgD does not appear to have a particular affinity for specialized antigens.

IgE binds to histamine-containing mast cells and basophils. It can mediate the release of histamine in immune response to parasites (helminths) and in some allergic con-

ditions. It is often called the reaginic antibody because of its involvement in immediate hypersensitivity reactions. Concentrations of it are low in the serum because the antibody is firmly fixed on tissue surfaces. Once activated by an antigen, it will trigger the release of the mast cell granules, resulting in the signs and symptoms of allergy and anaphylaxis.

## IMMUNITY

Links in the chain of the infectious disease may be broken at many points. One link can be broken by attacking the pathogen (human disease-causing organism) with antimicrobial or antiinfective therapy. Another can be broken by augmenting human resistance by using biologic agents such as vaccines and serums, which artificially supply antibodies or catalyze the ability of the immune system to produce its own. An immunologic reaction that destroys or resists foreign cells or their products (antigens) is termed **immunity.** The most successful antigens, or immunogens, are protein or polysaccharide macromolecules that are usually bacterial, viral, fungal, or rickettsial in origin.

The primary types of immunity are humoral immunity and cell-mediated immunity.

### Humoral Immunity

Antigens may be recognized by T helper cells that activate specific B cells, by a strong B cell response to the invasion of certain antigens (such as large polymers, *E. coli,* dex-

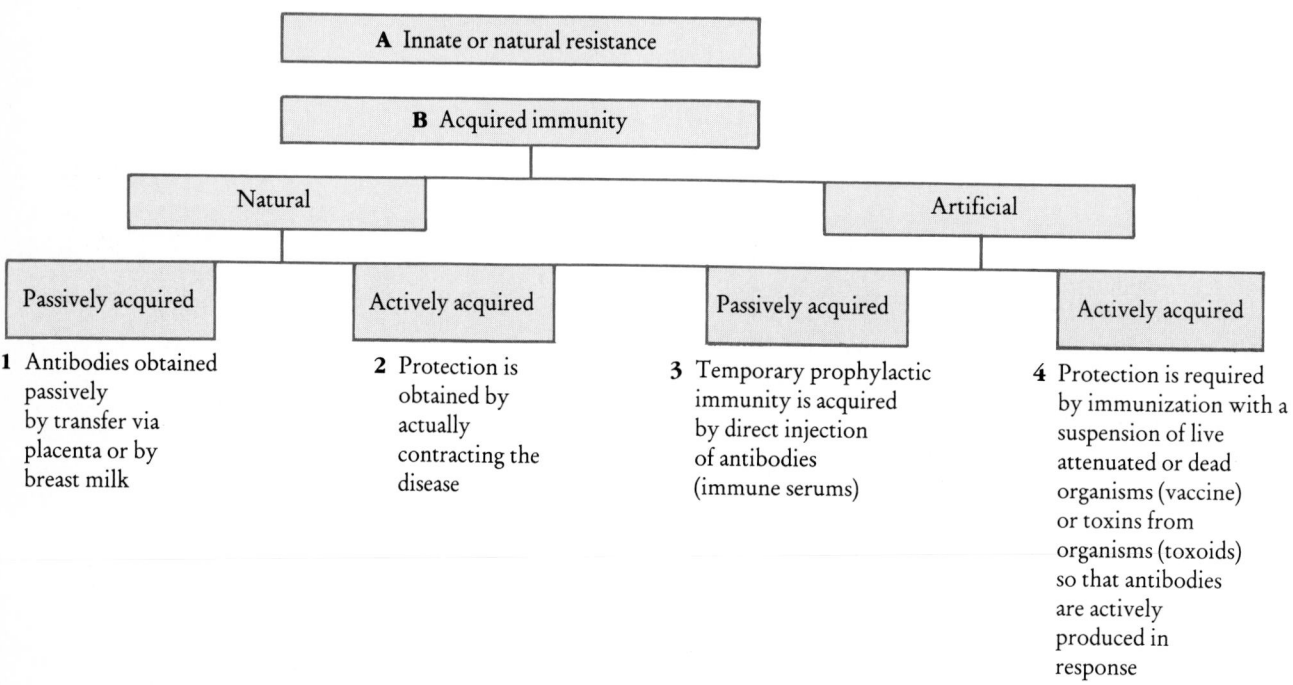

**FIGURE 64-3**  The process of immunity.

trans), or by a macrophage intermediary. Macrophage interactions often enhance the antigen recognition by both T and B cells in the body. Humoral response is described as primary or secondary immune response.

*Primary response.* The foreign antigen in the body will bind to specific B cells to produce specialized antibody-producing plasma cells. Usually within 6 days, antibodies that are specific to the antigen can be found in the blood. Initially the immunoglobulin is IgM, which increases in quantity for up to 2 weeks; then production declines so that very little IgM is present in a few weeks.

After the initial IgM evaluation, IgG antibodies start to appear at approximately day 10, peak in several weeks, and maintain high levels for a much longer time period.

*Secondary response.* This response is often called the memory response, because the immune system responds so much faster to the second exposure to the same antigen. Both T and B memory cells are involved in beginning immediate production of antibodies in large amounts.

The second part of humoral immunity is activation of the **complement system,** a series of approximately 20 proteins that circulate in the blood in an inactive form. When an antigen-antibody complex triggers complement, each component in the cascade is activated in precise order. (See Figure 64-2.) This reaction causes the mast cell release of substances that produces redness, increased heat, and edema of inflammation. It may also cause bacteria cell death and damage to normal tissue that surrounds the affected area.

## Cell-Mediated Immunity

Cell-mediated immunity is the result of contact between T cells and antigens. Receptors on the T cell surface are capable of recognizing foreign antigens, and antigen destruction may occur through one of two processes: (1) directly, by injecting chemical compounds into the target cell membrane (killer activity by cytotoxic T cells) or (2) by secreting lymphokines. The lymphokines can enhance or suppress the action of other lymphocytes, or they can create a chemotactic gradient in the area that will attract macrophages (and eosinophils, basophils, neutrophils) to the site. Cell-mediated immunity (delayed hypersensitivity) involves only the direct action of T cells without humoral assistance.

## Natural and Acquired Immunity

The body has certain inherited and innate abilities to resist encounters with antigens. This ability is known as **natural resistance** (or natural immunity, which is not to be confused with naturally acquired immunity). Some general defenses inherent to natural resistance come from factors familiar to the focus of nursing: for example, adequate rest, nutrition, exercise, and freedom from undue stress. Physiologic factors, which discourage proliferation of microbes, include the acidity of gastric secretions, respiratory tract cilia, and bactericidal lysozymes in tears. During a lifetime an individual may also acquire further immune capabilities through both natural and artificial means. This type of **acquired immunity** is conferred by either active or passive action (see Figure 64-3).

Unbroken skin is extremely effective in barring entry to microorganisms, but a barrage of defenses is mounted by the inflammatory response if invasion does succeed. The immune system identifies the threatening antigens or allergens and creates specific gamma globulins destructive to the particular species of antigen. These gamma globulins, or antibodies or immunoglobulins (Ig), are proteins that are chemically complementary and specifically configured to lock into the foreign antigen, inactivating it. Antibodies also activate cellular defenses to phagocytize the invading microorganisms. Custom-made gamma globulins, or antibodies, provide acquired immunity to the specific type of antigen for varying lengths of time. Those antibodies will then gradually disappear from the serum, but the potential for their rapid replication in response to a repeat challenge by that specific antigen continues to exist after the initial exposure. Consequently, the result is known as *naturally acquired immunity,* which is a process of *naturally acquired active immunity* because of the body's active involvement in creating the antibodies. Naturally acquired immunity can also result from a process of **passive immunity** when antibodies made by the mother's body are passively transferred by means of the placenta or by breast milk (especially colostrum, the breast milk produced shortly after delivery) to the fetus or infant.

On the other hand, artificial induction of the immune state, *artificially acquired immunity,* is initiated purposefully for protection of the susceptible individual. It may also be either induced actively or passively. Artificially acquired *active* immunity is evoked by the deliberate administration of antigens, either live partially modified organisms, killed organisms, or their toxins. The parenteral route is the predominant mode of administration. Periodic reactivation of actively acquired artificial immunity against certain organisms (by booster doses, e.g., tetanus) is sometimes necessary. Artificially acquired passive immunity is conferred by the parenteral administration of antibody-containing immune serum from immune humans or animals (Figure 64-3).

Artificially acquired active immunity generally secures protection for a longer duration than any kind of passive immunity and is usually the prophylactic treatment of choice for populations at potential risk. Side effects may include local pain at the injection site and headache with mild to moderate fever. Because of the agents used, *active* immunity results in fewer adverse effects than passive immunity. Artificially acquired *passive* immunity is often chosen for susceptible individuals following a known exposure. A combination of active and passive approaches is also occasionally used. A number of products used in artificial passive

**TABLE 64-1**   Comparison of active and passive immunity

|  | Active immunity | Passive immunity |
|---|---|---|
| Source | Self | Another human or animal |
| Effectiveness | High | Moderate to low |
| Method | Contracting disease itself (clinical or sublinical case) Immunization     Vaccines (killed or attenuated)     Toxoids | Administration of antibody itself by:     Injection     Maternal transplacental transfer     Breast milk |
| Time taken to develop | 5-14 days | Immediate effect |
| Duration | Relatively long (up to years) | Relatively short (few days or weeks) |
| Ease of reactivation | Easy, by booster dose | May be dangerous; possible anaphylaxis, especially if animal antiserum used |
| Purpose | Prophylactic | Prophylactic and therapeutic |

Modified from Barrett JT: Textbook of immunology, ed 3, St Louis, 1978, The CV Mosby Co.

immunization have caused adverse reactions because of individual hypersensitivities to animal products, especially horse serum or eggs, to the preservative used in a medication, or to an antibiotic. The products of bacterial metabolism are the agents responsible for other adverse reactions. Presence of a mild to moderate upper respiratory tract infection or pregnancy does not always prohibit immunization; however, an immunosuppressed state (as a result of cancer chemotherapy or disease) may. Current manufacturers' instructions should always be consulted. Table 64-1 makes a direct comparison of the capabilities and effects of active and passive immunities.

## SUMMARY

The immunologic system consists of lymphoid organs, the spleen, tonsils, lymph nodes and thymus, and immunocompetent cells, known as T lymphocytes (T cells) and B lymphocytes (B cells), which defend the body against invasion of foreign biologic and chemical substances. Antibodies are immunoglobulins that are specific for particular antigens. Immunity is the immunologic reaction that destroys or resists foreign cells or their products. It may be natural or artificial and actively or passively acquired. Pharmacologic therapy is usually aimed at strengthening the body's immunologic status for the prevention of disease.

## BIBLIOGRAPHY

Abernathy E. (1987). Immunology: how the immune system works, Amer J Nurs 87(4):456.

Barrett JT. (1988). Textbook of immunology: an introduction to immunochemistry and immunobiology, ed 5. St. Louis: The CV Mosby Co.

Bullock BL and Rosendahl PP. (1988). Pathophysiology: adaptations and alterations in function, ed 2. Glenview, Ill: Scott, Foresman and Co.

Dale MM and Foreman JC, eds. (1989). Textbook of immunopharmacology, ed 2. Oxford: Blackwell Scientific Publications.

Grady C. (1988). Host defense mechanisms: an overview, Semin Oncol Nurs 4(2):86.

Guyton AC. (1987). Human physiology and mechanisms of disease, ed. 4. Philadelphia: WB Saunders Co.

Guyton AC. (1990). Textbook of medical physiology, ed 8. Philadelphia: WB Saunders Co.

Ninnemann JL. (1987). Trauma, sepsis, and the immune response, J Burn Care Rehabil 8(6):462.

Petrucci KE et al. (1989). Aging, immunity, and critical care nursing, Crit Care Nurs Clin North Amer 1(4):787.

Reckling JB et al. (1987). Understanding immune system dysfunction, Nursing 17(9):34.

Tribett D. (1989). Immune system function: implications for critical care nursing practice, Crit Care Nurs Clin North Am 1(4):725.

Workman ML. (1989). Immunologic late effects in children and adults, Semin Oncol Nurs 5(1):36.

# 65 Serums, Vaccines, and Other Immunizing Agents

## CHAPTER OBJECTIVES

*After studying this chapter, you should be able to meet the following objectives and define the key terms.*

1. Discuss the present status and anticipated future developments of immunization.

2. State the appropriate immunization schedule for children until the age of two years.

3. Identify immunizations recommended for adults.

4. Describe the recommended use of tetanus toxoid and tetanus immune globulin in wound management.

5. Discuss the nursing management of immunotherapy.

6. List side effects/adverse reactions of immunizations and correlate with client education.

7. Compare the advantages and disadvantages of live attentuated and inactivated biologic products.

## KEY TERMS

**active immunization,** page 994

**antibody titer,** page 990

**endemic,** page 990

**immunoprophylaxis,** page 1003

**passive immunization,** page 1000

## INTRODUCTION

Intact skin and mucous membranes are the body's first defense against invasion by potentially lethal microorganisms (microbes). The antiinflammatory process and/or a competent immune system are the body's defense against microbes that break this barrier. Disease immunity exists when the body is capable of producing specific antibodies to combat infections caused by specific antigens or microbes. This immunity may be referred to as natural or acquired immunity in that a person who recovers from an infectious disease produces antibodies and memory cells against that specific antigen. The next time the body is in contact with the same antigen, the immune system will be primed to destroy the antigen. This is known as naturally active, acquired immunization.

A passively acquired immunity occurs when antibodies are transferred from a human or animal to the susceptible person. Newborn infants usually have passive acquired immunization that is naturally acquired from their mothers. But this type of immunity protects only for short periods of time (weeks to several months). Vaccines containing altered

989

microbes, dead or live (attenuated so that it does not induce the disease) whole or parts of microbes, may be administered to produce a specific immunity in the individual. Both vaccines will stimulate antibody production usually without inducing the specific disease state. The differences between these vaccines will be discussed in this chapter.

## THE PRESENT

The critical age period for immunization is 2 months of age through grade school entry and during the school years (several states now require maintenance of immunizations as a criterion for retention in the school system). Certain groups are found to be at high risk: adolescents, new parents (unimmunized or with waning immunity, exposed to childhood illness or vaccines), and health care providers. Other groups such as migrant workers and recent immigrants to the United States and Canada are predictably at high risk for infectious diseases.

International political and economic upheavals and the Indochinese and Cuban refugee influx to the United States all have pointed up the major problems these people encounter: diphtheria, measles deaths, hepatitis B, tuberculosis, and malaria carrier status. Immunization programs that are taken for granted in the United States and other countries are virtually unheard of in many others. As a group adolescents also seem to be at high risk for preventable infections. Of these, certain subgroups may be particularly in need of immunization, such as athletes, heavy drug users, runaways, foreign travelers, and those isolated from or rejecting traditional health care.

Several million children are not immunized against measles, polio, rubella (German measles), mumps, diphtheria, pertussis (whooping cough), and tetanus.

Newspapers and television news coverage have reported the adverse reactions associated with pertussis vaccine and some of the other vaccines, which have served to bias some viewers against vaccination. It is important to stress that the vaccines are not without some risks, but the serious risks associated with not being vaccinated and actually contracting the disease are greater still. Diphtheria, tetanus, polio, and the other diseases can cause crippling and death, and most are very contagious. Schedules for immunizations of these diseases have been developed as guidelines for the practitioner and for parents to ensure adequate protection for their children (Table 65-1).

A valid history of clinical disease or obtaining an **antibody titer** for some of these diseases is useful in determining disease exposure and immunity. However, proven exposure to the disease does not always guarantee immunity. Therefore timely immunizations are even more important if the potential for development of the disease is imminent or increased, as it is for persons traveling to foreign countries where some diseases are **endemic.** Required and recommended immunizations for foreign travel are constantly changing and are best obtained before travel from the local department of health.

Special assessments must be made when exposure, for example, to measles or tetanus has occurred. Measles can be prevented if exposure is followed within 72 hours by administration of the live measles vaccine. However, people who were vaccinated with the *killed*-virus measles vaccine between 1963 and 1967 and who have never had the disease have now been found to be at considerable risk. They are not protected from measles, and they are at serious risk of developing an atypical type of measles with fever spiking to 104° F (40° C), cough with abnormal infiltrates as seen on roentgenograms, a rash progressing paradoxically from the periphery, and occasionally cardiomegaly and a mild drop in the platelet count. Nurses should advise all individuals over 12 years of age who have not had the live measles vaccine or the disease itself to get immunized with the *live* measles vaccine. Other special immunizations recommended for adults 18 years and older are listed in Table 65-2.

Any time a traumatic wound (especially a puncture

**TABLE 65-1**   Recommended schedule for active immunization of normal infants and children

| Age | Vaccines | Special comments |
|---|---|---|
| 2 months | DPT-1,* OPV-1 | If necessary, may be given earlier if endemic to the area. |
| 4 months | DPT-2, OPV-2 | |
| 6 months | DPT-3 | A third dose of OPV is optional in areas of high endemicity of poliomyelitis. |
| 15 months | MMR, DPT-4, OPV-3 | May be given simultaneously. |
| 25 months | Hemophilus B polysaccharide vaccine | May be given between 18 to 23 months for infants at increased risk, i.e., those who attend daycare centers. |
| 4-6 years | DPT-5, OPV-4 | Given before or when entering the school system. |
| 14-16 years | Td | Repeat every 10 years during lifetime. |

From Immunization Practices Advisory Committee, Centers for Disease Control, MMWR, 1986.

*DPT, Diphtheria, tetanus toxoid, and pertussis vaccine; *OPV*, oral, attenuated poliovirus vaccine containing poliovirus types 1, 2, and 3; *MMR*, live measles, mumps, and rubella viruses; *Td*, adult tetanus toxoid and diphtheria toxoid in combination; this contains the same dose of tetanus toxoid as DPT or DT, but it has a reduced dose of diphtheria toxoid.

**TABLE 65-2**  Immunizations recommended for adults (18 and older)

| Immunizing agent | Indication(s)/dosage schedule |
|---|---|
| **For all adults routinely:** | |
| Tetanus toxoid | Management of wounds. IM booster dose every 10 years. |
| Diphtheria toxoid | As a preventive or to help in management of contacts with persons with diphtheria. IM dose every 10 years. |
| **For selected persons:** | |
| Influenza vaccine | Elderly persons or persons with chronic disease states. Adults living in high-risk situations: nursing home residents, medical personnel, or healthy persons 65 years and older. Annually. |
| Pneumococcal vaccine | High-risk persons, such as those with underlying health problems and healthy elderly persons 65 years and older. Once only. |
| **For adolescents and young persons:** | |
| Measles vaccine | For persons born after 1956 who have not had measles or have not previously received a live virus vaccine. SC schedule, 2 doses. |
| Rubella vaccine | For hospital workers, adolescent and adult females who are not immunized and have no laboratory evidence of immunity. SC once. |
| Hepatitis B vaccine | For persons at high risk of hepatitis exposure, such as health care personnel, hemodialysis patients, drug abusers, those exposed to a family member with hepatitis, and travelers. Three doses are the usual dosage schedule. |

Modified from Abramowicz M ed. (1990). Routine immunization for adults, The Medical Letter 32(819):54-56.

wound) is encountered, the individual's tetanus immunization status must be assessed. If the person has not been fully immunized within the past 10 years, or if the wound is contaminated and an immunization is more than 5 years old, a booster dose of tetanus toxoid may be in order (Table 65-3).

Most new parents today are too young to remember the fear engendered by the very mention of childhood illnesses a few decades ago. If parents are not convinced, outbreaks of diseases (e.g., poliomyelitis) may make the argument for us. Complacency about childhood illnesses and their current and potential threats must be shaken. The initial effects of childhood illnesses can be very serious, and more potential future hazards are currently being discovered (e.g., the possible association of mumps with eventual diabetes and of chickenpox with shingles).

A request for exemption from required immunizations for school entry on medical grounds can be obtained from the child's physician. A model form for exemption on religious grounds can be obtained from the Christian Science Committee on Publications. However, it is *theoretically* possible that the right to exempt certain children could interfere with "herd immunity" by sustaining a continued pool of susceptibles, thereby maintaining a hazard that would be unacceptable to other parents, who might apply legal and other pressures.

Community health nurses, school nurse-teachers, local public health departments, the Department of Health and Human Services, and the World Health Organization need to work together to share expertise in educating the public, in casefinding and reporting, in screening, and in mass immunization programs.

## CURRENT AND FUTURE DEVELOPMENTS

The overall picture of immunization shows that currently there is renewed evaluation of the effects and effectiveness of the "vaccine era" during which morbidity and mortality rates of infectious diseases (especially childhood illness, with the exception of pertussis) were significantly reduced by artificially acquired means. Refinements and developments in clinical immunology are advancing even as still more dilemmas arise.

**TABLE 65-3**  Guide to tetanus prophylaxis in wound management

| History of tetanus immunization (doses) | Clean, minor wounds | | All other wounds† | |
|---|---|---|---|---|
| | Td* | TIG | Td | TIG |
| Uncertain or less than 3 | Yes | No | Yes | Yes |
| 3 or more‡ | No§ | No | No‖ | No |

From the 1988 Report of the Committee on Infectious Diseases, ed 21. Published by the American Academy of Pediatrics, Elk Grove Village, Ill.

*Td = adult type tetanus and diphtheria toxoids. If the patient is less than 7 years old, DT or DTP is given (see text). TIG = tetanus immune globulin.

†Including but not limited to wounds contaminated with dirt, feces, soil, saliva; puncture wounds, avulsions, wounds resulting from missiles, crushing, burns, and frostbite.

‡If only three doses of *fluid* toxoid have been received, a fourth dose of toxoid, preferably an adsorbed toxoid, should be given.

§Yes, if more than 10 years since the last dose.

‖Yes, if more than 5 years since the last dose.

1. Live vaccine-related diseases have surfaced as problems. During the 1970s, in approximately 1 case in 11 million live poliovirus vaccinations, the vaccinee developed the disease itself. About 1 in 4 million of the vaccinees' contacts was found to develop polio of the vaccine type (versus the wild poliovirus type). This was thought to be an outstandingly safe record by comparison with some countries (e.g., the Soviet Union) and a deplorable record by comparison with others. Studies indicate the possibility that mutant strains of neurovirulent polioviruses (especially Type 3 virus) may be excreted in vaccinees' feces. There was some consideration of the renewed use of the inactivated poliovirus vaccine (IPV) of the 1950s or a new one being developed to avoid this eventuality. This approach must be weighed according to feasibility and risk versus benefits: the probability of a family returning for the necessary booster doses of IPV must be balanced against the probability of their contracting poliovirus as a result of vaccination with trivalent oral poliovirus vaccine (TOPV). Intensive campaigns to immunize infants and small children have since significantly reduced the number of susceptible individuals.

The whole question of vaccine safety seems to loom large in the decision-making process of the public. When questioned, only about half the parents interviewed at the close of the 1970s thought vaccines were *very* safe, and only one third thought they were moderately safe. This belief may partly account for the statistics that, at the same time, only about 68% of 10- to 14-year-olds were found to be adequately protected against the common infectious diseases. The other reason may be that childhood diseases are just not seen as significant anymore.

2. Immunization with the killed-virus measles vaccine given from 1963 to 1967 apparently left the vaccinee more vulnerable to an atypical measles virus with severe side effects. Increasingly a college-age person or parent is the subject of a relatively virulent form of some childhood disease for which he or she was much earlier immunized or whose antibody titers are waning.

3. Other secondary effects are surfacing: some booster injections (e.g., tetanus) seem to increase sensitivity to the antigen, resulting in severe reactions. Following the swine flu vaccination program, there were significant reports of apparently vaccine-related cases of Guillain-Barré syndrome. Since increasing numbers of liability claims against vaccine producers can be anticipated among our more astute population, children's health care practitioners can increasingly anticipate being objects of a lawsuit or being called as expert witnesses.

4. Poultry allergy is less of a potential threat than originally supposed, since only minute quantities of potential allergens are found in the vaccines and then only in those grown in egg embryo culture. Reactions to antibiotics and thimerosal allergy must still be dealt with, however.

5. Evidence is building that desired antibody formation from vaccines is subject to interference from concurrent passive transfer by way of immune serum or antitoxin, or by way of maternal transplacental or breast milk transfer of maternal antibodies, or interference when one single-virus vaccine is injected simultaneously with another virus vaccine. Such coincidences must be avoided through immunization schedules.

## AIDS Vaccine

Acquired immunodeficiency syndrome (AIDS), which results in often fatal, unusual malignancies and opportunistic infections, has been recognized as a new immunodeficiency state resulting from an infection with a human retrovirus, the human immunodeficiency virus or HIV-I. Investigators have intensified their search for a vaccine to protect high risk persons from developing this disease. A study from a Harvard University research team reported they found a vaccine that showed promise in protecting animals (rhesus monkeys) against the AIDS retrovirus. While this is promising news, it is considered preliminary because there is a significant difference between the strains of virus in humans and monkeys (Drug Research, 1989). Research is continuing with killed or attenuated HIV, recombinant vaccinia virus, and even subunit vaccines. Subunit vaccines are fragments of the viral proteins. A major potential problem with the search for an AIDS vaccine is that there are many currently identified HIV strains with new strains still being discovered (Baum RD, 1987). See Chapter 66, "Immunosuppressants and Immunomodulators."

## SIDE EFFECTS/ADVERSE REACTIONS

As important as protection from debilitating infectious disease is, even immunization is not without some risk. *Side*

---

### LIVE VS INACTIVATED PRODUCTS

The advantages of live attenuated-type immunization are the long-lasting immunity, and the similarity of the resistance that occurs to the disease to that produced by the natural disease. The disadvantages with the live immunization are an increased risk of inducing disease, plus the fact that a mild disease state is usually needed in order to induce immunity. One also has a higher risk of the vaccine being contaminated, and finally, the product is more labile, requiring special storage.

The inactivated (killed) biologic product is easier to ship and store. It is usually highly purified and has little risk of inducing a disease from infection. The disadvantage is that it provides a short-acting immunity so that the person often needs reimmunization. It may or may not simulate protective type factors, and it may not prevent a reinfection without the actual disease having been present.

*effects* (i.e., slight fever, sore injection site, or minor rash) are usually mild and transient; occasionally more *serious effects* (i.e., encephalitis and convulsions) are reported. Although serious, the incidence of these effects, when weighed against effects of diseases preventable through immunization, usually tips the balance in favor of immunization, particularly for those at high risk.

Joint pains and malaise may also be seen, especially after certain live and inactivated vaccines. Rarely allergy to the egg protein providing the culture medium for the organism involved, to antiserums or antitoxins, to the mercury preservative, or to contained antibiotics causes a reaction that is usually controllable by antihistamines. When any unusual or severe reaction occurs, the nurse should contact the practitioner and an informational form should be sent to the Centers for Disease Control. Vaccinees should be given a contact's name in case they become sick and visit a physician, hospital, or clinic within 4 weeks after immunization. Adverse reaction monitoring is part of a surveillance system to detect uncommon, severe, previously unrecognized, and rare reactions to vaccination. Past examples are the Guillain-Barré syndrome accompanying a small percentage of influenza vaccinations, encephalitis following measles vaccine, and peripheral neuropathy after rubella vaccinations; these are all *very* rare occurrences. Even though uncommon, a large number of benign, expected reactions could indicate a "hot" lot of vaccine. Data are collected by the Centers for Disease Control for comparison with national data and are published in the *Quarterly Adverse Reaction Report*.

Minor expected reactions can be treated with acetaminophen and rest. Severe fevers (more than 103° F) can be treated with acetaminophen and sponge baths to reduce the temperature; occasionally a convulsion may accompany a high temperature, and parents need to be advised. Serum sickness sometimes occurs after repeated serum injections; it consists of rash, urticaria, arthritis, adenopathy, and fever starting hours or even days after the injection. Treatment consists of analgesics, antihistamines, ephedrine, or corticosteroids. Rare but serious anaphylactic reactions can cause urticaria, dyspnea, cyanosis, shock, or unconsciousness that occurs within minutes of injection. This is not normal; it is an emergency situation. Therefore a nurse or someone responsible should observe any recipient of immunotherapy for up to half an hour after therapy. Treatment for anaphylaxis may involve epinephrine 1:1000 (0.01 ml/kg) in a 1:10 dilution subcutaneously or intramuscularly immediately, administered slowly in a physiologic saline solution. This may possibly be repeated and followed by intravenous administration of epinephrine. Vasopressors and intermittent positive pressure breathing (IPPB) oxygen, antihistamines, and corticosteroids may help. Immunization therapy may cautiously be resumed after all signs of anaphylaxis are gone.

Nurses often find themselves in charge of vaccination programs and clinics. Since nurses are often the first to be consulted by clients, keeping current about the changes in immunizations is important. A description of biologic agents (active and passive) used for immunization and their secondary effects may be found in Tables 65-4 and 65-5.

*Text continued on p. 999.*

**TABLE 65-4**   Vaccination during pregnancy

| | Vaccine | Indications for vaccination during pregnancy |
|---|---|---|
| **LIVE VIRUS VACCINES** | | |
| Measles | Live-attenuated | Contraindicated. |
| Mumps | | |
| Rubella | | |
| Yellow fever | Live-attenuated | Contraindicated except if exposure is unavoidable. |
| Poliomyelitis | Trivalent live-attenuated (OPV) | Persons at substantial risk of exposure may receive live-attenuated virus vaccine. |
| **INACTIVATED VIRUS VACCINES** | | |
| Hepatitis B | Plasma derived, purified hepatitis B surface antigen | Pregnancy is not a contraindication. |
| Influenza | Inactivated type A and type B virus vaccines | Usually recommended only for patients with serious underlying disease. It is prudent to avoid vaccination during the first trimester. Consult health authorities for current recommendations. |
| Poliomyelitis | Killed virus (IPV) | OPV, not IPV, is indicated when immediate protection of pregnant females is needed. |

From Health Information for International Travel, Atlanta, 1988, US Department of Health and Human Services, Centers for Disease Control.   *Continued.*

**TABLE 65-4** Vaccination during pregnancy—cont'd

| | Vaccine | Indications for vaccination during pregnancy |
|---|---|---|
| Rabies IG | Killed virus | Substantial risk of exposure |
| **INACTIVATED BACTERIAL VACCINES** | | |
| Cholera | Killed bacterial | Should reflect actual risks of disease and probable benefits of vaccine. |
| Typhoid | | |
| Plague | Killed bacterial | Selective vaccination of exposed persons. |
| Meningococcal | Polysaccharide | Only in unusual outbreak situations. |
| Pneumococcal | Polysaccharide | Only for high-risk persons. |
| **TOXOIDS** | | |
| Tetanus-diphtheria (Td) | Combined tetanus-diphtheria toxoids, adult formulation | Lack of primary series, or no booster within past 10 years. |
| **IMMUNE GLOBULINS, POOLED OR HYPERIMMUNE** | Immune globulin or specific globulin preparations | Exposure or anticipated unavoidable exposure to measles, hepatitis A, hepatitis B, rabies, or tetanus. |

**TABLE 65-5** Biological agents for active immunization

**Active immunization** uses either inactivated (K or killed) material or live (L) attenuated agents.
Advantages: Usually higher levels of antibody are induced and it is not necessary to repeat the procedure frequently.
Disadvantages: Adverse effects may occur, such as allergic reactions, that are not usually seen with passive immunization.
See box on p. 992 for advantages and disadvantages of live attenuated and inactivated biologic products.

| Product | Route of administration | Primary immunization schedule | Comments | Nursing assessment for contraindications and side effects/implementation |
|---|---|---|---|---|
| Cholera vaccine | (K) bacteria SC, IM | Two doses, 1-4 wk apart | Provides 50% protection for about 6 mo. | *Assessment.* Contraindications: acute illness; severe reaction or allergic response to previous dose; pregnancy evaluated individually. Precautions: review of hypersensitivity history. Side effects: redness, induration, pain at site; occasionally—malaise, headache, mild to moderate temperature elevations. *Implementation.* Administer IM in the deltoid muscle to adults and children over 3. Have epinephrine 1:1000 on hand. |
| Diphtheria toxoid | IM | Three doses, 4 or more wk apart; follow schedule in Table 66-1. | If seizures occur, use Td.* | *Assessment.* Contraindications: acute infection; reaction to initial dose, such as high fever, seizure, shock, purpura; preexisting neurologic disorder; immunosuppression; febrile states. Side effects: usual—local redness and possible tenderness; possible abscess; mild to moderate fever. |
| Hemophilus b polysaccharide vaccine (Hib) | SC | One dose to children 18-24 mo. | Efficacy improved if given to child over 2 years old. Should be given to high-risk infants at age 18 mo. | *Assessment.* Contraindicated in immunosuppression, acute illnesses, and febrile states. *Implementation.* Shake vial well. Store in medical refrigerator. May be given at the same time as DPT but at different sites. Reconstitute with diluent provided. Record date on vial. Refrigerate; stable 30 days. Have epinephrine 1:1000 available. |

*Td, Combination of tetanus toxoid and diphtheria toxoid. Less diphtheria toxoid is contained in Td as compared with diphtheria toxoid.

**TABLE 65-5**   Biological agents for active immunization—cont'd

| Product | Route of administration | Primary immunization schedule | Comments | Nursing assessment for contraindications and side effects/implementation |
|---|---|---|---|---|
| Hepatitis B | (K)-IM | Three doses. First two doses 1 mo apart, third at 6 mo. In immuno-compromized persons give double dosage. | Provides >90% protection. | *Assessment.* Contraindications/precautions: hypersensitivity. Safety and efficacy not yet established for children under 3 mo of age and in pregnant or breast-feeding women. Clinical judgment would probably weigh the risk of the disease higher then the potential risks caused by the vaccine's secondary effects. Delay giving vaccine in serious active infection or in presence of severely compromised cardiopulmonary status. Frequent handwashing, gloving (especially if any breaks in skin), and isolation modalities are essential for nurses in particular.<br>Side effects: 50% report various degrees of temporary injection site soreness; occasionally—101° F fevers are reported; infrequently—malaise, headache, nausea, myalgias, arthralgias.<br>*Implementation.* Shake before drawing up suspension; inspect for particles; do not dilute. Store opened and unopened vials in the refrigerator. |
| Influenza | (K)-IM | One dose. Split doses used in persons under 13 years old (lower incidence of side effects). | Give annually by November. | *Assessment.* Contraindications: hypersensitivity to egg products; individuals who are immunosuppressed; acute febrile illness; do not inject intravenously.<br>Precautions: pregnancy; keep epinephrine on hand; not effective against all possible strains of influenza virus; resterilize jet injection apparatus if contaminated with blood; complete immunizations by November. Toxic drug reactions may occur (especially with phenytoin, warfarin, or theophylline) following viral infection or vaccination.<br>Side effects: local tenderness, redness, induration; fever, malaise, myaglia; rare—allergic skin and respiratory reactions and Guillian-Barré syndrome; very rare—encephalopathy.<br>*Implementation.* Inject IM into deltoid or lateral mid-thigh or gluteus. Refrigerate. Have epinephrine 1:1000 available. |
| Measles virus vaccine | (L)-SC | One dose at 15 mo; earlier if epidemic occurs. | If given before 15 mo, may reimmunize. Also may prevent disease if given within 48 hr of exposure to measles. | *Assessment.* Contraindications: neomycin or chicken product hypersensitivity; active febrile infection; active untreated TB; immunosuppression or immunodeficiency; bone marrow or lymphatic deficiencies; pregnancy (pregnancy should also be avoided for 3 mo after vaccination).<br>Precautions: give no sooner than 3 mo after transfusion of blood/plasma/human ISG of more than 0.02 ml/lb body weight. Give with or after TB skin test. Do not give within 1 mo of immunization by other live virus vaccines except one of the M-M-R type or combination. |

*Continued.*

**TABLE 65-5** Biological agents for active immunization—cont'd

| Product | Route of administration | Primary immunization schedule | Comments | Nursing assessment for contraindications and side effects/implementation |
|---|---|---|---|---|
| | | | | Side effects: moderate fever to 102° F, rash (in 5-12 days); rare—fever more than 103° F with convulsions; 1 per million occurrences—encephalitis or subacute sclerosing panencephalitis; previous recipients of *killed* virus vaccine—local swelling, redness, vesiculation. *Implementation.* A 25-gauge ⅝-inch needle is recommended. Refrigerate before reconstitution and afterward. Use within 8 hr; avoid light at all times. Inject 0.5 ml reconstituted vaccine subcutaneously. Solution may be pink or yellow but must be clear. Discard cloudy solutions. Have epinephrine 1:1000 available. |
| Meningococcal meningitis vaccine | SC | One dose. If a household disease, antibiotic prophylaxis (rifampin) should be given for several days, since antibody response requires at least 5 days. | Used in epidemics. | *Assessment.* Obtain immunization and allergy history. Contraindications: immunosuppression; acute illness. Precautions: pregnancy. Side effects: mild, local erythema. *Implementation.* Administer in a single parenteral dose. Do not give IV. Have epinephrine 1:1000 available. |
| Mumps vaccine | (L)-SC | One dose | If administered before 1 year old, reimmunization may be necessary. | *Assessment.* Contraindications and precautions: same as for measles vaccine with following exceptions in side effects. Side effects: mild fever (uncommonly more than 103° F); low incidence of parotitis, orchitis, purpura, allergic reactions (urticaria); very rare—encephalitis and other nervous system reactions. *Implementation.* Same as measles vaccine. |
| Pertussis (in DPT and pertussis vaccine alone) | (K)-IM | As per DPT (see Table 65-1) | Not usually given after age 6. | *Assessment.* Contraindications: acute infection; previous reactions to an initial dose (all 3 antigens or only pertussis may be omitted then) such as fever greater than 103° F (39° C), convulsion, altered consciousness, focal neurologic signs, "screaming fits," shock/collapse, purpura; preexisting neurologic disorder; immunosuppression; older than 6 yr (give Td instead). Precautions: reactions to DPT call for reevaluation and possibly administration of Td only. Side effects: usual—local redness, induration, and possible tenderness; possible abscess; mild to moderate fever. *Implementation.* Administer IM into deltoid or thigh, varying site each time. Shake before using. Refrigerate. have epinephrine 1:1000 available. |
| Pneumococci polysaccharide vaccine | SC, IM | 0.5 ml | Not used in children under 2 yr old. | *Implementation.* Keep refrigerated. Inject into deltoid or midlateral thigh. Have epinephrine 1:1000 available. |

**TABLE 65-5**   Biological agents for active immunization—cont'd

| Product | Route of administration | Primary immunization schedule | Comments | Nursing assessment for contraindications and side effects/implementation |
|---|---|---|---|---|
| | | | | *Assessment.* Contraindications: hypersensitivity, revaccination, pregnancy, intradermal administration, and IV administration. Will not protect against specific antigens not included. Within 10 days of start of chemotherapy for Hodgkin's disease, vaccine is contraindicated. |
| | | | | Precautions: active infection; under 2 yr of age; immunosuppression; severely compromised cardiac or pulmonary function; history of pneumococcal infection. Keep epinephrine on hand. |
| | | | | Side effects: local redness and soreness, induration, fever greater than 100.9° F; rare—anaphylactoid reactions. |
| Poliomyelitis vaccine | (L)-Oral | Two doses, 6-8 wk apart (see Table 66-1). | | *Assessment.* Contraindications: never administered parenterally or in acute illness; advanced, debilitated condition; persistent vomiting or diarrhea; immunodeficient or immunosuppressed states. |
| | | | | Precautions: will not modify/prevent existing or incubating disease. |
| | | | | Side effects: rarely—paralytic disease after vaccination or after contact with vaccinee (advise unimmunized close contacts of vaccinee to seek immunization as needed). |
| | | | | *Implementation.* Store frozen, thaw before use, and agitate before giving 2 drops orally, in chlorine-free water, simple syrup, or milk, or on bread, cake, or cube sugar (usually dropper supplied). See package insert for specific storage advice. Change of color from pink to yellow is not remarkable. |
| Rabies vaccine | (K)-IM | Preexposure: two doses a week apart followed by a third dose in 14-21 days in endemic areas. Postexposure: five doses on days 1, 3, 7, 14, and 28. Give rabies immune globulin concurrently. | | *Assessment.* History of hypersensitivity dictates cautious use of rabies vaccine. *Implementation.* Flush and cleanse wound; possible initial prophylaxis with tetanus and antibiotic therapy. Have epinephrine 1:1000 available. Discontinue corticosteroids during immunization. |
| Rubella | (L)-SC | One dose. | Give after client 15 mo old. Do not give during pregnancy. Women must not become pregnant for 3 mo after injection. Contraceptive counseling may be needed. | *Assessment.* Contraindications and precautions as for Attenuvax with the following exceptions. Contraindications: postpubertal females with rubella titers of more than 1:8; pregnancy (pregnancy also to be avoided for 3 mo after vaccine). Precautions: theoretical possibility of live virus transmission from nose/throat of vaccinees. Side effects: occasionally—mild symptoms of naturally acquired rubella (lymphadenopathy, |

*Continued.*

**TABLE 65-5**   Biological agents for active immunization—cont'd

| Product | Route of administration | Primary immunization schedule | Comments | Nursing assessment for contraindications and side effects/implementation |
|---|---|---|---|---|
| | | | | urticaria, rash, malaise, sore throat, fever, headache, polyneuritis, arthralgias, local pain, swelling, redness; fever rarely more than 103°F); very rarely—encephalitis. *Implementation.* Same as for measles vaccine. |
| Smallpox vaccine | (L)-intradermal | One dose. | Today this vaccine is only indicated for the military and laboratory personnel who work with poxviruses.<br><br>No longer required for travel; production for local use was discontinued in 1983. | *Assessment.* Contraindications: not to be used for treatment of warts or recurrent herpes simplex infections; infants with "failure to thrive" syndrome; anyone with disturbed skin integrity; immunosuppression or immunodeficiency; pregnancy.<br>Precautions: blot off excess vaccine; vaccination equipment should be burned, boiled, or autoclaved before disposal.<br>Side effects: severe neurologic disorders; generalized rashes; local pyrogenic infections (see package insert for details).<br>*Implementation.* Injection is by needle punctures through a drop of vaccine on the skin; site should be inspected for presence of desired vesicle after 6-8 days. Store dry but refrigerated. |
| Tetanus toxoid | IM | Two doses 1 mo apart. Third dose 6-12 months after second dose. Included in DPT (see Table 65-1). | School children and adults receive fourth dose 6-12 mo after initial series. Duration of effect, 10 yr. | *Assessment.* Contraindications; not for *treatment* of an actual tetanus infection; any acute infection; immunosuppression.<br>Precautions: hypersensitivity; keep epinephrine on hand; history of cerebral damage, neurologic disorders, or febrile convulsions should be evaluated individually.<br>Side effects: occasionally—Arthus-type response to high levels of tetanus antibody (antitoxin) in those receiving regular or frequent tetanus toxoid boosters (thus the recommended 10-yr interval between Td booster). Response may include significant local symptoms of redness, edema resembling a giant "hive," axillary lymphadenopathy; systemic symptoms can include low fever, malaise, aches and pains, general urticaria, tachycardia, and hypotension. Prolonged intervals between primary immunizing doses has no effect on eventual immunity status.<br>*Implementation.* Shake well and give deep IM, avoiding blood vessels. Refrigerate, but do not freeze. have epinephrine 1:1000 available. |
| Tuberculosis BCG vaccine | (L)-SC or intradermal | One dose. | Because of questionable efficacy, this product is not commonly used in the U.S. | *Assessment.* Contraindications: altered immune states.<br>Precautions: pregnancy; postvaccination sensitivity may mimic positive reaction to tuberculin following a skin test for TB. Full, lasting protection from TB cannot be ensured postvaccination (great variance in efficacy among BCG products).<br>Side effects (can occur up to 1 yr later): severe local ulceration, lymphadenitis; very rare—osteomyelitis, lupoid reactions, disseminated BCG infection, death. |

**TABLE 65-5**  Biological agents for active immunization—cont'd

| Product | Route of administration | Primary immunization schedule | Comments | Nursing assessment for contraindications and side effects/implementation |
|---|---|---|---|---|
| | | | | *Implementation.* Reconstitute, do not shake, protect from light, and use within 8 hr. Halve dose on label for those under 28 days old and revaccinate with full dose after 1 yr old (intracutaneous route or follow label). Strains and efficacy vary among different preparations. |
| Typhoid vaccine | (K)-SC or intradermal | Two doses 1 mo or more apart. | Approximately 70% protective. Only recommended for travel, epidemics, or identified household carriers. | *Assessment.* Contraindications: acute infection; allergic reaction to previous dose. Precautions: get history of possible hypersensitivity. Keep current regarding recent literature. Side effects: local redness, induration, tenderness; malaise, headache, myalgia, elevated temperature. *Implementation.* Shake vial well before use. Keep refrigerated. Have epinephrine 1:1000 available. |
| Yellow fever vaccine | (L)-SC | One dose. | Only for persons living in or traveling to Africa and South America. | *Assessment.* Contraindications: pregnancy; altered immune states; hypersensitivity to eggs and certain contained antibiotics. Precautions: administer at least 1 mo apart from other live virus vaccines. Side effects: mild—headache, myalgia, fever; extremely rare—encephalitis. *Implementation.* Keep frozen. Reconstitute with sodium chloride without preservatives. Rotate vial; do not shake. Use within 1 hr; discard the rest. Have epinephrine 1:1000 available. |

## ▷NURSING MANAGEMENT: IMMUNOTHERAPY

***Assessment.*** Before an immunization is given, an interview with the client and family should take place. The individual's age, current physical condition and general resistance to disease, history of exposure to infectious diseases (both past and potential), and previous immunizations should be assessed. A list of the general contraindications to immunization follows:

1. Current acute or febrile illness
2. Immunosuppressive therapy in progress or immunodeficient state
3. Recent immune serum globulin (ISG), plasma, or blood transfusions
4. Pregnancy—"live" vaccines especially may prove to be teratogenic or may cause infection in the fetus and therefore need to be avoided or given with caution (see Table 65-6)
5. Certain malignancies that leave the individual infection-susceptible (e.g., leukemias, lymphomas)
6. Simultaneous administration of another *single* live virus, unless proved safe

7. Prior unusual or allergic reaction to the same or similar vaccine
8. Allergy to antibiotics in vaccine, thimerosal as a preservative, or other constituents

Minor afebrile infections such as the common cold are not usually contraindications to immunization.

Routinely assess individuals (especially children) for immune status. High-risk groups include adolescents, new parents, individuals not vaccinated with the live measles vaccine, migrant workers, or recent immigrants. Elderly individuals, especially those in nursing homes, as well as those with chronic health problems, are at particular risk for respiratory infections and should be encouraged to obtain annual influenza virus vaccinations. Individuals who have been exposed or are at risk of exposure to one of the childhood diseases or serious communicable diseases or who have incurred a traumatic wound are also candidates for immunization.

Be aware that a history of hypersensitivity reactions to the biologic agent or to any contained antibiotics or preservatives are contraindications to immunotherapy. Pregnancy may or may not be a contraindication, depending on

**TABLE 65-6**   Biological agents for passive immunization

**Passive immunization** is a transfer of antibodies from animal or human sources to a person incapable of forming antibodies OR to prevent disease when time does not allow for active immunization OR to treat a disease that is normally prevented by immunization OR for situations where active immunization is not available, such as snake bites.

| Product | Dosage | Comments | Nursing assessment for contraindications and side effects/ implementation |
|---|---|---|---|
| Black widow spider anti-venin, equine | One vial of 6000 units, IM or IV | Use is limited to children >15 kg. | *Assessment.* Do not proceed without hypersensitivity history, hypersensitivity skin test (0.02-0.03 ml of a 1:10 dilution of horse serum or anti-venin intracutaneously) with a control injection of sodium chloride in opposite extremity. *Implementation.* Give serum based on above results and individual evaluation of risks and benefits (see package insert for detailed instructions). Do not pack wound in ice; discontinue vaccine if there are any systemic reactions. Mix to reconstitute by swirling (to avoid foaming); have available epinephrine, oxygen, resuscitation equipment (airway, tourniquet, injectable antihistamines, corticosteroids, and injectable pressor amines); give first 5-10 ml of infusion slowly over a 3-5 min period and observe for reactions; if given by IM route, give into large muscle mass (e.g., gluteal); consider possible tetanus prophylaxis and antibiotics if local tissue damage is evident; treat shock with blood, plasma expanders; give aspirin or codeine as needed for pain; give sedative or tranquilizer as needed. |
| Botulism antitoxin | One vial IV and 1 vial IM. Repeat in 2-4 hr if client's symptoms get worse. | Available from CDC.* | *Implementation:* Follow directions closely on administration. Given only to asymptomatic individuals with unequivocal exposure. |
| Diphtheria antitoxin | 20,000 to 120,000 units IM. Same dose for adults, children. | Available from CDC. | *Assessment.* Observe contacts carefully; if symptoms occur, then administer antitoxin. *Implementation.* Active immunization and erythromycin prophylaxis preferred rather than antitoxin administration for nonimmune contacts of active cases. |

*CDC, Centers for Disease Control, Central number (404) 329-3311; (404) 329-2888 for nights, weekends, and holidays for emergencies only.

**TABLE 65-6**   Biological agents for passive immunization—cont'd

| Product | Dosage | Comments | Nursing assessment for contraindications and side effects/ implementation |
|---|---|---|---|
| Hepatitis B immune globulin | 0.06 ml/kg IM after exposure, preferably within 1 wk. A second injection should be given 25-30 days after first exposure except if this vaccine was given with HBIG. | | *Assessment.* Contraindications: hypersensitivity to this product or thimerosal. *Implementation.* Deltoid and buttocks are preferred injection sites. All exposures should be treated as if confirmed, and appropriate isolation procedures should be instituted. |
| Hepatitis non-A, non-B immune globulin Hypogammaglobulinemia immune globulin | 0.06 ml/kg IM immediately after exposure. 0.6 ml/kg IM every 21-28 days. | Should give double dose at onset of therapy. | *Assessment.* Contraindications: do not give IV; IgA deficiency (may develop possible anaphylactic reactions to blood products); coagulation disorder; allergy to thimerosal; do not give Gamastan to those with clinical signs of hepatitis A or if exposure within past 2 wk; vaccination for measles, mumps, polio, or rubella within 3 mo after IG Side effects: local pain, urticaria, angioedema; rare—anaphylaxis *Implementation.* Given to individuals with sera exposure to clients with hepatitis. IM route (gluteal is preferred site) in several muscle sites as needed. Do not inject more than 3 ml per site. Refrigerate; do not freeze; use before expiration date. Have epinephrine 1:1000 available. |
| Measles immune globulin | 0.25 ml/kg IM immediately after exposure. | | *Implementation.* Live vaccine usually prevents measles if given within 2 days of exposure. If immunoglobulin is given, do not administer the live vaccine for 3 mo. |
| Pertussis immune globulin | 1.25 ml/IM (child). | | Its effectiveness is questionable. |
| Poliomyelitis globulin | 0.15 ml/kg IM. | | *Implementation.* Use only for exposed, nonimmunized persons. After 2 to 3 mo, immunize with live or inactivated vaccine. |
| Rabies immune globulin | 20 IU/kg, up to ½ infiltrated locally at wound site and remainder of dose given IM. | Give immediately after bite or at scratches caused by bats, skunks, foxes, coyotes, raccoons, or other carnivores. | *Assessment.* Obtain specific history of animal bite. Do not give to anyone previously adequately immunized with rabies vaccine. Side effects: local soreness, slight fever; rare— angioneurotic edema, nephrotic syndrome, or anaphylaxis. |

*Continued.*

**TABLE 65-6**   Biological agents for passive immunization—cont'd

| Product | Dosage | Comments | Nursing assessment for contraindications and side effects/implementation |
|---|---|---|---|
| | | | *Implementation.* Administer 5 ml or less at each site; use different sites. Give intramuscularly only and never intravenously. Repeated doses may interfere with full development of active immunity. Flush and cleanse wound; possible initial prophylaxis with tetanus and antibiotic therapy. |
| Rh$_o$ (D) immune globulin | Treat Rh$_o$-negative woman; 1 dose IM within 3 days of abortion, delivery, or amniocentesis of Rh$_o$-positive infant, or transfusion Rh-positive blood. | For nonimmune women only. May administer after 3 days if necessary. | *Assessment.* Contraindicated in Rh$_o$ (D)-positive or D$^u$ positive individuals. *Implementation.* Keep refrigerated. |
| Rubella immune globulin | 20-40 ml IM at exposure. | Not recommended for pregnant women because it will protect the mother but not the fetus. | |
| Coral snake antivenin, equine | Minimum of 3-5 vials IV. | Use dosage sufficient to reverse symptoms of snakebite. | See nursing considerations for black widow spider antivenin, equine. |
| Tetanus immune globulin | Preventive: 250-500 units IM. Therapeutic: 3000-6000 units IM. | Given along with Td immunization, but administer in separate syringe at different IM sites. Use only for major or dirty wounds if the wound is more than 24 hours old and the person received less than 2 doses of toxoid in the past. | *Assessment.* Side effects: occasionally—local tenderness, stiffness, allergic or anaphylatic systemic reactions. *Implementation.* Do not give intravenously; avoid blood vessels. Have epinephrine available. |
| Vaccinia immune globulin | Preventive: 0.3 ml/kg IM. Therapeutic: 0.6 ml/kg IM. May repeat if necessary for treatment; in 1-wk intervals for prophylaxis. | Available from CDC. | |
| Varicella-zoster | 125 units/10 kg for persons up to 50 kg. 625 unit maximum for patients >50 kg. Give IM within 4 days of exposure. | For immunosuppressed or immunoincompetent children under 15 years old. | *Assessment.* Modifies the natural disease but may not prevent the development of the illness. (Costly; approximately $400 to treat one adult.) |

clinical judgment and manufacturers' instructions.

Always assess client's allergy history carefully and test for hypersensitivity before administering animal sera. Keep epinephrine on hand to counter any potentially dangerous event (such as anaphylaxis).

***Intervention.*** Immune antisera and globulin are administered intramuscularly unless otherwise noted. Passive immunization or **immunoprophylaxis** should always be administered as soon as possible after exposure to the agent.

Almost all immunotherapy is parenteral and must be given by the specified route and with the specified diluent to avoid either local reactions (especially seen when the intracutaneous route is used) or possible anaphylaxis (especially when the intravenous route is used). All needles should be changed after withdrawing the vaccine from the vial, if possible. Aspiration after insertion is, of course, also necessary to prevent the danger of depositing the dose into the bloodstream.

Be aware that a crying, wriggling baby or child presents a challenging moving target for injection and must be temporarily restrained. This can often be accomplished just as effectively in the warmth and security of another's arms (the mother's, if feasible) rather than on a hard table surface. Taking out the needle and syringe and explaining that "this may hurt for only a minute" *just before* the actual injection will lessen fear of pain.

Record the dates of immunization at the time of administration, and give a copy to the recipient or parents for permanent safekeeping. Explain that this record may be invaluable later when these dates may be required on applications to school, summer camp, or college.

Be aware that most products will lose potency at temperatures higher than 2° to 8° C (35.6° to 46.4° F) except for TOPV, which must be frozen. Most immunization agents should therefore be stored in a medical refrigerator, where a thermometer is placed nearby, and replaced immediately after use. They should not be stored near a radiator, on a window sill, or on a refrigerator door shelf because of unpredictable temperatures.

Apply and explain appropriate isolation precautions when caring for individuals with known or suspected exposure to the communicable diseases. Assuming that someone else will take this responsibility at the outset is unwise.

***Education.*** Perceptions and misconceptions concerning immunization must be clarified. The relative safety and merits of immunization versus risks of the disease process itself (both short- and long-range) should be discussed, using statistics where appropriate. The client and/or family should be told that a repeat immunization, if records are unclear, is usually not contraindicated; the risk is usually minimal, and future protection is ensured. Unimmunized parents should be identified and probably immunized before their children, especially when TOPV is administered.

Noncompletion of an immunization series may occasionally be prevented if vaccinees or their parents know that interruption of the series or a prolonged period between phases of immunization makes no difference to eventual antibody levels. A copy of the immunization schedule given to the patient or family also enhances compliance with the immunization series.

Complete, written, and accurate documentation of immunizations with dates is rare even in office records. Nonetheless, having access to these data is important. Therefore teaching parents or vaccinees to keep careful written records for each vaccination, especially in view of the high mobility of our population, is crucial. Simple blank forms are available for this purpose and should be given to parents or the vaccinee with an explanation and advice to keep them updated and in a safe place (e.g., with health record files at home or in the family Bible) and to bring them to each child's appointment.

Teach clients or their parents how to recognize and differentiate between anticipated side effects and serious adverse reactions. (See Tables 65-5 and 65-6). After any immunization, ask clients to remain in the area for up to half an hour for observation of any developing adverse reactions. Antipyretics may be taken for the not uncommon aches, local pain and swelling, or mild temperature elevations, which may occur within 24 hours. Recipients of immunotherapy should understand whom they are to contact if complications occur later.

***Evaluation.*** Because of the risk of anaphylaxis, clients should be observed for up to half an hour after administration.

Sources of information on immunization include primarily the Public Health Service Advisory Committee on Immunization Practices (ACIP), which advises the public health agencies, and the Committee on Control of Infectious Diseases (the Red Book Committee), which is drawn from the members of the American Academy of Pediatrics and advises the private health sector. The ACIP can be contacted through the Centers for Disease Control in Atlanta. Since the two groups maintain a slightly different perspective, minor inconsequential variations in recommendations may occasionally be noted. Other sources include local public health departments and printed package inserts included with the vaccine or serum. Biologic preparations and accompanying inserts are regulated by the Bureau of Biologics of the FDA. The state of the art of immunotherapy is in rapid flux. The only constant in immunization practice is change itself. To read, attend seminars, and consult with experts is to keep pace.

## SUMMARY

Immunization is available for a number of diseases for which prevalence has abruptly declined because of availability of vaccines and sera; such diseases include measles, polio, rubella, mumps, diphtheria, and tetanus. Vaccines are also available for yellow fever, hepatitis B, influenza, rabies, cholera, typhoid, plague, and other diseases. Smallpox has been eradicated because of a World Health Organization campaign of near universal vaccination. Although these preparations are available, nurses must still educate the public to minimize complacency regarding the diseases for which they provide protection and to promote immunization.

## BIBLIOGRAPHY

Abramowicz M, ed. (1990). Routine immunization for adults, The Medical Letter 32(819):54.

Ada GL. (1988). Vaccines and vaccination, World Health, July, p. 5.

Aggressive, persistent marketing gets staff to take Hbv vaccine, Hosp Employee Health 8(2):23.

Baum SG et al. (1989). Just who is at risk for mumps? Patient Care 23(4):48.

Baum RM. (1987). The search for vaccines, Chemical & Engineering News 65(47):27.

Clements J. (1987). Immunization is not enough, World Health, Dec, p. 21.

Cochi SL et al. (1988). Progress in haemophilus type b polysaccharide vaccine use in the United States, Pediatrics 81(1):166.

Cohen R. (1989). T-cell vaccination against autoimmune disease, Hosp Pract 24(2):57.

Drug research: vaccine protects animals. (1989). American Pharmacy NS29(10):15.

Eickhoff TC et al. (1988). When adult immunization is a must, Patient Care 22(6):137.

Fedson DS. (1986). Adult immunization: protocols and problems, Hosp Pract 21(7):143.

Few BJ. (1987). Pertussis vaccine, MCN 12(4):243.

Halpern JS. (1984). Rabies vaccine: reduced risks and fears, JEN 10(2):101.

Hedrick E. (1989). Hepatitis B vaccination implementation, Am J Infect Control 17(3):190.

Immunization: important for adults, too! (1988). Patient Care 22(6):187.

Kastrup EK, ed. (1991). Facts and comparisons. St Louis: JB Lippincott Co.

Katzung BG. (1987). Basic and clinical pharmacology, ed 3, Norwalk, Conn: Appleton & Lange.

Lancaster D et al. (1989). Immunogenicity of the intradermal route of hepatitis B vaccination with the use of recombinant hepatitis B vaccine, Am J Infect Control 17(3):126.

Lelyveld S. (1986). An update of immunization practices for the emergency physician, Top Emerg Med 8(1):76.

Longyear LA et al. (1987). Keeping children safe: the Haemophilus influenzae type b immunization, J Pediatr Health Care 1(2):73.

Poser CM. (1987). Vaccine, infection complications: neurologic syndromes that arise unpredictably, Consultant 27(1):45.

Rimar JM. (1986). Haemophilus influenzae type b polysaccharide vaccine, MCN 11(1):57.

Salerno MC et al. (1988). What does the National Childhood Vaccine Injury Act require of nurses? Am J Nurs 88(7):1019.

Shots for grownups. (1988). Harv Med Sch Health Letter 13(10):1.

Sieving RE. (1988). Measles vaccination timing: finding the right age, Int Nurs Rev 35(1):17.

Veatch RM. (1987). The ethics of promoting herd immunity, Fam Community Health 10(1):44.

Wahdan MH. (1989). Communicable diseases, World Health, July, p. 20.

Walker AM et al. (1987). Diphtheria-tetanus-pertussis immunization and sudden infant death syndrome, Am J Public Health 77(8):945.

West DJ. (1989). Clinical experience with hepatitis B vaccines, Am J Infect Control 17(3):172.

Williams WW et al. (1988). Immunization policies and vaccine coverage among adults: the risk for missed opportunities, Ann Intern Med 108(4):616.

Windom RE. (1987). Adult vaccination should be routine, too, Public Health Rep 102(3):245.

Wood SL et al. (1988). Advances in pediatric immunizations, Physician Assist 12(5):22.

Wyngaarden JB and Smith LH. (1988). Cecil's textbook of medicine, ed 18. Philadelphia: WB Saunders Co.

*Chapter*

# 66 Immunosuppressants and Immunomodulators

## CHAPTER OBJECTIVES

*After studying this chapter, you should be able to meet the following objectives and define the key terms.*

1. Identify the four primary components of the immune system that can lead to an immunocompromised state.

2. Discuss the general nursing management of the immunosuppressed client.

3. Identify three primary immunosuppressant drugs.

## KEY TERMS

**acquired immune deficiency syndrome (AIDS),** page 1009

**human immunodeficiency virus (HIV),** page 1009

**immunocompromised state,** page 1005

**immunomodulating agents,** page 1009

**immunosuppressant agents,** page 1005

## INTRODUCTION

The rejection of body organs in kidney, liver, and heart allogenic transplants has lead to the development of a new classification of medications, **immunosuppressant agents,** or agents that lessen or prevent an immune response. Immunodeficiency or immunosuppression may occur from a genetic or an acquired disorder of the immune system. While genetic disorders such as agammaglobulinemia or severe combined immune deficiency syndrome (SCIDS) are usually diagnosed shortly after birth, acquired disorders may occur at any time throughout life. The acquired immunodeficiency may be induced by a variety of drugs such as chemotherapeutic and immunosuppressant agents, radiation therapy, or through viral infections such as acquired immune deficiency syndrome (AIDS). Because the latter often has devastating complications and a fatal outcome, much research interest has been directed toward the development of immunomodulating or immunostimulating medications.

An **immunocompromised state** can be the result of one or more of four primary components of the immune system: (1) inhibition of granulocyte formation leading to severe neutropenia; (2) defect in complement synthesis and antibody production, which often occurs after chemotherapy; (3) loss of mucocutaneous barriers that will permit bacteria or microorganisms access to internal organs. This may occur in a variety of therapeutic situations, such as following the use of medical devices (central venous catheters, Foley catheters, endotracheal tubes) or after chemotherapy. (4) Impairment of cellular immunity (macrophages and T-cell lymphocytes) is usually seen in clients who receive immunosuppressive agents (corticosteroids, cyclosporine, and others), persons with certain types of cancer (Hodgkin's lymphoma), or those who receive an organ transplant.

**1005**

In the majority of clients, combinations of these defects are common, because several immune functions may be affected at the same time. For example, chronic therapy with antineoplastic medications will affect granulocytes and cellular immunity. Chemotherapy may result in the loss of mucocutaneous barriers or the development of mucositis and ulcers in the mouth and gastrointestinal tract. Such impaired clients are at a greater risk for the development of bacterial, fungal, or viral infections. This chapter will review some of the primary agents that suppress or have the potential to modify or stimulate the human immune system.

## ▷NURSING MANAGEMENT: THE IMMUNOSUPPRESSED CLIENT

The care of the client with a secondary immunodeficiency, immunosuppression caused by the therapeutic regimen, focuses on the treatment of the underlying condition and the immunotherapy.

*Assessment.* The client should be assessed for understanding of the condition and his or her feelings about the illness. The availability of supportive others should be considered. Nutritional status should be assessed, as well as the client's likes and dislikes so that nutritional counseling will be effective, since these clients have usually had some weight loss or require a modified diet. Level of comfort should be determined with regard to activity tolerance and participation in therapies. Objectively, the client should be examined for skin and mucous membrane integrity. Respiratory status should be ascertained and the frequency and character of stools determined.

With the administration of immunosuppressive agents, the client is at risk for the following nursing diagnoses: anxiety; altered bowel pattern (diarrhea); ineffective breathing pattern; altered comfort; high risk for infection; altered nutrition (less than body requirements); altered mucous membranes; impaired skin integrity; and social isolation.

Monitor the client's vital signs, daily weight, and intake and output ratios. WBCs are monitored for the drug's effectiveness; dosage is usually titrated on the leukocyte and platelet counts.

*Intervention.* Careful medical asepsis is a priority with the immunosuppressed client. Thorough handwashing, avoiding other persons with infection, and promoting the client's own resources to prevent infection are essential nursing interventions to be taken. Injections should be avoided when possible; if necessary, the skin should be cleansed with povidone-iodine and allowed to dry for 30 seconds. Irrigating solutions, vases, and other standing collections of water in which organisms may breed need to be avoided.

*Education.* Advise a well-balanced diet and a fluid intake of at least 1500 ml daily to minimize the risk of tissue dehydration and a urinary tract infection associated with low urinary output. Instruct the client to avoid trauma (e.g., breaks in the skin), and to seek medical treatment for wounds that do not heal quickly. Encourage meticulous oral hygiene, including cautious use of toothbrushes, dental floss, and toothpicks, and regular dental care to minimize gingival inflammation and early detection of altered oral mucous membranes. Alcohol and aspirin ingestion should be avoided to minimize the risk of gastrointestinal bleeding.

Instruct the client to report any signs and symptoms of infection (sore throat, malaise, headache, fever, dysuria, urinary frequency), bleeding gums, bruising, or signs and symptoms of hepatic dysfunction (abdominal pain, jaundice, pruritis, clay-colored stools). Advise the client to consult with health care provider before taking any OTC medications including aspirin or receiving any vaccinations while taking these medications. Reinforce the importance of physician appointments for follow-up care and laboratory examinations.

The client and family should be taught to monitor the client's blood pressure at home. Instruct the client to report any significant changes in the blood pressure, hematuria, cloudy urine, decreased urinary output, sudden weight gain, edema of the face or ankles, headache, or unusual fatigue.

If the immunosuppressant is taken to prevent transplant rejection, emphasize the importance of lifelong therapy.

*Evaluation.* Immunosuppression of the client should occur without the rejection of the transplanted tissue, the presence of infection, or impaired skin integrity. The client should also be able to describe methods of preventing infection and the need to maintain optimal nutrition.

## IMMUNOSUPPRESSANTS

The primary immunosuppressant drugs available in 1990 include azathioprine (Imuran), cyclosporine (Sandimmune), and Muromonab-CD3 (Orthoclone OKT3).

### azathioprine (Imuran)

Azathioprine is indicated as an adjunct medication to prevent rejection in organ transplants and as a disease modifier for the treatment of severe rheumatoid arthritis in the client who has not responded to other therapies. Investigationally, it is also used to treat other immunologic diseases, including ulcerative colitis, chronic active hepatitis and biliary cirrhosis, systemic lupus erythematosus (SLE), glomerulonephritis, nephrotic syndrome, myasthenia gravis, and pemphigus.

Its mechanism of action as an immunosuppressant is unknown although it does antagonize purine metabolism, may decrease DNA, RNA, and protein synthesis, and may block cellular metabolism and inhibit mitosis. In combination with steroids, it appears to have a steroid-conserving effect; that is, a lower dose of steroid is necessary to treat chronic inflammatory processes when it is given with azathioprine.

Azathioprine is available orally and parenterally. Orally it is well absorbed from the intestinal tract, has a half-life of 3 hours, and has an onset of action in 6 to 8 weeks in rheumatoid arthritis and perhaps 4 to 8 weeks for other inflammatory disease states. It is metabolized in the liver to active metabolites (6-mercaptopurine and 6-thioinosinic acid) with further metabolism by xanthine oxidase. It is excreted via bile or the biliary system.

The most frequent side effects reported are anorexia, and nausea or vomiting. Frequent adverse reactions seen are leukopenia or infection and megaloblastic anemia. The client is usually asymptomatic but may also have fever, chills, cough, low back or side pain, pain on urination, or increased weakness. The risk of hepatotoxicity is greater when doses administered are greater than 2.5 mg/kg daily. Thrombocytopenia may occur infrequently, and hypersensitivity, pancreatitis, pneumonitis, and mouth and lip sores are rarely encountered.

***Significant drug interactions.*** When azathioprine is given with the following drugs, the following significant drug interactions may occur:

| Drug | Possible Effect and Management |
|---|---|
| allopurinol | Allopurinol inhibits xanthine oxidase which may result in increased azathioprine activity and toxicity. Avoid concurrent use, especially in renal transplant clients. If it is absolutely necessary to give both drugs concurrently, reduce the dose of azathioprine to one fourth to one third of the usually prescribed dose; monitoring closely and adjust dosage as needed. |
| immunosuppressant agents, other (glucocorticoids, cyclophosphamide, cyclosporine) | May increase the risk for developing infections and/or neoplasms. |
| vaccines, live virus | Immunization with live vaccines should be postponed in persons receiving this drug and also in close family members. The use of a live virus vaccine in immunosuppressed clients may result in increased replication of the vaccine virus, may increase side effects/adverse reactions to the vaccine virus and possibly cause a decrease in the client's antibody response to the vaccine. |

***Dosage and administration.*** The pediatric and adult dose as an immunosuppressant agent for the prevention of organ transplant rejection is 3 to 5 mg/kg orally, 1 to 3 days before or at the time of surgery, or if given intravenously, before, during, or immediately after surgery. Maintenance dose is 1 to 2 mg/kg orally or intravenously. As a disease modifier for rheumatoid arthritis, the oral dose is 0.5 to 1 mg/kg daily.

***Pregnancy safety.*** Azathioprine is not recommended for use in pregnant women.

▷ **Nursing Management:
Azathioprine Therapy**

In addition to the general nursing management of the immunosuppressed client (p. 1006), clients receiving azathioprine therapy require the following nursing care:

***Assessment.*** If administered for rheumatoid arthritis, assess the client's range of motion, status of affected joints (swelling, pain, and strength), and ability to accomplish activities of daily living before and periodically during therapy.

Hematologic function should be monitored before therapy is initiated, weekly during the first month, twice a month for the next 2 to 3 months, and monthly thereafter. Notify the physician if the leukocyte count is less than 3000/mm³ or platelets less than 100,000/mm³; the dosage may need to be reduced. A decrease in hemoglobin may be indicative of bone marrow suppression. Renal and hepatic function studies should be monitored with the same frequency. Increased alkaline phosphatase, bilirubin, SGOT (AST), SGPT (ALT), and amylase concentrations may indicate hepatotoxicity.

***Intervention.*** Administer oral doses of azathioprine with or after meals to minimize gastrointestinal distress. Reconstitute each 100 mg for intravenous use by adding 10 ml of sterile water for injection to the vial and swirling to dissolve. It may be administered by intravenous push or further diluted with 0.9% sodium chloride injection or 5% dextrose and 0.9% sodium chloride injection for intravenous infusion. It may be administered over a time period of 5 minutes to 8 hours. Once reconstituted, azathioprine is stable at room temperature for 24 hours. Do not mix.

***Education.*** If administered for rheumatoid arthritis, the client should be advised to continue physical therapy and other concurrent therapy (salicylates, NSAIDs, glucocorticoids) as prescribed. As azathioprine has teratogenic effects, advise the client of child-bearing age to practice contraception during the course of therapy and for at least 4 months after its completion.

***Evaluation.*** Effectiveness for rheumatoid arthritis is evidenced by decreased pain, stiffness, and swelling of affected joints in 6 to 8 weeks.

### cyclosporine (Sandimmune)

Cyclosporine (cyclosporin A) is a potent immunosuppressant used for the prevention and treatment of organ (renal, hepatic, or cardiac allografts) transplant rejection. Its mechanism of action is unknown, but studies indicate it reversibly inhibits T lymphocytes. T helper cells are the main target, but the T suppressor cell may also be affected. Cyclosporine also inhibits lymphokine production and release, especially interleukin-2 or the T cell growth factor. Interleukin-2 is required for the cytotoxic T lymphocytes response to alloantigenic challenge; thus it plays a role in both cellular and humoral (antibody production) immune type responses. It does not cause myelosuppression or bone marrow depression.

Cyclosporine is available in capsule and liquid oral formulations and also parenterally. Orally, its bioavailability is about 30%, which may improve with increasing doses and chronic administration. Absorption is usually decreased after a liver transplant or in clients with liver impairment or gastrointestinal dysfunction, such as diarrhea, or vomiting. It has a half-life of approximately 7 hours in children, and 19 hours in adults; it reaches peak serum levels in 3.5 hours. It is metabolized in the liver and excreted via bile and feces.

The most frequently reported side effects are closely related and include an increase in hair growth and trembling, which is dose related. With chronic therapy, nephrotoxicity (blood in urine, renal failure) may occur. This toxic response is usually dose dependent, may be irreversible, and generally occurs after 12 months of continuous therapy. Severe hypertension usually associated with 25- to 50-mg/kg doses of cyclosporine may also occur. Lymphomas and other lymphoproliferative-type disorders have been reported, but they usually regress when the drug is stopped. Gingival hyperplasia (bleeding, swollen gums) is also a common problem with the use of this drug. Generally, this is reversible about 6 months after cyclosporine is discontinued. Less commonly reported adverse reactions are anaphylaxis (with intravenous dosage form only), hyperkalemia, and pancreatitis.

***Significant Drug Interactions.*** The following significant drug interactions may occur when cyclosporine is given with the following drugs:

| Drug | Possible Effect and Management |
|------|-------------------------------|
| androgens, cimetidine, danazol, diltiazem, estrogens, erythromycin, ketoconazole, or miconazole | May result in increased serum levels of cyclosporine, increasing the potential risk for hepatotoxicity and nephrotoxicity. If drugs must be administered concurrently, use extreme caution and monitor closely. |
| diuretics, potassium sparing (amiloride, spironolactone, or triamterene) or potassium supplements or salt substitutes | May increase risk for hyperkalemia. Monitor serum levels and for signs and symptoms of hyperkalemia (confusion, irregular heart rate, paresthesias of hands, feet, or lips, respiratory difficulties, increased weakness, feeling of weak or heavy legs. |
| immunosuppressants, others | Increases risk of developing infection or lymphoproliferative type disorders (lymphomas, etc.) Use extreme caution if given concurrently. |
| lovastatin | When used in heart transplant clients, it may increase the risk of developing rhabdomyolysis and acute renal failure. Monitor closely if concurrent therapy is necessary. |
| vaccines, live virus | See azathoprine. |

***Dosage and administration.*** Pediatric and adult oral dose is 12 to 15 mg/kg daily, starting 4 to 12 hours before surgery and continuing for 7 to 14 days afterward. Then decrease dose by 5% weekly to maintenance dose of 5 to 10 mg/kg daily. Children may need higher or more frequent dosing as they appear to rapidly metabolize this drug. The intravenous dosage form is given by infusion at a rate of 2 to 6 mg/kg daily starting 4 to 12 hours before surgery and continuing after surgery until the client can take oral medication.

***Pregnancy safety.*** Pregnancy safety has been established at FDA category C.

## ▷ Nursing Management: Cyclosporine Therapy

In addition to the general nursing management of the immunosuppressed client (p. 1006), clients receiving cyclosporine therapy require the following nursing care:

***Assessment.*** Monitor the client for signs and symptoms of hypersensitivity (dyspnea, wheezing, hypotension) and have resuscitation equipment in the vicinity when the drug is administered intravenously.

Serum cyclosporine levels are evaluated periodically during a course of therapy and dosages adjusted accordingly. Renal and hepatic function studies are done before therapy is begun and periodically thereafter. Significant changes in function may necessitate a reduction or discontinuation of dosage. Serum potassium and lipid levels may also be increased.

***Intervention.*** Administer with meals. When administering the oral solution, use the calibrated measuring device supplied by the manufacturer. Since it is a mixture of alcohol and vegetable oil, thoroughly mix with chocolate milk or orange juice at room temperature and drink at once. Use a glass container so that the oil will adhere less, and rinse with additional juice or milk to ensure that the entire dose is taken. Wipe the measuring device dry; do not wash after use.

The intravenous infusion is begun 4 to 12 hours before surgery and continued postoperatively until the client can tolerate an oral dosage form. The drug is prepared for intravenous infusion by diluting each 1 ml in 20 to 100 ml of 0.9% sodium chloride injection or 5% dextrose injection. Glass containers are used to prevent the leaching of diethylhexylphthalate (DEHP) from the PVC infusion bags into the cyclosporine solution. Significant amounts of the drug are lost when it is administered through PVC tubing. Solution is stable for 24 hours in 5% dextrose injection. In 0.9% sodium chloride injection at room temperature, it is stable for 6 hours in a PVC container and for 12 hours in a glass container. Infuse over 2 to 6 hours using an infusion pump or continuously over 24 hours.

### muromonab-CD3 (Orthoclone OKT3)

Muromonab-CD3 is an interesting drug made by fusion of mouse myeloma cells to lymphocytes from immunized animals, resulting in the combination of an antibody-producing cell and a multiple myeloma cell (a hybridoma). The hybridoma secretes antigen-specific antibodies (murine monoclonal antibodies) and is capable of being a continuous source of antibody. Muromonab-CD3 is an immunoglobulin antibody that will react with a CD3 (T3) molecule or human T lymphocytes to block both the activation and functions of the T-cells in response to an antigenic challenge. This product does not cause myelosuppression.

Muromonab-CD3 is indicated for the treatment of organ transplant rejection and is usually given in combination with azathioprine, cyclosporine, and/or adrenocorticoids. It is available parenterally with an onset of action to reduce circulating CD3 positive T cells in minutes after administration. It reaches steady state plasma levels in about 3 days and has a duration of action of about 7 days. In other words, the number of circulating CD3 positive T cells will return to previous levels in about a week, after muromonab-CD3 is stopped.

The most frequent adverse reactions are a first-dose effect: within 30 minutes to 6 hours after the first dose, the client may experience lightheadedness, elevated temperature, chills, nausea, vomiting, chest pain, respiratory difficulties, and tremors and trembling. These effects may be repeated to a lesser degree after the second dose but are rarely encountered with later doses. Fever and chills after administration indicate infection. Adverse reactions rarely seen include aseptic meningitis syndrome and pulmonary edema.

The most significant drug interactions reported for muromonab-CD3 are with other immunosuppressant agents and with live virus vaccines. See the drug interactions listed for azathioprine for a description of these interactions.

The adult dose is 5 mg daily by rapid IV for 10 to 14 days. In children under 12 years old, the rapid IV dose is 0.1 mg/kg daily for 10 to 14 days.

Pregnancy safety has been established at FDA category C.

▷ **Nursing Management:**
 **Muromonab-CD3 Therapy**

In addition to the general nursing management for immunosuppressed clients (p. 1006), clients receiving muromonab-CD3 require the following nursing care:

***Assessment.*** The client's temperature should be taken before administration and frequently for several hours after administration, especially with the first two doses. A first-dose reaction may occur evidenced by fever and chills, chest pain, dizziness, syncope, nausea and vomiting, diarrhea, and dyspnea. These symptoms occur in most clients 30 minutes to 6 hours after the first dose and may last several hours. They may occur to a lesser extent after the second dose but rarely occur after that. Fever and chills occurring later in therapy may be caused by infection. The client should be assessed also for headache, stiff neck, and photosensitivity because aseptic meningitis syndrome may occur in the first 3 days of therapy. CBCs should be monitored periodically throughout the course of treatment. To assess the efficacy of the drug, monitor the assay for circulating T cells expressing the CD3 antigen.

***Intervention.*** Cardiopulmonary resuscitation equipment and medications should be immediately available during the administration of the first dose. Muromonab-CD3 should be administered by intravenous push over a period of less than 1 minute by a physician experienced in immunosuppressive

therapy. Methylprednisolone may be administered intravenously before the first dose to minimize first-dose reaction. Intravenous hydrocortisone sodium succinate may be given 30 minutes after the first and possibly the second dose for the same reason.

Muromonab-CD3 is prepared for intravenous administration by drawing the solution through a low protein-binding 0.2- or 0.22-μm filter, then discarding the filter and attaching the appropriate needle for administration. It is not administered by intravenous infusion or with other solutions.

***Education.*** The client should be prepared for the possibility of first-dose reaction and alerted to report any of the adverse signs and symptoms of that reaction or aseptic meningitis syndrome.

## IMMUNOMODULATING AGENTS

Biotechnology is a new and exciting area of research concentrating on the development of new agents that can either activate the body's immune defenses or modify a biologic response to an unwanted stimulus, such as an antitumor response. These agents are called **immunomodulating agents.** With the advent of recombinant DNA technology in the early 1980s, new agents were made available in larger quantities for clinical trials and investigations. While still in its infancy, this area of study has the potential of solving some of the mysteries about disease that have eluded researchers for centuries and may also provide pharmaceuticals that control the devastation, pain, and suffering induced by many viral diseases, acquired immune deficiency syndrome (AIDS), and cancer.

A new, pathogenic retrovirus known as **human immunodeficiency virus** (HIV) is the etiologic agent in **acquired immune deficiency syndrome (AIDS).** AIDS has been identified throughout the world, with over 250,000 cases reported in 138 countries. It has been estimated that 5 to 10 million persons are infected with this virus and that during the next 5 years another 1 million new cases will be diagnosed. It affects all races, all ages (about 90% of the cases are between 20 and 49 years old), both sexes, and unfortunately, at present, there is no cure. Thus while the search for a cure continues, the primary method to prevent transmission is prevention.

This virus is transmitted sexually, via blood/blood products, or from a mother with AIDS to her child during birth. Current evidence indicates that the AIDS virus is not transmitted by shaking hands, hugging, social kissing, coughing, sneezing, or by sharing meals. It is also not contracted from swimming pools, toilet seats, hot tubs, dishes, or via food prepared by persons infected with the AIDS virus. AIDS is only transmitted by intimate contact with body fluids of an infected person, which can occur through sex, sharing of contaminated needles and syringes (drug addicts), blood or blood product transfusions, and from mother to child, be-

## AIDS OVERVIEW

Human immunodeficiency virus (HIV).

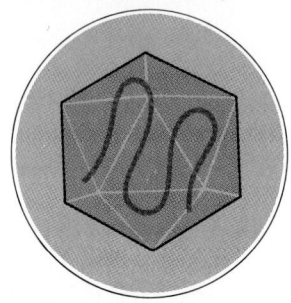

HIV virus enters T cells and macrophages, which, ironically, are the cells the body sent to destroy the virus. By reproduction the virus eventually kills them.

AIDS has no cure. Note that:
The HIV reproduces faster than any other virus.
It is present in the bloodstream in very small amounts; thus it is currently hard to target with medications.

AIDS has been diagnosed in:
All races
Men, women, and children
Homosexuals and heterosexuals

T cell and macrophage infiltration and destruction.

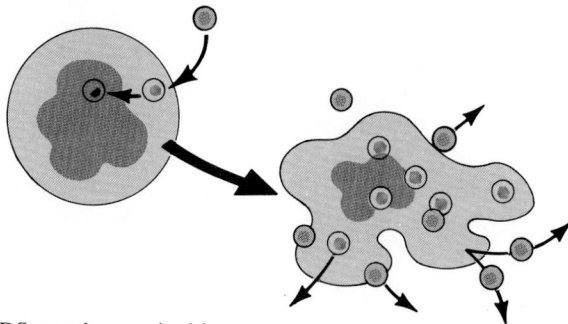

AIDS may be acquired by:
Intravenous drug use with an infected or contaminated needle.
Sexual contact with an infected person. The virus is transmitted in blood products, semen, and vaginal secretions. A small tear in the rectum lining or in the vagina can provide an entrance for the virus.

AIDS can be transmitted during birth or during breast-feeding, if the mother is AIDS infected.

AIDS-infected persons are not always sick, but they can still transmit the AIDS virus.

AIDS-related complex (ARC) symptoms may include:
Fever
Night sweats
Weight loss
Swollen glands (neck, armpits, groin)
Increased weakness
Skin infections
Fungal infection of mouth (thrush)

fore, during, or shortly after birth (Popescu, 1989). See the box above for overview of AIDS.

The HIV virus binds to protein on the cell membranes of the T4 helper lymphocytes and on macrophages. The T4 helper cells are destroyed by the virus, which leads to the immunodeficiency disease known as AIDS. The T4 cells are needed directly and indirectly for proper functioning of the human immune system. Both the humoral immune response, which involves B lymphocyte-produced antibodies, and cellular immune response, which involves stimulation of the cytotoxic T cells (or T8 cells) are mediated by the helper-inducer T cells. Therefore a severe decline or destruction of T4 cells by the HIV virus is responsible for the multiple symptoms of AIDS—severe suppression of the immune system leading to opportunistic infections and cancers. See the box for functions of a T4 helper cell and Figure 66-1 for T cell cellular effects.

## FUNCTIONS OF A T4 HELPER CELL

T4 cells are responsible for a variety of immune functions, some of which include:
1. Release of colony-stimulating factors and lymphokines to stimulate production of leukocytes, such as macrophages and eosinophils.
2. Activation of the natural killer cells (cytotoxic NK cells), which are large lymphocytes in the blood that have non–antigen specific antitumor and antibacterial properties.
3. T4 helper-inducer cells can activate the T8 suppressor cells, which will stop antibody production, or the T4 suppressor-inducers can activate T8 cytotoxic T cells and stimulate B cells to increase production of antibodies.

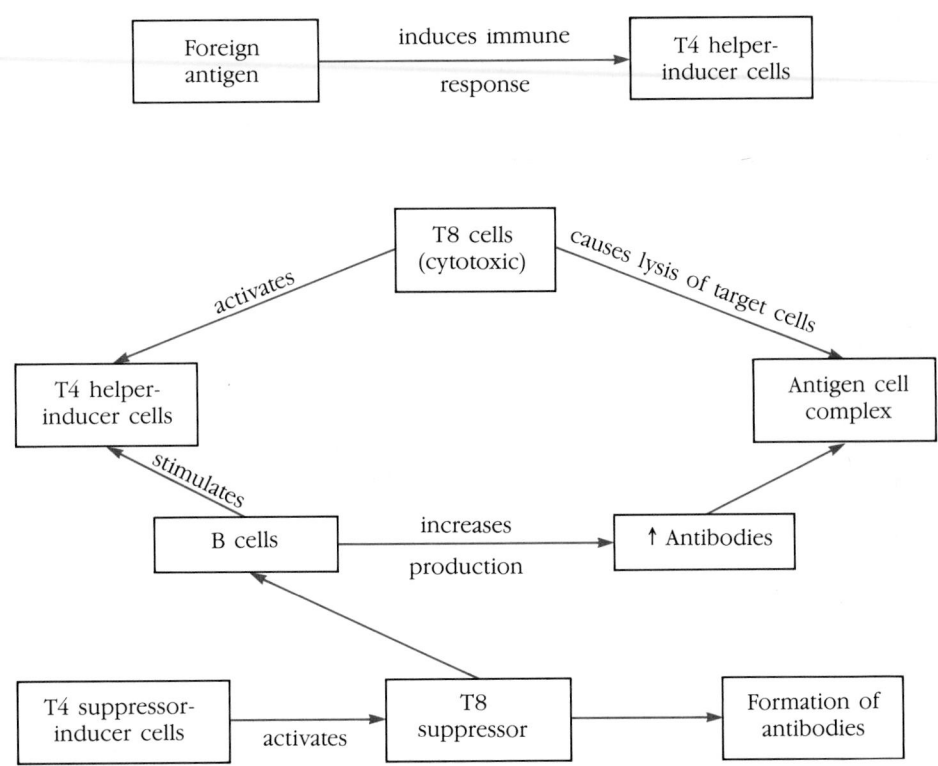

**FIGURE 66-1** T4 cell effects in the body. T4 cells are mainly the helper-inducer type of cells. They increase when antigens are present. T4 suppressor-inducer cells do not respond to antigens. They indirectly act to suppress antibody formation.

The Centers for Disease Control (CDC) has established a classification for the progression of HIV infection; see Table 66-1. The average time to progress from HIV positive to AIDS is about 8 to 10 years. In the later stages, the breakdown in cellular immunity results in the development of opportunistic infections in the body. See Table 66-2 for a list and treatment of the typical AIDS-related infections seen in the latter stages. Generally, in advanced stages of AIDS, most clients have a very low helper T cell count and the majority die within a few years.

A number of products are under study for the treatment of AIDS, AIDS-related complex (ARC) and AIDS-associated infections. These agents range from antiviral substances to immunomodulating drugs, but to date, only one product has been approved by the FDA for the treatment of AIDS, zidovudine (Retrovir). This drug is reviewed in Chapter 60.

Interferons, interleukins, and colony-stimulating factors are just a few of the substances under study for the treatment of various types of cancer. Interferons, natural body proteins

released in response to viral infections, have both cytotoxic and immune stimulation effects. These products are reviewed in Chapter 57, on antineoplastic agents.

Lymphokines (Interleukins 1 and 2) and colony-stimulating factors are involved with regulation of immune system functions. Lymphokines are protein substances released by sensitized lymphocytes when in contact with specific antigens. These substances activate macrophages, and they help to stimulate humoral and cellular immunity for the host. They have been referred to as the chemical messengers of immune cell communication. Interleukin-2 is believed to be T cell growth factor that induces long-term survival and growth of the T lymphocytes. It is necessary for continuing the immune response and is also involved in the rejection of transplanted organs. (Thus cyclosporine inhibits Interleukin-2 to prevent organ rejection.) Research involving immunomodulators such as Interleukin-2 is directed toward the AIDS, ARC, or HIV clients, to help boost their immune response.

Granulocyte macrophage colony-stimulating factor is an-

**TABLE 66-1**   CDC classification and progression of HIV infection

| Classification | Description |
|---|---|
| Group I | Acute HIV infection. Client may be asymptomatic or initially have a mononucleosis-type syndrome (i.e., fever, myalgias, malaise, arthralgias, rash, or lymphadenopathy). Usually occurs 1 to 12 weeks after exposure. Symptoms resolve in 7 to 14 days. |
| Group II | Asymptomatic carrier stage, may last weeks to several years. |
| Group III | Persistent, generalized lymphadenopathy at two or more extrainguinal sites for 3 months or longer in duration. |
| Group IV | Systemic presentation of HIV infection. Clients with AIDS or AIDS-related complex (ARC) are usually classified in group IV. Subgroups:<br>Group A—Person has constitutional disease or symptoms, such as an unexplained diarrhea or elevated temperature lasting more than a month, or a weight loss greater than 10% of baseline body weight.<br>Group B—Neurologic disorders such as dementia, sensory peripheral neuropathy, and myelopathy occur.<br>Group C—Secondary infections occur. This group has two subdivisions.<br>C1—The infected person may have one or more of the following primary opportunistic infections commonly reported: *Pneumocystis carinii* pneumonia, toxoplasmosis, cryptococcosis, cytomegalovirus infections, atypical mycobacteriosis, or disseminated herpes simplex.<br>C2—Persons in this category may have one or more of the following infections also seen in AIDS: oral hairy leukoplakia, tuberculosis, nocardiosis, oral candidiasis, recurrent salmonella infections, or multidermatomal herpes zoster.<br>Group D—Person may have one or more of the following AIDS-associated malignancies: Kaposi sarcoma, non-Hodgkin's lymphoma, or primary lymphoma of the brain.<br>Group E—Any other conditions not classified previously that may be attributed to HIV infection, such as chronic lymphoid interstitial pneumonitis, which is usually more prevalent in children. |

**TABLE 66-2**   Typical AIDS-related infections and treatments

| Disease | Syndrome | Examples of usual drug treatment |
|---|---|---|
| **VIRUSES** | | |
| Cytomegalovirus | Encephalitis, chorioretinitis, pneumonia, hepatitis, disseminated infection | Ganciclovir (Cytovene)—5 mg/kg by IV infusion.<br>Foscarnet, an investigational drug, also used. |
| Herpes simplex virus (HSV) | Persistent or recurrent, disseminated skin ulceration | Acyclovir (Zovirax)—5 mg/kg by IV infusion, every 8 hours for 1 week.<br>Vidarabine (Vira-A)—15 mg/kg daily by IV infusion for HSV encephalitis. |
| **PROTOZOAL INFECTIONS** | | |
| *Pneumocystis carinii* (PCP) | Pneumonia | Trimethoprim-sulfamethoxazole (TMP-SMZ, Bactrim, and others)—IV 15 to 20 mg (TMP) daily divided into 3 or 4 doses (given q 6 or 8 h) for 2 weeks or pentamidine isethionate (Pentam) 4 mg/kg IM or IV daily for 2 weeks. To prevent PCP, 300 mg by aerosol (via Respirgard II nebulizer) monthly. |
| *Toxoplasma gondii* | Encephalitis, brain abcesses | Sulfadiazine 1 g QID (or sulfapyrimidine), and pyrimethamine (Daraprim) 50 mg daily for 1-3 weeks. |
| **FUNGAL INFECTIONS** | | |
| *Candida albicans* (oral thrush) | Esophagitis, oropharyngitis, vaginitis | Nystatin 500,000 U as liquid, vaginal tablet (orally administered 4 to 6 times daily), or clotrimazole (Mycelex) 10 mg 5 times a day, or ketoconazole (Nizoral) 400 mg daily. |
| *Cryptococcus neoformans* | Major cause of meningitis in AIDS patients | Amphotericin B plus flucytosine (Ancoban) or alternate drug, fluconazole (Diflucan), oral or parenteral. Check current references for dosing recommendations. |
| **MYCOBACTERIAL INFECTIONS** | | |
| *Mycobacterium avium, M. intracellulare* | Disseminated infection, severe GI disease, massive intraabdominal lymphadenopathy | Requires multiple drug therapy, such as isoniazid, rifampin, ethambutol, streptomycin, cyclosporin, and many other drugs. Usually poor response to therapy. |
| *M. tuberculosis* | Pulmonary infection, meningitis | Also requires multiple drug therapies; many similar to above therapy. |

**TABLE 66-3**   Immunomodulator and antiviral investigational drugs

| Drug | Category | FDA status |
|---|---|---|
| ampligen (Poly IC12U) | Antiviral immunomodulator | Phase III AIDS |
| dideoxycytidine (HIVCID) | Antiviral | Phase II/III AIDS, ARC (orphan drug) |
| diethyl dithio carbamate (Imuthiol) | Immunomodulator | Phase II/II AIDS, ARC |
| Imreg-1 and Imreg-2 | Immunomodulator | Phase II/III AIDS, ARC, Kaposi |
| interferon, beta (Betaseron) | Antiviral | Phase III AIDS, ARC, Kaposi |
| isoprinosine (Inosine, Inosiplex) | Antiviral immunomodulator | Phase III ARC, HIV positive, asymptomatic |
| ribavirin (Virazole) | Antiviral | Phase II/III asymptomatic HIV positive, ARC |
| thymostimuline (TP-1) | Immunomodulator | Phase III AIDS |

other immunomodulator in phase II study with AIDS-infected clients. GM-CSF (Leukine), a recombinant human granulocyte macrophage colony-stimulating factor, and G-CSF (Neupogen), a recombinant human granulocyte colony-stimulating factor, are two products currently in investigational use in the United States. They both stimulate progenitor (parent) cells to mature along specific lines of differentiation. For example, G-CSF promotes the proliferation and maturation of neutrophil granulocytes and can also promote pre–B cell activation and growth. It can also act synergistically with Interleukin-3 to promote growth of other cell lines, especially megakaryocytes leading to the production of platelets.

GM-CSF promotes the proliferation and maturation of neutrophils, eosinophils, and monocytes. It inhibits neutrophil migration and increases the production of many cytokines, including tumor necrosis factor and Interleukin-1. It may be a more potent stimulator of macrophage cytotoxicity than G-CSF.

In clinical studies, both agents have demonstrated promise in many disease states, such as drug-induced bone marrow suppression. Thus they may be useful in bone marrow transplantation and improve survival or reduce morbidity when used concurrently with antineoplastic agents. The major side effect reported is bone pain that may be prevented by prior administration of acetaminophen. Further investigational studies with these agents are warranted as they have the potential for being very useful adjunct therapy in a number of disease states.

Many agents are in various phases of investigational study as antiviral agents or immunomodulators for the treatment of AIDS, HIV infection, or AIDS-related complications (see Table 66-3).

## SUMMARY

Immunosuppressants and immunomodulators are relatively new products used to lesson or modify an immune system response. Research is extensive and many new pharmacologic products are likely to be developed in the next few years. Nursing management centers on careful medical asepsis, proper diet and oral hygiene, and prevention of infec-

tion. As new drugs continue to undergo development, the role of the nurse in this important new therapy is likely to continue to expand.

## BIBLIOGRAPHY

American Hospital Formulary Service. (1991). AHFS drug information '91, Bethesda, Md: American Society of Hospital Pharmacists, Inc.

Baum RM. (1987). The molecular biology of AIDS, Chem Eng News 65(47):12.

Byram DA. (1989). Future expectations for critical care nurses: competence in immunotherapy, Crit Care Nurs Clin North Am 1(4):797.

Dale MM and Foreman JC. (1984). Textbook of immunopharmacology, Oxford: Blackwell Scientific Publications.

Dagani R. (1987). The quest for therapy—AIDS, Chem Eng News 65(47):41.

Dault LA et al. (1989). Reversing cardiac transplant rejection with Orthoclone OKT3, Am J Nurs 89(7):953.

DiPiro JT et al. (1989). Pharmacotherapy: a pathophysiologic approach, New York: Elsevier.

Futterman LG. (1988). Cardiac transplantation: a comprehensive nursing perspective, part 2, Heart Lung 17(6):631.

Gerbino PP. (No Date). AIDS: a public education priority. (Sponsored by the CAVDA Citizens AIDS Project and the American Pharamaceutical Association.)

Herfindal ET et al. (1988). Clinical pharmacy and therapeutics, ed 4, Baltimore: Williams & Wilkins.

Hutchings SM et al. (1989). Caring for the cardiac transplant patient, Crit Care Nurs Clin North Am 1(2):245.

Imperial FA et al. (1989). Cardiac transplantation, Crit Care Nurs Clin North Am (2):399.

Jones D et al. (1989). Care of the patient with HIV infection, Chapel Hill, NC: Health Sciences Consortium, Glaxo Inc.

Kastrup EK, ed. (1991). Facts and comparisons, St. Louis: JB Lippincott Co.

Malen JF et al. (1989). Nursing perspectives on lung transplantation, Crit Care Nurs Clin North Am 1(4):707.

Metzger JT et al. (1988). Cardiac transplantation: the changing faces of immunosuppression, Heart Lung 17(4):414.

Moir EJ. (1989). Nursing care of patients receiving Orthoclone OKT 3 . . . Orthoclone OKT 3 (murmonab-CD3) is an antirejection drug, ANNA J 16(5):327.

Mossingl
  velopm
  sociatic
Mossingl
  and va
  Associ
Muirhead
  Clin N
Popescu
  Americ
Robins E
  Care N
Rogers K
  rejectic
Rosentha
  care pa
Rothman
  (3):81.
Scutchfie
  Med 8!

If the skin problem is located on an elbow or knee and the site is sore and wet, then a dusting powder may be appropriate to reduce friction and help dry the area. Talcum or starch-type preparations may be used.

## SKIN DISORDERS

Reactions or disorders of the skin are manifested by symptoms such as itching, pain, or tingling and by signs such as swelling, redness, papules, pustules, blisters, and hives. Some common dermatologic disorders in the United States and Canada are:

Acne vulgaris (cystic acne and acne scars)
Atopic dermatitis
Dyshidrotic eczema
Folliculitis
Fungus infections (tinea pedis, tinea unguium, tinea versicolor, tinea cruris)
Hand eczema
Herpes simplex
Lichen simplex chronicus
Psoriasis
Seborrheic dermatitis
Verruca vulgaris
Vitiligo

A reaction of the skin that makes the individual uncomfortable or unsightly may be attributed to or related to sensitivity to drugs, allergy, infection, emotional conflict, genetic disease (e.g., atopic eczema, psoriasis), hormonal imbalance, or degenerative disease. Sometimes the cause of the skin disorder is unknown and the treatment may be empiric in the hope that the right remedy will be found.

Dermatologic diagnosis includes physical inspection, personal and family medical history, drug history including OTCs, and laboratory tests including blood and urine tests, cytodiagnosis, and biopsy. The physical examination of the skin sometimes includes the use of Wood's light. This instrument provides long-wave ultraviolet light, which is helpful in detecting hair and skin infected with fungi that fluoresce and in aiding in differentiation of hypopigmented areas and depigmented areas of the skin. The potassium hydroxide 10% (KOH) test aids in diagnosis of mycotic infection. The solution will disintegrate keratin, disclosing, under microscopic examination, mycelia (vegetative part as filaments), fungal elements, and hyphae (which acquire food). Other tests include the Tzanck test for epidermal giant cells (seen in herpes zoster viral infections, usually with inclusion bodies, and in pemphigus vulgaris without bodies), biopsy, and patch tests. The dermatophyte test medium is a fast-acting medium that creates a marked color change when a dermatophyte is grown in it.

When the nature of the lesion has been established, its characteristics should be defined according to size, shape, surface, and color. See the box below for different types of lesions and some of the conditions associated with them.

The next step is to discover the distribution of the condition. In some diseases the diagnosis can be made from the distribution alone, and in others, it provides some assistance. The inference should not be drawn, however, that because a disease is not found in its common pattern of

---

### DIFFERENT TYPES OF LESIONS AND SOME CONDITIONS ASSOCIATED WITH THEM

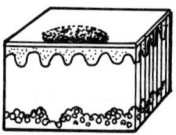

Macule: flat, nonpalpable, can vary in color
Examples: Addison's disease, drug eruptions, freckles, measles

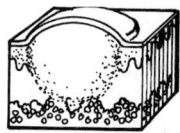

Nodule: raised, firm, palpable, 1 to 2 cm diameter, deeper in dermis
Examples: erythema induratum or nodosum, lipomas, syphilis, warts

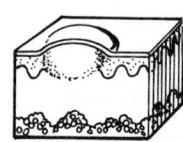

Papule: raised, palpable, firm, less than 1 cm diameter
Examples: acne, melanoma, warts, pigmented nevi

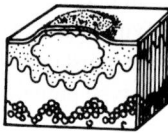

Plaques: raised, flat on top, hard, rough, larger than 1 cm diameter
Examples: atopic dermatitis, lichen planus, lupus erythematosus, psoriasis, seborrheic dermatitis

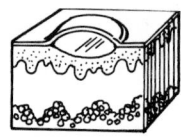

Vesicle: raised, circumscribed, filled with fluid, less than 1 cm diameter, blister
Examples: burns, chickenpox, herpes simplex or zoster, insect bites, scabies

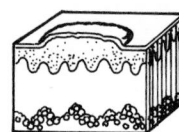

Wheals: raised, hard, area irregular shaped, edematous, diameter varies, usually pink in color
Examples: urticaria, insect bites

distribution that it can be excluded. For example, psoriasis is commonly found on the extensors, but occasionally it will be seen as a solitary lesion in the external ear. A basal cell carcinoma is most common on the face, but occasionally it occurs on the trunk. On the other hand, rosacea only attacks those areas of the face that flush.

The box on pp. 1022 to 1025 is a summary of the vast number of dermatologic reactions from drugs and their characteristic lesions and sequelae. Some may even be life-threatening. See Table 68-1 for the most common drugs involved. The nurse always needs to be cognizant of a client's drug history and current therapy to relate such lesions and sequelae to the appropriate cause; this often saves the client many unnecessary and uncomfortable diagnostic examinations and lessens the anxiety of the client and of the medical team. Simply discontinuing a particular drug often resolves a complicated dermatologic problem or sequelae of unknown origin.

Eczema and dermatitis are noninfectious inflammatory dermatoses. Contact dermatitis has clinical features that include skin rash with eczema (a red, thick, crusty, fissured, suppurating area) in various stages. The causes may be from contact with a primary irritant (acids, oils, soaps) in the environment, home, or work place or from a delayed allergic reaction (as seen with poison ivy contact).

Atopic dermatitis appears as a general eczema dermatitis frequently on the flexor body surfaces having genetic associations such as hay fever or asthma. Seborrheic dermatitis often appears on the scalp, eyebrows, ears, or sternum as a brown to red scaly rash.

Stasis dermatitis often preceding a venous stasis ulcer is found on the lower legs secondary to venous stasis and poor vascularity and is a brown eczematous area in appearance.

Papulosquamous eruptions are noninfectious inflammatory dermatoses that include uticaria (hives), psoriasis, pityriasis rosea, lichen planus, and exfoliative dermatitis. The nurse will see acute urticaria as an insidious-appearing, itchy erythematous wheal (which is a complement-mediated release of histamine from mast cells and basophils) resulting from an allergen. Chronic urticaria appears as a large hive without the sensation of itch or pruritis and is often accompanied by angioneurotic edema resulting from a genetic predisposition to diminished protease inhibitors (esterase).

Psoriasis often appears as erythematous plaques and orange-red-brown lesions covered with silvery scales. Psoriasis is often found on the scalp and extensor surfaces of the limbs and neck. Often thick, irregular nails are present.

Pityriasis rosea is a self-limited oval salmon-colored patch that follows the axis of skin cleavage lines. The major patches appear on the trunk, and smaller scales appear on the peripheral areas.

Infectious inflammatory dermatoses include viral diseases (**verruca** [wart], herpes simplex, varicella zoster/chickenpox), bacterial diseases (impetigo, folliculitis, **furuncle** [boil]) and fungal diseases (**tinea** [dermatophytosis], mucocutaneous candidiasis).

The verruca or wart is of various types, including the following: verruca vulgaris (commonly found on the hands and fingers); verruca plantaris (inward wart growth on the sole of the foot that may be covered with a callus or hyperkeratosis); verruca plana (found on the dorsa of the hands and face as a flat wart); condyloma acuminatum or venereal wart (cauliflower-like growth in the anogenital area often with hyperkeratosis).

**TABLE 68-1**   Life-threatening drug-induced skin eruptions

| Skin eruption | Description | Drugs involved |
|---|---|---|
| Exfoliative dermatitis | Entire surface of skin is red and scaly and will eventually slough off. Hair and nails may also be affected. Eruption may take weeks or months to resolve after causative agent is stopped. If not resolved, it may be fatal. | barbiturates carbamazepine demeclocycline furosemide gold griseofulvin penicillin phenothiazines phenytoin sulfonamides tetracyclines |
| Stevens-Johnson syndrome (erythema multiforme) | Severe form that involves widespread eruptions or lesions usually on face, neck, arms, legs, hands, and feet. May also involve mucosa, may produce fever and malaise. Syndrome may last months and is life-threatening. | May result from use of many drugs, especially phenytoin, sulfonamides, penicillin, carbamazepine, tetracyclines |
| Lupus erythematosus | Erythematous rash that may be flat or elevated, (butterfly) on cheek (malar), and across nose. Joint swelling and pain, rash, oral ulcers, serositis, renal, hematologic, pulmonary, and other systems may be affected. Reversible when drug is stopped. | procainamide, hydralazine, isoniazid, hydantoins, quinidine, trimethadione |

## COMMON DRUG-INDUCED DERMATOLOGIC CONDITIONS

### Drugs Causing an Acneform Reaction

ACTH
androgenic hormones
bromides
corticosteroids
cyanocobalamin
hydrantoins
iodides
methandrostenolone (Dianabol)
methyltestosterone (Metandren)
oral contraceptives

### Drugs Causing Purpura

ACTH
allopurinol (Zyloprim)
amitriptyline (Elavil, Endep)
anticoagulants
barbiturates
carbamides
chloral hydrate
chlorothiazide (Diuril)
chlorpropamide (Diabinese)
chlorpromazine (Thorazine)
corticosteroids
digitalis
fluoxymesterone
gold salts

griseofulvin (Grifulvin)
iodides
mepesulfate
meprobamate
penicillin
phenylbutazone (Butazolidin)
quinidine
rifampin (Rifadin, Rimac-
    tane, rifampicin)
sulfonamides
thiazides
trifluoperazine

### Drugs Causing Urticaria

ACTH
amitriptyline
barbiturates
bromides
chloramphenicol (Chloromy-
    cetin)
dextran
enzymes
erythromycin (Erythrocin,
    Ilotycin)
griseofulvin (Grifulvin)
hydantoins (Dilantin)
insulin
iodides
iodopyracet (Diodrast)
meperidine (Demerol)
meprobamate (Equanil,
    Miltown)

mercurials
nitrofurantoin (Furandantin)
novobiocin
opiates
penicillin
penicillinase
pentazocine (Talwin)
phenolphthalein
phenothiazines
propoxyphene (Darvon)
rifampin (Rifadin, Rimac-
    tane, rifampicin)
salicylates
serums
streptomycin
sulfonamides
tetracyclines
thiouracil

### Drugs Causing Alopecia

alkylating agents
anticoagulants
antimetabolites
bleomycin (Blenoxane)
mephenytoin (Mesantoin)
methimazole
methotrexate
norethindrone acetate
    (norinyl, Noriestrine, Ortho-Novum)
quinacrine
oral contraceptives
sodium warfarin (Coumadin)
trimethadione (Tridione)

### Drugs Causing Morbilliform Reactions

anticonvulsants
anticholinergics
antihistamines
barbiturates
chloral hydrate
chlordiazepoxide (Librium)
chlorothiazide (Diuril)
chlorpromazine (Thorazine)
gold salts
griseofulvin (Grifulvin)
hydantoins (Dilantin)
insulin
meprobamate

mercurials
methaminodiazepoxide
novobiocin
organic extracts
para-aminosalicylic acid
penicillin
phenothiazines
phenylbutazone (Butazolidin)
quinacrine (Atabrine)
salicylates
serums
streptomycin
sulfonamides
sulfones
tetracyclines
thiouracil

### Drugs Causing Lichenoid Reactions

aminphenazole (Daptazole)
chloroquine
gold salts compounds
organic arsenicals
para-aminosalicylic acid
quinacrine (Atabrine, mepacrine)
quinidine
thiazides

## COMMON DRUG-INDUCED DERMATOLOGIC CONDITIONS—cont'd

### Drugs Causing Fixed Eruptions

acetanilid
acetarsone
acetophenetidin
acetylsalicylic acid
aconite
acriflavine
aminopyrine
amobarbital
amodiaquine
amphetamine sulfate
anthralin
antimony potassium tartrate
antipyrine
arsphenamine
barbital
barbiturates
belladonna
bismuth salts
bromides
chloral hydrate
chlorguanide
chloroquine
chlorothiazide and sun
chlorpromazine
chlortetracycline
cinchophen
copaiba
dextroamphetamine
diacetyldiphenotisatin
diallybarbituric acid
diethylstilbestrol
digilanid
digitalis
dimenhydrinate (Dramamine)
dimethylamine acetarsone
diphenhydramine (Benadryl)

disulfiram and alcohol
eosin
ephedrine
epinephrine
ergot alkaloids
erythrocin
eucalyptus oil
formalin
frangula
gold compounds
griseofulvin (Grifulvin)
iodine
ipecac
ipomea
2-isopropyl-4-pentenoyl urea
    (Sedormid)
karaya gum
magnesium hydroxide
meprobamate
mercury salts
methenamine
neoarsphenamine
opium alkaloids
oxophenarsine
oxytetracycline (Terramycin)
para-aminosalicylic acid
penicillin
phenacetin
phenazone
phenobarbital
phenolphthalein
phenylbutazone (Butazolidin)
5-phenylethylhydantoin
phenylhydantoin
phenytoin (Dilantin)
phosphorus

potassium chlorate
pyramidine derivatives
quinacrine
quinidine
quinine
reserpine
salicylates
santonin
saccharin
scopolamine
sodium salicylate
sterculia gum
stramonium
streptomycin
strychnine
sulfadiazine
sulfaguanidine
sulfamerazine
sulfamethazine
sulfamethoxypyridazine (Kynex)
sulfapyridine
sulfarsphenamine
sulfathiazole
sulfisoxazole (Gantrisin)
sulfobromophthalein sodium
sulfonamides
tetracyclines
thiambutosine
thiram and alcohol
thonzylamine HCl (Neohetramine)
tripelennamine (Pyribenzamine)
trisodium arsphenamine sulfate
tryparsamide
urease
urginin
vaccines and immunizing agents

### Drugs Causing Contact Dermatitis

acriflavine
amethocaine
antazoline
antazoline and phenocide
antazoline and pyribenzamine
antihistamine
arsphenamine
atabrine
bacitracin (occupational)
benzocaine
benzoyl peroxide and chlorhy-
    droxyquinoline
bleomycin (Blenoxane)
cetrimide
chloramphenicol
chlorcyclizine

chlorhexidine
chlorhydroxyquinaline and benzoyl
    peroxide
chlorxylenol
chlorphenesin
chlorpromazine
colophony
crotamiton
cyclomethycaine
diphenhydramine
domiphen
ephedrine
formaldehyde
halogenated phenolic compounds
hedaquinium chloride

iodine
iodochlorhydroxyquinoline
isoniazid (occupational)
lanolin
meprobamate
mypyramine (Pyrilamine)
mercurials
mercury
neomycin
nitrofurazone
novobiocin
para-aminosalicylic acid
parabens
penicillin
peru balsam
phenindamine

*Continued.*

---

### COMMON DRUG-INDUCED DERMATOLOGIC CONDITIONS—cont'd

---

**Drugs Causing Contact Dermatitis—cont'd**

phenocide and antazoline
phenol
potassium hydroxyquinoline sulfate
procaine and other anesthetics
promethazine
propamidine
pyribenzamine and antazoline

quinacrine (Atabrine)
quinine
resorcin
spiramycin (occupational)
streptomycin

sulfonamides
sulfur and salicylic acid ointment
tetracylines
thiamine
thimerosal (Merthiolate)

**Photosensitizers**

acetohexamide (Dymelor)
acridine preparations (slight)
agave lechuguilla (amaryllis)
agrimony
9-aminoacridine
aminobenzoic acid
amitriptyline (Elavil)
anesthetics (procaine group)
angelica
anthracene
antimalarials
arsenicals
barbiturates
bavachi (corylifolia)
benzene
benzopyrine
bergamot (perfume)
bithionol (Actamer, Lorothidol)
blankophores (sulfa derivatives)
bulosemide (Jadit)
bromchlorsacylanilid
4-butyl-4-chlorosalicyanilide
carbamazepine (Tegretol)
carbinoxamine d-form (Twiston R-A)
carbutamide (Nadisan)
carrots, wild
cedar oil
celery
chlorophyll
chlorothiazide (Diuril)
chlorpromazine (Thorazine)
chlorpropamide (Diabinese)
chlortetracycline (Aureomycin)
citron oil
citrus fruits
clover
coal tar
contraceptives, oral
corticosteroids, topical
cyproheptadine

demeclocycline (Declomycin, deme-
    thylchlortetracycline)
desipramine (Norpramin, Pertofrane)
dibenzopyran derivatives
dicyanine-A
diethylstilbestrol
digalloyl trioleate (sunscreen)
dill
diphenhydramine hydrochloride
    (Benadryl)
disopyramide
doxycycline
dyes (methylene blue, toluidine blue)
eosin (slight)
estrone
fennel
fluorescein dyes
5-fluorouracil
furocoumarins (bergamot oil)
glyceryl p-aminobenzoate (sunscreen)
gold salts
grass (meadow)
griseofulvin (Fulvicin)
haloperidol
hematoporphyrin
hexachlorophene (rare)
hydrochlorothiazide (Esidrix,
    HydroDiuril)
imipramine HCI (Tofranil)
isothipencyl (Theruhistin)
isothipendyl (Theruhistin)
lady's thumb (tea)
lantinin
lavender oil
lime oil
meclothiazide (Enduron)
mepazine (Pacatal)

9-mercaptopurine
methotrimeprazine (Levoprome)
methoxsalen (Meloxine, Oxsoralen)
5-methoxypsoralen
8-methoxypsoralen
monoglycerol para-aminobenzoate
mustards
nalidixic acid (NegGram)
naphthalene
neuroleptics
nortriptyline (Aventyl)
oral contraceptives
oxytetracycline (Terramycin)
para-dimethylaminoazobenzene
paraphenylenediamine
parsley
parsnips
penicillin derivates (Griseofulvin)
perloline
perphenazine (Trilafon)
phenanthrene
phenazine dyes
phenolic compounds
phenothiazines
phenoxazines
phenylbutazone (Butazolidin)
phenytoin (Dilantin)
pitch and pitch fumes
porphyrins
prochlorperazine (Compazine)
promazine hydrochloride (Sparine)
profriptyline (Vivactil)
promethazine hydrochloride
    (Phenergan)
psoralens (perfume)
pyrathiazine hydrochloride (Pyrrolazote)
pyrazinamide
pyridine

---

### COMMON DRUG-INDUCED DERMATOLOGIC CONDITIONS—cont'd

**Photosensitizers—cont'd**

| | | |
|---|---|---|
| quinethazone (Hydromox) | sulfamerazine | trichlormethiazide (Metahydrin) |
| quinidine | sulfamethazine | tricyclic antidepressants |
| quinine | sulfapyridine | tridione |
| rose bengal perfume (slight) | sulfathiazole | triethylene melamine (TEM) |
| rue | sulfonamides | triflupromazine hydrochloride (Vesprin) |
| salicylanilides | sulfisomidine (Elkosin) | trimeprazine tartrate (Temaril) |
| salicylates | sulfonylureas (antidiabetics, oral | trimethadione (Tridione) |
| sandalwood oil (perfume) | hypoglycemics) | tripyrathiazine |
| silver salts | tetrachlorasalicylanilide (TCSA) | trypaflavine |
| smartweed (tea) | tetracyclines | trypan blue |
| stilbamidine isethionate | thiazides (Diuril, HydroDiuril) | vanillin oils |
| sulfacetamide | thiophene | water ash |
| sulfadiazine | thiopropazate dihydrochloride (Dartal) | xylene |
| sulfadimethoxine | tolbutamide (Orinase) | yarrow |
| sulfaguanidine | toluene | |
| sulfanilamide (slight) | tribromosalicylanilide (TBS) (deodorant soaps) | |

Herpes simplex and infectious inflammatory dermatoses appear as vesicles with an inflamed base and have an incubation period of up to 2 weeks in the primary infection. Late antibody development occurs. The herpes virus Type 1 affects skin and the oral cavity, and the herpes virus Type 2 affects the skin of neonates and genital mucosa. The recurrent infection is a reactivation of the older infection or new infection; antibodies appear early.

Fungal diseases, which include tinea or dermatophytosis, appear in the following various clinical classifications: tinea capitis (caused by either a *Trichophyton* or *microsporum* fungal infection as a nonfluorescent or fluorescent in children and in adults tinea barbae); tinea corporis (or *Microsporum* in children and *Trichophyton* in adults); tinea cruris *(Epidermophyton* or *Trichophyton);* and tinea pedis; onychomycosis *(Trichophyton);* and tinea versicolor *(Malassezia furfur).* Tinea or dermatophytosis often appear as a scaly erythematous circular lesion. Tinea versicolor appears as a brown discoloration. Breaking of the hair is seen in tinea capitis or barbae, and with onychomycosis the patient has thick, discolored nails.

## ▷NURSING MANAGEMENT: CARE OF THE CLIENT USING DERMATOLOGIC AGENTS

*Assessment.* Both a thorough history and an objective examination of the dermatologic condition are essential for the initial assessment and ongoing evaluation of nursing care. The nurse should elicit information regarding the onset of the problem; changes in the condition since onset; specific cause if known, or if not, recent exposures to new or different activities that might give a clue about cause; client-determined or physician-prescribed factors that may have alleviated the condition; and the client's psychologic response to the problem. Direct inspection and observation should be accomplished with a good light source. Palpation may be necessary, particularly in the instance of assessment of dark skin, where erythema may not be noticeable but warmth and edema of the involved area can be determined. Observations should be systematic and thorough, comparing the left side with the right. Descriptions need to be specific, using the metric system for measurement, and recorded. Recorded changes determine progress towards achieving the desired outcome of resolution of the dermatologic problem.

Clients receiving care with dermatologic agents may be at risk for a variety of nursing diagnoses. The nurse should consider some of the following: altered comfort related to pain, burning, or itching of the affected areas; risk for infection related to open skin areas; self-care deficits related to the location of the affected areas; and disturbance in self-concept related to perceived and actual disfigurement of the affected areas.

*Intervention.* Manufacturer's instructions should be followed in detail for application of the various preparations used for dermatological conditions. In addition, some conditions may be severe enough to require supportive therapy that is more systemic in nature. See also the boxes on skin absorption principles and general goals of therapy.

*Education.* If the etiology of the condition is known, unless it is genetic, the nurse should counsel the client on avoidance of exposure to the causative agent to prevent future episodes. Advise the client to maintain good hygiene of the unaffected areas of the body and to cleanse the affected area only in the prescribed fashion. Instruct the client not to touch affected areas and to dress to avoid or minimize contact with the involved area. Apply only prescribed preparations to the area and follow through with therapy even when the improvement may not be immediate. Avoid exposure of the involved areas to direct sunlight unless it is advised as a part of therapy. The client should be instructed to report any side effects or adverse reactions to the prescriber.

*Evaluation.* Observation and palpation are essential to evaluate progress of the resolution of the dermatologic condition. The lesions should decrease in size if the treatment is successful.

• • •

As previously stated, dermatologic products are so vast in number it would be difficult to cover them all in this chapter. For the sake of simplicity, this chapter will discuss three major groups of dermatologic products: general, prophylactic agents, and therapeutic agents. Some general dermatologic products include those previously discussed plus solutions, baths, soaps, wet dressings, and soaks. Prophylactic agents include sunscreens, protectives, and antiseptics and disinfectants. Therapeutic agents include the antiinfectives, and antiinflammatory corticosteroids, keratolytic agents, acne products, stimulants and irritants, topical anesthetics, burn products for second- and third-degree burns, antiaging products, and ectoparasiticidal topical drugs.

## GENERAL DERMATOLOGIC PREPARATIONS

This section refers to single and combination formulations used as bath preparations, cleansers, soaps, solutions and lotions, emollients, skin protectants, wet dressings and soaks, and rubs and liniments.

### Baths

Baths may be employed to cleanse the skin, to medicate it, or to reduce temperature. The usual method of cleansing the skin is by the use of soap and water, but this may not be tolerated in skin diseases. In some cases even water is not tolerated and inert oils must be substituted. Persons with dry skin should bathe less frequently than those with oily skin. It is possible to keep the skin clean without a daily bath. Nurses are sometimes accused of overbathing hospital patients, causing the client's skin to become dry and itchy. An oily lotion is preferable to alcohol (isopropyl or ethyl) for dry skin.

To render baths soothing in irritative conditions, oatmeal, starch, or gelatin may be added in the proportion of about 1 to 2 ounces per gallon of water. Oils such as Alpha-Keri, Lubath, and oilated oatmeal in a proportion of 1 ounce to the tub of water decrease the drying effect of water and thus help to relieve the itching of a sensitive, xerotic skin.

Lubricating topical medications or bland emollients should be applied immediately after the bath while skin is still moist. This increases absorption and hydration.

### Soaps

Ordinary soap is the sodium salt of palmitic, oleic, or stearic acids or mixtures of these. Soaps are prepared by saponifying fats or oils with the alkalies. The fats or oils used vary considerably. The oil used for castile soap is supposed to be olive oil. Some soaps are made with coconut oil to which the skin of some persons is sensitive. Soaps contain glycerin unless it has been removed from the preparation. The consistency of the soap depends on the predominating acid and alkali used.

Although all soaps are relatively alkaline, the presence

of an excess of free alkali or acid will constitute a potential source of skin irritation.

Medicated soaps contain antiseptics and other added substances, such as cresol, thymol, and sulfur, but soaps per se are antiseptic only insofar as they mechanically clean the skin.

Many people believe that soap and water are bad for the complexion. This is erroneous for the most part. A clean skin helps to promote a healthy skin. The soap used in maintaining a clean skin should be mild and contain a minimum of irritating materials. Perfumed or medicated soaps may be harmful if skin is extra sensitive to soap products, the soap is not adequately rinsed off the skin, if it stimulates excess production of natural skin oils, or if it excessively dries the skin.

Soaps are irritating to mucous membranes, and they are used in enemas mainly because of this action. They are also used in the manufacture of liniments and tooth powders. One of the mildest soaps is shaving soap.

## Solutions and Lotions

Soothing preparations may also be liquids that carry an insoluble powder or suspension, or they may be mild acid or alkaline solutions, such as boric acid solution, limewater, or aluminum subacetate used as wet dressings and soaks. The bismuth salts (the subcarbonate or subnitrate) and starch are also commonly used for their soothing effect.

**Aluminum acetate solution (Burow's solution, modified Burow's solution).** This mild protein precipitant astringent coagulates bacterial and serum protein and contains 545 ml aluminum subacetate solution and 15 ml glacial acetic acid in 1000 ml aqueous medium. It is diluted with 10 to 40 parts of water before application. This may be prepared from Domeboro or Bluboro products.

**Aluminum subacetate solution.** This preparation contains 145 g aluminum sulfate, 160 ml acetic acid, and 70 g precipitated calcium carbonate in 1000 ml aqueous medium. It is applied topically after dilution with 20 to 40 parts of water as a wet dressing.

**Calamine lotion.** Prepared calamine, zinc oxide, bentonite magma, glycerine, and calcium hydroxide solutions are included in this lotion. It is a soothing lotion used for the dermatitis caused by poison ivy, insect bites, prickly heat, and so on. It is patted on the involved skin area and is available with an antihistamine, diphenhydramine, as Caladryl lotion.

## Cleansers

Cleansers are usually soap free or modified soap products that are recommended for persons with sensitive, dry, or irritated skin or who may have had a previous reaction to soap product. These cleansers are less irritating, may contain an emollient substance, and may also have been adjusted to a slightly acidic or neutral pH. Included in this category are Aveeno Cleansing Bar, Lowila Cake, Keri Facial Cleanser, pHisoDerm, Spectro-Jel, Cetaphil, and Lobana Body Shampoo.

## Emollients

Emollients are fatty or oily substances that may be used to soften or soothe irritated skin and mucous membrane. An emollient is often used as a vehicle for other medicinal substances. Examples of emollients include lanolin, petroleum jelly (Vaseline), vitamin A and D ointment, vitamin E, and cold cream. Examples of emollient products on the market include Panthoderm; vitamin E oil, cream, ointment, or liquid; Aquacare; Nutraplus; vitamin A and D creams and ointments; Moisturel Lotion; Allercream Skin; Lubriderm; Dermassage; Nivea Skin; and many more.

## Skin Protectants

Skin protectants are used to coat minor skin irritations or to protect the person's skin from chemical irritants. Some commercially available products include AeroZoin, Benzoin, Kerodex, Hydropel, Covicone, and Benzoin Compound.

## Wet Dressings and Soaks

Wet dressings and soaks include some of the preparations discussed under solutions and lotions. These liquids are either a wet dressing or an astringent-type wet dressing used to treat inflammatory skin conditions, such as insect bites and poison ivy. Aluminum acetate solution (Burow's or modified Burow's solution), Bluboro powder, Domeboro Powder, and Pedi-Boro Soak Paks are available for this use.

A lime sulfur solution (Viem-Dome, Vlemasque, Vleminckx's) is often used as a soak or dressing for cystic acne, seborrheic dermatoses, and various types of pustular infections.

## Rubs and Liniments

Rubs and liniments are indicated for pain relief when the skin is intact. Pain caused by muscle aches, neuralgia, rheumatism, arthritis, and sprains are the types of pain that usually respond to these products. The ingredients in the preparations may include a counterirritant (e.g., cajuput oil, camphor, oil of cloves, methyl salicylate), an antiseptic (chloroxylenol, eugenol, thymol), local anesthetic (benzocain), or analgesics (salicylate-containing substances). The formulations are usually gels, creams, lotions, liniments, aerosols, or ointments. Examples from this category include Aspercreme, Myoflex Creme, infra-RUB Cream, Musterole

## Investigational Drug Update:
## NEURALGIA PAIN RELIEF

Capsaicin cream (Zostrix), a substance obtained from hot peppers, is under study for the treatment of chronic postherpetic neuralgia. Reported results state that it is both safe and effective and, in many instances, superior to other therapies. Capsaicin causes a release of substance P from nerve endings peripherally, thus an initial burning effect results in a temporary anesthetic effect. The skin becomes less sensitive to painful stimuli. This product was approved by the FDA under the orphan drug grant and several lower dose products are now available over the counter. A more concentrated formulation has been proposed for prescription status. It is currently under study for other painful conditions, such as diabetic neuropathy, reflex sympathetic dystrophy, and postmastectomy syndrome (Check, 1988).

Deep Strength Rub, Ben-Gay Ointment, Counterpain Rub, Vicks VapoRub, Doan's Backache Spray, Panalgesic Liniment, Banalg Liniment, and Sloan's Liniment.

## PROPHYLACTIC AGENTS

### Protectives

Protectives are soothing, cooling preparations that form a film on the skin. Protectives, to be useful, must not macerate the skin, must prevent drying of the tissues, and must keep out light, air, and dust. Nonabsorbable powders are usually listed as protectives, but they are not particularly useful because they stick to wet surfaces and have to be scraped off and do not stick to dry surfaces at all.

Collodion is a 5% solution of pyroxylin, or guncotton, in a mixture of ether and alcohol. When collodion is applied to the skin, the ether and alcohol evaporate, leaving a transparent film that adheres to the skin and protects it.

Flexible collodion is a mixture of collodion with 2% camphor and 3% castor oil. The addition of the latter makes the resulting film elastic and more tenacious. Styptic collodion contains 20% tannic acid and therefore is astringent, as well as protective.

Nonabsorbable powders include zinc stearate, zinc oxide, certain bismuth preparations, talcum powder, and aluminum silicate. The disadvantages associated with their use have been mentioned previously.

Although it is safe to say that no substances known at present can stimulate healing at a more rapid rate than is normal under optimal conditions, preparations that act as bland protectives may help by preventing crusting and trauma. In some instances they may reduce offensive odors.

## POTENCIES OF TOPICAL STEROID PRODUCTS

The following drug list compares the relative potency of the topical corticosteroid products. The fluorinated products (fluocinonide, betamethasone, halcinonide, triamcinolone, clobetasol, and others) are the most potent drugs and are less likely to cause sodium retention.

**Most Potent**

betamethasone dipropionate (Diprosone cream, ointment, 0.05%)
clobetasol propionate (Temovate cream, ointment, 0.05%)

**Very Potent**

amcinocide (Cyclocort cream, ointment, 0.1%)
betamethasone dipropionate (Diprosone lotion 0.05%)
desoximetasone (Topicort cream, ointment, 0.25%)
diflorasone diacetate (Florone cream, ointment, 0.05%)
fluocinolone (Synalar HP cream, 0.2%; Lidex and Lidex-E cream, gel, ointment, 0.05%)
halcinonide (Halog cream, ointment solution, 0.1%)
triamcinolone acetonide (Aristocort A), or Kenalog cream, ointment, 0.5%)

**Potent**

betamethasone (Benisone cream, gel, ointment, lotion, 0.025%)
betamethasone valerate (Valisone cream, ointment, lotion, 0.1%)
desoximetasone (Topicort LP; Topicort Gel, 0.05%)
flucinolone acetonide (Fluonid cream, ointment, 0.025%)
flurandrenolide (Cordran, Dordran SP cream, ointment, lotion, 0.025%)
halcinonide (Halog cream, 0.025%)
triamcinolone acetonide (Aristocort or Kenalog cream, ointment, lotion, 0.1%)

**Less Potent**

betamethasone valerate (Valisone, reduced strength cream, 0.01%)
clocortolone (Cloderm cream, 0.1%)
clocortolone (Cloderm cream, 0.1%)
desonide (Tridesiloncream, 0.05%)
fluocinolone acetonide (Synalar cream, 0.01%)
flurandrenolide (Cordran, Cordran SP cream, ointment, 0.025%)
hydrocortisone valerate (Westcort cream, ointment,) 0.2%
triamcinolone acetonide (Aristocort, Aristocort A, Kenalog cream, ointment, lotion, 0.025%)

**Least Potent**

dexamethasone (Decadron cream, 0.1%)
hydrocortisone (Cortef; Cort-Dome and others, cream, ointment, 2.5%)
methylprednisolone (Medrol ointment, 0.25%; 1%)

Data from Katcher, BS, Young, LY, and Koda-Kimble, MA: Applied therapeutics: the clinical use of drugs, ed 4, San Francisco, 1988, Applied Therapeutics, Inc, pp. 1404-1405.

## Sunscreen Preparations

Extended exposure to the sun, whether from sunbathing or as a normal consequence of an outdoor occupation, may lead to sunburn and/or premature aging of the skin (that is, loss of skin elasticity, resulting in an increase in wrinkling and dry skin). Certain chemicals (tetracyclines, sulfonamides, thiazides, phenothiazines, especially chlorpromazine, etc.,). plants, cosmetics, and soaps may cause photosensitivity or phototoxicity—that is, the substance causes an increased skin reaction to ultraviolet (UV) wavelengths, which is usually dose related and will appear as a sunburn on exposure (Feldman, 1990).

Persistent exposure to the sun may result in skin damage that progresses from minor irritations to a precancerous skin condition and, perhaps, to skin cancer later in life. Skin cancer is the most common type of cancer reported; it has been estimated to constitute one third of all malignancies, and it also has been reported that 40% to 50% of all Americans who reach 65 years of age will have at least one skin cancer in their lifetimes. (Lindley, 1988). The damaging ultraviolet radiation of sunlight is the major risk factor that causes sunburn and skin damage in the unprotected individual.

Sunscreen preparations are applied to either absorb or reflect the sun's harmful rays. Absorbing agents are chemicals such as amniobenzoic acid (formerly known as p-amniobenzoic acid, or PABA), benzophenones, cinnamates, and anthranilates, while the reflectors are physical agents such as titanium dioxide and zinc oxide. The latter agents are opaque (thick paste appearance) and must be heavily applied; thus they are not cosmetically acceptable to most persons.

The spectrum for ultraviolet radiation includes UV-A, UV-B, and UV-C. UV-A, or longwave radiation has a wavelength of 320 to 400 nm (nanometers). While sunlight exposure has focused more on UV-B, some recent evidence indicates that UV-A can penetrate deep into the skin, causing vascular damage. The long-term effects of UV-A are unknown at this time, but this evidence raises a concern about the potential for causing serious damage to underlying tissues. UV-A radiation can produce immediate or delayed pigment tanning (slow natural tan). It also is the range where most photosensitizing chemicals appear to be active, such as tetracyclines, thiazides, phenothiazines (especially chlorpromazine), and the psoralens.

UV-B (sunburn radiation) has a wavelength between 290 and 320 nm. This is the wavelength that causes erythema and is also associated with vitamin $D_3$ synthesis. UV-B has also been determined to be responsible for skin cancer induction, although the carcinogenic properties of UV-B appear to be augmented by UV-A. UV-C radiation from the sun does not appear to reach the earth's surface; therefore this type of radiation is usually emited by artificial ultraviolet sources. UV-C can cause some erythema but will not stimulate tanning.

The **sun protection factor (SPF)** is a ratio between the exposures to ultraviolet wavelengths required to cause erythema with and without a sunscreen. This is expressed as MED, or the minimal erythemal dose. Therefore if a person experiences 1 MED with 25 units of UV radiation (in an unprotected state), and after application of a sunscreen, the person requires 250 units of radiation to produce 1 MED, then this product would be given an SPF rating of 10. The higher the SPF, the longer it takes to develop a tan. If a person normally burned with 1 MED within 30 minutes, then applying a sunscreen with an SPF of 6 would allow that person to stay in the sun six times longer, or nearly 3 hours, before reaching 1 MED. The following is the recommended SPF for various skin types:

| Type | Description | SPF Recommended |
|---|---|---|
| 1 | Always burns, never tans, usually very fair complexion with red or blond hair and freckles | 8 or more |
| 2 | Burns easily, tans minimally, usually fair skinned | 6 to 7 |
| 3 | Sometimes burns but gradually tans | 4 to 5 |
| 4 | Minimal burning, always tans | 2 to 3 |
| 5 | Rarely ever burns, always tans | 2 |
| 6 | Never burns but tans darkly | — |

The best way to choose a sunscreen agent is according to your skin type, the length of time spent in the sun, the usual intensity of the sun's rays in your geographic area, and the type of preparation or formulation you prefer. The FDA has established the following degrees of protection according to a product's SPF:

| Degree of Protection Desired | SPF |
|---|---|
| Minimum sun protection | 2 to 4 |
| Medium sun protection | 4 to 6 |
| Extra sun protection | 6 to 8 |
| Maximum sun protection | 8 to 15 |
| Ultra sun protection | 15 or more |

The FDA advisory review panel has established three categories of sunscreens according to the products' active ingredients. Ingredients that absorb 95% or more of the radiation in the UV range of 290 to 320 nm are called sunscreen–sunburn preventive agents. If the active ingredient absorbs at least 85% of the radiation in the UV wavelength from 290 to 320 nm, then it is called a sunscreen-suntanning agent. An opaque agent that reflects or scatters all radiation in the UV range from 290 to 760 nm is a sunscreen–opaque sunblock agent. Most products are a combination of the first two types of agents, and the primary difference between a preventive agent and a suntanning agent might be the concentration of the active ingredient.

The nurse should advise clients appropriately on the selection and use of a sunscreen agent. Sunscreens should be liberally applied to all exposed body areas (except eyelids) and reapplied as frequently as recommended, in order to achieve the maximum effectiveness. Reapplication is usually every 2 to 3 hours. Refrain from being in the sun when the sun's rays are most direct and damaging,— that is, between 10 AM and 2 PM. Wear sunscreen and limit exposure on overcast or cloudy days. Very little UV radiation is blocked by the cloud cover, although infrared radiation that contributes to the sensation of heat is usually reduced. This heat reduction might give an individual a false sense of security against a sunburn. Be aware of reflective surfaces; the sun's rays can be reflected on skin from water, concrete, snow, and sand. Keep infants out of the sun— sunscreens should always be used on children over 6 months old. It has been projected that the use of an SPF 15 from 6 months of age through 18 years of age will result in a 78% reduction in the incidence of skin cancer over a person's lifetime (Feldmann, 1990).

See Table 68-2 for examples of sunscreen agents, including their SPFs and waterproof or water-resistant labels, if appropriate.

## THERAPEUTIC AGENTS

### Topical Antiinfectives

Antiinfectives include topical antibiotics, antiviral agents (for use with minor skin abrasions and superficial infected wounds), and antifungal agents.

### Antibiotics

The most frequent causative organisms of skin infections **(exodermas)** are *Streptococcus pyogenes* and *Staphylococcus aureus.* Folliculitis, impetigo, furuncles, carbuncles, and cellulitis often result from these organisms. These common skin disorders are infections for which topical prophylaxis antibiotics may be applied. Only some of the agents follow; other topical antibiotics will be discussed in sections on acne products, antifungals, and antivirals.

#### Bacitracin

Bacitracin is very useful in the local treatment of infectious lesions. Bacitracin is most often used in an ointment (Baciguent, over the counter), although it can be used to moisten wet dressings or as a dusting powder. It is odorless and nonstaining, and its use seldom results in sensitizing; however, allergic contact dermatitis has occurred.

#### Neomycin

Neomycin has been used successfully in the treatment of infections of skin and mucous membrane. It is applied topically (Myciguent, over the counter). It occasionally irritates the skin, and allergic contact dermatitis is reported especially when used on stasis ulcers. An ointment (Mycitracin, over the counter), which combines *neomycin, bacitracin, and polymyxin B,* may be more efficacious in mixed infections than when these agents are used singly.

In conditions where absorption of neomycin may occur (including burns and trophic ulceration), there is the potential of nephrotoxicity, ototoxicity, and neomycin hypersen-

**TABLE 68-2**   Sunscreen formulations

| Commercial name | SPF | Waterproof/water resistant |
|---|---|---|
| Hawaiian Tropic Baby Faces Sunblock | 25 | Water resistant |
| Sundown Sunscreen Ultra | 25 | Waterproof |
| Coppertone Moisturizing Sunblock | 15 | — |
| Ray Block | 15 | — |
| Block Out Clear by Sea & Ski | 15 | Water resistant |
| TI-Screen | 15 | Water resistant |
| PreSun 8 Creamy | 8 | Waterproof |
| PreSun 4 Creamy | 4 | Waterproof |
| Coppertone Lite Lotion | 4 | — |
| Coppertone Oil | 2 | — |
| Hawaiian Tropic Professional "Light" Tanning | 2 | — |
| **LIP BALM PROTECTANTS** | | |
| PreSun 15 Lip Protector | 15 | |
| Chapstick Sunblock 15 | 15 | |
| Lipkote by Coppertone | 15 | |
| Blistik | 10 | |

sitivity reactions. This risk is seen more frequently in persons with compromised renal function, in clients with extensive burns (over 20% of area), and in clients using other aminoglycoside antibiotics. Sensitization may occur to any of the antibiotic ingredients, and prolonged use may produce suprainfection as an over-growth of nonsuspective organisms such as fungi. Photosensitivity is reported with topical gentamicin.

The possibility of hypersensitivity occurs with chloramphenicol when used topically as does the additional risk of bone marrow hypoplasia, blood dyscrasias, itching, burning, angioneurotic edema, urticaria, and vesicular and maculopapular dermatitis. Tetracyclines may stain clothing and cause erythema, irritation, and swelling locally. See Table 68-3 for a list of topical antibiotics and their spectrum of activity.

Although erythromycin generally has activity against gram positive organisms, in the United States it is approved only for treatment of acne vulgaris caused by an anaerobe, *Propionibacterium acnes (Corynebacterium acnes).*

Mupirocin (Bactroban) is a topical antibacterial preparation indicated for the treatment of impetigo caused by *Staphylococcus aureus* and other beta-hemolytic strepto-

**TABLE 68-3**  Spectrum of antimicrobial activity of topical antibiotics

| Antibiotic | Gram + | Gram − | Broad spectrum |
|---|---|---|---|
| bacitracin ointment | | X | |
| chlortetracycline ointment | | | X |
| chloramphenicol cream | | | X |
| erythromycin liquid or ointment | X | | |
| gentamicin cream and ointment | | | X |
| neomycin cream and ointment | | | X |

cocci. Investigationally, it has also been used to treat infected eczema, folliculitis, and minor bacterial skin infections. It has a 2% concentration and is usually applied to affected areas, three times daily.

Topical preparations and antibiotic combinations available over the counter include all the above with the exception of chloramphenicol, erythromycin, and gentamicin.

The OTC products must be labeled as first aid products to help prevent infection in minor cuts, burns, or injuries. They cannot be recommended to treat known infections.

Prescription antibiotic ointments are generally indicated for the treatment of minor or surface bacteria infections.

### Antivirals
#### acyclovir (Zovirax Ointment 5%)

Acyclovir inhibits the viral enzymes necessary for DNA synthesis. It is used in the management of active initial infections of genital herpes genitalis and in limited, non−life threatening mucocutaneous herpes simplex infections (primarily herpes labialis) in immunocompromised patients.

Side effects/adverse reactions include vulvitis, mild skin pain, transient burning, stinging, pruritis, and rash. Dosage is adequate covering of the lesions with ointment every 3 hours six times daily for 7 days. Pregnancy safety has been established at FDA category C.

▷ **Nursing Management:**
**Acyclovir Therapy**

In addition to the nursing management of the care of the client using dermatologic agents, the following factors should be considered.

***Intervention.*** Dose per application will vary depending on lesion area; a 1/2-inch ribbon of ointment covers approximately 4 inches of surface area.

Store ointment at 15° C to 25° C (59° F to 78° F).

***Education.*** Instruct the client to use a finger cot or rubber glove when applying the ointment to prevent autoinoculation to other sites. Avoid contact with eyes.

Advise annual or more frequent Pap smears because women with herpes genitalis are more likely to develop cervical cancer.

Recommend the wearing of loose clothing and keeping affected areas clean and dry to prevent further irritation.

Advise the client to avoid sexual activity if lesions are active for either partner. Even if partner is asymptomatic, the disease may still be sexually transmitted; use of a condom probably will help prevent transmission of herpes.

### Antifungals

There are few fungi that produce keratinolytic enzymes to provide for their existence on skin. Three infectious fungi can cause local fungal infections without systemic effects: *Microsporum, Trichophyton,* and *Epidermophyton.* The possibility of a mixed infection with these fungi must never be overlooked.

Fungi exist in a moist, warm environment, preferably in dark areas (such as shoes and socks). Tinea pedis (athlete's foot, ringworm of the foot) is commonly encountered. Immunologic mechanisms may have an important role in fungal control. The triad for suspicion for fungal infections is an immunologic deficit, a specific fungi involvement, and the skin condition.

The stratum corneum is a layer of dead desquamated cells that are shed normally or are dissolved in sebum. The fungi invade this layer and cause inflammation and induce sensitivity when they penetrate the epidermis and dermis. Since the stratum corneum is shed daily, the ability to spread or transmit the fungi is by contact.

Most commonly reported side effects/adverse reactions include local irritation, pruritus, burning sensation, and scaling. Erythema, blistering, stinging, peeling, urticaria, pruritus, and general irritation may occur with products like clotrimazole.

Pregnancy safety has been noted only for the following antifungal agents: econazole (FDA category C), ciclopirox (FDA category B), clotrimazole (FDA category C), haloprogin (FDA category B), and ketoconazole (FDA category C).

The primary topical antifungal agents include undecylenic acid products, iodochlorhydroxyquin, miconazole nitrate, econazole nitrate, ciclopirox olamine, clotrimazole, triacetin, haloprogin, tolnaftate, nystatin, amphotericin B, gentian violet, ketoconazole, and a variety of antifungal combination ointments, powders and liquids. See Table 68-4 for the generic, trade name, status (OTC or prescription), and comments about the products.

▷ ***Nursing Management:***
***Antifungal Agent Therapy***

In addition to the nursing management of the care of the client using dermatologic agents, consider these points.

***Assessment.*** Carefully note skin characteristics, symptoms, and predisposing factors such as trauma, suppressed immunity, general health, hygiene practices, or exposure to infecting agent.

rected. In children give once or twice daily with steroids in potent or less potent drug category. Application frequency depends on site, response of the cutaneous eruption to medication, and application technique.

Pregnancy safety has been established at FDA category C.

### ▷ Nursing Management: Topical Corticosteroid Therapy

In addition to the nursing management of the care of the client using dermatologic agents, consider the following.

*Assessment.* The age of the skin affects absorption of the potent fluorinated corticosteroids; the very young and the very old have skin that is more permeable. If prolonged treatment is required, it is prudent for the physician to clinically monitor plasma cortisol levels monthly until the steroid is discontinued. Most side effects are temporary and are resolved when the topical steroid is discontinued. Taper therapy off gradually.

*Education.* To enhance client compliance the reasons for occlusive dressing procedure should be described to the patient. This technique intensifies percutaneous penetration of the topical steroid and concentrates the medication in the area where it is most needed.

*Evaluation.* Occlusive dressings may cause folliculitis from bacterial or candidal infection, hyperthermia from heat retention, or systemic effects related to increased drug absorption.

### Keratolytics

**Keratolytics** (keratin dissolvers) are drugs that soften scales and loosen the outer horny layer of the skin. Salicylic acid and resorcinol are drugs of choice. Their action makes possible the penetration of other medicinal substances by cleaning the lesions involved. Salicylic acid is particularly important for its keratolytic effect in local treatment of scalp conditions, warts, corns, fungous infections, acne, and chronic types of dermatitis. It is used up to 20% in ointments, plasters, or collodion for this purpose.

### Acne Products

Acne vulgaris involves an intrafollicular hyperkeratinization that leads to the formation of a keratin plug at the base of the pilosebaceous follicle; it affects 30% to 85% of adolescents. The reduction and removal of sebum and bacteria, specifically *Propionibacterium acnes*, are the target of acne vulgaris therapy. Treatment of acne therapy may include (1) removal of keratin plugs, (2) decreasing the amount of *P. acnes*, (3) lowering the amounts of free fatty acid and formation, (4) decreasing the sebum production, and (5) effectively improving the appearance of the individual for psychosocial benefits.

Grades of acne have been classified as follows. Grade I includes primarily sparse comedones; grade II has come-

dones, papules, and occasionally pustules; grade III has a predominance of papules and pustules with small cysts; grade IV has overt signs of cystic acne. Treatment varies with the needs of each grade.

Of the many treatment modalities in acne therapy, only the topical forms of benzoyl peroxide, tetracycline, erythromycin, clindamycin, and tretinoin will be discussed here.

### benzoyl peroxide

Benzoyl peroxide slowly and continuously liberates active oxygen, producing antibacterial, antiseptic, drying, and keratolytic actions. The release of oxygen into the philosebaceous and comedone area creates unfavorable growth conditions for *P. acnes* and reduces the release of the fatty acids from sebum. Additionally, the drying vehicle aids in shrinking the papules or pustules but does not have an effect on comedones or cysts. Benzoyl peroxide is used in the treatment of acne vulgaris.

Benzoyl peroxide is absorbed and metabolized in the skin to benzoic acid. Approximately 5% of the benzoic acid is absorbed and excreted in the kidneys. In 4 to 6 weeks improvement in acne is usually noted. Side effects occur infrequently and are rarely a problem. These include dry or peeling skin, red skin, or sensation of warmth of the skin. Adverse reactions that require medical intervention include: severe redness, pruritus, blisters, and burning or swelling of skin caused by an allergic reaction. No significant drug interactions are reported.

In adults and children 12 years and older, benzoyl peroxide is usually applied topically (5% or 10%): lotion, one to four times daily; cleansing bar, two or three times daily; cream or cleansing lotion, one to two times daily.

Pregnancy safety has been established at FDA category C.

### tretinoin (retinoic acid, vitamin A acid, Retin-A)

Tretinoin is an irritant that stimulates epidermal cell turnover, which causes skin peeling; this reduces the free fatty acids and horny cell adherence within the comedone. Tretinoin is used in the treatment of acne vulgaris in which comedones, pustules, and papules predominate.

Side effects/adverse reactions reported include excessively red and edematous blisters, crusted skin, temporary alterations in pigmentation of the skin.

Concomitant topical use with drying or peeling agents such as benzoyl peroxide, resorcinol, salicylic acid, and sulfur results in excessive keratolytic and peeling effects.

Apply each night by covering the area lightly before the person retires. Some clients require less frequent applications or use a lower percentage strength, and others may respond to the higher percentage dosage forms. Application should be done after thorough cleansing of area, allowing a minimum of 30 minutes for it to dry. If applied to wet skin, an increased drying effect and redness may occur.

Pregnancy safety has been established at FDA category B.

## ▷ Nursing Management:
### Tretinoin Therapy

See general nursing management of dermatologic agents, on p. 1025.

Clients with sunburned skin, skin sensitive to ultraviolet light, or skin exposed to weather extremes must exercise caution and avoid tretinoin until the skin has recovered.

The client must avoid medicated or abrasive cleansers, astringents, soaps, and cosmetics that have a drying effect and a high alcohol concentration.

The client will be excessively sensitive to sun and should wear SPF sunscreens during therapy.

Irritation and desquamation are most likely during the first 1 to 3 weeks of treatment.

### isotretinoin

Isotretinoin (Accutane) is an oral product indicated for the treatment of severe recalcitrant cystic acne. Women who are pregnant or are planning to become pregnant should not use this preparation. Many spontaneous abortions have been reported in pregnant women, as well as major abnormalities in the fetus at birth. Hydrocephalus, microcephalus, external ear abnormalities, facial dysmorphia, cleft palate, and cardiovascular problems have all been documented. This product is listed as contraindicated in pregnancy (FDA category X.)

Investigations are in progress to determine the status of this product. It will either have stronger restrictions placed on its use, or it may be removed from the market.

## ▷ Nursing Management:
### Isotretinoin Therapy

***Assessment.*** It should be ascertained that the client is not pregnant by a negative pregnancy test and an appropriate history and physical examination because isotretinion has been demonstrated to cause fetal abnormalities. The client of child-bearing age should be assessed for her capability to comply with mandatory contraceptive measures; these should be accomplished for at least 1 month before therapy, during therapy, and for 1 month after the end of therapy.

The client should receive a baseline CBC, serum electrolyte profile, blood lipid levels, blood glucose levels, and hepatic function studies. These should also be monitored throughout therapy.

The client receiving isotretinoin is at risk for the following nursing diagnoses: altered comfort related to joint tenderness, headache, inflammation of the eye, skin rash, optic neuritis, dryness of mouth, skin and eyes; impaired skin integrity (scaling, redness, inflammation of the lips) altered thought processes (depression); visual disturbances (cataracts, corneal opacities); and altered bowel patterns (diarrhea) related to inflammatory bowel disease or regional ileitis.

***Education.*** The client is to receive both oral and written instructions regarding the hazards of pregnancy and indicate her understanding and acceptance of the written warnings. The client receiving isotretinoin should be alerted not to donate blood during or for 30 days after therapy, because of risk to the fetus of a pregnant woman who may receive the blood. As isotretinoin may increase plasma triglyceride concentrations, those clients at particular cardiovascular risk should be cautioned: those with a history of high alcohol intake, obesity, or a history or family history of hypertriglyceridemia or diabetes mellitus.

Alert the client to avoid concurrent use of vitamin A, unless prescribed by a physician to minimize additive toxic effects. Avoid the ingestion of alcohol because of possible hypertriglyceridemia and consequent cardiovascular risks. Caution about a decrease in night vision; the client should alert the physician if this occurs. The client may also be intolerant of contact lens because of dryness of the eyes. Wearing the lens may need to be discontinued during the course of therapy if an ocular lubricant is not successful in the relief of the dryness. Sugar-free gum or candies or ice may be recommended to correct mouth dryness.

***Evaluation.*** Improvement in the cystic acne should occur after 1 to 2 months, but may require 4 to 5 months of therapy.

## *Topical Antibiotics*

Topical antibiotics used in the treatment of acne (clindamycin, erythromycin, tetracycline, meclocycline) have unknown mechanisms of action. Therefore the postulated mechanisms of action of these antibiotics are antiinflammatory or inhibitory or suppressive of acne-causing bacteria and the reduction of short-claim free fatty acids of the surface lipids.

### clindamycin phosphate (Cleocin T topical solution)

Topical clindamycin efficacy in the treatment of acne is reported to be equal to or better than oral tetracycline therapy and superior to topical erythromycin or topical tetracycline therapy. Skin phosphatases, by hydrolysis, convert the clindamycin phosphate to the antibacterial active clindamycin base.

Approximately 10% of a dose penetrates and is absorbed in the stratum corneum layer. Clindamycin has appeared in the urine without detectable activity in the plasma and with detectable activity in comedonal extracts. After topical application, there is an inhibition of acne-causing bacteria and reduction of free fatty acids on the skin surface.

This is one of the most widely used topical antibiotics indicated in the treatment of acne vulgaris.

The following side effects infrequently occur and rarely require physician intervention: dry, scaly and/or peeling of skin; a stinging or burning sensation. Medical intervention is necessary if a hypersensitivity skin reaction occurs.

For adults and children; apply a thin film twice daily to affected area.

Pregnancy safety has been established at FDA category B.

▷ **Nursing Management:**
**Clindamycin Therapy**

See general nursing management of dermatologic agents, on p. 1025.

Cross-resistance exists with lincomycin and antagonism with erythromycin. Contraindications demonstrated by hypersensitivity to any form of clindamycin or lincomycin may apply to the topical preparation. During the client interviews the nurse should inquire about any previous sensitivity not only to clindamycin but also to other antibiotics or allergens and a history of regional enteritis. Atopic patients should be questioned since some absorption may possibly occur through the skin.

**erythromycin topical solution (A/T/S, Eryderm)**

Erythromycin topical solution is indicated for the treatment of acne vulgaris.

With this product, suprainfection and an overgrowth of antibiotic-resistant organisms may occur. Skin reactions may be erythema, desquamation, tenderness, dryness, pruritus, burning, oiliness, and acne.

Erythromycin topical solution is applied with the fingertips and hands each morning and evening to the affected areas. These areas are to be washed and rinsed and patted dry; after application the hands and fingers should be washed.

Pregnancy safety has been established at FDA category C.

▷ **Nursing Management:**
**Erythromycin Topical Solution Therapy**

See general nursing management of dermatologic agents, on p. 1025.

Hypersensitivity to erythromycin or the other components of the solution (alcohol, propylene glycol, or acetone) is a containdication to its use. A cumulative irritant effect may occur with concomitant use of peeling, desquamating, or abrasive agents.

Caution the client that erythromycin solution should not be used near the eyes, nose, mouth, and other mucous membranes.

**meclocycline sulfosalicylate (Meclan) cream**

Meclocycline sulfosalicylate is a topical oxytetracycline derivative that is indicated in the treatment of acne vulgaris.

Acute contact dermatitis and skin irritation may occur with its use. Excessive application may result in temporary follicular staining and fabric staining.

This nonalcoholic vanishing cream is applied in the morning and evening or less often depending on client response. The cream contains formaldehyde and may cause allergic reactions.

Pregnancy safety has been established at FDA category B.

▷ **Nursing Management:**
**Meclocycling Sulfosalicylate Therapy**

The percutaneous absorption resulting from prolonged use of this tetracycline derivative necessitates cautious monitoring of clients with hepatic or renal dysfunctions. No adequate well-controlled studies have been made in pregnant women or nursing mothers.

**tetracycline topical solution (Topicycline)**

Topical tetracycline is used to treat acne vulgaris. It is directly applied to the pilosebaceous units (hair follicle and sebaceous gland), which are most numerous on the face, back, chest, and upper arms. Systemic tetracycline decreases the amount of free fatty acids present in acne lesions, but the mechanism by which topical tetracycline therapy improves acne is unknown.

Topical tetracycline by percutaneous absorption produces a serum level of 0.1 $\mu$g/ml, which is less than 7% of that produced by a 500 mg/day oral dose. Liver damage in clients with renal impairment using topical tetracycline is unlikely, but it should be considered in those with hepatorenal dysfunction. No data are available regarding the use of topical tetracyclines in pregnant women, and no established data are available concerning its use during lactation.

Transient stinging or burning may often occur. The slight yellow superficial coloring of the skin of light-complected clients may be washed off. Under a source of ultraviolet light (sun, sunlamp), the treated areas will fluoresce.

Tetracycline is generously applied twice daily (morning and evening) to affected areas until the skin is wet. Because of the 40% ethanol and other components, the eyes, nose, mouth, and mucous membrane areas should be avoided. Normal use of cosmetics is permitted. (See Chapter 59 for a more complete discussion.)

Pregnancy safety has been established at FDA category B.

## Burn Products

Approximately 6000 or more people die each year of thermal injury in the United States alone. The chief cause of death is shock, a fact of considerable significance in any effective plan of treatment.

Burns cause lesions of the skin accompanied by pain. The burn may be caused by heat (thermal burn), chemical cauterizing agents (chemical burns), or electricity (electrical burns). Sources may be friction, lightning, or electromagnetic energy sources (ultraviolet light, x-rays, lasers, or atomic explosion). The types of burns that result from various sources are relatively specific and diagnostic.

Consideration of what takes place in the damaged tissues clarifies many points of treatment. At first there is an altered capillary permeability in the local injured area. That is, the permeability is increased, resulting in a loss of plasma and weeping of the surface tissues. If the burn is at all extensive, considerable amounts of plasma fluid may be lost in a relatively short time. This depletes the blood volume and causes a decreased cardiac output and diminished blood flow. Unless the situation is rapidly brought under control, irreparable damage may result from the rapidly developing tissue anoxia. Lack of sufficient oxygen and the accumulation of waste products from inadequate oxidation result in loss of tone in the minute blood vessels, and the increased capillary permeability then extends to tissues remote from those suffering the initial injury. Thus a generalized edema often develops, and the vicious cycle once established tends to be self-perpetuating. One of the aims in the treatment of burns is therefore to stop the loss of plasma insofar as it is possible and replenish that which is lost as quickly as possible.

Partial- or full-thickness burns must be thought of as open wounds with the accompanying danger of infection. The infection must be prevented or treated. The treatment, however, must be such that it will not bring any further destruction of tissue or of the small islands of remaining epithelium from which growth and regeneration can take place.

When burns are divided into three degrees, they are classified by the depth of skin involved within a geographic designation. First-degree burns involve only the epidermis, causing erythema with characteristic dry, painful reddening and edema without blistering or vesiculation (e.g., overexposure to sun or flash burn). Second-degree burns involve the epidermis extending into the dermis and may be superficial or involve deep dermal necrosis. Epithelial regeneration may extend from the deep skin appendages such as hair follicles and sebaceous glands that penetrate the dermis. This burn is characterized by a moist, blistered, very painful surface (e.g., flash or scald burns from nonviscous liquids). Third-degree burns involve destruction of the entire dermis and epidermis characterized by white, lustrous, or opaque skin; dry, leathery skin; or coagulated, charred skin without sensation as a result of the destruction of nerve endings (e.g., flame burns or hot viscous liquids). Deep third-degree extend into subcutaneous fat, muscle, or bone; they cause scarring and may require skin grafting (see box).

The severity of electrical burns depends on the amount of voltage received, the condition of the skin (e.g., cuts, abrasions, and mositure, which lower resistance), and contraction of flexor muscles, which inhibits release from the power source. This may result in cardiac systole, ventricular fibrillation, or nervous system paralysis, which can lead to respiratory arrest. Electrical burns develop necrosis of more tissue than thermal burns. Electrical burns are of three types. In Type I, the electrical current causes effects on blood vessels such as occlusion, thrombosis, or tissue destruction. In Type II, electrical burns from high-tension currents (e.g., an electrical arc) produce a crater in the skin. Type III electrical burns are similar to flame burns because the arc flame ignites the person's clothes.

---

### BURN RATINGS

| Degree | Description |
| --- | --- |
| First | Superficial injury involving only the epidermis. Characterized by pain, red skin without blistering, and perhaps, swelling. This is a mild partial thickness burn that will heal without scarring. |
| Second | Burn extends from epidermis into the dermis area. Pain is intense, skin suface will be red, blistered, and may have a mottled appearance. This type burn usually has edema and blistering for 2 days after the initial burn injury. This is a partial thickness burn that generally leaves minimal scarring, if properly treated. |
| Third | This burn involves destruction of the epidermis and dermis and may extend into fat, muscle, or tissues. Some areas will be charred black, person will complain of severe pain or no pain at all if nerves have been destroyed. This is a full-thickness burn that may require skin grafting. Healing results in significant scarring. |

---

Chemical burns occur after contact with acid or alkali; the initial treatment is water irrigation of the affected area followed by neutralization. Chemical burns may occur in the mouth and appear as a white slough owing to necrosis of the epithelium and underlying connective tissues.

***First aid treatment of burns.*** An important first aid treatment for minor and major burns regardless of cause (chemical, electric, thermal) is to immediately cool the wound to remove irritants, decrease inflammation, and constrict blood vessels; this reduces the permeability of the blood vessels and checks edema formation. Cold tap water can be used to thoroughly flush the wound and to cool hot clothing. The more quickly the wound is cooled, the less tissue damage there is likely to be, and the more rapid will be the recovery. No greasy ointments, lard, butter, or dressings should be applied, since these agents will inhibit loss of heat from the burn, which will increase both discomfort and tissue damage. The burn may be left exposed to the air or cold wet compresses may be applied until the person can be transported for medical attention.

Burn victims treated in an emergency room or burn unit will be stabilized with intravenous fluids, given analgesics for pain, and sedated, if necessary. Such individuals are immunized with tetanus toxoid and/or tetanus immunoglobulin, depending on their immunization status. Catheterization may be necessary to measure urinary output, depending on client's status. Following stabilization, the burn wound is cleaned in a whirlpool (Hubbard) tank if available. Povidone-iodine (Betadine whirlpool concentrate) is usually added to the tank. Hair around the wound is shaved, loose skin is removed. Following the bath, topical antibiotic is started.

### silver sulfadiazine (Silvadene)

Silver sulfadiazine is an antiinfective agent with broad antimicrobial activity against many gram-negative and gram-positive bacteria and yeast. It is particularly effective against *Pseudomonas* organisms. It is produced by the reaction of silver nitrate with sulfadiazine. Silver sulfadiazine acts only on the cell membrane and cell wall to produce its bactericidal effect.

Silver sulfadiazine is used in second- and third-degree burns for the prevention and treatment of sepsis. Control of infection may prevent the conversion of infected second-degree burns resulting in necrosis. Since silver sulfadiazine is not a carbonic anhydrase inhibitor, it does not alter acid-base balance; neither does it alter electrolyte balance nor stain tissues, linen, or dressings. Silver sulfadiazine softens eschar, facilitating eschar removal and preparation of the wound for grafting.

Silver sulfadiazine is available as a 1% cream to be applied topically to cleansed, debrided burn wounds once or twice daily. It should be applied with a sterile gloved hand to a thickness of about $\frac{1}{16}$ inch. Burn wounds should be continuously covered with the cream. If the cream is removed by activity, it should be reapplied. Daily bathing and debriding are important. Dressings may or may not be used.

Therapy is usually continued until satisfactory healing has occurred or the wound is ready for grafting. Since silver sulfadiazine inhibits bacterial growth, delayed eschar separation may occur, necessitating escharotomy to prevent contractures.

Pain, burning, and itching occur infrequently following application of the silver sulfadiazine cream.

Silver sulfadiazine may cause a hypersensitivity reaction; if this occurs, the drug should be discontinued. Hemolysis may occur in persons with glucose-6-phosphate dehydrogenase deficiency.

When applied to extensive areas of the body, significant amounts of the drug may be absorbed, reaching therapeutic serum levels, producing adverse reactions characteristic of the sulfonamides. Renal function in these patients should be monitored and the urine examined for sulfa crystals.

Silver sulfadiazine may cause kernicterus. Although it is not recommended for pregnant women at term, premature neonates, or infants under 6 months, it is useful in pediatric burn clients. Proteolytic enzymes may be inactivated by this silver salt.

For nursing management consult Chapter 73.

### silver nitrate

An aqueous solution of silver nitrate 0.5% has been used extensively in some burn centers during the past few years. As a 0.5% solution it is a relatively safe antiseptic agent for gram-negative bacteria. Dressings soaked in silver nitrate 0.5% are applied early to the burn; the dressings must be kept moist and must not be allowed to dry, which would cause precipitation of silver salts into the wound and irritation. Concentrations of silver nitrate above 1% produce tissue necrosis; concentrations below 0.5% are not antiseptic. Silver nitrate stains anything with which it comes in contact. The brown or black tissue discoloration is usually not permanent. Silver nitrate solution 0.5% is a hypotonic solution, and when it is used on extensive burns or for extensive periods of time it may cause electrolyte imbalance. Serum electrolytes should be frequently determined and clients observed for symptoms of sodium or potassium depletion (such as change in behavior and confusion); blood sample color (brownish) is indicative of methemoglobinemia.

For nursing considerations, consult Chapter 73.

### mafenide acetate (Sulfamylon)

One of the most important therapeutic agents developed to combat burn infection in avascular tissue has been the discovery of mafenide acetate. Mafenide (a sulfonamide) is a water-soluble ointment (bacteriostatic to gram-negative and gram-positive organisms, including *Pseudomonas aeruginosa*) that is applied topically to the complete burn wound area with sterile gloves following wound cleansing and debridement. The exposure method of therapy is preferred, although occasionally thin-layer dressings may be applied; however, this may result in tissue maceration. Environmental pus, serum, or acidity do not affect the activity of this agent.

The ointment (applied with a sterile gloved hand) should always form a protective coating over the burn. It rapidly diffuses through partial (second-degree) and full-thickness (third-degree) burns and has proved to be one of the most effective means for preventing and retarding bacterial invasion in burn wounds. It has decreased deaths resulting from septicemia and decreased extension of the wound from infection. It has decreased the number of burn cases requiring plastic surgery or skin grafting. However, eschar separation is delayed.

Mafenide acetate is relatively nontoxic but has reported allergic reactions. It is rapidly metabolized to a metabolite and eliminated by way of the kidneys. Since this drug and metabolite are strong carbonic anhydrase inhibitors, acidosis (metabolic) may occur, usually compensated by hyperventilation. The client should be carefully observed for any signs resulting in respiratory alkalosis. If rapid or labored respirations occur, the ointment should be washed off the wound. Therapy can be interrupted for 2 to 3 days without impairing the bacterial control of the wound while continuing fluid therapy and acid-base restoration.

Mafenide may cause some discomfort when first applied (in $\frac{1}{16}$-inch layer once or twice daily)—a burning or pain sensation may occur that lasts from a few minutes to as long as an hour.

This is highly stable drug. It remains active for several years and does not need to be refrigerated except in tropical countries.

### gentamicin sulfate

Gentamicin sulfate (Garamycin) topical has been used to treat burns in some areas of the country. Many burn units have discontinued its use though, because of the development of bacterial resistance, especially *Pseudomonas* organisms. Silver sulfadiazine (Silvadene) is usually the preferred agent in many burn centers, although the other topical agents (Povidone iodine, mafenide acetate) are also commonly used.

## Topical Antipruritics

Antipruritics are drugs given to allay itching of skin and mucous membranes. There is less need for these preparations as the constitutional treatment of persons with skin disorders is better understood. Dilute solutions containing phenol, as well as tars, have been widely used. They may be applied as lotions, pastes, or ointments. Dressings wet with potassium permanganate 1:4000, aluminum subacetate 1:16, boric acid, or physiologic saline solution may cool and soothe and thus prevent itching. Lotions such as calamine or calamine with phenol (phenolated calamine) and cornstarch or oatmeal baths may also be used to relieve itching.

Local anesthetics such as dibucaine and benzocaine may decrease pruritus, but their use is not recommended because of their high sensitizing and irritating effects. The application of hydrocortisone in a lotion or ointment in a strength of 0.5% to 1% has proved to be one of the best methods of relieving pruritus and decreasing inflammation. It has the additional advantage of possessing a low sensitizing index.

## Topical Ectoparasiticidal Drugs

**Ectoparasites** are insects that live on the outer surface of the body. Ectoparasiticides are drugs used against those animal parasites. For human use these drugs are more frequently referred to as pediculicides and scabicides (miticides), reflecting the parasite treated with each group.

**Pediculosis** is a parasite infestation of lice on the skin of a human. Lice infestations have been increasing in North America and western Europe. It was once thought that pediculosis could be attributed to crowded dwellings and poor hygiene, but recently this assumption has proved not to be true. The lice are transmitted from one person to the next by close contact with infested persons, clothing, combs, and towels. There are three different varieties of the infestations: (1) pediculosis pubis, caused by *Phthbirus pubis* (pubic louse, or "crabs") (2) pediculosis corporis, caused by *Pediculus humanus* var. *corporis* (body louse), and (3) pedi-

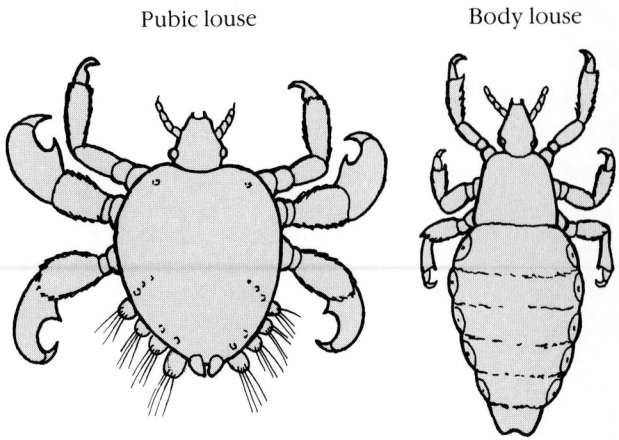

**FIGURE 68-1** Pubic louse *(Phthirus pubis), left,* and body louse *(Pediculus humanus), right).* Notice the first pair of legs on the pubic louse are thinner than the second and third pairs. Also, the abdomen is shorter. On the body louse, all legs are approximately the same length, and the abdomen is longer.

culosis capitis, caused by *P. humanus* var. *capitis* (head louse). See Figure 68-1.

Common findings in a person who is infested include pruritis, nits (eggs of louse) on hair shafts, lice on skin or clothes, and, when there are public lice, occasionally sky-blue macules on the inner thighs or lower abdomen. The drug of choice is the pediculicide lindane (gamma-benzene hexachloride).

A characteristic finding of pediculosis corporis, except in heavily infested individuals, is that the parasite is absent from the body but inhabits seams of clothing that come in contact with the axillae or that are in the beltline or collar.

**Scabies** is a parasitic infestation caused by the itch mite, *Sarcoptes scabiei.* It is transmitted from one person to the next by close contact, such as sleeping with an infested individual. It bores into the horny layers of the skin in cracks and folds, causing irritation and pruritus. Itching occurs almost exclusively at night. The infestation is usually generalized over the body except the head and neck regions. The drug of choice is the scabicide, crotamiton.

The first approach to the treatment of both pediculosis and scabies is identification of the source of infestation. Next, decontamination of clothing and personal articles used by the infested person is necessary. This can be done by washing clothing and bedding with hot, soapy water or by having items that cannot be washed dry-cleaned. Usually all persons involved, such as the whole family, are treated to prevent reinfestation. Table 68-6 summarizes the various topical pediculicides and scabicides used in the treatment of these parasitic infestations.

### lindane (gamma-benzene hexachloride; Kwell)

Lindane is considered both a scabicide and a pediculicide because it is effective in the treatment of both lice and mite

**TABLE 68-6**  Drugs used in the treatment of ectoparasitic diseases

| Disease | Drug |
| --- | --- |
| Pediculosis (lice infestation) | |
| *Pediculus humanus* var. *capitis* (head louse) | lindane (gamma-benzene hexachloride) malathion (0.5% Prioderm) |
| *Pediculus humanus* var. *corporis* (body louse) | pyrethrins with piperonylbutoxide |
| *Phthirus pubis* (pubic louse) | copper oleate, 0.03% |
| Scabies (mite infestation) *Sarcoptes scabiei* | crotamiton lindane (gamma-benzene hexachloride) benzyl benzoate, 12%-25% sulfur in petrolatum |

infestations. It is available in a 1% cream, lotion, and shampoo. For the treatment of pediculosis pubis and infestations of *Pediculus humanus* var. *capitis,* the cream or lotion is applied in a sufficient quantity to cover the skin and hair of the infected and surrounding areas. It is left on for 12 hours and then thoroughly washed. It seldom needs to be applied more than once. The shampoo is worked into the hair and left on for 4 minutes. Then the hair is rinsed and dried, and nits (eggs) are combed from the hair shafts. Retreatment is usually not necessary.

For the treatment of scabies, only the cream or lotion is used. If crusted lesions are present, a warm bath preceding the application of lindane is recommended. Lindane is applied over the entire body from the neck down. Again, it is left on for 8 to 12 hours and then washed off. Usually one application is sufficient. It is common to have pruritus after application, but this does not indicate a need for reapplication unless living mites can be demonstrated.

Lindane occasionally will cause an eczematous skin rash. It penetrates human skin and has a potential for central nervous system toxicity, especially in children. Rarely do convulsions or aplastic anemia occur with use of this drug.

### malathion (0.5% Prioderm)

The FDA has recently approved the use of malathion for the treatment of head lice and ova. In addition, the drug has been shown to destroy lindane-resistant lice. Research studies reveal that this agent is effective in lice-infested individuals within 24 hours after use. Also, the drug is well tolerated and no central nervous system toxicity has been reported. Malathion is a lotion that is rubbed into the scalp and left to air dry. Because the drug is flammable, the individual must be warned to avoid open flames and not to use a hairdryer. The hair should be shampooed 8 to 12 hours

after application; dead lice are combed out. If necessary, a second application may be tried 7 to 9 days later. Malathion is available only as a prescription in 2-ounce bottles.

### crotamiton (Eurax)

Crotamiton has scabicidal and antipruritic actions. It is massaged into the skin from the chin down, particularly in the folds and creases of the body. It is reapplied in 24 hours, and 48 hours after the second application it is washed from the body surface.

Two applications of crotamiton usually eradicate most mite infestations. In resistant cases it may be applied again 1 week later.

Crotamiton is available as a 10% cream or lotion. Occasionally a skin rash may occur with its application. Rarely allergic or irritant contact dermatitis occur.

## SUMMARY

Many dermatologic agents are available and used to treat the numerous skin disorders that occur. Three major groups of preparations were discussed: general, prophylactic, and therapeutic agents. General dermatologic preparations include bath substances, cleansers, soaps, solutions and emollients, skin protectants, wet dressings and soaks, and rubs and liniments. Many are soothing and used to promote comfort of the client with a dermatologic condition. Prophylactic agents form a film on the skin to keep out sun, light, air, or dust. Therapeutic agents may be antiinfectives (antibiotics, antivirals, and antifungals), corticosteroids, keratolytics, acne products, burn products, antipruritics, and ectoparasiticidal drugs. For all of the preparations, the nurse must correctly and safely apply them and instruct the client to do likewise if they are to be self-administered. Evaluating the effectiveness of dermatologic agents is related to the diminution of the affected areas without adverse effect.

## BIBLIOGRAPHY

Beck ML. (1988). Azulfidine (sulfasalazine, USP), SGA J 11(1):38.

Braunwald E et al. (1987). Harrison's principles of internal medicine, ed 11. New York: McGraw-Hill Book Co.

Castiglia PT. (1989). Acne, J Pediatr Health Care 3(5):259.

Check WA. (1988). Topical therapy for postherpetic-neuralgia pain, The Consultant Pharmacist 3(6):521.

Clore ER. (1989). Dispelling the common myths about pediculosis, J Pediatr Health Care 3(1):28.

Clore ER. (1988). Nursing management of pediculosis, Pediatr Nurs Forum 3(2):3.

Coody D. (1987). There is no such thing as a good tan, J Pediatr Health Care 1(3):125.

Davidson DE. (1986). Handbook of nonprescription drugs, ed 8. Washington, DC: American Pharmaceutical Association and The National Professional Society of Pharmacists.

Epstein JH et al. (1987). Blocking ultraviolet damage to the skin, Patient Care 21(12):26.

Ersek RA et al. (1988). Cross-linked silver-impregnated skin for burn wound management. J Burn Care Rehabil 9(5):476.

Feldmann, EG, editor. (1990). Handbook of nonprescription drugs, ed 9. Washington, DC: American Pharmaceutical Association.

Fuller FW et al. (1988). Leukopenia in non-septic burn patients receiving topical 1% silver sulfadiazine cream therapy: a survey, J Burn Care Rehabil 9(6):606.

Heinrich JJ. (1988). The role of topical treatment as a determinant of infection in outpatient burns, J Burn Care Rehabil 9(3):253.

Herfindal ET et al. (1988). Clinical pharmacy and therapeutics, ed 4. Baltimore: Williams & Wilkins.

Kastrup EK ed. (1991). Facts and comparisons. St Louis: JB Lippincott Co.

Knoben JE and Anderson PO. (1986). Handbook of clinical drug data, ed 5. Hamilton, Ill: Drug Intelligence Publications, Inc.

Lee JJ et al. (1988). Use of 5% sulfamylon (mafenide) solution after excision and grafting of burns, J Burn Care Rehabil 9(6):602.

Lindley, CM and Cronquist, SE. (1988). Skin cancers: detection, prevention, and therapeutics, American Pharm NS28(4):32.

Nicol NH. (1989). What's new with sunscreens? Pediatr Nurs 15(4):417.

Novotny J. (1989). Adolescents, acne, and the side-effects of accutane, J Pediatr Nurs 15(3):247.

Parker F. (1988). The skin and the elements: sun, plants, and stinging and biting organisms, Emerg Care Q 4(3):21.

Parks BR et al. (1989). Treatment of head lice and scabies infestations in children, Pediatr Nurs 15(5):522.

Pochi PE et al. (1989). An update on acne management, Patient Care 23(4):85.

Rosen T. (1989). Cutaneous fungal infections: dermaphytosis: practical tips for avoiding common mistakes, Consultant 29(8):29.

Rosen T. (1989). Cutaneous fungal infections: tinea versicolor and candidiasis: practical tips for avoiding common mistakes, part 2, Consultant 29(8):46.

10 ways to avoid sunburns, skin "aging," and skin cancer. (1987). Patient Care 21(12):197.

Thomson PD et al. (1989). Leukopenia in acute thermal injury: evidence against topical silver sulfadiazine as the causative agent, J Burn Care Rehabil 10(5):418.

Tolstoi LG. (1988). Drug-induced photosensitivity, Hospital Pharmacy 23(2):154.

United States Pharmacopeial Convention. (1991). Drug information for the health care provider, ed 11. Rockville, Md: The Convention.

Weiss SS et al. (1988). Topical trentinoin improves photo aged skin, JAMA 259(4):977.

*Chapter*

# 69 Debriding Agents

## CHAPTER OBJECTIVES

*After studying this chapter, you should be able to meet the following objectives and define the key terms.*

1. Use preventive and treatment measures to reduce the occurrence of decubitus ulcers.

2. Describe a classification system for grades of decubitus ulcers.

3. State the purpose of proteolytic enzyme preparations in the treatment of decubitus ulcers.

4. Discuss the nursing management of the administration of topical enzymatic agents.

5. Describe the mechanisms of action and the nursing management of nonenzymatic agent therapy for decubitus ulcers.

## KEY TERMS

**debridement,** page 1044

**decubitus ulcer,** page 1042

**proteolytic enzymes,** page 1044

## INTRODUCTION

The chapter covers debriding agents, which are agents used to remove dirt, foreign objects, damaged tissue, and cellular debris from a wound or burn to prevent infection and to promote healing. In treatment of a wound, debridement is the first step in cleansing it; debridement also allows thorough examination of the extent of the injury.

## DECUBITUS ULCERS

The **decubitus ulcer** (bedsore or pressure sore) is a break in the skin and underlying subcutaneous and muscle tissue caused by abnormal and sustained pressure or friction being exerted over the bony prominences of the body by the object on which the body part rests. It results in vascular insufficiency and ischemic necrosis, and it most frequently affects debilitated, comatose, immobilized, or paralyzed patients.

There are many contributing causes to this condition that must be treated. Among the local and systemic are the following: obesity or malnutrition; debilitation; a pressure and shearing force on the lower body if the head of the bed is raised more than 30 degrees; a loss of sensation of pressure or pain; muscle atrophy and motor paralysis; as a result of a reduction in the amount of adipose tissue between skin and underlying bone; emaciation and dehydration; poor nutrition because of vitamins, minerals, and trace elements (such as copper and zinc); friction; local anatomic defects; trauma; incontinence; edema; infections; heat and moisture (maceration); hypertension; septicemia; and local circulatory interference.

The bacterial flora of a decubitus ulcer are both gram-negative and gram-positive organisms, which include *Staphylococcus aureus,* streptococcus A and D, *Escherichia coli, Clostridium tetani,* and *Bacteroides, Proteus, Pseudomonas, Klebsiella,* and *Citrobacter* organisms. Parenteral antibiotics (adequate levels in granulating wounds are not reached) may be needed in difficult-to-treat infected decubitus ulcers as an adjunct to surgical management just before and at time of surgery.

An individual with a full thickness loss of skin may be a candidate for surgical intervention either to cover the ulcer area or to stabilize the wound. Surgical decisions include the underlying disease, the ability of the client to withstand surgery, and the ulcer condition or prognosis (especially those in which all soft tissue is destroyed, exposing bone).

## ▷NURSING MANAGEMENT: DECUBITUS ULCERS

Prevention and treatment of decubitus ulcers are centered around treatment of underlying causes, providing a well-balanced nutritional state, and minimizing or eliminating the pressure or friction causing tissue damage. The following are some preventive and treatment measures that the nurse may use to reduce the occurrence of impaired skin integrity.

1. Change the client's position frequently (every 1 to 2 hours day and night) for pressure relief.
2. Maintain a clean, dry, and wrinkle-free bed. Bedclothes should be smooth rather than coarse and should be changed frequently.
3. Provide active and passive exercise to increase muscle and skin tone and to improve vascularity, or use a whirlpool for hydrotherapy.
4. Position the client with pillows and pads, not exceeding a 30 degree elevation of the head.
5. Use hydrofloat devices, silica gel pads, polystyrene, and foam rubber pads and heel protectors to reduce pressure. Place them on a mattress in direct contact with the client's skin. The mattress should be free of surface bulges and indentations and have a uniform, flat surface to prevent friction or wrinkles.
6. Use an alternating pressure mattress pad covered with one layer of sheet to promote circulation and reduce the occurrence of tissue ischemia.
7. Massage the client's back with nonalcoholic skin lotion, covering and checking the bony prominences of the ankles, coccyx, elbows, heels, hips, knees, shoulders, and other areas having thin layers of subcutaneous tissue.
8. Provide meticulous skin hygiene with frequent inspections for abnormal alterations. Wash gently with warm water and, if needed, mild nondetergent soap, rinse, and blot dry with a soft towel. An emollient lubricating lotion may be used following washing to keep the skin soft.
9. Keep the skin of incontinent clients dry and clear of urine and fecal contamination, since maceration from moisture promotes tissue breakdown and predisposes patients to infection. Perspiration in the continent client is also cause of maceration. Trimmed nails prevent self-inflicted injury caused by scratching of the skin.
10. Maintain nutritional support for a positive nitrogen balance, tissue turgor, and adequate fluid intake with 3800 to 4600 cal/24 hours, a diet high in protein, vitamins, minerals, and trace elements. The client's hemoglobin level should be 12 g/100 ml or more and the serum protein above 6 mg/100 ml.
11. Necrotic decubitus ulcers often require debridement by surgical or drug methods and meticulous wound care.
12. Treatment regimens are based on the extent of skin involvement.
13. Assess the decubitus ulcer on a daily basis for gradual reduction in size, redness, and swelling; presence of granulation tissue; and signs and symptoms of infection (warmth, edema, and unusual drainage from site).

The preventive measures should be taught to clients, family members, or other caregivers of bedridden or other clients who are at risk for developing decubiti.

## PHARMACOLOGIC MANAGEMENT

A treatment plan for decubitus ulcers should take into consideration four basic principles: (1) assessment and interventions to improve the client's general health, which may help to reduce factors contributing to the problem, such as incontinence, anemia, or edema; (2) reducing pressure sites by positioning or the use of padding, special beds, and other items, thus increasing blood flow to the site; (3) maintaining a clean wound site; and (4) use of an appropriate agent for treatment or stimulation of granulation of tissue.

The treatment of decubitus ulcers depends on the stage of the ulcer and the condition of the wound bed. Topical antibiotics are only used when an infection is documented by a culture of the decubitus wound to identify the specific type of microorganisms present. When used, topical antibiotics are applied to the infected wound after cleaning and before application of the sterile dressing. However, they should be prescribed only for specific treatment regimens and for a limited period of time. Inflammation of the area, pus, or odor may indicate the need for a laboratory culture.

Decubitus or pressure sores have been classified into five grades or stages:

Stage I—A red area that overlies a bony or tendinous (tendons) site that remains even when the pressure is relieved (blanching erythema)

Stage II—A superficial ulceration (skin blister or break) into the dermis area (nonblanching erythema)

Stage III—Skin ulcer extends into exposed subcutaneous tissue; presence of blister and eschar formation

Stage IV—Deep skin ulcer that exposes muscle and bone; usually the body enzymes separate the eschar, sloughing of tissue results in an ulcer; generally, noninfectious

Stage V—Ulcer has extended into bursae, or joints, or into body cavities; or ulcer is the same as Stage IV with the addition of an infection

In addition to the nursing management previously reviewed, numerous treatment protocols have been applied. Decubitus ulcers are problem areas that generally do not

**TABLE 69-1**   Recommended treatment protocol for decubitus ulcers

| Staging | Typical treatment modalities |
|---|---|
| Stage I or II | Silicone spray, transparent or hydro-colloidal dressing |
| Stage III | Wet to dry dressings, debriding agent, hydrocolloidal dressing |
| Stage IV and V | Wet to dry dressings, debriding agent, surgical debridement |

**TABLE 69-2**   Effect of commonly used cleansing agents on healing rates

| Agent | Relative rate of healing (%)* |
|---|---|
| Liquid detergent | −28% |
| Povidone iodine | −10% |
| Hydrogen peroxide | −8% |
| Chlorhexidine | −7% |
| Dakin's solution (1%) | −6% |

Adapted from Alvarez et al, 1989.
*Compared with untreated control.

have widely accepted, standard treatment programs. Therefore, depending of the evaluation of the wound, the physician and local practice, the treatment approach can vary considerably. Table 69-1 is a recommended treatment protocol based on the previous staging system.

## Proteolytic Enzyme Preparations

In stage IV or V, debriding agents are often used to remove sloughing tissue and to help facilitate granulation of the wound. Although commonly used for debridement, wet-to-dry dressings can be irritating, painful, and disruptive to healthy tissue. Both betadine and Dakin's solution used for chemical debridement may cause damage to granulation tissue (Baxter and Rodeheaver, 1989). Chemical debridement is performed with proteolytic enzymes. In very serious ulceration, or if complications are present (osteomyelitis), surgical debridement may be required. The focus of this section will be limited to the use of proteolytic enzymes.

Proteolytic enzymes digest or liquefy necrotic tissue and purulent exudate without affecting fat, keratin, fibrin, or granulation tissues. The drawback with these preparations is that 2 or 3 days are usually needed to get rid of an eschar, and some physicians believe this should be done more quickly. Sutilains (Travase) debrides a new or fresh burn effectively, but enzymes that debride an ischemic decubitus ulcer are lacking, according to some specialists (Sawyer, PN and others, 1980). See Table 69-2 for the effect of commonly used cleansing agents on healing rates.

Enzymes are usually unable to penetrate eschar or remove large amounts of tissue. Many of the enzyme products are also inactivated by soaps or heavy metal ions, which further limits their usefulness (Knight, 1988).

Most enzymes contain the suffix "ase" in their name plus the name of the substrate on which they act. For example, collagenase acts on and degrades collagen; hyaluronidase acts on hyaluronic acid, a ground substance of connective tissue. Enzymes are also grouped according to the reactions they catalyze. For example, **proteolytic enzymes** hasten the hydrolysis of proteins.

Since enzymes are proteins, they may be antigenic and cause toxic reactions of an immunologic type.

The enzymes discussed in this chapter are used topically for *medical* or *chemical* **debridement**—i.e., the removal, by enzymatic digestion, of necrotic and injured tissue, clotted blood, purulent exudates, or fibrinous accumulations in wounds. This action cleans the wounds and facilitates healing. Systemic antibiotic therapy and topical antibiotic or antiseptic therapy may be used in conjunction with enzymatic debridement to control or inhibit infection.

## ▷Nursing Management: Proteolytic Enzyme Therapy

The following are aspects of care for clients being treated with topically applied enzymatic drugs (not the nonenzymatic agents). These are in addition to those aspects of care previously discussed in nursing management of decubitus ulcers. Before topical aseptic application of enzymes, the wound should be thoroughly cleansed (flushing away necrotic debris and fibrinous exudates) with a solution that does not inactivate the enzyme (e.g., physiologic saline or sterile distilled water). Solutions containing metal or acidic ions should be avoided to prevent inactivation of the enzymes. As much nectrotic tissue should be removed with forceps and scissors as can be readily removed. All previously applied ointment should be removed before new ointment is applied to the substrate.

- Dense, dry, and thick eschar should be crosshatched by the physician with a No. 10 or 11 blade for adequate contact of enzyme to the substrate of necrotic debris.
- Ointment should be applied directly to the wound with a tongue depressor or spatula and then covered with sterile petrolatum gauze or sterile gauze (or other non-adhering dressing), or it can be applied with a sterile gauze pad that is then placed over the wound. A bandage and/or tape should then be used to hold the dressing in place.
- Ointment or jelly preparations should be confined to the wound. The surrounding healthy tissue (or skin) should be protected from the enzyme (e.g., zinc oxide paste can be used).
- The treated lesion should be kept moist and protected from drying.

- The enzyme must be in direct contact with the wound for a sufficient length of time, usually about 4 days.
- To avoid delayed healing, the enzyme should be discontinued when the wound is cleaned and debrided.
- Secondary skin closure or grafting may follow optimal debridement.
- Debilitated clients should be carefully monitored, since debriding enzymes increase the risk of bacterial infection.
- Clients should be observed for allergic or sensitivity reactions (e.g., dermatitis and febrile reactions).

### collagenase (Santyl, Biozyme-C)

Collagenase is an enzymatic debriding agent that is capable of degrading both denatured and undenatured collagen. Other proteolytic enzymes act only on denatured collagen. Thus it is claimed that collagenase produces more effective debridement by acting on collagen at the wound edges, where necrotic slough is anchored. These actions promote the formation of granulation tissue and the epithelization of dermal ulcers and burned tissue.

This ointment should be applied only within the area of the lesion, since a transient erythema has been reported as a cutaneous reaction on the wound surface or the area adjacent to the lesion. This reaction may be prevented by applying a protectant (e.g., zinc oxide paste) around the lesion.

Topical enzymes used for debriding may increase the risk of bacteremia in the debilitated individual; this may necessitate monitoring of these clients for systemic bacterial infections.

***Significant drug interactions.*** The following interactions may occur if collagenase is used in conjunction with the drugs below:

| Drug | Possible Effect and Management |
|------|-------------------------------|
| Burow's solution and other acidic solutions | Collagenase can be inactivated by irrigating the lesion with acidic solutions such as Burow's (pH 3.6 to 4.4). The optimal pH range for collagenase is 6 to 8; a local pH alteration outside this range will decrease the enzymes' activity. |
| detergents, soaps, cleansing agents, hexachlorophene, heavy metal ions (as found in antiseptics, iodine, thimerosal, mercury compounds, silver nitrate), boric acid | Activity of collagenase is adversely affected. |

### ▷ Nursing Management: Collagenase Therapy

See p. 1043 for nursing management of decubitus ulcer.
Before collagenase is applied, the area is cleansed of debris by gentle irrigation with sterile normal saline. The ulcer should be patted dry with a clean gauze pad. If infection is present, a topical antibacterial agent (e.g., neomycinbacitracin-polymyxin B solution or powder) is applied directly to the ulcer surface before collagenase.

Collagenase should be applied once daily. If the wound is deep, it should be applied directly with a wooden tongue depressor or spatula. The application should be repeated if the dressing area is soiled (e.g., because of incontinence).

The average time for complete debridement of dermal ulcers and decubiti with collangenase is about 11 days. This time permits debridement of necrotic tissue and establishment of granulation tissue. Careful observation of wound bed is indicated. Enzyme should be stopped when granulation tissue is evident.

The ointment does not have to be refrigerated; it is stored at room temperature.

### fibrinolysin and desoxyribonuclease (Elase)

The proteolytic enzymes fibrinolysin and desoxyribonuclease have individual effects; desoxyribonuclease attacks deoxyribonucleic acid, and fibrinolysin (plasmin) acts on fibrin of blood clots and fibrinous exudates. The mechanism of action is fibrinolytic activity on denatured proteins (devitalized tissue); protein elements of living cells are unaffected.

An ointment product that contains the two enzymes in combination with chloromycetin is also available. The added bacteriostatic properties inhibit bacterial protein synthesis by interfering with transfer of activated amino acids from soluble ribonucleic acid to ribosomes in infected lesions. Systemic antibiotics are also indicated when clinical infection has been verified by positive culture results.

This product is used to debride inflamed and or infected lesions, including surgical wounds, ulcerative lesions (trophic, decubitus, stasis, arteriosclerotic), second- and third-degree burns, and wounds resulting from circumcision or episiotomy. The combination product with antibiotic is preferred for infected lesions. This product is also used for treatment of vaginitis and cervicitis (intravaginal use) and irrigation of infected wounds and superficial hematomas not adjacent to or near fatty tissue.

Allergic reactions have been observed in persons who are sensitive to bovine source materials, mercury compounds (thimerosal, a mercury derivative, is used as a preservative in the ointment base of Elase), or chloromycetin.

### ▷ Nursing Management: Fibrinolysin and Desoxyribonuclease Therapy

The topical solution (use within 24 hours following reconstitution) may be used in a spray or a wet dressing. Elase is also available as a dry powder in vials. Dressing should be changed at least once a day or preferably, two or three times daily. After 24 hours, this product is practically inactive. See p. 1043 for additional nursing management of decubitus ulcer.

## sutilains (Travase)

Sutilains is a sterile preparation of proteolytic enzymes that digests necrotic soft tissues and purulent exudates. It aids in the selective removal of only nonviable or undenatured protein in necrotic soft tissue and purulent exudate from open wounds and ulcers (which may impair granulation tissue formation and wound healing) resulting from second-and-third-degree burns, decubiti, peripheral vascular disease, and wounds (incisions, trauma, pyogens).

Side effects are mild; they include mild, transient pain (managed with a mild analgesic), local paresthesia, bleeding, and transient dermatitis.

***Significant drug interactions.*** The following interactions may occur if sutilains is used in conjunction with the drugs below:

| Drug | Possible Effect and Management |
| --- | --- |
| Antiseptics (benzalkonium chloride, hexachlorophene, iodine, nitrofurazone) and detergents | Concomitant use should be avoided because of possible inactivation of enzyme activity. |
| Compounds containing metallic ions, such as silver sulfaciazine, silver nitrate, or thimerosal | Interfere adversely with the action of the enzyme. |

▷ **Nursing Management:**
**Sutilains Therapy**

See also the general nursing management for topical enzymatic agents, on p. 1044.

***Assessment.*** Sutilains should not be applied to wounds communicating with major body cavities, wounds with exposed major nerves or nerve tissue, neoplastic ulcers, or wounds in women of childbearing age.

***Intervention.*** Sutilains is prepared as an ointment containing 82,000 casein units/g ointment base (15-g tubes). It must be refrigerated at a temperature between 2° C and 10° C.

A wound should be thoroughly cleansed (including removal of antiseptics) with water or isotonic sodium chloride solution and left moist or wet before a thin layer of sutilains ointment is applied up to ½ inch beyond the area needing debriding. When used for extensive burns, the ointment should only be used on 10% to 15% of the burned area at one time. The area should then be covered with loose, wet dressings.

This procedure should be repeated three or four times daily. A moist environment is necessary for this agent's enzymatic activity.

In concomitant use with topical antibiotics, apply sutilains first.

This drug must be kept away from the eyes; if contact occurs, the eyes should be rinsed with copious amounts of sterile water.

***Evaluation.*** If dissolution does not occur in 24 to 48 hours, the drug should be discontinued.

If bleeding or dermatitis occurs, the drug should be discontinued.

Although systemic allergic reactions have not been reported, the drug is capable of causing an antibody response.

### Topical Enzyme Combination Products

Trypsin and papain (proteolytic enzymes), balsam Peru (mild antibacterial agent that aids in improving circulation in the wound area by stimulating the capillary bed), castor oil (protective covering, improves epithelialization), urea (emollient and keratolytic), and chlorophyll derivatives (aid in controling wound odor and healing) have been formulated into various combinations and marketed. For example, Granulex contains trypsin, balsam Peru, and castor oil, whereas Panafil contains papain, urea and chlorophyll derivatives.

Such products may be ordered for administration once or twice daily. The wound area should be cleaned by flushing with physiologic saline before application each time. Be aware that hydrogen peroxide solution can inactivate papain activity.

### Nonenzymatic Agents

#### dextranomer (Debrisan)

Dextranomer is a hydrophilic dextran polymer in the form of small beads (0.1 to 0.3 mm in diameter); it is used for cleansing only a wet or secreting wound (not dry wounds). Each gram of beads absorbs about 4 ml of fluid (swelling to four times in size) from a secreting lesion or wounds. This rapid action continues until all the beads are saturated. The assumption of a grayish yellow color by the beads indicates that they are saturated and ready for removal. The spaces between the beads produce a powerful dehydrating suction force and capillary action in the area. Low-molecular-weight substances (bacteria and bacterial forms) in the secretions of wound exudates (e.g., toxins, peptides) are drawn up (absorbed) within the beads. The higher molecular weight substances (plasma, protein, fibrinogen, fibrin, split products) are absorbed in the spaces between adjacent swollen beads, and this removal retards eschar formation.

Application of dextranomer to the surface of a secreting wound removes exudates and particles that impede tissue repair and increase wound healing time and reduces edema and inflammation. Secreting or exudative wounds for which dextranomer can be used include (clean wet ulcer) venous stasis ulcers, decubitus ulcers, infected traumatic and surgical wounds, and infected burns.

▷ **Nursing Management:**
**Dextranomer**

Dextranomer is available in 4-g packages and 60- and 120-g containers and paste form. The contents of each container should be used for only one person to limit cross-contamination.

To initially prepare the wound, it should be irrigated with sterile water or saline and the area should be left moist. The beads should cover the wound surface to a depth of 3 mm to 6 mm (⅛ to ¼ inch) (e.g., 4 g of beads covers a wound or ulcer 1½ × 1½ inches). A paste mixture is often used for areas that are either irregular body surfaces or are difficult to reach. If the premade paste dosage form is not available (10-g foil packets) then the nurse may mix the beads with glycerin (only glycerin) and dress the wound in the usual manner. The beads or paste must be reapplied every 12 hours or more often while reducing the number of applications as the exudate diminishes.

If the wound is a cratered decubitus ulcer, the nurse should allow for expansion of the beads by not packing the wound tightly.

The wound should be lightly bandaged on all four sides to hold the beads in place and prevent maceration from occlusion. The degree of wound secretion determines the number of dressing changes (usually one or two daily profuse secretions may necessitate three or four dressing changes). Changes are done before encrustation or full saturation of the beads (grayish yellow color) to prevent drying and to facilitate bead removal by irrigation (e.g., sterile water, saline). During the first few days, as the edema is reduced, the wound itself may appear larger in size than it did before treatment. Therapy should be discontinued when healthy granulation is established. Treatment of an underlying pathologic condition (such as venous or arterial flow or pressure) is concurrent. Diabetic and immunosuppressed patients may be susceptible to severe infections.

A client occasionally may have some minor pain during dressing changes. The nurse should be aware that if the beads are spilled on the floor, the floor becomes slippery, creating a work hazard. Dextranomer should be used only in body areas where complete removal is possible (not deep fistulas or sinus tracts).

### flexible hydroactive dressings and granules (Duo-Derm)

These moisture-reactive dressings for pressure sores and leg ulcers remain in place for 1 to 7 days, and by interacting with the available skin moisture, a bond is created that keeps them in place. While in place over the wound, the moisture-reactive particles imbedded in a polymer base interact with the wound fluid exudate, creating a soft moist gel over the wound, which eases dressing removal with minimal damage to newly formed regenerating tissues. The control of wound fluid exudate absorption is a function of the rate at which the dressing interacts with the exudate.

These dressings are indicated for necrotic wounds only after the thick eschar at the wound margin is removed. Local management of venous stasis ulcers, ulcers secondary to arterial insufficiency, diabetes mellitus, trauma, pressure sores, and superficial wounds. The granule form is for local management of exudating dermal ulcers in association with the dressings.

▷ **Nursing Management:**
**Flexible Hydroactive Dressings and Granules**

***Assessment.*** Use in the following dermal conditions should be avoided: tissue of muscle, tendon, or bone, ulcers with infection (tuberculosis, syphilis, or deep fungal infections), active vasculitis (periarteritis nodosa, systemic lupus erythematosus, and cryoglobulinemia).

***Intervention.*** The liquefied material left in the wound (seen when the dressing is removed) has the appearance of pus and should be washed away before further wound evaluation proceeds.

Clean the wound site before applying this product. Follow the specific instructions outlined in the package labeling.

The characteristic disagreeable dermal ulcer odor, apparent when the dressing is removed or from wound leakage, may be diminished with the use of the granule dosage form during excess exudation periods.

***Evaluation.*** During the initial phase of treatment, the wound increases in size and depth because of the cleaning away of the necrotic debris.

During periods of infection, the dressings or granules should be discontinued and antibiotic treatment started until infection is completely treated.

Excessive exudate, when present, may necessitate the granule dosage form application into the wound to prevent leakage and allow the dressing to remain in place longer and reduce dressing changes.

### metronidazole (Flagyl)

Metronidazole is an oral agent used to treat amebiasis and trichomoniasis. A metronidazole solution (1%) has been prepared and used topically to treat deep, infected decubiti with extremely foul odors that are associated with anaerobic infection and necrosis. This is not currently an FDA approved use, but reports state that the results were quite favorable in eliminating the odor completely, within 1 to 2 days (Burnakis, 1989).

## SUMMARY

Decubitus ulcers add greatly to the length and cost of a hospital stay. They are best prevented, but when they do occur, they are then treated with proteolytic enzyme or non-enzymatic preparations, depending on the cause and extent of the ulcer.

## BIBLIOGRAPHY

Alterescu V et al. (1988). Etiology and treatment of pressure ulcers, Decubitus 1(1):28.

Alvarez O et al. (1989). Moist environment for healing: matching the dressing to the wound, Wounds: A Compendium of Clinical Research and Practice 1(1):35.

Barnes SH. (1987). Patient/family education for the patient with a pressure necrosis, Nurs Clin North Am 22(2):463.

Bergtoom N. (1987). A clinical trial of the braden scale for predicting pressure sore risk, Nurs Clin North Am 22(2):417.

Bobel LM. (1987). Nutritional implications in the patient with pressure sores, Nurs Clin North Am 22(2):379.

Brown-Etris M et al. (1989). A strategy for the management of pressure ulcers in nursing homes, Ostomy Wound Manage 22:28.

Burnakis TG. (1989). Topical metronidazole for decubitus ulcers, Hospital Pharmacy 24(11):961.

Dermal wounds: pressure sores . . . standards of care, J Enterostom Ther 15(1):4.

Dimant J et al. (1988). Pressure sore prevention and management, J Gerontol Nurs 14(8):18.

Doughty D. (1988). Management of pressure sores, J Enterostom Ther 15(1):39.

Fowler EM. (1987). Equipment and products used in management and treatment of pressure ulcers, Nurs Clin North Am 22(2):449.

Gesnell DJ. (1987). Assessment and evaluation of pressure sores, Nurs Clin North Am 22(2):399.

Hamilton L et al. (1989). Pressure ulcers: an interdisciplinary protocol for prevention and treatment, Perspectives 13(1):9.

Hamilton L. (1987). A pressure sore monitoring program: just the beginning, Perspectives 11(1):6.

Jeter KF et al. (1988). Principles of wound cleaning and wound care, J Home Health Care Pract 1(1):43.

Kastrup EK, ed. (1991). Facts and comparisons. St Louis: JB Lippincott Co.

Knight AL. (1988). Medical management of pressure sores, J Family Pract 27(1):95.

Moolten SE. (1987). Prevention and treatment of decubitus ulcers, Hosp Med 23(8):123.

Moriarty MB. (1987). How color can clarify wound care, RN 51(9):49.

Oot-Giromini B et al. (1989). Pressure ulcer prevention versus treatment, comparative product cost study, Decubitus 2(3):52.

Preston KM. (1987). Dermal ulcers: simplifying a complex problem, Rehabil Nurs 12(1):17.

Shannon ML et al. (1988). Pressure sore treatment: a case in point. This hydrocolloid dressing promoted rapid wound healing and time- and cost-efficiency, Geriatr Nurs 9(3):154.

Thomas S. (1988). Pressure points . . . assessing sores and modern methods of treatment, Community Outlook, Oct, p. 20.

United States Pharmacopeial Convention. (1991). Drug information for the health care provider, ed 11. Rockville, Md: The Convention.

# Intravenous and Nutritional Therapy

# 70  Vitamins and Minerals

## CHAPTER OBJECTIVES

*After studying this chapter, you should be able to meet the following objectives and define the key terms.*

1. Review the recommended daily allowances of vitamins and minerals.

2. Discuss factors that might contribute to inadequate intake of vitamins and minerals.

3. Describe the difference between fat-soluble and water-soluble vitamins.

4. Cite the results of a deficiency or excess of each vitamin.

5. Identify the nursing management essential to the administration of vitamins.

6. Compare the contents of OTC vitamin and mineral preparations with recommended daily allowances.

## KEY TERMS

**ascorbic acid,** page 1061
**avitaminosis,** page 1051
**fat-soluble vitamins,** page 1051
**hypervitaminosis,** page 1051
**water-soluble vitamins,** page 1051

## INTRODUCTION

Under usual circumstances, nutritional needs are best met by adequate oral ingestion of fluids and regular, balanced meals. Breast milk or formula meets the normal nutrition needs of the infant; strained and chopped table foods are added to the diet as tolerated by the growing child. Throughout life, challenges to nutrition status can occur that necessitate nutrient, vitamin, mineral, electrolyte, and fluid replacement or supplementation.

Debilitation from nutritional deprivation may impair wound healing; reduce collagen, hormone, and enzyme synthesis; and decrease essential protein production, reducing circulating albumin, fibrinogen, and hemoglobin. Malnutrition or mild to moderate starvation produces serious cellular biochemical changes, including diminished liver glycogen stores starting the first day of deprivation. Diminished protein stores are supplemented via gluconeogenesis, since amino acids are converted into glucose as an energy source. Tissue proteins are depleted and short-lived in the intestinal mucous membranes, liver, pancreas, and kidney tubular epithelia. Muscle proteins are converted to provide energy, and adipose tissues are metabolized to produce free fatty acids for energy substrates. The byproducts of fatty acid oxidation (ketones) are used as energy for the brain if starvation is prolonged.

Unusual or abnormal circumstances necessitating administration of the various nutritional modalities such as vitamin replacement and enteral or parenteral feedings are discussed in the following sections.

## VITAMINS

Adequate vitamin intake is of critical biochemical importance because vitamins help maintain normal metabolic functions, growth, and repair of tissue. Mechanisms of action, specific indications for use, and pharmacokinetics are not well understood for all vitamins, nor have dosages been established for all vitamins. However, vitamin supplement therapy may be essential during periods of nutrition challenge, typically during rapid growth, pregnancy, lactation, or convalescence. Other challenges to nutrition occur with inadequate nutrient ingestion or absorption and inordinate nutrient drain caused by neoplastic disorders; cancer thus has been called the "nitrogen trap."

Insufficient dietary intake of vitamins and other essential nutrients occasionally may be traced to impoverished diets resulting from cultural, religious, or personal beliefs; fad diets; alcoholism; poverty; ignorance; or lack of available foodstuffs. Mild forms of **avitaminosis** (vitamin deficiency), however, are more common in the United States and Canada (often as a result of alcoholism) than the pronounced deficiency states of beriberi, pellagra, rickets, or scurvy. The potential for iatrogenic starvation, however, exists because of ignorance or oversight on the part of health care personnel who routinely fail to assess their clients' nutrition status or do not know how to correct it when necessary. Many medical procedures also may potentiate client malnutrition. In addition, clients often are kept from oral intake or on a restricted diet for too long.

The ubiquitous IV D5W infusion only delivers 170 calories/L—and purely in the form of a carbohydrate. Multiple cleansing enemas or prolonged gastrointestinal suction rob the body of essential electrolytes. Only perfunctory medical assessment may be made of the effects of intraoperative blood losses or of wound drainage on nutrition needs, and surgery always is accompanied by increased nitrogen excretion. Also, common nursing problems that result when the client does not, cannot, or will not eat are often not given adequate medical attention to enable satisfactory nursing care. Vitamin preparations and other, more aggressive, supportive nutrition therapies are needed for the hospitalized patient more often than recognized.

Few vitamins are synthesized by the body. Vitamin K is formed by bacteria in the gut; vitamin D is produced when skin is exposed to sunlight; and small, insufficient amounts of vitamin B also are made in the gut. Thus most vitamins must either be ingested in food or taken as dietary supplements. Although the average American diet contains adequate vitamins, vitamin sales in the United States constitute a multimillion-dollar industry, largely because of advertising. Widespread vitamin use is often an unjustified effort to improve on normal health. **Hypervitaminosis,** or toxic amounts of one or more vitamins, is an occasional result.

Tables 70-1 and 70-2 list recommended daily dietary allowances (RDAs) for various vitamins and minerals.

The Food and Drug Administration issues a vitamin dosage listing known as the "U.S. Recommended Daily Allowance" (U.S. RDA) for labeling purposes. This listing is the common reference used in pharmacist-client teaching. Also the latter values are usually higher than the RDA values. See Table 70-3.

Vitamins are classified as being fat soluble or water soluble. **Fat-soluble vitamins** are A, D, E, and K. They are stored in the liver and fatty tissue in large amounts, and a deficiency in these vitamins occurs only after long deprivation from an adequate supply or disorders preventing their absorption. **Water-soluble vitamins** include the B-complex group and C. These vitamins are not stored in the body in large amounts, and short periods of inadequate intake can lead to a deficiency. Vitamins are important components of enzyme systems that catalyze the reactions for protein, fat, and carbohydrate metabolism.

The FDA proposes regulations dividing vitamin mineral products into three categories.

1. *Supplement*—all ingredients are within established limits
2. *Over-the-counter proprietary*—vitamin-mineral contents exceed the limits established for supplement use, but not excessively
3. *Prescription status*—contents exceed the upper limit for over-the-counter proprietary products

Many multivitamin capsules and tablets vary in their contents. Some contain ingredients such as biotin and pantothenic acid, for which evidence about their essential role in human nutrition is inconclusive.

"Optional vitamins" (E, $B_6$, folic acid, pantothenic acid, and $B_{12}$) may or may not be included as ingredients in OTC multivitamin preparations. However, the most popular OTC multivitamin preparations contain all vitamins needed by humans. Most OTC vitamin preparations are designed to fulfill daily body needs completely without regard for the amounts of various vitamins contained in the daily diet.

## ▷NURSING MANAGEMENT: VITAMIN THERAPY

Good nutrition is essential for good health. The nurse's participation in health promotion includes the provision of information regarding all aspects of nutrition. With the many misconceptions regarding vitamins and their function in health and the prevention of illness prevalent today, the nurse has an important role in the provision of accurate dietary couseling with regard to vitamins.

*Assessment.* A dietary history for the client will provide the nurse with insights into the client's eating patterns (e.g., the last 24-hour period). This will enable the nurse to be more specific with the client regarding his or her dietary needs. Assess for signs of the specific vitamin deficiency throughout therapy.

*Intervention.* Use the calibrated measuring device provided by the manufacturer for accurate dosing. Chewable tablets should be thoroughly chewed or crushed before swallowing. Use caution in administering fat-soluble vitamins to children, since they are more sensitive to high doses.

*Education.* Discussions with the client regarding vitamins should cover their function in the body, signs of vi-

**TABLE 70-1**  Recommended daily dietary allowances (designed for the maintenance of good nutrition of practically all healthy people in the United States)*

| | Age (years) | Weight | | Height | | Protein (g) | Fat-soluble vitamins | | |
|---|---|---|---|---|---|---|---|---|---|
| | | kg | lb | cm | in | | Vitamin A (μg RE)† | Vitamin D (μg)‡ | Vitamin E (mg α TE)§ |
| Infants | 0-0.5 | 6 | 13 | 60 | 24 | 13 | 375 | 7.5 | 3 |
| | 0.5-1.0 | 9 | 20 | 71 | 28 | 14 | 375 | 10 | 4 |
| Children | 1-3 | 13 | 29 | 90 | 35 | 16 | 400 | 10 | 6 |
| | 4-6 | 20 | 44 | 112 | 44 | 24 | 500 | 10 | 7 |
| | 7-10 | 28 | 62 | 132 | 52 | 28 | 700 | 10 | 7 |
| Males | 11-14 | 45 | 99 | 157 | 62 | 45 | 1000 | 10 | 10 |
| | 15-18 | 66 | 145 | 176 | 69 | 59 | 1000 | 10 | 10 |
| | 19-24 | 70 | 154 | 177 | 70 | 58 | 1000 | 10 | 10 |
| | 25-50 | 70 | 154 | 178 | 70 | 63 | 1000 | 5 | 10 |
| | 51 + | 70 | 154 | 178 | 70 | 63 | 1000 | 5 | 10 |
| Females | 11-14 | 46 | 101 | 157 | 62 | 46 | 800 | 10 | 8 |
| | 15-18 | 55 | 120 | 163 | 64 | 44 | 800 | 10 | 8 |
| | 19-22 | 55 | 120 | 163 | 64 | 46 | 800 | 10 | 8 |
| | 23-50 | 55 | 120 | 163 | 64 | 50 | 800 | 5 | 8 |
| | 51 + | 55 | 120 | 163 | 64 | 50 | 800 | 5 | 8 |
| Pregnant | | | | | | 60 | 1300 | 10 | 10 |
| Lactating | | | | | | 65 | 1200 | 10 | 12 |

From Food and Nutrition Board, National Academy of Sciences–National Research Council, Washington, DC, 1989.

*The allowances are intended to provide for individual variations among most normal persons as they live in the United States under usual environmental stresses. Diets should be based on a variety of common foods in order to provide other nutrients for which human requirements have been less well defined.

†Retinol equivalents. 1 Retinol equivalent = 1 μg retinol or 6 μg β carotene.

‡As cholecalciferol, 10 μg cholecalciferol = 400 IU vitamin D.

§α-Tocopherol equivalents. 1 mg d-α-tocopherol = 1 α TE.

**TABLE 70-2**  Estimated safe and adequate daily intakes of additional selected vitamins and minerals*

| | Age (years) | Vitamins | | | Trace elements† | |
|---|---|---|---|---|---|---|
| | | Vitamin K (μg) | Biotin (μg) | Pantothenic acid (mg) | Copper (mg) | Manganese (mg) |
| Infants | 0-0.5 | | 10 | 3 | 0.4-0.6 | 0.3-0.6 |
| | 0.5-1 | | 15 | 3 | 0.6-0.7 | 0.6-1 |
| Children | 1-3 | | 20 | 3 | 0.7-1 | 1.0-1.5 |
| | 4-6 | | 25 | 3-4 | 1-1.5 | 1.5-2 |
| | 7-10 | | 30 | 4-5 | 1-1.2 | 2.0-3 |
| Adolescents | 11 + | | 30:100 | 4-7 | 1.5-2.5 | 2-5 |
| Adults | | 70-140 | 20:100 | 4-7 | 1.5-3 | 2-5 |

From Feldman, 1990.

*Because there is less information on which to base allowances, these figures are not given in the main tables of the RDA and are provided here in the form of ranges of recommended intakes.

†Since the toxic levels for many trace elements may be only several times usual intakes, the upper levels for the trace elements given in this table should not be habitually exceeded.

| Water-soluble vitamins | | | | | | | Minerals | | | | | |
|---|---|---|---|---|---|---|---|---|---|---|---|---|
| Vitamin C (mg) | Thiamin (mg) | Riboflavin (mg) | Niacin (mg NE)|| | Vitamin B₆ (mg) | Folacin¶ (µg) | Vitamin B₁₂# (µg) | Calcium (mg) | Phosphorus (mg) | Magnesium (mg) | Iron (mg) | Zinc (mg) | Iodine (µg) |
| 35 | 0.3 | 0.4 | 6 | 0.3 | 30 | 0.5 | 360 | 240 | 50 | 10 | 3 | 40 |
| 35 | 0.5 | 0.6 | 8 | 0.6 | 45 | 1.5 | 540 | 360 | 70 | 15 | 5 | 50 |
| 45 | 0.7 | 0.8 | 9 | 0.9 | 100 | 2.0 | 800 | 800 | 150 | 15 | 10 | 70 |
| 45 | 0.9 | 1.0 | 11 | 1.3 | 200 | 2.5 | 800 | 800 | 200 | 10 | 10 | 90 |
| 45 | 1.2 | 1.4 | 16 | 1.6 | 300 | 3.0 | 800 | 800 | 250 | 10 | 10 | 120 |
| 50 | 1.4 | 1.6 | 18 | 1.8 | 400 | 3.0 | 1200 | 1200 | 350 | 18 | 15 | 150 |
| 60 | 1.4 | 1.7 | 18 | 2 | 400 | 3.0 | 1200 | 1200 | 400 | 18 | 15 | 150 |
| 60 | 1.5 | 1.7 | 19 | 2.2 | 400 | 3.0 | 800 | 800 | 350 | 10 | 15 | 150 |
| 60 | 1.4 | 1.6 | 18 | 2.2 | 400 | 3.0 | 800 | 800 | 350 | 10 | 15 | 150 |
| 60 | 1.2 | 1.4 | 16 | 2.2 | 400 | 3.0 | 800 | 800 | 350 | 10 | 15 | 150 |
| 50 | 1.1 | 1.3 | 15 | 1.8 | 400 | 3.0 | 1200 | 1200 | 300 | 18 | 15 | 150 |
| 60 | 1.1 | 1.3 | 14 | 2 | 400 | 3.0 | 1200 | 1200 | 300 | 18 | 15 | 150 |
| 60 | 1.1 | 1.3 | 14 | 2 | 400 | 3.0 | 800 | 800 | 300 | 18 | 15 | 150 |
| 60 | 1.0 | 1.2 | 13 | 2 | 400 | 3.0 | 800 | 800 | 300 | 18 | 15 | 150 |
| 60 | 1.0 | 1.2 | 13 | 2 | 400 | 3.0 | 800†† | 800 | 300 | 10 | 15 | 150 |
| +20 | +0.4 | +0.3 | +2 | +0.6 | +400 | +1.0 | +400 | +400 | +150 | ** | +5 | +25 |
| +40 | +0.5 | +0.5 | +5 | +0.5 | +100 | +1.0 | +400 | +400 | +150 | ** | +10 | +50 |

||NE (niacin equivalent) is equal to 1 mg of niacin or 60 mg of dietary tryptophan.

¶The folacin allowances refer to dietary sources as determined by *Lactobacillus casei* assay after treatment with enzymes ("conjugates") to make polyglutamyl forms of the vitamin available for the test organism.

#The RDA for vitamin B₁₂ in infants is based on average concentration of the vitamin in human milk. The allowances after weaning are based on energy intake (as recommended by the American Academy of Pediatrics) and consideration of other factors such as intestinal absorption.

**The increased requirement during pregnancy cannot be met by the iron content of habitual American diets nor by the existing iron stores of many women; therefore the use of 30-60 mg of supplemental iron is recommended. Iron needs during lactation are not substantially different from those of nonpregnant women, but continued supplementation of the mother for 2-3 months after parturition is advisable to replenish stores depleted by pregnancy.

††New recommendations may be adopted to prevent postmenopausal osteoporosis in this age group.

| Trace elements† | | | | Electrolytes | | |
|---|---|---|---|---|---|---|
| Fluoride (mg) | Chromium (mg) | Selenium (mg) | Molybdenum (mg) | Sodium (mg) | Potassium (mg) | Chloride (mg) |
| 0.1-0.5 | 0.001-0.04 | 0.01-0.04 | 0.03-0.06 | 115-350 | 350-925 | 295-700 |
| 0.2-1 | 0.02-0.06 | 0.02-0.06 | 0.04-0.08 | 250-750 | 425-1275 | 400-1200 |
| 0.5-1.5 | 0.02-0.08 | 0.02-0.08 | 0.05-0.1 | 325-975 | 550-1650 | 500-1500 |
| 1-2.5 | 0.03-0.12 | 0.03-0.12 | 0.06-0.15 | 450-1350 | 775-2325 | 700-2100 |
| 1.5-2.5 | 0.05-0.2 | 0.05-0.2 | 0.1-0.3 | 600-1800 | 1000-3000 | 925-2775 |
| 1.5-2.5 | 0.05-0.2 | 0.05-0.2 | 0.15-0.5 | 900-2700 | 1525-4575 | 1400-4200 |
| 1.5-4 | 0.05-0.2 | 0.05-0.2 | 0.15-0.5 | 1100-3300 | 1875-5625 | 1700-5100 |

**TABLE 70-3**  U.S. recommended daily allowances for labeling purposes

| Vitamins, minerals | Infants | Children under 4 | Adults and children 4 years and older | Pregnant† lactating women |
|---|---|---|---|---|
| vitamin A | 1500 IU | 2500 IU | 5,000 IU | 8,000 IU |
| vitamin D | 400 IU | 400 IU | 400 IU | 400 IU |
| vitamin E | 5 IU | 10 IU | 30 IU | 30 IU |
| vitamin C | 35 mg | 40 mg | 60 mg | 60 mg |
| folacin* | 0.1 mg | 0.2 mg | 0.4 mg | 0.8 mg |
| thiamine | 0.5 mg | 0.7 mg | 1.5 mg | 1.7 mg |
| riboflavin | 0.6 mg | 0.8 mg | 1.7 mg | 2.0 mg |
| niacin | 8 mg | 9 mg | 20 mg | 20 mg |
| pyridoxine | 0.4 mg | 0.7 mg | 2 mg | 2.5 mg |
| cyanocobalamin | 2 μg | 3 μg | 6 μg | 8 μg |
| pantothenic acid | 3 mg | 5 mg | 10 mg | 10 mg |
| calcium | 0.6 g | 0.8 g | 1 g | 1.3 g |
| phosphorus | 0.5 g | 0.8 g | 1 g | 1.3 g |
| iodine | 45 μg | 70 μg | 150 μg | 150 μg |
| iron | 15 mg | 10 mg | 18 mg | 18 mg |
| magnesium | 70 mg | 200 mg | 400 mg | 450 mg |
| manganese† | 0.5 mg | 1 mg | 4 mg | 4 mg |
| copper | 0.6 mg | 1 mg | 2 mg | 2 mg |
| zinc | 5 mg | 8 mg | 15 mg | 15 mg |
| biotin | 0.05 mg | 0.15 mg | 0.3 mg | 0.3 mg |

*Folacin refers to all folic acid derivatives that have vitamin activity.
†Proposed U.S. RDA values. (Feldman, 1990)

tamin deficiency, and unproven uses. Diet is the treatment of choice in vitamin deficiencies; vitamins are not a substitute for a balanced diet. Instruct the client in the four basic food groups and, in particular, specific foods that supply the vitamin in which he or she is deficient. Supplements are only needed if the dietary intake is insufficient to meet body requirements. Megadoses are not recommended, and there is the risk of toxicity with chronic overdoses. The RDA should not be exceeded.

## Fat-Soluble Vitamins

### vitamin A (Alphalin, Aquasol A)

Vitamin A, the fat-soluble, growth-promoting vitamin, is essential for growth in the younger age-groups for maintenance of health at all ages. The chemistry of this vitamin is related to the carotenoid pigments of plants, especially carotene; the term *vitamin A* may be applied to vitamin A, α-carotene, β-carotene, γ-carotene, and cryptoxanthin. The last four factors are formed in plants and are precursors of vitamin A in the body; β-carotene is hydrolyzed in the body to form two molecules of vitamin A.

Vitamin A may be found in spinach. Plant carotene also supplies the provitamin from which the body tissues prepare vitamin A. The amount of chlorophyll in the plant is a rough indication of the amount of carotene present. Animal fats, such as those found in butter, milk, eggs, and fish liver, are sources of the carotenoids that were originally derived from plants and stored in animal tissues.

Vitamin A is essential in promoting normal growth and development of bones and teeth and maintaining the health of epithelial tissues of the body. Its function in relation to normal vision and the prevention of night blindness has been studied carefully. Vitamin A actually is part of one of the major retinal pigments, rhodopsin, and thus is required for normal "rod vision" in the retina of human beings and many animals.

Vitamin A also has a function in the conversion processes resulting in corticosterone and cholesterol.

Vitamin A has the following indications:

1. It is used to treat or relieve symptoms associated with a deficiency of vitamin A, such as night blindness (nyctalopia), hyperkeratosis, retarded growth, xerophthalmia, keratomalacia, weakness, and increased susceptibility of mucous membranes to infection.
2. Certain analogs are used to treat acne (see Chapter 68).
3. The diet low in vitamin A should be corrected with foods rather than with drugs. It appears that large doses of vitamin A may cause neurologic and skin damage in adults, and excessive doses are known to produce highly toxic effects in rats and in young children.
4. At times vitamin A concentrates have a legitimate use as dietary supplements. Increased need occurs during pregnancy and lactation, in infancy, and in conditions characterized by lack of normal absorption and storage of vitamin A.

Vitamin A has not been found effective in the treatment of dry or wrinkled skin or to prevent or treat colds or infections that are not associated with a vitamin A deficiency. While vitamin A has been recommended for dozens of illnesses, there is currently no evidence of proven effectiveness

**TABLE 70-4**   Vitamins: significant side effects/adverse reactions

| Vitamin | Side effects | Adverse reactions |
|---|---|---|
| vitamin A | — | Acute overdose: Diplopia, severe headaches, increased agitation, skin peeling on lips and palms, severe vomiting, gum bleeding, mouth soreness, confusion or enhanced excitability, diarrhea, sedation, dizziness, convulsions. In babies, may see a bulging spot on the head and hydrocephalus. Older children and adults may have an increase in intracranial pressure.<br>Toxicity appears approximately 6 hours after an overdose. Reversible if vitamin ingestion is discontinued.<br>Chronic overdose: May result in pain in bones and joints, elevated temperature, feeling of weakness, headaches, anorexia, alopecia, abdominal pain, vomiting, increased irritability, increased frequency of urination (especially at night), skin photosensitivity, yellow-orange color discoloration on soles of feet, palms of hands or skin near nose and lips. May also see hepatotoxicity, intracranial and portal hypertension, anemia, hemolysis, and papilledema.<br>Toxicity is slowly reversible on discontinuing vitamin A. |
| vitamin D | — | Early signs of toxicity associated with hypercalcemia: Diarrhea, constipation seen more often in children and adolescents, dry mouth, continuous headaches, thirst, anorexia, metallic taste in mouth, nausea or vomiting—more often seen in children and adolescents. Increased weakness. Later signs of vitamin D toxicity associated with hypercalcemia: bone pain, elevated blood pressure, pruritus, increased urinary frequency (especially at night), eye irritation or increased sensitivity of eyes to lights, cloudy urine, mood alterations, nausea or vomiting, severe abdominal pain, convulsions, weight loss, irregular heart rate.<br>Severe toxicity is manifested by vascular and soft tissue calcification that may result in hypertension or renal failure. Growth in children may be arrested. Death can occur because of renal or heart failure. |
| vitamin E | Large doses: Visual disturbances, diarrhea, headaches, flu symptoms, nausea, abdominal cramps, severe weakness, lightheadedness, breast enlargement in both sexes | Very large doses (over 800 units/day for long time periods)—altered hormone metabolism such as thyroid, adrenal, and pituitary; altered immunity; increased bleeding problems in vitamin K—deficient persons. |
| niacin | Less frequent with niacin only: Feeling flush or warm, red skin especially in face and neck areas; headaches. Large doses: Diarrhea, lightheadedness, dry skin, nausea or vomiting, abdominal pain | Less frequent with niacin only: rash, pruritus or wheezing (with IV administration).<br>Large doses may also result in elevated serum levels of glucose and uric acid, liver toxicity, and cardiac arrhythmias. |
| ascorbic acid | Less frequent/rare: Lightheadedness (with IV injection). With high doses: Diarrhea (in oral daily doses of more than 1 g); red, flushing of skin, headaches, nausea or vomiting, increased urination in doses more than 600 mg/day, abdominal cramps | Dose-related effects: Side or back (lower) pain because of oxalate stones in urinary tract. |

in these conditions. The approved indication for use of vitamin A is for the prevention and treatment of vitamin A deficiency that may result in xerophthalmia, keratomalacia, and nyctalopia (night blindness).

Vitamin A and carotene are readily absorbed from the normal gastrointestinal tract. Efficient absorption depends on fat absorption and therefore on the presence of adequate bile salts in the intestine. Certain conditions, such as obstructive jaundice, some infectious diseases, and the presence of mineral oil in the intestine, may result in vitamin

A deficiency in spite of the amount ingested being normal.

Vitamin A is stored to a greater extent in the liver than elsewhere. The liver also functions in changing carotene to vitamin A; this function is inhibited in liver diseases and in diabetes. The amount of vitamin A stored depends on the dietary intake. When intake is high or excessive, the stores formed in the liver may be sufficient to last a long time. Vitamin A is metabolized by the liver and excreted by the feces and kidneys.

For side effects/adverse reactions, see Table 70-4.

---

### VITAMIN D PREPARATIONS

| Generic Name | Trade Name |
|---|---|
| calcifediol | (Calderol) |
| calcitriol | (Rocaltrol, Calcijex) |
| dihydrotachysterol | (Hytakerol, DHT) |
| ergocalciferol | (Deltalin, Drisdol, Osto-forte ✤) |
| ergocalciferol | (Calciferol) |

---

When vitamin A is given concurrently with isotretinoin, an additive increase in side effects may result. Avoid concurrent administration if possible. If not, monitor closely.

Adult dose in deficiency states is 10,000 to 25,000 units daily for 7 to 14 days or until the client demonstrates improvement. For xerophthalmia, the oral dose is 25,000 to 50,000 units daily. The pediatric dose for deficiency is 5,000 units/kg daily. For parenteral dosing with vitamin A, see current package insert or USP-DI.

### vitamin D

The term *vitamin D* is applied to two or more substances that affect the proper utilization of calcium and phosphorus in the body. Two forms of naturally occurring vitamin D have been isolated. One is obtained as a product of irradiated ergosterol and is known as vitamin $D_2$ or ergocalciferol. Ergosterol has therefore been shown to be a precursor of vitamin D. Further investigation has shown that several precursors can be changed by irradiation into compounds that have vitamin D activity. Irradiation of 7-dehydrocholesterol results in the formation of vitamin $D_3$ (cholecalciferol), which is stored in the body. It also is formed in skin exposed to sunlight. Irradiated ergosterol (calciferol) is the active constituent in various vitamin preparations, such as viosterol and irradiated yeast. See the box above for various preparations of vitamin D.

Vitamins $D_2$ and $D_3$, as well as other products of irradiated ergosterol, are capable of antirachitic activity.

Although an essential vitamin, vitamin D is contained in only a few foods (milk, bread, cereals, animal livers) of the average American diet. Small amounts are present in herring, sardines, salmon, tuna fish, eggs, and butter. Vitamin D is found in high concentrations in a number of fish oils (cod, halibut).

At present, milk is the chief commercial food product fortified by the addition of vitamin D concentrate. By federal regulation, milk products are standardized at 400 IUg of vitamin D/quart, which represents a day's requirement.

The exact mechanism by which vitamin D functions in the metabolism of calcium and phosphorus is not known. Evidence suggests that a complex relationship exists between vitamin D and parathyroid hormone, but this is not yet conclusive. The vitamin seems to be involved directly with the absorption of calcium and phosphorus from the intestinal tract and their deposition in bone and teeth. In the absence of vitamin D, the amount of these substances absorbed from the bowel is diminished to such an extent that even though the calcium and phosphate intake is adequate, rickets results in the child and osteomalacia in the adult.

When skin is exposed to the ultraviolet rays in sunlight, cholecalciferol (vitamin $D_3$) is formed. Ergocalciferol (calciferol, vitamin $D_2$) is usually found in vitamin preparations, and cholecalciferol is added to vitamin D–fortified milk. Both cholecalciferol and ergocalciferol are metabolized in the liver to calcifediol (25-hydroxychole-calciferol), which is then transported to the kidney where it is converted to calcitriol (1,25-dihydroxycholecalciferol, which is believed to be the most active analog). Dihydrotachysterol is a synthetic product of ergocalciferol that has only weak antirachitic activity; it is activated metabolically in the liver. Calcifediol appears to have intrinsic vitamin D activity in addition to its conversion to the active metabolite.

Calcitriol, which appears to bind to a receptor in the intestinal mucosa, is incorporated into the cell nucleus, resulting in the formation of a calcium-binding protein that increases calcium absorption from the intestine. Parathyroid hormone and calcitriol both act to control the transfer of calcium ions from bones into the extracellular fluid; therefore they maintain a calcium homeostasis effect in the extracellular fluid.

**Indications.** Vitamin D is indicated for the prevention and treatment of rickets. The incidence of rickets is low in the United States but it can occur in young children who are restricted to vegetarian diets without milk supplementation or in infants who are breast fed by mothers who did not take prenatal vitamins nor drink milk. It is primarily caused by a vitamin D deficiency that results in an inadequate intake and perhaps, an excessive loss of calcium from the body. Rickets results in soft bones, deformed joints, and bone deformities.

Vitamin D is used for the treatment of chronic hypocalcemia, hypophosphatemia, and osteodystrophy, for the treatment of osteomalacia in adults, and for the prevention and treatment of vitamin D deficiency states caused by improper nutrition or intestinal malabsorption conditions. It is also used for the prevention and treatment of tetany. (Dihydrotachysterol is the preferred product for acute, chronic, or latent types of postsurgical tetany and idiopathic tetany.)

**Pharmacokinetics**

*Absorption.* Absorption is best from the small intestine. Cholecalciferol is absorbed better than ergocalciferol because the latter requires the presence of bile salts for absorption.

*Protein binding.* Transported by specific alpha globulins.

*Storage.* In the liver and in fat.

*Metabolism.* See the discussion above. Both cholecalciferol and ergocalciferol require two steps for metabolic activation, that is the liver and kidneys. Calcifediol is activated by the kidneys, whereas dihydrotachysterol is activated in the liver. Calcitriol does not require any special metabolic activation. The kidneys are also responsible in part for degradation of these substances.

*Serum half-life.* Calcifediol: 10 to 22 days (usually 16 days); calcitriol: within 3 to 8 hours; ergocalciferol: within 19 to 48 hours, but it can be stored in fat sites for longer time periods

*Onset of action.* Hypercalcemic effect: calcitriol—orally within 2 to 6 hours; dihydrotachysterol—within hours, although maximum effect is seen in 7 to 14 days; ergocalciferol—within 12 to 24 hours, although therapeutic response may not be seen until 10 to 14 days later

*Time to peak serum concentration.* Calcifediol: in about 4 hours; calcitriol: orally in approximately 2 hours

*Duration of effect following oral administration.* Calcifediol: 15 to 20 days (in renal failure this can be increased 2 or 3 times); calcitriol: in 24 to 48 hours; dihydrotachysterol: up to 9 weeks; ergocalciferol: up to 6 months

*Excretion.* In bile and by the kidneys.

**Side effects/adverse reactions.** See Table 70-4.

**Significant drug interactions.** The following interactions may occur when vitamin D products are given concurrently with the drugs listed below:

| Drug | Possible Effect and Management |
|---|---|
| antacids containing magnesium | If given with calcifediol or calcitriol, hypermagnesemia may result, especially in clients with chronic renal failure. Avoid concurrent administration if possible; if not, monitor closely. |
| vitamin D, other products | Not recommended because of additive effects resulting in an increased risk of toxicity. |

**Dosage and administration.** The adult and adolescent dose for calcifediol is 50 to 100 μg (0.05 to 0.1 mg) orally daily. For children up to 2 years old, 20 to 50 μg orally daily; children 2 to 10 years old, 50 μg daily. For calcitriol, the adult and adolescent dose is 0.25 mg orally daily initially, which may be increased every 2 to 4 weeks if necessary. The pediatric dose varies according to the specific indication; therefore please refer to a current package insert or USP-DI for dosing instructions.

The usual dihydrotachysterol dose for the adult and adolescent is 125 μg to 2 mg orally daily. The pediatric dose for hypoparathyroidism is 1 to 5 mg orally initially for 4 days, which is then continued or decreased to one fourth of the dose thereafter. Maintenance dose is between 0.5 and 1.5 mg daily. Ergocalciferol adult and adolescent dose for vitamin D deficiency is 1,000 to 2,000 units orally daily, reduced when appropriate to 400 units daily. For vitamin D–dependent rickets, the dose is 10,000 to 60,000 units

daily while in vitamin D–resistant rickets, the dose is 12,000 to 500,000 units per day. For other indications, check a current package insert. The pediatric dose in vitamin D deficiency is 1,000 to 4,000 units daily, reduced to 400 units daily when appropriate. For vitamin D–dependent rickets the dose is 3,000 to 10,000 units orally daily.

▷**Nursing Management:
Vitamin D Therapy**

See the nursing management of vitamin therapy.

**Assessment.** The administration of vitamin D is contraindicated in clients with hypercalcemia and hypervitaminosis D. The nurse's assessment should rule out these conditions before initiation of vitamin D therapy. Other conditions for which caution should be used in the administration of vitamin D are arteriosclerosis, hyperphosphatemia, hypersensitivity to vitamin D, and renal or cardiac impairment.

Along with periodic evaluations of renal function, serum calcium levels should be monitored, particularly in the early weeks of therapy, to assist in the determination of the appropriate dosage levels. Serum calcium values should be in the 8 to 9 mg/100 ml range and the calcium times phosphorus product (Ca × P in milligrams per 100 ml) should not be greater than 58. Other examinations may be required according to the client's response to therapy.

Children should have their growth measurements monitored over the course of therapy. Growth may be inhibited by prolonged administration of the drug.

Assess for signs of toxicity: altered bowel elimination (constipation); and altered comfort related to anorexia, nausea, and vomiting, metallic taste and dryness in the mouth, and headache.

**Education.** Stress the importance of regular visits to the health care provider to monitor progress. Review with the client any instructions for a special diet or for a calcium supplement, if prescribed. Foods high in vitamin D include fish and fish liver oils, as well as vitamin D–fortified milk.

The client should be cautioned not to use any OTC products that contain calcium, phosphorus, or vitamin D unless approved by the physician. Clients taking calcifediol or calcitriol should avoid the use of antacids containing magnesium.

**vitamin E (tocopherol):
vitamin E capsules (Aquasol E; E-Ferol; Eprolin)**

Vitamin E is a fat-soluble vitamin, the richest source of which is wheat germ oil. Vitamin E also occurs in other vegetable oils, such as cottonseed oil and peanut oil, and is found in green, leafy vegetables.

Several compounds have been found that exhibit vitamin E activity. The most active of these are the tocopherols, of which three are naturally occurring compounds known as α-, β-, and γ-tocopherol. The most biologically potent of these compounds is α-tocopherol.

A vitamin E deficiency was seen in the late 1960s, induced in premature infants that were fed a formula that lacked vitamin E. The symptoms exhibited were hemolysis of erythrocytes, thrombocytosis, and edema that cleared up with administration of vitamin E. Since infant formulations now are supplemented with this vitamin, a vitamin E deficiency in infants is probably remote.

In adults, neuropathies in clients with biliary disease and cystic fibrosis have reportedly responded to vitamin E therapy. Interestingly, animals suffer severe symptoms (muscular dystrophy, sterility, cardiac lesions, and others) from a deficiency in this vitamin that are not recorded in human beings. The reason for this is unknown.

Vitamin E is an essential nutrient, but its exact function is unknown. It has antioxidant properties; when combined with dietary selenium, vitamin E will prevent the effects of peroxidase on unsaturated bonds in the cell membranes and will also protect red blood cells from hemolysis. It is also known to be a cofactor for several enzyme systems in the body.

Vitamin E is indicated for the prevention and treatment of vitamin E deficiency. About 20% to 80% is absorbed from the duodenum. Absorption requires the presence of bile salts and dietary fats. Vitamin E binds to beta lipoproteins in the blood and is stored in all body tissues but especially in fat depots (which contain up to a 4-year requirement of this vitamin). It is metabolized in the liver and excreted in bile and kidneys. For side effects/adverse reactions, see Table 70-4.

When vitamin E is given concurrently with iron supplements, iron's therapeutic effect for iron deficiency anemia may be impaired. Also, large daily doses of iron may result in an increased requirement for vitamin E. If given concurrently, monitor closely to determine an appropriate intervention.

When administered to adults to prevent vitamin E deficiency, give 30 units orally daily. To treat a vitamin E deficiency, give 60 to 75 units orally per day.

When administered to children to treat deficiency give 1 unit/kg orally daily or four to five times the RDA orally daily. If premature infants are receiving formulas that are high in polyunsaturated fatty acids, then add 15 to 25 units per day of vitamin E (or 7 units per liter of formula). In normal-birth-weight infants, add 5 units per liter of formula.

▷**Nursing Management:**
**Vitamin E Therapy**

See also the nursing management of vitamin therapy.
**Assessment.** Before the initiation of vitamin E therapy, it should be ascertained whether the client has hypoprothrombinemia as a result of vitamin K deficiency or iron

deficiency anemia because vitamin E will aggravate the former and interfere with the hematologic response to iron therapy in the latter.

**Intervention.** Water-miscible forms are more readily absorbed from the gastrointestinal tract, but parenteral administration may be necessary if the malabsorption syndrome is severe.

The client taking large doses of vitamin E for prolonged periods of time should be assessed for signs of toxicity: dizziness and drowsiness; impaired vision; breast enlargement; and flulike symptoms.

**Education.** Although vitamin E deficiency is infrequent, dietary instruction for clients may be necessary. Foods high in vitamin E are vegetable oils, wheat germ, whole-grain cereals, egg yolk, and liver.

### vitamin K

Vitamin K is a fat-soluble vitamin. (See Chapter 30 for drug monograph.)

## Water-Soluble Vitamins

The water-soluble vitamins are ascorbic acid (vitamin C) and the vitamin B complex. The vitamin B complex refers to a group of vitamins that often are found together in food, although they are chemically dissimilar and have different metabolic functions. They are grouped together largely on the historic basis of their having been discovered in sequential order. They have little in common other than their sources and their water solubility. A sensible and increasingly popular trend promotes discarding such names as vitamin $B_1$ and $B_2$ and referring to these vitamins as thiamine and riboflavin. The vitamin B complex includes thiamin, riboflavin, nicotinic acid, pyridoxine, folic acid, pantothenic acid, biotin, choline, inositol, and vitamin $B_{12}$ (cyanocobalamin).

This discussion will be limited to the B vitamins that are associated with deficiency states and for which information on therapeutic application is available: thiamine hydrochloride (vitamin $B_1$), riboflavin (vitamin $B_2$), niacin (nicotinic acid), pyridoxine hydrochloride (vitamin $B_6$), vitamin $B_{12}$ (cyanocobalamin), and folic acid.

### thiamine (vitamin $B_1$):
### thiamine hydrochloride (Betalin S, Bewon)

Thiamine combines with adenosine triphosphate (ATP) to form thiamine pyrophosphate coenzyme. This is necessary for carbohydrate metabolism.

Thiamine is used to prevent and treat thiamine deficiency, which can result in beriberi or Wernicke's encephalopathy.

Thiamine is well absorbed from the duodenum except in malabsorption syndrome. Alcohol inhibits thiamine absorption. Thiamine is metabolized in the liver and excreted by the kidneys. Side effects are usually rare. Skin rash, pruritus, or respiratory difficulties (wheezing) may occur rarely after a large intravenous dose is administered (anaphylactic reaction).

The adult dose of thiamine as a nutritional supplement is as follows: for beriberi, 5 to 10 mg three times daily, usually administered in a multivitamin formulation; for thiamine deficiency, 5 to 10 mg orally three times daily until client improves, then reduce to RDA dose; for alcohol-induced deficiency, 40 mg orally daily.

The pediatric dose is 10 to 50 mg daily, depending on the degree of the deficiency. As a dietary supplement, infants should receive 0.3 to 0.5 mg orally daily; children, 0.5 mg to 1 mg orally daily.

▷**Nursing Management:**
**Thiamine Therapy**

Also see nursing management of vitamin therapy.

***Assessment.*** Thiamine rarely causes toxicity in individuals with normal renal function. Skin rash or wheezing may occur as signs of hypersensitivity. Since it is infrequent that a deficiency of a single B vitamin would occur, the client needs to be assessed for multiple deficiencies.

***Intervention.*** In most instances the vitamin is administered in an oral preparation; however, if this is not acceptable or possible, parenteral forms are available.

***Education.*** Instruction for the client should include sources that are high in thiamine, such as whole grain or enriched cereals and meats, particularly pork.

### riboflavin (vitamin B₂)

In the body riboflavin is converted into two coenzymes—flavin mononucleotide (FMN) and flavin adenine dinucleotide (FAD)—that are necessary to normal tissue respiration. Riboflavin is also necessary for pyridoxine activation and may also be connected to maintenance of erythrocyte integrity.

Riboflavin is indicated for the prevention and treatment of riboflavin deficiency; usually this deficiency does not occur in healthy persons but may be detected as a result of malnutrition or intestinal malabsorption.

Riboflavin is very well absorbed from the intestinal tract, except for malabsorption states. It is metabolized in the liver and excreted by the kidneys. Side effects are rare. The use of alcohol may result in impairment of the absorption of riboflavin.

The adult dose to treat riboflavin deficiency is 5 to 30 mg orally daily in divided doses, which may be reduced in several days to 1 to 4 mg daily. For children 12 years and older, the dose is 3 to 10 mg orally daily for several days, then reduced to 0.6 mg/1000 calories ingested daily thereafter.

▷**Nursing Management:**
**Riboflavin Therapy**

Also see nursing management of vitamin therapy.

***Assessment.*** Vitamins that are water-soluble rarely cause toxicity in individuals with normal kidney function.

***Education.*** Alert the client that large doses of riboflavin may cause the urine to become yellow in color. The best food sources of riboflavin are milk and dairy products, meats, and green, leafy vegetables.

### niacin (nicotinic acid):
### niacin extended-release capsules
### (Nicobid, Tr-B3 ✳)
### niacin extended-release tablets (Span-Niacin)
### niacinamide injection

Niacin is converted to niacinamide in the body; then it is a part of two coenzymes, nicotinamide adenine dinucleotide (NAD) and nicotinamide adenine dinucleotide phosphate (NADP), which are necessary for glycogenolysis, tissue respiration, and lipid or fat metabolism.

As an antihyperlipid agent, niacin lowers serum cholesterol and triglyceride levels. Niacinamide does not possess these effects.

Niacin is indicated for the prevention and treatment of vitamin B₃ deficiency conditions. Niacin deficiency may result in pellagra. Niacin only is a treatment adjunct for hyperlipidemia. Its usefulness may be limited by its side effects, especially its vasodilating effects.

Niacin is readily absorbed orally, with the exception of persons with malabsorption. Half-life is 45 minutes, while onset of action to reduce cholesterol is several days; to reduce triglyceride serum levels, several hours. It is metabolized by the liver and excreted in the kidneys. For side effects/adverse reactions, see Table 70-4. No significant drug interactions are reported with its use.

The adult vitamin dose is up to 500 mg orally daily. As an antihyperlipidemic agent, the initial dose is 1 g orally three times daily; increase the dose by 500-mg increments every 2 to 4 weeks as necessary. The pediatric vitamin dose is up to 300 mg daily. Niacin is also available in liquid, extended-release tablets, and parenteral dosage forms.

The adult niacinamide vitamin dose is up to 500 mg orally daily. Niacinamide is not recommended for use in children. Niacinamide is also available in parenteral dosage form and is given 50 to 100 mg IM five times a day or more for pellagra or 25 to 100 mg by slow intravenous administration several times daily.

▷**Nursing Management:**
**Niacin Therapy**

Also consult nursing management of vitamin therapy.

***Assessment.*** Before large doses, it should be determined if the client has arterial bleeding, diabetes mellitus (niacin only), peptic ulcer, or hepatic disease, since all these conditions will be aggravated by niacin and niacinamide.

*Intervention.* Administer with milk or food to help prevent gastrointestinal distress. Oral administration of niacin is preferred. Parenteral niacin is used only when the oral route is not acceptable or possible. If administered intravenously, do not exceed a rate of 2 mg/minute.

If individuals are receiving large doses of niacin or niacinamide for prolonged periods, blood glucose and hepatic function should be monitored.

*Education.* Alert the client that for the first 2 weeks of therapy to expect a feeling of warmth, a flushing of the skin of the face and neck shortly after taking the tablets. This sensation may be reduced by starting with a low dosage and gradually increasing to the therapeutic dose. Niacinamide is preferred because it lacks this blushing effect.

Stress the importance of regular visits to the health care provider to monitor the effectiveness of the medication and the client's progress.

Since one of the adverse effects is dizziness, caution the client to avoid hazardous tasks that require mental alertness until the response to the medication has been determined.

The best food sources of niacin are meats, eggs, milk, and other dairy products.

### pyridoxine (vitamin B₆):
### pyridoxine hydrochloride (Hexa-Betalin, Rodex)

Pyridoxine is taken up by erythrocytes and converted into pyridoxal phosphate. This is a coenzyme necessary for many metabolic functions that affect proteins, carbohydrates, and lipid utilization in the body. Pyridoxine is also involved with the conversion of tryptophan to niacin or serotonin.

Pyridoxine is indicated to prevent or treat pyridoxine deficiency. A deficiency state can lead to sideroblastic anemia, neurologic disturbances, seborrheic dermatitis, cheilosis, and xanthurenic aciduria.

Oral pyridoxine is well absorbed from the jejunum. It is converted in erythrocytes to pyridoxal phosphate, which is totally protein bound in the plasma. Pyridoxal phosphate is a coenzyme for many metabolic functions that affect protein, carbohydrate, and lipid utilization. Pyridoxine is also necessary for the conversion of tryptophan to niacin or to serotonin. It has a half-life of 15 to 20 days and is metabolized by the liver and excreted in the kidneys.

Side effects and adverse reactions are very rare. Side effects are seen only when dosages of 200 mg/day are given for more than a month, resulting in a dependency-type syndrome. Megadoses also can cause severe sensory neuropathy such as ataxia, numb feet, clumsiness. It is reversible when pyridoxine is stopped.

When pyridoxine is given with levodopa, the antiparkinsonian effects of levodopa may be reduced or reversed. This effect is not reported with the carbidopa-levodopa combination.

As a dietary supplement, the adult dose is 10 to 20 mg orally daily for 3 weeks, followed by 2 to 5 mg daily for several additional weeks. For pyridoxine dependency syndrome, the dose is 30 to 600 mg orally daily. For other dosage recommendations, see a current package insert or USP-DI. The pediatric dosage has not been determined.

## ▷Nursing Management: Pyridoxine Therapy

Also consult nursing management of vitamin therapy.

*Assessment.* Initial assessment should determine whether the client has Parkinson's disease, which is treated with levodopa. Pyridoxine reverses the antiparkinsonian effects of levodopa.

*Education.* Large doses of pyridoxine for a period of several months may result in sensory neuropathy affecting gait and causing numbness of the hands and feet.

Best food sources of pyridoxine are meats, bananas, potatoes, lima beans, and whole grain cereals.

### cyanocobalamin (vitamin B₁₂):
### hydroxocobalamin (Acti-B₁₂✳),
### alphaREDISOL)

Cyanocobalamin is a coenzyme for a variety of metabolic functions that include fat and carbohydrate metabolism and protein synthesis. It is also needed for growth, cell replication, hematopoiesis, and nucleoprotein and myelin synthesis.

Cyanocobalamin is used to treat pernicious anemia (caused by lack of intrinsic factor) or to prevent and treat vitamin B₁₂ deficiency caused by malabsorption or strict vegetarianism. Vitamin B₁₂ deficiency can lead to megaloblastic anemia and irreversible neurologic damage.

For vitamin B₁₂ to be absorbed orally, the intrinsic factor must be present in the intestinal tract. It is highly protein bound, has a half-life of 6 days, and a time to peak serum level of 8 to 12 hours. It is stored and also metabolized by the liver and excreted in bile and urine. Side effects are rare. After parenteral injection, anaphylactic reactions are rarely seen. Less frequently seen are diarrhea and pruritus. No significant drug interactions are reported.

The adult dose as a nutritional supplement is 1 μg orally daily (up to 25 μg daily if necessary). For children up to 1 year old, the oral dose is 0.3 μg daily; for children 1 year and older, the dose is 1 μg daily. The parenteral dose to treat a vitamin B₁₂ deficiency is 100 μg IM or deep subcutaneous daily for 1 week, followed by 100 μg every other day for seven doses. If desired response is obtained, then 100 μg every 3 or 4 days for 2 to 3 more weeks is ordered. Maintenance dose is 100 to 200 μg. IM monthly for clients with pernicious anemia and also for clients following a total gastrectomy and extensive ileal resection. In such cases, the medication is continued for life.

The pediatric dose is 30 to 50 μg IM or by deep subcutaneous injection daily for 2 or more weeks, to a total dose of 1 to 5 mg. Maintenance dose is 100 μg IM or by deep subcutaneous injection monthly as necessary, depending on the diagnosis, (pernicious anemia, total gastrectomy, and others, same as adult).

▷**Nursing Management:**
**Cyanocobalamin Therapy**

See also nursing management of vitamin therapy.

***Assessment.*** The administration of cyanocobalamin is contraindicated in Leber's disease because the levels of the substance are already elevated. Caution should be used if the client has a history of gout.

Plasma vitamin $B_{12}$ levels should be determined before therapy begins and on about the sixth day of therapy. Diagnosis of vitamin $B_{12}$ deficiency should be confirmed by the lab or the initiation of $B_{12}$ therapy will mask a folic acid deficiency. During the first 48 hours of therapy, serum potassium should be monitored closely for the possibility of severe hypokalemia.

Hypersensitivity, which occurs rarely, is demonstrated by skin rash and, after parenteral administration, wheezing.

***Education.*** Stress compliance with the medication regimen if the client is on life-long therapy following a gastrectomy or ileal resection, or for pernicious anemia. For these conditions the drug is administered intramuscularly.

Best food sources for vitamin $B_{12}$ are meats, seafood, egg yolk, milk, and fermented cheeses.

**folic acid (vitamin B₉):**
**folic acid (Apo-Folic ✳, Folvite)**

Folic acid is converted to tetrahydrofolic acid in the body, which is then utilized for normal erythropoiesis and nucleoprotein synthesis.

Folic acid is used to prevent and treat folic acid deficiency. Folic acid should not be administered until pernicious anemia has been ruled out as a potential diagnosis. Folic acid will correct the hemotologic changes and mask pernicious anemia while the underlying neurologic damage progresses.

A folic acid deficiency may result in megaloblastic and macrocytic anemias and glossitis.

Folic acid is absorbed mostly from the upper duodenum, even in the presence of malabsorption (tropical sprue). But food folate absorption would be impaired in malabsorption syndromes. It is highly protein bound, stored and metabolized in and by the liver, and excreted by the kidneys. Folic acid in the presence of vitamin C (ascorbic acid) is converted in the liver and serum to its active form, tetrahydrofolic acid, by dihydrofolate reductase.

Side effects/adverse reactions are rare. Allergic reaction (elevated temperature and rash) or yellow discoloration of urine may occur. No significant drug interactions are reported.

The adult dose as a nutritional supplement is 100 μg orally daily, up to 1 mg daily in pregnancy. From 3 to 15 mg daily is used to treat tropical sprue. Folic acid deficiency is treated with 250 μg to 1 mg daily orally until the desired hematologic response is noted. Maintenance dose is 0.4 mg orally daily.

The pediatric dose as a nutritional supplement is 100 μg daily, increased to 500 μg or 1 mg daily, according to the individual's requirements. To treat folic acid deficiency, the dose is 0.25 mg to 1 mg orally daily, until the desired hematologic response is noted. Deficiency state is treated with 0.25 mg to 1 mg daily. Maintenance dosing varies with the age of the child. See a current package insert for dosing instructions.

▷**Nursing Management:**
**Folic Acid Therapy**

See also nursing management of vitamin therapy.

***Assessment.*** It should be determined if the client has pernicious anemia because folic acid will reverse hematologic abnormalities, but the neurologic aspects of the disease will continue to progress. The only side effect reported with folic acid, even with large doses, is allergic rash and fever.

***Education.*** Alert the client that large doses of folic acid may turn the urine yellow. The best food sources of folic acid are vegetables, fruits, and organ meats.

**ascorbic acid**

The well-known effects of lemon and orange juices in curing scurvy led to the discovery of vitamin C or **ascorbic acid.** Scurvy only occurs in humans and a few other species because ascorbic acid cannot be produced in the body. Today it is a very rare disease in the United States, only seen when all ascorbic acid intake is discontinued for 3 to 5 months. See the box below for the various forms of ascorbic acid, or vitamin C.

Although less is known about its function when compared to other water-soluble vitamins, ascorbic acid is involved in the formation of collagen in all fibrous tissue, including bone, and in the development of teeth, blood vessels, and blood cells. It also plays a role in carbohydrate metabolism. It is believed to stimulate the fibroblasts of connective tissue and thus promote tissue repair and the healing of wounds. It is thought to help maintain the integrity of the intercellular

---

**FORMS OF VITAMIN C**

ascorbic acid (Apo-C ✳, Cevalin)
ascorbic acid and sodium ascorbate chewable tablets (Apo-C)
ascorbic acid injection (Cetane, Cevalin)
sodium ascorbate injection (Cenolate, Redoxon ✳)

substance in the walls of blood vessels, and the capillary fragility associated with scurvy is explained on this basis. It is also involved in phenylalanine, tyrosine, folic acid, and iron metabolism.

When given as an adjunct to deferoxamine for a chronic iron overdose, it may serve to improve the chelating effect of deferoxamine, thus increasing the amount of iron excreted from the body (an unapproved indication).

The effectiveness of ascorbic acid in preventing or relieving cold symptoms is also an unapproved indication. Many studies have been performed over the years that have not substantiated the claims that megadoses of vitamin C reduce or eliminate cold symptoms (Davidson, 1986).

Ascorbic acid is well absorbed from the jejunum, which may be reduced if large doses are administered. It is stored in plasma and cells, with the highest concentration found in glandular sites. Metabolism is in the liver, and it is excreted by the kidneys. For side effects/adverse reactions, see Table 70-4. No significant drug interactions have been reported.

The adult dose as a nutritional supplement is 50 to 100 mg daily. To treat a vitamin deficiency the dose is 100 to 250 mg from one to three times daily. For infants and children under 4 years, the dose as a nutritional supplement is 20 to 50 mg daily. To treat vitamin deficiency, the dose is 100 to 300 mg daily in divided doses.

▷**Nursing Management:**
**Ascorbic Acid Therapy**

See also nursing management of vitamin therapy.

*Assessment.* Because of the risk of the formation of urinary stones when large doses of vitamin C are given to persons with the following conditions, it should be determined that the client does not have cystinuria, oxalosis, or a history of gout or urate renal stones.

Large doses may also precipitate a crisis in sickle cell anemia. Clients with diabetes mellitus may find interference with glucose testing with large doses of vitamin C.

If the purpose of administering vitamin C is to acidify the urine, urinary pHs will need to be monitored to determine effectiveness of the drug.

*Education.* Clients taking more than 600 mg daily may have a small increase in urination; more than 1 g daily, diarrhea; and more than 2 to 3 g daily of prolonged therapy, withdrawal scurvy.

The best food sources of vitamin C are citrus fruits, tomatoes, strawberries, cantaloupe, and raw peppers.

**Multiple-Vitamin Preparations**

Numerous multivitamin preparations are available in the United States and Canada. Supplemental preparations should provide 100% of the U.S. RDA to meet the needs of the vast majority of clients. Extra-potency or high-

potency vitamins are rarely necessary for routine supplementation. In addition, the nurse should be aware that many preparations contain chemicals that are not yet known to be associated with any known deficiency states.

## MINERALS

Oral sources of minerals are available commercially either as single sources or in combination with other minerals or multiple-vitamin preparations. The U.S. RDA is noted in Table 70-3.

Although many minerals are available, this section will be limited to iron, the most commonly prescribed mineral for iron-deficiency anemia. Other minerals are reviewed in other sections of this book.

### iron

Iron is an essential mineral for the proper functioning of all biological systems in the body. It functions as an oxygen carrier in hemoglobin and myoglobin, for tissue respiration, and for many enzyme reactions in the body. It is also stored in various body sites, such as the liver, spleen and bone marrow. Iron deficiency is the most common nutritional deficiency in the United States resulting in anemia. Young children and women, especially pregnant women, are most frequently affected.

Iron is supplied through diet (meats and certain vegetables and grains) and iron supplements. Ingested iron is converted to the ferrous state by gastric juices, which are then more readily absorbed in the body. The absorption of iron is affected by many substances, though; for example, ascorbic acid (vitamin C), orange juice, veal, and fish all potentiate iron absorption. Eggs, corn, beans, and many cereal products (containing phytates) inhibit iron absorption.

Iron is indicated for the treatment of iron deficiency anemia. The absorption of iron is mainly in the duodenum and proximal jejunum. In iron deficiency, between 20% to 30% of iron is absorbed. In normal individuals, 3% to 10% is usually absorbed. The quantity absorbed is approximately equivalent to the deficiency. Ferrous iron is better absorbed than the ferric dosage form.

Protein binding is high. Iron is not eliminated physiologically by the body. Excess iron intake can result in accumulation and iron toxicity. Small amounts are lost daily in shedding of skin, nails, hair, breast milk, urine, and menstrual blood. In healthy adults, the daily iron loss is approximately 1 mg per day for males and postmenopausal females and 1.5 mg per day in premenopausal females.

For side effects/adverse reactions, see Table 70-5.

*Significant drug interactions.* The following interactions may occur when iron salts are given concurrently with these drugs:

| Drug | Possible Effect and Management |
|---|---|
| acetohydroxamic acid | Iron may be chelated by the acetohydroxamic acid resulting in reduced absorption of both drugs. If iron therapy is necessary |

**TABLE 70-5**  Iron supplements: side effects/adverse reactions

| | Side effects | Adverse reactions |
|---|---|---|
| iron salts: ferrous fumarate, ferrous gluconate, ferrous sulfate, iron-polysaccharide | Most frequent: nausea, vomiting.<br>Less frequent: dark urine, constipation, diarrhea, teeth staining with liquid dosage formulations. | Most frequent: stomach cramps, pain.<br>Less frequent/rare: pain on swallowing, bloody stools.<br>*Iron toxicity:*<br>*Early signs of*<br>*acute toxicity:*<br>Diarrhea that may contain blood, elevated temperature, severe abdominal cramps or pain, vomiting.<br>*Late signs:*<br>Pale, cold skin, convulsions, increased weakness, sedation, blue lips, fingernails, palms of hands, irregular heart rate (weak and tachycardic). |

**TABLE 70-6**  Iron supplements

| Drug | Dosage and administration* | Percent iron |
|---|---|---|
| ferrous fumarate (Feostat, Palafer ✿) | Adults: 200 mg orally 3-4 times daily.<br>Children: 3 mg/kg 3 times daily. May be increased to 6 mg/kg if necessary. | 33 |
| ferrous gluconate (Fergon, Simron) | Adults: 325 mg orally, 4 times daily. May be increased to 650 mg 4 times daily if necessary.<br>Children (2 yrs and over): 16 mg/kg orally 3 times daily. | 11.6 |
| ferrous sulfate (Feosol, Mol-Iron) | Adults: 300 mg orally 2 times daily. May be increased to 4 times daily, if necessary.<br>Children: 10 mg/kg orally 3 times daily. | 20 |
| extended release tablets (Fero-Grad, Fero-Gradumet) | Adults: 160 to 525 mg orally 1 or 2 times daily.<br>Children: 160 mg orally daily. | |
| iron polysaccharide† (Hytinic, Nu-Iron) | Adults: 150 mg orally 2 times daily. May be increased to 150 mg 4 times daily, if necessary.<br>Children: therapeutic dosage not available. | Ferric, percentage depends on product. |

*Dosages are therapeutic recommendations, that is, for the treatment of iron deficiency anemia.
†Contains a water soluble complex of elemental ferric ion.

| Drug | Possible Effect and Management |
|---|---|
| | for a client receiving acetohydroxamic acid, it is suggested that iron be administered parenterally. |
| calcium supplements, milk or dairy products, coffee, fiber or selected food products (see previous section) | Decreased iron absorption may result. Schedule iron supplements at least 1 hour before or 2 hours after administration of these substances. |
| tetracyclines, oral administration | Decreases absorption of tetracycline, which may result in reduced antibiotic effectiveness. Avoid concurrent vitamin E. May impair hematologic effectiveness of the iron supplement. Avoid concurrent administration. |
| vitamin E | Concurrent administration with iron may reduce the client's hematologic response to iron therapy. If larger iron doses are ad- |

| Drug | Possible Effect and Management |
|---|---|
| | ministered, vitamin E requirements may also need to be increased. Close monitoring is suggested when concurrent therapy is administered. |

***Dosage and administration.*** For dosing recommendations, see Table 70-6.

▷ **Nursing Management:**
**Iron Therapy**

***Assessment.*** Complete a thorough dietary history and assess the client's nutritional status to ascertain the possible causes of the anemia and the need for client education.

Iron should be administered for iron deficiency anemias specifically rather than all anemias in general. Some anemic conditions such as thalassemias may actually result in excess deposits of iron in the body.

It should be determined that the client does not have a disorder of iron metabolism such as hemochromatosis, which causes an excess deposition of iron in the tissues, skin pigmentation, cirrhosis of the liver, and decreased carbohydrate tolerance; or hemosiderosis, an increase in tissue iron stores without associated tissue damage.

Some elderly clients may need larger doses of iron than the usual daily adult dose for iron deficiency anemia, for the reduction of gastric secretions and achlorhydria as a consequence of aging inhibits the ability to absorb iron.

*Intervention.* The ferrous rather than ferric preparation of iron provides for the most efficient absorption of iron. Iron is best administered on an empty stomach. When taken with food, its absorption may be decreased by as much as a half to a third. Administer with a full glass of water to prevent staining of the teeth with liquid iron preparations. A drinking straw or a dropper may be used to place the dose well back on the tongue to prevent contact with the teeth. Oral preparations of iron should be discontinued before parenteral iron therapy begins.

Anaphylaxis has been known to occur up to 24 hours after parenteral administration. Epinephrine should be available during injection of iron dextran, particularly in clients with asthma and known allergies. A test dose of 25 mg should be administered, intramuscularly or intravenously, to all clients at least 1 hour or longer before their first therapeutic parenteral dose.

For intravenous administration of iron dextran, do not mix with other medications or add it to parenteral nutrition solutions. It should be administered undiluted and at a rate of not more than 1 mL/minute. Flush the intravenous line with normal saline for injection. Maintain the client in a recumbent position for 30 minutes in case orthostatic hypotension should occur.

It is recommended that iron dextran be administered by the Z-track technique (see Chapter 6) using a 2- to 3-inch, 19- or 20-gauge needle, into the muscle mass of the upper outer quadrant of the buttock. It is never to be injected into the upper arm or any other exposed area because of the possibility of the preparation staining the skin dark brown.

To minimize staining use a separate needle to withdraw the drug from the vial.

*Education.* The client should be alerted that iron preparations cause black stools, which are medically insignificant. However, if the client experiences other symptoms of internal blood loss, such as bloody streaks in the stool, abdominal tenderness, cramping, or pain, the physician should be notified.

Instruct the client to maintain a diet rich in sources of iron, such as liver, green leafy vegetables, potatoes, dried peas and beans, dried fruit, and enriched flour, bread, and cereals.

*Evaluation.* The hemoglobin, hematocrit, reticulocyte count, and plasma iron values should be monitored at three weekly intervals during the first 2 months of oral iron therapy or a few days after the initiation of parenteral therapy. It usually takes 1 to 2 months for the hemoglobin concentration of a person with iron deficiency anemia to reach normal levels on oral therapy.

## SUMMARY

Nutritional requirements are best met by oral ingestion of adequate fluids and regular, balanced meals. When clients experience altered nutrition, less than the body requires, the nurse may participate in various nutritional modalities, such as vitamin replacement and enteral or parenteral feedings. Vitamins are essential to help maintain normal metabolic functions, growth, and repair of tissue. Most vitamin deficiencies are not singular, but multiple because of impoverished diets resulting from alcoholism, poverty, fads, or ignorance. Replacement therapy is available for the water-soluble vitamins—C and the B complex group—as well as the fat soluble ones—A, D, E, and K. Water-soluble vitamins are not stored in the body, so deficiencies can appear after short periods of inadequate intake. Fat-soluble vitamins, on the other hand, are stored in the liver and fatty tissue in large amounts so deficiencies occur only after long deprivation. However, toxic levels then are easier to reach with vitamin supplements. Iron deficiency is the most common nutritional deficiency in the United States and Canada, especially in young children and women. Supplement therapy is practical, but as in all nutritional deficiencies the best remedy is dietary intake.

## BIBLIOGRAPHY

American Hospital Formulary Service. (1991). AHFS: drug information '91. Bethesda, Md: American Society of Hospital Pharmacists.

Austen C. (1986). Vitamin chart no. 10: biotin, Nutr Support Serv 6(8):28.

Bailey LB. (1986). Vitamin chart no. 8: vitamin $B_6$, Nutr Support Serv 6(6):28.

Baumgartner TS et al. (1986). Vitamin chart no. 11: folic acid, part 1, Nutr Support Serv 6(9):33.

Baumgartner TS et al. (1986). Vitamin chart no. 11: folic acid, part 2, Nutr Support Serv 6(10):25.

Blair KA. (1986). Vitamin supplementation and mega doses, Nurse Pract 11(7):19.

Borderline $B_{12}$: a clue to pernicious anemia. (1989). Emerg Med 21(11):102.

Bowman BB. (1986). Vitamin chart no. 5: vitamin $B_1$, Nutr Support Serv 6(2):52.

Bowman BB. (1986). Vitamin chart no. 7: niacin, Nutr Support Serv 6(6):38.

Dawson-Hughes B. (1986). Vitamin chart no. 2: vitamin D, Nutr Support Serv 5(10):51.

Feldman EG. ed. (1990). Handbook of nonprescription drugs, ed 9. Washington, DC: American Pharmaceutical Association and The National Professional Society of Pharmacists.

Flink EB. (1987). Magnesium deficiency: causes and effects, Hosp Pract 22(2):116A.

Froberg JH. (1989). The anemias: causes and courses of action, RN 52(1):24.

Gardner SS. (1987). Vitamin $B_{12}$ deficiency anemia, SGA J 9(3):126.

Gums JG. (1987). Clinical significance of magnesium: a review, Drug Intell Clin Pharm 21(3):240.

Katzung BG. (1987). Basic and clinical pharmacology, ed 3. Norwalk, Conn: Appleton & Lange.

Krasinski SD. (1986). Vitamin chart no. 4: vitamin K, Nutr Support Serv 6(1):46.

Margen S et al. (1989). Vitamin supplementation: fact and fancy, Hosp Med 25(4):102.

Noerr B. (1990). Vitamin E (alphatocopherol), Neonat Netw 8(6):85.

Rolig EC. (1986). Vitamins: physiology and deficiency states, Nurse Pract 11(7):38.

Solomons N. (1986). Vitamin chart no. 6: vitamin $B_2$, Nutr Support Serv 6(3):30.

Solomons NW. (1985). Nutrient chart no. 13: adverse and toxic effects of excessive intakes of mineral nutrients, Nutr Support Serv 5(6):39.

Tsallas G et al. (1988). Vitamins, part 1 CINA J 4(2):4.

United States Pharmacopeial Convention. (1991). USP DI '90 drug information for the health care provider, ed 11. Rockville, Md: The Convention.

*Chapter*

# ➶71 Fluids and Electrolytes

## CHAPTER OBJECTIVES

*After studying this chapter, you should be able to meet the following objectives and define the key terms.*

1. Identify the various therapeutic reasons for the infusion of intravenous solutions.

2. Describe the role of water in human physiology.

3. Explain water transport in the body.

4. Describe the four categories of parenteral solutions, and give examples of particular solutions in each category.

5. Identify abnormal states of fluid-electrolyte balance.

6. Describe the symptoms of hypertonic dehydration by clinical grading.

7. State the normal requirements, dietary sources, specific functions, and problems associated with an excess or deficiency of sodium, potassium, calcium, and magnesium.

8. Develop a nursing plan for the client with potential complications from intravenous therapy.

## KEY TERMS

## INTRODUCTION

Injecting substances, including blood, into the bloodstream of animals or humans has been the subject of experiments since the seventeenth century. Although a few successes were recorded, the majority of cases resulted in complications, infections, and/or death.

In the early 1900s, it was discovered that all human blood was not the same and that sodium citrate could be safely added to blood to prevent it from clotting. From this point on, rapid advances were made in blood administration.

The administration of parenteral fluids intravenously has become more prevalent during the past 50 years. The problems associated with the use of unsafe solutions because of pyrogens had to first be resolved. This was first recognized in 1923; throughout the years advances in scientific knowledge and pharmaceutical technology have resulted in products that have significantly improved patient safety. See the box "Intravenous Therapy: 1930s to Today," which outlines nursing progress in intravenous therapy since the early 1930s.

## CURRENT OVERVIEW

Approximately 25% of all clients in hospitals today receive some type of intravascular therapy. There has also been a vast increase in outpatient and home administration of IV medications, hyperalimentations, and fluids. New, sophisticated delivery systems have been developed and different methods of application are constantly being conceived. Intravenous solutions are infused for various therapeutic reasons; some examples are listed here:

To replace fluids and electrolytes

To correct acid-base imbalance

To administer medications

To maintain ready access to the venous system if any of the first three measures is anticipated

To measure changes in venous pressure

To measure the kidneys' excretory capabilities by diagnostic test

To administer essential nutrients

Blood and its components are transfused intravenously to (1) replace blood volume or plasma fractions; (2) restore the blood's capabilities for oxygen carrying, clotting, or oncotic pressure; or (3) cleanse the plasma of harmful constituents by exchanges. Intravenous hyperalimentation or parenteral nutrition solutions are infused to complement or supplement dietary intake of individuals in deprived nutrition states.

## FLUIDS

Water comprises from 45% to 75% of the total human body weight, depending on the amount of adipose tissue present. Infants and young children have more water per unit of body weight than adults, and female adults have less water content than male adults. The greatest amount of body water (up to 45% of body weight) is to be found in the **intracellular fluid,** the fluid inside the cells. In this fluid the chemical reactions of all metabolism so essential to life occur. The remainder of body water is located in the **extracellular fluid,** the fluid surrounding the cells. This extracellular fluid consists of plasma, interstitial fluid, and lymph, as well as extracellular portions of dense connective tissue, cartilage, and bone. The volume of fluid in the two body fluid compartments varies with age and differs in the sexes. In this fluid, metabolic exchanges between cells and tissues and the external environment occur.

---

**INTRAVENOUS THERAPY: 1930s TO TODAY**

**Early 1930s**

Intravenous injections were reserved for only seriously ill clients.

Only a physician could perform the venipuncture.

**1940s**

Massachusetts General Hospital became one of the first hospitals to assign a nurse to intravenous therapy.

The job description included administering intravenous solutions and blood transfusions, cleaning the infusion sets for reuse, and cleaning and sharpening needles for reuse.

Primary responsibility was of a technical nature: administering and maintaining the infusions and keeping the equipment clean and functional.

**1950s to 1990s**

Improvements and innovations in equipment (such as pumps and monitors) needles (Intracaths, and so forth), tubing, development of plastic and disposable equipment, and an increased variety of commercially prepared intravenous fluids increase the safety of intravenous therapy.

The development of intravenous filters prevents particulate matter, bacteria, or fungus from entering the bloodstream.

Intravenous route is used to administer many medications and hyperalimentation fluids, in addition to intravenous fluids.

The development of intravenous nurse specialists, intravenous departments or teams in the hospital, standards for client care, and professional organizations to promote intravenous therapy as a speciality area in nursing.

---

The importance of body water is highlighted by two facts: (1) it is the medium in which all metabolic reactions occur, and (2) precise regulation of volume and composition of body fluid is essential to health. In the healthy individual, body water remains remarkably constant, maintained by a balance between intake and excretion—the water gained each day is equal to the water lost. If the water gained exceeds the water lost, water excess, or **overhydration,** and edema will occur. If the water lost exceeds the water gained, water deficit, or **dehydration**, will occur. If 20% to 25% of body water is lost, death usually occurs.

Water is an excellent solvent that permits many substances to be dispersed through it. It also has a high dielectric constant, which permits ionization of electrolytes. These electrolytes are important in maintaining any physiologic processes and body fluid volume and distribution. They include the cations sodium ($Na^+$) for extracellular fluid, and potassium ($K^+$) and magnesium ($Mg^{++}$) for intracellular fluid; and the anions chloride ($Cl^-$) and bicarbonate ($HCO_3$) for extracellular fluid, and phosphate ($PO_4^{--}$) and protein for intracellular fluid. Intracellular ions also occur in the extracellular fluid but in smaller amounts. Water is also an excellent lubricant between membranes, and it functions well as a heat insulator and heat exchanger.

Daily intake of water in some form is essential to maintain water balance. During starvation, human beings can go several weeks without food but can survive only a few days without water. The average volumes of water consumed daily are as follows: 120 to 150 ml/kg body weight in neonates and infants, 120 to 130 ml/kg in children, and 30 ml/kg in adults.

Thirst, the subjective desire to ingest water, helps maintain water balance. Although thirst is complex and not well understood, a decrease in saliva and dryness of the mouth and throat induce it. Dehydration of thirst receptors may lead to their stimulation.

Water intake occurs primarily by (1) drinking fluids, (2) ingesting food containing moisture (most foods contain a high percentage of water), and (3) absorbing water formed by the oxidation of hydrogen in the food during metabolic processes, which produces about 0.5 L of water per day.

Water is lost from the body in five principal ways: (1) by way of the kidneys as urine, (2) through the skin as insensible perspiration and sweat, (3) through expired air as water vapor, (4) through feces, and (5) through the excretion of tears and saliva. Urine excretion accounts for 50% to 60% of the total daily water loss. Urine output, of course, varies with the amount of water ingested.

Water loss by the kidney varies with the solute (molecular ions or particles) load and the antidiuretic hormone (ADH or vasopressin) level. The kidney excretes sufficient urine to transport the solutes into the bladder if an increase in solute load occurs, as in diabetes mellitus or following ingestion of excessive amounts of food (especially those that generate solutes, such as sodium from salty foods). The reabsorption of water in the distal convoluted tubules is controlled by ADH. An increase in ADH levels will lead to an increase in water reabsorption, which produces a more concentrated urine. ADH (vasopressin) is secreted by the posterior pituitary gland. This secretion is regulated by osmoreceptors located in the supraoptic nucleus. ADH has an action on specific vasopressin receptors on the medullary tubular cell to stimulate cyclic AMP (cAMP) production in this cell. The cAMP activates an enzyme that alters protein structure in the cell membrane to increase tubular cell permeability to water. This will increase water resorption and increase urine osmolality.

## Water Transport in the Body

Water travels from less concentrated areas to areas with higher concentrations of solutes or dissolved substances (**osmosis**). The solutes may be electrolytes, such as potassium chloride or sodium chloride, which, when dissolved in water, yield potassium cations and chloride anions (a chemical

**TABLE 71-1** Normal body electrolyte distribution*

| Electrolytes | Extracellular (mEq/L) | | Intracellular (mEq/l) |
|---|---|---|---|
| | Plasma | Interstitial | |
| sodium ($Na^+$) | 142 | 146 | 15 |
| potassium ($K^+$) | 5 | 5 | 150 |
| calcium ($Ca^{++}$) | 5 | 3 | 2 |
| magnesium ($Mg^{++}$) | 2 | 1 | 27 |
| chloride ($Cl^-$) | 103 | 114 | 1 |
| bicarbonate ($HCO_3^-$) | 27 | 30 | 10 |

*In addition, phosphates, sulfates, and other substances are located in the extracellular and intracellular fluids.

balance that is maintained) or nonelectrolytes, such as dextrose, urea, or creatinine. Each fluid compartment in the body—intracellular and extracellular compartments—has its own electrolyte composition. (See Table 71-1 for electrolyte composition in body compartments.) Disturbances in electrolyte composition can be reflected in clinical symptoms in the client.

Osmolality refers to the total solute concentration usually expressed per liter of serum. The osmotic pressure is decided by the number of solutes in solution. For example, if the extracellular fluid contained a large amount of dissolved particles and the intracellular fluid had a small amount of dissolved particles, then the osmotic pressure from the intracellular fluid would force water to pass from the less concentrated area to the more concentrated extracellular area. This would occur until both concentrations were equal. Therefore deciding on the appropriate intravenous therapy for a client would necessitate knowing the electrolyte values. The level of sodium, the principal electrolyte in the extracellular fluid, is essential to know, although potassium levels are also important, along with serum osmolality, current disease state or illnesses, specific laboratory values if appropriate, and the initial signs and symptoms.

## Parenteral Solutions

Parenteral solutions generally may be divided into four categories: (1) hydrating solutions, (2) isotonic solutions, (3) maintenance solutions, and (4) hypertonic solutions. See Table 71-2 for examples of the four categories of parenteral solutions.

*Hydrating solutions* include dextrose 2.5%, 5%, or higher in water or in 0.2% to 0.5% normal saline. (Hypotonic saline—note that full strength normal saline is not included in this category.) Hydrating solutions are used to hydrate or to prevent dehydration. They are often used to assess kidney status before specific electrolytes are ordered as replacement and maintenance therapy and also to help increase diuresis in dehydrated individuals.

**TABLE 71-2**   Four categories of selected parenteral solutions*

| | Na$^+$ | K$^+$ | Mg$^{++}$ | Ca$^{++}$ | Cl$^-$ | Osmolarity$^+$ |
|---|---|---|---|---|---|---|
| **HYDRATING SOLUTIONS** | | | | | | |
| dextrose 2.5%, 5%, 10% | | | | | | 126, 252, 505 |
| dextrose 2.5% in 0.45% NaCl injection† | 56 | | | | 56 | 280 |
| dextrose 5% in 0.45% NaCl injection‡ | 7 | | | | 77 | 405 |
| **ISOTONIC SOLUTIONS** | | | | | | |
| normal saline or sodium chloride injection (0.9% NaCl) | 154 | | | | 154 | 310 |
| Ringer's injection | 147 | 4 | | 4 | 155 | 310 |
| lactated Ringer's injection | 130 | 4 | | 3 | 109 | 275 |
| **MAINTENANCE SOLUTIONS** | | | | | | |
| Plasmalyte 56 | 40 | 13 | 3 | | 40 | 111 |
| Plasmalyte 148 (or Normosol-R, Isolyte S) | 140 | 5 | | 3 | 98 | 295 |
| **HYPERTONIC SOLUTIONS** | | | | | | |
| sodium chloride, 3% injection | 513 | | | | 513 | 1025 |
| sodium chloride, 5% injection | 855 | | | | 855 | 1710 |

*Normal plasma contains Na$^+$ (136-145), K$^+$ (3.5-5), Mg$^{++}$ (1.5-2.5), Ca$^{++}$ (4.3-5.3), Cl$^-$ (100-106), HCO$_3$ (27); osmolarity (280-300 mOsm).
$^+$electrolytes given as mEq/L; osmolarity as mOsm/L.
†Dextrose 2.5% = 25 g dextrose/L or 85 calories.
‡Dextrose 5% = 50 g dextrose/L or 170 calories.

Dextrose is a source of calories (one liter of 5% dextrose = approximately 170 calories) and is rapidly metabolized in the body. The monohydrate form of dextrose is used in parenteral solutions and it provides 3.4 calories/g (DiPiro, 1989). Therefore, although considered isotonic or more than isotonic in the bottle, in the body dextrose is metabolized leaving water that decreases the osmotic pressure of the plasma and easily transfers to body cells, providing water immediately to dehdyrated tissues.

*Isotonic solutions* are usually prescribed to replace extracellular fluid losses that occur from blood loss, severe vomiting episodes, or any situation in which the chloride loss is equal to or greater than the sodium loss. Isotonic or normal saline is also used before and after a blood transfusion. The reason is that hemolysis of red blood cells, which occurs with dextrose in water, is avoided by utilizing this product.

Isotonic sodium chloride is also used to treat metabolic alkalosis, especially when it occurs in the presence of fluid loss. The increased administration of chloride ions will help to decrease the number of bicarbonate ions in the individual. Other solutions considered isotonic preparations include Ringer's injection and lactated Ringer's injection. A major difference between Ringer's injection and lactated Ringer's injection is the 28 mEq of lactate, a precursor of bicarbonate, in the lactated injection. Thus lactated Ringer's is preferred for patients with metabolic acidosis perhaps caused by burns

or infections. Ringer's injection, however, has more chloride ions; thus it is more useful in treating dehydration from reduced water intake, vomiting, or diarrhea or for patients with hypochloremia.

*Maintenance solutions* or multiple electrolyte solutions have been formulated to replace daily electrolyte and extracellular needs and water. Such solutions may also be indicated to replace electrolytes and water loss from severe vomiting or diarrhea. With these preparations, the extracellular replacement is usually achieved within 2 days (usually 1 to 3 L/day is administered) and this should be closely monitored by laboratory tests. If maintenance solutions are continued after the client's deficits have been corrected, the excess sodium may lead to circulatory overload, pulmonary edema, and heart failure. Examples of maintenance solutions include PlasmaLyte and Normosol.

*Hypertonic solutions* are used to treat hypotonic expansion (water intoxication) when the increased body fluid volume is caused by water only. This can happen under several different circumstances: (1) hospitalized patients that receive large amounts of dextrose 5% in water or electrolyte-free solutions to replace fluid and electrolytes lost from vomiting, diarrhea, diuresis, or gastric suction, or (2) it is most apt to occur in elderly clients during the postoperative period when water is retained in response to stress (endocrine response to stress).

When behavioral changes, such as lethargy, confusion,

and perhaps, disorientation occur postoperatively in the elderly person, overhydration or hypotonic expansion should be considered. Central nervous system signs and symptoms such as increased tiredness, muscle twitching, headaches, nausea, vomiting, and even seizures have been noted. Weight gain is always present and the blood pressure may be normal or elevated.

In milder cases, the treatment usually includes withholding all fluids until excess fluids are excreted. In severe cases of hyponatremia, small quantities of hypertonic sodium chloride are administered to (1) increase the osmotic pressure, (2) increase the water flow from body cells to the extracellular compartment, and (3) to enhance excretion of the fluids by the kidneys.

The typical hypertonic saline is a 3% or 5% solution that when ordered, must be administered slowly with close supervision, (to prevent pulmonary edema) and requires close monitoring of laboratory tests for electrolytes.

## Fluid-Electrolyte Balances

A dynamic relationship exists in the human body between water and sodium, and abnormal states of hydration can be classified as (1) dehydration (volume depletion), (2) overhydration (hypervolemia or volume excess), (3) loss of water in excess of sodium (hypernatremia), and (4) loss of sodium in excess of water (hyponatremia). The second abnormal state—overhydration or volume excess—was reviewed previously, under the description of hypertonic solutions in the preceding section. The other three abnormal states may be viewed as various types of dehydration.

### Dehydration

Table 71-3 illustrates the differences between the three types of dehydration. Note that the causes of the three dehydration states are different, as are the effects on fluid compartments in the body and some of the initial signs and laboratory values, especially sodium concentration. This is very important information because it will aid the physician not only in diagnosing the initial condition but also in choosing an appropriate intravenous therapy for the individual client.

Hypertonic dehydration caused by heat exhaustion resulting from water depletion can occur on land or sea. Many cases of boaters lost at sea running out of water or refugees fleeing their countries in the Caribbean (Haiti, Cuba) and running out of water for days before being rescued or reaching land have been reported. Such persons require intensive care for their dehydration, and some may die from this deprivation. See Table 71-4 for the symptoms of hypertonic dehydration by clinical grading.

The nurse should be aware that geriatric clients with decreased renal function will be more vulnerable to dehydration and electrolyte imbalance. Also, due to the aging process, the additional physiologic changes experienced by the elderly may make them more susceptible to the adverse effects of fluid and electrolyte administration, such as overhydration or decreased renal excretion of exogenous potassium or magnesium with resultant toxic accumulation in the body.

## ELECTROLYTES

The major electrolytes in the body are sodium, potassium, calcium, and magnesium. This section will review the nor-

**TABLE 71-3**   Differences among three types of dehydration

|  | Hypotonic | Isotonic | Hypertonic |
|---|---|---|---|
| Cause | Loss of salt (NaCl) | Blood loss | Water loss or lack of sufficient fluid intake |
| Effect on ICF and ECF compartments | Volume ICF ↑<br>Volume ECF ↓ | Decrease in ECF volume | Decrease in ICF and ECF volume |
| Significant signs:<br>Rate of water elimination | Increased | Decreased | Decreased |
| Thirst | — | — | Early warning, because of cell dehydration |
| Pulse rate | Increased, weak, thready | Regular | Regular in early stages |
| Behavioral signs | May see vomiting, abdominal cramps | — | Confusion, irritability, agitation |
| Late stages | Skin turgor<br>Weak pulse, lethargy, confusion, death owing to circulatory failure | Shock, weak<br>Weak, thready | Skin turgor<br>Dry, furrowed tongue; death |
| Clinical lab results:<br>Hematocrit<br>Hemoglobin | Increased<br>Increased | Increased<br>Increased | Increased<br>Increased |
| Sodium levels | Decreased | — | Increased |

mal requirements, sources, specific functions, and problems associated with an excess or deficiency of the electrolyte.

## Sodium

*Sodium* is the major electrolyte in the extracellular fluid; the normal range is from 136 to 145 mEq/L of plasma. The sodium content in the body is regulated by sodium consumption (dietary) and sodium excretion by the kidneys. In the average person with normal renal function, sodium excretion will closely match sodium intake. This aids in keeping sodium content in the body at a level constant even if sodium intake is somewhat varied (Braunwald, 1987). Major dietary sources of sodium are table salt (sodium chloride), catsup, mustard, cured meats and fish, cheese, peanut butter, pickles, olives, potato chips, and popcorn. The recommended dietary allowance for sodium is from 1100 mg (women, 23 to 50 years old) to 3300 mg (men 23 to 50 years old). Sodium is necessary for control of body water; for the electrophysiology of nerve, muscle, and gland cells; and for the regulation of pH and isotonicity.

### Hyponatremia

**Hyponatremia** may be detected when the serum level falls below 135 mEq/L. It is induced by excessive sweating with replacement of only the water; infusion of large quantities of nonelectrolyte parenteral fluids; adrenal insufficiency or gastrointestinal suctioning with replacement fluids limited to water by mouth.

Symptoms include lethargy, hypotension, stomach cramps, vomiting, diarrhea, and possibly, seizures. Defi-

**TABLE 71-4**   Hypertonic dehydration symptoms

| Clinical grading | Symptoms |
| --- | --- |
| Mild or early | Increased thirst. Usually a 2% body weight loss. |
| Moderate to severe | Very dry mouth, difficulty in swallowing, scant urine output (highly concentrated urine), increased pulse rate and body temperature, poor skin turgor; an approximate 6% body weight loss. |
| Extreme or very severe | All previous symptoms plus impaired mental and physical capabilities, rectal temperature very high, respiratory difficulties (hyperventilation that may lead to tetany), cyanosis, severe oliguria or anuria, circulatory failure, loss of more than 7% in body weight. Usually coma and death occur when approximately 15% of body weight is lost. |

ciency states are usually treated with Ringer's solution or normal saline injection.

### Hypernatremia

**Hypernatremia** is seen when the serum sodium levels are higher than normal. This excess may be induced by excessive use of saline infusions, inadequate water consumption (as described previously), or excess fluid loss without a corresponding loss of sodium.

Signs and symptoms include edema; hypertonicity; red, flushed skin; dry, sticky mucous membranes; increase in thirst; temperature elevation; and a decrease in or absence of urination. Treatment includes reducing salt intake and using dextrose in water intravenously to promote diuresis and increase the excretion of both salt and water from the blood.

## Potassium

Potassium is the major electrolyte in the intracellular fluids. The amount of potassium in the intracellular fluid is approximately 150 mEq/L, whereas the amount in the plasma is between 3.5 and 5 mEq/L. Even though this plasma amount appears to be low, it is of great importance, since serum potassium must be maintained between 3.5 and 5 mEq/L for survival. The diet of most individuals contains from 35 to 100 mEq of potassium daily. Normally, any excess potassium is excreted by the kidney in the urine. Potassium plays an important part of (1) muscle contraction, (2) conduction of nerve impulses, (3) enzyme action, and (4) cell membrane function.

### Hypokalemia

**Hypokalemia** or potassium deficit may be caused by chronic administration of intravenous solutions containing little or no potassium; diuretic therapy with potassium-depleting medications; reduced dietary intake as in persons on "starvation diets"; poor absorption because of steatorrhea, regional enteritis, or short bowel syndrome; loss of gastrointestinal secretions, which are very rich in potassium, because of vomiting, diarrhea, gastrointestinal suction or fistula drainage; extensive burn conditions, and in the presence of excessive amounts of adrenocortical hormone.

Unlike sodium, which is reabsorbed when the serum sodium level is low, potassium ions continue to be excreted in the urine when the serum potassium level is low. As potassium loss continues, the individual's condition deteriorates unless potassium intake is increased and normal levels are reestablished.

With hypokalemia, impaired muscle function occurs. Impairment of skeletal muscle function may cause profound weakness or paralysis, including paralysis of the respiratory muscles. Impaired smooth muscle function may result in ileus.

Cardiac effects of hypokalemia include increased sensitivity to digitalis with potential toxicity and ECG changes such as ST segment depression, U waves, and T wave flattening, depression, or inversion. For example, early potassium deficiency may be detected by the use of the electrocardiogram. The T wave tends to flatten when serum potassium levels are below 3.5 mEq/L. The T wave tends to elongate vertically when the serum potassium level is 5.8 mEq/L or higher. Atrioventricular block and cardiac arrest may occur.

Hypokalemia also causes movement of Na$^+$ and H$^+$ from extracellular fluid and the excretion of H$^+$. This elevates the plasma pH, which results in **metabolic alkalosis.** Other effects are decreased water reabsorption in the renal tubule, resulting in polyuria, and hypochloremia.

Hypokalemia is treated by replacing potassium orally or parenterally. A hazard of parenteral correction of potassium deficit is the production of potassium poisoning, or hyperkalemia.

***Parenteral or intravenous administration.*** The dosage of potassium supplements depends on the individual requirements of the client, and it requires close monitoring of laboratory values. Intravenous potassium solutions must always be *diluted* and administered slowly. Potassium generally is only given to individuals with a documented adequate urine flow. In dehydrated clients, it is best to give a potassium-free fluid first to hydrate the client and determine urinary output.

It has been generally recommended (AHFS, 1991) that parenteral fluids should not contain more than 40 mEq/L of potassium and the rate of administration should not be more than 20 mEq/hour. Whenever possible, the oral preparations or consumption of foods high in potassium should replace the intravenous potassium solutions (see Chapter 33, Diuretics).

The parenteral potassium salts are available as potassium chloride, potassium acetate, and potassium phosphate. Generally, the potassium chloride is the preferred preparation, since the chloride ion is present also to correct the hypochloremia that often is seen with hypokalemia. The alkalinizing potassium salts (potassium bicarbonate, potassium acetate, potassium citrate, or potassium gluconate) may be necessary to treat hypokalemia associated with metabolic acidosis (a rare situation).

***Oral administration.*** Potassium acetate, potassium bicarbonate, potassium chloride, potassium citrate, and potassium gluconate are available alone or in combinations for oral administration. Liquid preparations are generally preferred for oral therapy and most contain 10, 20, or 40 mEq of potassium/15 ml. These preparations must be diluted with fruit juice or water before ingestion and taken after meals with a full glass of water to minimize the gastrointestinal irritation. For powder preparations, closely follow the manufacturer's instructions. See Table 71-5 for a listing of oral potassium preparations.

The uncoated and enteric-coated dosage forms of potassium have caused intestinal and gastric ulcers with bleeding episodes. Although still available, they are rarely used medically. Instead, liquid, effervescent preparations, powders, and extended-release dosage forms (wax matrix, microencapsulated) are the currently available preferred products. The nurse should be aware that ulceration has also been reported with the extended-release products (although much less frequently than with the other products), and these preparations should be reserved for clients that cannot or will not take the liquid or effervescent potassium.

If the client complains of stomach pain, swelling, or severe vomiting, or gastrointestinal bleeding is noted, the extended-release potassium should be stopped immediately and the physician should be contacted. Potassium supplements are contraindicated in clients with severe renal impairment, untreated chronic adrenocortical insufficiency (Addison's disease), hyperkalemia, and severe burn conditions or acute dehydration. They should also be avoided or used with extreme caution in persons taking potassium sparing diuretics or angiotensin-converting enzyme (ACE) inhibitors. Solid dosage forms of potassium should not be administered to clients with esophageal compression caused by an enlarged left atrium or other anatomic variation resulting in increased compression in this area. In such cases, ingestion of potassium-rich foods may also be helpful.

Approximately 45 mEq of potassium may be added to the diet by consuming 2 medium-sized bananas and 8 ounces of orange juice; 40 mEq of potassium may be derived from eating 20 large dried apricots, and a cup of dates will yield 36 mEq. A salt substitute (KCl) may provide 60 mEq of potassium/level teaspoon.

The dosage of potassium supplements depends on individual requirements. The approximate daily allowance for adults is 40 to 50 mEq; for infants, about 2 to 3 mEq/kg body weight daily. Oral dosage usually is increased gradually over a 3- to 7-day period to avoid producing hyperkalemia.

### Hyperkalemia

**Hyperkalemia,** or potassium excess, can be caused by acute or chronic renal failure; the release of large amounts of intracellular potassium in burns, crush injuries or severe infections; overtreatment with potassium salts; or metabolic acidosis, including diabetic ketoacidosis, which causes a shift of potassium from the cells into the extracellular fluids.

Hyperkalemia causes interference with neuromuscular function, which can produce weakness and paralysis. Abdominal distention and diarrhea also occur. Cardiac effects caused by hyperkalemia result from impaired conduction. The ECG shows widening and slurring of the QRS complexes, peaked T waves, depressed ST segments, and possibly disappearance of P waves. Ventricular fibrillation and cardiac arrest may occur.

The treatment of hyperkalemia depends on the serum level

**TABLE 71-5** Oral potassium preparations

| Products | Strength | Additional information |
|---|---|---|
| **LIQUIDS** | | |
| potassium chloride | 10 mEq/15 ml | (5% KCl solution) |
| Potassine | 15 mEq/15 ml | Contains saccharin |
| potassium chloride | | |
| Cena-K | | Contains saccharin |
| Kaochlor 10% | | Contains 5% alcohol, tartrazine, and saccharin, sucrose |
| Kaochlor S-F | | Contains 5% alcohol and saccharin |
| Kay Ciel | 20 mEq/15 ml | Contains 4% alcohol and saccharin |
| Klorvess 10% | | Contains 0.75% alcohol, saccharin; sodium benzoate, sucrose |
| Potachlor 10% | | Contains 5% alcohol; tartrazine |
| potassium chloride | 30 mEq/15 ml | |
| Rum-K | | Alcohol free; butter rum flavor |
| potassium chloride | | |
| Kaon-Cl 20% | | Contains 5% alcohol and saccharin |
| Potachlor 20% | 40 mEq/15 ml | Alcohol free; cherry flavor |
| potassium gluconate | 20 mEq/15 ml | |
| Kaon | | Contains 5% alcohol, saccharin |
| Kaylixir | | Contains 5% alcohol, saccharin |
| K-G Elixir | | Contains 5% alcohol |
| Combinations | | |
| Trikates (Tri-k) | 45 mEq/15 ml K (from K acetate, K bicarbonate, K citrate) | Contains saccharin |
| Twin-K | 20 mEq Potassium gluconate and citrate | Contains sorbitol, saccharin |
| Twin-K-Cl | 15 mEq/K and 4 mEq Cl/15 ml (K gluconate, K citrate and ammonium chloride) | Contains sorbitol, saccharin |
| Kolyum | 20 mEq/K and 3.4 mEq Cl/15 ml (from K gluconate and KCl) | |
| **POWDERS** | | |
| K-Lor | 15 mEq KCl/pkt and 20 mEq KCl | Saccharin; fruit flavor |
| Klor-Con | | Saccharin; fruit flavor |
| Klor-Con/25 | 25 mEq KCl/pkt | Contains saccharin; fruit flavor |
| K-Lyte/Cl | 25 mEq KCl | Contains fruit punch flavor |
| Klorvess Effervescent Granules | 20 mEq each K and Cl (from potassium chloride, bicarbonate, citrate, and lysine HCl)/pkt | Sodium free; saccharin |
| **EFFERVESCENT TABLETS** (must be dissolved in water) | | |
| Klorvess | 20 mEq KCl (from potassium chloride, bicarbonate) | Sodium free; contains saccharin |
| K-Lyte/Cl | 25 mEq KCl (from potassium chloride and bicarbonate, 1-lysine monohydrochloride and citric acid) | Contains saccharin; fruit punch or citrus flavor |
| K-Lyte/Cl 50 | 50 mEq K (same as above) | |
| Effer-K | 25 mEq K (bicarbonate and citrate) | Saccharin; orange flavor |
| K-Lyte | | Contains saccharin; orange or lime flavor |
| K-Lyte DS | 50 mEq K (as bicarbonate and citrate) | Contains saccharin; orange or lime flavor |
| **CAPSULES AND TABLETS** | | |
| potassium chloride tablets | 1.33 mEq, 8 mEq, 10 mEq | |
| Kaon-Cl | Controlled-release tablets (6.7 mEq (500 mg) KCl in wax matrix | Contains tartrazine |
| Klor-Con 8; Slow-K | Controlled-release tablets, 8 mEq (600 mg) KCl in wax matrix | Contains sodium benzoate, sucrose |
| Kaon Cl-10; Klor-Con-10 | Controlled-release tablets, 10 mEq (750) KCl in wax matrix | |
| Klotrix | Same as previous | |
| K-Tab | Same as previous | |
| K-Dur, Ten-K | Controlled-release tablets, microcrystalloids; 10 mEq (750 mg) KCl | |

of potassium and the electrocardiogram (ECG) patterns. If the serum level is below 6.5 mEq/L and the ECG changes are limited to peaking of the T waves, then this may be considered mild hyperkalemia. If the serum level of potassium is between 6.5 and 8 mEq/L with ECG changes limited to peaking of the T waves, then this is moderate hyperkalemia. Severe hyperkalemia is described as a serum level of potassium above 8 Eq/L with an ECG pattern of absent P waves, widened QRS complex or ventricular dysrhythmias.

For mild hypokalemia treatment includes removing or treating the cause. For example, if the client is receiving potassium supplements or diuretics with a potassium-sparing property, stop the medications. If metabolic acidosis is present, then treat this condition.

Moderate to severe hyperkalemia may require more aggressive therapy. Infusing hypertonic dextrose solutions will help shift potassium into the cells. Insulin has been used, especially in diabetic clients with hyperkalemia; it also reduces potassium serum levels by 1 to 2 mEq/L for hours. Sodium bicarbonate parenterally will also help shift serum potassium into the cells. Calcium gluconate intravenously is administered under constant ECG monitoring for the client who has severe cardiac toxicity. The calcium helps counteract the adverse effects of potassium on the neuromuscular membranes, so this is a temporary measure only. Lowering of the potassium levels is critical to reversing this situation.

All of the above-described methods do not remove potassium from the body. Sodium polystyrene sulfonate (Kayexalate) is a cation exchange resin that can be given orally or rectally to reduce potassium serum levels. A single enema can reduce the serum of potassium by 0.5 to 2 mEq/L within 1 hour. Additional enemas can be given if necessary.

The potassium is eliminated with feces or enema. Laxatives must be used when the drug is given orally. Since its action is considered slow, the previously discussed treatments are indicated if ECG changes indicate severe potassium intoxication. Administration should be discontinued when the serum potassium level falls to 4 or 5 mEq/L.

Side effects of sodium polystyrene sulfonate treatment include anorexia, nausea, vomiting, constipation, hypokalemia, and hypocalcemia. Fecal impaction has also been reported; it can be prevented with the use of laxatives.

The oral dose of sodium polystyrene sulfonate for adults is 15 g, one to four times daily in 20 to 100 ml of water or syrup. Add sorbitol to reduce the possibility of constipation. The rectal dose for adults is 25 to 100 g of the resin suspended in 100 ml of sorbitol or 10% dextrose in water. This dose may be administered every 6 hours. The solution should be retained rectally for several hours, if possible. Then, to remove the resin, administer a cleansing enema.

## Calcium

Calcium ($Ca^{++}$) is essential for growth and bone ossification, neuromuscular transmission, cell membrane permeability, the maintenance of excitability in nerve fibers, hormone secretion and action, muscle contraction, maintenance of cardiac and vascular tone, many enzyme activities, and the normal coagulation of blood.

Almost all of the 1000 to 1200 g calcium in the normal adult is in the skeletal tissue, and only about 1% of the total body calcium is in solution in body fluids. About half the calcium in plasma is bound to complex organic anions (e.g., bicarbonate and phosphate). Almost all unbound serum calcium is ionized. Normal serum calcium concentration is 4.5 to 5.5 mEq/L or 9 to 11 mg/100 ml.

The recommended dietary allowance of calcium for adults is 800 to 1200 mg daily. Pregnant or lactating women need 1.2 g; children 6 to 18 years of age need 0.8 to 1.2 g. The intake of calcium in a balanced diet is sufficient for normal body needs. Absorption of calcium depends on how well it is kept in solution in the digestive tract. An acid medium favors calcium solubility; thus calcium is absorbed mainly in the upper intestinal tract. Absorption is decreased by the presence of alkalis and large amounts of fatty acids, with which the calcium forms insoluble soaps. Adequate intake of vitamin D appears to promote calcium absorption. Calcium is excreted in the urine and feces, as well as in perspiration. Estrogen deficiency promotes calcium loss.

Maintenance of normal concentration of serum calcium depends on the interactions of three agents: parathyroid hormone, vitamin D, and calcitonin. Parathyroid hormone and vitamin D mobilize the removal of calcium from bone, the principal source of calcium for extracellular fluids. Parathyroid hormone also promotes renal tubular reabsorption of calcium and a slight increase in intestinal absorption of calcium. Calcitonin is synthesized in the thyroid gland; it moderates or decreases the rate of removal of calcium from the bone.

### Hypocalcemia

**Hypocalcemia,** a decrease in serum calcium, results from (1) hypoparathyroidism, (2) chronic renal insufficiency, (3) hypoalbuminemia, (4) malabsorption syndrome, and (5) deficiency of vitamin D. Hypoparathyroidism may follow thyroidectomy, since several parathyroid glands frequently are removed with this surgery. If the function of the remaining gland(s) is impaired, the result is depressed parathyroid activity.

Individuals who are bedridden tend to develop a negative calcium balance because the ion is lost from bones and is excreted. This effect is likely to be serious when long immobilization of the patient is necessary.

Hypocalcemia causes increased excitability of the nerves and neuromuscular junction, which leads to muscle cramps, muscle twitching, and tetany. Numbness and tingling of the fingers, toes, and lips occur. The hypertonicity of muscle may cause tonic contractions of the hands and feet (carpopedal spasm). The increased neural excitability may cause convulsions, abnormal behavior, and personality changes. In children, prolonged hypocalcemia has resulted in mental

**TABLE 71-6**  Calcium content of various calcium salts

| | Percent calcium | Amount calcium/amount salt per tablet | Tablets needed for 1 g calcium |
|---|---|---|---|
| calcium carbonate | 40 | 250 mg/625 mg | 4 |
| calcium gluconate | 9 | 45 mg/500 mg | 22 |
| calcium lactate | 13 | 42 mg/325 mg | 24 |
| calcium phosphate dibasic | 23 | 115 mg/500 mg | 9 |
| calcium phosphate tribasic | 38 | 304 mg/800 mg | 4 |

retardation. Other effects of hypocalcemia include dyspnea, laryngeal spasm, diplopia, abdominal cramps, and urinary frequency. Diminished cardiac contractility may occur. The ECG shows a prolonged QT interval and an inverted T wave. In prolonged hypocalcemia, defects can occur in the nails, skin, and teeth; cataracts may appear; and calcification of the basal ganglia may occur.

Regardless of the underlying cause, severe hypocalcemia is treated initially with intravenous administration of rapidly available calcium ions. For latent tetany, mild symptoms of hypocalcemia, and maintenance therapy, a calcium salt is given orally. Vitamin D may be given. Parathyroid injection is now considered obsolete and is not used for therapy; its biologic activity is uncertain. Overdosage of calcium may cause hypercalcemia, which results in anorexia, nausea, vomiting, weakness, depression, polyuria, and polydipsia. Calcium must be administered cautiously to clients on digitalis therapy, since calcium potentiates the effect of digitalis and may precipitate dysrhythmias. ECG monitoring of the client is recommended when parenteral calcium is administered.

Calcium salts are used as a nutritional supplement, particularly during pregnancy and lactation. They are specific in the treatment of hypocalcemic tetany. They have also been used for their antispasmodic effects in cases of abdominal pain, tenesmus, and colic resulting from disease of the gallbladder or painful contractions of the ureters. The basic salts of calcium are also used as antacids. Although controversial, approximately 1 to 1.5 g calcium per day has been recommended to prevent postmenopausal bone loss or osteoporosis.

The most widely used calcium salt is calcium carbonate. It requires an acid medium to form soluble calcium salts, since it is nearly insoluble in water. Absorption of or dissolution of calcium phosphate and calcium sulfate are also pH dependent, whereas calcium lactate, calcium citrate, and calcium gluconate are considered pH independent. In elderly persons and postmenopausal women, an impaired stomach acid production is noted. The higher stomach pH or achlorhydric state will result in a decreased solubility of the pH-dependent calcium salts.

Since the different calcium salts have different amounts of calcium present, many professionals choose the calcium salt with the highest percentage of calcium per gram present

**TABLE 71-7**  Foods with high calcium content

| Food | Calcium content |
|---|---|
| Yogurt, low fat (1 cup) | 400 mg |
| Skim milk (1 cup) | 300 mg |
| Cheese, Swiss (1 ounce) | 250 mg |
| Cheese, cottage (1 cup) | 215 mg |
| Cheese, cheddar (1 ounce) | 200 mg |
| Broccoli, raw | 100 mg |
| Ice cream (½ cup) | 100 mg |

because it would then require a smaller quantity of drug to be administered. For example, if the recommended daily dose of calcium is 1000 mg/day, then it would be necessary to administer nearly 10 g calcium gluconate to reach this amount; whereas only 2.5 g calcium carbonate per day would be required. This would require the consumption of smaller quantities of tablets to obtain the same amount of calcium. This, of course, is assuming all the present calcium is soluble under the conditions present in the client (See Table 71-6).

To improve the solubility of calcium carbonate tablets, especially in individuals that might be achlorhydric, it is recommended that the tablets be taken with meals, when acid secretion is highest. Avoid taking the tablets on an empty stomach or at night because these are times when acid secretions are minimal. Calcium phosphates and tricalcium phosphate have little usefulness in possible achlorhydric states and perhaps, even in the normal person. Both products have a very poor dissolution rate or pattern, thus reducing the possibility of calcium absorption. Perhaps in clients with known achlorhydric states, the soluble calcium salts (lactate or citrate) might be the appropriate form to use even though it will be necessary to use more tablets to provide sufficient quantities of calcium.

Selected food consumption is another source for calcium. See Table 71-7 for foods with a high calcium content.

### Hypercalcemia

**Hypercalcemia,** or elevated serum calcium levels, may be caused by neoplasms with or without bone metastases. Carcinoma of the ovary, kidney, or lung can synthesize and secrete a parathyroid-like hormone, causing hypercalcemia. Other common causes are hyperparathyroidism, thiazide or diuretic therapy, multiple myeloma, sarcoidosis, and vitamin D intoxication.

Clinical manifestations of hypercalcemia are highly variable and involve many organ systems. Calcium may be deposited in various body tissues.

Gastrointestinal symptoms are anorexia, nausea and vomiting, constipation, and abdominal pain.

Central nervous system symptoms include apathy, depression, amnesia, headaches, and drowsiness. In severe cases, disorientation, syncope, hallucinations, and coma may occur.

Renal symptoms include polyuria and polydipsia, which occur from loss of renal-concentrating ability. Kidney stones may be formed. Nephrocalcinosis may occur, seriously impairing renal function. This may lead to edema, uremia, and hypertension, which may be irreversible.

In the neuromuscular system, neural excitability is diminished, causing weakness and muscle flaccidity.

Cardiovascular symptoms include elevated serum calcium, which causes increased cardiac contractility, ventricular extrasystoles, and heart block. ECG changes include a short QT segment and characteristic signs of heart block. In severe calcium toxicity, cardiac arrest in systole may occur.

Treatment is variable and aimed at controlling the underlying disease. If hypercalcemia is caused by thiazide diuretic therapy, the diuretic is discontinued; the serum calcium returns to normal levels in about 1 month.

Renal excretion of calcium can be promoted with several drugs. Infusions of sodium chloride may be given to increase sodium excretion, which in turn increases calcium excretion. Natriuretic drugs, such as furosemide (Lasix) or ethacrynic acid (Edecrin), may be used. Chelating (binding) agents, such as disodium edetate, increase renal excretion of calcium by forming soluble complexes with the calcium that are not reabsorbed by the renal tubules. Inorganic phosphates may be given orally or intravenously to foster deposition of calcium in bone, thereby decreasing serum levels. An antineoplastic drug, mithramycin, also reduces serum calcium levels.

## Magnesium

Magnesium ($Mg^{++}$) is an important ion for the function of many enzyme systems.

### Hypomagnesemia

**Hypomagnesemia,** a deficit of magnesium, may be encountered in chronic alcoholism, severe malabsorption, starvation, diarrhea, prolonged gastrointestinal suction, vigorous diuresis, diseases causing hypocalcemia and hypokalemia, acute pancreatitis, and primary aldosteronism.

Hypomagnesemia is characterized by increased irritability of the nervous system, which may lead to disorientation and convulsions. Increased neuromuscular irritability and contractility also occur. Coarse tremor, muscle spasm, delirium, athetoid movements, and nystagmus may appear. Tetany may occur. Hypomagnesemia also causes tachycardia, hypertension, and vasomotor changes and can increase the risk of digitalis toxicity in persons taking cardiac glycosides.

Hypomagnesemia is treated with intravenous fluids containing magnesium, 10 to 40 mEq/day for severe deficit, followed by 10 mEq/day for maintenance. The use of intravenous fluids containing from 3 to 5 mEq magnesium/L may avert magnesium deficiency that arises from prolonged administration of intravenous solutions that do not contain magnesium.

### Hypermagnesemia

**Hypermagnesemia** occurs primarily in individuals with chronic renal insufficiency. An excess of magnesium causes depression of the central nervous system, which leads to sedation and confusion. Blockade of the myoneural junction occurs by inhibiting acetylcholine release and diminishing muscle cell excitability. This causes muscle weakness. Respiratory muscle paralysis may occur, causing death. Hypermagnesemia also causes blockade of sympathetic ganglia and has a direct vasodilating effect that causes decreased blood pressure.

Excess magnesium has a cardiac inhibitory effect. Conduction time is increased, and the ECG shows a lengthened PR segment and a prolonged QRS complex. If the $Mg^{++}$ concentration continues to increase, cardiac arrest in diastole may occur. Third-degree atrioventricular block may also occur.

An excess of $Mg^{++}$ may require dialysis. Since calcium acts as an antagonist to $Mg^{++}$, calcium salts may be given parenterally. Normal serum concentration is 1.5 to 2.5 mEq/L, with one third bound to protein and two thirds as free cation. A toxic blood level is greater than 4 mEq/L. About 50% of the total body magnesium exists in an insoluble state in bone, 45% is intracellular cation, and 5% extracellular cation. The normal dietary intake of magnesium has a range of approximately 8 to 24 mEq/24 hours in the adult (recommended dietary allowance is 300 to 400 mg daily). Magnesium is excreted by way of the kidney. Magnesium has physiologic effects on the nervous system similar to those of calcium.

## Additional Single-Salt Solutions

In addition to the previously discussed salt preparations, ammonium chloride injection and sodium lactate injection are also available for use.

Ammonium chloride injection is indicated to treat hypochloremia and metabolic alkalosis (not associated with severe liver disease) to prevent tetany or renal damage. Most cases will respond to sodium chloride solution, but for the rare, nonresponsive situation, ammonium chloride is available. Ammonium chloride has been used as a urinary acidifier (to promote excretion of alkaline substances). This product is most often required for infants that have severe, protracted vomiting caused by pyloric obstruction. It is available as a 2.14% solution (0.4 mEq/ml) and must be infused slowly to allow for metabolism of the ammonium ions by the liver to avoid ammonia toxicity.

Sodium lactate injection is available as a ⅙ molar solution containing 167 mEq/L each of sodium and lactate ions. It is used to treat metabolic acidosis when no evidence of an elevated lactic acid level exists. Sodium lactate is converted to sodium bicarbonate in the liver. In persons with lactic acidosis or impaired liver function, sodium bicarbonate should be administered.

## ▷NURSING MANAGEMENT: INTRAVENOUS THERAPY

With the increasing prevalence of clients receiving some type of intravascular therapy in hospitals, as well as in home settings, the role of the nurse in intravenous therapy has also grown and developed.

*Assessment.* Assessment begins with an understanding of the purpose of the particular client's intravenous therapy and his or her potential risks. Every individual with an intravenous infusion runs the risk of circulatory overload, iatrogenic starvation or dehydration, infiltration, phlebitis, air embolism, infection of the site, or sepsis. Because of their smaller body size, infants and children are especially at risk for overhydration. Those who are debilitated, have a renal or cardiovascular problem, are prone to infection, or have badly sclerosed veins are particularly at risk. Continued reassessments of laboratory data reports are essential for patients receiving electrolyte replacement therapy. Serum electrolytes should not exceed the following accepted ranges during intravenous therapy:

| | |
|---|---|
| Sodium | 135 to 145 mEq/L |
| Chlorides | 95 to 108 mEq/L |
| Potassium | 3.5 to 5 mEq/L |
| Calcium | 4.5 to 5.8 mEq/L |
| Magnesium | 1.5 to 2.5 mEq/L |

Note that fluctuations in potassium, calcium, and magnesium must be watched carefully during intravenous electrolyte therapy, since even a small deviation in these creates a much greater risk than in those electrolytes with a wider range of normal values. Understanding that milliequivalents (mEq) are not related to milligrams also is important; "mEq" does not reflect a measure of weight. **Milliequivalents** measure the number of chemically active ions in solution, which is a more precise measure of the relative potency of an electrolyte solution than weight-by-volume measurements. (See Chapter 6 for equipment and technical aspects of intravenous therapy.)

Remember that ongoing assessment of client response is essential to preventing complications from intravenous therapy. The entire intravenous system should be monitored from fluid container down to the client's infusion site. Such assessments are made frequently in some critical care units. Calculating the need for hourly changes in intravenous flow rates based on patient fluid output may be your responsibility. You may titrate infusion fluid intake according to the amount of hourly urine, gastric, or other outputs over specified periods.

*Complications.* Ongoing assessment of the client receiving intravenous therapy should include observations for the following complications:

*Infiltration.* Infiltration occurs when the needle is dislodged from the vein, permitting the solution to enter the surrounding tissues, which causes pain and edema. Clients or family members should be informed to notify the nurse if pain or swelling occurs at the infusion site. In addition, nurses should check the infusion site frequently for signs of infiltration and stop the infusion if infiltration occurs. Restarting intravenous therapy usually requires a new infusion site.

Infiltration is especially serious when infusions of vasopressors (e.g., norepinephrine, dopamine) or vesicants (e.g., many antineoplastic agents) are involved. See "necrosis" on p. 1078.

*Thrombosis.* An intravascular blood clot occurs when platelets agglutinate and fibrin strands and red and white blood cells adhere to the platelet mass. A thrombus may form any time a blood vessel is injured, including injury by venipuncture. A thrombus may form in or around the needle or catheter, plugging the lumen; if this occurs, the infusion stops. The infusion should be restarted at a new site with a new needle or catheter. Attempts to unplug the needle by forcing a bolus of solution in a syringe through the needle into the vein is unwise and unsafe. The thrombus may become an embolus and lodge in a vital organ, causing more serious complications such as pulmonary embolus.

*Thrombophlebitis.* Blood clot formation and inflammation of the vein may result from several factors: prolonged duration of infusion, use of contaminated equipment or contaminated solutions, irritation from drugs in the infusion, toxicity and pH of the solution, the use of leg vein as site of administration, and infection. Thrombophlebitis is manifested by pain, heat, swelling, redness along the vein's course, and loss of motion of the affected part. When this occurs, the infusion should be stopped, the needle withdrawn, and the condition reported and recorded immediately. Treatment usually consists of applying moist heat to the affected area and resting the body part; anticoagulant therapy also may be ordered.

Nurses should take the necessary precautions to prevent thrombophlebitis by doing the following:

- Using sterile aseptic technique with proper cleansing of skin before insertion of the needle
- Being certain equipment is not contaminated
- Checking solutions for precipitation, debris, sediment, or change in color before and during intravenous therapy
- Ascertaining that no intravenous bottle or tubing is left in place for more than 24 hours, since some organisms proliferate at room temperature in intravenous fluids
- Changing the intravenous setup every 24 hours to reduce the possibility of sepsis
- Administering irritating drugs slowly
- Avoiding intravenous needle infusion into leg veins or small veins

*Pain at administration site.* Pain occurs when (1) the needle touches the venous wall, (2) too much tension is put on the needle or tubing, and (3) irritating drugs are administered too rapidly. Adjusting the needle, relieving the tension by readjusting the needle support or relaxing the pull on the tubing, and administering irritating drugs at a slow rate may alleviate the pain and discomfort.

*Necrosis.* Death and sloughing of tissue can occur when irritating drugs or solutions, such as epinephrine or levarterenol, infiltrate into the tissues. The infusion should be stopped *immediately*. If the infiltration contains levarterenol, the antidote phentolamine (Regitine) may be injected subcutaneously in minute amounts immediately at many sites in the edematous area.

*Pulmonary edema.* Pulmonary edema occurs when the circulatory system is overloaded with fluids. Careful monitoring of flow rate and of urinary output is necessary. Central venous pressure monitoring, particularly in clients with cardiac disease, can help to prevent this hazardous complication.

*Pyrogenic reactions.* Pyrogenic reactions occur when pyrogens, or fever-producing substances, are introduced into the circulatory system. Bacterial pyrogens are filtrable, thermostable products of bacterial origin and activity that may accumulate and tend to cause a severe rigor when injected into the body. Pyrogenic reactions are characterized by fever and chills, malaise, headache, nausea, and vomiting. The infusion should be stopped *at once*. The solution should not be discarded but instead sent to the pharmacist. Pyrogenic reactions must be reported and recorded. The stock number should be noted, since an entire batch of solutions may be contaminated.

• • •

Note that the recommended system for surveillance and reporting of problems with large-volume parenteral solutions in hospitals has been delegated to the National Coordinating Committee on Large-Volume Parenterals. The Committee is composed of legally recognized standards-setting bodies, enforcement agencies, and national groups with a major influence over the manufacture and use of large-volume parenteral solutions. Organizations represented on the committee are the American Hospital Association, American Medical Association, American Nurses' Association, American Society of Hospital Pharmacists, Centers for Disease Control, Food and Drug Administration, Joint Commission on Accreditation of Hospitals, National Association of Boards of Pharmacy, National Association for Practical Nurse Education and Service, Parenteral Drug Association, The United States Pharmacopeial Convention, and major large-volume parenteral manufacturers (Abbott, Cutter, McGraw, Travenol). The committee's mission is to find workable solutions to those large-volume parenteral problems judged to have the greatest clinical significance. The National Intravenous Therapy Association is composed largely of intravenous team nurses who make procedure and policy recommendations. The recommendations relate to problems with large-volume parenteral solutions in health care facilities, methods for compounding intravenous admixtures in hospitals, labeling of large-volume parenteral solutions, and procedures for in-use testing for contamination or adverse reactions and for filter selection.

***Intervention.*** Intravenous fluid and dextrose or electrolyte replacement by infusion continues to be the most common application of intravascular therapy. Although the dosage and choice of solution is tailored to the client's needs by the physician according to the disorder and body surface area, monitoring the therapy is the nurse's responsibility. A member of the therapy team, the nurse, or the physician may be responsible for initiating therapy by inserting the necessary needle or catheter.

Consider intravascular therapy a closed-system, sterile procedure. It is invasive, and its effects are relatively irreversible. Therefore take care to perform and maintain it precisely. Maintain a steady, even flow at the rate ordered; do not speed up rates to make up for lost time (watch the literature, however, for a resolution of the question about slowed rates being more compatible with basal metabolic rates during the before-dawn hours). Use every aid to facilitate therapy, such as calculating drops to be infused per minute and then time-taping the container. Do not allow containers to empty completely, since air in the tubing could be driven into the vein when another full container is attached. Throughout all client activities keep containers about 3 feet above the site. If too high, the solution will infuse too rapidly; if too low, blood may find its way into the needle or tubing and clot there. Consult agency infusion specialists such as members of the intravenous therapy team, when available, if you encounter difficulties.

Be aware of the options available in selecting a filter for the intravenous infusion. Several different intravenous filter products are designed for different filtration needs. Filters are available in a range of sizes and in add-on or in-line form:

- A 5 μm filter removes *particulate* material and is designed to filter gross particulate matter. The smallest particle visible to the unaided eye is approximately 30 μm across.
- A 0.5 μm filter is considered a *bacteria-retention* filter, which is designed to prevent passage of most particulate matter and certain fungi and bacteria. A yeast cell is approximately 3 μm in diameter.
- The 0.22 μm filter is called a *sterilizing* filter, since it is designed to prevent passage of virtually all particulate matter and most bacteria for at least 24 hours. Bacteria range in size from 0.2 to 2 μm in diameter. Travenol Laboratories and other manufacturers provide these filters for use with the add-on or in-line systems. Select a 0.22 μm filter for parenteral nutrition solutions.

***Education.*** If your client is a child, keep in mind that intravenous therapy may be a frightening experience.

Instruct the client receiving intravenous therapy to report to the nurse any symptoms of the complications previously mentioned.

## SUMMARY

The administration of intravenous fluids and electrolytes has become commonplace in the experience of hospitalized clients. They are administered for a variety of reasons: to replace fluids and electrolytes, to correct acid-base imbalance, to administer medications, to maintain access to the venous system, to measure changes in the venous pressure, to measure renal function, and to administer essential nutrients. With the increased prevalence of intravascular therapy, the role of the nursing management in intravenous therapy has also grown and developed.

## BIBLIOGRAPHY

Abramowicz M, ed. (1987). Prevention and treatment of postmenopausal osteoporosis, The Medical Letter 29:746.

American Hospital Formulary Service. (1991). AHFS drug information '91. Bethesda, Md: American Society of Hospital Pharmacists.

Barker C. (1989). Is it drug toxicity—or something else? Nursing 19(4):84.

Barrus DH et al. (1987). Should you irrigate an occluded I.V. line? Nursing 17(3):63.

Beckwith N. (1987). Fundamentals of fluid resuscitation, Nursinglife 7(3):49.

Bryan CS. (1987). "CDC says . . .": the case of IV tubing replacement, Infect Control 8(6):255.

Buckalew VM Jr. (1986). Hyponatremia: pathogenesis and management, Hosp Pract 21(11):49.

Coward DD. (1986). Cancer-induced hypercalcemia, Cancer Nurs 9(3):125.

Davidson ED. (1986). Handbook of nonprescription drugs, ed 8.

Washington, DC: American Pharmaceutical Association and The National Professional Society of Pharmacists.

DiPiro JT et al. (1989). Pharmacotherapy: a pathophysiologic approach. New York: Elsevier.

Farley JM. (1989). Myths and facts . . . about electrolytes, Nursing 19(10):80.

Felver L et al. (1989). Home study program: electrolyte imbalances . . . intraoperative risk factors, AORN J 49(4):989.

Flink EB. (1987). Magnesium deficiency: causes and effects, Hosp Pract 22(2):116A.

Gaspario L et al. (1989). IV solutions: which one's right for your patient? Nursing 19(4):62.

Gilman AG et al, eds. (1990). Goodman & Gilman's the pharmacological basis of therapeutics, ed 8. New York: Macmillan Publishing Co.

Goodinson SM. (1990). The risks of IV therapy, Prof Nurse 5(5):235.

Hinkle AJ. (1989). Pediatric blood and fluid therapy, part 1, Curr Rev Nurse Anesth 12(6):43.

Hinkle AJ. (1989). Pediatric blood and fluid therapy, part 2, Curr Rev Nurse Anesth 12(7):51.

Holder C et al. (1990). A new and improved guide to IV therapy . . . protocols for intravenous therapy, Am J Nurs 90(2):43.

Kastrup EK, ed. (1991). Facts and comparisons. St Louis: JB Lippincott Co.

Lenox AC. (1990). IV therapy: reducing the risk of infection, Nursing 20(3):60.

Ley SJ et al. (1990). Crystalloid versus colloid fluid therapy after cardiac surgery, Heart Lung 19(1):31.

Linas SL. (1988). Potassium: weighing the evidence for supplementation, Hosp Pract 23(12):73.

Lunger DG. (1988). Potassium supplementation: how and why? Focus Crit Care 15(5):56.

Mahon SM. (1989). Signs and symptoms associated with malignancy-induced hypercalcemia, Cancer Nurs 12(3):153.

Mathewson M. (1989). Intravenous therapy, Crit Care Nurse 9(2):21.

Miller SF. (1988). Review. Calculation of fluid therapy: electrolyte disorders, J Burn Care Rehabil 9(4):413.

Persons CB. (1987). Preventing infection from intravascular devices, Nursing 17(4):75.

Pfister SM et al. (1988). Arterial blood gas evaluation: metabolic acidemia, Crit Care Nurse 8(8):14.

Pierson MG et al. (1989). Technology versus clinical evaluation for fluid management decisions in CABG patients, Image J Nurs Sch 21(4):192.

Rice V. (1983). Magnesium, calcium, and phosphate imbalances: their clinical significance . . . home study program, Crit Care Nurse 3(3):90.

Roberts SL. (1988). Cardiogenic shock: decreased coronary artery tissue perfusion, DCCN 7(4):196.

Roberts MK. (1989). Fluid resuscitation in the adult trauma patient, Orthop Nurs 8(6):41.

Rutherford C. (1989). Fluid and electrolyte therapy: considerations for patient care, J Intravenous Nurs 12(3):173.

Sommers M. (1990). Rapid fluid resuscitation: how to correct dangerous deficits, Nursing 20(1):52.

Stanaszek WF et al. (1985). Current approaches to the management of potassium deficiency, Drug Intell Clin Pharm 19(3):176.

*Chapter*

# 72 Enteral and Parenteral Nutrition

## CHAPTER OBJECTIVES

*After studying this chapter you should be able to meet the following objectives and define the key terms.*

1. Describe common techniques used for the delivery of enteral feedings.

2. Distinguish among elemental, polymeric, modular, and altered amino acid formulations for enteral feedings.

3. Identify major drug-food interactions to be aware of when enteral nutrient formulations are being administered.

4. Develop a nursing care plan for a client receiving enteral formulations.

5. Describe central hyperalimentation and the indications for its use.

6. Identify the components of total parenteral nutrition solutions and the function of each element in the attainment of the body's requirement.

7. Cite possible complications and related nursing management of parenteral nutrition therapy.

## KEY TERMS

**enteral nutrition,** page 1081

**essential amino acids,** page 1086

**hyperalimentation,** page 1085

**nonessential amino acids,** page 1086

**semiessential amino acids,** page 1086

**total parenteral nutrition (TPN),** page 1085

## INTRODUCTION

Pioneers in parenteral hyperalimentation in the late 1960s to the 1970s were Drs. Stanley Dudrick and Jonathan Rhoads. As surgeons and researchers, they were concerned about the tremendous weight loss in acutely ill individuals, so they performed animal studies, and later human studies, to prove their theory that a positive nitrogen balance could be achieved by providing nutrients intravenously.

Since then, many advances have been recorded in the fields of both enteral and parenteral nutrition. Clinical nutrition is now a recognized and active entity for improving health care in all settings, including the client's home, long-term care facilities, and hospitals. Today nutritional programs or specific products have even been developed for individuals with specific disease states or illnesses. In this chapter, enteral and parenteral nutrition will be reviewed, along with selected disease states and criteria for use of the specific nutritional systems.

## ENTERAL NUTRITION

The high incidence of reported malnutrition among hospitalized persons and nursing home residents is associated with such complications as muscle atrophy, slow wound healing, impaired immunocompetence, sepsis, and death. Other signs include peripheral edema caused by reduced plasma proteins, dry and flaky skin, and hair loss. Nearly half of hospitalized patients have some degree of malnutrition; 5% to 10% have severe protein-calorie deficiencies. Malnutrition is reflected in reduced total lymphocyte count, serum albumin and transferin levels, or iron-binding capacity; increased 24-hour urine urea nitrogen concentration reflects protein catabolism.

Stress in relation to hospitalization may alter a client's usual eating habits. Unfamiliar foods and general malaise resulting from illness cause patients to lose their appetites. Oral intake may be inadequate or be impossible because of oropharyngeal surgery, trauma, neoplasm, paralysis, or esophageal fistula. Fasting before surgery or for diagnostic workup also may be depleting. When sepsis, trauma, major surgery, inflammation or infection, or severe burns supervene, energy needs may be doubled. If the gastrointestinal tract is functional, however, enteral or tube feedings may effectively supply essential nutrition. **Enteral nutrition** is the oral or tube feeding of an individual, usually via a nasogastric, nasoduodenal, or esophagostomic tube. The cost per person for tube feedings is about equal to a regular hospital diet and provides more complete control and assessment of intake. Tube feedings also may be used to supplement parenteral nutrition as it is being tapered. Enteral feedings generally are contraindicated in individuals who are capable of oral intake or who have adynamic ileus, intestinal obstruction, intractable vomiting, or esophageal fistulas.

Enteral feedings may be administered by bolus doses, typically 250 to 400 ml of formula every 4 to 6 hours; by intermittent feedings by means of a 20- to 30-minute drip; or by continuous gravity or enteral pumps. The continuous method, for 16 to 24 hours, has had more success because it helps prevent complications such as the dumping syndrome (nausea, vomiting, cramping, diarrhea, and malabsorption caused by sudden influxes of undigested feedings of high osmolality into the small intestine) and obviates the need for frequent tube irrigations. Enteral feedings can be administered by the following routes: nasogastric, nasoduodenal, esophagostomy, gastrostomy, and jejunostomy. The last three are more invasive, requiring surgically created stomas, and thus are less preferred routes. Nasogastric, esophagostomy, and gastrostomy feedings allow for more natural digestion in the stomach and preclude the risk of the dumping syndrome. Aspiration, however, is more likely because gastric reflux can occur, since only the gastroesophageal sphincter is operant. Although feedings administered directly into the small intestine avoid this problem, hypoglycemia and the dumping syndrome may develop because of the sudden influx. Skin excoriation and infection are potential risks in gastrostomies and jejunostomies because the surgical opening penetrates the peritoneum. These com-

plications are avoided in the cervical esophagostomy, a surgically created, skin-lined canal tunneled from the lower neck border and extending to below the cervical esophagus.

The selection of tube feeding formula depends on the client's nutrition needs, organ or metabolic disorders, lactose intolerance, and gastrointestinal competence, as well as on convenience, feasibility, and cost. Nutritional assessment may be based on anthropometric parameters, biochemical data, and physical findings, as well as on medical, diet, drug, and socioeconomic histories. Ideal weight can be obtained from tables or by estimation:

*Men:* 106 pounds (48 kg) for the first 5 feet (150 cm) plus 6 pounds (2.7 kg) per inch (2.5 cm) over 5 feet (plus or minus 10%)

*Women:* 100 pounds (45 kg) for the first 5 feet plus 5 pounds (2.2 kg) per inch over 5 feet (plus or minus 10%)

## Enteral Formulations

Over 80 enteral formulations are available in the U.S. These products can be divided into elemental (monomeric), polymeric, modular, and altered amino acid formulations.

1. Elemental formulations contain dipeptides and tripeptides and/or crystalline amino acids, glucose oligosaccharides, and vegetable oil or the medium-chain triglycerides. This formula requires minimum digestion from the client. The residue is also minimal.

   Elemental formulations are indicated for persons with partial bowel obstruction, inflammatory bowel disease, radiation enteritis, bowel fistulas, and short bowel syndrome.

2. Polymeric formulations contain complex nutrients: protein (e.g., casein and soy protein); carbohydrate (e.g., corn syrup solid, maltodextrins); and fat (vegetable oil or milk fat).

   Polymeric formulas are preferred to elemental formulations for patients with a fully functional gastrointestinal tract who have few or no specialized nutrient requirements. These formulas are preferred because the hyperosmolarity of the elemental formulas causes more gastrointestinal problems than the polymeric formulations. It should not be used in clients with a malabsorption problem.

3. Modular formulations are single-nutrient formulas, i.e., protein, carbohydrate, or fat. Such a formula can be added to a monomeric or polymeric formulation to provide a more individual specialized nutrient formulation.

4. Altered amino acid formulations are indicated for clients with genetic errors of metabolism (e.g., phenylketonuria, homocystinuria, maple syrup urine disease), for clients with acquired disorders of nitrogen accumulation (e.g., cirrhosis or chronic renal failure), and in clients who are catabolic because of injuries or

**TABLE 72-1** Selected commercial enteral formulations

| | Comments |
| --- | --- |
| **ELEMENTAL FORMULATIONS*** | |
| Flexical | Approximately 30% of the calories are from fat. Proteins are short-chain peptides. Lactose free. |
| Vital | Proteins are short-chain peptides. Lower osmolatlity than others. Lactose free. |
| Vivonex | Proteins are amino acids. Lactose free. |
| Vivonex HN | Less fat content than Vivonex. Its higher osmolality necessitates dilution and slower infusion to avoid complaints of cramping. Lactose free. |
| **POLYMERIC FORMULATIONS** | |
| Compleat-B | For tube feedings only. Contains lactose. |
| Ensure | Lactose free. |
| Ensure-Plus | Higher caloric formula. Lactose free. |
| Isocal | For tube feedings only. Lactose free. Low osmolality. |
| Magnacal | Good for clients with sodium or water restrictions. Has a high caloric formula (2 calories/ml). |
| Meritene | High protein formula. Contains lactose. |
| Osmolite | An isotonic formula. Lactose free. |
| Portagen | Used in malabsorption syndromes because the fat content is from MCT oil. Lactose free. |
| Precision LR | Lactose free. Low in fat and residue. |
| Sustacal | Contains a high protein content and lactose. |
| **MODULAR FORMULATIONS** | |
| Carbohydrate | |
|   Controlyte | A carbohydrate supplement. Has low sodium; no vitamins, minerals, or lactose. |
|   Polycose | Unflavored carbohydrate supplement. 2 calories/ml. |
| Fat | |
|   MCT Oil | Fat supplement. Used in malabsorption, GI alterations, and pancreatitis. Contains 94% medium-chain triglyceride. |
| Microlipid | Fat supplement. Is a concentrated source for calories, i.e., it contains 4.5 calories/ml. |
| Proteins | |
|   Amin-aid | Contains a high biologic protein and has high caloric formula (1.9 calories/ml). Used for clients with renal failure (acute and chronic). |
|   Casec | A protein supplement for use in severe burns or trauma, fistulas, and complicated surgery. Contains milk but no vitamins, minerals, or lactose. |
|   Hepatic-Aid Instant Drink Powder, Hepatic-Aid II Instant Drink Powder | Contains high concentrations of branched-chain amino acids and low concentrations of aromatic amino acids to correct for the abnormal serum amino acid profiles. Use in chronic liver disease. |
|   Travasorb Renal Powder | Contains amino acids, glucose, and sucrose and MCT (medium-chain triglycerides). 1.35 calories/ml. For renal failure. |
|   Traum-Aid HBC Powder | Contains amino acids (high BCAA), carbohydrates, and fats (MCT, soybean oil). For trauma and sepsis clients. |
|   Stresstein Powder | Amino acids (BCAA), carbohydrates (maltodextrins), and fats (MCT, soybean oil). Indicated for severe trauma and stress. |
| **ALTERED AMINO ACID FORMULATIONS** | |
| For chronic renal failure: see Amin-aid above. | |
| For pre-eclampsia, congestive heart failure: | |
|   Lonalac | Protein supplement used for low sodium requirements. It has vitamins, trace elements, and lactose. |
| For genetic disorders: | |
|   Phenylketonuria: diet prescribed is low in phenylalanine. Tyrosine may need to be supplemented. | |
|   Homocystinuria: diet low in methionine and cystine | |
|   Maple syrup urine disease: diet low in leucine, isoleucine, and valine | |

*All these elemental formulations contain vitamins and trace elements. They also have 1 calorie/ml.

Chapter 72  Enteral and Parenteral Nutrition    **1083**

infection. (For selected examples of the four categories, see Table 72-1.)

## Drug-Food Interactions

A number of drug-food (nutrient) interactions have been identified, but this possibility is often overlooked when enteral nutrient formulations are being administered. Since the interactions can be clinically significant, the major ones are listed in Table 72-2.

## ▷NURSING MANAGEMENT: ENTERAL NUTRITION THERAPY

*Assessment.* Assess periodically for residual gastric volume and tube placement, particularly before each feeding or before administering a dose of a medication into the feeding tube. For continuous feedings, simply stop the feeding and measure the residual by aspirating the stomach contents with a bulb syringe. It is not necessary to clamp off the tube and wait for an interval of time because these feedings should move through the system continuously. If the residual is greater than 50% of an hour's volume, return the aspirate and notify the physician. For cyclic administration, measure residual volume halfway between feedings.

If the residual is more than 50% of the volume of the previous feeding, return the aspirate and consult with the physician. In both of these instances, a reduction in the volume of the feeding may be necessary.

Monitor bowel sounds to ensure that the client has good bowel function. Fluid intake and output should be carefully documented. If the client develops diarrhea, the physician needs to be consulted.

Many types of enteral formulas are lactose-free (non-milk proteins are the base) for clients who lack sufficient lactase in intestinal brush bodies for lactose absorption. Blacks, Orientals, American Indians, and Jews are particularly prone to lactase deficiency. Lactose ingestion causes varying degrees of diarrhea, abdominal cramps, bloating, and flatulence. Isotonic formulas may be useful to prevent the dumping syndrome.

*Intervention.* Although the gastrointestinal tract is the optimal route for nutrient administration, in many ill clients the normal ingestion of food is difficult, if not nearly impossible, to achieve. The availability of many enteral nutrient preparations was designed for such persons. These formulations may be given by the nasoenteral route through thin, flexible tubing that is generally well tolerated by the client. These feeding tubes are now made from silicone or polyurethane compounds and have much smaller lumen

**TABLE 72-2**  Drug-food interactions

| Drug(s) | Food or nutrient | Possible effect/management |
|---|---|---|
| ampicillin | Decrease in serum levels by food. | Administer on an empty stomach. |
| aspirin | Absorption prolonged by food. | Administer with milk or crackers; avoid giving on a full stomach. |
| cephalosporins (cefamandole, cefaperazone, moxalactam) | Absorption prolonged by food. May produce disulfiram reaction if alcohol is present. | Administer on schedule. Avoid alcohol-containing medications, beverages, sauces and topical preparations. |
| doxycycline | Iron will reduce serum levels of antibiotic. | Schedule iron preparations and doxycycline about 3 hr apart. |
| oxacillin | Absorption prolonged and serum levels decreased. | Administer on an empty stomach. |
| tetracyclines (with exception of doxycycline and minocycline) | Milk, dairy items, eggs, cereals, and divalent and trivalent cautions. | Administer on an empty stomach. |
| digoxin | Absorption prolonged or delayed if given with food. | Be consistent; give digoxin with or without food. This will reduce problems with bioavailability. |
| griseofulvin | Absorption is increased in presence of fats. | If client appears to have an inadequate absorption, consider giving the drug with a high fat meal. |
| levodopa | High protein diets will delay and prolong absorption. | Schedule apart from a high protein meal. |
| metoprolol, propranolol, phenytoin | Food will increase absorption and bioavailability. | Be consistent; give medication with or without food. This will reduce problems of fluctation in bioavailability. |
| warfarin | Foods with high vitamin K will reduce the anticoagulant action. | Avoid excessive consumption of foods with high vitamin K content (broccoli, spinach, and other green, leafy vegetables). |

sizes, No. 5 through 10 French. These are much preferred to the older, thicker rubber or polyvinyl chloride types (Salem pump, Levin tube) that stiffen in contact with digestive juices. Aspiration for residual gastrointestinal contents and irrigation of these small-lumen tubes, however, may be more difficult than with the older, larger types.

Small-diameter feeding tubes also get clogged more easily. To prevent this formula residue buildup, some suggest flushing tubes every 4 hours (and each time feeding is interrupted) with 20 ml of cranberry juice followed by 10 ml of water. Acidity of the juice breaks up the formula residue, and the water prevents sugar from crystallizing.

Transnasal tube placement in the intestine requires the use of longer, mercury- or tungsten-weighted feeding tubes that gradually are passed by peristalsis. This takes about 24 hours, and radiographic confirmation of tube placement must be made.

If tube feedings must be administered for long time periods, then the surgical placement of a gastrostomy (G) tube or a jejunostomy (J) tube can surgically be instituted. This will help reduce the need for the frequent flushing and replacement of the nasoenteral tube. A newer procedure in use today is the placement of a G tube percutaneously by using endoscopic guidance; this is known as the percutaneous endoscopic gastrostomy (PEG).

Initially, the infusion of enteral formulas is begun at half-strength concentrations and given at a rate of 50 ml/hour. This rate and strength can then be titrated according to the client's tolerance to the formulation. For example, the rate may be increased 25 ml/hour and the concentration increased to three-quarter strength, which eventually will be increased to the full-strength formulation. The desired calories and total volume ordered will then be administered, assuming the client can tolerate the full-strength preparation. To avoid inducing vomiting or diarrhea, the increases in

rate and fluid concentration should not be made simultaneously. The more rapid the feeding, the more likely is hyperglycemia or the dumping syndrome. However, nursing efforts should be maintained to encourage intake because the milk-based formulas, for example, contain 1 kcal/ml, and the client must take 1000 to 2000 ml of formula to obtain all the RDAs for the vitamins and minerals.

The enteral preparation may be given continuously or be cyclic administration. Cyclic feedings are similar to a person's normal feeding cycle and are the preferred method in some settings. If the client cannot or does not drink additional water while on the formulations, it is suggested that additional water be added to the enteral formulations. In general, enteral formulations that have 1 kcal/ml usually contain approximately 80% water, whereas the formulations with more concentrated kcal per ml have less than 70% water.

In the case of accidental aspiration after a tube feeding into the stomach, the tube may be advanced through the pyloric sphincter to prevent future regurgitation. Resultant hyperosmolality, however, potentiates hyperglycemia or the dumping syndrome. Physiologic osmolality is approximately 280 mOsm/L, but some preparations are greater than 400 mOsm/L.

The state of the art of enteral feedings is in rapid evolution. One source for current information is Ross Laboratories, 625 Clinton Ave, Columbus, OH 43216.

***Education.*** Tube feedings self-administered at home are now possible with the advent of smaller tubes and infusion instrumentation that incorporates improved human engineering features. Necessary preparation of the client and another family member should begin 5 to 7 days before discharge. Individualized instruction with return demonstrations of learning take about 3 to 6 hours, perhaps more if it includes learning insertion and removal of the tube for

**TABLE 72-3**  Most common secondary effects of tube feedings

| Condition | Cause | Action |
|---|---|---|
| Aspiration | Impaired gag reflex | Put head of bed at 30-60 degrees for feedings and for 1 hour after |
| | Uncuffed tracheostomy tube | Stop; suction trachea; inflate cuff before feedings |
| | Decreased gastric motility | Check for residual of feedings and tube placement |
| | Misplaced tube | Check taping of tube<br>Advance tube through pyloric sphincter |
| Obstructed tube | Plugged tube end-ports | Flush tubing before and after feedings or instillation of medications<br>Shake or mix formula well |
| Hyperglycemia, dumping syndrome: nausea, vomiting, diaphoresis, cramping | Osmotic intolerance to hyperosmolar load of feeding, rapid rate, or high concentration; ice-cold feeding | Change volume or rate of delivery and dilute feeding temporarily<br>Allow feedings to warm slightly |

nocturnal administration. Incorrect tube placement is signified by coughing, choking, difficulty in speaking, or cyanosis. Written and verbal instructions related to possible complications are also necessary (see Table 72-3). Resumption of daily activities at home is more inconvenient for the tube-fed ostomy patient who must loosen clothing or undress for each feeding.

Clients receiving tube feedings are deprived of the usual personal and social gratifications of the eating act. They may feel "different" and alienated from others. To some, it may be symbolic of a rapidly deteriorating state of health and a last resort for survival. They especially need to understand the procedure, its rationale, and what to expect from it. Once given the opportunity to discuss its meaning, many can go on to participate actively in their own feedings and to express greater satisfaction.

## PARENTERAL NUTRITION

Parenteral nutrition is the treatment of choice for selected clients who cannot eat, will not eat, should not eat, or cannot eat enough. Often called **hyperalimentation** or **total parenteral nutrition (TPN),** it is the intravenous approach to complete nutrition. TPN can supply all the calories, dextrose, amino acids, fats, trace elements, and other essential nutrients needed for growth, weight gain, wound healing, convalescence, immunocompetence, and other health-sustaining functions, and TPN provides these components in the ratio of a regular diet. It promotes anabolism by supplying all necessary nutrients in excess of those needed for energy expenditure, and it may be infused through a central vein, a peripheral vein, or both, simultaneously. Although related nomenclature has not yet been standardized, partial parenteral nutrition has come to denote parenteral nutrition therapy by intravenous solutions that are lacking some essential elements, notably fats, of the regular diet. Insulin and heparin have been added to parenteral nutrition preparations, but many other medications are avoided as admixtures because they may present potential incompatibilities with the nutrients in the solution. The three major parenteral systems for nutritional support are these:

1. Protein-sparing nutrition
2. Peripheral-vein total parenteral nutrition (PTPN)
3. Central-line venous hyperalimentation

### Protein-Sparing Nutrition

This type of nutrition is usually reserved for the client who has minimal protein deficiencies and sufficient fat stores. A 3% to 5% isotonic amino acid is mixed with carbohydrate-free fluids, vitamins, minerals, and electrolytes that are administered by peripheral vein. The solution will provide approximately 400 to 600 calories/day. The individual will meet many energy requirements by using the free fatty acids and ketones derived from their endogenous adipose tissue, thereby preserving their protein compartment in the body. This type usually is used for short-term periods for clients who are not nutritionally compromised and are not in a hypermetabolic state.

### Peripheral-Vein Total Parenteral Nutrition

Peripheral-vein total parenteral nutrition (PTPN) is ordered for clients needing nutritional support, but at the time, insertion of a central venous line for total parenteral nutrition may not be possible or necessary. The individual may be nutritionally healthy or have slight to moderate nutritional deficits without being in a hypermetabolic state. Their current medical situation indicates that a nutritional deficit will probably occur if nutritional therapy is not instituted.

It is considered a temporary measure, an attempt to provide an approximate nitrogen balance in clients who have mild deficits or in NPO clients who have a slightly elevated metabolic rate. It may be prescribed to precede a procedure that imposes restrictions on oral feedings; or for gastrointestinal illnesses that prevent oral food ingestion; or for anorexia caused by radiation or chemotherapy in cancer treatment programs; or following surgery, if the individual's nutritional deficits are minimal but oral food consumption will not be instituted for 5 or more days. It is not indicated for nutritionally depleted clients with a hypermetabolic state. If used in such persons, it should be a temporary measure until central vein hyperalimentation can be initiated.

The solution is composed of a 3% to 5% isotonic amino acid, which is mixed with a carbohydrate solution, vitamins, minerals, and electrolytes for administration through a peripheral vein. The solution will provide between 500 and 700 calories/day. The major advancement in this therapy is the use of a lipid as a nonprotein source of calories. Dextrose, when administered peripherally, must be limited to a 10% solution to avoid sclerosing of the veins. Peripherally administered lipid preparations or intravenous fat emulsions (Liposyn, Travamulsion, Intralipid, and Soyacal) are a source of additional calories for the individual.

### Central Hyperalimentation

A catheter is placed in a central vein, the subclavian vein most commonly, in order to administer solutions that contain hypertonic glucose and amino acids. Because of its blood flow, the central vein can accept the high-osmolar concentrated solutions. Central hyperalimentation or total parenteral nutrition (TPN) is usually composed of the three major nutrients—dextrose, crystalline amino acids, and lipid emulsions—plus vitamins, minerals, trace elements, electrolytes, and water. The solutions may vary according to the individual's requirements and, in general, according to the supplier of the basic amino acid solution. Special preparations of amino acids are also available for the client with a specific disease state.

The primary indications for central hyperalimentation are the following:

1. Malnutrition or a weight loss of more than 10% of body weight is present in a person before or after surgery.
2. Individuals with conditions of short bowel syndrome; acute pancreatitis; enteric or enterocutaneous fistulas; gastrointestinal tract obstructions; major trauma or burns when enteral feedings are not possible; clients with cancer, who are undergoing treatment and cannot maintain an adequate nutrition; comatose clients or persons with neurologic illnesses that interfere with eating (pseudobulbar palsy); or in selected persons with renal, cardiac, or liver failure.

## Components of Solutions

### Amino Acids

Amino acids are necessary to promote the production of proteins (anabolism), to reduce protein breakdown (catabolism), and to help promote healing of wounds. A healthy adult usually requires approximately 0.9 g protein/kg, whereas an infant or child needs from 1.4 to 2.2 g/kg. In undernourished or traumatized persons, this requirement can increase substantially.

The protein must be of high biologic value. This requirement is significantly increased (almost six times) in a traumatized or a seriously ill individual, since this patient's daily need is approximately 3 g/kg body weight. A nonprotein source of calories must be provided with the amino acids to offset their use as an energy source.

Protein is composed of amino acids, which are identified as essential and nonessential (see Table 72-4). **Essential amino acids** cannot be synthesized by the body. **Nonessential amino acids** can be synthesized from a nitrogen source (amino acids, ammonium salts, urea). All natural amino acids are needed for growth and development and must be present concurrently in the proper amounts for protein synthesis to occur. The adult can synthesize all but eight of these amino acids; these eight therefore are considered essential in adults. To the extent that oral intake of amino acids is limited, protein synthesis depends on an exogenous source. The **semiessential amino acids** (histidine, arginine) are not synthesized in adequate amounts during growth periods; thus 10 amino acids are considered essential in infants.

**amino acids, crystalline (Aminosyn 3.5%, 5%, 10%; FreeAmine III 8.5%, 10%); also available with electrolytes**

Amino acid crystalline solutions contain synthetic amino acids but not peptides. This is the preferred form of amino acid because most persons are able to tolerate this formulation.

**TABLE 72-4**   Classification of amino acids

| Essential | Nonessential | Semiessential |
|---|---|---|
| isoleucine | alanine | arginine |
| leucine | aspartic acid | histidine |
| lysine | cysteine | |
| methionine | glutamic acid | |
| phenylalanine | glycine | |
| threonine | proline | |
| tryptophan | serine | |
| valine | tyrosine | |

Dextrose usually is administered with these solutions because of the protein-sparing action of carbohydrates. If the protein is administered without adequate calories in the form of carbohydrate, the protein will be used for the body's caloric need rather than for repair and regeneration of tissue.

### Carbohydrates

Generally, dextrose is the primary source of carbohydrate in nutritional preparations. Both carbohydrate and lipids are used as sources of calories. One gram of d-glucose provides 3.4 calories, whereas fat supplies 9 calories/g and protein supplies 4 calories/g. Concentrations of dextrose solutions above 10% are hyperosmolar and too irritating to be given continuously peripherally, thus they should be administered through central venous catheters. Centrally, the concentration of dextrose solutions infused is usually between 25% and 35%.

When dextrose is administered without lipids as the primary source of calories, then hyperglycemia may occur. As dextrose requires insulin for utilization, using a combination of caloric sources, dextrose and lipids, will help decrease the potential for hyperglycemia and extra need for insulin in some individuals. Also, dextrose alone increases the rate of metabolism and production of carbon dioxide, which may increase the person's respiratory demands. Administering a combination caloric preparation of dextrose and lipids will reduce the increase in ventilatory demands.

Other sources of calories available, although not as prevalent in usage, include alcohol in dextrose solution, fructose (Levulose) in water, and invert sugar in water. Fructose is a carbohydrate normally found in the blood that does not require insulin for peripheral utilization. But fructose administration has resulted in elevated lactic acid levels, and deaths have occurred in persons with hereditary fructose intolerance.

The dextrose used in formulations is derived from corn sugar; however, a very small portion of the population may be sensitive to corn derivatives. For such persons, invert sugar derived from cane or beet sugar is an alternative.

Alcohol is another substrate providing 7 kcal/g, and it does not require insulin for peripheral utilization. Providing enough calories would necessitate a quantity of alcohol that would produce a potential for intoxication and hepatotoxicity. Since dextrose is inexpensive and readily available, it is often the preferred product for administration.

## Fats

### lipid emulsions (Intralipid 10%, 20%; Liposyn 10%, 20%)

Fat constitutes 40% to 50% of the total calories supplied in the average North American diet. Fat emulsions are derived from either soybean or safflower oil, which provides a mixture of neutral triglycerides and unsaturated fatty acids. The two functions of intravenous fat emulsions in parenteral nutrition are to supply essential fatty acids and to be a source of energy or calories (9 calories/g).

Linoleic, linolenic, and arachidonic acids are essential in humans. Linoleic acid cannot be synthesized in the body, and it is the precursor to both linolenic and arachidonic acid (a tetraene). If it is not available or if a deficiency of linoleic acid is present, then the enzyme system will act on oleic acid to synthesize eicosatrienoic acid (a triene), which is incapable of functioning like arachidonic acid. Essential fatty acid deficiency (EFAD) with clinical signs of hair loss, scaly dermatitis, retardation of growth, reduced wound healing, decreased platelets and fatty liver is noted when the triene-to-tetraene ratio is greater than 0.4. This necessitates the intravenous administration of a fat emulsion to correct the biochemical alteration.

The fat emulsions may be administered peripherally or by central veins. Fat emulsions break down when mixed with amino acids and dextrose solutions, but they may be coinfused from separate containers that flow into the same vein as the dextrose and amino acid solutions, by means of a Y connector positioned just in front of the infusion site. The lipid infusion line should be higher than the dextrose-amino acid line because the lipid emulsion has a lower specific gravity. If it is not administered in this order, the lipid emulsion may retract into the amino-dextrose line.

The fat emulsions currently available are either safflower oil (Liposyn) or soybean oil (Intralipid) or a combination of both (Liposyn II).

Daily intake may be 2 L (which provides 1980 calories) or 2.5 L (which provides 2475 calories). Or if administered with 500 ml Liposyn 10%, the 2 L fluid plus the Liposyn equals 2530 calories; if given with the 2.5 L fluid, it will provide 3025 calories. Larger amounts of liposyn may be administered, which in turn will increase caloric intake. The formula is modified according to the client's condition and individual needs.

Fat emulsion particles are thought to be metabolized from the bloodstream in a manner similar to that of the chylomicrons, which appear in the blood postprandially. No more than 60% of the total daily caloric needs of the individual should be provided by fat emulsions. The fat emulsions may prevent hyperglycemia, hyperinsulinemia, and hyperos-

molar syndrome, which often occurs in clients given dextrose as the only source of parenteral caloric nutrition. Fat emulsions pose some dangers for persons with severe liver disease, pulmonary disease, anemia, or blood coagulation disorders and for acutely ill patients with elevated serum concentrations of C-reactive protein. Fat emboli and accumulation of intravascular fat may occur in lungs of premature, preterm, or low-birth-weight infants (infusion rate not to exceed 1 g/kg in 4 hours). A normal diet should be 40% fat, 40% protein, and 20% carbohydrate.

## Trace Elements and Electrolytes

Although some of the commercial parenteral nutrition solutions contain trace elements, or minerals, persons placed on long-term administration should be evaluated for trace element deficiencies. Trace element solutions are available individually (zinc, copper, manganese, molybdenum, chromium, selenium, and iodine) and in combination formulations (M.T.E. 4, 5, or 6 Concentrated and others). Several trace metal formulations are also available in combination with electrolytes (Tracelyte, Tracelyte with Double Electrolytes, and others).

Examples of the signs and symptoms of trace element deficiency, normal serum levels, and primary excretion sites are noted in Table 72-5. It is also critical to monitor electrolyte serum levels, especially the cations sodium, potassium, calcium, and magnesium and the anions of chloride, phosphate, bicarbonate, and acetate. Combination of electrolyte concentrates are available for administration to large volume parentral solutions, such as Hyperlyte, Lypholyte, TPN Electrolytes, and others. Such preparations are usually used only in compounding of preparations in the pharmacy.

If iron replacement is necessary, it can be given by intramuscular injection by way of the Z track technique or injection or by intravenous injection or infusion. Do not mix iron with other drugs or add it to parenteral nutrition solutions. For additional information on iron (Iron Dextran), the reader is referred to a current package insert or current reference book.

## Vitamins

The client receiving parenteral feedings will need additional vitamins. Usually a combination of multivitamin infusion (MVI) and, perhaps, additional vitamins will be given on alternate days to meet the client's needs for vitamins A and D and the water-soluble vitamins (B and C). Such preparations can be added to the parenteral nutrition solution. Vitamin K and vitamin $B_{12}$ may be given at 3-week intervals, whereas folate (folic acid) is usually given on a weekly basis. The specific dose and frequency for vitamin regimens depend primarily on the individual client's needs and the usual protocols of the prescribing physician. See Table 72-6 for a typical daily total parenteral nutrition formulation for adults without any cardiac, liver, or kidney complications.

**TABLE 72-5**   Trace elements

| Elements | Normal serum levels | Excretion sites | Deficiency symptoms |
|---|---|---|---|
| copper | 80-163 μg/dl | Bile (80%), intestinal wall (16%) | Decrease in red and white blood cells, hair and skeletal abnormalities, defective tissue growth |
| chromium | 1-5 μg/L | Kidneys, bile | Neuropathy, confusion, impaired glucose tolerance, ataxia |
| iodine | 0.5-1.5 μg/dl | Kidneys, bile | Goiter, cretinism, impaired thyroid functioning |
| manganese | 6-12 μg/L | Bile | Defective growth, nausea, vomiting, weight loss, skin rash, CNS alterations (ataxia, seizures) |
| molybdenum | — | Mainly kidneys, some bile | Increased heart rate, tachypnea, headache, nausea, vomiting, edema, malaise, disorientation, coma, also may see hypouricemia, hypouricosuria, and hypermethioninemia |
| selenium | 10-37 μg/dl | Kidneys, feces | Muscle aches, pain, or tenderness, cardiomyopathy, kwashiorkor |
| zinc | 100 ± μg/dl | Stool (90%)kidneys, sweat | Nausea, vomiting, diarrhea, weakness, anorexia, growth retardation, anemia, hepatosplenomegaly, hypogeusia, rash, depression, defective wound healing, eye lesions |

**TABLE 72-6**   Typical daily TPN formulation for adults without heart, liver, or kidney compromise

| Calories | dextrose | 60%-80% of total energy needs |
|---|---|---|
| | lipids | 20%-40% of total energy needs |
| | protein (amino acids, crystalline) | 100% of individual's requirement |

An example of a typical formulation is (per unit or bottle):
   amino acids (Aminosyn 7%)—500 ml
   dextrose 50%—500 ml
   TPN electrolytes—20 ml
   multivitamins, including vitamin A, D, and E—10 ml
   trace metals—5 ml
   potassium phosphate (3 mMP/ml)—4 ml (12 mM P)
This formulation would provide the following per bottle or unit:
   water—1039 ml
   calories—990 Kcal
   nitrogen—5.5 g
   protein equivalent—35 g
   sodium—35 mEq
   potassium—40 mEq
   chloride—35 mEq
   magnesium—5 mEq
   calcium—4.5 mEq
   phosphorus—12 nM
   acetate—82 mEq

## Special Formulations

Specially formulated amino acid preparations are available for clients in renal failure, those with high metabolic stress, and those in liver failure or encephalopathy (see Table 72-7).

## ▷NURSING MANAGEMENT: PARENTERAL NUTRITION THERAPY

***Assessment.*** Close, ongoing reassessment of clients' responses to this complex therapy is essential. In particular, developing circulatory overload of fluids or electrolytes should be monitored by assessments of vital signs and fluid intake and output. A uniform infusion rate should be maintained at all times. Infusion instrumentation does not eliminate the need for alert nursing care, since it has the same potential for malfunction as all equipment does.

Some level of glucosuria may occur, particularly at initiation of therapy, since insulin response is challenged by the glucose load. The urine should be tested for glucosuria, and blood glucose may be tested at 6-hour intervals. The client's daily weight must be taken accurately and recorded. Blood urea nitrogen (BUN) is tested daily for 3 to 5 days, then every other day as needed. A sequential multichannel antoanalyzer (SMA) 12/60 procedure should be done weekly with tests for protein, partial thromboplastin time (PTT), and complete blood count (CBC). Serum electrolytes should be monitored daily.

Daily recording of the data and communication of atypical values to the attending physician are critical. These data include blood glucose in excess of 200 mg/100 ml; weight loss; urine glucose in excess of 1+ (glucosuria); and increase in pulse and blood pressure and sweating; elevated temperature; swelling and edema over the puncture site or on the head, neck, or face; low serum electrolytes; distended veins in the neck, arms, and hands; convulsions; coma; or other radical changes in the client's condition.

Complications of parenteral nutrition therapy include infection; hyperglycemia/hypoglycemia; dehydration; hypervolemia; depressed levels of the electrolytes potassium,

**TABLE 72-7**   Amino acid preparations

| Preparation | Use |
|---|---|
| Aminosyn-RF, NephrAmine, and RenAmin | Contains essential amino acids and hypertonic dextrose to promote protein synthesis. These preparations decrease the rise of urea nitrogen in the blood, allowing it to be recycled to glutamate (a precursor for the synthesis of nonessential amino acids). The latter aids in reducing many azotemic symptoms. Indicated for persons in renal failure. Since NephrAmine does not contain arginine, its use in infants would increase the risk of developing hyperammonemia. The other two preparations contain arginine. |
| FreAmine HBC | A mixture of essential and nonessential amino acids with a high concentration of branched-chain amino acids (BCAA). It is used to prevent nitrogen loss or to treat a negative nitrogen balance in adults when (a) the gastrointestinal tract cannot or should not be used to obtain an adequate protein intake, (b) the absorption of protein by the gastrointestinal tract is impaired, or (c) in severe trauma or sepsis, the nitrogen balance is significantly impaired. This formulation provides approximately 1.5 g/kg of amino acids for adults. This is a high metabolic stress formulation. |
| HepatAmine | This is a mixture of essential and nonessential amino acids with a high concentration of BCAA. It is indicated to treat hepatic failure and encephalopathy. In studies the BCAA reversed the abnormal plasma–amino acid levels in liver failure. The shift to normalization of amino acids was reflected by an improved mental status and EEG tests. Nitrogen balance was improved and mortality decreased in the reports. |

phosphate, calcium, or magnesium; EFAD, caused by prolonged fat-free hyperalimentation therapy, and trace element deficiencies (see the box). Because these balanced nutritional solutions provide an excellent medium for growth of microorganisms, strict asepsis must be employed when preparing solutions (usually done by pharmacists, ideally under a laminar flow hood) and when handling solutions or the insertion site.

**Intervention.**   Hickman or Broviac catheters are two central venous catheters that can be used for intermittent infusions of drugs, parenteral feedings, and other adjunctive therapies. These catheters are designed so that the ends may be capped between infusions. Heparinized saline is instilled at the completion of infusions, and the tube is recapped. Except during lipid infusions, in-line filters may be used to trap air and bacteria. Parenteral lines are reserved for feedings.

Parenteral nutrition intake may begin at a rate less than 1 L/12 hours for the first 2 days. If tolerated, the rate may be increased gradually during the first 5 days to 3 L/day. Ideally, the rate of parenteral nutrition solutions should be regulated by infusion pump for steady flow with no oscillations.

Do not shake lipid emulsion infusions that have separated in solution to mix them; instead discard them. Fats in these lipid emulsions have been found to leach out the plasticizer DEHP in polyvinyl chloride tubing. Since the toxic potential for DEHP is not known, it is wise to use the administration sets provided by the manufacturer for use with fat emulsions in parenteral nutrition therapy. As noted, the fat emulsion arm of the Y connector must be 6 inches higher than the other arm; otherwise the lower density of the fat emulsion will cause it to run up into the other arm of the tubing.

Dressings should be changed if they become wet or dislodged; they are designed to be air-occlusive. Protocols for

## COMPLICATIONS OF PARENTERAL NUTRITION

### Complications Arising From Infection and Sepsis
Catheter seeding from bloodborne or distant infection
Contamination of catheter entrance site during insertion or long-term catheter placement
Solution contamination

### Complications That Are Metabolic in Origin
Azotemia
Cholelithiasis (children under 15 years)
Dehydration from osmotic diuresis
Electrolyte imbalance
Hyperammonemia
Hyperosmolar, hyperglycemic, nonketotic coma (HHNC)
Hyperphosphatemia and hypophosphatemia
Hypocalcemia
Hypomagnesemia
Rebound hypoglycemia or sudden cessation of parenteral nutrition
Trace element deficiencies

### Complications Arising From Subclavian Catheterization
Air embolism
Arteriovenous fistula
Brachial plexus injury
Cardiac perforation, tamponade
Catheter embolism
Catheter misplacement
Central vein thrombophlebitis
Endocarditis
Hemothorax
Hydromediastinum
Hydrothorax
Pneumothorax
Subclavian artery injury
Subclavian hematoma
Subcutaneous emphysema
Tension pneumothorax
Thoracic duct injury

dressing changes can be found in selected references. If a client's temperature becomes elevated, it must be reported immediately. Cultures (fungal, bacterial) should be taken of the insertion site, tubing, and parenteral solutions. Peripheral vein sites should be changed routinely every 10 to 12 hours.

Air embolism is a potential hazard with central venous lines because of the low pressure in the venous system. Tubing connections must be kept taped to prevent their separation. When necessary, tubing should be changed quickly with the client in a supine position and executing Valsalva's maneuver (forced exhalation against a closed glottis). Insertions should be accomplished in Trendelenburg's position.

**Education.** Parenteral nutrition can now be continued at home for indefinite periods for those who need ongoing nutritional support and who meet the criteria. Education of the client and family is essential with regard to the purposes and techniques of the following: preventing infection, care of the solution and flow rate regulation, daily weights, recording of intake and output, and the need for close contact with community health nurses and other personnel. The client must understand infusion pump monitoring before taking on full responsibility for this technology. Every attempt should be made to resume the usual activities of daily living and to integrate this therapy into the client's lifestyle.

**Evaluation.** The client should be weighed on a daily basis at the same time of day, wearing the same type of clothing and on the same scale, preferably the first thing in the morning after voiding and before breakfast. Weight increases of 2 to 3 pounds a week can be expected if therapy is successful, until the client's weight is within normal limits for age, height, and weight. The client should also evidence improved strength and activity tolerance, and healthy gums and oral mucous membranes. Laboratory values should be within normal limits for BUN and serum albumin, protein, hematocrit, hemoglobin, vitamin $B_{12}$, folic acid, cholesterol, and lymphocyte and transferrin levels.

## SUMMARY

Starvation among the general population usually is associated with poverty. Alert nursing assessments of all clients' nutrition states is the key to avoiding the need for any of the complex regimens discussed. Nutrition by natural means is always more successful. If necessary, oral or tube feedings should be the first choice; parenteral nutrition should be employed when these are impossible or ineffective.

## BIBLIOGRAPHY

American Hospital Formulatory Service. (1991). AHFS drug information '91. Bethesda, Md: American Society of Hospital Pharamacists, Inc.

Berger R et al. (1989). Nutritional support in the critical care setting, part 2, Chest 96(2):372.

Birdsall C. (1987). Do total nutritional admixtures benefit your patients? Am J Nurs 87(1):14.

Bowman M et al. (1989). Effect of tube-feeding osmolality on serum sodium levels, Crit Care Nurse 9(1):22.

Bradley J. (1988). Principles of enteral nutrition, Hosp Pharm 23(2):197.

Braunwald E et al, eds. (1987). Harrison's principles of internal medicine, ed. 11. New York: McGraw-Hill Book Co.

Drescher MR. (1985). Advances in peripheral vein nutrition, NITA 8(6):533.

Edes TE et al. Diarrhea in tube-fed patients: feeding formula not necessarily the cause, Am J Med 88(2):91.

Eisenberg P. (1989). Enteral nutrition: indications, formulas, and delivery techniques, Nurs Clin North Am 24(2):315.

Flynn KT et al. (1987). Enteral tube feeding: indications, practices and outcomes, Image J Nurs Sch 19(1):16.

Fox B. et al. (1985). Take precautions now . . . patients receiving total parenteral nutrition, Nursing 15(5):48.

Grant M et al. (1989). Nutritional management in the head and neck cancer patient, Semin Oncol Nurs 5(3):195.

Guthrie P et al. (1986). Peripheral and central nutritional support, NITA 9(5):393.

Haynes-Johnson V. (1986). Tube feeding complications: causes, prevention, and therapy, Nutr Support Serv 6(3):17.

Horbal-Shuster M et al. (1987). Keeping enteral nutrition on track, Am J Nurs 87(4):523.

Kastrup EK, ed. (1991). Facts and comparisons. St Louis: JB Lippincott Co.

Kohn CL et al. (1989). Enteral nutrition: potential complications and patient monitoring, Nurs Clin North Am 24(2):339.

LaFranco M. (1988). Drug-food interactions, Parenterals 6(1):6.

Leider Z et al. (1986). Intermittent tube feedings: pros and cons, Nutr Support Serv 6(2):47.

Lyman B. et al. (1987). The role of the nutritional support team in preventing and identifying complications of parenteral and enteral nutrition, QRB 13(7):232.

Marvin JA. (1988). Nutritional support of the critically injured patient, Crit Care Nurs Q 11(2):21.

Matthews L. (1986). Enteral nutrition in the geriatric stroke patient, Nutr Support Serv 6(11):22.

Miller LS et al. (1986). Enteral and parenteral nutrition in the critically ill patient, Hosp Formul 21(6):672.

Munro-Black J. (1984). The ABCs of total parenteral nutrition, Nursing 14(2):50.

Murphy JI. (1990). Tube feeding problems and solutions, Adv Clin Care 5(2):7.

Olson GB et al. (1985). Balanced parenteral nutrition, Nutr Support Serv 5(6):16.

Petrosino BM et al. (1989). Implications of selected problems with nasoenteral tube feedings, Crit Care Nurs Q 12(3):1.

Rutherford C. (1986). Peripheral parenteral nutrition, NITA 9(3):232.

Standards for nutrition support: hospitalized pediatric patients. (1989). Nutr Clin Pract 4(1):33.

Vega GL et al. (1988). Metabolism of fat emulsions by thermally injured patients, J Burn Care Rehab 9(1):31.

Woolrige J. (1989). Nursing diagnosis: potential for aspiration, Classif Nurs Diagn Proc Eighth Conf, p. 429.

Worthington PH et al. (1989). Total parenteral nutrition, Nurs Clin North Am 24(2):355.

Wyngaarden JB and Smith LH. (1988). Cecil's textbook of medicine, ed 18. Philadelphia: WB Saunders Co.

*Unit 19*

# Miscellaneous Agents

*Chapter*

# 73 Antiseptics, Disinfectants, and Sterilant Agents

## CHAPTER OBJECTIVES

*After studying this chapter, you should be able to meet the following objectives and define the key terms.*

1. Compare nosocomial infections and community- or home-acquired infections.

2. Differentiate between medical asepsis and surgical asepsis.

3. Describe the characteristics of an ideal antiseptic/disinfectant.

4. Describe the mechanism of action of antiseptics and disinfectants.

5. List the indications for use of common antiseptics and disinfectants.

6. Identify the uses and limitations of silver nitrate and silver sulfadiazine.

7. Describe the effectiveness of iodine compounds and iodophors.

8. Explain the mechanism of action of oxidizing agents.

9. Describe the current uses of sterilants.

10. Identify nursing management for the safe and effective use of antiseptics, disinfectants, and sterilants.

## KEY TERMS

**asepsis,** page 1093
**bactericidal,** page 1094
**bacteriostatic,** page 1094
**community- or home-acquired infections,** page 1092
**germicides,** page 1094
**nosocomial infections,** page 1092
**sterilization,** page 1093

## INTRODUCTION

Infections and infectious diseases, although differing in type and character, occur in people in all settings—hospitals, institutions, the community at large, and the home.

**Community- or home-acquired infections** are usually fairly benign and relatively responsive to treatment. Characteristic examples are appendicitis, animal bites, lacerations, and foreign bodies.

**Nosocomial infections** are those that are acquired in a hospital. Between 2 to 4 million of the 40 million persons hospitalized yearly in the United States develop an infection that was not present or incubating upon admission to the hospital. Such nosocomial infections are responsible for an estimated 30,000 to 60,000 deaths. They also lead to extra hospitalization, resulting in approximately a $5 billion economic burden. Nosocomial infections have been called one of the most significant current ecologic problems in the United States. They are occasionally caused by virulent microorganisms resistant to antibiotics.

The emergence of antibiotic-resistant bacteria has become an increasingly important problem, especially in health care agencies. Relative virulence of strains of these bacteria tends to change over time. Before 1940 and the introduction of antibiotics, group A streptococci represented the major microbial problem. By the mid-1950s, when antibiotics were beginning to proliferate, coagulase-positive *Staphylococcus aureus* predominated. Subsequently, the problem became more complex, with the frequent appearance of aerobic gram-negative bacilli (such as *Pseudomonas*) fungi or yeast such as *Candida albicans,* and herpes virus hominis. *Serratia marcescens* has also rather quickly become a challenge. Anaerobic organisms such as *Clostridia, Bacteroides,* and *Peptostreptococcus* are increasingly common, but the organisms now most frequently responsible for hospital-acquired infections include *Staphylococcus aureus, Escherichia coli, Klebsiella, Enterobacter, Pseudomonas, Proteus, Serratia, Providencia, Actinetobacter,* and species of *Flavobacterium.* All are common, can survive at room temperature or under refrigeration, and have potential to develop resistance to antibiotics.

Urinary tract infections and postoperative wound infections account for the majority (approximately 70% or more) of the nosocomial infections detected in a hospital setting. The high-risk areas, such as critical care units, burn units, and dialysis units, usually have the highest incidence of infection outbreaks and of antibiotic resistance in the hospital. Nurses must be aware of the problem and of methods used to reduce the incidence of nosocomial infections in their practice.

## MEDICAL AND SURGICAL ASEPSIS

Medical **asepsis**, and surgical asepsis are used in health care to reduce the number and spread of organisms. These approaches presume the presence of pathogens (organisms capable of inducing disease or infection in human beings) or potential pathogens in the immediate environment and seek to limit their transmission (Figure 73-1). Methods in surgical asepsis destroy *all* microorganisms including spores; in medical asepsis, only *pathogens* are destroyed or inhibited. The focus in surgical asepsis is to keep *all* organisms out of a designated area (e.g., fresh wound), but in medical asepsis it is to remove or destroy the pathogens in the area and to contain the remaining nonpathogens there by conscious efforts. The former uses "sterile technique" (use of sterile equipment or sterile fields) and the latter uses "clean technique" (such as hygienic measures, cleaning agents, antiseptics, disinfectants, and barrier fields). Which is applied in any given situation depends largely on the susceptibility of the host, the organism's virulence, and other factors in the infectious cycle.

## Sterilization

An object is sterile if it is free of all forms and types of life. **Sterilization** is a process that destroys all forms of life on an instrument or utensil, in a liquid, or within a substance. Living tissue (of clients, nurses, or surgeons) cannot be sterilized by any known means without damage to that tissue; therefore the process known as sterilization is only applied to objects. It is also important to grasp the concept put forth by the Council on Pharmacy and Chemistry that use of the terms "sterile," "sterilizer," and "sterilization" can be used only in the absolute sense; there is no acceptable concept of relative sterility. However, just because a piece of equipment is labeled "sterilizer" does not mean that is totally and permanently effective for sterilizing. Nor does the term "sterilized" testify to an item's current condition of purity.

Several acceptable and practicable sterilization methods now exist. Steam under pressure (autoclaving) is preferred as the most effective. Ethylene oxide is a gas sterilant used for heat-labile materials, for sharp-edged instruments that could be dulled by steam, for electrical and anesthesia equipment, and for bedding. Hot air ovens are used to sterilize glassware. Chemical sterilants are also employed when necessary.

## ANTISEPTICS AND DISINFECTANTS

Antiseptics and disinfectants are agents, usually chemical, used to kill many of the pathogens within a given population of microorganisms. Their mechanisms of action are generally not very effective against spores of bacteria and fungi, many viruses, and some very resistant bacterial strains. As

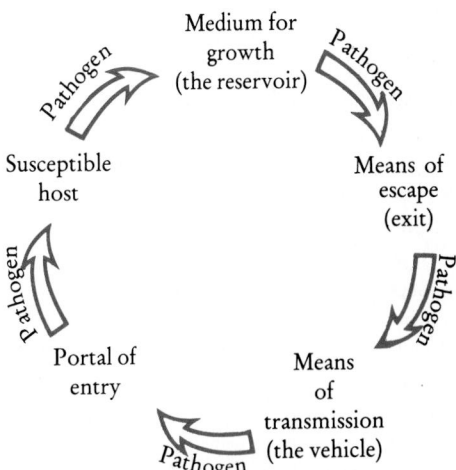

**FIGURE 73-1** Model of an infection process. Process is vulnerable to interruption with antiseptics, disinfectants, sterilants, and other medical or surgical aseptic techniques. Immunization increases host's resistance to the infection.

a group, the effects of disinfectants and antiseptics differ from sterilization largely in the degree and type of organisms destroyed. Disinfectants and antiseptics kill only pathogens, but sterilizing kills all types of organisms.

Although some of the literature uses the terms "disinfectant" and "antiseptic" interchangeably, this is erroneous and confusing. Disinfectants differ from antiseptics in the matter on which they are used and in their degree of ability to destroy organisms. Disinfectants are used only on nonliving objects; they are toxic to living tissue. Antiseptics are chemicals typically applied only to living tissue, so they must be less potent or made more dilute to prevent cell damage. Such lessening of potency, although crucial to viable tissue, decreases effectiveness accordingly. Some definitions of antiseptics emphasize their inhibiting rather than destructive effects. The narrow range of tolerance by tissues to antiinfective topical preparations tends to limit the variety and number of acceptable antiseptic agents available. Therefore antiseptics may differ markedly from disinfectants in chemical composition or may simply be a dilute version of a disinfectant for use on intact tissue. Thus some chemical substances may be used either as an antiseptic or as a disinfectant, depending on concentration.

Antiseptics and disinfectants are further categorized as **bacteriostatic** or **bactericidal** in character. Antiseptics are most often bacteriostatic; that is, they act to retard only the growth and replication of bacteria but do not kill off the entire bacteria population. Disinfectants, as bactericides, actually kill bacteria but perhaps not all types (depending on the disinfectant, its specificity, and so on) and often not fungi, viruses, or spores. Other disinfectants—fungicides, virucides, and sporicides—act specifically on these organisms. **Germicides** is an all-encompassing term for agents that work against many types of "germs"—bacteria, fungi, viruses, and spores.

Organisms vary in sensitivity to disinfectants and antiseptics in general (see box). However, factors such as the dormant and impervious spore forms of some bacteria, the waxy envelopes of the tubercle bacilli, certain properties of some types of gram-positive bacteria (staphylococci and enterococci), some gram-negative bacteria (*Salmonella* and *Pseudomonas* species), and hepatitis viruses make them highly refractory to many forms of disinfectants or antiseptics.

The ideal all-around antiseptic/disinfectant does not yet exist. Such an ideal agent would have to do the following:
1. Be destructive to all forms of microorganisms without being toxic to human cells
2. Have a low incidence of hypersensitivity
3. Be active in the presence of organic matter and soaps
4. Be stable, noncorrosive, nonstaining, and inexpensive

The current criteria for an effective disinfectant, however, includes the ability to destroy within 10 minutes all vegetative bacteria (but not spores) and fungi, tubercle bacilli, animal parasites, and viruses (but not hepatitis viruses).

---

## SENSITIVITY OF ORGANISMS TO DISINFECTANTS AND ANTISEPTICS*

| Least resistant | Bacteria |
|---|---|
| | Gram-positive and gram-negative |
| | Vegetative forms |
| | Fungi |
| | Viruses, lipophilic |
| | Influenza |
| | Herpes |
| | Vaccinia |
| | Rubella |
| | Mumps |
| | Varicella |
| | Tubercle bacilli |
| | Viruses, hydrophilic |
| | Enteroviruses |
| | Rhinoviruses |
| | Hepatitis viruses, A and B |
| Most resistant | Bacterial and fungal spores |

*May vary with concentration of compound and other factors.

---

Many variables affect the relative efficiency of a product. These include the ingredients' abilities to dissolve, mix, work in the presence of organic matter such as blood or other exudate, and penetrate into recesses. Other properties include chemical composition, concentration, pH, ionization, surface tension, temperature, and length of time required for action. Thus in actual clinical use, there may be extreme variability in the effectiveness of any given product, depending on the specific application and the situation. Although several standard tests for efficacy of these products are available, the results are subject to the same variables and, in several cases, are unwieldy to administer.

Currently, there are few established guidelines for specific approved use of any particular disinfectant: a disinfectant is considered a disinfectant whether it is to be used on corridor floors or on surgical instruments. This method of classifying permits widespread practices such as the common use of iodophor solutions as disinfectants when they have earned FDA approval as antiseptics. Antiseptics are not required to be as potent as disinfectants. Relative usefulness of various antiseptics can be compared based on their therapeutic index. This index is the relationship between the specific antiseptic concentration that is proved effective against microorganisms without irritating tissues or interfering with healing. Other decisive factors are the potential for causing hypersensitivity reactions or systemic absorption. *Thorough handwashing still predominates as the most effective measure for controlling the spread of infection.*

To place the concepts of sterilization, disinfection, and antisepsis in perspective, it should be clear that these processes differ in the degree to which they destroy organisms. Thus anything that is sterile can also be considered both disinfected and antiseptic. (The converse is, of course, not true.) All of these processes correctly begin with hand-washing, even when gloves are worn. It has been repeatedly demonstrated that clean, washed hands are crucial deterrents to microorganism growth, reproduction, and transmission in any environment.

Antiseptics and disinfectants may act in three ways.

1. They may bring about a change in the structure of the protein of the microbial cell (denaturation), which often proceeds to coagulation of protein with increased concentration of the chemical agent.
2. They may lower the surface tension of the aqueous medium of the parasitic cell. This increases the permeability of the plasma membrane, and the cellular constituents are destroyed by lysis. The cell is unable to maintain its equilibrium in its environment. (The surface-active agents are thought to act this way.)
3. They may interfere with some metabolic processes of the microbial cells in such ways as to interfere with the cell's ability to survive and multiply.

Table 73-1 is an overview of typical indications of selected disinfectants, antiseptics, and sterilants. In practice, applications may vary depending on the concentration of the solution and its purpose.

## Phenolic Compounds

### cresol, carbolic acid, Lysol

A 50% solution of cresol in vegetable oil (saponified, a milky emulsion) in 2% to 5% strength is known as Lysol. Phenols denature microbial protein structures and, in high concentrations, will precipitate cellular proteins. The actions of these compounds are relatively unaffected by the presence of organic matter or heavy bacterial inocula. Cresol is used for disinfecting excreta, sinks, bedpans, toilets, and equipment.

Solutions of phenol are antiseptic, bactericidal, or escharotic, depending on the strength of the concentration used. In aqueous solutions, from 1% to 2% of carbolic acid kills all but the hepatitis virus and bacterial or fungal spores within 20 minutes; it destroys even spores after 12 hours of contact. Cresol is two to five times as effective as phenol but no more toxic. Although it is only slightly soluble in water, it is soluble in liquid soaps. All phenols are deadly poisons if taken internally or applied topically to abraded skin. They are also corrosive to equipment.

▷ **Nursing Management:**
**Phenol Use**

Carbolic acid, cresol, and Lysol are intended for disinfectant use only. These phenolic compounds should not be applied to the skin in concentrations stronger than 2%; they should never be applied to broken skin. If accidental skin contact is made or if a burning sensation is noted, the area should be washed with copious amounts of water.

### hexachlorophene (pHisoHex, Septisol)

Hexachlorophene is a bacteriostatic agent that was incorporated into detergent creams, soaps, lotions, shampoos, and other topical products to reduce the incidence of pathogenic bacteria on the skin. Because of its toxicity, especially in infants, it is currently available only by prescription for surgical scrub purposes and as a bacteriostatic skin cleanser.

Hexachlorophene is a bacteriostatic agent effective against staphylococci and other gram-positive bacteria.

A surgical scrub and bacteriostatic skin cleansing agent, hexachlorophene is used to control gram-positive infection outbreaks when other methods have been unsuccessful.

This product is a cumulative antibacterial agent, especially with repeated use. It is also reported to be resistant to removal by many soaps and detergents, sometimes for several days.

This is a topical agent that is toxic if taken orally; ingestion results in gastric symptoms and central nervous system signs because of increased intracranial pressure. It is less toxic to tissues than phenol, but concentrations of 3% or more have a narrow margin of safety.

Daily topical use on newborns or application several times daily to the skin or vagina in adults has resulted in confusion, diplopia, lethargy, convulsions, respiratory arrest, and death. It is usually not routinely used or recommended for bathing infants. It also should not be used on mucous membranes or burned or denuded skin or for any prolonged skin contact without rinsing. Dermatitis and photosensitivity are also reported.

For surgical hand scrubs without a brush, a preliminary wash of 20 to 30 seconds, adding only a small amount of water, is followed by a sudsy 2 to 4 minute scrub and a thorough rinsing.

When a brush is used, a first scrub is followed by a scrub of varying length (see manufacturer's instructions), depending on the frequency of previous pHisoHex hand scrubs.

▷ **Nursing Management:**
**Hexachlorophene Use**

***Assessment.*** Observe clients with prolonged exposure for signs of CNS toxicity: change in sensorium, double vision, lethargy, and seizures.

***Intervention.*** These products are highly toxic if ingested and easily absorbed even through intact skin if not thoroughly rinsed. Do not leave in contact with skin or mucous membranes, as in occlusive dressings, wet packs, lotions, or vaginal packs. Avoid contact with the eyes. Most authoritative sources recommend against the use of pHisoHex for bathing infants or in pregnant or hypersensitive persons. Use should be discontinued if gastric or central nervous signs appear.

pHisoHex is most effective for handwashing when no other antiseptic or solvent follows the rinse, since its antibacterial effects are progressive and cumulative with repeated use. If used for a preoperative preparation, scrub the operative site and surrounding areas every day for 3 days for optimal effectiveness. pHisoHex may turn brown when exposed to light, but this does not affect its action. Dispensers should be cleaned every 1 to 2 weeks.

### resorcinol

Resorcinol is bactericidal and fungicidal and is about one third as effective as phenol. It is a protein precipitant and is keratolytic. Resorcinol is used for treatment of acne, ringworm, eczema, psoriasis, seborrheic dermatitis, and similar skin lesions. Its efficacy is said to be variable or erratic in these disorders. If systemically absorbed, this topical agent has a toxicity similar to phenol except that there is no prominent CNS stimulation. Usually marketed as an ointment, cream, or lotion in 1% to 10% concentrations.

▷ **Nursing Management:
Resorcinol Therapy**

Observe the application site for erythema, swelling, and peeling. Discontinue applications and notify the health care provider. Treatment on alternate days is suggested when used concomitantly with tretinoin for acne vulgaris to avoid excessive skin dryness or irritation.

### hexylresorcinol

Hexylresorcinol is a stainless and odorless antiseptic. Although quite irritating to body tissues, diluted solutions of hexylresorcinol are used to cleanse skin wounds and are also used in mouthwashes or pharyngeal antiseptic preparations. Occasionally a marked hypersensitivity reaction may occur. A 1:1000 solution of hexylresorcinol in glycerin and water is marketed for use as a mouthwash and gargle.

▷ **Nursing Management:
Hexylresorcinol Therapy**

Watch for and advise discontinuation of this product if there are signs of inflammation or irritation, which may indicate hypersensitivity rather than simple dermal irritation.

## Dyes

Rosaniline dyes are a group of basic dyes only used occasionally today as antiseptic or antiprotozoal agents. This group includes crystal violet, gentian violet, methyl violet, brilliant green, and fuchsin (red). Very few of these dyes continue to be used with any frequency, mainly because of their cosmetic effects (staining of skin, tissues, and clothing). Even gentian violet has largely been replaced by newer topical agents.

### gentian violet

Gentian violet is bactericidal to gram-positive organisms and bacteriostatic to *Monilia, Epidermophyton,* and *Trichophyton*. It is an antibacterial and antifungal dye. It is used as a topical antiinfective. Permanent purple staining may result if gentian violet solution is applied to granulation tissue. These agents are not intended for oral ingestion. Gentian violet solutions are available as 1% and 2% preparations. It also is available as gentian violet tampons, 5 mg, for intravaginal use in vulvitis.

▷ **Nursing Management:
Gentian Violet Application**

*Assessment.* Assessment of the rate and quality of healing lesions may be difficult because of discoloration of the involved skin areas. Although healing may be slow and require repeated treatments, these agents produce fewer adverse effects than some other antiseptic agents, which is a distinct advantage in the treatment of some complex dermatologic conditions.

*Intervention.* Question an order to apply to facial wounds or other frequently exposed body areas, since permanent staining may result. Suggest another topical antiseptic as a substitute. Use nonocclusive dressings. Do not apply to granulation tissue, since permanent discoloration or tattooing may occur.

*Education.* Alert clients that permanent staining of treated areas and clothing may occur. Advise clients to avoid use of occlusive dressing. Caution parents that children are attracted to these colorful solutions and will drink them if they are accessible.

## Heavy Metals

### *Mercury Compounds*
**ammoniated mercury ointment/lotion;
merbromin (Mercurochrome); thimerosal
(Merthiolate)**

The therapeutic effectiveness of mercurial antiseptics is quite low. These antiseptics are primarily bacteriostatic agents whose individual effectiveness in some cases is surpassed by the accompanying vehicle in the particular compound. Inorganic mercury compounds such as ammoniated mercury ointment may owe their effectiveness primarily to the vehicles in the compounds, which permit sustained action of the agent. Organic mercurial agents (e.g., thimerosal) are more bacteriostatic, less irritating, and less toxic than the inorganic mercurials, yet they also have a relatively low therapeutic index. Merbromin is the least effective of the common mercurial antiseptics.

The mercurial antiseptics probably act by inhibiting bacterial sulfhydryl enzymes. However, they inhibit tissue enzymes as well, which reduces their usefulness. Mercurial antiseptics are relatively slow acting, and organisms may revive if they come into contact with open wounds or body fluids. Bacterial spores will resume activity even after prolonged application of a mercurial antiseptic. Tissue and fluid proteins may compete for the mercury, leaving less free mercury for activity against microorganisms.

**Indications.** Ammoniated mercury is used for psoriasis, seborrheic dermatitis, impetigo contagiosa, dermatomycoses, pediculosis pubis, and superficial pyodermas. Since resistance to mercury has been demonstrated and because more effective, less toxic preparations are available, the use of this product is not often recommended.

Merbromin (25% mercury and 20% bromine; Mercurochrome) is used as an antiseptic and first aid product. Thimerosal (Merthiolate) aerosol pump is used to treat contaminated wounds after cleansing; for antisepsis of intact skin, pustular topical dermatoses, and dermatomycoses; also for preoperative and postoperative use.

In addition, thimerosal is available in the following forms:

Glycerite: used for local application to vagina and cervix area and also to irrigate open wounds

Solution: used whenever the tincture is contraindicated; a 1:5000 dilution is used in the eye, nose, throat, or genitourinary tract

Tincture: for skin antisepsis before surgery, for first aid treatment in contaminated wounds, and as an antifungal agent in athlete's foot infections

**Side effects/adverse reactions.** Skin irritations are reported with its use. For ammoniated mercury, prolonged use may lead to mercury poisoning. This product should not be used in infants or young children. Hypersensitivity reactions or allergic reactions have been reported with ammoniated mercury and thimerosal.

**Dosage and administration.** Apply ammoniated mercury ointment once or twice daily when using merbromin (Mercurochrome), clean injury first with soap and water; then apply freely until injury is healed. Apply thimerosal (merthiolate) topically one to three times daily.

▷ **Nursing Management:**
**Mercury Compounds**

**Assessment.** Before using, assess if client has a history of hypersensitivity to mercury compounds. Observe site of application for contact allergy dermatitis.

**Intervention.** Cleanse wound thoroughly before applying agent. Let dry before dressing wound. Thimerosal will sting when applied. Do not apply to large areas of abrasions, since the mercury may be absorbed systemically and cause toxicity.

**Education.** Make consumers aware of the very limited value of these products as antiseptics and disinfectants in comparison to their potential risks as poisons and allergens. There may be unwarranted reliance on them in the home, since they are relatively inexpensive. Children especially seem to like the pretty red stain left on the skin as evidence

of germicidal effectiveness. These products should be stored out of reach of children.

*Silver Compounds*
  **silver nitrate; silver protein, mild; silver sulfadiazine (Silvadene)**

Locally applied, many inorganic silver compounds have antiseptic qualities. Those silver salts that are highly ionizable and soluble produce astringent or caustic actions.

Release of free silver ions precipitates bacterial cellular proteins, resulting in bactericidal effects because of disruption of cell walls and plasma membranes. Effectiveness of these agents is directly proportional to their concentration and duration of contact time. There is an immediate bactericidal effect when silver solutions are applied to tissue. The silver proteinate that is formed slowly liberates small amounts of ionic silver, which provides continued bacteriostatic action. An unexplained strongly bactericidal quality resides in distilled water when it is in contact with metallic silver. Silver nitrate reacts with soluble chloride, iodides, and bromides to form insoluble salts, stopping the action of silver nitrate. Thus its action can be halted if necessary to irrigation of the area by sodium chloride solutions. This chemical characteristic explains why solutions of silver salts penetrate tissues slowly; apparently chlorides there precipitate the silver ions and inactivate them.

**Indications.** *Silver nitrate 1% solution* is used to prevent gonorrheal ophthalmia neonatorum, and *10% ointment* is used in podiatry to treat neurovascular helomas, to cauterize and seal small nerve endings and blood vessels, and as a protective cover after corns and calluses have been removed. *10% solution* is used to treat impetigo vulgaris and pruritus and in podiatry *25% solution* is used to treat pruritus; in podiatry, it is used to treat plantar warts. Use *50% solution* primarily in podiatry for plantar warts, papillomatous growths, and other selected problems. *Silver protein, mild (Argyrol S.S. 10%)* is used to treat local mild inflammation in the eye, ear, nose, throat, rectum, urethra, and vagina. Finally, *Silver sulfadiazine (Silvadene)* is bactericidal for many gram-positive and gram-negative organisms and yeast. It also inhibits bacteria that is resistant to other agents and is considered superior to sulfadiazine alone. It is used to prevent and treat infections in second and third degree burns.

**Side effects/adverse reactions**
*Silver nitrate 1% solution.* Eye redness or irritation.
*Other silver nitrate preparations.* Skin irritation. With long-term use, it can cause permanent discoloration of the skin because of the deposit of reduced silver (argyria). In higher concentrations it is limited to podiatric supervision because it is a strong caustic and escharotic agent, so tissues and membranes can be affected or damaged.
*Silver protein, mild.* Prolonged use can result in permanent skin discoloration and conjunctival argyria.

*Silver sulfadiazine (Silvadene).* Allergic skin reaction. Other adverse effects are difficult to attribute directly to this product, since other therapeutic drugs are usually being administered concurrently. Leukopenia and perhaps systemic sulfonamide adverse reactions may occur.

### Dosage and administration

*Silver nitrate 1% solution.* Following birth, the eyelids of infants are cleaned with sterile water and sterile cotton or gauze. Then 2 drops of this solution are instilled and allowed to remain in the eyes for no longer than 30 seconds. In many hospitals, topical erythromycin or tetracycline preparations are used because of their activity against chlamydia and also because silver nitrate may result in a chemical conjunctivitis in the newborn (DiPiro, JT, 1989).

*Other silver nitrate preparations.* 10% ointment: applied to lesion or affected area as needed, for up to 5 days. 10% solution: applied by cotton applicator to affected area or lesion two or three times a week for 2 to 3 weeks, as necessary. Stronger preparations: podiatric use only.

*Silver protein, mild (Argyrol S.S.).* For infections, instill 1 to 3 drops in eye(s) every 3 to 4 hours for several days. For preoperative use, place 2 or 3 drops in eye(s), then rinse with a sterile irrigating solution.

*Silver sulfadiazine (Silvadene).* Apply with a sterile gloved hand once or twice daily to a $\frac{1}{16}$-inch thickness. Keep burn areas covered with this product at all times.

**Pregnancy safety.** For silver sulfadiazine, has been established at FDA category B.

▷ **Nursing Management:**
**Silver Compound Therapy**

**Assessment.** Question client about hypersensitivity to silver (or sulfonamides in Silvadene Cream) or a glucose-6-phosphate dehydrogenase deficiency; these preclude treatment with these compounds. The effects in children and in pregnant or breast-feeding women are not known.

**Intervention.** Store silver nitrate solutions at temperatures between 15° and 30° C (59° to 86° F) and protected from light. Do not use Silvadene Cream if its white color has darkened.

Use only the appropriate concentrations of antiseptic solutions for antiseptic purposes to avoid irritation and burns to tissue. Sodium chloride can be used to flood the area should this occur accidentally.

Store silver nitrate solutions out of reach of children and never take internally. Since sulfadiazine may be absorbed from Silvadene Cream, clients should increase their fluid intake to prevent crystalluria.

Although application of silver sulfadiazine is not painful, application of silver nitrate in solution may be quite painful, especially when applied to burns. Therefore give clients analgesics before dressing changes.

Cleanse wounds before treatment to remove exudate, debris, and blood; this will prevent premature inactivation of these products.

Dressings are not necessary over silver sulfadiazine.

Take care with silver solutions to keep spills and stains to a minimum. Gloves are advised when working with silver solutions. Most tissue stains caused by Silvadene gradually disappear. Stains may be removed from linens, clothing, and shoes by applying household chlorine bleach.

**Evaluation.** Evaluate affected skin areas daily and note any changes. Perform ongoing evaluation of clients treated with these compounds to limit adverse effects related to hypersensitivities, crystalluria, or electrolyte imbalances because of absorbed drug components. If silver sulfadiazine is used in the treatment of extensive burns, monitor clients for serum sulfa concentrations, crystalluria, and renal function.

## Halogens

### Chlorine Compounds
#### chlorine

Chlorine, a nonmetallic element, is a greenish yellow gas with an intensely disagreeable odor. It is corrosive in all forms and acts as a bleaching agent. One part of chlorine in 10,000 parts of air causes respiratory tract irritation progressing to laryngospasm, unconsciousness, and, after 5 minutes, death.

Although chlorine can be bactericidal (though it is ineffective against acid-fast bacteria), sporicidal, viricidal, and amebicidal, the elemental form of chlorine itself has limited usefulness as a disinfectant because the gas is difficult to handle. The antibacterial action of chlorine is said to be caused by the formation of hypochlorous acid, which results when chlorine reacts with water. Hypochlorous acid is rapidly antibacterial, depending on the amount of organic matter, the size of the inoculum, the acidity of the medium, and the warmth of the solution's temperature. Prepared solutions decompose fairly rapidly and in a short time become markedly less microbicidal.

Several chlorine compounds act by slowly yielding hypochlorous acid when combined in various concentrations with water.

1. *Sodium hypochlorite solutions* in common use include the 5% solution, which is limited to the disinfection of utensils, walls, furniture, floors, and swimming pools, and to Dakin's solution, which is a 0.5% concentration used as an antiseptic for fungous infections (e.g., athlete's foot). These solutions are of limited usefulness for wound irrigations, except for debridement purposes, because they are irritating to the skin and delay the clotting process. Common household bleaches are usually 5.25% solutions of sodium hypochlorite. Therapeutic solutions are unstable and must be freshly prepared before use.
2. *Chloramines* are compounds in which chlorine in wa-

ter is linked chemically with nitrogen to release hypochlorous acid. Chloramines are more stable, less irritating, slower and more prolonged in action, and less readily affected by organic matter than hypochlorite solutions. Halazone is the only important chloramine used in the United States. It is available in tablet form for sanitizing drinking water. All pathogens usually found in water will be killed in 30 to 60 minutes by adding 1 or 2 tablets per liter of water.

Chlorine compounds are toxic if taken internally and are harmful to delicate tissues and mucous membranes. Over a period of time they are corrosive to equipment.

▷ **Nursing Management: Chlorine**

Store chlorine products in marked containers out of the reach of children. If a chlorine agent is swallowed, a poison control center should be contacted and emergency treatment sought. Small amounts of fluids may be given, but not so much that vomiting occurs.

Store these products away from light and in airtight containers, if possible. Therapeutic solutions should be prepared just before use. Avoid spills on skin or delicate tissues because it will cause irritation. Avoid spills on clothing or contact with hair because of its bleaching properties. Rinse thoroughly with clear water if a spill occurs.

*Iodine Compounds and Iodophors*
**iodine tincture, povidone-iodine solution (Betadine)**

Iodine is a heavy, bluish black, crystalline solid that has a metallic luster and a characteristic odor. It is slightly soluble in water but is soluble in alcohol and in aqueous solutions of sodium and potassium iodide. Iodine is volatile, and solutions should not be exposed to air except during use. In its elemental form, iodine is very rapidly bactericidal, viricidal, fungicidal, and lethal to protozoa; it is less effective against spores. It is one of the most efficient chemical disinfectants and antiseptics currently in use. Some of the iodine compounds are believed to be superior to other antiseptics, including hexachlorophene scrubs. This is controversial in view of the short life of topical iodine's effectiveness in comparison to that of hexachlorophene. All types of bacteria are destroyed at a single concentration of iodine. It is effective over a wide range of pH.

Organic matter interferes with the potency of iodine only when it is first applied; later, effectiveness increases because of diffusion as the iodine complexes dissociate. This initial delayed effect in the presence of organic material may also be offset by the increased strengths of the solution concentrations now on the market.

**Indications.** Iodine compounds are used chiefly for treatment of minor wounds, abrasions, infected wounds, indwelling urethral catheter care, skin preparation before invasive procedures, Hickman catheter and parenteral nutri-

tion dressing changes, and intravenous needle insertions. They are also used for disinfecting indwelling catheters for peritoneal dialysis and for sanitizing water and air. An aqueous solution of 5% iodine and 10% potassium iodide (Lugol's solution) can also be given orally in the treatment of goiter. Various iodine compounds are marketed for antisepsis and disinfection.

*Iodine topical solution (2% iodine), iodine tincture (2% iodine in alcohol solution), strong iodine solution (5% iodine in water), strong iodine tincture (7% iodine in alcohol).* These are used preoperatively to disinfect the skin. They are applied topically for antimicrobial effects against bacteria, fungi, viruses, protozoa, and yeasts.

*Povidone-iodine (Betadine, Operand, Pharmadine).* This water-soluble iodine combined with povidone releases approximately 10% free iodine. It has the same germicidal action of iodine without producing irritation to skin and mucous membranes. Povidone-iodines (Betadine, Isodine) are available in many formulations, such as 10% applicator solution, 2% scrub, spray, foam, vaginal gel, ointment, mouthwash, perineal wash, or whirlpool concentrate. With iodine tincture, the area cannot be bandaged. Povidone-iodine areas may be bandaged if necessary.

*Tincture of iodine.* Iodine tincture, the most commonly used iodine antiseptic, contains 2% iodine and 2.4% sodium iodide in 46% ethyl alcohol. This is frequently employed for cutaneous infections caused by bacteria and fungi. Even a 1% tincture will kill almost an entire bacterial population in 1½ minutes. Three drops of iodine tincture added to a quart of drinking water will reduce ameba and bacterial counts in 15 minutes without impairing palatability.

*Aqueous iodine solution.* This aqueous solution contains 2% iodine and 2.4% sodium iodide in water. Aqueous solutions are thought to be as effective as tincture of iodine for similar therapeutic purposes. They are also less irritating and therefore are used for abraded skin areas.

*Solution of iodine (2%) in glycerin.* This solution is the treatment of choice for application to mucous membranes.

*Iodophors (Betadine, Prepodyne).* Iodophors have become widely used as *antiseptics*. This is the only purpose for which they have been approved by the FDA, although in practice they continue to be used for disinfection of certain equipment. Iodophors are a group of iodine compounds that are combined with a carrier or agent, which increases the water solubility of iodine and provides a sustained-release pool of iodine. Studies show that *as a group* the iodophors are approximately equivalent in germicidal effectiveness but less effective than iodine tinctures or solutions because of their lower concentrations. However, iodophors have been shown to be more effective than chlorhexidine when hands are contaminated with gram-negative organisms.

Poloxamer-iodines (Prepodyne, Septodyne) are available as solutions containing 0.75% and 1% of available iodine, among other forms. Iodophors may also be combined with a detergent (e.g., Wescodyne), adding the power of a surface-acting agent. It is said that Wescodyne kills tubercle bacilli, as well as iodine's usual repertoire of organisms. However, detergents in iodophors for surgical scrubs have been associated with increased toxicity; povidone-iodine by itself is relatively low in tissue toxicity. Iodophor solutions have also been found to be susceptible to contamination within the container according to two reports circulated by the Centers for Disease Control (CDC).

***Side effects / adverse reactions.*** Iodine is toxic if taken internally. It is locally corrosive to gastrointestinal tissues but is inactivated by gastrointestinal contents. Iodine tinctures may be transiently quite painful when applied to open skin areas, but the aqueous solution form stings only slightly. Neonates have developed hypothyroidism following topical application of povidone-iodine. Marked hypersensitivity reactions do occur occasionally even with topical application. These are manifested by severe systemic reactions of fever and generalized skin eruptions.

▷ **Nursing Management:**
**Iodine Compounds and Iodophors**

***Assessment.*** Before iodine compounds and iodophors are applied, ask clients about any past allergic reactions to iodine, shellfish, or iodine-containing diagnostic agents. If there is doubt substitute another product. If irritation develops, wash the skin.

Do not use povidone-iodine as vaginal douche during pregnancy.

***Intervention.*** These products are exceptionally valuable because of their efficiency, low toxicity, and low cost.

Do not bandage or tape areas treated with tincture of iodine; if treated with povidone-iodine, a cover dressing may be applied.

Iodophors will stain only starched linen or clothing. Tinctures and solutions of iodine may stain more freely.

Soap and water cleansing of fingertips before skin puncture for blood glucose monitoring by some reagent strips is recommended. Artificially elevated blood glucose determinations have been noted when povidone-iodine swabs were used for skin preparation.

If appropriate, give the client medication for pain before iodine tinctures are applied.

***Education.*** Advise the client to purchase iodine preparations in very small quantities and discard routinely after a short time, since evaporation of the solvent or vehicle will leave a concentrated iodine preparation that may burn tissues on application.

## Oxidizing Agents

### hydrogen peroxide

Hydrogen peroxide is a colorless, odorless antiseptic that deteriorates readily to form water and oxygen. When hydrogen peroxide comes into contact with organic matter such as tissues, enzymatic reactions cause decomposition of hy-

drogen peroxide and rapid formation of oxygen bubbles. Solutions have a high surface tension. Because of this and the resulting effervescence, there is limited penetrability. Although the antiseptic action of hydrogen peroxide is fairly fast acting, it is short lived. It acts as an antibacterial only as long as the bubbling action continues.

***Indications.*** Oxygen that is released is particularly suited for destroying anerobic microorganisms, but effects vary depending on the type of organism. Several products containing hydrogen peroxide are marketed.

*Hydrogen peroxide topical solution.* This is a 3% solution of hydrogen peroxide in water, which is used to irrigate suppurating wounds and some extensive traumatic wounds. It should not be instilled into closed body spaces because of its effervescence. It is also used for wound cleansing, before Hickman catheter dressing changes, for surgical repair of cleft lip, as irrigations following some radical head and neck surgeries, for some oral lesions, for oral cleansing (Peroxyl mouthrinse), and for removal of collections of mucus from the inner cannula of tracheostomy tubes. It is used with caution, if at all, for ear irrigations to remove excess cerumen because of damage to the tympanic membrane.

The official solution should be further diluted with water into a half-strength or 1:4 strength for most applications.

*Medicinal zinc peroxide.* This peroxide, a combination of zinc and hydrogen peroxide, yields hydrogen peroxide. The residue of zinc oxide is mildly astringent. It is used topically for antisepsis and deodorizing of wounds, especially those infected with anerobes.

*Benzoyl peroxide.* Benzoyl peroxide is used as a topical antiseptic, keratolytic, antiseborrheic, and mild irritant to treat acne. (See Chapter 67.)

***Side effects / adverse reactions.*** If small amounts of dilute hydrogen peroxide solutions are swallowed, rapid decomposition of the substances in the stomach into relatively harmless molecular oxygen and water occurs. Repeated use as a mouthwash may cause hypertrophied papillae of the tongue ("hairy tongue"), a reversible condition. Some products may cause contact dermatitis and bleaching of clothing.

▷ **Nursing Management:**
**Oxidizing Agents**

To delay deterioration of the contents, store solutions in tightly capped, amber containers to protect from light and air. Solutions in containers should be discarded freqently, and fresh solutions should be used. The rapidity and vigor with which bubbling occurs may be used as a general guide to the freshness of the solution.

The bubbling action makes hydrogen peroxide useful for removing mucus secretions from equipment (i.e., inner cannulae of tracheostomy tubes).

Do not leave paper cups containing hydrogen peroxide where clients can reach them. Because the solution looks like water, clients have mistakenly drunk it despite the unusual taste. Although very small amounts will not be harmful, large amounts in the stomach could be harmful because of resultant effervescence in the stomach, a closed cavity. These compounds, like all medications, should be kept secured and out of children's reach.

## Biguanides

### chlorhexidine (Hibiclens, Hibitane Tincture)

Chlorhexidine gluconate is a biguanide with antiseptic activity. It is effective against both gram-positive and gram-negative bacteria. Chlorhexidine acts by disrupting the bacterial cell's plasma membrane (particularly gram-positive organisms).

Hibiclens is a bactericidal skin cleansing solution containing chlorhexidine gluconate. It is useful as a surgical scrub, a handwashing agent for personnel, and a skin wound cleanser. It is also used for the treatment of aphthous ulcers in the mouth and the prevention of dental caries.

Orally ingested, chlorhexidine is believed to have low toxicity; however, low concentrations in the bloodstream can cause hemolysis. There have been reports of deafness occurring when these products came into contact with the middle ear through a perforated eardrum. Rare secondary effects include dermatitis, photosensitivity, and irritation of mucosal tissue. Physiochemical properties of these agents suggest that absorption through the skin is minimal.

The action of chlorhexidine is not affected by the presence of blood or exudate, but effectiveness may be directly related to the concentration of the solution. Hibiclens (the 4% solution) is more effective than Hibitane (1% aqueous solution), according to studies. Studies comparing Hibiclens and povidone-iodone produced equivocal results. As a handwash, Hibiclens is applied, water added, and friction applied for 15 seconds. Skin wounds should be washed gently with Hibiclens and rinsed. For surgical scrubs hands and forearms are scrubbed with approximately 5 ml Hibiclens for 3 minutes without water, while using a brush or sponge. After hands and forearms are rinsed, washing is repeated for 3 more minutes. Hibitane Tincture should be applied liberally to the surgical site, swabbed for 2 minutes or more, and the area then air-dried. Pooled Hibitane has caused skin burns during electrocautery. The tinctures are said to have a persistent bactericidal effect against many gram-positive and gram-negative bacteria (some of the latter are completely resistant to chlorhexidine, however). Furthermore, there have been a few reports of epidemic infections caused by *Pseudomonas maltophilia* and *P. cepacia* that were traced to diluted solutions in 0.05% to 0.2%.

## ▷ Nursing Management: Chlorhexidine

*Intervention.* Use judgment when diluting these agents, since their effectiveness may be greatly reduced in proportion to the dilution. Certain solutions less than 4% may

actually support bacterial growth. Chlorhexidine-treated areas should not be wiped with alcohol, which will neutralize the intended residual action. Do not use chlorhexidine on delicate tissues such as eyes and mucous membranes. The area should be rinsed promptly if this occurs.

*Education.* Advise clients not to swallow chlorhexidine compounds (especially when used for mouth care).

## Surface-Active Agents

### benzalkonium chloride (Zephiran Chloride)

As wetting agents, emulsifiers, or detergents, surface-acting agents are considered superior to soaps because they can be used in hard water, are stable in acid or alkaline solutions, decrease surface tension more effectively, and are less irritating to the skin. Benzalkonium chloride is a cationic (bearing a positive electric charge on the active portion of the agent) quaternary ammonium compound used in solution as a topical antiseptic or as a disinfectant. It is generally believed that benzalkonium chloride is not very reliable in either role.

The mechanism of action is not known for certain, but it is thought that this agent and others like it have primary effects on the cell, causing increased permeability of bacterial cell membranes.

Indications include:
1. Used in an aqueous solution as an antiseptic for skin, mucous membranes, wounds, and preoperative skin preparation of personnel and patients.
2. Used to immersion-store sterile instruments and equipment. However, its documented ability to support the growth of contaminants has caused the CDC to recommend the substitution of other agents, such as iodophors and alcohols.

Chemical burns may occur if benzalkonium chloride is allowed to stay in contact with tissues, as in wet packs or occlusive dressings. The tincture and the spray formulations are flammable. Delicate tissues may be injured if specified dilution recommendations are not used. Ingestion only rarely causes toxicity. Hypersensitivity reactions can occur.

This agent is slow acting in comparison to iodine. Therapeutic effects are thought to be in direct relation to the concentration of the solution used. Depending of the purpose and tissues or equipment to be treated, recommended dilutions range from 1:750 to 1:5000 or 1:10,000. A variety of gram-positive and gram-negative organisms and many fungi and viruses (not hepatitis) are said to be susceptible. Bacterial spores and *Pseudomonas cepacia* are resistant, and *Mycobacterium tuberculosis* is relatively resistant to Zephiran chloride. Organic materials inactivate benzalkonium chloride. Tap water that contains metallic ions, organic matter, or resin-deionized water may reduce its effectiveness. Many materials, soaps, and anionic detergents may absorb the active ingredient, rendering it weak for many purposes.

▷ **Nursing Management:**
**Benzalkonium Chloride**

*Assessment.* If any of these compounds have been used, continue to monitor the area or utensil critically for contamination.

*Intervention.* In view of the highly questionable efficacy of surface-active agents, especially benzalkonium chloride, question an order or a suggestion to use them as antiseptics or disinfectants. Suggest the substitution of an iodophor, alcohol, or other compound. Use only the concentration recommended for each specified area. Do not use with occlusive dressings.

Do not apply these compounds to areas previously treated with soaps or anionic agents. Do not apply to delicate tissues. Flood the area with water if these agents are accidentally introduced. Do not reuse solutions after soaking cotton balls, dressings, or instruments. Avoid using Zephiran to disinfect thermometers. If it must be used, use not less than the recommended 1:750 concentration. Do not use the tincture or spray formulations near an open flame.

## Miscellaneous Agents

### nitrofurazone (Furacin)

Nitrofurazone is a broad antibacterial topical agent active against many bacteria that cause local infections, including *Staphylococcus aureus, Streptococcus, E. coli,* and others. Indications include:
1. Used mainly as adjunct therapy to clients with second and third degree burns when bacterial resistance to other agents is a problem.
2. Also used during skin grafting when bacterial contamination may result in graft rejection or a donor site infection.

Rash, itching, local edema (dermatitis), and allergic reactions have been reported. Hypersensitivity occurs early in the treatment of a few individuals. Furacin is not absorbed significantly through mucosal or burned tissues, and systemic toxicity is rare. However, its propylethylene glycol base may be absorbed and challenge the client with renal dysfunction. Bacterial and fungal suprainfections may occur. Clients with glucose-6-phosphate dehydrogenase deficiency should avoid the use of nitrofurazone if possible.

Nitrofurazone may inhibit the effectiveness of the enzyme sutilains (Travase).

The 0.2% powder, cream, ointment, soluble dressing, or topical solution may be applied directly on the area or to a gauze dressing for application. The soluble dressing form is useful as a preparatory antiseptic for skin graft areas. The solution is bacteriostatic in concentrations of 1:100,000 to 1:200,000 and bactericidal at twice these concentrations. Efficacy is reduced in the presence of heavy microbial contamination, plasma, or blood. Resistance seldom develops.

Pregnancy safety has been established at FDA category C.

▷ **Nursing Management:**
**Nitrofurazone Therapy**

*Assessment.* Watch for dermatitis or other manifestations of hypersensitivity to this product. Severe skin reactions may require topically applied steroids. Pregnant women should avoid use of this product until it has been proved safe; persons with glucose-6-phosphate dehydrogenase deficiency are likewise cautioned to avoid Furacin. Judgment should be used in treating individuals who have renal disorders with preparations that include polyethylene glycol. Clients should be alerted to these adverse reactions.

*Intervention.* Cleanse the affected area before each dressing change. Treatment by Furacin may be suggested in instances of burn or wound infections resistant to other medications. Treatment for a developing secondary infection may become necessary. Meticulous sterile technique is essential during dressing changes and when opening and withdrawing Furacin-saturated dressings from their sterile packets.

*Evaluation.* Evaluate affected areas daily. Areas that do not seem to be responding to treatment by Furacin or any areas becoming inflamed because of hypersensitivity should continue to be assessed for discontinuance.

## Alcohols

### ethanol (ethyl alcohol); isopropanol (isopropyl alcohol)

A 70% alcohol solution is antiseptic. Alcohol may also inhibit growth of bacteria; therefore it is often used as a preservative of biologic specimens and in some prepackaged injectables and medications. Alcohols may precipitate cellular proteins.

*Indications*
1. Alcohols are variably effective in topical application for the destruction of gram-positive and gram-negative bacteria, fungi, lipophilic viruses, and tubercle bacilli.
2. In topical application alcohols are commonly used to prepare skin for minor invasive procedures (using commercially packaged skin wipes), such as before parenteral injections, in combination with iodine for the same purpose, or for disinfection of vial tops and thermometers.
3. Alcohols are also used for disinfection of heat-labile instruments, polyethylene tubing, catheters, implants, prostheses, smooth hard-surfaced objects, hinged instruments, and inhalation and anesthesia equipment.
4. Because of their rapid evaporation rate, dilute solutions of alcohols are still occasionally used as sponge baths to reduce fever, although systemic absorption may be especially harmful to neonates and children.
5. Alcohols are also used as preservatives in solutions, used as diluents or to dissolve other drugs, and in combination with many other drugs for over-the-counter purchase (often without rationale).

6. Ethyl alcohol is also ingested purposefully as an intoxicating beverage.

*Side effects/adverse reactions.* Essentially, all of the alcohols are poisonous drugs when taken internally, depending on the dose. Isopropyl alcohol is inherently highly poisonous; ethyl alcohol, pure alcohol made from vegetables, fruits, canes, and grains, is the alcohol of alcoholic beverages. The degree to which fractional distillation is carried out determines the resultant concentration. When continuously inhaled or absorbed through the skin, alcohols can cause intoxication. Ethyl alcohol is irritating if left in contact with skin for prolonged periods. If ethyl alcohol is applied to open skin, a film that can harbor microorganisms develops. Isopropyl alcohol causes subcutaneous vasodilation, which can cause needle sites and incisions to bleed somewhat more freely.

*Dosage and administration.* Ethyl alcohol is slightly less effective as an antiseptic than isopropyl alcohol. Efficacy may depend highly on the concentration used and the amount of mechanical friction applied. The most effective solutions of ethyl alcohol are concentrations of 50% to 70%; stronger solutions are less effective. At concentrations of 70%, almost 90% of the bacteria on skin are killed within 2 minutes if the wet surface is allowed to dry naturally. Inadequate disinfection may occasionally result even if friction is conscientiously applied to surfaces.

Isopropyl alcohol is employed in aqueous solutions of 70% concentration or undiluted as 99% concentration (isopropyl rubbing alcohol). It may be combined with other disinfectants such as iodine and formaldehyde to improve efficiency.

▷**Nursing Management: Ethanol**

*Intervention.* Leave on the skin for at least 2 minutes. Allow to dry without fanning. Do not use with open wounds.

Cleanse thermometers before placing them to soak in an alcohol solution, because any adherent organic matter will inhibit the solution's action. Alcohol solutions themselves may harbor organisms and may rust instruments; therefore, they are often not the best solution for disinfecting or for sterile storage of equipment.

When alcohol is used as a disinfectant or antiseptic, its effectiveness is heightened when friction in applied and when it is allowed to dry naturally (without fanning with the hand or other object) before proceeding. Nonetheless, studies show that the sterility of tops of freshly uncapped vials is maintained whether or not alcohol swabs are applied to the tops, *unless* the alcohol itself is contaminated. Sterile tops of medication containers such as vials should not be wiped with a disinfectant before using, unless they have become contaminated or have remained uncovered too long.

Be prepared to apply more pressure and possibly a small pressure dressing after giving an injection or discontinuing an intravenous infusion if alcohol has been applied to the site. If the individual is also receiving anticoagulant therapy, the bleeding may be extensive.

*Education.* Make personnel, clients, and parents aware that all alcohols are inherently or potentially poisonous and that intoxication or dangerous poisoning can occur as a result of their absorption, inhalation, or ingestion. Keep alcohols secured and out of the reach of children.

## Acids

### acetic acid (vinegar); benzoic acid; lactic acid; boric acid

Various acids have been used as antiseptics or cauterizing agents. Of these, vinegar is the most commonly used, especially in community health nursing, because of its practicality, availability, and low cost. Other acids that are employed as antiseptics include benzoic acid (0.1%), which prevents bacterial and fungous growth; lactic acid, which is used primarily as a component of spermatocides in the United States (and as a topical antiseptic elsewhere); and boric acid, which is so mild that it is used in eye and ear preparations. Of these other acids, most have lost credibility as effective antiseptics. Specifically, boric acid has been implicated in cases of serious systemic intoxication by absorption.

Vinegar (acetic acid) provides an acid medium that inhibits the growth of organisms dependent on a neutral or alkaline medium.

In a 5% concentration, acetic acid is germicidal to many organisms. It is bacteriostatic at lower concentrations. A mild vinegar solution is often recommended as a vaginal douche for antisepsis in the prevention or suppression of vaginal infections caused by *Trichomonas*, *Candida*, and *Gardnerella vaginalis* organisms and for spermatocidal purposes. Acetic acid may also be used as a mild antiseptic-deodorant for many other applications, such as for instillation into the collection container of indwelling urinary drainage catheters, bladder irrigation (0.25% concentration), and diaper soaks. The 1% concentration may be used as a topical antiseptic for certain surgical wounds and burns since it is particularly effective against *Pseudomonas aeruginosa*. When applied to skin graft donor sites, a 0.25% acetic acid solution does not interfere with healing.

The residual pungent odor of acetic acid may be a deterrent to its use. Ingestion may produce laryngospasm. Preservatives that are incorporated in vinegar may be responsible for some hypersensitivity reactions.

▷**Nursing Management: Acetic Acid**

A mildly effective, soothing vaginal douche can be prepared by adding 1 to 2 tablespoons of white household vinegar (5%) to 1 quart of warm water. Stronger concentrations are no more effective and may irritate mucosal tissues.

Antiseptics instilled in urinary collection bags should be of concentrations that are not injurious to bladder mucosa in case the bag is inadvertently raised so that contents reflux into the bladder.

## STERILANTS
### Aldehydes
#### formaldehyde solution

Formaldehyde solution is a 37% concentration of formalin (by weight). It is a clear, colorless disinfectant liquid that, on exposure to air, liberates a pungent, irritating gas. It is effective against bacteria, fungi, and viruses. Proteins are precipitated by strong formaldehyde concentrations.

Indications include:
1. When formaldehyde is combined with isopropyl alcohol or hexachlorophene, it is probably the most potent germicidal solution currently available.
2. Preparations that combine formaldehyde solution, isopropyl alcohol, and antirust agents for the disinfection of instruments and heat-labile articles are used for "cold sterilization." Hemodialysis equipment is often cleaned with formaldehyde solutions. The solution may be applied as a strong astringent.
3. It is also used as a preservative for sputum and other types of specimens and in certain medicinals and biologicals, such as toxoid vaccines.
4. It is also used commercially to make clothing crease-resistant.

Personnel who are in frequent contact with formaldehyde compounds are at great risk. In the past only the adverse reactions of itchy and watery eyes, runny noses, coughing, dermatitis, and browning and blistering of hands were noted. Increasing attention is being paid to formaldehyde's confirmed mutagenicity and possible carcinogenicity. Studies show that formaldehyde may not only inhibit the repair of DNA that has been damaged by x-rays but also actually potentiate this damage. When hydrogen chloride fumes and formaldehyde fumes combine in moist air, the product may be associated with increased risk of lung cancer.

A report from the National Institute for Occupational Safety and Health (NIOSH) states that formaldehyde should be considered and handled as a potential occupational carcinogen and recommends that appropriate controls be developed and implemented accordingly. Currently, standards set by the Occupational Safety and Health Administration (OSHA) limit an 8-hour concentration limit to 3 parts per million (ppm), along with other specific limitations related to air concentration. In view of its latest findings, NIOSH recommends that exposure be limited to a concentration no more than 1 ppm for any 30-minute period.

The action of formaldehyde is slow. It is usually employed in 2% to 8% solutions as a disinfectant. Even at 8% concentrations, formaldehyde takes 18 hours to destroy bacterial spores.

▷ **Nursing Management: Formaldehyde Solution**

Help disseminate important information to other workers about the dangers of exposure to formaldehyde. Wear gloves when handling formaldehyde. All who work with formaldehyde should see that adequate ventilation is maintained in work areas and that goggles and filter masks are available and in good condition for use whenever fumes are strong enough to cause respiratory and eye irritations. Always dilute the 37% solution.

#### glutaraldehyde (Cidex)

Glutaraldehyde is considered to be a more effective disinfectant sterilant than formaldehyde. Glutaraldehyde is less volatile than formaldehyde; therefore it is less musty, and fewer irritating fumes generally occur.

At a pH of 7.5 to 8.5, glutaraldehyde is a very effective antibacterial agent with potent bactericidal, tuberculocidal, fungicidal, sporicidal, and virucidal action. This effectiveness is recorded even in the presence of organic material (blood, tissue, mucus).

Glutaraldehyde is a germicidal agent used to disinfect and sterilize plastic and rubber equipment (respiratory, anesthesia), surgical and dental instruments, catheters, thermometers, and other hard-surfaced, heat-labile equipment.

Glutaraldehyde is irritating to skin or mucous membranes. It is also a severe eye irritant, and fumes may irritate the respiratory tract. It should be used cautiously in a well-ventilated area.

Glutaraldehyde is used in disinfection of instruments: Immerse instruments in glutaraldehyde solution for 10 minutes. Rinse equipment before use.

Sterilization: Immerse equipment or instruments for a minimum of 10 hours to destroy pathogenic spores. Use sterile technique in removing the items from the solution and rinse thoroughly with sterile water. Flush all lumens and cannulas and dry the items before use.

▷ **Nursing Management: Glutaraldehde**

Do not use this disinfectant-sterilant on living tissue. If accidentally exposed, thoroughly rinse the area.

When feasible, consider steam under pressure, gas, or heat in preference to sterilization by glutaraldehyde.

To prepare a glutaraldehyde solution, add the specified activator powder, which contains a rust inhibitor.

Completely cover articles with the solution for the entire prescribed time. (The time necessary depends on the purpose for which the solution is used—for disinfection or for chemical sterilization.) During the immersion period, cap the container to prevent escape of fumes. Remove articles from the immersion fluid with sterile forceps and thoroughly air dry.

Post instructions for use in full view of personnel. Also instruct them in the use of glutaraldehyde. Ongoing inservice education should be maintained.

## Ethylene Oxide

Ethylene oxide is a colorless gas at ordinary temperatures. Its use is more dangerous, more complex, more expensive, and less reliable than steam under pressure. It is highly toxic, flammable, and thought to be mutagenic and carcinogenic as well. Carboxide is a combination of 10% ethylene oxide and 90% carbon dioxide; other combinations include gases such as Freon (to reduce flammability and explosive hazards). External exhaust systems are recommended when ethylene oxide is used.

Ethylene oxide is an alkylating agent, which allows it to unite chemically with components of living cells (proteins, nucleic acids), thereby interfering with cellular metabolism and destroying the cells.

Indications include:
1. Used for gaseous sterilization of materials that cannot be subjected to intense heat or pressure, such as plastic machinery parts, optical instruments, or prosthetic devices (i.e., artificial hip replacements and pacemakers).
2. It is highly penetrating and is destructive to all types of microorganisms, including viruses, tubercle bacilli, and spores.
3. Articles removed from gas sterilizers should be allowed adequate time for residual gases to be diffused from internal parts before they are removed and used.

Careful studies by the National Institute for Occupational Safety and the American Hospital Supply Corporation have correlated ethylene oxide exposure with chromosomal defects, low sperm counts, spontaneous abortion, and leukemia and other cancers in factory workers. Other toxic effects include respiratory, eye, and skin irritation, anemia, vomiting, and diarrhea. Studies recommended that "ethylene oxide be regarded in the workplace as a potential occupational carcinogen, and that appropriate controls be used to reduce worker exposure."* It has now been ruled that current minimal standards relating to exposure be changed so that workers are exposed to no more than 1 ppm in the air as an 8-hour time-weighted average and that those who work with ethylene oxide be provided with ongoing medical surveillance. The Occupational Safety and Health Administration has jurisdiction over standard setting. It was found that white blood cells of hospital workers who had been exposed to currently allowable levels of ethylene oxide for as little as 4 minutes/day for 6 months showed the same anomalous chromatid breaks and rejoinings that are used as criteria for determining genetic risk for mutagenesis and carcinogenesis.

---

*See Coene, RF: Bulletin No. 35, Washington, DC, 1981, US Government Printing Office.

**TABLE 73-1**   Antiseptics, disinfectants, and sterilants

| Agent | Indication |
|---|---|
| **PHENOLIC COMPOUNDS** | |
| Cresol, Lysol, carbolic acid | Disinfectant |
| Hexachlorophene | Antiseptic |
| Resorcinol | Antiseptic |
| Hexylresorcinol | Antiseptic |
| **DYES** | |
| Gentian violet | Antiseptic |
| Carbol-fuchsin solution | Antiseptic |
| **HEAVY METALS** | |
| *Mercurials* | |
| Ammoniated mercury ointment | Antiseptic |
| Merbromin (Mercurochrome) | Antiseptic |
| Thimerosal (Merthiolate) | Antiseptic |
| *Silver compounds* | |
| Silver nitrate, silver sulfadiazine | Antiseptic |
| **HALOGENS** | |
| *Chlorine compounds* | |
| Sodium hypochlorite | Disinfectant, antiseptic |
| *Chloramines* | |
| Halazone | Disinfectant |
| **IODINE COMPOUNDS** | |
| Tincture of iodine | Disinfectant, antiseptic |
| Aqueous iodine solution | Disinfectant, antiseptic |
| Iodophors | Antiseptic |
| **OXIDIZING AGENTS** | |
| Hydrogen peroxide | Disinfectant*, antiseptic |
| Zinc peroxide | Antiseptic |
| Benzoyl peroxide | Antiseptic |
| **BIGUANIDES** | |
| *Chlorhexidine gluconate* | |
| Hibiclens, Hibitane | Antiseptic |
| **SURFACE-ACTIVE AGENTS** | |
| *Benzalkonium chloride* | |
| Zephiran chloride | Antiseptic* |
| **NITROFURAZONE** | |
| Furacin | Antiseptic |
| **ALCOHOLS** | |
| Ethanol | Disinfectant, antiseptic |
| Isopropranol | Disinfectant, antiseptic |
| **ALDEHYDES** | |
| Formaldehyde | Sterilant, disinfectant |
| Glutaraldehyde | Sterilant, disinfectant |
| **ACIDS** | |
| Acetic | Disinfectant, antiseptic |
| Benzoic | Antiseptic |
| Lactic | Antiseptic |
| Boric | Antiseptic* |
| **ETHYLENE OXIDE** | Sterilant |

*This property of compound is questionable.

▷ **Nursing Management:**
   **Ethylene Oxide**

*Assessment.* If badges to monitor ambient air concentrations of ethylene oxide are issued, employees and nurses should wear them. Monthly level checks by facility engineers are recommended.

All who are frequently exposed (central supply room workers, operating room nurses, employees of manufacturers, and other users) should have routine follow-up examinations. Nurses and nurse practitioners may want to include questions related to industrial exposure in taking health histories of those with repeated respiratory tract conditions.

Women in their childbearing years should avoid prolonged exposure, especially early in pregnancy.

*Intervention.* Substitute other forms of sterilization for ethylene oxide, if feasible. There may be no other acceptable forms of sterilization for the specific applications, however. Implementation of recommended standards may compromise client's care and possibly place an inordinate financial burden on hospitals not now suitably equipped.

If ethylene oxide sterilization is frequently employed, hospital workers should be actively working with the hospital administration to have steps taken to monitor the ambient air levels of ethylene oxide during the use of gas sterilizers and to install air-exhaust systems that vent to the outside.

Post instructions for the preparation and use of ethylene oxide and gas sterilizers where they are used and where they are manufactured. Risks are incurred when articles are transferred from the ethylene oxide sterilizer to the aerator, when aeration time guidelines are not followed, or when the aerator malfunctions.

Monitor court proceedings, which will probably result in new standards for exposure, and disseminate findings to those in the occupational nursing field.

## SUMMARY

Medical asepsis and surgical asepsis are used in health care settings to reduce the number and spread of organisms. Although thorough handwashing is still the best method for accomplishing this reduction, antiseptics, disinfectants, and sterilants need to be utilized. Antiseptics are chemicals typically applied to living tissue to decrease the microbial population, whereas disinfectants are used only on nonliving objects, since they are caustic to living tissue. Antiseptics and disinfectants may be either bacteriostatic or bactericidal, or they may be both, depending on the concentrations employed. Sterilants free objects of all forms and types of life. Although these substances are used for therapeutic purposes, they still are caustic and so require careful handling to prevent irritation and injury.

## BIBLIOGRAPHY

Aly R et al. (1988). Comparative antibacterial efficacy of a 2-minute surgical scrub with chlorhexidine gluconate, providone-iodine, and chloroxylenol sponge-brushes, Am J Infect Control 16(4):173.

Amount of antiseptic soap used is important factor in cleansing. (1987). Hosp Employee Health 6(11):147.

Anderson RL. (1989). Iodophor antiseptics: intrinsic microbial contamination with resistant bacteria, Infect Control Hosp Epidemiol 10(10):443.

Beck WC (1988). Handwashing, Semmelweis, and chlorine. (1988). Infect Control Hosp Epidemiol 9(8):366.

Chatburn RL. (1989). Decontamination of respiratory care equipment: what can be done, what should be done, Respir Care 34(2):98.

Cronin WA et al. (1989). A no-rinse alcohol antiseptic and a no-touch dispenser for hand decontamination, Infect Control Hosp Epidemiol 10(2):80.

Devine A. (1989). Two minutes? Four minutes? Ten minutes? A discussion on current recommendations of disinfection policies for gastroscope, Natnews 26(4):12.

DiPiro JT et al, (eds) (1989). Pharmacotherapy: a pathophysiologic approach. New York: Elsevier.

Gilman AG et al. (1990). Goodman & Gilman's the pharmacologic basis of therapeutics, ed 8. New York: MacMillan, Inc.

Goetz A et al. (1989). *Pseudomonas aeruginosa* infections associated with use of providone-iodine in patients receiving continuous ambulatory peritoneal dialysis, Infect Control Hosp Epidemiol 10(10):447.

Gurevich I. (1989). Preventing central-line sepsis requires multi-faceted approach, Hosp Infect Control 16(8):104.

Hargiss CO and Larson E. (1981). Guidelines for prevention of hospital acquired infections, Am J Nurs 81(11):2175.

Herfindal ET and Hirschman JL (1988). Clinical pharmacy and therapeutics, ed 4. Baltimore: Williams & Wilkins.

Johnson A. (1988). Wound care: the cleansing ethic, Community Outlook Feb, p 9.

Kastrup EK, (ed.) (1991). Facts and comparisons. St Louis: JB Lippincott Co.

Katzung BG. (1987). Basic and clinical pharmacology, ed 3. Norwalk, Conn: Appleton & Lange.

Larson E. (1988). APIC guidelines for infection control practice: guidelines for use of topical antimicrobial agents, Am J Infect Control 46(6):253.

Larson E et al. (1989). Influence of two handwashing frequencies on reduction in colonizing flora with three handwashing products used by health care personnel, Am J Infect Control 17(2):83.

Larson EL et al. (1987). Quantity of soap as a variable in handwashing, Infect Control 8(9):371.

Leibovici L. (1989). Daily change of an antiseptic dressing does not prevent infusion phlebitis: a controlled trial, Am J Infect Control 17(1):23.

Morison MJ. (1989). Wound cleansing: which solution? Prof Nurse 4(5):220.

Morrison RT et al. (1978). Organic chemistry, ed 3. Boston: Allyn & Bacon, Inc.

Perkins J. (1982). Principles and methods of sterilization in the hospital, ed 3. Springfield, Ill: Charles C Thomas, Publisher.

Reddish GF, (ed.) (1978). Antiseptics, disinfectants, fungicides, and chemical and physical sterilization. Philadelphia: Lea & Febiger.

Robins EV. (1989). Immunosuppression of the burned patient, Crit Care Nurs Clin North Am 1(4):767.

Rutala WA. (1989). Draft guidelines for selection and use of disinfectants, Am J Infect Control 17(1):24A.

Speight TM, (ed.) (1987). Avery's drug treatment, ed 3. Baltimore: Williams & Wilkins.

Thomason SS. (1989). Front-line antiseptics, Geriatr Nurs 10(5):235.

United States Pharmacopeial Convention. (1991). Drug information for the health care provider, ed 11. Rockville, Md: The Convention.

# 74 Diagnostic Agents

## INTRODUCTION

Diagnostic agents are considered drugs in the sense that they are chemical substances used to diagnose or monitor a condition or disease. As diagnostic agents, certain secondary chemical characteristics are used to confirm a diagnosis or prognosis or to guide therapy. For example, one type of diagnostic agent may interact with a bodily fluid specimen as a reagent to produce one or another color as an indicant, or it may induce an inflammatory response or an enhancement of a particular gland's functioning. Other agents act by contrasting and enhancing visibility on x-ray film of the lumens or cavities of internal body structures. Some, because of a special affinity and uptake by certain organs, permit critical assessment of organ function. Diagnostic agents may also have side effects and adverse reactions, just like any drug. Thus it is necessary that the nurse know the agent used, its mechanism of action, and indications. Secondary effects are equally important, since many agents have a somewhat narrow range of safety. In some instances, nurses are responsible for correctly collecting and testing specimens and interpreting the results. Specialized training and professional education are necessary to administer some kinds of agents; others are packaged in simple kit form for over-the-counter sale. Because the field of diagnostics and its products is burgeoning, manufacturers' instructions should always be consulted to be assured of current information.

Products used for diagnostic testing are categorized in various ways. In this chapter they are organized by their diagnostic applications and presented primarily in tables:

- For assessment of the size, location, and integrity of structures, such as those of the gastrointestinal tract, gallbladder, kidneys, blood vessels, spleen, and joints, or as an adjunct to computed tomography examinations.
- For functional assessment of organ systems, for example, the heart, pancreas, stomach, liver, pituitary, adrenal cortex, thyroid, or gallbladder.
- For assessment of sensitivities to specific substances, as in allergy states, tuberculosis, mumps, coccidioidomycosis, blastomycosis, or histoplasmosis.
- For assessment of glandular responsivity to provocative challenge by certain agents.
- For screening assessments or monitoring of indicative components in urine, blood, or feces.

## RADIOPAQUE AGENTS FOR VISUALIZING ORGAN STRUCTURE

***Mechanism of action.*** When injected or instilled, radiopaque contrast agents make the body cavity or compartment more radiographically dense or opaque than neighboring anatomic structures. They are used when the structural integrity of a soft-tissue organ system is under study. Ordinary x-ray examinations are useful only for studies of dense materials such as bone. Radiopaque contrast media may also permit visualization of organs' functional dynamics as part of associated diagnostic tests. (See Table 74-1.)

Many of these agents contain molecular iodine in the radiopaque contrast medium to provide the opacity necessary for outlining internal organ cavities, lumens, or ducts that would otherwise be invisible by x-ray examination or fluoroscopy.

Barium contrast media do not contain iodine compounds. Instead, they consist of barium sulfate powder and a vehicle such as hydrosol gum for mixing with prescribed volumes of water to provide a suspension for oral or rectal administration. Additives may include compounds for coloring and flavoring. Iodinated radiopaque agents consist of substituted, triiodinated, benzoic acid derivatives or water-sol-

**TABLE 74-1**   Common diagnostic tests using barium sulfate and iodinated contrast media

| | Cholangiography/Cholecystography — Oral | Cholangiography/Cholecystography — IV | Computerized tomographic enhancement | Angiography | Myelography | Lymphography | Arthrography | Discography | Urography — IV | Urography — Retrograde | Hysterosalpingography | GI Radiography | FDA pregnancy category |
|---|---|---|---|---|---|---|---|---|---|---|---|---|---|
| **ORAL CHOLECYSTOGRAPHICS** | | | | | | | | | | | | | |
| iocetamic acid (Cholebrine) | ✔ | | | | | | | | | | | | B |
| iopanoic acid (Telepaque) | ✔ | | | | | | | | | | | | C |
| ipodate salts (Oragrafin sodium) | ✔ | | | | | | | | | | | | U* |
| tyropanoate sodium (Bilopaque) | ✔ | | | | | | | | | | | | C |
| **INTRAVENOUS AGENTS** | | | | | | | | | | | | | |
| diatrizoate salts (Hypaque Sodium 50%) | | ✔ | ✔ | ✔ | | | | | ✔ | | ✔ | | C |
| iodamide meglumine (Renovue 65) | | | | | | | | | ✔ | | | | U |
| iodamide meglumine (Cholegrafin) | | ✔ | | | | | | | | | | | U |
| iothalamate salts (Conray 60) | | ✔ | ✔ | ✔ | | | | | | | | | B |
| metrizamide (Amipaque) | | | ✔ | ✔ | ✔ | | | | | | | | B |
| **ORAL GASTROINTESTINAL AGENTS** | | | | | | | | | | | | | |
| diatrizoate salts (Hypaque sodium) | | | | | | | | | | | | ✔ | B |
| barium sulfate (Barotrast) | | | | | | | | | | | | ✔ | U |

*U, unclassified.

uble, triiodinated, benzoic acid salts. Manufacturers' instructions should always be reviewed.

The physician should be consulted when a client reports a history of idiosyncratic response or hypersensitivity to iodine, shellfish, or contrast media, or a history of multiple radiographic or radionuclide studies. The most common radiopaque contrast agents are barium sulfate suspensions and iodinated contrast materials.

### Indications

1. Barium-containing preparations are typically used to opacify the gastrointestinal tract. Radiographic techniques of upper gastrointestinal tract and colon examinations are generally performed when ulcers, inflammatory bowel disease, or cancer is suspected. One of the most common uses of barium contrast media is in "double-contrast" studies for gastrointestinal tract evaluation.

2. The most frequent clinical use of iodinated contrast media include intravenous urography and angiography. Iodinated contrast media are often used during computed tomography (CT) of the head and body to visualize vascular structures and to detect tumors.

### Pharmacokinetics.
Radiopaque agents may be administered by the oral, vaginal, rectal, intravenous, or intraarterial routes. They may also be instilled into other body cavities.

Orally administered iodinated agents for visualization of the gallbladder are absorbed across the gastrointestinal mucosa and enter the systemic circulation through the portal venous system. Orally or rectally administered iodinated media for delineation of the gastrointestinal tract are absorbed only minimally, but enough so that the renal tract may also be visualized. Barium sulfate preparations are not absorbed. They are metabolized by the liver and gallbladder and excreted by the kidneys.

### Side effects / adverse reactions.
These products are not without risk. Effects are diverse, are mild to moderate in severity, and usually occur within 1 to 3 minutes. However, delayed reactions may occur up to 1 hour after injection. Urticarial lesions may occur in minutes to hours of drug exposure and may be the first sign of anaphylaxis. Upper respiratory tract symptoms such as itching of eyes, sneezing, eyes tearing, nasal discharge, and throat irritation may occur within minutes of oral administration or inhalation of the substance (DiPiro et al, 1989).

Intravenous cholangiography has caused the highest number of reactions and has therefore been largely replaced by radionuclide diagnostics and retrograde duodenal examination. Excretory urography is performed frequently with only rare serious reactions. Milder reactions result from administration of oral cholecystographic agents. Certain agents are more likely to cause secondary effects than others; manufacturers' information should be consulted.

A history of allergy puts the client at twice the risk of reaction to contrast media, although, paradoxically, these are not true hypersensitivity reactions. Those with a previous reaction to contrast media are at three times the risk. Certain individualized reactions may occasionally have serious results. Death occurs in less than 0.01% of patients, and most of these are attributable to cardiac arrest associated with predisposing cardiovascular disease. Barium sulfate preparations, since they are not absorbed internally, are only potentially hazardous when administered to persons with bowel perforations or fistulas. If allowed to remain in the colon, barium sulfate may cause constipation. Hospitalization and close observation during the procedures are recommended for persons who have high potential for reactions or complications.

Isosulfan blue (for lymphography) should be administered *only subcutaneously*. Certain iothalamate, meglumine, or diatrizoate sodium compounds *are not for injection;* they are for instillation only.

Cardiovascular reactions commonly include reports of "feeling warm" and isolation. However, most clients have no sensation or discomfort. The most common reactions are nausea or flushing, with feelings of warmth over the abdomen and chest. Severely dehydrated patients, the elderly, infants, and the seriously ill tolerate these hemodynamic and hyperosmolar changes less well than others do. Rare adverse reactions include cerebral hematomas, hemodynamic alterations, sinus bradycardia, transient ECG changes, ventricular fibrillation, and petechiae. Individuals with pheochromocytoma may have hypertensive crises. Circulatory blood supply is temporarily increased, which may be detrimental in clients with congestive heart failure if agents are administered intravascularly.

Gastrointestinal effects may include nausea, vomiting, and parotid gland and submaxillary gland swellings.

Central nervous system symptoms may include paresthesias, dizziness, convulsions, paralysis, shock, or coma.

Skin lesions may result: urticaria, necrosis, or pain at the injection site (especially in urography).

Hematologic signs may include thrombocytopenia, leukopenia, or anemia. Diazoate salts inhibit all stages of coagulation. Platelet aggregation is inhibited by several of the agents. Exacerbations of sickle cell disease may attend intravascular injections of contrast media.

Renal system involvement may be manifested by nephrosis of proximal tubular cells in excretory urography, which may proceed to renal failure.

Respiratory signs may include rhinitis, cough, dyspnea, bronchospasm, asthma, laryngeal or pulmonary edema, and subclinical pulmonary emboli. Overt signs of pulmonary emboli and infarction may attend lymphography with ethiodized oil.

Special senses may be impaired: distorted taste sensations; irritated, itching, tearing eyes, or conjunctivitis.

Hypersensitivity reactions and others may include anaphylaxis. Incidence of paradoxic reactions is highest in the 20- to 40-year-old group. History of allergy predisposes to reactions to contrast media. Almost 20% of those who had had a previous reaction to some characteristic of contrast media (not iodine) again experienced a reaction. Although these reactions (primarily urticaria) may be similar to hypersensitivity reactions, they do not seem to be associated with allergy to iodine compounds. The cause is not known. Almost 13% of the remaining group had an iodine allergy history. About 25% of the rest of those with allergy histories had reactions to contrast media.

*Significant drug interactions.* The following interactions may occur when the oral cholecystographic agents are given with the drugs listed below.

| Drug | Possible Effect and Management |
|---|---|
| cholestyramine (Cuemid, Questran) | The cholestyramine will adsorb the cholecystographic agents, thus interfering with the test. Avoid concurrent administration for at least 8 hours or more when these tests are scheduled. |
| iodipamide meglumine IV | Prior administration of the oral agents may block liver metabolism and excretion of this drug. Administration of both drugs, within 24 hours is not recommended. |
| urographic agents | Renal toxicity has been reported in clients with abnormal liver function when these tests were given following the oral agents. Avoid concurrent administration. |

The following interactions may occur when the radiopaque parenteral agents are given with the drugs listed below.

| Drug | Possible Effect and Management |
|---|---|
| aspirin, nonsteroidal antiinflammatory drugs, and other antiplatelet agents | May enhance the antiplatelet effect, since high levels of iodipamide meglumine, diatrizoate sodium, and diaztrizoate meglumine all inhibit platelet aggregation. Monitor closely. |
| inotropic agents | May result in a paradoxic cardiac depressant effect, which is dangerous if client has an ischemic myocardium. Monitor closely if agents must be administered concurrently. |

*Dosage and administration.* Manufacturers' instructions for dose preparation and administration should be followed.

Iodinated radiopaque agents may be variously administered orally (tablets, paste, granules, or suspensions), rectally (enema), parenterally or instilled. Four to six of the tablet formulations may be taken over a short interval the morning before the test, with nothing else but water after that. Barium sulfate compounds are noniodinated, and most are prepared from powders for suspensions to be taken orally or rectally. The volume of orally administered reconstituted agents is about 8 ounces; the enema volume may range from 500 ml to 1,500 ml. Intravenous injection volumes vary according to the agent, from 20 to 300 ml. Direct injection of certain high concentrations of iothalamate solutions should never be made into carotid or vertebral arteries. Elderly patients should be hydrated before barium tests.

## ▷NURSING MANAGEMENT: RADIOPAQUE AGENTS

*Assessment.* Radiographic examinations are not without hazard to the client or to personnel. Risk/benefit ratios must be established on an individual basis. Reactions may arise from either physical or chemical properties of the compounds used. Almost any organ system may be affected. (See side effects/adverse reactions.) Conduct a careful history related to kidney, thyroid, or liver disease. Take an allergy history with particular attention to previous reactions to contrast media or iodine-containing foods, such as shellfish or iodized table salt. Pretreatment with prednisone, diphenhydramine, and ephedrine for clients with a history of iodine hypersensitivity and those with a generally positive allergy history may minimize but not prevent hypersensitivity reactions. This pretreatment regimen reduced the incidence of adverse reactions in one study from 35% to 3%. Do not mix these medications for concurrent administration with the contrast media; they are incompatible.

Maintain radiologic histories. Apprise clients and all those working in an environment of ionizing radiation that there may be current and long-term effects of radiation and of the fact that these effects are cumulative. Since there is no established safe dosage, single or cumulative, keep exposure to a minimum. The risks to benefits of each procedure should be weighed carefully by the clinician and the informed client.

It is recommended that radiography, fluoroscopy, or computed tomography not be performed in a female client if the woman is pregnant or after the first 10 days after menses.

Nurses should ask for lead shielding devices and client-supporting devices before participating in radiographic examinations. If frequently involved, monitor the individual cumulative exposure by wearing a film badge that is checked monthly or quarterly. Wear it outside any shields; obtain reports. Transport as necessary along with the client to the department a bedpan, an emesis basin, tissues, and a warm blanket (room temperatures and equipment in radiologic units are often noted to be cold).

Assist in making the decision to administer anesthesia to restless or agitated clients, especially children. Closely monitor the condition of anesthetized patients; they are at higher risk for adverse reactions than unanesthetized patients.

*Intervention.* Prepare clients appropriately for their examinations using protocols from the radiology department. If visualization is sufficiently impaired because of inadequate bowel preparation or because tablets were not taken as directed, or because foods and fluids other than water were not withheld, it may necessitate a repeat preparation and examination.

Have drugs, equipment, and medical assistance readily

available in case of an emergency such as cardiac arrest. Monitor levels of consciousness and vital signs during the procedure as feasible and afterward for at least 1 hour.

Obtain an order for clear enemas or laxatives as necessary after the procedure or similarly instruct the client.

*Education.* Instruct the client, as appropriate, to prepare by taking the agent with water the night before the procedure or to administer effective enemas or to ingest nothing but water until the test is completed. Explain as appropriate that the procedure may include the administration of about 8 ounces of a fairly thick oral suspension or a retention enema and that position changes may be necessary during the procedure.

## AGENTS FOR EVALUATING ORGAN FUNCTION

Some diagnostic agents can be used to track and visualize the functional processes of organ systems. Inferences can be made about organ function by measurement of the degree or rate at which the agent is distributed, taken up, sequestered, secreted, or excreted from the target organ system or by measurement of the volumes or flow rates. Some of these diagnostic agents are radionuclides (a species of radioactive atom characterized by higher atomic number than bodily tissues) whose gamma-ray emissions can be tracked or

whose residues can be sampled. Other nonradioactive agents are dyes, polysaccharides, or other substances whose dissemination may be traced by color changes or chemical analysis.

### Radioactive Agents

A **radionuclide** is an unstable form of a chemical element. Radiopharmaceutical agents are those in which one of the nonradioactive atoms has been replaced by a radioactive atom. They are either of natural origin or are produced by particle accelerators or generators. The process of neutron activation used in nuclear medicine to produce radionuclides describes the capture of a slow neutron into a stable nucleus with the subsequent emission of a gamma ray. Transmutation is a similar operation, using instead a fast neutron. After injection or ingestion of the resultant nuclide, its pharmacokinesis can be followed by a gamma-ray detector combined with either a rectilinear scanner, scintillation camera, Bender-Blau camera, or other radiation-display device. For nonemitters (such as glucose $^{14}$C), air, blood, lymph, spinal fluids, urine, or biopsy specimens may be collected and the residual radioactivity analyzed or counted as it is excreted. These data are used to make inferences about organ disorders and the body's ability to absorb, metabolize, or excrete substances. See Table 74-2.

**TABLE 74-2**   Common diagnostic tests using radioactive tracer and imaging agents

| Indications | Agent |
| --- | --- |
| Addison's disease, intestinal absorption | cyanocobalamin Co 57, Co 58, Co 60, oral/injectable (Racobalamin-57 kit, Rubatrope-57) |
| Blood iron studies | ferrous citrate (Fe 59), injectable |
| Blood plasma volume determinations or blood pool imaging | radioiodinated (I 125) serum albumin (RISA-125-H, Albumotope I 125), radioiodinated (I 131) serum albumin (RISA-131-H, Albumotope I 131, sodium pertechnetate Tc 99m solution (Pertscan-99m), pertechnetate sodium Tc 99m (Technetium Tc 99m Generator Solution) (see above) |
| Brain imaging | chlormerodrin Hg 197 injection<br>chlormerodrin Hg 203 injection<br>Sodium pertechnetate Tc 99m solution (Pertscan-99m)<br>Ytterbium (Yb) pentetate sodium (for cisternography); previously called DTPA (penetetic acid) |
| Brain, thyroid, and salivary gland imaging; placental localization; blood pool imaging | pertechnetate sodium Tc 99m (Technetium Tc 99m (Generator Solution, Elutek, Mektec 99, Minitec, ScintiCheck, Technetope) |
| Bone imaging | fluorine F 18 injection<br>strontium Sr 87m generator solution<br>strontium nitrate Sr 85, injection (Strotope, Stronscam-85)<br>technetium Tc 99m etidronate sodium kit (osteoscan, Hedspa)<br>technetium Tc 99m stannous pyrophosphate kit (TechneScan PYP kit, Phosphotec, Pyrolite) |
| Cardiac abnormalities, cerebral blood flow, pulmonary function, muscle blood flow studies | xenon Xe 133 injection (Xeneisol Xe 133 Injection)<br>xenon Xe 133 gas (not used for diagnosis of cardiac abnormalities) |
| Deep vein thrombosis | radio-iodinated I 125 fibrinogen injection (Ibrin) |
| Fats, fatty acid absorption (estimations) | triolein I 131, oral/injection oleic acid I 125, oral |
| Gastrointestinal protein loss, hypoproteinemia | chromium (Cr 51) serum albumin (human), injection (Chromalbin) |

***Ionizing radiation.*** Much can be learned through the use of radiation that could not otherwise be discovered or diagnosed. Like any other diagnostic technique, a risk-benefit ratio must be determined.

Ionizing radiation has the ability to knock electrons out of atoms, creating electrically charged ions. It may be defined as electromagnetic radiation (x-rays and gamma rays) or particulate radiation (electrons, occasionally beta particles, protons, neutrons, or atomic nuclei with kinetic energy).

Impact by emitted radiation energy may disrupt bonds between atoms in such crucial biologic molecules as DNA. Disruption can lead to cell death, mutations, or defective mitosis. Energy that is absorbed by tissues can lead to acute effects (as in radiotherapy or radiation accidents) or chronic effects (as from multiple low radiation doses). Effects may appear only after long periods (like cataracts) or in subsequent generations.

The amount of radiation absorbed by tissues during radiologic tests is determined by the dose administered, the half-life of the radionuclide, the energy, the mode of decay, and the length of time the agent dwells within the body. There is no known safe dosage of ionizing radiation despite limits set by the Nuclear Regulatory Commission and the National Council on Radiation, Protection and Measurements.

Estimations of the amount of radiation emitted, the effect, and the dose absorbed may be denoted by the following terms. A **roentgen** is the amount of gamma or x radiation that creates 1 electrostatic unit of ions in 1 ml of air at 0° C. A **rem** is the predicted effect on the human body of a 1-roentgen dose. A **rad** is a unit of measurement of absorbed ionizing radiation energy. One rad = 100 ergs of radiation energy per gram of matter.

Although arbitrary, annual limits for the general population and for any single gestational period have been set

**TABLE 74-2**  Common diagnostic tests using radioactive tracer and imaging agents—cont'd

| Indications | Agent |
| --- | --- |
| Heart blood pool, pericardial effusion, ventricular aneurysms | technetium Tc 99m serum albumin kit |
| Intestinal absorption | cyanocobalamin (see Addison's disease, above), oral/injection |
| Hodgkin's disease, lymphomas, bronchogenic carcinoma | gallium citrate Ga 67 |
| Liver function and liver imaging | sodium rose bengal I 125 injection (Robengatope)<br>sodium rose bengal I 131 injection<br>technetium Tc 99m sulfur colloid kit (Tesuloid, Techne-Coll)<br>technetium Tc 99m sulfur colloid injection |
| Ocular or cerebral tumors (localization) | sodium phosphate P 32, oral/injection (Phosphotope) (Also used in the treatment of polycythemia vera and chronic leukemia) |
| Pancreatic imaging | selenomethionine Se 75 injection (Sethotope) |
| Placental localization | chromated (Cr 51) serum albumin (human) (Chromalbin)<br>technetium Tc 99m (see above for brand names) |
| Pulmonary emboli, pulmonary carcinoma, pneumonitis, emphysema, tuberculosis; congenital heart disease, pulmonary vascular obliteration, pulmonary emboli, diffuse pulmonary disorders | iodinated I 131 aggregated albumin (Macroscan-131, MAA I 131) (Albumotope L-S, used for diagnosing disorders following the semicolon)<br>technetium Tc 99m aggregated albumin kit (Macrotec, TechneScan MAA, MAA kit, Pulmolite: Technetated Albumin Lungaggregate, Instant Microspheres) |
| Red blood cell volume, mass, or survival times; evaluation of blood loss | sodium chromate Cr 51 injection (Rachromate-51, Chromitope Sodium) |
| Reduction of Tc 99m accumulation in choroid plexus and in salivary and thyroid glands | potassium perchlorate, oral (Perchloracap) |
| Renal and urinary tract function | chlormerodrin Hg 197 injection<br>sodium ortho-iodohippurate, iodohippurate sodium, I 131 injection (Hippuran-131, Hipputope)<br>sodium iothalamate I 125 (Glofil-125)<br>technetium Tc 99m pertechnetate sodium kit (Renotec; previously called DTPA) |
| Thyroid function and imaging | sodium iodide I 125 (MPI Iodine 123)<br>sodium iodide I 125 oral solution, sodium iodide I 131 oral solution (Iodotope) (latter also used for treatment of hyperthyroidism or selected thyroid carcinomas)<br>sodium pertechnetate Tc 99m (Pertscan-99m)<br>technetium Tc 99m (see thyroid above) |

at 0.5 rem (for x rays, 1 rem is equal to 1 rad) and for closely monitored occupational workers at about 3 rem/year. Most nurses, physicians, and other health personnel are not routinely monitored for radiation exposure unless assigned to an area with high potential for exposure. Their risk for cumulative exposure is nonetheless higher than that of the general population.

Very little is known about the full effects of radiation. Certain increased risks are associated, however, as follows: infertility, birth defects, potential for certain malignant neoplasms, and manifestations of aging. Exposure to low-level ionizing radiation, such as that from radiographic examinations, and agents containing radionuclides add to the individual's total radiation history. Effects may be insidious, perhaps manifesting themselves in crucial enzyme defects many years after exposure. There is some evidence of the body's ability to repair chromosomal damage, but the scope of this ability is unknown.

"Excessive radiation exposure" is any unnecessary exposure above natural background levels. Although natural background radiation adds to the cumulative risk, medical and dental therapies account for the largest proportion of artificially generated exposure.

**Indications.** Most radionuclides in use today in radiology are for imaging of organs, evaluating organ function, or detecting or treating cancer. The role of nuclear imaging is gradually diminishing because there is increased reliance on computed tomography, ultrasound, and magnetic resonance imaging. Radionuclides are used as tracers to evaluate physiologic and biochemical functioning of organ systems. Extremely sensitive radioactivity sensing devices make it possible to detect, count, and visualize by imaging methods and to analyze minute amounts of radionuclides. Uniquely useful applications of nuclear imagery include the following (see Table 74-2 for specifics):

1. Thyroid enlargement or disease. Agents currently used include $^{131}$I, $^{125}$I, and $^{123}$I. All are isotopes of iodine that emit a type of radiation that can be mapped externally. Usually a 24-hour uptake study is employed to determine the extent and areas of thyroid activity. A scan is then performed to evaluate any thyroid mass or enlargement. "Cold" tumors have a 20% to 25% probability of representing a thyroid cancer. Tumors that localize the radionuclide well are usually benign.
2. Screening individuals with diagnosed malignancies for metastases. Many clients treated for breast cancer, colon cancer, malignant melanoma, lymphoma, prostate cancer, and lung cancer, among others, are often successfully evaluated periodically by scintigrams of the liver, spleen, and skeletal system. The risk-benefit ratio is very high, and information about new or recurrent disease can help the oncologist make crucial decisions about goals, management, prognosis, and so forth.
3. Evaluation of heart disease. This is a primary application of nuclear imagery. Computers are used to analyze data from the images to detect the extent of myo-

cardial damage and wall motion abnormalities and to estimate the ejection fraction of the ventricles. Underlying coronary artery disease can also be estimated before catheterization or other invasive procedures by the use of radionuclides.
4. Tracking physiologic substances and assessment of the status of an organ (e.g., renal function and—more recently by new products—biliary excretion).

In addition to diagnostic uses, some radiopharmaceuticals may be administered therapeutically to deliver radiation to internal body tissues (e.g., iodine 131 for destruction of thyroid tissue in hyperthyroidism). Radioactive tracer substances may also be incorporated into a nonradioactive drug to track the second drug's pharmacokinetics for research purposes.

**Computed tomography (CT)** scans body parts in a series of contiguous slices with pencil-thin x-ray beams, which, after passing through the body, produce data from detectors positioned diametrically across from the beam source. Huge amounts of collected data are integrated and displayed by computer as a video image. CT presents a series of two-dimensional images representing a reconstructed "slice" in the axial plane. By viewing a series of these images, one can perceive the anatomy in a three-dimensional sense. CT therefore often conveys more information than other modalities about lesion density, location, and size. CT has largely replaced older techniques such as pneumoencephalography and angiography in the diagnosis of intracranial disease, though angiography is still used in this application. CT may eliminate the need for other x-ray examinations, but it is not considered a first-line, or screening, technique. Radionuclide scans continue to be used for initial diagnostic screening and for specific tests where their results are more fruitful. Radiation exposure from CT varies depending on the equipment used and the frequency of testing, but it is said to be equal to or sometimes considerably higher than with ordinary x-ray techniques or radionuclides. Although CT is considered to be a noninvasive procedure, intravenous contrast material is frequently injected to enhance structures for differential diagnosis (Figure 74-1). This is referred to as CT with infusion.

**Ultrasound** is a nonradioactive diagnostic tool with cardiovascular, abdominal, obstetric, and other applications. It is used with anatomic and physiologic information obtained by other nuclear medicine techniques. Ultrasound examinations yield data about organ contours and tissue consistency or, in the case of Doppler scanning, blood flow patterns. Results can be distorted in the presence of bone or gases in the body. The secondary effects of high-frequency sound waves on cellular structures and functions are not fully known, though such tests are considered to be noninvasive and innocuous by many in the field.

**Nuclear magnetic resonance imaging (MRI)** is a diagnostic modality that uses radio waves and a magnet, not radiation, drugs, biopsy specimens, or body fluids (Figure 74-2). Like CT, MRI provides sectioned imagery but gives

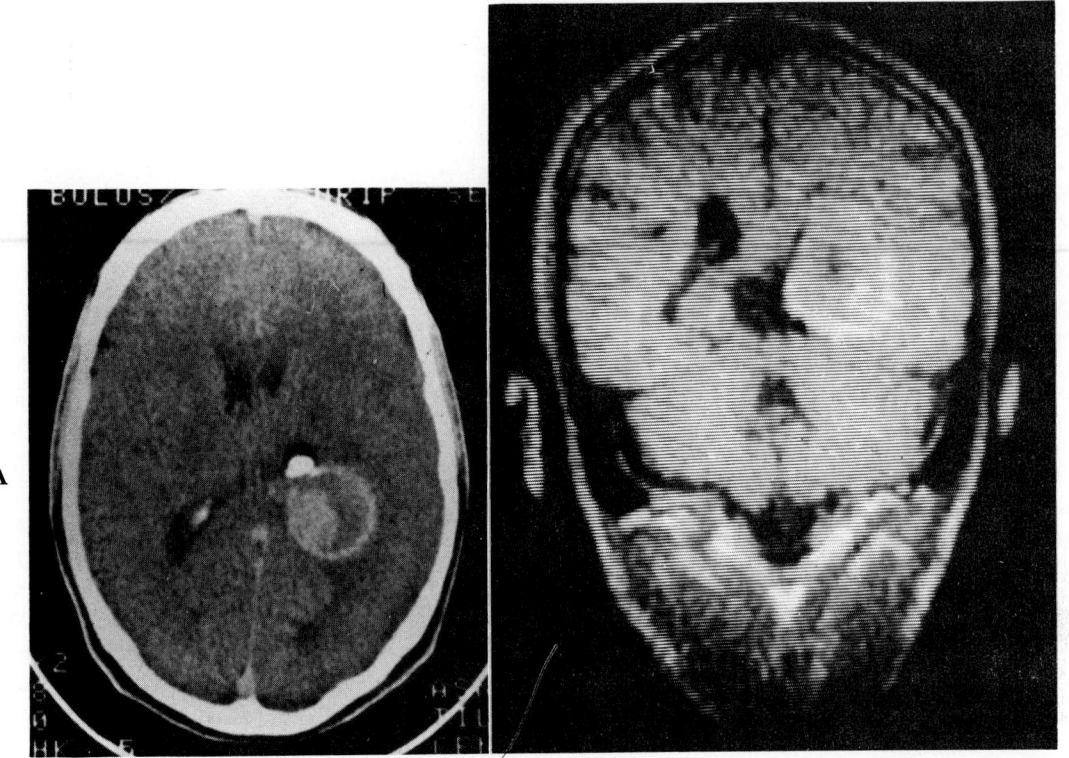

**FIGURE 74-1   A,** This CT scan shows a high-density mass in the left hemisphere, representing a hematoma. **B,** Coronal NMR saturation-recovery scan shows a high-density mass with a high-intensity rim and low-intensity center, representing the hematoma. *(From Alfidi RJ and others: [1982]. Radiology 143:175.)*

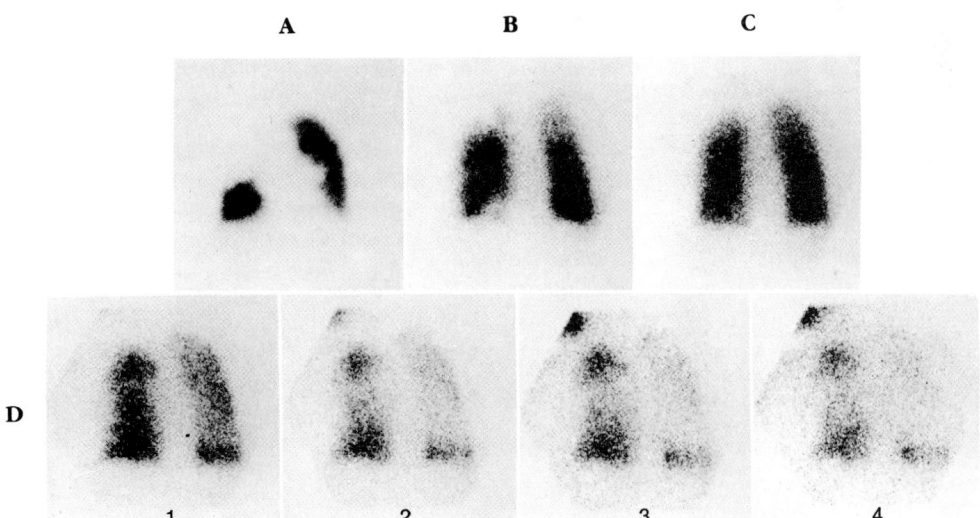

**FIGURE 74-2**   Client, 74 years of age, with moderately severe COPD (emphysema) and history of acute chest pain, increasing shortness of breath. **A,** Posterior perfusion lung image reveals absent perfusion in left upper lobe and superior left lower lobe, as well as in mediastinal region of right lung. **B,** Xe 133 ventilation study (posterior position). Inhalation phase—note ventilation of left lung and mediastinal portion of right lung. **C,** Xe 133 equilibrium phase. Even distribution of Xe 133 throughout both lung fields. **D,** Washout phase. Note delayed washout of Xe 133 from areas of increased dead air space (emphysema). Combined studies infer that client has pulmonary embolization superimposed on COPD. *(From Early PJ and Sodee DB: [1985]. Principles and practice of nuclear medicine. St. Louis: The CV Mosby Co.)*

*Singer CM et al. (1989). Exposure of emergency medicine personnel to ionizing radiation during cervical spine radiography, Ann Emerg Med 18(8):822.

---

### Nursing Research

The potential hazard of ionizing radiation exposure to health care workers who routinely stabilize the necks of trauma patients during cervical spine radiography was studied by Singer et al.* Using an artificial torso, they placed a radiation monitor where a health worker's fingers, hands, arms, and thyroid gland would be, and standard cervical spine radiographs were taken. If the simulated exposures were indicative of actual patient situations, a health care worker who holds the head of a trauma patient four times each week with unshielded hands would receive more than twice the maximum allowable annual occupational radiation exposure to the extremities recommended by the National Council of Radiation Protection and Measurements. It was concluded that health workers who routinely stabilize the necks of trauma patients during cervical spine radiography may incur a radiation risk and that 0.5-mm lead-equivalent gloves provide an effective barrier to ionizing radiation.

---

more than the gross anatomic information gained by CT scanning. MRI supplies extremely detailed images of internal heart and brain structures, for example, and is capable of imaging areas of the spine, abdomen, and extremities. It can differentiate between lesions and normal tissue. MRI is now FDA approved and is rapidly becoming integrated into the radiologist's armamentarium. Those ineligible for diagnostics by MRI include persons with metal prostheses or pacemakers, because the strong magnetic field surrounding the client may move some metallic devices, or a metallic object may result in a distorted test image.

*Pharmacokinetics.* Each type of radionuclide emits alpha or beta particles or gamma rays, or a combination of these. This spontaneous emission of charged particles is termed radioactive decay and eventually results in disintegration of the nucleus. The time it takes for the original radioactivity to decay to one half its original value is known as the physical or radioactive *half-life* of the particular radionuclide. Like a drug, the rate at which a tracer substance is excreted from the body also influences its effects, both valuable and undesirable.

*Dosage and administration.* Manufacturers' current directions should be reviewed. Dosages are not detailed here because they vary with individual needs.

The major considerations in radionuclide dosing are the amount of radioactivity that is administered to produce effective readings and the secondary effects of that radioactivity. While the radioactive material is in the body, it is irradiating even after the study has been completed, whereas x-rays irradiate from an external source and do so only while the body is exposed during the examination. The radionuclide dosage unit for imaging or nonimaging doses of radionuclides is a **microcurie** (one millionth of a curie). A **curie** is a specified measure of radioactivity associated with a specific amount of a radioactive substance, e.g., a radionuclide. Recommended dosages are spelled out in manufacturers' literature. The client's absorbed dose of each radionuclide has been predicted for each procedure with the following three factors being taken into account:

1. The biologic parameters that describe the uptake, distribution, retention, and release of the radiopharmaceutical in the body
2. The energy released by the radionuclide and whether it is penetrating or nonpenetrating
3. The fraction of the emitted energy that is absorbed by the target

The ultimate radiation dose to both the target organ and the whole body is somewhat less in radionuclide nonimaging procedures than in imaging procedures. It is considerably more in radiation therapy (not discussed here).

Shielding is a practical method to prevent or reduce excess radiation exposure of staff or patients during certain diagnostic examinations. Shielding acts to reduce radiation intensity to acceptable limits in body areas not intended for exposure during the radiologic examination. Alpha and beta radiation require very little shielding. An alpha particle can be blocked by the thickness of a sheet of paper, a beta particle by an inch of wood, but several feet of concrete or several inches of lead are necessary to stop gamma or x radiation. Half-value layer is the term describing the thickness of any material required to reduce the intensity of an x-ray or gamma-ray beam to half its original value. Because of its characteristic density, lead is the material typically used in radiation shielding equipment and coverings such as aprons and gloves.

### ▷Nursing Management: Radioactive Agents

*Assessment.* As in the nursing management for individuals receiving radiopaque contrast media, assessments should include appropriate histories related to allergies to iodine or iodine-containing foods, previous exposures to ionizing radiation, and menstrual histories.

*Intervention.* The basic principles of radiation exposure safety are relative to the source of radiation: *time* spent in the radioactive field, *distance* from the source, and *shielding*. The amount of radiation absorbed is directly proportional to the time spent in a radioactive field and inversely related to the distance from the source of radioactive emission. Thus quality nursing care requires careful planning so that sensible limitations on time spent in the radioactive field do not reduce the quality of client care.

Wear rubber or plastic gloves when handling bedpans, urine specimens, or continuous drainage bags of clients within a day or two after nuclear medicine procedures. Wherever radionuclides are used, one person, designated the radiation safety officer, has the responsibility for safety in case of spills or accidents with radioactive materials. This officer should be consulted if there is a break in safety procedures or if, for example, linen has been contaminated by vomitus or excreta within 24 hours of administration of a radiopharmaceutical. Although it may be determined that unusual precautions are not needed, it is wise to seek consultation as needed.

Follow instructions by radiopharmaceutical manufacturers about radionuclide storage (some require refrigeration), dosage, and technique. Errors in technique must not be tolerated, especially with regard to the handling of radiopharmaceuticals, disposal of contaminated equipment, and proper shielding of all present for radiologic and imaging procedures. Monitoring badges should be issued and worn by those regularly participating in these procedures. Protection should be assured for those who are unfamiliar with these procedures. Women of child-bearing age who are more than 10 days after menses or who are pregnant should not assist. (*Radiation therapy* requires other precautions.)

*Education.* Clients' anxieties may be heightened by the uncertainty of unknown diagnosis, fear of radiation, and cold or unfamiliar surroundings. Clients may be introduced to the personnel, surroundings, and the large equipment some time before scheduled examinations and given opportunity for questions and explanations. They should know that there may be some discomfort at the site of injection, taste alterations, or a feeling of warmth or discomfort in various parts of the body if the administered agent contains an iodine preparation. If a counter or rectilinear scanner is used, clients should be advised that it may typically emit irregular clicks as it collects data; it does not emit radiation. Since clients may be required to maintain a single position on a hard surface for extended periods or may be briefly restrained, supply foam wedge supports and coverings as necessary. Explain that personnel may wear strange-looking gray or green apparel to shield them from excess radiation and that clients too will be protected by protocols that have been established. Then adhere to them.

Give clients written instructions, especially about the specific time they should return for the examination after the nuclide dose. Explain that the test must be performed at a

**TABLE 74-3** Common nonradioactive compounds for visualization of organ function

| Compound | Indications | Secondary effects | Nursing management |
|---|---|---|---|
| aminohippurate sodium (PAH) | Renal function tests, especially of renal plasma flow | Considered safe; some reports of feelings of warmth and nausea<br>High-protein diet, penicillin, salicylates, phenolsulfonphthalein, and diuretics inhibit PAH secretion in the tubules<br>Procaine and sulfonamides may interfere with laboratory test results | Give intravenously at constant rate<br>Handle blood samples carefully without agitating<br>Observe site for hematoma or phlebitis |
| indocyanine green (Cardio-Green) | Liver function tests; blood flow, uptake, storage, and excretion<br>Renal blood flow in anuric patients<br>Cardiac output studies by the indicator dilution method | No reported toxicities<br>Half-life decreased by phenytoin, phenobarbitol, haloperidol, and other drugs; check package insert | The dye is unstable and must be dissolved and used within 10 hours |
| inulin (Alantin) | Glomerular filtration rate | Renal clearance may be altered in pregnancy | Intravenous injections |
| mannitol (Osmitrol) | Glomerular filtration rate<br>Used also for treatment of oliguria, cerebral edema, chemical poisoning, congestive glaucoma | Dry mouth, thirst, headache, acidosis, dehydration<br>Contraindicated in congestive heart failure, pulmonary edema, persistent renal disease after initial dose<br>Edetate may increase absorption of mannitol | Intravenous infusion<br>Monitor vital signs and urinary output closely |
| sodium indigotindisulfonate (Indigo Carmine) | Renal function tests and for locating ureteral orifices during cystoscopy | | Intramuscular or intravenous use<br>Replaced by more specific agents |

very specific time after the medication is administered (at the point of a specific half-life).

## Nonradioactive Agents

### Nonradioactive Agents for Evaluating Organ Function via Volumes and Flows

These relatively biologically inert and nonradioactive substances are commonly used to measure flow rates, fluid volumes, diffusion, concentration ability, and organ function. These compounds are mostly dyes, polysaccharides, or other substances that can be assayed chemically or detected by characteristic colors after administration. Many of the dye tests determine the rate of plasma clearance of the dye by the organ under study. The ability to measure certain parameters against known normal values at defined points in the procedure makes these compounds useful as diagnostic aids. They are used variously for evaluation of cardiac output, liver or kidney function or blood flows, circulation time, intestinal absorption, and so forth (see box, "Selected Multiple Urine Tests").

These compounds are administered primarily by the intravenous or intramuscular routes. They are rapidly absorbed by the organ system under examination and are usually excreted by that system.

These drugs are relatively pharmacologically inert and are used to permit measurement of specific physiologic func-

tions without themselves significantly altering those functions (Table 74-3).

### Nonradioactive Agents for Challenging Glandular Response

Certain compounds are used diagnostically to challenge a particular system, often glandular, to produce measurable responses. Secretory responses indicate whether there is functional integrity within the secreting gland or system. Many of these agents are protein substances that mimic the action of naturally occurring bodily chemicals such as secretagogues for exocrine gland response and stimulants for endocrine secretion.

Since most are administered intramuscularly or intravenously, these agents move rapidly to the site of action. Degradation of these agents is equally rapid.

Nonradioactive agents are used to evaluate or enhance capabilities such as hypothalamic-pituitary function, thyroid secretion, gallbladder contraction, insulin response, gastric acid secretory function, alkalinity of pancreatic juice, or titrated responses to angiotensin II.

These compounds act on the targeted gland or site as releasing factors. Thus secondary effects may be as widespread and disruptive to bodily chemical balance as a large dose of the secretion or hormone itself (Table 74-4). Epi-

**TABLE 74-4** Common nonradioactive agents for challenging glandular/body system response

| Compound | Indications and secondary effects | Nursing management |
|---|---|---|
| corticotropin (ACTH) | Adrenocortical functioning<br>Contraindications: scleroderma, osteoporosis, systemic fungal infections, ocular herpes simplex, postoperative status, congestive heart failure, hypertension, allergy to pork<br>Secondary effects: fluid-electrolyte imbalances, muscle weakness, GI ulceration, hypertension, increased intracranial pressure, infections, hypersensitivity | Withhold food and restrict activity for 12 hr before test<br>Low-carbohydrate diet for 2 days before test (usually); rest for 30 min before test<br>Withhold medications; corticosteroids, estrogens, calcium gluconate, amphetamines, spironolactone, ethanol, lithium (as feasible)<br>Test results may be altered by radioactive scanning examinations administered within the week before test |
| edrophonium chloride (Tensilon) | Differential diagnosis of myasthenia gravis<br>Contraindications: hypersensitivity, mechanical obstructions of the intestinal or urinary tracts<br>Secondary effects: severe cholinergic reactions—bradycardia or cardiac standstill; dysrhythmias; cholinergic reactions of the eye, CNS, respiratory, GI, or muscular systems | A placebo may be administered first as if it were the test dose to evaluate baseline muscular capabilities<br>Withhold medications: procainamide, muscle relaxants, prednisone, quinidine, and anticholinergics (for at least 8 hr)<br>Observe for developing signs of adverse effects<br>Keep available a syringe containing 1 mg atropine sulfate for IV use to reverse severe cholinergic reactions |
| gonadorelin (Factrel) | Anterior pituitary function; differential diagnosis of anterior pituitary from hypothalamic dysfunction; induction or inhibition of ovulation (investigational use)<br>Secondary effects: hypersensitivity, headache, lightheadedness, nausea; pain, pruritus, or rash at injection site | Withhold medications affecting pituitary secretion of gonadotrophins: androgens, estrogens, progestins, and glucocorticoids<br>Avoid interacting drugs: spironolactone, levodopa, digoxin, phenothiazines, and dopamine antagonists |

**TABLE 74-4**  Common nonradioactive agents for challenging glandular/body system response—cont'd

| Compound | Indications and secondary effects | Nursing management |
|---|---|---|
| histamine phosphate | Ability of gastric mucosa to produce hydrochloric acid and to diagnose pheochromocytoma<br>Contraindications: asthma and allergies; hypotension; severe cardiac, pulmonary, or renal disease<br>Secondary effects: flushing, dizziness, headache, dyspnea, asthma, urticaria, hypotension or hypertension, tachycardia, GI distress, or convulsions | Withhold food for 12 hr and fluids and smoking for 8 hr before test<br>Withhold medications: antacids, anticholinergics, alcohol, cimetidine, reserpine, adrenergic blockers, corticosteroids<br>Instruct client to expectorate excess saliva to prevent mixing it with specimen<br>Keep epinephrine available for severe hypotension |
| pentagastrin (Peptavlon) | Gastric acid secretory function in pernicious anemia, atrophic gastritis, gastric carcinoma, duodenal ulcers, Zollinger-Ellison tumors and to evaluate effectiveness of acid-reducing surgery<br>Secondary effects: hypersensitivity, stimulation of pancreatic secretion, GI distress or bleeding; effects less likely than with histamine or betazole | Withhold food, liquids, and smoking after midnight before test<br>Inform client that a nasogastric tube will be passed<br>Withhold medications: antacids, anticholinergics, adrenergic blockers, cimetidine, reserpine<br>After test, observe for GI distress<br>Usual diet and medications may be resumed |
| protirelin (Thypinone) | Thyroid function response to therapy; pituitary or hypothalamic dysfunction<br>Secondary effects are usually transitory and minor but occur in 50%: blood pressure swings, breast engorgement in lactating women, nausea, urinary urgency, lightheadedness, flushing, bad taste, headache, mouth dryness | Measure blood pressure every 15 min during test, especially for increases of up to 20 to 30 mm Hg<br>Administered by IV bolus over 15 to 30 sec with the patient supine |
| secretin (Secretin-Kabi) | Diagnosis of pancreatic exocrine disorders; gastrinoma; as an aid in collecting pancreatic cells for microscopic examination<br>Contraindications: acute pancreatitis attack, pregnancy<br>Hypersensitivity reactions may occur | Withhold food overnight before test (12 to 15 hr)<br>Prepare patient for discomfort of double-lumen oral tube |
| sincalide (Kinevac) | For gallbladder contraction to make possible aspiration of bile from the duodenum for assessment of cholesterol saturation<br>Used also as adjunct to secretin for pancreatic evaluation<br>Secondary effects: hypersensitivity, GI symptoms (not necessarily indicating biliary tract abnormality), dizziness, or flushing | Use solution within 24 hr |
| thyrotropin, TSH (Thytropar) | Differential diagnosis of source of myxedema: thyroid or pituitary; monitoring of drug therapy<br>Given with $^{131}$I to enhance uptake of $^{131}$I<br>Secondary effects: hypersensitivity, coronary thrombosis, exacerbation of Addison's disease, headache, hypotension, menstrual irregularities, fever, nausea, vomiting, urticaria, cardiac dysrhythmias | Used for 1-3 days to determine thyroid status; to diagnose thyroid cancer after surgery, usually given for 3-7 days<br>Blood may be drawn between 6 and 8 AM<br>Withhold all steroids and thyroid hormones for 2 days before test |
| Tolbutamide sodium (Orinase Diagnostic) | Diagnosis of islet cell adenomas differentiated from functional hypoglycemia<br>Secondary effect: severe hypoglycemia; may be falsely positive or unsafe for pregnant woman, for fetus, or for children<br>Contraindications: severe renal or liver disease<br>Rarely: burning sensations in shoulder or arm; thrombophlebitis | Instruct patients to adhere to a 150-300 g/day carbohydrate diet for 3 days before test and to fast overnight<br>Avoid smoking during the fast and the test<br>Withhold medications: dicumarol, salicylates, sulfonamides, oxyphenbutazone, phenylbutazone, probenecid, MAO inhibitors, beta blockers, and chloramphenicol for 3 days before test<br>Use drug solution within 1 hr after preparation<br>If severe hypoglycemia occurs, obtain a blood sample, stop the test, and prepare an IV glucose solution |

nephrine, antihistamines, corticoids, and a tourniquet should be readily available for all tests in case of severe reactions. Analgesics, nasogastric suction equipment, vasodilators (for histamine agents), intravenous glucose solutions (for tolbutamide sodium), and atropine (for edrophonium chloride) should also be kept available.

Manufacturers' instructions should be followed very closely because almost all these compounds are administered parenterally and in very small dosages.

## AGENTS FOR SCREENING AND MONITORING DISORDERS AND IMMUNE STATUS

Various screening and monitoring agents may be extracts of common allergens (ragweed, grasses, trees, molds, animal dander, and foods), purified derivatives or concentrates of microbial antigens, hormones, or animal cellular antigens, or they may be chemical reagents. Many chemical reagents for common diagnostic purposes are packaged in simple kit form for over-the-counter or prescribed purchase; they may also be used routinely in institutions and physicians' offices.

***Mechanism of action, pharmacokinetics.*** Antigens applied topically or intradermally cause antigen-antibody reactions, which may be manifested by a local inflammatory response at the test site. The test site is assessed after a prescribed time interval. A positive response is indicated by the presence of erythema, the typical "wheal and flare" response, and induration (a firm lump under the skin). In the case of microbial antigen challenge, this positive response may merely indicate a previous exposure to the microbe or its products, but not necessarily the presence of an active disease process. False negative results may also occur, and further investigation may be necessary. The size of the erythematous area or induration may be measured to estimate the degree of the person's sensitivity or immune response. These responses may be short lived or of lifelong duration. (See also Chapter 65.) Persons who are in an immunosuppressed state because of cancer chemotherapy or radiation treatments, malnutrition, debilitation, or congenital or acquired immune deficiency syndrome (AIDS) may demonstrate no response (anergy) when tested with a prescribed battery of antigen challenges. These persons are extremely vulnerable to infection and may need metabolic support and precautions to avoid infection. Test results may not be reliable in those who have viral infections, are febrile or uremic, or have recently received live viral vaccinations. In vitro tests of body fluids and the like are usually performed by addition of antigens, reagents, or agglutinating substances to the specimen and by interpretation of results based on established phenomena such as the presence or absence of agglutination.

***Indications.*** Some diagnostic agents measure a person's physiologic response or hypersensitivity to the agent as a specific chemical challenge. They are typically used in sim-

## SELECTED MULTIPLE URINE TESTS

| Measures | Chemstrip GP | Combistix | HemaCombistix | Uristix-4 | Keto-Diastix | Chemstrip 5L | Labstix | BiliLabstix | Multistix SG* | Multistix 7 | Multistix 10 SG* | Chemstrip 9 | Multistix 9 | Chemstrip LN | Multistix 2 |
|---|---|---|---|---|---|---|---|---|---|---|---|---|---|---|---|
| glucose | X | X | X | X | X | X | X | X | X | X | X | X | X | | |
| protein | X | X | X | X | | X | X | X | X | X | X | X | X | | |
| pH | | X | X | | | X | X | X | X | X | X | X | X | | |
| blood | | | X | | | X | X | X | X | X | X | X | X | | |
| ketones | | | | | X | X | X | X | X | X | X | X | X | | |
| bilirubin | | | | | | | | X | X | | X | X | X | | |
| urobilinogen | | | | | | | | | X | | X | X | X | | |
| nitrite | | | | X | | | | | | X | X | X | X | X | X |
| leukocytes | | | | X | | X | | | | X | 9 | X | X | X | X |

Modified and adapted from Facts and comparisons, St Louis, 1988, JB Lippincott.
*Also measures specific gravity.

ple baseline screening procedures as part of the initial diagnostic workup. Some are used in skin tests by patch, prick, scratch, or intradermal injection for assessment of hypersensitivity (allergy), anergy (congenital or acquired inability to develop a cell-mediated reaction), cellular immunity, or antibody response. (See Table 74-5.) Others are used as reagents in specimens of blood, urine, and bodily discharges for detection of the levels of certain components to facilitate diagnosis or to monitor known conditions. (See Table 74-6 and the box on p. 1120 on urine tests.)

***Side effects / adverse reactions.*** Local reactions to skin tests do not usually cause discomfort. Occasionally a highly positive reaction will result in vesiculation and necrosis of overlying skin; corticosteroids may be ordered. Transient tachycardia, malaise, or low-grade fever may occur separately. Occasionally, a person may report systemic allergic reactions of urticaria, sneezing, or dyspnea. Rarely an overwhelming antigen-antibody response may occur, an anaphylactic response, calling for emergency measures such as the administration of epinephrine and respiratory and circulatory support. All these secondary effects are more likely if hyposensitization therapy is begun, since this includes a well-controlled program of increasing dosages of the allergen in question.

***Dosage and administration.*** For certain standardized tests such as that for as coccidioidomycosis, the dosage is fixed (0.1 ml of a 1:100 dilution). Dosages for allergy testing are also very small (0.02 to 0.05 ml) but may be individualized. Manufacturers' instructions for all these diagnostic agents should be followed carefully.

**TABLE 74-5**   Biologic agents for diagnostic tests

| Biologic product | Purpose, preparation, and storage | Alerts |
|---|---|---|
| **BIOLOGIC DIAGNOSTIC TESTS** | | |
| Tuberculin, old; tine test | Multiple-puncture, disposable test device for the detection of tuberculin reactivity; especially useful in mass screening; initial test should be done at or before rubeola immunization, thereafter annually or biannually or as indicated by individual risk of exposure (repeated testing may increase the size of reaction but will not sensitize to tuberculin). Apply the disk with its 4 coated prongs quickly and firmly to the volar surface of the forearm so that puncture sites and disk impression are seen. Reaction read 48-72 hr (criteria for positive reaction—extent of induration or vesiculation as per enclosed ruler in package—2 mm or greater). Store unrefrigerated below 30° C (86° F) | Precautions: test with caution those with active tuberculosis (possible activation of quiescent lesions); hypersensitivity to acacia gum; immunosuppression or recent vaccination with live virus vaccines may suppress reactivity; doubtful or positive reaction—further test using Mantoux, chest roentgenogram, sputum culture<br>Side effects: local vesicles, ulceration, or necrosis in highly sensitive persons; pain or pruritus may be relieved by cold packs |
| Tuberculin purified protein derivatives—PPD test (Mantoux) (Aplitest, multipuncture) | Solution obtained from human strain of *Mycobacterium tuberculosis* for more conclusive results than the tine test. Given intradermally 0.1 ml strength either 1 US unit (for those who are highly sensitized), 5 US units, or 250 US units (for those failing to react), which should never be used as initial dose. Given intracutaneously. Positive reaction when read 48-72 hr later: an induration 10 mm or more; 5-9 mm is "doubtful" reaction except in case of known exposure. Positive reaction only indicates previous exposure to tuberculosis, not necessarily active disease; further testing for diagnosis is thus required. Store at 2°-8° C. | Contraindications: never inject a 250 US unit/ 0.1 ml dose as initial test<br>Precautions: immunosuppression or concurrent or recent immunization with certain virus vaccines or recent viral infection (may cause suppressed reactivity). Those over 55 yr may need second testing<br>Side effects: see package insert for details |
| **ALLERGENIC EXTRACTS** | Several hundred individual purified fluid allergens for diagnosis and hyposensitization for specific allergies: pollens, poison ivy/oak, foods, dusts, skin contactants, insects, fungi, yeasts, autogenous bacteria, based on intracutaneous skin test responses. Treatment is periodic subcutaneous injection of gradually increasing potency of dilutions of specific allergen(s); schedule and dosages highly individualized | Contraindications: severe anaphylaxis<br>Precautions: severe anaphylaxis (reduce dose); keep on hand epinephrine, antihistamines, oxygen, etc.<br>Side effects (grass allergens most reactive of all): local—edema, redness, pain (reduce dose); systemic—urticaria, sneezing, dyspnea (give epinephrine, antihistamines, steroids; reduce dose) |

**TABLE 74-6** Common tests for screening selected conditions

| Preparation | Condition monitored or detected | Procedure |
|---|---|---|
| Acetone tests (Acetest, Chemstrip K, Ketostix) | Tests of urine or blood for ketones, in diabetes mellitus | Tablets, papers, or strips |
| Albumin (Albustix) | Protein detection in urine | Strips |
| Bacteria in urine tests (Microstix-Nitrite; Microstix-3 Strips, Uricult) | Tests for nitrite to detect bacteria in urine | Strips |
| Bilirubin test (Ictotest) | Tests for bilirubin in urine | Tablets |
| Blood urea nitrogen test (Azostix) | Tests for urea nitrogen in blood | Strips |
| C-reactive protein (LAtest-CRP) | Serum test for acute inflammation | Kit |
| *Chlamydia trachomatis* Test (Micro Trak *Chlamydia trachomatis* Direct Specimen Test) | Tests of tissue specimens for *Chlamydia trachomatis* | Slide test |
| Gastrointestinal tests (Entero-Test, Entero-Test Pediatric) | Upper gastrointestinal fluid used to test for bleeding, parasites, pH differences, achlorhydria, and esophageal reflux | Capsules |
| Gastro-Test | Test for stomach pH to help locate/diagnose gastrointestinal bleeding | |
| Glucose blood tests (Chemstrip bG, Dextrostix, Glucostix, Visidex II) | Measure of blood glucose | Strips |
| Glucose urine tests (Clinitest, Chemstrip uG, Clinistix, Diastix, Tes-Tape) | Detection of urine glucose | Tablets, strips |
| Gonorrhea tests (Gonodecten, Biocult-GC) | Screen of discharges or swabs of urethral, rectal, pharyngeal, and endocervical areas for *Neisseria gonorrhoeae* | Kit |
| Mononucleosis tests (Mono-Chek, Mono-Diff, Monospot, Monosticon, Monosticon Dri-Dot, Mono-Sure, Mono-Test) | Physician office use, tests for antibodies to diagnose infectious mononucleosis | Kits |
| Occult blood screening CS-T, Early Detector, EZ-Detect, Fleet Detecatest | Home testing for blood in feces | Tests |
| Hemoccult II | Fecal sample from home sent to laboratory for check | Kit |
| Gastroccult | Tests of gastric content for blood | Kit |
| Coloscreen, Coloscreen/VPI, Hema-Chek, Hematest, Hemoccult, Hemastix | Tests of feces for blood | Tablets, slides, strips |
| Ovulation tests | Prediction of ovulation | Test, kit |
| (Clearplan, OvuStick) | Home tests | |
| (First Response Ovulation Predictor, Fortel Ovulation, OvuSTICK Urine hLH) | Immunoassay test for hLH in urine | |
| Pregnancy tests—home kits (Advance Test, Answer, Answer 2, Answer Plus, Answer Plus 2, Clearblue, Daisy 2, e.p.t. Plus, e.p.t. Stick test, Fact) | Urine testing | Kits |
| Pregnancy tests—for professional use only | | |
| (Pregnate Clone Slide, Pregnosis, Pregnosticon Dri-Dot, UCG Slide Test, Nimbus, Pregnospia) | Tests of urine for chorionic gonadotropins | Test |
| Rheumatoid factor test (LAtest-RF kit, Rheumanosticon Dri-Dot) | Test of blood for rheumatoid factor | Kit |
| Sickle cell test—for professional use only | | |
| Sickledex Test | Detection of hemoglobin S | Test |
| Streptococci tests—for professional use only | | |
| (Culturette 10 minute Group A Strep ID, Insta Kit, Rapid Test Strep) | A latex slide agglutination test for Group A streptococci | |
| Taste function | | |
| Accusens T | Measure of taste function and dysfunction | Kit |
| Virus tests | | |
| Abbott HTLV III EIA | Tests for antibody to human T-lymphotrepic virus type III in blood | Kit |
| Micro Trak HSV 1/HSV 2 culture/typing | Identification of herpes simplex in tissue cultures | Kit |
| Rotalex Test | Detection of rotavirus in feces | Kit |
| Rubacell II | Detection of antibody to rubella virus in serum | Test |

## ▷NURSING MANAGEMENT: SCREENING AGENTS

**Assessment.** Administer these preparations with care because of their propensity to trigger allergic reactions. Question the client regarding any previous reactions to skin testing. Dilute test doses of less than one tenth the usual concentration may then be administered.

**Intervention.** Inspect the liquid extract for clarity; do not use it if particles are seen. As appropriate, use one of the following methods for administering these diagnostic test agents.

A sterile needle or other instrument may be used to prick or scratch the skin after a drop of the extract is placed on the skin. Depending on the approach used, the results may be read directly or after the testing patch has been removed.

Intradermal injections are commonly made into the ventral surface of the forearm. Use a tuberculin syringe with a 25- to 27-gauge needle. Inject intradermally with the needle nearly parallel to the skin surface, making certain that the needle does not penetrate deeper, into subcutaneous tissue. This will increase the precision with which the results may be interpreted; in tuberculin tests it will also prevent febrile reactions. A correctly administered intradermal injection will immediately raise a small, colorless bleb or lump. Stop inserting the needle as soon as the tip of the needle, bevel up, has entered the skin but is still visible. Then inject the antigen with steady pressure.

Be prepared for major allergic manifestations such as angioedema, urticaria, serum sickness, or anaphylactic shock, which can occur. Have the person wait for 30 minutes to observe for development of an allergic reaction. Have available medications for emergency administration: antihistamines such as diphenhydramine and epinephrine, 0.2 ml for subcutaneous use. Equipment for full circulatory and respiratory support should also be available.

**Evaluation.** After the injection, there is a prescribed wait, often 20 minutes or several days (depending on the antigen), before the local reaction should be assessed for erythema and induration. A positive reaction to some antigens is determined by the presence of induration alone; erythema is not always a criterion. **Erythema** is categorized as follows:

| | |
|---|---|
| "tr" (trace) | Faint discoloration |
| + (one plus) | Pink |
| + + | Red |
| + + + | Purplish red |
| + + + + | Vesiculation or necrosis |

Measure the single largest induration or the largest coalesced induration. Induration can be measured with precision in the following way: Placing your index, middle, and ring fingers together, stroke the test site to determine the presence of induration. To delimit the indurated area, using a ballpoint pen, draw a line *toward* the indurated area in four

directions. Edges of the induration can easily be perceived as the ball-point tip touches them. Stop each marking when the edge is perceived. Then measure the diameter of the remaining unmarked indurated area in millimeters. Or use the following criteria for indurations:

| | |
|---|---|
| "tr" (trace) | Barely palpable |
| + | Palpable, but not visible |
| + + | Easily palpable and visible; indurated area buckles when squeezed gently |
| + + + | Easily palpable and visible; does not buckle when squeezed gently |
| + + + + | Vesiculation or necrosis |

Criteria used to categorize Mantoux tuberculin test results according to induration diameter are as follows.
- Less than 5 mm is a negative result.
- 5 to 9 mm is a questionable result, retesting by another method may be necessary.
- More than 9 mm is a positive result.

Indurations resulting from multiple puncture tuberculin testing devices are interpreted as positive if more than 2 mm in diameter. Results are considered less reliable than results of Mantoux tests.

## SUMMARY

Diagnostic agents are chemical substances used to diagnose or monitor a condition or disease. Just like other drugs, they may also have side effects and adverse reactions. It is essential then that the nurse know the agent used, its mechanism of action, and indications, and how to prevent or minimize any adverse effects.

## BIBLIOGRAPHY

American Hospital Formulary Service. (1991). AHFS drug information '91. Betheseda, Md: American Society of Hospital Pharmacists, Inc.

Cerne F. (1988). Computed tomography alive and well, Hospitals 62(21):65.

Christman NJ. (1990). Uncertainty and adjustment during radiotherapy, Nurs Research 39(1):17.

DiPiro JT, Talbert RL, et al, eds. (1989). Pharmacotherapy: a pathophysiologic approach. New York: Elsevier.

Dudjak LA. (1987). Mouth care for mucositis due to radiation therapy, Cancer Nurs 10(3):131.

Early PJ and Sodee DB. (1991). Principles and practice of nuclear medicine, ed 2, St Louis: Mosby–Year Book, Inc.

Erickson S et al. (1990). Intraoperative radiotherapy, Dimens Oncol Nurs 3(4):5.

Fraser MC et al. (1989). Second malignancies following cancer therapy, Semin Oncol Nurs 5(1):43.

Freeman J. (1988). Management of stomatitis symptoms, Dimens Oncol Nurs 2(3):14.

Haaga JR and Alfidi RJ. (1988). Computed tomography of the whole body, ed 2, St Louis: The CV Mosby Co.

Hobbie WL et al. (1989). Endocrine late effects among survivors of cancer, Semin Oncol Nurs 5(1):14.

Johnson JE et al. (1989). Process of coping with radiation therapy, J Consult Clin Psychol 57(3):358.

Kastrup EK, ed. (1991). Facts and comparisons. St Louis: JB Lippincott Co.

Kramer J et al. (1989). Late effects of cancer therapy on the central nervous system, Semin Oncol Nurs 5(1):22.

McGowan KL. (1989). Radiation therapy: saving your patient's skin, RN 52(6):24.

Monroe D. (1989). Patient teaching for x-ray and other diagnostic, RN 52(9):50.

Moshang T Jr et al. (1988). Late effects: disorders of growth and sexual maturation associated with the treatment of childhood cancer, J Assoc Pediatr Oncol Nurses 5(4):14.

Oakley K. (1990). Making sense of . . . x-ray precautions, Nursing Times 86(6):50.

Orsted H. (1989). Radiation skin reaction, Can Nurse 85(9):30.

Pape LH. (1988). Therapy-related acute leukemia: an overview, Cancer Nurs 11(5):295.

Radiation therapy: adverse effects. (1989). Nursing 19(9):73.

Radiocontrast nephrotoxicity: ionic vs nonionic compounds, NDA 13(5):37.

Ruccione K et al. (1989). Late effects in multiple body systems, Semin Oncol Nurs 5(1):4.

Sartoris DJ et al. (1989). Computed tomography of rheumatologic disorders, Hosp Pract 24(8):169.

Stang PE. (1988). Diagnostic and therapeutic concerns in head-injured patients, J Am Acad Physician Assist 1(2):112.

Strohl RA. (1989). Radiation therapy for head and neck cancers, Semin Oncol Nurs 5(3):166.

Weck E. (1989). A primer on medical imaging, part 2, FDA Consum 23(4):12.

*Chapter*

# 75  Poisons and Antidotes

## INTRODUCTION

Over 100 million emergency calls are made to poison control centers annually in America. Of these calls, the majority involve accidental ingestions of drugs or chemicals by children under 5 years old. Hospital emergency rooms treat more than 130,000 children for toxic substance ingestion, and more than 10% of them require hospital admission. While the majority of children's ingestions are accidental, most drug overdoses in adults are intentional, the result of a suicide attempt or drug abuse. The substances most commonly ingested by children are listed in Table 75-1. The most frequently ingested pharmaceutical in this age group is flavored chewable vitamins (14%). The most frequent adult poison is a medication, most often a tranquilizer or sedative. The most common agents of drug abuse or drug overdose leading to emergency room visits or a medical examiner's review were listed previously in Chapter 9. Criminal poisonings are rare, possibly because of the sophisticated poison detection capabilities of police toxicologic laboratories. Industrial poisonings may be more wide-

**TABLE 75-1**   Substances most commonly ingested by children under 5*

| Substance | Approximate percent of total ingestions |
| --- | --- |
| Pharmaceuticals (flavored chewable vitamins, analgesics, etc. | 40 |
| Polishes, household cleansers | 14 |
| Plants | 13 |
| Cosmetics | 10 |
| Pesticides | 5.5 |
| Paints, solvents | 4 |
| Petroleum products | 3 |
| Gases (fumes) | 0.2 |
| Unknown | 10 |

*Young and Koda-Kimble, 1988.

spread than previously suspected, since both the sources of toxic agents in the environment and their effects can be insidious. Common sources include chemical waste disposal sites (e.g., dioxin) or transport systems (e.g., radioactive substances), exhaust gases, insecticides, and fumigants.

Morbidity and mortality from accidental poisonings in children under age 5 have dropped, partly because of public awareness of the potential hazards in children's environments, the effectiveness of poison control centers, and child-proof containers. Unfortunately, this encouraging trend is not reproduced in other age-groups—a cause for continuing concern.

An unusual type of poisoning has resulted from the proliferation of battery-operated games, cameras, hearing aids, calculators, and watches. An estimated 500 to 600 miniature button or disk batteries are swallowed each year by persons of all ages. Their major component is aqueous potassium hydroxide, which also is used to unclog pipes. Children can mistake small batteries for candy; adults may mistake them for medication tablets. Batteries that lodge in the esophagus, cecum, or other areas of the gastrointestinal tract present two problems: (1) they are locally corrosive to mucosa, causing ulceration or perforation in 1 to 2 hours; and (2) they may cause mercury poisoning when certain battery contents leak. Endoscopic or surgical removal is necessary if the battery remains in the stomach for more than 24 hours, if gastric or peritoneal irritation develops, if radiologic evidence shows the battery lodging or leaking in the gastro-intestinal tract, or if the particular type of battery is prone to leakage.

## DETECTION OF POISONS

**Toxicology** is the study of poisons, their action and effects, methods of their detection, and diagnosis and treatment of poisoning. A **poison** can be defined as any substance that in relatively small amounts can cause death or serious bodily harm. All drugs are potential poisons when used improperly or in excess dosage. Poisoning may be acute or chronic. In **acute poisoning** the effects are immediate. In **chronic poisoning** the effects are insidious because of cumulative effects of small amounts of poison absorbed over a prolonged period. Chronic poisoning causes chronic illness, which may or may not be reversible.

Nurses may be confronted with a suspected poisoning in many ways. A mother may call, upset that her small child has taken one of her contraceptive pills; a patient may accidentally drink the glass of peroxide mixture intended as a mouthwash; or a teenager who cannot be aroused may be brought into the emergency room.

Cues that typically point to poisoning include sudden, violent symptoms of severe nausea, vomiting, diarrhea, collapse, or convulsions. If possible, it is important to find out what poison has been taken and how much. Additional information that might prove helpful to the physician in making a diagnosis includes answers to questions or reports of observed phenomena, with the nurse noting the following:

1. Any reports of poison contact by the victim
2. Poisoning in the "at-risk" age-group of children 1 to 5 years old
3. Report of a history of previous poisonings or ingestion of foreign substances
4. Diverse symptoms or signs referable to multiple organ system involvement that defy diagnosis
5. A history of suicidal intent or thought
6. Symptoms appearing suddenly in an otherwise healthy individual or a number of persons becoming ill about the same time, as might occur in food poisoning
7. Anything unusual about the person, the clothing, or the surroundings; evidence of burns about the lips and mouth; discolored gums; needle (hypodermic) pricks, pustules, or scars on the exposed and accessible surface of the body or dilated or constricted pupils, as may be seen in drug addicts; any skin rash or discoloration
8. The odor of the breath, the rate of respiration, any difficulty in respiration, and cyanosis
9. The quality and rate of the pulse
10. Appearance and odor of vomitus, if any, as well as accompanying diarrhea or abdominal pain
11. Any abnormalities of stool and urine, any change in color or the presence of blood
12. For signs of involvement of the nervous system, the presence of excitement, muscular twitching, delirium, difficulty in speech, stupor, coma, constriction or dilation of the pupils, and elevated or subnormal temperature

Coma caused by drug overdose is characterized by the following categories:

**TABLE 75-2**  Signs of coma of toxic origin vs. structural neurologic damage

| | | |
|---|---|---|
| Motor activity | Spasticity | Flaccidity |
| Pupillary reactions | Absent or variable | Present |
| Toe-to-head progression of signs | Yes | No |
| Blood pressure | May increase early; may decrease later | Usually decreases |

*Grade I*—patient asleep but easily aroused, reacts to painful stimuli, deep tendon reflexes present, pupils normal and reactive, ocular movements present, and vital signs stable

*Grade II*—pain response absent, deep tendon reflexes depressed, pupils slightly dilated but reactive, and vital signs stable

*Grade III*—deep tendon and pupillary reflexes absent and vital signs stable

*Grade IV*—respiration and circulation depressed

Table 75-2 further differentiates the signs of coma of toxic origin from those of coma resulting from structural neurologic damage. The nurse should *refrigerate in a covered container all specimens* of vomitus, urine, or stool in case the physician wishes to examine them and turn them over to the proper authority for analysis. This is of particular importance not only in making or confirming a diagnosis, but also in the event that the case has medicolegal significance.

Any of the signs listed earlier should be noted carefully for report to the position control center or physician in charge. However, full reliance on signs and symptoms for clear-cut diagnosis and poison identification is fraught with danger, since these incidents may occur concurrently with an episode of acute disease, especially in children (e.g., aspirin intoxication), and symptoms may be similar or otherwise confusing. Also, more than one substance may be responsible for the signs of poisoning observed.

Not all substances commonly ingested accidentally are toxic if small amounts are taken only once. Poison control centers define a small amount as the quantity of a substance contained in "a taste," "one bite," or "a small piece," as opposed to "a mouthful." Although subjective, this is typical of data received when taking a poisoning history. A list of some frequently ingested products that are usually systematically nontoxic if taken in small amounts follows:

Abrasives, bleaches (sodium hypochlorite, less than 5%)
Chalk
Cigarettes, cigarette ash, cigars
Cosmetics, perfume, cologne, deodorants
Crayons (if labelled C.P., A.P., or C.S., -130-46)
Glues, rubber cement
Hydrogen peroxide (medicinal, 3%)
Indelible pen or magic markers
Ink in full cartridge of a ballpoint pen
Paint (latex)

### Nursing Research:
## POISON PREVENTION PACKAGING

Although the Poison Prevention Packaging Act (PPPA) of 1970 has resulted in a 65% decline in ingestion of products (such as lye and antifreeze) packaged in child-resistant containers, ingestion of prescription drugs by children has declined by only 36%. In their epidemiologic study, King and Palmisano* found that toddlers between their second and third birthdays are the predominant victims of accidental prescription drug ingestions. These authors also found that only about 25% of all solid prescription drugs are enclosed in PPPA child-resistant containers, that more than 40% of the drugs are in ordinary containers or improperly used child-resistant containers, and that 30% are in no container at all. The investigators recommended a dual-closure scheme: requiring prescription drugs to be dispensed in plastic unit dose cells that are, in turn, enclosed in standard child-proof containers, particularly for a small selection of the most dangerous drugs (i.e., iron salts, cyclic antidepressants, clonidine, Lomotil, and opiates).

*King WD and Palmisano PA. (1989). Ingestion of prescription drugs by children: an epidemiologic study, South Med J 82(12):1468.

Pencil (graphite or coloring)
Play-Doh
Saccharin and cyclamates
Safety matches (ingestion of less than 20 books of matches)
Soaps, liquid shampoos, household detergents (except dishwasher detergents)
Toothpaste (unless heavy ingestion of fluorides)
Vitamins (in amounts usually available for a single overdose, unless containing iron)

Ingestion of small amounts of these nonedible substances may produce mild gastric irritation but not systemic poisoning. However, contact with a poison control center or physician is important (essential, if symptoms exist), since no produce or drug is entirely safe for ingestion, and hypersensitivity reactions can occur.

In assisting with poisoning diagnosis and toxic substance identification, nurses (especially emergency room nurses and nurse practitioners) should familiarize themselves with certain clusters of signs associated with common drug poisonings or overdoses. These have been called **toxidromes** and are listed in Table 75-3. Other common single signs and their associated causative toxins are listed in Table 75-4.

## POISON CONTROL CENTERS

There are about 600 poison control centers in the continental United States, Hawaii, Alaska, the Virgin Islands, Guam, Puerto Rico, the Canal Zone, and the District of Columbia. Most are located near hospitals or in emergency rooms of large community hospitals. Their telephone numbers are listed in the local telephone book or may be obtained from a pharmacist. The address of the coordinating agency for all poison control centers is: National Clearinghouse for Poison Control Centers, US Department of Health and Human Services, Food and Drug Administration, 5660 Fishers Lane, Room 1345, Rockville, MD 20857. Also, the *Physicians' Desk Reference* (PDR) includes a list of certified poison control centers and a guide to management of a drug overdose. Many centers are open 24 hours every day and are staffed to (1) answer specific questions from the public or from professionals about identification of ingredients in trade-named products, (2) estimate their toxicity, and (3) suggest specific treatment for poisonings.

Poison control centers can be highly instrumental in reducing the number of poisonings (aside from treatment). They provide annual nationwide statistical analyses of poisonings by category, which help clarify the magnitude of the problem.

Other sources of information include the *Poisindex,* a microfiche or microcomputer data base of computer-generated information describing nearly all known substances, including product ingredients. It is updated every 3 months. Another source is *Drugdex,* a compendium of information specifically about drugs that includes their ranges of toxicity. It is well referenced for efficient use.

## CLASSIFICATION OF ACTION OF POISONS

The classification of poisons is as broad as the classification of drugs, since any drug is a potential poison when used in excess. Poisons may be classified in various ways. They

---

**TABLE 75-3** Toxidromes*

**atropine, scopolamine, anticholinergics:** dry skin, tachycardia, beet-red skin color, agitation, dilated pupils, delirium, hyperthermia, hallucinations, coma

**barbiturates, sedative-hypnotics, tranquilizers:** ataxia, drowsiness, slurred speech (without an alcohol breath odor), respiratory depression, hypotension

**cholinergics** (such as organophosphates), **mushrooms** *(Amanita or Galerina):* salivation, lacrimation, involuntary urination and defecation, miosis, pulmonary congestion, seizures

**opioids:** miosis, respiratory depression, hypotension, slow respiration, coma

**salicylates:** fever, vomiting, hyperglycemia, mixed respiratory alkalosis and metabolic acidosis, hyperpnea

**tricyclic antidepressants:** anticholinergic signs and symptoms, plus dysrhythmias (prolonged QRS duration on ECG report), convulsions, coma

*The drugs or drug types in bold are followed by clusters of signs of poisonings.

---

**TABLE 75-4** Single signs that suggest presence of certain toxins

| Sign | Inference | Sign | Inference |
|---|---|---|---|
| Abdominal colic | black widow spider bite | Pulse rate changes | |
| | heavy metals | Increased | alcohol |
| | withdrawal from narcotic depressant | | amphetamines |
| | | | atropine |
| Ataxia | alcohol | | ephedrine |
| | barbiturates | Slowed | digitalis |
| | bromides | | lily-of-the-valley |
| | carbon monoxide | | narcotic depressants |
| | hallucinogens | | |
| | heavy metals | Pupillary changes | |
| | organic solvents | Dilated | amphetamines |
| | phenytoin (Dilantin) | | antihistamines |
| | tranquilizers | | atropine |
| | | | barbiturates (when combined with coma) |
| Coma and drowsiness | alcohol (ethyl) | | cocaine |
| | antihistamines | | ephedrine |
| | barbiturates, other hypnotics | | LSD (occasionally) |
| | carbon monoxide | | methanol |
| | opiates | | withdrawal from narcotic depressants (occasionally) |
| | salicylates | | |
| | tranquilizers | | |

**TABLE 75-4**   Single signs that suggest presence of certain toxins—cont'd

| Sign | Inference | Sign | Inference |
|---|---|---|---|
| Convulsions or muscle twitching | alcohol<br>amphetamines<br>antihistamines<br>boric acid<br>camphor<br>chlorinated hydrocarbon insecticides (DDT)<br>cyanide<br>lead<br>organophosphate insecticides<br>plants (azalea, iris, lily-of-the-valley, water hemlock)<br>salicylates<br>strychnine<br>withdrawal from drugs: barbiturates, benzodiazepines (Valium, Librium), meprobamate | Nystagmus on lateral gaze | barbiturates<br>minor tranquilizers (meprobamate, benzodiazepines), phenytoin (Dilantin) |
|  |  | Pinpoint pupils | mushrooms (muscarinic)<br>opiates<br>organophosphate insecticides |
|  |  | Respiratory alterations<br>  Increased | amphetamines<br>barbiturates (early sign)<br>carbon monoxide<br>methanol<br>petroleum distillates<br>salicylates |
|  |  | Paralysis | botulism<br>organophosphate insecticides |
| Paralysis | botulism<br>heavy metals<br>plants (poison hemlock, etc.)<br>triorthocresyl phosphate (plasticizer) | Slowed or depressed | alcohol (late sign)<br>barbiturates (late sign)<br>opiates<br>tranquilizers |
| Oliguria/anuria | carbon tetrachloride<br>ethylene glycol (antifreeze)<br>heavy metals<br>hemolysis caused by naphthalene, plants, and so on<br>methanol<br>mushrooms<br>oxylates<br>petroleum distillates<br>solvents | Wheezing/pulmonary edema | mushrooms (muscarinic)<br>opiates<br>organophosphate insecticides<br>petroleum distilates |
|  |  | Skin color changes<br>  Jaundice | aniline dyes/coal tar colors<br>arsenic<br>carbon tetrachloride<br>castor bean<br>fava bean<br>mushroom<br>naphthalene (moth repellent/insecticide)<br>yellow phosphorus |
| Oral signs<br>  Breath odors<br>    Acetone | acetone<br>alcohol (methyl or isopropyl)<br>phenol<br>salicylates | Red flush | alcohol<br>antihistamines<br>atropine<br>boric acid<br>carbon monoxide<br>nitrites<br>tricyclic antidepressants |
|     Alcohol<br>    Bitter almonds<br>    Coal gas<br>    Garlic | ethyl alcohol<br>cyanide<br>carbon monoxide<br>arsenic<br>dimethyl sulfoxide (DMSO)<br>phosphorus<br>organophosphate insecticides<br>thallium | Cyanosis | aniline dyes<br>carbon monoxide<br>cyanide<br>nitrites<br>strychnine |
|     Oil of wintergreen<br>    Petroleum<br>    Violets<br>  Dryness | methyl salicylate<br>petroleum distillates<br>turpentine<br>amphetamines<br>antihistamines<br>atropine<br>narcotic depressants<br>tricyclic antidepressants | Violent emesis (with or without hematemesis) | aminophylline<br>bacterial food poisoning<br>boric acid<br>corrosives<br>fluoride<br>heavy metals<br>phenol<br>salicylates |
|   Salivation | arsenic<br>corrosive substances<br>mercury<br>mushrooms<br>organophosphate insecticides<br>thallium |  |  |

may be grouped according to chemical classifications as organic and inorganic poisons; as alkaloids, glycosides, and resins; or as acids, alkalis, heavy metals, oxidizing agents, halogenated hydrocarbons, and so on. Poisons also may be classified according to the organ or tissue of the body in which the most damaging effects are produced. Some poisons injure all cells they contact. Such chemical substances are sometimes called protoplasmic poisons or cytotoxins. Others have more effect on the kidney (nephrotoxins), the liver (hepatotoxins), or the blood-forming organs.

Poisons that affect chiefly the nervous system are called neurotoxins or neurotropic poisons. They must be studied separately because different symptoms characterize each one. Symptoms of toxicity are mentioned with each of these drugs in previous chapters. Although symptoms of this group of poisons are to some extent specific, certain symptoms are encountered repeatedly and are associated with many poisons. Drowsiness, dizziness, headache, delirium, coma, and convulsive seizures always indicate central nervous system involvement. On the other hand, dry mouth, dilated pupils, and difficult swallowing are associated with overdosage of atropine or one of the atropine-like drugs; ringing in the ears, excessive perspiration, and gastric upset are associated with salicylate overdosage.

Many times the precise mechanism of action is not known; death may be caused by respiratory failure, but exactly what happens to cause depression of the respiratory center may not be known.

Central nervous system stimulants such as pentylenetetrazol and strychnine in toxic amounts cause convulsive seizures, exhaustion, and depression of vital centers.

The human body depends on a constant supply of oxygen if various physiologic functions are to proceed satisfactorily. Anything that interferes with the use of oxygen by the cells or with the transportation of oxygen will produce damaging effects faster in some cells than in others. Carbon monoxide from automobile engines and unvented gas heaters is one of the most widely distributed toxic agents. It poisons by producing hypoxia and finally asphyxia. Carbon monoxide has a great affinity for hemoglobin and forms carboxyhemoglobin. Thus the production of oxyhemoglobin and the free transport of oxygen is interfered with; oxygen deficiency soon develops in the cells. Unless exposure to the carbon monoxide is terminated before 40% of hemoglobin has been changed to carboxyhemoglobin, anoxia may produce serious brain damage. Death occurs when 60% of the hemoglobin has been changed to carboxyhemoglobin.

The cyanides act somewhat similarly in that they bring about cellular anoxia, but they do so differently. They inactivate certain tissue enzymes so that cells are unable to utilize oxygen. Death may occur very rapidly. Curare and the curariform drugs in toxic amounts bring about paralysis of the diaphragm, and again the victim dies from lack of oxygen.

Certain drugs have a direct effect on muscle tissue from the body, such as that of the myocardium, or the smooth muscle of the blood vessels. Death results from the failure of circulation or cardiac arrest. The nitrites, potassium salts, and digitalis drugs may exert such toxic effects.

Strong acids and alkalis denature and destroy cellular proteins. Examples of corrosive acids are hydrochloric, nitric, and sulfuric. Sodium, potassium, and ammonium hydroxides are examples of strong and caustic alkalis. Locally, these substances cause destruction of tissue, and death may result from hemorrhage, perforation, or shock. Corrosive poisons may also cause death by altering the pH of the blood or other body fluids, or they may produce marked degenerative changes on vital organs such as the liver or kidney.

## SPECIFIC POISONS, SYMPTOMS, AND SUGGESTED EMERGENCY TREATMENT

Since the emphasis is on *prompt* treatment, health care may be best served by quick action by informed bystanders at the scene who apply first-aid measures while help is sought from the poison control center and while transportation to a hospital, clinic, or physician's office is arranged. A first-aid chart that offers instruction for various poisoning emergencies is included in the box on p. 1131 as an example to delineate specific actions for different poisonings.

The caller to the poison control center should have the following information, if available:
1. Physical appearance of the substance
2. Odor, color, and texture; distinguishing characteristics of the substance
3. Trade name or chemical name, if known
4. Purpose or how the substance was meant to be used
5. Label statements relating to "poison" content or flammability

After the events of the suspected poisoning have been assessed thoroughly and problems analyzed, including the identification of the substance if possible, prompt medical interventions must be instituted. Nursing management will therefore be guided by the four major goals.
1. Vital functions (respirations, circulation, and others) will be maintained, supported, or restored.
2. The toxic substance will be removed or eliminated from the system as soon as possible.
3. The action of certain specific poisons may be counteracted, reversed, or antagonized by specific antidotes.
4. Recurrences will be reduced or prevented.

### Support of Vital Functions

Basic to the treatment of poisoning is intensive supportive therapy, good nursing care, and minimal dangerous invasive interventions. Nursing care of the poisoned patient should focus on restoration, support, and maintenance of such vital functions as ventilation, circulation, and acid-base and fluid-

---

### FIRST AID FOR POSSIBLE POISONING

**Remember: Any Nonfood Substance May Be Poisonous.**

1. Keep all potential poisons—household products and medicines—out of children's reach.
2. Use "safety caps" (child-resistant containers) to avoid accidents.
3. Have 1 ounce of ipecac syrup in your home and in your first-aid kit for camping, travel, and so on.
4. Keep your poison center's and your physician's phone number handy.

**If You Think an Accidental Ingestion Has Occurred:**

1. Keep calm. Do not wait for symptoms—call for help promptly.
2. Find out if the substance is toxic; your poison control center or your physician can tell you if a risk exists and what you should do.
3. Have the product's container or label with you at the phone.
   a. If a poison is on the skin:
      Immediately remove affected clothing.
      Flood involved parts of body with water, wash with soap or detergent, and rinse thoroughly.
   b. If a poison is in the eye:
      Immediately flush the eye with water for up to 20 minutes.
   c. If a poison is inhaled:
      Immediately get the victim to fresh air. Give mouth-to-mouth resuscitation if necessary.
   d. If vomiting has been recommended:
      Give 1 tablespoon of ipecac syrup followed by at least one glass (8 ounces) of clear liquid. If the patient does not vomit within 15 to 20 minutes, give 1 more tablespoon of ipecac and more water. Do *not* use salt water.

**Never Induce Vomiting If:**

1. The victim is in a *coma* (unconscious).
2. The victim is *convulsing* (having a seizure).
3. The victim has swallowed a *caustic* or *corrosive* (e.g., lye).

**For Reemphasis:**

1. Always call to be certain of possible toxicity before undertaking treatment.
2. Never induce vomiting until you are instructed to do so.
3. Do not rely on the label's antidote information, since it may be out of date. Call instead.
4. If you have to go to an emergency room, take the tablets, capsules, container, and/or label with you.
5. Do not hesitate to call your poison center or your physician a second time if the victim seems to be getting worse.

Adapted from American Association of Poison Control Centers, William O Robertson, MD, Secretary. Copyright © Physician's desk reference for nonprescription drugs, 1981 edition. Published by Medical Economics Co., Inc., Oradell, NJ 07649. Also adapted from Feldmann EG, ed. (1990). Handbook of nonprescription drugs, ed 9. Washington, DC: American Pharmaceutical Association.

---

electrolyte balance. Emotional support for the client and others involved in this crisis is crucial.

A general assessment and history should be performed quickly and competently to determine the extent of any impairments of body systems or particular susceptibilities. Expert nursing care is essential to observe the following for information indicating impending complications:

1. Level of consciousness
2. Vital signs. Temperature may be elevated with certain central nervous system (CNS) stimulants and salicylates and depressed with others. Transient cardiac dysrhythmias may occur; anticipate obtaining an electrocardiogram. Pulmonary congestion, airway obstruction, or apnea is common; aspiration of vomitus can occur.

Implemented plans may include:

1. Turning, deep breathing, coughing, and suctioning
2. Auscultation to demonstrate a need for chest x-ray examination, suctioning, tracheostomy, endotracheal intubation, blood gas determinations, supplemental oxygen and a respirator/ventilator

It is also essential that the victim be positioned to prevent aspiration of vomitus and that mouth care be attended to promptly after emesis. Moderate amounts of plain water by mouth (if a gag or swallow reflex is present) may be all that is needed to dilute or effectively inactivate many ingested poisons.

Close attention to developing problems and responsive intervention can often fend off the need for more aggressive medical therapies that tax the already tenuous condition of the poisoned individual.

### Removal or Elimination of Poison

Careful evaluation of the patient who has been affected by a toxic substance is essential to determine which of the foregoing steps take priority and by which route the poison should be removed or eliminated, if necessary. The route is largely determined by the manner of the poisoning. Removal of ingested substances can be attempted in several ways: (1) by directly removing it from the stomach, if the poisoning is discovered early; (2) by increasing the rate of transit of the poison through the colon, even though little or no absorption occurs there and thus may not be effective; or (3) if the substance has probably already been assimilated into the system or was injected, by attempting to remove or filter it from the bloodstream. Contact poisons may be flushed from the skin, eyes, and other external areas by copious volumes of plain, flowing water from a pitcher or other container. Inhaled toxins are treated by removing the patient to fresh air and administering artificial respiration or oxygen and other supportive measures as necessary.

Various methods exist for the removal or elimination of poisons from the gastrointestinal tract or systemic circulation: emesis, gastric lavage, cathartics, diuretics, dialysis, or occasionally blood exchange transfusions or hemoperfusion through charcoal or exchange resins.

### Emesis

Generally, if more than 4 hours have elapsed since a poison ingestion, emptying the stomach will be ineffective. Exceptions are poisonings by anticholinergic drugs, which slow gastric motility, and by salicylates, which promote pyloric spasm. Some drugs, such as ethanol, are absorbed too rapidly to be recovered after 1 hour. However, when situations have warranted emptying the stomach, whole tablets have occasionally been recovered even a day later. Because of this, some recommend emptying the stomach even after a delay.

The most effective method for removing ingested toxins is usually the most natural one—emesis, done as soon as possible. In some instances, however, emesis is contraindicated (see box). If vomiting does not or cannot occur naturally, either ipecac syrup or apomorphine is usually administered. However, neither emetic may be effective if the ingested substance is a sedative-hypnotic, a phenothiazine, or a tricyclic antidepressant, all of which have antiemetic properties.

#### ipecac syrup

The most commonly used emetic is ipecac syrup. (Fluid extract of ipecac, which is about 14 times more concentrated and has caused a number of deaths, *should never be used*.) Ipecac syrup tastes bitter-sweet. It probably acts both centrally and locally by directly stimulating the vomiting center, and by irritating the gastric mucosa. The usual dose for adults is 15 to 30 ml, followed by 200 to 300 ml of water, or fruit juice or as much fluid as the patient can drink. For children under 1 year of age, a 5- to 10-ml dose is given; children 1 to 12 years old, a 15-ml dose.

Vomiting usually occurs in 15 to 30 minutes. The dose may be repeated once after 20 minutes if the first dose is not effective. If vomiting does not occur within 30 minutes, gastric lavage should be performed, since ipecac is a cardiotoxic if absorbed and may cause conduction disturbances, atrial fibrillation, or myocarditis.

Ipecac syrup is available without a prescription in 1-ounce (30-ml) bottles bearing the following instructions:

1. For emergency use to cause vomiting in poisoning. Before using, call physician, poison control center, or hospital emergency room immediately for advice.
2. Warning—Keep out of reach of children. Do not use if strychnine, corrosives such as alkalis (lye) and strong acids, or petroleum distillates such as kerosene, gasoline, fuel oil, coal oil, paint thinner, or cleaning fluid have been ingested.

#### apomorphine

Apomorphine, although more dangerous to use, may be used to induce vomiting when more rapid emesis is necessary; it is effective within 1 to 15 minutes after administration. **Apomorphine** is a narcotic emetic that causes a reflex action of the vomiting center in the brainstem. It can cause severe, protracted emesis and should be used with extreme caution. Dose range is 2 to 6 mg. Naloxone hydrochloride (Narcan) should be on hand to counteract any respiratory depression due to opioid toxicity. The adult dose is 0.1 to 0.2 mg/kg, IV, IM or SC (0.4 to 2 mg). IV dose may be repeated every 2 to 3 minutes as needed. Children receive 0.01 mg/kg dose IV, which may be repeated every 2 to 3 minutes until the proper response is achieved.

If the patient is conscious, drug-induced vomiting is usually preferable to gastric lavage, particularly in children, since aspiration of vomitus is less likely to occur. Nurses should employ the necessary measures to reduce the likelihood of aspiration of vomitus (e.g., proper positioning of patient). Occasionally, induction of vomiting may be facilitated by stimulating the pharynx, but time should not be wasted in repeated futile attempts.

### Gastric Lavage

If emesis cannot be induced, **gastric lavage** should be begun *except* under most of the same contraindicating conditions (e.g., untreated convulsions, absent reflexes, corrosives). Lavage *may* be preferred treatment for pregnant women and for patients who have ingested more than 2 ml/kg body weight of a petroleum distillate and who should have endotracheal intubation to protect the airway. Lavage may be contraindicated in the presence of cardiac dysrhythmias.

An Ewald orogastric tube, no. 16 to 30 French, may be used to lavage children; tube sizes for adult lavage range

---

**CONTRAINDICATIONS FOR INDUCED EMESIS IN POISONINGS**

Infants up to 1 year of age
Comatose or convulsing patient
Absent gag and cough reflexes
Ingestion of:
   Convulsion-inducing substances
   Sharp objects (e.g., glass, nails) along with toxic substance
   Central nervous system (CNS) poisons (e.g., camphor, strychnine), which must be removed more quickly by lavage
   Acids, alkalis, or petroleum distillates
Ingestion of a petroleum distillate, such as kerosene, gasoline, or paint thinner, etc.
Patients who have already vomited copiously
During pregnancy (decision may depend on clinical judgment)

Modified with permission from Howard C. Mofenson: Poison control manual, 1979, unpublished material.

from no. 34 to 42. The newer, clear-plastic Lavacuator tube also may be used. A standard nasogastric tube is too narrow for extraction of particulate matter such as intact tablets (Figure 75-1). Stomach contents should be aspirated first and saved for toxicologic analysis if necessary. Several liters of half-strength saline solution may be used in increments of 50 to 100 ml for children and 150 to 200 ml for adults during repeated lavages until return flows are clear. (Remember that dead space in the tube itself accounts for 20 to 25 ml of the fluid instilled.) Neither emesis nor lavage is guaranteed to empty the stomach completely.

## Activated Charcoal

Following emesis or lavage, activated charcoal may be instilled or swallowed to act as an absorbent. Activated charcoal should be given as soon after poison ingestion as feasible, but not after ipecac and emesis, since it will adsorb the ipecac. Activated charcoal adsorbs many substances, thus it is used as an adjunct in the treatment of oral poisonings with heavy metals, mercuric chloride, strychnine, phenol, atropine, phenolphthalein, oxalic acid, poisonous mushrooms, aspirin, and most drugs. It is not effective for poisoning with cyanide, DDT, ethanol, methanol, caustic alkalis, ferrous sulfate, boric acid, organophosphates, or carbonate. The charcoal mixture need not be removed from the stomach afterward because no known adverse effects exist. Activated charcoal can also serve as a stool marker to indicate when further gastrointestinal absorption of the ingested poison has ended. Tablets or capsules of charcoal should not be used for treatment of poisoning, since they are less effective than the powder.

Administration of activated charcoal and ion exchange resins such as cholestyramine and colestipol, if given within 1 hour, may prevent intestinal reabsorption of some drugs that normally undergo recycling through the liver and thus may facilitate intestinal elimination. Paraquat, which is a lethal weed killer that is extremely rapidly absorbed from the gastrointestinal tract, is known to bind strongly to Fuller's earth and bentonite, but these adsorbents must be given too early to be practical. Cholestyramine binds to acidic drugs such as acetaminophen, but again, it must be given almost immediately.

## Other Treatments

Other ways used to block or eliminate toxins from the system include forced diuresis, cathartics and enemas, dialysis, hemoperfusion, and exchange transfusions. These methods should be reserved as treatment under certain conditions and for specific poisons; they are not universally effective and are much less commonly used than emesis or lavage.

In addition, changing the pH of the urine may enhance excretion of certain drugs. Alkalinization by administering sodium bicarbonate or other bases is particularly effective in salicylate overdoses and probably in phenobarbital and

**FIGURE 75-1** The two tubes on the left are used in various lavage techniques. The Ewald tube (left) has a single lumen. The orogastric hose, or Lavacuator (middle), has numerous openings up the side of the distal end and a double lumen. Note the sizes of the tablets in comparison to the nearby tubes. Standard nasogastric tubes (right) have no role in lavage of the poisoned patient since the tube is too narrow to enable evacuation of whole drug forms or even large particles *(From Goldfrank L: [1982]. Toxicologic emergencies, ed 2. New York: Appleton-Century-Crofts.)*

2,4-dichlorophenoxyacetic acid (weed killer, 2,4-D). It is reported to be questionably effective for some barbiturates and amitriptyline. Forced acid diuresis is probably more potentially hazardous but is often recommended for poisoning with amphetamines, quinine, and fenfluramine (Pondimin), despite lack of full documentation of efficacy.

Clearance of poisons directly from the bloodstream by peritoneal dialysis or hemodialysis, hemoperfusion, or transfusion is occasionally done to augment other measures previously discussed. These more complex methods may be ineffective, overly taxing to the poisoned patient, unnecessary, or even harmful in some instances. Not enough well-controlled studies have been done to prove efficacy. The degree to which they may be useful depends in part on the properties of the substance (i.e., whether it freely circulates or whether it is bound to plasma proteins or to tissues). Various lists of substances amenable to dialysis exist; some substances for which dialysis has *not* proved useful are as follows*:

amitriptyline (Elavil)
anticholinergics
antidepressants
antihistamines
atropine
chlordiazepoxide (Librium)
desipramine hydrochloride (Pertofrane)
diazepam (Valium)
digitalis
diphenoxylate hydrochloride (Lomotil)
glutethimide (Doriden)
hallucinogens
imipramine (Tofranil)
methaqualone (Quaalude)
methyprylon (Noludar)
narcotic opiate depressants (e.g., heroin)
nortriptyline (Aventyl)
oxazepam (Serax)
phenelzine sulfate (Nardil)
propoxyphene (Darvon)

The following are some common criteria for considering dialysis:

1. Presence of potentially lethal levels of a dialyzable substance
2. Presence of high levels of a substance that breaks down into dialyzable poisons
3. When usual supportive or corrective measures will not suffice to prevent further damage (e.g., coma, apnea, shock, hyperthermia)
4. When major degradation or excretion routes are damaged, blocked, or otherwise dysfunctional (e.g., renal or liver failure)
5. Often when the patient is pregnant (hemodialysis)

*Modified from Krupp MA and Chatton MJ: Current medical diagnosis and treatment, 1979, Los Altos, Calif, 1979, Lange Medical Publications; USP-DI 1990.

Although hemodialysis is more efficient for short-term dialysis, peritoneal dialysis may be less hazardous and may be continued over a longer period. Hemoperfusion is a more promising technique. Studies seem to show that more efficient removal of drugs occurs when heparinized blood can be passed through a column packed with adsorbents such as activated charcoal or, better yet, newer exchange resins such as polacrilin (Amberlite). Possible complications include embolism; loss of white cells, platelets, and fibrinogen; and hemorrhage.

Table 75-5 lists some selected poisons, with associated symptoms and antidotes.

## PREVENTION OF POISONING

The focus of nursing on primary care and its corollary, prevention, applies readily to poisonings. Prevention has always been emphasized by the nursing profession, and now other disciplines are beginning to take part. Combined efforts with drug information centers and other health professionals and creative approaches have already had an impact on the frequency of certain categories of drug poisoning, notably aspirin poisoning.

Various creative graphic symbols appear on labels of poisonous substances to alert the adult and/or nonreading child to the potential hazard contained therein. "Mr Yuk," an ugly, green-faced, scowling image, is one of these. Tricky-to-open caps appear to delay if not totally prevent children's indiscriminate use of medicines. Others who have no need for these caps can request medication in the familiar easy-to-open caps.

There is much to learn about toxins in our environment, both apparent and potential, and therefore much to do in the way of poison prevention, but concerted, thoughtful efforts have already had a positive effect on statistics.

## ANTIDOTES

The number of antidotes for specific toxins is minimal (Table 75-6); as no widely accepted "universal antidote" exists. Nevertheless, some general statements can be made about antidotes.

Antidotes are more effective after the stomach is empty. The correct dose to reverse toxicity depends on the specific drug involved, its half-life, and the severity of toxicity shown. Antidotes work by any of the following mechanisms: (1) antagonizing or stimulating receptor sites that have been rendered hyperfunctional or dysfunctional by the poison; (2) interfering with enzyme inhibition; (3) administering the product of metabolism that has been interfered with; (4) inhibiting the biotransformation of a substance to a poisonous metabolite; (5) giving an agent that inactivates the toxic product; (6) chelation (forming highly stable complexes, tying up the substance—usually a heavy metal such as iron); (7) producing immunotherapy—the use of antidrug anti-

**TABLE 75-5**   Selected poisons, symptoms, and antidotes

| Poison | Symptoms | Antidote |
|---|---|---|
| anticholinergics | See toxidrome | physostigmine |
| arsenic | Faint odor of garlic on breath, nausea, severe vomiting, difficulty swallowing, thirst, mouth and stomach pain, oliguria, hematuria, cold clammy skin, skeletal muscle cramps, collapse, and death | dimercaprol (BAL) |
| cyanide | sedation, tachycardia, seizures, headaches (see cyanide section, this chapter) | cyanide antidote kit (amyl nitrite, sodium nitrite, sodium thiosulfate) |
| dioxin, digitoxin | Noncardiac effects: stomach pain, anorexia, nausea, vomiting, photophobia, yellow-green vision or hazy vision, fatigue, weakness, dizziness<br>Cardiac effects: various arrhythmias (atrial, ventricular, AV block, sinoatrial) | digoxin immune FAB (Digibind) |
| lead | Acute: burning sensation in mouth, colic, GI upset, mental alterations, paralysis of extremities<br>Chronic: anorexia, anemia, increased irritability that progresses to acute form | Ca-EDTA (calcium disodium edetate) this antidote also used to treat cadmium, manganese, copper, and zinc poisoning |
| opioids (heroin, codeine, morphine, propoxyphene [Darvon], pentazocine [Talwin], etc.) | Respiratory depression, pulmonary edema, hypotension, seizures, coma, death | naloxone (Narcan) |

**TABLE 75-6**   Antidotes for specific drugs and poisons

| Poison | Specific antidote |
|---|---|
| Acetaminophen (Tylenol, Datril, in over-the-counter cold preparations) | N-acetylcysteine (Mucomyst)* |
| Alcohol (methanol) and ethylene glycol (antifreeze) | Alcohol (ethanol) |
| Anticholinergics (atropine) | Physostigmine salicylate |
| Carbon monoxide | Oxygen administered under high pressure |
| Coumarin anticoagulants | Vitamin K, clotting factors |
| Cyanide | Amyl nitrite, sodium nitrite, sodium thiosulfate |
| Heavy metals:<br>Arsenic | Dimercaprol (BAL) |
| Copper | Penicillamine (Cuprimine) |
| Iron | Deferoxamine (Desferal) |
| Lead | Dimercaprol, penicillamine, calcium disodium edetate (CaEDTA) |
| Mercury | Dimercaprol, deferoxamine |
| Narcotics | Naloxone |
| Nitrates and nitrites | Methylene blue |
| Opiates | Naloxone (Narcan) |
| Organophosphates (insecticides) | Atropine sulfate, pralidoxime (2-PAM) |
| Tricyclic antidepressants | Physostigmine salicylate |

Adapted with permission from Howard C. Mofenson, Poison control manual, 1979, unpublished data.
*Not yet FDA approved (see text).

bodies to bind and inactivate drugs (for example, there is a report of severe digoxin poisoning reversed with sheep digoxin—specific antibodies).

## ▷NURSING MANAGEMENT: CARE OF THE CLIENT WITH POISONING

***Assessment.*** An assessment should be done quickly to determine what substance is involved so that immediate action can be taken to prevent or minimize its effects. Symptoms may include, depending on the causative agent, nausea and vomiting, abdominal cramping, convulsions, change in the level of consciousness, and a decreased rate of pulse and respiration.

To assist in the determination of the agent, the lips and mouth are checked for excessive salivation, burns, or difficulty swallowing. The breath should be assessed for its odor. Some petroleum and cleaning products have distinctive smells which can be identified. The pupils should be checked for dilation or constriction, which may also help to indicate the substance.

If the patient is conscious, he should be questioned as to what substance and what quantity was taken. With the unconscious person, identification of the substance is facilitated by clues in the environment. Empty containers, open bottles or medication containers, or syringes should be gathered and taken to the hospital with the patient. Often the containers will list the ingredients of the substance to assist the medical staff in the choice of treatment or antidote.

***Intervention.*** Immediate action is required in the case of poisoning to prevent the absorption of the substance. If the person is unconscious, he should be transported as soon as possible to a hospital. If the individual is conscious, a physician and/or the poison control center should be contacted immediately. The telephone number of the nearest poison control center is usually listed in the front of the telephone directory with other emergency numbers for the community.

If the poison has been inhaled, such as a toxic gas or carbon monoxide, the individual should be removed from the source to the fresh air and oxygen administered if available. Cardiopulmonary resuscitation should be started if indicated. The victim will need to be transported to the hospital.

If the substance is a contact poison, absorbed through the skin and mucous membranes, the individual should be rinsed off immediately with copious amounts of water. The clothing should then be removed and the skin rinsed again. A shower would then be the best method of removal of the agent from the skin.

If the poison is ingested, the objective is to prevent absorption of the substance either by inducing vomiting or by lavage to remove the agent or by administering an agent to inactivate the poisonous substance. The most recommended method of inducing vomiting is to have the patient take 15 ml of syrup of ipecac followed by a full glass of water. This procedure may be repeated in 20 minutes if necessary. If lavage is attempted and the patient is unconscious, it should be done while a cuffed endotracheal tube is in place to prevent aspiration. Vomiting or lavage should not be attempted with the ingestion of caustic substances or hydrocarbons, found in petroleum products. Care for the ingestion of these substances is to give nothing by mouth and urgently seek medical assistance.

If the substance has a known antidote, it will be administered by the physician.

Other nursing interventions relate to the supportive care of the acutely ill client. Monitor vital signs and report changes immediately. If respirations are depressed, administer oxygen and suction. Maintain intravenous fluids as ordered. Observe the client for nausea, vomiting, diarrhea, and abdominal cramping. The client's vomitus, stool, and urine should be observed for abnormalities such as the presence of blood. Keep the client warm and turn frequently to promote drainage from the respiratory tract.

If the poisoning was intentional, as a suicide attempt, safety precautions should be instituted to protect the client from further self-destructive behavior and a psychiatric referral should be considered.

***Education.*** All medications should be clearly labeled with type, dosage, and storage requirements, and the client's ability to safely self-medicate should be assessed before there is an expectation for self-medication.

In interactions with clients, nurses should be alert to the presence of anger, depression, withdrawal, and faulty judg-

ment that might precede intentional or unintentional poisoning.

Clients should be cautioned that toxic substances are not to be stored in food containers, containers that are not properly labeled, or stored in a place that is accessible to children. Medication should not be stored beyond the date of expiration. Poisonous plants should not be kept in households where there are small children.

Syrup of ipecac is a necessary ingredient in a household first aid container, as well as the appropriate directions for its use.

***Evaluation.*** To prevent accidental poisoning, families should be assisted to evaluate environmental hazards in the home.

Clients should be monitored as with other life-threatening illness and specific interventions taken. Regression of the symptoms would indicate the successful elimination and inactivation of the poison.

## COMMON POISONS
### Acetaminophen

Acetaminophen is an analgesic-antipyretic ingredient in over 200 prescription and nonprescription drug formulations used therapeutically in adults and children. The drug is sold as a "safe substitute" for aspirin. However, when taken in massive overdose (greater than 15 g, the equivalent of 15 to 20 "extra-strength" capsules), acetaminophen can produce acute hepatic damage. When overdosage is promptly diagnosed and treated with a specific antidote, clients readily recover with no permanent ill effects. However, if not treated, hepatic coma and death may occur. Acute acetaminophen intoxication has four stages. Initial symptoms in patients with potentially hepatotoxic blood concentrations include nausea, vomiting, anorexia, and diaphoresis, accompanied by overwhelming malaise, which begins 4 to 14 hours after ingestion. The second stage begins 24 to 72 hours after ingestion. During this time the client seems to improve and have a feeling of well-being. However indices of impaired liver function begin to occur including increased serum hepatic enzymes (SGOT, SGPT) and bilirubin, and prolongation of prothrombin time. The right upper quadrant abdominal area becomes tender to palpation. Stage 3 begins 3 to 7 days after ingestion with signs of hepatic necrosis characterized by abdominal discomfort, jaundice, dramatically increased prothrombin times, hypoglycemia, hepatic encephalopathy, and death. Should the client survive, stage 4 is the return of normal liver function within several weeks. At therapeutic doses, the plasma half-life ($t\frac{1}{2}$, time required to eliminate half of the amount of drug present in plasma) is 2 to 4 hours. In overdoses in which hepatoxicity develops, half-life increases to 6 to 10 hours. Half-lives of greater than 10 hours indicate severe damage and possible hepatic coma. Blood is drawn for acetaminophen analysis 4 hours after ingestion; concentrations drawn before this time may

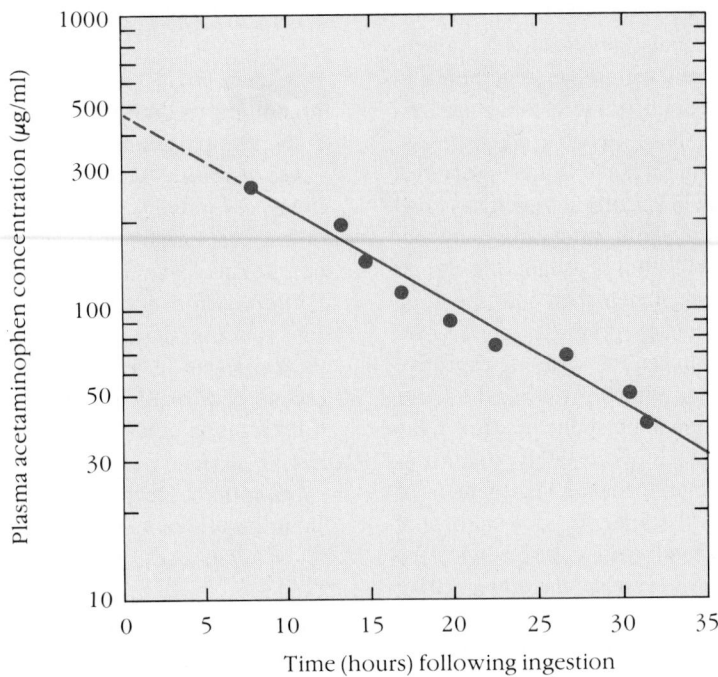

**FIGURE 75-2** Decrease in patient plasma acetaminophen concentration during treatment of acetaminophen overdose (t½ = 9 hr). *(Redrawn from Melethil S, Poklis A, and Schwartz HS: [1981]. Vet Hum Toxicol 23(6):422.)*

be misleading, since peak plasma concentrations may not occur before 4 hours after ingestion.

If the acetaminophen serum level is 100 μg/ml at 6 hours, 70 μg/ml at 8 hours, 50 μg/ml at 10 hours, 20 μg/ml at 15 hours, 8 μg/ml at 20 hours, or 3.5 μg/ml at 24 hours after the acetaminophen overdose, then an increased risk for hepatotoxicity is present. If the serum level is below these amounts at the times indicated, discontinuance of acetylcysteine therapy can be considered. Preferably, two serum levels below the previously stated levels should be obtained before stopping the acetylcysteine. Figure 75-2 presents multiple plasma concentrations determined in a patient with acetaminophen hepatotoxicity (SGOT, 4040 units/ml, 24 hours, postingestion) and a plasma half-life of 9 hours.

The development of potentially fatal liver damage in cases of acetaminophen overdose is caused by alterations in the drug's biotransformation (Chapter 4).

Antidotal therapy for acetaminophen poisoning is based on the administration of sulfur-containing glutathione as a receptor for the toxic product of acetaminophen biotransformation by pathway 3. Glutathione itself is not an effective antidote because it is readily broken down in plasma, and although normally synthesized in the liver cells, it is not taken up by the cells from external sources. In the United States the oral administration of *N*-acetyl-L-cysteine (Mucomyst) at a loading dose of 140 mg/kg followed by 70 mg/kg every 4 hours for a total of 17 doses, is the rec-

ommended antidote. It is administered orally in orange juice or soft drinks. To prevent hepatotoxicity, acetylcystein should be started within 10 to 12 hours after acetaminophen overdose. Some benefit may be obtained if it is instituted within the first 24 hours.

▷**Nursing Management:
Acetaminophen Poisoning**

In addition to the nursing management of the care of the client with poisoning on p. 1135:

***Assessment.*** Perform all procedures usually associated with treatment for ingested poisons before administering acetylcysteine: assess patient condition and vital signs, institute emesis or lavage, and so forth.

***Intervention.*** Avoid spilling acetylcysteine on materials such as iron, copper, and rubber because a reaction will occur. Note that prolonged, chronic contact with this agent may result in dermal eruptions, which may indicate a hypersensitivity reaction. Nursing staff are probably at higher risk than patients and should take appropriate precautions. Consider an occasional light purple coloration of the solution in an opened vial a harmless chemical reaction in its approved application. However, since no antimicrobial agent exists in the solution, refrigerate and discard opened containers if not used within 96 hours. Store unopened vials at controlled room temperature.

## Alcohols

The low molecular weight alcohols (isopropanol and methanol) are relatively weak poisons themselves, but their metabolites are lethal. Lethal doses of these alcohols are relatively large. Unfortunately, these alcohols are tasteless. Although they share many physical and chemical properties with ethanol (Chapter 9), and low molecular weight, small molecular size, and miscibility with water, they are not euphorigenic, and severe intoxication is usually life threatening. They do share a dehydrogenase to their corresponding aldehyde or ketone. The resultant aldehydes are rapidly converted by aldehyde dehydrogenase to their respective acids. However, unlike ethanol, which gives rise to acetic acid that may be utilized in normal metabolic processes, the other alcohols produce toxic acids. Fortunately, this metabolic interrelationship may be used for the management of their intoxication. Ethanol is the antidote for isopropanol and methanol poisoning. Ethanol will compete with the other alcohols for alcohol dehydrogenase, thereby blocking or significantly slowing their conversion to their respective aldehydes and ultimately their toxic acids.

The alcoholic client is particularly susceptible to exposure to these other alcohols for a variety of reasons. Either deliberately or accidentally, the alcoholic may ingest methanol or isopropanol to alter his mental status. It is not unusual for alcoholics to resort to drinking inexpensive products such as rubbing alcohol (isopropanol) when ethanol is not available. The early stages of poisonings from these agents produce a clinical picture much like ethanol intoxication: nausea, vomiting, motor incoordination, and impaired mental function. A history of ingestion of these other alcohols is often not obtained, either because the client conceals it or is too intoxicated to be interviewed or is in coma. In such instances a misdiagnosis of ethanol intoxication may be made. Laboratory testing for both ethanol and serum chemistries may clarify this picture.

## ▷Nursing Management: Alcohol Poisoning

In addition to the nursing management of the care of the client with poisoning on p. 1135:

**Assessment.** Make baseline assessment of level of consciousness initially; reassess frequently.

Note that emesis or lavage may be unsuccessful because these toxins leave the stomach very rapidly.

**Intervention.** Perform continuous assessment of vital signs and emergency supportive measures. Monitor blood glucose levels to assess for hypoglycemia or ketoacidosis frequently. Monitor intravenous infusion flow rates carefully to keep blood ethanol levels at approximately 100 mg 100 ml.

**Education.** Keep clients and concerned others informed about the progress of recovery and treatment measures.

### Isopropanol (Isopropyl Alcohol)

Isopropanol ($CH_3CHOHCH_3$) is a colorless, volatile, and flammable liquid present in numerous household products including disinfectants, cosmetics, solvents, liniments, and cleaning solutions. Most commonly, it is available in a 70% solution as a rubbing alcohol. Isopropanol poisoning is more common than generally recognized. It is often ingested by debilitated alcoholics because it is cheaper than alcohol. Accidental ingestion by children is also common. Isopropanol is approximately twice as toxic as ethanol but less toxic than methanol. The lethal dose in adults is considered to be 240 ml; however, as little as 20 ml has caused intoxication.

Isopropanol is rapidly absorbed from the alimentary tract and the lungs. Percutaneous absorption is minimal. Following absorption, like other alcohols, it is evenly distributed in the body water. Most of an absorbed dose is slowly excreted by the kidneys and lungs. Only about 15% is ox-

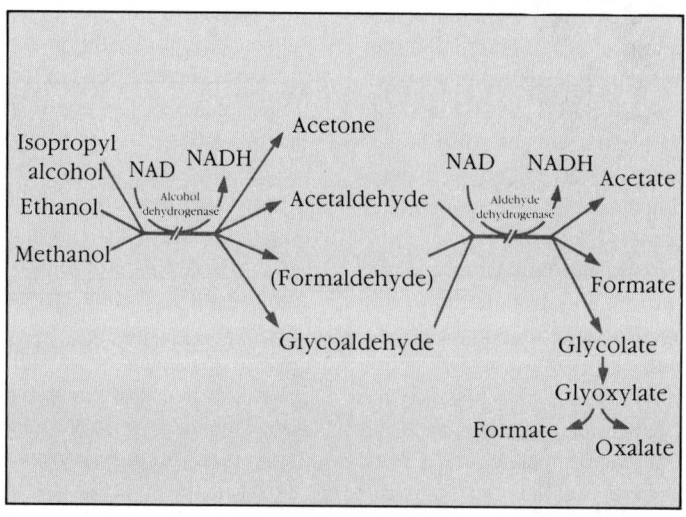

**FIGURE 75-3** Summary of the metabolism of alcohols.

idized to acetone by alcohol dehydrogenase (Figure 75-3). Acetone itself is very slowly excreted. This accounts for the prolonged effects of isopropanol poisoning and the characteristic acetone odor of the patient's breath. Although isopropanol and ethanol share the same metabolic pathway, ethanol has proved clinically ineffective as an antidote, since only a small fraction of isopropanol is converted to acetone.

The signs and symptoms of isopropanol poisoning are similar to those of ethanol; however, because of its slower metabolism and excretion, the symptoms of isopropanol intoxication persist two to four times longer than those of ethanol. Following ingestion, nausea, vomiting, gastritis, and severe abdominal pain may occur. Absorption is rapid, and dizziness, headache, lack of coordination, mental confusion, and stupor progressing to central nervous system depression and coma may occur within a few hours of ingestion. Cardiac dysrhythmia and severe hypotension progressing to cardiopulmonary collapse may occur. Dehydration and hemorrhagic gastritis are common features of isopropanol intoxication. Isopropanol poisoning may be differentiated from that of other alcohols by the presence of metabolic ketosis and a serum anion gap without metabolic acidosis. The determination of serum isopropanol and acetone concentration confirms the diagnosis. Serum values in excess of 150 mg/dl are usually associated with coma.

Treatment for isopropanol intoxication involves supportive therapy. If serum values are elevated, hemodialysis is indicated.

▷ *Nursing Management:*
*Isopropanol Poisoning*

See the general nursing management of the care of the client with poisoning, on p. 1135.

*Methanol (Methyl Alcohol)*

Methanol ($CH_3OH$) is a colorless liquid prepared either by the destructive distillation of wood or by chemical synthesis. The two products are chemically and physiologically identical. Methanol is widely used in commercial and industrial processes and is found in numerous home and garage products such as varnish and paint solvent, windshield wiper solution, and gas line de-icer. It is also used as a canned fuel (Sterno) and as an adulterant to make ethanol unfit to drink when sold as a cleaning disinfectant (denatured alcohol).

Most cases of acute methanol poisoning are associated with the accidental or deliberate ingestion of adulterated ethanolic beverages. During World War II, 6% of all cases of blindness in the U.S. armed forces were caused by ingestion of methanol itself or in adulterated ethanol. As little as 15 ml of methanol has proven fatal in some individuals; however, 80 ml is generally considered a fatal dose.

Methanol is absorbed from the alimentary tract and the lungs. Once absorbed, it is evenly distributed in the body water. Only small amounts of methanol are excreted by the kidney; as little as 3% is found unchanged in the urine. As described above, methanol is primarily biotransformed by alcohol dehydrogenase to formaldehyde and ultimately to formate. (Figure 75-3).

The most common presentation of methanol poisoning consists of a triad of symptoms relating to the gastrointestinal tract, the eyes, and metabolic acidosis. The onset of symptoms after ingestion ranges from 30 minutes to 72 hours. Like other aliphatic alcohols, methanol is a central nervous system depressant, but depression is rarely fatal. Gastrointestinal irritation is much greater with methanol than ethanol; vomiting, gastrointestinal bleeding, and severe abdominal pain are common symptoms. Following gastric symptoms, weakness, lethargy, and a general malaise, not unlike symptoms of an ethanol hangover, occur. These conditions may rapidly proceed to mental confusion, convulsions, coma, and death.

Two primary features of methanol poisoning are caused by its metabolite, formic acid. The conversion of methanol to formic acid in the liver causes a profound metabolic acidosis, which may cause the victim to become short of breath and tachypneic and in severe cases result in shock, multisystem failure, and death. Accumulation of formic acid in the retinal nerve fibers and their ganglion cells results in optic disc swelling. Ocular symptoms generally may develop as early as 2 minutes or as late as 3 days after methanol ingestion; they include blurred vision, photophobia, constructed visual fields, "spots before the eyes," "snow vision," and blindness. Good visual recovery slowly unfolds following mild intoxications; however, complete recovery from optic neuritis is rare.

Laboratory tests are critical in establishing a correct diagnosis and in guiding therapy. If the client has ingested methanol within the previous 4 hours, the stomach should be emptied by administration of syrup of ipecac or gastric lavage. To block the conversion of methanol to toxic metabolites, an intravenous injection of a 10% ethanol solution in a loading dose of 10 ml/kg, followed by an infusion of 1.5 ml/kg/h, is administered. Should serum methanol concentrations exceed 50 mg/dl, hemodialysis, in addition to ethanol therapy, is indicated. In such cases, a maintenance infusion of 3.0 ml/kg/h ethanol is necessary during hemodialysis. Both ethanol and methanol serum concentrations should be frequently monitored. These regimens will result in blood ethanol concentrations of 100 to 130 mg/dl, which appears optimal for inhibition of alcohol dehydrogenase. The affinity of ethanol for the enzyme is at least seven times greater than that of methanol. A serum profile of a client successfully treated for methanol poisoning by both ethanol infusion and hemodialysis is presented in Figure 75-4.

To correct metabolic acidosis, sodium bicarbonate is given intravenously; however, although bicarbonate may neutralize serum formic acid, it may not prevent optic nerve damage. Severe acidosis may require hemodialysis to re-

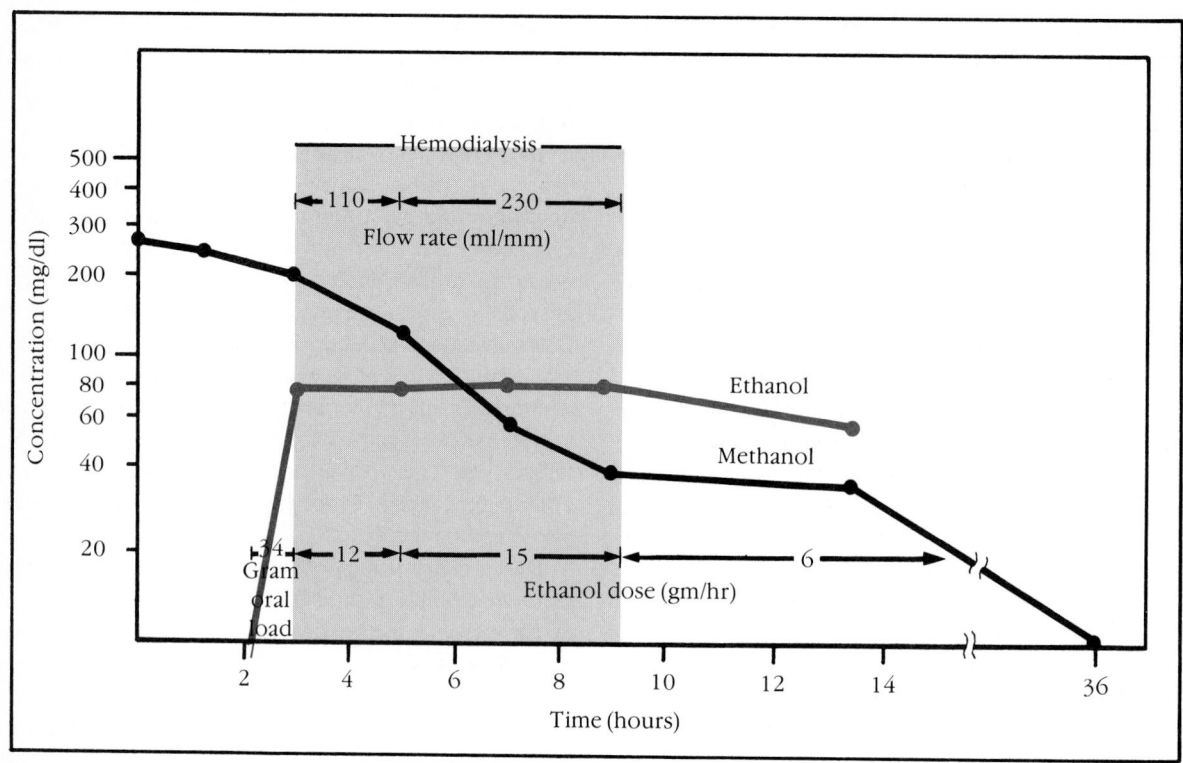

**FIGURE 75-4**   Blood methanol (black line) and blood ethanol (colored line) concentrations before, during, and after hemodialysis. Methanol elimination has enhanced during hemodialysis (shaded area).

move methanol and formic acid. When large concentrations of formic acid are present, the tetrahydrofolic acid becomes depleted. The administration of sodium folate replaces the depleted folic acid and accelerates the normal conversion of formic acid to carbon dioxide and water, thus preventing optic neuritis and blindness. The optimum dosage of sodium folate in man is yet to be determined; however, presently 50 mg intravenously every 4 hours is recommended. This antidote is sufficiently safe to warrant its use in all methanol-intoxicated patients. If sodium folate is unavailable, leucovorin, an active form of folate, may be substituted.

▷*Nursing Management:*
  *Methanol Poisoning*

See the general nursing management of care of the client with poisoning on p. 1135.

## Carbon Monoxide

Carbon monoxide (CO) is an odorless, colorless, tasteless gas produced by the incomplete combustion of carbon or carbonaceous materials. Any flame or combustion device is likely to emit CO. Sources of the gas include improperly maintained heating systems, improperly ventilated charcoal cookers or fireplaces, and industrial furnaces such as those in steel mills. Automobile exhaust contains 3% to 7% CO.

No other poison causes as many deaths in the United States as does CO. Inhalation of automobile exhaust is a common method of suicide. Accidental home and industrial exposure to CO is much more common than generally appreciated.

Poisoning by CO results from pulmonary absorption of the gas. CO readily combines with hemoglobin to form carboxyhemoglobin. Not only does CO replace oxygen in hemoglobin, thus lowering available oxygen carried by the blood to the body tissues, but with the addition of each CO molecule the oxygen molecules remaining on the hemoglobin become so tightly bound that they are not readily released to the oxygen starved tissues. CO is measured in blood as the percent carboxyhemoglobin (%HbCO). Additionally, CO gas dissolved in blood but not bound to hemoglobin diffuses into the body tissues and poisons cytochrome enzymes necessary for cellular utilization of oxygen.

The symptoms of CO poisoning are generally related to %HbCO. Clinically, only mild if any symptoms occur at 10% HbCO. Cigarette smokers may have CO up to this level. The initial signs of poisoning usually occur at 10% to 30% HbCO; these signs include throbbing headache, nausea, vomiting, dizziness, weakness, and visual disturbances. These early symptoms of intoxication are nonspecific and may be attributed to a number of other causes unless a history of CO is available or laboratory tests demonstrate elevated %HbCO. At 40% to 50% HbCO, syncope, tachycardia, tightness in the chest, and tachypnea occur. HbCO has a cherry pink color rather than the red color of oxyhemoglobin; therefore the patient may have a cherry pink coloration of the skin. Percent HbCO in excess of 50% causes life-threatening convulsions, coma, dangerously compromised cardiopulmonary function, and possible death. Fatalities from suicide or victims of fires often have %HbCO of 60% to 80%.

Treatment for CO poisoning is based on the patient's symptoms and %HbCO. Hyperbaric oxygen is the antidote of choice as oxygen under pressure is capable of replacing CO from hemoglobin and the iron containing respiratory cytochrome enzymes in the tissues. Ninety-five percent of absorbed CO is excreted by the lungs; however, once removed from the source of exposure, the half-life (t½) of CO in normal ambient air is 4 hours. If 100% oxygen is administered, the half-life decreases to 40 minutes. Hyperbaric oxygen at 3 atm decreases the t½ of CO to only 23 minutes. In severe poisoning, cardiopulmonary support is maintained throughout therapy. Additional drug therapy to control dysrhythmias, cerebral edema, and convulsions may be indicated.

▷**Nursing Management:**
**Carbon Monoxide Poisoning**

See the general nursing management for poisoning on p. 1135.

## Cyanide

Few poisons are as lethal as cyanide; large doses can produce death in minutes. Numerous industrial processes, including electroplating, chemical and dye syntheses, and extraction of precious metals, utilize cyanide or its salts. Cyanide is also commonly used as a fumigant-rodenticide in grain elevators, railway cars, and ship holds. It is available to the general public in photographic supplies, pesticides, and metal polishes. Certain seeds, particularly of the *genus Prunus* (wild cherry, bitter almonds, and others) contain cyanide-liberating glycosides.

Cyanide salts are often used as homocidal or suicidal agents. Numerous accidental poisonings arise from use of cyanide compounds in agriculture and industry. The popularity of the supposed antineoplastic agent laetrile has been responsible for a number of acute and subacute cyanide poisonings. Laetrile is usually amygdalin, a cyanide-containing glycoside that releases cyanide when metabolized by the body. Cigarette smoke contains HCN, (hydrogen cyanide) and smokers have a significantly higher blood concentration of cyanide than nonsmokers. In the stomach large ingested doses of cyanide salts produce a corrosive necrosis. Cyanide is biotransformed in the body to cyanate and thio-

cyanate and excreted in the urine. This conversion of cyanide is rapid enough to permit the continuous inhalation of low concentrations (less than 30 ppm) of HCN for 8 hours.

After absorption, the cyanide ($CN^-$) rapidly binds to and inactivates certain oxidative enzymes of all tissues. CN has a particular affinity for compounds containing oxidized iron ($Fe^{+3}$). Cytochrome oxidase and other respiratory enzymes containing oxidized iron are commonly inactivated. One part CN per 100 million parts of solution blocks all cytochrome oxidase activity. This inhibition prevents tissue utilization of oxygen, and rapid death follows. Another deadly effect of CN is the reflex stimulation of respiration by action of the sensory nerves ending in the carotid body. When cyanide vapor is inhaled, the carotid body and medullary stimulation cause a deep breath to be taken, thus allowing greater quantities of the poison to be inhaled.

The onset of symptoms of cyanide poisoning is rapid and dramatic. Cyanide poisoning initially causes headache, sweating, ataxia, and varying degrees of mental confusion, which may quickly progress to coma. Cyanosis or, as with carbon monoxide poisoning, a cherry pink coloration of the skin may be noted. Vomiting frequently occurs, and the pupils are dilated. Depending on the degree of poisoning, convulsions and involuntary micturition and defecation may occur. Circulatory function may be strong or weak; the pulse is often decreased initially, then becomes rapid. Death resulting from asphyxia may occur within minutes of exposure; either circulation or respiration may fail first. The average fatal dose of sodium or potassium cyanide is 0.25 g; however, as little as 0.06 g has caused death. HCN is twice as toxic as its salts. Generally, death ensues when only a small fraction of an ingested dose is absorbed.

The classical treatment of cyanide poisoning is the administration of sodium nitrite and sodium thiosulfate (Figure 75-5). Sodium nitrite is given to convert the reduced iron (ferrous, $Fe^{+2}$) in hemoglobin to the oxidized (ferric, $Fe^{+3}$) state thus forming methemoglobin. Because of cyanide's great affinity for iron in the ferric state, cyanide combines immediately with methemoglobin to form cyanomethemoglobin, thus competing with respiratory enzymes such as cythochrome oxidase for CN and restoring normal cellular function. As much as 40% of the blood hemoglobin may be converted to methemoglobin without hindering normal oxygen transport and body respiration by the remaining normal hemoglobin. As mentioned above, cyanide is normally detoxified in the body to thiocyanate (SCN), which is excreted in the urine. This metabolic conversion requires thiosulfate (or reducing sulfur) as a sulfur donor. In overdose situations the normal body stores of reducing sulfur are exhausted by the excess cyanide, thereby limiting the amount cyanide that can be detoxified. Sodium thiosulfate is administered to provide a source of reducing sulfur for the enzyme transsulfurase (rhodanese) to convert cyanomethemoglobin to thiocyanate, which is subsequently ex-

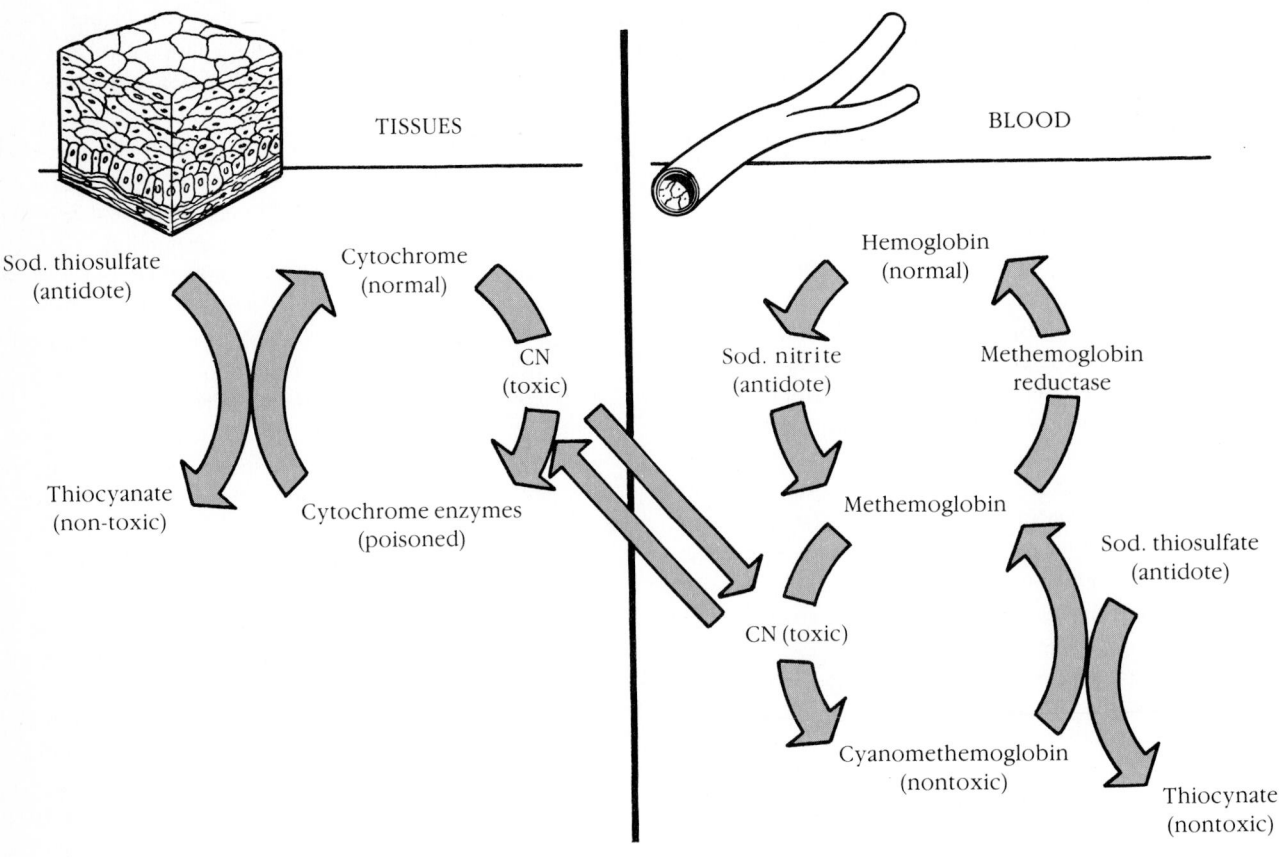

**FIGURE 75-5**  Mechanism of antidotal treatment for cyanide poisoning.

creted in the urine. The remaining methemoglobin is then reconverted to hemoglobin by the enzyme system, methemoglobin reductase, which is present in the red blood cells.

Amyl nitrite is immediately administered by inhalation from several "pearls" or capsules broken into gauze, followed by 300 mg of sodium nitrite intravenous. Amyl nitrite converts 5% of hemoglobin to methemoglobin, whereas the sodium nitrite converts 25% to 30%. Sodium thiosulfate, 12.5 mg, is then slowly administered intravenously. Excessive methemoglobineurea with this dose is rare in adults; however, children develop severe or even fatal methemoglobineurea if adult doses are given. For children weighing less than 60 lbs (25 kg), sodium nitrite doses should be based on blood hemoglobin; however, if hemoglobin values are not readily available, 10 mg/kg may be initially administered. The concurrent administration of oxygen with nitrite-thiosulfate therapy enhances the antidotal effects of the combination.

▷**Nursing Management:**
  **Cyanide Poisoning**

See the general nursing management for poisoning on p. 1135.

*Assessment.* Do not delay initiating treatment; rapid, competent care is essential in cyanide poisoning. Perform a baseline assessment of (1) vital signs, with particular attention to quality, rate, and rhythm of apical pulse, and (2) blood pressure; measure these parameters repeatedly throughout treatment.

*Intervention.* Initiate removal of ingested cyanide from stomach immediately by using rapid-acting emetic or lavage.

If poison has been inhaled, client must be moved to fresh air and may be given oxygen.

Be prepared to have blood drawn and to record the time and results; determinations of hemoglobin level and methemoglobinemia probably will be needed repeatedly to titrate antidote dosages. Advise against administration of methylene blue for excessive methemoglobinemia resulting from this therapy. Blood products should be ordered and available in case a transfusion is necessary.

Note that the client will be uncomfortable, with headache, feelings of chest constriction, and dyspnea.

**Iron**

Iron deficiency is a primary cause of anemia in both infants and adults. Thus iron is often added to infant formulas and foods and is available in over 100 commercial products for adults, including multiple and prenatal vitamins. Available products use a number of forms of iron, various salts and chelates. The toxic effects of iron are caused by its elemental form; therefore the relative toxicity of iron salts is related to the percent of elemental iron. For example, ferrous fumerate (33% iron) is more toxic on a weight basis than ferrous gluconate (12% iron). The accidental ingestion of iron preparations is a common form of pediatric poisoning, and suicidal ingestion of iron salts by adults is not uncommon. Though rarely fatal, iron overdose can result in profound mental retardation.

Once ingested, large amounts of iron cause local corrosive actions on the gastric and duodenal mucosa and upper gastrointestinal tract. Thus initial symptoms of iron poisoning include nausea, vomiting, upper abdominal pain, and bloody diarrhea. The corrosive action destroys the normal mucosal barrier to iron absorption, allowing rapid absorption of large amounts of iron into the general circulation. These overdose concentrations of iron exceed the binding capacity of transferrin, the iron-carrying protein of the blood. The excess free iron readily diffuses into various tissues and binds to the sulfhydryl (SH) radicals of numerous enzymes and structural proteins. This binding of iron to compounds necessary for normal cellular function poisons the tissue cells. Thus 6 to 24 hours after ingestion symptoms of systemic intoxication—cyanosis, pulmonary edema, and possible cardiovascular collapse—start to occur. Within a few days, coagulation defects, hepatic necrosis, and renal failure may develop. As with adults, the initial symptoms of pediatric iron poisoning are characterized by repeated vomiting, abdominal pain, and diarrhea. However, frequently a latent phase occurs when the initial symptoms abate and the child appears well for a 6- to 12-hour period, which is followed by rapid illness and the development of shock. The determination of serum iron will indicate the severity of the intoxication and prevent the possible dangerous misinterpretation of this latency period. Additionally, serum iron values will indicate the necessity of the initiation of antidotal therapy. Serum iron concentrations of 350 μg/dl or less are rarely associated with clinical illness. Concentrations between 350 and 500 μg/dl call for observation of the patient for the development of clinical signs of intoxication. For concentrations above 500 μg/dl, deferoxamine (an iron chelating agent) therapy is recommended. The prognosis of clients with serum iron of 500-2000 μg/dl is reasonably good; however, concentrations exceeding 10,000 μg/dl are indicative of severe hepatic and renal damage. Heroic measures are required in such instances.

The treatment for iron poisoning includes general supportive measures, and a specific antidote to precipitate or chelate the ingested iron. Emesis may be induced to expel unabsorbed iron tablets in the stomach; also, sodium bicarbonate lavage is indicated, since bicarbonate converts ferrous iron to ferrous carbonate, which is poorly absorbed. After lavage, 200 to 300 ml of the bicarbonate solution

should be left in the stomach. When indicated by toxic serum iron concentrations (+500 mg/dl), deferoxamine, a chelating agent, should be administered. Deferoxamine is a specific chelator that binds free serum iron and iron associated with hepatic and splenic stores. Deferoxamine does not bind with zinc, copper, or other trace metals. The deferoxamine-iron complex is nontoxic and freely excreted by the kidneys.

▷**Nursing Management:**
**Iron Poisoning**

In addition to the nursing management of the care of the client with poisoning on p. 1135:

**Assessment.** Take careful history of elicit possibility of pregnancy. Advise against the use of deferoxamine if client is pregnant, or may have severe renal impairment. Perform baseline assessments, including attention to vital signs, especially blood pressure and apical pulse.

**Intervention.** Institute emesis or gastric lavage as soon as possible. Initiate supportive measures, including maintenance of clear airway and interventions related to presence of shock and to acidosis. Administer deferoxamine using long needle and Z-track method; may add 0.2 to 0.3 ml of air to medication in syringe to prevent pain and induration at site of injections. Carefully controlled, slow intravenous infusion rates may be equally effective in preventing such pain.

**Education.** Tell client to expect reddish brown coloration of urine and stools.

## Organophosphate Insecticides

Organophosphate compounds are highly effective insecticides. Their chemical structure is unstable, resulting in their disintegration into nontoxic radicals within days after their application. Therefore they do not persist or accumulate in the environment or animal tissues as do the chlorinated insecticides such as DDT. This accounts for their addition to numerous commercial products from flea collars, bug bombs, and flypapers to most home and commercial insect sprays. This popularity accounts for the high potential for accidental poisoning by organophosphates. Popular organophosphate insecticides and their relative toxicity are presented in Table 75-7.

Organophosphate compounds are powerful inhibitors of the enzyme acetylcholinesterase (ACHE), which breaks down the neurohumeral transmitter acetylcholine (ACh) (Chapter 20). Organophosphates were developed during World War II as nerve gases, and much of our knowledge of their actions and effects is related to work on the poison gases sarin, tabun, and soman. They are rapidly absorbed into the body by all routes, respiratory, dermal, gastrointestinal, and ocular. However, individual organophosphates display wide variation in their ability to penetrate the skin,

**TABLE 75-7** Toxicity of organophosphates

| Organophosphate | Relative toxicity Oral LD$_{50}$ (mg/kg rates) |
|---|---|
| TEPP | 1.5 |
| Paraoxon (metabolite of parathion) | 2.5 |
| Parathion | 6 |
| EPN | 40 |
| Leptophos | 46 |
| Dichlorvos (DDVP) | 80 |
| Diazinon | 200 |
| Dichlofenthion | 270 |
| Malaoxon (metabolite of malathion) | 308 |
| Malathion | 1375 |

Reprinted with permission from Eto M: Organophosphorous pesticides: organic and biological chemistry, Cleveland, 1974, CRC Press, pp 234-297. Copyright CRC Press, Inc., Boca Raton, Fla.

in their oral absorption, and thus in their toxicity. For example, malathion does not penetrate the skin well and its oral toxicity is low, making it a popular insecticide for use in home products (Table 75-7).

The signs and symptoms of organophosphate insecticide poisoning are related to inhibition of AChE, which results in an accumulation of ACh in the parasympathetic nervous system. Hence, all organs acted on by ACh are overstimulated. The expected results of organophosphate poisoning are as follows: bradycardia, hypotension, dyspnea, wheezing, miosis, blurred vision, convulsions, muscular fasciculations, and profuse sweating. A common mnemonic for symptoms of organophosphate intoxication is **SLUDGE:** *s*alivation, *l*acrimation, *u*rination, *d*efecation, *g*astrointestinal distress, and *e*mesis. The usual mode of death is respiratory arrest caused by bronchospasm, decreased pulmonary muscle strength, and finally depression of central nervous system control of respiration. The sequence in which specific systems develop is related to the route of exposure. Respiratory tract effects appear first after inhalation, whereas gastrointestinal effects appear initially after ingestion. Skin absorption results in immediate profuse sweating and muscle weakness.

Therapy for organophosphate poisoning involves the support of cardiopulmonary function, clearance of respiratory tract secretions to maintain a clear airway, and the use of appropriate antidotes, atropine and 2-PAM (Pralidoxamine, Protopam). Atropine competitively antagonizes the action of ACh at muscarinic receptors on organs innervated by postganglionic parasympathetic nerves and cholinergic sympathetic nerves (Chapter 20). An initial dose of 2 to 4 mg is given every 3 to 8 minutes to increase heart rate and decrease secretions. If these effects do not occur, an insufficient dose has been given. Patients poisoned with organophosphates may be particularly resistant to atropine. There-

fore repeated larger doses may be necessary. Doses of 50 mg/24 hrs up to 2 to 4 g over a week have been safely administered in severe poisoning. The dangers of prolonged organophosphate intoxication exceed the risk of atropine overdose.

Atropine is effective in blocking muscarinic symptoms of bradycardia, bronchoconstriction, and excess secretions; however, muscular fasciculations are refractory to this antidote. These involuntary contractions and twitchings and respiratory paralysis are best treated with 2-PAM, a cholinesterase reactivator that removes organophosphates bound to AChE. This then frees AChE to break down the accumulated ACh, thereby resuming normal activity at the neuromuscular junction. 2-PAM also directly detoxifies certain organophosphates. The initial dose of 2-PAM is 1 to 2 g intravenously in 100 ml of saline over 15 to 30 minutes. For children the dose is 20 to 40 mg/kg. Doses are repeated every 3 to 8 hours if muscle weakness persists. Side effects of 2-PAM include dizziness, nausea, headache, and tachycardia.

▷**Nursing Management: Organophosphate Poisoning**

In addition to the management of care of the client with poisoning on p. 1135:

***Assessment.*** If there is cyanosis, establish and maintain an airway first. Copious secretions may necessitate nearly continuous suctioning at first; anticipate supplemental oxygen therapy.

Induce vomiting or perform gastric lavage if poison was ingested.

Cleanse skin of any insecticide contaminant if present.

Closely monitor both respiratory status and secretion production, since doses of atropine may be predicated on this information.

If signs of excessive atropinization appear, plan for treatment with physostigmine to antagonize atropine.

Anticipate need to administer pralidoxime (Protopam) if poisoning is severe.

Plan to monitor client's status closely for 72 hours.

**SUMMARY**

Poisoning, accidental or intentional, is a commonplace reason for admission to a hospital emergency room. Children make up the majority of the accidental poisoning population, whereas intentional poisoning is more likely to be the result of a suicide attempt or an abused substance overdose. No matter how poisonings are classified, the care provided focuses on prompt treatment, the identification of the substance, if possible, the support of vital functions, the removal or elimination of the poison, and the prevention of future occurrences.

# BIBLIOGRAPHY

Aronson JK. (1989). The treatment of self-poisoning, Emerg Med Serv 18(5):51.

Bibb J. (1988). Environmental emergencies, Emerg Care Q 4(3):61.

Cooper K. (1989). Drug overdose, Am J Nurs 89(9):1146.

Dailey MA. (1989). Carbon monoxide poisoning, J Emerg Nurs 15(2):120.

Davidson L et al. (1989). Medical emergencies in the pediatric patient, part 3, JEMS 14(6):74.

Davis NM et al. (1989). Today's poisonings: how to keep them from killing your patients, Nursing 19(1):49.

Done AK. (1988). The encephalopathic presentation, Emerg Med 20(17):154.

Done AK. (1988). The hepatotoxic presentation, Emerg Med 20(21):51.

Drug screening after the OD. (1988). Emerg Med 20(17):115.

Fein AM. (1989). Toxic gas inhalation, Emerg Med 21(7):53.

Feldmann EG, ed. (1990). Handbook of nonprescription drugs, ed 9. Washington, DC: American Pharmaceutical Association.

Flomenbaum NE et al. (1990). GI evacuation: is it still worthwhile? Emerg Med 22(2):80.

Gilman AG et al, eds. (1990). Goodman and Gilman's the pharmacological basis of therapeutics, ed 8. New York: Macmillan Publishing Co.

Goldberg MJ et al. (1986). An approach to the management of the poisoned patient, Arch Intern Med 146(7):1381.

Goldfrank LR. (1982). Toxicologic emergencies, ed 2. New York: Appleton-Century-Crofts.

Haddad LM and Winchester JF, eds. Clinical management of poisoning and drug overdose. Philadelphia: WB Saunders Co.

Halpern JS. (1989). Chronic occult carbon monoxide poisoning, J Emerg Nurs 15(2):101.

Herfindal ET et al. (1988). Clinical pharmacy and therapeutics, ed 4. Baltimore: Williams & Wilkins.

Identifying heavy metal poisoning. (1989). Emerg Med 21(8):81.

Izor-Povenmire K et al. (1989). Acute crack cocaine intoxications: a case study. Focus Crit Care 16(2):112.

Johnson RB et al. (1989). Tricyclic antidepressant overdose: a toxicologic emergency, J Am Acad Physician Assist 2(1):16.

Jones J et al. (1988). Holiday's hidden hazards, JEMS 13(12):34.

Kastrup EK, ed. (1991). Facts and comparisons. St Louis: JB Lippincott Co.

King WD and Palmisano PA. (1989). Ingestion of prescription drugs by children: an epidemiologic study, South Med J 82(12):1468.

Levy DB. (1988). A breath of dead air, Emergency 20(11):18.

Martindale LG. (1989). Carbon monoxide poisoning: the rest of the story, J Emerg Nurs 15(2):107.

Meyer D. (1988). Ethylene glycol poisoning, Focus Crit Care 15(6):54.

Meyer D. (1989). Action STAT! ethylene glycol poisoning, Nursing 19(11):33.

Molinaro J. (1989). A primary care approach to heavy metal poisoning, J Am Acad Physician Assist 2(4):261.

Poison prevention materials list. (1988). Directory of United States Poison Control Centers and Services. Washington, DC: US Department of Health and Human Services.

Physicians' desk reference, ed 45. (1991). Oradell, NJ: Medical Economics Co.

Poisoning among children: United States. (1984). MMWR 33:129.

Rich J. (1989). Action STAT! Acute alcohol intoxication, Nursing 19(9):33.

Special report: button batteries. (1983). Pittsburgh: National Poison Control Center.

Throckmorton, K et al. (1988). Pills, plants, and poisonings, Emergency 20(10):52.

United States Pharmacopeial Convention. (1991). USP-DI: drug information for the health care provider. Rockville Md: The Convention.

When ipecac is unnecessary. (1989). Emerg Med 21(14):154.

Young LY and Koda-Kimble MA. (1988). Applied therapeutics: the clinical use of drugs, ed 4. Vancouver: Applied Therapeutics, Inc.

# APPENDIXES

# A Commonly Used Medications: Generic to Trade Name Listing

The following is an alphabetical listing, by generic name, of selected prescription and over-the-counter medications.

| Generic Name | Trade Name |
|---|---|
| acetaminophen | Tylenol, Datril, Anacin-3 |
| acetazolamide | Diamox, Diamox Sequels |
| acetohexamide | Dymelor |
| acetylcysteine | Mucomyst |
| acetylsalicylic acid (ASA) | aspirin |
| acyclovir | Zovirax |
| albuterol | Proventil, Ventolin |
| allopurinol | Zyloprim |
| alprazolam | Xanax |
| aluminum hydroxide gel | Amphogel |
| aluminum-magnesium suspension | Maalox, Mylanta, Gelusil |
| amantadine | Symmetrel |
| ambenonium | Mytelase |
| amikacin | Amikin |
| amiloride | Midamor |
| aminocaproic acid | Amicar |
| aminoglutethimide | Cytadren |
| amitriptyline | Elavil, Endep |
| amobarbital | Amytal |
| amoxicillin | Amoxil, Larotid, Polymox |
| amoxicillin and clavulanate | Augmentin |
| amphotericin B | Fungizone |
| ampicillin | Amcil, Omnipen, Polycillin |
| ampicillin and sulbactam | Unasyn |
| ascorbic acid | Vitamin C |
| asparaginase | Elspar |
| aspirin, buffered | Bufferin |
| aspirin, enteric coated | Ecotrin |
| astemizole | Hismanal |

| Generic Name | Trade Name |
|---|---|
| atenolol | Tenormin |
| atracurium besylate | Tracrium |
| azatadine maleate | Trinalin, Optimine |
| azathioprine | Imuran |
| aztreonam | Azactam |
| baclofen | Lioresal |
| beclomethasone | Vanceril, Beclovent |
| belladonna alkaloids and phenobarbital | Donnatal |
| benzocaine | Americaine, Hurricaine |
| benzquinamide | Emeta-Con |
| benztropine | Cogentin |
| betamethasone | Celestone, Valisone |
| bethanechol chloride | Urecholine |
| biperiden | Akineton |
| bisacodyl | Dulcolax |
| bleomycin | Blenoxane |
| bretylium tosylate | Bretylol |
| bromocriptine | Parlodel |
| brompheniramine | Dimetane |
| buffered aspirin | Bufferin, Ascriptin |
| bumetanide | Bumex |
| buprenorphine | Buprenex |
| buspirone | Buspar |
| busulfan | Myleran |
| butabarbital | Butisol |
| butorphanol | Stadol |
| calcitonin | Calcimar |
| calcium carbonate | Tums, Titralac, Alka-2 |

| Generic Name | Trade Name | Generic Name | Trade Name |
|---|---|---|---|
| camphorated tincture of opium | Paregoric | clotrimazole | Lotrimin, Myclex |
| captopril | Capoten | colestipol | Colestid |
| caramiphen and phenylpropanolamine | Tuss-Ornade | conjugated estrogens | Premarin |
| | | corticotropin | ACTH, Acthar |
| carbamazepine | Tegretol | cortisone acetate | Cortone |
| carbenicillin | Geocillin, Geopen, Pyopen | cromolyn | Intal |
| carbidopa | Lodosyn | cyclizine | Marezine |
| carbidopa and levodopa | Sinemet | cyclobenzaprine | Flexeril |
| carmustine | BiCNU | cyclophosphamide | Cytoxan |
| cefaclor | Ceclor | cyproheptadine | Periactin |
| cefadroxil | Duricef | dactinomycin | Cosmegen |
| cefamandol | Mandol | danazol | Danocrine |
| cefapirin | Cefatrex | dantrolene sodium | Dantrium |
| cefazolin | Ancef, Kefzol | demeclocycline | Declomycin |
| cefixime | Suprax | desipramine | Norpramin, Pertofrane |
| cefoperazone | Cefobid | deslanoside | Cedilanid-D |
| cefotaxime | Claforan | dexamethasone | Decadron, Hexadrol |
| cefoxitin | Mefoxin | diazepam | Valium |
| ceftizoxime | Cefizox | diazoxide | Hyperstat, Proglycem |
| ceftriaxone | Rocephin | dibucaine | Nupercaine, Nupercainal |
| cefuroxime | Ceftin | diclofenac | Voltaren |
| cephalexin | Keflex | dicyclomine | Bentyl |
| cephalothin | Keflin | diethylstilbestrol | Stilbestrol, DES |
| cephapirin | Cefadyl | diflunisal | Dolobid |
| cephazolin | Ancef, Kefzol | digitoxin | Crystodigin |
| cephradine | Anspor, Velosef | digoxin | Lanoxin |
| chloral hydrate | Noctec | dimenhydrinate | Dramamine |
| chlorambucil | Leukeran | diocytl calcium sulfosuccinate (DOCS) | Surfak |
| chloramphenicol | Chloromycetin, Chloroptic | diocytl sodium sulfosuccinate (DSS) | Colace |
| chlorazepate, dipotassium | Tranxene | | |
| chlorazepate, monopotassium | Azene | dioctyl sodium sulfosuccinate with casanthranol | Pericolace |
| chlordiazepoxide | Librium, Libritab | | |
| chlordiazepoxide and amitriptyline | Limbitrol | diphenhydramine | Benadryl |
| chlordiazepoxide and clidinium | Limbrax | diphenoxylate HCL with atropine | Lomotil |
| chloroquine | Aralen | dipyridamole | Persantine |
| chlorothiazide | Diuril | disopyramide | Norpace |
| chlorotrianisene | Tace | disulfiram | Antabuse |
| chlorpheniramine | Chlortrimeton | dobutamine | Dobutrex |
| chlorpromazine | Thorazine | docusate calcium | Surfak |
| chlorpropamide | Diabinese | docusate sodium (DSS) | Colace |
| chlorprothixene | Taractan | dopamine | Intropin |
| chlorthalidone | Hygroton | doxapram | Dopram |
| cholestyramine | Questran | doxepin HCl | Adapin, Sinequan |
| cimetidine | Tagamet | doxorubicin HCl | Adriamycin |
| cinoxacin | Cinobac | doxycycline | Vibramycin |
| cisplatin | Platinol | dyphylline | Lufyllin |
| clemastine | Tavist | edrophonium | Tensilon |
| clidinium | Quarzan | enalapril | Vasotec |
| clindamycin | Cleocin-T | encainide | Enkaid |
| clofibrate | Atromid-S | enteric coated aspirin | Ecotrin |
| clomiphene | Clomid | ephedrine | Vaponefrin |
| clonazepam | Klonopin | epinephrine | Adrenalin, Sus-Phrine |
| clonidine | Catapres | ergoloid mesylates | Hydergine |

| Generic Name | Trade Name | Generic Name | Trade Name |
|---|---|---|---|
| ergonovine | Ergotrate | hydromorphone and guaifenesin | Dilaudin cough syrup |
| ergotamine | Ergomar, Ergostat | hydroxyzine HCl | Atarax |
| erythromycin | Erythrocin, Ilotycin | hydroxyzine pamoate | Vistaril |
| erythromycin estolate | Ilosone | ibuprofen | Advil, Motrin, Rufen |
| estrogens, conjugated | Premarin | idoxuridine | Stoxil, Herplex |
| ethacrynic acid | Edecrin | imipenem-cilastatin | Primaxin |
| ethchlorvynol | Placidyl | imipramine | Tofranil |
| etidronate | Didronel | indomethacin | Indocin |
| etoposide | Vepesid | INH (isoniazid) | Nydrazid |
| famotidine | Pepcid | ipratropium | Atrovent |
| fenoprofen | Nalfon | iron dextran | Imferon |
| fentanyl | Sublimaze | isoetharine HCl | Bronkosol |
| ferrous fumarate | Femiron | isoproterenol | Isuprel |
| ferrous gluconate | Fergon | isosorbide dinitrate | Isordil, Sorbitrate |
| ferrous sulfate | Mol–iron, Feosol | isotretinoin | Accutane |
| flecainide | Tambocor | isoxsuprine HCl | Vasodilan |
| flucytosine | Ancobon | kanamycin | Kantrex |
| fludrocortisone | Florinef | kaolin-pectin | Kaopectate |
| fluocinolone acetonide | Synalar | ketoconazole | Nizoral |
| fluocinonide | Lidex | ketoprofen | Orudis |
| fluoxetine | Prozac | labetalol | Normodyne, Trandate |
| fluphenazine | Prolixin | lactulose syrup | Chronulac |
| flurazepam | Dalmane | lanatoside C | Cedilanid |
| flurbiprofen | Ansaid | leucovorin | Wellcovorin |
| folic acid | Folvite | levarterenol | Levophed |
| folinic acid | Leucovorin calcium | levodopa | Dopar, Larodopa |
| furosemide | Lasix | levorphanol | Levo-Dromoran |
| gemfibrozil | Lopid | levothyroxine | Synthroid |
| gentamicin | Garamycin | lidocaine | Xylocaine |
| glutethimide | Doriden | lindane | Kwell |
| glyburide | Diabeta, Micronase | liothyronine | Cytomel |
| glycopyrrolate | Robinul | liotrix | Euthroid, Thyrolar |
| griseofulvin | Fulvicin P/G | lisinopril | Prinivil, Zestril |
| guaifenesin (glyceryl guaiacolate) | Robitussin | lithium carbonate | Lithane, Lithobid |
| guanabenz | Wytensin | lomustine | Cee Nu |
| guanethidine | Ismelin | loperamide | Imodium |
| guanfacine | Tenex | lorazepam | Ativan |
| haloperidol | Haldol | lovastatin | Mevacor |
| haloprogin | Halotex | loxapine succinate | Loxitane |
| halothane | Fluothane | lypressin | Diapid |
| heparin | Lipo-Hepin, Liquaemin | magaldrate | Riopan |
| hetacillin | Versapen | magnesium sulfate | Epsom salt |
| hyaluronidase | Wydase | maprotiline | Ludiomil |
| hydralazine | Apresoline | mazindol | Sanorex |
| hydrochlorothiazide | HydroDiuril, Esidrex | mebendazole | Vermox |
| hydrochlorothiazide and spironolactone | Aldactazide | mecamylamine | Inversine |
| hydrochlorothiazide and timolol | Timolide | mechlorethamine | Mustargen, Nitrogen Mustard |
| hydrochlorothiazide and triamterene | Dyazide | meclizine | Antivert, Bonine |
| | | meclofenamate | Meclomen |
| hydrocodone | Dicodid | medroxyprogesterone | Provera |
| hydrocodone and homatropine | Hycodan | megestrol | Megace |
| hydrocortisone | Solu-Cortef | melphalan | Alkeran |
| hydromorphone | Dilaudid | menadiol | Synkayvite, vitamin K |
| | | meperidine | Demerol |

| Generic Name | Trade Name | Generic Name | Trade Name |
|---|---|---|---|
| mephenytoin | Mesantoin | nylidrin | Arlidin |
| mephobarbital | Mebaral | nystatin | Mycostatin, Nilstat |
| meprobamate | Miltown, Equanil | orphendrine | Norflex |
| mesoridazine | Serentil | oxacillin | Prostaphlin |
| metaproterenol | Alupent | oxazepam | Serax |
| metaraminol | Aramine | oxtriphylline | Choledyl |
| methadone | Dolophine | oxycodone, ASA | Percodan |
| methandrostenolone | Dianabol | oxycodone, acetaminophen | Percocet, Tylox |
| methenamine hippurate | Hiprex, Urex | oxymetazoline, nasal | Afrin, Dristan Long Lasting |
| methenamine mandelate | Mandelamine | oxymorphone | Numorphan |
| methicillin | Staphcillin | oxyphenbutazone | Tandearil |
| methimazole | Tapazole | oxytetracycline | Terramycin |
| methocarbamol | Robaxin | oxytocin | Pitocin |
| methoxyflurane | Penthrane | pancrelipase | Cotazym, Viokase |
| methyldopa | Aldomet | pancuronium | Pavulon |
| methylphenidate | Ritalin | papaverine | Pavabid, Cerespan |
| methyprylon | Noludar | paraldehyde | Paral |
| methysergide | Sansert | pargyline | Eutonyl |
| metoclopramide | Reglan | pemoline | Cylert |
| metolazone | Zaroxolyn | penicillamine | Cuprimine |
| metoprolol | Lopressor | penicillin and benzathine | Bicillin |
| metronidazole | Flagyl | penicillin G potassium | Pfizepen, Pentid |
| mexiletine | Mexitil | penicillin procaine | Duracillin, crysticillin, Wycillin |
| mezlocillin | Mezlin | penicillin V potassium | Pen-Vee K, V-cillin K |
| miconazole | Monistat | pentaerythritol tetranitrate | Peritrate |
| milk of magnesia (MOM) | Magnesium Hydroxide | pentamidine isethionate | Pentam |
| mineral oil emulsion | Kondremul | pentazocine | Talwin |
| minocycline | Minocin | pentobarbital | Nembutal |
| minoxidil | Loniten | perphenazine | Trilafon |
| misoprostol | Cytotec | phenazopyridine HCl | Pyridium |
| mithramycin | Mithracin | phenazopyridine and sulfisoxazole | Azo-Gantrisin |
| mitotane | Lysodren | phenelzine sulfate | Nardil |
| molindone | Moban | pentoxifylline | Trental |
| morphine sulfate | Roxanol, Duramorph | phenmetrazine | Preludin |
| moxalactam | Moxam | phenobarbital | Luminal |
| nadolol | Corgard | phenolphthalein | Ex-Lax, Feen-A-Mint |
| nalbuphine | Nubain | phenoxymethyl penicillin | V-Cillin, Penicillin VK |
| nalidixic acid | Neg Gram | phentolamine | Regitine |
| naloxone | Narcan | phenylbutazone | Butazolidin, Azolid-A |
| naproxen | Naprosyn | phenylephrine | Neosynephrine |
| naproxen sodium | Anaprox | phenytoin | Dilantin |
| neostigmine | Prostigmin | phosphate enema | Fleet enema |
| niacin (nicotinic acid) | Nicobid, Nicolar | phosphated carbohydrate solution | Emetrol |
| nicardipine | Cardene | physostigmine | Antilirium |
| nifedipine | Procardia | phytonadione (vitamin $K_1$) | Mephyton, Aquamephyton |
| nitrofurantoin | Furadantin | pilocarpine | Isoptocarpine |
| nitrogen mustard | Mustargen | pindolol | Visken |
| nitroglycerin | Nitrobid, Nitrospan, Nitrostat | piperacillin | Pipracil |
| nitroprusside | Nipride | piroxicam | Feldene |
| nizatidine | Axid | potassium chloride | K-Lor, Kaon, Cl, Slow K, Micro K, Klorvess |
| norepinephrine | Levophed | | |
| norethindrone | Norlutin | potassium gluconate | Kaon |
| norethindrone acetate | Norlutate | povidone-iodine | Betadine |
| norfloxacin | Noroxin | prazosin | Minipress |
| nortriptyline | Aventyl, Pamelor | prednisolone | Meticortelone, Delta Cortef |

| Generic Name | Trade Name | Generic Name | Trade Name |
|---|---|---|---|
| primidone | Mysoline | tetanus immune globulin | Hyper-tet |
| probenecid | Benemid | tetracaine | Pontocaine |
| probucol | Lorelco | tetracycline | Achromycin, Sumycin |
| procainamide | Pronestyl | theophylline | Elixophyllin, Theo-Dur |
| procaine | Novocain | thiethylperzine | Torecan |
| procarbazine | Matulane | thioridazine | Mellaril |
| prochlorperazine | Compazine | thiothixene | Navane |
| procyclidine | Kemadrin | thyroglobulin | Proloid |
| promazine | Sparine | ticarcillin | Ticar |
| promethazine | Phenergan | ticarcillin disodium | Clavulanate-Timentin |
| propantheline | Probanthine | timolol maleate | Blocadren, Timoptic |
| propoxyphene | Darvon | tobramycin | Nebcin, Tobrex |
| propoxyphene, napsylate, acetaminophen | Davocet-N | tocainide | Tonocard |
| | | tolazamide | Tolinase |
| propranolol | Inderal | tolbutamide | Orinase |
| psyllium hydrocolloid | Effersyllium | t-PA | Activase |
| pyridostigmine | Mestinon | tranylcypromine sulfate | Parnate |
| pyrimethamine | Daraprim | trazodone | Desyrel |
| quinacrine | Atabrine | triamcinolone | Kenacort, Aristocort |
| quinidine gluconate | Quinaglute | triamterene | Dyrenium |
| quinidine sulfate | Quinora | triamterene and hydrochloro- thiazide | Dyazide, Maxzide |
| quinine sulfate | Quinamm | | |
| racepinephrine | Vaponefrin, Asthmanefin | triazolam | Halcion |
| ranitidine | Zantac | trifluoperazine | Stelazine |
| rauwolfia serpentina | Raudixin | trihexphenidyl HCl | Artane, Tremin |
| reserpine | Serpasil | trimeprazone | Temaril |
| ribavirin | Virazole | trimethadione | Tridione |
| rifampin | Rimactane, Rifadin | trimethaphan | Arfonad |
| ritodrine | Yutopar | trimethobenzamide | Tigan |
| salsalate | Disalcid | trimethoprim | Proloprim, Trimpex |
| scopolamine | Transderm-Scop | tripelennamine | Pyribenzamine (PBZ) |
| secobarbital | Seconal | triprolidine | Actidil |
| selenium sulfide | Selsun Blue, Selsun | triprolidine and pseudoephedrine | Actifed |
| senna | Senokot | undecylenic acid | Desenex |
| silver sulfadiazine | Silvadene | urokinase | Abbokinase |
| simethicone | Mylicon | ursodiol | Actigall |
| sodium polystyrene sulfonate | Kayexalate | valproic acid | Depakene |
| spironolactone | Aldactone | vancomycin | Vancocin |
| spironolactone and hydrochlorothiazide | Aldactazide | vasopressin | Pitressin |
| | | verapamil | Calan, Isoptin |
| streptokinase | Streptase | vidarabine | Vira-A |
| succinylcholine | Anectine | vinblastine | Velban |
| sucralfate | Carafate | vincristine | Oncovin |
| sufentanil | Sufenta | vitamin $B_1$ | Thiamine |
| sulfamethoxazole | Gantanol | vitamin $B_2$ | Riboflavin |
| sulfamethoxazole and trimethoprim | Bactrim, Septra | vitamin $B_3$ | Niacin, Nicotinic Acid |
| | | vitamin $B_6$ | Pyridoxine, Hexabetalin |
| sulfasalazine | Azulfidine | vitamin $B_{12}$ | Cyanocobalamin, Redisol |
| sulfisoxazole | Gantrisin | vitamin C | Ascorbic acid |
| sulfisoxazole and phenazopyridine | Azo-Gantrisin | vitamin D | Deltalin |
| sulindac | Clinoril | vitamin $K_1$ | Phytonadione |
| tamoxifen | Nolvadex | vitamin $K_2$ | Menadione |
| temazepam | Restoril | warfarin | Coumadin |
| terbutaline | Brethine, Bricanyl | wellbutrin | Bupropion |
| terfenadine | Seldane | zidovudine | Retrovir, AZT |

# B Drug Interferences with Laboratory Tests

Drugs may modify the results of laboratory tests by:

1. Changing the color of urine or stool, which may result in masking other abnormal circumstances, interfering with specific laboratory tests (colorimetric, photometric, and others), or causing undue concern for the uninformed client.
2. Direct chemical interference with the testing procedure.
3. Specific damage to a body organ, such as the liver or kidneys, or by specific metabolic alterations within the body. Often the reason for the laboratory test interference is unknown. The following sections will note the drugs that may cause test alterations, the type of changes induced (increased or decreased) and specific drug-test interferences when applicable.

## DRUGS THAT CHANGE URINE OR STOOL COLOR

Medications that may alter urine color

| Drug | Possible color changes |
|---|---|
| amitriptyline (Elavil) | Blue-green |
| anticoagulants (coumarin and others) | Pink, red, or dark brown (indicative of systemic bleeding) |
| cascara | In acid urine, brown; basic urine, yellow to pink; on standing, black |
| iron salts, dextran, and others | Brown to black |
| laxatives (danthron, senna) | Pink to red or brown |
| laxatives (phenolphthalein) | Pink to red |
| levodopa (Laradopa, Dopar) | May cause dark urine and sweat |

Medications that may alter urine color—cont'd

| Drug | Possible color changes |
|---|---|
| methyldopa (Aldomet, Dopamet ✿) | Pink, amber to dark urine |
| metronidazole (Flagyl) | Dark urine |
| nitrofurantoins (Furadantin, Macrodantin, Novofuran ✿) | Yellow to rusty brown urine |
| phenazopyridine (Pyridium, Phenazo ✿) | Orange red urine; may stain clothing |
| phenytoin (Dilantin) | Red-brown or darkening of urine |
| phenothiazines (chlorpromazine, or Thorazine, and others) | Pink, red, or orange urine |
| rifampin (Rifadin, Rofact ✿) | Red, orange, or brown urine, stool, saliva, sweat, and tears |

Medications that may alter stool color

| Drug | Possible color changes |
|---|---|
| antacids with aluminum salts (Maalox, Mylanta, and others) | White specks or discoloration of stools |
| anticoagulants (coumarin and others) | Red, orange, to black because of internal bleeding |
| bismuth or iron salts | Black |
| laxative (phenolphthalein) | Red |
| laxative (senna) | Yellow, orange to brown |
| phenazopyridine (Pyridium and others) | Orange, red |

# DIRECT CHEMICAL INTERFERENCES

Selected examples of direct chemical interference with laboratory tests*

| Test | Testing method | Possible result |
|---|---|---|
| **IN THE PRESENCE OF ACETAMINOPHEN (TYLENOL AND OTHERS)** | | |
| Blood glucose | Glucose oxidase/peroxidase method | False decrease |
| Pancreatic function testing | Bentiromide | False increase |
| Serum uric acid | Phosphotungstate uric acid test | False increase |
| **IN THE PRESENCE OF ANTICONVULSANTS, SUCH AS PHENYTOIN (DILANTIN), ETHOTOIN (PEGANONE), MEPHENYTOIN (MESANTOIN)** | | |
| Thyroid test | Protein-bound iodine (PBI) | False decrease |
| **IN THE PRESENCE OF ANTIHISTAMINES** | | |
| Skin testing | Allergen extracts | False negative |
| **IN THE PRESENCE OF NONSTEROIDAL ANTIINFLAMMATORY AGENTS (NSAIDs)** | | |
| Urinary bile | Diazo tablets | False positive with mefenamic acid (Ponstel) |
| Urinary 5-hydroxyindoleacetic acid (5-HIAA) and urinary steroid determinations | Various assays-m-dinitro-benzene | False increase |
| **IN THE PRESENCE OF THE ANTIMUSCARINIC, ATROPINE** | | |
| Urine test | phenolsulfonphthalein (PSP) excretion test | False decrease |
| **IN THE PRESENCE OF MEGADOSING WITH ASCORBIC ACID (VITAMIN C)** | | |
| Occult blood in stool | | False negative |
| Liver test, LDH and serum transaminases | Auto-analyzer | Interference |
| Urine glucose | Glucose oxidase test (Tes-tape) | False decrease |
| **IN THE PRESENCE OF COFFEE, TEA, COLA DRINKS, CHOCOLATE, AND ACETAMINOPHEN** | | |
| Theophylline test (clients receiving aminophylline, oxtriphylline, and theophylline) | Spectrophotometric | False increase |
| **IN THE PRESENCE OF CEPHALOSPORIN ANTIBIOTIC** | | |
| Blood glucose | Ferricyanide test | False negative with cefuroxime |
| Antiglobuline test | Combs test, direct | False positive in neonates when mother received cephalosporins or cephamycins before delivery |
| Urine glucose | Copper sulfate tests (Benedict's or Fehling's) | False positive or increase |
| Bleeding time (coagulation) | Prothrombin time (PT) | Increased or prolonged with cefamandole, cefoperazone, and cefotetan; may require therapeutic intervention with vitamin K |
| **IN THE PRESENCE OF HEPARIN** | | |
| Thyroid test | Resin $T_3$ uptake and, possibly, other thyroid test | Increase in serum thyroxine |

*For additional drug-test interferences, see appendix bibliography.

## DRUGS THAT CAUSE SPECIFIC DAMAGE TO A BODY ORGAN

Following are examples of drugs altering laboratory tests because of unwanted or adverse effects on the liver (hepatotoxic) or kidneys (nephrotoxic). For each section, generic names or general drug categories are listed. (Examples of registered trade names that are usually available in the United States or trade names generally available in Canada[✽] follow most of the entries.)

### Drugs That Are Hepatotoxic

acetaminophen (Tylenol and others) with chronic, high-dose therapy or in an acute overdose situation

4-aminoquinolines or chloroquine (Aralen), hydroxychloroquine (Plaquenil)

amiodarone (Cordarone)

anabolic steroid agents such as dromostanolone (Drolban), ethylestrenol (Maxibolin), nandrolone (Anabolin IM, Durabolin), and others

antithyroid agents (Tapazole)

asparaginase (Elspar)

azlocillin (Azlin)

carbamazepine (Tegretol, Mazepine ✽)

carmustine (BCNU)

contraceptives, estrogen containing, oral

dantrolene (Dantrium)

daunorubicin (Cerubidine)

disulfiram (Antabuse)

divalproex (Depakote, Epival ✽)

erythromycin (most often with estolate form, Ilosone)

estrogens (DES, conjugated estrogens and others)

etretinate (Tegison)

gold compounds (Ridaura and others)

halothane (Fluothane, Somnothane)

isoniazid (INH, Nydrazid, Rimifon ✽)

ketoconazole, oral (Nizoral)

mercaptopurine (Purinethol)

methotrexate (Mexate, Folex)

methyldopa (Aldomet)

mezlocillin (Mezlin, Baypen ✽)

naltrexone, chronic high-dose therapy (Trexan)

nitrofurans (Furadantin, Macrodantin, Novofuran✽ )

phenothiazines (Thorazine, Largactil ✽, and others)

phenytoin (Dilantin)

pipercillin (Pipracil)

plicamycin (Mithracin)

rifampin (Rifadin, Rimactane, Rofact ✽)

sulfonamides, systemic (Gantrisin, Gantanol, and others)

tetracycline, intravenous, high-dose therapy, especially in pregnant women

valproic acid (Depakene, Depakote, Epival ✽)

### Drugs That Are Nephrotoxic

acyclovir, parenteral (Zovirax)

aminoglycosides antibiotics (Garamycin, Nebcin, and others)

amphotericin B, parenteral (Fungizone)

analgesic combinations with acetaminophen and aspirin or salicylates used chronically in high-dose therapy (Excedrin, Trigesic, and others.)

antiinflammatory analgesics, nonsteroidal (NSAID)

capreomycin (Capastat)

captopril (Capoten)

cisplatin (Platinol)

cyclosporine (Sandimmune)

demeclocycline (Declomycin)

edetate calcium disodium, high doses (Calcium Disodium Versenate)

enalapril (Vasotec)

gold compounds (Ridaura and others)

lithium (Eskalith, Lithane, and others)

methotrexate, high doses (Mexate, Folex)

methoxyflurane (Penthrane)

neomycin, oral (Mycifradin)

penicillamine (Cuprimine, Distamine ✽)

pentamidine (Pentam, Lomidine ✽)

plicamycin (Mithracin)

rifampin (Rifadin, Rofact ✽)

streptozocin (Zanosar)

sulfonamides, systemic (Gantrisin, Gantanol, and others)

tetracyclines (with exception of doxycycline and minocycline)

vancomycin, parenteral (Vancocin I.V., Diatracin ✽)

## Selected Drug Effects on Specific Blood Substances*

| Drugs | Glucose | K+ | Na+ | PT | SGOT/ SGPT | Uric acid | BUN | Bilirubin |
|---|---|---|---|---|---|---|---|---|
| aminoglycosides (garamycin, and others) | | (−) | (−) | | (+) | | (+) | (+) |
| anticonvulsants (phenytoin, mephenytoin) | (+) | | | | | | | |
| antidepressants, tricyclic (amitriptyline, and others) | (+/ −) | | | | | | | |
| antiinflammatory analgesics, nonsteroidal (NSAID) (ibuprofen/piroxicam) | (−) | | | | | | | |
| mefenamic acid | | | | (+) | | | | |
| diflunisal | | | | | | (−) | | |
| all agents | | | | | (+) | | | |
| Beta adrenergic blocking agents (propranolol and others) | | (+) | | | (+) esp. with la- betalol | (+) | (+) | |
| carbamazepine (Tegretol) | | | | | (+) | | (+) | (+) |
| carbidopa/levodopa (Sine- met) | | | | | (+) | | (+) | (+) |
| cephalosporins (cefaman- dole, cefoperazone, cefox- itin, moxalactam) | | | | (+) | | | | |
| majority of cephalosporins | | | | | (+) | | | |
| cinoxacin (Cinobac) | | | | | (+) | | (+) | |
| cisplatin (Platinol) | | (−) | | | | (+) | (+) | |
| diuretics, loop (bumetanide, furosemide, ethacrynic acid) | (+) | (−) | (−) | | | (+) | (+) | |
| diuretics, thiazides (hydro- chlorothiazide and others). | (+) | (−) | (−) | | | (+) | | (+) |
| diuretics, potassium-sparing (amiloride, spironolac- tone, triamterene) | (+) | (+) | (−) | | | (+) | (+) | |
| methyldopa (Aldomet) | | (+) | (+) | | (+) | (+) | (+) | (+) |
| norfloxacin (Noroxin) | | | | | (+) | | (+) | |
| propoxyphene (Darvon and others) | | | | | (+) | | | (+) |
| Penicillin G-K | | (+) | | | | | | |
| injectable azlocillin, carbeni- cillin, mezlocillin, pipera- cillin, or ticarcillin | | | (+) | | | | | |

*Specific blood substances: serum glucose, potassium, sodium prothrombin time (PT), SGOT/SGPT (serum glutamic-oxaloacetic transaminase, glutamic-pyruvic transami-nase), serum uric acid, blood urea nitrogen (BUN), bilirubin. The possible effects of the drugs on laboratory tests are noted as follows: *blank spaces*, no reported effect; *(+)*, possible increase; *(−)*, possible decrease.

## Selected Drug Effects on Specific Blood Substances—cont'd

| Drugs | Glucose | K⁺ | Na⁺ | PT | SGOT/ SGPT | Uric acid | BUN | Bilirubin |
|---|---|---|---|---|---|---|---|---|
| azlocillin, ticarcillin | | | | | | (−) | | |
| azlocillin, mezlocillin, piper-acillin, ticarcillin | | | | | | | | (+) |
| majority of penicillins | | | | | (+) except methicillin, nafi-cillin, penicillin G-V | | | |
| prazosin (Minipress) | | | (+) | | | | | |
| rifampin (Rifadin and others) | | | | | (+) | (+) | (+) | (+) |
| trimethoprim (Proloprim) | | | | | (+) | | (+) | (+) |
| tetracyclines (Terramycin, and others) | | | | | | | (+) except doxycyc-line minocy-cline | (+) |
| valproic acid (Depakene, Depakote) | | | | | (+) | | | (+) |

*Appendix*

# C Food-Drug Interactions

| Drug category/medication | Foods to avoid | Rationale |
|---|---|---|
| **ANTACIDS** | | |
| calcium carbonate (Tums) | Avoid large amounts of dairy products. | Milk or cream may increase acid secretion. |
| | If used as a calcium supplement, avoid concurrent administration of bran and whole grain breads or cereals. | Reduces absorption of calcium |
| **ANTIBIOTICS** | | |
| erythromycin, penicillins* | Meals, acidic fruit juices, citrus fruits, or acidic beverages, such as cola drinks | The antibiotics are acid labile (reduced absorption). Take medication 1 hour before meals or apart from acidic foods or 2 hours after meals. |
| tetracyclines | Calcium-containing foods: milk, ice cream, yogurt, cheeses, and others | Calcium may complex with tetracycline, resulting in reduced absorption of the antibiotic. Most tetracyclines, with the exception of doxycycline and minocycline, should be administered 1 hour before or 2 hours after meals. |
| **ANTICOAGULANTS** | | |
| warfarin (Coumadin), dicumarol, heparin | Beef liver and green leafy vegetables contain vitamin K (spinach, cabbage, brussel sprouts) | Vitamin K can counteract therapeutic action of anticoagulants. A normal, balanced diet will not interfere with this medication. Fad or extreme diets with foods high in vitamin K can affect anticoagulant activity. |
| **LAXATIVE** | | |
| mineral oil (Agoral plain, Mineral Oil) | Take 2 hours apart from food. | May decrease absorption of vitamins A, D, E, and K. Also reduces absorption of calcium. |
| | Do not administer at bedtime. | Aspiration of mineral oil may induce lipid pneumonitis. |
| **MAO INHIBITORS** | | |
| isocarboxazid (Marplan), phenelzine (Nardil), tranylcypromine (Parnate) | Foods with high tyramine content, such as aged cheese, (brie, cheddar, processed American, camembert, and others), aged meat, sour cream, yogurt, pickled herring, chicken liver, canned figs, raisins, bananas, avocados, soy sauce, yeast extract, meat tenderizers, alcoholic beverages such as beer and wine (chianti, sherry, or hearty red wines), sausages, chocolate, anchovies | Concurrent use may result in severe headache, nosebleed, chest pain, eyes sensitive to light, or severe hypertension which may result in a hypertensive crisis. |

---

*Erythromycin base (E-Mycin, Ery-Tab, E-Mycin Eryc) or stearates (Erypar, Erythrocin Stearate, Ethril, Wyamycin S) are best absorbed in the fasting state. Erythromycin ethylsuccinate (E.E.S.), estolate (Ilosone), and enteric-coated erythromycin may be given before or with meals. Penicillin, such as penicillin G, ampicillin, cloxacillin, cyclacillin, dicloxacillin, nafcillin, and oxacillin may have decreased absorption if given with food or acidic-type products.

# D Time to Draw Blood Levels for Specific Medications

Serum drug levels are used to aid the physician (1) in determining dosage adjustments for drugs that have a narrow range between therapeutic effect and toxicity, thus ensuring drug efficacy and decreasing the potential for toxicity, and (2) to providing information to help evaluate a suspected toxicity or noncompliance.

Blood samples are usually drawn according to the pharmacokinetics of the individual drug. For example, to obtain a steady state (SS) serum level, the blood sample should be drawn at approximately 5 half-lives after therapy was instituted. For theophylline and phenytoin (Dilantin), the time to withdraw blood would be just before a dose, after at least 2 days of drug therapy.

Gentamicin (Garamycin) has a relatively short half-life; therefore peak and trough levels are usually ordered to ensure adequate therapy. The peak serum level (P) is usually obtained 15 to 30 minutes after an intravenous dose or 1 hour after an intramuscular dose. The trough (Tr) serum level should be drawn 15 minutes before the next scheduled dose. Trough serum levels are used to predict the risk of adverse reactions; a rising trough level or levels above 2 μg/ml have been associated with increased toxicity.

## Therapeutic Ranges of Serum Drug Concentrations

| Drug | Serum concentration | | Time for blood sampling (hours after last dose)* |
|------|------|------|------|
| | Ther (μg/ml) | Tr (μg/ml) | |
| **ANTIBIOTICS** | | | |
| amikacin (Amikin) | 15-25 | 5 | See previous discussion on gentamicin |
| gentamicin (Garamycin) | 4-10 | 2 | See previous discussion on gentamicin |
| netilmicin (Netromycin) | 6-10 | 4 | See previous discussion on gentamicin |
| tobramycin (Nebcin) | 4-10 | 2 | See previous discussion on gentamicin |
| **ANTICONVULSANTS** | | | |
| carbamazepine (Tegretol) | 4-12 | | SS 1-2 wk. Before next dose (Tr). |
| phenobarbital | 15-40 | | SS 10-30 days Before next dose (Tr). |
| phenytoin (Dilantin) | 10-20 | | SS 1-2 wk. Oral (Tr). before next dose; IV, 2-4 hr after loading dose. |
| primidone (Mysoline) | 5-12 | | SS 2-3 days for primidone; phenobarbital as above. Before next dose (Tr). |
| valproic acid (Depakene, Depakote) | 50-100 | | SS 1-2 days. Before next dose (Tr). |
| **CARDIOVASCULAR DRUGS** | | | |
| digoxin (Lanoxin) | 0.9-2 ng/ml | | SS 1 wk. Before next dose (Tr). at least 6 hr after last dose to allow for drug distribution in the body. |
| lidocaine (Xylocaine) | 1.5-5 | | SS 6-12 hr. Anytime during IV infusion. |
| procainamide (Pronestyl) | 4-10 | | SS 12-24 hr. Before next dose (Tr.) |
| quinidine (various drugs) | 2.3-5 | | SS 1.5 days. Before next dose (Tr.) |
| **RESPIRATORY DRUGS** | | | |
| theophylline (various drugs) | asthma 10-20 | | SS 1-2 days in adults, up to 1 week in neonates. IV infusion, anytime; oral, before next dose (Tr). |

*SS, Time to reach drug steady state. The SS time is noted first, then the suggested appropriate time of blood sampling for the specific drug. *Tr*, Trough.

*Appendix*

# Sulfite-Containing Food and Drug Products

A large number of sulfite sensitivity reactions (including deaths) have been reported to the FDA. Sulfites are used to preserve fresh foods, and are in prescription and nonprescription medications. As most of the reported cases of sensitivity were due to ingestion of restaurant meals, especially salad bars and other foods, the FDA has banned the use of sulfites in these areas. But sulfites are still present in some foods, prescription drugs which must bear warning labels and nonprescription drug products. The following are some of the foods known to contain sulfites (Saint Margaret Hospital, 1985; for complete reference see Chapter 5).

| | |
|---|---|
| Beer/Wine | Dried onion/green pepper |
| Cheese and mixtures: | Gelatin |
| American | Fruit juices |
| Brie | Hot roll mix |
| Lite Line | French fries/potato chips |
| Slim Line | Pickles/sauerkraut |
| Velveeta | Sweet and sour sauce |
| Cheese sauce | Potatoes, raw (frozen) |
| Cheese Whiz | Salad dressings made with vinegar |
| Snack Mate | Vinegar |
| Corn bread/muffin mix | Shellfish |
| Corn/pancake syrup | Clams |
| Cider | Crabs |
| Cordials | Lobsters |
| Dried fruits/vegetables | Oysters |
| Dried soup mixes/peas | Shrimp |

## Appendix Bibliography

Brown CH. (1990). Handbook of drug therapy monitoring. Baltimore: Williams & Wilkins.

Carey KW and Goldberg KE, eds. (1987). Clinical pocket manual: medications and I.V.s. Springhouse, Pa. Nursing 87 Books.

Elenbaas RM. (1986). When to monitor blood drug levels, Hosp Ther 11(7):27.

Hahn NH and Nissen JC. (1988). Compatibility of pre-op medications mixed in a syringe, Parenterals 6(2):7.

Knoben JE and Anderson PO. (1983). Handbook of clinical drug data, ed 5. Hamilton, Ill: Drug Intelligence Publications, Inc.

Powers DE and Moore AO. (1986). Food medication interactions, ed 5. Phoenix: Food-Medication Interactions.

Riemer WE. (1982). The laboratory manual. Miami, Fla: Baptist Hospital of Miami, Inc.

Trissel LA. (1986). ASHP handbook on injectable drugs. Bethesda, Md: American Society of Hospital Pharmacists, Inc.

United States Pharmacopeial Convention. (1991). Drug information for the health care provider, vols IA, IB, and II, ed 11. Rockville, Md: The Convention.

Wallach J. (1986). Interpretation of diagnostic tests, ed 4. Boston: Little, Brown & Co.

Zwiebel N. (1990). Brand-generic comparison handbook. Rockford, Ill: UDL Laboratories, Inc.

# Index

Page numbers in *italics* indicate boxed material
and illustrations. Page numbers followed by *t*
indicate tables.

## FDA PREGNANCY SAFETY CATEGORIES

**Category A:**

Studies indicate no risk to the fetus.

**Category B:**

Animal reproductive studies indicate no risk to the fetus; adequate and well-controlled studies in pregnant women are unavailable.

**Category C:**

Animal reproductive studies indicate an adverse effect on the fetus, but adequate and well-controlled studies in pregnant women are not available. Potential benefit to risk must be evaluated, as it may be warranted to use drug in selected pregnant women at risk.

**Category D:**

Human data or studies exhibit positive evidence of human fetal risk, but potential benefit to risk may warrant the use of the drug in pregnant women.

**Category X:**

Fetal abnormalities and positive evidence of fetal risk in humans are available from animal or human studies or from marketing reports. The risks of using this drug far outweigh the benefits; thus such drugs should not be used in pregnant women.

## CONTROLLED SUBSTANCES CHART

| Schedule | Characteristics | Examples |
|---|---|---|
| I | High abuse potential<br>No accepted medical use—for research, analysis, or instruction only<br>May lead to severe dependence | Heroin, marijuana (cannabis), tetrahydrocannabinols, LSD, mescaline, peyote, psilocybin, methaqualone |
| II | High abuse potential<br>Accepted medical uses<br>May lead to severe physical and/or psychologic dependence | Opium, morphine, hydromorphone, meperidine, codeine, oxycodone, methadone, secobarbital, pentobarbital, amphetamine, methylphenidate, cocaine, and others |
| III | Less abuse potential than drugs in Schedules I and II<br>Accepted medical uses<br>May lead to moderate/low physical dependence or high psychologic dependence | Preparations containing limited quantities of, or combined with, one or more active ingredients that are noncontrolled substances: codeine, hydrocodone, morphine, dihydrocodeine or ethylmorphine, and nonnarcotic drugs such as derivatives of barbituric acid except those that are listed in another schedule, glutethimide, methyprylon, chlorphentermine, paregoric, and others |
| IV | Lower abuse potential compared to Schedule III<br>Accepted medical uses<br>May lead to limited physical or psychologic dependence | Barbital, phenobarbital, chloral hydrate, meprobamate, fenfluramine, chlordiazepoxide, diazepam, oxazepam, clorazepate, flurazepam, lorazepam, dextropropoxyphene, pentazocine, mazindol, alprazolam, and others |
| V | Low abuse potential compared to Schedule IV<br>Accepted medical uses<br>May lead to limited physical or psychologic dependence | Medications, generally for relief of coughs or diarrhea, containing limited quantities of certain opioid controlled substances |